HOMEWOOD PUBLIC LIBRARY DISTRICT

3 1311 00454 3066

S0-BZP-178

Edu. Res.
650.0711
Pet

Peterson's
MBA
Programs
2009

PETERSON'S

A **nelnet** COMPANY

HOMEWOOD PUBLIC LIBRARY

OCT - - 2008

About Peterson's, a Nelnet company

Peterson's (www.petersons.com) is a leading provider of education information and advice, with books and online resources focusing on education search, test preparation, and financial aid. Its Web site offers searchable databases and interactive tools for contacting educational institutions, online practice tests and instruction, and planning tools for securing financial aid. Peterson's serves 110 million education consumers annually.

For more information, contact Peterson's, 2000 Lenox Drive, Lawrenceville, NJ 08648; 800-338-3282; or find us on the World Wide Web at www.petersons.com/about.

© 2008 Peterson's, a Nelnet company

Previous editions © 1995, 1996, 1997, 1998, 1999, 2000, 2001, 2002, 2003, 2004, 2005, 2006, 2007

Stephen Clemente, President; Fern A. Oram, Content Director; Bernadette Webster, Operations Director; Roger S. Williams, Sales and Marketing; Therese DeAngelis, Editor; Mark D. Snider, Production Editor; Bret Bollmann, Michael Haines, Sally Ross, Pam Sullivan, Valerie Bolus Vaughan, Copy Editors; Ken Britschge, Research Project Manager; Phyllis Johnson, Programmer; Ray Golaszewski, Manufacturing Manager; Linda M. Williams, Composition Manager; Janet Garwo, Mimi Kaufman, Danielle Vreeland, Client Relations Representatives; Charlotte Thomas, Richard Woodland, Contributing Editors

Peterson's makes every reasonable effort to obtain accurate, complete, and timely data from reliable sources. Nevertheless, Peterson's and the third-party data suppliers make no representation or warranty, either expressed or implied, as to the accuracy, timeliness, or completeness of the data or the results to be obtained from using the data, including, but not limited to, its quality, performance, merchantability, or fitness for a particular purpose, non-infringement or otherwise.

Neither Peterson's nor the third-party data suppliers warrant, guarantee, or make any representations that the results from using the data will be successful or will satisfy users' requirements. The entire risk to the results and performance is assumed by the user.

ALL RIGHTS RESERVED. No part of this work covered by the copyright herein may be reproduced or used in any form or by any means—graphic, electronic, or mechanical, including photocopying, recording, taping, Web distribution, or information storage and retrieval systems—without the prior written permission of the publisher.

For permission to use material from this text or product, complete the Permission Request Form at http://www.petersons.com/permissions.

ISSN 1080-2533
ISBN-13: 978-0-7689-2553-1
ISBN-10: 0-7689-2553-3

Printed in the United States of America

10 9 8 7 6 5 4 3 2 1   10 09 08

Fourteenth Edition

Contents

A Note from the Peterson's Editors

If you're thinking about applying to one of the myriad institutions around the world that offer advanced studies in the field of business, you're not alone. Over the past few decades, advanced business degrees have become the most viable and popular of graduate degrees. More than 100,000 graduate-level business degrees are awarded annually in the U.S. alone.

Because advanced study in business is so popular, the types of schools offering these courses of study run the gamut from small private colleges with business schools enrolling only a few hundred students to large state schools whose student bodies can number in the tens of thousands. These days, you can even join the increasing number of students who take distance learning courses from their own home or attend a "virtual university," where opportunities for learning are shared over the Internet. If you're already employed, perhaps your company is one of the increasing number of firms that offer on-site business courses in cooperation with local colleges. The choices are limitless. *Peterson's MBA Programs 2009* is the perfect tool to help you narrow your choices and choose the right program for you.

The **Secrets to Earning Your Graduate-Level Business Degree** section provides expert insight into the following:

- Understanding future trends in advanced business study

- Choosing the right program for your career needs

- Surviving the application process

- Deciding whether to study abroad

- Getting admitted to and paying for the program of your choice

The "How to Use This Guide" article provides in-depth explanations about each element contained in the **Profiles**, the criteria used to select the programs included in this guide, and data collection procedures.

Finally, there are two **Indexes** in the back of the book that provide page numbers for the schools' **Profiles** and **Close-Ups**. One lists the schools alphabetically by name, and one lists the schools by the areas of concentrations they offer—making it easy to identify which schools offer programs in your area of interest.

Like anything worthwhile, you'll get out of your graduate-level business study what you put into it. Usually the enthusiasm and dedication of the student are more important to his or her eventual success than the reputation or ranking of any one program.

Peterson's publishes a full line of resources to help guide you through the admission process. Peterson's publications can be found at your local bookstore or library; you can access us online at www.petersons.com.

We welcome any comments or suggestions you may have about this publication and invite you to complete our online survey at www.petersons.com/booksurvey. Or you can fill out the survey at the back of this book, tear it out, and mail it to us at:

Publishing Department
Peterson's, a Nelnet company
2000 Lenox Drive
Lawrenceville, NJ 08648

Your feedback will help us to make your education dreams possible.

The editors at Peterson's wish you the best of luck in your search for the perfect graduate-level business program for you!

SECRETS TO EARNING YOUR GRADUATE-LEVEL BUSINESS DEGREE

Why a Graduate-Level Business Degree? Uncovering Trends and Opportunities

John C. Hallenborg
Business Consultant

What's Hot in the Office Is Hot in the Classroom . . . and Vice Versa

Ambitious graduate-level business candidates, looking forward to their careers or perhaps to the exciting prospect of entrepreneurship, cannot afford to presume that every graduate-level business program will meet the educational requirements specific to an industry or profession. In today's job market the advanced business graduate is expected to deliver both technical and non-technical skills in every business and industrial sector. As in other areas of graduate study and related employment, the focus is on specialized expertise in business management. For businesses, opportunities exist to work with universities to create new graduate-level business programs that prepare candidates to fulfill an array of specialized leadership roles. For schools, this phenomenon continues to spur on the revamping of curricula almost annually to keep pace with the real-world demands that are placed upon future advanced business graduates.

Master's degree holders of all types are on the rise, allowing employers to be quite discriminating in hiring. Of course, the weight assigned to the graduate-level business degree by prospective employers varies considerably, depending on the industry, company, and job assignment. For a programmer at a software development company, the firm's in-house technical training would provide more valuable background than a graduate-level business degree. Conversely, someone applying for a middle-management job in the finance department at a midsize company may find a graduate-level business degree indispensable. The point is the two jobs might be represented on the same salary tier, so it is still a maxim in the transitional process from M.B.A. school to the workplace that the degree's importance is job-specific.

If you're holding down a job, it is always prudent to map out your time wisely. The working M.B.A. candidate may, for example, distribute a course load to accommodate a work schedule. An M.B.A. candidate will also need to consider employer assistance whereby the candidate's choice of school or program might be determined solely by which programs are endorsed and subsidized by the candidate's employer.

Holders of a newly minted graduate-level business degree bring new ways of thinking and innovative approaches to problem solving, leadership skills and experience, and the confidence that they can change things and make a difference. For many graduates, acquiring an advanced business degree may signal the difference between a lackluster occupation and a robust, life-affirming career full of welcome challenges and even more welcome rewards.

Two-Year Versus One-Year

Is it safe to presume that the recruitment managers at most major companies are aware of the changing makeup of the leading business school programs? The answer is most definitely yes, and it is apparent in the variety of degree options, concentrations, and alternative courses of study available to today's M.B.A. student. Certainly for the past thirty years or so, benchmark companies and top graduate schools have worked intensively to match academic programs to corporate needs. By all accounts, the composition of the graduate-level business degree and how it is acquired will continue to evolve in the coming years. The trend in graduate-level business programs is toward increased fragmentation and segmentation designed around students' specific needs.

How the degree can be obtained today also closely mirrors current business trends—the expectation of an early return on investment, preferably within one to two years. Future graduate-level business programs will likely continue to reflect the choices seen today: the one-year degree, which often dispenses with core programs in favor of specialized courses tailored to specific career paths, and the more traditional two-year and extended graduate-level business programs, which have been the basis of graduate business degrees for decades.

The upsurge in one-year degrees has been driven, for the most part, by corporate demand. Although two-year programs are still the norm in most business schools, accelerated and specialized one-year degree programs are seeing increases in enrollment.

The primary difference between one-year and traditional two-year programs is that with the shorter version, there is little, if any, overlap with undergraduate business curricula. Thus, it is highly recommended that students who decide on a one-year program enroll soon after receiving their undergraduate degrees and are able to satisfy all core business course requirements. However, some one-year programs require anywhere from two to five years' work experience in lieu of the traditional first-year M.B.A. core study courses. Many one-year programs are dedicated to serving experienced professionals and recent undergraduates with some work experience. One-year elective courses are all but tailored to the applicant's career, so that the graduate can reenter the workforce as quickly as possible. Classic two-year programs most often focus on elective and specialized course work in the second year after completion of core requirements in the first year.

A number of emerging realities highlight the one-year M.B.A. degree: technology-based information media replaces class time in many cases, fewer faculty members may be required as schools combine resources to teach fewer classes to more students, and distance learning replaces some on-campus classes. For most schools and students of the future, technology will certainly dictate the learning medium.

Business schools that have been adversely affected by the trend toward one-year programs are offering degree options that combine an undergraduate business degree with an M.B.A. in a five-year program. The proliferation of all these programs makes the choices more complex for the person considering an advanced business degree.

Corporations have generally been neutral about recruiting one-year program versus two-year program graduates. Part of the consideration comes down to a job applicant's reasons for pursuing a one-year versus a two-year program. Is it someone with plenty of work experience who is looking to advance her skills? Or is the graduate someone who is pursuing an advanced business degree because he is switching careers? Subjectivity on the question of whether an employer has a bias concerning graduates of two-year or one-year graduate-level business programs can come down to the hiring manager.

Albert W. Niemi Jr., dean of Southern Methodist University's Edwin L. Cox School of Business, explains: "I don't see, in the data that we have collected—in terms of starting salaries—that there is any difference in the way one-year people are treated by industry. One-year grads do as well as two-year grads in terms of earning power in the marketplace." Despite Niemi's findings, the proportion of one-year programs is still relatively small compared to the total number of graduate-level business programs offered nationwide.

Traditional Course Work Versus In-House Training

Rather than sending employees off site for their education, many companies choose to hire competent teachers as staff members to provide in-house training—a cost-effective alternative to traditional graduate-level business programs. The one-year M.B.A. and in-house training represent new models for graduate education. "Our dynamic economy is forcing change on all of us, if we are to be competitive and meet new challenges," says William K. Laidlaw Jr., former professor for the Practice of Management at the Weatherhead School of Management at Case Western Reserve University and former executive vice president of AACSB International.

Among the programs on the horizon are those directed at problem solving within a limited number of companies or even a single company. These programs are tailored to specific company issues. Typically, collaborative tutoring teams are composed of university professors and corporate upper management.

Changes in the Financial Sector

In the top tiers of the financial markets, there have been many changes following the scandals and management excesses of the 1990s. Because it was closely associated with these events, the reputation of the advanced business degree was somewhat tainted, directly or by implication. Today's graduates are under scrutiny to improve the standing of the degree in the academic and corporate worlds. The emphasis is on social skills such as communications, leadership, and teamwork, which has superseded the goal of attaining personal glory in most corporate environments. The financial community is no exception.

There has been a considerable shakeout in the better sectors of the financial job market, and many large financial organizations are as vigilant in maintaining a positive public image as they are about profit levels. Any M.B.A. candidate seeking a spot at one of the top investment banks, for example, will have to be aware of issues of public relations in addition to more predictable questions about money markets. Expect this sensitivity to public opinion to remain high for many years. In fact, a reputation for aboveboard dealings is nearly as important as bottom-line performance in today's financial sphere.

While the advanced business degree is still key in the world of investment banking, fewer M.B.A. graduates reported employment at investment banking firms upon graduation in 2003 than in 2000, according to a survey conducted by Duke University's Fuqua School of Business. The biggest gains were registered in marketing and management, where 41 percent of new M.B.A. graduates reported taking positions in these career fields versus 29 percent in the 2000 survey.

The New Attitude

How does this job market realignment affect the M.B.A. holder's chances for a lucrative career in finance? For one thing, M.B.A. graduates may find more opportunities in non-investment banking finance positions. Many small- and mid-sized companies that are doing quite well have neither the staff nor the inclination to recruit on campuses. They prefer to engage executive search firms to ferret out good candidates. It's up to applicants to make themselves known to these employers and their headhunters. Once M.B.A. graduates have their foot in the door, they should heed the message of employers: Bring us good grades from a good school but also bring along maturity and a problem-solving attitude. Despite the fact that compensation at the higher levels in banking is very bonus-oriented, the fresh M.B.A. graduate should avoid being a self-serving maverick. The advanced business degree holder of tomorrow, more than ever before, will have to display strengths in leadership, teamwork, problem solving, and communication. Upper management will be looking for well-rounded individuals who offer a balanced perspective and are ready and able to apply their education in a real-life setting.

Big Possibilities at Smaller Companies

The ideal of a "secure job forever" has been replaced by the reality that most Americans will have two or three careers in their lifetimes and may even change jobs every five years or so. Small and middle-market corporations continue to be fertile ground for M.B.A. recruitment. In the 2003 Fuqua survey, only 56 percent of M.B.A. graduates reported that they would be joining companies with revenue in excess of $1 billion. Twenty-two percent reported they would be joining firms with $100 million to $1 billion in revenue. The remaining 22 percent accepted offers to join companies with revenue below $100 million.

Once again, preparation for a specific industry niche or, better yet, a specific company or companies, is key to landing those choice spots that feature a daunting 50:1 or 500:1 applicant:position ratio. Most competing M.B.A.'s are aware that the key to landing the desired job is to positively differentiate oneself from other equally qualified candidates. Some graduate-level business students have gone so far as to research potential employers at the beginning of their course work, studying the details of annual reports, product brochures, etc., for the duration of the typical two-year M.B.A. program.

Skills learned in M.B.A. core and specialized courses can be especially valuable in helping to transform technical ideas and concepts into tangible, marketable products. In both large and small businesses in the future, managers will certainly be expected to bring not only technical expertise to the table but also the ability to translate new ideas into profit-sustaining products and services. The small- and mid-sized firm is often the perfect venue for such creative expression coupled with pragmatic implementation.

Tomorrow's Entrepreneur

There will always be a place for the ambitious M.B.A. holder who cannot wait for others to bring his or her ideas to the marketplace. For many fearless graduates, starting or buying a business may be a quicker and more lucrative route to success. Those with the best chance of making it this way will most likely combine prior experience raising money for and operating a start-up with the marketing and financial knowledge acquired with a graduate-level business degree. Graduate-level business programs are designing support systems for graduates who face the critical test of success within three to five years of launching their companies. This is when most businesses fail. Schools are involving alumni in the education process, developing communities among them to provide ongoing support, as well as bringing them back to teach and mentor current students.

Still, the appeal of running a small business does not get as much media coverage as it should, if a review of Harvard Business School alumni is any indication. M.B.A. graduates have founded such diverse and successful businesses as Intuit, United Bank of Africa, Donaldson, Lufkin & Jenrette, Bloomberg, Software Arts, Staples, Boston Concessions, and the Weather Channel.

Opportunities in the Twenty-First Century

Because management and finance are functions common to every conceivable type of business or industry, it is difficult to make predictions about job growth for M.B.A.s in particular markets. However, Gary Lindblad, assistant dean and director of The Paul Merage School of Business at the University of California, Irvine, mentions that their school's redesigned curriculum emphasizes the three critical drivers of the innovation economy: strategic innovation, information technology, and analytical decision making.

For advanced business students who intend to further their careers in the technology sector, M.B.A. programs with a technology focus may be the answer. These programs combine finance, operations, and marketing courses with a solid technical background. Candidates to these programs often have engineering and computer sciences backgrounds. Schools that rank high among recruiters include Northeastern University in Boston, University of Texas at Austin, University of Maryland at College Park, University of Alabama at Tuscaloosa, and University of California at Irvine.

A significant amount of future growth may come from overseas operations of domestic corporations. With the continued advance of telecommunications as the primary medium for data transfer, banks and corporations have permanently erased many commercial barriers between nations. This borderless, global market is an exciting prospect for the ambitious M.B.A. The Internet in particular has created opportunities for companies to outsource a broad array of operations to other countries with lower cost structures. Once content to move manufacturing to other countries, U.S. companies are now looking abroad to skilled, low-wage workforces to carry out certain operations, such as software development and bill processing. Graduate-level business students who graduate with an understanding of how to manage operations that are carried out in countries in different time zones with diverse cultures will find themselves in demand. Clearly, the cosmopolitan M.B.A. will be the first to reap the rewards from emerging international markets in the twenty-first century.

Postgraduate Tips

With the hiring of M.B.A. graduates trending away from investment banking and consulting, schools have been significantly reengineering their career services. Many institutions that were once content to stage recruitment fairs must now work closely with candidates to design a career journey strategy. Counselors are advising prospective graduates to approach alumni, involve themselves in student network groups, and undertake very heavy networking among any contacts they may have in the business community. Zero in on three to five companies that are very attractive, firms wherein you could happily spend the next three to ten years working hard to establish yourself in the business community. If you are a strong writer, parlay your skill by writing a detailed letter expressing your knowledge of the industry and the company and why you would be an asset to that company.

In the case of public companies, get their latest annual report, analyze it, and have your own views on the company's future ready to share with your interviewer. Do not make the mistake of blindly agreeing with everything the interviewer offers about the firm. If you disagree on a point, assert yourself with an explanation of your perspective on the issue. Never shy away from creating polarized discussion during an interview if you truly believe your position to be correct. Hopefully, your interviewer will recognize your willingness to defend your viewpoint as a trait of a successful executive.

What to Look for in Today's Reinvented Programs

Carter A. Prescott
Management Communications Consultant

Your team's assignment: Help the members of a rural dairy cooperative find a cheaper way to bring their products to market. Sound like typical M.B.A. fare? If you answered yes, you pass.

Today's graduate business programs are undergoing what some experts tout as nothing less than revolutionary change. In response to new competitive demands on corporations and increasing globalization—both of which require tomorrow's business leaders to be flexible and manage workforces and internal structures that cross cultural and political lines—graduate-level business programs are diversifying and redefining themselves. You'll still graduate with a firm grounding in the staples of business education—finance, strategy, operations management, marketing, and the like—but you'll also learn how to work in teams, how to motivate others, and how to see the "big picture" when solving problems. Strong communication and interpersonal skills are just as important in today's new graduate-level business programs as technical knowledge and the ability to "crunch numbers."

"There's more churning going on right now in management education than at any other time in thirty-eight years," says Charles Hickman, executive director, Northeast Ohio Council on Higher Education and former director of projects and services at AACSB International, which accredits M.B.A. programs in the United States. "The nature of M.B.A. programs and the supply/demand for them are interrelated. In the domestic market, the demand for M.B.A. programs has not been growing in recent years at pace with the growth from the 1970s to the 1990s. The emphasis today is changing from teaching to learning. The front-end-load module, where you dump two years of education into a student's head and then sew it up, is over. Many of today's M.B.A. programs have core curriculum requirements and provide students with more flexibility in creating their own curriculum. The pressure is on schools to differentiate programs from competitors and to try to identify particular niches in student or corporate markets in which they can position their programs. While there is still a cadre of ten to thirty high-end, full-time M.B.A. programs that attract national, and even global, pools of students, there is growth in the market for programs that offer a specialty or curriculum emphasis in a discipline. For instance, if you are interested in bioscience, which is now a course of study that some business schools have picked up on, you'll find dozens of these programs. Additionally, there is an emphasis on non-cognitive skills, such as content knowledge. There is growth in accelerated programs for full-time students who want to finish in less than two years. And certainly lots of growth has occurred in the part-time market, highlighted by growth in online learning, which the for-profit programs and the entrepreneurial conventional schools have pioneered. Students can get online M.B.A.s or blended programs that are part in person and part online."

The days when M.B.A. graduates could dazzle their bosses with only a few mentions of decision trees, regression analysis, net present value, and agency theory are gone. You'll still learn these concepts, but you'll be synthesizing them into a broader skill set. Dennis J. Weidenaar, Emeritus Professor of Economics and former dean of the Krannert Graduate School of Management at Purdue University, calls it the "new management environment." He says it is characterized by "teamwork and alliances, continuous changes in technologies, globalization, and networks that are in instantaneous communication with each other."

How, specifically, do today's advanced business programs prepare you to succeed in this environment? Here are ten primary ways.

1. Cross-Functional, Interdisciplinary Curricula

You'll hear these words so often they'll sound like a mantra. Across the country, graduate-level business schools are reshaping curricula to teach students the importance of solving problems by synthesizing a variety of subjects, such as combining marketing courses with information technology to prepare marketing managers for using data mining, customer relationship management, and other IT-based tools. Faculty members from different disciplines coordinate their syllabi and teach in teams to students who work in teams. Stanford's recently added course in human resources management, for example, was designed by professors of organizational behavior and economics. Cross-functional approaches have also proved resoundingly popular with students, who give them the thumbs-up in surveys.

2. New Programs

Whether they are specific sequences or subjects woven into the fabric of an M.B.A. curriculum, you'll find strong elements of entrepreneurship, ethics, innovation, and leadership development in nearly all basic advanced business programs. All first-year Purdue students, for example, attend the Leadership & Ethics Series during the year, with speakers discussing a variety of topics. Many also participate in the school's

Management Volunteer Program, in which M.B.A. students perform services, such as planting trees and maintenance in the local community. Harvard has a new course called Leadership and Corporate Accountability in which students examine the legal, ethical, and economic responsibilities of corporate leaders and how personal values play a critical role in effective leadership.

An emphasis on entrepreneurship reflects the reality that "the majority of M.B.A. graduates will not work in Fortune 500 companies, because they have been downsizing the most," notes Charles Hickman. For those who do work inside large organizations, a new perspective has emerged: intrapreneurship. Employees with breakthrough ideas are being encouraged to establish new businesses in-house by developing them as separate ventures under the corporate roof. Schools are also placing greater emphasis on social entrepreneurship, preparing managers to bring their business skills to the nonprofit sector.

On an individual level, the trend in curricula has been toward flexibility. Graduate-level business programs are introducing initiatives to personalize the management development process. If a student's skills are underdeveloped in a certain area, such as finance, she will have the opportunity to take courses that will address that weakness.

3. Global Perspectives

Part of the globalization of graduate-level business studies is the proliferation of super alliances among institutions in different countries. Several examples include the OneMBA® degree, which is attained through a twenty-one-month program designed by five schools on four continents: Kenan-Flagler (United States), Rotterdam School of Management (The Netherlands), Monterrey Tech (Mexico), Fundação Getulio Vargas (Brazil), and Chinese University of Hong Kong (China). Core courses are designed by faculty members from the five universities. Students attend classes at the institution that is nearest to them and also participate in regional courses. They are expected to have at least seven years of managerial experience before entering the program. The Trium global executive M.B.A. is offered in conjunction with New York University, London School of Economics, and HEC Paris. In the course of the sixteen-month program, the students, who are expected to have ten years work experience and at least fifteen years to be exempt from GMAT, travel to the schools for two-week periods.

4. Increased Student and Faculty Diversity

Business schools have realized that the best way to teach tomorrow's managers to tap into the talents of an increasingly diverse workforce is to surround students with a heterogeneous student body. They're also recruiting more faculty members who reflect out-of-the-box thinking and come from a variety of ethnic backgrounds. Students from diverse cultures are viewed as a resource that complements what faculty members know and what other students bring to the program. Almost across the board, graduate-level business programs in the U.S. are placing greater emphasis on international studies. The result is a rich exchange of students and faculty members with partner schools in other parts of the world.

5. Teamwork, Teamwork, and More Teamwork

Schools are working hard to encourage the same environment of teamwork that graduates will experience in the working world. "Cohort structures," for example, have gained in popularity. In a cohort structure, you are placed with a specified number of fellow students—deliberately chosen for their diversity—either for the first few weeks of class or for the entire first year. Together with other members of your cohort, you'll solve problems as a team, resolve conflicts, sustain morale, achieve accountability and, it is hoped, learn to reach your goals by becoming interdependent, just as you would in a corporate setting.

Reinvented graduate-level business programs are learning to "pit students against the curriculum and not against one another," says Sam Lundquist, vice president for development and alumni relations at Bucknell University. Stanford says its cooperative learning environment is a significant factor in the program's "joy coefficient," as George Parker, Dean Witter Distinguished Professor of Finance Emeritus, describes it. At MIT's Sloan School of Management, graduate-level business students learn to work together from the beginning when they are put into "core teams" in their first semester. Even the facilities in which students are taught increasingly reflect the teamwork needed in today's business environment. Many now offer breakout rooms for team sessions and have re-configured their classrooms so that students face each other rather than the front of the room.

6. Richer Learning Environment

Hand in hand with curriculum improvements, business schools are finding new ways to strengthen teaching and foster improved student-faculty relationships. Indeed, the most exciting part of Wharton's cross-functional curriculum, Lundquist says, is that teams of faculty teach the same students for the entire first year, which "drastically improves the quality of relationships between students and faculty members."

As advanced business programs bolster the quality of the learning experience, they are focusing a laser beam on how well professors help students learn. Pace University views faculty members as the managers of the student learning process. As a result, all programs and courses have objectives that are measured by student exit surveys, faculty question-naires, and yearly performance evaluations for faculty members. Any underperforming teachers are coached at the school's Center for Faculty Development and Teaching Effectiveness, where their syllabi are reviewed and their classes videotaped.

Teaching methods continue to evolve, employing not only the traditional tools of lectures and case studies but computer simulations, collaborations with local entrepreneurs, and group projects involving other schools. Harvard's curriculum reform was notable for adopting alternative teaching methods in addition to its reliance on the traditional case-study approach and for developing ways to have faculty members spend less time teaching basics.

7. Greater Use of Learning Technologies

Advanced business programs are making increasing use of distance learning, which uses interactive cable television and computers to take courses directly to students' homes. The University of Maryland University College (UMUC), for instance, uses distance learning to provide working adults with the flexibility to balance their job and family responsibilities while pursuing their educational goals. The M.B.A. program features courses taught by teams of faculty who focus their professional and academic expertise to help students apply business and management theories and practices in the context of their organizations. Distance learning also is favored heavily in Europe, where virtually all programs are part-time, according to Roger McCormick, former director general of the Association of M.B.A.'s in the United Kingdom. Distance learning allows students to learn at their own pace, which is especially helpful for remedial courses and quantitative work, he says.

The quality of distance learning programs covers a wide range. Those that garner the most respect from the business community are usually offered by institutions that also have a residency-based M.B.A. program. In such cases, the institution has already established its reputation and is using distance learning to leverage its brand.

In addition to interactive cable television, business schools are avidly employing other technologies. Projects that involve other schools move forward with the help of videoconferencing. The Internet is often the primary medium of communication among students, faculty members, and remote facilities. Students also make use of collaborative software, wireless networking, and Web-based document exchange.

Classroom facilities are being redesigned to accommodate the growing use of technology in the classroom. Case Western Reserve University's business school boasts the fastest academic broadband, which can be accessed from any desk. The building's infrastructure also supports multimedia and videoconferencing, enabling students to communicate with organizations in other parts of the world. The school's highly innovative design is the work of famed architect Frank Gehry. Classrooms are interspersed among faculty offices, imitating a real-world environment where workers interact daily with their bosses.

8. More Applied Learning

In most programs, there is some version of a "capstone" course that pulls together everything that students have learned throughout their M.B.A. degree studies. It is usually offered late in the program. With these so-called living cases, teams of students are assigned to an organization. For example, they may help a U.S. company enter the European market. When you are evaluating graduate-level business programs, ask about the capstone courses they have recently offered and the projects' outcomes.

9. Strategic Alliances

To better leverage their resources, schools are joining forces to teach students and to conduct postgraduate training for corporate executives. New York University, for example, develops executive Corporate Degree Programs whose curricula are customized to companies' employees. Corporate advisory boards, long a staple of most graduate-level business programs, are increasingly relied on to provide advice on curricula as well as hiring opportunities. Corporate partners also contribute other sorely needed resources. Purdue has one of the most extensive computing labs of any business school, thanks to the generosity of such high-tech partners as AT&T, Hewlett-Packard, IBM, Microsoft, and PictureTel. "The business environment is moving fast, and even elite schools don't have all the money they need to access new markets, technology, and faculty expertise," says Charles Hickman.

10. Customer Focus

It's not uncommon to hear business school professors routinely refer to students and companies as customers—and to treat their needs with the same respect. Many schools are applying the very business principles taught in those institutions to operating the schools themselves. They're becoming more customer-focused, reducing the cycle time for admissions processing and curriculum development, and becoming more efficient in lowering tuition or in keeping it from rising quickly. Seattle University, for example, brings classes closer to customers by holding identical evening courses on two campuses that straddle either side of the lake, making it easier for employees at Seattle's biggest companies to reach their classes.

With such evolution occurring day by day at business schools, more than ever before, today's reinvented advanced business programs aim to prepare you for the real world of work, where you will work in teams, take a global view, and analyze problems from a multitude of perspectives. To accomplish these goals, advanced business programs intend to equip you with the ability to embrace change, accept ambiguity, and lead others with the vision and confidence gained from continuous learning.

With a newly minted M.B.A. degree, you are better qualified to enter new fields, better able to leverage your prior work experience, and more likely to sustain higher earnings over the course of your career. Equally important, you'll have the opportunity to make a significant difference on as broad a scale as you wish. With finely honed analytical skills, the ability to work well with people, and the desire to keep learning, today's M.B.A. graduates can succeed in a broad range of general management positions and add more value than ever before.

Choosing the Right Program for Your Career Needs

Dr. Richard L. White
Director of Career Services
Rutgers University

In recent senior surveys, approximately 80 percent of Rutgers University students have indicated that they intend to pursue graduate study at some point in the future. Many are thinking about a graduate-level business degree. The intentions of Rutgers students reflect a national trend: More and more students want additional education, and, in fact, many feel they will need it to achieve their fullest career potential.

From your first thoughts about graduate school to your actual admission and decision to attend a school, you are engaged in an extensive, complex, competitive process. The emphasis of the program you select will greatly influence the direction of your career. In selecting a graduate-level business degree program, it is critical to match your strengths, interests, and goals with the specific offerings of the school and program.

To organize and manage the process, develop a strategy for evaluating your choices and developing a detailed action plan. At the heart of your action plan are four basic questions that are simple to ask but require self-exploration and research to answer.

1. Why Pursue an Advanced Business Degree?

You are probably thinking about pursuing an advanced business degree for these basic reasons:

- Your chosen profession demands further skills.

- You want to enhance your marketability and salary.

- You want to change careers.

- You are committed to further study in your current discipline or a new discipline.

Most applicants fit one of these profiles:

- You're currently working with an employer that you would like to stay with for the long term. You've talked to your boss and colleagues, and they believe that your getting an M.B.A. will improve your business and technical knowledge and thus increase your performance and promotional opportunities with the employer. You understand that there probably won't be a big jump in salary when you complete your degree, but in the long term it will pay off. In addition, your employer will pick up the tab through its tuition reimbursement program.

- You're currently working with an employer who doesn't fit into your long-term plans. You're planning to leave in the near future. You see your M.B.A. as the key to opening new opportunities in the same field or a new field and to increasing your salary prospects. You realize that you're on your own financially (no employer assistance), but you see the short-term investment paying off in the long run.

- You're a senior in college. You've surveyed the job market, but you're really leaning toward an advanced business degree program. You're very interested in pursuing your business education, especially because your bachelor's degree is not in business. You understand that the best business schools accept only a small percentage of applicants directly from undergraduate programs, but you have a strong academic record and some good internship and part-time work experience.

Whatever your profile may be, make sure you can articulate your reasons for pursuing an M.B.A. clearly, succinctly, and persuasively both orally and in writing. Review the evolution of your thinking from first thoughts about an M.B.A. to major influences such as people, courses, positions, and research.

To understand your motivation for pursuing an M.B.A., follow these five action steps:

1. Take notes on yourself.

2. Write or revise your resume.

3. Develop a generic personal statement (two or three typed pages), indicating what makes you special and why you want an advanced business degree. This will serve as the basis of the personal statement that will accompany your applications.

4. Request a sampling of M.B.A. applications and begin crafting sample answers to the questions, using parts of your generic personal statement.

5. Determine job prospects for graduate-level business students in your intended field—both short-term and long-term. The best resources for short-term job prospects are individual placement reports from business schools, which are available online or through the admissions offices. For long-term prospects, talk to relatives, family friends, or professors. Another great source is alumni, if your school has an alumni career network.

2. When and How Do You Want to Pursue Your Advanced Business Degree?

There are four fairly clear-cut options about when and how to pursue your advanced business degree:

1. *Full-time beginning in the fall after your graduation from college.* Keep in mind that graduate-level business programs typically look for candidates with at least one to two years of full-time work experience. If you are a student early in your undergraduate career, one option to explore is a five-year dual-degree (B.S./M.B.A.) program.

2. *Full-time beginning after a year or more of work.* Graduate-level business programs value the diversity and quality of candidates' work experiences, which bring "real-world" perspectives and new ideas into the classroom. Moreover, many graduate-level business students indicate that their course work has even more significance after they continue their professional and career development.

3. *Part-time while working.* In most cases, you will take evening classes. As part of your preliminary research, find out if your employer provides full or partial tuition remission. Also explore whether or not your employer values an advanced business degree and whether it will really contribute to your long-term promotability. Finally, try to determine how flexible your employer may be if, for example, you need to take a 4:30 class or need one or two days off to complete a school project.

4. *Part-time while not working.* If you're not working, you can take either day or evening classes. But if you're looking for a daytime job, bear in mind that you might want to remain flexible during the day and therefore take your classes at night. The reverse is true if you have a part-time evening job.

To sort out the different possibilities, take these three action steps:

1. Research the schools of your choice, using this guide. Compare these five key elements: percentage of full-time versus part-time enrollees; percentage of incoming M.B.A.s who came directly from undergraduate programs; average age; average work experience; and costs.

2. Research the profession and prospective employers, utilizing corporate recruiters, friends in the corporate world, career services and admissions professionals, professional associations, alumni networks, professors, and publications. Consider these elements: availability of tuition remission programs; value of the advanced business degree within the profession or company; and balance between a company's B.A./B.S. hiring and M.B.A. hiring.

3. Balance all of the above elements with your personal lifestyle and the lifestyle of the people closest to you.

3. Where Do You Want to Pursue Your Advanced Business Degree?

This is the most complex step in the process, because there are many variables. However, by taking these five action steps, you can gain firm control of the process and manage it to your advantage.

Note that these steps are in no specific order. It would be helpful to put them in rank order in terms of importance for you—or at least group them by "very important," "important," and "less important."

1. Determine the availability of degree programs in your specific field. For example, if you are thinking about an M.B.A. in international business, this guide will tell you which schools offer that program.

2. Determine the quality and reputation of the programs of your choice. This is a crucial element. Employers often base their recruiting decisions on quality and reputation, and you will be associated with the name of your M.B.A. school for the remainder of your career. Three key factors in assessing quality and reputation are faculty, facilities, and student body. In addition to utilizing this guide and perhaps other resources, talk to professors and professionals and "read between the lines" of the admissions literature and placement reports. Feel free to consult various national rankings, but don't take them too seriously. These are often based on journalistic endeavors rather than hard research and often overlook the special offerings of individual programs.

3. Determine the costs of graduate programs—the simple part—and your ability to pay through loans, income, savings, financial aid, and parental support—the not-so-simple part. Pursue those programs that are affordable. Consult the "Paying for Your Advanced Business Degree" article for an overview of the financing process.

4. Determine the locations of your preferred graduate programs. Do you prefer urban, suburban, or rural locations? Do you have any personal geographical restrictions or preferences? Think about the time and cost of commuting and travel.

5. Determine the size of the programs and the institutions. Most graduate-level business programs are relatively small but the size of institutions varies considerably. Many institutions enhance the breadth of their programs by partnering with other U.S. and international institutions offering programs. Size is critical to the overall environment, character, academic resources, and student-faculty ratios and relationships.

4. What Schools and Programs Are Right for You?

Here, you are putting it all together and generating a list of five to ten schools where you intend to apply. Typically, you will want one or two "stretch" schools, a handful of "good bets," and one or two "safety" schools. Rank your preferences at the outset of the admissions process, but remain flexible. As you receive admissions decisions, your preferences will probably change and need to change.

Once your acceptances are in hand, how do you make the final important decision? Consider the following steps.

Rank the five most important features of the graduate-level business experience for you. You might also want a second-tier group of five additional features. Focus on these ten features (feel free to add others to the list):

1. Career and placement services (placement report, number of employers recruiting on campus, overall quality of operation)

2. Class offerings (day, evening, summer, weekend)

3. Cost (tuition, room, board, travel, living expenses)

4. Curricular focus (ethics, diversity, international)

5. Facilities (dorms, classrooms, libraries)

6. Faculty (general quality, individual faculty members)

7. Location (geographic, urban, rural)

8. Personal considerations (spouse, family, friends)

9. Quality and reputation (general comments)

10. Teaching methodology (lectures, case studies, team projects)

Systematically compare each school and each feature. Rank schools within each feature, assigning a score if you wish.

Once you have completed your analysis, make sure your heart agrees with your head. If it's a toss-up, go with your instincts. They're probably right.

How to Get Top ROI from Your M.B.A.

An Interview with Dr. Randal Pinkett
Partner, President & Chief Executive Officer
BCT Partners

When facing a critical decision that could seriously impact the bottom line, savvy business leaders gather information, assess the input, make their choice, and move forward. When making a decision about where to invest thousands of dollars in getting your M.B.A., you, too, will want to gather as much information as you can about the program and its return on investment (ROI) for your career.

What if you got information from someone who started his first business while in college, established a multimillion dollar management, technology, and public policy consulting firm, was a Rhodes Scholar, graduated in two years from a top M.B.A. program with a dual master's, continued for his Ph.D., and—oh, by the way—after competing with 18 other skilled contestants, won a high-level job with Donald Trump on NBC TV's hit reality show *The Apprentice*?

You might not have seen Dr. Randal Pinkett accept a six-figure position in the final episode of the 2005 season of *The Apprentice*, but his resume puts him in a position to offer astute advice about choosing an M.B.A. program. Having overseen a $110 million renovation of three Trump properties in Atlantic City as a result of winning *The Apprentice*, he now speaks and writes about entrepreneurship, innovations in technology, career management, and succeeding in academia. His corporate experience includes General Electric, AT&T Bell Laboratories, and Lucent Technologies. Since graduating from college, Pinkett has packed plenty of experience into his education and career.

Wanting an M.B.A. is one thing; being accepted into the program that closely matches your experience, skills, and goals and getting the most out of it is another. Pinkett has plenty to share about all these aspects and about using the knowledge he gained. After receiving his M.B.A. in 1998, he launched BCT Partners, LLC, a management, information technology, and policy consulting company with clientele from corporations, government agencies, and nonprofit organizations. As its president and C.E.O. he oversees a full-time staff of 20 and expanded the company from $15K to more than $2 million in revenue in the first four years with no start-up capital. With those credentials, and looking back at his M.B.A. experience, Pinkett offers salient advice—and a few caveats.

The Best Time to Work Toward an M.B.A.

Looking back on the timing of his decision to get an M.B.A., Pinkett says, "As a general rule of thumb, you should go for the degree early in your career after you've had a chance to get your feet wet in business." His reasoning is that the later in life you pursue an M.B.A., the more likely you will have acquired skills and experience on the job and will have less need for the degree. The cost benefit decreases as your experience

---

Think an M.B.A Could Keep You from Hearing the Words "You're Fired"?

NBC's reality show, *The Apprentice*, pitted talented contestants who fiercely competed for thirteen weeks to win a one-year apprenticeship and six-figure salary working for Donald Trump. With limited time and resources, teams completed projects for companies such as Microsoft and Best Buy that tested their business acumen, creativity, and ability to lead and execute decisions. Every week, someone (or in some cases, more than one person) heard the dreaded words that Trump made famous: "You're fired."

How do you think you would do on these projects?

- Design an interactive display to promote a new DVD and video game based on a movie poised to hit the screen

- With the help of songwriters, write and produce an original song for a radio station to play on the air

- To promote a new fragrance, create a one-day promotion that will entice people on New York City streets to call an 800 number for more information

- For a software giant, produce a 60-second video to advertise the benefits of its new program, which links people from different locations to collaborate on one document

---

increases. "An M.B.A. early in your career provides a boost to your knowledge base and learning potential and your exposure to concepts and people," he reasons.

Applying to an M.B.A. Program

What are your goals?

Pinkett's search for the right program began with his quest to understand what he wanted to accomplish with the degree. "Early in my career as an aspiring entrepreneur, I envisioned the M.B.A. as a great tool belt," he says. Having already started one business venture before applying to an M.B.A. program and having launched another while in the program, he was most interested in focusing on entrepreneurship, but he notes that an M.B.A. can be the means to change careers, too. "Some students come in as English majors and come out as investment bankers," he says. "The benefit of an M.B.A. is that you have the chance to explore what it means to be in a business environment and to possibly pursue an entirely new career."

While he attended Rutgers University, New Brunswick, New Jersey, in the electrical engineering department, Pinkett's entrepreneurial bent was already in full swing. He co-founded MBS Enterprises, which sold CDs and tapes to provide funding for high school student outreach programs and workshops. After college, he entered the University of Oxford as a Rhodes Scholar to study computer science.

With a technical background and entrepreneurial experience, Pinkett chose to apply to MIT's Sloan School of Management because it had one of the strongest engineering and business programs in the country. "It was a combination of factors," he recalls. "My background in engineering gave me a leg up and a strong position." He entered as a double major, getting his master's in electrical engineering at the same time.

What differentiates you from other brilliant applicants?

When Pinkett applied to Sloan, he came with a 3.9 undergraduate GPA, a successful start-up business, and the prestige of having received a Rhodes Scholarship. But he wasn't the only one to bring a stellar list of accomplishments to the admissions table. "M.B.A. applicants compete against other very smart people, which can come as a shock when they are used to being at the top of their fields," Pinkett warns. He found the admissions process extremely competitive, and he surmises that it's even more so today. With limited enrollment and many applicants, M.B.A. programs seek the exact fit. Pinkett urges applicants to be prepared to outline what unique qualities and experiences they can offer to the admissions office.

Do the program's strengths and areas of expertise fit yours?

In selecting a program, Pinkett saw rankings as a starting point, but he took off from there. "I wanted to see which programs were strong in a particular area," he says. He used many sources to gather information, including word-of-mouth assessments, which provided a well-rounded picture of each program. Pinkett explains that some programs are strong in consulting, while others focus on banking or finance. "It's not that those are the program's exclusive areas of focus, but they gain a reputation for strength in a particular area or for a particular business environment," he explains.

He tracked down graduates of the programs he was considering and talked with them. He looked through publications for school profiles and compiled statistics about its graduates. Scrutinizing each program carefully allowed him to dig beneath the surface of name brands and top-ten lists. Today, the Internet provides additional resources which, Pinkett explains, weren't as readily available in 1996 as they are now.

Does your background match what the M.B.A. program is looking for?

The fact that Pinkett already had entrepreneurial experience was consistent with the program Sloan was in the process of building at that time. But Pinkett knew that admissions was looking for well-rounded people, not just technical whizzes and start-up geniuses, so he also emphasized his public speaking at seminars and his negotiation skills. "The fact that I wasn't a

A Low Point in an M.B.A. Experience

"The most difficult time for me was transitioning into the program. I had done the research, talked to students, and knew about the level and rigor of academic work expected of me. But in my first round of exams I did poorly because I underestimated what would be asked of me. More often than not in undergraduate school, teachers ask you to demonstrate what you were taught to show that you comprehend the material. At MIT, we were expected to take what we learned and apply it. It is assumed that you know the concept—here's what you've learned, now, solve this problem using that knowledge. I had to adjust my study habits and orientation toward the material to master it and be able to apply it in other domains. I had just returned from Oxford and thought I had done well, so I came in thinking getting an M.B.A. would be business as usual. Luckily I bounced back and graduated with a 4.9 out of 5.0."

stereotypical technologist but brought some communication skills to the program was a plus," he notes.

Many applicants take into account only the experience they gleaned from jobs, but Pinkett advises you to look at the skills and abilities you've garnered outside of work—even as far back as your undergraduate years. "Community or civic activities are relevant to the lessons you learned and how those experiences strengthen you as a business person and round you out. Your contextual experience adds to the class and makes it more fruitful," he says.

Will you do better in a competitive environment or in one that emphasizes teamwork?

While competition is fundamental to many M.B.A. programs, Pinkett advises prospective students to look closely at how students interact with each other. "Find out if the program encourages a supportive [environment] or . . . [one] in which students must fend for themselves," he cautions, recommending that you ask yourself whether having the support of peers meshes with your own style. How do you normally conduct yourself in business? Many people thrive in tough competition. Comparing his own experience to what he sees today, he believes that many programs are emphasizing teamwork to "mitigate some of the competitiveness" that up to now has been the standard of M.B.A. programs. He illustrates this argument by pointing out that, from day one at Sloan, he was assigned to a team, and he worked with teams throughout the first semester. He recalls that from the beginning it felt like a good fit for him.

Succeeding in an M.B.A. Program

The hurdles of actually being in an M.B.A. program are as daunting as getting accepted. Pinkett's experience was doubly so, because he simultaneously completed two degrees, his M.B.A. and Master of Science in Electrical Engineering from the MIT Leaders for Manufacturing Program and the MIT Center for Innovation in Product Development.

Randal Pinkett's Goal? Head Up a Multibillion Dollar Company

"When I was younger, my goal was to run a multimillion dollar company. Now it is to run a multibillion dollar company. As I've grown older and have been exposed to individuals like Bob Johnson (founder and chief executive of Black Entertainment Television), Donald Trump (business executive, real estate developer, founder, CEO of Trump Organization of the USA), and Earl Graves (founder and publisher of *Black Enterprise* magazine) and other accomplished business people, and now with the opportunities presented to me, I have every reason to shoot for the sky and not be limited."

What will be expected of you?

With his background in engineering and business start-ups, Pinkett had the advantage of a thorough familiarity with math. Many programs will assume you've had some calculus and have been exposed to some of the disciplines of business, such as sales, accounting, and communication. "More often than not, professors ask you to speak to your experience in a case study or to draw from your technical or math skills," Pinkett says. The sheer amount of work in an M.B.A. program didn't overwhelm him because he had sufficient orientation. Despite this, Pinkett says "It was still challenging."

What do you want to focus on?

"There are a lot of directions a program can pull you," Pinkett says of the necessity to drill down to the lower levels of program focus such as extracurricular activities, courses, and areas of specialization. "Focus is a major consideration driving your course selection and ultimately your job search." On the other hand, some students come into a program to explore different options. For instance, they might be deciding between consulting and investment banking. Pinkett calls having a razor-sharp focus at the beginning of the program a "preferred luxury," but he believes it is not a requirement. He cautions that focus is a benefit only to the extent that students are absolutely clear about their goals. If not, "You could be focused on the wrong thing," he says.

Can you manage your time well?

If you aren't already adept at juggling projects, setting priorities, and dealing with overlapping deadlines, be fore-warned. "Getting an M.B.A. is very demanding in terms of time and rigor," Pinkett observes. "If your heart is in it and you are willing to put time in to get the work done, it is very rewarding." The key for Pinkett was learning what aspects of study deserved his full attention and what he could just skim. "If you try to do it all, you will bite off more than you can chew," he says, noting the difference between required and recommended reading.

The Added Bonus of the M.B.A. Experience

Learn from your fellow students

"It's what makes an M.B.A. so powerful and rich," says Pinkett. "This is a two-year period in which you can share experiences, debate concepts, and bring what you have learned to your classmates." The interaction between students and professors was a powerful learning tool for Pinkett. He was fascinated by the diverse environment in which he worked with someone who had been in the fashion industry and a person who was considering getting a legal degree following the M.B.A. "I was able to glean so much and hear war stories," he mentions, recalling that one story was the behind-the-scenes details about the merger and acquisition of two multinational organizations.

Take full advantage of your M.B.A. experience

Pinkett expected to learn new aspects of business, but he also learned a lot from the experiences of his classmates, both in class and in social and networking functions. "My M.B.A. experience wasn't just exposure to new ideas but to new opportunities," he states. With the volume of work that is demanded of M.B.A. students, it's easy to forego activities outside the classroom. Pinkett views the classroom experience as just one way to learn. "I encourage M.B.A candidates to certainly focus on the demands of the classroom but don't let that limit them to the other possibilities they will have to enrich and enhance their experience."

The Apprentice Takes on His First Assignment

"I am overseeing a $110 million renovation of our three properties, namely: Trump Taj Mahal, Trump Plaza, and Trump Marina. Furthermore, I manage an information technology project that involves upgrading the computer systems for our 1,200 employees.

NOTE: *At the conclusion of his one-year term as an apprentice for Donald Trump, Randal Pinkett returned to his company, BCT Partners, and maintains a close connection to his partners and a capable executive team. He is also writing several books, and he frequently speaks at engagements around the country.*

Getting Admitted to Business Programs

Samuel T. Lundquist
Vice President for Development and Alumni Relations
Bucknell University

Applicants to graduate-level business programs often spend more time trying to figure out how to get into business school than researching the program itself. Hence, the prospective student has made the first critical error of the admissions process—seeking the elusive "admissions formula" versus making a quality presentation that demonstrates knowledge of self and graduate business education.

There really is no formula that can guarantee admission to a graduate-level business program. Business school applicants must enter the selection process understanding the difference between being admissible and being admitted. The distinction between the two varies considerably among business schools, depending on the level of selectivity in the admissions process. While some advanced business degree programs admit all qualified students, others may deny admission to four of every five applicants who are qualified to be admitted. Understanding this difference is the first step to a successful application.

The Evaluative Process

Applicants to graduate-level business programs should understand how they will be evaluated during the admissions process. In general, presentation, academic profile, professional work experience, and personal qualities will be the four areas in which each applicant will be evaluated. Admissions officers generally evaluate the factors influencing applicants' educational and professional decisions and the corresponding outcomes. Admissions committees do not spend a lot of time evaluating the labels that tend to categorize applicants into special groups. For instance, candidates for admission often assume that the quality of the undergraduate institution that they attended will affect the outcome of their application. A common misconception is that applicants with undergraduate degrees from Ivy League schools are always more desirable candidates for business schools. In fact, the undergraduate institution one attended may be an insignificant variable in the admissions process at some business schools.

Applicants are evaluated as individuals. The environment in which they have studied or worked is relevant only when it is given meaning in the context of their life experiences. How the culture of a campus or workplace has influenced one's success is interesting and important to the admissions committee's ability to fully evaluate an application. Therefore, applicants who provide only factual information about their academic and professional profile miss the opportunity to present the most compelling and distinguishing characteristics of their candidacy.

The M.B.A. degree is not a professional license that is required to practice management. Therefore, people of all ages are known to pursue the degree. Older applicants (32 and older) often fear that because they are not typical traditional graduate school students they will be less desirable to business schools. On the contrary, older students offer professional experience, maturity, and perspective that are highly valued in the classroom. The admissions committee does expect older applicants to have highly developed reasons for pursuing the M.B.A. at this stage of their lives. Post-M.B.A. goals are expected to be more defined than those of their younger counterparts.

Applicants have much more control of the admissions process than they realize. Prospective students determine all of the information that is presented in the application forms, essays, and interviews. They even get to select the people who will serve as references to support their candidacy. The only aspect of the process that an applicant does not control is the competition. It is the competition that will determine the threshold between admissibility and acceptance.

Presentation is obviously one of the most important factors in admission. Four other areas are evaluated during the evaluative process. They include academic profile, GMAT score, professional work experience, and personal qualities.

Academic Profile

Business schools seek students who can survive the demands of a rigorous program, and the best way to show your intellectual strength is to demonstrate strong classroom achievement and high aptitude. Your ability to excel as an undergraduate student is directly related to your ability to succeed in a graduate program.

Your undergraduate specialization will have little effect on admission to business school. It is not necessary to take undergraduate courses in business administration because most graduate-level business programs offer or require a core curriculum of basic business courses as part of the graduate degree. However, it is advisable to have basic skills in economics, calculus, and statistics in preparation for graduate study in business.

The Graduate Management Admission Test (GMAT®)

Most business schools require applicants to submit the results of their Graduate Management Admission Test (GMAT®). The importance of the GMAT® in admissions will vary depending on the school. Minimum score requirements do not exist at some business schools. Test scores are certainly not the sole criterion for admission to a graduate-level business program, but to one degree or another, most business schools use them as part of the admissions process.

The GMAT® uses a standardized set of criteria to evaluate the basic skills of college graduates, which allows graduate schools to compare and judge applicants. The test measures general verbal and math skills so that schools can assess an applicant's ability to succeed in a graduate-level environment.

- Quantitative section—This section measures mathematical skills and the ability to solve quantitative problems.

- Qualitative section—This section focuses on verbal skills, the ability to understand and interpret written materials, and basic English writing skills.

- Scoring—Total scores range from 200 to 800, but scores lower than 300 and higher than 700 are unusual.

- Analytical Writing Assessment—This section requires test-takers to write two essays that measure the ability to think critically and communicate complex ideas through writing in English. This section is scored on a scale of 0 to 6, but scores lower than 2 and higher than 5 are unusual.

- Taking the test—Since January 2006, the GMAT® computer-adaptive test (CAT) has been available around the world. The test is now completely computerized and is no longer available on paper. For more information, contact:

  GMAC®, Graduate Management Admission Council
  1600 Tysons Boulevard, Suite 1400
  McLean, Virginia 22102
  Phone: 866-505-6559 (toll-free in the U.S and Canada)
  Fax: 703-749-0169
  Web site: http://www.gmac.com

Professional Work Experience

Admission to selective, international business programs usually requires full-time, professional work experience prior to enrollment. While professional work experience is needed to provide a context for the interpretation and use of classroom material, students must also be able to contribute to class discussions and group projects in meaningful ways. Career success is the most effective way to prove your potential for leadership in a managerial capacity.

Personal Qualities

Graduate-level business programs want to enroll students who can lead people. The admissions committee seeks men and women who will eventually be responsible for the management of entire organizations. Leadership is one of the basic ingredients for success. Communication skills, initiative, and motivation can become the most important aspects of the admissions process. Personal qualities set the tone for the entire review of an application. It is the one part of an application that is most likely to distinguish a candidate in a compelling way.

The Interview

The interview is the one aspect of the admissions process that varies the most among schools. Some schools require all applicants to interview prior to admission. Others do not interview any of their applicants. Most schools leave the decision to interview up to the applicant. It is one more part of the admissions process that the applicant can control. For those prospective students who do have the interview available to them, it is highly recommended. It is also a great opportunity to take initiative in the admissions process.

If an interview is part of the admissions process, it can be an invaluable opportunity for the applicant to show the strengths and leadership qualities that most business schools are seeking in M.B.A. candidates. The most effective and interesting interviews are those discussions that go beyond the information provided in the written application. Too often interviews remain focused solely on the candidate's resume. The meeting becomes nothing more than a redundancy in the evaluation of a candidacy. It is up to both the interviewer and the applicant to create an exchange of information that solicits useful information that will help the admissions committee understand the context of the choices that the applicant has made throughout life.

The Greatest Impact

Categories and labels do not play as significant a role in the process as most applicants assume. Prospective graduate-level business students should take a high level of initiative during the admissions process, while exercising discretion when determining what information is most important for a school to properly evaluate their candidacy.

These guidelines are the first step in understanding the nature of the admissions process from the perspective of an admissions officer. It is vital to recognize that each school has its own policies and procedures in admissions. Careful research and communication will, fundamentally, have the greatest impact on the success of an M.B.A. application.

Surviving the Application Process

Michele F. Kornegay

So far, we've discussed the action plan leading up to your decision to apply to business school. Now it's time to move on to the really hard part—submitting applications to the programs you've chosen. What, you thought it was all downhill from here? Far from it. How you prepare your business school application makes all the difference when it comes to getting accepted at your dream school.

Timing and Deadlines

Different programs have different deadlines, so you'll need to stay organized throughout the application process. As you receive applications, you may want to file them in separate folders and note the program name and the deadline where you can see it easily. Be sure to note whether the program has a rolling deadline, in which applications are reviewed as they are received and spots are filled until the program is full—or a firm deadline, for which your application must be submitted by a certain date.

Most schools and most business programs have a filing period for applications of about six to eight months. During this time, the department accepts applications, reviews them, and offers attractive candidates a spot in their program. With such a large window, are you better off applying earlier or later in the cycle?

Most admissions counselors advise that, when it comes to filing your application, earlier is better. In their opinion, an early application has a better chance for admission for several reasons. Most importantly, submitting your application early shows that you are really interested in the program—a surefire way to impress admissions committees.

Although it may not necessarily be the case, if you wait until the last minute to send in your application, it may leave the impression that you see the program as a last resort. If you take it down to the wire, there's also a greater chance that you may have to prepare your application hastily, something any admissions committee worth its salt is sure to notice, and view negatively. Remember, these people are professionals; they've reviewed thousands of applications over the years, so they'll be sure to recognize if you've rushed to complete the application. This will not reflect well on your candidacy. The best applications are those that show readers that you have a well-thought-out plan for your future. A rushed application will make you look scattered and not very serious about the program.

Other good reasons for applying early: At the beginning of the process, there are more spots available. Inevitably, the majority of candidates wait until later on in the admissions window to apply, so as the deadline nears, you'll be competing for the (fewer) remaining spots with a greater number of applicants. Also, at the beginning of the application process, admissions directors have no idea about who will be applying to the program, so they're not very sure about how selective they can be about admissions. This could work in your favor, since early on, your application will be judged more on its own merit than on how it compares with others.

To How Many Schools Should You Apply?

The business school application process can be fairly arduous, so you want to be sure that you apply to just the right number of schools. Too few and you may not be accepted to any; too many and you may go crazy filling out all those forms and writing all those essays! Make realistic choices. Look at the criteria of the schools in which you're interested and at your qualifications, and be honest with yourself. By all means, don't rule out your dream program if your GMAT is 10 points below their stated cutoff; however, if your GMAT is 50 points below the cutoff, your GPA is a point below their cutoff, and you don't have any real work experience, you might want to save yourself the effort.

You may want to place the schools that you've chosen into three categories—reach schools, probable schools, and safety schools—and then go from there. Apply to a few reach schools (those that are longshots based on your academic record and other application materials), send more applications to probable schools (those to which you have a reasonable, realistic, and better-than-average chance of getting admitted), and send a few applications to your safety schools (those where you're sure you'll be accepted). Generally, safety schools won't be your first choices, but you may need to rely on them if you don't get accepted at your reach and probable schools. Don't, however, apply to any school that you wouldn't attend happily.

How Do Business Schools Pick Students?

When business schools review applications, they do not follow a magical formula, where GMAT + GPA + Work Experience + Personal Statement = Admissions. Most schools are looking to enroll an ideal community of students who will work well together in the program and benefit from the program's goals, so not just the straight-A students with high GMAT scores will be offered admission. Globalization in the field of business itself means that programs are looking for a more diverse student body that includes older students, women, minorities, international students, and students from small schools, big schools, Ivy League schools, and so on. This might all sound a little nebulous, but admissions directors want to enroll students that will be a good fit with their program, and every program has a different definition of what that good fit will be, based on a mix of professional, academic, and personal interests. If you've done your homework and are applying to those programs that you've determined will fulfill your career and personal goals, you're off to the right start. In other words, don't be discouraged from applying to a program that you feel is perfect for you just because your GMAT score falls slightly below their stated requirement. If all the other elements of your application show that you will be a valuable member of their team, your chances for admission will be favorable. By the same token, if you're an older applicant (more than 32 years old), you may feel that your chances for admission are lower because you do not represent the "typical" graduate student. On the contrary, in business school, older students are seen as offering professional experience, maturity, and real-world perspective—all highly valued in the business world.

So remember this when you're applying: at most schools, no single factor will count more than any other. As the old saying goes, "The whole is greater than the sum of its parts," and that's especially true in business school applications. Your tests scores, GPA, work experience, essays, and recommendations put together create a complete picture of your interests, strengths, and accolades. Weaknesses are overshadowed easily by strengths in other areas, so be sure to show off those strengths.

The Elements of an Application

Form and Fee

Application forms can be downloaded from a school's Web site, obtained through the mail, or submitted online. When filling out your application, whatever form it takes, remember that accuracy and neatness count. If you must handwrite it (and you should try at all costs to avoid this), make sure that your handwriting is legible. If you type your application, check and double-check for typos, errors of alignment, and other potentially embarrassing gaffs. You don't want to start off on the wrong foot with the admissions committee. You may want to photocopy the blank form several times and fill out a few drafts before you complete the copy that you'll submit.

Before you send the application, make a copy for your own records. Remember the fee. Ridiculous as it seems, admissions committees regularly receive lovingly prepared applications—presented in beautiful folders or professionally bound—from well-meaning applicants who've forgotten to include the fee. No matter how well the rest of the application is prepared, this oversight simply doesn't look good.

Test Scores

Most business schools (but not all) require that prospective applicants submit scores from standardized tests, most often the GMAT, and the TOEFL, if you're an international student. When you take these tests, you'll be able to pick which schools you'd like your scores to be sent to; if you decide later on that you'd like your scores submitted to other schools, you'll need to make the proper arrangements to get them there.

Transcripts and Resume

You'll need to provide each program with a copy of your academic transcript from every school that you've attended. Don't forget to include transcripts from summer school programs, graduate work, or any classes you have taken since graduation. Allow at least a month to receive your transcript, and be ready to pay for each copy. Review your transcripts carefully to make sure that there are no mistakes, and remember to keep a copy for yourself.

Some programs will also ask you to include your resume or curriculum vitae (CV) as a summary of your work history. If you haven't updated your resume or CV lately, take the time to do so now. Include information about articles you have published or papers you have presented, volunteer work, and memberships and positions in professional societies. Have someone else review it for accuracy and spelling. Your resume or CV should highlight your accomplishments, responsibilities, and career progression, if applicable. If possible, show evidence of managerial and leadership skills while portraying yourself as a team player.

Letters of Recommendation

Most business programs will require you to submit two or three letters of recommendation from your present employer or professors. If you're not comfortable asking these people, you can submit recommendations from a co-worker, a former boss, or someone else who can vouch for the quality of your work. When requesting recommendations, be sure to provide the recommendation writers with a summary of your accomplishments—perhaps your resume or academic transcripts—as well as some details about which programs you're applying to and the criteria by which you'll be judged. Supply them with labeled envelopes so they can seal the recommendations upon completing them. Give your recommendation writers plenty of time to write recommendations, as much as two or three months. Check in with them a month before the recommendations are due, and collect the recommendations from them yourselves; don't make them go to the trouble of mailing them for you.

Essays

By and large, all business programs ask candidates to respond to essay questions. The number varies from program to program; some ask candidates to provide just one personal statement that discusses their past and their goals, while others require candidates to respond to as many as five or more essay questions on separate topics. In general, admissions committees are looking for you to show them why you want to be admitted to their particular program, review your personal background and goals for the future, describe your accomplishments (and failures) and how they shaped you, and discuss activities that you enjoy outside of work and school.

Obviously, with some of these elements, you won't be able to exercise much control. The information you include on the form is basic general information about you—your stats, so to speak. Your transcripts and test scores, too, are what they are. You can't go back and change the grades you got in college (wouldn't it be great if we could do that?) or the scores you got on the GMAT (although you can take the test a few times, chances are that you won't improve you score that significantly with each try). How, then, can you show the admissions committees who you really are—the brilliant person behind the so-so GPA from that little-known college in rural Any Town, USA? With your recommendations and your essays, that's how. You have total control over these elements. By choosing the perfect people to toot your horn and by doing some tooting of your own, you can turn an average application into an outstanding one and swing those admissions committees in your favor.

What Your Applications Should Show about You

Academic Profile

Business programs want to admit those who can survive the rigors of their program. For this reason, they look at your undergraduate GPA, which reflects classroom achievement, and your GMAT score, which is an indicator of your aptitude. However, having a high GPA and GMAT score don't necessarily guarantee admission, nor does a lower GPA or GMAT score take you out of the picture. When reviewing your transcript, admissions committees will look not only at your overall GPA but also at the progression of your grades and the kinds of courses you took as an undergraduate. Did you work hard to improve your grades after a slow start—or did you lose steam in your final years? Did you take advanced courses as electives—or did you take easy introductory courses to beef up your GPA? Admissions committees will take note of this. They will also look to see if you've had any notable academic achievements or won any awards as an undergraduate or in the workplace. If this is the case, be sure that it's reflected on your application—if not in your transcripts, then in your essay, letters of recommendation, or resume.

Your undergraduate degree will have little effect on your chances for admission to most business schools, so don't think that your B.A. in English literature will be a hindrance. Remember that most advanced business degree programs offer or even require a core curriculum of basic business courses as part of the degree. However, you should be able to show that you have general skills in economics, calculus, and statistics. If you didn't take these courses as an undergraduate, show on your application that you are planning to do so before being admitted to the program.

Personal Qualities

Admissions committees want to see that you are a clear-headed individual who has taken the time to think about your future and your goals. For that reason, make sure that your application is consistent throughout—in what you're trying to say about yourself and your plans for the future. You'll be judged less favorably if you don't show a clear purpose or if you jump from idea to idea.

Along those lines, your application is a direct reflection of your ability to communicate with others—think of it as a high-level sales pitch. Communication skills are essential for business leaders. Your application is your only chance to show admissions committees how well you can communicate; this makes the essays especially important.

Your application should show that you have the motivation and commitment to complete graduate work in business.

Business programs are also looking for leaders who are capable of working as part of a team, so you'll need to show on your application that you have the right combination of initiative, ability to follow instructions, and capacity to work well with others.

Work Experience

The large majority of business programs want to see that you have a few years of solid work experience. In business school, you'll be called upon to contribute to class discussions and projects in meaningful ways, and work experience will provide a context for your interpretation of what you'll learn in the classroom. When reviewing your application, business schools will want to see not only *where* you worked, but *what* you did while you were there. Did you move up? Did you take initiative? How did your contributions to the companies you worked for make you invaluable to them? Obviously, if you rose up over the years from the mail room to the board room, this will show admissions committees that you've got what it takes to succeed not only in business but also in their program—initiative, drive, energy, and dedication. Committees also want to know about your membership in professional organizations and your positions within these organizations and about research you've done in the field. All of this will paint a clear picture of you as a worker and, by extension, as a student.

Organization/Presentation

When you enter the world of business, you'll be called upon to present your ideas and the ideas of your company. How well you present yourself in your application will be an indication of how well you'll do at this task. Are you thorough? Did you supply the requested materials and the proper fee? Is everything spelled correctly? Check and double-check all the materials to make sure you haven't inadvertently sent the materials for another school. This is a huge mistake that will put a giant black mark on your application. Thoroughness and accuracy are key.

The Essays

We've included a special section on essays because business schools put a lot of stock in the quality of the essays that they receive from their applicants. Admissions committees count on essays to show them the *real you*, beyond the numbers and stats shown in the other elements of your application. In your essay, you show why you're serious about getting an advanced degree in business, exhibit what you can contribute to a particular program, and elaborate on what you've achieved on a personal, professional, and academic level. It's also the perfect opportunity to demonstrate that you are a clear thinker and that you can express yourself well. While essays are just a part of the overall admissions process, stellar essays can propel an otherwise average application into the "accept" pile, and poorly written essays may drop you to the bottom of the list.

Before You Begin

By now, you should have carefully thought about your motivations for wanting to go to business school and what you want to get out of it. Even before you begin to write your essays, you should have a clear understanding of where you've been and where you're going. And not just in your professional life, either. How have your experiences—all of them, personal and professional—shaped you into the person that you are? And how does that relate to the course of study and profession you are choosing to pursue? This is what the admissions committees want to know. So before you begin writing your essays, take stock of your background, your experiences, your abilities, and your goals. In each of these four areas, think about not just your professional experience but about your academic accomplishments and personal life as well. Keep in mind that doing a self-assessment helps you understand how your background led you to apply to business school—a must-have piece of information that will tell admissions committees why you want to and *should* attend their program. If you don't know how to begin, the following questions will get you thinking about where you've been and where you're going:

- What were my strongest subjects as an undergraduate? How did my academic experiences influence my choice of major and my decision to apply to business school?

- When did my interest in the profession that I hope to enter after leaving business school first develop?

- What do I want to be doing in five years?

- What are my favorite extracurricular activities? Why do these mean so much to me?

Essay-Writing Tips

GIVE YOURSELF PLENTY OF TIME
As soon as you receive each application, take note of the essay questions. How many are there? What questions are being asked? You want to be sure that you have plenty of time to thoughtfully answer each question before you return the application. The entire process of assessing the question, deciding on a structure for the essay and creating an outline, writing the first draft, and revising could literally take you months to accomplish. If you need to brush up on your writing skills, give yourself even more time.

DO YOUR RESEARCH
Before writing your essays, refresh your memory about the school and program. You don't want to regurgitate their pamphlet back to them, but you should show that you know your audience—in other words, what their program is all about. Don't go on about your dreams to pursue a career in the field of health-care management if the program doesn't offer course work in that area. This would make it look like you're applying to a completely different program! Look for key words in their literature that appeal to you. Do they stress teamwork, communication, or leadership? Why does this appeal to you, and what can you say about your history that would demonstrate this?

FOLLOW THE DIRECTIONS
Whatever you do, don't let your essays run longer than the requested length. Admissions committees want to see that you can respond to their questions in a concise way and that you follow instructions. In your essay, get to the point quickly and then state your message succinctly. If you follow these guidelines, you'll have no problem meeting word limitations. If there's anything else that you feel you must say, incorporate it into another question or save it for your interview.

Another sticking point with admissions committees: not answering the question that's been asked. Some applicants think that they can submit the same essay to several different programs, reasoning that the questions aren't all that different from program to program and that they can save themselves some time this way. Try to avoid this. If you look closely at the questions from program to program, you'll find that there are many subtle and not-so-subtle differences. Unless each program that you're applying to is asking the standard "Why do you want a business degree?" question (and the likelihood of this is fairly rare), your essays should be tailor-made for the program to which you're applying. Admissions directors are often well aware of the questions that other programs are asking, so they'll recognize it if you're answering a question that's not their own.

BE YOURSELF
When responding to questions, be sure to take a stand that means something to you personally. If you get bogged down in telling the committee what you think they want to hear and don't really believe in what you're saying, your essay will be less effective and will sound hollow. Across the board, admissions committees say that they "just know" when an applicant isn't being genuine. They've read enough essays to recognize those that do and don't ring true. Seek a personal connection to the question and go from there. Don't worry about what you *should* be saying. Remember, there's no right answer. Your essays should distinguish you from the crowd and show what's distinctive and important about you; only by answering the questions honestly can you do that.

DON'T MAKE EXCUSES
Your essays can be an ideal place to address shortcomings in the rest of your application, but be sure that you do it the right way. Make your explanations short and to the point, and avoid sounding like a victim. Whatever you do, don't say, for example, "My professors in undergraduate school didn't like me; that's why my grades were so low." Take responsibility for your failures, and show what you've learned from them. Don't overemphasize the negative; turn them into challenges that you've conquered and from which you've moved on.

REVISE
Revising and re-revising will take your essays to a new level. Once you've written your first draft, put it away for a while and return to it later. Does the essay say what you really wanted to say? Read it again for focus and purpose. Make sure that it answers the question clearly and concisely. Will an outside reader be able to get to your point quickly and be persuaded by your argument? After you've reviewed your essay at this level, look at every sentence carefully. Each paragraph should convey only one theme. If it doesn't, you're trying to fit too many thoughts into one paragraph. Each

sentence should follow smoothly from the one before it and should lead into the one following. Check to make sure that you've maintained a consistent voice throughout—you want to make sure it's you that's speaking, not the program's brochure or your undergraduate business professor. Make sure that your tone is appropriate for the circumstances. You want to sing your own praises without sounding boastful, and you don't want to be whiny. Finally, correct run-on sentences, grammatical errors, and passive constructions. Remember, how you tell your story is just as important as what the story says.

PROOFREAD, PROOFREAD, PROOFREAD!

We can't stress this enough—before you send out your application, you absolutely, positively must make sure that you haven't made any basic mistakes. A spelling error in the first line of an essay that describes how you're a perfectionist is self-sabotage, plain and simple. Of course, you have a spell-checker built into your word-processing software, but under no circumstance should you depend on it to catch all the errors you may have made. In this case, you must resort to the tried-and-true methods used in days of yore (i.e., the days before computers). Print out your essays and read them forward and backward; challenge yourself to look for mistakes—rest assured, you'll find them. Read your essays several times, taking time between each reading. Ask someone who's a whiz at grammar and spelling to review your essays.

USE OUTSIDE READERS

Family, friends, colleagues, and professors will be invaluable assets as you write your application essays. Show them your essays (as well as the questions being asked), and ask for their honest opinions about the clarity and construction of the work. If the people closest to you can't understand what you're saying, no admissions committee will be able to either. Ask friends and family whether the essays show the real you, not just somebody who's read up on the program. Colleagues and supervisors at work will be able to tell you if you've stressed the right points about the field you want to pursue. Some applicants go so far as to hire professionals to help them write their essays. In general, admissions directors do not think highly of this practice. Remember what we said before about consistency? An essay that doesn't jibe with the tone of the rest of your application is a dead give-away that you haven't written it yourself. Admissions committees are pros at picking out canned essays. Do the work yourself (with the help of those closest to you, not those who expect payment for the service), and your true voice will emerge. This is what admissions committees look for.

Answering Specific Types of Essay Questions

QUESTIONS ABOUT YOUR CAREER GOALS

Almost every business program will ask you to evaluate your career thus far and discuss your career goals for the future. You should have no problem discussing what's already happened in the past and how this has affected you, but how can you clearly state what you want from your future? Begin by basing your goals in the experiences that you've already had. This will give you a good jumping-off point. If you love what you do and

---

What the Admissions Committee Wants to Learn from Your Essays

Who are you? This is your chance to tell them all about yourself—about your interests, your past, and your goals. In your essays, you should fill in the blanks of your application to provide a full-color portrait of yourself.

What can you bring to the program? Tell the committee why you're a great candidate for their program. Highlight the qualities that you possess that will benefit the program as well as your fellow students. Show them that you will be able to contribute to the school in a meaningful way.

Why do you want an advanced degree in business from this program in particular? Discuss those elements of the school's program that are appealing to you and the ways that they complement your goals. Of the hundreds and hundreds of programs offered, theirs was one of the most attractive. Be sure to tell them why you are interested in their program above all the others.

How have your experiences shaped you? Your life thus far has led you up to this point, and you've made the decision to apply to business school based on a variety of experiences that you've had and lessons that you've learned along the way. Describe the impact of these experiences and lessons—what you've gained, how you've changed, and what you've resolved because of them.

Where have your abilities taken you thus far? Where will they take you in the future? The approach here is twofold: First, you want to discuss those distinctive characteristics of yours that have helped you overcome adversity and have brought you success. Second, you want to describe how these same characteristics will help you not only succeed in the program but also contribute to your chosen field in the future.

---

want to take it a step further, begin by stating something like, "I've been interested in pursuing investment banking ever since I began my career as an assistant to a junior broker on Wall Street upon graduating from college." Two excellent approaches to organizing an essay are: (1) Outline the points you want to cover, then expand them; or (2) Jot down ideas as they come to you, then move them around until you create a logical sequence. If you're not already in a business field but find that you're drawn to a certain aspect of business, you may want to describe how you came to this conclusion: "I knew after beginning my career as a computer programmer that it wasn't the job for me; it can be very solitary and isolating, and I enjoy working as part of a group. When I realized that my interest in technology could be parlayed into a career in information systems management, I knew that the next step would be to pursue a degree in business." The key here is to *personalize* your goals and make them more interesting to your readers. You may want to break down your goals into short-term and long-term goals to make them sound more thoughtful and realistic about where your degree will take you. Or you can identify certain areas of interest to you—strategy, marketing, or leadership—and how they could be translated into a future career.

QUESTIONS ABOUT THE SOCIAL YOU

Believe it or not, business school isn't just about learning the art of wheeling and dealing and then moving on to a high-paying job; it's also about spending time with people, about really getting to know your colleagues and professors, about creating a *community*. Business schools ask you to write essays about your extracurricular interests because they want to know whether you'll fit in and what you'll contribute to the community. Business school, and the world of business as a whole for that matter, is a very social experience. You'll probably be asked to work in teams for presentations and group projects. Will you be able to get along with others in the group? Are you a participator? An initiator? More importantly, you need to show that you're a well-rounded person who knows how to mediate that fine line between work and play. You have to show that you have a "big picture" approach to the world. In today's job market, businesspeople need to be flexible. Show the admissions committee that you can roll with the punches.

QUESTIONS ABOUT THE "REAL" YOU

Questions like these usually manifest themselves in the form of: "Here's your chance to tell us something about yourself that we haven't asked yet." Be creative; after all, the school is giving you free rein to tell them what you want. Use this opportunity to tell them something truly unique about you that no other candidate can bring to the table. Relate an experience that really shaped your development or talk about someone you admire and why. However, stay within the guidelines of common sense. Don't talk about politics; don't talk about religion. Don't express any wildly out-of-the-norm viewpoints. Use humor if you wish, but only if you're comfortable doing so and it's in good taste.

QUESTIONS ABOUT YOUR ETHICS

Reacting to business scandals such as Enron, many business school programs now ask applicants about ethics. Questions about your perspective on ethics (e.g., "Relate an ethical problem you have faced and how you handled it") are aimed at determining whether you are honorable, whether you know the difference between right and wrong, and whether you're going for a degree in business just to make a quick buck. In short, you must show that you abide by a certain value system, both in your career and in your personal life. This can be a very sensitive subject for many; after all, ethics can be relative to the situation at hand. If you're asked a question about ethics, state your beliefs firmly. Waffling could show a susceptibility toward weakness, which will make you a less attractive candidate.

Sample Business School Admissions Essays

On the following pages is a series of essays from a successful applicant to Columbia Business School in New York City. As

---

Sample Business School Essay Topics

Describe the progression of your career to date. Why are you seeking a business degree at this point?

What are your career goals? How will an advanced degree in business help you achieve these goals?

Why do you want to obtain your degree from our particular program?

How has your background, experiences, and education influenced the person you are today?

In reviewing the last five years, describe one or two accomplishments in which you demonstrated leadership.

Discuss a nonacademic personal failure. In what way were you disappointed in yourself? What did you learn from the experience?

Discuss your involvement in a community or extracurricular organization. Include an explanation of how you became involved in the organization and how you help(ed) the organization meet its goals.

---

you read these essays, think about the points we've raised. What makes this candidate's essays stand out? Note how this candidate successfully makes his real-life experiences—in his career, in his personal life, and in his academic life—relevant to his desire to attend business school.

Question #1 asked the candidate to describe his career goals, how an advanced business degree would help him achieve these goals, and his reasons for applying to Columbia Business School (limit 1000 words).

The business world is full of many interesting opportunities and a vast array of sectors in which one can specialize. This financial world has global implications that are constantly changing, and therefore may leave a business leader feeling lost without a formulated plan of action. One needs to develop definitive paths and goals in order to remain focused. As a working member of the New York City financial world for the last three years, I have established certain goals that I am currently striving for as I journey on in my continuing career at Ernst & Young.

One such goal is the ability to manage people effectively and efficiently. I believe that in any line of work, the key to a successful business is how well that business is managed from a personal development perspective. Employees of any company must be given pertinent direction, sound training, and proper feedback from their managers to be more productive in their defined job roles and responsibilities. In order to provide employees with this development, job experience supplemented with a further academic education is extremely important. I feel that an advanced business degree will help me to attain this vital mix and provide me with the essentials of being a successful manager in the various engagements I encounter throughout my career at Ernst & Young.

A second career goal is to further expand my horizons and take a look at the whole picture. When I first began working in the "real world" as an auditor for Ernst & Young, I was placed on the Morgan Stanley engagement, which was one of the largest and most complex financial service engagements in our office. I was given job responsibilities that focused on such a small part of the ultimate goal. I was not privy to many of the other components that allowed my team to meet the client's demands and expectations. This was due to the fact that I lacked any prior experience in the financial service industry and that I was new to the engagement. As I continued on the engagement for the next three years, I was given more responsibilities and began to see more of the big picture. I began to develop a greater interest in financial services and wanted to see more aspects of the business. Thus far, I have been given the opportunity to see a vast array of areas at Morgan Stanley and at my current client, Lehman Brothers. These areas include front office trading operations on the fixed income and financing desks, middle office functions in fixed income cash and derivative instruments, back office operations on various trading desks, and multiple SEC filings. As I continue along in my career endeavors at Ernst & Young, I want to learn more about the financial industry and be able to look at the business from a much broader realm rather than from the individual components for which I have been responsible. As I have much more to learn, I believe an advanced business degree will provide me with a window to see various new ideas and avenues from both a domestic as well as a global perspective. This will allow me to communicate more effectively to my clients and indicate to them specific inefficiencies in their business processes for which I may be able to provide recommendations and assistance in improving.

Another goal is to continue developing my own experience and knowledge with the help of others. While experience in the work place is extremely important in attaining this goal, I believe it can only be enhanced in an academic arena where professors and other students can share their own work experiences with each other. This would provide me with different perspectives in looking at my own experiences and current job responsibilities. Also, the ability to work with these people in an academic setting (e.g., through various class assignments that require group participation) would allow me to bounce my own ideas off others, while at the same time provide me with the opportunity to listen to what others have to say. The wealth of knowledge and personal resources available in the process of obtaining an advanced business degree is an endeavor I feel is too worthwhile to forgo.

The goals I have established above in furthering my career can be accomplished at most business schools. However, one of the distinguishing attributes of obtaining my advanced business degree at Columbia University is the New York element. As mentioned previously, for the last three years I have been working as an auditor for Ernst & Young in New York City, primarily on financial service companies, including Morgan Stanley Group and Lehman Brothers, both highly reputable and profitable companies centralized in New York.

The experience I have received from working on these engagements has made me realize the advantage of being in New York, as I truly believe I would not have obtained as unique an experience anywhere else. Columbia, itself a highly reputable and professional business school, has that same advantage, which would allow me to strengthen the New York business experience while at the same time bring people from many different business backgrounds to the New York arena. The contacts I would make at Columbia, from the versatile faculty to my educated peers, would help me develop into a more knowledgeable member of the domestic and global business communities.

Question #2 asked the applicant to describe an accomplishment in which he demonstrated leadership (limit 500 words).

When I was a senior in high school, I decided to try something unique. As a music aficionado for many years with piano lessons and countless 45s, I decided to try out for the spring musical *Grease*. I had never sung before, but decided to give it a try. Even though this was not Broadway, I was still in shock when I was given a part in the show and had to sing. The show went surprisingly well, and I decided that I wanted to continue my singing endeavors as a hobby when I went to college the following year.

I attended Boston College in the fall of the following year. I discovered a group called the Boston College Chorale, which was a highly talented choral group of approximately 150 men and women. The big attraction to the group was that it traveled abroad for a week in the spring to perform, which included Italy, where the group attended a papal audience to sing. I found this intriguing, and I decided to try out during my first semester. I was accepted into the group and met many diverse and interesting people during my first year.

In my second year, I became more and more involved with the group. An interesting facet of the group was that it was led by students. There were eight officers, comprised of college juniors and seniors, who had various group responsibilities. Toward the end of my second year in the group, the annual elections for new officers was held. Because of my increased interest in and commitment to the group, I decided to run and became one of four officers elected. The officer positions were two-year commitments, and each year the officers would vote on new titles for each officer.

At the end of my first year as an officer, the internal elections for the officer titles were held again. I was voted president of the group for my senior year. I knew this role would be quite challenging and time consuming, but I accepted it gladly and was ready to face the numerous responsibilities for the upcoming year.

I had to make various decisions for the group with the efforts of the other officers. I was ultimately responsible for ensuring that the concerts were planned and advertised in a timely manner, the university funding provided to our group was properly utilized, the annual trip abroad was in order from the accommodations to the performances, and the social events were organized. I felt the year went smoothly and that the group of officers worked well together. I was able to demonstrate my leadership role to the best of my abilities. Members of the group showed their appreciation to me and to the other officers at the end of the year. I had an overwhelming sense of accomplishment at the end of the year as I graduated from Boston College, ready to face further challenges that would require my leadership abilities.

Question #3 asked the applicant to discuss a nonacademic personal failure, describing how he was disappointed in himself and what he learned from the experience (limit 500 words).

About a year and a half ago, my then-fiancée and I were returning from my college roommate's wedding in Rhode Island. It had been a long day for us, and we were taking turns driving back to New Jersey. When we got to New York, I told my fiancée that I would drive the rest of the way home to give her a chance to rest.

As I began my part of the drive, I was attempting to make a left-hand turn to get back on the highway. I did not see the car coming from the opposite direction until I had already started to make the turn, and our car was struck on the passenger's side. The sound was chilling. My fiancée's window had completely shattered, and I noticed that there was blood on her forehead. She said she was alright, except that her lower body was in pain. Medical help seemed to come instantaneously. The paramedics slowly removed her from the vehicle, and she was sent to the nearest hospital.

The whole experience put me in shock. I had this horrid sense of guilt and failure. I felt I had let her down tremendously with my mistake. After the doctors examined her, the final diagnosis was that she needed a few stitches on her forehead and that she had fractured her pelvis, which would require several weeks of bed rest until it healed on its own. She was going to be fine, which relieved me. The feelings of remorse, however, were still overwhelming. I sat down by her side after the doctors had left for the night and looked into her eyes and told her that I was so sorry for doing this to her. She grabbed me and told me that there was no reason to apologize. This was an accident, and the experience made her realize that she could not wait to spend the rest of her life with someone who cared so much for her.

I was in disbelief. How could she stay so calm after all I had done to her? I did not understand why she was not more angry with me. Over the next few months the scenes from the accident would play over and over again in my head. "If only" would be said in my thoughts repeatedly. I was angry with myself, and I felt that I was incapable of protecting my future wife.

My fiancée recovered fully, and we continued with our wedding plans for the next summer. I began to realize that since the accident, our faith in one another strengthened. The bond between us dispelled any doubts in the trust we had for one another. My feelings of guilt began to dissipate. When I realized how much she trusted me after the accident, I knew that any feelings of failure I would have in the future would be comforted with this trust.

Question #4 asked the applicant to discuss his involvement in a community or extracurricular organization, including an expla-

nation of how he became involved in the organization and how he helped the organization meet its goals (limit 250 words).

I am currently involved in a community service organization sponsored by my company, Ernst & Young, called the "One-To-One Mentoring Program." I learned about the organization from other people at Ernst & Young involved in the program. The goal of the program is to develop a relationship between a member of the Ernst & Young community and a high school student from the Bronx.

These students do not have much direction, nor do they have an abundance of opportunities. Many of them come from single-family homes with very little money. The program is voluntary on their end as well as ours, which makes the relationship one of choice from the very beginning. As present members of the working community, we are to share our experiences with the students and try to motivate them to continue on in their education. In addition, we are to be a friend who will listen to any of their problems or concern.

My current mentee is a sophomore who is bright but lacks motivation. I try to stress to him the importance of doing other activities after school, where he can make new friends and strive for additional goals. I also explain to him how important it is to complete his education. I use my own experiences in high school to help make him realize the importance of achieving goals. His grades have begun to improve, and he has started to look for part-time employment after school. In this respect I believe I have helped in meeting certain goals of the organization as our mentor/mentee relationship continues to strengthen.

Interviews

Many schools require that you interview with admissions committees and faculty members before you are admitted to the program. If you're asked for an interview, you should be glad, since chances are that you've made it to the program's short list of candidates. Even if the program doesn't require it, going on an interview is another great way to take some initiative and swing the vote in your favor.

While interviewing, don't simply rehash your resume and transcripts. This is the perfect chance to tell the admissions committee something they *don't* know about you from your application. Before you go on the interview, think about the questions that you might be asked and how you'll answer them, especially the biggie: "Why do you want to go to school *here*?" Think about those things that you want the interviewer to remember about you. However, try not to prepare speeches, as this won't sound natural when you're sitting face-to-face with the interviewer. The interviewer wants to see that you'll fit into the program, so be yourself. You'll be more natural and appealing if you don't try to put on an act. However, even in a casual interview, certain things are *always* off limits: profanity, tasteless jokes, discussions of sex or your love life. And please don't talk about mom and dad—remember, you're in the adult world now.

Show the interviewer that you're well-versed about the program, and describe what you plan to contribute to it. Bring a copy of your resume or CV, your application (especially your essays), and any examples of your work that you feel are important. Don't ask about financial aid; the interview is not the time to discuss these details. Be proactive—before the interview, think of some questions that you'd like the interviewer to answer. Finally, dress professionally and be on time. The simplest rules are usually the most important. After you leave, be sure to write a thank-you note to the interviewer.

Deciding Which School Is Right for You

You've waged the battle, and the offers for admission are pouring in. Now it's time for you to decide which program you'll attend. With any number of attractive choices, you will face a daunting task. First, try to separate the hype from the reality. The programs that accept you will likely barrage you with phone calls, letters, and e-mails from admissions counselors, students, and faculty members. When they call, ask the questions that you've been dying to ask but could not in your interview. Now that they want you, the ball is in your court. Review the strategies that helped you pick schools. Of the schools for which you've been accepted, which meet the criteria you originally found most important? Have your criteria changed at all through the admissions process? Revisit each campus where you've been accepted, and really take a good look around. Attend special on-campus events that you've been invited to, and pick the brains of those in attendance. What do they like about the school? Do they think you'd be a good match there? Be sure to find out *all* the details about the costs of the program—and about any available sources of aid to help you pay for it—before you sign on the dotted line. Resist making a hasty decision; be sure that you've weighed all the facts before you make your final choice.

Fifteen Tough Interview Questions

1. Why an advanced business degree now?

2. Tell me why you think our program is the one that's right for you.

3. Describe some examples of how you've demonstrated leadership.

4. What are your career aspirations?

5. What do you do to relax?

6. Give three words that best describe you.

7. Why did you choose your undergraduate major? Do you regret it?

8. Describe instances where you've worked as a member of a team to get a job done.

9. What is your definition of success?

10. Describe someone who's been an inspiration to you.

11. Where do you see yourself five years from now? Ten years from now?

12. What do you find most frustrating about your present job?

13. Tell me about your biggest failure and how you rebounded from it.

14. What will you do if you're not accepted to this program?

15. So, tell me a little more about yourself. . . .

Paying for Your Advanced Business Degree

Now that you've made a commitment to getting your advanced business degree, the next question is likely to be: "How will I pay for it?"

The first thing you will have to decide is whether you will go to school as a full-time or part-time student. About two-thirds of business students work toward their degree as part-time students while they continue working full-time. Although it will take you longer to earn your degree this way, the costs are more manageable and the amount of money you'll need to borrow can be significantly reduced. Another consideration is whether you work for a company that offers full or partial tuition reimbursement to its employees. This benefit will greatly reduce your costs and help in career advancement in the organization.

Some graduate-level business programs are available only to full-time students. If you attend one of these schools, it will be not be feasible for you to work full-time. You will need to consider alternatives to finance your education expenses.

The good news is that whether you attend full-time or part-time, funding for your graduate business education is readily available. For most students, the primary source of funding is through the various student loan programs. Students in the more expensive programs can incur significant student loan debt. However, most students view these costs as an investment in their future earnings potential, and the research consistently supports this claim. According to a recent salary survey conducted by the National Association of Colleges and Employers, average starting salary offers for M.B.A.'s is 25 to 40 percent higher than for non-M.B.A. graduates. Besides the economic benefits, adults with advanced degrees are more fulfilled in their careers and often enjoy better quality of life.

Determining Your Costs

Now let's look at the cost of getting your advanced business degree. Your most important expense is tuition and fees. A survey conducted by the National Association of Student Financial Aid Administrators (NASFAA) using 2003–04 data, the most recent available, estimated that the average total cost of attendance for full-time graduate-level business students was about $22,015 at public institutions and $32,936 at private institutions. For part-time programs, the mean cost was $10,572 at public institutions and $15,587 at private institutions. Remember, these are averages, so check with the programs you are considering for more specific costs. It is safe to assume that these charges increase about 5 percent per year.

Most business school students pay more for books and supplies than they did as undergraduates. While the amount will differ at each school, you should expect to pay approximately $1,000 or more. Owning your own computer is now a must, and many business schools make computers available to their students at discounted rates, so be sure to check with the school before you purchase a computer.

There are other indirect costs you must consider when developing your expense budget. Whether you will commute, live in campus-provided housing, or live off campus will be a major consideration. Most business schools can tell you what the average cost of living will be in the area and may offer subsidized housing or provide a housing office to help you find a place to live. Other indirect costs include travel expenses, miscellaneous personal expenses, and expenses such as car loan payments and insurance, child care, summer tuition, and medical expenses. As a student, you will need to budget your expenses as carefully as you do your time. Living the life of a student can be quite different from having a regular paycheck.

Types of Financial Aid and Payment Plans

GIFT AID (money you do not have to pay back)
- Individual grants, scholarships, and fellowships (merit-based or need-based)
  Sources: business schools, foundations, private companies, community groups
- Tuition waivers awarded by individual business schools
- Company employee education benefits
- Federal grants (very limited and based on need)
- State grants (very limited)

SELF-HELP AID (money you must earn)
- Federal Work-Study Program (need-based and awarded by business school)
  Source: Federal government
- Teaching assistantships
  Source: business school
- Resident assistantships
  Source: business school
- Research assistantships
  Source: business school

LOANS
- Federal Perkins Loan (need-based, lender is business school)
- Subsidized Federal Stafford Student Loan (need-based, lender is a bank, savings & loan, etc.)
- Unsubsidized Federal Stafford Student Loan (non-need-based; lender is federal government)
- Federal Direct Loan (similar to Stafford Loans; lender is the federal government)
- Private loan programs (lenders are private companies or organizations)

PAYMENT PLANS
- Private and institutional tuition payment plans that spread the payments over ten to twelve months. There is usually an annual fee for these plans.

Financial Aid

Once you've calculated your total expenses for attending business school and have determined the personal resources you can make available from current income and savings, you will need to consider financing options.

Financial aid is significantly different at the graduate level than it is for undergraduates. Most importantly, all graduate students are considered independent for the purpose of federal financial aid. This means your parents are not required to assist you financially or complete the Free Application for Federal Student Aid (FAFSA). Also, grant and scholarship money is limited at M.B.A. schools. Information from the 2003–04 NASFAA study reports that 13 percent of full-time M.B.A. students received a fellowship, grant, and/or tuition waiver, while another 9 percent received assistantships. However, 31 percent of full-time and 45 percent of part-time students received assistance from their employers, far higher than any other graduate program. Looking at the 2003–04 graduating class, 56 percent of public and 62 percent of private school students reported having student loan debt, averaging $25,563 and $38,499 respectively. Even students who have substantial savings often choose to use student loans and preserve some of their savings.

Many business schools offer fellowships, scholarships, and teaching and research assistantships to their students. Some of these positions and awards are based on your previous academic and employment record (merit-based) and some based on need. You should contact the admissions office or the dean's office to determine if these programs are available and how you can apply.

Applying for Financial Aid

To qualify for federal aid, every student is required to complete the FAFSA, either in paper or electronic form. The paper form is available in both business school and undergraduate school financial aid offices. You are strongly encouraged to file using FAFSA on the Web at www.fafsa.ed.gov. You will need your federal PIN number, easily accessible from this site.

Soon after January 1, before the period you plan to enroll, you should complete the FAFSA, which asks about your prior (or base-year) income and assets. Be sure to check with the school for their specific filing deadline dates.

Some business schools require that you complete an additional application called the Financial Aid PROFILE® form from the College Board. If your school requires this additional form, you need to complete this in October or November prior to your enrollment. The PROFILE® application is available from the financial aid office and is also available online at www.collegeboard.com. You can also call 305-829-9793 and register your information, including the business schools to which you are applying. You must pay an initial registration fee of $5 plus $18 for each school listed. A few weeks later you will receive your customized PROFILE® application containing all the questions you are required to answer.

To determine if your school requires the PROFILE®, check the PROFILE® registration packet for the list of schools that require this supplemental form. Remember, you still must file the FAFSA.

A number of business schools may have their own aid application or may use another data collection form called Need Access. This information will be noted in the brochures they send to you, so be sure to check the literature. Make certain you know the specific deadlines when applying for financial aid. Applying after a deadline can hurt your chances of qualifying for aid.

Once you have submitted the proper application, the business schools you have designated will receive information showing the amount you are expected to contribute to your education, a calculation based on your income and assets. This is called the Expected Family Contribution (EFC). The EFC from the federal form is the official amount that determines whether you will qualify for certain types of federal aid. If this amount is less than the total cost of attendance, you have demonstrated need and will qualify for aid—usually low-cost, government-subsidized loans. The PROFILE® calculation will give the school an expected contribution based on the additional criteria you provided. This contribution will be used by schools to award their own institutional funds.

Even if your family contribution is higher than the cost of attendance, you may still qualify for assistance. The EFC is based on your previous year's income, which will likely change significantly if you attend school on a full-time basis. You can

---

Table 1: Estimated Loan Repayment Schedule
Monthly Payments for Every $1000 Borrowed

Rate	5 years	10 years	15 years	20 years	25 years
5%	$18.87	$10.61	$ 7.91	$ 6.60	$ 5.85
8%	20.28	12.13	9.56	8.36	7.72
9%	20.76	12.67	10.14	9.00	8.39
10%	21.74	13.77	10.75	9.65	9.09
12%	22.24	14.35	12.00	11.01	10.53
14%	23.27	15.53	13.32	12.44	12.04

To estimate your monthly payment, choose the closest interest rate and multiply the amount of the payment listed by the total amount of your loan and then divide by 1,000. For example, for a total loan of $15,000 at 9% to be paid back over 10 years, multiply $12.67 by 15,000 (190,050) divided by 1,000. This yields $190.05 per month.

appeal to the financial aid office and ask them to recalculate your need based on the amount you will have available when you go to school, rather than on your previous year's income. Also, there are governmental, institutional, and private loans available to students regardless of whether they demonstrate need (such as the Federal Unsubsidized Stafford Loan, state loans and other private loans). The financial aid office is your best source of information for guiding you through this process and providing advice on these alternative loan programs.

Your Credit History

Since most business students have to borrow to pay for their education, making sure you qualify for a loan is critical. This means that your credit record must be free of default or serious delinquency. You are strongly encouraged to check your credit history with one or more of the following credit bureaus and clear up any adverse credit problems that might appear. All credit reporting agencies are required to provide this information at no charge to you at least once a year, and the information is available on the Internet.

Equifax Credit Information Services, Inc.
P.O. Box 740241
Atlanta, GA 30374
800-685-1111 (toll-free)
Web site: http://www.equifax.com

TransUnion
P.O. Box 105281
Atlanta, GA 30348-5281
877-322-8228 (toll-free)
Web site: http://www.transunion.com

Experian
475 Anton Blvd.
Costa Mesa, CA 92626
866-200-6020 (toll-free)
Web site: http://www.experian.com

Debt Management

Although the maximum limits on borrowing from federal programs are high, you will want to make sure you are not borrowing more than you will later be able to repay. Refer to Table 1 to estimate your school loan monthly payments. After having estimated your income and the total amount you'll need to borrow for your education, you can use Table 2 to determine whether your loan payments are affordable.

International Students

Costs of U.S. business schools for international students are usually the same as U.S. citizens at private institutions. However, international students are required to pay the out-of-state tuition rate at most public institutions. A Certificate of Eligibility for a student visa will serve as proof of sufficient funds. International students should make sure they have obtained the necessary funds from their own resources, including their home government. There may be institutional aid available for international students. Students should contact the financial aid office for possible funding sources. International students are not eligible for federal loans. International students usually need a U.S. co-signer for private (alternative) loans. The financial aid office can guide you through the process of finding lenders that offer loans to international students.

Additional Information

For more information about financing your business education, check with the personnel office at the company where you work and the financial aid office at the business school you plan to attend. You can find additional financial aid resources at www.petersons.com/finaid. Many financial aid offices have a preferred lender list to assist you with securing federal and private loans. However, students are free to borrow from any lender whom they feel offers the best terms and conditions. You are not required to borrow from any specific lender.

Table 2: Debt Management Guide

Total Outstanding Loan	Years in Repayment	Monthly Payment	Suggested Minimum Monthly Income
$10,000	10	$126	$ 840
20,000	10	253	1,687
30,000	10	380	2,533
40,000	10	506	3,373
50,000	10	633	4,220
20,000	20	179	1,193
30,000	20	270	1,800
40,000	20	360	2,400
50,000	20	450	3,000

Going Abroad

Richard Edelstein

Students are increasingly going abroad to obtain their graduate-level business education. Why? Individuals seeking a management career must prepare themselves to function in international contexts on a global scale. Studying abroad is one of the most effective ways of obtaining knowledge and developing skills that respond to these new demands. In large measure, this reflects the changing nature of business, where the globalization of markets and companies is forcing a rethinking of the types of education and experience necessary to pursue a successful career as a manager.

Technical skills remain critical, but international mobility, cross-cultural skills, and foreign language proficiency are increasingly appreciated by companies. Choosing to pursue your M.B.A. education abroad is an excellent way to acquire knowledge and skills that are necessary for the global economy.

This trend of attaching increased value to international experience is most noteworthy in transnational companies that have operations and management responsibility distributed in numerous countries.

An indication of increased demand for managers with specialized international experience and skills is the growth in importance of the so-called "transitional economies" like Brazil, China, India, Indonesia, Mexico, and South Africa. Many firms want to develop joint ventures or start-up operations in these countries but are constrained by a lack of personnel who can effectively manage in such diverse cultural and linguistic contexts. Demand is high for M.B.A.s who have experience operating overseas and possess a willingness to master foreign language skills.

One of the keys to a career as a successful manager is the capacity to develop networks of individuals whom you can work with and learn from. These professional networks may be within your present employer, with colleagues in other firms and, increasingly, in other nations. By choosing to pursue an advanced business degree abroad, you should recognize that you will build different professional networks than you would in the United States. Alumni associations that are a fixture in American universities and business schools tend to be somewhat underdeveloped in other countries.

International Recognition of the Advanced Business Degree

Many countries have significantly different educational and career paths for their managers. This is important to consider if you have particular aspirations to work in countries where an advanced business degree may not have the same recognition that it does in the United States. It is also useful information for anyone who plans to work in a multinational enterprise where professional colleagues may come from any country. For example, the most common educational qualification for future managers in Middle Eastern countries is an engineering degree. Another educational qualification for a business career quite common in other nations is a law degree.

Despite these caveats, the graduate-level business degree is becoming recognized internationally as the lingua franca of the business community. In places as diverse as Turkey and South Africa, the graduate-level business degree is highly regarded, especially for senior-level managers. In the United States, the largest growth segment in graduate-level business programs is international students. According to data collected by the Association to Advance Collegiate Schools of Business (AACSB International) from its 480 member schools, 32 percent of full-time M.B.A. enrollments and 6 percent of part-time M.B.A. enrollments are international students.

The advanced business degree is no longer a North American phenomenon. To demonstrate how widespread M.B.A. programs have become in recent years, the AACSB International list accredited programs in twenty-eight countries, including Argentina, China, Egypt, Ireland, Japan, Kuwait, Mexico, New Zealand, Singapore, Spain, Taiwan, and Turkey. In the People's Republic of China alone, there are now more than ninety. The ever-increasing number of graduate-level business programs in other countries further attests to the degree's growing stature throughout the world as a primary qualification for future managers.

Markets, Hierarchies, and Prestige

Not all advanced business degrees are created equal. Individuals must make compromises between where they would like to pursue their degree and where they have a serious chance of being accepted. This is true whether you are applying to institutions in your home country or abroad.

Prestige alone does not assure you of an education that is best suited to your individual needs. Students applying to American schools from abroad frequently assume that the only schools worth attending are the most elite schools with international reputations. In fact, the number of schools offering high-quality graduate-level business programs ranges far beyond the top twenty institutions that make it on the *BusinessWeek* survey. Reputation and prestige are important factors to consider when planning your graduate-level business education, but the best schools for you are those that meet your abilities and your professional goals.

Making the Decision to Study Abroad

Why go abroad for your advanced business degree when you can just as easily enter an American program that has an international dimension built into the program? The answer for many people is that they want and need a more intensive experience abroad that allows them to acquire foreign language and cultural skills and to build professional networks that cannot be obtained through an American program. Traveling and becoming a "citizen of the world" are also appealing reasons for some students. Before you decide to pursue your advanced business degree in another country, however, it is important to consider a few key points.

Personal Goals

Personal attributes will define whether or not studying abroad for an advanced business degree is the right choice for you. Have you already had extensive experiences abroad? If so, maybe you think that doing your graduate business studies abroad will add little value. But what about building on the skills you acquired in your previous experience, developing higher levels of language competence, and honing your knowledge in the country or region where you would like to study?

Studying abroad is clearly a more intensive international experience than anything you could pursue in the United States. In the end, it is this intensity that distinguishes getting the M.B.A. abroad from getting it at home. If you are doubtful about the need for this intensity of international experience, then you may want to consider staying in the United States and entering a program that includes an international emphasis.

Foreign Language Ability

A distinction should be made between international graduate-level business programs taught in English and national graduate-level business programs taught in the local language. Each has its market niche and serves different needs. The United Kingdom, Australia, New Zealand, Hong Kong, and Singapore have M.B.A. programs in English, although many of them are oriented toward a national employment market.

Although foreign language proficiency can be a defining criterion in deciding whether to study abroad, English is becoming the universal language for business. Schools outside the United States are being challenged to offer advanced business programs in English. Many European English-language advanced business programs are actually targeted to foreign nationals and include few students from the home country.

Be aware, however, that in international schools offering both English-language and local-language advanced business programs, the "flagship" management studies program may be the one taught in the local language. The latter program will limit admission, of course, to students who can demonstrate language proficiency. SDA Bocconi in Italy, for example, created an English-language international M.B.A. that responds to the needs of students who seek to develop an international career. However, the traditional Bocconi degree program is taught in Italian. It is more prestigious and has an international reputation for training managers, especially for the Italian market. In considering which program to apply to, an American needs to consider both foreign language proficiency and personal needs and goals.

Structure

With the globalization of business, M.B.A.s not only in the United States but also in other countries need to operate in many different environments. For instance, students in the one-year, full-time trinational European M.B.A. program have sequential study periods at the Bristol Business School at the University of West England in the United Kingdom, the Institut Commercial de Nancy at the Université Nancy 2 in France, and the University of Applied Sciences in Nürnberg, Germany. Another similar program, the European M.B.A., combines online learning with face-to-face residential weeks in six European countries. That consortium includes the Universiteit Maastricht Business School, Open University of the Netherlands, IAE Aix-en-Provence, AUDENCIA Nantes Ecole de Management, EADA Barcelona, and three associate partners: University College Dublin and Leon Kozminski Academy of Entrepreneurship and Management EQUIS, Akademie für Weiterbildung e.V., and EuroStudyCentre North-West Germany.

This is only one example where advanced business students coming from the United States should be aware that international programs may be structured differently. In the United Kingdom, for example, M.B.A. programs are typically only one-year long.

Whatever the length of the program, it may have somewhat different course requirements and curricula. Frequently, teaching approaches are also different. Sometimes they are closely tied to the patterns of university education in the host country. Increasing attention is being paid to teaching skills related to teamwork and working in cross-national groups.

Another point to consider is the tendency of off-shore advanced business programs to be less tied to the research faculty, which means that international institutions may not publish as frequently as their United States counterparts. If it is important for you to be enrolled at an institution that actively adds to the body of knowledge of business education, you may want to look closer to home.

Cost of Programs Abroad

The cost of advanced business programs outside the United States is generally quite competitive, even when you consider the added cost of airfare. Tuition costs for graduate education in the United States, especially at elite private universities, are among the highest in the world. All in all, you may find the cost of an advanced business program abroad surprisingly reasonable by comparison. Keep in mind that there is significant variation among schools and that the U.S. dollar may be weak against an institution's local currency, which will drive up your tuition, room and board, and ancillary spending costs.

The American Advantage

In some cases, Americans have some advantages when it comes to applying to advanced business programs abroad. Since the M.B.A. is essentially an American invention, one of the most significant ways of gaining credibility for an advanced business program outside the United States is to begin attracting American students who might otherwise attend an American institution. All things being equal, Americans sometimes have an advantage in the selection process at some schools. This may not continue to be true for very long as more Americans begin enrolling in foreign programs. But for the time being, many M.B.A. programs abroad are interested in recruiting Americans.

Cultural Adjustment

Reactions to living in another culture vary considerably depending on the person and on the culture but, as noted earlier, acquiring the skill to work and learn in more than one culture is a primary reason for wanting to study abroad. Still, do not assume this is an easy adjustment. It takes a serious commitment to self-improvement and a willingness to be open to entirely new situations to succeed in cross-cultural settings.

Finding the Right Program

Where Do You Want to Work?

One obvious reason for choosing to study for an advanced business degree abroad is to increase your chances of obtaining employment outside the United States. Do some research about the schools you are considering. Learn about their status in the prestige hierarchy and the types of companies that are likely to employ their graduates. If you have your heart set on living and working in France or Indonesia, then it makes sense to seriously consider attending an institution in that country. This is especially true if you select a school and program linked to the national employment market. While global markets are certainly a long-term trend, national employment markets are still the norm for most firms, and doing your studies in a particular country will generally enhance your chances of obtaining employment in that country.

This is accomplished in two ways. First, your degree and school/university will be more easily recognized and probably held in high standing in that national employment market. Second, the school may have placement services, alumni relations, and other ways of connecting graduates with the labor market for management positions. Even if you elect to work for a transnational firm, there are significant benefits to being able to access this national network of business professionals.

Which Country?

Graduate-level business degrees have become prevalent in most European countries. France has some of the top M.B.A. schools, such as INSEAD with campuses in France and Singapore and faculty members from thirty-one countries. Austria, Germany, and Switzerland offer about 120 institutions and 150 programs. In the United Kingdom, M.B.A. programs number more than 170—double the number ten years ago.

In Latin America (outside of Mexico), pure graduate-level business options are much more limited and often involve only one or two institutions in the country. Still, Latin American countries have created a number of good business schools that offer graduate-level business programs boasting international standing. Fundação Getulio Vargas in São Paulo, ESAN in Peru, IESE in Venezuela, and INCAE in Costa Rica are

examples of institutions that offer programs that may interest prospective American students. The options become numerous if one includes university-based programs in business and economics.

In Asia and the Pacific Rim, options are opening up but still remain somewhat limited. This is partly because of distinctly different educational systems that reflect different recruitment practices for managers. For example, Japan is well known for a manager recruitment structure that relies on in-company training rather than a professional university education. This pattern can also be found in other Asian countries, though to a somewhat lesser degree. In Japan, the language barrier can be significant, because very few Japanese universities have programs in English. Combined with the cultural tendency toward in-company education, Japan becomes especially difficult for foreigners to penetrate. One noteworthy exception is the IUJ, the International University of Japan, which does offer an M.B.A. program in English.

Hong Kong, Australia, and New Zealand have M.B.A. programs that are open to Americans and are taught in English. Most are university-based business schools that follow either the American or British models of university education. The Hong Kong programs tend to be focused on special needs of Hong Kong and China. The Australian programs are frequently oriented toward doing business in Asia, especially Southeast Asia. Schools in the Philippines, Indonesia, Malaysia, Singapore, and Thailand may also be of interest to those interested in working in one of these developing dynamic economies in the midst of transition and rapid growth. The English-based M.B.A. courses are very limited, however, and careful research needs to be done to ensure that the program is up to international standards.

Foreign language requirements can be significant, even at schools that teach in English. Since the study of foreign languages is more commonplace outside the United States, you should be prepared to study a foreign language even if you are entering an English language–based program. Be sure to learn about foreign language requirements before entering a program, as this may be an important consideration in preparing for your experience.

Evaluating Quality

When evaluating the quality of a school, you need to dig deeper than the promotional material typically sent to prospective students. Are the school and degree accredited by the Ministry of Education in the country where the degree is offered? Too often the school may be licensed by the department of commerce or industry as a business, but its degrees are not recognized by the country's university-level education authority, usually the Ministry of Education. If a program is not recognized as academically legitimate in the country where it operates, it is doubtful that its graduates have credibility in the international employment market. The embassy or consulate of the country in which an institution is located can also provide useful information.

Keep in mind when you are evaluating international institutions that there are no regulations on what constitutes an M.B.A. program. It is a good idea to check on an institution's standing with an accrediting organization. Two of the most prominent are AACSB International and the European Foundation for Management Development. The organizations accredit both institutions and M.B.A. programs, evaluating such components as curriculum standards, faculty qualifications, student support and retention, resources, improvement objectives, and other defined criteria.

Aside from looking into a program's accreditation, a close, commonsense look at the program is important. Are faculty members qualified to teach at the advanced level of a graduate-level business program by virtue of their education and experience? How many are full-time permanent faculty? How many are part-time or "contact only" faculty? How many faculty members hold a doctoral degree in the field in which they teach? Be cautious of schools that claim to prefer only part-time instructors. This can be a ploy to avoid paying qualified full-time people who demand higher salary levels. Have faculty members done any research or published any articles? Do they have corporate or professional experience related to the course work?

It is always useful to speak with graduates of the school prior to making a commitment to enroll to hear what they have to say about its advanced business program? Schools will usually provide you with the names of several graduates whom you can contact about their business educational experience. Ask how courses were structured, what the atmosphere in the classroom was, how your interviewee would rate the faculty, and what kind of placement services the institution provided. If it is possible to visit the school and meet with current students, this is even better.

Financing Your International Advanced Business Degree

Tuition costs abroad are rarely more than those found among leading graduate-level business programs in the United States. That is not saying much, however, since the average cost in the United States for a degree from an accredited, full-time M.B.A. program is about $33,774. Still, you are likely to find that graduate-level business programs abroad compare favorably in most cost/benefit analyses. This is especially true for some of the lesser-known programs that may be outside major capital cities, as well as for those programs that are less than two years long. European M.B.A. programs last only fourteen to sixteen months and high-end tuition is about $58,000 for the entire program.

Where you may run into problems is in obtaining federally subsidized loans such as those that are commonly available through many American university financial aid offices. Most of these loans have eligibility restrictions on the status of institutions and programs you may attend. Although some loan programs are more flexible than others in allowing foreign study, you should check with your bank or lender regarding regulations.

Some institutions have their own loan programs and scholarships to defray the cost of tuition. Less common are work opportunities, because graduate-level business programs generally require a full-time commitment. Still, it is worth asking the school about the potential for working on campus or assisting in research or consulting activity.

Other major costs to consider are round-trip air travel and the costs of living abroad. In some countries, especially in Europe and Asia, the cost of housing and food could be significantly higher than in the United States, depending on the specific location.

Studying and Living Abroad

Living abroad requires adaptability, an adventurous spirit, and a willingness to adjust to another culture. You will acquire a set of skills and experiences that will contribute to your preparation as a manager and give you a deeper understanding of your strengths, weaknesses, and values, even if you already have some cross-cultural experience.

Knowing something about the history, geography, politics, and culture of the country where you study is critical to adapting to your new environment, so do plenty of reading before your departure. You might also explore the Internet for chat groups that share information on studying and working abroad.

You should also consider joining local organizations such as churches, university clubs, and alumni groups in that country to replace American colleagues as your support system while living abroad.

Cross-cultural experiences can sometimes be challenging, but they always present opportunities. The important thing to remember is that you will not only need energy and effort to adapt to the rigors of pursuing an advanced business degree, but you will also be coping with the acculturation required of a foreign visitor. But this is precisely the reason for pursuing an advanced business degree abroad in the first place.

International Programs at U.S. Schools

If you still have doubts as to whether studying for an advanced business degree abroad is right for you, consider attending one of the many graduate-level business programs in the United States that incorporate some international experience into the curriculum. While this option cannot compare to living abroad, it may be preferable depending upon your needs and goals.

This guide includes information on a range of graduate-level business programs that have international dimensions built into their programs.

An increasing number of M.B.A. programs include an international track or international fellows program that require an internship abroad and offer foreign language courses, in addition to the requirements of the traditional M.B.A. program. The University of Chicago fits this description. The University of Washington offers a one-year Global M.B.A. Program that requires undergraduate business courses, international work experience, and favors advanced foreign language competence. The University of Southern California has a strong international focus and requires a course that includes a trip abroad. It also offers students a considerable number of international exchange and internship opportunities. Language courses offered through the International Business Education and Research program provide opportunities for students to improve foreign language skills.

A few graduate-level business programs include joint-degree or double-degree options in conjunction with a business school in another country. The University of Texas at Austin has several double-degree programs that allow a student to pursue a Texas M.B.A. and, with a year abroad, also acquire a Spanish, German, Peruvian, Brazilian, Chilean, or Mexican degree at the same time. NYU's Stern School has one of the most extensive exchange programs with foreign business schools of any U.S. university. Also available are joint-degree programs that combine an M.B.A. with a master's or doctoral degree in an area specialty such as Asian studies or Eastern European studies. The University of Pittsburgh and the University of Michigan are among the business schools that offer this type of option.

Many other graduate-level business programs include international exchange, internships, and group projects outside the United States as a major component of their programs. The University of Pennsylvania's Wharton School offers a traditional student exchange program in partnership with multiple international schools. Wharton also offers a Global Immersion Program, enabling students to engage in study projects that focus on one of three regions of the world. In addition, the business school sponsors the Global Consulting Practicum through which students take on consulting assignments to help business processes at institutions in other countries. Students can also participate in the Wharton International Volunteer Project, spending two weeks of their summer vacation consulting to businesses in other parts of the world. This is only one example of the many graduate-level business programs in the United States that have "gone global."

Does the trend in American graduate-level business programs to integrate an international component make the case for going abroad for the advanced business degree any less compelling? Probably not. An advanced business program in the United States can never match the intense learning experience of spending a year or two in another country studying business. Moreover, the personal and professional contacts you make while abroad enable you to create an international network that cannot be easily duplicated by studying in most American graduate-level business programs. In the end, you need to weigh the benefits of gaining an in-depth international experience along with other factors, such as the quality and prestige of the institutions you are considering.

Returning to School

Barbara B. Reinhold, Ed.D.
Former Director, Career Development and Executive Education for Women
Smith College

Some decisions can be made and implemented quickly—you can often choose a new car, a new place to live, or even a new relationship rather impetuously and have it work out just fine. For the returning student, however, the process of deciding on and applying to school, and then earning an advanced business degree is seldom simple. It has to be done with a great deal of forethought.

The good news about being a mature student is that you'll probably get much more out of it, because there is more of you to take to the classroom—more experience, better judgment, clearer goals, and a greater appreciation for learning. The bad news is that your life will be more "squeezed" than it would have been before you took on all of life's responsibilities, particularly balancing work and family. In general, however, later is often better than sooner when it comes to getting a graduate-level business degree.

For mature women and men alike, there are many things to consider before upending your life to pursue an advanced business degree. First, be sure you really need one. It is silly to waste your time and resources being "retooled" in a graduate-level business program if your career goals could be accomplished just as easily by taking targeted courses, getting more training and supervision through your employer, or using your connections to enter a different field or organization and move up. If you are trying to determine whether an advanced business degree is really the key to where you want to go, find ways to network with people whose lives and career goals are similar to yours. You might discover that a variety of routes could lead you to your desired goal.

It's essential that you make your own decision about whether and where to apply, using a blend of logic and intuition. Though an advanced business degree requires strong quantitative skills, you'll also need good organizational, decision-making, and communication skills. For returning students, success in an advanced business degree program is often due more to life and work experience than technical knowledge alone. You have more information, more common sense, and more self-awareness at your disposal than you did as an undergraduate student. Use these assets along with your intuition in deciding whether this is really the right step for you.

It's also important to be an informed and demanding customer at the front end of the process. Be sure to ask hard questions about how well a school is prepared to respond to the particular concerns you might have, such as cultural openness, support for students who are also parents, and flexibility and accommodations of various types. The ball will be in their court later; in the first half of the game, however, be aggressive

Ten Tips for Returning Students

DECIDING

1. Be sure an advanced business degree is the best route to where you're going—don't embark on a trip until your destination is clear.

2. Make your own decision, using a blend of logic and intuition.

3. Be a discerning customer; ask hard questions about which programs best meet your specific needs.

ARRIVING

4. Learn to market yourself; don't launch the campaign until you're ready.

5. Be sure your support system is in order—at home and at work.

6. Review your skills—technical, quantitative, written, and oral. If you're not really ready, take an extra year to polish those skills.

7. Measure your confidence level—if it's low, consider counseling to learn how to manage your anxieties and self- doubts.

8. Get your life in shape before you begin—paying attention to nutrition, exercise, relationships, and all the other things you'll need to sustain you.

THRIVING

9. Ascertain your most effective learning style and design routines and study regimens that best fit that style.

10. Find a group of friends/colleagues right away; collaboration is the key to success and good health through one of the most demanding experiences you'll ever have.

about getting the information you need. For more mature students, the philosophy, resources, and services of the school can be much more important than ranking or reputation.

The application stage is also a great time to practice your marketing skills. This may be the first of many times when you'll have to convince someone of your worth. For returning students this is often frightening. Some have been out of the job market for awhile, while others either want to change careers or are feeling stuck at a career plateau. Any of these situations is likely to leave you feeling less than competitive. This is a good time to figure out what you really have to offer to a particular school and to adjust to the notion of lifelong self-advocacy.

As you begin the difficult task of self-assessment, be honest about your strengths and weaknesses. If your technical, quantitative, or communication competencies are not what they should be in order for you to begin course work in a confident frame of mind, spend a year or so getting up to speed in these areas. You'll be expected to be familiar with the basics of accounting. Much of your work may be online and you'll be required to use programs such as Excel, Access, and PowerPoint. So use the time after you have completed your applications to do some studying on your own and become confortable with these disciplines before you even enroll!

Once enrolled, you can do two things to make your life easier. First, take an honest look at your own learning style. Try to determine which methods work best for you; use methods that fit your personality—outlines, memorizing, listening to tapes, discussing concepts with other people, etc. Be proactive and establish a routine. As a returning student with many other responsibilities, you'll need to take a different approach to studying than you did in undergraduate school.

You'll also find that connecting with classmates is a critical part of doing well. You may be assigned to project teams, but it's a good idea to seek out your own support group as well. Join study groups and relevant student organizations, even though it may seem you can't spare the time. In business school, as in business itself, collaboration and networking are everything!

Becoming a student again is a great adventure—earning an advanced business degree will tax you, test you, stretch you, and reward you. But only you can know if it's right for you. When you applied to college as a high school student, you thought you had all the answers. What's different now is that, although you still don't have all the answers, you probably know much more than you think.

Advice from Admissions Directors

In this section, admissions directors from three schools give you their perspectives on the value of an advanced degree in business, what you should look for when choosing a business program, and what they look for when reviewing business school applications. To gather responses, we asked business school admissions officers around the world to respond to an e-mail questionnaire; those who responded are included here. Admissions officers responded to as many questions as they chose of those that were posed:

- When is the right time for prospective students to start thinking about business school? Upon graduating from college? After a few years in the job market? Why?

- What is the value of an advanced degree in business—in today's society and in the future?

- What are the most important factors that a prospective student should consider when researching business programs? Some of these could include future career plans; reputation of faculty and school; cost of program; geographic location; availability of part-time, full-time, and distance options; and so on.

- How heavily does your program weigh the following five admissions criteria? (1) undergraduate grades, (2) GMAT scores, (3) work experience, (4) letters of recommendation, and (5) essays. Why do you place the emphasis where you do?

- How many essays does your program require the student to write? What kinds of questions do you ask? In your opinion, what is the difference between a good essay and a bad one? What do you look for when you read admissions essays?

- What kind of work experience do you look for? Does it necessarily have to be in a business field?

- What advice would you give students about whom to ask to write letters of recommendation?

- When you look at transcripts, do undergraduate business majors have an advantage over those with majors in other fields? If someone's major wasn't in a business or related field (economics, for example), what would your advice be?

- How important is timing in the admissions process? In other words, do students who apply early have an advantage over those who just meet the deadlines?

- What words of wisdom do you have for students who are considering applying to business school? This can cover any topic that you wish.

Julie R. Barefoot
Assistant Dean of Admissions
Goizueta Business School
Emory University
Atlanta, GA
http://goizueta.emory.edu

It is ideal if candidates begin considering business school while they are still in college. By doing so, they can begin to prepare by taking courses, such as business statistics and/or calculus. This is beneficial because such courses help students to develop analytical skills—even if they aren't business, math, or science majors. Also, it is typically easier to take these classes while in college, when one's quantitative skills are still strong. Along those lines, I encourage college seniors to take the GMAT prior to graduation. The test is valid for five years, and most applicants apply to business school within this time frame. Again, this usually helps an applicant because most individuals do not use the math skills that they learned in college when they are on the job.

Since I have an M.B.A. myself (University of North Carolina, '83) and have worked in admissions at Goizueta since 1988, I obviously feel passionately about the long-term value of the M.B.A. degree. I could speak about this topic for hours, but in a nutshell, the beauty of the M.B.A. degree is that it teaches you the business analytical skills that you need to operate in today's global business environment. The M.B.A. degree gives candidates the tools needed to address business problems and also the confidence to take on challenges at work. Our M.B.A. program is particularly strong in exposing candidates to the international perspective so critical in making business decisions. Goizueta also immerses them in the technological aspects of business operations today, and our faculty members share with them what they can anticipate in the years ahead. The M.B.A. is an amazingly flexible degree because it gives its holders the ability to transition between positions and industries. Just this week, I've received e-mails from two different M.B.A. alumni who previously were working in brand management roles in the consumer product industry; now they're both moving to e-business firms to work on corporate marketing strategies!

In judging prospective students' applications, the most important factor we look for is the quality of their work experience. Because our program is highly interactive, we expect that students will learn as much from classroom discussions and group work as they will from faculty lectures. Clearly, the only way that this will happen is if each applicant brings something to the table in terms of enriching our program's classroom experience. A close second in terms of our review process is our assessment of the applicant's ability to perform well academically in our program. Our program is rigorous and requires not only strong quantitative skills (as demonstrated in the GMAT quantitative score and in grades received on any quantitative course work, such as statistics or calculus) but also the ability to effectively juggle multiple courses and group projects. Candidates' undergraduate transcripts give us a track record of how they perform in an academic setting as well as a sense of their preparation for analytical work and of their leadership experiences; we very much like to see evidence of extracurricular activity and personal initiative in college and afterward.

You may rightly ask where the essays, interview, and letters of recommendation fit into this process. These components are also key pieces of the puzzle. Essays give us more information about the applicant's work responsibilities as well as a sense of what they might contribute to class discussions. Letters of recommendation give us firsthand insight into how the candidate is regarded either in a work or a social setting—again, critical information for the admissions committee to consider. Our program strongly recommends a personal interview so that we can gain a much clearer picture of the applicant's interpersonal skills and the quality of his or her work experience by asking more in-depth questions about career progression and challenges. All of this data is reviewed so that we can make the best decision possible for the applicant and Goizueta.

At a minimum, an applicant's essays should answer the question posed on the application. Goizueta asks four questions. The first relates to the applicant's most significant experience. For this question, we expect the applicant to discuss a work-related example; it is not viewed favorably if the applicant discusses something that happened in college, unless it was extraordinary (a fraternity presidency or the like, for example, is *not* considered extraordinary). The second question asks the applicant to discuss his or her post-M.B.A. plans and the remaining two essays are one-page sentence completions such as: "My family is unique because . . ." or "The greatest lesson I have learned is . . ." In addition to answering the questions, the essays should be well-written and well-organized and should have a strong and/or thoughtful conclusion. In the essays, we look for a deeper sense of the applicant's personality, and we like to see some "spark"—a sense of humor and some insightful comments about what applicants have learned on the job, in their family life, or through their collegiate studies, for example. Goizueta students are known for wanting to "make a difference," and we look for evidence of that in the applicant's prior life experiences.

We have a very diverse class in terms of the work experience they bring—when we evaluate an applicant's work experience, we're not looking for a specific type of job, but we do look for the following: evidence of career progression (in other words, is this person valued at their company, and has he or she been given more responsibility since beginning employment?) and evidence that the job was responsible and in some sense required the use of good organizational or strategic thinking skills. Clearly, if the job required strong analytical skills, that is a plus. Applicants should know that a great deal depends on how they explain their work experience in their essays and personal interview and how their letters of recommendation (if they are work-related) confirm the quality

of their work. At Goizueta, we have candidates with engineering backgrounds, candidates who are CPAs, candidates who have worked for the Peace Corps, candidates who are AIDS researchers, candidates who are pharmaceutical sales reps, and candidates who are financial analysts—we value many, many types of work experience.

Applicants whose undergraduate background is not in business are not at a disadvantage in the admissions process. I say that with the following caveat: liberal arts majors who did not take quantitative course work must fully demonstrate (through the GMAT quantitative score or a statistics course grade) that they can handle the rigor of the analytical courses that they'll take in business school. Obviously, when we review the transcript of a business major, they will have a number of quantitative classes that we can review (in addition to the GMAT) when making this assessment.

The timing of an application is not critically important at Goizueta, meaning that we try very hard to be consistent throughout the selection process. Having said that, if applicants want to be reviewed for the merit-based scholarships that we offer, they must apply by our scholarship deadline (February 15) or risk seriously damaging their opportunity for a full review for these awards.

My words of wisdom? Seriously consider the programs to which you apply; remember, you will be working intimately with these classmates for the duration of your program of study, and they will become your network for your business career. I urge candidates to look beyond rankings numbers and to visit the program and experience the learning and living environment being offered.

Dr. Daniel M. Gropper
Associate Dean for M.B.A. Programs, Associate
    Professor of Business Economics Programs
Auburn University College of Business
Auburn, Alabama
http://www.mba.business.auburn.edu

While some people could reasonably consider an M.B.A. coming straight from an undergraduate program (particularly if they are in a technical undergraduate program), most people will get the greatest gain after a couple of years of full-time work. It helps to have a good focus on what you want the program to do for you, although you should be open to changes of plans while you are in school. Also, the focus and maturity provided by a couple of years in the work force are needed by most people.

With an advanced degree in business, you get a broad perspective on managing people and organizations. You are challenged to think innovatively and to consider points of view that will be new to you. An M.B.A. also typically enhances one's professional opportunities. The "return on investment" for many M.B.A. programs, in many cases particularly those outside the "elite" range, is generally very high.

What should you look at when researching business programs? In one word, *fit*. Does the program meet your needs? Do you feel comfortable when you talk to people from the school? Is the program likely to allow you to do the things you want to do? I also think one should consider any program based on the program's reputation and a return on investment calculation. Consider the cost of tuition, books, living expenses, and so on, as well as your lost earnings while in school. Then look at the differential between your earnings now and when you graduate. While money isn't everything, it is a shame to invest two years of your life, perhaps take out $60,000 in student loans, and maybe give up $80,000 to $100,000 in lost earnings if you are not going to improve your professional situation when you graduate.

At Auburn, we weigh undergraduate grades fairly heavily, and we also consider the applicant's major and university or college attended. We actually prefer students from nonbusiness fields, particularly engineers. We also weigh GMAT scores, both verbal and quantitative, fairly heavily; we consider the AWA less so than other scores. Work experience is considered less so than grades and GMAT scores, except for Executive M.B.A. students, for whom work experience is absolutely critical. Exceptional work experience will cause an applicant to stand out, and may offset scores elsewhere. We look for students who bring a balance of skills and experiences to our classes. Unless we know the source of an applicant's recommendations and they are unusually good, we don't weigh them as heavily as undergraduate grades and GMAT scores. And unless something in them is really striking we don't place quite as much emphasis on essays as we do on grades, GMAT scores, and work experience although they are all important.

Applicants write two essays, in which we ask them to discuss, first, their backgrounds and what they bring to the program; then, their goals; and finally, plans for what they will do after the program. We look for organization, focus, clear writing, and reasonableness. Bad essays are ones with "pat" answers and bad writing. Good essays are crisp, to the point, well-organized, and have reasonable, well-supported goals.

When looking for recommenders, ask someone who can say something specific about what you did. Avoid someone too high up in the organization just because they have a better title, unless you did something specific for that person. Avoid a letter from the CEO if it would be generic; for example, "Jane was a superb employee and a great person" doesn't really tell us too much. Far better is a recommendation with specific accomplishments and examples of superb performance.

When applying, avoid the last-minute rush, and make sure everything is in on time. Do not call and harass people about the status of your application.

Words of wisdom? "Begin with the end in mind." Not original with me, but still good advice. Know what you want to get out of this, and commit to doing what needs to be done. Be focused and work hard, but take time to have fun, too. Business school can be one of the most fun and challenging educational experiences of your life.

Debbie Pierce
Evening M.B.A. Program Manager
Florida International University
Chapman Graduate School of Business
http://business.fiu.edu

The FIU Chapman Graduate School of Business Evening M.B.A. program has three entry dates. We welcome applicants with an undergraduate degree in any discipline from an accredited university. However, it is strongly recommended that applicants have a high level of quantitative and analytical skills. In addition, good computer skills are required.

Applicants are reviewed based upon their application. GMAT or GRE score, undergraduate GPA, TOEFL score (if applicable), letters of recommendation, work experience, and a statement of purpose. We prefer two years of significant work experience; however, we do not emphasize business experience over other kinds of work experience. A one-page statement of purpose should explain why the applicant wants to obtain a business degree at Florida International University.

Searching for Graduate-Level Business Programs Online

Thinking about an advanced business degree? The Internet can be a great tool for gathering information about institutions and their graduate-level business programs. Among the many worthwhile sites ready to help guide you through the selection process is Peterson's M.B.A. Channel at www.petersons.com/mba.

How Peterson's M.B.A. Channel Can Help

Whether you are a recent college graduate or a working professional thinking about earning your advanced business degree, Peterson's has everything you need to know—connecting you with some of the most respected providers of advanced business education. Choosing an advanced business program involves a serious commitment of time and resources. It is important to have the most up-to-date information about prospective institutions and their programs at your fingertips. Peterson's M.B.A. Channel is a great place to start the process!

M.B.A. Programs Detailed Search

Explore more than 1,000 institutions offering nearly 4,000 graduate-level business programs. Find a program by selecting from more than 120 program concentrations or search by name or keyword. To select more than one area of concentration, hold down the CTRL key and click on multiple entries.

Once you have selected your search criteria, you will be asked to refine your search by choosing an average GMAT score. These scores are restricted to the schools that meet your previous selections. Once you have chosen a GMAT average score, you can continue refining your search by choosing a location.

When you find a program of your choice, simply click on it to get more in-depth information, including admissions requirements, after-graduation employment data, degrees awarded, financial aid, international student information and contacts, and application fees deadlines.

Get Free Info

If you still have questions, you can send an e-mail directly to the admissions department of a school. Click on the "Get Free Info" button and send your message. If you keep your questions short and to the point, you will usually receive an answer in no time at all.

Visit School Web Site

For institutions that have provided information about their Web sites, simply click on the "School Web Site" button to be taken directly to that institution's Web page. Once you arrive at the school's Web site, look around and get a feel for the place. Often, schools offer virtual tours of the campus, complete with photos and commentary. If you have specific questions about the school, a visit to a school's Web site will often yield an answer.

Prepare for the GMAT®

You can prepare for the GMAT by registering for Peterson's full-length computer-adaptive practice test, which includes real-time essay scoring. Great scores on the GMAT, although they are no guarantee of acceptance, certainly help your chances of getting into the graduate school of your choice. Visit Peterson's Prep Central (www.petersons.com/testprep) to learn more.

Write Admissions Essays

This year, 200,000 business school applicants will write 200,000 different answers to essay questions. One-half will be rejected everywhere they apply, while a select 7 percent will gain admission to the nation's top schools. Setting yourself apart requires more than just blockbuster GMAT scores and glowing recommendations—it requires powerful, well-reasoned application essays. Named "the World's premier application essay editing service" by the *New York Times* Learning Network and "one of the best essay services on the Internet" by the *Washington Post*, EssayEdge (www.essayedge.com) has helped more applicants write successful personal statements than any other company in the world. Learn more about EssayEdge and how it can give you an edge over hundreds of applicants with comparable academic credentials.

Learn More About M.B.A. Programs

Peterson's M.B.A. Channel offers prospective students a wealth of information in online articles that cover every aspect of earning your degree, from tips on writing a great admissions essay to a review of the new types of programs being offered at institutions around the country. To read any article, simply click on the title listed on the right under "Related MBA Schools Articles" at www.petersons.com/mba.

Use the Tools to Your Advantage

Choosing an M.B.A. program is a complicated process. The tools available to you on www.petersons.com/mba can help you to be more productive in this process. So what are you waiting for? Fire up your computer; your advanced business degree is just a click away!

How to Use This Guide

Profiles of Graduate-Level Business Programs

Profiles begin with the official school name, the name of the business unit (if applicable), and location of the school.

Program Overview

This portion of each **Profile** features the business unit's *Phone, Fax, E-mail,* and *Business Program(s) Web Site* and the following key information for quick reference and comparison: *Graduate Business Unit Enrollment*—the number of full and part-time students enrolled, the number of men and women enrolled, the number of international students enrolled, and the average age of enrolled students. *Graduate Business Faculty*—the number of full- and part-time faculty members in the graduate business unit. *Admissions*—how many applications were received, how many students were offered admission, and how many students actually enrolled in the graduate business unit in fall 2007. It also includes the average GMAT score of entering students and the average GPA of entering students. *Academic Calendar*—the number and length of terms required to graduate. *Accreditation*—whether the institution is accredited by AACSB International or by ACBSP. *After Graduation*—the percentage of 2006–07 graduates who were employed within three months of graduation and their average starting salary.

Degrees

This section provides information pertaining to the basic graduate-level business programs offered by the institution and business school described. Information on other graduate management and master's-level degrees that are considered comparable or equivalent to an M.B.A., such as a Master of Science (M.S.), is also provided here.

Keep in mind that basic programs at different schools may vary considerably in academic focus, philosophy, and degree requirements, although each is offering an M.B.A. degree or equivalent graduate-level business program. Always contact schools directly for details on their programs, curricula, and individual approaches.

Also note that for consistency and data-management purposes, the names of degree concentrations reported by institutions were sometimes translated to fit under a more generalized name. For example, concentrations such as internal communications, management communication, survey of professional communication, business communication, and business writing would all be placed under the general category of business communications.

Details in this section include whether the program is offered full-time, part-time, or both; whether a distance learning option is available; the number of credits required; the minimum and maximum length of the program in months or years; special application requirements, if applicable; and areas of concentration or specializations offered (accounting/finance, economics, marketing, operations, etc.).

Supplementary **Announcements** submitted by deans, chairs, and other administrators who wish to offer an additional statement to readers may be supplied at the end of this section.

Resources and Services

Information about online services, personal computer policies, library resources, international exchange programs, internship programs, and placement services can be found here.

Expenses

Information on tuition, fees, and room and board is provided in this section. Tuition expenses may be indicated separately for full-time or part-time study. Tuition and fees are expressed as dollar amounts per course, credit hour, hour, quarter hour, semester hour, unit, quarter, semester, trimester, term, academic year, or degree program, as specified by the institution. For public institutions in which tuition differs according to residence, separate figures are given for area or state residents and for nonresidents. Some non-U.S. institutions have chosen to report figures in currencies other than U.S. dollars. In these instances, readers should refer to current exchange rates in determining equivalents in U.S. dollars.

Average room and board expenses are indicated in either U.S. dollars or non-U.S. currencies. Both room and board and room only costs may be indicated, depending upon the types of housing provided and whether or not institutions provided this data.

Financial Aid

Financial aid information includes the number of graduate-level business students who received college-administered financial aid in 2007–08; what types of aid were granted (grants, scholarships, work-study, loans, etc.); whether or not aid is awarded to part-time students; deadlines for submission of financial aid applications; and contact information, including name, address, phone, fax, and e-mail address.

International Students

An international student is defined, in this guide, as a person who is not a citizen of the country in which a particular college, university, or other institution is located but is in that country on a visa or temporary basis and does not have the right to remain indefinitely.

This section provides information regarding entrance and application requirements for international students, international student enrollment as a percentage of the total number of students enrolled in the business school, special services or facilities available to international students, availability of international student housing, and the availability of financial aid.

Application requirements for international students may include minimum acceptable TOEFL (Test of English as a Foreign Language) score, minimum acceptable IELT (International English Language Test), TWE (Test of Written English), or TSE (Test of Spoken English) scores, proof of adequate funds, and proof of health immunizations.

Where applicable, the name, address, phone, fax, and e-mail address of the on-campus adviser or other person responsible for working with international students or exchange students are provided.

Application

Specific application requirements and what is recommended, application deadlines, and the name, title, mailing address, telephone number, fax number, and e-mail address of the person who should receive applications for admission are described here.

Application requirements may include letters of recommendation, a written essay, an interview, copies of transcripts of previous college study, a resume/curriculum vitae, a personal statement, work experience, or other specific requirements. Application deadlines for spring, fall, or other admission are provided by most schools. Some may process applications on a continuous or rolling basis.

Recommended items to accompany or enhance the application may include submission of GMAT (Graduate Management Admission Test) scores, minimum GPA (grade point average), minimum acceptable TOEFL score, minimum acceptable IELT score, proof of adequate funds, proof of health immunizations (for non-U.S. applicants), and previous work experience.

Close-Ups

In addition, some schools may have provided narratives that appear in the **Close-Ups of Graduate-Level Business Programs** section immediately following the **Profiles of Graduate-Level Business Programs.** These descriptions provide additional information about institutions and their programs.

Indexes

There are two **Indexes.** The first, Areas of Concentration, lists schools in alphabetical order under the specific areas of study within the business program. The second, Alphabetical Listing of Schools, gives page references for all colleges and universities in the guide.

Data Collection Procedures

Information contained in the **Profiles of Graduate-Level Business Programs** and **Indexes** sections of this book was collected through *Peterson's Survey of M.B.A. and Other Master's-level Business Degree Programs.* The online survey was administered to more than 1,500 U.S. and international institutions offering M.B.A. and equivalent master's-level business programs. Information was requested from program department contacts, admissions officers, or other appropriate personnel within these institutions in order to ensure accuracy.

With minor exceptions, data for those colleges or schools that responded to the survey were submitted by officials at the schools themselves. All usable information received in time for publication has been included. In the handful of instances in which no information regarding an eligible M.B.A. or master's-level business program was submitted, the name, location, and some general information regarding the program appear in the **Profile** section to indicate the existence of the program. Because of the extensive system of checks performed on the data collected by Peterson's, we believe that the information presented in this guide is accurate. Nonetheless, errors and omissions are possible in a data collection and processing endeavor of this scope. Also, facts and figures, such as tuition and fees, can suddenly change. Therefore, students should check at the time of application with a specific college or university to verify all pertinent information.

Criteria for Inclusion in This Book

Peterson's MBA Programs 2009 includes detailed information about institutions offering nearly 4,000 programs of study leading to a Master of Business Administration (M.B.A.) degree or an equivalent graduate-level business degree. These programs are offered by accredited colleges in the United States and its territories and by international institutions.

PROFILES OF GRADUATE-LEVEL BUSINESS PROGRAMS

U.S. and U.S. Territories

ALABAMA

Andrew Jackson University

Brian Tracy College of Business and Entrepreneurship

Birmingham, Alabama

Phone: 800-429-9300 Ext. 201 **Fax:** 800-321-9694 **E-mail:** info@aju.edu

Business Program(s) Web Site: http://www.aju.edu

DEGREES MBA • MPA

MBA—Master of Business Administration Part-time. Distance learning option. 36 total credits required. 9 to 60 months to complete program. *Concentration:* management.

MBA—Master of Business Administration Full-time and part-time. Distance learning option. 36 total credits required. 9 to 60 months to complete program. *Concentration:* entrepreneurship.

MBA—Master of Business Administration Full-time and part-time. Distance learning option. 36 total credits required. 9 to 60 months to complete program. *Concentration:* marketing.

MBA—Master of Business Administration Full-time and part-time. Distance learning option. 36 total credits required. 9 to 60 months to complete program. *Concentration:* strategic management.

MBA—Master of Business Administration Full-time and part-time. Distance learning option. 36 total credits required. 9 to 60 months to complete program. *Concentration:* human resources management.

MBA—Master of Business Administration Full-time and part-time. Distance learning option. 36 total credits required. 9 to 60 months to complete program. *Concentration:* health administration.

MBA—Master of Business Administration Full-time and part-time. Distance learning option. 36 total credits required. 9 to 60 months to complete program. *Concentration:* finance.

MPA—Master of Public Administration Part-time. Distance learning option. 36 total credits required. 9 to 60 months to complete program. *Concentration:* public policy and administration.

RESOURCES AND SERVICES Access to Internet/World Wide Web, online (class) registration, and online grade reports available. *Personal computer requirements:* Graduate business students are required to have a personal computer.

Application Contact Betty J. Howell, Director, Student Affairs, 2919 John Hawkins Parkway, Birmingham, AL 35244. *Phone:* 800-429-9300 Ext. 201. *Fax:* 800-321-9694. *E-mail:* info@aju.edu.

Auburn University

College of Business

Auburn University, Alabama

Phone: 334-844-4060 **Fax:** 334-844-2964 **E-mail:** mbainfo@auburn.edu

Business Program(s) Web Site: http://www.mba.business.auburn.edu/

Graduate Business Unit Enrollment *Total:* 532 (160 women). *Average Age:* 25.

Graduate Business Faculty 70 full-time.

Admissions *Applied:* 153. *Admitted:* 45. *Enrolled:* 35. *Average GMAT:* 636. *Average GPA:* 3.32

Academic Calendar Semesters.

Accreditation AACSB—The Association to Advance Collegiate Schools of Business.

After Graduation (Class of 2006–07) *Employed within 3 months of graduation:* 80%. *Average starting salary:* $61,648.

DEGREES MBA

MBA—Executive Master of Business Administration Part-time. Distance learning option. July 1st: Special application procedures for cohort classes which begin each fall semester. At least 36 total credits required. 21 to 60 months to complete program. *Concentrations:* executive programs, health administration, technology management.

MBA—On-Campus Full-Time Master of Business Administration Full-time. Co-hort entry; lock-step academic model; fall semester entry only. At least 36 total credits required. 17 to 60 months to complete program. *Concentrations:* agribusiness, developmental economics, economics, finance, general MBA, health care, management information systems, marketing, operations management, production management, sports/entertainment management, supply chain management, technology management.

MBA—Online/Video Outreach Master of Business Administration Part-time. Distance learning option. Application deadlines: March 1 (Fall entry); September 1 (Spring entry). At least 36 total credits required. 17 to 60 months to complete program. *Concentrations:* economics, finance, health care, management information systems, marketing, operations management, production management, supply chain management, technology management.

MBA—Physician's Executive Master of Business Administration Part-time. Distance learning option. July 1st: Special application procedures for cohort classes which begin each fall semester. At least 36 total credits required. 21 to 60 months to complete program. *Concentration:* executive programs.

RESOURCES AND SERVICES 120 on-campus PCs are available to graduate business students. Access to Internet/World Wide Web, online (class) registration, and online grade reports available. *Personal computer requirements:* Graduate business students are strongly recommended to purchase or lease a personal computer. *Special opportunities include:* An international exchange program and an internship program are available. *Placement services include:* Alumni network, career placement, job search course, career counseling/planning, electronic job bank, resume referral, career fairs, and resume preparation.

EXPENSES *Tuition (state resident):* Full-time: $5834. Part-time: $217 per credit hour. *Tuition (nonresident):* Full-time: $16,334. Part-time: $651 per credit hour. *Tuition (international):* Full-time: $16,518. *Required fees:* Full-time: $4800. Tuition and/or fees vary by number of courses or credits taken and academic program.

FINANCIAL AID (2007–08) 100 students received aid, including fellowships, loans, research assistantships, scholarships, and teaching assistantships. *Financial aid application deadline:* 4/15.

Financial Aid Contact Mr. Mike Reynolds, Executive Director, Student Financial Aid, 203 Mary Martin Hall, Auburn University, AL 36849. *Phone:* 334-844-4634. *Fax:* 334-844-3757. *E-mail:* finaid7@auburn.edu.

INTERNATIONAL STUDENTS *Services and facilities:* Counseling/support services, ESL/language courses, Housing location assistance, International student organization, Orientation, Visa Services, International education office. Financial aid is available to international students. *Required with application:* TOEFL with recommended score of 213 (computer), 550 (paper), or 79 (Internet); proof of adequate funds; proof of health/immunizations.

International Student Contact Dr. Ken McNabb, Director, International Education, 201 Hargis Hall, Auburn University, AL 36849. *Phone:* 334-844-5766. *Fax:* 334-844-4983. *E-mail:* intled2@auburn.edu.

APPLICATION *Required:* GMAT, application form, baccalaureate/first degree, essay, interview, 3 letters of recommendation, personal statement, resume/curriculum vitae, transcripts of college work. *Recommended:* 2 years of work experience. *Application fee:* $25, $50 (international). *Deadlines:* 3/1 for fall, 3/1 for fall (international).

Auburn University (continued)

Application Contact Ms. Katie Brock, Interim Director of MBA Admissions, MBA Program Office, 415 West Magnolia Avenue, Suite 503, Lowder Business Building, Auburn University, AL 36849. *Phone:* 334-844-4060. *Fax:* 334-844-2964. *E-mail:* mbainfo@auburn.edu.

See full description on page 568.

Auburn University Montgomery
School of Business
Montgomery, Alabama

Phone: 334-244-3587 **Fax:** 334-244-3137 **E-mail:** jtaylor5@mail.aum.edu

Business Program(s) Web Site: http://www-biz.aum.edu/graduate.htm

Graduate Business Unit Enrollment *Total:* 168.

Graduate Business Faculty *Total:* 38 (37 full-time; 1 part-time).

Admissions *Applied:* 62. *Admitted:* 55. *Enrolled:* 53. *Average GMAT:* 500. *Average GPA:* 3.0

Academic Calendar Semesters.

Accreditation AACSB—The Association to Advance Collegiate Schools of Business.

After Graduation (Class of 2006–07) *Employed within 3 months of graduation:* 99%. *Average starting salary:* $36,000.

DEGREE MBA

MBA—Master of Business Administration Full-time and part-time. 30 to 47 total credits required. 12 to 60 months to complete program. *Concentrations:* accounting, economics, finance, general MBA, human resources management, information systems, management, marketing.

RESOURCES AND SERVICES 40 on-campus PCs are available to graduate business students. Access to Internet/World Wide Web and online grade reports available. *Personal computer requirements:* Graduate business students are not required to have a personal computer. *Special opportunities include:* An international exchange program and an internship program are available. *Placement services include:* Alumni network, career placement, career counseling/planning, resume referral, career fairs, job interviews arranged, resume preparation, and career library.

EXPENSES *Tuition (state resident):* Full-time: $5670. Part-time: $189 per credit hour. *Tuition (nonresident):* Full-time: $14,796. Part-time: $548 per credit hour. *Tuition (international):* Full-time: $14,796. Part-time: $548 per credit hour. *Required fees:* Full-time: $297. Tuition and/or fees vary by number of courses or credits taken and academic program. *Graduate housing:* Room and board costs vary by campus location, number of occupants, and type of accommodation. *Typical cost:* $2000 (room only).

FINANCIAL AID (2007–08) Loans, research assistantships, and scholarships. Aid is available to part-time students.

Financial Aid Contact Mr. Anthony Richey, Director, Financial Aid, PO Box 244023, Montgomery, AL 36124. *Phone:* 334-244-3126. *E-mail:* arichey@mail.aum.edu.

INTERNATIONAL STUDENTS *Services and facilities:* Counseling/ support services, ESL/language courses, International student housing, International student organization. Financial aid is not available to international students. *Required with application:* TOEFL with recommended score of 500 (paper); proof of adequate funds; proof of health/immunizations.

International Student Contact Mr. Ron Blaesing, International Student Advisor, PO Box 244023, Montgomery, AL 36124. *Phone:* 334-244-3758. *Fax:* 334-244-3795. *E-mail:* rblaesin@mail.aum.edu.

APPLICATION *Required:* GMAT, application form, baccalaureate/first degree, transcripts of college work. *Application fee:* $25. Applications for domestic and international students are processed on a rolling basis.

Application Contact Ms. Jennifer M. Taylor, Graduate Advisor/ Evaluator, PO Box 244023, Montgomery, AL 36124. *Phone:* 334-244-3587. *Fax:* 334-244-3137. *E-mail:* jtaylor5@mail.aum.edu.

Birmingham-Southern College
Program in Public and Private Management
Birmingham, Alabama

Phone: 205-226-4803 **Fax:** 205-226-4843 **E-mail:** bdurham@bsc.edu

Business Program(s) Web Site: http://www.bsc.edu/mppm

Graduate Business Unit Enrollment *Total:* 62 (62 full-time; 30 women).

Graduate Business Faculty *Total:* 18 (12 full-time; 6 part-time).

Admissions *Applied:* 19. *Admitted:* 16. *Enrolled:* 16. *Average GPA:* 3.0

Academic Calendar Semesters.

Accreditation AACSB—The Association to Advance Collegiate Schools of Business.

After Graduation (Class of 2006–07) *Employed within 3 months of graduation:* 99%. *Average starting salary:* $65,000.

DEGREE MA

MA—Master of Arts in Public and Private Management Full-time and part-time. At least 16 total credits required. 24 to 60 months to complete program. *Concentration:* public and private management.

RESOURCES AND SERVICES 114 on-campus PCs are available to graduate business students. Access to Internet/World Wide Web and online grade reports available. *Personal computer requirements:* Graduate business students are strongly recommended to purchase or lease a personal computer. *Placement services include:* Alumni network, career placement, career counseling/planning, electronic job bank, career fairs, and career library.

FINANCIAL AID (2007–08) 2 students received aid, including grants, loans, and scholarships. Aid is available to part-time students.

Financial Aid Contact Mr. Fred Carter, Director of Financial Aid, Box 549016, Birmingham, AL 35254. *Phone:* 205-226-4670. *Fax:* 205-226-3082. *E-mail:* fcarter@bsc.edu.

INTERNATIONAL STUDENTS *Services and facilities:* Counseling/ support services, Housing location assistance, Orientation. Financial aid is available to international students. *Required with application:* TOEFL with recommended score of 213 (computer) or 550 (paper); proof of adequate funds; proof of health/immunizations.

International Student Contact Brenda D. Durham, Director of MPPM Admission, Box 549052, 900 Arkadelphia Road, Birmingham, AL 35254. *Phone:* 205-226-4803. *Fax:* 205-226-4843. *E-mail:* predbdurham@ bsc.edu.

APPLICATION *Required:* Application form, baccalaureate/first degree, essay, interview, 2 letters of recommendation, personal statement, resume/curriculum vitae, transcripts of college work, 1 year of work experience. School will accept GMAT and GRE. *Application fee:* $25. Applications for domestic and international students are processed on a rolling basis.

Application Contact Brenda D. Durham, Director of MPPM Admission, Box 549052, 900 Arkadelphia Road, Birmingham, AL 35254. *Phone:* 205-226-4803. *Fax:* 205-226-4843. *E-mail:* bdurham@bsc.edu.

Columbia Southern University
MBA Program
Orange Beach, Alabama

Phone: 251-981-3771 Ext. 521 **Fax:** 251-981-3815 **E-mail:** admissions@columbiasouthern.edu

Business Program(s) Web Site: http://www.columbiasouthern.edu

Graduate Business Unit Enrollment *Total:* 1,126 (1,126 part-time). *Average Age:* 35.

Graduate Business Faculty *Total:* 32 (8 full-time; 24 part-time).

Admissions *Applied:* 740. *Admitted:* 702. *Enrolled:* 413. *Average GPA:* 3.5

Academic Calendar Continuous.

After Graduation (Class of 2006–07) *Employed within 3 months of graduation:* 98%. *Average starting salary:* $68,000.

DEGREE MBA

MBA—MBA Program Full-time and part-time. Distance learning option. 19 to 37 total credits required. 12 to 48 months to complete program. *Concentrations:* electronic commerce (E-commerce), finance, general MBA, health administration, hospitality management, human resources management, international management, marketing, project management, public policy and administration, sports/entertainment management.

RESOURCES AND SERVICES Access to Internet/World Wide Web, online (class) registration, and online grade reports available. *Personal computer requirements:* Graduate business students are strongly recommended to purchase or lease a personal computer. *Placement services include:* Alumni network, resume preparation, and career library.

EXPENSES *Tuition:* Full-time: $4500. Part-time: $250 per credit hour. *Tuition (international):* Full-time: $4500. Part-time: $250 per credit hour. *Required fees:* Full-time: $125. Part-time: $125 per year.

FINANCIAL AID (2007–08) 269 students received aid, including loans and scholarships. Aid is available to part-time students.

Financial Aid Contact Admissions Department, 25326 Canal Road, PO Box 3110, Orange Beach, AL 36561. *Phone:* 251-981-3771 Ext. 521. *Fax:* 251-981-3815. *E-mail:* admissions@columbiasouthern.edu.

INTERNATIONAL STUDENTS *Services and facilities:* Counseling/support services, Orientation. Financial aid is available to international students. *Required with application:* TOEFL with recommended score of 173 (computer), 500 (paper), or 61 (Internet).

International Student Contact Admissions Department, 25326 Canal Road, PO Box 3110, Orange Beach, AL 36561. *Phone:* 251-981-3771 Ext. 521. *Fax:* 251-981-3815. *E-mail:* admissions@columbiasouthern.edu.

APPLICATION *Required:* Application form, baccalaureate/first degree, resume/curriculum vitae, transcripts of college work. *Recommended:* Work experience. *Application fee:* $25, $50 (international). Applications for domestic and international students are processed on a rolling basis.

Application Contact Admissions Department, 25326 Canal Road, PO Box 3110, Orange Beach, AL 36561. *Phone:* 251-981-3771 Ext. 521. *Fax:* 251-981-3815. *E-mail:* admissions@columbiasouthern.edu.

DEGREE MBA

MBA—Master of Business Administration Full-time and part-time. Distance learning option. 30 to 33 total credits required. 18 to 72 months to complete program. *Concentration:* accounting.

RESOURCES AND SERVICES 300 on-campus PCs are available to graduate business students. Access to Internet/World Wide Web, online (class) registration, and online grade reports available. *Personal computer requirements:* Graduate business students are not required to have a personal computer. *Special opportunities include:* An internship program is available. *Placement services include:* Alumni network, career placement, career counseling/planning, electronic job bank, career fairs, job interviews arranged, and resume preparation.

EXPENSES *Tuition (state resident):* Full-time: $4050. Part-time: $225 per credit hour. *Tuition (nonresident):* Full-time: $8100. Part-time: $450 per credit hour. *Tuition (international):* Full-time: $8100. Part-time: $450 per credit hour. *Graduate housing:* Room and board costs vary by number of occupants, type of accommodation, and type of board plan. *Typical cost:* $1000 (room only).

FINANCIAL AID (2007–08) 47 students received aid, including loans, research assistantships, scholarships, teaching assistantships, and work study. Aid is available to part-time students. *Financial aid application deadline:* 3/15.

Financial Aid Contact Ms. Vicky Adams, Director of Financial Aid, 700 Pelham Road, North, Jacksonville, AL 36265-1602. *Phone:* 256-782-5006.

INTERNATIONAL STUDENTS 17% of students enrolled are international students. *Services and facilities:* Counseling/support services, ESL/language courses, Housing location assistance, International student housing, International student organization, Orientation, Visa Services. Financial aid is available to international students. *Required with application:* TOEFL with recommended score of 173 (computer), 550 (paper), or 61 (Internet); proof of adequate funds; proof of health/immunizations.

International Student Contact Dr. Jay Ketterer, Director of the Office of International Programs and Studies, 700 Pelham Road N, Jacksonville, AL 36265. *Phone:* 256-782-8304. *E-mail:* jkettere@jsu.edu.

APPLICATION *Required:* GMAT, application form, baccalaureate/first degree, 3 letters of recommendation, personal statement, resume/curriculum vitae, transcripts of college work. *Application fee:* $30. Applications for domestic and international students are processed on a rolling basis.

Application Contact Dr. Louise J Clark, Associate Dean and MBA Director, 700 Pelham Road, North, Jacksonville, AL 36265-9982. *Phone:* 256-782-5780. *Fax:* 256-782-8420. *E-mail:* lclark@jsu.edu.

Jacksonville State University
College of Commerce and Business Administration

Jacksonville, Alabama

Phone: 256-782-5780 **Fax:** 256-782-8420 **E-mail:** lclark@jsu.edu

Business Program(s) Web Site: http://www.jsu.edu/depart/graduate/bulletin/business.htm

Graduate Business Unit Enrollment *Total:* 75 (10 full-time; 65 part-time; 39 women; 13 international). *Average Age:* 27.

Graduate Business Faculty 21 full-time.

Admissions *Applied:* 40. *Admitted:* 25. *Enrolled:* 20. *Average GMAT:* 484. *Average GPA:* 3.27

Academic Calendar Semesters.

Accreditation AACSB—The Association to Advance Collegiate Schools of Business.

Samford University
School of Business

Birmingham, Alabama

Phone: 205-726-2931 **Fax:** 205-726-4555 **E-mail:** lcharper@samford.edu

Business Program(s) Web Site: http://www.samford.edu/business

Graduate Business Unit Enrollment *Total:* 126 (3 full-time; 123 part-time; 47 women; 3 international). *Average Age:* 26.

Graduate Business Faculty 21 full-time.

Admissions *Applied:* 70. *Admitted:* 55. *Enrolled:* 45. *Average GMAT:* 525. *Average GPA:* 3.0

Academic Calendar 4-1-4.

Accreditation AACSB—The Association to Advance Collegiate Schools of Business.

After Graduation (Class of 2006–07) *Employed within 3 months of graduation:* 100%.

Samford University (continued)

DEGREES JD/M Acc • JD/MBA • M Acc • MBA • MBA/M Acc • MBA/M Div • MBA/MSN

JD/M Acc—Juris Doctor/Master of Accountancy Full-time. 99 to 117 total credits required. 36 to 48 months to complete program. *Concentrations:* accounting, combined degrees, law.

JD/MBA—Juris Doctor/Master of Business Administration Full-time. 99 to 117 total credits required. 36 to 84 months to complete program. *Concentrations:* combined degrees, law, management.

M Acc—Master of Accountancy Full-time and part-time. 30 total credits required. 12 to 84 months to complete program. *Concentration:* accounting.

MBA—Master of Business Administration Full-time and part-time. 30 to 48 total credits required. 12 to 84 months to complete program. *Concentration:* management.

MBA/M Acc—Master of Business Administration/Master of Accounting Full-time and part-time. 45 to 63 total credits required. 17 to 84 months to complete program. *Concentrations:* accounting, combined degrees, general MBA.

MBA/M Div—Master of Business Administration/Master of Divinity Full-time and part-time. 115 to 133 total credits required. 36 to 84 months to complete program. *Concentrations:* combined degrees, general MBA.

MBA/MSN—Master of Business Administration/Master of Science in Nursing Full-time and part-time. 106 to 118 total credits required. 24 to 84 months to complete program. *Concentrations:* combined degrees, general MBA.

RESOURCES AND SERVICES 154 on-campus PCs are available to graduate business students. Access to Internet/World Wide Web, online (class) registration, and online grade reports available. *Personal computer requirements:* Graduate business students are not required to have a personal computer. *Special opportunities include:* An internship program is available. *Placement services include:* Alumni network, career placement, career counseling/planning, electronic job bank, resume referral, career fairs, job interviews arranged, resume preparation, and career library.

EXPENSES *Tuition:* Full-time: $15,600. Part-time: $1560 per course. *Tuition (international):* Full-time: $15,600. Part-time: $1560 per course. *Typical graduate housing cost:* $8000 (including board), $4000 (room only).

FINANCIAL AID (2007–08) 10 students received aid, including loans, scholarships, and work study. Aid is available to part-time students. *Financial aid application deadline:* 3/1.

Financial Aid Contact Ms. Melba E. Maudlin, Assistant Director of Financial Aid, 800 Lakeshore Drive, Financial Aid Office, Birmingham, AL 35229. *Phone:* 205-726-2445. *Fax:* 205-726-2738. *E-mail:* memaudli@samford.edu.

INTERNATIONAL STUDENTS 2% of students enrolled are international students. *Services and facilities:* Counseling/support services, Visa Services. Financial aid is not available to international students. *Required with application:* Proof of adequate funds; proof of health/immunizations. *Recommended with application:* TOEFL with recommended score of 213 (computer) or 550 (paper).

International Student Contact Mr. Larron C. Harper, Director, Graduate and Executive Education Programs, 800 Lakeshore Drive, Birmingham, AL 35229. *Phone:* 205-726-2931. *Fax:* 205-726-4555. *E-mail:* lcharper@samford.edu.

APPLICATION *Required:* GMAT, application form, baccalaureate/first degree, 1 letter of recommendation, personal statement, resume/curriculum vitae, transcripts of college work. *Recommended:* Work experience. *Application fee:* $25. Applications for domestic and international students are processed on a rolling basis.

Application Contact Mr. Larron C. Harper, Director of Graduate and Executive Education Programs/Assistant Professor, 800 Lakeshore Drive, Birmingham, AL 35229. *Phone:* 205-726-2931. *Fax:* 205-726-4555. *E-mail:* lcharper@samford.edu.

Spring Hill College
Division of Business and Management
Mobile, Alabama

Phone: 251-380-3094 **Fax:** 251-460-2190 **E-mail:** grad@shc.edu

Business Program(s) Web Site: http://www.shc.edu/graduate-and-adult-programs/graduate/mba

Graduate Business Unit Enrollment *Total:* 20 (1 full-time; 19 part-time; 10 women). *Average Age:* 32.

Graduate Business Faculty *Total:* 3 (2 full-time; 1 part-time).

Academic Calendar Semesters.

Accreditation ACBSP—The American Council of Business Schools and Programs.

After Graduation (Class of 2006–07) *Employed within 3 months of graduation:* 100%.

DEGREE MBA

MBA—Master of Business Administration Full-time and part-time. At least 36 total credits required. 24 to 72 months to complete program. *Concentration:* general MBA.

RESOURCES AND SERVICES 194 on-campus PCs are available to graduate business students. Access to Internet/World Wide Web, online (class) registration, and online grade reports available. *Personal computer requirements:* Graduate business students are not required to have a personal computer. *Placement services include:* Alumni network, career counseling/planning, resume preparation, and career library.

EXPENSES *Tuition:* Full-time: $6930. Part-time: $385 per semester hour. *Tuition (international):* Full-time: $6930. Part-time: $385 per semester hour.

FINANCIAL AID (2007–08) 13 students received aid, including grants and loans. Aid is available to part-time students.

Financial Aid Contact Ellen Foster, Director of Financial Aid, 4000 Dauphin Street, Mobile, AL 36608-1791. *Phone:* 251-380-3460. *Fax:* 251-460-2176. *E-mail:* efoster@shc.edu.

INTERNATIONAL STUDENTS *Services and facilities:* Counseling/support services, Orientation, Visa Services. Financial aid is available to international students. *Required with application:* TOEFL with recommended score of 213 (computer), 550 (paper), or 80 (Internet); proof of adequate funds; proof of health/immunizations.

International Student Contact Anna I. Gaw, Coordinator for Students in Transition, 4000 Dauphin Street, Mobile, AL 36608-1791. *Phone:* 251-380-3470. *Fax:* 251-460-2187. *E-mail:* agaw@shc.edu.

APPLICATION *Required:* GMAT, application form, baccalaureate/first degree, transcripts of college work. *Recommended:* Interview. *Application fee:* $25, $35 (international). Applications for domestic and international students are processed on a rolling basis.

Application Contact Joyce Genz, Dean of Continuing Studies and Director of Graduate Programs, 4000 Dauphin Street, Mobile, AL 36608-1791. *Phone:* 251-380-3094. *Fax:* 251-460-2190. *E-mail:* grad@shc.edu.

Troy University
College of Business
Troy, Alabama

Phone: 334-670-3188 **Fax:** 334-670-3774 **E-mail:** bcamp@troy.edu

Business Program(s) Web Site: http://spectrum.troyst.edu/~mba/

Graduate Business Unit Enrollment *Total:* 321 (149 full-time; 172 part-time; 131 women; 73 international). *Average Age:* 24.

Graduate Business Faculty *Total:* 21 (19 full-time; 2 part-time).

Admissions *Applied:* 120. *Admitted:* 115. *Enrolled:* 105. *Average GMAT:* 490. *Average GPA:* 3.0

Academic Calendar Semesters.

Accreditation ACBSP—The American Council of Business Schools and Programs.

DEGREES MBA • MHR • MSM

MBA—Executive Master of Business Administration Part-time. Distance learning option. 5 years post-bachelor's work experience required. At least 39 total credits required. 24 to 96 months to complete program. *Concentrations:* accounting, information management, management.

MBA—Master of Business Administration Full-time and part-time. Distance learning option. At least 36 total credits required. 15 to 96 months to complete program. *Concentrations:* accounting, information systems, management.

MHR—Human Resources Management Full-time and part-time. Distance learning option. At least 36 total credits required. 15 to 96 months to complete program. *Concentration:* human resources management.

MSM—Master of Science in Management Full-time and part-time. Distance learning option. At least 36 total credits required. 15 to 96 months to complete program. *Concentrations:* information systems, leadership.

RESOURCES AND SERVICES 155 on-campus PCs are available to graduate business students. Access to Internet/World Wide Web, online (class) registration, and online grade reports available. *Personal computer requirements:* Graduate business students are strongly recommended to purchase or lease a personal computer. *Special opportunities include:* An internship program is available. *Placement services include:* Career placement, career counseling/planning, electronic job bank, resume referral, career fairs, job interviews arranged, resume preparation, and career library.

EXPENSES *Tuition (state resident):* Full-time: $4368. *Tuition (nonresident):* Full-time: $8736. *Tuition (international):* Full-time: $8736. Tuition and/or fees vary by class time, number of courses or credits taken, campus location, and academic program.

FINANCIAL AID (2007–08) 17 students received aid, including fellowships and research assistantships. *Financial aid application deadline:* 4/30.

Financial Aid Contact Ms. Carol Supri, Director, Financial Aid, 133 Adams Administration Building, Troy, AL 36082. *Phone:* 334-670-3186.

INTERNATIONAL STUDENTS 23% of students enrolled are international students. *Services and facilities:* Counseling/support services, ESL/language courses, Housing location assistance, International student housing, International student organization, Language tutoring, Orientation, Visa Services, Transcript evaluation. Financial aid is available to international students. *Required with application:* TOEFL with recommended score of 197 (computer) or 525 (paper); TWE with recommended score of 4; proof of adequate funds; proof of health/immunizations. *Recommended with application:* IELT with recommended score of 5.5.

International Student Contact Curtis Porter, Dean, International Programs, 131 Pace Hall, Troy, AL 36082. *Phone:* 334-670-3335. *Fax:* 334-670-3735. *E-mail:* cporter@trojan.troyst.edu.

APPLICATION *Required:* Application form, baccalaureate/first degree, 1 letter of recommendation, transcripts of college work. School will accept GMAT and GRE. *Recommended:* Work experience. *Application fee:* $50. Applications for domestic and international students are processed on a rolling basis.

Application Contact Brenda Campbell, Director, Graduate Admissions, 134 Adams Administration Building, Troy, AL 36082. *Phone:* 334-670-3188. *Fax:* 334-670-3774. *E-mail:* bcamp@troy.edu.

Troy University Dothan
College of Business Administration
Dothan, Alabama

Phone: 334-983-6556 Ext. 230 **Fax:** 334-983-6322 **E-mail:** phamm@troy.edu

Business Program(s) Web Site: http://troy.edu/

Graduate Business Unit Enrollment *Total:* 69 (21 full-time; 48 part-time; 43 women).

Graduate Business Faculty *Total:* 30 (18 full-time; 12 part-time).

Admissions *Applied:* 27. *Admitted:* 22. *Enrolled:* 16. *Average GMAT:* 500. *Average GPA:* 3.0

Academic Calendar Semesters.

Accreditation ACBSP—The American Council of Business Schools and Programs.

After Graduation (Class of 2006–07) *Employed within 3 months of graduation:* 95%. *Average starting salary:* $35,000.

DEGREES MBA • MS

MBA—Master of Business Administration Full-time and part-time. Distance learning option. At least 36 total credits required. 12 to 96 months to complete program. *Concentrations:* accounting, human resources management, management, management information systems.

MS—Master of Science in Human Resources Management Full-time and part-time. At least 36 total credits required. 12 to 96 months to complete program. *Concentration:* human resources management.

RESOURCES AND SERVICES 120 on-campus PCs are available to graduate business students. Access to Internet/World Wide Web, online (class) registration, and online grade reports available. *Personal computer requirements:* Graduate business students are strongly recommended to purchase or lease a personal computer. *Special opportunities include:* An internship program is available. *Placement services include:* Alumni network, career placement, career counseling/planning, resume referral, career fairs, job interviews arranged, resume preparation, and career library.

FINANCIAL AID (2007–08) 10 students received aid, including loans and scholarships. Aid is available to part-time students. *Financial aid application deadline:* 5/1.

Financial Aid Contact Ms. Sussan Green, Director of Financial Aid, PO Box 8368, Dothan, AL 36304-0368. *Phone:* 334-983-6556 Ext. 255. *Fax:* 334-983-6322. *E-mail:* sgreen@troy.edu.

INTERNATIONAL STUDENTS *Services and facilities:* Counseling/support services, Language tutoring, tutoring. Financial aid is not available to international students. *Required with application:* TOEFL with recommended score of 213 (computer) or 550 (paper); proof of adequate funds; proof of health/immunizations.

International Student Contact Keith Seagle, Director of Counseling Services, PO Box 8368, Dothan, AL 36304-0368. *Phone:* 334-983-6556 Ext. 221. *Fax:* 334-983-6322. *E-mail:* kseagle@tsud.edu.

APPLICATION *Required:* Application form, baccalaureate/first degree, 1 letter of recommendation, transcripts of college work. School will accept GMAT and GRE. *Application fee:* $20. Applications for domestic and international students are processed on a rolling basis.

Application Contact P J Hamm, Director of Graduate Admissions and Records, PO Box 8368, Dothan, AL 36304-0368. *Phone:* 334-983-6556 Ext. 230. *Fax:* 334-983-6322. *E-mail:* phamm@troy.edu.

The University of Alabama
Manderson Graduate School of Business
Tuscaloosa, Alabama

Phone: 205-348-9122 **Fax:** 205-348-4504 **E-mail:** bbledsole@cba.ua.edu

The University of Alabama (continued)

Business Program(s) Web Site: http://mba.cba.ua.edu

Graduate Business Unit Enrollment *Total:* 399 (349 full-time; 50 part-time; 139 women; 62 international). *Average Age:* 25.

Graduate Business Faculty *Total:* 118 (93 full-time; 25 part-time).

Admissions *Applied:* 415. *Admitted:* 340. *Enrolled:* 327. *Average GMAT:* 620. *Average GPA:* 3.4

Academic Calendar Semesters.

Accreditation AACSB—The Association to Advance Collegiate Schools of Business.

After Graduation (Class of 2006–07) *Employed within 3 months of graduation:* 92%. *Average starting salary:* $62,000.

DEGREES JD/MBA • M Ac • MA • MBA • MBA/MSN • MSC • MTA

JD/MBA—Juris Doctor/Master of Business Administration Full-time. At least 108 total credits required. 48 months to complete program. *Concentration:* combined degrees.

M Ac—Master of Accountancy Full-time. At least 30 total credits required. Minimum of 12 months to complete program. *Concentration:* accounting.

MA—Master of Arts in Banking and Finance Full-time and part-time. At least 30 total credits required. 12 to 24 months to complete program. *Concentrations:* banking, finance.

MA—Master of Arts in Economics Full-time and part-time. At least 30 total credits required. 12 to 24 months to complete program. *Concentrations:* economics, financial economics, international economics.

MA—Master of Arts in Human Resources Management Part-time. At least 30 total credits required. 24 to 60 months to complete program. *Concentration:* management.

MA—Master of Arts in Management Science Full-time and part-time. At least 30 total credits required. 24 to 36 months to complete program. *Concentrations:* management science, manufacturing management, production management.

MA—Master of Arts in Marketing Full-time. At least 30 total credits required. 10 to 60 months to complete program. *Concentrations:* international business, marketing, marketing research.

MBA—Executive Master of Business Administration Part-time. Must have at least 5 years post undergraduate experience. At least 48 total credits required. Minimum of 17 months to complete program. *Concentration:* executive programs.

MBA—Master of Business Administration Full-time. At least 49 total credits required. 24 months to complete program. *Concentrations:* accounting, business policy/strategy, combined degrees, decision sciences, entrepreneurship, finance, general MBA, health care, human resources management, information management, information systems, international business, management information systems, marketing, operations management, production management, quality management, quantitative analysis, real estate, risk management, statistics, strategic management.

MBA/MSN—Master of Business Administration/Master of Science in Nursing Full-time. At least 54 total credits required. Minimum of 24 months to complete program. *Concentration:* combined degrees.

MSC—Master of Science in Commerce Full-time and part-time. At least 30 total credits required. 24 to 36 months to complete program. *Concentrations:* management science, manufacturing management, production management.

MSC—Master of Science in Commerce Full-time. At least 30 total credits required. 12 to 24 months to complete program. *Concentrations:* banking, finance.

MSC—Master of Science in Commerce Full-time. At least 30 total credits required. 12 to 24 months to complete program. *Concentrations:* economics, financial economics, international economics.

MTA—Master of Tax Accounting Full-time. At least 31 total credits required. Minimum of 12 months to complete program. *Concentration:* accounting.

RESOURCES AND SERVICES 250 on-campus PCs are available to graduate business students. Access to Internet/World Wide Web, online (class) registration, and online grade reports available. *Personal computer requirements:* Graduate business students are required to have a personal computer. *Special opportunities include:* An international exchange program and an internship program are available. *Placement services include:* Alumni network, career placement, job search course, career counseling/planning, electronic job bank, resume referral, career fairs, job interviews arranged, resume preparation, and career library.

EXPENSES *Tuition (state resident):* Full-time: $5700. *Tuition (nonresident):* Full-time: $16,518. *Tuition (international):* Full-time: $16,518. *Required fees:* Full-time: $2000. Tuition and/or fees vary by number of courses or credits taken and local reciprocity agreements. *Graduate housing:* Room and board costs vary by campus location, number of occupants, type of accommodation, and type of board plan. *Typical cost:* $5320 (including board), $4670 (room only).

FINANCIAL AID (2007–08) 210 students received aid, including fellowships, grants, loans, research assistantships, scholarships, teaching assistantships, and work study. Aid is available to part-time students. *Financial aid application deadline:* 2/15.

Financial Aid Contact Ms. Martha Carroll, Program Assistant, Box 870223, 101 Bidgood Hall, Tuscaloosa, AL 35487. *Phone:* 205-348-4077. *Fax:* 205-348-4504. *E-mail:* mcarroll@cba.ua.edu.

INTERNATIONAL STUDENTS 16% of students enrolled are international students. *Services and facilities:* Counseling/support services, ESL/language courses, Housing location assistance, International student housing, International student organization, Language tutoring, Orientation, Visa Services. Financial aid is available to international students. *Required with application:* TOEFL with recommended score of 575 (paper); proof of adequate funds; proof of health/immunizations.

International Student Contact Mary S. Williams, Graduate International Admissions Officer, Box 870118, Tuscaloosa, AL 35487. *Phone:* 205-348-5923. *Fax:* 205-348-0400.

APPLICATION *Required:* Application form, baccalaureate/first degree, interview, 3 letters of recommendation, personal statement, transcripts of college work. School will accept GMAT and GRE. *Recommended:* Essay, resume/curriculum vitae, work experience. *Application fee:* $30. Applications for domestic and international students are processed on a rolling basis.

Application Contact Mr. Blake Bedsole, Manager of Admissions and Student Services, Box 870223, Tuscaloosa, AL 35487. *Phone:* 205-348-9122. *Fax:* 205-348-4504. *E-mail:* bbledsole@cba.ua.edu.

The University of Alabama at Birmingham

School of Business

Birmingham, Alabama

Phone: 205-934-8227 **Fax:** 205-934-8413 **E-mail:** inquire@gradschool.huc.uab.edu

Business Program(s) Web Site: http://www.business.uab.edu/

Accreditation AACSB—The Association to Advance Collegiate Schools of Business.

DEGREES MAC • MBA • MBA/MPH • MBA/MS • MBA/MSN

MAC—Master of Accountancy Full-time and part-time. At least 30 total credits required. 12 to 84 months to complete program. *Concentration:* accounting.

MBA—MBA for Scientists Full-time and part-time. Master's degree or higher in science field or professional degree in medicine, dentistry, etc. 45 total credits required. 12 to 48 months to complete program.

MBA—Master of Business Administration Full-time and part-time. 36 to 51 total credits required. 12 to 84 months to complete program. *Concentrations:* finance, general MBA, health care, information technology.

MBA/MPH—Master of Business Administration/Master of Public Health Full-time and part-time. At least 72 total credits required. 24 to 84 months to complete program. *Concentration:* combined degrees.

MBA/MS—Master of Business Administration/Master of Science in Health Administration Full-time. At least 72 total credits required. 33 months to complete program. *Concentration:* combined degrees.

MBA/MSN—Master of Business Administration/Master of Science in Nursing Full-time and part-time. Distance learning option. Must have a Bachelor of Science in Nursing. At least 79 total credits required. 24 to 84 months to complete program. *Concentration:* health care.

RESOURCES AND SERVICES 100 on-campus PCs are available to graduate business students. Access to Internet/World Wide Web, online (class) registration, and online grade reports available. *Personal computer requirements:* Graduate business students are strongly recommended to purchase or lease a personal computer. *Special opportunities include:* An internship program is available. *Placement services include:* Alumni network, career placement, job search course, career counseling/planning, electronic job bank, resume referral, career fairs, job interviews arranged, resume preparation, and career library.

Application Contact Sha'Niethia Johnson, Student Services Assistant, 1400 University Boulevard, HUC 511, Birmingham, AL 35294-1150. *Phone:* 205-934-8227. *Fax:* 205-934-8413. *E-mail:* inquire@ gradschool.huc.uab.edu.

The University of Alabama in Huntsville

College of Business Administration

Huntsville, Alabama

Phone: 256-824-6198 **Fax:** 256-824-6405 **E-mail:** graddean@uah.edu

Business Program(s) Web Site: http://www.cba.uah.edu/

Graduate Business Unit Enrollment *Total:* 197 (42 full-time; 155 part-time; 80 women; 12 international). *Average Age:* 30.

Graduate Business Faculty *Total:* 24 (18 full-time; 6 part-time).

Admissions *Applied:* 75. *Admitted:* 54. *Enrolled:* 44. *Average GMAT:* 540. *Average GPA:* 3.1

Academic Calendar Semesters.

Accreditation AACSB—The Association to Advance Collegiate Schools of Business.

After Graduation (Class of 2006–07) *Employed within 3 months of graduation:* 97%.

DEGREES M Acc • M Sc • MBA

M Acc—Master of Accountancy Full-time and part-time. 30 to 33 total credits required. 12 to 72 months to complete program. *Concentration:* accounting.

M Sc—Master of Science in Management Information Systems Full-time and part-time. 30 to 33 total credits required. 12 to 72 months to complete program. *Concentration:* management information systems.

MBA Full-time and part-time. 33 to 48 total credits required. 12 to 72 months to complete program. *Concentration:* technology management.

RESOURCES AND SERVICES 170 on-campus PCs are available to graduate business students. Access to Internet/World Wide Web, online (class) registration, and online grade reports available. *Personal computer requirements:* Graduate business students are not required to have a personal computer. *Special opportunities include:* An internship program is available. *Placement services include:* Career placement, career counseling/planning, electronic job bank, resume referral, career fairs, job interviews arranged, resume preparation, and career library.

EXPENSES *Tuition (state resident):* Full-time: $9114. *Tuition (nonresident):* Full-time: $18,732. *Tuition (international):* Full-time: $18,732. *Typical graduate housing cost:* $3205 (including board), $2330 (room only).

FINANCIAL AID (2007–08) Grants, loans, and scholarships. *Financial aid application deadline:* 3/1.

Financial Aid Contact Mr. Andy Weaver, Director of Student Financial Services, UC 212, 301 Sparkman Drive, Huntsville, AL 35899. *Phone:* 256-824-6241. *Fax:* 256-824-6212. *E-mail:* finaid@uah.edu.

INTERNATIONAL STUDENTS 6% of students enrolled are international students. *Services and facilities:* Counseling/support services, ESL/language courses, Housing location assistance, International student housing, International student organization, Language tutoring, Orientation, Visa Services. Financial aid is not available to international students. *Required with application:* TOEFL with recommended score of 213 (computer) or 550 (paper); proof of adequate funds; proof of health/immunizations.

International Student Contact Ms. Kathy Biggs, Manager of Graduate Admissions, MSB C206, 301 Sparkman Drive, Huntsville, AL 35899. *Phone:* 256-824-6198. *Fax:* 256-824-6405. *E-mail:* graddean@uah.edu.

APPLICATION *Required:* GMAT, application form, baccalaureate/first degree, transcripts of college work. *Application fee:* $40. Applications for domestic and international students are processed on a rolling basis.

Application Contact Ms. Kathy Biggs, Manager of Graduate Admissions, MSB C206, 301 Sparkman Drive, Huntsville, AL 35899. *Phone:* 256-824-6198. *Fax:* 256-824-6405. *E-mail:* graddean@uah.edu.

University of Mobile

School of Business

Mobile, Alabama

Phone: 251-442-2219 **Fax:** 251-442-2523 **E-mail:** jblocke@umobile.edu

Business Program(s) Web Site: http://www.umobile.edu

Graduate Business Unit Enrollment *Total:* 30 (4 full-time; 26 part-time; 12 women; 3 international). *Average Age:* 30.

Graduate Business Faculty *Total:* 13 (10 full-time; 3 part-time).

Admissions *Average GMAT:* 447. *Average GPA:* 3.0

Academic Calendar Semesters.

Accreditation ACBSP—The American Council of Business Schools and Programs.

After Graduation (Class of 2006–07) *Employed within 3 months of graduation:* 100%. *Average starting salary:* $40,000.

DEGREE MBA

MBA—Master of Business Administration Full-time and part-time. At least 40 total credits required. 12 to 60 months to complete program. *Concentration:* general MBA.

RESOURCES AND SERVICES 110 on-campus PCs are available to graduate business students. Access to Internet/World Wide Web, online (class) registration, and online grade reports available. *Personal computer requirements:* Graduate business students are strongly recommended to purchase or lease a personal computer. *Placement services include:* Alumni network, career counseling/planning, career fairs, and resume preparation.

EXPENSES *Tuition:* Full-time: $6840. Part-time: $380 per semester hour. *Tuition (international):* Full-time: $21,140. Part-time: $380 per semester hour. *Required fees:* Full-time: $98. *Typical graduate housing cost:* $7140 (including board), $4260 (room only).

FINANCIAL AID (2007–08) Loans.

University of Mobile (continued)

Financial Aid Contact Ms. Marie Batson, Director of Financial Aid, 5735 College Parkway, Mobile, AL 36613-2842. *Phone:* 251-442-2370. *Fax:* 251-442-2507. *E-mail:* mariet@mail.umobile.edu.

INTERNATIONAL STUDENTS 10% of students enrolled are international students. *Services and facilities:* Counseling/support services, Orientation. Financial aid is not available to international students. *Required with application:* TOEFL with recommended score of 213 (computer), 550 (paper), or 80 (Internet); proof of adequate funds; proof of health/immunizations.

International Student Contact Ms. Hali Givens, Assistant Director of Admissions for Recruitment, 5735 College Parkway, Mobile, AL 36613-2842. *Phone:* 251-442-2221. *Fax:* 251-442-2498. *E-mail:* halig@umobile.edu.

APPLICATION *Required:* GMAT, application form, baccalaureate/first degree, transcripts of college work. *Recommended:* Work experience. *Application fee:* $40, $50 (international). Applications for domestic and international students are processed on a rolling basis.

Application Contact Mrs. J.B. Locke, Director of Administrative Services, 5735 College Parkway, Mobile, AL 36613-2842. *Phone:* 251-442-2219. *Fax:* 251-442-2523. *E-mail:* jblocke@umobile.edu.

University of North Alabama
College of Business

Florence, Alabama

Phone: 256-760-4447 **Fax:** 256-760-4349 **E-mail:** admissions@una.edu

Business Program(s) Web Site: http://www.una.edu

Graduate Business Unit Enrollment *Total:* 600 (125 full-time; 475 part-time; 275 women; 175 international). *Average Age:* 28.

Graduate Business Faculty *Total:* 31 (28 full-time; 3 part-time).

Admissions *Applied:* 180. *Admitted:* 145. *Enrolled:* 110. *Average GMAT:* 475. *Average GPA:* 3.0

Academic Calendar Semesters.

Accreditation ACBSP—The American Council of Business Schools and Programs.

After Graduation (Class of 2006–07) *Employed within 3 months of graduation:* 95%.

DEGREE MBA

MBA—Master of Business Administration Full-time and part-time. Distance learning option. At least 33 total credits required. 12 to 96 months to complete program. *Concentrations:* accounting, finance, general MBA, international business, management, management information systems, marketing.

RESOURCES AND SERVICES 275 on-campus PCs are available to graduate business students. Access to Internet/World Wide Web, online (class) registration, and online grade reports available. *Personal computer requirements:* Graduate business students are strongly recommended to purchase or lease a personal computer. *Placement services include:* Alumni network, career placement, career counseling/planning, electronic job bank, career fairs, job interviews arranged, resume preparation, and career library.

EXPENSES *Tuition (state resident):* Full-time: $3060. Part-time: $510 per course. *Tuition (nonresident):* Full-time: $6120. Part-time: $1020 per course. *Tuition (international):* Full-time: $7120. *Required fees:* Full-time: $944. Part-time: $157 per course. Tuition and/or fees vary by academic program. *Graduate housing:* Room and board costs vary by number of occupants, type of accommodation, and type of board plan. *Typical cost:* $5600 (including board), $3000 (room only).

FINANCIAL AID (2007–08) 200 students received aid, including grants, loans, scholarships, and work study. Aid is available to part-time students. *Financial aid application deadline:* 4/1.

Financial Aid Contact Ben Baker, Director of Student Financial Services, University Station, Florence, AL 35632-0001. *Phone:* 256-760-4278.

INTERNATIONAL STUDENTS 29% of students enrolled are international students. *Services and facilities:* Counseling/support services, ESL/language courses, Housing location assistance, International student organization, Orientation. Financial aid is not available to international students. *Required with application:* TOEFL with recommended score of 550 (paper); proof of adequate funds; proof of health/immunizations.

International Student Contact Dr. Evan Ward, Director, Office of International Student Services, Box 5058, Florence, AL 35632-0001. *Phone:* 256-765-4756. *E-mail:* erward@una.edu.

APPLICATION *Required:* Application form, baccalaureate/first degree, transcripts of college work. School will accept GMAT and GRE. *Application fee:* $25. *Deadlines:* 7/15 for fall (international), 11/15 for spring (international). Applications for domestic students are processed on a rolling basis.

Application Contact Mrs. Carolyn Austin, Graduate Admissions Record Specialist, Box 5011, Florence, AL 35632. *Phone:* 256-760-4447. *Fax:* 256-760-4349. *E-mail:* admissions@una.edu.

University of South Alabama
Mitchell College of Business

Mobile, Alabama

Phone: 334-460-6418 **Fax:** 334-460-6529 **E-mail:** jgamble@usouthal.edu

Business Program(s) Web Site: http://www.southalabama.edu/mba

Graduate Business Unit Enrollment *Total:* 105 (105 full-time; 50 women; 10 international).

Graduate Business Faculty *Total:* 53 (45 full-time; 8 part-time).

Admissions *Average GMAT:* 550. *Average GPA:* 3.4

Academic Calendar Semesters.

Accreditation AACSB—The Association to Advance Collegiate Schools of Business.

DEGREES M Acc • MBA

M Acc—Master of Accounting Full-time and part-time. 30 to 57 total credits required. 24 to 84 months to complete program. *Concentration:* accounting.

MBA—Mitchell MBA Full-time and part-time. 42 total credits required. 24 to 84 months to complete program. *Concentration:* general MBA.

RESOURCES AND SERVICES 155 on-campus PCs are available to graduate business students. Access to Internet/World Wide Web, online (class) registration, and online grade reports available. *Personal computer requirements:* Graduate business students are required to have a personal computer. *Special opportunities include:* An internship program is available. *Placement services include:* Alumni network, career placement, job search course, career counseling/planning, electronic job bank, resume referral, career fairs, job interviews arranged, resume preparation, and career library.

EXPENSES *Tuition (state resident):* Full-time: $1164. Part-time: $582 per course. *Tuition (nonresident):* Full-time: $2328. Part-time: $1164 per course. *Tuition (international):* Full-time: $2328. Part-time: $1164 per course. *Required fees:* Full-time: $551. Part-time: $363 per course. *Graduate housing:* Room and board costs vary by number of occupants, type of accommodation, and type of board plan. *Typical cost:* $5600 (including board), $3000 (room only).

FINANCIAL AID (2007–08) 9 students received aid, including research assistantships. *Financial aid application deadline:* 6/1.

Financial Aid Contact Mr. Grady Collins, Director, AD 260, 307 University Boulevard, Mobile, AL 36688. *Phone:* 334-460-6231.

INTERNATIONAL STUDENTS 10% of students enrolled are international students. *Services and facilities:* Counseling/support services,

ESL/language courses, International student organization, Language tutoring, Orientation, Visa Services. Financial aid is not available to international students. *Required with application:* TOEFL with recommended score of 525 (paper); proof of adequate funds; proof of health/immunizations.

International Student Contact Ms. Brenda Hinson, Director, International Admissions, 307 North University Boulevard, Mobile, AL 36688. *Phone:* 334-460-6050.

APPLICATION *Required:* GMAT, application form, baccalaureate/first degree, transcripts of college work. *Application fee:* $35. *Deadlines:* 7/15 for fall, 6/15 for fall (international).

Application Contact Dr. John Gamble, Associate Dean, 307 North University Boulevard, Mobile, AL 36688. *Phone:* 334-460-6418. *Fax:* 334-460-6529. *E-mail:* jgamble@usouthal.edu.

ALASKA

Alaska Pacific University
Business Administration Department
Anchorage, Alaska

Phone: 907-564-8248 **Fax:** 907-564-8317 **E-mail:** admissions@alaskapacific.edu

Business Program(s) Web Site: http://www.alaskapacific.edu/

Graduate Business Unit Enrollment *Total:* 59 (7 full-time; 52 part-time; 26 women; 3 international). *Average Age:* 37.

Graduate Business Faculty *Total:* 10 (3 full-time; 7 part-time).

Admissions *Applied:* 29. *Admitted:* 24. *Enrolled:* 19. *Average GMAT:* 493. *Average GPA:* 3.38

Academic Calendar Semesters.

DEGREES MBA

MBA—Executive MBA Full-time and part-time. At least 36 total credits required. 12 to 84 months to complete program. *Concentration:* executive programs.

MBA—Global Finance Part-time. At least 36 total credits required. 12 to 84 months to complete program. *Concentration:* international finance.

MBA—MBA Concentration in Health Services Administration Full-time and part-time. At least 36 total credits required. 12 to 84 months to complete program. *Concentration:* health administration.

MBA—Master of Business Administration Full-time and part-time. At least 36 total credits required. 12 to 84 months to complete program. *Concentration:* general MBA.

RESOURCES AND SERVICES 40 on-campus PCs are available to graduate business students. Access to Internet/World Wide Web, online (class) registration, and online grade reports available. *Personal computer requirements:* Graduate business students are strongly recommended to purchase or lease a personal computer. *Special opportunities include:* An internship program is available. *Placement services include:* Alumni network, career counseling/planning, career fairs, resume preparation, and career library.

EXPENSES *Tuition:* Full-time: $10,800. Part-time: $600 per credit hour. *Required fees:* Full-time: $220. Part-time: $110 per semester. *Graduate housing:* Room and board costs vary by number of occupants. *Typical cost:* $7700 (including board).

FINANCIAL AID (2007–08) 32 students received aid, including grants, loans, research assistantships, teaching assistantships, and work study. Aid is available to part-time students. *Financial aid application deadline:* 6/1.

Financial Aid Contact Mrs. Louise Driver, Director of Student Financial Services, 4101 University Drive, Anchorage, AK 99508. *Phone:* 907-564-8342. *Fax:* 907-564-8317. *E-mail:* ldriver@alaskapacific.edu.

INTERNATIONAL STUDENTS 5% of students enrolled are international students. *Services and facilities:* Counseling/support services, International student organization. Financial aid is available to international students. *Required with application:* TOEFL with recommended score of 550 (paper) or 79 (Internet); proof of adequate funds.

International Student Contact Ekaterina Kingry, International Admissions Counselor, 4101 University Drive, Anchorage, AK 99508-4672. *Phone:* 907-564-8248. *Fax:* 907-564-8317. *E-mail:* kat@alaskapacific.edu.

APPLICATION *Required:* Application form, baccalaureate/first degree, essay, 2 letters of recommendation, resume/curriculum vitae, transcripts of college work. School will accept GMAT and GRE. *Recommended:* Work experience. *Application fee:* $25. Applications for domestic and international students are processed on a rolling basis.

Application Contact Jennifer Jensen, Director of Admissions, 4101 University Drive, Anchorage, AK 99508-4672. *Phone:* 907-564-8248. *Fax:* 907-564-8317. *E-mail:* admissions@alaskapacific.edu.

University of Alaska Anchorage
College of Business and Public Policy
Anchorage, Alaska

Phone: 907-786-4129 **Fax:** 907-786-4119 **E-mail:** pat.lee@uaa.alaska.edu

Business Program(s) Web Site: http://www.cbpp.uaa.alaska.edu/busadmissions.asp

Graduate Business Unit Enrollment *Total:* 153 (42 full-time; 111 part-time; 91 women; 15 international). *Average Age:* 34.

Graduate Business Faculty 17 full-time.

Admissions *Applied:* 94. *Admitted:* 65. *Average GPA:* 3.0

Academic Calendar Semesters.

Accreditation AACSB—The Association to Advance Collegiate Schools of Business.

DEGREE MBA

MBA—Master of Business Administration Full-time and part-time. 36 total credits required. 12 to 84 months to complete program. *Concentration:* management.

RESOURCES AND SERVICES 200 on-campus PCs are available to graduate business students. Access to Internet/World Wide Web, online (class) registration, and online grade reports available. *Personal computer requirements:* Graduate business students are strongly recommended to purchase or lease a personal computer. *Special opportunities include:* An international exchange program and an internship program are available. *Placement services include:* Electronic job bank, career fairs, resume preparation, and career library.

EXPENSES *Tuition (state resident):* Part-time: $301 per credit hour. *Tuition (nonresident):* Part-time: $615 per credit hour. *Required fees:* Part-time: $158 per semester. *Graduate housing:* Room and board costs vary by number of occupants, type of accommodation, and type of board plan. *Typical cost:* $8880 (including board), $5680 (room only).

FINANCIAL AID (2007–08) Grants, loans, and scholarships. Aid is available to part-time students.

Financial Aid Contact Mr. Ted Malone, Student Financial Aid Director, 3211 Providence Drive, Anchorage, AK 99508-8060. *Phone:* 907-786-1520. *Fax:* 907-786-6122. *E-mail:* antem2@uaa.alaska.edu.

INTERNATIONAL STUDENTS 10% of students enrolled are international students. *Services and facilities:* Counseling/support services, ESL/language courses, International student housing, International student organization, Orientation, Visa Services. Financial aid is available to

University of Alaska Anchorage (continued)

international students. *Required with application:* TOEFL with recommended score of 550 (paper); proof of adequate funds; proof of health/immunizations.

International Student Contact Mrs. Doni Williams, International Student Advisor, 3211 Providence Drive, Anchorage, AK 99508-8060. *Phone:* 907-786-1573. *Fax:* 907-786-4888. *E-mail:* doni@uaa.alaska.edu.

APPLICATION *Required:* Application form, baccalaureate/first degree, transcripts of college work. School will accept GMAT. *Recommended:* Interview. *Application fee:* $60. *Deadlines:* 6/1 for fall (international), 10/15 for spring (international). Applications for domestic students are processed on a rolling basis.

Application Contact Mrs. Pat Lee, MBA Program Assistant, 3211 Providence Drive, Anchorage, AK 99508-8060. *Phone:* 907-786-4129. *Fax:* 907-786-4119. *E-mail:* pat.lee@uaa.alaska.edu.

University of Alaska Fairbanks
School of Management

Fairbanks, Alaska

Phone: 907-474-7500 **Fax:** 907-474-5379 **E-mail:** admissions@uaf.edu

Business Program(s) Web Site: http://www.uafsom.com/

Graduate Business Unit Enrollment *Total:* 24 (11 full-time; 13 part-time; 13 women; 6 international). *Average Age:* 31.

Graduate Business Faculty 8 full-time.

Admissions *Applied:* 13. *Admitted:* 12. *Enrolled:* 12. *Average GMAT:* 557. *Average GPA:* 3.26

Academic Calendar Semesters.

Accreditation AACSB—The Association to Advance Collegiate Schools of Business.

After Graduation (Class of 2006–07) *Employed within 3 months of graduation:* 63%. *Average starting salary:* $44,000.

DEGREE MBA

MBA—Master of Business Administration Full-time and part-time. 30 to 54 total credits required. 18 to 84 months to complete program. *Concentrations:* finance, management.

RESOURCES AND SERVICES 146 on-campus PCs are available to graduate business students. Access to Internet/World Wide Web, online (class) registration, and online grade reports available. *Personal computer requirements:* Graduate business students are not required to have a personal computer. *Special opportunities include:* An internship program is available. *Placement services include:* Alumni network, career placement, career counseling/planning, career fairs, and resume preparation.

FINANCIAL AID (2007–08) Loans, scholarships, and teaching assistantships. Aid is available to part-time students. *Financial aid application deadline:* 2/15.

Financial Aid Contact Ms. Deanna Dieringer, Director of Financial Aid, PO Box 756360, Fairbanks, AK 99775-6360. *Phone:* 907-474-7256. *Fax:* 907-474-7065. *E-mail:* financialaid@uaf.edu.

INTERNATIONAL STUDENTS 25% of students enrolled are international students. *Services and facilities:* Counseling/support services, Housing location assistance, International student organization, Orientation, Visa Services. Financial aid is available to international students. *Required with application:* TOEFL with recommended score of 213 (computer) or 550 (paper); proof of adequate funds; proof of health/immunizations.

International Student Contact Dr. John Lehman, Director of International Programs, PO Box 757760, International Programs, Fairbanks, AK 99775. *Phone:* 907-474-5327. *Fax:* 907-474-5979. *E-mail:* fyoip@uaf.edu.

APPLICATION *Required:* Application form, baccalaureate/first degree, 3 letters of recommendation, personal statement, resume/curriculum vitae, transcripts of college work. School will accept GMAT and GRE. *Application fee:* $50. Applications for domestic and international students are processed on a rolling basis.

Application Contact Ms. Nancy Dix, Director, Admissions Office, PO Box 757480, Fairbanks, AK 99775-7480. *Phone:* 907-474-7500. *Fax:* 907-474-5379. *E-mail:* admissions@uaf.edu.

ARIZONA

Argosy University, Phoenix
College of Business

Phoenix, Arizona

Phone: 602-216-2600 **Fax:** 602-216-3151

Business Program(s) Web Site: http://www.argosy.edu/phoenix

DEGREES DBA • MBA

DBA—Doctor of Business Administration (DBA) *Concentrations:* accounting, information systems, international business, management, marketing.

MBA—Master of Business Administration (MBA) *Concentrations:* finance, health administration, information systems, international business, management, marketing.

RESOURCES AND SERVICES *Personal computer requirements:* Graduate business students are not required to have a personal computer.

Financial Aid Contact Director of Admissions, 2233 West Dunlap Avenue, Phoenix, AZ 85021. *Phone:* 602-216-2600. *Fax:* 602-216-3151.

International Student Contact Director of Admissions, 2233 West Dunlap Avenue, Phoenix, AZ 85021. *Phone:* 602-216-2600. *Fax:* 602-216-3151.

Application Contact Director of Admissions, 2233 West Dunlap Avenue, Phoenix, AZ 85021. *Phone:* 602-216-2600. *Fax:* 602-216-3151.

See full description on page 566.

Arizona State University
W.P. Carey School of Business

Tempe, Arizona

Phone: 480-965-3332 **Fax:** 480-965-8569 **E-mail:** wpcareymba@asu.edu

Business Program(s) Web Site: http://wpcareymba.asu.edu

Academic Calendar Four 8-week terms.

Accreditation AACSB—The Association to Advance Collegiate Schools of Business.

DEGREES JD/MBA • MBA • MBA/M Acc • MBA/MHSA • MBA/MIM • MBA/MS • MBA/MTAX

JD/MBA—Master of Business Administration/Juris Doctorate Full-time. Students must complete a separate application for each degree. At least 117 total credits required. 48 to 60 months to complete program. *Concentrations:* combined degrees, law.

MBA—Full-Time Master of Business Administration Full-time. At least 58 total credits required. 22 to 24 months to complete program.

Concentrations: finance, health administration, information management, management, marketing, sports/entertainment management, supply chain management.

MBA—Master of Business Administration—Evening Program Part-time. At least 48 total credits required. 22 to 36 months to complete program. *Concentration:* general MBA.

MBA—Master of Business Administration—Executive Program Part-time. At least 48 total credits required. 22 to 24 months to complete program. *Concentration:* executive programs.

MBA—Master of Business Administration—Global Executive Program Part-time. Distance learning option. At least 48 total credits required. Minimum of 22 months to complete program. *Concentration:* general MBA.

MBA—Master of Business Administration—Online Program Part-time. Distance learning option. At least 48 total credits required. Minimum of 22 months to complete program. *Concentration:* general MBA.

MBA—Master of Business Administration—Technology Program Part-time. At least 48 total credits required. 24 to 36 months to complete program. *Concentrations:* general MBA, technology management.

MBA/M Acc—Master of Business Administration/Master of Accountancy and Information Systems Full-time. Students must complete a separate application for each degree. At least 63 total credits required. Minimum of 24 months to complete program. *Concentrations:* accounting, combined degrees, information systems.

MBA/MHSA—Master of Business Administration/Master of Health Sector Management Full-time. Students must complete a separate application for each degree. At least 72 total credits required. 22 to 24 months to complete program. *Concentrations:* combined degrees, health administration.

MBA/MIM—Master of Business Administration/Thunderbird Master of International Management Full-time. Students must complete a separate application for each degree. At least 66 total credits required. Minimum of 22 months to complete program. *Concentrations:* combined degrees, international management.

MBA/MS—Master of Business Administration/Master of Science in Economics Full-time. Students must complete a separate application for each degree. At least 66 total credits required. 22 to 24 months to complete program. *Concentrations:* combined degrees, economics.

MBA/MTAX—Master of Business Administration/Master of Science in Taxation Full-time. Students must complete a separate application for each degree. At least 63 total credits required. 22 to 24 months to complete program. *Concentrations:* combined degrees, taxation.

RESOURCES AND SERVICES Access to Internet/World Wide Web and online grade reports available. *Personal computer requirements:* Graduate business students are required to have a personal computer. *Special opportunities include:* An international exchange program and an internship program are available. *Placement services include:* Alumni network, career placement, job search course, career counseling/planning, electronic job bank, resume referral, career fairs, job interviews arranged, resume preparation, and career library.

FINANCIAL AID (2007–08) Fellowships, loans, research assistantships, scholarships, and teaching assistantships. Aid is available to part-time students. *Financial aid application deadline:* 3/1.

Financial Aid Contact Senior Coordinator, Financial Aid and Recruitment, PO Box 874906, Tempe, AZ 85287-4906. *Phone:* 480-965-6890. *Fax:* 480-965-8569. *E-mail:* wpcareymba.finaid@asu.edu.

INTERNATIONAL STUDENTS *Services and facilities:* Counseling/support services, ESL/language courses, International student housing, International student organization, Orientation, Visa Services. Financial aid is available to international students. *Required with application:* TOEFL with recommended score of 237 (computer) or 580 (paper); proof of adequate funds; proof of health/immunizations. *Recommended with application:* TWE.

International Student Contact Carol Takao, Director of Educational Development, International Student Office, Student Services Building, Room 265, Tempe, AZ 85287-0512. *Phone:* 480-965-3366. *Fax:* 480-965-9608. *E-mail:* carol.takao@asu.edu.

APPLICATION *Required:* GMAT, application form, baccalaureate/first degree, essay, interview, 2 letters of recommendation, personal statement, resume/curriculum vitae, transcripts of college work, 2 years of work experience. *Application fee:* $50. Applications for domestic and international students are processed on a rolling basis.

Application Contact W. P. Carey MBA Admissions, PO Box 874906, Tempe, AZ 85287-4906. *Phone:* 480-965-3332. *Fax:* 480-965-8569. *E-mail:* wpcareymba@asu.edu.

Arizona State University at the West campus

School of Global Management and Leadership

Phoenix, Arizona

Phone: 602-543-6239 **Fax:** 602-543-6249 **E-mail:** doris.fagin@asu.edu

Business Program(s) Web Site: http://sgml.asu.edu/programs/graduate/

Graduate Business Unit Enrollment *Total:* 319 (81 full-time; 238 part-time; 150 women; 10 international). *Average Age:* 33.

Graduate Business Faculty *Total:* 39 (36 full-time; 3 part-time).

Admissions *Applied:* 59. *Admitted:* 26. *Enrolled:* 18. *Average GMAT:* 585. *Average GPA:* 3.2

Academic Calendar Semesters.

Accreditation AACSB—The Association to Advance Collegiate Schools of Business.

DEGREES M Acc • MLM • MMR • UA Undergraduate Associate

M Acc—Master of Accountancy Full-time and part-time. Distance learning option. 30 total credits required. 12 to 60 months to complete program. *Concentration:* accounting.

MLM—Master of Applied Leadership and Management Full-time and part-time. 30 total credits required. 12 to 60 months to complete program. *Concentrations:* leadership, management.

MMR—MS in Customer Centric Innovation and Marketing Research Full-time and part-time. 30 total credits required. 12 to 60 months to complete program. *Concentration:* marketing research.

UA Undergraduate Associate—MS in Financial Analysis and Portfolio Management Full-time and part-time. 30 total credits required. 12 to 60 months to complete program. *Concentrations:* finance, investments and securities.

RESOURCES AND SERVICES 150 on-campus PCs are available to graduate business students. Access to Internet/World Wide Web, online (class) registration, and online grade reports available. *Personal computer requirements:* Graduate business students are strongly recommended to purchase or lease a personal computer. *Placement services include:* Alumni network, career counseling/planning, career fairs, and resume preparation.

EXPENSES *Tuition (state resident):* Full-time: $15,000. Part-time: $1500 per course. *Tuition (nonresident):* Full-time: $25,050. Part-time: $2505 per course. *Tuition (international):* Full-time: $25,050. Part-time: $2505 per course. *Required fees:* Full-time: $10,000. Part-time: $1000 per course. Tuition and/or fees vary by number of courses or credits taken.

FINANCIAL AID (2007–08) 75 students received aid, including loans, research assistantships, scholarships, and teaching assistantships. Aid is available to part-time students.

Financial Aid Contact Ms. Leah Samudio, Manager, Financial Aid Services, PO Box 37100, Phoenix, AZ 85069-7100. *Phone:* 602-543-8176. *Fax:* 602-543-8108. *E-mail:* leah.samudio@asu.edu.

INTERNATIONAL STUDENTS 3% of students enrolled are international students. *Services and facilities:* Counseling/support services, Visa Services. Financial aid is not available to international students. *Required*

Arizona State University at the West campus (continued)

with application: TOEFL with recommended score of 250 (computer) or 600 (paper); proof of adequate funds; proof of health/immunizations.

International Student Contact International Student Office, Arizona State University, PO Box 870512, Tempe, AZ 85287-0512. *Phone:* 480-965-7451. *E-mail:* iso@asu.edu.

APPLICATION *Required:* GMAT, GRE, application form, baccalaureate/first degree, 2 letters of recommendation, personal statement, resume/curriculum vitae, transcripts of college work. *Recommended:* Work experience. *Application fee:* $65, $85 (international). Applications for domestic and international students are processed on a rolling basis.

Application Contact Ms. Doris Fagin, Student Services Coordinator, PO Box 37100, Phoenix, AZ 85069-7100. *Phone:* 602-543-6239. *Fax:* 602-543-6249. *E-mail:* doris.fagin@asu.edu.

DeVry University
Keller Graduate School of Management

Phoenix, Arizona

Phone: 602-870-0117 **Fax:** 602-870-0022

Business Program(s) Web Site: http://www.devry.edu

Academic Calendar Semesters.

DEGREES MAFM • MBA • MHRM • MIS • MPA • MPM

MAFM—Master of Accounting and Financial Management Full-time and part-time. Distance learning option. At least 44 total credits required. 18 to 60 months to complete program. *Concentrations:* accounting, financial management/planning.

MBA—Master of Business Administration Full-time and part-time. Distance learning option. At least 48 total credits required. 18 to 60 months to complete program. *Concentration:* management.

MHRM—Master of Human Resource Management Full-time and part-time. Distance learning option. At least 45 total credits required. 18 to 60 months to complete program. *Concentration:* human resources management.

MIS—Master of Information Systems Management Full-time and part-time. Distance learning option. At least 45 total credits required. 18 to 60 months to complete program. *Concentration:* information systems.

MPA—Master of Public Administration Full-time and part-time. Distance learning option. At least 45 total credits required. 18 to 60 months to complete program. *Concentration:* public policy and administration.

MPM—Master of Project Management Full-time and part-time. Distance learning option. At least 42 total credits required. 18 to 60 months to complete program. *Concentration:* project management.

RESOURCES AND SERVICES *Personal computer requirements:* Graduate business students are not required to have a personal computer.

APPLICATION *Required:* Application form, baccalaureate/first degree, interview, transcripts of college work. Applications for domestic and international students are processed on a rolling basis.

Application Contact Admissions Office, Phoenix Campus, 2149 West Dunlap Avenue, Phoenix, AZ 85021. *Phone:* 602-870-0117. *Fax:* 602-870-0022.

Grand Canyon University
College of Business

Phoenix, Arizona

Phone: 866-969-9096

Business Program(s) Web Site: http://www.gcu.edu/petersons

Accreditation ACBSP—The American Council of Business Schools and Programs.

DEGREES EMBA • MBA • MBA/MS • MBA/MSN • MS

EMBA—Executive Master of Business Administration Full-time and part-time. Distance learning option. At least 39 total credits required. 12 months to complete program. *Concentration:* executive programs.

MBA—MBA with Emphasis in Management of Information Systems Full-time and part-time. Distance learning option. 36 to 51 total credits required. *Concentration:* information systems.

MBA—Master of Business Administration: Accounting Full-time and part-time. Distance learning option. 36 to 51 total credits required. *Concentration:* accounting.

MBA—Master of Business Administration: Finance Full-time and part-time. Distance learning option. 36 to 51 total credits required. *Concentration:* finance.

MBA—Master of Business Administration: General Management Full-time and part-time. Distance learning option. 36 to 51 total credits required. *Concentration:* administration.

MBA—Master of Business Administration: Health System Management Full-time and part-time. Distance learning option. 36 to 51 total credits required. *Concentration:* health care.

MBA—Master of Business Administration: Leadership Full-time and part-time. Distance learning option. 36 to 51 total credits required. *Concentration:* leadership.

MBA—Master of Business Administration: Marketing Full-time and part-time. Distance learning option. 36 to 51 total credits required. *Concentration:* marketing.

MBA—Master of Business Administration: Six Sigma Emphasis Full-time and part-time. Distance learning option. 36 to 51 total credits required. *Concentration:* other.

MBA/MS—Master of Business Administration and Master of Science in Leadership Full-time and part-time. Distance learning option. Up to 69 total credits required. *Concentration:* leadership.

MBA/MSN—Master of Business Administration and Master of Science in Nursing: Nursing Leadership in Health Care Systems Full-time and part-time. Distance learning option. Up to 69 total credits required. *Concentration:* health administration.

MS—Master of Science in Leadership Full-time and part-time. Distance learning option. At least 36 total credits required. *Concentration:* leadership.

MS—Master of Science in Leadership with an Emphasis in Disaster Preparedness and Crisis Management Full-time and part-time. Distance learning option. Up to 36 total credits required. *Concentration:* leadership.

RESOURCES AND SERVICES 64 on-campus PCs are available to graduate business students. Access to Internet/World Wide Web, online (class) registration, and online grade reports available. *Personal computer requirements:* Graduate business students are strongly recommended to purchase or lease a personal computer. *Special opportunities include:* An international exchange program is available. *Placement services include:* Alumni network, career placement, career counseling/planning, career fairs, and resume preparation.

Application Contact MBA Enrollment Team, 3300 West Camelback Road, PO Box 11097, Phoenix, AZ 85017-3030. *Phone:* 866-969-9096.

Northcentral University
MBA Program

Prescott Valley, Arizona

Phone: 888-327-2877 Ext. 8072 **Fax:** 928-541-7817 **E-mail:** pkeegan@ncu.edu

Business Program(s) Web Site: http://www.ncu.edu

DEGREES MBA

MBA—Applied Computer Science Part-time. Distance learning option. Up to 36 total credits required. *Concentration:* information technology.

MBA—Criminal Justice Part-time. Distance learning option. Up to 36 total credits required. *Concentrations:* law, legal administration.

MBA—Homeland Security Part-time. Distance learning option. Up to 36 total credits required. *Concentration:* public policy and administration.

MBA—Master of Business Administration Part-time. Distance learning option. At least 36 total credits required. *Concentrations:* electronic commerce (E-commerce), financial management/planning, general MBA, health administration, human resources management, international business, management, management information systems, public policy and administration, sports/entertainment management, technology management.

RESOURCES AND SERVICES Access to Internet/World Wide Web, online (class) registration, and online grade reports available. *Personal computer requirements:* Graduate business students are required to have a personal computer. *Placement services include:* Alumni network.

Application Contact Ms. Poppy Keegan, Admissions Counselor, 505 West Whipple Street, Prescott, AZ 86301. *Phone:* 888-327-2877 Ext. 8072. *Fax:* 928-541-7817. *E-mail:* pkeegan@ncu.edu.

Northern Arizona University
College of Business Administration
Flagstaff, Arizona

Phone: 928-523-7342 **Fax:** 928-523-7996 **E-mail:** mba@nau.edu

Business Program(s) Web Site: http://www.cba.nau.edu/mba/

Graduate Business Unit Enrollment *Total:* 21 (19 full-time; 2 part-time; 5 women; 3 international). *Average Age:* 25.

Graduate Business Faculty *Total:* 15 (13 full-time; 2 part-time).

Admissions *Applied:* 36. *Admitted:* 29. *Enrolled:* 21. *Average GMAT:* 534. *Average GPA:* 3.36

Academic Calendar Semesters.

Accreditation AACSB—The Association to Advance Collegiate Schools of Business.

DEGREES MBA • MBA/Diploma

MBA Full-time. At least 31 total credits required. 10 to 36 months to complete program. *Concentrations:* accounting, finance, management, marketing.

MBA/Diploma—MBA-ACC Accounting Full-time. Undergraduate degree in Accounting. At least 31 total credits required. 10 to 36 months to complete program. *Concentration:* accounting.

RESOURCES AND SERVICES 200 on-campus PCs are available to graduate business students. Access to Internet/World Wide Web, online (class) registration, and online grade reports available. *Personal computer requirements:* Graduate business students are not required to have a personal computer. *Placement services include:* Alumni network, career placement, career counseling/planning, electronic job bank, resume referral, career fairs, job interviews arranged, and resume preparation.

EXPENSES *Tuition (state resident):* Full-time: $6917. *Tuition (nonresident):* Full-time: $17,079. *Tuition (international):* Full-time: $17,079. *Required fees:* Full-time: $3500. *Graduate housing:* Room and board costs vary by number of occupants, type of accommodation, and type of board plan. *Typical cost:* $10,862 (including board), $7730 (room only).

FINANCIAL AID (2007–08) 12 students received aid, including fellowships, loans, research assistantships, scholarships, teaching assistantships, and work study.

Financial Aid Contact Ms. Jane Thompson, Director, MBA Program, The W. A. Franke College of Business, MBA Program Office, PO Box 15066, Flagstaff, AZ 86011-5066. *Phone:* 928-523-7342. *Fax:* 928-523-7996. *E-mail:* mba@nau.edu.

INTERNATIONAL STUDENTS 14% of students enrolled are international students. *Services and facilities:* Counseling/support services, ESL/language courses, Housing location assistance, International student organization, Language tutoring, Orientation, Visa Services. Financial aid is available to international students. *Required with application:* IELT with recommended score of 7; TOEFL with recommended score of 250 (computer), 600 (paper), or 95 (Internet); proof of adequate funds; proof of health/immunizations.

International Student Contact Mr. Matthew Geisler, Senior Program Coordinator, Center for International Education, Box 5598, Tinsley Hall, Room 102, Flagstaff, AZ 86011. *Phone:* 928-523-2409. *Fax:* 928-523-2409. *E-mail:* cie@nau.edu.

APPLICATION *Required:* GMAT, application form, baccalaureate/first degree, essay, interview, 2 letters of recommendation, personal statement, resume/curriculum vitae, transcripts of college work. *Recommended:* 2 years of work experience. *Application fee:* $50. Applications for domestic and international students are processed on a rolling basis.

Application Contact Ms. Jane Thompson, Director, MBA Program, MBA Program Office, PO Box 15066, Flagstaff, AZ 86011-5066. *Phone:* 928-523-7342. *Fax:* 928-523-7996. *E-mail:* mba@nau.edu.

Ottawa University
Graduate Studies-Arizona
Phoenix, Arizona

Phone: 602-371-1188 **Fax:** 602-371-0035 **E-mail:** tony.muscia@ottawa.edu

Business Program(s) Web Site: http://www.ottawa.edu/mba

DEGREES MA • MBA

MA—Master of Arts Full-time and part-time. Distance learning option. At least 36 total credits required. 18 to 60 months to complete program. *Concentrations:* human resources management, organizational management.

MA—Master of Arts Full-time and part-time. Distance learning option. At least 36 total credits required. *Concentration:* human resources development.

MBA—Master of Business Administration Full-time and part-time. Distance learning option. At least 36 total credits required. 18 to 60 months to complete program. *Concentrations:* finance, general MBA, human resources management, information technology, international business, leadership, marketing.

RESOURCES AND SERVICES 40 on-campus PCs are available to graduate business students. Access to Internet/World Wide Web, online (class) registration, and online grade reports available. *Personal computer requirements:* Graduate business students are strongly recommended to purchase or lease a personal computer. *Placement services include:* Alumni network.

Application Contact Dr. Tony Muscia, Director, Enrollment Management, 10020 North 25th Avenue, Phoenix, AZ 85021. *Phone:* 602-371-1188. *Fax:* 602-371-0035. *E-mail:* tony.muscia@ottawa.edu.

Thunderbird School of Global Management
Graduate Programs
Glendale, Arizona

Phone: 602-978-7596 **Fax:** 602-439-5432 **E-mail:** admissions@thunderbird.edu

ARIZONA

Thunderbird School of Global Management (continued)

Business Program(s) Web Site: http://www.thunderbird.edu

Graduate Business Unit Enrollment *Total:* 1,194 (583 full-time; 611 part-time; 336 women; 665 international). *Average Age:* 28.

Graduate Business Faculty *Total:* 49 (46 full-time; 3 part-time).

Admissions *Applied:* 595. *Admitted:* 430. *Enrolled:* 253. *Average GMAT:* 598. *Average GPA:* 3.3

Academic Calendar Trimesters.

Accreditation AACSB—The Association to Advance Collegiate Schools of Business.

After Graduation (Class of 2006–07) *Employed within 3 months of graduation:* 69%. *Average starting salary:* $80,979.

DEGREES EMBA • GMBA • M Sc • MA • MBA • MIM

EMBA—Executive Master of Business Administration in International Management Part-time. Distance learning option. At least 50 total credits required. Minimum of 23 months to complete program. *Concentration:* international management.

GMBA—Global Master of Business Administration—On Demand Program Part-time. Distance learning option. 47 total credits required. Minimum of 19 months to complete program. *Concentration:* international management.

GMBA—Global Master of Business Administration for Latin American Managers Part-time. Distance learning option. At least 46 total credits required. Minimum of 21 months to complete program. *Concentration:* Latin American business studies.

M Sc—Global Management Full-time. At least 45 total credits required. Minimum of 12 months to complete program. *Concentration:* international management.

MA—Global Affairs and Management Full-time. At least 45 total credits required. Minimum of 12 months to complete program. *Concentration:* international management.

MBA—Master of Business Administration in Global Management Full-time. 2 years of managerial/business experience. 48 to 60 total credits required. 12 to 20 months to complete program. *Concentrations:* international development management, international finance, international marketing.

MIM—Dual Degree—Master of Global Management Full-time. Distance learning option. 30 total credits required. *Concentration:* international management.

MIM—Post-MBA—Master of Global Management Full-time. Distance learning option. 30 total credits required. *Concentrations:* entrepreneurship, international finance, international management, international marketing.

RESOURCES AND SERVICES 141 on-campus PCs are available to graduate business students. Access to Internet/World Wide Web, online (class) registration, and online grade reports available. *Personal computer requirements:* Graduate business students are required to have a personal computer. *Special opportunities include:* An international exchange program and an internship program are available. *Placement services include:* Alumni network, career placement, job search course, career counseling/planning, electronic job bank, resume referral, career fairs, job interviews arranged, resume preparation, and career library.

EXPENSES *Tuition:* Full-time: $37,740. Part-time: $1258 per credit hour. *Tuition (international):* Full-time: $37,740. Part-time: $1258 per credit hour. *Required fees:* Full-time: $1255. *Typical graduate housing cost:* $1950 (including board), $1275 (room only).

FINANCIAL AID (2007–08) 383 students received aid, including grants, scholarships, and work study. *Financial aid application deadline:* 2/15.

Financial Aid Contact Ms. Catherine King-Todd, Director of Financial Aid, 15249 North 59th Avenue, Glendale, AZ 85306. *Phone:* 602-978-7888. *Fax:* 602-439-5432. *E-mail:* catherine.king-todd@thunderbird.edu.

INTERNATIONAL STUDENTS 56% of students enrolled are international students. *Services and facilities:* Counseling/support services, ESL/language courses, Housing location assistance, International student housing, International student organization, Orientation, Newsletter. Financial aid is available to international students. *Required with application:* TOEFL with recommended score of 250 (computer), 621 (paper), or 100 (Internet); proof of adequate funds.

International Student Contact Ms. Felicia Welch, Director, Academic and International Services, 15249 North 59th Avenue, Student Services and Program Support, Glendale, AZ 85306. *Phone:* 602-978-7544. *Fax:* 602-547-1356. *E-mail:* felicia.welch@thunderbird.edu.

APPLICATION *Required:* GMAT, application form, baccalaureate/first degree, essay, 2 letters of recommendation, personal statement, resume/ curriculum vitae, transcripts of college work, 3 years of work experience. *Application fee:* $125. Applications for domestic and international students are processed on a rolling basis.

Application Contact Ms. Judith Johnson, Associate Vice President, Admissions/Financial Aid, 15249 North 59th Avenue, Glendale, AZ 85306. *Phone:* 602-978-7596. *Fax:* 602-439-5432. *E-mail:* admissions@ thunderbird.edu.

The University of Arizona
Eller College of Management
Tucson, Arizona

Phone: 520-621-4008 **Fax:** 520-621-2606 **E-mail:** mba_admissions@eller.arizona.edu

Business Program(s) Web Site: http://www.ellermba.arizona.edu

Graduate Business Unit Enrollment *Total:* 329 (119 full-time; 210 part-time; 91 women; 86 international). *Average Age:* 30.

Graduate Business Faculty *Total:* 131 (117 full-time; 14 part-time).

Admissions *Applied:* 398. *Admitted:* 264. *Enrolled:* 190. *Average GMAT:* 603. *Average GPA:* 3.33

Academic Calendar Traditional 21-month full-time program; continuous 14-month executive program with classes every other Friday and Saturday; and continuous 18-month evening program with classes once weekly.

Accreditation AACSB—The Association to Advance Collegiate Schools of Business.

After Graduation (Class of 2006–07) *Employed within 3 months of graduation:* 80%. *Average starting salary:* $75,003.

DEGREES JD/MBA • MBA • MBA/MIM • MBA/MS • Pharm D/MBA

JD/MBA—Juris Doctor/Master of Business Administration Full-time. Must apply to both the MBA program and the JD program separately. At least 90 total credits required. 45 months to complete program. *Concentrations:* entrepreneurship, finance, human resources management, legal administration, management, management information systems, marketing, marketing research, operations management.

MBA—Master of Business Administration Full-time and part-time. GMAT required for full-time and evening programs; TOEFL is required for international students. 55 to 60 total credits required. 14 to 21 months to complete program. *Concentrations:* accounting, entrepreneurship, executive programs, finance, general MBA, management information systems, marketing.

MBA/MIM—Master of Business Administration/Master of International Management Full-time. Must apply to both the Eller School and Thunderbird. At least 75 total credits required. 38 to 41 months to complete program. *Concentrations:* entrepreneurship, finance, human resources management, international and area business studies, international banking, international business, international development management, international economics, international finance, international logistics, international management, international marketing, international trade, management, management information systems, marketing, marketing research, operations management.

MBA/MS—Master of Business Administration/Master of Science in Management Information Systems Full-time. Must apply to both the

MBA program and the MS programs separately. At least 75 total credits required. 38 to 41 months to complete program. *Concentrations:* accounting, finance, management information systems.

Pharm D/MBA—Doctor of Pharmacy/Master of Business Administration Full-time and part-time. Up to 209 total credits required. Minimum of 60 months to complete program. *Concentrations:* accounting, economics, entrepreneurship, executive programs, finance, general MBA, management information systems, marketing, operations management.

RESOURCES AND SERVICES 60 on-campus PCs are available to graduate business students. Access to Internet/World Wide Web, online (class) registration, and online grade reports available. *Personal computer requirements:* Graduate business students are strongly recommended to purchase or lease a personal computer. *Special opportunities include:* An international exchange program and an internship program are available. *Placement services include:* Alumni network, career placement, job search course, career counseling/planning, electronic job bank, resume referral, career fairs, job interviews arranged, resume preparation, and career library.

EXPENSES *Tuition (state resident):* Full-time: $15,267.84. *Tuition (nonresident):* Full-time: $26,075. *Tuition (international):* Full-time: $26,074.84. Tuition and/or fees vary by class time, number of courses or credits taken, and academic program.

FINANCIAL AID (2007–08) 58 students received aid, including fellowships, grants, loans, research assistantships, scholarships, and teaching assistantships. *Financial aid application deadline:* 4/15.

Financial Aid Contact Ms. Cindy Quick, Senior Program Coordinator, Financial Aid, Administration 203, PO Box 210066, Tucson, AZ 85721. *Phone:* 520-626-8583. *Fax:* 520-621-9473. *E-mail:* quick1@ email.arizona.edu.

INTERNATIONAL STUDENTS 26% of students enrolled are international students. *Services and facilities:* Counseling/support services, ESL/language courses, International student organization, Orientation, Visa Services. Financial aid is available to international students. *Required with application:* TOEFL with recommended score of 250 (computer), 600 (paper), or 100 (Internet); proof of adequate funds; proof of health/ immunizations.

International Student Contact International Student Programs and Services, 915 North Tyndall Avenue, PO Box 210441, Tucson, AZ 85721. *Phone:* 520-621-4627. *Fax:* 520-621-4069.

APPLICATION *Required:* GMAT, application form, baccalaureate/first degree, essay, interview, 2 letters of recommendation, personal statement, resume/curriculum vitae, transcripts of college work, 2 years of work experience. *Application fee:* $50. Applications for domestic and international students are processed on a rolling basis.

Application Contact Ms. Marisa Cox, Director, MBA Admissions, McClelland Hall 210, Box 210108, Tucson, AZ 85721-0108. *Phone:* 520-621-4008. *Fax:* 520-621-2606. *E-mail:* mba_admissions@ eller.arizona.edu.

University of Phoenix

College of Graduate Business and Management

Phoenix, Arizona

Phone: 480-317-6200 **Fax:** 480-643-1479 **E-mail:** beth.barilla@phoenix.edu

Business Program(s) Web Site: http://www.uoponline.com

DEGREES   M Mgt • MA • MBA

M Mgt—Master of Management Full-time. Distance learning option. Up to 39 total credits required. *Concentration:* organizational management.

M Mgt—Master of Management/Human Resource Management Full-time. Distance learning option. Up to 45 total credits required. *Concentration:* human resources management.

M Mgt—Master of Management/International Full-time. Distance learning option. Up to 30 total credits required. *Concentration:* international business.

M Mgt—Master of Management/Public Administration Full-time. Distance learning option. Up to 45 total credits required. *Concentration:* public policy and administration.

MA—Master of Arts in Organizational Management Full-time. Distance learning option. At least 40 total credits required. *Concentration:* organizational management.

MBA—Master of Business Administration/Human Resource Management Full-time. Distance learning option. Up to 45 total credits required. *Concentration:* human resources development.

MBA—Master of Business Administration in Accounting Full-time. Distance learning option. At least 54 total credits required. *Concentration:* accounting.

MBA—Master of Business Administration in Global Management Full-time. Distance learning option. At least 45 total credits required. *Concentration:* international management.

MBA—Master of Business Administration in e-Business Full-time. Distance learning option. At least 45 total credits required. *Concentration:* administration of technological information.

MBA—Master of Business Administration/Marketing Full-time. Distance learning option. Up to 45 total credits required. *Concentration:* marketing.

MBA—Master of Business Administration/Public Administration Full-time. Distance learning option. Up to 45 total credits required. *Concentration:* public policy and administration.

MBA—Master of Business Administration Full-time. Distance learning option. At least 39 total credits required. *Concentration:* administration.

RESOURCES AND SERVICES Access to online (class) registration and online grade reports available. *Personal computer requirements:* Graduate business students are strongly recommended to purchase or lease a personal computer. *Placement services include:* Alumni network.

Application Contact Beth Barilla, Associate Vice President of Student Admissions and Services, Mail Stop AA-K101, 4615 East Elwood Street, Phoenix, AZ 85040-1958. *Phone:* 480-317-6200. *Fax:* 480-643-1479. *E-mail:* beth.barilla@phoenix.edu.

University of Phoenix–Phoenix Campus

College of Graduate Business and Management

Phoenix, Arizona

Phone: 480-317-6200 **Fax:** 480-643-1479 **E-mail:** beth.barilla@phoenix.edu

Business Program(s) Web Site: http://www.phoenix.edu

DEGREES   EMBA • MA • MBA • MM

EMBA—Executive Master of Business Administration Full-time. At least 30 total credits required. *Concentration:* strategic management.

MA—Organizational Management Full-time. At least 40 total credits required. *Concentration:* organizational management.

MBA—Global Management Full-time. At least 45 total credits required. *Concentration:* international management.

MBA—Master of Business Administration/Accounting Full-time. At least 51 total credits required. *Concentration:* accounting.

MBA—e-Business Full-time. At least 46 total credits required. *Concentration:* electronic commerce (E-commerce).

MBA—Master of Business Administration Full-time. At least 45 total credits required. *Concentration:* administration.

University of Phoenix–Phoenix Campus (continued)

MM—Master of Management Full-time. At least 39 total credits required. *Concentration:* management.

RESOURCES AND SERVICES Access to online grade reports available. *Personal computer requirements:* Graduate business students are strongly recommended to purchase or lease a personal computer. *Placement services include:* Alumni network.

Application Contact Beth Barilla, Associate Vice President of Student Admissions and Services, Mail Stop AA-K101, 4615 East Elwood Street, Phoenix, AZ 85040-1958. *Phone:* 480-317-6200. *Fax:* 480-643-1479. *E-mail:* beth.barilla@phoenix.edu.

University of Phoenix–Southern Arizona Campus

College of Graduate Business and Management

Tucson, Arizona

Phone: 480-317-6200 **Fax:** 480-643-1479 **E-mail:** beth.barilla@phoenix.edu

Business Program(s) Web Site: http://www.phoenix.edu

DEGREES M Mgt • MA • MBA • MM

M Mgt—Human Resource Management Full-time. At least 39 total credits required. *Concentration:* human resources management.

MA—Organizational Management Full-time. At least 40 total credits required. *Concentration:* organizational management.

MBA—Accounting Full-time. At least 54 total credits required. *Concentration:* accounting.

MBA—Global Management Full-time. At least 45 total credits required. *Concentration:* international management.

MBA—Human Resource Management Full-time. At least 54 total credits required. *Concentration:* human resources management.

MBA—Marketing Full-time. At least 45 total credits required. *Concentration:* marketing.

MBA—e-Business Full-time. At least 45 total credits required. *Concentration:* electronic commerce (E-commerce).

MBA—Master of Business Administration Full-time. At least 45 total credits required. *Concentration:* administration.

MM—Master of Management Full-time. At least 39 total credits required. *Concentration:* management.

RESOURCES AND SERVICES Access to online grade reports available. *Personal computer requirements:* Graduate business students are strongly recommended to purchase or lease a personal computer. *Placement services include:* Alumni network.

Application Contact Beth Barilla, Associate Vice President of Student Admissions and Services, Mail Stop AA-K101, 4615 East Elwood Street, Phoenix, AZ 85040-1958. *Phone:* 480-317-6200. *Fax:* 480-643-1479. *E-mail:* beth.barilla@phoenix.edu.

Western International University

Graduate Programs in Business

Phoenix, Arizona

Phone: 602-943-2311 Ext. 1063 **E-mail:** karen.janitell@apollogrp.edu

Business Program(s) Web Site: http://www.wintu.edu

Graduate Business Unit Enrollment *Total:* 730 (730 full-time; 375 women; 105 international). *Average Age:* 35.

Graduate Business Faculty 149 part-time.

Admissions *Average GPA:* 3.0

Academic Calendar Continuous.

DEGREES MA • MBA • MPA • MS

MA—Innovative Leadership Full-time and part-time. Distance learning option. 33 to 39 total credits required. 12 to 72 months to complete program. *Concentration:* leadership.

MBA—Master of Business Administration in Finance Full-time. Distance learning option. 33 to 48 total credits required. 12 to 72 months to complete program. *Concentration:* finance.

MBA—Master of Business Administration in Information Technology Full-time. Distance learning option. 33 to 48 total credits required. 12 to 72 months to complete program. *Concentration:* management information systems.

MBA—Master of Business Administration in International Business Full-time. Distance learning option. 33 to 48 total credits required. 12 to 72 months to complete program. *Concentration:* international business.

MBA—Master of Business Administration in Management Full-time. Distance learning option. 33 to 48 total credits required. 12 to 72 months to complete program. *Concentration:* management.

MBA—Master of Business Administration in Marketing Full-time. Distance learning option. 33 to 48 total credits required. 12 to 72 months to complete program. *Concentration:* marketing.

MBA—Program in Organization Development Full-time. *Concentration:* organizational management.

MBA—Master of Business Administration Full-time. *Concentration:* general MBA.

MPA—Master of Public Administration Full-time. 33 to 48 total credits required. 12 to 72 months to complete program. *Concentration:* public policy and administration.

MS—Master of Science in Information Systems Engineering Full-time and part-time. Distance learning option. 33 to 48 total credits required. 12 to 72 months to complete program. *Concentration:* system management.

RESOURCES AND SERVICES 240 on-campus PCs are available to graduate business students. Access to Internet/World Wide Web, online (class) registration, and online grade reports available. *Personal computer requirements:* Graduate business students are strongly recommended to purchase or lease a personal computer. *Placement services include:* Alumni network.

EXPENSES *Tuition:* Full-time: $10,200. Part-time: $425 per credit. *Tuition (international):* Full-time: $10,200.

FINANCIAL AID (2007–08) 103 students received aid, including grants and scholarships. Aid is available to part-time students.

Financial Aid Contact Roger Walton, Director of Finance, 9215 North Black Canyon Highway, Phoenix, AZ 85021. *Phone:* 602-943-2311 Ext. 1050. *Fax:* 602-331-7091. *E-mail:* roger.walton@apollogrp.edu.

INTERNATIONAL STUDENTS 14% of students enrolled are international students. *Services and facilities:* Counseling/support services, ESL/language courses, Housing location assistance, International student organization, Orientation, Visa Services. Financial aid is not available to international students. *Required with application:* IELT with recommended score of 6.5; TOEFL with recommended score of 213 (computer) or 550 (paper); TWE with recommended score of 5; proof of adequate funds; proof of health/immunizations.

International Student Contact Ms. Hue Haslim, Director of International Operations/Registrar, 9215 North Black Canyon Highway, Phoenix, AZ 85021-2718. *Phone:* 602-943-2311 Ext. 1078. *Fax:* 602-371-8708. *E-mail:* hue.haslim@apollogrp.edu.

APPLICATION *Required:* Application form, baccalaureate/first degree, transcripts of college work. *Application fee:* $85, $100 (international). Applications for domestic and international students are processed on a rolling basis.

Application Contact Karen Janitell, Director of Enrollment, 9215 North Black Canyon Highway, Phoenix, AZ 85021-2718. *Phone:* 602-943-2311 Ext. 1063. *E-mail:* karen.janitell@apollogrp.edu.

ARKANSAS

Arkansas State University
College of Business

Jonesboro, State University, Arkansas

Phone: 870-972-3035 **Fax:** 870-972-3744 **E-mail:** broe@astate.edu

Business Program(s) Web Site: http://business.astate.edu/

Graduate Business Unit Enrollment *Total:* 170 (57 full-time; 113 part-time; 80 women; 24 international). *Average Age:* 30.

Graduate Business Faculty *Total:* 33 (31 full-time; 2 part-time).

Admissions *Applied:* 71. *Admitted:* 58. *Enrolled:* 49. *Average GMAT:* 554. *Average GPA:* 3.4

Academic Calendar Semesters.

Accreditation AACSB—The Association to Advance Collegiate Schools of Business.

After Graduation (Class of 2006–07) *Employed within 3 months of graduation:* 90%. *Average starting salary:* $52,000.

DEGREES EMBA • MAC • MBA • MS

EMBA—Executive Master of Business Administration Full-time and part-time. *Concentration:* executive programs.

MAC—Master of Accountancy Full-time and part-time. 31 total credits required. 12 to 24 months to complete program. *Concentration:* accounting.

MBA—Master of Business Administration Full-time and part-time. 34 total credits required. 12 to 72 months to complete program. *Concentrations:* economics, finance, management.

MS—Master of Science in Information Systems and e-Commerce Full-time and part-time. 36 total credits required. 18 to 24 months to complete program. *Concentrations:* electronic commerce (E-commerce), information systems.

RESOURCES AND SERVICES 120 on-campus PCs are available to graduate business students. Access to Internet/World Wide Web, online (class) registration, and online grade reports available. *Personal computer requirements:* Graduate business students are not required to have a personal computer. *Special opportunities include:* An international exchange program and an internship program are available. *Placement services include:* Alumni network, career placement, career counseling/planning, electronic job bank, resume referral, career fairs, job interviews arranged, resume preparation, and career library.

EXPENSES *Tuition (state resident):* Full-time: $3528. Part-time: $196 per hour. *Tuition (nonresident):* Full-time: $8928. Part-time: $496 per hour. *Required fees:* Full-time: $842. Part-time: $44 per hour. Tuition and/or fees vary by number of courses or credits taken and academic program. *Typical graduate housing cost:* $4636 (room only).

FINANCIAL AID (2007–08) Grants and scholarships. *Financial aid application deadline:* 7/1.

Financial Aid Contact Financial Aid Office, PO Box 2220, State University, AR 72467. *Phone:* 870-972-2310. *Fax:* 870-972-2794. *E-mail:* finaid@astate.edu.

INTERNATIONAL STUDENTS 14% of students enrolled are international students. *Services and facilities:* Counseling/support services, ESL/language courses, Housing location assistance, International student organization, Language tutoring, Orientation, Visa Services. Financial aid is available to international students. *Required with application:* TOEFL with recommended score of 213 (computer) or 550 (paper); proof of adequate funds; proof of health/immunizations.

International Student Contact C. William Roe, Associate Dean, PO Box 239, State University, AR 72467. *Phone:* 870-972-3035. *Fax:* 870-972-3648. *E-mail:* broe@astate.edu.

APPLICATION *Required:* GMAT, GRE, MAT, application form, baccalaureate/first degree, letter(s) of recommendation, transcripts of college work. *Recommended:* Interview. *Application fee:* $30, $40 (international). Applications for domestic and international students are processed on a rolling basis.

Application Contact C. William Roe, Associate Dean, PO Box 239, State University, AR 72467-1630. *Phone:* 870-972-3035. *Fax:* 870-972-3744. *E-mail:* broe@astate.edu.

Harding University
College of Business Administration

Searcy, Arkansas

Phone: 501-279-4523 **Fax:** 501-279-4805 **E-mail:** mba@harding.edu

Business Program(s) Web Site: http://www.harding.edu/mba

Graduate Business Unit Enrollment *Total:* 220 (121 full-time; 99 part-time; 94 women; 60 international). *Average Age:* 29.

Graduate Business Faculty 30 part-time.

Admissions *Applied:* 71. *Admitted:* 71. *Enrolled:* 69. *Average GPA:* 3.1

Academic Calendar Semesters.

Accreditation ACBSP—The American Council of Business Schools and Programs.

DEGREE MBA

MBA—Master of Business Administration Full-time and part-time. Distance learning option. 36 to 42 total credits required. Minimum of 12 months to complete program. *Concentrations:* accounting, health care, information technology, international business, organizational management.

RESOURCES AND SERVICES 100 on-campus PCs are available to graduate business students. Access to Internet/World Wide Web, online (class) registration, and online grade reports available. *Personal computer requirements:* Graduate business students are strongly recommended to purchase or lease a personal computer. *Placement services include:* Alumni network, career counseling/planning, resume referral, career fairs, job interviews arranged, and resume preparation.

EXPENSES *Tuition:* Full-time: $11,640. Part-time: $485 per credit hour. *Tuition (international):* Full-time: $11,640. Part-time: $485 per credit hour. *Required fees:* Full-time: $420. Part-time: $21 per credit hour. *Graduate housing:* Room and board costs vary by type of accommodation and type of board plan.

FINANCIAL AID (2007–08) 92 students received aid, including loans, scholarships, and work study. *Financial aid application deadline:* 7/30.

Financial Aid Contact Mr. Jon Roberts, Director of Student Financial Services, Box 12282, Searcy, AR 72149. *Phone:* 501-279-4257. *Fax:* 501-279-5438. *E-mail:* financialaid@harding.edu.

INTERNATIONAL STUDENTS 27% of students enrolled are international students. *Services and facilities:* Counseling/support services, ESL/language courses, Housing location assistance, International student organization, Orientation. Financial aid is available to international students. *Required with application:* TOEFL with recommended score of 213 (computer), 550 (paper), or 80 (Internet); proof of adequate funds; proof of health/immunizations.

International Student Contact Dr. Nicky Boyd, Director of International Student Services, Box 10822, Searcy, AR 72149. *Phone:* 501-279-4023. *Fax:* 501-279-4109. *E-mail:* admissions@harding.edu.

APPLICATION *Required:* Application form, baccalaureate/first degree, essay, 2 letters of recommendation, resume/curriculum vitae, transcripts of

Harding University (continued)

college work. *Recommended:* Interview, personal statement, work experience. *Application fee:* $35. Applications for domestic and international students are processed on a rolling basis.

Application Contact Mrs. Jill Hatcher, Marketing Manager, Box 10774, Searcy, AR 72149. *Phone:* 501-279-4523. *Fax:* 501-279-4805. *E-mail:* mba@harding.edu.

University of Arkansas
Sam M. Walton College of Business Administration

Fayetteville, Arkansas

Phone: 479-575-2851 **Fax:** 479-575-8721 **E-mail:** gsb@walton.uark.edu

Business Program(s) Web Site: http://gsb.uark.edu

Graduate Business Unit Enrollment *Total:* 137 (63 full-time; 74 part-time; 45 women; 25 international). *Average Age:* 29.

Graduate Business Faculty 65 full-time.

Admissions *Applied:* 264. *Admitted:* 174. *Enrolled:* 137. *Average GMAT:* 623. *Average GPA:* 3.5

Academic Calendar Semesters.

Accreditation AACSB—The Association to Advance Collegiate Schools of Business.

After Graduation (Class of 2006–07) *Employed within 3 months of graduation:* 90%.

DEGREES M Acc • MA • MBA • MIS

M Acc—Master of Accountancy Full-time. At least 30 total credits required. 9 months to complete program. *Concentration:* accounting.

MA—Master of Arts in Economics Full-time. GRE required. 30 total credits required. 12 months to complete program. *Concentration:* economics.

MBA—Managerial Master of Business Administration Part-time. Distance learning option. At least 38 total credits required. 24 months to complete program. *Concentration:* general MBA.

MBA—Master of Business Administration Full-time. GMAT or GRE accepted. At least 48 total credits required. 18 months to complete program. *Concentrations:* entrepreneurship, finance, logistics, marketing, supply chain management.

MIS—Professional Master of Information Systems Part-time. 30 to 36 total credits required. 24 months to complete program. *Concentrations:* information management, other, telecommunications management.

MIS—Master of Information Systems Full-time. 30 total credits required. 12 months to complete program. *Concentrations:* information management, information technology, other, telecommunications management.

RESOURCES AND SERVICES 400 on-campus PCs are available to graduate business students. Access to Internet/World Wide Web, online (class) registration, and online grade reports available. *Personal computer requirements:* Graduate business students are required to have a personal computer. *Special opportunities include:* An international exchange program and an internship program are available. *Placement services include:* Alumni network, career placement, career counseling/planning, electronic job bank, resume referral, career fairs, job interviews arranged, resume preparation, and career library.

EXPENSES *Tuition (state resident):* Part-time: $607 per hour. *Tuition (nonresident):* Part-time: $607 per hour. *Tuition (international):* Part-time: $607 per hour. *Typical graduate housing cost:* $13,986 (including board).

FINANCIAL AID (2007–08) 119 students received aid, including fellowships, loans, research assistantships, and scholarships. Aid is available to part-time students.

Financial Aid Contact Graduate School of Business, WCOB-WJWH 310, 1 University of Arkansas, 191 Harmon Avenue, Fayetteville, AR 72701. *Phone:* 479-575-2851. *Fax:* 479-575-8721. *E-mail:* gsb@walton.uark.edu.

INTERNATIONAL STUDENTS 18% of students enrolled are international students. *Services and facilities:* Counseling/support services, ESL/language courses, International student organization, Language tutoring, Orientation, Visa Services. *Required with application:* TOEFL with recommended score of 213 (computer), 550 (paper), or 80 (Internet); proof of adequate funds; proof of health/immunizations. *Recommended with application:* IELT with recommended score of 6.5.

International Student Contact International Admissions, 747 West Dickson Street #8, DICX 180, Fayetteville, AR 72701. *Phone:* 479-575-6246. *Fax:* 479-575-5055. *E-mail:* iao@uark.edu.

APPLICATION *Required:* GMAT, application form, baccalaureate/first degree, essay, 3 letters of recommendation, personal statement, resume/curriculum vitae, transcripts of college work. School will accept GRE. *Recommended:* Interview, 2 years of work experience. *Application fee:* $40, $50 (international). Applications for domestic and international students are processed on a rolling basis.

Application Contact Dr. Rebel Smith, Assistant Director, Graduate School of Business, WCOB-WJWH 310, 1 University of Arkansas, Fayetteville, AR 72701. *Phone:* 479-575-2851. *Fax:* 479-575-8721. *E-mail:* gsb@walton.uark.edu.

University of Central Arkansas
College of Business

Conway, Arkansas

Phone: 501-450-3411 **Fax:** 501-450-5302 **E-mail:** davidk@uca.edu

Business Program(s) Web Site: http://www.business.uca.edu/

Graduate Business Unit Enrollment *Total:* 61 (31 full-time; 30 part-time; 19 women; 6 international). *Average Age:* 27.

Graduate Business Faculty 12 full-time.

Admissions *Applied:* 33. *Admitted:* 25. *Enrolled:* 19. *Average GMAT:* 524. *Average GPA:* 3.27

Academic Calendar Semesters.

Accreditation AACSB—The Association to Advance Collegiate Schools of Business.

DEGREES M Acc • MBA

M Acc—Master of Accountancy At least 30 total credits required. 12 to 72 months to complete program. *Concentration:* accounting.

MBA—Master of Business Administration Full-time and part-time. 30 to 54 total credits required. 12 to 72 months to complete program. *Concentration:* general MBA.

RESOURCES AND SERVICES 210 on-campus PCs are available to graduate business students. Access to Internet/World Wide Web, online (class) registration, and online grade reports available. *Personal computer requirements:* Graduate business students are not required to have a personal computer. *Special opportunities include:* An international exchange program and an internship program are available. *Placement services include:* Alumni network, career placement, job search course, career counseling/planning, resume referral, and career fairs.

EXPENSES *Tuition (state resident):* Full-time: $4320. *Tuition (nonresident):* Full-time: $7920. *Tuition (international):* Full-time: $7920. *Required fees:* Full-time: $98. *Graduate housing:* Room and board costs vary by campus location, number of occupants, type of accommodation, and type of board plan. *Typical cost:* $6000 (including board), $4000 (room only).

FINANCIAL AID (2007–08) 5 students received aid, including grants, loans, research assistantships, scholarships, and work study. Aid is available to part-time students. *Financial aid application deadline:* 8/1.

Financial Aid Contact Mrs. Julia Robison, Associate Director of Financial Aid, 201 Donaghey Avenue, McCastlain 001, Conway, AR 72035-0001. *Phone:* 501-450-3140. *E-mail:* juliar@uca.edu.

INTERNATIONAL STUDENTS 10% of students enrolled are international students. *Services and facilities:* Counseling/support services, ESL/language courses, Housing location assistance, International student housing, International student organization, Language tutoring, Orientation, Immigration advising. Financial aid is available to international students. *Required with application:* TOEFL with recommended score of 173 (computer) or 550 (paper); proof of adequate funds; proof of health/immunizations.

International Student Contact Ms. Lisa Shoemake, Immigration Advisor, 201 Donaghey Avenue, Torreyson Library 304, Conway, AR 72035. *Phone:* 501-450-3445. *Fax:* 501-450-5095. *E-mail:* lisas@uca.edu.

APPLICATION *Required:* GMAT, application form, baccalaureate/first degree, essay, 2 letters of recommendation, personal statement, resume/curriculum vitae, transcripts of college work. *Application fee:* $25, $40 (international). *Deadlines:* 8/1 for fall, 12/1 for spring, 5/1 for summer, 8/1 for fall (international), 12/1 for spring (international), 5/1 for summer (international).

Application Contact Dr. David Kim, MBA Director, 201 Donaghey Avenue, Conway, AR 72035. *Phone:* 501-450-3411. *Fax:* 501-450-5302. *E-mail:* davidk@uca.edu.

University of Phoenix–Little Rock Campus

College of Graduate Business and Management

Little Rock, Arkansas

Phone: 480-317-6200 **Fax:** 480-643-1479 **E-mail:** beth.barilla@phoenix.edu

---

DEGREES   M Mgt • MBA

M Mgt—Master of Management Full-time. At least 39 total credits required. *Concentration:* management.

MBA—Master of Business Administration Full-time. At least 45 total credits required. *Concentration:* administration.

RESOURCES AND SERVICES Access to online grade reports available. *Personal computer requirements:* Graduate business students are strongly recommended to purchase or lease a personal computer. *Placement services include:* Alumni network.

Application Contact Beth Barilla, Associate Vice President of Student Admissions and Services, Mail Stop AA-K101, 4615 East Elwood Street, Phoenix, AZ 85040-1958. *Phone:* 480-317-6200. *Fax:* 480-643-1479. *E-mail:* beth.barilla@phoenix.edu.

CALIFORNIA

Alliant International University

Marshall Goldsmith School of Management

San Diego, California

Phone: 858-635-4544 **Fax:** 858-635-4739 **E-mail:** smusson@alliant.edu

Business Program(s) Web Site: http://www.alliant.edu/usicb

DEGREES   MBA • MIBA

MBA—Master of Business Administration Full-time and part-time. *Concentrations:* finance, information management, management information systems, marketing, strategic management.

MBA—Master of Business Administration Full-time and part-time. *Concentration:* finance.

MIBA—Master of International Business Administration Full-time and part-time. *Concentrations:* finance, information management, management information systems, marketing, strategic management.

MIBA—Master of International Business Administration Full-time and part-time. *Concentration:* finance.

RESOURCES AND SERVICES 146 on-campus PCs are available to graduate business students. Access to Internet/World Wide Web, online (class) registration, and online grade reports available. *Personal computer requirements:* Graduate business students are strongly recommended to purchase or lease a personal computer. *Special opportunities include:* An international exchange program and an internship program are available. *Placement services include:* Alumni network, career placement, job search course, career counseling/planning, resume referral, career fairs, and resume preparation.

Application Contact Ms. Stephanie Musson, Admissions Counselor, 10455 Pomerado Road, San Diego, CA 92131-1799. *Phone:* 858-635-4544. *Fax:* 858-635-4739. *E-mail:* smusson@alliant.edu.

American InterContinental University

Program in Business Administration

Los Angeles, California

Phone: 310-302-2421 **Fax:** 310-302-2001 **E-mail:** rdoten@la.aiuniv.edu

---

DEGREE   MBA

MBA—Master of Business Administration Full-time and part-time. At least 48 total credits required. 10 to 12 months to complete program. *Concentrations:* health care, human resources management, international marketing, management.

RESOURCES AND SERVICES 50 on-campus PCs are available to graduate business students. Access to Internet/World Wide Web available. *Personal computer requirements:* Graduate business students are required to have a personal computer. *Placement services include:* Career placement, job search course, career counseling/planning, electronic job bank, resume referral, career fairs, job interviews arranged, resume preparation, and career library.

Application Contact Randy Doten, Director of Admissions, 12655 West Jefferson Boulevard, Los Angeles, CA 90066. *Phone:* 310-302-2421. *Fax:* 310-302-2001. *E-mail:* rdoten@la.aiuniv.edu.

See full description on page 564.

American Jewish University

David Lieber School of Graduate Studies

Bel Air, California

Phone: 310-440-1260 **Fax:** 310-471-3657 **E-mail:** egrice@ajula.edu

Business Program(s) Web Site: http://www.ajula.edu/mba

Graduate Business Unit Enrollment *Total:* 46 (15 full-time; 31 part-time; 38 women).

Graduate Business Faculty *Total:* 14 (1 full-time; 13 part-time).

Admissions *Applied:* 18. *Admitted:* 15. *Enrolled:* 14. *Average GMAT:* 500. *Average GPA:* 3.5

Academic Calendar Semesters.

American Jewish University (continued)

After Graduation (Class of 2006–07) *Employed within 3 months of graduation:* 99%. *Average starting salary:* $65,000.

DEGREES   MA • MBA

MA—Master of Arts in Jewish Communal Service Full-time and part-time. At least 53 total credits required. 53 months to complete program. *Concentrations:* accounting, administration, business ethics, marketing, nonprofit management, nonprofit organization.

MA—Master of Arts in Nonprofit Management Full-time and part-time. At least 32 total credits required. Minimum of 12 months to complete program. *Concentrations:* business ethics, conflict resolution management, marketing, nonprofit management, nonprofit organization, resources management.

MBA—Master of Business Administration in Nonprofit Management Full-time and part-time. At least 53 total credits required. Minimum of 24 months to complete program. *Concentrations:* marketing, nonprofit management, nonprofit organization, resources management.

RESOURCES AND SERVICES 26 on-campus PCs are available to graduate business students. Access to Internet/World Wide Web available. *Personal computer requirements:* Graduate business students are strongly recommended to purchase or lease a personal computer. *Special opportunities include:* An internship program is available. *Placement services include:* Alumni network, career counseling/planning, electronic job bank, resume referral, resume preparation, and career library.

EXPENSES *Tuition:* Full-time: $21,408. Part-time: $892 per unit. *Tuition (international):* Full-time: $21,408. Part-time: $892 per unit. *Graduate housing:* Room and board costs vary by number of occupants, type of accommodation, and type of board plan. *Typical cost:* $10,658 (including board), $5808 (room only).

FINANCIAL AID (2007–08) 30 students received aid, including grants, loans, and scholarships. Aid is available to part-time students. *Financial aid application deadline:* 4/1.

Financial Aid Contact Ms. Larissa Zadoyen, Director of Financial Aid, 15600 Mulholland Drive, Los Angeles, CA 90077. *Phone:* 310-440-1252. *Fax:* 310-471-3657. *E-mail:* finaid@ajula.edu.

INTERNATIONAL STUDENTS *Services and facilities:* Counseling/support services, Housing location assistance, International student housing, Orientation. Financial aid is available to international students. *Required with application:* TOEFL with recommended score of 213 (computer) or 550 (paper); proof of adequate funds; proof of health/immunizations.

International Student Contact Ms. Tosha Petronicolos, MBA Program Coordinator, 15600 Mulholland Drive, Los Angeles, CA 90077-1599. *Phone:* 310-476-9777 Ext. 279. *Fax:* 310-471-3657. *E-mail:* tpetronicolos@ajula.edu.

APPLICATION *Required:* Application form, baccalaureate/first degree, essay, interview, 2 letters of recommendation, personal statement, transcripts of college work. School will accept GMAT and GRE. *Recommended:* Resume/curriculum vitae, work experience. *Application fee:* $50. Applications for domestic and international students are processed on a rolling basis.

Application Contact Mr. Edward Grice, Assistant Dean, 15600 Mulholland Drive, Los Angeles, CA 90077-1599. *Phone:* 310-440-1260. *Fax:* 310-471-3657. *E-mail:* egrice@ajula.edu.

Antioch University Los Angeles

Program in Organizational Management

Culver City, California

Phone: 310-578-1080 **Fax:** 310-822-4824 **E-mail:** admissions@antiochla.edu

Business Program(s) Web Site: http://www.antiochla.edu

DEGREE   MA

MA—Master of Arts in Organizational Management Full-time and part-time. At least 60 total credits required. 15 to 60 months to complete program. *Concentrations:* human resources management, leadership, organizational behavior/development, organizational management.

RESOURCES AND SERVICES 15 on-campus PCs are available to graduate business students. Access to Internet/World Wide Web available. *Personal computer requirements:* Graduate business students are strongly recommended to purchase or lease a personal computer. *Special opportunities include:* An internship program is available. *Placement services include:* Career counseling/planning and resume preparation.

Application Contact Admissions Office, 400 Corporate Way, Culver City, CA 90230-7615. *Phone:* 310-578-1080. *Fax:* 310-822-4824. *E-mail:* admissions@antiochla.edu.

Antioch University Santa Barbara

Program in Organizational Management

Santa Barbara, California

Phone: 805-962-8179 Ext. 330 **Fax:** 805-962-4786 **E-mail:** rborgioli@antiochsb.edu

Business Program(s) Web Site: http://www.antiochsb.edu/programs/programs-maom.html

Graduate Business Unit Enrollment *Total:* 40 (38 full-time; 2 part-time; 19 women; 21 international).

Graduate Business Faculty 7 full-time.

Academic Calendar Quarters.

DEGREE   MA

MA—Master of Arts in Organizational Management Full-time and part-time. Distance learning option. At least 60 total credits required. Minimum of 15 months to complete program. *Concentrations:* business ethics, human resources management, international business, international management, management, managerial economics, nonprofit management, nonprofit organization, public and private management, technology management.

RESOURCES AND SERVICES 14 on-campus PCs are available to graduate business students. Access to Internet/World Wide Web, online (class) registration, and online grade reports available. *Personal computer requirements:* Graduate business students are strongly recommended to purchase or lease a personal computer. *Special opportunities include:* An international exchange program and an internship program are available.

FINANCIAL AID (2007–08) 12 students received aid, including grants, loans, scholarships, and work study. Aid is available to part-time students. *Financial aid application deadline:* 4/15.

Financial Aid Contact Cecilia Schneider, Director of Financial Aid, 801 Garden Street, Suite 101, Santa Barbara, CA 93101-1581. *Phone:* 805-962-8179 Ext. 108. *Fax:* 805-962-4786. *E-mail:* cschneider@antiochsb.edu.

INTERNATIONAL STUDENTS 53% of students enrolled are international students. *Services and facilities:* Counseling/support services, Housing location assistance, Orientation, Visa Services. Financial aid is available to international students. *Required with application:* Proof of adequate funds.

International Student Contact Esther Elena Lopez-Mulnix, PhD, Director of International Programs, 801 Garden Street, Suite 101, Santa Barbara, CA 93101-1581. *Phone:* 805-962-8179 Ext. 335. *Fax:* 805-962-4786. *E-mail:* emulnix@antiochsb.edu.

APPLICATION *Required:* Application form, baccalaureate/first degree, essay, interview, 2 letters of recommendation, personal statement, resume/curriculum vitae, transcripts of college work, 2 years of work experience. *Application fee:* $60. Applications for domestic and international students are processed on a rolling basis.

Application Contact Ms. Rebecca Borgioli, Admissions Counselor, 801 Garden Street, Suite 101, Santa Barbara, CA 93101-1581. *Phone:* 805-962-8179 Ext. 330. *Fax:* 805-962-4786. *E-mail:* rborgioli@antiochsb.edu.

Argosy University, Inland Empire
College of Business
San Bernardino, California

Phone: 909-915-3800 **Fax:** 909-915-3810

Business Program(s) Web Site: http://www.argosy.edu/inlandempire

DEGREES DBA • MBA

DBA—Doctor of Business Administration (DBA) *Concentrations:* accounting, information systems, international business, management, marketing.

MBA—Master of Business Administration (MBA) *Concentrations:* finance, health care, information systems, international business, management, marketing, public management.

Financial Aid Contact Director of Admissions, 636 East Brier Drive, Suite 120, San Bernardino, CA 92408. *Phone:* 909-915-3800. *Fax:* 909-915-3810.

International Student Contact Director of Admissions, 636 East Brier Drive, Suite 120, San Bernardino, CA 92408. *Phone:* 909-915-3800. *Fax:* 909-915-3810.

Application Contact Director of Admissions, 636 East Brier Drive, Suite 120, San Bernardino, CA 92408. *Phone:* 909-915-3800. *Fax:* 909-915-3810.

See full description on page 566.

Argosy University, Los Angeles
College of Business
Santa Monica, California

Phone: 310-866-4000 **Fax:** 310-452-8720

Business Program(s) Web Site: http://www.argosy.edu/losangeles

DEGREES DBA • MBA • MSM

DBA—Doctor of Business Administration (DBA) *Concentrations:* accounting, information systems, international business, management, marketing.

MBA—Master of Business Administration (MBA) *Concentrations:* finance, health administration, information systems, international business, management, marketing, public management.

MSM—Master of Science in Management (MSM) *Concentration:* management.

Financial Aid Contact Director of Admissions, 2950 31st Street, Santa Monica, CA 90405. *Phone:* 310-866-4000. *Fax:* 310-452-8720.

International Student Contact Director of Admissions, 2950 31st Street, Santa Monica, CA 90405. *Phone:* 310-866-4000. *Fax:* 310-452-8720.

Application Contact Director of Admissions, 2950 31st Street, Santa Monica, CA 90405. *Phone:* 310-866-4000. *Fax:* 310-452-8720.

See full description on page 566.

Argosy University, Orange County
College of Business
Santa Ana, California

Phone: 714-338-6200 **Fax:** 714-437-1697

Business Program(s) Web Site: http://www.argosy.edu/orangecounty

DEGREES DBA • MBA • MSM

DBA—Doctor of Business Administration (DBA) *Concentrations:* accounting, information systems, international business, management, marketing.

MBA—Master of Business Administration (MBA) *Concentrations:* finance, health administration, information systems, international business, management, marketing, public policy and administration.

MSM—Master of Science in Management (MSM) *Concentration:* management.

Financial Aid Contact Director of Admissions, 3501 West Sunflower Avenue, Suite 110, Santa Ana, CA 92704. *Phone:* 714-338-6200. *Fax:* 714-437-1697.

International Student Contact Director of Admissions, 3501 West Sunflower Avenue, Suite 110, Santa Ana, CA 92704. *Phone:* 714-338-6200. *Fax:* 714-437-1697.

Application Contact Director of Admissions, 3501 West Sunflower Avenue, Suite 110, Santa Ana, CA 92704. *Phone:* 714-338-6200. *Fax:* 714-437-1697.

See full description on page 566.

Argosy University, San Diego
College of Business
San Diego, California

Phone: 619-321-3000 **Fax:** 619-321-3005

Business Program(s) Web Site: http://www.argosy.edu/sandiego

DEGREES DBA • MBA • MS

DBA—Doctor of Business Administration (DBA) *Concentrations:* accounting, information systems, international business, management, marketing.

MBA—Master of Business Administration (MBA) *Concentrations:* finance, information systems, international business, management, marketing, public policy and administration.

MS—Master of Science in Management (MSM) *Concentration:* management.

Financial Aid Contact Director of Admissions, 1615 Murray Canyon Road, Suite 100, San Diego, CA 92108. *Phone:* 619-321-3000. *Fax:* 619-321-3005.

International Student Contact Director of Admissions, 1615 Murray Canyon Road, Suite 100, San Diego, CA 92108. *Phone:* 619-321-3000. *Fax:* 619-321-3005.

Application Contact Director of Admissions, 1615 Murray Canyon Road, Suite 100, San Diego, CA 92108. *Phone:* 619-321-3000. *Fax:* 619-321-3005.

See full description on page 566.

Argosy University, San Francisco Bay Area

College of Business

Alameda, California

Phone: 510-217-4700 **Fax:** 519-217-4806

Business Program(s) Web Site: http://www.argosy.edu/sanfrancisco

---

DEGREES DBA • MBA • MSM

DBA—Doctor of Business Administration (DBA) *Concentrations:* accounting, information systems, international business, management, marketing.

MBA—Master of Business Administration (MBA) *Concentrations:* finance, health administration, information systems, international business, management, marketing, public policy and administration.

MSM—Master of Science in Management (MSM) *Concentration:* management.

Financial Aid Contact Director of Admissions, 1005 Atlantic Avenue, Alameda, CA 94501. *Phone:* 510-217-4700. *Fax:* 519-217-4806.

International Student Contact Director of Admissions, 1005 Atlantic Avenue, Alameda, CA 94501. *Phone:* 510-217-4700. *Fax:* 519-217-4806.

Application Contact Director of Admissions, 1005 Atlantic Avenue, Alameda, CA 94501. *Phone:* 510-217-4700. *Fax:* 519-217-4806.

See full description on page 566.

Azusa Pacific University

School of Business and Management

Azusa, California

Phone: 626-815-3835 **Fax:** 626-815-2023 **E-mail:** hbutler@apu.edu

Business Program(s) Web Site: http://www.apu.edu/sbm/

Graduate Business Unit Enrollment *Total:* 202 (18 full-time; 184 part-time; 64 women; 14 international).

Graduate Business Faculty *Total:* 14 (7 full-time; 7 part-time).

Admissions *Average GMAT:* 500. *Average GPA:* 3.3

Academic Calendar 9 week terms.

DEGREES MA • MBA

MA—Master of Arts in Human and Organizational Development Full-time and part-time. At least 36 total credits required. 12 to 96 months to complete program. *Concentration:* organizational behavior/development.

MBA—Master of Business Administration Full-time and part-time. 38 to 50 total credits required. 12 to 96 months to complete program. *Concentrations:* finance, international business, management information systems, marketing, organizational behavior/development, strategic management.

RESOURCES AND SERVICES 285 on-campus PCs are available to graduate business students. Access to Internet/World Wide Web, online (class) registration, and online grade reports available. *Personal computer requirements:* Graduate business students are strongly recommended to purchase or lease a personal computer. *Special opportunities include:* An internship program is available. *Placement services include:* Alumni network, career counseling/planning, electronic job bank, career fairs, resume preparation, and career library.

EXPENSES *Tuition:* Part-time: $625 per credit. *Tuition (international):* Part-time: $625 per credit. *Required fees:* Full-time: $80.

FINANCIAL AID (2007–08) Loans and scholarships. Aid is available to part-time students. *Financial aid application deadline:* 6/30.

Financial Aid Contact Debbie Serrano, Associate Director of Graduate Student Financial Services, 901 East Alosta Avenue, PO Box 7000, Azusa, CA 91702-7000. *Phone:* 626-815-4567. *Fax:* 626-815-4571. *E-mail:* dserrano@apu.edu.

INTERNATIONAL STUDENTS 7% of students enrolled are international students. *Services and facilities:* Counseling/support services, ESL/language courses, Housing location assistance, International student organization, Orientation, Visa Services. Financial aid is available to international students. *Required with application:* TOEFL with recommended score of 250 (computer) or 600 (paper); proof of adequate funds; proof of health/immunizations.

International Student Contact Mary Grams, Director, International Student Services, 901 East Alosta Avenue, PO Box 7000, Azusa, CA 91702-7000. *Phone:* 626-815-6000 Ext. 3055. *Fax:* 626-815-3801. *E-mail:* mgrams@apu.edu.

APPLICATION *Required:* Application form, baccalaureate/first degree, essay, 3 letters of recommendation, resume/curriculum vitae, transcripts of college work. School will accept GMAT and GRE. *Recommended:* Personal statement, 3 years of work experience. *Application fee:* $45, $65 (international). *Deadlines:* 8/1 for fall (international), 12/1 for spring (international), 4/1 for summer (international). Applications for domestic students are processed on a rolling basis.

Application Contact Heidi Anderson Butler, Marketing and Internship Director, Graduate School of Business and Management, 901 East Alosta Avenue, Azusa, CA 91702. *Phone:* 626-815-3835. *Fax:* 626-815-2023. *E-mail:* hbutler@apu.edu.

Biola University

Crowell School of Business

La Mirada, California

Phone: 562-777-4015 **Fax:** 562-906-4545 **E-mail:** mba@biola.edu

Business Program(s) Web Site: http://www.biola.edu/mba/

Graduate Business Unit Enrollment *Total:* 31 (31 part-time; 14 women). *Average Age:* 33.

Graduate Business Faculty *Total:* 10 (6 full-time; 4 part-time).

Admissions *Applied:* 25. *Admitted:* 15. *Enrolled:* 10. *Average GMAT:* 500. *Average GPA:* 3.3

Academic Calendar Trimesters.

Accreditation ACBSP—The American Council of Business Schools and Programs.

After Graduation (Class of 2006–07) *Employed within 3 months of graduation:* 100%.

DEGREE MBA

MBA—Master of Business Administration Part-time. 36 to 51 total credits required. 24 to 36 months to complete program. *Concentration:* general MBA.

RESOURCES AND SERVICES 15 on-campus PCs are available to graduate business students. Access to Internet/World Wide Web and online grade reports available. *Personal computer requirements:* Graduate business students are strongly recommended to purchase or lease a personal computer. *Placement services include:* Alumni network.

FINANCIAL AID (2007–08) 18 students received aid, including grants and loans. Aid is available to part-time students. *Financial aid application deadline:* 4/30.

INTERNATIONAL STUDENTS *Services and facilities:* Counseling/support services. Financial aid is available to international students. *Required with application:* TOEFL with recommended score of 250 (computer) or 600 (paper); proof of adequate funds; proof of health/immunizations.

International Student Contact Mr. James Hampson, Graduate Admissions Counselor, 13800 Biola Avenue, La Mirada, CA 90639. *Phone:* 562-903-4752. *Fax:* 562-903-4709. *E-mail:* james.hampson@biola.edu.

APPLICATION *Required:* GMAT, application form, baccalaureate/first degree, essay, interview, 3 letters of recommendation, personal statement, resume/curriculum vitae, transcripts of college work, 3 years of work experience. *Application fee:* $45. Applications for domestic and international students are processed on a rolling basis.

Application Contact Mrs. Bob Harriman, MBA Program Administrator, 13800 Biola Avenue, La Mirada, CA 90639. *Phone:* 562-777-4015. *Fax:* 562-906-4545. *E-mail:* mba@biola.edu.

California Baptist University

Program in Business Administration

Riverside, California

Phone: 951-343-4249 **Fax:** 951-351-1808 **E-mail:** gronveau@calbaptist.edu

Business Program(s) Web Site: http://www.calbaptist.edu/business/mba.htm

Graduate Business Unit Enrollment *Total:* 55 (50 full-time; 5 part-time; 30 women; 10 international). *Average Age:* 38.

Graduate Business Faculty *Total:* 10 (5 full-time; 5 part-time).

Admissions *Applied:* 55. *Admitted:* 40. *Enrolled:* 32. *Average GPA:* 3.5

Academic Calendar Trimesters.

Accreditation ACBSP—The American Council of Business Schools and Programs.

After Graduation (Class of 2006–07) *Employed within 3 months of graduation:* 100%. *Average starting salary:* $85,000.

DEGREE MBA

MBA—Master of Business Administration Full-time and part-time. *Concentrations:* general MBA, management.

RESOURCES AND SERVICES 160 on-campus PCs are available to graduate business students. Access to Internet/World Wide Web, online (class) registration, and online grade reports available. *Personal computer requirements:* Graduate business students are strongly recommended to purchase or lease a personal computer. *Placement services include:* Alumni network, career placement, job search course, career counseling/planning, resume referral, career fairs, job interviews arranged, and resume preparation.

FINANCIAL AID (2007–08) 30 students received aid, including loans and scholarships. Aid is available to part-time students.

Financial Aid Contact Rebecca Sanchez, Director of Financial Aid, 8432 Magnolia Avenue, Riverside, CA 92504. *Phone:* 951-343-4236. *Fax:* 951-343-4518. *E-mail:* finaid@calbaptist.edu.

INTERNATIONAL STUDENTS 18% of students enrolled are international students. *Services and facilities:* Counseling/support services, ESL/language courses, Visa Services. Financial aid is not available to international students. *Required with application:* Proof of adequate funds; proof of health/immunizations.

International Student Contact Mr. Jonathan Bello, Director of International Student Services, 8432 Magnolia Avenue, Riverside, CA 92504. *Phone:* 951-343-4721. *E-mail:* jbello@calbaptist.edu.

APPLICATION *Required:* Application form, baccalaureate/first degree, essay, interview, 2 letters of recommendation, personal statement, resume/curriculum vitae, transcripts of college work. School will accept GMAT and GRE. *Recommended:* 2 years of work experience. *Application fee:* $45. Applications for domestic and international students are processed on a rolling basis.

Application Contact Mrs. Gail Ronveaux, Dean of Graduate Enrollment, 8432 Magnolia Avenue, Riverside, CA 92504. *Phone:* 951-343-4249. *Fax:* 951-351-1808. *E-mail:* gronveau@calbaptist.edu.

California Lutheran University

School of Business

Thousand Oaks, California

Phone: 805-493-3128 **Fax:** 805-493-3542 **E-mail:** hanney@clunet.edu

Business Program(s) Web Site: http://www.callutheran.edu

DEGREES IMBA • MBA

IMBA—International Master of Business Administration Full-time and part-time. 42 to 48 total credits required. 12 to 84 months to complete program. *Concentration:* international business.

MBA—Master of Business Administration Full-time and part-time. 45 to 48 total credits required. 15 to 84 months to complete program. *Concentrations:* finance, financial management/planning, information management, management, marketing, organizational behavior/development.

RESOURCES AND SERVICES 252 on-campus PCs are available to graduate business students. Access to Internet/World Wide Web, online (class) registration, and online grade reports available. *Personal computer requirements:* Graduate business students are strongly recommended to purchase or lease a personal computer. *Special opportunities include:* An international exchange program and an internship program are available. *Placement services include:* Alumni network, career placement, job search course, career counseling/planning, electronic job bank, resume referral, career fairs, job interviews arranged, resume preparation, and career library.

Application Contact Mrs. Anita Hanney, MBA Admission Counselor, Graduate Enrollment Services, 60 West Olsen Road, #2200, Thousand Oaks, CA 91360-2700. *Phone:* 805-493-3128. *Fax:* 805-493-3542. *E-mail:* hanney@clunet.edu.

California National University for Advanced Studies

College of Business Administration

Northridge, California

Phone: 800-782-2422 **Fax:** 818-830-2418 **E-mail:** dlisell@mail.cnuas.edu

Business Program(s) Web Site: http://www.cnuas.edu/

DEGREES MBA • ME/MM • MHRM

MBA—Master of Business Administration Full-time and part-time. Distance learning option. 36 to 45 total credits required. 18 to 24 months to complete program. *Concentrations:* accounting, economics, finance, health care, human resources management, international business, management, management information systems, marketing, quality management.

ME/MM—Master of Engineering/Master of Management Full-time and part-time. Distance learning option. 36 to 39 total credits required. 18 to 21 months to complete program. *Concentrations:* business policy/strategy, engineering, financial management/planning, management, management information systems, quality management, quantitative analysis.

MHRM—Master of Human Resources Management Full-time and part-time. Distance learning option. At least 36 total credits required. 18 to 24 months to complete program. *Concentrations:* human resources management, organizational behavior/development, training and development.

MHRM—Master of Human Resources Management Full-time and part-time. Distance learning option. 18 to 36 total credits required. 18 to 36 months to complete program. *Concentrations:* human resources development, human resources management, management, management information systems, manpower administration.

California National University for Advanced Studies (continued)

RESOURCES AND SERVICES Access to Internet/World Wide Web, online (class) registration, and online grade reports available. *Personal computer requirements:* Graduate business students are required to have a personal computer. *Placement services include:* Alumni network.

Application Contact Ms. Dawn Lisell, Admissions Representative, 8550 Balboa Boulevard, Suite 210, Northridge, CA 91325. *Phone:* 800-782-2422. *Fax:* 818-830-2418. *E-mail:* dlisell@mail.cnuas.edu.

California Polytechnic State University, San Luis Obispo

Orfalea College of Business

San Luis Obispo, California

Phone: 805-756-2637 **Fax:** 805-756-0110 **E-mail:** vwalls@calpoly.edu

Business Program(s) Web Site: http://www.cob.calpoly.edu/

Graduate Business Unit Enrollment *Total:* 94 (86 full-time; 8 part-time; 25 women; 3 international). *Average Age:* 26.

Graduate Business Faculty *Total:* 103 (61 full-time; 42 part-time).

Admissions *Applied:* 177. *Admitted:* 107. *Enrolled:* 84. *Average GMAT:* 620. *Average GPA:* 3.32

Academic Calendar Quarters.

Accreditation AACSB—The Association to Advance Collegiate Schools of Business.

After Graduation (Class of 2006–07) *Employed within 3 months of graduation:* 97%. *Average starting salary:* $85,000.

DEGREES MBA • MBA/MS • MS

MBA—Master of Business Administration Full-time and part-time. At least 60 total credits required. Minimum of 10 months to complete program. *Concentrations:* combined degrees, general MBA, management, other, student designed.

MBA—Master of Business Administration—Architecture Management Track Full-time. Available only to those students who are enrolled in California Polytechnic's Bachelor of Architecture program. At least 60 total credits required. *Concentrations:* architecture, city/urban administration, combined degrees, general MBA, management, other.

MBA—Master of Business Administration—Landscape Architecture Management Track Full-time. Available only to students who are enrolled in California Polytechnic's Bachelor of Landscape Architecture program. At least 60 total credits required. *Concentrations:* architecture, combined degrees, general MBA, management, other.

MBA—Master of Business Administration in Agribusiness Specialization Full-time and part-time. At least 64 total credits required. Minimum of 10 months to complete program. *Concentrations:* agribusiness, combined degrees, general MBA, management, other.

MBA—Master of Business Administration in Graphic Communication Full-time and part-time. At least 64 total credits required. Minimum of 10 months to complete program. *Concentrations:* general MBA, management, management communication, other.

MBA/MS—Master of Business Administration/Master of Science Full-time and part-time. At least 93 total credits required. *Concentrations:* agribusiness, agricultural economics, combined degrees, engineering, facilities management, general MBA, industrial administration/management, management, manufacturing management, operations management, other, production management, supply chain management, transportation management.

MBA/MS—Master of Business Administration/Master of Science in Engineering Management Full-time and part-time. At least 90 total credits required. *Concentrations:* combined degrees, engineering, general MBA, management, manufacturing management, other.

MS—Accounting—Taxation Full-time. At least 45 total credits required. *Concentrations:* accounting, taxation.

MS—Master of Science in Industrial and Technical Studies Full-time and part-time. At least 45 total credits required. Minimum of 10 months to complete program. *Concentrations:* facilities management, industrial administration/management, manufacturing management, operations management, other, production management.

RESOURCES AND SERVICES 1,880 on-campus PCs are available to graduate business students. Access to Internet/World Wide Web, online (class) registration, and online grade reports available. *Personal computer requirements:* Graduate business students are strongly recommended to purchase or lease a personal computer. *Special opportunities include:* An international exchange program and an internship program are available. *Placement services include:* Alumni network, career placement, career counseling/planning, electronic job bank, resume referral, career fairs, job interviews arranged, resume preparation, and career library.

EXPENSES *Tuition (state resident):* Full-time: $15,351. *Tuition (nonresident):* Full-time: $21,995. *Tuition (international):* Full-time: $21,995. *Required fees:* Full-time: $1500. *Graduate housing:* Room and board costs vary by number of occupants and type of accommodation. *Typical cost:* $8793 (including board).

FINANCIAL AID (2007–08) Grants, loans, research assistantships, scholarships, and teaching assistantships. Aid is available to part-time students. *Financial aid application deadline:* 3/2.

Financial Aid Contact Lois Kelly, Director, Financial Aid Office, San Luis Obispo, CA 93407-0201. *Phone:* 805-756-5893. *Fax:* 805-756-7243. *E-mail:* lkelly@calpoly.edu.

INTERNATIONAL STUDENTS 3% of students enrolled are international students. *Services and facilities:* Counseling/support services, Housing location assistance, International student organization, Orientation. Financial aid is not available to international students. *Required with application:* TOEFL with recommended score of 213 (computer) or 550 (paper); TWE with recommended score of 4.5; proof of adequate funds; proof of health/immunizations.

International Student Contact Barbara Andre, Associate Director, International Education and Programs, San Luis Obispo, CA 93407-0721. *Phone:* 805-756-5837. *Fax:* 805-756-5484. *E-mail:* bandre@calpoly.edu.

APPLICATION *Required:* GMAT, application form, baccalaureate/first degree, 2 letters of recommendation, personal statement, resume/curriculum vitae, transcripts of college work. *Recommended:* Work experience. *Application fee:* $55. Applications for domestic and international students are processed on a rolling basis.

Application Contact Victoria Walls, Assistant Director, Graduate Programs, OCOB, Graduate Programs, San Luis Obispo, CA 93407-0300. *Phone:* 805-756-2637. *Fax:* 805-756-0110. *E-mail:* vwalls@calpoly.edu.

California State University, Bakersfield

School of Business and Public Administration

Bakersfield, California

Phone: 661-664-3099 **Fax:** 661-664-3486 **E-mail:** tmishoe@csub.edu

Business Program(s) Web Site: http://www.csubbpa.com/

Graduate Business Unit Enrollment *Total:* 84 (43 full-time; 41 part-time; 36 women; 11 international). *Average Age:* 25.

Graduate Business Faculty 10 full-time.

Admissions *Applied:* 76. *Admitted:* 43. *Enrolled:* 32. *Average GMAT:* 532. *Average GPA:* 3.14

Academic Calendar Quarters.

Accreditation AACSB—The Association to Advance Collegiate Schools of Business.

MBA—Master of Business Administration Full-time and part-time. At least 58 total credits required. 24 to 84 months to complete program. *Concentration:* general MBA.

RESOURCES AND SERVICES 75 on-campus PCs are available to graduate business students. Access to Internet/World Wide Web, online (class) registration, and online grade reports available. *Personal computer requirements:* Graduate business students are not required to have a personal computer. *Placement services include:* Career placement, career counseling/planning, electronic job bank, career fairs, and resume preparation.

EXPENSES *Tuition (state resident):* Full-time: $3102. Part-time: $1800 per year. *Tuition (nonresident):* Full-time: $6780. Part-time: $3390 per year. *Tuition (international):* Full-time: $6780. Part-time: $3390 per year. *Required fees:* Full-time: $880. Part-time: $880 per year. *Graduate housing:* Room and board costs vary by type of board plan. *Typical cost:* $13,534 (including board).

FINANCIAL AID (2007–08) 4 students received aid, including scholarships. *Financial aid application deadline:* 4/30.

Financial Aid Contact Financial Aid Office, 9001 Stockdale Highway, Bakersfield, CA 93311-1099. *Phone:* 661-664-3016. *Fax:* 661-664-6800.

INTERNATIONAL STUDENTS 13% of students enrolled are international students. *Services and facilities:* Counseling/support services, ESL/language courses, International student organization, Language tutoring, Orientation. Financial aid is not available to international students. *Required with application:* TOEFL with recommended score of 213 (computer) or 550 (paper); proof of adequate funds; proof of health/immunizations.

International Student Contact Claudia Pereyra, Advisor, International Students and Programs, 9001 Stockdale Highway, Bakersfield, CA 93311-1099. *Phone:* 661-664-2350. *Fax:* 661-664-6924. *E-mail:* cpereyra@cub.edu.

APPLICATION *Required:* Application form, baccalaureate/first degree, 2 letters of recommendation, personal statement, resume/curriculum vitae, transcripts of college work. School will accept GMAT and GRE. *Recommended:* Interview, 3 years of work experience. *Application fee:* $55. Applications for domestic and international students are processed on a rolling basis.

Application Contact Thomas P. Mishoe, Director of Student Services, 9001 Stockdale Highway, Bakersfield, CA 93311-1099. *Phone:* 661-664-3099. *Fax:* 661-664-3486. *E-mail:* tmishoe@csub.edu.

California State University, Dominguez Hills

College of Business Administration and Public Policy

Carson, California

Phone: 310-243-3465 **Fax:** 310-516-4178 **E-mail:** ehall@csudh.edu

Business Program(s) Web Site: http://cbapp.csudh.edu

Accreditation ACBSP—The American Council of Business Schools and Programs.

DEGREES MBA

MBA—Online Master of Business Administration Full-time and part-time. Distance learning option. 30 to 42 total credits required. Maximum of 15 months to complete program. *Concentrations:* finance, general MBA, human resources management, information technology, international business, management, marketing.

MBA—Master of Business Administration Full-time and part-time. Distance learning option. 30 to 57 total credits required. 12 to 24 months

to complete program. *Concentrations:* finance, general MBA, human resources management, information technology, international business, management, marketing.

RESOURCES AND SERVICES 311 on-campus PCs are available to graduate business students. Access to Internet/World Wide Web, online (class) registration, and online grade reports available. *Personal computer requirements:* Graduate business students are not required to have a personal computer. *Placement services include:* Alumni network, career placement, career counseling/planning, career fairs, job interviews arranged, resume preparation, and career library.

Application Contact Ms. Eileen Hall, MBA Coordinator, 1000 East Victoria Street, Carson, CA 90747-0001. *Phone:* 310-243-3465. *Fax:* 310-516-4178. *E-mail:* ehall@csudh.edu.

California State University, East Bay

College of Business and Economics

Hayward, California

Phone: 510-885-3364 **Fax:** 510-885-2176 **E-mail:** doris.duncan@csueastbay.edu

Business Program(s) Web Site: http://www.cbegrad.csueastbay.edu

Graduate Business Unit Enrollment *Total:* 646 (342 women; 280 international). *Average Age:* 28.

Graduate Business Faculty *Total:* 69 (52 full-time; 17 part-time).

Admissions *Applied:* 384. *Admitted:* 268. *Enrolled:* 233. *Average GMAT:* 539. *Average GPA:* 3.19

Academic Calendar Quarters.

Accreditation AACSB—The Association to Advance Collegiate Schools of Business.

DEGREES MA • MBA • MS

MA—Master of Arts in Economics Part-time. At least 45 total credits required. 12 to 60 months to complete program. *Concentration:* economics.

MBA—Master of Business Administration Part-time. At least 45 total credits required. 12 to 60 months to complete program. *Concentrations:* accounting, economics, electronic commerce (E-commerce), entrepreneurship, finance, human resources management, information technology, international business, management, marketing, operations management, strategic management, supply chain management, taxation.

MS—Master of Science in Business Administration: Information Technology Management Part-time. At least 45 total credits required. 12 to 60 months to complete program. *Concentration:* information technology.

MS—Master of Science in Taxation Part-time. At least 45 total credits required. 12 to 60 months to complete program. *Concentration:* taxation.

RESOURCES AND SERVICES Access to Internet/World Wide Web, online (class) registration, and online grade reports available. *Personal computer requirements:* Graduate business students are strongly recommended to purchase or lease a personal computer. *Special opportunities include:* An internship program is available. *Placement services include:* Career placement, career counseling/planning, electronic job bank, resume referral, career fairs, job interviews arranged, and resume preparation.

EXPENSES *Tuition (state resident):* Full-time: $5316. Part-time: $851 per quarter hour. *Tuition (nonresident):* Full-time: $12,548. Part-time: $1755 per quarter hour. *Tuition (international):* Full-time: $12,548. *Graduate housing:* Room and board costs vary by campus location, number of occupants, type of accommodation, and type of board plan. *Typical cost:* $10,152 (including board).

FINANCIAL AID (2007–08) 175 students received aid, including fellowships, grants, loans, scholarships, teaching assistantships, and work study. Aid is available to part-time students. *Financial aid application deadline:* 3/1.

California State University, East Bay (continued)

Financial Aid Contact Rhonda Johnson, Director, Financial Aid, 25800 Carlos Bee Boulevard, Warren Hall, Room 267, Hayward, CA 94542-3000. *Phone:* 510-885-3018. *Fax:* 510-885-4059. *E-mail:* rhonda.johnson@csueastbay.edu.

INTERNATIONAL STUDENTS 43% of students enrolled are international students. *Services and facilities:* Counseling/support services, ESL/language courses, Housing location assistance, International student housing, International student organization, Orientation, Visa Services, employment assistance. Financial aid is not available to international students. *Required with application:* TOEFL with recommended score of 213 (computer) or 550 (paper); proof of adequate funds; proof of health/immunizations.

International Student Contact Ray Wallace, Executive Director, International Programs, 25800 Carlos Bee Boulevard, Student Service Hub, Room 1336, Hayward, CA 94542. *Phone:* 510-885-4038. *Fax:* 510-885-2787. *E-mail:* ray.wallace@csueastbay.edu.

APPLICATION *Required:* GMAT, application form, baccalaureate/first degree, personal statement, transcripts of college work. *Application fee:* $55. Applications for domestic and international students are processed on a rolling basis.

Application Contact Dr. Doris Duncan, MBA Director, 25800 Carlos Bee Boulevard, Valley Business and Technology, Room 429, Hayward, CA 94542. *Phone:* 510-885-3364. *Fax:* 510-885-2176. *E-mail:* doris.duncan@csueastbay.edu.

California State University, Fresno
Craig School of Business

Fresno, California

Phone: 559-278-2107 **Fax:** 559-278-4911 **E-mail:** mbainfo@csufresno.edu

Business Program(s) Web Site: http://www.craig.csufresno.edu/mba/

Accreditation AACSB—The Association to Advance Collegiate Schools of Business.

DEGREES EMBA • MBA

EMBA—Executive Master of Business Administration Full-time. GPA 2.5, 10 years of experience, 3 years in upper management. 36 total credits required. 18 to 60 months to complete program. *Concentration:* general MBA.

MBA—Master of Business Administration Full-time and part-time. GMAT 550+, GPA 2.5+. 36 to 51 total credits required. 18 to 60 months to complete program. *Concentrations:* entrepreneurship, finance, general MBA, human resources management, international business, management, management information systems, marketing.

RESOURCES AND SERVICES 700 on-campus PCs are available to graduate business students. Access to Internet/World Wide Web, online (class) registration, and online grade reports available. *Personal computer requirements:* Graduate business students are strongly recommended to purchase or lease a personal computer. *Special opportunities include:* An international exchange program and an internship program are available. *Placement services include:* Alumni network, career placement, job search course, career counseling/planning, electronic job bank, resume referral, career fairs, job interviews arranged, resume preparation, and career library.

Application Contact Nee Lehman, Administrative Assistant, 5245 North Backer Avenue, Fresno, CA 93740-0008. *Phone:* 559-278-2107. *Fax:* 559-278-4911. *E-mail:* mbainfo@csufresno.edu.

California State University, Fullerton
College of Business and Economics

Fullerton, California

Phone: 714-278-2417 **Fax:** 714-278-7101 **E-mail:** dmazzey@fullerton.edu

Business Program(s) Web Site: http://business.fullerton.edu/

Graduate Business Unit Enrollment *Total:* 619 (619 part-time; 281 women; 164 international).

Graduate Business Faculty *Total:* 50 (44 full-time; 6 part-time).

Admissions *Applied:* 729. *Admitted:* 340. *Enrolled:* 190. *Average GMAT:* 558. *Average GPA:* 3.35

Academic Calendar Semesters.

Accreditation AACSB—The Association to Advance Collegiate Schools of Business.

DEGREES MA • MBA • MSA • MSIS • MSIT • MST

MA—Economics Full-time and part-time. Total minimum score of 1000 on the Verbal and Quantitative sections combined on the GRE General Test required. At least 30 total credits required. 12 to 60 months to complete program. *Concentration:* economics.

MBA—MBA—CSUF Irvine Institute Part-time. Fall admission only. 30 to 48 total credits required. 16 to 60 months to complete program. *Concentrations:* accounting, economics, electronic commerce (E-commerce), entrepreneurship, finance, general MBA, information systems, international business, management, management science, marketing.

MBA—Master of Business Administration Full-time and part-time. 33 to 48 total credits required. 12 to 60 months to complete program. *Concentrations:* accounting, economics, electronic commerce (E-commerce), entrepreneurship, finance, general MBA, international business, management, management information systems, management science, marketing.

MSA—Master of Science in Accountancy Full-time and part-time. At least 30 total credits required. 12 to 60 months to complete program. *Concentration:* accounting.

MSIS—Master of Science in Information Systems Full-time and part-time. At least 30 total credits required. 12 to 60 months to complete program. *Concentrations:* decision sciences, electronic commerce (E-commerce).

MSIT—Master of Science in Information Technology—Online Part-time. Distance learning option. Fall admission only. 30 total credits required. 20 to 60 months to complete program. *Concentration:* information technology.

MST—Master of Science in Taxation Full-time and part-time. 30 total credits required. 12 to 60 months to complete program. *Concentration:* taxation.

MST—Master of Science in Taxation—CSUF Irvine Institute Part-time. 30 total credits required. 22 to 60 months to complete program. *Concentration:* taxation.

RESOURCES AND SERVICES 800 on-campus PCs are available to graduate business students. Access to Internet/World Wide Web, online (class) registration, and online grade reports available. *Personal computer requirements:* Graduate business students are not required to have a personal computer. *Special opportunities include:* An internship program is available. *Placement services include:* Alumni network, career placement, career counseling/planning, electronic job bank, career fairs, job interviews arranged, resume preparation, and career library.

EXPENSES *Tuition (nonresident):* Full-time: $8136. Part-time: $4068 per semester. *Tuition (international):* Full-time: $8136. Part-time: $4068 per semester. *Required fees:* Full-time: $4024. Part-time: $2690 per year. Tuition and/or fees vary by number of courses or credits taken and academic program. *Graduate housing:* Room and board costs vary by number of occupants and type of accommodation. *Typical cost:* $4356 (room only).

FINANCIAL AID (2007–08) 50 students received aid, including fellowships, grants, loans, research assistantships, scholarships, teaching assistantships, and work study. Aid is available to part-time students. *Financial aid application deadline: 3/2.*

Financial Aid Contact Ms. Deborah McCracken, Director of Financial Aid, 800 North State College Boulevard, UH-164, Fullerton, CA 92834-6804. *Phone:* 714-278-3128. *Fax:* 714-278-7090. *E-mail:* fa@ fullerton.edu.

INTERNATIONAL STUDENTS 26% of students enrolled are international students. *Services and facilities:* Counseling/support services, ESL/language courses, Housing location assistance, International student organization, Language tutoring, Orientation, Visa Services, Employment assistance. Financial aid is available to international students. *Required with application:* TOEFL with recommended score of 230 (computer) or 570 (paper); proof of adequate funds; proof of health/immunizations.

International Student Contact Robert Erickson, Director of International Education and Exchange, 800 North State College Boulevard, CP-1060-3, Fullerton, CA 92834-6830. *Phone:* 714-278-2787. *Fax:* 714-278-7292. *E-mail:* bericksen@fullerton.edu.

APPLICATION *Required:* GMAT, application form, baccalaureate/first degree, essay, personal statement, transcripts of college work. *Recommended:* Letter(s) of recommendation, resume/curriculum vitae. *Application fee:* $55. Applications for domestic and international students are processed on a rolling basis.

Application Contact Diane Mazzey, Graduate Programs Advisor, 800 North State College Boulevard, SGMH-3280-E, Fullerton, CA 92834-6848. *Phone:* 714-278-2417. *Fax:* 714-278-7101. *E-mail:* dmazzey@ fullerton.edu.

California State University, Long Beach

College of Business Administration

Long Beach, California

Phone: 562-985-8627 **Fax:** 562-985-5590 **E-mail:** marifree@csulb.edu

Business Program(s) Web Site: http://www.csulb.edu/mba

Graduate Business Unit Enrollment *Total:* 340 (88 full-time; 252 part-time; 161 women; 79 international).

Graduate Business Faculty *Total:* 39 (32 full-time; 7 part-time).

Admissions *Applied:* 350. *Admitted:* 120. *Enrolled:* 80. *Average GMAT:* 560. *Average GPA:* 3.3

Academic Calendar Semesters.

Accreditation AACSB—The Association to Advance Collegiate Schools of Business.

DEGREES MBA

MBA—Accelerated MBA Full-time. 36 to 48 total credits required. Maximum of 12 months to complete program. *Concentration:* general MBA.

MBA—Fully-Employed Master of Business Administration Part-time. 36 to 48 total credits required. Maximum of 24 months to complete program. *Concentration:* general MBA.

MBA—Self-Paced Evening MBA Full-time and part-time. 36 to 48 total credits required. 18 to 84 months to complete program. *Concentrations:* accounting, finance, health care, human resources management, management, management information systems, marketing.

RESOURCES AND SERVICES 250 on-campus PCs are available to graduate business students. Access to Internet/World Wide Web, online (class) registration, and online grade reports available. *Personal computer requirements:* Graduate business students are strongly recommended to purchase or lease a personal computer. *Placement services include:* Alumni network, career counseling/planning, electronic job bank, career fairs, and resume preparation.

EXPENSES *Tuition (state resident):* Full-time: $4100. Part-time: $2522 per semester. *Tuition (nonresident):* Full-time: $6134. Part-time: $4556 per semester. *Tuition (international):* Full-time: $6134. Part-time: $4556 per semester.

FINANCIAL AID (2007–08) Loans, teaching assistantships, and work study. Aid is available to part-time students. *Financial aid application deadline: 6/30.*

Financial Aid Contact Financial Aid Office, 1250 Bellflower Boulevard, BH-101, Long Beach, CA 90840-0119. *Phone:* 562-985-7497. *Fax:* 562-985-4973.

INTERNATIONAL STUDENTS 23% of students enrolled are international students. *Services and facilities:* Counseling/support services, ESL/language courses, Housing location assistance, International student housing, Orientation, Visa Services. Financial aid is not available to international students. *Required with application:* TOEFL with recommended score of 213 (computer), 550 (paper), or 80 (Internet); proof of adequate funds.

International Student Contact Emiko Kawashima, Director, International Admissions, 1250 Bellflower Boulevard, BH-201, Long Beach, CA 90840-0119. *Phone:* 562-985-8426. *Fax:* 562-985-1725. *E-mail:* esallows@ csulb.edu.

APPLICATION *Required:* GMAT, application form, baccalaureate/first degree, 2 letters of recommendation, personal statement, resume/ curriculum vitae, transcripts of college work. *Recommended:* Work experience. *Application fee:* $55. Applications for domestic and international students are processed on a rolling basis.

Application Contact Marina Freeman, Admissions Manager, 1250 Bellflower Boulevard, Long Beach, CA 90840-0119. *Phone:* 562-985-8627. *Fax:* 562-985-5590. *E-mail:* marifree@csulb.edu.

California State University, Los Angeles

College of Business and Economics

Los Angeles, California

Phone: 323-343-5156 **Fax:** 323-343-5480 **E-mail:** ppartow@calstatela.edu

Business Program(s) Web Site: http://cbe.calstatela.edu/mba/index.htm

Graduate Business Unit Enrollment *Total:* 337 (111 full-time; 226 part-time; 142 international).

Graduate Business Faculty *Total:* 114 (75 full-time; 39 part-time).

Admissions *Applied:* 320. *Admitted:* 175. *Enrolled:* 152. *Average GMAT:* 560. *Average GPA:* 3.24

Academic Calendar Quarters.

Accreditation AACSB—The Association to Advance Collegiate Schools of Business.

DEGREES MA • MBA • MS

MA—Master of Arts in Economics Full-time and part-time. At least 45 total credits required. 18 to 48 months to complete program. *Concentrations:* financial economics, international economics.

MBA—Master of Business Administration Full-time and part-time. At least 48 total credits required. 18 to 48 months to complete program. *Concentrations:* accounting, business information science, economics, finance, health care, international business, management, marketing.

MS—Master of Science in Accountancy Full-time and part-time. At least 45 total credits required. 18 to 48 months to complete program. *Concentration:* accounting.

California State University, Los Angeles (continued)

MS—Master of Science in Business Administration Full-time and part-time. At least 45 total credits required. 18 to 48 months to complete program. *Concentrations:* economics, finance, international business, management, management information systems, marketing.

MS—Master of Science in Health Care Management Full-time and part-time. At least 45 total credits required. 18 to 48 months to complete program. *Concentration:* health care.

MS—Master of Science in Information Systems Full-time and part-time. At least 45 total credits required. 18 to 48 months to complete program. *Concentration:* management information systems.

RESOURCES AND SERVICES 600 on-campus PCs are available to graduate business students. Access to Internet/World Wide Web, online (class) registration, and online grade reports available. *Personal computer requirements:* Graduate business students are not required to have a personal computer. *Placement services include:* Alumni network, career counseling/planning, career fairs, and resume preparation.

FINANCIAL AID (2007–08) 14 students received aid, including research assistantships, scholarships, teaching assistantships, and work study. Aid is available to part-time students. *Financial aid application deadline:* 3/4.

Financial Aid Contact Mr. Benny Rios, Financial Aid Advisor, 5151 State University Drive, Los Angeles, CA 90032-4221. *Phone:* 323-343-6260. *Fax:* 323-343-3166. *E-mail:* brios@calstatela.edu.

INTERNATIONAL STUDENTS 42% of students enrolled are international students. *Services and facilities:* Counseling/support services, ESL/language courses, International student housing, International student organization, Language tutoring, Orientation, Visa Services. Financial aid is not available to international students. *Required with application:* TOEFL with recommended score of 213 (computer), 550 (paper), or 80 (Internet); proof of adequate funds; proof of health/immunizations.

International Student Contact Ms. Wai Fun (Chirstina) Wong, International Student Advisor, International Program and Services, 5151 State University Drive, Los Angeles, CA 90032-4221. *Phone:* 323-343-3170. *Fax:* 323-343-6478. *E-mail:* wwong@cslanet.calstatela.edu.

APPLICATION *Required:* GMAT, application form, baccalaureate/first degree, essay, 3 letters of recommendation, personal statement, resume/ curriculum vitae, transcripts of college work, 2 years of work experience. *Application fee:* $55. *Deadlines:* 3/1 for fall (international), 9/1 for winter (international), 10/1 for spring (international). Applications for domestic students are processed on a rolling basis.

Application Contact Dr. Parviz Partow, Graduate Program Director, Graduate Program Office, 5151 State University Drive, Los Angeles, CA 90032-8120. *Phone:* 323-343-5156. *Fax:* 323-343-5480. *E-mail:* ppartow@ calstatela.edu.

California State University, Northridge
College of Business and Economics
Northridge, California

Phone: 818-677-3625 **Fax:** 818-677-3188 **E-mail:** mba@csun.edu

Business Program(s) Web Site: http://www.csun.edu/mba

Accreditation AACSB—The Association to Advance Collegiate Schools of Business.

DEGREE MBA

MBA—Evening Master of Business Administration Full-time and part-time. 33 to 48 total credits required. 18 to 60 months to complete program. *Concentrations:* business law, economics, finance, international business, management, management information systems, management science, marketing.

RESOURCES AND SERVICES 100 on-campus PCs are available to graduate business students. Access to Internet/World Wide Web, online

(class) registration, and online grade reports available. *Personal computer requirements:* Graduate business students are strongly recommended to purchase or lease a personal computer. *Placement services include:* Alumni network, career counseling/planning, electronic job bank, and career fairs.

Application Contact Dr. Oscar W. DeShields, Jr., Director of Graduate Programs and PACE, 18111 Nordhoff Street, Juniper Hall, 3109D, Northridge, CA 91330-8380. *Phone:* 818-677-3625. *Fax:* 818-677-3188. *E-mail:* mba@csun.edu.

California State University, Sacramento
College of Business Administration
Sacramento, California

Phone: 916-278-6772 **Fax:** 916-278-4233 **E-mail:** cbagrad@csus.edu

Business Program(s) Web Site: http://www.cba.csus.edu/mba

Graduate Business Unit Enrollment *Total:* 231 (71 full-time; 160 part-time; 92 women; 25 international). *Average Age:* 29.

Graduate Business Faculty *Total:* 24 (23 full-time; 1 part-time).

Admissions *Applied:* 360. *Admitted:* 220. *Enrolled:* 54. *Average GMAT:* 553. *Average GPA:* 3.16

Academic Calendar Semesters.

Accreditation AACSB—The Association to Advance Collegiate Schools of Business.

After Graduation (Class of 2006–07) *Average starting salary:* $45,000.

DEGREES EMBA • M Sc • MBA • MSBA

EMBA—Master of Business Administration for Executives Part-time. Please visit our Website (www.cba.csus.edu/emba) for specific admission criteria. 41 total credits required. 15 months to complete program. *Concentration:* executive programs.

M Sc—Master of Science in Accountancy Part-time. Distance learning option. Applicants may substitute the CPA for the GMAT if they have not previously taken the GMAT (a GMAT score of 500 is given for the CPA). 30 to 40 total credits required. 18 to 84 months to complete program. *Concentration:* accounting.

MBA—Master of Business Administration Full-time and part-time. 33 to 52 total credits required. 12 to 84 months to complete program. *Concentrations:* accounting, city/urban administration, finance, human resources management, management information systems, marketing.

MSBA—Master of Science in Management Information Science Full-time and part-time. Resume and letters of recommendation are required for this program. 30 to 49 total credits required. 18 to 84 months to complete program. *Concentration:* management information systems.

MSBA—Master of Science in Urban Land Development Full-time and part-time. Two letters of recommendation required and GRE allowed. 33 to 42 total credits required. 18 to 48 months to complete program. *Concentrations:* city/urban administration, public policy and administration.

RESOURCES AND SERVICES 516 on-campus PCs are available to graduate business students. Access to Internet/World Wide Web, online (class) registration, and online grade reports available. *Personal computer requirements:* Graduate business students are strongly recommended to purchase or lease a personal computer. *Special opportunities include:* An international exchange program and an internship program are available. *Placement services include:* Alumni network, career placement, job search course, career counseling/planning, electronic job bank, resume referral, career fairs, job interviews arranged, resume preparation, and career library.

FINANCIAL AID (2007–08) Grants, research assistantships, scholarships, teaching assistantships, and work study. Aid is available to part-time students. *Financial aid application deadline:* 3/1.

Financial Aid Contact Mike Dear, Assistant Director, Financial Aid, 6000 J Street, Sacramento, CA 95819-6044. *Phone:* 916-278-6554. *Fax:* 916-278-6082. *E-mail:* dearm@csus.edu.

INTERNATIONAL STUDENTS 11% of students enrolled are international students. *Services and facilities:* Counseling/support services, ESL/language courses, Housing location assistance, Language tutoring, Orientation, Visa Services. Financial aid is not available to international students. *Required with application:* TOEFL with recommended score of 213 (computer) or 550 (paper); proof of adequate funds; proof of health/immunizations.

International Student Contact Mlima Wells, Coordinator, International Admissions, 6000 J Street, Sacramento, CA 95819-6012. *Phone:* 916-278-7772. *Fax:* 916-278-5603. *E-mail:* intladm@csus.edu.

APPLICATION *Required:* GMAT, application form, baccalaureate/first degree, 3 letters of recommendation, personal statement, resume/curriculum vitae, transcripts of college work. *Application fee:* $55. *Deadlines:* 4/1 for fall, 10/1 for spring, 4/1 for fall (international), 10/1 for spring (international).

Application Contact Jeanie Williams, Graduate Academic Director, 6000 J Street, Sacramento, CA 95819-6088. *Phone:* 916-278-6772. *Fax:* 916-278-4233. *E-mail:* cbagrad@csus.edu.

California State University, San Bernardino

College of Business and Public Administration

San Bernardino, California

Phone: 909-537-5703 **Fax:** 909-537-7582 **E-mail:** bflynn@csusb.edu

Business Program(s) Web Site: http://www.csusb.edu/mba/

Graduate Business Unit Enrollment *Total:* 325 (182 full-time; 143 part-time; 130 women; 112 international). *Average Age:* 29.

Graduate Business Faculty *Total:* 30 (28 full-time; 2 part-time).

Admissions *Applied:* 264. *Admitted:* 189. *Enrolled:* 121. *Average GMAT:* 527. *Average GPA:* 3.2

Academic Calendar Quarters.

Accreditation AACSB—The Association to Advance Collegiate Schools of Business.

After Graduation (Class of 2006–07) *Employed within 3 months of graduation:* 85%. *Average starting salary:* $55,000.

DEGREE MBA

MBA—Master of Business Administration Full-time and part-time. At least 48 total credits required. 15 to 84 months to complete program. *Concentrations:* accounting, entrepreneurship, finance, information management, management, marketing, other, supply chain management.

RESOURCES AND SERVICES 400 on-campus PCs are available to graduate business students. Access to Internet/World Wide Web, online (class) registration, and online grade reports available. *Personal computer requirements:* Graduate business students are not required to have a personal computer. *Special opportunities include:* An international exchange program and an internship program are available. *Placement services include:* Alumni network, career placement, job search course, career counseling/planning, electronic job bank, resume referral, career fairs, job interviews arranged, resume preparation, and career library.

EXPENSES *Tuition (state resident):* Full-time: $4161. Part-time: $2729 per year. *Tuition (nonresident):* Full-time: $12,297. Part-time: $5441 per year. *Tuition (international):* Full-time: $12,297. Tuition and/or fees vary by number of courses or credits taken. *Graduate housing:* Room and

board costs vary by number of occupants, type of accommodation, and type of board plan. *Typical cost:* $10,000 (including board), $7200 (room only).

FINANCIAL AID (2007–08) 122 students received aid, including grants, loans, research assistantships, scholarships, teaching assistantships, and work study. Aid is available to part-time students. *Financial aid application deadline:* 3/1.

Financial Aid Contact Ms. Roseanna Ruiz, Director of Financial Aid, Financial Aid UH 150, 5500 University Parkway, San Bernardino, CA 94207-2392. *Phone:* 909-880-7800 Ext. 3. *Fax:* 909-537-7024. *E-mail:* rruiz@csusb.edu.

INTERNATIONAL STUDENTS 34% of students enrolled are international students. *Services and facilities:* Counseling/support services, ESL/language courses, Housing location assistance, International student housing, International student organization, Language tutoring, Orientation, Visa Services. Financial aid is available to international students. *Required with application:* TOEFL with recommended score of 213 (computer), 550 (paper), or 79 (Internet); proof of adequate funds; proof of health/immunizations.

International Student Contact Cynthia Shum, Assistant Director, International Admissions, 5500 University Parkway, UH 112, San Bernardino, CA 92407-2397. *Phone:* 909-537-5212. *Fax:* 909-537-7354. *E-mail:* cshum@csusb.edu.

APPLICATION *Required:* GMAT, application form, baccalaureate/first degree, essay, personal statement, transcripts of college work. *Recommended:* Resume/curriculum vitae. *Application fee:* $55.

Application Contact Ms. Beth A. Flynn, MBA Program Director, 5500 University Parkway JB 282, San Bernardino, CA 92407-2397. *Phone:* 909-537-5703. *Fax:* 909-537-7582. *E-mail:* bflynn@csusb.edu.

California State University, San Marcos

College of Business Administration

San Marcos, California

Phone: 760-750-4267 **Fax:** 760-750-4263 **E-mail:** mba@csusm.edu

Business Program(s) Web Site: http://www.csusm.edu/mba

Graduate Business Unit Enrollment *Total:* 59 (59 part-time; 19 women).

Graduate Business Faculty *Total:* 50 (30 full-time; 20 part-time).

Admissions *Average GMAT:* 593. *Average GPA:* 3.19

Academic Calendar Semesters.

After Graduation (Class of 2006–07) *Employed within 3 months of graduation:* 90%.

DEGREE MBA

MBA—Fully-Employed Master of Business Administration Part-time. Minimum GPA of 3.0 in the last 60 semester units, minimum GMAT score of 500 (with a minimum 30th percentile in both Verbal and Quantitative) required. 56 to 64 total credits required. 33 to 60 months to complete program. *Concentration:* management.

RESOURCES AND SERVICES 250 on-campus PCs are available to graduate business students. Access to Internet/World Wide Web, online (class) registration, and online grade reports available. *Personal computer requirements:* Graduate business students are strongly recommended to purchase or lease a personal computer. *Placement services include:* Alumni network, career placement, job search course, career counseling/planning, electronic job bank, career fairs, resume preparation, and career library.

EXPENSES *Tuition (state resident):* Part-time: $2008 per term. *Tuition (nonresident):* Part-time: $4712 per term.

California State University, San Marcos (continued)

FINANCIAL AID (2007–08) Loans and scholarships. Aid is available to part-time students. *Financial aid application deadline:* 3/1.

Financial Aid Contact Director of Financial Aid, 333 South Twin Oaks Valley Road, San Marcos, CA 92096-0001. *Phone:* 760-750-4850. *Fax:* 760-750-3047. *E-mail:* finaid@csusm.edu.

INTERNATIONAL STUDENTS *Services and facilities:* Counseling/ support services, ESL/language courses, Housing location assistance, International student organization, Language tutoring, Orientation, Visa Services. Financial aid is not available to international students. *Required with application:* TOEFL with recommended score of 213 (computer), 550 (paper), or 80 (Internet); proof of health/immunizations. *Recommended with application:* IELT with recommended score of 6.

International Student Contact Miss Julie Pick, College Operations Administrator, 333 South Twin Oaks Valley Road, San Marcos, CA 92096-0001. *Phone:* 760-750-4267. *Fax:* 760-750-4263. *E-mail:* mba@ csusm.edu.

APPLICATION *Required:* GMAT, application form, baccalaureate/first degree, essay, 3 letters of recommendation, resume/curriculum vitae, transcripts of college work, 3 years of work experience. *Application fee:* $55. Applications for domestic and international students are processed on a rolling basis.

Application Contact Miss Julie Pick, College Operations Administrator, 333 South Twin Oaks Valley Road, San Marcos, CA 92096-0001. *Phone:* 760-750-4267. *Fax:* 760-750-4263. *E-mail:* mba@csusm.edu.

California State University, Stanislaus

College of Business Administration

Turlock, California

Phone: 209-667-3280 **Fax:** 209-667-3080 **E-mail:** rbrown@csustan.edu

Business Program(s) Web Site: http://www.csustan.edu/mba/dept/index.html

Graduate Business Unit Enrollment *Total:* 110 (25 full-time; 85 part-time; 52 women).

Graduate Business Faculty *Total:* 18 (14 full-time; 4 part-time).

Admissions *Applied:* 40. *Admitted:* 35. *Enrolled:* 35. *Average GMAT:* 490. *Average GPA:* 2.96

Academic Calendar Semesters.

Accreditation AACSB—The Association to Advance Collegiate Schools of Business.

After Graduation (Class of 2006–07) *Employed within 3 months of graduation:* 90%. *Average starting salary:* $56,000.

DEGREE MBA

MBA—Master of Business Administration Full-time and part-time. Distance learning option. 33 to 54 total credits required. 12 to 84 months to complete program. *Concentration:* general MBA.

RESOURCES AND SERVICES 110 on-campus PCs are available to graduate business students. Access to Internet/World Wide Web, online (class) registration, and online grade reports available. *Personal computer requirements:* Graduate business students are strongly recommended to purchase or lease a personal computer. *Placement services include:* Alumni network, career counseling/planning, resume referral, career fairs, job interviews arranged, resume preparation, and career library.

EXPENSES *Tuition (state resident):* Full-time: $3570. Part-time: $1992 per semester. *Tuition (nonresident):* Full-time: $6621. Part-time: $4026 per semester. *Tuition (international):* Full-time: $6621. Part-time: $4026 per semester.

FINANCIAL AID (2007–08) 44 students received aid, including fellowships, loans, and work study. *Financial aid application deadline:* 3/2.

Financial Aid Contact Joan Hillery, Director, Financial Aid, One University Circle, Turlock, CA 95382. *Phone:* 209-667-3336. *Fax:* 209-667-3080. *E-mail:* jhillery@stan.csustan.edu.

INTERNATIONAL STUDENTS *Services and facilities:* Counseling/ support services, ESL/language courses, International student housing, Visa Services. Financial aid is not available to international students. *Required with application:* TOEFL with recommended score of 213 (computer) or 550 (paper); proof of adequate funds; proof of health/immunizations.

International Student Contact Dette Silbaugh, Coordinator of International Student Programs, One University Circle, Turlock, CA 95382. *Phone:* 209-667-3381. *Fax:* 209-667-3585. *E-mail:* bsantos@ stan.csustan.edu.

APPLICATION *Required:* GMAT, application form, baccalaureate/first degree, 3 letters of recommendation, personal statement, transcripts of college work, 2 years of work experience. School will accept GRE. *Recommended:* Essay, interview, resume/curriculum vitae. *Application fee:* $55. *Deadlines:* 5/31 for fall, 11/1 for spring, 4/30 for summer, 5/31 for fall (international), 10/15 for spring (international), 3/30 for summer (international).

Application Contact Dr. Randall Brown, Director, MBA Programs, One University Circle, Turlock, CA 95382. *Phone:* 209-667-3280. *Fax:* 209-667-3080. *E-mail:* rbrown@csustan.edu.

Chapman University

The George L. Argyros School of Business and Economics

Orange, California

Phone: 714-997-6745 **Fax:** 714-997-6757 **E-mail:** gonda@chapman.edu

Business Program(s) Web Site: http://www.chapman.edu/argyros

Graduate Business Unit Enrollment *Total:* 190 (77 full-time; 113 part-time; 68 women; 16 international). *Average Age:* 33.

Graduate Business Faculty *Total:* 55 (39 full-time; 16 part-time).

Admissions *Applied:* 143. *Admitted:* 101. *Enrolled:* 65. *Average GMAT:* 550. *Average GPA:* 3.15

Academic Calendar Semesters.

Accreditation AACSB—The Association to Advance Collegiate Schools of Business.

After Graduation (Class of 2006–07) *Employed within 3 months of graduation:* 93%. *Average starting salary:* $57,875.

DEGREES JD/MBA • MA/MBA • MBA

JD/MBA—Juris Doctor/Master of Business Administration Full-time. At least 125 total credits required. Minimum of 48 months to complete program. *Concentration:* combined degrees.

MA/MBA—Master of Fine Arts/Master of Business Administration At least 89 total credits required. Minimum of 36 months to complete program. *Concentration:* combined degrees.

MBA—Day-Time Accelerated Full-time. Interview required. At least 52 total credits required. 16 months to complete program. *Concentration:* general MBA.

MBA—Evening Flex Part-time. At least 52 total credits required. 16 to 84 months to complete program. *Concentration:* general MBA.

MBA—Executive Master of Business Administration Part-time. At least 49 total credits required. Minimum of 21 months to complete program. *Concentration:* executive programs.

RESOURCES AND SERVICES 175 on-campus PCs are available to graduate business students. Access to Internet/World Wide Web, online

(class) registration, and online grade reports available. *Personal computer requirements:* Graduate business students are strongly recommended to purchase or lease a personal computer. *Special opportunities include:* An internship program is available. *Placement services include:* Alumni network, career placement, job search course, career counseling/planning, electronic job bank, resume referral, career fairs, job interviews arranged, resume preparation, and career library.

EXPENSES *Tuition:* Full-time: $29,535. *Tuition (international):* Full-time: $29,535. Tuition and/or fees vary by number of courses or credits taken and academic program. *Graduate housing:* Room and board costs vary by number of occupants and type of accommodation. *Typical cost:* $10,059 (room only).

FINANCIAL AID (2007–08) Fellowships, loans, research assistantships, and scholarships. Aid is available to part-time students. *Financial aid application deadline:* 7/1.

Financial Aid Contact Greg Ball, Director, Financial Aid, Orange, CA 92866. *Phone:* 714-997-6741. *Fax:* 714-997-6743.

INTERNATIONAL STUDENTS 8% of students enrolled are international students. *Services and facilities:* Counseling/support services, ESL/language courses, Housing location assistance, International student organization, Orientation, Visa Services. Financial aid is available to international students. *Required with application:* TOEFL with recommended score of 216 (computer), 550 (paper), or 80 (Internet); proof of adequate funds. *Recommended with application:* Proof of health/immunizations.

International Student Contact Mrs. Susan Sams, International Student Services Coordinator, One University Drive, Orange, CA 92866. *Phone:* 714-997-6829. *E-mail:* sams@chapman.edu.

APPLICATION *Required:* GMAT, application form, baccalaureate/first degree, essay, interview, 2 letters of recommendation, personal statement, transcripts of college work. *Recommended:* Resume/curriculum vitae, work experience. *Application fee:* $50. Applications for domestic and international students are processed on a rolling basis.

Application Contact Mrs. Debra Gonda, Associate Director, One University Drive, Beckman Hall, 303 North, Orange, CA 92866. *Phone:* 714-997-6745. *Fax:* 714-997-6757. *E-mail:* gonda@chapman.edu.

See full description on page 586.

Claremont Graduate University

Peter F. Drucker and Masatoshi Ito Graduate School of Management

Claremont, California

Phone: 909-607-7811 **Fax:** 909-607-9104 **E-mail:** drucker@cgu.edu

Business Program(s) Web Site: http://www.drucker.cgu.edu

Graduate Business Unit Enrollment *Total:* 158 (117 full-time; 41 part-time; 57 women; 43 international). *Average Age:* 28.

Graduate Business Faculty *Total:* 28 (14 full-time; 14 part-time).

Admissions *Applied:* 181. *Admitted:* 96. *Enrolled:* 41. *Average GMAT:* 635. *Average GPA:* 3.18

Academic Calendar Semesters.

Accreditation AACSB—The Association to Advance Collegiate Schools of Business.

After Graduation (Class of 2006–07) *Employed within 3 months of graduation:* 78%. *Average starting salary:* $63,988.

DEGREES EMBA • MA • MBA • MBA/MA • MBA/MS • MS • PhD/MBA

EMBA—Executive Management Full-time and part-time. Applicants are not required to take the GMAT. At least 48 total credits required. 24 to 60 months to complete program. *Concentrations:* leadership, strategic management.

MA—Arts and Cultural Management Full-time and part-time. Either GRE or GMAT required. At least 48 total credits required. 18 to 60 months to complete program. *Concentration:* arts administration/management.

MA—Executive Management Full-time and part-time. Applicants are not required to take the GMAT. At least 32 total credits required. 12 to 60 months to complete program. *Concentrations:* executive programs, leadership, strategic management.

MBA—Management Full-time and part-time. At least 60 total credits required. 18 to 72 months to complete program. *Concentrations:* arts administration/management, entrepreneurship, finance, financial engineering, general MBA, human resources management, international management, leadership, management, marketing, strategic management.

MBA/MA—Management/Economics Full-time and part-time. At least 96 total credits required. 24 to 72 months to complete program. *Concentrations:* entrepreneurship, finance, general MBA, international management, leadership, management, strategic management.

MBA/MA—Management/Politics and Policy Full-time and part-time. At least 96 total credits required. 36 to 72 months to complete program. *Concentrations:* entrepreneurship, finance, general MBA, international management, marketing, strategic management.

MBA/MA—Management/Psychology Full-time and part-time. At least 84 total credits required. 24 to 72 months to complete program. *Concentrations:* entrepreneurship, general MBA, leadership, management, organizational behavior/development, organizational management, strategic management.

MBA/MS—Management/Human Resources Design Full-time and part-time. At least 84 total credits required. 24 to 72 months to complete program. *Concentrations:* entrepreneurship, general MBA, human resources management, industrial administration/management, leadership, management.

MBA/MS—Management/Information Sciences Full-time and part-time. At least 80 total credits required. 24 to 72 months to complete program. *Concentrations:* entrepreneurship, finance, general MBA, information systems, international business, leadership, management.

MS—Executive Management Full-time and part-time. Applicants are not required to take the GMAT. At least 32 total credits required. 12 to 72 months to complete program. *Concentrations:* executive programs, leadership, management, strategic management.

MS—Financial Engineering Full-time and part-time. Applicants are required to take the GRE. At least 48 total credits required. 18 to 60 months to complete program. *Concentration:* financial engineering.

PhD/MBA—Economics/Management Full-time and part-time. At least 120 total credits required. 60 to 84 months to complete program. *Concentrations:* economics, entrepreneurship, finance, international business, strategic management.

PhD/MBA—Financial Engineering/Management Full-time and part-time. At least 120 total credits required. 60 to 84 months to complete program. *Concentrations:* entrepreneurship, finance, general MBA, international business, leadership, management, strategic management.

PhD/MBA—Politics and Policy/Management Full-time and part-time. At least 120 total credits required. 60 to 84 months to complete program. *Concentrations:* entrepreneurship, finance, general MBA, international business, international economics, leadership, management, strategic management.

RESOURCES AND SERVICES 32 on-campus PCs are available to graduate business students. Access to Internet/World Wide Web, online (class) registration, and online grade reports available. *Personal computer requirements:* Graduate business students are strongly recommended to purchase or lease a personal computer. *Special opportunities include:* An international exchange program and an internship program are available. *Placement services include:* Alumni network, career placement, job search course, career counseling/planning, electronic job bank, resume referral, career fairs, resume preparation, and career library.

EXPENSES *Tuition:* Full-time: $31,640. Part-time: $1376 per credit. *Tuition (international):* Full-time: $31,640. Part-time: $1376 per credit. *Required fees:* Full-time: $290. Part-time: $290 per year. *Graduate*

Claremont Graduate University (continued)

housing: Room and board costs vary by campus location, number of occupants, and type of accommodation. *Typical cost:* $10,000 (including board), $8100 (room only).

FINANCIAL AID (2007–08) 75 students received aid, including fellowships, grants, loans, research assistantships, scholarships, teaching assistantships, and work study. Aid is available to part-time students. *Financial aid application deadline:* 2/15.

Financial Aid Contact Mr. Jack Millis, Director, Office of Financial Aid, 170 East 10th Street, Claremont, CA 91711. *Phone:* 909-621-8337. *Fax:* 909-607-7285. *E-mail:* finaid@cgu.edu.

INTERNATIONAL STUDENTS 27% of students enrolled are international students. *Services and facilities:* Counseling/support services, ESL/language courses, Housing location assistance, International student housing, International student organization, Language tutoring, Orientation, Visa Services, International Fellows Program (Pre-MBA program). Financial aid is available to international students. *Required with application:* TOEFL with recommended score of 250 (computer), 600 (paper), or 100 (Internet); proof of adequate funds; proof of health/immunizations.

International Student Contact Ms. Nusha Shishegar, International Student Director, 160 East 10th Street, East Harper Hall, Claremont, CA 91711. *Phone:* 909-607-3371. *Fax:* 909-607-7285. *E-mail:* nusha.shishegar@cgu.edu.

APPLICATION *Required:* GMAT, application form, baccalaureate/first degree, essay, interview, 2 letters of recommendation, personal statement, resume/curriculum vitae, transcripts of college work. *Recommended:* 4 years of work experience. *Application fee:* $60. Applications for domestic and international students are processed on a rolling basis.

Application Contact Mr. Brandon Tuck, Admissions Coordinator, 1021 North Dartmouth Avenue, Claremont, CA 91711. *Phone:* 909-607-7811. *Fax:* 909-607-9104. *E-mail:* drucker@cgu.edu.

See full description on page 590.

DeVry University
Keller Graduate School of Management
Fremont, California

Phone: 510-574-1250

DEGREES MAFM • MBA • MHRM • MIS • MPA • MPM

MAFM—Master of Accounting and Financial Management Full-time and part-time. Distance learning option. At least 44 total credits required. 18 to 60 months to complete program. *Concentrations:* accounting, financial management/planning.

MBA—Master of Business Administration Full-time and part-time. Distance learning option. At least 48 total credits required. 18 to 60 months to complete program. *Concentration:* management.

MHRM—Master of Human Resources Management Full-time and part-time. Distance learning option. At least 45 total credits required. 18 to 60 months to complete program. *Concentration:* human resources management.

MIS—Master of Information Systems Management Full-time and part-time. Distance learning option. At least 45 total credits required. 18 to 60 months to complete program. *Concentration:* information systems.

MPA—Master of Public Administration Full-time and part-time. Distance learning option. At least 45 total credits required. 18 to 60 months to complete program. *Concentration:* public policy and administration.

MPM—Master of Project Management Full-time and part-time. Distance learning option. At least 42 total credits required. 18 to 60 months to complete program. *Concentration:* project management.

Application Contact Admissions Office, Fremont Center, 6600 Dumbarton Circle, Fremont, CA 94555. *Phone:* 510-574-1250.

DeVry University
Keller Graduate School of Management
Long Beach, California

Phone: 562-988-0162

DEGREES MAFM • MBA • MHRM • MIS • MPA • MPM

MAFM—Master of Accounting and Financial Management Full-time and part-time. Distance learning option. At least 44 total credits required. 18 to 60 months to complete program. *Concentrations:* accounting, financial management/planning.

MBA—Master of Business Administration Full-time and part-time. Distance learning option. At least 48 total credits required. 18 to 60 months to complete program. *Concentration:* management.

MHRM—Master of Human Resources Management Full-time and part-time. Distance learning option. At least 45 total credits required. 18 to 60 months to complete program. *Concentration:* human resources management.

MIS—Master of Information Systems Management Full-time and part-time. Distance learning option. At least 45 total credits required. 18 to 60 months to complete program. *Concentration:* information systems.

MPA—Master of Public Administration Full-time and part-time. Distance learning option. At least 45 total credits required. 18 to 60 months to complete program. *Concentration:* public policy and administration.

MPM—Master of Project Management Full-time and part-time. Distance learning option. At least 42 total credits required. 18 to 60 months to complete program. *Concentration:* project management.

Application Contact Admissions Office, Long Beach Campus, 3880 Kilroy Airport Way, Long Beach, CA 90806. *Phone:* 562-988-0162.

DeVry University
Keller Graduate School of Management
Palmdale, California

Phone: 866-986-9388

DEGREES MAFM • MBA • MHRM • MPM

MAFM—Master of Accounting and Financial Management Full-time and part-time. Distance learning option. At least 44 total credits required. 18 to 60 months to complete program. *Concentrations:* accounting, financial management/planning.

MBA—Master of Business Administration Full-time and part-time. Distance learning option. At least 48 total credits required. 18 to 60 months to complete program. *Concentration:* management.

MHRM—Master of Human Resources Management Full-time and part-time. Distance learning option. At least 45 total credits required. 18 to 60 months to complete program. *Concentration:* human resources management.

MPM—Master of Project Management Full-time and part-time. Distance learning option. At least 42 total credits required. 18 to 60 months to complete program. *Concentration:* project management.

Application Contact Admissions Office, Palmdale Center, 38256 Sierra Highway, Suite D, Palmdale, CA 93550. *Phone:* 866-986-9388.

DeVry University

Keller Graduate School of Management

Pomona, California

Phone: 909-868-4240

DEGREES MAFM • MBA • MHRM • MIS • MPA • MPM

MAFM—Master of Accounting and Financial Management Full-time and part-time. Distance learning option. At least 44 total credits required. 18 to 60 months to complete program. *Concentrations:* accounting, financial management/planning.

MBA—Master of Business Administration Full-time and part-time. Distance learning option. At least 48 total credits required. 18 to 60 months to complete program. *Concentration:* management.

MHRM—Master of Human Resources Management Full-time and part-time. Distance learning option. At least 45 total credits required. 18 to 60 months to complete program. *Concentration:* human resources management.

MIS—Master of Information Systems Management Full-time and part-time. Distance learning option. At least 45 total credits required. 18 to 60 months to complete program. *Concentration:* information systems.

MPA—Master of Public Administration Full-time and part-time. Distance learning option. At least 45 total credits required. 18 to 60 months to complete program. *Concentration:* public policy and administration.

MPM—Master of Project Management Full-time and part-time. Distance learning option. At least 42 total credits required. 18 to 60 months to complete program. *Concentration:* project management.

Application Contact Admissions Office, Pomona Center, 901 Corporate Center Drive, Suite 125, Pomona, CA 91768. *Phone:* 909-868-4240.

DeVry University

Keller Graduate School of Management

San Diego, California

Phone: 619-683-2446

DEGREES MAFM • MBA • MHRM • MIS • MPA • MPM

MAFM—Master of Accounting and Financial Management Full-time and part-time. Distance learning option. At least 44 total credits required. 18 to 60 months to complete program. *Concentrations:* accounting, financial management/planning.

MBA—Master of Business Administration Full-time and part-time. Distance learning option. At least 48 total credits required. 18 to 60 months to complete program. *Concentration:* management.

MHRM—Master of Human Resources Management Full-time and part-time. Distance learning option. At least 45 total credits required. 18 to 60 months to complete program. *Concentration:* human resources management.

MIS—Master of Information Systems Management Full-time and part-time. Distance learning option. At least 45 total credits required. 18 to 60 months to complete program. *Concentration:* information systems.

MPA—Master of Public Administration Full-time and part-time. Distance learning option. At least 45 total credits required. 18 to 60 months to complete program. *Concentration:* public policy and administration.

MPM—Master of Project Management Full-time and part-time. Distance learning option. At least 42 total credits required. 18 to 60 months to complete program. *Concentration:* project management.

Application Contact Admissions Office, San Diego Center, 2655 Camino Del Rio North, Suite 201, San Diego, CA 92108. *Phone:* 619-683-2446.

Dominican University of California

Division of Business and International Studies

San Rafael, California

Phone: 415-458-3765 **E-mail:** hoppe@dominican.edu

Business Program(s) Web Site: http://www.dominican.edu/academics/businesslead/business/mba.1.html

Graduate Business Unit Enrollment *Total:* 151 (93 full-time; 58 part-time; 93 women; 21 international). *Average Age:* 34.

Graduate Business Faculty *Total:* 14 (4 full-time; 10 part-time).

Admissions *Applied:* 168. *Admitted:* 97. *Enrolled:* 73.

Academic Calendar Semesters.

DEGREES MBA

MBA—Global Strategic Management (MBA-GSM) Full-time and part-time. At least 36 total credits required. 12 to 36 months to complete program. *Concentrations:* international business, international marketing.

MBA—Green MBA Full-time and part-time. At least 48 total credits required. 12 to 36 months to complete program. *Concentrations:* environmental economics/management, general MBA.

MBA—Strategic Leadership Part-time. At least 36 total credits required. 12 to 36 months to complete program. *Concentration:* leadership.

RESOURCES AND SERVICES 260 on-campus PCs are available to graduate business students. Access to Internet/World Wide Web available. *Personal computer requirements:* Graduate business students are not required to have a personal computer. *Special opportunities include:* An international exchange program and an internship program are available. *Placement services include:* Alumni network, career placement, career counseling/planning, electronic job bank, resume referral, resume preparation, and career library.

FINANCIAL AID (2007–08) 56 students received aid, including grants, loans, research assistantships, scholarships, and work study. Aid is available to part-time students. *Financial aid application deadline:* 7/1.

Financial Aid Contact Mary-Frances Causey, Director of Financial Aid, 50 Acacia Avenue, San Rafael, CA 94901-2298. *Phone:* 415-257-1302. *E-mail:* mary-frances.causey@dominican.edu.

INTERNATIONAL STUDENTS 14% of students enrolled are international students. *Services and facilities:* Counseling/support services, ESL/language courses, Housing location assistance, International student housing, Orientation, Tutoring. Financial aid is available to international students. *Required with application:* TOEFL with recommended score of 213 (computer) or 550 (paper); proof of adequate funds; proof of health/immunizations.

International Student Contact Vaolele Stawiarski, International Student Advisor, 50 Acacia Avenue, San Rafael, CA 94901-2298. *Phone:* 415-458-3767. *E-mail:* vaolele.stawiarski@dominican.edu.

APPLICATION *Required:* Application form, baccalaureate/first degree, interview, 2 letters of recommendation, personal statement, resume/curriculum vitae, transcripts of college work. School will accept GMAT and GRE. *Recommended:* Work experience. *Application fee:* $40. Applications for domestic and international students are processed on a rolling basis.

Application Contact Jody Hoppe, Director, Admissions Operations, 50 Acacia Avenue, San Rafael, CA 94901-2298. *Phone:* 415-458-3765. *E-mail:* hoppe@dominican.edu.

Fielding Graduate University

Programs in Organizational Management and Organizational Development

Santa Barbara, California

Phone: 805-898-4001 **Fax:** 805-687-9793 **E-mail:** admission@fielding.edu

Fielding Graduate University (continued)

Business Program(s) Web Site: http://www.fielding.edu

Graduate Business Unit Enrollment *Total:* 126 (63 full-time; 63 part-time; 89 women; 6 international). *Average Age:* 41.

Graduate Business Faculty *Total:* 11 (5 full-time; 6 part-time).

Admissions *Applied:* 50. *Admitted:* 46. *Enrolled:* 37. *Average GPA:* 3.2

Academic Calendar Trimesters.

DEGREE MA

MA—Master of Arts in Organization Management and Development Full-time and part-time. Distance learning option. At least 40 total credits required. 20 to 44 months to complete program. *Concentration:* organizational management.

RESOURCES AND SERVICES Access to Internet/World Wide Web, online (class) registration, and online grade reports available. *Personal computer requirements:* Graduate business students are required to have a personal computer. *Placement services include:* Alumni network.

EXPENSES *Tuition:* Full-time: $13,625. Part-time: $2725 per course. *Tuition (international):* Full-time: $13,625. Part-time: $2725 per course. Tuition and/or fees vary by number of courses or credits taken.

FINANCIAL AID (2007–08) 43 students received aid, including fellowships, grants, research assistantships, scholarships, and teaching assistantships. Aid is available to part-time students. *Financial aid application deadline:* 5/15.

Financial Aid Contact Sally Glasgow, Financial Aid Assistant, 2112 Santa Barbara Street, Santa Barbara, CA 93105. *Phone:* 805-898-4041. *Fax:* 805-687-9793. *E-mail:* seglasgow@fielding.edu.

INTERNATIONAL STUDENTS 5% of students enrolled are international students. *Services and facilities:* Orientation, online orientation. Financial aid is available to international students.

International Student Contact Admissions Counselor, 2112 Santa Barbara Street, Santa Barbara, CA 93105. *Phone:* 805-898-4054. *Fax:* 805-687-9793. *E-mail:* admission@fielding.edu.

APPLICATION *Required:* Application form, baccalaureate/first degree, 1 letter of recommendation, personal statement, resume/curriculum vitae, transcripts of college work. *Recommended:* Work experience. *Application fee:* $75. Applications for domestic and international students are processed on a rolling basis.

Application Contact Admissions Counselor, 2112 Santa Barbara Street, Santa Barbara, CA 93105. *Phone:* 805-898-4001. *Fax:* 805-687-9793. *E-mail:* admission@fielding.edu.

See full description on page 616.

Fresno Pacific University
Graduate Programs

Fresno, California

Phone: 559-253-7202 **Fax:** 559-252-4800 **E-mail:** duane.ruth-heffelbower@fresno.edu

Business Program(s) Web Site: http://www.fresno.edu/grad

Graduate Business Unit Enrollment *Total:* 88 (88 part-time; 56 women; 2 international). *Average Age:* 40.

Graduate Business Faculty *Total:* 4 (2 full-time; 2 part-time).

Admissions *Applied:* 6. *Admitted:* 5. *Enrolled:* 1.

Academic Calendar Semesters.

After Graduation (Class of 2006–07) *Employed within 3 months of graduation:* 100%.

DEGREE MA

MA—Master of Arts in Leadership and Organizational Studies Full-time and part-time. At least 37 total credits required. 16 to 36 months to complete program. *Concentrations:* leadership, organizational management.

RESOURCES AND SERVICES 90 on-campus PCs are available to graduate business students. Access to Internet/World Wide Web, online (class) registration, and online grade reports available. *Personal computer requirements:* Graduate business students are not required to have a personal computer. *Placement services include:* Alumni network, career counseling/planning, electronic job bank, job interviews arranged, resume preparation, and career library.

EXPENSES *Tuition:* Full-time: $7470. Part-time: $415 per unit. *Tuition (international):* Full-time: $7470. Part-time: $415 per unit.

FINANCIAL AID (2007–08) 46 students received aid, including grants, loans, and scholarships. Aid is available to part-time students.

Financial Aid Contact Joshua Blair, Financial Aid Counselor, Degree Completion and Graduate, 1717 South Chestnut Avenue, Fresno, CA 93702. *Phone:* 559-453-3685. *Fax:* 559-453-5595. *E-mail:* joshua.blair@fresno.edu.

INTERNATIONAL STUDENTS 2% of students enrolled are international students. *Services and facilities:* Counseling/support services, ESL/language courses, Language tutoring. Financial aid is available to international students. *Required with application:* TOEFL with recommended score of 213 (computer) or 550 (paper); proof of adequate funds; proof of health/immunizations.

International Student Contact Arnie P. Prieb, Director of International Programs and Services, 1717 South Chestnut Avenue, Fresno, CA 93702. *Phone:* 559-453-2128. *Fax:* 559-453-2007. *E-mail:* apprieb@fresno.edu.

APPLICATION *Required:* Application form, baccalaureate/first degree, essay, interview, 3 letters of recommendation, personal statement, transcripts of college work, 2 years of work experience. School will accept GMAT, GRE, and MAT. *Application fee:* $90. Applications for domestic and international students are processed on a rolling basis.

Application Contact Duane Ruth-Heffelbower, Leadership and Organizational Studies Program Director, 1717 South Chestnut Avenue, Fresno, CA 93702. *Phone:* 559-253-7202. *Fax:* 559-252-4800. *E-mail:* duane.ruth-heffelbower@fresno.edu.

Golden Gate University
Ageno School of Business

San Francisco, California

Phone: 415-442-7800 **Fax:** 415-442-7807 **E-mail:** info@ggu.edu

Business Program(s) Web Site: http://www.ggu.edu/school_of_business

Graduate Business Unit Enrollment *Total:* 1,069 (320 full-time; 749 part-time; 563 women; 856 international). *Average Age:* 34.

Graduate Business Faculty *Total:* 196 (21 full-time; 175 part-time).

Admissions *Applied:* 666. *Admitted:* 454. *Enrolled:* 233.

Academic Calendar 16-week trimesters and 8-week terms.

DEGREES JD/MBA • M Ac • M Sc • MBA • MPA • MS

JD/MBA—Juris Doctor/Master of Business Administration Full-time and part-time. Distance learning option. Admission to School of Law required. At least 48 total credits required. Maximum of 72 months to complete program. *Concentration:* law.

M Ac—Master of Accountancy Full-time and part-time. Distance learning option. 30 to 51 total credits required. 18 to 72 months to complete program. *Concentration:* accounting.

M Sc—Master of Science in Integrated Marketing Communications Full-time and part-time. Distance learning option. 45 total credits required. 12 to 36 months to complete program. *Concentrations:* marketing, public relations.

MBA—Executive Master of Business Administration Full-time. 8 years experience with 5 years at managerial level, professional or entrepreneur preferred; interview; one letter of recommendation; personal statement; resume/curriculum vitae required. At least 36 total credits required. 12 months to complete program. *Concentration:* executive programs.

MBA—Master of Business Administration Full-time and part-time. Distance learning option. 48 total credits required. 15 to 72 months to complete program. *Concentrations:* accounting, finance, general MBA, human resources management, information technology, international business, management, marketing, operations management.

MPA—Executive Master of Public Administration Full-time and part-time. Distance learning option. At least 36 total credits required. 12 to 36 months to complete program. *Concentration:* public policy and administration.

MS—Information Technology Management Full-time and part-time. Distance learning option. 33 total credits required. 12 to 48 months to complete program. *Concentration:* information technology.

MS—Master of Science Full-time and part-time. Distance learning option. 30 to 48 total credits required. 12 to 72 months to complete program. *Concentrations:* finance, financial management/planning, human resources management, information technology, marketing, taxation.

RESOURCES AND SERVICES 500 on-campus PCs are available to graduate business students. Access to Internet/World Wide Web, online (class) registration, and online grade reports available. *Personal computer requirements:* Graduate business students are strongly recommended to purchase or lease a personal computer. *Special opportunities include:* An internship program is available. *Placement services include:* Alumni network, career counseling/planning, electronic job bank, career fairs, resume preparation, and career library.

EXPENSES *Tuition:* Full-time: $16,320. Part-time: $680 per unit.

FINANCIAL AID (2007–08) Grants, loans, scholarships, and work study. Aid is available to part-time students. *Financial aid application deadline:* 6/30.

Financial Aid Contact Mr. Lou Riccardi, Director of Financial Aid and Registrar, 536 Mission Street, San Francisco, CA 94105-2968. *Phone:* 415-442-7270. *Fax:* 415-442-7819. *E-mail:* info@ggu.edu.

INTERNATIONAL STUDENTS 80% of students enrolled are international students. *Services and facilities:* Counseling/support services, ESL/language courses, Housing location assistance, International student organization, Orientation. Financial aid is available to international students. *Required with application:* TOEFL with recommended score of 213 (computer) or 550 (paper); proof of adequate funds; proof of health/immunizations. *Recommended with application:* IELT with recommended score of 6.5.

International Student Contact Ms. Tosie Baba, Associate Director, International Admissions and Advising Services, 536 Mission Street, San Francisco, CA 94105-2968. *Phone:* 415-442-7290. *Fax:* 415-442-7807.

APPLICATION *Required:* GMAT, application form, baccalaureate/first degree, transcripts of college work. *Recommended:* Interview, personal statement, resume/curriculum vitae, work experience. *Application fee:* $55, $90 (international). Applications for domestic and international students are processed on a rolling basis.

Application Contact Louis Riccardi, Director of Admissions, 536 Mission Street, San Francisco, CA 94105-2968. *Phone:* 415-442-7800. *Fax:* 415-442-7807. *E-mail:* info@ggu.edu.

Holy Names University
Department of Business
Oakland, California

Phone: 510-436-1351 **Fax:** 510-436-1325 **E-mail:** archambeau@hnu.edu
Business Program(s) Web Site: http://www.hnu.edu

DEGREE MBA

MBA—Master of Business Administration Full-time and part-time. At least 36 total credits required. 15 to 84 months to complete program. *Concentrations:* finance, management, marketing.

RESOURCES AND SERVICES 49 on-campus PCs are available to graduate business students. Access to Internet/World Wide Web available. *Personal computer requirements:* Graduate business students are not required to have a personal computer. *Placement services include:* Career counseling/planning, resume referral, career fairs, resume preparation, and career library.

Application Contact Ms. Kathleen Archambeau, Adult and Graduate Admission Counselor, 3500 Mountain Boulevard, Oakland, CA 94619-1699. *Phone:* 510-436-1351. *Fax:* 510-436-1325. *E-mail:* archambeau@hnu.edu.

Hope International University
Program in Business Administration
Fullerton, California

Phone: 800-762-1294 Ext. 2244 **Fax:** 714-681-7198 **E-mail:** anmativo@hiu.edu

Business Program(s) Web Site: http://www.hiu.edu/sgs/academics/programs/

Graduate Business Unit Enrollment *Total:* 47 (15 full-time; 32 part-time; 16 women; 16 international). *Average Age:* 36.

Graduate Business Faculty *Total:* 66 (7 full-time; 59 part-time).

Admissions *Applied:* 47. *Admitted:* 39. *Enrolled:* 34. *Average GPA:* 3.0

Academic Calendar Semesters.

DEGREES MBA • MS

MBA—Management Full-time and part-time. Distance learning option. 36 to 42 total credits required. *Concentrations:* administration, international development management, management, nonprofit management, theology/divinity.

MS—Master of Science in Management Full-time and part-time. Distance learning option. 30 total credits required. *Concentrations:* administration, executive programs, international development management, management, nonprofit management.

RESOURCES AND SERVICES 53 on-campus PCs are available to graduate business students. Access to Internet/World Wide Web, online (class) registration, and online grade reports available. *Personal computer requirements:* Graduate business students are strongly recommended to purchase or lease a personal computer. *Placement services include:* Alumni network and resume preparation.

EXPENSES *Tuition:* Full-time: $9072. *Tuition (international):* Full-time: $9072. *Required fees:* Full-time: $2170. Part-time: $2170 per year. Tuition and/or fees vary by number of courses or credits taken. *Graduate housing:* Room and board costs vary by number of occupants and type of board plan. *Typical cost:* $6330 (including board), $3500 (room only).

FINANCIAL AID (2007–08) 16 students received aid, including grants, loans, and scholarships. Aid is available to part-time students. *Financial aid application deadline:* 3/2.

Financial Aid Contact Rhoda Posey, Director, Financial Aid, 2500 East Nutwood Avenue, Fullerton, CA 92831-3104. *Phone:* 800-762-1294 Ext. 2638. *Fax:* 714-681-7421. *E-mail:* finaid@hiu.edu.

INTERNATIONAL STUDENTS 34% of students enrolled are international students. *Services and facilities:* Counseling/support services, ESL/language courses, Housing location assistance, International student housing, International student organization, Orientation, Visa Services. Financial aid is available to international students. *Required with application:* TOEFL with recommended score of 213 (computer), 550 (paper), or 86 (Internet); proof of adequate funds; proof of health/immunizations.

Hope International University (continued)

International Student Contact Kelem DeMissie, Management Program Coordinator, 2500 East Nutwood Avenue, Fullerton, CA 92831. *Phone:* 888-352-HOPE Ext. 2641. *Fax:* 714-681-7450. *E-mail:* kdemissie@hiu.edu.

APPLICATION *Required:* Application form, baccalaureate/first degree, essay, 2 letters of recommendation, personal statement, transcripts of college work. *Application fee:* $75. Applications for domestic and international students are processed on a rolling basis.

Application Contact Annette Mativo, Assistant Director of Admissions, Graduate and Adult Programs, 2500 East Nutwood Avenue, Fullerton, CA 92831-3104. *Phone:* 800-762-1294 Ext. 2244. *Fax:* 714-681-7198. *E-mail:* anmativo@hiu.edu.

Humboldt State University
School of Business

Arcata, California

Phone: 707-826-6022 **Fax:** 707-826-6666 **E-mail:** mft5@humboldt.edu

Business Program(s) Web Site: http://humboldt.edu/~sbe/

Graduate Business Unit Enrollment *Total:* 29 (21 full-time; 8 part-time; 17 women; 3 international). *Average Age:* 31.

Admissions *Applied:* 32. *Admitted:* 24. *Enrolled:* 20. *Average GMAT:* 575. *Average GPA:* 3.2

Academic Calendar Semesters.

DEGREE MBA

MBA—Master of Business Administration Full-time and part-time. At least 32 total credits required. 12 to 84 months to complete program. *Concentration:* general MBA.

RESOURCES AND SERVICES 54 on-campus PCs are available to graduate business students. Access to Internet/World Wide Web, online (class) registration, and online grade reports available. *Personal computer requirements:* Graduate business students are strongly recommended to purchase or lease a personal computer. *Special opportunities include:* An international exchange program and an internship program are available. *Placement services include:* Alumni network, career placement, job search course, career counseling/planning, electronic job bank, resume referral, career fairs, job interviews arranged, resume preparation, and career library.

EXPENSES *Tuition (nonresident):* Full-time: $4485. Part-time: $339 per unit.

FINANCIAL AID (2007–08) Fellowships and work study. Aid is available to part-time students. *Financial aid application deadline:* 3/1.

Financial Aid Contact Kim Coughlin-Lamphear, Director, Financial Aid, Student Business Services, Room 231, 1 Harpst Street, Arcata, CA 95521-8299. *Phone:* 707-826-5381. *Fax:* 707-826-5360. *E-mail:* coughlin@humboldt.edu.

INTERNATIONAL STUDENTS 10% of students enrolled are international students. *Services and facilities:* Counseling/support services, ESL/language courses, Housing location assistance, International student organization, Language tutoring, Orientation, Visa Services. Financial aid is available to international students. *Required with application:* TOEFL with recommended score of 173 (computer) or 500 (paper); proof of adequate funds; proof of health/immunizations.

International Student Contact International Student Admissions Officer, Student Business Services, Room 133, 1 Harpst Street, Arcata, CA 95521-8299. *Phone:* 707-826-6210. *Fax:* 707-826-6194.

APPLICATION *Required:* Application form, baccalaureate/first degree, transcripts of college work. School will accept GMAT and GRE. *Application fee:* $55. Applications for domestic and international students are processed on a rolling basis.

Application Contact Dr. Mike Thomas, MBA Program Director, 123 Siemens Hall, Arcata, CA 95521-8299. *Phone:* 707-826-6022. *Fax:* 707-826-6666. *E-mail:* mft5@humboldt.edu.

Lincoln University
Business Administration Program

Oakland, California

Phone: 510-628-8010 **Fax:** 510-628-8012 **E-mail:** adminofficer@lincolnuca.edu

Business Program(s) Web Site: http://www.lincolnuca.edu/

Graduate Business Unit Enrollment *Total:* 319 (298 full-time; 21 part-time; 169 women; 287 international). *Average Age:* 26.

Graduate Business Faculty *Total:* 28 (11 full-time; 17 part-time).

Admissions *Applied:* 336. *Admitted:* 312. *Enrolled:* 114. *Average GPA:* 3.0

Academic Calendar Semesters.

After Graduation (Class of 2006–07) *Employed within 3 months of graduation:* 75%. *Average starting salary:* $40,000.

DEGREE MA/MBA

MA/MBA—Master of Arts/Master of Business Administration Full-time and part-time. 36 to 57 total credits required. 12 to 36 months to complete program. *Concentrations:* financial management/planning, international business, management, management information systems.

RESOURCES AND SERVICES 29 on-campus PCs are available to graduate business students. Access to Internet/World Wide Web available. *Personal computer requirements:* Graduate business students are not required to have a personal computer. *Special opportunities include:* An internship program is available. *Placement services include:* Alumni network, career counseling/planning, resume referral, career fairs, resume preparation, and career library.

EXPENSES *Tuition:* Full-time: $6590. Part-time: $3295 per semester. *Tuition (international):* Full-time: $6590. Part-time: $3295 per semester.

FINANCIAL AID (2007–08) 12 students received aid, including loans and scholarships. Aid is available to part-time students. *Financial aid application deadline:* 6/30.

Financial Aid Contact Mr. James Peterson, Chief Financial Aid Officer, 401 15th Street, Oakland, CA 94612. *Phone:* 510-628-8023. *Fax:* 510-628-8012. *E-mail:* jep548@aol.com.

INTERNATIONAL STUDENTS 90% of students enrolled are international students. *Services and facilities:* ESL/language courses, Housing location assistance, Language tutoring, Orientation, Visa Services, Internships, Airport pick-up. Financial aid is available to international students. *Required with application:* TOEFL with recommended score of 196 (computer), 525 (paper), or 69 (Internet); proof of adequate funds. *Recommended with application:* Proof of health/immunizations.

International Student Contact Ms. Peggy Au, Director of Admissions, 401 15th Street, Oakland, CA 94612. *Phone:* 510-628-8010. *Fax:* 510-628-8012. *E-mail:* registrar@lincolnuca.edu.

APPLICATION *Required:* Application form, baccalaureate/first degree, transcripts of college work. *Recommended:* 1 letter of recommendation, personal statement. *Application fee:* $75. Applications for domestic and international students are processed on a rolling basis.

Application Contact Ms. Helen Zhu, Admissions Officer, 401 15th Street, Oakland, CA 94612. *Phone:* 510-628-8010. *Fax:* 510-628-8012. *E-mail:* adminofficer@lincolnuca.edu.

Loyola Marymount University
College of Business Administration

Los Angeles, California

Phone: 310-338-2848 **Fax:** 310-338-2899 **E-mail:** mbapc@lmu.edu

Business Program(s) Web Site: http://mba.lmu.edu

Graduate Business Unit Enrollment *Total:* 303 (72 full-time; 231 part-time; 122 women; 15 international). *Average Age:* 26.

Graduate Business Faculty *Total:* 58 (53 full-time; 5 part-time).

Admissions *Applied:* 283. *Admitted:* 163. *Enrolled:* 99. *Average GMAT:* 573. *Average GPA:* 3.23

Academic Calendar Semesters.

Accreditation AACSB—The Association to Advance Collegiate Schools of Business.

DEGREES EMBA • JD/MBA • MBA • MBA/M Eng

EMBA—Executive Master of Business Administration Part-time. 6 years of work experience required; June application deadline; no concentrations. At least 54 total credits required. 21 months to complete program. *Concentration:* executive programs.

JD/MBA—Juris Doctor/Master of Business Administration Full-time. Must complete first year of law studies at Loyola Law School. Must complete application process for MBA program, including GMAT. 21 to 60 total credits required. 12 to 48 months to complete program. *Concentration:* business law.

MBA—Master of Business Administration Full-time and part-time. 30 to 60 total credits required. 12 to 36 months to complete program. *Concentrations:* accounting, entrepreneurship, finance, human resources management, international business, management, management information systems, marketing.

MBA/M Eng—Systems Engineering Leadership Program Part-time. Must be admitted to Engineering and MBA programs separately. 39 to 66 total credits required. 24 to 60 months to complete program. *Concentrations:* engineering, system management.

RESOURCES AND SERVICES 200 on-campus PCs are available to graduate business students. Access to Internet/World Wide Web, online (class) registration, and online grade reports available. *Personal computer requirements:* Graduate business students are strongly recommended to purchase or lease a personal computer. *Special opportunities include:* An international exchange program and an internship program are available. *Placement services include:* Alumni network, career placement, career counseling/planning, electronic job bank, resume referral, career fairs, job interviews arranged, resume preparation, and career library.

FINANCIAL AID (2007–08) Grants, loans, research assistantships, scholarships, and work study. Aid is available to part-time students.

Financial Aid Contact Ms. Crystal Dootson, Graduate Financial Aid Counselor, 1 LMU Drive, Los Angeles, CA 90045. *Phone:* 310-338-1810. *Fax:* 310-338-2793. *E-mail:* cdootson@lmu.edu.

INTERNATIONAL STUDENTS 5% of students enrolled are international students. *Services and facilities:* Counseling/support services, Housing location assistance, International student organization, Orientation, Visa Services. Financial aid is available to international students. *Required with application:* TOEFL with recommended score of 250 (computer), 600 (paper), or 100 (Internet); proof of adequate funds; proof of health/immunizations.

International Student Contact Ms. Denise Folga, Director, International Student Services, 1 LMU Drive, Los Angeles, CA 90045. *Phone:* 310-338-2937. *Fax:* 310-338-5976. *E-mail:* dfolga@lmu.edu.

APPLICATION *Required:* GMAT, application form, baccalaureate/first degree, essay, 2 letters of recommendation, personal statement, resume/curriculum vitae, transcripts of college work. *Recommended:* Work experience. *Application fee:* $50. Applications for domestic and international students are processed on a rolling basis.

Application Contact Ms. Elynar Moreno, MBA Program Coordinator, 1 LMU Drive, MS 8387, Los Angeles, CA 90045-8387. *Phone:* 310-338-2848. *Fax:* 310-338-2899. *E-mail:* mbapc@lmu.edu.

Mills College
Graduate School of Business

Oakland, California

Phone: 510-430-3309 **Fax:** 510-430-2159 **E-mail:** grad-studies@mills.edu

Business Program(s) Web Site: http://www.mills.edu/mba

Graduate Business Unit Enrollment *Total:* 72 (47 full-time; 25 part-time; 72 women; 9 international). *Average Age:* 30.

Graduate Business Faculty *Total:* 24 (6 full-time; 18 part-time).

Admissions *Average GPA:* 3.3

Academic Calendar Semesters.

After Graduation (Class of 2006–07) *Employed within 3 months of graduation:* 70%.

DEGREES MBA

MBA—BA/MBA 4+1 Full-time. Foundation courses are completed at Mills as an undergraduate for entrance to this Program. 8 to 10 total credits required. 9 months to complete program. *Concentrations:* finance, general MBA, international business, marketing, nonprofit management.

MBA—Fast-Track Full-time. Foundation courses must have been completed for entrance to this Program. 8 to 10 total credits required. 9 months to complete program. *Concentrations:* finance, general MBA, international business, marketing, nonprofit management.

MBA—Flex-Track Full-time and part-time. Satisfaction of Foundation courses are required to complete the degree in two semesters. 8 to 18 total credits required. 9 to 24 months to complete program. *Concentrations:* finance, general MBA, international business, marketing, nonprofit management.

RESOURCES AND SERVICES 52 on-campus PCs are available to graduate business students. Access to Internet/World Wide Web, online (class) registration, and online grade reports available. *Personal computer requirements:* Graduate business students are strongly recommended to purchase or lease a personal computer. *Special opportunities include:* An internship program is available. *Placement services include:* Alumni network, career placement, job search course, career counseling/planning, electronic job bank, resume referral, career fairs, resume preparation, and career library.

FINANCIAL AID (2007–08) 72 students received aid, including loans and scholarships. *Financial aid application deadline:* 2/1.

Financial Aid Contact Ms. Judy Baldwin, Administrative Assistant, 5000 MacArthur Boulevard, Oakland, CA 94613. *Phone:* 510-430-3358. *Fax:* 510-430-2159. *E-mail:* grad-studies@mills.edu.

INTERNATIONAL STUDENTS 13% of students enrolled are international students. *Services and facilities:* Counseling/support services, ESL/language courses, Housing location assistance, International student housing, International student organization, Orientation, Visa Services. Financial aid is available to international students. *Required with application:* TOEFL with recommended score of 250 (computer), 600 (paper), or 85 (Internet); proof of adequate funds; proof of health/immunizations.

International Student Contact Ms. Katherine Perry, Program Coordinator, 5000 MacArthur Boulevard, Oakland, CA 94613. *Phone:* 510-430-3173. *Fax:* 510-430-2304. *E-mail:* mba@mills.edu.

APPLICATION *Required:* Application form, baccalaureate/first degree, essay, 3 letters of recommendation, personal statement, resume/curriculum vitae, transcripts of college work. School will accept GMAT and GRE.

Mills College (continued)

Recommended: Interview, work experience. *Application fee:* $50. Applications for domestic and international students are processed on a rolling basis.

Application Contact Ms. Linda Guzman, Administrative Assistant, Office of Graduate Studies, 5000 MacArthur Boulevard, Oakland, CA 94613. *Phone:* 510-430-3309. *Fax:* 510-430-2159. *E-mail:* grad-studies@mills.edu.

Monterey Institute of International Studies

Fisher Graduate School of International Business

Monterey, California

Phone: 831-647-4123 **Fax:** 831-647-6405 **E-mail:** admit@miis.edu

Business Program(s) Web Site: http://fisher.miis.edu/

Graduate Business Unit Enrollment *Total:* 81 (78 full-time; 3 part-time; 33 women; 37 international). *Average Age:* 27.

Graduate Business Faculty *Total:* 25 (10 full-time; 15 part-time).

Admissions *Applied:* 100. *Admitted:* 87. *Enrolled:* 39. *Average GMAT:* 552. *Average GPA:* 3.31

Academic Calendar Semesters.

Accreditation AACSB—The Association to Advance Collegiate Schools of Business.

After Graduation (Class of 2006–07) *Employed within 3 months of graduation:* 78%. *Average starting salary:* $64,000.

DEGREES MBA

MBA—Advanced Entry Master of Business Administration Full-time. Requires 30 credits of undergraduate business prerequisites and advanced language skills. At least 42 total credits required. 12 months to complete program. *Concentrations:* accounting, administration of technological information, Asian business studies, business ethics, business policy/strategy, Chinese business studies, combined degrees, commerce, conflict resolution management, decision sciences, electronic commerce (E-commerce), entrepreneurship, environmental economics/management, finance, international and area business studies, international banking, international business, international development management, international economics, international finance, international management, international marketing, international trade, marketing, nonprofit management, nonprofit organization, supply chain management.

MBA—International Master of Business Administration (with Peace Corps) Full-time. Enrolled students spend 2 years in Peace Corps during MBA program. Advanced language skills are required. At least 64 total credits required. 39 to 51 months to complete program. *Concentrations:* Asian business studies, conflict resolution management, decision sciences, electronic commerce (E-commerce), entrepreneurship, environmental economics/management, finance, international and area business studies, international banking, international business, international development management, international economics, international finance, international management, international marketing, international trade, marketing, nonprofit management.

MBA—Master of Business Administration Full-time. Applicants must have 4 semesters of undergraduate language study or must apply to MBA and Summer Intensive Language Program. At least 64 total credits required. 16 to 24 months to complete program. *Concentrations:* Asian business studies, conflict resolution management, decision sciences, electronic commerce (E-commerce), entrepreneurship, environmental economics/management, finance, international and area business studies, international banking, international business, international development

management, international economics, international finance, international management, international marketing, international trade, marketing, nonprofit management.

RESOURCES AND SERVICES 125 on-campus PCs are available to graduate business students. Access to Internet/World Wide Web available. *Personal computer requirements:* Graduate business students are strongly recommended to purchase or lease a personal computer. *Special opportunities include:* An international exchange program and an internship program are available. *Placement services include:* Alumni network, career placement, job search course, career counseling/planning, electronic job bank, resume referral, career fairs, job interviews arranged, resume preparation, and career library.

EXPENSES *Tuition:* Full-time: $29,356. *Tuition (international):* Full-time: $29,356. *Required fees:* Full-time: $56.

FINANCIAL AID (2007–08) 68 students received aid, including grants, loans, research assistantships, scholarships, and work study. Aid is available to part-time students. *Financial aid application deadline:* 3/15.

Financial Aid Contact Ms. Regina Lomboy, Director of Financial Aid, 460 Pierce Street, Monterey, CA 93940. *Phone:* 831-647-4119. *Fax:* 831-647-6685. *E-mail:* finaid@miis.edu.

INTERNATIONAL STUDENTS 46% of students enrolled are international students. *Services and facilities:* Counseling/support services, ESL/language courses, Housing location assistance, International student housing, International student organization, Language tutoring, Orientation, Visa Services. Financial aid is available to international students. *Required with application:* TOEFL with recommended score of 213 (computer), 550 (paper), or 80 (Internet); TWE with recommended score of 4; proof of adequate funds. *Recommended with application:* Proof of health/immunizations.

International Student Contact Ms. Kathy Sparaco, Manager of International Services, 460 Pierce Street, Monterey, CA 93940-2691. *Phone:* 831-647-3088. *Fax:* 831-647-3570. *E-mail:* kathy.sparaco@miis.edu.

APPLICATION *Required:* GMAT, application form, baccalaureate/first degree, 2 letters of recommendation, personal statement, resume/curriculum vitae, transcripts of college work. *Recommended:* Interview, 2 years of work experience. *Application fee:* $50. Applications for domestic and international students are processed on a rolling basis.

Application Contact Admissions Office, 460 Pierce Street, Monterey, CA 93940-2691. *Phone:* 831-647-4123. *Fax:* 831-647-6405. *E-mail:* admit@miis.edu.

See full description on page 660.

National University

School of Business and Management

La Jolla, California

Phone: 800-628-8648 **Fax:** 858-642-8709 **E-mail:** advisor@nu.edu

Business Program(s) Web Site: http://www.nu.edu/Academics/Schools/SOBM.html

Graduate Business Unit Enrollment *Total:* 1,456 (473 full-time; 983 part-time; 676 women; 184 international). *Average Age:* 35.

Graduate Business Faculty *Total:* 460 (33 full-time; 427 part-time).

Admissions *Applied:* 643. *Admitted:* 643. *Enrolled:* 643.

Academic Calendar One month course format.

DEGREES EMBA • MA Sc • MA • MBA • MPA • MS • MST

EMBA—Executive Master of Business Administration Full-time and part-time. Distance learning option. 54 total credits required. 12 to 84 months to complete program. *Concentrations:* business ethics, business information science, business policy/strategy, business studies, decision sciences, electronic commerce (E-commerce), general MBA, international and area business studies, international business, marketing, organizational management.

EMBA—Executive Master of Business Administration—Spanish Version Full-time and part-time. Distance learning option. 54 total credits required. 12 to 84 months to complete program. *Concentrations:* business ethics, business policy/strategy, business studies, decision sciences, electronic commerce (E-commerce), executive programs, general MBA, international and area business studies, international business.

MA—MA in Human Resource Management and Organizational Development Full-time and part-time. Distance learning option. 54 total credits required. 12 to 84 months to complete program. *Concentrations:* human resources management, industrial/labor relations, organizational behavior/development.

MA Sc—MA in Management Full-time and part-time. Distance learning option. 54 total credits required. 12 to 84 months to complete program. *Concentrations:* actuarial science, business ethics, business information science, business policy/strategy, business studies, conflict resolution management, decision sciences, executive programs, human resources development, human resources management, industrial administration/management, information management, international management, leadership, management, management communication, management consulting, management information systems, management science, manpower administration, new venture management, operations management, organizational behavior/development, organizational management.

MBA—Master of Business Administration Full-time and part-time. Distance learning option. 63 total credits required. 14 to 84 months to complete program. *Concentrations:* accounting, conflict resolution management, electronic commerce (E-commerce), financial management/planning, general MBA, human resources management, international business, marketing, organizational management.

MPA—Master of Public Administration Full-time and part-time. Distance learning option. 54 total credits required. 12 to 84 months to complete program. *Concentrations:* conflict resolution management, human resources management, organizational management, public finance.

MS—Corporate and International Finance Full-time and part-time. 72 total credits required. 16 to 84 months to complete program. *Concentrations:* finance, financial economics, financial engineering, financial information systems, financial management/planning, international and area business studies, international banking, international business, international development management, international economics, international finance, international logistics, international management, international marketing, investments and securities, leadership.

MS—Forensics Full-time and part-time. Distance learning option. 54 total credits required. 12 to 84 months to complete program. *Concentrations:* forensic accounting, law, legal administration.

MS—MS in Electronic Business Full-time and part-time. Distance learning option. 54 total credits required. 12 to 84 months to complete program. *Concentrations:* business information science, business studies, decision sciences, electronic commerce (E-commerce), entrepreneurship, European business studies, general MBA, industrial administration/management, information technology, international business, leadership, management science.

MST—MS in Taxation Full-time and part-time. Distance learning option. 54 total credits required. 12 to 84 months to complete program. *Concentration:* taxation.

RESOURCES AND SERVICES 3,109 on-campus PCs are available to graduate business students. Access to Internet/World Wide Web, online (class) registration, and online grade reports available. *Personal computer requirements:* Graduate business students are not required to have a personal computer. *Placement services include:* Alumni network, career counseling/planning, electronic job bank, career fairs, resume preparation, and career library.

EXPENSES *Tuition:* Full-time: $11,016. *Tuition (international):* Full-time: $11,016. *Required fees:* Full-time: $60. *Typical graduate housing cost:* $1968 (including board), $1413 (room only).

FINANCIAL AID (2007–08) Fellowships, grants, loans, and scholarships. Aid is available to part-time students. *Financial aid application deadline:* 6/30.

Financial Aid Contact Valerie Ryan, Director of Financial Aid, 11355 North Torrey Pines Road, La Jolla, CA 92037-1011. *Phone:* 858-642-8512. *Fax:* 858-642-8720. *E-mail:* vryan@nu.edu.

INTERNATIONAL STUDENTS 13% of students enrolled are international students. *Services and facilities:* Counseling/support services, ESL/language courses, Housing location assistance, Language tutoring, Orientation, Visa Services. Financial aid is not available to international students. *Required with application:* IELT with recommended score of 6; TOEFL with recommended score of 213 (computer) or 550 (paper); proof of adequate funds; proof of health/immunizations.

International Student Contact Rebecca Smith, Manager, International Programs, 9388 Lightwave Avenue, San Diego, CA 92123. *Phone:* 858-541-7960. *E-mail:* ipo@nu.edu.

APPLICATION *Required:* Application form, baccalaureate/first degree, interview, transcripts of college work. *Application fee:* $60, $65 (international). Applications for domestic and international students are processed on a rolling basis.

Application Contact Mr. Dominick Giovanniello, Associate Regional Dean, 11355 North Torrey Pines Road, La Jolla, CA 92037. *Phone:* 800-628-8648. *Fax:* 858-642-8709. *E-mail:* advisor@nu.edu.

Naval Postgraduate School
School of Business and Public Policy
Monterey, California

Phone: 831-656-1062 **Fax:** 831-656-2891 **E-mail:** manderse@nps.edu

Business Program(s) Web Site: http://www.nps.edu/academics/gsbpp

Graduate Business Unit Enrollment *Total:* 713 (315 full-time; 398 part-time; 100 women; 41 international). *Average Age:* 30.

Graduate Business Faculty *Total:* 87 (66 full-time; 21 part-time).

Academic Calendar Quarters.

Accreditation AACSB—The Association to Advance Collegiate Schools of Business.

After Graduation (Class of 2006–07) *Employed within 3 months of graduation:* 100%.

DEGREES EMBA • MBA • MS

EMBA—Executive Master of Business Administration Part-time. Distance learning option. Must be an active duty military officer or a federal government employee. 54 total credits required. 24 months to complete program. *Concentration:* general MBA.

MBA—Defense-Focused Master of Business Administration Full-time. Must be an active duty military officer or a federal government employee. 58 to 98 total credits required. 18 months to complete program. *Concentrations:* contract management, financial management/planning, logistics, management, management information systems, project management, supply chain management, transportation management.

MS—Master of Science in Contract Management Part-time. Distance learning option. Must be an active duty military officer or a federal government employee. At least 50 total credits required. Minimum of 27 months to complete program. *Concentration:* contract management.

MS—Master of Science in Management Full-time. Must be an active duty military officer or a federal government employee. 54 to 102 total credits required. 18 to 21 months to complete program. *Concentration:* manpower administration.

MS—Master of Science in Program Management Part-time. Distance learning option. Must be an active duty military officer or a federal government employee. At least 48 total credits required. Minimum of 24 months to complete program. *Concentration:* resources management.

Naval Postgraduate School (continued)

RESOURCES AND SERVICES 150 on-campus PCs are available to graduate business students. Access to Internet/World Wide Web, online (class) registration, and online grade reports available. *Personal computer requirements:* Graduate business students are strongly recommended to purchase or lease a personal computer. *Placement services include:* Alumni network, career placement, and career counseling/planning.

INTERNATIONAL STUDENTS 6% of students enrolled are international students. *Services and facilities:* Counseling/support services, ESL/language courses, Housing location assistance, International student housing, International student organization, Language tutoring, Orientation, Visa Services, writing courses. Financial aid is not available to international students. *Required with application:* TOEFL with recommended score of 220 (computer), 560 (paper), or 83 (Internet); proof of health/immunizations.

International Student Contact Col. Gary Roser, Assistant Dean of the School of International Graduate Studies, 699 Dyer Road, M-5, Monterey, CA 93943. *Phone:* 831-656-2186. *Fax:* 831-656-3064. *E-mail:* groser@nps.edu.

APPLICATION *Required:* Baccalaureate/first degree, transcripts of college work, 5 years of work experience. Applications for domestic and international students are processed on a rolling basis.

Application Contact Mr. Michael Anderson, Registrar/Director, One University Drive, Building 220, Room HE-022B, Monterey, CA 93943. *Phone:* 831-656-1062. *Fax:* 831-656-2891. *E-mail:* manderse@nps.edu.

Northwestern Polytechnic University
School of Business and Information Technology

Fremont, California

Phone: 510-657-5914 **Fax:** 510-657-8975 **E-mail:** shilpa@npu.edu

Business Program(s) Web Site: http://www.npu.edu/business/business_index.html

Graduate Business Unit Enrollment *Total:* 225 (187 full-time; 38 part-time; 116 women; 171 international). *Average Age:* 28.

Graduate Business Faculty *Total:* 21 (10 full-time; 11 part-time).

Admissions *Applied:* 220. *Admitted:* 202. *Enrolled:* 86. *Average GMAT:* 500. *Average GPA:* 3.1

Academic Calendar Trimesters.

After Graduation (Class of 2006–07) *Employed within 3 months of graduation:* 80%. *Average starting salary:* $42,000.

DEGREE MBA

MBA—Master of Business Administration Full-time and part-time. At least 36 total credits required. *Concentrations:* accounting, information technology, international development management, marketing, project management.

RESOURCES AND SERVICES 200 on-campus PCs are available to graduate business students. Access to Internet/World Wide Web, online (class) registration, and online grade reports available. *Personal computer requirements:* Graduate business students are strongly recommended to purchase or lease a personal computer. *Special opportunities include:* An international exchange program and an internship program are available. *Placement services include:* Alumni network, career placement, career counseling/planning, electronic job bank, resume referral, career fairs, job interviews arranged, resume preparation, and career library.

EXPENSES *Tuition:* Full-time: $11,340. Part-time: $5040 per year. *Tuition (international):* Full-time: $11,340. *Required fees:* Full-time: $210. Part-time: $210 per year. *Graduate housing:* Room and board costs vary by number of occupants. *Typical cost:* $4800 (room only).

FINANCIAL AID (2007–08) 12 students received aid, including teaching assistantships and work study. Aid is available to part-time students.

Financial Aid Contact Dr. Bill Wu, Director of Business Affairs, 47671 Westinghouse Drive, Fremont, CA 94539-7482. *Phone:* 510-657-5994. *Fax:* 510-657-8975. *E-mail:* wjw@npu.edu.

INTERNATIONAL STUDENTS 76% of students enrolled are international students. *Services and facilities:* Counseling/support services, ESL/language courses, Housing location assistance, International student housing, International student organization, Language tutoring, Orientation, Visa Services, placement advice and service. Financial aid is available to international students. *Required with application:* Proof of adequate funds; proof of health/immunizations. *Recommended with application:* IELT; TOEFL with recommended score of 213 (computer), 550 (paper), or 79 (Internet); TWE with recommended score of 5.

International Student Contact Ms. Wen Hsieh, Designated International Student Advisor, 47671 Westinghouse Drive, Fremont, CA 94539-7482. *Phone:* 510-360-0281. *Fax:* 510-657-8975. *E-mail:* wen@npu.edu.

APPLICATION *Required:* GMAT, application form, baccalaureate/first degree, transcripts of college work. *Recommended:* Interview, letter(s) of recommendation, resume/curriculum vitae. *Application fee:* $60. Applications for domestic and international students are processed on a rolling basis.

Application Contact Ms. Shilpa Eguvanti, Admissions Staff, 47671 Westinghouse Drive, Fremont, CA 94539-7482. *Phone:* 510-657-5914. *Fax:* 510-657-8975. *E-mail:* shilpa@npu.edu.

Notre Dame de Namur University
Department of Business Administration

Belmont, California

Phone: 650-508-3600 **Fax:** 650-508-3426 **E-mail:** grad.admit@ndnu.edu

Business Program(s) Web Site: http://www.ndnu.edu/business/index.html

Graduate Business Unit Enrollment *Total:* 172 (28 full-time; 144 part-time; 111 women; 12 international). *Average Age:* 33.

Graduate Business Faculty *Total:* 13 (7 full-time; 6 part-time).

Admissions *Applied:* 64. *Admitted:* 56. *Enrolled:* 40. *Average GMAT:* 450. *Average GPA:* 3.1

Academic Calendar Trimesters.

After Graduation (Class of 2006–07) *Employed within 3 months of graduation:* 95%.

DEGREES MBA • MPA • MS

MBA—Master of Business Administration Full-time and part-time. Work experience preferred. At least 36 total credits required. 12 to 60 months to complete program. *Concentrations:* electronic commerce (E-commerce), finance, human resources management, management information systems, marketing.

MPA—Master of Public Administration Full-time and part-time. At least 30 total credits required. 12 to 60 months to complete program. *Concentrations:* administration, health care, human resources management, public management.

MS—Master of Science in Management Full-time and part-time. Work experience required. At least 36 total credits required. 12 to 60 months to complete program. *Concentrations:* electronic commerce (E-commerce), information systems, project management.

RESOURCES AND SERVICES 60 on-campus PCs are available to graduate business students. Access to Internet/World Wide Web, online (class) registration, and online grade reports available. *Personal computer requirements:* Graduate business students are strongly recommended to purchase or lease a personal computer. *Special opportunities include:* An internship program is available. *Placement services include:* Alumni network, career counseling/planning, electronic job bank, career fairs, and resume preparation.

EXPENSES *Tuition:* Part-time: $699 per unit. *Tuition (international):* Part-time: $699 per unit. *Required fees:* Part-time: $35 per semester. *Graduate housing:* Room and board costs vary by number of occupants, type of accommodation, and type of board plan. *Typical cost:* $10,680 (including board).

FINANCIAL AID (2007–08) 77 students received aid, including loans, scholarships, and work study. Aid is available to part-time students. *Financial aid application deadline:* 3/1.

Financial Aid Contact Ms. Susan Pace, Director of Student Financing, 1500 Ralston Avenue, Belmont, CA 94002-1908. *Phone:* 650-508-3580. *Fax:* 650-508-3635. *E-mail:* space@ndnu.edu.

INTERNATIONAL STUDENTS 7% of students enrolled are international students. *Services and facilities:* Counseling/support services, ESL/language courses, International student housing, International student organization, Language tutoring, Orientation, Visa Services. Financial aid is available to international students. *Required with application:* TOEFL with recommended score of 213 (computer), 550 (paper), or 79 (Internet); proof of adequate funds. *Recommended with application:* Proof of health/immunizations.

International Student Contact Ms. Shannon Morton, Graduate Recruiter/Marketing Coordinator, 1500 Ralston Avenue, Belmont, CA 94002-1908. *Phone:* 650-508-3600. *Fax:* 650-508-3426. *E-mail:* grad.admit@ndnu.edu.

APPLICATION *Required:* GMAT, application form, baccalaureate/first degree, 2 letters of recommendation, transcripts of college work. *Recommended:* 1 year of work experience. *Application fee:* $60. Applications for domestic and international students are processed on a rolling basis.

Application Contact Ms. Helen Valine, Director for Graduate Admission, 1500 Ralston Avenue, Belmont, CA 94002-1908. *Phone:* 650-508-3600. *Fax:* 650-508-3426. *E-mail:* grad.admit@ndnu.edu.

Pacific States University
College of Business
Los Angeles, California

Phone: 323-731-2383 **Fax:** 323-731-7276 **E-mail:** admission@psuca.edu

Graduate Business Unit Enrollment *Total:* 172 (167 full-time; 5 part-time; 76 women; 157 international). *Average Age:* 31.

Graduate Business Faculty *Total:* 32 (5 full-time; 27 part-time).

Admissions *Applied:* 80. *Admitted:* 72. *Enrolled:* 70. *Average GPA:* 2.5

Academic Calendar Quarters.

DEGREES MBA

MBA—Master of Business Administration in Accounting Full-time and part-time. 60 to 76 total credits required. 18 to 30 months to complete program. *Concentration:* accounting.

MBA—Master of Business Administration in Finance Full-time and part-time. 60 to 76 total credits required. 18 to 30 months to complete program. *Concentration:* finance.

MBA—Master of Business Administration in International Business Full-time and part-time. Distance learning option. 60 to 76 total credits required. 18 to 30 months to complete program. *Concentration:* international business.

MBA—Master of Business Administration in Management of Information Technology Full-time and part-time. 60 to 80 total credits required. 18 to 30 months to complete program. *Concentration:* information technology.

MBA—Master of Business Administration in Real Estate Management Full-time and part-time. 60 to 76 total credits required. 18 to 30 months to complete program. *Concentration:* real estate.

RESOURCES AND SERVICES 85 on-campus PCs are available to graduate business students. Access to Internet/World Wide Web available. *Personal computer requirements:* Graduate business students are not required to have a personal computer. *Placement services include:* Alumni network, career counseling/planning, resume referral, resume preparation, and career library.

EXPENSES *Tuition:* Full-time: $13,400. Part-time: $235 per credit hour. *Tuition (international):* Full-time: $13,400. Part-time: $235 per credit hour. *Required fees:* Full-time: $1600. Part-time: $100 per course. Tuition and/or fees vary by number of courses or credits taken and academic program. *Graduate housing:* Room and board costs vary by number of occupants and type of accommodation. *Typical cost:* $9000 (including board), $5400 (room only).

FINANCIAL AID (2007–08) 4 students received aid, including grants, loans, scholarships, and work study.

Financial Aid Contact Dr. Min Sang Kim, Financial Aid Advisor, 1516 South Western Avenue, Los Angeles, CA 90006. *Phone:* 323-731-2383 Ext. 202. *Fax:* 323-731-7276. *E-mail:* mskim@psuca.edu.

INTERNATIONAL STUDENTS 91% of students enrolled are international students. *Services and facilities:* Counseling/support services, ESL/language courses, Housing location assistance, International student housing, International student organization, Language tutoring, Orientation. Financial aid is available to international students. *Required with application:* Proof of adequate funds. *Recommended with application:* TOEFL with recommended score of 133 (computer) or 450 (paper); proof of health/immunizations.

International Student Contact Ms. SeoHee Yang, Student Service Advisor, 1516 South Western Avenue, Los Angeles, CA 90006. *Phone:* 323-731-2383. *Fax:* 323-731-7276. *E-mail:* syang@psuca.edu.

APPLICATION *Required:* Application form, baccalaureate/first degree, transcripts of college work. School will accept GMAT. *Recommended:* Essay, 2 letters of recommendation, personal statement, resume/curriculum vitae, work experience. *Application fee:* $380. Applications for domestic and international students are processed on a rolling basis.

Application Contact Ms. Marina Miller, Assistant to the Admissions Director, 1516 South Western Avenue, Los Angeles, CA 90006. *Phone:* 323-731-2383. *Fax:* 323-731-7276. *E-mail:* admission@psuca.edu.

Pepperdine University
Graziadio School of Business and Management
Los Angeles, California

Phone: 310-568-5500 **Fax:** 310-568-5779 **E-mail:** gsbmadm@pepperdine.edu

Business Program(s) Web Site: http://bschool.pepperdine.edu/

Accreditation AACSB—The Association to Advance Collegiate Schools of Business.

DEGREES JD/MBA • MBA • MBA/MPP • MIB

JD/MBA—Juris Doctor/Master of Business Administration Full-time. Must be admitted to law school. At least 130 total credits required. 45 months to complete program. *Concentrations:* finance, marketing, strategic management.

MBA—Executive Master of Business Administration Part-time. 7 years of work experience (including 2 years of mid-to upper-level management) required. At least 50 total credits required. 20 months to complete program. *Concentration:* strategic management.

MBA—Master of Business Administration Full-time. 3 years of full-time work experience and an undergraduate degree in business for the 12-month track required. 48 to 60 total credits required. 12 to 15 months to complete program. *Concentrations:* finance, international business, management, marketing, public policy and administration, strategic management.

Pepperdine University (continued)

MBA—Presidential/Key Executive Master of Business Administration Part-time. 10 years of work experience (at least 2 years in a senior-level position) required. At least 50 total credits required. 20 months to complete program. *Concentration:* strategic management.

MBA—Professional Master of Business Administration Full-time and part-time. 49 to 60 total credits required. 24 to 84 months to complete program. *Concentrations:* entrepreneurship, finance, general MBA, international business, leadership, management, marketing, strategic management.

MBA—Two-Year Master of Business Administration Full-time. 60 to 64 total credits required. 20 months to complete program. *Concentrations:* electronic commerce (E-commerce), finance, international business, management, marketing, strategic management, technology management.

MBA/MPP—Master of Business Administration/Master of Public Policy Full-time. Must apply separately to School of Public Policy. At least 96 total credits required. 32 months to complete program. *Concentrations:* finance, Latin American business studies, marketing, public policy and administration.

MIB—IMBA—International MBA Full-time. Intermediate level of foreign language proficiency in French, German, or Spanish recommended as a minimum. 56 to 72 total credits required. 20 months to complete program. *Concentrations:* European business studies, finance, international finance, international marketing, Latin American business studies, marketing, strategic management.

RESOURCES AND SERVICES Access to Internet/World Wide Web, online (class) registration, and online grade reports available. *Personal computer requirements:* Graduate business students are strongly recommended to purchase or lease a personal computer. *Special opportunities include:* An international exchange program and an internship program are available. *Placement services include:* Alumni network, career placement, job search course, career counseling/planning, electronic job bank, resume referral, career fairs, job interviews arranged, resume preparation, and career library.

Application Contact Mr. Darrell Eriksen, Director of Admissions, 6100 Center Drive, Los Angeles, CA 90045. *Phone:* 310-568-5500. *Fax:* 310-568-5779. *E-mail:* gsbmadm@pepperdine.edu.

Point Loma Nazarene University

Program in Business Administration

San Diego, California

Phone: 619-563-2856 **Fax:** 619-563-2898 **E-mail:** mba@ptloma.edu

Business Program(s) Web Site: http://www.pointloma.edu/mba

Accreditation ACBSP—The American Council of Business Schools and Programs.

DEGREES MA/MBA • MBA

MA/MBA—Master of Arts/Master of Business Administration Part-time. 42 total credits required. 18 to 24 months to complete program. *Concentration:* student designed.

MBA—MBA Corporate Part-time. 42 total credits required. 18 to 24 months to complete program. *Concentration:* business policy/strategy.

MBA—MBA Organizational Leadership Part-time. 42 total credits required. 18 to 24 months to complete program. *Concentration:* organizational behavior/development.

MBA—Master of Business Administration Part-time. 42 total credits required. 24 months to complete program. *Concentration:* general MBA.

RESOURCES AND SERVICES 50 on-campus PCs are available to graduate business students. Access to Internet/World Wide Web and online grade reports available. *Personal computer requirements:* Graduate business students are required to have a personal computer. *Placement services include:* Alumni network, career placement, career counseling/

planning, electronic job bank, resume referral, job interviews arranged, resume preparation, and career library.

Application Contact Dejon Davis, Graduate Enrollment Counselor, Graduate Administrative Services, PLNU Mission Valley, 4007 Camino del Rio South STE 300, San Diego, CA 92108. *Phone:* 619-563-2856. *Fax:* 619-563-2898. *E-mail:* mba@ptloma.edu.

San Diego State University

College of Business Administration

San Diego, California

Phone: 619-594-1108 **Fax:** 619-594-1863 **E-mail:** shira.scott@sdsu.edu

Business Program(s) Web Site: http://www.sdsu.edu/business

Graduate Business Unit Enrollment *Total:* 809 (391 full-time; 418 part-time; 356 women; 186 international). *Average Age:* 27.

Graduate Business Faculty *Total:* 123 (87 full-time; 36 part-time).

Admissions *Applied:* 945. *Admitted:* 495. *Enrolled:* 301. *Average GMAT:* 591. *Average GPA:* 3.3

Academic Calendar Semesters.

Accreditation AACSB—The Association to Advance Collegiate Schools of Business.

DEGREES JD/MBA • MA/MS • MBA • MBA/MA • MS

JD/MBA—Juris Doctor/Master of Business Administration Full-time. 98 to 113 total credits required. 48 months to complete program. *Concentration:* combined degrees.

MA/MS—Master of Science in Business Administration Full-time and part-time. 30 total credits required. 12 to 84 months to complete program. *Concentrations:* entrepreneurship, finance, financial management/planning, human resources management, information systems, international business, management, marketing, operations management, taxation.

MBA—MBA for Executives in Life Sciences Up to 48 total credits required. Maximum of 20 months to complete program. *Concentrations:* executive programs, general MBA, other.

MBA—Master of Business Administration Full-time and part-time. 30 to 48 total credits required. 24 to 84 months to complete program. *Concentrations:* accounting, electronic commerce (E-commerce), entrepreneurship, finance, health care, information systems, international business, management, marketing, operations management, real estate.

MBA/MA—Master of Business Administration/Master of Arts in Latin American Studies Full-time. 54 to 72 total credits required. 36 to 84 months to complete program. *Concentration:* combined degrees.

MS—Master of Science in Accountancy Full-time and part-time. At least 30 total credits required. 12 to 84 months to complete program. *Concentration:* accounting.

RESOURCES AND SERVICES 313 on-campus PCs are available to graduate business students. Access to Internet/World Wide Web, online (class) registration, and online grade reports available. *Personal computer requirements:* Graduate business students are strongly recommended to purchase or lease a personal computer. *Special opportunities include:* An international exchange program and an internship program are available. *Placement services include:* Alumni network, career counseling/planning, electronic job bank, career fairs, job interviews arranged, resume preparation, and career library.

EXPENSES *Tuition (state resident):* Full-time: $4070. Part-time: $2636 per year. *Tuition (nonresident):* Full-time: $12,206. Part-time: $6704 per year. *Tuition (international):* Full-time: $12,206. Part-time: $6704 per year. *Graduate housing:* Room and board costs vary by number of occupants, type of accommodation, and type of board plan. *Typical cost:* $10,904 (including board).

FINANCIAL AID (2007–08) Loans, research assistantships, scholarships, and teaching assistantships.

Financial Aid Contact Financial Aid Office, 5500 Campanile Drive, San Diego, CA 92182-7436. *Phone:* 619-594-6323. *Fax:* 619-594-4268. *E-mail:* fao@mail.sdsu.edu.

INTERNATIONAL STUDENTS 23% of students enrolled are international students. *Services and facilities:* Counseling/support services, ESL/language courses, Housing location assistance, International student organization, Orientation, Visa Services, Multicultural activities. *Required with application:* TOEFL with recommended score of 213 (computer) or 550 (paper); proof of adequate funds; proof of health/immunizations.

International Student Contact Director ISC, Director of International Student Center, 5500 Campanile Drive, San Diego, CA 92182-5101. *Phone:* 619-594-1982. *Fax:* 619-594-1973. *E-mail:* isc.reception@sdsu.edu.

APPLICATION *Required:* GMAT, application form, baccalaureate/first degree, transcripts of college work. *Recommended:* 3 letters of recommendation, personal statement, resume/curriculum vitae, work experience. *Application fee:* $55. Applications for domestic and international students are processed on a rolling basis.

Application Contact Mrs. Shira Scott, Program Coordinator, 5500 Campanile Drive, San Diego, CA 92182-8228. *Phone:* 619-594-1108. *Fax:* 619-594-1863. *E-mail:* shira.scott@sdsu.edu.

San Francisco State University
College of Business

San Francisco, California

Phone: 415-817-4314 **Fax:** 415-817-4340 **E-mail:** mba@sfsu.edu

Business Program(s) Web Site: http://mba.sfsu.edu

Graduate Business Unit Enrollment *Total:* 601 (210 full-time; 391 part-time; 293 women; 198 international). *Average Age:* 28.

Graduate Business Faculty *Total:* 68 (57 full-time; 11 part-time).

Admissions *Applied:* 566. *Admitted:* 289. *Enrolled:* 146. *Average GMAT:* 560. *Average GPA:* 3.3

Academic Calendar Semesters.

Accreditation AACSB—The Association to Advance Collegiate Schools of Business.

After Graduation (Class of 2006–07) *Employed within 3 months of graduation:* 95%. *Average starting salary:* $75,000.

DEGREES EVEMBA • MBA • MSBA

EVEMBA—Executive MBA Part-time. Evening or Saturday cohorts contact emba@sfsu.edu for more information; professional work experience is required. Tuition is $885 per unit. Most terms are 15 weeks long and include 2 courses. 48 total credits required. 23 months to complete program. *Concentration:* management.

MBA—Master of Business Administration Full-time and part-time. 30 to 64 total credits required. 12 to 48 months to complete program. *Concentrations:* accounting, decision sciences, electronic commerce (E-commerce), entrepreneurship, finance, general MBA, information systems, international business, management, marketing, operations management, other.

MSBA—Master of Science in Business Administration Full-time and part-time. 30 to 64 total credits required. 12 to 48 months to complete program. *Concentrations:* accounting, decision sciences, electronic commerce (E-commerce), entrepreneurship, finance, hospitality management, information systems, international business, management, marketing, operations management.

RESOURCES AND SERVICES 40 on-campus PCs are available to graduate business students. Access to Internet/World Wide Web, online (class) registration, and online grade reports available. *Personal computer requirements:* Graduate business students are strongly recommended to purchase or lease a personal computer. *Special opportunities include:* An international exchange program and an internship program are available.

Placement services include: Alumni network, career counseling/planning, electronic job bank, career fairs, and resume preparation.

EXPENSES *Tuition (state resident):* Full-time: $6868. Part-time: $4292 per semester. *Tuition (nonresident):* Full-time: $15,004. Part-time: $8360 per semester. *Tuition (international):* Full-time: $15,004. Tuition and/or fees vary by number of courses or credits taken and academic program. *Graduate housing:* Room and board costs vary by number of occupants and type of accommodation. *Typical cost:* $9688 (room only).

FINANCIAL AID (2007–08) 50 students received aid, including loans, scholarships, and work study. Aid is available to part-time students. *Financial aid application deadline:* 3/1.

Financial Aid Contact Ms. Barbara Hubler, Director, Financial Aid, Student Services Building, SSB 302, 1600 Holloway Avenue, San Francisco, CA 94132-1722. *Phone:* 415-338-7000. *Fax:* 415-338-0949. *E-mail:* finaid@sfsu.edu.

INTERNATIONAL STUDENTS 33% of students enrolled are international students. *Services and facilities:* Counseling/support services, ESL/language courses, International student housing, International student organization, Language tutoring, Orientation, Visa Services. Financial aid is available to international students. *Required with application:* TOEFL with recommended score of 230 (computer), 570 (paper), or 88 (Internet); TWE with recommended score of 4; proof of adequate funds; proof of health/immunizations. *Recommended with application:* IELT with recommended score of 6.5.

International Student Contact Ms. Patrice Mulholland, Assistant Director, International Outreach Services, Office of International Programs, 1600 Holloway Avenue, Administration Building 450, San Francisco, CA 94132. *Phone:* 415-338-1293. *Fax:* 415-338-6234. *E-mail:* oip@sfsu.edu.

APPLICATION *Required:* GMAT, application form, baccalaureate/first degree, 2 letters of recommendation, personal statement, resume/curriculum vitae, transcripts of college work. *Recommended:* 3 years of work experience. *Application fee:* $55. Applications for domestic and international students are processed on a rolling basis.

Application Contact Ms. Armaan Moattari, Assistant Director, 835 Market Street, Suite 550, San Francisco, CA 94103. *Phone:* 415-817-4314. *Fax:* 415-817-4340. *E-mail:* mba@sfsu.edu.

San Jose State University
Lucas Graduate School of Business

San Jose, California

Phone: 408-924-3420 **Fax:** 408-924-3426 **E-mail:** mba@cob.sjsu.edu

Business Program(s) Web Site: http://www.cob.sjsu.edu/graduate

Accreditation AACSB—The Association to Advance Collegiate Schools of Business.

DEGREES MBA • MBA/M Eng • MS

MBA—Accelerated Off-Campus Master of Business Administration Part-time. 3 prerequisites—Intro to Microeconomics; Intro to Macroeconomics; Business Statistics. 42 total credits required. 18 to 84 months to complete program. *Concentration:* general MBA.

MBA—MBA-One Full-time. 42 total credits required. 12 months to complete program. *Concentration:* general MBA.

MBA—Master of Business Administration, On-Campus Full-time and part-time. 3 prerequisites—Intro to Microeconomics; Intro to Macroeconomics; Business Statistics. 42 total credits required. 24 to 84 months to complete program. *Concentration:* general MBA.

MBA/M Eng—Master of Business Administration/Master of Science in Engineering Part-time. 54 total credits required. 32 months to complete program. *Concentration:* combined degrees.

MS—Master of Science in Accountancy Full-time. 57 total credits required. 12 months to complete program. *Concentration:* accounting.

San Jose State University (continued)

MS—Master of Science in Taxation Full-time and part-time. 30 to 48 total credits required. 9 to 48 months to complete program. *Concentration:* taxation.

MS—Master of Science in Transportation Management Part-time. Distance learning option. 30 total credits required. 24 to 36 months to complete program. *Concentration:* transportation management.

RESOURCES AND SERVICES 71 on-campus PCs are available to graduate business students. Access to Internet/World Wide Web, online (class) registration, and online grade reports available. *Personal computer requirements:* Graduate business students are strongly recommended to purchase or lease a personal computer. *Special opportunities include:* An international exchange program and an internship program are available. *Placement services include:* Alumni network, career counseling/planning, electronic job bank, career fairs, resume preparation, and career library.

Application Contact Margaret Farmer, Admissions Coordinator, One Washington Square, San Jose, CA 95192-0162. *Phone:* 408-924-3420. *Fax:* 408-924-3426. *E-mail:* mba@cob.sjsu.edu.

Santa Clara University
Leavey School of Business

Santa Clara, California

Phone: 408-554-4539 **Fax:** 408-554-4571 **E-mail:** mbaadmissions@scu.edu

Business Program(s) Web Site: http://www.scu.edu/business/graduates

Graduate Business Unit Enrollment *Total:* 1,118 (243 full-time; 875 part-time; 369 women; 257 international). *Average Age:* 31.

Graduate Business Faculty *Total:* 104 (70 full-time; 34 part-time).

Admissions *Applied:* 470. *Admitted:* 303. *Enrolled:* 266. *Average GMAT:* 620. *Average GPA:* 3.13

Academic Calendar Quarters.

Accreditation AACSB—The Association to Advance Collegiate Schools of Business.

After Graduation (Class of 2006–07) *Employed within 3 months of graduation:* 90%. *Average starting salary:* $93,617.

DEGREES JD/MBA • M Sc • MBA

JD/MBA—Juris Doctor/Master of Business Administration—Law Program Full-time. Permission of the Law School required. 121 to 133 total credits required. 48 to 72 months to complete program. *Concentrations:* accounting, agribusiness, entrepreneurship, finance, international business, leadership, marketing, supply chain management, technology management.

M Sc—Master of Science in Information Systems Full-time and part-time. Knowledge of a programming language required. 45 to 54 total credits required. 27 to 72 months to complete program. *Concentration:* management information systems.

MBA—Executive Master of Business Administration Full-time. 10 years of work experience required. 54 to 59 total credits required. 17 months to complete program. *Concentration:* executive programs.

MBA—Weekend Accelerated MBA Program Full-time and part-time. 67 total credits required. 21 months to complete program. *Concentrations:* finance, marketing.

MBA—Master of Business Administration Full-time and part-time. 49 to 70 total credits required. 15 to 72 months to complete program. *Concentrations:* accounting, agribusiness, entrepreneurship, finance, international business, leadership, marketing, supply chain management, technology management.

RESOURCES AND SERVICES 200 on-campus PCs are available to graduate business students. Access to Internet/World Wide Web, online (class) registration, and online grade reports available. *Personal computer requirements:* Graduate business students are strongly recommended to purchase or lease a personal computer. *Special opportunities include:* An international exchange program and an internship program are available. *Placement services include:* Alumni network, job search course, career counseling/planning, electronic job bank, career fairs, resume preparation, and career library.

EXPENSES *Tuition:* Full-time: $26,604. Part-time: $739 per credit. *Tuition (international):* Full-time: $26,604. Part-time: $739 per credit. *Required fees:* Full-time: $165. Part-time: $55 per quarter. Tuition and/or fees vary by class time, number of courses or credits taken, and academic program.

FINANCIAL AID (2007–08) 70 students received aid, including fellowships, loans, research assistantships, scholarships, and work study. Aid is available to part-time students. *Financial aid application deadline:* 7/1.

Financial Aid Contact Jennifer W. Taylor, Director, Graduate Business Admissions, 500 El Camino Real, 116 Lucas Hall, Santa Clara, CA 95053-0001. *Phone:* 408-554-4539. *Fax:* 408-554-4571. *E-mail:* mbaadmissions@scu.edu.

INTERNATIONAL STUDENTS 23% of students enrolled are international students. *Services and facilities:* Counseling/support services, Housing location assistance, International student organization, Orientation, Visa Services. Financial aid is not available to international students. *Required with application:* TOEFL with recommended score of 250 (computer), 600 (paper), or 100 (Internet); proof of adequate funds; proof of health/immunizations.

International Student Contact Ms. Jennifer W. Taylor, Director, Graduate Business Admissions, 500 El Camino Real, 116 Lucas Hall, Santa Clara, CA 95053. *Phone:* 408-554-4539. *Fax:* 408-554-4571. *E-mail:* mbaadmissions@scu.edu.

APPLICATION *Required:* GMAT, GRE, application form, baccalaureate/first degree, essay, 2 letters of recommendation, resume/curriculum vitae, transcripts of college work. *Recommended:* Interview, 3 years of work experience. *Application fee:* $75, $100 (international). Applications for domestic and international students are processed on a rolling basis.

Application Contact Jennifer W. Taylor, Director, Graduate Business Admissions, 500 El Camino Real, 116 Lucas Hall, Santa Clara, CA 95053-0001. *Phone:* 408-554-4539. *Fax:* 408-554-4571. *E-mail:* mbaadmissions@scu.edu.

Stanford University
Graduate School of Business

Stanford, California

Phone: 650-723-2766 **Fax:** 650-725-7831 **E-mail:** mba@gsb.stanford.edu

Business Program(s) Web Site: http://www.gsb.stanford.edu/

Graduate Business Unit Enrollment *Total:* 897 (897 full-time; 307 women; 312 international).

Graduate Business Faculty *Total:* 160 (95 full-time; 65 part-time).

Admissions *Applied:* 5,741. *Admitted:* 455. *Enrolled:* 362. *Average GMAT:* 721. *Average GPA:* 3.61

Academic Calendar Quarters.

Accreditation AACSB—The Association to Advance Collegiate Schools of Business.

After Graduation (Class of 2006–07) *Employed within 3 months of graduation:* 94%. *Average starting salary:* $117,681.

DEGREES JD/MBA • MBA • MBA/ME • MBA/MPP • MBA/MS • MS

JD/MBA—Stanford JD-MBA Program Full-time. 47 months to complete program. *Concentrations:* combined degrees, general MBA.

MBA—Stanford MBA Full-time. At least 100 total credits required. 21 months to complete program. *Concentrations:* general MBA, international management, public management.

MBA/ME—Stanford MBA-M Ed Program Full-time. At least 119 total credits required. 21 to 27 months to complete program. *Concentrations:* combined degrees, general MBA.

MBA/MPP—Stanford MBA-MPP Program At least 145 total credits required. 33 months to complete program. *Concentrations:* combined degrees, general MBA.

MBA/MS—MBA/MS IPER Program includes Interdisciplinary Graduate Program in Environment and Resources. At least 129 total credits required. 27 to 30 months to complete program. *Concentrations:* combined degrees, general MBA.

MS—Stanford Sloan Master's Program Full-time. At least 57 total credits required. 10 months to complete program. *Concentrations:* leadership, management.

RESOURCES AND SERVICES 450 on-campus PCs are available to graduate business students. Access to Internet/World Wide Web, online (class) registration, and online grade reports available. *Personal computer requirements:* Graduate business students are not required to have a personal computer. *Special opportunities include:* An international exchange program and an internship program are available. *Placement services include:* Alumni network, career placement, job search course, career counseling/planning, electronic job bank, resume referral, career fairs, job interviews arranged, resume preparation, and career library.

EXPENSES *Tuition:* Full-time: $45,921. *Tuition (international):* Full-time: $45,921. *Required fees:* Full-time: $1845. *Graduate housing:* Room and board costs vary by campus location, number of occupants, type of accommodation, and type of board plan. *Typical cost:* $19,137 (including board).

FINANCIAL AID (2007–08) 548 students received aid, including fellowships and loans. *Financial aid application deadline:* 7/14.

Financial Aid Contact Mr. Jack Edwards, Director of Financial Aid, 518 Memorial Way, Stanford, CA 94305-5015. *Phone:* 650-723-3282. *Fax:* 650-725-3328. *E-mail:* finaid@gsb.stanford.edu.

INTERNATIONAL STUDENTS 35% of students enrolled are international students. *Services and facilities:* Counseling/support services, ESL/language courses, Housing location assistance, International student organization, Orientation, Visa Services, Career placement counselor. Financial aid is available to international students. *Required with application:* TOEFL with recommended score of 250 (computer) or 600 (paper); proof of adequate funds; proof of health/immunizations.

International Student Contact Derrick Bolton, Director of Admissions, 518 Memorial Way, Stanford, CA 94305-5015. *Phone:* 650-723-2766. *Fax:* 650-725-7831. *E-mail:* mba@gsb.stanford.edu.

APPLICATION *Required:* GMAT, application form, essay, interview, 3 letters of recommendation, resume/curriculum vitae, transcripts of college work. School will accept GRE. *Recommended:* Baccalaureate/first degree. *Application fee:* $250. *Deadlines:* 10/22 for fall, 1/7 for winter, 3/21 for spring, 10/22 for fall (international), 1/7 for winter (international), 3/21 for spring (international).

Application Contact Derrick Bolton, Director of Admissions, 518 Memorial Way, Stanford, CA 94305-5015. *Phone:* 650-723-2766. *Fax:* 650-725-7831. *E-mail:* mba@gsb.stanford.edu.

TUI University

College of Business Administration

Cypress, California

Phone: 714-816-0366 Ext. 2033 **Fax:** 714-816-0367 **E-mail:** registration@tuiu.edu

Business Program(s) Web Site: http://www.tuiu.edu/cba/mba.htm

Graduate Business Unit Enrollment *Total:* 2,310.

Graduate Business Faculty *Total:* 184 (28 full-time; 156 part-time).

Admissions *Applied:* 570. *Admitted:* 465. *Enrolled:* 457. *Average GPA:* 3.3

Academic Calendar Four 12-week sessions (semesters).

DEGREE MBA

MBA—Master of Business Administration Full-time and part-time. Distance learning option. At least 44 total credits required. Minimum of 15 months to complete program. *Concentrations:* conflict resolution management, entrepreneurship, finance, general MBA, human resources management, information management, international business, logistics, public and private management, strategic management.

RESOURCES AND SERVICES Access to Internet/World Wide Web, online (class) registration, and online grade reports available. *Personal computer requirements:* Graduate business students are required to have a personal computer.

EXPENSES *Tuition:* Part-time: $300 per credit hour. *Tuition (international):* Part-time: $300 per credit hour.

FINANCIAL AID (2007–08) Grants and loans. Aid is available to part-time students. *Financial aid application deadline:* 5/31.

Financial Aid Contact Renita Verner, Coordinator of Financial Aid, 5665 Plaza Drive, 3rd Floor, Cypress, CA 90630. *Phone:* 714-816-0366 Ext. 2047. *Fax:* 714-816-0367. *E-mail:* rverner@tuiu.edu.

INTERNATIONAL STUDENTS *Services and facilities:* Counseling/ support services. Financial aid is not available to international students. *Required with application:* TOEFL with recommended score of 550 (paper).

International Student Contact Ms. Wei Ren, Registrar, 5665 Plaza Drive, 3rd Floor, Cypress, CA 90630. *Phone:* 714-816-0366 Ext. 2033. *Fax:* 714-816-0367. *E-mail:* registration@tuiu.edu.

APPLICATION *Required:* Application form, baccalaureate/first degree, transcripts of college work. *Application fee:* $75. Applications for domestic and international students are processed on a rolling basis.

Application Contact Ms. Wei Ren, Registrar, 5665 Plaza Drive, 3rd Floor, Cypress, CA 90630. *Phone:* 714-816-0366 Ext. 2033. *Fax:* 714-816-0367. *E-mail:* registration@tuiu.edu.

University of California, Berkeley

Haas School of Business

Berkeley, California

Phone: 510-642-1405 **Fax:** 510-643-6659 **E-mail:** mbaadm@haas.berkeley.edu

Business Program(s) Web Site: http://www.haas.berkeley.edu/

Graduate Business Unit Enrollment *Total:* 1,545 (645 full-time; 900 part-time; 414 women; 333 international). *Average Age:* 29.

Graduate Business Faculty *Total:* 217 (77 full-time; 140 part-time).

Admissions *Applied:* 4,661. *Admitted:* 931. *Enrolled:* 618. *Average GMAT:* 710. *Average GPA:* 3.57

Academic Calendar Semesters.

Accreditation AACSB—The Association to Advance Collegiate Schools of Business.

After Graduation (Class of 2006–07) *Employed within 3 months of graduation:* 95.6%. *Average starting salary:* $101,859.

DEGREES EMBA • JD/MBA • MBA • MBA/MIAS • MBA/MPH • MQF • PhD/Mphil

---

EMBA—Berkeley-Columbia Executive MBA Program Part-time. EMBA students have a median age of 36. They bring an average of 12 years working experience from a variety of industries and job functions. More information at http://www.berkeley.columbia.edu. At least 48 total credits required. 19 months to complete program. *Concentrations:* business policy/strategy, electronic commerce (E-commerce), entrepreneurship, finance, financial economics, general MBA, information management, international and area business studies, international business,

University of California, Berkeley (continued)

international finance, international management, management, management information systems, marketing, new venture management, operations management, organizational behavior/development, strategic management, technology management.

JD/MBA—Juris Doctor/Master of Business Administration Full-time. At least 118 total credits required. 45 months to complete program. *Concentrations:* business information science, entrepreneurship, finance, financial economics, information management, international and area business studies, international business, management, management information systems, marketing, nonprofit management, operations management, organizational behavior/development, real estate, strategic management, technology management.

MBA—Evening and Weekend Master of Business Administration Program Part-time. The Evening and Weekend MBA Program accommodates the schedules of working professionals. The average age is 32, average work experience is 8 years. More information at http:// ewmba.haas.berkeley.edu. At least 42 total credits required. 28 to 45 months to complete program. *Concentrations:* electronic commerce (E-commerce), entrepreneurship, finance, financial economics, information management, management, management information systems, marketing, organizational behavior/development, real estate, strategic management, technology management.

MBA—Full-Time Master of Business Administration Program Full-time. More information at http://mba.haas.berkeley.edu/. At least 51 total credits required. 22 months to complete program. *Concentrations:* accounting, business policy/strategy, electronic commerce (E-commerce), entrepreneurship, finance, financial economics, health administration, health care, human resources management, information management, international and area business studies, international business, international finance, international management, management, management information systems, marketing, new venture management, nonprofit management, operations management, organizational behavior/development, real estate, strategic management, technology management.

MBA/MIAS—Master of Business Administration/Master of International Area Studies Full-time. At least 75 total credits required. 34 months to complete program. *Concentrations:* accounting, Asian business studies, entrepreneurship, European business studies, finance, financial economics, information management, international and area business studies, international business, international development management, international finance, international management, Japanese business studies, management, management information systems, marketing, nonprofit management, operations management, organizational behavior/development, real estate, strategic management, technology management.

MBA/MPH—Master of Business Administration/Master of Public Health in Health Services Management Full-time. At least 80 total credits required. 29 to 34 months to complete program. *Concentrations:* health care, management, nonprofit management, nonprofit organization.

MQF—Master of Financial Engineering Full-time. MFE students have a strong quantitative background. Applicants average 29 years of age and some already hold advanced degrees. More information at http:// mfe.haas.berkeley.edu/. 28 to 32 total credits required. 12 months to complete program. *Concentrations:* banking, business policy/strategy, economics, finance, financial economics, financial engineering, financial information systems, financial management/planning, international finance, managerial economics, quantitative analysis, risk management, statistics.

PhD/Mphil—Haas PhD Program Full-time. PhD students choose one of five subjects: accounting, business and public policy, finance, marketing, organizational behavior, or real estate. More information at http:// www.haas.berkeley.edu/Phd/. At least 48 total credits required. Minimum of 48 months to complete program. *Concentrations:* accounting, finance, marketing, organizational behavior/development, public policy and administration, real estate.

RESOURCES AND SERVICES 180 on-campus PCs are available to graduate business students. Access to Internet/World Wide Web, online (class) registration, and online grade reports available. *Personal computer requirements:* Graduate business students are required to have a personal computer. *Special opportunities include:* An international exchange

program and an internship program are available. *Placement services include:* Alumni network, career placement, job search course, career counseling/planning, electronic job bank, resume referral, career fairs, job interviews arranged, resume preparation, and career library.

EXPENSES *Tuition (state resident):* Full-time: $26,880. Part-time: $27,370 per year. *Tuition (nonresident):* Full-time: $37,949. Part-time: $27,370 per year. *Tuition (international):* Full-time: $37,949. Part-time: $27,370 per year. Tuition and/or fees vary by number of courses or credits taken and academic program. *Graduate housing:* Room and board costs vary by campus location, number of occupants, and type of accommodation. *Typical cost:* $15,104 (including board), $10,038 (room only).

FINANCIAL AID (2007–08) Fellowships, grants, loans, research assistantships, scholarships, and teaching assistantships. Aid is available to part-time students. *Financial aid application deadline:* 3/2.

INTERNATIONAL STUDENTS 22% of students enrolled are international students. *Services and facilities:* Counseling/support services, ESL/language courses, Housing location assistance, International student housing, International student organization, Orientation, Visa Services. Financial aid is available to international students. *Required with application:* TOEFL with recommended score of 230 (computer), 570 (paper), or 68 (Internet); proof of adequate funds.

International Student Contact Full-Time MBA Admissions, 430 Student Services Building, #1902, Berkeley, CA 94720-1902. *Phone:* 510-642-1405. *Fax:* 510-643-6659. *E-mail:* mbaadm@haas.berkeley.edu.

APPLICATION *Required:* GMAT, application form, baccalaureate/first degree, essay, 2 letters of recommendation, personal statement, resume/ curriculum vitae, transcripts of college work, 2 years of work experience. *Application fee:* $175. *Deadline:* 1/31 for fall.

Application Contact Full-Time MBA Admissions, 430 Student Services Building, #1902, Berkeley, CA 94720-1902. *Phone:* 510-642-1405. *Fax:* 510-643-6659. *E-mail:* mbaadm@haas.berkeley.edu.

University of California, Davis
Graduate School of Management

Davis, California

Phone: 530-752-7658 **Fax:** 530-754-9355 **E-mail:** admissions@gsm.ucdavis.edu

Business Program(s) Web Site: http://www.gsm.ucdavis.edu/

Graduate Business Unit Enrollment *Total:* 481 (120 full-time; 361 part-time; 153 women; 47 international). *Average Age:* 30.

Graduate Business Faculty *Total:* 49 (29 full-time; 20 part-time).

Admissions *Applied:* 585. *Admitted:* 274. *Enrolled:* 199. *Average GMAT:* 674. *Average GPA:* 3.4

Academic Calendar Quarters.

Accreditation AACSB—The Association to Advance Collegiate Schools of Business.

After Graduation (Class of 2006–07) *Employed within 3 months of graduation:* 89%. *Average starting salary:* $85,555.

DEGREES MBA

MBA—Working Professional MBA Program Part-time. At least 72 total credits required. 24 to 48 months to complete program. *Concentrations:* accounting, entrepreneurship, finance, general MBA, leadership, management, management information systems, marketing, organizational behavior/development, technology management.

MBA—Master of Business Administration Full-time. At least 72 total credits required. 21 to 48 months to complete program. *Concentrations:* accounting, entrepreneurship, finance, general MBA, leadership, management, management information systems, marketing, organizational behavior/development, technology management.

RESOURCES AND SERVICES 25 on-campus PCs are available to graduate business students. Access to Internet/World Wide Web, online

(class) registration, and online grade reports available. *Personal computer requirements:* Graduate business students are strongly recommended to purchase or lease a personal computer. *Special opportunities include:* An international exchange program and an internship program are available. *Placement services include:* Alumni network, career placement, job search course, career counseling/planning, electronic job bank, resume referral, career fairs, job interviews arranged, resume preparation, and career library.

EXPENSES *Tuition (state resident):* Full-time: $0. Part-time: $2550 per course. *Tuition (nonresident):* Full-time: $12,245. Part-time: $2550 per course. *Tuition (international):* Full-time: $12,245. Part-time: $2550 per course. *Required fees:* Full-time: $22,629. Tuition and/or fees vary by campus location and academic program. *Graduate housing:* Room and board costs vary by number of occupants and type of accommodation. *Typical cost:* $13,349 (including board).

FINANCIAL AID (2007–08) 100 students received aid, including fellowships, grants, loans, research assistantships, scholarships, teaching assistantships, and work study. Aid is available to part-time students. *Financial aid application deadline:* 3/1.

Financial Aid Contact Holly Bishop-Green, Associate Director, Admissions and Student Services, One Shields Avenue, AOB IV, Room 106, Davis, CA 95616. *Phone:* 530-752-7363. *Fax:* 530-752-2924. *E-mail:* hbbishopgreen@ucdavis.edu.

INTERNATIONAL STUDENTS 10% of students enrolled are international students. *Services and facilities:* Counseling/support services, ESL/language courses, Housing location assistance, International student housing, International student organization, Language tutoring, Orientation, Visa Services. Financial aid is available to international students. *Required with application:* IELT with recommended score of 7; TOEFL with recommended score of 250 (computer), 600 (paper), or 100 (Internet); proof of adequate funds; proof of health/immunizations.

International Student Contact Kathy Gleed, Director, Admissions and Student Services, One Shields Avenue, 105 AOB IV, Davis, CA 95616. *Phone:* 530-754-5476. *Fax:* 530-754-9355. *E-mail:* krgleed@ucdavis.edu.

APPLICATION *Required:* GMAT, application form, baccalaureate/first degree, essay, 2 letters of recommendation, resume/curriculum vitae, transcripts of college work. *Recommended:* Interview, work experience. *Application fee:* $125. Applications for domestic and international students are processed on a rolling basis.

Application Contact James R. Stevens, Assistant Dean of Student Affairs, One Shields Avenue, 107 AOB IV, Davis, CA 95616. *Phone:* 530-752-7658. *Fax:* 530-754-9355. *E-mail:* admissions@gsm.ucdavis.edu.

University of California, Irvine
The Paul Merage School of Business
Irvine, California

Phone: 949-824-4MBA **Fax:** 949-824-2235 **E-mail:** mba@merage.uci.edu

Business Program(s) Web Site: http://www.merage.uci.edu/

Graduate Business Unit Enrollment *Total:* 655 (200 full-time; 455 part-time). *Average Age:* 28.

Graduate Business Faculty *Total:* 90 (44 full-time; 46 part-time).

Admissions *Applied:* 594. *Admitted:* 255. *Enrolled:* 104. *Average GMAT:* 670. *Average GPA:* 3.3

Academic Calendar Quarters.

Accreditation AACSB—The Association to Advance Collegiate Schools of Business.

After Graduation (Class of 2006–07) *Employed within 3 months of graduation:* 92%. *Average starting salary:* $76,407.

DEGREES MBA

MBA—Executive Master of Business Administration Part-time. At least 92 total credits required. 24 months to complete program. *Concentration:* executive programs.

MBA—Fully-Employed Master of Business Administration Part-time. At least 92 total credits required. 33 to 36 months to complete program. *Concentration:* general MBA.

MBA—Health Care Executive Master of Business Administration Part-time. At least 92 total credits required. 24 months to complete program. *Concentrations:* executive programs, health care.

MBA—Master of Business Administration Full-time. At least 92 total credits required. 21 to 24 months to complete program. *Concentration:* general MBA.

RESOURCES AND SERVICES 10 on-campus PCs are available to graduate business students. Access to Internet/World Wide Web, online (class) registration, and online grade reports available. *Personal computer requirements:* Graduate business students are required to have a personal computer, the cost of which is included in tuition or other required fees. *Special opportunities include:* An international exchange program and an internship program are available. *Placement services include:* Alumni network, career placement, job search course, career counseling/planning, electronic job bank, resume referral, career fairs, job interviews arranged, resume preparation, and career library.

EXPENSES *Tuition (state resident):* Full-time: $27,814.50. Part-time: $8441 per quarter. *Tuition (nonresident):* Full-time: $38,949. Part-time: $8441 per quarter. *Tuition (international):* Full-time: $38,948.50. Part-time: $8441 per quarter. *Graduate housing:* Room and board costs vary by number of occupants and type of accommodation. *Typical cost:* $12,274 (including board).

FINANCIAL AID (2007–08) 102 students received aid, including fellowships, grants, loans, research assistantships, scholarships, teaching assistantships, and work study. Aid is available to part-time students. *Financial aid application deadline:* 6/1.

Financial Aid Contact Ms. Mary Morris, Financial Aid Counselor, 110 MPAA, Irvine, CA 92697-3130. *Phone:* 949-824-5728. *Fax:* 949-824-2235. *E-mail:* mkmorris@uci.edu.

INTERNATIONAL STUDENTS *Services and facilities:* Counseling/support services, ESL/language courses, Housing location assistance, International student housing, International student organization, Language tutoring, Orientation, Visa Services, International career counseling. Financial aid is available to international students. *Required with application:* TOEFL with recommended score of 250 (computer), 600 (paper), or 100 (Internet); proof of adequate funds; proof of health/immunizations.

International Student Contact Christine Hoyt, Assistant Director, Recruitment and Admissions, Full-Time MBA Program, SB 220, Irvine, CA 92697-3125. *Phone:* 949-824-4MBA. *Fax:* 949-824-2235. *E-mail:* mba@merage.uci.edu.

APPLICATION *Required:* GMAT, application form, baccalaureate/first degree, essay, interview, 2 letters of recommendation, resume/curriculum vitae, transcripts of college work. *Recommended:* 2 years of work experience. *Application fee:* $150. Applications for domestic and international students are processed on a rolling basis.

Application Contact Deena Raval, Admissions Coordinator, Full-Time MBA Program, SB 220, Irvine, CA 92697-3125. *Phone:* 949-824-4MBA. *Fax:* 949-824-2235. *E-mail:* mba@merage.uci.edu.

University of California, Los Angeles
UCLA Anderson School of Management
Los Angeles, California

Phone: 310-825-6944 **Fax:** 310-825-8582 **E-mail:** mba.admissions@anderson.ucla.edu

Business Program(s) Web Site: http://www.anderson.ucla.edu/

University of California, Los Angeles (continued)

Graduate Business Unit Enrollment *Total:* 1,425 (721 full-time; 704 part-time; 435 women). *Average Age:* 28.

Graduate Business Faculty *Total:* 109 (70 full-time; 39 part-time).

Admissions *Applied:* 3,891. *Admitted:* 1,036. *Enrolled:* 612. *Average GMAT:* 704. *Average GPA:* 3.5

Academic Calendar Quarters.

Accreditation AACSB—The Association to Advance Collegiate Schools of Business.

After Graduation (Class of 2006–07) *Employed within 3 months of graduation:* 93%. *Average starting salary:* $99,237.

DEGREES EMBA • JD/MBA • MBA • MBA/MA • MBA/MRP • MBA/MS • MD/MBA

EMBA—UCLA-NUS Global Executive MBA Program Part-time. Laptop computer required. At least 72 total credits required. 15 to 60 months to complete program. *Concentration:* executive programs.

JD/MBA—Juris Doctor/Master of Business Administration Full-time. At least 185 total credits required. 45 to 48 months to complete program. *Concentrations:* accounting, entrepreneurship, finance, human resources management, industrial/labor relations, international business, international economics, international finance, international management, international marketing, management, management information systems, management science, managerial economics, marketing, nonprofit management, operations management, organizational behavior/development, production management, real estate, strategic management, technology management.

MBA—Executive Master of Business Administration Part-time. Laptop computer required. At least 66 total credits required. 23 months to complete program. *Concentration:* executive programs.

MBA—Full-Time Master of Business Administration Full-time. Laptop computer required. At least 96 total credits required. 21 to 24 months to complete program. *Concentrations:* accounting, combined degrees, economics, entrepreneurship, finance, human resources management, international business, international economics, international finance, international management, international marketing, leadership, management, management information systems, management science, managerial economics, marketing, new venture management, operations management, organizational behavior/development, real estate, sports/entertainment management, strategic management, supply chain management, technology management.

MBA—Fully-Employed Master of Business Administration Part-time. Laptop computer required. At least 84 total credits required. 28 to 34 months to complete program. *Concentrations:* accounting, decision sciences, economics, entrepreneurship, finance, general MBA, human resources management, international business, international management, international marketing, leadership, management, management information systems, managerial economics, marketing, new venture management, operations management, organizational behavior/development, real estate, sports/entertainment management, strategic management, supply chain management, technology management.

MBA/MA—Master of Business Administration/Master of Arts in Latin American Studies Full-time. At least 120 total credits required. 30 to 36 months to complete program. *Concentrations:* accounting, entrepreneurship, finance, human resources management, industrial/labor relations, international business, international economics, international finance, international management, international marketing, management, management information systems, management science, managerial economics, marketing, nonprofit management, operations management, organizational behavior/development, production management, real estate, strategic management, technology management.

MBA/MA—Master of Business Administration/Master of Arts in Urban Studies Full-time. At least 144 total credits required. 33 to 36 months to complete program. *Concentrations:* accounting, entrepreneurship, finance, human resources management, industrial/labor relations, international business, international economics, international finance, international management, international marketing, management, manage-ment information systems, management science, managerial economics, marketing, nonprofit management, operations management, organizational behavior/development, production management, real estate, strategic management, technology management.

MBA/MRP—MBA/Master of Urban Planning Full-time. Laptop computer required. At least 96 total credits required. 21 to 24 months to complete program. *Concentrations:* accounting, city/urban administration, combined degrees, entrepreneurship, finance, general MBA, human resources management, information systems, international business, international management, international marketing, leadership, management, management information systems, managerial economics, marketing, new venture management, operations management, organizational behavior/development, real estate, sports/entertainment management, supply chain management, technology management.

MBA/MS—Master of Business Administration/Master of Science in Computer Science Full-time. At least 96 total credits required. 33 to 36 months to complete program. *Concentrations:* accounting, entrepreneurship, finance, human resources management, industrial/labor relations, international business, international economics, international finance, international management, international marketing, management, management information systems, management science, managerial economics, marketing, nonprofit management, operations management, organizational behavior/development, production management, real estate, strategic management, technology management.

MBA/MS—Master of Business Administration/Master of Science in Public Health Full-time. At least 132 total credits required. 33 to 36 months to complete program. *Concentrations:* accounting, entrepreneurship, finance, human resources management, industrial/labor relations, international business, international economics, international finance, international management, international marketing, management, management information systems, management science, managerial economics, marketing, nonprofit management, operations management, organizational behavior/development, production management, real estate, strategic management, technology management.

MD/MBA—Doctor of Medicine/Master of Business Administration Full-time. At least 96 total credits required. 60 to 63 months to complete program. *Concentrations:* accounting, entrepreneurship, finance, human resources management, industrial/labor relations, international business, international economics, international finance, international management, international marketing, management, management information systems, management science, managerial economics, marketing, nonprofit management, operations management, organizational behavior/development, production management, real estate, strategic management, technology management.

RESOURCES AND SERVICES Access to Internet/World Wide Web, online (class) registration, and online grade reports available. *Personal computer requirements:* Graduate business students are required to have a personal computer. *Special opportunities include:* An international exchange program and an internship program are available. *Placement services include:* Alumni network, career placement, job search course, career counseling/planning, electronic job bank, resume referral, career fairs, job interviews arranged, resume preparation, and career library.

EXPENSES *Tuition (state resident):* Full-time: $36,860. Part-time: $30,000 per year. *Tuition (nonresident):* Full-time: $39,050. Part-time: $30,000 per year.

FINANCIAL AID (2007–08) Fellowships, grants, loans, research assistantships, scholarships, teaching assistantships, and work study. Aid is available to part-time students. *Financial aid application deadline:* 3/2.

Financial Aid Contact Ms. Marta Peterson, Financial Aid Director, 110 Westwood Plaza, Box 951481, Los Angeles, CA 90095-1481. *Phone:* 310-825-0629. *Fax:* 310-825-8582. *E-mail:* mba.admissions@ anderson.ucla.edu.

INTERNATIONAL STUDENTS *Services and facilities:* Counseling/ support services, ESL/language courses, Housing location assistance, International student housing, Orientation, Visa Services. Financial aid is available to international students. *Required with application:* Proof of adequate funds; proof of health/immunizations. *Recommended with application:* TOEFL with recommended score of 260 (computer) or 600 (paper).

International Student Contact Mae Jennifer Shores, Assistant Dean and Director, MBA Admissions/Financial Aid, 110 Westwood Plaza, Box 951481, Los Angeles, CA 90095-1481. *Phone:* 310-825-6944. *Fax:* 310-825-8582. *E-mail:* mba.admissions@anderson.ucla.edu.

APPLICATION *Required:* GMAT, application form, baccalaureate/first degree, essay, 3 letters of recommendation, personal statement, transcripts of college work. *Recommended:* Interview, work experience. *Application fee:* $175. Applications for domestic and international students are processed on a rolling basis.

Application Contact Mae Jennifer Shores, Assistant Dean and Director of MBA Admissions/Financial Aid, 110 Westwood Plaza, Box 951481, Los Angeles, CA 90095-1481. *Phone:* 310-825-6944. *Fax:* 310-825-8582. *E-mail:* mba.admissions@anderson.ucla.edu.

See full description on page 696.

University of California, Riverside
A. Gary Anderson Graduate School of Management

Riverside, California

Phone: 951-827-6200 **Fax:** 951-827-3970 **E-mail:** mba@ucr.edu

Business Program(s) Web Site: http://www.agsm.ucr.edu

Graduate Business Unit Enrollment *Total:* 127 (115 full-time; 12 part-time; 69 women; 75 international). *Average Age:* 27.

Graduate Business Faculty *Total:* 48 (33 full-time; 15 part-time).

Admissions *Applied:* 317. *Admitted:* 126. *Enrolled:* 64. *Average GMAT:* 573. *Average GPA:* 3.4

Academic Calendar Quarters.

Accreditation AACSB—The Association to Advance Collegiate Schools of Business.

After Graduation (Class of 2006–07) *Employed within 3 months of graduation:* 62%. *Average starting salary:* $48,600.

DEGREE MBA

MBA—Master of Business Administration Full-time and part-time. Statement of Purpose required. 80 total credits required. 24 months to complete program. *Concentrations:* accounting, entrepreneurship, finance, human resources management, international management, management, management information systems, management science, marketing, operations management, organizational behavior/development, production management.

RESOURCES AND SERVICES 200 on-campus PCs are available to graduate business students. Access to Internet/World Wide Web, online (class) registration, and online grade reports available. *Personal computer requirements:* Graduate business students are not required to have a personal computer. *Special opportunities include:* An international exchange program and an internship program are available. *Placement services include:* Alumni network, career placement, career counseling/planning, electronic job bank, resume referral, career fairs, job interviews arranged, resume preparation, and career library.

EXPENSES *Tuition (state resident):* Full-time: $0. Part-time: $0 per year. *Tuition (nonresident):* Full-time: $14,694. Part-time: $7347 per year. *Tuition (international):* Full-time: $14,694. Part-time: $7347 per year. *Required fees:* Full-time: $10,108. Part-time: $6241 per year. *Graduate housing:* Room and board costs vary by number of occupants, type of accommodation, and type of board plan. *Typical cost:* $12,405 (including board).

FINANCIAL AID (2007–08) 70 students received aid, including fellowships, loans, research assistantships, scholarships, and teaching assistantships. Aid is available to part-time students. *Financial aid application deadline:* 5/1.

Financial Aid Contact Cindy Roulette, MBA Student Affairs Officer, Anderson Hall, Riverside, CA 92521-0203. *Phone:* 951-827-2513. *Fax:* 951-827-3970. *E-mail:* mba@ucr.edu.

INTERNATIONAL STUDENTS 59% of students enrolled are international students. *Services and facilities:* Counseling/support services, ESL/language courses, Housing location assistance, International student housing, International student organization, Language tutoring, Orientation, Visa Services. Financial aid is available to international students. *Required with application:* TOEFL with recommended score of 213 (computer), 550 (paper), or 80 (Internet); proof of adequate funds.

International Student Contact Gary Kuzas, MBA Student Recruiter, Anderson Hall, Riverside, CA 92521-0203. *Phone:* 951-827-6200. *Fax:* 951-827-3970. *E-mail:* mba@ucr.edu.

APPLICATION *Required:* GMAT, application form, baccalaureate/first degree, essay, 3 letters of recommendation, personal statement, resume/curriculum vitae, transcripts of college work. *Recommended:* Interview. *Application fee:* $70, $85 (international). Applications for domestic and international students are processed on a rolling basis.

Application Contact Gary Kuzas, MBA Student Recruiter, Anderson Hall, Riverside, CA 92521-0203. *Phone:* 951-827-6200. *Fax:* 951-827-3970. *E-mail:* mba@ucr.edu.

See full description on page 698.

University of California, San Diego
Rady School of Management

La Jolla, California

Phone: 858-534-0684 **Fax:** 858-822-5896 **E-mail:** mbaadmissions@ucsd.edu

Business Program(s) Web Site: http://rady.ucsd.edu/

Graduate Business Unit Enrollment *Total:* 225 (114 full-time; 111 part-time; 63 women). *Average Age:* 30.

Graduate Business Faculty 18 full-time.

Admissions *Applied:* 346. *Admitted:* 161. *Enrolled:* 117. *Average GMAT:* 675. *Average GPA:* 3.4

Academic Calendar Quarters.

After Graduation (Class of 2006–07) *Employed within 3 months of graduation:* 84%. *Average starting salary:* $80,333.

DEGREES EMBA • MBA • PhD/MBA

EMBA—FlexEvening MBA Part-time. Work experience and laptop required. At least 92 total credits required. Minimum of 30 months to complete program. *Concentrations:* entrepreneurship, general MBA, information management, information systems, information technology, management, management information systems, new venture management, pharmaceutical management, research and development administration, system management, technology management, telecommunications management.

EMBA—FlexWeekend MBA Part-time. Work experience and laptop required. At least 92 total credits required. Minimum of 24 months to complete program. *Concentrations:* entrepreneurship, executive programs, general MBA, information management, information systems, information technology, management, management information systems, new venture management, pharmaceutical management, research and development administration, system management, technology management, telecommunications management.

MBA—Full-Time MBA Full-time. Work experience recommended but not required. A laptop is required. At least 92 total credits required. Minimum of 21 months to complete program. *Concentrations:* entrepreneurship, general MBA, information management, information systems, information technology, management, management information systems, new venture management, pharmaceutical management, research and development administration, system management, technology management, telecommunications management.

University of California, San Diego (continued)

PhD/MBA—Concurrent PhD in Oceanography/MBA Full-time. Must be admitted to the UC San Diego Scripps Institution of Oceanography PhD program prior to applying to the MBA program. Work experience recommended but not required. Laptop required. *Concentrations:* entrepreneurship, general MBA, information systems, information technology, new venture management, other, pharmaceutical management, research and development administration, student designed, system management, technology management, telecommunications management.

RESOURCES AND SERVICES Access to Internet/World Wide Web, online (class) registration, and online grade reports available. *Personal computer requirements:* Graduate business students are required to have a personal computer. *Special opportunities include:* An international exchange program and an internship program are available. *Placement services include:* Alumni network, career placement, job search course, career counseling/planning, electronic job bank, resume referral, career fairs, job interviews arranged, resume preparation, and career library.

EXPENSES *Tuition (state resident):* Full-time: $26,000. Part-time: $870 per credit hour. *Tuition (nonresident):* Full-time: $37,000. Part-time: $870 per credit hour. *Tuition (international):* Full-time: $37,000. Part-time: $870 per credit hour.

FINANCIAL AID (2007–08) 31 students received aid, including fellowships, grants, loans, scholarships, and teaching assistantships. Aid is available to part-time students. *Financial aid application deadline:* 3/3.

Financial Aid Contact Margie Frazee, Director, MBA Recruitment and Admissions, 9500 Gilman Drive, MC 0554, Otterson Hall, 2nd Floor, La Jolla, CA 92093-0554. *Phone:* 858-822-6462. *Fax:* 858-822-5896. *E-mail:* mfrazee@ucsd.edu.

INTERNATIONAL STUDENTS *Services and facilities:* Counseling/support services, ESL/language courses, Housing location assistance, International student organization, Orientation, Visa Services. Financial aid is available to international students. *Required with application:* TOEFL with recommended score of 213 (computer), 550 (paper), or 80 (Internet); proof of adequate funds; proof of health/immunizations. *Recommended with application:* IELT with recommended score of 7.

International Student Contact Debra Aviila, Assistant Director, MBA Recruitment and Admissions, Otterson Hall, 2nd Floor, 9500 Gilman Drive, MC 0554, La Jolla, CA 92093-0554. *Phone:* 858-534-0864. *Fax:* 858-822-5896. *E-mail:* mbaadmissions@ucsd.edu.

APPLICATION *Required:* GMAT, application form, baccalaureate/first degree, essay, interview, 2 letters of recommendation, resume/curriculum vitae, transcripts of college work. *Application fee:* $150. Applications for domestic and international students are processed on a rolling basis.

Application Contact MBA Admissions Team, 9500 Gilman Drive, MC 0554, Otterson Hall, 2nd Floor, La Jolla, CA 92093-0554. *Phone:* 858-534-0684. *Fax:* 858-822-5896. *E-mail:* mbaadmissions@ucsd.edu.

See full description on page 700.

University of La Verne

College of Business and Public Management

La Verne, California

Phone: 909-593-3511 Ext. 4211 **Fax:** 909-392-2704 **E-mail:** heloua@ulv.edu

Business Program(s) Web Site: http://www.ulv.edu/cbpm/

Graduate Business Unit Enrollment *Total:* 805 (315 full-time; 490 part-time; 427 women; 227 international). *Average Age:* 35.

Graduate Business Faculty *Total:* 62 (25 full-time; 37 part-time).

Admissions *Applied:* 475. *Admitted:* 412. *Enrolled:* 377. *Average GMAT:* 520. *Average GPA:* 3.2.

Academic Calendar Four 10-week terms.

After Graduation (Class of 2006–07) *Employed within 3 months of graduation:* 93%. *Average starting salary:* $67,000.

DEGREES JD/MBA • MBA • MS

JD/MBA—Juris Doctor/Master of Business Administration Full-time and part-time. 98 to 110 total credits required. 48 to 96 months to complete program. *Concentrations:* accounting, contract management, finance, health care, information management, leadership, legal administration, management, marketing.

MBA—Career Master of Business Administration Full-time and part-time. 36 to 54 total credits required. 12 to 60 months to complete program. *Concentrations:* accounting, finance, health care, information management, international business, leadership, management, marketing, supply chain management.

MBA—Master of Business Administration for Experienced Professionals Full-time and part-time. Distance learning option. 33 to 48 total credits required. 12 to 60 months to complete program. *Concentrations:* accounting, finance, health care, information management, international business, leadership, management, marketing, supply chain management.

MS—Master of Science in Business Organizational Management Full-time and part-time. 36 total credits required. 24 to 60 months to complete program. *Concentrations:* health care, human resources management.

RESOURCES AND SERVICES 250 on-campus PCs are available to graduate business students. Access to Internet/World Wide Web, online (class) registration, and online grade reports available. *Personal computer requirements:* Graduate business students are strongly recommended to purchase or lease a personal computer. *Special opportunities include:* An international exchange program and an internship program are available. *Placement services include:* Alumni network, career placement, job search course, career counseling/planning, electronic job bank, resume referral, career fairs, job interviews arranged, resume preparation, and career library.

FINANCIAL AID (2007–08) 15 students received aid, including fellowships, loans, research assistantships, scholarships, and work study. Aid is available to part-time students.

Financial Aid Contact Ms. Leatha Webster, Director of Financial Aid, 1950 Third Street, La Verne, CA 91750. *Phone:* 909-593-3511 Ext. 4135. *Fax:* 909-392-2703. *E-mail:* websterl@ulv.edu.

INTERNATIONAL STUDENTS 28% of students enrolled are international students. *Services and facilities:* Counseling/support services, ESL/language courses, Housing location assistance, International student housing, International student organization, Language tutoring, Orientation, Visa Services, International student center. Financial aid is available to international students. *Required with application:* IELT with recommended score of 6.5; TOEFL with recommended score of 213 (computer), 550 (paper), or 80 (Internet); proof of adequate funds.

International Student Contact Ms. Rina Lazarian, Marketing Director, 1950 Third Street, La Verne, CA 91750. *Phone:* 909-593-3511 Ext. 4819. *Fax:* 909-392-2704. *E-mail:* lazarian@ulv.edu.

APPLICATION *Required:* Application form, baccalaureate/first degree, essay, 2 letters of recommendation, personal statement, resume/curriculum vitae, transcripts of college work. School will accept GMAT and GRE. *Recommended:* 3 years of work experience. *Application fee:* $50. Applications for domestic and international students are processed on a rolling basis.

Application Contact Ibrahim Helou, Associate Dean, 1950 Third Street, La Verne, CA 91750-4443. *Phone:* 909-593-3511 Ext. 4211. *Fax:* 909-392-2704. *E-mail:* heloua@ulv.edu.

University of Phoenix–Bay Area Campus

College of Graduate Business and Management

Pleasanton, California

Phone: 480-317-6200 **Fax:** 480-643-1479 **E-mail:** beth.barilla@phoenix.edu

Business Program(s) Web Site: http://www.phoenix.edu

DEGREES EMBA • M Mgt • MA • MBA

EMBA—Executive Master of Business Administration Full-time. At least 30 total credits required. *Concentration:* executive programs.

M Mgt—Human Resource Management Full-time. At least 39 total credits required. *Concentration:* human resources management.

M Mgt—Public Administration Full-time. At least 39 total credits required. *Concentration:* public policy and administration.

M Mgt—Master of Management Full-time. At least 39 total credits required. *Concentration:* management.

MA—Master of Arts in Organizational Management Full-time. At least 40 total credits required. *Concentration:* organizational management.

MBA—Accounting Full-time. At least 54 total credits required. *Concentration:* accounting.

MBA—Global Management Full-time. At least 45 total credits required. *Concentration:* international management.

MBA—Human Resource Management Full-time. At least 45 total credits required. *Concentration:* human resources management.

MBA—Marketing Full-time. At least 45 total credits required. *Concentration:* marketing.

MBA—Public Administration Full-time. At least 45 total credits required. *Concentration:* public policy and administration.

MBA—e-Business Full-time. At least 45 total credits required. *Concentration:* electronic commerce (E-commerce).

MBA—Master of Business Administration Full-time. At least 45 total credits required. *Concentration:* administration.

RESOURCES AND SERVICES Access to online grade reports available. *Personal computer requirements:* Graduate business students are strongly recommended to purchase or lease a personal computer. *Placement services include:* Alumni network.

Application Contact Beth Barilla, Associate Vice President of Student Admissions and Services, Mail Stop AA-K101, 4615 East Elwood Street, Phoenix, AZ 85040-1958. *Phone:* 480-317-6200. *Fax:* 480-643-1479. *E-mail:* beth.barilla@phoenix.edu.

University of Phoenix–Sacramento Valley Campus

College of Graduate Business and Management

Sacramento, California

Phone: 480-317-6200 **Fax:** 480-643-1479 **E-mail:** beth.barilla@phoenix.edu

Business Program(s) Web Site: http://www.phoenix.edu

DEGREES M Mgt • MA • MBA

M Mgt—Human Resource Management Full-time. At least 39 total credits required. *Concentration:* human resources management.

M Mgt—Master of Management Full-time. At least 39 total credits required. *Concentration:* management.

MA—Master of Arts in Organizational Management Full-time. At least 40 total credits required. *Concentration:* organizational management.

MBA—Accounting Full-time. At least 54 total credits required. *Concentration:* accounting.

MBA—Global Management Full-time. At least 45 total credits required. *Concentration:* international business.

MBA—Human Resource Management Full-time. At least 45 total credits required. *Concentration:* human resources management.

MBA—Marketing Full-time. At least 45 total credits required. *Concentration:* marketing.

MBA—Public Administration Full-time. At least 45 total credits required. *Concentration:* public policy and administration.

MBA—e-Business Full-time. At least 45 total credits required. *Concentration:* electronic commerce (E-commerce).

MBA—Master of Business Administration Full-time. At least 45 total credits required. *Concentration:* administration.

RESOURCES AND SERVICES Access to online grade reports available. *Personal computer requirements:* Graduate business students are strongly recommended to purchase or lease a personal computer. *Placement services include:* Alumni network.

Application Contact Beth Barrilla, Associate Vice President of Student Admissions and Services, Mail Stop AA-K101, 4615 East Elwood Street, Phoenix, AZ 85040-1958. *Phone:* 480-317-6200. *Fax:* 480-643-1479. *E-mail:* beth.barilla@phoenix.edu.

University of Phoenix–San Diego Campus

College of Graduate Business and Management

San Diego, California

Phone: 480-317-6200 **Fax:** 480-643-1479 **E-mail:** beth.barilla@phoenix.edu

Business Program(s) Web Site: http://www.phoenix.edu

DEGREES EMBA • M Mgt • MA • MBA

EMBA—Executive Master of Business Administration Full-time. At least 30 total credits required. *Concentration:* strategic management.

M Mgt—Human Resource Management Full-time. At least 39 total credits required. *Concentration:* human resources management.

M Mgt—Master of Management Full-time. At least 39 total credits required. *Concentration:* management.

MA—Master of Arts in Organizational Management Full-time. At least 40 total credits required. *Concentration:* organizational management.

MBA—Accounting Full-time. At least 54 total credits required. *Concentration:* accounting.

MBA—Global Management Full-time. At least 45 total credits required. *Concentration:* international management.

MBA—Human Resource Management Full-time. At least 45 total credits required. *Concentration:* human resources management.

MBA—Marketing Full-time. At least 45 total credits required. *Concentration:* marketing.

MBA—Public Administration Full-time. At least 45 total credits required. *Concentration:* public policy and administration.

MBA—e-Business Full-time. At least 46 total credits required. *Concentration:* electronic commerce (E-commerce).

MBA—Master of Business Administration Full-time. At least 45 total credits required. *Concentration:* administration.

RESOURCES AND SERVICES Access to online grade reports available. *Personal computer requirements:* Graduate business students are strongly recommended to purchase or lease a personal computer. *Placement services include:* Alumni network.

Application Contact Beth Barilla, Associate Vice President of Student Admissions and Services, Mail Stop AA-K101, 4615 East Elwood Street, Phoenix, AZ 85040-1958. *Phone:* 480-317-6200. *Fax:* 480-643-1479. *E-mail:* beth.barilla@phoenix.edu.

University of Phoenix–Southern California Campus

College of Graduate Business and Management

Costa Mesa, California

Phone: 480-317-6200 **Fax:** 480-643-1479 **E-mail:** beth.barilla@phoenix.edu

Business Program(s) Web Site: http://www.phoenix.edu

DEGREES M Mgt • MA • MBA

M Mgt—Human Resource Management Full-time. At least 39 total credits required. *Concentration:* human resources management.

M Mgt—Master of Management Full-time. At least 39 total credits required. *Concentration:* management.

MA—Master of Arts in Organizational Management Full-time. At least 40 total credits required. *Concentration:* organizational management.

MBA—Accounting Full-time. At least 54 total credits required. *Concentration:* accounting.

MBA—Global Management Full-time. At least 45 total credits required. *Concentration:* international management.

MBA—Human Resource Management Full-time. At least 45 total credits required. *Concentration:* human resources management.

MBA—Marketing Full-time. At least 45 total credits required. *Concentration:* marketing.

MBA—Public Administration Full-time. At least 45 total credits required. *Concentration:* public policy and administration.

MBA—e-Business Full-time. At least 45 total credits required. *Concentration:* electronic commerce (E-commerce).

MBA—Master of Business Administration Full-time. At least 45 total credits required. *Concentration:* administration.

RESOURCES AND SERVICES Access to online grade reports available. *Personal computer requirements:* Graduate business students are strongly recommended to purchase or lease a personal computer. *Placement services include:* Alumni network.

Application Contact Beth Barilla, Associate Vice President of Student Admissions and Services, Mail Stop AA-K101, 4615 East Elwood Street, Phoenix, AZ 85040-1958. *Phone:* 480-317-6200. *Fax:* 480-643-1479. *E-mail:* beth.barilla@phoenix.edu.

University of Redlands

School of Business

Redlands, California

Phone: 888-748-8752 **E-mail:** schoolofbusiness@redlands.edu

Business Program(s) Web Site: http://www.redlands.edu/x32677.xml

Graduate Business Unit Enrollment *Total:* 747 (747 full-time; 318 women; 8 international). *Average Age:* 36.

Graduate Business Faculty *Total:* 131 (23 full-time; 108 part-time).

Academic Calendar Continuous.

DEGREES MA • MBA • MS

MA—Master of Arts in Management Part-time. 35 total credits required. 18 months to complete program. *Concentration:* management.

MBA—Master of Business Administration Part-time. 46 total credits required. 24 months to complete program. *Concentrations:* finance, general MBA, information management, international business, management information systems.

MS—Master of Science in Information Technology Part-time. 48 total credits required. 24 months to complete program. *Concentration:* information technology.

RESOURCES AND SERVICES 712 on-campus PCs are available to graduate business students. Access to Internet/World Wide Web and online grade reports available. *Personal computer requirements:* Graduate business students are not required to have a personal computer. *Special opportunities include:* An international exchange program is available. *Placement services include:* Alumni network, job search course, career counseling/planning, electronic job bank, career fairs, resume preparation, and career library.

EXPENSES *Tuition:* Part-time: $670 per credit. *Required fees:* Part-time: $20 per course.

FINANCIAL AID (2007–08) Grants, loans, and scholarships. Aid is available to part-time students.

Financial Aid Contact Financial Aid, 1200 East Colton Avenue, PO Box 3080, Redlands, CA 92373-0999. *Phone:* 909-748-8047. *Fax:* 909-335-5399. *E-mail:* financialaid@redlands.edu.

INTERNATIONAL STUDENTS 1% of students enrolled are international students. *Services and facilities:* Counseling/support services. Financial aid is not available to international students. *Required with application:* TOEFL with recommended score of 213 (computer) or 550 (paper).

International Student Contact Gerald Groshek, Professor, 1200 East Colton Avenue, PO Box 3080, Redlands, CA 92373-0999. *Phone:* 909-748-8770. *Fax:* 909-335-4009. *E-mail:* gerald_groshek@redlands.edu.

APPLICATION *Required:* Application form, baccalaureate/first degree, essay, resume/curriculum vitae, transcripts of college work, 5 years of work experience. School will accept GMAT and GRE. *Recommended:* Letter(s) of recommendation. *Application fee:* $0. Applications for domestic and international students are processed on a rolling basis.

Application Contact Enrollment Services, 1200 East Colton Avenue, PO Box 3080, Redlands, CA 92373-0999. *Phone:* 888-748-8752. *E-mail:* schoolofbusiness@redlands.edu.

University of San Diego

School of Business Administration

San Diego, California

Phone: 619-260-4860 **E-mail:** mba@sandiego.edu

Business Program(s) Web Site: http://sandiego.edu/business

Graduate Business Unit Enrollment *Total:* 459 (202 full-time; 257 part-time; 152 women; 54 international). *Average Age:* 31.

Graduate Business Faculty *Total:* 52 (36 full-time; 16 part-time).

Admissions *Applied:* 465. *Admitted:* 298. *Enrolled:* 196.

Academic Calendar Semesters.

Accreditation AACSB—The Association to Advance Collegiate Schools of Business.

DEGREES IMBA • JD/IMBA • JD/MBA • MBA • MBA/MSN • MS • MTAX

IMBA—International Master of Business Administration Full-time. At least 50 total credits required. *Concentrations:* finance, management, marketing, new venture management, real estate, supply chain management.

JD/IMBA—Juris Doctor/International Master of Business Administration Full-time and part-time. At least 133 total credits required. *Concentration:* combined degrees.

JD/MBA—Juris Doctor/Master of Business Administration Full-time and part-time. At least 133 total credits required. *Concentration:* combined degrees.

MBA—Master of Business Administration Full-time and part-time. At least 50 total credits required. *Concentrations:* finance, international business, marketing, new venture management, real estate, supply chain management.

MBA/MSN—Master of Business Administration/Master of Science in Nursing Full-time and part-time. At least 60 total credits required. *Concentration:* combined degrees.

MS—Master of Science in Accounting and Financial Management Full-time and part-time. Strong undergraduate background in accounting. At least 30 total credits required. *Concentrations:* accounting, corporate accounting, financial management/planning.

MS—Master of Science in Executive Leadership Part-time. 5 years of work experience required. At least 36 total credits required. *Concentration:* leadership.

MS—Master of Science in Global Leadership Part-time. Distance learning option. At least 31 total credits required. *Concentration:* leadership.

MS—Master of Science in Real Estate Full-time. At least 32 total credits required. *Concentration:* real estate.

MS—Master of Science in Supply Chain Management Part-time. Distance learning option. At least 36 total credits required. *Concentration:* supply chain management.

MTAX—Master of Science in Taxation Full-time and part-time. At least 30 total credits required. *Concentration:* taxation.

RESOURCES AND SERVICES Access to Internet/World Wide Web, online (class) registration, and online grade reports available. *Personal computer requirements:* Graduate business students are strongly recommended to purchase or lease a personal computer. *Special opportunities include:* An international exchange program and an internship program are available. *Placement services include:* Alumni network, career counseling/planning, electronic job bank, resume referral, career fairs, job interviews arranged, and resume preparation.

EXPENSES *Tuition:* Full-time: $26,280. Part-time: $13,140 per year. *Required fees:* Full-time: $154. *Graduate housing:* Room and board costs vary by campus location, number of occupants, type of accommodation, and type of board plan. *Typical cost:* $10,960 (including board).

FINANCIAL AID (2007–08) 179 students received aid, including fellowships, grants, loans, research assistantships, and scholarships. Aid is available to part-time students. *Financial aid application deadline:* 5/1.

Financial Aid Contact Ms. Judith Lewis Logue, Director of Financial Aid Services, 5998 Alcala Park, San Diego, CA 92110-2492. *Phone:* 619-260-4720. *Fax:* 619-260-7508. *E-mail:* jllogue@sandiego.edu.

INTERNATIONAL STUDENTS 12% of students enrolled are international students. *Services and facilities:* Counseling/support services, ESL/language courses, International student organization, Orientation, Visa Services. Financial aid is available to international students. *Required with application:* TOEFL with recommended score of 237 (computer) or 580 (paper); TWE with recommended score of 4.5; proof of adequate funds; proof of health/immunizations.

International Student Contact Ms. Kacy Kilner, Admissions Director, MBA Programs, 5998 Alcala Park, San Diego, CA 92110-2492. *Phone:* 619-260-4860. *E-mail:* mba@sandiego.edu.

APPLICATION *Required:* GMAT, application form, baccalaureate/first degree, 3 letters of recommendation, personal statement, resume/curriculum vitae, transcripts of college work. *Recommended:* 2 years of work experience. *Application fee:* $45. Applications for domestic and international students are processed on a rolling basis.

Application Contact Ms. Kacy Kilner, Admissions Director, MBA Programs, 5998 Alcala Park, San Diego, CA 92110-2492. *Phone:* 619-260-4860. *E-mail:* mba@sandiego.edu.

University of San Francisco
Masagung Graduate School of Management

San Francisco, California

Phone: 415-422-2221 **Fax:** 415-422-6315 **E-mail:** ghtan@usfca.edu
Business Program(s) Web Site: http://www.usfca.edu/mba

Graduate Business Unit Enrollment *Total:* 307 (203 full-time; 104 part-time; 140 women; 112 international). *Average Age:* 28.

Graduate Business Faculty *Total:* 86 (45 full-time; 41 part-time).

Admissions *Applied:* 416. *Admitted:* 254. *Enrolled:* 122. *Average GMAT:* 570. *Average GPA:* 3.1

Academic Calendar Semesters.

Accreditation AACSB—The Association to Advance Collegiate Schools of Business.

After Graduation (Class of 2006–07) *Employed within 3 months of graduation:* 44%. *Average starting salary:* $84,000.

DEGREES DDS/MBA • EMBA • JD/MBA • MA/MBA • MBA • MBA/MAPS • MBA/MS • MBA/MSF

DDS/MBA—DDS (from UCSF)/MBA Part-time. Must be a current UCSF dental student to apply. 48 to 60 months to complete program. *Concentration:* combined degrees.

EMBA—MBA for Executives Part-time. Minimum 7 years' work experience with 2 years in a managerial position and interview required. Up to 50 total credits required. 19 months to complete program. *Concentration:* executive programs.

JD/MBA Full-time. LSAT, JD minimum GPA of 2.5 (must be current USF Law School student to apply). At least 128 total credits required. 48 to 60 months to complete program. *Concentration:* combined degrees.

MA/MBA—Intensive One-Year MBA Full-time. Undergraduate degree in accredited business school within the last 5 years required. At least 48 total credits required. 12 to 60 months to complete program. *Concentrations:* entrepreneurship, finance, international business, marketing.

MA/MBA—Intensive Part-Time MBA Part-time. Undergraduate degree in accredited business school within the last 5 years required. At least 48 total credits required. 21 to 60 months to complete program. *Concentrations:* entrepreneurship, finance, international business, marketing.

MA/MBA—Part-Time MBA Part-time. At least 56 total credits required. 33 to 60 months to complete program. *Concentrations:* entrepreneurship, finance, international business, marketing.

MBA—Full-Time MBA Full-time. At least 56 total credits required. 21 to 60 months to complete program. *Concentrations:* entrepreneurship, finance, international business, marketing.

MBA/MAPS—MAPS/MBA Full-time and part-time. GRE and GMAT required. At least 76 total credits required. 36 to 48 months to complete program. *Concentration:* combined degrees.

MBA/MS—MS in Environmental Management/MBA Full-time and part-time. At least 74 total credits required. 36 to 48 months to complete program. *Concentration:* combined degrees.

MBA/MSF—MSFA/MBA Full-time and part-time. Minimum GPA for first 19 units of MSFA program is 3.0 (must be current USF MSFA student to apply). At least 68 total credits required. 36 to 48 months to complete program. *Concentration:* combined degrees.

RESOURCES AND SERVICES 225 on-campus PCs are available to graduate business students. Access to Internet/World Wide Web, online (class) registration, and online grade reports available. *Personal computer requirements:* Graduate business students are strongly recommended to purchase or lease a personal computer. *Placement services include:* Alumni network, career placement, job search course, career counseling/planning, electronic job bank, resume referral, career fairs, job interviews arranged, resume preparation, and career library.

EXPENSES *Tuition:* Part-time: $1125 per credit. *Tuition (international):* Part-time: $1125 per credit. *Required fees:* Full-time: $150. Tuition and/or fees vary by class time, number of courses or credits taken, and academic program. *Graduate housing:* Room and board costs vary by number of occupants and type of accommodation.

FINANCIAL AID (2007–08) 15 students received aid, including loans and scholarships.

Financial Aid Contact Susan Murphy, Financial Aid Director, 2130 Fulton Street, San Francisco, CA 94117. *Phone:* 415-422-6303.

University of San Francisco (continued)

INTERNATIONAL STUDENTS 36% of students enrolled are international students. *Services and facilities:* Counseling/support services, ESL/language courses, Housing location assistance, International student housing, International student organization, Language tutoring, Orientation, Visa Services, Multicultural and international student services. Financial aid is available to international students. *Required with application:* IELT with recommended score of 7; TOEFL with recommended score of 250 (computer), 600 (paper), or 100 (Internet); proof of adequate funds; proof of health/immunizations.

International Student Contact Ms. Lisa Kosiewicz, Assistant Director, International Student Services, 2130 Fulton Street, University Center 402, San Francisco, CA 94117-1080. *Phone:* 415-422-2654. *Fax:* 415-422-2412. *E-mail:* lkosiewicz@usfca.edu.

APPLICATION *Required:* GMAT, application form, baccalaureate/first degree, essay, 2 letters of recommendation, personal statement, resume/curriculum vitae, transcripts of college work, 2 years of work experience. *Application fee:* $55. Applications for domestic and international students are processed on a rolling basis.

Application Contact Ms. Grace Tan, Associate Director, MBA Admissions, 2130 Fulton Street, San Francisco, CA 94117. *Phone:* 415-422-2221. *Fax:* 415-422-6315. *E-mail:* ghtan@usfca.edu.

University of Southern California

School of Business

Los Angeles, California

Phone: 213-740-7846 **Fax:** 213-749-8520 **E-mail:** marshallmba@marshall.usc.edu

Business Program(s) Web Site: http://www.marshall.usc.edu

Graduate Business Unit Enrollment *Total:* 1,957 (1,145 full-time; 812 part-time; 612 women; 334 international). *Average Age:* 28.

Graduate Business Faculty *Total:* 150 (137 full-time; 13 part-time).

Admissions *Applied:* 2,959. *Admitted:* 1,160. *Enrolled:* 753. *Average GMAT:* 689. *Average GPA:* 3.3

Academic Calendar Semesters.

Accreditation AACSB—The Association to Advance Collegiate Schools of Business.

After Graduation (Class of 2006–07) *Employed within 3 months of graduation:* 94%. *Average starting salary:* $88,841.

DEGREES DDS/MBA • EMBA • EdD/MBA • JD/MBA • JD/MBTax • M Acc • MBA • MBA/MA • MBA/MPI • MBA/MRED • MBA/MS • MBA/MSW • MBT • MD/MBA • MM • MS • Pharm D/MBA

DDS/MBA—Doctor of Dental Surgery/Master of Business Administration Full-time. Successful completion of first year of dental school. At least 229 total credits required. Minimum of 57 months to complete program. *Concentration:* combined degrees.

EMBA—Executive Master of Business Administration Part-time. At least 60 total credits required. 22 to 60 months to complete program. *Concentration:* management.

EMBA—Global Executive Master of Business Administration Part-time. Program is taught in Shanghai. At least 60 total credits required. 21 to 60 months to complete program. *Concentration:* international management.

EdD/MBA—MBA/Doctor of Education Full-time and part-time. At least 90 total credits required. 36 to 60 months to complete program. *Concentration:* combined degrees.

JD/MBA—Juris Doctor/Master of Business Administration Full-time. At least 91 total credits required. 48 to 60 months to complete program. *Concentration:* combined degrees.

JD/MBTax—Juris Doctor/Master of Business Taxation Full-time. Distance learning option. 89 to 119 total credits required. 48 to 60 months to complete program. *Concentration:* combined degrees.

M Acc—Master of Accounting Full-time. 33 to 48 total credits required. 9 to 60 months to complete program. *Concentration:* accounting.

MBA—International Business Education and Research (IBEAR) MBA Full-time. At least 56 total credits required. 11 to 60 months to complete program. *Concentration:* international business.

MBA—MBA for Professionals and Managers Part-time. At least 63 total credits required. 33 to 60 months to complete program. *Concentrations:* entrepreneurship, finance, financial management/planning, health administration, information management, information systems, international and area business studies, international business, management, management consulting, management information systems, marketing, new venture management, operations management, real estate, strategic management, technology management.

MBA—Marshall MBA Full-time. At least 63 total credits required. 21 to 60 months to complete program. *Concentrations:* entrepreneurship, finance, financial management/planning, health administration, information management, information systems, international and area business studies, international business, management, management consulting, management information systems, marketing, new venture management, operations management, real estate, strategic management, technology management.

MBA/MA—Master of Business Administration/Master of Arts in East Asian Area Studies Full-time and part-time. Distance learning option. At least 72 total credits required. 36 to 60 months to complete program. *Concentration:* combined degrees.

MBA/MA—Master of Business Administration/Master of Arts in Jewish Communal Service Full-time and part-time. At least 95 total credits required. 27 to 60 months to complete program. *Concentration:* combined degrees.

MBA/MPI—Master of Business Administration/Master of Planning Full-time and part-time. At least 84 total credits required. 36 to 60 months to complete program. *Concentration:* combined degrees.

MBA/MRED—Master of Business Administration/Master of Real Estate Development Full-time and part-time. At least 82 total credits required. 36 to 60 months to complete program. *Concentration:* combined degrees.

MBA/MS—Master of Business Administration/Master of Science in Gerontology Full-time and part-time. At least 78 total credits required. 36 to 60 months to complete program. *Concentration:* combined degrees.

MBA/MS—Master of Business Administration/Master of Science in Industrial and Systems Engineering Full-time and part-time. At least 66 total credits required. 24 to 60 months to complete program. *Concentration:* combined degrees.

MBA/MSW—Master of Business Administration/Master of Social Work Full-time and part-time. At least 96 total credits required. 36 to 60 months to complete program. *Concentration:* combined degrees.

MBT—Master of Business Taxation Full-time and part-time. At least 33 total credits required. 9 to 60 months to complete program. *Concentration:* taxation.

MD/MBA—Doctor of Medicine/Master of Business Administration Full-time. Successful completion of the first two years in the Keck School of Medicine. At least 48 total credits required. Minimum of 66 months to complete program. *Concentration:* combined degrees.

MM—Master of Medical Management Part-time. 33 total credits required. 17 months to complete program. *Concentrations:* health administration, management.

MS—Master of Science in Business Administration Full-time and part-time. MBA degree from an AACSB-accredited institution. At least 26 total credits required. 9 to 60 months to complete program. *Concentrations:* accounting, entrepreneurship, finance, financial management/planning, health administration, information management, information systems, international and area business studies, international business, international finance, management, management consulting, management information systems, marketing, new venture management, operations management, real estate, strategic management, student designed, supply chain management, taxation, technology management.

Pharm D/MBA—Doctor of Pharmacy/Master of Business Administration Full-time. Successful completion of the first year in the School of Pharmacy. At least 156 total credits required. Minimum of 57 months to complete program. *Concentration:* combined degrees.

RESOURCES AND SERVICES 1,372 on-campus PCs are available to graduate business students. Access to Internet/World Wide Web, online (class) registration, and online grade reports available. *Personal computer requirements:* Graduate business students are strongly recommended to purchase or lease a personal computer. *Special opportunities include:* An international exchange program and an internship program are available. *Placement services include:* Alumni network, career placement, job search course, career counseling/planning, electronic job bank, resume referral, career fairs, job interviews arranged, resume preparation, and career library.

EXPENSES *Tuition:* Full-time: $35,212. Part-time: $1217 per credit. *Tuition (international):* Full-time: $35,212. Part-time: $1217 per credit. *Required fees:* Full-time: $598. Tuition and/or fees vary by number of courses or credits taken and academic program. *Graduate housing:* Room and board costs vary by campus location, number of occupants, type of accommodation, and type of board plan. *Typical cost:* $17,000 (including board), $8200 (room only).

FINANCIAL AID (2007–08) Fellowships, grants, loans, research assistantships, scholarships, teaching assistantships, and work study. Aid is available to part-time students. *Financial aid application deadline:* 2/1.

Financial Aid Contact Ms. Grace Kim, Senior Associate Director of MBA Admissions, Popovich Hall 308, Los Angeles, CA 90089-2633. *Phone:* 213-740-7846. *Fax:* 213-749-8520. *E-mail:* gkim@marshall.usc.edu.

INTERNATIONAL STUDENTS 17% of students enrolled are international students. *Services and facilities:* Counseling/support services, ESL/language courses, Housing location assistance, International student housing, International student organization, Language tutoring, Orientation, Visa Services, International loan program. Financial aid is available to international students. *Required with application:* TOEFL with recommended score of 600 (paper) or 100 (Internet); proof of adequate funds; proof of health/immunizations.

International Student Contact Ms. Veronica Ho, Associate Director of MBA Admissions, Popovich Hall 308, Los Angeles, CA 90089-2633. *Phone:* 213-740-7846. *Fax:* 213-740-8520. *E-mail:* veronica.ho@marshall.usc.edu.

APPLICATION *Required:* GMAT, application form, baccalaureate/first degree, essay, 2 letters of recommendation, personal statement, resume/curriculum vitae, transcripts of college work. *Recommended:* Interview, work experience. *Application fee:* $150. *Deadlines:* 12/1 for fall, 1/15 for winter, 2/15 for spring, 4/1 for summer, 1/15 for fall (international).

Application Contact Mr. Keith Vaughn, Assistant Dean of MBA Admissions, Popovich Hall 308, Los Angeles, CA 90089-2633. *Phone:* 213-740-7846. *Fax:* 213-749-8520. *E-mail:* marshallmba@marshall.usc.edu.

University of the Pacific
Eberhardt School of Business
Stockton, California

Phone: 209-946-2629 **Fax:** 209-946-2586 **E-mail:** mba@pacific.edu

Business Program(s) Web Site: http://www.pacific.edu/mba

Graduate Business Unit Enrollment *Total:* 51 (42 full-time; 9 part-time; 15 women; 5 international). *Average Age:* 24.

Graduate Business Faculty *Total:* 22 (20 full-time; 2 part-time).

Admissions *Applied:* 54. *Admitted:* 30. *Enrolled:* 21. *Average GMAT:* 552. *Average GPA:* 3.39

Academic Calendar Semesters.

Accreditation AACSB—The Association to Advance Collegiate Schools of Business.

After Graduation (Class of 2006–07) *Employed within 3 months of graduation:* 71%. *Average starting salary:* $45,308.

DEGREES JD/MBA • MBA • Pharm D/MBA

JD/MBA Full-time. Must apply and be accepted for both degree programs. 52 total credits required. 48 to 60 months to complete program. *Concentrations:* entrepreneurship, finance, management, marketing.

MBA—Full-Time MBA Full-time. 52 total credits required. 16 to 60 months to complete program. *Concentrations:* entrepreneurship, finance, management, marketing.

MBA—Peace Corps/MBA (Master's International) Full-time. Must apply and be accepted for MBA and by Peace Corps for service. 52 total credits required. 40 to 60 months to complete program. *Concentrations:* entrepreneurship, finance, management, marketing.

Pharm D/MBA—PharmD/ MBA Full-time. Must apply and be accepted for by both degree programs. 52 total credits required. 48 to 60 months to complete program. *Concentrations:* entrepreneurship, finance, management, marketing.

RESOURCES AND SERVICES 24 on-campus PCs are available to graduate business students. Access to Internet/World Wide Web, online (class) registration, and online grade reports available. *Personal computer requirements:* Graduate business students are strongly recommended to purchase or lease a personal computer. *Special opportunities include:* An international exchange program and an internship program are available. *Placement services include:* Alumni network, career placement, job search course, career counseling/planning, electronic job bank, resume referral, career fairs, job interviews arranged, resume preparation, and career library.

EXPENSES *Tuition:* Full-time: $30,557. *Tuition (international):* Full-time: $30,557. *Required fees:* Full-time: $300. *Graduate housing:* Room and board costs vary by number of occupants, type of accommodation, and type of board plan. *Typical cost:* $9500 (including board).

FINANCIAL AID (2007–08) 16 students received aid, including loans, research assistantships, and scholarships. *Financial aid application deadline:* 5/1.

Financial Aid Contact Financial Aid Office, 3601 Pacific Avenue, Stockton, CA 95211-0197. *Phone:* 209-946-2421. *Fax:* 209-946-2758. *E-mail:* financialaid@pacific.edu.

INTERNATIONAL STUDENTS 10% of students enrolled are international students. *Services and facilities:* Counseling/support services, International student housing, International student organization, Orientation, Visa Services. Financial aid is available to international students. *Required with application:* TOEFL with recommended score of 213 (computer) or 550 (paper); proof of adequate funds; proof of health/immunizations.

International Student Contact Office of International Programs and Services, 3601 Pacific Avenue, Stockton, CA 95211-0197. *Phone:* 209-946-2246. *Fax:* 209-946-2094. *E-mail:* ips@pacific.edu.

APPLICATION *Required:* GMAT, application form, baccalaureate/first degree, essay, interview, 2 letters of recommendation, personal statement, resume/curriculum vitae, transcripts of college work. *Recommended:* 2 years of work experience. *Application fee:* $75. Applications for domestic and international students are processed on a rolling basis.

Application Contact Mr. Christopher Lozano, Director of Student Recruitment, MBA Program Office, 3601 Pacific Avenue, Stockton, CA 95211-0197. *Phone:* 209-946-2629. *Fax:* 209-946-2586. *E-mail:* mba@pacific.edu.

See full description on page 752.

University of the West
Department of Business Administration
Rosemead, California

Phone: 626-656-2120 **Fax:** 626-571-1413 **E-mail:** graceh@uwest.edu
Business Program(s) Web Site: http://www.uwest.edu

University of the West (continued)

DEGREES EMBA • MBA

EMBA—Executive Master of Business Administration Full-time and part-time. At least 42 total credits required. Minimum of 12 months to complete program. *Concentrations:* finance, information technology, international business, nonprofit organization.

MBA—Master of Business Administration Full-time and part-time. At least 39 total credits required. Minimum of 24 months to complete program. *Concentrations:* finance, information technology, international business, nonprofit management.

RESOURCES AND SERVICES 20 on-campus PCs are available to graduate business students. Access to Internet/World Wide Web and online (class) registration available. *Personal computer requirements:* Graduate business students are strongly recommended to purchase or lease a personal computer. *Special opportunities include:* An international exchange program and an internship program are available. *Placement services include:* Alumni network, career placement, career counseling/planning, electronic job bank, resume referral, career fairs, and resume preparation.

Application Contact Ms. Grace Hsiao, Registrar, 1409 North Walnut Grove Avenue, Rosemead, CA 91770. *Phone:* 626-656-2120. *Fax:* 626-571-1413. *E-mail:* graceh@uwest.edu.

Vanguard University of Southern California

School of Business and Management

Costa Mesa, California

Phone: 714-556-3610 Ext. 4141 **E-mail:** dlevasheff@vanguard.edu

Business Program(s) Web Site: http://www.vanguard.edu/mba

Graduate Business Unit Enrollment *Total:* 20 (14 full-time; 6 part-time; 6 women; 1 international). *Average Age:* 35..

Graduate Business Faculty *Total:* 6 (2 full-time; 4 part-time).

Admissions *Applied:* 15. *Admitted:* 12. *Enrolled:* 12. *Average GPA:* 3.2

Academic Calendar Trimesters.

DEGREE MBA

MBA—Master of Business Administration Full-time and part-time. 20 to 60 months to complete program. *Concentration:* general MBA.

RESOURCES AND SERVICES 40 on-campus PCs are available to graduate business students. Access to Internet/World Wide Web, online (class) registration, and online grade reports available. *Personal computer requirements:* Graduate business students are not required to have a personal computer. *Placement services include:* Career counseling/planning.

EXPENSES *Tuition:* Full-time: $17,850. Part-time: $8925 per year.

FINANCIAL AID (2007–08) 1 student received aid, including loans, scholarships, and work study. Aid is available to part-time students. *Financial aid application deadline:* 3/2.

Financial Aid Contact Robyn Fournier, Director of Financial Aid, 55 Fair Drive, Costa Mesa, CA 92626. *Phone:* 714-556-3610 Ext. 4250. *E-mail:* rfournier@vanguard.edu.

INTERNATIONAL STUDENTS 5% of students enrolled are international students. *Services and facilities:* Counseling/support services, Visa Services. Financial aid is available to international students. *Required with application:* TOEFL with recommended score of 213 (computer) or 550 (paper); proof of adequate funds.

International Student Contact Drake Levasheff, Director of Graduate Admissions, 55 Fair Drive, Costa Mesa, CA 92626. *Phone:* 714-556-3610 Ext. 4141. *E-mail:* dlevasheff@vanguard.edu.

APPLICATION *Required:* Application form, baccalaureate/first degree, essay, interview, 2 letters of recommendation, personal statement, resume/curriculum vitae, transcripts of college work, 5 years of work experience. School will accept GMAT and MAT. *Application fee:* $45. Applications for domestic and international students are processed on a rolling basis.

Application Contact Drake Levasheff, Director of Graduate Admissions, 55 Fair Drive, Costa Mesa, CA 92626. *Phone:* 714-556-3610 Ext. 4141. *E-mail:* dlevasheff@vanguard.edu.

Woodbury University

School of Business and Management

Burbank, California

Phone: 818-767-0888 Ext. 224 **Fax:** 818-767-7520 **E-mail:** frank.frias@woodbury.edu

Business Program(s) Web Site: http://www.woodbury.edu

Accreditation ACBSP—The American Council of Business Schools and Programs.

DEGREE MBA

MBA—Master of Business Administration Full-time and part-time. Undergraduate degree from accredited university required. Accelerated MBA requires 5 years work experience. 36 to 52 total credits required. 24 to 36 months to complete program. *Concentrations:* accounting, economics, electronic commerce (E-commerce), finance, information technology, international business, management, marketing.

RESOURCES AND SERVICES 270 on-campus PCs are available to graduate business students. Access to Internet/World Wide Web, online (class) registration, and online grade reports available. *Personal computer requirements:* Graduate business students are strongly recommended to purchase or lease a personal computer. *Placement services include:* Alumni network, career placement, job search course, career counseling/planning, electronic job bank, resume referral, career fairs, job interviews arranged, resume preparation, and career library.

Application Contact Frank Frias, Director of MBA Recruitment, 7500 Glenoaks Boulevard, Burbank, CA 91510-7846. *Phone:* 818-767-0888 Ext. 224. *Fax:* 818-767-7520. *E-mail:* frank.frias@woodbury.edu.

COLORADO

Argosy University, Denver

College of Business

Denver, Colorado

Phone: 303-248-2700 **Fax:** 303-248-2715

Business Program(s) Web Site: http://www.argosy.edu/denver

DEGREES DBA • MBA • MS

DBA—Doctor of Business Administration (DBA) *Concentrations:* accounting, information systems, international business, management, marketing.

MBA—Master of Business Administration (MBA) *Concentrations:* finance, health administration, information systems, international business, management, marketing, public management.

MS—Master of Science in Management (MSM) *Concentration:* management.

Financial Aid Contact Director of Admissions, 1200 Lincoln Street, Denver, CO 80203. *Phone:* 303-248-2700. *Fax:* 303-248-2715.

International Student Contact Director of Admissions, 1200 Lincoln Street, Denver, CO 80203. *Phone:* 303-248-2700. *Fax:* 303-248-2715.

Application Contact Director of Admissions, 1200 Lincoln Street, Denver, CO 80203. *Phone:* 303-248-2700. *Fax:* 303-248-2715.

See full description on page 566.

College for Financial Planning
Program in Financial Planning

Greenwood Village, Colorado

Phone: 303-220-1200 Ext. 4992 **Fax:** 303-220-4811 **E-mail:** julianna.sanchez@apollogrp.edu

Business Program(s) Web Site: http://www.cffp.edu

Graduate Business Unit Enrollment *Total:* 850 (850 part-time).

Graduate Business Faculty *Total:* 20 (10 full-time; 10 part-time).

Admissions *Applied:* 150. *Admitted:* 135. *Enrolled:* 117. *Average GPA:* 3.3

Academic Calendar Five 8-week semesters.

After Graduation (Class of 2006–07) *Employed within 3 months of graduation:* 95%. *Average starting salary:* $180,000.

DEGREES   MS • MS/MS

MS—Master of Science Financial Analysis Part-time. Distance learning option. At least 45 total credits required. Minimum of 24 months to complete program. *Concentrations:* finance, financial management/planning.

MS—Master of Science in Financial Planning Part-time. Distance learning option. At least 36 total credits required. Minimum of 18 months to complete program. *Concentrations:* finance, financial management/planning.

MS/MS—Finance Part-time. Distance learning option. 36 to 48 total credits required. 18 to 24 months to complete program. *Concentration:* finance.

RESOURCES AND SERVICES Access to Internet/World Wide Web, online (class) registration, and online grade reports available. *Personal computer requirements:* Graduate business students are required to have a personal computer.

EXPENSES *Tuition:* Part-time: $295 per semester hour. *Tuition (international):* Part-time: $295 per semester hour.

FINANCIAL AID (2007–08) 5 students received aid, including scholarships. Aid is available to part-time students. *Financial aid application deadline:* 4/1.

INTERNATIONAL STUDENTS Financial aid is available to international students. *Required with application:* TOEFL with recommended score of 213 (computer) or 550 (paper).

International Student Contact Ms. Viviane Price, Registrar, Administrative Offices, 8000 East Maplewood Avenue, Suite 200, Greenwood Village, CO 80111. *Phone:* 303-220-1200 Ext. 4868. *Fax:* 303-220-4811. *E-mail:* viviane.price@apollogrp.edu.

APPLICATION *Required:* Application form, baccalaureate/first degree, essay, personal statement, transcripts of college work. *Recommended:* Resume/curriculum vitae, work experience. *Application fee:* $75.

Application Contact Ms. JuliAnna Sanchez, Senior Director of Enrollment, Administrative Offices, 8000 East Maplewood Avenue, Suite 200, Greenwood Village, CO 80111. *Phone:* 303-220-1200 Ext. 4992. *Fax:* 303-220-4811. *E-mail:* julianna.sanchez@apollogrp.edu.

Colorado Christian University
Program in Business Administration

Lakewood, Colorado

Phone: 303-963-3300 **Fax:** 303-963-3301 **E-mail:** agsadmission@ccu.edu

Business Program(s) Web Site: http://luke.ccu.edu/mba/

DEGREE   MBA

MBA—Master of Business Administration Full-time and part-time. Distance learning option. GMAT, 3 essays, 2 letters of recommendation, a resume and a transcript are required. 33 to 39 total credits required. 18 to 48 months to complete program. *Concentration:* general MBA.

RESOURCES AND SERVICES 94 on-campus PCs are available to graduate business students. Access to Internet/World Wide Web, online (class) registration, and online grade reports available. *Personal computer requirements:* Graduate business students are strongly recommended to purchase or lease a personal computer. *Special opportunities include:* An internship program is available. *Placement services include:* Alumni network, career counseling/planning, resume referral, career fairs, and resume preparation.

Application Contact College of Adult and Graduate Studies, Master of Business Administration Program, 8787 West Alameda Avenue, Lakewood, CO 80226. *Phone:* 303-963-3300. *Fax:* 303-963-3301. *E-mail:* agsadmission@ccu.edu.

Colorado State University
College of Business

Fort Collins, Colorado

Phone: 970-491-3704 **Fax:** 970-491-3481 **E-mail:** rachel.stoll@colostate.edu

Business Program(s) Web Site: http://www.CSUdistanceMBA.com

Graduate Business Unit Enrollment *Total:* 835 (835 part-time; 292 women; 84 international). *Average Age:* 34.

Graduate Business Faculty *Total:* 66 (52 full-time; 14 part-time).

Admissions *Applied:* 403. *Admitted:* 343. *Enrolled:* 317. *Average GMAT:* 580. *Average GPA:* 3.2

Academic Calendar Semesters.

Accreditation AACSB—The Association to Advance Collegiate Schools of Business.

DEGREES   M Acc • M Mgt • MBA • MS • MSBA

M Acc—Master of Accountancy (MAcc) Full-time and part-time. Preparation for the CPA. 32 total credits required. 12 to 36 months to complete program. *Concentration:* accounting.

M Mgt—Master of Management Practice (MMP) Full-time. 4+1 program focusing on business minors in undergraduate studies. 30 total credits required. 12 months to complete program. *Concentration:* business education.

MBA—Denver Executive MBA Part-time. 8+ years of professional work experience required. At least 40 total credits required. Minimum of 21 months to complete program. *Concentration:* executive programs.

MBA—Distance MBA Program Part-time. Distance learning option. 4+ years of professional experience required. At least 36 total credits required. 21 to 60 months to complete program. *Concentration:* general MBA.

MBA—Professional MBA Part-time. 4+ years of professional experience required. At least 36 total credits required. Minimum of 21 months to complete program. *Concentration:* general MBA.

Colorado State University (continued)

MS—MSBA—CIS Full-time and part-time. At least 30 total credits required. Minimum of 12 months to complete program. *Concentration:* management information systems.

MSBA—Global Social and Sustainable Enterprises (GSSE) Summer program bringing economic sustainability projects to developing countries. 39 total credits required. 18 months to complete program. *Concentration:* international economics.

RESOURCES AND SERVICES 250 on-campus PCs are available to graduate business students. Access to Internet/World Wide Web, online (class) registration, and online grade reports available. *Personal computer requirements:* Graduate business students are required to have a personal computer. *Placement services include:* Alumni network, career placement, career counseling/planning, electronic job bank, resume referral, career fairs, job interviews arranged, resume preparation, and career library.

FINANCIAL AID (2007–08) 40 students received aid, including fellowships, loans, research assistantships, and scholarships. Aid is available to part-time students. *Financial aid application deadline:* 6/1.

Financial Aid Contact Ms. Eileen Griego, Student Financial Services Program Coordinator, 103 Administration Annex, 8024 Campus Delivery, Fort Collins, CO 80523-8024. *Phone:* 970-491-6321. *Fax:* 970-491-5010. *E-mail:* eileen.griego@colostate.edu.

INTERNATIONAL STUDENTS 10% of students enrolled are international students. *Services and facilities:* Counseling/support services, ESL/language courses, Housing location assistance, International student housing, International student organization, Language tutoring, Orientation, Visa Services. Financial aid is available to international students. *Required with application:* IELT with recommended score of 6.5; TOEFL with recommended score of 267 (computer), 565 (paper), or 86 (Internet); proof of adequate funds; proof of health/immunizations.

International Student Contact Ms. Rachel Stoll, Graduate Admissions Coordinator, 164 Rockwell Hall, 1270 Campus Delivery, Fort Collins, CO 80523-1270. *Phone:* 970-491-3704. *Fax:* 970-491-3481. *E-mail:* rachel.stoll@colostate.edu.

APPLICATION *Required:* GMAT, application form, baccalaureate/first degree, 3 letters of recommendation, personal statement, resume/curriculum vitae, transcripts of college work, 4 years of work experience. School will accept GRE. *Application fee:* $50. Applications for domestic and international students are processed on a rolling basis.

Application Contact Ms. Rachel Stoll, Graduate Admissions Coordinator, 164 Rockwell Hall, 1270 Campus Delivery, Fort Collins, CO 80523-1270. *Phone:* 970-491-3704. *Fax:* 970-491-3481. *E-mail:* rachel.stoll@colostate.edu.

See full description on page 596.

Colorado State University–Pueblo

Malik and Seeme Hasan School of Business

Pueblo, Colorado

Phone: 719-549-2997 **Fax:** 719-549-2419 **E-mail:** jon.valdez@colostate-pueblo.edu

Business Program(s) Web Site: http://www.hsb.colostate-pueblo.edu/

Graduate Business Unit Enrollment *Total:* 96 (45 full-time; 51 part-time; 40 women; 23 international).

Graduate Business Faculty 9 full-time.

Admissions *Average GMAT:* 490. *Average GPA:* 3.3

Academic Calendar Semesters.

Accreditation AACSB—The Association to Advance Collegiate Schools of Business.

After Graduation (Class of 2006–07) *Employed within 3 months of graduation:* 75%. *Average starting salary:* $55,000.

DEGREE MBA

MBA—Master of Business Administration Full-time and part-time. Minimum GMAT score of 450 and undergraduate GPA of 3.0 required. At least 36 total credits required. 12 to 72 months to complete program. *Concentration:* management.

RESOURCES AND SERVICES 600 on-campus PCs are available to graduate business students. Access to Internet/World Wide Web, online (class) registration, and online grade reports available. *Personal computer requirements:* Graduate business students are strongly recommended to purchase or lease a personal computer. *Special opportunities include:* An international exchange program and an internship program are available. *Placement services include:* Career placement, job search course, career counseling/planning, resume referral, career fairs, job interviews arranged, resume preparation, and career library.

FINANCIAL AID (2007–08) 11 students received aid, including loans, research assistantships, scholarships, and teaching assistantships. Aid is available to part-time students.

Financial Aid Contact Ofelia Morales, Director, Student Financial Services, 2200 Bonforte Boulevard, Pueblo, CO 81001-4901. *Phone:* 719-549-2753. *Fax:* 719-549-2088. *E-mail:* ofelia.morales@colostate-pueblo.edu.

INTERNATIONAL STUDENTS 24% of students enrolled are international students. *Services and facilities:* Counseling/support services, ESL/language courses, Housing location assistance, International student housing, International student organization, Language tutoring, Orientation, Visa Services. Financial aid is not available to international students. *Required with application:* TOEFL with recommended score of 550 (paper); proof of adequate funds; proof of health/immunizations.

International Student Contact Annie Williams, Coordinator of the International Student Center, 2200 Bonforte Boulevard, Pueblo, CO 81001-4901. *Phone:* 719-549-2116. *Fax:* 719-549-2938. *E-mail:* annie.williams@colostate-pueblo.edu.

APPLICATION *Required:* GMAT, application form, baccalaureate/first degree, transcripts of college work. *Application fee:* $35. Applications for domestic and international students are processed on a rolling basis.

Application Contact Mr. Jon Valdez, Program Assistant, 2200 Bonforte Boulevard, Pueblo, CO 81001-4901. *Phone:* 719-549-2997. *Fax:* 719-549-2419. *E-mail:* jon.valdez@colostate-pueblo.edu.

DeVry University

Keller Graduate School of Management

Colorado Springs, Colorado

Phone: 719-632-3000

DEGREES MAFM • MBA • MHRM • MISM • MPA • MPM

MAFM—Master of Accounting and Financial Management *Concentrations:* accounting, financial management/planning.

MBA—Master of Business Administration *Concentration:* general MBA.

MHRM—Master of Human Resources Management *Concentration:* human resources management.

MISM—Master of Information Systems Management *Concentration:* information systems.

MPA—Master of Public Administration *Concentration:* public policy and administration.

MPM—Master of Project Management *Concentration:* project management.

Application Contact Admissions Office, Colorado Springs Center, 1175 Kelly Johnson Boulevard, Colorado Springs, CO 80920. *Phone:* 719-632-3000.

Jones International University
Graduate School of Business Administration

Centennial, Colorado

Phone: 303-784-8274 **Fax:** 303-799-0966 **E-mail:** ecadman@jones.com

Business Program(s) Web Site: http://www.jonesinternational.edu/

DEGREES MA • MBA

MA—Master of Arts in Business Communication Full-time and part-time. Distance learning option. 2.5 GPA on all previous coursework and documented proficiency in public speaking and business writing required. At least 36 total credits required. 3 to 60 months to complete program. *Concentrations:* business studies, entrepreneurship, leadership, project management.

MBA—Master of Business Administration Full-time and part-time. Distance learning option. 2.5 GPA on all previous coursework required. At least 42 total credits required. 3 to 60 months to complete program. *Concentrations:* accounting, conflict resolution management, entrepreneurship, finance, health care, information technology, international management, project management.

RESOURCES AND SERVICES Access to Internet/World Wide Web, online (class) registration, and online grade reports available. *Personal computer requirements:* Graduate business students are strongly recommended to purchase or lease a personal computer. *Placement services include:* Alumni network and career library.

Application Contact Mr. Eric Cadman, Manager of Admissions, 9697 East Mineral Avenue, Centennial, CO 80112. *Phone:* 303-784-8274. *Fax:* 303-799-0966. *E-mail:* ecadman@jones.com.

Mesa State College
Department of Business

Grand Junction, Colorado

Phone: 970-248-1778 **Fax:** 970-248-1730 **E-mail:** jsandova@mesastate.edu

Business Program(s) Web Site: http://www.mesastate.edu/schools/sbps/mba/index.htm

Graduate Business Faculty 18 full-time.

Admissions *Applied:* 12. *Admitted:* 12. *Enrolled:* 4. *Average GMAT:* 477. *Average GPA:* 3.2

Academic Calendar Semesters.

After Graduation (Class of 2006–07) *Employed within 3 months of graduation:* 98%. *Average starting salary:* $35,000.

DEGREE MBA

MBA—Master of Business Administration Full-time and part-time. 36 total credits required. *Concentration:* general MBA.

RESOURCES AND SERVICES 178 on-campus PCs are available to graduate business students. Access to Internet/World Wide Web, online (class) registration, and online grade reports available. *Personal computer requirements:* Graduate business students are not required to have a personal computer. *Placement services include:* Alumni network, career placement, job search course, career counseling/planning, electronic job bank, resume referral, career fairs, job interviews arranged, resume preparation, and career library.

EXPENSES *Tuition (state resident):* Full-time: $3000. Part-time: $495 per course. *Tuition (nonresident):* Full-time: $9072. Part-time: $1512 per course.

FINANCIAL AID (2007–08) Grants and loans. Aid is available to part-time students. *Financial aid application deadline:* 3/1.

Financial Aid Contact Mr. Curt Martin, Associate Director of Financial Aid, 1100 North Avenue, Grand Junction, CO 81501-3122. *Phone:* 970-248-1065. *Fax:* 970-248-1191. *E-mail:* cumartin@mesastate.edu.

INTERNATIONAL STUDENTS *Services and facilities:* Counseling/support services, ESL/language courses, Housing location assistance, International student organization, Orientation, Visa Services. Financial aid is not available to international students. *Required with application:* TOEFL with recommended score of 207 (computer) or 550 (paper); proof of adequate funds; proof of health/immunizations.

International Student Contact Mr. Jared L. Meier, Admissions Counselor of International Admissions (DSO), 1100 North Avenue, Grand Junction, CO 81501-3122. *Phone:* 970-248-1613. *Fax:* 970-248-1973. *E-mail:* jmeier@mesastate.edu.

APPLICATION *Required:* Application form, baccalaureate/first degree, essay, 2 letters of recommendation, transcripts of college work. School will accept GMAT, GRE, and MAT. *Recommended:* Interview. *Application fee:* $50. Applications for domestic and international students are processed on a rolling basis.

Application Contact Ms. Jane Sandoval, EBI/MBA Coordinator, 1100 North Avenue, Grand Junction, CO 81501-3122. *Phone:* 970-248-1778. *Fax:* 970-248-1730. *E-mail:* jsandova@mesastate.edu.

Regis University
College for Professional Studies

Denver, Colorado

Phone: 800-677-9270 **Fax:** 303-964-5134 **E-mail:** gradmaster@regis.edu

Business Program(s) Web Site: http://www.regis.edu/spsgrad

Graduate Business Unit Enrollment *Total:* 2,644 (924 full-time; 1,720 part-time; 1,362 women; 151 international). *Average Age:* 36.

Graduate Business Faculty *Total:* 545 (82 full-time; 463 part-time).

Admissions *Applied:* 600. *Average GMAT:* 500. *Average GPA:* 3.2

Academic Calendar 8-week sessions.

After Graduation (Class of 2006–07) *Employed within 3 months of graduation:* 90%.

DEGREES MBA • MNM • MS

MBA—Master of Business Administration Full-time and part-time. Distance learning option. GMAT required for international students. 30 to 45 total credits required. 18 to 72 months to complete program. *Concentrations:* accounting, electronic commerce (E-commerce), finance, general MBA, health administration, human resources management, information technology, international business, leadership, management, marketing, nonprofit management, operations management, project management, strategic management.

MNM—Master of Nonprofit Management Full-time and part-time. Distance learning option. Non-profit experience required. At least 36 total credits required. 24 to 72 months to complete program. *Concentrations:* nonprofit management, nonprofit organization.

MS—Master of Science in Computer Information Systems Full-time and part-time. Distance learning option. At least 36 total credits required. 24 to 72 months to complete program. *Concentrations:* information management, management information systems, system management, technology management.

MS—Master of Science in Organization Leadership Full-time and part-time. Distance learning option. 2 admissions essays and 3 years of supervisory/administrative experience required. GMAT is required for international students. At least 30 total credits required. 24 to 72 months to complete program. *Concentrations:* human resources management, leadership, management, management science.

RESOURCES AND SERVICES 337 on-campus PCs are available to graduate business students. Access to Internet/World Wide Web, online

Regis University (continued)

(class) registration, and online grade reports available. *Personal computer requirements:* Graduate business students are strongly recommended to purchase or lease a personal computer. *Placement services include:* Alumni network, job search course, career counseling/planning, electronic job bank, resume referral, career fairs, and resume preparation.

FINANCIAL AID (2007–08) Fellowships, grants, loans, and scholarships. Aid is available to part-time students.

Financial Aid Contact Enrollment Services, 3333 Regis Boulevard, A-8, Denver, CO 80221. *Phone:* 303-458-4126 Ext. 5. *Fax:* 303-964-5449. *E-mail:* enrollsvc@regis.edu.

INTERNATIONAL STUDENTS 6% of students enrolled are international students. *Services and facilities:* Visa Services, Admissions advisor. Financial aid is not available to international students. *Required with application:* TOEFL with recommended score of 213 (computer) or 550 (paper); TWE with recommended score of 5; proof of adequate funds.

International Student Contact Rebecca Bloomfield, Administrative Manager, Marketing and New Student Enrollment, 3333 Regis Boulevard, M-6, ALX—Adult Learning Center Annex, Room 2, Denver, CO 80221-1099. *Phone:* 800-944-7667 Ext. 5377. *Fax:* 303-964-5134. *E-mail:* rbloomfi@regis.edu.

APPLICATION *Required:* Application form, baccalaureate/first degree, essay, interview, 2 letters of recommendation, resume/curriculum vitae, transcripts of college work, 2 years of work experience. School will accept GMAT. *Application fee:* $75. Applications for domestic and international students are processed on a rolling basis.

Application Contact Admissions Office, 3333 Regis Boulevard, M-6, Denver, CO 80221. *Phone:* 800-677-9270. *Fax:* 303-964-5134. *E-mail:* gradmaster@regis.edu.

University of Colorado at Boulder
Leeds School of Business
Boulder, Colorado

Phone: 303-492-1084 **Fax:** 303-492-1727 **E-mail:** anne.sandoe@colorado.edu

Business Program(s) Web Site: http://mbaep.colorado.edu/index.html

Graduate Business Unit Enrollment *Total:* 240 (128 full-time; 112 part-time; 60 women; 26 international). *Average Age:* 29.

Graduate Business Faculty *Total:* 40 (35 full-time; 5 part-time).

Admissions *Applied:* 373. *Admitted:* 196. *Enrolled:* 124. *Average GMAT:* 630. *Average GPA:* 3.3

Academic Calendar Semesters.

Accreditation AACSB—The Association to Advance Collegiate Schools of Business.

After Graduation (Class of 2006–07) *Employed within 3 months of graduation:* 81%. *Average starting salary:* $68,500.

DEGREES JD/MBA • MA/MBA • MBA • MBA/MS • MS

JD/MBA—Juris Doctor/Master of Business Administration Full-time. Applicants must submit separate applications to both MBA and School of Law. At least 141 total credits required. 48 months to complete program. *Concentrations:* combined degrees, decision sciences, entrepreneurship, finance, information management, information systems, management, marketing, operations management, organizational management, real estate, technology management.

MA/MBA—Master of Business Administration/Master of Arts Fine Arts Full-time. Applicants must apply to MBA program and MA program separately. At least 69 total credits required. 36 to 60 months to complete program. *Concentrations:* combined degrees, decision sciences, entrepreneurship, finance, general MBA, information management, information

systems, management, management information systems, marketing, operations management, organizational management, real estate, technology management.

MA/MBA—Master of Business Administration/Master of Arts in Anthropology Full-time. Applicants must apply to MBA program and MA program separately. At least 73 total credits required. 36 to 60 months to complete program. *Concentrations:* combined degrees, decision sciences, entrepreneurship, finance, general MBA, information management, information systems, management, management information systems, marketing, operations management, organizational management, real estate, technology management.

MA/MBA—Master of Business Administration/Master of Arts in Germanic Languages Full-time. Distance learning option. Applicants must apply to MBA program and MA program separately. At least 70 total credits required. 36 to 60 months to complete program. *Concentrations:* combined degrees, decision sciences, entrepreneurship, finance, general MBA, information management, information systems, management, management information systems, marketing, operations management, organizational management, real estate, technology management.

MA/MBA—Master of Business Administration/Master of Arts in Theatre and Dance Full-time. Applicants must apply to the MBA program and the MA program separately. At least 67 total credits required. 36 to 72 months to complete program. *Concentrations:* combined degrees, decision sciences, entrepreneurship, finance, general MBA, information management, information systems, management, management information systems, marketing, organizational management, real estate, technology management.

MBA—Evening Master of Business Administration Part-time. At least 50 total credits required. 33 months to complete program. *Concentration:* general MBA.

MBA—Master of Business Administration Full-time. At least 55 total credits required. 21 months to complete program. *Concentrations:* decision sciences, entrepreneurship, finance, information management, information systems, management, management information systems, marketing, operations management, organizational management, real estate, technology management.

MBA/MS—Master of Business Administration/Master of Science in Computer Sciences Full-time. Applicants must apply to MBA and MS programs separately. At least 73 total credits required. 36 to 60 months to complete program. *Concentrations:* combined degrees, decision sciences, entrepreneurship, finance, general MBA, information management, information systems, management, management communication, marketing, operations management, organizational management, real estate, technology management.

MBA/MS—Master of Business Administration/Master of Science in Environmental Sciences Full-time. Applicants must apply to MBA program and MS program separately. At least 79 total credits required. 36 to 60 months to complete program. *Concentrations:* combined degrees, decision sciences, entrepreneurship, finance, general MBA, information management, information systems, management, management information systems, marketing, operations management, organizational management, real estate, technology management.

MBA/MS—Master of Business Administration/Master of Science in Telecommunications Full-time. Applicants must submit separate applications to both MBA and telecommunications programs. At least 72 total credits required. 36 to 60 months to complete program. *Concentrations:* combined degrees, decision sciences, entrepreneurship, finance, information management, information systems, management, management information systems, marketing, operations management, organizational management, real estate, technology management, telecommunications management.

MS—Master of Science in Business Administration Full-time and part-time. At least 30 total credits required. 12 to 60 months to complete program. *Concentrations:* accounting, taxation.

RESOURCES AND SERVICES 100 on-campus PCs are available to graduate business students. Access to Internet/World Wide Web, online (class) registration, and online grade reports available. *Personal computer requirements:* Graduate business students are required to have a personal computer. *Special opportunities include:* An international exchange program and an internship program are available. *Placement services include:* Alumni network, career placement, job search course, career counseling/planning, electronic job bank, resume referral, career fairs, job interviews arranged, and resume preparation.

EXPENSES *Tuition (state resident):* Full-time: $10,500. *Tuition (nonresident):* Full-time: $24,700. *Tuition (international):* Full-time: $24,700. *Required fees:* Full-time: $1300. Tuition and/or fees vary by class time, academic program, and local reciprocity agreements. *Graduate housing:* Room and board costs vary by campus location, number of occupants, type of accommodation, and type of board plan.

FINANCIAL AID (2007–08) 58 students received aid, including fellowships, grants, loans, and work study. *Financial aid application deadline:* 2/1.

Financial Aid Contact Evan Icolari, Associate Director, Financial Aid, Office of Financial Aid, 77 UCB, Regent Administrative Center, Room 175, Boulder, CO 80309-0077. *Phone:* 303-492-7913. *Fax:* 303-492-0838. *E-mail:* finaid@colorado.edu.

INTERNATIONAL STUDENTS 11% of students enrolled are international students. *Services and facilities:* Counseling/support services, ESL/language courses, Housing location assistance, International student housing, International student organization, Language tutoring, Orientation, Visa Services, pre-MBA program. Financial aid is available to international students. *Required with application:* TOEFL with recommended score of 250 (computer), 600 (paper), or 80 (Internet); proof of adequate funds; proof of health/immunizations. *Recommended with application:* IELT with recommended score of 7.

International Student Contact Jeannine Bell, Assistant Director, Admissions, International Admissions, Campus Box 552, Boulder, CO 80309-0552. *Phone:* 303-735-2437. *Fax:* 303-492-7115. *E-mail:* jeannine.bell@colorado.edu.

APPLICATION *Required:* GMAT, application form, baccalaureate/first degree, essay, interview, 3 letters of recommendation, personal statement, resume/curriculum vitae, transcripts of college work. *Recommended:* 2 years of work experience. *Application fee:* $70. *Deadlines:* 4/1 for fall, 2/1 for fall (international).

Application Contact Emily Burks, Assistant Director for Admissions, MBA Programs, UCB 419, 995 Regent Drive, Boulder, CO 80309-0419. *Phone:* 303-492-1084. *Fax:* 303-492-1727. *E-mail:* anne.sandoe@colorado.edu.

See full description on page 702.

University of Colorado at Colorado Springs
Graduate School of Business Administration
Colorado Springs, Colorado

Phone: 719-262-3122 **Fax:** 719-262-3100 **E-mail:** mbacred@uccs.edu

Business Program(s) Web Site: http://www.uccs.edu/mba

Graduate Business Unit Enrollment *Total:* 234 (234 part-time; 103 women; 4 international). *Average Age:* 30.

Graduate Business Faculty 24 full-time.

Admissions *Applied:* 117. *Admitted:* 90. *Enrolled:* 75. *Average GMAT:* 550. *Average GPA:* 3.05

Academic Calendar Semesters.

Accreditation AACSB—The Association to Advance Collegiate Schools of Business.

DEGREE MBA

MBA—Master of Business Administration Part-time. Distance learning option. 36 to 50 total credits required. 18 to 60 months to complete program. *Concentrations:* accounting, finance, general MBA, health care,

information systems, international business, management, marketing, operations management, project management, technology management.

RESOURCES AND SERVICES 200 on-campus PCs are available to graduate business students. Access to Internet/World Wide Web, online (class) registration, and online grade reports available. *Personal computer requirements:* Graduate business students are strongly recommended to purchase or lease a personal computer. *Special opportunities include:* An internship program is available. *Placement services include:* Alumni network, career counseling/planning, and career fairs.

EXPENSES *Tuition (state resident):* Part-time: $607 per credit hour. *Tuition (nonresident):* Part-time: $1129 per credit hour. *Tuition (international):* Part-time: $1129 per credit hour. *Required fees:* Part-time: $40 per year.

FINANCIAL AID (2007–08) Fellowships, grants, loans, research assistantships, scholarships, and work study. Aid is available to part-time students. *Financial aid application deadline:* 4/1.

Financial Aid Contact Office of Financial Aid, 1420 Austin Bluffs Parkway, Colorado Springs, CO 80918. *Phone:* 719-262-3460. *Fax:* 719-262-3650. *E-mail:* finaidse@uccs.edu.

INTERNATIONAL STUDENTS 2% of students enrolled are international students. *Services and facilities:* Counseling/support services, Housing location assistance, International student organization, Orientation. Financial aid is not available to international students. *Required with application:* TOEFL with recommended score of 213 (computer), 550 (paper), or 79 (Internet); proof of adequate funds; proof of health/immunizations.

International Student Contact Ms. Irene Martinez, International Student Services Coordinator, International Student Services, 1420 Austin Bluffs Parkway, Colorado Springs, CO 80918. *Phone:* 719-262-3819. *Fax:* 719-262-3198. *E-mail:* imartine@uccs.edu.

APPLICATION *Required:* GMAT, application form, baccalaureate/first degree, personal statement, resume/curriculum vitae, transcripts of college work. School will accept GRE. *Recommended:* Essay, letter(s) of recommendation. *Application fee:* $60, $75 (international). Applications for domestic and international students are processed on a rolling basis.

Application Contact Tamara McCollough, MBA Admissions Coordinator, 1420 Austin Bluffs Parkway, Colorado Springs, CO 80918. *Phone:* 719-262-3122. *Fax:* 719-262-3100. *E-mail:* mbacred@uccs.edu.

See full description on page 704.

University of Colorado Denver
Business School
Denver, Colorado

Phone: 303-556-5900 **Fax:** 303-556-5904 **E-mail:** grad.business@cudenver.edu

Business Program(s) Web Site: http://www.business.cudenver.edu

Graduate Business Unit Enrollment *Total:* 1,059 (274 full-time; 785 part-time; 442 women; 119 international). *Average Age:* 33.

Graduate Business Faculty *Total:* 98 (67 full-time; 31 part-time).

Admissions *Applied:* 663. *Admitted:* 420. *Enrolled:* 225. *Average GMAT:* 560. *Average GPA:* 3.04

Academic Calendar Semesters.

Accreditation AACSB—The Association to Advance Collegiate Schools of Business.

After Graduation (Class of 2006–07) *Employed within 3 months of graduation:* 90%. *Average starting salary:* $62,069.

DEGREES EMBA • MBA • MBA-H • MBA/MIM • MBA/MS • MS

EMBA—Executive Master of Business Administration Part-time. At least 48 total credits required. 22 months to complete program. *Concentration:* executive programs.

University of Colorado Denver (continued)

MBA—Eleven-Month Accelerated Master of Business Administration
Full-time. At least 48 total credits required. 11 months to complete program. *Concentration:* general MBA.

MBA—Master of Business Administration Full-time and part-time. Distance learning option. At least 48 total credits required. 16 to 60 months to complete program. *Concentration:* general MBA.

MBA-H—Master of Business Administration with an Emphasis in Health Administration Full-time and part-time. Distance learning option. 2 letters of recommendation required. At least 48 total credits required. 16 to 60 months to complete program. *Concentration:* health care.

MBA/MIM—Master of Business Administration/Master of International Management Full-time and part-time. Distance learning option. At least 66 total credits required. 24 to 36 months to complete program. *Concentration:* international business.

MBA/MS—Master of Business Administration/Master of Science Full-time and part-time. Distance learning option. At least 66 total credits required. 27 to 86 months to complete program. *Concentrations:* accounting, finance, health administration, information management, information systems, international business, management, marketing.

MS—Master of Science Full-time and part-time. Distance learning option. 30 to 48 total credits required. 9 to 60 months to complete program. *Concentrations:* accounting, finance, health administration, information systems, international business, management, marketing.

RESOURCES AND SERVICES 230 on-campus PCs are available to graduate business students. Access to Internet/World Wide Web, online (class) registration, and online grade reports available. *Personal computer requirements:* Graduate business students are strongly recommended to purchase or lease a personal computer. *Special opportunities include:* An international exchange program and an internship program are available. *Placement services include:* Alumni network, job search course, career counseling/planning, electronic job bank, resume referral, career fairs, job interviews arranged, resume preparation, and career library.

EXPENSES *Tuition (state resident):* Full-time: $11,280. *Tuition (nonresident):* Full-time: $26,832. *Tuition (international):* Full-time: $26,832. *Required fees:* Full-time: $755. Tuition and/or fees vary by number of courses or credits taken, campus location, academic program, and local reciprocity agreements. *Graduate housing:* Room and board costs vary by number of occupants, type of accommodation, and type of board plan.

FINANCIAL AID (2007–08) 725 students received aid, including grants, loans, research assistantships, scholarships, teaching assistantships, and work study. Aid is available to part-time students. *Financial aid application deadline:* 4/1.

Financial Aid Contact Kaye Orten, Director of Financial Aid, Campus Box 125, PO Box 173364, Denver, CO 80217-3364. *Phone:* 303-556-2886. *Fax:* 303-556-6726. *E-mail:* finaid@cudenver.edu.

INTERNATIONAL STUDENTS 11% of students enrolled are international students. *Services and facilities:* Counseling/support services, ESL/language courses, Housing location assistance, International student housing, International student organization, Language tutoring, Orientation, Visa Services. Financial aid is available to international students. *Required with application:* TOEFL with recommended score of 195 (computer), 525 (paper), or 71 (Internet); proof of adequate funds.

International Student Contact Derrick Alex, Associate Director, International Admissions, Campus Box 185, PO Box 173364, Denver, CO 80217-3364. *Phone:* 303-315-2234. *Fax:* 303-315-2246. *E-mail:* derrick.alex@cudenver.edu.

APPLICATION *Required:* GMAT, application form, baccalaureate/first degree, essay, personal statement, resume/curriculum vitae, transcripts of college work. School will accept GRE. *Recommended:* Letter(s) of recommendation, work experience. *Application fee:* $50, $75 (international). Applications for domestic and international students are processed on a rolling basis.

Application Contact Shelly Townley, Director of Graduate Admissions, Campus Box 165, PO Box 173364, Denver, CO 80217-3364. *Phone:* 303-556-5900. *Fax:* 303-556-5904. *E-mail:* grad.business@cudenver.edu.

See full description on page 706.

University of Denver
Daniels College of Business
Denver, Colorado

Phone: 303-871-3416 **Fax:** 303-871-4466 **E-mail:** daniels@du.edu

Business Program(s) Web Site: http://www.daniels.du.edu

Graduate Business Unit Enrollment *Total:* 852 (384 full-time; 468 part-time; 284 women; 103 international). *Average Age:* 29.

Graduate Business Faculty *Total:* 127 (85 full-time; 42 part-time).

Admissions *Applied:* 887. *Admitted:* 660. *Enrolled:* 333. *Average GMAT:* 588. *Average GPA:* 3.09

Academic Calendar Quarters.

Accreditation AACSB—The Association to Advance Collegiate Schools of Business.

After Graduation (Class of 2006–07) *Employed within 3 months of graduation:* 59%. *Average starting salary:* $64,026.

DEGREES IMBA • JD/IMBA • JD/MBA • M Acc • M Mktg • M Sc • MBA • MS

IMBA—International Master of Business Administration Full-time and part-time. Requires second language proficiency by graduation. 72 to 88 total credits required. 21 to 60 months to complete program. *Concentrations:* accounting, construction management, electronic commerce (E-commerce), entrepreneurship, finance, general MBA, information management, information technology, leadership, marketing, other, real estate, strategic management, supply chain management.

JD/IMBA—Juris Doctor/International Master of Business Administration Full-time and part-time. 136 to 162 total credits required. 42 to 60 months to complete program. *Concentrations:* accounting, construction management, corporate accounting, entrepreneurship, finance, general MBA, hospitality management, human resources management, information management, information technology, leadership, marketing, other, real estate, strategic management, supply chain management, travel industry/tourism management.

JD/MBA—Juris Doctor/Master of Business Administration Full-time and part-time. 136 to 162 total credits required. 42 to 60 months to complete program. *Concentrations:* accounting, combined degrees, construction management, corporate accounting, entrepreneurship, finance, general MBA, information management, information technology, leadership, marketing, other, real estate, strategic management, supply chain management.

M Acc—Master of Accountancy Full-time and part-time. 50 total credits required. 12 to 60 months to complete program. *Concentrations:* accounting, information technology, taxation.

M Mktg—Master of Science in Marketing Full-time and part-time. 54 total credits required. 16 to 60 months to complete program. *Concentrations:* marketing, marketing research, supply chain management.

M Sc—Executive Master's of Real Estate and Construction Management Full-time and part-time. Distance learning option. 10 years of relevant work experience required. 50 total credits required. 12 to 60 months to complete program. *Concentrations:* construction management, executive programs, real estate.

MBA—Executive Master of Business Administration Part-time. 10 years of relevant work experience with at least 8 years in a progressively responsible management role required. At least 60 total credits required. Maximum of 18 months to complete program. *Concentration:* executive programs.

MBA—Master of Business Administration Full-time and part-time. 80 total credits required. 21 months to complete program. *Concentrations:* accounting, business ethics, construction management, electronic commerce (E-commerce), entrepreneurship, finance, general MBA, information management, information technology, marketing, other, real estate, supply chain management.

MS—Master of Science in Finance Full-time and part-time. 62 total credits required. 15 to 60 months to complete program. *Concentration:* finance.

MS—Master of Science in Real Estate and Construction Management Full-time and part-time. 50 total credits required. 12 to 60 months to complete program. *Concentrations:* construction management, real estate.

MS—Master's in Business Intelligence Full-time and part-time. 58 total credits required. 12 to 60 months to complete program. *Concentrations:* business information science, information management, information systems, information technology, management information systems.

RESOURCES AND SERVICES 25 on-campus PCs are available to graduate business students. Access to Internet/World Wide Web, online (class) registration, and online grade reports available. *Personal computer requirements:* Graduate business students are required to have a personal computer. *Special opportunities include:* An international exchange program and an internship program are available. *Placement services include:* Alumni network, career placement, job search course, career counseling/planning, electronic job bank, resume referral, career fairs, job interviews arranged, resume preparation, and career library.

EXPENSES *Tuition:* Full-time: $34,920. Part-time: $873 per credit. *Tuition (international):* Full-time: $34,920. Part-time: $873 per credit. *Required fees:* Full-time: $755. Part-time: $1510 per degree program. Tuition and/or fees vary by academic program. *Graduate housing:* Room and board costs vary by campus location, number of occupants, type of accommodation, and type of board plan. *Typical cost:* $10,782 (including board).

FINANCIAL AID (2007–08) 535 students received aid, including grants, loans, research assistantships, scholarships, teaching assistantships, and work study. Aid is available to part-time students. *Financial aid application deadline:* 3/15.

Financial Aid Contact Student Services, Rifkin Center for Student Services, 2101 South University Boulevard, Room 255, Denver, CO 80208. *Phone:* 303-871-3416. *Fax:* 303-871-4466. *E-mail:* daniels@du.edu.

INTERNATIONAL STUDENTS 12% of students enrolled are international students. *Services and facilities:* Counseling/support services, ESL/language courses, Housing location assistance, International student organization, Language tutoring, Orientation, Visa Services. Financial aid is available to international students. *Required with application:* TOEFL with recommended score of 230 (computer) or 570 (paper); proof of adequate funds; proof of health/immunizations. *Recommended with application:* IELT with recommended score of 6.5.

International Student Contact Student Services, Rifkin Center for Student Services, 2101 South University Boulevard, Room 255, Denver, CO 80208. *Phone:* 303-871-3416. *Fax:* 303-871-4466. *E-mail:* daniels@du.edu.

APPLICATION *Required:* GMAT, application form, baccalaureate/first degree, essay, 2 letters of recommendation, resume/curriculum vitae, transcripts of college work. *Recommended:* Interview, work experience. *Application fee:* $100. Applications for domestic and international students are processed on a rolling basis.

Application Contact Student Services, Rifkin Center for Student Services, 2101 South University Boulevard, Room 255, Denver, CO 80208. *Phone:* 303-871-3416. *Fax:* 303-871-4466. *E-mail:* daniels@du.edu.

University of Phoenix–Denver Campus

College of Graduate Business and Management

Lone Tree, Colorado

Phone: 480-317-6200 **Fax:** 480-643-1479 **E-mail:** beth.barilla@phoenix.edu

Business Program(s) Web Site: http://www.phoenix.edu

DEGREES EMBA • MA • MBA • MM

EMBA—X-MBA Full-time. At least 30 total credits required. *Concentration:* executive programs.

MA—Master of Arts in Organizational Management Full-time. At least 40 total credits required. *Concentration:* organizational management.

MBA—Accounting Full-time. At least 54 total credits required. *Concentration:* accounting.

MBA—Global Management Full-time. At least 41 total credits required. *Concentration:* international management.

MBA—Human Resource Management Full-time. At least 45 total credits required. *Concentration:* human resources management.

MBA—e-Business Full-time. At least 46 total credits required. *Concentration:* electronic commerce (E-commerce).

MBA—Master of Business Administration Full-time. At least 45 total credits required. *Concentration:* administration.

MM—Master of Management Full-time. At least 39 total credits required. *Concentration:* management.

RESOURCES AND SERVICES Access to online grade reports available. *Personal computer requirements:* Graduate business students are strongly recommended to purchase or lease a personal computer. *Placement services include:* Alumni network.

Application Contact Beth Barilla, Associate Vice President of Student Admissions and Services, Mail Stop AA-K101, 4615 East Elwood Street, Phoenix, AZ 85040-1958. *Phone:* 480-317-6200. *Fax:* 480-643-1479. *E-mail:* beth.barilla@phoenix.edu.

University of Phoenix–Southern Colorado Campus

College of Graduate Business and Management

Colorado Springs, Colorado

Phone: 480-317-6200 **Fax:** 480-643-1479 **E-mail:** beth.barilla@phoenix.edu

Business Program(s) Web Site: http://www.phoenix.edu

DEGREES EMBA • M Mgt • MA • MBA • MM

EMBA—Executive Master of Business Administration Full-time. At least 30 total credits required. *Concentration:* strategic management.

M Mgt—Human Resource Management Full-time. At least 39 total credits required. *Concentration:* human resources management.

MA—Master of Arts in Organizational Management Full-time. At least 40 total credits required. *Concentration:* organizational management.

MBA—Accounting Full-time. At least 54 total credits required. *Concentration:* accounting.

MBA—Global Management Full-time. At least 45 total credits required. *Concentration:* international management.

MBA—Human Resource Management Full-time. At least 45 total credits required. *Concentration:* human resources management.

MBA—e-Business Full-time. At least 46 total credits required. *Concentration:* electronic commerce (E-commerce).

MBA—Master of Business Administration Full-time. At least 45 total credits required. *Concentration:* administration.

MM—Master of Management Full-time. At least 39 total credits required. *Concentration:* management.

RESOURCES AND SERVICES Access to online grade reports available. *Personal computer requirements:* Graduate business students

University of Phoenix–Southern Colorado Campus (continued)

are strongly recommended to purchase or lease a personal computer. *Placement services include:* Alumni network.

Application Contact Beth Barilla, Associate Vice President of Student Admissions and Services, Mail Stop AA-K101, 4615 East Elwood Street, Phoenix, AZ 85040-1958. *Phone:* 480-317-6200. *Fax:* 480-643-1479. *E-mail:* beth.barilla@phoenix.edu.

CONNECTICUT

Albertus Magnus College

Program in Management

New Haven, Connecticut

Phone: 203-773-8068 Ext. **Fax:** 203-773-8525 **E-mail:** jdonohue@albertus.edu

Business Program(s) Web Site: http://www.albertus.edu/index.html

Graduate Business Unit Enrollment *Total:* 316 (311 full-time; 5 part-time; 149 women; 4 international). *Average Age:* 35.

Graduate Business Faculty *Total:* 33 (7 full-time; 26 part-time).

Admissions *Applied:* 175. *Admitted:* 158. *Enrolled:* 158. *Average GPA:* 3.0

Academic Calendar Continuous.

After Graduation (Class of 2006–07) *Employed within 3 months of graduation:* 100%.

DEGREES   MBA • MBA/MS • MSM

MBA—Master of Business Administration Full-time and part-time. 36 to 48 total credits required. 24 to 48 months to complete program. *Concentration:* general MBA.

MBA/MS—New Dimensions Program Full-time. At least 57 total credits required. 24 to 36 months to complete program. *Concentration:* management.

MSM—Master of Science in Management Full-time. At least 36 total credits required. 18 to 24 months to complete program. *Concentration:* management.

RESOURCES AND SERVICES 130 on-campus PCs are available to graduate business students. Access to Internet/World Wide Web, online (class) registration, and online grade reports available. *Personal computer requirements:* Graduate business students are strongly recommended to purchase or lease a personal computer. *Placement services include:* Career counseling/planning and career fairs.

EXPENSES *Tuition:* Part-time: $1692 per course. *Tuition (international):* Part-time: $1692 per course.

FINANCIAL AID (2007–08) Loans. Aid is available to part-time students.

Financial Aid Contact Mr. Andrew Foster, Director of Financial Aid, 700 Prospect Street, New Haven, CT 06511. *Phone:* 203-773-8508 Ext.. *Fax:* 203-773-8972. *E-mail:* afoster@albertus.edu.

INTERNATIONAL STUDENTS 1% of students enrolled are international students. Financial aid is not available to international students. *Required with application:* TOEFL with recommended score of 550 (paper).

International Student Contact Ms. Eileen Perillo, Registrar, 700 Prospect Street, New Haven, CT 06511. *Phone:* 203-773-8514. *Fax:* 203-773-3117.

APPLICATION *Required:* Application form, baccalaureate/first degree, essay, letter(s) of recommendation, personal statement, transcripts of

college work. *Application fee:* $35. Applications for domestic and international students are processed on a rolling basis.

Application Contact Dr. John P. Donohue, Vice President for Academic Affairs, 700 Prospect Street, New Haven, CT 06511. *Phone:* 203-773-8068 Ext.. *Fax:* 203-773-8525. *E-mail:* jdonohue@albertus.edu.

Eastern Connecticut State University

School of Education and Professional Studies/Graduate Division

Willimantic, Connecticut

Phone: 860-465-5292 **Fax:** 860-465-4538 **E-mail:** graduateadmissions@easternct.edu

Business Program(s) Web Site: http://www.easternct.edu/depts/graduate/

Graduate Business Unit Enrollment *Total:* 37 (3 full-time; 34 part-time; 22 women; 1 international). *Average Age:* 42.

Admissions *Applied:* 5. *Admitted:* 5. *Enrolled:* 5.

Academic Calendar Semesters.

After Graduation (Class of 2006–07) *Employed within 3 months of graduation:* 100%.

DEGREE   MS

MS—Master of Science in Organizational Management Full-time and part-time. 21 to 36 total credits required. 21 to 36 months to complete program. *Concentration:* organizational management.

RESOURCES AND SERVICES 637 on-campus PCs are available to graduate business students. Access to Internet/World Wide Web, online (class) registration, and online grade reports available. *Personal computer requirements:* Graduate business students are not required to have a personal computer. *Placement services include:* Alumni network, career placement, job search course, career counseling/planning, electronic job bank, resume referral, career fairs, job interviews arranged, resume preparation, and career library.

EXPENSES *Tuition (state resident):* Full-time: $4169. Part-time: $361 per credit hour. *Tuition (nonresident):* Full-time: $11,614. Part-time: $361 per credit hour. *Tuition (international):* Full-time: $11,614. Part-time: $361 per credit hour. *Required fees:* Full-time: $3615. Part-time: $2000 per semester. *Typical graduate housing cost:* $8855 (including board).

FINANCIAL AID (2007–08) 1 student received aid, including grants, loans, scholarships, and work study. Aid is available to part-time students. *Financial aid application deadline:* 3/15.

Financial Aid Contact Office of Financial Aid, Wood Support Services Center, 83 Windham Street, Willimantic, CT 06226. *Phone:* 860-465-5205. *Fax:* 860-465-2811. *E-mail:* financialaid@easternct.edu.

INTERNATIONAL STUDENTS 3% of students enrolled are international students. *Services and facilities:* Counseling/support services, International student organization. Financial aid is available to international students. *Required with application:* TOEFL with recommended score of 213 (computer) or 550 (paper); proof of adequate funds; proof of health/immunizations.

International Student Contact Dr. Paul A. Bryant, Dean of Students and Student Affairs, Wood Support Services Center, Room 207, Willimantic, CT 06226. *Phone:* 860-465-5247. *Fax:* 860-465-4440. *E-mail:* bryantpa@easternct.edu.

APPLICATION *Required:* GMAT, application form, baccalaureate/first degree, essay, 2 letters of recommendation, personal statement, transcripts of college work, 3 years of work experience. *Recommended:* Resume/curriculum vitae. *Application fee:* $50. Applications for domestic and international students are processed on a rolling basis.

Application Contact Graduate Division, 83 Windham Street, Willimantic, CT 06226. *Phone:* 860-465-5292. *Fax:* 860-465-4538. *E-mail:* graduateadmissions@easternct.edu.

Fairfield University
Charles F. Dolan School of Business

Fairfield, Connecticut

Phone: 203-254-4184 **Fax:** 203-254-4073 **E-mail:** gradadmis@mail.fairfield.edu

Business Program(s) Web Site: http://www.fairfield.edu/mba

Graduate Business Unit Enrollment *Total:* 213 (49 full-time; 164 part-time; 79 women; 9 international).

Graduate Business Faculty *Total:* 45 (42 full-time; 3 part-time).

Admissions *Applied:* 149. *Admitted:* 93. *Enrolled:* 79. *Average GMAT:* 535. *Average GPA:* 3.3

Academic Calendar Semesters.

Accreditation AACSB—The Association to Advance Collegiate Schools of Business.

After Graduation (Class of 2006–07) *Employed within 3 months of graduation:* 100%.

DEGREES M Sc • MBA • MS

M Sc—Master of Science in Accounting Full-time. 30 total credits required. *Concentration:* accounting.

M Sc—Taxation Part-time. 30 total credits required. *Concentration:* taxation.

MBA—Master of Business Administration Full-time and part-time. Minimum undergraduate GPA of 3.0 and minimum GMAT score of 500; prerequisite coursework in college-level math, microeconomics, macroeconomics and statistics required. 36 to 54 total credits required. 18 to 60 months to complete program. *Concentrations:* accounting, finance, human resources management, international business, management, management information systems, marketing, taxation.

MS—Master of Science in Finance Full-time and part-time. Minimum undergraduate GPA of 3.0 and minimum GMAT score of 500; prerequisite coursework in college-level math, microeconomics, macroeconomics, and statistics required. Up to 30 total credits required. 12 to 60 months to complete program. *Concentration:* finance.

RESOURCES AND SERVICES 150 on-campus PCs are available to graduate business students. Access to Internet/World Wide Web and online grade reports available. *Personal computer requirements:* Graduate business students are not required to have a personal computer. *Special opportunities include:* An international exchange program is available. *Placement services include:* Alumni network, career counseling/planning, electronic job bank, resume referral, resume preparation, and career library.

EXPENSES *Tuition:* Part-time: $660 per credit hour. *Tuition (international):* Part-time: $660 per credit hour. Tuition and/or fees vary by academic program.

FINANCIAL AID (2007–08) 10 students received aid, including loans, research assistantships, and scholarships. *Financial aid application deadline:* 4/15.

Financial Aid Contact Erin Chiaro, Interim Director of Financial Aid, 1073 North Benson Road, Fairfield, CT 06824. *Phone:* 203-254-4000 Ext. 4125. *E-mail:* echiaro@mail.fairfield.edu.

INTERNATIONAL STUDENTS 4% of students enrolled are international students. *Services and facilities:* Counseling/support services, Housing location assistance, International student organization, Orientation, Visa Services. Financial aid is available to international students. *Required with application:* TOEFL with recommended score of 213 (computer), 550 (paper), or 85 (Internet); TWE; proof of adequate funds; proof of health/immunizations. *Recommended with application:* IELT with recommended score of 6.

International Student Contact Dr. Dana A. Wilkie, Assistant Dean and Director of Graduate Programs, 1073 North Benson Road, Fairfield, CT 06824. *Phone:* 203-254-4000 Ext. 2662. *Fax:* 203-254-4029. *E-mail:* dwilkie@mail.fairfield.edu.

APPLICATION *Required:* GMAT, application form, baccalaureate/first degree, essay, 2 letters of recommendation, personal statement, transcripts of college work. *Recommended:* Interview, resume/curriculum vitae, 3 years of work experience. *Application fee:* $60. Applications for domestic and international students are processed on a rolling basis.

Application Contact Marianne L. Gumpper, Director of Graduate and Continuing Studies Admission, 1073 North Benson Road, Fairfield, CT 06824. *Phone:* 203-254-4184. *Fax:* 203-254-4073. *E-mail:* gradadmis@mail.fairfield.edu.

Quinnipiac University
School of Business

Hamden, Connecticut

Phone: 800-462-1944 **Fax:** 203-582-3443 **E-mail:** graduate@quinnipiac.edu

Business Program(s) Web Site: http://www.quinnipiac.edu

Graduate Business Unit Enrollment *Total:* 209 (62 full-time; 147 part-time; 82 women; 19 international). *Average Age:* 28.

Graduate Business Faculty *Total:* 25 (19 full-time; 6 part-time).

Admissions *Applied:* 145. *Admitted:* 107. *Enrolled:* 67. *Average GMAT:* 550. *Average GPA:* 3.26

Academic Calendar Semesters.

Accreditation AACSB—The Association to Advance Collegiate Schools of Business.

DEGREES JD/MBA • MBA • MIS • MSA

JD/MBA—Juris Doctor/Master of Business Administration Full-time and part-time. LSAT required; Separate Law School application. 110 total credits required. 48 to 60 months to complete program. *Concentrations:* general MBA, health care, law.

MBA—Chartered Financial Analyst (CFA) Track Full-time and part-time. 46 total credits required. 18 to 24 months to complete program. *Concentration:* finance.

MBA—MBA in Health Care Management Full-time and part-time. 52 total credits required. 24 to 36 months to complete program. *Concentration:* health care.

MBA—Master of Business Administration Full-time and part-time. 46 total credits required. 15 to 24 months to complete program. *Concentrations:* accounting, economics, finance, general MBA, health care, international business, management, management information systems, marketing.

MIS—Master of Science in Computer Information Systems Full-time and part-time. 2 semesters each of accounting, management, and computer language programming required. At least 36 total credits required. 12 to 24 months to complete program. *Concentration:* information systems.

MSA—Master of Science in Accounting Full-time and part-time. Bachelor of Science in Accounting or BS and fulfillment of prerequisites. 30 total credits required. 12 to 24 months to complete program. *Concentration:* accounting.

RESOURCES AND SERVICES 355 on-campus PCs are available to graduate business students. Access to Internet/World Wide Web, online (class) registration, and online grade reports available. *Personal computer requirements:* Graduate business students are not required to have a personal computer. *Special opportunities include:* An international exchange program and an internship program are available. *Placement services include:* Alumni network, career counseling/planning, career fairs, resume preparation, and career library.

EXPENSES *Tuition:* Full-time: $12,150. Part-time: $675 per semester hour. *Tuition (international):* Full-time: $12,150. Part-time: $675 per semester hour. *Required fees:* Full-time: $540. Part-time: $30 per credit.

Quinnipiac University (continued)

FINANCIAL AID (2007–08) 171 students received aid, including loans. Aid is available to part-time students. *Financial aid application deadline:* 4/15.

Financial Aid Contact Ms. Heather Hamilton, Director of Graduate Financial Aid, Office of Graduate Admissions and Financial Aid, 275 Mount Carmel Avenue, Hamden, CT 06518. *Phone:* 203-582-8588. *Fax:* 203-582-3443. *E-mail:* heather.hamilton@quinnipiac.edu.

INTERNATIONAL STUDENTS 9% of students enrolled are international students. *Services and facilities:* Counseling/support services, Housing location assistance, Orientation, Visa Services, International student advisor. Financial aid is not available to international students. *Required with application:* IELT with recommended score of 6.5; TOEFL with recommended score of 233 (computer), 575 (paper), or 90 (Internet); proof of adequate funds; proof of health/immunizations.

International Student Contact Mr. Patrick Frazier, Director of International Education, Office of International Education, 275 Mount Carmel Avenue, Mail Drop CS-CSV, Hamden, CT 06518. *Phone:* 203-582-8425. *Fax:* 203-582-8796. *E-mail:* patrick.frazier@quinnipiac.edu.

APPLICATION *Required:* GMAT, application form, baccalaureate/first degree, essay, 2 letters of recommendation, personal statement, resume/curriculum vitae, transcripts of college work. *Recommended:* Interview, 3 years of work experience. *Application fee:* $45. Applications for domestic and international students are processed on a rolling basis.

Application Contact Ms. Jennifer Boutin, Assistant Director of Graduate Admissions, Office of Graduate Admissions, 275 Mount Carmel Avenue, AB-GRD, Hamden, CT 06518. *Phone:* 800-462-1944. *Fax:* 203-582-3443. *E-mail:* graduate@quinnipiac.edu.

Rensselaer at Hartford

Lally School of Management and Technology

Hartford, Connecticut

Phone: 860-548-7881 **Fax:** 860-548-7823 **E-mail:** info@ewp.rpi.edu

Business Program(s) Web Site: http://www.ewp.rpi.edu

Graduate Business Unit Enrollment *Total:* 356 (16 full-time; 340 part-time; 115 women; 9 international). *Average Age:* 30.

Graduate Business Faculty *Total:* 19 (11 full-time; 8 part-time).

Admissions *Applied:* 101. *Admitted:* 94. *Enrolled:* 70. *Average GPA:* 3.0

Academic Calendar Semesters.

After Graduation (Class of 2006–07) *Employed within 3 months of graduation:* 98%.

DEGREES MBA • MS

MBA—Master of Business Administration Full-time and part-time. Distance learning option. At least 60 total credits required. 24 to 60 months to complete program. *Concentrations:* entrepreneurship, finance, management information systems, operations management, technology management.

MS—Master of Science Full-time and part-time. Distance learning option. At least 30 total credits required. 24 to 60 months to complete program. *Concentrations:* entrepreneurship, finance, management information systems, operations management, technology management.

RESOURCES AND SERVICES 125 on-campus PCs are available to graduate business students. Access to Internet/World Wide Web, online (class) registration, and online grade reports available. *Personal computer requirements:* Graduate business students are strongly recommended to purchase or lease a personal computer. *Placement services include:* Alumni network, career counseling/planning, and resume referral.

EXPENSES *Tuition:* Part-time: $1167 per credit hour. *Tuition (international):* Part-time: $1167 per credit hour.

FINANCIAL AID (2007–08) 25 students received aid, including loans. Aid is available to part-time students. *Financial aid application deadline:* 8/5.

Financial Aid Contact Mr. John Gonyea, Student Services and Financial Aid Administrator, 275 Windsor Street, Hartford, CT 06120. *Phone:* 860-548-2406. *Fax:* 860-548-7823. *E-mail:* gonyej@rpi.edu.

INTERNATIONAL STUDENTS 3% of students enrolled are international students. *Services and facilities:* Counseling/support services. Financial aid is not available to international students. *Required with application:* TOEFL with recommended score of 250 (computer) or 600 (paper); proof of adequate funds; proof of health/immunizations.

International Student Contact John Gonyea, Student Services and Financial Aid Administrator, 275 Windsor Street, Hartford, CT 06120. *Phone:* 860-548-2406. *Fax:* 860-548-7823. *E-mail:* gonyej@rpi.edu.

APPLICATION *Required:* Application form, baccalaureate/first degree, 2 letters of recommendation, personal statement, resume/curriculum vitae, transcripts of college work. School will accept GMAT. *Application fee:* $75. Applications for domestic and international students are processed on a rolling basis.

Application Contact Ms. Kristin Galligan, Director, Enrollment Management and Marketing, 275 Windsor Street, Hartford, CT 06120. *Phone:* 860-548-7881. *Fax:* 860-548-7823. *E-mail:* info@ewp.rpi.edu.

Sacred Heart University

John F. Welch College of Business

Fairfield, Connecticut

Phone: 203-365-4716 **Fax:** 203-365-4732 **E-mail:** woerzm@sacredheart.edu

Business Program(s) Web Site: http://www.sacredheart.edu/graduate/mba

Graduate Business Unit Enrollment *Total:* 183 (26 full-time; 157 part-time; 88 women). *Average Age:* 28.

Graduate Business Faculty *Total:* 47 (35 full-time; 12 part-time).

Admissions *Applied:* 75. *Admitted:* 61. *Enrolled:* 55. *Average GMAT:* 500. *Average GPA:* 3.1

Academic Calendar Trimesters.

Accreditation AACSB—The Association to Advance Collegiate Schools of Business.

After Graduation (Class of 2006–07) *Employed within 3 months of graduation:* 85%.

DEGREE MBA

MBA—Master of Business Administration Full-time and part-time. Distance learning option. None. 36 to 60 total credits required. 12 to 72 months to complete program. *Concentrations:* accounting, finance, management.

RESOURCES AND SERVICES 200 on-campus PCs are available to graduate business students. Access to Internet/World Wide Web, online (class) registration, and online grade reports available. *Personal computer requirements:* Graduate business students are strongly recommended to purchase or lease a personal computer. *Special opportunities include:* An international exchange program and an internship program are available. *Placement services include:* Alumni network, career placement, job search course, career counseling/planning, electronic job bank, resume referral, career fairs, job interviews arranged, resume preparation, and career library.

EXPENSES *Tuition:* Part-time: $650 per credit. *Tuition (international):* Part-time: $650 per credit. *Required fees:* Part-time: $125 per term. Tuition and/or fees vary by number of courses or credits taken and academic program.

FINANCIAL AID (2007–08) 43 students received aid, including loans, research assistantships, scholarships, teaching assistantships, and work study. Aid is available to part-time students.

Financial Aid Contact Linda Kirby, Director of Graduate and Part-Time Financial Assistance, 5151 Park Avenue, Fairfield, CT 06432-1000. *Phone:* 203-371-7983. *Fax:* 203-365-7608. *E-mail:* kirby1@sacredheart.edu.

INTERNATIONAL STUDENTS *Services and facilities:* Counseling/support services, ESL/language courses, Housing location assistance, International student organization, Orientation, Visa Services. Financial aid is not available to international students. *Required with application:* TOEFL with recommended score of 80 (Internet); proof of adequate funds; proof of health/immunizations.

International Student Contact Karima Ummah, Coordinator of International/Multicultural Affairs, 5151 Park Avenue, Fairfield, CT 06432-1000. *Phone:* 203-365-7614. *Fax:* 203-365-4780. *E-mail:* ummahk@sacredheart.edu.

APPLICATION *Required:* Application form, baccalaureate/first degree, essay, 2 letters of recommendation, personal statement, resume/curriculum vitae, transcripts of college work. School will accept GMAT and GRE. *Recommended:* Interview, work experience. *Application fee:* $50, $100 (international). Applications for domestic and international students are processed on a rolling basis.

Application Contact Meredith E. Woerz, Director of Graduate Admissions, 5151 Park Avenue, Fairfield, CT 06432-1000. *Phone:* 203-365-4716. *Fax:* 203-365-4732. *E-mail:* woerzm@sacredheart.edu.

Southern Connecticut State University
School of Business
New Haven, Connecticut

Phone: 203-392-7030 **Fax:** 203-392-7055 **E-mail:** nodoushanio1@southernct.edu

Business Program(s) Web Site: http://www.southernct.edu/mba/

Graduate Business Unit Enrollment *Total:* 334 (127 full-time; 207 part-time; 169 women; 84 international). *Average Age:* 28.

Graduate Business Faculty *Total:* 40 (34 full-time; 6 part-time).

Admissions *Applied:* 156. *Admitted:* 98. *Enrolled:* 89. *Average GMAT:* 440. *Average GPA:* 3.0

Academic Calendar Trimesters.

After Graduation (Class of 2006–07) *Employed within 3 months of graduation:* 100%. *Average starting salary:* $65,000.

DEGREE MBA

MBA—Master of Business Administration Full-time and part-time. Distance learning option. 36 to 51 total credits required. 12 to 24 months to complete program. *Concentration:* general MBA.

RESOURCES AND SERVICES 200 on-campus PCs are available to graduate business students. Access to Internet/World Wide Web, online (class) registration, and online grade reports available. *Personal computer requirements:* Graduate business students are strongly recommended to purchase or lease a personal computer. *Placement services include:* Alumni network, career counseling/planning, resume referral, career fairs, and job interviews arranged.

EXPENSES *Tuition (state resident):* Full-time: $3983. Part-time: $506 per credit. *Tuition (nonresident):* Full-time: $8531. Part-time: $506 per credit. *Tuition (international):* Full-time: $8531. *Required fees:* Full-time: $55. Part-time: $55 per year. Tuition and/or fees vary by academic program.

FINANCIAL AID (2007–08) 203 students received aid, including fellowships, loans, research assistantships, and work study. Aid is available to part-time students. *Financial aid application deadline:* 4/15.

Financial Aid Contact Mr. Lewis DeLuca, Financial Aid Office, 501 Crescent Street, New Haven, CT 06515. *Phone:* 203-392-5222. *Fax:* 203-392-5229. *E-mail:* delucal1@southernct.edu.

INTERNATIONAL STUDENTS 25% of students enrolled are international students. *Services and facilities:* Counseling/support services, Housing location assistance, International student housing, Orientation, Visa Services, MBA Students Association. Financial aid is available to international students. *Required with application:* TOEFL with recommended score of 550 (paper); proof of adequate funds; proof of health/immunizations.

International Student Contact Ms. Aliya Amin, International Student Advisor, 501 Crescent Street, New Haven, CT 06515. *Phone:* 203-392-6821. *Fax:* 203-392-6947. *E-mail:* amina1@southernct.edu.

APPLICATION *Required:* GMAT, application form, baccalaureate/first degree, 2 letters of recommendation, resume/curriculum vitae, transcripts of college work, 2 years of work experience. *Recommended:* Essay, interview, personal statement. *Application fee:* $50. Applications for domestic and international students are processed on a rolling basis.

Application Contact Dr. Omid Nodoushani, Director, MBA and Professor of Management, 501 Crescent Street, New Haven, CT 06515-1355. *Phone:* 203-392-7030. *Fax:* 203-392-7055. *E-mail:* nodoushanio1@southernct.edu.

University of Bridgeport
School of Business
Bridgeport, Connecticut

Phone: 203-576-4363 **Fax:** 203-576-4388 **E-mail:** mba@bridgeport.edu

Business Program(s) Web Site: http://www.bridgeport.edu

Graduate Business Unit Enrollment *Total:* 441 (304 full-time; 137 part-time; 198 women; 348 international). *Average Age:* 29.

Graduate Business Faculty *Total:* 25 (13 full-time; 12 part-time).

Admissions *Applied:* 993. *Admitted:* 599. *Enrolled:* 138. *Average GMAT:* 540. *Average GPA:* 3.1

Academic Calendar Semesters.

Accreditation ACBSP—The American Council of Business Schools and Programs.

DEGREES EMBA • MBA

EMBA—Executive MBA Full-time and part-time. 30 to 54 total credits required. 12 to 60 months to complete program. *Concentrations:* accounting, finance, international business, management, management information systems, marketing.

MBA—Master of Business Administration Full-time and part-time. 30 to 54 total credits required. 12 to 60 months to complete program. *Concentrations:* accounting, finance, international business, management, management information systems, marketing.

RESOURCES AND SERVICES 300 on-campus PCs are available to graduate business students. Access to Internet/World Wide Web, online (class) registration, and online grade reports available. *Personal computer requirements:* Graduate business students are not required to have a personal computer. *Special opportunities include:* An internship program is available. *Placement services include:* Alumni network, career placement, job search course, career counseling/planning, electronic job bank, resume referral, career fairs, job interviews arranged, resume preparation, and career library.

EXPENSES *Tuition:* Part-time: $610 per credit hour. *Tuition (international):* Part-time: $610 per credit hour. *Required fees:* Part-time: $75 per

University of Bridgeport (continued)

semester. Tuition and/or fees vary by academic program. *Graduate housing:* Room and board costs vary by number of occupants. *Typical cost:* $10,600 (including board).

FINANCIAL AID (2007–08) 45 students received aid, including fellowships, grants, loans, research assistantships, scholarships, teaching assistantships, and work study. Aid is available to part-time students. *Financial aid application deadline:* 6/1.

Financial Aid Contact Ms. Kathleen E. Gailor, Director of Financial Aid, 126 Park Avenue, Bridgeport, CT 06604. *Phone:* 203-576-4568. *Fax:* 203-576-4570. *E-mail:* finaid@bridgeport.edu.

INTERNATIONAL STUDENTS 79% of students enrolled are international students. *Services and facilities:* Counseling/support services, ESL/language courses, Housing location assistance, International student organization, Language tutoring, Orientation. Financial aid is available to international students. *Required with application:* TOEFL with recommended score of 575 (paper); proof of adequate funds; proof of health/immunizations.

International Student Contact Ms. Yumin Wang, Director of International Affairs, 126 Park Avenue, Bridgeport, CT 06604. *Phone:* 203-576-4395. *Fax:* 203-576-4461. *E-mail:* yuminw@bridgeport.edu.

APPLICATION *Required:* GMAT, application form, baccalaureate/first degree, essay, 2 letters of recommendation, personal statement, resume/curriculum vitae, transcripts of college work. *Recommended:* Interview, work experience. Applications for domestic and international students are processed on a rolling basis.

Application Contact Dr. Ward L. Thrasher, Director of the MBA Program, 230 Park Avenue, Bridgeport, CT 06604. *Phone:* 203-576-4363. *Fax:* 203-576-4388. *E-mail:* mba@bridgeport.edu.

University of Connecticut

School of Business

Storrs, Connecticut

Phone: 860-486-0319 **Fax:** 860-486-5222 **E-mail:** uconnmba@business.uconn.edu

Business Program(s) Web Site: http://www.business.uconn.edu

Graduate Business Unit Enrollment *Total:* 1,355 (204 full-time; 1,151 part-time; 472 women; 146 international). *Average Age:* 29.

Graduate Business Faculty *Total:* 137 (104 full-time; 33 part-time).

Admissions *Applied:* 1,011. *Admitted:* 665. *Enrolled:* 512. *Average GMAT:* 634. *Average GPA:* 3.4

Academic Calendar Semesters.

Accreditation AACSB—The Association to Advance Collegiate Schools of Business.

After Graduation (Class of 2006–07) *Employed within 3 months of graduation:* 88%. *Average starting salary:* $85,750.

DEGREES JD/MBA • MBA • MBA/MA • MBA/MIM • MBA/MS • MBA/MSW • MD/MBA

JD/MBA—Juris Doctor/Master of Business Administration Full-time and part-time. At least 116 total credits required. 48 to 60 months to complete program. *Concentration:* combined degrees.

MBA—Executive Master of Business Administration Part-time. At least 48 total credits required. Minimum of 21 months to complete program. *Concentration:* executive programs.

MBA—Full-Time Master of Business Administration Full-time. At least 57 total credits required. Minimum of 21 months to complete program. *Concentrations:* finance, health care, management consulting, marketing, operations management, real estate.

MBA—Master of Business Administration Part-time. At least 57 total credits required. 21 to 72 months to complete program. *Concentrations:*

accounting, finance, health care, international business, management, marketing, real estate, technology management.

MBA/MA—Master of Business Administration/Master of Arts in African Studies Full-time. At least 72 total credits required. Minimum of 30 months to complete program. *Concentration:* combined degrees.

MBA/MA—Master of Business Administration/Master of Arts in European Studies Full-time. At least 72 total credits required. Minimum of 30 months to complete program. *Concentrations:* Asian business studies, European business studies.

MBA/MA—Master of Business Administration/Master of Arts in Latin American Full-time. At least 72 total credits required. Minimum of 30 months to complete program. *Concentration:* combined degrees.

MBA/MIM—Master of Business Administration/Master of International Management Full-time. At least 60 total credits required. 24 to 72 months to complete program. *Concentration:* combined degrees.

MBA/MS—Master of Business Administration/Master of Science in Nursing Full-time and part-time. At least 63 total credits required. 18 to 60 months to complete program. *Concentration:* combined degrees.

MBA/MSW—Master of Business Administration/Master of Social Work Full-time and part-time. At least 57 total credits required. Minimum of 30 months to complete program. *Concentration:* combined degrees.

MD/MBA—Doctor of Medicine/Master of Business Administration Full-time and part-time. Maximum of 60 months to complete program. *Concentration:* combined degrees.

RESOURCES AND SERVICES 500 on-campus PCs are available to graduate business students. Access to Internet/World Wide Web, online (class) registration, and online grade reports available. *Personal computer requirements:* Graduate business students are required to have a personal computer. *Special opportunities include:* An international exchange program and an internship program are available. *Placement services include:* Alumni network, career placement, career counseling/planning, electronic job bank, resume referral, career fairs, job interviews arranged, resume preparation, and career library.

EXPENSES *Tuition (state resident):* Full-time: $8442. Part-time: $565 per credit. *Tuition (nonresident):* Full-time: $21,924. Part-time: $565 per credit. *Tuition (international):* Full-time: $21,924. Part-time: $565 per credit. *Required fees:* Full-time: $1610. *Graduate housing:* Room and board costs vary by campus location, number of occupants, type of accommodation, and type of board plan. *Typical cost:* $9304 (including board), $5344 (room only).

FINANCIAL AID (2007–08) 402 students received aid, including fellowships, loans, research assistantships, and scholarships. Aid is available to part-time students. *Financial aid application deadline:* 3/1.

Financial Aid Contact Ms. Jean Main, Student Financial Aid Office, 233 Glenbrook Road, Wilbur Cross Building, Unit 4116, Storrs, CT 06269-4116. *Phone:* 860-486-2819. *Fax:* 860-486-0945. *E-mail:* financialaid@uconn.edu.

INTERNATIONAL STUDENTS 11% of students enrolled are international students. *Services and facilities:* Counseling/support services, ESL/language courses, International student housing, International student organization, Language tutoring, Orientation, Visa Services. Financial aid is available to international students. *Required with application:* TOEFL with recommended score of 233 (computer), 575 (paper), or 90 (Internet); proof of adequate funds; proof of health/immunizations.

International Student Contact Ms. Laine Kingo, Program Administrator, 2100 Hillside Road, Unit 1041, Storrs, CT 06269-1041. *Phone:* 860-486-0319. *Fax:* 860-486-5222. *E-mail:* uconnmba@business.uconn.edu.

APPLICATION *Required:* GMAT, application form, baccalaureate/first degree, essay, 2 letters of recommendation, personal statement, resume/curriculum vitae, transcripts of college work, 2 years of work experience. *Recommended:* Interview. *Application fee:* $55. *Deadlines:* 4/1 for fall, 1/31 for fall (international).

Application Contact Ms. Laine Kingo, Program Administrator, 2100 Hillside Road, Unit 1041, Storrs, CT 06269-1041. *Phone:* 860-486-0319. *Fax:* 860-486-5222. *E-mail:* uconnmba@business.uconn.edu.

See full description on page 708.

University of Hartford
Barney School of Business

West Hartford, Connecticut

Phone: 860-768-4900 **Fax:** 860-768-4821 **E-mail:** csilver@hartford.edu

Business Program(s) Web Site: http://barney.hartford.edu

Graduate Business Unit Enrollment *Total:* 544 (116 full-time; 428 part-time; 224 women; 53 international). *Average Age:* 32.

Graduate Business Faculty *Total:* 72 (39 full-time; 33 part-time).

Admissions *Applied:* 178. *Admitted:* 140. *Enrolled:* 74. *Average GMAT:* 530. *Average GPA:* 3.0

Academic Calendar Semesters.

Accreditation AACSB—The Association to Advance Collegiate Schools of Business.

After Graduation (Class of 2006–07) *Employed within 3 months of graduation:* 86%. *Average starting salary:* $65,000.

DEGREES MBA • ME/MBA • MS

MBA—Accelerated MBA Full-time and part-time. At least 51 total credits required. 12 to 84 months to complete program. *Concentration:* general MBA.

MBA—Executive Master of Business Administration for the Health Care Professional Part-time. At least 48 total credits required. 21 to 84 months to complete program. *Concentration:* health care.

MBA—Master of Business Administration Full-time and part-time. At least 51 total credits required. 12 to 84 months to complete program. *Concentrations:* accounting, finance, insurance, international business, management, management information systems, marketing, organizational behavior/development, public management, taxation.

ME/MBA—Master of Engineering/Master of Business Administration Full-time and part-time. At least 13 total credits required. 18 to 84 months to complete program. *Concentration:* management.

MS—Accelerated Master of Science in Professional Accountancy Full-time. At least 48 total credits required. 15 to 84 months to complete program. *Concentration:* accounting.

MS—Master of Science in Accounting and Taxation Full-time and part-time. At least 30 total credits required. 12 to 84 months to complete program. *Concentrations:* accounting, taxation.

RESOURCES AND SERVICES 400 on-campus PCs are available to graduate business students. Access to Internet/World Wide Web and online (class) registration available. *Personal computer requirements:* Graduate business students are not required to have a personal computer. *Special opportunities include:* An international exchange program and an internship program are available. *Placement services include:* Alumni network, career placement, career counseling/planning, resume referral, career fairs, job interviews arranged, and resume preparation.

EXPENSES *Tuition:* Part-time: $595 per credit hour. *Tuition (international):* Part-time: $595 per credit hour.

FINANCIAL AID (2007–08) 102 students received aid, including fellowships, loans, research assistantships, and scholarships. Aid is available to part-time students. *Financial aid application deadline:* 5/1.

Financial Aid Contact Director of Student Financial Assistance, 200 Bloomfield Avenue, West Hartford, CT 06117-1500. *Phone:* 860-768-4904. *Fax:* 860-768-4961. *E-mail:* speters@hartford.edu.

INTERNATIONAL STUDENTS 10% of students enrolled are international students. *Services and facilities:* Counseling/support services, ESL/language courses, Housing location assistance, International student housing, International student organization, Language tutoring, Orientation, Visa Services. Financial aid is available to international students. *Required with application:* TOEFL with recommended score of 213 (computer) or 550 (paper); proof of adequate funds; proof of health/immunizations.

International Student Contact Richard Lazzerini, Associate Director of International Programs, 200 Bloomfield Avenue, West Hartford, CT 06117-1500. *Phone:* 860-768-4873. *Fax:* 860-768-4726. *E-mail:* lazzerini@hartford.edu.

APPLICATION *Required:* GMAT, application form, baccalaureate/first degree, 2 letters of recommendation, personal statement, resume/curriculum vitae, transcripts of college work. *Application fee:* $45. Applications for domestic and international students are processed on a rolling basis.

Application Contact Claire Silverstein, Director of MBA Program, Academic Services, 200 Bloomfield Avenue, West Hartford, CT 06117-1500. *Phone:* 860-768-4900. *Fax:* 860-768-4821. *E-mail:* csilver@hartford.edu.

University of New Haven
School of Business

West Haven, Connecticut

Phone: 203-932-7449 **Fax:** 203-932-7135 **E-mail:** gradinfo@newhaven.edu

Business Program(s) Web Site: http://www.mba.newhaven.edu

Graduate Business Unit Enrollment *Total:* 620.

Graduate Business Faculty *Total:* 104 (39 full-time; 65 part-time).

Admissions *Average GMAT:* 500. *Average GPA:* 3.2

Academic Calendar Continuous.

DEGREES MBA • MBA/MPA • MPA • MS

MBA—Executive Master of Business Administration Part-time. At least 30 total credits required. 22 months to complete program. *Concentration:* executive programs.

MBA—Master of Business Administration Full-time and part-time. 48 to 54 total credits required. 12 to 60 months to complete program. *Concentrations:* accounting, business policy/strategy, finance, human resources management, international business, management, marketing, sports/entertainment management.

MBA/MPA—Master of Business Administration/Master of Public Administration Full-time and part-time. At least 72 total credits required. 24 to 60 months to complete program. *Concentrations:* general MBA, public policy and administration.

MPA—Master of Public Administration Full-time and part-time. At least 42 total credits required. 15 to 60 months to complete program. *Concentration:* public policy and administration.

MS—Master of Science in Health Care Administration Full-time and part-time. At least 42 total credits required. 15 to 60 months to complete program. *Concentration:* health care.

MS—Master of Science in Labor Relations Full-time and part-time. At least 39 total credits required. 12 to 60 months to complete program. *Concentration:* public relations.

MS—Master of Science in Taxation Full-time and part-time. At least 36 total credits required. 15 to 60 months to complete program. *Concentration:* taxation.

RESOURCES AND SERVICES 300 on-campus PCs are available to graduate business students. Access to Internet/World Wide Web, online (class) registration, and online grade reports available. *Personal computer requirements:* Graduate business students are strongly recommended to purchase or lease a personal computer. *Special opportunities include:* An internship program is available. *Placement services include:* Alumni network, career placement, career counseling/planning, electronic job bank, career fairs, job interviews arranged, resume preparation, and career library.

FINANCIAL AID (2007–08) Fellowships, loans, research assistantships, and teaching assistantships. Aid is available to part-time students. *Financial aid application deadline:* 8/1.

University of New Haven (continued)

Financial Aid Contact Karen Flynn, Director of Financial Aid, 300 Orange Avenue, West Haven, CT 06516-1916. *Phone:* 800-342-5864 Ext. 7315. *Fax:* 203-932-7137. *E-mail:* finaid@newhaven.edu.

INTERNATIONAL STUDENTS *Services and facilities:* Counseling/support services, ESL/language courses, Housing location assistance, International student housing. Financial aid is not available to international students. *Required with application:* TOEFL with recommended score of 220 (computer) or 500 (paper); proof of adequate funds; proof of health/immunizations.

International Student Contact Joseph Spellman, Director, International Admissions, 300 Boston Post Road, West Haven, CT 06516. *Phone:* 800-DIAL-UNH Ext. 7134. *Fax:* 203-932-7137. *E-mail:* jspellman@newhaven.edu.

APPLICATION *Required:* GMAT, application form, baccalaureate/first degree, 2 letters of recommendation, transcripts of college work. *Recommended:* Resume/curriculum vitae, 2 years of work experience. *Application fee:* $50. Applications for domestic and international students are processed on a rolling basis.

Application Contact Eloise Gormley, Director of Graduate Admissions, 300 Boston Post Road, West Haven, CT 06516-1916. *Phone:* 203-932-7449. *Fax:* 203-932-7135. *E-mail:* gradinfo@newhaven.edu.

See full description on page 728.

Western Connecticut State University

Ancell School of Business

Danbury, Connecticut

Phone: 203-837-9005 **Fax:** 203-837-8326 **E-mail:** shanklec@wcsu.edu

Business Program(s) Web Site: http://www.wcsu.edu/asb/

Graduate Business Unit Enrollment *Total:* 89 (4 full-time; 85 part-time; 31 women; 5 international). *Average Age:* 31.

Graduate Business Faculty *Total:* 14 (13 full-time; 1 part-time).

Admissions *Average GMAT:* 490. *Average GPA:* 3.2

Academic Calendar Semesters.

DEGREES MBA • MHA

MBA—Master of Business Administration Part-time. 30 to 54 total credits required. 21 to 96 months to complete program. *Concentration:* general MBA.

MHA—Master of Health Administration Part-time. At least 36 total credits required. 24 to 72 months to complete program. *Concentration:* health care.

RESOURCES AND SERVICES 50 on-campus PCs are available to graduate business students. Access to Internet/World Wide Web, online (class) registration, and online grade reports available. *Personal computer requirements:* Graduate business students are strongly recommended to purchase or lease a personal computer. *Special opportunities include:* An internship program is available. *Placement services include:* Alumni network, career placement, career counseling/planning, career fairs, and resume preparation.

EXPENSES *Tuition (state resident):* Part-time: $363 per credit hour. *Tuition (nonresident):* Part-time: $363 per credit hour. *Tuition (international):* Part-time: $363 per credit hour. *Required fees:* Part-time: $60 per semester. Tuition and/or fees vary by number of courses or credits taken and academic program.

FINANCIAL AID (2007–08) Work study. Aid is available to part-time students.

Financial Aid Contact Melissa Stephens, Assistant Director of Financial Aid, Office of Financial Aid and Veterans Affairs, WCSU, 181 White Street, Danbury, CT 06810-6885. *Phone:* 203-837-8582. *Fax:* 203-837-8528. *E-mail:* bartonn@wcsu.edu.

INTERNATIONAL STUDENTS 6% of students enrolled are international students. *Required with application:* TOEFL with recommended score of 213 (computer) or 550 (paper); proof of adequate funds; proof of health/immunizations.

International Student Contact Mr. Chris Shankle, Associate Director of Graduate Admissions, Graduate Studies Office, 181 White Street, Danbury, CT 06810. *Phone:* 203-837-9005. *Fax:* 203-837-8326. *E-mail:* shanklec@wcsu.edu.

APPLICATION *Required:* GMAT, application form, baccalaureate/first degree, interview, 2 letters of recommendation, transcripts of college work. *Recommended:* Personal statement, resume/curriculum vitae, work experience. *Application fee:* $50. Applications for domestic and international students are processed on a rolling basis.

Application Contact Mr. Chris Shankle, Associate Director of Graduate Admissions, Graduate Studies Office, 181 White Street, Danbury, CT 06810-6885. *Phone:* 203-837-9005. *Fax:* 203-837-8326. *E-mail:* shanklec@wcsu.edu.

Yale University

Yale School of Management

New Haven, Connecticut

Phone: 203-432-5932 **Fax:** 203-432-7004 **E-mail:** mba.admissions@yale.edu

Business Program(s) Web Site: http://mba.yale.edu

Graduate Business Unit Enrollment *Total:* 395 (395 full-time; 143 women; 83 international). *Average Age:* 28.

Graduate Business Faculty *Total:* 80 (58 full-time; 22 part-time).

Admissions *Applied:* 2,776. *Admitted:* 407. *Enrolled:* 178. *Average GMAT:* 700. *Average GPA:* 3.5

Academic Calendar Semesters.

Accreditation AACSB—The Association to Advance Collegiate Schools of Business.

After Graduation (Class of 2006–07) *Employed within 3 months of graduation:* 88%. *Average starting salary:* $99,307.

DEGREES JD/MBA • MBA • MBA equivalent combined degree • MBA/M Arch • MBA/M Div • MBA/MA • MBA/MF • MBA/MPH • MBA/MSN • MD/MBA

JD/MBA—Juris Doctor/Master of Business Administration Full-time. Students must apply to each school independently. Minimum of 48 months to complete program. *Concentration:* combined degrees.

MBA—Master of Business Administration Full-time. Minimum of 24 months to complete program. *Concentrations:* finance, leadership, marketing, nonprofit management, operations management, public management, strategic management.

MBA equivalent combined degree—Business and Drama Full-time. Students must apply to each school independently. Minimum of 48 months to complete program. *Concentration:* combined degrees.

MBA/M Arch—Master of Business Administration/Master of Architecture Full-time. Students must apply to each school independently. Minimum of 48 months to complete program. *Concentration:* combined degrees.

MBA/M Div—Master of Business Administration/Master of Divinity Full-time. Students must apply to each school independently. Minimum of 36 months to complete program. *Concentration:* combined degrees.

MBA/MA—East Asian Studies Full-time. Students must apply to each school independently. Minimum of 36 months to complete program. *Concentration:* combined degrees.

MBA/MA—Master of Business Administration/Master of Arts in International Development Economics Full-time. Students must apply to each school independently. Minimum of 36 months to complete program. *Concentration:* combined degrees.

MBA/MA—Master of Business Administration/Master of Arts in International Relations Full-time. Students must apply to each school independently. Minimum of 36 months to complete program. *Concentration:* combined degrees.

MBA/MA—Master of Business Administration/Master of Arts in Russian and East European Studies Full-time. Students must apply to each school independently. Minimum of 36 months to complete program. *Concentration:* combined degrees.

MBA/MF—Master of Business Administration/Master of Forestry Full-time. Students must apply to each school independently. Minimum of 36 months to complete program. *Concentration:* combined degrees.

MBA/MPH—Master of Business Administration/Master of Public Health Full-time. Students must apply to each school independently. Minimum of 36 months to complete program. *Concentration:* combined degrees.

MBA/MSN—Master of Business Administration/Master of Science in Nursing Full-time. Students must apply to each school independently. Minimum of 36 months to complete program. *Concentration:* combined degrees.

MD/MBA—Doctor of Medicine/Master of Business Administration Full-time. Students must apply to each school independently. Minimum of 60 months to complete program. *Concentration:* combined degrees.

RESOURCES AND SERVICES Access to Internet/World Wide Web, online (class) registration, and online grade reports available. *Personal computer requirements:* Graduate business students are required to have a personal computer. *Special opportunities include:* An international exchange program and an internship program are available. *Placement services include:* Alumni network, career placement, job search course, career counseling/planning, electronic job bank, resume referral, career fairs, job interviews arranged, resume preparation, and career library.

FINANCIAL AID (2007–08) Fellowships, grants, loans, research assistantships, scholarships, and teaching assistantships.

Financial Aid Contact Karen Wellman, Financial Aid Administrator, Box 208200, New Haven, CT 06520-8200. *Phone:* 203-432-5173. *Fax:* 203-432-9916. *E-mail:* karen.wellman@yale.edu.

INTERNATIONAL STUDENTS 21% of students enrolled are international students. *Services and facilities:* Counseling/support services, ESL/language courses, Housing location assistance, International student housing, International student organization, Orientation, Visa Services, Writing tutor. Financial aid is available to international students. *Required with application:* TOEFL with recommended score of 250 (computer) or 600 (paper); proof of adequate funds; proof of health/immunizations.

International Student Contact Dean of Student Affairs, 135 Prospect Street, PO Box 208200, New Haven, CT 06520. *Phone:* 203-432-6012. *Fax:* 203-432-9916.

APPLICATION *Required:* GMAT, application form, baccalaureate/first degree, essay, 2 letters of recommendation, personal statement, resume/curriculum vitae, transcripts of college work. *Recommended:* Interview, work experience. *Application fee:* $200. *Deadlines:* 10/24 for fall, 1/9 for winter, 3/12 for spring, 10/24 for fall (international), 1/9 for winter (international), 3/12 for spring (international).

Application Contact Mr. Bruce DelMonico, Director, Admissions, 135 Prospect Street, PO Box 208200, New Haven, CT 06520-8200. *Phone:* 203-432-5932. *Fax:* 203-432-7004. *E-mail:* mba.admissions@yale.edu.

DELAWARE

Delaware State University
Program in Business Administration
Dover, Delaware

Phone: 302-857-6978 **Fax:** 302-857-6945 **E-mail:** ksheth@desu.edu

Business Program(s) Web Site: http://www.desu.edu/som/mba/index.php

Graduate Business Unit Enrollment *Total:* 135 (120 full-time; 15 part-time; 35 women; 54 international). *Average Age:* 29.

Graduate Business Faculty *Total:* 15 (10 full-time; 5 part-time).

Admissions *Applied:* 90. *Admitted:* 74. *Enrolled:* 62. *Average GMAT:* 400. *Average GPA:* 3.0

Academic Calendar Semesters.

Accreditation AACSB—The Association to Advance Collegiate Schools of Business.

After Graduation (Class of 2006–07) *Employed within 3 months of graduation:* 90%.

DEGREE MBA

MBA Full-time and part-time. 36 to 48 total credits required. 12 to 60 months to complete program. *Concentrations:* finance, information systems.

RESOURCES AND SERVICES 112 on-campus PCs are available to graduate business students. Access to Internet/World Wide Web, online (class) registration, and online grade reports available. *Personal computer requirements:* Graduate business students are not required to have a personal computer. *Special opportunities include:* An internship program is available. *Placement services include:* Alumni network, career placement, job search course, career counseling/planning, resume referral, career fairs, job interviews arranged, and resume preparation.

EXPENSES *Tuition (state resident):* Full-time: $12,000. *Tuition (nonresident):* Full-time: $24,000. *Tuition (international):* Full-time: $26,000. *Required fees:* Full-time: $2000. *Graduate housing:* Room and board costs vary by campus location, number of occupants, type of accommodation, and type of board plan. *Typical cost:* $9000 (including board), $7680 (room only).

FINANCIAL AID (2007–08) 20 students received aid, including loans, research assistantships, scholarships, and teaching assistantships.

Financial Aid Contact Yaw A. Badu, Associate Dean, 1200 North Dupont Highway, Dover, DE 19901. *Phone:* 302-857-6950. *Fax:* 302-857-6251. *E-mail:* ybadu@dsc.edu.

INTERNATIONAL STUDENTS 40% of students enrolled are international students. *Services and facilities:* Counseling/support services, Housing location assistance, International student housing, Orientation, Visa Services. Financial aid is available to international students. *Required with application:* TOEFL with recommended score of 80 (Internet); proof of adequate funds; proof of health/immunizations.

International Student Contact Candace Moore, Assistant Director, International Students, 1200 North Dupont Highway, Dover, DE 19901. *Phone:* 302-857-6474. *Fax:* 302-857-6567. *E-mail:* cmoore@desu.edu.

APPLICATION *Required:* GMAT, application form, baccalaureate/first degree, essay, 3 letters of recommendation, personal statement, resume/curriculum vitae, transcripts of college work. *Application fee:* $40. Applications for domestic and international students are processed on a rolling basis.

Application Contact Kishor C. Sheth, MBA Director, 1200 North Dupont Highway, Dover, DE 19901-2277. *Phone:* 302-857-6978. *Fax:* 302-857-6945. *E-mail:* ksheth@desu.edu.

Goldey-Beacom College

Graduate Program

Wilmington, Delaware

Phone: 302-225-6289 **Fax:** 302-996-5408 **E-mail:** ebylw@gbc.edu

Business Program(s) Web Site: http://www.gbc.edu/admissions/grad.html

Graduate Business Unit Enrollment *Total:* 350 (20 full-time; 330 part-time; 150 women; 200 international). *Average Age:* 30.

Graduate Business Faculty *Total:* 20 (15 full-time; 5 part-time).

Admissions *Average GMAT:* 450. *Average GPA:* 3.05

Academic Calendar Semesters.

Accreditation ACBSP—The American Council of Business Schools and Programs.

After Graduation (Class of 2006–07) *Employed within 3 months of graduation:* 95%.

DEGREES M Mgt • MBA

M Mgt—Master of Management Full-time and part-time. 36 total credits required. 12 to 24 months to complete program. *Concentration:* management.

MBA—Master of Business Administration Full-time and part-time. 36 total credits required. 12 to 24 months to complete program. *Concentrations:* finance, general MBA, human resources management, information management, marketing.

RESOURCES AND SERVICES 129 on-campus PCs are available to graduate business students. Access to Internet/World Wide Web, online (class) registration, and online grade reports available. *Personal computer requirements:* Graduate business students are not required to have a personal computer. *Special opportunities include:* An internship program is available. *Placement services include:* Alumni network, career placement, career counseling/planning, electronic job bank, career fairs, and resume preparation.

EXPENSES *Tuition:* Full-time: $27,252. Part-time: $13,626 per term. *Tuition (international):* Full-time: $27,252. Part-time: $13,626 per term. *Required fees:* Full-time: $360. Part-time: $180 per term.

FINANCIAL AID (2007–08) 300 students received aid, including loans and scholarships. Aid is available to part-time students.

Financial Aid Contact Ms. Jane Lysle, Dean of Enrollment Management, 4701 Limestone Road, Wilmington, DE 19808. *Phone:* 302-225-6265. *Fax:* 302-998-8631. *E-mail:* lyslej@gbc.edu.

INTERNATIONAL STUDENTS 57% of students enrolled are international students. *Services and facilities:* Counseling/support services, International student organization, Visa Services. Financial aid is not available to international students. *Required with application:* TOEFL with recommended score of 195 (computer) or 525 (paper); proof of adequate funds; proof of health/immunizations.

International Student Contact Mr. Kevin Barrett, International Graduate Admissions Representative, 4701 Limestone Road, Wilmington, DE 19808. *Phone:* 302-225-6383. *Fax:* 302-996-5408. *E-mail:* barrett@gbc.edu.

APPLICATION *Required:* Application form, baccalaureate/first degree, 2 letters of recommendation, personal statement, transcripts of college work. School will accept GMAT, GRE, and MAT. *Recommended:* Interview, resume/curriculum vitae, work experience. *Application fee:* $30. Applications for domestic and international students are processed on a rolling basis.

Application Contact Mr. Larry Eby, Acting Director of Admissions, 4701 Limestone Road, Wilmington, DE 19808. *Phone:* 302-225-6289. *Fax:* 302-996-5408. *E-mail:* ebylw@gbc.edu.

University of Delaware

Alfred Lerner College of Business and Economics

Newark, Delaware

Phone: 302-831-2221 **Fax:** 302-831-3329 **E-mail:** mbaprogram@udel.edu

Business Program(s) Web Site: http://www.mba.udel.edu

Graduate Business Unit Enrollment *Total:* 390 (72 full-time; 318 part-time; 138 women; 108 international). *Average Age:* 30.

Graduate Business Faculty *Total:* 51 (44 full-time; 7 part-time).

Admissions *Applied:* 186. *Admitted:* 127. *Enrolled:* 112. *Average GMAT:* 533. *Average GPA:* 3.2

Academic Calendar Semesters.

Accreditation AACSB—The Association to Advance Collegiate Schools of Business.

After Graduation (Class of 2006–07) *Employed within 3 months of graduation:* 100%. *Average starting salary:* $44,000.

DEGREES M Sc • MBA • MBA/MA • MS • MSA

M Sc—Finance Full-time and part-time. 30 total credits required. 9 to 60 months to complete program. *Concentration:* finance.

M Sc—Hospitality Information Mgmt Full-time. 36 total credits required. 24 months to complete program. *Concentration:* hospitality management.

M Sc—Master of Science in Information Systems and Technology Management Part-time. 36 total credits required. 24 to 60 months to complete program. *Concentrations:* information systems, information technology, management information systems, technology management.

MBA—Executive Master of Business Administration Full-time. 48 total credits required. 19 months to complete program. *Concentration:* executive programs.

MBA—Master of Business Administration Full-time and part-time. 36 to 48 total credits required. 12 to 60 months to complete program. *Concentrations:* accounting, arts administration/management, economics, finance, information management, international business, management, marketing, operations management, sports/entertainment management, technology management.

MBA/MA—Master of Arts in Economics/Master of Business Administration Full-time and part-time. 57 total credits required. 20 to 60 months to complete program. *Concentrations:* accounting, arts administration/management, economics, finance, general MBA, international business, logistics, management, management information systems, marketing.

MS—Master of Science in Organizational Effectiveness, Development and Change Full-time and part-time. Up to 36 total credits required. Maximum of 18 months to complete program. *Concentration:* organizational behavior/development.

MSA—Master of Science in Accounting Full-time and part-time. 36 to 48 total credits required. 11 to 60 months to complete program. *Concentration:* accounting.

RESOURCES AND SERVICES 200 on-campus PCs are available to graduate business students. Access to Internet/World Wide Web, online (class) registration, and online grade reports available. *Personal computer requirements:* Graduate business students are strongly recommended to purchase or lease a personal computer. *Special opportunities include:* An international exchange program and an internship program are available. *Placement services include:* Alumni network, career placement, career counseling/planning, electronic job bank, resume referral, career fairs, job interviews arranged, resume preparation, and career library.

EXPENSES *Tuition (state resident):* Full-time: $9000. Part-time: $500 per semester hour. *Tuition (nonresident):* Full-time: $18,500. Part-time: $1033 per semester hour. *Tuition (international):* Full-time: $18,500. Part-time: $1033 per semester hour. *Required fees:* Full-time: $650.

Part-time: $25 per semester. Tuition and/or fees vary by number of courses or credits taken and academic program.

FINANCIAL AID (2007–08) 40 students received aid, including fellowships, research assistantships, scholarships, and teaching assistantships. *Financial aid application deadline:* 2/1.

Financial Aid Contact Denise Waters, Director, Recruitment and Admissions, 110 Alfred Lerner Hall, Newark, DE 19716. *Phone:* 302-831-2221. *Fax:* 302-831-3329. *E-mail:* mbaprogram@udel.edu.

INTERNATIONAL STUDENTS 28% of students enrolled are international students. *Services and facilities:* Counseling/support services, ESL/language courses, Housing location assistance, International student organization, Language tutoring, Orientation, Visa Services. Financial aid is available to international students. *Required with application:* TOEFL with recommended score of 260 (computer) or 600 (paper); proof of adequate funds; proof of health/immunizations.

International Student Contact Mary E. Politakis, Staff Assistant, Foreign Student and Scholar Services, 30 Lovett Avenue, Newark, DE 19716. *Phone:* 302-831-2115. *Fax:* 302-831-2123. *E-mail:* maryp@udel.edu.

APPLICATION *Required:* GMAT, application form, baccalaureate/first degree, essay, interview, 2 letters of recommendation, personal statement, resume/curriculum vitae, transcripts of college work, 2 years of work experience. *Application fee:* $60. Applications for domestic and international students are processed on a rolling basis.

Application Contact Denise Waters, Director, Recruitment and Admissions, 110 Alfred Lerner Hall, Newark, DE 19716. *Phone:* 302-831-2221. *Fax:* 302-831-3329. *E-mail:* mbaprogram@udel.edu.

See full description on page 712.

Wesley College
Business Program
Dover, Delaware

Phone: 302-736-2343 **Fax:** 302-736-2343 **E-mail:** myersgr@wesley.edu

Business Program(s) Web Site: http://www.wesley.edu

Graduate Business Unit Enrollment *Total:* 105 (90 full-time; 15 part-time; 51 women; 5 international). *Average Age:* 35.

Graduate Business Faculty *Total:* 20 (10 full-time; 10 part-time).

Admissions *Applied:* 55. *Admitted:* 45. *Enrolled:* 42. *Average GPA:* 3.35

Academic Calendar Continuous.

After Graduation (Class of 2006–07) *Employed within 3 months of graduation:* 100%.

DEGREE MBA

MBA—Master of Business Administration Full-time and part-time. 36 total credits required. *Concentrations:* leadership, management.

RESOURCES AND SERVICES 100 on-campus PCs are available to graduate business students. Access to Internet/World Wide Web and online grade reports available. *Personal computer requirements:* Graduate business students are strongly recommended to purchase or lease a personal computer. *Special opportunities include:* An internship program is available. *Placement services include:* Career placement.

EXPENSES *Tuition (international):* Part-time: $1020 per course.

FINANCIAL AID (2007–08) Teaching assistantships and work study.

Financial Aid Contact Mr. James Marks, Director of Student Financial Planning, 120 North State Street, Dover, DE 19901. *Phone:* 302-736-2417. *E-mail:* marksjam@wesley.edu.

INTERNATIONAL STUDENTS 5% of students enrolled are international students. *Services and facilities:* Counseling/support services, ESL/language courses, International student organization, Orientation. *Required with application:* TOEFL with recommended score of 550 (paper).

International Student Contact Mr. Steven D. Clark, Director of International Programs, 120 North State Street, Dover, DE 19901. *Phone:* 302-736-2557. *E-mail:* clarkst@mail.wesley.edu.

APPLICATION *Required:* Application form, baccalaureate/first degree, interview, 2 letters of recommendation, resume/curriculum vitae, transcripts of college work. *Recommended:* 3 years of work experience. Applications for domestic and international students are processed on a rolling basis.

Application Contact Mr. G. R. Myers, Associate Director of Graduate Enrollment, 120 North State Street, Dover, DE 19901. *Phone:* 302-736-2343. *Fax:* 302-736-2343. *E-mail:* myersgr@wesley.edu.

Wilmington University
Division of Business
New Castle, Delaware

Phone: 302-295-1148 **Fax:** 302-655-7360

Business Program(s) Web Site: http://www.wilmu.edu/business/mba_program.html

Graduate Business Unit Enrollment *Total:* 791 (233 full-time; 558 part-time; 453 women).

Graduate Business Faculty *Total:* 77 (18 full-time; 59 part-time).

Admissions *Applied:* 329. *Admitted:* 329. *Enrolled:* 188.

Academic Calendar Semesters.

DEGREES MBA • MS

MBA—Master of Business Administration Full-time and part-time. At least 36 total credits required. 12 to 60 months to complete program. *Concentrations:* finance, health care, management information systems, marketing, transportation management.

MS—Master of Science in Management Full-time and part-time. At least 36 total credits required. 12 to 60 months to complete program. *Concentrations:* health care, human resources management, organizational management, public policy and administration, transportation management.

RESOURCES AND SERVICES 600 on-campus PCs are available to graduate business students. Access to Internet/World Wide Web, online (class) registration, and online grade reports available. *Personal computer requirements:* Graduate business students are not required to have a personal computer. *Special opportunities include:* An internship program is available. *Placement services include:* Alumni network, career placement, career counseling/planning, career fairs, and resume preparation.

EXPENSES *Tuition:* Full-time: $6246. Part-time: $3123 per year. Tuition and/or fees vary by campus location.

FINANCIAL AID (2007–08) Grants, loans, and scholarships. Aid is available to part-time students.

Financial Aid Contact Trudy Yingling, Director, Student Financial Services, 320 North DuPont Highway, New Castle, DE 19720. *Phone:* 302-328-9407 Ext. 106. *Fax:* 302-328-5902. *E-mail:* trudy.e.yingling@wilmcoll.edu.

INTERNATIONAL STUDENTS *Services and facilities:* Housing location assistance, Orientation. Financial aid is not available to international students. *Required with application:* TOEFL with recommended score of 173 (computer) or 500 (paper); proof of adequate funds; proof of health/immunizations.

International Student Contact Mrs. Stephen Buchanan, International Student Advisor, 320 North DuPont Highway, New Castle, DE 19720-6491. *Phone:* 302-328-9407 Ext. 186. *Fax:* 302-328-5902.

APPLICATION *Required:* Application form, baccalaureate/first degree, interview, 2 letters of recommendation, personal statement, transcripts of college work. *Recommended:* Resume/curriculum vitae, 3 years of work

Wilmington University (continued)

experience. *Application fee:* $25. Applications for domestic and international students are processed on a rolling basis.

Application Contact Clinton D. Robertson, Coordinator of MBA Program, 31 Read's Way, New Castle, DE 19720. *Phone:* 302-295-1148. *Fax:* 302-655-7360.

DISTRICT OF COLUMBIA

American University
Kogod School of Business
Washington, District of Columbia

Phone: 202-885-1913 **Fax:** 202-885-1078 **E-mail:** kogodmba@american.edu

Business Program(s) Web Site: http://www.kogod.american.edu/

Graduate Business Unit Enrollment *Total:* 391 (152 full-time; 239 part-time; 164 women; 64 international). *Average Age:* 28.

Graduate Business Faculty 54 full-time.

Admissions *Applied:* 556. *Admitted:* 334. *Enrolled:* 152. *Average GMAT:* 560. *Average GPA:* 3.07

Academic Calendar Semesters.

Accreditation AACSB—The Association to Advance Collegiate Schools of Business.

After Graduation (Class of 2006–07) *Employed within 3 months of graduation:* 97.8%. *Average starting salary:* $74,714.

DEGREES MBA • MS • MSA

MBA—Master of Business Administration Full-time and part-time. 42 to 51 total credits required. 18 to 24 months to complete program. *Concentrations:* accounting, electronic commerce (E-commerce), entrepreneurship, finance, international business, international finance, international management, international marketing, management information systems, marketing, real estate, taxation.

MS—Master of Science in Finance Full-time and part-time. 30 total credits required. 12 to 22 months to complete program. *Concentration:* finance.

MS—Master of Science in Taxation Part-time. 30 total credits required. 12 to 24 months to complete program. *Concentration:* taxation.

MSA—MS in Accounting Full-time and part-time. 30 total credits required. Minimum of 12 months to complete program. *Concentration:* accounting.

RESOURCES AND SERVICES 55 on-campus PCs are available to graduate business students. Access to Internet/World Wide Web, online (class) registration, and online grade reports available. *Personal computer requirements:* Graduate business students are strongly recommended to purchase or lease a personal computer. *Special opportunities include:* An international exchange program and an internship program are available. *Placement services include:* Alumni network, career placement, job search course, career counseling/planning, electronic job bank, resume referral, career fairs, job interviews arranged, resume preparation, and career library.

EXPENSES *Tuition:* Full-time: $28,226. Part-time: $1079 per credit hour. *Required fees:* Full-time: $95. Part-time: $90 per year. Tuition and/or fees vary by number of courses or credits taken. *Graduate housing:* Room and board costs vary by type of accommodation. *Typical cost:* $20,000 (including board).

FINANCIAL AID (2007–08) 129 students received aid, including fellowships, grants, loans, research assistantships, scholarships, and work study. *Financial aid application deadline:* 2/1.

Financial Aid Contact Damon Caldwell, Senior Director of Enrollment Management, 4400 Massachusetts Avenue, NW, Washington, DC 20016. *Phone:* 202-885-1913. *Fax:* 202-885-1078. *E-mail:* kogodmba@american.edu.

INTERNATIONAL STUDENTS 16% of students enrolled are international students. *Services and facilities:* Counseling/support services, Housing location assistance, International student housing, International student organization, Orientation, Visa Services. Financial aid is available to international students. *Required with application:* TOEFL with recommended score of 250 (computer) or 600 (paper); proof of adequate funds; proof of health/immunizations.

International Student Contact Damon Caldwell, Senior Director of Enrollment Management, 4400 Massachusetts Avenue, NW, Washington, DC 20016. *Phone:* 202-885-1913. *Fax:* 202-885-1078. *E-mail:* kogodmba@american.edu.

APPLICATION *Required:* GMAT, application form, baccalaureate/first degree, essay, interview, 2 letters of recommendation, personal statement, resume/curriculum vitae, transcripts of college work, 2 years of work experience. *Application fee:* $75. Applications for domestic and international students are processed on a rolling basis.

Application Contact Damon Caldwell, Senior Director of Enrollment Management, 4400 Massachusetts Avenue, NW, Washington, DC 20016. *Phone:* 202-885-1913. *Fax:* 202-885-1078. *E-mail:* kogodmba@american.edu.

The Catholic University of America
Metropolitan College
Washington, District of Columbia

Phone: 202-319-5057 **Fax:** 202-318-6533 **E-mail:** cua-admissions@cua.edu

Business Program(s) Web Site: http://metro.cua.edu/masters

Graduate Business Unit Enrollment *Total:* 58 (10 full-time; 48 part-time; 40 women; 8 international). *Average Age:* 37.

Graduate Business Faculty *Total:* 16 (2 full-time; 14 part-time).

Admissions *Applied:* 44. *Admitted:* 30. *Enrolled:* 25. *Average GPA:* 3.15

Academic Calendar Semesters.

After Graduation (Class of 2006–07) *Employed within 3 months of graduation:* 95%.

DEGREES MA • MS

MA—Master of Arts in Human Resources Management Full-time and part-time. GRE/GMAT not required—Evening classes. 36 total credits required. 18 to 84 months to complete program. *Concentrations:* human resources management, public management.

MS—Master of Science in Management Full-time and part-time. GMAT/GRE not required—Evening classes—Additional concentration: Professional Communication. 36 total credits required. 18 to 84 months to complete program. *Concentrations:* leadership, management, other.

RESOURCES AND SERVICES 100 on-campus PCs are available to graduate business students. Access to Internet/World Wide Web, online (class) registration, and online grade reports available. *Personal computer requirements:* Graduate business students are strongly recommended to purchase or lease a personal computer. *Placement services include:* Alumni network, career placement, career counseling/planning, electronic job bank, resume referral, career fairs, job interviews arranged, and resume preparation.

EXPENSES *Tuition:* Part-time: $750 per credit hour. *Tuition (international):* Part-time: $750 per credit hour. *Required fees:* Part-time: $120 per degree program.

FINANCIAL AID (2007–08) Loans, scholarships, and work study. Aid is available to part-time students.

Financial Aid Contact Office of Financial Aid, McMahon Hall, Room 6, Washington, DC 20064. *Phone:* 202-319-5307. *Fax:* 202-319-5573. *E-mail:* cua-finaid@cua.edu.

INTERNATIONAL STUDENTS 14% of students enrolled are international students. *Services and facilities:* Counseling/support services, ESL/language courses, Housing location assistance, International student housing, Visa Services. *Required with application:* TOEFL with recommended score of 237 (computer) or 92 (Internet); proof of adequate funds; proof of health/immunizations.

International Student Contact Ms. Julie Schwing, Director, Graduate Admissions, 620 Michigan Avenue NE, Washington, DC 20064. *Phone:* 202-319-5057. *Fax:* 202-319-6171. *E-mail:* cua-admissions@cua.edu.

APPLICATION *Required:* Application form, baccalaureate/first degree, essay, 3 letters of recommendation, resume/curriculum vitae, transcripts of college work. *Recommended:* Personal statement, work experience. *Application fee:* $55. Applications for domestic and international students are processed on a rolling basis.

Application Contact Graduate Admissions, 620 Michigan Avenue NE, McMahon Hall, Washington, DC 20064. *Phone:* 202-319-5057. *Fax:* 202-318-6533. *E-mail:* cua-admissions@cua.edu.

Georgetown University
McDonough School of Business

Washington, District of Columbia

Phone: 202-687-4200 **Fax:** 202-687-7809 **E-mail:** mba@georgetown.edu

Business Program(s) Web Site: http://msb.georgetown.edu

Graduate Business Unit Enrollment *Total:* 715 (490 full-time; 225 part-time; 236 women; 157 international). *Average Age:* 28.

Graduate Business Faculty *Total:* 78 (73 full-time; 5 part-time).

Admissions *Applied:* 2,094. *Admitted:* 706. *Enrolled:* 450. *Average GMAT:* 677. *Average GPA:* 3.26

Academic Calendar 7-week modules and four 1-week integrative courses.

Accreditation AACSB—The Association to Advance Collegiate Schools of Business.

After Graduation (Class of 2006–07) *Employed within 3 months of graduation:* 97.8%. *Average starting salary:* $90,082.

DEGREES JD/MBA • MBA • MBA/MPP • MBA/MS • MD/MBA

JD/MBA—Juris Doctor/Master of Business Administration Full-time. At least 122 total credits required. Minimum of 48 months to complete program. *Concentration:* combined degrees.

MBA—International Executive Master of Business Administration Full-time. At least 60 total credits required. Minimum of 18 months to complete program. *Concentration:* executive programs.

MBA—MBA Evening Program Part-time. At least 60 total credits required. Minimum of 36 months to complete program. *Concentration:* general MBA.

MBA—MBA Full-Time Program Full-time. At least 60 total credits required. Minimum of 21 months to complete program. *Concentration:* general MBA.

MBA/MPP—Master of Business Administration/Master of Public Policy Full-time. At least 87 total credits required. Minimum of 36 months to complete program. *Concentration:* combined degrees.

MBA/MS—Master of Business Administration/Master of Science in Foreign Service Full-time. At least 90 total credits required. Minimum of 36 months to complete program. *Concentration:* combined degrees.

MD/MBA—Doctor of Medicine/Master of Business Administration Full-time. Minimum of 60 months to complete program. *Concentration:* combined degrees.

RESOURCES AND SERVICES 100 on-campus PCs are available to graduate business students. Access to Internet/World Wide Web, online (class) registration, and online grade reports available. *Personal computer requirements:* Graduate business students are required to have a personal computer. *Special opportunities include:* An international exchange program is available. *Placement services include:* Alumni network, career placement, job search course, career counseling/planning, electronic job bank, resume referral, career fairs, job interviews arranged, resume preparation, and career library.

EXPENSES *Tuition:* Full-time: $39,984. *Tuition (international):* Full-time: $39,984. *Required fees:* Full-time: $1950. *Typical graduate housing cost:* $14,330 (including board).

FINANCIAL AID (2007–08) Loans, research assistantships, scholarships, teaching assistantships, and work study. *Financial aid application deadline:* 1/16.

Financial Aid Contact Ms. Theresa Torres, Graduate Program Director of Financial Services, G-19 Healy Building, Washington, DC 20057. *Phone:* 202-687-4547. *Fax:* 202-687-6542.

INTERNATIONAL STUDENTS 26% of students enrolled are international students. *Services and facilities:* Counseling/support services, ESL/language courses, Housing location assistance, International student organization, Orientation, Visa Services. Financial aid is available to international students. *Required with application:* IELT with recommended score of 7.5; TOEFL with recommended score of 250 (computer), 600 (paper), or 100 (Internet); proof of adequate funds; proof of health/immunizations.

International Student Contact MBA Student Services, Coordinator, International Programs and Student Services, 3520 Prospect Street, NW, Suite 211, Washington, DC 20007. *Phone:* 202-687-7638. *Fax:* 202-687-7809. *E-mail:* mbastudentservices@georgetown.edu.

APPLICATION *Required:* GMAT, application form, baccalaureate/first degree, essay, interview, 2 letters of recommendation, resume/curriculum vitae, transcripts of college work, 2 years of work experience. *Recommended:* Personal statement. *Application fee:* $175. *Deadlines:* 11/7 for fall, 1/16 for winter, 4/3 for spring, 11/7 for fall (international), 1/16 for winter (international), 4/3 for spring (international).

Application Contact Ms. Kelly R. Wilson, Assistant Dean/Director of Admissions, 3520 Prospect Street, NW, Suite 215, Washington, DC 20007. *Phone:* 202-687-4200. *Fax:* 202-687-7809. *E-mail:* mba@georgetown.edu.

The George Washington University
School of Business

Washington, District of Columbia

Phone: 202-994-5536 **Fax:** 202-994-3571 **E-mail:** mbaft@gwu.edu

Business Program(s) Web Site: http://business.gwu.edu/grad

Graduate Business Unit Enrollment *Total:* 2,214 (799 full-time; 1,415 part-time; 939 women; 421 international). *Average Age:* 31.

Graduate Business Faculty *Total:* 230 (113 full-time; 117 part-time).

Admissions *Applied:* 2,215. *Admitted:* 1,356. *Enrolled:* 731. *Average GMAT:* 618. *Average GPA:* 3.2

Academic Calendar Semesters.

Accreditation AACSB—The Association to Advance Collegiate Schools of Business.

After Graduation (Class of 2006–07) *Employed within 3 months of graduation:* 87%. *Average starting salary:* $76,188.

DEGREES JD/MBA • M Acc • MBA • MBA/MA • MBA/MSF • MSF • MSIST • MSPM • MTA

JD/MBA—Juris Doctor/Master of Business Administration Full-time and part-time. GMAT, LSAT, and dual application required. Must complete first year with law school. At least 108 total credits required. 45 months to complete program. *Concentrations:* accounting, business

---

The George Washington University (continued)

policy/strategy, decision sciences, electronic commerce (E-commerce), entrepreneurship, environmental economics/management, finance, health care, human resources management, information management, international business, logistics, management, management consulting, management information systems, management science, marketing, marketing research, operations management, organizational behavior/development, public policy and administration, real estate, sports/entertainment management, strategic management, supply chain management, travel industry/tourism management.

M Acc—Master of Accountancy Full-time and part-time. 35 to 40 total credits required. 12 to 60 months to complete program. *Concentrations:* accounting, taxation.

MBA—Accelerated Master of Business Administration Part-time. Interview and 4 years of work experience typically required. 40 to 48 total credits required. 24 months to complete program. *Concentrations:* accounting, business policy/strategy, decision sciences, electronic commerce (E-commerce), entrepreneurship, environmental economics/management, finance, health care, human resources management, information management, international business, logistics, management, management consulting, management information systems, management science, marketing, marketing research, operations management, organizational behavior/development, public policy and administration, real estate, sports/entertainment management, strategic management, supply chain management, travel industry/tourism management.

MBA—Executive Master of Business Administration Part-time. Designed for mid to senior level professionals. Organizational experience of 10 years or more with 5 years or more in a managerial capacity strongly preferred. Interview required. GMAT may be waived. 56 total credits required. 21 months to complete program. *Concentrations:* executive programs, general MBA, leadership, strategic management.

MBA—Global Master of Business Administration Full-time. 3-5 years of work experience preferred. 51 to 57 total credits required. 16 to 60 months to complete program. *Concentrations:* accounting, advertising, business ethics, business policy/strategy, city/urban administration, combined degrees, conflict resolution management, decision sciences, developmental economics, economics, electronic commerce (E-commerce), entrepreneurship, environmental economics/management, European business studies, executive programs, finance, general MBA, health administration, health care, human resources management, information management, international business, international development management, international economics, international finance, Latin American business studies, logistics, management, management consulting, management information systems, management science, marketing, marketing research, new venture management, nonprofit management, operations management, organizational behavior/development, project management, public policy and administration, real estate, sports/entertainment management, strategic management, student designed, supply chain management, travel industry/tourism management.

MBA—Part-Time Master of Business Administration Part-time. Must be fully employed. 40 to 48 total credits required. 36 to 60 months to complete program. *Concentration:* management.

MBA/MA—Master of Business Administration/Master of Arts in International Affairs Full-time and part-time. GMAT, GRE, and an application to the joint degree program are required. At least 56 total credits required. 20 to 60 months to complete program. *Concentration:* international business.

MBA/MSF—MBA/MSF Joint Degree Full-time. Applicants must apply to both programs simultaneously and meet the admission standards of both programs. Fall entry only. 80 to 84 total credits required. 24 to 36 months to complete program. *Concentration:* finance.

MSF—Master of Science in Finance Full-time and part-time. GRE or GMAT required; interview preferred. 48 to 69 total credits required. 12 to 24 months to complete program. *Concentration:* finance.

MSIST—Master of Science in Information Systems Technology Full-time and part-time. GRE required for applicants without related undergraduate degree. 30 to 33 total credits required. 12 to 60 months to complete program. *Concentrations:* management information systems, project management, technology management.

MSPM—Master of Science in Project Management Full-time and part-time. Distance learning option. GRE or GMAT required; interview recommended. 27 to 36 total credits required. 12 to 60 months to complete program. *Concentration:* project management.

MTA—Master of Tourism Administration Full-time and part-time. Distance learning option. GMAT or GRE required. At least 36 total credits required. Minimum of 12 months to complete program. *Concentration:* travel industry/tourism management.

RESOURCES AND SERVICES 200 on-campus PCs are available to graduate business students. Access to Internet/World Wide Web, online (class) registration, and online grade reports available. *Personal computer requirements:* Graduate business students are strongly recommended to purchase or lease a personal computer. *Special opportunities include:* An international exchange program and an internship program are available. *Placement services include:* Alumni network, career placement, career counseling/planning, electronic job bank, resume referral, career fairs, job interviews arranged, resume preparation, and career library.

EXPENSES *Tuition:* Full-time: $28,555. *Tuition (international):* Full-time: $28,555. *Required fees:* Full-time: $26. Part-time: $12 per credit hour. Tuition and/or fees vary by class time and number of courses or credits taken.

FINANCIAL AID (2007–08) 200 students received aid, including fellowships, grants, loans, research assistantships, scholarships, teaching assistantships, and work study. Aid is available to part-time students. *Financial aid application deadline:* 2/1.

Financial Aid Contact Mr. Daniel Small, Director, Student Financial Assistance, 2121 Eye Street, NW, Suite 310, Washington, DC 20052. *Phone:* 202-994-6620. *Fax:* 202-994-0906. *E-mail:* finaid@gwu.edu.

INTERNATIONAL STUDENTS 19% of students enrolled are international students. *Services and facilities:* Counseling/support services, ESL/language courses, Housing location assistance, International student housing, International student organization, Language tutoring, Orientation, Visa Services, Presentations and written communications workshops. Financial aid is available to international students. *Required with application:* TOEFL with recommended score of 250 (computer) or 600 (paper); TWE; proof of adequate funds; proof of health/immunizations. *Recommended with application:* IELT with recommended score of 7.

International Student Contact Laraine Q. Philiotis, Director, International Programs, 2201 G Street, NW, Suite 550, Washington, DC 20052. *Phone:* 202-994-1212. *Fax:* 202-994-3571. *E-mail:* mbaft@gwu.edu.

APPLICATION *Required:* GMAT, application form, baccalaureate/first degree, essay, 2 letters of recommendation, personal statement, resume/curriculum vitae, transcripts of college work, 3 years of work experience. *Recommended:* Interview. *Application fee:* $60. Applications for domestic and international students are processed on a rolling basis.

Application Contact Mr. Albert Razick, Director of MBA Admissions, 2201 G Street, NW, Suite 550, Washington, DC 20052. *Phone:* 202-994-5536. *Fax:* 202-994-3571. *E-mail:* mbaft@gwu.edu.

See full description on page 622.

Howard University
School of Business
Washington, District of Columbia

Phone: 202-806-1725 **Fax:** 202-986-4435 **E-mail:** mba_bschool@howard.edu

Business Program(s) Web Site: http://www.bschool.howard.edu

Graduate Business Unit Enrollment *Total:* 131 (101 full-time; 30 part-time; 64 women; 34 international). *Average Age:* 28.

Graduate Business Faculty *Total:* 37 (32 full-time; 5 part-time).

Admissions *Applied:* 164. *Admitted:* 76. *Enrolled:* 42. *Average GMAT:* 533. *Average GPA:* 3.14

Academic Calendar Semesters.

Accreditation AACSB—The Association to Advance Collegiate Schools of Business.

After Graduation (Class of 2006–07) *Employed within 3 months of graduation:* 88.6%. *Average starting salary:* $81,475.

DEGREES JD/MBA • MBA • MD/MBA • Pharm D/MBA

JD/MBA—Juris Doctor/Master of Business Administration Full-time. Applicant must apply to both MBA and JD programs separately and gain acceptance to both schools. 127 to 142 total credits required. 42 to 48 months to complete program. *Concentration:* combined degrees.

MBA—BBA/MBA—Five-Year Accounting/Master of Business Administration Full-time. Program restricted to Howard University undergraduate accounting majors. 158 total credits required. 60 months to complete program. *Concentration:* accounting.

MBA—BSE/MBA—Bachelor of Science in Engineering/Master of Business Administration Full-time. Program restricted to Howard University undergraduate engineering students. 167 to 182 total credits required. 66 to 72 months to complete program. *Concentration:* combined degrees.

MBA—Master of Business Administration Full-time and part-time. Minimum 48 credit hours is based upon acceptance of up to 6 credit hours of graduate coursework from an AACSB-accredited business school. Accelerated Part-time Program offered for 2.5 to 3 years. 48 to 54 total credits required. 24 to 72 months to complete program. *Concentrations:* entrepreneurship, finance, general MBA, human resources management, international business, management information systems, marketing, supply chain management.

MD/MBA—Doctor of Medicine/Master of Business Administration Full-time. Program restricted to Howard University Doctor of Medicine students. 229 to 244 total credits required. 60 to 66 months to complete program. *Concentration:* combined degrees.

Pharm D/MBA—Doctor of Pharmacy/Master of Business Administration Full-time. Program restricted to Howard University Doctor of Pharmacy students. 176 to 191 total credits required. 60 to 66 months to complete program. *Concentration:* combined degrees.

RESOURCES AND SERVICES 500 on-campus PCs are available to graduate business students. Access to Internet/World Wide Web, online (class) registration, and online grade reports available. *Personal computer requirements:* Graduate business students are strongly recommended to purchase or lease a personal computer. *Special opportunities include:* An internship program is available. *Placement services include:* Alumni network, career placement, career counseling/planning, electronic job bank, resume referral, career fairs, job interviews arranged, resume preparation, and career library.

EXPENSES *Tuition:* Full-time: $16,175. Part-time: $899 per credit. *Tuition (international):* Full-time: $16,175. Part-time: $899 per credit. *Required fees:* Full-time: $805. Part-time: $805 per year. Tuition and/or fees vary by class time and academic program. *Graduate housing:* Room and board costs vary by campus location, number of occupants, type of accommodation, and type of board plan. *Typical cost:* $13,372 (including board), $10,512 (room only).

FINANCIAL AID (2007–08) 115 students received aid, including fellowships, loans, research assistantships, scholarships, teaching assistantships, and work study. Aid is available to part-time students. *Financial aid application deadline:* 2/15.

Financial Aid Contact Marcus DeCosta, Associate Director of Financial Aid, Scholarships, and Student Employment, 2400 Sixth Street, NW, Administration Building, Room 205, Washington, DC 20059. *Phone:* 202-806-2840. *Fax:* 202-806-2818. *E-mail:* finaid@howard.edu.

INTERNATIONAL STUDENTS 26% of students enrolled are international students. *Services and facilities:* Counseling/support services, ESL/language courses, Housing location assistance, International student organization, Language tutoring, Orientation, Visa Services. Financial aid is available to international students. *Required with application:* TOEFL with recommended score of 213 (computer) or 550 (paper); proof of adequate funds; proof of health/immunizations.

International Student Contact Mrs. Grace Ansah-Birikorang, PhD, Director of International Student Services, Office of International Student Services, Room 119, Blackburn University Center, Washington, DC 20059. *Phone:* 202-806-7517. *Fax:* 202-806-9194. *E-mail:* gansah-binkorang@howard.edu.

APPLICATION *Required:* GMAT, application form, baccalaureate/first degree, essay, 3 letters of recommendation, personal statement, resume/curriculum vitae, transcripts of college work, 2 years of work experience. *Recommended:* Interview. *Application fee:* $65. Applications for domestic and international students are processed on a rolling basis.

Application Contact Donna Mason, Administrative Assistant, Office of Graduate Programs, 2600 Sixth Street, NW, Suite 236, Washington, DC 20059-0002. *Phone:* 202-806-1725. *Fax:* 202-986-4435. *E-mail:* mba_bschool@howard.edu.

Southeastern University
College of Graduate Studies
Washington, District of Columbia

Phone: 202-478-8200 Ext. 255 **Fax:** 202-488-8093 **E-mail:** admissions@seu.edu

Business Program(s) Web Site: http://www.seu.edu

Graduate Business Unit Enrollment *Total:* 246 (116 full-time; 130 part-time; 153 women; 64 international). *Average Age:* 35.

Graduate Business Faculty 15 part-time.

Admissions *Applied:* 83. *Admitted:* 54. *Enrolled:* 44. *Average GPA:* 3.47

Academic Calendar Quarters.

After Graduation (Class of 2006–07) *Employed within 3 months of graduation:* 64%. *Average starting salary:* $45,000.

DEGREES MBA • MPA • MS

MBA—Master of Business Administration Full-time and part-time. At least 45 total credits required. 12 to 84 months to complete program. *Concentrations:* accounting, economics, entrepreneurship, financial management/planning, information management, management, marketing, taxation.

MPA—Master of Public Administration Full-time and part-time. At least 45 total credits required. 12 to 84 months to complete program. *Concentrations:* health administration, nonprofit management.

MS—Master of Science Full-time and part-time. At least 45 total credits required. 12 to 84 months to complete program. *Concentration:* information technology.

RESOURCES AND SERVICES 160 on-campus PCs are available to graduate business students. Access to Internet/World Wide Web, online (class) registration, and online grade reports available. *Personal computer requirements:* Graduate business students are not required to have a personal computer. *Special opportunities include:* An internship program is available. *Placement services include:* Career counseling/planning, career fairs, resume preparation, and career library.

EXPENSES *Tuition:* Full-time: $10,230. Part-time: $340 per credit hour. *Tuition (international):* Full-time: $10,230. Part-time: $340 per credit hour. *Required fees:* Full-time: $1050. Part-time: $350 per quarter. Tuition and/or fees vary by number of courses or credits taken.

FINANCIAL AID (2007–08) 104 students received aid, including grants, loans, scholarships, and work study. Aid is available to part-time students. *Financial aid application deadline:* 9/1.

Financial Aid Contact Hope Gibbs, Director of Financial Aid, 501 I Street, SW, Washington, DC 20024. *Phone:* 202-478-8200 Ext. 260. *Fax:* 202-488-8093. *E-mail:* hgibbs@seu.edu.

INTERNATIONAL STUDENTS 26% of students enrolled are international students. *Services and facilities:* Counseling/support services, ESL/language courses, Orientation, Visa Services. Financial aid is not available to international students. *Required with application:* TOEFL

Southeastern University (continued)

with recommended score of 213 (computer), 550 (paper), or 79 (Internet); proof of adequate funds; proof of health/immunizations.

International Student Contact Miss Hanan Adnan, International Student Advisor, 501 I Street, SW, Washington, DC 20024. *Phone:* 202-478-8200 Ext. 365. *Fax:* 202-488-8093. *E-mail:* hadnan@seu.edu.

APPLICATION *Required:* Application form, baccalaureate/first degree, 2 letters of recommendation, personal statement, resume/curriculum vitae, transcripts of college work. *Recommended:* Essay, 3 years of work experience. *Application fee:* $50. *Deadlines:* 6/1 for fall (international), 10/1 for winter (international), 1/1 for spring (international), 4/1 for summer (international). Applications for domestic students are processed on a rolling basis.

Application Contact Dean Dorothy Harris, Associate Dean of Enrollment Management, 501 I Street, SW, Washington, DC 20024. *Phone:* 202-478-8200 Ext. 255. *Fax:* 202-488-8093. *E-mail:* admissions@seu.edu.

University of the District of Columbia

School of Business and Public Administration

Washington, District of Columbia

Phone: 202-274-7040 **Fax:** 202-274-7022 **E-mail:** hmakhlouf@udc.edu

Business Program(s) Web Site: http://Hmakhlouf@udc.edu

Accreditation ACBSP—The American Council of Business Schools and Programs.

DEGREES MBA • MPA

MBA—Master of Business Administration Full-time and part-time. At least 36 total credits required. 18 to 60 months to complete program. *Concentrations:* accounting, finance, international business, management, marketing.

MPA—Master of Public Administration Full-time and part-time. At least 36 total credits required. 24 to 60 months to complete program. *Concentrations:* public management, public policy and administration.

RESOURCES AND SERVICES 100 on-campus PCs are available to graduate business students. Access to Internet/World Wide Web available. *Personal computer requirements:* Graduate business students are not required to have a personal computer. *Special opportunities include:* An internship program is available. *Placement services include:* Career counseling/planning, resume referral, career fairs, job interviews arranged, and resume preparation.

Application Contact Hany Makhlouf, Director of MBA and MPA, 4200 Connecticut Avenue, NW, Washington, DC 20008-1175. *Phone:* 202-274-7040. *Fax:* 202-274-7022. *E-mail:* hmakhlouf@udc.edu.

FLORIDA

American InterContinental University

School of Business

Weston, Florida

Phone: 954-446-6341 **E-mail:** kgeorge@aiufl.edu

Business Program(s) Web Site: http://www.aiufl.edu/academic_programs/business.asp

DEGREES MBA • MIT

MBA—Master of Business Administration Full-time and part-time. Distance learning option. *Concentration:* general MBA.

MIT—Master of Information Technology Full-time and part-time. *Concentration:* information technology.

Application Contact Kris George, Vice President, Admissions and Marketing, 2250 North Commerce Parkway, Weston, FL 33326. *Phone:* 954-446-6341. *E-mail:* kgeorge@aiufl.edu.

See full description on page 564.

Argosy University, Sarasota

College of Business

Sarasota, Florida

Phone: 941-379-0404 **Fax:** 941-379-5964

Business Program(s) Web Site: http://www.argosy.edu/sarasota

DEGREES DBA • MBA • MSM

DBA—Doctor of Business Administration (DBA) *Concentrations:* accounting, information systems, international business, management, marketing.

MBA—Master of Business Administration (MBA) *Concentrations:* finance, health administration, information systems, international business, management, marketing.

MSM—Master of Science in Management (MSM) *Concentration:* management.

Financial Aid Contact Director of Admissions, 5250 17th Street, Sarasota, FL 34235. *Phone:* 941-379-0404. *Fax:* 941-379-5964.

International Student Contact Director of Admissions, 5250 17th Street, Sarasota, FL 34235. *Phone:* 941-379-0404. *Fax:* 941-379-5964.

Application Contact Director of Admissions, 5250 17th Street, Sarasota, FL 34235. *Phone:* 941-379-0404. *Fax:* 941-379-5964.

See full description on page 566.

Argosy University, Tampa

College of Business

Tampa, Florida

Phone: 813-393-5290 **Fax:** 813-874-1989

Business Program(s) Web Site: http://www.argosy.edu/tampa

DEGREES DBA • MBA • MSM

DBA—Doctor of Business Administration (DBA) *Concentrations:* accounting, information systems, international business, management, marketing.

MBA—Master of Business Administration (MBA) *Concentrations:* finance, health administration, information systems, international business, management, marketing, public policy and administration.

MSM—Master of Science in Management (MSM) *Concentration:* management.

Financial Aid Contact Director of Admissions, Parkside at Tampa Bay Park, 4401 North Himes Avenue, Suite 150, Tampa, FL 33614. *Phone:* 813-393-5290. *Fax:* 813-874-1989.

International Student Contact Director of Admissions, Parkside at Tampa Bay Park, 4401 North Himes Avenue, Suite 150, Tampa, FL 33614. *Phone:* 813-393-5290. *Fax:* 813-874-1989.

Application Contact Director of Admissions, Parkside at Tampa Bay Park, 4401 North Himes Avenue, Suite 150, Tampa, FL 33614. *Phone:* 813-393-5290. *Fax:* 813-874-1989.

See full description on page 566.

Barry University
Andreas School of Business
Miami Shores, Florida

Phone: 305-899-3535 **Fax:** 305-892-6412

Business Program(s) Web Site: http://www.barry.edu/business

Graduate Business Unit Enrollment *Total:* 126 (48 full-time; 78 part-time; 57 women; 25 international). *Average Age:* 30.

Graduate Business Faculty 21 full-time.

Admissions *Average GMAT:* 496. *Average GPA:* 3.09

Academic Calendar Semesters.

Accreditation AACSB—The Association to Advance Collegiate Schools of Business.

DEGREES M Sc • MBA • MBA/MS • MS

M Sc—Master of Science in Management Full-time and part-time. 30 total credits required. 20 to 60 months to complete program. *Concentration:* management.

MBA—Doctor of Podiatry/Master of Business Administration Full-time. Medical College Admissions Test and TOEFL score of 600 required. At least 205 total credits required. 20 to 60 months to complete program. *Concentration:* combined degrees.

MBA—Master of Business Administration Full-time and part-time. 36 to 39 total credits required. 20 to 60 months to complete program. *Concentrations:* accounting, finance, general MBA, health care, international business, management, management information systems, marketing.

MBA/MS—Master of Business Administration/Master of Science in Nursing Part-time. At least 69 total credits required. Maximum of 84 months to complete program. *Concentration:* combined degrees.

MBA/MS—Master of Business Administration/Master of Science in Sport Management Part-time. At least 57 total credits required. 32 to 84 months to complete program. *Concentrations:* international business, management information systems.

MBA/MS—Master of Science in Human Resource Development/Master of Business Administration Full-time and part-time. 60 to 75 total credits required. 20 to 60 months to complete program. *Concentration:* human resources management.

MS—Program in Accounting Full-time and part-time. At least 30 total credits required. 20 to 60 months to complete program. *Concentration:* accounting.

RESOURCES AND SERVICES 262 on-campus PCs are available to graduate business students. Access to Internet/World Wide Web, online (class) registration, and online grade reports available. *Personal computer requirements:* Graduate business students are strongly recommended to purchase or lease a personal computer. *Special opportunities include:* An internship program is available. *Placement services include:* Alumni network, career placement, career counseling/planning, electronic job bank, resume referral, career fairs, job interviews arranged, resume preparation, and career library.

FINANCIAL AID (2007–08) Grants and scholarships. Aid is available to part-time students.

Financial Aid Contact Assistant Director, Graduate Financial Aid, 11300 Northeast Second Avenue, Miami Shores, FL 33161-6695. *Phone:* 305-899-3664. *Fax:* 305-899-3104.

INTERNATIONAL STUDENTS 20% of students enrolled are international students. *Services and facilities:* Counseling/support services, ESL/language courses, Housing location assistance, International student housing, International student organization, Orientation, Visa Services. Financial aid is available to international students. *Required with application:* TOEFL with recommended score of 213 (computer) or 550 (paper); proof of adequate funds; proof of health/immunizations.

International Student Contact Director, Intercultural Center, 11300 Northeast Second Avenue, Miami Shores, FL 33161-6695. *Phone:* 305-899-3082. *Fax:* 305-899-3083.

APPLICATION *Required:* GMAT, application form, baccalaureate/first degree, 2 letters of recommendation, transcripts of college work. School will accept GRE and MAT. *Application fee:* $30. Applications for domestic and international students are processed on a rolling basis.

Application Contact Assistant Dean for Marketing, 11300 Northeast Second Avenue, Miami Shores, FL 33161-6695. *Phone:* 305-899-3535. *Fax:* 305-892-6412.

Carlos Albizu University, Miami Campus
Graduate Programs
Miami, Florida

Phone: 305-593-1223 Ext. 134 **E-mail:** pcohen@albizu.edu

Business Program(s) Web Site: http://mia.albizu.edu/web/academic_programs/business/master_of_business_administration_mba.asp

Graduate Business Unit Enrollment *Total:* 31 (29 full-time; 2 part-time; 17 women; 3 international). *Average Age:* 29.

Graduate Business Faculty *Total:* 14 (2 full-time; 12 part-time).

Admissions *Applied:* 27. *Admitted:* 19. *Enrolled:* 14. *Average GPA:* 3.3

Academic Calendar Semesters.

After Graduation (Class of 2006–07) *Employed within 3 months of graduation:* 87%.

DEGREE MBA

MBA—Master of Business Administration Full-time and part-time. 36 total credits required. 16 months to complete program. *Concentrations:* entrepreneurship, nonprofit organization, organizational management.

RESOURCES AND SERVICES 102 on-campus PCs are available to graduate business students. Access to Internet/World Wide Web and online grade reports available. *Personal computer requirements:* Graduate business students are strongly recommended to purchase or lease a personal computer. *Special opportunities include:* An international exchange program is available. *Placement services include:* Alumni network, career placement, career counseling/planning, resume referral, career fairs, and resume preparation.

EXPENSES *Tuition:* Full-time: $13,635. Part-time: $505 per credit. *Tuition (international):* Full-time: $13,635. Part-time: $505 per credit. *Required fees:* Full-time: $298.

FINANCIAL AID (2007–08) Grants, loans, scholarships, and work study.

INTERNATIONAL STUDENTS 10% of students enrolled are international students. *Services and facilities:* Counseling/support services, ESL/language courses, Orientation, Visa Services. *Required with application:* Proof of adequate funds; proof of health/immunizations.

International Student Contact Peter Cohen, Admissions Counselor, 2173 NW 99th Avenue, Miami, FL 33172. *Phone:* 305-593-1223 Ext. 134. *E-mail:* pcohen@albizu.edu.

APPLICATION *Required:* Application form, baccalaureate/first degree, interview, 3 letters of recommendation, personal statement, resume/

Carlos Albizu University, Miami Campus (continued)

curriculum vitae, transcripts of college work. *Recommended:* 5 years of work experience. *Application fee:* $50. Applications for domestic and international students are processed on a rolling basis.

Application Contact Peter Cohen, Admissions Counselor, 2173 NW 99th Avenue, Miami, FL 33172. *Phone:* 305-593-1223 Ext. 134. *E-mail:* pcohen@albizu.edu.

DeVry University
Keller Graduate School of Management

Miami, Florida

Phone: 786-425-1113

DEGREES   MAFM • MBA • MHRM • MIS • MPA • MPM

MAFM—Master of Accounting and Financial Management Full-time and part-time. Distance learning option. At least 44 total credits required. 18 to 60 months to complete program. *Concentrations:* accounting, financial management/planning.

MBA—Master of Business Administration Full-time and part-time. Distance learning option. At least 48 total credits required. 18 to 60 months to complete program. *Concentration:* management.

MHRM—Master of Human Resources Management Full-time and part-time. Distance learning option. At least 45 total credits required. 18 to 60 months to complete program. *Concentration:* human resources management.

MIS—Master of Information Systems Management Full-time and part-time. Distance learning option. At least 45 total credits required. 18 to 60 months to complete program. *Concentration:* information systems.

MPA—Master of Public Administration Full-time and part-time. Distance learning option. At least 45 total credits required. 18 to 60 months to complete program. *Concentration:* public policy and administration.

MPM—Master of Project Management Full-time and part-time. Distance learning option. At least 42 total credits required. 18 to 60 months to complete program. *Concentration:* project management.

Application Contact Admissions Office, Miami Center, 1111 Brickell Avenue, 11th Floor, Miami, FL 33131. *Phone:* 786-425-1113.

DeVry University
Keller Graduate School of Management

Miramar, Florida

Phone: 954-499-9900

DEGREES   MAFM • MBA • MHRM • MIS • MPA • MPM

MAFM—Master of Accounting and Financial Management Full-time and part-time. Distance learning option. At least 44 total credits required. 18 to 60 months to complete program. *Concentrations:* accounting, financial management/planning.

MBA—Master of Business Administration Full-time and part-time. Distance learning option. At least 48 total credits required. 18 to 60 months to complete program. *Concentration:* management.

MHRM—Master of Human Resources Management Full-time and part-time. Distance learning option. At least 45 total credits required. 18 to 60 months to complete program. *Concentration:* human resources management.

MIS—Master of Information Systems Management Full-time and part-time. Distance learning option. At least 45 total credits required. 18 to 60 months to complete program. *Concentration:* information systems.

MPA—Master of Public Administration Full-time and part-time. Distance learning option. At least 45 total credits required. 18 to 60 months to complete program. *Concentration:* public policy and administration.

MPM—Master of Project Management Full-time and part-time. Distance learning option. At least 42 total credits required. 18 to 60 months to complete program. *Concentration:* project management.

Application Contact Admissions Office, Miramar Center, 2300 Southwest 145th Avenue, Miramar, FL 33027. *Phone:* 954-499-9900.

DeVry University
Keller Graduate School of Management

Orlando, Florida

Phone: 407-903-5900

DEGREES   MAFM • MBA • MHRM • MIS • MPA • MPM

MAFM—Master of Accounting and Financial Management Full-time and part-time. Distance learning option. At least 44 total credits required. 18 to 60 months to complete program. *Concentrations:* accounting, financial management/planning.

MBA—Master of Business Administration Full-time and part-time. Distance learning option. At least 48 total credits required. 18 to 60 months to complete program. *Concentration:* management.

MHRM—Master of Human Resources Management Full-time and part-time. Distance learning option. At least 45 total credits required. 18 to 60 months to complete program. *Concentration:* human resources management.

MIS—Master of Information Systems Management Full-time and part-time. Distance learning option. At least 45 total credits required. 18 to 60 months to complete program. *Concentration:* information systems.

MPA—Master of Public Administration Full-time and part-time. Distance learning option. At least 45 total credits required. 18 to 60 months to complete program. *Concentration:* public policy and administration.

MPM—Master of Project Management Full-time and part-time. Distance learning option. At least 42 total credits required. 18 to 60 months to complete program. *Concentration:* project management.

Application Contact Admissions Office, Orlando Campus, 4000 Millennia Boulevard, Suite 117.1, Orlando, FL 32839. *Phone:* 407-903-5900.

DeVry University
Keller Graduate School of Management

Tampa, Florida

Phone: 813-288-8994

DEGREES   MAFM • MBA • MHRM • MIS • MPA • MPM

MAFM—Master of Accounting and Financial Management Full-time and part-time. Distance learning option. At least 44 total credits required. 18 to 60 months to complete program. *Concentrations:* accounting, financial management/planning.

MBA—Master of Business Administration Full-time and part-time. Distance learning option. At least 48 total credits required. 18 to 60 months to complete program. *Concentration:* management.

MHRM—Master of Human Resources Management Full-time and part-time. Distance learning option. At least 45 total credits required. 18 to 60 months to complete program. *Concentration:* human resources management.

MIS—Master of Information Systems Management Full-time and part-time. Distance learning option. At least 45 total credits required. 18 to 60 months to complete program. *Concentration:* information systems.

MPA—Master of Public Administration Full-time and part-time. Distance learning option. At least 45 total credits required. 18 to 60 months to complete program. *Concentration:* public policy and administration.

MPM—Master of Project Management Full-time and part-time. Distance learning option. At least 42 total credits required. 18 to 60 months to complete program. *Concentration:* project management.

Application Contact Admissions Office, Tampa Bay Center, 3030 North Rocky Point Drive West, Suite 100, Tampa, FL 33607. *Phone:* 813-288-8994.

Embry-Riddle Aeronautical University

College of Business

Daytona Beach, Florida

Phone: 386-226-7178 **Fax:** 386-226-7070 **E-mail:** graduate.admissions@erau.edu

Business Program(s) Web Site: http://www.embryriddle.edu

Graduate Business Unit Enrollment *Total:* 134 (85 full-time; 49 part-time; 32 women; 33 international). *Average Age:* 30.

Graduate Business Faculty 12 full-time.

Admissions *Applied:* 79. *Admitted:* 42. *Enrolled:* 32. *Average GMAT:* 546. *Average GPA:* 3.45

Academic Calendar Semesters.

Accreditation ACBSP—The American Council of Business Schools and Programs.

After Graduation (Class of 2006–07) *Employed within 3 months of graduation:* 97%. *Average starting salary:* $62,328.

DEGREE MBA

MBA—Master of Business Administration in Aviation Full-time and part-time. Distance learning option. 36 to 39 total credits required. 16 to 84 months to complete program. *Concentration:* aviation management.

RESOURCES AND SERVICES 1,001 on-campus PCs are available to graduate business students. Access to Internet/World Wide Web, online (class) registration, and online grade reports available. *Personal computer requirements:* Graduate business students are not required to have a personal computer. *Special opportunities include:* An internship program is available. *Placement services include:* Alumni network, career placement, career counseling/planning, electronic job bank, resume referral, career fairs, job interviews arranged, resume preparation, and career library.

EXPENSES *Tuition:* Full-time: $12,720. Part-time: $1100 per credit hour. *Tuition (international):* Full-time: $12,720. Part-time: $1100 per credit hour. *Required fees:* Full-time: $1096. Part-time: $548 per year. *Typical graduate housing cost:* $6614 (including board), $4566 (room only).

FINANCIAL AID (2007–08) 37 students received aid, including fellowships, loans, research assistantships, scholarships, teaching assistantships, and work study. Aid is available to part-time students. *Financial aid application deadline:* 6/30.

Financial Aid Contact Barbara Dryden, Director, Financial Aid, 600 South Clyde Morris Boulevard, Daytona Beach, FL 32114-3900. *Phone:* 386-226-6300. *Fax:* 386-226-6307. *E-mail:* dbfinaid@erau.edu.

INTERNATIONAL STUDENTS 25% of students enrolled are international students. *Services and facilities:* Counseling/support services, ESL/language courses, Housing location assistance, International student organization. Financial aid is not available to international students.

Required with application: TOEFL with recommended score of 213 (computer) or 550 (paper); proof of adequate funds; proof of health/immunizations.

International Student Contact Judith Assad, Director, International Student Services, 600 South Clyde Morris Boulevard, Daytona Beach, FL 32114-3900. *Phone:* 386-226-6579. *Fax:* 386-226-7920. *E-mail:* assadj@erau.edu.

APPLICATION *Required:* GMAT, application form, baccalaureate/first degree, 3 letters of recommendation, personal statement, transcripts of college work. *Recommended:* Resume/curriculum vitae. *Application fee:* $50. *Deadlines:* 7/1 for fall, 11/1 for spring, 3/1 for summer, 6/1 for fall (international), 10/1 for spring (international), 2/1 for summer (international).

Application Contact Director, International and Graduate Admissions, 600 South Clyde Morris Boulevard, Daytona Beach, FL 32114-3900. *Phone:* 386-226-7178. *Fax:* 386-226-7070. *E-mail:* graduate.admissions@erau.edu.

See full description on page 604.

Embry-Riddle Aeronautical University Worldwide

Department of Management

Daytona Beach, Florida

Phone: 386-226-6909 **Fax:** 386-226-6984 **E-mail:** ecinfo@erau.edu

Business Program(s) Web Site: http://www.embryriddle.edu

Graduate Business Unit Enrollment *Total:* 781 (357 full-time; 424 part-time; 181 women; 7 international). *Average Age:* 37.

Admissions *Applied:* 357. *Admitted:* 266. *Enrolled:* 209.

Academic Calendar Varies by location.

Accreditation ACBSP—The American Council of Business Schools and Programs.

After Graduation (Class of 2006–07) *Employed within 3 months of graduation:* 94%. *Average starting salary:* $74,547.

DEGREES MBA • MS • MSM

MBA—Master of Business Administration in Aviation Management Full-time and part-time. Distance learning option. 39 total credits required. Maximum of 84 months to complete program. *Concentration:* aviation management.

MS—Master of Science in Project Management Full-time and part-time. Distance learning option. 36 total credits required. Maximum of 84 months to complete program. *Concentration:* project management.

MS—Master of Science in Technical Management Full-time and part-time. Distance learning option. 42 total credits required. Maximum of 84 months to complete program. *Concentration:* technology management.

MSM—Master of Science in Management Full-time and part-time. Distance learning option. 36 total credits required. Maximum of 84 months to complete program. *Concentration:* aviation management.

RESOURCES AND SERVICES Access to Internet/World Wide Web and online grade reports available. *Personal computer requirements:* Graduate business students are not required to have a personal computer. *Placement services include:* Alumni network, career placement, career counseling/planning, electronic job bank, resume referral, career fairs, job interviews arranged, resume preparation, and career library.

EXPENSES *Tuition:* Full-time: $3828. Part-time: $319 per credit hour. *Tuition (international):* Full-time: $3828. Part-time: $319 per credit hour.

FINANCIAL AID (2007–08) 8 students received aid, including loans. Aid is available to part-time students. *Financial aid application deadline:* 6/30.

Embry-Riddle Aeronautical University Worldwide (continued)

Financial Aid Contact Barbara Dryden, Director, Financial Aid, 600 South Clyde Morris Boulevard, Daytona Beach, FL 32114-3900. *Phone:* 386-226-6300. *Fax:* 386-226-6307. *E-mail:* dbfinaid@erau.edu.

INTERNATIONAL STUDENTS 0.9% of students enrolled are international students. *Services and facilities:* Counseling/support services, ESL/language courses. Financial aid is not available to international students. *Required with application:* TOEFL with recommended score of 213 (computer) or 550 (paper); proof of adequate funds.

International Student Contact Pam Thomas, Director of Admissions and Records, 600 South Clyde Morris Boulevard, Daytona Beach, FL 32114. *Phone:* 386-226-6909. *Fax:* 386-226-6984. *E-mail:* ecinfo@erau.edu.

APPLICATION *Required:* GMAT, application form, baccalaureate/first degree, 3 letters of recommendation, transcripts of college work. *Recommended:* Interview. *Application fee:* $50. Applications for domestic and international students are processed on a rolling basis.

Application Contact Pam Thomas, Director of Admissions and Records, 600 South Clyde Morris Boulevard, Daytona Beach, FL 32114-3900. *Phone:* 386-226-6909. *Fax:* 386-226-6984. *E-mail:* ecinfo@erau.edu.

Everest University
Graduate School of Business
Clearwater, Florida

Phone: 727-725-2688 Ext. 116 **Fax:** 727-725-3827 **E-mail:** kbuskirk@cci.edu

Business Program(s) Web Site: http://www.mbaatfmu.com

DEGREE MBA

MBA—Master of Business Administration Full-time and part-time. Distance learning option. 56 total credits required. Minimum of 18 months to complete program. *Concentrations:* accounting, human resources management, international business.

RESOURCES AND SERVICES 58 on-campus PCs are available to graduate business students. Access to Internet/World Wide Web, online (class) registration, and online grade reports available. *Personal computer requirements:* Graduate business students are required to have a personal computer, the cost of which is included in tuition or other required fees. *Special opportunities include:* An international exchange program and an internship program are available. *Placement services include:* Alumni network, career placement, career counseling/planning, resume referral, career fairs, and resume preparation.

Application Contact Mr. Buskirk Kevin, Director of Admissions, 2471 McMullen Booth Road, Clearwater, FL 33759. *Phone:* 727-725-2688 Ext. 116. *Fax:* 727-725-3827. *E-mail:* kbuskirk@cci.edu.

Everest University
Program in Business Administration
Lakeland, Florida

Academic Calendar Quarters.

DEGREE MBA

MBA—Master of Business Administration *Concentrations:* accounting, human resources management, international business.

RESOURCES AND SERVICES Access to Internet/World Wide Web available. *Personal computer requirements:* Graduate business students are not required to have a personal computer.

Application Contact Admissions, 995 East Memorial Boulevard, Suite 110, Lakeland, FL 33801.

Everest University
Program in Business Administration
Orlando, Florida

Phone: 407-851-2525 **Fax:** 407-851-1477 **E-mail:** acloin@cci.edu

Business Program(s) Web Site: http://www.everest.edu

Graduate Business Faculty 5 part-time.

Admissions *Average GPA:* 3.0

Academic Calendar Quarters.

After Graduation (Class of 2006–07) *Employed within 3 months of graduation:* 85%.

DEGREE MBA

MBA—Master of Business Administration Full-time and part-time. Distance learning option. At least 56 total credits required. Minimum of 18 months to complete program. *Concentrations:* accounting, general MBA, human resources management, international management.

RESOURCES AND SERVICES Access to Internet/World Wide Web available. *Personal computer requirements:* Graduate business students are required to have a personal computer. *Placement services include:* Alumni network, career placement, career counseling/planning, electronic job bank, career fairs, and resume preparation.

EXPENSES *Tuition:* Full-time: $14,720. Part-time: $7360 per term. Tuition and/or fees vary by academic program.

FINANCIAL AID (2007–08) Loans, scholarships, and work study.

INTERNATIONAL STUDENTS *Services and facilities:* Counseling/support services, Housing location assistance, International student organization. Financial aid is not available to international students. *Required with application:* TOEFL.

APPLICATION *Required:* Application form, baccalaureate/first degree, interview, resume/curriculum vitae, transcripts of college work. School will accept GMAT, GRE, and MAT. *Application fee:* $25. Applications for domestic and international students are processed on a rolling basis.

Application Contact Annette Cloin, Director of Admissions, 9200 South Park Center Loop, Orlando, FL 32819. *Phone:* 407-851-2525. *Fax:* 407-851-1477. *E-mail:* acloin@cci.edu.

Florida Atlantic University
College of Business
Boca Raton, Florida

Phone: 561-297-3196 **Fax:** 561-297-1315 **E-mail:** ftaylor@fau.edu

Business Program(s) Web Site: http://business.fau.edu

Graduate Business Unit Enrollment *Total:* 944 (300 full-time; 644 part-time; 481 women; 196 international). *Average Age:* 32.

Graduate Business Faculty *Total:* 216 (141 full-time; 75 part-time).

Admissions *Applied:* 679. *Admitted:* 351. *Enrolled:* 254. *Average GMAT:* 540. *Average GPA:* 3.3

Academic Calendar Semesters.

Accreditation AACSB—The Association to Advance Collegiate Schools of Business.

After Graduation (Class of 2006–07) *Employed within 3 months of graduation:* 90%. *Average starting salary:* $55,000.

DEGREES M Econ • M Tax • MAC • MBA • MHA • MS

M Econ—Master of Science with a Major in Economics Full-time and part-time. 30 total credits required. 12 to 60 months to complete program. *Concentrations:* economics, finance, international business.

M Tax—Executive Master of Taxation Part-time. Distance learning option. 30 to 36 total credits required. 24 months to complete program. *Concentration:* taxation.

M Tax—Master of Taxation Full-time and part-time. 30 to 42 total credits required. 12 to 60 months to complete program. *Concentration:* taxation.

MAC—Executive Master of Accounting in Forensic Accounting Part-time. Distance learning option. 30 to 36 total credits required. 24 months to complete program. *Concentration:* forensic accounting.

MAC—Master of Accounting Full-time and part-time. Distance learning option. 30 to 51 total credits required. 12 to 60 months to complete program. *Concentration:* accounting.

MBA—Executive Master of Business Administration Full-time. At least 46 total credits required. 20 months to complete program. *Concentrations:* finance, general MBA, international business, operations management.

MBA—Master of Business Administration Full-time and part-time. Distance learning option. 40 to 52 total credits required. 12 to 84 months to complete program. *Concentrations:* accounting, entrepreneurship, finance, financial management/planning, general MBA, health administration, information technology, international business, marketing, operations management, real estate, sports/entertainment management.

MBA—Sport Management Full-time. Personal interview and essay required. 40 to 52 total credits required. 24 months to complete program. *Concentration:* sports/entertainment management.

MBA—Weekend Master of Business Administration Full-time. At least 40 total credits required. 16 months to complete program. *Concentrations:* finance, general MBA, international business, operations management.

MHA—Master of Health Administration Full-time and part-time. 30 to 42 total credits required. 12 to 60 months to complete program. *Concentration:* health administration.

MS—MS in Music Business Full-time and part-time. 36 total credits required. 24 months to complete program. *Concentration:* arts administration/management.

RESOURCES AND SERVICES 500 on-campus PCs are available to graduate business students. Access to Internet/World Wide Web, online (class) registration, and online grade reports available. *Personal computer requirements:* Graduate business students are strongly recommended to purchase or lease a personal computer. *Special opportunities include:* An international exchange program and an internship program are available. *Placement services include:* Alumni network, career placement, career counseling/planning, electronic job bank, resume referral, career fairs, job interviews arranged, resume preparation, and career library.

EXPENSES *Tuition (state resident):* Full-time: $5760. Part-time: $256 per credit hour. *Tuition (nonresident):* Full-time: $12,308. Part-time: $547 per credit hour. *Tuition (international):* Full-time: $12,308. Part-time: $547 per credit hour.

FINANCIAL AID (2007–08) 50 students received aid, including fellowships, grants, loans, research assistantships, scholarships, teaching assistantships, and work study. Aid is available to part-time students. *Financial aid application deadline:* 3/1.

Financial Aid Contact Carole Pfeilsticker, Director of Student Financial Aid, Student Financial Aid, 777 Glades Road, Boca Raton, FL 33431-0991. *Phone:* 561-297-3530. *Fax:* 561-297-3517. *E-mail:* pfeilsti@fau.edu.

INTERNATIONAL STUDENTS 21% of students enrolled are international students. *Services and facilities:* Counseling/support services, ESL/language courses, Housing location assistance, International student housing, International student organization, Orientation, Visa Services. Financial aid is available to international students. *Required with application:* TOEFL with recommended score of 250 (computer) or 600 (paper); proof of adequate funds; proof of health/immunizations.

International Student Contact Ingrid Jones, Director, Student Affairs, International Students and Scholars, International Students and Scholar Services, 777 Glades Road, SO 301, Boca Raton, FL 33431-0991. *Phone:* 561-297-3049. *Fax:* 561-297-2446. *E-mail:* ijones@fau.edu.

APPLICATION *Required:* GMAT, application form, baccalaureate/first degree, transcripts of college work. School will accept GRE. *Recommended:* Resume/curriculum vitae, work experience. *Application fee:* $30. Applications for domestic and international students are processed on a rolling basis.

Application Contact Mr. Fredrick G. Taylor, Admissions Coordinator, 101 Fleming West Building, Office of Masters Studies, 777 Glades Road, Boca Raton, FL 33461-0991. *Phone:* 561-297-3196. *Fax:* 561-297-1315. *E-mail:* ftaylor@fau.edu.

Florida Gulf Coast University
Lutgert College of Business
Fort Myers, Florida

Phone: 239-590-7351 **Fax:** 239-590-7330 **E-mail:** amacdiar@fgcu.edu

Business Program(s) Web Site: http://www.fgcu.edu/cob/grad

Graduate Business Unit Enrollment *Total:* 150 (104 full-time; 46 part-time; 69 women; 29 international). *Average Age:* 28.

Graduate Business Faculty *Total:* 54 (48 full-time; 6 part-time).

Admissions *Applied:* 102. *Admitted:* 77. *Enrolled:* 47. *Average GMAT:* 525. *Average GPA:* 3.09

Academic Calendar Semesters.

Accreditation AACSB—The Association to Advance Collegiate Schools of Business.

After Graduation (Class of 2006–07) *Employed within 3 months of graduation:* 80%.

DEGREE MBA

MBA—Master of Business Administration Full-time and part-time. Distance learning option. 30 to 54 total credits required. 12 to 84 months to complete program. *Concentrations:* finance, information systems, management, marketing, student designed.

RESOURCES AND SERVICES 80 on-campus PCs are available to graduate business students. Access to Internet/World Wide Web, online (class) registration, and online grade reports available. *Personal computer requirements:* Graduate business students are strongly recommended to purchase or lease a personal computer. *Special opportunities include:* An international exchange program and an internship program are available. *Placement services include:* Alumni network, career placement, career counseling/planning, electronic job bank, resume referral, career fairs, job interviews arranged, resume preparation, and career library.

EXPENSES *Tuition (state resident):* Full-time: $4542. Part-time: $243.38 per credit. *Tuition (nonresident):* Full-time: $19,449. Part-time: $543.18 per credit. *Tuition (international):* Full-time: $19,449. Part-time: $543.18 per credit. *Typical graduate housing cost:* $8267 (including board).

FINANCIAL AID (2007–08) 88 students received aid, including loans, research assistantships, and work study. Aid is available to part-time students. *Financial aid application deadline:* 4/1.

Financial Aid Contact Mr. Andrew MacDiarmid, Academic Advisor, 10501 FGCU Boulevard South, Fort Myers, FL 33965-6565. *Phone:* 239-590-7351. *Fax:* 239-590-7330. *E-mail:* amacdiar@fgcu.edu.

INTERNATIONAL STUDENTS 19% of students enrolled are international students. *Services and facilities:* Counseling/support services, Housing location assistance, International student organization, Orientation, Visa Services. Financial aid is available to international students. *Required with application:* TOEFL with recommended score of 213 (computer), 550 (paper), or 79 (Internet); proof of adequate funds; proof of health/immunizations.

International Student Contact Mr. Andrew MacDiarmid, Academic Advisor, 10501 FGCU Boulevard South, Fort Myers, FL 33965-6565. *Phone:* 239-590-7351. *Fax:* 239-590-7330. *E-mail:* amacdiar@fgcu.edu.

APPLICATION *Required:* GMAT, application form, baccalaureate/first degree, transcripts of college work. *Recommended:* Letter(s) of recom-

Florida Gulf Coast University (continued)

mendation, personal statement. *Application fee:* $30. Applications for domestic and international students are processed on a rolling basis.

Application Contact Mr. Andrew MacDiarmid, Academic Advisor, 10501 FGCU Boulevard South, Fort Myers, FL 33965-6565. *Phone:* 239-590-7351. *Fax:* 239-590-7330. *E-mail:* amacdiar@fgcu.edu.

Florida Institute of Technology
College of Business
Melbourne, Florida

Phone: 321-674-7577 **Fax:** 321-723-9468 **E-mail:** tshea@fit.edu

Business Program(s) Web Site: http://cob.fit.edu

Graduate Business Unit Enrollment *Total:* 75 (15 full-time; 60 part-time; 33 women; 9 international). *Average Age:* 31.

Graduate Business Faculty *Total:* 31 (13 full-time; 18 part-time).

Admissions *Applied:* 78. *Admitted:* 48. *Enrolled:* 12. *Average GMAT:* 439. *Average GPA:* 3.72

Academic Calendar Semesters.

After Graduation (Class of 2006–07) *Employed within 3 months of graduation:* 100%. *Average starting salary:* $65,000.

DEGREE MBA

MBA—Master of Business Administration Full-time and part-time. At least 36 total credits required. Minimum of 12 months to complete program. *Concentration:* general MBA.

RESOURCES AND SERVICES 400 on-campus PCs are available to graduate business students. Access to Internet/World Wide Web, online (class) registration, and online grade reports available. *Personal computer requirements:* Graduate business students are not required to have a personal computer. *Special opportunities include:* An internship program is available. *Placement services include:* Alumni network, career placement, career counseling/planning, electronic job bank, resume referral, career fairs, job interviews arranged, resume preparation, and career library.

EXPENSES *Tuition:* Full-time: $17,010. Part-time: $945 per credit hour. *Tuition (international):* Full-time: $17,010. Part-time: $945 per credit hour. Tuition and/or fees vary by campus location. *Graduate housing:* Room and board costs vary by campus location, number of occupants, type of accommodation, and type of board plan. *Typical cost:* $7770 (including board), $3400 (room only).

FINANCIAL AID (2007–08) 25 students received aid, including loans, research assistantships, and scholarships. Aid is available to part-time students.

Financial Aid Contact Mr. John Lally, Director, Financial Aid, 150 West University Boulevard, Melbourne, FL 32901-6975. *Phone:* 800-666-4348. *Fax:* 321-724-2778. *E-mail:* jlally@fit.edu.

INTERNATIONAL STUDENTS 12% of students enrolled are international students. *Services and facilities:* Counseling/support services, ESL/language courses, International student organization, Orientation, International friendship program. Financial aid is available to international students. *Required with application:* TOEFL with recommended score of 213 (computer) or 550 (paper); proof of adequate funds; proof of health/immunizations.

International Student Contact Ms. Judith Brooke, International Student and Scholar Services Director, 150 West University Boulevard, Melbourne, FL 32901-6975. *Phone:* 321-674-8053. *Fax:* 321-728-4570. *E-mail:* jbrooke@fit.edu.

APPLICATION *Required:* GMAT, application form, baccalaureate/first degree, transcripts of college work. *Application fee:* $50.

Application Contact Thomas M. Shea, Director, Graduate Admissions, 150 West University Boulevard, Melbourne, FL 32901-6975. *Phone:* 321-674-7577. *Fax:* 321-723-9468. *E-mail:* tshea@fit.edu.

Florida International University
Alvah H. Chapman, Jr. Graduate School of Business
Miami, Florida

Phone: 305-348-7398 **Fax:** 305-348-2368 **E-mail:** pietrasa@fiu.edu

Business Program(s) Web Site: http://chapman.fiu.edu

Graduate Business Unit Enrollment *Total:* 1,068 (124 full-time; 944 part-time; 489 women; 201 international). *Average Age:* 32.

Graduate Business Faculty *Total:* 153 (118 full-time; 35 part-time).

Admissions *Applied:* 1,275. *Admitted:* 580. *Enrolled:* 430. *Average GMAT:* 536. *Average GPA:* 3.28

Academic Calendar Semesters.

Accreditation AACSB—The Association to Advance Collegiate Schools of Business.

After Graduation (Class of 2006–07) *Employed within 3 months of graduation:* 47%. *Average starting salary:* $39,313.

DEGREES EMBA • EMST • EVEMBA • IMBA • JD/MBA • M Acc • MBA/MIB • MBA/MS • MBA/MSF • MBA/MSMIS • MIB • MS • MS/MS • MSF • MSHR • MSMIS

EMBA—Executive Master of Business Administration Part-time. Interview and 8+ years of management experience required. 42 total credits required. 20 months to complete program. *Concentration:* executive programs.

EMST—Executive Master of Science in Taxation Part-time. 30 total credits required. 10 months to complete program. *Concentrations:* executive programs, taxation.

EVEMBA—Evening Master of Business Administration Full-time and part-time. 55 total credits required. 24 to 36 months to complete program. *Concentrations:* accounting, entrepreneurship, finance, human resources management, international business, management, management information systems, marketing.

IMBA—International Master of Business Administration Full-time. 42 total credits required. 12 months to complete program. *Concentrations:* international business, international management.

JD/MBA—Juris Doctor/Master of Business Administration Full-time and part-time. 54 to 84 months to complete program. *Concentrations:* general MBA, law.

M Acc—Master of Accounting Part-time. 30 total credits required. 10 months to complete program. *Concentration:* accounting.

MBA/MIB—Master of Business Administration/Master of International Business 79 total credits required. 36 to 72 months to complete program. *Concentration:* international business.

MBA/MS—Human Resource Management 76 total credits required. 36 to 72 months to complete program. *Concentration:* human resources management.

MBA/MS—International Real Estate 70 total credits required. 36 to 72 months to complete program. *Concentration:* real estate.

MBA/MSF—Master of Business Administration/Master of Science in Finance Full-time and part-time. 73 total credits required. 24 to 36 months to complete program. *Concentration:* combined degrees.

MBA/MSMIS—Master of Business Administration/Master of Science in Management Information Systems Full-time and part-time. 76 total credits required. 24 to 36 months to complete program. *Concentration:* combined degrees.

MIB—Master of International Business Full-time and part-time. Undergraduate degree in business administration or related work experience required. 36 total credits required. 12 to 36 months to complete program. *Concentration:* international business.

MS—International Real Estate Part-time. 30 total credits required. 12 months to complete program. *Concentration:* real estate.

MS/MS—MS in Finance/MS in International Real Estate 60 total credits required. 24 months to complete program. *Concentrations:* finance, financial management/planning, international banking, investments and securities, real estate.

MSF—Master of Science in Finance Part-time. 33 total credits required. 12 months to complete program. *Concentrations:* finance, financial management/planning, international banking, investments and securities.

MSHR—Master of Science in Human Resources Part-time. 36 total credits required. 12 months to complete program. *Concentration:* human resources management.

MSMIS—Master of Science in Management Information Systems Part-time. 36 total credits required. 12 months to complete program. *Concentration:* management information systems.

RESOURCES AND SERVICES 150 on-campus PCs are available to graduate business students. Access to Internet/World Wide Web, online (class) registration, and online grade reports available. *Personal computer requirements:* Graduate business students are not required to have a personal computer. *Special opportunities include:* An international exchange program and an internship program are available. *Placement services include:* Alumni network, career placement, job search course, career counseling/planning, electronic job bank, resume referral, career fairs, job interviews arranged, and resume preparation.

EXPENSES *Tuition (state resident):* Full-time: $30,490. *Tuition (nonresident):* Full-time: $35,490. *Tuition (international):* Full-time: $35,490. *Required fees:* Full-time: $450.25. Part-time: $450.25 per year. Tuition and/or fees vary by number of courses or credits taken and academic program. *Graduate housing:* Room and board costs vary by number of occupants, type of accommodation, and type of board plan. *Typical cost:* $9800 (including board), $7000 (room only).

FINANCIAL AID (2007–08) 680 students received aid, including grants, loans, research assistantships, and scholarships. Aid is available to part-time students. *Financial aid application deadline:* 3/1.

Financial Aid Contact Mellissa Hew, Coordinator, Financial Aid Office, 11200 Southwest 8th Street, CBC 201, Miami, FL 33199. *Phone:* 305-348-1647. *Fax:* 305-348-2346.

INTERNATIONAL STUDENTS 19% of students enrolled are international students. *Services and facilities:* Counseling/support services, ESL/language courses, Housing location assistance, International student housing, International student organization, Language tutoring, Orientation. Financial aid is available to international students. *Required with application:* IELT with recommended score of 6.3; TOEFL with recommended score of 213 (computer), 550 (paper), or 80 (Internet); proof of adequate funds; proof of health/immunizations.

International Student Contact Ana Sippin, Director, International Student Services, 11200 Southwest 8th Street, GC 242, Miami, FL 33199. *Phone:* 305-348-2421. *Fax:* 305-348-1521. *E-mail:* sippina@fiu.edu.

APPLICATION *Required:* GMAT, GRE, application form, baccalaureate/first degree, essay, personal statement, resume/curriculum vitae, transcripts of college work. *Recommended:* 2 letters of recommendation, 2 years of work experience. *Application fee:* $30. Applications for domestic and international students are processed on a rolling basis.

Application Contact Anna Pietraszek, Associate Director of Admissions, Chapman Graduate School, 11200 Southwest 8th Street, CBC 201, Miami, FL 33199. *Phone:* 305-348-7398. *Fax:* 305-348-2368. *E-mail:* pietrasa@fiu.edu.

See full description on page 618.

Florida State University
College of Business
Tallahassee, Florida

Phone: 850-644-6455 **Fax:** 850-644-0588 **E-mail:** gradprog@cob.fsu.edu

Business Program(s) Web Site: http://www.cob.fsu.edu/grad/

Graduate Business Unit Enrollment *Total:* 609 (221 full-time; 388 part-time; 234 women; 48 international). *Average Age:* 29.

Graduate Business Faculty *Total:* 113 (112 full-time; 1 part-time).

Admissions *Applied:* 812. *Admitted:* 443. *Enrolled:* 293. *Average GMAT:* 570. *Average GPA:* 3.4

Academic Calendar Semesters.

Accreditation AACSB—The Association to Advance Collegiate Schools of Business.

After Graduation (Class of 2006–07) *Employed within 3 months of graduation:* 45%. *Average starting salary:* $61,790.

DEGREES JD/MBA • M Acc • MBA • MS • MSF • MSM

JD/MBA—Juris Doctor/Master of Business Administration Full-time. At least 113 total credits required. 48 to 84 months to complete program. *Concentration:* general MBA.

M Acc—Master of Accounting Full-time and part-time. At least 33 total credits required. 12 to 84 months to complete program. *Concentrations:* accounting, corporate accounting, information systems, taxation.

MBA—Master of Business Administration Full-time and part-time. 42 to 43 total credits required. 12 to 84 months to complete program. *Concentrations:* finance, general MBA, hospitality management, management information systems, marketing, real estate, supply chain management.

MBA—Online Master of Business Administration Part-time. Distance learning option. At least 42 total credits required. 24 to 84 months to complete program. *Concentrations:* general MBA, hospitality management, real estate.

MS—Master of Science in Management Information Systems Full-time and part-time. At least 32 total credits required. 12 to 84 months to complete program. *Concentration:* management information systems.

MSF—Master of Science in Finance Full-time. At least 32 total credits required. 12 to 84 months to complete program. *Concentration:* finance.

MSM—Risk Management and Insurance Part-time. Distance learning option. At least 33 total credits required. 24 to 84 months to complete program. *Concentrations:* insurance, real estate, risk management.

RESOURCES AND SERVICES 30 on-campus PCs are available to graduate business students. Access to Internet/World Wide Web, online (class) registration, and online grade reports available. *Personal computer requirements:* Graduate business students are required to have a personal computer. *Special opportunities include:* An internship program is available. *Placement services include:* Alumni network, career placement, job search course, career counseling/planning, electronic job bank, resume referral, career fairs, job interviews arranged, resume preparation, and career library.

EXPENSES *Tuition (state resident):* Full-time: $6700. Part-time: $3350 per year. *Tuition (nonresident):* Full-time: $23,748. Part-time: $11,874 per year. *Tuition (international):* Full-time: $23,748. Part-time: $11,874 per year.

FINANCIAL AID (2007–08) 30 students received aid, including fellowships, research assistantships, scholarships, and teaching assistantships. *Financial aid application deadline:* 1/15.

Financial Aid Contact Mr. Darryl A. Marshall, Director of Student Financial Aid, Office of Financial Aid, A4474 University Center, Tallahassee, FL 32306-2430. *Phone:* 850-644-5716. *Fax:* 850-644-6404. *E-mail:* dmarshall@admin.fsu.edu.

INTERNATIONAL STUDENTS 8% of students enrolled are international students. *Services and facilities:* Counseling/support services, ESL/language courses, Housing location assistance, International student housing, International student organization, Language tutoring, Orientation, Visa Services, Practical training search assistance. Financial aid is available to international students. *Required with application:* TOEFL with recommended score of 250 (computer), 600 (paper), or 100 (Internet); proof of adequate funds; proof of health/immunizations.

Florida State University (continued)

International Student Contact Ms. Cynthia Green, Director of International Center, International Student Center, 945 Learning Way, Tallahassee, FL 32306-4240. *Phone:* 850-644-3050. *Fax:* 850-644-9951. *E-mail:* cagreen@admin.fsu.edu.

APPLICATION *Required:* GMAT, application form, baccalaureate/first degree, 2 letters of recommendation, personal statement, resume/curriculum vitae, transcripts of college work. *Recommended:* Work experience. *Application fee:* $30. Applications for domestic and international students are processed on a rolling basis.

Application Contact Ms. Lisa Beverly, Director of Graduate Admissions, Graduate Office, Room 215 RBA, Tallahassee, FL 32306-1110. *Phone:* 850-644-6455. *Fax:* 850-644-0588. *E-mail:* gradprog@cob.fsu.edu.

Lynn University
School of Business
Boca Raton, Florida

Phone: 561-237-7900 Ext. 7803 **Fax:** 561-237-7100 **E-mail:** admissionpm@lynn.edu

Business Program(s) Web Site: http://www.lynn.edu

DEGREE MBA

MBA—Master of Business Administration Full-time and part-time. Distance learning option. At least 36 total credits required. 12 to 48 months to complete program. *Concentrations:* aviation management, electronic commerce (E-commerce), health care, hospitality management, international business, marketing, media administration, sports/entertainment management.

RESOURCES AND SERVICES 160 on-campus PCs are available to graduate business students. Access to Internet/World Wide Web, online (class) registration, and online grade reports available. *Personal computer requirements:* Graduate business students are not required to have a personal computer. *Special opportunities include:* An international exchange program and an internship program are available. *Placement services include:* Alumni network, career placement, career counseling/planning, electronic job bank, resume referral, career fairs, job interviews arranged, resume preparation, and career library.

Application Contact Dr. Larissa Baia, Assistant Director of Graduate Admissions, 3601 North Military Trail, Admissions Office, Boca Raton, FL 33431-5598. *Phone:* 561-237-7900 Ext. 7803. *Fax:* 561-237-7100. *E-mail:* admissionpm@lynn.edu.

Nova Southeastern University
H. Wayne Huizenga School of Business and Entrepreneurship
Fort Lauderdale, Florida

Phone: 800-672-7223 Ext. 5119 **Fax:** 954-262-3822 **E-mail:** sumulong@nsu.nova.edu

Business Program(s) Web Site: http://www.huizenga.nova.edu

Graduate Business Unit Enrollment *Total:* 3,652 (1,491 full-time; 2,161 part-time; 2,208 women). *Average Age:* 33.

Graduate Business Faculty *Total:* 254 (54 full-time; 200 part-time).

Admissions *Applied:* 892. *Admitted:* 663. *Enrolled:* 481. *Average GMAT:* 500. *Average GPA:* 3.0

Academic Calendar Semesters.

After Graduation (Class of 2006–07) *Employed within 3 months of graduation:* 89%.

DEGREES M Acc • MBA • MIBA • MPA • MS • MTX

M Acc—Master of Accounting Part-time. Distance learning option. At least 40 total credits required. 18 to 60 months to complete program. *Concentration:* accounting.

MBA—Master of Business Administration Full-time and part-time. Distance learning option. At least 43 total credits required. 12 to 60 months to complete program. *Concentrations:* accounting, entrepreneurship, finance, human resources management, international business, marketing.

MIBA—Master of International Business Administration Full-time and part-time. Distance learning option. At least 43 total credits required. 12 to 60 months to complete program. *Concentration:* international business.

MPA—Master of Public Administration Full-time and part-time. Distance learning option. At least 40 total credits required. 12 to 60 months to complete program. *Concentration:* public policy and administration.

MS—Master of Science in Human Resource Management Full-time and part-time. Distance learning option. At least 43 total credits required. 18 to 60 months to complete program. *Concentration:* human resources management.

MS—Master of Science in Leadership Full-time and part-time. Distance learning option. At least 40 total credits required. 12 to 60 months to complete program. *Concentration:* leadership.

MTX—Master of Taxation Part-time. Distance learning option. At least 36 total credits required. 18 to 60 months to complete program. *Concentration:* taxation.

RESOURCES AND SERVICES 80 on-campus PCs are available to graduate business students. Access to Internet/World Wide Web, online (class) registration, and online grade reports available. *Personal computer requirements:* Graduate business students are strongly recommended to purchase or lease a personal computer. *Special opportunities include:* An internship program is available. *Placement services include:* Alumni network, job search course, career counseling/planning, electronic job bank, resume referral, career fairs, job interviews arranged, resume preparation, and career library.

EXPENSES *Tuition:* Full-time: $27,778. Part-time: $13,680 per year. *Tuition (international):* Full-time: $27,778. Part-time: $13,680 per year. *Required fees:* Full-time: $830. Part-time: $830 per year. Tuition and/or fees vary by class time and number of courses or credits taken. *Graduate housing:* Room and board costs vary by campus location, number of occupants, and type of accommodation. *Typical cost:* $13,200 (room only).

FINANCIAL AID (2007–08) 1500 students received aid, including loans, research assistantships, scholarships, and work study. Aid is available to part-time students. *Financial aid application deadline:* 4/1.

Financial Aid Contact Ms. Liza Sumulong, Recruiter III, DeSantis Building, 3301 College Avenue, Fort Lauderdale-Davie, FL 33314-7796. *Phone:* 800-522-3243 Ext. 5119. *Fax:* 954-262-3822. *E-mail:* sumulong@nsu.nova.edu.

INTERNATIONAL STUDENTS *Services and facilities:* Counseling/support services, ESL/language courses, Housing location assistance, International student organization, Orientation, Visa Services. Financial aid is not available to international students. *Required with application:* TOEFL with recommended score of 213 (computer) or 550 (paper); proof of adequate funds. *Recommended with application:* Proof of health/immunizations.

International Student Contact Ms. Liza Sumulong, Recruiter III, DeSantis Building, 3301 College Avenue, Fort Lauderdale-Davie, FL 33314-7796. *Phone:* 800-541-6682 Ext. 5119. *Fax:* 954-262-3822. *E-mail:* sumulong@nsu.nova.edu.

APPLICATION *Required:* Application form, baccalaureate/first degree, transcripts of college work. School will accept GMAT and GRE. *Application fee:* $50. Applications for domestic and international students are processed on a rolling basis.

Application Contact Ms. Liza Sumulong, Recruiter III, DeSantis Building, 3301 College Avenue, Fort Lauderdale-Davie, FL 33314-7796. *Phone:* 800-672-7223 Ext. 5119. *Fax:* 954-262-3822. *E-mail:* sumulong@nsu.nova.edu.

See full description on page 666.

Palm Beach Atlantic University

Rinker School of Business

West Palm Beach, Florida

Phone: 561-803-2120 **Fax:** 561-803-2115 **E-mail:** genevieve_potrekus@pba.edu

Business Program(s) Web Site: http://www.pba.edu

Graduate Business Unit Enrollment *Total:* 85 (16 full-time; 69 part-time; 31 women; 13 international).

Graduate Business Faculty 6 full-time.

Admissions *Applied:* 135. *Admitted:* 130. *Enrolled:* 125. *Average GMAT:* 474. *Average GPA:* 3.0

Academic Calendar Semesters.

DEGREE MBA

MBA—Master of Business Administration Part-time. At least 36 total credits required. Minimum of 36 months to complete program. *Concentrations:* international business, management, management information systems, marketing.

RESOURCES AND SERVICES 200 on-campus PCs are available to graduate business students. Access to Internet/World Wide Web, online (class) registration, and online grade reports available. *Personal computer requirements:* Graduate business students are strongly recommended to purchase or lease a personal computer. *Special opportunities include:* An internship program is available. *Placement services include:* Alumni network, career placement, job search course, career counseling/planning, electronic job bank, resume referral, career fairs, job interviews arranged, resume preparation, and career library.

EXPENSES *Tuition:* Part-time: $445 per credit hour. *Tuition (international):* Part-time: $445 per credit hour.

FINANCIAL AID (2007–08) 1 student received aid, including scholarships and work study. Aid is available to part-time students. *Financial aid application deadline:* 9/29.

Financial Aid Contact Mrs. Becky Moore, Interim Director of Student Financial Planning, PO Box 24708, West Palm Beach, FL 33416-4708. *Phone:* 561-803-2127. *Fax:* 561-803-2130. *E-mail:* becky_moore@pba.edu.

INTERNATIONAL STUDENTS 15% of students enrolled are international students. *Services and facilities:* Counseling/support services, ESL/language courses. Financial aid is available to international students. *Required with application:* TOEFL with recommended score of 550 (paper); proof of adequate funds; proof of health/immunizations.

International Student Contact Ms. Judy Consentino, Coordinator, Graduate Studies, PO Box 24708, West Palm Beach, FL 33416-4708. *Phone:* 561-803-2120. *E-mail:* genevieve_potrekus@pba.edu.

APPLICATION *Required:* GMAT, application form, baccalaureate/first degree, essay, interview, 3 letters of recommendation, resume/curriculum vitae, transcripts of college work. *Deadlines:* 8/15 for fall, 12/15 for winter. Applications for international students are processed on a rolling basis.

Application Contact Ms. Judy Consentino, Coordinator, Graduate Studies, PO Box 24708, West Palm Beach, FL 33416-4708. *Phone:* 561-803-2120. *Fax:* 561-803-2115. *E-mail:* genevieve_potrekus@pba.edu.

Rollins College

Crummer Graduate School of Business

Winter Park, Florida

Phone: 407-646-2236 **Fax:** 407-646-2522 **E-mail:** lpuritz@rollins.edu

Business Program(s) Web Site: http://www.crummer.rollins.edu

Graduate Business Unit Enrollment *Total:* 472 (274 full-time; 198 part-time; 197 women; 22 international). *Average Age:* 28.

Graduate Business Faculty *Total:* 31 (24 full-time; 7 part-time).

Admissions *Applied:* 547. *Admitted:* 340. *Enrolled:* 240. *Average GMAT:* 580. *Average GPA:* 3.2

Academic Calendar Semesters.

Accreditation AACSB—The Association to Advance Collegiate Schools of Business.

After Graduation (Class of 2006–07) *Employed within 3 months of graduation:* 93%. *Average starting salary:* $55,000.

DEGREES MBA

MBA—Corporate Master of Business Administration Full-time. Requires at least ten years of full-time work experience. At least 53 total credits required. 21 to 60 months to complete program. *Concentrations:* entrepreneurship, management, marketing.

MBA—Early Advantage Master of Business Administration Full-time. Especially designed for younger students with little or no work experience. At least 62 total credits required. 21 to 60 months to complete program. *Concentrations:* entrepreneurship, finance, international and area business studies, management, marketing.

MBA—Professional Master of Business Administration Part-time. Especially designed for executives that want to attend class in the evening. At least 53 total credits required. 32 to 60 months to complete program. *Concentrations:* entrepreneurship, finance, international and area business studies, management, marketing.

MBA—Saturday Master of Business Administration Full-time. 5 or more years of significant work experience required. At least 53 total credits required. 20 to 60 months to complete program. *Concentrations:* entrepreneurship, finance, international and area business studies, management, marketing.

RESOURCES AND SERVICES 5 on-campus PCs are available to graduate business students. Access to Internet/World Wide Web, online (class) registration, and online grade reports available. *Personal computer requirements:* Graduate business students are required to have a personal computer, the cost of which is included in tuition or other required fees. *Special opportunities include:* An international exchange program and an internship program are available. *Placement services include:* Alumni network, career placement, job search course, career counseling/planning, electronic job bank, resume referral, career fairs, job interviews arranged, resume preparation, and career library.

EXPENSES *Tuition:* Full-time: $28,300. Part-time: $928 per credit hour. *Tuition (international):* Full-time: $28,300. Part-time: $928 per credit hour. Tuition and/or fees vary by academic program.

FINANCIAL AID (2007–08) 82 students received aid, including research assistantships, scholarships, and work study. Aid is available to part-time students.

Financial Aid Contact Mr. Steve Booker, Director of Financial Aid, 1000 Holt Avenue—2395, Winter Park, FL 32789-4499. *Phone:* 407-646-2395. *Fax:* 407-646-2173. *E-mail:* sbooker@rollins.edu.

INTERNATIONAL STUDENTS 5% of students enrolled are international students. *Services and facilities:* Counseling/support services, Housing location assistance, International student housing, International student organization, Orientation, Visa Services. Financial aid is available to international students. *Required with application:* TOEFL with recommended score of 250 (computer), 600 (paper), or 100 (Internet); proof of adequate funds.

Rollins College (continued)

International Student Contact Ms. Jackie Brito, Director of Full-time MBA Program and Career Management, 1000 Holt Avenue—2722, Winter Park, FL 32789-4499. *Phone:* 407-628-6320. *Fax:* 407-646-2311. *E-mail:* jbrito@rollins.edu.

APPLICATION *Required:* GMAT, application form, baccalaureate/first degree, essay, interview, 2 letters of recommendation, personal statement, resume/curriculum vitae, transcripts of college work, work experience. School will accept GRE and MAT. *Application fee:* $50. Applications for domestic and international students are processed on a rolling basis.

Application Contact Linda Puritz, Assistant Director, Full-time MBA Admissions, 1000 Holt Avenue—2722, Winter Park, FL 32789-4499. *Phone:* 407-646-2236. *Fax:* 407-646-2522. *E-mail:* lpuritz@rollins.edu.

See full description on page 674.

Saint Leo University
Graduate Business Studies

Saint Leo, Florida

Phone: 800-707-8846 **Fax:** 352-588-7873 **E-mail:** grad.admissions@saintleo.edu

Business Program(s) Web Site: http://www.saintleo.edu/

Graduate Business Unit Enrollment *Total:* 852 (320 full-time; 532 part-time; 517 women; 10 international). *Average Age:* 37.

Graduate Business Faculty *Total:* 48 (17 full-time; 31 part-time).

Academic Calendar Semesters.

After Graduation (Class of 2006–07) *Employed within 3 months of graduation:* 100%.

DEGREES MBA

MBA—MBA Master of Business Administration Full-time and part-time. Distance learning option. At least 36 total credits required. 12 to 60 months to complete program. *Concentration:* human resources management.

MBA—MBA with Concentration in Criminal Justice Full-time and part-time. Distance learning option. At least 36 total credits required. 12 to 60 months to complete program. *Concentration:* law.

MBA—MBA with Concentration in Health Care Administration Full-time and part-time. Distance learning option. At least 39 total credits required. 12 to 60 months to complete program. *Concentration:* health administration.

MBA—MBA with Concentration in Information Security Management Full-time and part-time. Distance learning option. At least 36 total credits required. 12 to 60 months to complete program. *Concentration:* information management.

MBA—MBA with Concentration in Sport Business Full-time and part-time. Distance learning option. At least 42 total credits required. 12 to 60 months to complete program. *Concentration:* sports/entertainment management.

MBA—Master of Business Administration Full-time and part-time. Distance learning option. At least 36 total credits required. 12 to 60 months to complete program. *Concentration:* management.

MBA—Master of Business Administration Full-time and part-time. Distance learning option. At least 36 total credits required. 12 to 60 months to complete program. *Concentration:* accounting.

MBA—Master of Business Administration with Concentration in Criminal Justice Full-time and part-time. Distance learning option. At least 36 total credits required. 12 to 60 months to complete program. *Concentration:* general MBA.

RESOURCES AND SERVICES 91 on-campus PCs are available to graduate business students. Access to Internet/World Wide Web, online (class) registration, and online grade reports available. *Personal computer*

requirements: Graduate business students are not required to have a personal computer. *Placement services include:* Alumni network, career counseling/planning, electronic job bank, resume referral, career fairs, job interviews arranged, resume preparation, and career library.

EXPENSES *Tuition:* Full-time: $10,296. Part-time: $572 per semester hour. *Tuition (international):* Full-time: $10,296. Part-time: $572 per semester hour. Tuition and/or fees vary by campus location. *Graduate housing:* Room and board costs vary by number of occupants, type of accommodation, and type of board plan. *Typical cost:* $8430 (including board), $4450 (room only).

FINANCIAL AID (2007–08) 48 students received aid, including grants and scholarships. Aid is available to part-time students.

Financial Aid Contact Financial Aid Counselor, PO Box 6665, MC 2228, Saint Leo, FL 33574-6665. *Phone:* 800-240-7658. *Fax:* 352-588-8403. *E-mail:* finaid@saintleo.edu.

INTERNATIONAL STUDENTS 1% of students enrolled are international students. *Services and facilities:* Counseling/support services, International student organization, Visa Services. Financial aid is available to international students. *Required with application:* TOEFL with recommended score of 213 (computer) or 550 (paper); proof of adequate funds; proof of health/immunizations.

International Student Contact Mr. Jared Welling, Director, Office of Admission for Graduate Studies and Adult Enrollment, MC 2248, PO Box 6665, Saint Leo, FL 33574-6665. *Phone:* 800-707-8846. *Fax:* 352-588-7873. *E-mail:* grad.admissions@saintleo.edu.

APPLICATION *Required:* Application form, baccalaureate/first degree, essay, interview, 2 letters of recommendation, personal statement, resume/curriculum vitae, transcripts of college work, 5 years of work experience. School will accept GMAT. *Application fee:* $45. Applications for domestic and international students are processed on a rolling basis.

Application Contact Mr. Jared Welling, Director, Office of Admission for Graduate Studies and Adult Enrollment, MC 2248, PO Box 6665, Saint Leo, FL 33574-6665. *Phone:* 800-707-8846. *Fax:* 352-588-7873. *E-mail:* grad.admissions@saintleo.edu.

St. Thomas University
Department of Business Administration

Miami Gardens, Florida

Phone: 305-628-6589 **E-mail:** mcarallosa@stu.edu

Business Program(s) Web Site: http://www.stu.edu/busadm/

Graduate Business Unit Enrollment *Total:* 171 (64 full-time; 107 part-time; 108 women; 20 international). *Average Age:* 32.

Graduate Business Faculty *Total:* 23 (15 full-time; 8 part-time).

Admissions *Applied:* 81. *Admitted:* 61. *Enrolled:* 51. *Average GPA:* 3.25

Academic Calendar Semesters.

DEGREES MAC • MBA • MIB • MS • MSM

MAC—Accounting Full-time and part-time. Two letters of recommendation; undergraduate degree in accounting (or its equivalent) with a GPA of 2.75 or higher in upper-division accounting, business and economics courses. At least 30 total credits required. 18 to 60 months to complete program. *Concentration:* accounting.

MBA—Master of Business Administration Full-time and part-time. Official transcripts, two letters of recommendation; current resume detailing work experience and education; formal writing assessment exam. At least 42 total credits required. 18 to 60 months to complete program. *Concentrations:* accounting, health administration, human resources management, international business, management, sports/entertainment management.

MIB—Master of International Business Full-time and part-time. Two letters of recommendation; transcripts. At least 30 total credits required. 12 to 60 months to complete program. *Concentration:* international business.

MS—Master of Science in Management Full-time and part-time. Official transcripts, two letters of recommendation; current resume detailing work experience and education; interview. At least 36 total credits required. 12 to 60 months to complete program. *Concentrations:* accounting, health administration, human resources management, international business, management, public management.

MS—Master of Science in Sports Administration Full-time and part-time. Typed statement of goals that includes career objectives; official transcripts; 3 letters of recommendation; overall GPA of 2.75 for all undergraduate course work; interview. At least 36 total credits required. 12 to 60 months to complete program. *Concentration:* sports/entertainment management.

MSM—Master of Science in Management Full-time and part-time. Up to 36 total credits required. 12 to 60 months to complete program. *Concentrations:* accounting, health administration, human resources management, international business.

RESOURCES AND SERVICES 200 on-campus PCs are available to graduate business students. Access to Internet/World Wide Web, online (class) registration, and online grade reports available. *Personal computer requirements:* Graduate business students are strongly recommended to purchase or lease a personal computer. *Special opportunities include:* An internship program is available. *Placement services include:* Alumni network, career placement, career counseling/planning, electronic job bank, resume referral, career fairs, job interviews arranged, resume preparation, and career library.

EXPENSES *Tuition:* Full-time: $11,808. Part-time: $656 per credit. *Tuition (international):* Full-time: $11,808. Part-time: $656 per credit. Tuition and/or fees vary by academic program. *Graduate housing:* Room and board costs vary by number of occupants and type of accommodation. *Typical cost:* $4200 (including board).

FINANCIAL AID (2007–08) Loans, research assistantships, scholarships, and work study. *Financial aid application deadline:* 5/1.

Financial Aid Contact Ms. Anh Do, Director of Financial Aid, 16401 Northwest 37th Avenue, Miami, FL 33054-6459. *Phone:* 305-628-6725. *Fax:* 305-628-6754. *E-mail:* ado@stu.edu.

INTERNATIONAL STUDENTS 12% of students enrolled are international students. *Services and facilities:* Counseling/support services, ESL/language courses, Housing location assistance, International student organization, Orientation, Visa Services. Financial aid is not available to international students. *Required with application:* TOEFL with recommended score of 213 (computer); proof of adequate funds; proof of health/immunizations.

International Student Contact Ms. Cristina Torres, Assistant Director of Admissions, 16401 Northwest 37th Avenue, Miami Gardens, FL 33054. *Phone:* 305-628-6709. *E-mail:* cjtorres@stu.edu.

APPLICATION *Required:* Application form, baccalaureate/first degree, essay, interview, 2 letters of recommendation, personal statement, resume/curriculum vitae, transcripts of college work. School will accept GMAT and GRE. *Recommended:* Work experience. *Application fee:* $40. Applications for domestic and international students are processed on a rolling basis.

Application Contact Ms. Marilyn Carballosa, Assistant Director, 16401 Northwest 37th Avenue, Miami Gardens, FL 33054. *Phone:* 305-628-6589. *E-mail:* mcarallosa@stu.edu.

Schiller International University
MBA Programs, Florida
Largo, Florida

Phone: 727-736-5082 Ext. 240 **Fax:** 727-734-0359 **E-mail:** admissions@schiller.edu

Business Program(s) Web Site: http://www.schiller.edu/

Graduate Business Unit Enrollment *Total:* 449 (124 full-time; 325 part-time; 99 women; 422 international). *Average Age:* 24.

Graduate Business Faculty *Total:* 13 (3 full-time; 10 part-time).

Academic Calendar Semesters.

After Graduation (Class of 2006–07) *Employed within 3 months of graduation:* 97%.

DEGREES MBA

MBA—Master of Business Administration in International Business Full-time and part-time. Distance learning option. At least 45 total credits required. 12 to 24 months to complete program. *Concentration:* international business.

MBA—Master of Business Administration in International Hotel and Tourism Management Full-time and part-time. At least 45 total credits required. 12 to 24 months to complete program. *Concentrations:* hospitality management, travel industry/tourism management.

MBA—Master of Business Administration in Management of Information Technology Full-time and part-time. Distance learning option. At least 45 total credits required. 12 to 24 months to complete program. *Concentration:* management information systems.

RESOURCES AND SERVICES 40 on-campus PCs are available to graduate business students. Access to Internet/World Wide Web available. *Personal computer requirements:* Graduate business students are required to have a personal computer. *Special opportunities include:* An international exchange program and an internship program are available. *Placement services include:* Alumni network, career placement, career counseling/planning, electronic job bank, resume referral, career fairs, job interviews arranged, resume preparation, and career library.

EXPENSES *Tuition:* Full-time: $18,750. Part-time: $1560 per course. *Tuition (international):* Full-time: $18,750. Part-time: $1560 per course. *Required fees:* Full-time: $595. Part-time: $595 per year.

FINANCIAL AID (2007–08) Grants, loans, scholarships, and work study. *Financial aid application deadline:* 4/1.

Financial Aid Contact Ms. Jennifer Fraser, Financial Aid Officer, 300 East Bay Drive, Largo, FL 33770. *Phone:* 727-736-5082 Ext. 253. *Fax:* 727-738-8405. *E-mail:* financial_aid@schiller.edu.

INTERNATIONAL STUDENTS 94% of students enrolled are international students. *Services and facilities:* Counseling/support services, ESL/language courses, Housing location assistance, International student housing, Language tutoring, Orientation, Visa Services. Financial aid is available to international students. *Required with application:* Proof of adequate funds. *Recommended with application:* TOEFL with recommended score of 213 (computer) or 550 (paper).

International Student Contact Ms. Stephanie Givens, Assistant Director of Admissions, 300 East Bay Drive, Largo, FL 33770. *Phone:* 727-736-5082 Ext. 411. *Fax:* 727-734-0359. *E-mail:* admissions@schiller.edu.

APPLICATION *Required:* Application form, baccalaureate/first degree, essay, transcripts of college work. *Recommended:* Personal statement, resume/curriculum vitae, work experience. *Application fee:* $65. Applications for domestic and international students are processed on a rolling basis.

Application Contact Ms. Kamala Dontamsetti, Assistant Director of Admissions, 300 East Bay Drive, Largo, FL 33770. *Phone:* 727-736-5082 Ext. 240. *Fax:* 727-734-0359. *E-mail:* admissions@schiller.edu.

See full description on page 684.

University of Central Florida
College of Business Administration
Orlando, Florida

Phone: 407-823-5693 **Fax:** 407-823-6442 **E-mail:** vblanco@mail.ucf.edu

Business Program(s) Web Site: http://www.bus.ucf.edu

University of Central Florida (continued)

Graduate Business Unit Enrollment *Total:* 1,011 (490 full-time; 521 part-time; 444 women; 116 international). *Average Age:* 33.

Graduate Business Faculty 103 full-time.

Admissions *Applied:* 724. *Admitted:* 465. *Enrolled:* 366. *Average GMAT:* 575. *Average GPA:* 3.4

Academic Calendar Semesters.

Accreditation AACSB—The Association to Advance Collegiate Schools of Business.

After Graduation (Class of 2006–07) *Employed within 3 months of graduation:* 78%. *Average starting salary:* $53,500.

DEGREES EMBA • MBA • MS • MSM

EMBA—Executive Master of Business Administration Full-time. 39 total credits required. 21 months to complete program. *Concentration:* executive programs.

MBA—One-Year MBA Cohort Full-time. At least 39 total credits required. 12 months to complete program. *Concentration:* general MBA.

MBA—Master of Business Administration Part-time. At least 39 total credits required. 24 to 33 months to complete program. *Concentrations:* accounting, economics, entrepreneurship, finance, human resources management, international and area business studies, management information systems, marketing.

MS—Business Sport Management Full-time. 47 to 57 total credits required. 20 to 23 months to complete program. *Concentration:* sports/entertainment management.

MS—Master of Science in Accounting Full-time and part-time. At least 30 total credits required. 12 to 24 months to complete program. *Concentration:* accounting.

MS—Master of Science in Economics Full-time. At least 30 total credits required. 24 months to complete program. *Concentration:* economics.

MS—Master of Science in Taxation Full-time and part-time. At least 30 total credits required. 12 to 24 months to complete program. *Concentration:* taxation.

MSM—Master of Science in Management Information Systems Full-time and part-time. At least 30 total credits required. 12 to 36 months to complete program. *Concentration:* management information systems.

RESOURCES AND SERVICES 2,300 on-campus PCs are available to graduate business students. Access to Internet/World Wide Web, online (class) registration, and online grade reports available. *Personal computer requirements:* Graduate business students are strongly recommended to purchase or lease a personal computer. *Special opportunities include:* An internship program is available. *Placement services include:* Alumni network, career placement, job search course, career counseling/planning, electronic job bank, resume referral, career fairs, job interviews arranged, resume preparation, and career library.

EXPENSES *Tuition (state resident):* Full-time: $6484. *Tuition (nonresident):* Full-time: $23,938. *Tuition (international):* Full-time: $23,938.

FINANCIAL AID (2007–08) 130 students received aid, including fellowships, research assistantships, scholarships, and teaching assistantships. *Financial aid application deadline:* 1/15.

Financial Aid Contact Mary McKinney, Executive Director, Student Financial Assistance, PO Box 25000, MH 120, Orlando, FL 32816. *Phone:* 407-823-2827. *E-mail:* mckinney@mail.ucf.edu.

INTERNATIONAL STUDENTS 11% of students enrolled are international students. *Services and facilities:* Counseling/support services, ESL/language courses, Housing location assistance, International student organization, Language tutoring, Orientation, Visa Services. Financial aid is available to international students. *Required with application:* TOEFL with recommended score of 233 (computer), 575 (paper), or 91 (Internet); proof of adequate funds; proof of health/immunizations.

International Student Contact Nataly Chandia, Director, International Services Center, PO Box 25000, Orlando, FL 32816. *Phone:* 407-823-2337. *Fax:* 407-823-2526. *E-mail:* chandia@mail.ucf.edu.

APPLICATION *Required:* GMAT, application form, baccalaureate/first degree, essay, 3 letters of recommendation, personal statement, resume/curriculum vitae, transcripts of college work. *Recommended:* Work experience. *Application fee:* $30. Applications for domestic and international students are processed on a rolling basis.

Application Contact Ms. Vanessa Blanco, Graduate Admissions, PO Box 160112, Orlando, FL 32816. *Phone:* 407-823-5693. *Fax:* 407-823-6442. *E-mail:* vblanco@mail.ucf.edu.

University of Florida
Hough Graduate School of Business
Gainesville, Florida

Phone: 352-392-7992 Ext. 1200 **Fax:** 352-392-8791 **E-mail:** floridamba@cba.ufl.edu

Business Program(s) Web Site: http://www.floridamba.ufl.edu

Graduate Business Unit Enrollment *Total:* 894 (143 full-time; 751 part-time; 228 women; 145 international). *Average Age:* 27.

Graduate Business Faculty *Total:* 112 (100 full-time; 12 part-time).

Admissions *Applied:* 639. *Admitted:* 363. *Enrolled:* 277. *Average GMAT:* 680. *Average GPA:* 3.4

Academic Calendar Semesters.

Accreditation AACSB—The Association to Advance Collegiate Schools of Business.

After Graduation (Class of 2006–07) *Employed within 3 months of graduation:* 93%. *Average starting salary:* $61,380.

DEGREES JD/MBA • MBA • MBA/MESS • MBA/MS • MD/MBA • PhD/MBA • Pharm D/MBA

JD/MBA—Juris Doctor/Master of Business Administration Full-time. At least 111 total credits required. Minimum of 46 months to complete program. *Concentrations:* business information science, business policy/strategy, electronic commerce (E-commerce), entrepreneurship, finance, financial management/planning, general MBA, human resources management, international business, Latin American business studies, management, management information systems, marketing, real estate, sports/entertainment management, supply chain management, technology management.

MBA—Executive Master of Business Administration Full-time. 8 years of professional work experience required. 48 total credits required. 20 months to complete program. *Concentration:* general MBA.

MBA—Internet (1-year option) Part-time. Distance learning option. Undergraduate degree in business completed within 7 years prior to the start of the program. 32 total credits required. 16 months to complete program. *Concentration:* general MBA.

MBA—Internet MBA (2-year option) Part-time. Distance learning option. 48 total credits required. 27 months to complete program. *Concentration:* general MBA.

MBA—Master of Business Administration for Professionals (1-year option) Part-time. Undergraduate degree in business completed within 7 years prior to the start of the program. 32 total credits required. 16 months to complete program. *Concentration:* general MBA.

MBA—Master of Business Administration for Professionals (2-year option) Part-time. 48 total credits required. 27 months to complete program. *Concentration:* general MBA.

MBA—Professional MBA in South Florida Part-time. 48 total credits required. 24 months to complete program. *Concentration:* general MBA.

MBA—Traditional 1-year Master of Business Administration Full-time. At least 48 total credits required. 12 months to complete program. *Concentrations:* business information science, business policy/strategy, electronic commerce (E-commerce), entrepreneurship, finance, financial management/planning, general MBA, human resources management, international business, Latin American business studies, management,

management information systems, marketing, real estate, sports/entertainment management, supply chain management, technology management.

MBA—Traditional 1-year Master of Business Administration Full-time. Undergraduate degree in business completed within 7 years prior to the start of the program. At least 32 total credits required. 10 months to complete program. *Concentrations:* business information science, business policy/strategy, electronic commerce (E-commerce), entrepreneurship, finance, financial management/planning, general MBA, human resources management, international business, Latin American business studies, management, management information systems, marketing, real estate, sports/entertainment management, supply chain management, technology management.

MBA—Traditional Master of Business Administration (2-year option) Full-time. At least 48 total credits required. 21 months to complete program. *Concentrations:* business information science, business policy/strategy, electronic commerce (E-commerce), entrepreneurship, finance, financial management/planning, general MBA, human resources management, international business, Latin American business studies, management, management information systems, marketing, real estate, sports/entertainment management, supply chain management, technology management.

MBA/MESS—Master of Business Administration/Master of Exercise and Sport Science Full-time. At least 66 total credits required. Minimum of 34 months to complete program. *Concentrations:* business information science, business policy/strategy, electronic commerce (E-commerce), entrepreneurship, finance, financial management/planning, general MBA, human resources management, international business, Latin American business studies, management, management information systems, marketing, real estate, sports/entertainment management, supply chain management, technology management.

MBA/MS—Master of Business Administration/Master of Science in Biotechnology Full-time. At least 68 total credits required. Minimum of 34 months to complete program. *Concentrations:* business information science, business policy/strategy, electronic commerce (E-commerce), entrepreneurship, finance, financial management/planning, general MBA, human resources management, international business, Latin American business studies, management, management information systems, marketing, real estate, sports/entertainment management, supply chain management, technology management.

MD/MBA—Doctor of Medicine/Master of Business Administration Full-time. At least 207 total credits required. Minimum of 60 months to complete program. *Concentrations:* business information science, business policy/strategy, electronic commerce (E-commerce), entrepreneurship, finance, financial management/planning, general MBA, human resources management, international business, Latin American business studies, management, management information systems, marketing, real estate, sports/entertainment management, supply chain management, technology management.

PhD/MBA—Doctor of Philosophy in Biotechnology/Master of Business Administration Full-time. At least 114 total credits required. Minimum of 58 months to complete program. *Concentrations:* business information science, business policy/strategy, electronic commerce (E-commerce), entrepreneurship, finance, financial management/planning, general MBA, human resources management, international business, Latin American business studies, management, management information systems, marketing, real estate, sports/entertainment management, supply chain management, technology management.

Pharm D/MBA—Doctor of Pharmacy/Master of Business Administration Full-time. At least 164 total credits required. Minimum of 58 months to complete program. *Concentrations:* business information science, business policy/strategy, electronic commerce (E-commerce), entrepreneurship, finance, financial management/planning, general MBA, human resources management, international business, Latin American business studies, management, management information systems, marketing, real estate, sports/entertainment management, supply chain management, technology management.

RESOURCES AND SERVICES Access to Internet/World Wide Web, online (class) registration, and online grade reports available. *Personal computer requirements:* Graduate business students are required to have a personal computer. *Special opportunities include:* An international exchange program and an internship program are available. *Placement services include:* Alumni network, career placement, career counseling/planning, electronic job bank, resume referral, career fairs, job interviews arranged, resume preparation, and career library.

EXPENSES *Tuition (state resident):* Full-time: $7729. Part-time: $28,000 per degree program. *Tuition (nonresident):* Full-time: $22,853. Part-time: $28,000 per degree program. *Tuition (international):* Full-time: $22,853. Part-time: $28,000 per degree program. *Required fees:* Full-time: $750. Part-time: $750 per degree program.

FINANCIAL AID (2007–08) 73 students received aid, including loans, scholarships, and teaching assistantships. *Financial aid application deadline:* 4/15.

Financial Aid Contact Connie Reed, MBA Coordinator, Student Financial Affairs, 107 Criser Hall, PO Box 114025, Gainesville, FL 32611. *Phone:* 352-392-1275. *Fax:* 352-392-2861. *E-mail:* clreed@ufl.edu.

INTERNATIONAL STUDENTS 16% of students enrolled are international students. *Services and facilities:* Counseling/support services, ESL/language courses, International student organization, Language tutoring, Orientation, Visa Services. Financial aid is available to international students. *Required with application:* TOEFL with recommended score of 250 (computer) or 600 (paper); proof of adequate funds; proof of health/immunizations.

International Student Contact Admissions, 134 Bryan Hall, PO Box 117152, Gainesville, FL 32611. *Phone:* 352-392-7992. *Fax:* 352-392-8791. *E-mail:* floridamba@cba.ufl.edu.

APPLICATION *Required:* GMAT, application form, baccalaureate/first degree, essay, interview, 2 letters of recommendation, personal statement, resume/curriculum vitae, transcripts of college work, 2 years of work experience. *Application fee:* $30. Applications for domestic and international students are processed on a rolling basis.

Application Contact MBA Admissions, 134 Bryan Hall, PO Box 117152, Gainesville, FL 32611. *Phone:* 352-392-7992 Ext. 1200. *Fax:* 352-392-8791. *E-mail:* floridamba@cba.ufl.edu.

University of Miami
School of Business Administration
Coral Gables, Florida

Phone: 305-284-4607 **Fax:** 305-284-5905 **E-mail:** mba@miami.edu

Business Program(s) Web Site: http://www.bus.miami.edu/grad

Graduate Business Unit Enrollment *Total:* 715 (682 full-time; 33 part-time; 256 women; 121 international). *Average Age:* 30.

Graduate Business Faculty 105 full-time.

Admissions *Applied:* 520. *Admitted:* 359. *Enrolled:* 156. *Average GMAT:* 630. *Average GPA:* 3.2

Academic Calendar Semesters.

Accreditation AACSB—The Association to Advance Collegiate Schools of Business.

After Graduation (Class of 2006–07) *Employed within 3 months of graduation:* 74%. *Average starting salary:* $61,655.

DEGREES EMBA • JD/MBA • M Sc • MA • MBA • MBA/MS • MPA • MS

EMBA—Executive Master of Business Administration in Health Administration and Policy Full-time. Full-time employment required. 48 total credits required. 23 months to complete program. *Concentration:* health administration.

JD/MBA—Juris Doctor/Master of Business Administration Full-time. Students must apply to both the School of Business and the School of Law. Letter of admission from the School of Law must be submitted with

University of Miami (continued)

application. At least 136 total credits required. 36 to 72 months to complete program. *Concentration:* law.

M Sc—Master of Science in Professional Management Full-time. Offered in Spanish to executives and professionals. 36 total credits required. 12 months to complete program. *Concentration:* management.

MA—Master of Arts in Economics Full-time and part-time. At least 30 total credits required. 12 to 72 months to complete program. *Concentration:* economics.

MBA—Executive Master of Business Administration Full-time. Full-time employment required. 48 total credits required. 23 months to complete program. *Concentrations:* international business, management.

MBA—Two-Year MBA Program Full-time. 48 total credits required. 21 months to complete program. *Concentrations:* accounting, finance, information systems, international business, management, management science, marketing.

MBA/MS—Master of Business Administration/Master of Science in Industrial Engineering Full-time. Full-time employment required. At least 60 total credits required. 25 months to complete program. *Concentration:* combined degrees.

MPA—Master of Public Administration Full-time and part-time. 36 to 48 total credits required. 12 to 72 months to complete program. *Concentration:* public policy and administration.

MPA—Master of Professional Accountancy Full-time and part-time. At least 30 total credits required. 12 to 72 months to complete program. *Concentration:* accounting.

MS—Management Science Full-time and part-time. At least 30 total credits required. 12 to 72 months to complete program. *Concentrations:* quality management, statistics, supply chain management.

MS—Master of Science in Taxation Full-time and part-time. At least 30 total credits required. 12 to 72 months to complete program. *Concentration:* taxation.

RESOURCES AND SERVICES 150 on-campus PCs are available to graduate business students. Access to Internet/World Wide Web and online grade reports available. *Personal computer requirements:* Graduate business students are strongly recommended to purchase or lease a personal computer. *Special opportunities include:* An internship program is available. *Placement services include:* Alumni network, career placement, career counseling/planning, electronic job bank, resume referral, career fairs, job interviews arranged, resume preparation, and career library.

EXPENSES *Tuition:* Full-time: $32,400. *Tuition (international):* Full-time: $32,400. *Required fees:* Full-time: $234. *Graduate housing:* Room and board costs vary by number of occupants, type of accommodation, and type of board plan. *Typical cost:* $9800 (including board), $5800 (room only).

FINANCIAL AID (2007–08) 372 students received aid, including loans, scholarships, and work study. *Financial aid application deadline:* 3/1.

Financial Aid Contact James M. Bauer, Director, Financial Assistance Services, PO Box 248187, Coral Gables, FL 33124-5240. *Phone:* 305-284-5212. *Fax:* 305-284-4082. *E-mail:* ofas@miami.edu.

INTERNATIONAL STUDENTS 17% of students enrolled are international students. *Services and facilities:* Counseling/support services, ESL/language courses, Housing location assistance, International student organization, Orientation, Visa Services. Financial aid is available to international students. *Required with application:* TOEFL with recommended score of 213 (computer), 550 (paper), or 59 (Internet); proof of adequate funds; proof of health/immunizations. *Recommended with application:* IELT with recommended score of 6.5.

International Student Contact Teresa De la Guardia, Director, International Student Services, Building 21-F, Coral Gables, FL 33124-5550. *Phone:* 305-284-2928. *Fax:* 305-284-3409. *E-mail:* tdelaguardia@miami.edu.

APPLICATION *Required:* GMAT, GRE, application form, baccalaureate/first degree, essay, 1 letter of recommendation, personal statement, resume/curriculum vitae, transcripts of college work. *Recommended:*

Work experience. *Application fee:* $50. *Deadlines:* 10/17 for fall, 12/1 for winter, 2/2 for spring, 4/1 for summer, 10/17 for fall (international), 12/1 for winter (international), 2/2 for spring (international), 4/1 for summer (international).

Application Contact Cristina Raecke, Director, Graduate Business Programs, Graduate Business Programs, PO Box 248505, Coral Gables, FL 33124-6524. *Phone:* 305-284-4607. *Fax:* 305-284-5905. *E-mail:* mba@miami.edu.

See full description on page 718.

University of North Florida
Coggin College of Business
Jacksonville, Florida

Phone: 904-620-1354 **Fax:** 904-620-1362 **E-mail:** kiersten.jarvis@unf.edu

Business Program(s) Web Site: http://www.unf.edu/coggin

Graduate Business Unit Enrollment *Total:* 536 (163 full-time; 373 part-time; 237 women; 28 international). *Average Age:* 30.

Graduate Business Faculty *Total:* 95 (76 full-time; 19 part-time).

Admissions *Applied:* 321. *Admitted:* 196. *Enrolled:* 153. *Average GMAT:* 530. *Average GPA:* 3.15

Academic Calendar Semesters.

Accreditation AACSB—The Association to Advance Collegiate Schools of Business.

After Graduation (Class of 2006–07) *Employed within 3 months of graduation:* 95%. *Average starting salary:* $45,644.

DEGREES GMBA • M Acc • MBA

GMBA—Global Master of Business Administration Full-time. Minimum GMAT score of 500 required. 66 to 78 total credits required. *Concentration:* international business.

M Acc—Master of Accountancy Full-time and part-time. 33 to 81 total credits required. 11 to 27 months to complete program. *Concentrations:* accounting, taxation.

MBA—Master of Business Administration Full-time and part-time. 36 to 48 total credits required. 12 to 16 months to complete program. *Concentrations:* accounting, construction management, economics, finance, human resources management, international business, logistics, management, marketing.

RESOURCES AND SERVICES 120 on-campus PCs are available to graduate business students. Access to Internet/World Wide Web, online (class) registration, and online grade reports available. *Personal computer requirements:* Graduate business students are strongly recommended to purchase or lease a personal computer. *Special opportunities include:* An international exchange program and an internship program are available. *Placement services include:* Alumni network, career placement, job search course, career counseling/planning, electronic job bank, resume referral, career fairs, job interviews arranged, resume preparation, and career library.

EXPENSES *Tuition (state resident):* Full-time: $6390. *Tuition (nonresident):* Full-time: $20,583. *Tuition (international):* Full-time: $20,583. *Required fees:* Full-time: $600. Tuition and/or fees vary by academic program. *Graduate housing:* Room and board costs vary by number of occupants, type of accommodation, and type of board plan. *Typical cost:* $7071 (including board), $4080 (room only).

FINANCIAL AID (2007–08) 190 students received aid, including fellowships, grants, loans, research assistantships, scholarships, teaching assistantships, and work study. Aid is available to part-time students. *Financial aid application deadline:* 3/15.

Financial Aid Contact Ms. Anissa Cameron, Director, Financial Aid, 1 UNF Drive, Jacksonville, FL 32224-2645. *Phone:* 904-620-2681. *Fax:* 904-620-2414. *E-mail:* anissa.cameron@unf.edu.

INTERNATIONAL STUDENTS 5% of students enrolled are international students. *Services and facilities:* Counseling/support services, ESL/language courses, Housing location assistance, International student housing, International student organization, Language tutoring, Orientation, Visa Services. Financial aid is available to international students. *Required with application:* TOEFL with recommended score of 213 (computer), 550 (paper), or 80 (Internet); proof of adequate funds; proof of health/immunizations.

International Student Contact Tim Robinson, Director, International Student Affairs, 1 UNF Drive, Jacksonville, FL 32224-2645. *Phone:* 904-626-2768. *Fax:* 904-620-3925. *E-mail:* trobinso@unf.edu.

APPLICATION *Required:* GMAT, application form, baccalaureate/first degree, transcripts of college work. *Application fee:* $30. Applications for domestic and international students are processed on a rolling basis.

Application Contact Ms. Kiersten Jarvis, Graduate Coordinator, 1 UNF Drive, Jacksonville, FL 32224-2645. *Phone:* 904-620-1354. *Fax:* 904-620-1362. *E-mail:* kiersten.jarvis@unf.edu.

University of Phoenix–Central Florida Campus

College of Graduate Business and Management

Maitland, Florida

Phone: 480-317-6200 **Fax:** 480-643-1479 **E-mail:** beth.barilla@phoenix.edu

Business Program(s) Web Site: http://www.phoenix.edu

DEGREES EMBA • MA • MBA • MM

EMBA—X-MBA Full-time. At least 30 total credits required. *Concentration:* executive programs.

MA—Master of Arts in Organizational Management Full-time. At least 40 total credits required. *Concentration:* organizational management.

MBA—Accounting Full-time. At least 54 total credits required. *Concentration:* accounting.

MBA—Global Management Full-time. At least 45 total credits required. *Concentration:* international business.

MBA—Human Resource Management Full-time. At least 45 total credits required. *Concentration:* human resources management.

MBA—Marketing Full-time. At least 45 total credits required. *Concentration:* marketing.

MBA—Public Administration Full-time. At least 45 total credits required. *Concentration:* public policy and administration.

MBA—e-Business Full-time. At least 45 total credits required. *Concentration:* electronic commerce (E-commerce).

MBA—Master of Business Administration Full-time. At least 45 total credits required. *Concentration:* administration.

MM—Master of Management Full-time. At least 39 total credits required. *Concentration:* management.

RESOURCES AND SERVICES Access to online grade reports available. *Personal computer requirements:* Graduate business students are strongly recommended to purchase or lease a personal computer. *Placement services include:* Alumni network.

Application Contact Beth Barilla, Associate Vice President of Student Admissions and Services, Mail Stop AA-K101, 4615 East Elwood Street, Phoenix, AZ 85040-1958. *Phone:* 480-317-6200. *Fax:* 480-643-1479. *E-mail:* beth.barilla@phoenix.edu.

University of Phoenix–North Florida Campus

College of Graduate Business and Management

Jacksonville, Florida

Phone: 480-317-6200 **Fax:** 480-643-1479 **E-mail:** beth.barilla@phoenix.edu

Business Program(s) Web Site: http://www.phoenix.edu/

DEGREES EMBA • MA • MBA

EMBA—X-MBA Full-time. At least 30 total credits required. *Concentration:* executive programs.

MA—Master of Arts in Organizational Management Full-time. At least 40 total credits required. *Concentration:* organizational management.

MBA—Accounting Full-time. At least 54 total credits required. *Concentration:* accounting.

MBA—Global Management Full-time. At least 45 total credits required. *Concentration:* international business.

MBA—Human Resource Management Full-time. At least 45 total credits required. *Concentration:* human resources management.

MBA—Marketing Full-time. At least 45 total credits required. *Concentration:* marketing.

MBA—Public Administration Full-time. At least 45 total credits required. *Concentration:* public policy and administration.

MBA—e-Business Full-time. At least 45 total credits required. *Concentration:* electronic commerce (E-commerce).

MBA—Master of Business Administration Full-time. At least 45 total credits required. *Concentration:* administration.

RESOURCES AND SERVICES Access to online grade reports available. *Personal computer requirements:* Graduate business students are strongly recommended to purchase or lease a personal computer. *Placement services include:* Alumni network.

Application Contact Beth Barilla, Associate Vice President of Student Admissions and Services, Mail Stop AA-K101, 4615 East Elwood Street, Phoenix, AZ 85040-1958. *Phone:* 480-317-6200. *Fax:* 480-643-1479. *E-mail:* beth.barilla@phoenix.edu.

University of Phoenix–South Florida Campus

College of Graduate Business and Management

Fort Lauderdale, Florida

Phone: 480-317-6200 **Fax:** 480-643-1479 **E-mail:** beth.barilla@phoenix.edu

Business Program(s) Web Site: http://www.phoenix.edu

DEGREES M Mgt • MBA

M Mgt—Human Resource Management Full-time. At least 39 total credits required. *Concentration:* human resources management.

M Mgt—Master of Management Full-time. At least 40 total credits required. *Concentration:* management.

MBA—Accounting Full-time. At least 54 total credits required. *Concentration:* accounting.

University of Phoenix–South Florida Campus (continued)

MBA—Master of Business Administration in Global Management Full-time. At least 45 total credits required. *Concentration:* international management.

MBA—Master of Business Administration in Human Resource Management Full-time. At least 45 total credits required. *Concentration:* human resources management.

MBA—Master of Business Administration in Marketing Full-time. At least 45 total credits required. *Concentration:* marketing.

MBA—Public Administration Full-time. At least 45 total credits required. *Concentration:* public policy and administration.

MBA—e-Business Full-time. At least 45 total credits required. *Concentration:* electronic commerce (E-commerce).

MBA—Master of Business Administration Full-time. At least 45 total credits required. *Concentration:* administration.

RESOURCES AND SERVICES Access to online grade reports available. *Personal computer requirements:* Graduate business students are strongly recommended to purchase or lease a personal computer. *Placement services include:* Alumni network.

Application Contact Beth Barilla, Associate Vice President of Student Admissions and Services, Mail Stop AA-K101, 4615 East Elwood Street, Phoenix, AZ 85040-1958. *Phone:* 480-317-6200. *Fax:* 480-643-1479. *E-mail:* beth.barilla@phoenix.edu.

University of Phoenix–West Florida Campus

College of Graduate Business and Management

Temple Terrace, Florida

Phone: 480-317-6200 **Fax:** 480-643-1479 **E-mail:** beth.barilla@phoenix.edu

Business Program(s) Web Site: http://www.phoenix.edu

DEGREES   M Mgt • MA • MBA

M Mgt—Human Resource Management Full-time. At least 39 total credits required. *Concentration:* human resources management.

M Mgt—Master of Management Full-time. At least 39 total credits required. *Concentration:* management.

MA—Organizational Management Full-time. At least 40 total credits required. *Concentration:* organizational management.

MBA—Accounting Full-time. At least 54 total credits required. *Concentration:* accounting.

MBA—Global Management Full-time. At least 45 total credits required. *Concentration:* international management.

MBA—Marketing Full-time. At least 45 total credits required. *Concentration:* marketing.

MBA—Public Administration Full-time. At least 45 total credits required. *Concentration:* public policy and administration.

MBA—e-Business Full-time. At least 46 total credits required. *Concentration:* electronic commerce (E-commerce).

MBA—Master of Business Administration Full-time. At least 45 total credits required. *Concentration:* administration.

RESOURCES AND SERVICES Access to online grade reports available. *Personal computer requirements:* Graduate business students are strongly recommended to purchase or lease a personal computer. *Placement services include:* Alumni network.

Application Contact Beth Barilla, Associate Vice President of Student Admissions and Services, Mail Stop AA-K101, 4615 East Elwood Street, Phoenix, AZ 85040-1958. *Phone:* 480-317-6200. *Fax:* 480-643-1479. *E-mail:* beth.barilla@phoenix.edu.

University of South Florida

College of Business Administration

Tampa, Florida

Phone: 813-974-3335 **Fax:** 813-974-4518 **E-mail:** mwarfel@coba.usf.edu

Business Program(s) Web Site: http://www.coba.usf.edu/programs

Graduate Business Unit Enrollment *Total:* 803 (389 full-time; 414 part-time; 316 women; 121 international). *Average Age:* 28.

Graduate Business Faculty *Total:* 152 (110 full-time; 42 part-time).

Admissions *Applied:* 705. *Admitted:* 406. *Enrolled:* 229. *Average GMAT:* 540. *Average GPA:* 3.2

Academic Calendar Semesters.

Accreditation AACSB—The Association to Advance Collegiate Schools of Business.

After Graduation (Class of 2006–07) *Employed within 3 months of graduation:* 64%. *Average starting salary:* $55,000.

DEGREES   M Acc • M Sc • MA • MBA • MS • MSM

M Acc—Master of Accountancy Full-time and part-time. Seehttp://www.coba.usf.edu/departments/accounting/programs/master.html. At least 30 total credits required. Minimum of 12 months to complete program. *Concentration:* accounting.

M Sc—MS Finance Full-time and part-time. See http://www.coba.usf.edu/departments/finance/programs/program.html. 30 to 42 total credits required. 12 to 60 months to complete program. *Concentration:* finance.

M Sc—Marketing Full-time and part-time. At least 32 total credits required. Minimum of 12 months to complete program. *Concentration:* marketing.

MA—Master of Arts in Economics Full-time and part-time. Seehttp://www.coba.usf.edu/departments/economics/programs/master.html. At least 30 total credits required. Minimum of 12 months to complete program. *Concentration:* economics.

MBA—Executive Master of Business Administration Full-time. 5 years of managerial experience required; sponsored by employer; see http://www.emba.usf.edu. At least 48 total credits required. 20 months to complete program. *Concentration:* executive programs.

MBA—Master of Business Administration Full-time and part-time. See http://www.mba.usf.edu; 2 years post-baccalaureate work experience preferred. 37 to 48 total credits required. 12 to 60 months to complete program. *Concentrations:* business ethics, entrepreneurship, finance, international business, management, management information systems, marketing.

MS—Entrepreneurship Full-time and part-time. See http://www.ce.usf.edu/. At least 30 total credits required. Minimum of 12 months to complete program. *Concentration:* entrepreneurship.

MSM—Master of Science in Management Full-time and part-time. Seehttp://www.coba.usf.edu/departments/management/programs/msm/master.html. At least 32 total credits required. Minimum of 12 months to complete program. *Concentration:* leadership.

MSM—Master of Science in Management Information Systems Full-time and part-time. Seehttp://www.coba.usf.edu/departments/isds/programs/master.html. At least 32 total credits required. Minimum of 12 months to complete program. *Concentration:* management information systems.

RESOURCES AND SERVICES 637 on-campus PCs are available to graduate business students. Access to Internet/World Wide Web, online (class) registration, and online grade reports available. *Personal computer*

requirements: Graduate business students are strongly recommended to purchase or lease a personal computer. *Special opportunities include:* An international exchange program is available. *Placement services include:* Alumni network, career counseling/planning, electronic job bank, resume referral, career fairs, job interviews arranged, and resume preparation.

EXPENSES *Tuition (state resident):* Full-time: $6050. Part-time: $275.11 per credit hour. *Tuition (nonresident):* Full-time: $21,530. Part-time: $919.04 per credit hour. *Tuition (international):* Full-time: $21,530. Part-time: $919.04 per credit hour. *Required fees:* Full-time: $74. Part-time: $37 per semester. Tuition and/or fees vary by campus location. *Graduate housing:* Room and board costs vary by campus location, number of occupants, type of accommodation, and type of board plan. *Typical cost:* $8620 (including board).

FINANCIAL AID (2007–08) 50 students received aid, including fellowships, research assistantships, scholarships, and teaching assistantships. *Financial aid application deadline:* 5/15.

Financial Aid Contact Financial Aid Office, 4202 East Fowler Avenue, SVC 1072, Tampa, FL 33620-5500. *Phone:* 813-974-4700.

INTERNATIONAL STUDENTS 15% of students enrolled are international students. *Services and facilities:* Counseling/support services, ESL/language courses, International student organization, Orientation, Visa Services. Financial aid is not available to international students. *Required with application:* TOEFL with recommended score of 213 (computer), 550 (paper), or 79 (Internet); proof of adequate funds; proof of health/immunizations.

International Student Contact Graduate Admissions, 4202 East Fowler Avenue, BEH 304, Tampa, FL 33620-5500. *Phone:* 813-974-8800. *Fax:* 813-974-8044.

APPLICATION *Required:* GMAT, application form, baccalaureate/first degree, 2 letters of recommendation, personal statement, resume/curriculum vitae, transcripts of college work, 2 years of work experience. School will accept GRE. *Application fee:* $30. Applications for domestic and international students are processed on a rolling basis.

Application Contact Molly Warfel, Manager of Recruiting, 4202 East Fowler Avenue, BSN 3403, Tampa, FL 33620-5500. *Phone:* 813-974-3335. *Fax:* 813-974-4518. *E-mail:* mwarfel@coba.usf.edu.

The University of Tampa
John H. Sykes College of Business

Tampa, Florida

Phone: 813-258-7409 **Fax:** 813-259-5403 **E-mail:** fnolasco@ut.edu

Business Program(s) Web Site: http://ut.edu/graduate

Graduate Business Unit Enrollment *Total:* 565 (189 full-time; 376 part-time; 221 women; 86 international). *Average Age:* 30.

Graduate Business Faculty *Total:* 76 (63 full-time; 13 part-time).

Admissions *Applied:* 509. *Admitted:* 291. *Enrolled:* 207. *Average GMAT:* 530. *Average GPA:* 3.4

Academic Calendar Semesters.

Accreditation AACSB—The Association to Advance Collegiate Schools of Business.

After Graduation (Class of 2006–07) *Employed within 3 months of graduation:* 86%. *Average starting salary:* $67,000.

DEGREES MBA • MS • MSA

MBA—Saturday MBA Part-time. Relevant work experience required. 37 total credits required. 24 months to complete program. *Concentration:* general MBA.

MBA—Master of Business Administration Full-time and part-time. 37 to 52 total credits required. 16 to 84 months to complete program. *Concentrations:* accounting, economics, entrepreneurship, finance, information management, international business, management, marketing, nonprofit management.

MS—Finance Full-time and part-time. 30 to 40 total credits required. 16 to 84 months to complete program. *Concentration:* finance.

MS—Marketing Full-time and part-time. 30 to 42 total credits required. 16 to 84 months to complete program. *Concentration:* marketing.

MS—Master of Science in Innovation Management Part-time. 5 years of relevant work experience with two years in a management position and 2 letters of recommendation required. At least 34 total credits required. 21 months to complete program. *Concentration:* technology management.

MSA—MS Accounting Full-time and part-time. 30 to 48 total credits required. 16 to 84 months to complete program. *Concentration:* accounting.

RESOURCES AND SERVICES 1,000 on-campus PCs are available to graduate business students. Access to Internet/World Wide Web, online (class) registration, and online grade reports available. *Personal computer requirements:* Graduate business students are not required to have a personal computer. *Special opportunities include:* An international exchange program and an internship program are available. *Placement services include:* Alumni network, career placement, job search course, career counseling/planning, electronic job bank, resume referral, career fairs, job interviews arranged, resume preparation, and career library.

EXPENSES *Tuition:* Full-time: $7200. *Tuition (international):* Full-time: $7200. *Required fees:* Full-time: $70. Part-time: $70 per year. Tuition and/or fees vary by academic program. *Graduate housing:* Room and board costs vary by number of occupants, type of accommodation, and type of board plan. *Typical cost:* $7616 (including board), $4076 (room only).

FINANCIAL AID (2007–08) 91 students received aid, including grants, loans, and research assistantships. Aid is available to part-time students.

Financial Aid Contact John Marsh, Director, Financial Aid, 401 West Kennedy Boulevard, Plant Hall 427, Tampa, FL 33606-1490. *Phone:* 813-253-6219. *Fax:* 813-258-7439. *E-mail:* jmarsh@ut.edu.

INTERNATIONAL STUDENTS 15% of students enrolled are international students. *Services and facilities:* Counseling/support services, Housing location assistance, International student housing, International student organization, Language tutoring, Orientation, Visa Services, Career services. Financial aid is available to international students. *Required with application:* IELT with recommended score of 7; TOEFL with recommended score of 230 (computer) or 577 (paper); proof of adequate funds; proof of health/immunizations.

International Student Contact Sally Moorehead, Assistant Director, International Programs, 401 West Kennedy Boulevard, Box 70F, Tampa, FL 33606-1490. *Phone:* 813-258-7433 Ext. 3659. *Fax:* 813-258-7404. *E-mail:* smoorehead@ut.edu.

APPLICATION *Required:* GMAT, application form, baccalaureate/first degree, 2 letters of recommendation, personal statement, resume/curriculum vitae, transcripts of college work. School will accept GRE. *Recommended:* Interview, work experience. *Application fee:* $40. Applications for domestic and international students are processed on a rolling basis.

Application Contact Fernando Nolasco, Director, Graduate Studies, 401 West Kennedy Boulevard, Box O, Tampa, FL 33606-1490. *Phone:* 813-258-7409. *Fax:* 813-259-5403. *E-mail:* fnolasco@ut.edu.

See full description on page 742.

University of West Florida
College of Business

Pensacola, Florida

Phone: 850-474-2230 **Fax:** 850-857-6043 **E-mail:** admissions@uwf.edu

Business Program(s) Web Site: http://uwf.edu/cob/

Graduate Business Unit Enrollment *Total:* 171 (38 full-time; 133 part-time; 74 women; 25 international). *Average Age:* 34.

Graduate Business Faculty *Total:* 24 (18 full-time; 6 part-time).

University of West Florida (continued)

Admissions *Applied:* 89. *Admitted:* 49. *Enrolled:* 37. *Average GMAT:* 548. *Average GPA:* 3.4

Academic Calendar Semesters.

Accreditation AACSB—The Association to Advance Collegiate Schools of Business.

DEGREES   M Acc • MBA

M Acc—Master of Accounting Full-time and part-time. At least 30 total credits required. Minimum of 12 months to complete program. *Concentration:* accounting.

MBA—Master of Business Administration Full-time and part-time. At least 30 total credits required. Minimum of 12 months to complete program. *Concentration:* general MBA.

RESOURCES AND SERVICES 225 on-campus PCs are available to graduate business students. Access to Internet/World Wide Web, online (class) registration, and online grade reports available. *Personal computer requirements:* Graduate business students are not required to have a personal computer. *Special opportunities include:* An international exchange program is available. *Placement services include:* Alumni network, career placement, career counseling/planning, resume referral, career fairs, job interviews arranged, resume preparation, and career library.

EXPENSES *Tuition (state resident):* Full-time: $4900. Part-time: $245 per semester hour. *Tuition (nonresident):* Full-time: $17,700. Part-time: $885 per semester hour. *Tuition (international):* Full-time: $17,700. Part-time: $885 per semester hour. Tuition and/or fees vary by number of courses or credits taken, campus location, and local reciprocity agreements. *Typical graduate housing cost:* $6600 (including board).

FINANCIAL AID (2007–08) 99 students received aid, including fellowships, grants, loans, research assistantships, scholarships, and work study. Aid is available to part-time students. *Financial aid application deadline:* 4/15.

Financial Aid Contact Cathy R. Brown, Director, Student Financial Aid, 11000 University Parkway, Pensacola, FL 32514-5750. *Phone:* 850-474-2400. *E-mail:* cbrown@uwf.edu.

INTERNATIONAL STUDENTS 15% of students enrolled are international students. *Services and facilities:* Counseling/support services, ESL/language courses, International student organization, Orientation, Visa Services, Mentoring. Financial aid is available to international students. *Required with application:* TOEFL with recommended score of 213 (computer) or 550 (paper); proof of adequate funds; proof of health/immunizations.

International Student Contact Ms. Brenda Akers, Admissions Coordinator, 11000 University Parkway, Pensacola, FL 32514-5750. *Phone:* 850-474-2115. *Fax:* 850-474-3360. *E-mail:* admissions@uwf.edu.

APPLICATION *Required:* GMAT, application form, baccalaureate/first degree, essay, interview, 2 letters of recommendation, personal statement, resume/curriculum vitae, transcripts of college work. *Recommended:* Work experience. *Application fee:* $30. Applications for domestic and international students are processed on a rolling basis.

Application Contact vacant vacant, Director of Admissions, 11000 University Parkway, Pensacola, FL 32514-5750. *Phone:* 850-474-2230. *Fax:* 850-857-6043. *E-mail:* admissions@uwf.edu.

Warner Southern College
School of Business
Lake Wales, Florida

Phone: 863-638-7212 Ext. 7212 **Fax:** 863-638-7290 **E-mail:** roej@warner.edu

Business Program(s) Web Site: http://www.warner.edu/admissions/graduate

DEGREES   MBA • MSM

MBA—Master of Business Administration Full-time and part-time. 40 total credits required. 20 to 40 months to complete program. *Concentration:* general MBA.

MSM— Full-time and part-time. Distance learning option. 36 total credits required. 24 to 48 months to complete program. *Concentration:* management.

RESOURCES AND SERVICES 78 on-campus PCs are available to graduate business students. Access to Internet/World Wide Web available. *Personal computer requirements:* Graduate business students are required to have a personal computer. *Placement services include:* Alumni network, job search course, career counseling/planning, electronic job bank, resume referral, career fairs, resume preparation, and career library.

Application Contact Mr. Jason Roe, Director of Admissions, 13895 Highway 27, Lake Wales, FL 33859. *Phone:* 863-638-7212 Ext. 7212. *Fax:* 863-638-7290. *E-mail:* roej@warner.edu.

Webber International University
Graduate School of Business
Babson Park, Florida

Phone: 863-638-2927 **Fax:** 863-638-1591 **E-mail:** mba@webber.edu

Business Program(s) Web Site: http://www.webber.edu

Graduate Business Unit Enrollment *Total:* 64 (45 full-time; 19 part-time; 33 women; 16 international). *Average Age:* 30.

Graduate Business Faculty 8 full-time.

Admissions *Applied:* 45. *Admitted:* 36. *Enrolled:* 31. *Average GPA:* 3.31

Academic Calendar Quarters.

After Graduation (Class of 2006–07) *Employed within 3 months of graduation:* 90%.

DEGREES   IMBA • MBA

IMBA—Security Management Full-time and part-time. Distance learning option. At least 36 total credits required. 19 to 96 months to complete program. *Concentrations:* information systems, international management.

MBA—Master of Business Administration Full-time and part-time. At least 36 total credits required. 19 to 94 months to complete program. *Concentration:* sports/entertainment management.

MBA—Master of Business Administration Full-time and part-time. At least 36 total credits required. 19 to 94 months to complete program. *Concentration:* accounting.

MBA—Master of Business Administration Full-time and part-time. At least 36 total credits required. 19 to 94 months to complete program. *Concentration:* management.

RESOURCES AND SERVICES 90 on-campus PCs are available to graduate business students. Access to Internet/World Wide Web available. *Personal computer requirements:* Graduate business students are not required to have a personal computer. *Placement services include:* Alumni network, career placement, career counseling/planning, electronic job bank, resume referral, career fairs, job interviews arranged, resume preparation, and career library.

EXPENSES *Tuition:* Full-time: $11,640. Part-time: $485 per credit hour. *Tuition (international):* Full-time: $11,640. Part-time: $485 per credit hour. *Typical graduate housing cost:* $7796 (including board), $4800 (room only).

FINANCIAL AID (2007–08) 25 students received aid, including loans and work study. *Financial aid application deadline:* 5/15.

Financial Aid Contact Mrs. Kathy Wilson, Financial Aid Director, 1201 North Scenic Highway, PO Box 96, Babson Park, FL 33827. *Phone:* 863-638-2930. *Fax:* 863-638-1317. *E-mail:* registrar@webber.edu.

INTERNATIONAL STUDENTS 25% of students enrolled are international students. *Services and facilities:* Counseling/support services, ESL/language courses, Housing location assistance, International student housing, International student organization, Orientation, Visa Services. Financial aid is not available to international students. *Required with application:* TOEFL with recommended score of 213 (computer) or 550 (paper); proof of adequate funds; proof of health/immunizations. *Recommended with application:* IELT with recommended score of 5.5.

International Student Contact Ms. Julie R. Ragans, Director of Admissions, MBA Program, 1201 North Scenic Highway, PO Box 96, Babson Park, FL 33827. *Phone:* 863-638-2927. *Fax:* 863-638-1591. *E-mail:* mba@webber.edu.

APPLICATION *Required:* Application form, baccalaureate/first degree, essay, 3 letters of recommendation, resume/curriculum vitae, transcripts of college work. School will accept GMAT. *Recommended:* Interview, work experience. *Application fee:* $50, $75 (international). *Deadlines:* 5/15 for fall, 12/1 for spring.

Application Contact Ms. Julie R. Ragans, Director of Admissions, MBA Program, 1201 North Scenic Highway, PO Box 96, Babson Park, FL 33827. *Phone:* 863-638-2927. *Fax:* 863-638-1591. *E-mail:* mba@webber.edu.

See full description on page 762.

GEORGIA

American InterContinental University Buckhead Campus

School of Business

Atlanta, Georgia

Phone: 404-965.5797 **E-mail:** tina.rowe@buckhead.aiuniv.edu

Business Program(s) Web Site: http://buckhead.aiuniv.edu/academic_programs/business.asp

Academic Calendar Quarters.

DEGREE MBA

MBA—Master of Business Administration Full-time and part-time. Distance learning option. *Concentration:* general MBA.

RESOURCES AND SERVICES Access to Internet/World Wide Web, online (class) registration, and online grade reports available. *Personal computer requirements:* Graduate business students are strongly recommended to purchase or lease a personal computer. *Placement services include:* Alumni network, career placement, career counseling/planning, career fairs, job interviews arranged, and resume preparation.

FINANCIAL AID (2007–08) Grants, loans, and scholarships. Aid is available to part-time students.

Financial Aid Contact Shalanda F. Jones, Executive Director of Financial Services, 3330 Peachtree Road, NE, Atlanta, GA 30326-1016. *Phone:* 888-999-4248 Ext. 5861. *E-mail:* shalanda.jones@buckhead.aiuniv.edu.

INTERNATIONAL STUDENTS *Services and facilities:* Counseling/support services, Housing location assistance, International student organization, Orientation, Visa Services.

International Student Contact Annie Mincey, International Admissions Advisor, 3330 Peachtree Road, NE, Atlanta, GA 30326-1016. *Phone:* 888-999-4248 Ext. 5805. *E-mail:* annie.mincey@buckhead.aiuniv.edu.

APPLICATION *Required:* Application form, baccalaureate/first degree, essay, interview, personal statement, resume/curriculum vitae, transcripts of college work. *Application fee:* $50. Applications for domestic and international students are processed on a rolling basis.

Application Contact Tina Rowe, Director of Admissions, 3330 Peachtree Road, NE, Atlanta, GA 30326. *Phone:* 404-965.5797. *E-mail:* tina.rowe@buckhead.aiuniv.edu.

See full description on page 564.

American InterContinental University Dunwoody Campus

School of Business

Atlanta, Georgia

Phone: 404-965-8029 **E-mail:** knorwood@aiuniv.edu

Business Program(s) Web Site: http://dunwoody.aiuniv.edu/

Academic Calendar Quarters.

DEGREES MBA • MIT

MBA—Master of Business Administration Full-time and part-time. Distance learning option. *Concentration:* general MBA.

MIT—Master of Information Technology Full-time and part-time. Distance learning option. *Concentration:* information technology.

RESOURCES AND SERVICES Access to Internet/World Wide Web, online (class) registration, and online grade reports available. *Personal computer requirements:* Graduate business students are required to have a personal computer, the cost of which is included in tuition or other required fees. *Placement services include:* Alumni network, career counseling/planning, career fairs, job interviews arranged, and resume preparation.

FINANCIAL AID (2007–08) Grants, loans, and scholarships. Aid is available to part-time students.

Financial Aid Contact Shalanda Jones, Executive Director of Financial Services, 6600 Peachtree-Dunwoody Road, 500 Embassy Row, Atlanta, GA 30328. *Phone:* 404-965-6486. *E-mail:* shalanda.jones@buckhead.aiuniv.edu.

INTERNATIONAL STUDENTS *Services and facilities:* Counseling/support services, Housing location assistance, International student organization, Orientation, Visa Services.

International Student Contact Charmaine Campbell, Admissions Advisor, 6600 Peachtree-Dunwoody Road, 500 Embassy Row, Atlanta, GA 30328. *Phone:* 404-965-8094. *E-mail:* ccampbell@aiuniv.edu.

APPLICATION *Required:* Application form, baccalaureate/first degree, essay, interview, personal statement, resume/curriculum vitae, transcripts of college work. *Application fee:* $50. Applications for domestic and international students are processed on a rolling basis.

Application Contact Knitra Norwood, Senior Director of Admissions, 6600 Peachtree-Dunwoody Road, 500 Embassy Row, Atlanta, GA 30328. *Phone:* 404-965-8029. *E-mail:* knorwood@aiuniv.edu.

See full description on page 564.

Argosy University, Atlanta

College of Business

Atlanta, Georgia

Phone: 770-671-1200 **Fax:** 770-671-9055

Business Program(s) Web Site: http://www.argosy.edu/atlanta

DEGREES DBA • MBA • MSM

DBA—Doctor of Business Administration (DBA) *Concentrations:* accounting, information systems, international business, management, marketing.

Argosy University, Atlanta (continued)

MBA—Master of Business Administration (MBA) *Concentrations:* finance, health care, information systems, international business, management, marketing.

MSM—Master of Science in Management *Concentration:* management.

Financial Aid Contact Director of Admissions, 980 Hammond Drive, Suite 100, Atlanta, GA 30328. *Phone:* 770-671-1200. *Fax:* 770-671-9055.

International Student Contact Director of Admissions, 980 Hammond Drive, Suite 100, Atlanta, GA 30328. *Phone:* 770-671-1200. *Fax:* 770-671-9055.

Application Contact Director of Admissions, 980 Hammond Drive, Suite 100, Atlanta, GA 30328. *Phone:* 770-671-1200. *Fax:* 770-671-9055.

See full description on page 566.

Augusta State University
Hull College of Business
Augusta, Georgia

Phone: 706-737-1565 **Fax:** 706-667-4064 **E-mail:** mbainfo@aug.edu

Business Program(s) Web Site: http://www.aug.edu/coba

Graduate Business Unit Enrollment *Total:* 87 (30 full-time; 57 part-time; 36 women; 9 international). *Average Age:* 30.

Graduate Business Faculty 16 full-time.

Admissions *Applied:* 26. *Admitted:* 18. *Enrolled:* 15. *Average GMAT:* 500. *Average GPA:* 3.13

Academic Calendar Semesters.

Accreditation AACSB—The Association to Advance Collegiate Schools of Business.

After Graduation (Class of 2006–07) *Employed within 3 months of graduation:* 90%.

DEGREE MBA

MBA—Master of Business Administration Full-time and part-time. 36 to 54 total credits required. 16 to 72 months to complete program. *Concentration:* general MBA.

RESOURCES AND SERVICES 250 on-campus PCs are available to graduate business students. Access to Internet/World Wide Web, online (class) registration, and online grade reports available. *Personal computer requirements:* Graduate business students are not required to have a personal computer. *Placement services include:* Career placement, career counseling/planning, resume referral, career fairs, job interviews arranged, resume preparation, and career library.

EXPENSES *Tuition (state resident):* Full-time: $2520. Part-time: $140 per semester hour. *Tuition (nonresident):* Full-time: $10,080. Part-time: $560 per semester hour. *Tuition (international):* Full-time: $10,080. Part-time: $560 per semester hour. *Required fees:* Full-time: $546. Part-time: $546 per year.

FINANCIAL AID (2007–08) 15 students received aid, including loans, research assistantships, and scholarships. Aid is available to part-time students.

Financial Aid Contact Willene C. Holmes, Director of Financial Aid, Financial Aid Office, 2500 Walton Way, Augusta, GA 30904-2200. *Phone:* 706-737-1431. *Fax:* 706-737-1777. *E-mail:* finaid@aug.edu.

INTERNATIONAL STUDENTS 10% of students enrolled are international students. *Services and facilities:* Counseling/support services, ESL/language courses, Housing location assistance, International student organization, Orientation. Financial aid is available to international students. *Required with application:* TOEFL with recommended score of 213 (computer), 550 (paper), or 80 (Internet); proof of adequate funds; proof of health/immunizations.

International Student Contact Miyoko Jackson, Degree Program Specialist, 2500 Walton Way, Augusta, GA 30904-2200. *Phone:* 706-737-1565. *Fax:* 706-667-4064. *E-mail:* mbainfo@aug.edu.

APPLICATION *Required:* GMAT, application form, baccalaureate/first degree, transcripts of college work. *Recommended:* Work experience. *Application fee:* $30. Applications for domestic and international students are processed on a rolling basis.

Application Contact Miyoko Jackson, Graduate Degree Program Specialist, 2500 Walton Way, Augusta, GA 30904-2200. *Phone:* 706-737-1565. *Fax:* 706-667-4064. *E-mail:* mbainfo@aug.edu.

Berry College
Campbell School of Business
Mount Berry, Georgia

Phone: 706-238-5835 **Fax:** 706-233-4082 **E-mail:** njohnston@berry.edu

Business Program(s) Web Site: http://www.campbell.berry.edu/

Graduate Business Unit Enrollment *Total:* 25 (25 part-time; 8 women; 4 international). *Average Age:* 27.

Graduate Business Faculty *Total:* 20 (19 full-time; 1 part-time).

Admissions *Applied:* 10. *Admitted:* 8. *Enrolled:* 5. *Average GMAT:* 508. *Average GPA:* 3.13

Academic Calendar Semesters.

Accreditation AACSB—The Association to Advance Collegiate Schools of Business.

After Graduation (Class of 2006–07) *Employed within 3 months of graduation:* 100%.

DEGREE MBA

MBA—Master of Business Administration Part-time. 30 total credits required. 24 to 72 months to complete program. *Concentration:* general MBA.

RESOURCES AND SERVICES 103 on-campus PCs are available to graduate business students. Access to Internet/World Wide Web, online (class) registration, and online grade reports available. *Personal computer requirements:* Graduate business students are strongly recommended to purchase or lease a personal computer. *Special opportunities include:* An international exchange program and an internship program are available. *Placement services include:* Alumni network, career placement, career counseling/planning, resume referral, career fairs, job interviews arranged, resume preparation, and career library.

EXPENSES *Tuition:* Part-time: $370 per credit hour. *Tuition (international):* Part-time: $370 per credit hour. *Required fees:* Part-time: $25 per semester.

FINANCIAL AID (2007–08) 5 students received aid, including loans, research assistantships, scholarships, and work study. Aid is available to part-time students.

Financial Aid Contact Mr. Ron Elmore, Director of Financial Aid, Office of Financial Aid, PO Box 495007, Mount Berry, GA 30149-5007. *Phone:* 706-236-2276. *E-mail:* relmore@berry.edu.

INTERNATIONAL STUDENTS 16% of students enrolled are international students. *Services and facilities:* Counseling/support services, International student organization, Orientation, Visa Services. Financial aid is not available to international students. *Required with application:* TOEFL with recommended score of 213 (computer), 550 (paper), or 79 (Internet); proof of adequate funds; proof of health/immunizations.

International Student Contact Dr. Clarice Ford, Associate Dean of Students, PO Box 495039, Mount Berry, GA 30149-5039. *Phone:* 706-238-7833. *Fax:* 706-368-5645. *E-mail:* cford@berry.edu.

APPLICATION *Required:* GMAT, application form, baccalaureate/first degree, essay, 2 letters of recommendation, personal statement, resume/ curriculum vitae, transcripts of college work. *Recommended:* Interview, 2

years of work experience. *Application fee:* $25, $30 (international). Applications for domestic and international students are processed on a rolling basis.

Application Contact Nancy Johnston, Assistant Dean/Director of MBA Marketing and Admissions, PO Box 5024, Mount Berry, GA 30149-5024. *Phone:* 706-238-5835. *Fax:* 706-233-4082. *E-mail:* njohnston@berry.edu.

Brenau University
School of Business and Mass Communication
Gainesville, Georgia

Phone: 770-538-4390 **Fax:** 770-538-4701 **E-mail:** mleavell@brenau.edu

Business Program(s) Web Site: http://www.brenau.edu

Graduate Business Unit Enrollment *Total:* 239 (67 full-time; 172 part-time; 149 women; 7 international).

Graduate Business Faculty *Total:* 26 (12 full-time; 14 part-time).

Admissions *Applied:* 139. *Admitted:* 75. *Enrolled:* 61.

Academic Calendar Semesters.

DEGREES   M Sc • MBA

M Sc—Master of Science in Organizational Development Part-time. At least 30 total credits required. *Concentrations:* organizational behavior/development, organizational management.

MBA—Master of Business Administration in Accounting Full-time and part-time. Distance learning option. At least 36 total credits required. *Concentration:* accounting.

MBA—Master of Business Administration in Health Care Management Full-time and part-time. Distance learning option. At least 33 total credits required. *Concentration:* health care.

MBA—Master of Business Administration in Management Full-time and part-time. Distance learning option. At least 30 total credits required. *Concentration:* management.

MBA—Project Management Full-time and part-time. Distance learning option. At least 36 total credits required. *Concentration:* project management.

RESOURCES AND SERVICES 100 on-campus PCs are available to graduate business students. Access to Internet/World Wide Web, online (class) registration, and online grade reports available. *Personal computer requirements:* Graduate business students are required to have a personal computer. *Placement services include:* Alumni network, career counseling/planning, career fairs, and resume preparation.

EXPENSES *Tuition:* Full-time: $11,400. Part-time: $380 per credit hour. *Tuition (international):* Full-time: $11,400. Part-time: $380 per credit hour. *Required fees:* Full-time: $150. Part-time: $150 per year. Tuition and/or fees vary by campus location.

FINANCIAL AID (2007–08) Grants and loans. Aid is available to part-time students.

Financial Aid Contact Pam Barrett, Director of Scholarships and Financial Assistance, 500 Washington Street, SE, Gainesville, GA 30501-3697. *Phone:* 770-534-6152. *Fax:* 770-538-4306. *E-mail:* pbarrett@lib.brenau.edu.

INTERNATIONAL STUDENTS 3% of students enrolled are international students. *Services and facilities:* Counseling/support services, ESL/language courses, International student organization, Orientation, Visa Services. Financial aid is not available to international students. *Required with application:* TOEFL with recommended score of 550 (paper); proof of adequate funds. *Recommended with application:* Proof of health/immunizations.

International Student Contact Ms. Michelle Leavell, Graduate Admissions Coordinator, 500 Washington Street, SC, Gainesville, GA 30501. *Phone:* 770-534-6299. *Fax:* 770-538-4701. *E-mail:* mleavell@brenau.edu.

APPLICATION *Required:* Application form, baccalaureate/first degree, interview, resume/curriculum vitae. School will accept GMAT, GRE, and MAT. *Application fee:* $35. Applications for domestic and international students are processed on a rolling basis.

Application Contact Ms. Michelle Leavell, Graduate Admissions Coordinator, 500 Washington Street, SE, Gainesville, GA 30501. *Phone:* 770-538-4390. *Fax:* 770-538-4701. *E-mail:* mleavell@brenau.edu.

Clark Atlanta University
School of Business Administration
Atlanta, Georgia

Phone: 404-880-8479 **Fax:** 404-880-6159 **E-mail:** sfleming@cau.edu

Business Program(s) Web Site: http://www.sbus.cau.edu

Accreditation AACSB—The Association to Advance Collegiate Schools of Business.

DEGREES   M Acc • MBA

M Acc—Master of Accounting Full-time. 12 months to complete program. *Concentration:* accounting.

MBA—Working Professional Program Full-time. Requires a personal interview and minimum of 5 years work experience. Friday night and Saturday classes only. At least 54 total credits required. 24 to 60 months to complete program. *Concentrations:* decision sciences, finance, marketing.

MBA—Master of Business Administration Full-time. At least 60 total credits required. 21 to 60 months to complete program. *Concentrations:* decision sciences, finance, marketing.

RESOURCES AND SERVICES 25 on-campus PCs are available to graduate business students. Access to Internet/World Wide Web, online (class) registration, and online grade reports available. *Personal computer requirements:* Graduate business students are strongly recommended to purchase or lease a personal computer. *Special opportunities include:* An internship program is available. *Placement services include:* Alumni network, career placement, job search course, career counseling/planning, resume referral, career fairs, job interviews arranged, resume preparation, and career library.

Application Contact Ms. Sarbeth J. Fleming, Director of Admissions and Student Affairs, 223 James P. Brawley Drive, S.W., Atlanta, GA 30314. *Phone:* 404-880-8479. *Fax:* 404-880-6159. *E-mail:* sfleming@cau.edu.

Columbus State University
College of Business
Columbus, Georgia

Phone: 706-568-5058 **Fax:** 706-568-2184 **E-mail:** daniels_michael@colstate.edu

Business Program(s) Web Site: http://mba.colstate.edu

DEGREE   MBA

MBA—Master of Business Administration Full-time and part-time. At least 30 total credits required. 18 to 72 months to complete program. *Concentration:* general MBA.

RESOURCES AND SERVICES 200 on-campus PCs are available to graduate business students. Access to Internet/World Wide Web, online (class) registration, and online grade reports available. *Personal computer requirements:* Graduate business students are not required to have a personal computer. *Placement services include:* Alumni network, career placement, job search course, career counseling/planning, electronic job bank, resume referral, career fairs, job interviews arranged, resume preparation, and career library.

Columbus State University (continued)

Application Contact Dr. Michael Daniels, MBA Program Director, 4225 University Avenue, Columbus, GA 31907-5645. *Phone:* 706-568-5058. *Fax:* 706-568-2184. *E-mail:* daniels_michael@colstate.edu.

DeVry University
Keller Graduate School of Management
Alpharetta, Georgia

Phone: 770-521-0118 **Fax:** 770-521-0134

Business Program(s) Web Site: http://www.devry.edu

Academic Calendar Semesters.

DEGREES MAFM • MBA • MHRM • MIS • MPA • MPM

MAFM—Master of Accounting and Financial Management Full-time and part-time. Distance learning option. At least 44 total credits required. 18 to 60 months to complete program. *Concentrations:* accounting, financial management/planning.

MBA—Master of Business Administration Full-time and part-time. Distance learning option. At least 48 total credits required. 18 to 60 months to complete program. *Concentrations:* accounting, electronic commerce (E-commerce), finance, general MBA, health care, human resources management, information systems, international and area business studies, marketing, project management, public policy and administration.

MHRM—Master of Human Resources Management Full-time and part-time. Distance learning option. At least 45 total credits required. 18 to 60 months to complete program. *Concentration:* human resources management.

MIS—Master of Information Systems Management Full-time and part-time. Distance learning option. At least 45 total credits required. 18 to 60 months to complete program. *Concentration:* information systems.

MPA—Master of Public Administration Full-time and part-time. Distance learning option. At least 45 total credits required. 18 to 60 months to complete program. *Concentrations:* health administration, nonprofit management.

MPM—Master of Project Management Full-time and part-time. Distance learning option. At least 42 total credits required. 18 to 60 months to complete program. *Concentration:* project management.

RESOURCES AND SERVICES *Personal computer requirements:* Graduate business students are not required to have a personal computer.

APPLICATION *Required:* Application form, baccalaureate/first degree, interview, transcripts of college work.

Application Contact Admissions Office, Alpharetta Center, 2555 Northwinds Parkway, Alpharetta, GA 30004. *Phone:* 770-521-0118. *Fax:* 770-521-0134.

DeVry University
Keller Graduate School of Management
Atlanta, Georgia

Phone: 404-296-7400 **Fax:** 404-240-0227

Business Program(s) Web Site: http://www.devry.edu

Academic Calendar Semesters.

DEGREES MAFM • MBA • MHRM • MISM • MPA • MPM

MAFM—Master of Accounting and Financial Management Full-time and part-time. Distance learning option. At least 44 total credits required. 18 to 60 months to complete program. *Concentrations:* accounting, financial management/planning.

MBA—Master of Business Administration Full-time and part-time. Distance learning option. At least 48 total credits required. 18 to 60 months to complete program. *Concentration:* general MBA.

MHRM—Master of Human Resource Management Full-time and part-time. Distance learning option. At least 45 total credits required. 18 to 60 months to complete program. *Concentration:* human resources management.

MISM—Master of Information Systems Management Full-time and part-time. Distance learning option. At least 45 total credits required. 18 to 60 months to complete program. *Concentration:* information systems.

MPA—Master of Public Administration Full-time and part-time. Distance learning option. At least 45 total credits required. 18 to 60 months to complete program. *Concentration:* public policy and administration.

MPM—Master of Project Management Full-time and part-time. Distance learning option. At least 42 total credits required. 18 to 60 months to complete program. *Concentration:* project management.

RESOURCES AND SERVICES *Personal computer requirements:* Graduate business students are not required to have a personal computer.

APPLICATION *Required:* Application form, baccalaureate/first degree, interview. Applications for domestic and international students are processed on a rolling basis.

Application Contact Admissions Office, Atlanta/Buckhead Center, Fifteen Piedmont Center, Plaza Level 100, 3575 Piedmont Road N.E., Atlanta, GA 30305. *Phone:* 404-296-7400. *Fax:* 404-240-0227.

DeVry University
Keller Graduate School of Management
Decatur, Georgia

Phone: 404-298-9444

DEGREES MAFM • MBA • MHRM • MIS • MPA • MPM

MAFM—Master of Accounting and Financial Management Full-time and part-time. Distance learning option. At least 44 total credits required. 18 to 60 months to complete program. *Concentrations:* accounting, financial management/planning.

MBA—Master of Business Administration Full-time and part-time. Distance learning option. At least 48 total credits required. 18 to 60 months to complete program. *Concentration:* management.

MHRM—Master of Human Resources Management Full-time and part-time. Distance learning option. At least 45 total credits required. 18 to 60 months to complete program. *Concentration:* human resources management.

MIS—Master of Information Systems Management Full-time and part-time. Distance learning option. At least 45 total credits required. 18 to 60 months to complete program. *Concentration:* information systems.

MPA—Master of Public Administration Full-time and part-time. Distance learning option. At least 45 total credits required. 18 to 60 months to complete program. *Concentration:* public policy and administration.

MPM—Master of Project Management Full-time and part-time. Distance learning option. At least 42 total credits required. 18 to 60 months to complete program. *Concentration:* project management.

Application Contact Admissions Office, Decatur Center, 250 North Arcadia Avenue, Decatur, GA 30030. *Phone:* 404-298-9444.

DeVry University

Keller Graduate School of Management

Duluth, Georgia

Phone: 678-380-9780

DEGREES MAFM • MBA • MHRM • MIS • MPA • MPM

MAFM—Master of Accounting and Financial Management Full-time and part-time. Distance learning option. At least 44 total credits required. 18 to 60 months to complete program. *Concentrations:* accounting, financial management/planning.

MBA—Master of Business Administration Full-time and part-time. Distance learning option. At least 48 total credits required. 18 to 60 months to complete program. *Concentration:* management.

MHRM—Master of Human Resources Management Full-time and part-time. Distance learning option. At least 45 total credits required. 18 to 60 months to complete program. *Concentration:* human resources management.

MIS—Master of Information Systems Management Full-time and part-time. Distance learning option. At least 45 total credits required. 18 to 60 months to complete program. *Concentration:* information systems.

MPA—Master of Public Administration Full-time and part-time. Distance learning option. At least 45 total credits required. 18 to 60 months to complete program. *Concentration:* public policy and administration.

MPM—Master of Project Management Full-time and part-time. Distance learning option. At least 42 total credits required. 18 to 60 months to complete program. *Concentration:* project management.

Application Contact Admissions Office, Gwinnett Center, 3505 Koger Boulevard, Suite 170, Duluth, GA 30096. *Phone:* 678-380-9780.

Emory University

Roberto C. Goizueta Business School

Atlanta, Georgia

Phone: 404-727-6311 **Fax:** 404-727-4612 **E-mail:** admissions@bus.emory.edu

Business Program(s) Web Site: http://www.goizueta.emory.edu

Accreditation AACSB—The Association to Advance Collegiate Schools of Business.

DEGREES JD/MBA • MBA • MBA/M Div • MBA/MPH

JD/MBA—Juris Doctor/Master of Business Administration Full-time. At least 127 total credits required. 45 months to complete program. *Concentration:* combined degrees.

MBA—Daytime Master of Business Administration Full-time. 68 total credits required. 21 months to complete program. *Concentrations:* accounting, entrepreneurship, finance, human resources management, international business, management, management information systems, marketing, operations management, organizational behavior/development, quantitative analysis, real estate, strategic management.

MBA—Evening Master of Business Administration Part-time. At least 55 total credits required. 28 to 36 months to complete program. *Concentration:* general MBA.

MBA—Modular Executive Master of Business Administration Part-time. Distance learning option. 52 total credits required. 20 months to complete program. *Concentration:* general MBA.

MBA—One-Year Master of Business Administration Full-time. Academic coursework in business is strongly preferred. At least 50 total credits required. 12 months to complete program. *Concentrations:* accounting, entrepreneurship, finance, human resources management, international business, management, management information systems, marketing, operations management, organizational behavior/development, quantitative analysis, real estate, strategic management.

MBA—Weekend Executive Master of Business Administration Part-time. At least 54 total credits required. 16 months to complete program. *Concentration:* general MBA.

MBA/M Div—Master of Business Administration/Master of Divinity Full-time. At least 120 total credits required. 45 months to complete program. *Concentration:* combined degrees.

MBA/MPH—Master of Business Administration/Master of Public Health Full-time and part-time. At least 80 total credits required. 28 months to complete program. *Concentration:* combined degrees.

RESOURCES AND SERVICES 95 on-campus PCs are available to graduate business students. Access to Internet/World Wide Web, online (class) registration, and online grade reports available. *Personal computer requirements:* Graduate business students are strongly recommended to purchase or lease a personal computer. *Special opportunities include:* An international exchange program and an internship program are available. *Placement services include:* Alumni network, career placement, job search course, career counseling/planning, electronic job bank, resume referral, career fairs, job interviews arranged, resume preparation, and career library.

Application Contact Julie Barefoot, Assistant Dean of MBA Admissions, 1300 Clifton Road, NE, Atlanta, GA 30322-2710. *Phone:* 404-727-6311. *Fax:* 404-727-4612. *E-mail:* admissions@bus.emory.edu.

See full description on page 606.

Georgia College & State University

The J. Whitney Bunting School of Business

Milledgeville, Georgia

Phone: 478-445-5115 **Fax:** 478-445-5249 **E-mail:** lynn.hanson@gcsu.edu

Business Program(s) Web Site: http://www.gcsu.edu/graduate/

Graduate Business Unit Enrollment *Total:* 128 (23 full-time; 105 part-time; 52 women; 10 international). *Average Age:* 27.

Graduate Business Faculty *Total:* 55 (43 full-time; 12 part-time).

Admissions *Applied:* 100. *Admitted:* 55. *Enrolled:* 34. *Average GMAT:* 490.

Academic Calendar Semesters.

Accreditation AACSB—The Association to Advance Collegiate Schools of Business.

DEGREES M Acc • MBA • MMIS

M Acc—Master of Accountancy Full-time and part-time. 30 to 57 total credits required. 12 to 84 months to complete program. *Concentration:* accounting.

MBA—MBA with Accounting Concentration Full-time and part-time. 36 to 69 total credits required. 18 to 84 months to complete program. *Concentration:* accounting.

MBA—MBA with Health Services Concentration Full-time and part-time. 35 to 49 total credits required. 18 to 84 months to complete program. *Concentration:* health administration.

MBA—MBA with Management Information Systems Concentration Full-time and part-time. 36 to 48 total credits required. 18 to 84 months to complete program. *Concentration:* information systems.

MBA—Master of Business Administration Full-time and part-time. 36 to 48 total credits required. 18 to 84 months to complete program. *Concentration:* general MBA.

MMIS—Master of Management Information Systems Full-time and part-time. 30 to 39 total credits required. 12 to 84 months to complete program. *Concentration:* accounting.

Georgia College & State University (continued)

RESOURCES AND SERVICES 180 on-campus PCs are available to graduate business students. Access to Internet/World Wide Web, online (class) registration, and online grade reports available. *Personal computer requirements:* Graduate business students are not required to have a personal computer. *Special opportunities include:* An international exchange program and an internship program are available. *Placement services include:* Alumni network, career placement, career counseling/planning, electronic job bank, resume referral, career fairs, job interviews arranged, and resume preparation.

EXPENSES *Tuition (state resident):* Full-time: $3726. Part-time: $207 per semester hour. *Tuition (nonresident):* Full-time: $14,868. Part-time: $826 per semester hour. *Tuition (international):* Full-time: $14,868. Part-time: $826 per semester hour. *Required fees:* Full-time: $828. Tuition and/or fees vary by class time, number of courses or credits taken, and campus location. *Graduate housing:* Room and board costs vary by number of occupants, type of accommodation, and type of board plan. *Typical cost:* $7380 (including board), $3990 (room only).

FINANCIAL AID (2007–08) Loans, research assistantships, and scholarships. Aid is available to part-time students. *Financial aid application deadline:* 7/1.

Financial Aid Contact Ms. Cathy Crawley, Director of Financial Aid, CBX 030, Milledgeville, GA 31061. *Phone:* 478-445-5149. *Fax:* 478-445-0729. *E-mail:* cathy.crawley@gcsu.edu.

INTERNATIONAL STUDENTS 8% of students enrolled are international students. *Services and facilities:* Counseling/support services, ESL/language courses, Housing location assistance, International student organization, Orientation, Visa Services. Financial aid is available to international students. *Required with application:* Proof of adequate funds; proof of health/immunizations. *Recommended with application:* TOEFL with recommended score of 213 (computer), 550 (paper), or 79 (Internet).

International Student Contact Dr. Dwight Call, Assistant Vice President for International Education, Campus Box 49, Milledgeville, GA 31061. *Phone:* 478-445-4789. *Fax:* 478-445-2623. *E-mail:* dwight.call@gcsu.edu.

APPLICATION *Required:* GMAT, application form, baccalaureate/first degree, transcripts of college work. *Application fee:* $35. Applications for domestic and international students are processed on a rolling basis.

Application Contact Lynn Hanson, Director, Graduate Programs in Business, Campus Box 19, Milledgeville, GA 31061. *Phone:* 478-445-5115. *Fax:* 478-445-5249. *E-mail:* lynn.hanson@gcsu.edu.

Georgia Institute of Technology
College of Management

Atlanta, Georgia

Phone: 404-894-8722 **Fax:** 404-894-4199 **E-mail:** mba@mgt.gatech.edu

Business Program(s) Web Site: http://www.mgt.gatech.edu

Graduate Business Unit Enrollment *Total:* 282 (218 full-time; 64 part-time; 85 women; 94 international). *Average Age:* 27.

Graduate Business Faculty *Total:* 82 (72 full-time; 10 part-time).

Admissions *Applied:* 504. *Admitted:* 211. *Enrolled:* 137. *Average GMAT:* 665. *Average GPA:* 3.4

Academic Calendar Semesters.

Accreditation AACSB—The Association to Advance Collegiate Schools of Business.

After Graduation (Class of 2006–07) *Employed within 3 months of graduation:* 98%. *Average starting salary:* $81,000.

DEGREES EMBA • MBA • MS

EMBA—EMBA—Management of Technology 19 months to complete program. *Concentrations:* executive programs, technology management.

EMBA—Global Executive MBA 17 months to complete program. *Concentrations:* executive programs, general MBA, international business.

MBA—Evening MBA Part-time. 54 total credits required. 22 to 60 months to complete program. *Concentrations:* accounting, entrepreneurship, finance, information technology, international business, operations management, organizational behavior/development, strategic management.

MBA Full-time. 54 total credits required. 22 months to complete program. *Concentrations:* accounting, entrepreneurship, finance, information technology, international business, marketing, operations management, organizational behavior/development, strategic management.

MS—Quantitative and Computational Finance Full-time. 36 total credits required. 22 months to complete program. *Concentrations:* finance, quantitative analysis.

RESOURCES AND SERVICES 20 on-campus PCs are available to graduate business students. Access to Internet/World Wide Web, online (class) registration, and online grade reports available. *Personal computer requirements:* Graduate business students are required to have a personal computer. *Special opportunities include:* An international exchange program and an internship program are available. *Placement services include:* Alumni network, career placement, job search course, career counseling/planning, electronic job bank, resume referral, career fairs, job interviews arranged, resume preparation, and career library.

EXPENSES *Tuition (state resident):* Full-time: $7218. Part-time: $650 per semester hour. *Tuition (nonresident):* Full-time: $28,870. Part-time: $1200 per semester hour. *Tuition (international):* Full-time: $28,870. Part-time: $1200 per semester hour. *Required fees:* Full-time: $573. Part-time: $573 per semester. Tuition and/or fees vary by class time and academic program. *Graduate housing:* Room and board costs vary by campus location, number of occupants, type of accommodation, and type of board plan. *Typical cost:* $12,000 (including board).

FINANCIAL AID (2007–08) 50 students received aid, including fellowships, loans, and research assistantships. *Financial aid application deadline:* 1/15.

Financial Aid Contact Student Financial Planning Services, 225 North Avenue, NW, Atlanta, GA 30332-0460. *Phone:* 404-894-4160. *Fax:* 404-894-7140. *E-mail:* finaid@success.gatech.edu.

INTERNATIONAL STUDENTS 33% of students enrolled are international students. *Services and facilities:* Counseling/support services, ESL/language courses, Housing location assistance, International student housing, International student organization, Orientation, Visa Services. Financial aid is available to international students. *Required with application:* TOEFL with recommended score of 250 (computer), 600 (paper), or 100 (Internet); proof of adequate funds; proof of health/immunizations.

International Student Contact International Student Services, 225 North Avenue, NW, Atlanta, GA 30332-0284. *Phone:* 404-894-7475. *Fax:* 404-894-7682. *E-mail:* info@oie.gatech.edu.

APPLICATION *Required:* GMAT, application form, baccalaureate/first degree, essay, interview, 3 letters of recommendation, personal statement, resume/curriculum vitae, transcripts of college work, 2 years of work experience. *Application fee:* $50. Applications for domestic and international students are processed on a rolling basis.

Application Contact Graduate Office, 800 West Peachtree Street, NW, Suite 302, Atlanta, GA 30332-0520. *Phone:* 404-894-8722. *Fax:* 404-894-4199. *E-mail:* mba@mgt.gatech.edu.

See full description on page 624.

Georgia Southern University
College of Business Administration

Statesboro, Georgia

Phone: 912-681-5767 **Fax:** 912-486-7480 **E-mail:** mmcdonal@georgiasouthern.edu

Business Program(s) Web Site: http://coba.georgiasouthern.edu/

Graduate Business Unit Enrollment *Total:* 250 (110 full-time; 140 part-time; 120 women; 24 international). *Average Age:* 26.

Graduate Business Faculty *Total:* 55 (40 full-time; 15 part-time).

Admissions *Applied:* 125. *Admitted:* 93. *Enrolled:* 63. *Average GMAT:* 490. *Average GPA:* 3.1

Academic Calendar Semesters.

Accreditation AACSB—The Association to Advance Collegiate Schools of Business.

DEGREES M Acc • MBA

M Acc—Master of Accounting Full-time and part-time. 30 to 61 total credits required. 24 to 36 months to complete program. *Concentration:* forensic accounting.

M Acc—Master of Accounting Full-time and part-time. 30 to 51 total credits required. 24 to 36 months to complete program. *Concentration:* accounting.

MBA—Evening Master of Business Administration Program Full-time and part-time. Distance learning option. 30 to 51 total credits required. 24 to 36 months to complete program. *Concentrations:* accounting, health care, information systems, international business.

MBA—General Full-time and part-time. 30 to 51 total credits required. 24 to 36 months to complete program. *Concentration:* general MBA.

MBA—Web Master of Business Administration Full-time. Distance learning option. 30 to 54 total credits required. 24 months to complete program. *Concentration:* general MBA.

RESOURCES AND SERVICES 175 on-campus PCs are available to graduate business students. Access to Internet/World Wide Web, online (class) registration, and online grade reports available. *Personal computer requirements:* Graduate business students are not required to have a personal computer. *Placement services include:* Alumni network, career placement, career counseling/planning, electronic job bank, resume referral, career fairs, job interviews arranged, and resume preparation.

EXPENSES *Tuition (state resident):* Part-time: $172 per credit. *Tuition (nonresident):* Part-time: $686 per credit hour. *Tuition (international):* Part-time: $686 per credit hour. *Required fees:* Part-time: $532 per term. *Graduate housing:* Room and board costs vary by campus location, number of occupants, type of accommodation, and type of board plan. *Typical cost:* $3666 (including board).

FINANCIAL AID (2007–08) 180 students received aid, including loans, research assistantships, scholarships, teaching assistantships, and work study. *Financial aid application deadline:* 4/15.

Financial Aid Contact Connie Murphey, Director of Financial Aid, PO Box 8065, Statesboro, GA 30460-8065. *Phone:* 912-681-5413. *Fax:* 912-681-0573.

INTERNATIONAL STUDENTS 10% of students enrolled are international students. *Services and facilities:* Counseling/support services, ESL/language courses, Housing location assistance, International student housing, International student organization, Language tutoring, Orientation, Visa Services. Financial aid is not available to international students. *Required with application:* TOEFL with recommended score of 213 (computer) or 550 (paper); proof of adequate funds; proof of health/immunizations.

International Student Contact Nancy Shumaker, Director, International Student Program, PO Box 8106, Statesboro, GA 30460-8106. *Phone:* 912-681-0382. *Fax:* 912-681-0694.

APPLICATION *Required:* GMAT, application form, baccalaureate/first degree, transcripts of college work. *Application fee:* $50. Applications for domestic and international students are processed on a rolling basis.

Application Contact J. Michael McDonald, Director of Graduate Studies, PO Box 8050, College of Business Administration Building, Room 1133, Statesboro, GA 30460. *Phone:* 912-681-5767. *Fax:* 912-486-7480. *E-mail:* mmcdonal@georgiasouthern.edu.

Georgia Southwestern State University
School of Business Administration
Americus, Georgia

Phone: 229-931-2090 **Fax:** 229-931-2092 **E-mail:** marthaw@canes.gsw.edu

Business Program(s) Web Site: http://www.business.gsw.edu

Graduate Business Unit Enrollment *Total:* 54 (54 part-time; 33 women; 6 international). *Average Age:* 28.

Graduate Business Faculty *Total:* 16 (14 full-time; 2 part-time).

Admissions *Applied:* 38. *Admitted:* 22. *Enrolled:* 22. *Average GMAT:* 400. *Average GPA:* 2.8

Academic Calendar Semesters.

Accreditation ACBSP—The American Council of Business Schools and Programs.

After Graduation (Class of 2006–07) *Employed within 3 months of graduation:* 100%. *Average starting salary:* $45,000.

DEGREE MBA

MBA—Master of Business Administration Part-time. 36 to 60 total credits required. Minimum of 18 months to complete program. *Concentration:* general MBA.

RESOURCES AND SERVICES 300 on-campus PCs are available to graduate business students. Access to Internet/World Wide Web, online (class) registration, and online grade reports available. *Personal computer requirements:* Graduate business students are strongly recommended to purchase or lease a personal computer. *Special opportunities include:* An internship program is available. *Placement services include:* Alumni network, career placement, career counseling/planning, electronic job bank, career fairs, resume preparation, and career library.

EXPENSES *Tuition (state resident):* Full-time: $4000. *Tuition (nonresident):* Full-time: $14,000. *Tuition (international):* Full-time: $14,000. *Typical graduate housing cost:* $6694 (including board), $4370 (room only).

Financial Aid Contact Freida Jones, Director of Financial Aid, 800 Wheatley Street, Americus, GA 31709. *Phone:* 229-928-1378. *E-mail:* fjjones@canes.gsw.edu.

INTERNATIONAL STUDENTS 11% of students enrolled are international students. *Services and facilities:* Counseling/support services, ESL/language courses, Housing location assistance, International student housing, International student organization, Orientation. Financial aid is not available to international students. *Required with application:* TOEFL with recommended score of 193 (computer) or 523 (paper); proof of adequate funds; proof of health/immunizations.

International Student Contact Dr. Michael Fathi, MBA Director, 800 GSW State University Drive, Americus, GA 30709. *Phone:* 229-931-2090. *Fax:* 229-931-2092. *E-mail:* mmf@canes.gsw.edu.

APPLICATION *Required:* GMAT, GRE, application form, baccalaureate/first degree, 3 letters of recommendation, transcripts of college work. *Recommended:* Interview, resume/curriculum vitae. *Application fee:* $25. Applications for domestic and international students are processed on a rolling basis.

Application Contact Martha E. Crimes, Administrative Assistant to the Dean of Graduate Admission, 800 Georgia Southwestern State University Drive, Americus, GA 31709-4693. *Phone:* 229-931-2090. *Fax:* 229-931-2092. *E-mail:* marthaw@canes.gsw.edu.

Georgia State University
J. Mack Robinson College of Business
Atlanta, Georgia

Phone: 404-413-7130 **Fax:** 404-413-7162 **E-mail:** mastersadmissions@gsu.edu

Georgia State University (continued)

Business Program(s) Web Site: http://robinson.gsu.edu/

Graduate Business Unit Enrollment *Total:* 1,799 (892 full-time; 907 part-time; 706 women; 283 international).

Graduate Business Faculty *Total:* 198 (177 full-time; 21 part-time).

Admissions *Applied:* 1,182. *Admitted:* 528. *Enrolled:* 363. *Average GMAT:* 602. *Average GPA:* 3.37

Academic Calendar Semesters.

Accreditation AACSB—The Association to Advance Collegiate Schools of Business.

DEGREES JD/MBA • JD/MHA • MAS • MBA • MBA/MHA • MIB • MPA • MS • MTX

JD/MBA—Juris Doctor/Master of Business Administration Full-time and part-time. 39 to 51 total credits required. 12 to 96 months to complete program. *Concentration:* combined degrees.

JD/MHA—Master of Science in Health Administration/Juris Doctor Full-time and part-time. 36 total credits required. 12 to 60 months to complete program. *Concentrations:* combined degrees, health administration, law.

MAS—Master of Actuarial Science Full-time. 24 to 30 total credits required. 15 to 60 months to complete program. *Concentration:* actuarial science.

MBA—Executive Master of Business Administration Full-time. At least 48 total credits required. 18 months to complete program. *Concentration:* executive programs.

MBA—Global Partners MBA Full-time. 51 total credits required. 14 months to complete program. *Concentrations:* international business, international management.

MBA—Professional Master of Business Administration Full-time and part-time. Candidate interview required. 39 to 54 total credits required. 24 to 60 months to complete program. *Concentrations:* accounting, actuarial science, decision sciences, economics, entrepreneurship, finance, financial management/planning, general MBA, health administration, hospitality management, human resources management, information systems, insurance, international business, management, marketing, operations management, organizational management, real estate, risk management.

MBA—Master of Business Administration Full-time and part-time. 24 to 57 total credits required. 12 to 60 months to complete program. *Concentrations:* accounting, actuarial science, decision sciences, economics, entrepreneurship, finance, financial management/planning, general MBA, health administration, hospitality management, human resources management, information systems, international business, management, marketing, operations management, organizational management, real estate, risk management.

MBA/MHA—Master of Business Administration/Master of Health Administration Full-time. 57 to 72 total credits required. 36 to 60 months to complete program. *Concentration:* combined degrees.

MIB—Master of International Business Full-time and part-time. 24 to 33 total credits required. 12 to 60 months to complete program. *Concentration:* international business.

MPA—Master of Professional Accountancy Full-time and part-time. 24 to 30 total credits required. 12 to 60 months to complete program. *Concentration:* accounting.

MS—Master of Science in Health Administration Full-time and part-time. 24 to 36 total credits required. 12 to 60 months to complete program. *Concentration:* health administration.

MS—Master of Science in Real Estate Full-time and part-time. 30 to 36 total credits required. 12 to 60 months to complete program. *Concentration:* real estate.

MS—Master of Science Full-time and part-time. 24 to 36 total credits required. 12 to 60 months to complete program. *Concentrations:* decision sciences, economics, finance, financial management/planning, human resources management, information systems, insurance, management, marketing, operations management, organizational management, project management, risk management.

MTX—Master of Taxation Full-time and part-time. At least 33 total credits required. 12 to 60 months to complete program. *Concentration:* taxation.

RESOURCES AND SERVICES 505 on-campus PCs are available to graduate business students. Access to Internet/World Wide Web, online (class) registration, and online grade reports available. *Personal computer requirements:* Graduate business students are strongly recommended to purchase or lease a personal computer. *Special opportunities include:* An international exchange program and an internship program are available. *Placement services include:* Alumni network, career placement, job search course, career counseling/planning, electronic job bank, resume referral, career fairs, job interviews arranged, resume preparation, and career library.

EXPENSES *Tuition (state resident):* Full-time: $6744. Part-time: $281 per credit hour. *Tuition (nonresident):* Full-time: $24,456. Part-time: $1019 per credit hour. *Tuition (international):* Full-time: $24,456. Part-time: $1019 per credit hour. *Required fees:* Full-time: $988. Part-time: $494 per semester. Tuition and/or fees vary by number of courses or credits taken, campus location, and academic program. *Graduate housing:* Room and board costs vary by campus location, number of occupants, type of accommodation, and type of board plan. *Typical cost:* $8500 (including board), $7000 (room only).

FINANCIAL AID (2007–08) 559 students received aid, including loans, research assistantships, and scholarships. Aid is available to part-time students. *Financial aid application deadline:* 5/1.

Financial Aid Contact Office of Student Financial Aid, PO Box 4040, Atlanta, GA 30303-4040. *Phone:* 404-413-2400. *Fax:* 404-413-2102.

INTERNATIONAL STUDENTS 16% of students enrolled are international students. *Services and facilities:* Counseling/support services, ESL/language courses, International student housing, International student organization, Language tutoring, Orientation, Visa Services. Financial aid is available to international students. *Required with application:* TOEFL with recommended score of 255 (computer), 610 (paper), or 101 (Internet); proof of adequate funds; proof of health/immunizations. *Recommended with application:* TWE.

International Student Contact Douglas Podoll, Director, International Student Services, International Programs, PO Box 3987, Atlanta, GA 30302-3987. *Phone:* 404-413-2070. *Fax:* 404-413-2072. *E-mail:* dougpodoll@gsu.edu.

APPLICATION *Required:* GMAT, application form, baccalaureate/first degree, essay, transcripts of college work. School will accept GRE. *Recommended:* 3 letters of recommendation, resume/curriculum vitae, work experience. *Application fee:* $50. Applications for domestic and international students are processed on a rolling basis.

Application Contact Graduate Admissions and Student Services, PO Box 3989, Atlanta, GA 30302-3989. *Phone:* 404-413-7130. *Fax:* 404-413-7162. *E-mail:* mastersadmissions@gsu.edu.

See full description on page 626.

Kennesaw State University
Michael J. Coles College of Business
Kennesaw, Georgia

Phone: 770-423-6472 **Fax:** 770-423-6141 **E-mail:** melissa_booth@kennesaw.edu

Business Program(s) Web Site: http://www.colesmba.com

Graduate Business Unit Enrollment *Total:* 755 (206 full-time; 549 part-time; 302 women; 50 international). *Average Age:* 35.

Graduate Business Faculty 60 full-time.

Admissions *Applied:* 242. *Admitted:* 127. *Enrolled:* 84. *Average GMAT:* 535. *Average GPA:* 3.3

Academic Calendar Semesters.

Accreditation AACSB—The Association to Advance Collegiate Schools of Business.

After Graduation (Class of 2006–07) *Employed within 3 months of graduation:* 97%.

DEGREES   M Acc • MBA

M Acc—Master of Accounting Full-time and part-time. 30 to 56 total credits required. 12 to 72 months to complete program. *Concentration:* accounting.

MBA—Coles Master of Business Administration Part-time. 36 to 39 total credits required. 12 to 72 months to complete program. *Concentration:* general MBA.

MBA—Master of Business Administration for Experienced Professionals Part-time. 5 years of managerial or professional experience required. 36 total credits required. 18 months to complete program. *Concentration:* general MBA.

MBA—WebMBA Part-time. Distance learning option. 30 total credits required. 21 months to complete program. *Concentration:* general MBA.

RESOURCES AND SERVICES 800 on-campus PCs are available to graduate business students. Access to Internet/World Wide Web, online (class) registration, and online grade reports available. *Personal computer requirements:* Graduate business students are strongly recommended to purchase or lease a personal computer. *Special opportunities include:* An international exchange program and an internship program are available. *Placement services include:* Alumni network, career placement, job search course, career counseling/planning, electronic job bank, resume referral, career fairs, job interviews arranged, resume preparation, and career library.

EXPENSES *Tuition (state resident):* Part-time: $153 per credit. *Tuition (nonresident):* Part-time: $612 per credit. *Tuition (international):* Part-time: $612 per credit. *Required fees:* Part-time: $2113 per year. Tuition and/or fees vary by class time, number of courses or credits taken, campus location, and academic program.

FINANCIAL AID (2007–08) Loans, research assistantships, and scholarships. Aid is available to part-time students. *Financial aid application deadline:* 4/1.

Financial Aid Contact Dr. Michael Roberts, Director, Student Financial Aid, 1000 Chastain Road, #0119, Kennesaw Hall Building #1, Room 1304, Kennesaw, GA 30144-5591. *Phone:* 770-423-6074. *Fax:* 770-423-6708. *E-mail:* mroberts@kennesaw.edu.

INTERNATIONAL STUDENTS 7% of students enrolled are international students. *Services and facilities:* Counseling/support services, ESL/language courses, Housing location assistance, International student housing, International student organization, Language tutoring, Orientation. Financial aid is available to international students. *Required with application:* TOEFL with recommended score of 213 (computer) or 550 (paper); proof of adequate funds; proof of health/immunizations.

International Student Contact David Baugher, Director, Graduate Admissions, 1000 Chastain Road, #0115, Kennesaw Hall Building #1, Room 3401, Kennesaw, GA 30144-5591. *Phone:* 770-420-4377. *Fax:* 770-420-4435. *E-mail:* dbaugher@kennesaw.edu.

APPLICATION *Required:* GMAT, application form, baccalaureate/first degree, resume/curriculum vitae, transcripts of college work, 2 years of work experience. *Recommended:* Letter(s) of recommendation. *Application fee:* $50. Applications for domestic and international students are processed on a rolling basis.

Application Contact Melissa Booth, Assistant Director, Graduate Business Programs, 1000 Chastain Road, Mail Drop #3306, KSU Center Building, Room 33, Kennesaw, GA 30144-5591. *Phone:* 770-423-6472. *Fax:* 770-423-6141. *E-mail:* melissa_booth@kennesaw.edu.

Mercer University
Eugene W. Stetson School of Business and Economics
Atlanta, Georgia

Phone: 678-547-6400 **Fax:** 678-547-6367 **E-mail:** atlbusadm@mercer.edu

Business Program(s) Web Site: http://www2.mercer.edu/business

Accreditation AACSB—The Association to Advance Collegiate Schools of Business.

DEGREES   EMBA • MBA • MBA equivalent • MBA equivalent combined degree • Pharm D/MBA

EMBA—Executive Master of Business Administration in International Business Part-time. 5 years of work experience, personal statement, 2 recommendations, transcripts, math test and interview required; GMAT not required. At least 48 total credits required. Minimum of 16 months to complete program. *Concentration:* international business.

MBA—Master of Business Administration Full-time and part-time. GMAT, transcripts, and resume. 36 to 48 total credits required. 12 to 60 months to complete program. *Concentration:* general MBA.

MBA equivalent—Professional Master of Business Administration Part-time. 4 years of work experience, personal statement, 2 recommendations, transcripts, math test and interview required; GMAT may be waived. 48 total credits required. 16 months to complete program. *Concentration:* international business.

MBA equivalent combined degree—Joint Master of Business Administration and Master of Divinity Full-time. GMAT, Admission to Schools of Theology and Business. 120 to 132 total credits required. 48 to 50 months to complete program. *Concentration:* general MBA.

Pharm D/MBA—Joint Master of Business Administration and Doctor of Pharmacy Full-time. Admission to School of Pharmacy, 128 semester hours college credit, GMAT. 179 to 185 total credits required. Minimum of 60 months to complete program. *Concentration:* general MBA.

RESOURCES AND SERVICES 40 on-campus PCs are available to graduate business students. Access to Internet/World Wide Web, online (class) registration, and online grade reports available. *Personal computer requirements:* Graduate business students are strongly recommended to purchase or lease a personal computer. *Placement services include:* Alumni network, career placement, career counseling/planning, electronic job bank, resume referral, career fairs, job interviews arranged, resume preparation, and career library.

Application Contact Ms. Jackie Thompson, Coordinator of Admissions, 3001 Mercer University Drive, Atlanta, GA 30341-4155. *Phone:* 678-547-6400. *Fax:* 678-547-6367. *E-mail:* atlbusadm@mercer.edu.

Piedmont College
School of Business
Demorest, Georgia

Phone: 706-778-3000 Ext. 1181 **Fax:** 706-776-6635 **E-mail:** ckokesh@piedmont.edu

Business Program(s) Web Site: http://www.piedmont.edu

Graduate Business Unit Enrollment *Total:* 89 (59 full-time; 30 part-time; 32 women).

Graduate Business Faculty *Total:* 21 (15 full-time; 6 part-time).

Academic Calendar Semesters.

Accreditation ACBSP—The American Council of Business Schools and Programs (candidate).

DEGREES   MB • MBA

Piedmont College (continued)

MB—Master of Business Full-time and part-time. *Concentrations:* finance, leadership.

MBA—Master of Business Administration Full-time and part-time. *Concentration:* health care.

RESOURCES AND SERVICES 75 on-campus PCs are available to graduate business students. Access to Internet/World Wide Web available. *Personal computer requirements:* Graduate business students are strongly recommended to purchase or lease a personal computer.

EXPENSES *Tuition:* Full-time: $6120. Part-time: $340 per credit. *Tuition (international):* Full-time: $6120. Part-time: $340 per credit.

FINANCIAL AID (2007–08) 1 student received aid, including work study. *Financial aid application deadline:* 8/1.

Financial Aid Contact Ms. Kimberly S. Lovell, Director of Financial Aid, PO Box 10, Demorest, GA 30535. *Phone:* 706-778-3000 Ext. 1191. *Fax:* 706-776-2811. *E-mail:* klovell@piedmont.edu.

INTERNATIONAL STUDENTS Financial aid is not available to international students. *Required with application:* TOEFL with recommended score of 213 (computer) or 550 (paper).

International Student Contact Mr. Anthony Cox, PDSO/International Students, Graduate Admissions Office, PO Box 10, Demorest, GA 30535. *Phone:* 706-778-3000 Ext. 1118. *Fax:* 706-776-6635. *E-mail:* acox@piedmont.edu.

APPLICATION *Required:* Application form, baccalaureate/first degree, 3 letters of recommendation, transcripts of college work. School will accept GMAT, GRE, and MAT. *Recommended:* Work experience. *Application fee:* $30, $100 (international). Applications for domestic and international students are processed on a rolling basis.

Application Contact Ms. Carol Kokesh, Director of Graduate Admissions, Graduate Admissions Office, PO Box 10, Demorest, GA 30535. *Phone:* 706-778-3000 Ext. 1181. *Fax:* 706-776-6635. *E-mail:* ckokesh@piedmont.edu.

Shorter College
School of Business
Rome, Georgia

Phone: 678-260-3547 **Fax:** 770-951-9590 **E-mail:** frances.tamboli@apollogrp.edu

Business Program(s) Web Site: http://www.shorter.edu/pro_studies/degrees.htm

Graduate Business Unit Enrollment *Total:* 244 (244 full-time; 169 women; 1 international). *Average Age:* 39.

Graduate Business Faculty *Total:* 144 (9 full-time; 135 part-time).

Academic Calendar Continuous.

DEGREES MA • MBA

MA—Master of Arts in Leadership Full-time. At least 33 total credits required. Minimum of 16 months to complete program. *Concentration:* leadership.

MBA—Master of Business Administration Full-time. At least 36 total credits required. Minimum of 18 months to complete program. *Concentration:* general MBA.

RESOURCES AND SERVICES 10 on-campus PCs are available to graduate business students. Access to Internet/World Wide Web and online grade reports available. *Personal computer requirements:* Graduate business students are required to have a personal computer, the cost of which is included in tuition or other required fees.

EXPENSES *Tuition:* Full-time: $11,070. Part-time: $443 per credit hour. *Tuition (international):* Full-time: $11,070. Part-time: $443 per credit hour.

FINANCIAL AID (2007–08) 114 students received aid, including grants and loans.

Financial Aid Contact Ms. Tara Jones, Director of Financial Aid, 315 Shorter Avenue, Rome, GA 30165. *Phone:* 706-233-7337. *Fax:* 706-233-7314. *E-mail:* tjones@shorter.edu.

INTERNATIONAL STUDENTS 0.4% of students enrolled are international students. *Services and facilities:* Visa Services. Financial aid is not available to international students. *Required with application:* TOEFL with recommended score of 213 (computer) or 550 (paper); proof of adequate funds; proof of health/immunizations.

International Student Contact Ms. Linda Palumbo Olszanski, Director of Campus Globalization, 315 Shorter Avenue, Rome, GA 30165. *Phone:* 706-233-7459. *Fax:* 706-233-7458. *E-mail:* lpalumbo@shorter.edu.

APPLICATION *Required:* Application form, baccalaureate/first degree, essay, personal statement, resume/curriculum vitae, transcripts of college work, 3 years of work experience. School will accept GMAT. *Recommended:* Letter(s) of recommendation. *Application fee:* $50. Applications for domestic and international students are processed on a rolling basis.

Application Contact Ms. Frances Tamboli, Director of Enrollment, 6151 Powers Ferry Road, NW, Suite 170, Atlanta, GA 30339. *Phone:* 678-260-3547. *Fax:* 770-951-9590. *E-mail:* frances.tamboli@apollogrp.edu.

Southern Polytechnic State University
Department of Business Administration
Marietta, Georgia

Phone: 678-915-4276 **Fax:** 678-915-7292 **E-mail:** npalamio@spsu.edu

Business Program(s) Web Site: http://www.spsu.edu/mba/

Graduate Business Unit Enrollment *Total:* 99 (41 full-time; 58 part-time; 41 women; 35 international). *Average Age:* 24-43.

Graduate Business Faculty *Total:* 11 (8 full-time; 3 part-time).

Admissions *Applied:* 74. *Admitted:* 37. *Enrolled:* 27. *Average GMAT:* 386. *Average GPA:* 3.0

Academic Calendar Semesters.

Accreditation ACBSP—The American Council of Business Schools and Programs.

After Graduation (Class of 2006–07) *Average starting salary:* $43,500.

DEGREE MBA

MBA—Master of Business Administration Full-time and part-time. Distance learning option. At least 36 total credits required. 12 to 60 months to complete program. *Concentrations:* management information systems, marketing, operations management, technology management.

RESOURCES AND SERVICES 800 on-campus PCs are available to graduate business students. Access to Internet/World Wide Web, online (class) registration, and online grade reports available. *Personal computer requirements:* Graduate business students are strongly recommended to purchase or lease a personal computer. *Placement services include:* Alumni network, career placement, career counseling/planning, electronic job bank, resume referral, career fairs, job interviews arranged, resume preparation, and career library.

EXPENSES *Tuition (state resident):* Full-time: $3242. Part-time: $135 per credit hour. *Tuition (nonresident):* Full-time: $12,960. Part-time: $540 per credit hour. *Tuition (international):* Full-time: $12,960. Part-time: $540 per credit hour. *Required fees:* Full-time: $630. Part-time: $630 per year. *Graduate housing:* Room and board costs vary by number of occupants, type of accommodation, and type of board plan. *Typical cost:* $5780 (including board), $3310 (room only).

FINANCIAL AID (2007–08) 33 students received aid, including loans, research assistantships, and teaching assistantships. *Financial aid application deadline: 5/1.*

Financial Aid Contact Mr. Gary W. Bush, Director of Financial Aid, 1100 South Marietta Parkway, Marietta, GA 30060-2896. *Phone:* 678-915-7290. *Fax:* 678-915-4227. *E-mail:* gbush@spsu.edu.

INTERNATIONAL STUDENTS 35% of students enrolled are international students. *Services and facilities:* Counseling/support services, Housing location assistance, International student organization, Orientation, Visa Services. Financial aid is not available to international students. *Required with application:* TOEFL with recommended score of 213 (computer), 550 (paper), or 79 (Internet); proof of adequate funds; proof of health/immunizations.

International Student Contact Ms. Lititia DeNard, Coordinator of International Student Services, 1100 South Marietta Parkway, Marietta, GA 30060-2896. *Phone:* 678-915-7938. *Fax:* 678-915-7913. *E-mail:* ldenard@spsu.edu.

APPLICATION *Required:* GMAT, application form, baccalaureate/first degree, 3 letters of recommendation, transcripts of college work. *Recommended:* Work experience. *Application fee:* $20. Applications for domestic and international students are processed on a rolling basis.

Application Contact Ms. Nikki Palamiotis, Director of Graduate Studies, 1100 South Marietta Parkway, Marietta, GA 30060-2896. *Phone:* 678-915-4276. *Fax:* 678-915-7292. *E-mail:* npalamio@spsu.edu.

University of Georgia
Terry College of Business

Athens, Georgia

Phone: 706-542-5671 **Fax:** 706-583-8277 **E-mail:** terrymba@terry.uga.edu

Business Program(s) Web Site: http://www.terry.uga.edu

Graduate Business Unit Enrollment *Total:* 890 (360 full-time; 530 part-time; 286 women; 132 international). *Average Age:* 28.

Graduate Business Faculty *Total:* 137 (108 full-time; 29 part-time).

Admissions *Applied:* 832. *Admitted:* 411. *Enrolled:* 309. *Average GMAT:* 653. *Average GPA:* 3.4

Academic Calendar Semesters.

Accreditation AACSB—The Association to Advance Collegiate Schools of Business.

After Graduation (Class of 2006–07) *Employed within 3 months of graduation:* 82%. *Average starting salary:* $71,908.

DEGREES JD/MBA • M Acc • MA • MBA • MIT • MMR

JD/MBA—Juris Doctor/Master of Business Administration Full-time. 122 total credits required. 45 months to complete program. *Concentrations:* accounting, economics, electronic commerce (E-commerce), entrepreneurship, finance, insurance, international business, management information systems, marketing, materials management, operations management, organizational management, production management, real estate, risk management.

M Acc—Master of Accountancy Full-time and part-time. 30 total credits required. 9 to 24 months to complete program. *Concentrations:* accounting, taxation.

MA—Master of Arts in Economics Full-time. 30 to 36 total credits required. 9 to 36 months to complete program. *Concentrations:* economics, financial economics, international economics.

MBA—EMBA—Executive Master of Business Administration Part-time. Distance learning option. 48 total credits required. 18 months to complete program. *Concentration:* general MBA.

MBA—Evening Master of Business Administration Part-time. 48 total credits required. 24 to 72 months to complete program. *Concentration:* general MBA.

MBA—Full-Time Master of Business Administration Full-time. 41 to 66 total credits required. 11 to 22 months to complete program. *Concentrations:* accounting, economics, electronic commerce (E-commerce), entrepreneurship, finance, insurance, international business, management information systems, marketing, materials management, operations management, organizational management, production management, real estate, risk management.

MIT—MIT—Master of Internet Technology Part-time. 32 total credits required. 20 months to complete program. *Concentration:* information technology.

MMR—Master of Marketing Research Full-time. 40 total credits required. 12 months to complete program. *Concentration:* marketing research.

RESOURCES AND SERVICES 1,000 on-campus PCs are available to graduate business students. Access to Internet/World Wide Web, online (class) registration, and online grade reports available. *Personal computer requirements:* Graduate business students are required to have a personal computer. *Special opportunities include:* An international exchange program and an internship program are available. *Placement services include:* Alumni network, career placement, job search course, career counseling/planning, electronic job bank, resume referral, career fairs, job interviews arranged, resume preparation, and career library.

EXPENSES *Tuition (state resident):* Full-time: $8182. Part-time: $650 per credit hour. *Tuition (nonresident):* Full-time: $27,036. Part-time: $1358 per credit hour. *Tuition (international):* Full-time: $27,036. Part-time: $650 per credit hour. *Required fees:* Full-time: $1126. Part-time: $105 per semester. Tuition and/or fees vary by number of courses or credits taken, campus location, and academic program. *Graduate housing:* Room and board costs vary by number of occupants, type of accommodation, and type of board plan. *Typical cost:* $7992 (including board), $4995 (room only).

FINANCIAL AID (2007–08) 93 students received aid, including research assistantships and scholarships. *Financial aid application deadline:* 5/12.

Financial Aid Contact Student Financial Aid, Academic Building, Athens, GA 30602-6114. *Phone:* 706-542-6147. *E-mail:* osfa@arches.uga.edu.

INTERNATIONAL STUDENTS 15% of students enrolled are international students. *Services and facilities:* Counseling/support services, ESL/language courses, Housing location assistance, International student housing, International student organization, Orientation, Visa Services. Financial aid is available to international students. *Required with application:* TOEFL with recommended score of 250 (computer), 600 (paper), or 95 (Internet); proof of adequate funds; proof of health/immunizations.

International Student Contact Foreign Student Advisors, Office of International Education, 201 Barrow Hall, Athens, GA 30602-2407. *Phone:* 706-542-7903. *Fax:* 706-542-6622. *E-mail:* oie@terry.uga.edu.

APPLICATION *Required:* GMAT, application form, baccalaureate/first degree, essay, 2 letters of recommendation, resume/curriculum vitae, transcripts of college work, 2 years of work experience. *Recommended:* Interview. *Application fee:* $62. Applications for domestic and international students are processed on a rolling basis.

Application Contact Anne Cooper, Director, MBA Admissions, 361 Brooks Hall, Athens, GA 30602-6264. *Phone:* 706-542-5671. *Fax:* 706-583-8277. *E-mail:* terrymba@terry.uga.edu.

University of Phoenix–Atlanta Campus
College of Graduate Business and Management

Sandy Springs, Georgia

Phone: 480-317-6200 **Fax:** 480-643-1479 **E-mail:** beth.barilla@phoenix.edu

University of Phoenix–Atlanta Campus (continued)

Business Program(s) Web Site: http://www.phoenix.edu

DEGREES EMBA • M Mgt • MBA

EMBA—Executive Master of Business Administration Full-time. At least 30 total credits required. *Concentration:* strategic management.

M Mgt—Master of Management/Human Resource Management Full-time. Up to 39 total credits required. *Concentration:* human resources management.

MBA—Master of Business Administration Full-time. At least 45 total credits required. *Concentration:* administration.

MBA—Master of Business Administration in Global Management Full-time. At least 45 total credits required. *Concentration:* international business.

MBA—Master of Business Administration in Human Resource Management Full-time. At least 45 total credits required. *Concentration:* human resources management.

MBA—Master of Management Full-time. At least 39 total credits required. *Concentration:* management.

RESOURCES AND SERVICES Access to online grade reports available. *Personal computer requirements:* Graduate business students are strongly recommended to purchase or lease a personal computer. *Placement services include:* Alumni network.

Application Contact Beth Barilla, Associate Vice President of Student Admissions and Services, Mail Stop AA-K101, 4615 East Elwood Street, Phoenix, AZ 85040-1958. *Phone:* 480-317-6200. *Fax:* 480-643-1479. *E-mail:* beth.barilla@phoenix.edu.

University of Phoenix–Columbus Georgia Campus

College of Graduate Business and Management

Columbus, Georgia

Phone: 480-317-6200 **Fax:** 480-643-1479 **E-mail:** beth.barilla@phoenix.edu

---

DEGREES M Mgt • MBA

M Mgt—Human Resource Management Full-time. At least 39 total credits required. *Concentration:* human resources management.

M Mgt—Master of Organizational Management Full-time. At least 40 total credits required. *Concentration:* organizational management.

M Mgt—Master of Management Full-time. At least 39 total credits required. *Concentration:* management.

MBA—Accounting Full-time. At least 54 total credits required. *Concentration:* accounting.

MBA—Master of Business Administration Full-time. At least 45 total credits required. *Concentration:* administration.

MBA—Master of Business Administration in Global Management Full-time. At least 45 total credits required. *Concentration:* international business.

MBA—Master of Business Administration in Human Resource Management Full-time. At least 45 total credits required. *Concentration:* human resources management.

MBA—Master of Business Administration in Marketing Full-time. At least 45 total credits required. *Concentration:* marketing.

MBA—e-Business Full-time. At least 45 total credits required. *Concentration:* electronic commerce (E-commerce).

MBA—Master of Business Administration Full-time. At least 39 total credits required. *Concentration:* administration.

RESOURCES AND SERVICES Access to online grade reports available. *Personal computer requirements:* Graduate business students are strongly recommended to purchase or lease a personal computer. *Placement services include:* Alumni network.

Application Contact Beth Barilla, Associate Vice President of Student Admissions and Services, Mail Stop AA-K101, 4615 East Elwood Street, Phoenix, AZ 85040-1958. *Phone:* 480-317-6200. *Fax:* 480-643-1479. *E-mail:* beth.barilla@phoenix.edu.

University of West Georgia

Richards College of Business

Carrollton, Georgia

Phone: 678-839-6419 **Fax:** 678-839-5949 **E-mail:** cclark@westga.edu

Business Program(s) Web Site: http://www.westga.edu/~busn/MBA.html

Graduate Business Unit Enrollment *Total:* 73 (17 full-time; 56 part-time; 36 women; 6 international). *Average Age:* 29.

Graduate Business Faculty *Total:* 17 (10 full-time; 7 part-time).

Admissions *Average GMAT:* 477. *Average GPA:* 3.08

Academic Calendar Semesters.

Accreditation AACSB—The Association to Advance Collegiate Schools of Business.

DEGREES MBA • MPA

MBA—Business Administration Full-time and part-time. Distance learning option. 54 to 57 total credits required. *Concentration:* general MBA.

MPA—Professional Accounting Full-time and part-time. 30 to 84 total credits required. *Concentration:* accounting.

RESOURCES AND SERVICES 745 on-campus PCs are available to graduate business students. Access to Internet/World Wide Web, online (class) registration, and online grade reports available. *Personal computer requirements:* Graduate business students are not required to have a personal computer. *Special opportunities include:* An internship program is available. *Placement services include:* Career placement, career counseling/planning, electronic job bank, resume referral, career fairs, job interviews arranged, resume preparation, and career library.

EXPENSES *Tuition (state resident):* Full-time: $2448. Part-time: $136 per credit hour. *Tuition (nonresident):* Full-time: $9774. Part-time: $543 per credit hour. *Tuition (international):* Full-time: $9774. Part-time: $543 per credit hour. *Required fees:* Full-time: $960. Tuition and/or fees vary by number of courses or credits taken. *Graduate housing:* Room and board costs vary by number of occupants, type of accommodation, and type of board plan. *Typical cost:* $5406 (including board), $2620 (room only).

FINANCIAL AID (2007–08) 37 students received aid, including loans, research assistantships, scholarships, and work study. Aid is available to part-time students. *Financial aid application deadline:* 4/1.

Financial Aid Contact Mrs. Kimberly Jordan, Director for Financial Aid, 1601 Maple Street, Carrollton, GA 30118. *Phone:* 678-839-6421. *Fax:* 678-839-6422. *E-mail:* kjordan@westga.edu.

INTERNATIONAL STUDENTS 8% of students enrolled are international students. *Services and facilities:* Counseling/support services, Housing location assistance, International student housing, International student organization, Orientation, Visa Services. Financial aid is available to international students. *Required with application:* TOEFL with recommended score of 213 (computer) or 550 (paper); proof of adequate funds; proof of health/immunizations.

International Student Contact Ms. Sylvia E. Shortt, Assistant Director for Student Development, Office of Student Development, 1601 Maple Street, Carrollton, GA 30118. *Phone:* 678-839-6428. *Fax:* 678-839-6429. *E-mail:* sshortt@westga.edu.

APPLICATION *Required:* GMAT, GRE, application form, baccalaureate/first degree, 3 letters of recommendation, transcripts of college work. *Application fee:* $30. Applications for domestic and international students are processed on a rolling basis.

Application Contact Dr. Charles W. Clark, Interim Dean of Graduate School, Graduate School, 1601 Maple Street, Carrollton, GA 30118. *Phone:* 678-839-6419. *Fax:* 678-839-5949. *E-mail:* cclark@westga.edu.

Valdosta State University
Langdale College of Business Administration
Valdosta, Georgia

Phone: 229-245-2233 **Fax:** 229-245-2795 **E-mail:** mba@valdosta.edu

Business Program(s) Web Site: http://www.valdosta.edu/lcoba/grad/

Graduate Business Unit Enrollment *Total:* 30 (30 part-time; 14 women; 4 international). *Average Age:* 33.

Graduate Business Faculty 10 full-time.

Admissions *Applied:* 25. *Admitted:* 5. *Enrolled:* 5. *Average GMAT:* 530. *Average GPA:* 3.3

Academic Calendar Semesters.

Accreditation AACSB—The Association to Advance Collegiate Schools of Business.

After Graduation (Class of 2006–07) *Employed within 3 months of graduation:* 100%. *Average starting salary:* $55,000.

DEGREES   MBA

MBA—Georgia WebMBA Part-time. Distance learning option. 30 total credits required. *Concentration:* general MBA.

MBA—Master of Business Administration Part-time. At least 30 total credits required. 24 to 84 months to complete program. *Concentration:* general MBA.

RESOURCES AND SERVICES 55 on-campus PCs are available to graduate business students. Access to Internet/World Wide Web, online (class) registration, and online grade reports available. *Personal computer requirements:* Graduate business students are strongly recommended to purchase or lease a personal computer. *Placement services include:* Career placement, career counseling/planning, resume referral, career fairs, and resume preparation.

FINANCIAL AID (2007–08) Loans and work study.

Financial Aid Contact Mr. Douglas Tanner, Director of Financial Aid, Office of Financial Aid, Valdosta, GA 31698. *Phone:* 229-333-5935. *Fax:* 229-333-5430. *E-mail:* dtanner@valdosta.edu.

INTERNATIONAL STUDENTS 13% of students enrolled are international students. *Services and facilities:* Counseling/support services, ESL/language courses, Housing location assistance, International student organization, Orientation, Visa Services. Financial aid is not available to international students. *Required with application:* TOEFL with recommended score of 193 (computer) or 523 (paper); proof of adequate funds; proof of health/immunizations.

International Student Contact Mr. David Starling, Foreign Student Advisor, Office of International Programs, Valdosta, GA 31698-0005. *Phone:* 229-333-7410. *Fax:* 229-245-3849. *E-mail:* dstarlin@valdosta.edu.

APPLICATION *Required:* GMAT, application form, baccalaureate/first degree, essay, personal statement, resume/curriculum vitae, transcripts of college work. *Recommended:* 2 years of work experience. *Application fee:* $40. Applications for domestic and international students are processed on a rolling basis.

Application Contact Ms. Georgia Whalen, MBA Secretary, Room 206 Pound Hall, Valdosta, GA 31698-0075. *Phone:* 229-245-2233. *Fax:* 229-245-2795. *E-mail:* mba@valdosta.edu.

HAWAII

Argosy University, Hawai'i
College of Business
Honolulu, Hawaii

Phone: 808-536-5555 **Fax:** 808-536-5505

Business Program(s) Web Site http://www.argosy.edu/hawaii

DEGREES   DBA • MBA

DBA—Doctor of Business Administration (DBA) *Concentrations:* accounting, information systems, international business, management, marketing.

MBA—Master of Business Administration (MBA) *Concentrations:* finance, health administration, information systems, international business, management, marketing.

Financial Aid Contact Director of Admissions, 400 ASB Tower, 1001 Bishop Street, Honolulu, HI 96813. *Phone:* 808-536-5555. *Fax:* 808-536-5505.

International Student Contact Director of Admissions, 400 ASB Tower, 1001 Bishop Street, Honolulu, HI 96813. *Phone:* 808-536-5555. *Fax:* 808-536-5505.

Application Contact Director of Admissions, 400 ASB Tower, 1001 Bishop Street, Honolulu, HI 96813. *Phone:* 808-536-5555. *Fax:* 808-536-5505.

See full description on page 566.

Hawai'i Pacific University
College of Business Administration
Honolulu, Hawaii

Phone: 808-544-1135 **Fax:** 808-544-0280 **E-mail:** dlam@hpu.edu

Business Program(s) Web Site: http://www.hpu.edu/mba

Graduate Business Unit Enrollment *Total:* 473 (280 full-time; 193 part-time; 223 women; 219 international). *Average Age:* 29.

Graduate Business Faculty *Total:* 70 (40 full-time; 30 part-time).

Admissions *Applied:* 204. *Admitted:* 194. *Enrolled:* 110. *Average GMAT:* 459.

Academic Calendar Semesters.

After Graduation (Class of 2006–07) *Employed within 3 months of graduation:* 76%. *Average starting salary:* $78,000.

DEGREES   MA • MBA • MS

MA—Master of Arts in Global Leadership and Sustainable Development Full-time and part-time. At least 2 years of professional experience is required. At least 42 total credits required. Minimum of 18 months to complete program. *Concentration:* leadership.

MA—Master of Arts in Human Resource Management Full-time and part-time. At least 42 total credits required. Minimum of 18 months to complete program. *Concentration:* human resources management.

MA—Master of Arts in Organizational Change Full-time and part-time. At least 42 total credits required. Minimum of 18 months to complete program. *Concentration:* organizational behavior/development.

MBA—Executive Master of Business Administration Full-time and part-time. At least 42 total credits required. Minimum of 18 months to complete program. *Concentration:* executive programs.

MBA—Master of Business Administration Full-time and part-time. At least 42 total credits required. Minimum of 18 months to complete program. *Concentrations:* accounting, economics, electronic commerce (E-commerce), finance, human resources management, information systems, international business, management, marketing, organizational management, other, travel industry/tourism management.

MS—Master of Science in Information Systems Full-time and part-time. Distance learning option. At least 36 total credits required. Minimum of 18 months to complete program. *Concentrations:* information management, other, technology management.

RESOURCES AND SERVICES 376 on-campus PCs are available to graduate business students. Access to Internet/World Wide Web, online (class) registration, and online grade reports available. *Personal computer requirements:* Graduate business students are strongly recommended to purchase or lease a personal computer. *Special opportunities include:* An international exchange program and an internship program are available. *Placement services include:* Alumni network, career placement, career counseling/planning, electronic job bank, resume referral, career fairs, job interviews arranged, resume preparation, and career library.

EXPENSES *Tuition:* Full-time: $14,760. *Tuition (international):* Full-time: $14,760. Tuition and/or fees vary by number of courses or credits taken and academic program. *Graduate housing:* Room and board costs vary by number of occupants and type of accommodation. *Typical cost:* $10,280 (room only).

FINANCIAL AID (2007–08) 107 students received aid, including loans, research assistantships, scholarships, and work study. Aid is available to part-time students. *Financial aid application deadline:* 3/1.

Financial Aid Contact Financial Aid, 1164 Bishop Street, Suite 201, Honolulu, HI 96813. *Phone:* 808-544-0253. *Fax:* 808-544-0884.

INTERNATIONAL STUDENTS 46% of students enrolled are international students. *Services and facilities:* Counseling/support services, ESL/language courses, Housing location assistance, International student organization, Language tutoring, Orientation, Visa Services. Financial aid is available to international students. *Required with application:* Proof of adequate funds; proof of health/immunizations. *Recommended with application:* IELT with recommended score of 6; TOEFL with recommended score of 213 (computer), 550 (paper), or 80 (Internet); TWE with recommended score of 5.

International Student Contact Rumi Yoshida, Associate Director of Graduate Admissions, 1132 Bishop Street, Suite 911, Honolulu, HI 96813. *Phone:* 808-544-1417. *Fax:* 808-544-0280. *E-mail:* ryoshida@hpu.edu.

APPLICATION *Required:* GMAT, application form, baccalaureate/first degree, essay, 2 letters of recommendation, personal statement, transcripts of college work. School will accept GRE. *Recommended:* Resume/curriculum vitae, work experience. *Application fee:* $50. Applications for domestic and international students are processed on a rolling basis.

Application Contact Mr. Danny Lam, Assistant Director of Graduate Admissions, 1164 Bishop Street, Suite 911, Honolulu, HI 96813. *Phone:* 808-544-1135. *Fax:* 808-544-0280. *E-mail:* dlam@hpu.edu.

See full description on page 630.

University of Hawaii at Manoa
Shidler College of Business

Honolulu, Hawaii

Phone: 808-956-8266 **Fax:** 808-956-2657 **E-mail:** tutak@hawaii.edu

Business Program(s) Web Site: http://www.shidler.hawaii.edu

Graduate Business Unit Enrollment *Total:* 476 (288 full-time; 188 part-time; 205 women; 142 international). *Average Age:* 28.

Graduate Business Faculty *Total:* 77 (61 full-time; 16 part-time).

Admissions *Applied:* 531. *Admitted:* 344. *Enrolled:* 307. *Average GMAT:* 632. *Average GPA:* 3.3

Academic Calendar Semesters.

Accreditation AACSB—The Association to Advance Collegiate Schools of Business.

After Graduation (Class of 2006–07) *Employed within 3 months of graduation:* 87%.

DEGREES EMBA • JD/MBA • M Acc • MBA • MHRM • PhD/MBA

EMBA—Executive Master of Business Administration Full-time. 5 years of full-time work experience and an interview are required. 48 total credits required. 22 months to complete program. *Concentration:* executive programs.

EMBA—Vietnam Executive Master of Business Administration Full-time. Distance learning option. 4 years of full-time post bachelor's work experience, interview and writing sample required. 48 total credits required. 22 months to complete program. *Concentrations:* executive programs, international and area business studies.

JD/MBA—Juris Doctor/Master of Business Administration Full-time and part-time. Must submit separate applications and be admitted to both programs. 122 to 128 total credits required. 60 to 84 months to complete program. *Concentrations:* international and area business studies, law.

M Acc—Master of Accountancy Full-time and part-time. Distance learning option. Completion of ACC 201 and 202 required. 39 to 42 total credits required. 15 to 48 months to complete program. *Concentrations:* accounting, international business.

MBA—China International Master of Business Administration Full-time. At least 2 years of post-baccalaureate work experience required. 48 total credits required. 21 months to complete program. *Concentrations:* Chinese business studies, international and area business studies.

MBA—Japan-Focused Master of Business Administration Full-time. At least 2 years of post-baccalaureate work experience required. 48 total credits required. 21 months to complete program. *Concentrations:* international and area business studies, Japanese business studies.

MBA Full-time and part-time. At least 2 years of full-time post-baccalaureate professional work experience preferred. 48 total credits required. 21 to 84 months to complete program. *Concentrations:* accounting, entrepreneurship, information management, international and area business studies, management, marketing.

MHRM—Master's in Human Resource Management Full-time. A writing sample and an interview are required. 30 total credits required. 16 months to complete program. *Concentration:* human resources management.

PhD/MBA—International Management Full-time. Master's degree or Bachelor's degree, foundation courses in business or accounting obtained at an accredited school and a minimum GMAT score of 600 required. 60 to 120 total credits required. 48 to 120 months to complete program. *Concentrations:* accounting, Asian business studies, finance, international management, international marketing, management information systems.

RESOURCES AND SERVICES 125 on-campus PCs are available to graduate business students. Access to Internet/World Wide Web, online (class) registration, and online grade reports available. *Personal computer requirements:* Graduate business students are strongly recommended to purchase or lease a personal computer. *Special opportunities include:* An international exchange program and an internship program are available. *Placement services include:* Alumni network, career placement, job search course, career counseling/planning, electronic job bank, resume referral, career fairs, job interviews arranged, resume preparation, and career library.

EXPENSES *Tuition (state resident):* Full-time: $13,920. Part-time: $580 per credit. *Tuition (nonresident):* Full-time: $21,480. Part-time: $895 per credit. *Tuition (international):* Full-time: $21,480. Part-time: $895 per credit.

FINANCIAL AID (2007–08) 72 students received aid, including grants, loans, and scholarships. Aid is available to part-time students. *Financial aid application deadline:* 3/1.

Financial Aid Contact Mr. Dean Nushida, Financial Aid Officer, 2600 Campus Road, Student Services Center, Room 112, Honolulu, HI 96822. *Phone:* 808-956-3986. *Fax:* 808-956-3985. *E-mail:* nushida@hawaii.edu.

INTERNATIONAL STUDENTS 30% of students enrolled are international students. *Services and facilities:* Counseling/support services, ESL/language courses, International student organization, Orientation, Visa Services. Financial aid is available to international students. *Required with application:* TOEFL with recommended score of 250 (computer), 600 (paper), or 100 (Internet); proof of adequate funds; proof of health/immunizations.

International Student Contact Ms. Linda Duckworth, Director, International Student Services, 2600 Campus Road, Student Services Center, Room 308, Honolulu, HI 96822. *Phone:* 808-956-4739. *Fax:* 808-956-5076. *E-mail:* lindaduc@hawaii.edu.

APPLICATION *Required:* GMAT, application form, baccalaureate/first degree, essay, interview, 2 letters of recommendation, personal statement, resume/curriculum vitae, transcripts of college work, 2 years of work experience. *Application fee:* $50. Applications for domestic and international students are processed on a rolling basis.

Application Contact Ms. Jennifer Tutak, MBA Admissions Director, 2404 Maile Way, G-202, Honolulu, HI 96822. *Phone:* 808-956-8266. *Fax:* 808-956-2657. *E-mail:* tutak@hawaii.edu.

University of Phoenix–Hawaii Campus
College of Graduate Business and Management

Honolulu, Hawaii

Phone: 480-317-6200 **Fax:** 480-643-1479 **E-mail:** beth.barilla@phoenix.edu

Business Program(s) Web Site: http://www.phoenix.edu

DEGREES EMBA • M Mgt • MA • MBA • MIBA

EMBA—Executive Master of Business Administration At least 45 total credits required. *Concentration:* strategic management.

M Mgt—Human Resource Management Full-time. At least 45 total credits required. *Concentration:* human resources management.

M Mgt—Public Administration Full-time. At least 45 total credits required. *Concentration:* public policy and administration.

M Mgt—Master of Management Full-time. At least 39 total credits required. *Concentration:* management.

MA—Master of Arts in Organizational Management Full-time. At least 40 total credits required. *Concentration:* organizational management.

MBA—Accounting Full-time. At least 54 total credits required. *Concentration:* accounting.

MBA—Human Resource Management Full-time. At least 45 total credits required. *Concentration:* human resources management.

MBA—Marketing Full-time. At least 45 total credits required. *Concentration:* marketing.

MBA—Public Administration Full-time. At least 45 total credits required. *Concentration:* public policy and administration.

MBA—e-Business Full-time. At least 45 total credits required. *Concentration:* electronic commerce (E-commerce).

MBA—Master of Business Administration Full-time. At least 45 total credits required. *Concentration:* administration.

MIBA—Global Management Full-time. At least 45 total credits required. *Concentration:* international business.

RESOURCES AND SERVICES Access to online grade reports available. *Personal computer requirements:* Graduate business students are strongly recommended to purchase or lease a personal computer. *Placement services include:* Alumni network.

Application Contact Beth Barilla, Associate Vice President of Student Admissions and Services, Mail Stop AA-K101, 4615 East Elwood Street, Phoenix, AZ 85040-1958. *Phone:* 480-317-6200. *Fax:* 480-643-1479. *E-mail:* beth.barilla@phoenix.edu.

IDAHO

Boise State University
College of Business and Economics

Boise, Idaho

Phone: 208-426-3116 **Fax:** 208-426-1135 **E-mail:** graduatebusiness@boisestate.edu

Business Program(s) Web Site: http://cobe.boisestate.edu/graduate

Graduate Business Unit Enrollment *Total:* 200 (108 full-time; 92 part-time; 73 women; 14 international). *Average Age:* 35.

Graduate Business Faculty *Total:* 47 (43 full-time; 4 part-time).

Admissions *Applied:* 163. *Admitted:* 71. *Enrolled:* 34. *Average GMAT:* 589. *Average GPA:* 3.36

Academic Calendar Semesters.

Accreditation AACSB—The Association to Advance Collegiate Schools of Business.

After Graduation (Class of 2006–07) *Employed within 3 months of graduation:* 99%. *Average starting salary:* $64,500.

DEGREES EMBA • MBA • MS

EMBA—Executive Master of Business Administration Part-time. 6 or more years of mid- to senior-level managerial or professional experience required. 40 total credits required. 21 months to complete program. *Concentration:* strategic management.

MBA—MBA in Information Technology Management Full-time and part-time. GMAT; undergraduate technical degree or 5 years work experience in a technical field required. 36 to 48 total credits required. 24 to 72 months to complete program. *Concentrations:* information technology, technology management.

MBA—Master of Business Administration Full-time and part-time. GMAT required. 37 to 49 total credits required. 18 to 84 months to complete program. *Concentrations:* accounting, conflict resolution management, engineering, entrepreneurship, finance, financial management/planning, general MBA, health administration, information technology, management, marketing, organizational management, public policy and administration, supply chain management, taxation, technology management, training and development.

MS—Accountancy Full-time and part-time. GMAT or current CPA license required. 30 total credits required. 12 to 84 months to complete program. *Concentrations:* accounting, conflict resolution management, taxation.

MS—Taxation Full-time and part-time. GMAT or current CPA license required. 30 total credits required. 12 to 84 months to complete program. *Concentrations:* conflict resolution management, taxation.

RESOURCES AND SERVICES 300 on-campus PCs are available to graduate business students. Access to Internet/World Wide Web, online (class) registration, and online grade reports available. *Personal computer requirements:* Graduate business students are strongly recommended to purchase or lease a personal computer. *Special opportunities include:* An international exchange program and an internship program are available. *Placement services include:* Alumni network, career placement, career counseling/planning, electronic job bank, career fairs, job interviews arranged, resume preparation, and career library.

Boise State University (continued)

EXPENSES *Tuition (state resident):* Full-time: $6470. Part-time: $272 per credit hour. *Tuition (nonresident):* Full-time: $14,638. Part-time: $272 per credit hour. *Tuition (international):* Full-time: $14,638. Part-time: $272 per credit hour. Tuition and/or fees vary by number of courses or credits taken. *Graduate housing:* Room and board costs vary by number of occupants, type of accommodation, and type of board plan. *Typical cost:* $6380 (including board), $3900 (room only).

FINANCIAL AID (2007–08) 32 students received aid, including loans, research assistantships, scholarships, teaching assistantships, and work study. Aid is available to part-time students. *Financial aid application deadline:* 2/1.

Financial Aid Contact Mrs. J. Renee Anchustegui, Program Coordinator, Graduate Business Studies, 1910 University Drive, B318, Boise, ID 83725-1600. *Phone:* 208-426-3116. *Fax:* 208-426-1135. *E-mail:* graduatebusiness@boisestate.edu.

INTERNATIONAL STUDENTS 7% of students enrolled are international students. *Services and facilities:* Counseling/support services, ESL/language courses, Housing location assistance, International student housing, International student organization, Language tutoring, Orientation, Visa Services, Area tours, Internships, Minimal academic advising, Cross-cultural training, Extracurricular activities and trips. Financial aid is available to international students. *Required with application:* TOEFL with recommended score of 240 (computer), 587 (paper), or 95 (Internet); proof of adequate funds. *Recommended with application:* IELT with recommended score of 6; proof of health/immunizations.

International Student Contact Ms. Sally Pittman, Foreign Student Services Coordinator, Enrollment Services, 1910 University Drive, Boise, ID 83725-1320. *Phone:* 208-426-1757. *Fax:* 208-426-3765. *E-mail:* spittman@boisestate.edu.

APPLICATION *Required:* GMAT, application form, baccalaureate/first degree, essay, 2 letters of recommendation, personal statement, resume/ curriculum vitae, transcripts of college work, 2 years of work experience. *Recommended:* Interview. *Application fee:* $55. Applications for domestic and international students are processed on a rolling basis.

Application Contact Mrs. J. Renee Anchustegui, Program Administrator and Academic Advisor, Graduate Business Studies, 1910 University Drive, B318, Boise, ID 83725-1600. *Phone:* 208-426-3116. *Fax:* 208-426-1135. *E-mail:* graduatebusiness@boisestate.edu.

Idaho State University
College of Business
Pocatello, Idaho

Phone: 208-282-2966 **Fax:** 208-282-4367 **E-mail:** seeljean@isu.edu

Business Program(s) Web Site: http://cob.isu.edu/mba/

Graduate Business Unit Enrollment *Total:* 118 (44 full-time; 74 part-time; 33 women; 10 international). *Average Age:* 32.

Graduate Business Faculty 36 full-time.

Admissions *Applied:* 91. *Admitted:* 52. *Enrolled:* 44. *Average GMAT:* 583. *Average GPA:* 3.5

Academic Calendar Semesters.

Accreditation AACSB—The Association to Advance Collegiate Schools of Business.

After Graduation (Class of 2006–07) *Employed within 3 months of graduation:* 95%.

DEGREES MBA

MBA—Master of Business Administration Full-time and part-time. 30 to 51 total credits required. 12 to 60 months to complete program. *Concentration:* general MBA.

MBA—Master of Business Administration in Accounting Full-time and part-time. 33 to 51 total credits required. Minimum of 12 months to complete program. *Concentrations:* accounting, finance, health care, management, management information systems, marketing.

RESOURCES AND SERVICES 100 on-campus PCs are available to graduate business students. Access to Internet/World Wide Web, online (class) registration, and online grade reports available. *Personal computer requirements:* Graduate business students are not required to have a personal computer. *Special opportunities include:* An international exchange program and an internship program are available. *Placement services include:* Alumni network, career placement, career counseling/ planning, career fairs, job interviews arranged, resume preparation, and career library.

EXPENSES *Tuition (state resident):* Full-time: $6206. Part-time: $259 per credit. *Tuition (nonresident):* Full-time: $14,890. Part-time: $379 per credit. *Tuition (international):* Full-time: $14,890. Part-time: $379 per credit. *Graduate housing:* Room and board costs vary by campus location, number of occupants, type of accommodation, and type of board plan.

FINANCIAL AID (2007–08) Fellowships, grants, loans, research assistantships, scholarships, teaching assistantships, and work study. *Financial aid application deadline:* 4/15.

Financial Aid Contact Mr. Douglas Severs, Director of Financial Aid and Scholarships, Campus Box 8077, Pocatello, ID 83209-8077. *Phone:* 208-282-2981. *Fax:* 208-282-4755. *E-mail:* sevedoug@isu.edu.

INTERNATIONAL STUDENTS 8% of students enrolled are international students. *Services and facilities:* Counseling/support services, ESL/language courses, Housing location assistance, International student housing, International student organization, Orientation. Financial aid is available to international students. *Required with application:* TOEFL with recommended score of 213 (computer) or 550 (paper); proof of adequate funds; proof of health/immunizations.

International Student Contact Ms. Kay Durman, International Student Advisor, Box 8075, Pocatello, ID 83209. *Phone:* 208-282-2270. *Fax:* 208-282-4847. *E-mail:* durmkay@isu.edu.

APPLICATION *Required:* GMAT, application form, baccalaureate/first degree, 2 letters of recommendation, personal statement, resume/ curriculum vitae, transcripts of college work. *Application fee:* $55. Applications for domestic and international students are processed on a rolling basis.

Application Contact Jeanette Seeley, MBA Director, 921 South 8th Avenue, Stop 8020, Pocatello, ID 83209. *Phone:* 208-282-2966. *Fax:* 208-282-4367. *E-mail:* seeljean@isu.edu.

University of Idaho
College of Business and Economics
Moscow, Idaho

Phone: 208-885-4001 **Fax:** 208-885-4406 **E-mail:** gadms@uidaho.edu

Business Program(s) Web Site: http://www.uidaho.edu/cbe/college/

Graduate Business Unit Enrollment *Total:* 28 (27 full-time; 1 part-time; 21 women; 11 international). *Average Age:* 25.

Graduate Business Faculty 7 full-time.

Admissions *Applied:* 23. *Admitted:* 21. *Enrolled:* 17. *Average GMAT:* 541. *Average GPA:* 3.5

Academic Calendar Semesters.

Accreditation AACSB—The Association to Advance Collegiate Schools of Business.

After Graduation (Class of 2006–07) *Employed within 3 months of graduation:* 100%. *Average starting salary:* $43,000.

DEGREES JD/M Acc • M Acct

JD/M Acc—Juris Doctor/Master of Accountancy Full-time and part-time. At least 30 total credits required. 9 to 24 months to complete program. *Concentration:* combined degrees.

M Acct—Master of Accountancy Full-time and part-time. At least 30 total credits required. *Concentration:* accounting.

RESOURCES AND SERVICES 100 on-campus PCs are available to graduate business students. Access to Internet/World Wide Web, online (class) registration, and online grade reports available. *Personal computer requirements:* Graduate business students are strongly recommended to purchase or lease a personal computer. *Special opportunities include:* An internship program is available. *Placement services include:* Alumni network, career placement, career counseling/planning, career fairs, job interviews arranged, and resume preparation.

EXPENSES *Tuition (state resident):* Full-time: $4950. Part-time: $239 per credit. *Tuition (nonresident):* Full-time: $15,030. Part-time: $387 per credit. *Tuition (international):* Full-time: $15,030. Part-time: $387 per credit. *Required fees:* Full-time: $1298. Part-time: $1298 per year. *Graduate housing:* Room and board costs vary by number of occupants, type of accommodation, and type of board plan. *Typical cost:* $8700 (including board).

FINANCIAL AID (2007–08) 28 students received aid, including fellowships, loans, research assistantships, scholarships, and teaching assistantships. Aid is available to part-time students.

Financial Aid Contact Student Financial Aid, SUB 101, Moscow, ID 83844-4291. *Phone:* 208-885-6312. *Fax:* 208-885-5592. *E-mail:* finaid@uidaho.edu.

INTERNATIONAL STUDENTS 39% of students enrolled are international students. *Services and facilities:* Counseling/support services, ESL/language courses, Housing location assistance, International student organization, Language tutoring, Orientation, Visa Services. Financial aid is available to international students. *Required with application:* TOEFL with recommended score of 213 (computer), 550 (paper), or 70 (Internet); proof of adequate funds.

International Student Contact International Programs Office, LLC Building 3, Moscow, ID 83844-1250. *Phone:* 208-885-8984. *Fax:* 208-885-2859. *E-mail:* ipo@uidaho.edu.

APPLICATION *Required:* GMAT, application form, baccalaureate/first degree, 3 letters of recommendation, personal statement, transcripts of college work. School will accept GRE. *Application fee:* $55, $60 (international). *Deadlines:* 7/1 for fall, 11/1 for spring, 4/1 for summer, 6/1 for fall (international), 10/1 for spring (international), 3/15 for summer (international).

Application Contact Graduate Admissions Office, SUB 137, Box 444266, Moscow, ID 83844-4266. *Phone:* 208-885-4001. *Fax:* 208-885-4406. *E-mail:* gadms@uidaho.edu.

University of Phoenix–Idaho Campus

College of Graduate Business and Management

Meridian, Idaho

Phone: 480-317-6200 **Fax:** 480-643-1479 **E-mail:** beth.barilla@phoenix.edu

Business Program(s) Web Site: http://www.phoenix.edu

DEGREES   MA • MBA

MA—Organizational Management Full-time. At least 40 total credits required. *Concentration:* organizational management.

MBA—Accounting Full-time. At least 45 total credits required. *Concentration:* accounting.

MBA—Global Management Full-time. At least 45 total credits required. *Concentration:* international business.

MBA—Human Resource Management Full-time. At least 45 total credits required. *Concentration:* human resources management.

MBA—Marketing Full-time. At least 45 total credits required. *Concentration:* marketing.

MBA—Master of Business Administration Full-time. At least 45 total credits required. *Concentration:* administration.

MBA—Public Administration Full-time. At least 45 total credits required. *Concentration:* public policy and administration.

MBA—e-Business Full-time. At least 45 total credits required. *Concentration:* electronic commerce (E-commerce).

RESOURCES AND SERVICES Access to online (class) registration and online grade reports available. *Personal computer requirements:* Graduate business students are strongly recommended to purchase or lease a personal computer. *Placement services include:* Alumni network.

Application Contact Beth Barilla, Associate Vice President of Student Admissions and Services, Mail Stop AA-K101, 4615 East Elwood Street, Phoenix, AZ 85040-1958. *Phone:* 480-317-6200. *Fax:* 480-643-1479. *E-mail:* beth.barilla@phoenix.edu.

ILLINOIS

American InterContinental University Online

Program in Business Administration

Hoffman Estates, Illinois

Phone: 877-701-3800 **E-mail:** info@aiuonline.edu

Business Program(s) Web Site: http://www.aiuonline.edu

Graduate Business Unit Enrollment *Total:* 1,513 (1,513 full-time; 948 women). *Average Age:* 36.

Graduate Business Faculty *Total:* 35 (5 full-time; 30 part-time).

Academic Calendar Quarters.

DEGREE   MBA

MBA—Master of Business Administration Full-time. Distance learning option. 48 total credits required. *Concentrations:* finance, health care, human resources management, international business, management, marketing, operations management, other, project management.

RESOURCES AND SERVICES Access to Internet/World Wide Web, online (class) registration, and online grade reports available. *Personal computer requirements:* Graduate business students are required to have a personal computer. *Placement services include:* Alumni network, career counseling/planning, electronic job bank, career fairs, and resume preparation.

EXPENSES *Tuition:* Full-time: $30,976. *Tuition (international):* Full-time: $30,976.

FINANCIAL AID (2007–08) Grants, loans, and scholarships.

Financial Aid Contact Mr. Matthew Reahm, Vice President of Financial Aid, 5550 Prairie Stone Parkway, Suite 400, Hoffman Estates, IL 60192. *Phone:* 877-701-3800. *E-mail:* info@aiuonline.edu.

INTERNATIONAL STUDENTS *Services and facilities:* Counseling/support services, Orientation. Financial aid is available to international students. *Recommended with application:* TOEFL with recommended score of 213 (computer) or 550 (paper).

APPLICATION *Required:* Application form, baccalaureate/first degree, essay, interview, personal statement, resume/curriculum vitae, transcripts of college work. *Recommended:* Work experience. *Application fee:* $50. Applications for domestic and international students are processed on a rolling basis.

American InterContinental University Online (continued)

Application Contact Mr. Richard Kennedy, Vice President of Admissions, 5550 Prairie Stone Parkway, Suite 400, Hoffman Estates, IL 60192. *Phone:* 877-701-3800. *E-mail:* info@aiuonline.edu.

Argosy University, Chicago
College of Business

Chicago, Illinois

Phone: 312-777-7600 **Fax:** 312-777-7748

Business Program(s) Web Site: http://www.argosy.edu/chicago

DEGREES DBA • MBA • MSM

DBA—Doctor of Business Administration (DBA) *Concentrations:* accounting, information systems, international business, management, marketing.

MBA—Master of Business Administration (MBA) Distance learning option. *Concentrations:* finance, health administration, information systems, international business, management, marketing.

MSM—Master of Science in Management Distance learning option. *Concentration:* management.

Financial Aid Contact Director of Admissions, 225 North Michigan Avenue, Suite 1300, Chicago, IL 60601. *Phone:* 312-777-7600. *Fax:* 312-777-7748.

International Student Contact Director of Admissions, 225 North Michigan Avenue, Suite 1300, Chicago, IL 60601. *Phone:* 312-777-7600. *Fax:* 312-777-7748.

Application Contact Director of Admissions, 225 North Michigan Avenue, Suite 1300, Chicago, IL 60601. *Phone:* 312-777-7600. *Fax:* 312-777-7748.

See full description on page 566.

Argosy University, Schaumburg
College of Business

Schaumburg, Illinois

Phone: 847-969-4900 **Fax:** 847-969-4999

Business Program(s) Web Site: http://www.argosy.edu/schaumburg

---

DEGREES DBA • MBA • MSM

DBA—Doctor of Business Administration (DBA) *Concentrations:* accounting, information systems, international business, management, marketing.

MBA—Master of Business Administration (MBA) *Concentrations:* finance, health administration, information systems, international business, management.

MSM—Master of Science in Management (MSM) *Concentration:* management.

Financial Aid Contact Director of Admissions, 999 North Plaza Drive, Suite 111, Schaumburg, IL 60173-5403. *Phone:* 847-969-4900. *Fax:* 847-969-4999.

International Student Contact Director of Admissions, 999 North Plaza Drive, Suite 111, Schaumburg, IL 60173-5403. *Phone:* 847-969-4900. *Fax:* 847-969-4999.

Application Contact Director of Admissions, 999 North Plaza Drive, Suite 111, Schaumburg, IL 60173-5403. *Phone:* 847-969-4900. *Fax:* 847-969-4999.

See full description on page 566.

Aurora University
Dunham School of Business

Aurora, Illinois

Phone: 630-844-8879 **Fax:** 630-844-5535 **E-mail:** eberg@aurora.edu

Business Program(s) Web Site: http://www.aurora.edu/mba

Graduate Business Unit Enrollment *Total:* 155 (45 full-time; 110 part-time; 82 women; 1 international). *Average Age:* 33.

Graduate Business Faculty *Total:* 19 (12 full-time; 7 part-time).

Admissions *Applied:* 72. *Admitted:* 70. *Enrolled:* 33. *Average GPA:* 3.0

Academic Calendar 5 eight week modules per year.

Accreditation ACBSP—The American Council of Business Schools and Programs.

After Graduation (Class of 2006–07) *Employed within 3 months of graduation:* 98%.

DEGREE MBA

MBA—Master of Business Administration Full-time and part-time. 36 to 42 total credits required. 18 to 60 months to complete program. *Concentrations:* accounting, general MBA, human resources management, leadership, operations management, other.

RESOURCES AND SERVICES 100 on-campus PCs are available to graduate business students. Access to Internet/World Wide Web and online grade reports available. *Personal computer requirements:* Graduate business students are strongly recommended to purchase or lease a personal computer. *Special opportunities include:* An internship program is available. *Placement services include:* Alumni network, career placement, career counseling/planning, electronic job bank, resume referral, career fairs, job interviews arranged, resume preparation, and career library.

EXPENSES *Tuition:* Full-time: $10,170. Part-time: $565 per semester hour. *Tuition (international):* Full-time: $10,170. Part-time: $565 per semester hour. Tuition and/or fees vary by campus location.

FINANCIAL AID (2007–08) 86 students received aid, including grants, loans, and scholarships. Aid is available to part-time students. *Financial aid application deadline:* 5/15.

Financial Aid Contact Ms. Katie O'Connor, Graduate Financial Services Representative, 347 South Gladstone Avenue, Aurora, IL 60506-4892. *Phone:* 630-844-4948. *Fax:* 630-844-5535. *E-mail:* koconnor@aurora.edu.

INTERNATIONAL STUDENTS 0.6% of students enrolled are international students. *Services and facilities:* Counseling/support services. Financial aid is not available to international students. *Required with application:* TOEFL with recommended score of 213 (computer) or 550 (paper); proof of adequate funds; proof of health/immunizations.

International Student Contact Ms. Peg Arendt, Adult and Graduate Enrollment Coordinator, 347 South Gladstone Avenue, Aurora, IL 60506-4892. *Phone:* 630-844-5294. *Fax:* 630-844-6854. *E-mail:* parendt@aurora.edu.

APPLICATION *Required:* Application form, baccalaureate/first degree, 3 letters of recommendation, transcripts of college work, 2 years of work experience. *Recommended:* Interview. *Application fee:* $25. Applications for domestic and international students are processed on a rolling basis.

Application Contact Miss Emily Berg, Adult and Corporate Recruiter, 347 South Gladstone Avenue, Aurora, IL 60506-4892. *Phone:* 630-844-8879. *Fax:* 630-844-5535. *E-mail:* eberg@aurora.edu.

Benedictine University
Graduate Programs

Lisle, Illinois

Phone: 630-829-6303 **Fax:** 630-829-6584 **E-mail:** cbenford@ben.edu

Business Program(s) Web Site: http://www.ben.edu/

DEGREES MBA • MBA/MPH • MBA/MSMIS • MBA/MSMOB

MBA—Accelerated Cohort Master of Business Administration Part-time. At least 64 total credits required. 22 months to complete program. *Concentrations:* general MBA, information technology.

MBA—Evening Master of Business Administration Full-time and part-time. 48 to 64 total credits required. 12 to 72 months to complete program. *Concentrations:* accounting, combined degrees, entrepreneurship, finance, general MBA, health care, human resources management, international business, leadership, management, management consulting, management information systems, marketing, operations management, technology management.

MBA—Executive Master of Business Administration Part-time. At least 64 total credits required. 18 months to complete program. *Concentration:* executive programs.

MBA—Webflex Master of Business Administration Full-time and part-time. Distance learning option. At least 64 total credits required. 12 to 72 months to complete program. *Concentrations:* accounting, entrepreneurship, finance, health administration, human resources management, information systems, international business, marketing, operations management, project management, technology management.

MBA/MPH—Master of Business Administration/Master of Public Health Full-time and part-time. At least 96 total credits required. 24 to 72 months to complete program. *Concentrations:* accounting, electronic commerce (E-commerce), entrepreneurship, finance, general MBA, health care, human resources management, international business, leadership, management, management consulting, management information systems, marketing, operations management, technology management.

MBA/MSMIS—Master of Business Administration/Master of Science in Management Information Systems Full-time and part-time. At least 96 total credits required. 24 to 72 months to complete program. *Concentrations:* accounting, electronic commerce (E-commerce), entrepreneurship, finance, general MBA, health care, human resources management, international business, leadership, management, management consulting, management information systems, marketing, operations management, technology management.

MBA/MSMOB—Master of Business Administration/Master of Science in Management and Organizational Behavior Full-time and part-time. At least 96 total credits required. 24 to 72 months to complete program. *Concentrations:* accounting, electronic commerce (E-commerce), entrepreneurship, finance, general MBA, health care, human resources management, international business, leadership, management, management consulting, management information systems, marketing, operations management, technology management.

RESOURCES AND SERVICES 120 on-campus PCs are available to graduate business students. Access to Internet/World Wide Web and online grade reports available. *Personal computer requirements:* Graduate business students are strongly recommended to purchase or lease a personal computer. *Special opportunities include:* An international exchange program and an internship program are available. *Placement services include:* Alumni network, career placement, job search course, career counseling/planning, electronic job bank, resume referral, career fairs, job interviews arranged, resume preparation, and career library.

Application Contact Mr. Charles Benford, Leads Manager, Graduate Programs, 5700 College Road, Enrollment Center—Lownik Hall, Lisle, IL 60532-0900. *Phone:* 630-829-6303. *Fax:* 630-829-6584. *E-mail:* cbenford@ben.edu.

Bradley University

Foster College of Business Administration

Peoria, Illinois

Phone: 309-677-2256 **Fax:** 309-677-3374 **E-mail:** sgawor@bradley.edu

Business Program(s) Web Site: http://www.bradley.edu/grad

Graduate Business Unit Enrollment *Total:* 207 (67 full-time; 140 part-time).

Graduate Business Faculty *Total:* 76 (53 full-time; 23 part-time).

Admissions *Applied:* 82. *Admitted:* 54. *Average GMAT:* 577. *Average GPA:* 3.28

Academic Calendar 7-week sessions.

Accreditation AACSB—The Association to Advance Collegiate Schools of Business.

After Graduation (Class of 2006–07) *Employed within 3 months of graduation:* 99%.

DEGREES MBA • MS

MBA—Master of Business Administration Full-time and part-time. 33 to 46 total credits required. 12 to 60 months to complete program. *Concentrations:* accounting, finance, management, marketing.

MS—Master of Science in Accounting Full-time and part-time. At least 30 total credits required. 12 to 60 months to complete program. *Concentration:* accounting.

RESOURCES AND SERVICES 194 on-campus PCs are available to graduate business students. Access to Internet/World Wide Web, online (class) registration, and online grade reports available. *Personal computer requirements:* Graduate business students are not required to have a personal computer. *Special opportunities include:* An international exchange program and an internship program are available. *Placement services include:* Alumni network, career placement, job search course, career counseling/planning, electronic job bank, resume referral, career fairs, job interviews arranged, resume preparation, and career library.

EXPENSES *Tuition:* Full-time: $14,000. Part-time: $7000 per year. *Tuition (international):* Full-time: $15,000. Part-time: $7500 per year.

FINANCIAL AID (2007–08) 24 students received aid, including fellowships, loans, research assistantships, and scholarships. Aid is available to part-time students.

Financial Aid Contact Mr. David Pardieck, Director, Financial Assistance, 1501 West Bradley Avenue, Peoria, IL 61625. *Phone:* 309-677-3089. *Fax:* 309-677-2798. *E-mail:* dlp@bradley.edu.

INTERNATIONAL STUDENTS *Services and facilities:* Counseling/support services, ESL/language courses, Housing location assistance, International student organization, Language tutoring, Orientation, Visa Services. Financial aid is available to international students. *Required with application:* TOEFL with recommended score of 213 (computer), 550 (paper), or 79 (Internet); proof of adequate funds; proof of health/immunizations.

International Student Contact Ms. Lynne Franks, Director, Graduate International Admissions and Student Services, 1501 West Bradley Avenue, Peoria, IL 61625-0002. *Phone:* 309-677-2375. *Fax:* 309-677-3739. *E-mail:* bugrad2@bradley.edu.

APPLICATION *Required:* GMAT, application form, baccalaureate/first degree, essay, 2 letters of recommendation, personal statement, resume/curriculum vitae, transcripts of college work. *Application fee:* $40, $50 (international). Applications for domestic and international students are processed on a rolling basis.

Application Contact Ms. Susannah Gawor, Assistant Director of Graduate Programs, 1501 West Bradley Avenue, Peoria, IL 61625. *Phone:* 309-677-2256. *Fax:* 309-677-3374. *E-mail:* sgawor@bradley.edu.

DePaul University

Charles H. Kellstadt Graduate School of Business

Chicago, Illinois

Phone: 312-362-8810 **Fax:** 312-362-6677 **E-mail:** dcornwel@depaul.edu

DePaul University (continued)

Business Program(s) Web Site: http://www.kellstadt.depaul.edu

Graduate Business Unit Enrollment *Total:* 1,886 (57 full-time; 1,829 part-time; 759 women; 128 international). *Average Age:* 30.

Graduate Business Faculty *Total:* 292 (134 full-time; 158 part-time).

Admissions *Applied:* 1,209. *Admitted:* 691. *Enrolled:* 455. *Average GMAT:* 575. *Average GPA:* 3.2

Academic Calendar Quarters.

Accreditation AACSB—The Association to Advance Collegiate Schools of Business.

After Graduation (Class of 2006–07) *Employed within 3 months of graduation:* 89%. *Average starting salary:* $66,929.

DEGREES JD/MBA • M Acc • MBA • MS • MSA • MSF • MSHR • MST

JD/MBA—Juris Doctor/Master of Business Administration Full-time and part-time. 60 to 72 total credits required. 34 to 46 months to complete program. *Concentrations:* accounting, economics, electronic commerce (E-commerce), entrepreneurship, finance, financial management/planning, general MBA, health administration, human resources management, international business, leadership, management information systems, marketing, marketing research, operations management, real estate.

M Acc—Master of Accountancy Full-time and part-time. 45 total credits required. 18 to 72 months to complete program. *Concentration:* accounting.

MBA—Full-Time Master of Business Administration Full-time. Additional essay; interview required. 48 to 72 total credits required. 12 to 72 months to complete program. *Concentrations:* accounting, banking, combined degrees, economics, electronic commerce (E-commerce), entrepreneurship, finance, financial management/planning, general MBA, health administration, human resources management, international business, leadership, management information systems, marketing, marketing research, operations management, real estate.

MBA—Part-Time Master of Business Administration Full-time and part-time. 48 to 72 total credits required. 12 to 72 months to complete program. *Concentrations:* accounting, combined degrees, economics, electronic commerce (E-commerce), entrepreneurship, finance, financial management/planning, general MBA, health administration, human resources management, international business, leadership, management information systems, marketing, marketing research, operations management, real estate.

MBA—Weekend Master of Business Administration Part-time. 48 to 72 total credits required. 21 months to complete program. *Concentration:* financial management/planning.

MS—Master of Science in Business Information Technology Full-time and part-time. 52 total credits required. 24 to 72 months to complete program. *Concentration:* business information science.

MS—Master of Science in Marketing Analysis Full-time and part-time. 48 total credits required. 18 to 72 months to complete program. *Concentration:* marketing.

MS—Master of Science in e-Business 48 total credits required. 12 to 72 months to complete program. *Concentration:* electronic commerce (E-commerce).

MSA—Master of Science in Accountancy Full-time and part-time. 61 total credits required. 15 to 72 months to complete program. *Concentration:* accounting.

MSF—Master of Science in Finance Full-time and part-time. 48 total credits required. 18 to 72 months to complete program. *Concentration:* finance.

MSHR—Master of Science in Human Resources Full-time and part-time. GRE can be substituted for the GMAT in this program only. 48 total credits required. 18 to 72 months to complete program. *Concentration:* human resources management.

MST—Master of Science in Taxation Full-time and part-time. 45 to 48 total credits required. 18 to 72 months to complete program. *Concentration:* taxation.

RESOURCES AND SERVICES 156 on-campus PCs are available to graduate business students. Access to Internet/World Wide Web, online (class) registration, and online grade reports available. *Personal computer requirements:* Graduate business students are not required to have a personal computer. *Special opportunities include:* An international exchange program and an internship program are available. *Placement services include:* Alumni network, career placement, job search course, career counseling/planning, electronic job bank, resume referral, career fairs, job interviews arranged, resume preparation, and career library.

EXPENSES *Tuition:* Full-time: $35,952. Part-time: $749 per quarter hour. *Tuition (international):* Full-time: $35,952. Part-time: $749 per quarter hour. *Required fees:* Full-time: $150. Part-time: $50 per quarter.

FINANCIAL AID (2007–08) 318 students received aid, including research assistantships and scholarships. Aid is available to part-time students. *Financial aid application deadline:* 4/1.

Financial Aid Contact Financial Aid Office, 1 East Jackson Boulevard, Suite 9000, Chicago, IL 60604. *Phone:* 312-362-8091. *Fax:* 312-362-5748.

INTERNATIONAL STUDENTS 7% of students enrolled are international students. *Services and facilities:* Counseling/support services, ESL/language courses, Housing location assistance, International student organization, Language tutoring, Orientation, Visa Services. Financial aid is available to international students. *Required with application:* TOEFL with recommended score of 213 (computer) or 550 (paper); proof of adequate funds; proof of health/immunizations.

International Student Contact Ms. Rikki Eul, Assistant Director, International Admissions, 1 East Jackson Boulevard, Suite 7900, Chicago, IL 60604-2287. *Phone:* 312-362-8810. *Fax:* 312-362-6677. *E-mail:* reul@depaul.edu.

APPLICATION *Required:* GMAT, application form, baccalaureate/first degree, essay, 2 letters of recommendation, personal statement, resume/curriculum vitae, transcripts of college work. *Recommended:* Work experience. *Application fee:* $60. Applications for domestic and international students are processed on a rolling basis.

Application Contact Mr. Dustin Cornwell, Director of Recruitment and Admissions, 1 East Jackson Boulevard, Suite 7900, Chicago, IL 60604-2287. *Phone:* 312-362-8810. *Fax:* 312-362-6677. *E-mail:* dcornwel@depaul.edu.

DeVry University
Keller Graduate School of Management

Elgin, Illinois

Phone: 847-649-3980

DEGREES MAFM • MBA • MHRM • MIS • MPA • MPM

MAFM—Master of Accounting and Financial Management Full-time and part-time. Distance learning option. At least 44 total credits required. 18 to 60 months to complete program. *Concentrations:* accounting, financial management/planning.

MBA—Master of Business Administration Full-time and part-time. Distance learning option. At least 48 total credits required. 18 to 60 months to complete program. *Concentration:* management.

MHRM—Master of Human Resources Management Full-time and part-time. Distance learning option. At least 45 total credits required. 18 to 60 months to complete program. *Concentration:* human resources management.

MIS—Master of Information Systems Management Full-time and part-time. Distance learning option. At least 45 total credits required. 18 to 60 months to complete program. *Concentration:* information systems.

MPA—Master of Public Administration Full-time and part-time. Distance learning option. At least 45 total credits required. 18 to 60 months to complete program. *Concentration:* public policy and administration.

MPM—Master of Project Management Full-time and part-time. Distance learning option. At least 42 total credits required. 18 to 60 months to complete program. *Concentration:* project management.

Application Contact Admissions Office, Randall Point, 2250 Point Boulevard, Suite 250, Elgin, IL 60123. *Phone:* 847-649-3980.

DeVry University
Keller Graduate School of Management
Gurnee, Illinois

Phone: 847-855-2649

___

DEGREES MAFM • MBA • MHRM • MIS • MPA • MPM

___

MAFM—Master of Accounting and Financial Management Full-time and part-time. Distance learning option. At least 44 total credits required. 18 to 60 months to complete program. *Concentrations:* accounting, financial management/planning.

MBA—Master of Business Administration Full-time and part-time. Distance learning option. At least 48 total credits required. 18 to 60 months to complete program. *Concentration:* management.

MHRM—Master of Human Resources Management Full-time and part-time. Distance learning option. At least 45 total credits required. 18 to 60 months to complete program. *Concentration:* human resources management.

MIS—Master of Information Systems Management Full-time and part-time. Distance learning option. At least 45 total credits required. 18 to 60 months to complete program. *Concentration:* information systems.

MPA—Master of Public Administration Full-time and part-time. Distance learning option. At least 45 total credits required. 18 to 60 months to complete program. *Concentration:* public policy and administration.

MPM—Master of Project Management Full-time and part-time. Distance learning option. At least 42 total credits required. 18 to 60 months to complete program. *Concentration:* project management.

Application Contact Admissions Office, Gurnee Center, 1075 Tri-State Parkway, Suite 800, Gurnee, IL 60031. *Phone:* 847-855-2649.

DeVry University
Keller Graduate School of Management
Lincolnshire, Illinois

Phone: 847-940-7768

___

DEGREES MAFM • MBA • MHRM • MIS • MPA • MPM

___

MAFM—Master of Accounting and Financial Management Full-time and part-time. Distance learning option. At least 44 total credits required. 18 to 60 months to complete program. *Concentrations:* accounting, financial management/planning.

MBA—Master of Business Administration Full-time and part-time. Distance learning option. At least 48 total credits required. 18 to 60 months to complete program. *Concentration:* management.

MHRM—Master of Human Resources Management Full-time and part-time. Distance learning option. At least 45 total credits required. 18 to 60 months to complete program. *Concentration:* human resources management.

MIS—Master of Information Systems Management Full-time and part-time. Distance learning option. At least 45 total credits required. 18 to 60 months to complete program. *Concentration:* information systems.

MPA—Master of Public Administration Full-time and part-time. Distance learning option. At least 45 total credits required. 18 to 60 months to complete program. *Concentration:* public policy and administration.

MPM—Master of Project Management Full-time and part-time. Distance learning option. At least 42 total credits required. 18 to 60 months to complete program. *Concentration:* project management.

Application Contact Admissions Office, Lincolnshire Center, 25 Tri-State International Center, Suite 130, Lincolnshire, IL 60069. *Phone:* 847-940-7768.

DeVry University
Keller Graduate School of Management
Oakbrook Terrace, Illinois

Phone: 630-571-7700 Ext. 3243 **Fax:** 630-574-1969 **E-mail:** psimpson@keller.edu

Business Program(s) Web Site: http://www.devry.edu

Academic Calendar Semesters.

___

DEGREES MAFM • MBA • MHRM • MISM • MPA • MPM

___

MAFM—Master of Accounting and Financial Management Full-time and part-time. Distance learning option. At least 44 total credits required. 18 to 60 months to complete program. *Concentrations:* accounting, finance.

MBA—Master of Business Administration Full-time and part-time. Distance learning option. At least 48 total credits required. 18 to 60 months to complete program. *Concentrations:* accounting, electronic commerce (E-commerce), finance, health care, human resources management, information management, international business, management, marketing, project management, public policy and administration, telecommunications management.

MHRM—Master of Human Resources Management Full-time and part-time. Distance learning option. At least 45 total credits required. 18 to 60 months to complete program. *Concentration:* human resources management.

MISM—Master of Information Systems Management Full-time and part-time. Distance learning option. At least 45 total credits required. 18 to 60 months to complete program. *Concentration:* information systems.

MPA—Master of Public Administration Full-time and part-time. Distance learning option. At least 45 total credits required. 18 to 60 months to complete program. *Concentration:* public policy and administration.

MPM—Master of Project Management Full-time and part-time. Distance learning option. At least 42 total credits required. 18 to 60 months to complete program. *Concentration:* project management.

RESOURCES AND SERVICES *Personal computer requirements:* Graduate business students are not required to have a personal computer.

Financial Aid Contact Cheryl Jordan, Director of Financial Aid, 1 Tower Lane, Oakbrook Terrace, IL 60181. *Phone:* 630-706-3258. *Fax:* 630-574-1969. *E-mail:* cjordan@keller.edu.

INTERNATIONAL STUDENTS Financial aid is not available to international students.

International Student Contact Peggy Simpson, Director of Central Services, 1 Tower Lane, Oakbrook Terrace, IL 60181. *Phone:* 630-571-7700 Ext. 3243. *Fax:* 630-574-1969. *E-mail:* psimpson@keller.edu.

APPLICATION *Required:* Application form, baccalaureate/first degree, interview, transcripts of college work. Applications for domestic and international students are processed on a rolling basis.

DeVry University (continued)

Application Contact Peggy Simpson, Director of Central Services, 1 Tower Lane, Oakbrook Terrace, IL 60181. *Phone:* 630-571-7700 Ext. 3243. *Fax:* 630-574-1969. *E-mail:* psimpson@keller.edu.

See full description on page 650.

DeVry University
Keller Graduate School of Management
Schaumburg, Illinois

Phone: 847-330-0040

DEGREES MAFM • MBA • MHRM • MIS • MPA • MPM

MAFM—Master of Accounting and Financial Management Full-time and part-time. Distance learning option. At least 44 total credits required. 18 to 60 months to complete program. *Concentrations:* accounting, financial management/planning.

MBA—Master of Business Administration Full-time and part-time. Distance learning option. At least 48 total credits required. 18 to 60 months to complete program. *Concentration:* management.

MHRM—Master of Human Resources Management Full-time and part-time. Distance learning option. At least 45 total credits required. 18 to 60 months to complete program. *Concentration:* human resources management.

MIS—Master of Information Systems Management Full-time and part-time. Distance learning option. At least 45 total credits required. 18 to 60 months to complete program. *Concentration:* information systems.

MPA—Master of Public Administration Full-time and part-time. Distance learning option. At least 45 total credits required. 18 to 60 months to complete program. *Concentration:* public policy and administration.

MPM—Master of Project Management Full-time and part-time. Distance learning option. At least 42 total credits required. 18 to 60 months to complete program. *Concentration:* project management.

Application Contact Admissions Office, Woodfield Executive Plaza, 1051 Perimeter Drive, 9th Floor, Schaumburg, IL 60173. *Phone:* 847-330-0040.

DeVry University
Keller Graduate School of Management
Tinley Park, Illinois

Phone: 708-342-3750

DEGREES MAFM • MBA • MHRM • MIS • MPA • MPM

MAFM—Master of Accounting and Financial Management Full-time and part-time. Distance learning option. At least 44 total credits required. 18 to 60 months to complete program. *Concentrations:* accounting, financial management/planning.

MBA—Master of Business Administration Full-time and part-time. Distance learning option. At least 48 total credits required. 18 to 60 months to complete program. *Concentration:* management.

MHRM—Master of Human Resources Management Full-time and part-time. Distance learning option. At least 45 total credits required. 18 to 60 months to complete program. *Concentration:* human resources management.

MIS—Master of Information Systems Management *Concentration:* information systems.

MPA—Master of Public Administration Full-time and part-time. Distance learning option. At least 45 total credits required. 18 to 60 months to complete program. *Concentration:* public policy and administration.

MPM—Master of Project Management Full-time and part-time. Distance learning option. At least 42 total credits required. 18 to 60 months to complete program. *Concentration:* project management.

Application Contact Admissions Office, Tinley Park Center, Suite 1108, 18624 West Creek Drive, Tinley Park, IL 60477. *Phone:* 708-342-3750.

Dominican University
Edward A. and Lois L. Brennan School of Business
River Forest, Illinois

Phone: 708-524-6181 **Fax:** 708-524-6939 **E-mail:** abartzis@dom.edu

Business Program(s) Web Site: http://www.business.dom.edu

Graduate Business Unit Enrollment *Total:* 336 (171 full-time; 165 part-time; 135 women; 182 international). *Average Age:* 27.

Graduate Business Faculty *Total:* 33 (16 full-time; 17 part-time).

Admissions *Applied:* 115. *Admitted:* 77. *Enrolled:* 38. *Average GMAT:* 500. *Average GPA:* 3.2

Academic Calendar Semesters.

Accreditation ACBSP—The American Council of Business Schools and Programs.

DEGREES JD/MBA • MBA • MBA/MSLIS • MS • MSA • MSMIS

JD/MBA—Juris Doctor/Master of Business Administration Full-time and part-time. Students must be accepted at Dominican University and The John Marshall Law School. 27 to 45 total credits required. *Concentrations:* accounting, entrepreneurship, finance, health care, human resources management, international business, management, management information systems, marketing.

MBA—Master of Business Administration Full-time and part-time. 36 to 54 total credits required. *Concentrations:* accounting, entrepreneurship, finance, health care, human resources management, international business, management, management information systems, marketing.

MBA/MSLIS—Master of Business Administration/Master of Science in Library and Information Science Full-time and part-time. Students must be accepted into both the Graduate School of Business and the Graduate School of Library and Information Science for this joint degree program. 54 to 75 total credits required. *Concentrations:* accounting, entrepreneurship, finance, health care, human resources management, international business, management, management information systems, marketing.

MS—Master of Science in Computer Information Systems Full-time and part-time. 33 to 45 total credits required. *Concentration:* information systems.

MSA—Master of Science in Accounting Full-time and part-time. 30 to 51 total credits required. *Concentration:* accounting.

MSMIS—Master of Science in Management Information Systems Full-time and part-time. 33 to 51 total credits required. *Concentration:* management information systems.

RESOURCES AND SERVICES 625 on-campus PCs are available to graduate business students. Access to Internet/World Wide Web, online (class) registration, and online grade reports available. *Personal computer requirements:* Graduate business students are not required to have a personal computer. *Special opportunities include:* An international exchange program and an internship program are available. *Placement services include:* Alumni network, career placement, career counseling/planning, electronic job bank, resume referral, career fairs, job interviews arranged, resume preparation, and career library.

EXPENSES *Tuition:* Part-time: $2160 per course. *Tuition (international):* Full-time: $12,960. Part-time: $2160 per course. *Required fees:* Part-time: $10 per course. *Graduate housing:* Room and board costs vary by campus location, number of occupants, type of accommodation, and type of board plan. *Typical cost:* $7000 (including board), $3900 (room only).

FINANCIAL AID (2007–08) 150 students received aid, including loans, research assistantships, and scholarships. Aid is available to part-time students.

Financial Aid Contact Marie von Ebers, Associate Director of Financial Aid, 7900 West Division Street, River Forest, IL 60305. *Phone:* 708-524-6809. *Fax:* 708-366-6478. *E-mail:* finaid@dom.edu.

INTERNATIONAL STUDENTS 54% of students enrolled are international students. *Services and facilities:* Counseling/support services, ESL/language courses, Housing location assistance, International student housing, International student organization, Language tutoring, Orientation, Visa Services. Financial aid is available to international students. *Required with application:* TOEFL with recommended score of 213 (computer), 550 (paper), or 79 (Internet); proof of adequate funds; proof of health/immunizations.

International Student Contact Ms. Andrea Bartzis, Director of Admissions and International Programs, 7900 West Division Street, River Forest, IL 60305. *Phone:* 708-524-6181. *Fax:* 708-524-6939. *E-mail:* abartzis@dom.edu.

APPLICATION *Required:* GMAT, GRE, application form, baccalaureate/first degree, 2 letters of recommendation, personal statement, transcripts of college work. *Recommended:* Resume/curriculum vitae. *Application fee:* $25. Applications for domestic and international students are processed on a rolling basis.

Application Contact Andrea Bartzis, Assistant Director of Admissions, 7900 West Division Street, River Forest, IL 60305. *Phone:* 708-524-6181. *Fax:* 708-524-6939. *E-mail:* abartzis@dom.edu.

See full description on page 600.

Eastern Illinois University
Lumpkin College of Business and Applied Sciences

Charleston, Illinois

Phone: 217-581-3028 **Fax:** 217-581-6642 **E-mail:** mba@eiu.edu

Business Program(s) Web Site: http://www.eiu.edu/~mba/

Graduate Business Unit Enrollment *Total:* 151 (69 full-time; 82 part-time; 79 women; 11 international). *Average Age:* 27.

Graduate Business Faculty 13 full-time.

Admissions *Applied:* 73. *Admitted:* 66. *Enrolled:* 57. *Average GMAT:* 511. *Average GPA:* 3.39

Academic Calendar Semesters.

Accreditation AACSB—The Association to Advance Collegiate Schools of Business.

After Graduation (Class of 2006–07) *Employed within 3 months of graduation:* 90%.

DEGREES MBA

MBA—Master of Business Administration Full-time and part-time. Undergraduate degree in accounting required. At least 34 total credits required. 12 to 72 months to complete program. *Concentration:* accounting.

MBA—Master of Business Administration Full-time and part-time. At least 33 total credits required. 12 to 72 months to complete program. *Concentration:* general MBA.

RESOURCES AND SERVICES 145 on-campus PCs are available to graduate business students. Access to Internet/World Wide Web, online (class) registration, and online grade reports available. *Personal computer*

requirements: Graduate business students are strongly recommended to purchase or lease a personal computer. *Special opportunities include:* An international exchange program and an internship program are available. *Placement services include:* Career placement, career counseling/planning, resume referral, career fairs, job interviews arranged, resume preparation, and career library.

EXPENSES *Tuition (state resident):* Full-time: $6270. Part-time: $190 per semester hour. *Tuition (nonresident):* Full-time: $18,810. Part-time: $570 per semester hour. *Tuition (international):* Full-time: $18,810. Part-time: $570 per semester hour. *Required fees:* Full-time: $2400. Tuition and/or fees vary by class time, number of courses or credits taken, campus location, and academic program. *Graduate housing:* Room and board costs vary by number of occupants, type of accommodation, and type of board plan. *Typical cost:* $3794 (including board), $3367 (room only).

FINANCIAL AID (2007–08) 23 students received aid, including loans, research assistantships, scholarships, and teaching assistantships. *Financial aid application deadline:* 3/15.

Financial Aid Contact Ms. Jone Zieren, Director of Financial Aid, 600 Lincoln Avenue, Charleston, IL 61920-3099. *Phone:* 217-581-3713. *Fax:* 217-581-6422. *E-mail:* jazieren@eiu.edu.

INTERNATIONAL STUDENTS 7% of students enrolled are international students. *Services and facilities:* Counseling/support services, Housing location assistance, International student housing, International student organization, Language tutoring, Orientation, Visa Services. Financial aid is available to international students. *Required with application:* IELT with recommended score of 6.5; TOEFL with recommended score of 213 (computer), 550 (paper), or 79 (Internet); proof of adequate funds; proof of health/immunizations.

International Student Contact Marilyn Thomas, International Student Advisor, International Programs, 600 Lincoln Avenue, Charleston, IL 61920-3099. *Phone:* 217-581-2321. *Fax:* 217-581-7207. *E-mail:* msthomas@eiu.edu.

APPLICATION *Required:* GMAT, application form, baccalaureate/first degree, 2 letters of recommendation, personal statement, resume/curriculum vitae, transcripts of college work. *Recommended:* Work experience. *Application fee:* $30. Applications for domestic and international students are processed on a rolling basis.

Application Contact Dr. Cheryl L. Noll, Coordinator of Graduate Business Studies, 600 Lincoln Avenue, Charleston, IL 61920-3099. *Phone:* 217-581-3028. *Fax:* 217-581-6642. *E-mail:* mba@eiu.edu.

Elmhurst College
Program in Business Administration

Elmhurst, Illinois

Phone: 630-617-3069 **Fax:** 630-617-6471 **E-mail:** betsyk@elmhurst.edu

Business Program(s) Web Site: http://public.elmhurst.edu/mba

Graduate Business Unit Enrollment *Total:* 166 (3 full-time; 163 part-time; 74 women). *Average Age:* 26-43.

Graduate Business Faculty *Total:* 23 (6 full-time; 17 part-time).

Admissions *Applied:* 123. *Admitted:* 94. *Enrolled:* 85.

Academic Calendar Continuous.

After Graduation (Class of 2006–07) *Employed within 3 months of graduation:* 90%.

DEGREES MBA • MP Acc • MS

MBA—Master of Business Administration Part-time. 30 total credits required. 18 to 60 months to complete program. *Concentration:* general MBA.

MP Acc—Professional Accountancy Part-time. 30 total credits required. 24 to 60 months to complete program. *Concentration:* accounting.

Elmhurst College (continued)

MS—Supply Chain Management Part-time. 38 total credits required. 21 months to complete program. *Concentration:* supply chain management.

RESOURCES AND SERVICES 440 on-campus PCs are available to graduate business students. Access to Internet/World Wide Web, online (class) registration, and online grade reports available. *Personal computer requirements:* Graduate business students are strongly recommended to purchase or lease a personal computer. *Placement services include:* Alumni network, career counseling/planning, electronic job bank, and resume preparation.

EXPENSES *Tuition:* Part-time: $781 per hour. *Tuition (international):* Part-time: $781 per hour. *Required fees:* Part-time: $30 per term. Tuition and/or fees vary by academic program. *Graduate housing:* Room and board costs vary by number of occupants and type of accommodation. *Typical cost:* $6060 (room only).

FINANCIAL AID (2007–08) 12 students received aid, including loans and scholarships. Aid is available to part-time students. *Financial aid application deadline:* 5/1.

Financial Aid Contact Ms. Elizabeth Kuebler, Director, Adult and Graduate Admission, The School for Advanced Learning, 190 Prospect, Elmhurst, IL 60126. *Phone:* 630-617-3069. *Fax:* 630-617-6471. *E-mail:* betsyk@elmhurst.edu.

INTERNATIONAL STUDENTS *Services and facilities:* Counseling/support services, Housing location assistance, International student organization, Orientation. Financial aid is available to international students. *Required with application:* TOEFL with recommended score of 213 (computer) or 550 (paper); proof of adequate funds; proof of health/immunizations.

International Student Contact Ms. Alice Niziolek, Coordinator/Adviser, International Students, The School for Advanced Learning, 190 Prospect, Elmhurst, IL 60126. *Phone:* 630-617-3296. *Fax:* 630-617-3464. *E-mail:* alicen@elmhurst.edu.

APPLICATION *Required:* Application form, baccalaureate/first degree, essay, 3 letters of recommendation, personal statement, resume/curriculum vitae, transcripts of college work, 3 years of work experience. *Recommended:* Interview. *Application fee:* $25. Applications for domestic and international students are processed on a rolling basis.

Application Contact Ms. Elizabeth Kuebler, Director, Adult and Graduate Admission, The School for Advanced Learning, 190 Prospect Avenue, Elmhurst, IL 60126. *Phone:* 630-617-3069. *Fax:* 630-617-6471. *E-mail:* betsyk@elmhurst.edu.

Governors State University
College of Business and Public Administration

University Park, Illinois

Phone: 708-534-7059 **Fax:** 708-534-1640 **E-mail:** j-finn@govst.edu

Business Program(s) Web Site: http://www.govst.edu/users/gcbpa

Graduate Business Unit Enrollment *Total:* 454 (76 full-time; 378 part-time; 255 women; 34 international). *Average Age:* 36.

Graduate Business Faculty *Total:* 77 (36 full-time; 41 part-time).

Admissions *Applied:* 257. *Admitted:* 194. *Enrolled:* 112. *Average GMAT:* 450. *Average GPA:* 3.2

Academic Calendar Trimesters.

Accreditation ACBSP—The American Council of Business Schools and Programs.

DEGREE MBA

MBA—Master of Business Administration Full-time and part-time. 33 to 45 total credits required. 12 to 60 months to complete program.

Concentrations: accounting, health care, human resources management, international business, management, management information systems, marketing, public management.

RESOURCES AND SERVICES 88 on-campus PCs are available to graduate business students. Access to Internet/World Wide Web, online (class) registration, and online grade reports available. *Personal computer requirements:* Graduate business students are not required to have a personal computer. *Special opportunities include:* An international exchange program and an internship program are available. *Placement services include:* Alumni network, career counseling/planning, electronic job bank, resume referral, career fairs, job interviews arranged, resume preparation, and career library.

EXPENSES *Tuition (state resident):* Full-time: $3348. *Tuition (nonresident):* Full-time: $10,044. *Tuition (international):* Full-time: $10,044. *Required fees:* Full-time: $432.

FINANCIAL AID (2007–08) Fellowships, loans, research assistantships, scholarships, and work study. Aid is available to part-time students. *Financial aid application deadline:* 5/1.

Financial Aid Contact Freda Whisenton-Comer, Director of Financial Aid, 1 University Parkway, University Park, IL 60466-0975. *Phone:* 708-534-7649. *Fax:* 708-534-1172. *E-mail:* f-whisenton-comer@govst.edu.

INTERNATIONAL STUDENTS 7% of students enrolled are international students. *Services and facilities:* Counseling/support services, Housing location assistance, International student organization, Orientation, Visa Services. Financial aid is available to international students. *Required with application:* TOEFL with recommended score of 550 (paper); proof of adequate funds; proof of health/immunizations.

International Student Contact Vreni Mendoza, Coordinator, Office of International Services, Office of International Services, University Park, IL 60466-0975. *Phone:* 708-534-3087. *Fax:* 708-534-8951. *E-mail:* v-mendoz@govst.edu.

APPLICATION *Required:* GMAT, application form, baccalaureate/first degree, transcripts of college work. *Application fee:* $25. Applications for domestic and international students are processed on a rolling basis.

Application Contact Jennifer Finn, Assistant Director of Admissions, 1 University Parkway, University Park, IL 60466-0975. *Phone:* 708-534-7059. *Fax:* 708-534-1640. *E-mail:* j-finn@govst.edu.

Illinois Institute of Technology
Stuart School of Business

Chicago, Illinois

Phone: 312-906-6576 **Fax:** 312-906-6549 **E-mail:** admission@stuart.iit.edu

Business Program(s) Web Site: http://www.stuart.iit.edu/

Graduate Business Unit Enrollment *Total:* 534 (385 full-time; 149 part-time; 192 women; 376 international). *Average Age:* 28.

Graduate Business Faculty *Total:* 77 (31 full-time; 46 part-time).

Admissions *Applied:* 953. *Admitted:* 698. *Enrolled:* 205. *Average GMAT:* 622.

Academic Calendar Semesters.

Accreditation AACSB—The Association to Advance Collegiate Schools of Business.

DEGREES JD/MBA • JD/MS • MBA • MBA/MPA • MBA/MS • MBA/MSF • MMF • MS • MSF

JD/MBA—Juris Doctor/Master of Business Administration Full-time and part-time. 48 to 72 months to complete program. *Concentrations:* combined degrees, entrepreneurship, environmental economics/management, finance, financial management/planning, health care, information management, international business, law, management,

management science, marketing, operations management, quality management, risk management, strategic management, technology management.

JD/MS—Juris Doctor/Master of Science in Environmental Management Full-time and part-time. 48 to 66 months to complete program. *Concentrations:* combined degrees, environmental economics/management, law.

JD/MS—Juris Doctor/Master of Science in Financial Markets Full-time and part-time. 48 to 66 months to complete program. *Concentrations:* combined degrees, financial economics, financial engineering, financial management/planning, international finance, investments and securities, law, risk management.

MBA—Master of Business Administration Full-time and part-time. At least 58 total credits required. 12 to 72 months to complete program. *Concentrations:* entrepreneurship, environmental economics/management, finance, financial management/planning, general MBA, health care, information management, international business, management, management science, marketing, operations management, quality management, risk management, strategic management, technology management.

MBA/MPA—Master of Business Administration/Master of Public Administration Full-time and part-time. At least 105 total credits required. 24 to 72 months to complete program. *Concentrations:* combined degrees, entrepreneurship, environmental economics/management, finance, health care, information management, international business, management, management science, marketing, nonprofit management, operations management, other, public management, public policy and administration, quality management, risk management, strategic management, technology management.

MBA/MS—Master of Business Administration/Master of Science in Environmental Management Full-time and part-time. At least 105 total credits required. 24 to 72 months to complete program. *Concentrations:* combined degrees, entrepreneurship, environmental economics/management, finance, financial management/planning, health care, information management, international business, management, management science, marketing, operations management, quality management, risk management, strategic management, technology management.

MBA/MS—Master of Business Administration/Master of Science in Financial Markets Full-time and part-time. At least 105 total credits required. 24 to 72 months to complete program. *Concentrations:* combined degrees, entrepreneurship, environmental economics/management, finance, financial economics, financial engineering, financial management/planning, general MBA, health care, information management, international business, international finance, investments and securities, management, management science, marketing, operations management, quality management, risk management, strategic management, technology management.

MBA/MS—Master of Business Administration/Master of Science in Marketing Communication Full-time and part-time. At least 105 total credits required. 24 to 72 months to complete program. *Concentrations:* advertising, combined degrees, electronic commerce (E-commerce), entrepreneurship, environmental economics/management, finance, financial management/planning, health care, information management, international business, management, management science, marketing, marketing research, operations management, public relations, quality management, risk management, strategic management.

MBA/MSF—Master of Business Administration/Master of Science in Finance Full-time and part-time. At least 105 total credits required. 24 to 72 months to complete program. *Concentrations:* combined degrees, corporate accounting, entrepreneurship, environmental economics/management, finance, financial economics, financial engineering, financial information systems, financial management/planning, health care, information management, international business, international economics, international finance, management, management science, marketing, operations management, quality management, quantitative analysis, risk management, strategic management, technology management.

MMF—Master of Mathematical Finance Full-time and part-time. At least 40 total credits required. *Concentrations:* finance, financial economics, financial management/planning, information management, international finance, investments and securities, quantitative analysis, risk management.

MS—Master of Science in Environmental Management Full-time and part-time. At least 50 total credits required. 12 to 72 months to complete program. *Concentration:* environmental economics/management.

MS—Master of Science in Financial Markets Full-time and part-time. At least 50 total credits required. 12 to 72 months to complete program. *Concentrations:* financial economics, financial engineering, financial management/planning, international finance, investments and securities, risk management.

MS—Master of Science in Marketing Communication Full-time and part-time. At least 50 total credits required. 12 to 72 months to complete program. *Concentrations:* advertising, electronic commerce (E-commerce), marketing, marketing research, public relations.

MSF—Master of Science in Finance Full-time and part-time. At least 50 total credits required. 12 to 72 months to complete program. *Concentrations:* corporate accounting, finance, financial economics, financial engineering, financial information systems, financial management/planning, information management, international economics, international finance, quantitative analysis, risk management.

RESOURCES AND SERVICES 95 on-campus PCs are available to graduate business students. Access to Internet/World Wide Web, online (class) registration, and online grade reports available. *Personal computer requirements:* Graduate business students are not required to have a personal computer. *Special opportunities include:* An international exchange program and an internship program are available. *Placement services include:* Alumni network, job search course, career counseling/planning, electronic job bank, resume referral, career fairs, job interviews arranged, resume preparation, and career library.

EXPENSES *Graduate housing:* Room and board costs vary by campus location, number of occupants, type of accommodation, and type of board plan.

FINANCIAL AID (2007–08) 348 students received aid, including loans and scholarships. Aid is available to part-time students. *Financial aid application deadline:* 4/1.

Financial Aid Contact Ada Chin, Director of Financial Aid, 565 West Adams Street, Suite 230, Chicago, IL 60661-3691. *Phone:* 312-906-5180. *Fax:* 312-906-6549. *E-mail:* finaid@stuart.iit.edu.

INTERNATIONAL STUDENTS 70% of students enrolled are international students. *Services and facilities:* Counseling/support services, ESL/language courses, International student organization, Language tutoring, Orientation, Visa Services, Tuition scholarships, CPT and OPT Training Programs. Financial aid is available to international students. *Required with application:* Proof of adequate funds; proof of health/immunizations. *Recommended with application:* TOEFL with recommended score of 250 (computer), 600 (paper), or 100 (Internet).

International Student Contact Brian Jansen, Director of Graduate Admissions, 565 West Adams Street, 6th Floor, Chicago, IL 60661-3691. *Phone:* 312-906-6576. *Fax:* 312-906-6549. *E-mail:* admission@stuart.iit.edu.

APPLICATION *Required:* Application form, baccalaureate/first degree, essay, 2 letters of recommendation, personal statement, resume/curriculum vitae, transcripts of college work. School will accept GMAT and GRE. *Recommended:* Work experience. *Application fee:* $75. Applications for domestic and international students are processed on a rolling basis.

Application Contact Brian Jansen, Director of Graduate Admissions, 565 West Adams Street, 6th Floor, Chicago, IL 60661-3691. *Phone:* 312-906-6576. *Fax:* 312-906-6549. *E-mail:* admission@stuart.iit.edu.

Illinois State University
College of Business
Normal, Illinois

Phone: 309-438-8388 **Fax:** 309-438-7255 **E-mail:** isumba@ilstu.edu

Business Program(s) Web Site: http://www.mba.ilstu.edu

Illinois State University (continued)

Graduate Business Unit Enrollment *Total:* 235 (99 full-time; 136 part-time; 97 women; 38 international). *Average Age:* 22—37.

Graduate Business Faculty *Total:* 70 (69 full-time; 1 part-time).

Admissions *Applied:* 106. *Admitted:* 77. *Enrolled:* 61. *Average GMAT:* 560. *Average GPA:* 3.45

Academic Calendar Semesters.

Accreditation AACSB—The Association to Advance Collegiate Schools of Business.

After Graduation (Class of 2006–07) *Employed within 3 months of graduation:* 92%. *Average starting salary:* $59,300.

DEGREES MBA • MPA • MS

MBA—Master of Business Administration Full-time and part-time. 36 to 53 total credits required. 12 to 72 months to complete program. *Concentrations:* accounting, agribusiness, arts administration/management, finance, human resources management, insurance, management, management information systems, marketing, organizational behavior/development, project management.

MPA—Master of Professional Accounting Full-time and part-time. 150 total credits required. 60 to 84 months to complete program. *Concentration:* accounting.

MS—Master of Science in Accounting Full-time and part-time. 33 to 71 total credits required. 12 to 72 months to complete program. *Concentration:* accounting.

RESOURCES AND SERVICES 493 on-campus PCs are available to graduate business students. Access to Internet/World Wide Web, online (class) registration, and online grade reports available. *Personal computer requirements:* Graduate business students are strongly recommended to purchase or lease a personal computer. *Special opportunities include:* An international exchange program and an internship program are available. *Placement services include:* Alumni network, career placement, career counseling/planning, electronic job bank, resume referral, career fairs, job interviews arranged, resume preparation, and career library.

EXPENSES *Tuition (state resident):* Full-time: $4677. Part-time: $194 per credit hour. *Tuition (nonresident):* Full-time: $8457. Part-time: $404 per credit hour. *Tuition (international):* Full-time: $8457. Part-time: $404 per credit hour. *Required fees:* Full-time: $1185. Part-time: $57 per credit hour.

FINANCIAL AID (2007–08) 149 students received aid, including research assistantships, scholarships, and teaching assistantships. Aid is available to part-time students. *Financial aid application deadline:* 5/3.

Financial Aid Contact Ms. Jana Albrecht, Director, Financial Aid, Campus Box 2320, Normal, IL 61790-2320. *Phone:* 309-438-2231. *Fax:* 309-438-3755. *E-mail:* jlalbre2@ilstu.edu.

INTERNATIONAL STUDENTS 16% of students enrolled are international students. *Services and facilities:* Counseling/support services, ESL/language courses, International student housing, International student organization, Orientation, Visa Services, International host families. Financial aid is available to international students. *Required with application:* TOEFL with recommended score of 250 (computer), 600 (paper), or 83 (Internet); proof of adequate funds; proof of health/immunizations.

International Student Contact Ms. Sarah Jome, Associate Director, International Studies, International Studies, Campus Box 6120, Normal, IL 61790-6120. *Phone:* 309-438-5276. *Fax:* 309-438-3987. *E-mail:* sjjome@ilstu.edu.

APPLICATION *Required:* GMAT, application form, baccalaureate/first degree, essay, 2 letters of recommendation, personal statement, resume/curriculum vitae, transcripts of college work. *Recommended:* Interview, work experience. *Application fee:* $40. Applications for domestic and international students are processed on a rolling basis.

Application Contact Dr. SJ Chang, Associate Dean for MBA and Undergraduate Programs, Campus Box 5570, Normal, IL 61790-5570. *Phone:* 309-438-8388. *Fax:* 309-438-7255. *E-mail:* isumba@ilstu.edu.

See full description on page 638.

Lake Forest Graduate School of Management
MBA Program
Lake Forest, Illinois

Phone: 800-737-4MBA **Fax:** 847-295-3656 **E-mail:** admiss@lfgsm.edu

Business Program(s) Web Site: http://www.lakeforestmba.edu

Graduate Business Unit Enrollment *Total:* 750 (750 part-time; 278 women). *Average Age:* 37.

Graduate Business Faculty 150 part-time.

Admissions *Average GMAT:* 500. *Average GPA:* 3.1

Academic Calendar Quarters.

After Graduation (Class of 2006–07) *Employed within 3 months of graduation:* 100%.

DEGREE MBA

MBA—Evening/Weekend Master of Business Administration Part-time. 4 years of professional work experience required. At least 64 total credits required. 24 to 72 months to complete program. *Concentrations:* general MBA, health care, international business, organizational behavior/development.

RESOURCES AND SERVICES 28 on-campus PCs are available to graduate business students. Access to Internet/World Wide Web and online grade reports available. *Personal computer requirements:* Graduate business students are required to have a personal computer. *Placement services include:* Alumni network, career counseling/planning, and electronic job bank.

EXPENSES *Tuition:* Part-time: $2585 per unit.

FINANCIAL AID (2007–08) 230 students received aid, including loans and scholarships. Aid is available to part-time students.

Financial Aid Contact Ms. Terry Hamlin, Alternative Financing Coordinator, 1905 West Field Court, Lake Forest, IL 60045. *Phone:* 847-574-5184. *Fax:* 847-295-3666. *E-mail:* thamlin@lfgsm.edu.

INTERNATIONAL STUDENTS Financial aid is not available to international students.

APPLICATION *Required:* Application form, baccalaureate/first degree, essay, interview, 2 letters of recommendation, personal statement, resume/curriculum vitae, transcripts of college work, 4 years of work experience. School will accept GMAT. *Application fee:* $0. Applications for domestic students are processed on a rolling basis.

Application Contact Ms. Angel Fournier, Director of Admissions Operations, 1905 West Field Court, Lake Forest, IL 60045. *Phone:* 800-737-4MBA. *Fax:* 847-295-3656. *E-mail:* admiss@lfgsm.edu.

See full description on page 652.

Lewis University
College of Business
Romeoville, Illinois

Phone: 815-836-5384 **Fax:** 815-838-3330 **E-mail:** gsm@lewisu.edu

Business Program(s) Web Site: http://www.lewisu.edu/academics/gsm/

Graduate Business Unit Enrollment *Total:* 310 (10 full-time; 300 part-time; 153 women; 16 international). *Average Age:* 34.

Graduate Business Faculty *Total:* 64 (18 full-time; 46 part-time).

Admissions *Applied:* 80. *Admitted:* 57. *Enrolled:* 57. *Average GPA:* 3.16

Academic Calendar Semesters.

DEGREES M Mgt • MBA • MBA/MS • MF

M Mgt—Master of Science in Management Part-time. 33 to 36 total credits required. 12 to 60 months to complete program. *Concentration:* management.

MBA—Master of Business Administration Full-time and part-time. 36 to 54 total credits required. 12 to 60 months to complete program. *Concentrations:* accounting, electronic commerce (E-commerce), finance, health care, human resources management, international business, management information systems, marketing, operations management, project management.

MBA/MS—Master of Business Administration/Master of Science in Nursing Full-time and part-time. At least 60 total credits required. 30 to 84 months to complete program. *Concentration:* combined degrees.

MF—Master of Science in Finance Part-time. 24 to 39 total credits required. 12 to 60 months to complete program. *Concentration:* finance.

RESOURCES AND SERVICES 100 on-campus PCs are available to graduate business students. Access to Internet/World Wide Web, online (class) registration, and online grade reports available. *Personal computer requirements:* Graduate business students are strongly recommended to purchase or lease a personal computer. *Placement services include:* Alumni network, career placement, job search course, career counseling/planning, electronic job bank, resume referral, career fairs, job interviews arranged, resume preparation, and career library.

EXPENSES *Tuition:* Part-time: $720 per credit hour. *Tuition (international):* Part-time: $720 per credit hour.

FINANCIAL AID (2007–08) Loans. Aid is available to part-time students. *Financial aid application deadline:* 5/1.

Financial Aid Contact Ms. Janeen Decharinte, Director of Financial Aid, One University Parkway, Romeoville, IL 60446. *Phone:* 815-838-0500 Ext. 5263. *Fax:* 815-838-9456. *E-mail:* decharja@lewisu.edu.

INTERNATIONAL STUDENTS 5% of students enrolled are international students. *Services and facilities:* Counseling/support services, ESL/language courses, Housing location assistance, International student organization, Orientation, Visa Services, International student services. Financial aid is not available to international students. *Required with application:* TOEFL with recommended score of 213 (computer) or 550 (paper); proof of adequate funds; proof of health/immunizations.

International Student Contact Mr. Roberto Suarez, Coordinator for Latino and International Admission, One University Parkway, Romeoville, IL 60446-2200. *Phone:* 815-836-5567. *Fax:* 815-838-5002. *E-mail:* suarezro@lewisu.edu.

APPLICATION *Required:* Application form, baccalaureate/first degree, interview, 2 letters of recommendation, personal statement, resume/curriculum vitae, transcripts of college work. *Application fee:* $40. Applications for domestic and international students are processed on a rolling basis.

Application Contact Ms. Michele King, Director of Admissions, Graduate School of Management, One University Parkway, Romeoville, IL 60446-2200. *Phone:* 815-836-5384. *Fax:* 815-838-3330. *E-mail:* gsm@lewisu.edu.

Loyola University Chicago
Graduate School of Business
Chicago, Illinois

Phone: 312-915-8908 **Fax:** 312-915-7207 **E-mail:** gsb@luc.edu

Business Program(s) Web Site: http://www.gsb.luc.edu

Graduate Business Unit Enrollment *Total:* 744 (246 full-time; 498 part-time; 387 women; 67 international). *Average Age:* 27.

Graduate Business Faculty *Total:* 87 (68 full-time; 19 part-time).

Admissions *Applied:* 755. *Admitted:* 550. *Enrolled:* 332. *Average GMAT:* 550. *Average GPA:* 3.2

Academic Calendar Quarters.

Accreditation AACSB—The Association to Advance Collegiate Schools of Business.

After Graduation (Class of 2006–07) *Employed within 3 months of graduation:* 65%. *Average starting salary:* $68,465.

DEGREES EMBA • JD/MBA • MBA • MBA-H • MBA/MSIMC • MBA/MSISM • MBA/MSN • MS • MSA • MSF • MSIMC • MSISM

EMBA—MBA for Executives Part-time. 48 total credits required. 18 months to complete program. *Concentration:* executive programs.

JD/MBA—Juris Doctor/Master of Business Administration Full-time and part-time. Must apply separately to each program: MBA and JD. 128 to 140 total credits required. 48 to 96 months to complete program. *Concentrations:* accounting, business ethics, business law, finance, health care, international business, management, management information systems, managerial economics, marketing, operations management, strategic management.

MBA—Master of Business Administration Full-time and part-time. 42 to 57 total credits required. 12 to 60 months to complete program. *Concentrations:* accounting, business ethics, economics, entrepreneurship, finance, health care, international business, management, management information systems, marketing, operations management, risk management, sports/entertainment management, strategic management.

MBA-H—MBA in Health Care Management Full-time and part-time. 48 total credits required. 24 months to complete program. *Concentration:* health care.

MBA/MSIMC—Master of Business Administration/Master of Science in Integrated Marketing Communication Full-time and part-time. 66 to 78 total credits required. 21 to 60 months to complete program. *Concentrations:* accounting, business ethics, economics, entrepreneurship, finance, health care, human resources management, international business, management, management information systems, marketing, operations management, risk management, sports/entertainment management, strategic management.

MBA/MSISM—Master of Business Administration/Master of Science in Information Systems Management Full-time and part-time. 69 to 81 total credits required. 21 to 60 months to complete program. *Concentrations:* accounting, business ethics, economics, entrepreneurship, finance, health care, international business, management, management information systems, marketing, operations management, risk management, sports/entertainment management, strategic management.

MBA/MSN—Master of Business Administration/Master of Science in Nursing Full-time and part-time. Must apply separately to each program: MBA and MSN. 69 to 81 total credits required. 36 to 84 months to complete program. *Concentrations:* accounting, business ethics, economics, entrepreneurship, finance, health care, international business, management, management information systems, marketing, operations management, risk management, sports/entertainment management, strategic management.

MS—Master of Science in Human Resources Full-time and part-time. 36 to 39 total credits required. 12 to 60 months to complete program. *Concentrations:* human resources management, industrial/labor relations, organizational behavior/development.

MSA—Master of Science in Accounting Full-time and part-time. At least 36 total credits required. 12 to 60 months to complete program. *Concentration:* accounting.

MSF—Master of Science in Finance Full-time and part-time. 42 to 54 total credits required. 12 to 60 months to complete program. *Concentrations:* finance, risk management.

MSIMC—Master of Science in Integrated Marketing Communications Full-time and part-time. 42 to 54 total credits required. 12 to 60 months to complete program. *Concentration:* marketing.

MSISM—Master of Science in Information Systems Management Full-time and part-time. 36 to 48 total credits required. 12 to 60 months to complete program. *Concentration:* information systems.

RESOURCES AND SERVICES 172 on-campus PCs are available to graduate business students. Access to Internet/World Wide Web, online (class) registration, and online grade reports available. *Personal computer*

Loyola University Chicago (continued)

requirements: Graduate business students are not required to have a personal computer. *Special opportunities include:* An international exchange program and an internship program are available. *Placement services include:* Alumni network, career counseling/planning, electronic job bank, resume referral, career fairs, job interviews arranged, resume preparation, and career library.

EXPENSES *Tuition:* Full-time: $28,269. Part-time: $3141 per course. *Tuition (international):* Full-time: $28,269. Part-time: $3141 per course. *Required fees:* Full-time: $300. Part-time: $300 per year. *Graduate housing:* Room and board costs vary by campus location, number of occupants, type of accommodation, and type of board plan. *Typical cost:* $16,206 (including board), $13,300 (room only).

FINANCIAL AID (2007–08) 647 students received aid, including loans, research assistantships, scholarships, and work study. Aid is available to part-time students. *Financial aid application deadline:* 3/1.

Financial Aid Contact Rodney Lumpkins, Assistant Director, Student Financial Assistance, 6525 North Sheridan Road, Chicago, IL 60626-5208. *Phone:* 312-915-6673. *Fax:* 773-508-3397. *E-mail:* gradfinaid@luc.edu.

INTERNATIONAL STUDENTS 9% of students enrolled are international students. *Services and facilities:* Counseling/support services, ESL/language courses, International student housing, International student organization, Language tutoring, Orientation, Visa Services. Financial aid is available to international students. *Required with application:* TOEFL with recommended score of 213 (computer) or 550 (paper); proof of adequate funds; proof of health/immunizations.

International Student Contact Mary Thies, Associate Director, International Affairs, Sullivan Center for Student Services, 6339 North Sheridan Road, Chicago, IL 60626-5208. *Phone:* 773-508-3899. *Fax:* 773-508-7125. *E-mail:* mtheis@luc.edu.

APPLICATION *Required:* GMAT, application form, baccalaureate/first degree, essay, 2 letters of recommendation, personal statement, resume/curriculum vitae, transcripts of college work. *Recommended:* 5 years of work experience. *Application fee:* $50. Applications for domestic and international students are processed on a rolling basis.

Application Contact Olivia Heath, Enrollment Advisor, 1 East Pearson, Room 224, Maguire Hall, Chicago, IN 60611-2045. *Phone:* 312-915-8908. *Fax:* 312-915-7207. *E-mail:* gsb@luc.edu.

National-Louis University
College of Management and Business
Chicago, Illinois

Phone: 847-475-1100 Ext. 5111 **E-mail:** nluinfo@nl.edu

Business Program(s) Web Site: http://www.nl.edu/nlu_cmb/programs/index.html

---

DEGREES MBA • MS

MBA—Master of Business Administration Full-time and part-time. Distance learning option. At least 37 total credits required. 22 months to complete program. *Concentration:* general MBA.

MS—Master of Science in Managerial Leadership Full-time and part-time. Distance learning option. At least 33 total credits required. 18 months to complete program. *Concentration:* management.

RESOURCES AND SERVICES *Personal computer requirements:* Graduate business students are required to have a personal computer. *Placement services include:* Career placement, job search course, career counseling/planning, electronic job bank, and career fairs.

Application Contact Office of Graduate Admissions, 122 South Michigan Avenue, Chicago, IL 60603. *Phone:* 847-475-1100 Ext. 5111. *E-mail:* nluinfo@nl.edu.

North Central College
Department of Business
Naperville, Illinois

Phone: 630-637-5840 **Fax:** 630-637-5819 **E-mail:** klnorthcutt@noctrl.edu

Business Program(s) Web Site: http://www.northcentralcollege.edu

Graduate Business Unit Enrollment *Total:* 147 (46 full-time; 101 part-time; 63 women; 3 international). *Average Age:* 31.

Graduate Business Faculty *Total:* 30 (17 full-time; 13 part-time).

Admissions *Applied:* 106. *Admitted:* 68. *Enrolled:* 50. *Average GMAT:* 470. *Average GPA:* 2.85

Academic Calendar Quarters.

After Graduation (Class of 2006–07) *Employed within 3 months of graduation:* 98%.

DEGREES MBA • MS

MBA—One-Year Professional MBA Full-time. Must have received undergraduate degree within the last 5 years and have completed prerequisites with a "B-" or better. 30 total credits required. *Concentration:* management.

MBA—Master of Business Administration Full-time and part-time. 30 to 48 total credits required. 12 to 60 months to complete program. *Concentrations:* business ethics, business information science, financial management/planning, human resources management, information management, leadership, management, marketing.

MS—Master of Science in Management Information Systems Full-time and part-time. 9.5 hours of undergraduate computer science coursework required. 42 to 51 total credits required. 12 to 60 months to complete program. *Concentration:* management information systems.

N*orth Central College in Naperville, Illinois, provides an education that exceeds the high standards of today's business world.*

The Master of Business Administration (M.B.A.) program is designed with today's complex business environment in mind and allows students to develop an individualized program of study targeted at their personal career goals. With many specialized areas of concentration, such as change management, leadership, and finance, North Central's M.B.A. combines traditional knowledge with skills deemed important for effective management within today's work environment.

A newly established alternative, the Professional Management M.B.A. program, which can be completed in one year, is designed for highly motivated students who already hold an undergraduate business degree. This program offers a coordinated and cohesive set of courses that balances management theory with applications in a broad spectrum of organizational settings.

No matter which alternative a student chooses, distinguished professors challenge students to develop their quantitative and analytical skills, while emphasizing an interdisciplinary, cutting-edge approach to understanding the intricacies of today's organizations. Faculty members are deeply committed to providing students with the tools they need to excel. Students come away from this program knowing they have received a tremendous education that immediately applies to real-world situations.

North Central College students enjoy the advantages of a small college centered in a high-tech corridor offering internship and employment opportunities.

The M.B.A. program at North Central College is characterized by a high level of excellence and integrity, one-on-one teaching, and a classroom atmosphere where learning is interactive.

RESOURCES AND SERVICES 36 on-campus PCs are available to graduate business students. Access to Internet/World Wide Web, online

(class) registration, and online grade reports available. *Personal computer requirements:* Graduate business students are strongly recommended to purchase or lease a personal computer. *Placement services include:* Alumni network, career placement, career counseling/planning, electronic job bank, resume referral, career fairs, resume preparation, and career library.

EXPENSES *Tuition:* Full-time: $16,248. Part-time: $677 per credit. *Tuition (international):* Full-time: $16,248. Part-time: $677 per credit. *Required fees:* Full-time: $75. Part-time: $20 per quarter. Tuition and/or fees vary by number of courses or credits taken and academic program.

FINANCIAL AID (2007–08) Loans and work study. Aid is available to part-time students. *Financial aid application deadline:* 9/15.

Financial Aid Contact Mr. Marty Rossman, Director of Financial Aid, 30 North Brainard Street, PO Box 3063, Naperville, IL 60566-7063. *Phone:* 630-637-5600. *Fax:* 630-637-5608. *E-mail:* finaid@noctrl.edu.

INTERNATIONAL STUDENTS 2% of students enrolled are international students. *Services and facilities:* Counseling/support services, International student organization, Language tutoring, Orientation, Visa Services. Financial aid is not available to international students. *Required with application:* TOEFL with recommended score of 250 (computer), 600 (paper), or 90 (Internet); proof of adequate funds; proof of health/immunizations. *Recommended with application:* TWE.

International Student Contact Ms. Kara Northcutt, Graduate and Continuing Education Admission Counselor, 30 North Brainard Street, Naperville, IL 60540. *Phone:* 630-637-5840. *Fax:* 630-637-5819. *E-mail:* grad@noctrl.edu.

APPLICATION *Required:* Application form, baccalaureate/first degree, personal statement, transcripts of college work. School will accept GMAT. *Recommended:* Resume/curriculum vitae, 3 years of work experience. *Application fee:* $25. Applications for domestic and international students are processed on a rolling basis.

Application Contact Miss Kara Northcutt, Graduate and Continuing Education Admission Counselor, 30 North Brainard Street, PO Box 3063, Naperville, IL 60566-7063. *Phone:* 630-637-5840. *Fax:* 630-637-5819. *E-mail:* klnorthcutt@noctrl.edu.

Northeastern Illinois University
College of Business and Management
Chicago, Illinois

Phone: 773-442-6106 **Fax:** 773-442-6110 **E-mail:** a-shub@neiu.edu

Business Program(s) Web Site: http://www.neiu.edu/~bschool/

Graduate Business Unit Enrollment *Total:* 110 (43 full-time; 67 part-time; 53 women; 26 international). *Average Age:* 31.

Graduate Business Faculty *Total:* 37 (24 full-time; 13 part-time).

Admissions *Applied:* 112. *Admitted:* 84. *Enrolled:* 80. *Average GMAT:* 550. *Average GPA:* 3.1

Academic Calendar Semesters.

DEGREES MBA • MSA

MBA—Master of Business Administration Full-time and part-time. 33 to 58 total credits required. 15 to 60 months to complete program. *Concentration:* general MBA.

MSA—Master of Science in Accounting Full-time and part-time. Distance learning option. 33 to 51 total credits required. 15 to 60 months to complete program. *Concentration:* accounting.

RESOURCES AND SERVICES Access to Internet/World Wide Web, online (class) registration, and online grade reports available. *Personal computer requirements:* Graduate business students are strongly recommended to purchase or lease a personal computer. *Special opportunities include:* An international exchange program and an internship program are available.

EXPENSES *Tuition (state resident):* Full-time: $2406. Part-time: $804 per course. *Tuition (nonresident):* Full-time: $4386. Part-time: $1464 per course. *Tuition (international):* Full-time: $4386. Part-time: $1464 per course. Tuition and/or fees vary by academic program.

FINANCIAL AID (2007–08) 20 students received aid, including grants, loans, research assistantships, scholarships, teaching assistantships, and work study. Aid is available to part-time students.

Financial Aid Contact Dr. Allen Shub, Coordinator, Graduate Program in Business Administration, 5500 North Saint Louis Avenue, Chicago, IL 60625. *Phone:* 773-442-6106. *Fax:* 773-442-6110. *E-mail:* a-shub@ neiu.edu.

INTERNATIONAL STUDENTS 24% of students enrolled are international students. *Services and facilities:* ESL/language courses, International student organization, Visa Services. Financial aid is available to international students. *Required with application:* TOEFL with recommended score of 213 (computer), 550 (paper), or 80 (Internet); proof of adequate funds.

International Student Contact Dr. Allen Shub, Coordinator, Graduate Program in Business Administration, 5500 North Saint Louis Avenue, Chicago, IL 60625. *Phone:* 773-442-6106. *Fax:* 773-442-6110. *E-mail:* a-shub@neiu.edu.

APPLICATION *Required:* GMAT, application form, baccalaureate/first degree, essay, 2 letters of recommendation, personal statement, transcripts of college work. *Recommended:* Resume/curriculum vitae, work experience. Applications for domestic and international students are processed on a rolling basis.

Application Contact Dr. Allen Shub, Coordinator, Graduate Program in Business Administration, 5500 North Saint Louis Avenue, Chicago, IL 60625. *Phone:* 773-442-6106. *Fax:* 773-442-6110. *E-mail:* a-shub@ neiu.edu.

Northern Illinois University
College of Business
De Kalb, Illinois

Phone: 866-NIU-MBA1 **Fax:** 815-753-3300 **E-mail:** cobgrads@niu.edu

Business Program(s) Web Site: http://www.cob.niu.edu/grad/

Graduate Business Unit Enrollment *Total:* 848 (179 full-time; 669 part-time; 330 women; 84 international). *Average Age:* 30.

Graduate Business Faculty *Total:* 107 (88 full-time; 19 part-time).

Admissions *Applied:* 620. *Admitted:* 572. *Enrolled:* 449. *Average GMAT:* 523. *Average GPA:* 3.24

Academic Calendar Semesters.

Accreditation AACSB—The Association to Advance Collegiate Schools of Business.

After Graduation (Class of 2006–07) *Employed within 3 months of graduation:* 96%. *Average starting salary:* $88,542.

DEGREES MAS • MBA • MS • MST

MAS—Master of Accounting Science Full-time and part-time. Minimum GMAT score of 475 required. 30 to 66 total credits required. 12 to 72 months to complete program. *Concentration:* accounting.

MBA—Evening Master of Business Administration Full-time and part-time. 2 years post-undergraduate work experience preferred and a minimum GMAT score of 450 required. 30 to 48 total credits required. 12 to 72 months to complete program. *Concentration:* general MBA.

MBA—Executive Master of Business Administration Full-time. 5 years of work experience and minimum GMAT score of 450 required. At least 51 total credits required. 24 months to complete program. *Concentration:* executive programs.

MBA—Professional Master of Business Administration Part-time. 5 years of work experience and minimum GMAT score of 450 required.

Northern Illinois University (continued)

Must have bachelor's degree in business or related field for consideration. At least 30 total credits required. 12 months to complete program. *Concentration:* general MBA.

MS—Master of Science in Management Information Systems Full-time and part-time. Minimum GMAT score of 500 required. 30 to 51 total credits required. 12 to 72 months to complete program. *Concentration:* management information systems.

MST—Master of Science in Taxation At least 30 total credits required. 12 to 72 months to complete program. *Concentration:* taxation.

RESOURCES AND SERVICES 1,100 on-campus PCs are available to graduate business students. Access to Internet/World Wide Web, online (class) registration, and online grade reports available. *Personal computer requirements:* Graduate business students are strongly recommended to purchase or lease a personal computer. *Special opportunities include:* An internship program is available. *Placement services include:* Alumni network, career placement, career counseling/planning, electronic job bank, resume referral, career fairs, resume preparation, and career library.

EXPENSES *Tuition (state resident):* Part-time: $553 per credit hour. *Tuition (nonresident):* Part-time: $807 per credit hour. *Tuition (international):* Part-time: $807 per credit hour. *Required fees:* Part-time: $50 per semester. Tuition and/or fees vary by class time, number of courses or credits taken, campus location, and academic program.

FINANCIAL AID (2007–08) Fellowships, loans, research assistantships, teaching assistantships, and work study. Aid is available to part-time students.

Financial Aid Contact Kathleen Brunson, Director, Student Financial Aid Office, Swen Parsons 245, DeKalb, IL 60115-2872. *Phone:* 815-753-1395. *Fax:* 815-753-9475. *E-mail:* kbrunson@niu.edu.

INTERNATIONAL STUDENTS 10% of students enrolled are international students. *Services and facilities:* Counseling/support services, ESL/language courses, Housing location assistance, International student organization, Orientation, Visa Services. Financial aid is available to international students. *Required with application:* TOEFL with recommended score of 213 (computer), 550 (paper), or 24 (Internet); proof of adequate funds; proof of health/immunizations. *Recommended with application:* IELT with recommended score of 6.5.

International Student Contact Susan Minas, International Specialist, Graduate School, Adams Hall, DeKalb, IL 60115. *Phone:* 815-753-9409. *Fax:* 815-753-6366. *E-mail:* sminas@niu.edu.

APPLICATION *Required:* GMAT, application form, baccalaureate/first degree, interview, 2 letters of recommendation, personal statement, resume/curriculum vitae, transcripts of college work, 2 years of work experience. *Application fee:* $30. Applications for domestic and international students are processed on a rolling basis.

Application Contact Mona L. Salmon, Assistant Director, Office of MBA Programs, Barsema 203, DeKalb, IL 60115-2897. *Phone:* 866-NIU-MBA1. *Fax:* 815-753-3300. *E-mail:* cobgrads@niu.edu.

North Park University
School of Business and Nonprofit Management
Chicago, Illinois

Phone: 773-244-5518 **Fax:** 773-279-7996 **E-mail:** cnicholson@northpark.edu

Business Program(s) Web Site: http://www.northpark.edu/sbnm

Graduate Business Unit Enrollment *Total:* 430 (10 full-time; 420 part-time; 249 women; 25 international). *Average Age:* 34.

Graduate Business Faculty *Total:* 58 (13 full-time; 45 part-time).

Admissions *Applied:* 120. *Admitted:* 97. *Enrolled:* 88. *Average GMAT:* 570. *Average GPA:* 3.2

Academic Calendar 7-week terms.

After Graduation (Class of 2006–07) *Employed within 3 months of graduation:* 95%.

DEGREES M Mgt • MBA • MBA/MA • MBA/MS • MHRM • MM • MNM

M Mgt—Master of Management Full-time and part-time. Distance learning option. 32 to 36 total credits required. 12 to 72 months to complete program. *Concentrations:* conflict resolution management, economics, finance, health care, human resources management, international business, leadership, marketing, nonprofit management, operations management, organizational behavior/development.

MBA—Master of Business Administration Full-time and part-time. Distance learning option. 32 to 36 total credits required. 12 to 72 months to complete program. *Concentrations:* combined degrees, conflict resolution management, economics, finance, health care, human resources management, international business, leadership, marketing, nonprofit management, nonprofit organization, operations management, organizational behavior/development.

MBA/MA—Master of Business Administration/Master of Arts in Theological Studies Full-time and part-time. At least 114 total credits required. 36 to 72 months to complete program. *Concentration:* combined degrees.

MBA/MS—Master of Business Administration/Master of Science in Nursing Full-time and part-time. At least 62 total credits required. 24 to 72 months to complete program. *Concentration:* combined degrees.

MHRM—Master of Human Resources Full-time and part-time. 32 to 36 total credits required. 12 to 72 months to complete program. *Concentrations:* economics, finance, health administration, human resources management, leadership, marketing, nonprofit management, operations management, organizational management.

MM—Master of Higher Education Administration Full-time and part-time. Distance learning option. 32 to 36 total credits required. 24 to 72 months to complete program. *Concentrations:* conflict resolution management, health administration, leadership, nonprofit management, organizational management.

MNM—Master of Nonprofit Administration Full-time and part-time. Distance learning option. 32 to 36 total credits required. 12 to 72 months to complete program. *Concentrations:* conflict resolution management, health administration, human resources management, leadership, nonprofit management, nonprofit organization.

RESOURCES AND SERVICES 200 on-campus PCs are available to graduate business students. Access to Internet/World Wide Web, online (class) registration, and online grade reports available. *Personal computer requirements:* Graduate business students are strongly recommended to purchase or lease a personal computer. *Special opportunities include:* An international exchange program and an internship program are available. *Placement services include:* Alumni network, career placement, job search course, career counseling/planning, resume referral, career fairs, resume preparation, and career library.

EXPENSES *Tuition:* Part-time: $1750 per course. *Tuition (international):* Full-time: $14,000.

FINANCIAL AID (2007–08) 250 students received aid, including grants, loans, and scholarships. Aid is available to part-time students.

Financial Aid Contact Christopher Nicholson, Director of Admissions, Graduate and Continuing Education, 3225 West Foster Avenue, Chicago, IL 60625-4895. *Phone:* 773-244-5518. *Fax:* 773-279-7996. *E-mail:* cnicholson@northpark.edu.

INTERNATIONAL STUDENTS 6% of students enrolled are international students. *Services and facilities:* Counseling/support services, ESL/language courses, Housing location assistance, Orientation, Visa Services. Financial aid is available to international students. *Required with application:* TOEFL with recommended score of 250 (computer), 600 (paper), or 90 (Internet); proof of adequate funds; proof of health/immunizations.

International Student Contact Ms. Ann Helen Anderson, Director, Office of International Studies, 3225 West Foster Avenue, Chicago, IL 60625-4895. *Phone:* 773-244-5571. *E-mail:* aanderson@northpark.edu.

APPLICATION *Required:* Application form, baccalaureate/first degree, essay, 2 letters of recommendation, resume/curriculum vitae, transcripts of college work. School will accept GMAT and GRE. *Recommended:* Work experience. *Application fee:* $30. Applications for domestic and international students are processed on a rolling basis.

Application Contact Christopher Nicholson, Director of Admissions, Graduate and Continuing Education, 3225 West Foster Avenue, Chicago, IL 60625-4895. *Phone:* 773-244-5518. *Fax:* 773-279-7996. *E-mail:* cnicholson@northpark.edu.

Northwestern University
Kellogg School of Management

Evanston, Illinois

Phone: 847-491-3308 **Fax:** 847-491-4960 **E-mail:** mbaadmissions@kellogg.northwestern.edu

Business Program(s) Web Site: http://www.kellogg.northwestern.edu

Graduate Business Unit Enrollment *Total:* 2,450 (1,200 full-time; 1,250 part-time; 833 women; 646 international). *Average Age:* 28.

Graduate Business Faculty *Total:* 230 (163 full-time; 67 part-time).

Admissions *Applied:* 4,148. *Average GMAT:* 704. *Average GPA:* 3.5

Academic Calendar Quarters.

Accreditation AACSB—The Association to Advance Collegiate Schools of Business.

After Graduation (Class of 2006–07) *Employed within 3 months of graduation:* 97%. *Average starting salary:* $103,652.

DEGREES JD/MBA • MBA • MBA/MEM • MD/MBA

JD/MBA—Juris Doctor/Master of Business Administration Full-time. *Concentrations:* accounting, decision sciences, entrepreneurship, finance, health care, international business, management, managerial economics, marketing, media administration, nonprofit management, operations management, organizational behavior/development, other, real estate, technology management.

MBA—One-Year MBA Full-time. *Concentrations:* accounting, decision sciences, entrepreneurship, finance, health administration, international business, management, managerial economics, manufacturing management, marketing, media administration, nonprofit management, operations management, organizational behavior/development, other, real estate, strategic management, technology management.

MBA—Two-Year MBA Full-time and part-time. *Concentrations:* accounting, decision sciences, entrepreneurship, finance, health administration, international business, management, managerial economics, manufacturing management, marketing, media administration, nonprofit management, operations management, organizational behavior/development, other, real estate, strategic management, technology management.

MBA/MEM—MMM Full-time. At least 23 total credits required. *Concentrations:* accounting, decision sciences, entrepreneurship, finance, health care, international business, management, managerial economics, manufacturing management, marketing, media administration, nonprofit management, operations management, organizational behavior/development, real estate, technology management.

MD/MBA—Doctor of Medicine/Master of Business Administration Full-time. Distance learning option. *Concentrations:* accounting, decision sciences, electronic commerce (E-commerce), entrepreneurship, finance, health care, international business, management, managerial economics, marketing, media administration, nonprofit management, operations management, organizational behavior/development, real estate, technology management.

RESOURCES AND SERVICES 145 on-campus PCs are available to graduate business students. Access to Internet/World Wide Web, online (class) registration, and online grade reports available. *Personal computer requirements:* Graduate business students are required to have a personal computer. *Special opportunities include:* An international exchange

program and an internship program are available. *Placement services include:* Alumni network, career placement, job search course, career counseling/planning, electronic job bank, resume referral, career fairs, job interviews arranged, resume preparation, and career library.

EXPENSES *Tuition:* Full-time: $46,791. *Graduate housing:* Room and board costs vary by campus location, number of occupants, type of accommodation, and type of board plan. *Typical cost:* $14,475 (including board).

FINANCIAL AID (2007–08) Grants, loans, and scholarships. Aid is available to part-time students. *Financial aid application deadline:* 5/20.

Financial Aid Contact Office of Admissions and Financial Aid, 2001 Sheridan Road, Evanston, IL 60208-2001. *Phone:* 847-491-3308. *Fax:* 847-491-4960. *E-mail:* mbaadmissions@kellogg.northwestern.edu.

INTERNATIONAL STUDENTS 26% of students enrolled are international students. *Services and facilities:* Counseling/support services, ESL/language courses, Housing location assistance, International student organization, Orientation. Financial aid is available to international students. *Required with application:* TOEFL.

International Student Contact Office of Admissions and Financial Aid, 2001 Sheridan Road, Evanston, IL 60208-2001. *Phone:* 847-491-3308. *Fax:* 847-491-4960. *E-mail:* mbaadmissions@kellogg.northwestern.edu.

APPLICATION *Required:* GMAT, application form, baccalaureate/first degree, essay, interview, 2 letters of recommendation, resume/curriculum vitae, transcripts of college work. *Recommended:* Work experience. *Application fee:* $225. *Deadlines:* 10/17 for fall, 1/12 for winter, 3/9 for spring, 10/17 for fall (international), 1/12 for winter (international), 3/9 for spring (international).

Application Contact Office of Admissions and Financial Aid, 2001 Sheridan Road, Evanston, IL 60208-2001. *Phone:* 847-491-3308. *Fax:* 847-491-4960. *E-mail:* mbaadmissions@kellogg.northwestern.edu.

Rockford College
Program in Business Administration

Rockford, Illinois

Phone: 815-226-4178 **Fax:** 815-226-4119 **E-mail:** jfahrenwald@rockford.edu

Business Program(s) Web Site: http://www.rockford.edu/mba/mba.htm

Graduate Business Unit Enrollment *Total:* 110 (14 full-time; 96 part-time; 45 women; 10 international). *Average Age:* 25-40.

Graduate Business Faculty *Total:* 15 (12 full-time; 3 part-time).

Admissions *Applied:* 20. *Admitted:* 18. *Enrolled:* 18. *Average GMAT:* 510. *Average GPA:* 3.3

Academic Calendar Semesters.

After Graduation (Class of 2006–07) *Employed within 3 months of graduation:* 95%.

DEGREE MBA

MBA—Master of Business Administration Full-time and part-time. 36 to 50 total credits required. 15 to 60 months to complete program. *Concentrations:* accounting, finance, general MBA, management, marketing, nonprofit organization, public management, strategic management.

RESOURCES AND SERVICES 150 on-campus PCs are available to graduate business students. Access to Internet/World Wide Web, online (class) registration, and online grade reports available. *Personal computer requirements:* Graduate business students are not required to have a personal computer. *Special opportunities include:* An internship program is available. *Placement services include:* Alumni network, career placement, career counseling/planning, electronic job bank, resume referral, career fairs, resume preparation, and career library.

EXPENSES *Tuition:* Part-time: $625 per credit hour. *Tuition (international):* Part-time: $625 per credit hour. *Required fees:* Full-time: $200.

Rockford College (continued)

Part-time: $100 per semester. *Graduate housing:* Room and board costs vary by number of occupants and type of board plan.

FINANCIAL AID (2007–08) 20 students received aid, including grants, loans, research assistantships, and work study. Aid is available to part-time students. *Financial aid application deadline:* 6/30.

Financial Aid Contact Ellen Hamrick, Assistant Director and Financial Specialist, 5050 East State Street, Rockford, IL 61108-2393. *Phone:* 815-226-3396. *Fax:* 815-394-5174. *E-mail:* ehamrick@rockford.edu.

INTERNATIONAL STUDENTS 9% of students enrolled are international students. *Services and facilities:* Counseling/support services, ESL/language courses, Housing location assistance, International student housing, International student organization, Language tutoring, Orientation, Visa Services. Financial aid is available to international students. *Required with application:* TOEFL with recommended score of 550 (paper); proof of adequate funds; proof of health/immunizations.

International Student Contact Mr. Jeff Fahrenwald, Director, MBA Program, 5050 East State Street, Rockford, IL 61108-2393. *Phone:* 815-226-4040. *Fax:* 815-394-3706. *E-mail:* jfahrenwald@rockford.edu.

APPLICATION *Required:* GMAT, application form, baccalaureate/first degree, essay, 3 letters of recommendation, personal statement, transcripts of college work. *Recommended:* Interview, resume/curriculum vitae, 5 years of work experience. *Application fee:* $50. Applications for domestic and international students are processed on a rolling basis.

Application Contact Mr. Jeffrey Fahrenwald, Director, MBA Program, 5050 East State Street, Rockford, IL 61108-2393. *Phone:* 815-226-4178. *Fax:* 815-226-4119. *E-mail:* jfahrenwald@rockford.edu.

Roosevelt University
Walter E. Heller College of Business Administration
Chicago, Illinois

Phone: 312-281-3250 **Fax:** 312-281-3356 **E-mail:** jcanhel@roosevelt.edu

Business Program(s) Web Site: http://www.roosevelt.edu/

Graduate Business Unit Enrollment *Total:* 807 (120 full-time; 687 part-time; 476 women; 41 international). *Average Age:* 32.

Graduate Business Faculty *Total:* 74 (28 full-time; 46 part-time).

Admissions *Applied:* 497. *Admitted:* 351. *Enrolled:* 196. *Average GMAT:* 500. *Average GPA:* 3.29

Academic Calendar Semesters.

Accreditation ACBSP—The American Council of Business Schools and Programs.

After Graduation (Class of 2006–07) *Employed within 3 months of graduation:* 90%.

DEGREES MBA • MS

MBA—Master of Business Administration Full-time and part-time. At least 37 total credits required. 16 to 72 months to complete program. *Concentrations:* accounting, advertising, economics, finance, forensic accounting, health administration, health care, hospitality management, human resources management, information systems, international business, leadership, management, management information systems, marketing, nonprofit management, organizational behavior/development, public policy and administration, public relations, real estate, strategic management, student designed, training and development.

MS—Master of Science in Accounting Full-time and part-time. At least 31 total credits required. 12 to 72 months to complete program. *Concentration:* accounting.

MS—Master of Science in Human Resources Management Full-time and part-time. At least 31 total credits required. 12 to 72 months to complete program. *Concentration:* human resources management.

MS—Master of Science in Information Systems Full-time and part-time. At least 31 total credits required. 12 to 72 months to complete program. *Concentration:* information systems.

MS—Master of Science in International Business Full-time and part-time. 3 years of relevant business experience required. At least 37 total credits required. 16 to 72 months to complete program. *Concentrations:* accounting, economics, finance, health administration, human resources management, information systems, leadership, management, management information systems, marketing, real estate, student designed.

MS—Master of Science in Real Estate Full-time and part-time. 31 total credits required. 12 to 72 months to complete program. *Concentration:* real estate.

RESOURCES AND SERVICES 400 on-campus PCs are available to graduate business students. Access to Internet/World Wide Web, online (class) registration, and online grade reports available. *Personal computer requirements:* Graduate business students are strongly recommended to purchase or lease a personal computer. *Special opportunities include:* An international exchange program and an internship program are available. *Placement services include:* Alumni network, career placement, career counseling/planning, electronic job bank, resume referral, career fairs, job interviews arranged, resume preparation, and career library.

EXPENSES *Tuition:* Full-time: $14,176. Part-time: $688 per credit hour. *Tuition (international):* Full-time: $14,176. Part-time: $688 per credit hour. *Required fees:* Full-time: $350. Part-time: $350 per year. Tuition and/or fees vary by number of courses or credits taken. *Graduate housing:* Room and board costs vary by number of occupants and type of accommodation. *Typical cost:* $10,572 (including board), $7548 (room only).

FINANCIAL AID (2007–08) Grants, loans, research assistantships, scholarships, and work study. Aid is available to part-time students. *Financial aid application deadline:* 6/15.

Financial Aid Contact Mr. Walter O'Neill, Director of Financial Aid, 430 South Michigan Avenue, Chicago, IL 60605-1394. *Phone:* 312-341-3566. *Fax:* 312-341-3545. *E-mail:* woneill@roosevelt.edu.

INTERNATIONAL STUDENTS 5% of students enrolled are international students. *Services and facilities:* Counseling/support services, ESL/language courses, International student housing, International student organization, Language tutoring, Orientation, Visa Services. Financial aid is not available to international students. *Required with application:* TWE with recommended score of 4.5; proof of adequate funds; proof of health/immunizations. *Recommended with application:* TOEFL with recommended score of 213 (computer) or 550 (paper).

International Student Contact Ms. Rubee Fuller, Director, Office of International Programs, 430 South Michigan Avenue, Chicago, IL 60605-1394. *Phone:* 312-341-3531. *Fax:* 312-341-6377. *E-mail:* internat@roosevelt.edu.

APPLICATION *Required:* GMAT, application form, baccalaureate/first degree, transcripts of college work. *Recommended:* Essay, letter(s) of recommendation, personal statement, resume/curriculum vitae. *Application fee:* $25, $35 (international). Applications for domestic and international students are processed on a rolling basis.

Application Contact Ms. Joanne Canyon-Heller, Coordinator, Graduate Admissions, 430 South Michigan Avenue, Chicago, IL 60605-1394. *Phone:* 312-281-3250. *Fax:* 312-281-3356. *E-mail:* jcanhel@roosevelt.edu.

See full description on page 676.

Rush University
Department of Health Systems Management
Chicago, Illinois

Phone: 312-942-5402 **Fax:** 312-942-4957 **E-mail:** daniel_gentry@rush.edu

Business Program(s) Web Site: http://www.rushu.rush.edu/hsm

Graduate Business Unit Enrollment *Total:* 46 (32 full-time; 14 part-time; 30 women; 3 international). *Average Age:* 27.

Graduate Business Faculty *Total:* 45 (5 full-time; 40 part-time).

Admissions *Applied:* 49. *Admitted:* 27. *Enrolled:* 23. *Average GMAT:* 597. *Average GPA:* 3.3

Academic Calendar Quarters.

After Graduation (Class of 2006–07) *Employed within 3 months of graduation:* 95%. *Average starting salary:* $55,000.

DEGREE MSHCM

MSHCM—Health Systems Management Full-time and part-time. Completion of undergraduate courses in statistics and accounting required. At least 80 total credits required. 21 to 60 months to complete program. *Concentration:* health administration.

RESOURCES AND SERVICES 100 on-campus PCs are available to graduate business students. Access to Internet/World Wide Web available. *Personal computer requirements:* Graduate business students are not required to have a personal computer. *Special opportunities include:* An international exchange program and an internship program are available. *Placement services include:* Alumni network, career placement, job search course, career counseling/planning, electronic job bank, resume referral, career fairs, and resume preparation.

EXPENSES *Tuition:* Full-time: $21,300. Part-time: $621 per credit hour. *Tuition (international):* Full-time: $21,300. Part-time: $621 per credit hour.

FINANCIAL AID (2007–08) 25 students received aid, including grants, loans, scholarships, and work study. Aid is available to part-time students.

Financial Aid Contact David Nelson, Interim Director of Student Financial Aid, 600 South Paulina Street, Suite 440, Chicago, IL 60612. *Phone:* 312-942-6256. *Fax:* 312-942-2219. *E-mail:* financial_aid@rush.edu.

INTERNATIONAL STUDENTS 7% of students enrolled are international students. *Services and facilities:* Counseling/support services, Housing location assistance, Orientation, Visa Services. Financial aid is not available to international students. *Required with application:* TOEFL with recommended score of 230 (computer), 570 (paper), or 88 (Internet); proof of adequate funds; proof of health/immunizations.

International Student Contact Helen Lavelle, Director, International Services, 600 South Paulina Street, Suite 440, Chicago, IL 60612. *Phone:* 312-942-2030. *Fax:* 312-942-2310. *E-mail:* helen_lavelle@rush.edu.

APPLICATION *Required:* Application form, baccalaureate/first degree, essay, interview, 3 letters of recommendation, transcripts of college work. School will accept GMAT and GRE. *Recommended:* Personal statement, resume/curriculum vitae. *Application fee:* $50, $100 (international). Applications for domestic and international students are processed on a rolling basis.

Application Contact Daniel Gentry, PhD, Program Director, 1700 West Van Buren Street, Suite 126B, Chicago, IL 60612. *Phone:* 312-942-5402. *Fax:* 312-942-4957. *E-mail:* daniel_gentry@rush.edu.

Saint Xavier University

Graham School of Management

Chicago, Illinois

Phone: 773-298-3059 **Fax:** 773-298-3951 **E-mail:** graduateadmission@sxu.edu

Business Program(s) Web Site: http://www.sxu.edu/gsm/default.asp

Graduate Business Unit Enrollment *Total:* 576 (152 full-time; 424 part-time; 326 women; 9 international). *Average Age:* 35.

Graduate Business Faculty *Total:* 48 (18 full-time; 30 part-time).

Admissions *Applied:* 280. *Admitted:* 165. *Enrolled:* 156.

Academic Calendar Quarters.

Accreditation ACBSP—The American Council of Business Schools and Programs.

DEGREES MBA • MBA/MS • MS

MBA—Master of Business Administration Full-time and part-time. 36 to 45 total credits required. 12 to 60 months to complete program. *Concentrations:* finance, financial management/planning, forensic accounting, general MBA, health care, management, marketing, nonprofit management, public and private management, training and development.

MBA/MS—Master of Business Administration/Master of Science in Nursing Full-time and part-time. 54 to 63 total credits required. 12 to 60 months to complete program. *Concentrations:* finance, health care, management, marketing.

MS—Master of Science Full-time and part-time. 36 to 45 total credits required. 12 to 60 months to complete program. *Concentrations:* finance, health care, management, nonprofit management, public and private management.

RESOURCES AND SERVICES 312 on-campus PCs are available to graduate business students. Access to Internet/World Wide Web, online (class) registration, and online grade reports available. *Personal computer requirements:* Graduate business students are strongly recommended to purchase or lease a personal computer. *Special opportunities include:* An internship program is available. *Placement services include:* Alumni network, career placement, career counseling/planning, electronic job bank, resume referral, career fairs, resume preparation, and career library.

EXPENSES *Tuition:* Full-time: $11,700. *Tuition (international):* Full-time: $11,700. *Required fees:* Full-time: $120. Part-time: $120 per year.

FINANCIAL AID (2007–08) 249 students received aid, including loans, research assistantships, and work study. Aid is available to part-time students. *Financial aid application deadline:* 3/1.

Financial Aid Contact Ms. Susan Swisher, Assistant Vice President of Student Financial Services and Director of Financial Aid, 3700 West 103rd Street, Chicago, IL 60655-3105. *Phone:* 773-298-3070. *Fax:* 773-298-3084. *E-mail:* swisher@sxu.edu.

INTERNATIONAL STUDENTS 2% of students enrolled are international students. *Services and facilities:* Counseling/support services, Housing location assistance, International student organization. Financial aid is available to international students. *Required with application:* TOEFL; proof of adequate funds; proof of health/immunizations.

International Student Contact Ms. Amy Lapinski, Assistant Director, Office of Graduate Admissions, 3700 West 103rd Street, Chicago, IL 60655-3105. *Phone:* 773-298-3059. *Fax:* 773-298-3951. *E-mail:* lapinski@sxu.edu.

APPLICATION *Required:* GMAT, application form, baccalaureate/first degree, 2 letters of recommendation, personal statement, resume/curriculum vitae, transcripts of college work. School will accept GRE and MAT. *Recommended:* Work experience. *Application fee:* $35. Applications for domestic and international students are processed on a rolling basis.

Application Contact Amy Lapinski, Assistant Director, Office of Graduate Admissions, 3700 West 103rd Street, Chicago, IL 60655-3105. *Phone:* 773-298-3059. *Fax:* 773-298-3951. *E-mail:* graduateadmission@sxu.edu.

Southern Illinois University Carbondale

College of Business and Administration

Carbondale, Illinois

Phone: 618-453-3030 **Fax:** 618-453-7961 **E-mail:** mbagp@cba.siu.edu

Business Program(s) Web Site: http://www.cba.siu.edu/mba

Graduate Business Unit Enrollment *Total:* 205 (190 full-time; 15 part-time; 83 women; 89 international).

Southern Illinois University Carbondale (continued)

Graduate Business Faculty 41 full-time.

Admissions *Average GMAT:* 529. *Average GPA:* 3.45

Academic Calendar Semesters.

Accreditation AACSB—The Association to Advance Collegiate Schools of Business.

After Graduation (Class of 2006–07) *Employed within 3 months of graduation:* 75%. *Average starting salary:* $55,000.

DEGREES EMBA • JD/MBA • MBA • MBA/MA • MBA/MS

EMBA—Executive Master of Business Administration Part-time. 5 years of managerial experience required. At least 33 total credits required. 18 months to complete program. *Concentration:* executive programs.

JD/MBA—Juris Doctor/Master of Business Administration Full-time. At least 105 total credits required. 36 to 48 months to complete program. *Concentration:* combined degrees.

MBA—Master of Business Administration Full-time and part-time. At least 33 total credits required. 12 to 24 months to complete program. *Concentrations:* accounting, finance, international business, management, management information systems, marketing, organizational behavior/development, production management.

MBA/MA—Master of Business Administration/Master of Arts in Mass Communication Full-time and part-time. At least 51 total credits required. 12 to 30 months to complete program. *Concentration:* combined degrees.

MBA/MS—Master of Business Administration/Master of Science in Agribusiness Economics Full-time and part-time. At least 51 total credits required. 12 to 30 months to complete program. *Concentration:* combined degrees.

RESOURCES AND SERVICES 80 on-campus PCs are available to graduate business students. Access to Internet/World Wide Web and online grade reports available. *Personal computer requirements:* Graduate business students are strongly recommended to purchase or lease a personal computer. *Special opportunities include:* An international exchange program and an internship program are available. *Placement services include:* Alumni network, career placement, career counseling/planning, electronic job bank, resume referral, career fairs, job interviews arranged, resume preparation, and career library.

EXPENSES *Tuition (state resident):* Full-time: $6600. Part-time: $275 per credit hour. *Tuition (nonresident):* Full-time: $16,500. Part-time: $687.50 per credit hour. *Tuition (international):* Full-time: $16,500. Part-time: $687.50 per credit hour. *Required fees:* Full-time: $2545. Tuition and/or fees vary by number of courses or credits taken and academic program. *Graduate housing:* Room and board costs vary by campus location, number of occupants, type of accommodation, and type of board plan. *Typical cost:* $6750 (including board), $3600 (room only).

FINANCIAL AID (2007–08) 40 students received aid, including fellowships, loans, research assistantships, scholarships, and teaching assistantships. *Financial aid application deadline:* 3/15.

Financial Aid Contact Ms. Pamela Britton, Director, Financial Aid, Woody Hall B326, Carbondale, IL 62901. *Phone:* 618-453-4334. *Fax:* 618-453-7305. *E-mail:* pbritton@siu.edu.

INTERNATIONAL STUDENTS 43% of students enrolled are international students. *Services and facilities:* Counseling/support services, ESL/language courses, Housing location assistance, International student organization, Language tutoring, Orientation, Visa Services. Financial aid is available to international students. *Required with application:* TOEFL with recommended score of 213 (computer), 550 (paper), or 80 (Internet); proof of adequate funds; proof of health/immunizations. *Recommended with application:* TWE.

International Student Contact Graduate Programs Office, 133 Rehn Hall, Mailstop 4625, Carbondale, IL 62901-4625. *Phone:* 618-453-3030. *Fax:* 618-453-7961. *E-mail:* mbagp@cba.siu.edu.

APPLICATION *Required:* GMAT, application form, baccalaureate/first degree, essay, 3 letters of recommendation, personal statement, transcripts of college work. *Recommended:* Resume/curriculum vitae. *Application fee:* $50. Applications for domestic and international students are processed on a rolling basis.

Application Contact Julie Virgo, Graduate Programs Office, 133 Rehn Hall, Mailstop 4625, Carbondale, IL 62901-4625. *Phone:* 618-453-3030. *Fax:* 618-453-7961. *E-mail:* mbagp@cba.siu.edu.

Southern Illinois University Edwardsville
School of Business
Edwardsville, Illinois

Phone: 618-650-3412 **Fax:** 618-650-3979 **E-mail:** jjoplin@siue.edu

Business Program(s) Web Site: http://www.siue.edu/business/

Graduate Business Unit Enrollment *Total:* 299 (299 part-time).

Graduate Business Faculty *Total:* 82 (53 full-time; 29 part-time).

Admissions *Average GMAT:* 512. *Average GPA:* 3.16

Academic Calendar 10-week semesters, six week option, weekend options.

Accreditation AACSB—The Association to Advance Collegiate Schools of Business.

After Graduation (Class of 2006–07) *Employed within 3 months of graduation:* 85%.

DEGREES MA • MBA • MBA/MIS • MS

MA—Master of Arts in Economics and Finance Full-time and part-time. 30 to 51 total credits required. 12 to 72 months to complete program. *Concentrations:* economics, finance, financial economics.

MBA—Master of Business Administration Part-time. 42 total credits required. 12 to 72 months to complete program. *Concentrations:* business information science, decision sciences, economics, finance, human resources management, information management, international business, management, manpower administration, marketing, organizational management, project management.

MBA—Master of Business Administration *Concentration:* general MBA.

MBA/MIS—Master of Business Administration with Management Information Systems Specialization Full-time and part-time. 30 to 55 total credits required. 12 to 72 months to complete program. *Concentrations:* business information science, decision sciences, economics, electronic commerce (E-commerce), finance, human resources management, international business, management, manpower administration, marketing, organizational management.

MS—Master of Science in Accountancy Full-time and part-time. 30 to 48 total credits required. 12 to 72 months to complete program. *Concentration:* accounting.

MS—Master of Science in Computing and Information Systems Full-time and part-time. 31 to 58 total credits required. 12 to 72 months to complete program. *Concentrations:* business information science, management information systems, management systems analysis, project management, system management.

MS—Master of Science in Economics and Finance Full-time and part-time. 30 to 51 total credits required. 12 to 72 months to complete program. *Concentrations:* economics, finance, financial economics.

MS—Master of Science in Marketing Research Full-time and part-time. 36 to 54 total credits required. 12 to 72 months to complete program. *Concentrations:* marketing, marketing research.

The School of Business at Southern Illinois University Edwardsville prepares students to be leaders in today's global economy. The central objective of the curriculum is to enhance quality and innovation in the analysis, interpretation, and use of information for

formulating, communicating, and implementing managerial decisions in business organizations. The M.B.A. program, consisting of ten required and four elective courses, requires 42 hours. The required courses include Quantitative Analysis, Decision Making in Organizations, Negotiation and Interpersonal Skills for Managers, Accounting for MBAs, Marketing Analysis and Applications for Managerial Decision Making, Information Systems and Technology, Corporate Finance, Managerial Economics, Operations Management and Process Analysis, and Strategic Management. Electives are available in finance, management information systems, and marketing, with additional electives available in accounting, economics, and management. A specialization in management information systems (MIS) and a project management concentration are also available. Evening and weekend formats permit flexible completion of the degree program with courses meeting one night a week for ten weeks or courses that are concentrated into three weekends. The School also offers master's degrees in accounting, computer management and information systems, economics and finance, and marketing research. For additional information, please refer to http://www.siue.edu/business/mba.

RESOURCES AND SERVICES 400 on-campus PCs are available to graduate business students. Access to Internet/World Wide Web, online (class) registration, and online grade reports available. *Personal computer requirements:* Graduate business students are not required to have a personal computer. *Special opportunities include:* An international exchange program and an internship program are available. *Placement services include:* Alumni network, career placement, job search course, career counseling/planning, electronic job bank, resume referral, career fairs, job interviews arranged, resume preparation, and career library.

FINANCIAL AID (2007–08) Fellowships, loans, research assistantships, scholarships, and work study. Aid is available to part-time students. *Financial aid application deadline:* 3/1.

Financial Aid Contact Sharon Berry, Director of Student Financial Aid, Box 1060, Edwardsville, IL 62026. *Phone:* 618-650-3880. *Fax:* 618-650-3885. *E-mail:* shaberr@siue.edu.

INTERNATIONAL STUDENTS *Services and facilities:* Counseling/ support services, ESL/language courses, International student housing, International student organization. Financial aid is not available to international students. *Required with application:* TOEFL with recommended score of 213 (computer) or 550 (paper); proof of adequate funds; proof of health/immunizations.

International Student Contact Debbie Bayne, Advisor, Box 1616, Edwardsville, IL 62026. *Phone:* 618-650-3785. *E-mail:* dbayne@sine.edu.

APPLICATION *Required:* GMAT, application form, baccalaureate/first degree, transcripts of college work. *Application fee:* $30. Applications for domestic and international students are processed on a rolling basis.

Application Contact Dr. Janice Joplin, Associate Dean for Academic Affairs, Box 1051, Edwardsville, IL 62026-1051. *Phone:* 618-650-3412. *Fax:* 618-650-3979. *E-mail:* jjoplin@siue.edu.

University of Chicago
Graduate School of Business
Chicago, Illinois

Phone: 773-702-7369 **Fax:** 773-702-9085 **E-mail:** admissions@chicagogsb.edu

Business Program(s) Web Site: http://ChicagoGSB.edu

Graduate Business Unit Enrollment *Total:* 3,252 (1,119 full-time; 2,133 part-time). *Average Age:* 28.

Graduate Business Faculty *Total:* 187 (140 full-time; 47 part-time).

Admissions *Average GMAT:* 710. *Average GPA:* 3.5

Academic Calendar Quarters.

Accreditation AACSB—The Association to Advance Collegiate Schools of Business.

After Graduation (Class of 2006–07) *Employed within 3 months of graduation:* 95.3%. *Average starting salary:* $100,000.

DEGREES IMBA • MBA

IMBA—International Master of Business Administration Full-time. Must first be admitted to the full-time MBA program. 30 to 60 months to complete program. *Concentrations:* accounting, economics, entrepreneurship, finance, human resources management, international business, management, managerial economics, marketing, operations management, production management, strategic management.

MBA—Evening Master of Business Administration Part-time. 30 to 60 months to complete program. *Concentrations:* accounting, economics, entrepreneurship, finance, human resources management, international business, management, marketing, operations management, statistics.

MBA—Executive Master of Business Administration Asia Part-time. 10 years of work experience required. 21 months to complete program. *Concentration:* management.

MBA—Executive Master of Business Administration Europe Part-time. 10 years of work experience required. 21 months to complete program. *Concentration:* executive programs.

MBA—Executive Master of Business Administration North America Part-time. 10 years of work experience required. 21 months to complete program. *Concentration:* executive programs.

MBA—Full-Time Master of Business Administration Program Full-time and part-time. 30 to 60 months to complete program. *Concentrations:* accounting, economics, entrepreneurship, finance, human resources management, international business, management, marketing, operations management, organizational behavior/development, strategic management.

MBA—Weekend Master of Business Administration Part-time. 30 to 60 months to complete program. *Concentrations:* accounting, economics, entrepreneurship, finance, human resources management, international business, management, marketing, operations management, strategic management.

RESOURCES AND SERVICES 200 on-campus PCs are available to graduate business students. Access to Internet/World Wide Web and online (class) registration available. *Personal computer requirements:* Graduate business students are not required to have a personal computer. *Special opportunities include:* An international exchange program and an internship program are available. *Placement services include:* Alumni network, career placement, job search course, career counseling/planning, electronic job bank, resume referral, career fairs, job interviews arranged, resume preparation, and career library.

EXPENSES *Tuition:* Full-time: $47,260. Part-time: $4655 per course. *Tuition (international):* Full-time: $47,260. Part-time: $4655 per course. *Required fees:* Full-time: $639. Tuition and/or fees vary by class time, number of courses or credits taken, and academic program.

FINANCIAL AID (2007–08) Loans and scholarships.

Financial Aid Contact Priscilla Parker, Director of Financial Aid, 5807 South Woodlawn Avenue, Chicago, IL 60637. *Phone:* 773-702-3076. *Fax:* 773-834-1355. *E-mail:* priscilla.parker@chicagogsb.edu.

INTERNATIONAL STUDENTS *Services and facilities:* Counseling/ support services, Housing location assistance, International student housing, International student organization, Orientation, Visa Services, Regional international business clubs. *Required with application:* IELT; TOEFL with recommended score of 250 (computer) or 600 (paper); proof of adequate funds; proof of health/immunizations.

International Student Contact Ms. Kari Nysather, Director, International Programs, 5807 South Woodlawn Avenue, Chicago, IL 60637. *Phone:* 773-702-7369. *Fax:* 773-702-9085. *E-mail:* admissions@chicagogsb.edu.

APPLICATION *Required:* GMAT, application form, baccalaureate/first degree, essay, interview, 2 letters of recommendation, personal statement, resume/curriculum vitae, transcripts of college work. *Recommended:* Work experience. *Application fee:* $200. *Deadlines:* 10/17 for fall, 1/9 for winter, 3/12 for spring, 10/17 for fall (international), 1/9 for winter (international), 3/12 for spring (international).

University of Chicago (continued)

Application Contact Rosemaria Martinell, Associate Dean for Student Recruitment and Admissions, 5807 South Woodlawn Avenue, Chicago, IL 60637. *Phone:* 773-702-7369. *Fax:* 773-702-9085. *E-mail:* admissions@ chicagogsb.edu.

University of Illinois at Chicago
Liautaud Graduate School of Business

Chicago, Illinois

Phone: 312-996-4573 **Fax:** 312-413-0338 **E-mail:** ritarack@uic.edu

Business Program(s) Web Site: http://www.lgsb.uic.edu

Graduate Business Unit Enrollment *Total:* 966 (642 full-time; 324 part-time; 412 women; 439 international). *Average Age:* 28.

Graduate Business Faculty *Total:* 102 (97 full-time; 5 part-time).

Admissions *Applied:* 888. *Admitted:* 360. *Enrolled:* 195. *Average GMAT:* 610. *Average GPA:* 3.18

Academic Calendar Semesters.

Accreditation AACSB—The Association to Advance Collegiate Schools of Business.

DEGREES MA • MBA • MSA • MSMIS

MA—Master of Arts in Real Estate Full-time and part-time. A minimum of one undergraduate accounting course is required as a prerequisite. 36 to 40 total credits required. 18 to 60 months to complete program. *Concentrations:* business studies, other.

MBA Full-time and part-time. At least 54 total credits required. 24 to 72 months to complete program. *Concentrations:* accounting, entrepreneurship, finance, management, management information systems, marketing, real estate, student designed.

MSA—MS in Accounting Full-time and part-time. Prerequisites are required. 32 to 48 total credits required. 12 to 60 months to complete program. *Concentration:* accounting.

MSMIS—MS in Management Information Systems Full-time and part-time. Prerequisites are required. 32 to 48 total credits required. 12 to 60 months to complete program. *Concentration:* management information systems.

RESOURCES AND SERVICES 770 on-campus PCs are available to graduate business students. Access to Internet/World Wide Web, online (class) registration, and online grade reports available. *Personal computer requirements:* Graduate business students are strongly recommended to purchase or lease a personal computer. *Special opportunities include:* An internship program is available. *Placement services include:* Alumni network, career placement, career counseling/planning, electronic job bank, resume referral, career fairs, job interviews arranged, resume preparation, and career library.

EXPENSES *Tuition (state resident):* Full-time: $15,098. *Tuition (nonresident):* Full-time: $30,218. *Tuition (international):* Full-time: $30,218. *Required fees:* Full-time: $3122. Part-time: $2758 per semester. Tuition and/or fees vary by number of courses or credits taken. *Graduate housing:* Room and board costs vary by number of occupants. *Typical cost:* $11,250 (including board).

FINANCIAL AID (2007–08) 30 students received aid, including fellowships, loans, research assistantships, scholarships, teaching assistantships, and work study. Aid is available to part-time students.

Financial Aid Contact Timothy A. Opgenorth, Director, Student Financial Aid, 1200 West Harrison Street, Suite 1892, Chicago, IL 60607. *Phone:* 312-996-5563. *Fax:* 312-996-3385. *E-mail:* timothy1@uic.edu.

INTERNATIONAL STUDENTS 45% of students enrolled are international students. *Services and facilities:* Counseling/support services, ESL/language courses, Housing location assistance, International student organization, Orientation, Visa Services. Financial aid is available to international students. *Required with application:* TOEFL with recommended score of 250 (computer) or 600 (paper); proof of adequate funds; proof of health/immunizations.

International Student Contact Rita Bieliauskas, Director of Admissions, 815 West Van Buren Street, Suite 220, Chicago, IL 60607. *Phone:* 312-996-4573. *Fax:* 312-413-0338. *E-mail:* ritarack@uic.edu.

APPLICATION *Required:* GMAT, GRE, application form, baccalaureate/first degree, essay, interview, 2 letters of recommendation, personal statement, resume/curriculum vitae, transcripts of college work, 2 years of work experience. *Application fee:* $50, $60 (international). Applications for domestic and international students are processed on a rolling basis.

Application Contact Rita Bieliauskas, Director of Admissions, 815 West Van Buren Street, Suite 220, Chicago, IL 60607. *Phone:* 312-996-4573. *Fax:* 312-413-0338. *E-mail:* ritarack@uic.edu.

University of Illinois at Urbana–Champaign
College of Business

Champaign, Illinois

Phone: 217-244-2953 **Fax:** 217-333-1156 **E-mail:** jjwilson@uiuc.edu

Business Program(s) Web Site: http://www.mba.uiuc.edu/

Graduate Business Unit Enrollment *Total:* 926 (862 full-time; 64 part-time; 353 women; 402 international). *Average Age:* 27.

Graduate Business Faculty *Total:* 140 (108 full-time; 32 part-time).

Admissions *Applied:* 537. *Admitted:* 223. *Enrolled:* 103. *Average GMAT:* 627. *Average GPA:* 3.4

Academic Calendar Semesters.

Accreditation AACSB—The Association to Advance Collegiate Schools of Business.

After Graduation (Class of 2006–07) *Employed within 3 months of graduation:* 97%. *Average starting salary:* $82,693.

DEGREES EMBA • JD/MBA • MAS • MBA • MBA/MA • MBA/ME • MBA/MS • MD/MBA • MS • MSA • MSF • MST

EMBA Part-time. 72 total credits required. 19 months to complete program. *Concentrations:* executive programs, general MBA, management.

JD/MBA Full-time. *Concentration:* combined degrees.

MAS—Master of Accounting Science Full-time. Must begin the program during the Summer term, which starts around June 10th. Minimum of 12 months to complete program. *Concentration:* accounting.

MBA—Illinois MBA Full-time. 72 total credits required. Minimum of 21 months to complete program. *Concentrations:* finance, information technology, management, marketing, operations management.

MBA—Part-Time Evening MBA for Working Professionals Part-time. 72 total credits required. Minimum of 30 months to complete program. *Concentration:* management.

MBA/MA—Master of Business Administration/Master of Arts in Architecture Full-time. *Concentration:* combined degrees.

MBA/MA—Master of Business Administration/Master of Arts in Journalism Full-time. *Concentration:* combined degrees.

MBA/ME Full-time. *Concentration:* combined degrees.

MBA/MS—Master of Business Administration/Master of Science in Civil Engineering Full-time. *Concentration:* combined degrees.

MBA/MS—Master of Business Administration/Master of Science in Computer Science Full-time. *Concentration:* combined degrees.

MBA/MS—Master of Business Administration/Master of Science in Electrical Engineering Full-time. *Concentration:* combined degrees.

MBA/MS—Master of Business Administration/Master of Science in General Engineering Full-time. *Concentration:* combined degrees.

MBA/MS—Master of Business Administration/Master of Science in Industrial Engineering Full-time. *Concentration:* combined degrees.

MBA/MS—Master of Business Administration/Master of Science in Mechanical Engineering Full-time. *Concentration:* combined degrees.

MD/MBA Full-time. *Concentration:* combined degrees.

MS—Master of Science in Business Administration Full-time. 3-5 years of work experience required. Minimum of 12 months to complete program. *Concentrations:* decision sciences, human resources management, information management, international business, management, management information systems, management science, marketing, operations management, organizational behavior/development, production management, strategic management.

MSA—MS—Accountancy Full-time. Minimum of 12 months to complete program. *Concentration:* accounting.

MSF Full-time. *Concentration:* finance.

MST—MS—Tax Full-time. Minimum of 12 months to complete program. *Concentrations:* accounting, taxation.

RESOURCES AND SERVICES Access to Internet/World Wide Web, online (class) registration, and online grade reports available. *Personal computer requirements:* Graduate business students are required to have a personal computer. *Special opportunities include:* An international exchange program and an internship program are available. *Placement services include:* Alumni network, career placement, job search course, career counseling/planning, electronic job bank, resume referral, career fairs, job interviews arranged, resume preparation, and career library.

EXPENSES *Tuition (state resident):* Full-time: $17,500. Part-time: $17,875 per year. *Tuition (nonresident):* Full-time: $26,500. *Tuition (international):* Full-time: $26,500. *Required fees:* Full-time: $2410. Tuition and/or fees vary by class time, number of courses or credits taken, campus location, and academic program. *Graduate housing:* Room and board costs vary by campus location, number of occupants, type of accommodation, and type of board plan. *Typical cost:* $14,196 (including board).

FINANCIAL AID (2007–08) 41 students received aid, including loans, scholarships, and work study. Aid is available to part-time students. *Financial aid application deadline:* 3/15.

Financial Aid Contact Dan Mann, Director of Student Financial Aid, 620 East John Street, MC 303, Champaign, IL 61820. *Phone:* 217-244-2024. *E-mail:* danmann@uiuc.edu.

INTERNATIONAL STUDENTS 43% of students enrolled are international students. *Services and facilities:* Counseling/support services, ESL/language courses, Housing location assistance, International student housing, International student organization, Language tutoring, Orientation, Visa Services. Financial aid is available to international students. *Required with application:* TOEFL; proof of adequate funds; proof of health/immunizations.

International Student Contact Jaquilin J. Wilson, Director of MBA Admissions, 1407 West Gregory Drive, 405 David Kinley Hall, MC 706, Urbana, IL 61801. *Phone:* 217-244-2953. *Fax:* 217-333-1156. *E-mail:* jjwilson@uiuc.edu.

APPLICATION *Required:* GMAT, application form, baccalaureate/first degree, essay, 3 letters of recommendation, resume/curriculum vitae, transcripts of college work. *Recommended:* Interview, work experience. *Application fee:* $60, $75 (international). Applications for domestic and international students are processed on a rolling basis.

Application Contact Jaquilin J. Wilson, Director of MBA Admissions, 1407 West Gregory Drive, 405 David Kinley Hall, MC 706, Urbana, IL 61801. *Phone:* 217-244-2953. *Fax:* 217-333-1156. *E-mail:* jjwilson@uiuc.edu.

University of Phoenix–Chicago Campus
College of Graduate Business and Management

Schaumburg, Illinois

Phone: 480-371-6200 **Fax:** 480-643-1479 **E-mail:** beth.barilla@phoenix.edu

DEGREES M Mgt • MA • MBA

M Mgt—Master of Management Full-time. Up to 39 total credits required. *Concentration:* management.

MA—Master of Arts in Organizational Management Full-time. At least 40 total credits required. *Concentration:* organizational management.

MBA—Master of Business Administration Full-time. At least 45 total credits required. *Concentration:* administration.

MBA—Master of Business Administration in Global Management Full-time. At least 45 total credits required. *Concentration:* international business.

MBA—Master of Business Administration in e-Business Full-time. At least 45 total credits required. *Concentration:* electronic commerce (E-commerce).

MBA—Master of Business Administration/Human Resource Management Full-time. Up to 45 total credits required. *Concentration:* human resources management.

RESOURCES AND SERVICES Access to online grade reports available. *Personal computer requirements:* Graduate business students are strongly recommended to purchase or lease a personal computer. *Placement services include:* Alumni network.

Application Contact Beth Barilla, Associate Vice President of Student Admissions and Services, Mail Stop AA-K101, 4615 East Elwood Street, Phoenix, AZ 85040-1958. *Phone:* 480-371-6200. *Fax:* 480-643-1479. *E-mail:* beth.barilla@phoenix.edu.

University of St. Francis
College of Business

Joliet, Illinois

Phone: 800-735-7500 **Fax:** 815-740-5032 **E-mail:** ssloka@stfrancis.edu

Business Program(s) Web Site: http://www.stfrancis.edu/cob

Graduate Business Unit Enrollment *Total:* 158 (35 full-time; 123 part-time; 96 women). *Average Age:* 38.

Graduate Business Faculty *Total:* 14 (6 full-time; 8 part-time).

Admissions *Applied:* 84. *Admitted:* 60. *Enrolled:* 46. *Average GPA:* 3.48

Academic Calendar Semesters.

After Graduation (Class of 2006–07) *Employed within 3 months of graduation:* 100%.

DEGREES MBA • MS

MBA—Master of Business Administration Full-time and part-time. Distance learning option. 2 years of management experience or GMAT required. 36 to 48 total credits required. 12 to 96 months to complete program. *Concentrations:* health care, management, organizational behavior/development.

MS—Master of Science in Management Full-time and part-time. Distance learning option. 2 years of management experience required. 36 total credits required. 12 to 96 months to complete program. *Concentrations:* health care, management, organizational behavior/ development.

University of St. Francis (continued)

RESOURCES AND SERVICES 365 on-campus PCs are available to graduate business students. Access to Internet/World Wide Web, online (class) registration, and online grade reports available. *Personal computer requirements:* Graduate business students are strongly recommended to purchase or lease a personal computer. *Special opportunities include:* An internship program is available. *Placement services include:* Alumni network, career counseling/planning, electronic job bank, resume referral, career fairs, job interviews arranged, resume preparation, and career library.

EXPENSES *Tuition:* Part-time: $670 per credit. *Tuition (international):* Part-time: $670 per credit. Tuition and/or fees vary by academic program. *Graduate housing:* Room and board costs vary by number of occupants, type of accommodation, and type of board plan. *Typical cost:* $7610 (including board).

FINANCIAL AID (2007–08) 76 students received aid, including scholarships. Aid is available to part-time students.

Financial Aid Contact Ms. Mary Shaw, Director, Financial Aid Services, 500 Wilcox Street, Joliet, IL 60435. *Phone:* 866-890-8331. *Fax:* 815-740-3822. *E-mail:* mshaw@stfrancis.edu.

INTERNATIONAL STUDENTS *Services and facilities:* Counseling/support services, Housing location assistance. Financial aid is not available to international students. *Required with application:* TOEFL with recommended score of 213 (computer) or 550 (paper); proof of adequate funds; proof of health/immunizations.

International Student Contact Ms. Sandi Miller, Registrar, 500 Wilcox Street, Joliet, IL 60435. *Phone:* 815-740-5040. *Fax:* 815-740-5084. *E-mail:* smiller@stfrancis.edu.

APPLICATION *Required:* Application form, baccalaureate/first degree, essay, 2 letters of recommendation, personal statement, transcripts of college work, 2 years of work experience. *Application fee:* $30. Applications for domestic and international students are processed on a rolling basis.

Application Contact Ms. Sandra Sloka, Director, Graduate/Degree Completion Admissions, 500 Wilcox Street, Joliet, IL 60435. *Phone:* 800-735-7500. *Fax:* 815-740-5032. *E-mail:* ssloka@stfrancis.edu.

Western Illinois University
College of Business and Technology

Macomb, Illinois

Phone: 309-298-2442 **Fax:** 309-298-1039 **E-mail:** lc-wall@wiu.edu

Business Program(s) Web Site: http://www.wiu.edu/

Graduate Business Unit Enrollment *Total:* 105 (50 full-time; 55 part-time; 48 women; 14 international).

Graduate Business Faculty 80 full-time.

Admissions *Applied:* 79. *Admitted:* 65. *Enrolled:* 48. *Average GMAT:* 530. *Average GPA:* 3.28

Academic Calendar Semesters.

Accreditation AACSB—The Association to Advance Collegiate Schools of Business.

After Graduation (Class of 2006–07) *Employed within 3 months of graduation:* 28%.

DEGREE MBA

MBA—Master of Business Administration Full-time and part-time. 33 to 60 total credits required. 12 to 24 months to complete program. *Concentrations:* accounting, agribusiness, economics, finance, information management, international business, management, marketing, statistics, supply chain management, taxation.

RESOURCES AND SERVICES 600 on-campus PCs are available to graduate business students. Access to Internet/World Wide Web, online (class) registration, and online grade reports available. *Personal computer*

requirements: Graduate business students are strongly recommended to purchase or lease a personal computer. *Special opportunities include:* An international exchange program and an internship program are available. *Placement services include:* Alumni network, career placement, career counseling/planning, electronic job bank, resume referral, career fairs, job interviews arranged, and career library.

EXPENSES *Tuition (state resident):* Full-time: $6500. Part-time: $270.97 per credit hour. *Tuition (nonresident):* Full-time: $11,700. Part-time: $487.67 per credit hour. *Tuition (international):* Full-time: $11,700. *Graduate housing:* Room and board costs vary by number of occupants and type of board plan. *Typical cost:* $6898 (including board), $4148 (room only).

FINANCIAL AID (2007–08) 23 students received aid, including loans, research assistantships, and scholarships. *Financial aid application deadline:* 3/31.

Financial Aid Contact Mr. William Bushaw, Director of Financial Aid, 1 University Circle, Macomb, IL 61455-1390. *Phone:* 309-298-2446. *Fax:* 309-298-2353.

INTERNATIONAL STUDENTS 13% of students enrolled are international students. *Services and facilities:* Counseling/support services, ESL/language courses, Housing location assistance, International student housing, International student organization, Orientation, Visa Services. Financial aid is not available to international students. *Required with application:* TOEFL with recommended score of 550 (paper); proof of adequate funds; proof of health/immunizations.

International Student Contact Ms. Jeanette Zotz, Director of International Admissions, School of Graduate and International Studies, 1 University Circle, Macomb, IL 61455-1309. *Phone:* 309-298-2501. *E-mail:* jy-zotz@wiu.edu.

APPLICATION *Required:* GMAT, application form, baccalaureate/first degree, transcripts of college work. *Application fee:* $30. Applications for domestic and international students are processed on a rolling basis.

Application Contact Dr. Larry C. Wall, Director of MBA Program, 1 University Circle, Macomb, IL 61455-1390. *Phone:* 309-298-2442. *Fax:* 309-298-1039. *E-mail:* lc-wall@wiu.edu.

INDIANA

Anderson University
Falls School of Business

Anderson, Indiana

Phone: 765-641-4188 **Fax:** 765-641-4356 **E-mail:** mba@anderson.edu

Business Program(s) Web Site: http://www.anderson.edu/mba

Graduate Business Unit Enrollment *Total:* 349 (323 full-time; 26 part-time). *Average Age:* 32.

Graduate Business Faculty *Total:* 27 (20 full-time; 7 part-time).

Academic Calendar Trimesters.

Accreditation ACBSP—The American Council of Business Schools and Programs.

DEGREE MBA

MBA—Master of Business Administration Full-time and part-time. 37 total credits required. 22 to 29 months to complete program. *Concentration:* general MBA.

RESOURCES AND SERVICES 15 on-campus PCs are available to graduate business students. Access to Internet/World Wide Web and online grade reports available. *Personal computer requirements:* Graduate business students are required to have a personal computer. *Placement*

services include: Alumni network, career placement, career counseling/planning, electronic job bank, and resume preparation.

FINANCIAL AID (2007–08) Loans.

Financial Aid Contact Kenneth Nieman, Student Financial Services Director, 1100 East Fifth Street, Anderson, IN 46012. *Phone:* 765-641-4182. *Fax:* 765-641-3831. *E-mail:* kfnieman@anderson.edu.

INTERNATIONAL STUDENTS *Services and facilities:* Counseling/support services, Housing location assistance, International student organization, Orientation, Visa Services. Financial aid is not available to international students. *Required with application:* TOEFL; proof of adequate funds; proof of health/immunizations.

International Student Contact Dr. Jeffrey M. Buck, MBA Programs Director, 1303 East Fifth Street, Anderson, IN 46012. *Phone:* 765-641-4188. *Fax:* 765-641-4356. *E-mail:* mba@anderson.edu.

APPLICATION *Required:* GMAT, application form, baccalaureate/first degree, 3 letters of recommendation, transcripts of college work, 2 years of work experience. *Recommended:* Interview, resume/curriculum vitae. *Application fee:* $30. Applications for domestic and international students are processed on a rolling basis.

Application Contact Dr. Jeffrey M. Buck, MBA Programs Director, 1303 East Fifth Street, Anderson, IN 46012. *Phone:* 765-641-4188. *Fax:* 765-641-4356. *E-mail:* mba@anderson.edu.

Ball State University
Miller College of Business
Muncie, Indiana

Phone: 765-285-5329 **Fax:** 765-285-8818 **E-mail:** mba@bsu.edu

Business Program(s) Web Site: http://www.bsu.edu/mba

Graduate Business Unit Enrollment *Total:* 153 (48 full-time; 105 part-time; 42 women; 10 international). *Average Age:* 29.

Graduate Business Faculty 28 full-time.

Admissions *Applied:* 120. *Admitted:* 69. *Enrolled:* 58. *Average GMAT:* 534. *Average GPA:* 3.34

Academic Calendar Semesters.

Accreditation AACSB—The Association to Advance Collegiate Schools of Business.

DEGREE MBA

MBA—Master of Business Administration Full-time and part-time. Distance learning option. At least 30 total credits required. 12 to 72 months to complete program. *Concentrations:* entrepreneurship, finance, general MBA, operations management.

RESOURCES AND SERVICES 600 on-campus PCs are available to graduate business students. Access to Internet/World Wide Web, online (class) registration, and online grade reports available. *Personal computer requirements:* Graduate business students are not required to have a personal computer. *Special opportunities include:* An internship program is available. *Placement services include:* Alumni network, career placement, career counseling/planning, electronic job bank, resume referral, career fairs, job interviews arranged, resume preparation, and career library.

EXPENSES *Tuition (state resident):* Full-time: $8920. Part-time: $315 per credit hour. *Tuition (nonresident):* Full-time: $22,302. Part-time: $583 per credit hour. *Required fees:* Full-time: $679.

FINANCIAL AID (2007–08) Loans, research assistantships, and scholarships. Aid is available to part-time students. *Financial aid application deadline:* 3/1.

Financial Aid Contact Robert M. Zellers, Director of Scholarships and Financial Aid, Scholarships and Financial Aid, LU 245, Muncie, IN 47306. *Phone:* 765-285-5600. *Fax:* 765-285-2464. *E-mail:* finaid@bsu.edu.

INTERNATIONAL STUDENTS 7% of students enrolled are international students. *Services and facilities:* Counseling/support services, ESL/language courses, Housing location assistance, International student organization, Orientation, Visa Services. Financial aid is available to international students. *Required with application:* TOEFL with recommended score of 213 (computer) or 550 (paper); proof of adequate funds; proof of health/immunizations.

International Student Contact Vicki Villarreal, International Admissions Administrator, Student Center, Room 105, Muncie, IN 47306. *Phone:* 765-285-5422. *Fax:* 765-285-3710. *E-mail:* intadmit@bsu.edu.

APPLICATION *Required:* GMAT, application form, baccalaureate/first degree, resume/curriculum vitae, transcripts of college work. *Recommended:* Personal statement. *Application fee:* $35, $40 (international). Applications for domestic and international students are processed on a rolling basis.

Application Contact Dr. Gayle Hartleroad, Director, Student Services, WB 147, Muncie, IN 47306. *Phone:* 765-285-5329. *Fax:* 765-285-8818. *E-mail:* mba@bsu.edu.

Bethel College
Program in Business Administration
Mishawaka, Indiana

Phone: 574-257-3363 **Fax:** 574-257-7616 **E-mail:** smithb@bethelcollege.edu

Business Program(s) Web Site: http://www.bethelcollege.edu/academics/graduate/mba/

Graduate Business Unit Enrollment *Total:* 46 (4 full-time; 42 part-time; 22 women). *Average Age:* 40.

Graduate Business Faculty *Total:* 9 (6 full-time; 3 part-time).

Admissions *Applied:* 40. *Admitted:* 24. *Enrolled:* 17. *Average GMAT:* 450. *Average GPA:* 3.34

Academic Calendar Modules.

DEGREE MBA

MBA—Master of Business Administration Full-time and part-time. At least 36 total credits required. 24 to 48 months to complete program. *Concentration:* management.

RESOURCES AND SERVICES 40 on-campus PCs are available to graduate business students. Access to Internet/World Wide Web and online grade reports available. *Personal computer requirements:* Graduate business students are strongly recommended to purchase or lease a personal computer. *Placement services include:* Alumni network, career counseling/planning, and resume preparation.

EXPENSES *Tuition:* Part-time: $340 per credit hour. *Tuition (international):* Part-time: $340 per credit hour.

FINANCIAL AID (2007–08) Loans, research assistantships, and work study. Aid is available to part-time students.

Financial Aid Contact Mr. Guy Fisher, Director of Financial Aid, 1001 West McKinley Avenue, Mishawaka, IN 46545-5591. *Phone:* 574-257-3317. *Fax:* 574-257-3326. *E-mail:* fisherg@bethelcollege.edu.

INTERNATIONAL STUDENTS *Services and facilities:* Counseling/support services, Visa Services. Financial aid is not available to international students. *Required with application:* TOEFL with recommended score of 207 (computer) or 540 (paper); proof of adequate funds; proof of health/immunizations.

International Student Contact Ms. Krista Wong, Director of Admissions, 1001 West McKinley Avenue, Mishawaka, IN 46545-5591. *Phone:* 574-257-3323. *Fax:* 574-257-3335. *E-mail:* wongk@bethelcollege.edu.

APPLICATION *Required:* GMAT, application form, baccalaureate/first degree, interview, personal statement, transcripts of college work, 2 years of work experience. School will accept GRE. *Application fee:* $25.

Bethel College (continued)

Deadlines: 5/1 for fall (international), 10/1 for spring (international). Applications for domestic students are processed on a rolling basis.

Application Contact Dr. Bradley Smith, Graduate Dean/Director of MBA Program, 1001 West McKinley Avenue, Mishawaka, IN 46545-5591. *Phone:* 574-257-3363. *Fax:* 574-257-7616. *E-mail:* smithb@bethelcollege.edu.

Butler University
College of Business Administration
Indianapolis, Indiana

Phone: 888-940-8100 **Fax:** 317-940-8150 **E-mail:** admissions@butler.edu

Business Program(s) Web Site: http://www.butler.edu/mba

Graduate Business Unit Enrollment *Total:* 217 (40 full-time; 177 part-time; 81 women; 23 international). *Average Age:* 30.

Graduate Business Faculty *Total:* 23 (13 full-time; 10 part-time).

Admissions *Applied:* 94. *Admitted:* 81. *Enrolled:* 55. *Average GMAT:* 570. *Average GPA:* 3.3

Academic Calendar Semesters.

Accreditation AACSB—The Association to Advance Collegiate Schools of Business.

After Graduation (Class of 2006–07) *Employed within 3 months of graduation:* 95%.

DEGREES M Acc • MBA

M Acc—Master of Professional Accountancy Full-time and part-time. 30 total credits required. 12 to 60 months to complete program. *Concentration:* accounting.

MBA—Master of Business Administration Full-time and part-time. 33 to 34 total credits required. 12 to 60 months to complete program. *Concentrations:* finance, international business, leadership, marketing.

RESOURCES AND SERVICES 125 on-campus PCs are available to graduate business students. Access to Internet/World Wide Web, online (class) registration, and online grade reports available. *Personal computer requirements:* Graduate business students are not required to have a personal computer. *Placement services include:* Alumni network, career counseling/planning, electronic job bank, resume referral, resume preparation, and career library.

EXPENSES *Tuition:* Full-time: $11,000. Part-time: $500 per credit hour. *Tuition (international):* Full-time: $11,000. Part-time: $500 per credit hour. *Required fees:* Full-time: $470. Tuition and/or fees vary by class time, number of courses or credits taken, and academic program. *Graduate housing:* Room and board costs vary by number of occupants, type of accommodation, and type of board plan. *Typical cost:* $8960 (including board), $5860 (room only).

FINANCIAL AID (2007–08) 33 students received aid, including loans. Aid is available to part-time students. *Financial aid application deadline:* 3/1.

Financial Aid Contact Richard Bellows, Executive Director, Office of Financial Aid, 4600 Sunset Avenue, Indianapolis, IN 46208-3485. *Phone:* 877-940-8200. *Fax:* 317-940-8250. *E-mail:* finaid@butler.edu.

INTERNATIONAL STUDENTS 11% of students enrolled are international students. *Services and facilities:* Counseling/support services, Housing location assistance, Visa Services. Financial aid is available to international students. *Required with application:* TOEFL with recommended score of 213 (computer) or 550 (paper); proof of adequate funds; proof of health/immunizations.

International Student Contact Jerry Dueweke, Assistant Director, International Admissions, 4600 Sunset Avenue, Indianapolis, IN 46208-3185. *Phone:* 888-940-8100. *Fax:* 317-940-8150. *E-mail:* intadmission@butler.edu.

APPLICATION *Required:* GMAT, application form, baccalaureate/first degree, 2 letters of recommendation, resume/curriculum vitae, transcripts of college work. *Recommended:* Personal statement, 3 years of work experience. *Application fee:* $35. Applications for domestic and international students are processed on a rolling basis.

Application Contact Pam Bender, Graduate Admissions Office, 4600 Sunset Avenue, Indianapolis, IN 46208-3485. *Phone:* 888-940-8100. *Fax:* 317-940-8150. *E-mail:* admissions@butler.edu.

DeVry University
Keller Graduate School of Management
Indianapolis, Indiana

Phone: 317-581-8854

DEGREES MAFM • MBA • MHRM • MIS • MPA • MPM

MAFM—Master of Accounting and Financial Management Full-time and part-time. Distance learning option. At least 44 total credits required. 18 to 60 months to complete program. *Concentrations:* accounting, financial management/planning.

MBA—Master of Business Administration Full-time and part-time. Distance learning option. At least 48 total credits required. 18 to 60 months to complete program. *Concentration:* management.

MHRM—Master of Human Resources Management Full-time and part-time. Distance learning option. At least 45 total credits required. 18 to 60 months to complete program. *Concentration:* human resources management.

MIS—Master of Information Systems Management Full-time and part-time. Distance learning option. At least 45 total credits required. 18 to 60 months to complete program. *Concentration:* information systems.

MPA—Master of Public Administration Full-time and part-time. Distance learning option. At least 45 total credits required. 18 to 60 months to complete program. *Concentration:* public policy and administration.

MPM—Master of Project Management Full-time and part-time. Distance learning option. At least 42 total credits required. 18 to 60 months to complete program. *Concentration:* project management.

Application Contact Admissions Office, Indianapolis Center, 9100 Keystone Crossing, Suite 350, Indianapolis, IN 46240. *Phone:* 317-581-8854.

DeVry University
Keller Graduate School of Management
Merrillville, Indiana

Phone: 219-736-7440

DEGREES MAFM • MBA • MHRM • MIS • MPA • MPM

MAFM—Master of Accounting and Financial Management Full-time and part-time. Distance learning option. At least 44 total credits required. 18 to 60 months to complete program. *Concentrations:* accounting, financial management/planning.

MBA—Master of Business Administration Full-time and part-time. Distance learning option. At least 48 total credits required. 18 to 60 months to complete program. *Concentration:* management.

MHRM—Master of Human Resources Management Full-time and part-time. Distance learning option. At least 45 total credits required. 18 to 60 months to complete program. *Concentration:* human resources management.

MIS—Master of Information Systems Management Full-time and part-time. Distance learning option. At least 45 total credits required. 18 to 60 months to complete program. *Concentration:* information systems.

MPA—Master of Public Administration Full-time and part-time. Distance learning option. At least 45 total credits required. 18 to 60 months to complete program. *Concentration:* public policy and administration.

MPM—Master of Project Management Full-time and part-time. Distance learning option. At least 42 total credits required. 18 to 60 months to complete program. *Concentration:* project management.

Application Contact Admissions Office, Merrillville Center Twin Towers, 1000 East 80th Place, Suite 222 Mall, Merrillville, IN 46410. *Phone:* 219-736-7440.

Indiana State University
College of Business

Terre Haute, Indiana

Phone: 812-237-2002 **Fax:** 812-237-8720 **E-mail:** mba@indstate.edu

Business Program(s) Web Site: http://web.indstate.edu/schbus/mba.html

Graduate Business Unit Enrollment *Total:* 55 (51 full-time; 4 part-time; 15 women; 35 international). *Average Age:* 27.

Graduate Business Faculty *Total:* 32 (30 full-time; 2 part-time).

Admissions *Average GMAT:* 530. *Average GPA:* 3.1

Academic Calendar Trimesters.

Accreditation AACSB—The Association to Advance Collegiate Schools of Business.

After Graduation (Class of 2006–07) *Employed within 3 months of graduation:* 90%. *Average starting salary:* $42,000.

DEGREE MBA

MBA—Master of Business Administration Full-time and part-time. Satisfactory GMAT scores. 33 to 62 total credits required. 18 to 60 months to complete program. *Concentrations:* accounting, electronic commerce (E-commerce), financial management/planning.

RESOURCES AND SERVICES 400 on-campus PCs are available to graduate business students. Access to Internet/World Wide Web, online (class) registration, and online grade reports available. *Personal computer requirements:* Graduate business students are required to have a personal computer. *Placement services include:* Career counseling/planning, career fairs, job interviews arranged, resume preparation, and career library.

EXPENSES *Tuition (state resident):* Part-time: $294 per credit hour. *Tuition (nonresident):* Part-time: $584 per credit hour. *Tuition (international):* Part-time: $584 per credit hour. *Required fees:* Part-time: $100 per semester.

FINANCIAL AID (2007–08) 25 students received aid, including fellowships, research assistantships, and scholarships. *Financial aid application deadline:* 4/1.

Financial Aid Contact Dale Varble, Associate Dean and Director, MBA Program, Terre Haute, IN 47809-5402. *Phone:* 812-237-2002. *Fax:* 812-237-8720. *E-mail:* mba@indstate.edu.

INTERNATIONAL STUDENTS 64% of students enrolled are international students. *Services and facilities:* Counseling/support services, ESL/language courses, Housing location assistance, International student organization, Language tutoring, Orientation, Visa Services, Academic advising. Financial aid is available to international students. *Required with application:* TOEFL with recommended score of 213 (computer) or 550 (paper); proof of adequate funds; proof of health/immunizations.

International Student Contact El-Houcin Chaqra, Associate Director, International Student and Scholar Services, Erickson Hall 617, Terre Haute, IN 47809-1401. *Phone:* 812-237-2440. *Fax:* 812-237-3085. *E-mail:* iac@indstate.edu.

APPLICATION *Required:* GMAT, application form, baccalaureate/first degree, personal statement, transcripts of college work. School will accept GRE. *Recommended:* 3 letters of recommendation, work experience. *Application fee:* $35. Applications for domestic and international students are processed on a rolling basis.

Application Contact Dale Varble, Associate Dean and Director, MBA Program, Terre Haute, IN 47809-5402. *Phone:* 812-237-2002. *Fax:* 812-237-8720. *E-mail:* mba@indstate.edu.

Indiana Tech
Program in Business Administration

Fort Wayne, Indiana

Phone: 260-422-5561 Ext. 2278 **Fax:** 260-422-1518 **E-mail:** slbradley@indianatech.edu

Business Program(s) Web Site: http://www.indianatech.edu/

Graduate Business Unit Enrollment *Total:* 305 (178 full-time; 127 part-time; 145 women). *Average Age:* 36.

Graduate Business Faculty *Total:* 41 (10 full-time; 31 part-time).

Academic Calendar Continuous.

DEGREES MBA • MSM

MBA—Master of Business Administration Full-time and part-time. 39 to 45 total credits required. 12 to 24 months to complete program. *Concentrations:* accounting, human resources management, management, marketing.

MSM—Master of Science in Management Full-time and part-time. 36 to 45 total credits required. 12 to 18 months to complete program. *Concentration:* management.

RESOURCES AND SERVICES 330 on-campus PCs are available to graduate business students. Access to Internet/World Wide Web, online (class) registration, and online grade reports available. *Personal computer requirements:* Graduate business students are strongly recommended to purchase or lease a personal computer. *Placement services include:* Alumni network, career placement, career counseling/planning, electronic job bank, resume referral, career fairs, and resume preparation.

EXPENSES *Tuition:* Full-time: $7020. Part-time: $390 per credit hour. *Tuition (international):* Full-time: $7020. Part-time: $390 per credit hour.

FINANCIAL AID (2007–08) 228 students received aid, including loans. *Financial aid application deadline:* 3/10.

Financial Aid Contact Ms. Teresa Vasquez, Director of Financial Aid, 1600 East Washington Boulevard, Fort Wayne, IN 46803. *Phone:* 260-422-5561 Ext. 2208. *Fax:* 260-422-1578. *E-mail:* tmvasquez@indianatech.edu.

INTERNATIONAL STUDENTS *Services and facilities:* Counseling/support services, Housing location assistance, International student organization, Visa Services. Financial aid is not available to international students. *Required with application:* TOEFL with recommended score of 213 (computer) or 550 (paper); proof of adequate funds.

International Student Contact Mr. Yiani Demitsas, Admissions Counselor, 1600 East Washington Boulevard, Fort Wayne, IN 46803. *Phone:* 260-422-5561 Ext. 2261. *Fax:* 260-422-1518. *E-mail:* ydemitsas@indianatech.edu.

APPLICATION *Required:* Application form, baccalaureate/first degree, 3 letters of recommendation, personal statement, transcripts of college work, 2 years of work experience. *Recommended:* Resume/curriculum vitae. *Application fee:* $25, $35 (international). *Deadlines:* 9/3 for fall (international), 1/8 for spring (international), 6/11 for summer (international). Applications for domestic students are processed on a rolling basis.

Application Contact Ms. Sandra Bradley, Campus Director-Fort Wayne, College of Professional Studies, 1600 East Washington Boulevard, Fort Wayne, IN 46803. *Phone:* 260-422-5561 Ext. 2278. *Fax:* 260-422-1518. *E-mail:* slbradley@indianatech.edu.

Indiana University Bloomington

Kelley School of Business

Bloomington, Indiana

Phone: 812-855-8006 **Fax:** 812-855-9039 **E-mail:** mbaoffice@indiana.edu

Business Program(s) Web Site: http://kelley.iu.edu/ksb_global/

Graduate Business Unit Enrollment *Total:* 444 (444 full-time; 120 women; 178 international). *Average Age:* 28.

Graduate Business Faculty *Total:* 218 (204 full-time; 14 part-time).

Admissions *Applied:* 1,227. *Admitted:* 422. *Enrolled:* 236. *Average GMAT:* 656. *Average GPA:* 3.37

Academic Calendar Semesters.

Accreditation AACSB—The Association to Advance Collegiate Schools of Business.

After Graduation (Class of 2006–07) *Employed within 3 months of graduation:* 96%. *Average starting salary:* $88,644.

DEGREES JD/MBA • MBA • MBA/MA • MBA/MS

JD/MBA—Juris Doctor/Master of Business Administration Full-time. At least 121 total credits required. 48 to 84 months to complete program. *Concentrations:* accounting, entrepreneurship, finance, management, marketing, operations management, supply chain management.

MBA—Master of Business Administration Full-time. At least 54 total credits required. 18 to 84 months to complete program. *Concentrations:* accounting, entrepreneurship, finance, management, marketing, operations management, supply chain management.

MBA/MA—Master of Business Administration/Master of Arts in Telecommunications Full-time. At least 69 total credits required. 36 to 84 months to complete program. *Concentrations:* accounting, entrepreneurship, finance, management, marketing, operations management, supply chain management.

MBA/MS—Master of Business Administration/Master of Science in East Asian Studies Full-time. At least 66 total credits required. 36 to 84 months to complete program. *Concentrations:* accounting, entrepreneurship, finance, management, marketing, operations management, supply chain management.

MBA/MS—Master of Business Administration/Master of Science in Latin American and Caribbean Studies Full-time. At least 66 total credits required. 36 to 84 months to complete program. *Concentrations:* accounting, entrepreneurship, finance, management, marketing, operations management, supply chain management.

MBA/MS—Master of Business Administration/Master of Science in Russian and East European Studies Full-time. At least 66 total credits required. 36 to 84 months to complete program. *Concentrations:* accounting, entrepreneurship, finance, management, marketing, operations management, supply chain management.

MBA/MS—Master of Business Administration/Master of Science in Telecommunications Full-time. At least 75 total credits required. 36 to 84 months to complete program. *Concentrations:* accounting, entrepreneurship, finance, management, marketing, operations management, supply chain management.

MBA/MS—Master of Business Administration/Master of Science in West European Studies Full-time. At least 66 total credits required. 36 to 84 months to complete program. *Concentrations:* accounting, entrepreneurship, finance, management, marketing, operations management, supply chain management.

RESOURCES AND SERVICES 280 on-campus PCs are available to graduate business students. Access to Internet/World Wide Web, online (class) registration, and online grade reports available. *Personal computer requirements:* Graduate business students are required to have a personal computer. *Special opportunities include:* An international exchange program is available. *Placement services include:* Alumni network, career placement, job search course, career counseling/planning, electronic job bank, resume referral, career fairs, job interviews arranged, resume preparation, and career library.

EXPENSES *Tuition (state resident):* Full-time: $16,796. *Tuition (nonresident):* Full-time: $33,414. *Tuition (international):* Full-time: $33,414. *Required fees:* Full-time: $1437. *Graduate housing:* Room and board costs vary by number of occupants, type of accommodation, and type of board plan. *Typical cost:* $9150 (including board), $5850 (room only).

FINANCIAL AID (2007–08) 420 students received aid, including fellowships, loans, research assistantships, scholarships, and teaching assistantships. *Financial aid application deadline:* 3/1.

Financial Aid Contact Tim Smith, Senior Associate Director of Admissions and Financial Aid, MBA Program, Graduate and Executive Education Center, Room 2010, 1275 East Tenth Street, Bloomington, IN 47405. *Phone:* 812-855-8006. *Fax:* 812-855-9039. *E-mail:* smithtim@indiana.edu.

INTERNATIONAL STUDENTS 40% of students enrolled are international students. *Services and facilities:* Counseling/support services, ESL/language courses, Housing location assistance, International student housing, International student organization, Language tutoring, Orientation, Visa Services. Financial aid is available to international students. *Required with application:* TOEFL with recommended score of 250 (computer), 600 (paper), or 100 (Internet); proof of adequate funds; proof of health/immunizations.

International Student Contact Amanda Bannon, Assistant Director of Graduate Student Services, MBA Program, Graduate and Executive Education Center, Room 2010, 1275 East Tenth Street, Bloomington, IN 47405. *Phone:* 812-855-8006. *Fax:* 812-855-9039. *E-mail:* abannon@indiana.edu.

APPLICATION *Required:* GMAT, application form, baccalaureate/first degree, essay, 2 letters of recommendation, personal statement, resume/curriculum vitae, transcripts of college work. *Recommended:* Interview, work experience. *Application fee:* $75. *Deadlines:* 4/15 for fall, 1/15 for fall (international).

Application Contact James Holmen, Director of Admissions and Financial Aid, MBA Program, Graduate and Executive Education Center, Room 2010, 1275 East Tenth Street, Bloomington, IN 47405. *Phone:* 812-855-8006. *Fax:* 812-855-9039. *E-mail:* mbaoffice@indiana.edu.

Indiana University Kokomo

School of Business

Kokomo, Indiana

Phone: 765-455-9471 **Fax:** 765-455-9348 **E-mail:** lficht@iuk.edu

Business Program(s) Web Site: http://www.iuk.edu/majors/mba.shtml

Graduate Business Unit Enrollment *Total:* 53 (11 full-time; 42 part-time; 18 women; 5 international). *Average Age:* 37.

Graduate Business Faculty 14 full-time.

Admissions *Applied:* 21. *Admitted:* 21. *Enrolled:* 17. *Average GMAT:* 506. *Average GPA:* 3.1

Academic Calendar Semesters.

Accreditation AACSB—The Association to Advance Collegiate Schools of Business.

DEGREE MBA

MBA—Master of Business Administration Full-time and part-time. 30 to 54 total credits required. 12 to 72 months to complete program. *Concentration:* management.

RESOURCES AND SERVICES 50 on-campus PCs are available to graduate business students. Access to Internet/World Wide Web, online (class) registration, and online grade reports available. *Personal computer requirements:* Graduate business students are not required to have a personal computer. *Special opportunities include:* An international

---

exchange program is available. *Placement services include:* Alumni network, career placement, resume referral, resume preparation, and career library.

EXPENSES *Tuition (state resident):* Full-time: $8124. Part-time: $270.80 per credit hour. *Tuition (nonresident):* Full-time: $18,258. Part-time: $608.60 per credit hour. *Tuition (international):* Full-time: $18,258. Part-time: $608.60 per credit hour. *Required fees:* Full-time: $261.15. Part-time: $140.55 per year. Tuition and/or fees vary by number of courses or credits taken and academic program.

FINANCIAL AID (2007–08) 4 students received aid, including grants and scholarships. Aid is available to part-time students. *Financial aid application deadline:* 3/31.

Financial Aid Contact Mr. David Campbell, Director, Financial Aid, 2300 South Washington, PO Box 9003, Kokomo, IN 46904-9003. *Phone:* 765-455-9216. *Fax:* 765-455-9537. *E-mail:* dcampbel@iuk.edu.

INTERNATIONAL STUDENTS 9% of students enrolled are international students. *Services and facilities:* Counseling/support services, Visa Services. Financial aid is not available to international students. *Required with application:* TOEFL with recommended score of 213 (computer), 550 (paper), or 80 (Internet); proof of adequate funds; proof of health/immunizations.

International Student Contact Dr. Christopher Viers, Associate Vice President for International Services, Franklin Hall 306, 601 East Kirkwood Avenue, Bloomington, IN 47405. *Phone:* 812-855-9086. *Fax:* 812-855-4418. *E-mail:* intlserv@indiana.edu.

APPLICATION *Required:* GMAT, application form, baccalaureate/first degree, essay, personal statement, transcripts of college work. *Application fee:* $40, $60 (international). Applications for domestic and international students are processed on a rolling basis.

Application Contact Dr. Linda S. Ficht, Assistant Dean/MBA Director/Assistant Professor of Business Law, 2300 South Washington, PO Box 9003, Kokomo, IN 46904-9003. *Phone:* 765-455-9471. *Fax:* 765-455-9348. *E-mail:* lficht@iuk.edu.

Indiana University Northwest
School of Business and Economics

Gary, Indiana

Phone: 219-980-6635 **Fax:** 219-980-6916 **E-mail:** jagibson@iun.edu

Business Program(s) Web Site: http://www.iun.edu/~busnw/

Graduate Business Unit Enrollment *Total:* 130 (130 part-time; 70 women). *Average Age:* 34.

Graduate Business Faculty 17 full-time.

Admissions *Average GMAT:* 490. *Average GPA:* 3.1

Academic Calendar Semesters.

Accreditation AACSB—The Association to Advance Collegiate Schools of Business.

After Graduation (Class of 2006–07) *Employed within 3 months of graduation:* 100%. *Average starting salary:* $45,000.

DEGREES MBA

MBA—Fast-Track Master of Business Administration Full-time and part-time. 30 to 45 total credits required. 30 to 45 months to complete program. *Concentration:* management.

MBA—Weekend MBA for Professionals Full-time and part-time. Distance learning option. 45 total credits required. 45 months to complete program. *Concentration:* general MBA.

RESOURCES AND SERVICES 200 on-campus PCs are available to graduate business students. Access to Internet/World Wide Web, online (class) registration, and online grade reports available. *Personal computer requirements:* Graduate business students are not required to have a personal computer. *Placement services include:* Alumni network, career

placement, career counseling/planning, electronic job bank, resume referral, career fairs, resume preparation, and career library.

EXPENSES *Tuition (state resident):* Full-time: $7500. Part-time: $236.90 per credit hour. *Tuition (nonresident):* Full-time: $16,667. Part-time: $555.90 per credit hour. *Tuition (international):* Full-time: $16,667. Part-time: $555.90 per credit hour. *Required fees:* Full-time: $250. Tuition and/or fees vary by number of courses or credits taken and academic program.

FINANCIAL AID (2007–08) 10 students received aid, including loans, research assistantships, scholarships, and work study. Aid is available to part-time students. *Financial aid application deadline:* 7/15.

Financial Aid Contact Harold Burtley, Director, Financial Aid, 3400 Broadway, Gary, IN 46408-1197. *Phone:* 219-980-6539. *Fax:* 219-981-5622. *E-mail:* hburtley@iun.edu.

INTERNATIONAL STUDENTS *Services and facilities:* Counseling/support services, Orientation, Visa Services. Financial aid is not available to international students. *Required with application:* TOEFL with recommended score of 550 (paper); proof of adequate funds; proof of health/immunizations.

International Student Contact Anne Palmer, Senior Director of International Admissions, International Admissions, 300 North Jordan, Bloomington, IN 47405. *Phone:* 812-855-4306.

APPLICATION *Required:* GMAT, application form, baccalaureate/first degree, 1 letter of recommendation, personal statement, transcripts of college work. *Recommended:* Interview, resume/curriculum vitae, work experience. *Application fee:* $25, $55 (international). Applications for domestic and international students are processed on a rolling basis.

Application Contact John Gibson, Director, Undergraduate and Graduate Programs, 3400 Broadway, Gary, IN 46408-1197. *Phone:* 219-980-6635. *Fax:* 219-980-6916. *E-mail:* jagibson@iun.edu.

Indiana University–Purdue University Fort Wayne
School of Business and Management Sciences

Fort Wayne, Indiana

Phone: 260-481-6498 **Fax:** 260-481-6879 **E-mail:** moore@ipfw.edu

Business Program(s) Web Site: http://www.ipfw.edu/academics/programs/graduate/business

Graduate Business Unit Enrollment *Total:* 162 (27 full-time; 135 part-time; 62 women; 22 international). *Average Age:* 30.

Graduate Business Faculty 29 full-time.

Admissions *Applied:* 70. *Admitted:* 58. *Enrolled:* 51. *Average GMAT:* 541. *Average GPA:* 3.28

Academic Calendar Semesters.

Accreditation AACSB—The Association to Advance Collegiate Schools of Business.

DEGREE MBA

MBA—Master of Business Administration Full-time and part-time. GMAT-minimum score of 450 (contact department for certain groups of applicants who are not required to submit GMAT score). At least 33 total credits required. 18 to 48 months to complete program. *Concentration:* general MBA.

RESOURCES AND SERVICES 472 on-campus PCs are available to graduate business students. Access to Internet/World Wide Web, online (class) registration, and online grade reports available. *Personal computer requirements:* Graduate business students are not required to have a personal computer. *Placement services include:* Alumni network, career counseling/planning, career fairs, job interviews arranged, resume preparation, and career library.

Indiana University–Purdue University Fort Wayne (continued)

EXPENSES *Tuition (state resident):* Full-time: $4669.20. Part-time: $259.40 per credit. *Tuition (nonresident):* Full-time: $10,228. Part-time: $568.20 per credit. *Tuition (international):* Full-time: $10,227.60. Part-time: $568.20 per credit. *Required fees:* Full-time: $466.20. Part-time: $25.90 per credit. Tuition and/or fees vary by number of courses or credits taken. *Graduate housing:* Room and board costs vary by number of occupants. *Typical cost:* $5140 (room only).

FINANCIAL AID (2007–08) 48 students received aid, including grants, loans, and teaching assistantships. Aid is available to part-time students. *Financial aid application deadline:* 3/1.

Financial Aid Contact Judith Cramer, Director of Financial Aid, 2101 East Coliseum Boulevard, Kettler Hall 102B, Fort Wayne, IN 46805-1499. *Phone:* 260-481-6820. *Fax:* 260-481-4159. *E-mail:* cramerj@ipfw.edu.

INTERNATIONAL STUDENTS 14% of students enrolled are international students. *Services and facilities:* Counseling/support services, ESL/language courses, Housing location assistance, International student housing, International student organization, Orientation, Visa Services. Financial aid is not available to international students. *Required with application:* TOEFL with recommended score of 250 (computer) or 600 (paper); proof of adequate funds; proof of health/immunizations.

International Student Contact Tarek Elshayeb, Director of International Student Services, 2101 East Coliseum Boulevard, Kettler Hall 104, Fort Wayne, IN 46805-1499. *Phone:* 260-481-6034. *Fax:* 260-481-6880. *E-mail:* internationalstudents@ipfw.edu.

APPLICATION *Required:* GMAT, application form, baccalaureate/first degree, essay, 2 letters of recommendation, personal statement, transcripts of college work. *Recommended:* Resume/curriculum vitae. *Application fee:* $30. Applications for domestic and international students are processed on a rolling basis.

Application Contact James Moore, Business Administration Program Director, 2101 East Coliseum Boulevard, Neff Hall 366, Fort Wayne, IN 46805-1499. *Phone:* 260-481-6498. *Fax:* 260-481-6879. *E-mail:* moore@ipfw.edu.

Indiana University–Purdue University Indianapolis
Kelley School of Business

Indianapolis, Indiana

Phone: 317-274-4895 **Fax:** 317-274-2483 **E-mail:** mbaindy@iupui.edu

Business Program(s) Web Site: http://kelley.iupui.edu

Accreditation AACSB—The Association to Advance Collegiate Schools of Business.

DEGREES JD/MBA • MBA • MBA/MHA • MBA/MPA • MBA/MS • MD/MBA • MPA

JD/MBA—Juris Doctor/Master of Business Administration Full-time. Applicant must apply to School of Law and Kelley School of Business separately. At least 119 total credits required. 48 to 60 months to complete program. *Concentration:* management.

MBA—Direct-Online MBA Program Distance learning option. At least 48 total credits required. 24 months to complete program. *Concentrations:* business information science, management.

MBA—Evening MBA Program Part-time. 2 years of work experience required. At least 51 total credits required. 30 to 60 months to complete program. *Concentrations:* accounting, finance, management, marketing, new venture management.

MBA/MHA—Master of Business Administration/Master of Health Administration Full-time and part-time. Student must apply to Kelley School of Business and School of Public and Environmental Affairs separately. At least 72 total credits required. 36 to 60 months to complete program. *Concentrations:* health care, management.

MBA/MPA—Master of Business Administration/Master of Professional Accounting Full-time and part-time. Student required to apply to both schools separately. 66 total credits required. 36 months to complete program. *Concentrations:* accounting, management.

MBA/MS—Master of Business Administration/Master of Science Full-time and part-time. 66 total credits required. 32 to 36 months to complete program. *Concentration:* combined degrees.

MD/MBA—Doctor of Medicine/Master of Business Administration Full-time and part-time. Students must apply to Kelley School of Business and School of Medicine separately. Minimum of 48 months to complete program. *Concentration:* combined degrees.

MPA—Master of Professional Accountancy Full-time and part-time. At least 30 total credits required. 12 to 60 months to complete program. *Concentration:* accounting.

RESOURCES AND SERVICES 100 on-campus PCs are available to graduate business students. Access to Internet/World Wide Web, online (class) registration, and online grade reports available. *Personal computer requirements:* Graduate business students are required to have a personal computer. *Special opportunities include:* An internship program is available. *Placement services include:* Alumni network, career placement, job search course, career counseling/planning, electronic job bank, resume referral, career fairs, job interviews arranged, resume preparation, and career library.

Application Contact Darrell E. Brown, PhD, Admissions, Evening MBA Program, 801 West Michigan Street, #3024L, Indianapolis, IN 46202-5151. *Phone:* 317-274-4895. *Fax:* 317-274-2483. *E-mail:* mbaindy@iupui.edu.

Indiana University South Bend
School of Business and Economics

South Bend, Indiana

Phone: 574-520-4138 **Fax:** 574-520-4866 **E-mail:** speterso@iusb.edu

Business Program(s) Web Site: http://www.iusb.edu/~buse/grad/

Graduate Business Unit Enrollment *Total:* 239 (43 full-time; 196 part-time; 85 women; 52 international).

Graduate Business Faculty *Total:* 36 (30 full-time; 6 part-time).

Admissions *Applied:* 61. *Admitted:* 59. *Enrolled:* 39. *Average GMAT:* 511. *Average GPA:* 3.06

Academic Calendar Semesters.

Accreditation AACSB—The Association to Advance Collegiate Schools of Business.

DEGREES MBA • MS • MSA

MBA—Master of Business Administration Full-time and part-time. 36 to 57 total credits required. 24 to 60 months to complete program. *Concentration:* general MBA.

MS—Master of Science in Management Information Technology Full-time and part-time. 38 to 48 total credits required. 24 to 60 months to complete program. *Concentration:* management information systems.

MSA—Master of Science in Accounting Full-time and part-time. 30 to 57 total credits required. 24 to 60 months to complete program. *Concentration:* accounting.

RESOURCES AND SERVICES 300 on-campus PCs are available to graduate business students. Access to Internet/World Wide Web, online (class) registration, and online grade reports available. *Personal computer requirements:* Graduate business students are strongly recommended to purchase or lease a personal computer. *Placement services include:* Alumni network, career placement, career counseling/planning, electronic job bank, resume referral, career fairs, resume preparation, and career library.

EXPENSES *Tuition (state resident):* Full-time: $4700. Part-time: $3100 per year. *Tuition (nonresident):* Full-time: $11,250. Part-time: $7500 per year. *Tuition (international):* Full-time: $11,250. *Graduate housing:* Room and board costs vary by number of occupants and type of accommodation. *Typical cost:* $7000 (including board), $2000 (room only).

FINANCIAL AID (2007–08) Grants, loans, scholarships, and work study. Aid is available to part-time students. *Financial aid application deadline:* 5/1.

Financial Aid Contact Ms. Melissa Pace, Secretary, Financial Aid Office, PO Box 7111, South Bend, IN 46634-7111. *Phone:* 574-520-4357. *Fax:* 574-520-5561. *E-mail:* mepace@iusb.edu.

INTERNATIONAL STUDENTS 22% of students enrolled are international students. *Services and facilities:* Counseling/support services, ESL/language courses, Housing location assistance, International student housing, International student organization, Orientation, Visa Services. Financial aid is not available to international students. *Required with application:* TOEFL with recommended score of 213 (computer), 550 (paper), or 79 (Internet); proof of adequate funds. *Recommended with application:* TWE; proof of health/immunizations.

International Student Contact Ms. Julie Williams, Director, Office of International Student Services, Office of International Student Services, 1700 Mishawaka Avenue, South Bend, IN 46634. *Phone:* 574-520-4419. *Fax:* 574-520-4590. *E-mail:* jwilliam@iusb.edu.

APPLICATION *Required:* GMAT, application form, baccalaureate/first degree, essay, 2 letters of recommendation, personal statement, transcripts of college work. *Recommended:* Interview, resume/curriculum vitae, 3 years of work experience. *Application fee:* $45, $55 (international). *Deadlines:* 7/1 for fall, 11/1 for spring, 4/1 for summer. Applications for international students are processed on a rolling basis.

Application Contact Ms. Sharon Peterson, Graduate Student Recorder, PO Box 7111, 1700 Mishawaka Ave, South Bend, IN 46634-7111. *Phone:* 574-520-4138. *Fax:* 574-520-4866. *E-mail:* speterso@iusb.edu.

ITT Technical Institute
Online MBA Program
Indianapolis, Indiana

Phone: 888-488-0007

Business Program(s) Web Site: http://www.itt-tech.edu/onlineprograms/mba.cfm

DEGREE MBA

MBA—Business Administration (Online Master's Program) Part-time. Distance learning option. At least 56 total credits required. *Concentration:* general MBA.

RESOURCES AND SERVICES *Personal computer requirements:* Graduate business students are required to have a personal computer.

Application Contact Online Admissions Department, 9511 Angola Court, Indianapolis, IN 46268. *Phone:* 888-488-0007.

Oakland City University
School of Adult and Extended Learning
Oakland City, Indiana

Phone: 812-749-1542 **Fax:** 812-749-1294 **E-mail:** nreynolds@oak.edu

Business Program(s) Web Site: http://www.oak.edu/

Graduate Business Unit Enrollment *Total:* 88 (88 full-time; 41 women).

Graduate Business Faculty 21 part-time.

Admissions *Average GPA:* 3.2

Academic Calendar Continuous.

After Graduation (Class of 2006–07) *Employed within 3 months of graduation:* 100%.

DEGREE MBA

MBA—Master of Business Administration Full-time. 27 to 36 total credits required. 18 months to complete program. *Concentration:* general MBA.

RESOURCES AND SERVICES 35 on-campus PCs are available to graduate business students. Access to Internet/World Wide Web and online grade reports available. *Personal computer requirements:* Graduate business students are strongly recommended to purchase or lease a personal computer. *Placement services include:* Alumni network, career placement, career counseling/planning, and career fairs.

EXPENSES *Tuition:* Full-time: $6300. *Tuition (international):* Full-time: $6300.

FINANCIAL AID (2007–08) Loans. *Financial aid application deadline:* 3/1.

Financial Aid Contact Mrs. Caren Richeson, Director, Financial Aid, 143 North Lucretia Street, Oakland City, IN 47660. *Phone:* 812-749-1224. *Fax:* 812-749-1438. *E-mail:* cricheson@oak.edu.

INTERNATIONAL STUDENTS *Services and facilities:* Counseling/support services, International student housing, Orientation. Financial aid is not available to international students. *Required with application:* TOEFL with recommended score of 500 (paper); proof of adequate funds. *Recommended with application:* Proof of health/immunizations.

International Student Contact Dr. Patricia Swails, Dean of Academic Affairs, 143 North Lucretia Street, Oakland City, IN 47660. *Phone:* 812-749-1238. *Fax:* 812-749-1511. *E-mail:* pswails@oak.edu.

APPLICATION *Required:* Application form, baccalaureate/first degree, 3 letters of recommendation, resume/curriculum vitae, transcripts of college work. School will accept GMAT, GRE, and MAT. *Recommended:* 3 years of work experience. *Application fee:* $35. Applications for domestic and international students are processed on a rolling basis.

Application Contact Norman Reynolds, Dean, School of Accelerated Adult Degrees, 143 North Lucretia Street, Oakland City, IN 47660-1099. *Phone:* 812-749-1542. *Fax:* 812-749-1294. *E-mail:* nreynolds@oak.edu.

Purdue University
Krannert School of Management
West Lafayette, Indiana

Phone: 765-494-0773 **Fax:** 765-494-9841 **E-mail:** masters@krannert.purdue.edu

Business Program(s) Web Site: http://www.krannert.purdue.edu/

Accreditation AACSB—The Association to Advance Collegiate Schools of Business.

DEGREES EMBA • IMBA/MBA • MBA • MS

EMBA—Executive Master of Business Administration Part-time. Distance learning option. At least 48 total credits required. 22 months to complete program. *Concentration:* executive programs.

IMBA/MBA—IMM Part-time. Distance learning option. 5 Years work experience. At least 48 total credits required. Minimum of 48 months to complete program.

MBA—Master of Business Administration Full-time. At least 60 total credits required. Minimum of 60 months to complete program. *Concentrations:* accounting, business policy/strategy, electronic commerce (E-commerce), finance, general MBA, human resources management, industrial administration/management, information systems, international business, logistics, management, management information systems, manufacturing management, marketing, operations management, organizational behavior/development, strategic management, supply chain management.

Purdue University (continued)

MBA—Weekend MBA Program Part-time. Distance learning option. At least 48 total credits required. Minimum of 48 months to complete program.

MS—Master of Science in Human Resource Management Full-time. At least 61 total credits required. Minimum of 24 months to complete program. *Concentrations:* human resources management, organizational behavior/development.

MS—Master of Science in Industrial Administration Full-time. At least 48 total credits required. Minimum of 11 months to complete program. *Concentrations:* industrial administration/management, management.

RESOURCES AND SERVICES 147 on-campus PCs are available to graduate business students. Access to Internet/World Wide Web, online (class) registration, and online grade reports available. *Personal computer requirements:* Graduate business students are strongly recommended to purchase or lease a personal computer. *Special opportunities include:* An international exchange program and an internship program are available. *Placement services include:* Alumni network, career placement, career counseling/planning, electronic job bank, resume referral, career fairs, job interviews arranged, resume preparation, and career library.

Application Contact Ms. Carmen Castro-Rivera, Director of Admissions, 100 South Grant Street, Rawls Hall, Suite 2020, West Lafayette, IN 47907-2076. *Phone:* 765-494-0773. *Fax:* 765-494-9841. *E-mail:* masters@krannert.purdue.edu.

Purdue University Calumet
School of Management
Hammond, Indiana

Phone: 219-989-2425 **Fax:** 219-989-3158 **E-mail:** pmcgrat@calumet.purdue.edu

Business Program(s) Web Site: http://www.calumet.purdue.edu

Graduate Business Unit Enrollment *Total:* 231 (25 full-time; 206 part-time; 99 women; 38 international). *Average Age:* 29.

Graduate Business Faculty *Total:* 33 (30 full-time; 3 part-time).

Admissions *Applied:* 55. *Admitted:* 53. *Enrolled:* 52. *Average GMAT:* 551. *Average GPA:* 2.6

Academic Calendar Semesters.

After Graduation (Class of 2006–07) *Employed within 3 months of graduation:* 100%. *Average starting salary:* $75,000.

DEGREES M Acc • MBA

M Acc—Master of Accountancy Part-time. At least 30 total credits required. Minimum of 24 months to complete program. *Concentration:* accounting.

MBA—Executive Master of Business Administration Part-time. 5 years of business experience and interview required. At least 42 total credits required. Minimum of 18 months to complete program. *Concentration:* executive programs.

MBA—Master of Business Administration Full-time and part-time. 36 to 51 total credits required. 30 to 42 months to complete program. *Concentration:* general MBA.

RESOURCES AND SERVICES 500 on-campus PCs are available to graduate business students. Access to Internet/World Wide Web, online (class) registration, and online grade reports available. *Personal computer requirements:* Graduate business students are not required to have a personal computer. *Placement services include:* Alumni network, career placement, career counseling/planning, electronic job bank, resume referral, career fairs, and resume preparation.

EXPENSES *Tuition (state resident):* Full-time: $9000. Part-time: $233 per credit hour. *Tuition (nonresident):* Full-time: $18,000. Part-time: $466 per credit hour. *Tuition (international):* Full-time: $18,000. Part-time:

$466 per credit hour. *Required fees:* Full-time: $500. Part-time: $13 per credit hour. Tuition and/or fees vary by academic program.

FINANCIAL AID (2007–08) Loans. *Financial aid application deadline:* 3/1.

Financial Aid Contact Mary Ann Bishel, Director of Financial Aid, Hammond, IN 46323-2094. *Phone:* 219-989-2301. *Fax:* 219-989-2771. *E-mail:* finaid@calumet.purdue.edu.

INTERNATIONAL STUDENTS 16% of students enrolled are international students. *Services and facilities:* Counseling/support services, ESL/language courses, Housing location assistance, International student housing, International student organization, Visa Services. Financial aid is not available to international students. *Required with application:* TOEFL with recommended score of 213 (computer), 550 (paper), or 84 (Internet); proof of adequate funds.

International Student Contact Marsha Gordon, Coordinator of Graduate School, Hammond, IN 46323-2094. *Phone:* 219-989-2559. *Fax:* 219-989-2581. *E-mail:* gordon@calumet.purdue.edu.

APPLICATION *Required:* GMAT, application form, baccalaureate/first degree, essay, 3 letters of recommendation, personal statement, resume/curriculum vitae, transcripts of college work. *Application fee:* $55. Applications for domestic and international students are processed on a rolling basis.

Application Contact Dr. Paul McGrath, MBA Advisor, 2200 169th Street, Hammond, IN 46323-2094. *Phone:* 219-989-2425. *Fax:* 219-989-3158. *E-mail:* pmcgrat@calumet.purdue.edu.

Taylor University Fort Wayne
Master of Business Administration Program
Fort Wayne, Indiana

Phone: 260-399-1624 **Fax:** 260-492-4052 **E-mail:** mba@tayloru.edu

Business Program(s) Web Site: http://www.taylor.edu/mba

DEGREE MA/MBA

MA/MBA—Master of Business Administration Full-time. 36 total credits required. 16 months to complete program. *Concentration:* general MBA.

RESOURCES AND SERVICES 20 on-campus PCs are available to graduate business students. Access to Internet/World Wide Web and online grade reports available. *Personal computer requirements:* Graduate business students are required to have a personal computer. *Placement services include:* Alumni network.

Application Contact Mrs. Nancy J. Johnson, MBA Program Assistant, 3201 Stellhorn Road, Fort Wayne, IN 46815. *Phone:* 260-399-1624. *Fax:* 260-492-4052. *E-mail:* mba@tayloru.edu.

University of Indianapolis
Graduate Business Programs
Indianapolis, Indiana

Phone: 317-788-3340 **Fax:** 317-788-3300 **E-mail:** mba@uindy.edu

Business Program(s) Web Site: http://mba.uindy.edu

Graduate Business Unit Enrollment *Total:* 315 (85 full-time; 230 part-time; 123 women; 25 international). *Average Age:* 32.

Graduate Business Faculty *Total:* 20 (8 full-time; 12 part-time).

Admissions *Average GMAT:* 523. *Average GPA:* 3.2

Academic Calendar Semesters.

Accreditation ACBSP—The American Council of Business Schools and Programs.

After Graduation (Class of 2006–07) *Employed within 3 months of graduation:* 90%.

DEGREES MBA

MBA—Executive Master of Business Administration Part-time. At least 42 total credits required. 24 months to complete program. *Concentration:* executive programs.

MBA—Master of Business Administration Part-time. 37 to 45 total credits required. 24 to 60 months to complete program. *Concentrations:* finance, general MBA, information technology, leadership, management, marketing.

RESOURCES AND SERVICES 120 on-campus PCs are available to graduate business students. Access to Internet/World Wide Web, online (class) registration, and online grade reports available. *Personal computer requirements:* Graduate business students are strongly recommended to purchase or lease a personal computer. *Special opportunities include:* An international exchange program and an internship program are available. *Placement services include:* Alumni network, career placement, career counseling/planning, electronic job bank, resume referral, career fairs, resume preparation, and career library.

EXPENSES *Tuition:* Part-time: $425 per credit hour. *Tuition (international):* Part-time: $425 per credit hour. Tuition and/or fees vary by academic program.

FINANCIAL AID (2007–08) Loans, research assistantships, and work study.

Financial Aid Contact Mrs. Linda Handy, Director of Financial Aid, 1400 East Hanna Avenue, Indianapolis, IN 46227. *Phone:* 317-788-3217. *Fax:* 317-788-3300.

INTERNATIONAL STUDENTS 8% of students enrolled are international students. *Services and facilities:* Counseling/support services, ESL/language courses, Housing location assistance, International student housing, International student organization, Language tutoring, Orientation, Visa Services. Financial aid is available to international students. *Required with application:* TOEFL with recommended score of 213 (computer), 550 (paper), or 80 (Internet); proof of adequate funds; proof of health/immunizations.

International Student Contact Ms. Mimi Chase, International Student Officer, 1400 East Hanna Avenue, Indianapolis, IN 46227. *Phone:* 317-788-3394. *Fax:* 317-788-3300.

APPLICATION *Required:* GMAT, application form, baccalaureate/first degree, 2 letters of recommendation, transcripts of college work. School will accept GRE. *Application fee:* $50. Applications for domestic and international students are processed on a rolling basis.

Application Contact Stephen Anthony Tokar, Sr., Director of Graduate Business Programs, 1400 East Hanna Avenue, Indianapolis, IN 46227. *Phone:* 317-788-3340. *Fax:* 317-788-3300. *E-mail:* mba@uindy.edu.

University of Notre Dame
Mendoza College of Business

Notre Dame, Indiana

Phone: 574-631-8488 **Fax:** 574-631-8800 **E-mail:** blohr@nd.edu

Business Program(s) Web Site: http://mba.nd.edu

Graduate Business Unit Enrollment *Total:* 731 (697 full-time; 34 part-time; 191 women; 85 international). *Average Age:* 29.

Graduate Business Faculty *Total:* 139 (112 full-time; 27 part-time).

Admissions *Applied:* 1,275. *Admitted:* 616. *Enrolled:* 378.

Academic Calendar 7-1-7 modules and semesters.

Accreditation AACSB—The Association to Advance Collegiate Schools of Business.

DEGREES JD/MBA • MBA • MS

JD/MBA—Juris Doctor/Master of Business Administration Full-time. At least 123 total credits required. Minimum of 48 months to complete program. *Concentrations:* entrepreneurship, finance, investments and securities, management, manufacturing management, marketing, other.

MBA—Executive Master of Business Administration Full-time. Distance learning option. At least 50 total credits required. 18 to 21 months to complete program. *Concentration:* executive programs.

MBA—One-Year Master of Business Administration Full-time. At least 44 total credits required. Minimum of 11 months to complete program. *Concentrations:* entrepreneurship, finance, investments and securities, management, manufacturing management, marketing, other.

MBA—Two-Year Master of Business Administration Full-time. 2 years of work experience required (3 or more preferred). Up to 63 total credits required. Maximum of 21 months to complete program. *Concentrations:* entrepreneurship, finance, management, manufacturing management, marketing, other.

MS—Master of Nonprofit Administration Full-time and part-time. Distance learning option. GRE required. At least 42 total credits required. 14 to 50 months to complete program. *Concentration:* nonprofit management.

MS—Master of Science in Accountancy Full-time. 30 to 36 total credits required. Minimum of 9 months to complete program. *Concentrations:* accounting, taxation.

RESOURCES AND SERVICES Access to Internet/World Wide Web, online (class) registration, and online grade reports available. *Personal computer requirements:* Graduate business students are strongly recommended to purchase or lease a personal computer. *Placement services include:* Alumni network, career placement, career counseling/planning, electronic job bank, resume referral, career fairs, job interviews arranged, resume preparation, and career library.

Financial Aid Contact Mr. Brian T. Lohr, Director of MBA Admissions, 276 College of Business, Notre Dame, IN 46556. *Phone:* 574-631-8488. *Fax:* 574-631-8800. *E-mail:* blohr@nd.edu.

INTERNATIONAL STUDENTS 12% of students enrolled are international students. *Services and facilities:* Counseling/support services, Housing location assistance, International student organization, Orientation, Visa Services. *Required with application:* TOEFL with recommended score of 250 (computer) or 600 (paper); proof of adequate funds; proof of health/immunizations.

International Student Contact Ms. Bethany Heet, Director of International Student Affairs, 204A LaFortune Student Center, Notre Dame, IN 46556. *Phone:* 574-631-3825. *Fax:* 574-631-3162. *E-mail:* heet.1@nd.edu.

APPLICATION *Required:* Application form, baccalaureate/first degree. *Recommended:* Work experience. Applications for domestic and international students are processed on a rolling basis.

Application Contact Mr. Brian T. Lohr, Director of MBA Admissions, 276 College of Business, Notre Dame, IN 46556. *Phone:* 574-631-8488. *Fax:* 574-631-8800. *E-mail:* blohr@nd.edu.

University of Phoenix–Indianapolis Campus
College of Graduate Business and Management

Indianapolis, Indiana

Phone: 480-317-6200 **Fax:** 480-643-1479 **E-mail:** beth.barilla@phoenix.edu

---

DEGREES MBA

MBA—Accounting Full-time. At least 54 total credits required. *Concentration:* accounting.

University of Phoenix–Indianapolis Campus (continued)

MBA—Global Management Full-time. At least 45 total credits required. *Concentration:* international management.

MBA—Human Resource Management Full-time. At least 45 total credits required. *Concentration:* human resources management.

MBA—Marketing Full-time. At least 45 total credits required. *Concentration:* marketing.

MBA—Master of Business Administration Full-time. At least 45 total credits required. *Concentration:* administration.

RESOURCES AND SERVICES Access to online grade reports available. *Personal computer requirements:* Graduate business students are strongly recommended to purchase or lease a personal computer. *Placement services include:* Alumni network.

Application Contact Beth Barilla, Associate Vice President of Student Admissions and Services, Mail Stop AA-K101, 4615 East Elwood Street, Phoenix, AZ 85040-1958. *Phone:* 480-317-6200. *Fax:* 480-643-1479. *E-mail:* beth.barilla@phoenix.edu.

Valparaiso University
College of Business Administration
Valparaiso, Indiana

Phone: 219-465-7952 **Fax:** 219-464-5789 **E-mail:** mba@valpo.edu

Business Program(s) Web Site: http://www.valpo.edu/mba

Graduate Business Unit Enrollment *Total:* 69. *Average Age:* 29.

Graduate Business Faculty 15 full-time.

Admissions *Average GMAT:* 580. *Average GPA:* 3.4

Academic Calendar Quarters.

Accreditation AACSB—The Association to Advance Collegiate Schools of Business.

After Graduation (Class of 2006–07) *Employed within 3 months of graduation:* 99%.

DEGREE MBA

MBA—Master of Business Administration Full-time and part-time. 38 to 52 total credits required. 12 to 60 months to complete program. *Concentrations:* accounting, law.

RESOURCES AND SERVICES 250 on-campus PCs are available to graduate business students. Access to Internet/World Wide Web, online (class) registration, and online grade reports available. *Personal computer requirements:* Graduate business students are not required to have a personal computer. *Special opportunities include:* An international exchange program and an internship program are available. *Placement services include:* Alumni network, career placement, job search course, career counseling/planning, electronic job bank, resume referral, career fairs, job interviews arranged, resume preparation, and career library.

EXPENSES *Tuition:* Part-time: $570 per credit.

FINANCIAL AID (2007–08) Loans. Aid is available to part-time students.

Financial Aid Contact Ms. Phyllis Schroeder, Associate Director, B33 Kretzmann Hall, Valparaiso, IN 46383. *Phone:* 219-464-5015. *E-mail:* phyllis.schroeder@valpo.edu.

INTERNATIONAL STUDENTS *Services and facilities:* Counseling/support services, ESL/language courses, Housing location assistance, International student housing, International student organization, Language tutoring, Orientation, Visa Services. Financial aid is not available to international students. *Required with application:* TOEFL with recommended score of 230 (computer) or 575 (paper); proof of adequate funds; proof of health/immunizations. *Recommended with application:* TWE.

International Student Contact Mr. Holly Singh, Assistant Director, International Studies, 137 Meier Hall, Valparaiso, IN 46383. *Phone:* 219-464-5333. *E-mail:* holly.singh@valpo.edu.

APPLICATION *Required:* GMAT, application form, baccalaureate/first degree, 2 letters of recommendation, personal statement, resume/curriculum vitae, transcripts of college work. *Application fee:* $30. Applications for domestic and international students are processed on a rolling basis.

Application Contact Admissions Office, 1909 Chapel Drive, 104 Urschel Hall, Valparaiso, IN 46383. *Phone:* 219-465-7952. *Fax:* 219-464-5789. *E-mail:* mba@valpo.edu.

IOWA

Clarke College
Program in Business Administration
Dubuque, Iowa

Phone: 563-588-8113 **Fax:** 563-588-6789 **E-mail:** wanda.ryan@clarke.edu

Business Program(s) Web Site: http://www.clarke.edu/academics/graduate/MBA/index.htm

Graduate Business Unit Enrollment *Total:* 67 (31 full-time; 36 part-time; 27 women).

Graduate Business Faculty *Total:* 11 (5 full-time; 6 part-time).

Admissions *Applied:* 25. *Admitted:* 22. *Enrolled:* 20. *Average GMAT:* 555. *Average GPA:* 3.2

Academic Calendar Semesters.

DEGREE MBA

MBA—Master of Business Administration Full-time and part-time. 36 total credits required. *Concentration:* general MBA.

RESOURCES AND SERVICES 236 on-campus PCs are available to graduate business students. Access to Internet/World Wide Web, online (class) registration, and online grade reports available. *Personal computer requirements:* Graduate business students are strongly recommended to purchase or lease a personal computer. *Special opportunities include:* An internship program is available. *Placement services include:* Alumni network, career placement, career counseling/planning, electronic job bank, career fairs, job interviews arranged, resume preparation, and career library.

EXPENSES *Tuition:* Full-time: $10,332. Part-time: $574 per credit hour. *Required fees:* Full-time: $180. Tuition and/or fees vary by academic program.

FINANCIAL AID (2007–08) Loans. Aid is available to part-time students. *Financial aid application deadline:* 7/1.

Financial Aid Contact Ms. Sharon Willenborg, Director of Financial Aid, 1550 Clarke Drive, Dubuque, IA 52001. *Phone:* 563-588-6327. *Fax:* 563-588-6789. *E-mail:* sharon.willenborg@clarke.edu.

INTERNATIONAL STUDENTS *Services and facilities:* Counseling/support services, ESL/language courses, International student housing, International student organization, Language tutoring, Orientation. Financial aid is not available to international students. *Required with application:* TOEFL with recommended score of 213 (computer) or 550 (paper); proof of adequate funds; proof of health/immunizations.

International Student Contact Mrs. Carrie Kirk, Graduate Studies Program Coordinator, 1550 Clarke Drive, Dubuque, IA 52001. *Phone:* 563-588-6635. *E-mail:* carrie.kirk@clarke.edu.

APPLICATION *Required:* GMAT, application form, baccalaureate/first degree, interview, 2 letters of recommendation, resume/curriculum vitae, transcripts of college work. *Recommended:* Essay, personal statement, work experience. *Application fee:* $35. Applications for domestic and international students are processed on a rolling basis.

Application Contact Dr. Wanda Ryan, Chair of MBA Program, 1550 Clarke Drive, Dubuque, IA 52001. *Phone:* 563-588-8113. *Fax:* 563-588-6789. *E-mail:* wanda.ryan@clarke.edu.

Drake University
College of Business and Public Administration

Des Moines, Iowa

Phone: 515-271-2188 **Fax:** 515-271-2187 **E-mail:** cbpa.gradprograms@drake.edu

Business Program(s) Web Site: http://www.cbpa.drake.edu/

Graduate Business Unit Enrollment *Total:* 515 (59 full-time; 456 part-time; 288 women; 28 international). *Average Age:* 21-41.

Graduate Business Faculty *Total:* 28 (23 full-time; 5 part-time).

Admissions *Applied:* 183. *Admitted:* 167. *Enrolled:* 117. *Average GMAT:* 530. *Average GPA:* 3.3

Academic Calendar Semesters.

Accreditation AACSB—The Association to Advance Collegiate Schools of Business.

After Graduation (Class of 2006–07) *Employed within 3 months of graduation:* 95%.

DEGREES JD/MBA • JD/MPA • M Acc • MBA • MBA equivalent • MBA equivalent combined degree • MF • MPA • Pharm D/MBA

JD/MBA—Juris Doctor/Master of Business Administration Full-time. Admission to Law School required. 111 total credits required. 36 to 72 months to complete program. *Concentration:* combined degrees.

JD/MPA—Juris Doctor/Master of Public Administration Full-time. Admission to Law School required. 108 total credits required. 36 to 72 months to complete program. *Concentration:* combined degrees.

M Acc—Master of Accounting Full-time and part-time. 30 to 54 total credits required. 12 to 60 months to complete program. *Concentration:* accounting.

MBA—Master of Business Administration Full-time and part-time. 39 to 42 total credits required. 16 to 60 months to complete program. *Concentrations:* accounting, entrepreneurship, finance, health care, human resources management, leadership, nonprofit management.

MBA equivalent—MCL—Master of Communication Leadership Part-time. 30 to 36 total credits required. 24 to 60 months to complete program. *Concentration:* leadership.

MBA equivalent combined degree—PharmD/MPA—Doctor of Pharmacy/Master of Public Administration Full-time. 215 total credits required. 72 to 108 months to complete program. *Concentrations:* combined degrees, pharmaceutical management, public policy and administration.

MF—Master of Finance Part-time. 33 to 36 total credits required. 18 to 60 months to complete program. *Concentration:* finance.

MPA—Master of Public Administration Full-time and part-time. 36 total credits required. 16 to 60 months to complete program. *Concentrations:* finance, health care, human resources management, leadership, public policy and administration.

Pharm D/MBA—Doctor of Pharmacy/Master of Business Administration Full-time. Admission to Pharmacy program required. 215 total credits required. 72 to 108 months to complete program. *Concentration:* combined degrees.

RESOURCES AND SERVICES 86 on-campus PCs are available to graduate business students. Access to Internet/World Wide Web, online (class) registration, and online grade reports available. *Personal computer requirements:* Graduate business students are strongly recommended to purchase or lease a personal computer. *Placement services include:*

Alumni network, career placement, career counseling/planning, electronic job bank, career fairs, resume preparation, and career library.

EXPENSES *Tuition:* Full-time: $8460. Part-time: $470 per credit hour. *Tuition (international):* Full-time: $8460. Part-time: $470 per credit hour. *Required fees:* Full-time: $206. Part-time: $40 per semester. Tuition and/or fees vary by number of courses or credits taken and academic program. *Graduate housing:* Room and board costs vary by type of accommodation and type of board plan. *Typical cost:* $6920 (including board), $3500 (room only).

FINANCIAL AID (2007–08) Loans, scholarships, and work study. Aid is available to part-time students. *Financial aid application deadline:* 8/1.

Financial Aid Contact Thomas Delahunt, Dean, Student Financial Planning, 2507 University Avenue, Carnegie Hall, Des Moines, IA 50311-4516. *Phone:* 515-271-2905. *E-mail:* tdelahunt@iona.edu.

INTERNATIONAL STUDENTS 5% of students enrolled are international students. *Services and facilities:* Counseling/support services, ESL/language courses, Housing location assistance, International student housing, International student organization, Orientation, Visa Services. Financial aid is not available to international students. *Required with application:* TOEFL with recommended score of 213 (computer), 550 (paper), or 80 (Internet); proof of adequate funds; proof of health/immunizations.

International Student Contact Ms. Ann Martin, Graduate Admission Coordinator, 2507 University Avenue, Office of Graduate Admission, Des Moines, IA 50311. *Phone:* 515-271-3871. *Fax:* 515-271-2831. *E-mail:* ann.martin@drake.edu.

APPLICATION *Required:* Application form, baccalaureate/first degree, 2 letters of recommendation, resume/curriculum vitae, transcripts of college work. School will accept GMAT and GRE. *Recommended:* Essay, work experience. *Application fee:* $25. Applications for domestic and international students are processed on a rolling basis.

Application Contact Danette Kenne, Director of Graduate Programs, 2507 University Avenue, Des Moines, IA 50311-4516. *Phone:* 515-271-2188. *Fax:* 515-271-2187. *E-mail:* cbpa.gradprograms@drake.edu.

Iowa State University of Science and Technology
College of Business

Ames, Iowa

Phone: 515-294-8118 **Fax:** 515-294-2446 **E-mail:** busgrad@iastate.edu

Business Program(s) Web Site: http://www.bus.iastate.edu/grad/

Graduate Business Unit Enrollment *Total:* 226 (73 full-time; 153 part-time; 87 women; 32 international).

Graduate Business Faculty *Total:* 89 (68 full-time; 21 part-time).

Admissions *Applied:* 189. *Admitted:* 122. *Enrolled:* 91. *Average GMAT:* 613. *Average GPA:* 3.49

Academic Calendar Semesters.

Accreditation AACSB—The Association to Advance Collegiate Schools of Business.

After Graduation (Class of 2006–07) *Employed within 3 months of graduation:* 97%. *Average starting salary:* $57,848.

DEGREES M Acc • MBA • MSIS

M Acc—Master of Accounting Full-time and part-time. 30 total credits required. 12 to 36 months to complete program. *Concentration:* accounting.

MBA—Full-Time Master of Business Administration Full-time. At least 48 total credits required. 21 months to complete program. *Concentrations:* accounting, agribusiness, finance, financial management/planning, international business, management information systems, marketing, supply chain management.

Iowa State University of Science and Technology (continued)

MBA—Part-Time Master of Business Administration Part-time. At least 48 total credits required. 24 to 31 months to complete program. *Concentrations:* accounting, agribusiness, finance, financial management/planning, international business, management information systems, marketing, supply chain management.

MSIS—Master of Science in Information Systems Full-time and part-time. 30 to 40 total credits required. 12 to 36 months to complete program. *Concentration:* information systems.

RESOURCES AND SERVICES 93 on-campus PCs are available to graduate business students. Access to Internet/World Wide Web, online (class) registration, and online grade reports available. *Personal computer requirements:* Graduate business students are not required to have a personal computer. *Special opportunities include:* An internship program is available. *Placement services include:* Alumni network, career placement, job search course, career counseling/planning, electronic job bank, resume referral, career fairs, job interviews arranged, resume preparation, and career library.

EXPENSES *Tuition (state resident):* Full-time: $6446. Part-time: $467 per credit hour. *Tuition (nonresident):* Full-time: $17,330. Part-time: $1071 per credit hour. *Tuition (international):* Full-time: $17,330. Part-time: $1071 per credit hour. *Required fees:* Full-time: $525. Part-time: $375 per year. Tuition and/or fees vary by class time and academic program. *Graduate housing:* Room and board costs vary by number of occupants, type of accommodation, and type of board plan. *Typical cost:* $7821 (including board).

FINANCIAL AID (2007–08) Loans, research assistantships, scholarships, and teaching assistantships. *Financial aid application deadline:* 6/1.

Financial Aid Contact Ms. Roberta Johnson, Director, Student Financial Aid Office, 0210 Beardshear Hall, Ames, IA 50011. *Phone:* 515-294-2223. *Fax:* 515-294-0851.

INTERNATIONAL STUDENTS 14% of students enrolled are international students. *Services and facilities:* Counseling/support services, ESL/language courses, Housing location assistance, International student housing, International student organization, Language tutoring, Orientation, Visa Services. Financial aid is available to international students. *Required with application:* TOEFL with recommended score of 250 (computer), 600 (paper), or 100 (Internet); proof of adequate funds.

International Student Contact Mr. James Dorsett, Director, International Students and Scholars Office, 3242 Memorial Union, Ames, IA 50011. *Phone:* 515-294-1120. *Fax:* 515-294-8263. *E-mail:* intlserv@iastate.edu.

APPLICATION *Required:* GMAT, application form, baccalaureate/first degree, essay, 3 letters of recommendation, resume/curriculum vitae, transcripts of college work. *Recommended:* 3 years of work experience. *Application fee:* $30, $70 (international). Applications for domestic and international students are processed on a rolling basis.

Application Contact Mr. Ronald Ackerman, Director of Graduate Admissions, 1360 Gerdin, Ames, IA 50011-1350. *Phone:* 515-294-8118. *Fax:* 515-294-2446. *E-mail:* busgrad@iastate.edu.

See full description on page 644.

St. Ambrose University
Program in Business Administration

Davenport, Iowa

Phone: 563-333-6270 **Fax:** 563-333-6268 **E-mail:** mba@sau.edu

Business Program(s) Web Site: http://www.sau.edu/mba

Graduate Business Unit Enrollment *Total:* 438 (74 full-time; 364 part-time; 209 women; 9 international). *Average Age:* 34.

Graduate Business Faculty *Total:* 45 (24 full-time; 21 part-time).

Admissions *Applied:* 136. *Admitted:* 128. *Enrolled:* 74. *Average GMAT:* 467. *Average GPA:* 3.4

Academic Calendar Semesters.

Accreditation ACBSP—The American Council of Business Schools and Programs.

After Graduation (Class of 2006–07) *Employed within 3 months of graduation:* 98%. *Average starting salary:* $33,949.

DEGREES M Acc • MBA

M Acc—Master of Accountancy Part-time. At least 30 total credits required. 30 to 60 months to complete program. *Concentrations:* accounting, management information systems.

MBA—Master of Business Administration Full-time and part-time. Distance learning option. At least 45 total credits required. 12 to 60 months to complete program. *Concentrations:* finance, human resources management, management information systems, marketing, nonprofit organization.

MBA—Master of Business Administration in Health Care Part-time. Distance learning option. At least 45 total credits required. 30 to 60 months to complete program. *Concentration:* health care.

RESOURCES AND SERVICES 190 on-campus PCs are available to graduate business students. Access to Internet/World Wide Web, online (class) registration, and online grade reports available. *Personal computer requirements:* Graduate business students are strongly recommended to purchase or lease a personal computer. *Special opportunities include:* An international exchange program and an internship program are available. *Placement services include:* Alumni network, career placement, job search course, career counseling/planning, electronic job bank, resume referral, career fairs, job interviews arranged, resume preparation, and career library.

EXPENSES *Tuition:* Part-time: $672 per credit hour. *Tuition (international):* Part-time: $672 per credit hour. Tuition and/or fees vary by academic program. *Graduate housing:* Room and board costs vary by campus location, number of occupants, type of accommodation, and type of board plan. *Typical cost:* $7825 (including board), $3988 (room only).

FINANCIAL AID (2007–08) 70 students received aid, including research assistantships. *Financial aid application deadline:* 3/1.

Financial Aid Contact Mrs. Julie Haack, Director of Financial Aid, Financial Aid Office, 518 West Locust Street, Davenport, IA 52803-2898. *Phone:* 563-333-6314. *Fax:* 563-333-6297. *E-mail:* finaid@sau.edu.

INTERNATIONAL STUDENTS 2% of students enrolled are international students. *Services and facilities:* Counseling/support services, ESL/language courses, Housing location assistance, International student organization, Visa Services. Financial aid is not available to international students. *Required with application:* TOEFL with recommended score of 213 (computer) or 550 (paper); proof of adequate funds; proof of health/immunizations.

International Student Contact Ms. Sherri L. Spillman, Director of International Student Programs, International Student Programs, 518 West Locust Street, Davenport, IA 52803-2898. *Phone:* 563-333-6309. *Fax:* 563-333-6243. *E-mail:* spillmansherri@sau.edu.

APPLICATION *Required:* GMAT, application form, baccalaureate/first degree, 2 letters of recommendation, personal statement, transcripts of college work. *Application fee:* $25. Applications for domestic and international students are processed on a rolling basis.

Application Contact Elizabeth Loveless, Director of MBA Student Recruitment, 518 West Locust Street, Davenport, IA 52803-2898. *Phone:* 563-333-6270. *Fax:* 563-333-6268. *E-mail:* mba@sau.edu.

University of Dubuque
School of Business

Dubuque, Iowa

Phone: 319-589-3300 **Fax:** 319-589-3184 **E-mail:** cknockle@dbq.edu

Business Program(s) Web Site: http://www.dbq.edu

Graduate Business Unit Enrollment *Total:* 85 (35 full-time; 50 part-time; 40 women; 35 international). *Average Age:* 34.

Graduate Business Faculty *Total:* 9 (4 full-time; 5 part-time).

Admissions *Applied:* 39. *Admitted:* 23. *Enrolled:* 23. *Average GPA:* 3.2

Academic Calendar Semesters.

After Graduation (Class of 2006–07) *Employed within 3 months of graduation:* 99%.

DEGREE MBA

MBA—Master of Business Administration Full-time and part-time. At least 36 total credits required. 12 to 96 months to complete program. *Concentration:* general MBA.

RESOURCES AND SERVICES 150 on-campus PCs are available to graduate business students. Access to Internet/World Wide Web and online grade reports available. *Personal computer requirements:* Graduate business students are strongly recommended to purchase or lease a personal computer. *Placement services include:* Alumni network, career placement, career counseling/planning, electronic job bank, resume referral, career fairs, job interviews arranged, and resume preparation.

FINANCIAL AID (2007–08) 8 students received aid, including loans, research assistantships, teaching assistantships, and work study. Aid is available to part-time students. *Financial aid application deadline:* 3/2.

Financial Aid Contact Timothy Kremer, Director of Student Financial Planning, 2000 University Avenue, Dubuque, IA 52001-5099. *Phone:* 563-589-3396. *Fax:* 563-589-3690. *E-mail:* tkremer@dbq.edu.

INTERNATIONAL STUDENTS 41% of students enrolled are international students. *Services and facilities:* Counseling/support services, ESL/language courses, Housing location assistance, International student housing, International student organization, Language tutoring, Orientation, Visa Services. Financial aid is not available to international students. *Required with application:* Proof of adequate funds; proof of health/immunizations.

International Student Contact Ms. Carol Knockle, Graduate Program Coordinator, 2000 University Avenue, Dubuque, IA 52001-5099. *Phone:* 563-589-3300. *Fax:* 563-589-3184. *E-mail:* cknockle@dbq.edu.

APPLICATION *Required:* Application form, baccalaureate/first degree, essay, 2 letters of recommendation, transcripts of college work. *Recommended:* Interview, personal statement, resume/curriculum vitae, work experience. *Application fee:* $25. Applications for domestic and international students are processed on a rolling basis.

Application Contact Ms. Carol Knockle, Graduate Program Coordinator, 2000 University Avenue, Dubuque, IA 52001-5099. *Phone:* 319-589-3300. *Fax:* 319-589-3184. *E-mail:* cknockle@dbq.edu.

The University of Iowa
Henry B. Tippie College of Business

Iowa City, Iowa

Phone: 319-335-1039 **Fax:** 319-335-3604 **E-mail:** mary-spreen@uiowa.edu

Business Program(s) Web Site: http://www.biz.uiowa.edu/

Graduate Business Unit Enrollment *Total:* 1,040 (277 full-time; 763 part-time; 321 women; 129 international). *Average Age:* 30.

Graduate Business Faculty *Total:* 155 (99 full-time; 56 part-time).

Admissions *Applied:* 438. *Admitted:* 294. *Enrolled:* 251. *Average GMAT:* 652. *Average GPA:* 3.34

Academic Calendar Semesters.

Accreditation AACSB—The Association to Advance Collegiate Schools of Business.

After Graduation (Class of 2006–07) *Employed within 3 months of graduation:* 90%. *Average starting salary:* $73,702.

DEGREES JD/MBA • M Ac • MBA • MBA/MA • MBA/MHA • MBA/MS • MD/MBA

JD/MBA—Juris Doctor/Master of Business Administration Full-time. At least 123 total credits required. 48 months to complete program. *Concentration:* combined degrees.

M Ac—Master of Accountancy Full-time and part-time. 30 to 69 total credits required. 9 to 24 months to complete program. *Concentration:* accounting.

MBA—Executive Master of Business Administration Part-time. 10 years of work experience required. At least 50 total credits required. 21 months to complete program. *Concentration:* executive programs.

MBA—Full-Time Program Full-time. 60 total credits required. 21 months to complete program. *Concentration:* general MBA.

MBA—Master of Business Administration for Professionals and Managers Part-time. At least 45 total credits required. 30 to 120 months to complete program. *Concentration:* general MBA.

MBA/MA—Master of Business Administration/Master of Arts in Library Science and Information Science Full-time. Minimum of 36 months to complete program. *Concentration:* combined degrees.

MBA/MHA—Master of Business Administration/Master of Hospital Administration Full-time. At least 75 total credits required. 28 to 36 months to complete program. *Concentration:* health care.

MBA/MS—Master of Business Administration/Master of Science in Nursing Full-time and part-time. At least 61 total credits required. Minimum of 36 months to complete program. *Concentration:* combined degrees.

MD/MBA—Doctor of Medicine/Master of Business Administration Full-time. At least 196 total credits required. Minimum of 60 months to complete program. *Concentration:* combined degrees.

RESOURCES AND SERVICES 232 on-campus PCs are available to graduate business students. Access to Internet/World Wide Web, online (class) registration, and online grade reports available. *Personal computer requirements:* Graduate business students are strongly recommended to purchase or lease a personal computer. *Special opportunities include:* An international exchange program and an internship program are available. *Placement services include:* Alumni network, career placement, job search course, career counseling/planning, electronic job bank, resume referral, career fairs, job interviews arranged, resume preparation, and career library.

EXPENSES *Tuition (state resident):* Full-time: $13,162. Part-time: $486 per credit hour. *Tuition (nonresident):* Full-time: $24,142. *Tuition (international):* Full-time: $778. Tuition and/or fees vary by class time, number of courses or credits taken, campus location, and academic program. *Graduate housing:* Room and board costs vary by number of occupants, type of accommodation, and type of board plan. *Typical cost:* $8420 (including board), $6060 (room only).

FINANCIAL AID (2007–08) 69 students received aid, including fellowships, research assistantships, scholarships, teaching assistantships, and work study. *Financial aid application deadline:* 4/15.

Financial Aid Contact Mary Spreen, Director of MBA Admissions and Financial Aid, 100 Pomerantz Center, Suite E442, Iowa City, IA 52242-1000. *Phone:* 319-335-1039. *Fax:* 319-335-3604. *E-mail:* mary-spreen@uiowa.edu.

INTERNATIONAL STUDENTS 12% of students enrolled are international students. *Services and facilities:* Counseling/support services, ESL/language courses, Housing location assistance, International student organization, Language tutoring, Orientation. Financial aid is available to international students. *Required with application:* TOEFL with recommended score of 250 (computer) or 600 (paper); proof of adequate funds; proof of health/immunizations.

International Student Contact Ann Knudson, Assistant Director, Iowa Institute for International Business, 108 Pappajohn Business Building, Suite W308, Iowa City, IA 52242-1000. *Phone:* 319-335-1379. *Fax:* 319-335-3604. *E-mail:* ann-knudson@uiowa.edu.

APPLICATION *Required:* GMAT, application form, baccalaureate/first degree, essay, interview, 3 letters of recommendation, resume/curriculum vitae, transcripts of college work, 3 years of work experience. *Application fee:* $60, $85 (international). Applications for domestic and international students are processed on a rolling basis.

The University of Iowa (continued)

Application Contact Mary Spreen, Director of MBA Admissions and Financial Aid, 100 Pomerantz Center, Suite E442, Iowa City, IA 52242-1000. *Phone:* 319-335-1039. *Fax:* 319-335-3604. *E-mail:* maryspreen@uiowa.edu.

See full description on page 714.

University of Northern Iowa
College of Business Administration

Cedar Falls, Iowa

Phone: 319-273-6243 **Fax:** 319-273-6230 **E-mail:** wilsonl@uni.edu

Business Program(s) Web Site: http://www.cba.uni.edu/dbweb/pages/programs/graduate-bus-admin.cfm

Graduate Business Unit Enrollment *Total:* 74 (7 full-time; 67 part-time; 26 women; 38 international). *Average Age:* 29.

Graduate Business Faculty 33 full-time.

Admissions *Applied:* 66. *Admitted:* 33. *Enrolled:* 29. *Average GMAT:* 580. *Average GPA:* 3.3

Academic Calendar Trimesters.

Accreditation AACSB—The Association to Advance Collegiate Schools of Business.

After Graduation (Class of 2006–07) *Employed within 3 months of graduation:* 57%. *Average starting salary:* $50,000.

DEGREES   MAC • MBA

MAC—Master of Accounting Full-time and part-time. At least 30 total credits required. 10 to 84 months to complete program. *Concentration:* accounting.

MBA—Master of Business Administration Full-time and part-time. Addendum to application form required. At least 31 total credits required. 10 to 70 months to complete program. *Concentration:* management.

RESOURCES AND SERVICES 150 on-campus PCs are available to graduate business students. Access to Internet/World Wide Web, online (class) registration, and online grade reports available. *Personal computer requirements:* Graduate business students are not required to have a personal computer. *Special opportunities include:* An international exchange program is available. *Placement services include:* Alumni network, career placement, job search course, career counseling/planning, electronic job bank, resume referral, career fairs, job interviews arranged, resume preparation, and career library.

EXPENSES *Tuition (state resident):* Full-time: $6246. Part-time: $347 per credit hour. *Tuition (nonresident):* Full-time: $14,554. Part-time: $347 per credit hour. *Tuition (international):* Full-time: $14,554. Part-time: $347 per credit hour. *Required fees:* Full-time: $838. Part-time: $59.50 per credit hour. *Graduate housing:* Room and board costs vary by campus location, number of occupants, type of accommodation, and type of board plan. *Typical cost:* $5730 (including board), $3537 (room only).

FINANCIAL AID (2007–08) 22 students received aid, including research assistantships, scholarships, and work study. Aid is available to part-time students. *Financial aid application deadline:* 2/1.

Financial Aid Contact Roland Carrillo, Financial Aid Director, Lower Level, Maucker Union, Game Room, Cedar Falls, IA 50614-0024. *Phone:* 319-273-2700. *Fax:* 319-273-6950. *E-mail:* roland.carrillo@uni.edu.

INTERNATIONAL STUDENTS 51% of students enrolled are international students. *Services and facilities:* Counseling/support services, ESL/language courses, Housing location assistance, International student housing, International student organization, Language tutoring, Orientation, Visa Services. Financial aid is not available to international students. *Required with application:* TOEFL with recommended score of 250 (computer) or 600 (paper); proof of adequate funds; proof of health/immunizations.

International Student Contact Ross Schupbach, Director, International Student Office, International Admissions, 113 Maucker Union, Cedar Falls, IA 50614-0164. *Phone:* 319-273-6421. *Fax:* 319-273-6103. *E-mail:* international.admissions@uni.edu.

APPLICATION *Required:* GMAT, application form, baccalaureate/first degree, essay, personal statement, transcripts of college work. *Recommended:* 2 letters of recommendation, resume/curriculum vitae, 2 years of work experience. *Application fee:* $30, $50 (international). Applications for domestic and international students are processed on a rolling basis.

Application Contact Leslie K. Wilson, Associate Dean, Suite 325, Curris Business Building, Cedar Falls, IA 50614-0123. *Phone:* 319-273-6243. *Fax:* 319-273-6230. *E-mail:* wilsonl@uni.edu.

Upper Iowa University
Online Master's Programs

Fayette, Iowa

Phone: 866-225-2208 **Fax:** 515-369-7777 **E-mail:** hannumd@uiu.edu

Business Program(s) Web Site: http://www.uiu.edu

Graduate Business Unit Enrollment *Total:* 255 (255 full-time; 170 women; 3 international).

Graduate Business Faculty *Total:* 26 (1 full-time; 25 part-time).

Admissions *Applied:* 127. *Admitted:* 108. *Enrolled:* 64. *Average GPA:* 3.0

Academic Calendar Six 8-week terms.

After Graduation (Class of 2006–07) *Employed within 3 months of graduation:* 88%. *Average starting salary:* $50,000.

DEGREE   MBA

MBA—Master of Business Administration Full-time and part-time. Distance learning option. 39 total credits required. 24 to 60 months to complete program. *Concentrations:* accounting, financial management/planning, human resources management, international and area business studies, organizational behavior/development, public policy and administration, quality management.

RESOURCES AND SERVICES Access to Internet/World Wide Web available. *Personal computer requirements:* Graduate business students are required to have a personal computer. *Placement services include:* Alumni network, job search course, career counseling/planning, electronic job bank, resume referral, career fairs, job interviews arranged, resume preparation, and career library.

FINANCIAL AID (2007–08) 153 students received aid. Aid is available to part-time students.

Financial Aid Contact Financial Aid Office, 605 Washington Street, PO Box 1859, Fayette, IA 52142-1857. *Phone:* 563-425-5393. *E-mail:* financialaid@uiu.edu.

INTERNATIONAL STUDENTS 1% of students enrolled are international students. *Services and facilities:* Counseling/support services. Financial aid is not available to international students. *Required with application:* TOEFL with recommended score of 230 (computer) or 570 (paper); proof of adequate funds.

International Student Contact Dr. James Skertich, MBA Program Coordinator, 605 Washington Street, PO Box 1857, Fayette, IA 52142. *Phone:* 866-559-0756. *Fax:* 770-267-1299. *E-mail:* skertichj@uiu.edu.

APPLICATION *Required:* Application form, baccalaureate/first degree, transcripts of college work. School will accept GMAT and GRE. *Application fee:* $50. Applications for domestic and international students are processed on a rolling basis.

Application Contact Mr. David W. Hannum, Online Recruiter, 1119 5th Street, West Des Moines, IA 50265. *Phone:* 866-225-2208. *Fax:* 515-369-7777. *E-mail:* hannumd@uiu.edu.

KANSAS

Baker University
School of Professional and Graduate Studies
Baldwin City, Kansas

Phone: 913-491-4432 **Fax:** 913-491-0470 **E-mail:** lephraim@bakeru.edu

Business Program(s) Web Site: http://www.bakerU.edu/

Graduate Business Unit Enrollment *Total:* 727 (162 full-time; 565 part-time; 345 women). *Average Age:* 33.

Graduate Business Faculty *Total:* 221 (4 full-time; 217 part-time).

Admissions *Average GPA:* 3.0

Academic Calendar Continuous lock step.

Accreditation ACBSP—The American Council of Business Schools and Programs.

DEGREES MA • MBA • MS

MA—Master of Arts in Conflict Management and Dispute Resolution Full-time. At least 37 total credits required. 18 to 72 months to complete program. *Concentration:* conflict resolution management.

MBA—Master of Business Administration Full-time. Distance learning option. At least 43 total credits required. 22 to 72 months to complete program. *Concentrations:* finance, human resources management, information systems, international business, marketing.

MS—Master of Science in Management Full-time. At least 36 total credits required. 18 to 72 months to complete program. *Concentrations:* finance, human resources management, information systems, international business, marketing.

RESOURCES AND SERVICES Access to Internet/World Wide Web and online grade reports available. *Personal computer requirements:* Graduate business students are required to have a personal computer, the cost of which is included in tuition or other required fees. *Placement services include:* Alumni network, resume referral, and resume preparation.

EXPENSES Tuition and/or fees vary by academic program.

FINANCIAL AID (2007–08) 400 students received aid, including loans. Aid is available to part-time students.

Financial Aid Contact Ms. Sylvia Ellis, Associate Director of Financial Aid, 8001 College Boulevard, Suite 100, Overland Park, KS 66210. *Phone:* 913-491-4432. *Fax:* 913-491-0470. *E-mail:* sellis@bakeru.edu.

INTERNATIONAL STUDENTS Financial aid is not available to international students. *Required with application:* TOEFL with recommended score of 250 (computer), 600 (paper), or 100 (Internet); proof of adequate funds; proof of health/immunizations.

International Student Contact Ms. Hannah Eckes, Academic Records Specialist, 8001 College Boulevard, Suite 100, Overland Park, KS 66210. *Phone:* 913-491-4432. *Fax:* 913-491-0470. *E-mail:* heckes@bakeru.edu.

APPLICATION *Required:* Application form, baccalaureate/first degree, 2 letters of recommendation, transcripts of college work, 2 years of work experience. *Application fee:* $45. Applications for domestic and international students are processed on a rolling basis.

Application Contact Ms. Lisa Ephraim, Enrollment Manager, 8001 College Boulevard, Suite 100, Overland Park, KS 66210. *Phone:* 913-491-4432. *Fax:* 913-491-0470. *E-mail:* lephraim@bakeru.edu.

Benedictine College
Executive Master of Business Administration Program
Atchison, Kansas

Phone: 800-467-5340 Ext. 7589 **Fax:** 913-360.7301 **E-mail:** emba@benedictine.edu

Business Program(s) Web Site: http://www.benedictine.edu/emba

Graduate Business Unit Enrollment *Total:* 98 (28 full-time; 70 part-time). *Average Age:* 38.

Graduate Business Faculty *Total:* 12 (3 full-time; 9 part-time).

Admissions *Applied:* 121. *Admitted:* 104. *Enrolled:* 98. *Average GMAT:* 380. *Average GPA:* 3.2

Academic Calendar 12-month cohort.

After Graduation (Class of 2006–07) *Employed within 3 months of graduation:* 100%. *Average starting salary:* $45,000.

DEGREES EMBA • MBA

EMBA—Executive Master of Business Administration Full-time and part-time. At least 33 total credits required. 12 to 24 months to complete program. *Concentration:* executive programs.

MBA—Traditional MBA Full-time and part-time. GMAT scores required. Up to 33 total credits required. 24 to 72 months to complete program. *Concentrations:* accounting, business studies.

RESOURCES AND SERVICES 25 on-campus PCs are available to graduate business students. Access to Internet/World Wide Web and online grade reports available. *Personal computer requirements:* Graduate business students are required to have a personal computer. *Placement services include:* Alumni network, career counseling/planning, and electronic job bank.

EXPENSES *Tuition:* Full-time: $21,000. *Tuition (international):* Full-time: $21,000.

FINANCIAL AID (2007–08) 15 students received aid, including loans and scholarships. Aid is available to part-time students. *Financial aid application deadline:* 3/1.

Financial Aid Contact Tony Tanking, Director, Financial Aid, 1020 North 2nd Street, Atchison, KS 66002. *Phone:* 913-367-5340. *E-mail:* ttanking@benedictine.edu.

INTERNATIONAL STUDENTS *Services and facilities:* Counseling/support services, ESL/language courses, Housing location assistance, Visa Services. Financial aid is not available to international students. *Required with application:* TOEFL with recommended score of 550 (paper); proof of adequate funds; proof of health/immunizations.

International Student Contact Donna Bonnel, Administrative Specialist, 1020 North 2nd Street, Atchison, KS 66002. *Phone:* 913-360-7589. *Fax:* 913-360-7301. *E-mail:* emba@benedictine.edu.

APPLICATION *Required:* Application form, baccalaureate/first degree, essay, interview, 2 letters of recommendation, personal statement, resume/curriculum vitae, transcripts of college work, 5 years of work experience. *Application fee:* $100. *Deadlines:* 6/15 for fall (international), 4/1 for summer (international). Applications for domestic students are processed on a rolling basis.

Application Contact Donna Bonnel, Administrative Specialist, 1020 North 2nd Street, Atchison, KS 66002. *Phone:* 800-467-5340 Ext. 7589. *Fax:* 913-360.7301. *E-mail:* emba@benedictine.edu.

Emporia State University
School of Business
Emporia, Kansas

Phone: 620-341-5456 **Fax:** 620-341-6523 **E-mail:** mba@emporia.edu

Business Program(s) Web Site: http://www.emporia.edu/grad/prog.htm

Graduate Business Unit Enrollment *Total:* 117 (91 full-time; 26 part-time; 60 women; 40 international). *Average Age:* 28.

Graduate Business Faculty 19 full-time.

Admissions *Applied:* 48. *Admitted:* 39. *Enrolled:* 39. *Average GMAT:* 498. *Average GPA:* 3.32

Academic Calendar Semesters.

Emporia State University (continued)

Accreditation AACSB—The Association to Advance Collegiate Schools of Business.

After Graduation (Class of 2006–07) *Employed within 3 months of graduation:* 80%. *Average starting salary:* $42,855.

DEGREE MBA

MBA—Master of Business Administration Full-time and part-time. At least 36 total credits required. 12 to 84 months to complete program. *Concentrations:* accounting, general MBA, information systems.

RESOURCES AND SERVICES 200 on-campus PCs are available to graduate business students. Access to Internet/World Wide Web and online grade reports available. *Personal computer requirements:* Graduate business students are not required to have a personal computer. *Placement services include:* Alumni network, career placement, career counseling/planning, electronic job bank, resume referral, career fairs, job interviews arranged, resume preparation, and career library.

EXPENSES *Tuition (state resident):* Full-time: $4554. Part-time: $204 per credit hour. *Tuition (nonresident):* Full-time: $12,186. Part-time: $522 per credit hour. *Tuition (international):* Full-time: $12,186. Part-time: $522 per credit hour. *Typical graduate housing cost:* $6600 (including board).

FINANCIAL AID (2007–08) 25 students received aid, including research assistantships and teaching assistantships.

Financial Aid Contact Elaine Henrie, Director of Financial Aid, 1200 Commercial Street, ESU Box 4038, Emporia, KS 66801. *Phone:* 620-341-5457. *Fax:* 620-341-6088. *E-mail:* ehenrie@emporia.edu.

INTERNATIONAL STUDENTS 34% of students enrolled are international students. *Services and facilities:* Counseling/support services, ESL/language courses, Housing location assistance, International student housing, International student organization, Orientation, Visa Services. *Required with application:* Proof of adequate funds; proof of health/immunizations. *Recommended with application:* TOEFL with recommended score of 575 (paper).

International Student Contact James Harter, Assistant Vice President for International Education, 1200 Commercial Street, ESU Box 4041, Emporia, KS 66801-5087. *Phone:* 620-341-5374. *Fax:* 620-341-5918. *E-mail:* oisa@emporia.edu.

APPLICATION *Required:* GMAT, application form, baccalaureate/first degree, transcripts of college work. *Recommended:* 3 letters of recommendation, personal statement, resume/curriculum vitae. *Application fee:* $40, $75 (international). Applications for domestic and international students are processed on a rolling basis.

Application Contact Donald S. Miller, Director, MBA Program, 1200 Commercial Street, ESU Box 4059, Emporia, KS 66801. *Phone:* 620-341-5456. *Fax:* 620-341-6523. *E-mail:* mba@emporia.edu.

Kansas State University

College of Business Administration

Manhattan, Kansas

Phone: 785-532-7190 **Fax:** 785-532-7809 **E-mail:** gradbusiness@ksu.edu

Business Program(s) Web Site: http://www.cba.k-state.edu/departments/gradstudies/index.htm

Graduate Business Unit Enrollment *Total:* 101 (85 full-time; 16 part-time; 46 women; 19 international). *Average Age:* 28.

Graduate Business Faculty *Total:* 32 (31 full-time; 1 part-time).

Admissions *Applied:* 100. *Admitted:* 70. *Enrolled:* 55. *Average GMAT:* 550. *Average GPA:* 3.55

Academic Calendar Semesters.

Accreditation AACSB—The Association to Advance Collegiate Schools of Business.

After Graduation (Class of 2006–07) *Employed within 3 months of graduation:* 75%. *Average starting salary:* $55,000.

DEGREES M Acc • MBA

M Acc—Master of Accountancy Full-time. Bachelor's degree in Accounting or equivalent required. At least 30 total credits required. 12 to 18 months to complete program. *Concentration:* accounting.

MBA—Master of Business Administration Full-time and part-time. 40 to 52 total credits required. 24 months to complete program. *Concentrations:* finance, general MBA, human resources management, information technology, operations management.

RESOURCES AND SERVICES 1,000 on-campus PCs are available to graduate business students. Access to Internet/World Wide Web, online (class) registration, and online grade reports available. *Personal computer requirements:* Graduate business students are strongly recommended to purchase or lease a personal computer. *Special opportunities include:* An international exchange program and an internship program are available. *Placement services include:* Career placement, career counseling/planning, electronic job bank, resume referral, career fairs, job interviews arranged, resume preparation, and career library.

FINANCIAL AID (2007–08) 20 students received aid, including grants, loans, research assistantships, scholarships, and teaching assistantships. *Financial aid application deadline:* 2/1.

Financial Aid Contact Lawrence E. Moeder, Director of Student Financial Assistance, 104 Fairchild Hall, Manhattan, KS 66506-0501. *Phone:* 785-532-6420. *Fax:* 785-532-7629. *E-mail:* ksusfa@ksu.edu.

INTERNATIONAL STUDENTS 19% of students enrolled are international students. *Services and facilities:* Counseling/support services, ESL/language courses, Housing location assistance, International student housing, International student organization, Language tutoring, Orientation, Visa Services. Financial aid is available to international students. *Required with application:* TOEFL with recommended score of 213 (computer), 550 (paper), or 79 (Internet); proof of adequate funds; proof of health/immunizations.

International Student Contact Dr. Jeff Katz, Director of Graduate Studies, 107 Calvin Hall, Manhattan, KS 66506-0501. *Phone:* 785-532-7190. *Fax:* 785-532-7809. *E-mail:* gradbusiness@ksu.edu.

APPLICATION *Required:* GMAT, application form, baccalaureate/first degree, 3 letters of recommendation, personal statement, resume/curriculum vitae, transcripts of college work. *Recommended:* Work experience. *Application fee:* $50, $60 (international). Applications for domestic and international students are processed on a rolling basis.

Application Contact Dr. Jeffrey P. Katz, Director of Graduate Studies, 107 Calvin Hall, Manhattan, KS 66506-0501. *Phone:* 785-532-7190. *Fax:* 785-532-7809. *E-mail:* gradbusiness@ksu.edu.

Newman University

School of Business

Wichita, Kansas

Phone: 316-942-4291 Ext. 2230 **E-mail:** graduate@newman.edu

Business Program(s) Web Site: http://www.newmanu.edu

Graduate Business Unit Enrollment *Total:* 132 (132 part-time; 61 women; 31 international). *Average Age:* 30.

Graduate Business Faculty *Total:* 21 (6 full-time; 15 part-time).

Admissions *Applied:* 82. *Admitted:* 75. *Enrolled:* 71. *Average GPA:* 3.2

Academic Calendar Semesters.

After Graduation (Class of 2006–07) *Employed within 3 months of graduation:* 95%.

DEGREES MBA

MBA—Master of Business Administration Part-time. At least 32 total credits required. *Concentrations:* leadership, management, management information systems.

MBA—Master of Business Administration *Concentration:* international business.

MBA—Master of Business Administration *Concentration:* finance.

RESOURCES AND SERVICES 40 on-campus PCs are available to graduate business students. Access to Internet/World Wide Web, online (class) registration, and online grade reports available. *Personal computer requirements:* Graduate business students are strongly recommended to purchase or lease a personal computer. *Placement services include:* Alumni network, career counseling/planning, career fairs, resume preparation, and career library.

EXPENSES *Tuition:* Part-time: $431 per credit hour. *Tuition (international):* Part-time: $431 per credit hour. *Required fees:* Part-time: $10 per course. *Graduate housing:* Room and board costs vary by campus location, number of occupants, type of accommodation, and type of board plan. *Typical cost:* $8450 (including board), $6900 (room only).

Financial Aid Contact Ms. Brenda Krehbiel, Director of Financial Aid, 3100 McCormick Avenue, Wichita, KS 67213-2097. *Phone:* 316-942-4291 Ext. 2306. *E-mail:* krehbielb@newmanu.edu.

INTERNATIONAL STUDENTS 23% of students enrolled are international students. *Services and facilities:* Counseling/support services, Housing location assistance, International student organization. Financial aid is not available to international students. *Required with application:* TOEFL with recommended score of 550 (paper); proof of adequate funds. *Recommended with application:* IELT.

International Student Contact Ms. Ami Larrea Adams, Advisor, 3100 McCormick Avenue, Wichita, KS 67213. *Phone:* 316-942-4291 Ext. 2487. *E-mail:* larreaa@newmanu.edu.

APPLICATION *Required:* Application form, baccalaureate/first degree, 3 letters of recommendation, transcripts of college work. *Recommended:* Interview, resume/curriculum vitae. *Application fee:* $25, $40 (international). Applications for domestic and international students are processed on a rolling basis.

Application Contact Director of Graduate Admissions, 3100 McCormick Avenue, 67213-2084. *Phone:* 316-942-4291 Ext. 2230. *E-mail:* graduate@newman.edu.

Ottawa University
Graduate Studies-Kansas City
Overland Park, Kansas

Phone: 913-451-1431

Business Program(s) Web Site: http://www.ottawa.edu

DEGREES MA • MBA

MA—Master of Arts in Human Resources Full-time and part-time. Distance learning option. At least 36 total credits required. Minimum of 18 months to complete program. *Concentrations:* human resources management, management, organizational management.

MBA—Master of Business Administration Full-time and part-time. Distance learning option. At least 36 total credits required. Minimum of 18 months to complete program. *Concentration:* general MBA.

RESOURCES AND SERVICES *Personal computer requirements:* Graduate business students are strongly recommended to purchase or lease a personal computer.

INTERNATIONAL STUDENTS *Required with application:* TOEFL with recommended score of 213 (computer) or 550 (paper).

APPLICATION *Required:* 3 letters of recommendation, resume/curriculum vitae. *Application fee:* $65. Applications for domestic and international students are processed on a rolling basis.

Pittsburg State University
Kelce College of Business
Pittsburg, Kansas

Phone: 620-235-4598 **Fax:** 620-235-4578 **E-mail:** mba@pittstate.edu

Business Program(s) Web Site: http://www.pittstate.edu/kelce/

Graduate Business Unit Enrollment *Total:* 125 (95 full-time; 30 part-time; 59 women; 55 international). *Average Age:* 27.

Graduate Business Faculty 28 full-time.

Admissions *Applied:* 220. *Admitted:* 178. *Enrolled:* 48. *Average GMAT:* 500. *Average GPA:* 3.5

Academic Calendar Semesters.

Accreditation AACSB—The Association to Advance Collegiate Schools of Business.

After Graduation (Class of 2006–07) *Employed within 3 months of graduation:* 90%. *Average starting salary:* $44,567.

DEGREES MBA

MBA—General Administration Full-time and part-time. 34 to 64 total credits required. 12 to 72 months to complete program. *Concentration:* general MBA.

MBA—MBA—International Business Full-time and part-time. 34 to 73 total credits required. 12 to 72 months to complete program. *Concentration:* international business.

MBA—Master of Business Administration Full-time and part-time. Foreign transcripts must be evaluated by a Third-Party (FACS, etc.). 34 to 82 total credits required. 12 to 72 months to complete program. *Concentrations:* accounting, management.

RESOURCES AND SERVICES 320 on-campus PCs are available to graduate business students. Access to Internet/World Wide Web, online (class) registration, and online grade reports available. *Personal computer requirements:* Graduate business students are strongly recommended to purchase or lease a personal computer. *Special opportunities include:* An international exchange program and an internship program are available. *Placement services include:* Career placement, career counseling/planning, electronic job bank, resume referral, career fairs, job interviews arranged, resume preparation, and career library.

EXPENSES *Tuition (state resident):* Full-time: $4590. Part-time: $194 per semester hour. *Tuition (nonresident):* Full-time: $11,254. Part-time: $472 per semester hour. *Tuition (international):* Full-time: $11,254. Part-time: $472 per semester hour. *Required fees:* Full-time: $1000. Part-time: $1000 per year. *Graduate housing:* Room and board costs vary by number of occupants, type of accommodation, and type of board plan. *Typical cost:* $5088 (including board).

FINANCIAL AID (2007–08) 32 students received aid, including research assistantships, scholarships, teaching assistantships, and work study. *Financial aid application deadline:* 4/1.

Financial Aid Contact Ms. Marilyn Haverly, Director, Financial Aid, 1701 South Broadway, Pittsburg, KS 66762. *Phone:* 620-235-4240. *Fax:* 620-235-7515. *E-mail:* mhaverly@pittstate.edu.

INTERNATIONAL STUDENTS 44% of students enrolled are international students. *Services and facilities:* Counseling/support services, ESL/language courses, Housing location assistance, International student organization, Language tutoring, Orientation. Financial aid is available to international students. *Required with application:* TOEFL with recommended score of 213 (computer), 550 (paper), or 79 (Internet); proof of adequate funds. *Recommended with application:* IELT with recommended score of 6.

International Student Contact Chuck Olcese, Director, International Student Services, 1701 South Broadway, Pittsburg, KS 66762. *Phone:* 620-235-4680. *Fax:* 620-235-4962. *E-mail:* colcese@pittstate.edu.

Pittsburg State University (continued)

APPLICATION *Required:* GMAT, application form, baccalaureate/first degree, transcripts of college work. *Application fee:* $30, $60 (international). Applications for domestic and international students are processed on a rolling basis.

Application Contact Michael I. Muoghalu, Director of MBA Program, Pittsburg, KS 66762. *Phone:* 620-235-4598. *Fax:* 620-235-4578. *E-mail:* mba@pittstate.edu.

Southwestern College
Professional Studies Programs

Wichita, Kansas

Phone: 888-684-5335 Ext. 203 **E-mail:** gail.cullen@sckans.edu

Business Program(s) Web Site: http://www.southwesterncollege.org

Graduate Business Unit Enrollment *Total:* 119 (119 part-time; 54 women; 1 international). *Average Age:* 36.

Graduate Business Faculty 77 part-time.

Admissions *Applied:* 40. *Admitted:* 35. *Enrolled:* 35. *Average GPA:* 3.7

Academic Calendar Accelerated degree completion.

DEGREES M Div/MS • M Mgt • MBA • MM • MSM

M Div/MS—Specialized Ministries Full-time and part-time. Distance learning option. Bachelor's degree. At least 33 total credits required. Minimum of 12 months to complete program. *Concentration:* management.

M Mgt—Security Management Full-time and part-time. Distance learning option. Bachelor's degree. At least 39 total credits required. Minimum of 12 months to complete program. *Concentration:* management.

MBA Full-time and part-time. Distance learning option. Bachelor's degree. At least 36 total credits required. Minimum of 12 months to complete program. *Concentration:* administration.

MM—Leadership Full-time and part-time. Distance learning option. Bachelor's degree. At least 36 total credits required. Minimum of 12 months to complete program. *Concentration:* management.

MSM—Management Full-time and part-time. Distance learning option. Bachelor's degree. At least 36 total credits required. Minimum of 12 months to complete program. *Concentration:* risk management.

RESOURCES AND SERVICES 20 on-campus PCs are available to graduate business students. Access to Internet/World Wide Web, online (class) registration, and online grade reports available. *Personal computer requirements:* Graduate business students are strongly recommended to purchase or lease a personal computer.

EXPENSES *Tuition:* Full-time: $11,394. Part-time: $422 per credit hour. *Tuition (international):* Full-time: $11,394. Part-time: $422 per credit hour. Tuition and/or fees vary by class time, campus location, and academic program.

FINANCIAL AID (2007–08) 69 students received aid, including grants and loans.

INTERNATIONAL STUDENTS 0.8% of students enrolled are international students. *Required with application:* TOEFL with recommended score of 213 (computer) or 550 (paper); proof of adequate funds; proof of health/immunizations.

APPLICATION *Required:* Application form, baccalaureate/first degree, essay, interview, 2 letters of recommendation, transcripts of college work, 3 years of work experience. *Application fee:* $0. Applications for domestic and international students are processed on a rolling basis.

Application Contact Ms. Gail Cullen, Director of Academic Affairs, 2040 South Rock Road, Wichita, KS 67207. *Phone:* 888-684-5335 Ext. 203. *E-mail:* gail.cullen@sckans.edu.

University of Kansas
School of Business

Lawrence, Kansas

Phone: 913-897-8587 **Fax:** 785-864-5376 **E-mail:** bschoolgrad@ku.edu

Business Program(s) Web Site: http://www.business.ku.edu

Accreditation AACSB—The Association to Advance Collegiate Schools of Business.

DEGREES M Acct • MBA • MS

M Acct—Master of Accounting Full-time. Undergraduate degree in accounting or business required. At least 30 total credits required. 12 to 24 months to complete program. *Concentrations:* accounting, information systems, taxation.

MBA—Evening Master of Business Administration Part-time. At least 48 total credits required. 24 to 72 months to complete program. *Concentrations:* finance, general MBA, human resources management, information management, international business, management, marketing, strategic management.

MBA—In-Residence Master of Business Administration Full-time. At least 52 total credits required. 18 to 24 months to complete program. *Concentrations:* entrepreneurship, finance, human resources management, information management, international business, management, marketing, strategic management.

MS—Master of Science in Business, Finance Concentration Full-time and part-time. At least 30 total credits required. 12 to 24 months to complete program. *Concentration:* finance.

RESOURCES AND SERVICES 500 on-campus PCs are available to graduate business students. Access to Internet/World Wide Web, online (class) registration, and online grade reports available. *Personal computer requirements:* Graduate business students are strongly recommended to purchase or lease a personal computer. *Special opportunities include:* An international exchange program and an internship program are available. *Placement services include:* Alumni network, career placement, job search course, career counseling/planning, electronic job bank, resume referral, career fairs, job interviews arranged, resume preparation, and career library.

Application Contact Mr. Jeff Morrow, Masters Recruiting Coordinator, 1300 Sunnyside Avenue, 206 Summerfield Hall, Lawrence, KS 66045-7585. *Phone:* 913-897-8587. *Fax:* 785-864-5376. *E-mail:* bschoolgrad@ku.edu.

University of Phoenix–Wichita Campus
College of Graduate Business and Management

Wichita, Kansas

Phone: 480-317-6200 **Fax:** 480-643-1479 **E-mail:** beth.barilla@phoenix.edu

DEGREES MBA

MBA—Global Management Full-time. At least 45 total credits required. *Concentration:* international business.

MBA—Master of Business Administration Full-time. At least 45 total credits required. *Concentration:* administration.

RESOURCES AND SERVICES Access to online grade reports available. *Personal computer requirements:* Graduate business students are strongly recommended to purchase or lease a personal computer. *Placement services include:* Alumni network.

Application Contact Beth Barilla, Associate Vice President of Student Admissions and Services, Mail Stop AA-K101, 4615 East Elwood Street, Phoenix, AZ 85040-1958. *Phone:* 480-317-6200. *Fax:* 480-643-1479. *E-mail:* beth.barilla@phoenix.edu.

Washburn University
School of Business
Topeka, Kansas

Phone: 785-670-2047 **Fax:** 785-670-1063 **E-mail:** bob.boncella@washburn.edu

Business Program(s) Web Site: http://www.washburn.edu/business/mba/

Graduate Business Unit Enrollment *Total:* 67 (16 full-time; 51 part-time; 41 women; 5 international). *Average Age:* 29.

Graduate Business Faculty *Total:* 17 (14 full-time; 3 part-time).

Admissions *Applied:* 49. *Admitted:* 31. *Enrolled:* 31. *Average GMAT:* 535. *Average GPA:* 3.29

Academic Calendar Semesters.

Accreditation AACSB—The Association to Advance Collegiate Schools of Business.

After Graduation (Class of 2006–07) *Employed within 3 months of graduation:* 95%. *Average starting salary:* $52,200.

DEGREE MBA

MBA—Master of Business Administration Full-time and part-time. 30 to 55 total credits required. 12 to 72 months to complete program. *Concentration:* general MBA.

The mission of the Washburn University Master of Business Administration Program is to provide management education of recognized high quality through an evening M.B.A. program for current and future business professionals. It is designed for men and women who are seeking new career opportunities or who want stay in their current organizations and sharpen their managerial and leadership skills. Washburn M.B.A. students learn concepts and decision-making tools that are directly relevant to the work place.

Class schedules can vary to accommodate work and family obligations, allowing students to work at their own pace. To permit maximum flexibility, M.B.A. courses are scheduled one evening per week. Washburn's graduate faculty members are dedicated teachers whose professional interests include practical research. Their job is to be on the cutting edge and to know what current best practices are and where systems might be going.

Washburn is intimately connected to the business community it serves and is committed to the highest standards of quality and professionalism. The program's goal is to assure that the students have the knowledge and skills to enable them to succeed in general management and leadership roles and to contribute to the success of their organizations and of their local and regional economies.

RESOURCES AND SERVICES 100 on-campus PCs are available to graduate business students. Access to Internet/World Wide Web, online (class) registration, and online grade reports available. *Personal computer requirements:* Graduate business students are strongly recommended to purchase or lease a personal computer. *Placement services include:* Alumni network, career placement, job search course, career counseling/planning, electronic job bank, resume referral, career fairs, job interviews arranged, resume preparation, and career library.

EXPENSES *Tuition (state resident):* Part-time: $320 per credit hour. *Tuition (nonresident):* Part-time: $520 per credit hour. *Tuition (international):* Part-time: $520 per credit hour. *Graduate housing:* Room and board costs vary by number of occupants and type of board plan. *Typical cost:* $7000 (including board).

FINANCIAL AID (2007–08) 23 students received aid, including loans, scholarships, and work study. Aid is available to part-time students. *Financial aid application deadline:* 2/15.

Financial Aid Contact Ms. Annita Huff, Director, Financial Aid, 1700 Southwest College Avenue, Topeka, KS 66621. *Phone:* 785-670-1151. *Fax:* 785-670-1079. *E-mail:* annita.huff@washburn.edu.

INTERNATIONAL STUDENTS 7% of students enrolled are international students. *Services and facilities:* Counseling/support services, ESL/language courses, Housing location assistance, International student housing, International student organization, Language tutoring, Orientation, Visa Services. Financial aid is not available to international students. *Required with application:* TOEFL with recommended score of 213 (computer), 550 (paper), or 80 (Internet); TWE with recommended score of 5; proof of adequate funds; proof of health/immunizations. *Recommended with application:* IELT.

International Student Contact Baili Zhang, Director of International Student Services, 1700 Southwest College Avenue. *Phone:* 785-670-1051. *Fax:* 785-670-1067. *E-mail:* iip@washburn.edu.

APPLICATION *Required:* GMAT, application form, baccalaureate/first degree, 2 letters of recommendation, resume/curriculum vitae, transcripts of college work. *Recommended:* Interview, personal statement, work experience. *Application fee:* $40, $60 (international). Applications for domestic and international students are processed on a rolling basis.

Application Contact Dr. Robert J. Boncella, Director of MBA Program, 1700 Southwest College Avenue, Topeka, KS 66621. *Phone:* 785-670-2047. *Fax:* 785-670-1063. *E-mail:* bob.boncella@washburn.edu.

Wichita State University
W. Frank Barton School of Business
Wichita, Kansas

Phone: 316-978-3230 **Fax:** 316-978-3767 **E-mail:** nedra.henry@wichita.edu

Business Program(s) Web Site: http://www.wichita.edu/mba

Graduate Business Unit Enrollment *Total:* 198 (72 women; 23 international). *Average Age:* 27.

Graduate Business Faculty 54 full-time.

Admissions *Applied:* 142. *Admitted:* 89. *Enrolled:* 53. *Average GMAT:* 559. *Average GPA:* 3.35

Academic Calendar Semesters.

Accreditation AACSB—The Association to Advance Collegiate Schools of Business.

After Graduation (Class of 2006–07) *Employed within 3 months of graduation:* 80%. *Average starting salary:* $48,000.

DEGREES MBA • MBA/MS

MBA—Executive Master of Business Administration Part-time. 5-10 years of managerial work experience is required. At least 36 total credits required. 22 months to complete program. *Concentration:* executive programs.

MBA—Master of Business Administration Full-time and part-time. 36 to 48 total credits required. 12 to 72 months to complete program. *Concentrations:* entrepreneurship, finance, general MBA, health administration, international business, marketing, operations management.

MBA/MS—Master of Science in Business/Master of Science in Nursing Full-time and part-time. At least 63 total credits required. 36 to 72 months to complete program. *Concentration:* combined degrees.

RESOURCES AND SERVICES 500 on-campus PCs are available to graduate business students. Access to Internet/World Wide Web, online (class) registration, and online grade reports available. *Personal computer requirements:* Graduate business students are strongly recommended to purchase or lease a personal computer. *Special opportunities include:* An international exchange program and an internship program are available.

Wichita State University (continued)

Placement services include: Alumni network, career placement, career counseling/planning, electronic job bank, resume referral, career fairs, job interviews arranged, resume preparation, and career library.

EXPENSES *Tuition (state resident):* Full-time: $1855.80. Part-time: $206.20 per credit hour. *Tuition (nonresident):* Full-time: $5005. Part-time: $556.10 per credit hour. *Tuition (international):* Full-time: $5004.90. Part-time: $556.10 per credit hour. *Required fees:* Full-time: $233. Part-time: $188 per semester. *Graduate housing:* Room and board costs vary by number of occupants, type of accommodation, and type of board plan. *Typical cost:* $5860 (including board), $3245 (room only).

FINANCIAL AID (2007–08) 20 students received aid, including fellowships, loans, and research assistantships. Aid is available to part-time students. *Financial aid application deadline:* 3/30.

Financial Aid Contact Deb Byers, Director, Financial Planning and Assistance, 1845 North Fairmount, Wichita, KS 67260-0024. *Phone:* 800-522-2978. *Fax:* 316-978-3396. *E-mail:* deb.byers@wichita.edu.

INTERNATIONAL STUDENTS 12% of students enrolled are international students. *Services and facilities:* Counseling/support services, ESL/language courses, Housing location assistance, International student housing, International student organization, Orientation, Visa Services. Financial aid is available to international students. *Required with application:* TOEFL with recommended score of 230 (computer), 570 (paper), or 88 (Internet); proof of adequate funds. *Recommended with application:* IELT with recommended score of 7; proof of health/immunizations.

International Student Contact Vince Altum, Coordinator of Recruiting, 1845 North Fairmount, Wichita, KS 67260-0122. *Phone:* 316-978-3232. *Fax:* 316-978-3777. *E-mail:* vince.altum@wichita.edu.

APPLICATION *Required:* GMAT, application form, baccalaureate/first degree, essay, 2 letters of recommendation, personal statement, resume/curriculum vitae, transcripts of college work. *Recommended:* Work experience. *Application fee:* $35, $50 (international). Applications for domestic and international students are processed on a rolling basis.

Application Contact Nedra Henry, Administrative Coordinator, 1845 North Fairmount, Wichita, KS 67260-0048. *Phone:* 316-978-3230. *Fax:* 316-978-3767. *E-mail:* nedra.henry@wichita.edu.

KENTUCKY

Bellarmine University
W. Fielding Rubel School of Business

Louisville, Kentucky

Phone: 502-452-8258 **Fax:** 502-452-8013 **E-mail:** lrichardson@bellarmine.edu

Business Program(s) Web Site: http://www.bellarmine.edu

Graduate Business Unit Enrollment *Total:* 232 (94 full-time; 138 part-time; 93 women; 4 international). *Average Age:* 29.

Graduate Business Faculty *Total:* 18 (14 full-time; 4 part-time).

Admissions *Applied:* 125. *Admitted:* 120. *Enrolled:* 109. *Average GMAT:* 485. *Average GPA:* 3.2

Academic Calendar Semesters.

Accreditation AACSB—The Association to Advance Collegiate Schools of Business.

After Graduation (Class of 2006–07) *Employed within 3 months of graduation:* 99%.

DEGREES MBA

MBA—Executive Master of Business Administration Full-time. At least 48 total credits required. 16 months to complete program. *Concentration:* executive programs.

MBA—Weekend Master of Business Administration Full-time. At least 48 total credits required. 16 to 22 months to complete program. *Concentration:* general MBA.

MBA—Weeknight Master of Business Administration Part-time. At least 48 total credits required. 30 to 72 months to complete program. *Concentration:* general MBA.

RESOURCES AND SERVICES 430 on-campus PCs are available to graduate business students. Access to Internet/World Wide Web available. *Personal computer requirements:* Graduate business students are not required to have a personal computer. *Placement services include:* Alumni network, career placement, career counseling/planning, career fairs, job interviews arranged, and career library.

FINANCIAL AID (2007–08) Loans. Aid is available to part-time students. *Financial aid application deadline:* 8/15.

Financial Aid Contact Heather Boutell, Associate Director of Financial Aid, 2001 Newburg Road, Louisville, KY 40205-0671. *Phone:* 502-452-8131. *Fax:* 502-452-8002. *E-mail:* hboutell@bellarmine.edu.

INTERNATIONAL STUDENTS 2% of students enrolled are international students. *Services and facilities:* Counseling/support services, Orientation. Financial aid is not available to international students. *Required with application:* TOEFL with recommended score of 213 (computer) or 550 (paper); proof of adequate funds.

International Student Contact Laura Richardson, Director, MBA Programs, 2001 Newburg Road, Louisville, KY 40205-0671. *Phone:* 502-452-8258. *Fax:* 502-452-8013. *E-mail:* lrichardson@bellarmine.edu.

APPLICATION *Required:* GMAT, application form, baccalaureate/first degree, essay, 2 letters of recommendation, transcripts of college work. *Recommended:* Interview, personal statement, resume/curriculum vitae, work experience. *Application fee:* $25.

Application Contact Laura Richardson, Director, MBA Programs, 2001 Newburg Road, Louisville, KY 40205-0671. *Phone:* 502-452-8258. *Fax:* 502-452-8013. *E-mail:* lrichardson@bellarmine.edu.

Brescia University
Program in Management

Owensboro, Kentucky

Phone: 270-686-4241 **Fax:** 270-686-4134 **E-mail:** admissions@brescia.edu

Business Program(s) Web Site: http://www.brescia.edu

Graduate Business Unit Enrollment *Total:* 26 (26 full-time; 11 women; 6 international). *Average Age:* 38.

Graduate Business Faculty *Total:* 5 (4 full-time; 1 part-time).

Admissions *Applied:* 26. *Admitted:* 26. *Enrolled:* 26. *Average GMAT:* 420. *Average GPA:* 3.4

Academic Calendar Quarters.

After Graduation (Class of 2006–07) *Employed within 3 months of graduation:* 100%.

DEGREE MSM

MSM—Master of Science in Management Full-time and part-time. Minimum 2.5 undergraduate GPA required. At least 32 total credits required. 22 to 72 months to complete program. *Concentrations:* human resources management, international business, international economics, leadership, organizational management, strategic management.

RESOURCES AND SERVICES 45 on-campus PCs are available to graduate business students. Access to Internet/World Wide Web and online grade reports available. *Personal computer requirements:* Graduate business students are strongly recommended to purchase or lease a personal computer. *Placement services include:* Alumni network, career placement, career counseling/planning, electronic job bank, career fairs, resume preparation, and career library.

EXPENSES *Tuition:* Part-time: $325 per credit hour. *Tuition (international):* Part-time: $325 per credit hour. *Required fees:* Part-time: $80 per year.

FINANCIAL AID (2007–08) Loans.

Financial Aid Contact Ms. Marcie Tillett, Student Financial Aid Director, 717 Frederica Street, Owensboro, KY 42301-3023. *Phone:* 270-686-4241. *Fax:* 270-686-4314. *E-mail:* marcie.tillett@brescia.edu.

INTERNATIONAL STUDENTS 23% of students enrolled are international students. *Services and facilities:* Counseling/support services, ESL/language courses, Housing location assistance, International student organization, Orientation. Financial aid is not available to international students. *Required with application:* TOEFL with recommended score of 213 (computer) or 550 (paper); proof of adequate funds.

International Student Contact Dean Chris Houk, Dean of Enrollment, 717 Frederica Street, Owensboro, KY 42301-3023. *Phone:* 270-686-4241. *Fax:* 270-686-4134. *E-mail:* admissions@brescia.edu.

APPLICATION *Required:* Application form, baccalaureate/first degree, interview, 2 letters of recommendation, personal statement, resume/ curriculum vitae, transcripts of college work. School will accept GMAT and GRE. *Recommended:* Work experience. *Application fee:* $50. Applications for domestic and international students are processed on a rolling basis.

Application Contact Dean Chris Houk, Dean of Enrollment, 717 Frederica Street, Admissions Office, Owensboro, KY 42301-3023. *Phone:* 270-686-4241. *Fax:* 270-686-4134. *E-mail:* admissions@brescia.edu.

Campbellsville University
School of Business and Economics
Campbellsville, Kentucky

Phone: 270-789-5078 Ext. 5078 **Fax:** 270-789-5050 **E-mail:** rtargo@campbellsville.edu

Business Program(s) Web Site: http://www.campbellsville.edu

Graduate Business Unit Enrollment *Total:* 37 (1 full-time; 36 part-time; 19 women; 2 international).

Graduate Business Faculty *Total:* 6 (4 full-time; 2 part-time).

Admissions *Applied:* 30. *Admitted:* 18. *Enrolled:* 8. *Average GMAT:* 450. *Average GPA:* 3.2

Academic Calendar Trimesters.

After Graduation (Class of 2006–07) *Employed within 3 months of graduation:* 90%. *Average starting salary:* $40,000.

DEGREE MBA

MBA—Master of Business Administration Distance learning option. 36 total credits required. 18 to 60 months to complete program. *Concentration:* general MBA.

RESOURCES AND SERVICES 125 on-campus PCs are available to graduate business students. Access to Internet/World Wide Web, online (class) registration, and online grade reports available. *Personal computer requirements:* Graduate business students are strongly recommended to purchase or lease a personal computer. *Special opportunities include:* An internship program is available. *Placement services include:* Career placement, job search course, career counseling/planning, electronic job bank, resume referral, career fairs, job interviews arranged, and resume preparation.

EXPENSES *Tuition:* Full-time: $6570. Part-time: $365 per credit hour. *Tuition (international):* Full-time: $6570. Part-time: $365 per credit hour. *Required fees:* Full-time: $250. Part-time: $125 per semester. *Typical graduate housing cost:* $6410 (including board).

FINANCIAL AID (2007–08) 28 students received aid, including grants, loans, research assistantships, and scholarships. Aid is available to part-time students. *Financial aid application deadline:* 6/30.

Financial Aid Contact Christi Tolson, Director of Financial Aid, 1 University Drive, UPO 1305, Campbellsville, KY 42718. *Phone:* 270-789-5013. *Fax:* 270-789-5050. *E-mail:* ctolson@campbellsvil.edu.

INTERNATIONAL STUDENTS 5% of students enrolled are international students. *Services and facilities:* Counseling/support services, ESL/language courses, Housing location assistance, Language tutoring, Orientation. Financial aid is available to international students. *Required with application:* TOEFL with recommended score of 213 (computer) or 550 (paper). *Recommended with application:* Proof of adequate funds; proof of health/immunizations.

International Student Contact Ms. Karla Deaton, Graduate Admissions, 1 University Drive, UPO 1299, Campbellsville, KY 42718. *Phone:* 270-789-5078 Ext. 5078. *Fax:* 270-789-5050. *E-mail:* krdeaton@ campbellsville.edu.

APPLICATION *Required:* GRE, application form, baccalaureate/first degree, essay, 2 letters of recommendation, personal statement, resume/ curriculum vitae, transcripts of college work, 3 years of work experience. School will accept GMAT. *Application fee:* $25. Applications for domestic and international students are processed on a rolling basis.

Application Contact Ms. Karla Deaton, Graduate Admissions, 1 University Drive, UPO 1299, Campbellsville, KY 42718. *Phone:* 270-789-5078 Ext. 5078. *Fax:* 270-789-5050. *E-mail:* rtargo@ campbellsville.edu.

Eastern Kentucky University
College of Business and Technology
Richmond, Kentucky

Phone: 859-622-1775 **Fax:** 859-622-1382 **E-mail:** mba@eku.edu

Business Program(s) Web Site: http://www.mba.eku.edu/

Graduate Business Unit Enrollment *Total:* 74 (13 full-time; 61 part-time; 36 women; 16 international). *Average Age:* 41.

Graduate Business Faculty 20 full-time.

Admissions *Applied:* 38. *Admitted:* 30. *Enrolled:* 27. *Average GMAT:* 520. *Average GPA:* 3.23

Academic Calendar Semesters.

Accreditation AACSB—The Association to Advance Collegiate Schools of Business.

DEGREES MBA

MBA Full-time and part-time. Distance learning option. 30 to 36 total credits required. 12 to 84 months to complete program. *Concentration:* general MBA.

MBA—MBA with Accounting Option Full-time and part-time. Distance learning option. Undergraduate degree in accounting required. 30 to 36 total credits required. 12 to 84 months to complete program. *Concentration:* accounting.

MBA—MBA with Integrated Communications Option Full-time and part-time. Distance learning option. 33 to 39 total credits required. 12 to 84 months to complete program. *Concentration:* general MBA.

RESOURCES AND SERVICES 165 on-campus PCs are available to graduate business students. Access to Internet/World Wide Web, online (class) registration, and online grade reports available. *Personal computer requirements:* Graduate business students are not required to have a personal computer. *Placement services include:* Career counseling/ planning, career fairs, and resume preparation.

EXPENSES *Tuition (state resident):* Full-time: $6140. Part-time: $341 per credit hour. *Tuition (nonresident):* Full-time: $8419. Part-time: $935 per credit hour. *Tuition (international):* Full-time: $8419. Part-time: $935 per credit hour. *Required fees:* Full-time: $25. Tuition and/or fees vary by

Eastern Kentucky University (continued)

local reciprocity agreements. *Graduate housing:* Room and board costs vary by number of occupants, type of accommodation, and type of board plan. *Typical cost:* $2780 (including board), $2358 (room only).

FINANCIAL AID (2007–08) 12 students received aid, including loans, research assistantships, teaching assistantships, and work study.

Financial Aid Contact Shelley Park, Director, Financial Assistance, SSB CPO 59, Richmond, KY 40475-3102. *Phone:* 859-622-2361. *Fax:* 859-622-1020. *E-mail:* shelley.park@eku.edu.

INTERNATIONAL STUDENTS 22% of students enrolled are international students. *Services and facilities:* Counseling/support services, ESL/language courses, International student organization, Orientation. Financial aid is available to international students. *Required with application:* TOEFL with recommended score of 550 (paper); proof of adequate funds; proof of health/immunizations.

International Student Contact Neil Wright, Director of International Education, Case Annex, Room 181, Richmond, KY 40475. *Phone:* 859-622-1478. *Fax:* 859-622-1020. *E-mail:* neil.wright@.eku.edu.

APPLICATION *Required:* GMAT, application form, baccalaureate/first degree, 3 letters of recommendation, personal statement, resume/curriculum vitae, transcripts of college work. *Application fee:* $35. Applications for domestic and international students are processed on a rolling basis.

Application Contact Dr. Judith W. Spain, MBA Director, BTC 257, 521 Lancaster Avenue, Richmond, KY 40475-3102. *Phone:* 859-622-1775. *Fax:* 859-622-1382. *E-mail:* mba@eku.edu.

Morehead State University
College of Business
Morehead, Kentucky

Phone: 606-783-2969 **Fax:** 606-783-5025 **E-mail:** k.moore@morehead-st.edu

Business Program(s) Web Site: http://www.moreheadstate.edu/mba

Graduate Business Unit Enrollment *Total:* 163 (21 full-time; 142 part-time; 85 women). *Average Age:* 34.

Graduate Business Faculty 26 full-time.

Admissions *Applied:* 157. *Admitted:* 93. *Enrolled:* 57. *Average GMAT:* 488. *Average GPA:* 3.4

Academic Calendar Semesters.

Accreditation AACSB—The Association to Advance Collegiate Schools of Business. ACBSP—The American Council of Business Schools and Programs.

DEGREE MBA

MBA—Master of Business Administration Full-time and part-time. Distance learning option. 36 to 54 total credits required. *Concentration:* general MBA.

RESOURCES AND SERVICES 830 on-campus PCs are available to graduate business students. Access to Internet/World Wide Web, online (class) registration, and online grade reports available. *Personal computer requirements:* Graduate business students are strongly recommended to purchase or lease a personal computer. *Placement services include:* Alumni network, career placement, career counseling/planning, electronic job bank, resume referral, career fairs, resume preparation, and career library.

EXPENSES *Tuition (state resident):* Full-time: $2835. Part-time: $225 per credit hour. *Tuition (nonresident):* Full-time: $7371. Part-time: $585 per credit hour. *Graduate housing:* Room and board costs vary by type of accommodation and type of board plan.

FINANCIAL AID (2007–08) Loans, research assistantships, and work study. *Financial aid application deadline:* 4/1.

Financial Aid Contact Ms. Carol Becker, Director of Financial Aid, Admissions Center 100, Morehead, KY 40351. *Phone:* 606-783-2011. *Fax:* 606-783-2293. *E-mail:* finaid@morehead-st.edu.

INTERNATIONAL STUDENTS *Services and facilities:* Counseling/support services, ESL/language courses, International student organization, Language tutoring, Orientation, Visa Services. Financial aid is available to international students. *Required with application:* TOEFL with recommended score of 525 (paper); proof of adequate funds.

International Student Contact Ms. Pamela Jaisingh, International Student Coordinator, 225 Raider Hall, Morehead, KY 40351. *Phone:* 606-783-9305. *E-mail:* p.jaisingh@morehead-st.edu.

APPLICATION *Required:* GMAT, application form, baccalaureate/first degree, transcripts of college work. *Recommended:* Work experience. *Deadlines:* 8/1 for fall, 12/1 for spring, 4/15 for summer.

Application Contact Dr. Keith D. Moore, MBA Program Director, 213 Combs Building, Morehead, KY 40351. *Phone:* 606-783-2969. *Fax:* 606-783-5025. *E-mail:* k.moore@morehead-st.edu.

Murray State University
College of Business and Public Affairs
Murray, Kentucky

Phone: 270-762-6970 **Fax:** 270-762-3482 **E-mail:** cbpa@murraystate.edu

Business Program(s) Web Site: http://www.murraystate.edu/cbpa

Graduate Business Unit Enrollment *Total:* 185 (109 full-time; 76 part-time; 100 women; 31 international). *Average Age:* 24.

Graduate Business Faculty 24 full-time.

Admissions *Applied:* 181. *Admitted:* 146. *Enrolled:* 80. *Average GMAT:* 490. *Average GPA:* 3.31

Academic Calendar Semesters.

Accreditation AACSB—The Association to Advance Collegiate Schools of Business.

DEGREES M Pr A • MA • MBA • MS

M Pr A—Master of Professional Accountancy Full-time and part-time. 30 to 150 total credits required. *Concentration:* accounting.

MA—Organizational Communication Full-time and part-time. 30 total credits required. 12 to 96 months to complete program. *Concentration:* management communication.

MBA—Master of Business Administration Full-time and part-time. Distance learning option. 30 total credits required. 12 to 96 months to complete program. *Concentrations:* accounting, economics, electronic commerce (E-commerce), finance, management, marketing.

MS—Master of Science in Economics Full-time and part-time. At least 30 total credits required. 18 to 96 months to complete program. *Concentration:* economics.

MS—Master of Science in Organizational Communication Full-time and part-time. 30 total credits required. 12 to 96 months to complete program. *Concentration:* management communication.

MS—Master of Science in Telecommunications Systems Management Full-time and part-time. At least 36 total credits required. 18 to 96 months to complete program. *Concentration:* telecommunications management.

RESOURCES AND SERVICES 1,200 on-campus PCs are available to graduate business students. Access to Internet/World Wide Web and online grade reports available. *Personal computer requirements:* Graduate business students are not required to have a personal computer. *Special opportunities include:* An international exchange program is available. *Placement services include:* Alumni network, career placement, career counseling/planning, electronic job bank, resume referral, career fairs, job interviews arranged, resume preparation, and career library.

EXPENSES *Tuition (state resident):* Full-time: $6156. Part-time: $435 per credit hour. *Tuition (nonresident):* Full-time: $17,316. Part-time: $962 per credit hour. *Tuition (international):* Full-time: $17,316. Part-time: $962 per credit hour. *Required fees:* Full-time: $120. Part-time: $40 per credit hour. Tuition and/or fees vary by number of courses or credits taken and academic program. *Graduate housing:* Room and board costs vary by number of occupants, type of accommodation, and type of board plan. *Typical cost:* $3605 (including board).

FINANCIAL AID (2007–08) 30 students received aid, including research assistantships, scholarships, and teaching assistantships. *Financial aid application deadline:* 4/1.

Financial Aid Contact Mr. Charles Vinson, Director, Student Financial Aid, PO Box 9, Murray, KY 42071. *Phone:* 270-762-2596. *Fax:* 270-762-3050. *E-mail:* charles.vinson@murraystate.edu.

INTERNATIONAL STUDENTS 17% of students enrolled are international students. *Services and facilities:* Counseling/support services, ESL/language courses, Housing location assistance, International student organization, Language tutoring, Orientation, Visa Services. Financial aid is available to international students. *Required with application:* TOEFL with recommended score of 297 (computer) or 525 (paper); proof of adequate funds; proof of health/immunizations.

International Student Contact Michael Basile, Director, Institute for International Programs, PO Box 9, Murray, KY 42071. *Phone:* 270-762-4411. *Fax:* 270-762-3237. *E-mail:* michael.basile@murraystate.edu.

APPLICATION *Required:* GMAT, application form, baccalaureate/first degree, transcripts of college work. School will accept GRE. *Application fee:* $25. Applications for domestic and international students are processed on a rolling basis.

Application Contact Dr. Nkombo Muuka, MBA Director, 109 Business Building, Murray, KY 42071. *Phone:* 270-762-6970. *Fax:* 270-762-3482. *E-mail:* cbpa@murraystate.edu.

Northern Kentucky University
College of Business
Highland Heights, Kentucky

Phone: 859-572-6336 **Fax:** 859-572-6177 **E-mail:** mbusiness@nku.edu

Business Program(s) Web Site: http://co.nku.edu/mba

Graduate Business Unit Enrollment *Total:* 336 (51 full-time; 285 part-time; 148 women; 13 international). *Average Age:* 30.

Graduate Business Faculty *Total:* 30 (22 full-time; 8 part-time).

Admissions *Applied:* 105. *Admitted:* 78. *Enrolled:* 48. *Average GMAT:* 527. *Average GPA:* 3.1

Academic Calendar Semesters.

Accreditation AACSB—The Association to Advance Collegiate Schools of Business.

After Graduation (Class of 2006–07) *Employed within 3 months of graduation:* 95%. *Average starting salary:* $55,000.

DEGREES JD/MBA • M Acc • MBA • MBA equivalent

JD/MBA—Juris Doctor/Master of Business Administration Full-time and part-time. Separate admission to the College of Law required. 110 to 119 total credits required. 54 to 120 months to complete program. *Concentration:* combined degrees.

M Acc—Master of Accountancy Full-time and part-time. Undergraduate degree in accounting with a minimum GPA of 2.9 in accounting required. 30 total credits required. 12 to 72 months to complete program. *Concentration:* accounting.

MBA—Master of Business Administration Full-time and part-time. A GMAT score of 450, and a minimum undergraduate GPA 2.5. 39 to 51 total credits required. 24 to 72 months to complete program. *Concentrations:* entrepreneurship, finance, international business, management information systems, marketing, project management.

MBA equivalent—Master of Business Informatics Full-time and part-time. 30 to 42 total credits required. 12 to 84 months to complete program. *Concentration:* information systems.

RESOURCES AND SERVICES 300 on-campus PCs are available to graduate business students. Access to Internet/World Wide Web, online (class) registration, and online grade reports available. *Personal computer requirements:* Graduate business students are not required to have a personal computer. *Special opportunities include:* An international exchange program is available. *Placement services include:* Career placement, career counseling/planning, electronic job bank, resume referral, career fairs, job interviews arranged, resume preparation, and career library.

EXPENSES *Graduate housing:* Room and board costs vary by campus location, number of occupants, type of accommodation, and type of board plan.

FINANCIAL AID (2007–08) 15 students received aid, including loans, research assistantships, scholarships, and work study. Aid is available to part-time students. *Financial aid application deadline:* 3/1.

Financial Aid Contact Dr. Peg Griffin, Director of Graduate Programs, 333 Natural Science Building, Highland Heights, KY 41099. *Phone:* 859-572-6364. *Fax:* 859-572-6670. *E-mail:* griffinp@nku.edu.

INTERNATIONAL STUDENTS 4% of students enrolled are international students. *Services and facilities:* Counseling/support services, Housing location assistance, International student housing, International student organization, Language tutoring, Orientation, Visa Services, liaison with agencies involved with educational exchange. Financial aid is available to international students. *Required with application:* TOEFL with recommended score of 213 (computer) or 550 (paper); proof of adequate funds; proof of health/immunizations.

International Student Contact Mr. Adam Widanski, Director, International Student Affairs Office, University Center 366, Louie B. Nunn Drive, Highland Heights, KY 41099. *Phone:* 859-572-6517. *Fax:* 859-572-6178. *E-mail:* isa@nku.edu.

APPLICATION *Required:* GMAT, application form, baccalaureate/first degree, transcripts of college work. School will accept GRE. *Recommended:* Essay, 2 years of work experience. *Application fee:* $25. *Deadlines:* 8/1 for fall, 12/1 for spring, 5/1 for summer, 6/1 for fall (international), 10/1 for spring (international).

Application Contact Dr. Greg W Farfsing, MBA Program Director, BEP Center 401, Highland Heights, KY 41099. *Phone:* 859-572-6336. *Fax:* 859-572-6177. *E-mail:* mbusiness@nku.edu.

Thomas More College
Program in Business Administration
Crestview Hills, Kentucky

Phone: 859-344-3602 **Fax:** 859-344-3686 **E-mail:** nathan.hartman@thomasmore.edu

Business Program(s) Web Site: http://www.thomasmore.edu

Graduate Business Unit Enrollment *Total:* 85 (85 full-time; 35 women; 2 international). *Average Age:* 32.

Graduate Business Faculty *Total:* 13 (11 full-time; 2 part-time).

Admissions *Applied:* 69. *Admitted:* 47. *Enrolled:* 44.

Academic Calendar Continuous.

After Graduation (Class of 2006–07) *Employed within 3 months of graduation:* 100%. *Average starting salary:* $50,000.

DEGREE MBA

MBA—Accelerated Master of Business Administration Full-time. 45 total credits required. 22 months to complete program. *Concentration:* general MBA.

RESOURCES AND SERVICES 115 on-campus PCs are available to graduate business students. Access to Internet/World Wide Web and online

Thomas More College (continued)

grade reports available. *Personal computer requirements:* Graduate business students are strongly recommended to purchase or lease a personal computer. *Placement services include:* Career counseling/planning, resume referral, career fairs, and resume preparation.

EXPENSES *Tuition:* Full-time: $10,555. *Tuition (international):* Full-time: $10,555.

FINANCIAL AID (2007–08) 80 students received aid, including loans. *Financial aid application deadline:* 3/15.

Financial Aid Contact Mary Givhan, Director of Financial Aid, 333 Thomas More Parkway, Crestview Hills, KY 41017-3495. *Phone:* 859-344-3531. *Fax:* 859-344-3638. *E-mail:* mary.givhan@thomasmore.edu.

INTERNATIONAL STUDENTS 2% of students enrolled are international students. *Services and facilities:* Counseling/support services, International student organization, Visa Services. Financial aid is available to international students. *Required with application:* TOEFL with recommended score of 250 (computer), 600 (paper), or 100 (Internet); proof of adequate funds; proof of health/immunizations.

International Student Contact Jennifer Mason, International Student Coordinator, 333 Thomas More Parkway, Crestview Hills, KY 41017-3495. *Phone:* 859-344-3307. *Fax:* 859-344-3444. *E-mail:* jennifer.mason@thomasmore.edu.

APPLICATION *Required:* GMAT, application form, baccalaureate/first degree, essay, 3 letters of recommendation, personal statement, resume/curriculum vitae, transcripts of college work, 2 years of work experience. *Application fee:* $25. Applications for domestic and international students are processed on a rolling basis.

Application Contact Nathan Hartman, Director of Lifelong Learning, 333 Thomas More Parkway, Crestview Hills, KY 41017-3495. *Phone:* 859-344-3602. *Fax:* 859-344-3686. *E-mail:* nathan.hartman@thomasmore.edu.

University of Kentucky

Gatton College of Business and Economics

Lexington, Kentucky

Phone: 859-257-7722 **Fax:** 859-323-9971 **E-mail:** kemper@uky.edu

Business Program(s) Web Site: http://gatton.uky.edu/academic/mba/index.html

Graduate Business Unit Enrollment *Total:* 295 (183 full-time; 112 part-time; 96 women; 46 international). *Average Age:* 27.

Graduate Business Faculty 68 full-time.

Admissions *Applied:* 212. *Admitted:* 136. *Enrolled:* 109. *Average GMAT:* 609. *Average GPA:* 3.4

Academic Calendar Continuous.

Accreditation AACSB—The Association to Advance Collegiate Schools of Business.

After Graduation (Class of 2006–07) *Employed within 3 months of graduation:* 65%. *Average starting salary:* $46,991.

DEGREES JD/MBA • MBA • MBA/INR • MD/MBA • MS • Pharm D/MBA

JD/MBA—Juris Doctor/Master of Business Administration Full-time. Apply independently to both Law School and MBA program. At least 111 total credits required. 48 to 96 months to complete program. *Concentration:* combined degrees.

MBA—Evening MBA Program Full-time and part-time. Minimum of two years of relevant work experience. At least 36 total credits required. 18 to 96 months to complete program. *Concentrations:* accounting, banking, finance, information management, international business, marketing, real estate.

MBA—One-Year MBA Full-time. At least 44 total credits required. Minimum of 11 months to complete program. *Concentration:* general MBA.

MBA/INR—Master of Business Administration/Master of International Relations Full-time. Apply independently to both MBA Program and School of Diplomacy. At least 57 total credits required. *Concentrations:* combined degrees, European business studies, international and area business studies, international banking, international business, international development management, international economics, international finance, international management, international marketing, international trade.

MD/MBA—Doctor of Medicine/Master of Business Administration Full-time. Apply independently to both Medical School and MBA program. At least 204 total credits required. 60 to 96 months to complete program. *Concentration:* combined degrees.

MS—Master of Science in Accountancy Full-time and part-time. At least 30 total credits required. 12 to 96 months to complete program. *Concentration:* accounting.

Pharm D/MBA—Doctor of Pharmacy/Master of Business Administration Full-time. Apply independently to both Pharmacy school and MBA program. At least 148 total credits required. Minimum of 48 months to complete program. *Concentration:* combined degrees.

RESOURCES AND SERVICES 150 on-campus PCs are available to graduate business students. Access to Internet/World Wide Web, online (class) registration, and online grade reports available. *Personal computer requirements:* Graduate business students are strongly recommended to purchase or lease a personal computer. *Special opportunities include:* An international exchange program and an internship program are available. *Placement services include:* Alumni network, career placement, job search course, career counseling/planning, electronic job bank, resume referral, career fairs, job interviews arranged, resume preparation, and career library.

EXPENSES *Tuition (state resident):* Full-time: $8212. Part-time: $468.43 per credit hour. *Tuition (nonresident):* Full-time: $16,700. Part-time: $1046.43 per credit hour. *Tuition (international):* Full-time: $16,700. Part-time: $1046.43 per credit hour. *Required fees:* Full-time: $6000. Part-time: $750 per unit. Tuition and/or fees vary by academic program. *Graduate housing:* Room and board costs vary by type of accommodation. *Typical cost:* $7200 (room only).

FINANCIAL AID (2007–08) 31 students received aid, including fellowships, research assistantships, scholarships, and work study. *Financial aid application deadline:* 4/1.

Financial Aid Contact Ms. Beverly Kemper, MBA Student Advisor, MBA Center, Lexington, KY 40506-0034. *Phone:* 859-257-7722. *Fax:* 859-323-9971. *E-mail:* kemper@uky.edu.

INTERNATIONAL STUDENTS 16% of students enrolled are international students. *Services and facilities:* Counseling/support services, ESL/language courses, Housing location assistance, International student housing, International student organization, Language tutoring, Orientation, Visa Services, Host family program. Financial aid is available to international students. *Required with application:* TOEFL with recommended score of 213 (computer), 550 (paper), or 79 (Internet); TWE with recommended score of 4.5; proof of adequate funds; proof of health/immunizations.

International Student Contact Ms. Karen Slaymaker, Assistant Director for International Student Services, Office of International Affairs, 204 Bradley Hall, Lexington, KY 40506-0058. *Phone:* 859-257-4067 Ext. 237. *Fax:* 859-323-1026. *E-mail:* kmslay0@uky.edu.

APPLICATION *Required:* GMAT, application form, baccalaureate/first degree, essay, 3 letters of recommendation, personal statement, resume/curriculum vitae, transcripts of college work. *Recommended:* 2 years of work experience. *Application fee:* $40, $55 (international). Applications for domestic and international students are processed on a rolling basis.

Application Contact Ms. Beverly Kemper, MBA Program Advisor, MBA Center, Lexington, KY 40506-0034. *Phone:* 859-257-7722. *Fax:* 859-323-9971. *E-mail:* kemper@uky.edu.

See full description on page 716.

University of Louisville
College of Business
Louisville, Kentucky

Phone: 502-852-2169 **Fax:** 502-852-4901 **E-mail:** kevin.kane@louisville.edu

Business Program(s) Web Site: http://business.louisville.edu

Graduate Business Unit Enrollment *Total:* 303 (119 full-time; 184 part-time; 119 women; 17 international). *Average Age:* 28.

Graduate Business Faculty *Total:* 37 (30 full-time; 7 part-time).

Admissions *Applied:* 195. *Admitted:* 89. *Enrolled:* 84. *Average GMAT:* 578. *Average GPA:* 3.4

Academic Calendar Five- and six-week modules or semesters/modules.

Accreditation AACSB—The Association to Advance Collegiate Schools of Business.

After Graduation (Class of 2006–07) *Employed within 3 months of graduation:* 71%. *Average starting salary:* $63,000.

DEGREES JD/MBA • M Acc • MBA • MBA/M Acc • ME/MBA

JD/MBA—Juris Doctor/Master of Business Administration Part-time. Students must be admitted to both the JD and MBA programs; credit hours reflect 39 hours MBA, with 9 hours substituted from Law plus a minimum 81 hours required in Law. Length reflects MBA only. At least 120 total credits required. Minimum of 24 months to complete program. *Concentrations:* combined degrees, general MBA, law.

M Acc—Master of Accountancy Part-time. At least 30 total credits required. Minimum of 12 months to complete program. *Concentration:* accounting.

MBA—IMBA—The MBA for Entrepreneurial Thinking Part-time. This program admits annually in the summer. 49 to 50 total credits required. 24 months to complete program. *Concentration:* entrepreneurship.

MBA—Master of Business Administration Part-time. Lock-step, cohort based program. Options include two nights per week or Saturday formats. 48 total credits required. 24 months to complete program. *Concentration:* general MBA.

MBA/M Acc—MBA/MAC Part-time. Students must be admitted to the MBA and MAC programs; 9 hours from MAC substituted toward MBA requirements and 9 hours from MBA substituted toward MAC degree. Total minimum hours are for both degrees. At least 60 total credits required. Minimum of 24 months to complete program. *Concentrations:* accounting, combined degrees, general MBA.

ME/MBA—Master of Engineering/Master of Business Administration Part-time. Students must be admitted to both the Meng and MBA programs; credit hours reflect MBA hours only, with 9 hours substituted from Engineering toward the total 48 hours. At least 39 total credits required. 24 months to complete program. *Concentrations:* combined degrees, engineering, general MBA.

RESOURCES AND SERVICES 150 on-campus PCs are available to graduate business students. Access to Internet/World Wide Web, online (class) registration, and online grade reports available. *Personal computer requirements:* Graduate business students are strongly recommended to purchase or lease a personal computer. *Special opportunities include:* An international exchange program and an internship program are available. *Placement services include:* Alumni network, career placement, career counseling/planning, electronic job bank, resume referral, career fairs, job interviews arranged, resume preparation, and career library.

EXPENSES *Tuition (state resident):* Part-time: $14,000 per year. *Tuition (nonresident):* Part-time: $14,000 per year. *Tuition (international):* Part-time: $14,000 per year. *Required fees:* Full-time: $202. Part-time: $202 per year. Tuition and/or fees vary by academic program. *Graduate housing:* Room and board costs vary by campus location, type of accommodation, and type of board plan. *Typical cost:* $6000 (including board).

FINANCIAL AID (2007–08) 147 students received aid, including grants, loans, research assistantships, scholarships, and work study. Aid is available to part-time students. *Financial aid application deadline:* 3/15.

Financial Aid Contact Patricia Arauz, Director of Financial Aid, Financial Aid Office, Louisville, KY 40292. *Phone:* 502-852-5517. *Fax:* 502-852-0182. *E-mail:* p.arauz@louisville.edu.

INTERNATIONAL STUDENTS 6% of students enrolled are international students. *Services and facilities:* Counseling/support services, ESL/language courses, Housing location assistance, International student housing, International student organization, Orientation, Visa Services. Financial aid is available to international students. *Required with application:* TOEFL with recommended score of 213 (computer) or 550 (paper); proof of adequate funds; proof of health/immunizations.

International Student Contact Ms. Sharolyn Pepper, International Student Coordinator, International Center, Louisville, KY 40292. *Phone:* 502-852-6602. *Fax:* 502-852-7216. *E-mail:* pepper@louisville.edu.

APPLICATION *Required:* GMAT, application form, baccalaureate/first degree, interview, 2 letters of recommendation, personal statement, resume/curriculum vitae, transcripts of college work, 3 years of work experience. School will accept GRE. *Application fee:* $50. Applications for domestic and international students are processed on a rolling basis.

Application Contact Mr. Kevin J. Kane, Administrative Director, Masters Programs, MBA Programs Office, 2301 South 3rd Street, Louisville, KY 40292. *Phone:* 502-852-2169. *Fax:* 502-852-4901. *E-mail:* kevin.kane@louisville.edu.

Western Kentucky University
Gordon Ford College of Business
Bowling Green, Kentucky

Phone: 877-WKU-1MNA **Fax:** 270-745-3893 **E-mail:** paula.newby@wku.edu

Business Program(s) Web Site: http://www.wku.edu/mba

Graduate Business Unit Enrollment *Total:* 125 (44 full-time; 81 part-time; 66 women; 43 international). *Average Age:* 28.

Graduate Business Faculty *Total:* 26 (24 full-time; 2 part-time).

Admissions *Applied:* 103. *Admitted:* 66. *Enrolled:* 38. *Average GMAT:* 538. *Average GPA:* 3.4

Academic Calendar Semesters.

Accreditation AACSB—The Association to Advance Collegiate Schools of Business.

DEGREE MBA

MBA—Full-Time, Professional, or Online Options Full-time and part-time. Distance learning option. TheProfessional Options (accelerated) requires 5 years mid- to upper-managerial or professional experience. 33 to 51 total credits required. 12 to 72 months to complete program. *Concentration:* general MBA.

RESOURCES AND SERVICES 700 on-campus PCs are available to graduate business students. Access to Internet/World Wide Web, online (class) registration, and online grade reports available. *Personal computer requirements:* Graduate business students are strongly recommended to purchase or lease a personal computer. *Special opportunities include:* An international exchange program is available. *Placement services include:* Alumni network, career placement, job search course, career counseling/planning, electronic job bank, resume referral, career fairs, job interviews arranged, resume preparation, and career library.

EXPENSES *Tuition (state resident):* Full-time: $7014. Part-time: $351 per credit hour. *Tuition (nonresident):* Full-time: $7678. Part-time: $384 per credit hour. *Tuition (international):* Full-time: $8674. Part-time: $434 per credit hour. Tuition and/or fees vary by class time and academic program. *Graduate housing:* Room and board costs vary by campus location, number of occupants, and type of accommodation.

Western Kentucky University (continued)

FINANCIAL AID (2007–08) 9 students received aid, including loans, research assistantships, and teaching assistantships.

Financial Aid Contact Ms. Nancy Alfonso, Student Financial Assistance Coordinator, 317 Potter Hall, 1906 College Heights Boulevard, Bowling Green, KY 42101. *Phone:* 270-745-2755. *Fax:* 270-745-6586. *E-mail:* nancy.alfonso@wku.edu.

INTERNATIONAL STUDENTS 34% of students enrolled are international students. *Services and facilities:* Counseling/support services, ESL/language courses, International student organization, Language tutoring, Orientation. Financial aid is available to international students. *Required with application:* TOEFL with recommended score of 213 (computer) or 550 (paper); proof of adequate funds.

International Student Contact Mr. Derick B Strode, International Student Advisor, Sofia-Downing International Center, 1906 College Heights Boulevard, Bowling Green, KY 42101. *Phone:* 270-745-4353. *Fax:* 270-745-6144. *E-mail:* derick.strode@wku.edu.

APPLICATION *Required:* GMAT, application form, baccalaureate/first degree, 1 letter of recommendation, personal statement, resume/ curriculum vitae, transcripts of college work. *Recommended:* Work experience. *Application fee:* $35. *Deadlines:* 4/15 for fall, 10/15 for winter, 11/15 for spring, 4/1 for fall (international), 9/1 for spring (international), 1/10 for summer (international).

Application Contact Ms. Paula Newby, MBA Program Director of Admissions, 1906 College Heights Boulevard #11056, Bowling Green, KY 42101-1056. *Phone:* 877-WKU-1MNA. *Fax:* 270-745-3893. *E-mail:* paula.newby@wku.edu.

LOUISIANA

Centenary College of Louisiana

Frost School of Business

Shreveport, Louisiana

Phone: 318-869-5141 **Fax:** 318-869-5139 **E-mail:** mba@centenary.edu

Business Program(s) Web Site: http://www.centenary.edu/mba

Graduate Business Unit Enrollment *Total:* 40 (40 part-time). *Average Age:* 35.

Graduate Business Faculty *Total:* 13 (9 full-time; 4 part-time).

Admissions *Average GMAT:* 500. *Average GPA:* 3.0

Academic Calendar Five 10-week modules.

After Graduation (Class of 2006–07) *Employed within 3 months of graduation:* 100%.

DEGREE MBA

MBA—Executive MBA Program Part-time. Employment in leadership position required. Up to 45 total credits required. *Concentrations:* entrepreneurship, executive programs, strategic management.

RESOURCES AND SERVICES 300 on-campus PCs are available to graduate business students. Access to Internet/World Wide Web and online grade reports available. *Personal computer requirements:* Graduate business students are strongly recommended to purchase or lease a personal computer. *Placement services include:* Alumni network, career counseling/planning, resume referral, resume preparation, and career library.

EXPENSES *Tuition:* Part-time: $820 per course. *Tuition (international):* Part-time: $820 per course. *Required fees:* Part-time: $300 per degree program.

FINANCIAL AID (2007–08) Grants and loans. Aid is available to part-time students.

Financial Aid Contact Mary Sue Rix, Financial Aid Director, Office of Financial Aid, 2911 Centenary Boulevard, Shreveport, LA 71134. *Phone:* 318-869-5137. *E-mail:* msrix@centenary.edu.

INTERNATIONAL STUDENTS Financial aid is not available to international students. *Required with application:* Proof of adequate funds; proof of health/immunizations.

APPLICATION *Required:* GMAT, application form, baccalaureate/first degree, essay, interview, 1 letter of recommendation, personal statement, resume/curriculum vitae, transcripts of college work, 5 years of work experience. *Application fee:* $20. Applications for domestic and international students are processed on a rolling basis.

Application Contact Pat Gallion, Executive MBA Coordinator, PO Box 41188, Shreveport, LA 71134-1188. *Phone:* 318-869-5141. *Fax:* 318-869-5139. *E-mail:* mba@centenary.edu.

Louisiana State University and Agricultural and Mechanical College

E. J. Ourso College of Business

Baton Rouge, Louisiana

Phone: 225-578-8892 **Fax:** 225-578-2421 **E-mail:** shedge@lsu.edu

Business Program(s) Web Site: http://mba.lsu.edu/

Graduate Business Unit Enrollment *Total:* 600 (449 full-time; 151 part-time; 272 women; 86 international). *Average Age:* 22 to 37.

Graduate Business Faculty *Total:* 110 (108 full-time; 2 part-time).

Admissions *Applied:* 253. *Admitted:* 163. *Enrolled:* 141. *Average GMAT:* 637. *Average GPA:* 3.43

Academic Calendar Semesters.

Accreditation AACSB—The Association to Advance Collegiate Schools of Business.

After Graduation (Class of 2006–07) *Employed within 3 months of graduation:* 91.4%. *Average starting salary:* $61,707.

DEGREES MBA • MPA • MS

MBA—Executive MBA Program Part-time. 42 total credits required. 17 months to complete program. *Concentration:* executive programs.

MBA—Master of Business Administration Full-time. At least 52 total credits required. 22 months to complete program. *Concentrations:* Chinese business studies, entrepreneurship, finance, human resources management, law, management information systems, marketing, project management, real estate.

MBA—Professional MBA Program—Track 1 Part-time. 42 total credits required. 24 months to complete program. *Concentration:* general MBA.

MBA—Professional MBA Program—Track 2 Part-time. 42 total credits required. 33 months to complete program. *Concentration:* general MBA.

MPA—Master of Public Administration Full-time and part-time. At least 42 total credits required. 24 to 60 months to complete program. *Concentration:* public policy and administration.

MS—Master of Science Full-time and part-time. At least 36 total credits required. 12 to 60 months to complete program. *Concentrations:* accounting, economics, finance, information systems.

RESOURCES AND SERVICES 350 on-campus PCs are available to graduate business students. Access to Internet/World Wide Web, online (class) registration, and online grade reports available. *Personal computer requirements:* Graduate business students are not required to have a personal computer. *Special opportunities include:* An internship program is available. *Placement services include:* Alumni network, career placement, job search course, career counseling/planning, electronic job bank, resume referral, career fairs, job interviews arranged, resume preparation, and career library.

EXPENSES *Tuition (state resident):* Full-time: $2981.50. *Tuition (nonresident):* Full-time: $11,281. *Tuition (international):* Full-time: $11,281. Tuition and/or fees vary by class time, number of courses or credits taken, and academic program. *Graduate housing:* Room and board costs vary by number of occupants, type of accommodation, and type of board plan. *Typical cost:* $6852 (including board), $4130 (room only).

FINANCIAL AID (2007–08) 52 students received aid, including fellowships, loans, research assistantships, scholarships, and teaching assistantships. *Financial aid application deadline:* 5/15.

Financial Aid Contact Mary G. Parker, Executive Director, Office of Undergraduate Admission and Student Aid, Office of Undergraduate Admission and Student Aid, 146 Pleasant Hall, Baton Rouge, LA 70803. *Phone:* 225-578-3103. *Fax:* 225-578-6300. *E-mail:* financialaid@lsu.edu.

INTERNATIONAL STUDENTS 14% of students enrolled are international students. *Services and facilities:* Counseling/support services, ESL/language courses, Housing location assistance, International student organization, Language tutoring, Orientation, Visa Services. Financial aid is available to international students. *Required with application:* TOEFL with recommended score of 213 (computer), 550 (paper), or 79 (Internet); proof of adequate funds; proof of health/immunizations.

International Student Contact Natalie Rigby, Director, International Services Office, International Services Office, 116 Hatcher Hall, Baton Rouge, LA 70803-6302. *Phone:* 225-578-3191. *Fax:* 225-578-1413. *E-mail:* nrigby@lsu.edu.

APPLICATION *Required:* GMAT, application form, baccalaureate/first degree, essay, interview, personal statement, resume/curriculum vitae, transcripts of college work. *Recommended:* Letter(s) of recommendation, work experience. *Application fee:* $25. Applications for domestic and international students are processed on a rolling basis.

Application Contact Stephanie Cancienne Hedge, Associate Director for Enrollment and Administration, Flores MBA Program, 3176 A Patrick F. Taylor Hall, Baton Rouge, LA 70803-6302. *Phone:* 225-578-8892. *Fax:* 225-578-2421. *E-mail:* shedge@lsu.edu.

Louisiana Tech University
College of Administration and Business
Ruston, Louisiana

Phone: 318-257-4528 Fax: 318-257-4253 E-mail: sstrick@latech.edu

Business Program(s) Web Site: http://www.cab.latech.edu/public/index.htm

Graduate Business Unit Enrollment *Total:* 112 (106 full-time; 6 part-time; 57 women; 22 international).

Graduate Business Faculty *Total:* 49 (39 full-time; 10 part-time).

Admissions *Applied:* 67. *Admitted:* 43. *Enrolled:* 30. *Average GMAT:* 520. *Average GPA:* 3.2

Academic Calendar Quarters.

Accreditation AACSB—The Association to Advance Collegiate Schools of Business.

After Graduation (Class of 2006–07) *Employed within 3 months of graduation:* 92%.

DEGREES MBA • MPA

MBA—Master of Business Administration Full-time and part-time. Distance learning option. At least 30 total credits required. 12 to 72 months to complete program. *Concentrations:* accounting, economics, finance, management, marketing, quantitative analysis.

MPA—Master of Professional Accountancy Full-time and part-time. At least 30 total credits required. 12 to 72 months to complete program. *Concentration:* accounting.

RESOURCES AND SERVICES 100 on-campus PCs are available to graduate business students. Access to Internet/World Wide Web, online (class) registration, and online grade reports available. *Personal computer*

requirements: Graduate business students are not required to have a personal computer. *Placement services include:* Career placement, career counseling/planning, career fairs, job interviews arranged, and resume preparation.

EXPENSES *Tuition (state resident):* Part-time: $374 per quarter hour. *Tuition (nonresident):* Part-time: $1792 per quarter hour. *Tuition (international):* Part-time: $1792 per quarter hour. *Required fees:* Full-time: $3000. Part-time: $1500 per year. Tuition and/or fees vary by campus location and academic program. *Graduate housing:* Room and board costs vary by number of occupants, type of accommodation, and type of board plan. *Typical cost:* $5880 (including board), $3080 (room only).

FINANCIAL AID (2007–08) 35 students received aid, including fellowships, grants, loans, research assistantships, and teaching assistantships. Aid is available to part-time students. *Financial aid application deadline:* 2/1.

Financial Aid Contact Mr. Roger Vick, Director of Financial Aid, PO Box 7925 TS, Ruston, LA 71272. *Phone:* 318-257-2641. *Fax:* 318-257-2628.

INTERNATIONAL STUDENTS 20% of students enrolled are international students. *Services and facilities:* Counseling/support services, Housing location assistance, International student organization, Language tutoring, Orientation, Visa Services. Financial aid is available to international students. *Required with application:* TOEFL with recommended score of 213 (computer) or 550 (paper); proof of adequate funds; proof of health/immunizations.

International Student Contact Mr. Daniel Erickson, International Student Advisor, PO Box 3177 TS, Ruston, LA 71272. *Phone:* 318-257-4321. *Fax:* 318-257-4750. *E-mail:* daniel@vm.cc.latech.edu.

APPLICATION *Required:* GMAT, application form, baccalaureate/first degree, transcripts of college work. *Application fee:* $30, $40 (international). Applications for domestic and international students are processed on a rolling basis.

Application Contact Sally W. Strickland, Administrative Coordinator for Graduate Studies and Research, PO Box 10318, Ruston, LA 71272. *Phone:* 318-257-4528. *Fax:* 318-257-4253. *E-mail:* sstrick@latech.edu.

Loyola University New Orleans
Joseph A. Butt, S.J., College of Business
New Orleans, Louisiana

Phone: 504-864-7965 Fax: 504-864-7970 E-mail: smans@loyno.edu

Business Program(s) Web Site: http://www.business.loyno.edu/mba

Graduate Business Unit Enrollment *Total:* 71 (22 full-time; 49 part-time; 31 women; 6 international). *Average Age:* 25.

Graduate Business Faculty *Total:* 20 (18 full-time; 2 part-time).

Admissions *Applied:* 41. *Admitted:* 39. *Enrolled:* 23. *Average GMAT:* 527. *Average GPA:* 3.3

Academic Calendar Semesters.

Accreditation AACSB—The Association to Advance Collegiate Schools of Business.

After Graduation (Class of 2006–07) *Average starting salary:* $53,000.

DEGREES JD/MBA • MBA

JD/MBA—Juris Doctor/Master of Business Administration Full-time and part-time. Must apply separately to both the Law School and the Business School. 105 to 130 total credits required. 42 to 84 months to complete program. *Concentration:* combined degrees.

MBA—Evening MBA—Master of Business Administration Full-time and part-time. 39 to 54 total credits required. 12 to 84 months to complete program. *Concentration:* general MBA.

RESOURCES AND SERVICES 130 on-campus PCs are available to graduate business students. Access to Internet/World Wide Web, online

Loyola University New Orleans (continued)

(class) registration, and online grade reports available. *Personal computer requirements:* Graduate business students are strongly recommended to purchase or lease a personal computer. *Special opportunities include:* An international exchange program and an internship program are available. *Placement services include:* Alumni network, career placement, job search course, career counseling/planning, electronic job bank, resume referral, career fairs, job interviews arranged, resume preparation, and career library.

EXPENSES *Tuition:* Full-time: $18,264. Part-time: $761 per credit hour. *Tuition (international):* Full-time: $18,264. Part-time: $761 per credit hour. *Required fees:* Full-time: $906. Part-time: $175 per semester. *Graduate housing:* Room and board costs vary by campus location, number of occupants, type of accommodation, and type of board plan. *Typical cost:* $8628 (including board), $5428 (room only).

FINANCIAL AID (2007–08) 12 students received aid, including grants, loans, research assistantships, and scholarships. Aid is available to part-time students. *Financial aid application deadline:* 6/15.

Financial Aid Contact Mrs. Catherine Simoneaux, Director of Scholarships and Financial Aid, 6363 Saint Charles Avenue, Box 206, New Orleans, LA 70118. *Phone:* 504-865-3231. *Fax:* 504-865-3233. *E-mail:* cmsimone@loyno.edu.

INTERNATIONAL STUDENTS 8% of students enrolled are international students. *Services and facilities:* Counseling/support services, International student housing, International student organization, Language tutoring, Orientation, Visa Services. Financial aid is available to international students. *Required with application:* TOEFL with recommended score of 237 (computer), 580 (paper), or 92 (Internet); proof of adequate funds; proof of health/immunizations.

International Student Contact Ms. Stephanie Mansfield, MBA Marketing and Communications Coordinator, 6363 Saint Charles Avenue, Box 15, New Orleans, LA 70118. *Phone:* 504-864-7965. *Fax:* 504-864-7970. *E-mail:* smans@loyno.edu.

APPLICATION *Required:* GMAT, application form, baccalaureate/first degree, essay, 2 letters of recommendation, resume/curriculum vitae, transcripts of college work. *Recommended:* Work experience. *Application fee:* $50. Applications for domestic and international students are processed on a rolling basis.

Application Contact Ms. Stephanie Mansfield, MBA Marketing and Communications Coordinator, 6363 Saint Charles Avenue, Box 15, New Orleans, LA 70118. *Phone:* 504-864-7965. *Fax:* 504-864-7970. *E-mail:* smans@loyno.edu.

McNeese State University
College of Business

Lake Charles, Louisiana

Phone: 337-475-5576 **Fax:** 337-475-5986 **E-mail:** mbaprog@mcneese.edu

Business Program(s) Web Site: http://www.mcneese.edu/colleges/bus/

Graduate Business Unit Enrollment *Total:* 80 (53 full-time; 27 part-time; 26 women; 29 international). *Average Age:* 28.

Graduate Business Faculty 15 full-time.

Admissions *Applied:* 48. *Admitted:* 43. *Enrolled:* 21. *Average GMAT:* 470. *Average GPA:* 3.2

Academic Calendar Semesters.

Accreditation AACSB—The Association to Advance Collegiate Schools of Business.

After Graduation (Class of 2006–07) *Employed within 3 months of graduation:* 90%. *Average starting salary:* $35,500.

DEGREE MBA

MBA—Master of Business Administration Full-time and part-time. 33 to 51 total credits required. 18 to 72 months to complete program. *Concentrations:* accounting, general MBA.

RESOURCES AND SERVICES 330 on-campus PCs are available to graduate business students. Access to Internet/World Wide Web, online (class) registration, and online grade reports available. *Personal computer requirements:* Graduate business students are not required to have a personal computer. *Placement services include:* Career placement, career counseling/planning, and career fairs.

EXPENSES *Tuition (state resident):* Full-time: $3156. Part-time: $505.25 per course. *Tuition (nonresident):* Full-time: $7836. *Tuition (international):* Full-time: $7836. Tuition and/or fees vary by number of courses or credits taken and local reciprocity agreements. *Graduate housing:* Room and board costs vary by number of occupants, type of accommodation, and type of board plan.

FINANCIAL AID (2007–08) 29 students received aid, including loans and research assistantships. Aid is available to part-time students. *Financial aid application deadline:* 5/1.

Financial Aid Contact Ms. Taina Savoit, Director of Financial Aid, Box 93260, Lake Charles, LA 70609. *Phone:* 337-475-5065. *Fax:* 337-475-5068. *E-mail:* tsavoit@mcneese.edu.

INTERNATIONAL STUDENTS 36% of students enrolled are international students. *Services and facilities:* Counseling/support services, ESL/language courses, International student organization. Financial aid is available to international students. *Required with application:* TOEFL with recommended score of 183 (computer) or 550 (paper); proof of adequate funds; proof of health/immunizations.

International Student Contact Ms. Christine Kay, International Student Affairs, Box 92495, Lake Charles, LA 70609. *Phone:* 337-475-5243. *Fax:* 337-475-5151. *E-mail:* ckay@mcneese.edu.

APPLICATION *Required:* GMAT, application form, baccalaureate/first degree, transcripts of college work. *Application fee:* $20, $30 (international). *Deadlines:* 5/1 for fall (international), 10/1 for spring (international), 3/1 for summer (international). Applications for domestic students are processed on a rolling basis.

Application Contact Dr. Cam Caldwell, MBA Program Director, Box 91660, Lake Charles, LA 70609. *Phone:* 337-475-5576. *Fax:* 337-475-5986. *E-mail:* mbaprog@mcneese.edu.

Nicholls State University
College of Business Administration

Thibodaux, Louisiana

Phone: 985-448-4241 **Fax:** 985-448-4922 **E-mail:** chuck.viosca@nicholls.edu

Business Program(s) Web Site: http://www.nicholls.edu/mba

Graduate Business Unit Enrollment *Total:* 99 (44 full-time; 55 part-time; 54 women).

Graduate Business Faculty 23 full-time.

Admissions *Applied:* 53. *Admitted:* 53. *Enrolled:* 36. *Average GMAT:* 469. *Average GPA:* 3.17

Academic Calendar Semesters.

Accreditation AACSB—The Association to Advance Collegiate Schools of Business.

DEGREES EMBA • MBA

EMBA—Executive Master of Business Administration Full-time. Distance learning option. Bachelor degree, 3 or more years of full-time professional experience & meet formula. Up to 33 total credits required. Maximum of 17 months to complete program. *Concentration:* general MBA.

MBA—Master of Business Administration Full-time and part-time. 33 to 57 total credits required. 18 to 72 months to complete program. *Concentration:* general MBA.

RESOURCES AND SERVICES 40 on-campus PCs are available to graduate business students. Access to Internet/World Wide Web, online (class) registration, and online grade reports available. *Personal computer requirements:* Graduate business students are not required to have a personal computer. *Special opportunities include:* An international exchange program is available. *Placement services include:* Career placement, career counseling/planning, electronic job bank, resume referral, career fairs, job interviews arranged, resume preparation, and career library.

FINANCIAL AID (2007–08) 16 students received aid, including research assistantships. *Financial aid application deadline:* 3/31.

Financial Aid Contact Colette M. LaGarde, Director of Financial Aid, PO Box 2005, Thibodaux, LA 70310. *Phone:* 985-448-4048. *Fax:* 985-448-4124. *E-mail:* colette.lagarde@nicholls.edu.

INTERNATIONAL STUDENTS *Services and facilities:* Counseling/support services, Housing location assistance, International student organization, Orientation, Visa Services. Financial aid is available to international students. *Required with application:* TOEFL with recommended score of 213 (computer) or 550 (paper); proof of adequate funds; proof of health/immunizations.

International Student Contact Mrs. Marilyn Gonzalez, Assistant Director, International Students, PO Box 2004, Thibodaux, LA 70310. *Phone:* 985-449-7038. *Fax:* 985-448-4124. *E-mail:* marilyn.gonzalez@ nicholls.edu.

APPLICATION *Required:* GMAT, application form, baccalaureate/first degree, transcripts of college work. *Application fee:* $20, $30 (international). Applications for domestic and international students are processed on a rolling basis.

Application Contact Dr. Chuck Viosca, Assistant Dean for Graduate Studies in Business, PO Box 2015, 104 White Hall, Thibodaux, LA 70310. *Phone:* 985-448-4241. *Fax:* 985-448-4922. *E-mail:* chuck.viosca@ nicholls.edu.

Southeastern Louisiana University
College of Business
Hammond, Louisiana

Phone: 985-549-5619 **Fax:** 985-549-5632 **E-mail:** smeyers@selu.edu

Business Program(s) Web Site: http://www.selu.edu/acad_research/colleges/bus

Graduate Business Unit Enrollment *Total:* 147 (117 full-time; 30 part-time; 64 women; 15 international). *Average Age:* 27.

Graduate Business Faculty 24 full-time.

Admissions *Applied:* 44. *Admitted:* 43. *Enrolled:* 36. *Average GMAT:* 480. *Average GPA:* 3.2

Academic Calendar Semesters.

Accreditation AACSB—The Association to Advance Collegiate Schools of Business.

DEGREE MBA

MBA—Master of Business Administration Full-time and part-time. At least 33 total credits required. 12 to 72 months to complete program. *Concentrations:* accounting, general MBA, health care, management information systems, marketing.

RESOURCES AND SERVICES 882 on-campus PCs are available to graduate business students. Access to Internet/World Wide Web, online (class) registration, and online grade reports available. *Personal computer requirements:* Graduate business students are not required to have a personal computer. *Special opportunities include:* An international exchange program is available. *Placement services include:* Alumni

network, career placement, career counseling/planning, electronic job bank, resume referral, career fairs, job interviews arranged, resume preparation, and career library.

EXPENSES *Tuition (state resident):* Full-time: $2216. Part-time: $123 per credit hour. *Tuition (nonresident):* Full-time: $6716. Part-time: $373 per credit hour. *Tuition (international):* Full-time: $6716. Part-time: $373 per credit hour. *Required fees:* Full-time: $1105. Part-time: $61 per credit hour. Tuition and/or fees vary by number of courses or credits taken. *Graduate housing:* Room and board costs vary by number of occupants, type of accommodation, and type of board plan. *Typical cost:* $5990 (including board), $3780 (room only).

FINANCIAL AID (2007–08) 99 students received aid, including loans, scholarships, and work study. Aid is available to part-time students. *Financial aid application deadline:* 5/1.

Financial Aid Contact Director, Financial Aid, SLU 10768, Hammond, LA 70402. *Phone:* 985-549-2244. *Fax:* 985-549-5077. *E-mail:* finaid@ selu.edu.

INTERNATIONAL STUDENTS 10% of students enrolled are international students. *Services and facilities:* Counseling/support services, ESL/language courses, International student housing, International student organization, Language tutoring, Orientation, Visa Services. Financial aid is available to international students. *Required with application:* TOEFL with recommended score of 195 (computer), 525 (paper), or 70 (Internet); proof of adequate funds; proof of health/immunizations.

International Student Contact Dr. Rusty Juban, Coordinator, Graduate Business Programs, SLU 10735, Hammond, LA 70402. *Phone:* 985-549-2146. *Fax:* 985-549-3977. *E-mail:* rjuban@selu.edu.

APPLICATION *Required:* GMAT, application form, baccalaureate/first degree, transcripts of college work. *Application fee:* $20, $30 (international). Applications for domestic and international students are processed on a rolling basis.

Application Contact Mrs. Sandra Meyers, Graduate Admissions Analyst, SLU 10752, Hammond, LA 70402. *Phone:* 985-549-5619. *Fax:* 985-549-5632. *E-mail:* smeyers@selu.edu.

Tulane University
A. B. Freeman School of Business
New Orleans, Louisiana

Phone: 504-865-5410 **Fax:** 504-865-6770 **E-mail:** abfadmit@tulane.edu

Business Program(s) Web Site: http://freeman.tulane.edu

Graduate Business Unit Enrollment *Total:* 442 (262 full-time; 180 part-time; 140 women; 85 international). *Average Age:* 25.

Graduate Business Faculty *Total:* 129 (64 full-time; 65 part-time).

Admissions *Applied:* 330. *Admitted:* 209. *Enrolled:* 167. *Average GMAT:* 656. *Average GPA:* 3.34

Academic Calendar Semesters.

Accreditation AACSB—The Association to Advance Collegiate Schools of Business.

After Graduation (Class of 2006–07) *Employed within 3 months of graduation:* 93%. *Average starting salary:* $88,000.

DEGREES JD/M Acc • JD/MBA • M Acc • MAF • MBA • MBA/M Acc • MBA/MA • MBA/MPH

JD/M Acc—Juris Doctor/Master of Accountancy Full-time. Admittance to Law School is required. At least 106 total credits required. 39 to 84 months to complete program. *Concentrations:* accounting, management information systems, taxation.

JD/MBA—Juris Doctor/Master of Business Administration Full-time. Admittance to Law School is required. At least 127 total credits required. 48 to 84 months to complete program. *Concentrations:* accounting, finance, international management, management, management information systems, marketing, organizational behavior/development.

Tulane University (continued)

M Acc—Master of Accounting Full-time. At least 30 total credits required. 9 to 84 months to complete program. *Concentrations:* accounting, management information systems, taxation.

MAF—Master of Finance Full-time. At least 34 total credits required. 12 to 84 months to complete program. *Concentrations:* finance, financial economics, financial information systems, financial management/planning.

MBA—Asia Executive Master of Business Administration Part-time. 5 years of management experience and English language proficiency required. At least 48 total credits required. 13 to 36 months to complete program. *Concentration:* management.

MBA—Chile Executive Master of Business Administration Part-time. Required: joint admission to Universidad de Chile and Tulane; work and management experience; English proficiency. At least 48 total credits required. 21 to 84 months to complete program. *Concentration:* management.

MBA—Houston Executive Master of Business Administration Part-time. At least 48 total credits required. Minimum of 18 months to complete program. *Concentration:* management.

MBA—New Orleans Executive Master of Business Administration Part-time. 7 years of work experience with at least 5 years in management required. At least 48 total credits required. Minimum of 18 months to complete program. *Concentration:* management.

MBA—Professional Master of Business Administration Part-time. At least 55 total credits required. 36 to 84 months to complete program. *Concentrations:* accounting, finance, international management, management, management information systems, marketing, organizational behavior/development.

MBA—Master of Business Administration Full-time. At least 60 total credits required. 21 to 84 months to complete program. *Concentrations:* accounting, finance, international management, management, management information systems, marketing, organizational behavior/development.

MBA/M Acc—Master of Business Administration/Master of Accounting Full-time. Admission to joint program. At least 75 total credits required. 24 to 84 months to complete program. *Concentrations:* accounting, finance, international management, management, management information systems, marketing, organizational behavior/development, taxation.

MBA/MA—Master of Business Administration/Master of Arts in Latin American Studies Full-time. Admittance to Master of Arts Program required. At least 72 total credits required. 28 to 84 months to complete program. *Concentrations:* accounting, finance, international management, management, management information systems, marketing, organizational behavior/development.

MBA/MA—Master of Business Administration/Master of Arts in Political Science Full-time. Admittance to Master of Arts program required. At least 75 total credits required. 28 to 84 months to complete program. *Concentrations:* accounting, finance, international management, management, management information systems, marketing, organizational behavior/development.

MBA/MPH—Master of Business Administration/Master of Public Health in Health Systems Management Full-time. Admittance to School of Public Health and Tropical Medicine required. At least 90 total credits required. 33 to 84 months to complete program. *Concentrations:* accounting, finance, international management, management, management information systems, marketing, organizational behavior/development.

RESOURCES AND SERVICES 255 on-campus PCs are available to graduate business students. Access to Internet/World Wide Web, online (class) registration, and online grade reports available. *Personal computer requirements:* Graduate business students are required to have a personal computer. *Special opportunities include:* An international exchange program and an internship program are available. *Placement services include:* Alumni network, career placement, job search course, career counseling/planning, electronic job bank, resume referral, career fairs, job interviews arranged, resume preparation, and career library.

EXPENSES *Tuition:* Full-time: $37,000. Part-time: $1300 per contact hour. *Tuition (international):* Full-time: $37,000. Part-time: $1300 per contact hour. *Required fees:* Full-time: $1650. Tuition and/or fees vary by class time and academic program. *Typical graduate housing cost:* $12,000 (including board), $6000 (room only).

FINANCIAL AID (2007–08) 111 students received aid, including fellowships, research assistantships, scholarships, teaching assistantships, and work study. *Financial aid application deadline:* 5/15.

Financial Aid Contact Bill Sandefer, Director of Graduate Admissions and Financial Aid, 7 McAlister Drive, Suite 410, New Orleans, LA 70118-5669. *Phone:* 504-865-5410. *Fax:* 504-865-6770. *E-mail:* abfadmit@tulane.edu.

INTERNATIONAL STUDENTS 19% of students enrolled are international students. *Services and facilities:* Counseling/support services, ESL/language courses, Housing location assistance, International student housing, International student organization, Language tutoring, Orientation, Visa Services. Financial aid is available to international students. *Required with application:* TOEFL with recommended score of 250 (computer) or 600 (paper); proof of adequate funds; proof of health/immunizations.

International Student Contact Bill Sandefer, Director of Graduate Admissions and Financial Aid, 7 McAlister Drive, Suite 410, New Orleans, LA 70118-5669. *Phone:* 504-865-5410. *Fax:* 504-865-6770. *E-mail:* abfadmit@tulane.edu.

APPLICATION *Required:* GMAT, application form, baccalaureate/first degree, essay, interview, 2 letters of recommendation, resume/curriculum vitae, transcripts of college work. *Recommended:* 2 years of work experience. *Application fee:* $125. Applications for domestic and international students are processed on a rolling basis.

Application Contact Bill Sandefer, Director of Graduate Admissions and Financial Aid, 7 McAlister Drive, Suite 410, New Orleans, LA 70118-5669. *Phone:* 504-865-5410. *Fax:* 504-865-6770. *E-mail:* abfadmit@tulane.edu.

University of Louisiana at Lafayette
Graduate School

Lafayette, Louisiana

Phone: 337-482-6965 **Fax:** 337-482-6195 **E-mail:** palmer@louisiana.edu

Business Program(s) Web Site: http://moody.louisiana.edu

Graduate Business Unit Enrollment *Total:* 184 (36 full-time; 148 part-time; 89 women; 20 international). *Average Age:* 28.

Graduate Business Faculty *Total:* 60 (46 full-time; 14 part-time).

Admissions *Applied:* 1,342. *Admitted:* 71. *Enrolled:* 52. *Average GMAT:* 537. *Average GPA:* 3.38

Academic Calendar Semesters.

Accreditation AACSB—The Association to Advance Collegiate Schools of Business.

After Graduation (Class of 2006–07) *Employed within 3 months of graduation:* 100%. *Average starting salary:* $54,000.

DEGREES MBA

MBA—Master of Business Administration in Health Care Administration Full-time and part-time. 39 to 54 total credits required. 18 to 72 months to complete program. *Concentrations:* accounting, economics, finance, health care, management, marketing.

MBA—Master of Business Administration Full-time and part-time. 33 to 48 total credits required. 18 to 72 months to complete program. *Concentrations:* accounting, economics, finance, management, marketing.

RESOURCES AND SERVICES 525 on-campus PCs are available to graduate business students. Access to Internet/World Wide Web, online (class) registration, and online grade reports available. *Personal computer*

requirements: Graduate business students are strongly recommended to purchase or lease a personal computer. *Special opportunities include:* An international exchange program and an internship program are available. *Placement services include:* Alumni network, career placement, job search course, career counseling/planning, electronic job bank, career fairs, job interviews arranged, and resume preparation.

EXPENSES *Tuition (state resident):* Full-time: $3360. *Tuition (nonresident):* Full-time: $9446. *Tuition (international):* Full-time: $9582. *Required fees:* Full-time: $538. Tuition and/or fees vary by number of courses or credits taken. *Graduate housing:* Room and board costs vary by number of occupants, type of accommodation, and type of board plan.

FINANCIAL AID (2007–08) 32 students received aid, including fellowships, loans, research assistantships, and scholarships. Aid is available to part-time students. *Financial aid application deadline:* 5/1.

Financial Aid Contact Dr. C. E. Palmer, Dean, Box 44610, Lafayette, LA 70504-4610. *Phone:* 337-482-6965. *Fax:* 337-482-6195. *E-mail:* palmer@louisiana.edu.

INTERNATIONAL STUDENTS 11% of students enrolled are international students. *Services and facilities:* Counseling/support services, ESL/language courses, Housing location assistance, International student housing, International student organization, Orientation, Visa Services. Financial aid is available to international students. *Required with application:* TOEFL with recommended score of 213 (computer), 550 (paper), or 81 (Internet); proof of adequate funds; proof of health/immunizations.

International Student Contact Rose Honegger, Director, Box 43932, Lafayette, LA 70504-3932. *Phone:* 337-482-6819. *E-mail:* roseh@louisiana.edu.

APPLICATION *Required:* GMAT, application form, baccalaureate/first degree, 3 letters of recommendation, personal statement, resume/curriculum vitae, transcripts of college work. *Recommended:* Work experience. *Application fee:* $25, $30 (international). Applications for domestic and international students are processed on a rolling basis.

Application Contact Dr. C. E. Palmer, Dean, Box 44610, Lafayette, LA 70504-4610. *Phone:* 337-482-6965. *Fax:* 337-482-6195. *E-mail:* palmer@louisiana.edu.

University of Louisiana at Monroe
College of Business Administration
Monroe, Louisiana

Phone: 318-342-1100 **Fax:** 318-342-1101 **E-mail:** perez@ulm.edu

Business Program(s) Web Site: http://ele.ulm.edu/mba.html

Graduate Business Unit Enrollment *Total:* 69 (35 full-time; 34 part-time; 13 international).

Graduate Business Faculty 22 full-time.

Admissions *Average GMAT:* 510. *Average GPA:* 3.08

Academic Calendar Semesters.

Accreditation AACSB—The Association to Advance Collegiate Schools of Business.

DEGREES MBA

MBA—Managerial Master of Business Administration Part-time. Distance learning option. At least 3 years of decision-making managerial experience is required. 30 to 60 total credits required. Minimum of 30 months to complete program. *Concentration:* management.

MBA—Master of Business Administration Full-time and part-time. 30 to 66 total credits required. 12 to 72 months to complete program. *Concentration:* health administration.

RESOURCES AND SERVICES 250 on-campus PCs are available to graduate business students. Access to Internet/World Wide Web, online (class) registration, and online grade reports available. *Personal computer requirements:* Graduate business students are not required to have a

personal computer. *Special opportunities include:* An international exchange program is available. *Placement services include:* Alumni network, career placement, career counseling/planning, resume referral, career fairs, job interviews arranged, resume preparation, and career library.

EXPENSES *Tuition (state resident):* Full-time: $3400. *Tuition (nonresident):* Full-time: $9200. *Typical graduate housing cost:* $1500 (including board).

FINANCIAL AID (2007–08) 50 students received aid, including research assistantships, teaching assistantships, and work study. *Financial aid application deadline:* 7/1.

Financial Aid Contact Teresa H. Smith, Director of Financial Aid, 700 University Avenue, Monroe, LA 71209-0100. *Phone:* 318-342-5320. *E-mail:* finaid@ulm.edu.

INTERNATIONAL STUDENTS 19% of students enrolled are international students. *Services and facilities:* Counseling/support services, ESL/language courses, International student organization, Language tutoring, Orientation. Financial aid is available to international students. *Required with application:* TOEFL with recommended score of 250 (computer), 600 (paper), or 61 (Internet); proof of adequate funds; proof of health/immunizations.

International Student Contact Dr. Mara Loeb, Director, International Student Programs, 700 University Avenue, Monroe, LA 71209. *Phone:* 318-342-5225. *E-mail:* international@ulm.edu.

APPLICATION *Required:* GMAT, application form, baccalaureate/first degree, transcripts of college work. *Recommended:* Interview, letter(s) of recommendation, personal statement, resume/curriculum vitae, work experience. *Application fee:* $20, $30 (international).

Application Contact Mr. Miguel Perez, MBA Program Coordinator, 700 University Avenue, Monroe, LA 71209-0100. *Phone:* 318-342-1100. *Fax:* 318-342-1101. *E-mail:* perez@ulm.edu.

University of New Orleans
College of Business Administration
New Orleans, Louisiana

Phone: 504-280-7013 **Fax:** 504-280-5522 **E-mail:** rjhensle@uno.edu

Business Program(s) Web Site: http://business.uno.edu/mba/

Accreditation AACSB—The Association to Advance Collegiate Schools of Business.

DEGREES MBA • MS

MBA—Executive Master of Business Administration Full-time. 5 years of work experience required. At least 48 total credits required. 17 months to complete program. *Concentration:* executive programs.

MBA—Master of Business Administration Full-time and part-time. 33 to 57 total credits required. 14 to 96 months to complete program. *Concentrations:* finance, general MBA, health care, human resources management, international business, management information systems, marketing, technology management, travel industry/tourism management.

MS—Executive Master of Science in Health Care Management Full-time. 5 years of work experience required. At least 33 total credits required. 15 months to complete program. *Concentration:* health care.

MS—Master of Science in Accounting Full-time and part-time. 30 to 75 total credits required. 12 to 96 months to complete program. *Concentration:* accounting.

MS—Master of Science in Health Care Management Full-time and part-time. At least 33 total credits required. 14 to 96 months to complete program. *Concentration:* health care.

MS—Master of Science in Hospitality and Tourism Management Full-time and part-time. 30 to 33 total credits required. 16 to 96 months to complete program. *Concentrations:* hospitality management, travel industry/tourism management.

University of New Orleans (continued)

MS—Master of Science in Taxation Full-time and part-time. 30 to 69 total credits required. 12 to 96 months to complete program. *Concentration:* taxation.

RESOURCES AND SERVICES 367 on-campus PCs are available to graduate business students. Access to Internet/World Wide Web, online (class) registration, and online grade reports available. *Personal computer requirements:* Graduate business students are not required to have a personal computer. *Special opportunities include:* An international exchange program and an internship program are available. *Placement services include:* Alumni network, career placement, job search course, career counseling/planning, electronic job bank, resume referral, career fairs, job interviews arranged, resume preparation, and career library.

Application Contact Robert J. Hensley, Jr., Director of Admissions, Room AD-103, Lakefront, New Orleans, LA 70148. *Phone:* 504-280-7013. *Fax:* 504-280-5522. *E-mail:* rjhensle@uno.edu.

University of Phoenix–Louisiana Campus
College of Graduate Business and Management

Metairie, Louisiana

Phone: 480-317-6200 **Fax:** 480-643-1479 **E-mail:** beth.barilla@phoenix.edu

DEGREES M Mgt • MA • MB • MBA • MM

M Mgt—Master of Management Full-time. At least 39 total credits required. *Concentration:* management.

MA—Organizational Management Full-time. At least 40 total credits required. *Concentration:* organizational management.

MB—Master of Business Administration Full-time. At least 45 total credits required. *Concentration:* administration.

MBA—Accounting Full-time. At least 51 total credits required. *Concentration:* accounting.

MBA—Global Management Full-time. At least 45 total credits required. *Concentration:* international management.

MBA—Human Resource Management Full-time. At least 45 total credits required. *Concentration:* human resources management.

MBA—Marketing Full-time. At least 45 total credits required. *Concentration:* marketing.

MBA—e-Business Full-time. At least 45 total credits required. *Concentration:* electronic commerce (E-commerce).

MM—Human Resources Management Full-time. At least 39 total credits required. *Concentrations:* human resources management, management.

RESOURCES AND SERVICES Access to online grade reports available. *Personal computer requirements:* Graduate business students are strongly recommended to purchase or lease a personal computer. *Placement services include:* Alumni network.

Application Contact Beth Barilla, Associate Vice President of Student Admissions and Services, Mail Stop AA-K101, 4615 East Elwood Street, Phoenix, AZ 85040-1958. *Phone:* 480-317-6200. *Fax:* 480-643-1479. *E-mail:* beth.barilla@phoenix.edu.

MAINE

Maine Maritime Academy
Department of Graduate Studies

Castine, Maine

Phone: 207-326-2212 **Fax:** 207-326-2411 **E-mail:** info.ls@mma.edu

Business Program(s) Web Site: http://ibl.mainemaritime.edu

Graduate Business Unit Enrollment *Total:* 21 (16 full-time; 5 part-time; 7 women; 5 international). *Average Age:* 25.

Graduate Business Faculty *Total:* 11 (6 full-time; 5 part-time).

Admissions *Applied:* 36. *Admitted:* 26. *Enrolled:* 19. *Average GPA:* 3.4

Academic Calendar Semesters.

After Graduation (Class of 2006–07) *Employed within 3 months of graduation:* 100%. *Average starting salary:* $50,000.

DEGREES MS

MS—Global Supply Chain Logistics Full-time and part-time. Distance learning option. 36 total credits required. Minimum of 10 months to complete program. *Concentrations:* information management, international trade, logistics, management systems analysis, materials management, operations management, organizational behavior/development, supply chain management, transportation management.

MS—Maritime Management Full-time and part-time. Distance learning option. 36 total credits required. Minimum of 10 months to complete program. *Concentrations:* international business, international logistics, international trade, logistics, port/maritime management.

RESOURCES AND SERVICES 15 on-campus PCs are available to graduate business students. Access to Internet/World Wide Web, online (class) registration, and online grade reports available. *Personal computer requirements:* Graduate business students are strongly recommended to purchase or lease a personal computer. *Special opportunities include:* An international exchange program and an internship program are available. *Placement services include:* Alumni network, career placement, career counseling/planning, electronic job bank, resume referral, career fairs, job interviews arranged, resume preparation, and career library.

EXPENSES *Tuition (state resident):* Full-time: $13,300. Part-time: $370 per credit hour. *Tuition (nonresident):* Full-time: $19,900. Part-time: $555 per credit hour. *Tuition (international):* Full-time: $23,800. Part-time: $665 per credit hour. *Required fees:* Full-time: $820. Tuition and/or fees vary by local reciprocity agreements. *Graduate housing:* Room and board costs vary by type of board plan. *Typical cost:* $15,000 (including board), $1000 (room only).

FINANCIAL AID (2007–08) 2 students received aid, including fellowships, loans, research assistantships, teaching assistantships, and work study. *Financial aid application deadline:* 4/15.

Financial Aid Contact Ms. Kathy Heath, Director of Financial Aid, Financial Aid Office, Castine, ME 04420. *Phone:* 207-326-2206. *Fax:* 207-326-2515. *E-mail:* kheath@mma.edu.

INTERNATIONAL STUDENTS 24% of students enrolled are international students. *Services and facilities:* Counseling/support services, Housing location assistance, International student housing, Orientation, Visa Services. Financial aid is not available to international students. *Required with application:* IELT; TOEFL; proof of adequate funds; proof of health/immunizations.

International Student Contact Mr. Tom Sawyer, Registrar, Castine, ME 04420. *Phone:* 207-326-2441. *Fax:* 207-326-2510. *E-mail:* tsawyer@mma.edu.

APPLICATION *Required:* Application form, baccalaureate/first degree, 2 letters of recommendation, personal statement, resume/curriculum vitae, transcripts of college work. School will accept GMAT and GRE.

Recommended: Essay, interview, work experience. *Application fee:* $40. Applications for domestic and international students are processed on a rolling basis.

Application Contact Patrick Haugen, Administrative Assistant, Graduate Studies, Loeb-Sullivan School of International Business and Logistics, Castine, ME 04420. *Phone:* 207-326-2212. *Fax:* 207-326-2411. *E-mail:* info.ls@mma.edu.

Saint Joseph's College of Maine
Program in Business Administration

Standish, Maine

Phone: 800-752-4723 **Fax:** 207-892-7480 **E-mail:** info@sjcme.edu

Business Program(s) Web Site: http://www.sjcme.edu/gps/programs/mba.htm

Graduate Business Unit Enrollment *Total:* 125 (125 part-time; 70 women). *Average Age:* 43.

Graduate Business Faculty 15 part-time.

Admissions *Applied:* 71. *Admitted:* 66. *Enrolled:* 61.

Academic Calendar Continuous.

DEGREE MBA

MBA—The Leadership MBA Part-time. Distance learning option. Minimum undergraduate GPA of 2.5, essay required. 42 total credits required. 24 to 60 months to complete program. *Concentration:* leadership.

RESOURCES AND SERVICES 10 on-campus PCs are available to graduate business students. Access to Internet/World Wide Web available. *Personal computer requirements:* Graduate business students are required to have a personal computer. *Placement services include:* Alumni network, career counseling/planning, resume referral, resume preparation, and career library.

EXPENSES *Tuition:* Part-time: $400 per credit.

Financial Aid Contact Andrea Cross, Director of Financial Aid, 278 Whites Bridge Road, Standish, ME 04084. *Phone:* 207-893-7841 Ext. 6612. *Fax:* 207-893-7862. *E-mail:* across@sjcme.edu.

INTERNATIONAL STUDENTS Financial aid is not available to international students. *Required with application:* TOEFL with recommended score of 161 (computer) or 485 (paper). *Recommended with application:* Proof of adequate funds; proof of health/immunizations.

International Student Contact Lynne Robinson, Director of Admission, 278 Whites Bridge Road, Standish, ME 04084. *Phone:* 207-893-7841. *Fax:* 207-892-7480. *E-mail:* info@sjcme.edu.

APPLICATION *Required:* Application form, baccalaureate/first degree, essay, transcripts of college work, 2 years of work experience. *Recommended:* Resume/curriculum vitae. *Application fee:* $50. Applications for domestic and international students are processed on a rolling basis.

Application Contact Lynne Robinson, Director of Admission, 278 Whites Bridge Road, Standish, ME 04084. *Phone:* 800-752-4723. *Fax:* 207-892-7480. *E-mail:* info@sjcme.edu.

Thomas College
Programs in Business

Waterville, Maine

Phone: 207-859-1102 **Fax:** 207-859-1114 **E-mail:** grad@thomas.edu

Business Program(s) Web Site: http://www.thomas.edu/grad

Graduate Business Unit Enrollment *Total:* 185 (1 full-time; 184 part-time; 115 women). *Average Age:* 35.

Graduate Business Faculty *Total:* 30 (13 full-time; 17 part-time).

Admissions *Applied:* 50. *Admitted:* 48. *Enrolled:* 48. *Average GMAT:* 510. *Average GPA:* 3.2

Academic Calendar Trimesters.

After Graduation (Class of 2006–07) *Employed within 3 months of graduation:* 97.5%.

DEGREES MBA

MBA—Human Resource Management Part-time. At least 36 total credits required. *Concentration:* human resources management.

MBA—Master of Business Administration Part-time. At least 36 total credits required. *Concentration:* general MBA.

RESOURCES AND SERVICES 60 on-campus PCs are available to graduate business students. Access to Internet/World Wide Web, online (class) registration, and online grade reports available. *Personal computer requirements:* Graduate business students are strongly recommended to purchase or lease a personal computer. *Placement services include:* Career counseling/planning, career fairs, and resume preparation.

EXPENSES *Tuition:* Part-time: $825 per course.

FINANCIAL AID (2007–08) Loans and scholarships. Aid is available to part-time students.

Financial Aid Contact Jeannine Bossie, Director of Student Financial Services, 180 West River Road, Waterville, ME 04901. *Phone:* 207-859-1112 Ext. 112. *Fax:* 207-859-1114. *E-mail:* sfsdir@thomas.edu.

INTERNATIONAL STUDENTS Financial aid is not available to international students. *Required with application:* TOEFL with recommended score of 530 (paper); proof of adequate funds; proof of health/immunizations.

APPLICATION *Required:* Application form, baccalaureate/first degree, 2 letters of recommendation, transcripts of college work. School will accept GMAT, GRE, and MAT. *Application fee:* $50. Applications for domestic students are processed on a rolling basis.

Application Contact Libby LaRochelle, Administrative Assistant, 180 West River Road, Waterville, ME 04901. *Phone:* 207-859-1102. *Fax:* 207-859-1114. *E-mail:* grad@thomas.edu.

University of Maine
The Maine Business School

Orono, Maine

Phone: 207-581-1973 **Fax:** 207-581-1930 **E-mail:** mba@maine.edu

Business Program(s) Web Site: http://www.umaine.edu/business/

Graduate Business Unit Enrollment *Total:* 89 (60 full-time; 29 part-time; 38 women; 10 international). *Average Age:* 30.

Graduate Business Faculty *Total:* 22 (21 full-time; 1 part-time).

Admissions *Applied:* 39. *Admitted:* 28. *Enrolled:* 15. *Average GMAT:* 560. *Average GPA:* 3.24

Academic Calendar Semesters.

Accreditation AACSB—The Association to Advance Collegiate Schools of Business.

After Graduation (Class of 2006–07) *Employed within 3 months of graduation:* 85%. *Average starting salary:* $49,700.

DEGREES MBA • MSA

MBA—Master of Business Administration Full-time and part-time. 42 to 120 total credits required. 18 to 72 months to complete program. *Concentrations:* finance, management.

MSA—Master of Science in Accounting Full-time and part-time. 30 to 66 total credits required. 12 to 72 months to complete program. *Concentrations:* health care, management, nonprofit management, public policy and administration.

University of Maine (continued)

RESOURCES AND SERVICES 200 on-campus PCs are available to graduate business students. Access to Internet/World Wide Web, online (class) registration, and online grade reports available. *Personal computer requirements:* Graduate business students are strongly recommended to purchase or lease a personal computer. *Special opportunities include:* An international exchange program and an internship program are available. *Placement services include:* Alumni network, career placement, career counseling/planning, electronic job bank, resume referral, career fairs, job interviews arranged, resume preparation, and career library.

EXPENSES *Tuition (state resident):* Full-time: $7497. Part-time: $357 per credit. *Tuition (nonresident):* Full-time: $21,588. Part-time: $1028 per credit. *Tuition (international):* Full-time: $21,588. Part-time: $1028 per credit. *Required fees:* Full-time: $971. Part-time: $201 per credit.

FINANCIAL AID (2007–08) 8 students received aid, including research assistantships, scholarships, and work study. *Financial aid application deadline:* 2/15.

Financial Aid Contact Peggy Crawford, Director of Student Financial Aid, 5781 Wingate Hall, Orono, ME 04469-5781. *Phone:* 207-581-1324. *Fax:* 207-581-3261. *E-mail:* umfinaid@maine.edu.

INTERNATIONAL STUDENTS 11% of students enrolled are international students. *Services and facilities:* Counseling/support services, ESL/language courses, Housing location assistance, International student housing, International student organization, Orientation, Visa Services, Intensive English Institute (fee). Financial aid is available to international students. *Required with application:* TOEFL with recommended score of 213 (computer), 550 (paper), or 79 (Internet); proof of adequate funds; proof of health/immunizations.

International Student Contact Karen Boucias, Director of International Programs, 100 Winslow Hall, Orono, ME 04469-5782. *Phone:* 207-581-2905. *Fax:* 207-581-2920. *E-mail:* umintprg@maine.edu.

APPLICATION *Required:* GMAT, application form, baccalaureate/first degree, essay, 3 letters of recommendation, personal statement, resume/curriculum vitae, transcripts of college work. *Recommended:* Work experience. *Application fee:* $60. Applications for domestic and international students are processed on a rolling basis.

Application Contact Dr. Nory Jones, Director, 5723 D. P. Corbett Business Building, Orono, ME 04469-5723. *Phone:* 207-581-1973. *Fax:* 207-581-1930. *E-mail:* mba@maine.edu.

RESOURCES AND SERVICES 400 on-campus PCs are available to graduate business students. Access to Internet/World Wide Web, online (class) registration, and online grade reports available. *Personal computer requirements:* Graduate business students are strongly recommended to purchase or lease a personal computer. *Special opportunities include:* An international exchange program and an internship program are available. *Placement services include:* Alumni network, career counseling/planning, electronic job bank, career fairs, job interviews arranged, resume preparation, and career library.

EXPENSES *Tuition (state resident):* Part-time: $297 per credit hour. *Tuition (nonresident):* Part-time: $844 per credit hour. *Tuition (international):* Part-time: $844 per credit hour. *Required fees:* Full-time: $678. Tuition and/or fees vary by academic program. *Graduate housing:* Room and board costs vary by number of occupants and type of board plan. *Typical cost:* $12,000 (including board).

FINANCIAL AID (2007–08) Loans, research assistantships, scholarships, teaching assistantships, and work study. Aid is available to part-time students. *Financial aid application deadline:* 1/15.

Financial Aid Contact Mr. Keith Dubois, Financial Aid Director, 37 College Avenue, Gorham, ME 04038. *Phone:* 207-780-5250. *Fax:* 207-780-5143. *E-mail:* fin-aid@usm.maine.edu.

INTERNATIONAL STUDENTS 6% of students enrolled are international students. *Services and facilities:* Counseling/support services, ESL/language courses, International student housing, International student organization, Orientation, Visa Services. Financial aid is available to international students. *Required with application:* TOEFL with recommended score of 213 (computer), 550 (paper), or 79 (Internet); proof of adequate funds; proof of health/immunizations.

International Student Contact Domenica Cipollone, Director, International Programs, PO Box 9300, Portland, ME 04104-9300. *Phone:* 207-780-4954. *Fax:* 207-780-4933. *E-mail:* domenica@usm.maine.edu.

APPLICATION *Required:* Application form, baccalaureate/first degree, essay, 3 letters of recommendation, resume/curriculum vitae, transcripts of college work. School will accept GMAT and GRE. *Application fee:* $50. Applications for domestic and international students are processed on a rolling basis.

Application Contact Ms. Alice Cash, Assistant Dean for Student Affairs, PO Box 9300, 96 Falmouth Street, Portland, ME 04104-9300. *Phone:* 207-780-4184. *Fax:* 207-780-4662. *E-mail:* mba@usm.maine.edu.

University of Southern Maine
School of Business
Portland, Maine

Phone: 207-780-4184 **Fax:** 207-780-4662 **E-mail:** mba@usm.maine.edu

Business Program(s) Web Site: http://www.usm.maine.edu/sb/

Graduate Business Unit Enrollment *Total:* 162 (40 full-time; 122 part-time; 78 women; 9 international). *Average Age:* 29.

Graduate Business Faculty *Total:* 24 (22 full-time; 2 part-time).

Admissions *Applied:* 80. *Admitted:* 60. *Enrolled:* 49. *Average GMAT:* 564. *Average GPA:* 3.42

Academic Calendar Semesters.

Accreditation AACSB—The Association to Advance Collegiate Schools of Business.

DEGREES MBA • MSA

MBA—Master of Business Administration Full-time and part-time. 39 to 54 total credits required. 18 to 72 months to complete program. *Concentration:* general MBA.

MSA—Master of Science in Accounting Full-time and part-time. 30 to 55 total credits required. 12 to 72 months to complete program. *Concentration:* accounting.

MARYLAND

Capitol College
Graduate Programs
Laurel, Maryland

Phone: 800-950-1992 **E-mail:** gradadmit@capitol-college.edu

Business Program(s) Web Site: http://www.capitol-college.edu/

Graduate Business Unit Enrollment *Total:* 300 (50 full-time; 250 part-time; 110 women; 5 international). *Average Age:* 34.

Graduate Business Faculty *Total:* 15 (3 full-time; 12 part-time).

Admissions *Applied:* 75. *Admitted:* 68. *Enrolled:* 53.

Academic Calendar Semesters.

DEGREE MBA

MBA—Master of Business Administration Full-time and part-time. Distance learning option. 36 to 42 total credits required. Maximum of 7 months to complete program. *Concentration:* general MBA.

RESOURCES AND SERVICES Access to Internet/World Wide Web, online (class) registration, and online grade reports available. *Personal*

computer requirements: Graduate business students are required to have a personal computer. *Special opportunities include:* An internship program is available. *Placement services include:* Alumni network, career fairs, and resume preparation.

EXPENSES *Tuition:* Part-time: $540 per credit. *Tuition (international):* Part-time: $540 per credit.

INTERNATIONAL STUDENTS 2% of students enrolled are international students. *Required with application:* TOEFL with recommended score of 500 (paper) or 82 (Internet).

APPLICATION *Required:* Application form, baccalaureate/first degree, essay, transcripts of college work. *Application fee:* $0. Applications for domestic and international students are processed on a rolling basis.

Columbia Union College
MBA Program
Takoma Park, Maryland

Phone: 301-891-4072 **Fax:** 301-891-4023 **E-mail:** jdcasey@cuc.edu

Business Program(s) Web Site: http://www.cuc.edu/mba

Graduate Business Unit Enrollment *Total:* 80 (80 part-time).

Graduate Business Faculty 15 part-time.

Admissions *Average GPA:* 3.0

Academic Calendar Continuous.

After Graduation (Class of 2006–07) *Employed within 3 months of graduation:* 100%.

DEGREE MBA

MBA—Master of Business Administration Part-time. 36 total credits required. 12 to 24 months to complete program. *Concentrations:* accounting, general MBA.

RESOURCES AND SERVICES 100 on-campus PCs are available to graduate business students. Access to Internet/World Wide Web and online grade reports available. *Personal computer requirements:* Graduate business students are strongly recommended to purchase or lease a personal computer. *Placement services include:* Alumni network, resume preparation, and career library.

EXPENSES *Tuition:* Part-time: $520 per credit hour. *Tuition (international):* Part-time: $520 per credit hour. *Required fees:* Part-time: $275 per degree program.

FINANCIAL AID (2007–08) 80 students received aid, including loans. Aid is available to part-time students.

Financial Aid Contact Graduate Student Services, School of Graduate and Professional Studies, 7600 Flower Avenue, Takoma Park, MD 20912. *E-mail:* mba@cuc.edu.

INTERNATIONAL STUDENTS *Services and facilities:* Visa Services. Financial aid is not available to international students. *Required with application:* IELT with recommended score of 5; TOEFL with recommended score of 213 (computer) or 550 (paper); proof of adequate funds; proof of health/immunizations.

International Student Contact Mr. Emile John, Director of Admissions, Office of Admissions, 7600 Flower Avenue, Takoma Park, MD 20912. *Phone:* 301-891-4079. *Fax:* 301-891-4230. *E-mail:* ejohn@cuc.edu.

APPLICATION *Required:* Application form, baccalaureate/first degree, essay, interview, personal statement, resume/curriculum vitae, transcripts of college work. *Recommended:* Work experience. *Application fee:* $50. Applications for domestic and international students are processed on a rolling basis.

Application Contact Ms. Joy Daquila-Casey, Director, MBA Program, School of Graduate and Professional Studies, 7600 Flower Avenue, Takoma Park, MD 20912-7796. *Phone:* 301-891-4072. *Fax:* 301-891-4023. *E-mail:* jdcasey@cuc.edu.

Frostburg State University
College of Business
Frostburg, Maryland

Phone: 301-687-7053 **Fax:** 301-687-4597 **E-mail:** vmmazer@frostburg.edu

Business Program(s) Web Site: http://www.frostburg.edu/dept/mba/home.htm

Graduate Business Unit Enrollment *Total:* 353 (74 full-time; 279 part-time; 156 women; 14 international).

Graduate Business Faculty 40 full-time.

Admissions *Applied:* 152. *Admitted:* 141. *Enrolled:* 113. *Average GMAT:* 510. *Average GPA:* 2.96

Academic Calendar Semesters.

Accreditation AACSB—The Association to Advance Collegiate Schools of Business.

After Graduation (Class of 2006–07) *Employed within 3 months of graduation:* 95%.

DEGREES MBA • MBA equivalent combined degree • MBA/MS

MBA—Master of Business Administration Full-time and part-time. 36 to 46 total credits required. 12 to 72 months to complete program. *Concentration:* management.

MBA equivalent combined degree—Bachelor of Science in Accounting/Master of Business Administration Full-time and part-time. Applicant must be a declared accounting major at Frostburg State University. Student must complete 2 MBA courses during the final semester of the undergraduate senior year. 150 total credits required. 12 to 72 months to complete program. *Concentrations:* accounting, management.

MBA/MS—Master of Business Administration/Master of Science in Nursing Administration Full-time and part-time. Distance learning option. Must fulfill admissions process and standards criteria for MBA program and the University of Maryland Baltimore's MS in Nursing Administration program. 36 to 72 total credits required. 24 to 72 months to complete program. *Concentrations:* health administration, management.

RESOURCES AND SERVICES 150 on-campus PCs are available to graduate business students. Access to Internet/World Wide Web, online (class) registration, and online grade reports available. *Personal computer requirements:* Graduate business students are strongly recommended to purchase or lease a personal computer. *Placement services include:* Alumni network, career placement, career counseling/planning, electronic job bank, career fairs, resume preparation, and career library.

EXPENSES *Tuition (state resident):* Full-time: $4728. Part-time: $394 per credit. *Tuition (nonresident):* Full-time: $5292. Part-time: $441 per credit. *Tuition (international):* Full-time: $5292. Part-time: $441 per credit. *Graduate housing:* Room and board costs vary by type of accommodation and type of board plan.

FINANCIAL AID (2007–08) 15 students received aid, including fellowships, grants, loans, research assistantships, scholarships, and work study. *Financial aid application deadline:* 3/15.

Financial Aid Contact Vickie Mazer, Director of Graduate Services, Pullen Hall, Frostburg, MD 21532. *Phone:* 301-687-7053. *Fax:* 301-687-4597. *E-mail:* vmmazer@frostburg.edu.

INTERNATIONAL STUDENTS 4% of students enrolled are international students. *Services and facilities:* Counseling/support services, Orientation, Visa Services. Financial aid is available to international students. *Required with application:* IELT with recommended score of 6; TOEFL with recommended score of 213 (computer), 550 (paper), or 79 (Internet); proof of adequate funds; proof of health/immunizations.

International Student Contact Ms. Vickie Mazer, Director of Graduate Services, Pullen Hall, Frostburg, MD 21532. *Phone:* 301-687-7053. *Fax:* 301-687-4597. *E-mail:* vmmazer@frostburg.edu.

APPLICATION *Required:* Application form, baccalaureate/first degree, transcripts of college work. School will accept GMAT and GRE.

Frostburg State University (continued)

Recommended: Resume/curriculum vitae, 2 years of work experience. *Application fee:* $30. Applications for domestic and international students are processed on a rolling basis.

Application Contact Vickie Mazer, Director, Graduate Services, Frostburg, MD 21532-1099. *Phone:* 301-687-7053. *Fax:* 301-687-4597. *E-mail:* vmmazer@frostburg.edu.

Hood College

Department of Economics and Management

Frederick, Maryland

Phone: 301-696-3811 **Fax:** 301-696-3597 **E-mail:** gofurther@hood.edu

Business Program(s) Web Site: http://www.hood.edu/graduate

Graduate Business Unit Enrollment *Total:* 193 (30 full-time; 163 part-time; 106 women; 22 international). *Average Age:* 33.

Graduate Business Faculty *Total:* 13 (4 full-time; 9 part-time).

Admissions *Applied:* 85. *Admitted:* 74. *Enrolled:* 47.

Academic Calendar Semesters.

DEGREE MBA

MBA—Master of Business Administration Full-time and part-time. 36 to 54 total credits required. Maximum of 84 months to complete program. *Concentrations:* accounting, finance, human resources management, information management, marketing, public management.

RESOURCES AND SERVICES 212 on-campus PCs are available to graduate business students. Access to Internet/World Wide Web, online (class) registration, and online grade reports available. *Personal computer requirements:* Graduate business students are strongly recommended to purchase or lease a personal computer. *Placement services include:* Alumni network, career placement, job search course, career counseling/planning, electronic job bank, resume referral, career fairs, job interviews arranged, resume preparation, and career library.

EXPENSES *Tuition:* Full-time: $6480. Part-time: $360 per credit. *Tuition (international):* Full-time: $6480. Part-time: $360 per credit. *Required fees:* Full-time: $70. Part-time: $35 per semester. *Graduate housing:* Room and board costs vary by number of occupants and type of board plan. *Typical cost:* $8542 (including board), $4462 (room only).

Financial Aid Contact Ms. Margherite Powell, Director of Financial Aid, 401 Rosemont Avenue, Frederick, MD 21701. *Phone:* 301-696-3411. *Fax:* 301-696-3812. *E-mail:* powellm@hood.edu.

INTERNATIONAL STUDENTS 11% of students enrolled are international students. *Services and facilities:* Counseling/support services, International student organization, Visa Services. Financial aid is not available to international students. *Required with application:* TOEFL with recommended score of 231 (computer), 575 (paper), or 89 (Internet); TWE with recommended score of 4; proof of adequate funds.

International Student Contact Dr. Kiran Chadda, Director, Multi-Cultural Affairs, 401 Rosemont Avenue, Frederick, MD 21701-8578. *Phone:* 301-696-3577. *Fax:* 301-696-3771. *E-mail:* chadda@hood.edu.

APPLICATION *Required:* Application form, baccalaureate/first degree, transcripts of college work. *Recommended:* Essay, interview, letter(s) of recommendation, resume/curriculum vitae, work experience. *Application fee:* $35. Applications for domestic and international students are processed on a rolling basis.

Application Contact Dr. Kathleen C. Bands, Dean of the Graduate School, 401 Rosemont Avenue, Frederick, MD 21701-8575. *Phone:* 301-696-3811. *Fax:* 301-696-3597. *E-mail:* gofurther@hood.edu.

The Johns Hopkins University

Carey Business School

Baltimore, Maryland

Phone: 410-516-4234 **Fax:** 410-516-0826 **E-mail:** careyinfo@jhu.edu

Business Program(s) Web Site: http://carey.jhu.edu

Graduate Business Unit Enrollment *Total:* 2,182 (399 full-time; 1,783 part-time; 950 women; 299 international). *Average Age:* 34.

Graduate Business Faculty *Total:* 225 (25 full-time; 200 part-time).

Admissions *Applied:* 826. *Admitted:* 486. *Enrolled:* 385. *Average GMAT:* 600. *Average GPA:* 3.2

Academic Calendar Semesters.

After Graduation (Class of 2006–07) *Employed within 3 months of graduation:* 93%.

DEGREES MBA • MBA/MPH • MBA/MS • MBA/MSN • MS • MSF

MBA—Master of Business Administration Full-time and part-time. 39 to 54 total credits required. 24 to 72 months to complete program. *Concentrations:* electronic commerce (E-commerce), finance, general MBA, human resources management, information systems, information technology, management, management information systems, marketing, technology management.

MBA—Medical Services Management Full-time and part-time. 39 to 54 total credits required. 24 to 72 months to complete program. *Concentration:* medicine.

MBA/MPH—Master of Business Administration/Master of Public Health Full-time. Up to 82 total credits required. Maximum of 18 months to complete program. *Concentration:* combined degrees.

MBA/MS—MBA/MS in Information and Telecommunication Systems Full-time and part-time. Up to 66 total credits required. Maximum of 72 months to complete program. *Concentrations:* general MBA, information systems.

MBA/MS—Master of Business Administration/Master of Science in Biotechnology Part-time. 65 to 67 total credits required. Maximum of 72 months to complete program. *Concentration:* combined degrees.

MBA/MSN—Master of Business Administration/Master of Science in Nursing Full-time and part-time. 56 to 57 total credits required. Maximum of 72 months to complete program. *Concentration:* combined degrees.

MS—Master of Science in Information and Telecommunications Systems Full-time and part-time. At least 48 total credits required. Maximum of 72 months to complete program. *Concentrations:* electronic commerce (E-commerce), information systems, telecommunications management.

MS—Master of Science in Marketing Full-time and part-time. At least 48 total credits required. Maximum of 72 months to complete program. *Concentration:* marketing.

MS—Master of Science in Organization Development and Strategic Human Resources Full-time and part-time. 37 to 42 total credits required. Maximum of 72 months to complete program. *Concentrations:* human resources management, organizational behavior/development.

MS—Master of Science in Real Estate Full-time and part-time. At least 40 total credits required. *Concentration:* real estate.

MSF—Master of Science in Finance Full-time and part-time. At least 36 total credits required. Maximum of 72 months to complete program. *Concentration:* finance.

RESOURCES AND SERVICES 275 on-campus PCs are available to graduate business students. Access to Internet/World Wide Web, online (class) registration, and online grade reports available. *Personal computer requirements:* Graduate business students are required to have a personal computer. *Placement services include:* Alumni network, career placement, job search course, career counseling/planning, electronic job bank, resume referral, career fairs, job interviews arranged, resume preparation, and career library.

EXPENSES Tuition and/or fees vary by campus location.

FINANCIAL AID (2007–08) 427 students received aid, including loans and scholarships. Aid is available to part-time students. *Financial aid application deadline:* 6/1.

Financial Aid Contact Laura Donnelly, Director of Financial Aid, 6740 Alexander Bell Drive, Suite 110, Columbia, MD 21046. *Phone:* 410-516-9808. *Fax:* 410-516-9799. *E-mail:* onestop.finaid@jhu.edu.

INTERNATIONAL STUDENTS 14% of students enrolled are international students. *Services and facilities:* Counseling/support services, ESL/language courses, International student organization, Orientation, Visa Services. Financial aid is available to international students. *Required with application:* TOEFL with recommended score of 250 (computer), 600 (paper), or 100 (Internet); proof of adequate funds; proof of health/immunizations.

International Student Contact Ann Roeder, Assistant Director, International and Disability Services, 10 North Charles Street, Baltimore, MD 21201. *Phone:* 410-516-9740. *Fax:* 410-516-9748. *E-mail:* onestop.intl@jhu.edu.

APPLICATION *Required:* GMAT, application form, baccalaureate/first degree, essay, 2 letters of recommendation, personal statement, resume/curriculum vitae, transcripts of college work. School will accept GRE. *Recommended:* Interview, work experience. *Application fee:* $70. *Deadlines:* 5/1 for fall (international), 10/15 for spring (international). Applications for domestic students are processed on a rolling basis.

Application Contact Sondra Smith, Director of Admissions, 100 North Charles Street, 7th Floor, Baltimore, MD 21201. *Phone:* 410-516-4234. *Fax:* 410-516-0826. *E-mail:* careyinfo@jhu.edu.

See full description on page 646.

Loyola College in Maryland
Sellinger School of Business and Management

Baltimore, Maryland

Phone: 410-617-5020 **Fax:** 410-617-2002 **E-mail:** graduate@loyola.edu

Business Program(s) Web Site: http://sellinger.loyola.edu/

Graduate Business Unit Enrollment *Total:* 994 (196 full-time; 798 part-time; 382 women; 22 international). *Average Age:* 31.

Graduate Business Faculty *Total:* 95 (60 full-time; 35 part-time).

Admissions *Applied:* 619. *Admitted:* 439. *Enrolled:* 352. *Average GMAT:* 536. *Average GPA:* 3.34

Academic Calendar Semesters.

Accreditation AACSB—The Association to Advance Collegiate Schools of Business.

After Graduation (Class of 2006–07) *Employed within 3 months of graduation:* 98%. *Average starting salary:* $42,000.

DEGREES MBA • MSF

MBA—Evening Program Full-time and part-time. 33 to 53 total credits required. 15 to 84 months to complete program. *Concentrations:* accounting, finance, general MBA, international business, management, management information systems, marketing.

MBA—Executive Master of Business Administration Part-time. 51 total credits required. 21 months to complete program. *Concentration:* executive programs.

MBA—Executive Master of Business Administration Fellows Program Part-time. 51 total credits required. 30 months to complete program. *Concentration:* executive programs.

MSF—Master of Science in Finance Part-time. 30 to 40 total credits required. 12 to 84 months to complete program. *Concentration:* finance.

RESOURCES AND SERVICES 377 on-campus PCs are available to graduate business students. Access to Internet/World Wide Web, online (class) registration, and online grade reports available. *Personal computer*

requirements: Graduate business students are strongly recommended to purchase or lease a personal computer. *Placement services include:* Alumni network, career placement, job search course, career counseling/planning, electronic job bank, resume referral, career fairs, job interviews arranged, resume preparation, and career library.

EXPENSES *Tuition:* Full-time: $11,700. Part-time: $650 per credit. *Tuition (international):* Full-time: $11,700. Part-time: $650 per credit. *Required fees:* Full-time: $50. Part-time: $25 per semester.

FINANCIAL AID (2007–08) 173 students received aid, including grants, loans, and scholarships.

Financial Aid Contact Mr. Mark Lindenmeyer, Director of Financial Aid, 4501 North Charles Street, Baltimore, MD 21210-2699. *Phone:* 410-617-2576. *Fax:* 410-617-5149.

INTERNATIONAL STUDENTS 2% of students enrolled are international students. *Services and facilities:* Counseling/support services, ESL/language courses, Orientation, Visa Services. Financial aid is not available to international students. *Required with application:* TOEFL with recommended score of 213 (computer) or 550 (paper); proof of adequate funds; proof of health/immunizations.

International Student Contact Andre Colombat, Director, International Program, 4501 North Charles Street, Baltimore, MD 21210-2699. *Phone:* 410-617-2910. *E-mail:* international@loyola.edu.

APPLICATION *Required:* GMAT, application form, baccalaureate/first degree, essay, personal statement, resume/curriculum vitae, transcripts of college work. *Recommended:* Letter(s) of recommendation, work experience. *Application fee:* $50. Applications for domestic and international students are processed on a rolling basis.

Application Contact Scott Greatorex, Director, Graduate Admissions, 4501 North Charles Street, Baltimore, MD 21210-2699. *Phone:* 410-617-5020. *Fax:* 410-617-2002. *E-mail:* graduate@loyola.edu.

Mount St. Mary's University
Program in Business Administration

Emmitsburg, Maryland

Phone: 301-447-5396 **Fax:** 301-447-5335 **E-mail:** forgang@msmary.edu

Business Program(s) Web Site: http://www.msmary.edu/mba

Graduate Business Unit Enrollment *Total:* 213 (40 full-time; 173 part-time; 98 women; 6 international). *Average Age:* 33.

Graduate Business Faculty *Total:* 20 (12 full-time; 8 part-time).

Admissions *Applied:* 73. *Admitted:* 65. *Enrolled:* 41.

Academic Calendar Continuous cycle of 8 week sessions.

DEGREE MBA

MBA—Master of Business Administration Full-time and part-time. At least 36 total credits required. 12 to 60 months to complete program. *Concentrations:* accounting, finance, management, marketing.

RESOURCES AND SERVICES 150 on-campus PCs are available to graduate business students. Access to Internet/World Wide Web, online (class) registration, and online grade reports available. *Personal computer requirements:* Graduate business students are strongly recommended to purchase or lease a personal computer. *Placement services include:* Alumni network, career counseling/planning, resume referral, career fairs, job interviews arranged, resume preparation, and career library.

EXPENSES *Tuition:* Full-time: $7560. Part-time: $420 per credit hour. *Tuition (international):* Full-time: $7560. Part-time: $420 per credit hour.

FINANCIAL AID (2007–08) 71 students received aid, including loans and research assistantships.

Financial Aid Contact David C. Reeder, Director of Financial Aid, 16300 Old Emmitsburg Road, Emmitsburg, MD 21727. *Phone:* 301-447-5207. *Fax:* 301-447-5915. *E-mail:* reeder@msmary.edu.

Mount St. Mary's University (continued)

INTERNATIONAL STUDENTS 3% of students enrolled are international students. *Services and facilities:* International student organization, International student adviser. Financial aid is available to international students. *Required with application:* TOEFL with recommended score of 213 (computer) or 550 (paper); proof of adequate funds; proof of health/immunizations.

International Student Contact Dr. Gertrude Conway, Professor of Philosophy, 16300 Old Emmitsburg Road, Emmitsburg, MD 21727. *Phone:* 301-447-5368. *Fax:* 301-447-5806. *E-mail:* conway@msmary.edu.

APPLICATION *Required:* Application form, baccalaureate/first degree, personal statement, transcripts of college work. *Recommended:* Resume/curriculum vitae, work experience. *Application fee:* $35. Applications for domestic and international students are processed on a rolling basis.

Application Contact William Forgang, Chairperson, Business Department, 16300 Old Emmitsburg Road, Emmitsburg, MD 21727. *Phone:* 301-447-5396. *Fax:* 301-447-5335. *E-mail:* forgang@msmary.edu.

Salisbury University
Franklin P. Perdue School of Business
Salisbury, Maryland

Phone: 410-548-3983 **Fax:** 410-548-2908 **E-mail:** srharrington@salisbury.edu

Business Program(s) Web Site: http://mba.salisbury.edu

Graduate Business Unit Enrollment *Total:* 84 (50 full-time; 34 part-time; 43 women; 14 international).

Graduate Business Faculty 26 full-time.

Admissions *Applied:* 54. *Admitted:* 29. *Enrolled:* 26. *Average GMAT:* 510. *Average GPA:* 3.3

Academic Calendar Semesters.

Accreditation AACSB—The Association to Advance Collegiate Schools of Business.

DEGREE MBA

MBA—Master of Business Administration Full-time and part-time. 30 to 54 total credits required. 12 to 84 months to complete program. *Concentration:* general MBA.

RESOURCES AND SERVICES 100 on-campus PCs are available to graduate business students. Access to Internet/World Wide Web, online (class) registration, and online grade reports available. *Personal computer requirements:* Graduate business students are not required to have a personal computer. *Special opportunities include:* An international exchange program and an internship program are available. *Placement services include:* Alumni network, career placement, career counseling/planning, electronic job bank, resume referral, career fairs, job interviews arranged, resume preparation, and career library.

EXPENSES *Tuition (state resident):* Part-time: $260 per credit. *Tuition (nonresident):* Part-time: $556 per credit hour. *Tuition (international):* Part-time: $556 per credit hour. *Required fees:* Full-time: $175. Part-time: $175 per year. Tuition and/or fees vary by class time.

FINANCIAL AID (2007–08) 8 students received aid, including loans and research assistantships. *Financial aid application deadline:* 5/1.

Financial Aid Contact Ms. Elizabeth Zimmerman, Director, Financial Aid, 1101 Camden Avenue, Salisbury, MD 21801-6837. *Phone:* 410-543-6165. *Fax:* 410-543-6138. *E-mail:* finaid@salisbury.edu.

INTERNATIONAL STUDENTS 17% of students enrolled are international students. *Services and facilities:* Counseling/support services, Housing location assistance, International student organization, Language tutoring, Orientation. Financial aid is available to international students.

Required with application: TOEFL with recommended score of 213 (computer) or 550 (paper); proof of adequate funds; proof of health/immunizations.

International Student Contact Ms. Sharon Harrington, MBA Director, 1101 Camden Avenue, Salisbury, MD 21801-6837. *Phone:* 410-548-3983. *Fax:* 410-548-2908. *E-mail:* srharrington@salisbury.edu.

APPLICATION *Required:* GMAT, application form, baccalaureate/first degree, essay, 2 letters of recommendation, personal statement, resume/curriculum vitae, transcripts of college work. *Recommended:* 2 years of work experience. *Application fee:* $45. *Deadlines:* 3/1 for fall, 3/1 for fall (international).

Application Contact Ms. Sharon Harrington, MBA Director, 1101 Camden Avenue, Salisbury, MD 21801-6837. *Phone:* 410-548-3983. *Fax:* 410-548-2908. *E-mail:* srharrington@salisbury.edu.

University of Baltimore
Merrick School of Business
Baltimore, Maryland

Phone: 877-277-5982 **Fax:** 410-837-6565 **E-mail:** gradadmissions@ubalt.edu

Business Program(s) Web Site: http://business.ubalt.edu/

Graduate Business Unit Enrollment *Total:* 677 (160 full-time; 517 part-time; 330 women; 98 international). *Average Age:* 29.

Graduate Business Faculty *Total:* 45 (36 full-time; 9 part-time).

Admissions *Applied:* 591. *Admitted:* 258. *Enrolled:* 213. *Average GMAT:* 520. *Average GPA:* 3.2

Academic Calendar Semesters.

Accreditation AACSB—The Association to Advance Collegiate Schools of Business.

DEGREES JD/MBA • MBA • MBA/MS • MS • PhD/MBA • Pharm D/MBA

JD/MBA—Juris Doctor/UB/Towson Master of Business Administration Full-time and part-time. MBA application in online. 102 to 123 total credits required. 36 to 84 months to complete program. *Concentrations:* entrepreneurship, finance, human resources management, international business, management, management information systems, marketing, technology management.

MBA—UB/Towson Web Master of Business Administration Full-time and part-time. Distance learning option. Online. At least 48 total credits required. 24 months to complete program. *Concentration:* management.

MBA/MS—UB/Towson Master of Business Administration/Master of Science in Nursing Full-time and part-time. MBA application is online. At least 66 total credits required. 24 to 84 months to complete program. *Concentration:* health care.

MS—Master of Science in Accounting and Business Advisory Services Full-time and part-time. 30 to 51 total credits required. 12 to 84 months to complete program. *Concentration:* accounting.

MS—Master of Science in Taxation Full-time and part-time. At least 30 total credits required. 12 to 84 months to complete program. *Concentration:* taxation.

PhD/MBA—Doctor of Philosophy in Nursing/UB/Towson Master of Business Administration Full-time and part-time. MBA application is online. At least 85 total credits required. 24 to 84 months to complete program. *Concentration:* health care.

Pharm D/MBA—Doctorate of Pharmacy/UB/Towson Master of Business Administration Full-time and part-time. MBA application is online. At least 155 total credits required. 24 to 84 months to complete program. *Concentration:* health care.

RESOURCES AND SERVICES 250 on-campus PCs are available to graduate business students. Access to Internet/World Wide Web, online (class) registration, and online grade reports available. *Personal computer*

requirements: Graduate business students are strongly recommended to purchase or lease a personal computer. *Special opportunities include:* An international exchange program and an internship program are available. *Placement services include:* Alumni network, career placement, job search course, career counseling/planning, electronic job bank, resume referral, career fairs, job interviews arranged, resume preparation, and career library.

EXPENSES *Tuition (state resident):* Part-time: $536 per credit hour. *Tuition (nonresident):* Part-time: $751 per credit hour. *Tuition (international):* Part-time: $751 per credit hour. *Required fees:* Part-time: $235 per course.

FINANCIAL AID (2007–08) Loans, research assistantships, scholarships, and work study. Aid is available to part-time students. *Financial aid application deadline:* 4/1.

Financial Aid Contact Barbara Miller, Director of Financial Aid, 1420 North Charles Street, Baltimore, MD 21201-5779. *Phone:* 410-837-4763. *Fax:* 410-837-4820. *E-mail:* financial-aid@ubalt.edu.

INTERNATIONAL STUDENTS 14% of students enrolled are international students. *Services and facilities:* Counseling/support services, Housing location assistance, International student organization, Orientation, Visa Services. Financial aid is available to international students. *Required with application:* TOEFL with recommended score of 213 (computer), 550 (paper), or 79 (Internet); proof of adequate funds. *Recommended with application:* Proof of health/immunizations.

International Student Contact Wendy Burgess, Director, International Services, 1420 North Charles Street, Baltimore, MD 21201-5779. *Phone:* 410-837-4756. *Fax:* 410-837-6676. *E-mail:* intladms@ubalt.edu.

APPLICATION *Required:* GMAT, application form, baccalaureate/first degree, essay, 2 letters of recommendation, personal statement, resume/ curriculum vitae, transcripts of college work. School will accept GRE. *Recommended:* Work experience. *Application fee:* $30. Applications for domestic and international students are processed on a rolling basis.

Application Contact Wendy Bolyard, Director of Graduate Admissions, 1420 North Charles Street, Baltimore, MD 21201-5779. *Phone:* 877-277-5982. *Fax:* 410-837-6565. *E-mail:* gradadmissions@ubalt.edu.

University of Baltimore/Towson University

Joint University of Baltimore/Towson University (UB/Towson) MBA Program

Baltimore, Maryland

Phone: 410-837-6565 **Fax:** 410-837-4793 **E-mail:** mba@towson.ubalt.edu

Business Program(s) Web Site: http://www.ubtowsonmba.com

Graduate Business Unit Enrollment *Total:* 556 (424 full-time; 132 part-time; 257 women; 62 international). *Average Age:* 29.

Graduate Business Faculty *Total:* 45 (36 full-time; 9 part-time).

Admissions *Applied:* 443. *Admitted:* 192. *Enrolled:* 157. *Average GMAT:* 520. *Average GPA:* 3.12

Academic Calendar Semesters.

DEGREE MBA

MBA—UB/Towson MBA Full-time and part-time. Distance learning option. 33 to 51 total credits required. 18 to 84 months to complete program. *Concentrations:* entrepreneurship, finance, general MBA, health care, human resources management, international business, leadership, management information systems, marketing, sports/entertainment management.

RESOURCES AND SERVICES 250 on-campus PCs are available to graduate business students. Access to Internet/World Wide Web, online (class) registration, and online grade reports available. *Personal computer*

requirements: Graduate business students are strongly recommended to purchase or lease a personal computer. *Special opportunities include:* An internship program is available. *Placement services include:* Alumni network, career placement, job search course, career counseling/planning, electronic job bank, resume referral, career fairs, job interviews arranged, resume preparation, and career library.

EXPENSES *Tuition (state resident):* Part-time: $536 per credit. *Tuition (nonresident):* Part-time: $751 per credit. *Tuition (international):* Part-time: $751 per credit. *Required fees:* Part-time: $235 per course.

FINANCIAL AID (2007–08) Grants, loans, scholarships, and work study. Aid is available to part-time students. *Financial aid application deadline:* 4/1.

Financial Aid Contact UB/Towson MBA Program Office of Financial Aid, 1420 North Charles Street, Baltimore, MD 21201-5779. *Phone:* 410-837-4763. *Fax:* 410-837-5493.

INTERNATIONAL STUDENTS 11% of students enrolled are international students. *Services and facilities:* Counseling/support services, ESL/language courses, Housing location assistance, International student organization, Orientation, Visa Services. Financial aid is available to international students. *Required with application:* TOEFL with recommended score of 213 (computer), 550 (paper), or 79 (Internet); proof of adequate funds; proof of health/immunizations.

International Student Contact Wendy Burgess, Director of International Services, 1420 North Charles Street, Baltimore, MD 21201-5779. *Phone:* 410-837-4756. *Fax:* 410-837-6676. *E-mail:* intladms@ubalt.edu.

APPLICATION *Required:* GMAT, application form, baccalaureate/first degree, essay, 2 letters of recommendation, personal statement, resume/ curriculum vitae, transcripts of college work. School will accept GRE. *Application fee:* $30. Applications for domestic and international students are processed on a rolling basis.

Application Contact UB/Towson MBA Office of Admissions, 1420 North Charles Street, Baltimore, MD 21201-5779. *Phone:* 410-837-6565. *Fax:* 410-837-4793. *E-mail:* mba@towson.ubalt.edu.

University of Maryland, College Park

Robert H. Smith School of Business

College Park, Maryland

Phone: 301-405-2559 **Fax:** 301-314-9862 **E-mail:** mba_info@rhsmith.umd.edu

Business Program(s) Web Site: http://www.rhsmith.umd.edu

Graduate Business Unit Enrollment *Total:* 1,534 (570 full-time; 964 part-time; 504 women; 282 international). *Average Age:* 29.

Graduate Business Faculty *Total:* 147 (136 full-time; 11 part-time).

Admissions *Applied:* 1,684. *Admitted:* 880. *Enrolled:* 558. *Average GMAT:* 619. *Average GPA:* 3.32

Academic Calendar Semesters.

Accreditation AACSB—The Association to Advance Collegiate Schools of Business.

After Graduation (Class of 2006–07) *Employed within 3 months of graduation:* 92%. *Average starting salary:* $99,433.

DEGREES EMBA • JD/MBA • MBA • MBA/MPP • MBA/MS • MBA/MSW • MS

EMBA—Robert H. Smith School of Business Executive MBA 18 months to complete program. *Concentration:* executive programs.

JD/MBA—Juris Doctor/Master of Business Administration Full-time and part-time. Must apply separately to the School of Law at University of Maryland, Baltimore and the School of Business. At least 108 total credits required. 36 to 60 months to complete program. *Concentration:* combined degrees.

University of Maryland, College Park (continued)

MBA—Master of Business Administration Full-time and part-time. At least 54 total credits required. 18 to 60 months to complete program. *Concentrations:* decision sciences, electronic commerce (E-commerce), entrepreneurship, finance, financial engineering, general MBA, information systems, international business, leadership, logistics, management consulting, management information systems, management science, marketing, other, supply chain management.

MBA/MPP—Master of Business Administration/Master of Public Policy Full-time and part-time. Must apply separately to the Smith School of Business and the School of Public Policy. 66 total credits required. 28 to 60 months to complete program. *Concentration:* combined degrees.

MBA/MS—Master of Business Administration/Master of Science Full-time and part-time. At least 66 total credits required. 21 to 60 months to complete program. *Concentration:* finance.

MBA/MSW—Master of Business Administration/Master of Social Work Full-time and part-time. Must apply separately to the School of Social Work at University of Maryland, Baltimore and the Smith School of Business. At least 88 total credits required. 28 to 60 months to complete program. *Concentration:* social work.

MS—Robert H. Smith School of Business MS in Business: Accounting Full-time and part-time. 30 total credits required. 15 to 60 months to complete program. *Concentration:* accounting.

RESOURCES AND SERVICES 1,800 on-campus PCs are available to graduate business students. Access to Internet/World Wide Web, online (class) registration, and online grade reports available. *Personal computer requirements:* Graduate business students are strongly recommended to purchase or lease a personal computer. *Special opportunities include:* An international exchange program is available. *Placement services include:* Alumni network, career placement, job search course, career counseling/planning, electronic job bank, resume referral, career fairs, job interviews arranged, resume preparation, and career library.

EXPENSES *Tuition (state resident):* Full-time: $14,454. Part-time: $803 per credit. *Tuition (nonresident):* Full-time: $23,814. Part-time: $803 per credit. *Tuition (international):* Full-time: $23,814. Part-time: $803 per credit. *Required fees:* Full-time: $14,761. Tuition and/or fees vary by class time, number of courses or credits taken, campus location, and academic program.

FINANCIAL AID (2007–08) 136 students received aid, including fellowships, grants, research assistantships, scholarships, and teaching assistantships. *Financial aid application deadline:* 1/15.

Financial Aid Contact Malina Heng, Financial Aid Counselor, 0102 Lee Building, College Park, MD 20742. *Phone:* 301-314-9859. *Fax:* 301-314-9587. *E-mail:* mheng@umd.edu.

INTERNATIONAL STUDENTS 18% of students enrolled are international students. *Services and facilities:* Counseling/support services, ESL/language courses, International student organization, Orientation, Visa Services. Financial aid is available to international students. *Required with application:* IELT with recommended score of 6.5; TOEFL with recommended score of 250 (computer), 600 (paper), or 84 (Internet); proof of adequate funds; proof of health/immunizations.

International Student Contact Valerie Woolston, Director of International Education Services, Mitchell Building, 3rd Floor, College Park, MD 20742. *Phone:* 301-314-7740. *Fax:* 301-314-9347. *E-mail:* vwoolsto@deans.umd.edu.

APPLICATION *Required:* GMAT, application form, baccalaureate/first degree, essay, interview, 2 letters of recommendation, resume/curriculum vitae, transcripts of college work. *Recommended:* Work experience. *Application fee:* $60. *Deadlines:* 3/1 for fall, 3/1 for fall (international).

Application Contact LeAnne Dagnall, Associate Director, MBA/MS Admission, 2417 Van Munching Hall, College Park, MD 20742. *Phone:* 301-405-2559. *Fax:* 301-314-9862. *E-mail:* mba_info@rhsmith.umd.edu.

University of Maryland University College

Graduate School of Management and Technology

Adelphi, Maryland

Phone: 800-888-UMUC **E-mail:** emteam@umuc.edu

Business Program(s) Web Site: http://www.umuc.edu/

Graduate Business Unit Enrollment *Total:* 7,121 (192 full-time; 6,929 part-time; 4,128 women; 250 international). *Average Age:* 34.

Graduate Business Faculty *Total:* 406 (88 full-time; 318 part-time).

Admissions *Applied:* 1,176. *Admitted:* 1,176. *Enrolled:* 890.

Academic Calendar Semesters.

DEGREES   EMBA • MAFM • MAIS • MBA • MIM • MS

EMBA—Executive Master of Business Administration Part-time. 5 years of business or management experience required. At least 42 total credits required. 21 to 60 months to complete program. *Concentration:* executive programs.

MAFM—Master of Accounting and Financial Management Full-time and part-time. Distance learning option. 36 to 39 total credits required. 16 to 84 months to complete program. *Concentration:* accounting.

MAIS—Master of Science in Accounting and Information Technology Full-time and part-time. Distance learning option. 36 to 39 total credits required. 16 to 84 months to complete program. *Concentration:* accounting.

MBA—Master of Business Administration Full-time and part-time. Distance learning option. Internet access required. At least 43 total credits required. 24 to 60 months to complete program. *Concentration:* general MBA.

MIM—Master of International Management Full-time and part-time. Distance learning option. 36 to 39 total credits required. 16 to 84 months to complete program. *Concentrations:* international finance, international marketing, international trade.

MS—Executive Master of Science in Technology Management Part-time. 5 years of mid- or senior-level management experience required. At least 36 total credits required. 18 to 60 months to complete program. *Concentration:* technology management.

MS—Master of Science in Computer Systems Management Full-time and part-time. Distance learning option. 36 to 39 total credits required. 16 to 84 months to complete program. *Concentration:* information management.

MS—Master of Science in Management Full-time and part-time. Distance learning option. 36 to 39 total credits required. 16 to 84 months to complete program. *Concentrations:* accounting, electronic commerce (E-commerce), information management, management, system management.

MS—Master of Science in Technology Management Full-time and part-time. Distance learning option. 36 to 39 total credits required. 16 to 84 months to complete program. *Concentration:* technology management.

MS—Master of Science in Telecommunications Management Full-time and part-time. Distance learning option. 36 to 39 total credits required. 16 to 84 months to complete program. *Concentration:* telecommunications management.

RESOURCES AND SERVICES 138 on-campus PCs are available to graduate business students. Access to Internet/World Wide Web, online (class) registration, and online grade reports available. *Personal computer requirements:* Graduate business students are strongly recommended to purchase or lease a personal computer. *Placement services include:* Alumni network, job search course, career counseling/planning, electronic job bank, career fairs, and career library.

EXPENSES *Tuition (state resident):* Part-time: $412 per credit hour. *Tuition (nonresident):* Part-time: $659 per credit hour. *Tuition (international):* Part-time: $659 per credit hour.

FINANCIAL AID (2007–08) Grants, loans, scholarships, and work study. Aid is available to part-time students. *Financial aid application deadline:* 6/1.

INTERNATIONAL STUDENTS 4% of students enrolled are international students. *Services and facilities:* Counseling/support services, Orientation, Visa Services. Financial aid is not available to international students. *Required with application:* TOEFL with recommended score of 233 (computer) or 575 (paper); TWE with recommended score of 4; proof of adequate funds.

APPLICATION *Required:* Application form, baccalaureate/first degree, personal statement, transcripts of college work. *Recommended:* Work experience. *Application fee:* $50. Applications for domestic and international students are processed on a rolling basis.

University of Phoenix–Maryland Campus

College of Graduate Business and Management

Columbia, Maryland

Phone: 480-317-6200 **Fax:** 480-643-1479 **E-mail:** beth.barilla@phoenix.edu

Business Program(s) Web Site: http://www.phoenix.edu

DEGREES M Mgt • MA • MBA

M Mgt—Master of Management Full-time. At least 39 total credits required. *Concentration:* management.

MA—Organizational Management Full-time. At least 40 total credits required. *Concentration:* organizational management.

MBA—Global Management Full-time. At least 45 total credits required. *Concentration:* international management.

MBA—e-Business Full-time. At least 45 total credits required. *Concentration:* electronic commerce (E-commerce).

MBA—Master of Business Administration Full-time. At least 45 total credits required. *Concentration:* administration.

RESOURCES AND SERVICES Access to online grade reports available. *Personal computer requirements:* Graduate business students are strongly recommended to purchase or lease a personal computer. *Placement services include:* Alumni network.

Application Contact Beth Barilla, Associate Vice President of Student Admissions and Services, Mail Stop AA-K101, 4615 East Elwood Street, Phoenix, AZ 85040-1958. *Phone:* 480-317-6200. *Fax:* 480-643-1479. *E-mail:* beth.barilla@phoenix.edu.

MASSACHUSETTS

Anna Maria College

Program in Business Administration

Paxton, Massachusetts

Phone: 508-849-3360 **Fax:** 508-849-3362 **E-mail:** admission@annamaria.edu

Business Program(s) Web Site: http://www.annamaria.edu/graduate/business

Graduate Business Unit Enrollment *Total:* 48 (11 full-time; 37 part-time; 27 women; 2 international). *Average Age:* 32.

Graduate Business Faculty *Total:* 10 (2 full-time; 8 part-time).

Admissions *Average GMAT:* 550. *Average GPA:* 2.7

Academic Calendar Five 9-week semesters.

After Graduation (Class of 2006–07) *Employed within 3 months of graduation:* 90%. *Average starting salary:* $40,000.

DEGREES MBA

MBA—Master of Business Administration in Health Care Administration Full-time and part-time. 45 total credits required. 18 to 60 months to complete program. *Concentration:* business studies.

MBA—Master of Business Administration Full-time and part-time. 45 total credits required. 18 to 60 months to complete program. *Concentrations:* accounting, entrepreneurship, finance, human resources management, leadership, marketing, operations management, quality management, strategic management.

RESOURCES AND SERVICES 45 on-campus PCs are available to graduate business students. Access to Internet/World Wide Web and online grade reports available. *Personal computer requirements:* Graduate business students are strongly recommended to purchase or lease a personal computer. *Special opportunities include:* An internship program is available. *Placement services include:* Alumni network, career placement, job search course, career counseling/planning, resume referral, career fairs, job interviews arranged, resume preparation, and career library.

EXPENSES *Tuition:* Part-time: $1272 per course.

FINANCIAL AID (2007–08) Grants and loans.

Financial Aid Contact Ms. Laurie Peltier, Director of Financial Aid, 50 Sunset Lane, Paxton, MA 01612-1198. *Phone:* 508-849-3366. *Fax:* 508-849-3362. *E-mail:* finaid@annamaria.edu.

INTERNATIONAL STUDENTS 4% of students enrolled are international students. *Services and facilities:* Counseling/support services, ESL/language courses. Financial aid is not available to international students. *Required with application:* TOEFL with recommended score of 500 (paper); proof of adequate funds; proof of health/immunizations. *Recommended with application:* TWE.

International Student Contact Bernard Wood, Director of Business Programs, 50 Sunset Lane, Paxton, MA 01612-1198. *Phone:* 508-849-3307. *Fax:* 508-849-3362. *E-mail:* bwood@annamaria.edu.

APPLICATION *Required:* Application form, baccalaureate/first degree, personal statement, resume/curriculum vitae, transcripts of college work. *Recommended:* Interview. *Application fee:* $40. Applications for domestic and international students are processed on a rolling basis.

Application Contact Crystal Letendre, Admissions Coordinator, 50 Sunset Lane, Paxton, MA 01612-1198. *Phone:* 508-849-3360. *Fax:* 508-849-3362. *E-mail:* admission@annamaria.edu.

Assumption College

Department of Business Studies

Worcester, Massachusetts

Phone: 508-767-7365 **Fax:** 508-767-7030 **E-mail:** adumas@assumption.edu

Business Program(s) Web Site: http://www.assumption.edu/gradce/grad/mba/mba1.html

Graduate Business Unit Enrollment *Total:* 152 (15 full-time; 137 part-time; 78 women; 3 international). *Average Age:* 27.

Graduate Business Faculty *Total:* 16 (6 full-time; 10 part-time).

Admissions *Applied:* 90. *Admitted:* 87. *Enrolled:* 75. *Average GPA:* 3.07

Assumption College (continued)

Academic Calendar Semesters.

DEGREE MBA

MBA—Master of Business Administration Part-time. 36 to 48 total credits required. 16 to 84 months to complete program. *Concentrations:* accounting, economics, finance, human resources management, international business, management, marketing.

RESOURCES AND SERVICES 50 on-campus PCs are available to graduate business students. Access to Internet/World Wide Web available. *Personal computer requirements:* Graduate business students are not required to have a personal computer. *Placement services include:* Career counseling/planning, resume referral, and career library.

EXPENSES *Tuition:* Part-time: $1350 per course. *Tuition (international):* Part-time: $1350 per course.

FINANCIAL AID (2007–08) 47 students received aid, including loans. Aid is available to part-time students. *Financial aid application deadline:* 6/1.

Financial Aid Contact Ms. Arlene Tatro, Graduate Financial Aid Counselor, 500 Salisbury Street, Worcester, MA 01609-1296. *Phone:* 508-767-7154. *Fax:* 508-767-7346. *E-mail:* atatro@assumption.edu.

INTERNATIONAL STUDENTS 2% of students enrolled are international students. *Services and facilities:* Counseling/support services, Housing location assistance, Academic support center. Financial aid is not available to international students. *Required with application:* IELT with recommended score of 6; TOEFL with recommended score of 200 (computer), 540 (paper), or 78 (Internet); proof of adequate funds; proof of health/immunizations.

International Student Contact Mr. Robert Ravenelle, Dean of Students, 500 Salisbury Street, Worcester, MA 01609-1296. *Phone:* 508-767-7325. *Fax:* 508-767-7098. *E-mail:* rravenel@assumption.edu.

APPLICATION *Required:* Application form, baccalaureate/first degree, essay, 3 letters of recommendation, personal statement, resume/curriculum vitae, transcripts of college work. *Application fee:* $30. Applications for domestic and international students are processed on a rolling basis.

Application Contact Ms. Adrian O. Dumas, Director of Graduate Enrollment, 500 Salisbury Street, Worcester, MA 01609-1296. *Phone:* 508-767-7365. *Fax:* 508-767-7030. *E-mail:* adumas@assumption.edu.

Babson College
F. W. Olin Graduate School of Business

Wellesley, Babson Park, Massachusetts

Phone: 781-239-5591 **Fax:** 781-239-4194 **E-mail:** mbaoutreach@babson.edu

Business Program(s) Web Site: http://www.babson.edu/mba/

Graduate Business Unit Enrollment *Total:* 1,635 (409 full-time; 1,226 part-time; 434 women; 316 international). *Average Age:* 32.

Graduate Business Faculty *Total:* 171 (132 full-time; 39 part-time).

Admissions *Applied:* 566. *Admitted:* 320. *Enrolled:* 156. *Average GMAT:* 631. *Average GPA:* 3.21

Academic Calendar Semesters.

Accreditation AACSB—The Association to Advance Collegiate Schools of Business.

After Graduation (Class of 2006–07) *Employed within 3 months of graduation:* 92%. *Average starting salary:* $89,161.

DEGREES MBA • MSM

MBA—Evening Master of Business Administration Full-time and part-time. 60 to 64 total credits required. 24 to 96 months to complete program. *Concentration:* general MBA.

MBA—Fast-Track Master of Business Administration Full-time and part-time. Distance learning option. At least 46 total credits required. 24 months to complete program. *Concentration:* general MBA.

MBA—One-Year Master of Business Administration Full-time. Undergraduate degree in business required. At least 45 total credits required. Minimum of 12 months to complete program. *Concentration:* general MBA.

MBA—Two-Year Master of Business Administration Full-time. At least 62 total credits required. Minimum of 21 months to complete program. *Concentration:* general MBA.

MSM—Master of Science in Management with a Concentration in Technological Entrepreneurship Full-time. This is a dual degree program in conjunction with Instituto Tecnologico y de Estudios Superiores de Monterrey in Mexico. 30 total credits required. 13 months to complete program. *Concentrations:* entrepreneurship, management, technology management.

*L*everaging its world leadership role in entrepreneurial management education, Babson weaves innovation into all that it does. Students learn how to recognize and define the changes that are critical to growing businesses in a competitive, global marketplace. Graduates launch start-ups or lead global enterprises, driving the inspiration to develop new products, processes, and markets.

Babson offers a diverse community that values differences and cherishes opportunities to interact with others in order to enhance creativity, productivity, innovation, and quality of life.

Babson's M.B.A. program is a recognized leader in the academic and business communities. Business Week *ranked Babson among the top 38 U.S. M.B.A. programs. For the fourteenth consecutive year,* U.S. News & World Report *ranked Babson as the top M.B.A. program in the country for entrepreneurship. The* Princeton Review *has rated Babson's M.B.A. program as a top 10 program for women for four consecutive years, and* America Economia *ranked Babson the number 20 M.B.A. program among U.S. business schools.*

RESOURCES AND SERVICES 100 on-campus PCs are available to graduate business students. Access to Internet/World Wide Web, online (class) registration, and online grade reports available. *Personal computer requirements:* Graduate business students are strongly recommended to purchase or lease a personal computer. *Special opportunities include:* An international exchange program and an internship program are available. *Placement services include:* Alumni network, career placement, job search course, career counseling/planning, electronic job bank, resume referral, career fairs, job interviews arranged, resume preparation, and career library.

EXPENSES *Tuition:* Full-time: $35,110. *Tuition (international):* Full-time: $35,110. Tuition and/or fees vary by number of courses or credits taken and academic program. *Typical graduate housing cost:* $10,125 (including board), $10,125 (room only).

FINANCIAL AID (2007–08) Fellowships, grants, loans, research assistantships, scholarships, and work study. *Financial aid application deadline:* 4/15.

Financial Aid Contact Ms. Melissa Shaak, Associate Dean, Undergraduate School and Director, Student Financial Services, Hollister Hall, Babson Park, MA 02457-0310. *Phone:* 781-239-4219. *Fax:* 781-239-5510. *E-mail:* sfs@babson.edu.

INTERNATIONAL STUDENTS 19% of students enrolled are international students. *Services and facilities:* Counseling/support services, Housing location assistance, International student housing, International student organization, Orientation, Visa Services, Office of International Programs. Financial aid is available to international students. *Required with application:* TOEFL with recommended score of 250 (computer), 600 (paper), or 100 (Internet); proof of adequate funds; proof of health/immunizations.

International Student Contact Ms. Karen Pabon, International Student and Scholar Advisor, Babson Park, MA 02457-0130. *Phone:* 781-239-4565. *Fax:* 781-239-5232. *E-mail:* kpabon@babson.edu.

APPLICATION *Required:* GMAT, application form, baccalaureate/first degree, essay, interview, 2 letters of recommendation, resume/curriculum vitae, transcripts of college work, 2 years of work experience. *Application fee:* $100. *Deadlines:* 4/15 for fall, 1/15 for fall (international).

Application Contact Mr. Dennis Nations, Director, Graduate Admissions, Olin Hall, Babson Park, MA 02457. *Phone:* 781-239-5591. *Fax:* 781-239-4194. *E-mail:* mbaoutreach@babson.edu.

See full description on page 570.

Bentley College
The Elkin B. McCallum Graduate School of Business

Waltham, Massachusetts

Phone: 781-891-2108 **Fax:** 781-891-2464 **E-mail:** shill@bentley.edu

Business Program(s) Web Site: http://www.bentley.edu/graduate

Graduate Business Unit Enrollment *Total:* 1,393 (378 full-time; 1,015 part-time; 617 women; 210 international). *Average Age:* 30.

Graduate Business Faculty *Total:* 285 (170 full-time; 115 part-time).

Admissions *Applied:* 1,130. *Admitted:* 879. *Enrolled:* 493. *Average GMAT:* 585. *Average GPA:* 3.52

Academic Calendar Semesters.

Accreditation AACSB—The Association to Advance Collegiate Schools of Business.

After Graduation (Class of 2006–07) *Employed within 3 months of graduation:* 98%. *Average starting salary:* $60,000.

DEGREES MBA • MS

MBA—Master of Business Administration and Master of Science in Human Factors in Information Design Full-time. Interview required. 51 to 66 total credits required. 22 to 36 months to complete program. *Concentration:* combined degrees.

MBA—Master of Business Administration and Master of Science in Information Technology Full-time. Interview required. 51 to 66 total credits required. 22 to 36 months to complete program. *Concentration:* combined degrees.

MBA—Master of Business Administration, Day Program Full-time. Interview required. 45 to 60 total credits required. 22 to 24 months to complete program. *Concentrations:* accounting, business ethics, combined degrees, economics, entrepreneurship, finance, financial management/planning, information technology, international business, management, management information systems, marketing, other, quantitative analysis, real estate, risk management, taxation.

MBA—Master of Business Administration, Evening Program Full-time and part-time. 36 to 54 total credits required. 16 to 84 months to complete program. *Concentrations:* accounting, business ethics, combined degrees, economics, entrepreneurship, finance, financial management/planning, information technology, international business, management, management information systems, marketing, operations management, other, quantitative analysis, real estate, risk management, taxation.

MS—Master of Science in Accountancy Full-time and part-time. 30 to 36 total credits required. 12 to 84 months to complete program. *Concentration:* accounting.

MS—Master of Science in Finance Full-time and part-time. May submit GRE in place of GMAT. 30 to 42 total credits required. 12 to 84 months to complete program. *Concentrations:* finance, quantitative analysis.

MS—Master of Science in Financial Planning Full-time and part-time. Distance learning option. 30 total credits required. 12 to 60 months to complete program. *Concentration:* finance.

MS—Master of Science in Human Factors in Information Design Full-time and part-time. Distance learning option. May submit GRE in place of GMAT. 30 total credits required. 12 to 60 months to complete program. *Concentration:* information management.

MS—Master of Science in Information Technology Full-time and part-time. May submit GRE in place of GMAT. 30 total credits required. 12 to 84 months to complete program. *Concentration:* information systems.

MS—Master of Science in Marketing Analytics Full-time and part-time. 30 to 38 total credits required. 12 to 84 months to complete program. *Concentration:* marketing.

MS—Master of Science in Real Estate Management Full-time and part-time. Distance learning option. 30 to 48 total credits required. 12 to 84 months to complete program. *Concentration:* real estate.

MS—Master of Science in Taxation Full-time and part-time. Distance learning option. 30 total credits required. 12 to 60 months to complete program. *Concentration:* taxation.

RESOURCES AND SERVICES 120 on-campus PCs are available to graduate business students. Access to Internet/World Wide Web, online (class) registration, and online grade reports available. *Personal computer requirements:* Graduate business students are required to have a personal computer. *Special opportunities include:* An internship program is available. *Placement services include:* Alumni network, career placement, job search course, career counseling/planning, electronic job bank, resume referral, career fairs, job interviews arranged, resume preparation, and career library.

EXPENSES *Tuition:* Full-time: $23,664. Part-time: $2958 per course. *Tuition (international):* Full-time: $23,664. Part-time: $2958 per course. *Required fees:* Full-time: $404. Part-time: $105 per year. Tuition and/or fees vary by number of courses or credits taken. *Graduate housing:* Room and board costs vary by number of occupants, type of accommodation, and type of board plan. *Typical cost:* $12,865 (including board), $8465 (room only).

FINANCIAL AID (2007–08) 239 students received aid, including grants, research assistantships, scholarships, and work study. Aid is available to part-time students. *Financial aid application deadline:* 3/1.

Financial Aid Contact Ms. Donna Kendall, Executive Director, 175 Forest Street, Waltham, MA 02452. *Phone:* 781-891-3441. *Fax:* 781-891-2448. *E-mail:* finaid@bentley.edu.

INTERNATIONAL STUDENTS 15% of students enrolled are international students. *Services and facilities:* Counseling/support services, Housing location assistance, International student housing, International student organization, Language tutoring, Orientation, Visa Services, One-on-one tutoring. Financial aid is available to international students. *Required with application:* TOEFL with recommended score of 250 (computer), 600 (paper), or 100 (Internet); proof of adequate funds.

International Student Contact Ms. Barbara Lombardi, Assistant Director, International Students, 175 Forest Street, Waltham, MA 02452. *Phone:* 781-891-2767. *Fax:* 781-891-2819. *E-mail:* blombardi@bentley.edu.

APPLICATION *Required:* GMAT, application form, baccalaureate/first degree, essay, 2 letters of recommendation, personal statement, resume/curriculum vitae, transcripts of college work. *Recommended:* Interview. *Application fee:* $50. Applications for domestic and international students are processed on a rolling basis.

Application Contact Sharon Hill, Assistant Dean and Director of Graduate Admission, 175 Forest Street, Waltham, MA 02452. *Phone:* 781-891-2108. *Fax:* 781-891-2464. *E-mail:* shill@bentley.edu.

See full description on page 578.

Boston College
The Carroll School of Management

Chestnut Hill, Massachusetts

Phone: 617-552-3920 **Fax:** 617-552-8078 **E-mail:** bcmba@bc.edu

Business Program(s) Web Site: http://www.bc.edu/schools/csom/

Boston College (continued)

Graduate Business Unit Enrollment *Total:* 980 (345 full-time; 635 part-time; 313 women; 134 international). *Average Age:* 27.

Graduate Business Faculty *Total:* 64 (42 full-time; 22 part-time).

Admissions *Applied:* 1,884. *Admitted:* 591. *Enrolled:* 370. *Average GMAT:* 651. *Average GPA:* 3.35

Academic Calendar Semesters.

Accreditation AACSB—The Association to Advance Collegiate Schools of Business.

After Graduation (Class of 2006–07) *Employed within 3 months of graduation:* 98.4%. *Average starting salary:* $87,468.

DEGREES JD/MBA • MBA • MBA/MA • MBA/MS • MBA/MSF • MBA/MSW • MS • PhD/MBA

JD/MBA—Juris Doctor/Master of Business Administration Full-time. Must take LSAT and apply to both programs. 110 to 116 total credits required. 40 to 45 months to complete program. *Concentration:* combined degrees.

MBA—Master of Business Administration Full-time and part-time. 56 total credits required. 24 to 60 months to complete program. *Concentrations:* accounting, entrepreneurship, finance, international management, management, management consulting, management information systems, marketing, operations management, organizational behavior/development, strategic management.

MBA/MA—Master of Business Administration/Master of Arts in French Studies Full-time. Must apply to both programs. 67 to 85 total credits required. 28 to 33 months to complete program. *Concentration:* combined degrees.

MBA/MA—Master of Business Administration/Master of Arts in Higher Education Full-time. Must apply to both programs. 67 to 85 total credits required. 28 to 33 months to complete program. *Concentration:* combined degrees.

MBA/MA—Master of Business Administration/Master of Arts in Hispanic Studies Full-time. Must apply to both programs. 67 to 85 total credits required. 28 to 33 months to complete program. *Concentration:* combined degrees.

MBA/MA—Master of Business Administration/Master of Arts in Italian Studies Full-time. Must apply to both programs. 67 to 85 total credits required. 28 to 33 months to complete program. *Concentration:* combined degrees.

MBA/MA—Master of Business Administration/Master of Arts in Linguistics Full-time. Must apply to both programs. 67 to 85 total credits required. 28 to 33 months to complete program. *Concentration:* combined degrees.

MBA/MA—Master of Business Administration/Master of Arts in Mathematics Full-time. Must apply to both programs. 67 to 85 total credits required. 28 to 33 months to complete program. *Concentration:* combined degrees.

MBA/MA—Master of Business Administration/Master of Arts in Political Science Full-time. Must apply to both programs. 67 to 85 total credits required. 28 to 33 months to complete program. *Concentration:* combined degrees.

MBA/MA—Master of Business Administration/Master of Arts in Russian Full-time. Must apply to both programs. 67 to 85 total credits required. 28 to 33 months to complete program. *Concentration:* combined degrees.

MBA/MA—Master of Business Administration/Master of Arts in Slavic Studies Full-time. Must apply to both programs. 67 to 85 total credits required. 28 to 33 months to complete program. *Concentration:* combined degrees.

MBA/MS—Master of Business Administration/Master of Science in Biology Full-time. Must apply to both programs. 67 to 85 total credits required. 28 to 33 months to complete program. *Concentration:* combined degrees.

MBA/MS—Master of Business Administration/Master of Science in Geology/Geophysics Full-time. Must apply to both programs. 67 to 85 total credits required. 28 to 33 months to complete program. *Concentration:* combined degrees.

MBA/MS—Master of Business Administration/Master of Science in Nursing Full-time. Must apply to both programs. 74 to 92 total credits required. 33 to 36 months to complete program. *Concentration:* combined degrees.

MBA/MSF—Master of Business Administration/Master of Science in Finance Full-time and part-time. Must apply to both programs. 67 to 85 total credits required. 28 to 33 months to complete program. *Concentration:* combined degrees.

MBA/MSW—Master of Business Administration/Master of Social Work Full-time. Must apply to both programs. 104 to 110 total credits required. 28 to 33 months to complete program. *Concentration:* combined degrees.

MS—Master of Science in Accounting Full-time and part-time. 30 to 45 total credits required. 14 to 20 months to complete program. *Concentration:* accounting.

MS—Master of Science in Finance Full-time and part-time. 24 to 30 total credits required. 11 to 36 months to complete program. *Concentration:* finance.

PhD/MBA—Doctor of Philosophy in Sociology/Master of Business Administration Full-time. Must apply to both programs. 77 to 95 total credits required. 52 to 57 months to complete program. *Concentration:* combined degrees.

RESOURCES AND SERVICES 165 on-campus PCs are available to graduate business students. Access to Internet/World Wide Web, online (class) registration, and online grade reports available. *Personal computer requirements:* Graduate business students are strongly recommended to purchase or lease a personal computer. *Special opportunities include:* An international exchange program and an internship program are available. *Placement services include:* Alumni network, career placement, job search course, career counseling/planning, electronic job bank, resume referral, career fairs, job interviews arranged, resume preparation, and career library.

EXPENSES *Tuition:* Full-time: $31,528. Part-time: $1126 per credit hour. *Tuition (international):* Full-time: $31,528. Part-time: $1126 per credit hour.

FINANCIAL AID (2007–08) 183 students received aid, including fellowships, grants, loans, scholarships, and work study. *Financial aid application deadline:* 2/15.

Financial Aid Contact Mr. Robert Carpenter, Program Director for Student Employment, 140 Commonwealth Avenue, Lyons Hall 120, Chestnut Hill, MA 02467-3808. *Phone:* 617-552-3300. *Fax:* 617-552-4889. *E-mail:* robert.carpenter@bc.edu.

INTERNATIONAL STUDENTS 14% of students enrolled are international students. *Services and facilities:* Counseling/support services, ESL/language courses, Housing location assistance, International student organization, Language tutoring, Orientation, Visa Services. Financial aid is available to international students. *Required with application:* TOEFL with recommended score of 250 (computer) or 600 (paper); proof of adequate funds; proof of health/immunizations.

International Student Contact Ms. Adrienne Nussbaum, Director, Office of International Students and Scholars, 21 Campanella Way, Suite 249, Chestnut Hill, MA 02467. *Phone:* 617-552-8005. *Fax:* 617-552-2190. *E-mail:* adrienne.nussbaum.1@bc.edu.

APPLICATION *Required:* GMAT, application form, baccalaureate/first degree, essay, 2 letters of recommendation, resume/curriculum vitae, transcripts of college work. *Recommended:* Interview, work experience. *Application fee:* $100. *Deadlines:* 3/15 for fall, 2/15 for fall (international).

Application Contact Ms. Shelley Burt, Director, Graduate Management Enrollment, 140 Commonwealth Avenue, Fulton Hall 315, Chestnut Hill, MA 02467-3808. *Phone:* 617-552-3920. *Fax:* 617-552-8078. *E-mail:* bcmba@bc.edu.

See full description on page 580.

Boston University

School of Management

Boston, Massachusetts

Phone: 617-353-2670 **Fax:** 617-353-7368 **E-mail:** mba@bu.edu

Business Program(s) Web Site: http://management.bu.edu/

Graduate Business Unit Enrollment *Total:* 992 (418 full-time; 574 part-time; 374 women; 187 international). *Average Age:* 32.

Graduate Business Faculty *Total:* 103 (68 full-time; 35 part-time).

Admissions *Applied:* 1,773. *Admitted:* 774. *Enrolled:* 410. *Average GMAT:* 668. *Average GPA:* 3.38

Academic Calendar Semesters.

Accreditation AACSB—The Association to Advance Collegiate Schools of Business.

After Graduation (Class of 2006–07) *Employed within 3 months of graduation:* 95%. *Average starting salary:* $85,277.

DEGREES EMBA • JD/MBA • MBA • MBA/MA • MBA/MPH • MBA/MS • MD/MBA • MS

EMBA Full-time. 10 years of work experience and company sponsorship required. At least 64 total credits required. 17 months to complete program. *Concentration:* executive programs.

JD/MBA Full-time. LSAT required. At least 116 total credits required. 36 to 72 months to complete program. *Concentrations:* combined degrees, law, management.

MBA—International Management MBA—China and Japan Full-time. At least 64 total credits required. 14 to 21 months to complete program. *Concentrations:* international business, international management.

MBA Full-time and part-time. At least 64 total credits required. 21 to 72 months to complete program. *Concentrations:* entrepreneurship, finance, general MBA, health administration, international management, marketing, nonprofit management, strategic management.

MBA/MA—MBA/MA in Economics Full-time and part-time. At least 80 total credits required. 24 to 72 months to complete program. *Concentration:* combined degrees.

MBA/MA—MBA/MA in International Relations Full-time and part-time. At least 80 total credits required. 24 to 72 months to complete program. *Concentration:* combined degrees.

MBA/MA—MBA/MA in Medical Science Full-time and part-time. At least 80 total credits required. 24 to 72 months to complete program. *Concentration:* combined degrees.

MBA/MPH—MBA/MPH in Management and Public Health Full-time and part-time. At least 80 total credits required. 27 to 72 months to complete program. *Concentrations:* combined degrees, health care, management.

MBA/MS—MBA/MS in Manufacturing Engineering and Management Full-time and part-time. At least 80 total credits required. 24 to 72 months to complete program. *Concentration:* combined degrees.

MBA/MS—MBA/MS in Television Management Full-time and part-time. At least 80 total credits required. 24 to 72 months to complete program. *Concentration:* combined degrees.

MBA/MS—MS/MBA Full-time. At least 84 total credits required. 21 to 72 months to complete program. *Concentrations:* combined degrees, management, management information systems.

MD/MBA Full-time. At least 114 total credits required. *Concentrations:* combined degrees, management, medicine.

MS—MSIM Part-time. At least 38 total credits required. 17 months to complete program. *Concentration:* finance.

RESOURCES AND SERVICES 131 on-campus PCs are available to graduate business students. Access to Internet/World Wide Web, online (class) registration, and online grade reports available. *Personal computer requirements:* Graduate business students are strongly recommended to purchase or lease a personal computer. *Special opportunities include:* An internship program is available. *Placement services include:* Alumni network, career placement, job search course, career counseling/planning, electronic job bank, resume referral, career fairs, job interviews arranged, resume preparation, and career library.

EXPENSES *Tuition:* Full-time: $34,930. Part-time: $1092 per credit. *Required fees:* Full-time: $440. Part-time: $140 per year.

FINANCIAL AID (2007–08) 252 students received aid, including loans, research assistantships, scholarships, and work study. Aid is available to part-time students. *Financial aid application deadline:* 3/15.

Financial Aid Contact Nicola Melton, Assistant Director, Financial Aid, 595 Commonwealth Avenue, Boston, MA 02215. *Phone:* 617-353-3584. *Fax:* 617-353-9498. *E-mail:* mba@bu.edu.

INTERNATIONAL STUDENTS 19% of students enrolled are international students. *Services and facilities:* Counseling/support services, ESL/language courses, Housing location assistance, International student housing, International student organization, Language tutoring, Orientation, Visa Services. Financial aid is available to international students. *Required with application:* TOEFL with recommended score of 250 (computer) or 600 (paper); proof of adequate funds; proof of health/immunizations.

International Student Contact Hayden Estrada, Assistant Dean for Graduate Admissions, 595 Commonwealth Avenue, Boston, MA 02215. *Phone:* 617-353-2670. *Fax:* 617-353-7368. *E-mail:* mba@bu.edu.

APPLICATION *Required:* GMAT, application form, baccalaureate/first degree, essay, interview, 2 letters of recommendation, resume/curriculum vitae, transcripts of college work, 2 years of work experience. *Application fee:* $125. *Deadlines:* 3/15 for fall, 11/15 for spring, 3/15 for fall (international), 11/15 for spring (international).

Application Contact Hayden Estrada, Assistant Dean for Graduate Admissions, 595 Commonwealth Avenue, Boston, MA 02215. *Phone:* 617-353-2670. *Fax:* 617-353-7368. *E-mail:* mba@bu.edu.

Brandeis University

The Heller School for Social Policy and Management

Waltham, Massachusetts

Phone: 781-736-3820 **Fax:** 781-736-2774 **E-mail:** helleradmissions@brandeis.edu

Business Program(s) Web Site: http://heller.brandeis.edu

DEGREES MA/MBA • MBA

MA/MBA—Master of Arts/Master of Business Administration Full-time. Minimum of 16 months to complete program. *Concentrations:* combined degrees, leadership, nonprofit management.

MBA—Master of Business Administration in Mission-Driven Management Full-time. Minimum of 16 months to complete program. *Concentrations:* health care, nonprofit management, public policy and administration.

RESOURCES AND SERVICES 100 on-campus PCs are available to graduate business students. Access to Internet/World Wide Web, online (class) registration, and online grade reports available. *Personal computer requirements:* Graduate business students are strongly recommended to purchase or lease a personal computer. *Placement services include:* Alumni network, job search course, career counseling/planning, electronic job bank, resume referral, career fairs, resume preparation, and career library.

Application Contact Mr. James Sabourin, Assistant Dean for Admissions and Recruitment, The Heller School for Social Policy and Management, Brandeis University, MS 035, 415 South Street, Waltham, MA 02454-9110. *Phone:* 781-736-3820. *Fax:* 781-736-2774. *E-mail:* helleradmissions@brandeis.edu.

Brandeis University

International Business School

Waltham, Massachusetts

Phone: 781-736-2252 **Fax:** 781-736-2263 **E-mail:** admission@lemberg.brandeis.edu

Business Program(s) Web Site: http://www.brandeis.edu/global

Admissions *Average GMAT:* 585. *Average GPA:* 3.3

Academic Calendar Semesters.

After Graduation (Class of 2006–07) *Employed within 3 months of graduation:* 85%. *Average starting salary:* $84,000.

DEGREES MA • MBA • MS

MA—Master of Arts in International Economics and Finance Full-time. At least 64 total credits required. Minimum of 21 months to complete program. *Concentrations:* economics, international business, international economics, international finance.

MBA—International Master of Business Administration Full-time. 2-3 years of work experience recommended. At least 64 total credits required. Minimum of 21 months to complete program. *Concentrations:* finance, international and area business studies, international banking, international business, international economics, international finance, international management.

MS—Master of Science in Finance Full-time and part-time. 2-3 years of work experience recommended. 32 to 40 total credits required. Minimum of 12 months to complete program. *Concentrations:* accounting, executive programs, finance, financial economics, international banking, international finance.

RESOURCES AND SERVICES 85 on-campus PCs are available to graduate business students. Access to Internet/World Wide Web, online (class) registration, and online grade reports available. *Personal computer requirements:* Graduate business students are strongly recommended to purchase or lease a personal computer. *Special opportunities include:* An international exchange program and an internship program are available. *Placement services include:* Alumni network, career placement, job search course, career counseling/planning, electronic job bank, resume referral, career fairs, job interviews arranged, resume preparation, and career library.

EXPENSES *Tuition:* Full-time: $36,122. Part-time: $3350 per course. *Tuition (international):* Full-time: $36,122. Part-time: $3350 per course. *Required fees:* Full-time: $1500. Part-time: $35 per course.

FINANCIAL AID (2007–08) Fellowships, grants, loans, research assistantships, scholarships, teaching assistantships, and work study. *Financial aid application deadline:* 2/15.

Financial Aid Contact Ms. Holly Chase, Assistant Dean for Admission and Financial Aid, 415 South Street, MS 032, Waltham, MA 02454-9110. *Phone:* 781-736-2252. *Fax:* 781-736-2263. *E-mail:* admission@lemberg.brandeis.edu.

INTERNATIONAL STUDENTS *Services and facilities:* Counseling/support services, ESL/language courses, Housing location assistance, International student housing, International student organization, Language tutoring, Orientation, Visa Services. Financial aid is available to international students. *Required with application:* IELT with recommended score of 7; TOEFL with recommended score of 250 (computer) or 600 (paper); proof of adequate funds; proof of health/immunizations.

International Student Contact Ms. David Elwell, Director, Kutz Hall, 415 South Street, Waltham, MA 02454-9110. *Phone:* 781-736-3480. *Fax:* 781-736-3484. *E-mail:* elwell@brandeis.edu.

APPLICATION *Required:* Application form, baccalaureate/first degree, essay, 3 letters of recommendation, personal statement, resume/curriculum vitae, transcripts of college work, 2 years of work experience. School will accept GMAT and GRE. *Recommended:* Interview. *Application fee:* $55. Applications for domestic and international students are processed on a rolling basis.

Application Contact Ms. Holly Chase, Assistant Dean for Admission and Financial Aid, 415 South Street, MS 032, Waltham, MA 02454-9110. *Phone:* 781-736-2252. *Fax:* 781-736-2263. *E-mail:* admission@lemberg.brandeis.edu.

See full description on page 582.

Clark University

Graduate School of Management

Worcester, Massachusetts

Phone: 508-793-7406 **Fax:** 508-421-3825 **E-mail:** clarkmba@clarku.edu

Business Program(s) Web Site: http://www.clarku.edu/gsom

Graduate Business Unit Enrollment *Total:* 326 (153 women; 173 international). *Average Age:* 27.

Graduate Business Faculty *Total:* 30 (19 full-time; 11 part-time).

Admissions *Applied:* 486. *Admitted:* 286. *Enrolled:* 102. *Average GMAT:* 552. *Average GPA:* 3.25

Academic Calendar Semesters.

Accreditation AACSB—The Association to Advance Collegiate Schools of Business.

After Graduation (Class of 2006–07) *Employed within 3 months of graduation:* 70%. *Average starting salary:* $64,750.

DEGREES MBA • MSF

MBA—Master of Business Administration Full-time and part-time. *Concentrations:* accounting, environmental economics/management, finance, general MBA, international business, international development management, management, management information systems, marketing.

MSF—Master of Science in Finance Full-time. *Concentration:* finance.

RESOURCES AND SERVICES 135 on-campus PCs are available to graduate business students. Access to Internet/World Wide Web, online (class) registration, and online grade reports available. *Personal computer requirements:* Graduate business students are strongly recommended to purchase or lease a personal computer. *Special opportunities include:* An international exchange program and an internship program are available. *Placement services include:* Alumni network, career placement, job search course, career counseling/planning, electronic job bank, resume referral, career fairs, job interviews arranged, resume preparation, and career library.

EXPENSES *Tuition:* Full-time: $21,140. Part-time: $3020 per course. *Tuition (international):* Full-time: $21,140. *Required fees:* Full-time: $1410. Tuition and/or fees vary by number of courses or credits taken. *Graduate housing:* Room and board costs vary by number of occupants and type of accommodation.

FINANCIAL AID (2007–08) 80 students received aid, including research assistantships, scholarships, and teaching assistantships. Aid is available to part-time students. *Financial aid application deadline:* 4/1.

Financial Aid Contact Lynn Davis, Director of Enrollment and Marketing, 950 Main Street, Worcester, MA 01610-1477. *Phone:* 508-793-7406. *Fax:* 508-421-3825. *E-mail:* clarkmba@clarku.edu.

INTERNATIONAL STUDENTS 53% of students enrolled are international students. *Services and facilities:* Counseling/support services, ESL/language courses, Housing location assistance, International student housing, International student organization, Language tutoring, Orientation, Visa Services. Financial aid is available to international students. *Required with application:* TOEFL with recommended score of 213 (computer), 550 (paper), or 80 (Internet); proof of adequate funds; proof of health/immunizations.

International Student Contact Amy Daly, Director, Intercultural Affairs Office, 950 Main Street, Worcester, MA 01610-1477. *Phone:* 508-793-7362. *Fax:* 508-421-3732. *E-mail:* adaly@clarku.edu.

APPLICATION *Required:* GMAT, application form, baccalaureate/first degree, essay, 2 letters of recommendation, personal statement, resume/

curriculum vitae, transcripts of college work. School will accept GRE. *Application fee:* $50. Applications for domestic and international students are processed on a rolling basis.

Application Contact Lynn Davis, Director of Enrollment and Marketing, 950 Main Street, Worcester, MA 01610-1477. *Phone:* 508-793-7406. *Fax:* 508-421-3825. *E-mail:* clarkmba@clarku.edu.

See full description on page 592.

Emmanuel College
Graduate and Professional Programs
Boston, Massachusetts

Phone: 617-735-9859 **Fax:** 617-735-9708 **E-mail:** bellma@emmanuel.edu

Business Program(s) Web Site: http://www.emmanuel.edu/gpp.html

Graduate Business Unit Enrollment *Total:* 129 (4 full-time; 125 part-time; 97 women).

Graduate Business Faculty 23 part-time.

Admissions *Applied:* 58. *Admitted:* 22. *Enrolled:* 20.

Academic Calendar Continuous.

DEGREES MS

MS—Master of Science in Human Resource Management Full-time and part-time. At least 36 total credits required. 24 to 30 months to complete program. *Concentration:* human resources management.

MS—Master of Science in Management Full-time and part-time. At least 36 total credits required. 24 to 60 months to complete program. *Concentrations:* leadership, management.

RESOURCES AND SERVICES 115 on-campus PCs are available to graduate business students. Access to Internet/World Wide Web, online (class) registration, and online grade reports available. *Personal computer requirements:* Graduate business students are strongly recommended to purchase or lease a personal computer. *Placement services include:* Alumni network, career counseling/planning, career fairs, and career library.

EXPENSES *Tuition:* Part-time: $1872 per course. *Tuition (international):* Part-time: $1872 per course.

FINANCIAL AID (2007–08) Loans. Aid is available to part-time students.

Financial Aid Contact Christina Broderick, Associate Director, Office of Student Financial Services, 400 The Fenway, Boston, MA 02115. *Phone:* 617-735-9928. *Fax:* 617-735-9939. *E-mail:* brodech@emmanuel.edu.

INTERNATIONAL STUDENTS *Services and facilities:* Counseling/ support services, International student housing, International student organization, Orientation, Visa Services. Financial aid is not available to international students. *Required with application:* TOEFL with recommended score of 223 (computer) or 550 (paper); proof of adequate funds; proof of health/immunizations.

International Student Contact Thomas Millington, Director of International Programs, 400 The Fenway, Boston, MA 02115. *Phone:* 617-735-9989. *Fax:* 617-735-9801. *E-mail:* millith@emmanuel.edu.

APPLICATION *Required:* Application form, baccalaureate/first degree, essay, interview, 2 letters of recommendation, personal statement, resume/curriculum vitae, transcripts of college work, 1 year of work experience. *Application fee:* $50. Applications for domestic and international students are processed on a rolling basis.

Application Contact Marjorie Bell, Enrollment Counselor, 400 The Fenway, Boston, MA 02115. *Phone:* 617-735-9859. *Fax:* 617-735-9708. *E-mail:* bellma@emmanuel.edu.

Endicott College
Program in Business Administration
Beverly, Massachusetts

Phone: 978-232-2744 **Fax:** 978-232-3000 **E-mail:** rbenedet@endicott.edu

Business Program(s) Web Site: http://www.endicott.edu/gps/mba

Graduate Business Unit Enrollment *Total:* 344 (106 full-time; 238 part-time; 227 women; 97 international). *Average Age:* 33.

Graduate Business Faculty *Total:* 37 (7 full-time; 30 part-time).

Admissions *Applied:* 25. *Admitted:* 23. *Enrolled:* 23.

Academic Calendar Continuous.

DEGREE MBA

MBA—Master of Business Administration *Concentration:* general MBA.

RESOURCES AND SERVICES 167 on-campus PCs are available to graduate business students. Access to Internet/World Wide Web available. *Personal computer requirements:* Graduate business students are not required to have a personal computer. *Special opportunities include:* An internship program is available. *Placement services include:* Career counseling/planning.

EXPENSES *Tuition:* Part-time: $441 per credit. *Tuition (international):* Part-time: $441 per credit. *Required fees:* Full-time: $1350. Part-time: $1350 per degree program.

FINANCIAL AID (2007–08) Loans.

Financial Aid Contact Marcia Toomey, Director, Financial Aid, 376 Hale Street, Beverly, MA 01915. *Phone:* 978-232-2060. *E-mail:* mtoomey@endicott.edu.

INTERNATIONAL STUDENTS 28% of students enrolled are international students. *Services and facilities:* Counseling/support services, Housing location assistance, International student housing, International student organization, Orientation, Visa Services. *Required with application:* TOEFL; proof of adequate funds; proof of health/immunizations.

International Student Contact April Burris, Dean of International Education, 376 Hale Street, Beverly, MA 01915. *Phone:* 978-232-2272. *E-mail:* aburris@endicott.edu.

APPLICATION *Required:* GMAT, application form, baccalaureate/first degree, essay, interview, 2 letters of recommendation, personal statement, resume/curriculum vitae, transcripts of college work, 7 years of work experience. *Application fee:* $50. Applications for domestic and international students are processed on a rolling basis.

Application Contact Richard Benedetto, Admissions, 376 Hale Street, Beverly, MA 01915. *Phone:* 978-232-2744. *Fax:* 978-232-3000. *E-mail:* rbenedet@endicott.edu.

Fitchburg State College
Division of Graduate and Continuing Education
Fitchburg, Massachusetts

Phone: 978-665-3144 **Fax:** 978-665-4540 **E-mail:** admissions@fsc.edu

Business Program(s) Web Site: http://www.fsc.edu/

Graduate Business Unit Enrollment *Total:* 78 (27 full-time; 51 part-time; 26 women; 34 international). *Average Age:* 28.

Graduate Business Faculty *Total:* 10 (6 full-time; 4 part-time).

Admissions *Applied:* 54. *Admitted:* 45. *Enrolled:* 38.

Academic Calendar Semesters.

Fitchburg State College (continued)

DEGREE MBA

MBA—Master of Business Administration Full-time and part-time. Distance learning option. Minimum undergraduate GPA of 2.8 and minimum GMAT score of 400 required. 30 to 54 total credits required. 24 to 72 months to complete program. *Concentrations:* accounting, human resources management, management.

RESOURCES AND SERVICES 50 on-campus PCs are available to graduate business students. Access to Internet/World Wide Web, online (class) registration, and online grade reports available. *Personal computer requirements:* Graduate business students are strongly recommended to purchase or lease a personal computer. *Special opportunities include:* An internship program is available. *Placement services include:* Alumni network, career counseling/planning, electronic job bank, resume referral, career fairs, job interviews arranged, resume preparation, and career library.

EXPENSES *Tuition (state resident):* Full-time: $2700. Part-time: $150 per credit. *Tuition (nonresident):* Full-time: $2700. Part-time: $150 per credit. *Tuition (international):* Full-time: $2700. Part-time: $150 per credit. *Required fees:* Full-time: $1958. Part-time: $109 per credit.

FINANCIAL AID (2007–08) Grants, loans, research assistantships, scholarships, and work study. Aid is available to part-time students. *Financial aid application deadline:* 3/1.

Financial Aid Contact Ms. Pamela McCafferty, Dean of Enrollment Management, 160 Pearl Street, Fitchburg, MA 01420-2697. *Phone:* 978-665-3435. *Fax:* 978-665-3559. *E-mail:* finaid@fsc.edu.

INTERNATIONAL STUDENTS 44% of students enrolled are international students. *Services and facilities:* Counseling/support services. Financial aid is not available to international students. *Required with application:* TOEFL with recommended score of 213 (computer) or 550 (paper); proof of adequate funds; proof of health/immunizations.

International Student Contact Dr. Clare M. O'Brien, Director of International Education, 160 Pearl Street, Fitchburg, MA 01420-2697. *Phone:* 978-665-3089. *Fax:* 978-665-4040. *E-mail:* cmobrien@fsc.edu.

APPLICATION *Required:* GMAT, application form, baccalaureate/first degree, 3 letters of recommendation, resume/curriculum vitae, transcripts of college work. *Application fee:* $25, $50 (international). Applications for domestic and international students are processed on a rolling basis.

Application Contact Ms. Pamela McCafferty, Dean of Enrollment Management, 160 Pearl Street, Fitchburg, MA 01420-2697. *Phone:* 978-665-3144. *Fax:* 978-665-4540. *E-mail:* admissions@fsc.edu.

Framingham State College
Program in Business Administration

Framingham, Massachusetts

Phone: 508-626-4550 **Fax:** 508-626-4030 **E-mail:** dgce@frc.mass.edu

Business Program(s) Web Site: http://www.framingham.edu/mba

Graduate Business Unit Enrollment *Total:* 32 (32 part-time; 11 women). *Average Age:* 31.

Graduate Business Faculty 4 full-time.

Admissions *Average GPA:* 3.13

Academic Calendar Semesters.

DEGREE MBA

MBA—Master of Business Administration Part-time. Distance learning option. 48 to 72 total credits required. 24 to 36 months to complete program. *Concentration:* general MBA.

RESOURCES AND SERVICES 500 on-campus PCs are available to graduate business students. Access to Internet/World Wide Web and online (class) registration available. *Personal computer requirements:* Graduate business students are required to have a personal computer. *Placement*

services include: Alumni network, career counseling/planning, electronic job bank, resume referral, resume preparation, and career library.

EXPENSES *Tuition (state resident):* Part-time: $975 per course. *Tuition (nonresident):* Part-time: $975 per course. Tuition and/or fees vary by number of courses or credits taken and academic program.

FINANCIAL AID (2007–08) Grants and loans. Aid is available to part-time students.

Financial Aid Contact Ms. Susan E. Lanzillo, Director of Financial Aid, 100 State Street, PO Box 9101, Framingham, MA 01701-9101. *Phone:* 508-626-4534. *Fax:* 508-626-4598. *E-mail:* finaid@frc.mass.edu.

INTERNATIONAL STUDENTS Financial aid is not available to international students.

APPLICATION *Required:* GMAT, application form, baccalaureate/first degree, essay, 2 letters of recommendation, resume/curriculum vitae, transcripts of college work. *Application fee:* $50. *Deadline:* 8/1 for fall.

Application Contact Dr. Ronald Sundberg, Associate Dean, 100 State Street, PO Box 9101, Framingham, MA 01701-9101. *Phone:* 508-626-4550. *Fax:* 508-626-4030. *E-mail:* dgce@frc.mass.edu.

Harvard University
Business School

Boston, Massachusetts

Phone: 617-495-6128 **Fax:** 617-496-8137 **E-mail:** admissions@hbs.edu

Business Program(s) Web Site: http://www.hbs.edu/

Graduate Business Unit Enrollment *Total:* 1,848 (1,848 full-time; 648 women; 610 international).

Graduate Business Faculty 205 full-time.

Admissions *Applied:* 7,411. *Admitted:* 1,021. *Enrolled:* 901. *Average GMAT:* 713. *Average GPA:* 3.6

Academic Calendar Semesters.

Accreditation AACSB—The Association to Advance Collegiate Schools of Business.

After Graduation (Class of 2006–07) *Employed within 3 months of graduation:* 94%. *Average starting salary:* $115,665.

DEGREES JD/MBA • MBA • MD/MBA

JD/MBA—Juris Doctor/Master of Business Administration Full-time. 48 months to complete program. *Concentration:* management.

MBA—Master of Business Administration Full-time. 18 months to complete program. *Concentration:* management.

MD/MBA—Doctor of Medicine/Master of Business Administration Full-time. 60 months to complete program. *Concentration:* management.

RESOURCES AND SERVICES Access to Internet/World Wide Web, online (class) registration, and online grade reports available. *Personal computer requirements:* Graduate business students are required to have a personal computer. *Special opportunities include:* An internship program is available. *Placement services include:* Alumni network, career placement, job search course, career counseling/planning, electronic job bank, resume referral, career fairs, job interviews arranged, resume preparation, and career library.

EXPENSES *Tuition:* Full-time: $41,900. *Tuition (international):* Full-time: $41,900. *Required fees:* Full-time: $6838. *Typical graduate housing cost:* $24,562 (including board).

FINANCIAL AID (2007–08) 1250 students received aid, including fellowships and loans. *Financial aid application deadline:* 6/11.

Financial Aid Contact MBA Financial Aid Office, Spangler Center, Soldiers Field, Boston, MA 02163. *Phone:* 617-495-6640. *Fax:* 617-496-3991. *E-mail:* finaid@hbs.edu.

INTERNATIONAL STUDENTS 33% of students enrolled are international students. *Services and facilities:* Counseling/support services,

ESL/language courses, Housing location assistance, International student housing, International student organization, Language tutoring, Orientation, Visa Services. Financial aid is available to international students. *Required with application:* TOEFL with recommended score of 267 (computer) or 630 (paper); proof of adequate funds; proof of health/immunizations. *Recommended with application:* TWE.

International Student Contact MBA Admissions, Dillon House, Soldiers Field, Boston, MA 02163. *Phone:* 617-495-6128. *Fax:* 617-496-8137. *E-mail:* admissions@hbs.edu.

APPLICATION *Required:* GMAT, application form, baccalaureate/first degree, essay, interview, 3 letters of recommendation, personal statement, resume/curriculum vitae, transcripts of college work. *Application fee:* $235. *Deadlines:* 3/3 for fall, 3/3 for fall (international).

Application Contact MBA Admissions, Dillon House, Soldiers Field, Boston, MA 02163. *Phone:* 617-495-6128. *Fax:* 617-496-8137. *E-mail:* admissions@hbs.edu.

Hult International Business School

Graduate Program

Cambridge, Massachusetts

Phone: 852-21582937 **Fax:** 852-21119551 **E-mail:** admissions@hult.edu

Business Program(s) Web Site: http://www.hult.edu

DEGREE MBA

MBA—One-Year Accelerated Master of Business Administration Full-time. Minimum 3 years experience, GMAT and English language proficiency. 60 to 63 total credits required. 12 months to complete program. *Concentrations:* accounting, business policy/strategy, economics, entrepreneurship, finance, general MBA, human resources management, industrial administration/management, international and area business studies, international business, international finance, international management, international marketing, leadership, management, management consulting, management science, marketing, operations management, organizational behavior/development, quantitative analysis, risk management, strategic management, student designed.

Founded in 1964, Hult International Business School is a top-ranked one-year U.S. M.B.A. program that the Economist Intelligence Unit *ranked the twenty-first best in the U.S. and number thirty-nine in the world in 2007. Recognizing the importance of a truly global perspective and the exciting career opportunities that are available in the world's fastest-growing economies, the Hult M.B.A. is offered across four key locations: Boston, London, Dubai, and Shanghai. No matter where Hult students choose to start their program, they are given the opportunity to study at the other Hult campuses to gain international exposures and unique insights into the world's key economies.*

Hult's highly ranked M.B.A. program is also distinguished by its diverse student body and Action Learning Curriculum. Hult's student body comprises experienced professionals from over forty countries. Averaging thirty years of age with seven years of professional experience, they are more mature than the usual M.B.A. student. Action learning is the cornerstone of the Hult M.B.A. program, which is oriented toward the real business world and is taught by professors who have significant experience in leading corporations and consulting firms. Students learn through case studies, group projects, and simulations of real business situations as well as the Action Learning Project. In this project, students have the opportunity to work with a client company to resolve real business problems.

Hult is accredited by New England Association of Schools and Colleges (NEASC) and Association of MBAs (AMBA).

RESOURCES AND SERVICES 5 on-campus PCs are available to graduate business students. Access to Internet/World Wide Web available. *Personal computer requirements:* Graduate business students are required to have a personal computer. *Special opportunities include:* An international exchange program and an internship program are available. *Placement services include:* Alumni network, career placement, job search course, career counseling/planning, electronic job bank, resume referral, career fairs, job interviews arranged, resume preparation, and career library.

Application Contact Ms. Carol Hung, Global Head of Recruiting and Marketing, 23/F, Shell Tower, Times Square, Causeway Bay, Hong Kong, Hong Kong. *Phone:* 852-21582937. *Fax:* 852-21119551. *E-mail:* admissions@hult.edu.

See full description on page 634.

Massachusetts Institute of Technology

Sloan School of Management

Cambridge, Massachusetts

Phone: 617-253-3730 **Fax:** 617-253-6405 **E-mail:** mbaadmissions@sloan.mit.edu

Business Program(s) Web Site: http://mitsloan.mit.edu/

Graduate Business Unit Enrollment *Total:* 781 (781 full-time; 242 women; 250 international). *Average Age:* 28.

Graduate Business Faculty 102 full-time.

Admissions *Applied:* 3,038. *Admitted:* 599. *Enrolled:* 392. *Average GMAT:* 710. *Average GPA:* 3.5

Academic Calendar Semesters.

Accreditation AACSB—The Association to Advance Collegiate Schools of Business.

After Graduation (Class of 2006–07) *Employed within 3 months of graduation:* 98%. *Average starting salary:* $107,990.

DEGREES MBA • MS • MS/MS

MBA—Fellows Program Full-time and part-time. 12 to 24 months to complete program. *Concentrations:* management, management information systems, management science, operations management, strategic management.

MBA—MBA Program Full-time. 24 months to complete program. *Concentrations:* entrepreneurship, finance, financial management/planning, management, management information systems, management science, new venture management, operations management, strategic management.

MS—Fellows Program Full-time. 12 to 24 months to complete program. *Concentrations:* management, management information systems, management science, operations management, strategic management, technology management.

MS/MS—Master of Science in Management/Master of Science in Engineering Full-time. 24 months to complete program. *Concentration:* combined degrees.

RESOURCES AND SERVICES 50 on-campus PCs are available to graduate business students. Access to Internet/World Wide Web, online (class) registration, and online grade reports available. *Personal computer requirements:* Graduate business students are required to have a personal computer. *Special opportunities include:* An international exchange program and an internship program are available. *Placement services include:* Alumni network, career placement, job search course, career counseling/planning, electronic job bank, resume referral, career fairs, job interviews arranged, resume preparation, and career library.

Massachusetts Institute of Technology (continued)

EXPENSES *Tuition:* Full-time: $44,556. *Tuition (international):* Full-time: $44,556. *Graduate housing:* Room and board costs vary by campus location, number of occupants, type of accommodation, and type of board plan.

FINANCIAL AID (2007–08) 410 students received aid, including fellowships, grants, loans, research assistantships, teaching assistantships, and work study. Aid is available to part-time students. *Financial aid application deadline:* 4/15.

Financial Aid Contact Ms. Liz Barnes, Financial Aid Representative, 77 Massachusetts Avenue, 5-119, Cambridge, MA 02139. *Phone:* 617-258-5775. *Fax:* 617-258-8301. *E-mail:* finaid@mit.edu.

INTERNATIONAL STUDENTS 32% of students enrolled are international students. *Services and facilities:* Counseling/support services, ESL/language courses, Housing location assistance, International student organization, Orientation, Visa Services. Financial aid is available to international students. *Required with application:* Proof of adequate funds; proof of health/immunizations.

International Student Contact Danielle Ashbrook Guichard, Acting Director and Associate Dean, 77 Massachusetts Avenue, 5-106, Cambridge, MA 02139. *Phone:* 617-253-3795. *Fax:* 617-258-5483. *E-mail:* iso-help@mit.edu.

APPLICATION *Required:* Application form, baccalaureate/first degree, essay, interview, 2 letters of recommendation, personal statement, resume/curriculum vitae, transcripts of college work. School will accept GMAT and GRE. *Recommended:* Work experience. *Application fee:* $230. *Deadlines:* 11/6 for fall, 1/7 for winter, 11/6 for fall (international), 1/7 for winter (international).

Application Contact Rod Garcia, Director of Master's Admissions, 50 Memorial Drive, E52-126, Cambridge, MA 02142. *Phone:* 617-253-3730. *Fax:* 617-253-6405. *E-mail:* mbaadmissions@sloan.mit.edu.

Nichols College
Graduate Program in Business Administration

Dudley, Massachusetts

Phone: 800-243-3844 **Fax:** 508-213-2490 **E-mail:** shannon.johnston@nichols.edu

Business Program(s) Web Site: http://www.nichols.edu/adultlearner

DEGREE MBA

MBA—Master of Business Administration Full-time and part-time. Distance learning option. 36 to 45 total credits required. 12 to 72 months to complete program. *Concentration:* general MBA.

RESOURCES AND SERVICES 30 on-campus PCs are available to graduate business students. Access to Internet/World Wide Web, online (class) registration, and online grade reports available. *Personal computer requirements:* Graduate business students are not required to have a personal computer. *Placement services include:* Alumni network, career placement, career counseling/planning, electronic job bank, career fairs, resume preparation, and career library.

Application Contact Shannon Johnston, Enrollment Services Coordinator, 129 Center Road, Dudley, MA 01571. *Phone:* 800-243-3844. *Fax:* 508-213-2490. *E-mail:* shannon.johnston@nichols.edu.

Northeastern University
Graduate School of Business Administration

Boston, Massachusetts

Phone: 617-373-3258 **Fax:** 617-373-8564 **E-mail:** e.tate@neu.edu

Business Program(s) Web Site: http://www.cba.neu.edu/graduate

Graduate Business Unit Enrollment *Total:* 668 (200 full-time; 468 part-time; 262 women; 83 international). *Average Age:* 30.

Graduate Business Faculty *Total:* 132 (115 full-time; 17 part-time).

Admissions *Applied:* 485. *Admitted:* 323. *Enrolled:* 182. *Average GMAT:* 589. *Average GPA:* 3.2

Academic Calendar Semesters.

Accreditation AACSB—The Association to Advance Collegiate Schools of Business.

After Graduation (Class of 2006–07) *Employed within 3 months of graduation:* 59%. *Average starting salary:* $66,300.

DEGREES JD/MBA • MBA • MBA/MS • MBA/MSF • MBA/MSN • MS • MSA • MSCIB • MST

JD/MBA Full-time. At least 126 total credits required. Minimum of 60 months to complete program. *Concentrations:* administration, business studies, combined degrees, general MBA, law, management.

MBA—Evening Master of Business Administration Part-time. At least 60 total credits required. 24 to 84 months to complete program. *Concentrations:* administration, business studies, entrepreneurship, finance, general MBA, information management, international business, management, marketing, supply chain management.

MBA—Executive Master of Business Administration Part-time. At least 60 total credits required. 16 months to complete program. *Concentrations:* administration, business studies, executive programs, general MBA, international business, management.

MBA—Full-Time Master of Business Administration Full-time. At least 60 total credits required. 24 months to complete program. *Concentrations:* administration, business studies, finance, general MBA, management, marketing, supply chain management.

MBA—High-Tech Master of Business Administration Part-time. At least 60 total credits required. 21 months to complete program. *Concentrations:* administration, business studies, general MBA, management, new venture management, technology management.

MBA—Online MBA Part-time. Distance learning option. 50 total credits required. 24 to 84 months to complete program. *Concentrations:* administration, business studies, entrepreneurship, finance, general MBA, health care, international management, management, marketing, supply chain management, technology management.

MBA/MS—Master of Business Administration/Master of Science in Accounting Full-time. At least 72 total credits required. 15 months to complete program. *Concentrations:* accounting, administration, business studies, combined degrees, general MBA, management.

MBA/MSF—Master of Business Administration/Master of Science in Finance Full-time and part-time. At least 72 total credits required. 24 to 84 months to complete program. *Concentrations:* administration, business studies, combined degrees, finance, financial management/planning, general MBA, management.

MBA/MSN—Master of Business Administration/Master of Science in Nursing Full-time and part-time. At least 68 total credits required. 30 to 84 months to complete program. *Concentrations:* administration, business studies, combined degrees, general MBA, health administration, health care, management, medicine.

MS—Master of Science in Finance Part-time. At least 30 total credits required. 12 to 48 months to complete program. *Concentrations:* finance, financial management/planning.

MSA—Master of Science in Accounting Part-time. At least 30 total credits required. 12 to 24 months to complete program. *Concentrations:* accounting, corporate accounting.

MSCIB—MS in International Business Full-time and part-time. At least 30 total credits required. 12 to 24 months to complete program. *Concentrations:* business studies, international and area business studies, international business, international management, management.

MST—Master of Science in Taxation Part-time. At least 30 total credits required. 24 to 48 months to complete program. *Concentration:* taxation.

RESOURCES AND SERVICES 72 on-campus PCs are available to graduate business students. Access to Internet/World Wide Web, online

(class) registration, and online grade reports available. *Personal computer requirements:* Graduate business students are strongly recommended to purchase or lease a personal computer. *Special opportunities include:* An international exchange program and an internship program are available. *Placement services include:* Alumni network, career placement, job search course, career counseling/planning, electronic job bank, resume referral, career fairs, job interviews arranged, resume preparation, and career library.

EXPENSES *Tuition:* Full-time: $33,000. Part-time: $1110 per credit. *Tuition (international):* Full-time: $33,000. Part-time: $1110 per credit. *Required fees:* Full-time: $402. Part-time: $37 per semester. Tuition and/or fees vary by number of courses or credits taken and academic program.

FINANCIAL AID (2007–08) 599 students received aid, including loans, scholarships, and work study. Aid is available to part-time students. *Financial aid application deadline:* 3/1.

Financial Aid Contact Brian Murphy Clinton, Associate Director, Graduate Financial Aid, 356 Richards Hall, Boston, MA 02115. *Phone:* 617-373-5899. *E-mail:* b.murphyclinton@neu.edu.

INTERNATIONAL STUDENTS 12% of students enrolled are international students. *Services and facilities:* Counseling/support services, ESL/language courses, Housing location assistance, International student organization, Language tutoring, Orientation, Visa Services. Financial aid is available to international students. *Required with application:* TOEFL with recommended score of 250 (computer), 600 (paper), or 100 (Internet); proof of adequate funds; proof of health/immunizations.

International Student Contact Salvatore Mazzone, Associate Director, International Student Office, 360 Huntington Avenue, 206 Ell Building, Boston, MA 02115. *Phone:* 617-373-2310. *Fax:* 617-373-8788.

APPLICATION *Required:* GMAT, application form, baccalaureate/first degree, essay, interview, 2 letters of recommendation, personal statement, resume/curriculum vitae, transcripts of college work. *Recommended:* 2 years of work experience. *Application fee:* $100. *Deadlines:* 4/15 for fall, 11/1 for winter, 11/1 for spring, 4/1 for summer, 2/1 for fall (international), 11/1 for winter (international), 11/1 for spring (international), 1/15 for summer (international).

Application Contact Evelyn Tate, Director, Recruitment and Admissions, 360 Huntington Avenue, 350 Dodge Hall, Boston, MA 02115. *Phone:* 617-373-3258. *Fax:* 617-373-8564. *E-mail:* e.tate@neu.edu.

Regis College

Department of Management and Leadership

Weston, Massachusetts

Phone: 781-768-7100 **Fax:** 781-768-7071 **E-mail:** gradmanagement@regiscollege.edu

Business Program(s) Web Site: http://regisnet.regiscollege.edu/management/ms.html

Graduate Business Unit Enrollment *Total:* 24 (24 part-time; 18 women). *Average Age:* 32.

Graduate Business Faculty *Total:* 7 (2 full-time; 5 part-time).

Admissions *Applied:* 7. *Admitted:* 5. *Enrolled:* 5. *Average GPA:* 3.0

Academic Calendar Semesters.

After Graduation (Class of 2006–07) *Employed within 3 months of graduation:* 100%. *Average starting salary:* $50,000.

DEGREE MS

MS—Master of Science in Leadership and Organizational Change Full-time and part-time. GRE. At least 33 total credits required. Minimum of 11 months to complete program. *Concentrations:* leadership, organizational management.

RESOURCES AND SERVICES 60 on-campus PCs are available to graduate business students. Access to Internet/World Wide Web, online (class) registration, and online grade reports available. *Personal computer*

requirements: Graduate business students are not required to have a personal computer. *Special opportunities include:* An internship program is available. *Placement services include:* Alumni network, career placement, career counseling/planning, career fairs, resume preparation, and career library.

EXPENSES *Tuition:* Part-time: $1920 per course. *Tuition (international):* Part-time: $1920 per course.

FINANCIAL AID (2007–08) 5 students received aid, including loans and scholarships. Aid is available to part-time students.

Financial Aid Contact Dee Ludwick, Director of Financial Aid, 235 Wellesley Street, Weston, MA 02493. *Phone:* 781-768-7180. *Fax:* 781-768-7225. *E-mail:* finaid@regiscollege.edu.

INTERNATIONAL STUDENTS *Services and facilities:* Counseling/support services, International student organization, Orientation. Financial aid is available to international students. *Required with application:* TOEFL with recommended score of 213 (computer) or 550 (paper); proof of health/immunizations.

International Student Contact Ms. Kathryn Anastasia, International Student Advisor, 235 Wellesley Street, Weston, MA 02493. *Phone:* 781-768-8360. *E-mail:* kathryn.anastasia@regiscollege.edu.

APPLICATION *Required:* Application form, baccalaureate/first degree, essay, interview, 2 letters of recommendation, personal statement, resume/curriculum vitae, transcripts of college work. School will accept GRE and MAT. *Recommended:* Work experience. *Application fee:* $50. Applications for domestic and international students are processed on a rolling basis.

Application Contact Claudia Pouravelis, Director of Graduate Admission, 235 Wellesley Street, Weston, MA 02493. *Phone:* 781-768-7100. *Fax:* 781-768-7071. *E-mail:* gradmanagement@regiscollege.edu.

Salem State College

Program in Business Administration

Salem, Massachusetts

Phone: 978-542-7006 **Fax:** 978-542-6027 **E-mail:** rluther@salemstate.edu

Business Program(s) Web Site: http://www.salemstate.edu/graduate/mba

Graduate Business Unit Enrollment *Total:* 143 (143 part-time; 59 women; 19 international). *Average Age:* 31.

Graduate Business Faculty *Total:* 34 (31 full-time; 3 part-time).

Admissions *Applied:* 42. *Admitted:* 28. *Enrolled:* 14. *Average GMAT:* 500. *Average GPA:* 3.2

Academic Calendar Semesters.

DEGREES MBA

MBA—Master of Business Administration Full-time and part-time. Distance learning option. 30 to 48 total credits required. 12 to 72 months to complete program. *Concentrations:* decision sciences, financial management/planning, marketing.

MBA—Master of Business Administration *Concentrations:* general MBA, international business.

RESOURCES AND SERVICES 394 on-campus PCs are available to graduate business students. Access to Internet/World Wide Web, online (class) registration, and online grade reports available. *Personal computer requirements:* Graduate business students are strongly recommended to purchase or lease a personal computer. *Special opportunities include:* An international exchange program and an internship program are available. *Placement services include:* Career counseling/planning, electronic job bank, career fairs, resume preparation, and career library.

EXPENSES *Tuition (state resident):* Part-time: $750 per course. *Tuition (nonresident):* Part-time: $1020 per course. *Tuition (international):* Part-time: $1020 per course.

Salem State College (continued)

FINANCIAL AID (2007–08) 5 students received aid, including loans, research assistantships, scholarships, teaching assistantships, and work study. Aid is available to part-time students. *Financial aid application deadline:* 4/1.

Financial Aid Contact Ms. Janet Lundstrom, Director of Administrative Services, Graduate School, Graduate School, 352 Lafayette Street, Salem, MA 01970-5353. *Phone:* 978-542-6310. *Fax:* 978-542-7215. *E-mail:* janet.lundstrom@salemstate.edu.

INTERNATIONAL STUDENTS 13% of students enrolled are international students. *Services and facilities:* Counseling/support services, ESL/language courses, Housing location assistance, International student organization, Language tutoring, Orientation, Visa Services, Cultural programming. Financial aid is available to international students. *Required with application:* TOEFL with recommended score of 213 (computer), 550 (paper), or 80 (Internet); proof of adequate funds; proof of health/immunizations.

International Student Contact Donald Ross, Director, Center for International Education, 352 Lafayette Street, Salem, MA 01970-5353. *Phone:* 978-542-6351. *Fax:* 978-542-7104. *E-mail:* donald.ross@salemstate.edu.

APPLICATION *Required:* GMAT, application form, baccalaureate/first degree, essay, 3 letters of recommendation, personal statement, resume/curriculum vitae, transcripts of college work. *Application fee:* $35. *Deadlines:* 7/1 for fall, 11/1 for winter, 11/1 for spring, 3/1 for summer, 7/1 for fall (international), 11/1 for winter (international), 11/1 for spring (international), 3/1 for summer (international).

Application Contact Dr. Raminder K. Luther, Coordinator, Graduate Programs in Business, Bertolon School of Business, 352 Lafayette Street, Salem, MA 01970-5353. *Phone:* 978-542-7006. *Fax:* 978-542-6027. *E-mail:* rluther@salemstate.edu.

Simmons College
Simmons School of Management

Boston, Massachusetts

Phone: 617-521-3840 **Fax:** 617-521-3880 **E-mail:** denise.haile@simmons.edu

Business Program(s) Web Site: http://www.simmons.edu/som

Graduate Business Unit Enrollment *Total:* 250 (50 full-time; 200 part-time; 250 women; 75 international). *Average Age:* 31.

Graduate Business Faculty *Total:* 31 (18 full-time; 13 part-time).

Admissions *Applied:* 102. *Admitted:* 98. *Enrolled:* 58. *Average GMAT:* 535. *Average GPA:* 3.2

Academic Calendar Trimesters.

After Graduation (Class of 2006–07) *Employed within 3 months of graduation:* 91%. *Average starting salary:* $75,000.

DEGREE MBA

MBA—Master of Business Administration Full-time and part-time. At least 48 total credits required. 12 to 60 months to complete program. *Concentrations:* entrepreneurship, general MBA, management.

RESOURCES AND SERVICES 60 on-campus PCs are available to graduate business students. Access to Internet/World Wide Web, online (class) registration, and online grade reports available. *Personal computer requirements:* Graduate business students are strongly recommended to purchase or lease a personal computer. *Special opportunities include:* An internship program is available. *Placement services include:* Alumni network, career placement, job search course, career counseling/planning, electronic job bank, resume referral, career fairs, job interviews arranged, resume preparation, and career library.

EXPENSES *Tuition:* Full-time: $49,680. Part-time: $1035 per credit. *Tuition (international):* Full-time: $49,680. Part-time: $1035 per credit. *Required fees:* Full-time: $1000. *Typical graduate housing cost:* $12,000 (including board).

FINANCIAL AID (2007–08) 225 students received aid, including fellowships, grants, loans, scholarships, and work study. Aid is available to part-time students. *Financial aid application deadline:* 5/1.

Financial Aid Contact Diane Hallesey, Director of Financial Aid, 300 The Fenway, Boston, MA 02115. *Phone:* 617-521-2001. *Fax:* 617-521-3195. *E-mail:* financialaid@simmons.edu.

INTERNATIONAL STUDENTS 30% of students enrolled are international students. *Services and facilities:* Counseling/support services, ESL/language courses, Housing location assistance, International student housing, International student organization, Language tutoring, Orientation, Visa Services. Financial aid is available to international students. *Required with application:* TOEFL with recommended score of 230 (computer), 550 (paper), or 90 (Internet); proof of adequate funds; proof of health/immunizations.

International Student Contact Denise Haile, Director of MBA Admissions, 409 Commonwealth Avenue, Boston, MA 02215. *Phone:* 617-521-3840. *Fax:* 617-521-3880. *E-mail:* denise.haile@simmons.edu.

APPLICATION *Required:* GMAT, application form, baccalaureate/first degree, essay, 2 letters of recommendation, resume/curriculum vitae, transcripts of college work, 2 years of work experience. *Recommended:* Interview. *Application fee:* $75. Applications for domestic and international students are processed on a rolling basis.

Application Contact Denise Haile, Director of MBA Admissions, 409 Commonwealth Avenue, Boston, MA 02215. *Phone:* 617-521-3840. *Fax:* 617-521-3880. *E-mail:* denise.haile@simmons.edu.

Suffolk University
Sawyer Business School

Boston, Massachusetts

Phone: 617-573-8302 **Fax:** 617-305-1733 **E-mail:** grad.admission@suffolk.edu

Business Program(s) Web Site: http://www/suffolk.edu/business/1196.html

Graduate Business Unit Enrollment *Total:* 1,068 (225 full-time; 843 part-time; 544 women; 165 international). *Average Age:* 30.

Graduate Business Faculty *Total:* 167 (107 full-time; 60 part-time).

Admissions *Applied:* 946. *Admitted:* 696. *Enrolled:* 334. *Average GMAT:* 499. *Average GPA:* 3.2

Academic Calendar Semesters.

Accreditation AACSB—The Association to Advance Collegiate Schools of Business.

After Graduation (Class of 2006–07) *Employed within 3 months of graduation:* 91%. *Average starting salary:* $63,800.

DEGREES GMBA • JD/MBA • MBA • MHA • MPA • MSA • MSF • MSFS • MST

GMBA—Global MBA Full-time and part-time. Distance learning option. Interview Required. 33 to 57 total credits required. 12 to 16 months to complete program. *Concentrations:* international finance, international marketing.

JD/MBA—Juris Doctor/Master of Business Administration Full-time and part-time. 115 total credits required. 36 to 60 months to complete program. *Concentration:* combined degrees.

MBA—Executive Master of Business Administration Part-time. Interview required. 51 total credits required. 18 months to complete program. *Concentrations:* executive programs, other.

MBA—Master of Business Administration Full-time and part-time. Distance learning option. 31 to 55 total credits required. 10 to 16 months to complete program. *Concentrations:* accounting, business law, combined degrees, entrepreneurship, finance, health administration, international business, marketing, nonprofit management, organizational behavior/ development, taxation.

MBA—Online Master of Business Administration Full-time and part-time. Distance learning option. 31 to 55 total credits required. 10 to 16 months to complete program. *Concentrations:* accounting, entrepreneurship, finance, information systems, marketing.

MHA—Master of Health Administration Full-time and part-time. 49 total credits required. 18 to 24 months to complete program. *Concentrations:* combined degrees, health administration.

MPA—Master of Public Administration Full-time and part-time. 49 total credits required. 16 to 24 months to complete program. *Concentrations:* combined degrees, health care, leadership, nonprofit management, other, public management.

MSA—Master of Science in Accounting Full-time and part-time. 30 to 57 total credits required. 10 to 16 months to complete program. *Concentrations:* accounting, combined degrees.

MSF—Master of Science in Finance Full-time and part-time. Interview Required. 30 to 44 total credits required. 15 months to complete program. *Concentrations:* banking, combined degrees, finance.

MSFS—Master of Science in Financial Services and Banking Full-time and part-time. 30 to 44 total credits required. 15 months to complete program. *Concentrations:* banking, finance.

MST—Master of Science in Taxation Full-time and part-time. 30 to 39 total credits required. 10 to 16 months to complete program. *Concentrations:* combined degrees, taxation.

RESOURCES AND SERVICES 1,288 on-campus PCs are available to graduate business students. Access to Internet/World Wide Web, online (class) registration, and online grade reports available. *Personal computer requirements:* Graduate business students are not required to have a personal computer. *Special opportunities include:* An internship program is available. *Placement services include:* Alumni network, career placement, job search course, career counseling/planning, electronic job bank, resume referral, career fairs, job interviews arranged, resume preparation, and career library.

FINANCIAL AID (2007–08) 521 students received aid, including fellowships, grants, loans, research assistantships, scholarships, and work study. Aid is available to part-time students. *Financial aid application deadline:* 3/1.

Financial Aid Contact Christine Perry, Director of Financial Aid/ Assistant Dean of Enrollment Management, 8 Ashburton Place, Boston, MA 02108-2770. *Phone:* 617-573-8470. *Fax:* 617-720-3579. *E-mail:* cperry@suffolk.edu.

INTERNATIONAL STUDENTS 15% of students enrolled are international students. *Services and facilities:* Counseling/support services, ESL/language courses, Housing location assistance, International student organization, Orientation, Visa Services, International student advising office. Financial aid is available to international students. *Required with application:* IELT with recommended score of 6.5; TOEFL with recommended score of 213 (computer) or 550 (paper); proof of adequate funds; proof of health/immunizations.

International Student Contact Daphne L. Durham, Director of Immigration Services and Advising, Center for International Education, 8 Ashburton Place, Boston, MA 02108-2770. *Phone:* 617-573-8154. *Fax:* 617-305-1751. *E-mail:* ddurham@suffolk.edu.

APPLICATION *Required:* GMAT, application form, baccalaureate/first degree, essay, 2 letters of recommendation, personal statement, resume/ curriculum vitae, transcripts of college work, 1 year of work experience. *Application fee:* $50. Applications for domestic and international students are processed on a rolling basis.

Application Contact Judith L. Reynolds, Director of Graduate Admission, 8 Ashburton Place, Boston, MA 02108-2770. *Phone:* 617-573-8302. *Fax:* 617-305-1733. *E-mail:* grad.admission@suffolk.edu.

University of Massachusetts Amherst
Isenberg School of Management

Amherst, Massachusetts

Phone: 413-545-5608 **Fax:** 413-577-2234 **E-mail:** gradprog@som.umass.edu

Business Program(s) Web Site: http://www.isenberg.umass.edu/mba

Graduate Business Unit Enrollment *Total:* 951 (176 full-time; 775 part-time; 317 women). *Average Age:* 28.

Graduate Business Faculty 76 full-time.

Admissions *Applied:* 596. *Admitted:* 415. *Enrolled:* 288. *Average GMAT:* 647. *Average GPA:* 3.3

Academic Calendar Semesters.

Accreditation AACSB—The Association to Advance Collegiate Schools of Business.

After Graduation (Class of 2006–07) *Employed within 3 months of graduation:* 97%. *Average starting salary:* $75,200.

DEGREES MAS • MBA • MBA/MHRIM • PhD/MBA

MAS—MSc in Accounting Full-time. Distance learning option. At least 30 total credits required. 15 months to complete program. *Concentration:* accounting.

MBA—Dual Degrees Full-time. At least 55 total credits required. Minimum of 24 months to complete program. *Concentrations:* engineering, public policy and administration, sports/entertainment management.

MBA—Full-Time MBA Full-time. At least 55 total credits required. 24 months to complete program. *Concentration:* general MBA.

MBA—Part-Time MBA Part-time. Distance learning option. At least 37 total credits required. 11 to 48 months to complete program. *Concentration:* general MBA.

MBA/MHRIM—MBA/MS in Hospitality Management Full-time. At least 55 total credits required. Minimum of 24 months to complete program. *Concentration:* hospitality management.

PhD/MBA—Doctor of Philosophy in Management/Master of Business Administration Full-time. At least 63 total credits required. 48 to 60 months to complete program. *Concentrations:* accounting, financial management/planning, management science, marketing, organizational behavior/development, sports/entertainment management, strategic management.

RESOURCES AND SERVICES 128 on-campus PCs are available to graduate business students. Access to Internet/World Wide Web, online (class) registration, and online grade reports available. *Personal computer requirements:* Graduate business students are strongly recommended to purchase or lease a personal computer. *Special opportunities include:* An international exchange program and an internship program are available. *Placement services include:* Alumni network, career placement, job search course, career counseling/planning, electronic job bank, resume referral, career fairs, job interviews arranged, resume preparation, and career library.

EXPENSES *Tuition (state resident):* Full-time: $3025. Part-time: $600 per credit hour. *Tuition (nonresident):* Full-time: $11,385. Part-time: $670 per credit hour. *Tuition (international):* Full-time: $11,385. Part-time: $670 per credit hour. *Required fees:* Full-time: $7103. Part-time: $45 per semester. Tuition and/or fees vary by class time, number of courses or credits taken, campus location, academic program, and local reciprocity agreements. *Graduate housing:* Room and board costs vary by number of occupants, type of accommodation, and type of board plan. *Typical cost:* $9500 (including board).

FINANCIAL AID (2007–08) 69 students received aid, including fellowships, grants, research assistantships, and scholarships. Aid is available to part-time students. *Financial aid application deadline:* 3/1.

Financial Aid Contact Anne B. Peramba, Financial Aid Services, 255 Whitmore Building, Amherst, MA 01003. *Phone:* 413-577-0555. *Fax:* 413-545-1722. *E-mail:* grads@finaid.umass.edu.

University of Massachusetts Amherst (continued)

INTERNATIONAL STUDENTS *Services and facilities:* Counseling/support services, ESL/language courses, Housing location assistance, International student housing, International student organization, Language tutoring, Orientation, Visa Services, Career services, Writing center. Financial aid is available to international students. *Required with application:* TOEFL with recommended score of 250 (computer) or 600 (paper); proof of adequate funds; proof of health/immunizations.

International Student Contact Patricia Vokbus, Foreign Student Advisor, William S. Clark International Center, Amherst, MA 01003. *Phone:* 413-545-2843. *Fax:* 413-545-1201. *E-mail:* vokbus@ipo.umass.edu.

APPLICATION *Required:* GMAT, application form, baccalaureate/first degree, 2 letters of recommendation, personal statement, resume/curriculum vitae, transcripts of college work, 3 years of work experience. *Recommended:* Interview. *Application fee:* $40, $65 (international). *Deadlines:* 2/1 for fall, 2/1 for fall (international).

Application Contact Director of MBA Admissions, 305 Isenberg School of Management, 121 Presidents Drive, Amherst, MA 01003. *Phone:* 413-545-5608. *Fax:* 413-577-2234. *E-mail:* gradprog@som.umass.edu.

University of Massachusetts Boston

College of Management

Boston, Massachusetts

Phone: 617-287-7720 **Fax:** 617-287-7725 **E-mail:** mba@umb.edu

Business Program(s) Web Site: http://www.management.umb.edu

Graduate Business Unit Enrollment *Total:* 475 (180 full-time; 295 part-time; 246 women; 86 international). *Average Age:* 32.

Graduate Business Faculty *Total:* 62 (51 full-time; 11 part-time).

Admissions *Applied:* 532. *Admitted:* 218. *Enrolled:* 136. *Average GMAT:* 581. *Average GPA:* 3.34

Academic Calendar Semesters.

Accreditation AACSB—The Association to Advance Collegiate Schools of Business.

After Graduation (Class of 2006–07) *Employed within 3 months of graduation:* 92%. *Average starting salary:* $77,200.

DEGREES MBA • MS • MSA • MSF • MSIT

MBA—Master of Business Administration Full-time and part-time. 33 to 57 total credits required. 12 to 60 months to complete program. *Concentrations:* accounting, electronic commerce (E-commerce), environmental economics/management, finance, health administration, human resources management, information technology, international management, management information systems, marketing, nonprofit management, operations management.

MS—International Management Full-time and part-time. 30 to 45 total credits required. 12 to 60 months to complete program. *Concentration:* international management.

MSA—Master of Science in Accounting Full-time and part-time. 30 to 45 total credits required. 12 to 60 months to complete program. *Concentration:* accounting.

MSF—Master of Science in Finance Full-time and part-time. 30 to 45 total credits required. 12 to 60 months to complete program. *Concentration:* finance.

MSIT—Master of Science in Information Technology Full-time and part-time. 30 to 45 total credits required. 12 to 60 months to complete program. *Concentration:* information technology.

RESOURCES AND SERVICES 200 on-campus PCs are available to graduate business students. Access to Internet/World Wide Web, online (class) registration, and online grade reports available. *Personal computer requirements:* Graduate business students are strongly recommended to purchase or lease a personal computer. *Special opportunities include:* An international exchange program and an internship program are available.

Placement services include: Alumni network, career placement, job search course, career counseling/planning, electronic job bank, resume referral, career fairs, job interviews arranged, resume preparation, and career library.

EXPENSES *Tuition (state resident):* Full-time: $10,200. Part-time: $1300 per course. *Tuition (nonresident):* Full-time: $21,300. Part-time: $2500 per course. *Tuition (international):* Full-time: $21,300. Part-time: $2500 per course. *Required fees:* Full-time: $150. Part-time: $75 per semester. Tuition and/or fees vary by class time.

FINANCIAL AID (2007–08) 52 students received aid, including loans, research assistantships, teaching assistantships, and work study. *Financial aid application deadline:* 5/1.

Financial Aid Contact Ms. Judy Keyes, Director of Financial Aid, 100 Morrissey Boulevard, Boston, MA 02125-3393. *Phone:* 617-287-6300. *Fax:* 617-287-6323. *E-mail:* judy.keyes@umb.edu.

INTERNATIONAL STUDENTS 18% of students enrolled are international students. *Services and facilities:* Counseling/support services, ESL/language courses, Housing location assistance, International student housing, International student organization, Language tutoring, Orientation, Visa Services. Financial aid is available to international students. *Required with application:* TOEFL with recommended score of 250 (computer), 600 (paper), or 90 (Internet); proof of adequate funds; proof of health/immunizations.

International Student Contact Suddi St. Ives, Admissions Officer, 100 Morrissey Boulevard, Boston, MA 02125-3393. *Phone:* 617-287-6401. *Fax:* 617-287-6236. *E-mail:* suddi.stives@umb.edu.

APPLICATION *Required:* GMAT, application form, baccalaureate/first degree, essay, 3 letters of recommendation, personal statement, resume/curriculum vitae, transcripts of college work. *Recommended:* Interview, 2 years of work experience. *Application fee:* $40, $60 (international). Applications for domestic and international students are processed on a rolling basis.

Application Contact William Koehler, PhD, Graduate Program Director, 100 Morrissey Boulevard, Boston, MA 02125-3393. *Phone:* 617-287-7720. *Fax:* 617-287-7725. *E-mail:* mba@umb.edu.

University of Massachusetts Dartmouth

Charlton College of Business

North Dartmouth, Massachusetts

Phone: 508-999-8604 **Fax:** 508-999-8183 **E-mail:** graduate@umassd.edu

Business Program(s) Web Site: http://www.umassd.edu/charlton/programs/mba.cfm

Graduate Business Unit Enrollment *Total:* 201 (50 full-time; 151 part-time; 97 women; 39 international). *Average Age:* 32.

Graduate Business Faculty *Total:* 81 (40 full-time; 41 part-time).

Admissions *Applied:* 152. *Admitted:* 123. *Enrolled:* 71. *Average GMAT:* 500.

Academic Calendar Semesters.

Accreditation AACSB—The Association to Advance Collegiate Schools of Business.

DEGREES JD/MBA • MBA

JD/MBA—Master of Business Administration/Juris Doctor Joint Degree Full-time and part-time. Applicants must apply to both schools. *Concentrations:* general MBA, law.

MBA—Master of Business Administration Full-time and part-time. At least 30 total credits required. 12 to 60 months to complete program. *Concentration:* general MBA.

RESOURCES AND SERVICES 650 on-campus PCs are available to graduate business students. Access to Internet/World Wide Web, online (class) registration, and online grade reports available. *Personal computer requirements:* Graduate business students are not required to have a personal computer. *Special opportunities include:* An internship program is available. *Placement services include:* Alumni network, career counseling/planning, electronic job bank, career fairs, job interviews arranged, resume preparation, and career library.

EXPENSES *Tuition (state resident):* Full-time: $9729. Part-time: $405 per credit. *Tuition (nonresident):* Full-time: $18,174. Part-time: $757 per credit. *Tuition (international):* Full-time: $18,174. Part-time: $757 per credit. Tuition and/or fees vary by class time, number of courses or credits taken, academic program, and local reciprocity agreements. *Graduate housing:* Room and board costs vary by number of occupants, type of accommodation, and type of board plan. *Typical cost:* $6405 (room only).

FINANCIAL AID (2007–08) 47 students received aid, including loans, research assistantships, and teaching assistantships. Aid is available to part-time students. *Financial aid application deadline:* 3/1.

Financial Aid Contact Mr. Bruce Palmer, Director of Financial Aid, 285 Old Westport Road, North Dartmouth, MA 02747-2300. *Phone:* 508-999-8632. *Fax:* 508-999-8935. *E-mail:* financialaid@umassd.edu.

INTERNATIONAL STUDENTS 19% of students enrolled are international students. *Services and facilities:* Counseling/support services, ESL/language courses, Housing location assistance, Orientation, Visa Services, International student office. Financial aid is not available to international students. *Required with application:* TOEFL with recommended score of 200 (computer) or 533 (paper); proof of adequate funds; proof of health/immunizations.

International Student Contact Tina Bruen, Director of International Students, 285 Old Westport Road, North Dartmouth, MA 02747-2300. *Phone:* 508-910-6633. *Fax:* 508-910-6411. *E-mail:* cbruen@umassd.edu.

APPLICATION *Required:* GMAT, application form, baccalaureate/first degree, essay, 2 letters of recommendation, resume/curriculum vitae, transcripts of college work. School will accept GRE. *Application fee:* $40, $60 (international). Applications for domestic and international students are processed on a rolling basis.

Application Contact Carol A. Novo, Staff Assistant, Graduate Admissions, 285 Old Westport Road, North Dartmouth, MA 02747-2300. *Phone:* 508-999-8604. *Fax:* 508-999-8183. *E-mail:* graduate@umassd.edu.

University of Massachusetts Lowell

College of Management

Lowell, Massachusetts

Phone: 978-934-2848 **Fax:** 978-934-4017 **E-mail:** kathleen_rourke@uml.edu

Business Program(s) Web Site: http://www.uml.edu/MBA

Graduate Business Unit Enrollment *Total:* 327 (12 full-time; 315 part-time; 104 women; 31 international). *Average Age:* 32.

Graduate Business Faculty *Total:* 30 (20 full-time; 10 part-time).

Admissions *Applied:* 115. *Admitted:* 67. *Enrolled:* 42. *Average GMAT:* 525. *Average GPA:* 3.2

Academic Calendar Semesters.

Accreditation AACSB—The Association to Advance Collegiate Schools of Business.

After Graduation (Class of 2006–07) *Employed within 3 months of graduation:* 95%. *Average starting salary:* $70,930.

DEGREE   MBA

MBA—Master of Business Administration Full-time and part-time. Distance learning option. 2 years business experience. 30 to 48 total credits required. 18 to 60 months to complete program. *Concentrations:* accounting, finance, general MBA, information systems.

RESOURCES AND SERVICES 400 on-campus PCs are available to graduate business students. Access to Internet/World Wide Web, online (class) registration, and online grade reports available. *Personal computer requirements:* Graduate business students are strongly recommended to purchase or lease a personal computer. *Placement services include:* Alumni network, career placement, career counseling/planning, electronic job bank, career fairs, job interviews arranged, and resume preparation.

EXPENSES *Tuition (state resident):* Full-time: $8429.22. Part-time: $468.29 per credit hour. *Tuition (nonresident):* Full-time: $17,160. Part-time: $953.35 per credit hour. *Tuition (international):* Full-time: $17,160.30. Part-time: $953.35 per credit hour. Tuition and/or fees vary by local reciprocity agreements. *Graduate housing:* Room and board costs vary by number of occupants, type of accommodation, and type of board plan. *Typical cost:* $7359 (including board), $4742 (room only).

FINANCIAL AID (2007–08) 7 students received aid, including loans, research assistantships, and teaching assistantships. *Financial aid application deadline:* 6/1.

Financial Aid Contact Ms. Carole King, Director, Financial Aid, Dudan Hall 102, Lowell, MA 01854-2881. *Phone:* 978-934-4237. *E-mail:* carole_king@uml.edu.

INTERNATIONAL STUDENTS 9% of students enrolled are international students. *Services and facilities:* Counseling/support services, Housing location assistance, International student organization, Visa Services. Financial aid is not available to international students. *Required with application:* TOEFL with recommended score of 250 (computer), 600 (paper), or 100 (Internet); proof of adequate funds; proof of health/immunizations.

International Student Contact Anne Dean, International Student Advisor, Graduate School International Office, Dugan Hall 110, Lowell, MA 01854-2881. *Phone:* 978-934-2386. *E-mail:* anne_dean@uml.edu.

APPLICATION *Required:* GMAT, application form, baccalaureate/first degree, 3 letters of recommendation, personal statement, resume/curriculum vitae, transcripts of college work, 2 years of work experience. *Recommended:* Interview. *Application fee:* $30, $60 (international). Applications for domestic and international students are processed on a rolling basis.

Application Contact Ms. Kathleen Rourke, Assistant to the Director of MBA Program, One University Avenue, PA 303, Lowell, MA 01854-2881. *Phone:* 978-934-2848. *Fax:* 978-934-4017. *E-mail:* kathleen_rourke@uml.edu.

University of Phoenix–Boston Campus

College of Graduate Business and Management

Braintree, Massachusetts

Phone: 480-317-6200 **Fax:** 480-643-1479 **E-mail:** beth.barilla@phoenix.edu

Business Program(s) Web Site: http://www.phoenix.edu

DEGREES   MBA

MBA—Master of Business Administration Full-time. Up to 45 total credits required. *Concentration:* administration.

MBA—Master of Business Administration in Global Management Full-time. At least 45 total credits required. *Concentration:* international business.

MBA—Master of Business Administration Full-time. At least 45 total credits required. *Concentration:* administration.

RESOURCES AND SERVICES Access to online grade reports available. *Personal computer requirements:* Graduate business students are strongly recommended to purchase or lease a personal computer. *Placement services include:* Alumni network.

University of Phoenix–Boston Campus (continued)

Application Contact Beth Barilla, Associate Vice President of Student Admissions and Services, Mail Stop AA-K101, 4615 East Elwood Street, Phoenix, AZ 85040-1958. *Phone:* 480-317-6200. *Fax:* 480-643-1479. *E-mail:* beth.barilla@phoenix.edu.

University of Phoenix–Central Massachusetts Campus

College of Graduate Business and Management

Westborough, Massachusetts

Phone: 480-317-6200 **Fax:** 480-643-1479 **E-mail:** beth.barilla@phoenix.edu

DEGREES   MA • MBA

MA—Master of Arts in Organizational Management Full-time. At least 40 total credits required. *Concentration:* organizational management.

MBA—Master of Business Administration Full-time. At least 45 total credits required. *Concentration:* administration.

MBA—Master of Business Administration in Global Management Full-time. At least 45 total credits required. *Concentration:* international business.

RESOURCES AND SERVICES Access to online grade reports available. *Personal computer requirements:* Graduate business students are strongly recommended to purchase or lease a personal computer. *Placement services include:* Alumni network.

Application Contact Beth Barilla, Associate Vice President of Student Admissions and Services, Mail Stop AA-K101, 4615 East Elwood Street, Phoenix, AZ 85040-1958. *Phone:* 480-317-6200. *Fax:* 480-643-1479. *E-mail:* beth.barilla@phoenix.edu.

Western New England College

School of Business

Springfield, Massachusetts

Phone: 413-782-1249 **Fax:** 413-782-1779 **E-mail:** jcadden@wnec.edu

Business Program(s) Web Site: http://www.wnec.edu

Accreditation AACSB—The Association to Advance Collegiate Schools of Business.

DEGREES   MBA • MS

MBA—Master of Business Administration in Sport Management Part-time. Distance learning option. 42 total credits required. 18 to 24 months to complete program. *Concentration:* sports/entertainment management.

MBA—Master of Business Administration Part-time. Distance learning option. 37 total credits required. 18 to 24 months to complete program. *Concentration:* general MBA.

MS—Master of Science in Accounting Part-time. Distance learning option. At least 30 total credits required. 12 to 18 months to complete program. *Concentration:* accounting.

RESOURCES AND SERVICES 489 on-campus PCs are available to graduate business students. Access to Internet/World Wide Web, online (class) registration, and online grade reports available. *Personal computer requirements:* Graduate business students are not required to have a personal computer. *Placement services include:* Alumni network, job search course, career counseling/planning, electronic job bank, resume referral, career fairs, resume preparation, and career library.

Application Contact Ms. Judy Cadden, Assistant Director, Student Services, 1215 Wilbraham Road, Springfield, MA 01119-2654. *Phone:* 413-782-1249. *Fax:* 413-782-1779. *E-mail:* jcadden@wnec.edu.

Worcester Polytechnic Institute

Department of Management

Worcester, Massachusetts

Phone: 508-831-5218 **Fax:** 508-831-5720 **E-mail:** gmp@wpi.edu

Business Program(s) Web Site: http://www.mgt.wpi.edu/Graduate

Graduate Business Unit Enrollment *Total:* 238 (37 full-time; 201 part-time; 57 women; 46 international). *Average Age:* 32.

Graduate Business Faculty *Total:* 24 (20 full-time; 4 part-time).

Admissions *Applied:* 158. *Admitted:* 113. *Enrolled:* 52. *Average GMAT:* 620. *Average GPA:* 3.35

Academic Calendar Semesters.

Accreditation AACSB—The Association to Advance Collegiate Schools of Business.

After Graduation (Class of 2006–07) *Employed within 3 months of graduation:* 100%. *Average starting salary:* $91,500.

DEGREES   M Sc • MBA • MS • MSIT

M Sc—Master of Science in Operations Design and Leadership Full-time and part-time. Distance learning option. 30 to 35 total credits required. 11 to 96 months to complete program. *Concentrations:* industrial administration/management, leadership, manufacturing management, operations management, organizational management, production management, project management, supply chain management, technology management.

MBA—Master of Business Administration Full-time and part-time. Distance learning option. 31 to 49 total credits required. 11 to 96 months to complete program. *Concentrations:* electronic commerce (E-commerce), entrepreneurship, general MBA, industrial administration/management, information systems, information technology, leadership, management, management information systems, manufacturing management, marketing, new venture management, operations management, organizational behavior/development, organizational management, production management, project management, supply chain management, technology management, telecommunications management.

MS—Master of Science in Marketing and Technological Innovation Full-time and part-time. Distance learning option. 30 to 32 total credits required. 11 to 96 months to complete program. *Concentrations:* electronic commerce (E-commerce), entrepreneurship, marketing, new venture management, technology management.

MSIT—Master of Science in Information Technology Full-time and part-time. Distance learning option. 30 to 35 total credits required. 11 to 96 months to complete program. *Concentrations:* information management, information systems, information technology, management information systems, technology management, telecommunications management.

RESOURCES AND SERVICES 350 on-campus PCs are available to graduate business students. Access to Internet/World Wide Web, online (class) registration, and online grade reports available. *Personal computer requirements:* Graduate business students are strongly recommended to purchase or lease a personal computer. *Special opportunities include:* An international exchange program and an internship program are available. *Placement services include:* Alumni network, career placement, job search course, career counseling/planning, electronic job bank, resume referral, career fairs, job interviews arranged, resume preparation, and career library.

EXPENSES *Tuition:* Full-time: $25,529. Part-time: $1042 per credit hour. *Tuition (international):* Full-time: $25,529. Part-time: $1042 per credit hour. *Required fees:* Full-time: $85. *Graduate housing:* Room and board costs vary by campus location, number of occupants, type of accommodation, and type of board plan. *Typical cost:* $8100 (including board), $4500 (room only).

FINANCIAL AID (2007–08) 24 students received aid, including fellowships, loans, and research assistantships. *Financial aid application deadline:* 2/15.

Financial Aid Contact Norm Wilkinson, Director of Graduate Management Programs, 100 Institute Road, Worcester, MA 01609-2280. *Phone:* 508-831-5218. *Fax:* 508-831-5720. *E-mail:* gmp@wpi.edu.

INTERNATIONAL STUDENTS 19% of students enrolled are international students. *Services and facilities:* Counseling/support services, ESL/language courses, Housing location assistance, International student housing, International student organization, Language tutoring, Orientation, Visa Services. Financial aid is available to international students. *Required with application:* TOEFL with recommended score of 250 (computer), 600 (paper), or 100 (Internet); proof of adequate funds; proof of health/immunizations.

International Student Contact Tom Thomsen, Director, International Students and Scholars, 28 Trowbridge Road, Worcester, MA 01609-2280. *Phone:* 508-831-6030. *Fax:* 508-831-6032. *E-mail:* hartvig@wpi.edu.

APPLICATION *Required:* GMAT, application form, baccalaureate/first degree, essay, 3 letters of recommendation, personal statement, resume/curriculum vitae, transcripts of college work. School will accept GRE. *Recommended:* Work experience. *Application fee:* $70. Applications for domestic and international students are processed on a rolling basis.

Application Contact Norm Wilkinson, Director of Graduate Management Programs, 100 Institute Road, Worcester, MA 01609-2280. *Phone:* 508-831-5218. *Fax:* 508-831-5720. *E-mail:* gmp@wpi.edu.

See full description on page 770.

MICHIGAN

Andrews University
School of Business
Berrien Springs, Michigan

Phone: 269-471-3339 **Fax:** 269-471-6158 **E-mail:** schwab@andrews.edu

Business Program(s) Web Site: http://www.andrews.edu/sba/

Graduate Business Unit Enrollment *Total:* 18 (13 full-time; 5 part-time; 9 women; 9 international). *Average Age:* 33.

Graduate Business Faculty *Total:* 11 (9 full-time; 2 part-time).

Admissions *Applied:* 19. *Admitted:* 13. *Enrolled:* 8. *Average GMAT:* 530. *Average GPA:* 3.15

Academic Calendar Semesters.

DEGREES MBA • MSA

MBA—Master of Business Administration Full-time and part-time. At least 33 total credits required. 12 to 72 months to complete program. *Concentration:* management.

MSA—Church Administration Emphasis Full-time and part-time. At least 33 total credits required. 12 to 72 months to complete program. *Concentration:* nonprofit management.

RESOURCES AND SERVICES 148 on-campus PCs are available to graduate business students. Access to Internet/World Wide Web, online (class) registration, and online grade reports available. *Personal computer requirements:* Graduate business students are not required to have a personal computer. *Placement services include:* Alumni network, career placement, career counseling/planning, resume referral, career fairs, job interviews arranged, and resume preparation.

EXPENSES *Tuition:* Full-time: $24,024. Part-time: $728 per credit. *Tuition (international):* Full-time: $24,024. Part-time: $728 per credit. *Required fees:* Full-time: $1600. Part-time: $650 per semester. Tuition and/or fees vary by class time and number of courses or credits taken. *Graduate housing:* Room and board costs vary by campus location, number of occupants, type of accommodation, and type of board plan. *Typical cost:* $8500 (including board), $6600 (room only).

FINANCIAL AID (2007–08) 10 students received aid, including grants, loans, scholarships, and teaching assistantships. Aid is available to part-time students. *Financial aid application deadline:* 7/15.

Financial Aid Contact Cynthia Schulz, Assistant Director of Financial Aid, Administration Building, Berrien Springs, MI 49104-0750. *Phone:* 800-253-2874 Ext. 3221. *Fax:* 269-471-3228. *E-mail:* schulz@andrews.edu.

INTERNATIONAL STUDENTS 50% of students enrolled are international students. *Services and facilities:* Counseling/support services, ESL/language courses, Housing location assistance, International student organization, Language tutoring, Orientation. Financial aid is available to international students. *Required with application:* TOEFL with recommended score of 213 (computer), 550 (paper), or 80 (Internet); proof of adequate funds; proof of health/immunizations.

International Student Contact Najeeb Nakhle, Director of International Student Affairs, Campus Center, Berrien Springs, MI 49104-0300. *Phone:* 800-253-2874 Ext. 6395. *Fax:* 269-471-6388. *E-mail:* nakhle@andrews.edu.

APPLICATION *Required:* GMAT, application form, baccalaureate/first degree, 2 letters of recommendation, personal statement, transcripts of college work. *Application fee:* $40. Applications for domestic and international students are processed on a rolling basis.

Application Contact Dr. Robert Schwab, Graduate Programs Director, Chan Shun Hall, Berrien Springs, MI 49104-0022. *Phone:* 269-471-3339. *Fax:* 269-471-6158. *E-mail:* schwab@andrews.edu.

Aquinas College
School of Management
Grand Rapids, Michigan

Phone: 616-632-2922 **Fax:** 616-732-4489 **E-mail:** vangecyn@aquinas.edu

Business Program(s) Web Site: http://www.aquinas.edu/management/index.html

Graduate Business Unit Enrollment *Total:* 75 (7 full-time; 68 part-time; 46 women; 2 international). *Average Age:* 31.

Graduate Business Faculty *Total:* 44 (30 full-time; 14 part-time).

Admissions *Applied:* 30. *Admitted:* 28. *Enrolled:* 23. *Average GMAT:* 463.

Academic Calendar Semesters.

After Graduation (Class of 2006–07) *Employed within 3 months of graduation:* 83%. *Average starting salary:* $45,000.

DEGREE MM

MM—Master of Management Full-time and part-time. At least 39 total credits required. 18 to 48 months to complete program. *Concentrations:* arts administration/management, health care, international business, marketing, organizational behavior/development.

RESOURCES AND SERVICES 140 on-campus PCs are available to graduate business students. Access to Internet/World Wide Web and online (class) registration available. *Personal computer requirements:* Graduate business students are strongly recommended to purchase or lease a personal computer. *Special opportunities include:* An internship program is available. *Placement services include:* Alumni network, career placement, job search course, career counseling/planning, electronic job bank, resume referral, career fairs, job interviews arranged, resume preparation, and career library.

Aquinas College (continued)

EXPENSES *Tuition:* Full-time: $12,258. Part-time: $454 per credit hour. *Tuition (international):* Full-time: $12,258. Part-time: $454 per credit hour.

FINANCIAL AID (2007–08) 28 students received aid, including loans and scholarships. Aid is available to part-time students. *Financial aid application deadline:* 6/15.

Financial Aid Contact Mr. David Steffee, Director of Financial Aid, 1607 Robinson Road, SE, Grand Rapids, MI 49506-1799. *Phone:* 616-632-2895. *Fax:* 616-732-4547. *E-mail:* steffdav@aquinas.edu.

INTERNATIONAL STUDENTS 3% of students enrolled are international students. *Services and facilities:* Counseling/support services, Housing location assistance, Visa Services. Financial aid is not available to international students. *Required with application:* TOEFL with recommended score of 213 (computer) or 550 (paper); proof of adequate funds; proof of health/immunizations.

International Student Contact Paula Meehan, Vice President for Enrollment Management, 1607 Robinson Road, SE, Grand Rapids, MI 49506-1799. *Phone:* 616-632-2852. *Fax:* 616-732-4469. *E-mail:* meehapau@aquinas.edu.

APPLICATION *Required:* GMAT, application form, baccalaureate/first degree, interview, 3 letters of recommendation, personal statement, transcripts of college work, 2 years of work experience. *Recommended:* Essay, resume/curriculum vitae. Applications for domestic and international students are processed on a rolling basis.

Application Contact Cynthia VanGelderen, Dean, 1607 Robinson Road, SE, Grand Rapids, MI 49506-1799. *Phone:* 616-632-2922. *Fax:* 616-732-4489. *E-mail:* vangecyn@aquinas.edu.

Baker College Center for Graduate Studies

Graduate Programs

Flint, Michigan

Phone: 810-766-4390 **Fax:** 810-766-4399 **E-mail:** cgurde01@baker.edu

Business Program(s) Web Site: http://www.baker.edu/graduate

Graduate Business Unit Enrollment *Total:* 1,010 (450 full-time; 560 part-time).

Graduate Business Faculty *Total:* 310 (10 full-time; 300 part-time).

Admissions *Applied:* 954. *Admitted:* 660. *Enrolled:* 601. *Average GMAT:* 520. *Average GPA:* 2.98

Academic Calendar Quarters.

After Graduation (Class of 2006–07) *Employed within 3 months of graduation:* 100%.

DEGREE MBA

MBA—Master of Business Administration Full-time and part-time. Distance learning option. At least 50 total credits required. 18 to 48 months to complete program. *Concentrations:* accounting, administration of technological information, finance, general MBA, health care, human resources management, industrial administration/management, international business, leadership, management, marketing.

RESOURCES AND SERVICES Access to Internet/World Wide Web, online (class) registration, and online grade reports available. *Personal computer requirements:* Graduate business students are required to have a personal computer. *Placement services include:* Alumni network, job search course, career counseling/planning, electronic job bank, resume referral, resume preparation, and career library.

EXPENSES *Tuition:* Full-time: $7920. Part-time: $330 per credit hour. *Tuition (international):* Full-time: $7920. Part-time: $330 per credit hour.

FINANCIAL AID (2007–08) 600 students received aid, including grants and loans. Aid is available to part-time students. *Financial aid application deadline:* 9/1.

Financial Aid Contact Mrs. Krista McGuire, Director of Financial Aid, 1116 West Bristol Road, Flint, MI 48507-5508. *Phone:* 800-469-3165. *Fax:* 810-766-4399. *E-mail:* krista.mcguire@baker.edu.

INTERNATIONAL STUDENTS Financial aid is not available to international students. *Required with application:* TOEFL with recommended score of 213 (computer) or 550 (paper); proof of adequate funds; proof of health/immunizations. *Recommended with application:* IELT; TWE.

International Student Contact Mr. Chuck J. Gurden, Vice President for Graduate Admissions, 1116 West Bristol Road, Flint, MI 48507-5508. *Phone:* 810-766-4390. *Fax:* 810-766-4399. *E-mail:* cgurde01@baker.edu.

APPLICATION *Required:* Application form, baccalaureate/first degree, essay, 3 letters of recommendation, personal statement, resume/curriculum vitae, transcripts of college work, 4 years of work experience. School will accept GMAT, GRE, and MAT. *Recommended:* Interview. *Application fee:* $25. Applications for domestic and international students are processed on a rolling basis.

Application Contact Mr. Chuck J. Gurden, Vice President for Graduate Admissions, 1116 West Bristol Road, Flint, MI 48507-5508. *Phone:* 810-766-4390. *Fax:* 810-766-4399. *E-mail:* cgurde01@baker.edu.

See full description on page 572.

Cleary University

Program in Business Administration

Ann Arbor, Michigan

Phone: 517-548-3670 **Fax:** 517-552-7805 **E-mail:** cbono@cleary.edu

Business Program(s) Web Site: http://www.cleary.edu

Graduate Business Unit Enrollment *Total:* 102 (1 full-time; 101 part-time; 56 women; 4 international). *Average Age:* 35.

Graduate Business Faculty *Total:* 19 (3 full-time; 16 part-time).

Admissions *Applied:* 38. *Admitted:* 37. *Enrolled:* 30. *Average GPA:* 3.0

Academic Calendar Quarters.

After Graduation (Class of 2006–07) *Employed within 3 months of graduation:* 98%.

DEGREE MBA

MBA—Master of Business Administration Full-time and part-time. Distance learning option. Accounting concentration requires an undergraduate degree in accounting. 52 total credits required. 19 to 22 months to complete program. *Concentrations:* accounting, management, nonprofit management.

RESOURCES AND SERVICES 60 on-campus PCs are available to graduate business students. Access to Internet/World Wide Web and online grade reports available. *Personal computer requirements:* Graduate business students are required to have a personal computer. *Placement services include:* Alumni network, job search course, career counseling/planning, electronic job bank, resume referral, career fairs, job interviews arranged, resume preparation, and career library.

EXPENSES *Tuition:* Full-time: $11,160. Part-time: $465 per credit hour. *Tuition (international):* Full-time: $11,160. Part-time: $465 per credit hour.

FINANCIAL AID (2007–08) 68 students received aid, including grants, loans, scholarships, and work study. Aid is available to part-time students. *Financial aid application deadline:* 8/15.

Financial Aid Contact Vesta Smith-Campbell, Director of Financial Aid, 3750 Cleary Drive, Howell, MI 48843. *Phone:* 517-548-3670 Ext. 2220. *Fax:* 517-552-8022. *E-mail:* vscampbell@cleary.edu.

INTERNATIONAL STUDENTS 4% of students enrolled are international students. Financial aid is not available to international students. *Required with application:* TOEFL with recommended score of 213 (computer) or 550 (paper); proof of adequate funds.

International Student Contact Rose Smith, 3601 Plymouth Road, Ann Arbor, MI 48105. *Phone:* 800-686-1883. *Fax:* 734-332-4646. *E-mail:* rosemsmith@cleary.edu.

APPLICATION *Required:* Application form, baccalaureate/first degree, essay, 3 letters of recommendation, personal statement, resume/curriculum vitae, transcripts of college work. *Recommended:* Interview. *Application fee:* $50. Applications for domestic and international students are processed on a rolling basis.

Application Contact Carrie Bonofiglio, Director of Student Recruiting, 3750 Cleary Drive, Howell, MI 48843. *Phone:* 517-548-3670. *Fax:* 517-552-7805. *E-mail:* cbono@cleary.edu.

Davenport University
Sneden Graduate School
Grand Rapids, Michigan

Phone: 616-698-7111 **Fax:** 616-698-0333 **E-mail:** darylkingrey@davenport.edu

Business Program(s) Web Site: http://www.davenport.edu

Graduate Business Unit Enrollment *Total:* 789 (495 full-time; 294 part-time; 459 women; 95 international). *Average Age:* 31.

Graduate Business Faculty *Total:* 74 (12 full-time; 62 part-time).

Admissions *Average GMAT:* 450. *Average GPA:* 3.62

Academic Calendar Semesters.

After Graduation (Class of 2006–07) *Employed within 3 months of graduation:* 93%.

DEGREES   MBA

MBA—Master of Business Full-time and part-time. Distance learning option. 39 to 60 total credits required. 12 to 72 months to complete program. *Concentration:* strategic management.

MBA—Master of Business Administration Full-time and part-time. Distance learning option. 39 to 60 total credits required. 12 to 72 months to complete program. *Concentration:* accounting.

MBA—Master of Business Administration Full-time and part-time. Distance learning option. 39 to 60 total credits required. 12 to 72 months to complete program. *Concentration:* human resources management.

MBA—Master of Business Administration Full-time and part-time. Distance learning option. 39 to 60 total credits required. 12 to 72 months to complete program. *Concentration:* finance.

MBA—Master of Business Administration in Health Care Management Full-time and part-time. Distance learning option. 39 to 60 total credits required. 12 to 72 months to complete program. *Concentration:* health care.

RESOURCES AND SERVICES 3,224 on-campus PCs are available to graduate business students. Access to Internet/World Wide Web, online (class) registration, and online grade reports available. *Personal computer requirements:* Graduate business students are not required to have a personal computer. *Placement services include:* Career placement, career counseling/planning, electronic job bank, career fairs, and resume preparation.

EXPENSES *Tuition:* Full-time: $8442. Part-time: $455 per credit. *Typical graduate housing cost:* $4750 (room only).

FINANCIAL AID (2007–08) 119 students received aid, including grants, loans, scholarships, and work study. Aid is available to part-time students. *Financial aid application deadline:* 9/1.

Financial Aid Contact Mr. David DeBoer, Executive Director of Financial Aid, 415 East Fulton Street, Grand Rapids, MI 49503. *Phone:* 616-451-3400. *Fax:* 616-732-1167. *E-mail:* david.deboer@davenport.edu.

INTERNATIONAL STUDENTS 12% of students enrolled are international students. *Services and facilities:* ESL/language courses, Housing location assistance. Financial aid is available to international students. *Required with application:* TOEFL with recommended score of 213 (computer) or 550 (paper); proof of adequate funds.

International Student Contact Mr. Alex Akulli, Senior Advisor for Study Abroad and International Students, International Office, 6191 Kraft Avenue SE, Grand Rapids, MI 49512. *Phone:* 616-698-7111 Ext. 5317. *Fax:* 616-554-5213. *E-mail:* international@davenport.edu.

APPLICATION *Required:* GMAT, application form, baccalaureate/first degree, essay, 2 letters of recommendation, resume/curriculum vitae, transcripts of college work, 2 years of work experience. *Recommended:* Interview. *Application fee:* $25. Applications for domestic and international students are processed on a rolling basis.

Application Contact Mr. Daryl Kingrey, Executive Director of Admissions, 6191 Kraft Avenue SE, Grand Rapids, MI 49512. *Phone:* 616-698-7111. *Fax:* 616-698-0333. *E-mail:* darylkingrey@davenport.edu.

Eastern Michigan University
College of Business
Ypsilanti, Michigan

Phone: 734-487-4444 **Fax:** 734-483-1316 **E-mail:** dawn.gaymer@emich.edu

Business Program(s) Web Site: http://www.cob.emich.edu/gr/

Graduate Business Unit Enrollment *Total:* 753 (279 full-time; 474 part-time; 394 women; 208 international). *Average Age:* 28.

Graduate Business Faculty *Total:* 120 (88 full-time; 32 part-time).

Admissions *Applied:* 502. *Admitted:* 302. *Enrolled:* 173. *Average GMAT:* 451. *Average GPA:* 3.01

Academic Calendar Semesters.

Accreditation AACSB—The Association to Advance Collegiate Schools of Business.

After Graduation (Class of 2006–07) *Employed within 3 months of graduation:* 80%. *Average starting salary:* $60,000.

DEGREES   MBA • MS • MSIMC

MBA—Master of Business Administration Full-time and part-time. 36 to 57 total credits required. 12 to 72 months to complete program. *Concentrations:* electronic commerce (E-commerce), entrepreneurship, finance, general MBA, human resources management, international business, management information systems, marketing, nonprofit management, organizational behavior/development, supply chain management.

MS—Master of Science in Accounting Full-time and part-time. 30 to 51 total credits required. 12 to 72 months to complete program. *Concentrations:* accounting, information systems, taxation.

MS—Master of Science in Human Resources and Organizational Development Full-time and part-time. 30 to 39 total credits required. 12 to 72 months to complete program. *Concentrations:* human resources management, organizational behavior/development.

MS—Master of Science in Information Systems Full-time and part-time. 30 to 48 total credits required. 12 to 72 months to complete program. *Concentration:* management information systems.

MSIMC—Master of Science in Integrated Marketing Communications Full-time and part-time. Distance learning option. 36 total credits required. 12 to 72 months to complete program. *Concentration:* marketing.

RESOURCES AND SERVICES 1,714 on-campus PCs are available to graduate business students. Access to Internet/World Wide Web, online (class) registration, and online grade reports available. *Personal computer*

Eastern Michigan University (continued)

requirements: Graduate business students are not required to have a personal computer. *Special opportunities include:* An international exchange program and an internship program are available. *Placement services include:* Alumni network, career placement, job search course, career counseling/planning, electronic job bank, career fairs, job interviews arranged, resume preparation, and career library.

EXPENSES *Tuition (state resident):* Full-time: $8388. *Tuition (nonresident):* Full-time: $14,899. *Tuition (international):* Full-time: $14,899. *Required fees:* Full-time: $1134. Tuition and/or fees vary by academic program. *Typical graduate housing cost:* $6942 (including board), $3260 (room only).

FINANCIAL AID (2007–08) 301 students received aid, including fellowships, grants, loans, research assistantships, scholarships, and work study. Aid is available to part-time students. *Financial aid application deadline:* 3/15.

Financial Aid Contact Ms. Cynthia Van Pelt, Associate Director, Office of Financial Aid, 403 Pierce Hall, Ypsilanti, MI 48197. *Phone:* 734-487-0455. *Fax:* 734-487-4281. *E-mail:* cynthia.vanpelt@emich.edu.

INTERNATIONAL STUDENTS 28% of students enrolled are international students. *Services and facilities:* Counseling/support services, ESL/language courses, Housing location assistance, International student organization, Orientation, Visa Services. Financial aid is available to international students. *Required with application:* TOEFL with recommended score of 213 (computer), 550 (paper), or 79 (Internet); proof of adequate funds; proof of health/immunizations. *Recommended with application:* IELT with recommended score of 6.5; TWE with recommended score of 4.

International Student Contact Ms. Esther L. Gunal, Associate Director, Office of International Students, 244 Student Center, Ypsilanti, MI 48197. *Phone:* 734-487-3116. *Fax:* 734-487-0303. *E-mail:* esther.gunel@emich.edu.

APPLICATION *Required:* GMAT, application form, baccalaureate/first degree, personal statement, transcripts of college work. School will accept GRE. *Recommended:* Letter(s) of recommendation, resume/curriculum vitae, work experience. *Application fee:* $35. Applications for domestic and international students are processed on a rolling basis.

Application Contact Dawn Gaymer, Assistant Dean, Graduate Business Programs, 404 Gary M. Owen Building, Ypsilanti, MI 48197. *Phone:* 734-487-4444. *Fax:* 734-483-1316. *E-mail:* dawn.gaymer@emich.edu.

Grand Valley State University
Seidman College of Business
Allendale, Michigan

Phone: 616-331-7387 **Fax:** 616-331-7389 **E-mail:** bajemac@gvsu.edu

Business Program(s) Web Site: http://www.gvsu.edu/business

Graduate Business Unit Enrollment *Total:* 390 (79 full-time; 311 part-time; 148 women; 18 international). *Average Age:* 29.

Graduate Business Faculty *Total:* 35 (21 full-time; 14 part-time).

Admissions *Applied:* 255. *Admitted:* 225. *Enrolled:* 184. *Average GMAT:* 567. *Average GPA:* 3.3

Academic Calendar Semesters.

Accreditation AACSB—The Association to Advance Collegiate Schools of Business.

After Graduation (Class of 2006–07) *Employed within 3 months of graduation:* 93%.

DEGREES JD/M Tax • JD/MBA • M Acc • MA/MBA • MBA/MSN • MS

JD/M Tax—Juris Doctor/Master of Taxation Full-time and part-time. Must be admitted to the MST program through the School of Business and to the JD program through the Michigan State University-Detroit College of Law. 97 to 111 total credits required. 48 to 60 months to complete program. *Concentration:* combined degrees.

JD/MBA—Juris Doctor/Master of Business Administration Full-time and part-time. Must be admitted to the MBA program through the School of Business and to the JD program through the Michigan State University College of Law. 97 to 114 total credits required. 48 to 60 months to complete program. *Concentration:* combined degrees.

M Acc—Master of Science in Accounting Full-time and part-time. 33 to 51 total credits required. 8 to 96 months to complete program. *Concentration:* accounting.

MA/MBA—Master of Arts/Master of Business Administration Full-time and part-time. 33 to 55 total credits required. 12 to 96 months to complete program. *Concentrations:* business studies, health administration, technology management.

MBA/MSN—Master of Business Administration/Master of Science in Nursing Full-time and part-time. Must be admitted by both the School of Business and the School of Nursing. 69 to 88 total credits required. 60 to 96 months to complete program. *Concentration:* combined degrees.

MS—Master of Science in Taxation Full-time and part-time. 33 to 45 total credits required. 12 to 96 months to complete program. *Concentration:* taxation.

RESOURCES AND SERVICES 1,800 on-campus PCs are available to graduate business students. Access to Internet/World Wide Web, online (class) registration, and online grade reports available. *Personal computer requirements:* Graduate business students are not required to have a personal computer. *Special opportunities include:* An international exchange program is available. *Placement services include:* Alumni network, career placement, career counseling/planning, resume referral, career fairs, resume preparation, and career library.

EXPENSES *Tuition (state resident):* Part-time: $385 per credit hour. *Tuition (nonresident):* Part-time: $610 per credit hour. *Tuition (international):* Part-time: $610 per credit hour. *Typical graduate housing cost:* $12,000 (including board).

FINANCIAL AID (2007–08) 104 students received aid, including fellowships, loans, research assistantships, scholarships, and work study. Aid is available to part-time students. *Financial aid application deadline:* 2/15.

Financial Aid Contact Mr. Ed Kerestly, Director, Financial Aid, 100 STU, Allendale, MI 49401. *Phone:* 616-331-3234. *Fax:* 616-331-3180. *E-mail:* kerestle@gvsu.edu.

INTERNATIONAL STUDENTS 5% of students enrolled are international students. *Services and facilities:* Counseling/support services, ESL/language courses, Housing location assistance, International student organization, Orientation, Visa Services. Financial aid is available to international students. *Required with application:* TOEFL with recommended score of 213 (computer), 550 (paper), or 80 (Internet); proof of adequate funds; proof of health/immunizations.

International Student Contact Chris Hendree, International Admissions, 300 STU, Allendale, MI 49401. *Phone:* 616-331-2025. *Fax:* 616-331-2000. *E-mail:* hendreec@gvsu.edu.

APPLICATION *Required:* GMAT, application form, baccalaureate/first degree, personal statement, transcripts of college work. *Application fee:* $30. Applications for domestic and international students are processed on a rolling basis.

Application Contact Ms. Claudia Bajema, Graduate Business Programs Director, 401 Fulton Street West, 306C DeVos, Grand Rapids, MI 49504. *Phone:* 616-331-7387. *Fax:* 616-331-7389. *E-mail:* bajemac@gvsu.edu.

Kettering University
Graduate School
Flint, Michigan

Phone: 810-762-7953 **Fax:** 810-762-9935 **E-mail:** afleming@kettering.edu

Business Program(s) Web Site: http://www.kettering.edu

Graduate Business Unit Enrollment *Total:* 465 (7 full-time; 458 part-time; 126 women; 4 international). *Average Age:* 33.

Graduate Business Faculty *Total:* 10 (8 full-time; 2 part-time).

Admissions *Applied:* 146. *Admitted:* 129. *Enrolled:* 90. *Average GPA:* 3.02

Academic Calendar Quarters.

Accreditation ACBSP—The American Council of Business Schools and Programs.

After Graduation (Class of 2006–07) *Employed within 3 months of graduation:* 100%.

DEGREES MBA • MS

MBA—Master of Business Administration Full-time and part-time. Distance learning option. Prerequisite coursework in accounting, statistics, economics, marketing, and management. At least 48 total credits required. *Concentrations:* engineering, general MBA, information technology.

MS—Master of Science in Engineering Management Full-time and part-time. Distance learning option. Prerequisite coursework in accounting, statistics, economics, marketing, and management. At least 40 total credits required. *Concentration:* engineering.

MS—Master of Science in Information Technology Full-time and part-time. Distance learning option. Prerequisite coursework in undergraduate programming or six months of professional experience as a programmer, plus completed coursework in accounting, marketing, and management. At least 40 total credits required. *Concentration:* information technology.

MS—Master of Science in Manufacturing Management Full-time and part-time. Distance learning option. Prerequisite coursework in accounting, statistics, economics, marketing, and management. At least 40 total credits required. *Concentration:* manufacturing management.

MS—Master of Science in Manufacturing Operations Full-time and part-time. Distance learning option. Two letters of recommendation are required as part of the application process. At least 40 total credits required. *Concentration:* manufacturing management.

MS—Master of Science in Operations Management Full-time and part-time. Distance learning option. Prerequisite coursework in accounting, statistics, economics, marketing, and management. At least 40 total credits required. *Concentration:* operations management.

RESOURCES AND SERVICES 180 on-campus PCs are available to graduate business students. Access to Internet/World Wide Web, online (class) registration, and online grade reports available. *Personal computer requirements:* Graduate business students are required to have a personal computer. *Special opportunities include:* An international exchange program is available.

EXPENSES *Tuition:* Part-time: $674 per credit hour. *Tuition (international):* Part-time: $674 per credit hour. Tuition and/or fees vary by class time, number of courses or credits taken, campus location, and academic program.

FINANCIAL AID (2007–08) 94 students received aid, including fellowships, grants, loans, research assistantships, scholarships, teaching assistantships, and work study. Aid is available to part-time students. *Financial aid application deadline:* 5/31.

Financial Aid Contact Diane Bice, Director of Financial Aid, 1700 West Third Avenue, Flint, MI 48504-4898. *Phone:* 810-762-7491. *Fax:* 810-762-9807. *E-mail:* dbice@kettering.edu.

INTERNATIONAL STUDENTS 0.9% of students enrolled are international students. *Services and facilities:* Counseling/support services, Housing location assistance, International student organization, Orientation, Visa Services, Scheduling assistance, Cultural exposure. Financial aid is not available to international students. *Required with application:* TOEFL with recommended score of 213 (computer) or 550 (paper); proof of adequate funds; proof of health/immunizations.

International Student Contact Heidi Schmoll, Coordinator, International Programs, 1700 West Third Avenue, Flint, MI 48504-4898. *Phone:* 810-762-9869. *Fax:* 810-762-9755. *E-mail:* hschmoll@kettering.edu.

APPLICATION *Required:* Application form, baccalaureate/first degree, transcripts of college work. *Application fee:* $0, $50 (international). Applications for domestic and international students are processed on a rolling basis.

Application Contact Allison Fleming, Graduate Admissions Assistant, 1700 West Third Avenue, Flint, MI 48504-4898. *Phone:* 810-762-7953. *Fax:* 810-762-9935. *E-mail:* afleming@kettering.edu.

Lawrence Technological University
College of Management
Southfield, Michigan

Phone: 248-204-3050 **Fax:** 248-204-3099 **E-mail:** mgtdean@ltu.edu

Business Program(s) Web Site: http://www.ltu.edu/management

Graduate Business Unit Enrollment *Total:* 819 (13 full-time; 806 part-time; 293 women; 181 international). *Average Age:* 35.

Graduate Business Faculty *Total:* 90 (15 full-time; 75 part-time).

Admissions *Applied:* 412. *Admitted:* 330. *Enrolled:* 193. *Average GPA:* 3.2

Academic Calendar Semesters.

Accreditation ACBSP—The American Council of Business Schools and Programs.

After Graduation (Class of 2006–07) *Employed within 3 months of graduation:* 90%. *Average starting salary:* $65,000.

DEGREES MBA • MS

MBA—Master of Business Administration Full-time and part-time. Distance learning option. 36 to 48 total credits required. 18 to 36 months to complete program. *Concentrations:* finance, human resources management, international business, management information systems, nonprofit management, operations management, project management.

MS—Master of Science in Information Systems Full-time and part-time. 30 to 42 total credits required. 18 to 36 months to complete program. *Concentrations:* project management, resources management.

MS—Master of Science in Operations Management Full-time and part-time. 30 to 32 total credits required. 15 to 36 months to complete program. *Concentrations:* manufacturing management, project management.

RESOURCES AND SERVICES 150 on-campus PCs are available to graduate business students. Access to Internet/World Wide Web, online (class) registration, and online grade reports available. *Personal computer requirements:* Graduate business students are strongly recommended to purchase or lease a personal computer. *Placement services include:* Alumni network, career placement, career counseling/planning, electronic job bank, resume referral, career fairs, job interviews arranged, resume preparation, and career library.

EXPENSES *Tuition:* Full-time: $10,221. *Tuition (international):* Full-time: $10,221. *Required fees:* Full-time: $220. Part-time: $220 per year. *Graduate housing:* Room and board costs vary by number of occupants, type of accommodation, and type of board plan. *Typical cost:* $7872 (including board), $5292 (room only).

FINANCIAL AID (2007–08) 453 students received aid, including grants, loans, and work study. Aid is available to part-time students. *Financial aid application deadline:* 3/1.

Financial Aid Contact Mark Martin, Director, Financial Aid, 21000 West Ten Mile Road, Southfield, MI 48075-1058. *Phone:* 248-204-2126. *Fax:* 248-204-2228. *E-mail:* m_martin@ltu.edu.

INTERNATIONAL STUDENTS 22% of students enrolled are international students. *Services and facilities:* Counseling/support services, ESL/language courses, Housing location assistance, International student housing, International student organization, Language tutoring, Orientation, Visa Services. Financial aid is available to international students. *Required with application:* TOEFL with recommended score of 213

Lawrence Technological University (continued)

(computer), 550 (paper), or 79 (Internet); proof of adequate funds. *Recommended with application:* TWE.

International Student Contact Chinling Lin, Chief Operating Officer, 21000 West Ten Mile Road, Southfield, MI 48075-1058. *Phone:* 248-204-3050. *Fax:* 248-204-3099. *E-mail:* c_lin@ltu.edu.

APPLICATION *Required:* Application form, baccalaureate/first degree, resume/curriculum vitae, transcripts of college work. *Recommended:* Interview, letter(s) of recommendation, work experience. *Application fee:* $50. Applications for domestic and international students are processed on a rolling basis.

Application Contact Mina Jena, Administrative Assistant, 21000 West Ten Mile Road, Southfield, MI 48075-1058. *Phone:* 248-204-3050. *Fax:* 248-204-3099. *E-mail:* mgtdean@ltu.edu.

See full description on page 654.

Madonna University
School of Business
Livonia, Michigan

Phone: 734-432-5666 **Fax:** 734-432-5862 **E-mail:** kellums@smtp.munet.edu

Business Program(s) Web Site: http://ww3.munet.edu/gradstdy

DEGREES MBA • MSBA

MBA—Master of Business Administration Full-time and part-time. 40 to 46 total credits required. 24 to 72 months to complete program. *Concentrations:* administration, business studies, electronic commerce (E-commerce), human resources management, information management, international and area business studies, international banking, international business, international finance, leadership, marketing, nonprofit management, operations management, quality management.

MSBA—Master of Science in Business Administration Full-time and part-time. Distance learning option. At least 36 total credits required. 24 to 72 months to complete program. *Concentration:* leadership.

MSBA—Master of Science in Business Administration in International Business Full-time and part-time. At least 36 total credits required. 24 to 72 months to complete program. *Concentrations:* international and area business studies, international economics, international finance, international management, international marketing, international trade.

MSBA—Master of Science in Business Administration in Quality and Operations Management Full-time and part-time. Distance learning option. At least 36 total credits required. 24 to 72 months to complete program. *Concentrations:* operations management, quality management.

MSBA—Master of Science in Business Administration/Master of Science in Nursing Full-time and part-time. At least 60 total credits required. 36 to 72 months to complete program. *Concentrations:* human resources management, information management, leadership, marketing, nonprofit management, operations management, quality management.

RESOURCES AND SERVICES 74 on-campus PCs are available to graduate business students. Access to Internet/World Wide Web and online (class) registration available. *Personal computer requirements:* Graduate business students are strongly recommended to purchase or lease a personal computer. *Placement services include:* Career placement, career fairs, and resume preparation.

Application Contact Sandra Kellums, Coordinator of Graduate Admissions and Records, 36600 Schoolcraft Road, Livonia, MI 48150-1173. *Phone:* 734-432-5666. *Fax:* 734-432-5862. *E-mail:* kellums@smtp.munet.edu.

Michigan State University
Eli Broad Graduate School of Management
East Lansing, Michigan

Phone: 517-355-7604 **Fax:** 517-353-1649

Business Program(s) Web Site: http://www.bus.msu.edu/graduate/

Academic Calendar Semesters.

Accreditation AACSB—The Association to Advance Collegiate Schools of Business.

DEGREES EMBA • MBA • MS

EMBA—Executive Master of Business Administration in Advanced Management Part-time. 8 years of work experience with minimum of 3-4 years management experience and employer nomination required. At least 45 total credits required. Maximum of 21 months to complete program. *Concentration:* general MBA.

MBA—Full-Time Master of Business Administration Full-time. Minimum GMAT raw verbal score of 25 and raw quantitative score of 33 required. At least 57 total credits required. Maximum of 21 months to complete program. *Concentrations:* accounting, business information science, finance, general MBA, hospitality management, human resources management, information systems, international business, international management, leadership, logistics, management, management information systems, marketing, operations management, organizational behavior/development, supply chain management, transportation management.

MBA—Weekend Master of Business Administration Program Part-time. 4 years of professional work experience and employer nomination required. At least 45 total credits required. Maximum of 17 months to complete program. *Concentration:* general MBA.

MS—Master of Science in Business Management of Manufacturing Full-time. At least 39 total credits required. Maximum of 21 months to complete program. *Concentration:* management.

MS—Master of Science in Food Service Management Full-time. At least 30 total credits required. Maximum of 21 months to complete program. *Concentration:* management.

MS—Master of Science in Logistics Part-time. At least 36 total credits required. 19 to 25 months to complete program. *Concentration:* logistics.

MS—Master of Science in Manufacturing and Innovation Part-time. At least 31 total credits required. 16 to 31 months to complete program. *Concentration:* manufacturing management.

MS—Master of Science in Professional Accounting Full-time. At least 31 total credits required. Maximum of 21 months to complete program. *Concentrations:* accounting, management information systems, taxation.

RESOURCES AND SERVICES Access to Internet/World Wide Web, online (class) registration, and online grade reports available. *Personal computer requirements:* Graduate business students are required to have a personal computer. *Special opportunities include:* An international exchange program and an internship program are available. *Placement services include:* Alumni network, career placement, career counseling/planning, electronic job bank, resume referral, career fairs, job interviews arranged, resume preparation, and career library.

FINANCIAL AID (2007–08) Fellowships, grants, loans, research assistantships, scholarships, teaching assistantships, and work study. *Financial aid application deadline:* 3/14.

Financial Aid Contact Office of Financial Aid, 252 Student Services Building, East Lansing, MI 48824-1113. *Phone:* 517-353-5940. *Fax:* 517-432-1155. *E-mail:* finaid@msu.edu.

INTERNATIONAL STUDENTS *Services and facilities:* Counseling/support services, ESL/language courses, Housing location assistance, International student housing, International student organization, Orientation, Visa Services. Financial aid is available to international students. *Required with application:* TOEFL with recommended score of 250 (computer) or 600 (paper); proof of adequate funds.

International Student Contact Office for International Students and Scholars, 103 International Center, East Lansing, MI 48824. *Phone:* 517-353-1720. *Fax:* 517-355-4657. *E-mail:* oiss@msu.edu.

APPLICATION *Required:* GMAT, application form, baccalaureate/first degree, essay, interview, 2 letters of recommendation, resume/curriculum vitae, transcripts of college work, 2 years of work experience. *Application fee:* $85. *Deadlines:* 11/1 for fall, 1/9 for winter, 3/16 for spring, 5/2 for summer, 11/1 for fall (international), 1/9 for winter (international), 3/16 for spring (international).

Application Contact Director, MBA Admissions, 215 Eppley Center, East Lansing, MI 48824-1121. *Phone:* 517-355-7604. *Fax:* 517-353-1649.

Michigan Technological University
School of Business and Economics
Houghton, Michigan

Phone: 906-487-3055 **Fax:** 906-487-2944 **E-mail:** mba@mtu.edu

Business Program(s) Web Site: http://www.mba.mtu.edu/

Graduate Business Unit Enrollment *Total:* 29 (16 full-time; 13 part-time; 14 women; 3 international). *Average Age:* 32.

Graduate Business Faculty *Total:* 29 (26 full-time; 3 part-time).

Admissions *Applied:* 24. *Admitted:* 20. *Enrolled:* 12. *Average GMAT:* 530. *Average GPA:* 3.4

Academic Calendar Semesters.

Accreditation AACSB—The Association to Advance Collegiate Schools of Business.

After Graduation (Class of 2006–07) *Employed within 3 months of graduation:* 100%. *Average starting salary:* $67,445.

DEGREES   MBA • MS

MBA—Master of Business Administration Full-time and part-time. GPA 2.9, GMAT 530, 6 undergraduate prerequisites (Accounting 1, Calculus, Economics 1, Economic Decision Analysis, Statistics, Quantitative Problem Solving). 36 total credits required. 12 to 60 months to complete program. *Concentration:* general MBA.

MS—Master of Science in Mineral Economics Full-time and part-time. 30 to 39 total credits required. 9 to 60 months to complete program. *Concentration:* resources management.

RESOURCES AND SERVICES 25 on-campus PCs are available to graduate business students. Access to Internet/World Wide Web, online (class) registration, and online grade reports available. *Personal computer requirements:* Graduate business students are not required to have a personal computer. *Placement services include:* Career placement, career counseling/planning, career fairs, job interviews arranged, resume preparation, and career library.

EXPENSES *Tuition (state resident):* Full-time: $19,260. Part-time: $535 per credit hour. *Tuition (nonresident):* Full-time: $19,260. Part-time: $535 per credit hour. *Tuition (international):* Full-time: $19,260. Part-time: $535 per credit hour. *Required fees:* Full-time: $848. *Graduate housing:* Room and board costs vary by number of occupants, type of accommodation, and type of board plan. *Typical cost:* $8686 (including board), $5059 (room only).

FINANCIAL AID (2007–08) 7 students received aid, including loans, research assistantships, scholarships, and teaching assistantships. *Financial aid application deadline:* 3/15.

Financial Aid Contact Dr. Sonia Goltz, Director, Business Graduate Program, 1400 Townsend Avenue, Houghton, MI 49931-1295. *Phone:* 906-487-3055. *Fax:* 906-487-2944. *E-mail:* mba@mtu.edu.

INTERNATIONAL STUDENTS 10% of students enrolled are international students. *Services and facilities:* Counseling/support services, ESL/language courses, International student organization, Orientation, Visa Services. Financial aid is available to international students. *Required*

with application: TOEFL with recommended score of 240 (computer) or 590 (paper); proof of adequate funds.

International Student Contact Saleha Suleman, Director, International Services, International Programs, 1400 Townsend Avenue, Houghton, MI 49931. *Phone:* 906-487-2160. *Fax:* 906-487-1891. *E-mail:* ssuleman@mtu.edu.

APPLICATION *Required:* GMAT, application form, baccalaureate/first degree, personal statement, transcripts of college work. School will accept GRE. *Recommended:* 3 letters of recommendation. *Application fee:* $0. Applications for domestic and international students are processed on a rolling basis.

Application Contact Dr. Sonia Goltz, Director, Business Graduate Program, 1400 Townsend Avenue, Houghton, MI 49931-1295. *Phone:* 906-487-3055. *Fax:* 906-487-2944. *E-mail:* mba@mtu.edu.

Northwood University
Richard DeVos Graduate School of Management
Midland, Michigan

Phone: 989-837-4475 **Fax:** 989-837-4800 **E-mail:** lake@northwood.edu

Business Program(s) Web Site: http://www.northwood.edu/graduate

DEGREES   MB • MBA

MB—Switzerland Program Full-time. Official TOEFL or IELTS Score required for students from non-English speaking countries unless undergrad degree was instructed in English. 56 total credits required. 12 months to complete program. *Concentration:* management.

MBA—Evening Program Part-time. Various levels of Professional/Managerial experience; No GMAT required. 39 total credits required. 27 months to complete program. *Concentration:* management.

MBA—Full-Time Master of Business Administration Full-time. 2 letters of recommendation required. 64 total credits required. 15 months to complete program. *Concentration:* general MBA.

RESOURCES AND SERVICES 215 on-campus PCs are available to graduate business students. Access to Internet/World Wide Web and online grade reports available. *Personal computer requirements:* Graduate business students are strongly recommended to purchase or lease a personal computer. *Special opportunities include:* An internship program is available. *Placement services include:* Alumni network, career placement, job search course, career counseling/planning, electronic job bank, resume referral, career fairs, job interviews arranged, resume preparation, and career library.

Application Contact Lake A. Hamilton, Director of Graduate Programs, 4000 Whiting Drive, Midland, MI 48640. *Phone:* 989-837-4475. *Fax:* 989-837-4800. *E-mail:* lake@northwood.edu.

Oakland University
School of Business Administration
Rochester, Michigan

Phone: 248-370-3287 **Fax:** 248-370-4964 **E-mail:** gbp@oakland.edu

Business Program(s) Web Site: http://www.sba.oakland.edu/grad/

Graduate Business Unit Enrollment *Total:* 574 (93 full-time; 481 part-time; 214 women; 58 international). *Average Age:* 28.

Graduate Business Faculty *Total:* 68 (59 full-time; 9 part-time).

Admissions *Applied:* 116. *Admitted:* 97. *Enrolled:* 87. *Average GMAT:* 535. *Average GPA:* 3.23

Academic Calendar Semesters.

Oakland University (continued)

Accreditation AACSB—The Association to Advance Collegiate Schools of Business.

After Graduation (Class of 2006–07) *Employed within 3 months of graduation:* 98%. *Average starting salary:* $70,000.

DEGREES EMBA • M Acc • MBA

EMBA—Executive Master of Business Administration in Health Care Management Part-time. 5 years of work experience in health care required. At least 39 total credits required. Minimum of 21 months to complete program. *Concentration:* health care.

M Acc—Master of Accounting Full-time and part-time. At least 30 total credits required. 12 to 72 months to complete program. *Concentration:* accounting.

MBA—Master of Business Administration Full-time and part-time. 36 to 48 total credits required. 12 to 72 months to complete program. *Concentrations:* accounting, economics, entrepreneurship, finance, financial information systems, human resources management, international business, management information systems, marketing, operations management.

RESOURCES AND SERVICES 288 on-campus PCs are available to graduate business students. Access to Internet/World Wide Web, online (class) registration, and online grade reports available. *Personal computer requirements:* Graduate business students are not required to have a personal computer. *Placement services include:* Alumni network, career placement, career counseling/planning, electronic job bank, resume referral, career fairs, job interviews arranged, resume preparation, and career library.

EXPENSES *Tuition (state resident):* Full-time: $8508. *Tuition (nonresident):* Full-time: $14,661. *Tuition (international):* Full-time: $14,661. *Typical graduate housing cost:* $7507 (including board), $7505 (room only).

FINANCIAL AID (2007–08) Loans, research assistantships, and work study. *Financial aid application deadline:* 4/1.

Financial Aid Contact Ms. Cindy L. Hermsen, Director, Financial Aid, 120 North Foundation Hall, Financial Aid Office, Rochester, MI 48309-4401. *Phone:* 248-370-2550. *Fax:* 248-370-4188. *E-mail:* hermsen@oakland.edu.

INTERNATIONAL STUDENTS 10% of students enrolled are international students. *Services and facilities:* Counseling/support services, ESL/language courses, Housing location assistance, Orientation, Visa Services. Financial aid is available to international students. *Required with application:* TOEFL with recommended score of 213 (computer), 550 (paper), or 79 (Internet); proof of adequate funds. *Recommended with application:* Proof of health/immunizations.

International Student Contact David J. Archbold, Director, International Students and Scholars, 157 North Foundation Hall, International Students and Scholars Office, Rochester, MI 48309-4401. *Phone:* 248-370-3358. *Fax:* 248-370-3351. *E-mail:* archbold@oakland.edu.

APPLICATION *Required:* GMAT, application form, baccalaureate/first degree, transcripts of college work. School will accept GRE. *Recommended:* 2 years of work experience. *Application fee:* $0. Applications for domestic and international students are processed on a rolling basis.

Application Contact Ms. Monica Milczarski, Program Assistant, Office of Graduate Business Programs, 432 Elliott Hall, Rochester, MI 48309-4493. *Phone:* 248-370-3287. *Fax:* 248-370-4964. *E-mail:* gbp@oakland.edu.

Saginaw Valley State University
College of Business and Management
University Center, Michigan

Phone: 989-964-4064 **Fax:** 989-964-7497 **E-mail:** jwetmore@svsu.edu

Business Program(s) Web Site: http://www.svsu.edu/mba

Graduate Business Unit Enrollment *Total:* 95 (37 full-time; 58 part-time; 46 women; 34 international). *Average Age:* 30.

Graduate Business Faculty 15 full-time.

Admissions *Applied:* 76. *Admitted:* 72. *Enrolled:* 42. *Average GMAT:* 505. *Average GPA:* 3.14

Academic Calendar Semesters.

Accreditation AACSB—The Association to Advance Collegiate Schools of Business.

DEGREE MBA

MBA—Master of Business Administration Full-time and part-time. Distance learning option. 35 to 46 total credits required. 12 to 72 months to complete program. *Concentrations:* accounting, economics, entrepreneurship, finance, general MBA, information technology, international business, management.

RESOURCES AND SERVICES 1,033 on-campus PCs are available to graduate business students. Access to Internet/World Wide Web, online (class) registration, and online grade reports available. *Personal computer requirements:* Graduate business students are not required to have a personal computer. *Special opportunities include:* An internship program is available. *Placement services include:* Alumni network, career placement, job search course, career counseling/planning, electronic job bank, resume referral, career fairs, job interviews arranged, resume preparation, and career library.

EXPENSES *Tuition (state resident):* Full-time: $6198.30. Part-time: $344.35 per credit hour. *Tuition (nonresident):* Full-time: $11,890. Part-time: $660.55 per credit hour. *Tuition (international):* Full-time: $11,889.90. Part-time: $660.55 per credit hour. *Required fees:* Full-time: $255.60. Part-time: $14.20 per credit hour. *Graduate housing:* Room and board costs vary by number of occupants, type of accommodation, and type of board plan. *Typical cost:* $6630 (including board), $3750 (room only).

FINANCIAL AID (2007–08) 37 students received aid, including grants, loans, research assistantships, scholarships, and work study. Aid is available to part-time students. *Financial aid application deadline:* 6/1.

Financial Aid Contact Robert Lemuel, Director of Scholarships and Financial Aid, 7400 Bay Road, 147 Wickes Hall, University Center, MI 48710. *Phone:* 989-964-4393. *Fax:* 989-790-0180. *E-mail:* lemuel@svsu.edu.

INTERNATIONAL STUDENTS 36% of students enrolled are international students. *Services and facilities:* Counseling/support services, ESL/language courses, Housing location assistance, International student organization, Language tutoring, Orientation, Visa Services. Financial aid is available to international students. *Required with application:* IELT with recommended score of 6; TOEFL with recommended score of 197 (computer), 525 (paper), or 71 (Internet); proof of adequate funds; proof of health/immunizations.

International Student Contact Stephen Kazar, Special Assistant to the President, International Programs, 7400 Bay Road, 163 Wickes Hall, University Center, MI 48710. *Phone:* 989-964-2167. *Fax:* 989-964-6066. *E-mail:* sjkazar@svsu.edu.

APPLICATION *Required:* GMAT, application form, baccalaureate/first degree, essay, 2 letters of recommendation, personal statement, transcripts of college work. *Recommended:* Resume/curriculum vitae. *Application fee:* $25, $60 (international). Applications for domestic and international students are processed on a rolling basis.

Application Contact Jill L. Wetmore, Assistant Dean, 7400 Bay Road, 320 Curtiss Hall, University Center, MI 48710. *Phone:* 989-964-4064. *Fax:* 989-964-7497. *E-mail:* jwetmore@svsu.edu.

Siena Heights University
Graduate College
Adrian, Michigan

Phone: 517-264-7606 **Fax:** 517-264-7704 **E-mail:** ppalmer@sienaheights.edu

Business Program(s) Web Site: http://www.sienaheights.edu

Graduate Business Unit Enrollment *Total:* 372 (12 full-time; 360 part-time; 230 women; 12 international).

Graduate Business Faculty *Total:* 18 (4 full-time; 14 part-time).

Admissions *Applied:* 105. *Admitted:* 103. *Enrolled:* 98. *Average GPA:* 3.1

Academic Calendar Semesters.

DEGREES MA

MA—Master of Arts in Leadership Full-time and part-time. At least 36 total credits required. 24 to 84 months to complete program. *Concentrations:* human resources management, leadership, nonprofit organization, organizational behavior/development, organizational management, public policy and administration, training and development.

MA—Master of Arts in Leadership Full-time and part-time. At least 36 total credits required. 24 to 84 months to complete program. *Concentration:* health administration.

RESOURCES AND SERVICES 78 on-campus PCs are available to graduate business students. Access to Internet/World Wide Web, online (class) registration, and online grade reports available. *Personal computer requirements:* Graduate business students are strongly recommended to purchase or lease a personal computer. *Special opportunities include:* An international exchange program and an internship program are available.

Financial Aid Contact Mr. Christopher Howard, Director of Financial Aid, 1247 East Siena Heights Drive, Adrian, MI 49221-1796. *Phone:* 517-264-7130. *Fax:* 517-264-7734. *E-mail:* choward@sienaheights.edu.

INTERNATIONAL STUDENTS 3% of students enrolled are international students. *Services and facilities:* Counseling/support services, ESL/language courses, Housing location assistance, International student housing, International student organization, Language tutoring, Orientation, Visa Services. Financial aid is not available to international students. *Required with application:* TOEFL with recommended score of 550 (paper); TWE with recommended score of 4; proof of adequate funds.

International Student Contact Dr. Hanson Jennifer, Coordinator of International Students, 1247 East Siena Heights Drive, Adrian, MI 49221-1796. *Phone:* 517-264-7665. *Fax:* 517-264-7714. *E-mail:* jhanson@sienaheights.edu.

APPLICATION *Required:* Application form, baccalaureate/first degree, essay, interview, 3 letters of recommendation, personal statement, resume/curriculum vitae, transcripts of college work, 5 years of work experience. Applications for domestic and international students are processed on a rolling basis.

Application Contact Dean C. Patrick Palmer, Associate Professor of Organizational Leadership, 1247 East Siena Heights, Adrian, MI 49221-1796. *Phone:* 517-264-7606. *Fax:* 517-264-7704. *E-mail:* ppalmer@sienaheights.edu.

Spring Arbor University
School of Business and Management
Spring Arbor, Michigan

Phone: 517-750-6703 Fax: 517-750-6614 E-mail: dglinz@arbor.edu

Business Program(s) Web Site: http://www.arbor.edu/graduate/programs/mba/index.aspx

Graduate Business Unit Enrollment *Total:* 88 (40 full-time; 48 part-time; 48 women; 5 international).

Graduate Business Faculty *Total:* 18 (9 full-time; 9 part-time).

Admissions *Applied:* 30. *Admitted:* 30. *Enrolled:* 22.

Academic Calendar Semesters.

After Graduation (Class of 2006–07) *Employed within 3 months of graduation:* 100%.

DEGREE MBA

MBA—Business Administration Full-time and part-time. Distance learning option. Minimum GPA of 3.0 for at least the last two years of bachelor's degree required. 36 to 54 total credits required. 18 to 72 months to complete program. *Concentration:* general MBA.

RESOURCES AND SERVICES 127 on-campus PCs are available to graduate business students. Access to Internet/World Wide Web, online (class) registration, and online grade reports available. *Personal computer requirements:* Graduate business students are strongly recommended to purchase or lease a personal computer. *Special opportunities include:* An internship program is available. *Placement services include:* Alumni network, career counseling/planning, and resume preparation.

EXPENSES *Tuition:* Full-time: $4560. Part-time: $380 per credit hour. *Required fees:* Full-time: $150. Part-time: $105 per year. Tuition and/or fees vary by number of courses or credits taken and academic program. *Graduate housing:* Room and board costs vary by type of accommodation and type of board plan. *Typical cost:* $5140 (including board), $3380 (room only).

FINANCIAL AID (2007–08) Grants, loans, and work study. Aid is available to part-time students.

Financial Aid Contact Lois Hardy, Director of Financial Aid, 106 East Main Street, Spring Arbor, MI 49283-9799. *Phone:* 517-750-1200 Ext. 1468. *Fax:* 517-750-6620. *E-mail:* loish@arbor.edu.

INTERNATIONAL STUDENTS 6% of students enrolled are international students. *Services and facilities:* Counseling/support services, ESL/language courses, Housing location assistance, International student housing, International student organization, Orientation. Financial aid is not available to international students. *Required with application:* TOEFL with recommended score of 220 (computer), 550 (paper), or 80 (Internet); proof of adequate funds; proof of health/immunizations.

International Student Contact Sharon Hastings, Director of International Students, 106 East Main Street, Spring Arbor, MI 49283-9799. *Phone:* 517-750-1200 Ext. 1334. *Fax:* 517-750-6620. *E-mail:* sharonh@arbor.edu.

APPLICATION *Required:* Application form, baccalaureate/first degree, 2 letters of recommendation, resume/curriculum vitae, transcripts of college work, 3 years of work experience. *Recommended:* Essay, personal statement. *Application fee:* $40. Applications for domestic and international students are processed on a rolling basis.

Application Contact Mr. Dale Glinz, Coordinator of Graduate Recruitment, 106 East Main Street, Spring Arbor, MI 49283-9799. *Phone:* 517-750-6703. *Fax:* 517-750-6614. *E-mail:* dglinz@arbor.edu.

University of Detroit Mercy
College of Business Administration
Detroit, Michigan

Phone: 313-993-1203 Fax: 313-993-1673 E-mail: naskibom@udmercy.edu

Business Program(s) Web Site: http://business.udmercy.edu/mba.htm

Graduate Business Unit Enrollment *Total:* 265 (87 full-time; 178 part-time; 110 women; 111 international). *Average Age:* 30.

Graduate Business Faculty *Total:* 27 (20 full-time; 7 part-time).

Admissions *Applied:* 56. *Admitted:* 50. *Enrolled:* 31. *Average GMAT:* 570. *Average GPA:* 3.38

Academic Calendar Semesters.

Accreditation AACSB—The Association to Advance Collegiate Schools of Business.

After Graduation (Class of 2006–07) *Employed within 3 months of graduation:* 95%. *Average starting salary:* $57,000.

DEGREES M Sc • MBA • MS

M Sc—Business Turnaround Management Part-time. 30 to 36 total credits required. 12 to 60 months to complete program. *Concentration:* business policy/strategy.

University of Detroit Mercy (continued)

MBA—Master of Business Administration Part-time. 36 to 54 total credits required. 12 to 60 months to complete program. *Concentrations:* accounting, decision sciences, developmental economics, economics, finance, human resources management, international and area business studies, international trade, management, management information systems, management science, marketing, operations management, quantitative analysis.

MS—Master of Science in Computer and Information Systems Part-time. 30 to 33 total credits required. 12 to 60 months to complete program. *Concentration:* information systems.

MS—UDM/MBA Weekend Cohort Part-time. GMAT not required, 5 years management experience required. At least 32 total credits required. Minimum of 15 months to complete program. *Concentration:* executive programs.

RESOURCES AND SERVICES 600 on-campus PCs are available to graduate business students. Access to Internet/World Wide Web, online (class) registration, and online grade reports available. *Personal computer requirements:* Graduate business students are strongly recommended to purchase or lease a personal computer. *Special opportunities include:* An international exchange program is available. *Placement services include:* Alumni network, career placement, job search course, career counseling/planning, electronic job bank, resume referral, career fairs, job interviews arranged, and resume preparation.

EXPENSES *Tuition:* Full-time: $16,830. Part-time: $935 per semester hour. *Tuition (international):* Full-time: $16,830. Part-time: $935 per semester hour. *Required fees:* Full-time: $570. Part-time: $370 per semester hour. *Graduate housing:* Room and board costs vary by number of occupants, type of accommodation, and type of board plan. *Typical cost:* $7550 (including board), $4470 (room only).

FINANCIAL AID (2007–08) Loans, research assistantships, and work study. Aid is available to part-time students. *Financial aid application deadline:* 8/15.

Financial Aid Contact Sandy Ross, Director of Financial Aid, 4001 West McNichols Road, Detroit, MI 48221. *Phone:* 313-993-3350. *Fax:* 313-993-3347. *E-mail:* rosssc@udmercy.edu.

INTERNATIONAL STUDENTS 42% of students enrolled are international students. *Services and facilities:* Counseling/support services, ESL/language courses, Housing location assistance, International student housing, International student organization, Language tutoring, Orientation, Visa Services. Financial aid is available to international students. *Required with application:* Proof of adequate funds; proof of health/immunizations.

International Student Contact Ms. Sharon Messinger, Director for International Admissions, 4001 West McNichols Road, Detroit, MI 48221. *Phone:* 313-993-1205. *Fax:* 313-993-1192.

APPLICATION *Required:* Application form, baccalaureate/first degree, transcripts of college work. *Recommended:* 2 letters of recommendation, personal statement, resume/curriculum vitae, work experience. *Application fee:* $30, $50 (international). Applications for domestic and international students are processed on a rolling basis.

Application Contact Bonnie Naski, Coordinator, Student Services, 4001 West McNichols Road, Detroit, MI 48221. *Phone:* 313-993-1203. *Fax:* 313-993-1673. *E-mail:* naskibom@udmercy.edu.

University of Michigan

Ross School of Business at the University of Michigan

Ann Arbor, Michigan

Phone: 734-763-5796 **Fax:** 734-763-7804 **E-mail:** rossmba@umich.edu

Business Program(s) Web Site: http://www.bus.umich.edu/

Graduate Business Unit Enrollment *Total:* 1,953 (1,193 full-time; 760 part-time; 523 women; 535 international).

Graduate Business Faculty *Total:* 120 (83 full-time; 37 part-time).

Admissions *Applied:* 2,983. *Admitted:* 609. *Enrolled:* 427. *Average GMAT:* 700. *Average GPA:* 3.3.

Academic Calendar Semesters.

Accreditation AACSB—The Association to Advance Collegiate Schools of Business.

After Graduation (Class of 2006–07) *Employed within 3 months of graduation:* 90%. *Average starting salary:* $99,265.

DEGREES JD/MBA • MBA • MBA/M Arch • MBA/MA • MBA/MEM • MBA/MHSA • MBA/MM • MBA/MPP • MBA/MS • MBA/MSW

JD/MBA—Juris Doctor/Master of Business Administration Full-time. At least 90 total credits required. 48 to 60 months to complete program. *Concentration:* combined degrees.

MBA—Evening Master of Business Administration Part-time. At least 60 total credits required. 36 to 120 months to complete program. *Concentrations:* accounting, Asian business studies, entrepreneurship, finance, human resources management, international and area business studies, international business, international management, management information systems, marketing, operations management, organizational behavior/development, production management, public policy and administration, real estate, strategic management.

MBA—Full-Time Master of Business Administration Full-time. At least 57 total credits required. 24 months to complete program. *Concentrations:* accounting, entrepreneurship, finance, general MBA, human resources management, international business, international management, management information systems, marketing, nonprofit organization, operations management, production management, real estate, strategic management.

MBA/M Arch—Master of Business Administration/Master of Architecture Full-time. At least 90 total credits required. 36 months to complete program. *Concentration:* combined degrees.

MBA/MA—Master of Business Administration/Master of Arts in Chinese Studies Full-time. At least 70 total credits required. 36 months to complete program. *Concentration:* combined degrees.

MBA/MA—Master of Business Administration/Master of Arts in Japanese Studies Full-time. At least 70 total credits required. 36 months to complete program. *Concentration:* combined degrees.

MBA/MA—Master of Business Administration/Master of Arts in Japanese Studies Full-time. At least 120 total credits required. 48 months to complete program. *Concentration:* combined degrees.

MBA/MA—Master of Business Administration/Master of Arts in Modern Middle Eastern and North African Studies Full-time. At least 81 total credits required. 36 months to complete program. *Concentration:* combined degrees.

MBA/MA—Master of Business Administration/Master of Arts in Russian and East European Studies Full-time. At least 75 total credits required. 30 to 36 months to complete program. *Concentration:* combined degrees.

MBA/MA—Master of Business Administration/Master of Arts in South and Southeast Asian Studies Full-time. At least 69 total credits required. 30 to 36 months to complete program. *Concentration:* combined degrees.

MBA/MEM—Master of Business Administration/Master of Engineering in Manufacturing Full-time. At least 66 total credits required. 30 months to complete program. *Concentration:* combined degrees.

MBA/MHSA—Master of Business Administration/Master of Health Services Administration Full-time. At least 90 total credits required. 36 months to complete program. *Concentration:* combined degrees.

MBA/MM—Master of Business Administration/Master of Music Full-time. At least 65 total credits required. 24 months to complete program. *Concentration:* combined degrees.

MBA/MPP—Master of Business Administration/Master of Public Policy Full-time. At least 84 total credits required. 36 months to complete program. *Concentration:* combined degrees.

MBA/MS—Master of Business Administration/Master of Science in Construction Engineering and Management Full-time. At least 69 total credits required. 30 months to complete program. *Concentration:* combined degrees.

MBA/MS—Master of Business Administration/Master of Science in Engineering Full-time. At least 69 total credits required. 24 to 30 months to complete program. *Concentration:* combined degrees.

MBA/MS—Master of Business Administration/Master of Science in Industrial and Operations Engineering Full-time. At least 65 total credits required. 30 months to complete program. *Concentration:* combined degrees.

MBA/MS—Master of Business Administration/Master of Science in Nursing Administration Full-time. At least 70 total credits required. 30 months to complete program. *Concentration:* combined degrees.

MBA/MSW—Master of Business Administration/Master of Social Work Full-time. At least 85 total credits required. 36 months to complete program. *Concentration:* combined degrees.

RESOURCES AND SERVICES 109 on-campus PCs are available to graduate business students. Access to Internet/World Wide Web, online (class) registration, and online grade reports available. *Personal computer requirements:* Graduate business students are strongly recommended to purchase or lease a personal computer. *Special opportunities include:* An international exchange program is available. *Placement services include:* Alumni network, career placement, job search course, career counseling/planning, electronic job bank, resume referral, career fairs, job interviews arranged, resume preparation, and career library.

EXPENSES *Tuition (state resident):* Full-time: $38,100. Part-time: $15,310 per semester. *Tuition (nonresident):* Full-time: $43,100. Part-time: $15,310 per semester. *Tuition (international):* Full-time: $43,100. Part-time: $15,310 per semester. *Required fees:* Full-time: $189.38. Part-time: $189.38 per year. *Typical graduate housing cost:* $10,884 (including board).

FINANCIAL AID (2007–08) 1676 students received aid, including fellowships, loans, research assistantships, scholarships, teaching assistantships, and work study. Aid is available to part-time students. *Financial aid application deadline:* 3/1.

Financial Aid Contact Diane Hunt, Manager, Financial Aid and Scholarships, 710 East University, K2336, Ann Arbor, MI 48109-1234. *Phone:* 734-764-5139. *Fax:* 734-763-7804. *E-mail:* rossfinaid@umich.edu.

INTERNATIONAL STUDENTS 27% of students enrolled are international students. *Services and facilities:* Counseling/support services, ESL/language courses, Housing location assistance, International student housing, International student organization, Language tutoring, Orientation, Visa Services. *Required with application:* TOEFL with recommended score of 250 (computer) or 600 (paper); proof of adequate funds.

APPLICATION *Required:* GMAT, application form, baccalaureate/first degree, essay, 2 letters of recommendation, personal statement, resume/curriculum vitae, transcripts of college work. *Recommended:* Interview, work experience. *Application fee:* $200. *Deadlines:* 11/1 for fall, 1/7 for winter, 3/1 for spring, 11/1 for fall (international), 1/7 for winter (international), 3/1 for spring (international).

Application Contact Soojin Kwon Koh, Director, Admissions, 710 East University, E2540, Ann Arbor, MI 48109-1234. *Phone:* 734-763-5796. *Fax:* 734-763-7804. *E-mail:* rossmba@umich.edu.

University of Michigan–Dearborn
School of Management

Dearborn, Michigan

Phone: 313-593-5460 **Fax:** 313-271-9838 **E-mail:** gradbusiness@umd.umich.edu

Business Program(s) Web Site: http://www.som.umd.umich.edu

Graduate Business Unit Enrollment *Total:* 560 (82 full-time; 478 part-time; 187 women; 91 international). *Average Age:* 31.

Graduate Business Faculty *Total:* 30 (24 full-time; 6 part-time).

Admissions *Applied:* 112. *Admitted:* 71. *Enrolled:* 54. *Average GMAT:* 535. *Average GPA:* 3.18

Academic Calendar Trimesters.

Accreditation AACSB—The Association to Advance Collegiate Schools of Business.

DEGREES MBA • MBA/MHSA • MBA/MS • MBA/MSF • MS

MBA—Master of Business Administration Full-time and part-time. Distance learning option. Two years of professional work experience. 36 to 63 total credits required. 16 to 84 months to complete program. *Concentrations:* accounting, finance, general MBA, human resources management, international business, management, management information systems, marketing, supply chain management.

MBA/MHSA—Master of Business Administration/Master of Health Services Administration Full-time and part-time. Distance learning option. Two years of professional work experience. 81 total credits required. 32 to 84 months to complete program. *Concentrations:* general MBA, health administration, management.

MBA/MS—Master of Business Administration/Master of Science in Engineering Full-time and part-time. Distance learning option. Two years of professional work experience. At least 66 total credits required. 24 to 84 months to complete program. *Concentrations:* accounting, finance, general MBA, human resources management, international business, management, management information systems, marketing, supply chain management.

MBA/MSF—Master of Business Administration/Master of Science in Finance Full-time and part-time. Distance learning option. Two years of professional work experience and Principles of Accounting I. 51 to 75 total credits required. 30 to 84 months to complete program. *Concentrations:* accounting, finance, general MBA, human resources management, international business, management, management information systems, marketing, supply chain management.

MS—Master of Science in Accounting Full-time and part-time. Principles of Accounting I and II, Cost Accounting, Asset Accounting, Equity Accounting, and Tax Accounting courses are required. 30 total credits required. 10 to 84 months to complete program. *Concentrations:* accounting, taxation.

MS—Master of Science in Finance Full-time and part-time. Distance learning option. Principles of Accounting I required. 30 total credits required. 10 to 84 months to complete program. *Concentration:* finance.

RESOURCES AND SERVICES 200 on-campus PCs are available to graduate business students. Access to Internet/World Wide Web, online (class) registration, and online grade reports available. *Personal computer requirements:* Graduate business students are strongly recommended to purchase or lease a personal computer. *Special opportunities include:* An international exchange program and an internship program are available. *Placement services include:* Alumni network, career placement, career counseling/planning, electronic job bank, resume referral, career fairs, job interviews arranged, resume preparation, and career library.

FINANCIAL AID (2007–08) Loans, scholarships, and work study. Aid is available to part-time students.

Financial Aid Contact Judy Benfield Tatum, Director Of Financial Aid And Scholarships, 4901 Evergreen Road, Room 1183, University Center, Dearborn, MI 48128. *Phone:* 313-593-5300. *Fax:* 313-593-5313. *E-mail:* ask-ofa@umd.umich.edu.

INTERNATIONAL STUDENTS 16% of students enrolled are international students. *Services and facilities:* Counseling/support services, ESL/language courses, Housing location assistance, Orientation, Visa Services. Financial aid is not available to international students. *Required with application:* TOEFL with recommended score of 220 (computer) or 560 (paper); proof of adequate funds; proof of health/immunizations.

University of Michigan–Dearborn (continued)

International Student Contact Graduate Programs Director, 19000 Hubbard Drive, Room 168, Fairlane Center South, Dearborn, MI 48126. *Phone:* 313-593-5460. *Fax:* 313-271-9838. *E-mail:* gradbusiness@umd.umich.edu.

APPLICATION *Required:* GMAT, application form, baccalaureate/first degree, 1 letter of recommendation, personal statement, resume/curriculum vitae, transcripts of college work, 2 years of work experience. *Application fee:* $60. Applications for domestic and international students are processed on a rolling basis.

Application Contact Christine Brzezinski, Graduate Admissions Coordinator, 19000 Hubbard Drive, Room 168, Fairlane Center South, Dearborn, MI 48126. *Phone:* 313-593-5460. *Fax:* 313-271-9838. *E-mail:* gradbusiness@umd.umich.edu.

University of Michigan–Flint
School of Management
Flint, Michigan

Phone: 866-UMF-MBA1 **Fax:** 810-237-6685 **E-mail:** umflintmba1@umich.edu

Business Program(s) Web Site: http://www.umflint.edu/departments/som/

Graduate Business Unit Enrollment *Total:* 180 (23 full-time; 157 part-time; 70 women; 15 international). *Average Age:* 32.

Graduate Business Faculty *Total:* 14 (11 full-time; 3 part-time).

Admissions *Applied:* 132. *Admitted:* 67. *Enrolled:* 53. *Average GMAT:* 514. *Average GPA:* 3.53

Academic Calendar Semesters.

Accreditation AACSB—The Association to Advance Collegiate Schools of Business.

DEGREE MBA

MBA—Traditional Master of Business Administration or NetPlus Master of Business Administration Part-time. Distance learning option. At least 48 total credits required. 24 to 84 months to complete program. *Concentrations:* accounting, finance, general MBA, health care, international business, organizational management.

RESOURCES AND SERVICES 887 on-campus PCs are available to graduate business students. Access to Internet/World Wide Web, online (class) registration, and online grade reports available. *Personal computer requirements:* Graduate business students are strongly recommended to purchase or lease a personal computer. *Placement services include:* Alumni network, career counseling/planning, electronic job bank, resume referral, career fairs, job interviews arranged, resume preparation, and career library.

EXPENSES *Tuition (state resident):* Full-time: $12,048. Part-time: $502 per credit. *Tuition (nonresident):* Full-time: $12,048. Part-time: $502 per credit. *Tuition (international):* Full-time: $12,048. Part-time: $502 per credit. *Required fees:* Full-time: $334. Part-time: $267 per year. Tuition and/or fees vary by academic program.

FINANCIAL AID (2007–08) 64 students received aid, including grants, loans, research assistantships, scholarships, and work study. Aid is available to part-time students. *Financial aid application deadline:* 3/15.

Financial Aid Contact Mrs. Lori Vedder, Financial Aid Director, 277 University Pavilion, Flint, MI 48502-1950. *Phone:* 810-762-3444. *Fax:* 810-766-6757. *E-mail:* lvedder@umflint.edu.

INTERNATIONAL STUDENTS 8% of students enrolled are international students. *Services and facilities:* Counseling/support services, Housing location assistance, International student organization, Language tutoring, Orientation, Visa Services. Financial aid is available to international students. *Required with application:* IELT with recom-

mended score of 6.5; TOEFL with recommended score of 220 (computer) or 560 (paper); proof of adequate funds.

International Student Contact Ms. Kim Butka, International Admissions Counselor, 303 East Kearsley Street, 245 University Pavilion, Flint, MI 48502-1950. *Phone:* 810-762-3302. *Fax:* 810-762-3272. *E-mail:* international@umflint.edu.

APPLICATION *Required:* GMAT, application form, baccalaureate/first degree, 3 letters of recommendation, personal statement, resume/curriculum vitae, transcripts of college work. *Recommended:* Work experience. *Application fee:* $55. Applications for domestic and international students are processed on a rolling basis.

Application Contact Ms. D. Nicol Taylor, MBA Program Coordinator, 303 East Kearsley Street, Flint, MI 48502-1950. *Phone:* 866-UMF-MBA1. *Fax:* 810-237-6685. *E-mail:* umflintmba1@umich.edu.

University of Phoenix–Metro Detroit Campus
College of Graduate Business and Management
Troy, Michigan

Phone: 480-317-6200 **Fax:** 480-643-1479 **E-mail:** beth.barilla@phoenix.edu

Business Program(s) Web Site: http://www.phoenix.edu

DEGREES M Mgt • MA • MBA

M Mgt—Human Resource Management Full-time. At least 45 total credits required. *Concentration:* human resources management.

M Mgt—Master of Management Full-time. At least 39 total credits required. *Concentration:* management.

MA—Master of Arts in Organizational Management Full-time. At least 40 total credits required. *Concentration:* organizational management.

MBA—Global Management Full-time. At least 45 total credits required. *Concentration:* international management.

MBA—Human Resource Management Full-time. At least 45 total credits required. *Concentration:* human resources management.

MBA—e-Business Full-time. At least 45 total credits required. *Concentration:* electronic commerce (E-commerce).

MBA—Master of Business Administration Full-time. At least 45 total credits required. *Concentration:* administration.

RESOURCES AND SERVICES Access to online grade reports available. *Personal computer requirements:* Graduate business students are strongly recommended to purchase or lease a personal computer. *Placement services include:* Alumni network.

Application Contact Beth Barilla, Associate Vice President of Student Admissions and Services, Mail Stop AA-K101, 4615 East Elwood Street, Phoenix, AZ 85040-1958. *Phone:* 480-317-6200. *Fax:* 480-643-1479. *E-mail:* beth.barilla@phoenix.edu.

University of Phoenix–West Michigan Campus
College of Graduate Business and Management
Walker, Michigan

Phone: 480-317-6200 **Fax:** 480-643-1479 **E-mail:** beth.barilla@phoenix.edu

Business Program(s) Web Site: http://www.phoenix.edu

DEGREES MA • MBA

MA—Organizational Management Full-time. At least 40 total credits required. *Concentration:* organizational management.

MBA—Accounting Full-time. At least 54 total credits required. *Concentration:* accounting.

MBA—Global Management Full-time. At least 45 total credits required. *Concentration:* international business.

MBA—Human Resource Management Full-time. At least 45 total credits required. *Concentration:* human resources management.

MBA—Marketing Full-time. At least 45 total credits required. *Concentration:* marketing.

MBA—Public Administration Full-time. At least 45 total credits required. *Concentration:* public policy and administration.

MBA—e-Business Full-time. At least 45 total credits required.

MBA—Master of Business Administration Full-time. At least 45 total credits required. *Concentration:* administration.

RESOURCES AND SERVICES Access to online grade reports available. *Personal computer requirements:* Graduate business students are strongly recommended to purchase or lease a personal computer. *Placement services include:* Alumni network.

Application Contact Beth Barilla, Associate Vice President of Student Admissions and Services, Mail Stop AA-K101, 4615 East Elwood Street, Phoenix, AZ 85040-1958. *Phone:* 480-317-6200. *Fax:* 480-643-1479. *E-mail:* beth.barilla@phoenix.edu.

Walsh College of Accountancy and Business Administration

Graduate Programs

Troy, Michigan

Phone: 248-823-1207 **Fax:** 248-823-1663 **E-mail:** vscavone@walshcollege.edu

Business Program(s) Web Site: http://www.walshcollege.edu

Graduate Business Unit Enrollment *Total:* 2,148 (88 full-time; 2,060 part-time; 1,067 women; 77 international). *Average Age:* 34.

Graduate Business Faculty *Total:* 185 (20 full-time; 165 part-time).

Admissions *Applied:* 573. *Admitted:* 523. *Enrolled:* 419. *Average GMAT:* 500. *Average GPA:* 3.07

Academic Calendar Semesters.

After Graduation (Class of 2006–07) *Employed within 3 months of graduation:* 100%. *Average starting salary:* $66,492.

DEGREES MBA • MIB • MS • MSIST

MBA—Master of Business Administration Full-time and part-time. Distance learning option. 36 to 57 total credits required. 12 to 60 months to complete program. *Concentrations:* accounting, economics, finance, human resources management, international business, marketing, project management, taxation.

MIB—MS in International Business Part-time. 24 to 42 total credits required. 12 to 60 months to complete program. *Concentration:* international business.

MS—Master of Science in Accountancy Full-time and part-time. 30 to 54 total credits required. 18 to 60 months to complete program. *Concentration:* accounting.

MS—Master of Science in Finance Full-time and part-time. 24 to 45 total credits required. 12 to 60 months to complete program. *Concentrations:* finance, financial management/planning.

MS—Master of Science in Taxation Full-time and part-time. 24 to 36 total credits required. 12 to 60 months to complete program. *Concentration:* taxation.

MSIST—MS in Information Systems Full-time and part-time. 21 to 42 total credits required. 12 to 60 months to complete program. *Concentration:* project management.

RESOURCES AND SERVICES 300 on-campus PCs are available to graduate business students. Access to Internet/World Wide Web, online (class) registration, and online grade reports available. *Personal computer requirements:* Graduate business students are strongly recommended to purchase or lease a personal computer. *Placement services include:* Alumni network, career placement, job search course, career counseling/planning, electronic job bank, resume referral, career fairs, job interviews arranged, resume preparation, and career library.

EXPENSES *Tuition:* Full-time: $9162. Part-time: $4581 per semester. *Tuition (international):* Full-time: $9162. Part-time: $4581 per semester. *Required fees:* Full-time: $360. Part-time: $360 per year.

FINANCIAL AID (2007–08) 492 students received aid, including grants, loans, scholarships, and work study. Aid is available to part-time students. *Financial aid application deadline:* 6/30.

Financial Aid Contact Mr. Howard Thomas, Director, Student Financial Resources, 3838 Livernois Road, PO Box 7006, Troy, MI 48007-7006. *Phone:* 248-823-1285. *Fax:* 248-524-2520. *E-mail:* hthomas@walshcollege.edu.

INTERNATIONAL STUDENTS 4% of students enrolled are international students. *Services and facilities:* Counseling/support services, International student organization, Orientation. Financial aid is available to international students. *Required with application:* TOEFL with recommended score of 213 (computer) or 550 (paper); proof of adequate funds; proof of health/immunizations.

International Student Contact Ms. Hamsa Daher, Associate Director of International Students and New Markets, 3838 Livernois Road, PO Box 7006, Troy, MI 48007-7006. *Phone:* 248-823-1610 Ext. 1363. *Fax:* 248-689-0938. *E-mail:* hdaher@walshcollege.edu.

APPLICATION *Required:* Application form, baccalaureate/first degree, resume/curriculum vitae, transcripts of college work, 2 years of work experience. School will accept GMAT. *Application fee:* $50. Applications for domestic and international students are processed on a rolling basis.

Application Contact Ms. Victoria Scavone, Assistant Vice President for Enrollment, 3838 Livernois Road, PO Box 7006, Troy, MI 48007-7006. *Phone:* 248-823-1207. *Fax:* 248-823-1663. *E-mail:* vscavone@walshcollege.edu.

Wayne State University

School of Business Administration

Detroit, Michigan

Phone: 313-577-4510 **Fax:** 313-577-5299 **E-mail:** l.s.zaddach@wayne.edu

Business Program(s) Web Site: http://www.busadm.wayne.edu/

Graduate Business Unit Enrollment *Total:* 1,255 (221 full-time; 1,034 part-time). *Average Age:* 27.

Graduate Business Faculty *Total:* 121 (58 full-time; 63 part-time).

Admissions *Applied:* 433. *Admitted:* 317. *Enrolled:* 216. *Average GMAT:* 550. *Average GPA:* 3.1

Academic Calendar Semesters.

Accreditation AACSB—The Association to Advance Collegiate Schools of Business.

After Graduation (Class of 2006–07) *Employed within 3 months of graduation:* 95%. *Average starting salary:* $85,000.

DEGREES MBA • MS • MSA

Wayne State University (continued)

MBA—Master of Business Administration Full-time and part-time. At least 36 total credits required. 12 to 72 months to complete program. *Concentrations:* accounting, entrepreneurship, finance, human resources management, industrial/labor relations, international business, management, management information systems, managerial economics, marketing, quality management, taxation.

MS—Master of Science in Taxation Full-time and part-time. At least 30 total credits required. 12 to 72 months to complete program. *Concentration:* taxation.

MSA—Master of Science in Accounting Program Full-time and part-time. At least 30 total credits required. 12 to 72 months to complete program. *Concentration:* accounting.

RESOURCES AND SERVICES 125 on-campus PCs are available to graduate business students. Access to Internet/World Wide Web, online (class) registration, and online grade reports available. *Personal computer requirements:* Graduate business students are not required to have a personal computer. *Special opportunities include:* An internship program is available. *Placement services include:* Career placement, career counseling/planning, resume referral, career fairs, job interviews arranged, resume preparation, and career library.

EXPENSES *Tuition (state resident):* Full-time: $9752. Part-time: $468 per semester hour. *Tuition (nonresident):* Full-time: $18,515. Part-time: $955 per semester hour. *Tuition (international):* Full-time: $18,515. Part-time: $955 per semester hour. *Required fees:* Full-time: $280. Part-time: $140 per semester.

FINANCIAL AID (2007–08) 50 students received aid, including research assistantships, scholarships, and work study. Aid is available to part-time students.

Financial Aid Contact Mr. Adam Hermsen, Jr., Director, Student Financial Aid, Welcome Center, 42 West Warren, Detroit, MI 48202. *Phone:* 313-577-4982. *Fax:* 313-577-0648. *E-mail:* dx4245@wayne.edu.

INTERNATIONAL STUDENTS *Services and facilities:* Counseling/support services, ESL/language courses, Housing location assistance, International student housing, International student organization, Orientation. Financial aid is not available to international students. *Required with application:* TOEFL with recommended score of 213 (computer) or 550 (paper); proof of adequate funds; proof of health/immunizations.

International Student Contact Linda Seatts, Director, International Services Office, 598 Student Center Building, Detroit, MI 48202. *Phone:* 313-577-3422. *Fax:* 313-577-2962. *E-mail:* ac5041@wayne.edu.

APPLICATION *Required:* GMAT, application form, baccalaureate/first degree, transcripts of college work. *Application fee:* $50. Applications for domestic and international students are processed on a rolling basis.

Application Contact Linda Zaddach, Assistant Dean of Student Affairs, 5201 Cass, Prentis Building, Room 200, Detroit, MI 48202. *Phone:* 313-577-4510. *Fax:* 313-577-5299. *E-mail:* l.s.zaddach@wayne.edu.

See full description on page 760.

Western Michigan University

Haworth College of Business

Kalamazoo, Michigan

Phone: 269-387-5075 **Fax:** 269-387-5796 **E-mail:** barb.caras-tomczak@wmich.edu

Business Program(s) Web Site: http://www.hcob.wmich.edu

Graduate Business Unit Enrollment *Total:* 398 (99 full-time; 299 part-time; 220 women; 62 international). *Average Age:* 30.

Graduate Business Faculty *Total:* 97 (82 full-time; 15 part-time).

Admissions *Applied:* 202. *Admitted:* 118. *Enrolled:* 94. *Average GMAT:* 530. *Average GPA:* 3.2

Academic Calendar Semesters.

Accreditation AACSB—The Association to Advance Collegiate Schools of Business.

After Graduation (Class of 2006–07) *Employed within 3 months of graduation:* 71%. *Average starting salary:* $62,410.

DEGREES MBA • MS

MBA—Master of Business Administration Full-time and part-time. 2.75 GPA and 500 GMAT. 36 to 48 total credits required. 15 to 72 months to complete program. *Concentrations:* finance, general MBA, international business, management, management information systems, marketing.

MS—Master of Science in Accountancy Full-time and part-time. 30 to 66 total credits required. 8 to 72 months to complete program. *Concentration:* accounting.

RESOURCES AND SERVICES 250 on-campus PCs are available to graduate business students. Access to Internet/World Wide Web, online (class) registration, and online grade reports available. *Personal computer requirements:* Graduate business students are strongly recommended to purchase or lease a personal computer. *Placement services include:* Alumni network, career placement, career counseling/planning, electronic job bank, resume referral, career fairs, job interviews arranged, resume preparation, and career library.

FINANCIAL AID (2007–08) 30 students received aid, including fellowships, research assistantships, teaching assistantships, and work study. *Financial aid application deadline:* 2/15.

Financial Aid Contact Ms. Rachel Colingsworth, Interim Director of Financial Aid, 1000 Oliver Street, Kalamazoo, MI 49008-5337. *Phone:* 269-387-6023. *Fax:* 269-387-6989. *E-mail:* finaid-info@wmich.edu.

INTERNATIONAL STUDENTS 16% of students enrolled are international students. *Services and facilities:* Counseling/support services, ESL/language courses, Housing location assistance, International student housing, International student organization, Orientation, Visa Services. Financial aid is available to international students. *Required with application:* TOEFL with recommended score of 213 (computer) or 550 (paper); proof of adequate funds; proof of health/immunizations. *Recommended with application:* IELT with recommended score of 7; TWE.

International Student Contact Ms. Rebecca Soloman, Director, International Student Services, 414 Ellsworth Hall, Kalamazoo, MI 49008-5246. *Phone:* 269-387-5865. *Fax:* 269-387-5899. *E-mail:* rebecca.soloman@wmich.edu.

APPLICATION *Required:* GMAT, application form, baccalaureate/first degree, transcripts of college work. *Recommended:* Letter(s) of recommendation, resume/curriculum vitae, 2 years of work experience. *Application fee:* $45, $55 (international). Applications for domestic and international students are processed on a rolling basis.

Application Contact Ms. Barbara Caras-Tomczak, Graduate Admissions Advisor, 2130 Schneider Hall, Kalamazoo, MI 49008-5411. *Phone:* 269-387-5075. *Fax:* 269-387-5796. *E-mail:* barb.caras-tomczak@wmich.edu.

MINNESOTA

Argosy University, Twin Cities

College of Business

Eagan, Minnesota

Phone: 651-846-2882 **Fax:** 651-994-7956

Business Program(s) Web Site: http://www.argosy.edu/twincities

DEGREES DBA • MBA • MSM

DBA—Doctor of Business Administration (DBA) *Concentrations:* accounting, information systems, international business, management, marketing.

MBA—Master of Business Administration (MBA) *Concentrations:* finance, health administration, information systems, international business, management, marketing, public policy and administration.

MSM—Master of Science in Management (MSM) *Concentration:* management.

Financial Aid Contact Director of Admissions, 1515 Central Parkway, Eagan, MN 55121. *Phone:* 651-846-2882. *Fax:* 651-994-7956.

International Student Contact Director of Admissions, 1515 Central Parkway, Eagan, MN 55121. *Phone:* 651-846-2882. *Fax:* 651-994-7956.

Application Contact Director of Admissions, 1515 Central Parkway, Eagan, MN 55121. *Phone:* 651-846-2882. *Fax:* 651-994-7956.

See full description on page 566.

College of St. Catherine
Program in Organizational Leadership

St. Paul, Minnesota

Phone: 651-690-6933 **Fax:** 651-690-6064 **E-mail:** swalexander@stkate.edu

Business Program(s) Web Site: http://minerva.stkate.edu/offices/academic/maol.nsf

Graduate Business Unit Enrollment *Total:* 146 (11 full-time; 135 part-time; 135 women; 2 international). *Average Age:* 41.

Graduate Business Faculty *Total:* 18 (8 full-time; 10 part-time).

Admissions *Applied:* 47. *Admitted:* 37. *Enrolled:* 34.

Academic Calendar Trimesters.

After Graduation (Class of 2006–07) *Employed within 3 months of graduation:* 100%.

DEGREES JD/MA • MA

JD/MA—Juris Doctor/Master of Arts in Organizational Leadership Full-time and part-time. At least 108 total credits required. *Concentration:* leadership.

MA—Master of Arts in Organizational Leadership Full-time and part-time. At least 32 total credits required. *Concentration:* strategic management.

MA—Master of Arts in Organizational Leadership Full-time and part-time. At least 35 total credits required. *Concentration:* information technology.

MA—Master of Arts in Organizational Leadership Full-time and part-time. At least 38 total credits required. *Concentration:* health care.

MA—Master of Arts in Organizational Leadership Full-time and part-time. At least 43 total credits required. *Concentration:* conflict resolution management.

MA—Master of Arts in Organizational Leadership Full-time and part-time. At least 38 total credits required. *Concentration:* leadership.

MA—Master of Arts in Organizational Leadership: Spirituality and Leadership Full-time and part-time. 38 to 39 total credits required. *Concentration:* other.

MA—Organizational Leadership: Accountancy Leadership Full-time and part-time. At least 39 total credits required. *Concentration:* accounting.

RESOURCES AND SERVICES 250 on-campus PCs are available to graduate business students. Access to Internet/World Wide Web, online (class) registration, and online grade reports available. *Personal computer requirements:* Graduate business students are strongly recommended to purchase or lease a personal computer. *Special opportunities include:* An internship program is available. *Placement services include:* Alumni network, job search course, career counseling/planning, career fairs, and resume preparation.

EXPENSES *Tuition:* Part-time: $648 per credit. *Tuition (international):* Part-time: $648 per credit. *Required fees:* Full-time: $60. Part-time: $20 per term. *Graduate housing:* Room and board costs vary by number of occupants, type of accommodation, and type of board plan. *Typical cost:* $6360 (including board), $5620 (room only).

FINANCIAL AID (2007–08) 60 students received aid, including grants, loans, and research assistantships. Aid is available to part-time students. *Financial aid application deadline:* 4/1.

Financial Aid Contact Elizabeth Stevens, Director of Financial Aid, Mail Stop F-11, 2004 Randolph Avenue, St. Paul, MN 55105-1789. *Phone:* 651-690-6540. *Fax:* 651-690-6765. *E-mail:* finaid@stkate.edu.

INTERNATIONAL STUDENTS 1% of students enrolled are international students. *Services and facilities:* Counseling/support services, ESL/language courses, International student organization, Orientation, Visa Services. Financial aid is available to international students. *Required with application:* TOEFL with recommended score of 250 (computer), 600 (paper), or 100 (Internet); proof of adequate funds; proof of health/immunizations.

International Student Contact Norah Hoff, Associate Director of International Programs and Services, 2004 Randolph Avenue, #F-29, St. Paul, MN 55105. *Phone:* 651-690-6014. *Fax:* 651-690-8824. *E-mail:* nvhoff@stkate.edu.

APPLICATION *Required:* Application form, baccalaureate/first degree, 2 letters of recommendation, personal statement, resume/curriculum vitae, transcripts of college work, 2 years of work experience. School will accept GMAT, GRE, and MAT. *Application fee:* $35. Applications for domestic and international students are processed on a rolling basis.

Application Contact Sylvia Alexander-Sedey, Senior Admission Counselor, 2004 Randolph Avenue, #4027, St. Paul, MN 55105-1789. *Phone:* 651-690-6933. *Fax:* 651-690-6064. *E-mail:* swalexander@stkate.edu.

The College of St. Scholastica
Department of Management

Duluth, Minnesota

Phone: 218-723-6651 **Fax:** 218-723-6150 **E-mail:** rhartl@css.edu

Business Program(s) Web Site: http://www.css.edu/x2113.xml

Graduate Business Unit Enrollment *Total:* 168 (84 full-time; 84 part-time; 106 women).

Graduate Business Faculty *Total:* 30 (6 full-time; 24 part-time).

Admissions *Applied:* 64. *Admitted:* 57. *Enrolled:* 43. *Average GPA:* 3.19.

Academic Calendar 8-week sessions.

DEGREES MA • MBA

MA—Master of Arts in Management Full-time and part-time. At least 39 total credits required. 12 to 84 months to complete program. *Concentrations:* health administration, human resources management, organizational behavior/development.

MBA—Master of Business Administration Full-time and part-time. 33 to 45 total credits required. *Concentration:* general MBA.

RESOURCES AND SERVICES 187 on-campus PCs are available to graduate business students. Access to Internet/World Wide Web, online (class) registration, and online grade reports available. *Personal computer requirements:* Graduate business students are strongly recommended to purchase or lease a personal computer. *Placement services include:* Alumni network, career counseling/planning, resume preparation, and career library.

FINANCIAL AID (2007–08) 53 students received aid, including grants, loans, scholarships, and work study. Aid is available to part-time students.

The College of St. Scholastica (continued)

Financial Aid Contact Jon Erickson, Director of Financial Aid, 1200 Kenwood Avenue, Duluth, MN 55811. *Phone:* 218-723-6725. *Fax:* 218-723-5991. *E-mail:* jerickso@css.edu.

INTERNATIONAL STUDENTS *Services and facilities:* Counseling/support services, Housing location assistance, International student organization, Language tutoring, Orientation, Visa Services. Financial aid is available to international students. *Required with application:* TOEFL with recommended score of 213 (computer) or 550 (paper); proof of adequate funds; proof of health/immunizations.

International Student Contact Oliver Meyer, Associate Director of Admissions, 1200 Kenwood Avenue, Duluth, MN 55811. *Phone:* 218-723-6045. *Fax:* 218-723-6290. *E-mail:* omeyer@css.edu.

APPLICATION *Required:* Application form, baccalaureate/first degree, essay, 2 letters of recommendation, transcripts of college work. *Application fee:* $50. Applications for domestic and international students are processed on a rolling basis.

Application Contact Mr. Robert Hartl, Program Director, Management Department, 1200 Kenwood Avenue, Duluth, MN 55811. *Phone:* 218-723-6651. *Fax:* 218-723-6150. *E-mail:* rhartl@css.edu.

Concordia University, St. Paul
College of Business and Organizational Leadership
St. Paul, Minnesota

Phone: 651-641-8489 **E-mail:** blahosky@csp.edu

Business Program(s) Web Site: http://www.csp.edu/Academics/Graduate/MBA/

Graduate Business Faculty *Total:* 30 (5 full-time; 25 part-time).

Academic Calendar Continuous.

DEGREES   MA • MBA

MA—Organizational Management Full-time. Distance learning option. Up to 40 total credits required. *Concentrations:* business studies, management, organizational management.

MA—Organizational Management: Human Resources Emphasis Full-time. Distance learning option. Up to 40 total credits required. *Concentrations:* human resources management, management, organizational behavior/development.

MA—Organizational Management: Sports Management Emphasis Full-time. Distance learning option. Up to 40 total credits required. *Concentrations:* organizational management, sports/entertainment management.

MBA—Master of Business Administration Full-time. Distance learning option. Up to 42 total credits required. *Concentrations:* general MBA, management.

RESOURCES AND SERVICES 6 on-campus PCs are available to graduate business students. Access to Internet/World Wide Web, online (class) registration, and online grade reports available. *Personal computer requirements:* Graduate business students are required to have a personal computer. *Placement services include:* Alumni network, career counseling/planning, and resume preparation.

Financial Aid Contact Financial Aid Office, 275 Syndicate Street, North, St. Paul, MN 55104. *Phone:* 651-641-8204. *E-mail:* bearcenter@csp.edu.

INTERNATIONAL STUDENTS *Services and facilities:* International student organization. Financial aid is not available to international students. *Required with application:* TOEFL; proof of adequate funds; proof of health/immunizations.

International Student Contact Bridget Blahosky, International Student Program, 275 Syndicate Street North, St. Paul, MN 55104. *Phone:* 651-641-8230. *E-mail:* blahosky@csp.edu.

APPLICATION *Required:* Application form, baccalaureate/first degree, essay, 2 letters of recommendation, resume/curriculum vitae, transcripts of college work, 5 years of work experience. *Application fee:* $50. Applications for domestic and international students are processed on a rolling basis.

Application Contact Bridget Blahosky, Graduate Admission Counselor, 275 Syndicate Street North, St. Paul, MN 55104. *Phone:* 651-641-8489. *E-mail:* blahosky@csp.edu.

Metropolitan State University
College of Management
St. Paul, Minnesota

Phone: 612-659-7258 **Fax:** 612-659-7268 **E-mail:** gloria.marcus@metrostate.edu

Business Program(s) Web Site: http://www.metrostate.edu/com/

Graduate Business Unit Enrollment *Total:* 553 (184 full-time; 369 part-time; 332 women; 18 international). *Average Age:* 38.

Graduate Business Faculty *Total:* 78 (21 full-time; 57 part-time).

Admissions *Applied:* 256. *Admitted:* 163. *Enrolled:* 131. *Average GMAT:* 500. *Average GPA:* 3.2

Academic Calendar Semesters.

After Graduation (Class of 2006–07) *Employed within 3 months of graduation:* 96%. *Average starting salary:* $65,000.

DEGREES   MBA • MBA/MSMIS • MPM

MBA—Master of Business Administration Full-time and part-time. Distance learning option. GMAT, two years professional work experience. At least 40 total credits required. 18 to 60 months to complete program. *Concentrations:* finance, management information systems, marketing, project management.

MBA/MSMIS—Master of Management Information Systems Full-time and part-time. Distance learning option. Diagnostic assessment required. At least 44 total credits required. 18 to 60 months to complete program. *Concentrations:* information management, system management.

MPM—Master of Public and Nonprofit Administration Full-time and part-time. Distance learning option. Diagnostic skills assessment required. At least 40 total credits required. 18 to 60 months to complete program. *Concentrations:* nonprofit organization, public management.

RESOURCES AND SERVICES 212 on-campus PCs are available to graduate business students. Access to Internet/World Wide Web, online (class) registration, and online grade reports available. *Personal computer requirements:* Graduate business students are strongly recommended to purchase or lease a personal computer. *Special opportunities include:* An internship program is available. *Placement services include:* Alumni network, career placement, career counseling/planning, resume referral, career fairs, resume preparation, and career library.

EXPENSES *Tuition (state resident):* Full-time: $4358.88. *Tuition (nonresident):* Full-time: $8391. *Tuition (international):* Full-time: $8390.88. *Required fees:* Full-time: $41.72. Part-time: $20.86 per credit. Tuition and/or fees vary by academic program and local reciprocity agreements.

FINANCIAL AID (2007–08) Loans, research assistantships, scholarships, and work study. Aid is available to part-time students. *Financial aid application deadline:* 6/14.

Financial Aid Contact Mr. Robert Bode, Director, Financial Aid, 700 East 7th Street, FH 110, St. Paul, MN 55106-5000. *Phone:* 651-793-1412. *Fax:* 651-793-1410. *E-mail:* finaid@metrostate.edu.

INTERNATIONAL STUDENTS 3% of students enrolled are international students. *Services and facilities:* Counseling/support services, International student organization, Orientation, Visa Services. Financial aid is not available to international students. *Required with application:*

TOEFL with recommended score of 213 (computer), 550 (paper), or 80 (Internet); proof of adequate funds; proof of health/immunizations.

International Student Contact Dr. Kamal Elbasher, Director, International Student Services, 700 East 7th Street, St. Paul, MN 55106-5000. *Phone:* 651-793-1219. *Fax:* 651-793-1546. *E-mail:* kamal.elbasher@metrostate.edu.

APPLICATION *Required:* GMAT, application form, baccalaureate/first degree, essay, 2 letters of recommendation, personal statement, resume/curriculum vitae, transcripts of college work, 2 years of work experience. School will accept GRE. *Application fee:* $20. *Deadlines:* 8/1 for fall, 12/1 for spring, 4/1 for summer, 5/1 for fall (international), 9/1 for spring (international).

Application Contact Gloria Marcus, Admissions Advisor/Recruiter, 1501 Hennepin Avenue, Minneapolis, MN 55403-1896. *Phone:* 612-659-7258. *Fax:* 612-659-7268. *E-mail:* gloria.marcus@metrostate.edu.

St. Cloud State University
G.R. Herberger College of Business

St. Cloud, Minnesota

Phone: 320-308-2112 **Fax:** 320-308-5371 **E-mail:** graduatestudies@stcloudstate.edu

Business Program(s) Web Site: http://cob.stcloudstate.edu/

Graduate Business Unit Enrollment *Total:* 169 (47 full-time; 122 part-time; 63 women; 25 international). *Average Age:* 31.

Graduate Business Faculty 39 full-time.

Admissions *Average GMAT:* 503. *Average GPA:* 3.25

Academic Calendar Semesters.

Accreditation AACSB—The Association to Advance Collegiate Schools of Business.

DEGREE MBA

MBA—Master of Business Administration Full-time and part-time. 33 to 36 total credits required. 15 to 96 months to complete program. *Concentrations:* economics, human resources management, management information systems.

RESOURCES AND SERVICES 150 on-campus PCs are available to graduate business students. Access to Internet/World Wide Web, online (class) registration, and online grade reports available. *Personal computer requirements:* Graduate business students are strongly recommended to purchase or lease a personal computer. *Special opportunities include:* An internship program is available. *Placement services include:* Alumni network, job search course, career counseling/planning, electronic job bank, career fairs, job interviews arranged, resume preparation, and career library.

EXPENSES *Tuition (state resident):* Part-time: $435 per credit. *Tuition (international):* Part-time: $435 per credit. *Required fees:* Part-time: $28.32 per credit. Tuition and/or fees vary by campus location, academic program, and local reciprocity agreements.

FINANCIAL AID (2007–08) Loans, research assistantships, scholarships, and teaching assistantships. *Financial aid application deadline:* 3/1.

Financial Aid Contact Joyce Heim, Office Manager, Financial Aid, 720 4th Avenue South, St. Cloud, MN 56301-4498. *Phone:* 320-308-2047. *Fax:* 320-308-5424. *E-mail:* finaid@stcloudstate.edu.

INTERNATIONAL STUDENTS 15% of students enrolled are international students. *Services and facilities:* Counseling/support services, ESL/language courses, Housing location assistance, International student organization, Language tutoring, Orientation. Financial aid is available to international students. *Required with application:* TOEFL with recommended score of 213 (computer), 550 (paper), or 79 (Internet); proof of adequate funds; proof of health/immunizations.

International Student Contact Assistant Vice President for Academic Affairs/International Studies, 720 4th Avenue South, St. Cloud, MN 56301-4498. *Phone:* 320-308-4287. *Fax:* 320-308-4223. *E-mail:* intstudy@stcloudstate.edu.

APPLICATION *Required:* GMAT, application form, baccalaureate/first degree, 3 letters of recommendation, personal statement, transcripts of college work. *Recommended:* Resume/curriculum vitae, work experience. *Application fee:* $35. *Deadlines:* 6/1 for fall, 10/1 for spring, 4/1 for fall (international), 8/1 for spring (international).

Application Contact Linda Krueger, Graduate Admissions Manager, 720 4th Avenue South, St. Cloud, MN 56301-4498. *Phone:* 320-308-2112. *Fax:* 320-308-5371. *E-mail:* graduatestudies@stcloudstate.edu.

Saint Mary's University of Minnesota
Schools of Graduate and Professional Programs

Minneapolis, Minnesota

Phone: 612-728-5198 **Fax:** 612-728-5121 **E-mail:** tc-admission@smumn.edu

Business Program(s) Web Site: http://www.smumn.edu/gradpro

DEGREES EMBA • M Sc • MA • MBA • MS

EMBA—PowerTrak Master of Business Administration—Executive Part-time. At least 38 total credits required. Maximum of 60 months to complete program. *Concentration:* executive programs.

M Sc—Project Management Full-time and part-time. At least 38 total credits required. 15 to 60 months to complete program. *Concentration:* project management.

MA—Arts Administration Full-time and part-time. 36 total credits required. 18 to 36 months to complete program. *Concentration:* arts administration/management.

MA—Human Resource Management Full-time and part-time. 38 total credits required. 24 to 36 months to complete program. *Concentration:* human resources management.

MA—International Business Full-time and part-time. 41 total credits required. 24 to 36 months to complete program. *Concentrations:* international and area business studies, international business.

MA—Master of Arts in International Business Full-time and part-time. GMAT required. At least 41 total credits required. 15 to 60 months to complete program. *Concentrations:* international and area business studies, international business, international management.

MA—Master of Arts in Management Full-time and part-time. At least 35 total credits required. 24 to 60 months to complete program. *Concentration:* management.

MA—Public Safety Administration Full-time and part-time. 36 total credits required. 3 months to complete program. *Concentrations:* administration, public and private management, public management, public policy and administration.

MBA—PowerTrak Master of Business Administration—Custom Part-time. At least 36 total credits required. Maximum of 60 months to complete program. *Concentrations:* business ethics, health administration, human resources management, international business, management, marketing, project management, telecommunications management.

MBA—PowerTrak Master of Business Administration—Specialized Part-time. Provides an in-depth specialty in Marketing or Finance. At least 44 total credits required. Maximum of 60 months to complete program. *Concentrations:* finance, marketing.

MS—Geographical Information Sciences Full-time and part-time. 37 total credits required. 24 to 36 months to complete program.

Saint Mary's University of Minnesota (continued)

MS—Telecommunications Full-time and part-time. 36 total credits required. 24 to 36 months to complete program. *Concentration:* telecommunications management.

RESOURCES AND SERVICES 50 on-campus PCs are available to graduate business students. Access to Internet/World Wide Web, online (class) registration, and online grade reports available. *Personal computer requirements:* Graduate business students are strongly recommended to purchase or lease a personal computer. *Placement services include:* Alumni network.

Application Contact Andrea Benedict, Office of Admission, 2500 Park Avenue, Minneapolis, MN 55404-4403. *Phone:* 612-728-5198. *Fax:* 612-728-5121. *E-mail:* tc-admission@smumn.edu.

University of Minnesota, Duluth
Labovitz School of Business and Economics

Duluth, Minnesota

Phone: 218-726-7523 **Fax:** 218-726-6970 **E-mail:** grad@d.umn.edu

Business Program(s) Web Site: http://www.d.umn.edu/sbe/degreeprogs/mba/

Graduate Business Unit Enrollment *Total:* 64 (64 part-time; 25 women; 4 international). *Average Age:* 32.

Graduate Business Faculty *Total:* 35 (33 full-time; 2 part-time).

Admissions *Applied:* 21. *Admitted:* 20. *Enrolled:* 19. *Average GMAT:* 553. *Average GPA:* 3.44

Academic Calendar Semesters.

Accreditation AACSB—The Association to Advance Collegiate Schools of Business.

After Graduation (Class of 2006–07) *Employed within 3 months of graduation:* 95%.

DEGREE MBA

MBA—Evening Master of Business Administration Full-time and part-time. GMAT required. At least 32 total credits required. 24 to 84 months to complete program. *Concentration:* general MBA.

RESOURCES AND SERVICES 500 on-campus PCs are available to graduate business students. Access to Internet/World Wide Web, online (class) registration, and online grade reports available. *Personal computer requirements:* Graduate business students are strongly recommended to purchase or lease a personal computer. *Placement services include:* Alumni network, career placement, career counseling/planning, career fairs, job interviews arranged, resume preparation, and career library.

EXPENSES *Tuition (state resident):* Part-time: $773 per credit. *Tuition (international):* Part-time: $773 per credit. *Required fees:* Part-time: $500 per semester. Tuition and/or fees vary by campus location, academic program, and local reciprocity agreements. *Graduate housing:* Room and board costs vary by number of occupants, type of accommodation, and type of board plan. *Typical cost:* $6000 (including board).

FINANCIAL AID (2007–08) 5 students received aid, including research assistantships. Aid is available to part-time students. *Financial aid application deadline:* 6/1.

Financial Aid Contact Ms. Brenda Herzig, Director of Financial Aid, 1117 University Drive, 21 Solon Campus Center, Duluth, MN 55812-3000. *Phone:* 218-726-8000. *Fax:* 218-726-8532. *E-mail:* finaid@d.umn.edu.

INTERNATIONAL STUDENTS 6% of students enrolled are international students. *Services and facilities:* Counseling/support services, ESL/language courses, Housing location assistance, International student organization, Orientation. Financial aid is not available to international students. *Required with application:* TOEFL with recommended score of 215 (computer) or 550 (paper); TWE with recommended score of 4; proof of adequate funds; proof of health/immunizations.

International Student Contact Ms. Karin Robbins, International Student Advisor, 60 Solon Campus Center, 1117 University Drive, Duluth, MN 55812-3000. *Phone:* 218-726-8962. *Fax:* 218-726-6244. *E-mail:* krobbin1@d.umn.edu.

APPLICATION *Required:* GMAT, application form, baccalaureate/first degree, personal statement, resume/curriculum vitae, transcripts of college work. *Recommended:* 3 years of work experience. *Application fee:* $55, $75 (international). Applications for domestic and international students are processed on a rolling basis.

Application Contact Ms. M. J. Leone, 1049 University Drive, 431 Darland Administration Building, Duluth, MN 55812-3011. *Phone:* 218-726-7523. *Fax:* 218-726-6970. *E-mail:* grad@d.umn.edu.

University of Minnesota, Twin Cities Campus
Carlson School of Management

Minneapolis, Minnesota

Phone: 612-625-5555 **Fax:** 612-625-1012 **E-mail:** full-timembainfo@csom.umn.edu

Business Program(s) Web Site: http://www.carlsonmba.umn.edu/

Accreditation AACSB—The Association to Advance Collegiate Schools of Business.

DEGREES EMBA • M Acc • MBA • MBT

EMBA—Executive Master of Business Administration Part-time. 8 years of work experience required, GMAT not required. At least 48 total credits required. Minimum of 20 months to complete program. *Concentration:* management.

M Acc—Master of Accountancy Full-time and part-time. UG degree in accounting or equivalent. At least 30 total credits required. 9 to 84 months to complete program. *Concentration:* accounting.

MBA—Full-Time Master of Business Administration Full-time. At least 63 total credits required. 21 months to complete program. *Concentrations:* accounting, entrepreneurship, finance, health care, information management, international business, marketing, operations management, strategic management, supply chain management.

MBA—Part-Time Master of Business Administration Part-time. 48 to 57 total credits required. 18 to 60 months to complete program. *Concentrations:* accounting, entrepreneurship, finance, health care, information management, international and area business studies, international business, international management, management information systems, management science, marketing, operations management, strategic management, supply chain management.

MBT—Master of Business Taxation Full-time and part-time. At least 30 total credits required. 12 to 84 months to complete program. *Concentration:* taxation.

RESOURCES AND SERVICES 258 on-campus PCs are available to graduate business students. Access to Internet/World Wide Web, online (class) registration, and online grade reports available. *Personal computer requirements:* Graduate business students are required to have a personal computer, the cost of which is included in tuition or other required fees. *Special opportunities include:* An international exchange program and an internship program are available. *Placement services include:* Alumni network, career placement, job search course, career counseling/planning, electronic job bank, resume referral, career fairs, job interviews arranged, resume preparation, and career library.

Application Contact Jeff Bieganek, Director of Admissions and Business Development, Suite 4-106, 321 19th Avenue South, Minneapolis, MN 55455. *Phone:* 612-625-5555. *Fax:* 612-625-1012. *E-mail:* full-timembainfo@csom.umn.edu.

University of St. Thomas

Opus College of Business

St. Paul, Minnesota

Phone: 651-962-8800 **Fax:** 651-962-4129 **E-mail:** ustmba@stthomas.edu

Business Program(s) Web Site: http://www.stthomas.edu/business/

Graduate Business Unit Enrollment *Total:* 1,760 (114 full-time; 1,646 part-time; 748 women; 62 international). *Average Age:* 33.

Graduate Business Faculty *Total:* 251 (83 full-time; 168 part-time).

Admissions *Applied:* 523. *Admitted:* 389. *Enrolled:* 278. *Average GMAT:* 558. *Average GPA:* 3.25

Academic Calendar Semesters.

After Graduation (Class of 2006–07) *Employed within 3 months of graduation:* 86%.

DEGREES MBA • MBC • MS

MBA—Evening UST MBA Part-time. Must be currently employed in a full-time position. At least 51 total credits required. 24 to 84 months to complete program. *Concentrations:* accounting, entrepreneurship, finance, financial management/planning, human resources management, information management, international management, management, manufacturing management, marketing, new venture management, nonprofit management, risk management.

MBA—Executive UST MBA Part-time. 5 years of management or leadership experience, class visit and interview required. At least 50 total credits required. 30 months to complete program. *Concentration:* executive programs.

MBA—Full-Time UST MBA Full-time. Interview required. At least 61 total credits required. 21 months to complete program. *Concentrations:* accounting, entrepreneurship, finance, health care, human resources management, information management, international management, management, manufacturing management, marketing, nonprofit management, risk management.

MBA—Health Care UST MBA Part-time. Distance learning option. 5 years of work experience and interview required. At least 54 total credits required. 27 months to complete program. *Concentration:* health care.

MBC—Master of Business Communication Part-time. 2 years of work experience and writing assessment required. At least 42 total credits required. 24 to 84 months to complete program. *Concentration:* management communication.

MS—Master of Science in Accountancy Full-time. A bachelor's degree in accounting or its equivalent required. At least 31 total credits required. 12 months to complete program. *Concentration:* accounting.

MS—Master of Science in Real Estate Part-time. At least 36 total credits required. 33 to 36 months to complete program. *Concentration:* real estate.

RESOURCES AND SERVICES 94 on-campus PCs are available to graduate business students. Access to Internet/World Wide Web, online (class) registration, and online grade reports available. *Personal computer requirements:* Graduate business students are strongly recommended to purchase or lease a personal computer. *Special opportunities include:* An internship program is available. *Placement services include:* Alumni network, career placement, job search course, career counseling/planning, electronic job bank, resume referral, career fairs, job interviews arranged, resume preparation, and career library.

EXPENSES *Tuition:* Full-time: $21,579. Part-time: $707.50 per credit. *Tuition (international):* Full-time: $21,579. Part-time: $707.50 per credit. *Required fees:* Full-time: $442. Part-time: $75 per semester. Tuition and/or fees vary by academic program.

FINANCIAL AID (2007–08) 584 students received aid, including grants, loans, research assistantships, scholarships, and work study. Aid is available to part-time students. *Financial aid application deadline:* 7/1.

Financial Aid Contact Mr. Chad R. Nosbusch, Associate Director of Financial Aid, 1000 LaSalle Avenue, TMH 110E, Minneapolis, MN 55403. *Phone:* 651-962-4051. *Fax:* 651-962-6599. *E-mail:* crnosbusch@stthomas.edu.

INTERNATIONAL STUDENTS 4% of students enrolled are international students. *Services and facilities:* Counseling/support services, ESL/language courses, Housing location assistance, International student organization, Orientation, Visa Services. Financial aid is available to international students. *Required with application:* TOEFL with recommended score of 213 (computer) or 550 (paper); proof of adequate funds; proof of health/immunizations.

International Student Contact Mr. Milyon Trulove, Admissions Director, 1000 LaSalle Avenue, TMH 100, Minneapolis, MN 55403. *Phone:* 651-962-8800. *Fax:* 651-962-4129. *E-mail:* ustmba@stthomas.edu.

APPLICATION *Required:* GMAT, application form, baccalaureate/first degree, essay, 2 letters of recommendation, personal statement, resume/curriculum vitae, transcripts of college work. *Recommended:* Interview, work experience. *Application fee:* $60, $90 (international). Applications for domestic and international students are processed on a rolling basis.

Application Contact Mr. Milyon Trulove, Admissions Director, 1000 LaSalle Avenue, TMH 100, Minneapolis, MN 55403. *Phone:* 651-962-8800. *Fax:* 651-962-4129. *E-mail:* ustmba@stthomas.edu.

See full description on page 738.

Walden University

School of Management

Minneapolis, Minnesota

Phone: 866-492-5336 **E-mail:** info@waldenu.edu

Business Program(s) Web Site: http://www.waldenu.edu/c/Schools/Schools_109.htm

Graduate Business Unit Enrollment *Total:* 3,147 (1,996 full-time; 1,151 part-time; 1,774 women; 49 international). *Average Age:* 36.

Academic Calendar Both semesters and quarters.

DEGREES MBA • MISM

MBA—Master of Business Administration Full-time and part-time. Distance learning option. Applicants must have a bachelor's degree from a regionally-accredited institution, and 2 years of professional experience in a public/non-profit setting. 40 to 68 total credits required. 18 to 24 months to complete program. *Concentrations:* entrepreneurship, finance, general MBA, human resources management, leadership, marketing, project management, risk management, technology management.

MISM—Master of Information Systems Management Full-time and part-time. Distance learning option. At least 33 total credits required. 18 to 24 months to complete program. *Concentrations:* business information science, information management, information technology, marketing, supply chain management.

RESOURCES AND SERVICES Access to Internet/World Wide Web, online (class) registration, and online grade reports available. *Personal computer requirements:* Graduate business students are required to have a personal computer. *Placement services include:* Alumni network, job search course, career counseling/planning, and resume preparation.

EXPENSES *Tuition:* Full-time: $14,064. Part-time: $442 per credit hour. *Tuition (international):* Full-time: $14,064. Part-time: $442 per credit hour. Tuition and/or fees vary by number of courses or credits taken and academic program.

FINANCIAL AID (2007–08) Fellowships, loans, and scholarships. Aid is available to part-time students.

INTERNATIONAL STUDENTS 2% of students enrolled are international students. *Services and facilities:* Counseling/support services, ESL/language courses, Orientation, writing center, online concierge.

Walden University (continued)

Required with application: IELT with recommended score of 6.5; TOEFL with recommended score of 213 (computer) or 550 (paper).

APPLICATION *Required:* Application form, baccalaureate/first degree, personal statement, resume/curriculum vitae, transcripts of college work, 2 years of work experience. *Application fee:* $50. Applications for domestic and international students are processed on a rolling basis.

Application Contact Enrollment Advisor, 1001 Fleet Street, Baltimore, MD 21202. *Phone:* 866-492-5336. *E-mail:* info@waldenu.edu.

MISSISSIPPI

Alcorn State University
School of Business
Natchez, Mississippi

Phone: 601-304-4309 **Fax:** 601-304-4350 **E-mail:** jwild@alcorn.edu

Business Program(s) Web Site: http://bschool.alcorn.edu

DEGREE MBA

MBA—Graduate Business Programs Full-time and part-time. Distance learning option. GMAT Score. 36 to 48 total credits required. 18 to 24 months to complete program. *Concentration:* general MBA.

RESOURCES AND SERVICES 24 on-campus PCs are available to graduate business students. Access to Internet/World Wide Web, online (class) registration, and online grade reports available. *Personal computer requirements:* Graduate business students are strongly recommended to purchase or lease a personal computer. *Special opportunities include:* An internship program is available. *Placement services include:* Alumni network, career placement, job search course, career counseling/planning, electronic job bank, resume referral, career fairs, job interviews arranged, resume preparation, and career library.

Application Contact Mr. Joe Wild, Director of Student Services and Recruitment, 9 Campus Drive, Natchez, MS 39120. *Phone:* 601-304-4309. *Fax:* 601-304-4350. *E-mail:* jwild@alcorn.edu.

Belhaven College
Program in Business
Jackson, Mississippi

Phone: 407-804-1424 **Fax:** 407-620-5210 **E-mail:** akelleher@belhaven.edu

Business Program(s) Web Site: http://www.belhaven.edu/academics.business/default.htm

Graduate Business Unit Enrollment *Total:* 233 (233 full-time; 159 women). *Average Age:* 33.

Graduate Business Faculty *Total:* 33 (17 full-time; 16 part-time).

Admissions *Applied:* 64. *Admitted:* 60. *Enrolled:* 35.

Academic Calendar Semesters.

DEGREE MBA/MPA

MBA/MPA—Master of Business Administration/Master of Public Administration Full-time. *Concentrations:* general MBA, public policy and administration.

RESOURCES AND SERVICES 30 on-campus PCs are available to graduate business students. Access to Internet/World Wide Web, online

(class) registration, and online grade reports available. *Personal computer requirements:* Graduate business students are not required to have a personal computer.

Financial Aid Contact Linda Phillips, Assistant Vice President for Institutional Advancement, 1500 Peachtree Street, Jackson, MS 39202. *Phone:* 601-968-5934. *E-mail:* lphillips@belhaven.edu.

INTERNATIONAL STUDENTS *Services and facilities:* Counseling/support services, ESL/language courses, International student organization, Language tutoring, Orientation, Visa Services. *Required with application:* TOEFL with recommended score of 173 (computer), 500 (paper), or 61 (Internet); proof of adequate funds; proof of health/immunizations.

International Student Contact Becky Sims, Administrative Assistant to Vice President for Institutional Advancement, 1500 Peachtree Street, Jackson, MS 39202. *Phone:* 601-968-8746. *E-mail:* bsims@belhaven.edu.

APPLICATION *Required:* GMAT, application form, baccalaureate/first degree, essay, resume/curriculum vitae, transcripts of college work, 2 years of work experience. School will accept GRE and MAT. *Application fee:* $25. Applications for domestic and international students are processed on a rolling basis.

Application Contact Dr. Audrey Kelleher, Vice President, Adult and Graduate Marketing and Development, Maitland 200 Suite 165, 2301 Maitland Center Parkway, Maitland, FL 32751. *Phone:* 407-804-1424. *Fax:* 407-620-5210. *E-mail:* akelleher@belhaven.edu.

Delta State University
College of Business
Cleveland, Mississippi

Phone: 662-846-4875 **Fax:** 662-846-4313 **E-mail:** tjackson@deltastate.edu

Business Program(s) Web Site: http://gradbusiness.deltastate.edu/

Graduate Business Unit Enrollment *Total:* 71 (47 full-time; 24 part-time; 45 women; 6 international). *Average Age:* 29.

Graduate Business Faculty *Total:* 22 (18 full-time; 4 part-time).

Admissions *Applied:* 46. *Admitted:* 30. *Enrolled:* 25. *Average GMAT:* 405. *Average GPA:* 3.28

Academic Calendar Semesters.

Accreditation ACBSP—The American Council of Business Schools and Programs.

After Graduation (Class of 2006–07) *Employed within 3 months of graduation:* 83%. *Average starting salary:* $36,000.

DEGREES MBA • MCA • MPA

MBA—Integrated Master of Business Administration Full-time. Distance learning option. Current resume required. At least 30 total credits required. 12 to 72 months to complete program. *Concentration:* management.

MBA—Master of Business Administration Full-time and part-time. At least 36 total credits required. 12 to 72 months to complete program. *Concentrations:* accounting, economics, finance, general MBA, information management, management, marketing, other.

MCA—Master of Commercial Aviation Full-time and part-time. Distance learning option. At least 30 total credits required. 12 to 72 months to complete program. *Concentration:* travel industry/tourism management.

MPA Full-time and part-time. At least 30 total credits required. 12 to 72 months to complete program. *Concentration:* accounting.

RESOURCES AND SERVICES 192 on-campus PCs are available to graduate business students. Access to Internet/World Wide Web, online (class) registration, and online grade reports available. *Personal computer requirements:* Graduate business students are strongly recommended to purchase or lease a personal computer. *Special opportunities include:* An international exchange program is available. *Placement services include:* Alumni network, career placement, career counseling/planning, resume referral, career fairs, job interviews arranged, and resume preparation.

EXPENSES *Tuition (state resident):* Full-time: $4450. Part-time: $247 per hour. *Tuition (nonresident):* Full-time: $11,182. Part-time: $621 per hour. *Tuition (international):* Full-time: $11,182. Part-time: $621 per hour. *Required fees:* Full-time: $700. Tuition and/or fees vary by number of courses or credits taken, campus location, and academic program. *Graduate housing:* Room and board costs vary by number of occupants and type of accommodation. *Typical cost:* $5546 (including board).

FINANCIAL AID (2007–08) 69 students received aid, including fellowships, loans, research assistantships, scholarships, and work study. Aid is available to part-time students. *Financial aid application deadline:* 7/1.

Financial Aid Contact Ms. Ann Margaret Mullins, Director of Student Financial Assistance, Kent Wyatt Hall 144, Cleveland, MS 38733. *Phone:* 662-846-4670. *Fax:* 662-846-4683. *E-mail:* amullins@deltastate.edu.

INTERNATIONAL STUDENTS 8% of students enrolled are international students. *Services and facilities:* Counseling/support services, ESL/language courses, International student organization, Orientation. Financial aid is not available to international students. *Required with application:* TOEFL with recommended score of 197 (computer) or 525 (paper); proof of adequate funds; proof of health/immunizations.

International Student Contact Mr. Norman House, International Student Advisor, Kent Wyatt Hall 161, Cleveland, MS 38733. *Phone:* 662-846-4151. *Fax:* 662-846-3446. *E-mail:* dhouse@deltastate.edu.

APPLICATION *Required:* GMAT, application form, baccalaureate/first degree, resume/curriculum vitae, transcripts of college work. School will accept GRE and MAT. *Application fee:* $25, $100 (international). Applications for domestic and international students are processed on a rolling basis.

Application Contact Dr. Tyrone Jackson, Interim Dean, Division of Graduate and Continuing Studies, DSU Box 3124, 239 Kent Wyatt Hall, Room 245, Cleveland, MS 38733. *Phone:* 662-846-4875. *Fax:* 662-846-4313. *E-mail:* tjackson@deltastate.edu.

Jackson State University
School of Business
Jackson, Mississippi

Phone: 601-979-4326 **Fax:** 601-979-3772 **E-mail:** jean-claude.assad@jsums.edu

Business Program(s) Web Site: http://www.jsums.edu/business/

Graduate Business Unit Enrollment *Total:* 95 (38 full-time; 57 part-time; 54 women; 9 international). *Average Age:* 29.

Graduate Business Faculty *Total:* 43 (39 full-time; 4 part-time).

Admissions *Applied:* 124. *Admitted:* 38. *Enrolled:* 24. *Average GMAT:* 380. *Average GPA:* 3.29

Academic Calendar Semesters.

Accreditation AACSB—The Association to Advance Collegiate Schools of Business.

After Graduation (Class of 2006–07) *Employed within 3 months of graduation:* 90%. *Average starting salary:* $35,000.

DEGREES MBA • MBE • MPA • MSSM

MBA—Master of Business Administration Full-time and part-time. At least 36 total credits required. 12 to 96 months to complete program. *Concentration:* general MBA.

MBE—Master of Business Education Full-time. At least 27 total credits required. 12 to 96 months to complete program. *Concentration:* business education.

MPA—Master of Professional Accountancy Full-time and part-time. At least 30 total credits required. 12 to 96 months to complete program. *Concentration:* accounting.

MSSM—Master of Science in Systems Management Full-time. Distance learning option. At least 32 total credits required. 12 to 96 months to complete program. *Concentration:* system management.

RESOURCES AND SERVICES 108 on-campus PCs are available to graduate business students. Access to Internet/World Wide Web, online (class) registration, and online grade reports available. *Personal computer requirements:* Graduate business students are not required to have a personal computer. *Placement services include:* Alumni network, career placement, career counseling/planning, electronic job bank, resume referral, career fairs, job interviews arranged, resume preparation, and career library.

EXPENSES *Required fees:* Full-time: $44. *Graduate housing:* Room and board costs vary by campus location, number of occupants, type of accommodation, and type of board plan. *Typical cost:* $5138 (including board), $3148 (room only).

FINANCIAL AID (2007–08) 30 students received aid, including fellowships, research assistantships, scholarships, and work study. *Financial aid application deadline:* 5/1.

Financial Aid Contact Dr. Jean-Claude Assad, Director of Graduate Programs, PO Box 17760, Jackson, MS 39217. *Phone:* 601-979-4326. *Fax:* 601-979-3772.

INTERNATIONAL STUDENTS 9% of students enrolled are international students. *Services and facilities:* Counseling/support services, ESL/language courses, Housing location assistance, International student housing, International student organization, Language tutoring, Orientation, Visa Services, Host family program. Financial aid is available to international students. *Required with application:* TOEFL with recommended score of 525 (paper); proof of adequate funds; proof of health/immunizations.

International Student Contact Ms. Kathy Sims, International Student Advisor, PO Box 17103, Jackson, MS 39217. *Phone:* 601-979-3794. *Fax:* 601-979-3388. *E-mail:* kathy.sims@jsums.edu.

APPLICATION *Required:* GMAT, application form, baccalaureate/first degree, 3 letters of recommendation, transcripts of college work. *Deadlines:* 3/1 for fall, 10/15 for spring, 3/15 for summer, 3/1 for fall (international), 10/15 for spring (international), 3/15 for summer (international).

Application Contact Dr. Jean-Claude Assad, Director of Graduate Programs, PO Box 17760, Jackson, MS 39217. *Phone:* 601-979-4326. *Fax:* 601-979-3772. *E-mail:* jean-claude.assad@jsums.edu.

Millsaps College
Else School of Management
Jackson, Mississippi

Phone: 601-974-1256 **Fax:** 601-974-1260 **E-mail:** meachms@millsaps.edu

Business Program(s) Web Site: http://www.millsaps.edu/esom

Graduate Business Unit Enrollment *Total:* 110 (52 full-time; 58 part-time; 41 women; 3 international). *Average Age:* 26.

Graduate Business Faculty *Total:* 20 (17 full-time; 3 part-time).

Admissions *Applied:* 86. *Admitted:* 79. *Enrolled:* 69. *Average GMAT:* 570. *Average GPA:* 3.4

Academic Calendar Semesters.

Accreditation AACSB—The Association to Advance Collegiate Schools of Business.

After Graduation (Class of 2006–07) *Employed within 3 months of graduation:* 90%. *Average starting salary:* $46,000.

DEGREES M Acc • MBA

Millsaps College (continued)

M Acc—Master of Accountancy Full-time and part-time. 30 to 48 total credits required. 12 to 72 months to complete program. *Concentration:* accounting.

MBA—Master of Business Administration Full-time and part-time. 30 to 48 total credits required. 12 to 72 months to complete program. *Concentrations:* accounting, decision sciences, finance, international business, management, marketing.

RESOURCES AND SERVICES 75 on-campus PCs are available to graduate business students. Access to Internet/World Wide Web available. *Personal computer requirements:* Graduate business students are strongly recommended to purchase or lease a personal computer. *Special opportunities include:* An internship program is available. *Placement services include:* Alumni network, career placement, job search course, career counseling/planning, electronic job bank, resume referral, career fairs, job interviews arranged, resume preparation, and career library.

EXPENSES *Tuition:* Part-time: $880 per hour. *Required fees:* Part-time: $16 per hour. *Typical graduate housing cost:* $8800 (including board), $5000 (room only).

FINANCIAL AID (2007–08) Grants, loans, research assistantships, scholarships, and work study. Aid is available to part-time students. *Financial aid application deadline:* 7/1.

Financial Aid Contact Ms. Melissa Meacham, Director of Graduate Business Admissions, 1701 North State Street, Jackson, MS 39210-0001. *Phone:* 601-974-1256. *Fax:* 601-974-1260. *E-mail:* meachms@ millsaps.edu.

INTERNATIONAL STUDENTS 3% of students enrolled are international students. *Services and facilities:* Counseling/support services, Housing location assistance, International student organization, Orientation, Visa Services, Advising, Outplacement services. Financial aid is available to international students. *Required with application:* TOEFL with recommended score of 220 (computer) or 550 (paper); proof of adequate funds. *Recommended with application:* Proof of health/immunizations.

International Student Contact Ms. Melissa Meacham, Director of Graduate Business Admissions, 1701 North State Street, Jackson, MS 39210-0001. *Phone:* 601-974-1256. *Fax:* 601-974-1260. *E-mail:* meachms@ millsaps.edu.

APPLICATION *Required:* GMAT, application form, baccalaureate/first degree, transcripts of college work. *Application fee:* $25. Applications for domestic and international students are processed on a rolling basis.

Application Contact Ms. Melissa Meacham, Director of Graduate Business Admissions, 1701 North State Street, Jackson, MS 39210-0001. *Phone:* 601-974-1256. *Fax:* 601-974-1260. *E-mail:* meachms@ millsaps.edu.

Mississippi College

School of Business Administration

Clinton, Mississippi

Phone: 601-925-3220 **Fax:** 601-925-3954 **E-mail:** glee@mc.edu

Business Program(s) Web Site: http://www.mc.edu

Accreditation ACBSP—The American Council of Business Schools and Programs.

DEGREES JD/MBA • MBA

JD/MBA—Juris Doctor/Master of Business Administration Full-time. At least 103 total credits required. Minimum of 42 months to complete program. *Concentrations:* accounting, commerce.

MBA—Master of Business Administration Full-time and part-time. At least 30 total credits required. 12 to 60 months to complete program. *Concentration:* accounting.

RESOURCES AND SERVICES 330 on-campus PCs are available to graduate business students. Access to Internet/World Wide Web available. *Personal computer requirements:* Graduate business students are strongly recommended to purchase or lease a personal computer. *Special opportunities include:* An international exchange program is available. *Placement services include:* Alumni network, career placement, career counseling/planning, electronic job bank, resume referral, career fairs, job interviews arranged, resume preparation, and career library.

Application Contact Dr. Gerald Lee, Director, MBA Program, Box 4014, Clinton, MS 39058. *Phone:* 601-925-3220. *Fax:* 601-925-3954. *E-mail:* glee@mc.edu.

Mississippi State University

College of Business and Industry

Mississippi State, Mississippi

Phone: 662-325-1891 **Fax:** 662-325-8161 **E-mail:** gsb@cobilan.msstate.edu

Business Program(s) Web Site: http://www.cbi.msstate.edu/gsb

Graduate Business Unit Enrollment *Total:* 400 (191 full-time; 209 part-time; 147 women; 46 international). *Average Age:* 29.

Graduate Business Faculty *Total:* 86 (66 full-time; 20 part-time).

Admissions *Applied:* 175. *Admitted:* 135. *Enrolled:* 90. *Average GMAT:* 520. *Average GPA:* 3.4

Academic Calendar Semesters.

Accreditation AACSB—The Association to Advance Collegiate Schools of Business.

DEGREES MA • MBA • MPA • MSBA • MSIS • MTX

MA—Master of Arts Full-time and part-time. At least 30 total credits required. 12 to 72 months to complete program. *Concentration:* economics.

MBA—Master of Business Administration Full-time and part-time. Distance learning option. At least 30 total credits required. 12 to 72 months to complete program. *Concentration:* general MBA.

MBA—Master of Business Administration in Project Management Full-time and part-time. Distance learning option. At least 32 total credits required. 12 to 72 months to complete program. *Concentration:* project management.

MPA—Master of Professional Accountancy Full-time and part-time. At least 30 total credits required. 12 to 72 months to complete program. *Concentration:* accounting.

MSBA—Master of Science in Business Administration Full-time and part-time. At least 30 total credits required. 12 to 72 months to complete program. *Concentration:* finance.

MSIS—Master of Science in Information Systems Full-time. At least 30 total credits required. 12 to 72 months to complete program. *Concentration:* information systems.

MTX—Master of Taxation Full-time and part-time. At least 30 total credits required. 12 to 72 months to complete program. *Concentration:* taxation.

RESOURCES AND SERVICES 448 on-campus PCs are available to graduate business students. Access to Internet/World Wide Web, online (class) registration, and online grade reports available. *Personal computer requirements:* Graduate business students are strongly recommended to purchase or lease a personal computer. *Special opportunities include:* An international exchange program is available. *Placement services include:* Alumni network, career placement, career counseling/planning, electronic job bank, resume referral, career fairs, resume preparation, and career library.

EXPENSES *Tuition (state resident):* Full-time: $7467. *Tuition (nonresident):* Full-time: $17,204. *Tuition (international):* Full-time: $17,204. *Graduate housing:* Room and board costs vary by number of occupants, type of accommodation, and type of board plan. *Typical cost:* $13,214 (including board), $8361 (room only).

FINANCIAL AID (2007–08) 256 students received aid, including fellowships, loans, research assistantships, scholarships, teaching assistantships, and work study. Aid is available to part-time students. *Financial aid application deadline:* 4/1.

Financial Aid Contact Mr. Bruce Crain, Director of Financial Aid, PO Box 6035, Mississippi State, MS 39762. *Phone:* 662-325-3990. *Fax:* 662-325-0702. *E-mail:* bruce@saffairs.msstate.edu.

INTERNATIONAL STUDENTS 12% of students enrolled are international students. *Services and facilities:* Counseling/support services, ESL/language courses, International student organization, Orientation. Financial aid is available to international students. *Required with application:* TOEFL with recommended score of 233 (computer), 575 (paper), or 91 (Internet); proof of adequate funds; proof of health/ immunizations.

International Student Contact Carol Walker, Immigration Advisor, PO Box 9742, 101 Montgomery Hall, Mississippi State, MS 39762-9742. *Phone:* 662-325-8929. *Fax:* 662-325-8583. *E-mail:* reception@ iso.msstate.edu.

APPLICATION *Required:* GMAT, GRE, application form, baccalaureate/ first degree, 3 letters of recommendation, personal statement, transcripts of college work. *Recommended:* Resume/curriculum vitae. *Application fee:* $30. Applications for domestic and international students are processed on a rolling basis.

Application Contact Dr. Barbara Spencer, Director of Graduate Studies in Business, PO Box 5288, Mississippi State, MS 39762. *Phone:* 662-325-1891. *Fax:* 662-325-8161. *E-mail:* gsb@cobilan.msstate.edu.

University of Mississippi
School of Business Administration
Oxford, University, Mississippi

Phone: 662-915-5483 **Fax:** 662-915-5821 **E-mail:** holleman@bus.olemiss.edu

Business Program(s) Web Site: http://www.olemissbusiness.com/

Accreditation AACSB—The Association to Advance Collegiate Schools of Business.

DEGREE MBA

MBA—Master of Business Administration Full-time and part-time. Distance learning option. 35 total credits required. 12 months to complete program. *Concentrations:* accounting, banking, economics, finance, financial management/planning, general MBA, human resources management, information management, insurance, international business, management, management information systems, managerial economics, marketing, operations management, organizational behavior/development, quantitative analysis, real estate, system management.

RESOURCES AND SERVICES Access to Internet/World Wide Web, online (class) registration, and online grade reports available. *Personal computer requirements:* Graduate business students are required to have a personal computer. *Special opportunities include:* An internship program is available. *Placement services include:* Alumni network, career placement, job search course, career counseling/planning, electronic job bank, resume referral, career fairs, job interviews arranged, resume preparation, and career library.

Application Contact Dr. John Holleman, Director of MBA Administration, 253 Holman Hall, University, MS 38677. *Phone:* 662-915-5483. *Fax:* 662-915-5821. *E-mail:* holleman@bus.olemiss.edu.

University of Southern Mississippi
College of Business
Hattiesburg, Mississippi

Phone: 601-266-4653 **Fax:** 601-266-5269 **E-mail:** mba@usm.edu

Business Program(s) Web Site: http://www.usm.edu/business/

Graduate Business Unit Enrollment *Total:* 126 (64 full-time; 62 part-time; 65 women; 6 international). *Average Age:* 27.

Graduate Business Faculty 13 full-time.

Admissions *Applied:* 95. *Admitted:* 60. *Enrolled:* 58. *Average GMAT:* 498. *Average GPA:* 3.24.

Academic Calendar Semesters.

Accreditation AACSB—The Association to Advance Collegiate Schools of Business.

After Graduation (Class of 2006–07) *Employed within 3 months of graduation:* 81%. *Average starting salary:* $43,780.

DEGREES MBA • MPA

MBA—Master of Business Administration Full-time and part-time. 30 to 48 total credits required. 12 to 72 months to complete program. *Concentrations:* accounting, finance, management, marketing.

MPA—Master of Professional Accountancy Full-time and part-time. 30 total credits required. 12 to 72 months to complete program. *Concentration:* accounting.

RESOURCES AND SERVICES 10 on-campus PCs are available to graduate business students. Access to Internet/World Wide Web, online (class) registration, and online grade reports available. *Personal computer requirements:* Graduate business students are not required to have a personal computer. *Placement services include:* Alumni network, career placement, career counseling/planning, resume referral, career fairs, job interviews arranged, resume preparation, and career library.

EXPENSES *Tuition (state resident):* Full-time: $4914. Part-time: $205 per credit hour. *Tuition (nonresident):* Full-time: $11,692. Part-time: $488 per credit hour. *Tuition (international):* Full-time: $11,692. Part-time: $488 per credit hour. *Graduate housing:* Room and board costs vary by campus location, number of occupants, type of accommodation, and type of board plan. *Typical cost:* $5040 (including board), $2826 (room only).

FINANCIAL AID (2007–08) 18 students received aid, including loans, research assistantships, scholarships, and work study. Aid is available to part-time students. *Financial aid application deadline:* 3/15.

Financial Aid Contact David Williamson, Director of Financial Aid, 118 College Drive #5101, Hattiesburg, MS 39406. *Phone:* 601-266-4774. *E-mail:* david.williamson@usm.edu.

INTERNATIONAL STUDENTS 5% of students enrolled are international students. *Services and facilities:* Counseling/support services, ESL/language courses, Housing location assistance, International student organization, Language tutoring, Orientation. Financial aid is available to international students. *Required with application:* TOEFL with recommended score of 250 (computer) or 550 (paper); proof of adequate funds; proof of health/immunizations.

International Student Contact Barbara Whitt Jackson, Administrator, International Student Affairs, 118 College Drive #5151, Hattiesburg, MS 39406. *Phone:* 601-266-4841. *Fax:* 601-266-5839. *E-mail:* barbara.whittjackson@usm.edu.

APPLICATION *Required:* GMAT, application form, baccalaureate/first degree, essay, 3 letters of recommendation, personal statement, resume/ curriculum vitae, transcripts of college work. *Recommended:* Interview, 2 years of work experience. *Application fee:* $30. Applications for domestic and international students are processed on a rolling basis.

Application Contact Ms. Machell Haynes, Assistant Director, Graduate Academic Services, 118 College Drive #5096, Hattiesburg, MS 39406. *Phone:* 601-266-4653. *Fax:* 601-266-5269. *E-mail:* mba@usm.edu.

William Carey University

School of Business

Hattiesburg, Mississippi

Phone: 601-318-6204 **Fax:** 601-318-6281 **E-mail:** frank.baugh@wmcarey.edu

Business Program(s) Web Site: http://www.wmcarey.edu

Graduate Business Unit Enrollment *Total:* 141.

Graduate Business Faculty 9 full-time.

Academic Calendar Trimesters.

After Graduation (Class of 2006–07) *Employed within 3 months of graduation:* 100%.

DEGREE MBA

MBA—Master of Business Administration Full-time and part-time. 30 to 51 total credits required. 12 to 48 months to complete program. *Concentration:* general MBA.

RESOURCES AND SERVICES 60 on-campus PCs are available to graduate business students. Access to Internet/World Wide Web available. *Personal computer requirements:* Graduate business students are not required to have a personal computer. *Placement services include:* Career counseling/planning, career fairs, and resume preparation.

FINANCIAL AID (2007–08) Loans, scholarships, and work study. Aid is available to part-time students. *Financial aid application deadline:* 6/15.

Financial Aid Contact Mr. Bill Curry, Director of Financial Aid, 498 Tuscan Avenue, Box 7, Hattiesburg, MS 39401-5499. *Phone:* 601-318-6153. *Fax:* 601-318-6154. *E-mail:* bill.curry@wmcarey.edu.

INTERNATIONAL STUDENTS *Services and facilities:* Counseling/support services, International student housing, International student organization, Language tutoring, Orientation. Financial aid is not available to international students. *Required with application:* TOEFL with recommended score of 213 (computer) or 550 (paper); proof of adequate funds; proof of health/immunizations.

International Student Contact Mr. Emerson Toledo, Director of International Admissions, Box 13, 498 Tuscan Avenue, Hattiesburg, MS 39401. *Phone:* 601-318-6564. *Fax:* 601-318-6765. *E-mail:* emerson.toledo@wmcarey.edu.

APPLICATION *Required:* GMAT, application form, baccalaureate/first degree, 2 letters of recommendation, transcripts of college work. *Application fee:* $25.

Application Contact Dr. Cheryl Dale, Dean, Box 18, 498 Tuscan Avenue, Hattiesburg, MS 39401. *Phone:* 601-318-6204. *Fax:* 601-318-6281. *E-mail:* frank.baugh@wmcarey.edu.

MISSOURI

Avila University

School of Business

Kansas City, Missouri

Phone: 816-501-3601 **Fax:** 816-501-2463 **E-mail:** joanna.giffin@avila.edu

Business Program(s) Web Site: http://www.avila.edu/mba

Graduate Business Unit Enrollment *Total:* 263 (139 full-time; 124 part-time; 158 women; 60 international). *Average Age:* 32.

Graduate Business Faculty *Total:* 27 (8 full-time; 19 part-time).

Admissions *Applied:* 78. *Admitted:* 63. *Enrolled:* 63. *Average GMAT:* 495. *Average GPA:* 3.3

Academic Calendar Trimesters.

DEGREE MBA

MBA—Master of Business Administration Full-time and part-time. 30 to 48 total credits required. 12 to 84 months to complete program. *Concentrations:* accounting, finance, health care, international business, management, management information systems, marketing.

RESOURCES AND SERVICES 50 on-campus PCs are available to graduate business students. Access to Internet/World Wide Web, online (class) registration, and online grade reports available. *Personal computer requirements:* Graduate business students are strongly recommended to purchase or lease a personal computer. *Special opportunities include:* An internship program is available. *Placement services include:* Alumni network, career placement, career counseling/planning, career fairs, and resume preparation.

EXPENSES *Tuition:* Part-time: $435 per credit hour. *Tuition (international):* Part-time: $435 per credit hour. *Required fees:* Part-time: $19 per credit hour. *Graduate housing:* Room and board costs vary by number of occupants and type of board plan. *Typical cost:* $5500 (including board), $4000 (room only).

FINANCIAL AID (2007–08) Loans. Aid is available to part-time students. *Financial aid application deadline:* 7/31.

Financial Aid Contact Edwin Harris, PhD, Vice President for Enrollment and Student Development, 11901 Wornall Road, Kansas City, MO 64145-1698. *Phone:* 816-501-3627.

INTERNATIONAL STUDENTS 23% of students enrolled are international students. *Services and facilities:* Counseling/support services, ESL/language courses, International student organization, Language tutoring. Financial aid is not available to international students. *Required with application:* TOEFL with recommended score of 550 (paper); proof of adequate funds; proof of health/immunizations.

International Student Contact Bruce Inwards, ILCP Coordinator and ESL Lecturer, 11901 Wornall Road, Kansas City, MO 64145-1698. *Phone:* 816-501-3772.

APPLICATION *Required:* GMAT, application form, baccalaureate/first degree, interview, personal statement, transcripts of college work. *Application fee:* $0. Applications for domestic and international students are processed on a rolling basis.

Application Contact JoAnna Giffin, MBA Admissions Director, 11901 Wornall Road, Kansas City, MO 64145-1698. *Phone:* 816-501-3601. *Fax:* 816-501-2463. *E-mail:* joanna.giffin@avila.edu.

Columbia College

Program in Business Administration

Columbia, Missouri

Phone: 573-875-7354 **Fax:** 573-875-7506 **E-mail:** rmmorin@ccis.edu

Business Program(s) Web Site: http://www.ccis.edu/graduate/academics/degrees.asp?488

DEGREE MBA

MBA—Master of Business Administration Full-time and part-time. Distance learning option. Baccalaureate earned in Business Administration or completion of core undergraduate courses required. At least 36 total credits required. Minimum of 15 months to complete program. *Concentration:* general MBA.

RESOURCES AND SERVICES 80 on-campus PCs are available to graduate business students. Access to Internet/World Wide Web, online (class) registration, and online grade reports available. *Personal computer requirements:* Graduate business students are not required to have a personal computer. *Placement services include:* Alumni network, career placement, career counseling/planning, electronic job bank, resume referral, career fairs, and resume preparation.

Application Contact Ms. Regina Morin, Director of Admissions, 1001 Rogers Street, Columbia, MO 65216. *Phone:* 573-875-7354. *Fax:* 573-875-7506. *E-mail:* rmmorin@ccis.edu.

DeVry University
Keller Graduate School of Management

Kansas City, Missouri

Phone: 816-221-1300

DEGREES MAFM • MBA • MHRM • MIS • MPA • MPM

MAFM—Master of Accounting and Financial Management Full-time and part-time. Distance learning option. At least 44 total credits required. 18 to 60 months to complete program. *Concentrations:* accounting, financial management/planning.

MBA—Master of Business Administration Full-time and part-time. Distance learning option. At least 48 total credits required. 18 to 60 months to complete program. *Concentration:* management.

MHRM—Master of Human Resources Management Full-time and part-time. Distance learning option. At least 45 total credits required. 18 to 60 months to complete program. *Concentration:* human resources management.

MIS—Master of Information Systems Management Full-time and part-time. Distance learning option. At least 45 total credits required. 18 to 60 months to complete program. *Concentration:* information systems.

MPA—Master of Public Administration Full-time and part-time. Distance learning option. At least 45 total credits required. 18 to 60 months to complete program. *Concentration:* public policy and administration.

MPM—Master of Project Management Full-time and part-time. Distance learning option. At least 42 total credits required. 18 to 60 months to complete program. *Concentration:* project management.

Application Contact Admissions Office, Kansas City Downtown, City Center Square, 1100 Main Street, Suite 118, Kansas City, MO 64105. *Phone:* 816-221-1300.

DeVry University
Keller Graduate School of Management

St. Louis, Missouri

Phone: 314-542-4222

DEGREES MAFM • MBA • MHRM • MIS • MPA • MPM

MAFM—Master of Accounting and Financial Management Full-time and part-time. Distance learning option. At least 44 total credits required. 18 to 60 months to complete program. *Concentrations:* accounting, financial management/planning.

MBA—Master of Business Administration Full-time and part-time. Distance learning option. At least 48 total credits required. 18 to 60 months to complete program. *Concentration:* management.

MHRM—Master of Human Resources Management Full-time and part-time. Distance learning option. At least 45 total credits required. 18 to 60 months to complete program. *Concentration:* human resources management.

MIS—Master of Information Systems Management Full-time and part-time. Distance learning option. At least 45 total credits required. 18 to 60 months to complete program. *Concentration:* information systems.

MPA—Master of Public Administration Full-time and part-time. Distance learning option. At least 45 total credits required. 18 to 60 months to complete program. *Concentration:* public policy and administration.

MPM—Master of Project Management Full-time and part-time. Distance learning option. At least 42 total credits required. 18 to 60 months to complete program. *Concentration:* project management.

Application Contact Admissions Office, St. Louis West Center, 1801 Park 270 Drive, Suite 260, St. Louis, MO 63146. *Phone:* 314-542-4222.

Drury University
Breech School of Business Administration

Springfield, Missouri

Phone: 417-873-7614 **Fax:** 417-873-7537 **E-mail:** dhiles@drury.edu

Business Program(s) Web Site: http://mba.drury.edu/

Graduate Business Unit Enrollment *Total:* 60 (5 full-time; 55 part-time; 30 women; 4 international).

Graduate Business Faculty 12 full-time.

Admissions *Applied:* 60. *Admitted:* 31. *Enrolled:* 29. *Average GMAT:* 530. *Average GPA:* 3.4

Academic Calendar Semesters.

Accreditation ACBSP—The American Council of Business Schools and Programs.

After Graduation (Class of 2006–07) *Employed within 3 months of graduation:* 100%.

DEGREE MBA

MBA—Master of Business Administration Full-time and part-time. 30 to 54 total credits required. 12 to 84 months to complete program. *Concentrations:* accounting, entrepreneurship, health care, strategic management.

RESOURCES AND SERVICES 120 on-campus PCs are available to graduate business students. Access to Internet/World Wide Web, online (class) registration, and online grade reports available. *Personal computer requirements:* Graduate business students are strongly recommended to purchase or lease a personal computer. *Special opportunities include:* An international exchange program and an internship program are available. *Placement services include:* Alumni network, career placement, career counseling/planning, resume referral, and resume preparation.

FINANCIAL AID (2007–08) 6 students received aid, including grants, loans, research assistantships, scholarships, and teaching assistantships. Aid is available to part-time students. *Financial aid application deadline:* 7/1.

Financial Aid Contact Dawn M. Hiles, Director, MBA Program, 900 North Benton Avenue, Springfield, MO 65802-3791. *Phone:* 417-873-7614. *Fax:* 417-873-7537. *E-mail:* dhiles@drury.edu.

INTERNATIONAL STUDENTS 7% of students enrolled are international students. *Services and facilities:* Counseling/support services, ESL/language courses, Housing location assistance, International student organization, Orientation, Visa Services. Financial aid is available to international students. *Required with application:* TOEFL with recommended score of 213 (computer) or 550 (paper); proof of adequate funds; proof of health/immunizations.

International Student Contact Jan Swann, Director of International Student Services, 900 North Benton Avenue, Springfield, MO 65802-3791. *Phone:* 417-873-7885. *E-mail:* jswann@drury.edu.

APPLICATION *Required:* GMAT, application form, baccalaureate/first degree, essay, letter(s) of recommendation, personal statement, resume/curriculum vitae, transcripts of college work. *Recommended:* Interview, work experience. *Application fee:* $25. Applications for domestic and international students are processed on a rolling basis.

Drury University (continued)

Application Contact Dawn M. Hiles, Director, MBA Program, 900 North Benton Avenue, Springfield, MO 65802-3791. *Phone:* 417-873-7614. *Fax:* 417-873-7537. *E-mail:* dhiles@drury.edu.

Fontbonne University
Department of Business Administration

St. Louis, Missouri

Phone: 314-863-2220 **Fax:** 314-719-3676 **E-mail:** malexander@fontbonne.edu

Business Program(s) Web Site: http://www.fontbonne.edu/GraduatePrograms

Graduate Business Unit Enrollment *Total:* 487 (376 full-time; 111 part-time; 292 women; 32 international). *Average Age:* 35.

Graduate Business Faculty *Total:* 86 (4 full-time; 82 part-time).

Admissions *Average GPA:* 3.3

Academic Calendar Semesters.

After Graduation (Class of 2006–07) *Employed within 3 months of graduation:* 96%. *Average starting salary:* $48,840.

DEGREES M Mgt • MBA • MS • MST

M Mgt—Options Accelerated Adult Master of Management Part-time. 3 years of work experience required. At least 36 total credits required. 18 to 19 months to complete program. *Concentration:* management.

MBA—Options Accelerated Master of Business Administration Part-time. 3 years of work experience required. At least 43 total credits required. 24 months to complete program. *Concentration:* general MBA.

MBA—Weekend Master of Business Administration Part-time. 36 to 48 total credits required. 12 to 72 months to complete program. *Concentration:* general MBA.

MS—Master of Science in Accounting Part-time. Minimum GPA of 2.75 and minimum GMAT score of 475. 36 to 57 total credits required. 12 to 72 months to complete program. *Concentration:* accounting.

MST—Master of Science in Taxation Part-time. 30 to 46 total credits required. 12 to 72 months to complete program. *Concentration:* taxation.

RESOURCES AND SERVICES 110 on-campus PCs are available to graduate business students. Access to Internet/World Wide Web, online (class) registration, and online grade reports available. *Personal computer requirements:* Graduate business students are required to have a personal computer, the cost of which is included in tuition or other required fees. *Placement services include:* Alumni network, career counseling/planning, career fairs, resume preparation, and career library.

EXPENSES *Tuition:* Full-time: $9720. Part-time: $540 per credit hour. *Tuition (international):* Full-time: $22,160. *Required fees:* Full-time: $288. Part-time: $16 per credit hour. Tuition and/or fees vary by number of courses or credits taken and academic program. *Graduate housing:* Room and board costs vary by campus location, number of occupants, type of accommodation, and type of board plan. *Typical cost:* $7210 (including board).

FINANCIAL AID (2007–08) 175 students received aid, including grants and loans. *Financial aid application deadline:* 7/1.

Financial Aid Contact Ms. Nicole Moore, Director of Financial Aid, 6800 Wydown Boulevard, St. Louis, MO 63105. *Phone:* 314-889-1496. *Fax:* 314-889-1451. *E-mail:* nmoore@fontbonne.edu.

INTERNATIONAL STUDENTS 7% of students enrolled are international students. *Services and facilities:* Counseling/support services, ESL/language courses, Housing location assistance, International student housing, Orientation, Visa Services. Financial aid is not available to international students. *Required with application:* TOEFL with recommended score of 173 (computer), 525 (paper), or 61 (Internet); proof of adequate funds; proof of health/immunizations.

International Student Contact Rebecca Bahan, Director of International Affairs, 6800 Wydown Boulevard, St. Louis, MO 63105-3098. *Phone:* 314-889-4509. *Fax:* 314-889-1451. *E-mail:* rbahan@fontbonne.edu.

APPLICATION *Required:* Application form, baccalaureate/first degree, interview, 2 letters of recommendation, personal statement, transcripts of college work. *Application fee:* $25. Applications for domestic and international students are processed on a rolling basis.

Application Contact Mark Alexander, Assistant Chair, Business Administration, 6800 Wydown Boulevard, St. Louis, MO 63105-3098. *Phone:* 314-863-2220. *Fax:* 314-719-3676. *E-mail:* malexander@fontbonne.edu.

Grantham University
Mark Skousen School of Business

Kansas City, Missouri

Phone: 800-955-2527 **Fax:** 816-595-5757 **E-mail:** admissions@grantham.edu

Business Program(s) Web Site: http://www.grantham.edu

Academic Calendar Continuous.

DEGREES MBA

MBA—General Full-time and part-time. Distance learning option. At least 36 total credits required. Minimum of 24 months to complete program. *Concentration:* general MBA.

MBA—Information Management Full-time and part-time. Distance learning option. At least 36 total credits required. Minimum of 24 months to complete program. *Concentration:* information management.

MBA—Project Management Full-time and part-time. Distance learning option. At least 36 total credits required. Minimum of 24 months to complete program. *Concentration:* project management.

RESOURCES AND SERVICES Access to Internet/World Wide Web, online (class) registration, and online grade reports available. *Personal computer requirements:* Graduate business students are strongly recommended to purchase or lease a personal computer. *Placement services include:* Alumni network, career counseling/planning, and resume preparation.

EXPENSES *Tuition:* Full-time: $4770. Part-time: $265 per credit hour. *Tuition (international):* Full-time: $4770. Part-time: $265 per credit hour.

FINANCIAL AID (2007–08) Scholarships. Aid is available to part-time students.

INTERNATIONAL STUDENTS Financial aid is available to international students. *Required with application:* TOEFL with recommended score of 500 (paper).

International Student Contact Ms. DeAnn Wandler, Director of Admissions, 7200 Northwest 86th Street, Kansas City, MO 64153. *Phone:* 800-955-2527. *Fax:* 816-595-5757. *E-mail:* admissions@grantham.edu.

APPLICATION *Required:* Application form, baccalaureate/first degree. *Application fee:* $0. Applications for domestic and international students are processed on a rolling basis.

Application Contact Ms. DeAnn Wandler, Director of Admissions, 7200 Northwest 86th Street, Kansas City, MO 64153. *Phone:* 800-955-2527. *Fax:* 816-595-5757. *E-mail:* admissions@grantham.edu.

Lincoln University
College of Business and Professional Studies

Jefferson City, Missouri

Phone: 573-681-5247 **Fax:** 573-681-5106 **E-mail:** bickell@lincolnu.edu

Business Program(s) Web Site: http://www.lincolnu.edu/pages/379.asp

Graduate Business Unit Enrollment *Total:* 48 (26 full-time; 22 part-time; 28 women; 10 international). *Average Age:* 33.

Graduate Business Faculty *Total:* 7 (1 full-time; 6 part-time).

Admissions *Applied:* 22. *Admitted:* 19. *Enrolled:* 14. *Average GPA:* 3.17

Academic Calendar Semesters.

Accreditation ACBSP—The American Council of Business Schools and Programs.

DEGREE MBA

MBA—Master of Business Administration Full-time and part-time. At least 36 total credits required. 12 to 60 months to complete program. *Concentrations:* accounting, entrepreneurship, management, public policy and administration.

RESOURCES AND SERVICES 250 on-campus PCs are available to graduate business students. Access to Internet/World Wide Web, online (class) registration, and online grade reports available. *Personal computer requirements:* Graduate business students are not required to have a personal computer. *Special opportunities include:* An internship program is available. *Placement services include:* Career counseling/planning, electronic job bank, career fairs, job interviews arranged, resume preparation, and career library.

EXPENSES *Tuition (state resident):* Full-time: $5376. Part-time: $224 per credit hour. *Tuition (nonresident):* Full-time: $10,032. Part-time: $418 per credit hour. *Tuition (international):* Full-time: $10,032. Part-time: $418 per credit. *Required fees:* Full-time: $480. Part-time: $15 per credit hour. Tuition and/or fees vary by number of courses or credits taken. *Graduate housing:* Room and board costs vary by number of occupants and type of board plan. *Typical cost:* $4590 (including board), $2358 (room only).

FINANCIAL AID (2007–08) 38 students received aid, including grants, loans, scholarships, and work study. Aid is available to part-time students. *Financial aid application deadline:* 3/1.

Financial Aid Contact Mr. Alfred L. Robinson, Director, 820 Chestnut Street, 103 Young Hall, Jefferson City, MO 65102-0029. *Phone:* 573-681-6156. *Fax:* 573-681-5871. *E-mail:* financialaid@lincolnu.edu.

INTERNATIONAL STUDENTS 21% of students enrolled are international students. *Services and facilities:* Counseling/support services, Housing location assistance, International student organization, Orientation, Visa Services. Financial aid is available to international students. *Required with application:* TOEFL with recommended score of 173 (computer) or 500 (paper); proof of adequate funds; proof of health/immunizations.

International Student Contact Mr. Mike Kosher, Director of Admissions, 820 Chestnut Street, B-7 Young Hall, Jefferson City, MO 65102-0029. *Phone:* 573-681-5017. *Fax:* 573-681-5889. *E-mail:* kosherm@lincolnu.edu.

APPLICATION *Required:* GMAT, application form, baccalaureate/first degree, 3 letters of recommendation, personal statement, transcripts of college work. *Application fee:* $20. Applications for domestic and international students are processed on a rolling basis.

Application Contact Dr. Linda Bickel, Dean, Graduate Studies, 820 Chestnut Street, 110 MLK Hall, Jefferson City, MO 65102-0029. *Phone:* 573-681-5247. *Fax:* 573-681-5106. *E-mail:* bickell@lincolnu.edu.

Lindenwood University

Division of Management

St. Charles, Missouri

Phone: 636-949-4366 **Fax:** 636-949-4697 **E-mail:** bbarger@lindenwood.edu

Business Program(s) Web Site: http://www.lindenwood.edu

Graduate Business Unit Enrollment *Total:* 920 (780 full-time; 140 part-time; 538 women; 134 international). *Average Age:* 33.

Graduate Business Faculty *Total:* 105 (39 full-time; 66 part-time).

Admissions *Applied:* 446. *Admitted:* 403. *Enrolled:* 369. *Average GPA:* 3.3

Academic Calendar 5-term program and quarter program.

Accreditation ACBSP—The American Council of Business Schools and Programs (candidate).

DEGREES MA • MBA • MS • MSA

MA—Master of Arts Full-time and part-time. At least 39 total credits required. 12 to 60 months to complete program. *Concentration:* sports/entertainment management.

MA—Specialized Fields Full-time and part-time. At least 39 total credits required. 12 to 60 months to complete program. *Concentrations:* arts administration/management, financial management/planning, human resources management, international business, leadership, management, marketing, organizational behavior/development, training and development.

MBA—Specialized Fields Full-time and part-time. At least 36 total credits required. 12 to 60 months to complete program. *Concentrations:* accounting, arts administration/management, entrepreneurship, finance, general MBA, human resources management, information technology, international business, management, management information systems, marketing, public management.

MBA—Master of Business Administration Full-time and part-time. At least 36 total credits required. 12 to 60 months to complete program. *Concentration:* general MBA.

MS—Master of Science in Health Management Full-time. At least 48 total credits required. 12 to 60 months to complete program. *Concentration:* health care.

MS—Master of Science in Human Resource Management Full-time and part-time. At least 48 total credits required. 12 to 60 months to complete program. *Concentration:* human resources management.

MS—Master of Science in Information Technology Full-time. At least 48 total credits required. 12 to 60 months to complete program. *Concentration:* information technology.

MS—Specialized Fields Full-time and part-time. At least 36 total credits required. 12 to 60 months to complete program. *Concentrations:* accounting, finance, human resources management, international business, management, management information systems, marketing, public management.

MSA—Master of Science in Administration Full-time and part-time. At least 45 total credits required. 12 to 60 months to complete program. *Concentrations:* management, marketing.

RESOURCES AND SERVICES 360 on-campus PCs are available to graduate business students. Access to Internet/World Wide Web available. *Personal computer requirements:* Graduate business students are strongly recommended to purchase or lease a personal computer. *Special opportunities include:* An international exchange program and an internship program are available. *Placement services include:* Alumni network, career placement, job search course, career counseling/planning, resume referral, career fairs, resume preparation, and career library.

EXPENSES *Tuition:* Full-time: $16,800. Part-time: $350 per credit hour. *Tuition (international):* Full-time: $16,800. Part-time: $350 per credit hour. *Typical graduate housing cost:* $6500 (including board), $3400 (room only).

FINANCIAL AID (2007–08) 749 students received aid, including grants, loans, scholarships, and work study. Aid is available to part-time students.

Financial Aid Contact Ms. Lori Bode, Director of Financial Aid, 209 South Kingshighway, St. Charles, MO 63301. *Phone:* 636-949-4925. *Fax:* 636-949-4924. *E-mail:* lbode@lindenwood.edu.

INTERNATIONAL STUDENTS 15% of students enrolled are international students. *Services and facilities:* Counseling/support services, Housing location assistance, International student housing, International student organization, Language tutoring, Orientation, Visa Services, Reading, writing, and mathematics development courses. Financial aid is available to international students. *Required with application:* TOEFL

Lindenwood University (continued)

with recommended score of 213 (computer), 550 (paper), or 80 (Internet); proof of adequate funds. *Recommended with application:* IELT.

International Student Contact Mr. Chris Burnette, International Admissions Counselor, 209 South Kingshighway, St. Charles, MO 63301. *Phone:* 636-949-4982. *Fax:* 636-949-4989. *E-mail:* cburnette@lindenwood.edu.

APPLICATION *Required:* Application form, baccalaureate/first degree, transcripts of college work. *Recommended:* Essay, interview, letter(s) of recommendation, personal statement, resume/curriculum vitae. *Application fee:* $30, $100 (international). Applications for domestic and international students are processed on a rolling basis.

Application Contact Mr. Brett Barger, Dean of Evening Admissions and Extension Campuses, 209 South Kingshighway, St. Charles, MO 63301. *Phone:* 636-949-4366. *Fax:* 636-949-4697. *E-mail:* bbarger@lindenwood.edu.

Maryville University of Saint Louis
The John E. Simon School of Business

St. Louis, Missouri

Phone: 800-627-9855 Ext. 9382 **Fax:** 314-529-9975 **E-mail:** business@maryville.edu

Business Program(s) Web Site: http://www.maryville.edu/academics/bu/MasterBusinessAdmin/

Graduate Business Unit Enrollment *Total:* 184 (19 full-time; 165 part-time; 108 women; 6 international). *Average Age:* 31.

Graduate Business Faculty *Total:* 20 (8 full-time; 12 part-time).

Admissions *Applied:* 87. *Admitted:* 55. *Enrolled:* 35. *Average GMAT:* 500. *Average GPA:* 3.56

Academic Calendar Semesters.

Accreditation ACBSP—The American Council of Business Schools and Programs.

After Graduation (Class of 2006–07) *Employed within 3 months of graduation:* 95%. *Average starting salary:* $60,000.

DEGREE MBA

MBA—Master of Business Administration Full-time and part-time. At least 36 total credits required. Maximum of 60 months to complete program. *Concentrations:* accounting, electronic commerce (E-commerce), management, marketing.

RESOURCES AND SERVICES 498 on-campus PCs are available to graduate business students. Access to Internet/World Wide Web, online (class) registration, and online grade reports available. *Personal computer requirements:* Graduate business students are not required to have a personal computer. *Special opportunities include:* An internship program is available. *Placement services include:* Career placement, career counseling/planning, electronic job bank, career fairs, job interviews arranged, resume preparation, and career library.

EXPENSES *Tuition:* Full-time: $18,600. Part-time: $580 per credit hour. *Tuition (international):* Full-time: $18,600. Part-time: $580 per credit hour. *Required fees:* Full-time: $300. Part-time: $150 per year. *Graduate housing:* Room and board costs vary by number of occupants, type of accommodation, and type of board plan. *Typical cost:* $7500 (including board).

FINANCIAL AID (2007–08) 69 students received aid, including loans and work study. *Financial aid application deadline:* 7/31.

Financial Aid Contact Ms. Martha Harbaugh, Director of Financial Aid, 650 Maryville University Drive, St. Louis, MO 63141-7299. *Phone:* 800-627-9855 Ext. 9360. *Fax:* 314-529-9199. *E-mail:* fin_aid@maryville.edu.

INTERNATIONAL STUDENTS 3% of students enrolled are international students. *Services and facilities:* Counseling/support services, Housing location assistance, International student housing, Orientation, Visa Services, Health services. Financial aid is not available to international students. *Required with application:* TOEFL with recommended score of 213 (computer) or 550 (paper); proof of adequate funds; proof of health/immunizations.

International Student Contact Dr. Marshall King, Interim Director of International Programs, 650 Maryville University Drive, St. Louis, MO 63141-7299. *Phone:* 800-627-9855 Ext. 9503. *Fax:* 314-529-9384. *E-mail:* intl@maryville.edu.

APPLICATION *Required:* Application form, baccalaureate/first degree, personal statement, transcripts of college work. *Application fee:* $35, $50 (international). Applications for domestic and international students are processed on a rolling basis.

Application Contact Ms. Kathy Dougherty, Director, Graduate Admissions and Enrollment, 650 Maryville University Drive, St. Louis, MO 63141-7299. *Phone:* 800-627-9855 Ext. 9382. *Fax:* 314-529-9975. *E-mail:* business@maryville.edu.

Missouri State University
College of Business Administration

Springfield, Missouri

Phone: 417-836-5335 **Fax:** 417-836-6888 **E-mail:** graduatecollege@missouristate.edu

Business Program(s) Web Site: http://www.coba.missouristate.edu/

Graduate Business Unit Enrollment *Total:* 570 (352 full-time; 218 part-time; 262 women; 154 international). *Average Age:* 25.

Graduate Business Faculty *Total:* 128 (120 full-time; 8 part-time).

Admissions *Applied:* 286. *Admitted:* 179. *Enrolled:* 121. *Average GMAT:* 498. *Average GPA:* 3.4

Academic Calendar Semesters.

Accreditation AACSB—The Association to Advance Collegiate Schools of Business.

After Graduation (Class of 2006–07) *Employed within 3 months of graduation:* 90%. *Average starting salary:* $46,900.

DEGREES MAC • MBA • MHA

MAC—Master of Accounting Full-time and part-time. Distance learning option. 33 to 57 total credits required. 12 to 96 months to complete program. *Concentration:* accounting.

MBA—Master of Business Administration Full-time and part-time. Distance learning option. 33 to 57 total credits required. 12 to 96 months to complete program. *Concentrations:* accounting, finance, financial management/planning, general MBA, information management, international business, management, management information systems, marketing, transportation management.

MHA—Master of Health Administration Full-time and part-time. Distance learning option. 42 to 60 total credits required. 24 to 96 months to complete program. *Concentration:* health care.

Missouri State University's M.B.A. degree, which is accredited by AACSB International–The Association to Advance Collegiate Schools of Business, integrates a variety of courses offered by the six departments of the College of Business Administration. The program is designed specifically for students who hold undergraduate degrees in the arts, the sciences, engineering, and law, as well as business administration. Students with little or no undergraduate work in business normally require five semesters to complete the program. Students possessing prior academic preparation in business and economics and a strong work ethic may complete the program in one calendar year.

A strength of the Missouri State M.B.A. program is its emphasis on the individual. The program empowers students to tailor their

educational experience according to their goals. Emphasis areas are available in traditional business disciplines such as marketing, management, accounting, and finance. The design of the program allows students to structure a concentration that is consistent with their individual career goals and needs. The program is designed to offer an outstanding combination of resources that provides students with unequaled educational value. Students and faculty members work closely together to build a cooperative environment that promotes continuous improvement and lifelong learning. M.B.A. faculty members recognize that their major responsibilities are teaching and working with students, but they are also actively involved in their areas of professional expertise.

State-of-the-art David D. Glass Hall, home of the College of Business Administration, includes a variety of special-purpose classrooms as well as eight computer laboratories.

RESOURCES AND SERVICES 350 on-campus PCs are available to graduate business students. Access to Internet/World Wide Web, online (class) registration, and online grade reports available. *Personal computer requirements:* Graduate business students are not required to have a personal computer. *Special opportunities include:* An international exchange program and an internship program are available. *Placement services include:* Alumni network, career placement, career counseling/planning, electronic job bank, resume referral, career fairs, job interviews arranged, resume preparation, and career library.

EXPENSES *Tuition (state resident):* Full-time: $3708. *Tuition (nonresident):* Full-time: $7236. *Tuition (international):* Full-time: $7236. *Required fees:* Full-time: $309. *Graduate housing:* Room and board costs vary by number of occupants, type of accommodation, and type of board plan. *Typical cost:* $3000 (including board).

FINANCIAL AID (2007–08) 287 students received aid, including loans, research assistantships, scholarships, teaching assistantships, and work study. Aid is available to part-time students. *Financial aid application deadline:* 1/31.

Financial Aid Contact Vicki Mattocks, Director of Financial Aid, Office of Student Financial Aid, 901 South National Avenue, Carrington Hall 101, Springfield, MO 65897. *Phone:* 417-836-5262. *Fax:* 417-836-8392. *E-mail:* financialaid@missouristate.edu.

INTERNATIONAL STUDENTS 27% of students enrolled are international students. *Services and facilities:* Counseling/support services, ESL/language courses, Housing location assistance, International student housing, International student organization, Language tutoring, Orientation, Visa Services, International friends hosting program. Financial aid is available to international students. *Required with application:* TOEFL with recommended score of 213 (computer) or 550 (paper); proof of adequate funds; proof of health/immunizations.

International Student Contact Diana Garland, Interim Director of International Student Services, 901 South National Avenue, Carrington Hall 302, Springfield, MO 65897. *Phone:* 417-836-6618. *Fax:* 417-836-7656. *E-mail:* internationalstudentservices@missouristate.edu.

APPLICATION *Required:* GMAT, application form, baccalaureate/first degree, personal statement, transcripts of college work. *Application fee:* $35. *Deadlines:* 7/20 for fall, 12/20 for spring, 5/20 for summer, 4/15 for fall (international), 9/1 for spring (international), 4/1 for summer (international).

Application Contact Tobin Bushman, Admissions and Recruitment Coordinator, 901 South National Avenue, Carrington Hall, Room 306, Springfield, MO 65897. *Phone:* 417-836-5335. *Fax:* 417-836-6888. *E-mail:* graduatecollege@missouristate.edu.

Northwest Missouri State University
Melvin and Valorie Booth College of Business and Professional Studies

Maryville, Missouri

Phone: 660-562-1144 **Fax:** 660-562-1484 **E-mail:** timmel@nwmissouri.edu

Business Program(s) Web Site: http://www.nwmissouri.edu/graduate/mba/index.htm

Graduate Business Unit Enrollment *Total:* 105 (64 full-time; 41 part-time; 45 women; 17 international). *Average Age:* 26.

Graduate Business Faculty *Total:* 15 (14 full-time; 1 part-time).

Admissions *Applied:* 66. *Admitted:* 65. *Enrolled:* 41. *Average GMAT:* 476. *Average GPA:* 3.12

Academic Calendar Trimesters.

Accreditation ACBSP—The American Council of Business Schools and Programs.

After Graduation (Class of 2006–07) *Employed within 3 months of graduation:* 95%.

DEGREES MBA

MBA—MBA—Quality Emphasis Full-time and part-time. GMAT of 500. 33 to 36 total credits required. 12 to 96 months to complete program. *Concentration:* quality management.

MBA—Master of Business Administration in Accounting Full-time and part-time. At least 33 total credits required. 12 to 96 months to complete program. *Concentration:* accounting.

MBA—Master of Business Administration in Agricultural Economics Full-time and part-time. At least 36 total credits required. 12 to 96 months to complete program. *Concentration:* agricultural economics.

MBA—Master of Business Administration in Management Information Systems Full-time and part-time. At least 33 total credits required. 12 to 96 months to complete program. *Concentration:* information technology.

MBA—Master of Business Administration Full-time and part-time. At least 33 total credits required. 12 to 96 months to complete program. *Concentration:* general MBA.

RESOURCES AND SERVICES 3,400 on-campus PCs are available to graduate business students. Access to Internet/World Wide Web, online (class) registration, and online grade reports available. *Personal computer requirements:* Graduate business students are strongly recommended to purchase or lease a personal computer. *Placement services include:* Alumni network, career placement, job search course, career counseling/planning, resume referral, career fairs, job interviews arranged, resume preparation, and career library.

EXPENSES *Tuition (state resident):* Part-time: $260 per credit hour. *Tuition (nonresident):* Part-time: $455 per credit hour. *Tuition (international):* Part-time: $455 per credit hour. *Required fees:* Part-time: $105 per trimester. *Graduate housing:* Room and board costs vary by campus location, type of accommodation, and type of board plan.

FINANCIAL AID (2007–08) Loans, research assistantships, scholarships, and work study. *Financial aid application deadline:* 3/1.

Financial Aid Contact Mr. Del Morley, Director of Financial Assistance, 800 University Drive, Maryville, MO 64468. *Phone:* 660-562-1363. *Fax:* 660-562-1900. *E-mail:* 0700277@nwmissouri.edu.

INTERNATIONAL STUDENTS 16% of students enrolled are international students. *Services and facilities:* Counseling/support services, ESL/language courses, International student organization, Orientation, Visa Services. Financial aid is not available to international students. *Required with application:* TOEFL with recommended score of 213 (computer), 550 (paper), or 79 (Internet); proof of adequate funds.

International Student Contact Mr. Jeff Foot, Coordinator IIC, 800 University Drive, Maryville, MO 64468. *Phone:* 660-562-1367. *Fax:* 660-562-1439. *E-mail:* jfoot@nwmissouri.edu.

APPLICATION *Required:* GMAT, application form, baccalaureate/first degree, personal statement, transcripts of college work. *Application fee:* $0, $50 (international). *Deadlines:* 7/1 for fall, 12/1 for spring, 5/1 for summer, 5/1 for fall (international), 11/1 for spring (international), 4/1 for summer (international).

Northwest Missouri State University (continued)

Application Contact Ms. Terri Immel, Graduate Records Specialist, 800 University Drive, Administration Building 270, Maryville, MO 64468. *Phone:* 660-562-1144. *Fax:* 660-562-1484. *E-mail:* timmel@nwmissouri.edu.

Park University
Program in Business Administration
Parkville, Missouri

Phone: 816-842-6182 Ext. 5522 **Fax:** 816-472-1173 **E-mail:** joslyn.creighton@park.edu

Business Program(s) Web Site: http://www.park.edu/mba

DEGREE MBA

MBA—Master of Business Administration Full-time and part-time. Distance learning option. 36 total credits required. 18 to 84 months to complete program. *Concentrations:* entrepreneurship, general MBA, health administration, information systems, international business.

RESOURCES AND SERVICES 34 on-campus PCs are available to graduate business students. Access to Internet/World Wide Web, online (class) registration, and online grade reports available. *Personal computer requirements:* Graduate business students are strongly recommended to purchase or lease a personal computer. *Placement services include:* Alumni network, career placement, career counseling/planning, electronic job bank, resume referral, career fairs, and resume preparation.

Application Contact Joslyn Creighton, Student Services Coordinator, Park University Graduate School, 911 Main Suite 900, Kansas City, MO 64105. *Phone:* 816-842-6182 Ext. 5522. *Fax:* 816-472-1173. *E-mail:* joslyn.creighton@park.edu.

Rockhurst University
Helzberg School of Management
Kansas City, Missouri

Phone: 816-501-4731 **Fax:** 816-501-4241 **E-mail:** ron.filipowicz@rockhurst.edu

Business Program(s) Web Site: http://www.rockhurst.edu/

Accreditation AACSB—The Association to Advance Collegiate Schools of Business.

DEGREES EMBA • MBA

EMBA—Executive Master of Business Administration Full-time. Company or organization sponsorship, letter of recommendation and 9+ years of mid-to-upper level management experience required. 48 total credits required. 24 months to complete program. *Concentration:* management.

MBA—Master of Business Administration Full-time and part-time. Distance learning option. 36 to 54 total credits required. 18 to 72 months to complete program. *Concentrations:* accounting, finance, health care, international business, management, marketing.

RESOURCES AND SERVICES 500 on-campus PCs are available to graduate business students. Access to Internet/World Wide Web, online (class) registration, and online grade reports available. *Personal computer requirements:* Graduate business students are not required to have a personal computer. *Placement services include:* Alumni network, career placement, job search course, career counseling/planning, electronic job bank, resume referral, career fairs, job interviews arranged, resume preparation, and career library.

Application Contact Ron Filipowicz, Director of Graduate Admission, 1100 Rockhurst Road, Kansas City, MO 64110-2561. *Phone:* 816-501-4731. *Fax:* 816-501-4241. *E-mail:* ron.filipowicz@rockhurst.edu.

Saint Louis University
John Cook School of Business
St. Louis, Missouri

Phone: 314-977-6221 **Fax:** 314-977-1416 **E-mail:** gradbiz@slu.edu

Business Program(s) Web Site: http://gradbiz.slu.edu

Graduate Business Unit Enrollment *Total:* 435 (76 full-time; 359 part-time; 162 women; 24 international). *Average Age:* 27.

Graduate Business Faculty *Total:* 98 (68 full-time; 30 part-time).

Admissions *Applied:* 314. *Admitted:* 254. *Enrolled:* 186. *Average GMAT:* 560. *Average GPA:* 3.3

Academic Calendar Semesters.

Accreditation AACSB—The Association to Advance Collegiate Schools of Business.

After Graduation (Class of 2006–07) *Employed within 3 months of graduation:* 78%. *Average starting salary:* $60,000.

DEGREES EMIB • JD/MBA • M Acc • MBA • MBA/MHA • MD/MBA • MSF

EMIB—Executive Master of International Business Part-time. 38 total credits required. 21 to 24 months to complete program. *Concentration:* international business.

JD/MBA—Juris Doctor/Master of Business Administration Full-time and part-time. 118 to 121 total credits required. 42 to 52 months to complete program. *Concentration:* combined degrees.

M Acc—Master of Accountancy Full-time and part-time. 30 to 51 total credits required. 12 to 60 months to complete program. *Concentration:* accounting.

MBA—Master of Business Administration Full-time and part-time. 33 to 53 total credits required. 12 to 60 months to complete program. *Concentrations:* accounting, economics, entrepreneurship, finance, international business, management, management information systems, marketing, supply chain management.

MBA/MHA—Master of Business Administration/Master of Health Administration Full-time. 81 total credits required. 24 months to complete program. *Concentration:* combined degrees.

MD/MBA—Doctor of Medicine/Master of Business Administration Full-time. 191 total credits required. 60 months to complete program. *Concentration:* combined degrees.

MSF—Master of Science in Finance Part-time. Not currently accepting applications; program under revision. 30 total credits required. 21 months to complete program. *Concentration:* finance.

*S*aint Louis University's (SLU) John Cook School of Business has a long and proud tradition of providing a sound academic foundation for the professional practice of business. The SLU M.B.A. program blends business knowledge with individual growth, allowing students to balance personal goals with professional achievement. For more than fifty years, SLU's M.B.A. program has provided students with important analytical skills and functional principles, but today's environment demands more. SLU M.B.A. students prepare for the business environment of tomorrow through an academically challenging, values-based curriculum that emphasizes adaptability to change, practical training, and personal and professional development.*

The Saint Louis University M.B.A. program is designed to produce professional business and organizational leaders who can adapt to perform effectively and ethically in a fast-changing, global environment. Through electives, students have the opportunity to select areas

of emphasis, which range from entrepreneurship to international business to a specialization in a functional area.

The John Cook School of Business now offers both a part-time Professional M.B.A. and a full-time One-Year M.B.A., so there has never been a better time to accept the challenge of an SLU M.B.A.

RESOURCES AND SERVICES 104 on-campus PCs are available to graduate business students. Access to Internet/World Wide Web, online (class) registration, and online grade reports available. *Personal computer requirements:* Graduate business students are strongly recommended to purchase or lease a personal computer. *Special opportunities include:* An international exchange program and an internship program are available. *Placement services include:* Alumni network, career placement, job search course, career counseling/planning, electronic job bank, resume referral, career fairs, job interviews arranged, resume preparation, and career library.

EXPENSES *Tuition:* Part-time: $860 per credit hour. *Tuition (international):* Part-time: $860 per credit hour. Tuition and/or fees vary by academic program. *Graduate housing:* Room and board costs vary by campus location, number of occupants, type of accommodation, and type of board plan.

FINANCIAL AID (2007–08) Loans, research assistantships, scholarships, and teaching assistantships. *Financial aid application deadline:* 4/15.

Financial Aid Contact Cari Wickliffe, Director, Student Financial Services, Office of Financial Aid, 221 North Grand, Saint Louis, MO 63103-9945. *Phone:* 314-977-2350. *Fax:* 314-977-3437. *E-mail:* finaid@slu.edu.

INTERNATIONAL STUDENTS 6% of students enrolled are international students. *Services and facilities:* Counseling/support services, ESL/language courses, Housing location assistance, International student housing, International student organization, Orientation, Visa Services, Graduate writing center, International intramural league. Financial aid is available to international students. *Required with application:* TOEFL with recommended score of 230 (computer), 570 (paper), or 88 (Internet); TWE with recommended score of 4.5; proof of adequate funds; proof of health/immunizations.

International Student Contact Ms. Cathy Donahue, Foreign Student Advisor, International Center, DuBourg Hall 150, 221 North Grand, Saint Louis, MO 63103-9945. *Phone:* 314-977-7148. *Fax:* 314-977-3412. *E-mail:* donahuec@slu.edu.

APPLICATION *Required:* GMAT, application form, baccalaureate/first degree, interview, 2 letters of recommendation, personal statement, resume/curriculum vitae, transcripts of college work. *Recommended:* 2 years of work experience. *Application fee:* $90. Applications for domestic and international students are processed on a rolling basis.

Application Contact Ms. Nancy Biscan, Program Coordinator, Graduate Business Programs, 3674 Lindell Boulevard, Suite 132, Saint Louis, MO 63108. *Phone:* 314-977-6221. *Fax:* 314-977-1416. *E-mail:* gradbiz@slu.edu.

After Graduation (Class of 2006–07) *Employed within 3 months of graduation:* 95%. *Average starting salary:* $50,000.

DEGREE MBA

MBA—Master of Business Administration Full-time and part-time. Distance learning option. 33 to 63 total credits required. 12 to 72 months to complete program. *Concentrations:* accounting, environmental economics/management, finance, health administration, industrial administration/management, international business, management.

RESOURCES AND SERVICES 1,000 on-campus PCs are available to graduate business students. Access to Internet/World Wide Web, online (class) registration, and online grade reports available. *Personal computer requirements:* Graduate business students are strongly recommended to purchase or lease a personal computer. *Special opportunities include:* An international exchange program and an internship program are available. *Placement services include:* Career placement, job search course, career counseling/planning, electronic job bank, resume referral, career fairs, job interviews arranged, resume preparation, and career library.

EXPENSES *Tuition (state resident):* Part-time: $225 per credit hour. *Tuition (nonresident):* Part-time: $396 per credit hour. *Tuition (international):* Part-time: $396 per credit hour. *Graduate housing:* Room and board costs vary by number of occupants, type of accommodation, and type of board plan. *Typical cost:* $5826 (including board), $3756 (room only).

FINANCIAL AID (2007–08) 35 students received aid, including loans, research assistantships, scholarships, and work study. Aid is available to part-time students. *Financial aid application deadline:* 3/1.

Financial Aid Contact Karen Walker, Director, Financial Aid Services, Financial Aid Office, Cape Girardeau, MO 63701. *Phone:* 573-651-2039. *Fax:* 573-651-5155. *E-mail:* financialaid@semovm.semo.edu.

INTERNATIONAL STUDENTS 15% of students enrolled are international students. *Services and facilities:* Counseling/support services, ESL/language courses, Housing location assistance, International student organization, Orientation, Visa Services. Financial aid is available to international students. *Required with application:* TOEFL with recommended score of 213 (computer), 550 (paper), or 79 (Internet); proof of adequate funds; proof of health/immunizations.

International Student Contact Kenneth Heischmidt, Director, MBA Program, MBA Office, One University Plaza, MS5890, Cape Girardeau, MO 63701. *Phone:* 573-651-2912. *Fax:* 573-651-5032. *E-mail:* kheischmidt@semo.edu.

APPLICATION *Required:* GMAT, application form, baccalaureate/first degree, transcripts of college work. *Application fee:* $20, $100 (international). Applications for domestic and international students are processed on a rolling basis.

Application Contact Kenneth Heischmidt, Director, MBA Program, MBA Office, 1 University Plaza, MS5890, Cape Girardeau, MO 63701. *Phone:* 573-651-5116. *Fax:* 573-651-5032. *E-mail:* mba@semo.edu.

Southeast Missouri State University

Harrison College of Business

Cape Girardeau, Missouri

Phone: 573-651-5116 **Fax:** 573-651-5032 **E-mail:** mba@semo.edu

Business Program(s) Web Site: http://www6.semo.edu/mba

Graduate Business Unit Enrollment *Total:* 117 (45 full-time; 72 part-time; 58 women; 17 international). *Average Age:* 27.

Graduate Business Faculty 45 full-time.

Admissions *Applied:* 62. *Admitted:* 53. *Enrolled:* 42. *Average GMAT:* 515. *Average GPA:* 3.56

Academic Calendar Semesters.

Accreditation AACSB—The Association to Advance Collegiate Schools of Business.

Southwest Baptist University

College of Business and Computer Science

Bolivar, Missouri

Phone: 417-328-2000 **Fax:** 417-328-1887 **E-mail:** mba@sbuniv.edu

Business Program(s) Web Site: http://www.sbuniv.edu/

Graduate Business Unit Enrollment *Total:* 67.

Graduate Business Faculty *Total:* 10 (3 full-time; 7 part-time).

Admissions *Applied:* 25. *Admitted:* 20. *Enrolled:* 18. *Average GPA:* 3.1

Academic Calendar Semesters.

Accreditation ACBSP—The American Council of Business Schools and Programs.

DEGREES MBA

Southwest Baptist University (continued)

MBA—Master of Business Administration Full-time and part-time. Distance learning option. At least 36 total credits required. 12 to 60 months to complete program. *Concentration:* administration.

MBA—Master of Business Administration in Health Administration Full-time and part-time. Distance learning option. At least 45 total credits required. 14 to 60 months to complete program. *Concentration:* health administration.

RESOURCES AND SERVICES 25 on-campus PCs are available to graduate business students. Access to Internet/World Wide Web and online grade reports available. *Personal computer requirements:* Graduate business students are not required to have a personal computer. *Special opportunities include:* An internship program is available. *Placement services include:* Alumni network, career placement, career counseling/ planning, career fairs, and resume preparation.

EXPENSES *Tuition:* Full-time: $12,000. Part-time: $300 per credit hour. *Tuition (international):* Full-time: $12,000. Part-time: $300 per credit hour.

FINANCIAL AID (2007–08) 50 students received aid, including loans.

Financial Aid Contact Brad Gamble, Director of Financial Assistance, 1600 University Avenue, Bolivar, MO 65613. *Phone:* 417-326-1820. *Fax:* 417-328-1514. *E-mail:* bgamble@sbuniv.edu.

INTERNATIONAL STUDENTS *Services and facilities:* Counseling/ support services. Financial aid is not available to international students. *Required with application:* TOEFL; proof of adequate funds.

International Student Contact Shelly Francka, Director of Graduate Studies in Business, 1600 University Avenue, Bolivar, MO 65613. *Phone:* 417-328-2000. *Fax:* 417-328-1887. *E-mail:* mba@sbuniv.edu.

APPLICATION *Required:* Application form, baccalaureate/first degree, essay, 3 letters of recommendation, personal statement, resume/curriculum vitae, transcripts of college work. *Recommended:* 3 years of work experience. *Application fee:* $25. Applications for domestic and international students are processed on a rolling basis.

Application Contact Shelly Francka, Director of Graduate Studies in Business, 1600 University Avenue, Bolivar, MO 65613-2597. *Phone:* 417-328-2000. *Fax:* 417-328-1887. *E-mail:* mba@sbuniv.edu.

Truman State University
School of Business

Kirksville, Missouri

Phone: 660-785-4378 **Fax:** 660-785-7471 **E-mail:** jromine@truman.edu

Business Program(s) Web Site: http://www2.truman.edu/gradinfo/

Accreditation AACSB—The Association to Advance Collegiate Schools of Business.

DEGREE M Acc

M Acc—Master of Accountancy Full-time and part-time. 30 to 42 total credits required. 12 to 24 months to complete program. *Concentrations:* accounting, taxation.

RESOURCES AND SERVICES 475 on-campus PCs are available to graduate business students. Access to Internet/World Wide Web, online (class) registration, and online grade reports available. *Personal computer requirements:* Graduate business students are strongly recommended to purchase or lease a personal computer. *Placement services include:* Alumni network, career placement, career counseling/planning, electronic job bank, resume referral, career fairs, job interviews arranged, resume preparation, and career library.

Application Contact Jeffrey Romine, Coordinator of Graduate Studies, 100 East Normal Street, Kirksville, MO 63501-4221. *Phone:* 660-785-4378. *Fax:* 660-785-7471. *E-mail:* jromine@truman.edu.

University of Central Missouri
Harmon College of Business Administration

Warrensburg, Missouri

Phone: 660-543-8617 **Fax:** 660-543-8350 **E-mail:** best@ucmo.edu

Business Program(s) Web Site: http://www.ucmo.edu/x6600.xml

Graduate Business Unit Enrollment *Total:* 139 (101 full-time; 38 part-time; 51 women; 60 international). *Average Age:* 25.

Graduate Business Faculty 30 full-time.

Admissions *Applied:* 114. *Admitted:* 82. *Enrolled:* 42. *Average GMAT:* 495. *Average GPA:* 3.3

Academic Calendar Semesters.

Accreditation AACSB—The Association to Advance Collegiate Schools of Business.

After Graduation (Class of 2006–07) *Employed within 3 months of graduation:* 90%. *Average starting salary:* $40,250.

DEGREES M Acc • MBA • MS

M Acc—Master of Arts in Accountancy Full-time and part-time. 32 to 45 total credits required. 18 to 96 months to complete program. *Concentration:* accounting.

MBA—Master of Business Administration Full-time and part-time. 33 to 64 total credits required. 12 to 96 months to complete program. *Concentrations:* accounting, finance, information management, marketing.

MS—Master of Science in Information Technology Full-time and part-time. 33 to 45 total credits required. 18 to 96 months to complete program. *Concentration:* information management.

RESOURCES AND SERVICES 275 on-campus PCs are available to graduate business students. Access to Internet/World Wide Web, online (class) registration, and online grade reports available. *Personal computer requirements:* Graduate business students are not required to have a personal computer. *Special opportunities include:* An internship program is available. *Placement services include:* Alumni network, career placement, career counseling/planning, job interviews arranged, and resume preparation.

EXPENSES *Tuition (state resident):* Full-time: $8682. *Tuition (nonresident):* Full-time: $16,459. *Tuition (international):* Full-time: $16,459. Tuition and/or fees vary by campus location. *Graduate housing:* Room and board costs vary by campus location, number of occupants, type of accommodation, and type of board plan. *Typical cost:* $5846 (including board), $3746 (room only).

FINANCIAL AID (2007–08) 40 students received aid, including fellowships, loans, research assistantships, scholarships, teaching assistantships, and work study. Aid is available to part-time students. *Financial aid application deadline:* 4/1.

Financial Aid Contact Dr. Roger Best, Director of Graduate Programs, Ward Edwards 1624, Warrensburg, MO 64093. *Phone:* 660-543-8617. *Fax:* 660-543-8350. *E-mail:* best@ucmo.edu.

INTERNATIONAL STUDENTS 43% of students enrolled are international students. *Services and facilities:* Counseling/support services, ESL/language courses, Housing location assistance, International student organization, Orientation, Visa Services. Financial aid is available to international students. *Required with application:* TOEFL with recommended score of 213 (computer), 550 (paper), or 79 (Internet); proof of adequate funds; proof of health/immunizations. *Recommended with application:* IELT with recommended score of 6.

International Student Contact Dr. Joy Stevenson, International Student Advisor, Ward Edwards 1200, Warrensburg, MO 64093. *Phone:* 660-543-4195. *Fax:* 660-543-4201. *E-mail:* stevenson@ucmo.edu.

APPLICATION *Required:* GMAT, application form, baccalaureate/first degree, transcripts of college work. *Recommended:* Letter(s) of recommendation, personal statement. *Application fee:* $30, $50 (international). Applications for domestic and international students are processed on a rolling basis.

Application Contact Dr. Roger Best, Director of Graduate Programs, Ward Edwards 1624, Warrensburg, MO 64093. *Phone:* 660-543-8617. *Fax:* 660-543-8350. *E-mail:* best@ucmo.edu.

University of Missouri–Columbia
Robert J. Trulaske, Sr. College of Business

Columbia, Missouri

Phone: 573-882-2750 **Fax:** 573-882-6838 **E-mail:** mba@missouri.edu

Business Program(s) Web Site: http://business.missouri.edu/

Graduate Business Unit Enrollment *Total:* 207 (207 full-time; 80 women; 61 international). *Average Age:* 25.

Graduate Business Faculty *Total:* 30 (24 full-time; 6 part-time).

Admissions *Applied:* 332. *Admitted:* 206. *Enrolled:* 110. *Average GMAT:* 630. *Average GPA:* 3.45

Academic Calendar Semesters.

Accreditation AACSB—The Association to Advance Collegiate Schools of Business.

After Graduation (Class of 2006–07) *Employed within 3 months of graduation:* 91%. *Average starting salary:* $56,400.

DEGREES JD/MBA • MBA • MBA/MHA • MBA/MS

JD/MBA—Juris Doctor/Master of Business Administration Full-time and part-time. Must apply and be accepted to each program separately. *Concentration:* combined degrees.

MBA—Master of Business Administration Full-time and part-time. 32 to 59 total credits required. 12 to 21 months to complete program. *Concentrations:* accounting, advertising, agribusiness, agricultural economics, banking, business education, business information science, combined degrees, economics, electronic commerce (E-commerce), engineering, European business studies, finance, general MBA, health administration, hospitality management, human resources development, human resources management, industrial administration/management, information management, information systems, information technology, international and area business studies, international business, investments and securities, management, management information systems, marketing, nonprofit management, nonprofit organization, public policy and administration, public relations, real estate, risk management, statistics.

MBA/MHA—Master of Business Administration/Master of Health Administration Full-time and part-time. Must apply and be accepted to each program separately. *Concentration:* combined degrees.

MBA/MS—Master of Business Administration/Master of Science in Industrial Engineering Full-time and part-time. Must apply and be accepted to each program separately. *Concentration:* combined degrees.

RESOURCES AND SERVICES 1,000 on-campus PCs are available to graduate business students. Access to Internet/World Wide Web, online (class) registration, and online grade reports available. *Personal computer requirements:* Graduate business students are strongly recommended to purchase or lease a personal computer. *Special opportunities include:* An international exchange program and an internship program are available. *Placement services include:* Alumni network, career placement, job search course, career counseling/planning, electronic job bank, resume referral, career fairs, job interviews arranged, resume preparation, and career library.

EXPENSES *Tuition (state resident):* Full-time: $8962.80. *Tuition (nonresident):* Full-time: $21,672. *Tuition (international):* Full-time: $21,672. *Required fees:* Full-time: $950. Tuition and/or fees vary by number of courses or credits taken and academic program. *Graduate housing:* Room and board costs vary by number of occupants, type of accommodation, and type of board plan. *Typical cost:* $8100 (including board).

FINANCIAL AID (2007–08) 120 students received aid, including loans, research assistantships, scholarships, teaching assistantships, and work study. *Financial aid application deadline:* 5/1.

Financial Aid Contact Barbara Schneider, Director of Admissions and Financial Aid, 213 Cornell Hall, Columbia, MO 65211. *Phone:* 573-882-2750. *Fax:* 573-882-6838. *E-mail:* mba@missouri.edu.

INTERNATIONAL STUDENTS 29% of students enrolled are international students. *Services and facilities:* Counseling/support services, ESL/language courses, Housing location assistance, International student housing, International student organization, Language tutoring, Orientation, Visa Services. Financial aid is available to international students. *Required with application:* TOEFL with recommended score of 213 (computer), 550 (paper), or 79 (Internet); proof of adequate funds; proof of health/immunizations.

International Student Contact Barbara Schneider, Director of Admissions and Financial Aid, 213 Cornell Hall, Columbia, MO 65211. *Phone:* 573-882-2750. *Fax:* 573-882-6838. *E-mail:* mba@missouri.edu.

APPLICATION *Required:* GMAT, application form, baccalaureate/first degree, resume/curriculum vitae, transcripts of college work. *Recommended:* Work experience. *Application fee:* $45, $60 (international). Applications for domestic and international students are processed on a rolling basis.

Application Contact Barbara Schneider, Director of Admissions and Financial Aid, 213 Cornell Hall, Columbia, MO 65211. *Phone:* 573-882-2750. *Fax:* 573-882-6838. *E-mail:* mba@missouri.edu.

See full description on page 720.

University of Missouri–Kansas City
Henry W. Bloch School of Business and Public Administration

Kansas City, Missouri

Phone: 816-235-1111 **Fax:** 816-235-5544 **E-mail:** admit@umkc.edu

Business Program(s) Web Site: http://www.bloch.umkc.edu

Graduate Business Unit Enrollment *Total:* 393 (393 part-time; 138 women; 26 international). *Average Age:* 30.

Graduate Business Faculty 36 full-time.

Admissions *Applied:* 307. *Admitted:* 180. *Enrolled:* 145. *Average GMAT:* 534. *Average GPA:* 2.92

Academic Calendar Semesters.

Accreditation AACSB—The Association to Advance Collegiate Schools of Business.

DEGREES MBA • MS

MBA—Executive Master of Business Administration Part-time. At least 48 total credits required. 21 months to complete program. *Concentration:* management.

MBA—Master of Business Administration Part-time. 30 to 48 total credits required. 12 to 84 months to complete program. *Concentrations:* entrepreneurship, finance, international business, leadership, management, management information systems, marketing, operations management.

MS—Master of Science in Accounting Part-time. 30 to 60 total credits required. 12 to 84 months to complete program. *Concentration:* accounting.

RESOURCES AND SERVICES 450 on-campus PCs are available to graduate business students. Access to Internet/World Wide Web, online (class) registration, and online grade reports available. *Personal computer requirements:* Graduate business students are not required to have a personal computer. *Special opportunities include:* An international exchange program and an internship program are available. *Placement services include:* Alumni network, career placement, job search course, career counseling/planning, electronic job bank, resume referral, career fairs, job interviews arranged, resume preparation, and career library.

EXPENSES *Tuition (state resident):* Full-time: $7077. Part-time: $235.90 per credit hour. *Tuition (nonresident):* Full-time: $17,733. Part-time:

University of Missouri–Kansas City (continued)

$591.10 per credit hour. *Tuition (international):* Full-time: $17,733. Part-time: $591.10 per credit hour. *Required fees:* Full-time: $869. Part-time: $30.81 per credit hour. *Graduate housing:* Room and board costs vary by number of occupants, type of accommodation, and type of board plan. *Typical cost:* $9560 (including board).

FINANCIAL AID (2007–08) 147 students received aid, including fellowships, loans, research assistantships, scholarships, teaching assistantships, and work study. Aid is available to part-time students. *Financial aid application deadline:* 3/1.

Financial Aid Contact Jan Brandow, Director of Financial Aid, 5100 Rockhill Road, Kansas City, MO 64110-2499. *Phone:* 816-235-1154. *Fax:* 816-235-5511.

INTERNATIONAL STUDENTS 7% of students enrolled are international students. *Services and facilities:* Counseling/support services, ESL/language courses, Housing location assistance, International student organization, Language tutoring, Orientation, Visa Services. Financial aid is available to international students. *Required with application:* TOEFL with recommended score of 213 (computer) or 550 (paper); proof of adequate funds; proof of health/immunizations.

International Student Contact Sandra Gault, Associate Director, International Student Affairs, 5235 Rockhill Road, Kansas City, MO 64110-2499. *Phone:* 816-235-1113. *Fax:* 816-235-6502. *E-mail:* isao@ umkc.edu.

APPLICATION *Required:* GMAT, application form, baccalaureate/first degree, personal statement, resume/curriculum vitae, transcripts of college work. School will accept GRE. *Recommended:* Work experience. *Application fee:* $35, $50 (international). Applications for domestic and international students are processed on a rolling basis.

Application Contact Jennifer DeHaemers, Director of Admissions, 5100 Rockhill Road, Kansas City, MO 64110-2499. *Phone:* 816-235-1111. *Fax:* 816-235-5544. *E-mail:* admit@umkc.edu.

University of Missouri–St. Louis
College of Business Administration

St. Louis, Missouri

Phone: 314-516-5885 **Fax:** 314-516-7202 **E-mail:** mba@umsl.edu

Business Program(s) Web Site: http://mba.umsl.edu

Accreditation AACSB—The Association to Advance Collegiate Schools of Business.

DEGREES M Acc • MBA • MS

M Acc—Master of Accounting Full-time and part-time. 30 to 69 total credits required. 18 to 72 months to complete program. *Concentration:* accounting.

MBA—Master of Business Administration Full-time and part-time. 39 to 54 total credits required. 18 to 72 months to complete program. *Concentrations:* accounting, finance, management, marketing, operations management, supply chain management.

MBA—Professional Master of Business Administration Part-time. 3 years of work experience required. At least 48 total credits required. 24 months to complete program. *Concentration:* general MBA.

MS—Master of Science in Information Systems Full-time and part-time. 30 to 48 total credits required. 18 to 72 months to complete program. *Concentrations:* electronic commerce (E-commerce), information systems, telecommunications management.

The M.B.A. program at the University of Missouri–St. Louis produces highly qualified business professionals and is flexible enough to accommodate the person who seeks a general base of knowledge in business administration as well as one who seeks to obtain a concentration in a specific discipline. Emphasis areas are available in accounting, finance, information systems, logistics and supply chain management, management, marketing, and operations management.

Graduate business programs at UM–St. Louis combine high-quality students with active, well-trained faculty members. The result is a challenging educational program with demanding instruction in state-of-the-art, research-based management education. Faculty members are nationally respected scholars who are widely published and engage in extensive real-world consulting. Program participants come from all walks of life and are employed at virtually every firm in the region. International students hail from all parts of the world. Program quality is reflected by the fact that all business programs have carried the prestigious AACSB International accreditation for nearly four decades.

Full-time students can complete the evening M.B.A. program in eighteen months to two years. Part-time students generally take three to five years to complete the program. The Professional M.B.A. is an Internet-enhanced weekend program that is completed in two years and is geared to the busy professional. The International M.B.A. is a unique two-year program in which students spend the first year studying overseas at a partner institution and the second year on-campus at UM–St. Louis.

RESOURCES AND SERVICES 300 on-campus PCs are available to graduate business students. Access to Internet/World Wide Web, online (class) registration, and online grade reports available. *Personal computer requirements:* Graduate business students are strongly recommended to purchase or lease a personal computer. *Special opportunities include:* An international exchange program and an internship program are available. *Placement services include:* Career placement, career counseling/planning, electronic job bank, resume referral, career fairs, job interviews arranged, resume preparation, and career library.

Application Contact Mr. Karl Kottemann, Associate Director, Graduate Programs in Business, One University Boulevard, St. Louis, MO 63121-4499. *Phone:* 314-516-5885. *Fax:* 314-516-7202. *E-mail:* mba@ umsl.edu.

University of Phoenix–Kansas City Campus
College of Graduate Business and Management

Kansas City, Missouri

Phone: 480-317-6200 **Fax:** 480-643-1479 **E-mail:** beth.barilla@phoenix.edu

---

DEGREES M Mgt • MBA

M Mgt—Human Resource Management Full-time. At least 45 total credits required. *Concentration:* human resources management.

M Mgt—Master of Management Full-time. At least 39 total credits required. *Concentration:* management.

M Mgt—Public Administration Full-time. At least 45 total credits required. *Concentration:* public policy and administration.

MBA—Accounting Full-time. At least 54 total credits required. *Concentration:* accounting.

MBA—Global Management Full-time. At least 45 total credits required. *Concentration:* international business.

MBA—Human Resource Management Full-time. At least 45 total credits required. *Concentration:* human resources management.

MBA—Public Administration Full-time. At least 45 total credits required. *Concentration:* public policy and administration.

MBA—e-Business Full-time. At least 45 total credits required. *Concentration:* electronic commerce (E-commerce).

MBA—Master of Business Administration Full-time. At least 45 total credits required. *Concentration:* administration.

RESOURCES AND SERVICES Access to online grade reports available. *Personal computer requirements:* Graduate business students are strongly recommended to purchase or lease a personal computer. *Placement services include:* Alumni network.

Application Contact Beth Barilla, Associate Vice President of Student Admissions and Services, Mail Stop AA-K101, 4615 East Elwood Street, Phoenix, AZ 85040-1958. *Phone:* 480-317-6200. *Fax:* 480-643-1479. *E-mail:* beth.barilla@phoenix.edu.

University of Phoenix–St. Louis Campus
College of Graduate Business and Management
St. Louis, Missouri

Phone: 480-317-6200 **Fax:** 480-643-1479 **E-mail:** beth.barilla@phoenix.edu

Business Program(s) Web Site: http://www.phoenix.edu

DEGREES M Mgt • MA • MBA

M Mgt—Human Resource Management Full-time. At least 39 total credits required. *Concentration:* human resources management.

M Mgt—Master of Management Full-time. At least 39 total credits required. *Concentration:* management.

MA—Organizational Management Full-time. At least 40 total credits required. *Concentration:* organizational management.

MBA—Global Management Full-time. At least 45 total credits required. *Concentration:* international business.

MBA—Human Resource Management Full-time. At least 45 total credits required. *Concentration:* human resources management.

MBA—e-Business Full-time. At least 46 total credits required. *Concentration:* electronic commerce (E-commerce).

MBA—Master of Business Administration Full-time. At least 45 total credits required. *Concentration:* administration.

RESOURCES AND SERVICES Access to online grade reports available. *Personal computer requirements:* Graduate business students are strongly recommended to purchase or lease a personal computer. *Placement services include:* Alumni network.

Application Contact Beth Barilla, Associate Vice President of Student Admissions and Services, Mail Stop AA-K101, 4615 East Elwood Street, Phoenix, AZ 85040-1958. *Phone:* 480-317-6200. *Fax:* 480-643-1479. *E-mail:* beth.barilla@phoenix.edu.

Washington University in St. Louis
Olin Business School
St. Louis, Missouri

Phone: 314-935-7301 **Fax:** 314-935-6309 **E-mail:** mba@wustl.edu

Business Program(s) Web Site: http://www.olin.wustl.edu/

Graduate Business Unit Enrollment *Total:* 999 (619 full-time; 380 part-time). *Average Age:* 28.

Graduate Business Faculty *Total:* 108 (65 full-time; 43 part-time).

Admissions *Applied:* 1,402. *Admitted:* 530. *Enrolled:* 313. *Average GMAT:* 674. *Average GPA:* 3.38

Academic Calendar Semesters.

Accreditation AACSB—The Association to Advance Collegiate Schools of Business.

After Graduation (Class of 2006–07) *Employed within 3 months of graduation:* 95%. *Average starting salary:* $85,583.

DEGREES JD/MBA • M Acc • MBA • MBA/M Arch • MBA/M Eng • MBA/MA • MBA/MSW • MSF

JD/MBA—MBA Dual Degree—Law Full-time. Distance learning option. Must apply to both programs separately. 48 to 60 months to complete program. *Concentrations:* combined degrees, law.

M Acc—Master of Accounting Full-time and part-time. 33 total credits required. 12 to 24 months to complete program. *Concentration:* accounting.

MBA—Executive Master of Business Administration Part-time. Preferred minimum of five years of managerial experience. Program options include every other weekend or once per month. 18 months to complete program. *Concentration:* executive programs.

MBA—Full-Time Master of Business Administration Full-time. At least 66 total credits required. 21 months to complete program. *Concentrations:* accounting, combined degrees, entrepreneurship, finance, general MBA, leadership, management, management consulting, marketing, organizational behavior/development, organizational management, strategic management, supply chain management.

MBA—Professional Master of Business Administration Part-time. Must be employed full-time, preferably with 2 years or more experience. At least 54 total credits required. 28 to 60 months to complete program. *Concentrations:* accounting, finance, general MBA, management, marketing, organizational behavior/development, strategic management, supply chain management.

MBA—Shanghai Executive Master of Business Administration Part-time. Program in partnership with Fudan University. Fluency in reading, writing and speaking English; minimum of 5 years of managerial experience required. 18 months to complete program. *Concentration:* executive programs.

MBA/M Arch—MBA Dual Degree—Architecture Full-time. Must apply to both programs separately. 36 to 60 months to complete program. *Concentrations:* architecture, combined degrees.

MBA/M Eng—MBA Dual Degree—Biomedical Engineering Full-time and part-time. Must apply to both programs separately. 36 to 60 months to complete program. *Concentration:* combined degrees.

MBA/MA—MBA Dual Degree—East Asian Studies Full-time. Must apply to both programs separately. 36 to 60 months to complete program. *Concentrations:* Asian business studies, combined degrees.

MBA/MSW—MBA Dual Degree—Social Work Full-time. Must apply to both programs separately. 36 to 60 months to complete program. *Concentrations:* combined degrees, social work.

MSF—MS in Finance Full-time and part-time. 33 to 39 total credits required. 12 to 24 months to complete program. *Concentrations:* finance, financial engineering, quantitative analysis.

RESOURCES AND SERVICES Access to Internet/World Wide Web, online (class) registration, and online grade reports available. *Personal computer requirements:* Graduate business students are required to have a personal computer. *Special opportunities include:* An international exchange program and an internship program are available. *Placement services include:* Alumni network, career placement, job search course, career counseling/planning, electronic job bank, resume referral, career fairs, job interviews arranged, resume preparation, and career library.

EXPENSES *Tuition:* Full-time: $37,900. Part-time: $1150 per credit hour. *Tuition (international):* Full-time: $37,900. Part-time: $1150 per credit hour. *Required fees:* Full-time: $836. Tuition and/or fees vary by class time, number of courses or credits taken, and academic program.

FINANCIAL AID (2007–08) Fellowships, loans, research assistantships, scholarships, teaching assistantships, and work study. Aid is available to part-time students. *Financial aid application deadline:* 5/1.

Washington University in St. Louis (continued)

Financial Aid Contact Kyle Cronan, Assistant Director of Financial Aid, 1 Brookings Drive, Campus Box 1133, St. Louis, MO 63130-4899. *Phone:* 314-935-7301. *Fax:* 314-935-6309. *E-mail:* mba@wustl.edu.

INTERNATIONAL STUDENTS *Services and facilities:* Counseling/support services, ESL/language courses, Housing location assistance, International student organization, Language tutoring, Orientation, Visa Services, Special mentoring program. Financial aid is available to international students. *Required with application:* TOEFL; proof of adequate funds; proof of health/immunizations.

International Student Contact Kathy Steiner-Lang, Director, International Office, 1 Brookings Drive, Campus Box 1083, St. Louis, MO 63130-4899. *Phone:* 314-935-5910. *Fax:* 314-935-4075. *E-mail:* stix@artsci.wustl.edu.

APPLICATION *Required:* GMAT, application form, baccalaureate/first degree, essay, personal statement, resume/curriculum vitae, transcripts of college work. *Recommended:* Interview, work experience. *Application fee:* $100. *Deadlines:* 11/5 for fall, 1/14 for winter, 3/3 for spring, 5/1 for summer, 11/5 for fall (international), 1/14 for winter (international), 3/3 for spring (international), 5/1 for summer (international).

Application Contact Evan Bouffides, Assistant Dean, MBA Admissions and Financial Aid, 1 Brookings Drive, Campus Box 1133, St. Louis, MO 63130-4899. *Phone:* 314-935-7301. *Fax:* 314-935-6309. *E-mail:* mba@wustl.edu.

Webster University
School of Business and Technology

St. Louis, Missouri

Phone: 314-968-7100 **Fax:** 314-968-7462 **E-mail:** gadmit@webster.edu

Business Program(s) Web Site: http://www.webster.edu/depts/business/

Graduate Business Unit Enrollment *Total:* 11,854 (2,591 full-time; 9,263 part-time; 5,704 women; 856 international). *Average Age:* 35.

Graduate Business Faculty *Total:* 1,316 (36 full-time; 1,280 part-time).

Admissions *Applied:* 2,548. *Admitted:* 2,506. *Enrolled:* 2,009.

Academic Calendar Five 9-week terms.

After Graduation (Class of 2006–07) *Employed within 3 months of graduation:* 96%. *Average starting salary:* $63,757.

DEGREES MA • MBA • MHA • MS

MA—Business and Organizational Security Management Full-time and part-time. Distance learning option. 36 total credits required. *Concentration:* other.

MA—Human Resources Development Full-time and part-time. 36 total credits required. *Concentration:* human resources development.

MA—Master of Arts in Business Full-time and part-time. At least 36 total credits required. *Concentration:* business studies.

MA—Master of Arts in Health Care Management Full-time and part-time. At least 36 total credits required. *Concentration:* health care.

MA—Master of Arts in Human Resources Management Full-time and part-time. Distance learning option. At least 36 total credits required. *Concentration:* human resources management.

MA—Master of Arts in Information Technology Management Full-time and part-time. At least 36 total credits required. *Concentration:* information management.

MA—Master of Arts in International Business Full-time and part-time. At least 36 total credits required. *Concentration:* international business.

MA—Master of Arts in Management and Leadership Full-time and part-time. Distance learning option. At least 36 total credits required. *Concentration:* management.

MA—Master of Arts in Marketing Full-time and part-time. At least 36 total credits required. *Concentration:* marketing.

MA—Master of Arts in Public Administration Full-time and part-time. At least 36 total credits required. *Concentration:* public policy and administration.

MA—Master of Arts in Telecommunications Management Full-time and part-time. At least 36 total credits required. *Concentration:* telecommunications management.

MA—Procurement and Acquisitions Management Full-time and part-time. Distance learning option. 36 total credits required. *Concentration:* materials management.

MBA—Master of Business Administration Full-time and part-time. Distance learning option. 36 to 48 total credits required. *Concentrations:* environmental economics/management, finance, general MBA, health care, human resources development, human resources management, information management, international business, management, marketing, media administration, telecommunications management.

MHA—Master of Health Administration Full-time and part-time. 36 total credits required. *Concentration:* health administration.

MS—Master of Science in Computer Science/Distributed Systems Full-time and part-time. At least 36 total credits required. *Concentration:* information systems.

MS—Master of Science in Finance Full-time and part-time. Distance learning option. At least 36 total credits required. Minimum of 36 months to complete program. *Concentration:* finance.

MS—Master of Science in Space Systems Operations Management Full-time and part-time. At least 36 total credits required. *Concentration:* management science.

RESOURCES AND SERVICES 1,185 on-campus PCs are available to graduate business students. Access to Internet/World Wide Web, online (class) registration, and online grade reports available. *Personal computer requirements:* Graduate business students are not required to have a personal computer. *Special opportunities include:* An international exchange program and an internship program are available. *Placement services include:* Alumni network, career counseling/planning, electronic job bank, resume referral, career fairs, job interviews arranged, resume preparation, and career library.

EXPENSES *Tuition:* Full-time: $12,480. Part-time: $520 per credit hour. *Tuition (international):* Full-time: $12,480. Part-time: $520 per credit hour. Tuition and/or fees vary by campus location. *Graduate housing:* Room and board costs vary by campus location, number of occupants, and type of accommodation. *Typical cost:* $6300 (room only).

FINANCIAL AID (2007–08) 5818 students received aid, including loans, scholarships, and work study. Aid is available to part-time students. *Financial aid application deadline:* 4/1.

Financial Aid Contact Jonathan Gruett, Director, Office of Financial Aid, 470 East Lockwood Avenue, St. Louis, MO 63119-3194. *Phone:* 314-968-6903. *Fax:* 314-968-7125. *E-mail:* gruettjo@webster.edu.

INTERNATIONAL STUDENTS 7% of students enrolled are international students. *Services and facilities:* Counseling/support services, ESL/language courses, Housing location assistance, International student organization, Language tutoring, Orientation, Visa Services, International student advisor, International credential specialist. Financial aid is available to international students. *Required with application:* TOEFL with recommended score of 230 (computer) or 575 (paper); proof of adequate funds; proof of health/immunizations. *Recommended with application:* TWE.

International Student Contact Calvin Smith, Director, International Recruitment and Services, International Enrollment Center, 470 East Lockwood Avenue, St. Louis, MO 63119-3194. *Phone:* 314-968-7049. *Fax:* 314-968-7119. *E-mail:* intlstudy@webster.edu.

APPLICATION *Required:* Application form, baccalaureate/first degree, interview, personal statement, resume/curriculum vitae, transcripts of college work, work experience. School will accept GMAT, GRE, and MAT. *Recommended:* Essay. *Application fee:* $35, $50 (international). Applications for domestic students are processed on a rolling basis.

Application Contact Matt Nolan, Director, Graduate and Evening Student Admissions, 470 East Lockwood Avenue, St. Louis, MO 63119-3194. *Phone:* 314-968-7100. *Fax:* 314-968-7462. *E-mail:* gadmit@webster.edu.

William Woods University
Graduate and Adult Studies

Fulton, Missouri

Phone: 573-592-1185 **Fax:** 573-592-1164 **E-mail:** lrembish@williamwoods.edu

Business Program(s) Web Site: http://www.williamwoods.edu/evening

---
DEGREE MBA

MBA—Master of Business Administration Full-time. Minimum undergraduate GPA of 2.5; coursework in accounting and economics required. A Bachelor degree in accounting and overall GPA of 2.5 is required for the Accounting concentration. 36 total credits required. 18 to 22 months to complete program. *Concentrations:* accounting, health care, human resources management.

RESOURCES AND SERVICES Access to Internet/World Wide Web and online grade reports available. *Personal computer requirements:* Graduate business students are strongly recommended to purchase or lease a personal computer. *Placement services include:* Alumni network.

Application Contact Ms. Linda Rembish, Administrative Assistant, One University Avenue, Fulton, MO 65251-1098. *Phone:* 573-592-1185. *Fax:* 573-592-1164. *E-mail:* lrembish@williamwoods.edu.

MONTANA

Montana State University
College of Business

Bozeman, Montana

Phone: 406-994-4683 **Fax:** 406-994-6206 **E-mail:** busgrad@montana.edu

Business Program(s) Web Site: http://www.montana.edu/acct/mpac.html

Accreditation AACSB—The Association to Advance Collegiate Schools of Business.

DEGREE MP Ac

MP Ac—Master of Professional Accountancy Full-time and part-time. At least 30 total credits required. 9 to 60 months to complete program. *Concentration:* accounting.

RESOURCES AND SERVICES 300 on-campus PCs are available to graduate business students. Access to Internet/World Wide Web, online (class) registration, and online grade reports available. *Personal computer requirements:* Graduate business students are strongly recommended to purchase or lease a personal computer. *Special opportunities include:* An internship program is available. *Placement services include:* Alumni network, career placement, career counseling/planning, electronic job bank, resume referral, career fairs, job interviews arranged, resume preparation, and career library.

Application Contact Pamela Shelden, Office of Student Services, 338 Reid Hall, PO Box 173040, Bozeman, MT 59717-3040. *Phone:* 406-994-4683. *Fax:* 406-994-6206. *E-mail:* busgrad@montana.edu.

NEBRASKA

Bellevue University
College of Business

Bellevue, Nebraska

Phone: 402-557-7245 **Fax:** 402-557-7245 **E-mail:** scott.bierman@bellevue.edu

Business Program(s) Web Site: http://www.bellevue.edu

Graduate Business Faculty *Total:* 26 (14 full-time; 12 part-time).

Academic Calendar Trimesters with 1 summer session.

DEGREES EMBA • M Sc • MA • MBA • MSMIS

EMBA—Executive Master of Business Administration Full-time. Distance learning option. Management and profits/loss management experience required. 36 total credits required. 36 months to complete program. *Concentration:* executive programs.

M Sc—Contract and Acquisition Management Full-time. Distance learning option. *Concentration:* contract management.

M Sc—Human Capital Management Full-time. Distance learning option. 36 total credits required. 36 months to complete program. *Concentration:* human resources management.

MA—Management Full-time and part-time. Distance learning option. 36 total credits required. 36 months to complete program. *Concentration:* arts administration/management.

MBA—Master of Business Administration Full-time and part-time. Distance learning option. 36 total credits required. 36 months to complete program. *Concentrations:* accounting, contract management, finance, general MBA, human resources development, information management, international management, logistics, management, marketing.

MSMIS—Management of Information Systems Full-time and part-time. Distance learning option. At least 36 total credits required. 36 months to complete program. *Concentrations:* business studies, health administration, information technology.

RESOURCES AND SERVICES 547 on-campus PCs are available to graduate business students. Access to Internet/World Wide Web, online (class) registration, and online grade reports available. *Personal computer requirements:* Graduate business students are strongly recommended to purchase or lease a personal computer. *Special opportunities include:* An internship program is available. *Placement services include:* Alumni network, career placement, career counseling/planning, resume referral, career fairs, resume preparation, and career library.

EXPENSES *Tuition:* Part-time: $405 per credit. *Tuition (international):* Part-time: $405 per credit. *Required fees:* Full-time: $150. Part-time: $150 per degree program.

FINANCIAL AID (2007–08) Scholarships. Aid is available to part-time students.

Financial Aid Contact Mr. Scott Klene, Senior Director, Student Financial Services, 1000 Galvin Road South, Bellevue, NE 68005. *Phone:* 402-557-7319. *E-mail:* scott.klene@bellevue.edu.

INTERNATIONAL STUDENTS *Services and facilities:* Counseling/support services, ESL/language courses, International student housing, International student organization, Orientation, Visa Services. Financial aid is available to international students. *Required with application:* TOEFL with recommended score of 190 (computer) or 520 (paper); proof of adequate funds.

International Student Contact Mr. Todd Betts, Associate Director, International Programs, 1000 Galvin Road South, Bellevue, NE 68005. *Phone:* 402-557-7278. *Fax:* 402-557-5423. *E-mail:* todd.betts@bellevue.edu.

Bellevue University (continued)

APPLICATION *Required:* Application form, baccalaureate/first degree, transcripts of college work. *Recommended:* 3 years of work experience. *Application fee:* $75. Applications for domestic and international students are processed on a rolling basis.

Application Contact Mr. Scott Bierman, Graduate Enrollment Director, 1000 Galvin Road South, Bellevue, NE 68005. *Phone:* 402-557-7245. *Fax:* 402-557-7245. *E-mail:* scott.bierman@bellevue.edu.

See full description on page 576.

Chadron State College
Department of Business and Economics
Chadron, Nebraska

Phone: 308-432-6214 **Fax:** 308-432-6454 **E-mail:** mburke@csc.edu

Business Program(s) Web Site: http://www.csc.edu

Graduate Business Unit Enrollment *Total:* 45 (18 full-time; 27 part-time; 21 women; 1 international). *Average Age:* 31.

Graduate Business Faculty *Total:* 16 (11 full-time; 5 part-time).

Admissions *Applied:* 15. *Admitted:* 15. *Enrolled:* 13. *Average GMAT:* 441.

Academic Calendar Semesters.

Accreditation ACBSP—The American Council of Business Schools and Programs.

After Graduation (Class of 2006–07) *Average starting salary:* $44,000.

DEGREE MBA

MBA—Master of Business Administration Full-time and part-time. Distance learning option. At least 36 total credits required. 12 to 84 months to complete program. *Concentration:* general MBA.

RESOURCES AND SERVICES 120 on-campus PCs are available to graduate business students. Access to Internet/World Wide Web, online (class) registration, and online grade reports available. *Personal computer requirements:* Graduate business students are not required to have a personal computer. *Special opportunities include:* An internship program is available. *Placement services include:* Career placement, career counseling/planning, electronic job bank, resume referral, career fairs, job interviews arranged, resume preparation, and career library.

EXPENSES *Tuition (state resident):* Full-time: $1896.75. Part-time: $210.75 per credit. *Tuition (nonresident):* Full-time: $1897. Part-time: $210.75 per credit. *Tuition (international):* Full-time: $1896.75. Part-time: $210.75 per credit. *Graduate housing:* Room and board costs vary by number of occupants, type of accommodation, and type of board plan. *Typical cost:* $4318 (including board), $2080 (room only).

FINANCIAL AID (2007–08) Grants, loans, research assistantships, scholarships, teaching assistantships, and work study. Aid is available to part-time students. *Financial aid application deadline:* 6/1.

Financial Aid Contact Ms. Sherry Douglas, Director of Financial Aid, 1000 Main Street, Chadron, NE 69337. *Phone:* 308-432-6230. *Fax:* 308-432-6229. *E-mail:* sdouglas@csc.edu.

INTERNATIONAL STUDENTS 2% of students enrolled are international students. *Services and facilities:* Counseling/support services, Orientation. Financial aid is available to international students. *Required with application:* TOEFL with recommended score of 213 (computer) or 550 (paper); proof of adequate funds; proof of health/immunizations.

International Student Contact Mr. Dale Williamson, Registrar, 1000 Main Street, Chadron, NE 69337. *Phone:* 308-432-6221. *Fax:* 308-432-6229. *E-mail:* dwilliamson@csc.edu.

APPLICATION *Required:* GMAT, application form, baccalaureate/first degree, essay, 3 letters of recommendation, personal statement, transcripts of college work. *Application fee:* $15. Applications for domestic and international students are processed on a rolling basis.

Application Contact Ms. Mary Burke, Graduate Office, 1000 Main Street, Chadron, NE 69337. *Phone:* 308-432-6214. *Fax:* 308-432-6454. *E-mail:* mburke@csc.edu.

Creighton University
Eugene C. Eppley College of Business Administration
Omaha, Nebraska

Phone: 402-280-2829 **Fax:** 402-280-2172 **E-mail:** cobagrad@creighton.edu

Business Program(s) Web Site: http://business.creighton.edu

Graduate Business Unit Enrollment *Total:* 160 (20 full-time; 140 part-time; 38 women; 17 international). *Average Age:* 27.

Graduate Business Faculty *Total:* 18 (13 full-time; 5 part-time).

Admissions *Applied:* 59. *Admitted:* 40. *Enrolled:* 36. *Average GMAT:* 560. *Average GPA:* 3.4

Academic Calendar Semesters.

Accreditation AACSB—The Association to Advance Collegiate Schools of Business.

After Graduation (Class of 2006–07) *Employed within 3 months of graduation:* 97%. *Average starting salary:* $45,000.

DEGREES JD/MBA • MBA • MBA/INR • MBA/MS • MS • MSISM • Pharm D/MBA

JD/MBA—Juris Doctor/Master of Business Administration Full-time and part-time. Applicants must apply to and be independently accepted by each program. At least 33 total credits required. 36 to 72 months to complete program. *Concentrations:* combined degrees, general MBA, law.

MBA—Master of Business Administration Full-time and part-time. 33 to 42 total credits required. 12 to 72 months to complete program. *Concentration:* general MBA.

MBA/INR—Master of Business Administration/Master of Arts in International Relations Full-time and part-time. Applicants must apply to and be independently accepted by each program. 54 to 77 total credits required. 24 to 72 months to complete program. *Concentrations:* combined degrees, general MBA, international business.

MBA/MS—Master of Business Administration/Master of Science in Information Technology Management Full-time and part-time. 48 to 60 total credits required. 24 to 72 months to complete program. *Concentrations:* general MBA, information management, management, management information systems, technology management.

MS—Master of Science in Information Technology Management Full-time and part-time. 33 to 45 total credits required. 12 to 72 months to complete program. *Concentrations:* information management, management information systems, technology management.

MS—Master of Security Analysis and Portfolio Management Full-time and part-time. 30 to 36 total credits required. 12 to 72 months to complete program. *Concentrations:* finance, financial management/planning, investments and securities.

MSISM—Master of Science in Information Technology Management/ Juris Doctor Full-time and part-time. Applicants must apply to and be independently accepted by each program. 33 to 45 total credits required. 36 to 72 months to complete program. *Concentrations:* combined degrees, information systems, information technology, law, management information systems.

Pharm D/MBA—Master of Business Administration/Doctor of Pharmacy Part-time. Applicants must apply to and be independently accepted by each program. At least 33 total credits required. 12 to 72 months to complete program. *Concentrations:* combined degrees, general MBA, pharmaceutical management.

RESOURCES AND SERVICES 42 on-campus PCs are available to graduate business students. Access to Internet/World Wide Web and online grade reports available. *Personal computer requirements:* Graduate business students are not required to have a personal computer. *Special opportunities include:* An internship program is available. *Placement services include:* Alumni network, career placement, career counseling/planning, electronic job bank, resume referral, career fairs, resume preparation, and career library.

FINANCIAL AID (2007–08) Research assistantships. *Financial aid application deadline:* 3/1.

Financial Aid Contact Robert Walker, Director, Financial Aid, Brandeis 213, 2500 California Plaza, Omaha, NE 68178. *Phone:* 402-280-2731. *Fax:* 402-280-2895. *E-mail:* rwalker@creighton.edu.

INTERNATIONAL STUDENTS 11% of students enrolled are international students. *Services and facilities:* Counseling/support services, ESL/language courses, Housing location assistance, International student organization, Orientation, Visa Services. Financial aid is available to international students. *Required with application:* TOEFL with recommended score of 213 (computer), 550 (paper), or 80 (Internet); proof of adequate funds; proof of health/immunizations.

International Student Contact Dr. Maria Krane, Director of International Programs, Becker G25, 2500 California Plaza, Omaha, NE 68178. *Phone:* 402-280-2221. *Fax:* 402-280-2211. *E-mail:* mkrane@creighton.edu.

APPLICATION *Required:* GMAT, application form, baccalaureate/first degree, 2 letters of recommendation, personal statement, resume/curriculum vitae, transcripts of college work. *Recommended:* Work experience. *Application fee:* $50. Applications for domestic and international students are processed on a rolling basis.

Application Contact Gail Hafer, Coordinator of Graduate Business Programs, College of Business Administration, 211C, 2500 California Plaza, Omaha, NE 68178. *Phone:* 402-280-2829. *Fax:* 402-280-2172. *E-mail:* cobagrad@creighton.edu.

Doane College
Program in Management
Crete, Nebraska

Phone: 402-466-4774 **Fax:** 402-466-4228 **E-mail:** susan.rocker@doane.edu

Business Program(s) Web Site: http://www.doane.edu

Graduate Business Unit Enrollment *Total:* 200 (200 full-time; 120 women; 3 international). *Average Age:* 35.

Graduate Business Faculty *Total:* 18 (3 full-time; 15 part-time).

Admissions *Applied:* 31. *Admitted:* 31. *Enrolled:* 31. *Average GPA:* 3.0

Academic Calendar Five 8-week terms.

Accreditation ACBSP—The American Council of Business Schools and Programs.

After Graduation (Class of 2006–07) *Employed within 3 months of graduation:* 100%.

DEGREE MA

MA—Master of Arts in Management Full-time and part-time. 42 to 45 total credits required. 18 to 72 months to complete program. *Concentrations:* arts administration/management, information management, international and area business studies, leadership.

RESOURCES AND SERVICES 70 on-campus PCs are available to graduate business students. Access to Internet/World Wide Web, online (class) registration, and online grade reports available. *Personal computer requirements:* Graduate business students are strongly recommended to purchase or lease a personal computer. *Placement services include:* Alumni network, job search course, career counseling/planning, career fairs, resume preparation, and career library.

EXPENSES *Tuition:* Full-time: $4050. *Tuition (international):* Full-time: $4050.

FINANCIAL AID (2007–08) 60 students received aid, including loans.

Financial Aid Contact Christina Bartels, Assistant Financial Aid Director, 303 North 52nd Street, Lincoln, NE 68504. *Phone:* 402-466-4774. *Fax:* 402-466-4228. *E-mail:* christina.bartels@doane.edu.

INTERNATIONAL STUDENTS 2% of students enrolled are international students. *Services and facilities:* Counseling/support services, Orientation, Visa Services. Financial aid is not available to international students. *Required with application:* TOEFL with recommended score of 600 (paper); proof of adequate funds; proof of health/immunizations.

International Student Contact Ms. Jan Willems, International Student Coordinator, 1014 Boswell Avenue, Crete, NE 68333. *Phone:* 402-826-8215. *Fax:* 402-826-8592. *E-mail:* jan.willems@doane.edu.

APPLICATION *Required:* Application form, baccalaureate/first degree, essay, interview, 3 letters of recommendation, personal statement, transcripts of college work. *Application fee:* $25. Applications for domestic and international students are processed on a rolling basis.

Application Contact Ms. Susan Rocker, Student Advisor, 303 North 52nd Street, Lincoln, NE 68504. *Phone:* 402-466-4774. *Fax:* 402-466-4228. *E-mail:* susan.rocker@doane.edu.

University of Nebraska at Kearney
College of Business and Technology
Kearney, Nebraska

Phone: 308-865-8346 **Fax:** 308-865-8114 **E-mail:** mbaoffice@unk.edu

Business Program(s) Web Site: http://www.unk.edu/acad/MBA/

Graduate Business Unit Enrollment *Total:* 78 (44 full-time; 34 part-time; 38 women; 9 international). *Average Age:* 25.

Graduate Business Faculty 29 full-time.

Admissions *Applied:* 16. *Admitted:* 13. *Enrolled:* 7. *Average GMAT:* 500. *Average GPA:* 3.36

Academic Calendar Semesters.

DEGREE MBA

MBA—Master of Business Administration Full-time and part-time. At least 30 total credits required. 12 to 120 months to complete program. *Concentrations:* accounting, general MBA, human resources management, information systems, other.

RESOURCES AND SERVICES 80 on-campus PCs are available to graduate business students. Access to Internet/World Wide Web, online (class) registration, and online grade reports available. *Personal computer requirements:* Graduate business students are not required to have a personal computer.

EXPENSES *Tuition (state resident):* Full-time: $3060. Part-time: $170 per credit hour. *Tuition (nonresident):* Full-time: $6332. Part-time: $351.75 per credit hour. *Tuition (international):* Full-time: $6332. Part-time: $351.75 per credit hour. *Required fees:* Full-time: $683.50. Part-time: $57.25 per credit hour. *Graduate housing:* Room and board costs vary by campus location, number of occupants, type of accommodation, and type of board plan. *Typical cost:* $6800 (including board), $3100 (room only).

FINANCIAL AID (2007–08) Loans, research assistantships, scholarships, and teaching assistantships.

Financial Aid Contact Financial Aid Office, MSAB, Kearney, NE 68849. *Phone:* 308-865-8520. *Fax:* 308-865-8096. *E-mail:* finaid1@unk.edu.

INTERNATIONAL STUDENTS 12% of students enrolled are international students. *Services and facilities:* Counseling/support services, ESL/language courses, International student housing, International student organization, Language tutoring, Orientation. *Required with application:* TOEFL with recommended score of 213 (computer) or 550 (paper); proof of adequate funds; proof of health/immunizations.

University of Nebraska at Kearney (continued)

International Student Contact Ms. Corliss Sullwold, Foreign Student Advisor, Welch Hall 114, 905 West 25th Street, Kearney, NE 68849. *Phone:* 308-865-8946. *Fax:* 308-865-8947. *E-mail:* sullwoldc@unk.edu.

APPLICATION *Required:* GMAT, application form, baccalaureate/first degree, 2 letters of recommendation, personal statement, transcripts of college work. *Recommended:* Resume/curriculum vitae, work experience. *Application fee:* $45. *Deadlines:* 5/1 for fall (international), 8/15 for spring (international), 2/1 for summer (international). Applications for domestic students are processed on a rolling basis.

Application Contact Dr. David K Palmer, MBA Director, WSTC 135C, 1917 West 24th Street, Kearney, NE 68849-4580. *Phone:* 308-865-8346. *Fax:* 308-865-8114. *E-mail:* mbaoffice@unk.edu.

University of Nebraska–Lincoln
College of Business Administration
Lincoln, Nebraska

Phone: 402-472-2338 **Fax:** 402-472-5997 **E-mail:** jshutts1@unl.edu

Business Program(s) Web Site: http://mba.unl.edu

Graduate Business Unit Enrollment *Total:* 438 (206 full-time; 232 part-time; 136 women; 111 international). *Average Age:* 26.

Graduate Business Faculty 64 full-time.

Admissions *Applied:* 262. *Admitted:* 177. *Enrolled:* 134. *Average GMAT:* 616. *Average GPA:* 3.49

Academic Calendar Semesters.

Accreditation AACSB—The Association to Advance Collegiate Schools of Business.

After Graduation (Class of 2006–07) *Employed within 3 months of graduation:* 75%. *Average starting salary:* $51,463.

DEGREES JD/MBA • MA • MBA • MBA/M Arch • MPA

JD/MBA—Juris Doctor/Master of Business Administration Full-time and part-time. At least 100 total credits required. 48 to 72 months to complete program. *Concentration:* law.

MA—Master of Arts in Business Full-time and part-time. At least 36 total credits required. 12 to 72 months to complete program. *Concentrations:* management, marketing.

MBA—Master of Business Administration Full-time and part-time. Distance learning option. At least 48 total credits required. 18 to 72 months to complete program. *Concentrations:* agribusiness, finance, human resources management, international business, management information systems, marketing, strategic management.

MBA/M Arch—Master of Business Administration/Master of Architecture Full-time and part-time. At least 72 total credits required. 36 to 60 months to complete program. *Concentration:* architecture.

MPA—Master of Professional Accountancy Full-time and part-time. At least 36 total credits required. 12 to 72 months to complete program. *Concentration:* accounting.

RESOURCES AND SERVICES 240 on-campus PCs are available to graduate business students. Access to Internet/World Wide Web, online (class) registration, and online grade reports available. *Personal computer requirements:* Graduate business students are not required to have a personal computer. *Special opportunities include:* An international exchange program and an internship program are available. *Placement services include:* Alumni network, career placement, career counseling/planning, electronic job bank, resume referral, career fairs, job interviews arranged, resume preparation, and career library.

EXPENSES *Tuition (state resident):* Full-time: $5376. Part-time: $1344 per semester. *Tuition (nonresident):* Full-time: $14,496. Part-time: $3624 per semester. *Tuition (international):* Full-time: $14,496. *Required fees:* Full-time: $810. Part-time: $233.05 per semester. *Graduate housing:*

Room and board costs vary by number of occupants, type of accommodation, and type of board plan. *Typical cost:* $7864 (including board).

FINANCIAL AID (2007–08) 58 students received aid, including fellowships, grants, loans, research assistantships, and scholarships. *Financial aid application deadline:* 3/1.

Financial Aid Contact Scholarships and Financial Aid, 16 Canfield Administration Building, Lincoln, NE 68588-0411. *Phone:* 402-472-2030. *Fax:* 402-472-9826. *E-mail:* finad@unl.edu.

INTERNATIONAL STUDENTS 25% of students enrolled are international students. *Services and facilities:* Counseling/support services, ESL/language courses, Housing location assistance, International student housing, International student organization, Orientation, Visa Services, Travel services. Financial aid is available to international students. *Required with application:* TOEFL with recommended score of 213 (computer), 550 (paper), or 80 (Internet); proof of adequate funds; proof of health/immunizations.

International Student Contact Janice P Hostetler, Director of Graduate Admission, 1100 Seaton Hall, Lincoln, NE 68588-0619. *Phone:* 402-472-2878. *Fax:* 402-472-0589. *E-mail:* jhostetler2@unl.edu.

APPLICATION *Required:* GMAT, application form, baccalaureate/first degree, 3 letters of recommendation, resume/curriculum vitae, transcripts of college work. *Recommended:* Work experience. *Application fee:* $45. Applications for domestic and international students are processed on a rolling basis.

Application Contact Judith Shutts, Graduate Advisor, PO Box 880405, CBA 125, Lincoln, NE 68588-0405. *Phone:* 402-472-2338. *Fax:* 402-472-5997. *E-mail:* jshutts1@unl.edu.

Wayne State College
School of Business and Technology
Wayne, Nebraska

Phone: 402-375-7587 **Fax:** 402-375-7434 **E-mail:** rhsebad1@wsc.edu

Business Program(s) Web Site: http://www.wsc.edu/mba

Graduate Business Unit Enrollment *Total:* 69 (69 part-time; 35 women; 2 international).

Graduate Business Faculty 19 full-time.

Admissions *Average GMAT:* 500. *Average GPA:* 3.3

Academic Calendar Semesters.

After Graduation (Class of 2006–07) *Employed within 3 months of graduation:* 95%.

DEGREE MBA

MBA—Master of Business Administration Full-time and part-time. Distance learning option. At least 30 total credits required. 18 to 84 months to complete program. *Concentration:* general MBA.

RESOURCES AND SERVICES 100 on-campus PCs are available to graduate business students. Access to Internet/World Wide Web, online (class) registration, and online grade reports available. *Personal computer requirements:* Graduate business students are strongly recommended to purchase or lease a personal computer. *Placement services include:* Alumni network, career placement, career counseling/planning, electronic job bank, resume referral, career fairs, job interviews arranged, resume preparation, and career library.

EXPENSES *Tuition (state resident):* Full-time: $3240. Part-time: $157 per credit hour. *Tuition (nonresident):* Full-time: $5750. Part-time: $157 per credit hour. *Tuition (international):* Full-time: $5750. Part-time: $157 per credit hour. *Graduate housing:* Room and board costs vary by number of occupants, type of accommodation, and type of board plan. *Typical cost:* $3200 (including board), $2280 (room only).

FINANCIAL AID (2007–08) 4 students received aid, including teaching assistantships. *Financial aid application deadline:* 2/1.

Financial Aid Contact Kyle Rose, Director of Financial Aid, 1111 Main Street, Wayne, NE 68787. *Phone:* 402-375-7000 Ext. 7230. *E-mail:* kyrose1@wsc.edu.

INTERNATIONAL STUDENTS 3% of students enrolled are international students. *Services and facilities:* Counseling/support services, International student organization. *Required with application:* TOEFL with recommended score of 550 (paper); proof of adequate funds; proof of health/immunizations.

International Student Contact Curt Frye, Vice President, Student Services, 1111 Main Street, Wayne, NE 68787. *Phone:* 402-375-7000 Ext. 7232. *E-mail:* cufrye1@wsc.edu.

APPLICATION *Required:* GMAT, application form, baccalaureate/first degree, 3 letters of recommendation, transcripts of college work. *Application fee:* $30. Applications for domestic and international students are processed on a rolling basis.

Application Contact Rhonda Sebade, MBA Coordinator, 1111 Main Street, Wayne, NE 68787. *Phone:* 402-375-7587. *Fax:* 402-375-7434. *E-mail:* rhsebad1@wsc.edu.

NEVADA

DeVry University
Keller Graduate School of Management

Henderson, Nevada

Phone: 702-933-9700

DEGREES MAFM • MBA • MHRM • MIS • MPA • MPM

MAFM—Master of Accounting and Financial Management Full-time and part-time. Distance learning option. At least 44 total credits required. 18 to 60 months to complete program. *Concentrations:* accounting, financial management/planning.

MBA—Master of Business Administration Full-time and part-time. Distance learning option. At least 48 total credits required. 18 to 60 months to complete program. *Concentration:* management.

MHRM—Master of Human Resources Management Full-time and part-time. Distance learning option. At least 45 total credits required. 18 to 60 months to complete program. *Concentration:* human resources management.

MIS—Master of Information Systems Management Full-time and part-time. Distance learning option. At least 45 total credits required. 18 to 60 months to complete program. *Concentration:* information systems.

MPA—Master of Public Administration Full-time and part-time. Distance learning option. At least 45 total credits required. 18 to 60 months to complete program. *Concentration:* public policy and administration.

MPM—Master of Project Management Full-time and part-time. Distance learning option. At least 42 total credits required. 18 to 60 months to complete program. *Concentration:* project management.

Application Contact Admissions Office, Henderson Center, 2490 Paseo Verde Parkway, Suite 150, Henderson, NV 89074. *Phone:* 702-933-9700.

University of Nevada, Las Vegas
College of Business

Las Vegas, Nevada

Phone: 702-895-3655 **Fax:** 702-895-4090 **E-mail:** cobmba@unlv.edu

Business Program(s) Web Site: http://business.unlv.edu/mba/

Graduate Business Unit Enrollment *Total:* 221 (114 full-time; 107 part-time; 96 women; 32 international). *Average Age:* 28.

Graduate Business Faculty 40 full-time.

Admissions *Applied:* 180. *Admitted:* 96. *Enrolled:* 60. *Average GMAT:* 590. *Average GPA:* 3.35

Academic Calendar Semesters.

Accreditation AACSB—The Association to Advance Collegiate Schools of Business.

After Graduation (Class of 2006–07) *Employed within 3 months of graduation:* 90%. *Average starting salary:* $65,000.

DEGREES DDS/MBA • EMBA • JD/MBA • MA • MBA • MBA/MIS • MS

DDS/MBA—Dual MBA/DDM Full-time. Must be admitted to the Dental School and the MBA program. 260 to 280 total credits required. 44 to 45 months to complete program. *Concentration:* combined degrees.

EMBA—Executive Master of Business Administration 7 years of work experience required including 3 years in a key decision-making role. 43 total credits required. 18 months to complete program. *Concentration:* executive programs.

JD/MBA—Dual MBA/JD Full-time and part-time. Must be admitted to the Boyd School of Law and the MBA program. 113 total credits required. 46 to 72 months to complete program. *Concentration:* combined degrees.

MA—Master of Arts in Economics Full-time and part-time. At least 30 total credits required. 12 to 72 months to complete program. *Concentration:* economics.

MBA—Master of Business Administration Full-time and part-time. At least 48 total credits required. 18 to 72 months to complete program. *Concentrations:* finance, management information systems, marketing, new venture management.

MBA—Master of Business Administration/Master of Science in Hotel Administration Full-time and part-time. At least 54 total credits required. 24 to 72 months to complete program. *Concentration:* combined degrees.

MBA/MIS—Dual MBA/MS in Management Information Systems Full-time and part-time. 54 total credits required. 24 to 60 months to complete program. *Concentration:* combined degrees.

MS—Master of Science in Accountancy Full-time and part-time. At least 30 total credits required. 12 to 72 months to complete program. *Concentration:* accounting.

MS—Master of Science in Management Information Systems Full-time and part-time. 36 to 52 total credits required. 18 to 72 months to complete program. *Concentration:* information systems.

RESOURCES AND SERVICES 700 on-campus PCs are available to graduate business students. Access to Internet/World Wide Web, online (class) registration, and online grade reports available. *Personal computer requirements:* Graduate business students are strongly recommended to purchase or lease a personal computer. *Special opportunities include:* An internship program is available. *Placement services include:* Alumni network, career placement, job search course, career counseling/planning, electronic job bank, resume referral, career fairs, job interviews arranged, resume preparation, and career library.

EXPENSES *Tuition (state resident):* Full-time: $4752. Part-time: $198 per credit. *Tuition (nonresident):* Full-time: $15,847. Part-time: $470 per credit. *Tuition (international):* Full-time: $15,847. Part-time: $470 per credit. *Required fees:* Full-time: $610. Part-time: $580 per year. Tuition and/or fees vary by academic program. *Graduate housing:* Room and board costs vary by type of board plan. *Typical cost:* $3576 (including board), $2822 (room only).

FINANCIAL AID (2007–08) 37 students received aid, including fellowships, research assistantships, and scholarships. *Financial aid application deadline:* 3/1.

Financial Aid Contact Mr. Norm Bedford, Director, Student Financial Services, 4505 South Maryland Parkway, Las Vegas, NV 89154-2016. *Phone:* 702-895-3424. *Fax:* 702-895-1353. *E-mail:* financialaid@unlv.edu.

University of Nevada, Las Vegas (continued)

INTERNATIONAL STUDENTS 14% of students enrolled are international students. *Services and facilities:* Counseling/support services, ESL/language courses, Housing location assistance, International student organization, Language tutoring, Orientation, Visa Services. Financial aid is available to international students. *Required with application:* TOEFL with recommended score of 213 (computer), 550 (paper), or 80 (Internet); proof of adequate funds; proof of health/immunizations.

International Student Contact Lisa Davis, MBA Recruitment Director, 4505 South Maryland Parkway, Las Vegas, NV 89154-6031. *Phone:* 702-895-3655. *Fax:* 702-895-4090. *E-mail:* cobmba@unlv.edu.

APPLICATION *Required:* GMAT, application form, baccalaureate/first degree, 2 letters of recommendation, personal statement, resume/ curriculum vitae, transcripts of college work. *Recommended:* 2 years of work experience. *Application fee:* $60, $75 (international). Applications for domestic and international students are processed on a rolling basis.

Application Contact Lisa Davis, MBA Recruitment Director, 4505 South Maryland Parkway, Las Vegas, NV 89154-6031. *Phone:* 702-895-3655. *Fax:* 702-895-4090. *E-mail:* cobmba@unlv.edu.

See full description on page 722.

University of Nevada, Reno
College of Business Administration

Reno, Nevada

Phone: 775-784-4912 **Fax:** 775-784-1773 **E-mail:** vkrentz@unr.edu

Business Program(s) Web Site: http://www.coba.unr.edu/

Graduate Business Unit Enrollment *Total:* 132 (37 full-time; 95 part-time; 51 women; 7 international).

Graduate Business Faculty *Total:* 19 (15 full-time; 4 part-time).

Admissions *Applied:* 79. *Admitted:* 51. *Enrolled:* 47. *Average GMAT:* 569. *Average GPA:* 3.1

Academic Calendar Semesters.

Accreditation AACSB—The Association to Advance Collegiate Schools of Business.

After Graduation (Class of 2006–07) *Employed within 3 months of graduation:* 95%. *Average starting salary:* $55,000.

DEGREES M Ac • MA • MBA • MS

M Ac—Master of Accountancy Part-time. At least 30 total credits required. 24 to 72 months to complete program. *Concentration:* accounting.

MA—Master of Arts in Economics Full-time and part-time. At least 32 total credits required. 24 to 72 months to complete program. *Concentration:* economics.

MBA—Master of Business Administration Part-time. Distance learning option. At least one year working requirement; minimum GMAT of 500, TOEFL 240, undergraduate GPA of 2.75. 30 to 51 total credits required. 24 to 72 months to complete program. *Concentration:* general MBA.

MS—Master of Science in Economics Part-time. At least 32 total credits required. 24 to 72 months to complete program. *Concentration:* economics.

RESOURCES AND SERVICES 150 on-campus PCs are available to graduate business students. Access to Internet/World Wide Web, online (class) registration, and online grade reports available. *Personal computer requirements:* Graduate business students are strongly recommended to purchase or lease a personal computer. *Special opportunities include:* An international exchange program and an internship program are available. *Placement services include:* Alumni network, career counseling/planning, resume referral, career fairs, job interviews arranged, and resume preparation.

EXPENSES *Tuition (state resident):* Part-time: $176 per credit hour. *Tuition (nonresident):* Full-time: $10,810. Part-time: $365 per credit hour. *Tuition (international):* Full-time: $10,810. Part-time: $365 per credit hour. *Required fees:* Full-time: $447. Part-time: $447 per year. *Graduate housing:* Room and board costs vary by campus location, number of occupants, type of accommodation, and type of board plan. *Typical cost:* $8000 (including board).

FINANCIAL AID (2007–08) 14 students received aid, including research assistantships and scholarships. Aid is available to part-time students. *Financial aid application deadline:* 2/1.

Financial Aid Contact Ms. Suzanne Bach, Coordinator, Student Financial Aid and Scholarships, MS 076, Reno, NV 89557. *Phone:* 775-784-4666. *Fax:* 775-784-1025. *E-mail:* bach@unr.nevada.edu.

INTERNATIONAL STUDENTS 5% of students enrolled are international students. *Services and facilities:* Counseling/support services, ESL/language courses, Housing location assistance, International student housing, International student organization, Language tutoring, Orientation. Financial aid is available to international students. *Required with application:* IELT; TOEFL with recommended score of 220 (computer) or 550 (paper); proof of adequate funds; proof of health/immunizations.

International Student Contact Ms. Pauline Filemoni, Advisor, International Students, Office of International Students and Scholars, MS 074, Reno, NV 89557. *Phone:* 775-784-6874. *Fax:* 775-327-5845. *E-mail:* filemoni@unr.edu.

APPLICATION *Required:* GMAT, application form, baccalaureate/first degree, essay, 2 letters of recommendation, personal statement, resume/ curriculum vitae, transcripts of college work, 2 years of work experience. *Application fee:* $60, $100 (international). Applications for domestic and international students are processed on a rolling basis.

Application Contact Ms. Vickie Krentz, Coordinator of Graduate Programs, MS 0024, Reno, NV 89557. *Phone:* 775-784-4912. *Fax:* 775-784-1773. *E-mail:* vkrentz@unr.edu.

University of Phoenix–Las Vegas Campus
College of Graduate Business and Management

Las Vegas, Nevada

Phone: 480-317-6200 **Fax:** 480-643-1479 **E-mail:** beth.barilla@phoenix.edu

Business Program(s) Web Site: http://www.phoenix.edu/

DEGREES M Mgt • MA • MBA

M Mgt—Public Administration Full-time. At least 45 total credits required. *Concentration:* public policy and administration.

M Mgt—Master of Management Part-time. Distance learning option. At least 39 total credits required. *Concentration:* management.

MA—Organizational Management Full-time. At least 40 total credits required. *Concentration:* organizational management.

MBA—Human Resource Management Full-time. At least 45 total credits required. *Concentration:* human resources management.

MBA—Public Administration Full-time. At least 45 total credits required. *Concentration:* public policy and administration.

MBA—e-Business Full-time. At least 45 total credits required. *Concentration:* electronic commerce (E-commerce).

MBA—Master of Business Administration Full-time. At least 45 total credits required. *Concentration:* administration.

RESOURCES AND SERVICES Access to online grade reports available. *Personal computer requirements:* Graduate business students are strongly recommended to purchase or lease a personal computer. *Placement services include:* Alumni network.

Application Contact Beth Barilla, Associate Vice President of Student Admissions and Services, Mail Stop AA-K101, 4615 East Elwood Street, Phoenix, AZ 85040-1958. *Phone:* 480-317-6200. *Fax:* 480-643-1479. *E-mail:* beth.barilla@phoenix.edu.

NEW HAMPSHIRE

Antioch University New England
Department of Organization and Management
Keene, New Hampshire

Phone: 603-357-3122 Ext. 2128 Fax: 603-357-0718 E-mail: loram@antiochne.edu

Business Program(s) Web Site: http://www.antiochne.edu

Graduate Business Unit Enrollment *Total:* 46 (39 full-time; 7 part-time; 31 women). *Average Age:* 40.

Graduate Business Faculty *Total:* 17 (6 full-time; 11 part-time).

Admissions *Applied:* 66. *Admitted:* 61. *Enrolled:* 52. *Average GPA:* 3.0

Academic Calendar Trimesters.

After Graduation (Class of 2006–07) *Employed within 3 months of graduation:* 95%. *Average starting salary:* $41,000.

DEGREES MBA • ME • MS

MBA—Master of Business Administration in Organizational and Environmental Sustainability Full-time and part-time. At least 45 total credits required. Minimum of 20 months to complete program. *Concentrations:* accounting, administration, economics, environmental economics/management, human resources development, leadership, management, nonprofit management.

ME—Master of Education in Administration and Supervision Full-time and part-time. At least 40 total credits required. Minimum of 20 months to complete program. *Concentrations:* leadership, management, management consulting, nonprofit management, organizational behavior/development, organizational management.

MS—Master of Science in Management Full-time and part-time. At least 40 total credits required. Minimum of 20 months to complete program. *Concentrations:* human resources management, leadership, management, management consulting, organizational behavior/development, organizational management.

RESOURCES AND SERVICES 18 on-campus PCs are available to graduate business students. Access to Internet/World Wide Web, online (class) registration, and online grade reports available. *Personal computer requirements:* Graduate business students are required to have a personal computer. *Special opportunities include:* An internship program is available. *Placement services include:* Alumni network and career counseling/planning.

EXPENSES *Tuition:* Full-time: $7000. *Tuition (international):* Full-time: $7000. *Required fees:* Full-time: $300. Tuition and/or fees vary by academic program.

FINANCIAL AID (2007–08) 40 students received aid, including fellowships, loans, scholarships, and work study. *Financial aid application deadline:* 8/2.

Financial Aid Contact Susan Howard, Director of Financial Aid, 40 Avon Street, Keene, NH 03431-3516. *Phone:* 603-357-3122 Ext. 2367. *Fax:* 603-357-0718. *E-mail:* susan_howard@antiochne.edu.

INTERNATIONAL STUDENTS *Services and facilities:* Counseling/support services, Housing location assistance, International student organization, Language tutoring, Orientation. Financial aid is available to international students. *Required with application:* TOEFL with recommended score of 250 (computer), 550 (paper), or 79 (Internet); proof of adequate funds; proof of health/immunizations.

International Student Contact Laura Andrews, Co-Director of Admissions, 40 Avon Street, Keene, NH 03431-3516. *Phone:* 603-357-3122 Ext. 2131. *Fax:* 603-357-0718. *E-mail:* landrews@antiochne.edu.

APPLICATION *Required:* GRE, application form, baccalaureate/first degree, essay, interview, 3 letters of recommendation, personal statement, resume/curriculum vitae, transcripts of college work. *Recommended:* 2 years of work experience. *Application fee:* $50. Applications for domestic and international students are processed on a rolling basis.

Application Contact Leatrice A. Oram, Co-Director of Admissions, 40 Avon Street, Keene, NH 03431-3516. *Phone:* 603-357-3122 Ext. 2128. *Fax:* 603-357-0718. *E-mail:* loram@antiochne.edu.

Dartmouth College
Tuck School of Business at Dartmouth
Hanover, New Hampshire

Phone: 603-646-3162 Fax: 603-646-1441 E-mail: tuck.admissions@dartmouth.edu

Business Program(s) Web Site: http://www.tuck.dartmouth.edu/

Graduate Business Unit Enrollment *Total:* 500 (500 full-time; 170 women; 177 international). *Average Age:* 28.

Graduate Business Faculty *Total:* 77 (46 full-time; 31 part-time).

Admissions *Applied:* 2,584. *Admitted:* 496. *Enrolled:* 255. *Average GMAT:* 713. *Average GPA:* 3.5

Academic Calendar Trimesters.

Accreditation AACSB—The Association to Advance Collegiate Schools of Business.

After Graduation (Class of 2006–07) *Employed within 3 months of graduation:* 96%. *Average starting salary:* $107,406.

DEGREES MBA • MBA/MEM • MBA/MPH • MD/MBA

MBA—Master of Business Administration Full-time. 21 to 60 months to complete program. *Concentration:* general MBA.

MBA/MEM—Master of Engineering Management/Master of Business Administration Full-time. 36 to 60 months to complete program. *Concentration:* combined degrees.

MBA/MPH—Master of Business Administration/Master of Public Health Full-time. 36 to 60 months to complete program. *Concentration:* combined degrees.

MD/MBA—Doctor of Medicine/Master of Business Administration Full-time. 60 to 84 months to complete program. *Concentration:* combined degrees.

RESOURCES AND SERVICES Access to Internet/World Wide Web, online (class) registration, and online grade reports available. *Personal computer requirements:* Graduate business students are required to have a personal computer, the cost of which is included in tuition or other required fees. *Special opportunities include:* An international exchange program and an internship program are available. *Placement services include:* Alumni network, career placement, job search course, career counseling/planning, electronic job bank, resume referral, career fairs, job interviews arranged, resume preparation, and career library.

EXPENSES *Tuition:* Full-time: $42,990. *Tuition (international):* Full-time: $42,990. *Required fees:* Full-time: $250. *Graduate housing:* Room and board costs vary by number of occupants and type of accommodation. *Typical cost:* $9725 (including board).

FINANCIAL AID (2007–08) 405 students received aid, including loans and scholarships. *Financial aid application deadline:* 4/16.

Financial Aid Contact Diane Bonin, Director of Financial Aid, 100 Tuck Hall, Hanover, NH 03755-9000. *Phone:* 603-646-0640. *Fax:* 603-646-1308. *E-mail:* diane.bonin@dartmouth.edu.

Dartmouth College (continued)

INTERNATIONAL STUDENTS 35% of students enrolled are international students. *Services and facilities:* Counseling/support services, ESL/language courses, Housing location assistance, International student housing, International student organization, Language tutoring, Orientation, Visa Services. Financial aid is available to international students. *Required with application:* TOEFL; proof of adequate funds; proof of health/immunizations.

International Student Contact Christie St. John, Senior Associate Director of Recruiting and Enrollment, 100 Tuck Hall, Hanover, NH 03755-9000. *Phone:* 603-646-3162. *Fax:* 603-646-1441. *E-mail:* tuck.admissions@dartmouth.edu.

APPLICATION *Required:* GMAT, application form, baccalaureate/first degree, essay, 2 letters of recommendation, personal statement, resume/curriculum vitae, transcripts of college work. *Recommended:* Interview, work experience. *Application fee:* $220. *Deadlines:* 10/10 for fall, 1/9 for winter, 4/2 for spring, 10/10 for fall (international), 1/9 for winter (international), 4/2 for spring (international).

Application Contact Dawna Clarke, Director of Admissions, 100 Tuck Hall, Hanover, NH 03755. *Phone:* 603-646-3162. *Fax:* 603-646-1441. *E-mail:* tuck.admissions@dartmouth.edu.

Franklin Pierce University
Graduate Studies
Rindge, New Hampshire

Phone: 800-325-1090 **E-mail:** stpierren@franklinpierce.edu

Business Program(s) Web Site: http://www.fpc.edu/pages/gps/gradstudies/gradstud.html

Graduate Business Unit Enrollment *Total:* 350 (120 full-time; 230 part-time; 110 women; 20 international).

Graduate Business Faculty *Total:* 28 (8 full-time; 20 part-time).

Admissions *Applied:* 75. *Admitted:* 75. *Enrolled:* 70.

Academic Calendar Quarters.

DEGREES   M Sc • MBA

M Sc—Information Technology Management Full-time and part-time. Programming language C++ or higher required. At least 39 total credits required. 21 to 96 months to complete program. *Concentration:* information management.

M Sc—Information Technology Management for Law Enforcement Full-time. Distance learning option. 40 total credits required. 16 months to complete program. *Concentration:* information management.

MBA—Health Practice Management Full-time and part-time. Distance learning option. 41 total credits required. 3 to 8 months to complete program. *Concentration:* health administration.

MBA—Master of Business Administration Full-time and part-time. Distance learning option. At least 40 total credits required. 21 to 96 months to complete program. *Concentrations:* human resources management, leadership.

RESOURCES AND SERVICES 90 on-campus PCs are available to graduate business students. Access to Internet/World Wide Web available. *Personal computer requirements:* Graduate business students are strongly recommended to purchase or lease a personal computer. *Placement services include:* Alumni network and career counseling/planning.

FINANCIAL AID (2007–08) Loans, scholarships, and teaching assistantships. Aid is available to part-time students.

Financial Aid Contact Ruth Barrieau, 5 Chennel Drive, Concord, NH 03301. *Phone:* 603-899-1155. *E-mail:* barrieaur@franklinpierce.edu.

INTERNATIONAL STUDENTS 6% of students enrolled are international students. Financial aid is not available to international students.

Required with application: TOEFL with recommended score of 195 (computer) or 550 (paper); proof of adequate funds; proof of health/immunizations.

APPLICATION *Required:* Application form, baccalaureate/first degree, essay, 3 letters of recommendation, personal statement, resume/curriculum vitae, transcripts of college work. *Recommended:* Interview, work experience. Applications for domestic and international students are processed on a rolling basis.

Application Contact Nicole St. Pierre, 5 Chenell Drive, Concord, NH 03301. *Phone:* 800-325-1090. *E-mail:* stpierren@franklinpierce.edu.

New England College
Program in Management
Henniker, New Hampshire

Business Program(s) Web Site: http://www.nec.edu

Graduate Business Unit Enrollment *Total:* 100 (20 full-time; 80 part-time; 70 women; 2 international).

Graduate Business Faculty *Total:* 30 (5 full-time; 25 part-time).

Admissions *Applied:* 48. *Admitted:* 38. *Enrolled:* 35. *Average GPA:* 3.3

Academic Calendar 7-week terms.

DEGREE   MS

MS—Master of Science in Management Full-time and part-time. Distance learning option. 36 total credits required. 14 to 24 months to complete program. *Concentrations:* health administration, health care, leadership, nonprofit management, organizational management, project management, strategic management.

RESOURCES AND SERVICES 60 on-campus PCs are available to graduate business students. Access to Internet/World Wide Web, online (class) registration, and online grade reports available. *Personal computer requirements:* Graduate business students are strongly recommended to purchase or lease a personal computer. *Special opportunities include:* An internship program is available. *Placement services include:* Alumni network.

EXPENSES *Tuition:* Full-time: $16,000. Part-time: $8000 per term. *Tuition (international):* Full-time: $16,000. Part-time: $8000 per term. *Required fees:* Full-time: $150. Tuition and/or fees vary by academic program.

FINANCIAL AID (2007–08) 100 students received aid, including grants, loans, research assistantships, and work study. Aid is available to part-time students. *Financial aid application deadline:* 6/1.

Financial Aid Contact Russell Stein, Director of Financial Aid, 15 Main Street, Henniker, NH 03242-3293. *Phone:* 603-428-2436. *Fax:* 603-428-2404. *E-mail:* rstein@nec.edu.

INTERNATIONAL STUDENTS 2% of students enrolled are international students. *Services and facilities:* Counseling/support services, ESL/language courses, Housing location assistance, International student housing, International student organization, Orientation, Visa Services. Financial aid is not available to international students. *Required with application:* Proof of adequate funds; proof of health/immunizations.

International Student Contact Dana Bolduc, Graduate Admissions Director, 15 Main Street, Henniker, NH 03242. *Phone:* 603-428-2297. *Fax:* 603-428-8123. *E-mail:* dbolduc@nec.edu.

APPLICATION *Required:* Application form, baccalaureate/first degree, 2 letters of recommendation, personal statement, resume/curriculum vitae, transcripts of college work. *Application fee:* $35. Applications for domestic and international students are processed on a rolling basis.

Plymouth State University

Department of Graduate Studies in Business

Plymouth, New Hampshire

Phone: 603-535-3020 **Fax:** 603-535-2648 **E-mail:** czamzow@plymouth.edu

Business Program(s) Web Site: http://mba.plymouth.edu

Graduate Business Unit Enrollment *Total:* 150 (25 full-time; 125 part-time; 75 women; 15 international).

Graduate Business Faculty *Total:* 27 (16 full-time; 11 part-time).

Admissions *Applied:* 40. *Admitted:* 35. *Enrolled:* 35. *Average GPA:* 3.2

Academic Calendar Quarters.

Accreditation ACBSP—The American Council of Business Schools and Programs.

DEGREE MBA

MBA—Master of Business Administration in General Management Full-time and part-time. Distance learning option. 30 total credits required. 9 to 36 months to complete program. *Concentration:* management.

RESOURCES AND SERVICES 300 on-campus PCs are available to graduate business students. Access to Internet/World Wide Web, online (class) registration, and online grade reports available. *Personal computer requirements:* Graduate business students are strongly recommended to purchase or lease a personal computer. *Placement services include:* Alumni network, career fairs, resume preparation, and career library.

FINANCIAL AID (2007–08) Fellowships, loans, scholarships, and teaching assistantships. Aid is available to part-time students. *Financial aid application deadline:* 4/15.

Financial Aid Contact Mr. Maurice Day, II, Financial Aid Officer, Speare Administration Building, Room 108, Plymouth, NH 03264-1595. *Phone:* 603-535-2873. *Fax:* 603-535-2627. *E-mail:* mday@plymouth.edu.

INTERNATIONAL STUDENTS 10% of students enrolled are international students. *Services and facilities:* Counseling/support services, Housing location assistance, Orientation, ESL services available. Financial aid is available to international students. *Required with application:* TOEFL with recommended score of 200 (computer) or 500 (paper); proof of adequate funds.

International Student Contact Cheryl B. Baker, Director of Recruitment and Outreach, 17 High Street, MSC 11, Plymouth, NH 03264-1595. *Phone:* 603-535-2737. *Fax:* 603-535-2572. *E-mail:* cbaker@plymouth.edu.

APPLICATION *Required:* Application form, baccalaureate/first degree, 3 letters of recommendation, personal statement, resume/curriculum vitae, transcripts of college work. *Application fee:* $75. Applications for domestic and international students are processed on a rolling basis.

Application Contact Craig Zamzow, MBA Admissions, 17 High Street, MSC 11, Plymouth, NH 03264-1595. *Phone:* 603-535-3020. *Fax:* 603-535-2648. *E-mail:* czamzow@plymouth.edu.

Rivier College

Department of Business Administration

Nashua, New Hampshire

Phone: 603-897-8519 **Fax:** 603-897-8810 **E-mail:** lroth@rivier.edu

Business Program(s) Web Site: http://www.rivier.edu

Graduate Business Unit Enrollment *Total:* 125 (15 full-time; 110 part-time; 75 women; 15 international).

Graduate Business Faculty *Total:* 33 (4 full-time; 29 part-time).

Admissions *Applied:* 30. *Admitted:* 25. *Enrolled:* 18. *Average GPA:* 3.2

Academic Calendar Semesters.

After Graduation (Class of 2006–07) *Employed within 3 months of graduation:* 95%. *Average starting salary:* $55,000.

DEGREES EMBA • MBA • MS

EMBA—Executive Master of Business Administration Part-time. 3 years of fulltime work experience. At least 39 total credits required. Minimum of 24 months to complete program. *Concentration:* organizational management.

MBA—MBA/Marketing Full-time and part-time. 36 total credits required. 12 to 60 months to complete program. *Concentration:* marketing.

MBA—Master of Business Administration Full-time and part-time. 36 total credits required. 12 to 60 months to complete program. *Concentrations:* general MBA, health care, marketing, quality management.

MS—Computer Information Systems Full-time and part-time. Distance learning option. 39 to 45 total credits required. 24 to 60 months to complete program. *Concentration:* management systems analysis.

RESOURCES AND SERVICES 100 on-campus PCs are available to graduate business students. Access to Internet/World Wide Web, online (class) registration, and online grade reports available. *Personal computer requirements:* Graduate business students are not required to have a personal computer. *Special opportunities include:* An internship program is available. *Placement services include:* Career placement, career counseling/planning, career fairs, job interviews arranged, resume preparation, and career library.

EXPENSES *Tuition:* Part-time: $425 per credit. *Tuition (international):* Part-time: $425 per credit. Tuition and/or fees vary by academic program.

FINANCIAL AID (2007–08) 23 students received aid, including loans, research assistantships, teaching assistantships, and work study. Aid is available to part-time students. *Financial aid application deadline:* 2/1.

Financial Aid Contact Valerie Patnaude, Director, 420 Main Street, Nashua, NH 03060-5086. *Phone:* 603-897-8510. *Fax:* 603-897-8890. *E-mail:* finaid@rivier.edu.

INTERNATIONAL STUDENTS 12% of students enrolled are international students. *Services and facilities:* Counseling/support services, ESL/language courses, International student organization, Language tutoring, Visa Services. Financial aid is not available to international students. *Required with application:* TOEFL with recommended score of 600 (paper); proof of adequate funds.

International Student Contact Prof. Maria Matarazzo, Associate Professor/Chair, 420 Main Street, Nashua, NH 03060. *Phone:* 603-897-8491. *Fax:* 603-897-8885. *E-mail:* mmatarazzo@rivier.edu.

APPLICATION *Required:* Application form, baccalaureate/first degree, interview, 1 letter of recommendation, personal statement, transcripts of college work. *Recommended:* Resume/curriculum vitae, work experience. *Application fee:* $25. Applications for domestic and international students are processed on a rolling basis.

Application Contact Linda Roth, Director, Graduate Admissions, 420 Main Street, Nashua, NH 03060-5086. *Phone:* 603-897-8519. *Fax:* 603-897-8810. *E-mail:* lroth@rivier.edu.

Southern New Hampshire University

School of Business

Manchester, New Hampshire

Phone: 603-644-3102 Ext. 3015 **Fax:** 603-644-3144 **E-mail:** e.cady@snhu.edu

Business Program(s) Web Site: http://www.snhu.edu

Graduate Business Unit Enrollment *Total:* 1,308 (549 full-time; 759 part-time; 667 women; 261 international). *Average Age:* 28.

Graduate Business Faculty *Total:* 120 (45 full-time; 75 part-time).

Southern New Hampshire University (continued)

Admissions *Applied:* 332. *Admitted:* 317. *Enrolled:* 180. *Average GMAT:* 520. *Average GPA:* 3.2

Academic Calendar Quarters.

Accreditation ACBSP—The American Council of Business Schools and Programs.

After Graduation (Class of 2006–07) *Employed within 3 months of graduation:* 92%. *Average starting salary:* $60,000.

DEGREES M Sc • MBA • MS • MSIT

M Sc—Operations Management 36 total credits required. 12 months to complete program. *Concentration:* operations management.

MBA—Master of Business Administration Full-time and part-time. Distance learning option. At least 42 total credits required. 14 months to complete program. *Concentrations:* accounting, combined degrees, finance, general MBA, hospitality management, human resources management, information management, information technology, international business, marketing, operations management, project management, sports/entertainment management, taxation, training and development.

MS—Marketing Full-time and part-time. 36 total credits required. 12 months to complete program. *Concentration:* marketing.

MS—Master of Science in Accounting Full-time and part-time. 36 to 42 total credits required. 12 to 14 months to complete program. *Concentration:* accounting.

MS—Master of Science in Finance Full-time and part-time. 36 to 39 total credits required. 12 to 13 months to complete program. *Concentration:* finance.

MS—Master of Science in International Business Full-time and part-time. Distance learning option. At least 36 total credits required. 12 to 36 months to complete program. *Concentration:* international business.

MS—Master of Science in Organizational Leadership Full-time and part-time. At least 36 total credits required. 12 months to complete program. *Concentrations:* accounting, combined degrees, finance, general MBA, hospitality management, human resources management, information management, information technology, international business, marketing, operations management, sports/entertainment management, taxation, training and development.

MS—Master of Science in Sport Management Full-time and part-time. At least 42 total credits required. 14 months to complete program. *Concentration:* sports/entertainment management.

MSIT—Information Technology Full-time and part-time. 36 total credits required. 12 months to complete program. *Concentration:* information technology.

RESOURCES AND SERVICES 700 on-campus PCs are available to graduate business students. Access to Internet/World Wide Web, online (class) registration, and online grade reports available. *Personal computer requirements:* Graduate business students are required to have a personal computer. *Special opportunities include:* An internship program is available. *Placement services include:* Alumni network, job search course, career counseling/planning, electronic job bank, resume referral, career fairs, job interviews arranged, resume preparation, and career library.

EXPENSES *Tuition:* Full-time: $20,076. *Tuition (international):* Full-time: $20,076. *Required fees:* Full-time: $650. *Graduate housing:* Room and board costs vary by number of occupants, type of accommodation, and type of board plan. *Typical cost:* $7240 (including board), $5480 (room only).

FINANCIAL AID (2007–08) 156 students received aid, including loans, scholarships, and work study. Aid is available to part-time students.

Financial Aid Contact Louisa Martin, Financial Aid Administrator, 2500 North River Road, Manchester, NH 03106-1045. *Phone:* 603-645-9645. *Fax:* 603-645-9665. *E-mail:* l.martin@snhu.edu.

INTERNATIONAL STUDENTS 20% of students enrolled are international students. *Services and facilities:* Counseling/support services, ESL/language courses, Housing location assistance, International student organization, Language tutoring, Orientation, Visa Services. Financial aid is available to international students. *Required with application:* IELT with

recommended score of 6.5; TOEFL with recommended score of 213 (computer) or 550 (paper); proof of adequate funds; proof of health/immunizations.

International Student Contact Dr. Steven Harvey, Director of International Admission, 2500 North River Road, Manchester, NH 03106-1045. *Phone:* 603-668-2211 Ext. 2388. *Fax:* 603-645-9603. *E-mail:* s.harvey@snhu.edu.

APPLICATION *Required:* Application form, baccalaureate/first degree, resume/curriculum vitae, transcripts of college work. *Recommended:* Work experience. *Application fee:* $25. Applications for domestic and international students are processed on a rolling basis.

Application Contact Ellen Cady, Associate Director of Graduate Admission, 2500 North River Road, Manchester, NH 03106-1045. *Phone:* 603-644-3102 Ext. 3015. *Fax:* 603-644-3144. *E-mail:* e.cady@snhu.edu.

See full description on page 690.

University of New Hampshire
Whittemore School of Business and Economics
Durham, New Hampshire

Phone: 603-862-1367 **Fax:** 603-862-4468 **E-mail:** wsbe.grad@unh.edu

Business Program(s) Web Site: http://wsbe.unh.edu/grad/

Graduate Business Unit Enrollment *Total:* 351 (116 full-time; 235 part-time; 118 women; 55 international). *Average Age:* 32.

Graduate Business Faculty *Total:* 30 (18 full-time; 12 part-time).

Admissions *Applied:* 264. *Admitted:* 228. *Enrolled:* 165. *Average GMAT:* 531. *Average GPA:* 3.17

Academic Calendar 5 terms.

Accreditation AACSB—The Association to Advance Collegiate Schools of Business.

After Graduation (Class of 2006–07) *Employed within 3 months of graduation:* 60%. *Average starting salary:* $52,704.

DEGREES EMBA • MA • MBA • MS • MSMOT

EMBA—Executive Master of Business Administration Full-time. 5 years of professional work experience and an interview are required. 51 total credits required. 19 months to complete program. *Concentrations:* entrepreneurship, general MBA, technology management.

MA—Master of Arts in Economics Full-time. 36 total credits required. 10 months to complete program. *Concentration:* economics.

MBA—Full-Time, One-Year Master of Business Administration Program Full-time. Interview required. 48 total credits required. 11 months to complete program. *Concentration:* general MBA.

MBA—Part-Time Evening Master of Business Administration Program Part-time. 39 to 48 total credits required. 22 to 72 months to complete program. *Concentrations:* entrepreneurship, finance, general MBA, supply chain management.

MS—Master of Science in Accounting Full-time and part-time. Students must have completed a series of prerequisite courses in accounting before beginning the program. Applicants without the prerequisites will be considered for the two-year full-time option. At least 30 total credits required. 10 to 72 months to complete program. *Concentration:* accounting.

MSMOT—Management of Technology 36 total credits required. 12 months to complete program. *Concentration:* technology management.

RESOURCES AND SERVICES 225 on-campus PCs are available to graduate business students. Access to Internet/World Wide Web, online (class) registration, and online grade reports available. *Personal computer requirements:* Graduate business students are required to have a personal computer. *Special opportunities include:* An internship program is available. *Placement services include:* Alumni network, career placement, career counseling/planning, electronic job bank, resume referral, career fairs, job interviews arranged, resume preparation, and career library.

EXPENSES *Tuition (state resident):* Full-time: $17,000. Part-time: $1740 per course. *Tuition (nonresident):* Full-time: $28,000. Part-time: $2043 per course. *Tuition (international):* Full-time: $28,000. *Required fees:* Full-time: $1550. Tuition and/or fees vary by class time, number of courses or credits taken, campus location, academic program, and local reciprocity agreements. *Graduate housing:* Room and board costs vary by number of occupants, type of accommodation, and type of board plan. *Typical cost:* $8780 (including board), $5654 (room only).

FINANCIAL AID (2007–08) 118 students received aid, including grants, loans, research assistantships, scholarships, teaching assistantships, and work study. Aid is available to part-time students. *Financial aid application deadline:* 3/1.

Financial Aid Contact George Abraham, Director, Graduate and Executive Programs, 15 College Road, McConnell Hall, Room 116, Durham, NH 03824-3593. *Phone:* 603-862-1367. *Fax:* 603-862-4468. *E-mail:* wsbe.grad@unh.edu.

INTERNATIONAL STUDENTS 16% of students enrolled are international students. *Services and facilities:* Counseling/support services, ESL/language courses, International student organization, Orientation, Visa Services. Financial aid is available to international students. *Required with application:* TOEFL with recommended score of 213 (computer) or 550 (paper); proof of adequate funds; proof of health/immunizations. *Recommended with application:* TWE.

International Student Contact Ms. Leila Paje-Manalo, Office for International Students and Scholars, Hood House, 89 Main Street, Durham, NH 03824. *Phone:* 603-862-1508. *Fax:* 603-862-0169. *E-mail:* oiss@unh.edu.

APPLICATION *Required:* GMAT, application form, baccalaureate/first degree, essay, interview, 3 letters of recommendation, personal statement, resume/curriculum vitae, transcripts of college work. *Recommended:* Work experience. *Application fee:* $60. Applications for domestic and international students are processed on a rolling basis.

Application Contact George Abraham, Director, Graduate and Executive Programs, 15 College Road, McConnell Hall, Room 116, Durham, NH 03824-3593. *Phone:* 603-862-1367. *Fax:* 603-862-4468. *E-mail:* wsbe.grad@unh.edu.

See full description on page 726.

NEW JERSEY

Caldwell College
Program in Business Administration
Caldwell, New Jersey

Phone: 973-618-3384 **Fax:** 973-618-3640 **E-mail:** lcorrao@caldwell.edu

Business Program(s) Web Site: http://www.caldwell.edu/graduate

Accreditation ACBSP—The American Council of Business Schools and Programs (candidate).

DEGREE MBA

MBA—Master of Business Administration Full-time and part-time. Distance learning option. 39 to 60 total credits required. *Concentration:* accounting.

RESOURCES AND SERVICES 235 on-campus PCs are available to graduate business students. Access to Internet/World Wide Web, online (class) registration, and online grade reports available. *Personal computer requirements:* Graduate business students are strongly recommended to purchase or lease a personal computer. *Special opportunities include:* An

internship program is available. *Placement services include:* Alumni network, career fairs, job interviews arranged, and resume preparation.

Application Contact Liana Corrao, Graduate Admissions Counselor, Office of Graduate Studies, 9 Ryerson Avenue, Caldwell, NJ 07006. *Phone:* 973-618-3384. *Fax:* 973-618-3640. *E-mail:* lcorrao@caldwell.edu.

Centenary College
Program in Business Administration
Hackettstown, New Jersey

Phone: 908-852-1400 Ext. 2494 **Fax:** 908-852-8515 **E-mail:** baysr@centenarycollege.edu

Business Program(s) Web Site: http://www.centenarycollege.edu

Graduate Business Unit Enrollment *Total:* 353 (338 full-time; 15 part-time).

Graduate Business Faculty *Total:* 10 (5 full-time; 5 part-time).

Admissions *Average GPA:* 2.8

Academic Calendar Semesters.

DEGREE MBA

MBA—Master of Business Administration Full-time and part-time. Distance learning option. 36 to 63 total credits required. 24 to 72 months to complete program. *Concentrations:* finance, human resources management, international management, management, marketing.

RESOURCES AND SERVICES 30 on-campus PCs are available to graduate business students. Access to Internet/World Wide Web, online (class) registration, and online grade reports available. *Personal computer requirements:* Graduate business students are strongly recommended to purchase or lease a personal computer. *Special opportunities include:* An international exchange program is available. *Placement services include:* Alumni network, career placement, career counseling/planning, career fairs, resume preparation, and career library.

EXPENSES *Tuition:* Part-time: $635 per credit hour.

FINANCIAL AID (2007–08) Loans.

Financial Aid Contact Mr. Michael Corso, Director of Financial Aid, Financial Aid Office, 400 Jefferson Street, Hackettstown, NJ 07840-2100. *Phone:* 908-852-1400 Ext. 2207. *E-mail:* corsom@centenarycollege.edu.

INTERNATIONAL STUDENTS *Services and facilities:* Counseling/support services, ESL/language courses, Housing location assistance, International student housing, International student organization, Language tutoring, Orientation, Visa Services. Financial aid is not available to international students. *Required with application:* TOEFL with recommended score of 213 (computer) or 550 (paper); proof of adequate funds; proof of health/immunizations.

International Student Contact Robert Frail, Director of International Studies, International Studies, 400 Jefferson Street, Hackettstown, NJ 07840-2100. *Phone:* 908-852-1984 Ext. 2067. *Fax:* 908-979-4351. *E-mail:* frail@centenarycollege.edu.

APPLICATION *Required:* Application form, baccalaureate/first degree, personal statement, transcripts of college work. *Application fee:* $30, $50 (international). Applications for domestic and international students are processed on a rolling basis.

Application Contact Ronald Bays, MBA Program Recruitment Coordinator, 400 Jefferson Street, Hackettstown, NJ 07840-2100. *Phone:* 908-852-1400 Ext. 2494. *Fax:* 908-852-8515. *E-mail:* baysr@centenarycollege.edu.

Fairleigh Dickinson University, College at Florham

Silberman College of Business

Madison, New Jersey

Phone: 201-692-2554 **Fax:** 201-692-2560 **E-mail:** sbrooman@fdu.edu

Business Program(s) Web Site: http://www.business.fdu.edu

Graduate Business Unit Enrollment *Total:* 438 (102 full-time; 336 part-time; 170 women; 28 international). *Average Age:* 29.

Graduate Business Faculty *Total:* 143 (61 full-time; 82 part-time).

Admissions *Applied:* 191. *Admitted:* 131. *Average GMAT:* 480. *Average GPA:* 3.3

Academic Calendar Semesters.

Accreditation AACSB—The Association to Advance Collegiate Schools of Business.

After Graduation (Class of 2006–07) *Employed within 3 months of graduation:* 90%.

DEGREES EMBA • HEMBA • MBA • MSA • MST

EMBA—Executive Master of Business Administration Full-time. 48 total credits required. *Concentration:* executive programs.

HEMBA—Executive MBA for Health Care and Sciences Professionals Full-time. 48 total credits required. *Concentration:* executive programs.

MBA—Master of Business Administration in Entrepreneurial Studies Full-time and part-time. 30 to 48 total credits required. *Concentration:* entrepreneurship.

MBA—Master of Business Administration in Finance Full-time and part-time. 30 to 48 total credits required. *Concentration:* finance.

MBA—Master of Business Administration in Global Management Full-time. 30 to 48 total credits required. 12 months to complete program. *Concentration:* general MBA.

MBA—Master of Business Administration in Human Resources Management Full-time and part-time. 30 to 48 total credits required. *Concentration:* human resources management.

MBA—Master of Business Administration in International Business Full-time and part-time. 30 to 48 total credits required. *Concentration:* international business.

MBA—Master of Business Administration in Management Full-time and part-time. 30 to 48 total credits required. *Concentration:* management.

MBA—Master of Business Administration in Management Information Systems Full-time and part-time. 30 to 48 total credits required. *Concentration:* management information systems.

MBA—Master of Business Administration in Marketing Full-time and part-time. 30 to 48 total credits required. *Concentration:* marketing.

MBA—Master of Business Administration in Pharmaceutical Management Full-time and part-time. 30 to 48 total credits required. *Concentration:* pharmaceutical management.

MSA—Master of Science in Accounting Full-time and part-time. 30 total credits required. *Concentration:* accounting.

MST—Master of Science in Taxation Full-time and part-time. 30 total credits required. *Concentration:* taxation.

RESOURCES AND SERVICES 200 on-campus PCs are available to graduate business students. Access to Internet/World Wide Web, online (class) registration, and online grade reports available. *Personal computer requirements:* Graduate business students are not required to have a personal computer. *Special opportunities include:* An internship program is available. *Placement services include:* Alumni network, career placement, job search course, career counseling/planning, electronic job bank, resume referral, career fairs, job interviews arranged, resume preparation, and career library.

EXPENSES *Tuition:* Full-time: $16,074. *Tuition (international):* Full-time: $16,074. *Required fees:* Full-time: $608. Part-time: $288 per semester. *Graduate housing:* Room and board costs vary by campus location, number of occupants, type of accommodation, and type of board plan. *Typical cost:* $9982 (including board), $6074 (room only).

FINANCIAL AID (2007–08) 11 students received aid, including fellowships, loans, research assistantships, and scholarships. *Financial aid application deadline:* 2/15.

Financial Aid Contact Vincent Tungstall, University Director of Financial Aid, 1000 River Road, T-KB1-04, Teaneck, NJ 07666. *Phone:* 201-692-2823. *Fax:* 201-692-2364.

INTERNATIONAL STUDENTS 6% of students enrolled are international students. *Services and facilities:* Counseling/support services, ESL/language courses, Housing location assistance, International student housing, International student organization, Language tutoring, Orientation, Visa Services, Conversation partners. Financial aid is available to international students. *Required with application:* TOEFL with recommended score of 213 (computer), 550 (paper), or 79 (Internet); proof of adequate funds; proof of health/immunizations. *Recommended with application:* IELT; TWE with recommended score of 6.

International Student Contact Heather Augar, Director of International Admissions, 1000 River Road, T-KB1-01, Teaneck, NJ 07666. *Phone:* 201-692-2205. *Fax:* 201-692-2560. *E-mail:* global@fdu.edu.

APPLICATION *Required:* GMAT, application form, baccalaureate/first degree, essay, transcripts of college work. *Recommended:* 3 letters of recommendation, personal statement, resume/curriculum vitae. *Application fee:* $40. *Deadlines:* 7/1 for fall (international), 12/1 for winter (international), 12/1 for spring (international), 4/15 for summer (international). Applications for domestic students are processed on a rolling basis.

Application Contact Susan Brooman, Director of Graduate Admissions, 1000 River Road, T-KB1-01, Teaneck, NJ 07666. *Phone:* 201-692-2554. *Fax:* 201-692-2560. *E-mail:* sbrooman@fdu.edu.

See full description on page 612.

Fairleigh Dickinson University, Metropolitan Campus

Silberman College of Business

Teaneck, New Jersey

Phone: 201-692-2554 **Fax:** 201-692-2560 **E-mail:** sbrooman@fdu.edu

Business Program(s) Web Site: http://business.fdu.edu/business/index.html

Graduate Business Unit Enrollment *Total:* 361 (210 full-time; 151 part-time; 166 women; 136 international). *Average Age:* 29.

Graduate Business Faculty *Total:* 143 (61 full-time; 82 part-time).

Admissions *Applied:* 334. *Admitted:* 209. *Average GMAT:* 485. *Average GPA:* 3.3

Academic Calendar Semesters.

Accreditation AACSB—The Association to Advance Collegiate Schools of Business.

After Graduation (Class of 2006–07) *Employed within 3 months of graduation:* 70%.

DEGREES EMBA • HEMBA • MBA • MSA • MST

EMBA—Executive Master of Business Administration Full-time. 48 total credits required. *Concentration:* executive programs.

HEMBA—Exec MBA for Healthcare and Sciences Professionals Full-time. 48 total credits required. *Concentration:* health administration.

MBA—Master of Business Administration in Entrepreneurship Full-time and part-time. 30 to 48 total credits required. *Concentration:* entrepreneurship.

MBA—Master of Business Administration in Finance Full-time and part-time. 30 to 48 total credits required. *Concentration:* finance.

MBA—Master of Business Administration in Global Management Full-time. 30 to 48 total credits required. 12 months to complete program. *Concentration:* general MBA.

MBA—Master of Business Administration in Human Resources Full-time and part-time. 30 to 48 total credits required. *Concentration:* human resources management.

MBA—Master of Business Administration in International Business Full-time and part-time. 30 to 48 total credits required. *Concentration:* international business.

MBA—Master of Business Administration in Management Full-time and part-time. 30 to 48 total credits required. *Concentration:* management.

MBA—Master of Business Administration in Management Information Systems Full-time and part-time. 30 to 48 total credits required. *Concentration:* management information systems.

MBA—Master of Business Administration in Marketing Full-time and part-time. 30 to 48 total credits required. *Concentration:* marketing.

MBA—Pharmaceutical Master of Business Administration Full-time and part-time. 30 to 48 total credits required. *Concentration:* pharmaceutical management.

MSA—Master of Science in Accounting Full-time and part-time. 30 total credits required. *Concentration:* accounting.

MST—Master of Science in Taxation Full-time and part-time. 30 total credits required. *Concentration:* system management.

RESOURCES AND SERVICES 190 on-campus PCs are available to graduate business students. Access to Internet/World Wide Web, online (class) registration, and online grade reports available. *Personal computer requirements:* Graduate business students are not required to have a personal computer. *Special opportunities include:* An internship program is available. *Placement services include:* Alumni network, career placement, job search course, career counseling/planning, electronic job bank, resume referral, career fairs, job interviews arranged, resume preparation, and career library.

EXPENSES *Tuition:* Full-time: $16,074. *Tuition (international):* Full-time: $16,074. *Required fees:* Full-time: $608. Part-time: $288 per semester. *Graduate housing:* Room and board costs vary by campus location, number of occupants, type of accommodation, and type of board plan. *Typical cost:* $11,854 (including board), $8240 (room only).

FINANCIAL AID (2007–08) 43 students received aid, including fellowships, loans, research assistantships, and scholarships. *Financial aid application deadline:* 2/15.

Financial Aid Contact Vincent Tungstall, University Director for Financial Aid, 1000 River Road, T-KB1-04, Teaneck, NJ 07666. *Phone:* 201-692-2823. *Fax:* 201-692-2364.

INTERNATIONAL STUDENTS 38% of students enrolled are international students. *Services and facilities:* Counseling/support services, ESL/language courses, Housing location assistance, International student housing, International student organization, Language tutoring, Orientation, Visa Services, Conversation partners. Financial aid is available to international students. *Required with application:* TOEFL with recommended score of 213 (computer), 550 (paper), or 79 (Internet); proof of adequate funds; proof of health/immunizations. *Recommended with application:* IELT; TWE with recommended score of 6.

International Student Contact Heather Augar, Director of International Admissions, 1000 River Road, T-KB1-01, Teaneck, NJ 07666. *Phone:* 201-692-2205. *Fax:* 201-692-2560. *E-mail:* global@fdu.edu.

APPLICATION *Required:* GMAT, application form, baccalaureate/first degree, essay, transcripts of college work. *Recommended:* 3 letters of recommendation, personal statement, resume/curriculum vitae. *Application fee:* $40. *Deadlines:* 7/1 for fall (international), 12/1 for winter (international), 12/1 for spring (international), 4/15 for summer (international). Applications for domestic students are processed on a rolling basis.

Application Contact Susan Brooman, Director of Graduate Admissions, 1000 River Road, T-KB1-01, Teaneck, NJ 07666. *Phone:* 201-692-2554. *Fax:* 201-692-2560. *E-mail:* sbrooman@fdu.edu.

See full description on page 612.

Felician College
Program in Business
Lodi, New Jersey

Phone: 201-559-6051 **Fax:** 201-559-6138 **E-mail:** lin-cookw@felician.edu

Business Program(s) Web Site: http://www.felician.edu/business/

Academic Calendar Continuous.

DEGREES MBA • MBA/M Acc

MBA—Accounting Full-time and part-time. Up to 36 total credits required. *Concentration:* accounting.

MBA—Entrepreneurship and Innovation Full-time and part-time. Up to 36 total credits required. *Concentration:* entrepreneurship.

MBA/M Acc—Accounting Full-time and part-time. Up to 36 total credits required. *Concentration:* accounting.

RESOURCES AND SERVICES Access to Internet/World Wide Web available. *Personal computer requirements:* Graduate business students are strongly recommended to purchase or lease a personal computer. *Placement services include:* Career placement, career counseling/planning, electronic job bank, career fairs, resume preparation, and career library.

EXPENSES *Tuition:* Part-time: $790 per credit. *Tuition (international):* Part-time: $790 per credit.

Financial Aid Contact Janet Merli, Director, 262 South Main Street, Lodi, NJ 07644. *Phone:* 201-559-6010. *E-mail:* merlij@felician.edu.

INTERNATIONAL STUDENTS *Services and facilities:* ESL/language courses, Language tutoring, Visa Services. *Required with application:* TOEFL with recommended score of 550 (paper).

International Student Contact Wendy Wen-Chun Lin-Cook, Dean, 262 South Main Street, Lodi, NJ 07644. *Phone:* 201-559-6051. *Fax:* 201-559-6138. *E-mail:* lin-cookw@felician.edu.

APPLICATION *Required:* GMAT, application form, baccalaureate/first degree, 2 letters of recommendation, personal statement, resume/curriculum vitae, transcripts of college work. *Application fee:* $40. Applications for domestic and international students are processed on a rolling basis.

Application Contact Wendy Wen-Chun Lin-Cook, Dean, 262 South Main Street, Lodi, NJ 07644. *Phone:* 201-559-6051. *Fax:* 201-559-6138. *E-mail:* lin-cookw@felician.edu.

See full description on page 614.

Georgian Court University
School of Business
Lakewood, New Jersey

Phone: 732-987-2770 **Fax:** 732-987-2000 **E-mail:** admissions@georgian.edu

Business Program(s) Web Site: http://www.georgian.edu/business

Graduate Business Unit Enrollment *Total:* 155 (19 full-time; 136 part-time; 108 women; 5 international). *Average Age:* 35.

Graduate Business Faculty *Total:* 27 (11 full-time; 16 part-time).

Admissions *Applied:* 80. *Admitted:* 69. *Enrolled:* 52. *Average GPA:* 3.04

Academic Calendar Semesters.

Accreditation ACBSP—The American Council of Business Schools and Programs.

DEGREE MBA

Georgian Court University (continued)

MBA—Master of Business Administration Full-time and part-time. At least 30 total credits required. *Concentrations:* executive programs, general MBA, health care, international business, management, marketing.

RESOURCES AND SERVICES 256 on-campus PCs are available to graduate business students. Access to Internet/World Wide Web, online (class) registration, and online grade reports available. *Personal computer requirements:* Graduate business students are strongly recommended to purchase or lease a personal computer. *Placement services include:* Alumni network, career counseling/planning, career fairs, and resume preparation.

EXPENSES *Tuition:* Full-time: $13,524. Part-time: $644 per credit. *Tuition (international):* Full-time: $13,524. Part-time: $644 per credit. *Required fees:* Full-time: $760. Part-time: $400 per year. Tuition and/or fees vary by campus location. *Graduate housing:* Room and board costs vary by number of occupants and type of board plan. *Typical cost:* $8136 (including board), $4882 (room only).

FINANCIAL AID (2007–08) 44 students received aid, including grants, loans, scholarships, and work study. Aid is available to part-time students. *Financial aid application deadline:* 4/15.

Financial Aid Contact Carol Strauss, Director of Financial Aid, 900 Lakewood Avenue, Lakewood, NJ 08701-2697. *Phone:* 732-987-2259. *Fax:* 732-987-2012. *E-mail:* financialaid@georgian.edu.

INTERNATIONAL STUDENTS 3% of students enrolled are international students. *Services and facilities:* Counseling/support services, ESL/language courses. Financial aid is available to international students. *Required with application:* TOEFL with recommended score of 213 (computer) or 550 (paper); proof of adequate funds; proof of health/immunizations.

International Student Contact Ms. Kathie DeBona Gallant, Director of Admissions, 900 Lakewood Avenue, Lakewood, NJ 08701-2697. *Phone:* 732-987-2760. *Fax:* 732-987-2000. *E-mail:* admissions@georgian.edu.

APPLICATION *Required:* GMAT, application form, baccalaureate/first degree, 3 letters of recommendation, personal statement, transcripts of college work. *Recommended:* Interview. *Application fee:* $40. Applications for domestic and international students are processed on a rolling basis.

Application Contact Mr. Eugene Soltys, Director of Graduate Admissions, 900 Lakewood Avenue, Lakewood, NJ 08701-2697. *Phone:* 732-987-2770. *Fax:* 732-987-2000. *E-mail:* admissions@georgian.edu.

Kean University
College of Business and Public Administration
Union, New Jersey

Phone: 908-737-7122 **Fax:** 908-737-3444 **E-mail:** dshani@kean.edu

Business Program(s) Web Site: http://www.kean.edu/~keangrad

Graduate Business Unit Enrollment *Total:* 61 (26 full-time; 35 part-time; 29 women; 17 international).

Graduate Business Faculty *Total:* 25 (10 full-time; 15 part-time).

Admissions *Applied:* 30. *Admitted:* 20. *Enrolled:* 15. *Average GMAT:* 485. *Average GPA:* 3.15

Academic Calendar Semesters.

DEGREES EMBA • GMBA • MBA • MPA • MS

EMBA—MBA Executive Option Part-time. Substantial business experience required. 42 to 48 total credits required. 20 to 24 months to complete program. *Concentrations:* accounting, finance, management, management information systems, marketing.

GMBA—MBA in Global Management Full-time and part-time. 42 to 60 total credits required. 20 to 72 months to complete program.

Concentrations: accounting, electronic commerce (E-commerce), finance, information management, information technology, management, marketing.

MBA—Global Management Full-time and part-time. Distance learning option. Second language proficiency. 42 to 60 total credits required. *Concentrations:* finance, information systems, management, marketing.

MPA—Public Administration Full-time and part-time. 42 to 48 total credits required. 24 to 72 months to complete program. *Concentrations:* combined degrees, environmental economics/management, health administration, nonprofit management.

MS—MS Accounting Full-time and part-time. 30 to 36 total credits required. 18 to 72 months to complete program. *Concentration:* accounting.

RESOURCES AND SERVICES 500 on-campus PCs are available to graduate business students. Access to Internet/World Wide Web, online (class) registration, and online grade reports available. *Personal computer requirements:* Graduate business students are strongly recommended to purchase or lease a personal computer. *Special opportunities include:* An international exchange program and an internship program are available. *Placement services include:* Alumni network, career counseling/planning, electronic job bank, career fairs, job interviews arranged, resume preparation, and career library.

EXPENSES *Tuition (state resident):* Full-time: $6000. Part-time: $500 per credit hour.

FINANCIAL AID (2007–08) 8 students received aid, including loans, research assistantships, scholarships, and work study. Aid is available to part-time students. *Financial aid application deadline:* 5/1.

Financial Aid Contact Mr. Charlie Xu, Office of Financial Aid, 1000 Morris Avenue, Administration Building, First Floor, Union, NJ 07083. *Phone:* 908-737-3190. *Fax:* 908-737-3200. *E-mail:* cxu@kean.edu.

INTERNATIONAL STUDENTS 28% of students enrolled are international students. *Services and facilities:* Counseling/support services, ESL/language courses, Housing location assistance, International student organization, Language tutoring, Orientation, Visa Services. Financial aid is available to international students. *Required with application:* TOEFL with recommended score of 80 (Internet); proof of adequate funds; proof of health/immunizations.

International Student Contact Ms. Lilliam Hodge-Banner, International Student Services, 1000 Morris Avenue, Downs D-122, Union, NJ 07083. *Phone:* 908-737-4860. *Fax:* 908-737-4865. *E-mail:* lbanner@kean.edu.

APPLICATION *Required:* Application form, baccalaureate/first degree, essay, 2 letters of recommendation, personal statement, transcripts of college work. School will accept GMAT and GRE. *Recommended:* Interview, resume/curriculum vitae, work experience. *Application fee:* $60, $150 (international). Applications for domestic and international students are processed on a rolling basis.

Application Contact Dr. David Shani, Program Director, 1000 Morris Avenue, Kean Hall K-225C, Union, NJ 07083. *Phone:* 908-737-7122. *Fax:* 908-737-3444. *E-mail:* dshani@kean.edu.

Monmouth University
School of Business Administration
West Long Branch, New Jersey

Phone: 732-571-3452 **Fax:** 732-263-5123 **E-mail:** kroane@monmouth.edu

Business Program(s) Web Site: http://www.monmouth.edu/~business/

Graduate Business Unit Enrollment *Total:* 229 (58 full-time; 171 part-time; 91 women; 12 international). *Average Age:* 30.

Graduate Business Faculty *Total:* 35 (32 full-time; 3 part-time).

Admissions *Applied:* 152. *Admitted:* 117. *Enrolled:* 78. *Average GMAT:* 518. *Average GPA:* 3.0

Academic Calendar Semesters.

Accreditation AACSB—The Association to Advance Collegiate Schools of Business.

DEGREES MA/MBA • MBA

MA/MBA—Finance Track Part-time. 36 to 51 total credits required. 12 to 60 months to complete program. *Concentration:* finance.

MBA—Accounting Track Part-time. 30 to 54 total credits required. 12 to 60 months to complete program. *Concentration:* accounting.

MBA—Concentration in Health Care Part-time. 33 to 54 total credits required. 12 to 60 months to complete program. *Concentration:* health care.

MBA—Real Estate Track Part-time. 36 to 51 total credits required. 12 to 60 months to complete program. *Concentration:* real estate.

MBA—Master of Business Administration Part-time. 30 to 48 total credits required. 12 to 60 months to complete program. *Concentration:* general MBA.

RESOURCES AND SERVICES 700 on-campus PCs are available to graduate business students. Access to Internet/World Wide Web, online (class) registration, and online grade reports available. *Personal computer requirements:* Graduate business students are strongly recommended to purchase or lease a personal computer. *Placement services include:* Alumni network, career placement, job search course, career counseling/planning, electronic job bank, career fairs, job interviews arranged, resume preparation, and career library.

EXPENSES *Tuition:* Full-time: $26,784. Part-time: $744 per credit. *Tuition (international):* Full-time: $26,784. Part-time: $744 per credit. *Required fees:* Full-time: $628. Part-time: $314 per term.

FINANCIAL AID (2007–08) 135 students received aid, including fellowships, grants, loans, research assistantships, scholarships, and work study. Aid is available to part-time students.

Financial Aid Contact Ms. Claire Alasio, Director, Financial Aid, 400 Cedar Avenue, West Long Branch, NJ 07764-1898. *Phone:* 732-571-3463. *Fax:* 732-263-5577. *E-mail:* calasio@monmouth.edu.

INTERNATIONAL STUDENTS 5% of students enrolled are international students. *Services and facilities:* Counseling/support services, Housing location assistance, International student organization, Orientation, Visa Services. Financial aid is available to international students. *Required with application:* TOEFL with recommended score of 213 (computer), 550 (paper), or 79 (Internet); proof of adequate funds; proof of health/immunizations.

International Student Contact Laurie Kuhn, Admission Counselor, 400 Cedar Avenue, West Long Branch, NJ 07764-1898. *Phone:* 732-571-3452. *Fax:* 732-263-5123. *E-mail:* lkuhn@monmouth.edu.

APPLICATION *Required:* GMAT, application form, baccalaureate/first degree, 2 letters of recommendation, transcripts of college work. *Application fee:* $50. Applications for domestic and international students are processed on a rolling basis.

Application Contact Kevin Roane, Director, Graduate Admission/Enrollment, 400 Cedar Avenue, West Long Branch, NJ 07764-1898. *Phone:* 732-571-3452. *Fax:* 732-263-5123. *E-mail:* kroane@monmouth.edu.

Montclair State University

School of Business

Montclair, New Jersey

Phone: 973-655-5147 **Fax:** 973-655-7869 **E-mail:** osullivanj@mail.montclair.edu

Business Program(s) Web Site: http://www.montclair.edu/mba

Graduate Business Unit Enrollment *Total:* 342 (83 full-time; 259 part-time; 148 women; 40 international). *Average Age:* 30.

Graduate Business Faculty *Total:* 107 (74 full-time; 33 part-time).

Admissions *Applied:* 184. *Admitted:* 93. *Enrolled:* 76. *Average GMAT:* 489. *Average GPA:* 3.2

Academic Calendar Semesters.

Accreditation AACSB—The Association to Advance Collegiate Schools of Business.

After Graduation (Class of 2006–07) *Employed within 3 months of graduation:* 95%. *Average starting salary:* $65,000.

DEGREE MBA

MBA—Master of Business Administration Full-time and part-time. 33 to 54 total credits required. 18 to 96 months to complete program. *Concentrations:* accounting, economics, finance, international business, management, management information systems, marketing.

RESOURCES AND SERVICES 450 on-campus PCs are available to graduate business students. Access to Internet/World Wide Web, online (class) registration, and online grade reports available. *Personal computer requirements:* Graduate business students are strongly recommended to purchase or lease a personal computer. *Special opportunities include:* An international exchange program is available. *Placement services include:* Alumni network.

EXPENSES *Tuition (state resident):* Full-time: $10,033.92. Part-time: $557.44 per semester hour. *Tuition (nonresident):* Full-time: $13,800. Part-time: $766.66 per semester hour. *Tuition (international):* Full-time: $13,799.88. Part-time: $766.66 per semester hour. *Required fees:* Full-time: $1199.60. Part-time: $105.65 per semester hour. *Graduate housing:* Room and board costs vary by number of occupants, type of accommodation, and type of board plan. *Typical cost:* $8650 (including board), $6000 (room only).

FINANCIAL AID (2007–08) 100 students received aid, including loans, research assistantships, scholarships, and work study. Aid is available to part-time students. *Financial aid application deadline:* 3/1.

Financial Aid Contact Financial Aid Office, 1 Normal Avenue, Montclair, NJ 07043-1624. *Phone:* 973-655-4461. *Fax:* 973-655-7712. *E-mail:* financialaid@montclair.edu.

INTERNATIONAL STUDENTS 12% of students enrolled are international students. *Services and facilities:* Counseling/support services, ESL/language courses, International student organization, Orientation, Visa Services. Financial aid is available to international students. *Required with application:* TOEFL with recommended score of 207 (computer), 380 (paper), or 83 (Internet); proof of adequate funds; proof of health/immunizations.

International Student Contact Ms. Jacqueline Leighton, Director, International Services, International Services, 22 Normal Avenue, Upper Montclair, NJ 07043-1624. *Phone:* 973-655-6862. *Fax:* 973-655-7726. *E-mail:* leightonj@mail.montclair.edu.

APPLICATION *Required:* GMAT, application form, baccalaureate/first degree, essay, 2 letters of recommendation, personal statement, transcripts of college work. *Recommended:* Interview, resume/curriculum vitae, work experience. *Application fee:* $60. Applications for domestic and international students are processed on a rolling basis.

Application Contact Ms. Jennifer O'Sullivan, Admissions Coordinator, The Office of Graduate Admissions, 203 College Hall, 1 Normal Avenue, Montclair, NJ 07043. *Phone:* 973-655-5147. *Fax:* 973-655-7869. *E-mail:* osullivanj@mail.montclair.edu.

New Jersey Institute of Technology

School of Management

Newark, New Jersey

Phone: 973-596-6378 **Fax:** 973-596-3074 **E-mail:** frazier@njit.edu

Business Program(s) Web Site: http://management.njit.edu

Graduate Business Unit Enrollment *Total:* 255 (153 full-time; 102 part-time; 58 women; 69 international). *Average Age:* 34.

New Jersey Institute of Technology (continued)

Graduate Business Faculty *Total:* 31 (29 full-time; 2 part-time).

Admissions *Applied:* 257. *Admitted:* 133. *Enrolled:* 86. *Average GMAT:* 530. *Average GPA:* 3.2

Academic Calendar Semesters.

Accreditation AACSB—The Association to Advance Collegiate Schools of Business.

After Graduation (Class of 2006–07) *Employed within 3 months of graduation:* 95%. *Average starting salary:* $80,000.

DEGREES MBA • MS

MBA—Executive Master of Business Part-time. 5 years of work experience and GMAT are required. 48 total credits required. 18 months to complete program. *Concentrations:* management information systems, strategic management.

MBA—Master of Business Administration in Management of Technology Full-time and part-time. Distance learning option. GMAT required. At least 48 total credits required. 18 to 36 months to complete program. *Concentrations:* electronic commerce (E-commerce), finance, logistics, management, management information systems, marketing, operations management, technology management.

MS—Master of Science in Management Full-time and part-time. Distance learning option. GMAT required. At least 30 total credits required. 12 to 30 months to complete program. *Concentrations:* electronic commerce (E-commerce), management information systems, organizational management, technology management.

RESOURCES AND SERVICES 1,500 on-campus PCs are available to graduate business students. Access to Internet/World Wide Web, online (class) registration, and online grade reports available. *Personal computer requirements:* Graduate business students are strongly recommended to purchase or lease a personal computer. *Special opportunities include:* An internship program is available. *Placement services include:* Alumni network, career placement, career counseling/planning, electronic job bank, career fairs, job interviews arranged, resume preparation, and career library.

EXPENSES *Tuition (state resident):* Full-time: $12,730. Part-time: $694 per credit hour. *Tuition (nonresident):* Full-time: $18,090. Part-time: $955 per credit hour. *Tuition (international):* Full-time: $18,090. Part-time: $955 per credit hour. Tuition and/or fees vary by class time, number of courses or credits taken, and local reciprocity agreements. *Graduate housing:* Room and board costs vary by campus location, number of occupants, type of accommodation, and type of board plan. *Typical cost:* $9246 (including board).

FINANCIAL AID (2007–08) 200 students received aid, including fellowships, loans, research assistantships, scholarships, teaching assistantships, and work study. *Financial aid application deadline:* 3/15.

Financial Aid Contact Ms. Ivon Nunez, Director, Financial Aid Department, University Heights, Newark, NJ 07102-1982. *Phone:* 973-596-3479.

INTERNATIONAL STUDENTS 27% of students enrolled are international students. *Services and facilities:* Counseling/support services, ESL/language courses, Housing location assistance, International student housing, International student organization, Language tutoring, Orientation, Visa Services. Financial aid is available to international students. *Required with application:* TOEFL with recommended score of 213 (computer) or 550 (paper); proof of adequate funds; proof of health/immunizations.

International Student Contact Jeffrey W. Grundy, Director, International Student and Faculty Services, University Heights, Newark, NJ 07102-1982. *Phone:* 973-596-2451. *E-mail:* jeffrey.w.grundy@njit.edu.

APPLICATION *Required:* GMAT, application form, baccalaureate/first degree, transcripts of college work. *Recommended:* 2 letters of recommendation, personal statement, resume/curriculum vitae, 2 years of work experience. *Application fee:* $60. Applications for domestic and international students are processed on a rolling basis.

Application Contact D. Elaine Frazier, Director, EMBA and Graduate Programs, University Heights, Newark, NJ 07102-1982. *Phone:* 973-596-6378. *Fax:* 973-596-3074. *E-mail:* frazier@njit.edu.

The Richard Stockton College of New Jersey

Program in Business Administration

Pomona, New Jersey

Phone: 609-626-3482 **Fax:** 609-626-6050 **E-mail:** annemari.tarsitano@stockton.edu

Business Program(s) Web Site: http://graduate.stockton.edu/mba.html

Graduate Business Unit Enrollment *Total:* 52 (8 full-time; 44 part-time; 29 women). *Average Age:* 32.

Graduate Business Faculty 9 full-time.

Admissions *Applied:* 26. *Admitted:* 20. *Enrolled:* 18. *Average GMAT:* 450. *Average GPA:* 3.0

Academic Calendar Semesters.

DEGREES MBA

MBA—Master of Business Administration Full-time and part-time. 33 total credits required. 12 to 36 months to complete program. *Concentration:* general MBA.

MBA—Master of Business Administration Full-time and part-time. 33 total credits required. 12 to 36 months to complete program. *Concentration:* accounting.

RESOURCES AND SERVICES 450 on-campus PCs are available to graduate business students. Access to Internet/World Wide Web, online (class) registration, and online grade reports available. *Personal computer requirements:* Graduate business students are strongly recommended to purchase or lease a personal computer. *Special opportunities include:* An internship program is available. *Placement services include:* Alumni network, career placement, job search course, career counseling/planning, electronic job bank, resume referral, career fairs, job interviews arranged, resume preparation, and career library.

EXPENSES *Tuition (state resident):* Full-time: $7895. Part-time: $439 per credit. *Tuition (nonresident):* Full-time: $11,931. *Required fees:* Full-time: $1881. Part-time: $104.50 per credit. Tuition and/or fees vary by number of courses or credits taken. *Typical graduate housing cost:* $8900 (including board), $6388 (room only).

FINANCIAL AID (2007–08) 9 students received aid, including work study. Aid is available to part-time students. *Financial aid application deadline:* 3/1.

Financial Aid Contact Ms. Jeanne Lewis, Director of Financial Aid, PO Box 195, Pomona, NJ 08240-0195. *Phone:* 609-652-4201. *Fax:* 609-748-5517. *E-mail:* iaprod91@stockton.edu.

INTERNATIONAL STUDENTS *Services and facilities:* Counseling/support services, Housing location assistance, International student organization, Orientation. Financial aid is available to international students. *Required with application:* TOEFL with recommended score of 216 (computer) or 550 (paper); proof of adequate funds; proof of health/immunizations.

International Student Contact MBA Director, PO Box 195, Pomona, NJ 08240-0195. *Phone:* 609-652-4501. *Fax:* 609-652-4858.

APPLICATION *Required:* GMAT, application form, baccalaureate/first degree, transcripts of college work. *Application fee:* $50. Applications for domestic and international students are processed on a rolling basis.

Application Contact Ms. Annemari Tarsitano, Assistant Director for Graduate Enrollment Management, Office of Enrollment Management, PO Box 195, Pomona, NJ 08240-0195. *Phone:* 609-626-3482. *Fax:* 609-626-6050. *E-mail:* annemari.tarsitano@stockton.edu.

Rider University

College of Business Administration

Lawrenceville, New Jersey

Phone: 609-896-5036 **Fax:** 609-895-5680 **E-mail:** grdsrv@rider.edu

Business Program(s) Web Site: http://www.rider.edu/mba

Graduate Business Unit Enrollment *Total:* 350 (87 full-time; 263 part-time; 161 women; 55 international).

Graduate Business Faculty *Total:* 30 (19 full-time; 11 part-time).

Admissions *Applied:* 143. *Admitted:* 89. *Enrolled:* 71. *Average GMAT:* 504. *Average GPA:* 3.29

Academic Calendar Semesters.

Accreditation AACSB—The Association to Advance Collegiate Schools of Business.

DEGREES EMBA • M Acc • MBA

EMBA—Executive Master of Business Administration Part-time. Distance learning option. Minimum of 5 years' work experience, 3 in management/supervisory experience, 2 work-related recommendations, objective statement, interview, and resume required. 51 total credits required. 21 months to complete program. *Concentration:* executive programs.

M Acc—Master of Accountancy Full-time and part-time. 30 to 57 total credits required. 10 to 60 months to complete program. *Concentrations:* entrepreneurship, finance, health care, information systems, international business, management, marketing.

MBA—Master of Business Administration Full-time and part-time. 30 to 51 total credits required. 10 to 60 months to complete program. *Concentrations:* entrepreneurship, finance, health care, information management, international business, management, marketing.

RESOURCES AND SERVICES 520 on-campus PCs are available to graduate business students. Access to Internet/World Wide Web, online (class) registration, and online grade reports available. *Personal computer requirements:* Graduate business students are strongly recommended to purchase or lease a personal computer. *Special opportunities include:* An internship program is available. *Placement services include:* Alumni network, career counseling/planning, electronic job bank, resume referral, career fairs, resume preparation, and career library.

EXPENSES *Tuition:* Full-time: $13,230. Part-time: $735 per credit. *Tuition (international):* Full-time: $13,230. Part-time: $735 per credit. *Required fees:* Full-time: $360. Part-time: $22 per credit.

FINANCIAL AID (2007–08) 129 students received aid, including loans and research assistantships. Aid is available to part-time students. *Financial aid application deadline:* 6/30.

Financial Aid Contact Mr. Drew Aromando, Acting Director, Student Financial Services, 2083 Lawrenceville Road, Lawrenceville, NJ 08648-3099. *Phone:* 609-896-5360. *Fax:* 609-219-4487. *E-mail:* aromando@rider.edu.

INTERNATIONAL STUDENTS 16% of students enrolled are international students. *Services and facilities:* Counseling/support services, ESL/language courses, Housing location assistance, Language tutoring, Orientation, Visa Services. Financial aid is available to international students. *Required with application:* TOEFL with recommended score of 213 (computer) or 550 (paper); proof of adequate funds; proof of health/immunizations.

International Student Contact Ms. Aimee Thomson, Senior Assistant Director, 2083 Lawrenceville Road, Lawrenceville, NJ 08648-3099. *Phone:* 609-896-5036. *Fax:* 609-895-5680. *E-mail:* athomson@rider.edu.

APPLICATION *Required:* GMAT, application form, baccalaureate/first degree, essay, resume/curriculum vitae, transcripts of college work. *Recommended:* Interview, letter(s) of recommendation, personal statement, work experience. *Application fee:* $50. *Deadlines:* 8/1 for fall, 12/1 for spring, 5/1 for summer, 6/1 for fall (international), 12/1 for spring (international), 5/1 for summer (international).

Application Contact Ms. Jamie Mitchell, Director, Graduate Admissions, 2083 Lawrenceville Road, Lawrenceville, NJ 08648-3099. *Phone:* 609-896-5036. *Fax:* 609-895-5680. *E-mail:* grdsrv@rider.edu.

Rowan University

William G. Rohrer College of Business

Glassboro, New Jersey

Phone: 856-256-4024 **Fax:** 856-256-4439 **E-mail:** mba@rowan.edu

Business Program(s) Web Site: http://www.rowan.edu/colleges/business/

Graduate Business Unit Enrollment *Total:* 84 (20 full-time; 64 part-time; 38 women; 15 international). *Average Age:* 27.

Graduate Business Faculty *Total:* 28 (25 full-time; 3 part-time).

Admissions *Applied:* 76. *Admitted:* 53. *Enrolled:* 40. *Average GMAT:* 501. *Average GPA:* 3.31

Academic Calendar Semesters.

Accreditation AACSB—The Association to Advance Collegiate Schools of Business.

After Graduation (Class of 2006–07) *Employed within 3 months of graduation:* 95%. *Average starting salary:* $50,000.

DEGREES MBA

MBA—Master of Business Administration Full-time and part-time. 36 to 57 total credits required. 18 to 72 months to complete program. *Concentrations:* accounting, entrepreneurship, finance, management, marketing.

MBA—Master of Business Administration Full-time and part-time. 36 to 57 total credits required. 18 to 72 months to complete program. *Concentration:* general MBA.

RESOURCES AND SERVICES 400 on-campus PCs are available to graduate business students. Access to Internet/World Wide Web, online (class) registration, and online grade reports available. *Personal computer requirements:* Graduate business students are not required to have a personal computer. *Special opportunities include:* An international exchange program and an internship program are available. *Placement services include:* Alumni network, career placement, career counseling/planning, electronic job bank, resume referral, career fairs, job interviews arranged, resume preparation, and career library.

EXPENSES *Tuition (state resident):* Full-time: $10,624. Part-time: $590 per semester hour. *Tuition (nonresident):* Full-time: $10,624. Part-time: $590 per semester hour. *Tuition (international):* Full-time: $10,624. Part-time: $590 per semester hour. *Required fees:* Full-time: $2058. Part-time: $115 per semester hour. *Graduate housing:* Room and board costs vary by campus location, number of occupants, type of accommodation, and type of board plan. *Typical cost:* $9235 (including board), $6250 (room only).

FINANCIAL AID (2007–08) Research assistantships and work study. Aid is available to part-time students.

Financial Aid Contact Financial Aid Office, Savitz Hall, 201 Mullica Hill Road, Glassboro, NJ 08028-1701. *Phone:* 856-256-4250. *Fax:* 856-256-4413. *E-mail:* financialaid@rowan.edu.

INTERNATIONAL STUDENTS 18% of students enrolled are international students. *Services and facilities:* Counseling/support services, ESL/language courses, Housing location assistance, International student organization, Orientation. Financial aid is not available to international students. *Required with application:* TOEFL with recommended score of 213 (computer), 550 (paper), or 79 (Internet); proof of adequate funds; proof of health/immunizations.

International Student Contact Mr. Craig Katz, Director, International Student Services, 201 Mullica Hill Road, Robinson Hall, Glassboro, NJ 08028-1701. *Phone:* 856-256-5238. *E-mail:* katz@rowan.edu.

APPLICATION *Required:* Application form, baccalaureate/first degree, essay, 2 letters of recommendation, personal statement, resume/curriculum

Rowan University (continued)

vitae, transcripts of college work. School will accept GMAT and GRE. *Recommended:* Work experience. *Application fee:* $50. Applications for domestic and international students are processed on a rolling basis.

Application Contact Dr. Daniel McFarland, MBA Program Director, 201 Mullica Hill Road, Bunce Hall, Glassboro, NJ 08028-1701. *Phone:* 856-256-4024. *Fax:* 856-256-4439. *E-mail:* mba@rowan.edu.

Rutgers, The State University of New Jersey

Rutgers Business School–Newark and New Brunswick

Newark and New Brunswick, New Jersey

Phone: 973-353-1234 **Fax:** 973-353-1592 **E-mail:** admit@business.rutgers.edu

Business Program(s) Web Site: http://www.business.rutgers.edu

Graduate Business Unit Enrollment *Total:* 1,540 (372 full-time; 1,168 part-time; 558 women; 197 international). *Average Age:* 28.

Graduate Business Faculty *Total:* 212 (130 full-time; 82 part-time).

Admissions *Applied:* 955. *Admitted:* 481. *Enrolled:* 272. *Average GMAT:* 637. *Average GPA:* 3.3

Academic Calendar Trimesters.

Accreditation AACSB—The Association to Advance Collegiate Schools of Business.

After Graduation (Class of 2006–07) *Employed within 3 months of graduation:* 86%. *Average starting salary:* $78,760.

DEGREES M Acc • MBA • MQF

M Acc—Master of Accountancy in Financial Accounting Full-time and part-time. Distance learning option. At least 30 total credits required. 10 to 24 months to complete program. *Concentration:* accounting.

M Acc—Master of Accountancy in Governmental Accounting Part-time. Distance learning option. GMAT waived for CPA holders. At least 30 total credits required. 12 to 30 months to complete program. *Concentration:* accounting.

M Acc—Master of Accountancy in Taxation Part-time. GMAT waived for CPA holders. 30 total credits required. 10 to 30 months to complete program. *Concentration:* taxation.

MBA—Executive Master of Business Administration Full-time. 10 years of work experience required. At least 54 total credits required. 20 months to complete program. *Concentrations:* finance, information technology, marketing, pharmaceutical management, supply chain management.

MBA—Master of Business Administration in Management Full-time and part-time. 60 to 75 total credits required. 20 to 96 months to complete program. *Concentrations:* arts administration/management, finance, general MBA, information technology, international business, management, marketing, pharmaceutical management, supply chain management.

MBA—Master of Business Administration in Professional Accounting Full-time. 62 to 75 total credits required. 14 months to complete program. *Concentration:* accounting.

MQF—Quantitative Financial Management Full-time and part-time. GRE or GMAT Accepted for 2008. 54 total credits required. 20 to 36 months to complete program. *Concentration:* finance.

RESOURCES AND SERVICES 100 on-campus PCs are available to graduate business students. Access to Internet/World Wide Web, online (class) registration, and online grade reports available. *Personal computer requirements:* Graduate business students are required to have a personal computer. *Special opportunities include:* An international exchange program and an internship program are available. *Placement services*

include: Alumni network, career placement, job search course, career counseling/planning, electronic job bank, resume referral, career fairs, job interviews arranged, resume preparation, and career library.

EXPENSES *Tuition (state resident):* Full-time: $18,825. Part-time: $780 per credit hour. *Tuition (nonresident):* Full-time: $30,027. Part-time: $1247 per credit hour. *Tuition (international):* Full-time: $30,027. *Required fees:* Full-time: $998. Part-time: $383 per course. Tuition and/or fees vary by number of courses or credits taken. *Graduate housing:* Room and board costs vary by campus location, number of occupants, type of accommodation, and type of board plan. *Typical cost:* $10,000 (room only).

FINANCIAL AID (2007–08) 17 students received aid, including fellowships, grants, loans, scholarships, and work study. Aid is available to part-time students. *Financial aid application deadline:* 4/1.

Financial Aid Contact Ms. Rita Galen, Director of Admissions, Office of Admissions, 190 University Avenue, Newark, NJ 07102-1813. *Phone:* 973-353-1234. *Fax:* 973-353-1592. *E-mail:* admit@business.rutgers.edu.

INTERNATIONAL STUDENTS 13% of students enrolled are international students. *Services and facilities:* Counseling/support services, ESL/language courses, Housing location assistance, International student housing, International student organization, Language tutoring, Orientation, Visa Services. Financial aid is not available to international students. *Required with application:* TOEFL with recommended score of 250 (computer) or 600 (paper); proof of adequate funds; proof of health/immunizations.

International Student Contact Rita Galen, Director of Admissions, 190 University Avenue, Office of Graduate Admissions, Newark, NJ 07102-1813. *Phone:* 973-353-1234. *Fax:* 973-353-1592. *E-mail:* admit@business.rutgers.edu.

APPLICATION *Required:* GMAT, application form, baccalaureate/first degree, essay, 2 letters of recommendation, resume/curriculum vitae, transcripts of college work, 2 years of work experience. *Application fee:* $60. Applications for domestic and international students are processed on a rolling basis.

Application Contact Rita Galen, Director of Admissions, Office of Graduate Admissions, 190 University Avenue, Newark, NJ 07102-1813. *Phone:* 973-353-1234. *Fax:* 973-353-1592. *E-mail:* admit@business.rutgers.edu.

See full description on page 678.

Rutgers, The State University of New Jersey, Camden

School of Business

Camden, New Jersey

Phone: 856-225-6452 **Fax:** 856-225-6231 **E-mail:** sambhary@camden.rutgers.edu

Business Program(s) Web Site: http://camden-sbc.rutgers.edu/ProspectiveStudent/grad/default.htm

Graduate Business Unit Enrollment *Total:* 259 (37 full-time; 222 part-time; 85 women; 57 international). *Average Age:* 28.

Graduate Business Faculty *Total:* 39 (34 full-time; 5 part-time).

Admissions *Applied:* 212. *Admitted:* 130. *Enrolled:* 57. *Average GMAT:* 557. *Average GPA:* 3.2

Academic Calendar Semesters.

Accreditation AACSB—The Association to Advance Collegiate Schools of Business.

After Graduation (Class of 2006–07) *Employed within 3 months of graduation:* 90%. *Average starting salary:* $88,438.

DEGREES JD/MBA • MBA

JD/MBA—Juris Doctor/Master of Business Administration Full-time and part-time. LSAT required. 108 to 120 total credits required. 36 to 57 months to complete program. *Concentrations:* business law, international business.

MBA—Master of Business Administration Full-time and part-time. 36 to 57 total credits required. 18 to 24 months to complete program. *Concentrations:* accounting, finance, health care, international business, management, management information systems, marketing, operations management.

RESOURCES AND SERVICES 158 on-campus PCs are available to graduate business students. Access to Internet/World Wide Web, online (class) registration, and online grade reports available. *Personal computer requirements:* Graduate business students are not required to have a personal computer. *Special opportunities include:* An internship program is available. *Placement services include:* Alumni network, career placement, job search course, career counseling/planning, electronic job bank, resume referral, career fairs, job interviews arranged, resume preparation, and career library.

FINANCIAL AID (2007–08) Loans, research assistantships, scholarships, and work study. Aid is available to part-time students. *Financial aid application deadline:* 8/1.

Financial Aid Contact Mr. Richard Woodland, Director, Financial Aid, Camden Campus, 311 North Fifth Street, Camden, NJ 08102-1401. *Phone:* 856-225-6039. *Fax:* 856-225-6074. *E-mail:* rwoodlan@ camden.rutgers.edu.

INTERNATIONAL STUDENTS 22% of students enrolled are international students. *Services and facilities:* Counseling/support services, Housing location assistance, International student housing, International student organization, Orientation, Visa Services. Financial aid is available to international students. *Required with application:* TOEFL with recommended score of 230 (computer); proof of adequate funds; proof of health/immunizations.

International Student Contact Ms. Janice Edwards, Associate Director of Graduate Admissions, Camden Campus, Office of Graduate Admissions, Camden, NJ 08102-1401. *Phone:* 856-225-6104. *Fax:* 856-225-6498. *E-mail:* edwards@ugadm.rutgers.edu.

APPLICATION *Required:* GMAT, application form, baccalaureate/first degree, essay, 2 letters of recommendation, personal statement, transcripts of college work. *Recommended:* Resume/curriculum vitae, 3 years of work experience. *Application fee:* $60. Applications for domestic and international students are processed on a rolling basis.

Application Contact Dr. Rakesh B Sambharya, Director, Graduate Programs, 227 Penn Street, Camden, NJ 08102-1401. *Phone:* 856-225-6452. *Fax:* 856-225-6231. *E-mail:* sambhary@camden.rutgers.edu.

Rutgers, The State University of New Jersey, New Brunswick
School of Management and Labor Relations

New Brunswick, New Jersey

Phone: 732-445-5973 **Fax:** 732-445-2830 **E-mail:** mhrm@rci.rutgers.edu

Business Program(s) Web Site: http://www.smlr.rutgers.edu

Graduate Business Unit Enrollment *Total:* 257 (121 full-time; 136 part-time; 186 women; 39 international). *Average Age:* 31.

Graduate Business Faculty *Total:* 34 (30 full-time; 4 part-time).

Admissions *Applied:* 228. *Admitted:* 160. *Enrolled:* 93. *Average GMAT:* 591. *Average GPA:* 3.23.

Academic Calendar Semesters.

After Graduation (Class of 2006–07) *Employed within 3 months of graduation:* 81%. *Average starting salary:* $77,000.

DEGREES MHRM • MLIR

MHRM—Master of Human Resources Management Full-time and part-time. 30 to 48 total credits required. 18 to 48 months to complete program. *Concentration:* human resources management.

MLIR—Master of Labor and Employment Relations Full-time and part-time. At least 39 total credits required. 12 to 60 months to complete program. *Concentration:* industrial/labor relations.

RESOURCES AND SERVICES 60 on-campus PCs are available to graduate business students. Access to Internet/World Wide Web, online (class) registration, and online grade reports available. *Personal computer requirements:* Graduate business students are strongly recommended to purchase or lease a personal computer. *Special opportunities include:* An internship program is available. *Placement services include:* Alumni network, career placement, job search course, career counseling/planning, electronic job bank, resume referral, career fairs, job interviews arranged, resume preparation, and career library.

EXPENSES *Tuition (state resident):* Full-time: $14,600. *Tuition (nonresident):* Full-time: $22,400. *Graduate housing:* Room and board costs vary by campus location, number of occupants, and type of accommodation.

FINANCIAL AID (2007–08) 31 students received aid, including fellowships, scholarships, and work study. *Financial aid application deadline:* 2/1.

Financial Aid Contact Office of Financial Aid, Records Hall, New Brunswick, NJ 08903. *Phone:* 732-932-7755. *Fax:* 732-932-7385.

INTERNATIONAL STUDENTS 15% of students enrolled are international students. *Services and facilities:* Counseling/support services, ESL/language courses, Housing location assistance, International student organization, Orientation, Visa Services. Financial aid is available to international students. *Required with application:* TOEFL with recommended score of 230 (computer) or 575 (paper); proof of adequate funds; proof of health/immunizations.

International Student Contact Marcy Cohen, Director, International Faculty and Student Services Center, 180 College Avenue, New Brunswick, NJ 08903. *Phone:* 732-932-7015. *Fax:* 732-932-7992. *E-mail:* marcohen@rci.rutgers.edu.

APPLICATION *Required:* Application form, baccalaureate/first degree, 3 letters of recommendation, personal statement, transcripts of college work. School will accept GMAT and GRE. *Recommended:* Resume/curriculum vitae, work experience. *Application fee:* $50. Applications for domestic and international students are processed on a rolling basis.

Application Contact Ms. Joanna Eriksen, Administrative Assistant, Janice H. Levin Building, 94 Rockafeller Road, Piscataway, NJ 08854-8054. *Phone:* 732-445-5973. *Fax:* 732-445-2830. *E-mail:* mhrm@ rci.rutgers.edu.

Saint Peter's College
MBA Programs

Jersey City, New Jersey

Phone: 201-915-9203 **Fax:** 201-432-6241 **E-mail:** camorino@spc.edu

Business Program(s) Web Site: http://grad.spc.edu

DEGREES MBA • MS

MBA—Master of Business Administration in Finance Full-time and part-time. At least 48 total credits required. 12 to 60 months to complete program. *Concentration:* finance.

MBA—Master of Business Administration in International Business Full-time and part-time. At least 48 total credits required. 12 to 60 months to complete program. *Concentration:* international business.

MBA—Master of Business Administration in Management Full-time and part-time. At least 48 total credits required. 12 to 60 months to complete program. *Concentration:* management.

Saint Peter's College (continued)

MBA—Master of Business Administration in Management Information Systems Full-time and part-time. At least 48 total credits required. 12 to 60 months to complete program. *Concentration:* management information systems.

MBA—Master of Business Administration in Marketing Full-time and part-time. At least 48 total credits required. 12 to 60 months to complete program. *Concentration:* marketing.

MS—Master of Science in Accountancy Full-time and part-time. At least 30 total credits required. 10 to 60 months to complete program. *Concentration:* accounting.

RESOURCES AND SERVICES 295 on-campus PCs are available to graduate business students. Access to Internet/World Wide Web available. *Personal computer requirements:* Graduate business students are not required to have a personal computer. *Placement services include:* Alumni network, job search course, career counseling/planning, electronic job bank, resume referral, career fairs, and resume preparation.

Application Contact Candace Amorino, Coordinator of Graduate Admissions, 2641 Kennedy Boulevard, Jersey City, NJ 07306-5997. *Phone:* 201-915-9203. *Fax:* 201-432-6241. *E-mail:* camorino@spc.edu.

See full description on page 682.

Seton Hall University
Stillman School of Business

South Orange, New Jersey

Phone: 973-761-9262 **Fax:** 973-761-9208 **E-mail:** busgrad@shu.edu

Business Program(s) Web Site: http://www.business.shu.edu/

Graduate Business Unit Enrollment *Total:* 465 (64 full-time; 401 part-time; 168 women; 15 international). *Average Age:* 27.

Graduate Business Faculty *Total:* 67 (53 full-time; 14 part-time).

Admissions *Applied:* 218. *Admitted:* 102. *Enrolled:* 96. *Average GMAT:* 560. *Average GPA:* 3.35

Academic Calendar Semesters.

Accreditation AACSB—The Association to Advance Collegiate Schools of Business.

After Graduation (Class of 2006–07) *Average starting salary:* $85,000.

DEGREES JD/MBA • MBA • MBA/INR • MBA/MSN • MS

JD/MBA—Juris Doctor/Master of Business Administration Full-time. Must apply and be accepted into Seton Hall Law School and receive permission from Seton Hall Law School to enter the joint JD/MBA program. 128 to 131 total credits required. 48 to 60 months to complete program. *Concentrations:* accounting, finance, international business, management, management information systems, marketing, pharmaceutical management, sports/entertainment management.

MBA—Master of Business Administration Full-time and part-time. 42 to 57 total credits required. 18 to 60 months to complete program. *Concentrations:* accounting, combined degrees, finance, international business, management, management information systems, marketing, pharmaceutical management, sports/entertainment management.

MBA/INR—MBA/MADIR Part-time. Must apply and be accepted into the MBA Program and the Whitehead School of Diplomacy and International Relations. 60 to 63 total credits required. 24 to 60 months to complete program. *Concentrations:* accounting, finance, international business, management, management information systems, marketing, pharmaceutical management, sports/entertainment management.

MBA/MSN—Master of Business Administration/Master of Science in Nursing Full-time and part-time. 54 total credits required. 24 to 60 months to complete program. *Concentration:* health administration.

MS—Master of Science in Accounting Full-time and part-time. 24 to 36 total credits required. 12 to 60 months to complete program. *Concentration:* accounting.

MS—Master of Science in Professional Accounting Full-time and part-time. This program is open only to students that hold a Bachelor of Science in Accounting. 24 to 30 total credits required. 12 to 60 months to complete program. *Concentration:* accounting.

MS—Master of Science in Taxation Full-time and part-time. Distance learning option. 24 to 30 total credits required. 12 to 60 months to complete program. *Concentration:* taxation.

RESOURCES AND SERVICES 250 on-campus PCs are available to graduate business students. Access to Internet/World Wide Web, online (class) registration, and online grade reports available. *Personal computer requirements:* Graduate business students are strongly recommended to purchase or lease a personal computer. *Special opportunities include:* An international exchange program and an internship program are available. *Placement services include:* Alumni network, career placement, career counseling/planning, electronic job bank, career fairs, job interviews arranged, resume preparation, and career library.

EXPENSES *Tuition:* Full-time: $21,336. *Tuition (international):* Full-time: $21,336. Part-time: $889 per credit. *Required fees:* Full-time: $610. Part-time: $185 per semester.

FINANCIAL AID (2007–08) 36 students received aid, including grants, loans, and research assistantships. Aid is available to part-time students. *Financial aid application deadline:* 6/1.

Financial Aid Contact LaSaundra Floyd, Director of Financial Aid, Financial Aid Office, Department of Enrollment Services/Bayley Hall, 400 South Orange Avenue, South Orange, NJ 07079. *Phone:* 973-761-9350. *Fax:* 973-761-7954. *E-mail:* floydlas@shu.edu.

INTERNATIONAL STUDENTS 3% of students enrolled are international students. *Services and facilities:* Counseling/support services, ESL/language courses, Housing location assistance, International student organization, Language tutoring, Orientation, Visa Services. Financial aid is available to international students. *Required with application:* TOEFL with recommended score of 254 (computer), 607 (paper), or 102 (Internet); proof of adequate funds; proof of health/immunizations. *Recommended with application:* IELT with recommended score of 6.

International Student Contact Maria Soares, Director, Office of International Programs, Office of International Programs, 400 South Orange Avenue, Fahey Hall Room 128, South Orange, NJ 07079. *Phone:* 973-761-9072. *Fax:* 973-275-2383. *E-mail:* oip@shu.edu.

APPLICATION *Required:* GMAT, application form, baccalaureate/first degree, essay, 1 letter of recommendation, personal statement, resume/curriculum vitae, transcripts of college work. *Recommended:* Work experience. *Application fee:* $75. Applications for domestic and international students are processed on a rolling basis.

Application Contact Catherine Bianchi, Director of Graduate Admissions, 400 South Orange Avenue, Jubilee Hall Room 515, South Orange, NJ 07079-2692. *Phone:* 973-761-9262. *Fax:* 973-761-9208. *E-mail:* busgrad@shu.edu.

See full description on page 686.

Stevens Institute of Technology
Wesley J. Howe School of Technology Management

Hoboken, New Jersey

Phone: 201-216-5550 **Fax:** 201-216-5385 **E-mail:** lex.mccusker@stevens.edu

Business Program(s) Web Site: http://howe.stevens.edu

Graduate Business Unit Enrollment *Total:* 1,463 (189 full-time; 1,274 part-time; 445 women; 326 international). *Average Age:* 33.

Graduate Business Faculty *Total:* 98 (42 full-time; 56 part-time).

Admissions *Applied:* 804. *Admitted:* 566. *Enrolled:* 403. *Average GMAT:* 580. *Average GPA:* 3.0

Academic Calendar Semesters.

DEGREES EMBA • MBA • MS • MSIS • MSM • MTM

EMBA—Executive Master of Business Administration in Technology Management Full-time and part-time. Distance learning option. 5 years of management experience required. 60 total credits required. 24 to 72 months to complete program. *Concentrations:* general MBA, information systems, other, technology management, telecommunications management.

MBA—Master of Business Administration in Technology Management Full-time and part-time. Distance learning option. GMAT. 60 total credits required. 24 to 72 months to complete program. *Concentrations:* entrepreneurship, financial engineering, financial information systems, general MBA, information management, information technology, other, pharmaceutical management, project management, technology management, telecommunications management.

MS—Master of Science in Telecommunications Management Full-time and part-time. Distance learning option. 2 semesters of calculus required. At least 36 total credits required. 12 to 36 months to complete program. *Concentrations:* combined degrees, other, project management, telecommunications management.

MSIS—Master of Science in Information Systems Full-time and part-time. Distance learning option. 1 to 2 years work experience. At least 36 total credits required. 12 to 36 months to complete program. *Concentrations:* combined degrees, electronic commerce (E-commerce), financial information systems, health care, information management, other, pharmaceutical management, project management, telecommunications management.

MSM—Master of Science in Management Full-time and part-time. Distance learning option. Microeconomics and introductory calculus required. At least 36 total credits required. 12 to 36 months to complete program. *Concentrations:* health care, information management, management, other, pharmaceutical management, project management, technology management.

MTM—Master of Technology Management Part-time. Distance learning option. 5-7 years of industry experience required. 42 total credits required. 21 months to complete program. *Concentration:* technology management.

RESOURCES AND SERVICES 35 on-campus PCs are available to graduate business students. Access to Internet/World Wide Web, online (class) registration, and online grade reports available. *Personal computer requirements:* Graduate business students are strongly recommended to purchase or lease a personal computer. *Special opportunities include:* An international exchange program and an internship program are available. *Placement services include:* Alumni network, career placement, career counseling/planning, electronic job bank, resume referral, career fairs, job interviews arranged, resume preparation, and career library.

EXPENSES *Tuition:* Full-time: $15,930. *Tuition (international):* Full-time: $15,930. *Required fees:* Full-time: $310. Part-time: $310 per year. *Graduate housing:* Room and board costs vary by number of occupants, type of accommodation, and type of board plan.

FINANCIAL AID (2007–08) Fellowships, grants, loans, research assistantships, scholarships, teaching assistantships, and work study.

Financial Aid Contact Annette Feliciano, Assistant Vice President of Student Services, Castle Point on the Hudson, Hoboken, NJ 07030. *Phone:* 201-216-8142. *Fax:* 201-216-8050. *E-mail:* annette.feliciano@stevens.edu.

INTERNATIONAL STUDENTS 22% of students enrolled are international students. *Services and facilities:* Counseling/support services, ESL/language courses, Housing location assistance, International student organization, Language tutoring, Visa Services. Financial aid is not available to international students. *Required with application:* TOEFL with recommended score of 210 (computer) or 550 (paper); proof of adequate funds; proof of health/immunizations.

International Student Contact Jennifer Marsalis, Director of International Student and Scholar Services, Castle Point on the Hudson, Hoboken, NJ 07030. *Phone:* 201-216-5189. *Fax:* 201-216-8333. *E-mail:* jmarsali@stevens.edu.

APPLICATION *Required:* Application form, baccalaureate/first degree, 2 letters of recommendation, transcripts of college work. School will accept GMAT. *Recommended:* Personal statement, resume/curriculum vitae, 2 years of work experience. *Application fee:* $60. Applications for domestic and international students are processed on a rolling basis.

Application Contact Dr. Lex McCusker, Dean, Castle Point on the Hudson, 408 Babbio Center, Hoboken, NJ 07030. *Phone:* 201-216-5550. *Fax:* 201-216-5385. *E-mail:* lex.mccusker@stevens.edu.

Thomas Edison State College
School of Business and Management
Trenton, New Jersey

Phone: 888-442-8372 **Fax:** 609-984-8447 **E-mail:** admissions@tesc.edu

Business Program(s) Web Site: http://www.tesc.edu/1485.php

Graduate Business Unit Enrollment *Total:* 298 (298 part-time; 116 women; 8 international). *Average Age:* 41.

Admissions *Applied:* 99.

Academic Calendar Semesters.

DEGREES MSHR • MSM

MSHR—Human Resource Management Full-time and part-time. Distance learning option. At least 36 total credits required. *Concentration:* human resources management.

MSM—Organizational Leadership Full-time and part-time. Distance learning option. At least 36 total credits required. *Concentration:* leadership.

MSM—Public Sector Auditing Full-time and part-time. Distance learning option. At least 36 total credits required. *Concentration:* general MBA.

MSM—Public Service Leadership Full-time and part-time. Distance learning option. At least 36 total credits required. *Concentration:* leadership.

RESOURCES AND SERVICES Access to online (class) registration and online grade reports available. *Personal computer requirements:* Graduate business students are strongly recommended to purchase or lease a personal computer. *Placement services include:* Alumni network.

EXPENSES *Tuition (state resident):* Part-time: $440 per credit. *Tuition (nonresident):* Part-time: $440 per credit. *Tuition (international):* Part-time: $440 per credit.

Financial Aid Contact Mr. James Owens, Director of Financial Aid and Veterans Affairs, 101 West State Street, Trenton, NJ 08608-1176. *Phone:* 609-633-9658. *Fax:* 609-633-6489. *E-mail:* finaid@tesc.edu.

INTERNATIONAL STUDENTS 3% of students enrolled are international students. Financial aid is not available to international students. *Required with application:* TOEFL with recommended score of 213 (computer) or 550 (paper).

International Student Contact Mr. David Hoftiezer, Director of Admissions, 101 West State Street, Trenton, NJ 08608-1176. *Phone:* 888-442-8372. *Fax:* 609-984-8447. *E-mail:* admissions@tesc.edu.

APPLICATION *Required:* Application form, baccalaureate/first degree, essay, 2 letters of recommendation, personal statement, resume/curriculum vitae, transcripts of college work, 3 years of work experience. *Application fee:* $75. *Deadlines:* 8/15 for fall, 11/15 for winter, 2/15 for spring, 5/15 for summer, 8/15 for fall (international), 11/15 for winter (international), 2/15 for spring (international), 5/15 for summer (international).

Application Contact Mr. David Hoftiezer, Director of Admissions, 101 West State Street, Trenton, NJ 08608-1176. *Phone:* 888-442-8372. *Fax:* 609-984-8447. *E-mail:* admissions@tesc.edu.

William Paterson University of New Jersey

Christos M. Cotsakos College of Business

Wayne, New Jersey

Phone: 973-720-2764 **Fax:** 973-720-2035 **E-mail:** adenirant@wpunj.edu

Business Program(s) Web Site: http://www.wpunj.edu/cob/COB_new/mbaprogram/geninformation.html

Graduate Business Unit Enrollment *Total:* 69 (23 full-time; 46 part-time; 29 women; 5 international).

Graduate Business Faculty 41 full-time.

Admissions *Applied:* 64. *Admitted:* 19. *Enrolled:* 11. *Average GMAT:* 500. *Average GPA:* 3.1

Academic Calendar Semesters.

Accreditation AACSB—The Association to Advance Collegiate Schools of Business.

DEGREES MBA

MBA—Master of Business Administration *Concentrations:* accounting, finance, marketing.

MBA—Master of Business Administration Full-time and part-time. Up to 48 total credits required. 24 to 72 months to complete program. *Concentration:* general MBA.

RESOURCES AND SERVICES Access to Internet/World Wide Web, online (class) registration, and online grade reports available. *Personal computer requirements:* Graduate business students are strongly recommended to purchase or lease a personal computer. *Special opportunities include:* An internship program is available. *Placement services include:* Alumni network, career placement, job search course, career counseling/planning, electronic job bank, resume referral, career fairs, job interviews arranged, resume preparation, and career library.

EXPENSES *Tuition (state resident):* Full-time: $9756. Part-time: $542 per credit hour. *Tuition (nonresident):* Full-time: $15,138. Part-time: $841 per credit hour. *Tuition (international):* Full-time: $15,138. Part-time: $841 per credit hour. *Typical graduate housing cost:* $9650 (including board), $6500 (room only).

FINANCIAL AID (2007–08) Grants, loans, research assistantships, and teaching assistantships. *Financial aid application deadline:* 4/1.

Financial Aid Contact Kenya Easley-Mosby, Assistant Director, 300 Pompton Road, Raubinger Hall, Wayne, NJ 07470-8420. *Phone:* 973-720-3578. *Fax:* 973-720-2035. *E-mail:* mosbyk@wpunj.edu.

INTERNATIONAL STUDENTS 7% of students enrolled are international students. *Services and facilities:* Counseling/support services, ESL/language courses, Housing location assistance, International student housing, International student organization, Orientation, Visa Services. Financial aid is available to international students. *Required with application:* TOEFL with recommended score of 213 (computer), 550 (paper), or 80 (Internet); proof of adequate funds; proof of health/immunizations.

International Student Contact Cinza Richardson, Director, Wayne Hall, 300 Pompton Road, Wayne, NJ 07470-8420. *Phone:* 973-720-2976. *Fax:* 973-720-2336. *E-mail:* richardsonc@wpunj.edu.

APPLICATION *Required:* GMAT, application form, baccalaureate/first degree, essay, 2 letters of recommendation, personal statement, resume/curriculum vitae, transcripts of college work. *Application fee:* $50. Applications for domestic and international students are processed on a rolling basis.

Application Contact Tinu O. Adeniran, Assistant Director, 300 Pompton Road, Raubinger Hall, Wayne, NJ 07470-8420. *Phone:* 973-720-2764. *Fax:* 973-720-2035. *E-mail:* adenirant@wpunj.edu.

NEW MEXICO

College of Santa Fe

Department of Business Administration

Santa Fe, New Mexico

Phone: 505-855-7281 **Fax:** 505-262-5595 **E-mail:** jsaya@csf.edu

Business Program(s) Web Site: http://www.csf.edu/evening_and_weekend

Graduate Business Unit Enrollment *Total:* 93.

Graduate Business Faculty *Total:* 28 (3 full-time; 25 part-time).

Academic Calendar Five 9-week terms.

DEGREE MBA

MBA—Master of Business Administration Full-time and part-time. At least 36 total credits required. 12 to 60 months to complete program. *Concentrations:* finance, human resources management.

RESOURCES AND SERVICES 84 on-campus PCs are available to graduate business students. Access to Internet/World Wide Web, online (class) registration, and online grade reports available. *Personal computer requirements:* Graduate business students are not required to have a personal computer. *Placement services include:* Alumni network, career counseling/planning, and resume preparation.

EXPENSES *Tuition:* Part-time: $385 per semester hour. *Tuition (international):* Part-time: $385 per semester hour. *Required fees:* Part-time: $25 per semester hour. *Typical graduate housing cost:* $8458 (including board), $4565 (room only).

FINANCIAL AID (2007–08) Scholarships. Aid is available to part-time students.

Financial Aid Contact Ms. Jill Robertson, Director, Student Financial Services, 1600 St. Michael's Drive, Santa Fe, NM 87505. *Phone:* 505-473-6454. *Fax:* 505-473-6464. *E-mail:* sfs@csf.edu.

INTERNATIONAL STUDENTS *Services and facilities:* Counseling/support services. Financial aid is available to international students. *Required with application:* TOEFL with recommended score of 213 (computer), 550 (paper), or 79 (Internet); proof of adequate funds.

International Student Contact Mr. Joseph Fitzpatrick, Interim Dean of Enrollment, 1600 St. Michael's Drive, Santa Fe, NM 87505-7634. *Phone:* 505-473-6133. *Fax:* 505-473-6129. *E-mail:* admissions@csf.edu.

APPLICATION *Required:* Application form, baccalaureate/first degree, interview, 2 letters of recommendation, transcripts of college work. *Recommended:* Work experience. *Application fee:* $35. Applications for domestic and international students are processed on a rolling basis.

Application Contact Mr. James Saya, Chair, Business Administration Department, 1600 St. Michael's Drive, Santa Fe, NM 87505-7634. *Phone:* 505-855-7281. *Fax:* 505-262-5595. *E-mail:* jsaya@csf.edu.

Eastern New Mexico University

College of Business

Portales, New Mexico

Phone: 505-562-2352 **Fax:** 505-562-2252 **E-mail:** john.stockmyer@enmu.edu

Business Program(s) Web Site: http://www.enmu.edu/academics/undergrad/colleges/business/graduate/index.shtml

Accreditation ACBSP—The American Council of Business Schools and Programs.

DEGREE MBA/Diploma

MBA/Diploma—Master of Business Administration Full-time and part-time. Distance learning option. 2 years of work experience preferred. At least 33 total credits required. 24 to 72 months to complete program. *Concentration:* general MBA.

RESOURCES AND SERVICES 200 on-campus PCs are available to graduate business students. Access to Internet/World Wide Web, online (class) registration, and online grade reports available. *Personal computer requirements:* Graduate business students are strongly recommended to purchase or lease a personal computer. *Placement services include:* Alumni network, career counseling/planning, electronic job bank, resume referral, career fairs, resume preparation, and career library.

Application Contact Dr. John L. Stockmyer, Assistant Professor of Marketing, Station 49, Portales, NM 88130. *Phone:* 505-562-2352. *Fax:* 505-562-2252. *E-mail:* john.stockmyer@enmu.edu.

New Mexico Highlands University

School of Business

Las Vegas, New Mexico

Phone: 505-454-3004 **Fax:** 505-454-3354 **E-mail:** charlesswim@nmhu.edu

Business Program(s) Web Site: http://www.nmhu.edu/business/

Graduate Business Unit Enrollment *Total:* 197 (87 full-time; 110 part-time; 114 women; 37 international).

Graduate Business Faculty *Total:* 16 (14 full-time; 2 part-time).

Admissions *Applied:* 155. *Admitted:* 147. *Enrolled:* 104. *Average GPA:* 3.3

Academic Calendar Semesters.

Accreditation ACBSP—The American Council of Business Schools and Programs.

After Graduation (Class of 2006–07) *Employed within 3 months of graduation:* 80%. *Average starting salary:* $35,000.

DEGREE MBA

MBA—Master of Business Administration Full-time and part-time. Distance learning option. Minimum of 37 months to complete program. *Concentrations:* human resources management, information technology, international business, nonprofit management.

RESOURCES AND SERVICES 42 on-campus PCs are available to graduate business students. Access to Internet/World Wide Web, online (class) registration, and online grade reports available. *Personal computer requirements:* Graduate business students are strongly recommended to purchase or lease a personal computer. *Special opportunities include:* An internship program is available. *Placement services include:* Alumni network, career placement, career counseling/planning, electronic job bank, resume referral, career fairs, job interviews arranged, resume preparation, and career library.

EXPENSES *Tuition (state resident):* Full-time: $2880. Part-time: $120 per credit hour. *Tuition (nonresident):* Full-time: $3660. Part-time: $120 per credit hour. *Tuition (international):* Full-time: $5300. Part-time: $120 per credit hour. *Graduate housing:* Room and board costs vary by number of occupants, type of accommodation, and type of board plan. *Typical cost:* $8000 (including board).

FINANCIAL AID (2007–08) 8 students received aid, including fellowships, loans, research assistantships, scholarships, teaching assistantships, and work study. *Financial aid application deadline:* 3/1.

Financial Aid Contact Eileen Sedillo, Director of Financial Aid, Felix Martinez Building, Las Vegas, NM 87701. *Phone:* 800-379-4038. *Fax:* 505-454-3398. *E-mail:* sedillo_e@nmhu.edu.

INTERNATIONAL STUDENTS 19% of students enrolled are international students. *Services and facilities:* Counseling/support services, ESL/language courses, Housing location assistance, International student organization, Orientation, Visa Services. Financial aid is available to

international students. *Required with application:* TOEFL with recommended score of 525 (paper); proof of adequate funds.

International Student Contact Tina Clayton, Director of International Programs, Office of International Studies, Las Vegas, NM 87701. *Phone:* 505-454-3058. *Fax:* 505-454-3511. *E-mail:* eclayton@nmhu.edu.

APPLICATION *Required:* Application form, baccalaureate/first degree, 2 letters of recommendation, personal statement, resume/curriculum vitae, transcripts of college work. *Recommended:* Essay, work experience. *Application fee:* $15. Applications for domestic and international students are processed on a rolling basis.

Application Contact Dr. Charles H Swim, Interim Dean, Box 9000, Las Vegas, NM 87701. *Phone:* 505-454-3004. *Fax:* 505-454-3354. *E-mail:* charlesswim@nmhu.edu.

New Mexico State University

College of Business

Las Cruces, New Mexico

Phone: 575-646-3025 **Fax:** 575-646-7977 **E-mail:** mba@nmsu.edu

Business Program(s) Web Site: http://mba.nmsu.edu/

Graduate Business Unit Enrollment *Total:* 329 (177 full-time; 152 part-time; 147 women; 58 international). *Average Age:* 33.

Graduate Business Faculty 52 full-time.

Admissions *Applied:* 169. *Admitted:* 143. *Enrolled:* 100. *Average GMAT:* 492. *Average GPA:* 3.73

Academic Calendar Semesters.

Accreditation AACSB—The Association to Advance Collegiate Schools of Business.

After Graduation (Class of 2006–07) *Employed within 3 months of graduation:* 11%. *Average starting salary:* $40,000.

DEGREES M Acct • MA • MBA • MS

M Acct—Master of Accountancy Full-time and part-time. *Concentrations:* accounting, information systems.

MA—Master of Arts in Economics *Concentration:* economics.

MBA—Master of Business Administration Full-time and part-time. Required: minimum GMAT score of 400 and minimum score of 1400 when GPA is combined with GMAT. 36 to 60 total credits required. 12 to 48 months to complete program. *Concentrations:* agribusiness, information systems, international business.

MS—Master of Experimental Statistics *Concentration:* statistics.

RESOURCES AND SERVICES 1,000 on-campus PCs are available to graduate business students. Access to Internet/World Wide Web, online (class) registration, and online grade reports available. *Personal computer requirements:* Graduate business students are strongly recommended to purchase or lease a personal computer. *Special opportunities include:* An international exchange program is available. *Placement services include:* Alumni network, career placement, job search course, career counseling/planning, electronic job bank, resume referral, career fairs, job interviews arranged, resume preparation, and career library.

FINANCIAL AID (2007–08) Fellowships, grants, loans, research assistantships, scholarships, teaching assistantships, and work study. Aid is available to part-time students. *Financial aid application deadline:* 3/1.

Financial Aid Contact Director, Financial Aid, PO Box 30001, Department 5100, Las Cruces, NM 88003. *Phone:* 575-646-2447. *Fax:* 575-646-7381.

INTERNATIONAL STUDENTS 18% of students enrolled are international students. *Services and facilities:* Counseling/support services, ESL/language courses, Housing location assistance, International student housing, International student organization, Language tutoring, Orientation, Visa Services, Sponsored student assistance. Financial aid is not

New Mexico State University (continued)

available to international students. *Required with application:* TOEFL with recommended score of 197 (computer) or 530 (paper).

International Student Contact Ms. Mary Jaspers, Assistant Director, Foreign Students Services, International Programs Office, Box 3567, Las Cruces, NM 88003. *Phone:* 575-646-3199. *Fax:* 575-646-2558. *E-mail:* marjaspe@nmsu.edu.

APPLICATION *Required:* GMAT, application form, baccalaureate/first degree, resume/curriculum vitae, transcripts of college work. *Application fee:* $30, $50 (international). *Deadlines:* 7/1 for fall, 11/1 for spring, 4/1 for summer, 3/1 for fall (international), 10/1 for spring (international).

Application Contact Bobbie Green, Director, MBA Program, 109D Guthrie Hall, Las Cruces, NM 88003. *Phone:* 575-646-3025. *Fax:* 575-646-7977. *E-mail:* mba@nmsu.edu.

University of New Mexico
Robert O. Anderson Graduate School of Management

Albuquerque, New Mexico

Phone: 505-277-3147 **Fax:** 505-277-9356 **E-mail:** chastain@mgt.unm.edu

Business Program(s) Web Site: http://www.mgt.unm.edu

Graduate Business Unit Enrollment *Total:* 652 (652 part-time; 304 women; 37 international). *Average Age:* 32.

Graduate Business Faculty *Total:* 98 (59 full-time; 39 part-time).

Admissions *Applied:* 305. *Admitted:* 193. *Enrolled:* 153. *Average GMAT:* 544. *Average GPA:* 3.5

Academic Calendar Semesters.

Accreditation AACSB—The Association to Advance Collegiate Schools of Business.

After Graduation (Class of 2006–07) *Employed within 3 months of graduation:* 85%. *Average starting salary:* $53,025.

DEGREES JD/MBA • MBA • MBA/MA • MS

JD/MBA—Juris Doctor/Master of Business Administration Full-time. At least 116 total credits required. 48 to 96 months to complete program. *Concentration:* management.

MBA—Executive Master of Business Administration Full-time. At least 50 total credits required. 24 months to complete program. *Concentration:* management.

MBA—Master of Business Administration Full-time and part-time. At least 48 total credits required. 12 to 84 months to complete program. *Concentrations:* accounting, business policy/strategy, entrepreneurship, finance, human resources management, information management, international business, Latin American business studies, management, management information systems, marketing, nonprofit management, operations management, organizational behavior/development, public policy and administration, taxation, technology management.

MBA/MA—Master of Business Administration/Master of Arts in Latin American Studies Full-time and part-time. At least 63 total credits required. 53 to 72 months to complete program. *Concentration:* international management.

MS—Master of Science in Accounting Full-time and part-time. 33 total credits required. 24 to 60 months to complete program. *Concentration:* accounting.

RESOURCES AND SERVICES 110 on-campus PCs are available to graduate business students. Access to Internet/World Wide Web, online (class) registration, and online grade reports available. *Personal computer requirements:* Graduate business students are not required to have a personal computer. *Special opportunities include:* An international exchange program and an internship program are available. *Placement services include:* Career placement, job search course, career counseling/planning, electronic job bank, resume referral, career fairs, job interviews arranged, resume preparation, and career library.

EXPENSES *Tuition (state resident):* Part-time: $265 per credit hour. *Tuition (nonresident):* Part-time: $696 per credit hour. *Tuition (international):* Part-time: $696 per credit hour. *Required fees:* Part-time: $170 per semester. *Graduate housing:* Room and board costs vary by campus location, number of occupants, type of accommodation, and type of board plan. *Typical cost:* $6800 (including board).

FINANCIAL AID (2007–08) 70 students received aid, including fellowships, loans, research assistantships, scholarships, and teaching assistantships. *Financial aid application deadline:* 5/1.

Financial Aid Contact Mr. Ron S. Martinez, Director, MSC 06 3610, 1 University of New Mexico, Albuquerque, NM 87131-0001. *Phone:* 505-277-5017. *Fax:* 505-277-6326. *E-mail:* ronm@unm.edu.

INTERNATIONAL STUDENTS 6% of students enrolled are international students. *Services and facilities:* Counseling/support services, ESL/language courses, Housing location assistance, International student organization, Orientation, Visa Services. Financial aid is not available to international students. *Required with application:* TOEFL with recommended score of 213 (computer) or 550 (paper); proof of adequate funds; proof of health/immunizations.

International Student Contact Ms. Cynthia Stuart, Director of Admissions, MSC 06 3720, 1 University of New Mexico, Albuquerque, NM 87131-0001. *Phone:* 505-277-5829. *Fax:* 505-277-6686. *E-mail:* cstuart@unm.edu.

APPLICATION *Required:* GMAT, application form, baccalaureate/first degree, essay, 3 letters of recommendation, personal statement, resume/curriculum vitae, transcripts of college work. *Recommended:* 2 years of work experience. *Application fee:* $50. Applications for domestic and international students are processed on a rolling basis.

Application Contact Ms. Loyola Chastain, Graduate Programs Manager, Albuquerque, NM 87131-1221. *Phone:* 505-277-3147. *Fax:* 505-277-9356. *E-mail:* chastain@mgt.unm.edu.

University of Phoenix–New Mexico Campus
College of Graduate Business and Management

Albuquerque, New Mexico

Phone: 480-317-6200 **Fax:** 480-643-1479 **E-mail:** beth.barilla@phoenix.edu

Business Program(s) Web Site: http://www.phoenix.edu

DEGREES M Mgt • MA • MBA

M Mgt—Human Resource Management Full-time. At least 45 total credits required. *Concentration:* human resources management.

M Mgt—Master of Management Full-time. At least 39 total credits required. *Concentration:* management.

MA—Master of Arts in Organizational Management Full-time. At least 40 total credits required. *Concentration:* organizational management.

MBA—Accounting Full-time. At least 54 total credits required. *Concentration:* accounting.

MBA—Global Management Full-time. At least 45 total credits required. *Concentration:* international management.

MBA—Human Resource Management Full-time. At least 45 total credits required. *Concentration:* human resources management.

MBA—Marketing Full-time. At least 45 total credits required. *Concentration:* marketing.

MBA—Public Administration Full-time. At least 45 total credits required. *Concentration:* public policy and administration.

MBA—e-Business Full-time. At least 45 total credits required. *Concentration:* electronic commerce (E-commerce).

MBA—Master of Business Administration Full-time. At least 45 total credits required. *Concentration:* administration.

RESOURCES AND SERVICES Access to online grade reports available. *Personal computer requirements:* Graduate business students are strongly recommended to purchase or lease a personal computer. *Placement services include:* Alumni network.

Application Contact Beth Barilla, Associate Vice President of Student Admissions and Services, Mail Stop AA-K101, 4615 East Elwood Street, Phoenix, AZ 85040-1958. *Phone:* 480-317-6200. *Fax:* 480-643-1479. *E-mail:* beth.barilla@phoenix.edu.

NEW YORK

Adelphi University
School of Business
Garden City, New York

Phone: 516-877-3050 **Fax:** 516-877-3244 **E-mail:** murphy2@adelphi.edu

Business Program(s) Web Site: http://business.adelphi.edu/gbus

Graduate Business Unit Enrollment *Total:* 292 (88 full-time; 204 part-time; 142 women; 54 international).

Graduate Business Faculty *Total:* 67 (36 full-time; 31 part-time).

Admissions *Applied:* 220. *Admitted:* 99. *Enrolled:* 78. *Average GMAT:* 460. *Average GPA:* 2.8

Academic Calendar Semesters.

After Graduation (Class of 2006–07) *Employed within 3 months of graduation:* 98%. *Average starting salary:* $70,000.

DEGREE MBA

MBA—Master of Business Administration Full-time and part-time. 33 to 66 total credits required. 12 to 72 months to complete program. *Concentrations:* electronic commerce (E-commerce), finance, health administration, human resources management, information systems, management, marketing.

RESOURCES AND SERVICES 598 on-campus PCs are available to graduate business students. Access to Internet/World Wide Web, online (class) registration, and online grade reports available. *Personal computer requirements:* Graduate business students are strongly recommended to purchase or lease a personal computer. *Special opportunities include:* An internship program is available. *Placement services include:* Alumni network, career placement, career counseling/planning, electronic job bank, resume referral, career fairs, job interviews arranged, resume preparation, and career library.

EXPENSES *Tuition:* Part-time: $850 per credit. *Tuition (international):* Part-time: $850 per credit. *Typical graduate housing cost:* $9000 (including board).

FINANCIAL AID (2007–08) 55 students received aid, including research assistantships and scholarships. Aid is available to part-time students. *Financial aid application deadline:* 6/1.

Financial Aid Contact Ms. Kathy Lemmon, Manager, Office of Student Financial Services, Collections, Garden City, NY 11530. *Phone:* 516-877-3073. *Fax:* 516-877-3039.

INTERNATIONAL STUDENTS 18% of students enrolled are international students. *Services and facilities:* Counseling/support services, ESL/language courses, Housing location assistance, International student organization, Orientation, Visa Services. Financial aid is available to international students. *Required with application:* IELT with recommended score of 6.5; TOEFL with recommended score of 213 (computer), 550 (paper), or 80 (Internet); proof of adequate funds; proof of health/immunizations.

International Student Contact Wendy Palczynski, Assistant Director, International Student Services, One South Avenue, Garden City, NY 11530. *Phone:* 516-877-4990. *E-mail:* palczynski@adelphi.edu.

APPLICATION *Required:* GMAT, application form, baccalaureate/first degree, essay, 2 letters of recommendation, transcripts of college work. School will accept GRE. *Recommended:* Personal statement, resume/curriculum vitae, work experience. *Application fee:* $50. Applications for domestic and international students are processed on a rolling basis.

Application Contact Mrs. Christine Murphy, Director of University Admissions, Office of Admission, 1 South Avenue, Garden City, NY 11530. *Phone:* 516-877-3050. *Fax:* 516-877-3244. *E-mail:* murphy2@adelphi.edu.

See full description on page 560.

Alfred University
College of Business
Alfred, New York

Phone: 607-871-2115 **Fax:** 607-871-2198

Business Program(s) Web Site: http://business.alfred.edu/mba.html

Graduate Business Unit Enrollment *Total:* 14 (8 full-time; 6 part-time; 6 women). *Average Age:* 28.

Graduate Business Faculty 10 full-time.

Admissions *Average GMAT:* 517. *Average GPA:* 3.06

Academic Calendar Semesters.

Accreditation AACSB—The Association to Advance Collegiate Schools of Business.

After Graduation (Class of 2006–07) *Employed within 3 months of graduation:* 95%. *Average starting salary:* $47,889.

DEGREE MBA

MBA—Master of Business Administration Full-time and part-time. 30 to 61 total credits required. 10 to 72 months to complete program. *Concentration:* general MBA.

RESOURCES AND SERVICES 390 on-campus PCs are available to graduate business students. Access to Internet/World Wide Web, online (class) registration, and online grade reports available. *Personal computer requirements:* Graduate business students are not required to have a personal computer. *Placement services include:* Alumni network, career counseling/planning, electronic job bank, resume referral, career fairs, resume preparation, and career library.

EXPENSES *Tuition:* Part-time: $680 per credit hour. *Required fees:* Full-time: $140.

FINANCIAL AID (2007–08) 8 students received aid, including research assistantships.

Financial Aid Contact Earl Pierce, Director of Student Financial Aid, 26 North Main Street, Alumni Hall, Alfred, NY 14802. *Phone:* 607-871-2159. *Fax:* 607-871-2198. *E-mail:* pierce@alfred.edu.

INTERNATIONAL STUDENTS *Services and facilities:* Counseling/support services, ESL/language courses, Housing location assistance, International student organization, Orientation. Financial aid is available to international students. *Required with application:* IELT with recommended score of 6.5; TOEFL with recommended score of 243 (computer), 590 (paper), or 90 (Internet); proof of adequate funds; proof of health/immunizations.

International Student Contact Dean of Students, One Saxon Drive, Alfred, NY 14802. *Phone:* 607-871-2133. *Fax:* 607-871-2339.

Alfred University (continued)

APPLICATION *Required:* GMAT, application form, baccalaureate/first degree, transcripts of college work. *Application fee:* $50. Applications for domestic and international students are processed on a rolling basis.

Application Contact Admissions Office, One Saxon Drive, Alfred, NY 14802. *Phone:* 607-871-2115. *Fax:* 607-871-2198.

See full description on page 562.

Bernard M. Baruch College of the City University of New York

Zicklin School of Business

New York, New York

Phone: 646-312-1300 **Fax:** 646-312-1301 **E-mail:** zicklingradadmissions@baruch.cuny.edu

Business Program(s) Web Site: http://zicklin.baruch.cuny.edu/

Graduate Business Unit Enrollment *Total:* 2,168 (607 full-time; 1,561 part-time; 1,019 women; 1171 international). *Average Age:* 28.

Graduate Business Faculty *Total:* 372 (197 full-time; 175 part-time).

Admissions *Applied:* 1,763. *Admitted:* 1,093. *Enrolled:* 670. *Average GMAT:* 585. *Average GPA:* 3.2

Academic Calendar Semesters.

Accreditation AACSB—The Association to Advance Collegiate Schools of Business.

After Graduation (Class of 2006–07) *Employed within 3 months of graduation:* 83.3%. *Average starting salary:* $75,775.

DEGREES EMBA • JD/MBA • MBA • MS

EMBA—Executive Master of Business Administration Full-time. 57 total credits required. 22 months to complete program. *Concentration:* strategic management.

JD/MBA—Juris Doctor/Master of Business Administration Full-time and part-time. Students must also be accepted into the corresponding programs at New York Law School or Brooklyn Law School. At least 134 total credits required. 42 to 72 months to complete program. *Concentration:* combined degrees.

MBA—Accelerated Part-Time Master of Business Administration Program Part-time. Fall entry only. 57 to 63 total credits required. 28 months to complete program. *Concentrations:* accounting, advertising, electronic commerce (E-commerce), entrepreneurship, finance, general MBA, human resources management, international business, international marketing, management information systems, marketing, marketing research, operations management.

MBA—Master of Business Administration Full-time and part-time. 57 to 75 total credits required. 24 to 72 months to complete program. *Concentrations:* accounting, advertising, economics, electronic commerce (E-commerce), entrepreneurship, finance, general MBA, health care, human resources management, international business, international marketing, management, management information systems, marketing, marketing research, operations management, organizational behavior/development, quantitative analysis, statistics, taxation.

MS—Executive Master of Science in Finance Full-time. At least 30 total credits required. 10 months to complete program. *Concentration:* finance.

MS—Executive Master of Science in Industrial and Labor Relations Part-time. 36 total credits required. 30 to 36 months to complete program. *Concentrations:* human resources management, industrial/labor relations.

MS—Master of Science in Accountancy Full-time and part-time. 31 to 76 total credits required. 18 to 72 months to complete program. *Concentration:* accounting.

MS—Master of Science in Business Computer Information Systems Full-time and part-time. 36 to 53 total credits required. 18 to 72 months to complete program. *Concentration:* information systems.

MS—Master of Science in Marketing Full-time and part-time. 30 total credits required. 18 to 72 months to complete program. *Concentrations:* electronic commerce (E-commerce), international marketing, marketing research.

MS—Master of Science in Quantitative Methods and Modeling Full-time and part-time. Will accept either the GMAT or GRE. 30 to 40 total credits required. 18 to 72 months to complete program. *Concentration:* quantitative analysis.

MS—Master of Science in Statistics Full-time and part-time. Will accept either the GMAT or GRE. 36 to 49 total credits required. 36 to 72 months to complete program. *Concentration:* statistics.

MS—Master of Science in Taxation Full-time and part-time. Will accept either the GMAT or GRE. 30 to 33 total credits required. 30 to 72 months to complete program. *Concentration:* taxation.

RESOURCES AND SERVICES 1,500 on-campus PCs are available to graduate business students. Access to Internet/World Wide Web, online (class) registration, and online grade reports available. *Personal computer requirements:* Graduate business students are strongly recommended to purchase or lease a personal computer. *Special opportunities include:* An international exchange program and an internship program are available. *Placement services include:* Alumni network, career placement, job search course, career counseling/planning, electronic job bank, resume referral, career fairs, job interviews arranged, resume preparation, and career library.

EXPENSES *Tuition (state resident):* Full-time: $8800. Part-time: $400 per credit. *Tuition (nonresident):* Full-time: $18,000. Part-time: $600 per credit. *Tuition (international):* Full-time: $18,000. Part-time: $600 per credit. *Required fees:* Full-time: $1813. Part-time: $156.50 per semester. Tuition and/or fees vary by number of courses or credits taken and academic program.

FINANCIAL AID (2007–08) 104 students received aid, including fellowships, grants, loans, research assistantships, scholarships, teaching assistantships, and work study. Aid is available to part-time students. *Financial aid application deadline:* 4/30.

Financial Aid Contact James Murphy, Director of Financial Aid, 1 Bernard Baruch Way, Box H-0725, New York, NY 10010. *Phone:* 646-312-1360. *Fax:* 646-312-1361. *E-mail:* financial_aid@baruch.cuny.edu.

INTERNATIONAL STUDENTS 54% of students enrolled are international students. *Services and facilities:* Counseling/support services, ESL/language courses, Housing location assistance, International student organization, Orientation, Visa Services, English Communication Immersion Program. Financial aid is available to international students. *Required with application:* TOEFL with recommended score of 250 (computer), 600 (paper), or 100 (Internet); TWE with recommended score of 5; proof of adequate funds; proof of health/immunizations.

International Student Contact Marisa Delacruz, Director, International Student Service Center, 1 Bernard Baruch Way, Box H-880, New York, NY 10010. *Phone:* 646-312-2050. *Fax:* 646-312-2051. *E-mail:* marisa_delacruz@baruch.cuny.edu.

APPLICATION *Required:* GMAT, application form, baccalaureate/first degree, essay, 2 letters of recommendation, personal statement, resume/curriculum vitae, transcripts of college work, 2 years of work experience. *Application fee:* $125. Applications for domestic and international students are processed on a rolling basis.

Application Contact Frances Murphy, Director of Graduate Admissions, 1 Bernard Baruch Way, Box H-820, New York, NY 10010-5585. *Phone:* 646-312-1300. *Fax:* 646-312-1301. *E-mail:* zicklingradadmissions@baruch.cuny.edu.

Canisius College

Richard J. Wehle School of Business

Buffalo, New York

Phone: 716-888-2140 **Fax:** 716-888-2145 **E-mail:** gradbus@canisius.edu

Business Program(s) Web Site: http://www.canisius.edu/mba

Graduate Business Unit Enrollment *Total:* 286 (85 full-time; 201 part-time; 127 women; 26 international). *Average Age:* 29.

Graduate Business Faculty *Total:* 51 (38 full-time; 13 part-time).

Admissions *Applied:* 145. *Admitted:* 106. *Enrolled:* 75. *Average GMAT:* 499. *Average GPA:* 3.06

Academic Calendar Semesters.

Accreditation AACSB—The Association to Advance Collegiate Schools of Business.

After Graduation (Class of 2006–07) *Employed within 3 months of graduation:* 85%. *Average starting salary:* $48,000.

DEGREES MBA

MBA—Master of Business Administration in Professional Accounting Full-time and part-time. 61 total credits required. 24 to 72 months to complete program. *Concentration:* accounting.

MBA—One-Year Master of Business Administration Full-time. 48 total credits required. 12 months to complete program. *Concentrations:* finance, general MBA, international business, marketing.

MBA—Master of Business Administration Full-time and part-time. 48 total credits required. 16 to 60 months to complete program. *Concentrations:* accounting, finance, general MBA, human resources management, information technology, international business, marketing, supply chain management.

RESOURCES AND SERVICES 500 on-campus PCs are available to graduate business students. Access to Internet/World Wide Web, online (class) registration, and online grade reports available. *Personal computer requirements:* Graduate business students are not required to have a personal computer. *Special opportunities include:* An international exchange program and an internship program are available. *Placement services include:* Alumni network, career placement, career counseling/planning, electronic job bank, career fairs, and resume preparation.

EXPENSES *Tuition:* Full-time: $32,574. Part-time: $651 per credit hour. *Required fees:* Full-time: $222. Part-time: $18.50 per credit hour. *Graduate housing:* Room and board costs vary by number of occupants, type of accommodation, and type of board plan. *Typical cost:* $8850 (including board), $7190 (room only).

FINANCIAL AID (2007–08) 10 students received aid, including loans, research assistantships, and scholarships. Aid is available to part-time students. *Financial aid application deadline:* 7/15.

Financial Aid Contact Mr. Curt Gaume, Director of Financial Aid, 2001 Main Street, Buffalo, NY 14208-1098. *Phone:* 716-888-2300. *E-mail:* gaume@canisius.edu.

INTERNATIONAL STUDENTS 9% of students enrolled are international students. *Services and facilities:* Counseling/support services, ESL/language courses, Housing location assistance, International student housing, International student organization, Language tutoring, Orientation, Visa Services. Financial aid is available to international students. *Required with application:* TOEFL with recommended score of 200 (computer) or 500 (paper); proof of adequate funds; proof of health/immunizations.

International Student Contact Esther Northman, Director, International Student Programs, 2001 Main Street, Buffalo, NY 14208-1098. *Phone:* 716-888-2784. *E-mail:* northman@canisius.edu.

APPLICATION *Required:* GMAT, application form, baccalaureate/first degree, essay, personal statement, resume/curriculum vitae, transcripts of college work. School will accept GRE. *Recommended:* Work experience. *Application fee:* $25. Applications for domestic and international students are processed on a rolling basis.

Application Contact Laura McEwen, Director of Graduate Business Programs, 2001 Main Street, Bagen Hall 201, Buffalo, NY 14208-1098. *Phone:* 716-888-2140. *Fax:* 716-888-2145. *E-mail:* gradubus@canisius.edu.

Clarkson University
School of Business
Potsdam, New York

Phone: 315-268-6613 **Fax:** 315-268-3810 **E-mail:** bkozsan@clarkson.edu

Business Program(s) Web Site: http://www.clarkson.edu/mba

Graduate Business Unit Enrollment *Total:* 58 (49 full-time; 9 part-time; 17 women). *Average Age:* 24.

Graduate Business Faculty *Total:* 34 (31 full-time; 3 part-time).

Admissions *Applied:* 155. *Admitted:* 96. *Enrolled:* 65. *Average GMAT:* 550. *Average GPA:* 3.3

Academic Calendar Semesters.

Accreditation AACSB—The Association to Advance Collegiate Schools of Business.

After Graduation (Class of 2006–07) *Employed within 3 months of graduation:* 90%. *Average starting salary:* $71,000.

DEGREE MBA

MBA—Master of Business Administration Full-time and part-time. At least 35 total credits required. 12 to 36 months to complete program. *Concentrations:* environmental economics/management, general MBA, new venture management, supply chain management.

RESOURCES AND SERVICES 75 on-campus PCs are available to graduate business students. Access to Internet/World Wide Web, online (class) registration, and online grade reports available. *Personal computer requirements:* Graduate business students are strongly recommended to purchase or lease a personal computer. *Special opportunities include:* An international exchange program is available. *Placement services include:* Alumni network, career placement, job search course, career counseling/planning, electronic job bank, resume referral, career fairs, job interviews arranged, resume preparation, and career library.

EXPENSES *Tuition:* Full-time: $35,385. Part-time: $1010 per credit hour. *Tuition (international):* Full-time: $35,385. Part-time: $1010 per credit hour. *Required fees:* Full-time: $215. Tuition and/or fees vary by number of courses or credits taken. *Graduate housing:* Room and board costs vary by campus location, number of occupants, type of accommodation, and type of board plan. *Typical cost:* $3020 (including board).

FINANCIAL AID (2007–08) Loans, scholarships, and teaching assistantships.

Financial Aid Contact Brenda R. Kozsan, Director, Graduate Business Programs, Box 5770, 8 Clarkson Avenue, Potsdam, NY 13699-5770. *Phone:* 315-268-6613. *Fax:* 315-268-3810. *E-mail:* bkozsan@clarkson.edu.

INTERNATIONAL STUDENTS *Services and facilities:* Counseling/support services, ESL/language courses, Housing location assistance, International student organization, Orientation, Visa Services, Career search workshops. Financial aid is available to international students. *Required with application:* TOEFL with recommended score of 250 (computer), 600 (paper), or 100 (Internet); proof of adequate funds; proof of health/immunizations.

International Student Contact Tess Casler, Director, International Students and Scholars Office (ISSO), 229 Price Hall, Box 5651, Potsdam, NY 13699. *Phone:* 315-268-7970. *Fax:* 315-268-7882. *E-mail:* tcasler@clarkson.edu.

APPLICATION *Required:* GMAT, GRE, application form, baccalaureate/first degree, essay, 3 letters of recommendation, resume/curriculum vitae, transcripts of college work. *Application fee:* $25, $35 (international). Applications for domestic and international students are processed on a rolling basis.

Application Contact Brenda R. Kozsan, Director, Graduate Business Program, Box 5770, 8 Clarkson Avenue, Potsdam, NY 13699-5770. *Phone:* 315-268-6613. *Fax:* 315-268-3810. *E-mail:* bkozsan@clarkson.edu.

The College of Saint Rose
School of Business

Albany, New York

Phone: 518-454-5143 **Fax:** 518-458-5479 **E-mail:** grad@strose.edu

Business Program(s) Web Site: http://www.strose.edu/Future_Students/Academics/School_of_Business/default.asp

Graduate Business Unit Enrollment *Total:* 207 (69 full-time; 138 part-time; 114 women; 18 international). *Average Age:* 29.

Graduate Business Faculty *Total:* 16 (14 full-time; 2 part-time).

Admissions *Applied:* 112. *Admitted:* 94. *Enrolled:* 65.

Academic Calendar Semesters.

Accreditation ACBSP—The American Council of Business Schools and Programs.

DEGREES JD/MBA • MBA • MBA equivalent combined degree • MS

JD/MBA—Juris Doctor/Master of Business Administration Full-time and part-time. Applicant must be an admitted law student at Albany Law School in order to be eligible. At least 102 total credits required. 48 to 72 months to complete program. *Concentration:* combined degrees.

MBA—MBA Plus+ Full-time and part-time. 45 total credits required. 18 to 72 months to complete program. *Concentrations:* financial management/planning, information systems, nonprofit management.

MBA—Master of Business Administration Full-time and part-time. At least 36 total credits required. 12 to 72 months to complete program. *Concentration:* general MBA.

MBA—One-Year Master of Business Administration Full-time. At least 36 total credits required. 12 months to complete program. *Concentration:* general MBA.

MBA equivalent combined degree—Bachelor of Science/Master of Business Administration Full-time and part-time. At least 138 total credits required. 60 to 84 months to complete program. *Concentration:* combined degrees.

MS—Master of Science in Accounting Full-time and part-time. At least 30 total credits required. 24 to 72 months to complete program. *Concentration:* accounting.

MS—Master of Science in Professional Accountancy Full-time and part-time. At least 150 total credits required. 48 to 72 months to complete program. *Concentration:* combined degrees.

RESOURCES AND SERVICES 543 on-campus PCs are available to graduate business students. Access to Internet/World Wide Web, online (class) registration, and online grade reports available. *Personal computer requirements:* Graduate business students are strongly recommended to purchase or lease a personal computer. *Special opportunities include:* An internship program is available. *Placement services include:* Alumni network, career placement, career counseling/planning, electronic job bank, resume referral, career fairs, job interviews arranged, resume preparation, and career library.

EXPENSES *Tuition:* Part-time: $560 per credit hour. *Tuition (international):* Part-time: $560 per credit hour.

FINANCIAL AID (2007–08) 26 students received aid, including grants, loans, research assistantships, and scholarships. Aid is available to part-time students. *Financial aid application deadline:* 6/1.

Financial Aid Contact Mr. Steven Dwire, Director of Financial Aid, 432 Western Avenue, Albany, NY 12203-1490. *Phone:* 518-454-5464. *Fax:* 518-454-2109. *E-mail:* dwires@strose.edu.

INTERNATIONAL STUDENTS 9% of students enrolled are international students. *Services and facilities:* Counseling/support services, Housing location assistance, International student organization, Orientation, Visa Services, International student health insurance, Assistance with preparation of appropriate tax forms. Financial aid is available to international students. *Required with application:* TOEFL with recommended score of 220 (computer), 550 (paper), or 80 (Internet); proof of adequate funds; proof of health/immunizations. *Recommended with application:* IELT with recommended score of 7.

International Student Contact Colleen Flynn Thapalia, Director of Graduate Admissions, 432 Western Avenue, Albany, NY 12203-1490. *Phone:* 518-454-5143. *Fax:* 518-458-5479. *E-mail:* thapalic@strose.edu.

APPLICATION *Required:* Application form, baccalaureate/first degree, essay, 2 letters of recommendation, personal statement, resume/curriculum vitae, transcripts of college work. *Recommended:* Interview. *Application fee:* $35. *Deadlines:* 6/1 for fall, 10/15 for spring, 3/15 for summer, 6/1 for fall (international), 10/15 for spring (international), 3/15 for summer (international).

Application Contact Susan Patterson, Assistant Vice President of Graduate Admissions, 432 Western Avenue, Albany, NY 12203-1490. *Phone:* 518-454-5143. *Fax:* 518-458-5479. *E-mail:* grad@strose.edu.

See full description on page 594.

Columbia University
Graduate School of Business

New York, New York

Phone: 212-854-1961 **Fax:** 212-662-6754 **E-mail:** apply@gsb.columbia.edu

Business Program(s) Web Site: http://www.gsb.columbia.edu

Graduate Business Unit Enrollment *Total:* 2,096 (2,096 full-time; 644 women; 730 international). *Average Age:* 28.

Graduate Business Faculty *Total:* 252 (136 full-time; 116 part-time).

Admissions *Applied:* 5,623. *Admitted:* 919. *Enrolled:* 711. *Average GMAT:* 707. *Average GPA:* 3.4

Academic Calendar Trimesters.

Accreditation AACSB—The Association to Advance Collegiate Schools of Business.

After Graduation (Class of 2006–07) *Employed within 3 months of graduation:* 93%. *Average starting salary:* $107,265.

DEGREES DDS/MBA • EMBA • JD/MBA • MBA • MBA/MIA • MBA/MPH • MBA/MS • MD/MBA

DDS/MBA—Doctor of Dental Surgery/Master of Business Administration Full-time. Students must apply and be admitted to both schools and complete 5 terms of full-time matriculation at the dental school prior to entering the business school. Minimum of 56 months to complete program. *Concentration:* combined degrees.

EMBA—Berkeley-Columbia Executive MBA Full-time. Company sponsorship in assured time off for all class days and 5 or more years of organizational experience required. At least 60 total credits required. Minimum of 19 months to complete program. *Concentration:* general MBA.

EMBA—EMBA—Global Full-time. Company sponsorship in assured time off for all class days and 5 or more years of organizational experience required. At least 60 total credits required. Minimum of 20 months to complete program. *Concentration:* general MBA.

EMBA—Executive Master of Business Administration Full-time. Company sponsorship in assured time off for all class days and 5 or more years of organizational experience required. At least 60 total credits required. Minimum of 20 months to complete program. *Concentration:* general MBA.

JD/MBA—Juris Doctor/Master of Business Administration Full-time. Must apply and be admitted to both schools. At least 118 total credits required. Minimum of 44 months to complete program. *Concentration:* combined degrees.

MBA—Master of Business Administration Full-time. At least 60 total credits required. 16 to 20 months to complete program. *Concentrations:* accounting, decision sciences, economics, entrepreneurship, finance, health care, human resources management, international business, leadership, management, marketing, media administration, nonprofit management, operations management, other, pharmaceutical management, public management, real estate, risk management.

MBA/MIA—Master of Business Administration/Master of International Affairs Full-time. Must apply and be admitted to both schools. At least 90 total credits required. Minimum of 32 months to complete program. *Concentration:* combined degrees.

MBA/MPH—Master of Business Administration/Master of Public Health Full-time. Must apply and be admitted to both schools. At least 80 total credits required. Minimum of 27 months to complete program. *Concentration:* combined degrees.

MBA/MS—Master of Business Administration/Master of Science in Engineering and Applied Science Full-time. Must apply and be admitted to both schools. 69 to 75 total credits required. Minimum of 27 months to complete program. *Concentration:* combined degrees.

MBA/MS—Master of Business Administration/Master of Science in Journalism Full-time. Must apply and be admitted to both schools. At least 75 total credits required. Minimum of 27 months to complete program. *Concentration:* combined degrees.

MBA/MS—Master of Business Administration/Master of Science in Nursing Full-time and part-time. Must apply and be admitted to both schools. At least 75 total credits required. Minimum of 27 months to complete program. *Concentration:* combined degrees.

MBA/MS—Master of Business Administration/Master of Science in Social Work Full-time. Must apply and be admitted to both schools. At least 90 total credits required. Minimum of 32 months to complete program. *Concentration:* combined degrees.

MBA/MS—Master of Business Administration/Master of Science in Urban Planning Full-time. Must apply and be admitted to both schools. At least 90 total credits required. Minimum of 32 months to complete program. *Concentration:* combined degrees.

MD/MBA—Doctor of Medicine/Master of Business Administration Full-time. Must apply and be admitted to both schools and begin matriculation at the medical school. Minimum of 57 months to complete program. *Concentration:* combined degrees.

RESOURCES AND SERVICES 423 on-campus PCs are available to graduate business students. Access to Internet/World Wide Web, online (class) registration, and online grade reports available. *Personal computer requirements:* Graduate business students are required to have a personal computer. *Special opportunities include:* An international exchange program and an internship program are available. *Placement services include:* Alumni network, job search course, career counseling/planning, electronic job bank, resume referral, career fairs, job interviews arranged, resume preparation, and career library.

EXPENSES *Tuition:* Full-time: $43,436. *Tuition (international):* Full-time: $43,436. *Required fees:* Full-time: $1986. Tuition and/or fees vary by number of courses or credits taken. *Typical graduate housing cost:* $18,900 (including board).

FINANCIAL AID (2007–08) 875 students received aid, including fellowships, grants, loans, research assistantships, scholarships, and teaching assistantships. *Financial aid application deadline:* 1/9.

Financial Aid Contact Ms. Marilena Botoulas, Director of Financial Aid, 218 Uris Hall, 3022 Broadway, New York, NY 10027. *Phone:* 212-854-4057. *Fax:* 212-854-1809. *E-mail:* finaid@gsb.columbia.edu.

INTERNATIONAL STUDENTS 35% of students enrolled are international students. *Services and facilities:* Counseling/support services, ESL/language courses, Housing location assistance, International student housing, International student organization, Orientation, Visa Services. Financial aid is available to international students. *Required with application:* TOEFL; proof of health/immunizations.

International Student Contact Ms. Linda B. Meehan, Assistant Dean of MBA Admissions, 216 Uris Hall, 3022 Broadway, New York, NY 10027. *Phone:* 212-854-1961. *Fax:* 212-662-6754. *E-mail:* apply@gsb.columbia.edu.

APPLICATION *Required:* GMAT, application form, baccalaureate/first degree, essay, 2 letters of recommendation, personal statement, resume/

curriculum vitae, transcripts of college work. *Application fee:* $250. Applications for domestic and international students are processed on a rolling basis.

Application Contact Ms. Linda B. Meehan, Assistant Dean of MBA Admissions, 216 Uris Hall, 3022 Broadway, New York, NY 10027. *Phone:* 212-854-1961. *Fax:* 212-662-6754. *E-mail:* apply@gsb.columbia.edu.

Cornell University

Johnson Graduate School of Management

Ithaca, New York

Phone: 607-255-8006 **Fax:** 607-255-0065 **E-mail:** rs348@cornell.edu

Business Program(s) Web Site: http://www.johnson.cornell.edu

Graduate Business Unit Enrollment *Total:* 563 (563 full-time; 143 women; 168 international). *Average Age:* 28.

Graduate Business Faculty *Total:* 82 (63 full-time; 19 part-time).

Admissions *Applied:* 2,290. *Admitted:* 611. *Enrolled:* 309. *Average GMAT:* 682. *Average GPA:* 3.31

Academic Calendar Semesters.

Accreditation AACSB—The Association to Advance Collegiate Schools of Business.

After Graduation (Class of 2006–07) *Employed within 3 months of graduation:* 96%. *Average starting salary:* $98,000.

DEGREES EMBA • JD/MBA • MBA • MBA/MA • MBA/MILR • MD/MBA • ME/MBA

EMBA—Cornell Queens Executive EMBA Part-time. 8 years of full-time professional and substantial management experience required. At least 60 total credits required. Minimum of 18 months to complete program. *Concentration:* executive programs.

JD/MBA—Juris Doctor/Master of Business Administration Full-time. At least 126 total credits required. Minimum of 48 months to complete program. *Concentration:* combined degrees.

MBA—Executive Master of Business Administration Part-time. 8 years of full-time professional and substantial management experience required. At least 60 total credits required. Minimum of 20 months to complete program. *Concentration:* executive programs.

MBA—MBA/MPS in Real Estate Full-time. *Concentration:* combined degrees.

MBA—Master of Business Administration Full-time. Graduate science or technical degree required. At least 60 total credits required. Minimum of 12 months to complete program. *Concentration:* general MBA.

MBA—Master of Business Administration Full-time. At least 60 total credits required. Minimum of 20 months to complete program. *Concentration:* general MBA.

MBA/MA—Master of Business Administration/Master of Arts in Asian Studies Full-time. At least 85 total credits required. 36 to 42 months to complete program. *Concentration:* combined degrees.

MBA/MILR—Master of Business Administration/Master of Industrial and Labor Relations Full-time. At least 76 total credits required. Minimum of 30 months to complete program. *Concentration:* combined degrees.

MD/MBA—MD/MBA Full-time. Currently available only to students of Weill Cornell Medical College. *Concentration:* combined degrees.

ME/MBA—Master of Engineering/Master of Business Administration Full-time. At least 75 total credits required. Minimum of 30 months to complete program. *Concentration:* combined degrees.

RESOURCES AND SERVICES Access to Internet/World Wide Web, online (class) registration, and online grade reports available. *Personal computer requirements:* Graduate business students are required to have a personal computer. *Special opportunities include:* An international

Cornell University (continued)

exchange program and an internship program are available. *Placement services include:* Alumni network, career placement, career counseling/planning, electronic job bank, resume referral, career fairs, job interviews arranged, resume preparation, and career library.

EXPENSES *Tuition:* Full-time: $44,950. *Tuition (international):* Full-time: $44,950. *Required fees:* Full-time: $1550.

FINANCIAL AID (2007–08) 181 students received aid, including fellowships, grants, loans, scholarships, and teaching assistantships. *Financial aid application deadline:* 1/9.

Financial Aid Contact Mr. Randall Sawyer, Director of Admissions and Financial Aid, Sage Hall, Ithaca, NY 14853-6201. *Phone:* 607-255-8006. *Fax:* 607-225-0065. *E-mail:* rs348@cornell.edu.

INTERNATIONAL STUDENTS 30% of students enrolled are international students. *Services and facilities:* Counseling/support services, ESL/language courses, Housing location assistance, International student organization, Language tutoring, Orientation, Visa Services. Financial aid is available to international students. *Required with application:* TOEFL with recommended score of 250 (computer) or 600 (paper); TWE; proof of adequate funds; proof of health/immunizations.

International Student Contact Christine Sneva, Assistant Director, Admissions and Financial Aid, 113 Sage Hall, Ithaca, NY 14853-6201. *Phone:* 607-255-0060. *E-mail:* ces255@cornell.edu.

APPLICATION *Required:* GMAT, application form, baccalaureate/first degree, essay, interview, 2 letters of recommendation, resume/curriculum vitae, transcripts of college work, 3 years of work experience. *Application fee:* $200. *Deadlines:* 10/8 for fall, 11/8 for winter, 1/8 for spring, 3/8 for summer, 10/8 for fall (international), 11/8 for winter (international), 1/8 for spring (international), 3/8 for summer (international).

Application Contact Mr. Randall Sawyer, Director of Admissions and Financial Aid, Sage Hall, Ithaca, NY 14853-6201. *Phone:* 607-255-8006. *Fax:* 607-255-0065. *E-mail:* rs348@cornell.edu.

See full description on page 598.

Dowling College
School of Business

Oakdale, New York

Phone: 631-244-3266 **Fax:** 631-244-5098 **E-mail:** loschiat@dowling.edu

Business Program(s) Web Site: http://www.dowling.edu/school_of_business.htm

Graduate Business Unit Enrollment *Total:* 938 (269 full-time; 669 part-time; 422 women). *Average Age:* 35.

Graduate Business Faculty *Total:* 85 (19 full-time; 66 part-time).

Admissions *Applied:* 408. *Admitted:* 330. *Enrolled:* 231. *Average GPA:* 3.0

Academic Calendar Semesters.

DEGREES MA/MBA • MBA

MA/MBA—MBA in Health Care Management Full-time and part-time. 36 total credits required. 12 to 36 months to complete program. *Concentration:* health care.

MBA—Master of Business Administration in Aviation Management Full-time and part-time. At least 36 total credits required. 12 to 36 months to complete program. *Concentration:* aviation management.

MBA—Master of Business Administration in Banking and Finance Full-time and part-time. At least 36 total credits required. 12 to 36 months to complete program. *Concentrations:* banking, finance, international banking, international finance.

MBA—Master of Business Administration in Corporate Finance Full-time and part-time. At least 36 total credits required. 12 to 36 months to complete program. *Concentration:* finance.

MBA—Master of Business Administration in General Management Full-time and part-time. At least 36 total credits required. 12 to 36 months to complete program. *Concentration:* management.

MBA—Master of Business Administration in Information Systems Management Full-time and part-time. Up to 36 total credits required. 12 to 36 months to complete program. *Concentration:* information management.

MBA—Master of Business Administration in Weekend Accelerated Full-time. At least 36 total credits required. 16 months to complete program. *Concentrations:* banking, finance, international banking, international finance, management.

RESOURCES AND SERVICES 100 on-campus PCs are available to graduate business students. Access to Internet/World Wide Web, online (class) registration, and online grade reports available. *Personal computer requirements:* Graduate business students are strongly recommended to purchase or lease a personal computer. *Special opportunities include:* An internship program is available. *Placement services include:* Alumni network, career placement, job search course, career counseling/planning, resume referral, career fairs, job interviews arranged, resume preparation, and career library.

EXPENSES *Tuition:* Part-time: $735 per credit. *Tuition (international):* Part-time: $735 per credit. *Required fees:* Full-time: $400. *Typical graduate housing cost:* $9140 (including board).

FINANCIAL AID (2007–08) Grants, loans, research assistantships, scholarships, and work study. Aid is available to part-time students. *Financial aid application deadline:* 6/30.

Financial Aid Contact Patricia Noren, Director of Financial Services, 150 Idle Hour Boulevard, Oakdale, NY 11769-1999. *Phone:* 800-244-3013. *Fax:* 631-244-1059. *E-mail:* norenpl@dowling.edu.

INTERNATIONAL STUDENTS *Services and facilities:* Counseling/support services, ESL/language courses, Housing location assistance, International student housing, International student organization, Orientation, Visa Services. Financial aid is available to international students. *Required with application:* Proof of adequate funds; proof of health/immunizations. *Recommended with application:* TOEFL with recommended score of 550 (paper); TWE.

International Student Contact Yu-Wan Wang, Director, 150 Idle Hour Boulevard, Enrollment Services, Fortunoff Hall 216, Oakdale, NY 11769-1999. *Phone:* 631-244-5097. *Fax:* 631-563-3827. *E-mail:* wangy@dowling.edu.

APPLICATION *Required:* Application form, baccalaureate/first degree, 2 letters of recommendation, resume/curriculum vitae, transcripts of college work. *Recommended:* Interview, work experience. *Application fee:* $25. Applications for domestic and international students are processed on a rolling basis.

Application Contact Antonia Loschiavo, Executive Director of Operations, 150 Idle Hour Boulevard, Oakdale, NY 11769-5098. *Phone:* 631-244-3266. *Fax:* 631-244-5098. *E-mail:* loschiat@dowling.edu.

D'Youville College
Department of Business

Buffalo, New York

Phone: 716-829-7676 **Fax:** 716-829-7790 **E-mail:** graduateadmissions@dyc.edu

Business Program(s) Web Site: http://www.dyc.edu/academics/business/index.asp

Graduate Business Unit Enrollment *Total:* 50 (33 full-time; 17 part-time; 28 women; 8 international). *Average Age:* 31.

Admissions *Applied:* 40. *Admitted:* 23. *Enrolled:* 19. *Average GMAT:* 550.

Academic Calendar Semesters.

DEGREE MS

MS—Master of Science in International Business Full-time and part-time. Distance learning option. 39 to 45 total credits required. 24 to 60 months to complete program. *Concentration:* international business.

RESOURCES AND SERVICES 60 on-campus PCs are available to graduate business students. Access to Internet/World Wide Web, online (class) registration, and online grade reports available. *Personal computer requirements:* Graduate business students are strongly recommended to purchase or lease a personal computer. *Special opportunities include:* An internship program is available. *Placement services include:* Alumni network, career counseling/planning, electronic job bank, resume referral, career fairs, resume preparation, and career library.

EXPENSES *Tuition:* Full-time: $17,145. Part-time: $635 per credit hour. *Tuition (international):* Full-time: $17,145. Part-time: $635 per credit hour. *Required fees:* Full-time: $200. Part-time: $48 per semester. *Typical graduate housing cost:* $8770 (including board), $7170 (room only).

FINANCIAL AID (2007–08) 21 students received aid, including grants, loans, research assistantships, scholarships, and work study. *Financial aid application deadline:* 4/15.

Financial Aid Contact Ms. Lorraine Metz, Director of Financial Aid, 320 Porter Avenue, Buffalo, NY 14201-1084. *Phone:* 716-829-7691. *Fax:* 716-829-7790. *E-mail:* financialaid@dyc.edu.

INTERNATIONAL STUDENTS 16% of students enrolled are international students. *Services and facilities:* Counseling/support services, Housing location assistance, International student organization, Orientation, Visa Services. Financial aid is available to international students. *Required with application:* TOEFL with recommended score of 173 (computer) or 550 (paper); proof of adequate funds; proof of health/immunizations.

International Student Contact Ms. Linda Fisher, Director of International Student Recruitment, 320 Porter Avenue, Buffalo, NY 14201-1084. *Phone:* 716-829-7600. *Fax:* 716-829-7790. *E-mail:* admissions@dyc.edu.

APPLICATION *Required:* Application form, baccalaureate/first degree, interview, letter(s) of recommendation, transcripts of college work. School will accept GMAT and GRE. *Recommended:* Essay, resume/curriculum vitae, work experience. *Application fee:* $25. *Deadlines:* 5/15 for fall (international), 9/15 for spring (international), 3/1 for summer (international). Applications for domestic students are processed on a rolling basis.

Application Contact Ms. Linda Fisher, Graduate Admissions Director, 320 Porter Avenue, Buffalo, NY 14201-1084. *Phone:* 716-829-7676. *Fax:* 716-829-7790. *E-mail:* graduateadmissions@dyc.edu.

European School of Economics
MBA Programme
New York, New York

Phone: 212-400-1440 **Fax:** 212-400-1441 **E-mail:** info@ese.edu

Business Program(s) Web Site: http://www.eselondon.ac.uk/campuses/new-york-city-business-school

Academic Calendar Four 10-12 week terms.

DEGREE MBA

MBA—Master of Business Administration Full-time and part-time. 12 to 18 months to complete program. *Concentrations:* general MBA, international finance, marketing.

RESOURCES AND SERVICES *Special opportunities include:* An internship program is available. *Placement services include:* Career placement, career counseling/planning, electronic job bank, job interviews arranged, and resume preparation.

FINANCIAL AID (2007–08) Fellowships and scholarships.

INTERNATIONAL STUDENTS *Required with application:* IELT; TOEFL. *Recommended with application:* Proof of adequate funds.

APPLICATION *Required:* GMAT, application form, essay, 2 letters of recommendation, resume/curriculum vitae, transcripts of college work, 2 years of work experience. *Application fee:* 50 British pounds. Applications for domestic and international students are processed on a rolling basis.

Application Contact Admissions Office, 350 Fifth Avenue, 33rd Floor, New York, NY 10018. *Phone:* 212-400-1440. *Fax:* 212-400-1441. *E-mail:* info@ese.edu.

See full description on page 608.

Excelsior College
School of Business and Technology
Albany, New York

Phone: 888-647-2388 Ext. 27 **E-mail:** admissions@excelsior.edu

Business Program(s) Web Site: http://www.mba.excelsior.edu

Graduate Business Unit Enrollment *Total:* 154 (154 part-time; 67 women). *Average Age:* 42.

Graduate Business Faculty *Total:* 20 (5 full-time; 15 part-time).

Admissions *Applied:* 140. *Admitted:* 90. *Enrolled:* 35.

Academic Calendar Continuous.

After Graduation (Class of 2006–07) *Employed within 3 months of graduation:* 100%. *Average starting salary:* $80,000.

DEGREE MBA

MBA—Master of Business Administration Part-time. Distance learning option. Up to 48 total credits required. *Concentration:* general MBA.

RESOURCES AND SERVICES Access to Internet/World Wide Web, online (class) registration, and online grade reports available. *Personal computer requirements:* Graduate business students are required to have a personal computer. *Placement services include:* Alumni network, electronic job bank, and resume preparation.

EXPENSES *Tuition:* Part-time: $410 per credit hour. *Tuition (international):* Part-time: $410 per credit hour. *Required fees:* Part-time: $275 per year. Tuition and/or fees vary by academic program.

Financial Aid Contact Donna Cooper, Financial Aid Manager, 7 Columbia Circle, Albany, NY 12203. *Phone:* 518-464-8632. *Fax:* 518-464-8777. *E-mail:* dcooper@excelsior.edu.

INTERNATIONAL STUDENTS Financial aid is not available to international students.

APPLICATION *Required:* Application form, baccalaureate/first degree, transcripts of college work. *Application fee:* $100. Applications for domestic students are processed on a rolling basis.

See full description on page 610.

Fordham University
Graduate School of Business Administration
New York, New York

Phone: 212-636-6200 **Fax:** 212-636-7076 **E-mail:** admissionsgb@fordham.edu

Business Program(s) Web Site: http://www.fordham.edu/business

Graduate Business Unit Enrollment *Total:* 1,548 (365 full-time; 1,183 part-time; 617 women; 69 international). *Average Age:* 28.

Graduate Business Faculty *Total:* 187 (92 full-time; 95 part-time).

Admissions *Applied:* 1,065. *Admitted:* 671. *Enrolled:* 384. *Average GMAT:* 603. *Average GPA:* 3.18

Fordham University (continued)

Academic Calendar Trimesters.

Accreditation AACSB—The Association to Advance Collegiate Schools of Business.

After Graduation (Class of 2006–07) *Average starting salary:* $80,900.

DEGREES JD/MBA • MBA • MBA/MS • MS • MSIS

JD/MBA—Juris Doctor/Master of Business Administration *Concentration:* law.

MBA—Accelerated Executive Master of Business Administration Part-time. At least 60 total credits required. 22 months to complete program. *Concentrations:* international business, management.

MBA—Deming Scholars Master of Business Administration Full-time. At least 60 total credits required. 18 months to complete program. *Concentration:* quality management.

MBA—Global Professional Master of Business Administration Full-time and part-time. 45 to 78 total credits required. 12 to 72 months to complete program. *Concentrations:* accounting, finance, information management, management, marketing, quality management.

MBA—Master of Business Administration Full-time and part-time. 45 to 72 total credits required. 15 to 72 months to complete program. *Concentrations:* accounting, electronic commerce (E-commerce), finance, information management, international business, management, marketing, quality management.

MBA/MS—Master of Business Administration in Accounting/Master of Science in Taxation Full-time and part-time. 90 to 99 total credits required. Maximum of 72 months to complete program. *Concentrations:* accounting, taxation.

MS—Master of Science in Media Management Full-time and part-time. 30 to 39 total credits required. 12 to 72 months to complete program. *Concentration:* media administration.

MS—Master of Science in Quantitative Finance Full-time. Demonstrated proficiency in quantitative problem-solving skills shown by previous training in mathematics, engineering, or other quantitative disciplines required. 55 total credits required. 18 months to complete program. *Concentration:* finance.

MS—Master of Science in Taxation Full-time and part-time. 39 to 54 total credits required. 12 to 72 months to complete program. *Concentration:* taxation.

MSIS—Master of Science in Information Systems Full-time and part-time. 30 to 39 total credits required. 12 to 72 months to complete program. *Concentration:* information systems.

RESOURCES AND SERVICES 125 on-campus PCs are available to graduate business students. Access to Internet/World Wide Web, online (class) registration, and online grade reports available. *Personal computer requirements:* Graduate business students are not required to have a personal computer. *Special opportunities include:* An international exchange program and an internship program are available. *Placement services include:* Alumni network, career placement, job search course, career counseling/planning, electronic job bank, resume referral, career fairs, job interviews arranged, resume preparation, and career library.

EXPENSES *Tuition:* Full-time: $32,775. Part-time: $950 per credit. *Tuition (international):* Full-time: $32,775. Part-time: $950 per credit. *Required fees:* Full-time: $340.

FINANCIAL AID (2007–08) 109 students received aid, including fellowships, grants, loans, research assistantships, and scholarships. Aid is available to part-time students. *Financial aid application deadline:* 9/1.

Financial Aid Contact Ms. Cynthia Perez, Director of MBA Admissions, 33 West 60th Street, Fourth Floor, New York, NY 10023. *Phone:* 212-636-6200. *Fax:* 212-636-7076. *E-mail:* admissionsgb@fordham.edu.

INTERNATIONAL STUDENTS 4% of students enrolled are international students. *Services and facilities:* Counseling/support services, ESL/language courses, Housing location assistance, International student organization, Language tutoring, Orientation, Visa Services. Financial aid is available to international students. *Required with application:* TOEFL with recommended score of 250 (computer), 600 (paper), or 100 (Internet); proof of adequate funds; proof of health/immunizations.

International Student Contact Mr. Salvatore Longarino, Director of International Students, 33 West 60th Street, Room 306, New York, NY 10023. *Phone:* 212-636-6270. *Fax:* 212-636-7368. *E-mail:* longarino@fordham.edu.

APPLICATION *Required:* GMAT, application form, baccalaureate/first degree, essay, 2 letters of recommendation, personal statement, resume/curriculum vitae, transcripts of college work. *Recommended:* Interview, 2 years of work experience. *Application fee:* $65. Applications for domestic and international students are processed on a rolling basis.

Application Contact Ms. Cynthia Perez, Director of MBA Admission, 33 West 60th Street, Fourth Floor, New York, NY 10023. *Phone:* 212-636-6200. *Fax:* 212-636-7076. *E-mail:* admissionsgb@fordham.edu.

See full description on page 620.

Hofstra University
Frank G. Zarb School of Business
Hempstead, New York

Phone: 516-463-4876 **Fax:** 516-463-4664 **E-mail:** gradstudent@hofstra.edu

Business Program(s) Web Site: http://www.hofstra.edu/gradbusiness

Graduate Business Unit Enrollment *Total:* 616 (186 full-time; 430 part-time; 253 women; 61 international). *Average Age:* 31.

Graduate Business Faculty *Total:* 54 (42 full-time; 12 part-time).

Admissions *Applied:* 699. *Admitted:* 340. *Enrolled:* 159. *Average GMAT:* 525. *Average GPA:* 3.14

Academic Calendar 4-1-4.

Accreditation AACSB—The Association to Advance Collegiate Schools of Business.

After Graduation (Class of 2006–07) *Employed within 3 months of graduation:* 94%. *Average starting salary:* $66,953.

DEGREES MBA • MS

MBA—Executive Master of Business Administration Full-time. 7 years of work experience required. 48 total credits required. 20 months to complete program. *Concentration:* management.

MBA—Master of Business Administration Full-time and part-time. 41 to 48 total credits required. 18 to 60 months to complete program. *Concentrations:* accounting, finance, international business, management, management information systems, marketing, other, quality management, sports/entertainment management, taxation.

MS—Master of Science in Marketing Research Full-time and part-time. 30 to 36 total credits required. 12 to 60 months to complete program. *Concentration:* marketing research.

MS—Master of Science Full-time and part-time. Bachelor of Arts in Accounting or equivalent required. 30 to 36 total credits required. 12 to 60 months to complete program. *Concentrations:* accounting, taxation.

MS—Master of Science Full-time and part-time. 30 to 33 total credits required. 12 to 60 months to complete program. *Concentrations:* finance, human resources management, management information systems, marketing.

RESOURCES AND SERVICES 1,694 on-campus PCs are available to graduate business students. Access to Internet/World Wide Web, online (class) registration, and online grade reports available. *Personal computer requirements:* Graduate business students are strongly recommended to purchase or lease a personal computer. *Special opportunities include:* An international exchange program and an internship program are available. *Placement services include:* Alumni network, career placement, job search course, career counseling/planning, electronic job bank, resume referral, career fairs, job interviews arranged, resume preparation, and career library.

EXPENSES *Tuition:* Full-time: $14,760. Part-time: $820 per credit hour. *Tuition (international):* Full-time: $14,760. Part-time: $820 per credit hour. *Required fees:* Full-time: $970. Part-time: $330 per credit hour. Tuition and/or fees vary by number of courses or credits taken and academic program. *Graduate housing:* Room and board costs vary by number of occupants, type of accommodation, and type of board plan. *Typical cost:* $10,400 (including board).

FINANCIAL AID (2007–08) 201 students received aid, including grants, loans, research assistantships, scholarships, and work study. Aid is available to part-time students. *Financial aid application deadline:* 2/15.

Financial Aid Contact Sandra A. Filbry, Associate Director of Financial Aid, 126 Hofstra University, Office of Financial Aid, Hempstead, NY 11549-1090. *Phone:* 516-463-4335. *Fax:* 516-463-4936. *E-mail:* sandra.a.filbry@hofstra.edu.

INTERNATIONAL STUDENTS 10% of students enrolled are international students. *Services and facilities:* Counseling/support services, ESL/language courses, International student housing, International student organization, Language tutoring, Orientation. Financial aid is available to international students. *Required with application:* TOEFL with recommended score of 213 (computer) or 550 (paper); proof of adequate funds; proof of health/immunizations.

International Student Contact Ryan Greene, Director of International Students, 200 Hofstra University, International Student Office, Hempstead, NY 11549. *Phone:* 516-467-6795. *Fax:* 516-463-5328. *E-mail:* international@hofstra.edu.

APPLICATION *Required:* GMAT, application form, baccalaureate/first degree, essay, 2 letters of recommendation, personal statement, resume/curriculum vitae, transcripts of college work. *Recommended:* Work experience. *Application fee:* $60. Applications for domestic and international students are processed on a rolling basis.

Application Contact Carol Drummer, Dean of Graduate Admissions, 126 Hofstra University, Office of Graduate Admissions, Hempstead, NY 11549-1090. *Phone:* 516-463-4876. *Fax:* 516-463-4664. *E-mail:* gradstudent@hofstra.edu.

Iona College
Hagan School of Business
New Rochelle, New York

Phone: 914-637-2708 Fax: 914-633-2012 E-mail: jfleurismond@iona.edu

Business Program(s) Web Site: http://www.iona.edu/hagan/

Graduate Business Unit Enrollment *Total:* 309 (60 full-time; 249 part-time; 134 women; 13 international). *Average Age:* 30.

Graduate Business Faculty *Total:* 30 (20 full-time; 10 part-time).

Admissions *Applied:* 128. *Admitted:* 107. *Enrolled:* 82. *Average GMAT:* 450. *Average GPA:* 3.25

Academic Calendar Trimesters.

Accreditation AACSB—The Association to Advance Collegiate Schools of Business.

DEGREE MBA

MBA—Master of Business Administration Full-time and part-time. Distance learning option. 33 to 57 total credits required. 15 to 72 months to complete program. *Concentrations:* accounting, finance, human resources management, management, management information systems, marketing.

RESOURCES AND SERVICES 627 on-campus PCs are available to graduate business students. Access to Internet/World Wide Web, online (class) registration, and online grade reports available. *Personal computer requirements:* Graduate business students are not required to have a personal computer. *Special opportunities include:* An international exchange program and an internship program are available. *Placement services include:* Alumni network, career placement, career counseling/

planning, electronic job bank, resume referral, career fairs, job interviews arranged, resume preparation, and career library.

EXPENSES *Tuition:* Full-time: $19,224. Part-time: $712 per credit. *Tuition (international):* Full-time: $19,224. Part-time: $712 per credit. *Required fees:* Full-time: $300.

FINANCIAL AID (2007–08) 75 students received aid, including loans, research assistantships, scholarships, and work study. Aid is available to part-time students. *Financial aid application deadline:* 4/15.

Financial Aid Contact Mary Grant, Director of Student Financial Services, 715 North Avenue, New Rochelle, NY 10801-1890. *Phone:* 914-633-2497. *Fax:* 914-633-2486. *E-mail:* mgrant@iona.edu.

INTERNATIONAL STUDENTS 4% of students enrolled are international students. *Services and facilities:* Counseling/support services, Visa Services. Financial aid is available to international students. *Required with application:* TOEFL with recommended score of 213 (computer), 550 (paper), or 79 (Internet); proof of adequate funds; proof of health/immunizations.

International Student Contact Mr. Kevin Cavanagh, Assistant Vice President for College Admissions, 715 North Avenue, New Rochelle, NY 10801. *Phone:* 914-633-2502. *Fax:* 914-633-2642. *E-mail:* kcavanagh@iona.edu.

APPLICATION *Required:* GMAT, application form, baccalaureate/first degree, essay, 2 letters of recommendation, personal statement, resume/curriculum vitae, transcripts of college work. *Recommended:* Interview, work experience. *Application fee:* $50. Applications for domestic and international students are processed on a rolling basis.

Application Contact Mr. Jude Fleurismond, Director of MBA Admissions, 715 North Avenue, New Rochelle, NY 10801-1890. *Phone:* 914-637-2708. *Fax:* 914-633-2012. *E-mail:* jfleurismond@iona.edu.

See full description on page 642.

Ithaca College
School of Business
Ithaca, New York

Phone: 607-274-3936 Fax: 607-274-1152 E-mail: eckrich@ithaca.edu

Business Program(s) Web Site: http://www.ithaca.edu/business/mba

Graduate Business Unit Enrollment *Total:* 24 (18 full-time; 6 part-time; 11 women; 2 international). *Average Age:* 27.

Graduate Business Faculty 20 full-time.

Admissions *Applied:* 33. *Admitted:* 28. *Enrolled:* 20. *Average GMAT:* 526. *Average GPA:* 3.2

Academic Calendar Semesters.

DEGREES MBA • MBA/M Acc

MBA—Master of Business Administration Full-time and part-time. Baccalaureate major in business or accounting or the equivalent required. 36 total credits required. 10 to 60 months to complete program. *Concentration:* management.

MBA/M Acc—MBA in Professional Accountancy Full-time and part-time. Baccalaureate degree with accounting major, concentration, or specialty. 36 total credits required. 10 to 60 months to complete program. *Concentration:* accounting.

RESOURCES AND SERVICES 685 on-campus PCs are available to graduate business students. Access to Internet/World Wide Web, online (class) registration, and online grade reports available. *Personal computer requirements:* Graduate business students are not required to have a personal computer. *Special opportunities include:* An international exchange program and an internship program are available. *Placement services include:* Alumni network, career counseling/planning, electronic job bank, resume referral, and career fairs.

Ithaca College (continued)

EXPENSES *Tuition:* Full-time: $23,400. Part-time: $650 per credit hour. *Tuition (international):* Full-time: $23,400. Part-time: $650 per credit hour.

FINANCIAL AID (2007–08) 6 students received aid, including scholarships and work study. Aid is available to part-time students. *Financial aid application deadline:* 4/15.

Financial Aid Contact Wendy Fonder, MBA Program Specialist, Room 309, Ithaca, NY 14850. *Phone:* 607-274-7308. *Fax:* 607-274-1152. *E-mail:* mba@ithaca.edu.

INTERNATIONAL STUDENTS 8% of students enrolled are international students. *Services and facilities:* Counseling/support services, Orientation. Financial aid is available to international students. *Required with application:* TOEFL with recommended score of 213 (computer), 550 (paper), or 79 (Internet); proof of adequate funds; proof of health/immunizations.

International Student Contact Sally Espinosa, Assistant to the Deans of Graduate and Professional Studies, Office of Graduate and Professional Studies, 111 Towers Concourse, Ithaca, NY 14850-7142. *Phone:* 607-274-3527. *Fax:* 607-274-1263. *E-mail:* gradstudies@ithaca.edu.

APPLICATION *Required:* GMAT, application form, baccalaureate/first degree, essay, 2 letters of recommendation, personal statement, transcripts of college work. *Application fee:* $40. Applications for domestic and international students are processed on a rolling basis.

Application Contact Dr. Donald W. Eckrich, Director of MBA Programs, Room 316, Ithaca, NY 14850-7172. *Phone:* 607-274-3936. *Fax:* 607-274-1152. *E-mail:* eckrich@ithaca.edu.

Keuka College
Program in Management

Keuka Park, New York

Phone: 866-255-3852 **Fax:** 315-279-5407 **E-mail:** jfarrell@mail.keuka.edu

Business Program(s) Web Site: http://www.keuka.edu/asap/msm.htm

DEGREE M Mgt

M Mgt—Master in Management Full-time. 33 total credits required. *Concentration:* management.

RESOURCES AND SERVICES 60 on-campus PCs are available to graduate business students. Access to Internet/World Wide Web available. *Personal computer requirements:* Graduate business students are required to have a personal computer. *Placement services include:* Alumni network, career placement, career counseling/planning, electronic job bank, career fairs, resume preparation, and career library.

Application Contact Mr. Jack Farrell, Director of Admissions, Keuka College, Center for Professional Studies & International Programs, Keuka Park, NY 14478. *Phone:* 866-255-3852. *Fax:* 315-279-5407. *E-mail:* jfarrell@mail.keuka.edu.

Le Moyne College
Division of Management

Syracuse, New York

Phone: 315-445-4265 **Fax:** 315-445-6027 **E-mail:** trapaskp@lemoyne.edu

Business Program(s) Web Site: http://www.lemoyne.edu/mba/

Graduate Business Unit Enrollment *Total:* 98 (3 full-time; 95 part-time; 44 women). *Average Age:* 31.

Graduate Business Faculty *Total:* 19 (18 full-time; 1 part-time).

Admissions *Applied:* 72. *Admitted:* 61. *Enrolled:* 61. *Average GMAT:* 500. *Average GPA:* 3.05

Academic Calendar Semesters.

After Graduation (Class of 2006–07) *Employed within 3 months of graduation:* 95%.

DEGREE MBA

MBA—Master of Business Administration Full-time and part-time. 36 to 51 total credits required. 15 to 72 months to complete program. *Concentration:* general MBA.

RESOURCES AND SERVICES 325 on-campus PCs are available to graduate business students. Access to Internet/World Wide Web, online (class) registration, and online grade reports available. *Personal computer requirements:* Graduate business students are not required to have a personal computer. *Special opportunities include:* An international exchange program and an internship program are available. *Placement services include:* Alumni network, career placement, career counseling/planning, electronic job bank, resume referral, career fairs, job interviews arranged, resume preparation, and career library.

EXPENSES *Tuition:* Full-time: $10,386. Part-time: $577 per credit hour. *Tuition (international):* Full-time: $10,386. Part-time: $577 per credit hour.

FINANCIAL AID (2007–08) 28 students received aid, including loans and scholarships. Aid is available to part-time students.

Financial Aid Contact Mr. William C. Cheetham, Director of Financial Aid, 1419 Salt Springs Road, Syracuse, NY 13214-1301. *Phone:* 315-445-4400. *Fax:* 315-445-4182. *E-mail:* cheethwc@lemoyne.edu.

INTERNATIONAL STUDENTS *Services and facilities:* Counseling/support services. *Required with application:* TOEFL with recommended score of 213 (computer), 550 (paper), or 79 (Internet); proof of adequate funds; proof of health/immunizations.

International Student Contact Mrs. Allison L. Farrell, Co-Director of Global Education, 1419 Salt Springs Road, Syracuse, NY 13214-1301. *Phone:* 315-445-4275. *Fax:* 315-445-6027. *E-mail:* cudaal@lemoyne.edu.

APPLICATION *Required:* GMAT, application form, baccalaureate/first degree, interview, 2 letters of recommendation, personal statement, resume/curriculum vitae, transcripts of college work. Applications for domestic and international students are processed on a rolling basis.

Application Contact Ms. Kristen P. Trapasso, Director of Graduate Admission, 1419 Salt Springs Road, Syracuse, NY 13214-1301. *Phone:* 315-445-4265. *Fax:* 315-445-6027. *E-mail:* trapaskp@lemoyne.edu.

Long Island University, Brooklyn Campus
School of Business, Public Administration and Information Sciences

Brooklyn, New York

Phone: 800-548-7526 **Fax:** 718-797-2399 **E-mail:** attend@liu.edu

Business Program(s) Web Site: http://www.liu.edu/

Graduate Business Unit Enrollment *Total:* 169 (20 full-time; 149 part-time; 101 women; 22 international).

Graduate Business Faculty *Total:* 52 (25 full-time; 27 part-time).

Admissions *Average GPA:* 3.2

Academic Calendar Semesters.

After Graduation (Class of 2006–07) *Employed within 3 months of graduation:* 85%. *Average starting salary:* $62,000.

DEGREES MBA • MPA • MS

MBA—Master of Business Administration Full-time and part-time. 36 to 60 total credits required. 18 to 72 months to complete program. *Concentrations:* accounting, finance, human resources management, international business, management, management information systems, marketing.

MPA—Master of Public Administration At least 48 total credits required. Minimum of 24 months to complete program. *Concentration:* health administration.

MS—Master of Science in Accounting At least 36 total credits required. Minimum of 24 months to complete program. *Concentration:* accounting.

MS—Master of Science in Human Resource Management At least 36 total credits required. Minimum of 24 months to complete program. *Concentration:* human resources management.

MS—Master of Science in Taxation At least 36 total credits required. Minimum of 24 months to complete program. *Concentration:* taxation.

RESOURCES AND SERVICES 200 on-campus PCs are available to graduate business students. Access to Internet/World Wide Web available. *Personal computer requirements:* Graduate business students are not required to have a personal computer. *Placement services include:* Alumni network, career placement, job search course, career counseling/planning, electronic job bank, resume referral, career fairs, job interviews arranged, and resume preparation.

FINANCIAL AID (2007–08) 25 students received aid, including fellowships, grants, loans, research assistantships, scholarships, and work study. Aid is available to part-time students.

Financial Aid Contact Ms. Rose Iannicelli, Director of Financial Aid, One University Plaza, Brooklyn, NY 11201-8423. *Phone:* 718-488-3320. *Fax:* 718-488-3343. *E-mail:* yanni@joshua.liu.edu.

INTERNATIONAL STUDENTS 13% of students enrolled are international students. *Services and facilities:* Counseling/support services, ESL/language courses, International student housing, Language tutoring, Orientation. Financial aid is available to international students. *Required with application:* TOEFL with recommended score of 500 (paper) or 61 (Internet); proof of adequate funds; proof of health/immunizations.

International Student Contact Steven Chin, Director of International Student Services, One University Plaza, Brooklyn, NY 11201-5372. *Phone:* 718-488-1216. *E-mail:* schin@hornet_liu.edu.

APPLICATION *Required:* GMAT, application form, baccalaureate/first degree, 2 letters of recommendation, personal statement, resume/curriculum vitae, transcripts of college work. *Recommended:* Work experience. *Application fee:* $30. *Deadlines:* 7/2 for fall (international), 12/2 for spring (international), 5/3 for summer (international). Applications for domestic students are processed on a rolling basis.

Application Contact Elizabeth Storinge, Dean of Admissions, One University Plaza, Brooklyn, NY 11201-8423. *Phone:* 800-548-7526. *Fax:* 718-797-2399. *E-mail:* attend@liu.edu.

Long Island University, C.W. Post Campus

College of Management

Brookville, New York

Phone: 516-299-2900 **Fax:** 516-299-2137 **E-mail:** enroll@cwpost.liu.edu

Business Program(s) Web Site: http://www.liu.edu/business

Graduate Business Unit Enrollment *Total:* 310 (119 full-time; 191 part-time; 122 women; 61 international). *Average Age:* 28.

Graduate Business Faculty *Total:* 49 (40 full-time; 9 part-time).

Admissions *Applied:* 143. *Admitted:* 94. *Enrolled:* 60. *Average GMAT:* 460. *Average GPA:* 3.1

Academic Calendar Semesters.

Accreditation AACSB—The Association to Advance Collegiate Schools of Business.

After Graduation (Class of 2006–07) *Employed within 3 months of graduation:* 85%.

DEGREES JD/MBA • MBA • MS

JD/MBA—Juris Doctor/Master of Business Administration Full-time and part-time. 102 to 119 total credits required. 48 to 72 months to complete program. *Concentration:* combined degrees.

MBA—Master of Business Administration Full-time and part-time. 36 to 48 total credits required. 12 to 60 months to complete program. *Concentration:* general MBA.

MS—Master of Science in Accountancy Full-time and part-time. 36 to 60 total credits required. 18 to 60 months to complete program. *Concentration:* accounting.

MS—Master of Science in Taxation Full-time and part-time. 36 to 60 total credits required. 18 to 60 months to complete program. *Concentrations:* accounting, taxation.

RESOURCES AND SERVICES 520 on-campus PCs are available to graduate business students. Access to Internet/World Wide Web and online grade reports available. *Personal computer requirements:* Graduate business students are strongly recommended to purchase or lease a personal computer. *Placement services include:* Alumni network, career placement, career counseling/planning, electronic job bank, resume referral, career fairs, resume preparation, and career library.

EXPENSES *Tuition:* Full-time: $7515. Part-time: $835 per credit. *Tuition (international):* Full-time: $7515. Part-time: $835 per credit. Tuition and/or fees vary by number of courses or credits taken. *Graduate housing:* Room and board costs vary by number of occupants, type of accommodation, and type of board plan. *Typical cost:* $9320 (including board), $6320 (room only).

FINANCIAL AID (2007–08) Grants, loans, research assistantships, scholarships, and work study. Aid is available to part-time students. *Financial aid application deadline:* 3/1.

Financial Aid Contact Ms. Karen Urdahl, Assistant Director, Financial Aid, 720 Northern Boulevard, Brookville, NY 11548-1300. *Phone:* 516-299-2338. *Fax:* 516-299-3833.

INTERNATIONAL STUDENTS 20% of students enrolled are international students. *Services and facilities:* Counseling/support services, ESL/language courses, Housing location assistance, International student housing, International student organization, Language tutoring, Orientation, Visa Services. Financial aid is available to international students. *Required with application:* TOEFL with recommended score of 197 (computer), 550 (paper), or 75 (Internet); proof of adequate funds; proof of health/immunizations.

International Student Contact Ms. Kathy Riley, Assistant Director, International Admissions, 720 Northern Boulevard, Brookville, NY 11548-1300. *Phone:* 516-299-2900. *Fax:* 516-299-2418. *E-mail:* kathy.riley@liu.edu.

APPLICATION *Required:* GMAT, application form, baccalaureate/first degree, essay, 2 letters of recommendation, personal statement, resume/curriculum vitae, transcripts of college work. *Recommended:* Work experience. *Application fee:* $30. Applications for domestic and international students are processed on a rolling basis.

Application Contact Ms. Carol Hafford, Director, Graduate Admissions, 720 Northern Boulevard, Brookville, NY 11548-1300. *Phone:* 516-299-2900. *Fax:* 516-299-2137. *E-mail:* enroll@cwpost.liu.edu.

Long Island University, Rockland Graduate Campus

Program in Business Administration

Orangeburg, New York

Phone: 845-359-7200 **Fax:** 845-359-7248 **E-mail:** rockland@liu.edu

Business Program(s) Web Site: http://www.liu.edu/rockland

Long Island University, Rockland Graduate Campus (continued)

DEGREE MBA

MBA—Master of Business Administration Full-time and part-time. 36 to 60 total credits required. Maximum of 60 months to complete program. *Concentrations:* finance, management.

RESOURCES AND SERVICES 40 on-campus PCs are available to graduate business students. Access to Internet/World Wide Web and online grade reports available. *Personal computer requirements:* Graduate business students are not required to have a personal computer. *Placement services include:* Alumni network, career counseling/planning, resume preparation, and career library.

Application Contact Maureen VerSchneider, Assistant Director of Admissions, 70 Route 340, Orangeburg, NY 10962. *Phone:* 845-359-7200. *Fax:* 845-359-7248. *E-mail:* rockland@liu.edu.

Manhattanville College
School of Graduate and Professional Studies

Purchase, New York

Phone: 914-323-5418 **Fax:** 914-694-3488 **E-mail:** fernandezn@mville.edu

Business Program(s) Web Site: http://www.manhattanville.edu/graduate

Graduate Business Unit Enrollment *Total:* 242 (170 women; 10 international).

Graduate Business Faculty *Total:* 49 (4 full-time; 45 part-time).

Admissions *Average GPA:* 3.1

Academic Calendar Quarters.

After Graduation (Class of 2006–07) *Employed within 3 months of graduation:* 99%.

DEGREES MS • MS/MS • MSCIB

MS—Master of Science in Leadership and Strategic Management Part-time. At least 39 total credits required. 24 to 60 months to complete program. *Concentrations:* leadership, strategic management.

MS—Master of Science in Organizational Management and Human Resource Development Part-time. At least 36 total credits required. 18 to 60 months to complete program. *Concentrations:* human resources management, organizational management.

MS—Sport Business Management Full-time and part-time. At least 36 total credits required. 12 to 60 months to complete program. *Concentration:* sports/entertainment management.

MS/MS—Master of Science in Management Communications Part-time. At least 36 total credits required. 18 to 60 months to complete program. *Concentrations:* management, management information systems.

MSCIB—Master of Science in International Management Part-time. 36 total credits required. 18 to 60 months to complete program. *Concentration:* international business.

RESOURCES AND SERVICES 291 on-campus PCs are available to graduate business students. Access to Internet/World Wide Web, online (class) registration, and online grade reports available. *Personal computer requirements:* Graduate business students are strongly recommended to purchase or lease a personal computer. *Special opportunities include:* An internship program is available. *Placement services include:* Alumni network, career placement, career counseling/planning, electronic job bank, resume referral, career fairs, resume preparation, and career library.

EXPENSES *Tuition:* Part-time: $655 per credit. *Tuition (international):* Part-time: $655 per credit. *Required fees:* Part-time: $40 per semester.

FINANCIAL AID (2007–08) 28 students received aid, including loans and work study. Aid is available to part-time students. *Financial aid application deadline:* 8/1.

Financial Aid Contact Darlene Huszar, Associate Director of Financial Aid, 2900 Purchase Street, Purchase, NY 10577-2132. *Phone:* 914-323-5357. *Fax:* 914-323-5382. *E-mail:* huszard@mville.edu.

INTERNATIONAL STUDENTS 4% of students enrolled are international students. *Services and facilities:* Counseling/support services, ESL/language courses, International student organization, International student advisor. Financial aid is not available to international students. *Required with application:* TOEFL with recommended score of 600 (paper); proof of adequate funds; proof of health/immunizations.

International Student Contact Ms. L.A. Adams, Director, International Student Services, 2900 Purchase Street, Purchase, NY 10577-2132. *Phone:* 914-323-5168. *Fax:* 914-323-5494. *E-mail:* oiss@mville.edu.

APPLICATION *Required:* Application form, baccalaureate/first degree, essay, interview, 2 letters of recommendation, personal statement, resume/curriculum vitae, transcripts of college work, 2 years of work experience. School will accept GMAT. *Application fee:* $65. Applications for domestic and international students are processed on a rolling basis.

Application Contact Natalia Fernandez, Director of Admissions, Graduate and Professional Studies, 2900 Purchase Street, Purchase, NY 10577-2123. *Phone:* 914-323-5418. *Fax:* 914-694-3488. *E-mail:* fernandezn@mville.edu.

Marist College
School of Management

Poughkeepsie, New York

Phone: 845-575-3800 **Fax:** 845-575-3166 **E-mail:** graduate@marist.edu

Business Program(s) Web Site: http://www.marist.edu/management/mba/

Graduate Business Unit Enrollment *Total:* 210 (210 part-time; 78 women; 1 international). *Average Age:* 30.

Graduate Business Faculty 23 full-time.

Admissions *Applied:* 67. *Admitted:* 57. *Enrolled:* 40. *Average GMAT:* 532. *Average GPA:* 3.42

Academic Calendar Semesters.

Accreditation AACSB—The Association to Advance Collegiate Schools of Business.

After Graduation (Class of 2006–07) *Employed within 3 months of graduation:* 100%. *Average starting salary:* $63,889.

DEGREE MBA

MBA—Master of Business Administration Full-time and part-time. Distance learning option. 30 to 51 total credits required. 12 to 84 months to complete program. *Concentration:* general MBA.

RESOURCES AND SERVICES 761 on-campus PCs are available to graduate business students. Access to Internet/World Wide Web, online (class) registration, and online grade reports available. *Personal computer requirements:* Graduate business students are strongly recommended to purchase or lease a personal computer. *Placement services include:* Alumni network, career placement, career counseling/planning, electronic job bank, resume referral, career fairs, resume preparation, and career library.

EXPENSES *Tuition:* Part-time: $665 per credit. *Tuition (international):* Part-time: $665 per credit.

FINANCIAL AID (2007–08) 43 students received aid, including grants, loans, and scholarships. Aid is available to part-time students. *Financial aid application deadline:* 8/15.

Financial Aid Contact Kelly Holmes, Director of Admission, 3399 North Road, Dyson 127, Poughkeepsie, NY 12601-1387. *Phone:* 845-575-3800. *Fax:* 845-575-3166. *E-mail:* graduate@marist.edu.

INTERNATIONAL STUDENTS 0.5% of students enrolled are international students. *Services and facilities:* Counseling/support services, ESL/language courses, Housing location assistance, International student organization, Language tutoring, Orientation, Visa Services. Financial aid is not available to international students. *Required with application:* TOEFL with recommended score of 213 (computer) or 550 (paper); proof of adequate funds; proof of health/immunizations. *Recommended with application:* IELT with recommended score of 6.

International Student Contact Kelly Holmes, Director of Admission, 3399 North Road, Dyson 127, Poughkeepsie, NY 12601-1387. *Phone:* 845-575-3800. *Fax:* 845-575-3166. *E-mail:* graduate@marist.edu.

APPLICATION *Required:* GMAT, application form, baccalaureate/first degree, essay, 2 letters of recommendation, personal statement, resume/curriculum vitae, transcripts of college work. *Recommended:* 5 years of work experience. *Application fee:* $50. Applications for domestic and international students are processed on a rolling basis.

Application Contact Kelly Holmes, Director of Admission, 3399 North Road, Dyson 127, Poughkeepsie, NY 12601-1387. *Phone:* 845-575-3800. *Fax:* 845-575-3166. *E-mail:* graduate@marist.edu.

Medaille College
Accelerated Learning Programs

Amherst, New York

Phone: 716-631-1061 Ext. 2541 **Fax:** 716-632-1811 **E-mail:** jacqueline.s.matheny@medaille.edu

Business Program(s) Web Site: http://www.medaille.edu

Graduate Business Unit Enrollment *Total:* 267 (267 full-time; 164 women). *Average Age:* 36.

Graduate Business Faculty *Total:* 90 (7 full-time; 83 part-time).

Admissions *Applied:* 162. *Admitted:* 159. *Enrolled:* 150. *Average GPA:* 3.0

Academic Calendar Continuous.

After Graduation (Class of 2006–07) *Employed within 3 months of graduation:* 100%. *Average starting salary:* $60,000.

DEGREES MA • MBA

MA—Organizational Leadership Full-time. Applicant essay on a given relevant issue; 3 years full-time work experience. 40 total credits required. 18 to 20 months to complete program. *Concentrations:* leadership, organizational behavior/development.

MBA—Master of Business Administration Accelerated Learning Programs Full-time. This program can be completed in 3 years (full-time). Post-secondary school work experience and 2 professional letters of recommendation are required. 48 total credits required. 22 to 25 months to complete program. *Concentration:* general MBA.

RESOURCES AND SERVICES 5 on-campus PCs are available to graduate business students. Access to Internet/World Wide Web available. *Personal computer requirements:* Graduate business students are required to have a personal computer, the cost of which is included in tuition or other required fees. *Placement services include:* Alumni network, career counseling/planning, career fairs, and resume preparation.

EXPENSES *Tuition:* Full-time: $14,760. Part-time: $615 per credit hour. *Typical graduate housing cost:* $8424 (including board).

FINANCIAL AID (2007–08) 208 students received aid, including work study.

Financial Aid Contact Ms. Phyllis G. Hart, Director of Financial Aid, 30 Wilson Road, Williamsville, NY 14221. *Phone:* 716-631-1061 Ext. 2597. *Fax:* 716-631-1380. *E-mail:* phart@medaille.edu.

INTERNATIONAL STUDENTS *Services and facilities:* Orientation, academic advisement. Financial aid is not available to international students. *Required with application:* TOEFL with recommended score of 213 (computer) or 550 (paper); proof of adequate funds; proof of health/immunizations.

International Student Contact Ms. Jacqueline S. Matheny, Executive Director of Marketing and Enrollment Management, School of Adult and Graduate Education, 30 Wilson Road, Williamsville, NY 14221. *Phone:* 716-631-1061 Ext. 2541. *Fax:* 716-632-1811. *E-mail:* jacqueline.s.matheny@medaille.edu.

APPLICATION *Required:* GMAT, application form, baccalaureate/first degree, personal statement, transcripts of college work, 3 years of work experience. *Application fee:* $100. Applications for domestic and international students are processed on a rolling basis.

Application Contact Ms. Jacqueline S. Matheny, Executive Director of Marketing and Enrollment Management, School of Adult and Graduate Education, 30 Wilson Road, Williamsville, NY 14221. *Phone:* 716-631-1061 Ext. 2541. *Fax:* 716-632-1811. *E-mail:* jacqueline.s.matheny@medaille.edu.

Mercy College
Division of Business and Accounting

Dobbs Ferry, New York

Phone: 914-674-7482 **Fax:** 914-674-7488 **E-mail:** wcioffari@mercy.edu

Business Program(s) Web Site: http://www.mercy.edu/

Graduate Business Unit Enrollment *Total:* 339 (110 full-time; 229 part-time; 234 women; 19 international). *Average Age:* 35.

Graduate Business Faculty *Total:* 52 (9 full-time; 43 part-time).

Admissions *Applied:* 86. *Admitted:* 46. *Enrolled:* 24. *Average GMAT:* 450. *Average GPA:* 3.29

Academic Calendar Quarters.

After Graduation (Class of 2006–07) *Employed within 3 months of graduation:* 97%. *Average starting salary:* $55,000.

DEGREES MBA • MS

MBA—Master of Business Administration Full-time and part-time. Distance learning option. 33 to 57 total credits required. 24 to 60 months to complete program. *Concentrations:* accounting, banking, finance, general MBA, human resources management, international business, leadership, management, marketing.

MS—Direct Marketing Full-time and part-time. Distance learning option. 30 to 36 total credits required. 24 to 60 months to complete program. *Concentrations:* business ethics, marketing, marketing research.

MS—Internet Business Systems Full-time and part-time. Distance learning option. 30 to 36 total credits required. 18 to 60 months to complete program. *Concentrations:* business ethics, information systems, management, marketing.

MS—Master of Science in Human Resource Management Full-time and part-time. At least 36 total credits required. 12 to 60 months to complete program. *Concentrations:* human resources management, organizational management.

MS—Organizational Leadership Full-time and part-time. Distance learning option. 30 to 36 total credits required. 12 to 24 months to complete program. *Concentrations:* business ethics, leadership, organizational behavior/development, organizational management.

MS—Public Accounting Full-time and part-time. 24 to 30 total credits required. 15 to 36 months to complete program. *Concentrations:* accounting, corporate accounting, finance, management, managerial economics, marketing.

RESOURCES AND SERVICES 588 on-campus PCs are available to graduate business students. Access to Internet/World Wide Web, online (class) registration, and online grade reports available. *Personal computer requirements:* Graduate business students are strongly recommended to purchase or lease a personal computer. *Special opportunities include:* An internship program is available. *Placement services include:* Alumni network, career placement, career counseling/planning, resume referral, career fairs, job interviews arranged, and resume preparation.

EXPENSES *Tuition:* Full-time: $12,150. Part-time: $675 per credit hour. *Tuition (international):* Full-time: $12,150. Part-time: $675 per credit

Mercy College (continued)

hour. *Required fees:* Full-time: $440. Part-time: $220 per year. Tuition and/or fees vary by number of courses or credits taken. *Graduate housing:* Room and board costs vary by number of occupants and type of board plan. *Typical cost:* $9820 (including board).

FINANCIAL AID (2007–08) Grants, loans, research assistantships, scholarships, and work study. Aid is available to part-time students. *Financial aid application deadline:* 2/15.

Financial Aid Contact SFS Office, Office of Student Financial Services, 555 Broadway, Dobbs Ferry, NY 10522. *Phone:* 888-464-6737.

INTERNATIONAL STUDENTS 6% of students enrolled are international students. *Services and facilities:* Counseling/support services, Housing location assistance, International student housing, International student organization, Visa Services. Financial aid is not available to international students. *Required with application:* TOEFL with recommended score of 600 (paper); proof of adequate funds; proof of health/immunizations.

International Student Contact Mr. Simeon-Dan Guisuraga, International Student Advisor, 555 Broadway, Dobbs Ferry, NY 10522. *Phone:* 914-674-7284. *Fax:* 914-674-7270. *E-mail:* sguisuraga@mercy.edu.

APPLICATION *Required:* GMAT, application form, baccalaureate/first degree, interview, transcripts of college work. *Recommended:* 2 letters of recommendation, personal statement. *Application fee:* $37. Applications for domestic and international students are processed on a rolling basis.

Application Contact Prof. Wayne Cioffari, Director, MBA Program, 555 Broadway, Dobbs Ferry, NY 10522-1189. *Phone:* 914-674-7482. *Fax:* 914-674-7488. *E-mail:* wcioffari@mercy.edu.

The New School: A University
Milano The New School for Management and Urban Policy

New York, New York

Phone: 212-229-5462 Ext. 1108 **Fax:** 212-627-2695 **E-mail:** escandom@newschool.edu

Business Program(s) Web Site: http://www.newschool.edu/milano

Graduate Business Unit Enrollment *Total:* 695 (449 women; 32 international).

Graduate Business Faculty *Total:* 78 (22 full-time; 56 part-time).

Admissions *Applied:* 388. *Admitted:* 299. *Enrolled:* 156. *Average GPA:* 3.2

Academic Calendar Semesters.

After Graduation (Class of 2006–07) *Employed within 3 months of graduation:* 90%. *Average starting salary:* $42,000.

DEGREES MS

MS—Master of Science in Health Services Management and Policy Full-time and part-time. Distance learning option. At least 42 total credits required. Minimum of 24 months to complete program. *Concentration:* health care.

MS—Master of Science in Nonprofit Management Full-time and part-time. Distance learning option. At least 42 total credits required. Minimum of 24 months to complete program. *Concentration:* nonprofit management.

MS—Master of Science in Organizational Change Management Full-time and part-time. Distance learning option. At least 42 total credits required. Minimum of 24 months to complete program. *Concentration:* organizational management.

MS—Master of Science in Urban Policy Analysis and Management Full-time and part-time. Distance learning option. At least 42 total credits required. Minimum of 24 months to complete program. *Concentration:* public policy and administration.

RESOURCES AND SERVICES 200 on-campus PCs are available to graduate business students. Access to Internet/World Wide Web, online (class) registration, and online grade reports available. *Personal computer requirements:* Graduate business students are strongly recommended to purchase or lease a personal computer. *Special opportunities include:* An international exchange program and an internship program are available. *Placement services include:* Alumni network, career placement, job search course, career counseling/planning, electronic job bank, resume referral, career fairs, job interviews arranged, resume preparation, and career library.

EXPENSES *Tuition:* Full-time: $24,150. *Tuition (international):* Full-time: $24,150.

FINANCIAL AID (2007–08) 215 students received aid, including fellowships, grants, loans, research assistantships, scholarships, teaching assistantships, and work study. Aid is available to part-time students. *Financial aid application deadline:* 3/1.

Financial Aid Contact Ms. Laurie Schaffler, Director of Graduate Financial Aid, 79 Fifth Avenue, New York, NY 10011. *Phone:* 212-229-8930. *Fax:* 212-229-5919. *E-mail:* financialaid@newschool.edu.

INTERNATIONAL STUDENTS 5% of students enrolled are international students. *Services and facilities:* Counseling/support services, ESL/language courses, Housing location assistance, International student housing, International student organization, Orientation, Visa Services. Financial aid is available to international students. *Required with application:* TOEFL with recommended score of 250 (computer), 600 (paper), or 78 (Internet); proof of adequate funds; proof of health/immunizations.

International Student Contact Mrs. Monique N. Nri, Director of International Student Services, 79 Fifth Avenue, International Student Services, New York, NY 10011. *Phone:* 212-229-5592. *Fax:* 212-229-8992. *E-mail:* iss@newschool.edu.

APPLICATION *Required:* Application form, baccalaureate/first degree, essay, 2 letters of recommendation, personal statement, resume/curriculum vitae, transcripts of college work. *Recommended:* Interview. *Application fee:* $50. Applications for domestic and international students are processed on a rolling basis.

Application Contact Merida Escandon, Director of Admissions, 72 Fifth Avenue, Third Floor, New York, NY 10011. *Phone:* 212-229-5462 Ext. 1108. *Fax:* 212-627-2695. *E-mail:* escandom@newschool.edu.

New York Institute of Technology
School of Management

Old Westbury, New York

Phone: 212-261-1706 **Fax:** 212-261-1593 **E-mail:** gkalyana@nyit.edu

Business Program(s) Web Site: http://www.nyit.edu

Graduate Business Unit Enrollment *Total:* 1,464 (621 full-time; 843 part-time; 546 women; 641 international). *Average Age:* 32.

Graduate Business Faculty *Total:* 91 (27 full-time; 64 part-time).

Admissions *Applied:* 1,039. *Admitted:* 915. *Enrolled:* 256. *Average GMAT:* 453. *Average GPA:* 2.95

Academic Calendar Semesters.

After Graduation (Class of 2006–07) *Employed within 3 months of graduation:* 75%.

DEGREES DO/MBA • MBA • MS

DO/MBA—Doctor of Osteopathy/Master of Business Administration Full-time and part-time. Distance learning option. Must be matriculated at NYCOM. MCAT scores accepted in lieu of GMAT. An undergraduate GPA of 2.75 or above and MCAT scores in the 50th percentile or above required. Minimum of 60 months to complete program. *Concentrations:* health care, management.

MBA—Executive Master of Business Administration Full-time and part-time. Distance learning option. 56 total credits required. *Concentrations:* accounting, business policy/strategy, electronic commerce (E-commerce), international business, international finance, management, management information systems, managerial economics, marketing.

MBA—Master of Business Administration Full-time and part-time. Distance learning option. 36 to 54 total credits required. 12 to 60 months to complete program. *Concentrations:* accounting, electronic commerce (E-commerce), finance, health care, international business, management, management information systems, marketing.

MS—Master of Science in Human Resource Management and Labor Relations Full-time and part-time. Distance learning option. 42 total credits required. 12 to 60 months to complete program. *Concentrations:* human resources management, industrial/labor relations.

RESOURCES AND SERVICES 815 on-campus PCs are available to graduate business students. Access to Internet/World Wide Web, online (class) registration, and online grade reports available. *Personal computer requirements:* Graduate business students are required to have a personal computer. *Special opportunities include:* An internship program is available. *Placement services include:* Alumni network, career placement, career counseling/planning, electronic job bank, career fairs, resume preparation, and career library.

EXPENSES *Tuition:* Full-time: $18,792. Part-time: $783 per credit hour. *Tuition (international):* Full-time: $18,792. Part-time: $783 per credit hour. *Graduate housing:* Room and board costs vary by campus location, number of occupants, type of accommodation, and type of board plan. *Typical cost:* $10,520 (including board).

FINANCIAL AID (2007–08) 208 students received aid, including fellowships, loans, research assistantships, and scholarships. Aid is available to part-time students. *Financial aid application deadline:* 2/1.

Financial Aid Contact Ms. Clain Jacobi, Director of Financial Aid, Northern Boulevard, Harry Schure Hall, Old Westbury, NY 11568-8000. *Phone:* 516-686-1085. *Fax:* 516-686-7997. *E-mail:* cjacobi@nyit.edu.

INTERNATIONAL STUDENTS 44% of students enrolled are international students. *Services and facilities:* Counseling/support services, ESL/language courses, Housing location assistance, International student housing, International student organization, Language tutoring, Orientation, Visa Services. Financial aid is available to international students. *Required with application:* TOEFL with recommended score of 550 (paper); proof of adequate funds; proof of health/immunizations.

International Student Contact Ms. Barbara Multari, Director, Office of International Education, Northern Boulevard, Theobald Hall, Room 317, Old Westbury, NY 11568-8000. *Phone:* 516-686-7585. *Fax:* 516-686-7802. *E-mail:* bmultari@nyit.edu.

APPLICATION *Required:* GMAT, application form, baccalaureate/first degree, essay, transcripts of college work. School will accept GRE. *Recommended:* Work experience. *Application fee:* $50. *Deadlines:* 6/1 for fall (international), 11/1 for spring (international). Applications for domestic students are processed on a rolling basis.

Application Contact Gurumurthy Kalyanaram, Director, MBA Program, 1855 Broadway, New York, NY 10023-7692. *Phone:* 212-261-1706. *Fax:* 212-261-1593. *E-mail:* gkalyana@nyit.edu.

New York University
Leonard N. Stern School of Business

New York, New York

Phone: 212-998-0600 **E-mail:** sternmba@stern.nyu.edu

Business Program(s) Web Site: http://www.stern.nyu.edu/

Admissions *Average GMAT:* 700. *Average GPA:* 3.4

Academic Calendar Semesters.

Accreditation AACSB—The Association to Advance Collegiate Schools of Business.

After Graduation (Class of 2006–07) *Employed within 3 months of graduation:* 94%. *Average starting salary:* $96,738.

DEGREES JD/MBA • MBA • MBA/MA • MBA/MPA • MBA/MS

JD/MBA—Juris Doctor/Master of Business Administration At least 122 total credits required. *Concentrations:* combined degrees, general MBA, law.

MBA—Executive Master of Business Administration *Concentrations:* finance, management.

MBA—MBA/MFA (Master of Fine Arts) Maximum of 36 months to complete program. *Concentrations:* combined degrees, general MBA, other.

MBA—Master of Business Administration *Concentrations:* accounting, banking, economics, electronic commerce (E-commerce), entrepreneurship, finance, financial economics, general MBA, international business, leadership, management information systems, marketing, media administration, operations management, organizational behavior/development, statistics, strategic management.

MBA/MA—MBA/MA in French Studies *Concentrations:* combined degrees, general MBA, other.

MBA/MA—MBA/MA in Politics Maximum of 36 months to complete program. *Concentrations:* combined degrees, general MBA, other.

MBA/MPA—Master of Business Administration/Master of Public Administration Maximum of 36 months to complete program. *Concentrations:* combined degrees, general MBA, public policy and administration.

MBA/MS—MBA/MS in Biology Maximum of 36 months to complete program. *Concentrations:* combined degrees, general MBA, other.

RESOURCES AND SERVICES *Personal computer requirements:* Graduate business students are not required to have a personal computer. *Placement services include:* Alumni network, career placement, job search course, career counseling/planning, electronic job bank, resume referral, career fairs, job interviews arranged, resume preparation, and career library.

EXPENSES *Tuition:* Full-time: $39,800. Part-time: $1440 per credit. *Tuition (international):* Full-time: $39,800. Part-time: $1440 per credit. *Required fees:* Full-time: $2022. *Graduate housing:* Room and board costs vary by campus location, number of occupants, and type of accommodation. *Typical cost:* $2822 (including board).

FINANCIAL AID (2007–08) Fellowships, loans, scholarships, and teaching assistantships. *Financial aid application deadline:* 3/15.

Financial Aid Contact Financial Aid Office, 44 West Fourth Street, 6th Floor, New York, NY 10012-1126. *E-mail:* fin-aid@stern.nyu.edu.

INTERNATIONAL STUDENTS *Services and facilities:* International student organization, Orientation. Financial aid is available to international students.

APPLICATION *Required:* GMAT, application form, baccalaureate/first degree, essay, letter(s) of recommendation, personal statement, resume/curriculum vitae, transcripts of college work, work experience. *Recommended:* Interview. *Application fee:* $200. *Deadlines:* 11/15 for fall, 1/15 for winter, 3/15 for spring.

Application Contact MBA Admissions Office, 44 West Fourth Street, Henry Kaufman Management Center, Suite 6-70, New York, NY 10012. *Phone:* 212-998-0600. *E-mail:* sternmba@stern.nyu.edu.

New York University
Robert F. Wagner Graduate School of Public Service

New York, New York

Phone: 212-998-7414 **Fax:** 212-995-4164 **E-mail:** wagner.admissions@nyu.edu

New York University (continued)

Business Program(s) Web Site: http://www.wagner.nyu.edu

Graduate Business Unit Enrollment *Total:* 881 (443 full-time; 438 part-time; 640 women; 93 international). *Average Age:* 28.

Graduate Business Faculty *Total:* 166 (38 full-time; 128 part-time).

Admissions *Applied:* 1,354. *Admitted:* 804. *Enrolled:* 303. *Average GPA:* 3.4

Academic Calendar Semesters.

Accreditation AACSB—The Association to Advance Collegiate Schools of Business.

After Graduation (Class of 2006–07) *Average starting salary:* $58,000.

DEGREES MBA equivalent • MPA • MS

MBA equivalent—MUP—Master of Urban Planning Full-time and part-time. 60 total credits required. 21 to 60 months to complete program. *Concentrations:* city/urban administration, developmental economics, environmental economics/management, transportation management.

MPA—Health Policy and Management Full-time and part-time. 60 total credits required. 21 to 60 months to complete program. *Concentrations:* health administration, health care.

MPA—Public and Nonprofit Management and Policy Full-time and part-time. 60 total credits required. 21 to 60 months to complete program. *Concentrations:* administration, arts administration/management, international development management, international management, nonprofit management, nonprofit organization, public management, public policy and administration.

MS—Management Full-time and part-time. Must have 5 to 7 years management experience. 36 total credits required. 9 to 60 months to complete program. *Concentrations:* administration, arts administration/management, city/urban administration, finance, health administration, health care, international development management, international finance, international management, leadership, management, nonprofit management, public finance, public policy and administration.

RESOURCES AND SERVICES Access to Internet/World Wide Web, online (class) registration, and online grade reports available. *Personal computer requirements:* Graduate business students are strongly recommended to purchase or lease a personal computer. *Special opportunities include:* An international exchange program and an internship program are available. *Placement services include:* Alumni network, career counseling/planning, electronic job bank, career fairs, resume preparation, and career library.

EXPENSES *Tuition:* Full-time: $27,840. Part-time: $870 per credit. *Tuition (international):* Full-time: $27,840. Part-time: $870 per credit. *Required fees:* Full-time: $1425. Part-time: $58 per credit. Tuition and/or fees vary by number of courses or credits taken and academic program. *Graduate housing:* Room and board costs vary by campus location, number of occupants, type of accommodation, and type of board plan. *Typical cost:* $17,355 (including board).

FINANCIAL AID (2007–08) 306 students received aid, including fellowships, loans, research assistantships, scholarships, and work study. Aid is available to part-time students. *Financial aid application deadline:* 1/15.

Financial Aid Contact Office of Enrollment and Student Services, The Puck Building, 295 Lafayette Street, New York, NY 10012. *Phone:* 212-998-7414. *Fax:* 212-995-4164. *E-mail:* wagner.admissions@nyu.edu.

INTERNATIONAL STUDENTS 11% of students enrolled are international students. *Services and facilities:* Counseling/support services, ESL/language courses, International student organization, Language tutoring, Orientation, Visa Services. Financial aid is available to international students. *Required with application:* TOEFL with recommended score of 250 (computer), 600 (paper), or 103 (Internet); TWE with recommended score of 4; proof of adequate funds; proof of health/immunizations.

International Student Contact Office of Enrollment and Student Services, The Puck Building, 295 Lafayette Street, 2nd Floor, New York, NY 10012. *Phone:* 212-998-7414. *Fax:* 212-995-4164. *E-mail:* wagner.admissions@nyu.edu.

APPLICATION *Required:* Application form, baccalaureate/first degree, 2 letters of recommendation, personal statement, resume/curriculum vitae, transcripts of college work. School will accept GMAT and GRE. *Recommended:* Essay, work experience. *Application fee:* $70. Applications for domestic and international students are processed on a rolling basis.

Application Contact Office of Enrollment and Student Services, The Puck Building, 295 Lafayette Street, 2nd Floor, New York, NY 10012. *Phone:* 212-998-7414. *Fax:* 212-995-4164. *E-mail:* wagner.admissions@nyu.edu.

Nyack College
School of Business
Nyack, New York

Phone: 212-625-0500 Ext. 262 **Fax:** 212-941-1575 **E-mail:** michele.ortiz@nyack.edu

Business Program(s) Web Site: http://www.nyackcollege.edu

DEGREES MBA

MBA—MBA Finance Full-time. At least 36 total credits required. Minimum of 16 months to complete program. *Concentration:* finance.

MBA—Master of Business Administration Full-time. At least 36 total credits required. Minimum of 16 months to complete program. *Concentration:* general MBA.

MBA—Master of Business Administration in Accounting Full-time. Students pursuing an MBA in Accounting must have an undergraduate degree in accounting. At least 36 total credits required. Minimum of 16 months to complete program. *Concentration:* accounting.

MBA—Master of Business Administration Full-time. Up to 36 total credits required. Maximum of 16 months to complete program. *Concentrations:* human resources management, information systems, international business, marketing.

RESOURCES AND SERVICES 50 on-campus PCs are available to graduate business students. Access to Internet/World Wide Web and online (class) registration available. *Personal computer requirements:* Graduate business students are required to have a personal computer. *Placement services include:* Alumni network and career fairs.

Application Contact Michele Ortiz, MBA Program Administrator, 93 Worth Street, New York, NY 10013. *Phone:* 212-625-0500 Ext. 262. *Fax:* 212-941-1575. *E-mail:* michele.ortiz@nyack.edu.

Pace University
Lubin School of Business
New York, New York

Phone: 212-346-1531 **Fax:** 212-346-1585 **E-mail:** gradnyc@pace.edu

Business Program(s) Web Site: http://www.pace.edu/lubin

Graduate Business Unit Enrollment *Total:* 1,035 (226 full-time; 809 part-time; 459 women; 295 international). *Average Age:* 29.

Graduate Business Faculty *Total:* 76 (55 full-time; 21 part-time).

Admissions *Applied:* 1,055. *Admitted:* 586. *Enrolled:* 238. *Average GMAT:* 547. *Average GPA:* 3.14

Academic Calendar Semesters.

Accreditation AACSB—The Association to Advance Collegiate Schools of Business.

After Graduation (Class of 2006–07) *Employed within 3 months of graduation:* 87%. *Average starting salary:* $57,608.

DEGREES JD/MBA • MBA • MS

JD/MBA—Juris Doctor/Master of Business Administration Full-time and part-time. Application must be made to the School of Business and the School of Law. 129 to 145 total credits required. 48 to 72 months to complete program. *Concentration:* combined degrees.

MBA—Executive Master of Business Administration Distance learning option. 5 years of managerial experience required. 54 total credits required. 23 months to complete program. *Concentration:* management.

MBA—Master of Business Administration Full-time and part-time. 52 total credits required. 24 to 60 months to complete program. *Concentrations:* accounting, electronic commerce (E-commerce), entrepreneurship, finance, financial management/planning, human resources management, information systems, international business, international economics, management, management science, marketing, organizational behavior/development, taxation.

MS—Master of Science Full-time and part-time. 30 to 60 total credits required. 12 to 60 months to complete program. *Concentrations:* accounting, economics, financial management/planning, human resources management, investments and securities, management science, taxation.

RESOURCES AND SERVICES 985 on-campus PCs are available to graduate business students. Access to Internet/World Wide Web, online (class) registration, and online grade reports available. *Personal computer requirements:* Graduate business students are strongly recommended to purchase or lease a personal computer. *Special opportunities include:* An international exchange program and an internship program are available. *Placement services include:* Alumni network, career placement, job search course, career counseling/planning, electronic job bank, resume referral, career fairs, job interviews arranged, resume preparation, and career library.

EXPENSES *Tuition:* Full-time: $27,000. Part-time: $900 per credit. *Tuition (international):* Full-time: $27,000. Part-time: $900 per credit. *Required fees:* Full-time: $725. Tuition and/or fees vary by number of courses or credits taken. *Graduate housing:* Room and board costs vary by campus location, number of occupants, type of accommodation, and type of board plan. *Typical cost:* $11,180 (including board).

FINANCIAL AID (2007–08) 559 students received aid, including grants, loans, research assistantships, scholarships, and work study. Aid is available to part-time students. *Financial aid application deadline:* 2/15.

Financial Aid Contact Mark Stephens, Director, Student Financial Aid, 861 Bedford Road, Pleasantville, NY 10570. *Phone:* 914-773-3486. *E-mail:* mstephens@pace.edu.

INTERNATIONAL STUDENTS 29% of students enrolled are international students. *Services and facilities:* Counseling/support services, ESL/language courses, Housing location assistance, International student housing, International student organization, Language tutoring, Orientation, Visa Services. Financial aid is not available to international students. *Required with application:* TOEFL with recommended score of 229 (computer) or 570 (paper); proof of adequate funds; proof of health/immunizations. *Recommended with application:* IELT with recommended score of 6.

International Student Contact Joanna Broda, Director of Admissions, Office of Graduate Admissions, One Pace Plaza, New York, NY 10038. *Phone:* 212-346-1531. *Fax:* 212-346-1585. *E-mail:* gradnyc@pace.edu.

APPLICATION *Required:* GMAT, application form, baccalaureate/first degree, essay, 2 letters of recommendation, personal statement, resume/curriculum vitae, transcripts of college work. *Application fee:* $65. Applications for domestic and international students are processed on a rolling basis.

Application Contact Joanna Broda, Director of Admissions, Office of Graduate Admissions, One Pace Plaza, New York, NY 10038. *Phone:* 212-346-1531. *Fax:* 212-346-1585. *E-mail:* gradnyc@pace.edu.

Rensselaer Polytechnic Institute
Lally School of Management and Technology
Troy, New York

Phone: 518-276-6565 **Fax:** 518-276-2665 **E-mail:** lallymba@rpi.edu

Business Program(s) Web Site: http://lallyschool.rpi.edu/

Graduate Business Unit Enrollment *Total:* 550 (100 full-time; 450 part-time; 177 women; 48 international). *Average Age:* 28.

Graduate Business Faculty *Total:* 53 (51 full-time; 2 part-time).

Admissions *Applied:* 350. *Admitted:* 278. *Enrolled:* 126. *Average GMAT:* 619. *Average GPA:* 3.2

Academic Calendar Semesters.

Accreditation AACSB—The Association to Advance Collegiate Schools of Business.

After Graduation (Class of 2006–07) *Employed within 3 months of graduation:* 67%. *Average starting salary:* $75,255.

DEGREES MBA • MS

MBA—Executive Master of Business Administration Full-time. 6 years of management experience required. 48 total credits required. 18 months to complete program. *Concentrations:* leadership, management, technology management.

MBA—Master of Business Administration Full-time and part-time. Pathfinders MBA requires one-year co-op between first and second years. 60 total credits required. 18 to 24 months to complete program. *Concentrations:* business information science, business policy/strategy, decision sciences, entrepreneurship, finance, financial information systems, information management, management, management consulting, management information systems, management science, manufacturing management, marketing, new venture management, operations management, production management, quality management, quantitative analysis, research and development administration, statistics, technology management.

MS—Master of Science in Management Full-time and part-time. Distance learning option. 30 total credits required. 9 to 18 months to complete program. *Concentrations:* business information science, business policy/strategy, decision sciences, entrepreneurship, finance, financial information systems, information management, management, management consulting, management information systems, management science, management systems analysis, marketing, new venture management, operations management, production management, quality management, quantitative analysis, statistics.

RESOURCES AND SERVICES 1,565 on-campus PCs are available to graduate business students. Access to Internet/World Wide Web, online (class) registration, and online grade reports available. *Personal computer requirements:* Graduate business students are required to have a personal computer. *Special opportunities include:* An international exchange program and an internship program are available. *Placement services include:* Alumni network, career placement, job search course, career counseling/planning, electronic job bank, resume referral, career fairs, job interviews arranged, resume preparation, and career library.

EXPENSES *Tuition:* Full-time: $36,950. Part-time: $1255 per credit hour. *Tuition (international):* Full-time: $36,950. *Required fees:* Full-time: $1830. *Graduate housing:* Room and board costs vary by number of occupants, type of accommodation, and type of board plan. *Typical cost:* $10,000 (including board).

FINANCIAL AID (2007–08) Fellowships, loans, scholarships, and teaching assistantships. *Financial aid application deadline:* 4/15.

Financial Aid Contact Ms. Jill M. Terry, Assistant Dean of Master's Programs, Pittsburgh Building, Room 3216, 110 Eighth Street, Troy, NY 12180-3590. *Phone:* 518-276-6565. *Fax:* 518-276-2665. *E-mail:* lallymba@rpi.edu.

Rensselaer Polytechnic Institute (continued)

INTERNATIONAL STUDENTS 9% of students enrolled are international students. *Services and facilities:* Counseling/support services, ESL/language courses, Housing location assistance, International student housing, International student organization, Language tutoring, Orientation, Visa Services, U.S. culture courses. Financial aid is available to international students. *Required with application:* TOEFL with recommended score of 250 (computer) or 600 (paper); proof of adequate funds; proof of health/immunizations. *Recommended with application:* IELT with recommended score of 7.

International Student Contact Jane Havis, Assistant Dean, International Student Services, RPI 4631 Academy Hall, 110 Eighth Street, Troy, NY 12180-3590. *Phone:* 518-276-6561. *Fax:* 518-276-4839. *E-mail:* havisj@rpi.edu.

APPLICATION *Required:* GMAT, application form, baccalaureate/first degree, essay, 2 letters of recommendation, personal statement, resume/curriculum vitae, transcripts of college work, 3 years of work experience. *Application fee:* $75. Applications for domestic and international students are processed on a rolling basis.

Application Contact Ms. Jill M. Terry, Assistant Dean of Master's Programs, Pittsburgh Building, Room 3216, 110 Eighth Street, Troy, NY 12180-3590. *Phone:* 518-276-6565. *Fax:* 518-276-2665. *E-mail:* lallymba@rpi.edu.

See full description on page 670.

Roberts Wesleyan College
Division of Business
Rochester, New York

Phone: 585-594-6904 **Fax:** 585-594-6444 **E-mail:** sullivan_susan@roberts.edu

Business Program(s) Web Site: http://www.roberts.edu/Academics/AcademicDivisions/BusinessManagement/

Graduate Business Unit Enrollment *Total:* 85 (84 full-time; 1 part-time; 55 women). *Average Age:* 41.

Graduate Business Faculty *Total:* 20 (7 full-time; 13 part-time).

Admissions *Applied:* 71. *Admitted:* 70. *Enrolled:* 62. *Average GPA:* 3.4

Academic Calendar Continuous.

After Graduation (Class of 2006–07) *Employed within 3 months of graduation:* 100%.

DEGREES MSMP • MSOL

MSMP—Master of Science in Strategic Marketing Full-time. At least 36 total credits required. Minimum of 16 months to complete program. *Concentration:* marketing.

MSOL—Master of Science in Strategic Leadership Full-time. At least 36 total credits required. Minimum of 17 months to complete program. *Concentration:* leadership.

RESOURCES AND SERVICES 85 on-campus PCs are available to graduate business students. Access to Internet/World Wide Web and online grade reports available. *Personal computer requirements:* Graduate business students are strongly recommended to purchase or lease a personal computer. *Placement services include:* Alumni network, career placement, career counseling/planning, career fairs, resume preparation, and career library.

FINANCIAL AID (2007–08) 63 students received aid, including loans and scholarships. *Financial aid application deadline:* 5/1.

Financial Aid Contact Mr. Steve Field, Director of Financial Aid, 2301 Westside Drive, Rochester, NY 14624-1997. *Phone:* 585-594-6150. *Fax:* 585-594-6036. *E-mail:* fields@roberts.edu.

INTERNATIONAL STUDENTS *Services and facilities:* Counseling/support services, ESL/language courses, Housing location assistance, Orientation, Visa Services. Financial aid is available to international students. *Required with application:* TOEFL with recommended score of 550 (paper); proof of adequate funds; proof of health/immunizations.

International Student Contact Ms. Gale Lynch, International Students Coordinator, 2301 Westside Drive, Rochester, NY 14624-1997. *Phone:* 585-594-6382. *Fax:* 585-594-6567. *E-mail:* lynchg@roberts.edu.

APPLICATION *Required:* Application form, baccalaureate/first degree, essay, 2 letters of recommendation, personal statement, resume/curriculum vitae, transcripts of college work, 2 years of work experience. *Application fee:* $35. Applications for domestic and international students are processed on a rolling basis.

Application Contact Susan J. Sullivan, Director of Marketing and Recruitment, 2301 Westside Drive, Rochester, NY 14624-1997. *Phone:* 585-594-6904. *Fax:* 585-594-6444. *E-mail:* sullivan_susan@roberts.edu.

Rochester Institute of Technology
E. Philip Saunders College of Business
Rochester, New York

Phone: 585-475-6916 **Fax:** 585-475-7450 **E-mail:** gradbus@rit.edu

Business Program(s) Web Site: http://www.ritmba.com

Graduate Business Unit Enrollment *Total:* 425 (247 full-time; 178 part-time; 165 women; 95 international). *Average Age:* 29.

Graduate Business Faculty 48 full-time.

Admissions *Applied:* 416. *Admitted:* 260. *Enrolled:* 136. *Average GMAT:* 576. *Average GPA:* 3.2

Academic Calendar Quarters.

Accreditation AACSB—The Association to Advance Collegiate Schools of Business.

DEGREES EMBA • MBA • MS • MSF

EMBA—Executive Master of Business Administration Part-time. 72 total credits required. 15 months to complete program. *Concentration:* executive programs.

MBA—Master of Business Administration Full-time and part-time. At least 72 total credits required. 12 to 84 months to complete program. *Concentrations:* accounting, corporate accounting, electronic commerce (E-commerce), engineering, entrepreneurship, finance, human resources management, international business, leadership, management, management information systems, manufacturing management, marketing, marketing research, other, public policy and administration, quality management, supply chain management, technology management, telecommunications management.

MS—Innovation Management Full-time and part-time. 48 total credits required. 12 to 84 months to complete program. *Concentration:* technology management.

MS—Management Full-time and part-time. At least 48 total credits required. 12 to 84 months to complete program. *Concentrations:* international business, technology management.

MSF—Master of Science in Finance Full-time and part-time. 48 total credits required. 12 to 84 months to complete program. *Concentration:* finance.

RESOURCES AND SERVICES 3,000 on-campus PCs are available to graduate business students. Access to Internet/World Wide Web, online (class) registration, and online grade reports available. *Personal computer requirements:* Graduate business students are strongly recommended to purchase or lease a personal computer. *Special opportunities include:* An internship program is available. *Placement services include:* Alumni network, career placement, job search course, career counseling/planning, electronic job bank, resume referral, career fairs, job interviews arranged, resume preparation, and career library.

EXPENSES *Tuition:* Full-time: $30,174. Part-time: $848 per credit hour. *Tuition (international):* Full-time: $30,174. *Required fees:* Full-time: $207. Tuition and/or fees vary by number of courses or credits taken.

Graduate housing: Room and board costs vary by number of occupants, type of accommodation, and type of board plan. *Typical cost:* $7500 (including board).

FINANCIAL AID (2007–08) 130 students received aid, including grants, research assistantships, and scholarships. Aid is available to part-time students. *Financial aid application deadline:* 8/1.

Financial Aid Contact Ms. Rupa Patel, Assistant Director, Admissions and Recruiting for Graduate Business Admissions, 105 Lomb Memorial Drive, Rochester, NY 14623-5604. *Phone:* 585-475-6916. *Fax:* 585-475-7450. *E-mail:* gradbus@saunders.rit.edu.

INTERNATIONAL STUDENTS 22% of students enrolled are international students. *Services and facilities:* Counseling/support services, ESL/language courses, Housing location assistance, International student housing, International student organization, Orientation, Visa Services. Financial aid is available to international students. *Required with application:* TOEFL with recommended score of 237 (computer), 580 (paper), or 92 (Internet); proof of adequate funds; proof of health/immunizations.

International Student Contact Mr. Jeffrey Cox, Program Coordinator, International Students, One Lomb Memorial Drive, Rochester, NY 14623-5604. *Phone:* 585-475-7433. *Fax:* 585-475-7419. *E-mail:* jwccst@rit.edu.

APPLICATION *Required:* GMAT, application form, baccalaureate/first degree, personal statement, transcripts of college work. *Recommended:* Letter(s) of recommendation, resume/curriculum vitae. *Application fee:* $50. Applications for domestic and international students are processed on a rolling basis.

Application Contact Ms. Rupa Patel, Assistant Director, Admissions and Recruiting for Graduate Business Admissions, 105 Lomb Memorial Drive, Rochester, NY 14623-5604. *Phone:* 585-475-6916. *Fax:* 585-475-7450. *E-mail:* gradbus@rit.edu.

Sage Graduate School

Department of Management

Troy, New York

Phone: 518-244-2443 **Fax:** 518-244-4571 **E-mail:** eastos@sage.edu

Business Program(s) Web Site: http://www.sage.edu

Graduate Business Unit Enrollment *Total:* 131 (21 full-time; 110 part-time; 99 women). *Average Age:* 32.

Graduate Business Faculty *Total:* 10 (3 full-time; 7 part-time).

Admissions *Applied:* 68. *Admitted:* 40. *Enrolled:* 28.

Academic Calendar Semesters.

After Graduation (Class of 2006–07) *Employed within 3 months of graduation:* 82%. *Average starting salary:* $40,000.

DEGREES JD/MBA • MBA • MBA/MS • MS

JD/MBA—Juris Doctor/Master of Business Administration Full-time and part-time. 75 to 87 total credits required. 48 to 72 months to complete program. *Concentrations:* human resources management, management, marketing, strategic management.

MBA—Professional Master of Business Administration Full-time and part-time. 36 to 48 total credits required. 24 to 72 months to complete program. *Concentrations:* finance, human resources management, management, marketing.

MBA/MS—Master of Business Administration/Master of Science in Nursing Full-time and part-time. 36 to 48 total credits required. 24 to 72 months to complete program. *Concentrations:* health care, management, marketing.

MS—Master of Science in Health Services Administration Full-time and part-time. At least 39 total credits required. 24 to 72 months to complete program. *Concentration:* health care.

RESOURCES AND SERVICES 183 on-campus PCs are available to graduate business students. Access to Internet/World Wide Web, online (class) registration, and online grade reports available. *Personal computer requirements:* Graduate business students are strongly recommended to purchase or lease a personal computer. *Special opportunities include:* An internship program is available. *Placement services include:* Alumni network, career placement, career counseling/planning, career fairs, resume preparation, and career library.

EXPENSES *Tuition:* Full-time: $9720. Part-time: $540 per credit hour. *Tuition (international):* Full-time: $9720. Part-time: $540 per credit hour. *Typical graduate housing cost:* $8950 (including board), $4650 (room only).

FINANCIAL AID (2007–08) Loans and research assistantships. Aid is available to part-time students.

Financial Aid Contact Lisa Kuban, Director of Financial Aid, 65 First Street, Troy, NY 12180. *Phone:* 518-244-2201. *Fax:* 518-244-2460. *E-mail:* kubanl@sage.edu.

INTERNATIONAL STUDENTS Financial aid is not available to international students. *Required with application:* TOEFL with recommended score of 213 (computer) or 550 (paper); proof of adequate funds; proof of health/immunizations.

International Student Contact Wendy Diefendorf, Director of Graduate and Adult Admission, 45 Ferry Street, Troy, NY 12180-4115. *Phone:* 518-244-2443. *Fax:* 518-244-4571. *E-mail:* eastos@sage.edu.

APPLICATION *Required:* Application form, baccalaureate/first degree, essay, 2 letters of recommendation, personal statement, resume/curriculum vitae, transcripts of college work. *Recommended:* Interview, 1 year of work experience. *Application fee:* $40. Applications for domestic and international students are processed on a rolling basis.

Application Contact Wendy Diefendorf, Director of Graduate and Adult Admission, 45 Ferry Street, Troy, NY 12180-4115. *Phone:* 518-244-2443. *Fax:* 518-244-4571. *E-mail:* eastos@sage.edu.

St. Bonaventure University

School of Business

St. Bonaventure, New York

Phone: 716-375-2021 **Fax:** 716-375-4015 **E-mail:** tdewe@sbu.edu

Business Program(s) Web Site: http://www.grad.sbu.edu

Accreditation AACSB—The Association to Advance Collegiate Schools of Business.

DEGREES M Sc • MBA

M Sc—Master of Science in Professional Leadership Full-time. 30 total credits required. 15 months to complete program. *Concentration:* leadership.

MBA—Evening Master of Business Administration Full-time and part-time. 30 to 51 total credits required. 12 to 72 months to complete program. *Concentrations:* accounting, finance, international business, management, marketing.

MBA—Master of Business Administration Full-time. 30 to 51 total credits required. Minimum of 12 months to complete program. *Concentrations:* accounting, finance, international business, management, marketing.

MBA—Weekend Master of Business Administration Full-time and part-time. 30 to 51 total credits required. 12 to 72 months to complete program. *Concentrations:* accounting, finance, international business, management, marketing.

RESOURCES AND SERVICES 125 on-campus PCs are available to graduate business students. Access to Internet/World Wide Web, online (class) registration, and online grade reports available. *Personal computer requirements:* Graduate business students are not required to have a personal computer. *Special opportunities include:* An internship program is available. *Placement services include:* Alumni network, career

St. Bonaventure University (continued)

placement, career counseling/planning, electronic job bank, career fairs, job interviews arranged, resume preparation, and career library.

Application Contact Tina Dewe, Administrative Assistant to Dean of Enrollment and Graduate Admissions, PO Box D, Graduate Admissions, St. Bonaventure, NY 14778. *Phone:* 716-375-2021. *Fax:* 716-375-4015. *E-mail:* tdewe@sbu.edu.

St. John Fisher College

The Ronald L. Bittner School of Business

Rochester, New York

Phone: 585-385-8045 **Fax:** 585-385-8344 **E-mail:** hsmith@sjfc.edu

Business Program(s) Web Site: http://www.sjfc.edu/bittner

Graduate Business Unit Enrollment *Total:* 93 (24 full-time; 69 part-time; 42 women). *Average Age:* 32.

Graduate Business Faculty *Total:* 13 (11 full-time; 2 part-time).

Admissions *Applied:* 54. *Admitted:* 43. *Enrolled:* 36. *Average GMAT:* 456. *Average GPA:* 3.17

Academic Calendar Semesters.

Accreditation AACSB—The Association to Advance Collegiate Schools of Business.

After Graduation (Class of 2006–07) *Employed within 3 months of graduation:* 100%.

DEGREES MBA

MBA—One-Year Master of Business Administration Full-time. Classes are held Wednesday evening and all day Saturday. At least 48 total credits required. 12 months to complete program. *Concentration:* general MBA.

MBA—Part-Time Master of Business Administration Full-time and part-time. At least 48 total credits required. 24 to 60 months to complete program. *Concentration:* general MBA.

RESOURCES AND SERVICES 424 on-campus PCs are available to graduate business students. Access to Internet/World Wide Web, online (class) registration, and online grade reports available. *Personal computer requirements:* Graduate business students are not required to have a personal computer. *Placement services include:* Alumni network, career counseling/planning, electronic job bank, resume referral, career fairs, job interviews arranged, resume preparation, and career library.

EXPENSES *Tuition:* Part-time: $803 per credit hour. *Tuition (international):* Part-time: $803 per credit hour. *Required fees:* Full-time: $50. Tuition and/or fees vary by academic program.

FINANCIAL AID (2007–08) 36 students received aid, including grants, loans, and scholarships. Aid is available to part-time students. *Financial aid application deadline:* 2/15.

Financial Aid Contact Mrs. Angela Monnat, Director of Financial Aid, 3690 East Avenue, Rochester, NY 14618-3597. *Phone:* 585-385-8042. *Fax:* 585-385-8044. *E-mail:* amonnat@sjfc.edu.

INTERNATIONAL STUDENTS *Services and facilities:* Counseling/ support services, Housing location assistance. Financial aid is not available to international students. *Required with application:* TOEFL with recommended score of 575 (paper); proof of adequate funds; proof of health/immunizations.

International Student Contact Nicole Forster, Academic Counselor, 3690 East Avenue, Rochester, NY 14618-3597. *Phone:* 585-385-8321. *Fax:* 585-385-8344. *E-mail:* nforster@sjfc.edu.

APPLICATION *Required:* GMAT, application form, baccalaureate/first degree, essay, 2 letters of recommendation, personal statement, resume/ curriculum vitae, transcripts of college work. *Recommended:* Interview, 5 years of work experience. *Application fee:* $30. Applications for domestic and international students are processed on a rolling basis.

Application Contact Ms. Holly Smith, Interim Director of Graduate Admissions, 3690 East Avenue, Rochester, NY 14618-3597. *Phone:* 585-385-8045. *Fax:* 585-385-8344. *E-mail:* hsmith@sjfc.edu.

St. John's University

The Peter J. Tobin College of Business

Queens, New York

Phone: 718-990-1345 **Fax:** 718-990-5242 **E-mail:** russells@stjohns.edu

Business Program(s) Web Site: http://www.stjohns.edu/tobincollege

Accreditation AACSB—The Association to Advance Collegiate Schools of Business.

DEGREES JD/MBA • MBA • MS

JD/MBA—Juris Doctor/Master of Business Administration Full-time. 115 to 143 total credits required. 48 to 60 months to complete program. *Concentrations:* accounting, decision sciences, economics, finance, international finance, management, management information systems, marketing, taxation.

MBA—Master of Business Administration in Accounting Full-time and part-time. 39 to 78 total credits required. 16 to 60 months to complete program. *Concentration:* accounting.

MBA—Master of Business Administration in Computer Information Systems Full-time and part-time. 36 to 54 total credits required. 12 to 60 months to complete program. *Concentration:* management information systems.

MBA—Master of Business Administration in Decision Sciences Full-time and part-time. 36 to 66 total credits required. 12 to 60 months to complete program. *Concentration:* decision sciences.

MBA—Master of Business Administration in Finance Full-time and part-time. 36 to 54 total credits required. 12 to 60 months to complete program. *Concentrations:* finance, international finance.

MBA—Master of Business Administration in International Business Full-time and part-time. 36 to 54 total credits required. 12 to 60 months to complete program. *Concentration:* international business.

MBA—Master of Business Administration in International Finance Full-time and part-time. 36 to 54 total credits required. 12 to 60 months to complete program. *Concentration:* international finance.

MBA—Master of Business Administration in Management Full-time and part-time. 36 to 54 total credits required. 12 to 60 months to complete program. *Concentration:* management.

MBA—Master of Business Administration in Marketing Management Full-time and part-time. 36 to 54 total credits required. 12 to 60 months to complete program. *Concentration:* marketing.

MBA—Master of Business Administration in Risk and Insurance Full-time and part-time. 36 to 54 total credits required. 12 to 60 months to complete program. *Concentrations:* insurance, risk management.

MBA—Master of Business Administration in Taxation Full-time and part-time. 39 to 76 total credits required. 16 to 60 months to complete program. *Concentration:* taxation.

MS—MS in Management of Risk Full-time and part-time. 36 to 45 total credits required. 12 to 36 months to complete program. *Concentration:* risk management.

MS—MS in Management of Risk Full-time and part-time. GRE or GMAT accepted for this program only. 36 to 45 total credits required. 12 to 36 months to complete program. *Concentration:* risk management.

MS—Master of Science in Taxation Full-time and part-time. Undergraduate degree in accounting or equivalent required. 31 to 34 total credits required. 12 to 60 months to complete program. *Concentration:* taxation.

RESOURCES AND SERVICES 908 on-campus PCs are available to graduate business students. Access to Internet/World Wide Web, online (class) registration, and online grade reports available. *Personal computer requirements:* Graduate business students are strongly recommended to

purchase or lease a personal computer. *Special opportunities include:* An international exchange program and an internship program are available. *Placement services include:* Alumni network, career placement, job search course, career counseling/planning, electronic job bank, resume referral, career fairs, job interviews arranged, resume preparation, and career library.

Application Contact Sheila Russell, Assistant Director of MBA Admissions, 8000 Utopia Parkway, Queens, NY 11439. *Phone:* 718-990-1345. *Fax:* 718-990-5242. *E-mail:* russells@stjohns.edu.

See full description on page 680.

St. Thomas Aquinas College
Division of Business Administration

Sparkill, New York

Phone: 845-398-4130 **Fax:** 845-359-8136 **E-mail:** acolsey@stac.edu

Business Program(s) Web Site: http://www.stac.edu/

Graduate Business Unit Enrollment *Total:* 59 (2 full-time; 57 part-time; 30 women; 1 international). *Average Age:* 30.

Graduate Business Faculty *Total:* 17 (7 full-time; 10 part-time).

Admissions *Applied:* 24. *Admitted:* 12. *Enrolled:* 10. *Average GPA:* 3.0

Academic Calendar Quarters.

After Graduation (Class of 2006–07) *Employed within 3 months of graduation:* 100%.

DEGREE MBA

MBA—Master of Business Administration Full-time and part-time. 33 to 57 total credits required. 12 to 60 months to complete program. *Concentrations:* finance, general MBA, management, marketing.

RESOURCES AND SERVICES 100 on-campus PCs are available to graduate business students. Access to Internet/World Wide Web, online (class) registration, and online grade reports available. *Personal computer requirements:* Graduate business students are not required to have a personal computer. *Special opportunities include:* An internship program is available. *Placement services include:* Alumni network, career placement, career counseling/planning, career fairs, resume preparation, and career library.

EXPENSES *Tuition:* Full-time: $10,980. Part-time: $610 per credit. *Tuition (international):* Full-time: $10,980. Part-time: $610 per credit. *Required fees:* Full-time: $40. Part-time: $40 per year. *Graduate housing:* Room and board costs vary by number of occupants, type of accommodation, and type of board plan. *Typical cost:* $10,000 (including board), $5680 (room only).

FINANCIAL AID (2007–08) 35 students received aid, including grants, loans, research assistantships, and work study. Aid is available to part-time students. *Financial aid application deadline:* 2/15.

Financial Aid Contact Ms. Anna Maria Chrissotimos, Director of Financial Aid, 125 Route 340, Sparkill, NY 10976-1050. *Phone:* 845-398-4097. *Fax:* 845-398-4114.

INTERNATIONAL STUDENTS 2% of students enrolled are international students. *Services and facilities:* Counseling/support services, Housing location assistance, International student housing, International student organization, Orientation, Visa Services. Financial aid is not available to international students. *Required with application:* TOEFL with recommended score of 213 (computer) or 550 (paper); proof of adequate funds; proof of health/immunizations.

International Student Contact Ms. Faride Rodriguez, Admissions Counselor/Special Program Advisor, 125 Route 340, Sparkill, NY 10976-1050. *Phone:* 845-398-4103. *Fax:* 845-398-4114. *E-mail:* frodrigu@stac.edu.

APPLICATION *Required:* Application form, baccalaureate/first degree, essay, 3 letters of recommendation, personal statement, resume/curriculum vitae, transcripts of college work. School will accept GMAT. *Recom-*

mended: Interview. *Application fee:* $30. Applications for domestic and international students are processed on a rolling basis.

Application Contact Alan Colsey, Director of MBA Program, 125 Route 340, Sparkill, NY 10976-1050. *Phone:* 845-398-4130. *Fax:* 845-359-8136. *E-mail:* acolsey@stac.edu.

State University of New York at Binghamton
School of Management

Binghamton, New York

Phone: 607-777-4236 **Fax:** 607-777-4872 **E-mail:** awheeler@binghamton.edu

Business Program(s) Web Site: http://som.binghamton.edu/

Graduate Business Unit Enrollment *Total:* 261 (261 full-time; 135 women; 188 international). *Average Age:* 24.

Graduate Business Faculty *Total:* 30 (22 full-time; 8 part-time).

Admissions *Applied:* 358. *Admitted:* 258. *Enrolled:* 120. *Average GMAT:* 615. *Average GPA:* 3.5

Academic Calendar Semesters.

Accreditation AACSB—The Association to Advance Collegiate Schools of Business.

After Graduation (Class of 2006–07) *Employed within 3 months of graduation:* 89%. *Average starting salary:* $59,000.

DEGREES EMBA • MBA • MS

EMBA—Executive Master of Business Administration Full-time. Up to 54 total credits required. Maximum of 21 months to complete program. *Concentrations:* executive programs, health care.

MBA—Fast-Track MBA Program for Business Majors Full-time. Must possess undergraduate business degree from AACSB-accredited program within five years. 38 total credits required. 9 months to complete program. *Concentrations:* finance, leadership, management information systems, marketing, operations management.

MBA—Fast-Track Professional MBA—New York City Full-time. Must possess undergraduate business degree from AACSB-accredited program within seven years. Up to 36 total credits required. 12 months to complete program. *Concentration:* general MBA.

MBA—Master of Business Administration Full-time and part-time. 36 to 68 total credits required. 9 to 57 months to complete program. *Concentrations:* accounting, finance, leadership, management information systems, marketing, operations management.

MS—Master of Science in Accounting Full-time and part-time. Students with bachelor's degree in accounting from U.S. AACSB-accredited program automatically eligible for one year program. 32 to 66 total credits required. 9 to 57 months to complete program. *Concentrations:* finance, leadership, management information systems, marketing, operations management.

RESOURCES AND SERVICES 63 on-campus PCs are available to graduate business students. Access to Internet/World Wide Web, online (class) registration, and online grade reports available. *Personal computer requirements:* Graduate business students are required to have a personal computer. *Special opportunities include:* An internship program is available. *Placement services include:* Alumni network, career placement, job search course, career counseling/planning, electronic job bank, resume referral, career fairs, job interviews arranged, resume preparation, and career library.

EXPENSES *Tuition (state resident):* Full-time: $7100. Part-time: $296 per credit hour. *Tuition (nonresident):* Full-time: $11,340. Part-time: $473 per credit hour. *Tuition (international):* Full-time: $11,340. Part-time: $473 per credit hour. *Required fees:* Full-time: $1091. Part-time: $143.35 per credit hour. Tuition and/or fees vary by academic program.

State University of New York at Binghamton (continued)

FINANCIAL AID (2007–08) 28 students received aid, including fellowships, grants, loans, research assistantships, scholarships, teaching assistantships, and work study. *Financial aid application deadline:* 3/15.

Financial Aid Contact Dennis Chavez, Director, Financial Aid Services, PO Box 6000, Binghamton, NY 13902-6000. *Phone:* 607-777-2470. *Fax:* 607-777-6897. *E-mail:* dchavez@binghamton.edu.

INTERNATIONAL STUDENTS 72% of students enrolled are international students. *Services and facilities:* Counseling/support services, ESL/language courses, Housing location assistance, International student organization, Language tutoring, Orientation, Visa Services. Financial aid is available to international students. *Required with application:* TOEFL with recommended score of 237 (computer) or 580 (paper); proof of adequate funds; proof of health/immunizations.

International Student Contact Ellen Badger, Director, International Student and Scholar Services, PO Box 6000, Binghamton, NY 13902-6000. *Phone:* 607-777-2510. *Fax:* 607-777-2889. *E-mail:* ebadger@binghamton.edu.

APPLICATION *Required:* GMAT, application form, baccalaureate/first degree, 2 letters of recommendation, personal statement, transcripts of college work. *Recommended:* Resume/curriculum vitae, work experience. *Application fee:* $60. Applications for domestic and international students are processed on a rolling basis.

Application Contact Alesia Wheeler-Wade, Assistant Director, MBA/MS Program, PO Box 6000, Binghamton, NY 13902-6000. *Phone:* 607-777-4236. *Fax:* 607-777-4872. *E-mail:* awheeler@binghamton.edu.

State University of New York at New Paltz

School of Business

New Paltz, New York

Phone: 845-257-2930 **Fax:** 845-257-3737 **E-mail:** mba@newpaltz.edu

Business Program(s) Web Site: http://mba.newpaltz.edu

Graduate Business Unit Enrollment *Total:* 129 (55 full-time; 74 part-time; 69 women; 36 international).

Graduate Business Faculty *Total:* 29 (26 full-time; 3 part-time).

Admissions *Applied:* 95. *Admitted:* 66. *Enrolled:* 29. *Average GMAT:* 474. *Average GPA:* 3.28

Academic Calendar Semesters.

After Graduation (Class of 2006–07) *Employed within 3 months of graduation:* 97%. *Average starting salary:* $40,000.

DEGREE MBA

MBA—Master of Business Administration Full-time and part-time. 36 to 57 total credits required. *Concentrations:* accounting, general MBA.

RESOURCES AND SERVICES 100 on-campus PCs are available to graduate business students. Access to Internet/World Wide Web, online (class) registration, and online grade reports available. *Personal computer requirements:* Graduate business students are strongly recommended to purchase or lease a personal computer. *Special opportunities include:* An international exchange program and an internship program are available. *Placement services include:* Alumni network, career placement, job search course, career counseling/planning, electronic job bank, resume referral, career fairs, job interviews arranged, resume preparation, and career library.

EXPENSES *Tuition (state resident):* Full-time: $7100. Part-time: $296 per credit hour. *Tuition (nonresident):* Full-time: $11,340. Part-time: $473 per credit hour. *Tuition (international):* Full-time: $11,340. Part-time: $473 per credit hour. *Required fees:* Full-time: $1313. Part-time: $30 per credit. *Graduate housing:* Room and board costs vary by type of board plan. *Typical cost:* $4035 (including board), $2600 (room only).

FINANCIAL AID (2007–08) Fellowships, grants, loans, scholarships, and teaching assistantships.

Financial Aid Contact Mr. Daniel Sistarenik, Director of Financial Aid, 1 Hawk Drive, New Paltz, NY 12561-2443. *Phone:* 845-257-3250. *Fax:* 845-257-3568. *E-mail:* sistared@newpaltz.edu.

INTERNATIONAL STUDENTS 28% of students enrolled are international students. *Services and facilities:* Counseling/support services, ESL/language courses, Housing location assistance, International student housing, International student organization, Language tutoring, Orientation, Visa Services. Financial aid is available to international students. *Required with application:* TOEFL with recommended score of 213 (computer), 550 (paper), or 80 (Internet); proof of adequate funds; proof of health/immunizations.

International Student Contact Hadi Salavitabar, Dean, 1 Hawk Drive, New Paltz, NY 12561-2443. *Phone:* 845-257-2930. *Fax:* 845-257-3737. *E-mail:* mba@newpaltz.edu.

APPLICATION *Required:* GMAT, application form, baccalaureate/first degree, essay, 3 letters of recommendation, personal statement, transcripts of college work. *Application fee:* $50. Applications for domestic and international students are processed on a rolling basis.

Application Contact Hadi Salavitabar, Dean, 1 Hawk Drive, New Paltz, NY 12561-2443. *Phone:* 845-257-2930. *Fax:* 845-257-3737. *E-mail:* mba@newpaltz.edu.

State University of New York at Oswego

School of Business

Oswego, New York

Phone: 315-312-3152 **Fax:** 315-312-3577 **E-mail:** gradoff@oswego.edu

Business Program(s) Web Site: http://www.oswego.edu/business/mba

Graduate Business Unit Enrollment *Total:* 66 (43 full-time; 23 part-time; 35 women; 19 international). *Average Age:* 30.

Graduate Business Faculty *Total:* 10 (7 full-time; 3 part-time).

Admissions *Applied:* 84. *Admitted:* 64. *Enrolled:* 31. *Average GMAT:* 520. *Average GPA:* 3.1

Academic Calendar Semesters.

Accreditation AACSB—The Association to Advance Collegiate Schools of Business.

After Graduation (Class of 2006–07) *Employed within 3 months of graduation:* 90%. *Average starting salary:* $41,000.

DEGREES MBA

MBA—Master of Business Administration/Accounting Full-time and part-time. At least 36 total credits required. 12 to 72 months to complete program. *Concentration:* accounting.

MBA—Master of Business Administration Full-time and part-time. 36 to 57 total credits required. 12 to 84 months to complete program. *Concentration:* general MBA.

RESOURCES AND SERVICES 300 on-campus PCs are available to graduate business students. Access to Internet/World Wide Web, online (class) registration, and online grade reports available. *Personal computer requirements:* Graduate business students are required to have a personal computer. *Special opportunities include:* An internship program is available. *Placement services include:* Alumni network, career placement, job search course, career counseling/planning, resume referral, career fairs, resume preparation, and career library.

EXPENSES *Tuition (state resident):* Full-time: $7100. Part-time: $296 per credit hour. *Tuition (nonresident):* Full-time: $11,340. Part-time: $473 per credit hour. *Tuition (international):* Full-time: $11,340. Part-time: $473 per credit hour. *Required fees:* Full-time: $775. Part-time: $775 per year. *Graduate housing:* Room and board costs vary by number of occupants and type of board plan. *Typical cost:* $8940 (including board), $5490 (room only).

FINANCIAL AID (2007–08) 25 students received aid, including fellowships, loans, research assistantships, teaching assistantships, and work study. Aid is available to part-time students. *Financial aid application deadline:* 4/1.

Financial Aid Contact Mark Humbert, Director of Financial Aid, 206 Culkin Hall, Oswego, NY 13126. *Phone:* 315-312-2248. *Fax:* 315-312-3696. *E-mail:* finaid@oswego.edu.

INTERNATIONAL STUDENTS 29% of students enrolled are international students. *Services and facilities:* Counseling/support services, ESL/language courses, Housing location assistance, International student housing, International student organization, Language tutoring, Orientation, Visa Services, Intensive Summer English Program. Financial aid is not available to international students. *Required with application:* TOEFL with recommended score of 213 (computer) or 550 (paper); proof of adequate funds; proof of health/immunizations.

International Student Contact Gerry Oliver, International Student Advisor, Office of International Studies, 201 Culkin Hall, Oswego, NY 13126. *Phone:* 315-312-5775. *Fax:* 315-312-2488. *E-mail:* oliver@oswego.edu.

APPLICATION *Required:* GMAT, application form, baccalaureate/first degree, essay, 2 letters of recommendation, personal statement, transcripts of college work. *Recommended:* Resume/curriculum vitae, work experience. *Application fee:* $50. *Deadlines:* 7/1 for fall, 11/1 for winter, 11/1 for spring, 4/1 for summer. Applications for international students are processed on a rolling basis.

Application Contact David King, Dean of Graduate Studies, 602 Culkin Hall, Oswego, NY 13126. *Phone:* 315-312-3152. *Fax:* 315-312-3577. *E-mail:* gradoff@oswego.edu.

State University of New York Institute of Technology

School of Business

Utica, New York

Phone: 315-792-7500 **Fax:** 315-792-7837 **E-mail:** smbl@sunyit.edu

Business Program(s) Web Site: http://web1.sunyit.edu/business

DEGREES MBA • MS

MBA—Master of Business Administration in Technology Management Full-time and part-time. Distance learning option. At least 48 total credits required. *Concentrations:* accounting, finance, health administration, human resources management, marketing.

MS—Master of Science in Accountancy Full-time and part-time. Distance learning option. At least 33 total credits required. *Concentration:* accounting.

MS—Master of Science in Health Services Administration Full-time and part-time. Distance learning option. 33 to 45 total credits required. *Concentration:* health administration.

RESOURCES AND SERVICES 380 on-campus PCs are available to graduate business students. Access to Internet/World Wide Web, online (class) registration, and online grade reports available. *Personal computer requirements:* Graduate business students are strongly recommended to purchase or lease a personal computer. *Placement services include:* Alumni network, career placement, career counseling/planning, electronic job bank, resume referral, career fairs, job interviews arranged, resume preparation, and career library.

Application Contact Ms. Marybeth Lyons, Director of Admissions, PO Box 3050, Utica, NY 13504-3050. *Phone:* 315-792-7500. *Fax:* 315-792-7837. *E-mail:* smbl@sunyit.edu.

State University of New York Maritime College

Program in International Transportation Management

Throggs Neck, New York

Phone: 718-409-7285 **Fax:** 718-409-7359 **E-mail:** gradschool@sunymaritime.edu

Business Program(s) Web Site: http://graduate.sunymaritime.edu

DEGREES MS • MS/MS

MS—Master of Science in International Transportation Management Full-time and part-time. Distance learning option. 33 to 57 total credits required. 18 to 60 months to complete program. *Concentrations:* insurance, international and area business studies, international business, international logistics, international trade, logistics, management, management information systems, supply chain management, transportation management.

MS/MS—Master of Science/Master of Science At least 39 total credits required.

RESOURCES AND SERVICES 80 on-campus PCs are available to graduate business students. Access to Internet/World Wide Web, online (class) registration, and online grade reports available. *Personal computer requirements:* Graduate business students are strongly recommended to purchase or lease a personal computer. *Special opportunities include:* An internship program is available. *Placement services include:* Alumni network, career placement, career counseling/planning, electronic job bank, resume referral, career fairs, job interviews arranged, resume preparation, and career library.

Application Contact Natalie Caesar, Assistant Director of Admissions, Graduate Program, 6 Pennyfield Avenue, Throggs Neck, NY 10465. *Phone:* 718-409-7285. *Fax:* 718-409-7359. *E-mail:* gradschool@sunymaritime.edu.

Stony Brook University, State University of New York

W. Averell Harriman School for Management and Policy

Stony Brook, New York

Phone: 631-632-7722 **Fax:** 631-632-8181 **E-mail:** oss@notes.cc.sunysb.edu

Business Program(s) Web Site: http://www.sunysb.edu/harriman/home.htm

Graduate Business Unit Enrollment *Total:* 261 (180 full-time; 81 part-time; 114 women; 74 international).

Graduate Business Faculty *Total:* 18 (8 full-time; 10 part-time).

Admissions *Applied:* 168. *Admitted:* 113. *Enrolled:* 87. *Average GMAT:* 550. *Average GPA:* 3.3

Academic Calendar Semesters.

DEGREES EMBA • MBA

EMBA Part-time. Distance learning option. 48 total credits required. Maximum of 5 months to complete program. *Concentrations:* finance, health care, human resources management, information systems, management, marketing.

Stony Brook University, State University of New York (continued)

MBA—Accelerated MBA Full-time and part-time. 48 total credits required. Maximum of 5 months to complete program. *Concentrations:* finance, health care, human resources management, information systems, management, marketing.

MBA—Master of Business Administration Full-time and part-time. 60 total credits required. Maximum of 5 months to complete program. *Concentrations:* finance, health care, human resources management, information systems, management, marketing.

RESOURCES AND SERVICES 28 on-campus PCs are available to graduate business students. Access to Internet/World Wide Web, online (class) registration, and online grade reports available. *Personal computer requirements:* Graduate business students are not required to have a personal computer. *Special opportunities include:* An internship program is available. *Placement services include:* Career placement, career counseling/planning, electronic job bank, resume referral, career fairs, job interviews arranged, resume preparation, and career library.

EXPENSES *Tuition (state resident):* Full-time: $7100. Part-time: $296 per credit hour. *Tuition (nonresident):* Full-time: $11,340. Part-time: $473 per credit hour. *Tuition (international):* Full-time: $11,340. Part-time: $473 per credit hour. *Required fees:* Full-time: $1983. Part-time: $40.20 per credit hour. Tuition and/or fees vary by number of courses or credits taken. *Graduate housing:* Room and board costs vary by campus location, number of occupants, type of accommodation, and type of board plan. *Typical cost:* $8815 (including board), $5000 (room only).

FINANCIAL AID (2007–08) 16 students received aid, including research assistantships, teaching assistantships, and work study. *Financial aid application deadline:* 3/1.

Financial Aid Contact Office of Financial Aid and Student Employment, Stony Brook, NY 11794-0851. *Phone:* 631-632-6840. *Fax:* 631-632-9525.

INTERNATIONAL STUDENTS 28% of students enrolled are international students. *Services and facilities:* Counseling/support services, ESL/language courses, International student housing, Orientation, Visa Services. Financial aid is available to international students. *Required with application:* TOEFL with recommended score of 213 (computer), 550 (paper), or 90 (Internet); proof of adequate funds; proof of health/immunizations.

International Student Contact Michelle Poole, Manager, Office of Student Services, Harriman Hall, Room 102, Stony Brook, NY 11794-3775. *Phone:* 631-632-7171. *Fax:* 631-632-8181. *E-mail:* oss@notes.cc.sunysb.edu.

APPLICATION *Required:* GMAT, application form, 3 letters of recommendation, personal statement, transcripts of college work. School will accept GRE. *Recommended:* Resume/curriculum vitae, work experience. *Application fee:* $60.

Application Contact Erica Hackley, Graduate Coordinator, Office of Student Services, Harriman Hall 102, Stony Brook, NY 11794-3775. *Phone:* 631-632-7722. *Fax:* 631-632-8181. *E-mail:* oss@notes.cc.sunysb.edu.

Syracuse University
Martin J. Whitman School of Management
Syracuse, New York

Phone: 315-443-9214 **Fax:** 315-443-9517 **E-mail:** mbainfo@syr.edu

Business Program(s) Web Site: http://whitman.syr.edu

Graduate Business Unit Enrollment *Total:* 379 (100 full-time; 279 part-time; 102 women; 63 international).

Graduate Business Faculty *Total:* 73 (71 full-time; 2 part-time).

Admissions *Applied:* 522. *Admitted:* 211. *Enrolled:* 99. *Average GMAT:* 619. *Average GPA:* 3.3

Academic Calendar Semesters.

Accreditation AACSB—The Association to Advance Collegiate Schools of Business.

After Graduation (Class of 2006–07) *Employed within 3 months of graduation:* 71%. *Average starting salary:* $62,700.

DEGREES JD/MBA • JD/MS • MBA • MS • MSA • MSF

JD/MBA—Juris Doctor/Master of Business Administration Full-time. 117 total credits required. 47 to 84 months to complete program. *Concentrations:* accounting, entrepreneurship, finance, general MBA, marketing, supply chain management.

JD/MS—Juris Doctor/Master of Science in Accounting Full-time. 96 to 126 total credits required. 38 to 84 months to complete program. *Concentration:* accounting.

MBA—Accelerated Master of Business Administration Full-time. Requires 4 years of full-time experience, business undergraduate degree from a U.S. institution, and GMAT of 650 or higher. 36 total credits required. 9 to 16 months to complete program. *Concentrations:* accounting, entrepreneurship, finance, general MBA, marketing, supply chain management.

MBA—Independent Study MBA Program (iMBA) Distance learning option. Requires a minimum of 5 years of full-time professional work experience. 54 total credits required. 24 to 72 months to complete program. *Concentration:* general MBA.

MBA—Master of Business Administration Full-time. 54 total credits required. 16 to 20 months to complete program. *Concentrations:* accounting, entrepreneurship, finance, general MBA, marketing, supply chain management.

MS—Master of Science in Media Management Full-time. 36 to 42 total credits required. 12 to 84 months to complete program. *Concentration:* media administration.

MSA—Independent Study MS in Accounting (iMSA) Part-time. Distance learning option. 30 total credits required. 9 to 42 months to complete program. *Concentration:* accounting.

MSA—Master of Science in Accounting Full-time and part-time. 30 to 63 total credits required. 9 to 42 months to complete program. *Concentration:* accounting.

MSF—Master of Science in Finance Full-time and part-time. 30 to 63 total credits required. 9 to 42 months to complete program. *Concentration:* finance.

RESOURCES AND SERVICES 500 on-campus PCs are available to graduate business students. Access to Internet/World Wide Web, online (class) registration, and online grade reports available. *Personal computer requirements:* Graduate business students are strongly recommended to purchase or lease a personal computer. *Special opportunities include:* An international exchange program and an internship program are available. *Placement services include:* Alumni network, career placement, career counseling/planning, electronic job bank, resume referral, career fairs, job interviews arranged, resume preparation, and career library.

FINANCIAL AID (2007–08) 21 students received aid, including fellowships, loans, scholarships, and work study. *Financial aid application deadline:* 3/1.

Financial Aid Contact Ms. Carol J. Swanberg, Director of Graduate Admissions and Financial Aid, 721 University Avenue, Suite 315, Syracuse, NY 13244-2450. *Phone:* 315-443-9214. *Fax:* 315-443-9517. *E-mail:* mbainfo@syr.edu.

INTERNATIONAL STUDENTS 17% of students enrolled are international students. *Services and facilities:* Counseling/support services, ESL/language courses, Housing location assistance, International student housing, International student organization, Language tutoring, Orientation, Visa Services. Financial aid is available to international students. *Required with application:* TOEFL with recommended score of 250 (computer) or 600 (paper); proof of adequate funds; proof of health/immunizations.

International Student Contact Ms. Carol J. Swanberg, Director of Graduate Admissions and Financial Aid, 721 University Avenue, Suite 315, Syracuse, NY 13244-2450. *Phone:* 315-443-9214. *Fax:* 315-443-9517. *E-mail:* mbainfo@syr.edu.

APPLICATION *Required:* GMAT, application form, baccalaureate/first degree, essay, 2 letters of recommendation, resume/curriculum vitae, transcripts of college work. *Recommended:* Interview, 2 years of work experience. *Application fee:* $75. Applications for domestic and international students are processed on a rolling basis.

Application Contact Ms. Carol J. Swanberg, Director of Graduate Admissions and Financial Aid, 721 University Avenue, Suite 315, Syracuse, NY 13244-2450. *Phone:* 315-443-9214. *Fax:* 315-443-9517. *E-mail:* mbainfo@syr.edu.

See full description on page 692.

Union Graduate College

School of Management

Schenectady, New York

Phone: 518-388-6238 **Fax:** 518-388-6686 **E-mail:** sheehanr@uniongraduatecollege.edu

Business Program(s) Web Site: http://www.uniongraduatecollege.edu

Graduate Business Unit Enrollment *Average Age:* 25.

Graduate Business Faculty *Total:* 27 (7 full-time; 20 part-time).

Admissions *Applied:* 100. *Admitted:* 80. *Enrolled:* 70. *Average GMAT:* 545. *Average GPA:* 3.3

Academic Calendar Trimesters.

Accreditation AACSB—The Association to Advance Collegiate Schools of Business.

After Graduation (Class of 2006–07) *Employed within 3 months of graduation:* 97%. *Average starting salary:* $65,000.

DEGREES MBA

MBA—Master of Business Administration in Health Systems Administration Full-time and part-time. At least 66 total credits required. 24 to 72 months to complete program. *Concentration:* health care.

MBA—Master of Business Administration Full-time and part-time. At least 66 total credits required. 24 to 72 months to complete program. *Concentrations:* general MBA, management.

RESOURCES AND SERVICES 50 on-campus PCs are available to graduate business students. Access to Internet/World Wide Web available. *Personal computer requirements:* Graduate business students are not required to have a personal computer. *Special opportunities include:* An internship program is available. *Placement services include:* Alumni network, career placement, career counseling/planning, electronic job bank, resume referral, career fairs, job interviews arranged, resume preparation, and career library.

EXPENSES *Tuition (state resident):* Full-time: $23,000. Part-time: $2300 per course. *Tuition (nonresident):* Full-time: $23,000. Part-time: $2300 per course. *Tuition (international):* Full-time: $23,000. Part-time: $230 per course.

FINANCIAL AID (2007–08) 60 students received aid, including loans, scholarships, and work study. Aid is available to part-time students.

Financial Aid Contact Nikki Gallucci, Director of Financial Aid, Lamont House, 807 Union Street, Schenectady, NY 12308. *Phone:* 518-388-8744. *Fax:* 518-388-6686. *E-mail:* galluccn@uniongraduatecollege.edu.

INTERNATIONAL STUDENTS *Services and facilities:* Counseling/support services, ESL/language courses, Housing location assistance, International student organization, Orientation, Visa Services. Financial aid is available to international students. *Required with application:* TOEFL with recommended score of 213 (computer) or 550 (paper); proof of adequate funds; proof of health/immunizations.

International Student Contact Rhonda Sheehan, Director of Graduate Admissions and Registrar, Lamont House, 807 Union Street, Schenectady, NY 12308. *Phone:* 518-388-6238. *Fax:* 518-388-6686. *E-mail:* sheehanr@uniongraduatecollege.edu.

APPLICATION *Required:* GMAT, application form, baccalaureate/first degree, essay, 3 letters of recommendation, transcripts of college work. *Recommended:* Interview, resume/curriculum vitae. *Application fee:* $60. Applications for domestic and international students are processed on a rolling basis.

Application Contact Rhonda Sheehan, Director of Graduate Admissions and Registrar, Lamont House, 807 Union Street, Schenectady, NY 12308. *Phone:* 518-388-6238. *Fax:* 518-388-6686. *E-mail:* sheehanr@uniongraduatecollege.edu.

University at Albany, State University of New York

School of Business

Albany, New York

Phone: 518-442-4961 **Fax:** 518-442-3944 **E-mail:** zlawrence@uamail.albany.edu

Business Program(s) Web Site: http://www.albany.edu/business

Graduate Business Unit Enrollment *Total:* 275 (100 full-time; 175 part-time; 105 women; 25 international). *Average Age:* 28.

Graduate Business Faculty *Total:* 35 (25 full-time; 10 part-time).

Admissions *Applied:* 260. *Admitted:* 145. *Enrolled:* 100. *Average GMAT:* 570. *Average GPA:* 3.4

Academic Calendar Semesters.

Accreditation AACSB—The Association to Advance Collegiate Schools of Business.

After Graduation (Class of 2006–07) *Employed within 3 months of graduation:* 97%. *Average starting salary:* $55,000.

DEGREES MBA • MS

MBA—Evening Master of Business Administration Part-time. 3 years of work experience required. 38 to 48 total credits required. 24 to 72 months to complete program. *Concentrations:* finance, information technology, management, marketing, new venture management, taxation.

MBA—Full-Time Master of Business Administration Full-time. 51 to 61 total credits required. 21 months to complete program. *Concentrations:* accounting, human resources management, management information systems.

MBA—Weekend Master of Business Administration Part-time. 3 years of work experience required. 48 total credits required. 22 months to complete program. *Concentration:* general MBA.

MS—Master of Science in Accounting Full-time. 51 to 61 total credits required. 21 months to complete program. *Concentration:* accounting.

MS—Master of Science in Accounting Full-time. Degree in accounting required. 30 total credits required. 9 months to complete program. *Concentrations:* accounting, information management.

MS—Master of Science in Taxation Full-time and part-time. 30 total credits required. 12 to 72 months to complete program. *Concentration:* taxation.

RESOURCES AND SERVICES 625 on-campus PCs are available to graduate business students. Access to Internet/World Wide Web, online (class) registration, and online grade reports available. *Personal computer requirements:* Graduate business students are strongly recommended to purchase or lease a personal computer. *Special opportunities include:* An internship program is available. *Placement services include:* Alumni network, career placement, job search course, career counseling/planning, electronic job bank, resume referral, career fairs, job interviews arranged, resume preparation, and career library.

EXPENSES *Tuition (state resident):* Full-time: $7100. Part-time: $296 per credit. *Tuition (nonresident):* Full-time: $11,340. Part-time: $473 per credit hour. *Tuition (international):* Full-time: $11,340. Part-time: $473 per credit hour. *Required fees:* Full-time: $600. Tuition and/or fees vary by

University at Albany, State University of New York (continued)

class time, number of courses or credits taken, and academic program. *Graduate housing:* Room and board costs vary by number of occupants and type of accommodation. *Typical cost:* $3352.50 (room only).

FINANCIAL AID (2007–08) 40 students received aid, including fellowships, research assistantships, and teaching assistantships. *Financial aid application deadline:* 3/1.

Financial Aid Contact Ms. Beth Post, Director of Financial Aid, CCB52, 1400 Washington Avenue, Albany, NY 12222. *Phone:* 518-442-5757. *Fax:* 518-442-5295. *E-mail:* bpost@uamail.albany.edu.

INTERNATIONAL STUDENTS 9% of students enrolled are international students. *Services and facilities:* Counseling/support services, ESL/language courses, Housing location assistance, International student housing, International student organization, Language tutoring, Orientation, Visa Services. Financial aid is not available to international students. *Required with application:* TOEFL with recommended score of 250 (computer), 600 (paper), or 100 (Internet); proof of adequate funds; proof of health/immunizations.

International Student Contact Margaret Reich, Director of International Student Services, LI 84, 1400 Washington Avenue, Albany, NY 12222. *Phone:* 518-442-5495. *Fax:* 518-442-5390. *E-mail:* mreich@uamail.albany.edu.

APPLICATION *Required:* GMAT, application form, baccalaureate/first degree, essay, 3 letters of recommendation, personal statement, resume/curriculum vitae, transcripts of college work. School will accept GRE. *Recommended:* Interview, work experience. *Application fee:* $75. Applications for domestic and international students are processed on a rolling basis.

Application Contact Zina Lawrence, Director of Graduate Student Services, 1400 Washington Avenue, BA 361A, Albany, NY 12222. *Phone:* 518-442-4961. *Fax:* 518-442-3944. *E-mail:* zlawrence@uamail.albany.edu.

University at Buffalo, the State University of New York

School of Management

Buffalo, New York

Phone: 716-645-3204 **Fax:** 716-645-2341 **E-mail:** davidf@buffalo.edu

Business Program(s) Web Site: http://mgt.buffalo.edu/

Graduate Business Unit Enrollment *Total:* 703 (499 full-time; 204 part-time; 266 women; 295 international). *Average Age:* 27.

Graduate Business Faculty *Total:* 101 (61 full-time; 40 part-time).

Admissions *Applied:* 1,145. *Admitted:* 496. *Enrolled:* 279. *Average GMAT:* 619. *Average GPA:* 3.3

Academic Calendar Semesters.

Accreditation AACSB—The Association to Advance Collegiate Schools of Business.

After Graduation (Class of 2006–07) *Employed within 3 months of graduation:* 75%. *Average starting salary:* $54,282.

DEGREES JD/MBA • MBA • MBA/M Arch • MBA/MPH • MBA/MS • MBA/MSW • MD/MBA • Pharm D/MBA

JD/MBA—Juris Doctor/Master of Business Administration Full-time. At least 96 total credits required. 48 to 72 months to complete program. *Concentrations:* accounting, finance, international business, management, management information systems, manufacturing management, marketing.

MBA—Doctor of Audiology/Master of Business Administration Full-time. GRE required for Audiology admissions and GMAT required for MBA admissions. 60 months to complete program. *Concentration:* management.

MBA—Executive Master of Business Administration Part-time. At least 48 total credits required. 22 months to complete program. *Concentration:* management.

MBA—Full-Time Master of Business Administration Full-time. At least 60 total credits required. 22 to 48 months to complete program. *Concentrations:* accounting, electronic commerce (E-commerce), finance, international business, management, management consulting, management information systems, manufacturing management, marketing.

MBA—Professional Master of Business Administration Part-time. 3 years of relevant post-baccalaureate work experience required. At least 48 total credits required. 33 to 60 months to complete program. *Concentration:* management.

MBA/M Arch—Master of Business Administration/Master of Architecture Full-time. At least 96 total credits required. 48 to 72 months to complete program. *Concentrations:* accounting, finance, international business, management, management information systems, manufacturing management, marketing.

MBA/MPH Full-time. 97 total credits required. 33 months to complete program. *Concentrations:* general MBA, health administration, public management.

MBA/MS—Master of Business Administration/Master of Science in Geography Full-time. At least 78 total credits required. 36 to 48 months to complete program. *Concentrations:* accounting, finance, international business, management, management information systems, manufacturing management, marketing.

MBA/MSW Full-time. 96 total credits required. 33 months to complete program. *Concentrations:* general MBA, social work.

MD/MBA—Doctor of Medicine/Master of Business Administration Full-time. At least 180 total credits required. 60 months to complete program. *Concentration:* combined degrees.

Pharm D/MBA—PharmD/MBA—Doctor of Pharmacy/Master of Business Administration Full-time. Apply separately to both schools. At least 231 total credits required. 84 months to complete program. *Concentration:* combined degrees.

RESOURCES AND SERVICES 450 on-campus PCs are available to graduate business students. Access to Internet/World Wide Web, online (class) registration, and online grade reports available. *Personal computer requirements:* Graduate business students are strongly recommended to purchase or lease a personal computer. *Special opportunities include:* An international exchange program and an internship program are available. *Placement services include:* Alumni network, career placement, job search course, career counseling/planning, electronic job bank, resume referral, career fairs, job interviews arranged, resume preparation, and career library.

EXPENSES *Tuition (state resident):* Full-time: $7100. *Tuition (nonresident):* Full-time: $11,340. *Tuition (international):* Full-time: $11,340. *Required fees:* Full-time: $2000. *Graduate housing:* Room and board costs vary by number of occupants, type of accommodation, and type of board plan. *Typical cost:* $7000 (including board), $5000 (room only).

FINANCIAL AID (2007–08) 35 students received aid, including fellowships, grants, loans, research assistantships, scholarships, teaching assistantships, and work study. *Financial aid application deadline:* 2/1.

Financial Aid Contact Student Response Center, 232 Capen Hall, Buffalo, NY 14260. *Phone:* 716-645-2450. *Fax:* 716-645-6566. *E-mail:* srcenter@buffalo.edu.

INTERNATIONAL STUDENTS 42% of students enrolled are international students. *Services and facilities:* Counseling/support services, ESL/language courses, International student organization, Language tutoring, Orientation, Visa Services. Financial aid is available to international students. *Required with application:* TOEFL with recommended score of 230 (computer), 570 (paper), or 100 (Internet); proof of adequate funds; proof of health/immunizations.

International Student Contact Ellen Dussourd, Director, International Student Scholar Services, 210 Talbert Hall, Buffalo, NY 14260. *Phone:* 716-645-2258. *Fax:* 716-645-6197. *E-mail:* disspird@acsu.buffalo.edu.

APPLICATION *Required:* GMAT, application form, baccalaureate/first degree, essay, interview, 2 letters of recommendation, personal statement, resume/curriculum vitae, transcripts of college work. *Recommended:* 2 years of work experience. *Application fee:* $50. Applications for domestic and international students are processed on a rolling basis.

Application Contact David W. Frasier, Assistant Dean and Administrative Director of the MBA Program, 203 Alfiero Center, Buffalo, NY 14260. *Phone:* 716-645-3204. *Fax:* 716-645-2341. *E-mail:* davidf@buffalo.edu.

University of Rochester
William E. Simon Graduate School of Business Administration
Rochester, New York

Phone: 585-275-3533 **Fax:** 585-271-3907 **E-mail:** admissions@simon.rochester.edu

Business Program(s) Web Site: http://www.simon.rochester.edu

Graduate Business Unit Enrollment *Total:* 959 (718 full-time; 241 part-time; 283 women; 398 international). *Average Age:* 26.

Graduate Business Faculty *Total:* 60 (48 full-time; 12 part-time).

Admissions *Applied:* 1,248. *Admitted:* 548. *Enrolled:* 310. *Average GMAT:* 673. *Average GPA:* 3.52

Academic Calendar Quarters.

Accreditation AACSB—The Association to Advance Collegiate Schools of Business.

After Graduation (Class of 2006–07) *Employed within 3 months of graduation:* 92.4%. *Average starting salary:* $84,137.

DEGREES MBA • MBA/MS • MD/MBA • MS • MSBA

MBA—Executive Master of Business Administration Full-time. At least 66 total credits required. 19 to 22 months to complete program. *Concentration:* executive programs.

MBA—Master of Business Administration Full-time and part-time. At least 67 total credits required. 18 to 22 months to complete program. *Concentrations:* accounting, electronic commerce (E-commerce), entrepreneurship, finance, health care, international management, management information systems, marketing, operations management, public policy and administration, strategic management.

MBA/MS—Master of Business Administration/Master of Science in Public Health Full-time. At least 85 total credits required. 24 to 28 months to complete program. *Concentrations:* accounting, economics, electronic commerce (E-commerce), entrepreneurship, finance, health care, international management, management information systems, marketing, operations management, public policy and administration, strategic management.

MD/MBA—Doctor of Medicine/Master of Business Administration Full-time. Minimum of 60 months to complete program. *Concentrations:* accounting, economics, electronic commerce (E-commerce), entrepreneurship, finance, health care, international management, management information systems, marketing, operations management, public policy and administration, strategic management.

MS—Accounting Full-time and part-time. At least 36 total credits required. Minimum of 9 months to complete program. *Concentrations:* accounting, corporate accounting.

MS—Business Administration in Finance Full-time and part-time. Two options, one with a prior MBA, one without. 36 to 43 total credits required. 9 to 11 months to complete program. *Concentration:* finance.

MS—Business Administration in Information Systems Management Full-time and part-time. At least 39 total credits required. Minimum of 9 months to complete program. *Concentration:* management information systems.

MS—Business Administration in Manufacturing Management Full-time and part-time. At least 39 total credits required. Minimum of 9 months to complete program. *Concentration:* manufacturing management.

MS—Business Administration in Marketing Full-time and part-time. At least 33 total credits required. Minimum of 10 months to complete program. *Concentrations:* advertising, marketing, marketing research.

MS—Business Administration in Medical Management Part-time. At least 30 total credits required. 15 months to complete program. *Concentrations:* health administration, health care, pharmaceutical management.

MS—Business Administration in Service Management Full-time and part-time. At least 39 total credits required. Minimum of 9 months to complete program. *Concentrations:* management, operations management.

MS—Business Administration in Technology Transfer and Commercialization Full-time and part-time. At least 39 total credits required. Minimum of 9 months to complete program. *Concentration:* administration of technological information.

MSBA—General Management Full-time and part-time. At least 39 total credits required. Minimum of 9 months to complete program. *Concentration:* management.

RESOURCES AND SERVICES 75 on-campus PCs are available to graduate business students. Access to Internet/World Wide Web, online (class) registration, and online grade reports available. *Personal computer requirements:* Graduate business students are required to have a personal computer. *Special opportunities include:* An international exchange program and an internship program are available. *Placement services include:* Alumni network, career placement, job search course, career counseling/planning, electronic job bank, resume referral, career fairs, resume preparation, and career library.

EXPENSES *Tuition:* Full-time: $39,030. Part-time: $1301 per credit hour. *Tuition (international):* Full-time: $39,030. Part-time: $1301 per credit hour. *Required fees:* Full-time: $975. Part-time: $45 per quarter. Tuition and/or fees vary by number of courses or credits taken and academic program. *Typical graduate housing cost:* $10,710 (including board), $6210 (room only).

FINANCIAL AID (2007–08) Fellowships, loans, research assistantships, and scholarships. *Financial aid application deadline:* 6/1.

Financial Aid Contact Gregory V. MacDonald, Executive Director for MBA Admissions and Administration, 305 Schlegel Hall, Rochester, NY 14627-0107. *Phone:* 585-275-3533. *Fax:* 585-271-3907. *E-mail:* admissions@simon.rochester.edu.

INTERNATIONAL STUDENTS 42% of students enrolled are international students. *Services and facilities:* Counseling/support services, ESL/language courses, Housing location assistance, International student organization, Orientation, Visa Services. Financial aid is available to international students. *Required with application:* TOEFL; proof of adequate funds; proof of health/immunizations.

International Student Contact Cary Jensen, Director, International Relations, Morey 2-213, Rochester, NY 14627-0447. *Phone:* 585-275-8928. *Fax:* 585-244-4503. *E-mail:* cjensen@iso.rochester.edu.

APPLICATION *Required:* GMAT, application form, baccalaureate/first degree, essay, 2 letters of recommendation, resume/curriculum vitae, transcripts of college work. *Recommended:* Interview. *Application fee:* $125. Applications for domestic and international students are processed on a rolling basis.

Application Contact Gregory V. MacDonald, Executive Director for MBA Admissions and Administration, 305 Schlegel Hall, Rochester, NY 14627-0107. *Phone:* 585-275-3533. *Fax:* 585-271-3907. *E-mail:* admissions@simon.rochester.edu.

See full description on page 736.

Wagner College
Department of Business Administration
Staten Island, New York

Phone: 718-390-3106 **Fax:** 718-390-3456 **E-mail:** graduate@wagner.edu

Wagner College (continued)

Business Program(s) Web Site: http://www.wagner.edu/graduate_programs/busadmin

Graduate Business Unit Enrollment *Total:* 138 (111 full-time; 27 part-time; 61 women; 4 international). *Average Age:* 27.

Graduate Business Faculty *Total:* 24 (8 full-time; 16 part-time).

Admissions *Applied:* 78. *Admitted:* 77. *Enrolled:* 71. *Average GMAT:* 520. *Average GPA:* 3.0

Academic Calendar Semesters.

Accreditation ACBSP—The American Council of Business Schools and Programs.

DEGREES MBA • MS

MBA—Accelerated MBA Full-time. Up to 46 total credits required. Maximum of 12 months to complete program. *Concentration:* business studies.

MBA—Executive Master of Business Administration Full-time. 5 years of management experience required. At least 45 total credits required. Minimum of 18 months to complete program. *Concentration:* executive programs.

MBA—Master of Business Administration Full-time and part-time. 45 to 51 total credits required. 18 to 60 months to complete program. *Concentrations:* finance, health administration, international business, management, marketing.

MS—Master of Science in Accounting Full-time and part-time. Part of a 5-year Accounting program; completion of a BS degree in business administration with a concentration in accounting from Wagner College or the equivalent from another institution. At least 30 total credits required. Minimum of 12 months to complete program. *Concentration:* accounting.

RESOURCES AND SERVICES 225 on-campus PCs are available to graduate business students. Access to Internet/World Wide Web and online (class) registration available. *Personal computer requirements:* Graduate business students are not required to have a personal computer. *Placement services include:* Alumni network, career counseling/planning, electronic job bank, career fairs, and resume preparation.

EXPENSES *Tuition:* Full-time: $15,570. Part-time: $5190 per semester. *Tuition (international):* Full-time: $15,570. Part-time: $5190 per semester. *Typical graduate housing cost:* $9250 (room only).

FINANCIAL AID (2007–08) 26 students received aid, including fellowships. *Financial aid application deadline:* 2/15.

Financial Aid Contact Ms. Theresa Weimer, Director of Financial Aid, One Campus Road, Staten Island, NY 10301. *Phone:* 718-390-3183. *Fax:* 718-390-3203. *E-mail:* finaid@wagner.edu.

INTERNATIONAL STUDENTS 3% of students enrolled are international students. *Services and facilities:* Orientation. Financial aid is not available to international students. *Required with application:* TOEFL with recommended score of 217 (computer), 550 (paper), or 79 (Internet); proof of adequate funds; proof of health/immunizations.

International Student Contact Ms. Susan Rosenberg, Coordinator for Graduate Studies, One Campus Road, Staten Island, NY 10301. *Phone:* 718-390-3106. *Fax:* 718-390-3456. *E-mail:* graduate@wagner.edu.

APPLICATION *Required:* GMAT, application form, baccalaureate/first degree, essay, 2 letters of recommendation, personal statement, transcripts of college work. School will accept GRE. *Recommended:* Interview, resume/curriculum vitae. *Application fee:* $50, $85 (international). Applications for domestic and international students are processed on a rolling basis.

Application Contact Ms. Susan Rosenberg, Coordinator for Graduate Studies, One Campus Road, Staten Island, NY 10301. *Phone:* 718-390-3106. *Fax:* 718-390-3456. *E-mail:* graduate@wagner.edu.

NORTH CAROLINA

Appalachian State University
John A. Walker College of Business

Boone, North Carolina

Phone: 828-262-2922 **Fax:** 828-262-8069 **E-mail:** mba@appstate.edu

Business Program(s) Web Site: http://www.mba.appstate.edu

Graduate Business Unit Enrollment *Total:* 22 (8 full-time; 14 part-time; 6 women).

Graduate Business Faculty 48 full-time.

Admissions *Applied:* 22. *Admitted:* 12. *Enrolled:* 8. *Average GMAT:* 540. *Average GPA:* 3.35

Academic Calendar Semesters.

Accreditation AACSB—The Association to Advance Collegiate Schools of Business.

DEGREES MBA • MS

MBA—Master of Business Administration Full-time. At least 32 total credits required. Minimum of 12 months to complete program. *Concentration:* general MBA.

MS—Master of Science in Accounting Full-time and part-time. At least 30 total credits required. 12 to 24 months to complete program. *Concentrations:* accounting, taxation.

RESOURCES AND SERVICES 100 on-campus PCs are available to graduate business students. Access to Internet/World Wide Web, online (class) registration, and online grade reports available. *Personal computer requirements:* Graduate business students are strongly recommended to purchase or lease a personal computer. *Placement services include:* Alumni network, career placement, career counseling/planning, electronic job bank, career fairs, job interviews arranged, and resume preparation.

EXPENSES *Tuition (state resident):* Full-time: $5738. *Tuition (nonresident):* Full-time: $17,274. *Tuition (international):* Full-time: $17,274. *Graduate housing:* Room and board costs vary by campus location, number of occupants, type of accommodation, and type of board plan. *Typical cost:* $4000 (including board), $3000 (room only).

FINANCIAL AID (2007–08) 7 students received aid, including loans, research assistantships, and scholarships. *Financial aid application deadline:* 3/1.

Financial Aid Contact Director, Financial Aid Office, John E. Thomas Academic Support, Boone, NC 28608. *Phone:* 828-262-2190. *Fax:* 828-262-2585.

INTERNATIONAL STUDENTS *Services and facilities:* Counseling/support services, ESL/language courses, Housing location assistance, International student housing, International student organization, Orientation, Visa Services. Financial aid is available to international students. *Required with application:* TOEFL with recommended score of 213 (computer) or 550 (paper); proof of adequate funds; proof of health/immunizations.

International Student Contact Mr. Robert White, Executive Director, International Programs, Office of International Programs, IG Greer, Boone, NC 28608. *Phone:* 828-262-2046. *E-mail:* whitera@appstate.edu.

APPLICATION *Required:* GMAT, application form, baccalaureate/first degree, 3 letters of recommendation, resume/curriculum vitae, transcripts of college work. *Application fee:* $45. Applications for domestic and international students are processed on a rolling basis.

Application Contact Program Assistant, MBA Program, PO Box 32037, Boone, NC 28608. *Phone:* 828-262-2922. *Fax:* 828-262-8069. *E-mail:* mba@appstate.edu.

Campbell University

Lundy-Fetterman School of Business

Buies Creek, North Carolina

Phone: 910-893-1318 **Fax:** 910-814-4718 **E-mail:** hupfeld@campbell.edu

Business Program(s) Web Site: http://www.campbell.edu

Graduate Business Unit Enrollment *Total:* 208 (47 full-time; 161 part-time; 85 women; 12 international). *Average Age:* 29.

Graduate Business Faculty *Total:* 18 (13 full-time; 5 part-time).

Admissions *Applied:* 114. *Admitted:* 79. *Enrolled:* 65. *Average GMAT:* 510. *Average GPA:* 3.1

Academic Calendar Semesters.

Accreditation ACBSP—The American Council of Business Schools and Programs (candidate).

After Graduation (Class of 2006–07) *Employed within 3 months of graduation:* 85%. *Average starting salary:* $40,000.

DEGREE MBA

MBA—Master of Business Administration Full-time and part-time. 36 to 54 total credits required. 12 to 60 months to complete program. *Concentration:* general MBA.

RESOURCES AND SERVICES 60 on-campus PCs are available to graduate business students. Access to Internet/World Wide Web, online (class) registration, and online grade reports available. *Personal computer requirements:* Graduate business students are not required to have a personal computer. *Placement services include:* Career placement, resume referral, job interviews arranged, and resume preparation.

EXPENSES *Required fees:* Full-time: $21,000. *Typical graduate housing cost:* $9000 (including board).

FINANCIAL AID (2007–08) 41 students received aid, including loans. Aid is available to part-time students. *Financial aid application deadline:* 4/15.

Financial Aid Contact Ms. Nancy Beasley, Director of Financial Aid, PO Box 36, Buies Creek, NC 27506. *Phone:* 910-893-1310. *Fax:* 910-893-1288. *E-mail:* beasley@campbell.edu.

INTERNATIONAL STUDENTS 6% of students enrolled are international students. *Services and facilities:* Counseling/support services, International student housing, International student organization, Orientation. Financial aid is not available to international students. *Required with application:* TOEFL with recommended score of 213 (computer), 550 (paper), or 63 (Internet); proof of adequate funds; proof of health/immunizations.

International Student Contact Allison Shell, Director of International Admissions, PO Box 249, Buies Creek, NC 27506. *Phone:* 910-893-1417. *Fax:* 910-814-4718. *E-mail:* shella@campbell.edu.

APPLICATION *Required:* GMAT, application form, baccalaureate/first degree, 3 letters of recommendation, transcripts of college work, 2 years of work experience. *Application fee:* $65. Applications for domestic and international students are processed on a rolling basis.

Application Contact Jim Farthing, Director of Graduate Admissions, PO Box 546G, Buies Creek, NC 27506. *Phone:* 910-893-1318. *Fax:* 910-814-4718. *E-mail:* hupfeld@campbell.edu.

DeVry University

Keller Graduate School of Management

Charlotte, North Carolina

Phone: 704-362-2345 **Fax:** 704-362-2668

Business Program(s) Web Site: http://www.devry.edu

Academic Calendar Semesters.

DEGREES MAFM • MBA • MHRM • MISM • MPA • MPM

MAFM—Master of Accounting and Financial Management Full-time and part-time. Distance learning option. At least 44 total credits required. 18 to 60 months to complete program. *Concentrations:* accounting, financial management/planning.

MBA—Master of Business Administration Full-time and part-time. Distance learning option. At least 48 total credits required. 18 to 60 months to complete program. *Concentration:* general MBA.

MHRM—Master of Human Resource Management Full-time and part-time. Distance learning option. At least 45 total credits required. 18 to 60 months to complete program. *Concentration:* human resources management.

MISM—Master of Information Systems Management Full-time and part-time. Distance learning option. At least 45 total credits required. 18 to 60 months to complete program. *Concentration:* information systems.

MPA—Master of Public Administration Full-time and part-time. Distance learning option. At least 45 total credits required. 18 to 60 months to complete program. *Concentration:* public policy and administration.

MPM—Master of Project Management Full-time and part-time. Distance learning option. At least 42 total credits required. 18 to 60 months to complete program. *Concentration:* project management.

RESOURCES AND SERVICES *Personal computer requirements:* Graduate business students are not required to have a personal computer.

APPLICATION *Required:* Application form, baccalaureate/first degree, interview, transcripts of college work. Applications for domestic and international students are processed on a rolling basis.

Application Contact Admissions Office, Charlotte Center, 4521 Sharon Road, Suite 145, Charlotte, NC 28211. *Phone:* 704-362-2345. *Fax:* 704-362-2668.

Duke University

The Fuqua School of Business

Durham, North Carolina

Phone: 919-660-7705 **Fax:** 919-681-8026 **E-mail:** admissions-info@fuqua.duke.edu

Business Program(s) Web Site: http://www.fuqua.duke.edu

Graduate Business Unit Enrollment *Total:* 1,617 (1,617 full-time; 432 women; 654 international). *Average Age:* 26-34.

Graduate Business Faculty *Total:* 146 (117 full-time; 29 part-time).

Admissions *Applied:* 3,519. *Admitted:* 1,327. *Enrolled:* 774. *Average GMAT:* 690. *Average GPA:* 3.4

Academic Calendar Quarters.

Accreditation AACSB—The Association to Advance Collegiate Schools of Business.

After Graduation (Class of 2006–07) *Employed within 3 months of graduation:* 85%. *Average starting salary:* $95,000.

DEGREES EMBA • MBA • MMS

EMBA—Cross Continent EMBA Full-time. 48 total credits required. 20 months to complete program. *Concentration:* general MBA.

EMBA—Duke Goethe EMBA Full-time. 45 total credits required. 22 months to complete program. *Concentration:* general MBA.

EMBA—Global Executive MBA Full-time. 51 total credits required. 18 months to complete program. *Concentrations:* general MBA, health administration.

Duke University (continued)

EMBA—Weekend Executive MBA Full-time. 51 total credits required. 20 months to complete program. *Concentrations:* general MBA, health administration.

MBA—Master of Business Administration Full-time. 79 total credits required. 22 months to complete program. *Concentrations:* accounting, decision sciences, entrepreneurship, finance, general MBA, health administration, leadership, marketing, operations management, strategic management.

MMS—Master of Management Studies Full-time. Joint degree program with Seoul National University. Students complete their first year of study at Seoul (SNU's Global MBA Program), and typically apply to Fuqua's MMS program after their first term. 40 total credits required. 12 months to complete program. *Concentrations:* accounting, decision sciences, entrepreneurship, finance, general MBA, health administration, leadership, marketing, operations management, strategic management.

RESOURCES AND SERVICES 150 on-campus PCs are available to graduate business students. Access to Internet/World Wide Web, online (class) registration, and online grade reports available. *Personal computer requirements:* Graduate business students are required to have a personal computer. *Special opportunities include:* An international exchange program and an internship program are available. *Placement services include:* Alumni network, career placement, career counseling/planning, electronic job bank, resume referral, career fairs, job interviews arranged, resume preparation, and career library.

EXPENSES *Tuition:* Full-time: $44,100. *Tuition (international):* Full-time: $44,100. *Required fees:* Full-time: $2703. Tuition and/or fees vary by class time, number of courses or credits taken, campus location, and academic program. *Typical graduate housing cost:* $6500 (including board).

FINANCIAL AID (2007–08) 610 students received aid, including fellowships, loans, scholarships, and work study.

Financial Aid Contact Mr. Lamar Richardson, Director of Financial Aid, Box 90120, Durham, NC 27708-0120. *Phone:* 919-660-7687. *Fax:* 919-681-6243. *E-mail:* lamar@duke.edu.

INTERNATIONAL STUDENTS 40% of students enrolled are international students. *Services and facilities:* Counseling/support services, ESL/language courses, Housing location assistance, International student organization, Language tutoring, Orientation, Visa Services. Financial aid is available to international students. *Required with application:* Proof of health/immunizations. *Recommended with application:* Proof of adequate funds.

International Student Contact Bertrand Guillotin, Director of the International Center, Box 90120, Durham, NC 27708-0120. *Phone:* 919-660-7931. *Fax:* 919-681-6245. *E-mail:* bertrand.guillotin@duke.edu.

APPLICATION *Required:* GMAT, application form, baccalaureate/first degree, essay, 2 letters of recommendation, personal statement, resume/curriculum vitae, transcripts of college work. *Recommended:* Interview, work experience. *Application fee:* $200.

Application Contact Ms. Liz Riley Hargrove, Associate Dean of Admissions, Box 90104, Durham, NC 27708-0104. *Phone:* 919-660-7705. *Fax:* 919-681-8026. *E-mail:* admissions-info@fuqua.duke.edu.

East Carolina University
College of Business
Greenville, North Carolina

Phone: 866-592-0835 **Fax:** 252-328-2106 **E-mail:** gradbus@ecu.edu

Business Program(s) Web Site: http://www.business.ecu.edu/grad

Graduate Business Unit Enrollment *Total:* 693 (318 full-time; 375 part-time; 322 women; 24 international).

Graduate Business Faculty *Total:* 110 (106 full-time; 4 part-time).

Admissions *Applied:* 305. *Admitted:* 269. *Enrolled:* 195. *Average GMAT:* 506. *Average GPA:* 3.12

Academic Calendar Semesters.

Accreditation AACSB—The Association to Advance Collegiate Schools of Business.

DEGREES MBA • MD/MBA • MSA

MBA—Master of Business Administration Full-time and part-time. Distance learning option. 30 to 60 total credits required. 10 to 72 months to complete program. *Concentrations:* city/urban administration, finance, general MBA, health care, hospitality management, international management, management information systems, sports/entertainment management, supply chain management, taxation.

MD/MBA—Doctor of Medicine/Master of Business Administration Full-time and part-time. Distance learning option. Must be enrolled in an accredited medical school, be a medical resident, or be a practicing physician. 42 total credits required. 12 to 48 months to complete program. *Concentrations:* general MBA, health care.

MSA—Master of Science in Accounting Full-time and part-time. 30 to 60 total credits required. 10 to 72 months to complete program. *Concentrations:* city/urban administration, finance, health care, international business, management information systems, sports/entertainment management, taxation.

RESOURCES AND SERVICES 1,425 on-campus PCs are available to graduate business students. Access to Internet/World Wide Web, online (class) registration, and online grade reports available. *Personal computer requirements:* Graduate business students are strongly recommended to purchase or lease a personal computer. *Special opportunities include:* An international exchange program and an internship program are available. *Placement services include:* Alumni network, career placement, career counseling/planning, electronic job bank, resume referral, career fairs, job interviews arranged, resume preparation, and career library.

EXPENSES *Tuition (state resident):* Full-time: $5780. *Tuition (nonresident):* Full-time: $16,096. *Tuition (international):* Full-time: $16,096.

FINANCIAL AID (2007–08) Loans, research assistantships, and scholarships. Aid is available to part-time students. *Financial aid application deadline:* 6/1.

Financial Aid Contact Maryann Jenkins, Assistant Director, Student Financial Aid, East Fifth Street, Greenville, NC 27858-4353. *Phone:* 252-328-6610. *Fax:* 252-328-4347. *E-mail:* faques@ecu.edu.

INTERNATIONAL STUDENTS 3% of students enrolled are international students. *Services and facilities:* Counseling/support services, Housing location assistance, International student organization, Orientation, Visa Services. Financial aid is available to international students. *Required with application:* IELT with recommended score of 6.5; TOEFL with recommended score of 213 (computer), 550 (paper), or 80 (Internet); proof of adequate funds; proof of health/immunizations.

International Student Contact Mr. Bill Mallett, Foreign Studies Advisor, International Affairs, International House, 306 East Ninth Street, Greenville, NC 27858-4353. *Phone:* 252-328-1939. *Fax:* 252-328-4813. *E-mail:* mallettw@ecu.edu.

APPLICATION *Required:* GMAT, application form, baccalaureate/first degree, resume/curriculum vitae, transcripts of college work. *Recommended:* Work experience. *Application fee:* $60. Applications for domestic and international students are processed on a rolling basis.

Application Contact Len Rhodes, Assistant Dean for Graduate Programs, 3203 Bate Building, Greenville, NC 27858-4353. *Phone:* 866-592-0835. *Fax:* 252-328-2106. *E-mail:* gradbus@ecu.edu.

See full description on page 602.

Elon University
Martha and Spencer Love School of Business
Elon, North Carolina

Phone: 336-278-7600 **Fax:** 336-278-7699 **E-mail:** afadde@elon.edu

Business Program(s) Web Site: http://www.elon.edu/mba

Graduate Business Unit Enrollment *Total:* 150 (150 part-time; 52 women; 7 international). *Average Age:* 32.

Graduate Business Faculty *Total:* 26 (23 full-time; 3 part-time).

Admissions *Applied:* 96. *Admitted:* 71. *Enrolled:* 61. *Average GMAT:* 523. *Average GPA:* 3.0

Academic Calendar Trimesters.

After Graduation (Class of 2006–07) *Employed within 3 months of graduation:* 100%. *Average starting salary:* $65,000.

DEGREES MBA

MBA—General Management *Concentration:* general MBA.

MBA—Master of Business Administration Full-time and part-time. At least 39 total credits required. 21 to 72 months to complete program. *Concentrations:* entrepreneurship, finance, health administration, leadership, marketing, project management.

RESOURCES AND SERVICES 835 on-campus PCs are available to graduate business students. Access to Internet/World Wide Web, online (class) registration, and online grade reports available. *Personal computer requirements:* Graduate business students are strongly recommended to purchase or lease a personal computer. *Special opportunities include:* An international exchange program is available. *Placement services include:* Alumni network, career counseling/planning, electronic job bank, resume referral, career fairs, and career library.

EXPENSES *Tuition:* Full-time: $10,000. Part-time: $5000 per year. *Tuition (international):* Full-time: $10,000. Part-time: $5000 per year.

FINANCIAL AID (2007–08) 28 students received aid, including loans. Aid is available to part-time students. *Financial aid application deadline:* 3/15.

Financial Aid Contact Pat Murphy, Director of Financial Planning, 100 Campus Drive, 2700 Campus Box, Elon, NC 27244. *Phone:* 800-334-8448 Ext. 2. *Fax:* 336-278-7639. *E-mail:* murphyp@elon.edu.

INTERNATIONAL STUDENTS 5% of students enrolled are international students. *Services and facilities:* Counseling/support services, Housing location assistance, International student organization, Language tutoring, Orientation, Visa Services, Writing center, Health care, International student advisor. Financial aid is not available to international students. *Required with application:* TOEFL with recommended score of 213 (computer), 550 (paper), or 79 (Internet); proof of adequate funds; proof of health/immunizations.

International Student Contact Art Fadde, Director of Graduate Admissions, 100 Campus Drive, 2750 Campus Box, Elon, NC 27244. *Phone:* 800-334-8448 Ext. 3. *Fax:* 336-278-7699. *E-mail:* afadde@elon.edu.

APPLICATION *Required:* GMAT, application form, baccalaureate/first degree, 3 letters of recommendation, personal statement, transcripts of college work, 2 years of work experience. *Recommended:* Interview, resume/curriculum vitae. *Application fee:* $50. Applications for domestic and international students are processed on a rolling basis.

Application Contact Art Fadde, Director of Graduate Admissions, Office of Graduate Admissions, 100 Campus Drive, 2750 Campus Box, Elon, NC 27244. *Phone:* 336-278-7600. *Fax:* 336-278-7699. *E-mail:* afadde@elon.edu.

Fayetteville State University

Program in Business Administration

Fayetteville, North Carolina

Phone: 910-672-1197 **Fax:** 910-672-1849 **E-mail:** atavakoli@uncfsu.edu

Business Program(s) Web Site: http://www.uncfsu.edu/mba

Graduate Business Unit Enrollment *Total:* 100 (10 full-time; 90 part-time; 51 women; 14 international). *Average Age:* 32.

Graduate Business Faculty *Total:* 44 (40 full-time; 4 part-time).

Admissions *Applied:* 100. *Admitted:* 80. *Enrolled:* 64. *Average GMAT:* 470. *Average GPA:* 3.2

Academic Calendar Semesters.

After Graduation (Class of 2006–07) *Employed within 3 months of graduation:* 90%. *Average starting salary:* $65,000.

DEGREE MBA

MBA—MBA Program Full-time and part-time. Distance learning option. 36 to 54 total credits required. 12 to 36 months to complete program. *Concentrations:* entrepreneurship, finance, general MBA, health care, management, project management.

RESOURCES AND SERVICES 50 on-campus PCs are available to graduate business students. Access to Internet/World Wide Web, online (class) registration, and online grade reports available. *Personal computer requirements:* Graduate business students are strongly recommended to purchase or lease a personal computer. *Special opportunities include:* An international exchange program and an internship program are available. *Placement services include:* Career placement, career counseling/planning, electronic job bank, career fairs, job interviews arranged, resume preparation, and career library.

EXPENSES *Tuition (state resident):* Full-time: $2118. *Tuition (nonresident):* Full-time: $11,708. *Tuition (international):* Full-time: $11,708. *Required fees:* Full-time: $1218. Tuition and/or fees vary by class time, number of courses or credits taken, and campus location. *Graduate housing:* Room and board costs vary by number of occupants, type of accommodation, and type of board plan. *Typical cost:* $6200 (including board), $4050 (room only).

FINANCIAL AID (2007–08) 3 students received aid, including loans, research assistantships, and work study. Aid is available to part-time students. *Financial aid application deadline:* 7/15.

Financial Aid Contact Lois N. McKoy, Director, Financial Aid Office, 1200 Murchison Road, Fayetteville, NC 28301. *Phone:* 910-486-1325. *Fax:* 910-486-1111. *E-mail:* lmckoy@uncfsu.edu.

INTERNATIONAL STUDENTS 14% of students enrolled are international students. *Services and facilities:* Counseling/support services, Housing location assistance, Orientation, Visa Services. Financial aid is not available to international students. *Required with application:* TOEFL with recommended score of 213 (computer) or 550 (paper); proof of adequate funds. *Recommended with application:* Proof of health/immunizations.

International Student Contact Asad A. Tavakoli, MBA Director, MBA Program, 1200 Murchison Road, Fayetteville, NC 28301. *Phone:* 910-672-1197. *Fax:* 910-672-1849. *E-mail:* atavakoli@uncfsu.edu.

APPLICATION *Required:* GMAT, application form, baccalaureate/first degree, 2 letters of recommendation, transcripts of college work. *Application fee:* $25. Applications for domestic and international students are processed on a rolling basis.

Application Contact Asad A. Tavakoli, MBA Director, MBA Program, 1200 Murchison Road, Fayetteville, NC 28301. *Phone:* 910-672-1197. *Fax:* 910-672-1849. *E-mail:* atavakoli@uncfsu.edu.

Gardner-Webb University

Graduate School of Business

Boiling Springs, North Carolina

Phone: 704-406-4489 **Fax:** 704-406-3895 **E-mail:** dknupp@gardner-webb.edu

Business Program(s) Web Site: http://www.gradbiz.gardner-webb.edu

Graduate Business Unit Enrollment *Total:* 400 (400 full-time; 228 women; 12 international). *Average Age:* 29.

Graduate Business Faculty 19 full-time.

Admissions *Applied:* 134. *Admitted:* 129. *Enrolled:* 104. *Average GMAT:* 523. *Average GPA:* 3.33

Gardner-Webb University (continued)

Academic Calendar Semesters.

Accreditation ACBSP—The American Council of Business Schools and Programs.

After Graduation (Class of 2006–07) *Employed within 3 months of graduation:* 95%.

DEGREES IMBA • M Acc • MBA

IMBA—International Master of Business Administration Full-time and part-time. At least 36 total credits required. 24 to 72 months to complete program. *Concentration:* international business.

M Acc—Master of Accountancy Full-time and part-time. Distance learning option. At least 30 total credits required. 18 to 72 months to complete program. *Concentrations:* accounting, taxation.

MBA—Master of Business Administration Full-time and part-time. Distance learning option. At least 36 total credits required. 24 to 72 months to complete program. *Concentrations:* accounting, finance, health care, human resources management, international business, management information systems.

RESOURCES AND SERVICES 300 on-campus PCs are available to graduate business students. Access to Internet/World Wide Web, online (class) registration, and online grade reports available. *Personal computer requirements:* Graduate business students are strongly recommended to purchase or lease a personal computer. *Placement services include:* Alumni network, career placement, career counseling/planning, electronic job bank, resume referral, career fairs, resume preparation, and career library.

FINANCIAL AID (2007–08) 38 students received aid, including loans and work study. Aid is available to part-time students.

Financial Aid Contact Deborah Hintz, Director of Financial Aid, Boiling Springs, NC 28017. *Phone:* 704-406-4497. *Fax:* 704-406-4102. *E-mail:* dhintz@gardner-webb.edu.

INTERNATIONAL STUDENTS 3% of students enrolled are international students. *Services and facilities:* Counseling/support services, International student housing, International student organization, I-20 processing. Financial aid is not available to international students. *Required with application:* TOEFL with recommended score of 170 (computer) or 500 (paper); proof of adequate funds; proof of health/immunizations.

International Student Contact Ms. Deborah Knupp, Director of Admissions, PO Box 5168, Boiling Springs, NC 28017. *Phone:* 704-406-4489. *Fax:* 704-406-3895. *E-mail:* dknupp@gardner-webb.edu.

APPLICATION *Required:* GMAT, application form, baccalaureate/first degree, essay, 3 letters of recommendation, personal statement, resume/curriculum vitae, transcripts of college work. School will accept GRE. *Application fee:* $40. Applications for domestic and international students are processed on a rolling basis.

Application Contact Ms. Deborah Knupp, Director of Admissions, PO Box 5168, Boiling Springs, NC 28017. *Phone:* 704-406-4489. *Fax:* 704-406-3895. *E-mail:* dknupp@gardner-webb.edu.

High Point University
Norcross Graduate School
High Point, North Carolina

Phone: 336-841-9198 **Fax:** 336-888-6378 **E-mail:** graduate@highpoint.edu

Business Program(s) Web Site: http://www.highpoint.edu/graduate

Graduate Business Unit Enrollment *Total:* 127 (18 full-time; 109 part-time; 62 women; 9 international). *Average Age:* 33.

Graduate Business Faculty 36 full-time.

Admissions *Applied:* 112. *Admitted:* 70. *Enrolled:* 66. *Average GPA:* 3.3

Academic Calendar Semesters.

Accreditation ACBSP—The American Council of Business Schools and Programs.

After Graduation (Class of 2006–07) *Employed within 3 months of graduation:* 100%.

DEGREE MBA

MBA—Master of Business Administration Full-time and part-time. 33 to 48 total credits required. 24 to 60 months to complete program. *Concentration:* general MBA.

RESOURCES AND SERVICES 150 on-campus PCs are available to graduate business students. Access to Internet/World Wide Web, online (class) registration, and online grade reports available. *Personal computer requirements:* Graduate business students are required to have a personal computer. *Placement services include:* Career counseling/planning and resume preparation.

EXPENSES *Tuition:* Full-time: $7725. Part-time: $515 per credit hour.

FINANCIAL AID (2007–08) 49 students received aid, including loans. Aid is available to part-time students. *Financial aid application deadline:* 3/1.

Financial Aid Contact Julie Setzer, Director of Student Financial Services, 833 Montlieu Avenue, High Point, NC 27262-3598. *Phone:* 336-841-9128. *Fax:* 336-841-4649. *E-mail:* jsetzer@highpoint.edu.

INTERNATIONAL STUDENTS 7% of students enrolled are international students. *Services and facilities:* Counseling/support services, Housing location assistance, International student organization, Orientation, Visa Services. Financial aid is not available to international students. *Required with application:* TOEFL with recommended score of 550 (paper); proof of adequate funds.

International Student Contact Alberta Haynes Herron, Dean, 833 Montlieu Avenue, High Point, NC 27262-3598. *Phone:* 336-841-9198. *Fax:* 336-888-6378. *E-mail:* graduate@highpoint.edu.

APPLICATION *Required:* GMAT, application form, baccalaureate/first degree, essay, 3 letters of recommendation, personal statement, resume/curriculum vitae, transcripts of college work. *Recommended:* Work experience. *Application fee:* $50. Applications for domestic and international students are processed on a rolling basis.

Application Contact Alberta Haynes Herron, Dean, 833 Montlieu Avenue, High Point, NC 27262-3598. *Phone:* 336-841-9198. *Fax:* 336-888-6378. *E-mail:* graduate@highpoint.edu.

Lenoir-Rhyne College
Charles M. Snipes School of Business
Hickory, North Carolina

Phone: 828-328-7300 **Fax:** 828-328-7378 **E-mail:** admission@lrc.edu

Business Program(s) Web Site: http://www.lrc.edu/bus/

Graduate Business Unit Enrollment *Total:* 28 (8 full-time; 20 part-time; 10 women; 1 international). *Average Age:* 30.

Graduate Business Faculty *Total:* 5 (4 full-time; 1 part-time).

Academic Calendar Semesters.

Accreditation ACBSP—The American Council of Business Schools and Programs.

DEGREE MBA

MBA—Master of Business Administration Full-time and part-time. At least 36 total credits required. 15 to 72 months to complete program. *Concentrations:* accounting, general MBA, international and area business studies, leadership.

RESOURCES AND SERVICES 112 on-campus PCs are available to graduate business students. Access to Internet/World Wide Web available. *Personal computer requirements:* Graduate business students are not required to have a personal computer. *Placement services include:* Alumni network, job search course, career counseling/planning, electronic job bank, resume referral, career fairs, resume preparation, and career library.

EXPENSES *Tuition:* Full-time: $5850. Part-time: $325 per credit hour. *Tuition (international):* Full-time: $5850. Part-time: $325 per credit hour. *Required fees:* Full-time: $50. Tuition and/or fees vary by number of courses or credits taken and academic program. *Graduate housing:* Room and board costs vary by number of occupants and type of accommodation. *Typical cost:* $7620 (including board), $3880 (room only).

FINANCIAL AID (2007–08) 13 students received aid, including grants, loans, scholarships, and teaching assistantships. Aid is available to part-time students. *Financial aid application deadline:* 3/1.

Financial Aid Contact Mr. Eric Brandon, Director of Admissions and Financial Aid, PO Box 7419, Hickory, NC 28603. *Phone:* 828-328-7300. *Fax:* 828-328-7039. *E-mail:* finaid@lrc.edu.

INTERNATIONAL STUDENTS 4% of students enrolled are international students. *Services and facilities:* Counseling/support services, ESL/language courses, Housing location assistance, International student organization, Language tutoring, Orientation, Visa Services, Pre-MBA Program. Financial aid is available to international students. *Required with application:* TOEFL with recommended score of 213 (computer) or 550 (paper); proof of adequate funds; proof of health/immunizations.

International Student Contact Lynda Kirby, Coordinator, Office for International Education, PO Box 7160, Hickory, NC 28603. *Phone:* 828-328-7160. *Fax:* 828-328-7365. *E-mail:* oie@lrc.edu.

APPLICATION *Required:* GMAT, application form, baccalaureate/first degree, essay, interview, 3 letters of recommendation, personal statement, transcripts of college work, 2 years of work experience. *Application fee:* $35. Applications for domestic and international students are processed on a rolling basis.

Application Contact Mr. Eric Brandon, Office of Admissions and Financial Aid, PO Box 7227, Hickory, NC 28603. *Phone:* 828-328-7300. *Fax:* 828-328-7378. *E-mail:* admission@lrc.edu.

Meredith College
John E. Weems Graduate School

Raleigh, North Carolina

Phone: 919-760-8212 **Fax:** 919-760-2898 **E-mail:** anthonya@meredith.edu

Business Program(s) Web Site: http://www.meredith.edu/mba

Graduate Business Unit Enrollment *Total:* 71 (29 full-time; 42 part-time; 59 women; 2 international). *Average Age:* 33.

Graduate Business Faculty 8 full-time.

Admissions *Average GMAT:* 500. *Average GPA:* 2.9

Academic Calendar Semesters.

DEGREE MBA

MBA—Master of Business Administration Full-time and part-time. 30 to 35 total credits required. 24 to 72 months to complete program. *Concentration:* general MBA.

RESOURCES AND SERVICES 120 on-campus PCs are available to graduate business students. Access to Internet/World Wide Web, online (class) registration, and online grade reports available. *Personal computer requirements:* Graduate business students are not required to have a personal computer. *Placement services include:* Alumni network, career counseling/planning, electronic job bank, resume referral, career fairs, resume preparation, and career library.

EXPENSES *Tuition:* Full-time: $6840. Part-time: $570 per credit hour. *Tuition (international):* Full-time: $6840. Part-time: $570 per credit hour. *Required fees:* Full-time: $150.

FINANCIAL AID (2007–08) Loans and scholarships. Aid is available to part-time students. *Financial aid application deadline:* 4/15.

Financial Aid Contact Kevin Michaelsen, Director of Financial Assistance, 3800 Hillsborough Street, Raleigh, NC 27607-5298. *Phone:* 919-760-8565. *Fax:* 919-760-2373. *E-mail:* michaelsen@meredith.edu.

INTERNATIONAL STUDENTS 3% of students enrolled are international students. *Services and facilities:* Counseling/support services, International student organization. Financial aid is available to international students. *Required with application:* TOEFL; proof of adequate funds; proof of health/immunizations.

International Student Contact Allison Anthony, MBA Recruiter, 3800 Hillsborough Street, Raleigh, NC 27607-5298. *Phone:* 919-760-8212. *Fax:* 919-760-2898. *E-mail:* mba@meredith.edu.

APPLICATION *Required:* GMAT, application form, baccalaureate/first degree, essay, interview, 2 letters of recommendation, resume/curriculum vitae, transcripts of college work, 2 years of work experience. *Application fee:* $50. Applications for domestic and international students are processed on a rolling basis.

Application Contact Allison Anthony, MBA Recruiter, 3800 Hillsborough Street, Raleigh, NC 27607-5298. *Phone:* 919-760-8212. *Fax:* 919-760-2898. *E-mail:* anthonya@meredith.edu.

Montreat College
School of Professional and Adult Studies

Montreat, North Carolina

Phone: 828-669-8012 Ext. 3782 **Fax:** 828-669-0120 **E-mail:** jhiggins@montreat.edu

Business Program(s) Web Site: http://www.montreat.edu/

DEGREE MBA

MBA—Master of Business Administration Full-time. 34 to 40 total credits required. Minimum of 24 months to complete program. *Concentration:* general MBA.

RESOURCES AND SERVICES 7 on-campus PCs are available to graduate business students. Access to Internet/World Wide Web and online grade reports available. *Personal computer requirements:* Graduate business students are required to have a personal computer. *Placement services include:* Alumni network, career counseling/planning, electronic job bank, career fairs, resume preparation, and career library.

Application Contact Mr. Joey Higgins, Dean of Admissions and Financial Aid, Office of Admissions, 310 Gaither Circle, Montreat, NC 28757-1267. *Phone:* 828-669-8012 Ext. 3782. *Fax:* 828-669-0120. *E-mail:* jhiggins@montreat.edu.

North Carolina Central University
School of Business

Durham, North Carolina

Phone: 919-530-7390 **Fax:** 919-530-7961 **E-mail:** fpollock@nccu.edu

Business Program(s) Web Site: http://www.nccu.edu/business

Graduate Business Unit Enrollment *Total:* 70 (33 full-time; 37 part-time; 38 women; 10 international). *Average Age:* 30.

Graduate Business Faculty *Total:* 13 (12 full-time; 1 part-time).

Admissions *Applied:* 39. *Admitted:* 25. *Enrolled:* 20. *Average GMAT:* 474. *Average GPA:* 3.1

Academic Calendar Semesters.

Accreditation AACSB—The Association to Advance Collegiate Schools of Business. ACBSP—The American Council of Business Schools and Programs.

After Graduation (Class of 2006–07) *Employed within 3 months of graduation:* 80%. *Average starting salary:* $71,000.

North Carolina Central University (continued)

DEGREES JD/MBA • MBA • MBA/MIS

JD/MBA—Juris Doctor/Master of Business Administration Full-time and part-time. 103 to 130 total credits required. 48 to 72 months to complete program. *Concentration:* combined degrees.

MBA—Master of Business Administration Full-time and part-time. 33 to 63 total credits required. 24 to 72 months to complete program. *Concentration:* general MBA.

MBA/MIS—Master of Business Administration/Master of Information Science Full-time and part-time. At least 48 total credits required. 36 to 72 months to complete program. *Concentration:* combined degrees.

RESOURCES AND SERVICES 40 on-campus PCs are available to graduate business students. Access to Internet/World Wide Web, online (class) registration, and online grade reports available. *Personal computer requirements:* Graduate business students are strongly recommended to purchase or lease a personal computer. *Special opportunities include:* An international exchange program and an internship program are available. *Placement services include:* Alumni network, career placement, job search course, career counseling/planning, electronic job bank, resume referral, career fairs, job interviews arranged, resume preparation, and career library.

EXPENSES *Tuition (state resident):* Full-time: $1033.88. Part-time: $344.63 per hour. *Tuition (nonresident):* Full-time: $4716. Part-time: $1572.25 per hour. *Tuition (international):* Full-time: $4716.25. Part-time: $1572.25 per hour. *Required fees:* Full-time: $783.65. Part-time: $535.87 per course. Tuition and/or fees vary by number of courses or credits taken and academic program. *Graduate housing:* Room and board costs vary by campus location, number of occupants, type of accommodation, and type of board plan. *Typical cost:* $3900 (including board), $1291 (room only).

FINANCIAL AID (2007–08) 45 students received aid, including loans, research assistantships, scholarships, and work study. *Financial aid application deadline:* 3/15.

Financial Aid Contact Sharon Oliver, Assistant Vice Chancellor for Scholarships and Student Aid, 1801 Fayetteville Street, 143 Student Services Building, Durham, NC 27707-3129. *Phone:* 919-530-6202. *Fax:* 919-530-7959. *E-mail:* soliver@nccu.edu.

INTERNATIONAL STUDENTS 14% of students enrolled are international students. *Services and facilities:* Counseling/support services, Housing location assistance, International student organization, Language tutoring, Orientation, Visa Services. Financial aid is available to international students. *Required with application:* TOEFL with recommended score of 173 (computer) or 500 (paper); proof of adequate funds; proof of health/immunizations.

International Student Contact Mrs. Emma L. Mosby, Assistant Dean of Student Affairs/Director of International Studies, PO Box 19406, 1801 Fayetteville Street, Durham, NC 27707. *Phone:* 919-530-7492. *Fax:* 919-530-7567. *E-mail:* emosby@nccu.edu.

APPLICATION *Required:* GMAT, application form, baccalaureate/first degree, interview, 3 letters of recommendation, personal statement, resume/curriculum vitae, transcripts of college work. *Recommended:* 2 years of work experience. *Application fee:* $40. Applications for domestic and international students are processed on a rolling basis.

Application Contact Dr. Frank Pollock, Director, MBA Program, 1801 Fayetteville Street, Durham, NC 27707-3129. *Phone:* 919-530-7390. *Fax:* 919-530-7961. *E-mail:* fpollock@nccu.edu.

North Carolina State University
College of Management
Raleigh, North Carolina

Phone: 919-515-5584 **Fax:** 919-515-5073 **E-mail:** mba@ncsu.edu

Business Program(s) Web Site: http://www.mgt.ncsu.edu/

Graduate Business Unit Enrollment *Total:* 373 (76 full-time; 297 part-time; 105 women; 65 international). *Average Age:* 31.

Graduate Business Faculty *Total:* 114 (98 full-time; 16 part-time).

Admissions *Applied:* 309. *Admitted:* 210. *Enrolled:* 145. *Average GMAT:* 584. *Average GPA:* 3.2

Academic Calendar Semesters.

Accreditation AACSB—The Association to Advance Collegiate Schools of Business.

After Graduation (Class of 2006–07) *Employed within 3 months of graduation:* 91%. *Average starting salary:* $72,568.

DEGREES M Acc • M Econ • MA • MBA • MS

M Acc—Master of Accounting Full-time and part-time. At least 36 total credits required. 12 to 72 months to complete program. *Concentrations:* accounting, information technology, risk management.

M Econ—Master of Economics Full-time and part-time. At least 30 total credits required. 12 to 72 months to complete program. *Concentration:* economics.

MA—Master of Arts in Economics Full-time and part-time. At least 30 total credits required. 12 to 72 months to complete program. *Concentration:* economics.

MBA—Master of Business Administration Full-time and part-time. At least 56 total credits required. 16 to 72 months to complete program. *Concentrations:* entrepreneurship, financial management/planning, marketing, pharmaceutical management, production management, supply chain management, technology management.

MS—Master of Science in Agricultural Economics Full-time and part-time. At least 30 total credits required. 12 to 72 months to complete program. *Concentration:* agricultural economics.

RESOURCES AND SERVICES 117 on-campus PCs are available to graduate business students. Access to Internet/World Wide Web, online (class) registration, and online grade reports available. *Personal computer requirements:* Graduate business students are required to have a personal computer. *Special opportunities include:* An international exchange program and an internship program are available. *Placement services include:* Alumni network, career placement, job search course, career counseling/planning, electronic job bank, resume referral, career fairs, job interviews arranged, resume preparation, and career library.

EXPENSES *Tuition (state resident):* Full-time: $10,893. Part-time: $3382 per semester. *Tuition (nonresident):* Full-time: $22,816. Part-time: $7853 per semester. *Tuition (international):* Full-time: $22,816. Part-time: $7853 per semester. *Required fees:* Full-time: $1368. Part-time: $456 per semester. Tuition and/or fees vary by class time, number of courses or credits taken, campus location, and academic program. *Graduate housing:* Room and board costs vary by number of occupants, type of accommodation, and type of board plan. *Typical cost:* $11,000 (including board).

FINANCIAL AID (2007–08) 52 students received aid, including fellowships, research assistantships, scholarships, and teaching assistantships. *Financial aid application deadline:* 3/1.

Financial Aid Contact Ms. Julie Rice Mallette, Director, Financial Aid, Box 7302, Raleigh, NC 27695. *Phone:* 919-515-2334. *Fax:* 919-515-8422. *E-mail:* julie_mallette@ncsu.edu.

INTERNATIONAL STUDENTS 17% of students enrolled are international students. *Services and facilities:* Counseling/support services, ESL/language courses, International student housing, International student organization, Language tutoring, Orientation, Visa Services. Financial aid is available to international students. *Required with application:* TOEFL with recommended score of 250 (computer), 600 (paper), or 100 (Internet); proof of adequate funds; proof of health/immunizations.

International Student Contact Michael Bustle, Director, International Student Office, Box 7222, Raleigh, NC 27695. *Phone:* 919-515-2961. *Fax:* 919-515-1402. *E-mail:* michael_bustle@ncsu.edu.

APPLICATION *Required:* GMAT, application form, baccalaureate/first degree, essay, interview, 3 letters of recommendation, personal statement, resume/curriculum vitae, transcripts of college work, 2 years of work experience. *Application fee:* $65, $75 (international). Applications for domestic and international students are processed on a rolling basis.

Application Contact Pamela Bostic, Director of MBA Admissions, Campus Box 8114, Raleigh, NC 27695-8114. *Phone:* 919-515-5584. *Fax:* 919-515-5073. *E-mail:* mba@ncsu.edu.

See full description on page 664.

Pfeiffer University
Program in Business Administration

Misenheimer, North Carolina

Phone: 704-945-7314 **Fax:** 704-521-8617 **E-mail:** tom.leitzel@pfeiffer.edu

Business Program(s) Web Site: http://www.pfeiffer.edu/graduate

Graduate Business Unit Enrollment *Total:* 876 (85 full-time; 791 part-time; 517 women; 57 international). *Average Age:* 34.

Graduate Business Faculty *Total:* 74 (26 full-time; 48 part-time).

Admissions *Applied:* 236. *Admitted:* 225. *Enrolled:* 220. *Average GMAT:* 525. *Average GPA:* 3.12

Academic Calendar Semesters.

DEGREES MBA • MBA/MHA • MBA/MOD • MHA • MS

MBA—Master of Business Administration Full-time and part-time. Distance learning option. At least 36 total credits required. 18 to 60 months to complete program. *Concentrations:* international business, management.

MBA/MHA—Master of Business Administration/Master of Health Administration Full-time and part-time. Distance learning option. At least 54 total credits required. 42 to 84 months to complete program. *Concentration:* health care.

MBA/MOD—Master of Business Administration/Master of Organizational Change and Leadership Full-time and part-time. Distance learning option. 54 total credits required. 42 to 84 months to complete program. *Concentrations:* leadership, organizational management.

MHA—Master of Health Administration Full-time and part-time. Distance learning option. At least 36 total credits required. 18 to 60 months to complete program. *Concentration:* health care.

MS—Master of Science in Organizational Change and Leadership Full-time and part-time. Distance learning option. At least 36 total credits required. 18 to 60 months to complete program. *Concentration:* organizational management.

RESOURCES AND SERVICES 50 on-campus PCs are available to graduate business students. Access to Internet/World Wide Web, online (class) registration, and online grade reports available. *Personal computer requirements:* Graduate business students are strongly recommended to purchase or lease a personal computer. *Special opportunities include:* An international exchange program and an internship program are available. *Placement services include:* Alumni network, career counseling/planning, career fairs, and resume preparation.

EXPENSES *Tuition:* Full-time: $14,580. Part-time: $7290 per year. *Tuition (international):* Full-time: $14,580. Part-time: $7290 per year. Tuition and/or fees vary by campus location.

FINANCIAL AID (2007–08) Loans. Aid is available to part-time students. *Financial aid application deadline:* 8/6.

Financial Aid Contact Ms. Amy Brown, Director of Financial Aid, PO Box 960, Misenheimer, NC 28109. *Phone:* 704-463-3046. *Fax:* 704-463-1363. *E-mail:* amy.brown@pfeiffer.edu.

INTERNATIONAL STUDENTS 7% of students enrolled are international students. *Services and facilities:* Counseling/support services, Orientation. Financial aid is not available to international students. *Required with application:* TOEFL with recommended score of 500 (paper); proof of adequate funds; proof of health/immunizations.

International Student Contact Mr. Jonatham C. Beam, Admissions Coordinator, 4701 Park Road, Charlotte, NC 28209. *Phone:* 704-945-7356. *Fax:* 704-521-8617. *E-mail:* jonathan.beam@pfeiffer.edu.

APPLICATION *Required:* Application form, baccalaureate/first degree, 3 letters of recommendation, transcripts of college work. School will accept GMAT, GRE, and MAT. *Recommended:* Interview, resume/curriculum vitae, 4 years of work experience. *Application fee:* $75. Applications for domestic and international students are processed on a rolling basis.

Application Contact Dr. Thomas C. Leitzel, Vice President for Enrollment Management, 4701 Park Road, Charlotte, NC 28209. *Phone:* 704-945-7314. *Fax:* 704-521-8617. *E-mail:* tom.leitzel@pfeiffer.edu.

Queens University of Charlotte
McColl Graduate School of Business

Charlotte, North Carolina

Phone: 704-337-2224 **Fax:** 704-337-2594 **E-mail:** mobleyr@rex.queens.edu

Business Program(s) Web Site: http://mccoll.queens.edu/

Graduate Business Unit Enrollment *Total:* 212 (61 full-time; 151 part-time; 80 women; 8 international). *Average Age:* 27.

Graduate Business Faculty *Total:* 16 (14 full-time; 2 part-time).

Admissions *Applied:* 68. *Admitted:* 57. *Enrolled:* 52. *Average GMAT:* 570. *Average GPA:* 2.9

Academic Calendar Trimesters.

Accreditation AACSB—The Association to Advance Collegiate Schools of Business. ACBSP—The American Council of Business Schools and Programs.

After Graduation (Class of 2006–07) *Employed within 3 months of graduation:* 99%.

DEGREES M Sc • MBA

M Sc—Master of Science Full-time and part-time. 5 year of professional work experience. 36 total credits required. 24 to 60 months to complete program. *Concentration:* organizational behavior/development.

MBA—Executive Master of Business Administration Full-time. 5-7 years of work/management experience required. 54 total credits required. 20 months to complete program. *Concentration:* executive programs.

MBA—Professional Master of Business Administration Full-time and part-time. 39 to 54 total credits required. 28 to 60 months to complete program. *Concentrations:* finance, general MBA, marketing.

RESOURCES AND SERVICES 40 on-campus PCs are available to graduate business students. Access to Internet/World Wide Web, online (class) registration, and online grade reports available. *Personal computer requirements:* Graduate business students are not required to have a personal computer. *Placement services include:* Alumni network, career counseling/planning, and resume preparation.

EXPENSES *Tuition:* Part-time: $750 per credit hour. *Tuition (international):* Part-time: $750 per credit hour.

FINANCIAL AID (2007–08) 72 students received aid, including fellowships and loans. Aid is available to part-time students.

Financial Aid Contact Ms. Michelle Thompson, Director of Student Financial Services, 1900 Selwyn Avenue, Charlotte, NC 28274-0001. *Phone:* 704-337-2561. *Fax:* 704-337-2416. *E-mail:* thompsonm@queens.edu.

INTERNATIONAL STUDENTS 4% of students enrolled are international students. *Services and facilities:* Orientation. Financial aid is not available to international students. *Required with application:* TOEFL with recommended score of 550 (paper); proof of adequate funds; proof of health/immunizations.

Queens University of Charlotte (continued)

International Student Contact Robert Mobley, Director of McColl School Admissions, 1900 Selwyn Avenue, Charlotte, NC 28274-0002. *Phone:* 704-337-2224. *Fax:* 704-337-2594. *E-mail:* mobleyr@queens.edu.

APPLICATION *Required:* Application form, baccalaureate/first degree, essay, 2 letters of recommendation, personal statement, resume/curriculum vitae, transcripts of college work. *Recommended:* 3 years of work experience. *Application fee:* $75. Applications for domestic and international students are processed on a rolling basis.

Application Contact Robert Mobley, Director of McColl School Admissions, 1900 Selwyn Avenue, Charlotte, NC 28274-0002. *Phone:* 704-337-2224. *Fax:* 704-337-2594. *E-mail:* mobleyr@rex.queens.edu.

The University of North Carolina at Chapel Hill

Kenan-Flagler Business School

Chapel Hill, North Carolina

Phone: 919-962-3236 **Fax:** 919-962-0898 **E-mail:** mba_info@unc.edu

Business Program(s) Web Site: http://www.kenan-flagler.unc.edu/

Graduate Business Unit Enrollment *Total:* 571 (571 full-time).

Graduate Business Faculty 102 full-time.

Admissions *Average GMAT:* 664. *Average GPA:* 3.3

Academic Calendar Semesters.

Accreditation AACSB—The Association to Advance Collegiate Schools of Business.

After Graduation (Class of 2006–07) *Average starting salary:* $92,505.

DEGREES EMBA • JD/MBA • MAC • MBA • MBA/MHA • MBA/MRP • MBA/MSIS

EMBA—OneMBA Full-time. 21 months to complete program. *Concentration:* executive programs.

JD/MBA—Juris Doctor/Master of Business Administration Full-time. At least 123 total credits required. Minimum of 48 months to complete program. *Concentration:* combined degrees.

MAC—Master of Accounting Full-time. At least 48 total credits required. 12 months to complete program. *Concentration:* accounting.

MBA—Evening MBA for Executives Program Full-time. At least 57 total credits required. Maximum of 24 months to complete program. *Concentration:* executive programs.

MBA—Weekend MBA for Executives Program Full-time. Maximum of 20 months to complete program. *Concentration:* executive programs.

MBA—Master of Business Administration Full-time. At least 59 total credits required. 21 months to complete program. *Concentrations:* electronic commerce (E-commerce), entrepreneurship, environmental economics/management, finance, international business, management, management consulting, marketing, new venture management, real estate, supply chain management.

MBA/MHA—Master of Business Administration/Master of Health Administration Full-time. At least 110 total credits required. Minimum of 36 months to complete program. *Concentration:* combined degrees.

MBA/MRP—Master of Business Administration/Master of Regional Planning Full-time. At least 107 total credits required. Minimum of 36 months to complete program. *Concentration:* combined degrees.

MBA/MSIS—Master of Business Administration/Master of Science in Information Sciences Full-time. Maximum of 36 months to complete program. *Concentration:* combined degrees.

RESOURCES AND SERVICES Access to Internet/World Wide Web and online (class) registration available. *Personal computer requirements:* Graduate business students are required to have a personal computer. *Special opportunities include:* An international exchange program and an internship program are available. *Placement services include:* Alumni network, career placement, job search course, career counseling/planning, electronic job bank, resume referral, career fairs, job interviews arranged, resume preparation, and career library.

EXPENSES *Tuition (state resident):* Full-time: $19,525. *Tuition (nonresident):* Full-time: $39,049. *Tuition (international):* Full-time: $39,049. *Required fees:* Full-time: $2851.

FINANCIAL AID (2007–08) Fellowships, grants, loans, and scholarships.

Financial Aid Contact Susan Brooks, MBA Financial Aid Officer, CB 3490 McColl Building, Chapel Hill, NC 27599-3490. *Phone:* 919-962-9491. *E-mail:* susan_brooks@unc.edu.

INTERNATIONAL STUDENTS *Services and facilities:* Counseling/support services, Housing location assistance, International student organization, Orientation, Visa Services, Honing Executive English Language Skills (HEELS) program in career management office. Financial aid is available to international students. *Required with application:* TOEFL with recommended score of 250 (computer) or 600 (paper); proof of adequate funds; proof of health/immunizations.

International Student Contact Alison Jesse, Associate Director, MBA Admissions and Student Services, CB 3490 McColl Building, Chapel Hill, NC 27599-3490. *Phone:* 919-962-9830. *Fax:* 919-962-0898. *E-mail:* mba_info@unc.edu.

APPLICATION *Required:* GMAT, application form, baccalaureate/first degree, essay, interview, 2 letters of recommendation, personal statement, resume/curriculum vitae, transcripts of college work, 2 years of work experience. *Application fee:* $135. *Deadlines:* 10/24 for fall, 12/5 for winter, 1/9 for spring, 3/13 for summer, 10/24 for fall (international), 12/5 for winter (international), 1/9 for spring (international), 3/13 for summer (international).

Application Contact Sherrylyn Wallace, Director, MBA Admissions, CB 3490 McColl Building, Chapel Hill, NC 27599-3490. *Phone:* 919-962-3236. *Fax:* 919-962-0898. *E-mail:* mba_info@unc.edu.

The University of North Carolina at Charlotte

Belk College of Business Administration

Charlotte, North Carolina

Phone: 704-687-7566 **Fax:** 704-687-2809 **E-mail:** jsnelson@uncc.edu

Business Program(s) Web Site: http://www.belkcollege.uncc.edu

Graduate Business Unit Enrollment *Total:* 672 (255 full-time; 417 part-time; 249 women; 208 international). *Average Age:* 29.

Graduate Business Faculty *Total:* 99 (79 full-time; 20 part-time).

Admissions *Applied:* 588. *Admitted:* 396. *Enrolled:* 270. *Average GMAT:* 591. *Average GPA:* 3.34

Academic Calendar Semesters.

Accreditation AACSB—The Association to Advance Collegiate Schools of Business.

After Graduation (Class of 2006–07) *Employed within 3 months of graduation:* 100%. *Average starting salary:* $64,797.

DEGREES EMBA • M Acc • MBA • MS

EMBA—Executive Master of Business Administration *Concentration:* executive programs.

M Acc—Master of Accountancy Full-time and part-time. At least 30 total credits required. *Concentrations:* accounting, taxation.

MBA—Sports Marketing and Management Full-time. *Concentration:* sports/entertainment management.

MBA—Master of Business Administration Full-time and part-time. At least 37 total credits required. 17 to 72 months to complete program.

Concentrations: accounting, economics, finance, general MBA, information technology, management, marketing, other, real estate.

MS—Master of Science At least 30 total credits required. *Concentrations:* economics, finance.

RESOURCES AND SERVICES 400 on-campus PCs are available to graduate business students. Access to Internet/World Wide Web, online (class) registration, and online grade reports available. *Personal computer requirements:* Graduate business students are strongly recommended to purchase or lease a personal computer. *Special opportunities include:* An international exchange program and an internship program are available. *Placement services include:* Alumni network, career placement, career counseling/planning, electronic job bank, resume referral, career fairs, job interviews arranged, resume preparation, and career library.

FINANCIAL AID (2007–08) 131 students received aid, including grants, loans, scholarships, and teaching assistantships. Aid is available to part-time students. *Financial aid application deadline:* 6/1.

Financial Aid Contact Mr. Tony Carter, Director, Financial Aid, Student Financial Aid Office, 106 Reese, 9201 University City Boulevard, Charlotte, NC 28223-0001. *Phone:* 704-687-2426. *Fax:* 704-687-3132. *E-mail:* acarte1@uncc.edu.

INTERNATIONAL STUDENTS 31% of students enrolled are international students. *Services and facilities:* Counseling/support services, ESL/language courses, Housing location assistance, International student housing, International student organization, Orientation, Visa Services. Financial aid is available to international students. *Required with application:* IELT with recommended score of 6.5; TOEFL with recommended score of 220 (computer) or 557 (paper); proof of adequate funds; proof of health/immunizations.

International Student Contact Allison B. Brinkley, International Admissions Office, 9201 University City Boulevard, Charlotte, NC 28223-0001. *Phone:* 704-687-2633. *Fax:* 704-687-6340. *E-mail:* abrinkley@uncc.edu.

APPLICATION *Required:* GMAT, application form, baccalaureate/first degree, 3 letters of recommendation, personal statement, transcripts of college work. *Recommended:* Resume/curriculum vitae, work experience. *Application fee:* $55. Applications for domestic and international students are processed on a rolling basis.

Application Contact Jeremiah Nelson, Associate MBA Director, 9201 University City Boulevard, 206A Friday Building, Charlotte, NC 28223. *Phone:* 704-687-7566. *Fax:* 704-687-2809. *E-mail:* jsnelson@uncc.edu.

See full description on page 730.

The University of North Carolina at Greensboro

Bryan School of Business and Economics

Greensboro, North Carolina

Phone: 336-334-5390 **Fax:** 336-334-4209 **E-mail:** tlkeller@uncg.edu

Business Program(s) Web Site: http://www.uncg.edu/bae/

Graduate Business Unit Enrollment *Total:* 400 (158 full-time; 242 part-time; 172 women; 50 international). *Average Age:* 31.

Graduate Business Faculty *Total:* 43 (35 full-time; 8 part-time).

Admissions *Applied:* 324. *Admitted:* 135. *Enrolled:* 100. *Average GMAT:* 555. *Average GPA:* 3.18

Academic Calendar Semesters.

Accreditation AACSB—The Association to Advance Collegiate Schools of Business.

After Graduation (Class of 2006–07) *Employed within 3 months of graduation:* 90%.

DEGREES MBA • MBA/MS • MBA/MSN

MBA—Day Master of Business Administration Full-time. 48 total credits required. 21 months to complete program. *Concentration:* general MBA.

MBA—Evening Master of Business Administration Full-time and part-time. 36 to 48 total credits required. 18 to 60 months to complete program. *Concentration:* general MBA.

MBA/MS—MBA/MS in Gerontology Full-time and part-time. 57 total credits required. 30 to 60 months to complete program. *Concentration:* combined degrees.

MBA/MSN—Master of Science in Nursing/Master of Business Administration Full-time and part-time. BSN degree, licensure in U.S., and 1 year of nursing experience required. 54 total credits required. 24 to 60 months to complete program. *Concentration:* combined degrees.

RESOURCES AND SERVICES 385 on-campus PCs are available to graduate business students. Access to Internet/World Wide Web, online (class) registration, and online grade reports available. *Personal computer requirements:* Graduate business students are required to have a personal computer. *Special opportunities include:* An international exchange program and an internship program are available. *Placement services include:* Alumni network, career placement, job search course, career counseling/planning, electronic job bank, resume referral, career fairs, job interviews arranged, resume preparation, and career library.

EXPENSES *Tuition (state resident):* Full-time: $6093. Part-time: $1824 per semester. *Tuition (nonresident):* Full-time: $17,143. Part-time: $5968 per semester. *Tuition (international):* Full-time: $17,143. Tuition and/or fees vary by number of courses or credits taken. *Graduate housing:* Room and board costs vary by number of occupants, type of accommodation, and type of board plan. *Typical cost:* $6396 (including board), $5134 (room only).

FINANCIAL AID (2007–08) 74 students received aid, including fellowships, loans, research assistantships, scholarships, and teaching assistantships. *Financial aid application deadline:* 3/15.

Financial Aid Contact Ms. Deborah Tollefson, Director, Financial Aid, 723 Kenilworth Street, Greensboro, NC 27412-5001. *Phone:* 336-334-5702. *Fax:* 336-334-3010. *E-mail:* deborah_tollefson@uncg.edu.

INTERNATIONAL STUDENTS 13% of students enrolled are international students. *Services and facilities:* Counseling/support services, ESL/language courses, Housing location assistance, International student housing, International student organization, Language tutoring, Orientation, Visa Services. Financial aid is available to international students. *Required with application:* TOEFL with recommended score of 213 (computer), 550 (paper), or 79 (Internet); proof of adequate funds; proof of health/immunizations.

International Student Contact Mr. Michael Elliott, Director of International Scholar and Student Services, International Programs Center, 127 McIver Street, PO Box 26170, Greensboro, NC 27402-6170. *Phone:* 336-334-5404. *Fax:* 336-334-5406. *E-mail:* int_programs@uncg.edu.

APPLICATION *Required:* GMAT, application form, baccalaureate/first degree, 3 letters of recommendation, personal statement, resume/curriculum vitae, transcripts of college work. *Application fee:* $45. Applications for domestic and international students are processed on a rolling basis.

Application Contact Mr. Thomas Keller, Director of Marketing, Bryan MBA Program, 220 Bryan Building, PO Box 26165, Greensboro, NC 27402-6165. *Phone:* 336-334-5390. *Fax:* 336-334-4209. *E-mail:* tlkeller@uncg.edu.

The University of North Carolina at Pembroke

Graduate Studies

Pembroke, North Carolina

Phone: 910-521-6271 **Fax:** 910-521-6751 **E-mail:** kathleen.hilton@uncp.edu

The University of North Carolina at Pembroke (continued)

Business Program(s) Web Site: http://www.uncp.edu/grad/

DEGREE MBA

MBA—Master of Business Administration Full-time and part-time. At least 36 total credits required. 12 to 60 months to complete program. *Concentration:* general MBA.

RESOURCES AND SERVICES 320 on-campus PCs are available to graduate business students. Access to Internet/World Wide Web, online (class) registration, and online grade reports available. *Personal computer requirements:* Graduate business students are strongly recommended to purchase or lease a personal computer. *Special opportunities include:* An international exchange program and an internship program are available. *Placement services include:* Alumni network, career placement, career counseling/planning, resume referral, career fairs, job interviews arranged, resume preparation, and career library.

Application Contact Kathleen C. Hilton, PhD, Dean, School of Graduate Studies, Office of Graduate Studies, PO Box 1510, Pembroke, NC 28372-1510. *Phone:* 910-521-6271. *Fax:* 910-521-6751. *E-mail:* kathleen.hilton@uncp.edu.

The University of North Carolina Wilmington

School of Business

Wilmington, North Carolina

Phone: 910-962-3903 **Fax:** 910-962-2184 **E-mail:** barnhillk@uncw.edu

Business Program(s) Web Site: http://www.csb.uncw.edu

Graduate Business Unit Enrollment *Total:* 169 (60 full-time; 109 part-time; 83 women; 15 international). *Average Age:* 28.

Graduate Business Faculty *Total:* 23 (21 full-time; 2 part-time).

Admissions *Applied:* 88. *Admitted:* 58. *Enrolled:* 49. *Average GMAT:* 560. *Average GPA:* 3.2

Academic Calendar Semesters.

Accreditation AACSB—The Association to Advance Collegiate Schools of Business.

After Graduation (Class of 2006–07) *Employed within 3 months of graduation:* 100%.

DEGREES IMBA/MBA • MBA • MSA

IMBA/MBA—MBA—International Option Full-time. Must have undergraduate degree in business. 30 to 36 total credits required. 12 to 15 months to complete program. *Concentration:* international business.

MBA—Master of Business Administration Part-time. 1 year of professional full-time work experience required. At least 48 total credits required. 24 months to complete program. *Concentrations:* entrepreneurship, finance, management information systems, manufacturing management, marketing, organizational behavior/development.

MSA Full-time. 32 total credits required. 10 to 12 months to complete program. *Concentration:* accounting.

RESOURCES AND SERVICES 250 on-campus PCs are available to graduate business students. Access to Internet/World Wide Web, online (class) registration, and online grade reports available. *Personal computer requirements:* Graduate business students are strongly recommended to purchase or lease a personal computer. *Special opportunities include:* An international exchange program and an internship program are available. *Placement services include:* Alumni network, job search course, career counseling/planning, electronic job bank, resume referral, career fairs, job interviews arranged, resume preparation, and career library.

EXPENSES *Tuition (state resident):* Part-time: $7000 per year. *Tuition (nonresident):* Part-time: $14,000 per year.

FINANCIAL AID (2007–08) 40 students received aid, including loans, research assistantships, scholarships, teaching assistantships, and work study. Aid is available to part-time students. *Financial aid application deadline:* 3/15.

Financial Aid Contact Patti B. Lewis, Financial Aid Officer, James Hall, 601 South College Road, Wilmington, NC 28403. *Phone:* 910-962-3177. *E-mail:* lewisp@uncw.edu.

INTERNATIONAL STUDENTS 9% of students enrolled are international students. *Services and facilities:* Counseling/support services, ESL/language courses, Housing location assistance, International student housing, Language tutoring, Orientation, Visa Services. Financial aid is not available to international students. *Required with application:* TOEFL with recommended score of 213 (computer) or 600 (paper); proof of adequate funds; proof of health/immunizations.

International Student Contact Prof. Denise DiPuccio, Director, International Programs, 601 South College Road, Wilmington, NC 28403. *Phone:* 910-962-3685. *Fax:* 910-962-7933. *E-mail:* gallovicm@uncw.edu.

APPLICATION *Required:* GMAT, application form, baccalaureate/first degree, 3 letters of recommendation, resume/curriculum vitae, transcripts of college work, 1 year of work experience. School will accept GRE. *Recommended:* Interview. *Application fee:* $45. *Deadlines:* 3/1 for spring, 3/1 for spring (international).

Application Contact Ms. Karen Barnhill, Graduate Programs Administrator, 601 South College Road, Wilmington, NC 28403. *Phone:* 910-962-3903. *Fax:* 910-962-2184. *E-mail:* barnhillk@uncw.edu.

University of Phoenix–Charlotte Campus

College of Graduate Business and Management

Charlotte, North Carolina

Phone: 480-317-6200 **Fax:** 480-643-1479 **E-mail:** beth.barilla@phoenix.edu

---

DEGREES MBA

MBA—Master of Business Administration Full-time. At least 45 total credits required. *Concentration:* administration.

MBA—Master of Business Administration in Accounting Full-time. At least 45 total credits required. *Concentration:* accounting.

MBA—Master of Business Administration in Global Management Full-time. At least 45 total credits required. *Concentration:* international business.

MBA—Master of Business Administration in e-Business Full-time. At least 45 total credits required. *Concentration:* electronic commerce (E-commerce).

RESOURCES AND SERVICES Access to online grade reports available. *Personal computer requirements:* Graduate business students are strongly recommended to purchase or lease a personal computer. *Placement services include:* Alumni network.

Application Contact Beth Barilla, Associate Vice President of Student Admissions and Services, Mail Stop AA-K101, 4615 East Elwood Street, Phoenix, AZ 85040-1958. *Phone:* 480-317-6200. *Fax:* 480-643-1479. *E-mail:* beth.barilla@phoenix.edu.

Wake Forest University

Babcock Graduate School of Management

Winston-Salem, North Carolina

Phone: 336-758-5422 **Fax:** 336-758-5830 **E-mail:** admissions@mba.wfu.edu

---

Business Program(s) Web Site: http://www.mba.wfu.edu/

Graduate Business Unit Enrollment *Total:* 515 (479 full-time; 36 part-time; 146 women; 51 international). *Average Age:* 31.

Graduate Business Faculty *Total:* 44 (33 full-time; 11 part-time).

Admissions *Average GMAT:* 632. *Average GPA:* 3.1

Academic Calendar Semesters.

Accreditation AACSB—The Association to Advance Collegiate Schools of Business.

After Graduation (Class of 2006–07) *Employed within 3 months of graduation:* 78.1%. *Average starting salary:* $81,012.

DEGREES JD/MBA • M Mgt • MBA • MBA/MS • MD/MBA • PhD/MBA

JD/MBA—Juris Doctor/Master of Business Administration Full-time. At least 123 total credits required. 44 months to complete program. *Concentration:* general MBA.

M Mgt—MA in Management Full-time. Interview required. At least 42 total credits required. 10 months to complete program. *Concentration:* management.

MBA—Evening Master of Business Administration—Charlotte Part-time. Interview required. At least 54 total credits required. 24 months to complete program. *Concentration:* general MBA.

MBA—Evening Master of Business Administration—Winston-Salem Part-time. Interview required. At least 56 total credits required. 24 months to complete program. *Concentration:* general MBA.

MBA—Fast-Track Executive Master of Business Administration—Winston-Salem Part-time. Interview required. At least 49 total credits required. 17 months to complete program. *Concentrations:* executive programs, general MBA.

MBA—Full-Time Master of Business Administration Full-time. An interview is required for all domestic applicants. Interviews are by invitation only for international applicants unless the international applicant can interview at a forum or on campus. At least 64 total credits required. 21 months to complete program. *Concentrations:* entrepreneurship, finance, general MBA, management consulting, marketing, operations management.

MBA—Saturday Master of Business Administration—Charlotte Part-time. Interview required. At least 54 total credits required. 24 months to complete program. *Concentration:* general MBA.

MBA/MS—MSA/MBA—Master of Science in Accountancy/Master of Business Administration Full-time. At least 172 total credits required. 65 months to complete program. *Concentration:* general MBA.

MD/MBA—Doctor of Medicine/Master of Business Administration Full-time. At least 230 total credits required. 56 months to complete program. *Concentration:* general MBA.

PhD/MBA—Doctor of Philosophy/Master of Business Administration Full-time and part-time. Enrolled students are full-time PhD students and part-time MBA students. Students complete 50 MBA credits plus PhD credits, which vary by area of study. Minimum of 60 months to complete program. *Concentration:* general MBA.

RESOURCES AND SERVICES 62 on-campus PCs are available to graduate business students. Access to Internet/World Wide Web, online (class) registration, and online grade reports available. *Personal computer requirements:* Graduate business students are required to have a personal computer, the cost of which is included in tuition or other required fees. *Special opportunities include:* An international exchange program and an internship program are available. *Placement services include:* Alumni network, career placement, job search course, career counseling/planning, electronic job bank, resume referral, career fairs, job interviews arranged, resume preparation, and career library.

EXPENSES *Tuition:* Full-time: $33,400. Part-time: $30,165 per year. *Tuition (international):* Full-time: $33,400. Part-time: $30,165 per year. *Required fees:* Full-time: $150. Tuition and/or fees vary by academic program.

FINANCIAL AID (2007–08) 361 students received aid, including loans, research assistantships, and scholarships. Aid is available to part-time students. *Financial aid application deadline:* 2/15.

Financial Aid Contact Donna Agee, Associate Director, Admissions and Financial Aid, Worrell Professional Center, Room 2119, 1834 Wake Forest Road, Winston-Salem, NC 27106. *Phone:* 336-758-4424. *Fax:* 336-758-5830. *E-mail:* donna.agee@mba.wfu.edu.

INTERNATIONAL STUDENTS 10% of students enrolled are international students. *Services and facilities:* Counseling/support services, ESL/language courses, Housing location assistance, International student housing, International student organization, Language tutoring, Orientation, Visa Services. Financial aid is available to international students. *Required with application:* TOEFL with recommended score of 250 (computer), 600 (paper), or 100 (Internet); proof of adequate funds; proof of health/immunizations.

International Student Contact Carrie Ross, Assistant Director, Full-Time Admissions, Worrell Professional Center, Room 2119, 1834 Wake Forest Road, Winston-Salem, NC 27106. *Phone:* 336-758-4331. *Fax:* 336-758-5830. *E-mail:* carrie.ross@mba.wfu.edu.

APPLICATION *Required:* GMAT, application form, baccalaureate/first degree, essay, interview, 2 letters of recommendation, resume/curriculum vitae, transcripts of college work. *Recommended:* Work experience. *Application fee:* $75. Applications for domestic and international students are processed on a rolling basis.

Application Contact Ginny Kerlin, Administrative Assistant, Admissions and Financial Aid, Worrell Professional Center, Room 2119, 1834 Wake Forest Road, Winston-Salem, NC 27106. *Phone:* 336-758-5422. *Fax:* 336-758-5830. *E-mail:* admissions@mba.wfu.edu.

Western Carolina University
College of Business
Cullowhee, North Carolina

Phone: 828-227-3588 **Fax:** 828-227-7414 **E-mail:** fdeitz@email.wcu.edu

Business Program(s) Web Site: http://www.wcu.edu/cob/graduate/index.htm

Graduate Business Unit Enrollment *Total:* 301 (69 full-time; 232 part-time; 123 women; 13 international). *Average Age:* 34.

Graduate Business Faculty *Total:* 45 (39 full-time; 6 part-time).

Admissions *Applied:* 196. *Admitted:* 158. *Enrolled:* 133. *Average GMAT:* 488. *Average GPA:* 3.45

Academic Calendar Semesters.

Accreditation AACSB—The Association to Advance Collegiate Schools of Business.

DEGREES M Acc • MBA • MBA equivalent • MEntr • MPM

M Acc—Master of Accountancy Full-time and part-time. 30 to 39 total credits required. 12 to 72 months to complete program. *Concentrations:* accounting, entrepreneurship.

MBA—Master of Business Administration Full-time and part-time. 36 to 48 total credits required. 16 to 72 months to complete program. *Concentrations:* entrepreneurship, general MBA, health care, human resources management, project management.

MBA equivalent—Master of Sport Management Full-time and part-time. 36 total credits required. 16 to 72 months to complete program. *Concentration:* sports/entertainment management.

MEntr—Master of Entrepreneurship Full-time and part-time. Distance learning option. 30 total credits required. 12 to 72 months to complete program. *Concentration:* entrepreneurship.

MPM—Master of Project Management Full-time and part-time. Distance learning option. Designed for professional project managers with

Western Carolina University (continued)

2+ years of experience. 36 total credits required. 16 to 72 months to complete program. *Concentration:* project management.

RESOURCES AND SERVICES 226 on-campus PCs are available to graduate business students. Access to Internet/World Wide Web, online (class) registration, and online grade reports available. *Personal computer requirements:* Graduate business students are required to have a personal computer. *Special opportunities include:* An international exchange program and an internship program are available. *Placement services include:* Alumni network, career placement, career counseling/planning, electronic job bank, resume referral, career fairs, job interviews arranged, resume preparation, and career library.

EXPENSES *Tuition (nonresident):* Full-time: $2314. Part-time: $1543 per year. *Tuition (international):* Full-time: $11,899. Part-time: $7933 per year. *Required fees:* Full-time: $2033. Part-time: $1355 per year. Tuition and/or fees vary by number of courses or credits taken. *Graduate housing:* Room and board costs vary by number of occupants, type of accommodation, and type of board plan. *Typical cost:* $5462 (including board), $2832 (room only).

FINANCIAL AID (2007–08) 31 students received aid, including fellowships, grants, loans, research assistantships, scholarships, teaching assistantships, and work study. Aid is available to part-time students. *Financial aid application deadline:* 3/31.

Financial Aid Contact Ms. Nancy B. Dillard, Director, Student Financial Aid, 118 Killian Annex, Cullowhee, NC 28723. *Phone:* 828-227-7290. *Fax:* 828-227-7042. *E-mail:* dillard@email.wcu.edu.

INTERNATIONAL STUDENTS 4% of students enrolled are international students. *Services and facilities:* Counseling/support services, Housing location assistance, International student organization, Orientation, Visa Services. Financial aid is not available to international students. *Required with application:* TOEFL with recommended score of 270 (computer), 550 (paper), or 79 (Internet); proof of adequate funds; proof of health/immunizations.

International Student Contact Dr. Lois Petrovich-Mwaniki, Director, International Programs and Services, 183 Belk Building, Cullowhee, NC 28723. *Phone:* 828-227-7494. *Fax:* 828-227-7080. *E-mail:* lmwaniki@email.wcu.edu.

APPLICATION *Required:* GMAT, GRE, application form, baccalaureate/first degree, 2 letters of recommendation, resume/curriculum vitae, transcripts of college work, 2 years of work experience. *Application fee:* $40. Applications for domestic and international students are processed on a rolling basis.

Application Contact Ms. Faye J. Deitz, Administrative Support Specialist, MBA Program, 379 Belk Building, Cullowhee, NC 28723. *Phone:* 828-227-3588. *Fax:* 828-227-7414. *E-mail:* fdeitz@email.wcu.edu.

Wingate University
Program in Business Administration

Wingate, North Carolina

Phone: 704-846-1404 **Fax:** 704-849-2468 **E-mail:** mbryant@wingate.edu

Business Program(s) Web Site: http://www.mba.wingate.edu

Graduate Business Unit Enrollment *Total:* 65 (65 part-time; 30 women). *Average Age:* 30.

Graduate Business Faculty *Total:* 13 (10 full-time; 3 part-time).

Admissions *Applied:* 28. *Admitted:* 24. *Enrolled:* 19. *Average GMAT:* 475. *Average GPA:* 3.0

Academic Calendar Semesters.

Accreditation ACBSP—The American Council of Business Schools and Programs.

After Graduation (Class of 2006–07) *Employed within 3 months of graduation:* 100%.

DEGREE MBA

MBA—Master of Business Administration Part-time. Two years professional experience required. At least 33 total credits required. 24 to 72 months to complete program. *Concentration:* management.

RESOURCES AND SERVICES 50 on-campus PCs are available to graduate business students. Access to Internet/World Wide Web and online grade reports available. *Personal computer requirements:* Graduate business students are strongly recommended to purchase or lease a personal computer. *Placement services include:* Career placement, career counseling/planning, and career fairs.

EXPENSES *Tuition:* Part-time: $400 per credit hour.

FINANCIAL AID (2007–08) Loans.

INTERNATIONAL STUDENTS Financial aid is not available to international students. *Required with application:* TOEFL with recommended score of 550 (paper); proof of adequate funds; proof of health/immunizations.

APPLICATION *Required:* GMAT, application form, baccalaureate/first degree, 2 letters of recommendation, personal statement, resume/curriculum vitae, transcripts of college work, 2 years of work experience. School will accept GRE. *Application fee:* $50. Applications for domestic and international students are processed on a rolling basis.

Application Contact Mark Bryant, Director, MBA Program, 110 Matthews Station Street, Suite 2D, PO Box 3549, Wingate, NC 28106. *Phone:* 704-846-1404. *Fax:* 704-849-2468. *E-mail:* mbryant@wingate.edu.

NORTH DAKOTA

Minot State University
College of Business

Minot, North Dakota

Phone: 701-858-3250 **Fax:** 701-858-4286 **E-mail:** brenda.anderson@minotstateu.edu

Business Program(s) Web Site: http://www.minotstateu.edu/business/

Graduate Business Unit Enrollment *Total:* 78 (35 full-time; 43 part-time; 40 women; 15 international). *Average Age:* 30.

Graduate Business Faculty 13 full-time.

Admissions *Applied:* 55. *Admitted:* 52. *Enrolled:* 42. *Average GPA:* 3.62

Academic Calendar Semesters.

After Graduation (Class of 2006–07) *Employed within 3 months of graduation:* 90%. *Average starting salary:* $45,000.

DEGREES MS • MSIS

MS—Master of Science in Management Full-time and part-time. Distance learning option. 30 total credits required. 16 to 72 months to complete program. *Concentration:* management.

MSIS—Master of Science in Information Systems Full-time and part-time. Distance learning option. 30 total credits required. 12 to 72 months to complete program. *Concentration:* information systems.

RESOURCES AND SERVICES 300 on-campus PCs are available to graduate business students. Access to Internet/World Wide Web, online (class) registration, and online grade reports available. *Personal computer requirements:* Graduate business students are strongly recommended to purchase or lease a personal computer. *Special opportunities include:* An international exchange program is available. *Placement services include:* Alumni network, career placement, career counseling/planning, electronic job bank, resume referral, career fairs, job interviews arranged, and resume preparation.

FINANCIAL AID (2007–08) 18 students received aid, including grants, loans, research assistantships, scholarships, and teaching assistantships. Aid is available to part-time students. *Financial aid application deadline:* 2/15.

Financial Aid Contact Mr. Dale Gehring, Financial Aid Director, 500 University Avenue West, Minot, ND 58707. *Phone:* 701-858-3862. *Fax:* 701-858-4310. *E-mail:* dale.gehring@minotstateu.edu.

INTERNATIONAL STUDENTS 19% of students enrolled are international students. *Services and facilities:* Counseling/support services, Housing location assistance, International student organization, Language tutoring, Orientation. Financial aid is available to international students. *Required with application:* IELT with recommended score of 6; TOEFL with recommended score of 213 (computer), 550 (paper), or 80 (Internet); proof of adequate funds; proof of health/immunizations.

International Student Contact Ms. Ronnie Walker, International Student Coordinator, 500 University Avenue West, Minot, ND 58707. *Phone:* 701-858-3348. *Fax:* 701-858-3888. *E-mail:* ronnie.walker@minotstateu.edu.

APPLICATION *Required:* GMAT, GRE, application form, baccalaureate/first degree, essay, 3 letters of recommendation, personal statement, resume/curriculum vitae, transcripts of college work. *Recommended:* Work experience. *Application fee:* $35. *Deadlines:* 4/15 for fall, 3/15 for fall (international).

Application Contact Ms. Brenda Anderson, Administrative Assistant, 500 University Avenue West, Minot, ND 58707. *Phone:* 701-858-3250. *Fax:* 701-858-4286. *E-mail:* brenda.anderson@minotstateu.edu.

North Dakota State University
College of Business
Fargo, North Dakota

Phone: 701-231-8808 **Fax:** 701-231-7508 **E-mail:** karen.froelich@ndsu.nodak.edu

Business Program(s) Web Site: http://www.ndsu.nodak.edu/

Graduate Business Unit Enrollment *Total:* 107 (23 full-time; 84 part-time; 52 women; 21 international). *Average Age:* 34.

Graduate Business Faculty 33 full-time.

Admissions *Applied:* 58. *Admitted:* 40. *Enrolled:* 35. *Average GMAT:* 550. *Average GPA:* 3.28

Academic Calendar Semesters.

Accreditation AACSB—The Association to Advance Collegiate Schools of Business.

After Graduation (Class of 2006–07) *Employed within 3 months of graduation:* 100%.

DEGREE MBA

MBA—Master of Business Administration Full-time and part-time. At least 30 total credits required. 12 to 84 months to complete program. *Concentrations:* accounting, finance, management, marketing.

RESOURCES AND SERVICES 600 on-campus PCs are available to graduate business students. Access to Internet/World Wide Web, online (class) registration, and online grade reports available. *Personal computer requirements:* Graduate business students are strongly recommended to purchase or lease a personal computer. *Special opportunities include:* An international exchange program is available. *Placement services include:* Alumni network, career counseling/planning, resume referral, career fairs, job interviews arranged, resume preparation, and career library.

FINANCIAL AID (2007–08) 18 students received aid, including loans, research assistantships, scholarships, and work study. Aid is available to part-time students. *Financial aid application deadline:* 4/15.

Financial Aid Contact Ms. Jeanette Enebo, Bison Connection, Memorial Union, Fargo, ND 58105. *Phone:* 701-231-6200. *E-mail:* ndsu.bisonconnection@ndsu.edu.

INTERNATIONAL STUDENTS 20% of students enrolled are international students. *Services and facilities:* Counseling/support services, ESL/language courses, Housing location assistance, International student organization, Orientation, Visa Services. Financial aid is available to international students. *Required with application:* TOEFL with recommended score of 550 (paper); proof of adequate funds; proof of health/immunizations.

International Student Contact Director of International Programs, Ceres Hall, Fargo, ND 58105. *Phone:* 701-231-7895. *Fax:* 701-231-1014.

APPLICATION *Required:* GMAT, application form, baccalaureate/first degree, 3 letters of recommendation, personal statement, transcripts of college work. *Application fee:* $45. Applications for domestic and international students are processed on a rolling basis.

Application Contact Dr. Karen Froelich, MBA Program Director, Box 5137, Putnam Hall, Fargo, ND 58105. *Phone:* 701-231-8808. *Fax:* 701-231-7508. *E-mail:* karen.froelich@ndsu.nodak.edu.

University of Mary
Program in Management
Bismarck, North Dakota

Phone: 701-355-8134 **Fax:** 701-255-7687 **E-mail:** wmaruska@umary.edu

Business Program(s) Web Site: http://www.umary.edu/

Graduate Business Unit Enrollment *Total:* 613 (334 full-time; 279 part-time; 316 women; 11 international). *Average Age:* 35.

Graduate Business Faculty 90 part-time.

Admissions *Applied:* 137. *Admitted:* 115. *Enrolled:* 105. *Average GPA:* 3.0

Academic Calendar Trimesters.

After Graduation (Class of 2006–07) *Employed within 3 months of graduation:* 99%.

DEGREES M Mgt • MBA

M Mgt—Master of Management Full-time and part-time. At least 30 total credits required. 15 to 84 months to complete program. *Concentrations:* health care, human resources management, information systems, management.

MBA Full-time and part-time. Distance learning option. At least 39 total credits required. Minimum of 18 months to complete program. *Concentrations:* accounting, executive programs, health care, human resources management, management.

RESOURCES AND SERVICES 60 on-campus PCs are available to graduate business students. Access to Internet/World Wide Web, online (class) registration, and online grade reports available. *Personal computer requirements:* Graduate business students are strongly recommended to purchase or lease a personal computer. *Special opportunities include:* An international exchange program is available. *Placement services include:* Alumni network, career placement, career counseling/planning, electronic job bank, resume referral, career fairs, and resume preparation.

EXPENSES *Tuition:* Part-time: $415 per credit hour. *Tuition (international):* Part-time: $415 per credit hour. *Required fees:* Full-time: $875.

FINANCIAL AID (2007–08) 165 students received aid, including loans. Aid is available to part-time students.

Financial Aid Contact Mrs. Brenda Zastoupil, Director of Financial Aid, 7500 University Drive, Bismarck, ND 58504. *Phone:* 701-255-7500 Ext. 325. *Fax:* 701-255-7687. *E-mail:* brendaz@umary.edu.

INTERNATIONAL STUDENTS 2% of students enrolled are international students. *Services and facilities:* Counseling/support services, Orientation. Financial aid is available to international students. *Required with application:* Proof of adequate funds; proof of health/immunizations. *Recommended with application:* TOEFL with recommended score of 550 (paper).

University of Mary (continued)

International Student Contact Wayne G. Maruska, Graduate Program Advisor, School of Accelerated and Distance Education, 7500 University Drive, Bismarck, ND 58504. *Phone:* 701-355-8134. *Fax:* 701-255-7687. *E-mail:* wmaruska@umary.edu.

APPLICATION *Required:* Application form, baccalaureate/first degree, essay, 2 letters of recommendation, personal statement, resume/curriculum vitae, transcripts of college work. *Recommended:* 3 years of work experience. *Application fee:* $40. Applications for domestic and international students are processed on a rolling basis.

Application Contact Wayne Maruska, Graduate Program Advisor, 7500 University Drive, Bismarck, ND 58504-9652. *Phone:* 701-355-8134. *Fax:* 701-255-7687. *E-mail:* wmaruska@umary.edu.

University of North Dakota
College of Business and Public Administration

Grand Forks, North Dakota

Phone: 701-777-4853 **Fax:** 701-777-2019 **E-mail:** michelle.garske@mail.business.und.edu

Business Program(s) Web Site: http://www.business.und.edu/

Graduate Business Unit Enrollment *Total:* 98 (39 full-time; 59 part-time; 39 women; 14 international). *Average Age:* 27.

Graduate Business Faculty 46 full-time.

Admissions *Applied:* 37. *Admitted:* 31. *Enrolled:* 22. *Average GMAT:* 525. *Average GPA:* 3.17

Academic Calendar Semesters.

Accreditation AACSB—The Association to Advance Collegiate Schools of Business.

After Graduation (Class of 2006–07) *Employed within 3 months of graduation:* 95%.

DEGREE MBA

MBA—Master of Business Administration Full-time and part-time. Distance learning option. At least 68 total credits required. 12 to 84 months to complete program. *Concentrations:* accounting, international business.

RESOURCES AND SERVICES 700 on-campus PCs are available to graduate business students. Access to Internet/World Wide Web, online (class) registration, and online grade reports available. *Personal computer requirements:* Graduate business students are not required to have a personal computer. *Special opportunities include:* An international exchange program and an internship program are available. *Placement services include:* Alumni network, career placement, career counseling/planning, electronic job bank, resume referral, career fairs, job interviews arranged, resume preparation, and career library.

EXPENSES *Tuition (state resident):* Full-time: $6510. Part-time: $335.44 per credit hour. *Tuition (nonresident):* Full-time: $15,537. Part-time: $711.56 per credit hour. *Tuition (international):* Full-time: $15,537. Part-time: $711.56 per credit hour. *Required fees:* Full-time: $1105.22. Part-time: $110.21 per credit hour. Tuition and/or fees vary by number of courses or credits taken, campus location, academic program, and local reciprocity agreements. *Graduate housing:* Room and board costs vary by campus location, number of occupants, type of accommodation, and type of board plan. *Typical cost:* $3980 (including board).

FINANCIAL AID (2007–08) 20 students received aid, including fellowships, grants, loans, research assistantships, scholarships, teaching assistantships, and work study. Aid is available to part-time students. *Financial aid application deadline:* 3/15.

Financial Aid Contact Ms. Robin Holden, Director of Financial Aid, Box 8371, Grand Forks, ND 58202-8371. *Phone:* 701-777-3121. *E-mail:* robin_holden@mail.und.nodak.edu.

INTERNATIONAL STUDENTS 14% of students enrolled are international students. *Services and facilities:* Counseling/support services, ESL/language courses, Housing location assistance, International student housing, International student organization, Orientation, Visa Services. Financial aid is available to international students. *Required with application:* TOEFL with recommended score of 213 (computer) or 550 (paper); proof of adequate funds; proof of health/immunizations.

International Student Contact Shannon Jolly, International Student Advisor, Box 7109, Grand Forks, ND 58202-7109. *Phone:* 701-777-4231. *Fax:* 701-777-4773. *E-mail:* internationalprograms@mail.und.nodak.edu.

APPLICATION *Required:* GMAT, application form, baccalaureate/first degree, essay, 3 letters of recommendation, transcripts of college work. *Application fee:* $35. Applications for domestic and international students are processed on a rolling basis.

Application Contact Michelle Garske, MBA Graduate Advisor, Box 8098, Grand Forks, ND 58202-8098. *Phone:* 701-777-4853. *Fax:* 701-777-2019. *E-mail:* michelle.garske@mail.business.und.edu.

OHIO

Antioch University McGregor
Program in Management

Yellow Springs, Ohio

Phone: 937-769-1816 **Fax:** 937-769-1804 **E-mail:** rmclaughlin@mcgregor.edu

Business Program(s) Web Site: http://www.mcgregor.edu/

Graduate Business Unit Enrollment *Total:* 49 (48 full-time; 1 part-time; 24 women). *Average Age:* 37.

Graduate Business Faculty *Total:* 25 (4 full-time; 21 part-time).

Admissions *Applied:* 23. *Admitted:* 20. *Enrolled:* 20.

Academic Calendar Quarters.

DEGREE MA

MA—Master of Arts in Management Full-time. At least 64 total credits required. 18 months to complete program. *Concentration:* management.

RESOURCES AND SERVICES 32 on-campus PCs are available to graduate business students. Access to Internet/World Wide Web and online grade reports available. *Personal computer requirements:* Graduate business students are strongly recommended to purchase or lease a personal computer. *Placement services include:* Alumni network.

EXPENSES *Tuition:* Full-time: $17,808. Part-time: $371 per credit hour. *Required fees:* Full-time: $600. Part-time: $150 per quarter.

FINANCIAL AID (2007–08) Loans.

Financial Aid Contact Ms. Kathy John, Financial Aid Director, 900 Dayton Street, Yellow Springs, OH 45387. *Phone:* 937-769-1840. *Fax:* 937-769-1804. *E-mail:* kjohn@mcgregor.edu.

INTERNATIONAL STUDENTS Financial aid is not available to international students.

International Student Contact Student Services, 900 Dayton Street, Yellow Springs, OH 45387. *Phone:* 937-769-1818. *Fax:* 937-769-1804. *E-mail:* sas@mcgregor.edu.

APPLICATION *Required:* Application form, baccalaureate/first degree, essay, interview, 2 letters of recommendation, personal statement, resume/curriculum vitae, transcripts of college work, 5 years of work experience. *Application fee:* $50. Applications for domestic students are processed on a rolling basis.

Application Contact Rob McLaughlin, Enrollment Services Manager, Student Services, 900 Dayton Street, Yellow Springs, OH 45387. *Phone:* 937-769-1816. *Fax:* 937-769-1804. *E-mail:* rmclaughlin@mcgregor.edu.

Ashland University
Dauch College of Business and Economics
Ashland, Ohio

Phone: 800-882-1548 Ext. 5236 **Fax:** 419-289-5910 **E-mail:** skrispin@ashland.edu

Business Program(s) Web Site: http://www.ashland.edu/mba/

Graduate Business Unit Enrollment *Total:* 550 (50 full-time; 500 part-time; 225 women; 25 international). *Average Age:* 34.

Graduate Business Faculty *Total:* 44 (24 full-time; 20 part-time).

Admissions *Applied:* 125. *Admitted:* 120. *Enrolled:* 90. *Average GPA:* 3.2

Academic Calendar Semesters.

Accreditation ACBSP—The American Council of Business Schools and Programs.

DEGREE MBA

MBA—Executive Master of Business Administration Part-time. 36 to 55 total credits required. 24 to 60 months to complete program. *Concentrations:* entrepreneurship, finance, human resources management, international business, management, project management.

RESOURCES AND SERVICES 125 on-campus PCs are available to graduate business students. Access to Internet/World Wide Web, online (class) registration, and online grade reports available. *Personal computer requirements:* Graduate business students are strongly recommended to purchase or lease a personal computer. *Placement services include:* Career placement, career counseling/planning, electronic job bank, resume referral, career fairs, job interviews arranged, resume preparation, and career library.

EXPENSES *Tuition:* Part-time: $544 per credit.

FINANCIAL AID (2007–08) Loans. Aid is available to part-time students.

Financial Aid Contact Mr. Steve Howell, Director, Financial Aid, 401 College Avenue, Ashland, OH 44805. *Phone:* 800-882-1548 Ext. 5002. *Fax:* 419-289-5333. *E-mail:* showell@ashland.edu.

INTERNATIONAL STUDENTS 5% of students enrolled are international students. *Services and facilities:* Counseling/support services, ESL/language courses, Housing location assistance, International student organization, Language tutoring, Orientation, Visa Services, Writing center. Financial aid is not available to international students. *Required with application:* TOEFL with recommended score of 213 (computer) or 550 (paper); proof of adequate funds; proof of health/immunizations.

International Student Contact Susan Rosa, Associate Director, International Student Services, 401 College Avenue, Ashland, OH 44805. *Phone:* 800-882-1548 Ext. 5926. *Fax:* 419-289-5629. *E-mail:* srosa@ashland.edu.

APPLICATION *Required:* Application form, baccalaureate/first degree, personal statement, resume/curriculum vitae, transcripts of college work, 2 years of work experience. *Application fee:* $30, $50 (international). Applications for domestic and international students are processed on a rolling basis.

Application Contact Stephen W. Krispinsky, Executive Director, MBA Program, 401 College Avenue, Ashland, OH 44805. *Phone:* 800-882-1548 Ext. 5236. *Fax:* 419-289-5910. *E-mail:* skrispin@ashland.edu.

Baldwin-Wallace College
Division of Business
Berea, Ohio

Phone: 800-773-4261 **Fax:** 440-826-3868 **E-mail:** graduate@bw.edu

Business Program(s) Web Site: http://www.bw.edu/academics/bus/mba/

Graduate Business Unit Enrollment *Total:* 471 (274 full-time; 197 part-time; 240 women; 23 international). *Average Age:* 33.

Graduate Business Faculty *Total:* 37 (19 full-time; 18 part-time).

Admissions *Applied:* 180. *Admitted:* 165. *Enrolled:* 110. *Average GMAT:* 503. *Average GPA:* 3.1

Academic Calendar Semesters.

DEGREES EMBA • IMBA • MBA • MBA-H

EMBA—Executive Master of Business Administration Part-time. An interview with the Director of the program required. 38 to 44 total credits required. 24 to 48 months to complete program. *Concentration:* executive programs.

IMBA—International Master of Business Administration Full-time and part-time. Foreign students need proof of English language proficiency evidenced in a TOEFL or IELTS test score. 40 to 46 total credits required. 12 to 48 months to complete program. *Concentration:* international management.

MBA—Master of Business Administration Full-time and part-time. 40 to 46 total credits required. 24 to 48 months to complete program. *Concentrations:* accounting, entrepreneurship, human resources management, system management.

MBA-H—Master of Business Administration in Health Care Part-time. An interview with the Director of the program and GMAT required. 38 to 44 total credits required. 24 to 48 months to complete program. *Concentration:* health care.

RESOURCES AND SERVICES 100 on-campus PCs are available to graduate business students. Access to Internet/World Wide Web, online (class) registration, and online grade reports available. *Personal computer requirements:* Graduate business students are strongly recommended to purchase or lease a personal computer. *Special opportunities include:* An internship program is available. *Placement services include:* Alumni network, career placement, job search course, career counseling/planning, electronic job bank, resume referral, career fairs, job interviews arranged, resume preparation, and career library.

EXPENSES *Tuition:* Full-time: $15,900. Part-time: $795 per credit. *Tuition (international):* Full-time: $15,900. Part-time: $795 per credit. *Required fees:* Full-time: $600. Tuition and/or fees vary by academic program. *Graduate housing:* Room and board costs vary by number of occupants and type of accommodation. *Typical cost:* $3348 (room only).

FINANCIAL AID (2007–08) 14 students received aid, including research assistantships and work study. *Financial aid application deadline:* 7/15.

Financial Aid Contact George Rolleston, Director of Financial Aid, 275 Eastland Road, Berea, OH 44017-2088. *Phone:* 440-826-2108. *Fax:* 440-826-8048. *E-mail:* grollest@bw.edu.

INTERNATIONAL STUDENTS 5% of students enrolled are international students. *Services and facilities:* Counseling/support services, ESL/language courses, Housing location assistance, International student housing, International student organization, Language tutoring, Orientation, Visa Services. Financial aid is available to international students. *Required with application:* TOEFL with recommended score of 193 (computer), 523 (paper), or 69 (Internet); proof of adequate funds.

International Student Contact Ms. Peggy Shepard, Graduate Business Coordinator, 275 Eastland Road, Berea, OH 44017-2088. *Phone:* 800-773-4261. *Fax:* 440-826-3868. *E-mail:* graduate@bw.edu.

APPLICATION *Required:* GMAT, application form, baccalaureate/first degree, 2 letters of recommendation, resume/curriculum vitae, transcripts of college work. School will accept GRE. *Recommended:* Interview, personal statement, 2 years of work experience. *Application fee:* $25. Applications for domestic and international students are processed on a rolling basis.

Application Contact Ms. Peggy Shepard, Graduate Business Coordinator, 275 Eastland Road, Berea, OH 44017-2088. *Phone:* 800-773-4261. *Fax:* 440-826-3868. *E-mail:* graduate@bw.edu.

Bowling Green State University

College of Business Administration

Bowling Green, Ohio

Phone: 419-372-2488 **Fax:** 419-372-2875 **E-mail:** mba-info@bgsu.edu

Business Program(s) Web Site: http://www.cba.bgsu.edu

Accreditation AACSB—The Association to Advance Collegiate Schools of Business.

DEGREES M Acc • MBA • MBA/MOD • MOD

M Acc—Master of Accountancy Full-time. At least 30 total credits required. 12 to 72 months to complete program. *Concentration:* accounting.

MBA—Executive Master of Business Administration Part-time. At least 36 total credits required. 18 to 72 months to complete program. *Concentration:* executive programs.

MBA—Full-Time Master of Business Administration Full-time. 48 to 62 total credits required. 14 to 18 months to complete program. *Concentrations:* accounting, finance, management information systems.

MBA—Part-Time Master of Business Administration Part-time. 36 to 48 total credits required. 36 to 72 months to complete program. *Concentration:* general MBA.

MBA/MOD—Master of Business Administration/Master of Organization Development Full-time and part-time. 38 to 69 total credits required. 30 to 72 months to complete program. *Concentration:* combined degrees.

MOD—Executive Master of Organization Development Part-time. At least 30 total credits required. 18 to 72 months to complete program. *Concentration:* organizational behavior/development.

MOD—Master of Organizational Development Full-time. Not accepting applications for 2007-2008. At least 33 total credits required. 18 to 72 months to complete program. *Concentration:* organizational behavior/ development.

RESOURCES AND SERVICES 500 on-campus PCs are available to graduate business students. Access to Internet/World Wide Web, online (class) registration, and online grade reports available. *Personal computer requirements:* Graduate business students are not required to have a personal computer. *Special opportunities include:* An international exchange program and an internship program are available. *Placement services include:* Alumni network, career placement, job search course, career counseling/planning, electronic job bank, resume referral, career fairs, job interviews arranged, resume preparation, and career library.

Application Contact Sheila K. Irving, Director, Graduate Studies in Business, 369 Business Administration Building, Bowling Green, OH 43403. *Phone:* 419-372-2488. *Fax:* 419-372-2875. *E-mail:* mba-info@ bgsu.edu.

DEGREES JD/MBA • MBA • MBA/LLM • MBA/MSN

JD/MBA—Juris Doctor/Master of Business Administration Full-time and part-time. Admission to both the Law School and the School of Management required. Minimum of 36 months to complete program. *Concentration:* combined degrees.

MBA—Master of Business Administration Part-time. At least 40 total credits required. 18 to 60 months to complete program. *Concentration:* general MBA.

MBA/LLM—Master of Business Administration/Master of Laws Part-time. Students must be admitted to both programs. *Concentration:* combined degrees.

MBA/MSN—Master of Business Administration/Master of Science in Nursing Full-time and part-time. At least 49 total credits required. Minimum of 18 months to complete program. *Concentrations:* combined degrees, health care.

RESOURCES AND SERVICES Access to Internet/World Wide Web, online (class) registration, and online grade reports available. *Personal computer requirements:* Graduate business students are strongly recommended to purchase or lease a personal computer. *Placement services include:* Alumni network, job search course, career counseling/planning, electronic job bank, resume referral, career fairs, job interviews arranged, and resume preparation.

EXPENSES *Tuition:* Part-time: $500 per credit hour. *Tuition (international):* Part-time: $500 per credit hour. Tuition and/or fees vary by number of courses or credits taken.

FINANCIAL AID (2007–08) Loans.

Financial Aid Contact Director of Financial Aid, 1 College and Main, Columbus, OH 43209-2394. *Phone:* 614-236-6511. *Fax:* 614-236-6820.

INTERNATIONAL STUDENTS *Services and facilities:* Counseling/ support services, ESL/language courses, International student organization, Orientation, Visa Services. Financial aid is not available to international students. *Required with application:* TOEFL with recommended score of 237 (computer), 580 (paper), or 80 (Internet); proof of adequate funds; proof of health/immunizations. *Recommended with application:* IELT with recommended score of 6.

International Student Contact Jennifer Adams, Director of International Education, 1 College and Main, Columbus, OH 43209-2394. *Phone:* 614-236-7102. *Fax:* 614-236-6170.

APPLICATION *Required:* GMAT, application form, baccalaureate/first degree, essay, 2 letters of recommendation, personal statement, resume/ curriculum vitae, transcripts of college work, 2 years of work experience. School will accept GRE. *Recommended:* Interview. *Application fee:* $25. Applications for domestic and international students are processed on a rolling basis.

Application Contact Emily Morris, 1 College and Main, Columbus, OH 43209. *Phone:* 614-236-6990. *Fax:* 614-236-6540. *E-mail:* mba@ capital.edu.

Capital University

School of Management

Columbus, Ohio

Phone: 614-236-6990 **Fax:** 614-236-6540 **E-mail:** mba@capital.edu

Business Program(s) Web Site: http://www.business.capital.edu

Graduate Business Unit Enrollment *Total:* 145 (145 part-time). *Average Age:* 31.

Graduate Business Faculty *Total:* 39 (18 full-time; 21 part-time).

Admissions *Average GMAT:* 530.

Academic Calendar Trimesters.

Accreditation ACBSP—The American Council of Business Schools and Programs.

Case Western Reserve University

Weatherhead School of Management

Cleveland, Ohio

Phone: 216-368-2030 **Fax:** 216-368-5548 **E-mail:** bizadmission@case.edu

Business Program(s) Web Site: http://weatherhead.case.edu

Graduate Business Unit Enrollment *Total:* 1,080 (603 full-time; 477 part-time; 449 women; 279 international). *Average Age:* 29.

Graduate Business Faculty *Total:* 78 (73 full-time; 5 part-time).

Admissions *Applied:* 286. *Admitted:* 193. *Enrolled:* 92. *Average GMAT:* 611. *Average GPA:* 3.2

Academic Calendar Semesters.

Accreditation AACSB—The Association to Advance Collegiate Schools of Business.

After Graduation (Class of 2006–07) *Employed within 3 months of graduation:* 73%. *Average starting salary:* $72,949.

DEGREES JD/MBA • M Acc • MBA • MBA/M Acc • MBA/MIS • MBA/MS • MBA/MSN • MD/MBA • MIM/MBA • MSM-ORM-OR/MBA • MSM-SC/MBA

JD/MBA—Juris Doctor/Master of Business Administration Full-time. 115 to 131 total credits required. 36 to 48 months to complete program. *Concentrations:* accounting, banking, economics, electronic commerce (E-commerce), entrepreneurship, finance, health care, human resources management, industrial/labor relations, international management, management, management information systems, marketing, nonprofit management, operations management, organizational behavior/development, supply chain management, technology management.

M Acc—Master of Accountancy Full-time and part-time. 36 to 48 total credits required. 11 to 21 months to complete program. *Concentrations:* accounting, taxation.

MBA—Accelerated Master of Business Administration Part-time. Distance learning option. Must have received an undergraduate degree in business within the last 2 years. At least 42 total credits required. 24 to 60 months to complete program. *Concentrations:* accounting, banking, economics, electronic commerce (E-commerce), entrepreneurship, finance, health care, human resources management, industrial/labor relations, international management, management, management information systems, marketing, nonprofit management, operations management, organizational behavior/development, supply chain management, technology management.

MBA—Executive Master of Business Administration Full-time. Minimum of 10 years of work experience and company sponsorship required. At least 45 total credits required. 24 months to complete program. *Concentration:* general MBA.

MBA—Master of Business Administration Full-time. At least 63 total credits required. 21 months to complete program. *Concentrations:* accounting, banking, economics, electronic commerce (E-commerce), entrepreneurship, finance, health care, human resources management, industrial/labor relations, international management, management, management information systems, marketing, nonprofit management, operations management, organizational behavior/development, other, supply chain management, technology management.

MBA—Master of Business Administration Full-time. Undergraduate degree in business granted within the last 10 years required. At least 47 total credits required. 11 months to complete program. *Concentrations:* accounting, banking, economics, electronic commerce (E-commerce), entrepreneurship, finance, health care, human resources management, industrial/labor relations, international management, management, management information systems, marketing, nonprofit management, operations management, organizational behavior/development, supply chain management, technology management.

MBA—Part-Time Master of Business Administration Part-time. Distance learning option. At least 48 total credits required. 36 to 60 months to complete program. *Concentrations:* accounting, banking, economics, electronic commerce (E-commerce), entrepreneurship, finance, health care, human resources management, industrial/labor relations, international management, management, management information systems, marketing, nonprofit management, operations management, organizational behavior/development, supply chain management, technology management.

MBA/M Acc—Master of Business Administration/Master of Accounting Full-time and part-time. At least 67 total credits required. 24 to 48 months to complete program. *Concentrations:* accounting, banking, economics, electronic commerce (E-commerce), health care, human resources management, industrial/labor relations, management, management information systems, marketing, nonprofit management, operations management, organizational behavior/development, supply chain management, technology management.

MBA/MIS—Master of Business Administration/Master of Management Information Systems Full-time and part-time. 63 total credits required. 21 months to complete program. *Concentrations:* accounting, business policy/strategy, economics, entrepreneurship, finance, health administration, human resources management, industrial/labor relations, information systems, information technology, international management, management information systems, marketing, nonprofit management, operations management, organizational behavior/development, other, supply chain management.

MBA/MS—Master of Business Administration/Master of Science in Applied Social Sciences Full-time and part-time. 93 to 105 total credits required. 36 to 48 months to complete program. *Concentrations:* accounting, arts administration/management, banking, economics, electronic commerce (E-commerce), entrepreneurship, finance, health care, human resources management, industrial/labor relations, international management, management, management information systems, marketing, nonprofit management, operations management, organizational behavior/development, supply chain management, technology management.

MBA/MSN—Master of Business Administration/Master of Science in Nursing Full-time and part-time. 78 to 104 total credits required. 29 to 48 months to complete program. *Concentrations:* accounting, banking, economics, electronic commerce (E-commerce), entrepreneurship, finance, health care, human resources management, industrial/labor relations, international management, management, management information systems, marketing, nonprofit management, operations management, organizational behavior/development, supply chain management, technology management.

MD/MBA—Doctor of Medicine/Master of Business Administration Full-time. 120 total credits required. 48 to 60 months to complete program. *Concentrations:* accounting, banking, economics, electronic commerce (E-commerce), entrepreneurship, health care, human resources management, industrial/labor relations, international management, management, management information systems, marketing, nonprofit management, operations management, organizational behavior/development, supply chain management, technology management.

MIM/MBA—Master of International Management/Master of Business Administration Full-time. 66 to 78 total credits required. 21 to 24 months to complete program. *Concentrations:* accounting, banking, economics, electronic commerce (E-commerce), entrepreneurship, finance, health care, human resources management, industrial/labor relations, international management, management, management information systems, marketing, nonprofit management, operations management, organizational behavior/development, supply chain management, technology management.

MSM-ORM-OR/MBA—Master of Science in Management in Operations Research/Master of Business Administration Full-time and part-time. At least 36 total credits required. 11 to 60 months to complete program. *Concentrations:* accounting, banking, economics, electronic commerce (E-commerce), entrepreneurship, finance, health care, human resources management, industrial/labor relations, international management, management, management information systems, marketing, nonprofit management, operations management, organizational behavior/development, supply chain management, technology management.

MSM-SC/MBA—Master of Science in Management in Supply Chain/Master of Business Administration Full-time and part-time. At least 36 total credits required. 11 to 60 months to complete program. *Concentrations:* accounting, banking, economics, electronic commerce (E-commerce), entrepreneurship, finance, health care, human resources management, industrial/labor relations, international management, management, management information systems, marketing, nonprofit management, operations management, organizational behavior/development, supply chain management, technology management.

RESOURCES AND SERVICES 125 on-campus PCs are available to graduate business students. Access to Internet/World Wide Web, online (class) registration, and online grade reports available. *Personal computer requirements:* Graduate business students are required to have a personal computer. *Special opportunities include:* An international exchange program and an internship program are available. *Placement services include:* Alumni network, career placement, job search course, career

Case Western Reserve University (continued)

counseling/planning, electronic job bank, resume referral, career fairs, job interviews arranged, resume preparation, and career library.

EXPENSES *Tuition:* Full-time: $33,650. Part-time: $1366 per credit hour. *Tuition (international):* Full-time: $33,650. Part-time: $1366 per credit hour. *Required fees:* Full-time: $1666. Tuition and/or fees vary by number of courses or credits taken and academic program.

FINANCIAL AID (2007–08) Fellowships, loans, scholarships, and work study. Aid is available to part-time students.

Financial Aid Contact Admissions, 10900 Euclid Avenue, 150 Peter B. Lewis Building, Cleveland, OH 44106-7235. *Phone:* 216-368-5548 Ext. 8907. *Fax:* 216-368-0703. *E-mail:* bizadmission@case.edu.

INTERNATIONAL STUDENTS 26% of students enrolled are international students. *Services and facilities:* Counseling/support services, ESL/language courses, Housing location assistance, International student organization, Orientation, Visa Services. Financial aid is available to international students. *Required with application:* TOEFL with recommended score of 250 (computer), 600 (paper), or 100 (Internet); proof of adequate funds; proof of health/immunizations.

International Student Contact Admissions, 10900 Euclid Avenue, 150 Peter B. Lewis Building, Cleveland, OH 44106-7235. *Phone:* 216-368-2030 Ext. 3315. *Fax:* 216-368-5548. *E-mail:* bizadmission@case.edu.

APPLICATION *Required:* GMAT, application form, baccalaureate/first degree, essay, 2 letters of recommendation, resume/curriculum vitae, transcripts of college work, 2 years of work experience. *Recommended:* Interview. *Application fee:* $50. *Deadlines:* 3/1 for fall, 12/1 for spring, 3/1 for summer, 3/1 for fall (international), 3/1 for summer (international).

Application Contact Admissions, 10900 Euclid Avenue, 150 Peter B. Lewis Building, Cleveland, OH 44106-7235. *Phone:* 216-368-2030. *Fax:* 216-368-5548. *E-mail:* bizadmission@case.edu.

Cleveland State University
Nance College of Business Administration
Cleveland, Ohio

Phone: 216-687-3730 **Fax:** 216-687-5311 **E-mail:** b.gottschalk@csuohio.edu

Business Program(s) Web Site: http://www.csuohio.edu/cba/mba

Graduate Business Unit Enrollment *Total:* 1,195 (211 full-time; 984 part-time; 478 women; 239 international). *Average Age:* 27.

Graduate Business Faculty *Total:* 104 (71 full-time; 33 part-time).

Admissions *Applied:* 1,234. *Admitted:* 833. *Enrolled:* 413. *Average GMAT:* 500. *Average GPA:* 3.1

Academic Calendar Semesters.

Accreditation AACSB—The Association to Advance Collegiate Schools of Business.

After Graduation (Class of 2006–07) *Employed within 3 months of graduation:* 79%. *Average starting salary:* $58,540.

DEGREES JD/MBA • M Acc • MBA • MCIS • MLRHR • MN/MBA

JD/MBA—Juris Doctor/Master of Business Administration Full-time and part-time. 112 to 139 total credits required. 42 to 72 months to complete program. *Concentrations:* legal administration, management.

M Acc—Master of Accountancy Full-time and part-time. 33 to 93 total credits required. 9 to 72 months to complete program. *Concentration:* accounting.

MBA—Accelerated Master of Business Administration Part-time. At least 31 total credits required. Minimum of 12 months to complete program. *Concentrations:* finance, human resources management, management, marketing, organizational behavior/development.

MBA—Executive Master of Business Administration Part-time. Up to 45 total credits required. Maximum of 19 months to complete program. *Concentration:* management.

MBA—Master of Business Administration in Health Administration Full-time and part-time. 34 to 66 total credits required. 12 to 72 months to complete program. *Concentrations:* organizational behavior/development, organizational management, public and private management, public management.

MBA—Master of Business Administration Full-time and part-time. 31 to 69 total credits required. 6 to 72 months to complete program. *Concentrations:* accounting, advertising, banking, finance, human resources management, industrial/labor relations, information management, international and area business studies, management, management information systems, marketing, operations management, organizational behavior/development, quality management, real estate.

MCIS—Master of Computer and Information Science Full-time and part-time. 31 to 66 total credits required. 12 to 72 months to complete program. *Concentrations:* business information science, information management, management information systems, technology management.

MLRHR—Master of Labor Relations and Human Resources Full-time and part-time. 34 to 46 total credits required. 12 to 72 months to complete program. *Concentrations:* human resources management, industrial/labor relations, management, organizational behavior/development, organizational management.

MN/MBA—Master of Nursing/Master of Business Administration Full-time and part-time. 53 to 74 total credits required. 30 to 72 months to complete program. *Concentrations:* administration, business policy/strategy, combined degrees, general MBA, health administration, management.

RESOURCES AND SERVICES 250 on-campus PCs are available to graduate business students. Access to Internet/World Wide Web, online (class) registration, and online grade reports available. *Personal computer requirements:* Graduate business students are not required to have a personal computer. *Special opportunities include:* An international exchange program and an internship program are available. *Placement services include:* Alumni network, career placement, job search course, career counseling/planning, electronic job bank, resume referral, career fairs, job interviews arranged, resume preparation, and career library.

EXPENSES *Tuition (state resident):* Full-time: $10,536. Part-time: $439 per credit hour. *Tuition (nonresident):* Full-time: $20,016. Part-time: $834 per credit hour. *Tuition (international):* Full-time: $20,016. Part-time: $834 per credit hour. *Required fees:* Full-time: $60. *Graduate housing:* Room and board costs vary by campus location, number of occupants, and type of board plan. *Typical cost:* $8200 (including board), $5000 (room only).

FINANCIAL AID (2007–08) 62 students received aid, including loans, research assistantships, scholarships, and work study. Aid is available to part-time students. *Financial aid application deadline:* 2/15.

Financial Aid Contact Rachel Schmidt, Director of Financial Aid, 2121 Euclid Avenue, University Center 560, Cleveland, OH 44115. *Phone:* 216-687-3764. *Fax:* 216-687-9247. *E-mail:* r.schmidt@csuohio.edu.

INTERNATIONAL STUDENTS 20% of students enrolled are international students. *Services and facilities:* Counseling/support services, ESL/language courses, Housing location assistance, International student organization, Language tutoring, Orientation, Visa Services. Financial aid is available to international students. *Required with application:* TOEFL with recommended score of 213 (computer), 550 (paper), or 79 (Internet); proof of adequate funds; proof of health/immunizations. *Recommended with application:* IELT with recommended score of 6.5; TWE.

International Student Contact George Burke, Director, Center for International Services and Programs, 2121 Euclid Avenue, University Center Room 302, Cleveland, OH 44115. *Phone:* 216-687-3910. *Fax:* 216-687-3965. *E-mail:* gburke@csuohio.edu.

APPLICATION *Required:* GMAT, GRE, application form, baccalaureate/first degree, transcripts of college work. *Application fee:* $30. Applications for domestic and international students are processed on a rolling basis.

Application Contact Bruce Gottschalk, Administrator, MBA Programs, 2121 Euclid Avenue, BU 219, Cleveland, OH 44115. *Phone:* 216-687-3730. *Fax:* 216-687-5311. *E-mail:* b.gottschalk@csuohio.edu.

DeVry University
Keller Graduate School of Management

Columbus, Ohio

Phone: 614-251-6969

DEGREES MAFM • MBA • MHRM • MIS • MPA • MPM

MAFM—Master of Accounting and Financial Management Full-time and part-time. Distance learning option. At least 44 total credits required. 18 to 60 months to complete program. *Concentrations:* accounting, financial management/planning.

MBA—Master of Business Administration Full-time and part-time. Distance learning option. At least 48 total credits required. 18 to 60 months to complete program. *Concentration:* management.

MHRM—Master of Human Resources Management Full-time and part-time. Distance learning option. At least 45 total credits required. 18 to 60 months to complete program. *Concentration:* human resources management.

MIS—Master of Information Systems Management Full-time and part-time. Distance learning option. At least 45 total credits required. 18 to 60 months to complete program. *Concentration:* information systems.

MPA—Master of Public Administration Full-time and part-time. Distance learning option. At least 45 total credits required. 18 to 60 months to complete program. *Concentration:* public policy and administration.

MPM—Master of Project Management Full-time and part-time. Distance learning option. At least 42 total credits required. 18 to 60 months to complete program. *Concentration:* project management.

Application Contact Admissions Office, Columbus Campus, 1350 Alum Creek Drive, Columbus, OH 43209. *Phone:* 614-251-6969.

DeVry University
Keller Graduate School of Management

Seven Hills, Ohio

Phone: 216-328-8754

DEGREES MAFM • MBA • MHRM • MIS • MPA • MPM

MAFM—Master of Accounting and Financial Management Full-time and part-time. Distance learning option. At least 44 total credits required. 18 to 60 months to complete program. *Concentrations:* accounting, financial management/planning.

MBA—Master of Business Administration Full-time and part-time. Distance learning option. At least 48 total credits required. 18 to 60 months to complete program. *Concentration:* management.

MHRM—Master of Human Resources Management Full-time and part-time. Distance learning option. At least 45 total credits required. 18 to 60 months to complete program. *Concentration:* human resources management.

MIS—Master of Information Systems Management Full-time and part-time. Distance learning option. At least 45 total credits required. 18 to 60 months to complete program. *Concentration:* information systems.

MPA—Master of Public Administration Full-time and part-time. Distance learning option. At least 45 total credits required. 18 to 60 months to complete program. *Concentration:* public policy and administration.

MPM—Master of Project Management Full-time and part-time. Distance learning option. At least 42 total credits required. 18 to 60 months to complete program. *Concentration:* project management.

Application Contact Admissions Office, Rockside Center, The Genesis Building, 6000 Lombardo Center, Suite 200, Seven Hills, OH 44131. *Phone:* 216-328-8754.

Franciscan University of Steubenville
Department of Business

Steubenville, Ohio

Phone: 740-284-5249 **Fax:** 740-284-5456 **E-mail:** mmcguire@franciscan.edu

Business Program(s) Web Site: http://www.franciscan.edu/home2/Content/Admissions/main.aspx?id=692ç=737

Graduate Business Unit Enrollment *Total:* 37 (11 full-time; 26 part-time; 16 women; 1 international). *Average Age:* 32.

Graduate Business Faculty *Total:* 8 (5 full-time; 3 part-time).

Admissions *Applied:* 19. *Admitted:* 12. *Enrolled:* 11. *Average GPA:* 3.46

Academic Calendar Trimesters.

After Graduation (Class of 2006–07) *Employed within 3 months of graduation:* 100%. *Average starting salary:* $37,000.

DEGREE MBA

MBA—Master of Business Administration Full-time and part-time. At least 40 total credits required. 15 to 84 months to complete program. *Concentration:* accounting.

RESOURCES AND SERVICES 126 on-campus PCs are available to graduate business students. Access to Internet/World Wide Web, online (class) registration, and online grade reports available. *Personal computer requirements:* Graduate business students are not required to have a personal computer. *Placement services include:* Alumni network, career counseling/planning, electronic job bank, career fairs, job interviews arranged, resume preparation, and career library.

EXPENSES *Tuition:* Full-time: $8370. Part-time: $310 per credit hour. *Tuition (international):* Full-time: $8370. Part-time: $310 per credit hour. *Required fees:* Full-time: $270. Part-time: $10 per credit hour.

FINANCIAL AID (2007–08) Grants, loans, scholarships, and work study. Aid is available to part-time students. *Financial aid application deadline:* 7/1.

Financial Aid Contact Mr. John Herrmann, Director of Student Financial Services, 1235 University Boulevard, Enrollment Services, Steubenville, OH 43952-1763. *Phone:* 740-284-5215. *Fax:* 740-284-5469. *E-mail:* jherrmann@franciscan.edu.

INTERNATIONAL STUDENTS 3% of students enrolled are international students. *Services and facilities:* Counseling/support services, Housing location assistance, International student organization, Orientation. Financial aid is available to international students. *Required with application:* TOEFL with recommended score of 213 (computer) or 550 (paper); proof of adequate funds. *Recommended with application:* Proof of health/immunizations.

International Student Contact Mrs. Juliana Deluca Daugherty, Director of Student Development and International Students, 1235 University Boulevard, Student Life Office, Steubenville, OH 43952-1763. *Phone:* 740-284-5867. *Fax:* 740-284-7225. *E-mail:* jdaugherty@franciscan.edu.

APPLICATION *Required:* GMAT, application form, baccalaureate/first degree, 3 letters of recommendation, personal statement, transcripts of college work. *Recommended:* Essay, interview, resume/curriculum vitae. *Application fee:* $20. Applications for domestic and international students are processed on a rolling basis.

Franciscan University of Steubenville (continued)

Application Contact Mark McGuire, Director of Graduate Enrollment, 1235 University Boulevard, Admissions Department, Steubenville, OH 43952-1763. *Phone:* 740-284-5249. *Fax:* 740-284-5456. *E-mail:* mmcguire@franciscan.edu.

Heidelberg College
Program in Business

Tiffin, Ohio

Phone: 419-448-2221 **Fax:** 419-448-2072 **E-mail:** hrennie@heidelberg.edu

Business Program(s) Web Site: http://www.heidelberg.edu

Graduate Business Unit Enrollment *Total:* 68 (3 full-time; 65 part-time; 32 women; 4 international).

Graduate Business Faculty *Total:* 10 (5 full-time; 5 part-time).

Admissions *Applied:* 50. *Admitted:* 30. *Enrolled:* 30. *Average GMAT:* 550. *Average GPA:* 3.2

Academic Calendar 8-week terms.

After Graduation (Class of 2006–07) *Employed within 3 months of graduation:* 100%.

DEGREE MBA

MBA—Master of Business Administration Full-time and part-time. At least 39 total credits required. 12 to 72 months to complete program. *Concentration:* management.

RESOURCES AND SERVICES 30 on-campus PCs are available to graduate business students. Access to Internet/World Wide Web, online (class) registration, and online grade reports available. *Personal computer requirements:* Graduate business students are strongly recommended to purchase or lease a personal computer. *Special opportunities include:* An international exchange program is available. *Placement services include:* Alumni network, career counseling/planning, career fairs, and job interviews arranged.

EXPENSES *Tuition:* Full-time: $19,695. Part-time: $1515 per course.

Financial Aid Contact Director of Financial Aid, 310 East Market Street, Tiffin, OH 44883. *Phone:* 419-448-2293. *Fax:* 419-448-2124.

INTERNATIONAL STUDENTS 6% of students enrolled are international students. *Services and facilities:* Counseling/support services, ESL/language courses, Housing location assistance, International student housing, International student organization, Language tutoring, Orientation. Financial aid is not available to international students. *Required with application:* TOEFL with recommended score of 550 (paper); TWE; proof of adequate funds.

International Student Contact Mark O'Reilly, Director, International Programs, 310 East Market Street, Tiffin, OH 44883. *Phone:* 419-448-2207. *E-mail:* lmiller@heidelberg.edu.

APPLICATION *Required:* Application form, baccalaureate/first degree, essay, personal statement, transcripts of college work. *Recommended:* Interview, work experience. *Application fee:* $25. Applications for domestic and international students are processed on a rolling basis.

Application Contact Henry Rennie, Director, Graduate Studies in Business, 310 East Market Street, Tiffin, OH 44883. *Phone:* 419-448-2221. *Fax:* 419-448-2072. *E-mail:* hrennie@heidelberg.edu.

John Carroll University
John M. and Mary Jo Boler School of Business

University Heights, Ohio

Phone: 216-397-1970 **Fax:** 216-397-1833 **E-mail:** gradbusiness@jcu.edu

Business Program(s) Web Site: http://www.jcu.edu/boler/grads

Graduate Business Unit Enrollment *Total:* 208 (67 full-time; 141 part-time; 87 women; 6 international). *Average Age:* 27.

Graduate Business Faculty *Total:* 64 (34 full-time; 30 part-time).

Admissions *Applied:* 111. *Admitted:* 110. *Enrolled:* 79. *Average GMAT:* 550. *Average GPA:* 3.1

Academic Calendar Semesters.

Accreditation AACSB—The Association to Advance Collegiate Schools of Business.

After Graduation (Class of 2006–07) *Employed within 3 months of graduation:* 90%.

DEGREES MBA • MSA

MBA—Master of Business Administration Part-time. 30 to 54 total credits required. 12 to 60 months to complete program. *Concentrations:* accounting, finance, international business, management, marketing.

MSA—Master of Science in Accountancy Part-time. 30 to 78 total credits required. 12 to 60 months to complete program. *Concentration:* accounting.

RESOURCES AND SERVICES 120 on-campus PCs are available to graduate business students. Access to Internet/World Wide Web, online (class) registration, and online grade reports available. *Personal computer requirements:* Graduate business students are strongly recommended to purchase or lease a personal computer. *Special opportunities include:* An internship program is available. *Placement services include:* Alumni network, career placement, career counseling/planning, electronic job bank, resume referral, career fairs, job interviews arranged, resume preparation, and career library.

EXPENSES *Tuition:* Part-time: $793 per credit hour. *Tuition (international):* Part-time: $793 per credit hour. Tuition and/or fees vary by academic program.

FINANCIAL AID (2007–08) 97 students received aid, including loans, research assistantships, and scholarships. Aid is available to part-time students. *Financial aid application deadline:* 7/15.

Financial Aid Contact Financial Aid Department, 20700 North Park Boulevard, University Heights, OH 44118-4581. *Phone:* 216-397-4248. *Fax:* 216-397-3098. *E-mail:* jcuofa@jcu.edu.

INTERNATIONAL STUDENTS 3% of students enrolled are international students. *Services and facilities:* Counseling/support services, Housing location assistance, International student organization, Language tutoring, Orientation, Visa Services. Financial aid is not available to international students. *Required with application:* TOEFL with recommended score of 213 (computer), 550 (paper), or 79 (Internet); proof of adequate funds; proof of health/immunizations.

International Student Contact Mr. Frank Congin, Assistant Director, Office of Global Education, 20700 North Park Boulevard, University Heights, OH 44118. *Phone:* 216-397-4357. *E-mail:* fcongin@jcu.edu.

APPLICATION *Required:* GMAT, application form, baccalaureate/first degree, essay, 1 letter of recommendation, personal statement, resume/curriculum vitae, transcripts of college work. *Recommended:* Work experience. *Application fee:* $25, $35 (international). Applications for domestic and international students are processed on a rolling basis.

Application Contact Ms. Gayle Bruno-Gannon, Assistant to the Dean, Graduate Business Programs, 20700 North Park Boulevard, University Heights, OH 44118-4581. *Phone:* 216-397-1970. *Fax:* 216-397-1833. *E-mail:* gradbusiness@jcu.edu.

Kent State University
Graduate School of Management

Kent, Ohio

Phone: 330-672-2282 **Fax:** 330-672-7303 **E-mail:** gradbus@kent.edu

Business Program(s) Web Site: http://business.kent.edu/grad

Graduate Business Unit Enrollment *Total:* 349 (196 full-time; 153 part-time; 162 women; 72 international). *Average Age:* 25.

Graduate Business Faculty *Total:* 63 (55 full-time; 8 part-time).

Admissions *Applied:* 174. *Admitted:* 156. *Enrolled:* 102. *Average GMAT:* 520. *Average GPA:* 3.36

Academic Calendar Semesters.

Accreditation AACSB—The Association to Advance Collegiate Schools of Business.

After Graduation (Class of 2006–07) *Employed within 3 months of graduation:* 75%. *Average starting salary:* $50,029.

DEGREES MA • MA/MBA • MBA • MBA/MLS • MBA/MS • MS

MA—Master of Arts in Economics Full-time and part-time. GMAT or GRE required. At least 30 total credits required. 12 to 72 months to complete program. *Concentrations:* economics, financial economics.

MA/MBA—Master of Architecture/Master of Business Administration Full-time. Bachelor of Architecture and GMAT or GRE required. 70 total credits required. 12 to 72 months to complete program. *Concentration:* combined degrees.

MBA—Executive Master of Business Administration Full-time. Interview, minimum of 5 years of work experience and GMAT required. 39 total credits required. 19 months to complete program. *Concentration:* executive programs.

MBA—Master of Business Administration Full-time and part-time. GMAT required. 39 to 54 total credits required. 15 to 72 months to complete program. *Concentrations:* accounting, finance, human resources management, international business, management information systems, marketing.

MBA/MLS—Master of Business Administration/Master of Library and Information Science Full-time and part-time. GMAT or GRE required. 70 total credits required. 36 to 72 months to complete program. *Concentration:* combined degrees.

MBA/MS—Master of Business Administration/Master of Science in Nursing Full-time and part-time. Bachelor of Science in Nursing and GMAT or GRE required. 64 total credits required. 36 to 72 months to complete program. *Concentration:* combined degrees.

MS—Master of Science in Accounting Full-time and part-time. GMAT required. 32 to 55 total credits required. 12 to 72 months to complete program. *Concentration:* accounting.

MS—Master of Science in Financial Engineering Full-time. GRE or GMAT required. 36 total credits required. 12 months to complete program. *Concentration:* finance.

RESOURCES AND SERVICES 125 on-campus PCs are available to graduate business students. Access to Internet/World Wide Web, online (class) registration, and online grade reports available. *Personal computer requirements:* Graduate business students are not required to have a personal computer. *Special opportunities include:* An international exchange program and an internship program are available. *Placement services include:* Alumni network, career placement, career counseling/planning, electronic job bank, resume referral, career fairs, job interviews arranged, resume preparation, and career library.

EXPENSES *Tuition (state resident):* Full-time: $8968. Part-time: $408 per credit hour. *Tuition (nonresident):* Full-time: $15,980. Part-time: $728 per credit hour. *Tuition (international):* Full-time: $15,980. Tuition and/or fees vary by number of courses or credits taken. *Graduate housing:* Room and board costs vary by number of occupants, type of accommodation, and type of board plan. *Typical cost:* $8690 (including board), $5900 (room only).

FINANCIAL AID (2007–08) Loans, research assistantships, and work study. *Financial aid application deadline:* 4/1.

Financial Aid Contact Mr. Mark Evans, Director, Office of Student Financial Aid, PO Box 5190, Kent, OH 44242-0001. *Phone:* 330-672-2972. *Fax:* 330-672-4014. *E-mail:* mevans@kent.edu.

INTERNATIONAL STUDENTS 21% of students enrolled are international students. *Services and facilities:* Counseling/support services, ESL/language courses, International student housing, International student

organization, Orientation, Visa Services. Financial aid is available to international students. *Required with application:* TOEFL with recommended score of 213 (computer) or 550 (paper); proof of adequate funds; proof of health/immunizations.

International Student Contact Mr. Ted McKown, II, Director for International Admissions, Office of International Affairs, PO Box 5190, Kent, OH 44242-0001. *Phone:* 330-672-7980. *Fax:* 330-672-2745. *E-mail:* tmckown@kent.edu.

APPLICATION *Required:* GMAT, application form, baccalaureate/first degree, essay, 3 letters of recommendation, personal statement, resume/curriculum vitae, transcripts of college work. *Application fee:* $30, $60 (international). Applications for domestic and international students are processed on a rolling basis.

Application Contact Ms. Louise Ditchey, Director, Master's Programs, PO Box 5190, Kent, OH 44242-0001. *Phone:* 330-672-2282. *Fax:* 330-672-7303. *E-mail:* gradbus@kent.edu.

Miami University
Farmer School of Business
Oxford, Ohio

Phone: 513-529-6643 **Fax:** 513-529-6992 **E-mail:** morrowrr@muohio.edu

Business Program(s) Web Site: http://mba.muohio.edu

Graduate Business Unit Enrollment *Total:* 77 (77 full-time; 35 women; 8 international). *Average Age:* 22-27.

Graduate Business Faculty *Total:* 30 (28 full-time; 2 part-time).

Admissions *Applied:* 177. *Admitted:* 103. *Enrolled:* 77. *Average GMAT:* 560. *Average GPA:* 3.2

Academic Calendar Semesters.

Accreditation AACSB—The Association to Advance Collegiate Schools of Business.

After Graduation (Class of 2006–07) *Employed within 3 months of graduation:* 88%. *Average starting salary:* $67,625.

DEGREES M Acc • MA • MBA

M Acc—Master of Accountancy Full-time. 30 total credits required. 10 months to complete program. *Concentration:* accounting.

MA—Master of Arts Full-time. 35 total credits required. 12 months to complete program. *Concentration:* economics.

MBA—Master of Business Administration Full-time. Minimum 2 years professional work experience required. 50 total credits required. 14 months to complete program. *Concentration:* management.

RESOURCES AND SERVICES 360 on-campus PCs are available to graduate business students. Access to Internet/World Wide Web, online (class) registration, and online grade reports available. *Personal computer requirements:* Graduate business students are required to have a personal computer. *Special opportunities include:* An internship program is available. *Placement services include:* Alumni network, career placement, career counseling/planning, electronic job bank, resume referral, career fairs, job interviews arranged, resume preparation, and career library.

EXPENSES *Tuition (state resident):* Full-time: $9000. *Tuition (nonresident):* Full-time: $21,860. *Tuition (international):* Full-time: $21,860. *Required fees:* Full-time: $2714. Tuition and/or fees vary by academic program. *Graduate housing:* Room and board costs vary by type of accommodation and type of board plan. *Typical cost:* $4740 (including board), $4601 (room only).

FINANCIAL AID (2007–08) 27 students received aid, including loans, research assistantships, and scholarships. *Financial aid application deadline:* 3/1.

Miami University (continued)

Financial Aid Contact Mr. Charles R Knepfle, Director of Student Financial Assistance, 121 Campus Avenue Building, Oxford, OH 45056. *Phone:* 513-529-8555. *Fax:* 513-529-8713. *E-mail:* knepflcr@muohio.edu.

INTERNATIONAL STUDENTS 10% of students enrolled are international students. *Services and facilities:* Counseling/support services, Housing location assistance, International student housing, International student organization, Orientation, Visa Services. Financial aid is not available to international students. *Required with application:* TOEFL with recommended score of 213 (computer), 550 (paper), or 80 (Internet); proof of adequate funds; proof of health/immunizations.

International Student Contact Ms. Rita R Morrow, Assistant Director of the MBA Program, 107 Laws Hall, Oxford, OH 45056. *Phone:* 513-529-6643. *Fax:* 513-529-6992. *E-mail:* morrowrr@muohio.edu.

APPLICATION *Required:* GMAT, GRE, application form, baccalaureate/first degree, essay, interview, 2 letters of recommendation, resume/curriculum vitae, transcripts of college work, 2 years of work experience. *Application fee:* $35.

Application Contact Rita R Morrow, Assistant Director of the MBA Program, 107 Laws Hall, Oxford, OH 45056. *Phone:* 513-529-6643. *Fax:* 513-529-6992. *E-mail:* morrowrr@muohio.edu.

The Ohio State University
Max M. Fisher College of Business

Columbus, Ohio

Phone: 614-292-2249 **Fax:** 614-292-9006 **E-mail:** merzel.1@osu.edu

Business Program(s) Web Site: http://fisher.osu.edu

Graduate Business Unit Enrollment *Total:* 874 (596 full-time; 278 part-time; 307 women; 196 international). *Average Age:* 27.

Graduate Business Faculty *Total:* 92 (71 full-time; 21 part-time).

Admissions *Applied:* 1,477. *Admitted:* 661. *Enrolled:* 446. *Average GMAT:* 661. *Average GPA:* 3.44

Academic Calendar Quarters.

Accreditation AACSB—The Association to Advance Collegiate Schools of Business.

After Graduation (Class of 2006–07) *Employed within 3 months of graduation:* 98%. *Average starting salary:* $84,674.

DEGREES M Acc • MBA • MBA/M Eng • MLHR

M Acc—Master of Accounting Full-time. At least 45 total credits required. 9 months to complete program. *Concentration:* accounting.

MBA—Executive MBA Full-time. 7 years professional experience. 60 total credits required. 18 months to complete program. *Concentration:* executive programs.

MBA—Full-Time Master of Business Administration Full-time. At least 98 total credits required. 18 to 22 months to complete program. *Concentrations:* accounting, finance, human resources management, international business, logistics, management consulting, management information systems, marketing, operations management, real estate.

MBA—Part-Time Master of Business Administration Full-time and part-time. 76 total credits required. 24 to 48 months to complete program. *Concentration:* general MBA.

MBA/M Eng—Master of Business Logistics Engineering Program Full-time. At least 45 total credits required. 9 to 15 months to complete program. *Concentrations:* engineering, logistics.

MLHR—Master of Labor and Human Resources Full-time and part-time. 76 total credits required. 18 months to complete program. *Concentration:* industrial/labor relations.

RESOURCES AND SERVICES 121 on-campus PCs are available to graduate business students. Access to Internet/World Wide Web, online

(class) registration, and online grade reports available. *Personal computer requirements:* Graduate business students are not required to have a personal computer. *Special opportunities include:* An international exchange program and an internship program are available. *Placement services include:* Alumni network, career placement, career counseling/planning, electronic job bank, resume referral, career fairs, job interviews arranged, resume preparation, and career library.

EXPENSES *Tuition (state resident):* Full-time: $20,346. Part-time: $678 per credit hour. *Tuition (nonresident):* Full-time: $34,500. Part-time: $1150 per credit hour. *Tuition (international):* Full-time: $34,500. Part-time: $1150 per credit hour. *Required fees:* Full-time: $837. Part-time: $47 per credit hour. Tuition and/or fees vary by number of courses or credits taken and academic program. *Typical graduate housing cost:* $7632 (including board), $4464 (room only).

FINANCIAL AID (2007–08) 204 students received aid, including fellowships, research assistantships, scholarships, and teaching assistantships.

Financial Aid Contact Ms. Alison Merzel, Director of Admissions, 2108 Neil Avenue, 100 Gerlach Hall, Columbus, OH 43210. *Phone:* 614-292-2246. *Fax:* 614-292-9006. *E-mail:* merzel.1@osu.edu.

INTERNATIONAL STUDENTS 22% of students enrolled are international students. *Services and facilities:* Counseling/support services, ESL/language courses, Housing location assistance, International student housing, International student organization, Language tutoring, Orientation, Visa Services, Career services specialist. Financial aid is available to international students. *Required with application:* TOEFL with recommended score of 250 (computer) or 600 (paper); proof of adequate funds; proof of health/immunizations.

International Student Contact Ms. Alison Merzel, Director of Admissions, 2108 Neil Avenue, 100 Gerlach Hall, Columbus, OH 43210. *Phone:* 614-292-8511. *Fax:* 614-292-9006. *E-mail:* mba@fisher.osu.edu.

APPLICATION *Required:* GMAT, application form, baccalaureate/first degree, essay, interview, 3 letters of recommendation, personal statement, resume/curriculum vitae, transcripts of college work. *Recommended:* Work experience. *Application fee:* $60, $70 (international). Applications for domestic and international students are processed on a rolling basis.

Application Contact Alison Merzel, Director of Admissions, 2108 Neil Avenue, 100 Gerlach Hall, Columbus, OH 43210. *Phone:* 614-292-2249. *Fax:* 614-292-9006. *E-mail:* merzel.1@osu.edu.

Ohio University
College of Business

Athens, Ohio

Phone: 740-593-2007 **Fax:** 740-593-1388 **E-mail:** rossj@ohiou.edu

Business Program(s) Web Site: http://www.cob.ohiou.edu/grad

Graduate Business Unit Enrollment *Total:* 127 (51 full-time; 76 part-time; 45 women; 19 international). *Average Age:* 30.

Graduate Business Faculty *Total:* 60 (55 full-time; 5 part-time).

Admissions *Applied:* 270. *Admitted:* 141. *Enrolled:* 127. *Average GMAT:* 560. *Average GPA:* 3.3

Academic Calendar Quarters.

Accreditation AACSB—The Association to Advance Collegiate Schools of Business.

After Graduation (Class of 2006–07) *Employed within 3 months of graduation:* 70%. *Average starting salary:* $65,000.

DEGREES MBA

MBA—Full-Time Master of Business Administration Full-time. 72 to 89 total credits required. 15 months to complete program. *Concentrations:* general MBA, health administration, sports/entertainment management.

MBA—Professional MBA Part-time. Distance learning option. At least 72 total credits required. 24 months to complete program. *Concentration:* general MBA.

RESOURCES AND SERVICES 150 on-campus PCs are available to graduate business students. Access to Internet/World Wide Web, online (class) registration, and online grade reports available. *Personal computer requirements:* Graduate business students are strongly recommended to purchase or lease a personal computer. *Special opportunities include:* An international exchange program is available. *Placement services include:* Alumni network, career placement, career counseling/planning, electronic job bank, resume referral, career fairs, job interviews arranged, resume preparation, and career library.

EXPENSES *Tuition (state resident):* Full-time: $12,504. Part-time: $387 per credit hour. *Tuition (nonresident):* Full-time: $23,160. Part-time: $718 per credit hour. *Tuition (international):* Full-time: $23,160. Part-time: $718 per credit hour. *Required fees:* Full-time: $4300. Tuition and/or fees vary by number of courses or credits taken, campus location, and academic program. *Graduate housing:* Room and board costs vary by campus location, number of occupants, type of accommodation, and type of board plan. *Typical cost:* $11,000 (including board), $6500 (room only).

FINANCIAL AID (2007–08) 40 students received aid, including loans, scholarships, and work study. *Financial aid application deadline:* 2/1.

Financial Aid Contact Jan Ross, Assistant Dean, Copeland Hall 514A, Athens, OH 45701-2979. *Phone:* 740-593-2007. *Fax:* 740-593-1388. *E-mail:* rossj@ohiou.edu.

INTERNATIONAL STUDENTS 15% of students enrolled are international students. *Services and facilities:* Counseling/support services, ESL/language courses, Housing location assistance, International student organization, Orientation. Financial aid is available to international students. *Required with application:* TOEFL with recommended score of 250 (computer) or 600 (paper); proof of adequate funds. *Recommended with application:* TWE.

International Student Contact Alan Boyd, Director, International Student and Faculty Services, Scott Quad 172, Athens, OH 45701-2979. *Phone:* 740-593-4330. *Fax:* 740-593-4328.

APPLICATION *Required:* GMAT, application form, baccalaureate/first degree, essay, interview, 3 letters of recommendation, resume/curriculum vitae, transcripts of college work. *Recommended:* Personal statement, 2 years of work experience. *Application fee:* $45, $55 (international). *Deadlines:* 2/1 for fall, 1/15 for fall (international).

Application Contact Jan Ross, Assistant Dean, Graduate Programs, Copeland Hall 514A, Athens, OH 45701-2979. *Phone:* 740-593-2007. *Fax:* 740-593-1388. *E-mail:* rossj@ohiou.edu.

Otterbein College

Department of Business, Accounting and Economics

Westerville, Ohio

Phone: 614-823-1096 **Fax:** 614-823-1014 **E-mail:** shasan@otterbein.edu

Business Program(s) Web Site: http://www.otterbein.edu/MBA

Graduate Business Unit Enrollment *Total:* 103 (53 full-time; 50 part-time; 46 women; 8 international). *Average Age:* 33.

Graduate Business Faculty *Total:* 15 (8 full-time; 7 part-time).

Admissions *Applied:* 23. *Admitted:* 14. *Enrolled:* 14. *Average GMAT:* 495. *Average GPA:* 3.27

Academic Calendar Quarters.

DEGREE MBA

MBA—Master of Business Administration Full-time and part-time. At least 48 total credits required. 18 to 60 months to complete program. *Concentrations:* actuarial science, finance, general MBA, human resources management, nonprofit management.

RESOURCES AND SERVICES 156 on-campus PCs are available to graduate business students. Access to Internet/World Wide Web, online (class) registration, and online grade reports available. *Personal computer requirements:* Graduate business students are strongly recommended to purchase or lease a personal computer. *Special opportunities include:* An international exchange program and an internship program are available. *Placement services include:* Alumni network, career counseling/planning, career fairs, resume preparation, and career library.

FINANCIAL AID (2007–08) 37 students received aid, including loans and research assistantships. Aid is available to part-time students.

Financial Aid Contact Mr. Philip E. Bovenizer, Assistant Director of Financial Aid, Office of Financial Aid, One Otterbein College, Westerville, OH 43081-2006. *Phone:* 614-823-1502. *E-mail:* pbovenizer@otterbein.edu.

INTERNATIONAL STUDENTS 8% of students enrolled are international students. *Services and facilities:* Counseling/support services, ESL/language courses, Housing location assistance, International student organization, Orientation, Visa Services. Financial aid is available to international students. *Required with application:* TOEFL with recommended score of 213 (computer) or 550 (paper); proof of adequate funds. *Recommended with application:* Proof of health/immunizations.

International Student Contact Mr. Charles Vedder, Director, International Student Programs, International Student Programs, One Otterbein College, Westerville, OH 43081-2006. *Phone:* 614-823-1312. *Fax:* 614-823-3299. *E-mail:* cvedder@otterbein.edu.

APPLICATION *Required:* GMAT, application form, baccalaureate/first degree, 2 letters of recommendation, personal statement, resume/curriculum vitae, transcripts of college work. *Recommended:* 2 years of work experience. *Application fee:* $35. Applications for domestic and international students are processed on a rolling basis.

Application Contact Dr. Shah Hasan, Director, MBA Program, MBA Program, One Otterbein College, Westerville, OH 43081-2006. *Phone:* 614-823-1096. *Fax:* 614-823-1014. *E-mail:* shasan@otterbein.edu.

Tiffin University

Program in Business Administration

Tiffin, Ohio

Phone: 800-968-6446 Ext. 3401 **Fax:** 419-443-5002 **E-mail:** grad@tiffin.edu

Business Program(s) Web Site: http://www.tiffin.edu/graduateprograms/

Graduate Business Unit Enrollment *Average Age:* 29.

Admissions *Average GPA:* 3.01

Academic Calendar Semesters.

Accreditation ACBSP—The American Council of Business Schools and Programs.

DEGREES MBA

MBA—MBA—General Management Full-time and part-time. Distance learning option. 36 total credits required. 18 to 72 months to complete program. *Concentration:* general MBA.

MBA—MBA—Leadership Full-time and part-time. Distance learning option. 36 total credits required. 18 to 72 months to complete program. *Concentration:* leadership.

MBA—MBA General Management Full-time and part-time. Distance learning option. 36 total credits required. 18 to 72 months to complete program. *Concentrations:* general MBA, management, organizational management.

MBA—Online Master of Business Administration Full-time and part-time. Distance learning option. 36 total credits required. 18 to 72 months to complete program. *Concentrations:* general MBA, leadership, management, organizational management, sports/entertainment management.

Tiffin University (continued)

RESOURCES AND SERVICES 50 on-campus PCs are available to graduate business students. Access to Internet/World Wide Web, online (class) registration, and online grade reports available. *Personal computer requirements:* Graduate business students are strongly recommended to purchase or lease a personal computer. *Special opportunities include:* An international exchange program is available. *Placement services include:* Alumni network, career placement, career counseling/planning, career fairs, resume preparation, and career library.

EXPENSES *Tuition:* Full-time: $14,000. *Tuition (international):* Full-time: $14,000. *Graduate housing:* Room and board costs vary by campus location, number of occupants, type of accommodation, and type of board plan. *Typical cost:* $7500 (including board).

FINANCIAL AID (2007–08) Loans, scholarships, and work study. Aid is available to part-time students.

Financial Aid Contact Cindy Little, Director of Financial Aid, 155 Miami Street, Tiffin, OH 44883-2161. *Phone:* 419-448-3415. *Fax:* 419-443-5006. *E-mail:* grad@tiffin.edu.

INTERNATIONAL STUDENTS *Services and facilities:* Counseling/support services, Housing location assistance, International student housing, International student organization, Orientation, Visa Services. Financial aid is available to international students. *Required with application:* TOEFL with recommended score of 213 (computer) or 550 (paper); proof of adequate funds; proof of health/immunizations.

International Student Contact Ryan Miller, Graduate Admissions Representative, 155 Miami Street, Tiffin, OH 44883-2161. *Phone:* 419-448-3310. *Fax:* 419-443-5002. *E-mail:* grad@tiffin.edu.

APPLICATION *Required:* Application form, baccalaureate/first degree, essay, personal statement, resume/curriculum vitae, transcripts of college work. Applications for domestic and international students are processed on a rolling basis.

Application Contact Ryan Miller, Graduate Admissions Representative, Office of Graduate Studies, 155 Miami Street, Tiffin, OH 44883. *Phone:* 800-968-6446 Ext. 3401. *Fax:* 419-443-5002. *E-mail:* grad@tiffin.edu.

The University of Akron
College of Business Administration

Akron, Ohio

Phone: 330-972-7043 **Fax:** 330-972-6588 **E-mail:** gradcba@uakron.edu

Business Program(s) Web Site: http://www.uakron.edu/cba/grad

Graduate Business Unit Enrollment *Total:* 438 (202 full-time; 236 part-time; 192 women; 116 international). *Average Age:* 29.

Graduate Business Faculty *Total:* 54 (38 full-time; 16 part-time).

Admissions *Applied:* 215. *Admitted:* 172. *Enrolled:* 89. *Average GMAT:* 548. *Average GPA:* 3.25

Academic Calendar Semesters.

Accreditation AACSB—The Association to Advance Collegiate Schools of Business.

After Graduation (Class of 2006–07) *Employed within 3 months of graduation:* 58%. *Average starting salary:* $58,528.

DEGREES JD/M Tax • JD/MBA • JD/MHR • M Tax • MBA • MSA • MSM

JD/M Tax—Juris Doctor/Master of Taxation Full-time and part-time. 98 to 104 total credits required. 36 to 96 months to complete program. *Concentrations:* combined degrees, law, taxation.

JD/MBA—Juris Doctor/Master of Business Administration Full-time and part-time. 103 to 124 total credits required. 36 to 96 months to complete program. *Concentrations:* combined degrees, finance, international business, law, management, marketing.

JD/MHR—Juris Doctor/Master of Human Resources Full-time and part-time. 103 to 121 total credits required. 36 to 96 months to complete program. *Concentrations:* combined degrees, human resources management, law.

M Tax—Master of Taxation Full-time and part-time. 30 to 36 total credits required. 12 to 72 months to complete program. *Concentration:* taxation.

MBA—Master of Business Administration Full-time and part-time. 34 to 58 total credits required. 12 to 72 months to complete program. *Concentrations:* electronic commerce (E-commerce), entrepreneurship, finance, general MBA, health care, international business, international finance, management, marketing, supply chain management, technology management.

MSA—Master of Science in Accountancy Full-time and part-time. 30 to 57 total credits required. 12 to 72 months to complete program. *Concentration:* accounting.

MSM—Master of Science in Management Full-time and part-time. 33 to 57 total credits required. 12 to 72 months to complete program. *Concentrations:* human resources management, management information systems.

RESOURCES AND SERVICES 266 on-campus PCs are available to graduate business students. Access to Internet/World Wide Web, online (class) registration, and online grade reports available. *Personal computer requirements:* Graduate business students are strongly recommended to purchase or lease a personal computer. *Special opportunities include:* An international exchange program and an internship program are available. *Placement services include:* Career placement, job search course, career counseling/planning, electronic job bank, resume referral, career fairs, job interviews arranged, resume preparation, and career library.

EXPENSES *Tuition (state resident):* Full-time: $12,067. *Tuition (nonresident):* Full-time: $19,418. *Tuition (international):* Full-time: $19,418. *Required fees:* Full-time: $900.

FINANCIAL AID (2007–08) 55 students received aid, including loans, research assistantships, and work study. *Financial aid application deadline:* 3/1.

Financial Aid Contact Myra Weakland, Assistant Director, Graduate Programs in Business, Graduate Programs in Business, Room 412, Akron, OH 44325-4805. *Phone:* 330-972-7043. *Fax:* 330-972-6588. *E-mail:* gradcba@uakron.edu.

INTERNATIONAL STUDENTS 26% of students enrolled are international students. *Services and facilities:* Counseling/support services, ESL/language courses, Housing location assistance, International student housing, International student organization, Language tutoring, Orientation, Visa Services. Financial aid is available to international students. *Required with application:* TOEFL with recommended score of 213 (computer), 550 (paper), or 79 (Internet); proof of adequate funds; proof of health/immunizations.

International Student Contact Ms. Theresa M. McCune, Coordinator, Graduate Admissions, Graduate School, Akron, OH 44325-2101. *Phone:* 330-972-7663. *Fax:* 330-972-6475. *E-mail:* gradschool@uakron.edu.

APPLICATION *Required:* GMAT, application form, baccalaureate/first degree, 2 letters of recommendation, personal statement, resume/curriculum vitae, transcripts of college work. *Recommended:* Essay, interview, work experience. *Application fee:* $30, $40 (international). Applications for domestic and international students are processed on a rolling basis.

Application Contact Myra Weakland, Assistant Director, Graduate Programs in Business, Graduate Programs in Business, Room 412, Akron, OH 44325-4805. *Phone:* 330-972-7043. *Fax:* 330-972-6588. *E-mail:* gradcba@uakron.edu.

University of Cincinnati
College of Business

Cincinnati, Ohio

Phone: 513-556-7024 **Fax:** 513-558-7006 **E-mail:** andrew.vogel@uc.edu

Business Program(s) Web Site: http://www.business.uc.edu/

Graduate Business Unit Enrollment *Total:* 666 (265 full-time; 401 part-time; 250 women; 196 international). *Average Age:* 30.

Graduate Business Faculty *Total:* 118 (70 full-time; 48 part-time).

Admissions *Applied:* 800. *Admitted:* 495. *Enrolled:* 251. *Average GMAT:* 567. *Average GPA:* 3.2

Academic Calendar Quarters.

Accreditation AACSB—The Association to Advance Collegiate Schools of Business.

After Graduation (Class of 2006–07) *Employed within 3 months of graduation:* 62%. *Average starting salary:* $58,450.

DEGREES   JD/MBA • M Sc • MBA • MBA/MA • MD/MBA

JD/MBA—Juris Doctor/Master of Business Administration Full-time. At least 134 total credits required. 48 to 84 months to complete program. *Concentration:* combined degrees.

M Sc—Master of Science Full-time and part-time. 45 to 57 total credits required. 12 to 84 months to complete program. *Concentrations:* accounting, information systems, marketing, quantitative analysis.

MBA—Master of Business Administration Full-time and part-time. 45 to 72 total credits required. 12 to 84 months to complete program. *Concentrations:* construction management, finance, information management, international business, management, marketing, operations management, quantitative analysis, real estate.

MBA/MA—Master of Business Administration/Master of Arts in Arts Administration Full-time and part-time. At least 90 total credits required. 24 to 84 months to complete program. *Concentration:* combined degrees.

MD/MBA—Doctor of Medicine/Master of Business Administration Full-time. At least 147 total credits required. 60 to 84 months to complete program. *Concentration:* combined degrees.

RESOURCES AND SERVICES 125 on-campus PCs are available to graduate business students. Access to Internet/World Wide Web, online (class) registration, and online grade reports available. *Personal computer requirements:* Graduate business students are strongly recommended to purchase or lease a personal computer. *Special opportunities include:* An international exchange program and an internship program are available. *Placement services include:* Alumni network, career placement, job search course, career counseling/planning, electronic job bank, resume referral, career fairs, job interviews arranged, resume preparation, and career library.

EXPENSES *Tuition (state resident):* Full-time: $21,868. Part-time: $457 per credit hour. *Tuition (nonresident):* Full-time: $27,380. Part-time: $457 per credit hour. *Tuition (international):* Full-time: $27,380. Part-time: $457 per credit hour. *Required fees:* Full-time: $2004. Part-time: $50 per quarter hour. Tuition and/or fees vary by number of courses or credits taken, academic program, and local reciprocity agreements. *Graduate housing:* Room and board costs vary by number of occupants, type of accommodation, and type of board plan. *Typical cost:* $13,020 (including board), $8328 (room only).

FINANCIAL AID (2007–08) 63 students received aid, including research assistantships, scholarships, and teaching assistantships. *Financial aid application deadline:* 2/15.

Financial Aid Contact Ms. Connie Williams, Student Financial Aid, PO Box 210125, Cincinnati, OH 45221-0125. *Phone:* 513-556-6982. *Fax:* 513-556-9171.

INTERNATIONAL STUDENTS 29% of students enrolled are international students. *Services and facilities:* Counseling/support services, ESL/language courses, Housing location assistance, International student organization, Language tutoring, Orientation, Visa Services, Social and cultural adjustment activities. Financial aid is available to international students. *Required with application:* TOEFL with recommended score of 250 (computer), 600 (paper), or 100 (Internet); proof of adequate funds; proof of health/immunizations.

International Student Contact Karen Mueller, Records Manager, PO Box 210020, Cincinnati, OH 45221. *Phone:* 513-556-7020. *Fax:* 513-558-7006. *E-mail:* karen.mueller@uc.edu.

APPLICATION *Required:* GMAT, application form, baccalaureate/first degree, essay, 2 letters of recommendation, personal statement, resume/curriculum vitae, transcripts of college work. *Recommended:* Work experience. *Application fee:* $40. *Deadlines:* 7/1 for fall, 4/1 for fall (international).

Application Contact Mr. Andrew Vogel, Associate Director of Admissions, PO Box 210020, Cincinnati, OH 45221-0020. *Phone:* 513-556-7024. *Fax:* 513-558-7006. *E-mail:* andrew.vogel@uc.edu.

University of Dayton
School of Business Administration
Dayton, Ohio

Phone: 937-229-3733 **Fax:** 937-229-3882 **E-mail:** mba@udayton.edu

Business Program(s) Web Site: http://www.sba.udayton.edu/mba/

Graduate Business Unit Enrollment *Total:* 450 (90 full-time; 360 part-time; 158 women; 58 international). *Average Age:* 29.

Graduate Business Faculty *Total:* 90 (63 full-time; 27 part-time).

Admissions *Applied:* 329. *Admitted:* 263. *Enrolled:* 210. *Average GMAT:* 563. *Average GPA:* 3.26

Academic Calendar Semesters.

Accreditation AACSB—The Association to Advance Collegiate Schools of Business.

After Graduation (Class of 2006–07) *Employed within 3 months of graduation:* 95%.

DEGREES   JD/MBA • MBA

JD/MBA—Juris Doctor/Master of Business Administration Full-time and part-time. 105 to 127 total credits required. 42 to 60 months to complete program. *Concentrations:* accounting, business information science, electronic commerce (E-commerce), entrepreneurship, finance, international business, management information systems, marketing, operations management.

MBA—Master of Business Administration Full-time and part-time. 30 to 52 total credits required. 12 to 60 months to complete program. *Concentrations:* accounting, business information science, electronic commerce (E-commerce), entrepreneurship, finance, international business, management information systems, marketing, operations management.

RESOURCES AND SERVICES 130 on-campus PCs are available to graduate business students. Access to Internet/World Wide Web, online (class) registration, and online grade reports available. *Personal computer requirements:* Graduate business students are strongly recommended to purchase or lease a personal computer. *Special opportunities include:* An international exchange program is available. *Placement services include:* Alumni network, career placement, career counseling/planning, electronic job bank, resume referral, career fairs, job interviews arranged, resume preparation, and career library.

EXPENSES *Tuition:* Full-time: $18,738. Part-time: $4164 per semester. *Tuition (international):* Full-time: $18,738. Part-time: $4164 per semester. *Required fees:* Full-time: $75. Part-time: $25 per semester.

FINANCIAL AID (2007–08) Fellowships, grants, loans, research assistantships, and scholarships. Aid is available to part-time students. *Financial aid application deadline:* 3/15.

Financial Aid Contact Mr. Jeff Daniels, Director, Office of Financial Aid, 300 College Park Avenue, Dayton, OH 45469-1305. *Phone:* 937-229-4311. *Fax:* 937-229-4545. *E-mail:* jdaniels@udayton.edu.

INTERNATIONAL STUDENTS 13% of students enrolled are international students. *Services and facilities:* Counseling/support services, ESL/language courses, Housing location assistance, International student organization, Language tutoring, Orientation, Visa Services. Financial aid is available to international students. *Required with application:* TOEFL

University of Dayton (continued)

with recommended score of 213 (computer), 550 (paper), or 79 (Internet); proof of adequate funds; proof of health/immunizations.

International Student Contact Mr. John Huart, International Student Advisor, 300 College Park Avenue, Dayton, OH 45469-1323. *Phone:* 937-229-2094. *E-mail:* jhuart@udayton.edu.

APPLICATION *Required:* GMAT, application form, baccalaureate/first degree, transcripts of college work. *Recommended:* Essay, 2 letters of recommendation, personal statement, resume/curriculum vitae, work experience. *Application fee:* $0. *Deadlines:* 3/1 for fall (international), 7/1 for winter (international), 1/1 for spring (international). Applications for domestic students are processed on a rolling basis.

Application Contact Jeffrey A. Carter, Assistant Director, MBA Program, 300 College Park Avenue, Dayton, OH 45469-2234. *Phone:* 937-229-3733. *Fax:* 937-229-3882. *E-mail:* mba@udayton.edu.

The University of Findlay
College of Business

Findlay, Ohio

Phone: 419-434-4640 **Fax:** 419-434-5517 **E-mail:** riffle@findlay.edu

Business Program(s) Web Site: http://www.findlay.edu/

Graduate Business Unit Enrollment *Total:* 707 (125 full-time; 582 part-time; 263 women; 489 international). *Average Age:* 25.

Graduate Business Faculty *Total:* 34 (19 full-time; 15 part-time).

Admissions *Applied:* 270. *Admitted:* 235. *Enrolled:* 212. *Average GMAT:* 475. *Average GPA:* 3.1

Academic Calendar Quarters.

After Graduation (Class of 2006–07) *Employed within 3 months of graduation:* 100%. *Average starting salary:* $35,000.

DEGREE MBA

MBA—Master of Business Administration Full-time and part-time. Distance learning option. At least 33 total credits required. 12 to 60 months to complete program. *Concentrations:* accounting, finance, health care, hospitality management, human resources management, international business, marketing, organizational management, public management.

RESOURCES AND SERVICES 210 on-campus PCs are available to graduate business students. Access to Internet/World Wide Web, online (class) registration, and online grade reports available. *Personal computer requirements:* Graduate business students are strongly recommended to purchase or lease a personal computer. *Special opportunities include:* An internship program is available. *Placement services include:* Alumni network, career placement, career counseling/planning, electronic job bank, career fairs, job interviews arranged, resume preparation, and career library.

EXPENSES *Tuition:* Full-time: $13,095. *Tuition (international):* Full-time: $13,095. *Required fees:* Full-time: $460. Part-time: $360 per term. Tuition and/or fees vary by number of courses or credits taken and academic program. *Typical graduate housing cost:* $8026 (including board), $4024 (room only).

FINANCIAL AID (2007–08) Loans, research assistantships, teaching assistantships, and work study. Aid is available to part-time students. *Financial aid application deadline:* 4/15.

Financial Aid Contact Arman Habegger, Financial Aid Director, 1000 North Main Street, Findlay, OH 45840-3653. *Phone:* 419-434-4791. *Fax:* 419-434-4898. *E-mail:* habegger@findlay.edu.

INTERNATIONAL STUDENTS 69% of students enrolled are international students. *Services and facilities:* Counseling/support services, ESL/language courses, Housing location assistance, International student housing, International student organization, Language tutoring, Orientation, Visa Services. Financial aid is not available to international students. *Required with application:* TOEFL with recommended score of 213

(computer) or 550 (paper); proof of adequate funds; proof of health/immunizations. *Recommended with application:* IELT with recommended score of 7.

International Student Contact Deborah VanAtta, Director of International Student Services, 1000 North Main Street, Findlay, OH 45840. *Phone:* 419-434-4558. *Fax:* 419-434-5507. *E-mail:* vanatta@findlay.edu.

APPLICATION *Required:* GMAT, application form, baccalaureate/first degree, transcripts of college work. School will accept GRE. *Recommended:* Interview. *Application fee:* $25. Applications for domestic and international students are processed on a rolling basis.

Application Contact Heather L. Riffle, Assistant to the Dean, Graduate and Professional Studies, 1000 North Main Street, Findlay, OH 45840-3653. *Phone:* 419-434-4640. *Fax:* 419-434-5517. *E-mail:* riffle@findlay.edu.

University of Phoenix–Cincinnati Campus
College of Graduate Business and Management

West Chester, Ohio

Phone: 480-317-6200 **Fax:** 480-643-1479 **E-mail:** beth.barilla@phoenix.edu

DEGREES M Mgt • MBA

M Mgt—Master of Management Full-time. Up to 40 total credits required. *Concentration:* organizational management.

MBA—Master of Business Administration Full-time. At least 45 total credits required. *Concentration:* administration.

MBA—Master of Business Administration/Accounting Full-time. Up to 46 total credits required. *Concentration:* accounting.

MBA—Master of Business Administration/Global Management Full-time. Up to 46 total credits required. *Concentration:* international business.

MBA—Master of Business Administration/Human Resource Management Full-time. Up to 45 total credits required. *Concentration:* human resources management.

MBA—Master of Business Administration/Marketing Full-time. Up to 45 total credits required. *Concentration:* marketing.

MBA—Master of Business Administration/Public Administration Full-time. Up to 45 total credits required. *Concentration:* public policy and administration.

MBA—Master of Business Administration/e-Business Full-time. Up to 46 total credits required. *Concentration:* electronic commerce (E-commerce).

RESOURCES AND SERVICES Access to online grade reports available. *Personal computer requirements:* Graduate business students are strongly recommended to purchase or lease a personal computer. *Placement services include:* Alumni network.

Application Contact Beth Barilla, Associate Vice President of Student Admissions and Services, Mail Stop AA-K101, 4615 East Elwood Street, Phoenix, AZ 85040-1958. *Phone:* 480-317-6200. *Fax:* 480-643-1479. *E-mail:* beth.barilla@phoenix.edu.

University of Phoenix–Cleveland Campus
College of Graduate Business and Management

Independence, Ohio

Phone: 480-317-6200 **Fax:** 480-643-1479 **E-mail:** beth.barilla@phoenix.edu

Business Program(s) Web Site: http://www.phoenix.edu

DEGREES M Mgt • MBA

M Mgt—Master of Management Full-time. Up to 40 total credits required. *Concentration:* organizational management.

MBA—Master of Business Administration Full-time. At least 45 total credits required. *Concentration:* administration.

MBA—Master of Business Administration/Human Resource Management Full-time. Up to 45 total credits required. *Concentration:* human resources management.

MBA—Master of Business Administration/Marketing Full-time. Up to 45 total credits required. *Concentration:* marketing.

MBA—Master of Business Administration/Public Administration Full-time. Up to 45 total credits required. *Concentration:* public policy and administration.

MBA—Master of Business Administration/e-Business Full-time. Up to 46 total credits required. *Concentration:* electronic commerce (E-commerce).

RESOURCES AND SERVICES Access to online grade reports available. *Personal computer requirements:* Graduate business students are strongly recommended to purchase or lease a personal computer. *Placement services include:* Alumni network.

Application Contact Beth Barilla, Associate Vice President of Student Admissions and Services, Mail Stop AA-K101, 4615 East Elwood Street, Phoenix, AZ 85040-1958. *Phone:* 480-317-6200. *Fax:* 480-643-1479. *E-mail:* beth.barilla@phoenix.edu.

University of Phoenix–Columbus Ohio Campus

College of Graduate Business and Management

Columbus, Ohio

Phone: 480-317-6200 **Fax:** 480-643-1479 **E-mail:** beth.barilla@phoenix.edu

DEGREES M Mgt • MBA

M Mgt—Master of Organizational Management Full-time. At least 40 total credits required. *Concentration:* organizational management.

MBA—Global Management Full-time. At least 45 total credits required. *Concentration:* international business.

MBA—Human Resource Management Full-time. At least 45 total credits required. *Concentration:* human resources management.

MBA—Marketing Full-time. At least 45 total credits required. *Concentration:* marketing.

MBA—Master of Business Administration Full-time. At least 39 total credits required. *Concentration:* administration.

MBA—Public Administration Full-time. At least 45 total credits required. *Concentration:* public policy and administration.

RESOURCES AND SERVICES Access to online grade reports available. *Personal computer requirements:* Graduate business students are strongly recommended to purchase or lease a personal computer. *Placement services include:* Alumni network.

Application Contact Beth Barilla, Associate Vice President of Student Admissions and Services, Mail Stop AA-K101, 4615 East Elwood Street, Phoenix, AZ 85040-1958. *Phone:* 480-317-6200. *Fax:* 480-643-1479. *E-mail:* beth.barilla@phoenix.edu.

The University of Toledo

College of Business Administration

Toledo, Ohio

Phone: 419-530-2513 **Fax:** 419-530-7260 **E-mail:** mba@utoledo.edu

Business Program(s) Web Site: http://www.utoledo.edu/business/COBAProspectiveStudents/GraduatePrograms.html

Graduate Business Unit Enrollment *Total:* 335 (48 full-time; 287 part-time; 113 women; 74 international). *Average Age:* 28.

Graduate Business Faculty *Total:* 79 (75 full-time; 4 part-time).

Admissions *Applied:* 166. *Admitted:* 147. *Enrolled:* 80. *Average GMAT:* 520. *Average GPA:* 3.2

Academic Calendar Semesters.

Accreditation AACSB—The Association to Advance Collegiate Schools of Business.

After Graduation (Class of 2006–07) *Employed within 3 months of graduation:* 97%. *Average starting salary:* $45,000.

DEGREES MBA • MS

MBA—Executive Master of Business Administration Full-time. Minimum 3-5 years professional work experience. At least 42 total credits required. Maximum of 15 months to complete program. *Concentrations:* entrepreneurship, management, technology management.

MBA—Traditional MBA Full-time and part-time. 36 to 54 total credits required. 12 to 72 months to complete program. *Concentrations:* administration, combined degrees, entrepreneurship, finance, information systems, international business, law, leadership, management, marketing, operations management.

MS—Master of Science in Accounting Full-time and part-time. At least 30 total credits required. 12 to 72 months to complete program. *Concentration:* accounting.

RESOURCES AND SERVICES 700 on-campus PCs are available to graduate business students. Access to Internet/World Wide Web, online (class) registration, and online grade reports available. *Personal computer requirements:* Graduate business students are strongly recommended to purchase or lease a personal computer. *Special opportunities include:* An internship program is available. *Placement services include:* Alumni network, career placement, career counseling/planning, electronic job bank, resume referral, career fairs, job interviews arranged, resume preparation, and career library.

EXPENSES *Tuition (state resident):* Full-time: $5377. Part-time: $448 per credit hour. *Tuition (nonresident):* Full-time: $9783. Part-time: $815 per credit hour. *Tuition (international):* Full-time: $9783. Part-time: $815 per credit hour. Tuition and/or fees vary by number of courses or credits taken, academic program, and local reciprocity agreements.

FINANCIAL AID (2007–08) 87 students received aid, including loans, research assistantships, and scholarships. Aid is available to part-time students. *Financial aid application deadline:* 3/1.

Financial Aid Contact Office of Student Financial Aid, 2801 West Bancroft Street, Rocket Hall, Mail Stop 314, Toledo, OH 43606-3398. *Phone:* 419-530-8700. *Fax:* 419-530-5835.

INTERNATIONAL STUDENTS 22% of students enrolled are international students. *Services and facilities:* Counseling/support services, ESL/language courses, Housing location assistance, International student housing, International student organization, Orientation, Visa Services. Financial aid is available to international students. *Required with application:* IELT with recommended score of 6; TOEFL with recommended score of 213 (computer), 550 (paper), or 80 (Internet); proof of adequate funds; proof of health/immunizations.

International Student Contact Ms. Michelle Arbogast, Manager of Support Services, Graduate Studies, University Hall 3240, Toledo, OH 43606-3390. *Phone:* 419-530-2283. *Fax:* 419-530-6137. *E-mail:* michelle.arbogast@utoledo.edu.

The University of Toledo (continued)

APPLICATION *Required:* GMAT, application form, baccalaureate/first degree, 3 letters of recommendation, personal statement, transcripts of college work. *Recommended:* Resume/curriculum vitae. *Application fee:* $45. Applications for domestic and international students are processed on a rolling basis.

Application Contact Robert R Detwiler, Adviser/Recruiter, 2801 West Bancroft, MS 103, Toledo, OH 43606-3390. *Phone:* 419-530-2513. *Fax:* 419-530-7260. *E-mail:* mba@utoledo.edu.

Walsh University

Program in Business Administration

North Canton, Ohio

Phone: 330-490-7171 **Fax:** 330-490-7165 **E-mail:** bfreshour@walsh.edu

Business Program(s) Web Site: http://www.walsh.edu

Graduate Business Unit Enrollment *Total:* 120 (13 full-time; 107 part-time; 57 women; 2 international). *Average Age:* 30.

Graduate Business Faculty *Total:* 13 (4 full-time; 9 part-time).

Admissions *Applied:* 58. *Admitted:* 57. *Enrolled:* 45. *Average GMAT:* 525. *Average GPA:* 3.2

Academic Calendar Trimesters.

DEGREE MBA

MBA—Master of Business Administration Full-time and part-time. At least 36 total credits required. 12 to 60 months to complete program. *Concentrations:* health administration, management, marketing.

RESOURCES AND SERVICES 335 on-campus PCs are available to graduate business students. Access to Internet/World Wide Web, online (class) registration, and online grade reports available. *Personal computer requirements:* Graduate business students are not required to have a personal computer. *Placement services include:* Alumni network, career placement, career counseling/planning, resume referral, career fairs, job interviews arranged, resume preparation, and career library.

EXPENSES *Tuition:* Full-time: $9270. Part-time: $515 per credit hour. *Tuition (international):* Full-time: $9270. Part-time: $515 per credit hour. *Graduate housing:* Room and board costs vary by number of occupants, type of accommodation, and type of board plan. *Typical cost:* $6680 (including board), $3670 (room only).

FINANCIAL AID (2007–08) 32 students received aid, including loans and research assistantships. Aid is available to part-time students. *Financial aid application deadline:* 3/1.

Financial Aid Contact Holly Van Gilder, Director of Financial Aid, 2020 East Maple Street, North Canton, OH 44720-3396. *Phone:* 330-490-7367. *Fax:* 330-490-7372. *E-mail:* hvangilder@walsh.edu.

INTERNATIONAL STUDENTS 2% of students enrolled are international students. *Services and facilities:* Counseling/support services, ESL/language courses, International student organization, Orientation. Financial aid is not available to international students. *Required with application:* TOEFL with recommended score of 173 (computer), 500 (paper), or 61 (Internet); proof of adequate funds. *Recommended with application:* Proof of health/immunizations.

International Student Contact Clark Harvey, Admissions Counselor, 2020 East Maple Street, North Canton, OH 44720-3396. *Phone:* 330-490-7349. *Fax:* 330-499-8518. *E-mail:* charvey@walsh.edu.

APPLICATION *Required:* GMAT, application form, baccalaureate/first degree, interview, resume/curriculum vitae, transcripts of college work. *Application fee:* $25. Applications for domestic and international students are processed on a rolling basis.

Application Contact Mr. Brett Freshour, Vice President of Enrollment Management, 2020 East Maple Street, North Canton, OH 44720-3396. *Phone:* 330-490-7171. *Fax:* 330-490-7165. *E-mail:* bfreshour@walsh.edu.

Wright State University

Raj Soin College of Business

Dayton, Ohio

Phone: 937-775-2437 **Fax:** 937-775-3545 **E-mail:** michael.evans@wright.edu

Business Program(s) Web Site: http://www.wright.edu/business/mba/

Accreditation AACSB—The Association to Advance Collegiate Schools of Business.

DEGREES M Acc • MBA • MBA/MS • MS

M Acc—Master of Accountancy Full-time and part-time. 45 to 108 total credits required. 12 to 60 months to complete program. *Concentration:* accounting.

MBA—Master of Business Administration Full-time and part-time. 48 to 64 total credits required. 12 to 60 months to complete program. *Concentrations:* economics, finance, international business, management, management information systems, marketing, project management, supply chain management.

MBA/MS—Master of Business Administration/Master of Science in Nursing Full-time and part-time. 90 to 104 total credits required. 24 to 60 months to complete program. *Concentration:* combined degrees.

MBA/MS—Master of Business Administration/Master of Science in Social and Applied Economics Full-time and part-time. 84 to 104 total credits required. 18 to 60 months to complete program. *Concentration:* combined degrees.

MS—Master of Science in Logistics Part-time. Distance learning option. 40 total credits required. 12 months to complete program. *Concentration:* supply chain management.

MS—Master of Science in Social and Applied Economics Full-time and part-time. 48 to 60 total credits required. 12 to 60 months to complete program. *Concentration:* economics.

RESOURCES AND SERVICES 60 on-campus PCs are available to graduate business students. Access to Internet/World Wide Web, online (class) registration, and online grade reports available. *Personal computer requirements:* Graduate business students are not required to have a personal computer. *Special opportunities include:* An international exchange program and an internship program are available. *Placement services include:* Alumni network, career placement, job search course, career counseling/planning, electronic job bank, resume referral, career fairs, job interviews arranged, resume preparation, and career library.

Application Contact Michael R. Evans, Director of MBA Programs, 110 Rike Hall, Dayton, OH 45435. *Phone:* 937-775-2437. *Fax:* 937-775-3545. *E-mail:* michael.evans@wright.edu.

Xavier University

Williams College of Business

Cincinnati, Ohio

Phone: 513-745-3525 **Fax:** 513-745-2929 **E-mail:** whelana@xavier.edu

Business Program(s) Web Site: http://www.xavier.edu/williams/

Graduate Business Unit Enrollment *Total:* 994 (994 part-time; 340 women; 25 international). *Average Age:* 27.

Graduate Business Faculty *Total:* 74 (57 full-time; 17 part-time).

Admissions *Applied:* 290. *Admitted:* 210. *Enrolled:* 163. *Average GMAT:* 550. *Average GPA:* 3.3

Academic Calendar Semesters.

Accreditation AACSB—The Association to Advance Collegiate Schools of Business.

After Graduation (Class of 2006–07) *Employed within 3 months of graduation:* 84%. *Average starting salary:* $69,628.

DEGREES MBA • MBA/Diploma • MBA/MHSA • MBA/MSN

MBA—Executive Master of Business Administration Part-time. At least 48 total credits required. 19 months to complete program. *Concentration:* executive programs.

MBA—Weekend Master of Business Administration Program Part-time. All foundation skill courses must be completed before entry. At least 36 total credits required. 24 months to complete program. *Concentration:* general MBA.

MBA—West Chester Part-time. 56 total credits required. 22 months to complete program. *Concentration:* general MBA.

MBA—Working Professionals Evening Master of Business Administration Program Full-time and part-time. 36 to 56 total credits required. 18 to 72 months to complete program. *Concentrations:* electronic commerce (E-commerce), finance, general MBA, information systems, international business, marketing.

MBA/Diploma—Deerfield MBA Part-time. 56 total credits required. 22 months to complete program. *Concentration:* general MBA.

MBA/MHSA—Master of Business Administration/Master of Health Services Administration Full-time and part-time. 92 to 105 total credits required. 36 to 72 months to complete program. *Concentration:* combined degrees.

MBA/MSN—Master of Business Administration/Master of Science in Nursing Full-time and part-time. 56 to 65 total credits required. 36 to 72 months to complete program. *Concentration:* combined degrees.

RESOURCES AND SERVICES 250 on-campus PCs are available to graduate business students. Access to Internet/World Wide Web, online (class) registration, and online grade reports available. *Personal computer requirements:* Graduate business students are not required to have a personal computer. *Special opportunities include:* An international exchange program and an internship program are available. *Placement services include:* Alumni network, job search course, career counseling/planning, electronic job bank, resume referral, career fairs, job interviews arranged, resume preparation, and career library.

EXPENSES *Tuition:* Part-time: $680 per credit hour. *Tuition (international):* Part-time: $680 per credit hour. Tuition and/or fees vary by campus location.

FINANCIAL AID (2007–08) 227 students received aid, including grants, loans, research assistantships, and scholarships. Aid is available to part-time students. *Financial aid application deadline:* 5/1.

Financial Aid Contact Mr. Paul Calme, Director, Financial Aid, 3800 Victory Parkway, Cincinnati, OH 45207-5411. *Phone:* 513-742-3142. *Fax:* 513-745-2806. *E-mail:* calme@xavier.edu.

INTERNATIONAL STUDENTS 3% of students enrolled are international students. *Services and facilities:* Counseling/support services, ESL/language courses, International student housing, International student organization, Orientation, Visa Services. Financial aid is available to international students. *Required with application:* TOEFL with recommended score of 213 (computer), 550 (paper), or 78 (Internet); proof of adequate funds; proof of health/immunizations.

International Student Contact Ms. Anna Marie Whelan, Assistant Director, MBA Enrollment Services, 3800 Victory Parkway, Cincinnati, OH 45207-3221. *Phone:* 513-745-3525. *Fax:* 513-714-2929. *E-mail:* whelana@xavier.edu.

APPLICATION *Required:* GMAT, application form, baccalaureate/first degree, resume/curriculum vitae, transcripts of college work. *Recommended:* 2 letters of recommendation, 3 years of work experience. *Application fee:* $35. *Deadlines:* 6/1 for fall (international), 10/1 for spring (international). Applications for domestic students are processed on a rolling basis.

Application Contact Ms. Anna Marie Whelan, Assistant Director, MBA Programs, 3800 Victory Parkway, Cincinnati, OH 45207-3221. *Phone:* 513-745-3525. *Fax:* 513-745-2929. *E-mail:* whelana@xavier.edu.

Youngstown State University
Warren P. Williamson Jr. College of Business Administration

Youngstown, Ohio

Phone: 330-941-3092 **Fax:** 330-941-1580 **E-mail:** jkweintz@ysu.edu

Business Program(s) Web Site: http://www.wcba.ysu.edu/mba.htm

Graduate Business Unit Enrollment *Total:* 105 (20 full-time; 85 part-time). *Average Age:* 27.

Graduate Business Faculty *Total:* 60 (40 full-time; 20 part-time).

Admissions *Applied:* 40. *Admitted:* 36. *Enrolled:* 22. *Average GMAT:* 523. *Average GPA:* 3.4

Academic Calendar Semesters.

Accreditation AACSB—The Association to Advance Collegiate Schools of Business.

DEGREE MBA

MBA—Master of Business Administration Full-time and part-time. Resume and letter of intent required. 30 to 48 total credits required. 12 to 72 months to complete program. *Concentrations:* accounting, finance, management, marketing.

RESOURCES AND SERVICES 1,200 on-campus PCs are available to graduate business students. Access to Internet/World Wide Web, online (class) registration, and online grade reports available. *Personal computer requirements:* Graduate business students are strongly recommended to purchase or lease a personal computer. *Special opportunities include:* An international exchange program and an internship program are available. *Placement services include:* Job search course, career counseling/planning, electronic job bank, career fairs, job interviews arranged, resume preparation, and career library.

EXPENSES *Tuition (state resident):* Full-time: $8727.84. Part-time: $363.66 per credit hour. *Tuition (nonresident):* Full-time: $8928. Part-time: $372 per credit hour. *Tuition (international):* Full-time: $8928. Part-time: $372 per credit hour. *Graduate housing:* Room and board costs vary by campus location.

FINANCIAL AID (2007–08) Fellowships, grants, loans, research assistantships, scholarships, teaching assistantships, and work study. *Financial aid application deadline:* 5/20.

Financial Aid Contact Elaine Ruse, Director, Jones Hall, One University Plaza, Youngstown, OH 44555-0002. *Phone:* 330-941-3399. *Fax:* 330-941-1659. *E-mail:* eruse@ysu.edu.

INTERNATIONAL STUDENTS *Services and facilities:* Counseling/support services, ESL/language courses, International student housing, International student organization, Language tutoring, Orientation. Financial aid is available to international students. *Required with application:* TOEFL with recommended score of 213 (computer) or 550 (paper); proof of adequate funds.

International Student Contact Ms. Terry Hjerpe, School of Graduate Studies International Admissions, Tod Hall, Youngstown, OH 44555. *Phone:* 330-941-7250. *Fax:* 330-941-1580. *E-mail:* graduateschool@cc.ysu.edu.

APPLICATION *Required:* GMAT, application form, baccalaureate/first degree, personal statement, resume/curriculum vitae, transcripts of college work. *Recommended:* Letter(s) of recommendation, work experience. *Application fee:* $30, $75 (international). Applications for domestic and international students are processed on a rolling basis.

Application Contact Ms. Tina Weintz, Admissions Director, School of Graduate Studies, One University Plaza, Youngstown, OH 44555-0002. *Phone:* 330-941-3092. *Fax:* 330-941-1580. *E-mail:* jkweintz@ysu.edu.

OKLAHOMA

Cameron University
Office of Graduate Studies

Lawton, Oklahoma

Phone: 580-581-2987 **Fax:** 580-581-5532 **E-mail:** graduate@cameron.edu

Business Program(s) Web Site: http://www.cameron.edu/

Accreditation ACBSP—The American Council of Business Schools and Programs.

DEGREES M Sc • MBA

M Sc—Entrepreneurial Studies Full-time and part-time. Distance learning option. 33 to 45 total credits required. 12 to 72 months to complete program. *Concentration:* entrepreneurship.

MBA—Master of Business Administration Full-time and part-time. Distance learning option. 33 to 45 total credits required. 12 to 72 months to complete program. *Concentration:* general MBA.

RESOURCES AND SERVICES 213 on-campus PCs are available to graduate business students. Access to Internet/World Wide Web and online grade reports available. *Personal computer requirements:* Graduate business students are not required to have a personal computer. *Placement services include:* Resume referral, career fairs, job interviews arranged, and resume preparation.

Application Contact Mrs. Teresa M. Enriquez, School of Graduate Studies, 2800 West Gore Boulevard, Lawton, OK 73505-6377. *Phone:* 580-581-2987. *Fax:* 580-581-5532. *E-mail:* graduate@cameron.edu.

Northeastern State University
College of Business and Technology

Tahlequah, Oklahoma

Phone: 918-456-5511 Ext. 5912 **Fax:** 918-458-2106 **E-mail:** edwar001@nsuok.edu

Business Program(s) Web Site: http://www.nsuok.edu

Graduate Business Unit Enrollment *Total:* 90 (90 part-time; 45 women; 5 international).

Graduate Business Faculty *Total:* 11 (10 full-time; 1 part-time).

Admissions *Applied:* 60. *Admitted:* 50. *Enrolled:* 50. *Average GMAT:* 450. *Average GPA:* 3.0

Academic Calendar Part-time evening program and hybrid evening co-hort.

Accreditation ACBSP—The American Council of Business Schools and Programs.

After Graduation (Class of 2006–07) *Employed within 3 months of graduation:* 95%. *Average starting salary:* $48,000.

DEGREES MBA

MBA—Master of Business Administration Part-time. Professional MBA—3 yrs past undergrad. 22 to 30 total credits required. 22 months to complete program. *Concentration:* leadership.

MBA—Master of Business Administration Full-time and part-time. 36 total credits required. 22 to 36 months to complete program. *Concentration:* management.

RESOURCES AND SERVICES 50 on-campus PCs are available to graduate business students. Access to Internet/World Wide Web and online grade reports available. *Personal computer requirements:* Graduate business students are strongly recommended to purchase or lease a

personal computer. *Placement services include:* Alumni network, career placement, career counseling/planning, electronic job bank, career fairs, job interviews arranged, and resume preparation.

FINANCIAL AID (2007–08) 10 students received aid, including loans, scholarships, and work study. Aid is available to part-time students. *Financial aid application deadline:* 3/1.

Financial Aid Contact Scott Medlin, Director, Student Financial Services, 600 North Grand, Tahlequah, OK 74464. *Phone:* 918-456-5511 Ext. 3410. *Fax:* 918-458-2150. *E-mail:* medlinsa@nsuok.edu.

INTERNATIONAL STUDENTS 6% of students enrolled are international students. *Services and facilities:* Counseling/support services, Housing location assistance, International student organization, Visa Services. Financial aid is not available to international students. *Required with application:* TOEFL with recommended score of 550 (paper); proof of adequate funds.

International Student Contact Kimbra Scott, International Student Coordinator, 2400 West Shawnee, PO Box 549, Muskogee, OK 74402. *Phone:* 918-456-5511 Ext. 5000. *Fax:* 918-458-2106. *E-mail:* ranallo@nsuok.edu.

APPLICATION *Required:* GMAT, application form, baccalaureate/first degree, transcripts of college work. *Recommended:* Essay, interview, letter(s) of recommendation, personal statement, resume/curriculum vitae, work experience. *Deadlines:* 7/1 for fall, 12/1 for winter, 1/1 for spring, 5/1 for summer, 7/1 for fall (international), 12/1 for winter (international), 1/1 for spring (international), 5/1 for summer (international).

Application Contact Dr. Sandra Edwards, MBA Program Director, 2400 West Shawnee, PO Box 549, Muskogee, OK 74402. *Phone:* 918-456-5511 Ext. 5912. *Fax:* 918-458-2106. *E-mail:* edwar001@nsuok.edu.

Oklahoma City University
Meinders School of Business

Oklahoma City, Oklahoma

Phone: 405-208-5050 **Fax:** 405-208-5946 **E-mail:** eprieto@okcu.edu

Business Program(s) Web Site: http://www.okcu.edu/business/

Graduate Business Faculty *Total:* 43 (29 full-time; 14 part-time).

Admissions *Average GPA:* 3.25

Academic Calendar Continuous.

Accreditation ACBSP—The American Council of Business Schools and Programs.

After Graduation (Class of 2006–07) *Employed within 3 months of graduation:* 100%. *Average starting salary:* $55,400.

DEGREES MBA • MSA

MBA—Executive Master of Business Administration Full-time and part-time. 36 to 39 total credits required. 20 to 60 months to complete program. *Concentration:* management.

MBA—Master of Business Administration Full-time and part-time. 36 to 39 total credits required. 20 to 60 months to complete program. *Concentrations:* arts administration/management, finance, health care, international finance, international marketing, management, management information systems, marketing.

MSA—Master of Science in Accounting Full-time and part-time. At least 30 total credits required. 20 to 60 months to complete program. *Concentration:* accounting.

RESOURCES AND SERVICES 264 on-campus PCs are available to graduate business students. Access to Internet/World Wide Web, online (class) registration, and online grade reports available. *Personal computer requirements:* Graduate business students are not required to have a personal computer. *Special opportunities include:* An international exchange program and an internship program are available. *Placement services include:* Alumni network, career placement, job search course, career counseling/planning, electronic job bank, resume referral, career fairs, job interviews arranged, resume preparation, and career library.

EXPENSES *Tuition:* Full-time: $14,040. Part-time: $780 per credit hour. *Tuition (international):* Full-time: $14,040. Part-time: $780 per credit hour. *Required fees:* Full-time: $920. Part-time: $124 per credit hour. *Graduate housing:* Room and board costs vary by number of occupants, type of accommodation, and type of board plan. *Typical cost:* $9100 (including board), $5300 (room only).

FINANCIAL AID (2007–08) Fellowships, loans, scholarships, and work study. *Financial aid application deadline:* 8/1.

Financial Aid Contact Denise Flis, Director of Financial Aid, 2501 North Blackwelder, Oklahoma City, OK 73106. *Phone:* 405-208-5211. *Fax:* 405-208-5466. *E-mail:* dflis@okcu.edu.

INTERNATIONAL STUDENTS *Services and facilities:* Counseling/support services, ESL/language courses, Housing location assistance, International student housing, International student organization, Language tutoring, Orientation, Visa Services. Financial aid is available to international students. *Required with application:* TOEFL with recommended score of 213 (computer) or 550 (paper); proof of adequate funds; proof of health/immunizations.

International Student Contact Julie Sinclair, Director of International Student Office, 2501 North Blackwelder, Oklahoma City, OK 73106. *Phone:* 405-208-5299. *Fax:* 405-208-5946. *E-mail:* jsinclair@okcu.edu.

APPLICATION *Required:* Application form, baccalaureate/first degree, 2 letters of recommendation, personal statement, transcripts of college work. *Recommended:* Interview, work experience. *Application fee:* $30, $70 (international). Applications for domestic and international students are processed on a rolling basis.

Application Contact Eduardo Prieto, Associate Vice President and Dean of Enrollment Services, 2501 North Blackwelder, Oklahoma City, OK 73106. *Phone:* 405-208-5050. *Fax:* 405-208-5946. *E-mail:* eprieto@okcu.edu.

Oklahoma Wesleyan University
Professional Studies Division
Bartlesville, Oklahoma

Phone: 918-728-6143 **E-mail:** jjones@okwu.edu

Business Program(s) Web Site: http://www.okwu.edu

DEGREE   MBA

MBA—Master of Business Administration Full-time. 38 to 40 total credits required. 20 to 22 months to complete program. *Concentrations:* finance, human resources management, management information systems, marketing.

RESOURCES AND SERVICES 47 on-campus PCs are available to graduate business students. Access to Internet/World Wide Web available. *Personal computer requirements:* Graduate business students are required to have a personal computer.

Application Contact Dr. Jody Jones, Director of Enrollment Services, 2201 South Silver Lake Road, Bartlesville, OK 74006. *Phone:* 918-728-6143. *E-mail:* jjones@okwu.edu.

Oral Roberts University
School of Business
Tulsa, Oklahoma

Phone: 918-495-6117 **Fax:** 918-495-7965 **E-mail:** rgunn@oru.edu

Business Program(s) Web Site: http://www.oru.edu/university/departments/schools/bus

Graduate Business Unit Enrollment *Total:* 85 (37 full-time; 48 part-time; 41 women; 18 international).

Graduate Business Faculty *Total:* 8 (7 full-time; 1 part-time).

Admissions *Applied:* 31. *Admitted:* 28. *Enrolled:* 22. *Average GPA:* 3.37

Academic Calendar Semesters.

Accreditation ACBSP—The American Council of Business Schools and Programs.

After Graduation (Class of 2006–07) *Average starting salary:* $39,000.

DEGREES   M Mgt • MBA

M Mgt—Master of Management Full-time and part-time. Distance learning option. 35 to 37 total credits required. Minimum of 18 months to complete program. *Concentrations:* nonprofit management, organizational management.

MBA—Master of Business Administration Full-time and part-time. At least 36 total credits required. Minimum of 18 months to complete program. *Concentrations:* accounting, entrepreneurship, finance, international business, management, marketing, nonprofit management.

RESOURCES AND SERVICES 375 on-campus PCs are available to graduate business students. Access to Internet/World Wide Web, online (class) registration, and online grade reports available. *Personal computer requirements:* Graduate business students are strongly recommended to purchase or lease a personal computer. *Special opportunities include:* An internship program is available. *Placement services include:* Alumni network, career placement, job search course, career counseling/planning, electronic job bank, resume referral, career fairs, job interviews arranged, resume preparation, and career library.

EXPENSES *Tuition:* Full-time: $8100. *Tuition (international):* Full-time: $8100. *Required fees:* Full-time: $500. Part-time: $250 per semester. Tuition and/or fees vary by academic program. *Graduate housing:* Room and board costs vary by number of occupants and type of board plan. *Typical cost:* $1720 (including board).

FINANCIAL AID (2007–08) 69 students received aid, including loans, scholarships, and work study. Aid is available to part-time students.

Financial Aid Contact Mr. Paul Foster, Financial Aid Coordinator, Adult Learning Service Center, 7777 South Lewis Avenue, Tulsa, OK 74171-0001. *Phone:* 918-495-6602. *Fax:* 918-495-7965. *E-mail:* pfoster@oru.edu.

INTERNATIONAL STUDENTS 21% of students enrolled are international students. *Services and facilities:* Counseling/support services, ESL/language courses, International student organization, Orientation, Visa Services. Financial aid is available to international students. *Required with application:* TOEFL with recommended score of 213 (computer) or 550 (paper); proof of adequate funds; proof of health/immunizations.

International Student Contact Director of International Admissions, 7777 South Lewis Avenue, Tulsa, OK 74171-0001. *Phone:* 800-678-8876. *Fax:* 918-495-6488. *E-mail:* admissions@oru.edu.

APPLICATION *Required:* Application form, baccalaureate/first degree, essay, 3 letters of recommendation, personal statement, transcripts of college work. School will accept GMAT. *Recommended:* Resume/curriculum vitae. *Application fee:* $35. Applications for domestic and international students are processed on a rolling basis.

Application Contact Mrs. Rebecca Gunn, Graduate Business Representative, 7777 South Lewis Avenue, Tulsa, OK 74171-0001. *Phone:* 918-495-6117. *Fax:* 918-495-7965. *E-mail:* rgunn@oru.edu.

Southeastern Oklahoma State University
School of Business
Durant, Oklahoma

Phone: 580-745-2200 **Fax:** 580-745-7474 **E-mail:** aramos@sosu.edu

Business Program(s) Web Site: http://www.sosu.edu

Southeastern Oklahoma State University (continued)

Accreditation ACBSP—The American Council of Business Schools and Programs.

DEGREE MBA

MBA—Master of Business Administration Full-time and part-time. Distance learning option. Successful completion of the GMAT is required prior to enrollment in MBA courses. At least 36 total credits required. 24 to 72 months to complete program. *Concentration:* general MBA.

RESOURCES AND SERVICES 25 on-campus PCs are available to graduate business students. Access to Internet/World Wide Web, online (class) registration, and online grade reports available. *Personal computer requirements:* Graduate business students are not required to have a personal computer. *Placement services include:* Alumni network, career placement, career counseling/planning, electronic job bank, resume referral, career fairs, job interviews arranged, and resume preparation.

Application Contact Dr. Doug McMillan, Dean, Graduate School, 1405 North 4th Avenue, PMB 4137, Durant, OK 74701. *Phone:* 580-745-2200. *Fax:* 580-745-7474. *E-mail:* aramos@sosu.edu.

Southern Nazarene University
School of Business

Bethany, Oklahoma

Phone: 405-491-6358 **Fax:** 405-491-6302 **E-mail:** jseyfert@snu.edu

Business Program(s) Web Site: http://www.snu.edu/graduate/departme/business/index.htm

Graduate Business Unit Enrollment *Total:* 170 (170 full-time; 99 women; 5 international). *Average Age:* 37.

Graduate Business Faculty *Total:* 18 (5 full-time; 13 part-time).

Academic Calendar Rolling semesters (non-traditional).

DEGREES EMBA • MBA • MS

EMBA—MBA—Ethical Leadership Full-time. Distance learning option. Minimum of five years middle-management experience. 40 total credits required. 18 to 19 months to complete program. *Concentration:* leadership.

MBA Full-time. 34 to 40 total credits required. 22 to 23 months to complete program. *Concentration:* management.

MS—Master of Science in Management Full-time. 31 total credits required. 17 to 18 months to complete program. *Concentration:* management.

RESOURCES AND SERVICES 35 on-campus PCs are available to graduate business students. Access to Internet/World Wide Web and online grade reports available. *Personal computer requirements:* Graduate business students are required to have a personal computer, the cost of which is included in tuition or other required fees. *Placement services include:* Alumni network, career counseling/planning, electronic job bank, career fairs, resume preparation, and career library.

EXPENSES Tuition and/or fees vary by academic program.

FINANCIAL AID (2007–08) Loans.

Financial Aid Contact Margaret Rohlmeier, Assistant Financial Aid Director, 6729 Northwest 39th Expressway, Bethany, OK 73008-2694. *Phone:* 405-491-6685. *Fax:* 405-491-6302. *E-mail:* mrohlmi@snu.edu.

INTERNATIONAL STUDENTS 3% of students enrolled are international students. Financial aid is not available to international students. *Required with application:* TOEFL with recommended score of 213 (computer), 550 (paper), or 79 (Internet); proof of adequate funds; proof of health/immunizations.

International Student Contact Ms. Lisa Carr, International Admissions Assistant, 6729 Northwest 39th Expressway, Bethany, OK 73008. *Phone:* 405-491-6386. *Fax:* 405-491-6320. *E-mail:* lcarr@snu.edu.

APPLICATION *Required:* Application form, baccalaureate/first degree, essay, resume/curriculum vitae, transcripts of college work. School will accept GMAT. *Recommended:* Work experience. *Application fee:* $35. Applications for domestic and international students are processed on a rolling basis.

Application Contact Mr. Jeff L. Seyfert, Assistant Director, Graduate Studies in Management, 6729 Northwest 39th Expressway, Bethany, OK 73008-2694. *Phone:* 405-491-6358. *Fax:* 405-491-6302. *E-mail:* jseyfert@snu.edu.

University of Central Oklahoma
College of Business Administration

Edmond, Oklahoma

Phone: 405-974-2422 **Fax:** 405-974-3821 **E-mail:** mba@ucok.edu

Business Program(s) Web Site: http://www.busn.ucok.edu/mba

Graduate Business Unit Enrollment *Total:* 164 (85 full-time; 79 part-time; 79 women; 32 international). *Average Age:* 29.

Graduate Business Faculty *Total:* 18 (16 full-time; 2 part-time).

Admissions *Applied:* 104. *Admitted:* 77. *Enrolled:* 55. *Average GMAT:* 522. *Average GPA:* 3.19

Academic Calendar Semesters.

Accreditation ACBSP—The American Council of Business Schools and Programs.

After Graduation (Class of 2006–07) *Average starting salary:* $31,825.

DEGREE MBA

MBA—Master of Business Administration Full-time and part-time. 35 total credits required. 35 months to complete program. *Concentration:* general MBA.

RESOURCES AND SERVICES 100 on-campus PCs are available to graduate business students. Access to Internet/World Wide Web, online (class) registration, and online grade reports available. *Personal computer requirements:* Graduate business students are not required to have a personal computer. *Special opportunities include:* An internship program is available. *Placement services include:* Alumni network, career placement, job search course, career counseling/planning, electronic job bank, resume referral, career fairs, job interviews arranged, resume preparation, and career library.

EXPENSES *Tuition (state resident):* Full-time: $3291. Part-time: $164.55 per credit hour. *Tuition (nonresident):* Full-time: $7906. Part-time: $395.30 per credit hour. *Tuition (international):* Full-time: $7906. Part-time: $395.30 per credit hour. *Required fees:* Full-time: $570. Part-time: $28.50 per credit hour. *Typical graduate housing cost:* $3200 (room only).

FINANCIAL AID (2007–08) 25 students received aid, including research assistantships, scholarships, teaching assistantships, and work study. Aid is available to part-time students. *Financial aid application deadline:* 2/15.

Financial Aid Contact Ms. Sheila Fugett, Director, Financial Aid, 100 North University Drive, Edmond, OK 73034-5209. *Phone:* 405-974-2303. *Fax:* 405-340-7658. *E-mail:* sfugett@ucok.edu.

INTERNATIONAL STUDENTS 20% of students enrolled are international students. *Services and facilities:* Counseling/support services, ESL/language courses, Housing location assistance, International student housing, International student organization, Language tutoring, Orientation, Visa Services. Financial aid is available to international students. *Required with application:* TOEFL with recommended score of 213 (computer), 550 (paper), or 79 (Internet); proof of adequate funds; proof of health/immunizations.

International Student Contact Mr. Timothy Kok, Assistant Director, International Student Services, 100 North University Drive, Box 163, Edmond, OK 73034. *Phone:* 405-974-2370. *Fax:* 405-974-3842. *E-mail:* jkok@ucok.edu.

APPLICATION *Required:* GMAT, application form, baccalaureate/first degree, 2 letters of recommendation, resume/curriculum vitae, transcripts of college work. *Application fee:* $25. Applications for domestic and international students are processed on a rolling basis.

Application Contact Ms. Dawna Terrell, Director, MBA Program, 100 North University Drive, Edmond, OK 73034-5209. *Phone:* 405-974-2422. *Fax:* 405-974-3821. *E-mail:* mba@ucok.edu.

University of Oklahoma
Michael F. Price College of Business

Norman, Oklahoma

Phone: 405-325-2074 **Fax:** 405-325-7753 **E-mail:** mkmorley@ou.edu

Business Program(s) Web Site: http://price.ou.edu/mba/

Graduate Business Unit Enrollment *Total:* 381 (227 full-time; 154 part-time; 120 women; 64 international).

Graduate Business Faculty *Total:* 43 (39 full-time; 4 part-time).

Admissions *Applied:* 262. *Admitted:* 197. *Enrolled:* 155. *Average GMAT:* 594. *Average GPA:* 3.42

Academic Calendar 8-week modules.

Accreditation AACSB—The Association to Advance Collegiate Schools of Business.

After Graduation (Class of 2006–07) *Employed within 3 months of graduation:* 97%. *Average starting salary:* $71,833.

DEGREES JD/MBA • M Acc • MBA • MSMIS

JD/MBA—Juris Doctor/Master of Business Administration Full-time. At least 118 total credits required. 48 to 60 months to complete program. *Concentration:* combined degrees.

M Acc—Master of Accountancy Full-time and part-time. 33 to 63 total credits required. 12 to 60 months to complete program. *Concentration:* accounting.

MBA—Master of Business Administration Full-time and part-time. 47 total credits required. 16 to 60 months to complete program. *Concentrations:* combined degrees, entrepreneurship, finance, general MBA, investments and securities, management information systems, risk management, supply chain management.

MSMIS—Master of Science in Management Information Systems Full-time and part-time. 33 to 39 total credits required. 12 to 60 months to complete program. *Concentration:* management information systems.

RESOURCES AND SERVICES 410 on-campus PCs are available to graduate business students. Access to Internet/World Wide Web, online (class) registration, and online grade reports available. *Personal computer requirements:* Graduate business students are strongly recommended to purchase or lease a personal computer. *Special opportunities include:* An internship program is available. *Placement services include:* Alumni network, career placement, job search course, career counseling/planning, resume referral, career fairs, job interviews arranged, resume preparation, and career library.

EXPENSES *Tuition (state resident):* Full-time: $8048.70. Part-time: $243.90 per credit hour. *Tuition (nonresident):* Full-time: $20,397. Part-time: $618.10 per credit hour. *Tuition (international):* Full-time: $20,397.30. Part-time: $618.10 per credit hour. *Required fees:* Full-time: $2810. Part-time: $357.50 per credit hour. Tuition and/or fees vary by campus location and academic program.

FINANCIAL AID (2007–08) 79 students received aid, including fellowships, loans, research assistantships, scholarships, and teaching assistantships. *Financial aid application deadline:* 7/1.

Financial Aid Contact Gina M. S. Amundson, Director of Graduate Programs, 1003 Asp Avenue, Suite 1040, Norman, OK 73019-4302. *Phone:* 405-325-4118. *Fax:* 405-325-7753. *E-mail:* gamundson@ou.edu.

INTERNATIONAL STUDENTS 17% of students enrolled are international students. *Services and facilities:* Counseling/support services, ESL/language courses, Housing location assistance, International student housing, International student organization, Language tutoring, Orientation, Visa Services. Financial aid is available to international students. *Required with application:* TOEFL with recommended score of 250 (computer), 600 (paper), or 100 (Internet); proof of adequate funds; proof of health/immunizations. *Recommended with application:* IELT with recommended score of 7.

International Student Contact Millie Audas, Director, Office of International Relations, International Relations, SCI 211, Norman, OK 73019. *Phone:* 405-325-1607. *E-mail:* maudas@ou.edu.

APPLICATION *Required:* GMAT, application form, baccalaureate/first degree, 3 letters of recommendation, personal statement, resume/curriculum vitae, transcripts of college work. *Recommended:* Interview, 2 years of work experience. *Application fee:* $40, $90 (international). Applications for domestic and international students are processed on a rolling basis.

Application Contact Kathy Morley, Academic Counselor, 1003 Asp Avenue, Suite 1040, Norman, OK 73019-4302. *Phone:* 405-325-2074. *Fax:* 405-325-7753. *E-mail:* mkmorley@ou.edu.

University of Phoenix–Oklahoma City Campus
College of Graduate Business and Management

Oklahoma City, Oklahoma

Phone: 480-317-6200 **Fax:** 480-643-1479 **E-mail:** beth.barilla@phoenix.edu

Business Program(s) Web Site: http://www.phoenix.edu

DEGREES M Mgt • MA • MBA

M Mgt—Master of Management Full-time. At least 39 total credits required. *Concentration:* management.

MA—Master of Arts in Organizational Management Full-time. At least 40 total credits required. *Concentration:* organizational management.

MBA—Accounting Full-time. At least 51 total credits required. *Concentration:* accounting.

MBA—Global Management Full-time. At least 45 total credits required. *Concentration:* international management.

MBA—Human Resource Management Full-time. At least 45 total credits required. *Concentration:* human resources management.

MBA—e-Business Full-time. At least 45 total credits required. *Concentration:* electronic commerce (E-commerce).

MBA—Master of Business Administration Full-time. At least 45 total credits required. *Concentration:* administration.

RESOURCES AND SERVICES Access to online grade reports available. *Personal computer requirements:* Graduate business students are strongly recommended to purchase or lease a personal computer. *Placement services include:* Alumni network.

Application Contact Beth Barilla, Associate Vice President of Student Admissions and Services, Mail Stop AA-K101, 4615 East Elwood Street, Phoenix, AZ 85040-1958. *Phone:* 480-317-6200. *Fax:* 480-643-1479. *E-mail:* beth.barilla@phoenix.edu.

University of Phoenix–Tulsa Campus
College of Graduate Business and Management

Tulsa, Oklahoma

Phone: 480-317-6200 **Fax:** 480-643-1479 **E-mail:** beth.barilla@phoenix.edu

University of Phoenix–Tulsa Campus (continued)

Business Program(s) Web Site: http://www.phoenix.edu

DEGREES MA • MBA

MA—Master of Arts in Organizational Management Full-time. At least 40 total credits required. *Concentration:* organizational management.

MBA—Accounting Full-time. At least 51 total credits required. *Concentration:* accounting.

MBA—Human Resource Management Full-time. At least 45 total credits required. *Concentration:* human resources management.

MBA—e-Business Full-time. At least 45 total credits required. *Concentration:* electronic commerce (E-commerce).

MBA—Master of Business Administration Full-time. At least 45 total credits required. *Concentration:* administration.

RESOURCES AND SERVICES Access to online grade reports available. *Personal computer requirements:* Graduate business students are strongly recommended to purchase or lease a personal computer. *Placement services include:* Alumni network.

Application Contact Beth Barilla, Associate Vice President of Student Admissions and Services, Mail Stop AA-K101, 4615 East Elwood Street, Phoenix, AZ 85040-1958. *Phone:* 480-317-6200. *Fax:* 480-643-1479. *E-mail:* beth.barilla@phoenix.edu.

University of Tulsa
College of Business Administration

Tulsa, Oklahoma

Phone: 918-631-2553 **Fax:** 918-631-2142 **E-mail:** candace-sitzer@utulsa.edu

Business Program(s) Web Site: http://www.cba.utulsa.edu/programs/graduate/

Graduate Business Unit Enrollment *Total:* 182 (78 full-time; 104 part-time; 114 women; 28 international). *Average Age:* 32.

Graduate Business Faculty 30 full-time.

Admissions *Applied:* 107. *Admitted:* 51. *Enrolled:* 41. *Average GMAT:* 569. *Average GPA:* 3.35

Academic Calendar Semesters.

Accreditation AACSB—The Association to Advance Collegiate Schools of Business.

After Graduation (Class of 2006–07) *Employed within 3 months of graduation:* 87%. *Average starting salary:* $59,405.

DEGREES JD/M Tax • JD/MBA • M Tax • MBA • MBA/MSF • MF • MS/MTax • MSF

JD/M Tax—JD/MTAX—Juris Doctor/Master of Taxation Full-time and part-time. Distance learning option. 103 total credits required. 36 to 60 months to complete program. *Concentration:* combined degrees.

JD/MBA—Juris Doctor/Master of Business Administration Full-time and part-time. 103 to 133 total credits required. 36 to 60 months to complete program. *Concentration:* combined degrees.

M Tax—Master of Taxation—Online Part-time. Distance learning option. 30 total credits required. 18 to 72 months to complete program. *Concentration:* taxation.

MBA—Master of Business Administration Full-time and part-time. 31 to 49 total credits required. 15 to 72 months to complete program. *Concentrations:* accounting, finance, management, management information systems, taxation.

MBA/MSF Full-time and part-time. 55 to 81 total credits required. 36 to 72 months to complete program. *Concentrations:* accounting, finance, financial engineering, financial management/planning, international finance, management, management information systems, risk management, taxation.

MF—Master of Science in Finance Full-time and part-time. 30 to 48 total credits required. 15 to 72 months to complete program. *Concentrations:* finance, financial engineering, financial management/planning, risk management.

MS/MTax—Master of Science/Master of Taxation Part-time. Distance learning option. 30 to 36 total credits required. 21 to 72 months to complete program. *Concentration:* taxation.

MSF—Master of Science in Finance/Master of Science in Applied Mathematics Full-time and part-time. 55 to 81 total credits required. 36 to 72 months to complete program. *Concentrations:* finance, financial engineering, financial management/planning, risk management.

RESOURCES AND SERVICES 216 on-campus PCs are available to graduate business students. Access to Internet/World Wide Web and online grade reports available. *Personal computer requirements:* Graduate business students are strongly recommended to purchase or lease a personal computer. *Special opportunities include:* An international exchange program and an internship program are available. *Placement services include:* Alumni network, career placement, career counseling/planning, electronic job bank, resume referral, career fairs, job interviews arranged, and resume preparation.

EXPENSES *Tuition:* Full-time: $14,004. Part-time: $778 per credit hour. *Tuition (international):* Full-time: $14,004. Part-time: $778 per credit hour. *Required fees:* Full-time: $54. Part-time: $3 per credit hour. *Graduate housing:* Room and board costs vary by number of occupants, type of accommodation, and type of board plan. *Typical cost:* $7404 (including board), $4090 (room only).

FINANCIAL AID (2007–08) 127 students received aid, including fellowships, loans, research assistantships, scholarships, and work study. Aid is available to part-time students. *Financial aid application deadline:* 3/1.

Financial Aid Contact Vicki A. Hendrickson, Director of Student Financial Services, Collins Hall, 800 South Tucker Drive, Tulsa, OK 74104-9700. *Phone:* 918-631-2526. *Fax:* 918-631-5105. *E-mail:* vicki-hendrickson@utulsa.edu.

INTERNATIONAL STUDENTS 15% of students enrolled are international students. *Services and facilities:* Counseling/support services, ESL/language courses, Housing location assistance, International student organization, Orientation. Financial aid is available to international students. *Required with application:* IELT with recommended score of 6.5; TOEFL with recommended score of 232 (computer), 575 (paper), or 90 (Internet); proof of adequate funds; proof of health/immunizations.

International Student Contact Pam Smith, Dean of International Services and Programs, Westby Hall, 800 South Tucker Drive, Tulsa, OK 74104-9700. *Phone:* 918-631-2329. *Fax:* 918-631-3322. *E-mail:* pamela-smith@utulsa.edu.

APPLICATION *Required:* GMAT, application form, baccalaureate/first degree, essay, 3 letters of recommendation, personal statement, resume/curriculum vitae, transcripts of college work. *Recommended:* Interview, work experience. *Application fee:* $40. Applications for domestic and international students are processed on a rolling basis.

Application Contact Candace Sitzer, Enrollment Coordinator, 800 South Tucker Drive, BAH 217, Tulsa, OK 74104-9700. *Phone:* 918-631-2553. *Fax:* 918-631-2142. *E-mail:* candace-sitzer@utulsa.edu.

OREGON

DeVry University
Keller Graduate School of Management

Portland, Oregon

Phone: 503-296-7468

DEGREES MAFM • MBA • MHRM • MIS • MPA • MPM

MAFM—Master of Accounting and Financial Management Full-time and part-time. Distance learning option. At least 44 total credits required. 18 to 60 months to complete program. *Concentrations:* accounting, financial management/planning.

MBA—Master of Business Administration Full-time and part-time. Distance learning option. At least 48 total credits required. 18 to 60 months to complete program. *Concentration:* management.

MHRM—Master of Human Resources Management Full-time and part-time. Distance learning option. At least 45 total credits required. 18 to 60 months to complete program. *Concentration:* human resources management.

MIS—Master of Information Systems Management Full-time and part-time. Distance learning option. At least 45 total credits required. 18 to 60 months to complete program. *Concentration:* information systems.

MPA—Master of Public Administration Full-time and part-time. Distance learning option. At least 45 total credits required. 18 to 60 months to complete program. *Concentration:* public policy and administration.

MPM—Master of Project Management Full-time and part-time. Distance learning option. At least 42 total credits required. 18 to 60 months to complete program. *Concentration:* project management.

Application Contact Admissions Office, Portland Center, Peterkort Center II, 9755 SW Barnes Road, Suite 150, Portland, OR 97225. *Phone:* 503-296-7468.

George Fox University

School of Management

Newberg, Oregon

Phone: 503-554-6123 **Fax:** 503-554-6111 **E-mail:** mba@georgefox.edu

Business Program(s) Web Site: http://www.georgefox.edu/som

Graduate Business Unit Enrollment *Total:* 214 (214 part-time; 67 women; 8 international). *Average Age:* 34.

Graduate Business Faculty *Total:* 17 (13 full-time; 4 part-time).

Admissions *Applied:* 51. *Admitted:* 38. *Enrolled:* 34. *Average GPA:* 3.25

Academic Calendar Trimesters.

After Graduation (Class of 2006–07) *Employed within 3 months of graduation:* 93%.

DEGREES EMBA • MBA

EMBA—Master of Business Administration Executive Track Part-time. Five or more years of executive responsibility required. 42 total credits required. Minimum of 26 months to complete program. *Concentration:* executive programs.

MBA—Master of Business Administration Professional Track Part-time. Five years work experience required including 2 years professional or managerial experience. 42 total credits required. Minimum of 26 months to complete program. *Concentrations:* general MBA, leadership, management.

RESOURCES AND SERVICES 17 on-campus PCs are available to graduate business students. Access to Internet/World Wide Web, online (class) registration, and online grade reports available. *Personal computer requirements:* Graduate business students are required to have a personal computer. *Placement services include:* Career counseling/planning, electronic job bank, resume referral, resume preparation, and career library.

FINANCIAL AID (2007–08) 57 students received aid, including loans. Aid is available to part-time students. *Financial aid application deadline:* 8/1.

Financial Aid Contact Heidi Thomason, Student Financial Services Counselor, 414 North Meridian, Newberg, OR 97132. *Phone:* 800-765-4369 Ext. 2232. *Fax:* 503-554-2232. *E-mail:* sfs@georgefox.edu.

INTERNATIONAL STUDENTS 4% of students enrolled are international students. *Services and facilities:* Counseling/support services, Visa Services. Financial aid is not available to international students. *Required with application:* TOEFL with recommended score of 213 (computer) or 550 (paper); proof of adequate funds; proof of health/immunizations.

International Student Contact Ms. Robin Halverson, MBA Admission Counselor, 12753 Southwest 68th Avenue, Portland, OR 97223. *Phone:* 503-554-6123. *Fax:* 503-554-6111. *E-mail:* mba@georgefox.edu.

APPLICATION *Required:* Application form, baccalaureate/first degree, essay, interview, 3 letters of recommendation, resume/curriculum vitae, transcripts of college work, 5 years of work experience. *Recommended:* Personal statement. *Application fee:* $40. Applications for domestic and international students are processed on a rolling basis.

Application Contact Ms. Robin Halverson, MBA Admission Counselor, 12753 Southwest 68th Avenue, Portland, OR 97223. *Phone:* 503-554-6123. *Fax:* 503-554-6111. *E-mail:* mba@georgefox.edu.

Marylhurst University

Department of Business Administration

Marylhurst, Oregon

Phone: 503-675-3960 **Fax:** 503-697-5597 **E-mail:** hmather@marylhurst.edu

Business Program(s) Web Site: http://www.marylhurst.edu/

Graduate Business Unit Enrollment *Total:* 336 (30 full-time; 306 part-time; 183 women; 13 international). *Average Age:* 36.

Graduate Business Faculty *Total:* 25 (1 full-time; 24 part-time).

Admissions *Average GMAT:* 435. *Average GPA:* 3.3

Academic Calendar Quarters.

After Graduation (Class of 2006–07) *Employed within 3 months of graduation:* 90%.

DEGREES MBA

MBA—Accelerated Online MBA Full-time and part-time. Distance learning option. GMAT or minimum GPA of 3.0 or 5+ years' work experience and interview. 48 total credits required. 18 months to complete program. *Concentrations:* general MBA, health care, management, nonprofit management, real estate.

MBA—Blended MBA—Online/On Campus Full-time and part-time. Distance learning option. GMAT or minimum GPA of 3.0 or 5+ years' work experience and interview. 48 to 52 total credits required. 12 to 60 months to complete program. *Concentrations:* finance, general MBA, management, marketing, organizational behavior/development.

MBA—MBA—Saturday Cohort MBA Full-time and part-time. GMAT or minimum GPA of 3.0 or 5+ years' work experience and interview. 52 total credits required. 24 months to complete program. *Concentrations:* general MBA, management.

RESOURCES AND SERVICES 35 on-campus PCs are available to graduate business students. Access to Internet/World Wide Web, online (class) registration, and online grade reports available. *Personal computer requirements:* Graduate business students are strongly recommended to purchase or lease a personal computer. *Special opportunities include:* An internship program is available. *Placement services include:* Alumni network, career placement, job search course, career counseling/planning, electronic job bank, job interviews arranged, resume preparation, and career library.

FINANCIAL AID (2007–08) 69 students received aid, including loans, scholarships, and work study. Aid is available to part-time students.

Marylhurst University (continued)

Financial Aid Contact Tracy Reisinger, Director, Financial Aid, 17600 Pacific Highway 43, PO Box 026, Marylhurst, OR 97036-0261. *Phone:* 503-699-6253. *Fax:* 503-635-6585. *E-mail:* finaid@marylhurst.edu.

INTERNATIONAL STUDENTS 4% of students enrolled are international students. *Services and facilities:* ESL/language courses, Visa Services. Financial aid is not available to international students. *Required with application:* TOEFL with recommended score of 213 (computer), 550 (paper), or 79 (Internet); proof of adequate funds; proof of health/immunizations.

International Student Contact Ms. Marie Gemender, International Admissions Specialist, 17600 Pacific Highway 43, PO Box 261, Marylhurst, OR 97036-0261. *Phone:* 503-699-6268. *Fax:* 503-697-5597. *E-mail:* studentinfo@marylhurst.edu.

APPLICATION *Required:* Application form, baccalaureate/first degree, essay, interview, 2 letters of recommendation, personal statement, resume/curriculum vitae, transcripts of college work. School will accept GMAT. *Recommended:* 5 years of work experience. *Application fee:* $40, $50 (international). Applications for domestic and international students are processed on a rolling basis.

Application Contact Heather Mather, Business Programs Advisor, 17600 Pacific Highway 43, PO Box 261, Marylhurst, OR 97036-0261. *Phone:* 503-675-3960. *Fax:* 503-697-5597. *E-mail:* hmather@marylhurst.edu.

Northwest Christian College
School of Business and Management

Eugene, Oregon

Phone: 877-463-6622 Ext. 7326 **Fax:** 541-684-7326 **E-mail:** kwilson@northwestchristian.edu

Business Program(s) Web Site: http://www.nwcc.edu/academics/grad/mba/

Graduate Business Unit Enrollment *Total:* 31 (31 part-time; 8 women; 2 international). *Average Age:* 36.

Graduate Business Faculty *Total:* 11 (6 full-time; 5 part-time).

Admissions *Applied:* 19. *Admitted:* 19. *Enrolled:* 18. *Average GMAT:* 590. *Average GPA:* 3.01

Academic Calendar Trimesters.

After Graduation (Class of 2006–07) *Employed within 3 months of graduation:* 100%.

DEGREE EVEMBA

EVEMBA—Evening Master of Business Administration Part-time. 36 total credits required. 24 to 30 months to complete program. *Concentration:* general MBA.

RESOURCES AND SERVICES 39 on-campus PCs are available to graduate business students. Access to Internet/World Wide Web and online grade reports available. *Personal computer requirements:* Graduate business students are strongly recommended to purchase or lease a personal computer. *Placement services include:* Alumni network, career counseling/planning, resume referral, career fairs, resume preparation, and career library.

EXPENSES *Tuition:* Part-time: $724 per credit hour. *Tuition (international):* Part-time: $724 per credit hour.

FINANCIAL AID (2007–08) Loans. Aid is available to part-time students. *Financial aid application deadline:* 3/15.

Financial Aid Contact Ms. Jocelyn Hubbs, Director, Financial Aid, 828 East 11th Avenue, Eugene, OR 97401. *Phone:* 877-463-6622 Ext. 7218. *Fax:* 541-684-7218. *E-mail:* jocelynh@northwestchristian.edu.

INTERNATIONAL STUDENTS 6% of students enrolled are international students. *Services and facilities:* Counseling/support services, Orientation. Financial aid is available to international students. *Required*

with application: TOEFL with recommended score of 213 (computer), 550 (paper), or 80 (Internet); proof of adequate funds; proof of health/immunizations.

International Student Contact Ms. Kathy Wilson, Admissions Counselor, 828 East 11th Avenue, Eugene, OR 97401. *Phone:* 877-463-6622 Ext. 7326. *Fax:* 541-684-7326. *E-mail:* kwilson@northwestchristian.edu.

APPLICATION *Required:* Application form, baccalaureate/first degree, essay, interview, personal statement, resume/curriculum vitae, transcripts of college work, 5 years of work experience. School will accept GMAT and GRE. *Application fee:* $35. *Deadlines:* 3/15 for fall, 3/15 for fall (international).

Application Contact Ms. Kathy Wilson, Admissions Counselor, 828 East 11th Avenue, Eugene, OR 97401. *Phone:* 877-463-6622 Ext. 7326. *Fax:* 541-684-7326. *E-mail:* kwilson@northwestchristian.edu.

OGI School of Science & Engineering at Oregon Health & Science University
Department of Management in Science and Technology

Beaverton, Oregon

Phone: 503-748-1028 **Fax:** 503-748-1285 **E-mail:** johnsamy@ohsu.edu

Business Program(s) Web Site: http://www.mst.ogi.edu

DEGREES MSM

MSM—Health Care Management Certificate Program Part-time. BA, BS or RN degree; two years healthcare experience at managerial level. 20 to 24 total credits required. 12 to 18 months to complete program.

MSM—Management in Science and Technology Full-time and part-time. Distance learning option. GMAT or GRE required if undergraduate GPA is less than 3.0. At least 52 total credits required. 18 to 60 months to complete program. *Concentrations:* business education, financial information systems, financial management/planning, health administration, industrial administration/management, international business, international management, leadership, management, manufacturing management, marketing, new venture management, operations management, organizational behavior/development, organizational management, project management, quality management, strategic management, supply chain management, technology management.

RESOURCES AND SERVICES Access to online (class) registration and online grade reports available. *Personal computer requirements:* Graduate business students are strongly recommended to purchase or lease a personal computer. *Placement services include:* Career counseling/planning, electronic job bank, career fairs, and resume preparation.

Application Contact Mrs. Amy Johnson, Graduate Education Director, 20000 Northwest Walker Road, Beaverton, OR 97006. *Phone:* 503-748-1028. *Fax:* 503-748-1285. *E-mail:* johnsamy@ohsu.edu.

Portland State University
School of Business Administration

Portland, Oregon

Phone: 503-725-2291 **E-mail:** jeffm@sba.pdx.edu

Business Program(s) Web Site: http://www.sba.pdx.edu/

Graduate Business Unit Enrollment *Total:* 445 (126 full-time; 319 part-time; 163 women; 60 international). *Average Age:* 32.

Graduate Business Faculty *Total:* 60 (31 full-time; 29 part-time).

Admissions *Applied:* 508. *Admitted:* 291. *Enrolled:* 225. *Average GMAT:* 600. *Average GPA:* 3.2

Academic Calendar Quarters.

Accreditation AACSB—The Association to Advance Collegiate Schools of Business.

After Graduation (Class of 2006–07) *Employed within 3 months of graduation:* 50%. *Average starting salary:* $51,515.

DEGREES MBA • MIM • UA Undergraduate Associate

MBA—Master of Business Administration Full-time and part-time. Distance learning option. 60 to 72 total credits required. 12 to 60 months to complete program. *Concentrations:* entrepreneurship, finance, general MBA, health care, international business, real estate, technology management.

MIM—Master of International Management Full-time and part-time. At least 70 total credits required. 12 to 24 months to complete program. *Concentrations:* international management, marketing, supply chain management.

UA Undergraduate Associate—Master of Science in Financial Analysis Full-time and part-time. Undergraduate degree in business required. 49 total credits required. 12 to 24 months to complete program. *Concentrations:* accounting, finance.

RESOURCES AND SERVICES 40 on-campus PCs are available to graduate business students. Access to Internet/World Wide Web, online (class) registration, and online grade reports available. *Personal computer requirements:* Graduate business students are not required to have a personal computer. *Special opportunities include:* An international exchange program and an internship program are available. *Placement services include:* Alumni network, career placement, job search course, career counseling/planning, electronic job bank, resume referral, career fairs, job interviews arranged, resume preparation, and career library.

FINANCIAL AID (2007–08) Grants, loans, research assistantships, scholarships, teaching assistantships, and work study. Aid is available to part-time students. *Financial aid application deadline:* 1/31.

Financial Aid Contact Phillip Rodgers, Executive Director of Financial Aid, Student Financial Aid Office, PO Box 751, Portland, OR 97207-0751. *Phone:* 503-725-3461. *E-mail:* prodgers@pdx.edu.

INTERNATIONAL STUDENTS 13% of students enrolled are international students. *Services and facilities:* Counseling/support services, ESL/language courses, Housing location assistance, International student housing, International student organization, Language tutoring, Orientation, Visa Services. Financial aid is available to international students. *Required with application:* TOEFL with recommended score of 213 (computer) or 550 (paper); proof of adequate funds; proof of health/immunizations.

International Student Contact Dawn White, Director, International Education Services, PO Box 751, Portland, OR 97207. *Phone:* 503-725-5075. *E-mail:* whited@pdx.edu.

APPLICATION *Required:* GMAT, application form, baccalaureate/first degree, essay, interview, 2 letters of recommendation, personal statement, resume/curriculum vitae, transcripts of college work, 2 years of work experience. *Application fee:* $50. Applications for domestic and international students are processed on a rolling basis.

Application Contact Jeff Millard, Graduate Programs Administrator, PO Box 751, Portland, OR 97207-0751. *Phone:* 503-725-2291. *E-mail:* jeffm@sba.pdx.edu.

Southern Oregon University
School of Business
Ashland, Oregon

Phone: 541-552-8283 **E-mail:** wilsonh@sou.edu
Business Program(s) Web Site: http://www.sou.edu/mim

DEGREES M Mgt • MBA

M Mgt—Master in Management Full-time and part-time. 45 to 51 total credits required. 18 to 84 months to complete program. *Concentration:* management.

MBA—Saturday MBA Part-time. Application Deadline is March 1 of the academic year prior to fall start. This is a cohort program. 45 total credits required. 18 to 21 months to complete program. *Concentration:* general MBA.

RESOURCES AND SERVICES Access to Internet/World Wide Web, online (class) registration, and online grade reports available. *Personal computer requirements:* Graduate business students are strongly recommended to purchase or lease a personal computer. *Placement services include:* Career fairs.

Application Contact Ms. Hart Wilson, MM, Program Manager, 1250 Siskiyou Boulevard, Ashland, OR 97520. *Phone:* 541-552-8283. *E-mail:* wilsonh@sou.edu.

University of Oregon
Charles H. Lundquist College of Business
Eugene, Oregon

Phone: 541-346-3376 **Fax:** 541-346-0073 **E-mail:** mdbrown@uoregon.edu

Business Program(s) Web Site: http://lcb.uoregon.edu/

Graduate Business Unit Enrollment *Total:* 165 (165 full-time; 75 women; 43 international). *Average Age:* 27.

Graduate Business Faculty *Total:* 50 (39 full-time; 11 part-time).

Admissions *Applied:* 199. *Admitted:* 110. *Enrolled:* 92. *Average GMAT:* 628. *Average GPA:* 3.43

Academic Calendar Quarters.

Accreditation AACSB—The Association to Advance Collegiate Schools of Business.

After Graduation (Class of 2006–07) *Employed within 3 months of graduation:* 81%. *Average starting salary:* $57,400.

DEGREES JD/MBA • M Acc • MBA

JD/MBA—Juris Doctor/Master of Business Administration Full-time. Applicants must be accepted to both the University of Oregon Lundquist College of Business and the School of Law. At least 135 total credits required. Minimum of 48 months to complete program. *Concentration:* combined degrees.

M Acc—Master of Accounting Full-time. At least 45 total credits required. Minimum of 9 months to complete program. *Concentration:* accounting.

MBA—Oregon MBA Program Full-time. Note: "other" & "supply chain management" are combined into a Sustainable Business Practices program; "accounting" & "finance" are combined into a Securities Analysis program. 46 to 81 total credits required. 9 to 21 months to complete program. *Concentrations:* accounting, entrepreneurship, finance, other, sports/entertainment management, supply chain management.

RESOURCES AND SERVICES 90 on-campus PCs are available to graduate business students. Access to Internet/World Wide Web, online (class) registration, and online grade reports available. *Personal computer requirements:* Graduate business students are strongly recommended to purchase or lease a personal computer. *Special opportunities include:* An international exchange program and an internship program are available. *Placement services include:* Alumni network, job search course, career counseling/planning, electronic job bank, resume referral, career fairs, job interviews arranged, resume preparation, and career library.

EXPENSES *Tuition (state resident):* Full-time: $11,592. *Tuition (nonresident):* Full-time: $16,344. *Tuition (international):* Full-time: $16,344. *Required fees:* Full-time: $1800. Tuition and/or fees vary by number of

University of Oregon (continued)

courses or credits taken and academic program. *Graduate housing:* Room and board costs vary by campus location, number of occupants, and type of accommodation. *Typical cost:* $7775 (room only).

FINANCIAL AID (2007–08) 130 students received aid, including fellowships, grants, loans, research assistantships, scholarships, teaching assistantships, and work study. *Financial aid application deadline:* 2/1.

Financial Aid Contact Ms. Elisabeth Bickford, Director of Student Financial Aid, Financial Aid and Scholarships, 1278 University of Oregon, Eugene, OR 97403-1278. *Phone:* 541-346-1192. *Fax:* 541-346-1175. *E-mail:* ebick@uoregon.edu.

INTERNATIONAL STUDENTS 26% of students enrolled are international students. *Services and facilities:* Counseling/support services, ESL/language courses, Housing location assistance, International student housing, International student organization, Language tutoring, Orientation, Visa Services. Financial aid is available to international students. *Required with application:* TOEFL with recommended score of 250 (computer), 600 (paper), or 93 (Internet); proof of adequate funds; proof of health/immunizations.

International Student Contact Ms. Perri McGee, Admissions Assistant, Graduate Programs, Lundquist College of Business, 1208 University of Oregon, Eugene, OR 97403-1208. *Phone:* 541-346-1462. *Fax:* 541-346-0073. *E-mail:* info@oregonmba.com.

APPLICATION *Required:* GMAT, application form, baccalaureate/first degree, essay, 2 letters of recommendation, resume/curriculum vitae, transcripts of college work, 2 years of work experience. *Recommended:* Interview. *Application fee:* $50. Applications for domestic and international students are processed on a rolling basis.

Application Contact Ms. Marilyn Brown, Admissions and Recruiting Coordinator, Graduate Programs, Lundquist College of Business, 1208 University of Oregon, Eugene, OR 97403-1208. *Phone:* 541-346-3376. *Fax:* 541-346-0073. *E-mail:* mdbrown@uoregon.edu.

See full description on page 732.

University of Phoenix–Oregon Campus

College of Graduate Business and Management

Tigard, Oregon

Phone: 480-317-6200 **Fax:** 480-643-1479 **E-mail:** beth.barilla@phoenix.edu

Business Program(s) Web Site: http://www.phoenix.edu

DEGREES   M Mgt • MA • MBA • MM

M Mgt—Human Resource Management Full-time. At least 39 total credits required. *Concentration:* human resources management.

MA—Organizational Management Full-time. At least 40 total credits required. *Concentration:* organizational management.

MBA—Accounting Full-time. At least 54 total credits required. *Concentration:* accounting.

MBA—Global Management Full-time. At least 45 total credits required. *Concentration:* international business.

MBA—Human Resource Management Full-time. At least 45 total credits required. *Concentration:* human resources management.

MBA—Marketing Full-time. At least 45 total credits required.

MBA—Public Administration Full-time. At least 45 total credits required. *Concentration:* public policy and administration.

MBA—e-Business Full-time. At least 45 total credits required. *Concentration:* electronic commerce (E-commerce).

MBA—Master of Business Administration Full-time. At least 45 total credits required. *Concentration:* administration.

MM—Master of Management Full-time. At least 39 total credits required. *Concentration:* management.

RESOURCES AND SERVICES Access to online grade reports available. *Personal computer requirements:* Graduate business students are strongly recommended to purchase or lease a personal computer. *Placement services include:* Alumni network.

Application Contact Beth Barilla, Associate Vice President of Student Admissions and Services, Mail Stop AA-K101, 4615 East Elwood Street, Phoenix, AZ 85040-1958. *Phone:* 480-317-6200. *Fax:* 480-643-1479. *E-mail:* beth.barilla@phoenix.edu.

University of Portland

Dr. Robert B. Pamplin, Jr. School of Business

Portland, Oregon

Phone: 503-943-7224 **Fax:** 503-943-8041 **E-mail:** mba-up@up.edu

Business Program(s) Web Site: http://business.up.edu/

Graduate Business Unit Enrollment *Total:* 138 (57 full-time; 81 part-time; 55 women; 39 international). *Average Age:* 29.

Graduate Business Faculty *Total:* 30 (27 full-time; 3 part-time).

Admissions *Applied:* 77. *Admitted:* 50. *Enrolled:* 31. *Average GMAT:* 540. *Average GPA:* 3.3

Academic Calendar Semesters.

Accreditation AACSB—The Association to Advance Collegiate Schools of Business.

DEGREE   MBA

MBA—Master of Business Administration Full-time and part-time. 30 to 54 total credits required. 12 to 60 months to complete program. *Concentrations:* entrepreneurship, finance, health care, international business, management, marketing.

RESOURCES AND SERVICES 200 on-campus PCs are available to graduate business students. Access to Internet/World Wide Web, online (class) registration, and online grade reports available. *Personal computer requirements:* Graduate business students are not required to have a personal computer. *Special opportunities include:* An international exchange program and an internship program are available. *Placement services include:* Alumni network, job search course, career counseling/planning, electronic job bank, resume referral, career fairs, job interviews arranged, resume preparation, and career library.

EXPENSES *Tuition:* Full-time: $13,950. Part-time: $775 per credit. *Tuition (international):* Full-time: $13,950. Part-time: $775 per credit. *Required fees:* Full-time: $630. Part-time: $35 per credit.

FINANCIAL AID (2007–08) 63 students received aid, including fellowships, grants, loans, research assistantships, scholarships, and work study. *Financial aid application deadline:* 6/30.

Financial Aid Contact Mr. Herald Johnson, Director of Financial Aid, 5000 North Willamette Boulevard, Portland, OR 97203-5798. *Phone:* 503-943-7311. *Fax:* 503-943-7399. *E-mail:* herald_johnson@up.edu.

INTERNATIONAL STUDENTS 28% of students enrolled are international students. *Services and facilities:* Counseling/support services, Housing location assistance, International student housing, International student organization, Orientation, Visa Services. Financial aid is available to international students. *Required with application:* TOEFL with recommended score of 230 (computer), 570 (paper), or 88 (Internet); proof of adequate funds; proof of health/immunizations.

International Student Contact Mr. Michael Pelley, Director of International Programs, 5000 North Willamette Boulevard, Portland, OR 97203-5798. *Phone:* 503-943-7367. *Fax:* 503-943-7399. *E-mail:* pelley@up.edu.

APPLICATION *Required:* GMAT, application form, baccalaureate/first degree, essay, 2 letters of recommendation, personal statement, resume/curriculum vitae, transcripts of college work. *Recommended:* Work experience. *Application fee:* $50. Applications for domestic and international students are processed on a rolling basis.

Application Contact Dr. Howard D. Feldman, Associate Dean and Director of Graduate Studies, 5000 North Willamette Boulevard, Portland, OR 97203-5798. *Phone:* 503-943-7224. *Fax:* 503-943-8041. *E-mail:* mba-up@up.edu.

Willamette University

George H. Atkinson Graduate School of Management

Salem, Oregon

Phone: 503-370-6167 **Fax:** 503-370-3011 **E-mail:** mba-admission@willamette.edu

Business Program(s) Web Site: http://www.willamette.edu/mba/

Graduate Business Unit Enrollment *Total:* 229 (131 full-time; 98 part-time; 88 women; 34 international). *Average Age:* 28.

Graduate Business Faculty *Total:* 26 (13 full-time; 13 part-time).

Admissions *Applied:* 194. *Admitted:* 172. *Enrolled:* 102. *Average GMAT:* 598. *Average GPA:* 3.3

Academic Calendar Semesters.

Accreditation AACSB—The Association to Advance Collegiate Schools of Business.

After Graduation (Class of 2006–07) *Employed within 3 months of graduation:* 89%. *Average starting salary:* $58,697.

DEGREES JD/MBA • MBA

JD/MBA—Juris Doctor/Master of Business Administration in Management and Law Full-time. Students must be admitted to both the MBA program and the College of Law. 126 total credits required. 48 months to complete program. *Concentrations:* accounting, entrepreneurship, finance, human resources management, management, marketing, nonprofit management, operations management, organizational behavior/development, public and private management, public management, public policy and administration.

MBA—Accelerated Option Full-time and part-time. Completed business degree from AACSB-accredited program within past 7 years, minimum cumulative GPA of 3.2, and 2 years of work experience required. 36 to 66 total credits required. 9 to 60 months to complete program. *Concentrations:* accounting, finance, human resources management, information management, international management, management, management science, marketing, organizational behavior/development, public management, public policy and administration, quantitative analysis.

MBA—Early Career MBA Full-time and part-time. 60 total credits required. 21 to 60 months to complete program. *Concentrations:* accounting, entrepreneurship, finance, human resources management, management, management science, marketing, nonprofit management, operations management, organizational behavior/development, public and private management, public management, public policy and administration.

MBA—MBA for Professionals Part-time. Designed for working professionals with a minimum of three years of professional experience. 48 total credits required. Minimum of 24 months to complete program. *Concentration:* general MBA.

RESOURCES AND SERVICES 6 on-campus PCs are available to graduate business students. Access to Internet/World Wide Web, online

(class) registration, and online grade reports available. *Personal computer requirements:* Graduate business students are required to have a personal computer. *Special opportunities include:* An international exchange program and an internship program are available. *Placement services include:* Alumni network, career placement, job search course, career counseling/planning, electronic job bank, resume referral, career fairs, job interviews arranged, resume preparation, and career library.

EXPENSES *Tuition:* Full-time: $25,200. Part-time: $840 per unit. *Tuition (international):* Full-time: $25,200. Part-time: $840 per unit. *Required fees:* Full-time: $80. Part-time: $40 per semester. Tuition and/or fees vary by class time, number of courses or credits taken, and academic program.

FINANCIAL AID (2007–08) 180 students received aid, including loans, research assistantships, scholarships, and work study. Aid is available to part-time students. *Financial aid application deadline:* 5/1.

Financial Aid Contact Katy Wilson, Senior Financial Aid Counselor, 900 State Street, Financial Aid Office, Salem, OR 97301. *Phone:* 503-370-6273. *Fax:* 503-370-6588. *E-mail:* gradaid@willamette.edu.

INTERNATIONAL STUDENTS 15% of students enrolled are international students. *Services and facilities:* Counseling/support services, Housing location assistance, International student organization, Orientation, Visa Services. Financial aid is available to international students. *Required with application:* TOEFL with recommended score of 230 (computer), 570 (paper), or 88 (Internet); proof of adequate funds; proof of health/immunizations.

International Student Contact Aimee Akimoff, Director of Recruitment, 900 State Street, Salem, OR 97301. *Phone:* 503-370-6167. *Fax:* 503-370-3011. *E-mail:* mba-admission@willamette.edu.

APPLICATION *Required:* GMAT, application form, baccalaureate/first degree, essay, interview, 2 letters of recommendation, personal statement, resume/curriculum vitae, transcripts of college work. School will accept GRE. *Application fee:* $50. Applications for domestic and international students are processed on a rolling basis.

Application Contact Aimee Akimoff, Director of Recruitment, 900 State Street, Salem, OR 97301. *Phone:* 503-370-6167. *Fax:* 503-370-3011. *E-mail:* mba-admission@willamette.edu.

See full description on page 768.

PENNSYLVANIA

Alvernia College

Department of Business

Reading, Pennsylvania

Phone: 610-796-8296 **Fax:** 610-796-8367 **E-mail:** clyde.weitkamp@alvernia.edu

Business Program(s) Web Site: http://www.alvernia.edu/graduate/mba.htm

Graduate Business Unit Enrollment *Total:* 187 (27 full-time; 160 part-time; 111 women; 1 international). *Average Age:* 36.

Graduate Business Faculty *Total:* 19 (8 full-time; 11 part-time).

Admissions *Applied:* 35. *Admitted:* 22. *Enrolled:* 21. *Average GMAT:* 590. *Average GPA:* 3.15

Academic Calendar Semesters.

Accreditation ACBSP—The American Council of Business Schools and Programs (candidate).

DEGREE MBA

MBA Full-time and part-time. Distance learning option. 36 to 45 total credits required. 15 to 60 months to complete program. *Concentrations:*

Alvernia College (continued)

entrepreneurship, general MBA, health care, human resources management, marketing, nonprofit organization.

RESOURCES AND SERVICES 279 on-campus PCs are available to graduate business students. Access to Internet/World Wide Web, online (class) registration, and online grade reports available. *Personal computer requirements:* Graduate business students are strongly recommended to purchase or lease a personal computer. *Placement services include:* Alumni network, career counseling/planning, resume referral, career fairs, job interviews arranged, resume preparation, and career library.

FINANCIAL AID (2007–08) 47 students received aid, including fellowships and loans. Aid is available to part-time students.

Financial Aid Contact Mr. Clyde Weitkamp, Graduate and Continuing Studies Counselor, 540 Upland Avenue, Reading, PA 19607. *Phone:* 610-796-8296. *Fax:* 610-796-8367. *E-mail:* clyde.weitkamp@ alvernia.edu.

INTERNATIONAL STUDENTS 0.5% of students enrolled are international students. *Services and facilities:* Visa Services. Financial aid is not available to international students. *Required with application:* Proof of adequate funds.

International Student Contact Dr. Tufan Tiglioglu, MBA Program Coordinator, 400 St. Bernardine Street, BusEd Building, Room 5, Reading, PA 19607. *Phone:* 610-796-8278. *Fax:* 610-796-8292. *E-mail:* tufan.tiglioglu@alvernia.edu.

APPLICATION *Required:* Application form, baccalaureate/first degree, 3 letters of recommendation, personal statement, transcripts of college work. School will accept GMAT, GRE, and MAT. *Recommended:* Resume/ curriculum vitae. *Application fee:* $50. Applications for domestic and international students are processed on a rolling basis.

Application Contact Mr. Clyde Weitkamp, Graduate Program Admissions, 540 Upland Street, Reading, PA 19607. *Phone:* 610-796-8296. *Fax:* 610-796-8367. *E-mail:* clyde.weitkamp@alvernia.edu.

The American College

Richard D. Irwin Graduate School

Bryn Mawr, Pennsylvania

Phone: 610-526-1366 **Fax:** 610-526-1359 **E-mail:** joanne.patterson@theamericancollege.edu

Business Program(s) Web Site: http://www.theamericancollege.edu

Graduate Business Unit Enrollment *Total:* 700 (700 part-time; 252 women; 8 international).

Graduate Business Faculty *Total:* 33 (15 full-time; 18 part-time).

Admissions *Applied:* 125. *Admitted:* 120. *Enrolled:* 120. *Average GPA:* 3.0

Academic Calendar Quarters.

DEGREES EMM • MS

EMM—Master of Science in Management with an Emphasis in Leadership Part-time. Distance learning option. Up to 30 total credits required. 12 months to complete program. *Concentration:* leadership.

MS—Master of Science in Financial Services Full-time and part-time. Distance learning option. At least 36 total credits required. Maximum of 84 months to complete program. *Concentration:* financial management/ planning.

RESOURCES AND SERVICES 4 on-campus PCs are available to graduate business students. Access to online (class) registration available. *Personal computer requirements:* Graduate business students are strongly recommended to purchase or lease a personal computer. *Placement services include:* Alumni network.

FINANCIAL AID (2007–08) Grants and scholarships. Aid is available to part-time students.

Financial Aid Contact Mr. Neal R. Fegely, Chief Operations Officer, 270 South Bryn Mawr Avenue, Bryn Mawr, PA 19010-2105. *Phone:* 610-526-1501. *Fax:* 610-526-1310. *E-mail:* neal.fegely@ theamericancollege.edu.

INTERNATIONAL STUDENTS 1% of students enrolled are international students. Financial aid is not available to international students.

International Student Contact Mr. Bud Drago, Director, Student Services, 270 South Bryn Mawr Avenue, Bryn Mawr, PA 19010. *Phone:* 610-526-1168. *Fax:* 610-526-1300. *E-mail:* bud.drago@ theamericancollege.edu.

APPLICATION *Required:* Application form, baccalaureate/first degree, personal statement, transcripts of college work. *Recommended:* Work experience. *Application fee:* $335. Applications for domestic and international students are processed on a rolling basis.

Application Contact Ms. Joanne F. Patterson, Associate Director, Graduate School Administration, 270 South Bryn Mawr Avenue, Bryn Mawr, PA 19010-2105. *Phone:* 610-526-1366. *Fax:* 610-526-1359. *E-mail:* joanne.patterson@theamericancollege.edu.

Bloomsburg University of Pennsylvania

College of Business

Bloomsburg, Pennsylvania

Phone: 570-389-4015 **Fax:** 570-389-3054 **E-mail:** jmatta@bloomu.edu

Business Program(s) Web Site: http://www.bloomu.edu/

Graduate Business Unit Enrollment *Total:* 61 (10 full-time; 51 part-time; 25 women; 9 international). *Average Age:* 25.

Graduate Business Faculty 21 full-time.

Admissions *Applied:* 22. *Admitted:* 15. *Enrolled:* 15. *Average GMAT:* 490. *Average GPA:* 3.14

Academic Calendar Semesters.

DEGREES MBA • MBE

MBA—Master of Business Administration Full-time and part-time. GMAT required. 36 to 51 total credits required. 12 to 72 months to complete program. *Concentration:* general MBA.

MBE—Master in Education Business Education Part-time. GRE and PRAXIS I and II required. 30 to 46 total credits required. 12 to 72 months to complete program. *Concentration:* business education.

RESOURCES AND SERVICES 500 on-campus PCs are available to graduate business students. Access to Internet/World Wide Web, online (class) registration, and online grade reports available. *Personal computer requirements:* Graduate business students are strongly recommended to purchase or lease a personal computer. *Placement services include:* Alumni network, career placement, career counseling/planning, electronic job bank, career fairs, resume preparation, and career library.

EXPENSES *Tuition (state resident):* Full-time: $5177. Part-time: $216 per credit. *Tuition (nonresident):* Full-time: $12,944. Part-time: $539 per credit. *Tuition (international):* Full-time: $12,944. Part-time: $539 per credit.

FINANCIAL AID (2007–08) 25 students received aid, including grants, loans, research assistantships, and work study. Aid is available to part-time students. *Financial aid application deadline:* 6/1.

Financial Aid Contact Thomas M. Lyons, 400 East Second Street, Bloomsburg, PA 17815-1905. *Phone:* 570-389-4279. *Fax:* 570-389-4795.

INTERNATIONAL STUDENTS 15% of students enrolled are international students. *Services and facilities:* Counseling/support services, Housing location assistance, International student housing, International student organization, Orientation, Visa Services. Financial aid is available to international students. *Required with application:* TOEFL with recommended score of 215 (computer) or 550 (paper); proof of adequate funds; proof of health/immunizations.

International Student Contact Dr. Madhau Sharma, Director, International Education, 400 East Second Street, Bloomsburg, PA 17815-1905. *Phone:* 570-389-4830. *E-mail:* msharma@bloomu.edu.

APPLICATION *Required:* GMAT, application form, baccalaureate/first degree, interview, 3 letters of recommendation, personal statement, resume/curriculum vitae, transcripts of college work. *Application fee:* $30. Applications for domestic and international students are processed on a rolling basis.

Application Contact Dr. James F. Matta, Dean, Graduate Studies and Research, 400 East Second Street, Bloomsburg, PA 17815-1905. *Phone:* 570-389-4015. *Fax:* 570-389-3054. *E-mail:* jmatta@bloomu.edu.

California University of Pennsylvania

School of Graduate Studies and Research

California, Pennsylvania

Phone: 724-938-4029 **Fax:** 724-938-5712 **E-mail:** powers_s@cup.edu

Business Program(s) Web Site: http://www.cup.edu/graduate

DEGREES MS • MSBA

MS—Master of Science in Business Administration Full-time and part-time. At least 36 total credits required. 12 to 72 months to complete program. *Concentration:* general MBA.

MSBA—Master of Science in Business Administration Full-time. Up to 36 total credits required. Maximum of 16 months to complete program. *Concentration:* technology management.

RESOURCES AND SERVICES 1,736 on-campus PCs are available to graduate business students. Access to Internet/World Wide Web, online (class) registration, and online grade reports available. *Personal computer requirements:* Graduate business students are strongly recommended to purchase or lease a personal computer. *Special opportunities include:* An internship program is available. *Placement services include:* Alumni network, career placement, job search course, career counseling/planning, electronic job bank, resume referral, career fairs, job interviews arranged, resume preparation, and career library.

Application Contact Suzanne C. Powers, Director of Graduate Recruitment and Admissions, 250 University Avenue, California, PA 15419-1394. *Phone:* 724-938-4029. *Fax:* 724-938-5712. *E-mail:* powers_s@cup.edu.

Carnegie Mellon University

Tepper School of Business

Pittsburgh, Pennsylvania

Phone: 412-268-2272 **Fax:** 412-268-4209 **E-mail:** mba-admissions@andrew.cmu.edu

Business Program(s) Web Site: http://www.tepper.cmu.edu

Graduate Business Unit Enrollment *Total:* 786 (420 full-time; 366 part-time; 190 women; 221 international). *Average Age:* 28.

Graduate Business Faculty *Total:* 121 (94 full-time; 27 part-time).

Admissions *Applied:* 1,502. *Admitted:* 532. *Enrolled:* 295. *Average GMAT:* 692. *Average GPA:* 3.38.

Academic Calendar Eight mini-semesters.

Accreditation AACSB—The Association to Advance Collegiate Schools of Business.

After Graduation (Class of 2006–07) *Employed within 3 months of graduation:* 94.85%. *Average starting salary:* $97,394.

DEGREES JD/MBA • MBA • MBA/MPM • MS

JD/MBA—Juris Doctor/Master of Business Administration Full-time. At least 247 total credits required. 48 months to complete program. *Concentration:* general MBA.

MBA—Master of Business Administration Full-time and part-time. Distance learning option. At least 64 total credits required. 16 to 36 months to complete program. *Concentrations:* accounting, economics, electronic commerce (E-commerce), entrepreneurship, finance, general MBA, international management, management information systems, marketing, operations management, organizational behavior/development, quantitative analysis, strategic management.

MBA/MPM—Master of Business Administration/Master of Public Management Full-time. *Concentrations:* general MBA, public management.

MS—Health Care Policy and Management Full-time. *Concentration:* health care.

MS—Master of Science in Civil Engineering and Management Minimum of 24 months to complete program. *Concentration:* engineering.

MS—Master of Science in Computational Finance Full-time and part-time. Distance learning option. At least 48 total credits required. 12 to 24 months to complete program. *Concentrations:* finance, quantitative analysis.

RESOURCES AND SERVICES on-campus PCs are available to graduate business students. Access Internet/World Wide Web, online (class) registration, and online grade reports available. *Personal computer requirements:* Graduate business students are required to have a personal computer. *Special opportunities include:* An internship program is available. *Placement services include:* Alumni network, career placement, career counseling/planning, electronic job bank, resume referral, career fairs, job interviews arranged, resume preparation, and career library.

EXPENSES *Tuition:* Full-time: $45,250. Part-time: $495 per unit. *Tuition (international):* Full-time: $45,250. Part-time: $495 per unit. *Required fees:* Full-time: $394. Part-time: $394 per year. *Typical graduate housing cost:* $13,500 (including board), $8400 (room only).

FINANCIAL AID (2007–08) Fellowships, loans, and scholarships.

Financial Aid Contact Ms. Janet Kaercher, Assistant Director of Financial Aid, Posner Hall, 5000 Forbes Avenue, Pittsburgh, PA 15213-3890. *Phone:* 412-268-4943. *Fax:* 412-268-4209. *E-mail:* janetk@andrew.cmu.edu.

INTERNATIONAL STUDENTS 28% of students enrolled are international students. *Services and facilities:* Counseling/support services, Housing location assistance, International student organization, Orientation, Visa Services. Financial aid is available to international students. *Required with application:* TOEFL with recommended score of 250 (computer) or 600 (paper).

International Student Contact Ms. Laurie Stewart, Executive Director, Admissions, Posner Hall 149, 5000 Forbes Avenue, Pittsburgh, PA 15213-3890. *Phone:* 412-268-2272. *Fax:* 412-268-4209. *E-mail:* mba-admissions@andrew.cmu.edu.

APPLICATION *Required:* GMAT, application form, baccalaureate/first degree, essay, 2 letters of recommendation, resume/curriculum vitae, transcripts of college work. *Application fee:* $100. *Deadlines:* 4/27 for fall, 3/9 for fall (international).

Application Contact Ms. Laurie Stewart, Executive Director of MBA Admissions, Posner Hall 149, 5000 Forbes Avenue, Pittsburgh, PA 15213-3890. *Phone:* 412-268-2272. *Fax:* 412-268-4209. *E-mail:* mba-admissions@andrew.cmu.edu.

See full description on page 584.

Chatham University

Program in Business Administration

Pittsburgh, Pennsylvania

Phone: 412-365-1825 **E-mail:** dperry@chatham.edu

Business Program(s) Web Site: http://www.chatham.edu/

Graduate Business Unit Enrollment *Total:* 64 (21 full-time; 43 part-time; 56 women; 1 international). *Average Age:* 32.

Graduate Business Faculty *Total:* 12 (5 full-time; 7 part-time).

Admissions *Applied:* 52. *Admitted:* 26. *Enrolled:* 23.

Academic Calendar 4-4-1.

After Graduation (Class of 2006–07) *Employed within 3 months of graduation:* 98%.

DEGREE MBA

MBA—Master of Business Administration Full-time and part-time. 36 to 46 total credits required. 12 to 60 months to complete program. *Concentrations:* general MBA, health care.

RESOURCES AND SERVICES 55 on-campus PCs are available to graduate business students. Access to Internet/World Wide Web, online (class) registration, and online grade reports available. *Personal computer requirements:* Graduate business students are not required to have a personal computer. *Special opportunities include:* An internship program is available. *Placement services include:* Alumni network, career placement, career counseling/planning, electronic job bank, resume referral, career fairs, job interviews arranged, resume preparation, and career library.

FINANCIAL AID (2007–08) Loans.

Financial Aid Contact Ms. Jennifer Burns, Director of Financial Aid, Woodland Road, Pittsburgh, PA 15232. *Phone:* 412-365-1849. *E-mail:* jburns@chatham.edu.

INTERNATIONAL STUDENTS 2% of students enrolled are international students. *Services and facilities:* Counseling/support services, ESL/language courses, Housing location assistance, International student housing, International student organization, Orientation, Visa Services. Financial aid is not available to international students. *Required with application:* TOEFL with recommended score of 600 (paper); proof of adequate funds; proof of health/immunizations.

International Student Contact Dr. Funwi Ayuninjam, Director for International Programs, Woodland Road, Pittsburgh, PA 15232. *Phone:* 412-365-1159. *E-mail:* fayuninjam@chatham.edu.

APPLICATION *Required:* Application form, baccalaureate/first degree, essay, 3 letters of recommendation, personal statement, resume/curriculum vitae, transcripts of college work. *Recommended:* Interview, 2 years of work experience. *Application fee:* $45. Applications for domestic and international students are processed on a rolling basis.

Application Contact Ms. Dory Perry, Associate Director, Graduate Admissions, Woodland Road, Pittsburgh, PA 15232. *Phone:* 412-365-1825. *E-mail:* dperry@chatham.edu.

Clarion University of Pennsylvania

College of Business Administration

Clarion, Pennsylvania

Phone: 814-393-2605 **Fax:** 814-393-1910 **E-mail:** mba@clarion.edu

Business Program(s) Web Site: http://www.clarion.edu/mba/

Graduate Business Unit Enrollment *Total:* 36 (31 full-time; 5 part-time; 13 women; 11 international). *Average Age:* 29.

Graduate Business Faculty *Total:* 20 full-time.

Admissions *Applied:* 36. *Admitted:* 31. *Enrolled:* 20. *Average GMAT:* 489. *Average GPA:* 3.57

Academic Calendar Semesters.

Accreditation AACSB—The Association to Advance Collegiate Schools of Business.

DEGREES MBA

MBA—Eleven-Month MBA Full-time. Designed for students who have completed all of the business foundation coursework. At least 33 total credits required. 11 months to complete program. *Concentrations:* accounting, economics, finance, general MBA, international business, management, marketing.

MBA—Full-Time or Part-Time Full-time and part-time. Distance learning option. At least 33 total credits required. 18 to 72 months to complete program. *Concentrations:* accounting, economics, finance, general MBA, international business, management, marketing.

MBA—Online Part-Time Part-time. Distance learning option. GMAT requirement may be exempted for qualifying applications. Designed for students who have completed all of the business foundation coursework. At least 33 total credits required. 30 to 72 months to complete program. *Concentrations:* accounting, economics, finance, general MBA, international business, management, marketing.

RESOURCES AND SERVICES 440 on-campus PCs are available to graduate business students. Access to Internet/World Wide Web, online (class) registration, and online grade reports available. *Personal computer requirements:* Graduate business students are strongly recommended to purchase or lease a personal computer. *Special opportunities include:* An internship program is available. *Placement services include:* Career placement, job search course, career counseling/planning, resume referral, career fairs, job interviews arranged, resume preparation, and career library.

EXPENSES *Tuition (state resident):* Full-time: $6430. Part-time: $1071 per course. *Tuition (nonresident):* Full-time: $10,288. Part-time: $1716 per course. *Tuition (international):* Full-time: $10,288. Part-time: $1716 per course. *Required fees:* Full-time: $2050. Part-time: $376 per course. Tuition and/or fees vary by number of courses or credits taken. *Graduate housing:* Room and board costs vary by number of occupants and type of board plan. *Typical cost:* $6068 (including board), $4140 (room only).

FINANCIAL AID (2007–08) 36 students received aid, including loans, research assistantships, scholarships, and work study. Aid is available to part-time students. *Financial aid application deadline:* 4/15.

Financial Aid Contact Mr. Kenneth Grugel, Director of Financial Aid, Egbert Hall, Clarion, PA 16214. *Phone:* 814-393-2315. *Fax:* 814-393-2520. *E-mail:* kgrugel@clarion.edu.

INTERNATIONAL STUDENTS 31% of students enrolled are international students. *Services and facilities:* Counseling/support services, Housing location assistance, International student housing, International student organization, Orientation. Financial aid is available to international students. *Required with application:* TOEFL with recommended score of 213 (computer) or 550 (paper); proof of adequate funds; proof of health/immunizations.

International Student Contact Ms. Linda Heineman, Foreign Student Advisor, International Programs Office, Clarion, PA 16214. *Phone:* 814-393-2340. *Fax:* 814-393-2341. *E-mail:* lheineman@clarion.edu.

APPLICATION *Required:* GMAT, application form, baccalaureate/first degree, 3 letters of recommendation, resume/curriculum vitae, transcripts of college work. *Recommended:* Personal statement. *Application fee:* $30. Applications for domestic and international students are processed on a rolling basis.

Application Contact Brenda Ponsford, PhD, Director of MBA Program, 302 Still Hall, Clarion, PA 16214. *Phone:* 814-393-2605. *Fax:* 814-393-1910. *E-mail:* mba@clarion.edu.

DeSales University
Department of Business

Center Valley, Pennsylvania

Phone: 610-282-1100 Ext. 1448 **Fax:** 610-282-2869 **E-mail:** mba@desales.edu

Business Program(s) Web Site: http://www.desales.edu/mba/

Graduate Business Unit Enrollment *Total:* 720.

Graduate Business Faculty *Total:* 48 (18 full-time; 30 part-time).

Admissions *Average GMAT:* 550. *Average GPA:* 3.2

Academic Calendar Three 12-week sessions and one 6-week session.

Accreditation ACBSP—The American Council of Business Schools and Programs.

After Graduation (Class of 2006–07) *Employed within 3 months of graduation:* 99%.

DEGREES MBA • MBA/MSN

MBA—Master of Business Administration Part-time. Distance learning option. 36 to 48 total credits required. 12 to 84 months to complete program. *Concentrations:* accounting, electronic commerce (E-commerce), finance, health care, management, marketing.

MBA/MSN—Master of Business Administration/Master of Science in Nursing Part-time. Distance learning option. Applicant must meet the admission requirements for both the MBA and MSN programs. At least 18 total credits required. 36 to 84 months to complete program. *Concentration:* combined degrees.

RESOURCES AND SERVICES 100 on-campus PCs are available to graduate business students. Access to Internet/World Wide Web, online (class) registration, and online grade reports available. *Personal computer requirements:* Graduate business students are strongly recommended to purchase or lease a personal computer. *Placement services include:* Alumni network and career library.

INTERNATIONAL STUDENTS *Services and facilities:* Counseling/support services, Orientation. Financial aid is not available to international students. *Required with application:* TOEFL; proof of adequate funds.

International Student Contact Rev. Peter Leonard, OSFS, Dean of Graduate Studies, 2755 Station Avenue, Center Valley, PA 18034. *Phone:* 610-282-1100 Ext. 1289. *Fax:* 610-282-2254. *E-mail:* peter.leonard@desales.edu.

APPLICATION *Required:* Application form, baccalaureate/first degree, 3 letters of recommendation, personal statement, transcripts of college work, 2 years of work experience. School will accept GMAT. *Recommended:* Interview, resume/curriculum vitae. *Application fee:* $50. Applications for domestic and international students are processed on a rolling basis.

Application Contact Mary Ann Falk, Associate Director, MBA Program, MBA Office, 2755 Station Avenue, Center Valley, PA 18034-9568. *Phone:* 610-282-1100 Ext. 1448. *Fax:* 610-282-2869. *E-mail:* mba@desales.edu.

DeVry University
Keller Graduate School of Management

Chesterbrook, Pennsylvania

Phone: 610-889-9980

DEGREES MAFM • MBA • MHRM • MIS • MPA • MPM

MAFM—Master of Accounting and Financial Management Full-time and part-time. Distance learning option. At least 44 total credits required. 18 to 60 months to complete program. *Concentrations:* accounting, financial management/planning.

MBA—Master of Business Administration Full-time and part-time. Distance learning option. At least 48 total credits required. 18 to 60 months to complete program. *Concentration:* management.

MHRM—Master of Human Resources Management Full-time and part-time. Distance learning option. At least 45 total credits required. 18 to 60 months to complete program. *Concentration:* human resources management.

MIS—Master of Information Systems Management Full-time and part-time. Distance learning option. At least 45 total credits required. 18 to 60 months to complete program. *Concentration:* information systems.

MPA—Master of Public Administration Full-time and part-time. Distance learning option. At least 45 total credits required. 18 to 60 months to complete program. *Concentration:* public policy and administration.

MPM—Master of Project Management Full-time and part-time. Distance learning option. At least 42 total credits required. 18 to 60 months to complete program. *Concentration:* project management.

Application Contact Admissions Office, Valley Forge Center, 701 Lee Road, Suite 103, Chesterbrook, PA 19087. *Phone:* 610-889-9980.

DeVry University
Keller Graduate School of Management

Fort Washington, Pennsylvania

Phone: 215-591-5900

DEGREES MAFM • MBA • MHRM • MIS • MPA • MPM

MAFM—Master of Accounting and Financial Management Full-time and part-time. Distance learning option. At least 44 total credits required. 18 to 60 months to complete program. *Concentrations:* accounting, financial management/planning.

MBA—Master of Business Administration Full-time and part-time. Distance learning option. At least 48 total credits required. 18 to 60 months to complete program. *Concentration:* management.

MHRM—Master of Human Resources Management Full-time and part-time. Distance learning option. At least 45 total credits required. 18 to 60 months to complete program. *Concentration:* human resources management.

MIS—Master of Information Systems Management Full-time and part-time. Distance learning option. At least 45 total credits required. 18 to 60 months to complete program. *Concentration:* information systems.

MPA—Master of Public Administration Full-time and part-time. Distance learning option. At least 45 total credits required. 18 to 60 months to complete program. *Concentration:* public policy and administration.

MPM—Master of Project Management Full-time and part-time. Distance learning option. At least 42 total credits required. 18 to 60 months to complete program. *Concentration:* project management.

Application Contact Admissions Office, Ft. Washington Campus, 1140 Virginia Drive, Ft. Washington, PA 19034. *Phone:* 215-591-5900.

DeVry University
Keller Graduate School of Management

Pittsburgh, Pennsylvania

Phone: 412-642-9072

DEGREES MAFM • MBA • MHRM • MIS • MPA • MPM

DeVry University (continued)

MAFM—Master of Accounting and Financial Management Full-time and part-time. Distance learning option. At least 44 total credits required. 18 to 60 months to complete program. *Concentrations:* accounting, financial management/planning.

MBA—Master of Business Administration Full-time and part-time. At least 48 total credits required. 18 to 60 months to complete program. *Concentration:* management.

MHRM—Master of Human Resources Management Full-time and part-time. Distance learning option. At least 45 total credits required. 18 to 60 months to complete program. *Concentration:* human resources management.

MIS—Master of Information Systems Management Full-time and part-time. Distance learning option. At least 45 total credits required. 18 to 60 months to complete program. *Concentration:* information systems.

MPA—Master of Public Administration Full-time and part-time. Distance learning option. At least 45 total credits required. 18 to 60 months to complete program. *Concentration:* public policy and administration.

MPM—Master of Project Management Full-time and part-time. Distance learning option. At least 42 total credits required. 18 to 60 months to complete program. *Concentration:* project management.

Application Contact Admissions Office, Pittsburgh Center, 210 Sixth Avenue, Suite 200, Pittsburgh, PA 15222. *Phone:* 412-642-9072.

Drexel University
LeBow College of Business
Philadelphia, Pennsylvania

Phone: 215-895-0562 **Fax:** 215-895-1012 **E-mail:** mba@drexel.edu

Business Program(s) Web Site: http://www.lebow.drexel.edu

Graduate Business Unit Enrollment *Total:* 1,060 (219 full-time; 841 part-time; 461 women; 162 international). *Average Age:* 30.

Graduate Business Faculty *Total:* 206 (110 full-time; 96 part-time).

Admissions *Applied:* 1,419. *Admitted:* 585. *Enrolled:* 320. *Average GMAT:* 580. *Average GPA:* 3.3

Academic Calendar Quarters.

Accreditation AACSB—The Association to Advance Collegiate Schools of Business.

After Graduation (Class of 2006–07) *Employed within 3 months of graduation:* 85%. *Average starting salary:* $75,000.

DEGREES EMBA • JD/MBA • MBA • MD/MBA • MS

EMBA Part-time. 51 total credits required. 22 months to complete program. *Concentrations:* general MBA, leadership, strategic management.

JD/MBA—Juris Doctor/Master of Business Administration Full-time. Separate admissions applications required for business school and law school (must be admitted to both programs). 45 total credits required. 12 to 36 months to complete program. *Concentrations:* general MBA, law.

MBA—LEAD Part-time. 51 total credits required. 24 months to complete program. *Concentrations:* engineering, entrepreneurship, finance, management information systems, marketing.

MBA—MBA Anywhere Part-time. Distance learning option. 60 total credits required. 24 months to complete program. *Concentrations:* engineering, entrepreneurship, finance, management information systems, marketing.

MBA—MBA in Pharmaceutical Management Part-time. Distance learning option. 51 total credits required. 28 months to complete program. *Concentration:* pharmaceutical management.

MBA—One-Year MBA Full-time. Can take additional courses for concentrations available in Two-Year MBA. 51 total credits required. 12 months to complete program. *Concentration:* general MBA.

MBA—Professional MBA Full-time and part-time. 45 to 51 total credits required. 15 to 81 months to complete program. *Concentrations:* accounting, economics, entrepreneurship, finance, general MBA, international business, management, management information systems, marketing, operations management, organizational management, production management.

MBA—Two-Year MBA Full-time. Internship required. 51 total credits required. 18 to 30 months to complete program. *Concentrations:* accounting, economics, entrepreneurship, finance, general MBA, international business, management information systems, marketing, operations management, organizational management, production management.

MD/MBA—Doctor of Medicine/Master of Business Administration Full-time. Must be admitted to Drexel Medical School prior to applying for MBA program; the MBA portion is the One-Year MBA program. 51 total credits required. 12 to 111 months to complete program. *Concentrations:* general MBA, medicine.

MS—Master of Science in Accounting Full-time and part-time. 54 to 60 total credits required. 12 to 84 months to complete program. *Concentration:* accounting.

MS—Master of Science in Finance Full-time and part-time. 54 to 60 total credits required. 12 to 84 months to complete program. *Concentration:* finance.

RESOURCES AND SERVICES 900 on-campus PCs are available to graduate business students. Access to Internet/World Wide Web, online (class) registration, and online grade reports available. *Personal computer requirements:* Graduate business students are required to have a personal computer. *Special opportunities include:* An internship program is available. *Placement services include:* Alumni network, career placement, job search course, career counseling/planning, electronic job bank, resume referral, career fairs, job interviews arranged, resume preparation, and career library.

EXPENSES *Tuition:* Full-time: $24,000. Part-time: $875 per credit. *Tuition (international):* Full-time: $24,000. Part-time: $875 per credit. *Required fees:* Full-time: $500. Part-time: $300 per quarter. Tuition and/or fees vary by academic program.

FINANCIAL AID (2007–08) 193 students received aid, including fellowships, loans, research assistantships, scholarships, teaching assistantships, and work study. Aid is available to part-time students. *Financial aid application deadline:* 1/5.

Financial Aid Contact Melissa Englund, Assistant Vice President, EM Planning/Retention, Main Building, 3141 Chestnut Street, Philadelphia, PA 19104-2875. *Phone:* 215-895-6395. *Fax:* 215-895-1012. *E-mail:* melissa.marie.englund@drexel.edu.

INTERNATIONAL STUDENTS 15% of students enrolled are international students. *Services and facilities:* Counseling/support services, ESL/language courses, International student organization, Language tutoring, Orientation, Visa Services, LeBow International Student Association. Financial aid is available to international students. *Required with application:* TOEFL with recommended score of 250 (computer), 600 (paper), or 100 (Internet); proof of adequate funds; proof of health/ immunizations.

International Student Contact Adrienne Kekec, Executive Director, International Students and Scholars Office, 3141 Chestnut Street, Creese Student Center, Room 210, Philadelphia, PA 19104. *Phone:* 215-895-2502. *Fax:* 215-895-6617. *E-mail:* intlprog@drexel.edu.

APPLICATION *Required:* GMAT, application form, baccalaureate/first degree, essay, 2 letters of recommendation, personal statement, resume/ curriculum vitae, transcripts of college work. *Recommended:* Work experience. *Application fee:* $100. Applications for domestic and international students are processed on a rolling basis.

Application Contact John Adamski, Director of Graduate Business Admissions, 207 Matheson Hall, 3141 Chestnut Street, Philadelphia, PA 19104-2875. *Phone:* 215-895-0562. *Fax:* 215-895-1012. *E-mail:* mba@drexel.edu.

Duquesne University

John F. Donahue Graduate School of Business

Pittsburgh, Pennsylvania

Phone: 412-396-6276 **Fax:** 412-396-1726 **E-mail:** moorep@duq.edu

Business Program(s) Web Site: http://www.business.duq.edu/grad

Graduate Business Unit Enrollment *Total:* 334 (113 full-time; 221 part-time; 138 women; 27 international).

Graduate Business Faculty *Total:* 70 (50 full-time; 20 part-time).

Admissions *Applied:* 205. *Admitted:* 118. *Enrolled:* 75. *Average GMAT:* 510. *Average GPA:* 3.1

Academic Calendar Semesters.

Accreditation AACSB—The Association to Advance Collegiate Schools of Business.

After Graduation (Class of 2006–07) *Employed within 3 months of graduation:* 80%. *Average starting salary:* $70,000.

DEGREES JD/MBA • M Acc • MBA • MBA/M Acc • MBA/MA • MBA/MHMS • MBA/MLS • MBA/MS • MS

JD/MBA—Juris Doctor/Master of Business Administration Full-time and part-time. Must apply to Graduate School of Business and Law School. At least 126 total credits required. 36 to 72 months to complete program. *Concentration:* combined degrees.

M Acc—Master of Accountancy Full-time and part-time. At least 30 total credits required. 12 to 72 months to complete program. *Concentration:* accounting.

MBA—MBA in Sustainability Full-time. 45 total credits required. 12 months to complete program. *Concentrations:* finance, supply chain management.

MBA—Master of Business Administration Full-time and part-time. 37 to 57 total credits required. 18 to 72 months to complete program. *Concentrations:* business ethics, environmental economics/management, finance, general MBA, health administration, human resources management, information systems, international business, logistics, management, management information systems, marketing, supply chain management.

MBA/M Acc—Master of Business Administration/Master of Accounting Full-time and part-time. At least 65 total credits required. 24 to 72 months to complete program. *Concentration:* combined degrees.

MBA/MA—Master of Business Administration/MA in Corporate Communication Full-time and part-time. Must apply to Graduate School of Business and Graduate School of Liberal Arts. At least 70 total credits required. 24 to 72 months to complete program. *Concentration:* combined degrees.

MBA/MA—Master of Business Administration/MA in Social and Public Policy Full-time and part-time. Must apply to Graduate School of Business and Graduate School of Liberal Arts. At least 59 total credits required. 24 to 72 months to complete program. *Concentration:* combined degrees.

MBA/MA—Master of Business Administration/Master of Arts in Liberal Studies Full-time and part-time. Must apply to Graduate School of Business and Graduate School of Liberal Arts. At least 75 total credits required. 24 to 72 months to complete program. *Concentration:* combined degrees.

MBA/MHMS—Master of Business Administration/Master of Health Management Systems Full-time and part-time. Must apply to Graduate School of Business and School of Health Sciences. At least 79 total credits required. 24 to 72 months to complete program. *Concentration:* combined degrees.

MBA/MLS—MBA/MLLS—Leadership Full-time and part-time. Must apply to Graduate School of Business and School of Leadership and Professional Advancement. At least 81 total credits required. 24 to 72 months to complete program. *Concentration:* combined degrees.

MBA/MS—Master of Business Administration/Master of Science in Environmental Science Management Full-time and part-time. Must apply to Graduate School of Business and Graduate School of Sciences. At least 67 total credits required. 24 to 72 months to complete program. *Concentration:* combined degrees.

MBA/MS—Master of Business Administration/Master of Science in Industrial Pharmacy Full-time. Must apply to Graduate School of Business and School of Pharmacy. At least 83 total credits required. 24 to 72 months to complete program. *Concentration:* combined degrees.

MBA/MS—Master of Business Administration/Master of Science in Information Systems Management Full-time and part-time. At least 81 total credits required. 24 to 72 months to complete program. *Concentrations:* accounting, business ethics, combined degrees, economics, environmental economics/management, finance, health care, human resources management, international business, international management, management information systems, marketing, real estate, supply chain management.

MBA/MS—Master of Business Administration/Master of Science in Nursing Full-time and part-time. Must apply to Graduate School of Business and School of Nursing. At least 82 total credits required. 24 to 72 months to complete program. *Concentration:* combined degrees.

MS—Master of Science in Information Systems Management Full-time and part-time. At least 54 total credits required. 18 to 72 months to complete program. *Concentration:* information systems.

RESOURCES AND SERVICES 350 on-campus PCs are available to graduate business students. Access to Internet/World Wide Web, online (class) registration, and online grade reports available. *Personal computer requirements:* Graduate business students are not required to have a personal computer. *Special opportunities include:* An international exchange program and an internship program are available. *Placement services include:* Alumni network, career placement, career counseling/planning, electronic job bank, resume referral, career fairs, job interviews arranged, resume preparation, and career library.

EXPENSES *Tuition:* Part-time: $774 per credit. *Tuition (international):* Part-time: $774 per credit. Tuition and/or fees vary by number of courses or credits taken and campus location. *Graduate housing:* Room and board costs vary by campus location, number of occupants, type of accommodation, and type of board plan. *Typical cost:* $8546 (including board), $4662 (room only).

FINANCIAL AID (2007–08) 37 students received aid, including fellowships, loans, and research assistantships. Aid is available to part-time students. *Financial aid application deadline:* 7/1.

Financial Aid Contact Mr. Richard Esposito, Director, Financial Aid, 600 Forbes Avenue, Pittsburgh, PA 15282. *Phone:* 412-396-6607. *Fax:* 412-396-5284. *E-mail:* financialaid@duq.edu.

INTERNATIONAL STUDENTS 8% of students enrolled are international students. *Services and facilities:* Counseling/support services, ESL/language courses, Housing location assistance, International student organization, Language tutoring, Orientation, Visa Services. Financial aid is not available to international students. *Required with application:* TOEFL with recommended score of 213 (computer), 550 (paper), or 80 (Internet); proof of adequate funds; proof of health/immunizations. *Recommended with application:* TWE with recommended score of 4.

International Student Contact Ms. Michele Janosko, Assistant Director, 601 Duquesne Union, Pittsburgh, PA 15282. *Phone:* 412-396-5812. *Fax:* 412-396-5178. *E-mail:* janosko@duq.edu.

APPLICATION *Required:* GMAT, application form, baccalaureate/first degree, essay, 2 letters of recommendation, personal statement, transcripts of college work. *Recommended:* Interview, resume/curriculum vitae, work experience. Applications for domestic and international students are processed on a rolling basis.

Application Contact Patricia Moore, Managing Director of Graduate Programs, 600 Forbes Avenue, Pittsburgh, PA 15282. *Phone:* 412-396-6276. *Fax:* 412-396-1726. *E-mail:* moorep@duq.edu.

Eastern University
Graduate Business Programs
St. Davids, Pennsylvania

Phone: 610-341-1704 **Fax:** 610-341-1468 **E-mail:** pjberol@eastern.edu

Business Program(s) Web Site: http://www.eastern.edu/academic/ccgps/

Graduate Business Unit Enrollment *Total:* 681 (618 full-time; 63 part-time; 373 women; 47 international).

Graduate Business Faculty 13 full-time.

Academic Calendar Semesters and Terms.

DEGREES M Div/MS • MBA • MBA/M Div • MBA/MS

M Div/MS—Master of Divinity/Master of Science in Economic Development Full-time and part-time. At least 116 total credits required. Maximum of 84 months to complete program. *Concentration:* combined degrees.

MBA—Fast-Track Master of Business Administration Full-time. At least 39 total credits required. Minimum of 22 months to complete program. *Concentration:* management.

MBA/M Div—Master of Business Administration/Master of Divinity Full-time and part-time. At least 116 total credits required. Maximum of 84 months to complete program. *Concentrations:* accounting, economics, finance, international development management, management.

MBA/MS—Fast-Track Executive Master of Business Administration/Master of Science in Health Administration Full-time and part-time. 5 years of full-time professional work experience or 3 years post-baccalaureate full-time professional work required. 33 to 39 total credits required. 22 to 84 months to complete program. *Concentration:* health care.

MBA/MS—Master of Business Administration/Master of Science in Economic Development Full-time and part-time. At least 39 total credits required. 18 to 84 months to complete program. *Concentration:* international development management.

MBA/MS—Master of Business Administration/Master of Science in Non-Profit Management Full-time and part-time. At least 36 total credits required. 24 to 84 months to complete program. *Concentration:* nonprofit management.

RESOURCES AND SERVICES 100 on-campus PCs are available to graduate business students. Access to Internet/World Wide Web, online (class) registration, and online grade reports available. *Personal computer requirements:* Graduate business students are strongly recommended to purchase or lease a personal computer. *Special opportunities include:* An internship program is available. *Placement services include:* Career counseling/planning, electronic job bank, resume referral, career fairs, resume preparation, and career library.

FINANCIAL AID (2007–08) Fellowships, grants, loans, research assistantships, scholarships, and teaching assistantships.

Financial Aid Contact Lauren Pizzo, Director of Financial Aid, 1300 Eagle Road, St. Davids, PA 19087-3696. *Phone:* 610-341-5843. *Fax:* 610-341-1492. *E-mail:* lpizzo@eastern.edu.

INTERNATIONAL STUDENTS 7% of students enrolled are international students. *Services and facilities:* Counseling/support services, International student organization. Financial aid is available to international students. *Required with application:* TOEFL with recommended score of 213 (computer) or 550 (paper); proof of adequate funds; proof of health/immunizations.

International Student Contact Rev. Kathy Kautz, Coordinator of International Student Services, 1300 Eagle Road, St. Davids, PA 19087-3696. *Phone:* 610-341-5870. *Fax:* 610-225-1705. *E-mail:* kkautz2@eastern.edu.

APPLICATION *Required:* Application form, baccalaureate/first degree, essay, 2 letters of recommendation, personal statement, resume/curriculum vitae, transcripts of college work. *Application fee:* $35. Applications for domestic and international students are processed on a rolling basis.

Application Contact Peter Berol, Director, Graduate Admissions, 1300 Eagle Road, St. Davids, PA 19087-3696. *Phone:* 610-341-1704. *Fax:* 610-341-1468. *E-mail:* pjberol@eastern.edu.

Gannon University
School of Business
Erie, Pennsylvania

Phone: 814-871-5819 **Fax:** 814-871-7210 **E-mail:** meszaros001@gannon.edu

Business Program(s) Web Site: http://www.gannon.edu/PROGRAMS/GRAD/mba.asp

Graduate Business Unit Enrollment *Total:* 130.

Graduate Business Faculty *Total:* 21 (16 full-time; 5 part-time).

Admissions *Average GMAT:* 503. *Average GPA:* 3.21

Academic Calendar Semesters.

Accreditation ACBSP—The American Council of Business Schools and Programs.

After Graduation (Class of 2006–07) *Employed within 3 months of graduation:* 100%.

DEGREES MBA • MPA

MBA—Master of Business Administration Full-time and part-time. 30 to 48 total credits required. 12 to 72 months to complete program. *Concentrations:* accounting, finance, general MBA, human resources management, information technology, marketing, public policy and administration.

MPA—Master of Public Administration Full-time and part-time. 36 to 37 total credits required. 12 to 36 months to complete program. *Concentrations:* accounting, finance, marketing, nonprofit management, public management, public policy and administration.

RESOURCES AND SERVICES Access to Internet/World Wide Web, online (class) registration, and online grade reports available. *Personal computer requirements:* Graduate business students are strongly recommended to purchase or lease a personal computer. *Special opportunities include:* An internship program is available. *Placement services include:* Alumni network, career placement, career counseling/planning, resume referral, career fairs, job interviews arranged, resume preparation, and career library.

EXPENSES *Tuition:* Part-time: $725 per semester hour. *Tuition (international):* Part-time: $725 per semester hour.

FINANCIAL AID (2007–08) Loans, research assistantships, scholarships, teaching assistantships, and work study.

Financial Aid Contact Director of Financial Aid, University Square, Erie, PA 16541. *Phone:* 814-871-7481.

INTERNATIONAL STUDENTS *Services and facilities:* Counseling/support services, ESL/language courses, Housing location assistance, Orientation. Financial aid is available to international students. *Required with application:* TOEFL with recommended score of 213 (computer) or 550 (paper); proof of adequate funds. *Recommended with application:* IELT; proof of health/immunizations.

International Student Contact Ms. Kimberly Hajec, Director of International Recruitment, University Square, Erie, PA 16541. *Phone:* 814-871-7474. *Fax:* 814-871-5827. *E-mail:* cfal@gannon.edu.

APPLICATION *Required:* GMAT, application form, baccalaureate/first degree, 3 letters of recommendation, personal statement, transcripts of college work. *Recommended:* Resume/curriculum vitae, work experience. *Application fee:* $25. Applications for domestic and international students are processed on a rolling basis.

Application Contact Ms. Debra Meszaros, Director of Graduate Recruitment, 109 University Square, Erie, PA 16541. *Phone:* 814-871-5819. *Fax:* 814-871-7210. *E-mail:* meszaros001@gannon.edu.

Geneva College

Department of Business, Accounting and Management

Beaver Falls, Pennsylvania

Phone: 724-847-6571 **Fax:** 724-847-6893 **E-mail:** lahartge@geneva.edu

Business Program(s) Web Site: http://www.geneva.edu/academics/graduate/mba/index.html

Graduate Business Unit Enrollment *Total:* 52 (4 full-time; 48 part-time; 20 women; 1 international). *Average Age:* 34.

Graduate Business Faculty *Total:* 10 (9 full-time; 1 part-time).

Admissions *Applied:* 16. *Admitted:* 15. *Enrolled:* 15. *Average GPA:* 3.1

Academic Calendar Continuous.

Accreditation ACBSP—The American Council of Business Schools and Programs.

After Graduation (Class of 2006–07) *Employed within 3 months of graduation:* 100%.

DEGREE MBA

MBA—Master of Business Administration Full-time and part-time. 36 to 45 total credits required. 12 to 84 months to complete program. *Concentration:* general MBA.

RESOURCES AND SERVICES 84 on-campus PCs are available to graduate business students. Access to Internet/World Wide Web, online (class) registration, and online grade reports available. *Personal computer requirements:* Graduate business students are strongly recommended to purchase or lease a personal computer. *Placement services include:* Career counseling/planning, career fairs, resume preparation, and career library.

FINANCIAL AID (2007–08) 10 students received aid, including loans.

Financial Aid Contact Mr. Steve Bell, Financial Aid Director, 3200 College Avenue, Beaver Falls, PA 15010-3599. *Phone:* 724-847-6530. *Fax:* 724-847-6776. *E-mail:* skbell@geneva.edu.

INTERNATIONAL STUDENTS 2% of students enrolled are international students. *Services and facilities:* Counseling/support services, ESL/language courses. Financial aid is not available to international students. *Required with application:* TOEFL with recommended score of 150 (computer) or 550 (paper); proof of adequate funds; proof of health/immunizations.

International Student Contact Ms. Lori Hartge, Graduate Student Support Specialist, 3200 College Avenue, Beaver Falls, PA 15010-3599. *Phone:* 724-847-6571. *Fax:* 724-847-6893. *E-mail:* lahartge@geneva.edu.

APPLICATION *Required:* Application form, baccalaureate/first degree, essay, 2 letters of recommendation, personal statement, resume/curriculum vitae, transcripts of college work. *Recommended:* 3 years of work experience. Applications for domestic and international students are processed on a rolling basis.

Application Contact Ms. Lori Hartge, Graduate Student Support Specialist, 3200 College Avenue, Beaver Falls, PA 15010-3599. *Phone:* 724-847-6571. *Fax:* 724-847-6893. *E-mail:* lahartge@geneva.edu.

Indiana University of Pennsylvania

Eberly College of Business and Information Technology

Indiana, Pennsylvania

Phone: 724-357-2522 **Fax:** 724-357-6232 **E-mail:** kjdavis@iup.edu

Business Program(s) Web Site: http://www.eberly.iup.edu/mba

Graduate Business Unit Enrollment *Total:* 239 (215 full-time; 24 part-time; 95 women; 123 international). *Average Age:* 26.

Graduate Business Faculty 40 full-time.

Admissions *Applied:* 456. *Admitted:* 319. *Enrolled:* 239. *Average GMAT:* 531. *Average GPA:* 3.13

Academic Calendar Semesters.

Accreditation AACSB—The Association to Advance Collegiate Schools of Business.

After Graduation (Class of 2006–07) *Employed within 3 months of graduation:* 72%. *Average starting salary:* $54,500.

DEGREES MBA • ME

MBA—Executive Master of Business Administration Part-time. 3 years of work experience required. 36 to 45 total credits required. 16 to 20 months to complete program. *Concentration:* executive programs.

MBA—Master of Business Administration Full-time and part-time. 36 to 45 total credits required. 12 to 24 months to complete program. *Concentration:* general MBA.

ME—Master of Education in Business Full-time and part-time. 30 to 45 total credits required. 12 to 18 months to complete program. *Concentration:* business education.

RESOURCES AND SERVICES 435 on-campus PCs are available to graduate business students. Access to Internet/World Wide Web, online (class) registration, and online grade reports available. *Personal computer requirements:* Graduate business students are strongly recommended to purchase or lease a personal computer. *Special opportunities include:* An international exchange program and an internship program are available. *Placement services include:* Alumni network, career placement, job search course, career counseling/planning, electronic job bank, resume referral, career fairs, job interviews arranged, resume preparation, and career library.

EXPENSES *Tuition (state resident):* Full-time: $7594. Part-time: $345 per credit. *Tuition (nonresident):* Full-time: $11,413. Part-time: $552 per credit. *Tuition (international):* Full-time: $11,413. Part-time: $552 per credit. *Required fees:* Full-time: $735. Part-time: $388 per semester. *Graduate housing:* Room and board costs vary by campus location, number of occupants, type of accommodation, and type of board plan. *Typical cost:* $5442 (including board), $3340 (room only).

FINANCIAL AID (2007–08) 46 students received aid, including fellowships, grants, loans, research assistantships, scholarships, and work study. *Financial aid application deadline:* 4/1.

Financial Aid Contact Dr. Krish Krishnan, Director, MBA Program, 301 Eberly Building, 664 Pratt Drive, Indiana, PA 15705. *Phone:* 724-357-2522. *Fax:* 724-357-6232. *E-mail:* krishnan@iup.edu.

INTERNATIONAL STUDENTS 51% of students enrolled are international students. *Services and facilities:* Counseling/support services, ESL/language courses, Housing location assistance, International student housing, International student organization, Language tutoring, Orientation. Financial aid is available to international students. *Required with application:* TOEFL with recommended score of 213 (computer) or 550 (paper); proof of adequate funds.

International Student Contact Ms. Karen Davis, MBA Program Secretary, 301 Eberly Building, 664 Pratt Drive, Indiana, PA 15705. *Phone:* 724-357-2522. *Fax:* 724-357-6232. *E-mail:* kjdavis@iup.edu.

APPLICATION *Required:* GMAT, GRE, application form, baccalaureate/first degree, essay, 2 letters of recommendation, personal statement, resume/curriculum vitae, transcripts of college work. *Recommended:* Work experience. *Application fee:* $30. Applications for domestic and international students are processed on a rolling basis.

Application Contact Ms. Karen Davis, Secretary, MBA Program, 301 Eberly Building, 664 Pratt Drive, Indiana, PA 15705. *Phone:* 724-357-2522. *Fax:* 724-357-6232. *E-mail:* kjdavis@iup.edu.

Kutztown University of Pennsylvania

College of Business

Kutztown, Pennsylvania

Phone: 610-683-4575 **Fax:** 610-683-4573 **E-mail:** ikem@kutztown.edu

Kutztown University of Pennsylvania (continued)

Business Program(s) Web Site: http://www.kutztown.edu/academics/business/mbaprograms/

Graduate Business Unit Enrollment *Total:* 95 (22 full-time; 73 part-time; 34 women; 7 international). *Average Age:* 31.

Graduate Business Faculty *Total:* 18 (16 full-time; 2 part-time).

Admissions *Applied:* 62. *Admitted:* 57. *Enrolled:* 54. *Average GMAT:* 510. *Average GPA:* 3.05

Academic Calendar Trimesters.

After Graduation (Class of 2006–07) *Employed within 3 months of graduation:* 99%.

DEGREE MBA

MBA—Master of Business Administration Full-time and part-time. At least 36 total credits required. 12 to 72 months to complete program. *Concentrations:* general MBA, human resources management, international business, logistics, marketing, supply chain management.

RESOURCES AND SERVICES 500 on-campus PCs are available to graduate business students. Access to Internet/World Wide Web, online (class) registration, and online grade reports available. *Personal computer requirements:* Graduate business students are strongly recommended to purchase or lease a personal computer. *Special opportunities include:* An international exchange program and an internship program are available. *Placement services include:* Alumni network, career placement, career counseling/planning, electronic job bank, resume referral, career fairs, job interviews arranged, resume preparation, and career library.

EXPENSES *Tuition (state resident):* Full-time: $3107. Part-time: $345 per semester hour. *Tuition (nonresident):* Full-time: $4972. Part-time: $552 per semester hour. *Tuition (international):* Full-time: $4972. Part-time: $552 per semester hour. *Required fees:* Full-time: $370. Part-time: $283 per semester.

FINANCIAL AID (2007–08) 14 students received aid, including grants, loans, research assistantships, scholarships, and work study.

Financial Aid Contact Ms. Joan Holleran, Interim Director of Financial Aid, 209 Stratton Administration Center, PO Box 730, Kutztown, PA 19530-0730. *Phone:* 610-683-4077. *Fax:* 610-683-1380. *E-mail:* holleran@kutztown.edu.

INTERNATIONAL STUDENTS 7% of students enrolled are international students. *Services and facilities:* Counseling/support services, International student housing, International student organization, Orientation, Visa Services. Financial aid is available to international students. *Required with application:* TOEFL with recommended score of 213 (computer) or 550 (paper); proof of adequate funds; proof of health/immunizations.

International Student Contact Ms. Sarah Wade, Director of International Initiatives and Student Services, 204 Stratton Administration Building, PO Box 730, Kutztown, PA 19530. *Phone:* 484-646-4256. *Fax:* 610-683-1356. *E-mail:* wade@kutztown.edu.

APPLICATION *Required:* GMAT, application form, baccalaureate/first degree, 2 letters of recommendation, personal statement, resume/curriculum vitae, transcripts of college work. *Recommended:* Work experience. *Application fee:* $35. Applications for domestic and international students are processed on a rolling basis.

Application Contact Dr. Fidelis M. Ikem, Interim Dean, 119 deFrancesco Building, Kutztown, PA 19530. *Phone:* 610-683-4575. *Fax:* 610-683-4573. *E-mail:* ikem@kutztown.edu.

La Roche College
School of Graduate Studies and Adult Education

Pittsburgh, Pennsylvania

Phone: 412-536-1266 **Fax:** 412-536-1283 **E-mail:** hope.schiffgens@laroche.edu

Business Program(s) Web Site: http://www.laroche.edu

Graduate Business Unit Enrollment *Total:* 73 (4 full-time; 69 part-time; 63 women; 2 international). *Average Age:* 35.

Graduate Business Faculty *Total:* 10 (2 full-time; 8 part-time).

Admissions *Applied:* 23. *Admitted:* 23. *Enrolled:* 15. *Average GMAT:* 430. *Average GPA:* 3.26

Academic Calendar Semesters.

Accreditation ACBSP—The American Council of Business Schools and Programs.

After Graduation (Class of 2006–07) *Employed within 3 months of graduation:* 90%.

DEGREE MS

MS—Master of Science in Human Resources Management Full-time and part-time. At least 36 total credits required. 12 to 72 months to complete program. *Concentration:* human resources management.

RESOURCES AND SERVICES 200 on-campus PCs are available to graduate business students. Access to Internet/World Wide Web, online (class) registration, and online grade reports available. *Personal computer requirements:* Graduate business students are not required to have a personal computer. *Placement services include:* Alumni network, career placement, career counseling/planning, resume referral, career fairs, job interviews arranged, resume preparation, and career library.

EXPENSES *Tuition:* Full-time: $10,440. Part-time: $580 per credit hour. *Tuition (international):* Full-time: $10,440. Part-time: $580 per credit hour. *Required fees:* Full-time: $252. Part-time: $14 per credit hour. *Typical graduate housing cost:* $7942 (including board), $4974 (room only).

FINANCIAL AID (2007–08) 50 students received aid, including loans. Aid is available to part-time students. *Financial aid application deadline:* 5/1.

Financial Aid Contact Ms. Sharon Platt, Director of Financial Aid, 9000 Babcock Boulevard, Pittsburgh, PA 15237-5898. *Phone:* 412-536-1120. *Fax:* 412-536-1072. *E-mail:* sharon.platt@laroche.edu.

INTERNATIONAL STUDENTS 3% of students enrolled are international students. *Services and facilities:* Counseling/support services, ESL/language courses, Housing location assistance, International student housing, International student organization, Language tutoring, Orientation, Visa Services. Financial aid is not available to international students. *Required with application:* Proof of adequate funds; proof of health/immunizations.

International Student Contact Natasha Garrett, Director of International Student Services, 9000 Babcock Boulevard, Pittsburgh, PA 15237. *Phone:* 412-536-1296. *Fax:* 412-536-1290. *E-mail:* crvenkn1@laroche.edu.

APPLICATION *Required:* Application form, baccalaureate/first degree, essay, 2 letters of recommendation, personal statement, resume/curriculum vitae, transcripts of college work. School will accept GMAT, GRE, and MAT. *Recommended:* Interview, work experience. *Application fee:* $50. *Deadlines:* 8/15 for fall (international), 12/15 for spring (international), 5/1 for summer (international). Applications for domestic students are processed on a rolling basis.

Application Contact Ms. Hope A. Schiffgens, Director of Graduate and Adult Education, 9000 Babcock Boulevard, Pittsburgh, PA 15237. *Phone:* 412-536-1266. *Fax:* 412-536-1283. *E-mail:* hope.schiffgens@laroche.edu.

La Salle University
School of Business

Philadelphia, Pennsylvania

Phone: 215-951-1057 **Fax:** 215-951-1886 **E-mail:** mba@lasalle.edu

Business Program(s) Web Site: http://www.lasalle.edu/mba

Accreditation AACSB—The Association to Advance Collegiate Schools of Business.

DEGREE MBA

MBA—Master of Business Administration Full-time and part-time. 33 to 48 total credits required. 12 to 84 months to complete program. *Concentrations:* accounting, finance, general MBA, human resources management, international business, management, management information systems, marketing.

RESOURCES AND SERVICES 135 on-campus PCs are available to graduate business students. Access to Internet/World Wide Web, online (class) registration, and online grade reports available. *Personal computer requirements:* Graduate business students are not required to have a personal computer. *Special opportunities include:* An international exchange program and an internship program are available. *Placement services include:* Alumni network, career placement, job search course, career counseling/planning, electronic job bank, resume referral, career fairs, job interviews arranged, resume preparation, and career library.

Application Contact Ms. Terry Jackson, Director, MBA Program, 1900 West Olney Avenue, Philadelphia, PA 19141. *Phone:* 215-951-1057. *Fax:* 215-951-1886. *E-mail:* mba@lasalle.edu.

Lebanon Valley College
Program in Business Administration
Annville, Pennsylvania

Phone: 717-867-6335 **Fax:** 717-867-6018 **E-mail:** b_raffie@lvc.edu

Business Program(s) Web Site: http://www.lvc.edu/mba

Graduate Business Unit Enrollment *Total:* 99 (99 part-time; 51 women).

Graduate Business Faculty *Total:* 16 (1 full-time; 15 part-time).

Admissions *Applied:* 14. *Admitted:* 12. *Enrolled:* 12. *Average GMAT:* 543. *Average GPA:* 3.28

Academic Calendar Semesters.

Accreditation ACBSP—The American Council of Business Schools and Programs (candidate).

After Graduation (Class of 2006–07) *Employed within 3 months of graduation:* 100%.

DEGREE MBA

MBA—Master of Business Administration Part-time. At least 36 total credits required. Maximum of 60 months to complete program. *Concentration:* general MBA.

RESOURCES AND SERVICES 94 on-campus PCs are available to graduate business students. Access to Internet/World Wide Web and online grade reports available. *Personal computer requirements:* Graduate business students are strongly recommended to purchase or lease a personal computer. *Placement services include:* Alumni network, career placement, career counseling/planning, resume referral, resume preparation, and career library.

EXPENSES *Tuition:* Part-time: $410 per credit hour.

Financial Aid Contact Vicki Cantrell, Assistant Director of Financial Aid, 101 North College Avenue, Annville, PA 17003-0501. *Phone:* 717-867-6181. *Fax:* 717-867-6026. *E-mail:* finaid@lvc.edu.

INTERNATIONAL STUDENTS Financial aid is not available to international students.

APPLICATION *Required:* Application form, baccalaureate/first degree, interview, resume/curriculum vitae, transcripts of college work, 2 years of work experience. School will accept GMAT. *Application fee:* $30. Applications for domestic students are processed on a rolling basis.

Application Contact Dr. Barney T Raffield, III, Coordinator, MBA Program, 101 North College Avenue, Annville, PA 17003-0501. *Phone:* 717-867-6335. *Fax:* 717-867-6018. *E-mail:* b_raffie@lvc.edu.

Lehigh University
College of Business and Economics
Bethlehem, Pennsylvania

Phone: 610-758-3418 **Fax:** 610-758-5283 **E-mail:** corinn.mcbride@lehigh.edu

Business Program(s) Web Site: http://www.lehigh.edu/business

Graduate Business Unit Enrollment *Total:* 374 (92 full-time; 282 part-time; 115 women). *Average Age:* 30.

Graduate Business Faculty 63 full-time.

Admissions *Average GMAT:* 633. *Average GPA:* 3.2

Academic Calendar Semesters.

Accreditation AACSB—The Association to Advance Collegiate Schools of Business.

After Graduation (Class of 2006–07) *Employed within 3 months of graduation:* 70%. *Average starting salary:* $76,000.

DEGREES M Econ • M Sc • MAS • MBA • MBA/M Eng • MBA/ME • MS

M Econ—MS—Health and Bio-Pharmaceutical Economics Full-time and part-time. Undergraduate degree in life sciences. 30 total credits required. 12 to 72 months to complete program. *Concentration:* health administration.

M Sc—Analytical Finance Full-time and part-time. GMAT or GRE. 33 total credits required. 12 to 72 months to complete program. *Concentration:* financial engineering.

MAS—Master of Science in Accounting and Information Analysis Full-time and part-time. GMAT required. At least 30 total credits required. 12 to 72 months to complete program. *Concentration:* accounting.

MBA—Master of Business Administration Full-time and part-time. Distance learning option. GMAT required. At least 36 total credits required. 12 to 72 months to complete program. *Concentrations:* entrepreneurship, finance, general MBA, information systems, international business, management, marketing, project management, supply chain management, technology management.

MBA/M Eng—Master of Business Administration and Engineering Full-time and part-time. Distance learning option. GMAT or GRE required depending on the engineering concentration. At least 45 total credits required. 24 to 72 months to complete program. *Concentrations:* engineering, general MBA, information systems, management, marketing, supply chain management.

MBA/ME—MBA/Master in Educational Leadership Full-time and part-time. GMAT. 45 total credits required. 24 to 72 months to complete program. *Concentration:* leadership.

MS—Master of Science in Economics Full-time and part-time. GMAT or GRE required. At least 30 total credits required. 12 to 72 months to complete program. *Concentration:* economics.

RESOURCES AND SERVICES 334 on-campus PCs are available to graduate business students. Access to Internet/World Wide Web, online (class) registration, and online grade reports available. *Personal computer requirements:* Graduate business students are strongly recommended to purchase or lease a personal computer. *Special opportunities include:* An international exchange program and an internship program are available. *Placement services include:* Alumni network, career placement, job search course, career counseling/planning, electronic job bank, resume referral, career fairs, job interviews arranged, resume preparation, and career library.

EXPENSES *Tuition:* Part-time: $700 per credit. *Tuition (international):* Part-time: $700 per credit.

FINANCIAL AID (2007–08) 86 students received aid, including fellowships, research assistantships, scholarships, and teaching assistantships. Aid is available to part-time students. *Financial aid application deadline:* 1/15.

Lehigh University (continued)

Financial Aid Contact Corinn McBride, Director of Recruitment and Admissions, Rauch Business Center, 621 Taylor Street, Bethlehem, PA 18015. *Phone:* 610-758-3418. *Fax:* 610-758-5283. *E-mail:* corinn.mcbride@lehigh.edu.

INTERNATIONAL STUDENTS *Services and facilities:* Counseling/support services, ESL/language courses, Housing location assistance, International student housing, International student organization, Language tutoring, Orientation, Visa Services. Financial aid is available to international students. *Required with application:* TOEFL with recommended score of 250 (computer), 600 (paper), or 94 (Internet); proof of adequate funds; proof of health/immunizations.

International Student Contact Giselle Nansteel, Director, International Students and Scholars Office, 32 Sayre Drive, Bethlehem, PA 18015. *Phone:* 610-758-4859. *E-mail:* gmn0@lehigh.edu.

APPLICATION *Required:* Application form, baccalaureate/first degree, essay, 2 letters of recommendation, personal statement, resume/curriculum vitae, transcripts of college work, 2 years of work experience. School will accept GMAT and GRE. *Recommended:* Interview. *Application fee:* $65. Applications for domestic and international students are processed on a rolling basis.

Application Contact Corinn McBride, Director of Recruitment and Admissions, Rauch Business Center, 621 Taylor Street, Bethlehem, PA 18015. *Phone:* 610-758-3418. *Fax:* 610-758-5283. *E-mail:* corinn.mcbride@lehigh.edu.

See full description on page 656.

Millersville University of Pennsylvania
Department of Business Administration

Millersville, Pennsylvania

Phone: 717-872-3030 **Fax:** 717-871-2022 **E-mail:** gradstu@millersville.edu

Business Program(s) Web Site: http://www.millersville.edu/~graduate

Graduate Business Unit Enrollment *Total:* 48 (6 full-time; 42 part-time; 19 women). *Average Age:* 30.

Graduate Business Faculty *Total:* 13 (10 full-time; 3 part-time).

Admissions *Applied:* 11. *Admitted:* 8. *Enrolled:* 8. *Average GMAT:* 464. *Average GPA:* 3.1

Academic Calendar Semesters.

Accreditation ACBSP—The American Council of Business Schools and Programs.

DEGREE MBA

MBA—Master of Business Administration Full-time and part-time. 36 total credits required. 14 to 60 months to complete program. *Concentration:* general MBA.

RESOURCES AND SERVICES Access to Internet/World Wide Web, online (class) registration, and online grade reports available. *Personal computer requirements:* Graduate business students are strongly recommended to purchase or lease a personal computer. *Placement services include:* Alumni network, career placement, career counseling/planning, career fairs, and resume preparation.

EXPENSES *Tuition (state resident):* Part-time: $1289 per course. *Tuition (nonresident):* Part-time: $1932 per course. *Tuition (international):* Part-time: $1289 per course.

FINANCIAL AID (2007–08) Work study. Aid is available to part-time students. *Financial aid application deadline:* 2/1.

INTERNATIONAL STUDENTS *Services and facilities:* Counseling/support services, ESL/language courses, Housing location assistance, International student organization, Orientation. Financial aid is available

to international students. *Required with application:* TOEFL with recommended score of 500 (paper); proof of adequate funds.

APPLICATION *Required:* GMAT, application form, baccalaureate/first degree, essay, 3 letters of recommendation, personal statement, resume/curriculum vitae, transcripts of college work. *Recommended:* Interview. *Application fee:* $40. Applications for domestic and international students are processed on a rolling basis.

Application Contact Office of Graduate Studies, 231 Lyle Hall, PO Box 1002, Millersville, PA 17551. *Phone:* 717-872-3030. *Fax:* 717-871-2022. *E-mail:* gradstu@millersville.edu.

Misericordia University
Division of Behavioral Science, Education, and Business

Dallas, Pennsylvania

Phone: 570-674-6451 **E-mail:** lbrown@misericordia.edu

Business Program(s) Web Site: http://www.misericordia.edu/misericordia_pg.cfm?page_id=737&subcat_id=146

Graduate Business Unit Enrollment *Total:* 139 (139 part-time; 91 women). *Average Age:* 37.

Graduate Business Faculty *Total:* 12 (4 full-time; 8 part-time).

Admissions *Applied:* 46. *Admitted:* 38. *Enrolled:* 35. *Average GPA:* 3.0

Academic Calendar Semesters.

DEGREES MBA • MS

MBA—Master of Business Administration Part-time. Distance learning option. 36 total credits required. *Concentrations:* accounting, human resources management, management.

MS—Master of Science in Organizational Management Part-time. Distance learning option. 36 total credits required. *Concentrations:* human resources management, information systems, management, marketing.

RESOURCES AND SERVICES 100 on-campus PCs are available to graduate business students. Access to Internet/World Wide Web, online (class) registration, and online grade reports available. *Personal computer requirements:* Graduate business students are strongly recommended to purchase or lease a personal computer. *Special opportunities include:* An internship program is available. *Placement services include:* Alumni network, career placement, job search course, career counseling/planning, resume referral, career fairs, job interviews arranged, resume preparation, and career library.

EXPENSES *Tuition:* Part-time: $495 per credit. *Tuition (international):* Part-time: $495 per credit.

FINANCIAL AID (2007–08) 89 students received aid, including grants and loans. Aid is available to part-time students.

Financial Aid Contact Jane Dessoye, Executive Director of Admissions and Financial Aid, 301 Lake Street, Dallas, PA 18612-1098. *Phone:* 570-674-6280. *E-mail:* jdessoye@misericordia.edu.

INTERNATIONAL STUDENTS Financial aid is not available to international students. *Required with application:* TOEFL with recommended score of 550 (paper).

International Student Contact Ms. Larree Brown, Assistant Director of Admissions, Data Management and Student Services, Office of Adult Education, 301 Lake Street, Dallas, PA 18612-1098. *Phone:* 570-674-6451.

APPLICATION *Required:* Application form, baccalaureate/first degree, 3 letters of recommendation, transcripts of college work. School will accept GMAT, GRE, and MAT. *Recommended:* Essay, interview, work experience. *Application fee:* $25. Applications for domestic and international students are processed on a rolling basis.

Application Contact Ms. Larree Brown, Assistant Director of Admissions, Data Management and Student Services, Office of Adult Education, 301 Lake Street, Dallas, PA 18612-1098. *Phone:* 570-674-6451. *E-mail:* lbrown@misericordia.edu.

Moravian College
The Moravian MBA
Bethlehem, Pennsylvania

Phone: 610-861-1400 **Fax:** 610-861-1466 **E-mail:** mba@moravian.edu

Business Program(s) Web Site: http://comenius.moravian.edu

Graduate Business Unit Enrollment *Total:* 69 (69 part-time; 35 women).

Graduate Business Faculty *Total:* 13 (5 full-time; 8 part-time).

Admissions *Applied:* 13. *Admitted:* 11. *Enrolled:* 10. *Average GMAT:* 481. *Average GPA:* 3.3

Academic Calendar Semesters.

After Graduation (Class of 2006–07) *Employed within 3 months of graduation:* 100%.

DEGREE MBA

MBA—Master of Business Administration Full-time and part-time. 30 to 48 total credits required. 12 to 84 months to complete program. *Concentrations:* general MBA, health administration, health care, information systems, information technology, management, supply chain management.

RESOURCES AND SERVICES 60 on-campus PCs are available to graduate business students. Access to Internet/World Wide Web, online (class) registration, and online grade reports available. *Personal computer requirements:* Graduate business students are strongly recommended to purchase or lease a personal computer. *Special opportunities include:* An internship program is available. *Placement services include:* Alumni network, electronic job bank, resume referral, and career library.

EXPENSES *Tuition:* Part-time: $1704 per course. *Tuition (international):* Part-time: $1704 per course. *Required fees:* Part-time: $40 per semester.

FINANCIAL AID (2007–08) 1 student received aid, including fellowships. Aid is available to part-time students.

Financial Aid Contact Ms. Linda J. Doyle, Information Contact, Moravian College Comenius Center, 1200 Main Street, Bethlehem, PA 18018. *Phone:* 610-861-1400. *Fax:* 610-861-1466. *E-mail:* mba@moravian.edu.

INTERNATIONAL STUDENTS *Services and facilities:* Counseling/support services, Housing location assistance, International student organization, Orientation. Financial aid is not available to international students. *Required with application:* TOEFL with recommended score of 213 (computer) or 550 (paper); proof of adequate funds; proof of health/immunizations.

International Student Contact Dr. William A. Kleintop, Associate Dean of Business and Management Programs, Moravian College Comenius Center, 1200 Main Street, Bethlehem, PA 18018. *Phone:* 610-861-1400. *Fax:* 610-861-1466. *E-mail:* mba@moravian.edu.

APPLICATION *Required:* Application form, baccalaureate/first degree, interview, 2 letters of recommendation, resume/curriculum vitae, transcripts of college work, 1 year of work experience. School will accept GMAT. *Application fee:* $40. Applications for domestic and international students are processed on a rolling basis.

Application Contact Ms. Linda J. Doyle, Information Contact, Moravian College Comenius Center, 1200 Main Street, Bethlehem, PA 18018. *Phone:* 610-861-1400. *Fax:* 610-861-1466. *E-mail:* mba@moravian.edu.

Penn State Great Valley
Graduate Studies
Malvern, Pennsylvania

Phone: 610-648-3248 **Fax:** 610-725-5296 **E-mail:** gvmba@psu.edu

Business Program(s) Web Site: http://www.gv.psu.edu/mba

DEGREES MBA • MBA/MSIS • MF • MLM

MBA—Master of Business Administration in Biotechnology and Health Industry Management Full-time and part-time. New students are admitted six times each year. 30 to 45 total credits required. 24 to 72 months to complete program. *Concentrations:* health administration, health care, pharmaceutical management.

MBA—Master of Business Administration in General Business Full-time and part-time. New students are admitted six times each year. 30 to 45 total credits required. 24 to 72 months to complete program. *Concentrations:* business ethics, business information science, entrepreneurship, finance, general MBA, health administration, health care, information management, information systems, leadership, management, management communication, management information systems, marketing, new venture management, pharmaceutical management.

MBA—Master of Business Administration in New Ventures and Entrepreneurial Studies Full-time and part-time. New students are admitted six times each year. 30 to 45 total credits required. 24 to 72 months to complete program. *Concentrations:* entrepreneurship, new venture management.

MBA—Master of Business Administration New students are admitted six times each year. *Concentrations:* business information science, information management, information systems, information technology, management information systems.

MBA/MSIS—Master of Business Administration/Master of Science in Information Science Full-time and part-time. New students are admitted six times each year. At least 66 total credits required. 36 to 72 months to complete program. *Concentrations:* business information science, combined degrees, entrepreneurship, finance, financial information systems, health administration, health care, information management, information systems, information technology, management, management information systems, management systems analysis, marketing, new venture management, pharmaceutical management, project management, system management, technology management.

MF—Finance Part-time. Applications should be submitted by October 31 for admission in January (spring semester) or by June 30 for admission in September (fall semester). 30 total credits required. 15 to 72 months to complete program. *Concentration:* finance.

MLM—Master of Leadership Development ((MLD) Part-time. Applicants should have at least five years of relevant work experience. 33 total credits required. 18 to 72 months to complete program. *Concentration:* leadership.

RESOURCES AND SERVICES 270 on-campus PCs are available to graduate business students. Access to Internet/World Wide Web, online (class) registration, and online grade reports available. *Personal computer requirements:* Graduate business students are strongly recommended to purchase or lease a personal computer. *Special opportunities include:* An internship program is available. *Placement services include:* Alumni network, career placement, career counseling/planning, electronic job bank, resume referral, career fairs, resume preparation, and career library.

Application Contact Ms. Susan Haldeman, Graduate Enrollment Coordinator, 30 East Swedesford Road, Malvern, PA 19355. *Phone:* 610-648-3248. *Fax:* 610-725-5296. *E-mail:* gvmba@psu.edu.

Penn State Harrisburg
School of Business Administration
Middletown, Pennsylvania

Phone: 717-948-6250 **Fax:** 717-948-6325 **E-mail:** rrl1@psu.edu

Business Program(s) Web Site: http://www.hbg.psu.edu/sbus

Penn State Harrisburg (continued)

Accreditation AACSB—The Association to Advance Collegiate Schools of Business.

DEGREES MBA • MS

MBA—Master of Business Administration Full-time and part-time. 30 to 48 total credits required. 18 to 72 months to complete program. *Concentration:* general MBA.

MS—Master of Science in Information Systems Full-time and part-time. 30 to 39 total credits required. 18 to 72 months to complete program. *Concentration:* management information systems.

RESOURCES AND SERVICES 230 on-campus PCs are available to graduate business students. Access to Internet/World Wide Web, online (class) registration, and online grade reports available. *Personal computer requirements:* Graduate business students are not required to have a personal computer. *Special opportunities include:* An internship program is available. *Placement services include:* Alumni network, career placement, career counseling/planning, electronic job bank, resume referral, career fairs, job interviews arranged, resume preparation, and career library.

Application Contact Admissions, 777 West Harrisburg Pike, Middletown, PA 17057-4898. *Phone:* 717-948-6250. *Fax:* 717-948-6325. *E-mail:* rrl1@psu.edu.

Penn State University Park
The Mary Jean and Frank P. Smeal College of Business Administration

State College, University Park, Pennsylvania

Phone: 814-863-0474 **Fax:** 814-863-8072 **E-mail:** smealmba@psu.edu

Business Program(s) Web Site: http://www.smeal.psu.edu/mba

Graduate Business Unit Enrollment *Total:* 171 (171 full-time; 52 women; 111 international). *Average Age:* 28.

Graduate Business Faculty 44 full-time.

Admissions *Applied:* 526. *Admitted:* 151. *Enrolled:* 86. *Average GMAT:* 650. *Average GPA:* 3.3

Academic Calendar 7 weeks—1 week—7 weeks.

Accreditation AACSB—The Association to Advance Collegiate Schools of Business.

After Graduation (Class of 2006–07) *Employed within 3 months of graduation:* 90%. *Average starting salary:* $83,098.

DEGREES JD/MBA • MBA • MMM

JD/MBA—Juris Doctor/Master of Business Administration Full-time. At least 88 total credits required. Minimum of 48 months to complete program. *Concentrations:* entrepreneurship, finance, financial management/planning, law, marketing, strategic management, supply chain management.

MBA—Full-Time Master of Business Administration Full-time. At least 60 total credits required. Minimum of 21 months to complete program. *Concentrations:* entrepreneurship, finance, financial management/planning, marketing, strategic management, supply chain management.

MBA—Master of Business Administration Full-time. At least 140 total credits required. Minimum of 60 months to complete program. *Concentrations:* entrepreneurship, finance, financial management/planning, marketing, strategic management, supply chain management.

MMM—Master of Quality and Manufacturing Management Full-time and part-time. At least 48 total credits required. Minimum of 21 months to complete program. *Concentrations:* manufacturing management, supply chain management.

RESOURCES AND SERVICES 40 on-campus PCs are available to graduate business students. Access to Internet/World Wide Web, online

(class) registration, and online grade reports available. *Personal computer requirements:* Graduate business students are required to have a personal computer. *Special opportunities include:* An international exchange program and an internship program are available. *Placement services include:* Alumni network, career placement, job search course, career counseling/planning, electronic job bank, resume referral, career fairs, job interviews arranged, resume preparation, and career library.

EXPENSES *Tuition (state resident):* Full-time: $17,110. *Tuition (nonresident):* Full-time: $28,712. *Tuition (international):* Full-time: $28,712. *Required fees:* Full-time: $1410. *Graduate housing:* Room and board costs vary by number of occupants and type of board plan. *Typical cost:* $9410 (including board), $6050 (room only).

FINANCIAL AID (2007–08) 130 students received aid, including fellowships, grants, loans, research assistantships, scholarships, and teaching assistantships. *Financial aid application deadline:* 2/1.

Financial Aid Contact Ms. Anna M. Griswold, Assistant Vice Provost for Student Aid, Office of Student Aid, 311 Shields Building, University Park, PA 16802. *Phone:* 814-865-0507. *Fax:* 814-863-0322. *E-mail:* amg5@psu.edu.

INTERNATIONAL STUDENTS 65% of students enrolled are international students. *Services and facilities:* Counseling/support services, ESL/language courses, Housing location assistance, International student organization, Language tutoring, Orientation, Visa Services. Financial aid is available to international students. *Required with application:* TOEFL with recommended score of 250 (computer), 600 (paper), or 100 (Internet); proof of adequate funds; proof of health/immunizations.

International Student Contact Ms. Masume Assaf, Associate Director, International Programs, 4100 Boucke Building, University Park, PA 16802. *Phone:* 814-865-6348. *Fax:* 814-865-3336. *E-mail:* assaf@psu.edu.

APPLICATION *Required:* GMAT, application form, baccalaureate/first degree, essay, interview, 2 letters of recommendation, resume/curriculum vitae, transcripts of college work. *Recommended:* Work experience. *Application fee:* $75. Applications for domestic and international students are processed on a rolling basis.

Application Contact Carrie Marcinkevage, Director of Admissions, 220 Business Building, University Park, PA 16802-3603. *Phone:* 814-863-0474. *Fax:* 814-863-8072. *E-mail:* smealmba@psu.edu.

Philadelphia Biblical University
School of Business and Leadership

Langhorne, Pennsylvania

Phone: 215-702-4260 **Fax:** 215-702-4844 **E-mail:** rferner@pbu.edu

Business Program(s) Web Site: http://www.pbu.edu/academic/bl/msol

Graduate Business Unit Enrollment *Total:* 24 (1 full-time; 23 part-time; 14 women; 22 international). *Average Age:* 39.

Graduate Business Faculty *Total:* 3 (2 full-time; 1 part-time).

Admissions *Applied:* 23. *Admitted:* 9. *Enrolled:* 8. *Average GPA:* 3.3

Academic Calendar Semesters.

After Graduation (Class of 2006–07) *Employed within 3 months of graduation:* 100%.

DEGREE MSOL

MSOL—Master of Science in Organizational Leadership Full-time and part-time. At least 44 total credits required. Minimum of 9 months to complete program. *Concentrations:* leadership, organizational behavior/development, organizational management.

RESOURCES AND SERVICES 40 on-campus PCs are available to graduate business students. Access to Internet/World Wide Web, online (class) registration, and online grade reports available. *Personal computer requirements:* Graduate business students are not required to have a personal computer. *Placement services include:* Career counseling/planning, resume referral, career fairs, resume preparation, and career library.

EXPENSES *Tuition:* Full-time: $8820. Part-time: $490 per credit. *Tuition (international):* Full-time: $8820. Part-time: $490 per credit. *Graduate housing:* Room and board costs vary by campus location, number of occupants, type of accommodation, and type of board plan. *Typical cost:* $10,702 (including board), $7452 (room only).

FINANCIAL AID (2007–08) 4 students received aid, including loans and scholarships. Aid is available to part-time students.

Financial Aid Contact Mr. William Kellaris, Director, Financial Aid, 200 Manor Avenue, Langhorne, PA 19047. *Phone:* 800-366-0049. *Fax:* 215-702-4248. *E-mail:* bkellaris@pbu.edu.

INTERNATIONAL STUDENTS 92% of students enrolled are international students. *Services and facilities:* Counseling/support services, Housing location assistance, International student housing, International student organization, Orientation, Visa Services. Financial aid is available to international students. *Required with application:* TOEFL with recommended score of 213 (computer) or 550 (paper); proof of adequate funds; proof of health/immunizations.

International Student Contact Mr. Eric Rivera, International Admissions Counselor, 200 Manor Avenue, Langhorne, PA 19047. *Phone:* 215-702-4241. *Fax:* 215-702-4248. *E-mail:* erivera@pbu.edu.

APPLICATION *Required:* Application form, baccalaureate/first degree, essay, 3 letters of recommendation, personal statement, transcripts of college work. *Recommended:* Interview. *Application fee:* $25. Applications for domestic and international students are processed on a rolling basis.

Application Contact Mr. Ron Ferner, Dean, 200 Manor Avenue, Langhorne, PA 19047. *Phone:* 215-702-4260. *Fax:* 215-702-4844. *E-mail:* rferner@pbu.edu.

Philadelphia University
School of Business Administration

Philadelphia, Pennsylvania

Phone: 215-951-2943 **Fax:** 215-951-2907 **E-mail:** klettj@philau.edu

Business Program(s) Web Site: http://www.philau.edu/graduate/

Graduate Business Unit Enrollment *Total:* 164 (47 full-time; 117 part-time; 85 women).

Graduate Business Faculty *Total:* 22 (12 full-time; 10 part-time).

Admissions *Applied:* 196. *Admitted:* 98. *Enrolled:* 58. *Average GMAT:* 459. *Average GPA:* 3.2

Academic Calendar Semesters.

DEGREES MBA • MBA/MS • MS

MBA—Master of Business Administration Full-time and part-time. Distance learning option. 33 to 52 total credits required. 12 to 84 months to complete program. *Concentrations:* finance, health care, international business, management, marketing, taxation.

MBA/MS—Master of Business Administration/Master of Science in Taxation Full-time and part-time. 53 to 72 total credits required. 30 to 84 months to complete program. *Concentrations:* accounting, taxation.

MS—Master of Science in Taxation Full-time and part-time. At least 30 total credits required. 18 to 84 months to complete program. *Concentration:* taxation.

RESOURCES AND SERVICES 675 on-campus PCs are available to graduate business students. Access to Internet/World Wide Web, online (class) registration, and online grade reports available. *Personal computer requirements:* Graduate business students are not required to have a personal computer. *Special opportunities include:* An internship program is available. *Placement services include:* Alumni network, career

placement, job search course, career counseling/planning, electronic job bank, resume referral, career fairs, job interviews arranged, resume preparation, and career library.

EXPENSES *Tuition:* Full-time: $13,428. Part-time: $746 per credit. *Tuition (international):* Full-time: $13,443.

FINANCIAL AID (2007–08) 30 students received aid, including scholarships. Aid is available to part-time students. *Financial aid application deadline:* 5/1.

Financial Aid Contact Ms. Lisa Cooper, Director of Financial Aid, School House Lane and Henry Avenue, Philadelphia, PA 19144. *Phone:* 215-951-2940. *Fax:* 215-951-2907. *E-mail:* cooperl@philau.edu.

INTERNATIONAL STUDENTS *Services and facilities:* Counseling/support services, Housing location assistance, International student organization, Orientation, Visa Services. Financial aid is available to international students. *Required with application:* TOEFL with recommended score of 213 (computer), 550 (paper), or 79 (Internet); proof of adequate funds; proof of health/immunizations.

International Student Contact Ms. Hannah Bar-Giora, International Student Advisor, School House Lane and Henry Avenue, Philadelphia, PA 19144. *Phone:* 215-951-2660. *E-mail:* bargiorah@philau.edu.

APPLICATION *Required:* GMAT, application form, baccalaureate/first degree, transcripts of college work. School will accept GRE and MAT. *Recommended:* Resume/curriculum vitae. *Application fee:* $35. Applications for domestic and international students are processed on a rolling basis.

Application Contact Jack Klett, Director of Graduate Admissions, School House Lane and Henry Avenue, Philadelphia, PA 19144. *Phone:* 215-951-2943. *Fax:* 215-951-2907. *E-mail:* klettj@philau.edu.

See full description on page 668.

Point Park University
School of Business

Pittsburgh, Pennsylvania

Phone: 412-392-3808 **Fax:** 412-392-6164 **E-mail:** kballas@pointpark.edu

Business Program(s) Web Site: http://www.pointpark.edu

Graduate Business Unit Enrollment *Total:* 298 (143 full-time; 155 part-time; 181 women; 27 international). *Average Age:* 32.

Graduate Business Faculty *Total:* 29 (12 full-time; 17 part-time).

Admissions *Applied:* 334. *Admitted:* 229. *Enrolled:* 162. *Average GPA:* 3.2

Academic Calendar Semesters.

DEGREES MA • MBA

MA—Organizational Leadership Full-time and part-time. 30 total credits required. 12 to 24 months to complete program. *Concentration:* leadership.

MBA—Master of Business Administration Full-time and part-time. 36 total credits required. 12 to 24 months to complete program. *Concentrations:* arts administration/management, information systems, international business, management, sports/entertainment management.

RESOURCES AND SERVICES 100 on-campus PCs are available to graduate business students. Access to Internet/World Wide Web and online (class) registration available. *Personal computer requirements:* Graduate business students are not required to have a personal computer. *Special opportunities include:* An internship program is available. *Placement services include:* Career placement, career counseling/planning, resume referral, career fairs, resume preparation, and career library.

EXPENSES *Tuition:* Full-time: $10,566. Part-time: $587 per credit. *Tuition (international):* Full-time: $10,566. Part-time: $587 per credit. *Required fees:* Full-time: $360. Part-time: $20 per credit. *Graduate*

Point Park University (continued)

housing: Room and board costs vary by number of occupants, type of accommodation, and type of board plan. *Typical cost:* $8440 (including board), $3980 (room only).

FINANCIAL AID (2007–08) Grants, loans, scholarships, and teaching assistantships. Aid is available to part-time students.

Financial Aid Contact Sandra Cronin, Director, Financial Aid, 201 Wood Street, Pittsburgh, PA 15222. *Phone:* 412-392-3930. *Fax:* 412-392-4795. *E-mail:* scronin@pointpark.edu.

INTERNATIONAL STUDENTS 9% of students enrolled are international students. *Services and facilities:* Counseling/support services, ESL/language courses, International student housing, International student organization, Orientation, Visa Services, International student services office. Financial aid is available to international students. *Required with application:* TOEFL with recommended score of 500 (paper); proof of adequate funds.

International Student Contact Mr. Aamir Anwar, Director, International Student Services and Enrollment, International Student Services and Enrollment Office, 201 Wood Street, Pittsburgh, PA 15222-1984. *Phone:* 412-392-3903. *Fax:* 412-391-1980. *E-mail:* anwar@pointpark.edu.

APPLICATION *Required:* Application form, baccalaureate/first degree, 2 letters of recommendation, transcripts of college work. *Recommended:* Resume/curriculum vitae. *Application fee:* $30. Applications for domestic and international students are processed on a rolling basis.

Application Contact Kathy Ballas, Director of Adult Enrollment, Office of Adult Enrollment, 201 Wood Street, Pittsburgh, PA 15222-1984. *Phone:* 412-392-3808. *Fax:* 412-392-6164. *E-mail:* kballas@pointpark.edu.

Robert Morris University
Program in Business Administration

Moon Township, Pennsylvania

Phone: 412-397-5200 **Fax:** 412-397-2425 **E-mail:** admissions@rmu.edu

Business Program(s) Web Site: http://www.rmu.edu/

Graduate Business Unit Enrollment *Total:* 252 (252 part-time; 115 women; 5 international). *Average Age:* 34.

Graduate Business Faculty *Total:* 28 (24 full-time; 4 part-time).

Admissions *Applied:* 104. *Admitted:* 85. *Enrolled:* 53.

Academic Calendar Semesters.

After Graduation (Class of 2006–07) *Employed within 3 months of graduation:* 95%. *Average starting salary:* $45,500.

DEGREES MBA • MS

MBA—Master of Business Administration Part-time. At least 36 total credits required. *Concentration:* general MBA.

MS—Master of Science Part-time. At least 30 total credits required. *Concentrations:* human resources management, nonprofit management, taxation.

RESOURCES AND SERVICES 360 on-campus PCs are available to graduate business students. Access to Internet/World Wide Web, online (class) registration, and online grade reports available. *Personal computer requirements:* Graduate business students are not required to have a personal computer. *Special opportunities include:* An internship program is available. *Placement services include:* Career placement, job search course, career counseling/planning, electronic job bank, resume referral, career fairs, job interviews arranged, resume preparation, and career library.

EXPENSES *Tuition:* Part-time: $700 per credit hour. *Tuition (international):* Part-time: $700 per credit hour. *Required fees:* Part-time: $15 per credit hour. Tuition and/or fees vary by academic program. *Graduate housing:* Room and board costs vary by type of accommodation and type of board plan. *Typical cost:* $9880 (including board), $4940 (room only).

FINANCIAL AID (2007–08) Loans and work study. Aid is available to part-time students. *Financial aid application deadline:* 5/1.

Financial Aid Contact Financial Aid Office, 6001 University Boulevard, Moon Township, PA 15108-1189. *Phone:* 412-397-6250. *Fax:* 412-397-2200. *E-mail:* finaid@rmu.edu.

INTERNATIONAL STUDENTS 2% of students enrolled are international students. *Services and facilities:* Counseling/support services, International student organization, Orientation, Health services, International student advisor. Financial aid is available to international students. *Required with application:* TOEFL with recommended score of 213 (computer) or 500 (paper); proof of adequate funds.

International Student Contact Ms. Kellie L. Laurenzi, Dean, Enrollment Services, 6001 University Boulevard, Moon Township, PA 15108-1189. *Phone:* 412-397-5200. *Fax:* 412-397-2425. *E-mail:* admissions@rmu.edu.

APPLICATION *Required:* GMAT, application form, baccalaureate/first degree, 2 letters of recommendation, transcripts of college work. *Recommended:* Interview. *Application fee:* $35. Applications for domestic and international students are processed on a rolling basis.

Application Contact Ms. Kellie L. Laurenzi, Dean, Enrollment Services, 6001 University Boulevard, Moon Township, PA 15108-1189. *Phone:* 412-397-5200. *Fax:* 412-397-2425. *E-mail:* admissions@rmu.edu.

See full description on page 672.

Rosemont College
Accelerated Program in Management

Rosemont, Pennsylvania

Phone: 888-276-7366 Ext. 2596 **Fax:** 610-526-2987 **E-mail:** asabol@rosemont.edu

Business Program(s) Web Site: http://www.rosemont.edu/

Graduate Business Unit Enrollment *Total:* 123 (16 full-time; 107 part-time; 96 women; 2 international). *Average Age:* 37.

Graduate Business Faculty 21 part-time.

Admissions *Applied:* 60. *Admitted:* 42. *Enrolled:* 30. *Average GPA:* 3.4

Academic Calendar Six 7-week sessions.

After Graduation (Class of 2006–07) *Employed within 3 months of graduation:* 100%. *Average starting salary:* $44,000.

DEGREES MBA • MS

MBA—Master of Business Administration Part-time. Distance learning option. 3 years of professional managerial experience required. At least 36 total credits required. 12 to 36 months to complete program. *Concentration:* general MBA.

MS—Master of Science in Management Part-time. Distance learning option. 3 years of progressive managerial experience required. At least 36 total credits required. 12 to 36 months to complete program. *Concentration:* management.

RESOURCES AND SERVICES 25 on-campus PCs are available to graduate business students. Access to Internet/World Wide Web and online (class) registration available. *Personal computer requirements:* Graduate business students are required to have a personal computer. *Placement services include:* Alumni network, career placement, career counseling/planning, career fairs, resume preparation, and career library.

EXPENSES *Tuition:* Full-time: $15,390. Part-time: $570 per credit. *Tuition (international):* Full-time: $15,390. Part-time: $570 per credit. *Required fees:* Full-time: $945. Part-time: $105 per credit. *Graduate housing:* Room and board costs vary by number of occupants and type of accommodation. *Typical cost:* $9980 (including board).

FINANCIAL AID (2007–08) Loans.

Financial Aid Contact Valerie Harding, Counselor, Financial Aid, 1400 Montgomery Avenue, Rosemont, PA 19010. *Phone:* 610-527-0200 Ext. 22221. *Fax:* 610-520-4399. *E-mail:* mreynolds@rosemont.edu.

INTERNATIONAL STUDENTS 2% of students enrolled are international students. *Services and facilities:* Counseling/support services, Housing location assistance, International student organization, Orientation, Visa Services. Financial aid is not available to international students. *Required with application:* TOEFL with recommended score of 550 (paper); proof of adequate funds; proof of health/immunizations.

International Student Contact Carmella D. Catrambone, Coordinator of International Support Services, 1400 Montgomery Avenue, Rosemont, PA 19010. *Phone:* 610-527-0200 Ext. 2975. *Fax:* 610-520-4399. *E-mail:* cdimartino@rosemont.edu.

APPLICATION *Required:* Application form, baccalaureate/first degree, essay, interview, 2 letters of recommendation, personal statement, resume/curriculum vitae, transcripts of college work, 3 years of work experience. *Application fee:* $50. Applications for domestic and international students are processed on a rolling basis.

Application Contact Ann Sabol, Enrollment Counselor, 1400 Montgomery Avenue, Rosemont, PA 19010-1699. *Phone:* 888-276-7366 Ext. 2596. *Fax:* 610-526-2987. *E-mail:* asabol@rosemont.edu.

Saint Francis University
Master of Business Administration Program
Loretto, Pennsylvania

Phone: 814-472-3026 **Fax:** 814-472-3369 **E-mail:** rhogue@francis.edu

Business Program(s) Web Site: http://www.francis.edu/graduate

Graduate Business Unit Enrollment *Total:* 197 (15 full-time; 182 part-time; 92 women; 1 international). *Average Age:* 35.

Graduate Business Faculty *Total:* 31 (11 full-time; 20 part-time).

Admissions *Applied:* 75. *Admitted:* 60. *Enrolled:* 56. *Average GMAT:* 520. *Average GPA:* 3.2

Academic Calendar Semesters.

After Graduation (Class of 2006–07) *Employed within 3 months of graduation:* 100%. *Average starting salary:* $45,000.

DEGREES MBA • MHRM

MBA—Master of Business Administration Full-time and part-time. 36 to 48 total credits required. 12 to 60 months to complete program. *Concentrations:* accounting, finance, health care, human resources management, industrial/labor relations, marketing.

MHRM—Master's of Human Resource Management Full-time and part-time. 33 total credits required. 12 to 60 months to complete program. *Concentration:* human resources management.

RESOURCES AND SERVICES 50 on-campus PCs are available to graduate business students. Access to Internet/World Wide Web, online (class) registration, and online grade reports available. *Personal computer requirements:* Graduate business students are strongly recommended to purchase or lease a personal computer. *Special opportunities include:* An internship program is available. *Placement services include:* Alumni network, career placement, job search course, career counseling/planning, electronic job bank, resume referral, career fairs, job interviews arranged, resume preparation, and career library.

EXPENSES *Tuition:* Full-time: $13,374. Part-time: $743 per credit. *Tuition (international):* Full-time: $13,374. Part-time: $743 per credit hour.

FINANCIAL AID (2007–08) 12 students received aid, including loans and research assistantships. *Financial aid application deadline:* 8/1.

Financial Aid Contact Jamie Kosh, Director, Financial Aid, 117 Evergreen Drive, PO Box 600, Loretto, PA 15940. *Phone:* 814-472-3010.

INTERNATIONAL STUDENTS 0.5% of students enrolled are international students. *Services and facilities:* Counseling/support services, Housing location assistance. Financial aid is available to international students. *Required with application:* TOEFL with recommended score of 550 (paper); proof of adequate funds; proof of health/immunizations.

APPLICATION *Required:* GMAT, application form, baccalaureate/first degree, essay, 2 letters of recommendation, transcripts of college work. *Recommended:* Interview, resume/curriculum vitae, 2 years of work experience. *Application fee:* $30. Applications for domestic and international students are processed on a rolling basis.

Application Contact Roxane L. Hogue, Coordinator, MBA and MHRM Programs, 117 Evergreen Drive, PO Box 600, Loretto, PA 15940. *Phone:* 814-472-3026. *Fax:* 814-472-3369. *E-mail:* rhogue@francis.edu.

Saint Joseph's University
Erivan K. Haub School of Business
Philadelphia, Pennsylvania

Phone: 610-660-1690 **Fax:** 610-660-1599 **E-mail:** sjacob01@sju.edu

Business Program(s) Web Site: http://www.sju.edu/hsb

Graduate Business Unit Enrollment *Total:* 975 (186 full-time; 789 part-time; 435 women). *Average Age:* 33.

Graduate Business Faculty *Total:* 63 (52 full-time; 11 part-time).

Admissions *Applied:* 477. *Admitted:* 269. *Enrolled:* 207. *Average GMAT:* 520. *Average GPA:* 3.2

Academic Calendar Semesters.

Accreditation AACSB—The Association to Advance Collegiate Schools of Business.

DEGREES EMBA • MBA • MS • MSIS

EMBA—Executive Master of Business Administration Full-time. Qualified candidates may substitute a structured interview in lieu of the GMAT requirement; 5 years of working experience required. 30 to 48 total credits required. 12 to 20 months to complete program. *Concentration:* executive programs.

MBA—Executive Pharmaceutical Master of Business Administration Part-time. Distance learning option. Four years of pharmaceutical work experience, GMAT or structured interview for qualified candidates. 33 to 48 total credits required. *Concentration:* pharmaceutical management.

MBA—MBA Executive Food Marketing Part-time. GMAT or structured interview; 4 years of industry experience required. At least 48 total credits required. 24 to 72 months to complete program. *Concentration:* marketing.

MBA—Professional MBA Program Full-time and part-time. International applicants must have WES evaluation of undergraduate work. 33 to 52 total credits required. 18 to 72 months to complete program. *Concentrations:* accounting, decision sciences, finance, general MBA, health care, human resources management, international business, international marketing, management, marketing, nonprofit management.

MS—Master of Science in Financial Services Full-time and part-time. Students who complete the appropriate coursework (six designated courses) will be eligible to sit for the CFP (R) exam. Students who hold a CPA, CFP or CFA certification do not need the GMAT exam. 30 to 44 total credits required. 18 to 72 months to complete program. *Concentration:* finance.

MS—Master of Science in Food Marketing Part-time. GMAT or structured interview and 4 years of industry experience required. At least 36 total credits required. 24 to 72 months to complete program. *Concentration:* marketing.

MS—Master of Science in Human Resource Management Full-time and part-time. 33 to 36 total credits required. 18 to 72 months to complete program. *Concentration:* human resources management.

MS—Master of Science in International Marketing Full-time and part-time. 30 to 39 total credits required. Minimum of 12 months to complete program. *Concentration:* international marketing.

Saint Joseph's University (continued)

MSIS—Master of Science in Decision and System Sciences Full-time and part-time. Candidates may take either the GMAT or GRE exam. 30 to 45 total credits required. 18 to 72 months to complete program. *Concentration:* system management.

RESOURCES AND SERVICES 130 on-campus PCs are available to graduate business students. Access to Internet/World Wide Web, online (class) registration, and online grade reports available. *Personal computer requirements:* Graduate business students are not required to have a personal computer. *Placement services include:* Alumni network, career placement, career counseling/planning, electronic job bank, resume referral, career fairs, and resume preparation.

EXPENSES *Tuition:* Part-time: $785 per credit. *Tuition (international):* Part-time: $785 per credit.

FINANCIAL AID (2007–08) Loans, research assistantships, scholarships, and teaching assistantships. Aid is available to part-time students. *Financial aid application deadline:* 5/1.

Financial Aid Contact Financial Aid Counselor, 5600 City Avenue, Philadelphia, PA 19131. *Phone:* 610-660-1555.

INTERNATIONAL STUDENTS *Services and facilities:* Counseling/support services, ESL/language courses, Housing location assistance, International student organization, Orientation, Visa Services. Financial aid is available to international students. *Required with application:* TOEFL with recommended score of 213 (computer), 550 (paper), or 79 (Internet); proof of adequate funds. *Recommended with application:* Proof of health/immunizations.

International Student Contact Coralee Dixon, Counselor, Graduate Admissions, 5600 City Avenue, Philadelphia, PA 19131. *Phone:* 610-660-1102. *E-mail:* cdixon01@sju.edu.

APPLICATION *Required:* GMAT, application form, baccalaureate/first degree, essay, 2 letters of recommendation, personal statement, resume/curriculum vitae, transcripts of college work. *Application fee:* $35. Applications for domestic and international students are processed on a rolling basis.

Application Contact Ms. Susan P. Jacobs, Assistant Director, Graduate Business Programs, 5600 City Avenue, Philadelphia, PA 19131. *Phone:* 610-660-1690. *Fax:* 610-660-1599. *E-mail:* sjacob01@sju.edu.

Saint Vincent College
Alex G. McKenna School of Business, Economics, and Government
Latrobe, Pennsylvania

Phone: 724-537-4540 **Fax:** 724-532-5069 **E-mail:** david.collins@email.stvincent.edu

Business Program(s) Web Site: http://www.stvincent.edu/graduate_programs5

Graduate Business Unit Enrollment *Total:* 18.

Academic Calendar Semesters.

Accreditation ACBSP—The American Council of Business Schools and Programs.

After Graduation (Class of 2006–07) *Employed within 3 months of graduation:* 100%. *Average starting salary:* $40,000.

DEGREES M Mgt • MS

M Mgt—Operational Excellence Part-time. GMAT. At least 36 total credits required. *Concentrations:* operations management, organizational management.

MS—Health Services Leadership Part-time. At least 36 total credits required. *Concentrations:* health administration, health care.

RESOURCES AND SERVICES 100 on-campus PCs are available to graduate business students. Access to Internet/World Wide Web, online

(class) registration, and online grade reports available. *Personal computer requirements:* Graduate business students are not required to have a personal computer. *Special opportunities include:* An internship program is available. *Placement services include:* Alumni network, career placement, career counseling/planning, electronic job bank, resume referral, career fairs, job interviews arranged, resume preparation, and career library.

FINANCIAL AID (2007–08) Grants, loans, and work study.

Financial Aid Contact Ms. Kimberly Woodley, Director of Financial Aid, 300 Fraser Purchase Road, Latrobe, PA 15650. *Phone:* 724-805-2500. *Fax:* 724-532-5069. *E-mail:* kimberly.woodley@email.stvincent.edu.

INTERNATIONAL STUDENTS *Services and facilities:* Counseling/support services, International student organization, Orientation. *Required with application:* TOEFL.

International Student Contact Mr. David Collins, Assistant Vice President for Admission, 300 Fraser Purchase Road, Latrobe, PA 15650. *Phone:* 724-537-4540. *Fax:* 724-532-5069. *E-mail:* david.collins@email.stvincent.edu.

APPLICATION *Required:* GMAT, application form, baccalaureate/first degree, letter(s) of recommendation, personal statement, transcripts of college work, 1 year of work experience. *Recommended:* Interview, resume/curriculum vitae. *Application fee:* $25. Applications for domestic and international students are processed on a rolling basis.

Application Contact Mr. David Collins, Assistant Vice President for Admission, 300 Fraser Purchase Road, Latrobe, PA 15650. *Phone:* 724-537-4540. *Fax:* 724-532-5069. *E-mail:* david.collins@email.stvincent.edu.

Seton Hill University
Program in Business Administration
Greensburg, Pennsylvania

Phone: 724-838-4221 **Fax:** 724-830-1891 **E-mail:** gadmit@setonhill.edu

Business Program(s) Web Site: http://www.setonhill.edu/mba

Graduate Business Unit Enrollment *Total:* 98 (34 full-time; 64 part-time; 33 women).

Graduate Business Faculty *Total:* 12 (4 full-time; 8 part-time).

Admissions *Applied:* 47. *Admitted:* 39. *Enrolled:* 33. *Average GPA:* 3.0

Academic Calendar Six 8-week sessions.

After Graduation (Class of 2006–07) *Employed within 3 months of graduation:* 95%. *Average starting salary:* $54,000.

DEGREE MBA

MBA—Master of Business Administration Full-time and part-time. 36 to 39 total credits required. 12 to 60 months to complete program. *Concentrations:* entrepreneurship, management.

RESOURCES AND SERVICES 150 on-campus PCs are available to graduate business students. Access to Internet/World Wide Web, online (class) registration, and online grade reports available. *Personal computer requirements:* Graduate business students are strongly recommended to purchase or lease a personal computer. *Special opportunities include:* An internship program is available. *Placement services include:* Alumni network, career placement, career counseling/planning, electronic job bank, career fairs, resume preparation, and career library.

EXPENSES *Tuition:* Full-time: $25,020. Part-time: $695 per credit. *Tuition (international):* Full-time: $25,020. Part-time: $695 per credit. *Required fees:* Full-time: $250. Part-time: $250 per year. *Graduate housing:* Room and board costs vary by campus location, number of occupants, type of accommodation, and type of board plan. *Typical cost:* $5225 (including board).

FINANCIAL AID (2007–08) Loans and scholarships. Aid is available to part-time students.

Financial Aid Contact Ms. Maryann Dudas, Director of Financial Aid, Seton Hill Drive, Greensburg, PA 15601. *Phone:* 724-838-4293. *Fax:* 724-830-1292. *E-mail:* dudas@setonhill.edu.

INTERNATIONAL STUDENTS *Services and facilities:* Counseling/support services, ESL/language courses, International student housing, International student organization, Orientation, Visa Services, On campus housing available. Financial aid is available to international students. *Required with application:* IELT; TOEFL; proof of adequate funds. *Recommended with application:* Proof of health/immunizations.

International Student Contact Ms. Christine E. Schaeffer, Director of Graduate and Adult Studies, Office of Graduate and Adult Studies, Seton Hill Drive Box 510F, Greensburg, PA 15601. *Phone:* 724-838-4221. *Fax:* 724-830-1891. *E-mail:* gadmit@setonhill.edu.

APPLICATION *Required:* Application form, baccalaureate/first degree, 3 letters of recommendation, personal statement, resume/curriculum vitae, transcripts of college work. *Recommended:* Work experience. *Application fee:* $35. Applications for domestic and international students are processed on a rolling basis.

Application Contact Christine E Schaeffer, Director of Graduate and Adult Studies, 1 Seton Hill Drive, Box 510F, Greensburg, PA 15601. *Phone:* 724-838-4221. *Fax:* 724-830-1891. *E-mail:* gadmit@setonhill.edu.

Shippensburg University of Pennsylvania
John L. Grove College of Business
Shippensburg, Pennsylvania

E-mail: admiss@ship.edu

Business Program(s) Web Site: http://webspace.ship.edu/mba

Graduate Business Unit Enrollment *Total:* 265 (15 full-time; 250 part-time).

Graduate Business Faculty 15 part-time.

Admissions *Applied:* 148. *Admitted:* 129. *Enrolled:* 115.

Academic Calendar Semesters.

Accreditation AACSB—The Association to Advance Collegiate Schools of Business.

DEGREE MBA

MBA—Master of Business Administration Part-time. Distance learning option. 30 total credits required. 24 months to complete program. *Concentration:* general MBA.

APPLICATION *Required:* GMAT, application form, baccalaureate/first degree, resume/curriculum vitae, transcripts of college work. *Recommended:* Letter(s) of recommendation, personal statement, work experience. *Application fee:* $30. Applications for domestic and international students are processed on a rolling basis.

Application Contact Admissions, Shippensburg, PA 17257. *E-mail:* admiss@ship.edu.

Temple University
Fox School of Business and Management
Philadelphia, Pennsylvania

Phone: 215-204-8732 **Fax:** 215-204-1632 **E-mail:** nbutto@temple.edu

Business Program(s) Web Site: http://www.fox.temple.edu/grad/

Graduate Business Unit Enrollment *Total:* 812 (421 full-time; 391 part-time; 307 women; 202 international). *Average Age:* 31.

Graduate Business Faculty *Total:* 76 (53 full-time; 23 part-time).

Admissions *Applied:* 794. *Admitted:* 525. *Enrolled:* 291. *Average GMAT:* 623. *Average GPA:* 3.33

Academic Calendar Semesters.

Accreditation AACSB—The Association to Advance Collegiate Schools of Business.

After Graduation (Class of 2006–07) *Employed within 3 months of graduation:* 89%. *Average starting salary:* $80,964.

DEGREES DDS/MBA • EMBA • IMBA • JD/MBA • MBA • MD/MBA • MS

DDS/MBA—Doctor of Dental Medicine/Master of Business Administration Part-time. Candidates must apply to both the School of Business and Management and the School of Dentistry. Credit hours are in addition to Dental School credits. Students study in the evening MBA Program. 51 total credits required. 36 months to complete program. *Concentration:* combined degrees.

EMBA—Executive Master of Business Administration Full-time. 48 total credits required. 22 months to complete program. *Concentration:* executive programs.

IMBA—Master of Business Administration in International Business Full-time. This program requires study in 3 countries. 48 total credits required. 12 months to complete program. *Concentration:* international management.

JD/MBA—Juris Doctor/Master of Business Administration Full-time and part-time. Candidates must apply to both the School of Business and Management and the School of Law. Credits are in addition to Law School credits. 42 total credits required. 48 months to complete program. *Concentration:* business law.

MBA—Fox MBA Full-time. 54 total credits required. 22 months to complete program. *Concentrations:* accounting, finance, general MBA, health care, human resources management, insurance, international business, management information systems, marketing, strategic management.

MBA—Fox Professional MBA Part-time. 54 total credits required. 36 to 72 months to complete program. *Concentrations:* accounting, finance, general MBA, health care, human resources management, information technology, international business, marketing, risk management.

MD/MBA—Doctor of Medicine/Master of Business Administration Full-time. Must apply to Temple University School of Medicine and be accepted prior to enrolling in the School of Business. Credit hours are in addition to the Medical School curriculum. 54 total credits required. 48 months to complete program. *Concentration:* health care.

MS—Master of Science Full-time and part-time. 30 to 48 total credits required. 12 to 72 months to complete program. *Concentrations:* accounting, actuarial science, finance, financial engineering, health care, human resources management, management information systems, marketing, statistics.

RESOURCES AND SERVICES 3,134 on-campus PCs are available to graduate business students. Access to Internet/World Wide Web, online (class) registration, and online grade reports available. *Personal computer requirements:* Graduate business students are required to have a personal computer. *Special opportunities include:* An international exchange program and an internship program are available. *Placement services include:* Alumni network, career placement, job search course, career counseling/planning, electronic job bank, resume referral, career fairs, job interviews arranged, resume preparation, and career library.

EXPENSES *Tuition (state resident):* Full-time: $17,010. Part-time: $574 per credit hour. *Tuition (nonresident):* Full-time: $25,245. Part-time: $851 per credit hour. *Tuition (international):* Full-time: $25,245. Part-time: $851 per credit hour. *Required fees:* Full-time: $1100. Tuition and/or fees vary by number of courses or credits taken and academic program.

FINANCIAL AID (2007–08) 53 students received aid, including fellowships, grants, research assistantships, scholarships, teaching assistantships, and work study. *Financial aid application deadline:* 1/15.

Temple University (continued)

Financial Aid Contact Mr. Natale A. Butto, Director, Graduate Admissions Operations, 1515 Market Street, Suite 400, Philadelphia, PA 19102. *Phone:* 215-204-8732. *Fax:* 215-204-1632. *E-mail:* nbutto@ temple.edu.

INTERNATIONAL STUDENTS 25% of students enrolled are international students. *Services and facilities:* Counseling/support services, ESL/language courses, Housing location assistance, International student organization, Orientation, Visa Services. Financial aid is available to international students. *Required with application:* IELT with recommended score of 7; TOEFL with recommended score of 250 (computer), 600 (paper), or 100 (Internet); proof of adequate funds; proof of health/immunizations.

International Student Contact Martyn Miller, Director, 203 Vivacqua Hall, PO Box 2843, Philadelphia, PA 19122-6083. *Phone:* 215-204-7708. *Fax:* 215-204-6166.

APPLICATION *Required:* GMAT, application form, baccalaureate/first degree, essay, interview, 2 letters of recommendation, personal statement, resume/curriculum vitae, transcripts of college work. School will accept GRE. *Recommended:* 2 years of work experience. *Application fee:* $50. Applications for domestic and international students are processed on a rolling basis.

Application Contact Mr. Natale A. Butto, Director, Graduate Admissions Operations, 1515 Market Street, Suite 400, Philadelphia, PA 19102. *Phone:* 215-204-8732. *Fax:* 215-204-1632. *E-mail:* nbutto@temple.edu.

University of Pennsylvania
Wharton School

Philadelphia, Pennsylvania

Phone: 215-898-6183 **Fax:** 215-898-0120 **E-mail:** mba.admissions@wharton.upenn.edu

Business Program(s) Web Site: http://mba.wharton.upenn.edu/mba

Graduate Business Unit Enrollment *Average Age:* 28.

Graduate Business Faculty 250 full-time.

Admissions *Applied:* 7,328. *Admitted:* 1,186. *Enrolled:* 797. *Average GMAT:* 712. *Average GPA:* 3.5

Academic Calendar Combination of quarters and semesters.

Accreditation AACSB—The Association to Advance Collegiate Schools of Business.

After Graduation (Class of 2006–07) *Employed within 3 months of graduation:* 94%.

DEGREES MBA • MBA/MA

MBA—Executive Master of Business Administration Full-time. 7-10 years of work experience and company sponsorship required. At least 19 total credits required. 24 months to complete program. *Concentration:* executive programs.

MBA—Master of Business Administration Full-time. At least 19 total credits required. Minimum of 20 months to complete program. *Concentrations:* accounting, economics, electronic commerce (E-commerce), entrepreneurship, environmental economics/management, finance, health care, human resources management, information management, insurance, international management, management, marketing, operations management, organizational management, public policy and administration, real estate, risk management, statistics, strategic management, student designed, technology management.

MBA/MA—Lauder Institute of Management and International Studies Full-time. 24 months to complete program. *Concentrations:* accounting, Asian business studies, Chinese business studies, electronic commerce (E-commerce), entrepreneurship, European business studies, finance, health care, human resources management, information management, insurance, international and area business studies, international

banking, international business, international economics, international finance, international management, international marketing, international trade, Japanese business studies, Latin American business studies, management, marketing, operations management, public policy and administration, real estate, statistics, strategic management.

RESOURCES AND SERVICES Access to Internet/World Wide Web, online (class) registration, and online grade reports available. *Personal computer requirements:* Graduate business students are strongly recommended to purchase or lease a personal computer. *Special opportunities include:* An international exchange program and an internship program are available. *Placement services include:* Alumni network, career placement, job search course, career counseling/planning, electronic job bank, resume referral, career fairs, job interviews arranged, resume preparation, and career library.

EXPENSES *Tuition:* Full-time: $41,950. *Tuition (international):* Full-time: $41,950. *Required fees:* Full-time: $4700. *Graduate housing:* Room and board costs vary by number of occupants, type of accommodation, and type of board plan. *Typical cost:* $18,054 (including board).

FINANCIAL AID (2007–08) 520 students received aid, including fellowships, grants, loans, research assistantships, scholarships, and teaching assistantships.

Financial Aid Contact Financial Aid Office, 3730 Walnut Street, 420 Jon M. Hunstman Hall, Philadelphia, PA 19104-6340. *E-mail:* mba.admissions@ wharton.upenn.edu.

INTERNATIONAL STUDENTS *Services and facilities:* Counseling/ support services, ESL/language courses, Housing location assistance, International student housing, International student organization, Language tutoring, Orientation, Visa Services. Financial aid is available to international students. *Required with application:* TOEFL; proof of health/immunizations.

International Student Contact Office of Admissions and Financial Aid, 3730 Walnut Street, 420 Jon M. Huntsman Hall, Philadelphia, PA 19104-6340. *Phone:* 215-898-6183. *Fax:* 215-898-0120. *E-mail:* mba.admissions@wharton.upenn.edu.

APPLICATION *Required:* GMAT, application form, baccalaureate/first degree, essay, interview, 2 letters of recommendation, resume/curriculum vitae, transcripts of college work. *Recommended:* Work experience. *Application fee:* $235. *Deadlines:* 10/9 for fall, 1/8 for winter, 3/5 for spring, 10/9 for fall (international), 1/8 for winter (international), 3/5 for spring (international).

Application Contact Office of MBA Admissions and Financial Aid, 3730 Walnut Street, 420 Jon M. Hunstman Hall, Philadelphia, PA 19104-6340. *Phone:* 215-898-6183. *Fax:* 215-898-0120. *E-mail:* mba.admissions@ wharton.upenn.edu.

University of Phoenix–Philadelphia Campus
College of Graduate Business and Management

Wayne, Pennsylvania

Phone: 480-317-6200 **Fax:** 480-643-1479 **E-mail:** beth.barilla@phoenix.edu

Business Program(s) Web Site: http://www.phoenix.edu

DEGREES M Mgt • MA • MBA

M Mgt—Master of Management Full-time. At least 39 total credits required. *Concentration:* management.

MA—Master of Arts in Organizational Management Full-time. Up to 40 total credits required. *Concentration:* organizational management.

MBA—Global Management Full-time. At least 45 total credits required. *Concentration:* international management.

MBA—e-Business Full-time. At least 45 total credits required. *Concentration:* electronic commerce (E-commerce).

MBA—Master of Business Administration Full-time. At least 45 total credits required. *Concentration:* administration.

RESOURCES AND SERVICES Access to online grade reports available. *Personal computer requirements:* Graduate business students are strongly recommended to purchase or lease a personal computer. *Placement services include:* Alumni network.

Application Contact Beth Barilla, Associate Vice President of Student Admissions and Services, Mail Stop AA-K101, 4615 East Elwood Street, Phoenix, AZ 85040-1958. *Phone:* 480-317-6200. *Fax:* 480-643-1479. *E-mail:* beth.barilla@phoenix.edu.

University of Phoenix–Pittsburgh Campus
College of Graduate Business and Management

Pittsburgh, Pennsylvania

Phone: 480-317-6200 **Fax:** 480-643-1479 **E-mail:** beth.barilla@phoenix.edu

Business Program(s) Web Site: http://www.phoenix.edu

DEGREES M Mgt • MA • MBA

M Mgt—Master of Management Full-time. At least 39 total credits required. *Concentration:* management.

MA—Master of Arts in Organizational Management Full-time. At least 40 total credits required. *Concentration:* organizational management.

MBA—Accounting Full-time. At least 54 total credits required. *Concentration:* accounting.

MBA—Global Management Full-time. At least 45 total credits required. *Concentration:* international management.

MBA—e-Business Full-time. At least 45 total credits required. *Concentration:* electronic commerce (E-commerce).

MBA—Master of Business Administration Full-time. At least 45 total credits required. *Concentration:* administration.

RESOURCES AND SERVICES Access to online grade reports available. *Personal computer requirements:* Graduate business students are strongly recommended to purchase or lease a personal computer. *Placement services include:* Alumni network.

Application Contact Beth Barilla, Associate Vice President of Student Admissions and Services, Mail Stop AA-K101, 4615 East Elwood Street, Phoenix, AZ 85040-1958. *Phone:* 480-317-6200. *Fax:* 480-643-1479. *E-mail:* beth.barilla@phoenix.edu.

University of Pittsburgh
Joseph M. Katz Graduate School of Business

Pittsburgh, Pennsylvania

Phone: 412-648-1700 **Fax:** 412-648-1659 **E-mail:** mba@katz.pitt.edu

Business Program(s) Web Site: http://www.katz.pitt.edu/

Graduate Business Unit Enrollment *Total:* 865 (348 full-time; 517 part-time; 294 women; 212 international). *Average Age:* 27.

Graduate Business Faculty *Total:* 99 (69 full-time; 30 part-time).

Admissions *Applied:* 1,016. *Admitted:* 509. *Enrolled:* 338. *Average GMAT:* 620. *Average GPA:* 3.3

Academic Calendar Trimesters.

Accreditation AACSB—The Association to Advance Collegiate Schools of Business.

After Graduation (Class of 2006–07) *Employed within 3 months of graduation:* 93%. *Average starting salary:* $72,000.

DEGREES JD/MBA • MBA • MBA/M Eng • MBA/MPIA • MBA/MS • MIB

JD/MBA—Juris Doctor/Master of Business Administration Full-time. At least 115 total credits required. Minimum of 115 months to complete program. *Concentration:* combined degrees.

MBA—Full-Time Master of Business Administration Full-time and part-time. At least 57 total credits required. Minimum of 57 months to complete program. *Concentrations:* accounting, finance, human resources management, management, management information systems, marketing, operations management.

MBA/M Eng—Master of Business Administration/Master in Bioengineering Full-time and part-time. At least 65 total credits required. Minimum of 65 months to complete program. *Concentration:* combined degrees.

MBA/M Eng—Master of Business Administration/Master of Science in Industrial Engineering Full-time and part-time. At least 65 total credits required. Minimum of 65 months to complete program. *Concentration:* combined degrees.

MBA/MPIA—Master of Business Administration/Master of International Business Full-time and part-time. At least 75 total credits required. Minimum of 75 months to complete program. *Concentration:* international business.

MBA/MS—Master of Business Administration/Master of Science in Management of Information Systems Full-time and part-time. At least 72 total credits required. Minimum of 72 months to complete program. *Concentration:* management information systems.

MIB—Master of Business Administration/Master of International Business Full-time and part-time. At least 71 total credits required. Minimum of 71 months to complete program. *Concentration:* international business.

RESOURCES AND SERVICES 100 on-campus PCs are available to graduate business students. Access to Internet/World Wide Web and online grade reports available. *Personal computer requirements:* Graduate business students are required to have a personal computer. *Special opportunities include:* An international exchange program and an internship program are available. *Placement services include:* Alumni network, career placement, job search course, career counseling/planning, electronic job bank, resume referral, career fairs, job interviews arranged, resume preparation, and career library.

EXPENSES *Tuition (state resident):* Full-time: $14,838. Part-time: $853 per credit. *Tuition (nonresident):* Full-time: $22,208. Part-time: $1409 per credit. *Tuition (international):* Full-time: $22,208. Part-time: $1409 per credit. *Required fees:* Full-time: $2650. Part-time: $265 per credit.

FINANCIAL AID (2007–08) 45 students received aid, including fellowships, loans, scholarships, and work study. *Financial aid application deadline:* 4/15.

Financial Aid Contact Kelly Wilson, Assistant Dean and Director of the Office of Enrollment Management, 276 Mervis Hall, Pittsburgh, PA 15260. *Phone:* 412-648-1700. *Fax:* 412-648-1659. *E-mail:* mba@katz.pitt.edu.

INTERNATIONAL STUDENTS 25% of students enrolled are international students. *Services and facilities:* Counseling/support services, ESL/language courses, Housing location assistance, International student organization, Language tutoring, Orientation, Visa Services. Financial aid is available to international students. *Required with application:* TOEFL with recommended score of 250 (computer) or 600 (paper); proof of adequate funds.

International Student Contact Kelly Wilson, Assistant Dean and Director of the Office of Enrollment Management, 276 Mervis Hall, Pittsburgh, PA 15260. *Phone:* 412-648-1700. *Fax:* 412-648-1659. *E-mail:* mba@katz.pitt.edu.

APPLICATION *Required:* GMAT, application form, baccalaureate/first degree, essay, 2 letters of recommendation, resume/curriculum vitae, transcripts of college work. *Recommended:* Interview, work experience. *Application fee:* $50. *Deadlines:* 11/1 for fall, 12/1 for winter, 1/15 for spring, 3/1 for summer, 11/1 for fall (international), 12/1 for winter (international), 1/15 for spring (international), 3/1 for summer (international).

Application Contact Kelly Wilson, Assistant Dean and Director of the Office of Enrollment Management, 276 Mervis Hall, Pittsburgh, PA 15260. *Phone:* 412-648-1700. *Fax:* 412-648-1659. *E-mail:* mba@katz.pitt.edu.

The University of Scranton
Program in Business Administration

Scranton, Pennsylvania

Phone: 570-941-6304 **Fax:** 570-941-5995 **E-mail:** goonanj1@scranton.edu

Business Program(s) Web Site: http://www.academic.scranton.edu/department/mba/

Graduate Business Unit Enrollment *Total:* 101 (34 full-time; 67 part-time; 34 women; 39 international). *Average Age:* 28.

Graduate Business Faculty 34 full-time.

Admissions *Applied:* 58. *Admitted:* 48. *Enrolled:* 29. *Average GMAT:* 520. *Average GPA:* 3.33

Academic Calendar 4-1-4.

Accreditation AACSB—The Association to Advance Collegiate Schools of Business.

After Graduation (Class of 2006–07) *Employed within 3 months of graduation:* 97%. *Average starting salary:* $53,000.

DEGREE MBA

MBA—Master of Business Administration Full-time and part-time. Distance learning option. Enterprise Management Technology available as a concentration. 36 to 48 total credits required. 18 to 72 months to complete program. *Concentrations:* accounting, finance, general MBA, international business, management information systems, marketing, operations management.

RESOURCES AND SERVICES 300 on-campus PCs are available to graduate business students. Access to Internet/World Wide Web, online (class) registration, and online grade reports available. *Personal computer requirements:* Graduate business students are not required to have a personal computer. *Special opportunities include:* An international exchange program and an internship program are available. *Placement services include:* Alumni network, career placement, job search course, career counseling/planning, electronic job bank, resume referral, career fairs, job interviews arranged, resume preparation, and career library.

EXPENSES *Tuition:* Full-time: $9300. Part-time: $775 per credit hour. *Tuition (international):* Full-time: $9300. Part-time: $775 per credit hour. Tuition and/or fees vary by campus location and academic program.

FINANCIAL AID (2007–08) 16 students received aid, including teaching assistantships and work study. *Financial aid application deadline:* 3/1.

Financial Aid Contact William R. Burke, Director of Financial Aid, Financial Aid Office, Scranton, PA 18510-4689. *Phone:* 570-941-7700. *Fax:* 570-941-6369. *E-mail:* burkew1@scranton.edu.

INTERNATIONAL STUDENTS 39% of students enrolled are international students. *Services and facilities:* Counseling/support services, ESL/language courses, Housing location assistance, International student housing, International student organization, Orientation. Financial aid is available to international students. *Required with application:* IELT with recommended score of 5.5; TOEFL with recommended score of 173 (computer), 500 (paper), or 61 (Internet); proof of adequate funds.

International Student Contact Peter J. Blazes, Director of International Student and Scholar Services, International Programs and Services, Scranton, PA 18510-4632. *Phone:* 570-941-7575. *Fax:* 570-941-5995. *E-mail:* blazesp1@scranton.edu.

APPLICATION *Required:* GMAT, application form, baccalaureate/first degree, 3 letters of recommendation, personal statement, transcripts of college work. *Recommended:* Resume/curriculum vitae. *Application fee:* $50. Applications for domestic and international students are processed on a rolling basis.

Application Contact James L. Goonan, Director of Graduate Admissions, College of Graduate and Continuing Education, Scranton, PA 18510-4632. *Phone:* 570-941-6304. *Fax:* 570-941-5995. *E-mail:* goonanj1@scranton.edu.

Villanova University
Villanova School of Business

Villanova, Pennsylvania

Phone: 610-519-4336 **Fax:** 610-519-6273 **E-mail:** simone.pollard@villanova.edu

Business Program(s) Web Site: http://www.gradbusiness.villanova.edu

Graduate Business Unit Enrollment *Total:* 679 (139 full-time; 540 part-time; 209 women). *Average Age:* 30.

Graduate Business Faculty *Total:* 137 (96 full-time; 41 part-time).

Admissions *Average GMAT:* 590. *Average GPA:* 3.12

Academic Calendar Semesters.

Accreditation AACSB—The Association to Advance Collegiate Schools of Business.

DEGREES EMBA • JD/MBA • MAC • MBA • MF • MT • MTM

EMBA—VSB Executive MBA Part-time. 21 months to complete program. *Concentration:* executive programs.

JD/MBA—JD/MBA Program Full-time and part-time. Distance learning option. 30 to 56 total credits required. 36 to 84 months to complete program. *Concentration:* combined degrees.

MAC—Master of Accountancy Full-time and part-time. Distance learning option. At least 30 total credits required. 14 months to complete program. *Concentration:* accounting.

MBA—FTE MBA (Full-Time Equivalent Master of Business Administration) Part-time. 24-month, evening, part-time, accelerated MBA Program. 44 total credits required. 24 months to complete program. *Concentration:* general MBA.

MBA—PMBA (Professional Master of Business Administration) Full-time and part-time. Distance learning option. 41 to 56 total credits required. 24 to 84 months to complete program. *Concentrations:* finance, health administration, international business, management information systems, marketing.

MF—Master of Science in Finance Full-time. At least 33 total credits required. Minimum of 12 months to complete program. *Concentration:* finance.

MT—Master of Taxation Full-time and part-time. Distance learning option. At least 24 total credits required. 12 to 60 months to complete program. *Concentration:* taxation.

MTM—Master of Technology Management Part-time. 46 total credits required. 30 to 84 months to complete program. *Concentrations:* engineering, information systems, information technology.

RESOURCES AND SERVICES 400 on-campus PCs are available to graduate business students. Access to Internet/World Wide Web, online (class) registration, and online grade reports available. *Personal computer requirements:* Graduate business students are strongly recommended to purchase or lease a personal computer. *Placement services include:*

Alumni network, career placement, career counseling/planning, electronic job bank, resume referral, career fairs, job interviews arranged, and career library.

EXPENSES *Tuition:* Part-time: $750 per credit. Tuition and/or fees vary by academic program.

FINANCIAL AID (2007–08) 23 students received aid, including research assistantships. Aid is available to part-time students. *Financial aid application deadline:* 3/31.

Financial Aid Contact Bonnie Behm, Director of Financial Assistance, Kennedy Hall, 800 Lancaster Avenue, Villanova, PA 19085. *Phone:* 610-519-6456. *Fax:* 610-519-7599. *E-mail:* bonnie.behm@villanova.edu.

INTERNATIONAL STUDENTS *Services and facilities:* Counseling/support services, Orientation. Financial aid is available to international students. *Required with application:* TOEFL with recommended score of 250 (computer), 600 (paper), or 100 (Internet); proof of adequate funds; proof of health/immunizations.

International Student Contact Stephen McWilliams, Director of International Student Services, 800 Lancaster Avenue, Villanova, PA 19085. *Phone:* 610-519-4095. *Fax:* 610-519-5203. *E-mail:* stephen.mcwilliams@villanova.edu.

APPLICATION *Required:* GMAT, application form, baccalaureate/first degree, essay, 2 letters of recommendation, personal statement, resume/curriculum vitae, transcripts of college work. *Recommended:* Interview, 5 years of work experience. *Application fee:* $50. Applications for domestic and international students are processed on a rolling basis.

Application Contact Simone L. Pollard, Assistant Dean, Graduate Business Programs, 800 Lancaster Avenue, Villanova, PA 19085. *Phone:* 610-519-4336. *Fax:* 610-519-6273. *E-mail:* simone.pollard@villanova.edu.

Waynesburg University
Graduate and Professional Studies

Waynesburg, Pennsylvania

Phone: 724-743-4420 **E-mail:** dmariner@waynesburg.edu

Business Program(s) Web Site: http://www.waynesburg.edu

Graduate Business Unit Enrollment *Total:* 482 (48 full-time; 434 part-time; 207 women; 2 international). *Average Age:* 33.

Graduate Business Faculty *Total:* 60 (5 full-time; 55 part-time).

Admissions *Applied:* 270. *Admitted:* 230. *Enrolled:* 202. *Average GPA:* 3.4

Academic Calendar 8-week sessions.

DEGREE MBA

MBA—Master of Business Administration Program Full-time and part-time. Minimum age of 25 required. At least 36 total credits required. 12 to 84 months to complete program. *Concentrations:* finance, health care, human resources development, leadership, marketing.

RESOURCES AND SERVICES 150 on-campus PCs are available to graduate business students. Access to Internet/World Wide Web, online (class) registration, and online grade reports available. *Personal computer requirements:* Graduate business students are strongly recommended to purchase or lease a personal computer. *Special opportunities include:* An internship program is available. *Placement services include:* Alumni network, career placement, career counseling/planning, career fairs, and resume preparation.

EXPENSES *Tuition:* Part-time: $500 per credit. *Tuition (international):* Part-time: $500 per credit.

FINANCIAL AID (2007–08) Loans. Aid is available to part-time students. *Financial aid application deadline:* 3/15.

Financial Aid Contact Mr. Matt Stokan, Director, Financial Aid, 51 West College Street, Waynesburg, PA 15370. *Phone:* 724-852-3227. *Fax:* 724-627-6416. *E-mail:* mstokan@waynesburg.edu.

INTERNATIONAL STUDENTS 0.4% of students enrolled are international students. *Services and facilities:* Counseling/support services, ESL/language courses, Housing location assistance, International student organization, Orientation. Financial aid is not available to international students. *Required with application:* TOEFL with recommended score of 550 (paper); proof of adequate funds; proof of health/immunizations.

International Student Contact Mr. Dave Mariner, Director of Admissions, 1001 Corporate Drive, Suite 100, Canonsburg, PA 15317. *Phone:* 724-852-3518. *Fax:* 724-627-6416. *E-mail:* dmariner@waynesburg.edu.

APPLICATION *Required:* Application form, baccalaureate/first degree, 2 letters of recommendation, personal statement, resume/curriculum vitae, transcripts of college work, 3 years of work experience. *Recommended:* Essay, interview. Applications for domestic and international students are processed on a rolling basis.

Application Contact Mr. Dave Mariner, Director of Admissions, 1001 Corporate Drive, Suite 100, Canonsburg, PA 15317. *Phone:* 724-743-4420. *E-mail:* dmariner@waynesburg.edu.

West Chester University of Pennsylvania
College of Business and Public Affairs

West Chester, Pennsylvania

Phone: 610-436-2608 **Fax:** 610-436-2439 **E-mail:** mba@wcupa.edu

Business Program(s) Web Site: http://www.wcumba.org

Graduate Business Faculty *Total:* 28 (20 full-time; 8 part-time).

Admissions *Average GMAT:* 525. *Average GPA:* 3.2

Academic Calendar 10-week terms.

After Graduation (Class of 2006–07) *Employed within 3 months of graduation:* 100%.

DEGREE MBA

MBA—Evening Master of Business Administration Full-time and part-time. 34 to 49 total credits required. 12 to 72 months to complete program. *Concentration:* general MBA.

RESOURCES AND SERVICES Access to Internet/World Wide Web, online (class) registration, and online grade reports available. *Personal computer requirements:* Graduate business students are required to have a personal computer. *Placement services include:* Alumni network, career placement, job search course, career counseling/planning, electronic job bank, resume referral, career fairs, job interviews arranged, resume preparation, and career library.

EXPENSES *Tuition (state resident):* Part-time: $1035 per course. *Tuition (nonresident):* Part-time: $1656 per course. *Tuition (international):* Part-time: $1656 per course. *Required fees:* Part-time: $147 per term.

FINANCIAL AID (2007–08) Research assistantships. Aid is available to part-time students. *Financial aid application deadline:* 3/1.

Financial Aid Contact Office of Financial Aid, University Avenue and High Street, West Chester, PA 19383. *Phone:* 610-436-2627. *Fax:* 610-436-2574. *E-mail:* finaid@wcupa.edu.

INTERNATIONAL STUDENTS *Services and facilities:* Counseling/support services, ESL/language courses, Visa Services. Financial aid is available to international students. *Required with application:* TOEFL with recommended score of 213 (computer), 550 (paper), or 80 (Internet); proof of adequate funds; proof of health/immunizations.

International Student Contact Lynn Kaiser, Director, University Avenue and High Street, West Chester, PA 19383. *Phone:* 610-436-3515. *Fax:* 610-436-3426. *E-mail:* international@wcupa.edu.

APPLICATION *Required:* GMAT, application form, baccalaureate/first degree, 3 letters of recommendation, personal statement, resume/curriculum vitae, transcripts of college work. *Recommended:* Work

West Chester University of Pennsylvania (continued)

experience. *Application fee:* $35. Applications for domestic and international students are processed on a rolling basis.

Application Contact Paul Christ, PhD, Director, MBA Program, Graduate Business Center, 1160 McDermott Drive, West Chester, PA 19383. *Phone:* 610-436-2608. *Fax:* 610-436-2439. *E-mail:* mba@wcupa.edu.

Widener University
School of Business Administration

Chester, Pennsylvania

Phone: 610-499-4305 **Fax:** 610-499-4615 **E-mail:** sbagradv@mail.widener.edu

Business Program(s) Web Site: http://www.widener.edu

Graduate Business Unit Enrollment *Total:* 125 (30 full-time; 95 part-time; 52 women; 6 international).

Graduate Business Faculty *Total:* 54 (34 full-time; 20 part-time).

Admissions *Applied:* 139. *Admitted:* 61. *Enrolled:* 50. *Average GMAT:* 532. *Average GPA:* 3.1

Academic Calendar Semesters.

Accreditation AACSB—The Association to Advance Collegiate Schools of Business.

DEGREES JD/MBA • MBA • ME/MBA • MS • Psy D/MBA • Psy D/MS

JD/MBA—Juris Doctor/Master of Business Administration Full-time and part-time. Must apply to School of Law as well as School of Business Administration. 105 to 120 total credits required. 48 to 84 months to complete program. *Concentration:* combined degrees.

MBA—Master of Business Administration in Health Care Management Full-time and part-time. GRE may be substituted for the GMAT. 32 to 44 total credits required. 12 to 60 months to complete program. *Concentration:* health administration.

MBA—Master of Business Administration Full-time and part-time. GRE may be substituted for the GMAT. 30 to 42 total credits required. 12 to 60 months to complete program. *Concentrations:* financial management/planning, general MBA, human resources management, management, management information systems, marketing, other.

ME/MBA—Master of Engineering/Master of Business Administration Full-time and part-time. Must apply to School of Engineering as well as School of Business Administration. 60 to 68 total credits required. 27 to 84 months to complete program. *Concentration:* combined degrees.

MS—Master of Science in Human Resource and Organizational Leadership Full-time and part-time. May substitute GRE for GMAT. 30 to 37 total credits required. 15 to 84 months to complete program. *Concentrations:* human resources development, human resources management, organizational management.

MS—Master of Science in Information Systems Full-time and part-time. GRE may be substituted for the GMAT. 30 to 39 total credits required. 15 to 84 months to complete program. *Concentrations:* accounting, management information systems.

MS—Master of Science in Taxation and Financial Planning Full-time and part-time. GMAT not required for Certified Public Accountants. 33 to 42 total credits required. 15 to 84 months to complete program. *Concentrations:* financial management/planning, taxation.

Psy D/MBA—Doctor of Clinical Psychology/Master of Business Administration Full-time. Must apply to the Institute for Graduate Clinical Psychology as well as School of Business Administration. 120 to 155 total credits required. 60 months to complete program. *Concentrations:* health care, management.

Psy D/MS—Doctor of Clinical Psychology/Master of Science in Human Resource and Organizational Leadership Full-time. Must apply to the Institute for Graduate Clinical Psychology as well as School of Business

Administration. 120 to 155 total credits required. 60 months to complete program. *Concentration:* human resources management.

RESOURCES AND SERVICES 500 on-campus PCs are available to graduate business students. Access to Internet/World Wide Web, online (class) registration, and online grade reports available. *Personal computer requirements:* Graduate business students are not required to have a personal computer. *Special opportunities include:* An internship program is available. *Placement services include:* Alumni network, career placement, career counseling/planning, electronic job bank, resume referral, career fairs, job interviews arranged, resume preparation, and career library.

FINANCIAL AID (2007–08) 31 students received aid, including loans, research assistantships, and work study. Aid is available to part-time students. *Financial aid application deadline:* 5/1.

Financial Aid Contact Thomas Malloy, Director, Financial Aid, One University Place, Chester, PA 19013-5792. *Phone:* 610-499-4174. *Fax:* 610-499-4687. *E-mail:* finaidmc@mail.widener.edu.

INTERNATIONAL STUDENTS 5% of students enrolled are international students. *Services and facilities:* Counseling/support services, ESL/language courses, Housing location assistance, International student organization, Orientation, Visa Services. Financial aid is not available to international students. *Required with application:* TOEFL with recommended score of 213 (computer) or 550 (paper); proof of adequate funds; proof of health/immunizations. *Recommended with application:* TWE with recommended score of 3.5.

International Student Contact Lois Fuller, Director, International Student Services, One University Place, Chester, PA 19013-5792. *Phone:* 610-499-4498. *Fax:* 610-499-4473. *E-mail:* ljfuller@mail.widener.edu.

APPLICATION *Required:* GMAT, application form, baccalaureate/first degree, essay, 2 letters of recommendation, transcripts of college work. School will accept GRE. *Recommended:* Resume/curriculum vitae, work experience. *Application fee:* $25, $300 (international). Applications for domestic and international students are processed on a rolling basis.

Application Contact Ann Seltzer, Graduate Enrollment Process Administrator, One University Place, Chester, PA 19013-5792. *Phone:* 610-499-4305. *Fax:* 610-499-4615. *E-mail:* sbagradv@mail.widener.edu.

See full description on page 764.

Wilkes University
College of Arts, Humanities and Social Sciences

Wilkes-Barre, Pennsylvania

Phone: 570-408-4238 **Fax:** 570-408-7846 **E-mail:** nichole.redmond@wilkes.edu

Business Program(s) Web Site: http://www.wilkes.edu/pages/457.asp

Graduate Business Unit Enrollment *Total:* 192 (59 full-time; 133 part-time; 95 women; 19 international). *Average Age:* 29.

Graduate Business Faculty *Total:* 16 (12 full-time; 4 part-time).

Admissions *Applied:* 78. *Admitted:* 75. *Enrolled:* 62. *Average GPA:* 3.0

Academic Calendar Trimesters.

Accreditation ACBSP—The American Council of Business Schools and Programs.

After Graduation (Class of 2006–07) *Employed within 3 months of graduation:* 99%.

DEGREE MBA

MBA—Master of Business Administration Full-time and part-time. 36 to 48 total credits required. 18 to 72 months to complete program. *Concentrations:* accounting, entrepreneurship, finance, health care, human resources management, international and area business studies, leadership, management, marketing.

RESOURCES AND SERVICES 125 on-campus PCs are available to graduate business students. Access to Internet/World Wide Web, online (class) registration, and online grade reports available. *Personal computer requirements:* Graduate business students are strongly recommended to purchase or lease a personal computer. *Placement services include:* Alumni network, career counseling/planning, electronic job bank, career fairs, job interviews arranged, resume preparation, and career library.

EXPENSES *Tuition:* Part-time: $715 per credit. *Tuition (international):* Part-time: $715 per credit. *Required fees:* Part-time: $60 per credit. *Graduate housing:* Room and board costs vary by number of occupants, type of accommodation, and type of board plan. *Typical cost:* $10,970 (including board), $6780 (room only).

FINANCIAL AID (2007–08) Loans, research assistantships, and work study.

Financial Aid Contact Mrs. Pamela Hoffman, Director, Student Services, 84 West South Street, Wilkes-Barre, PA 18766. *Phone:* 570-408-2000. *E-mail:* pamela.hoffman@wilkes.edu.

INTERNATIONAL STUDENTS 10% of students enrolled are international students. *Services and facilities:* Counseling/support services, ESL/language courses, Housing location assistance, International student organization, Language tutoring, Orientation, Visa Services. Financial aid is not available to international students. *Required with application:* TOEFL with recommended score of 205 (computer), 550 (paper), or 79 (Internet); proof of adequate funds; proof of health/immunizations.

International Student Contact Marcie Riebe, Assistant Director/Immigration Specialist, International Student and Faculty Services, 84 West South Street, Wilkes-Barre, PA 18766. *Phone:* 570-408-4106. *E-mail:* marcie.riebe@wilkes.edu.

APPLICATION *Required:* Application form, baccalaureate/first degree, 2 letters of recommendation, transcripts of college work. *Recommended:* Resume/curriculum vitae, work experience. *Application fee:* $45. Applications for domestic and international students are processed on a rolling basis.

Application Contact Nichole Redmond, Recruitment Retention Coordinator, 84 West South Street, Wilkes-Barre, PA 18766. *Phone:* 570-408-4238. *Fax:* 570-408-7846. *E-mail:* nichole.redmond@wilkes.edu.

York College of Pennsylvania
Department of Business Administration
York, Pennsylvania

Phone: 717-815-1491 **Fax:** 717-600-3999 **E-mail:** ehostler@ycp.edu

Business Program(s) Web Site: http://www.ycp.edu/mba

Graduate Business Unit Enrollment *Total:* 184 (39 full-time; 145 part-time).

Graduate Business Faculty *Total:* 16 (14 full-time; 2 part-time).

Admissions *Applied:* 56. *Admitted:* 49. *Enrolled:* 41.

Academic Calendar Semesters.

Accreditation ACBSP—The American Council of Business Schools and Programs.

DEGREE MBA

MBA—Master of Business Administration Full-time and part-time. At least 30 total credits required. 12 to 84 months to complete program. *Concentrations:* accounting, finance, general MBA, human resources management, management, marketing.

RESOURCES AND SERVICES 210 on-campus PCs are available to graduate business students. Access to Internet/World Wide Web, online (class) registration, and online grade reports available. *Personal computer requirements:* Graduate business students are strongly recommended to purchase or lease a personal computer. *Placement services include:* Alumni network, career placement, job search course, career counseling/

planning, electronic job bank, resume referral, career fairs, job interviews arranged, resume preparation, and career library.

EXPENSES *Tuition:* Part-time: $540 per credit hour. *Tuition (international):* Part-time: $540 per credit hour. *Required fees:* Full-time: $1250. Part-time: $278 per semester.

FINANCIAL AID (2007–08) 2 students received aid, including loans and scholarships. Aid is available to part-time students. *Financial aid application deadline:* 4/15.

Financial Aid Contact Mr. Calvin Williams, Director of Financial Aid, York, PA 17405-7199. *Phone:* 717-846-7788 Ext. 1226.

INTERNATIONAL STUDENTS *Services and facilities:* Counseling/support services. Financial aid is not available to international students. *Required with application:* TOEFL with recommended score of 200 (computer), 530 (paper), or 72 (Internet); proof of adequate funds; proof of health/immunizations.

International Student Contact Ms. Ines Ramirez, Associate Director of Admissions, York, PA 17405-7199. *Phone:* 717-846-7788 Ext. 1600.

APPLICATION *Required:* GMAT, application form, baccalaureate/first degree, essay, 2 letters of recommendation, personal statement, transcripts of college work. *Application fee:* $30.

Application Contact Dr. R. Eric Hostler, Director, MBA Program, York, PA 17405-7199. *Phone:* 717-815-1491. *Fax:* 717-600-3999. *E-mail:* ehostler@ycp.edu.

PUERTO RICO

Inter American University of Puerto Rico, San Germán Campus
Department of Business Administration
San Germán, Puerto Rico

Phone: 787-264-1912 Ext. 7357 **Fax:** 787-892-6350 **E-mail:** carlos.irizarry@sg.inter.edu

Business Program(s) Web Site: http://www.sg.inter.edu

Graduate Business Unit Enrollment *Total:* 239.

Graduate Business Faculty *Total:* 16 (12 full-time; 4 part-time).

Admissions *Applied:* 118. *Admitted:* 115. *Enrolled:* 115. *Average GPA:* 2.5

Academic Calendar Semesters.

DEGREE MBA

MBA—Master of Business Administration Full-time and part-time. At least 42 total credits required. 30 to 84 months to complete program. *Concentrations:* accounting, business education, finance, general MBA, human resources management, industrial administration/management, management information systems, marketing.

RESOURCES AND SERVICES 1,200 on-campus PCs are available to graduate business students. Access to Internet/World Wide Web, online (class) registration, and online grade reports available. *Personal computer requirements:* Graduate business students are strongly recommended to purchase or lease a personal computer. *Placement services include:* Alumni network, career placement, career counseling/planning, career fairs, and resume preparation.

EXPENSES *Tuition:* Full-time: $3384. Part-time: $188 per credit hour. *Tuition (international):* Full-time: $3384. Part-time: $188 per credit hour. *Required fees:* Full-time: $516. Part-time: $516 per year. *Graduate housing:* Room and board costs vary by number of occupants, type of accommodation, and type of board plan. *Typical cost:* $2500 (including board), $1000 (room only).

Inter American University of Puerto Rico, San Germán Campus (continued)

FINANCIAL AID (2007–08) Fellowships, loans, scholarships, teaching assistantships, and work study. *Financial aid application deadline:* 5/15.

Financial Aid Contact Mrs. María Lugo, Director of Financial Aid, PO Box 5100, San German, 00683-9801, Puerto Rico. *Phone:* 787-264-1912 Ext. 7252. *Fax:* 787-892-6350. *E-mail:* milugo@sg.inter.edu.

INTERNATIONAL STUDENTS *Services and facilities:* Counseling/support services, ESL/language courses, Orientation. Financial aid is not available to international students. *Required with application:* Proof of health/immunizations.

International Student Contact Mr. Efraín Angleró, Dean of Students, PO Box 5100, San German, 00683-9801, Puerto Rico. *Phone:* 787-264-1912 Ext. 7200. *Fax:* 787-892-6350. *E-mail:* eanglero@sg.inter.edu.

APPLICATION *Required:* Application form, baccalaureate/first degree, 2 letters of recommendation, transcripts of college work. School will accept GMAT and GRE. *Recommended:* Interview, resume/curriculum vitae. *Application fee:* $31. Applications for domestic and international students are processed on a rolling basis.

Application Contact Dr. Carlos Irizarry, Director of Graduate Center, PO Box 5100, San German, 00683-9801, Puerto Rico. *Phone:* 787-264-1912 Ext. 7357. *Fax:* 787-892-6350. *E-mail:* carlos.irizarry@sg.inter.edu.

Pontifical Catholic University of Puerto Rico

College of Business Administration

Ponce, Puerto Rico

Phone: 787-841-2000 Ext. 1004 **Fax:** 787-840-4295 **E-mail:** abonilla@pucpr.edu

Business Program(s) Web Site: http://www.pucpr.edu/

Graduate Business Unit Enrollment *Total:* 246 (155 full-time; 91 part-time; 145 women). *Average Age:* 34.

Graduate Business Faculty *Total:* 23 (5 full-time; 18 part-time).

Admissions *Applied:* 65. *Admitted:* 56. *Enrolled:* 38. *Average GPA:* 3.0

Academic Calendar Trimesters.

Accreditation ACBSP—The American Council of Business Schools and Programs.

After Graduation (Class of 2006–07) *Employed within 3 months of graduation:* 50%.

DEGREES JD/MBA • MBA • MBA equivalent combined degree • MS

JD/MBA—Juris Doctor/Master of Business Administration Full-time and part-time. At least 122 total credits required. 36 to 96 months to complete program. *Concentration:* combined degrees.

MBA—Accounting Full-time and part-time. At least 43 total credits required. 24 to 60 months to complete program. *Concentration:* accounting.

MBA—Administrative Office Full-time and part-time. At least 43 total credits required. 24 to 60 months to complete program. *Concentration:* administration of technological information.

MBA—Finance Full-time and part-time. At least 43 total credits required. 24 to 60 months to complete program. *Concentration:* finance.

MBA—General Business Full-time and part-time. At least 43 total credits required. 24 to 60 months to complete program. *Concentration:* business studies.

MBA—Human Resources Full-time and part-time. At least 43 total credits required. 24 to 60 months to complete program. *Concentration:* human resources development.

MBA—International Business Full-time and part-time. At least 43 total credits required. 24 to 60 months to complete program. *Concentration:* international business.

MBA—Management Full-time and part-time. At least 43 total credits required. 24 to 60 months to complete program. *Concentration:* management.

MBA—Management Information Systems Full-time and part-time. At least 43 total credits required. 24 to 60 months to complete program. *Concentration:* management information systems.

MBA—Marketing Full-time and part-time. At least 43 total credits required. 24 to 60 months to complete program. *Concentration:* marketing.

MBA equivalent combined degree—BBA General Business with Specialty in MBA General Business Full-time and part-time. At least 167 total credits required. 60 to 72 months to complete program. *Concentration:* combined degrees.

MBA equivalent combined degree—BBA in Accounting with Specialty in MBA in Accounting Full-time and part-time. At least 167 total credits required. 60 to 72 months to complete program. *Concentration:* combined degrees.

MBA equivalent combined degree—BBA in General Business with Specialty in MBA in Human Resources Full-time and part-time. At least 167 total credits required. 60 to 72 months to complete program. *Concentration:* combined degrees.

MBA equivalent combined degree—BBA in General Business with Specialty in MBA in Management Full-time and part-time. At least 167 total credits required. 60 to 72 months to complete program. *Concentration:* combined degrees.

MS—Administrative Office Full-time and part-time. At least 43 total credits required. 24 to 60 months to complete program. *Concentration:* administration of technological information.

RESOURCES AND SERVICES 120 on-campus PCs are available to graduate business students. Access to Internet/World Wide Web, online (class) registration, and online grade reports available. *Personal computer requirements:* Graduate business students are not required to have a personal computer. *Special opportunities include:* An international exchange program is available. *Placement services include:* Alumni network, career counseling/planning, and resume preparation.

EXPENSES *Tuition:* Part-time: $1800 per credit. *Tuition (international):* Part-time: $1800 per credit. *Required fees:* Full-time: $552. Part-time: $552 per year. *Typical graduate housing cost:* $4302 (including board), $1575 (room only).

FINANCIAL AID (2007–08) Loans, teaching assistantships, and work study. Aid is available to part-time students. *Financial aid application deadline:* 5/15.

Financial Aid Contact Rosalia Martinez, Student Financial Aid Director, 2250 Las Americas Avenue, Suite 549, Ponce, PR 00717-9777. *Phone:* 787-841-2000 Ext. 1054. *Fax:* 787-651-2000 Ext. 2041. *E-mail:* rmartinez@email.pucpr.edu.

INTERNATIONAL STUDENTS *Services and facilities:* Counseling/support services, International student organization. Financial aid is available to international students. *Required with application:* TOEFL; proof of adequate funds; proof of health/immunizations.

International Student Contact Yolanda Rentas, Interchange Students Program Coordinator, 2250 Las Americas Avenue, Suite 592, Ponce, PR 00717-9777. *Phone:* 787-841-2000 Ext. 1473. *Fax:* 787-651-2000 Ext. 2040. *E-mail:* yrentas@email.pucpr.edu.

APPLICATION *Required:* GRE, application form, baccalaureate/first degree, interview, 2 letters of recommendation, transcripts of college work. *Recommended:* Resume/curriculum vitae. *Application fee:* $25. *Deadlines:* 3/15 for fall, 8/15 for winter, 11/1 for spring, 4/1 for summer, 3/15 for fall (international), 8/15 for winter (international), 11/1 for spring (international), 4/1 for summer (international).

Application Contact Dr. Ana Bonilla, Director of Admissions, 2250 Las Americas Avenue, Suite 584, Ponce, PR 00717-9777. *Phone:* 787-841-2000 Ext. 1004. *Fax:* 787-840-4295. *E-mail:* abonilla@pucpr.edu.

University of Phoenix–Puerto Rico Campus

College of Graduate Business and Management

Guaynabo, Puerto Rico

Phone: 480-317-6200 **Fax:** 480-643-1479 **E-mail:** beth.barilla@phoenix.edu

Business Program(s) Web Site: http://www.phoenix.edu

DEGREES MBA

MBA—Accounting Full-time. At least 51 total credits required. *Concentration:* accounting.

MBA—Global Management Full-time. At least 45 total credits required. *Concentration:* international business.

MBA—Human Resource Management Full-time. At least 45 total credits required. *Concentration:* human resources management.

MBA—Marketing Full-time. At least 45 total credits required. *Concentration:* marketing.

MBA—e-Business Full-time. At least 45 total credits required. *Concentration:* electronic commerce (E-commerce).

MBA—Master of Business Administration Full-time. At least 45 total credits required. *Concentration:* administration.

RESOURCES AND SERVICES Access to online grade reports available. *Personal computer requirements:* Graduate business students are strongly recommended to purchase or lease a personal computer. *Placement services include:* Alumni network.

Application Contact Beth Barilla, Associate Vice President of Student Admissions and Services, Mail Stop AA-K101, 4615 East Elwood Street, Phoenix, AZ 85040-1958. *Phone:* 480-317-6200. *Fax:* 480-643-1479. *E-mail:* beth.barilla@phoenix.edu.

University of the Sacred Heart

Department of Business Administration

San Juan, Puerto Rico

Phone: 787-728-1515 Ext. 3237 **Fax:** 787-727-5890 **E-mail:** lhenriquez@sagrado.edu

Business Program(s) Web Site: http://www.sagrado.edu

Graduate Business Unit Enrollment *Total:* 241 (9 full-time; 232 part-time; 161 women). *Average Age:* 31.

Graduate Business Faculty *Total:* 22 (4 full-time; 18 part-time).

Admissions *Applied:* 60. *Admitted:* 60. *Enrolled:* 60.

Academic Calendar Trimesters.

DEGREES MBA

MBA—Master of Business Administration in Human Resource Management Full-time and part-time. At least 47 total credits required. 36 to 72 months to complete program. *Concentration:* human resources management.

MBA—Master of Business Administration in Management Information Systems Full-time and part-time. At least 48 total credits required. 36 to 72 months to complete program. *Concentration:* management information systems.

MBA—Master of Business Administration in Marketing Full-time and part-time. At least 47 total credits required. 36 to 72 months to complete program. *Concentration:* marketing.

MBA—Master of Business Administration in Taxation Full-time and part-time. At least 47 total credits required. 36 to 72 months to complete program. *Concentration:* taxation.

MBA—Master of Business Administration *Concentration:* general MBA.

RESOURCES AND SERVICES Access to Internet/World Wide Web available. *Personal computer requirements:* Graduate business students are not required to have a personal computer. *Special opportunities include:* An international exchange program is available.

FINANCIAL AID (2007–08) 77 students received aid, including grants, loans, scholarships, and work study. *Financial aid application deadline:* 5/31.

Financial Aid Contact Mr. Luis Diaz Rivera, Director, Financial Aid Office, PO Box 12383, San Juan, 00914-0383, Puerto Rico. *Phone:* 787-728-1515 Ext. 3605. *Fax:* 787-728-1515. *E-mail:* lrdiaz@sagrado.edu.

INTERNATIONAL STUDENTS Financial aid is not available to international students.

International Student Contact Ivette Lugo-Fabre, Co-op and Student Exchange Program Coordinator, PO Box 12383, San Juan, 00914-0383, Puerto Rico. *Phone:* 787-728-1515 Ext. 1218. *Fax:* 787-268-8843. *E-mail:* ilugo@sagrado.edu.

APPLICATION *Application fee:* $25. *Deadlines:* 6/30 for fall, 6/30 for fall (international).

Application Contact Luis Henriquez, Director of Admissions and Promotions Office, PO Box 12383, San Juan, 00914-0383, Puerto Rico. *Phone:* 787-728-1515 Ext. 3237. *Fax:* 787-727-5890. *E-mail:* lhenriquez@sagrado.edu.

RHODE ISLAND

Bryant University

Graduate School

Smithfield, Rhode Island

Phone: 401-232-6230 **Fax:** 401-232-6494 **E-mail:** gradprog@bryant.edu

Business Program(s) Web Site: http://www.bryant.edu/

Graduate Business Unit Enrollment *Total:* 439 (39 full-time; 400 part-time; 179 women; 18 international). *Average Age:* 31.

Graduate Business Faculty *Total:* 37 (30 full-time; 7 part-time).

Admissions *Applied:* 147. *Admitted:* 107. *Enrolled:* 82. *Average GMAT:* 516. *Average GPA:* 3.22

Academic Calendar Semesters.

Accreditation AACSB—The Association to Advance Collegiate Schools of Business.

DEGREES MBA • MSIS • MST

MBA—Master of Business Administration Full-time and part-time. 37 to 40 total credits required. 24 to 48 months to complete program. *Concentration:* general MBA.

MSIS—Master of Science in Information Systems Full-time and part-time. At least 30 total credits required. 12 to 72 months to complete program. *Concentration:* information systems.

MST—Master of Science in Taxation Part-time. At least 30 total credits required. 30 to 72 months to complete program. *Concentration:* taxation.

RESOURCES AND SERVICES 539 on-campus PCs are available to graduate business students. Access to Internet/World Wide Web, online (class) registration, and online grade reports available. *Personal computer requirements:* Graduate business students are not required to have a

Bryant University (continued)

personal computer. *Placement services include:* Alumni network, career counseling/planning, electronic job bank, resume preparation, and career library.

FINANCIAL AID (2007–08) Fellowships, loans, research assistantships, and work study.

Financial Aid Contact John B. Canning, Director of Financial Aid, 1150 Douglas Pike, Smithfield, RI 02917-1284. *Phone:* 401-232-6020. *Fax:* 401-232-6293. *E-mail:* jcanning@bryant.edu.

INTERNATIONAL STUDENTS 4% of students enrolled are international students. *Services and facilities:* International student organization, intercultural center (compliance requirements of immigration regulations). *Required with application:* TOEFL with recommended score of 237 (computer) or 580 (paper); proof of adequate funds; proof of health/immunizations.

International Student Contact Shontay D. King, Director, Intercultural Center, 1150 Douglas Pike, Smithfield, RI 02917-1284. *Phone:* 401-232-6448. *Fax:* 401-232-6362. *E-mail:* sdelalue@bryant.edu.

APPLICATION *Required:* GMAT, application form, baccalaureate/first degree, 1 letter of recommendation, personal statement, resume/curriculum vitae, transcripts of college work. *Recommended:* Interview, work experience. *Application fee:* $60, $80 (international). Applications for domestic and international students are processed on a rolling basis.

Application Contact Kristopher Sullivan, Director of Graduate Programs, 1150 Douglas Pike, Smithfield, RI 02917-1284. *Phone:* 401-232-6230. *Fax:* 401-232-6494. *E-mail:* gradprog@bryant.edu.

Johnson & Wales University
The Alan Shawn Feinstein Graduate School

Providence, Rhode Island

Phone: 401-598-1015 **Fax:** 401-598-1286 **E-mail:** admissions.grad@jwu.edu

Business Program(s) Web Site: http://www.jwu.edu/grad/index.htm

Graduate Business Unit Enrollment *Total:* 801 (646 full-time; 155 part-time; 391 women; 469 international). *Average Age:* 24.

Graduate Business Faculty *Total:* 21 (11 full-time; 10 part-time).

Admissions *Applied:* 581. *Admitted:* 437. *Enrolled:* 305. *Average GPA:* 3.36

Academic Calendar Trimesters.

After Graduation (Class of 2006–07) *Employed within 3 months of graduation:* 98%.

DEGREES MBA

MBA—Hospitality Full-time and part-time. 54 to 99 total credits required. *Concentrations:* finance, leadership, marketing.

MBA—Hospitality and Tourism Full-time and part-time. At least 54 total credits required. 12 to 18 months to complete program. *Concentrations:* finance, hospitality management, marketing.

MBA—Master of Business Administration in Global Business Full-time and part-time. At least 54 total credits required. 12 to 18 months to complete program. *Concentrations:* accounting, financial management/planning, international trade, management, marketing, organizational management.

MBA—Master of Business Administration Full-time and part-time. *Concentrations:* finance, hospitality management, human resources management.

RESOURCES AND SERVICES 600 on-campus PCs are available to graduate business students. Access to Internet/World Wide Web, online (class) registration, and online grade reports available. *Personal computer requirements:* Graduate business students are strongly recommended to purchase or lease a personal computer. *Placement services include:*

Alumni network, career placement, job search course, career counseling/planning, electronic job bank, resume referral, career fairs, job interviews arranged, resume preparation, and career library.

EXPENSES *Tuition:* Full-time: $8208. Part-time: $304 per quarter hour.

FINANCIAL AID (2007–08) 391 students received aid, including grants, loans, scholarships, and work study. Aid is available to part-time students.

Financial Aid Contact Lynn Robinson, Director, Student Financial Services, 8 Abbott Park Place, Providence, RI 02903-3703. *Phone:* 401-598-1468. *Fax:* 401-598-1040. *E-mail:* admissions.grad@jwu.edu.

INTERNATIONAL STUDENTS 59% of students enrolled are international students. *Services and facilities:* Counseling/support services, ESL/language courses, Housing location assistance, International student housing, International student organization, Orientation, Visa Services. Financial aid is available to international students. *Required with application:* TOEFL with recommended score of 210 (computer) or 550 (paper); proof of adequate funds; proof of health/immunizations. *Recommended with application:* IELT with recommended score of 6.5; TWE with recommended score of 5.

International Student Contact Dr. Allan Freedman, Director, Graduate Admissions, 8 Abbott Park Place, Providence, RI 02903-3703. *Phone:* 401-598-1015. *Fax:* 401-598-1286. *E-mail:* admissions.grad@jwu.edu.

APPLICATION *Required:* Application form, baccalaureate/first degree, 2 letters of recommendation, transcripts of college work. School will accept GMAT, GRE, and MAT. *Recommended:* Interview, personal statement, resume/curriculum vitae, work experience. Applications for domestic and international students are processed on a rolling basis.

Application Contact Dr. Allan Freedman, Director, Graduate Admissions, 8 Abbott Park Place, Providence, RI 02903-3703. *Phone:* 401-598-1015. *Fax:* 401-598-1286. *E-mail:* admissions.grad@jwu.edu.

See full description on page 648.

Providence College
School of Business

Providence, Rhode Island

Phone: 401-865-2333 **Fax:** 401-865-2978 **E-mail:** jshaw@providence.edu

Business Program(s) Web Site: http://www.providence.edu/grad/mba.html

Graduate Business Unit Enrollment *Total:* 220 (30 full-time; 190 part-time; 120 women; 30 international).

Graduate Business Faculty *Total:* 33 (25 full-time; 8 part-time).

Admissions *Applied:* 60. *Admitted:* 48. *Enrolled:* 44. *Average GMAT:* 520. *Average GPA:* 3.1

Academic Calendar Semesters.

DEGREE MBA

MBA—Graduate Business Administration Program Full-time and part-time. At least 36 total credits required. 12 to 60 months to complete program. *Concentrations:* accounting, economics, finance, health care, international business, management, management information systems, marketing.

RESOURCES AND SERVICES 250 on-campus PCs are available to graduate business students. Access to Internet/World Wide Web, online (class) registration, and online grade reports available. *Personal computer requirements:* Graduate business students are strongly recommended to purchase or lease a personal computer. *Special opportunities include:* An internship program is available. *Placement services include:* Alumni network, career placement, career counseling/planning, electronic job bank, and career fairs.

FINANCIAL AID (2007–08) 12 students received aid, including work study.

Financial Aid Contact Financial Aid Office, Harkins Hall 215, River and Eaton Streets, Providence, RI 02918. *Phone:* 401-865-2286. *Fax:* 401-865-2057.

INTERNATIONAL STUDENTS 14% of students enrolled are international students. *Services and facilities:* Counseling/support services, Orientation. *Required with application:* TOEFL; proof of adequate funds; proof of health/immunizations.

International Student Contact Dr. John J. Shaw, Director of MBA Program, Koffler Hall, River and Eaton Streets, Providence, RI 02918. *Phone:* 401-865-2333. *Fax:* 401-865-2978. *E-mail:* jshaw@providence.edu.

APPLICATION *Required:* GMAT, application form, baccalaureate/first degree, 2 letters of recommendation, personal statement, transcripts of college work. *Recommended:* Resume/curriculum vitae. *Application fee:* $55. Applications for domestic and international students are processed on a rolling basis.

Application Contact Dr. John J. Shaw, Director of MBA Program, Koffler Hall, River and Eaton Streets, Providence, RI 02918. *Phone:* 401-865-2333. *Fax:* 401-865-2978. *E-mail:* jshaw@providence.edu.

Salve Regina University
Graduate Studies

Newport, Rhode Island

Phone: 401-341-2153 **Fax:** 401-341-2973 **E-mail:** graduate_studies@salve.edu

Business Program(s) Web Site: http://www.salve.edu/graduatestudies/

Graduate Business Unit Enrollment *Total:* 143 (39 full-time; 104 part-time; 75 women). *Average Age:* 33.

Graduate Business Faculty *Total:* 15 (1 full-time; 14 part-time).

Admissions *Applied:* 141. *Admitted:* 101. *Enrolled:* 90.

Academic Calendar Semesters.

DEGREES MBA • MS

MBA—Master of Business Administration Program Full-time and part-time. Distance learning option. Undergraduate Accounting I & II, Economic Principles I & II, Quantitative Analysis and Calculus or Statistics. At least 36 total credits required. 24 to 60 months to complete program. *Concentrations:* business studies, general MBA, health administration, international and area business studies, leadership, rehabilitation administration.

MS—Master of Science in Management Full-time and part-time. Distance learning option. At least 36 total credits required. 24 to 60 months to complete program. *Concentrations:* health administration, international and area business studies, leadership, management, rehabilitation administration.

RESOURCES AND SERVICES 215 on-campus PCs are available to graduate business students. Access to Internet/World Wide Web, online (class) registration, and online grade reports available. *Personal computer requirements:* Graduate business students are strongly recommended to purchase or lease a personal computer. *Special opportunities include:* An internship program is available. *Placement services include:* Alumni network, career counseling/planning, career fairs, resume preparation, and career library.

EXPENSES *Tuition:* Part-time: $380 per credit. *Tuition (international):* Part-time: $380 per credit. *Required fees:* Part-time: $40 per term.

FINANCIAL AID (2007–08) 32 students received aid, including loans and scholarships. Aid is available to part-time students. *Financial aid application deadline:* 3/1.

Financial Aid Contact Aida Mirante, Director of Financial Aid and Veterans Affairs, 100 Ochre Point Avenue, Newport, RI 02840-4192. *Phone:* 401-341-2901. *Fax:* 401-341-2928. *E-mail:* mirantea@salve.edu.

INTERNATIONAL STUDENTS *Services and facilities:* Counseling/support services, ESL/language courses, International student organiza-

tion. Financial aid is available to international students. *Required with application:* Proof of adequate funds. *Recommended with application:* IELT with recommended score of 6.5; TOEFL with recommended score of 550 (paper).

International Student Contact Mrs. Tiffany McClanaghan, Admissions Counselor, 100 Ochre Point Avenue, Newport, RI 02840-4192. *Phone:* 401-341-2198. *Fax:* 401-341-2931. *E-mail:* tiffany.mcclanaghan@salve.edu.

APPLICATION *Required:* Application form, baccalaureate/first degree, 2 letters of recommendation, personal statement, transcripts of college work. School will accept GMAT, GRE, and MAT. *Recommended:* Resume/curriculum vitae. *Application fee:* $50. Applications for domestic and international students are processed on a rolling basis.

Application Contact Mrs. Tiffany McClanaghan, Admissions Counselor, 100 Ochre Point Avenue, Newport, RI 02840-4192. *Phone:* 401-341-2153. *Fax:* 401-341-2973. *E-mail:* graduate_studies@salve.edu.

University of Rhode Island
College of Business Administration

Kingston, Rhode Island

Phone: 401-874-4241 **Fax:** 401-874-4312 **E-mail:** mba@uri.edu

Business Program(s) Web Site: http://www.mba.uri.edu

Graduate Business Unit Enrollment *Total:* 170 (17 full-time; 153 part-time).

Graduate Business Faculty 37 full-time.

Admissions *Applied:* 87. *Admitted:* 77. *Enrolled:* 67. *Average GMAT:* 558. *Average GPA:* 3.24

Academic Calendar Semesters.

Accreditation AACSB—The Association to Advance Collegiate Schools of Business.

After Graduation (Class of 2006–07) *Average starting salary:* $70,000.

DEGREES MBA • MS

MBA—Full-Time Master of Business Administration Full-time. 45 total credits required. 12 months to complete program. *Concentrations:* finance, general MBA, management, marketing, supply chain management.

MBA—Part-Time Master of Business Administration Part-time. 36 to 45 total credits required. 24 to 56 months to complete program. *Concentrations:* finance, general MBA, management, marketing, supply chain management.

MS—Master of Science in Accounting Full-time and part-time. 30 to 69 total credits required. 12 to 48 months to complete program. *Concentration:* accounting.

RESOURCES AND SERVICES 200 on-campus PCs are available to graduate business students. Access to Internet/World Wide Web, online (class) registration, and online grade reports available. *Personal computer requirements:* Graduate business students are strongly recommended to purchase or lease a personal computer. *Special opportunities include:* An internship program is available. *Placement services include:* Alumni network, career placement, job search course, career counseling/planning, electronic job bank, resume referral, career fairs, job interviews arranged, resume preparation, and career library.

EXPENSES *Tuition (state resident):* Full-time: $12,711. Part-time: $385 per credit. *Tuition (nonresident):* Full-time: $34,914. Part-time: $1058 per credit. *Tuition (international):* Full-time: $34,914. Part-time: $1058 per credit. *Required fees:* Full-time: $1508. Part-time: $48 per credit. Tuition and/or fees vary by number of courses or credits taken and local reciprocity agreements.

FINANCIAL AID (2007–08) Loans and research assistantships. Aid is available to part-time students. *Financial aid application deadline:* 4/15.

University of Rhode Island (continued)

Financial Aid Contact Financial Aid Office, Roosevelt Hall, Kingston, RI 02881. *Phone:* 401-874-9500. *Fax:* 401-874-2002.

INTERNATIONAL STUDENTS *Services and facilities:* Counseling/support services, Housing location assistance, International student housing, International student organization, Orientation, Visa Services. Financial aid is available to international students. *Required with application:* TOEFL with recommended score of 233 (computer), 575 (paper), or 91 (Internet); proof of adequate funds; proof of health/immunizations.

International Student Contact International Students and Scholars Office, 37 Lower College Road, Kingston, RI 02881. *Phone:* 401-874-2395. *Fax:* 401-789-5298. *E-mail:* issoff@uriacc.uri.edu.

APPLICATION *Required:* GMAT, application form, baccalaureate/first degree, essay, 2 letters of recommendation, personal statement, resume/curriculum vitae, transcripts of college work. School will accept GRE. *Application fee:* $50. Applications for domestic and international students are processed on a rolling basis.

Application Contact Lisa Lancellotta, Coordinator, MBA Programs, Ballentine Hall, 7 Lippitt Road, Kingston, RI 02881-0802. *Phone:* 401-874-4241. *Fax:* 401-874-4312. *E-mail:* mba@uri.edu.

See full description on page 734.

SOUTH CAROLINA

Charleston Southern University

Program in Business

Charleston, South Carolina

Phone: 843-863-7050 **Fax:** 843-863-7070 **E-mail:** pthomas@csuniv.edu

Business Program(s) Web Site: http://www.charlestonsouthern.edu/academics/graduate/mba/mba_index.htm

Graduate Business Unit Enrollment *Total:* 325 (22 full-time; 303 part-time; 180 women; 18 international). *Average Age:* 34.

Graduate Business Faculty *Total:* 23 (16 full-time; 7 part-time).

Admissions *Applied:* 150. *Admitted:* 119. *Enrolled:* 110. *Average GMAT:* 525. *Average GPA:* 3.1

Academic Calendar 4-4-1.

After Graduation (Class of 2006–07) *Employed within 3 months of graduation:* 95%. *Average starting salary:* $45,000.

DEGREE MBA

MBA—Master of Business Administration Full-time and part-time. 30 to 36 total credits required. 12 to 72 months to complete program. *Concentrations:* accounting, finance, management information systems, organizational behavior/development.

RESOURCES AND SERVICES 300 on-campus PCs are available to graduate business students. Access to Internet/World Wide Web, online (class) registration, and online grade reports available. *Personal computer requirements:* Graduate business students are strongly recommended to purchase or lease a personal computer. *Placement services include:* Alumni network, career placement, career counseling/planning, electronic job bank, resume referral, career fairs, job interviews arranged, resume preparation, and career library.

EXPENSES *Tuition:* Full-time: $8810. Part-time: $320 per hour. *Tuition (international):* Full-time: $8810. Part-time: $320 per hour. Tuition and/or fees vary by number of courses or credits taken. *Typical graduate housing cost:* $3386 (including board).

FINANCIAL AID (2007–08) Loans and research assistantships. Aid is available to part-time students. *Financial aid application deadline:* 4/15.

Financial Aid Contact Ms. Chrissie Miller, Director of Admissions and Financial Aid, PO Box 118087, Charleston, SC 29423-8087. *Phone:* 843-863-7050. *Fax:* 843-863-7070. *E-mail:* cmiller@csuniv.edu.

INTERNATIONAL STUDENTS 6% of students enrolled are international students. *Services and facilities:* Counseling/support services, Visa Services, International luncheons. Financial aid is available to international students. *Required with application:* TOEFL with recommended score of 213 (computer) or 550 (paper); proof of adequate funds; proof of health/immunizations.

International Student Contact Barbara Mead, Assistant Dean of Students/International Services Director, PO Box 118087, Charleston, SC 29423-8087. *Phone:* 843-863-8009. *Fax:* 843-863-7021. *E-mail:* bmead@csuniv.edu.

APPLICATION *Required:* GMAT, application form, baccalaureate/first degree, 2 letters of recommendation, resume/curriculum vitae, transcripts of college work. *Application fee:* $30. *Deadlines:* 7/11 for fall (international), 12/6 for spring (international), 4/25 for summer (international). Applications for domestic students are processed on a rolling basis.

Application Contact Paula Thomas, Graduate Enrollment Counselor, PO Box 118087, Charleston, SC 29423-8087. *Phone:* 843-863-7050. *Fax:* 843-863-7070. *E-mail:* pthomas@csuniv.edu.

The Citadel, The Military College of South Carolina

Citadel Graduate College

Charleston, South Carolina

Phone: 843-953-5089 **Fax:** 843-953-7630 **E-mail:** cgc@citadel.edu

Business Program(s) Web Site: http://www.citadel.edu/csba/

Graduate Business Unit Enrollment *Total:* 251 (31 full-time; 220 part-time; 94 women; 6 international). *Average Age:* 29.

Graduate Business Faculty *Total:* 23 (16 full-time; 7 part-time).

Admissions *Applied:* 116. *Admitted:* 63. *Enrolled:* 53. *Average GMAT:* 496.

Academic Calendar Semesters.

Accreditation AACSB—The Association to Advance Collegiate Schools of Business.

DEGREE MBA

MBA—Master of Business Administration Full-time and part-time. Up to 48 total credits required. 24 to 72 months to complete program. *Concentration:* general MBA.

RESOURCES AND SERVICES Access to Internet/World Wide Web and online (class) registration available. *Personal computer requirements:* Graduate business students are not required to have a personal computer. *Placement services include:* Alumni network, career placement, career counseling/planning, electronic job bank, career fairs, job interviews arranged, resume preparation, and career library.

EXPENSES *Tuition (state resident):* Part-time: $280 per credit hour. *Tuition (nonresident):* Part-time: $458 per credit hour. *Tuition (international):* Part-time: $458 per credit hour. *Required fees:* Part-time: $15 per term.

FINANCIAL AID (2007–08) Loans and research assistantships. Aid is available to part-time students. *Financial aid application deadline:* 2/28.

Financial Aid Contact Lt. Col. Henry Fuller, Director of Financial Aid, Office of Financial Aid, 171 Moultrie Street, Charleston, SC 29409. *Phone:* 843-953-5187. *Fax:* 843-953-6759. *E-mail:* financial.aid@citadel.edu.

INTERNATIONAL STUDENTS 2% of students enrolled are international students. *Services and facilities:* Counseling/support services.

Financial aid is available to international students. *Required with application:* TOEFL with recommended score of 213 (computer) or 550 (paper); proof of adequate funds.

International Student Contact Maj. Robert Pickering, Jr., Student Services Coordinator, Multicultural Student Services, 171 Moultrie Street, Charleston, SC 29409. *Phone:* 843-953-5096. *Fax:* 843-953-7464. *E-mail:* robert.pickering@citadel.edu.

APPLICATION *Required:* GMAT, application form, baccalaureate/first degree, essay, 2 letters of recommendation, transcripts of college work, work experience. *Application fee:* $30. Applications for domestic and international students are processed on a rolling basis.

Application Contact Dr. Raymond Jones, Associate Dean, College of Graduate and Professional Studies, 171 Moultrie Street, Charleston, SC 29409. *Phone:* 843-953-5089. *Fax:* 843-953-7630. *E-mail:* cgc@citadel.edu.

Clemson University
College of Business and Behavioral Science
Clemson, South Carolina

Phone: 864-656-3975 **Fax:** 864-656-0947 **E-mail:** mba@clemson.edu

Business Program(s) Web Site: http://www.cbbs.clemson.edu/

Graduate Business Unit Enrollment *Total:* 383 (197 full-time; 186 part-time; 148 women; 52 international). *Average Age:* 28.

Graduate Business Faculty *Total:* 86 (84 full-time; 2 part-time).

Admissions *Applied:* 122. *Admitted:* 82. *Enrolled:* 46. *Average GMAT:* 595. *Average GPA:* 3.3

Academic Calendar Semesters.

Accreditation AACSB—The Association to Advance Collegiate Schools of Business.

After Graduation (Class of 2006–07) *Employed within 3 months of graduation:* 82.4%. *Average starting salary:* $69,333.

DEGREES MBA

MBA—Evening Master of Business Administration Full-time and part-time. 2 years of work experience required. 33 to 44 total credits required. 21 to 72 months to complete program. *Concentrations:* general MBA, health administration.

MBA—Full-Time Program Full-time. 2 years of work experience required for business majors and preferred for non-business majors. 62 to 64 total credits required. 17 to 21 months to complete program. *Concentrations:* accounting, combined degrees, engineering, entrepreneurship, finance, health administration, information management, information systems, international business, international trade, leadership, management information systems, marketing research, public policy and administration, real estate, statistics, supply chain management, taxation.

RESOURCES AND SERVICES 155 on-campus PCs are available to graduate business students. Access to Internet/World Wide Web, online (class) registration, and online grade reports available. *Personal computer requirements:* Graduate business students are required to have a personal computer. *Special opportunities include:* An international exchange program and an internship program are available. *Placement services include:* Alumni network, career placement, job search course, career counseling/planning, electronic job bank, resume referral, career fairs, job interviews arranged, resume preparation, and career library.

EXPENSES *Tuition (state resident):* Full-time: $7282. Part-time: $535 per credit hour. *Tuition (nonresident):* Full-time: $14,570. Part-time: $918 per credit hour.

FINANCIAL AID (2007–08) 84 students received aid, including fellowships, loans, and research assistantships. Aid is available to part-time students. *Financial aid application deadline:* 4/1.

Financial Aid Contact Financial Aid Office, G01 Sikes Hall, Clemson, SC 29634-5123. *Phone:* 864-656-2280. *Fax:* 864-656-1831. *E-mail:* finaid@clemson.edu.

INTERNATIONAL STUDENTS 14% of students enrolled are international students. *Services and facilities:* Counseling/support services, Housing location assistance, International student organization, Language tutoring, Orientation, International student orientation. Financial aid is available to international students. *Required with application:* TOEFL with recommended score of 250 (computer) or 600 (paper); proof of adequate funds; proof of health/immunizations.

International Student Contact International Programs and Services, East 208 Martin Hall, Clemson, SC 29634-5714. *Phone:* 864-656-3614. *Fax:* 864-656-4187. *E-mail:* isdp@clemson.edu.

APPLICATION *Required:* GMAT, application form, baccalaureate/first degree, interview, 2 letters of recommendation, personal statement, resume/curriculum vitae, transcripts of college work. School will accept GRE. *Recommended:* 2 years of work experience. *Application fee:* $55. Applications for domestic and international students are processed on a rolling basis.

Application Contact Director of Admissions, MBA Programs, 124 Sirrine Hall, Box 341315, Clemson, SC 29634-1315. *Phone:* 864-656-3975. *Fax:* 864-656-0947. *E-mail:* mba@clemson.edu.

College of Charleston
School of Business and Economics
Charleston, South Carolina

Phone: 843-953-5614 **Fax:** 843-953-1434 **E-mail:** hallatts@cofc.edu

Business Program(s) Web Site: http://www.cofc.edu/~accntncy

Graduate Business Unit Enrollment *Total:* 50 (39 full-time; 11 part-time; 28 women; 3 international). *Average Age:* 26.

Graduate Business Faculty 8 full-time.

Admissions *Applied:* 44. *Admitted:* 37. *Enrolled:* 30. *Average GMAT:* 554. *Average GPA:* 3.23

Academic Calendar Semesters.

Accreditation AACSB—The Association to Advance Collegiate Schools of Business.

After Graduation (Class of 2006–07) *Employed within 3 months of graduation:* 100%. *Average starting salary:* $47,200.

DEGREE MS

MS—Master of Science in Accountancy Full-time and part-time. At least 30 total credits required. 12 to 60 months to complete program. *Concentration:* accounting.

RESOURCES AND SERVICES Access to Internet/World Wide Web, online (class) registration, and online grade reports available. *Personal computer requirements:* Graduate business students are not required to have a personal computer. *Placement services include:* Alumni network, career placement, career counseling/planning, electronic job bank, resume referral, career fairs, job interviews arranged, resume preparation, and career library.

EXPENSES *Tuition (state resident):* Full-time: $8400. Part-time: $350 per credit. *Tuition (nonresident):* Full-time: $20,418. Part-time: $851 per credit. *Tuition (international):* Full-time: $20,418. Part-time: $851 per credit.

FINANCIAL AID (2007–08) 40 students received aid, including loans, research assistantships, scholarships, teaching assistantships, and work study. Aid is available to part-time students. *Financial aid application deadline:* 4/1.

Financial Aid Contact Mr. Donald Griggs, Director, Office of Financial Assistance and Veterans Affairs, Charleston, SC 29424-0001. *Phone:* 843-953-5540. *Fax:* 843-953-7192. *E-mail:* financialaid@cofc.edu.

College of Charleston (continued)

INTERNATIONAL STUDENTS 6% of students enrolled are international students. *Services and facilities:* Counseling/support services, ESL/language courses, Housing location assistance, International student housing, Language tutoring, Orientation, Visa Services. Financial aid is not available to international students. *Required with application:* TOEFL with recommended score of 550 (paper); proof of adequate funds; proof of health/immunizations.

International Student Contact Ms. Susan Hallatt, Assistant Director of Admissions, Randolph Hall, Suite 310, 66 George Street, Charleston, SC 29424-0001. *Phone:* 843-953-5614. *Fax:* 843-953-1434. *E-mail:* hallatts@cofc.edu.

APPLICATION *Required:* GMAT, application form, baccalaureate/first degree, 2 letters of recommendation, transcripts of college work. *Application fee:* $45. Applications for domestic and international students are processed on a rolling basis.

Application Contact Ms. Susan Hallatt, Assistant Director of Admissions, Randolph Hall, Suite 310, 66 George Street, Charleston, SC 29424-0001. *Phone:* 843-953-5614. *Fax:* 843-953-1434. *E-mail:* hallatts@cofc.edu.

Francis Marion University
School of Business
Florence, South Carolina

Phone: 843-661-1436 **Fax:** 843-661-1432 **E-mail:** bkyer@fmarion.edu

Business Program(s) Web Site: http://alpha1.fmarion.edu/~mba/

Graduate Business Unit Enrollment *Total:* 71 (10 full-time; 61 part-time; 33 women; 9 international).

Graduate Business Faculty 12 full-time.

Admissions *Applied:* 34. *Admitted:* 25. *Enrolled:* 25. *Average GMAT:* 450. *Average GPA:* 3.0

Academic Calendar Semesters.

Accreditation AACSB—The Association to Advance Collegiate Schools of Business.

After Graduation (Class of 2006–07) *Employed within 3 months of graduation:* 100%. *Average starting salary:* $45,000.

DEGREES MBA

MBA—Master of Business Administration in Health Management Full-time and part-time. Distance learning option. 36 to 42 total credits required. 24 to 72 months to complete program. *Concentrations:* health care, management.

MBA—Master of Business Administration Full-time and part-time. At least 36 total credits required. 18 to 72 months to complete program. *Concentration:* general MBA.

RESOURCES AND SERVICES 125 on-campus PCs are available to graduate business students. Access to Internet/World Wide Web available. *Personal computer requirements:* Graduate business students are strongly recommended to purchase or lease a personal computer. *Special opportunities include:* An internship program is available. *Placement services include:* Alumni network, career placement, career counseling/planning, electronic job bank, resume referral, career fairs, job interviews arranged, resume preparation, and career library.

EXPENSES *Tuition (state resident):* Full-time: $3300. Part-time: $330 per credit hour. *Tuition (nonresident):* Full-time: $6600. Part-time: $660 per credit hour.

FINANCIAL AID (2007–08) 5 students received aid, including research assistantships and scholarships. Aid is available to part-time students. *Financial aid application deadline:* 3/1.

Financial Aid Contact Kathryn Phillips, Director of Financial Assistance, Box 100547, Florence, SC 29501-0547. *Phone:* 843-661-1190. *E-mail:* kphillips@fmarion.edu.

INTERNATIONAL STUDENTS 13% of students enrolled are international students. *Services and facilities:* Counseling/support services, ESL/language courses, Housing location assistance, International student organization, Orientation, Visa Services. Financial aid is available to international students. *Required with application:* TOEFL with recommended score of 213 (computer) or 550 (paper); proof of adequate funds; proof of health/immunizations.

International Student Contact Barry O'Brien, Dean, Box 100547, Florence, SC 29501-0547. *Phone:* 843-661-1419. *Fax:* 843-661-1432. *E-mail:* bobrien@fmarion.edu.

APPLICATION *Required:* GMAT, application form, baccalaureate/first degree, essay, 2 letters of recommendation, personal statement, transcripts of college work. *Recommended:* Interview. *Application fee:* $30.

Application Contact Ben Kyer, Director, MBA Program, Box 100547, Florence, SC 29501-0547. *Phone:* 843-661-1436. *Fax:* 843-661-1432. *E-mail:* bkyer@fmarion.edu.

Southern Wesleyan University
Program in Management
Central, South Carolina

Phone: 800-737-1292 **Fax:** 803-739-4925 **E-mail:** bharper@swu.edu

Business Program(s) Web Site: http://www.swu.edu/ags

DEGREES MBA • MS

MBA—Master of Business Administration Full-time. Must have 3.0 GPA and take GRE, GMAT. 36 total credits required. 18 months to complete program. *Concentration:* management.

MS—Master of Science in Management Full-time. 36 total credits required. 18 months to complete program. *Concentration:* management.

RESOURCES AND SERVICES 22 on-campus PCs are available to graduate business students. Access to Internet/World Wide Web and online grade reports available. *Personal computer requirements:* Graduate business students are required to have a personal computer. *Placement services include:* Alumni network, career counseling/planning, and career fairs.

Application Contact Mr. Brooks Harper, Enrollment Manager, 1801Charleston Highway, Suite Q, Cayce, SC 29033. *Phone:* 800-737-1292. *Fax:* 803-739-4925. *E-mail:* bharper@swu.edu.

University of South Carolina
Moore School of Business
Columbia, South Carolina

Phone: 803-777-6749 **Fax:** 803-777-0414 **E-mail:** rlichten@moore.sc.edu

Business Program(s) Web Site: http://mooreschool.sc.edu

Graduate Business Unit Enrollment *Total:* 791 (406 full-time; 385 part-time; 275 women; 112 international). *Average Age:* 27.

Graduate Business Faculty 115 full-time.

Admissions *Applied:* 814. *Admitted:* 496. *Enrolled:* 370. *Average GMAT:* 638. *Average GPA:* 3.3

Academic Calendar Semesters.

Accreditation AACSB—The Association to Advance Collegiate Schools of Business.

After Graduation (Class of 2006–07) *Employed within 3 months of graduation:* 86%. *Average starting salary:* $75,402.

DEGREES IEMBA • IMBA • JD/IMBA • JD/M Acc • JD/MA • JD/MHR • M Acc • MA • MBA • MHR

IEMBA—EIMBA—Executive International MBA Full-time. 48 total credits required. 24 months to complete program. *Concentrations:* executive programs, international business.

IMBA—International Master of Business Administration Full-time. 2 years of work experience required. 48 to 72 total credits required. Minimum of 15 months to complete program. *Concentrations:* accounting, entrepreneurship, finance, international business, international finance, international management, international marketing, international trade, management, management information systems, management science, marketing, operations management, organizational management, strategic management.

JD/IMBA—Juris Doctor/International Master of Business Administration Full-time. 60 to 84 total credits required. 36 to 48 months to complete program. *Concentrations:* accounting, economics, entrepreneurship, finance, human resources management, information systems, information technology, international business, management information systems, marketing, operations management, real estate, statistics, supply chain management.

JD/M Acc—Juris Doctor/Master of Accountancy Full-time. 48 to 60 total credits required. 36 to 48 months to complete program. *Concentrations:* accounting, business law.

JD/MA—Juris Doctor/Master of Arts in Economics Full-time. 48 to 60 total credits required. 36 to 48 months to complete program. *Concentrations:* business law, economics.

JD/MHR—Juris Doctor/Master of Human Resources Full-time. 48 to 60 total credits required. 36 to 48 months to complete program. *Concentrations:* business law, human resources management, industrial administration/management, industrial/labor relations.

M Acc—Master of Accountancy Full-time. At least 30 total credits required. 12 to 18 months to complete program. *Concentration:* accounting.

MA—Master of Arts in Economics Full-time. At least 30 total credits required. 12 to 15 months to complete program. *Concentration:* economics.

MBA—Professional Master of Business Administration Part-time. Distance learning option. Up to 48 total credits required. Maximum of 31 months to complete program. *Concentrations:* accounting, economics, entrepreneurship, finance, human resources management, information management, information systems, information technology, international and area business studies, international business, international finance, management, management information systems, management science, marketing, operations management, organizational behavior/development, quantitative analysis, real estate, statistics, strategic management, supply chain management.

MHR—Master of Human Resources Full-time. At least 42 total credits required. 18 to 24 months to complete program. *Concentrations:* human resources management, industrial administration/management, industrial/labor relations.

The Moore School of Business' International M.B.A. (IMBA) is a comprehensive master's program with a global focus. The program prepares students for today's competitive business world through a blend of academic and real-world experience. In addition to experiencing an internationalized core curriculum, students gain practical experience during a required four-to six-month internship with a global company, typically overseas. IMBA students study in the Global Track or a Language Tracks (Arabic, Chinese, French, German, Italian, Japanese, Portuguese, or Spanish).

The Global Track focuses on political and economic factors affecting the investment climate of various regions throughout the world. The Language Track emphasizes these same issues, but in a specific language and culture. All foreign language instruction is conducted overseas at partner universities and institutes. Students also have the option of gaining even more international experience by attending classes at one of nineteen leading partner universities located abroad.

All told, IMBA students spend at least seven months living, studying, and working in a foreign country. This full-immersion experience teaches students to think and act globally as they gain highly valuable work experience.

RESOURCES AND SERVICES 300 on-campus PCs are available to graduate business students. Access to Internet/World Wide Web, online (class) registration, and online grade reports available. *Personal computer requirements:* Graduate business students are strongly recommended to purchase or lease a personal computer. *Special opportunities include:* An international exchange program and an internship program are available. *Placement services include:* Alumni network, career placement, job search course, career counseling/planning, electronic job bank, resume referral, career fairs, job interviews arranged, resume preparation, and career library.

FINANCIAL AID (2007–08) 300 students received aid, including fellowships, loans, research assistantships, scholarships, teaching assistantships, and work study. *Financial aid application deadline:* 12/1.

Financial Aid Contact Reena Lichtenfeld, Columbia, SC 29208. *Phone:* 803-777-6749. *Fax:* 803-777-0414. *E-mail:* rlichten@moore.sc.edu.

INTERNATIONAL STUDENTS 14% of students enrolled are international students. *Services and facilities:* Counseling/support services, ESL/language courses, Housing location assistance, International student housing, International student organization, Language tutoring, Orientation, Visa Services. Financial aid is available to international students. *Required with application:* TOEFL with recommended score of 250 (computer) or 600 (paper); proof of adequate funds; proof of health/immunizations.

International Student Contact Patricia Willer, Director of International Programs for Students, James F. Byrne Building, Suite 123, Columbia, SC 29208. *Phone:* 803-777-7461. *Fax:* 803-777-0462. *E-mail:* d800033@vm.sc.edu.

APPLICATION *Required:* Application form, baccalaureate/first degree, essay, 2 letters of recommendation, personal statement, resume/curriculum vitae, transcripts of college work. School will accept GMAT and GRE. *Recommended:* Interview, 2 years of work experience. *Application fee:* $50. Applications for domestic and international students are processed on a rolling basis.

Application Contact Ms. Reena Lichtenfeld, Director of Graduate Admissions and Enrollment Management, 1705 College Street, Columbia, SC 29208. *Phone:* 803-777-6749. *Fax:* 803-777-0414. *E-mail:* rlichten@moore.sc.edu.

See full description on page 740.

Winthrop University
College of Business Administration
Rock Hill, South Carolina

Phone: 803-323-2409 **Fax:** 803-323-2539 **E-mail:** hagerp@winthrop.edu

Business Program(s) Web Site: http://www.winthrop.edu/

Graduate Business Unit Enrollment *Total:* 249 (110 full-time; 139 part-time; 112 women; 32 international). *Average Age:* 28.

Graduate Business Faculty *Total:* 59 (51 full-time; 8 part-time).

Admissions *Applied:* 96. *Admitted:* 86. *Enrolled:* 74. *Average GMAT:* 510. *Average GPA:* 2.9

Academic Calendar Semesters.

Accreditation AACSB—The Association to Advance Collegiate Schools of Business.

After Graduation (Class of 2006–07) *Employed within 3 months of graduation:* 95%.

DEGREES MA/MBA • MBA • MS

Winthrop University (continued)

MA/MBA—MBA/Finance Concentration Full-time and part-time. At least 39 total credits required. Minimum of 18 months to complete program. *Concentration:* finance.

MA/MBA—MBA/International Concentration Full-time and part-time. Distance learning option. At least 39 total credits required. Minimum of 18 months to complete program. *Concentration:* international business.

MBA—Executive Master of Business Administration Full-time. At least 51 total credits required. Minimum of 24 months to complete program. *Concentration:* executive programs.

MBA—Master of Business Administration Full-time and part-time. Distance learning option. At least 39 total credits required. Minimum of 18 months to complete program. *Concentration:* general MBA.

MBA—Master of Business Administration Full-time and part-time. Distance learning option. At least 33 total credits required. Minimum of 18 months to complete program. *Concentration:* accounting.

MS—Master of Science in Software Development Full-time and part-time. 30 to 33 total credits required. *Concentration:* engineering.

RESOURCES AND SERVICES Access to Internet/World Wide Web, online (class) registration, and online grade reports available. *Personal computer requirements:* Graduate business students are not required to have a personal computer. *Special opportunities include:* An international exchange program and an internship program are available. *Placement services include:* Career placement, career counseling/planning, electronic job bank, resume referral, career fairs, job interviews arranged, resume preparation, and career library.

FINANCIAL AID (2007–08) 41 students received aid, including loans, research assistantships, scholarships, and work study. Aid is available to part-time students. *Financial aid application deadline:* 2/15.

Financial Aid Contact Ms. Betty C. Whalen, Director of Financial Resource Center, 117 Tillman, Rock Hill, SC 29733. *Phone:* 803-323-2189. *Fax:* 803-323-4528.

INTERNATIONAL STUDENTS 13% of students enrolled are international students. *Services and facilities:* Counseling/support services, International student organization, Orientation, Visa Services. Financial aid is available to international students. *Required with application:* TOEFL with recommended score of 550 (paper); proof of adequate funds; proof of health/immunizations.

International Student Contact Peggy Hager, Director of Graduate Studies, Rock Hill, SC 29733. *Phone:* 803-323-2409. *Fax:* 803-323-2539. *E-mail:* hagerp@winthrop.edu.

APPLICATION *Required:* GMAT, application form, baccalaureate/first degree, 2 letters of recommendation, personal statement, transcripts of college work. *Recommended:* Interview, resume/curriculum vitae, work experience. *Application fee:* $50. Applications for domestic and international students are processed on a rolling basis.

Application Contact Peggy Hager, Director of Graduate Studies, Rock Hill, SC 29733. *Phone:* 803-323-2409. *Fax:* 803-323-2539. *E-mail:* hagerp@winthrop.edu.

SOUTH DAKOTA

Black Hills State University

College of Business and Technology

Spearfish, South Dakota

Phone: 605-642-6093 **E-mail:** kristipearce@bhsu.edu

Business Program(s) Web Site: http://www.bhsu.edu

DEGREE MS

MS—Master of Science in Business Services Management Full-time and part-time. Distance learning option. At least 36 total credits required. 24 to 72 months to complete program. *Concentration:* travel industry/tourism management.

RESOURCES AND SERVICES 57 on-campus PCs are available to graduate business students. Access to Internet/World Wide Web, online (class) registration, and online grade reports available. *Personal computer requirements:* Graduate business students are strongly recommended to purchase or lease a personal computer. *Special opportunities include:* An internship program is available. *Placement services include:* Alumni network, career placement, career counseling/planning, electronic job bank, resume referral, career fairs, job interviews arranged, resume preparation, and career library.

Application Contact Dr. Kristi Pearce, Director of Graduate Studies/Assessment, 1200 University Street, Unit 9502, Spearfish, SD 57799-9502. *Phone:* 605-642-6093. *E-mail:* kristipearce@bhsu.edu.

University of Sioux Falls

John T. Vucurevich School of Business

Sioux Falls, South Dakota

Phone: 605-575-2068 **E-mail:** mba@usiouxfalls.edu

Business Program(s) Web Site: http://www.usiouxfalls.edu/mba

Graduate Business Unit Enrollment *Total:* 150 (150 part-time; 75 women; 2 international). *Average Age:* 28.

Graduate Business Faculty *Total:* 14 (7 full-time; 7 part-time).

Admissions *Applied:* 50. *Admitted:* 47. *Enrolled:* 47. *Average GPA:* 3.5

Academic Calendar Semesters.

After Graduation (Class of 2006–07) *Employed within 3 months of graduation:* 100%.

DEGREE MBA

MBA—Master of Business Administration Maximum of 24 months to complete program. *Concentrations:* accounting, general MBA, health care, management, marketing.

RESOURCES AND SERVICES 100 on-campus PCs are available to graduate business students. Access to Internet/World Wide Web, online (class) registration, and online grade reports available. *Personal computer requirements:* Graduate business students are strongly recommended to purchase or lease a personal computer. *Placement services include:* Career placement, career fairs, and resume preparation.

EXPENSES Tuition and/or fees vary by academic program.

FINANCIAL AID (2007–08) Scholarships. Aid is available to part-time students.

Financial Aid Contact Laura Olsen, Financial Aid Director, 1101 West 22nd Street, Sioux Falls, SD 57105. *Phone:* 605-331-5000.

INTERNATIONAL STUDENTS 1% of students enrolled are international students. Financial aid is not available to international students. *Required with application:* TOEFL with recommended score of 550 (paper). *Recommended with application:* Proof of adequate funds; proof of health/immunizations.

International Student Contact Prof. Rebecca T. Murdock, Director of MBA Program, 1101 West 22nd Street, Sioux Falls, SD 57105. *E-mail:* mba@usiouxfalls.edu.

APPLICATION *Required:* Application form, baccalaureate/first degree, 2 letters of recommendation, personal statement, transcripts of college work, 3 years of work experience. *Application fee:* $25. Applications for domestic students are processed on a rolling basis.

Application Contact Prof. Rebecca T. Murdock, Director of MBA Program, 1101 West 22nd Street, Sioux Falls, SD 57105. *Phone:* 605-575-2068. *E-mail:* mba@usiouxfalls.edu.

The University of South Dakota

School of Business

Vermillion, South Dakota

Phone: 866-890-1622 **Fax:** 605-677-5058 **E-mail:** alavin@usd.edu

Business Program(s) Web Site: http://www.usd.edu/business/mba

Accreditation AACSB—The Association to Advance Collegiate Schools of Business.

DEGREES MBA • MPA

MBA—Master of Business Administration Full-time and part-time. Distance learning option. 33 total credits required. 12 to 84 months to complete program. *Concentration:* health care.

MPA—Master of Professional Accountancy Full-time and part-time. 30 total credits required. 12 to 84 months to complete program. *Concentration:* accounting.

RESOURCES AND SERVICES 60 on-campus PCs are available to graduate business students. Access to Internet/World Wide Web, online (class) registration, and online grade reports available. *Personal computer requirements:* Graduate business students are not required to have a personal computer. *Placement services include:* Alumni network, career placement, career counseling/planning, electronic job bank, resume referral, career fairs, job interviews arranged, and resume preparation.

Application Contact Dr. Angeline Lavin, MBA Director, 414 East Clark Street, Vermillion, SD 57069-2390. *Phone:* 866-890-1622. *Fax:* 605-677-5058. *E-mail:* alavin@usd.edu.

TENNESSEE

Argosy University, Nashville

College of Business

Nashville, Tennessee

Phone: 615-525-2800 **Fax:** 615-525-2900

Business Program(s) Web Site: http://www.argosy.edu/nashville

DEGREES DBA • MBA • MSM

DBA—Doctor of Business Administration *Concentrations:* accounting, information systems, international business, management, marketing.

MBA—Master of Business Administration *Concentrations:* finance, health administration, information systems, international business, management, marketing.

MSM—Master of Science in Management *Concentration:* management.

Financial Aid Contact Director of Admissions, 100 Centerview Drive, Suite 225, Nashville, TN 37214. *Phone:* 615-525-2800. *Fax:* 615-525-2900.

International Student Contact Director of Admissions, 100 Centerview Drive, Suite 225, Nashville, TN 37214. *Phone:* 615-525-2800. *Fax:* 615-525-2900.

Application Contact Director of Admissions, 100 Centerview Drive, Suite 225, Nashville, TN 37214. *Phone:* 615-525-2800. *Fax:* 615-525-2900.

See full description on page 566.

Belmont University

Jack C. Massey Graduate School of Business

Nashville, Tennessee

Phone: 615-460-6480 **Fax:** 615-460-6353 **E-mail:** masseyadmissions@mail.belmont.edu

Business Program(s) Web Site: http://massey.belmont.edu

Graduate Business Unit Enrollment *Total:* 223 (223 part-time; 97 women; 6 international). *Average Age:* 30.

Graduate Business Faculty *Total:* 41 (34 full-time; 7 part-time).

Admissions *Applied:* 49. *Admitted:* 36. *Enrolled:* 27. *Average GMAT:* 553. *Average GPA:* 3.24

Academic Calendar Semesters.

Accreditation AACSB—The Association to Advance Collegiate Schools of Business.

After Graduation (Class of 2006–07) *Employed within 3 months of graduation:* 99%.

DEGREES M Acc • MBA

M Acc—Executive Master of Accountancy Part-time. At least 30 total credits required. 12 to 36 months to complete program. *Concentration:* accounting.

MBA—Evening Master of Business Administration Part-time. At least 34 total credits required. 18 to 48 months to complete program. *Concentrations:* accounting, entrepreneurship, finance, general MBA, health care, management, marketing.

RESOURCES AND SERVICES 120 on-campus PCs are available to graduate business students. Access to Internet/World Wide Web, online (class) registration, and online grade reports available. *Personal computer requirements:* Graduate business students are strongly recommended to purchase or lease a personal computer. *Special opportunities include:* An international exchange program and an internship program are available. *Placement services include:* Alumni network, career placement, career counseling/planning, electronic job bank, resume referral, career fairs, resume preparation, and career library.

EXPENSES *Tuition:* Part-time: $2135 per course. *Tuition (international):* Part-time: $2135 per course. *Required fees:* Part-time: $235 per semester.

FINANCIAL AID (2007–08) 20 students received aid, including research assistantships and scholarships. Aid is available to part-time students. *Financial aid application deadline:* 3/1.

Financial Aid Contact Financial Aid Office, 1900 Belmont Boulevard, Nashville, TN 37212-3757. *Phone:* 615-460-6403. *Fax:* 615-460-6141.

INTERNATIONAL STUDENTS 3% of students enrolled are international students. *Services and facilities:* ESL/language courses, International student organization. Financial aid is available to international students. *Required with application:* TOEFL with recommended score of 213 (computer) or 550 (paper); proof of adequate funds; proof of health/immunizations.

International Student Contact Kathy Skinner, Director of International Student Services, 1900 Belmont Boulevard, Nashville, TN 37212-3757. *Phone:* 615-460-5500. *Fax:* 615-460-5539. *E-mail:* skinnerk@mail.belmont.edu.

APPLICATION *Required:* GMAT, application form, baccalaureate/first degree, essay, interview, 2 letters of recommendation, personal statement, resume/curriculum vitae, transcripts of college work, 2 years of work experience. *Application fee:* $50. Applications for domestic and international students are processed on a rolling basis.

Application Contact Graduate Office, 1900 Belmont Boulevard, Nashville, TN 37212-3757. *Phone:* 615-460-6480. *Fax:* 615-460-6353. *E-mail:* masseyadmissions@mail.belmont.edu.

Christian Brothers University
School of Business

Memphis, Tennessee

Phone: 901-321-3291 **Fax:** 901-321-3575 **E-mail:** dmessing@cbu.edu

Business Program(s) Web Site: http://www.cbu.edu/business/

Graduate Business Unit Enrollment *Total:* 67 (65 full-time; 2 part-time).

Graduate Business Faculty *Total:* 17 (16 full-time; 1 part-time).

Admissions *Applied:* 132. *Admitted:* 121. *Enrolled:* 86. *Average GMAT:* 520. *Average GPA:* 3.12

Academic Calendar 8-week terms.

After Graduation (Class of 2006–07) *Employed within 3 months of graduation:* 100%.

DEGREE   MBA

MBA—Master of Business Administration Full-time. At least 34 total credits required. 22 to 60 months to complete program. *Concentrations:* accounting, banking, business ethics, finance, general MBA, health care, human resources management, information systems, international and area business studies, leadership, management, project management.

RESOURCES AND SERVICES 150 on-campus PCs are available to graduate business students. Access to Internet/World Wide Web, online (class) registration, and online grade reports available. *Personal computer requirements:* Graduate business students are strongly recommended to purchase or lease a personal computer. *Special opportunities include:* An internship program is available. *Placement services include:* Alumni network, career placement, career counseling/planning, resume referral, career fairs, job interviews arranged, resume preparation, and career library.

EXPENSES *Tuition:* Full-time: $9000. *Tuition (international):* Full-time: $14,300.

FINANCIAL AID (2007–08) 50 students received aid, including loans. Aid is available to part-time students.

Financial Aid Contact Mr. Jim Shannon, Student Financial Resources Director, 650 East Parkway South, Memphis, TN 38104-5581. *Phone:* 901-321-3306. *E-mail:* ushannon@cbu.edu.

INTERNATIONAL STUDENTS *Services and facilities:* Counseling/support services, International student organization, Orientation, Visa Services. Financial aid is not available to international students. *Required with application:* TOEFL with recommended score of 231 (computer), 550 (paper), or 79 (Internet); proof of adequate funds. *Recommended with application:* Proof of health/immunizations.

International Student Contact Ms. Karen Conway, Director, Student Services, 650 East Parkway South, Memphis, TN 38104-5581. *Phone:* 901-321-3566. *E-mail:* kconway@cbu.edu.

APPLICATION *Required:* GMAT, application form, baccalaureate/first degree, interview, 2 letters of recommendation, resume/curriculum vitae, transcripts of college work. School will accept GRE. *Recommended:* 3 years of work experience. *Application fee:* $50. Applications for domestic and international students are processed on a rolling basis.

Application Contact Mr. Daniel T. Messinger, Director of Graduate Programs, 650 East Parkway South, BOX T5, Memphis, TN 38104-5581. *Phone:* 901-321-3291. *Fax:* 901-321-3575. *E-mail:* dmessing@cbu.edu.

East Tennessee State University
College of Business and Technology

Johnson City, Tennessee

Phone: 423-439-5314 **Fax:** 423-439-5274 **E-mail:** business@etsu.edu

Business Program(s) Web Site: http://www.etsu.edu¢bat

Graduate Business Unit Enrollment *Total:* 170 (70 full-time; 100 part-time; 50 women; 20 international). *Average Age:* 29.

Graduate Business Faculty *Total:* 49 (37 full-time; 12 part-time).

Admissions *Applied:* 69. *Admitted:* 60. *Enrolled:* 55. *Average GMAT:* 535. *Average GPA:* 3.25

Academic Calendar Semesters.

Accreditation AACSB—The Association to Advance Collegiate Schools of Business.

After Graduation (Class of 2006–07) *Employed within 3 months of graduation:* 80%. *Average starting salary:* $40,000.

DEGREES   M Acc • MBA

M Acc—Master of Accounting Full-time and part-time. Distance learning option. At least 33 total credits required. 12 to 72 months to complete program. *Concentration:* accounting.

MBA—Master of Business Administration Full-time and part-time. Distance learning option. At least 36 total credits required. 16 to 72 months to complete program. *Concentration:* general MBA.

RESOURCES AND SERVICES 800 on-campus PCs are available to graduate business students. Access to Internet/World Wide Web, online (class) registration, and online grade reports available. *Personal computer requirements:* Graduate business students are not required to have a personal computer. *Special opportunities include:* An international exchange program and an internship program are available. *Placement services include:* Alumni network, career placement, career counseling/planning, electronic job bank, resume referral, career fairs, job interviews arranged, and resume preparation.

EXPENSES *Tuition (state resident):* Full-time: $3000. Part-time: $310 per credit hour. *Tuition (nonresident):* Full-time: $8000. Part-time: $800 per credit hour. *Tuition (international):* Full-time: $8000. Part-time: $800 per credit hour. *Required fees:* Full-time: $60. Part-time: $60 per semester. *Graduate housing:* Room and board costs vary by campus location, number of occupants, type of accommodation, and type of board plan. *Typical cost:* $3000 (including board), $1500 (room only).

FINANCIAL AID (2007–08) 60 students received aid, including research assistantships and scholarships. *Financial aid application deadline:* 5/15.

Financial Aid Contact Margaret Miller, Director of Financial Aid, PO Box 70722, Johnson City, TN 37614. *Phone:* 423-439-4300. *E-mail:* finaid@etsu.edu.

INTERNATIONAL STUDENTS 12% of students enrolled are international students. *Services and facilities:* Counseling/support services, ESL/language courses, Housing location assistance, International student organization, Orientation, Visa Services. Financial aid is available to international students. *Required with application:* TOEFL with recommended score of 213 (computer) or 550 (paper); proof of adequate funds; proof of health/immunizations. *Recommended with application:* IELT with recommended score of 6.5.

International Student Contact Ms. Maria Costa, International Student Counselor, PO Box 70668, Johnson City, TN 37614. *Phone:* 423-439-4429. *Fax:* 423-439-7131. *E-mail:* costa@etsu.edu.

APPLICATION *Required:* GMAT, application form, baccalaureate/first degree, essay, personal statement, transcripts of college work. *Recommended:* Letter(s) of recommendation, 2 years of work experience. *Application fee:* $25, $35 (international). Applications for domestic and international students are processed on a rolling basis.

Application Contact Dr. Martha M. Pointer, Associate Dean for Graduate Studies, PO Box 70699, Johnson City, TN 37614. *Phone:* 423-439-5314. *Fax:* 423-439-5274. *E-mail:* business@etsu.edu.

King College
School of Business and Economics

Bristol, Tennessee

Phone: 423-652-4773 **Fax:** 423-652-4793 **E-mail:** mrcrews@king.edu

Business Program(s) Web Site: http://www.king.edu/cgps

Graduate Business Unit Enrollment *Total:* 679 (425 full-time; 254 part-time; 367 women). *Average Age:* 36.

Graduate Business Faculty *Total:* 14 (11 full-time; 3 part-time).

Admissions *Applied:* 273. *Admitted:* 256. *Enrolled:* 238. *Average GMAT:* 550. *Average GPA:* 3.3

Academic Calendar Semesters.

After Graduation (Class of 2006–07) *Employed within 3 months of graduation:* 100%. *Average starting salary:* $40,000.

DEGREE MBA

MBA—Professional Master of Business Administration Part-time. Must have at least 2 years of significant work experience. 30 to 36 total credits required. 18 to 22 months to complete program. *Concentrations:* entrepreneurship, human resources management, international business.

RESOURCES AND SERVICES 100 on-campus PCs are available to graduate business students. Access to Internet/World Wide Web available. *Personal computer requirements:* Graduate business students are required to have a personal computer. *Special opportunities include:* An internship program is available. *Placement services include:* Alumni network, career placement, career counseling/planning, career fairs, resume preparation, and career library.

EXPENSES *Tuition:* Full-time: $9000. Part-time: $500 per semester hour. *Tuition (international):* Full-time: $9000. Part-time: $500 per semester hour.

FINANCIAL AID (2007–08) 40 students received aid, including loans. Aid is available to part-time students. *Financial aid application deadline:* 8/1.

Financial Aid Contact Mr. Micah R. Crews, Director of Recruitment for Graduate and Professional Studies, 1350 King College Road, Bristol, TN 37620. *Phone:* 423-652-4773. *Fax:* 423-652-4793. *E-mail:* mrcrews@king.edu.

INTERNATIONAL STUDENTS *Services and facilities:* Counseling/support services, ESL/language courses, International student organization, Language tutoring, Orientation, Visa Services. Financial aid is not available to international students. *Required with application:* TOEFL with recommended score of 225 (computer) or 550 (paper); proof of adequate funds; proof of health/immunizations.

International Student Contact Mr. Micah Crews, Director of Recruitment for Graduate and Professional Studies, 1359 King College Road, Bristol, TN 37620. *Phone:* 423-652-4773. *Fax:* 423-652-4793.

APPLICATION *Required:* Application form, baccalaureate/first degree, essay, 2 letters of recommendation, personal statement, transcripts of college work, 2 years of work experience. *Recommended:* Interview, resume/curriculum vitae. *Application fee:* $25. Applications for domestic and international students are processed on a rolling basis.

Application Contact Mr. Micah R. Crews, Director of Recruitment for Graduate and Professional Studies, 1350 King College Road, Bristol, TN 37620. *Phone:* 423-652-4773. *Fax:* 423-652-4793. *E-mail:* mrcrews@king.edu.

Lipscomb University
MBA Program

Nashville, Tennessee

Phone: 615-966-1833 **Fax:** 615-966-1818 **E-mail:** jackie.cash@lipscomb.edu

Business Program(s) Web Site: http://mba.lipscomb.edu and http://macc.lipscomb.edu

Graduate Business Unit Enrollment *Total:* 93 (37 full-time; 56 part-time; 40 women; 2 international). *Average Age:* 30.

Graduate Business Faculty *Total:* 24 (8 full-time; 16 part-time).

Admissions *Applied:* 61. *Admitted:* 36. *Enrolled:* 30. *Average GMAT:* 513. *Average GPA:* 3.29

Academic Calendar Semesters.

Accreditation ACBSP—The American Council of Business Schools and Programs.

After Graduation (Class of 2006–07) *Employed within 3 months of graduation:* 100%. *Average starting salary:* $59,125.

DEGREES M Acc • MBA

M Acc—MAcc Full-time and part-time. Requires completion of specific undergraduate accounting courses before enrollment. 30 to 40 total credits required. 12 to 24 months to complete program. *Concentration:* accounting.

MBA—Lipscomb MBA Full-time and part-time. 30 to 40 total credits required. 12 to 30 months to complete program. *Concentrations:* accounting, conflict resolution management, environmental economics/management, financial management/planning, general MBA, health care, leadership, nonprofit management.

MBA—Professional MBA Full-time and part-time. Minimum work experience requirement. Tuition for this program is higher and includes a global travel experience. 30 to 40 total credits required. 11 to 24 months to complete program. *Concentrations:* conflict resolution management, environmental economics/management, leadership.

RESOURCES AND SERVICES 218 on-campus PCs are available to graduate business students. Access to Internet/World Wide Web, online (class) registration, and online grade reports available. *Personal computer requirements:* Graduate business students are strongly recommended to purchase or lease a personal computer. *Special opportunities include:* An internship program is available. *Placement services include:* Alumni network, career placement, career counseling/planning, electronic job bank, resume referral, career fairs, job interviews arranged, resume preparation, and career library.

EXPENSES *Tuition:* Full-time: $24,450. Part-time: $815 per semester hour. *Tuition (international):* Full-time: $24,450. Part-time: $815 per semester hour. *Required fees:* Full-time: $200. Part-time: $200 per degree program. Tuition and/or fees vary by academic program. *Graduate housing:* Room and board costs vary by number of occupants, type of accommodation, and type of board plan. *Typical cost:* $8180 (including board), $5100 (room only).

FINANCIAL AID (2007–08) 12 students received aid, including loans, research assistantships, and scholarships. Aid is available to part-time students. *Financial aid application deadline:* 3/1.

Financial Aid Contact Mrs. Tamera Spivey, Financial Aid Counselor, 1 University Park Drive, Nashville, TN 37204-3951. *Phone:* 615-966-6202. *Fax:* 615-966-1804. *E-mail:* tamera.spivey@lipscomb.edu.

INTERNATIONAL STUDENTS 2% of students enrolled are international students. *Services and facilities:* Counseling/support services, ESL/language courses, Housing location assistance, Visa Services. Financial aid is not available to international students. *Required with application:* TOEFL with recommended score of 230 (computer) or 570 (paper); proof of adequate funds; proof of health/immunizations.

International Student Contact Mr. Ricky Holaway, Director of Admissions, 1 University Park Drive, Nashville, TN 37204-3951. *Phone:* 615-966-6133. *E-mail:* ricky.holaway@lipscomb.edu.

APPLICATION *Required:* GMAT, application form, baccalaureate/first degree, essay, interview, 2 letters of recommendation, resume/curriculum vitae, transcripts of college work. *Recommended:* Work experience. *Application fee:* $50, $75 (international). Applications for domestic and international students are processed on a rolling basis.

Application Contact Mrs. Jackie Cash, Assistant, Graduate Business Programs, 1 University Park Drive, Nashville, TN 37204-3951. *Phone:* 615-966-1833. *Fax:* 615-966-1818. *E-mail:* jackie.cash@lipscomb.edu.

Middle Tennessee State University
College of Business

Murfreesboro, Tennessee

Phone: 615-898-2964 **Fax:** 615-904-8491 **E-mail:** fester@mtsu.edu

Middle Tennessee State University (continued)

Business Program(s) Web Site: http://www.mtsu.edu/~business/index.html

Graduate Business Unit Enrollment *Total:* 406 (138 full-time; 268 part-time; 218 women; 61 international).

Graduate Business Faculty 132 full-time.

Admissions *Applied:* 128. *Admitted:* 113. *Enrolled:* 112. *Average GMAT:* 510. *Average GPA:* 3.1

Academic Calendar Semesters.

Accreditation AACSB—The Association to Advance Collegiate Schools of Business.

After Graduation (Class of 2006–07) *Employed within 3 months of graduation:* 95%. *Average starting salary:* $45,000.

DEGREE MBA

MBA—Master of Business Administration Full-time and part-time. At least 36 total credits required. 12 to 72 months to complete program. *Concentration:* general MBA.

RESOURCES AND SERVICES 98 on-campus PCs are available to graduate business students. Access to Internet/World Wide Web, online (class) registration, and online grade reports available. *Personal computer requirements:* Graduate business students are strongly recommended to purchase or lease a personal computer. *Special opportunities include:* An international exchange program and an internship program are available. *Placement services include:* Alumni network, career placement, career counseling/planning, electronic job bank, resume referral, career fairs, job interviews arranged, resume preparation, and career library.

FINANCIAL AID (2007–08) 36 students received aid, including fellowships, loans, research assistantships, and scholarships. Aid is available to part-time students. *Financial aid application deadline:* 5/1.

Financial Aid Contact Financial Aid Office, MTSU Box 290, Murfreesboro, TN 37132. *Phone:* 615-898-2830. *Fax:* 615-898-4736.

INTERNATIONAL STUDENTS 15% of students enrolled are international students. *Services and facilities:* Counseling/support services, Housing location assistance, International student organization, Language tutoring, Orientation. Financial aid is available to international students. *Required with application:* TOEFL with recommended score of 197 (computer) or 525 (paper); proof of adequate funds; proof of health/immunizations.

International Student Contact Tech Wubneh, Director, International Programs and Services Office, 202 Cope Administration Building, Murfreesboro, TN 37132. *Phone:* 615-898-2238. *Fax:* 615-898-5178. *E-mail:* twubnch@mtsu.edu.

APPLICATION *Required:* GMAT, application form, baccalaureate/first degree, transcripts of college work. *Application fee:* $25, $35 (international). Applications for domestic and international students are processed on a rolling basis.

Application Contact Troy Festervand, Associate Dean for Graduate and Executive Education, MTSU Box 290, Murfreesboro, TN 37132. *Phone:* 615-898-2964. *Fax:* 615-904-8491. *E-mail:* fester@mtsu.edu.

Rhodes College

Department of Economics/Business Administration

Memphis, Tennessee

Phone: 901-843-3920 **Fax:** 901-843-3736 **E-mail:** church@rhodes.edu

Business Program(s) Web Site: http://www.rhodes.edu

Graduate Business Unit Enrollment *Total:* 13 (13 full-time; 4 women). *Average Age:* 21.

Graduate Business Faculty *Total:* 6 (3 full-time; 3 part-time).

Admissions *Applied:* 14. *Admitted:* 14. *Enrolled:* 12.

Academic Calendar Semesters.

After Graduation (Class of 2006–07) *Employed within 3 months of graduation:* 100%. *Average starting salary:* $46,000.

DEGREE MS

MS—Master of Science in Accounting Full-time and part-time. At least 30 total credits required. 9 to 36 months to complete program. *Concentration:* accounting.

RESOURCES AND SERVICES 85 on-campus PCs are available to graduate business students. Access to Internet/World Wide Web, online (class) registration, and online grade reports available. *Personal computer requirements:* Graduate business students are strongly recommended to purchase or lease a personal computer. *Special opportunities include:* An internship program is available. *Placement services include:* Alumni network, career placement, job search course, career counseling/planning, electronic job bank, resume referral, career fairs, job interviews arranged, resume preparation, and career library.

FINANCIAL AID (2007–08) 13 students received aid, including loans and scholarships. Aid is available to part-time students. *Financial aid application deadline:* 3/1.

Financial Aid Contact Pam Church, Director of Master's Program, 2000 North Parkway, Memphis, TN 38152-1690. *Phone:* 901-843-3920. *Fax:* 901-843-3736. *E-mail:* church@rhodes.edu.

INTERNATIONAL STUDENTS *Services and facilities:* Counseling/support services, ESL/language courses, International student housing, Visa Services. Financial aid is available to international students. *Required with application:* TOEFL with recommended score of 550 (paper).

International Student Contact Katharine Owen-Richardson, Director of International Programs, 2000 North Parkway, Memphis, TN 38112-1690. *Phone:* 901-843-3403. *E-mail:* owen@rhodes.edu.

APPLICATION *Required:* GMAT, application form, baccalaureate/first degree, 2 letters of recommendation, transcripts of college work. *Recommended:* Interview, resume/curriculum vitae. *Application fee:* $25. *Deadlines:* 3/1 for fall, 3/1 for fall (international).

Application Contact Pam Church, Director of Master's Program, 2000 North Parkway, Memphis, TN 38112-1690. *Phone:* 901-843-3920. *Fax:* 901-843-3736. *E-mail:* church@rhodes.edu.

Southern Adventist University

School of Business and Management

Collegedale, Tennessee

Phone: 423-236-2751 **Fax:** 423-236-1527 **E-mail:** lwilhelm@southern.edu

Business Program(s) Web Site: http://www.business.southern.edu/

Graduate Business Unit Enrollment *Total:* 93 (8 full-time; 85 part-time; 48 women; 17 international). *Average Age:* 35-45.

Graduate Business Faculty *Total:* 9 (6 full-time; 3 part-time).

Admissions *Applied:* 33. *Admitted:* 28. *Enrolled:* 28. *Average GMAT:* 430. *Average GPA:* 3.5

Academic Calendar Semesters.

After Graduation (Class of 2006–07) *Employed within 3 months of graduation:* 95%. *Average starting salary:* $48,000.

DEGREES MBA • MBA/MSN • MF • MSA

MBA—Master of Business Administration in Accounting Full-time and part-time. At least 36 total credits required. 12 to 60 months to complete program. *Concentration:* accounting.

MBA—Master of Business Administration in Healthcare Administration Full-time and part-time. Distance learning option. At least 36 total credits required. 12 to 60 months to complete program. *Concentrations:* accounting, health care, management, marketing, nonprofit organization.

MBA—Master of Business Administration in Management Full-time and part-time. Distance learning option. At least 36 total credits required. 12 to 60 months to complete program. *Concentration:* management.

MBA—Master of Business Administration Full-time and part-time. At least 36 total credits required. 12 to 60 months to complete program. *Concentration:* nonprofit organization.

MBA—Master of Business Administration Full-time and part-time. At least 36 total credits required. 12 to 60 months to complete program. *Concentration:* marketing.

MBA/MSN—Master of Business Administration/Master of Science in Nursing Full-time and part-time. At least 56 total credits required. 18 to 72 months to complete program. *Concentrations:* health care, management.

MF—Master of Financial Services Full-time and part-time. 30 to 33 total credits required. 12 to 60 months to complete program. *Concentrations:* accounting, administration, finance.

MSA—Master of Science in Administration Full-time and part-time. 36 to 39 total credits required. 12 to 60 months to complete program. *Concentration:* administration.

RESOURCES AND SERVICES 45 on-campus PCs are available to graduate business students. Access to Internet/World Wide Web available. *Personal computer requirements:* Graduate business students are strongly recommended to purchase or lease a personal computer. *Placement services include:* Career fairs and resume preparation.

EXPENSES *Tuition:* Full-time: $15,696. *Tuition (international):* Full-time: $15,696.

FINANCIAL AID (2007–08) 2 students received aid, including loans and scholarships. Aid is available to part-time students.

Financial Aid Contact Financial Aid Office, PO Box 370, Collegedale, TN 37315. *Phone:* 423-236-2380. *Fax:* 423-236-1835. *E-mail:* magrundy@southern.edu.

INTERNATIONAL STUDENTS 18% of students enrolled are international students. *Services and facilities:* Counseling/support services, ESL/language courses, Housing location assistance, International student organization, Orientation, Visa Services. Financial aid is not available to international students. *Required with application:* TOEFL with recommended score of 600 (paper); proof of adequate funds; proof of health/immunizations.

International Student Contact Ms. Linda Wilhelm, Graduate Admissions Coordinator, PO Box 370, Collegedale, TN 37315. *Phone:* 800-SOUTHERN. *Fax:* 423-236-1527. *E-mail:* lwilhelm@southern.edu.

APPLICATION *Required:* GMAT, application form, baccalaureate/first degree, essay, 2 letters of recommendation, transcripts of college work. *Recommended:* Personal statement, resume/curriculum vitae. *Application fee:* $25. Applications for domestic and international students are processed on a rolling basis.

Application Contact Ms. Linda Wilhelm, Graduate Admissions Coordinator, PO Box 370, Collegedale, TN 37315. *Phone:* 423-236-2751. *Fax:* 423-236-1527. *E-mail:* lwilhelm@southern.edu.

Tennessee State University
College of Business
Nashville, Tennessee

Phone: 615-963-7170 **Fax:** 615-963-7139 **E-mail:** rrussell3@tnstate.edu

Business Program(s) Web Site: http://www.cob.tnstate.edu/

Graduate Business Unit Enrollment *Total:* 160 (40 full-time; 120 part-time; 60 women; 25 international).

Graduate Business Faculty 24 full-time.

Admissions *Applied:* 84. *Admitted:* 64. *Enrolled:* 45. *Average GMAT:* 520. *Average GPA:* 3.0

Academic Calendar Semesters.

Accreditation AACSB—The Association to Advance Collegiate Schools of Business.

MBA Full-time and part-time. Up to 36 total credits required. *Concentrations:* accounting, health care, management information systems, supply chain management.

RESOURCES AND SERVICES 100 on-campus PCs are available to graduate business students. Access to Internet/World Wide Web, online (class) registration, and online grade reports available. *Personal computer requirements:* Graduate business students are strongly recommended to purchase or lease a personal computer. *Special opportunities include:* An international exchange program is available. *Placement services include:* Career counseling/planning, career fairs, and job interviews arranged.

EXPENSES *Tuition (state resident):* Full-time: $6274. *Tuition (nonresident):* Full-time: $16,550.

FINANCIAL AID (2007–08) 9 students received aid, including research assistantships and work study. *Financial aid application deadline:* 6/1.

Financial Aid Contact Ms. Mary Chambliss, Director of Financial Aid, 3500 John A. Merritt Boulevard, Nashville, TN 37209-1561. *Phone:* 615-963-5772. *Fax:* 615-963-7540. *E-mail:* mchambliss@tnstate.edu.

INTERNATIONAL STUDENTS 16% of students enrolled are international students. *Services and facilities:* Counseling/support services, Housing location assistance, International student organization, Orientation. Financial aid is available to international students. *Required with application:* TOEFL with recommended score of 173 (computer), 500 (paper), or 61 (Internet); proof of adequate funds; proof of health/immunizations.

International Student Contact Gunter Mark, Director of Multicultural and International Affairs, 3500 John A. Merritt Boulevard, Nashville, TN 37209-1561. *Phone:* 615-963-5640. *E-mail:* mgunter@tnstate.edu.

APPLICATION *Required:* GMAT, application form, baccalaureate/first degree, transcripts of college work. *Application fee:* $25. Applications for domestic and international students are processed on a rolling basis.

Application Contact Raoul Russell, MBA Coordinator, 330 Tenth Avenue North, Nashville, TN 37203. *Phone:* 615-963-7170. *Fax:* 615-963-7139. *E-mail:* rrussell3@tnstate.edu.

Tennessee Technological University
College of Business
Cookeville, Tennessee

Phone: 931-372-3600 **Fax:** 931-372-6544 **E-mail:** mbastudies@tntech.edu

Business Program(s) Web Site: http://www.tntech.edu/mba

Graduate Business Unit Enrollment *Total:* 238 (93 full-time; 145 part-time; 98 women; 17 international). *Average Age:* 29.

Graduate Business Faculty 28 full-time.

Admissions *Applied:* 141. *Admitted:* 84. *Enrolled:* 75. *Average GMAT:* 528. *Average GPA:* 3.27

Academic Calendar Semesters.

Accreditation AACSB—The Association to Advance Collegiate Schools of Business.

After Graduation (Class of 2006–07) *Employed within 3 months of graduation:* 95%. *Average starting salary:* $46,178.

MBA—TTU MBA Full-time and part-time. Distance learning option. Minimum GMAT score of 450 required. 30 total credits required. 12 to 72 months to complete program. *Concentrations:* accounting, finance, human resources management, international business, management, management information systems, risk management.

RESOURCES AND SERVICES 375 on-campus PCs are available to graduate business students. Access to Internet/World Wide Web, online (class) registration, and online grade reports available. *Personal computer requirements:* Graduate business students are strongly recommended to purchase or lease a personal computer. *Special opportunities include:* An international exchange program is available. *Placement services include:* Alumni network, career placement, career counseling/planning, electronic job bank, resume referral, career fairs, job interviews arranged, resume preparation, and career library.

EXPENSES *Tuition (state resident):* Full-time: $9382. Part-time: $1224 per course. *Tuition (nonresident):* Full-time: $12,852. Part-time: $1338 per course. *Tuition (international):* Full-time: $12,852. Part-time: $1338 per course. *Required fees:* Full-time: $1308. Part-time: $177 per course. Tuition and/or fees vary by number of courses or credits taken and academic program. *Graduate housing:* Room and board costs vary by campus location, number of occupants, type of accommodation, and type of board plan. *Typical cost:* $6530 (including board).

FINANCIAL AID (2007–08) 59 students received aid, including fellowships, loans, research assistantships, and scholarships. *Financial aid application deadline:* 4/1.

Financial Aid Contact Dr. Bob G. Wood, Associate Dean, College of Business, TTU Box 5023, Cookeville, TN 38505. *Phone:* 931-372-3600. *Fax:* 931-372-6544. *E-mail:* mbastudies@tntech.edu.

INTERNATIONAL STUDENTS 7% of students enrolled are international students. *Services and facilities:* Counseling/support services, ESL/language courses, Housing location assistance, International student organization, Orientation, Visa Services. Financial aid is available to international students. *Required with application:* TOEFL with recommended score of 213 (computer) or 550 (paper); proof of adequate funds; proof of health/immunizations.

International Student Contact Charles Wilkerson, Director of International Student Affairs, TTU Box 5093, Cookeville, TN 38505. *Phone:* 931-372-3634. *Fax:* 931-372-6111. *E-mail:* cwilkerson@tntech.edu.

APPLICATION *Required:* GMAT, application form, baccalaureate/first degree, 1 letter of recommendation, transcripts of college work. *Recommended:* Interview, resume/curriculum vitae. *Application fee:* $25, $35 (international). *Deadlines:* 8/1 for fall, 12/1 for spring, 5/1 for summer, 7/1 for fall (international), 11/1 for spring (international), 4/1 for summer (international).

Application Contact Dr. Bob G Wood, Associate Dean, TTU Box 5023, Cookeville, TN 38505. *Phone:* 931-372-3600. *Fax:* 931-372-6544. *E-mail:* mbastudies@tntech.edu.

University of Memphis

Fogelman College of Business and Economics

Memphis, Tennessee

Phone: 901-678-3721 **Fax:** 901-678-4705 **E-mail:** fcbegp@cc.memphis.edu

Business Program(s) Web Site: http://fcbe.memphis.edu/

Graduate Business Unit Enrollment *Total:* 339 (177 full-time; 162 part-time; 141 women; 102 international).

Graduate Business Faculty *Total:* 88 (86 full-time; 2 part-time).

Admissions *Applied:* 291. *Admitted:* 166. *Enrolled:* 125. *Average GMAT:* 560. *Average GPA:* 3.2

Academic Calendar Semesters.

Accreditation AACSB—The Association to Advance Collegiate Schools of Business.

After Graduation (Class of 2006–07) *Employed within 3 months of graduation:* 75%. *Average starting salary:* $48,500.

DEGREES JD/MBA • MA • MBA • MS

JD/MBA—Juris Doctor/Master of Business Administration Full-time and part-time. 113 to 131 total credits required. 36 to 72 months to complete program. *Concentration:* combined degrees.

MA—Master of Arts in Economics Full-time and part-time. At least 33 total credits required. 12 to 72 months to complete program. *Concentration:* economics.

MBA—Executive Master of Business Administration Full-time. At least 48 total credits required. 22 months to complete program. *Concentration:* executive programs.

MBA—International Master of Business Administration Full-time. At least 56 total credits required. 24 months to complete program. *Concentration:* general MBA.

MBA—Master of Business Administration Full-time and part-time. 33 to 54 total credits required. 12 to 72 months to complete program. *Concentration:* general MBA.

MS—Master of Science in Accounting Full-time and part-time. 30 to 51 total credits required. 12 to 72 months to complete program. *Concentrations:* accounting, system management, taxation.

MS—Master of Science in Business Administration Full-time and part-time. At least 33 total credits required. 12 to 72 months to complete program. *Concentrations:* finance, management information systems, real estate.

RESOURCES AND SERVICES 700 on-campus PCs are available to graduate business students. Access to Internet/World Wide Web, online (class) registration, and online grade reports available. *Personal computer requirements:* Graduate business students are strongly recommended to purchase or lease a personal computer. *Special opportunities include:* An international exchange program and an internship program are available. *Placement services include:* Alumni network, career placement, career counseling/planning, electronic job bank, resume referral, career fairs, and job interviews arranged.

EXPENSES *Tuition (state resident):* Full-time: $8236. *Tuition (nonresident):* Full-time: $20,038. *Tuition (international):* Full-time: $20,038. *Required fees:* Full-time: $938.

FINANCIAL AID (2007–08) 137 students received aid, including fellowships, research assistantships, scholarships, and teaching assistantships. *Financial aid application deadline:* 3/1.

Financial Aid Contact Mr. Richard Ritzman, Director, Student Financial Aid, Student Financial Aid Office, Wilder Tower, Memphis, TN 38152. *Phone:* 901-678-4825. *Fax:* 901-678-3590. *E-mail:* rritzman@memphis.edu.

INTERNATIONAL STUDENTS 30% of students enrolled are international students. *Services and facilities:* Counseling/support services, ESL/language courses, International student organization, Orientation, Visa Services. Financial aid is not available to international students. *Required with application:* TOEFL with recommended score of 210 (computer) or 550 (paper); proof of adequate funds; proof of health/immunizations.

International Student Contact Dr. Carol Danehower, Associate Dean for Academic Programs, Dean's Office Room 426, Memphis, TN 38152. *Phone:* 901-678-3721. *Fax:* 901-678-4705. *E-mail:* fcbegp@cc.memphis.edu.

APPLICATION *Required:* Application form, baccalaureate/first degree, essay, personal statement, resume/curriculum vitae, transcripts of college work, 1 year of work experience. School will accept GMAT and GRE. *Recommended:* 2 letters of recommendation. *Application fee:* $35, $50 (international). *Deadlines:* 7/1 for fall, 12/1 for spring, 5/1 for summer, 5/1 for fall (international), 9/15 for spring (international), 2/1 for summer (international).

Application Contact Dr. Carol Danehower, Associate Dean for Academic Programs, Dean's Office, Room 426, Memphis, TN 38152. *Phone:* 901-678-3721. *Fax:* 901-678-4705. *E-mail:* fcbegp@cc.memphis.edu.

University of Phoenix–Nashville Campus

College of Graduate Business and Management

Nashville, Tennessee

Phone: 480-317-6200 **Fax:** 480-643-1479 **E-mail:** beth.barilla@phoenix.edu

DEGREES MBA

MBA—Human Resource Management Full-time. At least 45 total credits required. *Concentration:* human resources management.

MBA—Master of Business Administration Full-time. At least 45 total credits required. *Concentration:* administration.

MBA—e-Business Full-time. At least 45 total credits required. *Concentration:* electronic commerce (E-commerce).

RESOURCES AND SERVICES Access to online grade reports available. *Personal computer requirements:* Graduate business students are strongly recommended to purchase or lease a personal computer. *Placement services include:* Alumni network.

Application Contact Beth Barilla, Associate Vice President of Student Admissions and Services, Mail Stop AA-K101, 4615 East Elwood Street, Phoenix, AZ 85040-1958. *Phone:* 480-317-6200. *Fax:* 480-643-1479. *E-mail:* beth.barilla@phoenix.edu.

The University of Tennessee

College of Business Administration

Knoxville, Tennessee

Phone: 865-974-5033 **Fax:** 865-974-3826 **E-mail:** mba@utk.edu

Business Program(s) Web Site: http://bus.utk.edu/

Graduate Business Unit Enrollment *Total:* 536 (500 full-time; 36 part-time; 208 women; 87 international). *Average Age:* 22—31.

Graduate Business Faculty 115 full-time.

Admissions *Applied:* 232. *Admitted:* 137. *Enrolled:* 86. *Average GMAT:* 600. *Average GPA:* 3.35

Academic Calendar Semesters.

Accreditation AACSB—The Association to Advance Collegiate Schools of Business.

After Graduation (Class of 2006–07) *Employed within 3 months of graduation:* 88%. *Average starting salary:* $71,241.

DEGREES JD/MBA • M Acc • MA • MBA • ME/MBA • MS • MSHR

JD/MBA—Juris Doctor/Master of Business Administration Full-time. Must apply to both the MBA Program and the Law School. At least 121 total credits required. 48 to 58 months to complete program. *Concentrations:* finance, marketing, operations management, transportation management.

M Acc—Master of Accountancy Full-time. At least 30 total credits required. 12 to 16 months to complete program. *Concentrations:* accounting, information management, other, taxation.

MA—Economics Full-time. At least 30 total credits required. 12 to 16 months to complete program. *Concentration:* economics.

MBA—Aerospace Executive Master of Business Administration Part-time. Distance learning option. Several residency periods required. At least 45 total credits required. Minimum of 12 months to complete program. *Concentration:* executive programs.

MBA—Full-Time Master of Business Administration Full-time. At least 49 total credits required. 17 months to complete program. *Concentrations:* finance, marketing, operations management, transportation management.

MBA—Physician Executive Master of Business Administration Part-time. Distance learning option. Several residency periods required. At least 45 total credits required. Minimum of 12 months to complete program. *Concentration:* executive programs.

MBA—Professional Master of Business Administration Part-time. Distance learning option. Several residency periods required. At least 45 total credits required. Minimum of 17 months to complete program. *Concentration:* executive programs.

MBA—Senior Executive Master of Business Administration Part-time. Distance learning option. Several residency periods required. At least 45 total credits required. Minimum of 12 months to complete program. *Concentration:* executive programs.

ME/MBA—Master of Science in Engineering/Master of Business Administration Full-time. Must apply to both the MBA Program and the College of Engineering. At least 60 total credits required. Minimum of 24 months to complete program. *Concentrations:* manufacturing management, operations management, other, production management.

MS—Management Science Full-time and part-time. At least 44 total credits required. 18 to 24 months to complete program. *Concentrations:* finance, management science, operations management, other, production management, statistics.

MS—Master of Science in Statistics Full-time and part-time. At least 33 total credits required. Minimum of 21 months to complete program. *Concentration:* statistics.

MSHR—Master of Science in Human Resource Development Full-time and part-time. At least 39 total credits required. 18 to 72 months to complete program. *Concentration:* human resources management.

*T*he Master of Business Administration (M.B.A.) at the University of Tennessee begins with this simple question: "What does every global manager need to know?" It is a question that requires seventeen months of long days, longer nights, and many weekends to answer. The answer lies in action and hands-on, experiential learning. Furthermore, once mastered, the answer charts a new course for University of Tennessee graduates.

The School of Business offers an M.B.A. degree with concentrations in finance, innovation and entrepreneurship, logistics, marketing, and operations management. Support areas may include a variety of subjects including global business and information management. The program is geared toward full-time students, with admission in the fall semester only. An international trip and a summer internship are also required. A J.D./M.B.A. and an M.B.A./M.S. in engineering and M.B.A./M.S. in sport management are also offered. In addition, the University offers Aerospace Executive M.B.A., Physician's Executive M.B.A., Professional M.B.A., and Senior Executive M.B.A. programs.

Also offered by the College of Business Administration are master's programs in accounting, human resource development, management science, and statistics. Ph.D. programs in economics and management science are offered as well as a Ph.D. program in business administration with concentrations in accounting, finance, logistics, marketing, or statistics.

RESOURCES AND SERVICES 130 on-campus PCs are available to graduate business students. Access to Internet/World Wide Web, online (class) registration, and online grade reports available. *Personal computer requirements:* Graduate business students are required to have a personal computer. *Special opportunities include:* An international exchange program and an internship program are available. *Placement services include:* Alumni network, career placement, job search course, career counseling/planning, electronic job bank, resume referral, career fairs, job interviews arranged, resume preparation, and career library.

EXPENSES *Tuition (state resident):* Full-time: $12,054. *Tuition (nonresident):* Full-time: $24,296. *Tuition (international):* Full-time: $24,296. *Required fees:* Full-time: $1000. Tuition and/or fees vary by local reciprocity agreements.

The University of Tennessee (continued)

FINANCIAL AID (2007–08) 72 students received aid, including fellowships, grants, loans, research assistantships, scholarships, teaching assistantships, and work study. *Financial aid application deadline:* 2/1.

Financial Aid Contact Mr. Jeff Gerkin, Assistant Dean, Office of Financial Aid and Scholarships, 115 Student Services Building, Knoxville, TN 37996-0210. *Phone:* 865-974-3131. *Fax:* 865-974-2175. *E-mail:* finaid@utk.edu.

INTERNATIONAL STUDENTS 16% of students enrolled are international students. *Services and facilities:* Counseling/support services, ESL/language courses, International student housing, International student organization, Language tutoring, Orientation, Visa Services. Financial aid is available to international students. *Required with application:* TOEFL with recommended score of 250 (computer) or 600 (paper); proof of adequate funds.

International Student Contact Dr. Pia Wood, Director, Center for International Education, 1620 Melrose, Knoxville, TN 37996-3531. *Phone:* 865-974-3177. *Fax:* 865-974-2985. *E-mail:* pwood6@utk.edu.

APPLICATION *Required:* GMAT, application form, baccalaureate/first degree, essay, 2 letters of recommendation, resume/curriculum vitae, transcripts of college work. *Recommended:* Interview, personal statement, 4 years of work experience. *Application fee:* $35. Applications for domestic and international students are processed on a rolling basis.

Application Contact Donna L. Potts, MBA Admissions Director, 527 Stokely Management Center, Knoxville, TN 37996-0552. *Phone:* 865-974-5033. *Fax:* 865-974-3826. *E-mail:* mba@utk.edu.

See full description on page 744.

The University of Tennessee at Chattanooga

College of Business

Chattanooga, Tennessee

Phone: 423-425-4666 **E-mail:** yvonne-kilpatrick@utc.edu

Business Program(s) Web Site: http://www.utc.edu/Academic/Business/graduate

Graduate Business Unit Enrollment *Total:* 263 (263 part-time; 106 women; 6 international). *Average Age:* 29.

Graduate Business Faculty *Total:* 76 (51 full-time; 25 part-time).

Admissions *Applied:* 145. *Admitted:* 107. *Enrolled:* 67. *Average GMAT:* 516. *Average GPA:* 3.2

Academic Calendar Semesters.

Accreditation AACSB—The Association to Advance Collegiate Schools of Business.

DEGREES EMBA • M Ac • MBA

EMBA Part-time. Three to five year meaningful work experience and recommendation from employer required. 36 total credits required. 18 months to complete program. *Concentration:* executive programs.

M Ac—Master of Accountancy Part-time. 30 to 63 total credits required. 12 to 72 months to complete program. *Concentration:* accounting.

MBA—Master of Business Administration Part-time. 36 to 48 total credits required. 12 to 72 months to complete program. *Concentration:* general MBA.

RESOURCES AND SERVICES 100 on-campus PCs are available to graduate business students. Access to Internet/World Wide Web, online (class) registration, and online grade reports available. *Personal computer requirements:* Graduate business students are strongly recommended to purchase or lease a personal computer. *Placement services include:* Alumni network, career placement, career counseling/planning, electronic job bank, career fairs, and resume preparation.

EXPENSES *Tuition (state resident):* Part-time: $1009 per course. *Tuition (nonresident):* Part-time: $2668 per course. Tuition and/or fees vary by number of courses or credits taken and local reciprocity agreements. *Graduate housing:* Room and board costs vary by number of occupants, type of accommodation, and type of board plan. *Typical cost:* $5055 (room only).

FINANCIAL AID (2007–08) 47 students received aid, including loans and research assistantships. Aid is available to part-time students. *Financial aid application deadline:* 7/1.

Financial Aid Contact Ms. Rexann Bumpus, Director of Financial Aid, 615 McCallie Avenue, Department 4805, Chattanooga, TN 37403-2598. *Phone:* 423-425-4677. *Fax:* 423-425-2292. *E-mail:* rexann-bumpus@utc.edu.

INTERNATIONAL STUDENTS 2% of students enrolled are international students. *Services and facilities:* Counseling/support services, ESL/language courses, Housing location assistance, International student organization, Language tutoring, Orientation. Financial aid is not available to international students. *Required with application:* TOEFL with recommended score of 213 (computer) or 550 (paper); proof of adequate funds; proof of health/immunizations.

International Student Contact Nancy Amberson, Coordinator of International Students, 615 McCallie Avenue, Hooper Hall 258, Department 5305, Chattanooga, TN 37403-2598. *Phone:* 423-425-4573. *E-mail:* nancy-amberson@utc.edu.

APPLICATION *Required:* GMAT, application form, baccalaureate/first degree, transcripts of college work. *Application fee:* $30, $35 (international). Applications for domestic and international students are processed on a rolling basis.

Application Contact Yvonne Kilpatrick, Director of the Graduate School, The Graduate School, Department 5305, 615 McCallie Avenue, Chattanooga, TN 37403-2598. *Phone:* 423-425-4666. *E-mail:* yvonne-kilpatrick@utc.edu.

The University of Tennessee at Martin

College of Business and Public Affairs

Martin, Tennessee

Phone: 731-881-7236 **Fax:** 731-881-7241 **E-mail:** khammond@utm.edu

Business Program(s) Web Site: http://www.utm.edu/departments/cbpa

Graduate Business Unit Enrollment *Total:* 103 (26 full-time; 77 part-time; 47 women; 12 international). *Average Age:* 30.

Graduate Business Faculty 25 full-time.

Admissions *Applied:* 21. *Admitted:* 17. *Enrolled:* 14. *Average GMAT:* 485. *Average GPA:* 2.92

Academic Calendar Semesters.

Accreditation AACSB—The Association to Advance Collegiate Schools of Business.

After Graduation (Class of 2006–07) *Employed within 3 months of graduation:* 99%.

DEGREE MBA

MBA—Master of Business Administration Full-time and part-time. Distance learning option. At least 35 total credits required. 9 to 72 months to complete program. *Concentration:* general MBA.

RESOURCES AND SERVICES 200 on-campus PCs are available to graduate business students. Access to Internet/World Wide Web, online (class) registration, and online grade reports available. *Personal computer requirements:* Graduate business students are strongly recommended to purchase or lease a personal computer. *Placement services include:* Alumni network, career placement, career counseling/planning, and career fairs.

EXPENSES *Tuition (state resident):* Full-time: $2893. Part-time: $323 per credit hour. *Tuition (nonresident):* Full-time: $7913. Part-time: $881 per credit hour. *Tuition (international):* Full-time: $7913. Part-time: $881 per credit hour. Tuition and/or fees vary by number of courses or credits taken, academic program, and local reciprocity agreements. *Graduate housing:* Room and board costs vary by number of occupants, type of accommodation, and type of board plan. *Typical cost:* $2278 (including board), $1080 (room only).

FINANCIAL AID (2007–08) 15 students received aid, including research assistantships. Aid is available to part-time students. *Financial aid application deadline:* 3/1.

Financial Aid Contact Sandra J. Neel, Director of Student Financial Assistance, 205 Administration Building, Martin, TN 38238. *Phone:* 731-881-7040. *Fax:* 731-881-7036. *E-mail:* sneel@utm.edu.

INTERNATIONAL STUDENTS 12% of students enrolled are international students. *Services and facilities:* Counseling/support services, International student organization, Orientation. Financial aid is not available to international students. *Required with application:* TOEFL with recommended score of 197 (computer) or 525 (paper); proof of adequate funds; proof of health/immunizations.

International Student Contact Sandra Baker, Director, International Programs, 144 Gooch Hall, Martin, TN 38238-1000. *Phone:* 731-881-7340. *Fax:* 731-881-7322. *E-mail:* sbaker@utm.edu.

APPLICATION *Required:* GMAT, application form, baccalaureate/first degree, essay, resume/curriculum vitae, transcripts of college work. *Application fee:* $30, $80 (international). Applications for domestic and international students are processed on a rolling basis.

Application Contact Dr. Kevin L. Hammond, Professor of Marketing/Coordinator of Graduate Programs in Business, 314 Clement Hall, Martin, TN 38238-1015. *Phone:* 731-881-7236. *Fax:* 731-881-7241. *E-mail:* khammond@utm.edu.

Vanderbilt University

Owen Graduate School of Management

Nashville, Tennessee

Phone: 615-342-6469 **Fax:** 615-343-1175 **E-mail:** admissions@owen.vanderbilt.edu

Business Program(s) Web Site: http://www.owen.vanderbilt.edu/vanderbilt/

Graduate Business Unit Enrollment *Total:* 415 (415 full-time; 123 women; 92 international). *Average Age:* 28.

Graduate Business Faculty *Total:* 85 (48 full-time; 37 part-time).

Admissions *Applied:* 1,137. *Admitted:* 437. *Enrolled:* 260. *Average GMAT:* 644. *Average GPA:* 3.27

Academic Calendar Half-semester modules.

Accreditation AACSB—The Association to Advance Collegiate Schools of Business.

After Graduation (Class of 2006–07) *Employed within 3 months of graduation:* 84%. *Average starting salary:* $89,268.

DEGREES EMBA • JD/MBA • MAC • MBA • MBA/M Div • MBA/MA • MBA/MSN • MD/MBA • MSF

EMBA—Executive Master of Business Administration Full-time. Minimum 5 years of work experience (including management experience) required. At least 60 total credits required. 21 months to complete program. *Concentration:* management.

JD/MBA—Juris Doctor/Master of Business Administration Full-time. At least 125 total credits required. 40 months to complete program. *Concentrations:* accounting, business law, finance, health care, human resources management, management information systems, marketing, operations management, organizational behavior/development, strategic management.

MAC—Vanderbilt Master of Accountancy Full-time. At least 37 total credits required. 9 months to complete program. *Concentrations:* accounting, business education.

MBA—Master of Business Administration Full-time. At least 62 total credits required. 20 months to complete program. *Concentrations:* accounting, business law, finance, health care, human resources management, management information systems, marketing, operations management, organizational behavior/development, strategic management.

MBA/M Div—Master of Business Administration/Master of Divinity Full-time. At least 122 total credits required. 40 months to complete program. *Concentrations:* accounting, business law, finance, health care, human resources management, management information systems, marketing, operations management, organizational behavior/development, strategic management.

MBA/MA—Master of Business Administration/Master of Arts in Latin American Studies Program Full-time. Applicants to this joint degree program apply only to Owen. A copy of application is sent to CLAIS. Must be accepted to both schools. At least 72 total credits required. 25 to 30 months to complete program. *Concentrations:* accounting, business law, finance, health care, human resources management, management information systems, marketing, operations management, organizational behavior/development, strategic management.

MBA/MSN—Master of Business Administration/Master of Science in Nursing Full-time. At least 75 total credits required. 25 to 30 months to complete program. *Concentrations:* accounting, business law, finance, health care, human resources management, management information systems, marketing, operations management, strategic management.

MD/MBA—Doctor of Medicine/Master of Business Administration Full-time. Students must apply to the School of Medicine and Owen separately and be accepted by both programs to pursue the joint degree. At least 125 total credits required. 50 months to complete program. *Concentrations:* accounting, business law, finance, health care, human resources management, management information systems, marketing, operations management, organizational behavior/development, strategic management.

MSF—Master of Science in Finance Full-time. At least 32 total credits required. 9 months to complete program. *Concentration:* finance.

RESOURCES AND SERVICES 15 on-campus PCs are available to graduate business students. Access to Internet/World Wide Web, online (class) registration, and online grade reports available. *Personal computer requirements:* Graduate business students are required to have a personal computer. *Special opportunities include:* An international exchange program is available. *Placement services include:* Alumni network, career placement, job search course, career counseling/planning, electronic job bank, resume referral, career fairs, job interviews arranged, resume preparation, and career library.

EXPENSES *Tuition:* Full-time: $37,834. *Tuition (international):* Full-time: $37,834. *Required fees:* Full-time: $5086. Tuition and/or fees vary by academic program.

FINANCIAL AID (2007–08) 244 students received aid, including scholarships. *Financial aid application deadline:* 5/1.

Financial Aid Contact John Roeder, Director, MBA Admissions, 401 21st Avenue, South, Nashville, TN 37203. *Phone:* 615-322-6469. *Fax:* 615-343-1175. *E-mail:* admissions@owen.vanderbilt.edu.

INTERNATIONAL STUDENTS 22% of students enrolled are international students. *Services and facilities:* Counseling/support services, ESL/language courses, Housing location assistance, International student housing, International student organization, Language tutoring, Orientation, Visa Services. Financial aid is available to international students. *Required with application:* TOEFL with recommended score of 250 (computer), 600 (paper), or 100 (Internet); proof of adequate funds; proof of health/immunizations.

International Student Contact Mr. John Roeder, Director, MBA Admissions, 401 21st Avenue, South, Nashville, TN 37203. *Phone:* 615-322-6469. *Fax:* 615-343-1175. *E-mail:* admissions@owen.vanderbilt.edu.

Vanderbilt University (continued)

APPLICATION *Required:* GMAT, application form, baccalaureate/first degree, essay, interview, 2 letters of recommendation, resume/curriculum vitae, transcripts of college work. *Recommended:* 3 years of work experience. *Application fee:* $100. Applications for domestic and international students are processed on a rolling basis.

Application Contact John Roeder, Director, MBA Admissions, 401 21st Avenue, South, Nashville, TN 37203. *Phone:* 615-342-6469. *Fax:* 615-343-1175. *E-mail:* admissions@owen.vanderbilt.edu.

See full description on page 758.

TEXAS

Abilene Christian University
College of Business Administration
Abilene, Texas

Phone: 325-674-2080 **Fax:** 325-674-2564 **E-mail:** bill.fowler@coba.acu.edu

Business Program(s) Web Site: http://www.acu.edu/academics/coba.html

Graduate Business Unit Enrollment *Total:* 41 (36 full-time; 5 part-time; 15 women; 6 international). *Average Age:* 24.

Graduate Business Faculty 6 full-time.

Admissions *Applied:* 34. *Admitted:* 30. *Enrolled:* 30. *Average GPA:* 3.5

Academic Calendar Semesters.

Accreditation AACSB—The Association to Advance Collegiate Schools of Business. ACBSP—The American Council of Business Schools and Programs.

After Graduation (Class of 2006–07) *Employed within 3 months of graduation:* 100%. *Average starting salary:* $48,000.

DEGREE M Acc

M Acc—Master of Accountancy Full-time and part-time. At least 30 total credits required. 12 to 60 months to complete program. *Concentration:* accounting.

RESOURCES AND SERVICES 700 on-campus PCs are available to graduate business students. Access to Internet/World Wide Web, online (class) registration, and online grade reports available. *Personal computer requirements:* Graduate business students are not required to have a personal computer. *Placement services include:* Alumni network, career placement, career counseling/planning, career fairs, job interviews arranged, resume preparation, and career library.

EXPENSES *Tuition:* Full-time: $16,710. Part-time: $557 per credit hour. *Required fees:* Full-time: $700. Part-time: $33.50 per credit hour. Tuition and/or fees vary by number of courses or credits taken. *Graduate housing:* Room and board costs vary by number of occupants, type of accommodation, and type of board plan. *Typical cost:* $6350 (including board).

FINANCIAL AID (2007–08) 34 students received aid, including loans, scholarships, and teaching assistantships. Aid is available to part-time students. *Financial aid application deadline:* 3/1.

Financial Aid Contact Michael Lewis, Director of Student Financial Services, ACU Box 29007, Abilene, TX 79699-9007. *Phone:* 325-674-2643. *Fax:* 325-674-2130.

INTERNATIONAL STUDENTS 15% of students enrolled are international students. *Services and facilities:* Counseling/support services, ESL/language courses, International student organization, Visa Services. Financial aid is available to international students. *Required with application:* TOEFL with recommended score of 197 (computer) or 525 (paper); proof of adequate funds; proof of health/immunizations.

International Student Contact Mr. Kevin Kehl, Director for International and Intercultural Education, ACU Box 28226, Abilene, TX 79699. *Phone:* 325-674-2710. *Fax:* 325-674-2966. *E-mail:* kehlk@acu.edu.

APPLICATION *Required:* GMAT, baccalaureate/first degree, 2 letters of recommendation, personal statement, transcripts of college work. *Application fee:* $40, $45 (international). Applications for domestic and international students are processed on a rolling basis.

Application Contact Bill Fowler, Chair, Department of Accounting and Finance, ACU Box 29305, Abilene, TX 79699-9305. *Phone:* 325-674-2080. *Fax:* 325-674-2564. *E-mail:* bill.fowler@coba.acu.edu.

Amberton University
Department of Business Administration
Garland, Texas

Phone: 972-279-6511 Ext. 127 **Fax:** 972-279-9773 **E-mail:** advisor@amberton.edu

Business Program(s) Web Site: http://www.amberton.edu

Graduate Business Unit Enrollment *Total:* 396 (40 full-time; 356 part-time; 157 women).

Graduate Business Faculty *Total:* 61 (16 full-time; 45 part-time).

Admissions *Applied:* 325. *Admitted:* 320. *Enrolled:* 300. *Average GPA:* 3.0

Academic Calendar Four 10-week sessions.

After Graduation (Class of 2006–07) *Employed within 3 months of graduation:* 90%. *Average starting salary:* $45,000.

DEGREES MBA

MBA—Master of Business Administration in Management Full-time and part-time. Distance learning option. At least 36 total credits required. *Concentration:* management.

MBA—Master of Business Administration Full-time and part-time. Distance learning option. At least 36 total credits required. *Concentration:* general MBA.

RESOURCES AND SERVICES 25 on-campus PCs are available to graduate business students. Access to Internet/World Wide Web available. *Personal computer requirements:* Graduate business students are not required to have a personal computer.

EXPENSES *Tuition:* Part-time: $225 per semester hour. *Tuition (international):* Part-time: $225 per semester hour.

Financial Aid Contact Dr. Brent Bradshaw, Vice President for Administrative Services, 1700 Eastgate Drive, Garland, TX 75041. *Phone:* 972-279-6511 Ext. 141. *Fax:* 972-279-9773. *E-mail:* bbradshaw@amberton.edu.

INTERNATIONAL STUDENTS Financial aid is not available to international students. *Required with application:* Proof of adequate funds.

International Student Contact Mr. Bill Gilbreath, Director for Student Services, 1700 Eastgate Drive, Garland, TX 75041. *Phone:* 972-279-6511 Ext. 127. *Fax:* 972-279-9773. *E-mail:* advisor@amberton.edu.

APPLICATION *Required:* Application form, baccalaureate/first degree, transcripts of college work. *Application fee:* $0, $125 (international). Applications for domestic and international students are processed on a rolling basis.

Application Contact Mr. Bill Gilbreath, Director of Student Advising, 1700 Eastgate Drive, Garland, TX 75041. *Phone:* 972-279-6511 Ext. 127. *Fax:* 972-279-9773. *E-mail:* advisor@amberton.edu.

Angelo State University
Department of Management and Marketing
San Angelo, Texas

Phone: 325-942-2169 **Fax:** 325-942-2194 **E-mail:** graduate.school@angelo.edu

Business Program(s) Web Site: http://www.angelo.edu/dept/Management_marketing/mba.html

Graduate Business Unit Enrollment *Total:* 60 (19 full-time; 41 part-time; 33 women; 3 international). *Average Age:* 29.

Graduate Business Faculty 19 full-time.

Admissions *Applied:* 29. *Admitted:* 21. *Enrolled:* 16. *Average GMAT:* 485. *Average GPA:* 3.19

Academic Calendar Semesters.

Accreditation ACBSP—The American Council of Business Schools and Programs.

DEGREES   M Pr A • MBA

M Pr A—Professional Accountancy Full-time and part-time. At least 36 total credits required. 18 to 72 months to complete program. *Concentration:* accounting.

MBA—Master of Business Administration Full-time and part-time. At least 39 total credits required. 18 to 72 months to complete program. *Concentration:* administration.

MBA—Master of Business Administration in Accounting Full-time and part-time. At least 36 total credits required. 18 to 72 months to complete program. *Concentration:* accounting.

RESOURCES AND SERVICES 700 on-campus PCs are available to graduate business students. Access to Internet/World Wide Web, online (class) registration, and online grade reports available. *Personal computer requirements:* Graduate business students are not required to have a personal computer. *Special opportunities include:* An internship program is available. *Placement services include:* Alumni network, career placement, career counseling/planning, career fairs, job interviews arranged, resume preparation, and career library.

EXPENSES *Tuition (state resident):* Full-time: $3180. *Tuition (nonresident):* Full-time: $11,460. *Tuition (international):* Full-time: $11,460. *Required fees:* Full-time: $1100. Part-time: $418.85 per semester. *Graduate housing:* Room and board costs vary by number of occupants, type of accommodation, and type of board plan. *Typical cost:* $5314 (including board), $2167 (room only).

FINANCIAL AID (2007–08) 27 students received aid, including grants, loans, research assistantships, scholarships, teaching assistantships, and work study. Aid is available to part-time students. *Financial aid application deadline:* 2/1.

Financial Aid Contact Dr. Carol B. Diminnie, Graduate Dean, College of Graduate Studies, ASU Station #11025, San Angelo, TX 76909-1025. *Phone:* 325-942-2169. *Fax:* 325-942-2169. *E-mail:* carol.diminnie@angelo.edu.

INTERNATIONAL STUDENTS 5% of students enrolled are international students. *Services and facilities:* Counseling/support services, International student organization, Orientation. Financial aid is available to international students. *Required with application:* Proof of adequate funds; proof of health/immunizations. *Recommended with application:* IELT; TOEFL with recommended score of 213 (computer) or 550 (paper).

International Student Contact Meghan Pace, International Student Services Counselor, ASU Station #11035, ASU Station #11035, San Angelo, TX 76909-1014. *Phone:* 325-942-2083. *Fax:* 325-942-2084. *E-mail:* meghan.pace@angelo.edu.

APPLICATION *Required:* GMAT, application form, baccalaureate/first degree, essay, resume/curriculum vitae, transcripts of college work. *Application fee:* $40, $50 (international). Applications for domestic and international students are processed on a rolling basis.

Application Contact Dr. Carol B. Diminnie, Graduate Dean, College of Graduate Studies, ASU Station #11025, San Angelo, TX 76909-1025. *Phone:* 325-942-2169. *Fax:* 325-942-2194. *E-mail:* graduate.school@angelo.edu.

Argosy University, Dallas
College of Business
Dallas, Texas

Phone: 214-890-9900 **Fax:** 214-378-8555

Business Program(s) Web Site: http://www.argosy.edu/dallas

DEGREE   MBA

MBA—Master of Business Administration (MBA) *Concentrations:* finance, health administration, information systems, international business, management, marketing, public management.

Financial Aid Contact Director of Admissions, 8080 Park Lane, Suite 400A, Dallas, TX 75231. *Phone:* 214-890-9900. *Fax:* 214-378-8555.

International Student Contact Director of Admissions, 8080 Park Lane, Suite 400A, Dallas, TX 75231. *Phone:* 214-890-9900. *Fax:* 214-378-8555.

Application Contact Director of Admissions, 8080 Park Lane, Suite 400A, Dallas, TX 75231. *Phone:* 214-890-9900. *Fax:* 214-378-8555.

See full description on page 566.

Baylor University
Hankamer School of Business
Waco, Texas

Phone: 254-710-3718 **Fax:** 254-710-1066 **E-mail:** joanna_gaitros@baylor.edu

Business Program(s) Web Site: http://www.baylor.edu/mba

Graduate Business Unit Enrollment *Total:* 273. *Average Age:* 26.

Graduate Business Faculty 130 full-time.

Admissions *Applied:* 128. *Admitted:* 67. *Enrolled:* 44. *Average GMAT:* 595. *Average GPA:* 3.2

Academic Calendar Semesters.

Accreditation AACSB—The Association to Advance Collegiate Schools of Business.

After Graduation (Class of 2006–07) *Employed within 3 months of graduation:* 95%. *Average starting salary:* $61,100.

DEGREES   JD/MBA • MBA • MBA/ME • MBA/MSIS

JD/MBA—Juris Doctor/Master of Business Administration Full-time. Acceptance to both the Business School and the Law School required. 32 to 44 total credits required. 9 to 12 months to complete program. *Concentrations:* business law, law.

MBA—Executive Master of Business Administration—Austin Part-time. 5 years of work experience required. At least 48 total credits required. 21 months to complete program. *Concentration:* executive programs.

MBA—Executive Master of Business Administration—Dallas Part-time. 8 years of work experience required. At least 48 total credits required. 21 months to complete program. *Concentration:* executive programs.

MBA—Master of Business Administration Full-time. 53 to 65 total credits required. 16 to 21 months to complete program. *Concentrations:* entrepreneurship, finance, health care, information systems, international management.

Baylor University (continued)

MBA/ME—Master of Business Administration/Master of Engineering
Full-time. 44 total credits required. 12 months to complete program. *Concentrations:* business studies, engineering.

MBA/MSIS—Master of Business Administration/Master of Science in Information Systems Full-time. 71 to 83 total credits required. 21 to 24 months to complete program. *Concentrations:* information management, system management.

RESOURCES AND SERVICES 200 on-campus PCs are available to graduate business students. Access to Internet/World Wide Web, online (class) registration, and online grade reports available. *Personal computer requirements:* Graduate business students are required to have a personal computer. *Special opportunities include:* An international exchange program and an internship program are available. *Placement services include:* Alumni network, career placement, job search course, career counseling/planning, electronic job bank, resume referral, career fairs, resume preparation, and career library.

EXPENSES *Tuition:* Full-time: $11,832. Part-time: $986 per hour. *Tuition (international):* Full-time: $11,832. Part-time: $986 per hour. *Required fees:* Full-time: $2670. Tuition and/or fees vary by number of courses or credits taken and academic program. *Graduate housing:* Room and board costs vary by campus location, number of occupants, type of accommodation, and type of board plan. *Typical cost:* $3665 (including board), $2000 (room only).

FINANCIAL AID (2007–08) Fellowships, loans, research assistantships, scholarships, and work study. *Financial aid application deadline:* 4/15.

Financial Aid Contact Joanna Iturbe, Admissions Coordinator, Graduate Business Programs, One Bear Place #98013, Waco, TX 76798. *Phone:* 254-710-3718. *Fax:* 254-710-1066. *E-mail:* joanna_gaitros@baylor.edu.

INTERNATIONAL STUDENTS *Services and facilities:* Counseling/support services, Orientation, Membership in Graduate Business Association and Global Graduate Business Council. Financial aid is available to international students. *Required with application:* TOEFL with recommended score of 250 (computer), 600 (paper), or 100 (Internet); proof of adequate funds; proof of health/immunizations.

International Student Contact Alexine Burke, Advisor, International Students, One Bear Place #97381, Waco, TX 76798-7381. *Phone:* 254-710-1461. *Fax:* 254-710-1468. *E-mail:* international_programs_support@baylor.edu.

APPLICATION *Required:* GMAT, application form, baccalaureate/first degree, essay, 2 letters of recommendation, personal statement, resume/curriculum vitae, transcripts of college work. *Recommended:* Interview, 2 years of work experience. *Application fee:* $50. Applications for domestic and international students are processed on a rolling basis.

Application Contact Joanna Iturbe, Admissions Coordinator, Graduate Business Programs, One Bear Place #98013, Waco, TX 76798-8013. *Phone:* 254-710-3718. *Fax:* 254-710-1066. *E-mail:* joanna_gaitros@baylor.edu.

See full description on page 574.

Dallas Baptist University

Graduate School of Business

Dallas, Texas

Phone: 214-333-5242 **Fax:** 214-333-5579 **E-mail:** graduate@dbu.edu

Business Program(s) Web Site: http://www.dbu.edu

Graduate Business Unit Enrollment *Total:* 646 (154 full-time; 492 part-time; 360 women).

Graduate Business Faculty *Total:* 169 (55 full-time; 114 part-time).

Admissions *Applied:* 346. *Admitted:* 205. *Enrolled:* 143. *Average GPA:* 3.0

Academic Calendar 4-1-4.

Accreditation ACBSP—The American Council of Business Schools and Programs.

DEGREES MA • MBA

MA—Master of Arts in Organizational Management Full-time and part-time. Distance learning option. 36 to 45 total credits required. Maximum of 72 months to complete program. *Concentrations:* conflict resolution management, health care, human resources management, management.

MBA—Master of Business Administration Full-time and part-time. Distance learning option. 36 to 60 total credits required. Maximum of 72 months to complete program. *Concentrations:* accounting, conflict resolution management, electronic commerce (E-commerce), finance, health care, international business, management, management information systems, marketing, technology management.

RESOURCES AND SERVICES 201 on-campus PCs are available to graduate business students. Access to Internet/World Wide Web, online (class) registration, and online grade reports available. *Personal computer requirements:* Graduate business students are not required to have a personal computer. *Special opportunities include:* An internship program is available. *Placement services include:* Alumni network, career counseling/planning, electronic job bank, resume referral, career fairs, job interviews arranged, resume preparation, and career library.

EXPENSES *Tuition:* Full-time: $9144. Part-time: $508 per credit hour. *Tuition (international):* Full-time: $9144. Part-time: $508 per credit hour. *Typical graduate housing cost:* $5058 (including board).

FINANCIAL AID (2007–08) Grants, loans, scholarships, and work study. Aid is available to part-time students.

Financial Aid Contact Mr. Donald Zackary, Director of Financial Aid, 3000 Mountain Creek Parkway, Dallas, TX 75211-9299. *Phone:* 214-333-5363. *Fax:* 214-333-5586. *E-mail:* donz@dbu.edu.

INTERNATIONAL STUDENTS *Services and facilities:* Counseling/support services, ESL/language courses, Housing location assistance, International student housing, International student organization, Language tutoring, Orientation, Visa Services, Transportation to various places off campus. Financial aid is available to international students. *Required with application:* TOEFL with recommended score of 213 (computer) or 550 (paper); proof of adequate funds; proof of health/immunizations.

International Student Contact Mr. Timothy Watts, Assistant Director of International Student Services, 3000 Mountain Creek Parkway, Dallas, TX 75211-9299. *Phone:* 214-333-6905. *Fax:* 214-333-5409. *E-mail:* timothyw@dbu.edu.

APPLICATION *Required:* GMAT, application form, baccalaureate/first degree, 2 letters of recommendation, personal statement, resume/curriculum vitae, transcripts of college work. School will accept GRE. *Recommended:* 2 years of work experience. *Application fee:* $25. Applications for domestic and international students are processed on a rolling basis.

Application Contact Mrs. Kit P. Montgomery, Director of Graduate Programs, 3000 Mountain Creek Parkway, Dallas, TX 75211-9299. *Phone:* 214-333-5242. *Fax:* 214-333-5579. *E-mail:* graduate@dbu.edu.

DeVry University

Keller Graduate School of Management

Houston, Texas

Phone: 713-973-3200

DEGREES MAFM • MBA • MISM • MPM

MAFM—Master of Accounting and Financial Management *Concentrations:* accounting, financial management/planning.

MBA—Master of Business Administration *Concentration:* general MBA.

MISM—Master of Information Systems Management *Concentration:* information systems.

MPM—Master of Project Management *Concentration:* project management.

Application Contact Admissions Office, Houston Campus, 11125 Equity Drive, Houston, TX 77041. *Phone:* 713-973-3200.

DeVry University
Keller Graduate School of Management

Irving, Texas

Phone: 972-621-8520

DEGREES MAFM • MBA • MHRM • MIS • MPM

MAFM—Master of Accounting and Financial Management Full-time and part-time. Distance learning option. At least 44 total credits required. 18 to 60 months to complete program. *Concentrations:* accounting, financial management/planning.

MBA—Master of Business Administration Full-time and part-time. Distance learning option. At least 48 total credits required. 18 to 60 months to complete program. *Concentration:* management.

MHRM—Master of Human Resources Management Full-time and part-time. Distance learning option. At least 45 total credits required. 18 to 60 months to complete program. *Concentration:* human resources management.

MIS—Master of Information Systems Management Full-time and part-time. Distance learning option. At least 45 total credits required. 18 to 60 months to complete program. *Concentration:* information systems.

MPM—Master of Project Management Full-time and part-time. Distance learning option. At least 42 total credits required. 18 to 60 months to complete program. *Concentration:* project management.

Application Contact Admissions Office, Irving Center, 4800 Regent Boulevard, Irving, TX 75063. *Phone:* 972-621-8520.

Hardin-Simmons University
Kelley College of Business

Abilene, Texas

Phone: 325-670-1298 **Fax:** 325-670-1564 **E-mail:** gradoff@hsutx.edu

Business Program(s) Web Site: http://www.hsutx.edu/academics/graduate/programs/business/

Graduate Business Unit Enrollment *Total:* 28 (6 full-time; 22 part-time; 12 women). *Average Age:* 33.

Graduate Business Faculty *Total:* 6 (5 full-time; 1 part-time).

Admissions *Applied:* 16. *Admitted:* 15. *Enrolled:* 13. *Average GMAT:* 488. *Average GPA:* 3.4

Academic Calendar Semesters.

Accreditation ACBSP—The American Council of Business Schools and Programs.

DEGREES MBA

MBA—Master of Business Administration Non-Thesis Full-time and part-time. At least 45 total credits required. 12 to 60 months to complete program. *Concentration:* general MBA.

MBA—Master of Business Administration Thesis Full-time and part-time. At least 45 total credits required. 12 to 60 months to complete program. *Concentration:* general MBA.

RESOURCES AND SERVICES 234 on-campus PCs are available to graduate business students. Access to Internet/World Wide Web available.

Personal computer requirements: Graduate business students are not required to have a personal computer. *Placement services include:* Alumni network, career placement, career counseling/planning, electronic job bank, career fairs, job interviews arranged, and resume preparation.

EXPENSES *Tuition:* Full-time: $9810. Part-time: $545 per semester hour. *Tuition (international):* Full-time: $9810. Part-time: $545 per semester hour. *Required fees:* Full-time: $830. Part-time: $75 per semester. Tuition and/or fees vary by number of courses or credits taken and academic program. *Graduate housing:* Room and board costs vary by number of occupants, type of accommodation, and type of board plan. *Typical cost:* $4950 (including board), $2602 (room only).

FINANCIAL AID (2007–08) 21 students received aid, including fellowships, loans, research assistantships, scholarships, and work study. Aid is available to part-time students.

Financial Aid Contact Mr. Jim Jones, Director, Student Financial Aid, Financial Aid Office, Box 16050, Abilene, TX 79698. *Phone:* 325-670-1206. *Fax:* 325-670-5822. *E-mail:* jjones@hsutx.edu.

INTERNATIONAL STUDENTS *Services and facilities:* Counseling/support services, International student organization. Financial aid is available to international students. *Required with application:* TOEFL with recommended score of 232 (computer) or 600 (paper); proof of adequate funds; proof of health/immunizations.

International Student Contact Mrs. Meredith Aim, International Liaison, Office of Graduate Studies, Box 16210, Abilene, TX 79698. *Phone:* 325-670-1299. *Fax:* 325-670-1527. *E-mail:* maim@hsutx.edu.

APPLICATION *Required:* GMAT, application form, baccalaureate/first degree, essay, interview, resume/curriculum vitae, transcripts of college work. *Recommended:* Letter(s) of recommendation, personal statement, work experience. *Application fee:* $50, $100 (international). *Deadlines:* 4/1 for fall (international), 9/1 for spring (international). Applications for domestic students are processed on a rolling basis.

Application Contact Dr. Gary Stanlake, Dean of Graduate Studies, Office of Graduate Studies, Box 16210, Abilene, TX 79698. *Phone:* 325-670-1298. *Fax:* 325-670-1564. *E-mail:* gradoff@hsutx.edu.

Hardin-Simmons University
The Acton MBA in Entrepreneurship

Austin, Texas

Phone: 512-703-1231 **Fax:** 512-495-9480 **E-mail:** jblanchard@actonmba.org

Business Program(s) Web Site: http://www.actonmba.org

Graduate Business Unit Enrollment *Total:* 22 (22 full-time; 3 women; 4 international). *Average Age:* 30.

Graduate Business Faculty 11 full-time.

Admissions *Applied:* 51. *Admitted:* 27. *Enrolled:* 22. *Average GMAT:* 670. *Average GPA:* 3.1

Academic Calendar Semesters.

Accreditation ACBSP—The American Council of Business Schools and Programs.

After Graduation (Class of 2006–07) *Employed within 3 months of graduation:* 60%. *Average starting salary:* $70,000.

DEGREE MBA

MBA—The Acton MBA in Entrepreneurship Full-time. 36 total credits required. 9 months to complete program. *Concentration:* entrepreneurship.

RESOURCES AND SERVICES Access to Internet/World Wide Web available. *Personal computer requirements:* Graduate business students are required to have a personal computer. *Placement services include:* Alumni network, job search course, career counseling/planning, and resume preparation.

EXPENSES *Tuition:* Full-time: $35,000. *Tuition (international):* Full-time: $35,000.

Hardin-Simmons University (continued)

FINANCIAL AID (2007–08) 22 students received aid, including fellowships.

Financial Aid Contact Jessica Blanchard, Director of Enrollment, 515 Congress, Suite 1875, Austin, TX 78701. *Phone:* 512-703-1231. *Fax:* 512-495-9480. *E-mail:* jblanchard@actonmba.org.

INTERNATIONAL STUDENTS 18% of students enrolled are international students. Financial aid is available to international students. *Required with application:* TOEFL with recommended score of 260 (computer) or 620 (paper).

International Student Contact Jessica Blanchard, Director of Enrollment, 515 Congress, Suite 1875, Austin, TX 78701. *Phone:* 512-703-1231. *Fax:* 512-495-9480. *E-mail:* jblanchard@actonmba.org.

APPLICATION *Required:* GMAT, application form, baccalaureate/first degree, essay, interview, 3 letters of recommendation, resume/curriculum vitae, transcripts of college work. *Recommended:* 3 years of work experience. *Application fee:* $150. *Deadlines:* 11/15 for fall, 3/1 for winter, 4/15 for spring, 11/15 for fall (international), 3/1 for winter (international), 4/15 for spring (international).

Application Contact Jessica Blanchard, Director of Enrollment, 515 Congress, Suite 1875, Austin, TX 78701. *Phone:* 512-703-1231. *Fax:* 512-495-9480. *E-mail:* jblanchard@actonmba.org.

Houston Baptist University
College of Business and Economics
Houston, Texas

Phone: 281-649-3249 **Fax:** 281-649-3436 **E-mail:** dwilde@hbu.edu

Business Program(s) Web Site: http://www.hbu.edu/gradbusiness

Graduate Business Unit Enrollment *Total:* 82 (82 full-time; 36 women; 8 international). *Average Age:* 29.

Graduate Business Faculty *Total:* 31 (23 full-time; 8 part-time).

Admissions *Applied:* 78. *Admitted:* 39. *Enrolled:* 26. *Average GMAT:* 520. *Average GPA:* 3.07

Academic Calendar Semesters.

DEGREES MBA • MS

MBA—Master of Business Administration Part-time. 48 total credits required. 24 to 60 months to complete program. *Concentration:* general MBA.

MS—Master of Science in Human Resource Management Part-time. 48 total credits required. 24 to 60 months to complete program. *Concentration:* human resources management.

RESOURCES AND SERVICES Access to online (class) registration and online grade reports available. *Personal computer requirements:* Graduate business students are strongly recommended to purchase or lease a personal computer. *Special opportunities include:* An internship program is available. *Placement services include:* Career counseling/planning, career fairs, and resume preparation.

EXPENSES *Tuition:* Part-time: $18,000 per year. *Tuition (international):* Part-time: $18,000 per year.

FINANCIAL AID (2007–08) Grants and loans. Aid is available to part-time students. *Financial aid application deadline:* 4/1.

Financial Aid Contact Ms. Sherry Byrd, Director, Financial Aid, 7502 Fondren Road, Houston, TX 77074-3298. *Phone:* 281-649-3204. *Fax:* 281-649-3303. *E-mail:* sbyrd@hbu.edu.

INTERNATIONAL STUDENTS 10% of students enrolled are international students. *Services and facilities:* Counseling/support services, Orientation, Visa Services. Financial aid is not available to international students. *Required with application:* TOEFL with recommended score of 213 (computer), 550 (paper), or 80 (Internet); proof of adequate funds.

International Student Contact Harold Harris, Director of International Student Services, 7502 Fondren Road, Houston, TX 77074-3298. *Phone:* 281-649-3260. *E-mail:* hharris@hbu.edu.

APPLICATION *Required:* GMAT, application form, baccalaureate/first degree, 3 letters of recommendation, personal statement, resume/curriculum vitae, transcripts of college work. *Recommended:* Work experience. Applications for domestic and international students are processed on a rolling basis.

Application Contact Ms. Danya Wilde, Director of Graduate Recruiting, 7502 Fondren Road, Houston, TX 77074-3298. *Phone:* 281-649-3249. *Fax:* 281-649-3436. *E-mail:* dwilde@hbu.edu.

Lamar University
College of Business
Beaumont, Texas

Phone: 409-880-8604 **Fax:** 409-880-8605 **E-mail:** cob-mba@lamar.edu

Business Program(s) Web Site: http://mba.lamar.edu

Graduate Business Unit Enrollment *Total:* 92 (55 full-time; 37 part-time; 40 women; 12 international). *Average Age:* 28.

Graduate Business Faculty 26 full-time.

Admissions *Applied:* 59. *Admitted:* 35. *Enrolled:* 17. *Average GMAT:* 484. *Average GPA:* 3.28

Academic Calendar Semesters.

Accreditation AACSB—The Association to Advance Collegiate Schools of Business.

After Graduation (Class of 2006–07) *Employed within 3 months of graduation:* 99%. *Average starting salary:* $45,000.

DEGREE MBA

MBA—Master of Business Administration Full-time and part-time. 36 to 54 total credits required. 16 to 24 months to complete program. *Concentrations:* accounting, entrepreneurship, financial management/planning, health administration, management, management information systems.

RESOURCES AND SERVICES 326 on-campus PCs are available to graduate business students. Access to Internet/World Wide Web, online (class) registration, and online grade reports available. *Personal computer requirements:* Graduate business students are strongly recommended to purchase or lease a personal computer. *Special opportunities include:* An internship program is available. *Placement services include:* Alumni network, career placement, career counseling/planning, electronic job bank, resume referral, career fairs, job interviews arranged, resume preparation, and career library.

EXPENSES *Tuition (state resident):* Full-time: $4654. Part-time: $179 per credit hour. *Tuition (nonresident):* Full-time: $11,882. Part-time: $457 per credit hour. *Tuition (international):* Full-time: $11,882. Part-time: $457 per credit hour. *Required fees:* Full-time: $1421. Part-time: $168.80 per credit hour. *Typical graduate housing cost:* $5888 (including board).

FINANCIAL AID (2007–08) 57 students received aid, including grants, loans, scholarships, and work study. Aid is available to part-time students. *Financial aid application deadline:* 4/1.

Financial Aid Contact Jill Rowley, Director of Financial Aid, PO Box 10042, Beaumont, TX 77710. *Phone:* 409-880-8450.

INTERNATIONAL STUDENTS 13% of students enrolled are international students. *Services and facilities:* Counseling/support services, ESL/language courses, Housing location assistance, International student organization, Language tutoring, Orientation, Visa Services. *Required with application:* TOEFL with recommended score of 195 (computer), 525 (paper), or 71 (Internet); proof of adequate funds; proof of health/immunizations.

International Student Contact Ms. Sandy Drane, International Student Advisor, PO Box 10078, Beaumont, TX 77710. *Phone:* 409-880-8356.

APPLICATION *Required:* GMAT, application form, baccalaureate/first degree, essay, transcripts of college work. *Recommended:* Interview, letter(s) of recommendation, personal statement, resume/curriculum vitae. *Application fee:* $25, $75 (international). Applications for domestic and international students are processed on a rolling basis.

Application Contact Bradley Mayer, Associate Dean, PO Box 11612, Beaumont, TX 77710. *Phone:* 409-880-8604. *Fax:* 409-880-8605. *E-mail:* cob-mba@lamar.edu.

LeTourneau University
Graduate and Professional Studies
Longview, Texas

Phone: 903-233-4000 **Fax:** 903-233-4001 **E-mail:** chrisfontaine@letu.edu

Business Program(s) Web Site: http://www.letu.edu/

Graduate Business Unit Enrollment *Total:* 324 (324 full-time; 189 women). *Average Age:* 37.

Graduate Business Faculty *Total:* 42 (9 full-time; 33 part-time).

Academic Calendar Continuous.

DEGREES MBA • MBA/ME

MBA—Master of Business Administration Full-time and part-time. Distance learning option. Minimum age of 23 required. At least 39 total credits required. 20 to 60 months to complete program. *Concentrations:* electronic commerce (E-commerce), finance, human resources management, international business, management, marketing.

MBA/ME—Master of Educational Leadership Full-time and part-time. Distance learning option. At least 39 total credits required. 20 to 60 months to complete program. *Concentration:* leadership.

RESOURCES AND SERVICES 210 on-campus PCs are available to graduate business students. Access to Internet/World Wide Web, online (class) registration, and online grade reports available. *Personal computer requirements:* Graduate business students are strongly recommended to purchase or lease a personal computer. *Placement services include:* Alumni network, career placement, career counseling/planning, electronic job bank, resume referral, career fairs, job interviews arranged, resume preparation, and career library.

EXPENSES *Tuition:* Full-time: $11,000. Part-time: $551 per credit hour. *Tuition (international):* Full-time: $11,000. Part-time: $551 per credit hour. *Required fees:* Full-time: $975. Part-time: $50 per credit hour.

FINANCIAL AID (2007–08) Loans. Aid is available to part-time students.

Financial Aid Contact Ms. Lindy Hall, Senior Director of Enrollment Services and Financial Aid, PO Box 7001, Longview, TX 75607-7001. *Phone:* 903-233-4350. *Fax:* 903-233-4302. *E-mail:* lindyhall@letu.edu.

INTERNATIONAL STUDENTS Financial aid is not available to international students. *Required with application:* TOEFL with recommended score of 173 (computer) or 500 (paper).

International Student Contact Donald Connors, Assistant Vice President and Dean of Graduate Program, PO Box 7668, Longview, TX 75607-7668. *Phone:* 903-233-4000. *Fax:* 903-233-4001. *E-mail:* donconnors@letu.edu.

APPLICATION *Required:* GRE, application form, baccalaureate/first degree, essay, 2 letters of recommendation, resume/curriculum vitae, transcripts of college work, 3 years of work experience. *Application fee:* $50. Applications for domestic and international students are processed on a rolling basis.

Application Contact Chris Fontaine, Assistant Vice President of Enrollment Management and Market Research, PO Box 7668, Longview, TX 75607-7668. *Phone:* 903-233-4000. *Fax:* 903-233-4001. *E-mail:* chrisfontaine@letu.edu.

Midwestern State University
College of Business Administration
Wichita Falls, Texas

Phone: 940-397-6260 **Fax:** 940-397-4280 **E-mail:** david.wierschem@mwsu.edu

Business Program(s) Web Site: http://business.mwsu.edu/mba/index.asp

Graduate Business Unit Enrollment *Total:* 70 (20 full-time; 50 part-time; 30 women; 8 international).

Graduate Business Faculty *Total:* 26 (23 full-time; 3 part-time).

Admissions *Applied:* 20. *Admitted:* 18. *Enrolled:* 15. *Average GMAT:* 450. *Average GPA:* 3.0

Academic Calendar Semesters.

Accreditation ACBSP—The American Council of Business Schools and Programs.

After Graduation (Class of 2006–07) *Employed within 3 months of graduation:* 80%.

DEGREES MBA

MBA—MBA with a Major in Health Service Administration Full-time and part-time. 45 total credits required. 18 to 72 months to complete program. *Concentration:* health administration.

MBA—MBA with a Concentration in Management Information Systems Full-time and part-time. 36 total credits required. 12 to 72 months to complete program. *Concentration:* management information systems.

MBA—Master of Business Administration Full-time and part-time. Distance learning option. 33 to 60 total credits required. 12 to 72 months to complete program. *Concentration:* management.

RESOURCES AND SERVICES 200 on-campus PCs are available to graduate business students. Access to Internet/World Wide Web, online (class) registration, and online grade reports available. *Personal computer requirements:* Graduate business students are not required to have a personal computer. *Special opportunities include:* An international exchange program and an internship program are available. *Placement services include:* Career placement, career counseling/planning, career fairs, and resume preparation.

EXPENSES *Tuition (state resident):* Full-time: $4200. Part-time: $700 per course. *Tuition (nonresident):* Full-time: $6000. Part-time: $790 per course. *Tuition (international):* Full-time: $9600. Part-time: $1600 per course. *Required fees:* Full-time: $500. Part-time: $25 per course. *Graduate housing:* Room and board costs vary by campus location, number of occupants, type of accommodation, and type of board plan. *Typical cost:* $6000 (including board), $4000 (room only).

FINANCIAL AID (2007–08) 20 students received aid, including loans, research assistantships, scholarships, and work study. Aid is available to part-time students. *Financial aid application deadline:* 4/1.

Financial Aid Contact Dr. David Wierschem, Advisor, MBA Program, 3410 Taft Boulevard, Wichita Falls, TX 76308-2099. *Phone:* 940-397-6260. *Fax:* 940-397-4280. *E-mail:* david.wierschem@mwsu.edu.

INTERNATIONAL STUDENTS 11% of students enrolled are international students. *Services and facilities:* Counseling/support services, ESL/language courses, International student organization, Orientation. Financial aid is available to international students. *Required with application:* TOEFL with recommended score of 213 (computer) or 550 (paper); proof of adequate funds; proof of health/immunizations.

International Student Contact Ms. Kerrie Cale, International Student Advisor, International Programs, 3410 Taft Boulevard, Wichita Falls, TX 76308-2099. *Phone:* 940-397-4344. *E-mail:* kerrie.cale@mwsu.edu.

APPLICATION *Required:* GMAT, application form, baccalaureate/first degree, transcripts of college work. *Application fee:* $35. *Deadlines:* 8/7 for fall, 12/15 for spring, 5/15 for summer, 4/1 for fall (international), 8/1 for spring (international), 1/1 for summer (international).

Midwestern State University (continued)

Application Contact Dr. David Wierschem, Advisor, MBA Program, 3410 Taft Boulevard, Wichita Falls, TX 76308-2099. *Phone:* 940-397-6260. *Fax:* 940-397-4280. *E-mail:* david.wierschem@mwsu.edu.

Prairie View A&M University
College of Business
Prairie View, Texas

Phone: 936-261-9217 **Fax:** 936-261-9232 **E-mail:** jwdyck@pvamu.edu

Business Program(s) Web Site: http://www.pvamu.edu

Accreditation AACSB—The Association to Advance Collegiate Schools of Business.

DEGREES M Sc • MBA

M Sc—Master of Science Full-time and part-time. 30 to 54 total credits required. 18 to 72 months to complete program. *Concentration:* accounting.

MBA—Master of Business Administration Full-time and part-time. 36 to 57 total credits required. 18 to 72 months to complete program. *Concentration:* general MBA.

RESOURCES AND SERVICES 60 on-campus PCs are available to graduate business students. Access to Internet/World Wide Web, online (class) registration, and online grade reports available. *Personal computer requirements:* Graduate business students are strongly recommended to purchase or lease a personal computer. *Placement services include:* Alumni network, career placement, career counseling/planning, electronic job bank, career fairs, job interviews arranged, and resume preparation.

Application Contact Dr. John W. Dyck, Director, Graduate Programs in Business, PO Box 519, MS 2320, Prairie View, TX 77446-0638. *Phone:* 936-261-9217. *Fax:* 936-261-9232. *E-mail:* jwdyck@pvamu.edu.

Rice University
Jesse H. Jones Graduate School of Management
Houston, Texas

Phone: 888-844-4773 **Fax:** 713-348-6147 **E-mail:** ricemba@rice.edu

Business Program(s) Web Site: http://jonesgsm.rice.edu

Graduate Business Unit Enrollment *Total:* 229 (229 full-time; 73 women; 71 international). *Average Age:* 27.

Graduate Business Faculty *Total:* 93 (55 full-time; 38 part-time).

Admissions *Applied:* 566. *Admitted:* 223. *Enrolled:* 124. *Average GMAT:* 642. *Average GPA:* 3.27.

Academic Calendar Terms.

Accreditation AACSB—The Association to Advance Collegiate Schools of Business.

After Graduation (Class of 2006–07) *Employed within 3 months of graduation:* 95%. *Average starting salary:* $89,006.

DEGREES MBA • MD/MBA • ME/MBA

MBA—Executive Master of Business Administration Full-time. 10 years of work experience required. At least 60 total credits required. 22 months to complete program. *Concentration:* management.

MBA—Master of Business Administration Full-time. At least 60 total credits required. 22 months to complete program. *Concentrations:* corporate accounting, entrepreneurship, finance, international business, management, management consulting, marketing, other, real estate, strategic management.

MD/MBA—Doctor of Medicine/Master of Business Administration Full-time. Must be accepted into program at Baylor College of Medicine. At least 48 total credits required. 60 months to complete program. *Concentration:* management.

ME/MBA—Master of Engineering/Master of Business Administration Full-time. Undergraduate degree in engineering and GRE required. Must be accepted into Brown School of Engineering at Rice University. At least 63 total credits required. 22 months to complete program. *Concentration:* management.

RESOURCES AND SERVICES 50 on-campus PCs are available to graduate business students. Access to Internet/World Wide Web, online (class) registration, and online grade reports available. *Personal computer requirements:* Graduate business students are required to have a personal computer, the cost of which is included in tuition or other required fees. *Special opportunities include:* An international exchange program and an internship program are available. *Placement services include:* Alumni network, career placement, job search course, career counseling/planning, electronic job bank, resume referral, career fairs, job interviews arranged, resume preparation, and career library.

EXPENSES *Tuition:* Full-time: $36,000. *Tuition (international):* Full-time: $36,000. *Required fees:* Full-time: $2058.

FINANCIAL AID (2007–08) 192 students received aid, including loans and scholarships. *Financial aid application deadline:* 6/1.

Financial Aid Contact Student Financial Services, Office of Financial Aid, MS-12, PO Box 1892, Houston, TX 77251-1892. *Phone:* 713-348-4958. *Fax:* 713-348-2139. *E-mail:* fina@rice.edu.

INTERNATIONAL STUDENTS 31% of students enrolled are international students. *Services and facilities:* Counseling/support services, ESL/language courses, Housing location assistance, International student organization, Orientation, Visa Services, Pre-term international immersion. Financial aid is available to international students. *Required with application:* TOEFL with recommended score of 250 (computer) or 600 (paper); proof of adequate funds; proof of health/immunizations.

International Student Contact Adria Baker, Director, International Services, 6100 Main Street, MS 365, Houston, TX 77005-1892. *Phone:* 713-348-6095. *Fax:* 713-348-6058. *E-mail:* abaker@rice.edu.

APPLICATION *Required:* GMAT, application form, baccalaureate/first degree, essay, interview, 2 letters of recommendation, resume/curriculum vitae, transcripts of college work. *Recommended:* 2 years of work experience. *Application fee:* $100. Applications for domestic and international students are processed on a rolling basis.

Application Contact Melissa Blakeslee, Director of Admissions, PO Box 2932, Houston, TX 77252-2932. *Phone:* 888-844-4773. *Fax:* 713-348-6147. *E-mail:* ricemba@rice.edu.

St. Edward's University
The School of Management and Business
Austin, Texas

Phone: 512-448-8600 **Fax:** 512-428-1032 **E-mail:** gotograd@stedwards.edu

Business Program(s) Web Site: http://www.stedwards.edu/business/graduate

Graduate Business Unit Enrollment *Total:* 626 (68 full-time; 558 part-time; 337 women; 20 international). *Average Age:* 32.

Graduate Business Faculty *Total:* 61 (24 full-time; 37 part-time).

Admissions *Applied:* 164. *Admitted:* 120. *Enrolled:* 103.

Academic Calendar Trimesters.

DEGREES MBA • MBA equivalent

MBA—Master of Business Administration Full-time and part-time. 36 to 58 total credits required. 12 to 72 months to complete program. *Concentrations:* accounting, entrepreneurship, finance, human resources management, international business, management, management information systems, marketing, operations management.

MBA equivalent—Master of Business Administration in Digital Media Management Full-time. Letters of recommendation, interview, and GRE or GMAT are required. 54 total credits required. 20 to 72 months to complete program. *Concentration:* media administration.

RESOURCES AND SERVICES 678 on-campus PCs are available to graduate business students. Access to Internet/World Wide Web, online (class) registration, and online grade reports available. *Personal computer requirements:* Graduate business students are strongly recommended to purchase or lease a personal computer. *Placement services include:* Alumni network, job search course, career counseling/planning, electronic job bank, resume referral, career fairs, resume preparation, and career library.

EXPENSES *Tuition:* Full-time: $12,672. Part-time: $704 per credit hour. *Tuition (international):* Full-time: $12,672. Part-time: $704 per credit hour. Tuition and/or fees vary by number of courses or credits taken and academic program.

FINANCIAL AID (2007–08) 8 students received aid, including scholarships. Aid is available to part-time students.

Financial Aid Contact Doris Constantine, Director of Student Financial Services, 3001 South Congress Avenue, Austin, TX 78704. *Phone:* 512-448-8525. *Fax:* 512-416-5837. *E-mail:* dorisc@stedwards.edu.

INTERNATIONAL STUDENTS 3% of students enrolled are international students. *Services and facilities:* Counseling/support services, International student organization, Orientation, Visa Services. Financial aid is available to international students. *Required with application:* TOEFL with recommended score of 213 (computer), 550 (paper), or 79 (Internet); proof of adequate funds.

International Student Contact Ms. Erin Ray, Director, International Education Services, 3001 South Congress Avenue, Austin, TX 78704. *Phone:* 512-428-1051. *Fax:* 512-448-8492. *E-mail:* erinr@stedwards.edu.

APPLICATION *Required:* Application form, baccalaureate/first degree, essay, personal statement, resume/curriculum vitae, transcripts of college work. School will accept GMAT and GRE. *Recommended:* Letter(s) of recommendation, work experience. *Application fee:* $45, $50 (international). Applications for domestic and international students are processed on a rolling basis.

Application Contact Center for Academic Progress, Graduate Admission, 3001 South Congress Avenue, Austin, TX 78704. *Phone:* 512-448-8600. *Fax:* 512-428-1032. *E-mail:* gotograd@stedwards.edu.

St. Mary's University
Bill Greehey School of Business

San Antonio, Texas

Phone: 210-431-2027 **Fax:** 210-431-2115 **E-mail:** rmenger@stmarytx.edu

Business Program(s) Web Site: http://www.stmarytx.edu/mba

Graduate Business Unit Enrollment *Total:* 120 (24 full-time; 96 part-time; 65 women; 11 international). *Average Age:* 35.

Graduate Business Faculty *Total:* 30 (26 full-time; 4 part-time).

Admissions *Applied:* 62. *Admitted:* 25. *Enrolled:* 25. *Average GMAT:* 565. *Average GPA:* 3.65

Academic Calendar Semesters.

Accreditation AACSB—The Association to Advance Collegiate Schools of Business.

After Graduation (Class of 2006–07) *Employed within 3 months of graduation:* 90%. *Average starting salary:* $65,000.

DEGREES JD/MBA • MBA

JD/MBA—Juris Doctor/Master of Business Administration Full-time and part-time. Also must be accepted into the St. Mary's Law School. 108

to 111 total credits required. 36 to 60 months to complete program. *Concentrations:* accounting, financial management/planning, general MBA.

MBA—Financial Planning Full-time and part-time. May require an additional 6 hours of prerequisite courses. 30 to 36 total credits required. 12 to 36 months to complete program. *Concentration:* financial management/planning.

MBA—General Management Full-time and part-time. 30 total credits required. 12 to 36 months to complete program. *Concentration:* general MBA.

MBA—Professional Accountancy Full-time and part-time. Credits shown presume a previous BBA in Accounting. 30 total credits required. 12 to 36 months to complete program. *Concentration:* accounting.

RESOURCES AND SERVICES 50 on-campus PCs are available to graduate business students. Access to Internet/World Wide Web, online (class) registration, and online grade reports available. *Personal computer requirements:* Graduate business students are strongly recommended to purchase or lease a personal computer. *Special opportunities include:* An international exchange program and an internship program are available. *Placement services include:* Alumni network, career placement, career counseling/planning, electronic job bank, resume referral, career fairs, job interviews arranged, resume preparation, and career library.

EXPENSES *Tuition:* Full-time: $18,450. *Tuition (international):* Full-time: $18,450. *Required fees:* Full-time: $250. Part-time: $125 per semester. *Graduate housing:* Room and board costs vary by type of board plan. *Typical cost:* $6220 (including board), $4020 (room only).

FINANCIAL AID (2007–08) 12 students received aid, including grants, loans, research assistantships, and scholarships. Aid is available to part-time students. *Financial aid application deadline:* 3/15.

Financial Aid Contact David Krause, Director, Financial Assistance, Office of Financial Assistance, 1 Camino Santa Maria, San Antonio, TX 78228. *Phone:* 210-436-3141. *Fax:* 210-431-2221. *E-mail:* dkrause@stmarytx.edu.

INTERNATIONAL STUDENTS 9% of students enrolled are international students. *Services and facilities:* Counseling/support services, ESL/language courses, Housing location assistance, International student organization, Language tutoring, Orientation, Visa Services. Financial aid is available to international students. *Required with application:* IELT with recommended score of 6.5; TOEFL with recommended score of 230 (computer), 570 (paper), or 89 (Internet); proof of adequate funds; proof of health/immunizations.

International Student Contact Dr. Richard Menger, MBA Director, One Camino Santa Maria, San Antonio, TX 78228-8607. *Phone:* 210-431-2027. *Fax:* 210-431-2115. *E-mail:* rmenger@stmarytx.edu.

APPLICATION *Required:* GMAT, application form, baccalaureate/first degree, 2 letters of recommendation, resume/curriculum vitae, transcripts of college work. *Recommended:* Essay, interview, personal statement. Applications for domestic and international students are processed on a rolling basis.

Application Contact Dr. Richard A. Menger, MBA Director, One Camino Santa Maria, San Antonio, TX 78228-8607. *Phone:* 210-431-2027. *Fax:* 210-431-2115. *E-mail:* rmenger@stmarytx.edu.

Southern Methodist University
Cox School of Business

Dallas, Texas

Phone: 214-768-1214 **Fax:** 214-768-3956 **E-mail:** mbainfo@cox.smu.edu

Business Program(s) Web Site: http://www.cox.smu.edu/grad

Graduate Business Faculty 70 full-time.

Admissions *Applied:* 393. *Admitted:* 185. *Enrolled:* 81. *Average GMAT:* 640. *Average GPA:* 3.3

Academic Calendar 8-week modules within the semester schedule.

Southern Methodist University (continued)

Accreditation AACSB—The Association to Advance Collegiate Schools of Business.

After Graduation (Class of 2006–07) *Employed within 3 months of graduation:* 91%. *Average starting salary:* $88,701.

DEGREES JD/MBA • MBA • MBA/MA • MSA • MSM

JD/MBA—Juris Doctor/Master of Business Administration Full-time. At least 123 total credits required. Minimum of 48 months to complete program. *Concentrations:* accounting, electronic commerce (E-commerce), entrepreneurship, finance, management, management consulting, marketing, technology management.

MBA—Executive Master of Business Administration Full-time. 10 years of work experience required. At least 48 total credits required. Minimum of 21 months to complete program. *Concentrations:* accounting, business policy/strategy, electronic commerce (E-commerce), entrepreneurship, finance, management, marketing, operations management, strategic management, technology management.

MBA—Full-Time Master of Business Administration Full-time. At least 61 total credits required. 22 months to complete program. *Concentrations:* accounting, business policy/strategy, electronic commerce (E-commerce), entrepreneurship, finance, management, management consulting, marketing, operations management, organizational behavior/development, strategic management, technology management, telecommunications management.

MBA—Professional Master of Business Administration Part-time. Applicants must be employed. At least 48 total credits required. 24 months to complete program. *Concentrations:* accounting, business policy/strategy, electronic commerce (E-commerce), entrepreneurship, finance, information management, management, management consulting, marketing, operations management, organizational behavior/development, strategic management, technology management, telecommunications management.

MBA/MA—Master of Business Administration/Master of Arts in Administration Full-time. At least 75 total credits required. Minimum of 24 months to complete program. *Concentrations:* accounting, arts administration/management, electronic commerce (E-commerce), entrepreneurship, finance, management, management consulting, marketing, operations management, strategic management, technology management.

MSA—Master of Science in Accounting Program Full-time. At least 32 total credits required. 9 months to complete program. *Concentration:* accounting.

MSM—Master of Science in Management Part-time. 30 total credits required. 10 months to complete program. *Concentration:* management.

RESOURCES AND SERVICES 250 on-campus PCs are available to graduate business students. Access to Internet/World Wide Web, online (class) registration, and online grade reports available. *Personal computer requirements:* Graduate business students are required to have a personal computer. *Special opportunities include:* An international exchange program and an internship program are available. *Placement services include:* Alumni network, career placement, job search course, career counseling/planning, electronic job bank, resume referral, career fairs, job interviews arranged, resume preparation, and career library.

EXPENSES *Tuition:* Full-time: $35,530. *Tuition (international):* Full-time: $35,530. *Required fees:* Full-time: $3480. Tuition and/or fees vary by class time, number of courses or credits taken, and academic program.

FINANCIAL AID (2007–08) Loans, research assistantships, and scholarships. *Financial aid application deadline:* 3/1.

Financial Aid Contact Ms. Barbara Waters, Financial Aid Advisor, PO Box 750181, Dallas, TX 75275-0181. *Phone:* 214-768-2371. *E-mail:* bwaters@smu.edu.

INTERNATIONAL STUDENTS *Services and facilities:* Counseling/support services, ESL/language courses, Housing location assistance, International student organization, Orientation, Visa Services. Financial aid is available to international students. *Required with application:* TOEFL with recommended score of 250 (computer), 600 (paper), or 100 (Internet); proof of adequate funds; proof of health/immunizations.

International Student Contact Patti Cudney, Director of MBA Admissions, PO Box 750333, Dallas, TX 75275-0333. *Phone:* 214-768-1214. *Fax:* 214-768-3956. *E-mail:* mbainfo@cox.smu.edu.

APPLICATION *Required:* GMAT, application form, baccalaureate/first degree, essay, 2 letters of recommendation, personal statement, resume/curriculum vitae, transcripts of college work, 2 years of work experience. *Recommended:* Interview. *Application fee:* $75. Applications for domestic and international students are processed on a rolling basis.

Application Contact Patti Cudney, Director of MBA Admissions, PO Box 750333, Dallas, TX 75275-0333. *Phone:* 214-768-1214. *Fax:* 214-768-3956. *E-mail:* mbainfo@cox.smu.edu.

See full description on page 688.

Southwestern Adventist University
Business Department, Graduate Program
Keene, Texas

Phone: 817-556-4724 **Fax:** 817-556-4744 **E-mail:** yanezl@cosmic.swau.edu

Business Program(s) Web Site: http://business.swau.edu

Graduate Business Unit Enrollment *Total:* 35.

Graduate Business Faculty *Total:* 9 (5 full-time; 4 part-time).

Admissions *Applied:* 50. *Admitted:* 30. *Enrolled:* 25. *Average GMAT:* 450. *Average GPA:* 3.25

Academic Calendar Semesters.

After Graduation (Class of 2006–07) *Employed within 3 months of graduation:* 100%. *Average starting salary:* $55,000.

DEGREE MBA

MBA—MBA—Master of Business Administration Full-time and part-time. Distance learning option. We allow students to transfer three MBA courses from other universities. At least 36 total credits required. 12 to 60 months to complete program. *Concentrations:* accounting, general MBA, leadership, management.

RESOURCES AND SERVICES 70 on-campus PCs are available to graduate business students. Access to Internet/World Wide Web, online (class) registration, and online grade reports available. *Personal computer requirements:* Graduate business students are required to have a personal computer. *Special opportunities include:* An internship program is available. *Placement services include:* Alumni network, career placement, job search course, career counseling/planning, electronic job bank, resume referral, career fairs, job interviews arranged, and resume preparation.

EXPENSES *Tuition:* Full-time: $13,000. Part-time: $6500 per year. *Graduate housing:* Room and board costs vary by number of occupants, type of accommodation, and type of board plan. *Typical cost:* $3000 (room only).

FINANCIAL AID (2007–08) 25 students received aid, including grants, loans, scholarships, teaching assistantships, and work study. Aid is available to part-time students. *Financial aid application deadline:* 7/31.

Financial Aid Contact Patricia Norwood, Assistant Financial Vice President, 100 West Hillcrest, Keene, TX 76059. *Phone:* 817-645-3921 Ext. 223. *Fax:* 817-556-4744. *E-mail:* norwoodp@cosmic.swau.edu.

INTERNATIONAL STUDENTS *Services and facilities:* Counseling/support services, ESL/language courses, Housing location assistance, International student housing, Orientation, Visa Services. Financial aid is available to international students. *Required with application:* TOEFL with recommended score of 190 (computer), 550 (paper), or 68 (Internet); proof of adequate funds.

International Student Contact Dr. Karl Konrad, Vice President, Academic Administration, 100 West Hillcrest, Keene, TX 76059. *Phone:* 817-645-3921 Ext. 211. *Fax:* 817-556-4744. *E-mail:* konradk@swau.edu.

APPLICATION *Required:* Application form, baccalaureate/first degree, 2 letters of recommendation, transcripts of college work. School will accept

GMAT. *Application fee:* $0. Applications for domestic and international students are processed on a rolling basis.

Application Contact Ms. Laura Yanez, Graduate Studies Secretary, 100 West Hillcrest, Keene, TX 76059. *Phone:* 817-556-4724. *Fax:* 817-556-4744. *E-mail:* yanezl@cosmic.swau.edu.

Stephen F. Austin State University
College of Business
Nacogdoches, Texas

Phone: 936-468-3101 **Fax:** 936-468-1560 **E-mail:** mba@sfasu.edu

Business Program(s) Web Site: http://www.cob.sfasu.edu/

Graduate Business Unit Enrollment *Total:* 45 (20 full-time; 25 part-time; 15 women; 13 international).

Graduate Business Faculty *Total:* 72 (57 full-time; 15 part-time).

Admissions *Applied:* 25. *Admitted:* 21. *Enrolled:* 15. *Average GMAT:* 493. *Average GPA:* 3.0

Academic Calendar Semesters.

Accreditation AACSB—The Association to Advance Collegiate Schools of Business.

After Graduation (Class of 2006–07) *Employed within 3 months of graduation:* 100%. *Average starting salary:* $48,000.

DEGREES MBA • MPA

MBA—Master of Business Administration Full-time and part-time. Must have a GMAT exam score. 36 to 54 total credits required. 12 to 18 months to complete program. *Concentrations:* general MBA, management.

MPA—Master of Professional Accountancy Full-time and part-time. Must have a GMAT exam score. 36 to 54 total credits required. 15 to 18 months to complete program. *Concentration:* accounting.

RESOURCES AND SERVICES 360 on-campus PCs are available to graduate business students. Access to Internet/World Wide Web, online (class) registration, and online grade reports available. *Personal computer requirements:* Graduate business students are not required to have a personal computer. *Placement services include:* Alumni network, career placement, job search course, career counseling/planning, electronic job bank, resume referral, career fairs, job interviews arranged, resume preparation, and career library.

EXPENSES *Tuition (state resident):* Part-time: $600 per course. *Tuition (nonresident):* Part-time: $1150 per course. *Tuition (international):* Part-time: $1150 per course.

FINANCIAL AID (2007–08) 14 students received aid, including research assistantships, scholarships, teaching assistantships, and work study. *Financial aid application deadline:* 4/1.

Financial Aid Contact Michael O'Rear, Director of Financial Aid, PO Box 13052, Nacogdoches, TX 75962. *Phone:* 936-468-2403. *Fax:* 936-468-1048. *E-mail:* morear@sfasu.edu.

INTERNATIONAL STUDENTS 29% of students enrolled are international students. *Services and facilities:* Counseling/support services, ESL/language courses, International student organization, Language tutoring, Orientation, Visa Services, Office of International Student Assistance. Financial aid is available to international students. *Required with application:* TOEFL with recommended score of 213 (computer) or 550 (paper); TWE with recommended score of 3.5; proof of adequate funds; proof of health/immunizations.

International Student Contact Ms. Stacy Wilson, International Student Advisor, PO Box 13051, Nacogdoches, TX 75962. *Phone:* 936-468-2504. *Fax:* 936-468-3849. *E-mail:* swilson@sfasu.edu.

APPLICATION *Required:* GMAT, application form, baccalaureate/first degree, transcripts of college work. *Recommended:* 2 years of work experience. *Application fee:* $25, $50 (international). Applications for domestic and international students are processed on a rolling basis.

Application Contact Michael D. Stroup, MBA Director, PO Box 13004, Nacogdoches, TX 75962-3004. *Phone:* 936-468-3101. *Fax:* 936-468-1560. *E-mail:* mba@sfasu.edu.

Tarleton State University
College of Business Administration
Stephenville, Texas

Phone: 254-968-9104 **Fax:** 254-968-9670 **E-mail:** gradoffice@tarleton.edu

Business Program(s) Web Site: http://www.tarleton.edu

Graduate Business Unit Enrollment *Total:* 209 (49 full-time; 160 part-time; 112 women; 10 international). *Average Age:* 30.

Graduate Business Faculty *Total:* 32 (28 full-time; 4 part-time).

Admissions *Applied:* 99. *Admitted:* 83. *Average GMAT:* 435. *Average GPA:* 3.3

Academic Calendar Semesters.

Accreditation ACBSP—The American Council of Business Schools and Programs.

After Graduation (Class of 2006–07) *Average starting salary:* $35,000.

DEGREES MBA • MSHR • MSM

MBA—Master of Business Administration Full-time and part-time. Distance learning option. At least 36 total credits required. 12 to 72 months to complete program. *Concentrations:* accounting, agribusiness, finance, management, management information systems, marketing.

MSHR—Human Resource Management Full-time and part-time. Distance learning option. At least 36 total credits required. 12 to 72 months to complete program. *Concentrations:* accounting, finance, human resources management, management, management information systems, marketing.

MSM—Management and Leadership Full-time and part-time. Distance learning option. At least 36 total credits required. 12 to 72 months to complete program. *Concentrations:* accounting, finance, information systems, management, marketing.

RESOURCES AND SERVICES 100 on-campus PCs are available to graduate business students. Access to Internet/World Wide Web, online (class) registration, and online grade reports available. *Personal computer requirements:* Graduate business students are not required to have a personal computer. *Special opportunities include:* An international exchange program and an internship program are available. *Placement services include:* Career placement, career counseling/planning, electronic job bank, career fairs, and resume preparation.

EXPENSES *Tuition (state resident):* Full-time: $1170. Part-time: $130 per credit hour. *Tuition (international):* Full-time: $3582. Part-time: $398 per credit hour. *Required fees:* Full-time: $4802. Part-time: $52 per credit hour. Tuition and/or fees vary by campus location and academic program. *Graduate housing:* Room and board costs vary by campus location, number of occupants, type of accommodation, and type of board plan. *Typical cost:* $2932 (including board), $1617 (room only).

FINANCIAL AID (2007–08) 51 students received aid, including grants, loans, research assistantships, scholarships, and teaching assistantships. Aid is available to part-time students. *Financial aid application deadline:* 2/12.

Financial Aid Contact Ms. Betty Murray, Financial Aid Director, Box T-0310, Stephenville, TX 76402. *Phone:* 254-968-9070. *Fax:* 254-968-9600. *E-mail:* finaid@tarleton.edu.

INTERNATIONAL STUDENTS 5% of students enrolled are international students. *Services and facilities:* Counseling/support services, Housing location assistance, International student organization, Language tutoring, Orientation, Visa Services. Financial aid is available to

---

Tarleton State University (continued)

international students. *Required with application:* TOEFL with recommended score of 190 (computer) or 520 (paper); proof of adequate funds; proof of health/immunizations.

International Student Contact Fred Koestler, Director, Box T-0770, Tarleton Station, Stephenville, TX 76402. *Phone:* 254-968-9632. *Fax:* 254-968-9618. *E-mail:* koestler@tarleton.edu.

APPLICATION *Required:* Application form, baccalaureate/first degree, essay, transcripts of college work. School will accept GMAT and GRE. *Application fee:* $25. Applications for domestic and international students are processed on a rolling basis.

Application Contact Dr. Linda Jones, Graduate Office Dean, Box T-0350, Stephenville, TX 76402. *Phone:* 254-968-9104. *Fax:* 254-968-9670. *E-mail:* gradoffice@tarleton.edu.

Texas A&M International University
College of Business Administration

Laredo, Texas

Phone: 956-326-2202 **Fax:** 956-326-2199 **E-mail:** rosie@tamiu.edu

Business Program(s) Web Site: http://www.tamiu.edu/coba

Graduate Business Unit Enrollment *Total:* 279 (114 full-time; 165 part-time; 107 women; 170 international). *Average Age:* 28.

Graduate Business Faculty *Total:* 24 (20 full-time; 4 part-time).

Admissions *Applied:* 146. *Admitted:* 145. *Enrolled:* 79. *Average GMAT:* 436. *Average GPA:* 3.31

Academic Calendar Semesters.

Accreditation AACSB—The Association to Advance Collegiate Schools of Business.

DEGREES MBA • MPA • MS

MBA—Master of Business Administration in International Banking Full-time and part-time. At least 33 total credits required. 12 to 72 months to complete program. *Concentration:* international banking.

MBA—Master of Business Administration in International Trade Full-time and part-time. At least 33 total credits required. 12 to 72 months to complete program. *Concentration:* international trade.

MBA—Master of Business Administration in Spanish Full-time and part-time. Distance learning option. Program offered in Spanish. At least 30 total credits required. 12 to 72 months to complete program. *Concentration:* international business.

MBA—Master of Business Administration Full-time and part-time. At least 30 total credits required. 12 to 72 months to complete program. *Concentrations:* accounting, information systems, international business, international economics, international finance, logistics, management, marketing.

MPA—Master of Professional Accountancy Full-time and part-time. At least 30 total credits required. 12 to 72 months to complete program. *Concentration:* accounting.

MS—Master of Science in Information Systems Full-time and part-time. At least 30 total credits required. 12 to 72 months to complete program. *Concentration:* information systems.

RESOURCES AND SERVICES 120 on-campus PCs are available to graduate business students. Access to Internet/World Wide Web, online (class) registration, and online grade reports available. *Personal computer requirements:* Graduate business students are strongly recommended to purchase or lease a personal computer. *Special opportunities include:* An international exchange program and an internship program are available. *Placement services include:* Alumni network, career placement, career counseling/planning, electronic job bank, resume referral, career fairs, job interviews arranged, resume preparation, and career library.

EXPENSES *Tuition (state resident):* Full-time: $1950. Part-time: $390 per semester. *Tuition (nonresident):* Full-time: $10,290. Part-time: $2058 per semester. *Tuition (international):* Full-time: $10,290. Part-time: $2058 per semester. *Required fees:* Full-time: $3784. Part-time: $804 per semester. *Graduate housing:* Room and board costs vary by number of occupants and type of board plan. *Typical cost:* $6630 (including board).

FINANCIAL AID (2007–08) 114 students received aid, including fellowships, grants, loans, research assistantships, and scholarships. Aid is available to part-time students. *Financial aid application deadline:* 6/1.

Financial Aid Contact Ms. Laura Elizondo, Director of Financial Aid, 5201 University Boulevard, Laredo, TX 78041-1900. *Phone:* 956-326-2225. *Fax:* 956-326-2224. *E-mail:* laura@tamiu.edu.

INTERNATIONAL STUDENTS 61% of students enrolled are international students. *Services and facilities:* Counseling/support services, ESL/language courses, Housing location assistance, International student organization, Language tutoring, Orientation, Visa Services. Financial aid is available to international students. *Required with application:* TOEFL with recommended score of 213 (computer), 550 (paper), or 79 (Internet); proof of adequate funds. *Recommended with application:* Proof of health/immunizations.

International Student Contact Mr. Jaime Ortiz, Associate Vice President for International Programs, 5201 University Boulevard, Laredo, TX 78041-1900. *Phone:* 956-326-3068. *Fax:* 956-326-2279. *E-mail:* jortiz@tamiu.edu.

APPLICATION *Required:* Application form, baccalaureate/first degree, essay, 2 letters of recommendation, personal statement, resume/curriculum vitae, transcripts of college work. School will accept GMAT and GRE. *Application fee:* $25. Applications for domestic and international students are processed on a rolling basis.

Application Contact Ms. Rosie Espinoza, Director of Admissions, 5201 University Boulevard, Laredo, TX 78041-1900. *Phone:* 956-326-2202. *Fax:* 956-326-2199. *E-mail:* rosie@tamiu.edu.

Texas A&M University
Mays Business School

College Station, Texas

Phone: 979-845-4714 **Fax:** 979-862-2393 **E-mail:** maysmba@tamu.edu

Business Program(s) Web Site: http://mba.tamu.edu/

Graduate Business Unit Enrollment *Total:* 600 (600 full-time; 240 women; 168 international). *Average Age:* 26.

Graduate Business Faculty *Total:* 163 (149 full-time; 14 part-time).

Admissions *Applied:* 370. *Admitted:* 130. *Enrolled:* 76. *Average GMAT:* 665. *Average GPA:* 3.4

Academic Calendar Trimesters.

Accreditation AACSB—The Association to Advance Collegiate Schools of Business.

After Graduation (Class of 2006–07) *Employed within 3 months of graduation:* 100%. *Average starting salary:* $87,411.

DEGREES MBA • MBA/MIS • MBA/MSF • MS

MBA—Executive Master of Business Administration Part-time. At least 53 total credits required. 24 months to complete program. *Concentration:* general MBA.

MBA—Master of Business Administration Full-time. At least 48 total credits required. 16 to 21 months to complete program. *Concentrations:* accounting, agribusiness, finance, financial information systems, financial management/planning, general MBA, human resources management, information management, international and area business studies, international business, international management, leadership, management consulting, management information systems, manufacturing management, marketing, new venture management, operations management, organizational behavior/development, production management, public policy and administration, real estate, strategic management, supply chain management, technology management, telecommunications management.

MBA/MIS—MBA/MS Full-time. 85 total credits required. 24 to 30 months to complete program. *Concentrations:* information systems, management, management information systems.

MBA/MSF—MBA/MS in Finance Full-time. 85 total credits required. 24 to 30 months to complete program. *Concentrations:* administration, finance, management.

MS—Master of Science in Accounting Full-time. At least 36 total credits required. 12 to 24 months to complete program. *Concentrations:* accounting, taxation.

MS—Master of Science in Finance Full-time. At least 36 total credits required. 12 to 24 months to complete program. *Concentrations:* finance, real estate.

MS—Master of Science in Land Economics and Real Estate Full-time. At least 36 total credits required. 12 to 34 months to complete program. *Concentration:* real estate.

MS—Master of Science in Management Full-time. At least 36 total credits required. 12 to 24 months to complete program. *Concentrations:* human resources management, organizational behavior/development.

MS—Master of Science in Management Information Systems Full-time. At least 36 total credits required. 12 to 24 months to complete program. *Concentrations:* management information systems, management systems analysis, operations management, system management, technology management.

MS—Master of Science in Marketing Full-time. At least 36 total credits required. 12 to 24 months to complete program. *Concentrations:* marketing, marketing research.

RESOURCES AND SERVICES 360 on-campus PCs are available to graduate business students. Access to Internet/World Wide Web, online (class) registration, and online grade reports available. *Personal computer requirements:* Graduate business students are not required to have a personal computer. *Special opportunities include:* An international exchange program and an internship program are available. *Placement services include:* Alumni network, career placement, career counseling/planning, electronic job bank, resume referral, career fairs, job interviews arranged, resume preparation, and career library.

EXPENSES *Tuition (state resident):* Full-time: $7333. *Tuition (nonresident):* Full-time: $17,341. *Tuition (international):* Full-time: $17,341. *Required fees:* Full-time: $7982. *Graduate housing:* Room and board costs vary by number of occupants and type of accommodation. *Typical cost:* $9651 (including board), $6267 (room only).

FINANCIAL AID (2007–08) 112 students received aid, including fellowships, loans, research assistantships, scholarships, teaching assistantships, and work study.

Financial Aid Contact Wendy Flynn, Director, MBA Admissions, 390 Wehner, Mailstop 4117, College Station, TX 77843-4117. *Phone:* 979-845-4714. *Fax:* 979-862-2393. *E-mail:* maysmba@tamu.edu.

INTERNATIONAL STUDENTS 28% of students enrolled are international students. *Services and facilities:* Counseling/support services, ESL/language courses, Housing location assistance, International student housing, International student organization, Orientation, Visa Services. Financial aid is available to international students. *Required with application:* TOEFL with recommended score of 250 (computer) or 600 (paper); proof of adequate funds; proof of health/immunizations.

International Student Contact Mrs. Wendy Flynn, Director of MBA Admissions, 390 Wehner, Mailstop 4117, College Station, TX 77843-4117. *Phone:* 979-845-4714. *Fax:* 979-862-2393. *E-mail:* maysmba@tamu.edu.

APPLICATION *Required:* GMAT, application form, baccalaureate/first degree, essay, interview, 3 letters of recommendation, resume/curriculum vitae, transcripts of college work, 2 years of work experience. *Application fee:* $50, $75 (international). *Deadlines:* 11/1 for fall, 1/4 for winter, 2/28 for spring, 4/15 for summer, 11/1 for fall (international), 1/4 for winter (international), 2/28 for spring (international), 4/15 for summer (international).

Application Contact Wendy Flynn, Director of MBA Admissions, 390 Wehner, Mailstop 4117, College Station, TX 77843-4117. *Phone:* 979-845-4714. *Fax:* 979-862-2393. *E-mail:* maysmba@tamu.edu.

Texas A&M University–Commerce
College of Business and Technology
Commerce, Texas

Phone: 903-468-3197 **Fax:** 903-468-6011 **E-mail:** brenda_walker@tamu-commerce.edu

Business Program(s) Web Site: http://www.tamu-commerce.edu/graduateprograms

Graduate Business Unit Enrollment *Total:* 647 (561 full-time; 86 part-time; 288 women).

Graduate Business Faculty 36 full-time.

Admissions *Applied:* 4,212. *Admitted:* 3,397. *Enrolled:* 3,282. *Average GMAT:* 500. *Average GPA:* 3.2

Academic Calendar Semesters.

Accreditation AACSB—The Association to Advance Collegiate Schools of Business.

After Graduation (Class of 2006–07) *Employed within 3 months of graduation:* 79%. *Average starting salary:* $68,000.

DEGREE MBA

MBA—Master of Business Administration *Concentration:* general MBA.

RESOURCES AND SERVICES 120 on-campus PCs are available to graduate business students. Access to Internet/World Wide Web, online (class) registration, and online grade reports available. *Personal computer requirements:* Graduate business students are strongly recommended to purchase or lease a personal computer. *Special opportunities include:* An international exchange program is available. *Placement services include:* Career counseling/planning, resume referral, career fairs, job interviews arranged, resume preparation, and career library.

FINANCIAL AID (2007–08) Loans, research assistantships, scholarships, teaching assistantships, and work study.

Financial Aid Contact Ms. Gari Yelenik, Financial Aid Student Services, PO Box 3011, Commerce, TX 75429-3011. *Phone:* 903-886-5910. *Fax:* 903-886-5098. *E-mail:* gari_yelenik@tamu-commerce.edu.

INTERNATIONAL STUDENTS *Services and facilities:* Counseling/support services, Housing location assistance, International student housing, International student organization, Orientation, Visa Services. Financial aid is available to international students. *Required with application:* TOEFL with recommended score of 173 (computer), 500 (paper), or 61 (Internet); proof of adequate funds; proof of health/immunizations.

International Student Contact Mr. John Mark Jones, International Student Services Director, PO Box 3011, Commerce, TX 75429-3011. *Phone:* 903-886-8144. *Fax:* 903-468-3200. *E-mail:* john_jones@tamu-commerce.edu.

APPLICATION *Required:* GMAT, GRE, application form, baccalaureate/first degree, essay, 3 letters of recommendation, personal statement, resume/curriculum vitae, transcripts of college work. *Application fee:* $35, $50 (international). Applications for domestic and international students are processed on a rolling basis.

Application Contact Ms. Brenda Walker, Administrative Secretary, PO Box 3011, Commerce, TX 75429-3011. *Phone:* 903-468-3197. *Fax:* 903-468-6011. *E-mail:* brenda_walker@tamu-commerce.edu.

Texas A&M University–Corpus Christi

College of Business

Corpus Christi, Texas

Phone: 361-825-2655 **Fax:** 361-825-2725 **E-mail:** sharon.polansky@tamucc.edu

Business Program(s) Web Site: http://cob.tamucc.edu

Graduate Business Unit Enrollment *Total:* 194 (105 full-time; 89 part-time; 99 women; 64 international). *Average Age:* 30.

Graduate Business Faculty *Total:* 33 (32 full-time; 1 part-time).

Admissions *Applied:* 69. *Admitted:* 64. *Enrolled:* 58. *Average GMAT:* 459. *Average GPA:* 3.1

Academic Calendar Semesters.

Accreditation AACSB—The Association to Advance Collegiate Schools of Business.

DEGREES   M Acc • MBA

M Acc—Master of Accountancy Full-time and part-time. 30 to 72 total credits required. 12 to 72 months to complete program. *Concentration:* accounting.

MBA—Master of Business Administration Full-time and part-time. 30 to 48 total credits required. 12 to 72 months to complete program. *Concentrations:* general MBA, health care, international business.

RESOURCES AND SERVICES 84 on-campus PCs are available to graduate business students. Access to Internet/World Wide Web, online (class) registration, and online grade reports available. *Personal computer requirements:* Graduate business students are strongly recommended to purchase or lease a personal computer. *Placement services include:* Alumni network, career placement, job search course, career counseling/planning, electronic job bank, resume referral, career fairs, job interviews arranged, resume preparation, and career library.

EXPENSES *Tuition (state resident):* Full-time: $2583. Part-time: $1722 per year. *Tuition (nonresident):* Full-time: $7587. Part-time: $5058 per year. *Tuition (international):* Full-time: $7587. Part-time: $5058 per year. *Required fees:* Full-time: $1169.14. Part-time: $849.76 per year. Tuition and/or fees vary by number of courses or credits taken. *Graduate housing:* Room and board costs vary by number of occupants and type of accommodation. *Typical cost:* $5310 (room only).

FINANCIAL AID (2007–08) Grants, loans, and scholarships. Aid is available to part-time students.

Financial Aid Contact Ms. Jeannie Gage, Director, Financial Assistance, 6300 Ocean Drive, Corpus Christi, TX 78412. *Phone:* 361-825-2338. *Fax:* 361-825-6095. *E-mail:* jeannie.gage@tamucc.edu.

INTERNATIONAL STUDENTS 33% of students enrolled are international students. *Services and facilities:* Counseling/support services, Housing location assistance, International student organization, Orientation, Visa Services. Financial aid is available to international students. *Required with application:* TOEFL with recommended score of 213 (computer), 550 (paper), or 80 (Internet); proof of adequate funds; proof of health/immunizations.

International Student Contact Ms. Karin Griffith, International Advisor, 6300 Ocean Drive, Corpus Christi, TX 78412. *Phone:* 361-825-2258. *Fax:* 361-825-5887. *E-mail:* karin.griffith@tamucc.edu.

APPLICATION *Required:* GMAT, application form, baccalaureate/first degree, essay, 2 letters of recommendation, personal statement, resume/curriculum vitae, transcripts of college work. *Recommended:* Interview. *Application fee:* $40, $70 (international). Applications for domestic and international students are processed on a rolling basis.

Application Contact Ms. Sharon Polansky, Director of Master's Programs, 6300 Ocean Drive, Unit 5808, Corpus Christi, TX 78412-5808. *Phone:* 361-825-2655. *Fax:* 361-825-2725. *E-mail:* sharon.polansky@tamucc.edu.

Texas A&M University–Texarkana

College of Business

Texarkana, Texas

Phone: 903-223-3106 **Fax:** 903-223-3121 **E-mail:** edward.bashaw@tamut.edu

Business Program(s) Web Site: http://www.tamut.edu

Graduate Business Unit Enrollment *Total:* 197 (12 full-time; 185 part-time; 103 women; 3 international).

Graduate Business Faculty *Total:* 19 (11 full-time; 8 part-time).

Admissions *Applied:* 146. *Admitted:* 125. *Enrolled:* 118.

Academic Calendar Semesters.

DEGREES   MBA • MS • MSA

MBA—Master of Business Administration Full-time and part-time. At least 36 total credits required. Maximum of 36 months to complete program. *Concentration:* general MBA.

MS—Master of Science in Business Administration Full-time and part-time. At least 36 total credits required. Maximum of 36 months to complete program. *Concentration:* general MBA.

MSA—Master of Science in Accounting Full-time and part-time. At least 36 total credits required. Maximum of 36 months to complete program. *Concentration:* accounting.

RESOURCES AND SERVICES 150 on-campus PCs are available to graduate business students. Access to Internet/World Wide Web, online (class) registration, and online grade reports available. *Personal computer requirements:* Graduate business students are not required to have a personal computer. *Placement services include:* Alumni network, career placement, career counseling/planning, career fairs, and resume preparation.

EXPENSES *Tuition (state resident):* Full-time: $4337. *Tuition (nonresident):* Full-time: $10,148. *Tuition (international):* Full-time: $10,148.

FINANCIAL AID (2007–08) Grants, loans, and scholarships. Aid is available to part-time students. *Financial aid application deadline:* 3/1.

Financial Aid Contact Marilyn Raney, Director of Financial Aid and Veteran Services, 2600 North Robison Road, Texarkana, TX 75501. *Phone:* 903-223-3060. *Fax:* 903-832-8890. *E-mail:* marilyn.raney@tamut.edu.

INTERNATIONAL STUDENTS 2% of students enrolled are international students. Financial aid is not available to international students. *Required with application:* TOEFL with recommended score of 213 (computer) or 550 (paper); proof of adequate funds; proof of health/immunizations.

International Student Contact Carl Greig, Director of Student Services, PO Box 5518, Texarkana, TX 75503. *Phone:* 903-223-3062. *Fax:* 903-223-3140. *E-mail:* carl.greig@tamut.edu.

APPLICATION *Required:* GMAT, application form, baccalaureate/first degree, 3 letters of recommendation, personal statement, resume/curriculum vitae, transcripts of college work. *Application fee:* $0, $25 (international). Applications for domestic and international students are processed on a rolling basis.

Application Contact Dr. Edward R. Bashaw, Dean, PO Box 5518, Texarkana, TX 75505-5518. *Phone:* 903-223-3106. *Fax:* 903-223-3121. *E-mail:* edward.bashaw@tamut.edu.

Texas Christian University

The Neeley School of Business at TCU

Fort Worth, Texas

Phone: 817-257-7531 **Fax:** 817-257-6431 **E-mail:** mbainfo@tcu.edu

Business Program(s) Web Site: http://www.mba.tcu.edu/

Graduate Business Unit Enrollment *Total:* 384 (135 full-time; 249 part-time; 132 women; 27 international). *Average Age:* 27.

Graduate Business Faculty *Total:* 98 (69 full-time; 29 part-time).

Admissions *Applied:* 226. *Admitted:* 165. *Enrolled:* 108. *Average GMAT:* 608. *Average GPA:* 3.3

Academic Calendar Semesters.

Accreditation AACSB—The Association to Advance Collegiate Schools of Business.

After Graduation (Class of 2006–07) *Employed within 3 months of graduation:* 97%. *Average starting salary:* $70,477.

DEGREES EMBA • EdD/MBA • M Acc • MBA • MIM

EMBA—Executive Master of Business Administration Part-time. 8 years of work experience (at least 5 managerial) required. At least 47 total credits required. 16 months to complete program. *Concentration:* executive programs.

EdD/MBA—Doctor of Education/Master of Business Administration Full-time and part-time. At least 86 total credits required. 28 to 60 months to complete program. *Concentration:* combined degrees.

M Acc—Master of Accounting Full-time. At least 30 total credits required. 9 to 24 months to complete program. *Concentration:* accounting.

MBA—Accelerated Master of Business Administration Full-time. At least 36 total credits required. 12 months to complete program. *Concentrations:* accounting, finance, management, management consulting, marketing, supply chain management.

MBA—Full-Time Master of Business Administration Full-time. At least 54 total credits required. 21 months to complete program. *Concentrations:* accounting, finance, management, management consulting, marketing, supply chain management.

MBA—Professional Part-Time Master of Business Administration Part-time. At least 48 total credits required. 24 to 33 months to complete program. *Concentration:* general MBA.

MIM—Master of International Management Full-time. Undergraduate degree in business and fluency in English and Spanish required. At least 40 total credits required. 20 to 24 months to complete program. *Concentration:* international business.

RESOURCES AND SERVICES 200 on-campus PCs are available to graduate business students. Access to Internet/World Wide Web, online (class) registration, and online grade reports available. *Personal computer requirements:* Graduate business students are required to have a personal computer. *Special opportunities include:* An international exchange program and an internship program are available. *Placement services include:* Alumni network, career placement, job search course, career counseling/planning, electronic job bank, resume referral, career fairs, job interviews arranged, resume preparation, and career library.

EXPENSES *Tuition:* Full-time: $25,950. Part-time: $15,570 per year. *Tuition (international):* Full-time: $25,950. Part-time: $15,570 per year. *Required fees:* Full-time: $3350. Part-time: $1575 per year. Tuition and/or fees vary by academic program. *Graduate housing:* Room and board costs vary by number of occupants. *Typical cost:* $12,000 (including board), $7000 (room only).

FINANCIAL AID (2007–08) 84 students received aid, including fellowships, grants, loans, research assistantships, scholarships, and work study. Aid is available to part-time students. *Financial aid application deadline:* 5/1.

Financial Aid Contact Debbie Mar, Coordinator, Graduate Financial Aid, PO Box 297012, Fort Worth, TX 76129. *Phone:* 817-257-7872. *Fax:* 817-257-7462. *E-mail:* d.mar@tcu.edu.

INTERNATIONAL STUDENTS 7% of students enrolled are international students. *Services and facilities:* Counseling/support services, ESL/language courses, Housing location assistance, International student organization, Language tutoring, Orientation, Visa Services. Financial aid is available to international students. *Required with application:* TOEFL with recommended score of 213 (computer), 550 (paper), or 100 (Internet); proof of adequate funds; proof of health/immunizations.

International Student Contact John Singleton, Director of International Student Services, PO Box 297003, Fort Worth, TX 76129. *Phone:* 817-921-7292. *Fax:* 817-921-7333. *E-mail:* jsingleton@tcu.edu.

APPLICATION *Required:* GMAT, application form, baccalaureate/first degree, essay, interview, 3 letters of recommendation, resume/curriculum vitae, transcripts of college work. *Recommended:* 2 years of work experience. *Application fee:* $75. Applications for domestic and international students are processed on a rolling basis.

Application Contact Peggy Conway, Director of MBA Admissions, PO Box 298540, Fort Worth, TX 76129. *Phone:* 817-257-7531. *Fax:* 817-257-6431. *E-mail:* mbainfo@tcu.edu.

See full description on page 694.

Texas Southern University
Jesse H. Jones School of Business
Houston, Texas

Phone: 713-313-7309 **Fax:** 713-313-7705 **E-mail:** richardson_bj@tsu.edu

Business Program(s) Web Site: http://www.tsu.edu/academics/business/program/graduate.asp

Graduate Business Unit Enrollment *Total:* 136 (28 full-time; 108 part-time; 77 women; 34 international).

Graduate Business Faculty *Total:* 43 (36 full-time; 7 part-time).

Admissions *Applied:* 173. *Admitted:* 142. *Enrolled:* 136. *Average GMAT:* 457. *Average GPA:* 3.07

Academic Calendar Semesters.

Accreditation AACSB—The Association to Advance Collegiate Schools of Business.

After Graduation (Class of 2006–07) *Employed within 3 months of graduation:* 87%. *Average starting salary:* $41,000.

DEGREES JD/MBA • MBA • MBA-H • MSMIS

JD/MBA—Dual Degree in JD and MBA Full-time and part-time. Requires separate applications for JD and MBA degrees. At least 111 total credits required. 48 to 72 months to complete program. *Concentrations:* business studies, combined degrees, law.

MBA—Master of Business Administration Full-time and part-time. At least 39 total credits required. 24 to 72 months to complete program. *Concentration:* general MBA.

MBA-H—MBA with Concentration in Health Care Administration Full-time and part-time. At least 39 total credits required. 24 to 72 months to complete program. *Concentration:* health administration.

MSMIS—MS in Management Information Systems Full-time and part-time. At least 33 total credits required. 24 to 72 months to complete program. *Concentration:* information management.

RESOURCES AND SERVICES 125 on-campus PCs are available to graduate business students. Access to Internet/World Wide Web, online (class) registration, and online grade reports available. *Personal computer requirements:* Graduate business students are strongly recommended to purchase or lease a personal computer. *Special opportunities include:* An internship program is available. *Placement services include:* Alumni network, career placement, resume referral, career fairs, and job interviews arranged.

EXPENSES *Tuition (state resident):* Full-time: $1152. Part-time: $100 per credit hour. *Tuition (nonresident):* Full-time: $5966. Part-time: $800.40 per credit hour. *Tuition (international):* Full-time: $5966. Part-time: $800.40 per credit hour. *Required fees:* Full-time: $1850. Part-time: $447.40 per credit hour. Tuition and/or fees vary by number of courses or credits taken. *Graduate housing:* Room and board costs vary by number of occupants, type of accommodation, and type of board plan. *Typical cost:* $6664 (including board).

Texas Southern University (continued)

FINANCIAL AID (2007–08) 11 students received aid, including research assistantships and work study. *Financial aid application deadline:* 5/1.

Financial Aid Contact Mr. Albert Tezno, Director of Financial Aid, 3100 Cleburne Avenue, Houston, TX 77004. *Phone:* 713-313-4384. *Fax:* 713-313-1859. *E-mail:* aidaajtezno@tsu.edu.

INTERNATIONAL STUDENTS 25% of students enrolled are international students. *Services and facilities:* Counseling/support services, ESL/language courses, Housing location assistance, International student organization, Orientation. Financial aid is available to international students. *Required with application:* TOEFL with recommended score of 213 (computer) or 550 (paper); proof of adequate funds; proof of health/immunizations.

International Student Contact Ms. Patricia Luckett, Director, International Student Affairs, 3100 Cleburne Avenue, Houston, TX 77004-4584. *Phone:* 713-313-7930. *Fax:* 713-313-1878. *E-mail:* luckettph@tsu.edu.

APPLICATION *Required:* GMAT, application form, baccalaureate/first degree, essay, interview, 3 letters of recommendation, resume/curriculum vitae, transcripts of college work. *Application fee:* $50, $75 (international). Applications for domestic and international students are processed on a rolling basis.

Application Contact Ms. Bobbie Richardson, MBA Coordinator, 3100 Cleburne Avenue, Houston, TX 77004-4584. *Phone:* 713-313-7309. *Fax:* 713-313-7705. *E-mail:* richardson_bj@tsu.edu.

Texas Tech University
Jerry S. Rawls College of Business Administration

Lubbock, Texas

Phone: 806-742-0221 **Fax:** 806-742-3958 **E-mail:** patsy.fisher@ttu.edu

Business Program(s) Web Site: http://grad.ba.ttu.edu

Graduate Business Unit Enrollment *Total:* 623 (248 full-time; 375 part-time; 230 women; 73 international). *Average Age:* 27.

Graduate Business Faculty *Total:* 75 (70 full-time; 5 part-time).

Admissions *Applied:* 569. *Admitted:* 381. *Enrolled:* 314. *Average GMAT:* 528. *Average GPA:* 3.43

Accreditation AACSB—The Association to Advance Collegiate Schools of Business.

After Graduation (Class of 2006–07) *Employed within 3 months of graduation:* 68%. *Average starting salary:* $53,072.

DEGREES IMBA • JD/MBA • MBA • MBA/M Arch • MBA/MA • MBA/MS • MD/MBA • MS • MS/MS • MSA

IMBA—International Master of Business Administration Full-time and part-time. 49 total credits required. 16 to 72 months to complete program. *Concentration:* international business.

JD/MBA—Juris Doctor/Master of Business Administration Full-time and part-time. 109 to 112 total credits required. 36 to 72 months to complete program. *Concentration:* legal administration.

MBA—Master of Business Administration Full-time and part-time. 48 total credits required. 16 to 72 months to complete program. *Concentrations:* agribusiness, entrepreneurship, finance, financial management/planning, international business, management, management information systems, marketing, other.

MBA—Master of Business Administration in Health Organization Management Full-time and part-time. 51 to 54 total credits required. 16 to 72 months to complete program. *Concentration:* health care.

MBA/M Arch—Master of Business Administration/Master of Architecture Full-time and part-time. 72 total credits required. 24 to 72 months to complete program. *Concentration:* combined degrees.

MBA/MA—Master of Business Administration/Master of Arts in Foreign Language Full-time and part-time. 60 total credits required. 24 to 72 months to complete program. *Concentration:* combined degrees.

MBA/MS—Master of Business Administration/Master of Science in Environmental Toxicology Full-time and part-time. 62 total credits required. 24 to 72 months to complete program. *Concentration:* combined degrees.

MBA/MS—Master of Business Administration/Master of Science in Personal Financial Planning Full-time and part-time. 63 total credits required. 24 to 72 months to complete program. *Concentrations:* combined degrees, finance, financial management/planning.

MD/MBA—Doctor of Medicine/Master of Business Administration Full-time and part-time. 206 to 211 total credits required. 48 months to complete program. *Concentration:* health care.

MS—Master of Science in Business Administration Full-time and part-time. 36 to 62 total credits required. 12 to 72 months to complete program. *Concentrations:* finance, management information systems, production management, statistics.

MS/MS—Master of Science in Business Administration/Master of Science in Personal Financial Planning Full-time and part-time. 51 to 73 total credits required. 24 to 72 months to complete program. *Concentrations:* combined degrees, finance, financial management/planning.

MSA—Master of Science in Accounting Full-time and part-time. 36 to 84 total credits required. 12 to 72 months to complete program. *Concentration:* taxation.

MSA—Master of Science in Accounting/Juris Doctor Full-time and part-time. 102 to 148 total credits required. 36 to 72 months to complete program. *Concentrations:* legal administration, taxation.

RESOURCES AND SERVICES 481 on-campus PCs are available to graduate business students. Access to Internet/World Wide Web, online (class) registration, and online grade reports available. *Personal computer requirements:* Graduate business students are strongly recommended to purchase or lease a personal computer. *Special opportunities include:* An international exchange program and an internship program are available. *Placement services include:* Alumni network, career placement, job search course, career counseling/planning, electronic job bank, resume referral, career fairs, job interviews arranged, resume preparation, and career library.

EXPENSES *Tuition (state resident):* Full-time: $4650. Part-time: $195 per credit hour. *Tuition (nonresident):* Full-time: $11,320. Part-time: $475 per credit hour. *Tuition (international):* Full-time: $11,320. Part-time: $475 per credit hour. *Required fees:* Full-time: $3200. Part-time: $180 per credit hour. Tuition and/or fees vary by number of courses or credits taken and local reciprocity agreements. *Graduate housing:* Room and board costs vary by campus location, number of occupants, type of accommodation, and type of board plan. *Typical cost:* $7000 (including board).

FINANCIAL AID (2007–08) 120 students received aid, including research assistantships, scholarships, and teaching assistantships. *Financial aid application deadline:* 3/1.

Financial Aid Contact Ms. Becky Wilson, Director, Financial Aid, Box 45011, Lubbock, TX 79409-5011. *Phone:* 806-742-3681. *Fax:* 806-742-0880. *E-mail:* finaid.advisor@ttu.edu.

INTERNATIONAL STUDENTS 12% of students enrolled are international students. *Services and facilities:* Counseling/support services, ESL/language courses, Housing location assistance, International student organization, Language tutoring, Orientation, Visa Services, International Olympics. Financial aid is available to international students. *Required with application:* TOEFL with recommended score of 213 (computer) or 550 (paper); proof of adequate funds; proof of health/immunizations.

International Student Contact Bob Crosier, Director, International Student and Scholar Service, Box 45004, Lubbock, TX 79409-5004. *Phone:* 806-742-3667. *Fax:* 806-742-1286. *E-mail:* bob.crosier@ttu.edu.

APPLICATION *Required:* GMAT, application form, baccalaureate/first degree, resume/curriculum vitae, transcripts of college work. *Recommended:* Essay, letter(s) of recommendation, work experience. *Application*

fee: $50, $60 (international). Applications for domestic and international students are processed on a rolling basis.

Application Contact Mrs. Patsy Fisher, Assistant Director, Graduate Services Center, Box 42101, Lubbock, TX 79409-2101. *Phone:* 806-742-0221. *Fax:* 806-742-3958. *E-mail:* patsy.fisher@ttu.edu.

Texas Wesleyan University
School of Business
Fort Worth, Texas

Phone: 817-531-4422 **Fax:** 817-531-7515 **E-mail:** hkiser@txwes.edu

Business Program(s) Web Site: http://www.txwes.edu/

Graduate Business Unit Enrollment *Total:* 75 (20 full-time; 55 part-time; 41 women; 4 international). *Average Age:* 34.

Graduate Business Faculty *Total:* 9 (5 full-time; 4 part-time).

Admissions *Average GMAT:* 455. *Average GPA:* 3.2

Academic Calendar Semesters.

DEGREE MBA

MBA—Master of Business Administration Full-time and part-time. At least 36 total credits required. 30 to 36 months to complete program. *Concentrations:* accounting, human resources management, international business, management information systems, organizational management.

RESOURCES AND SERVICES 50 on-campus PCs are available to graduate business students. Access to Internet/World Wide Web, online (class) registration, and online grade reports available. *Personal computer requirements:* Graduate business students are strongly recommended to purchase or lease a personal computer. *Special opportunities include:* An internship program is available. *Placement services include:* Alumni network, career placement, career counseling/planning, resume referral, career fairs, job interviews arranged, and resume preparation.

EXPENSES *Tuition:* Full-time: $5004. Part-time: $499 per credit hour. *Tuition (international):* Full-time: $5004. Part-time: $499 per credit hour. *Required fees:* Full-time: $840. Part-time: $40 per credit hour. *Typical graduate housing cost:* $5870 (including board), $3320 (room only).

FINANCIAL AID (2007–08) 61 students received aid, including grants, loans, research assistantships, and scholarships. Aid is available to part-time students.

Financial Aid Contact Ms. Shanna Hollis, Director of Financial Aid, 1201 Wesleyan Street, Fort Worth, TX 76105-1536. *Phone:* 817-531-4420. *Fax:* 817-531-4231. *E-mail:* shollis@txwes.edu.

INTERNATIONAL STUDENTS 5% of students enrolled are international students. *Services and facilities:* Counseling/support services, International student housing, International student organization, Orientation, Visa Services, Special trips and planned events. Financial aid is available to international students. *Required with application:* TOEFL with recommended score of 190 (computer) or 520 (paper); proof of adequate funds; proof of health/immunizations.

International Student Contact Ms. Betsy Johnson, Director, 1201 Wesleyan Street, Fort Worth, TX 76105-1536. *Phone:* 817-531-4965. *E-mail:* ejohnson@txwes.edu.

APPLICATION *Required:* GMAT, application form, baccalaureate/first degree, essay, 3 letters of recommendation, personal statement, transcripts of college work. *Recommended:* Resume/curriculum vitae, work experience. *Application fee:* $50. Applications for domestic and international students are processed on a rolling basis.

Application Contact Ms. Holly Kiser, Director of Admissions, 1201 Wesleyan Street, Fort Worth, TX 76105-1536. *Phone:* 817-531-4422. *Fax:* 817-531-7515. *E-mail:* hkiser@txwes.edu.

Texas Woman's University
School of Management
Denton, Texas

Phone: 940-898-3047 **Fax:** 940-898-3079 **E-mail:** swheelerr@twu.edu

Business Program(s) Web Site: http://www.twu.edu/som/

Graduate Business Unit Enrollment *Total:* 722 (720 full-time; 2 part-time). *Average Age:* 35.

Graduate Business Faculty *Total:* 40 (21 full-time; 19 part-time).

Admissions *Applied:* 250. *Admitted:* 150. *Enrolled:* 150. *Average GPA:* 3.5

Academic Calendar Semesters.

DEGREE MBA

MBA—Master of Business Administration Full-time and part-time. Distance learning option. At least 36 total credits required. 12 to 36 months to complete program. *Concentration:* general MBA.

RESOURCES AND SERVICES Access to Internet/World Wide Web, online (class) registration, and online grade reports available. *Personal computer requirements:* Graduate business students are not required to have a personal computer. *Special opportunities include:* An international exchange program is available. *Placement services include:* Alumni network, career placement, job search course, career counseling/planning, electronic job bank, resume referral, career fairs, job interviews arranged, resume preparation, and career library.

EXPENSES Tuition and/or fees vary by campus location and academic program. *Graduate housing:* Room and board costs vary by number of occupants, type of accommodation, and type of board plan.

FINANCIAL AID (2007–08) Loans, research assistantships, scholarships, teaching assistantships, and work study. Aid is available to part-time students. *Financial aid application deadline:* 3/1.

Financial Aid Contact Mr. Governor Jackson, Director of Financial Aid, Box 425408, TWU Station, Denton, TX 76204. *Phone:* 940-898-3050. *Fax:* 940-898-3068. *E-mail:* gjackson@twu.edu.

INTERNATIONAL STUDENTS *Services and facilities:* Counseling/support services, ESL/language courses, International student organization, Orientation. Financial aid is available to international students. *Required with application:* TOEFL with recommended score of 550 (paper); proof of adequate funds; proof of health/immunizations.

International Student Contact Dr. Paula Ann Hughes, Director, Box 425738, TWU Station, Denton, TX 76204. *Phone:* 940-898-2105. *Fax:* 940-898-2121. *E-mail:* pahughes@twu.edu.

APPLICATION *Required:* Application form, baccalaureate/first degree, 3 letters of recommendation, resume/curriculum vitae, transcripts of college work. *Recommended:* Interview, 5 years of work experience. *Application fee:* $30, $35 (international). Applications for domestic and international students are processed on a rolling basis.

Application Contact Mr. Samuel Wheeler, Graduate Admissions Counselor, Box 425589, Denton, TX 76204. *Phone:* 940-898-3047. *Fax:* 940-898-3079. *E-mail:* swheelerr@twu.edu.

Trinity University
Department of Business Administration
San Antonio, Texas

Phone: 210-999-7296 **Fax:** 210-999-7296 **E-mail:** psandlin@trinity.edu

Business Program(s) Web Site: http://www.trinity.edu/departments/business_admin/acctgms2.htm

Accreditation AACSB—The Association to Advance Collegiate Schools of Business.

Trinity University (continued)

DEGREE MSA

MSA—Master of Science in Accounting Full-time and part-time. At least 30 total credits required. 9 to 54 months to complete program. *Concentration:* accounting.

RESOURCES AND SERVICES 60 on-campus PCs are available to graduate business students. Access to Internet/World Wide Web, online (class) registration, and online grade reports available. *Personal computer requirements:* Graduate business students are not required to have a personal computer. *Placement services include:* Career counseling/planning and resume preparation.

Application Contact Dr. Petrea K. Sandlin, Director of the Accounting Program, One Trinity Place, Director of the Accounting Program, San Antonio, TX 78212. *Phone:* 210-999-7296. *Fax:* 210-999-7296. *E-mail:* psandlin@trinity.edu.

University of Dallas
Graduate School of Management
Irving, Texas

Phone: 972-721-5356 **Fax:** 972-721-4009 **E-mail:** admiss@gsm.udallas.edu

Business Program(s) Web Site: http://www.thedallasmba.com/

Graduate Business Unit Enrollment *Total:* 1,356 (235 full-time; 1,121 part-time; 530 women; 231 international). *Average Age:* 34.

Graduate Business Faculty *Total:* 81 (30 full-time; 51 part-time).

Admissions *Applied:* 436. *Admitted:* 384. *Enrolled:* 237. *Average GMAT:* 467. *Average GPA:* 3.6

Academic Calendar Trimesters.

Accreditation ACBSP—The American Council of Business Schools and Programs.

After Graduation (Class of 2006–07) *Employed within 3 months of graduation:* 94%. *Average starting salary:* $50,000.

DEGREES M Mgt • MBA • MS

M Mgt—Master of Management Full-time and part-time. Distance learning option. At least 30 total credits required. 12 to 72 months to complete program. *Concentrations:* accounting, engineering, entrepreneurship, finance, financial management/planning, health care, human resources management, information management, information technology, international business, leadership, marketing, project management, sports/entertainment management, supply chain management, technology management, telecommunications management.

MBA—Master of Business Administration Full-time and part-time. Distance learning option. At least 49 total credits required. 12 to 72 months to complete program. *Concentrations:* accounting, engineering, entrepreneurship, finance, financial management/planning, health care, human resources management, information management, information technology, international business, leadership, management, marketing, nonprofit management, organizational behavior/development, project management, sports/entertainment management, supply chain management, telecommunications management.

MS—Master of Science Full-time and part-time. Distance learning option. At least 31 total credits required. 12 to 72 months to complete program. *Concentrations:* accounting, entrepreneurship, human resources management, information management, information technology, international business, project management.

RESOURCES AND SERVICES 125 on-campus PCs are available to graduate business students. Access to Internet/World Wide Web and online (class) registration available. *Personal computer requirements:* Graduate business students are not required to have a personal computer. *Special opportunities include:* An international exchange program and an internship program are available. *Placement services include:* Alumni network, career placement, job search course, career counseling/planning, electronic job bank, resume referral, career fairs, job interviews arranged, resume preparation, and career library.

EXPENSES *Tuition:* Part-time: $522 per credit hour. *Tuition (international):* Part-time: $522 per credit hour. *Required fees:* Full-time: $150. Tuition and/or fees vary by campus location.

FINANCIAL AID (2007–08) 450 students received aid, including grants, loans, scholarships, and work study. Aid is available to part-time students. *Financial aid application deadline:* 3/1.

Financial Aid Contact Laurie Rosenkrantz, Assistant Dean Financial Aid, 1845 East Northgate Drive, Irving, TX 75062-4736. *Phone:* 972-721-5266. *Fax:* 972-721-5017. *E-mail:* admiss@gsm.udallas.edu.

INTERNATIONAL STUDENTS 17% of students enrolled are international students. *Services and facilities:* Counseling/support services, ESL/language courses, Housing location assistance, International student housing, International student organization, Language tutoring, Orientation, Visa Services. Financial aid is not available to international students. *Required with application:* TOEFL with recommended score of 213 (computer) or 550 (paper); proof of adequate funds. *Recommended with application:* Proof of health/immunizations.

International Student Contact Pamela Jones, Executive Director, Admissions Executive for International Students, 1845 East Northgate Drive, Irving, TX 75062-4736. *Phone:* 972-721-5104. *Fax:* 972-721-5254. *E-mail:* pjones@gsm.udallas.edu.

APPLICATION *Required:* Application form, baccalaureate/first degree, 2 letters of recommendation, resume/curriculum vitae, transcripts of college work. School will accept GMAT and GRE. *Recommended:* Personal statement, 4 years of work experience. *Application fee:* $50, $100 (international). Applications for domestic and international students are processed on a rolling basis.

Application Contact Ms. Alounda Joseph, Director of Graduate School of Management Enrollment Process, 1845 East Northgate Drive, Irving, TX 75062-4736. *Phone:* 972-721-5356. *Fax:* 972-721-4009. *E-mail:* admiss@gsm.udallas.edu.

See full description on page 710.

University of Houston
Bauer College of Business
Houston, Texas

Phone: 713-743-5936 **Fax:** 713-743-4368 **E-mail:** smross@uh.edu

Business Program(s) Web Site: http://www.bauer.uh.edu/

Accreditation AACSB—The Association to Advance Collegiate Schools of Business.

DEGREES JD/MBA • MBA • MBA equivalent combined degree • MBA/MA • MBA/MIM • MBA/MS • MBA/MSW • MS

JD/MBA—Juris Doctor/Master of Business Administration Full-time and part-time. At least 111 total credits required. 48 to 72 months to complete program. *Concentration:* general MBA.

MBA—Evening Program Full-time and part-time. 48 total credits required. 16 to 60 months to complete program. *Concentration:* general MBA.

MBA—Executive Master of Business Administration—Global Energy Track Full-time. Interview required. 48 total credits required. 22 months to complete program. *Concentration:* general MBA.

MBA—Executive Master of Business Administration—Leadership Track Full-time. Interview required. 48 total credits required. 18 to 22 months to complete program. *Concentration:* general MBA.

MBA—Full-Time Day Program Full-time. 48 total credits required. 21 months to complete program. *Concentration:* general MBA.

MBA equivalent combined degree—MBA/MS-Master of Business Administration/Master of Science in Hospitality Management Full-time and part-time. At least 84 total credits required. 36 to 60 months to complete program. *Concentration:* hospitality management.

MBA/MA—Master of Business Administration/Master of Arts in Spanish Full-time and part-time. At least 60 total credits required. 24 to 60 months to complete program. *Concentration:* general MBA.

MBA/MIM—Master of Business Administration/Master of International Management Full-time and part-time. At least 66 total credits required. 36 to 60 months to complete program. *Concentration:* international business.

MBA/MS—Master of Business Administration/Master of Industrial Engineering Full-time and part-time. 60 to 72 total credits required. 24 to 60 months to complete program. *Concentration:* general MBA.

MBA/MSW—Master of Business Administration/Master of Social Work Full-time and part-time. 87 total credits required. 36 to 60 months to complete program. *Concentration:* general MBA.

MS—Master of Science in Accountancy Full-time and part-time. 36 to 75 total credits required. 18 to 60 months to complete program. *Concentration:* accounting.

MS—Master of Science in Finance Full-time and part-time. 27 to 36 total credits required. 16 to 60 months to complete program. *Concentration:* finance.

RESOURCES AND SERVICES 500 on-campus PCs are available to graduate business students. Access to Internet/World Wide Web, online (class) registration, and online grade reports available. *Personal computer requirements:* Graduate business students are strongly recommended to purchase or lease a personal computer. *Special opportunities include:* An international exchange program and an internship program are available. *Placement services include:* Alumni network, career placement, job search course, career counseling/planning, electronic job bank, resume referral, career fairs, job interviews arranged, resume preparation, and career library.

Application Contact Stephanie Ross, Director of MBA Admissions, MBA Program Office, 334 Melcher Hall, Room 275, Houston, TX 77204-6021. *Phone:* 713-743-5936. *Fax:* 713-743-4368. *E-mail:* smross@uh.edu.

University of Houston–Clear Lake
School of Business
Houston, Texas

Phone: 281-283-3112 **Fax:** 281-283-3951 **E-mail:** carter@uhcl.edu

Business Program(s) Web Site: http://wwwadmin.uhcl.edu/bpa/index.html

Graduate Business Unit Enrollment *Total:* 834 (420 full-time; 414 part-time; 387 women; 229 international). *Average Age:* 30.

Graduate Business Faculty *Total:* 72 (59 full-time; 13 part-time).

Admissions *Applied:* 504. *Admitted:* 259. *Enrolled:* 166. *Average GMAT:* 502. *Average GPA:* 3.15

Academic Calendar Semesters.

Accreditation AACSB—The Association to Advance Collegiate Schools of Business.

DEGREES M Sc • MA • MBA • MBA/MHA • MS

M Sc—Master of Science in Environmental Management Full-time and part-time. 36 to 48 total credits required. 24 to 60 months to complete program. *Concentration:* environmental economics/management.

MA—Master of Arts in Human Resource Management Full-time and part-time. 42 to 54 total credits required. 12 to 60 months to complete program. *Concentration:* human resources management.

MBA—Master of Business Administration Full-time and part-time. Distance learning option. 36 to 54 total credits required. 12 to 60 months

to complete program. *Concentrations:* environmental economics/management, finance, human resources management, international business, management information systems, marketing, other, technology management.

MBA/MHA—Master of Healthcare Administration/Master of Business Administration Full-time and part-time. Distance learning option. 57 to 78 total credits required. 24 to 60 months to complete program. *Concentration:* combined degrees.

MS—Master of Science in Accounting Full-time and part-time. 33 to 69 total credits required. 12 to 60 months to complete program. *Concentration:* accounting.

MS—Master of Science in Finance Full-time and part-time. 36 to 54 total credits required. 12 to 60 months to complete program. *Concentrations:* finance, health care.

MS—Master of Science in Management Information Systems Full-time and part-time. 36 to 48 total credits required. 12 to 60 months to complete program. *Concentration:* management information systems.

RESOURCES AND SERVICES 140 on-campus PCs are available to graduate business students. Access to Internet/World Wide Web, online (class) registration, and online grade reports available. *Personal computer requirements:* Graduate business students are not required to have a personal computer. *Special opportunities include:* An internship program is available. *Placement services include:* Alumni network, career placement, career counseling/planning, electronic job bank, resume referral, career fairs, job interviews arranged, resume preparation, and career library.

EXPENSES *Tuition (state resident):* Full-time: $3600. Part-time: $100 per credit hour. *Tuition (nonresident):* Full-time: $13,608. Part-time: $378 per credit hour. *Tuition (international):* Full-time: $13,608. Part-time: $378 per credit hour. *Required fees:* Full-time: $5256. Part-time: $146 per credit hour. *Graduate housing:* Room and board costs vary by number of occupants. *Typical cost:* $5238 (room only).

FINANCIAL AID (2007–08) 200 students received aid, including loans, scholarships, teaching assistantships, and work study. Aid is available to part-time students. *Financial aid application deadline:* 5/1.

Financial Aid Contact Ms. Lynda McKendree, Director of Financial Aid and Veterans Affairs, 2700 Bay Area Boulevard, Houston, TX 77058-1098. *Phone:* 281-283-2480. *Fax:* 281-283-2502. *E-mail:* uhcl_fao@uhcl.edu.

INTERNATIONAL STUDENTS 27% of students enrolled are international students. *Services and facilities:* Counseling/support services, ESL/language courses, Housing location assistance, International student housing, International student organization, Language tutoring, Orientation. Financial aid is not available to international students. *Required with application:* TOEFL with recommended score of 213 (computer) or 550 (paper); proof of adequate funds.

International Student Contact International Student Advisor, International Student Advisor, 2700 Bay Area Boulevard, Houston, TX 77058-1098. *Phone:* 281-283-2500. *Fax:* 281-283-2522. *E-mail:* intladmissions@uhcl.edu.

APPLICATION *Required:* GMAT, application form, baccalaureate/first degree, transcripts of college work. *Recommended:* Personal statement, resume/curriculum vitae. *Application fee:* $35, $75 (international). Applications for domestic and international students are processed on a rolling basis.

Application Contact Ms. Karen Carter, Academic Advisor, 2700 Bay Area Boulevard, Houston, TX 77058-1098. *Phone:* 281-283-3112. *Fax:* 281-283-3951. *E-mail:* carter@uhcl.edu.

University of Houston–Victoria
School of Business Administration
Victoria, Texas

Phone: 361-570-4122 **Fax:** 361-570-4114 **E-mail:** morgenrothk@uhv.edu

University of Houston–Victoria (continued)

Business Program(s) Web Site: http://www.uhv.edu/bus

Graduate Business Unit Enrollment *Total:* 825 (168 full-time; 657 part-time; 410 women; 58 international). *Average Age:* 35.

Graduate Business Faculty *Total:* 41 (28 full-time; 13 part-time).

Admissions *Applied:* 332. *Admitted:* 243. *Enrolled:* 186. *Average GMAT:* 456. *Average GPA:* 3.45

Academic Calendar Semesters.

Accreditation AACSB—The Association to Advance Collegiate Schools of Business.

After Graduation (Class of 2006–07) *Employed within 3 months of graduation:* 80%. *Average starting salary:* $55,600.

DEGREES MBA • MBA equivalent • MS

MBA—Fourth-Year Bridge Master of Business Administration Full-time and part-time. Distance learning option. Must have a 3 year baccalaureate degree from a Commonwealth university. 21 to 40 months to complete program. *Concentrations:* accounting, finance, international business, management, marketing.

MBA—Master of Business Administration Full-time and part-time. Distance learning option. Four-year baccalaureate degree from a regionally accredited institution required. At least 48 total credits required. 16 to 33 months to complete program. *Concentrations:* accounting, finance, international business, management, marketing.

MBA equivalent—Global Master of Business Administration Full-time and part-time. Distance learning option. 30 to 54 total credits required. 11 to 35 months to complete program. *Concentrations:* finance, management.

MS—Economic Development and Entrepreneurship Full-time and part-time. Distance learning option. At least 36 total credits required. 11 to 24 months to complete program. *Concentrations:* developmental economics, entrepreneurship.

RESOURCES AND SERVICES 77 on-campus PCs are available to graduate business students. Access to Internet/World Wide Web, online (class) registration, and online grade reports available. *Personal computer requirements:* Graduate business students are strongly recommended to purchase or lease a personal computer. *Placement services include:* Career placement, career counseling/planning, electronic job bank, resume referral, career fairs, job interviews arranged, resume preparation, and career library.

EXPENSES *Tuition (state resident):* Part-time: $568.50 per course. *Tuition (nonresident):* Part-time: $1252.50 per course. *Tuition (international):* Part-time: $1252.50 per course. *Required fees:* Part-time: $304.50 per course.

FINANCIAL AID (2007–08) 221 students received aid, including grants, loans, research assistantships, scholarships, and work study. Aid is available to part-time students. *Financial aid application deadline:* 4/15.

Financial Aid Contact Carolyn Mallory, Director of Financial Aid, 3007 North Ben Wilson, Victoria, TX 77901. *Phone:* 361-570-4130. *Fax:* 361-570-4132. *E-mail:* malloryc@uhv.edu.

INTERNATIONAL STUDENTS 7% of students enrolled are international students. *Services and facilities:* Housing location assistance, Orientation, Visa Services. Financial aid is not available to international students. *Required with application:* TOEFL with recommended score of 213 (computer), 550 (paper), or 79 (Internet); proof of adequate funds; proof of health/immunizations.

International Student Contact Elois Kraatz, International Student Coordinator, 3007 North Ben Wilson, Victoria, TX 77901. *Phone:* 361-570-4112. *Fax:* 361-570-4114. *E-mail:* kraatze@uhv.edu.

APPLICATION *Required:* GMAT, application form, baccalaureate/first degree, transcripts of college work. *Application fee:* $0. Applications for domestic and international students are processed on a rolling basis.

Application Contact Kristen Morgenroth, Admissions Analyst, 3007 North Ben Wilson, Victoria, TX 77901. *Phone:* 361-570-4122. *Fax:* 361-570-4114. *E-mail:* morgenrothk@uhv.edu.

University of Mary Hardin-Baylor
College of Business

Belton, Texas

Phone: 254-295-4647 **Fax:** 254-295-4651 **E-mail:** chrisann.merriman@umhb.edu

Business Program(s) Web Site: http://www.umhb.edu

DEGREE MBA

MBA—Master of Business Administration Full-time and part-time. At least 36 total credits required. 12 to 60 months to complete program. *Concentration:* management.

RESOURCES AND SERVICES Access to Internet/World Wide Web, online (class) registration, and online grade reports available. *Personal computer requirements:* Graduate business students are strongly recommended to purchase or lease a personal computer. *Placement services include:* Career placement, career counseling/planning, career fairs, job interviews arranged, and resume preparation.

Application Contact Dr. Chrisann Merriman, MBA Program Director, UMHB Station Box 8018, 900 College Street, Belton, TX 76513-2599. *Phone:* 254-295-4647. *Fax:* 254-295-4651. *E-mail:* chrisann.merriman@umhb.edu.

University of North Texas
College of Business Administration

Denton, Texas

Phone: 940-369-8977 **Fax:** 940-369-8978 **E-mail:** denise.galubenski@unt.edu

Business Program(s) Web Site: http://www.coba.unt.edu/advising/mba/

Graduate Business Unit Enrollment *Total:* 673 (429 full-time; 244 part-time; 299 women; 109 international). *Average Age:* 28.

Graduate Business Faculty *Total:* 118 (104 full-time; 14 part-time).

Admissions *Applied:* 529. *Admitted:* 268. *Enrolled:* 182. *Average GMAT:* 540. *Average GPA:* 3.35

Academic Calendar Semesters.

Accreditation AACSB—The Association to Advance Collegiate Schools of Business.

After Graduation (Class of 2006–07) *Employed within 3 months of graduation:* 85%. *Average starting salary:* $61,335.

DEGREES MBA • MBA/MS • MS

MBA—Master of Business Administration Full-time and part-time. Distance learning option. 36 total credits required. 18 to 72 months to complete program. *Concentrations:* decision sciences, finance, health administration, information technology, logistics, marketing, operations management, organizational behavior/development, strategic management, supply chain management.

MBA/MS—MBA in Operations and MS in Engineering Technology Full-time and part-time. Distance learning option. Must meet the admissions standards for both programs. 54 to 70 total credits required. 36 to 72 months to complete program. *Concentrations:* engineering, operations management.

MBA/MS—MBA in Operations and MS in Hospitality Management Full-time. Distance learning option. Must meet the admissions standards for both programs. 54 to 70 total credits required. 36 to 72 months to complete program. *Concentrations:* hospitality management, operations management.

MBA/MS—MBA in Operations and MS in Industrial, Technical, Merchandising and Fabric Analytics Full-time and part-time. Distance learning option. Must meet the admission standards of both programs. 54

to 70 total credits required. Maximum of 72 months to complete program. *Concentrations:* industrial administration/management, operations management.

MS—Master of Science in Taxation Full-time and part-time. At least 36 total credits required. Maximum of 72 months to complete program. *Concentration:* taxation.

MS—Master of Science with Various Concentrations Full-time and part-time. Distance learning option. 36 total credits required. 24 to 72 months to complete program. *Concentrations:* accounting, decision sciences, finance, information technology, real estate.

RESOURCES AND SERVICES 3,000 on-campus PCs are available to graduate business students. Access to Internet/World Wide Web, online (class) registration, and online grade reports available. *Personal computer requirements:* Graduate business students are not required to have a personal computer. *Special opportunities include:* An international exchange program and an internship program are available. *Placement services include:* Alumni network, career placement, job search course, career counseling/planning, electronic job bank, resume referral, career fairs, job interviews arranged, resume preparation, and career library.

EXPENSES *Tuition (state resident):* Full-time: $3862.08. Part-time: $160.92 per credit hour. *Tuition (nonresident):* Full-time: $11,932. Part-time: $441.92 per credit hour. *Tuition (international):* Full-time: $11,931.84. Part-time: $441.92 per credit hour. *Required fees:* Full-time: $638.85. Part-time: $356.85 per course. Tuition and/or fees vary by class time, campus location, and academic program. *Graduate housing:* Room and board costs vary by campus location, number of occupants, type of accommodation, and type of board plan. *Typical cost:* $5902.16 (including board), $3702 (room only).

FINANCIAL AID (2007–08) Fellowships, grants, loans, research assistantships, scholarships, teaching assistantships, and work study. Aid is available to part-time students. *Financial aid application deadline:* 2/22.

Financial Aid Contact Lisa Goodwin, Assistant Director, PO Box 311370, Denton, TX 76203-1370. *Phone:* 877-881-1014. *Fax:* 940-565-2738. *E-mail:* finaid@unt.edu.

INTERNATIONAL STUDENTS 16% of students enrolled are international students. *Services and facilities:* Counseling/support services, ESL/language courses, Housing location assistance, International student housing, International student organization, Language tutoring, Orientation, Visa Services. Financial aid is available to international students. *Required with application:* TOEFL with recommended score of 213 (computer) or 550 (paper); proof of adequate funds; proof of health/immunizations.

International Student Contact International Office, PO Box 311067, Denton, TX 76203-1067. *Phone:* 940-565-2442. *Fax:* 940-565-4822. *E-mail:* international@unt.edu.

APPLICATION *Required:* GMAT, application form, baccalaureate/first degree, essay, 3 letters of recommendation, resume/curriculum vitae, transcripts of college work. School will accept GRE. *Recommended:* Work experience. *Application fee:* $50, $75 (international). Applications for domestic and international students are processed on a rolling basis.

Application Contact Mrs. Denise Galubenski, Graduate Program Advisor, PO Box 311160, Denton, TX 76203-1160. *Phone:* 940-369-8977. *Fax:* 940-369-8978. *E-mail:* denise.galubenski@unt.edu.

University of Phoenix–Dallas Campus

College of Graduate Business and Management

Dallas, Texas

Phone: 480-317-6200 **Fax:** 480-643-1479 **E-mail:** beth.barilla@phoenix.edu

Business Program(s) Web Site: http://www.phoenix.edu

DEGREES MBA • MM

MBA—Accounting Full-time. At least 54 total credits required. *Concentration:* accounting.

MBA—Global Management Full-time. At least 45 total credits required. *Concentration:* international business.

MBA—Human Resource Management Full-time. At least 45 total credits required. *Concentration:* human resources management.

MBA—Marketing Full-time. At least 45 total credits required. *Concentration:* marketing.

MBA—Public Administration Full-time. At least 45 total credits required. *Concentration:* public policy and administration.

MBA—e-Business Full-time. At least 46 total credits required. *Concentration:* electronic commerce (E-commerce).

MBA—Master of Business Administration Full-time. At least 39 total credits required. *Concentration:* administration.

MM—Master of Management Full-time. At least 39 total credits required. *Concentration:* management.

RESOURCES AND SERVICES Access to online grade reports available. *Personal computer requirements:* Graduate business students are strongly recommended to purchase or lease a personal computer. *Placement services include:* Alumni network.

Application Contact Beth Barilla, Associate Vice President of Student Admissions and Services, Mail Stop AA-K101, 4615 East Elwood Street, Phoenix, AZ 85040-1958. *Phone:* 480-317-6200. *Fax:* 480-643-1479. *E-mail:* beth.barilla@phoenix.edu.

University of Phoenix–Houston Campus

College of Graduate Business and Management

Houston, Texas

Phone: 480-317-6200 **Fax:** 480-643-1479 **E-mail:** beth.barilla@phoenix.edu

Business Program(s) Web Site: http://www.phoenix.edu

DEGREES M Mgt • MA • MBA • MM

M Mgt—Master of Management Full-time. At least 39 total credits required. *Concentration:* management.

MA—Organizational Management Full-time. At least 40 total credits required. *Concentration:* organizational management.

MBA—Global Management Full-time. At least 45 total credits required. *Concentration:* international business.

MBA—Human Resource Management Full-time. At least 45 total credits required. *Concentration:* human resources management.

MBA—Public Administration Full-time. At least 45 total credits required. *Concentration:* public policy and administration.

MBA—e-Business Full-time. At least 45 total credits required. *Concentration:* electronic commerce (E-commerce).

MBA—Master of Business Administration Full-time. At least 45 total credits required. *Concentration:* administration.

MM—Human Resources Management Full-time. At least 39 total credits required. *Concentrations:* human resources management, management.

RESOURCES AND SERVICES Access to online grade reports available. *Personal computer requirements:* Graduate business students are strongly recommended to purchase or lease a personal computer. *Placement services include:* Alumni network.

University of Phoenix–Houston Campus (continued)

Application Contact Beth Barilla, Associate Vice President of Student Admissions and Services, Mail Stop AA-K101, 4615 East Elwood Street, Phoenix, AZ 85040-1958. *Phone:* 480-317-6200. *Fax:* 480-643-1479. *E-mail:* beth.barilla@phoenix.edu.

University of St. Thomas
Cameron School of Business
Houston, Texas

Phone: 713-525-2101 **Fax:** 713-525-2110 **E-mail:** flanags@stthom.edu

Business Program(s) Web Site: http://www.stthom.edu/bschool/index.html

Graduate Business Unit Enrollment *Total:* 535 (157 full-time; 378 part-time; 272 women; 103 international). *Average Age:* 31.

Graduate Business Faculty *Total:* 31 (20 full-time; 11 part-time).

Admissions *Applied:* 204. *Admitted:* 151. *Enrolled:* 103. *Average GMAT:* 464.

Academic Calendar Semesters.

Accreditation ACBSP—The American Council of Business Schools and Programs.

DEGREES MBA • MSA

MBA—Master of Business Administration Full-time and part-time. At least 36 total credits required. Maximum of 72 months to complete program. *Concentrations:* accounting, finance, international business, management information systems, marketing.

MSA—Master of Science in Accounting Full-time and part-time. At least 36 total credits required. Maximum of 72 months to complete program. *Concentration:* accounting.

RESOURCES AND SERVICES 367 on-campus PCs are available to graduate business students. Access to Internet/World Wide Web, online (class) registration, and online grade reports available. *Personal computer requirements:* Graduate business students are strongly recommended to purchase or lease a personal computer. *Special opportunities include:* An internship program is available. *Placement services include:* Career counseling/planning, electronic job bank, resume referral, career fairs, job interviews arranged, resume preparation, and career library.

EXPENSES *Tuition:* Full-time: $12,690. Part-time: $705 per credit. *Tuition (international):* Full-time: $12,690. Part-time: $705 per credit. *Required fees:* Full-time: $124.

FINANCIAL AID (2007–08) 185 students received aid, including grants, loans, and scholarships. Aid is available to part-time students. *Financial aid application deadline:* 3/1.

Financial Aid Contact Mr. Scott Moore, Dean of Scholarships and Financial Aid, 3800 Montrose Boulevard, Houston, TX 77006-4696. *Phone:* 713-942-3465. *Fax:* 713-525-2142. *E-mail:* finaid@stthom.edu.

INTERNATIONAL STUDENTS 19% of students enrolled are international students. *Services and facilities:* Counseling/support services, International student organization, Orientation, Visa Services. Financial aid is available to international students. *Required with application:* TOEFL with recommended score of 213 (computer) or 550 (paper); proof of adequate funds.

International Student Contact Ms. Shanna Guerra, International Student Advisor, 3800 Montrose Boulevard, Houston, TX 77006-4696. *Phone:* 713-525-3503. *Fax:* 713-525-6968. *E-mail:* sguerra@stthom.edu.

APPLICATION *Required:* GMAT, application form, baccalaureate/first degree, 3 letters of recommendation, transcripts of college work. School will accept GRE. *Application fee:* $35. *Deadlines:* 7/15 for fall, 11/3 for spring, 4/7 for summer, 6/30 for fall (international), 10/20 for spring (international), 3/30 for summer (international).

Application Contact Mr. Sandra Flanagan, Admissions Coordinator, 3800 Montrose Boulevard, Houston, TX 77006-4696. *Phone:* 713-525-2101. *Fax:* 713-525-2110. *E-mail:* flanags@stthom.edu.

The University of Texas at Arlington
College of Business Administration
Arlington, Texas

Phone: 817-272-3005 **Fax:** 817-272-5799 **E-mail:** admit@uta.edu

Business Program(s) Web Site: http://www2.uta.edu/gradbiz

Graduate Business Unit Enrollment *Total:* 1,322 (540 full-time; 782 part-time; 562 women; 353 international). *Average Age:* 31.

Graduate Business Faculty *Total:* 136 (106 full-time; 30 part-time).

Admissions *Applied:* 902. *Admitted:* 362. *Enrolled:* 296. *Average GMAT:* 540. *Average GPA:* 3.3

Academic Calendar Semesters.

Accreditation AACSB—The Association to Advance Collegiate Schools of Business.

DEGREES M Sc • MA • MBA • MPA • MS

M Sc—Master of Science in Quantitative Finance Full-time and part-time. 36 to 51 total credits required. 12 to 72 months to complete program. *Concentrations:* finance, financial economics, financial management/planning.

MA—Master of Arts in Economics Full-time and part-time. 30 to 36 total credits required. 12 to 72 months to complete program. *Concentration:* economics.

MBA—Online Master of Business Administration Part-time. Distance learning option. 36 to 48 total credits required. 14 to 72 months to complete program. *Concentration:* general MBA.

MBA—Professional Master of Business Administration Part-time. 45 total credits required. Maximum of 28 months to complete program. *Concentration:* general MBA.

MBA—Master of Business Administration Full-time and part-time. 36 to 45 total credits required. 12 to 72 months to complete program. *Concentrations:* accounting, decision sciences, economics, electronic commerce (E-commerce), finance, international business, management, management information systems, management science, management systems analysis, marketing, operations management, real estate, system management, technology management.

MPA—Master of Professional Accountancy Full-time and part-time. 39 to 60 total credits required. 14 to 72 months to complete program. *Concentration:* accounting.

MS—Master of Science in Accounting Full-time and part-time. 36 to 75 total credits required. 14 to 72 months to complete program. *Concentrations:* accounting, system management.

MS—Master of Science in Health Care Administration Full-time and part-time. 36 total credits required. 24 months to complete program. *Concentration:* health care.

MS—Master of Science in Human Resource Management Full-time and part-time. 30 to 57 total credits required. 12 to 72 months to complete program. *Concentrations:* human resources management, industrial/labor relations.

MS—Master of Science in Information Systems Full-time and part-time. 33 to 45 total credits required. 14 to 72 months to complete program. *Concentrations:* electronic commerce (E-commerce), information management, management information systems, management systems analysis, system management, technology management.

MS—Master of Science in Marketing Research Full-time and part-time. 36 to 67 total credits required. 12 to 72 months to complete program. *Concentration:* marketing research.

MS—Master of Science in Real Estate Full-time and part-time. 30 to 57 total credits required. 12 to 72 months to complete program. *Concentration:* real estate.

MS—Master of Science in Taxation Full-time and part-time. 36 to 75 total credits required. 14 to 72 months to complete program. *Concentration:* taxation.

RESOURCES AND SERVICES 835 on-campus PCs are available to graduate business students. Access to Internet/World Wide Web, online (class) registration, and online grade reports available. *Personal computer requirements:* Graduate business students are not required to have a personal computer. *Special opportunities include:* An international exchange program and an internship program are available. *Placement services include:* Alumni network, career placement, job search course, career counseling/planning, electronic job bank, resume referral, career fairs, job interviews arranged, resume preparation, and career library.

EXPENSES *Tuition (state resident):* Full-time: $7310. *Tuition (nonresident):* Full-time: $12,368. *Tuition (international):* Full-time: $12,538. *Graduate housing:* Room and board costs vary by campus location, number of occupants, type of accommodation, and type of board plan.

FINANCIAL AID (2007–08) 316 students received aid, including fellowships, loans, research assistantships, and scholarships. Aid is available to part-time students. *Financial aid application deadline:* 5/15.

Financial Aid Contact Karen Krause, Director of Financial Aid, UTA Box 19199, Arlington, TX 76019-0199. *Phone:* 817-272-3568. *Fax:* 817-272-3555. *E-mail:* fao@uta.edu.

INTERNATIONAL STUDENTS 27% of students enrolled are international students. *Services and facilities:* Counseling/support services, ESL/language courses, Housing location assistance, International student organization, Orientation, Visa Services. Financial aid is available to international students. *Required with application:* TOEFL with recommended score of 213 (computer) or 550 (paper); proof of adequate funds; proof of health/immunizations.

International Student Contact Judy Young, Director of International Office, UTA Box 19028, Arlington, TX 76019. *Phone:* 817-272-2355. *Fax:* 817-272-5005. *E-mail:* international@uta.edu.

APPLICATION *Required:* GMAT, application form, baccalaureate/first degree, essay, 3 letters of recommendation, personal statement, transcripts of college work. School will accept GRE. *Recommended:* Resume/curriculum vitae, 2 years of work experience. *Application fee:* $30, $60 (international). Applications for domestic and international students are processed on a rolling basis.

Application Contact Becky Neilson, Director for Graduate Business Services, UTA Box 19376, Arlington, TX 76019-0376. *Phone:* 817-272-3005. *Fax:* 817-272-5799. *E-mail:* admit@uta.edu.

See full description on page 746.

The University of Texas at Austin
Programs in MBA

Austin, Texas

Phone: 512-471-7698 **Fax:** 512-471-4131 **E-mail:** mccombsmba@mccombs.utexas.edu

Business Program(s) Web Site: http://mba.mccombs.utexas.edu

Graduate Business Unit Enrollment *Total:* 1,655 (1,438 full-time; 217 part-time; 490 women; 496 international). *Average Age:* 28.

Graduate Business Faculty *Total:* 147 (121 full-time; 26 part-time).

Admissions *Applied:* 2,550. *Admitted:* 1,046. *Enrolled:* 654. *Average GMAT:* 673. *Average GPA:* 3.38

Academic Calendar Semesters.

Accreditation AACSB—The Association to Advance Collegiate Schools of Business.

After Graduation (Class of 2006–07) *Employed within 3 months of graduation:* 94%. *Average starting salary:* $93,649.

DEGREES JD/MBA • MBA • MBA/MA • MBA/MPA • MBA/MS • MPA

JD/MBA—MBA/JD Full-time. At least 116 total credits required. 48 to 60 months to complete program. *Concentrations:* accounting, entrepreneurship, finance, information management, international business, investments and securities, management, marketing, operations management, other, strategic management.

MBA—Texas Evening MBA Part-time. 2 years of post-baccalaureate work experience required (average is 5.8 years). At least 48 total credits required. 33 months to complete program. *Concentration:* general MBA.

MBA—Texas Executive MBA Part-time. 5 years of business experience required (average is 11). At least 42 total credits required. 22 months to complete program. *Concentration:* executive programs.

MBA—Texas Executive MBA at Mexico City Part-time. 5 years of business experience required (average is 7). At least 42 total credits required. 22 months to complete program. *Concentration:* executive programs.

MBA—Texas MBA Full-time. 2 years of post-baccalaureate work experience required (average is 5 years). 60 total credits required. 21 months to complete program. *Concentrations:* accounting, entrepreneurship, finance, information management, international business, investments and securities, management, marketing, operations management, other, strategic management.

MBA—Texas MBA at Dallas/Fort Worth Part-time. 2 years of post-baccalaureate work experience required (average is 6.5 years). At least 48 total credits required. 22 months to complete program. *Concentration:* general MBA.

MBA—Texas MBA at Houston Part-time. 2 years of post-baccalaureate work experience required (average is 6.5 years). At least 48 total credits required. 22 months to complete program. *Concentration:* general MBA.

MBA/MA—MBA/MA in Advertising Full-time. 79 to 82 total credits required. 36 to 48 months to complete program. *Concentrations:* accounting, entrepreneurship, finance, information management, international business, investments and securities, management, marketing, operations management, other, strategic management.

MBA/MA—MBA/MA in Asian Studies Full-time. 79 to 82 total credits required. 36 to 48 months to complete program. *Concentrations:* accounting, entrepreneurship, finance, information management, international business, investments and securities, management, marketing, operations management, other, strategic management.

MBA/MA—MBA/MA in Communications Studies Full-time. 79 to 82 total credits required. 36 to 48 months to complete program. *Concentrations:* accounting, entrepreneurship, finance, information management, international business, investments and securities, management, marketing, operations management, other, strategic management.

MBA/MA—MBA/MA in Journalism Full-time. 79 to 82 total credits required. 36 to 48 months to complete program. *Concentrations:* accounting, entrepreneurship, finance, information management, international business, investments and securities, management, marketing, operations management, other, strategic management.

MBA/MA—MBA/MA in Latin American Studies Full-time. 79 to 82 total credits required. 36 to 48 months to complete program. *Concentrations:* accounting, entrepreneurship, finance, information management, international business, investments and securities, management, marketing, operations management, other, strategic management.

MBA/MA—MBA/MA in Middle Eastern Studies Full-time. 79 to 82 total credits required. 36 to 48 months to complete program. *Concentrations:* accounting, entrepreneurship, finance, information management, international business, investments and securities, management, marketing, operations management, other, strategic management.

MBA/MA—MBA/MA in Post-Soviet/Eastern European Studies Full-time. 79 to 82 total credits required. 36 to 48 months to complete program. *Concentrations:* accounting, entrepreneurship, finance, information management, international business, investments and securities, management, marketing, operations management, other, strategic management.

The University of Texas at Austin (continued)

MBA/MA—MBA/MA in Radio, TV and Film Full-time. 79 to 82 total credits required. 36 to 48 months to complete program. *Concentrations:* accounting, entrepreneurship, finance, information management, international business, investments and securities, management, marketing, operations management, other, strategic management.

MBA/MPA—MBA/Master of Public Affairs Full-time. At least 79 total credits required. 36 to 48 months to complete program. *Concentrations:* accounting, entrepreneurship, finance, information management, international business, investments and securities, management, marketing, operations management, other, strategic management.

MBA/MS—MBA/MS in Nursing Full-time. At least 82 total credits required. 36 to 48 months to complete program. *Concentrations:* accounting, entrepreneurship, finance, information management, international business, investments and securities, management, marketing, operations management, other, strategic management.

MPA—Master of Professional Accounting Full-time. 37 to 43 total credits required. 11 to 24 months to complete program. *Concentrations:* accounting, financial management/planning, taxation.

RESOURCES AND SERVICES 500 on-campus PCs are available to graduate business students. Access to Internet/World Wide Web, online (class) registration, and online grade reports available. *Personal computer requirements:* Graduate business students are required to have a personal computer. *Special opportunities include:* An international exchange program and an internship program are available. *Placement services include:* Alumni network, career placement, job search course, career counseling/planning, electronic job bank, resume referral, career fairs, job interviews arranged, resume preparation, and career library.

EXPENSES *Tuition (state resident):* Full-time: $14,882. *Tuition (nonresident):* Full-time: $31,686. *Tuition (international):* Full-time: $31,686. *Required fees:* Full-time: $7536.

FINANCIAL AID (2007–08) 275 students received aid, including fellowships, grants, loans, research assistantships, scholarships, teaching assistantships, and work study. Aid is available to part-time students. *Financial aid application deadline:* 3/31.

Financial Aid Contact Financial Aid Officer, 1 University Station, B6004, Austin, TX 78712-0205. *Phone:* 512-471-7698. *Fax:* 512-471-4131. *E-mail:* financialaid@mccombs.utexas.edu.

INTERNATIONAL STUDENTS 30% of students enrolled are international students. *Services and facilities:* Counseling/support services, ESL/language courses, International student organization, Language tutoring, Orientation, Visa Services. Financial aid is available to international students. *Required with application:* TOEFL with recommended score of 260 (computer), 620 (paper), or 100 (Internet); proof of adequate funds; proof of health/immunizations.

International Student Contact Ms. Teri Albrecht, Director, International Student and Scholar Services, International Office, PO Drawer A, Austin, TX 78713-8901. *Phone:* 512-471-2477. *Fax:* 512-471-8848. *E-mail:* teri@austin.utexas.edu.

APPLICATION *Required:* GMAT, application form, baccalaureate/first degree, essay, interview, 2 letters of recommendation, resume/curriculum vitae, transcripts of college work, 2 years of work experience. *Application fee:* $125. Applications for domestic and international students are processed on a rolling basis.

Application Contact Ms. Tina Mabley, Director of Admissions, MBA Program, 1 University Station, B6004, Austin, TX 78712-0205. *Phone:* 512-471-7698. *Fax:* 512-471-4131. *E-mail:* mccombsmba@mccombs.utexas.edu.

The University of Texas at Brownsville

School of Business

Brownsville, Texas

Phone: 956-882-7787 **E-mail:** mari.montelongo@utb.edu

Business Program(s) Web Site: http://www.utb.edu/vpaa/graduate

Graduate Business Unit Enrollment *Total:* 148 (8 full-time; 140 part-time; 26 international).

Graduate Business Faculty *Total:* 18 (17 full-time; 1 part-time).

Admissions *Applied:* 66. *Admitted:* 40. *Enrolled:* 37.

Academic Calendar Semesters.

DEGREES MBA • MBA/MPH

MBA—Master of Business Administration Full-time and part-time. Distance learning option. 30 to 51 total credits required. 12 to 84 months to complete program. *Concentration:* general MBA.

MBA/MPH—Master of Business Administration/Master of Public Health Part-time. 51 to 76 total credits required. *Concentration:* other.

RESOURCES AND SERVICES Access to Internet/World Wide Web, online (class) registration, and online grade reports available. *Personal computer requirements:* Graduate business students are strongly recommended to purchase or lease a personal computer.

FINANCIAL AID (2007–08) Aid is available to part-time students.

Financial Aid Contact Ms. Mari F. Chapa, Director of Financial Aid, Financial Aid Office, Tandy 206, 80 Fort Brown, Brownsville, TX 78520-4991. *Phone:* 956-544-8265. *Fax:* 956-544-8229. *E-mail:* mchapa@utb.edu.

INTERNATIONAL STUDENTS 18% of students enrolled are international students. Financial aid is not available to international students.

International Student Contact Ms. Mari Montelongo, Graduate Studies Specialist, 80 Fort Brown, Brownsville, TX 78520. *Phone:* 956-882-7787. *E-mail:* mari.montelongo@utb.edu.

APPLICATION *Application fee:* $35. Applications for domestic and international students are processed on a rolling basis.

Application Contact Mrs. Mari Montelongo, Graduate Studies Specialist, 80 Fort Brown, Brownsville, TX 78520-4991. *Phone:* 956-882-7787. *E-mail:* mari.montelongo@utb.edu.

The University of Texas at Dallas

School of Management

Richardson, Texas

Phone: 972-883-2701 **Fax:** 972-883-6425 **E-mail:** davidr@utdallas.edu

Business Program(s) Web Site: http://som.utdallas.edu/

Graduate Business Unit Enrollment *Total:* 2,335 (977 full-time; 1,358 part-time; 1,381 women; 650 international). *Average Age:* 32.

Graduate Business Faculty *Total:* 146 (112 full-time; 34 part-time).

Admissions *Applied:* 1,279. *Admitted:* 702. *Enrolled:* 629. *Average GMAT:* 586. *Average GPA:* 3.28

Academic Calendar Semesters.

Accreditation AACSB—The Association to Advance Collegiate Schools of Business.

After Graduation (Class of 2006–07) *Employed within 3 months of graduation:* 94%. *Average starting salary:* $73,334.

DEGREES MA • MBA • MS • MSIT

MA—Master of Arts in International Management Studies Full-time and part-time. Distance learning option. At least 36 total credits required. 12 to 60 months to complete program. *Concentrations:* international development management, international management.

MBA—Executive Master of Business Administration Part-time. At least 53 total credits required. 24 months to complete program. *Concentration:* executive programs.

MBA—Full-Time (Cohort) Master of Business Administration Full-time. At least 53 total credits required. 16 months to complete program. *Concentrations:* accounting, finance, management information systems, managerial economics, marketing, operations management, organizational behavior/development, strategic management, technology management.

MBA—Global Leadership Executive Master of Business Administration Part-time. Distance learning option. At least 53 total credits required. 24 months to complete program. *Concentration:* international management.

MBA—Global MBA Online Full-time and part-time. Distance learning option. At least 53 total credits required. 12 to 60 months to complete program. *Concentrations:* accounting, international business, management information systems.

MBA—Master of Business Administration in Project Management Part-time. Distance learning option. At least 53 total credits required. 24 months to complete program. *Concentration:* project management.

MBA—Professional MBA Full-time and part-time. Distance learning option. At least 53 total credits required. 12 to 60 months to complete program. *Concentrations:* accounting, finance, management information systems, managerial economics, marketing, operations management, organizational behavior/development, strategic management.

MS—Healthcare Management Full-time and part-time. Distance learning option. 18 to 36 total credits required. 12 to 60 months to complete program. *Concentrations:* accounting, finance, health care, information management, organizational behavior/development.

MS—Master of Science in Accounting and Information Management Full-time and part-time. At least 36 total credits required. 12 to 60 months to complete program. *Concentrations:* accounting, information management.

MS—Master of Science in Management and Administration Full-time and part-time. At least 36 total credits required. 12 to 60 months to complete program. *Concentrations:* electronic commerce (E-commerce), finance, organizational behavior/development, strategic management, supply chain management.

MSIT—Master of Science in Information Technology Management Full-time and part-time. At least 36 total credits required. 12 to 60 months to complete program. *Concentrations:* electronic commerce (E-commerce), information management, information technology, telecommunications management.

The University of Texas at Dallas School of Management (SOM) is a metropolitan research and teaching institution that offers master's programs ranging from a Cohort M.B.A. (full-time) to a highly popular professional M.B.A. (part-time) and Master of Science degrees in a variety of concentrations. In addition, the School offers a Master of Science in accountancy with an emphasis on management information systems, a Master of Science in information technology and management, a Master of Arts in international management, and extensive executive education programs.

Located in the North Dallas Telecom Corridor, the School's programs attract young, midlevel managers and upper-level executives seeking continuing management development. The curriculum focuses on global business issues, change management, and management of technology. SOM's active relationships with its Advisory Council and corporate partners enhance students' educational experiences and influence placement opportunities.

RESOURCES AND SERVICES 185 on-campus PCs are available to graduate business students. Access to Internet/World Wide Web, online (class) registration, and online grade reports available. *Personal computer requirements:* Graduate business students are strongly recommended to purchase or lease a personal computer. *Special opportunities include:* An international exchange program and an internship program are available. *Placement services include:* Alumni network, career placement, job search course, career counseling/planning, electronic job bank, resume referral, career fairs, job interviews arranged, resume preparation, and career library.

EXPENSES *Graduate housing:* Room and board costs vary by campus location, number of occupants, and type of accommodation. *Typical cost:* $6828 (including board).

FINANCIAL AID (2007–08) 80 students received aid, including grants, scholarships, and teaching assistantships. *Financial aid application deadline:* 3/31.

Financial Aid Contact Ms. Cathy Coursey, Associate Director of Financial Aid, 800 West Campbell Road, Mail Station MC12, Richardson, TX 75083-0688. *Phone:* 972-883-4027. *Fax:* 972-883-2947. *E-mail:* coursey@utdallas.edu.

INTERNATIONAL STUDENTS 28% of students enrolled are international students. *Services and facilities:* Counseling/support services, Housing location assistance, International student housing, International student organization, Orientation, Visa Services. Financial aid is available to international students. *Required with application:* TOEFL with recommended score of 213 (computer), 550 (paper), or 80 (Internet); proof of adequate funds; proof of health/immunizations.

International Student Contact Cristen Casey, Director of International Student Services, 800 West Campbell Road, Mail Station MC 36, Richardson, TX 75083-0688. *Phone:* 972-883-4189. *Fax:* 972-883-4010. *E-mail:* cristen@utdallas.edu.

APPLICATION *Required:* GMAT, application form, baccalaureate/first degree, 3 letters of recommendation, personal statement, transcripts of college work. School will accept GRE. *Recommended:* Resume/curriculum vitae, work experience. *Application fee:* $50, $150 (international). Applications for domestic and international students are processed on a rolling basis.

Application Contact David Ritchey, Associate Dean for Operations, 800 West Campbell Road, Mail Station SM 20, Richardson, TX 75083-0688. *Phone:* 972-883-2701. *Fax:* 972-883-6425. *E-mail:* davidr@utdallas.edu.

See full description on page 748.

The University of Texas at San Antonio
College of Business
San Antonio, Texas

Phone: 210-458-4641 **Fax:** 210-458-4398 **E-mail:** mbainfo@utsa.edu

Business Program(s) Web Site: http://business.utsa.edu/graduate

Graduate Business Unit Enrollment *Total:* 752 (318 full-time; 434 part-time; 288 women; 122 international). *Average Age:* 35.

Graduate Business Faculty *Total:* 106 (92 full-time; 14 part-time).

Admissions *Applied:* 306. *Admitted:* 211. *Enrolled:* 146. *Average GMAT:* 568. *Average GPA:* 3.21

Academic Calendar Semesters.

Accreditation AACSB—The Association to Advance Collegiate Schools of Business.

After Graduation (Class of 2006–07) *Average starting salary:* $54,129.

DEGREES MA • MBA • MS • MSMOT

MA—Master of Arts in Economics Full-time and part-time. 33 to 48 total credits required. 12 to 72 months to complete program. *Concentration:* economics.

MBA—Executive Master of Business Administration Full-time. At least 42 total credits required. 21 months to complete program. *Concentration:* executive programs.

MBA—Master of Business Administration in International Business Full-time and part-time. 39 to 63 total credits required. 12 to 72 months to complete program. *Concentration:* international business.

MBA—Master of Business Administration Full-time and part-time. 33 to 57 total credits required. 12 to 72 months to complete program. *Concentrations:* accounting, economics, finance, health care, management information systems, management science, marketing, project management, real estate, taxation, technology management, travel industry/tourism management.

The University of Texas at San Antonio (continued)

MS—Master of Accountancy Full-time and part-time. 30 to 60 total credits required. 12 to 72 months to complete program. *Concentrations:* accounting, taxation.

MS—Master of Science in Finance Full-time and part-time. 33 to 48 total credits required. 12 to 72 months to complete program. *Concentrations:* finance, real estate.

MS—Master of Science in Information Technology Full-time and part-time. 33 to 51 total credits required. 12 to 72 months to complete program. *Concentration:* information technology.

MS—Master of Science in Statistics Part-time. 36 to 42 total credits required. 12 to 72 months to complete program. *Concentration:* statistics.

MSMOT—Master of Science in Management of Technology Full-time and part-time. At least 39 total credits required. 12 to 72 months to complete program. *Concentration:* technology management.

RESOURCES AND SERVICES 550 on-campus PCs are available to graduate business students. Access to Internet/World Wide Web, online (class) registration, and online grade reports available. *Personal computer requirements:* Graduate business students are not required to have a personal computer. *Special opportunities include:* An international exchange program and an internship program are available. *Placement services include:* Alumni network, career placement, job search course, career counseling/planning, electronic job bank, resume referral, career fairs, job interviews arranged, resume preparation, and career library.

EXPENSES *Tuition (state resident):* Full-time: $6386.20. Part-time: $4389 per year. *Tuition (nonresident):* Full-time: $16,999. Part-time: $10,961 per year. *Tuition (international):* Full-time: $17,099.10. Part-time: $11,061 per year. Tuition and/or fees vary by academic program.

FINANCIAL AID (2007–08) Loans, research assistantships, scholarships, and teaching assistantships. Aid is available to part-time students. *Financial aid application deadline:* 3/31.

INTERNATIONAL STUDENTS 16% of students enrolled are international students. *Services and facilities:* Counseling/support services, ESL/language courses, Housing location assistance, International student housing, International student organization, Language tutoring, Orientation, Visa Services. Financial aid is available to international students. *Required with application:* TOEFL with recommended score of 173 (computer), 500 (paper), or 61 (Internet); proof of adequate funds. *Recommended with application:* Proof of health/immunizations.

APPLICATION *Required:* GMAT, application form, baccalaureate/first degree, personal statement, transcripts of college work. *Recommended:* Letter(s) of recommendation, resume/curriculum vitae. *Application fee:* $45, $80 (international). Applications for domestic and international students are processed on a rolling basis.

See full description on page 750.

The University of Texas at Tyler
College of Business and Technology

Tyler, Texas

Phone: 903-566-7433 **Fax:** 903-566-7372 **E-mail:** mary_fischer@mail.uttyl.edu

Business Program(s) Web Site: http://www.uttyler.edu/cbt/mba.htm

Accreditation AACSB—The Association to Advance Collegiate Schools of Business.

DEGREES MBA • MBA/MS • MS

MBA—Master of Business Administration Full-time and part-time. Distance learning option. At least 36 total credits required. 24 to 72 months to complete program. *Concentration:* health care.

MBA—Master of Business Administration Online Full-time and part-time. Distance learning option. 42 to 48 total credits required. 24 to 72 months to complete program. *Concentration:* general MBA.

MBA—Master of Business Administration Full-time and part-time. Distance learning option. At least 36 total credits required. 24 to 72 months to complete program. *Concentrations:* accounting, finance, management, marketing.

MBA/MS—Master of Science in Business Administration/Master of Science in Engineering Full-time and part-time. 36 to 60 total credits required. 24 to 72 months to complete program. *Concentrations:* administration, combined degrees, engineering.

MS—Master of Science in Technology Full-time and part-time. At least 36 total credits required. 12 to 45 months to complete program. *Concentration:* technology management.

RESOURCES AND SERVICES 45 on-campus PCs are available to graduate business students. Access to Internet/World Wide Web, online (class) registration, and online grade reports available. *Personal computer requirements:* Graduate business students are not required to have a personal computer. *Placement services include:* Career placement, career counseling/planning, and career fairs.

Application Contact Mary Fischer, Director of Graduate Programs in Business, 3900 University Boulevard, Tyler, TX 75799. *Phone:* 903-566-7433. *Fax:* 903-566-7372. *E-mail:* mary_fischer@mail.uttyl.edu.

The University of Texas of the Permian Basin
School of Business

Odessa, Texas

Phone: 915-552-2202 **Fax:** 915-552-2174 **E-mail:** gaulden_c@utpb.edu

Business Program(s) Web Site: http://www.utpb.edu

DEGREES MBA • MPA

MBA—Master of Business Administration in Management Full-time and part-time. Distance learning option. 36 to 48 total credits required. 18 to 96 months to complete program. *Concentration:* management.

MPA—Master of Professional Accountancy Full-time and part-time. 36 total credits required. 18 to 96 months to complete program. *Concentration:* accounting.

RESOURCES AND SERVICES 50 on-campus PCs are available to graduate business students. Access to Internet/World Wide Web, online (class) registration, and online grade reports available. *Personal computer requirements:* Graduate business students are strongly recommended to purchase or lease a personal computer. *Special opportunities include:* An internship program is available. *Placement services include:* Career placement, career counseling/planning, and career fairs.

Application Contact Corbett Gaulden, Jr., Coordinator of Graduate Business Studies, 4901 East University Boulevard, Odessa, TX 79762-8301. *Phone:* 915-552-2202. *Fax:* 915-552-2174. *E-mail:* gaulden_c@utpb.edu.

The University of Texas–Pan American
College of Business Administration

Edinburg, Texas

Phone: 956-381-3661 **Fax:** 956-381-2863 **E-mail:** delagarzaa@panam.edu

Business Program(s) Web Site: http://portal.utpa.edu/utpa_main/daa_home/coba_home/coba_mba

Graduate Business Unit Enrollment *Total:* 185 (42 full-time; 143 part-time; 90 women). *Average Age:* 33.

Graduate Business Faculty *Total:* 48 (47 full-time; 1 part-time).

Admissions *Applied:* 36. *Admitted:* 25. *Average GMAT:* 460. *Average GPA:* 3.1

Academic Calendar Semesters.

Accreditation AACSB—The Association to Advance Collegiate Schools of Business.

After Graduation (Class of 2006–07) *Employed within 3 months of graduation:* 90%.

DEGREE MBA

MBA—Master of Business Administration Full-time and part-time. Distance learning option. 36 to 48 total credits required. 18 to 84 months to complete program. *Concentrations:* accounting, general MBA.

RESOURCES AND SERVICES 55 on-campus PCs are available to graduate business students. Access to Internet/World Wide Web, online (class) registration, and online grade reports available. *Personal computer requirements:* Graduate business students are not required to have a personal computer. *Special opportunities include:* An international exchange program is available. *Placement services include:* Career placement, career counseling/planning, electronic job bank, resume referral, career fairs, job interviews arranged, and resume preparation.

EXPENSES *Tuition (state resident):* Full-time: $1512. Part-time: $84 per credit hour. *Tuition (nonresident):* Full-time: $6516. Part-time: $362 per credit hour. *Tuition (international):* Full-time: $6516. Part-time: $362 per credit hour. *Required fees:* Full-time: $2174. Part-time: $300 per credit hour. Tuition and/or fees vary by number of courses or credits taken and local reciprocity agreements. *Graduate housing:* Room and board costs vary by number of occupants, type of accommodation, and type of board plan. *Typical cost:* $6696 (including board).

FINANCIAL AID (2007–08) 8 students received aid, including fellowships and research assistantships. *Financial aid application deadline:* 7/1.

Financial Aid Contact Ms. Michelle Alverado, Director of Financial Aid, 1201 West University Drive, Edinburg, TX 78539. *Phone:* 956-381-2501. *Fax:* 956-381-2392. *E-mail:* michelle@panam.edu.

INTERNATIONAL STUDENTS *Services and facilities:* Counseling/support services, ESL/language courses, Housing location assistance, International student housing, International student organization, Language tutoring, Orientation, Visa Services. Financial aid is available to international students. *Required with application:* TOEFL with recommended score of 173 (computer) or 500 (paper); proof of adequate funds; proof of health/immunizations.

International Student Contact Mr. Philip Clay, International Student Advisor, 1201 West University Drive, Edinburg, TX 78539. *Phone:* 956-381-2647. *Fax:* 956-381-2661. *E-mail:* clayp@panam.edu.

APPLICATION *Required:* GMAT, application form, baccalaureate/first degree, transcripts of college work. *Recommended:* Letter(s) of recommendation, resume/curriculum vitae, work experience. *Application fee:* $35. Applications for domestic and international students are processed on a rolling basis.

Application Contact Adelita De La Garza, Administrative Clerk, Office of Graduate Admissions, 1201 West University Drive, Edinburg, TX 78539. *Phone:* 956-381-3661. *Fax:* 956-381-2863. *E-mail:* delagarzaa@panam.edu.

University of the Incarnate Word
H-E-B School of Business and Administration

San Antonio, Texas

Phone: 210-829-3924 **Fax:** 210-805-3564 **E-mail:** sdaly@uiwtx.edu

Business Program(s) Web Site: http://www.uiw.edu/heb/

Graduate Business Unit Enrollment *Total:* 425 (10 full-time; 415 part-time; 254 women; 40 international).

Graduate Business Faculty *Total:* 28 (17 full-time; 11 part-time).

Admissions *Average GMAT:* 400. *Average GPA:* 3.03

Academic Calendar Semesters.

Accreditation ACBSP—The American Council of Business Schools and Programs.

DEGREES MBA • MBA/MSN

MBA—Master of Business Administration *Concentrations:* general MBA, health care, international business, sports/entertainment management.

MBA/MSN—Master of Business Administration/Master of Science in Nursing Full-time and part-time. At least 66 total credits required. 24 to 86 months to complete program. *Concentration:* combined degrees.

RESOURCES AND SERVICES 225 on-campus PCs are available to graduate business students. Access to Internet/World Wide Web, online (class) registration, and online grade reports available. *Personal computer requirements:* Graduate business students are required to have a personal computer. *Special opportunities include:* An international exchange program is available. *Placement services include:* Alumni network, career placement, career counseling/planning, electronic job bank, resume referral, career fairs, job interviews arranged, resume preparation, and career library.

EXPENSES *Tuition:* Part-time: $605 per credit. *Tuition (international):* Part-time: $605 per credit. *Required fees:* Part-time: $32 per credit. *Graduate housing:* Room and board costs vary by number of occupants, type of accommodation, and type of board plan. *Typical cost:* $7040 (including board), $5440 (room only).

FINANCIAL AID (2007–08) 185 students received aid, including loans and work study. Aid is available to part-time students. *Financial aid application deadline:* 5/31.

Financial Aid Contact Ms. Amy Carcanagues, Director, Financial Assistance, 4301 Broadway, CPO#308, San Antonio, TX 78209. *Phone:* 210-829-6008. *Fax:* 210-283-5053. *E-mail:* amyc@uiwtx.edu.

INTERNATIONAL STUDENTS 9% of students enrolled are international students. *Services and facilities:* Counseling/support services, ESL/language courses, Housing location assistance, International student housing, International student organization, Language tutoring, Orientation, Visa Services. Financial aid is not available to international students. *Required with application:* TOEFL with recommended score of 220 (computer) or 560 (paper); proof of adequate funds; proof of health/immunizations.

International Student Contact Ms. Janet Kaufmann, Graduate Admissions Counselor, 4301 Broadway, CPO285, San Antonio, TX 78209. *Phone:* 210-805 3551. *Fax:* 210-829 3921. *E-mail:* jkaufman@uiwtx.edu.

APPLICATION *Required:* GMAT, application form, baccalaureate/first degree, transcripts of college work. School will accept GRE. *Recommended:* Interview, personal statement, resume/curriculum vitae, work experience. *Application fee:* $25. *Deadlines:* 6/1 for fall (international), 10/1 for spring (international), 2/1 for summer (international). Applications for domestic students are processed on a rolling basis.

Application Contact Dr. Shawn Daly, Dean, School of Business and Applied Arts and Sciences, UPO #123, 4301 Broadway, San Antonio, TX 78209. *Phone:* 210-829-3924. *Fax:* 210-805-3564. *E-mail:* sdaly@uiwtx.edu.

Wayland Baptist University
Graduate Programs

Plainview, Texas

Phone: 806-291-3414 **Fax:** 806-291-1950 **E-mail:** stantona@wbu.edu

Business Program(s) Web Site: http://www.wbu.edu

Wayland Baptist University (continued)

Graduate Business Unit Enrollment *Total:* 46 (4 full-time; 42 part-time; 20 women; 1 international). *Average Age:* 32.

Graduate Business Faculty 5 full-time.

Admissions *Applied:* 35. *Admitted:* 33. *Enrolled:* 15.

Academic Calendar Semesters.

DEGREES MA • MBA

MA—Master of Arts in Management Full-time and part-time. Distance learning option. At least 36 total credits required. 12 to 72 months to complete program. *Concentration:* management.

MBA—Master of Business Administration Full-time and part-time. At least 36 total credits required. 12 to 72 months to complete program. *Concentrations:* business studies, health care, human resources management, international management, management, management information systems.

RESOURCES AND SERVICES 47 on-campus PCs are available to graduate business students. Access to Internet/World Wide Web, online (class) registration, and online grade reports available. *Personal computer requirements:* Graduate business students are not required to have a personal computer. *Special opportunities include:* An internship program is available. *Placement services include:* Career placement, career counseling/planning, career fairs, job interviews arranged, resume preparation, and career library.

EXPENSES *Tuition:* Full-time: $5130. *Tuition (international):* Full-time: $5130. *Required fees:* Full-time: $600. Tuition and/or fees vary by campus location. *Graduate housing:* Room and board costs vary by type of accommodation and type of board plan. *Typical cost:* $3446 (including board), $1276 (room only).

FINANCIAL AID (2007–08) Grants, loans, scholarships, and work study. Aid is available to part-time students. *Financial aid application deadline:* 5/1.

Financial Aid Contact Mrs. Karen LaQuey, Director of Financial Aid, 1900 West 7th Street, CMB #597, Plainview, TX 79072-6998. *Phone:* 806-291-3520. *Fax:* 806-291-1956. *E-mail:* laquey@wbu.edu.

INTERNATIONAL STUDENTS 2% of students enrolled are international students. *Services and facilities:* Counseling/support services. Financial aid is available to international students. *Required with application:* TOEFL with recommended score of 173 (computer) or 500 (paper); proof of adequate funds; proof of health/immunizations.

International Student Contact Rosa Padilla, Admissions Representative, 1900 West 7th Street, CMB #712, Plainview, TX 79072. *Phone:* 806-291-3500. *E-mail:* admityou@wbu.edu.

APPLICATION *Required:* Application form, baccalaureate/first degree, personal statement, transcripts of college work. School will accept GMAT, GRE, and MAT. *Application fee:* $50. Applications for domestic and international students are processed on a rolling basis.

Application Contact Ms. Amanda Stanton, Graduate Services, 1900 West 7th Street, CMB #529, Plainview, TX 79072. *Phone:* 806-291-3414. *Fax:* 806-291-1950. *E-mail:* stantona@wbu.edu.

West Texas A&M University
College of Business

Canyon, Texas

Phone: 806-651-3866 **Fax:** 806-651-2927 **E-mail:** lmills@mail.wtamu.edu

Business Program(s) Web Site: http://www.wtamu.edu/academics/college-business.aspx

Graduate Business Unit Enrollment *Total:* 346 (97 full-time; 249 part-time; 148 women; 67 international). *Average Age:* 28.

Graduate Business Faculty 28 full-time.

Admissions *Applied:* 183. *Admitted:* 104. *Enrolled:* 87. *Average GMAT:* 525. *Average GPA:* 3.2

Academic Calendar Semesters.

Accreditation ACBSP—The American Council of Business Schools and Programs.

After Graduation (Class of 2006–07) *Employed within 3 months of graduation:* 90%. *Average starting salary:* $50,000.

DEGREES MBA • MPA • MS

MBA—Master of Business Administration Full-time and part-time. Distance learning option. 40 to 49 total credits required. 24 to 60 months to complete program. *Concentrations:* agribusiness, general MBA, health care, management, management information systems, marketing.

MPA—Master of Professional Accountancy Full-time and part-time. Distance learning option. 36 to 60 total credits required. 24 to 60 months to complete program. *Concentration:* accounting.

MS—Master of Science in Finance and Economics Full-time and part-time. Distance learning option. 36 to 60 total credits required. 24 to 60 months to complete program. *Concentrations:* economics, finance.

RESOURCES AND SERVICES 300 on-campus PCs are available to graduate business students. Access to Internet/World Wide Web, online (class) registration, and online grade reports available. *Personal computer requirements:* Graduate business students are strongly recommended to purchase or lease a personal computer. *Special opportunities include:* An international exchange program and an internship program are available. *Placement services include:* Career counseling/planning, career fairs, job interviews arranged, resume preparation, and career library.

EXPENSES *Tuition (state resident):* Full-time: $4042. *Tuition (nonresident):* Full-time: $9100. *Tuition (international):* Full-time: $9100. Tuition and/or fees vary by class time, number of courses or credits taken, and local reciprocity agreements. *Graduate housing:* Room and board costs vary by number of occupants, type of accommodation, and type of board plan. *Typical cost:* $5514 (including board), $3000 (room only).

FINANCIAL AID (2007–08) Grants, loans, research assistantships, scholarships, teaching assistantships, and work study. Aid is available to part-time students. *Financial aid application deadline:* 2/1.

Financial Aid Contact Jim Reed, Director of Student Financial Services, PO Box 60939, Canyon, TX 79016-0001. *Phone:* 806-651-2055. *Fax:* 806-651-2924. *E-mail:* financial@wtamu.edu.

INTERNATIONAL STUDENTS 19% of students enrolled are international students. *Services and facilities:* Counseling/support services, ESL/language courses, International student housing, International student organization, Orientation, Visa Services. Financial aid is available to international students. *Required with application:* TOEFL with recommended score of 550 (paper); proof of adequate funds; proof of health/immunizations.

International Student Contact Kristine Combs, Director of International Student Office, PO Box 60745, Canyon, TX 79016-0001. *Phone:* 806-651-2073. *Fax:* 806-651-2071. *E-mail:* kcombs@mail.wtamu.edu.

APPLICATION *Required:* GMAT, application form, baccalaureate/first degree, transcripts of college work. *Recommended:* Interview, resume/curriculum vitae. *Application fee:* $25, $75 (international). Applications for domestic and international students are processed on a rolling basis.

Application Contact Dr. LaVelle Mills, Associate Dean, PO Box 60768, Canyon, TX 79016-0001. *Phone:* 806-651-3866. *Fax:* 806-651-2927. *E-mail:* lmills@mail.wtamu.edu.

UTAH

Argosy University, Salt Lake City
College of Business

Draper, Utah

Phone: 801-601-5000 **Fax:** 801-601-4990

Business Program(s) Web Site: http://www.argosy.edu/saltlakecity

DEGREES DBA • MBA

DBA—Doctor of Business Administration (DBA) *Concentrations:* accounting, information systems, international business, management, marketing.

MBA—Master of Business Administration (MBA) *Concentrations:* finance, health administration, information systems, international business, management, marketing, public policy and administration.

Financial Aid Contact Director of Admissions, 121 Election Road, Suite 300, Draper, UT 84020. *Phone:* 801-601-5000. *Fax:* 801-601-4990.

International Student Contact Director of Admissions, 121 Election Road, Suite 300, Draper, UT 84020. *Phone:* 801-601-5000. *Fax:* 801-601-4990.

Application Contact Director of Admissions, 121 Election Road, Suite 300, Draper, UT 84020. *Phone:* 801-601-5000. *Fax:* 801-601-4990.

See full description on page 566.

Brigham Young University
Marriott School of Management

Provo, Utah

Phone: 801-422-3500 **Fax:** 801-422-0513 **E-mail:** mba@byu.edu

Business Program(s) Web Site: http://marriottschool.byu.edu

Accreditation AACSB—The Association to Advance Collegiate Schools of Business.

DEGREES JD/M Acc • JD/MBA • JD/MPA • M Acc • MBA • MBA/ MS • MISM • MPA

JD/M Acc—Juris Doctor/Master of Accountancy Full-time. Must apply and be admitted to both programs independently. At least 111 total credits required. 44 to 60 months to complete program. *Concentration:* combined degrees.

JD/MBA—Juris Doctor/Master of Business Administration Full-time. Must apply and be admitted to both programs independently. At least 132 total credits required. 44 to 60 months to complete program. *Concentration:* combined degrees.

JD/MPA—Juris Doctor/Master of Public Administration Full-time. Must apply and be admitted to both programs independently. At least 120 total credits required. 44 to 60 months to complete program. *Concentration:* combined degrees.

M Acc—Master of Accountancy Full-time. This program is an integrated 5-year Master's degree program for students who do their undergraduate work at Brigham Young University. It is a 2-year Master's degree for all others. At least 36 total credits required. 16 to 60 months to complete program. *Concentrations:* accounting, taxation.

MBA—Executive Master of Business Administration Part-time. 4 years of full-time professional work experience required. At least 53 total credits required. 22 months to complete program. *Concentration:* executive programs.

MBA—Master of Business Administration Full-time. At least 64 total credits required. 20 to 60 months to complete program. *Concentrations:* finance, marketing, organizational behavior/development, supply chain management.

MBA/MS—Interdisciplinary Product Development Master of Business Administration Full-time. Must apply and be admitted to both programs independently. At least 90 total credits required. 28 to 60 months to complete program. *Concentration:* combined degrees.

MISM—Master of Information Systems Management Full-time. At least 45 total credits required. 20 to 60 months to complete program. *Concentration:* management information systems.

MPA—Executive Master of Public Administration Part-time. Priority deadline is March 15 and final deadline is May 1. At least 45 total credits required. 34 to 60 months to complete program. *Concentration:* executive programs.

MPA—Master of Public Administration Full-time. At least 57 total credits required. 20 to 60 months to complete program. *Concentrations:* city/urban administration, financial management/planning, human resources management, nonprofit management.

RESOURCES AND SERVICES 1,281 on-campus PCs are available to graduate business students. Access to Internet/World Wide Web, online (class) registration, and online grade reports available. *Personal computer requirements:* Graduate business students are required to have a personal computer. *Special opportunities include:* An international exchange program and an internship program are available. *Placement services include:* Alumni network, career placement, career counseling/planning, electronic job bank, resume referral, career fairs, job interviews arranged, resume preparation, and career library.

Application Contact Mrs. Yvette Anderson, Admissions Coordinator, 640 TNRB, Provo, UT 84602-3184. *Phone:* 801-422-3500. *Fax:* 801-422-0513. *E-mail:* mba@byu.edu.

Southern Utah University
School of Business

Cedar City, Utah

Phone: 435-865-8157 **Fax:** 435-586-5493 **E-mail:** alger@suu.edu

Business Program(s) Web Site: http://www.suu.edu/business/

Graduate Business Unit Enrollment *Total:* 84 (59 full-time; 25 part-time; 26 women). *Average Age:* 29.

Graduate Business Faculty *Total:* 14 (12 full-time; 2 part-time).

Admissions *Applied:* 53. *Admitted:* 43. *Enrolled:* 41. *Average GMAT:* 500. *Average GPA:* 3.2

Academic Calendar Semesters.

Accreditation ACBSP—The American Council of Business Schools and Programs.

After Graduation (Class of 2006–07) *Employed within 3 months of graduation:* 100%.

DEGREES M Acc • MBA

M Acc—Master of Accountancy Full-time and part-time. At least 30 total credits required. 9 to 36 months to complete program. *Concentration:* accounting.

MBA—Master of Business Administration Full-time and part-time. 30 to 74 total credits required. *Concentration:* general MBA.

RESOURCES AND SERVICES 60 on-campus PCs are available to graduate business students. Access to Internet/World Wide Web, online (class) registration, and online grade reports available. *Personal computer requirements:* Graduate business students are not required to have a personal computer. *Special opportunities include:* An internship program is available. *Placement services include:* Alumni network, career placement, job search course, career counseling/planning, electronic job bank, resume referral, career fairs, job interviews arranged, resume preparation, and career library.

FINANCIAL AID (2007–08) Loans, research assistantships, scholarships, and work study.

Financial Aid Contact Ms. Dina Nielsen, Director of Financial Aid and Scholarships, 351 West Center Street, Cedar City, UT 84720. *Phone:* 435-586-7735. *Fax:* 435-586-7736. *E-mail:* nielsend@suu.edu.

INTERNATIONAL STUDENTS *Services and facilities:* Counseling/ support services, ESL/language courses, Visa Services. Financial aid is not available to international students. *Required with application:* Proof of adequate funds; proof of health/immunizations.

Southern Utah University (continued)

International Student Contact Lynne J. Brown, Director of Student Support Center, Sharwan Smith Student Center, 351 West Center Street, Cedar City, UT 84720. *Phone:* 435-586-7771. *Fax:* 435-586-8753. *E-mail:* brown_lj@suu.edu.

APPLICATION *Required:* GMAT, application form, baccalaureate/first degree, personal statement, transcripts of college work. *Application fee:* $50, $65 (international). Applications for domestic and international students are processed on a rolling basis.

Application Contact Paula Alger, Curriculum Coordinator and Adviser, Cedar City, UT 84720. *Phone:* 435-865-8157. *Fax:* 435-586-5493. *E-mail:* alger@suu.edu.

University of Phoenix–Utah Campus
College of Graduate Business and Management

Salt Lake City, Utah

Phone: 480-317-6200 **Fax:** 480-643-1479 **E-mail:** beth.barilla@phoenix.edu

Business Program(s) Web Site: http://www.phoenix.edu

DEGREES EMBA • M Mgt • MA • MBA

EMBA—Executive Master of Business Administration Full-time. At least 30 total credits required. *Concentration:* strategic management.

M Mgt—Human Resource Management Full-time. At least 39 total credits required. *Concentration:* human resources management.

M Mgt—Master of Management Full-time. At least 39 total credits required. *Concentration:* management.

MA—Organizational Management Full-time. At least 40 total credits required. *Concentration:* organizational management.

MBA—Accounting Full-time. At least 51 total credits required. *Concentration:* accounting.

MBA—Global Management Full-time. At least 45 total credits required. *Concentration:* international business.

MBA—Human Resource Management Full-time. At least 45 total credits required. *Concentration:* human resources management.

MBA—Marketing Full-time. At least 45 total credits required. *Concentration:* marketing.

MBA—Public Administration Full-time. At least 45 total credits required. *Concentration:* public policy and administration.

MBA—e-Business Full-time. At least 45 total credits required. *Concentration:* electronic commerce (E-commerce).

MBA—Master of Business Administration Full-time. At least 45 total credits required. *Concentration:* administration.

RESOURCES AND SERVICES Access to online grade reports available. *Personal computer requirements:* Graduate business students are strongly recommended to purchase or lease a personal computer. *Placement services include:* Alumni network.

Application Contact Beth Barilla, Associate Vice President of Student Admissions and Services, Mail Stop AA-K101, 4615 East Elwood Street, Phoenix, AZ 85040-1958. *Phone:* 480-317-6200. *Fax:* 480-643-1479. *E-mail:* beth.barilla@phoenix.edu.

Weber State University
John B. Goddard School of Business and Economics

Ogden, Utah

Phone: 801-626-7308 **Fax:** 801-626-7423 **E-mail:** mvaughan@weber.edu

Business Program(s) Web Site: http://goddard.weber.edu/

Graduate Business Unit Enrollment *Total:* 220 (93 full-time; 127 part-time; 52 women; 2 international). *Average Age:* 31.

Graduate Business Faculty *Total:* 10 (6 full-time; 4 part-time).

Admissions *Applied:* 138. *Admitted:* 118. *Enrolled:* 109. *Average GMAT:* 573. *Average GPA:* 3.43

Academic Calendar Semesters.

Accreditation AACSB—The Association to Advance Collegiate Schools of Business.

After Graduation (Class of 2006–07) *Employed within 3 months of graduation:* 76%.

DEGREES MBA • MS

MBA—Master of Business Administration Full-time and part-time. Distance learning option. At least 36 total credits required. 12 to 60 months to complete program. *Concentration:* general MBA.

MS—Master of Professional Accountancy Full-time and part-time. Distance learning option. At least 30 total credits required. 12 to 60 months to complete program. *Concentrations:* accounting, financial management/planning, taxation.

RESOURCES AND SERVICES 600 on-campus PCs are available to graduate business students. Access to Internet/World Wide Web, online (class) registration, and online grade reports available. *Personal computer requirements:* Graduate business students are not required to have a personal computer. *Special opportunities include:* An international exchange program and an internship program are available. *Placement services include:* Alumni network, career placement, job search course, career counseling/planning, electronic job bank, resume referral, career fairs, job interviews arranged, resume preparation, and career library.

EXPENSES *Tuition (state resident):* Full-time: $4225. Part-time: $2924 per year. *Tuition (nonresident):* Full-time: $11,096. Part-time: $7773 per year. *Tuition (international):* Full-time: $11,096. Part-time: $7773 per year. *Required fees:* Full-time: $574. Part-time: $423 per year. *Graduate housing:* Room and board costs vary by number of occupants, type of accommodation, and type of board plan. *Typical cost:* $6237 (including board), $2700 (room only).

FINANCIAL AID (2007–08) 29 students received aid, including research assistantships and scholarships. Aid is available to part-time students. *Financial aid application deadline:* 3/1.

Financial Aid Contact Michael Vaughan, Dean, School of Business and Economics, 3801 University Circle, Ogden, UT 84408-3801. *Phone:* 801-626-7308. *Fax:* 801-626-7423. *E-mail:* mvaughan@weber.edu.

INTERNATIONAL STUDENTS 0.9% of students enrolled are international students. *Services and facilities:* Counseling/support services, ESL/language courses, Housing location assistance, International student housing, International student organization, Language tutoring, Orientation, Visa Services. Financial aid is available to international students. *Required with application:* TOEFL with recommended score of 550 (paper); proof of adequate funds; proof of health/immunizations.

International Student Contact Morteza Emami, Coordinator, Services for International Students, 1107 University Circle, Ogden, UT 84408-1107. *Phone:* 801-626-7534. *Fax:* 801-626-7963. *E-mail:* memami@weber.edu.

APPLICATION *Required:* GMAT, application form, baccalaureate/first degree, essay, 3 letters of recommendation, personal statement, resume/curriculum vitae, transcripts of college work. *Recommended:* Work experience. *Application fee:* $60, $75 (international). *Deadlines:* 2/1 for fall, 11/1 for spring, 2/1 for fall (international), 11/1 for spring (international).

Application Contact Michael Vaughan, Dean, 3810 University Circle, Ogden, UT 84408-3801. *Phone:* 801-626-7308. *Fax:* 801-626-7423. *E-mail:* mvaughan@weber.edu.

Westminster College
The Bill and Vieve Gore School of Business

Salt Lake City, Utah

Phone: 801-832-2200 Ext. 2621 **E-mail:** amackin@westminstercollege.edu

Business Program(s) Web Site: http://www.westminstercollege.edu/mba/

Graduate Business Unit Enrollment *Total:* 387 (109 full-time; 278 part-time; 129 women; 9 international). *Average Age:* 32.

Graduate Business Faculty *Total:* 26 (17 full-time; 9 part-time).

Admissions *Applied:* 185. *Admitted:* 111. *Enrolled:* 103. *Average GMAT:* 550. *Average GPA:* 3.28

Academic Calendar 7-week modules.

Accreditation ACBSP—The American Council of Business Schools and Programs.

After Graduation (Class of 2006–07) *Employed within 3 months of graduation:* 96%. *Average starting salary:* $56,000.

DEGREES MBA

MBA—Master of Business Administration Full-time and part-time. At least 39 total credits required. *Concentrations:* accounting, economics, entrepreneurship, finance, general MBA, human resources management, information management, international business, marketing, organizational behavior/development, resources management.

MBA—Master of Business Administration in Technology Management Full-time and part-time. At least 39 total credits required. *Concentration:* technology management.

RESOURCES AND SERVICES 250 on-campus PCs are available to graduate business students. Access to Internet/World Wide Web, online (class) registration, and online grade reports available. *Personal computer requirements:* Graduate business students are strongly recommended to purchase or lease a personal computer. *Special opportunities include:* An international exchange program and an internship program are available. *Placement services include:* Alumni network, career placement, job search course, career counseling/planning, electronic job bank, career fairs, resume preparation, and career library.

EXPENSES *Tuition:* Full-time: $19,559. Part-time: $1003 per hour. *Tuition (international):* Full-time: $19,559. Part-time: $1003 per hour.

FINANCIAL AID (2007–08) 185 students received aid, including loans. Aid is available to part-time students. *Financial aid application deadline:* 4/15.

Financial Aid Contact Mr. Sean View, Director of Financial Aid, 1840 South 1300 East, Salt Lake City, UT 84105-3697. *Phone:* 801-832-2500 Ext. 2502. *E-mail:* sview@westminstercollege.edu.

INTERNATIONAL STUDENTS 2% of students enrolled are international students. *Services and facilities:* Counseling/support services, Housing location assistance, International student organization, Orientation. Financial aid is not available to international students. *Required with application:* TOEFL with recommended score of 213 (computer), 550 (paper), or 79 (Internet); proof of adequate funds.

International Student Contact Ms. Emily Edmonston, Assistant Director of Admission/International Recruiter, 1840 South 1300 East, Salt Lake City, UT 84105-3697. *Phone:* 801-832-2200 Ext. 2219. *E-mail:* eedmonston@westminstercollege.edu.

APPLICATION *Required:* Application form, baccalaureate/first degree, essay, 2 letters of recommendation, personal statement, resume/curriculum vitae, transcripts of college work. School will accept GMAT and GRE. *Recommended:* 3 years of work experience. *Application fee:* $40. Applications for domestic and international students are processed on a rolling basis.

Application Contact Mr. Ann Mackin, Director of Master of Business Administration, 1840 South 1300 East, Salt Lake City, UT 84105-3697. *Phone:* 801-832-2200 Ext. 2621. *E-mail:* amackin@westminstercollege.edu.

VERMONT

College of St. Joseph
Program in Master of Business Administration

Rutland, Vermont

Phone: 877-270-9998 **Fax:** 802-773-5900 **E-mail:** pryan@csj.edu

Business Program(s) Web Site: http://www.csj.edu

Graduate Business Unit Enrollment *Total:* 31 (2 full-time; 29 part-time; 10 women; 1 international). *Average Age:* 33.

Graduate Business Faculty *Total:* 12 (3 full-time; 9 part-time).

Admissions *Applied:* 14. *Admitted:* 13. *Enrolled:* 13. *Average GPA:* 3.1

Academic Calendar Continuous.

After Graduation (Class of 2006–07) *Employed within 3 months of graduation:* 100%.

DEGREE MBA

MBA—Master of Business Administration Full-time and part-time. 42 total credits required. 42 months to complete program. *Concentration:* general MBA.

RESOURCES AND SERVICES 34 on-campus PCs are available to graduate business students. Access to Internet/World Wide Web available. *Personal computer requirements:* Graduate business students are strongly recommended to purchase or lease a personal computer. *Special opportunities include:* An internship program is available. *Placement services include:* Alumni network, career counseling/planning, career fairs, resume preparation, and career library.

EXPENSES *Tuition:* Full-time: $6500. Part-time: $400 per credit hour.

FINANCIAL AID (2007–08) 4 students received aid, including loans. Aid is available to part-time students.

Financial Aid Contact Yvonne Payrits, Student Financial Service Coordinator, 71 Clement Road, Rutland, VT 05701. *Phone:* 802-773-5900 Ext. 3218. *Fax:* 802-773-3258. *E-mail:* finaid@csj.edu.

INTERNATIONAL STUDENTS 3% of students enrolled are international students. *Services and facilities:* Counseling/support services, ESL/language courses, Housing location assistance, Orientation, Visa Services. Financial aid is not available to international students. *Required with application:* TOEFL with recommended score of 213 (computer) or 550 (paper); proof of adequate funds; proof of health/immunizations.

International Student Contact Ms. Pat Ryan, Director of Marketing and Admissions, 71 Clement Road, Rutland, VT 05701. *Phone:* 877-270-9998 Ext. 3206. *Fax:* 802-773-5900. *E-mail:* pryan@csj.edu.

APPLICATION *Required:* Application form, baccalaureate/first degree, essay, 2 letters of recommendation, transcripts of college work. *Application fee:* $35. Applications for domestic and international students are processed on a rolling basis.

Application Contact Ms. Pat Ryan, Director of Marketing and Admissions, 71 Clement Road, Rutland, VT 05701. *Phone:* 877-270-9998. *Fax:* 802-773-5900. *E-mail:* pryan@csj.edu.

Norwich University
Distance MBA Program

Northfield, Vermont

Phone: 800-460-5597 Ext. 3367 **Fax:** 888-560-4934 **E-mail:** mba@grad.norwich.edu

Business Program(s) Web Site: http://www.graduate.norwich.edu/mba/

Norwich University (continued)

Graduate Business Unit Enrollment *Total:* 254 (254 full-time; 89 women).

Graduate Business Faculty *Total:* 40 (4 full-time; 36 part-time).

Admissions *Applied:* 450. *Admitted:* 75. *Enrolled:* 63. *Average GPA:* 3.1

Academic Calendar Continuous.

Accreditation ACBSP—The American Council of Business Schools and Programs.

After Graduation (Class of 2006–07) *Employed within 3 months of graduation:* 95%.

DEGREE MBA

MBA—Master of Business Administration Full-time. Distance learning option. At least 36 total credits required. Minimum of 18 months to complete program. *Concentration:* general MBA.

RESOURCES AND SERVICES Access to Internet/World Wide Web, online (class) registration, and online grade reports available. *Personal computer requirements:* Graduate business students are strongly recommended to purchase or lease a personal computer. *Placement services include:* Alumni network, career counseling/planning, electronic job bank, resume referral, and resume preparation.

EXPENSES *Tuition:* Full-time: $16,000. *Tuition (international):* Full-time: $16,000. *Required fees:* Full-time: $1600. Tuition and/or fees vary by academic program.

FINANCIAL AID (2007–08) Loans and scholarships.

Financial Aid Contact Sara Ball, Student Financial Planning, Student Financial Planning Office, 158 Harmon Drive, Northfield, VT 05663. *Phone:* 802-485-2019. *E-mail:* finaidgrad@norwich.edu.

INTERNATIONAL STUDENTS *Services and facilities:* Counseling/support services, Orientation. Financial aid is not available to international students. *Recommended with application:* TOEFL with recommended score of 213 (computer) or 550 (paper).

International Student Contact Mr. Anthony Broomfield, Admissions Advisor, School of Graduate Studies—MBA, PO Box 367, Northfield, VT 05663-0367. *Phone:* 800-460-5597 Ext. 3376. *Fax:* 888-560-4934. *E-mail:* mba@grad.norwich.edu.

APPLICATION *Required:* Application form, baccalaureate/first degree, 3 letters of recommendation, personal statement, resume/curriculum vitae, transcripts of college work, 2 years of work experience. *Application fee:* $50. Applications for domestic and international students are processed on a rolling basis.

Application Contact Mr. Anthony Broomfield, Admissions Advisor, PO Box 367, Northfield, VT 05663-0367. *Phone:* 800-460-5597 Ext. 3367. *Fax:* 888-560-4934. *E-mail:* mba@grad.norwich.edu.

Saint Michael's College
Program in Administration and Management
Colchester, Vermont

Phone: 802-654-2661 **Fax:** 802-654-2478 **E-mail:** polsen@smcvt.edu

Business Program(s) Web Site: http://www.smcvt.edu/gradprograms

Graduate Business Unit Enrollment *Total:* 62 (7 full-time; 55 part-time; 38 women; 5 international). *Average Age:* 38.

Graduate Business Faculty *Total:* 20 (9 full-time; 11 part-time).

Admissions *Applied:* 38. *Admitted:* 31. *Enrolled:* 28.

Academic Calendar Semesters.

DEGREE MSA

MSA—Master of Science in Administration Full-time and part-time. 37 to 43 total credits required. 24 to 84 months to complete program. *Concentrations:* business policy/strategy, human resources management,

international management, management, management information systems, marketing, nonprofit management, organizational behavior/development, organizational management.

RESOURCES AND SERVICES 150 on-campus PCs are available to graduate business students. Access to Internet/World Wide Web, online (class) registration, and online grade reports available. *Personal computer requirements:* Graduate business students are strongly recommended to purchase or lease a personal computer.

EXPENSES *Tuition:* Full-time: $13,650.

FINANCIAL AID (2007–08) Scholarships and work study. *Financial aid application deadline:* 4/15.

Financial Aid Contact Daniel Couture, Financial Aid Officer, One Winooski Park, Box 4, VT. *Phone:* 802-654-3244. *Fax:* 802-654-2591. *E-mail:* dcouture@smcvt.edu.

INTERNATIONAL STUDENTS 8% of students enrolled are international students. *Services and facilities:* ESL/language courses, Visa Services. Financial aid is available to international students. *Required with application:* IELT with recommended score of 6; TOEFL with recommended score of 213 (computer), 550 (paper), or 80 (Internet); proof of adequate funds; proof of health/immunizations.

International Student Contact Robert Letovsky, Director, Master of Science in Administration Program, One Winooski Park, Box 273, Colchester, VT 05439. *Phone:* 802-654-2477. *Fax:* 802-654-2478. *E-mail:* rletovsky@smcvt.edu.

APPLICATION *Required:* Application form, baccalaureate/first degree, transcripts of college work, 3 years of work experience. *Application fee:* $35. Applications for domestic and international students are processed on a rolling basis.

Application Contact Paul Olsen, Associate Director, Master of Science in Administration Program, One Winooski Park, Box 38, Colchester, VT 05439. *Phone:* 802-654-2661. *Fax:* 802-654-2478. *E-mail:* polsen@smcvt.edu.

SIT Graduate Institute
Master's Programs in Intercultural Service, Leadership, and Management
Brattleboro, Vermont

Phone: 800-336-1616 **Fax:** 802-258-3500 **E-mail:** admissions@sit.edu

Business Program(s) Web Site: http://www.sit.edu/

DEGREES MA/MS

MA/MS—Conflict Transformation Full-time. 40 to 43 total credits required. 24 to 60 months to complete program. *Concentration:* conflict resolution management.

MA/MS—Intercultural Service, Leadership, and Management Full-time. 40 to 43 total credits required. 24 to 60 months to complete program. *Concentrations:* combined degrees, international development management, international management, leadership, management, nonprofit management, organizational management, other.

MA/MS—International Education Full-time. 40 to 43 total credits required. 24 to 60 months to complete program. *Concentrations:* international management, nonprofit management, other.

MA/MS—Management Full-time. 45 to 48 total credits required. 24 to 60 months to complete program. *Concentrations:* international development management, management, management science, nonprofit management, nonprofit organization, organizational management.

MA/MS—Social Justice in Intercultural Relations Full-time. 40 to 43 total credits required. 24 to 60 months to complete program. *Concentrations:* international business, international development management, international management, nonprofit management, other.

MA/MS—Sustainable Development Full-time. 40 to 43 total credits required. 24 to 60 months to complete program. *Concentrations:* international development management, nonprofit management, other, resources management.

RESOURCES AND SERVICES 43 on-campus PCs are available to graduate business students. Access to Internet/World Wide Web available. *Personal computer requirements:* Graduate business students are not required to have a personal computer. *Special opportunities include:* An internship program is available. *Placement services include:* Alumni network, career placement, job search course, career counseling/planning, electronic job bank, resume referral, job interviews arranged, resume preparation, and career library.

Application Contact Graduate Admissions Receptionist, Kipling Road, PO Box 676, Brattleboro, VT 05302-0676. *Phone:* 800-336-1616. *Fax:* 802-258-3500. *E-mail:* admissions@sit.edu.

University of Vermont
School of Business Administration

Burlington, Vermont

Phone: 802-656-4119 **Fax:** 802-656-4078 **E-mail:** studentservices@bsad.uvm.edu

Business Program(s) Web Site: http://www.studentservices@bsad.uvm.edu

Graduate Business Unit Enrollment *Total:* 65 (20 full-time; 45 part-time; 29 women; 6 international). *Average Age:* 31.

Graduate Business Faculty *Total:* 28 (26 full-time; 2 part-time).

Admissions *Applied:* 46. *Admitted:* 35. *Enrolled:* 27. *Average GMAT:* 603. *Average GPA:* 3.24

Academic Calendar Semesters.

Accreditation AACSB—The Association to Advance Collegiate Schools of Business.

DEGREE MBA

MBA—Master of Business Administration Full-time and part-time. 30 to 48 total credits required. 12 to 60 months to complete program. *Concentration:* general MBA.

RESOURCES AND SERVICES 300 on-campus PCs are available to graduate business students. Access to Internet/World Wide Web, online (class) registration, and online grade reports available. *Personal computer requirements:* Graduate business students are not required to have a personal computer. *Special opportunities include:* An internship program is available. *Placement services include:* Alumni network, career placement, career counseling/planning, electronic job bank, resume referral, career fairs, job interviews arranged, and resume preparation.

EXPENSES *Tuition (state resident):* Full-time: $10,422. Part-time: $434 per credit hour. *Tuition (nonresident):* Full-time: $26,306. Part-time: $1096 per credit hour. *Tuition (international):* Full-time: $26,306. Part-time: $1096 per credit hour. *Required fees:* Full-time: $1632. Part-time: $58 per credit hour. Tuition and/or fees vary by class time, number of courses or credits taken, and academic program. *Graduate housing:* Room and board costs vary by number of occupants, type of accommodation, and type of board plan. *Typical cost:* $8534 (including board).

FINANCIAL AID (2007–08) 27 students received aid, including fellowships, loans, research assistantships, scholarships, and teaching assistantships. Aid is available to part-time students. *Financial aid application deadline:* 3/1.

Financial Aid Contact Cecelia Dry, Director of Financial Aid, 330 Waterman Building, Burlington, VT 05405. *Phone:* 802-656-1340. *Fax:* 802-656-4076. *E-mail:* cecelia.dry@uvm.edu.

INTERNATIONAL STUDENTS 9% of students enrolled are international students. *Services and facilities:* Counseling/support services, ESL/language courses, Housing location assistance, International student

housing, International student organization, Orientation, Visa Services. Financial aid is available to international students. *Required with application:* TOEFL with recommended score of 213 (computer) or 550 (paper); proof of adequate funds.

International Student Contact Ms. Sarah Curry, Advisor, International Students, B161 Living/Learning Center, Faculty Box 8, Burlington, VT 05405. *Phone:* 802-656-4296. *Fax:* 802-656-8553. *E-mail:* sarah.curry@uvm.edu.

APPLICATION *Required:* GMAT, application form, baccalaureate/first degree, 3 letters of recommendation, personal statement, resume/curriculum vitae, transcripts of college work. School will accept GRE. *Application fee:* $50. Applications for domestic and international students are processed on a rolling basis.

Application Contact Amelia Coleman, MBA Program Administrative Assistant, 55 Colchester Avenue, 101 Kalkin Hall, Burlington, VT 05405. *Phone:* 802-656-4119. *Fax:* 802-656-4078. *E-mail:* studentservices@bsad.uvm.edu.

VIRGIN ISLANDS

University of the Virgin Islands
Division of Business Administration

Saint Thomas, Virgin Islands

Phone: 340-693-1224 **Fax:** 340-693-1055 **E-mail:** ealexan@uvi.edu

Business Program(s) Web Site: http://www.uvi.edu/

Graduate Business Unit Enrollment *Total:* 39 (4 full-time; 35 part-time; 31 women; 2 international). *Average Age:* 35.

Graduate Business Faculty 7 full-time.

Admissions *Applied:* 45. *Admitted:* 33. *Enrolled:* 15. *Average GMAT:* 334. *Average GPA:* 2.91

Academic Calendar Semesters.

Accreditation ACBSP—The American Council of Business Schools and Programs (candidate).

DEGREE MBA

MBA—Master of Business Administration Full-time and part-time. At least 36 total credits required. 24 to 60 months to complete program. *Concentration:* general MBA.

RESOURCES AND SERVICES 26 on-campus PCs are available to graduate business students. Access to Internet/World Wide Web, online (class) registration, and online grade reports available. *Personal computer requirements:* Graduate business students are not required to have a personal computer. *Placement services include:* Career counseling/planning and resume preparation.

EXPENSES *Tuition, territory resident:* Full-time: $4950. Part-time: $275 per credit. *Tuition (nonresident):* Full-time: $9900. Part-time: $550 per credit. *Tuition (international):* Full-time: $9900. Part-time: $550 per credit. *Required fees:* Full-time: $300. Part-time: $300 per year.

FINANCIAL AID (2007–08) 3 students received aid, including loans and scholarships. Aid is available to part-time students. *Financial aid application deadline:* 6/1.

Financial Aid Contact Ms. Mavis Gilchrist, Director of Financial Aid, RR02—Box 10,000, Kingshill, St. Croix, 00850, U.S. Virgin Islands. *Phone:* 340-692-4186. *Fax:* 340-692-4145. *E-mail:* mgilchr@uvi.edu.

INTERNATIONAL STUDENTS 5% of students enrolled are international students. *Services and facilities:* Counseling/support services. Financial aid is not available to international students. *Required with*

University of the Virgin Islands (continued)

application: Proof of adequate funds; proof of health/immunizations. *Recommended with application:* TOEFL with recommended score of 213 (computer) or 550 (paper).

International Student Contact Dr. Judith Edwin, Vice Provost for Access and Enrollment Services, 2 John Brewers Bay, Charlotte Amalie, St. Thomas, 00802-9990, U.S. Virgin Islands. *Phone:* 340-693-1207. *Fax:* 340-693-1055. *E-mail:* jedwin@uvi.edu.

APPLICATION *Required:* GMAT, application form, baccalaureate/first degree, essay, transcripts of college work. School will accept GRE. *Recommended:* Letter(s) of recommendation, personal statement, resume/ curriculum vitae, work experience. *Application fee:* $30. *Deadlines:* 4/30 for fall, 10/30 for spring, 4/30 for fall (international), 10/30 for spring (international).

Application Contact Mr. Edward Alexander, Director of Admissions, 2 John Brewers Bay, Charlotte Amalie, St. Thomas, 00802-9990, U.S. Virgin Islands. *Phone:* 340-693-1224. *Fax:* 340-693-1055. *E-mail:* ealexan@uvi.edu.

VIRGINIA

Argosy University, Washington DC
College of Business

Arlington, Virginia

Phone: 703-526-5800 **Fax:** 703-526-5850

Business Program(s) Web Site: http://www.argosy.edu/washingtondc

---
DEGREES DBA • MBA • MSM

DBA—Doctor of Business Administration (DBA) *Concentrations:* accounting, information systems, international business, management, marketing.

MBA—Master of Business Administration (MBA) *Concentrations:* finance, health administration, information systems, international business, management, marketing.

MSM—Master of Science in Management (MSM) *Concentration:* management.

Financial Aid Contact Director of Admissions, 1550 Wilson Boulevard, Suite 600, Arlington, VA 22209. *Phone:* 703-526-5800. *Fax:* 703-526-5850.

International Student Contact Director of Admissions, 1550 Wilson Boulevard, Suite 600, Arlington, VA 22209. *Phone:* 703-526-5800. *Fax:* 703-526-5850.

Application Contact Director of Admissions, 1550 Wilson Boulevard, Suite 600, Arlington, VA 22209. *Phone:* 703-526-5800. *Fax:* 703-526-5850.

See full description on page 566.

Averett University
Program in Business Administration

Danville, Virginia

Phone: 434-791-5844 **Fax:** 434-791-5872 **E-mail:** kapappas@averett.edu

Business Program(s) Web Site: http://www.averett.edu/gps/mba.html

Graduate Business Unit Enrollment *Total:* 479 (120 full-time; 359 part-time; 288 women; 2 international). *Average Age:* 37.

Graduate Business Faculty *Total:* 53 (10 full-time; 43 part-time).

Admissions *Applied:* 54. *Admitted:* 54. *Enrolled:* 54. *Average GPA:* 3.02

Academic Calendar Continuous.

After Graduation (Class of 2006–07) *Employed within 3 months of graduation:* 100%.

DEGREE MBA

MBA—Master of Business Administration Full-time and part-time. Cumulative GPA of 3.0 for last 60 undergraduate credit hours required. At least 40 total credits required. 24 to 72 months to complete program. *Concentration:* management.

RESOURCES AND SERVICES 100 on-campus PCs are available to graduate business students. Access to Internet/World Wide Web and online grade reports available. *Personal computer requirements:* Graduate business students are not required to have a personal computer. *Special opportunities include:* An internship program is available. *Placement services include:* Alumni network, career placement, career counseling/ planning, electronic job bank, resume referral, career fairs, resume preparation, and career library.

EXPENSES *Tuition:* Part-time: $475 per credit. *Tuition (international):* Part-time: $475 per credit. *Required fees:* Part-time: $25 per degree program. Tuition and/or fees vary by number of courses or credits taken, campus location, and academic program.

FINANCIAL AID (2007–08) 190 students received aid, including loans. Aid is available to part-time students.

Financial Aid Contact Ms. Nicole Lathrop, Financial Aid Coordinator, 420 West Main Street, Danville, VA 24541. *Phone:* 434-791-5871. *Fax:* 434-791-5647. *E-mail:* nlathrop@averett.edu.

INTERNATIONAL STUDENTS 0.4% of students enrolled are international students. *Services and facilities:* Counseling/support services, Orientation. Financial aid is not available to international students. *Required with application:* TOEFL with recommended score of 250 (computer) or 600 (paper); proof of adequate funds; proof of health/immunizations.

International Student Contact Ms. Katherine Pappas-Smith, Marketing and Enrollment Manager, 420 West Main Street, Danville, VA 24541. *Phone:* 434-791-5844. *Fax:* 434-791-5872. *E-mail:* kapappas@ averett.edu.

APPLICATION *Required:* Application form, baccalaureate/first degree, 3 letters of recommendation, resume/curriculum vitae, transcripts of college work, 3 years of work experience. *Application fee:* $50. Applications for domestic and international students are processed on a rolling basis.

Application Contact Ms. Katherine Pappas-Smith, Marketing and Enrollment Manager, 420 West Main Street, Danville, VA 24541. *Phone:* 434-791-5844. *Fax:* 434-791-5872. *E-mail:* kapappas@averett.edu.

The College of William and Mary
Mason School of Business

Williamsburg, Virginia

Phone: 757-221-2900 **Fax:** 757-221-2958 **E-mail:** amy.hughes@mason.wm.edu

Business Program(s) Web Site: http://mason.wm.edu/

Graduate Business Unit Enrollment *Total:* 282 (131 full-time; 151 part-time; 75 women; 50 international). *Average Age:* 26.

Graduate Business Faculty *Total:* 54 (42 full-time; 12 part-time).

Admissions *Applied:* 303. *Admitted:* 178. *Enrolled:* 81. *Average GMAT:* 613. *Average GPA:* 3.4

Academic Calendar Semesters.

Accreditation AACSB—The Association to Advance Collegiate Schools of Business.

After Graduation (Class of 2006–07) *Employed within 3 months of graduation:* 83%. *Average starting salary:* $76,297.

DEGREES MBA

MBA—Flex Master of Business Administration Part-time. At least 54 total credits required. 36 to 72 months to complete program. *Concentrations:* entrepreneurship, finance, information management, marketing, operations management.

MBA—Full-Time Master of Business Administration Full-time. At least 63 total credits required. 21 months to complete program. *Concentrations:* entrepreneurship, finance, information management, marketing, operations management.

RESOURCES AND SERVICES 350 on-campus PCs are available to graduate business students. Access to Internet/World Wide Web, online (class) registration, and online grade reports available. *Personal computer requirements:* Graduate business students are required to have a personal computer. *Special opportunities include:* An internship program is available. *Placement services include:* Alumni network, career placement, job search course, career counseling/planning, electronic job bank, resume referral, career fairs, job interviews arranged, resume preparation, and career library.

EXPENSES *Tuition (state resident):* Full-time: $16,140. Part-time: $515 per credit hour. *Tuition (nonresident):* Full-time: $27,930. Part-time: $900 per credit hour. *Tuition (international):* Full-time: $27,930. Part-time: $900 per credit hour. Tuition and/or fees vary by class time, number of courses or credits taken, campus location, and academic program. *Graduate housing:* Room and board costs vary by number of occupants, type of accommodation, and type of board plan. *Typical cost:* $8330 (including board).

FINANCIAL AID (2007–08) 81 students received aid, including loans, research assistantships, and scholarships. *Financial aid application deadline:* 3/1.

Financial Aid Contact Amy Hughes, Interim Director of MBA Admissions, PO Box 8795, Williamsburg, VA 23187-8795. *Phone:* 757-221-2900. *Fax:* 757-221-2958. *E-mail:* amy.hughes@mason.wm.edu.

INTERNATIONAL STUDENTS 18% of students enrolled are international students. *Services and facilities:* Counseling/support services, ESL/language courses, Housing location assistance, International student housing, International student organization, Language tutoring, Orientation, Visa Services. Financial aid is available to international students. *Required with application:* TOEFL with recommended score of 250 (computer); proof of adequate funds; proof of health/immunizations.

International Student Contact Amy Hughes, Interim Director of MBA Admissions, PO Box 8795, Williamsburg, VA 23187-8795. *Phone:* 757-221-2900. *Fax:* 757-221-2958. *E-mail:* amy.hughes@mason.wm.edu.

APPLICATION *Required:* GMAT, application form, baccalaureate/first degree, essay, interview, 2 letters of recommendation, resume/curriculum vitae, transcripts of college work. *Recommended:* Work experience. *Application fee:* $100. Applications for domestic and international students are processed on a rolling basis.

Application Contact Amy Hughes, Interim Director of MBA Admissions, PO Box 8795, Williamsburg, VA 23187-8795. *Phone:* 757-221-2900. *Fax:* 757-221-2958. *E-mail:* amy.hughes@mason.wm.edu.

DeVry University
Keller Graduate School of Management
Arlington, Virginia

Phone: 703-415-0600 **Fax:** 703-415-0700

Business Program(s) Web Site: http://www.devry.edu

Academic Calendar Semesters.

DEGREES MAFM • MBA • MHRM • MISM • MPA • MPM

MAFM—Master of Accounting and Financial Management Full-time and part-time. Distance learning option. At least 44 total credits required. 18 to 60 months to complete program. *Concentrations:* accounting, financial management/planning.

MBA—Master of Business Administration Full-time and part-time. Distance learning option. At least 48 total credits required. 18 to 60 months to complete program. *Concentrations:* accounting, electronic commerce (E-commerce), finance, general MBA, health care, human resources management, information systems, international and area business studies, marketing, project management, public policy and administration.

MHRM—Master of Human Resource Management Full-time and part-time. Distance learning option. At least 45 total credits required. 18 to 60 months to complete program. *Concentration:* human resources management.

MISM—Master of Information Systems Management Full-time and part-time. Distance learning option. At least 45 total credits required. 18 to 60 months to complete program. *Concentration:* information systems.

MPA—Master of Public Administration Full-time and part-time. Distance learning option. At least 45 total credits required. 18 to 60 months to complete program. *Concentration:* public policy and administration.

MPM—Master of Project Management Full-time and part-time. Distance learning option. At least 42 total credits required. 18 to 60 months to complete program. *Concentration:* project management.

RESOURCES AND SERVICES *Personal computer requirements:* Graduate business students are not required to have a personal computer.

APPLICATION *Required:* Application form, baccalaureate/first degree, interview, transcripts of college work. Applications for domestic and international students are processed on a rolling basis.

Application Contact Admissions Office, Arlington Center, 2450 Crystal Drive, Arlington, VA 22202. *Phone:* 703-415-0600. *Fax:* 703-415-0700.

DeVry University
Keller Graduate School of Management
McLean, Virginia

Phone: 703-556-9669

DEGREES MAFM • MBA • MHRM • MIS • MPA • MPM

MAFM—Master of Accounting and Financial Management Full-time and part-time. Distance learning option. At least 44 total credits required. 18 to 60 months to complete program. *Concentrations:* accounting, financial management/planning.

MBA—Master of Business Administration Full-time and part-time. Distance learning option. At least 48 total credits required. 18 to 60 months to complete program. *Concentration:* management.

MHRM—Master of Human Resources Management Full-time and part-time. Distance learning option. At least 45 total credits required. 18 to 60 months to complete program. *Concentration:* human resources management.

MIS—Master of Information Systems Management Full-time and part-time. Distance learning option. At least 45 total credits required. 18 to 60 months to complete program. *Concentration:* information systems.

MPA—Master of Public Administration Full-time and part-time. Distance learning option. At least 45 total credits required. 18 to 60 months to complete program. *Concentration:* public policy and administration.

MPM—Master of Project Management Full-time and part-time. Distance learning option. At least 42 total credits required. 18 to 60 months to complete program. *Concentration:* project management.

Application Contact Admissions Office, Tysons Corner Center, 1751 Pinnacle Drive, Suite 250, McLean, VA 22102. *Phone:* 703-556-9669.

Eastern Mennonite University
Program in Business Administration

Harrisonburg, Virginia

Phone: 540-432-4000 **E-mail:** mba@emu.edu

Business Program(s) Web Site: http://www.emu.edu/

Graduate Business Unit Enrollment *Total:* 43 (43 part-time; 29 women; 40 international). *Average Age:* 36.

Graduate Business Faculty *Total:* 8 (5 full-time; 3 part-time).

Admissions *Applied:* 44. *Admitted:* 44. *Enrolled:* 43. *Average GMAT:* 520. *Average GPA:* 2.93

Academic Calendar Semesters.

DEGREE MBA

MBA—Master of Business Administration *Concentrations:* accounting, business law, economics, finance, human resources management, information systems, international business, management, marketing, operations management, production management, strategic management.

RESOURCES AND SERVICES 25 on-campus PCs are available to graduate business students. Access to Internet/World Wide Web and online grade reports available. *Personal computer requirements:* Graduate business students are strongly recommended to purchase or lease a personal computer. *Placement services include:* Alumni network and career counseling/planning.

EXPENSES *Tuition:* Part-time: $440 per credit hour. *Tuition (international):* Part-time: $440 per credit hour.

FINANCIAL AID (2007–08) Loans.

INTERNATIONAL STUDENTS 93% of students enrolled are international students. *Services and facilities:* Counseling/support services, ESL/language courses, International student organization, Orientation. Financial aid is not available to international students. *Required with application:* TOEFL with recommended score of 550 (paper); proof of adequate funds.

International Student Contact Jonathan Kratz, Director of International Student Services, 1200 Park Road, Harrisonburg, VA 22802. *Phone:* 540-432-4459. *E-mail:* kratzja@emu.edu.

APPLICATION *Required:* GMAT, application form, baccalaureate/first degree, interview, 2 letters of recommendation, personal statement, resume/curriculum vitae, transcripts of college work, 2 years of work experience. *Application fee:* $25.

Application Contact Admissions, 1200 Park Road, Harrisonburg, VA 22802-2462. *Phone:* 540-432-4000. *E-mail:* mba@emu.edu.

George Mason University
School of Management

Fairfax, Virginia

Phone: 703-993-2136 **Fax:** 703-993-1778 **E-mail:** mba@gmu.edu

Business Program(s) Web Site: http://www.som.gmu.edu

Graduate Business Unit Enrollment *Total:* 453 (109 full-time; 344 part-time; 163 women).

Graduate Business Faculty *Total:* 116 (73 full-time; 43 part-time).

Admissions *Applied:* 268. *Admitted:* 161. *Enrolled:* 84. *Average GMAT:* 583. *Average GPA:* 3.0

Academic Calendar Semesters.

Accreditation AACSB—The Association to Advance Collegiate Schools of Business.

DEGREES EMBA • MBA • MSA • MSTM

EMBA—Executive Master of Business Administration Part-time. Significant professional work experience required. All-inclusive tuition rates apply, including one overseas residency, three domestic residencies and a laptop. 54 total credits required. 18 months to complete program. *Concentration:* executive programs.

MBA—Master of Business Administration Full-time and part-time. Two years of full-time work experience required. Tuition includes cost of international residency. 24-month pace is a full-time course load. 48 total credits required. 24 to 72 months to complete program. *Concentrations:* accounting, entrepreneurship, finance, management information systems, marketing, project management.

MSA—Master of Science in Accounting Full-time and part-time. Students must have a bachelor's degree in accounting. Student can opt to continue on and complete MBA 12 additional credits. 30 to 42 total credits required. 18 to 72 months to complete program. *Concentration:* accounting.

MSTM—Master of Science in Technology Management Part-time. Three years of full-time professional work experience in the information technology field or industry required; executive format; tuition includes books and international residency. At least 36 total credits required. 18 months to complete program. *Concentration:* management information systems.

RESOURCES AND SERVICES 100 on-campus PCs are available to graduate business students. Access to Internet/World Wide Web, online (class) registration, and online grade reports available. *Personal computer requirements:* Graduate business students are strongly recommended to purchase or lease a personal computer. *Special opportunities include:* An international exchange program and an internship program are available. *Placement services include:* Alumni network, career placement, job search course, career counseling/planning, electronic job bank, career fairs, resume preparation, and career library.

EXPENSES *Tuition (state resident):* Full-time: $13,320. Part-time: $6660 per semester. *Tuition (nonresident):* Full-time: $23,640. Part-time: $11,820 per semester. *Tuition (international):* Full-time: $23,640. Part-time: $11,820 per semester.

FINANCIAL AID (2007–08) Grants, loans, research assistantships, scholarships, teaching assistantships, and work study. Aid is available to part-time students. *Financial aid application deadline:* 3/1.

Financial Aid Contact Ms. Jevita de Freitas, Director, Financial Aid, 4400 University Drive, Mail Stop 3B5, Fairfax, VA 22030. *Phone:* 703-993-2353. *Fax:* 703-993-2350. *E-mail:* finaid@gmu.edu.

INTERNATIONAL STUDENTS *Services and facilities:* Counseling/support services, ESL/language courses, Housing location assistance, International student organization, Language tutoring, Orientation, Visa Services. Financial aid is available to international students. *Required with application:* IELT with recommended score of 6.5; TOEFL with recommended score of 250 (computer), 650 (paper), or 93 (Internet); proof of adequate funds; proof of health/immunizations.

International Student Contact Ms. Judith Green, Director, International Programs and Services, 4400 University Drive, Mail Stop 4C3, Fairfax, VA 22030. *Phone:* 703-993-2970. *Fax:* 703-993-2966. *E-mail:* oips@gmu.edu.

APPLICATION *Required:* GMAT, application form, baccalaureate/first degree, essay, 2 letters of recommendation, personal statement, resume/curriculum vitae, transcripts of college work, 2 years of work experience. *Recommended:* Interview. *Application fee:* $60. Applications for domestic and international students are processed on a rolling basis.

Application Contact MBA Admissions Office, 4400 University Drive, Mail Stop 5A2, Fairfax, VA 22030. *Phone:* 703-993-2136. *Fax:* 703-993-1778. *E-mail:* mba@gmu.edu.

James Madison University
College of Business

Harrisonburg, Virginia

Phone: 540-568-3253 **Fax:** 540-568-3587 **E-mail:** dofflekd@jmu.edu

Business Program(s) Web Site: http://www.jmu.edu/mba/

Graduate Business Unit Enrollment *Total:* 130 (12 full-time; 118 part-time; 50 women; 15 international). *Average Age:* 27.

Graduate Business Faculty 40 full-time.

Admissions *Applied:* 35. *Admitted:* 27. *Enrolled:* 23. *Average GMAT:* 570. *Average GPA:* 3.2

Academic Calendar Semesters.

Accreditation AACSB—The Association to Advance Collegiate Schools of Business.

After Graduation (Class of 2006–07) *Employed within 3 months of graduation:* 90%.

DEGREES   MBA

MBA—Master of Business Administration in Information Security Part-time. Distance learning option. At least 42 total credits required. 27 months to complete program. *Concentration:* general MBA.

MBA—Master of Business Administration Full-time and part-time. At least 36 total credits required. 16 to 72 months to complete program. *Concentrations:* administration of technological information, general MBA, health care, information management.

RESOURCES AND SERVICES 225 on-campus PCs are available to graduate business students. Access to Internet/World Wide Web, online (class) registration, and online grade reports available. *Personal computer requirements:* Graduate business students are required to have a personal computer. *Placement services include:* Alumni network and career fairs.

EXPENSES *Tuition (state resident):* Full-time: $5040. Part-time: $280 per credit hour. *Tuition (nonresident):* Full-time: $14,328. Part-time: $796 per credit hour. *Tuition (international):* Full-time: $14,328. Part-time: $796 per credit hour. *Required fees:* Full-time: $55. Part-time: $55 per degree program. *Graduate housing:* Room and board costs vary by number of occupants, type of accommodation, and type of board plan.

FINANCIAL AID (2007–08) 23 students received aid, including research assistantships and work study. *Financial aid application deadline:* 4/10.

Financial Aid Contact Ms. Lisa Tumer, Director of Financial Aid, Harrisonburg, VA 22807. *Phone:* 540-568-7820. *Fax:* 540-568-7994. *E-mail:* tumerll@jmu.edu.

INTERNATIONAL STUDENTS 12% of students enrolled are international students. *Services and facilities:* Counseling/support services, ESL/language courses, International student organization, Orientation, Visa Services. Financial aid is not available to international students. *Required with application:* TOEFL with recommended score of 280 (computer), 500 (paper), or 80 (Internet); proof of adequate funds.

International Student Contact Ms. Kathy Thompson, College of Graduate and Professional Programs, MSC 2602, Harrisonburg, VA 22807. *Phone:* 540-568-7065. *Fax:* 540-568-6266. *E-mail:* thompskb@jmu.edu.

APPLICATION *Required:* GMAT, application form, baccalaureate/first degree, 2 letters of recommendation, resume/curriculum vitae, transcripts of college work, 2 years of work experience. *Application fee:* $55. Applications for domestic and international students are processed on a rolling basis.

Application Contact Ms. Krista Dofflemyer, MBA Program Office, MSC 0206, Harrisonburg, VA 22807. *Phone:* 540-568-3253. *Fax:* 540-568-3587. *E-mail:* dofflekd@jmu.edu.

Liberty University

School of Business

Lynchburg, Virginia

Phone: 800-424-9596 **Fax:** 800-628-7977 **E-mail:** lrapp@liberty.edu

Business Program(s) Web Site: http://www.luonline.com/index.cfm?PID=14279

Graduate Business Unit Enrollment *Total:* 2,800.

Admissions *Average GPA:* 3.3

Academic Calendar 8-week terms.

DEGREES   MBA • MSA • MSM

MBA—MBA—Accounting Full-time and part-time. Distance learning option. Up to 45 total credits required. *Concentration:* accounting.

MBA—MBA—General Full-time and part-time. Distance learning option. Up to 45 total credits required. *Concentration:* general MBA.

MBA—MBA—Human Resources Full-time and part-time. Distance learning option. Up to 45 total credits required. *Concentration:* human resources management.

MBA—MBA—International Business Full-time and part-time. Distance learning option. Up to 45 total credits required. *Concentration:* international business.

MBA—MBA—Leadership Full-time and part-time. Distance learning option. Up to 45 total credits required. *Concentration:* leadership.

MSA—Master of Science in Accounting Full-time and part-time. Distance learning option. Up to 30 total credits required. *Concentration:* accounting.

MSM—Master of Science in Management Full-time and part-time. Distance learning option. Up to 30 total credits required. *Concentration:* management.

RESOURCES AND SERVICES 257 on-campus PCs are available to graduate business students. Access to Internet/World Wide Web, online (class) registration, and online grade reports available. *Personal computer requirements:* Graduate business students are required to have a personal computer. *Placement services include:* Alumni network, job search course, career counseling/planning, resume preparation, and career library.

FINANCIAL AID (2007–08) Grants and loans. Aid is available to part-time students.

Financial Aid Contact Financial Aid Office, 1971 University Boulevard, Lynchburg, VA 24502. *Phone:* 800-424-9596. *Fax:* 800-628-7977. *E-mail:* financialaid@liberty.edu.

INTERNATIONAL STUDENTS *Services and facilities:* ESL/language courses, Housing location assistance, Orientation, Visa Services. Financial aid is not available to international students. *Required with application:* TOEFL with recommended score of 250 (computer) or 600 (paper); proof of adequate funds; proof of health/immunizations.

International Student Contact Dr. Bill Wegert, Director of International Admissions, 1971 University Boulevard, Lynchburg, VA 24502. *Phone:* 434-592-3025. *Fax:* 800-628-7977. *E-mail:* wewegert@liberty.edu.

APPLICATION *Required:* Application form, baccalaureate/first degree, transcripts of college work. *Application fee:* $50. Applications for domestic and international students are processed on a rolling basis.

Application Contact Leslee Rapp, Director of Admissions, 1971 University Boulevard, Lynchburg, VA 24502. *Phone:* 800-424-9596. *Fax:* 800-628-7977. *E-mail:* lrapp@liberty.edu.

Lynchburg College

School of Business and Economics

Lynchburg, Virginia

Phone: 804-544-8300 **Fax:** 434-544-8439 **E-mail:** bower.s@lynchburg.edu

Business Program(s) Web Site: http://www.lynchburg.edu/business/

Graduate Business Unit Enrollment *Total:* 53 (14 full-time; 39 part-time; 24 women; 5 international).

Graduate Business Faculty 7 full-time.

Admissions *Applied:* 23. *Admitted:* 18. *Enrolled:* 17. *Average GMAT:* 515. *Average GPA:* 3.18

Academic Calendar Semesters.

Lynchburg College (continued)

After Graduation (Class of 2006–07) *Employed within 3 months of graduation:* 100%.

DEGREE MBA

MBA—Master of Business Administration Full-time and part-time. 36 hour program all incoming students (with or without undergraduate business degree). 36 total credits required. 15 to 36 months to complete program. *Concentration:* general MBA.

RESOURCES AND SERVICES 240 on-campus PCs are available to graduate business students. Access to Internet/World Wide Web, online (class) registration, and online grade reports available. *Personal computer requirements:* Graduate business students are strongly recommended to purchase or lease a personal computer. *Special opportunities include:* An international exchange program and an internship program are available. *Placement services include:* Alumni network, career placement, job search course, career counseling/planning, electronic job bank, resume referral, career fairs, job interviews arranged, resume preparation, and career library.

EXPENSES *Tuition:* Full-time: $3375. Part-time: $375 per credit hour. *Tuition (international):* Full-time: $3375. Part-time: $375 per credit hour. *Required fees:* Full-time: $120. Part-time: $120 per year. *Graduate housing:* Room and board costs vary by number of occupants, type of accommodation, and type of board plan. *Typical cost:* $3485 (including board), $2055 (room only).

FINANCIAL AID (2007–08) 14 students received aid, including grants, loans, and research assistantships. Aid is available to part-time students. *Financial aid application deadline:* 5/1.

Financial Aid Contact Ms. Michelle Davis, Director of Financial Aid, 1501 Lakeside Drive, Lynchburg, VA 24501. *Phone:* 434-544-8228. *Fax:* 434-544-8653. *E-mail:* davis_m@lynchburg.edu.

INTERNATIONAL STUDENTS 9% of students enrolled are international students. *Services and facilities:* Counseling/support services, Housing location assistance, International student housing, International student organization, Orientation, Visa Services. Financial aid is not available to international students. *Required with application:* TOEFL with recommended score of 550 (paper); proof of adequate funds; proof of health/immunizations. *Recommended with application:* TWE.

International Student Contact Ms. Annette Stadtherr, International Student Advisor, 150 Lakeside Drive, Lynchburg, VA 24501. *Phone:* 800-426-8101. *Fax:* 434-544-8653. *E-mail:* stadtherr@lynchburg.edu.

APPLICATION *Required:* GMAT, application form, baccalaureate/first degree, essay, 3 letters of recommendation, personal statement, transcripts of college work. *Recommended:* Interview, work experience. *Application fee:* $30. Applications for domestic and international students are processed on a rolling basis.

Application Contact Ms. Sharon Walters-Bower, Director of Admissions, 1501 Lakeside Drive, Lynchburg, VA 24501-3199. *Phone:* 804-544-8300. *Fax:* 434-544-8439. *E-mail:* bower.s@lynchburg.edu.

Marymount University
School of Business Administration

Arlington, Virginia

Phone: 703-284-5901 **Fax:** 703-527-3815 **E-mail:** francesca.reed@marymount.edu

Business Program(s) Web Site: http://www.marymount.edu/academic/business/

Graduate Business Unit Enrollment *Total:* 424 (94 full-time; 330 part-time; 260 women; 37 international). *Average Age:* 33.

Graduate Business Faculty *Total:* 42 (23 full-time; 19 part-time).

Admissions *Applied:* 179. *Admitted:* 172. *Enrolled:* 108. *Average GMAT:* 433. *Average GPA:* 3.0

Academic Calendar Semesters.

Accreditation ACBSP—The American Council of Business Schools and Programs.

After Graduation (Class of 2006–07) *Employed within 3 months of graduation:* 82%.

DEGREES MA • MBA • MS

MA—Master of Arts in Human Resource Management Full-time and part-time. 2 years of substantial work experience strongly recommended. At least 36 total credits required. 12 to 60 months to complete program. *Concentration:* human resources management.

MA—Master of Arts in Legal Administration Full-time and part-time. 2 years of substantial work experience strongly recommended. At least 36 total credits required. 12 to 60 months to complete program. *Concentration:* legal administration.

MBA—Master of Business Administration Full-time and part-time. 2 years of substantial work experience strongly recommended. At least 45 total credits required. 24 to 60 months to complete program. *Concentrations:* finance, health care, human resources management, information technology, international business, legal administration, management, marketing.

MS—Master of Science in Health Care Management Full-time and part-time. 2 years of substantial work experience strongly recommended. At least 36 total credits required. 12 to 60 months to complete program. *Concentration:* health care.

MS—Master of Science in Information Technology Full-time and part-time. 2 years of substantial work experience strongly recommended. At least 36 total credits required. 12 to 60 months to complete program. *Concentrations:* information technology, technology management.

MS—Master of Science in Management Full-time and part-time. 2 years of substantial work experience strongly recommended. At least 36 total credits required. 12 to 60 months to complete program. *Concentrations:* leadership, management, organizational behavior/development, project management.

RESOURCES AND SERVICES 110 on-campus PCs are available to graduate business students. Access to Internet/World Wide Web, online (class) registration, and online grade reports available. *Personal computer requirements:* Graduate business students are not required to have a personal computer. *Special opportunities include:* An internship program is available. *Placement services include:* Alumni network, job search course, career counseling/planning, electronic job bank, resume referral, career fairs, resume preparation, and career library.

EXPENSES *Tuition:* Full-time: $11,790. Part-time: $655 per credit hour. *Tuition (international):* Full-time: $11,790. Part-time: $655 per credit hour. *Required fees:* Full-time: $121. Part-time: $6.70 per credit hour. Tuition and/or fees vary by number of courses or credits taken.

FINANCIAL AID (2007–08) 122 students received aid, including grants, loans, research assistantships, scholarships, and work study. Aid is available to part-time students.

Financial Aid Contact Ms. Debbie Raines, Director of Financial Aid, 2807 North Glebe Road, Arlington, VA 22207-4299. *Phone:* 703-284-1530. *Fax:* 703-516-4771. *E-mail:* debbie.raines@marymount.edu.

INTERNATIONAL STUDENTS 9% of students enrolled are international students. *Services and facilities:* Counseling/support services, International student organization, Orientation. Financial aid is available to international students. *Required with application:* TOEFL with recommended score of 250 (computer), 600 (paper), or 100 (Internet); proof of adequate funds; proof of health/immunizations.

International Student Contact Ms. Aline Orfali, Director of International Student Services, 2807 North Glebe Road, Arlington, VA 22207-4299. *Phone:* 703-526-6922. *Fax:* 703-284-5799. *E-mail:* aline.orfali@marymount.edu.

APPLICATION *Required:* Application form, baccalaureate/first degree, resume/curriculum vitae, transcripts of college work. School will accept GMAT and GRE. *Recommended:* 2 years of work experience. *Application fee:* $40. *Deadlines:* 7/1 for fall (international), 10/15 for spring (international), 3/15 for summer (international). Applications for domestic students are processed on a rolling basis.

Application Contact Francesca Reed, Director of Graduate Admissions, 2807 North Glebe Road, Arlington, VA 22207-4299. *Phone:* 703-284-5901. *Fax:* 703-527-3815. *E-mail:* francesca.reed@marymount.edu.

Old Dominion University
College of Business and Public Administration
Norfolk, Virginia

Phone: 757-683-3585 **Fax:** 757-683-5750 **E-mail:** mbainfo@odu.edu

Business Program(s) Web Site: http://bpa.odu.edu/

Graduate Business Unit Enrollment *Total:* 374 (120 full-time; 254 part-time; 146 women; 67 international). *Average Age:* 28.

Graduate Business Faculty *Total:* 136 (89 full-time; 47 part-time).

Admissions *Applied:* 328. *Admitted:* 256. *Enrolled:* 181. *Average GMAT:* 560. *Average GPA:* 3.3

Academic Calendar Semesters.

Accreditation AACSB—The Association to Advance Collegiate Schools of Business.

DEGREES MA • MBA • MPA • MSA

MA—Master of Arts in Economics Full-time and part-time. GRE is required if undergraduate GPA falls below a certain level. At least 30 total credits required. 20 to 72 months to complete program. *Concentration:* economics.

MBA—Master of Business Administration Full-time and part-time. GMAT required. At least 48 total credits required. Maximum of 72 months to complete program. *Concentrations:* economics, finance, general MBA, international business, management information systems, port/maritime management, public policy and administration.

MPA—Master of Public Administration Full-time and part-time. Essay required, GRE Required. 39 total credits required. 24 to 72 months to complete program. *Concentrations:* city/urban administration, decision sciences, financial management/planning, health care, human resources management, public management, public policy and administration.

MSA—Master of Science in Accounting Full-time and part-time. 30 total credits required. 24 to 72 months to complete program. *Concentrations:* accounting, corporate accounting, information technology, technology management.

RESOURCES AND SERVICES 600 on-campus PCs are available to graduate business students. Access to Internet/World Wide Web, online (class) registration, and online grade reports available. *Personal computer requirements:* Graduate business students are not required to have a personal computer. *Special opportunities include:* An international exchange program and an internship program are available. *Placement services include:* Alumni network, career placement, career counseling/planning, electronic job bank, resume referral, career fairs, job interviews arranged, and resume preparation.

EXPENSES *Tuition (state resident):* Full-time: $7704. Part-time: $321 per credit hour. *Tuition (nonresident):* Full-time: $19,104. Part-time: $796 per credit hour. *Tuition (international):* Full-time: $19,104. Part-time: $796 per credit hour. *Required fees:* Full-time: $255. Part-time: $39 per semester. Tuition and/or fees vary by number of courses or credits taken and campus location. *Graduate housing:* Room and board costs vary by number of occupants, type of accommodation, and type of board plan. *Typical cost:* $6856 (including board), $5356 (room only).

FINANCIAL AID (2007–08) 50 students received aid, including fellowships, grants, loans, research assistantships, scholarships, and teaching assistantships. Aid is available to part-time students. *Financial aid application deadline:* 4/15.

Financial Aid Contact Dr. Bruce Rubin, Director, MBA Program, 1026 Constant Hall, Norfolk, VA 23529. *Phone:* 757-683-3585. *Fax:* 757-683-5750. *E-mail:* mbainfo@odu.edu.

INTERNATIONAL STUDENTS 18% of students enrolled are international students. *Services and facilities:* Counseling/support services, ESL/language courses, Housing location assistance, International student housing, International student organization, Language tutoring, Orientation, Visa Services, airport pick-up. Financial aid is available to international students. *Required with application:* TOEFL with recommended score of 213 (computer), 550 (paper), or 80 (Internet); proof of adequate funds; proof of health/immunizations.

International Student Contact Steve Risch, Director, International Admissions, 220 Rollins Hall, Norfolk, VA 23529. *Phone:* 757-683-3701. *Fax:* 757-683-5196. *E-mail:* srisch@odu.edu.

APPLICATION *Required:* GMAT, application form, baccalaureate/first degree, essay, 1 letter of recommendation, personal statement, resume/curriculum vitae, transcripts of college work. *Recommended:* Work experience. *Application fee:* $40. Applications for domestic and international students are processed on a rolling basis.

Application Contact Dr. Bruce Rubin, Director, MBA Program, 1026 Constant Hall, Norfolk, VA 23529. *Phone:* 757-683-3585. *Fax:* 757-683-5750. *E-mail:* mbainfo@odu.edu.

Radford University
College of Business and Economics
Radford, Virginia

Phone: 540-831-5185 **Fax:** 540-831-6655 **E-mail:** rumba@radford.edu

Business Program(s) Web Site: http://rumba.asp.radford.edu/

Graduate Business Unit Enrollment *Total:* 79 (42 full-time; 37 part-time; 23 women; 8 international). *Average Age:* 25.

Graduate Business Faculty 7 full-time.

Admissions *Applied:* 70. *Admitted:* 56. *Enrolled:* 47. *Average GMAT:* 481. *Average GPA:* 3.24

Academic Calendar Semesters.

Accreditation AACSB—The Association to Advance Collegiate Schools of Business.

DEGREE MBA

MBA—Master of Business Administration Full-time and part-time. Distance learning option. At least 30 total credits required. 12 to 72 months to complete program. *Concentration:* general MBA.

RESOURCES AND SERVICES 550 on-campus PCs are available to graduate business students. Access to Internet/World Wide Web, online (class) registration, and online grade reports available. *Personal computer requirements:* Graduate business students are not required to have a personal computer. *Special opportunities include:* An internship program is available. *Placement services include:* Alumni network, career placement, career counseling/planning, electronic job bank, resume referral, career fairs, job interviews arranged, and resume preparation.

EXPENSES *Tuition (state resident):* Full-time: $2511. Part-time: $279 per credit hour. *Tuition (nonresident):* Full-time: $4671. Part-time: $519 per credit hour.

FINANCIAL AID (2007–08) 24 students received aid, including research assistantships and teaching assistantships. *Financial aid application deadline:* 3/1.

Financial Aid Contact Barbara A. Porter, Director, Financial Aid, PO Box 6905, Radford, VA 24142. *Phone:* 540-831-5408. *Fax:* 540-831-5138. *E-mail:* bporter@radford.edu.

INTERNATIONAL STUDENTS 10% of students enrolled are international students. *Services and facilities:* Counseling/support services, Housing location assistance, International student organization, Language tutoring, Orientation, Visa Services. Financial aid is available to

Radford University (continued)

international students. *Required with application:* TOEFL with recommended score of 213 (computer), 550 (paper), or 79 (Internet); proof of adequate funds; proof of health/immunizations.

International Student Contact Mr. Darrell Thorpe, Director, Multicultural and International Student Services, PO Box 6979, Radford, VA 24142. *Phone:* 540-831-5765. *Fax:* 540-831-5820. *E-mail:* dgthorpe@radford.edu.

APPLICATION *Required:* GMAT, application form, baccalaureate/first degree, 2 letters of recommendation, transcripts of college work. School will accept GRE. *Recommended:* Personal statement, resume/curriculum vitae. *Application fee:* $40. Applications for domestic and international students are processed on a rolling basis.

Application Contact Dr. Clarence C. Rose, Director, MBA Program, PO Box 6956, Radford, VA 24142. *Phone:* 540-831-5185. *Fax:* 540-831-6655. *E-mail:* rumba@radford.edu.

Regent University
School of Global Leadership and Entrepreneurship
Virginia Beach, Virginia

Phone: 757-226-4361 **Fax:** 757-226-4823 **E-mail:** jtotty@regent.edu

Business Program(s) Web Site: http://www.regent.edu/global

Graduate Business Unit Enrollment *Total:* 539 (291 full-time; 248 part-time; 221 women; 43 international). *Average Age:* 32.

Graduate Business Faculty *Total:* 27 (18 full-time; 9 part-time).

Admissions *Applied:* 250. *Admitted:* 109. *Enrolled:* 79. *Average GMAT:* 511. *Average GPA:* 3.3

Academic Calendar Trimesters.

DEGREES   MA • MBA • PhD/Mphil

MA—MOL—Master of Organizational Leadership Full-time and part-time. Distance learning option. 33 total credits required. 16 to 60 months to complete program. *Concentrations:* organizational management, other.

MA—MSF—Master of Strategic Foresight Full-time and part-time. Distance learning option. 33 total credits required. 18 to 48 months to complete program. *Concentration:* strategic management.

MBA—Master of Business Administration Full-time and part-time. Distance learning option. 42 total credits required. 16 to 60 months to complete program. *Concentration:* general MBA.

PhD/Mphil—PhD in Organizational Leadership Part-time. Distance learning option. 60 total credits required. 42 to 84 months to complete program. *Concentrations:* entrepreneurship, human resources development, leadership, other.

RESOURCES AND SERVICES 130 on-campus PCs are available to graduate business students. Access to Internet/World Wide Web, online (class) registration, and online grade reports available. *Personal computer requirements:* Graduate business students are strongly recommended to purchase or lease a personal computer. *Placement services include:* Alumni network, job search course, electronic job bank, and resume preparation.

EXPENSES *Tuition:* Part-time: $735 per credit hour. *Required fees:* Full-time: $400. Tuition and/or fees vary by academic program.

FINANCIAL AID (2007–08) Fellowships, grants, loans, research assistantships, and scholarships. Aid is available to part-time students. *Financial aid application deadline:* 4/15.

Financial Aid Contact Monica Bocarnea, Manager of Academic Services, 1000 Regent University Drive, CRB 324, Virginia Beach, VA 23464-9800. *Phone:* 757-226-4754. *Fax:* 757-226-4369. *E-mail:* moniboc@regent.edu.

INTERNATIONAL STUDENTS 8% of students enrolled are international students. *Services and facilities:* Counseling/support services, Housing location assistance, International student organization, Orientation, Visa Services. Financial aid is available to international students. *Required with application:* TOEFL with recommended score of 233 (computer), 577 (paper), or 90 (Internet); proof of adequate funds.

International Student Contact Amanda Leffel, International Admissions Coordinator, 1000 Regent University Drive, SC 218, Virginia Beach, VA 23464-9800. *Phone:* 757-226-4936. *Fax:* 757-226-4381. *E-mail:* aleffel@regent.edu.

APPLICATION *Required:* GMAT, GRE, application form, baccalaureate/first degree, essay, interview, personal statement, resume/curriculum vitae, transcripts of college work. *Recommended:* Letter(s) of recommendation, work experience. *Application fee:* $50. Applications for domestic and international students are processed on a rolling basis.

Application Contact Jessica Totty, Admissions Manager, 1000 Regent University Drive, Virginia Beach, VA 23464-9800. *Phone:* 757-226-4361. *Fax:* 757-226-4823. *E-mail:* jtotty@regent.edu.

Shenandoah University
Byrd School of Business
Winchester, Virginia

Phone: 540-665-4581 **Fax:** 540-665-4627 **E-mail:** danthony@su.edu

Business Program(s) Web Site: http://www.su.edu/bsb/

Graduate Business Unit Enrollment *Total:* 28 (18 full-time; 10 part-time; 7 women; 10 international). *Average Age:* 30.

Graduate Business Faculty *Total:* 21 (20 full-time; 1 part-time).

Admissions *Applied:* 25. *Admitted:* 19. *Enrolled:* 15. *Average GMAT:* 530. *Average GPA:* 3.0

Academic Calendar Trimesters.

Accreditation AACSB—The Association to Advance Collegiate Schools of Business.

After Graduation (Class of 2006–07) *Employed within 3 months of graduation:* 95%.

DEGREE   MBA

MBA—Master of Business Administration Full-time and part-time. 36 to 48 total credits required. 12 to 24 months to complete program. *Concentration:* general MBA.

RESOURCES AND SERVICES 50 on-campus PCs are available to graduate business students. Access to Internet/World Wide Web, online (class) registration, and online grade reports available. *Personal computer requirements:* Graduate business students are required to have a personal computer. *Special opportunities include:* An international exchange program and an internship program are available. *Placement services include:* Alumni network, career placement, career counseling/planning, electronic job bank, resume referral, career fairs, and resume preparation.

EXPENSES *Tuition:* Full-time: $12,000. Part-time: $640 per credit hour. *Tuition (international):* Full-time: $12,000. *Required fees:* Full-time: $1200. Part-time: $400 per trimester. *Graduate housing:* Room and board costs vary by number of occupants, type of accommodation, and type of board plan. *Typical cost:* $8000 (including board).

FINANCIAL AID (2007–08) 10 students received aid, including fellowships, grants, loans, research assistantships, and work study.

Financial Aid Contact Ms. Nancy Bragg, Director, Financial Aid, 1460 University Drive, Winchester, VA 22601-5195. *Phone:* 540-665-4538. *Fax:* 540-665-5433. *E-mail:* nbragg@su.edu.

INTERNATIONAL STUDENTS 36% of students enrolled are international students. *Services and facilities:* Counseling/support services, ESL/language courses, Housing location assistance, International student organization, Orientation. Financial aid is available to international students. *Required with application:* IELT with recommended score of 6.5;

TOEFL with recommended score of 213 (computer), 550 (paper), or 80 (Internet); proof of adequate funds; proof of health/immunizations.

International Student Contact Bethany R. Galipeau, International Admissions Counselor, 1460 University Drive, Winchester, VA 22601-5195. *Phone:* 540-665-4520. *Fax:* 540-665-4627. *E-mail:* bgalipea@su.edu.

APPLICATION *Required:* GMAT, application form, baccalaureate/first degree, essay, interview, 2 letters of recommendation, personal statement, resume/curriculum vitae, transcripts of college work. School will accept GRE and MAT. *Recommended:* Work experience. *Application fee:* $30. Applications for domestic and international students are processed on a rolling basis.

Application Contact David Anthony, Dean of Admissions, 1460 University Drive, Winchester, VA 22601-5195. *Phone:* 540-665-4581. *Fax:* 540-665-4627. *E-mail:* danthony@su.edu.

Stratford University

Graduate Business Programs

Falls Church, Virginia

Phone: 703-821-8570 Ext. 3211 **Fax:** 703-734-5339 **E-mail:** kevans@stratford.edu

Business Program(s) Web Site: http://www.stratford.edu

Graduate Business Unit Enrollment *Total:* 299 (281 full-time; 18 part-time; 120 women; 224 international). *Average Age:* 26.

Graduate Business Faculty *Total:* 124 (23 full-time; 101 part-time).

Admissions *Applied:* 500. *Admitted:* 266. *Enrolled:* 238. *Average GMAT:* 570. *Average GPA:* 3.3

Academic Calendar Quarters.

After Graduation (Class of 2006–07) *Employed within 3 months of graduation:* 99%. *Average starting salary:* $50,000.

DEGREES IMBA • MBA • MBA equivalent

IMBA—International MBA Full-time and part-time. Distance learning option. 54 total credits required. 15 to 23 months to complete program. *Concentrations:* entrepreneurship, finance, information technology, leadership, marketing.

MBA—Master of Business Administration Full-time and part-time. Distance learning option. BS/BA degree from an accredited college and one of the following: minimum GMAT score of 550 or GRE score of 1600 or 3 years business experience determined by an interview with the Dean. At least 90 total credits required. 25 to 37 months to complete program. *Concentrations:* entrepreneurship, finance, information systems, information technology, leadership, marketing, organizational behavior/development.

MBA equivalent—Enterprise Business Management Full-time and part-time. 54 total credits required. 15 to 23 months to complete program. *Concentration:* management.

RESOURCES AND SERVICES 315 on-campus PCs are available to graduate business students. Access to Internet/World Wide Web and online (class) registration available. *Personal computer requirements:* Graduate business students are strongly recommended to purchase or lease a personal computer. *Placement services include:* Alumni network, career placement, career counseling/planning, electronic job bank, resume referral, career fairs, job interviews arranged, resume preparation, and career library.

EXPENSES *Tuition:* Full-time: $9720. *Tuition (international):* Full-time: $9720.

FINANCIAL AID (2007–08) 15 students received aid, including grants, loans, scholarships, and work study.

Financial Aid Contact Ms. Tawonda Chase, Director of Financial Aid, 7777 Leesburg Pike, Falls Church, VA 22043. *Phone:* 703-821-8570 Ext. 3124. *Fax:* 703-734-5337. *E-mail:* tchase@stratford.edu.

INTERNATIONAL STUDENTS 75% of students enrolled are international students. *Services and facilities:* Counseling/support services, ESL/language courses, Housing location assistance, International student organization, Language tutoring, Orientation, Visa Services. Financial aid is not available to international students. *Required with application:* TOEFL with recommended score of 173 (computer) or 61 (Internet); proof of adequate funds.

International Student Contact Ms. Erica Rhodes, Assistant Director, International Programs, 7777 Leesburg Pike, Falls Church, VA 22043. *Phone:* 703-821-8570 Ext. 3031. *Fax:* 703-734-5339. *E-mail:* erhodes@stratford.edu.

APPLICATION *Required:* Application form, baccalaureate/first degree, interview, transcripts of college work. *Recommended:* Essay, letter(s) of recommendation, personal statement, resume/curriculum vitae, 3 years of work experience. *Application fee:* $50. Applications for domestic and international students are processed on a rolling basis.

Application Contact Mr. Keith Evans, Director of Admissions, 7777 Leesburg Pike, Falls Church, VA 22043. *Phone:* 703-821-8570 Ext. 3211. *Fax:* 703-734-5339. *E-mail:* kevans@stratford.edu.

University of Management and Technology

Graduate Business Programs

Arlington, Virginia

Phone: 703-516-0035 **Fax:** 703-516-0985 **E-mail:** admissions@umtweb.edu

Business Program(s) Web Site: http://www.umtweb.edu

Graduate Business Unit Enrollment *Total:* 2,000 (1,900 full-time; 100 part-time).

Academic Calendar Continuous.

After Graduation (Class of 2006–07) *Employed within 3 months of graduation:* 100%.

DEGREES MBA • MSM

MBA—Master of Business Administration Full-time and part-time. Distance learning option. 24 to 45 total credits required. 12 to 36 months to complete program. *Concentrations:* administration, contract management, general MBA, project management, public and private management, public policy and administration.

MSM—Master of Science in Management Full-time and part-time. Distance learning option. 18 to 33 total credits required. 12 to 36 months to complete program. *Concentrations:* contract management, information technology, international management, management, management information systems, other, public policy and administration, telecommunications management.

RESOURCES AND SERVICES Access to Internet/World Wide Web, online (class) registration, and online grade reports available. *Personal computer requirements:* Graduate business students are required to have a personal computer. *Special opportunities include:* An international exchange program and an internship program are available.

FINANCIAL AID (2007–08) 1200 students received aid, including scholarships. Aid is available to part-time students.

INTERNATIONAL STUDENTS *Services and facilities:* Counseling/support services, Orientation, Visa Services. Financial aid is available to international students. *Required with application:* TOEFL with recommended score of 213 (computer) or 550 (paper); proof of adequate funds; proof of health/immunizations. *Recommended with application:* TWE.

International Student Contact International Student Admissions, 1901 North Fort Myer Drive, Suite 700, Arlington, VA 22209. *Phone:* 703-516-0035. *Fax:* 703-516-0985. *E-mail:* admissions@umtweb.edu.

APPLICATION *Required:* Application form, baccalaureate/first degree, resume/curriculum vitae, transcripts of college work, 5 years of work

University of Management and Technology (continued)

experience. School will accept GMAT, GRE, and MAT. *Recommended:* Letter(s) of recommendation. *Application fee:* $30, $150 (international). Applications for domestic and international students are processed on a rolling basis.

Application Contact Admissions, 1901 North Fort Myer Drive, Suite 700, Arlington, VA 22209. *Phone:* 703-516-0035. *Fax:* 703-516-0985. *E-mail:* admissions@umtweb.edu.

University of Mary Washington
College of Graduate and Professional Studies
Fredericksburg, Virginia

Phone: 540-286-8017 **Fax:** 540-286-8085 **E-mail:** mmejia@umw.edu

Business Program(s) Web Site: http://www.umw.edu/cgps

Graduate Business Unit Enrollment *Total:* 157 (40 full-time; 117 part-time; 78 women; 2 international). *Average Age:* 35.

Graduate Business Faculty *Total:* 14 (11 full-time; 3 part-time).

Admissions *Applied:* 74. *Admitted:* 62. *Enrolled:* 55. *Average GMAT:* 550. *Average GPA:* 3.44

Academic Calendar Five 7-week terms.

After Graduation (Class of 2006–07) *Employed within 3 months of graduation:* 99%. *Average starting salary:* $70,000.

DEGREES MBA • MBA/MSMIS

MBA—Master of Business Administration Full-time and part-time. 36 to 70 total credits required. *Concentrations:* accounting, contract management, human resources development, insurance, management, organizational behavior/development, other, project management, public policy and administration, risk management, technology management.

MBA/MSMIS—Dual MBA/MSMIS Program Full-time and part-time. 60 to 91 total credits required. *Concentration:* combined degrees.

RESOURCES AND SERVICES 114 on-campus PCs are available to graduate business students. Access to Internet/World Wide Web, online (class) registration, and online grade reports available. *Personal computer requirements:* Graduate business students are strongly recommended to purchase or lease a personal computer. *Placement services include:* Alumni network, career counseling/planning, electronic job bank, career fairs, job interviews arranged, resume preparation, and career library.

EXPENSES *Tuition (state resident):* Part-time: $292 per credit hour. *Tuition (nonresident):* Part-time: $664 per credit hour. *Tuition (international):* Part-time: $664 per credit hour.

FINANCIAL AID (2007–08) 54 students received aid, including grants, loans, scholarships, and work study. Aid is available to part-time students.

Financial Aid Contact Debra J. Harber, Associate Dean of Financial Aid, 1301 College Avenue, Fredericksburg, VA 22401. *Phone:* 540-654-2468. *Fax:* 540-654-1858. *E-mail:* dharber@umw.edu.

INTERNATIONAL STUDENTS 1% of students enrolled are international students. *Services and facilities:* Counseling/support services, Orientation, Visa Services. Financial aid is not available to international students. *Required with application:* TOEFL with recommended score of 230 (computer), 550 (paper), or 100 (Internet); proof of adequate funds.

International Student Contact Christopher T. Musick, Director of International Academic Services, 1301 College Avenue, Fredericksburg, VA 22401. *Phone:* 540-654-1870. *Fax:* 540-654-1163. *E-mail:* cmusick@umw.edu.

APPLICATION *Required:* Application form, baccalaureate/first degree, 2 letters of recommendation, personal statement, resume/curriculum vitae, transcripts of college work. School will accept GMAT. *Recommended:* 3 years of work experience. *Application fee:* $45. *Deadlines:* 6/1 for fall, 10/1 for spring, 3/1 for summer, 5/1 for fall (international), 9/1 for spring (international), 2/1 for summer (international).

Application Contact Mr. Matt E. Mejia, Associate Dean of Admissions for Adult Programs, 121 University Boulevard, Fredericksburg, VA 22406. *Phone:* 540-286-8017. *Fax:* 540-286-8085. *E-mail:* mmejia@umw.edu.

University of Richmond
Richard S. Reynolds Graduate School
Richmond, University of Richmond, Virginia

Phone: 804-289-8553 **Fax:** 804-287-1228 **E-mail:** adavis@richmond.edu

Business Program(s) Web Site: http://business.richmond.edu/mba

Graduate Business Unit Enrollment *Total:* 148 (148 part-time; 67 women; 12 international). *Average Age:* 24-37.

Graduate Business Faculty *Total:* 65 (50 full-time; 15 part-time).

Admissions *Applied:* 83. *Admitted:* 64. *Enrolled:* 47. *Average GMAT:* 592. *Average GPA:* 3.24

Academic Calendar Semesters.

Accreditation AACSB—The Association to Advance Collegiate Schools of Business.

DEGREES JD/MBA • MBA

JD/MBA—Juris Doctor/Master of Business Administration Full-time. 95 to 140 total credits required. 36 to 48 months to complete program. *Concentration:* combined degrees.

MBA—Master of Business Administration Part-time. 54 total credits required. 18 to 60 months to complete program. *Concentration:* general MBA.

RESOURCES AND SERVICES 900 on-campus PCs are available to graduate business students. Access to Internet/World Wide Web, online (class) registration, and online grade reports available. *Personal computer requirements:* Graduate business students are not required to have a personal computer. *Placement services include:* Career placement, career counseling/planning, resume preparation, and career library.

EXPENSES *Tuition:* Full-time: $28,970. Part-time: $770 per credit hour. *Tuition (international):* Full-time: $28,970. Part-time: $770 per credit hour.

FINANCIAL AID (2007–08) 59 students received aid, including loans and research assistantships. Aid is available to part-time students. *Financial aid application deadline:* 5/1.

Financial Aid Contact Ms. Cynthia Deffenbaugh, Director, Financial Aid Office, Sarah Brunet Hall, Richmond, VA 23173. *Phone:* 804-289-8438. *Fax:* 804-289-6003. *E-mail:* cdeffenb@richmond.edu.

INTERNATIONAL STUDENTS 8% of students enrolled are international students. *Services and facilities:* Counseling/support services, International student organization, Orientation, Visa Services. Financial aid is available to international students. *Required with application:* TOEFL with recommended score of 250 (computer) or 600 (paper); proof of adequate funds; proof of health/immunizations.

International Student Contact Dr. Richard S. Coughlan, Associate Dean for Graduate and Executive Programs, MBA Program, Robins School of Business, Richmond, VA 23173. *Phone:* 804-289-8553. *Fax:* 804-287-1228. *E-mail:* mba@richmond.edu.

APPLICATION *Required:* GMAT, application form, baccalaureate/first degree, resume/curriculum vitae, transcripts of college work, 2 years of work experience. *Application fee:* $50. Applications for domestic and international students are processed on a rolling basis.

Application Contact Ms. Arlene H. Davis, Program Coordinator, Graduate Studies in Business, MBA Program, Robins School of Business, Richmond, VA 23173. *Phone:* 804-289-8553. *Fax:* 804-287-1228. *E-mail:* adavis@richmond.edu.

University of Virginia

Darden Graduate School of Business Administration

Charlottesville, Virginia

Phone: 434-924-7281 **Fax:** 434-243-5033 **E-mail:** darden@virginia.edu

Business Program(s) Web Site: http://www.darden.virginia.edu/

Graduate Business Unit Enrollment *Total:* 651 (651 full-time; 167 women; 196 international). *Average Age:* 28.

Graduate Business Faculty *Total:* 92 (69 full-time; 23 part-time).

Admissions *Applied:* 2,463. *Admitted:* 711. *Enrolled:* 318. *Average GMAT:* 688. *Average GPA:* 3.3

Academic Calendar Semesters.

Accreditation AACSB—The Association to Advance Collegiate Schools of Business.

After Graduation (Class of 2006–07) *Employed within 3 months of graduation:* 95%. *Average starting salary:* $100,575.

DEGREES EMBA • JD/MBA • MA/MBA • MBA • MBA/MA • MBA/MSN • ME/MBA • PhD/MBA

EMBA—MBA for Executives Full-time. Distance learning option. For more information please see http://www.darden.virginia.edu/MBAexec/. At least 60 total credits required. Maximum of 22 months to complete program. *Concentration:* management.

JD/MBA—Juris Doctor/Master of Business Administration Full-time. For degree information please visit http://www.darden.virginia.edu/mba/jointDegree.htm. Maximum of 48 months to complete program. *Concentration:* management.

MA/MBA—Master of Business Administration/Master of Arts in Government or Foreign Affairs Full-time. For degree information please visit http://www.darden.virginia.edu/mba/jointDegree.htm. *Concentration:* management.

MBA—Master of Business Administration Full-time. For more information please visit http://www.darden.virginia.edu/mba/. At least 60 total credits required. Maximum of 24 months to complete program. *Concentration:* management.

MBA/MA—Master of Business Administration/Master of Arts in East Asian Studies Full-time. For degree information please visit http://www.darden.virginia.edu/mba/jointDegree.htm. *Concentration:* management.

MBA/MSN—Master of Business Administration/Master of Science in Nursing Full-time. For more degree information please see http://www.darden.virginia.edu/mba/jointDegree.htm. *Concentration:* management.

ME/MBA—Master of Engineering/Master of Business Administration Full-time. For degree information please visit http://www.darden.virginia.edu/mba/jointDegree.htm. *Concentration:* management.

PhD/MBA—Doctor of Philosophy/Master of Business Administration Full-time. For degree information please visit http://www.darden.virginia.edu/doctoral/. *Concentration:* management.

RESOURCES AND SERVICES 22 on-campus PCs are available to graduate business students. Access to Internet/World Wide Web, online (class) registration, and online grade reports available. *Personal computer requirements:* Graduate business students are required to have a personal computer. *Special opportunities include:* An international exchange program and an internship program are available. *Placement services include:* Alumni network, career placement, job search course, career counseling/planning, electronic job bank, resume referral, career fairs, job interviews arranged, resume preparation, and career library.

EXPENSES *Tuition (state resident):* Full-time: $37,500. *Tuition (nonresident):* Full-time: $42,500. *Tuition (international):* Full-time: $42,600. *Required fees:* Full-time: $102. *Graduate housing:* Room and board costs vary by campus location, number of occupants, type of accommodation, and type of board plan. *Typical cost:* $17,200 (including board), $6480 (room only).

FINANCIAL AID (2007–08) 304 students received aid, including fellowships, grants, loans, and scholarships. *Financial aid application deadline:* 4/26.

Financial Aid Contact Laurence G. Mueller, Director of Financial Aid, PO Box 6550, Charlottesville, VA 22906. *Phone:* 434-924-7559. *Fax:* 434-243-5033. *E-mail:* muellerl@darden.virginia.edu.

INTERNATIONAL STUDENTS 30% of students enrolled are international students. *Services and facilities:* Counseling/support services, ESL/language courses, Housing location assistance, International student organization, Orientation, Visa Services, Focused student clubs. Financial aid is available to international students. *Required with application:* TOEFL with recommended score of 280 (computer) or 650 (paper); proof of adequate funds; proof of health/immunizations.

International Student Contact Ms. Cheryl Jones, Senior Assistant Director of Admissions, PO Box 6550, Charlottesville, VA 22906-6550. *Phone:* 434-924-7281. *Fax:* 434-243-5033. *E-mail:* darden@virginia.edu.

APPLICATION *Required:* GMAT, application form, essay, interview, 2 letters of recommendation, personal statement, resume/curriculum vitae, transcripts of college work. *Recommended:* Baccalaureate/first degree, work experience. *Application fee:* $190. Applications for domestic and international students are processed on a rolling basis.

Application Contact Ms. Sara Neher, Director of Admissions, PO Box 6550, Charlottesville, VA 22906. *Phone:* 434-924-7281. *Fax:* 434-243-5033. *E-mail:* darden@virginia.edu.

Virginia Commonwealth University

School of Business

Richmond, Virginia

Phone: 804-828-4622 **Fax:** 804-828-7174 **E-mail:** jpmcquaid@vcu.edu

Business Program(s) Web Site: http://www.gsib.vcu.edu

Graduate Business Unit Enrollment *Total:* 569 (235 full-time; 334 part-time; 213 women; 90 international). *Average Age:* 27.

Graduate Business Faculty *Total:* 104 (94 full-time; 10 part-time).

Admissions *Applied:* 454. *Admitted:* 289. *Enrolled:* 204. *Average GMAT:* 567. *Average GPA:* 3.2

Academic Calendar Semesters.

Accreditation AACSB—The Association to Advance Collegiate Schools of Business.

After Graduation (Class of 2006–07) *Employed within 3 months of graduation:* 95%.

DEGREES M Acc • M Sc • M Tax • MA • MBA • MBA/MSIS • MS • Pharm D/MBA

M Acc—Master of Accountancy Full-time and part-time. 30 to 54 total credits required. 12 to 60 months to complete program. *Concentration:* accounting.

M Sc—Master of Science Full-time and part-time. 30 to 45 total credits required. 12 to 60 months to complete program. *Concentrations:* decision sciences, finance, marketing, real estate.

M Tax—Master of Taxation Full-time and part-time. GMAT required for academic track. At least 30 total credits required. 12 to 60 months to complete program. *Concentration:* taxation.

MA—Master of Arts in Economics Full-time and part-time. GRE required. At least 30 total credits required. 12 to 60 months to complete program. *Concentrations:* economics, financial economics.

MBA—Fast-Track Master of Business Administration Part-time. At least 39 total credits required. Maximum of 20 months to complete program. *Concentration:* general MBA.

Virginia Commonwealth University (continued)

MBA—Master of Business Administration Full-time and part-time. 36 to 57 total credits required. 12 to 60 months to complete program. *Concentrations:* accounting, decision sciences, economics, finance, human resources management, management information systems, marketing, real estate, risk management.

MBA/MSIS—Master of Business Administration/Master of Science in Information Science Full-time and part-time. 42 to 56 total credits required. 12 to 60 months to complete program. *Concentration:* information management.

MS—Information Systems Full-time and part-time. 30 to 54 total credits required. 12 to 60 months to complete program. *Concentration:* information systems.

Pharm D/MBA—Doctor of Pharmacy/Master of Business Administration Full-time and part-time. 36 to 57 total credits required. 12 to 60 months to complete program. *Concentrations:* combined degrees, health care.

RESOURCES AND SERVICES 200 on-campus PCs are available to graduate business students. Access to Internet/World Wide Web, online (class) registration, and online grade reports available. *Personal computer requirements:* Graduate business students are strongly recommended to purchase or lease a personal computer. *Special opportunities include:* An international exchange program and an internship program are available. *Placement services include:* Alumni network, career placement, career counseling/planning, electronic job bank, career fairs, job interviews arranged, resume preparation, and career library.

EXPENSES *Tuition (state resident):* Full-time: $8904. Part-time: $465 per credit hour. *Tuition (nonresident):* Full-time: $17,752. Part-time: $954 per credit hour. Tuition and/or fees vary by class time and campus location. *Graduate housing:* Room and board costs vary by number of occupants, type of accommodation, and type of board plan. *Typical cost:* $8000 (including board).

FINANCIAL AID (2007–08) 30 students received aid, including loans, research assistantships, scholarships, and work study. Aid is available to part-time students. *Financial aid application deadline:* 7/15.

Financial Aid Contact Ms. Susan Kadir, Director, University Financial Aid, 901 West Franklin Street, Box 843026, Richmond, VA 23284-4000. *Phone:* 804-828-6669. *Fax:* 804-827-0060. *E-mail:* sfkadir@vcu.edu.

INTERNATIONAL STUDENTS 16% of students enrolled are international students. *Services and facilities:* Counseling/support services, ESL/language courses, Housing location assistance, International student organization, Language tutoring, Orientation, Visa Services. Financial aid is available to international students. *Required with application:* TOEFL with recommended score of 250 (computer), 600 (paper), or 100 (Internet); TWE; proof of adequate funds; proof of health/immunizations.

International Student Contact Dr. Blair W. Brown, Director, Office of International Education, 916 West Franklin Street, Box 843043, Richmond, VA 23284-3043. *Phone:* 804-828-6016. *Fax:* 804-828-1829. *E-mail:* bwbrown@vcu.edu.

APPLICATION *Required:* GMAT, application form, baccalaureate/first degree, essay, 3 letters of recommendation, personal statement, resume/curriculum vitae, transcripts of college work. School will accept GRE. *Recommended:* 2 years of work experience. *Application fee:* $50. Applications for domestic and international students are processed on a rolling basis.

Application Contact Ms. Jana P. McQuaid, Director, Graduate Studies in Business, 301 West Main Street, Box 844000, Richmond, VA 23284-4000. *Phone:* 804-828-4622. *Fax:* 804-828-7174. *E-mail:* jpmcquaid@vcu.edu.

Virginia Polytechnic Institute and State University

Pamplin College of Business

Blacksburg, Virginia

Phone: 540-231-6152 **Fax:** 540-231-4487 **E-mail:** awwebb@vt.edu
Business Program(s) Web Site: http://www.mba.vt.edu

Graduate Business Unit Enrollment *Total:* 1,126. *Average Age:* 27.

Graduate Business Faculty *Total:* 150 (131 full-time; 19 part-time).

Admissions *Applied:* 132. *Admitted:* 76. *Enrolled:* 39. *Average GMAT:* 629. *Average GPA:* 3.3

Academic Calendar Semesters.

Accreditation AACSB—The Association to Advance Collegiate Schools of Business.

After Graduation (Class of 2006–07) *Employed within 3 months of graduation:* 92%. *Average starting salary:* $64,921.

DEGREES M Acc • MBA

M Acc—Master of Accountancy Full-time. At least 30 total credits required. 18 to 48 months to complete program. *Concentrations:* accounting, management information systems.

MBA—Pamplin MBA Program at Virginia Tech Full-time and part-time. Data in this profile represents MBA program only. Pamplin College of Business offers graduate programs in many other areas. See www.pamplin.vt.edu. 48 to 52 total credits required. 21 to 48 months to complete program. *Concentrations:* combined degrees, executive programs, finance, investments and securities, management, system management.

RESOURCES AND SERVICES 45 on-campus PCs are available to graduate business students. Access to Internet/World Wide Web, online (class) registration, and online grade reports available. *Personal computer requirements:* Graduate business students are required to have a personal computer. *Special opportunities include:* An international exchange program and an internship program are available. *Placement services include:* Alumni network, career placement, job search course, career counseling/planning, electronic job bank, resume referral, career fairs, job interviews arranged, resume preparation, and career library.

EXPENSES *Tuition (state resident):* Full-time: $7361. Part-time: $456 per credit hour. *Tuition (nonresident):* Full-time: $13,556. Part-time: $809.25 per credit hour. *Tuition (international):* Full-time: $13,556. Part-time: $809.25 per credit hour. *Required fees:* Full-time: $1795. *Graduate housing:* Room and board costs vary by campus location, number of occupants, type of accommodation, and type of board plan. *Typical cost:* $6191 (including board), $3803 (room only).

FINANCIAL AID (2007–08) 63 students received aid, including fellowships, loans, research assistantships, scholarships, and teaching assistantships. *Financial aid application deadline:* 2/1.

Financial Aid Contact Ms. Angela Webb, Admissions Coordinator, 1044 Pamplin Hall (0209), Blacksburg, VA 24061. *Phone:* 540-231-6152. *Fax:* 540-231-4487. *E-mail:* awwebb@vt.edu.

INTERNATIONAL STUDENTS *Services and facilities:* Counseling/support services, ESL/language courses, Housing location assistance, International student organization, Language tutoring, Orientation, Visa Services. Financial aid is available to international students. *Required with application:* TOEFL with recommended score of 231 (computer), 550 (paper), or 80 (Internet); proof of adequate funds; proof of health/immunizations.

International Student Contact Ms. Zelma Harris, Immigration Advisor, Graduate School, Graduate Life Center at Donaldson Brown (0325), Blacksburg, VA 24061. *Phone:* 540-231-8486. *Fax:* 540-231-3714. *E-mail:* igss@vt.edu.

APPLICATION *Required:* GMAT, application form, baccalaureate/first degree, essay, interview, 2 letters of recommendation, resume/curriculum vitae, transcripts of college work. *Recommended:* Work experience. *Application fee:* $45. Applications for domestic and international students are processed on a rolling basis.

Application Contact Ms. Angela Webb, Admissions Coordinator, 1044 Pamplin Hall (0209), Blacksburg, VA 24061. *Phone:* 540-231-6152. *Fax:* 540-231-4487. *E-mail:* awwebb@vt.edu.

WASHINGTON

Argosy University, Seattle
College of Business

Seattle, Washington

Phone: 206-283-4500 **Fax:** 206-393-3592

Business Program(s) Web Site: http://www.argosy.edu/seattle

DEGREES DBA • MBA • MSM

DBA—Doctor of Business Administration (DBA) *Concentrations:* accounting, information systems, international business, management, marketing.

MBA—Master of Business Administration (MBA) *Concentrations:* finance, health administration, information systems, international business, management, marketing, public policy and administration.

MSM—Master of Science in Management (MSM) *Concentration:* management.

Financial Aid Contact Director of Admissions, 2601-A Elliott Avenue, Seattle, WA 98121. *Phone:* 206-283-4500. *Fax:* 206-393-3592.

International Student Contact Director of Admissions, 2601-A Elliott Avenue, Seattle, WA 98121. *Phone:* 206-283-4500. *Fax:* 206-393-3592.

Application Contact Director of Admissions, 2601-A Elliott Avenue, Seattle, WA 98121. *Phone:* 206-283-4500. *Fax:* 206-393-3592.

See full description on page 566.

City University of Seattle
School of Management

Bellevue, Washington

Phone: 425-637-1010 Ext. 5273 **Fax:** 425-709-5361 **E-mail:** mmecham@cityu.edu

Business Program(s) Web Site: http://www.cityu.edu/

Graduate Business Unit Enrollment *Total:* 1,155 (552 full-time; 603 part-time; 485 women; 154 international). *Average Age:* 34.

Graduate Business Faculty *Total:* 542 (9 full-time; 533 part-time).

Admissions *Applied:* 350. *Admitted:* 350. *Enrolled:* 259.

Academic Calendar Quarters.

DEGREES M Sc • MA • MBA • MS

M Sc—Technology Management Full-time and part-time. Distance learning option. 45 total credits required. *Concentration:* technology management.

MA—Leadership Full-time and part-time. Distance learning option. 45 total credits required. *Concentrations:* organizational behavior/development, organizational management.

MBA—Master of Business Administration Full-time and part-time. Distance learning option. At least 48 total credits required. *Concentration:* general MBA.

MS—Master of Science in Project Management Full-time and part-time. Distance learning option. At least 45 total credits required. *Concentration:* project management.

RESOURCES AND SERVICES 320 on-campus PCs are available to graduate business students. Access to Internet/World Wide Web, online (class) registration, and online grade reports available. *Personal computer requirements:* Graduate business students are required to have a personal computer. *Special opportunities include:* An international exchange

program is available. *Placement services include:* Alumni network, job search course, career counseling/planning, electronic job bank, resume preparation, and career library.

EXPENSES *Tuition:* Full-time: $13,152. Part-time: $548 per credit. *Tuition (international):* Full-time: $13,152. Part-time: $548 per credit. Tuition and/or fees vary by academic program.

FINANCIAL AID (2007–08) 378 students received aid, including grants, loans, scholarships, and work study. Aid is available to part-time students.

Financial Aid Contact Jean L. Roberts, Student Financial Services, 11900 Northeast First Street, Bellevue, WA 98005. *Phone:* 425-637-1010 Ext. 5251. *Fax:* 425-709-5263. *E-mail:* jroberts@cityu.edu.

INTERNATIONAL STUDENTS 13% of students enrolled are international students. *Services and facilities:* Counseling/support services, ESL/language courses, International student organization, Language tutoring, Orientation, Visa Services, Academic advising. Financial aid is not available to international students. *Required with application:* TOEFL with recommended score of 227 (computer) or 567 (paper); proof of adequate funds.

International Student Contact Ms. Sabine Csecsinovics, International Senior Advisor, 11900 Northeast First Street, Bellevue, WA 98005. *Phone:* 425-637-1010 Ext. 5308. *Fax:* 425-709-5319. *E-mail:* scsecsinovics@cityu.edu.

APPLICATION *Required:* Application form, baccalaureate/first degree, transcripts of college work. School will accept GMAT, GRE, and MAT. *Application fee:* $50. Applications for domestic and international students are processed on a rolling basis.

Application Contact Melissa Mecham, Vice President of Admissions, 11900 Northeast First Street, Bellevue, WA 98005. *Phone:* 425-637-1010 Ext. 5273. *Fax:* 425-709-5361. *E-mail:* mmecham@cityu.edu.

See full description on page 588.

DeVry University
Keller Graduate School of Management

Bellevue, Washington

Phone: 425-455-2242 **Fax:** 425-455-2322

Business Program(s) Web Site: http://www.devry.edu

Academic Calendar Semesters.

DEGREES MAFM • MBA • MHRM • MISM • MPA • MPM

MAFM—Master of Accounting and Financial Management Full-time and part-time. Distance learning option. At least 44 total credits required. 18 to 60 months to complete program. *Concentrations:* accounting, financial management/planning.

MBA—Master of Business Administration Full-time and part-time. Distance learning option. At least 48 total credits required. 18 to 60 months to complete program. *Concentration:* general MBA.

MHRM—Master of Human Resource Management Full-time and part-time. Distance learning option. At least 45 total credits required. 18 to 60 months to complete program. *Concentration:* human resources management.

MISM—Master of Information Systems Management Full-time and part-time. Distance learning option. At least 45 total credits required. 18 to 60 months to complete program. *Concentration:* information systems.

MPA—Master of Public Administration Full-time and part-time. Distance learning option. At least 45 total credits required. 18 to 60 months to complete program. *Concentration:* public policy and administration.

MPM—Master of Project Management Full-time and part-time. Distance learning option. At least 42 total credits required. 18 to 60 months to complete program. *Concentration:* project management.

RESOURCES AND SERVICES *Personal computer requirements:* Graduate business students are not required to have a personal computer.

DeVry University (continued)

APPLICATION *Required:* Application form, baccalaureate/first degree, interview, transcripts of college work. Applications for domestic and international students are processed on a rolling basis.

Application Contact Admissions Office, Bellevue Corporate Plaza, 600 108th Avenue, NE, Suite 230, Bellevue, WA 98004. *Phone:* 425-455-2242. *Fax:* 425-455-2322.

DeVry University
Keller Graduate School of Management

Federal Way, Washington

Phone: 253-943-2840

DEGREES MAFM • MBA • MHRM • MIS • MPA • MPM

MAFM—Master of Accounting and Financial Management Full-time and part-time. Distance learning option. At least 44 total credits required. 18 to 60 months to complete program. *Concentrations:* accounting, financial management/planning.

MBA—Master of Business Administration Full-time and part-time. Distance learning option. At least 48 total credits required. 18 to 60 months to complete program. *Concentration:* management.

MHRM—Master of Human Resources Management Full-time and part-time. Distance learning option. At least 45 total credits required. 18 to 60 months to complete program. *Concentration:* human resources management.

MIS—Master of Information Systems Management Full-time and part-time. Distance learning option. At least 45 total credits required. 18 to 60 months to complete program. *Concentration:* information systems.

MPA—Master of Public Administration Full-time and part-time. Distance learning option. At least 45 total credits required. 18 to 60 months to complete program. *Concentration:* public policy and administration.

MPM—Master of Project Management Full-time and part-time. Distance learning option. At least 42 total credits required. 18 to 60 months to complete program. *Concentration:* project management.

Application Contact Admissions Office, 3600 South 344th Way, Federal Way, WA 98001. *Phone:* 253-943-2840.

Eastern Washington University
College of Business and Public Administration

Cheney, Washington

Phone: 509-358-2270 **Fax:** 509-358-2267 **E-mail:** rbrooke@mail.ewu.edu

Business Program(s) Web Site: http://www.ewu.edu/mba

Graduate Business Unit Enrollment *Total:* 74 (34 full-time; 40 part-time; 31 women; 17 international). *Average Age:* 30.

Graduate Business Faculty 16 full-time.

Admissions *Applied:* 90. *Admitted:* 89. *Enrolled:* 74. *Average GMAT:* 511. *Average GPA:* 3.32

Academic Calendar Quarters.

Accreditation AACSB—The Association to Advance Collegiate Schools of Business.

After Graduation (Class of 2006–07) *Employed within 3 months of graduation:* 74%. *Average starting salary:* $30,000.

DEGREES MBA • MBA/MPA • MPA

MBA—Master of Business Administration Full-time and part-time. GMAT required. At least 49 total credits required. 12 to 72 months to complete program. *Concentrations:* accounting, entrepreneurship, general MBA, health care, international business, marketing.

MBA/MPA—Master of Business Administration/Master of Public Administration Full-time and part-time. GMAT required. 73 to 85 total credits required. 18 to 72 months to complete program. *Concentrations:* city/urban administration, nonprofit management, nonprofit organization, public policy and administration.

MPA—Master of Public Administration Full-time and part-time. GMAT not required. At least 60 total credits required. 12 to 72 months to complete program. *Concentration:* public policy and administration.

RESOURCES AND SERVICES 132 on-campus PCs are available to graduate business students. Access to Internet/World Wide Web, online (class) registration, and online grade reports available. *Personal computer requirements:* Graduate business students are strongly recommended to purchase or lease a personal computer. *Special opportunities include:* An international exchange program and an internship program are available. *Placement services include:* Alumni network, career placement, career counseling/planning, resume referral, career fairs, job interviews arranged, resume preparation, and career library.

EXPENSES *Tuition (state resident):* Full-time: $8640. *Tuition (nonresident):* Full-time: $15,800. *Tuition (international):* Full-time: $15,800. *Required fees:* Full-time: $75. *Graduate housing:* Room and board costs vary by number of occupants, type of accommodation, and type of board plan. *Typical cost:* $10,996 (including board), $9540 (room only).

FINANCIAL AID (2007–08) 4 students received aid, including loans, research assistantships, scholarships, teaching assistantships, and work study. *Financial aid application deadline:* 2/1.

Financial Aid Contact Bruce Defrates, Director, Financial Aid and Scholarships, 526 5th Street, 102 Sutton, Cheney, WA 99004-2431. *Phone:* 509-359-2314. *Fax:* 509-359-6153. *E-mail:* bruce.defrates@mail.ewu.edu.

INTERNATIONAL STUDENTS 23% of students enrolled are international students. *Services and facilities:* Counseling/support services, ESL/language courses, International student organization, Language tutoring, Orientation, Visa Services. Financial aid is not available to international students. *Required with application:* TOEFL with recommended score of 237 (computer), 580 (paper), or 92 (Internet); proof of adequate funds. *Recommended with application:* Proof of health/immunizations.

International Student Contact Ms. Susan Hales, Director, International Student Programs, 526 5th Street, 127 Showalter Hall, Cheney, WA 99004-2431. *Phone:* 509-359-2331. *Fax:* 509-359-4643. *E-mail:* esp@mail.ewu.edu.

APPLICATION *Required:* GMAT, application form, baccalaureate/first degree, personal statement, resume/curriculum vitae, transcripts of college work. *Recommended:* Interview, 3 letters of recommendation, work experience. *Application fee:* $100. Applications for domestic and international students are processed on a rolling basis.

Application Contact Ms. Roberta A. Brooke, Director, MBA Program, 668 North Riverpoint Boulevard, Suite A, Spokane, WA 99202-1677. *Phone:* 509-358-2270. *Fax:* 509-358-2267. *E-mail:* rbrooke@mail.ewu.edu.

Gonzaga University
School of Business Administration

Spokane, Washington

Phone: 509-313-4622 **Fax:** 509-313-5811 **E-mail:** chatman@gonzaga.edu

Business Program(s) Web Site: http://www.gonzaga.edu/MBA

Graduate Business Unit Enrollment *Total:* 304 (304 part-time; 113 women; 30 international). *Average Age:* 28.

Graduate Business Faculty *Total:* 40 (30 full-time; 10 part-time).

Admissions *Applied:* 207. *Admitted:* 142. *Enrolled:* 109. *Average GMAT:* 572. *Average GPA:* 3.43

Academic Calendar Semesters.

Accreditation AACSB—The Association to Advance Collegiate Schools of Business.

After Graduation (Class of 2006–07) *Employed within 3 months of graduation:* 90%. *Average starting salary:* $67,000.

DEGREES JD/M Acc • JD/MBA • M Acc • MBA

JD/M Acc—Juris Doctor/Master of Accountancy Full-time. Students must apply to the JD and MAcc programs separately. At least 111 total credits required. 36 to 60 months to complete program. *Concentrations:* accounting, taxation.

JD/MBA—Juris Doctor/Master of Business Administration Full-time. Students must apply to the JD and MBA programs separately. At least 114 total credits required. 36 to 60 months to complete program. *Concentrations:* accounting, business ethics, combined degrees, entrepreneurship, finance, management information systems, marketing, sports/entertainment management, supply chain management.

M Acc—Master of Accountancy Full-time and part-time. At least 30 total credits required. 12 to 60 months to complete program. *Concentrations:* accounting, taxation.

MBA—Master of Business Administration Full-time and part-time. Distance learning option. At least 33 total credits required. 12 to 60 months to complete program. *Concentrations:* accounting, business ethics, entrepreneurship, finance, general MBA, leadership, management information systems, marketing, sports/entertainment management, supply chain management.

RESOURCES AND SERVICES 500 on-campus PCs are available to graduate business students. Access to Internet/World Wide Web, online (class) registration, and online grade reports available. *Personal computer requirements:* Graduate business students are strongly recommended to purchase or lease a personal computer. *Special opportunities include:* An international exchange program and an internship program are available. *Placement services include:* Alumni network, career placement, job search course, career counseling/planning, electronic job bank, resume referral, career fairs, job interviews arranged, resume preparation, and career library.

EXPENSES *Tuition:* Full-time: $14,400. Part-time: $7200 per semester. *Tuition (international):* Full-time: $14,400. Part-time: $7200 per semester. *Required fees:* Full-time: $100. Part-time: $100 per year.

FINANCIAL AID (2007–08) 195 students received aid, including loans, research assistantships, scholarships, and work study. Aid is available to part-time students. *Financial aid application deadline:* 6/1.

Financial Aid Contact Sharon Griffith, Financial Aid Counselor, 502 East Boone Avenue, Spokane, WA 99258-0072. *Phone:* 509-313-4236. *Fax:* 509-313-5718. *E-mail:* griffith@gonzaga.edu.

INTERNATIONAL STUDENTS 10% of students enrolled are international students. *Services and facilities:* Counseling/support services, ESL/language courses, Housing location assistance, International student housing, International student organization, Language tutoring, Orientation. Financial aid is available to international students. *Required with application:* TOEFL with recommended score of 230 (computer) or 570 (paper); proof of adequate funds; proof of health/immunizations.

International Student Contact Stacey Chatman, Assistant Director for Graduate Admissions, 502 East Boone Avenue, Spokane, WA 99258-0009. *Phone:* 509-313-4622. *Fax:* 509-313-5811. *E-mail:* chatman@gonzaga.edu.

APPLICATION *Required:* GMAT, application form, baccalaureate/first degree, essay, 2 letters of recommendation, resume/curriculum vitae, transcripts of college work. *Recommended:* Interview, personal statement, work experience. *Application fee:* $50. Applications for domestic and international students are processed on a rolling basis.

Application Contact Stacey Chatman, Assistant Director for Graduate Admissions, 502 East Boone Avenue, Spokane, WA 99258-0009. *Phone:* 509-313-4622. *Fax:* 509-313-5811. *E-mail:* chatman@gonzaga.edu.

Leadership Institute of Seattle
School of Applied Behavioral Science

Kenmore, Washington

Phone: 425-939-8124 Ext. 120 **Fax:** 425-939-8110 **E-mail:** sharris@lios.org

Business Program(s) Web Site: http://www.lios.org/education/master_arts.cfm

---

DEGREE MOB/MA

MOB/MA—Leadership and Organization Development Full-time. Up to 64 total credits required. *Concentrations:* business education, business ethics, business policy/strategy, business studies, conflict resolution management, executive programs, human resources development, human resources management, leadership, management, management communication, management consulting, management science, management systems analysis, nonprofit management, nonprofit organization, organizational behavior/development, organizational management, quality management, strategic management, system management, training and development.

RESOURCES AND SERVICES Access to Internet/World Wide Web and online (class) registration available. *Personal computer requirements:* Graduate business students are strongly recommended to purchase or lease a personal computer. *Placement services include:* Alumni network, career counseling/planning, resume referral, career fairs, resume preparation, and career library.

Application Contact Scott Harris, Admissions Director, 14506 Juanita Drive, Kenmore, WA 98028-4966. *Phone:* 425-939-8124 Ext. 120. *Fax:* 425-939-8110. *E-mail:* sharris@lios.org.

Pacific Lutheran University
School of Business

Tacoma, Washington

Phone: 253-535-7330 **Fax:** 253-535-8723 **E-mail:** business@plu.edu

Business Program(s) Web Site: http://www.plu.edu/busa/

Graduate Business Unit Enrollment *Total:* 84 (84 part-time; 40 women; 19 international). *Average Age:* 29.

Graduate Business Faculty *Total:* 19 (15 full-time; 4 part-time).

Admissions *Applied:* 52. *Admitted:* 38. *Enrolled:* 26. *Average GMAT:* 530. *Average GPA:* 3.3

Academic Calendar 4-1-4.

Accreditation AACSB—The Association to Advance Collegiate Schools of Business.

After Graduation (Class of 2006–07) *Employed within 3 months of graduation:* 99%. *Average starting salary:* $75,000.

DEGREES MBA • MBA/MSN

MBA—Master of Business Administration Full-time and part-time. 40 to 48 total credits required. 20 to 84 months to complete program. *Concentrations:* entrepreneurship, general MBA, health administration, technology management.

MBA/MSN—MSN/MBA Full-time and part-time. Applicants must apply to the School of Nursing. 60 total credits required. 36 months to complete program. *Concentration:* combined degrees.

Pacific Lutheran University (continued)

RESOURCES AND SERVICES 240 on-campus PCs are available to graduate business students. Access to Internet/World Wide Web, online (class) registration, and online grade reports available. *Personal computer requirements:* Graduate business students are strongly recommended to purchase or lease a personal computer. *Special opportunities include:* An international exchange program and an internship program are available. *Placement services include:* Alumni network, career counseling/planning, electronic job bank, resume referral, career fairs, resume preparation, and career library.

EXPENSES *Tuition:* Full-time: $19,755. Part-time: $2634 per course. *Tuition (international):* Full-time: $19,755. Part-time: $2534 per course. Tuition and/or fees vary by number of courses or credits taken. *Graduate housing:* Room and board costs vary by number of occupants and type of board plan. *Typical cost:* $7774 (including board).

FINANCIAL AID (2007–08) 56 students received aid, including fellowships, grants, loans, research assistantships, scholarships, and work study. Aid is available to part-time students. *Financial aid application deadline:* 5/1.

Financial Aid Contact Kay Soltis, Director of Financial Aid, Tacoma, WA 98447. *Phone:* 253-535-7161. *Fax:* 253-535-8320. *E-mail:* finaid@plu.edu.

INTERNATIONAL STUDENTS 23% of students enrolled are international students. *Services and facilities:* Counseling/support services, ESL/language courses, Housing location assistance, International student housing, International student organization, Language tutoring, Orientation, Visa Services. Financial aid is available to international students. *Required with application:* IELT with recommended score of 6.5; TOEFL with recommended score of 230 (computer), 570 (paper), or 88 (Internet); proof of adequate funds; proof of health/immunizations.

International Student Contact David Gerry, Coordinator, International Student Services, International Student Services, Tacoma, WA 98447. *Phone:* 253-535-7194. *Fax:* 253-535-8752. *E-mail:* gerrydp@plu.edu.

APPLICATION *Required:* GMAT, application form, baccalaureate/first degree, 2 letters of recommendation, personal statement, resume/curriculum vitae, transcripts of college work. School will accept GRE. *Recommended:* Interview, 2 years of work experience. *Application fee:* $40. Applications for domestic and international students are processed on a rolling basis.

Application Contact Abby J. Wigstrom-Carlson, Director of Graduate Programs and External Relations, Tacoma, WA 98447. *Phone:* 253-535-7330. *Fax:* 253-535-8723. *E-mail:* business@plu.edu.

Saint Martin's University
Division of Economics and Business Administration
Lacey, Washington

Phone: 360-438-4512 **Fax:** 360-438-4522 **E-mail:** hwilson@stmartin.edu

Business Program(s) Web Site: http://www.stmartin.edu

Graduate Business Unit Enrollment *Total:* 125 (125 part-time; 77 women; 5 international).

Graduate Business Faculty *Total:* 14 (6 full-time; 8 part-time).

Admissions *Average GMAT:* 520. *Average GPA:* 3.45

Academic Calendar 5 terms.

After Graduation (Class of 2006–07) *Employed within 3 months of graduation:* 95%.

DEGREES MBA • MBA/M Acc

MBA—Master of Business Administration Full-time and part-time. At least 33 total credits required. 12 to 84 months to complete program. *Concentration:* general MBA.

MBA/M Acc—MBA in Accounting Full-time and part-time. Must have undergraduate accounting degree. At least 33 total credits required. 12 to 83 months to complete program. *Concentration:* accounting.

RESOURCES AND SERVICES 200 on-campus PCs are available to graduate business students. Access to Internet/World Wide Web, online (class) registration, and online grade reports available. *Personal computer requirements:* Graduate business students are strongly recommended to purchase or lease a personal computer. *Special opportunities include:* An internship program is available. *Placement services include:* Alumni network, career placement, career counseling/planning, electronic job bank, resume referral, career fairs, resume preparation, and career library.

FINANCIAL AID (2007–08) Loans and scholarships. Aid is available to part-time students.

Financial Aid Contact Ms. Laura Miller, Director of Financial Aid, 5300 Pacific Avenue, SE, Lacey, WA 98503-1297. *Phone:* 360-438-4397. *Fax:* 360-412-6189. *E-mail:* finaid@stmartin.edu.

INTERNATIONAL STUDENTS 4% of students enrolled are international students. *Services and facilities:* Counseling/support services, ESL/language courses, Visa Services. Financial aid is not available to international students. *Required with application:* TOEFL with recommended score of 193 (computer) or 525 (paper); proof of adequate funds.

International Student Contact Josephine Yung, Dean, Office of International Programs, 5300 Pacific Avenue, SE, Lacey, WA 98503. *Phone:* 360-438-4375. *E-mail:* jyung@stmartin.edu.

APPLICATION *Required:* GMAT, application form, baccalaureate/first degree, transcripts of college work. School will accept GRE. *Recommended:* Interview. *Application fee:* $35. Applications for domestic and international students are processed on a rolling basis.

Application Contact Dr. Riley Moore, MBA Director, 5300 Pacific Avenue, SE, Lacey, WA 98503. *Phone:* 360-438-4512. *Fax:* 360-438-4522. *E-mail:* hwilson@stmartin.edu.

Seattle Pacific University
School of Business and Economics
Seattle, Washington

Phone: 206-281-2753 **Fax:** 206-281-2733 **E-mail:** djwysom@spu.edu

Business Program(s) Web Site: http://www.spu.edu/sbe

Graduate Business Unit Enrollment *Total:* 134 (13 full-time; 121 part-time; 59 women; 8 international). *Average Age:* 31.

Graduate Business Faculty *Total:* 30 (20 full-time; 10 part-time).

Admissions *Applied:* 32. *Admitted:* 28. *Enrolled:* 12. *Average GMAT:* 530. *Average GPA:* 3.54

Academic Calendar Quarters.

Accreditation AACSB—The Association to Advance Collegiate Schools of Business.

After Graduation (Class of 2006–07) *Employed within 3 months of graduation:* 92%. *Average starting salary:* $65,100.

DEGREES MBA • MS

MBA—Master of Business Administration Full-time and part-time. Minimum GMAT score of 490 required. 45 to 72 total credits required. 24 to 72 months to complete program. *Concentrations:* electronic commerce (E-commerce), finance, human resources management, management, management information systems.

MS—Master of Science in Information Systems Management Full-time and part-time. GRE required. 45 to 51 total credits required. 24 to 72 months to complete program. *Concentration:* management information systems.

RESOURCES AND SERVICES 161 on-campus PCs are available to graduate business students. Access to Internet/World Wide Web, online (class) registration, and online grade reports available. *Personal computer requirements:* Graduate business students are strongly recommended to

purchase or lease a personal computer. *Placement services include:* Job search course, career counseling/planning, electronic job bank, resume referral, career fairs, job interviews arranged, resume preparation, and career library.

EXPENSES *Tuition:* Full-time: $15,000. Part-time: $625 per credit. *Tuition (international):* Full-time: $15,000. Part-time: $625 per credit. *Graduate housing:* Room and board costs vary by number of occupants, type of accommodation, and type of board plan. *Typical cost:* $9528 (including board), $8016 (room only).

FINANCIAL AID (2007–08) 3 students received aid, including research assistantships and scholarships. Aid is available to part-time students. *Financial aid application deadline:* 4/1.

Financial Aid Contact Jordan Grant, Director, Student Financial Services, 3307 Third Avenue, West, Seattle, WA 98119-1997. *Phone:* 206-281-2469. *E-mail:* grantj@spu.edu.

INTERNATIONAL STUDENTS 6% of students enrolled are international students. *Services and facilities:* Counseling/support services, ESL/language courses, Housing location assistance, Orientation. Financial aid is not available to international students. *Required with application:* TOEFL with recommended score of 225 (computer), 565 (paper), or 86 (Internet); proof of adequate funds.

International Student Contact Ms. Lori Hont Tongol, International Student Advisor, 3307 Third Avenue, West, Seattle, WA 98119. *Phone:* 206-281-2486. *Fax:* 206-281-2730. *E-mail:* tongol@spu.edu.

APPLICATION *Required:* GMAT, application form, baccalaureate/first degree, essay, 2 letters of recommendation, personal statement, resume/ curriculum vitae, transcripts of college work, 1 year of work experience. *Application fee:* $50. Applications for domestic and international students are processed on a rolling basis.

Application Contact Debra Wysomierski, Associate Graduate Director, 3307 Third Avenue, West, Suite 201, Seattle, WA 98119-1950. *Phone:* 206-281-2753. *Fax:* 206-281-2733. *E-mail:* djwysom@spu.edu.

Seattle University
Albers School of Business and Economics

Seattle, Washington

Phone: 206-296-2000 **Fax:** 206-296-5656 **E-mail:** grad-admissions@seattleu.edu

Business Program(s) Web Site: http://www.seattleu.edu/asbe/

Graduate Business Unit Enrollment *Total:* 920 (223 full-time; 697 part-time; 355 women; 105 international). *Average Age:* 28.

Graduate Business Faculty *Total:* 60 (51 full-time; 9 part-time).

Admissions *Applied:* 408. *Admitted:* 287. *Enrolled:* 202. *Average GMAT:* 575. *Average GPA:* 3.38

Academic Calendar Quarters.

Accreditation AACSB—The Association to Advance Collegiate Schools of Business.

After Graduation (Class of 2006–07) *Employed within 3 months of graduation:* 80%.

DEGREES EMBA • MBA • MIB • MPA • MSF

EMBA—Executive Master of Business Administration Full-time. At least 60 total credits required. Minimum of 21 months to complete program. *Concentration:* executive programs.

MBA—Master of Business Administration Full-time and part-time. 55 to 73 total credits required. 12 to 72 months to complete program. *Concentrations:* accounting, business law, economics, electronic commerce (E-commerce), entrepreneurship, finance, general MBA, international business, management, marketing.

MIB Full-time and part-time. 46 to 67 total credits required. 12 to 72 months to complete program. *Concentration:* international business.

MPA—Master of Professional Accounting Full-time and part-time. 46 to 91 total credits required. 12 to 72 months to complete program. *Concentration:* accounting.

MSF Full-time and part-time. 45 to 63 total credits required. 12 to 72 months to complete program. *Concentration:* finance.

RESOURCES AND SERVICES 272 on-campus PCs are available to graduate business students. Access to Internet/World Wide Web, online (class) registration, and online grade reports available. *Personal computer requirements:* Graduate business students are strongly recommended to purchase or lease a personal computer. *Special opportunities include:* An internship program is available. *Placement services include:* Alumni network, job search course, career counseling/planning, electronic job bank, resume referral, career fairs, resume preparation, and career library.

EXPENSES *Tuition:* Full-time: $17,415. *Tuition (international):* Full-time: $17,415. *Graduate housing:* Room and board costs vary by campus location, type of accommodation, and type of board plan. *Typical cost:* $8286 (including board), $6036 (room only).

FINANCIAL AID (2007–08) 27 students received aid, including loans, scholarships, and work study. Aid is available to part-time students. *Financial aid application deadline:* 2/1.

Financial Aid Contact Janet Cantelon, Director, Student Financial Services, Student Financial Services, 901 12th Avenue, USVC 105, PO Box 222000, Seattle, WA 98122-1090. *Phone:* 206-296-2000. *Fax:* 206-296-5755. *E-mail:* cantelon@seattleu.edu.

INTERNATIONAL STUDENTS 11% of students enrolled are international students. *Services and facilities:* Counseling/support services, ESL/language courses, International student organization, Language tutoring, Orientation, Visa Services. Financial aid is not available to international students. *Required with application:* TOEFL with recommended score of 237 (computer), 580 (paper), or 92 (Internet); proof of adequate funds.

International Student Contact Faizi Ghodsi, Director, International Student Center, 901 12th Avenue, Pavilion P160, Seattle, WA 98122-1090. *Phone:* 206-296-6260. *Fax:* 206-296-6262. *E-mail:* fghodsi@seattleu.edu.

APPLICATION *Required:* GMAT, application form, baccalaureate/first degree, resume/curriculum vitae, transcripts of college work, 2 years of work experience. *Recommended:* Letter(s) of recommendation. *Application fee:* $55. Applications for domestic and international students are processed on a rolling basis.

Application Contact Janet Shandley, Director of Admissions, Graduate Admissions, 901 12th Avenue, PO Box 222000, Seattle, WA 98122-1090. *Phone:* 206-296-2000. *Fax:* 206-296-5656. *E-mail:* grad-admissions@ seattleu.edu.

University of Phoenix–Eastern Washington Campus
College of Graduate Business and Management

Spokane Valley, Washington

Phone: 480-317-6200 **Fax:** 480-643-1479 **E-mail:** beth.barilla@phoenix.edu

DEGREES MBA

MBA—Accounting Full-time. At least 54 total credits required. *Concentration:* accounting.

MBA—Human Resource Management Full-time. At least 45 total credits required. *Concentration:* human resources management.

MBA—Marketing Full-time. At least 45 total credits required. *Concentration:* marketing.

MBA—Master of Business Administration Full-time. At least 45 total credits required. *Concentration:* administration.

University of Phoenix–Eastern Washington Campus (continued)

MBA—Public Administration Full-time. At least 45 total credits required. *Concentration:* public policy and administration.

RESOURCES AND SERVICES Access to online grade reports available. *Personal computer requirements:* Graduate business students are strongly recommended to purchase or lease a personal computer. *Placement services include:* Alumni network.

Application Contact Beth Barilla, Associate Vice President of Student Admissions and Services, Mail Stop AA-K101, 4615 East Elwood Street, Phoenix, AZ 85040-1958. *Phone:* 480-317-6200. *Fax:* 480-643-1479. *E-mail:* beth.barilla@phoenix.edu.

University of Phoenix–Washington Campus

College of Graduate Business and Management

Seattle, Washington

Phone: 480-317-6200 **Fax:** 480-643-1479 **E-mail:**
beth.barilla@phoenix.edu

Business Program(s) Web Site: http://www.phoenix.edu

DEGREES M Mgt • MBA • MM

M Mgt—Human Resource Management Full-time. At least 39 total credits required.

MBA—Accounting Full-time. At least 51 total credits required. *Concentration:* accounting.

MBA—Global Management Full-time. At least 45 total credits required. *Concentration:* international business.

MBA—Human Resource Management Full-time. At least 45 total credits required. *Concentration:* human resources management.

MBA—Marketing Full-time. At least 45 total credits required. *Concentration:* marketing.

MBA—e-Business Full-time. At least 45 total credits required. *Concentration:* electronic commerce (E-commerce).

MBA—Master of Business Administration Full-time. At least 45 total credits required. *Concentration:* administration.

MM—Master of Management Full-time. At least 39 total credits required. *Concentration:* management.

RESOURCES AND SERVICES Access to online grade reports available. *Personal computer requirements:* Graduate business students are strongly recommended to purchase or lease a personal computer. *Placement services include:* Alumni network.

Application Contact Beth Barilla, Associate Vice President of Student Admissions and Services, Mail Stop AA-K101, 4615 East Elwood Street, Phoenix, AZ 85040-1958. *Phone:* 480-317-6200. *Fax:* 480-643-1479. *E-mail:* beth.barilla@phoenix.edu.

University of Washington

Michael G. Foster School of Business

Seattle, Washington

Phone: 206-543-4661 **Fax:** 206-616-7351 **E-mail:**
mba@u.washington.edu

Business Program(s) Web Site: http://www.foster.washington.edu/mba

Graduate Business Unit Enrollment *Total:* 798 (325 full-time; 473 part-time; 215 women; 189 international). *Average Age:* 32.

Graduate Business Faculty *Total:* 148 (106 full-time; 42 part-time).

Admissions *Applied:* 1,478. *Admitted:* 645. *Enrolled:* 411. *Average GMAT:* 679. *Average GPA:* 3.34

Academic Calendar Quarters.

Accreditation AACSB—The Association to Advance Collegiate Schools of Business.

After Graduation (Class of 2006–07) *Employed within 3 months of graduation:* 91%. *Average starting salary:* $84,992.

DEGREES EMBA • GMBA • JD/MBA • M Pr A • MBA • MBA/MA • MBA/MHA • MPA

EMBA—Global Executive Master of Business Administration Full-time. At least 48 total credits required. 15 to 18 months to complete program. *Concentration:* general MBA.

GMBA—Global Master of Business Administration Full-time. At least 64 total credits required. 12 to 72 months to complete program. *Concentrations:* general MBA, international business.

JD/MBA—Juris Doctor/Master of Business Administration Full-time. At least 212 total credits required. 48 to 72 months to complete program. *Concentrations:* business law, legal administration.

M Pr A—Master of Professional Accounting in Auditing and Assurance Full-time. At least 48 total credits required. 12 to 72 months to complete program. *Concentration:* accounting.

MBA—Evening Master of Business Administration Part-time. At least 82 total credits required. 27 to 45 months to complete program. *Concentrations:* decision sciences, economics, entrepreneurship, finance, general MBA, information systems, international business, management, managerial economics, marketing.

MBA—Executive Master of Business Administration Part-time. At least 66 total credits required. 21 months to complete program. *Concentration:* management.

MBA—Technology Management Master of Business Administration Part-time. At least 59 total credits required. 18 to 72 months to complete program. *Concentration:* technology management.

MBA—Master of Business Administration Full-time. At least 90 total credits required. 18 to 72 months to complete program. *Concentrations:* accounting, decision sciences, economics, electronic commerce (E-commerce), entrepreneurship, finance, general MBA, health administration, human resources management, information management, international business, management, management information systems, managerial economics, marketing, operations management, organizational behavior/development, quantitative analysis, real estate, strategic management, technology management, transportation management.

MBA/MA—Master of Business Administration/Master of Arts in International Studies Full-time. At least 132 total credits required. 36 to 72 months to complete program. *Concentrations:* international and area business studies, international business, international economics, international finance, international logistics, international management, international marketing, international trade.

MBA/MHA—Master of Business Administration/Master of Health Administration Full-time. At least 112 total credits required. 24 to 72 months to complete program. *Concentration:* management.

MPA—Master of Professional Accounting in Taxation Full-time and part-time. At least 48 total credits required. 12 to 72 months to complete program. *Concentration:* taxation.

RESOURCES AND SERVICES 140 on-campus PCs are available to graduate business students. Access to Internet/World Wide Web, online (class) registration, and online grade reports available. *Personal computer requirements:* Graduate business students are required to have a personal computer. *Special opportunities include:* An international exchange program is available. *Placement services include:* Alumni network, career placement, job search course, career counseling/planning, electronic job bank, resume referral, career fairs, job interviews arranged, resume preparation, and career library.

EXPENSES *Tuition (state resident):* Full-time: $19,299. Part-time: $15,993 per year. *Tuition (nonresident):* Full-time: $29,000. Part-time: $15,993 per year. *Tuition (international):* Full-time: $29,000. Part-time:

$15,993 per year. *Required fees:* Full-time: $543. Part-time: $543 per year. Tuition and/or fees vary by class time, number of courses or credits taken, and academic program. *Graduate housing:* Room and board costs vary by campus location, number of occupants, type of accommodation, and type of board plan. *Typical cost:* $15,656 (including board).

FINANCIAL AID (2007–08) 186 students received aid, including fellowships, loans, research assistantships, scholarships, teaching assistantships, and work study. *Financial aid application deadline:* 3/15.

Financial Aid Contact Ms. Erin Ernst, Assistant Admissions Director, Box 353200, 110 Mackenzie Hall, Seattle, WA 98195-3200. *Phone:* 206-543-4661. *Fax:* 206-616-7351. *E-mail:* ee2@u.washington.edu.

INTERNATIONAL STUDENTS 24% of students enrolled are international students. *Services and facilities:* Counseling/support services, ESL/language courses, Housing location assistance, International student housing, International student organization, Orientation, Visa Services, Professional communications and presentation skill development. Financial aid is available to international students. *Required with application:* TOEFL with recommended score of 250 (computer), 600 (paper), or 100 (Internet); proof of adequate funds; proof of health/immunizations.

International Student Contact Ms. Erin Ernst, Assistant Admissions Director, MBA Program, Box 353200, 110 Mackenzie Hall, Seattle, WA 98195-3200. *Phone:* 206-543-4661. *Fax:* 206-616-7351. *E-mail:* ee2@u.washington.edu.

APPLICATION *Required:* GMAT, application form, baccalaureate/first degree, essay, interview, 2 letters of recommendation, personal statement, resume/curriculum vitae, transcripts of college work. *Recommended:* Work experience. *Application fee:* $75. Applications for domestic and international students are processed on a rolling basis.

Application Contact MBA Program Office, Box 353200, 110 Mackenzie Hall, Seattle, WA 98195-3200. *Phone:* 206-543-4661. *Fax:* 206-616-7351. *E-mail:* mba@u.washington.edu.

See full description on page 754.

Washington State University
College of Business
Pullman, Washington

Phone: 509-335-7617 **Fax:** 509-335-4735 **E-mail:** mba@wsu.edu

Business Program(s) Web Site: http://www.business.wsu.edu/graduate

Graduate Business Unit Enrollment *Total:* 125 (125 full-time). *Average Age:* 27.

Graduate Business Faculty *Total:* 24 (21 full-time; 3 part-time).

Admissions *Applied:* 124. *Admitted:* 59. *Enrolled:* 29. *Average GMAT:* 568. *Average GPA:* 3.35

Academic Calendar Semesters.

Accreditation AACSB—The Association to Advance Collegiate Schools of Business.

After Graduation (Class of 2006–07) *Employed within 3 months of graduation:* 93%. *Average starting salary:* $33,000.

DEGREES JD/MBA • M Acc • MBA

JD/MBA—Juris Doctor/Master of Business Administration Full-time. 45 months to complete program. *Concentration:* combined degrees.

M Acc—Master of Accounting Full-time. At least 34 total credits required. 12 to 24 months to complete program. *Concentration:* accounting.

MBA—Accelerated MBA Full-time. 39 total credits required. 12 months to complete program. *Concentration:* general MBA.

MBA—Master of Business Administration Full-time. 62 total credits required. 21 months to complete program. *Concentration:* general MBA.

RESOURCES AND SERVICES Access to Internet/World Wide Web, online (class) registration, and online grade reports available. *Personal*

computer requirements: Graduate business students are required to have a personal computer. *Special opportunities include:* An international exchange program and an internship program are available. *Placement services include:* Career placement, job search course, career counseling/planning, electronic job bank, resume referral, career fairs, job interviews arranged, resume preparation, and career library.

EXPENSES *Tuition (state resident):* Full-time: $11,126. *Tuition (nonresident):* Full-time: $22,118. *Tuition (international):* Full-time: $22,118. *Required fees:* Full-time: $526. Tuition and/or fees vary by campus location and academic program. *Typical graduate housing cost:* $8910 (including board), $5054 (room only).

FINANCIAL AID (2007–08) 23 students received aid, including loans, research assistantships, scholarships, teaching assistantships, and work study. *Financial aid application deadline:* 3/1.

Financial Aid Contact Chio Flores, Assistant Director, Financial Aid Office, Lighty Student Services Building, Room 380, Pullman, WA 99164-1068. *Phone:* 509-335-9711.

INTERNATIONAL STUDENTS *Services and facilities:* Counseling/support services, ESL/language courses, International student housing, International student organization, Language tutoring, Orientation, Visa Services. Financial aid is not available to international students. *Required with application:* TOEFL with recommended score of 237 (computer), 580 (paper), or 93 (Internet); proof of adequate funds; proof of health/immunizations. *Recommended with application:* IELT with recommended score of 7.

International Student Contact Furnari Mary, Assistant Director, International Programs, Pullman, WA 99164-5110. *Phone:* 509-335-4508. *Fax:* 509-335-2373. *E-mail:* mfurnai@wsu.edu.

APPLICATION *Required:* GMAT, application form, baccalaureate/first degree, 3 letters of recommendation, personal statement, resume/curriculum vitae, transcripts of college work. *Recommended:* Interview, work experience. *Application fee:* $50. Applications for domestic and international students are processed on a rolling basis.

Application Contact Ms. Cheryl Oliver, Director, PO Box 644744, Pullman, WA 99164-4744. *Phone:* 509-335-7617. *Fax:* 509-335-4735. *E-mail:* mba@wsu.edu.

Washington State University Tri-Cities
College of Business
Richland, Washington

Phone: 509-372-7360 **Fax:** 509-372-7512 **E-mail:** wwalters@tricity.wsu.edu

Business Program(s) Web Site: http://www.tricity.wsu.edu/business/

Graduate Business Unit Enrollment *Total:* 53 (2 full-time; 51 part-time; 17 women). *Average Age:* 35.

Graduate Business Faculty *Total:* 10 (8 full-time; 2 part-time).

Admissions *Applied:* 15. *Admitted:* 13. *Enrolled:* 13. *Average GMAT:* 571. *Average GPA:* 3.36

Academic Calendar Semesters.

After Graduation (Class of 2006–07) *Employed within 3 months of graduation:* 100%.

DEGREE MBA

MBA—Master of Business Administration Full-time and part-time. Minimum GMAT score of 550, minimum GPA of 3.0 in last 60 semester hours of undergraduate study. 32 to 53 total credits required. 12 to 72 months to complete program. *Concentrations:* entrepreneurship, general MBA, human resources management, management, management information systems, technology management.

Washington State University Tri-Cities (continued)

RESOURCES AND SERVICES 20 on-campus PCs are available to graduate business students. Access to Internet/World Wide Web, online (class) registration, and online grade reports available. *Personal computer requirements:* Graduate business students are strongly recommended to purchase or lease a personal computer. *Placement services include:* Career counseling/planning and career fairs.

EXPENSES *Tuition (state resident):* Full-time: $4034. Part-time: $403 per credit. *Tuition (nonresident):* Full-time: $9838. Part-time: $984 per credit.

FINANCIAL AID (2007–08) Loans.

Financial Aid Contact Ms. Mary Bauer, Financial Aid Coordinator, 2710 University Drive, Richland, WA 99354. *Phone:* 509-372-7228. *Fax:* 509-372-7100. *E-mail:* mbauer@tricity.wsu.edu.

INTERNATIONAL STUDENTS *Required with application:* TOEFL with recommended score of 237 (computer) or 580 (paper); proof of adequate funds; proof of health/immunizations.

APPLICATION *Required:* GMAT, application form, baccalaureate/first degree, 3 letters of recommendation, transcripts of college work. School will accept GRE. *Recommended:* Interview, work experience. *Application fee:* $50. *Deadlines:* 6/25 for fall, 11/5 for spring, 3/8 for summer, 3/1 for fall (international), 7/1 for spring (international).

Application Contact Mrs. Wanda Walters, Academic Coordinator Business Programs, Business Programs, 2710 University Drive, Richland, WA 99354. *Phone:* 509-372-7360. *Fax:* 509-372-7512. *E-mail:* wwalters@tricity.wsu.edu.

Washington State University Vancouver

Program in Business Administration

Vancouver, Washington

Phone: 360-546-9751 **E-mail:** mstender@vancouver.wsu.edu

Business Program(s) Web Site: http://www.vancouver.wsu.edu/programs/bus/mba3.html

Graduate Business Faculty *Total:* 8 (7 full-time; 1 part-time).

Academic Calendar Semesters.

DEGREE MA/MBA

MA/MBA—Master of Arts/Master of Business Administration Full-time and part-time. 35 total credits required. *Concentration:* general MBA.

RESOURCES AND SERVICES Access to Internet/World Wide Web, online (class) registration, and online grade reports available. *Personal computer requirements:* Graduate business students are not required to have a personal computer. *Placement services include:* Alumni network, career placement, career counseling/planning, career fairs, and resume preparation.

EXPENSES *Tuition (state resident):* Full-time: $10,162. Part-time: $2424 per semester. *Tuition (nonresident):* Full-time: $21,822. Part-time: $5904 per semester. *Tuition (international):* Full-time: $21,822. Tuition and/or fees vary by number of courses or credits taken and local reciprocity agreements.

FINANCIAL AID (2007–08) Loans and scholarships.

INTERNATIONAL STUDENTS *Services and facilities:* Counseling/support services. *Required with application:* TOEFL; proof of adequate funds.

APPLICATION *Required:* GMAT, application form, baccalaureate/first degree, 3 letters of recommendation, resume/curriculum vitae, transcripts of college work. *Recommended:* Interview, 2 years of work experience. *Application fee:* $50. *Deadlines:* 1/10 for fall, 7/1 for spring, 1/10 for summer, 1/10 for fall (international), 7/1 for spring (international), 1/10 for summer (international).

Application Contact Mary Stender, Academic Coordinator, Business Programs, 14204 NE Salmon Creek Avenue, Vancouver, WA 98686-9600. *Phone:* 360-546-9751. *E-mail:* mstender@vancouver.wsu.edu.

Western Washington University

College of Business and Economics

Bellingham, Washington

Phone: 360-650-3898 **Fax:** 360-650-4844 **E-mail:** mba@wwu.edu

Business Program(s) Web Site: http://www.cbe.wwu.edu/mba

Graduate Business Unit Enrollment *Total:* 62 (47 full-time; 15 part-time; 20 women; 12 international).

Graduate Business Faculty 50 full-time.

Admissions *Applied:* 86. *Admitted:* 74. *Enrolled:* 47. *Average GMAT:* 552. *Average GPA:* 3.37

Academic Calendar Quarters.

Accreditation AACSB—The Association to Advance Collegiate Schools of Business.

After Graduation (Class of 2006–07) *Average starting salary:* $50,000.

DEGREE MBA

MBA—Master of Business Administration Full-time and part-time. 60 to 92 total credits required. 12 to 27 months to complete program. *Concentration:* general MBA.

RESOURCES AND SERVICES 50 on-campus PCs are available to graduate business students. Access to Internet/World Wide Web, online (class) registration, and online grade reports available. *Personal computer requirements:* Graduate business students are not required to have a personal computer. *Special opportunities include:* An internship program is available. *Placement services include:* Career placement, job search course, career counseling/planning, resume referral, career fairs, job interviews arranged, resume preparation, and career library.

FINANCIAL AID (2007–08) 20 students received aid, including fellowships, loans, research assistantships, scholarships, teaching assistantships, and work study. Aid is available to part-time students. *Financial aid application deadline:* 3/31.

Financial Aid Contact Student Financial Resources, 516 High Street, Bellingham, WA 98225-9006. *Phone:* 360-650-3470. *Fax:* 360-650-7291. *E-mail:* financialaid@wwu.edu.

INTERNATIONAL STUDENTS 19% of students enrolled are international students. *Services and facilities:* Counseling/support services, ESL/language courses, International student housing, International student organization, Orientation, Visa Services. Financial aid is available to international students. *Required with application:* TOEFL with recommended score of 227 (computer) or 567 (paper); proof of adequate funds; proof of health/immunizations.

International Student Contact International Programs and Exchanges, 516 High Street, Bellingham, WA 98225-9046. *Phone:* 360-650-3298. *Fax:* 360-650-6572. *E-mail:* iep@wwu.edu.

APPLICATION *Required:* GMAT, application form, baccalaureate/first degree, essay, personal statement, resume/curriculum vitae, transcripts of college work. *Application fee:* $50. *Deadlines:* 5/2 for fall, 5/2 for summer, 2/2 for fall (international), 2/2 for summer (international).

Application Contact Dorothy E. McCoy, Program Manager, MBA Program, 516 High Street, Bellingham, WA 98225-9072. *Phone:* 360-650-3898. *Fax:* 360-650-4844. *E-mail:* mba@wwu.edu.

Whitworth University
School of Global Commerce and Management
Spokane, Washington

Phone: 509-777-4280 **Fax:** 509-777-3723 **E-mail:** malberts@whitworth.edu

Business Program(s) Web Site: http://www.whitworth.edu/sgcm

Graduate Business Unit Enrollment *Total:* 35 (14 full-time; 21 part-time; 16 women).

Graduate Business Faculty *Total:* 14 (7 full-time; 7 part-time).

Admissions *Applied:* 38. *Admitted:* 29. *Enrolled:* 27. *Average GMAT:* 524. *Average GPA:* 3.59

Academic Calendar 6-week modules (3 semesters, 8 modules).

After Graduation (Class of 2006–07) *Employed within 3 months of graduation:* 88%.

DEGREES   MBA • MIM

MBA—Master of Business Administration Full-time and part-time. GMAT Score, Essay, Resume, 2 Letters of Recommendation, Application, Bachelors Degree Transcript, $50 processing fee, TOEFL score for international students. At least 38 total credits required. 12 to 72 months to complete program. *Concentration:* administration.

MIM—Master of International Management Full-time and part-time. GMAT Score, Essay, Resume, 2 Letters of Recommendation, Application, Bachelors Degree Transcript, $50 processing fee, TOEFL score for international students. At least 38 total credits required. 12 to 72 months to complete program. *Concentrations:* international business, international management, nonprofit management.

RESOURCES AND SERVICES 88 on-campus PCs are available to graduate business students. Access to Internet/World Wide Web, online (class) registration, and online grade reports available. *Personal computer requirements:* Graduate business students are strongly recommended to purchase or lease a personal computer. *Special opportunities include:* An international exchange program is available. *Placement services include:* Alumni network, job search course, career counseling/planning, electronic job bank, resume referral, career fairs, resume preparation, and career library.

EXPENSES *Tuition:* Full-time: $22,724. Part-time: $598 per credit.

FINANCIAL AID (2007–08) 29 students received aid, including grants, loans, research assistantships, scholarships, teaching assistantships, and work study. Aid is available to part-time students.

Financial Aid Contact Mrs. Wendy Olson, Director of Financial Aid, 300 West Hawthorne Road, Spokane, WA 99251. *Phone:* 509-777-4306. *Fax:* 509-777-3725. *E-mail:* wolson@whitworth.edu.

INTERNATIONAL STUDENTS *Services and facilities:* Counseling/support services, ESL/language courses, Housing location assistance, International student organization, Language tutoring, Orientation, Visa Services. Financial aid is available to international students. *Required with application:* TOEFL with recommended score of 213 (computer) or 550 (paper); proof of adequate funds; proof of health/immunizations.

International Student Contact Mary A. Alberts, Director, 300 West Hawthorne Road, Spokane, WA 99251. *Phone:* 509-777-4280. *Fax:* 509-777-3723. *E-mail:* malberts@whitworth.edu.

APPLICATION *Required:* Application form, baccalaureate/first degree, essay, 2 letters of recommendation, resume/curriculum vitae, transcripts of college work. School will accept GMAT. *Recommended:* Interview, 2 years of work experience. *Application fee:* $35. Applications for domestic and international students are processed on a rolling basis.

Application Contact Mary A. Alberts, Director, 300 West Hawthorne Road, MS 2704, Spokane, WA 99251. *Phone:* 509-777-4280. *Fax:* 509-777-3723. *E-mail:* malberts@whitworth.edu.

WEST VIRGINIA

American Public University System
AMU/APU Graduate Programs
Charles Town, West Virginia

Phone: 304-724-3720 **Fax:** 304-724-3788 **E-mail:** tgrant@apus.edu

Business Program(s) Web Site: http://www.apus.edu

Graduate Business Unit Enrollment *Total:* 661 (58 full-time; 603 part-time). *Average Age:* 35.

Graduate Business Faculty *Total:* 37 (7 full-time; 30 part-time).

Admissions *Applied:* 133. *Admitted:* 133. *Enrolled:* 101.

Academic Calendar Continuous.

DEGREE   MA/MBA

MA/MBA—Master of Business Administration Full-time and part-time. Distance learning option. 30 to 36 total credits required. *Concentrations:* entrepreneurship, finance, information technology, organizational behavior/development, other.

RESOURCES AND SERVICES Access to Internet/World Wide Web, online (class) registration, and online grade reports available. *Personal computer requirements:* Graduate business students are strongly recommended to purchase or lease a personal computer. *Placement services include:* Alumni network, electronic job bank, resume preparation, and career library.

Financial Aid Contact Mr. Chip Woodward, Director of Financial Aid, 111 West Congress Street, Charles Town, WV 25414. *Phone:* 866-487-3692. *E-mail:* amu@finaidhelpdesk.com.

INTERNATIONAL STUDENTS *Services and facilities:* Counseling/support services, Orientation. Financial aid is not available to international students. *Required with application:* IELT with recommended score of 6.5; TOEFL with recommended score of 213 (computer), 550 (paper), or 79 (Internet); TWE with recommended score of 4.5.

International Student Contact Ms. Geanine Garcia-Poindexter, Director, Student Records, 10110 Battleview Parkway, Suite 114, Manassas, VA 20109. *Phone:* 877-755-2787. *Fax:* 703-330-5109. *E-mail:* gpoindexter@apus.edu.

APPLICATION *Required:* Application form, baccalaureate/first degree, transcripts of college work. *Application fee:* $0. Applications for domestic and international students are processed on a rolling basis.

Application Contact Ms. Terry Grant, Director, Enrollment Management, 111 West Congress Street, Charles Town, WV 25414. *Phone:* 304-724-3720. *Fax:* 304-724-3788. *E-mail:* tgrant@apus.edu.

Salem International University
School of Business
Salem, West Virginia

Phone: 304-326-1359 **Fax:** 304-325-1246 **E-mail:** admissions@salemu.edu

Business Program(s) Web Site: http://www.salemu.edu

Graduate Business Unit Enrollment *Total:* 82 (82 full-time; 29 women; 47 international). *Average Age:* 26.

Graduate Business Faculty *Total:* 8 (2 full-time; 6 part-time).

Admissions *Average GPA:* 3.0

Academic Calendar Modules.

Accreditation ACBSP—The American Council of Business Schools and Programs.

Salem International University (continued)

DEGREES MBA

MBA—International Master of Business Administration Part-time. Distance learning option. 36 total credits required. 3 months to complete program. *Concentration:* international business.

MBA—Master of Business Administration in Information Security Part-time. Distance learning option. 48 total credits required. 3 months to complete program. *Concentration:* other.

RESOURCES AND SERVICES 50 on-campus PCs are available to graduate business students. Access to Internet/World Wide Web, online (class) registration, and online grade reports available. *Personal computer requirements:* Graduate business students are not required to have a personal computer. *Special opportunities include:* An international exchange program and an internship program are available. *Placement services include:* Resume preparation and career library.

EXPENSES *Tuition:* Full-time: $13,500. Part-time: $450 per credit hour. *Tuition (international):* Full-time: $13,500. Part-time: $450 per credit hour. *Required fees:* Full-time: $1200. Part-time: $40 per credit hour. Tuition and/or fees vary by academic program. *Typical graduate housing cost:* $5420 (including board), $2050 (room only).

FINANCIAL AID (2007–08) Loans and scholarships. Aid is available to part-time students.

Financial Aid Contact Mrs. Pat Zinsmeister, Vice President for Financial Aid and Compliance, 223 West Main Street, PO Box 500, Salem, WV 26426. *Phone:* 304-326-1303 Ext.. *Fax:* 304-326-1299. *E-mail:* pzinsmeister@salemu.edu.

INTERNATIONAL STUDENTS 57% of students enrolled are international students. *Services and facilities:* Counseling/support services, ESL/language courses. Financial aid is available to international students. *Required with application:* Proof of adequate funds. *Recommended with application:* IELT with recommended score of 6.5; TOEFL with recommended score of 213 (computer) or 550 (paper).

International Student Contact Ms. Lynn Ning, International Recruitment Specialist, 223 West Main Street, PO Box 500, Salem, WV 26426. *Phone:* 304-326-1293. *Fax:* 304-326-1246. *E-mail:* lning@salemu.edu.

APPLICATION *Required:* Application form, baccalaureate/first degree, resume/curriculum vitae, transcripts of college work. *Recommended:* Work experience. *Application fee:* $25. Applications for domestic and international students are processed on a rolling basis.

Application Contact Ms. Gina Cossey, Vice President for Admissions and Marketing, 223 West Main Street, PO Box 500, Salem, WV 26426. *Phone:* 304-326-1359. *Fax:* 304-325-1246. *E-mail:* admissions@salemu.edu.

University of Charleston
Executive Business Administration Program

Charleston, West Virginia

Phone: 304-357-4752 **Fax:** 304-357-4872 **E-mail:** erinstuck@ucwv.edu

Business Program(s) Web Site: http://www.ucwv.edu/

Graduate Business Unit Enrollment *Total:* 70 (20 full-time; 50 part-time; 22 women; 7 international). *Average Age:* 35.

Graduate Business Faculty *Total:* 15 (5 full-time; 10 part-time).

Admissions *Applied:* 102. *Admitted:* 72. *Enrolled:* 49. *Average GMAT:* 500. *Average GPA:* 3.4

Academic Calendar 12-week sessions.

After Graduation (Class of 2006–07) *Employed within 3 months of graduation:* 100%. *Average starting salary:* $50,000.

DEGREE MBA

MBA—Executive Master of Business Administration Part-time. 5 years of management experience required. At least 40 total credits required. 15 months to complete program. *Concentration:* executive programs.

RESOURCES AND SERVICES 58 on-campus PCs are available to graduate business students. Access to Internet/World Wide Web, online (class) registration, and online grade reports available. *Personal computer requirements:* Graduate business students are strongly recommended to purchase or lease a personal computer. *Placement services include:* Alumni network, career placement, job search course, career counseling/planning, electronic job bank, resume referral, career fairs, job interviews arranged, resume preparation, and career library.

EXPENSES *Tuition:* Full-time: $22,000. *Tuition (international):* Full-time: $22,000.

FINANCIAL AID (2007–08) 12 students received aid, including grants, loans, teaching assistantships, and work study. Aid is available to part-time students.

Financial Aid Contact Ms. Jan Ruge, Director of Financial Aid, 2300 MacCorkle Avenue, SE, Charleston, WV 25304. *Phone:* 304-357-4760. *Fax:* 304-357-4769. *E-mail:* jruge@ucwv.edu.

INTERNATIONAL STUDENTS 10% of students enrolled are international students. *Services and facilities:* Counseling/support services, ESL/language courses, Housing location assistance, International student housing, International student organization, Language tutoring, Orientation, Visa Services. Financial aid is available to international students. *Required with application:* TOEFL with recommended score of 500 (paper).

International Student Contact Ms. Ginny Bennett-Helmick, Office of International Student Programs, 2300 MacCorkle Avenue, SE, Charleston, WV 25304. *Phone:* 304-357-4987. *Fax:* 304-357-4769. *E-mail:* ginnybennett-helmick@ucwv.edu.

APPLICATION *Required:* Application form, baccalaureate/first degree, essay, interview, 3 letters of recommendation, personal statement, resume/curriculum vitae, transcripts of college work, 5 years of work experience. School will accept GMAT. *Application fee:* $50. *Deadline:* 7/1 for fall (international). Applications for domestic students are processed on a rolling basis.

Application Contact Ms. Erin Stuck, Graduate Admissions, Office of Admissions, 2300 MacCorkle Avenue, SE, Charleston, WV 25304. *Phone:* 304-357-4752. *Fax:* 304-357-4872. *E-mail:* erinstuck@ucwv.edu.

West Virginia Wesleyan College
Department of Business and Economics

Buckhannon, West Virginia

Phone: 304-473-8622 **Fax:** 304-473-8479 **E-mail:** bellamys@wvwc.edu

Business Program(s) Web Site: http://www.wvwc.edu/aca2/dept/mba/

Graduate Business Unit Enrollment *Total:* 65 (56 full-time; 9 part-time; 35 women; 3 international). *Average Age:* 30.

Graduate Business Faculty *Total:* 13 (8 full-time; 5 part-time).

Admissions *Applied:* 23. *Admitted:* 16. *Enrolled:* 16. *Average GMAT:* 500. *Average GPA:* 3.4

Academic Calendar Semesters.

After Graduation (Class of 2006–07) *Employed within 3 months of graduation:* 80%.

DEGREE MBA

MBA—Master of Business Administration Full-time and part-time. At least 42 total credits required. 24 to 84 months to complete program. *Concentration:* general MBA.

RESOURCES AND SERVICES 25 on-campus PCs are available to graduate business students. Access to Internet/World Wide Web and online grade reports available. *Personal computer requirements:* Graduate business students are strongly recommended to purchase or lease a personal computer. *Placement services include:* Alumni network, career counseling/planning, career fairs, and resume preparation.

FINANCIAL AID (2007–08) Loans and work study.

Financial Aid Contact Director of Financial Aid, 59 College Avenue, Buckhannon, WV 26201. *Phone:* 304-473-8080.

INTERNATIONAL STUDENTS 5% of students enrolled are international students. *Services and facilities:* Counseling/support services, ESL/language courses, International student housing, International student organization. *Required with application:* TOEFL with recommended score of 500 (paper).

International Student Contact Chris Chavers, Intercultural Relations, 59 College Avenue, Buckhannon, WV 26201. *Phone:* 304-473-8163. *E-mail:* chavers_cs@wvwc.edu.

APPLICATION *Required:* GMAT, application form, baccalaureate/first degree, 2 letters of recommendation, personal statement, resume/curriculum vitae, transcripts of college work. School will accept GRE. *Application fee:* $30. Applications for domestic and international students are processed on a rolling basis.

Application Contact D. Scott Bellamy, Director of MBA Program, 59 College Avenue, Buckhannon, WV 26201. *Phone:* 304-473-8622. *Fax:* 304-473-8479. *E-mail:* bellamys@wvwc.edu.

Wheeling Jesuit University
Department of Business

Wheeling, West Virginia

Phone: 304-243-2250 **Fax:** 304-243-4441 **E-mail:** adulted@wju.edu

Business Program(s) Web Site: http://www.wju.edu/academics/business/gradprog.asp

Graduate Business Unit Enrollment *Total:* 52 (21 full-time; 31 part-time; 21 women; 2 international). *Average Age:* 30.

Graduate Business Faculty *Total:* 8 (6 full-time; 2 part-time).

Admissions *Applied:* 31. *Admitted:* 30. *Enrolled:* 19. *Average GMAT:* 443. *Average GPA:* 3.12

Academic Calendar Semesters.

Accreditation ACBSP—The American Council of Business Schools and Programs (candidate).

DEGREES MBA • MS

MBA—Master of Business Administration Full-time and part-time. 36 to 48 total credits required. 12 to 84 months to complete program. *Concentration:* general MBA.

MS—Master of Science in Accountancy Full-time and part-time. 30 total credits required. 12 to 84 months to complete program. *Concentration:* accounting.

RESOURCES AND SERVICES 90 on-campus PCs are available to graduate business students. Access to Internet/World Wide Web, online (class) registration, and online grade reports available. *Personal computer requirements:* Graduate business students are not required to have a personal computer. *Special opportunities include:* An internship program is available. *Placement services include:* Alumni network, career counseling/planning, electronic job bank, career fairs, job interviews arranged, resume preparation, and career library.

EXPENSES *Tuition:* Full-time: $9000. *Tuition (international):* Full-time: $9000. *Required fees:* Full-time: $370. Part-time: $370 per year. *Graduate housing:* Room and board costs vary by campus location, number of occupants, type of accommodation, and type of board plan. *Typical cost:* $6355 (including board), $4520 (room only).

FINANCIAL AID (2007–08) 29 students received aid, including loans, research assistantships, and work study. Aid is available to part-time students. *Financial aid application deadline:* 8/28.

Financial Aid Contact Ms. Christie Tomczyk, Director of Student Financial Planning, 316 Washington Avenue, Wheeling, WV 26003-6243. *Phone:* 304-243-2304. *Fax:* 304-243-4397. *E-mail:* ctomczyk@wju.edu.

INTERNATIONAL STUDENTS 4% of students enrolled are international students. *Services and facilities:* Counseling/support services, ESL/language courses, Housing location assistance, International student organization, Language tutoring, Orientation, Visa Services. Financial aid is not available to international students. *Required with application:* TOEFL with recommended score of 250 (computer), 600 (paper), or 80 (Internet); proof of adequate funds; proof of health/immunizations.

International Student Contact Mrs. Eileen Viglietta, International Student Advisor, 316 Washington Avenue, Wheeling, WV 26003-6243. *Phone:* 304-243-2346. *Fax:* 304-243-2397. *E-mail:* eileenv@wju.edu.

APPLICATION *Required:* GMAT, application form, baccalaureate/first degree, 3 letters of recommendation, resume/curriculum vitae, transcripts of college work. *Recommended:* Interview, work experience. *Application fee:* $25. Applications for domestic and international students are processed on a rolling basis.

Application Contact Ms. Becky Forney, Associate Dean, Adult and Continuing Education, 316 Washington Avenue, Wheeling, WV 26003-6243. *Phone:* 304-243-2250. *Fax:* 304-243-4441. *E-mail:* adulted@wju.edu.

WISCONSIN

Cardinal Stritch University
College of Business and Management

Milwaukee, Wisconsin

Phone: 800-347-8822 Ext. 4422 **Fax:** 414-410-4624 **E-mail:** pmrosenwald@stritch.edu

Business Program(s) Web Site: http://www.stritch.edu/College_of_Business_and_Management_Home.aspx

Graduate Business Unit Enrollment *Total:* 851 (851 full-time; 506 women; 25 international). *Average Age:* 35.9.

Graduate Business Faculty *Total:* 239 (9 full-time; 230 part-time).

Academic Calendar Continuous.

Accreditation ACBSP—The American Council of Business Schools and Programs.

After Graduation (Class of 2006–07) *Employed within 3 months of graduation:* 95%.

DEGREES MBA • MS

MBA—Master of Business Administration Full-time. Distance learning option. At least 36 total credits required. *Concentration:* general MBA.

MS—Master of Science in Management Full-time. At least 30 total credits required. *Concentration:* management.

RESOURCES AND SERVICES 167 on-campus PCs are available to graduate business students. Access to Internet/World Wide Web and online grade reports available. *Personal computer requirements:* Graduate business students are required to have a personal computer. *Placement services include:* Alumni network, career placement, career counseling/planning, electronic job bank, resume referral, career fairs, resume preparation, and career library.

EXPENSES *Tuition:* Full-time: $9450. Part-time: $450 per credit. *Required fees:* Full-time: $360. Tuition and/or fees vary by academic program.

FINANCIAL AID (2007–08) Loans, scholarships, and work study.

Financial Aid Contact Financial Aid Office, 6801 North Yates Road, Milwaukee, WI 53217-3985. *Phone:* 414-410-4046.

Cardinal Stritch University (continued)

INTERNATIONAL STUDENTS 3% of students enrolled are international students. *Services and facilities:* Counseling/support services. Financial aid is not available to international students. *Required with application:* TOEFL with recommended score of 600 (paper).

International Student Contact Program Representative, 6801 North Yates Road, Milwaukee, WI 53217. *Phone:* 800-347-8822 Ext. 4317. *Fax:* 414-410-4324.

APPLICATION *Required:* Application form, baccalaureate/first degree, resume/curriculum vitae, transcripts of college work, 3 years of work experience. *Application fee:* $25. Applications for domestic and international students are processed on a rolling basis.

Application Contact Patricia Rosenwald, Enrollment Representative, 6801 North Yates Road, Milwaukee, WI 53217. *Phone:* 800-347-8822 Ext. 4422. *Fax:* 414-410-4624. *E-mail:* pmrosenwald@stritch.edu.

Concordia University Wisconsin
Graduate Programs

Mequon, Wisconsin

Phone: 262-243-4298 **Fax:** 262-243-4585 **E-mail:** david.borst@cuw.edu

Business Program(s) Web Site: http://www.cuw.edu/

Graduate Business Unit Enrollment *Total:* 650 (150 international).

Graduate Business Faculty *Total:* 40 (8 full-time; 32 part-time).

Admissions *Average GPA:* 3.4

Academic Calendar 6 continuous terms.

After Graduation (Class of 2006–07) *Employed within 3 months of graduation:* 100%.

DEGREE MBA

MBA—Master of Business Administration Full-time and part-time. Distance learning option. 39 to 60 total credits required. 12 to 60 months to complete program. *Concentrations:* business education, finance, human resources management, international business, management, management information systems, marketing, nonprofit organization, public policy and administration, risk management.

RESOURCES AND SERVICES 120 on-campus PCs are available to graduate business students. Access to Internet/World Wide Web, online (class) registration, and online grade reports available. *Personal computer requirements:* Graduate business students are strongly recommended to purchase or lease a personal computer. *Special opportunities include:* An international exchange program and an internship program are available. *Placement services include:* Career placement, career counseling/planning, electronic job bank, resume referral, career fairs, resume preparation, and career library.

EXPENSES *Tuition:* Part-time: $495 per credit. *Tuition (international):* Part-time: $495 per credit. *Required fees:* Full-time: $9000. Part-time: $9000 per year. Tuition and/or fees vary by number of courses or credits taken. *Graduate housing:* Room and board costs vary by number of occupants and type of board plan. *Typical cost:* $7700 (including board).

FINANCIAL AID (2007–08) 6 students received aid, including grants, loans, research assistantships, scholarships, and work study.

Financial Aid Contact Steve Taylor, Director, Financial Aid, 12800 North Lake Shore Drive, Mequon, WI 53097. *Phone:* 262-243-4392. *E-mail:* steve. taylor@cuw.edu.

INTERNATIONAL STUDENTS 23% of students enrolled are international students. *Services and facilities:* Counseling/support services, ESL/language courses, Housing location assistance, International student housing, International student organization, Language tutoring, Orientation, Visa Services. Financial aid is available to international students. *Required with application:* TOEFL with recommended score of 213 (computer) or 550 (paper); proof of adequate funds.

International Student Contact Mrs. Heidi Englebert, Coordinator of International Admissions, 12800 North Lake Shore Drive, Mequon, WI 53097. *Phone:* 262-243-4294. *Fax:* 262-243-4585. *E-mail:* heidi.englebert@cuw.edu.

APPLICATION *Required:* Application form, baccalaureate/first degree, essay, 2 letters of recommendation, personal statement, resume/curriculum vitae, transcripts of college work. *Recommended:* 2 years of work experience. *Application fee:* $35. Applications for domestic and international students are processed on a rolling basis.

Application Contact Dr. David Borst, Dean, School of Business and Legal Studies, 12800 North Lake Shore Drive, Mequon, WI 53097-2402. *Phone:* 262-243-4298. *Fax:* 262-243-4585. *E-mail:* david.borst@cuw.edu.

Edgewood College
Program in Business

Madison, Wisconsin

Phone: 608-663-2294 **Fax:** 608-663-2214 **E-mail:** pomalley@edgewood.edu

Business Program(s) Web Site: http://www.edgewood.edu/academics/graduate/MBA/

Graduate Business Unit Enrollment *Total:* 156 (15 full-time; 141 part-time; 79 women; 7 international). *Average Age:* 38.

Graduate Business Faculty *Total:* 19 (15 full-time; 4 part-time).

Admissions *Applied:* 23. *Admitted:* 23. *Enrolled:* 17. *Average GMAT:* 517. *Average GPA:* 3.07

Academic Calendar Semesters.

Accreditation ACBSP—The American Council of Business Schools and Programs.

After Graduation (Class of 2006–07) *Employed within 3 months of graduation:* 97%. *Average starting salary:* $40,000.

DEGREE MBA

MBA—Master of Business Administration Full-time and part-time. 36 to 54 total credits required. 24 to 84 months to complete program. *Concentrations:* accounting, finance, general MBA, international business, management, marketing.

RESOURCES AND SERVICES 140 on-campus PCs are available to graduate business students. Access to Internet/World Wide Web, online (class) registration, and online grade reports available. *Personal computer requirements:* Graduate business students are strongly recommended to purchase or lease a personal computer. *Special opportunities include:* An international exchange program and an internship program are available. *Placement services include:* Alumni network, career placement, job search course, career counseling/planning, electronic job bank, resume referral, career fairs, resume preparation, and career library.

EXPENSES *Tuition:* Full-time: $11,790. *Tuition (international):* Full-time: $11,790.

FINANCIAL AID (2007–08) 54 students received aid, including loans, scholarships, and work study. Aid is available to part-time students. *Financial aid application deadline:* 3/1.

Financial Aid Contact Kari Gribble, Director of Financial Aid, 1000 Edgewood College Drive, Madison, WI 53711-1997. *Phone:* 608-663-2206. *Fax:* 608-663-3495. *E-mail:* kgribble@edgewood.edu.

INTERNATIONAL STUDENTS 4% of students enrolled are international students. *Services and facilities:* Counseling/support services, Housing location assistance, International student housing, International student organization, Language tutoring, Orientation, Visa Services. Financial aid is not available to international students. *Required with application:* TOEFL with recommended score of 213 (computer), 550 (paper), or 80 (Internet); proof of adequate funds.

International Student Contact Sara Friar, Director of Center for Global Education, 1000 Edgewood College Drive, Madison, WI 53711-1997. *Phone:* 608-663-2277. *E-mail:* sfriar@edgewood.edu.

APPLICATION *Required:* GMAT, application form, baccalaureate/first degree, 2 letters of recommendation, personal statement, transcripts of college work. *Recommended:* 2 years of work experience. *Application fee:* $25. Applications for domestic and international students are processed on a rolling basis.

Application Contact Paula O'Malley, Director of Graduate and Adult Admissions, 1000 Edgewood College Drive, Madison, WI 53711-1997. *Phone:* 608-663-2294. *Fax:* 608-663-2214. *E-mail:* pomalley@edgewood.edu.

Lakeland College
Graduate Studies Division
Sheboygan, Wisconsin

Phone: 920-565-1268 **Fax:** 920-565-1341 **E-mail:** thillcr@lakeland.edu

Business Program(s) Web Site: http://www.lakeland.edu

Graduate Business Unit Enrollment *Total:* 155 (25 full-time; 130 part-time; 85 women; 10 international).

Graduate Business Faculty *Total:* 65 (5 full-time; 60 part-time).

Admissions *Applied:* 17. *Admitted:* 15. *Enrolled:* 15. *Average GMAT:* 480.

Academic Calendar Semesters.

DEGREE MBA

MBA—Master of Business Administration Part-time. Distance learning option. At least 36 total credits required. 36 to 84 months to complete program. *Concentrations:* accounting, international and area business studies, marketing.

RESOURCES AND SERVICES 30 on-campus PCs are available to graduate business students. Access to Internet/World Wide Web, online (class) registration, and online grade reports available. *Personal computer requirements:* Graduate business students are strongly recommended to purchase or lease a personal computer. *Placement services include:* Alumni network, job search course, career counseling/planning, electronic job bank, resume referral, career fairs, resume preparation, and career library.

FINANCIAL AID (2007–08) Loans. Aid is available to part-time students.

Financial Aid Contact Patty Taylor, Director of Financial Aid, PO Box 359, Sheboygan, WI 53082-0359. *Phone:* 920-565-1298. *E-mail:* taylorpl@lakeland.edu.

INTERNATIONAL STUDENTS 6% of students enrolled are international students. *Services and facilities:* Counseling/support services, ESL/language courses, International student housing, International student organization, Orientation, Visa Services. Financial aid is available to international students. *Required with application:* TOEFL with recommended score of 550 (paper); proof of adequate funds.

International Student Contact Mr. Patrick Liu, International Students Advisor, PO Box 359, Sheboygan, WI 53082-0359. *Phone:* 920-565-1502. *Fax:* 920-565-1206. *E-mail:* liup@lakeland.edu.

APPLICATION *Required:* Application form, baccalaureate/first degree, 2 letters of recommendation, resume/curriculum vitae, transcripts of college work. Applications for domestic and international students are processed on a rolling basis.

Application Contact Ms. Cindy Thill, Online Counselor, PO Box 359, Sheboygan, WI 53082-0359. *Phone:* 920-565-1268. *Fax:* 920-565-1341. *E-mail:* thillcr@lakeland.edu.

Marquette University
Graduate School of Management
Milwaukee, Wisconsin

Phone: 414-288-8064 **Fax:** 414-288-8078 **E-mail:** debra.leutermann@marquette.edu

Business Program(s) Web Site: http://www.marquette.edu/mba

Graduate Business Unit Enrollment *Total:* 685 (197 full-time; 488 part-time).

Graduate Business Faculty *Total:* 45 (33 full-time; 12 part-time).

Admissions *Applied:* 255. *Admitted:* 230. *Enrolled:* 183. *Average GMAT:* 569. *Average GPA:* 3.22

Academic Calendar Semesters.

Accreditation AACSB—The Association to Advance Collegiate Schools of Business.

DEGREES EMBA • MBA • MS

EMBA—Executive Master of Business Administration Full-time and part-time. 5 years of managerial experience required. At least 50 total credits required. 17 months to complete program. *Concentrations:* executive programs, international business.

MBA—Master of Business Administration Full-time and part-time. 34 to 50 total credits required. 12 to 72 months to complete program. *Concentrations:* accounting, economics, finance, general MBA, human resources management, information management, international business, marketing, quality management.

MS—Master of Science in Accounting Full-time and part-time. 30 to 45 total credits required. 12 to 72 months to complete program. *Concentration:* accounting.

MS—Master of Science in Applied Economics Full-time and part-time. 30 to 42 total credits required. 12 to 72 months to complete program. *Concentrations:* financial economics, international economics, public policy and administration, real estate.

MS—Master of Science in Engineering Management Full-time and part-time. At least 36 total credits required. 12 to 72 months to complete program. *Concentration:* engineering.

MS—Master of Science in Human Resources Full-time and part-time. 36 to 48 total credits required. 12 to 72 months to complete program. *Concentration:* human resources management.

RESOURCES AND SERVICES 135 on-campus PCs are available to graduate business students. Access to Internet/World Wide Web, online (class) registration, and online grade reports available. *Personal computer requirements:* Graduate business students are not required to have a personal computer. *Special opportunities include:* An international exchange program is available. *Placement services include:* Alumni network, career placement, career counseling/planning, electronic job bank, resume referral, career fairs, job interviews arranged, resume preparation, and career library.

EXPENSES *Tuition:* Full-time: $14,400. Part-time: $800 per credit hour. *Tuition (international):* Full-time: $14,400. Part-time: $800 per credit hour.

FINANCIAL AID (2007–08) 108 students received aid, including research assistantships, scholarships, and teaching assistantships. Aid is available to part-time students. *Financial aid application deadline:* 2/15.

Financial Aid Contact Mr. Thomas Marek, Financial Aid Coordinator, Graduate School, PO Box 1881, Milwaukee, WI 53201-1881. *Phone:* 414-288-5325. *Fax:* 414-288-1902. *E-mail:* thomas.marek@marquette.edu.

INTERNATIONAL STUDENTS *Services and facilities:* Counseling/support services, ESL/language courses, Housing location assistance, International student organization, Orientation, Visa Services. Financial aid is available to international students. *Required with application:* TOEFL with recommended score of 213 (computer), 550 (paper), or 80 (Internet); proof of adequate funds; proof of health/immunizations.

Marquette University (continued)

International Student Contact Cheryl Nelson, Director of Student Services, PO Box 1881, GSM Straz Hall Suite 275, Milwaukee, WI 53201-1881. *Phone:* 414-288-7145. *Fax:* 414-288-8078. *E-mail:* cheryl.nelson@marquette.edu.

APPLICATION *Required:* GMAT, application form, baccalaureate/first degree, essay, personal statement, resume/curriculum vitae, transcripts of college work. *Recommended:* Letter(s) of recommendation, work experience. *Application fee:* \$50. Applications for domestic and international students are processed on a rolling basis.

Application Contact Mrs. Debra Leutermann, Admissions Coordinator, PO Box 1881, GSM Straz Hall Suite 275, Milwaukee, WI 53201-1881. *Phone:* 414-288-8064. *Fax:* 414-288-8078. *E-mail:* debra.leutermann@ marquette.edu.

Milwaukee School of Engineering
Rader School of Business

Milwaukee, Wisconsin

Phone: 414-277-6763 **Fax:** 414-277-7475 **E-mail:** schuster@msoe.edu

Business Program(s) Web Site: http://www.msoe.edu/Business

Graduate Business Unit Enrollment *Total:* 108 (4 full-time; 104 part-time; 16 women). *Average Age:* 34.

Graduate Business Faculty *Total:* 18 (3 full-time; 15 part-time).

Admissions *Applied:* 34. *Admitted:* 28. *Enrolled:* 22. *Average GPA:* 3.37

Academic Calendar Quarters.

After Graduation (Class of 2006–07) *Employed within 3 months of graduation:* 98%. *Average starting salary:* \$51,506.

DEGREE   MS

MS—Master of Science in Engineering Management Full-time and part-time. 48 to 51 total credits required. 36 to 84 months to complete program. *Concentrations:* marketing, operations management, project management, quality management.

RESOURCES AND SERVICES 127 on-campus PCs are available to graduate business students. Access to Internet/World Wide Web, online (class) registration, and online grade reports available. *Personal computer requirements:* Graduate business students are strongly recommended to purchase or lease a personal computer. *Placement services include:* Alumni network, career placement, career counseling/planning, electronic job bank, resume referral, career fairs, job interviews arranged, resume preparation, and career library.

EXPENSES *Tuition:* Part-time: \$548 per credit. *Tuition (international):* Part-time: \$548 per credit. *Graduate housing:* Room and board costs vary by campus location, number of occupants, type of accommodation, and type of board plan. *Typical cost:* \$2275 (including board), \$1460 (room only).

FINANCIAL AID (2007–08) 46 students received aid, including loans and research assistantships. Aid is available to part-time students. *Financial aid application deadline:* 3/15.

Financial Aid Contact Mr. Steve Midthun, Assistant Director of Student Financial Services, 1025 North Broadway, Milwaukee, WI 53202-3109. *Phone:* 414-277-7224. *Fax:* 414-277-6952. *E-mail:* midthun@msoe.edu.

INTERNATIONAL STUDENTS *Services and facilities:* Counseling/ support services, ESL/language courses, Housing location assistance, International student organization, Language tutoring, Orientation. Financial aid is not available to international students. *Required with application:* TOEFL with recommended score of 79 (Internet); proof of adequate funds; proof of health/immunizations.

International Student Contact Patrick Coffey, Vice President of Student Life, 1025 North Broadway, Milwaukee, WI 53202-3109. *Phone:* 414-277-7226. *Fax:* 414-277-7248. *E-mail:* coffey@msoe.edu.

APPLICATION *Required:* Application form, baccalaureate/first degree, 2 letters of recommendation, personal statement, transcripts of college work. School will accept GMAT and GRE. *Recommended:* 3 years of work experience. *Application fee:* \$35. Applications for domestic and international students are processed on a rolling basis.

Application Contact Julie A Schuster, Assistant Director of Admission, 1025 North Broadway, Milwaukee, WI 53202-3109. *Phone:* 414-277-6763. *Fax:* 414-277-7475. *E-mail:* schuster@msoe.edu.

Silver Lake College
Program in Management and Organizational Behavior

Manitowoc, Wisconsin

Phone: 800-236-4752 Ext. 186 **Fax:** 920-684-7082 **E-mail:** jgrant@silver.sl.edu

Business Program(s) Web Site: http://www.sl.edu

Graduate Business Unit Enrollment *Total:* 72 (11 full-time; 61 part-time; 49 women). *Average Age:* 36.

Graduate Business Faculty 24 part-time.

Admissions *Applied:* 31. *Admitted:* 21. *Enrolled:* 20. *Average GPA:* 3.0

Academic Calendar Semesters.

After Graduation (Class of 2006–07) *Employed within 3 months of graduation:* 100%. *Average starting salary:* \$45,000.

DEGREES   M Sc • MS

M Sc—Management and Organizational Behavior Full-time and part-time. 39 total credits required. 26 to 84 months to complete program. *Concentrations:* health care, international business, other, training and development.

MS—Master of Science in Management and Organizational Behavior Full-time and part-time. Students should have at least 3 years of work-related experience prior to pursuing their master's degree. At least 39 total credits required. 26 to 84 months to complete program. *Concentrations:* health care, international business, other, training and development.

RESOURCES AND SERVICES 25 on-campus PCs are available to graduate business students. Access to Internet/World Wide Web, online (class) registration, and online grade reports available. *Personal computer requirements:* Graduate business students are required to have a personal computer. *Placement services include:* Alumni network, career placement, career counseling/planning, career fairs, and resume preparation.

FINANCIAL AID (2007–08) Grants, scholarships, and work study. Aid is available to part-time students. *Financial aid application deadline:* 4/1.

Financial Aid Contact Ms. Michelle Leider, Associate Director, Student Financial Aid, 2406 South Alverno Road, Manitowoc, WI 54220-9319. *Phone:* 920-686-6122. *Fax:* 920-684-9072. *E-mail:* mlleider@ silver.sl.edu.

INTERNATIONAL STUDENTS *Services and facilities:* Counseling/ support services, Housing location assistance, Orientation, Visa Services. Financial aid is not available to international students. *Required with application:* TOEFL; proof of adequate funds; proof of health/ immunizations.

International Student Contact Ms. Jamie Grant, Associate Director of Admissions, 2406 South Alverno Road, Manitowoc, WI 54220. *Phone:* 920-686-6186. *Fax:* 920-684-7082. *E-mail:* jgrant@silver.sl.edu.

APPLICATION *Required:* Application form, baccalaureate/first degree, essay, 3 letters of recommendation, personal statement, resume/curriculum vitae, transcripts of college work, 3 years of work experience. School will accept GMAT and GRE. *Recommended:* Interview. *Application fee:* \$35. Applications for domestic and international students are processed on a rolling basis.

Application Contact Ms. Jamie Grant, Associate Director of Admissions, 2406 South Alverno Road, Manitowoc, WI 54220-9319. *Phone:* 800-236-4752 Ext. 186. *Fax:* 920-684-7082. *E-mail:* jgrant@silver.sl.edu.

University of Phoenix–Wisconsin Campus
College of Graduate Business and Management
Brookfield, Wisconsin

Phone: 480-317-6200 **Fax:** 408-643-1479 **E-mail:** beth.barilla@phoenix.edu

Business Program(s) Web Site: http://www.phoenix.edu

DEGREES M Mgt • MA • MBA

M Mgt—Master of Management Full-time. At least 39 total credits required. *Concentration:* management.

MA—Master of Arts in Organizational Management Full-time. At least 40 total credits required. *Concentration:* organizational management.

MBA—Accounting Full-time. At least 46 total credits required. *Concentration:* accounting.

MBA—Global Management Full-time. At least 45 total credits required. *Concentration:* international business.

MBA—Marketing Full-time. At least 46 total credits required. *Concentration:* marketing.

MBA—Master of Business Administration Full-time. At least 45 total credits required. *Concentration:* administration.

MBA—e-Business Full-time. At least 46 total credits required. *Concentration:* electronic commerce (E-commerce).

RESOURCES AND SERVICES Access to online grade reports available. *Personal computer requirements:* Graduate business students are strongly recommended to purchase or lease a personal computer. *Placement services include:* Alumni network.

Application Contact Beth Barilla, Associate Vice President of Student Admissions and Services, Mail Stop AA-K101, 4615 East Elwood Street, Phoenix, AZ 85040-1958. *Phone:* 480-317-6200. *Fax:* 408-643-1479. *E-mail:* beth.barilla@phoenix.edu.

University of Wisconsin–Eau Claire
College of Business
Eau Claire, Wisconsin

Phone: 715-836-6019 **Fax:** 715-836-3923 **E-mail:** erffmerc@uwec.edu

Business Program(s) Web Site: http://www.uwec.edu/cob/academics/mba/index.htm

Accreditation AACSB—The Association to Advance Collegiate Schools of Business.

DEGREE MBA

MBA—Master of Business Administration Full-time and part-time. Distance learning option. 30 total credits required. 22 to 84 months to complete program. *Concentrations:* accounting, finance, information management, management, marketing.

RESOURCES AND SERVICES 1,000 on-campus PCs are available to graduate business students. Access to Internet/World Wide Web, online (class) registration, and online grade reports available. *Personal computer requirements:* Graduate business students are strongly recommended to purchase or lease a personal computer. *Placement services include:*

Alumni network, career placement, career counseling/planning, electronic job bank, resume referral, career fairs, job interviews arranged, resume preparation, and career library.

Application Contact Dr. Robert Erffmeyer, MBA Program Director, PO Box 4004, Eau Claire, WI 54702-4004. *Phone:* 715-836-6019. *Fax:* 715-836-3923. *E-mail:* erffmerc@uwec.edu.

See full description on page 756.

University of Wisconsin–Green Bay
Program in Management
Green Bay, Wisconsin

Phone: 920-465-2520 **Fax:** 920-465-2123 **E-mail:** mccartnd@uwgb.edu

Business Program(s) Web Site: http://www.uwgb.edu/management/

Graduate Business Unit Enrollment *Total:* 41 (4 full-time; 37 part-time; 27 women; 2 international). *Average Age:* 32.

Graduate Business Faculty *Total:* 5 (3 full-time; 2 part-time).

Admissions *Applied:* 19. *Admitted:* 18. *Enrolled:* 13.

Academic Calendar Semesters.

DEGREE MS

MS—Master of Science in Management Full-time and part-time. At least 36 total credits required. *Concentrations:* human resources management, international management, leadership, management, organizational behavior/development, statistics.

RESOURCES AND SERVICES 600 on-campus PCs are available to graduate business students. Access to Internet/World Wide Web, online (class) registration, and online grade reports available. *Personal computer requirements:* Graduate business students are not required to have a personal computer. *Special opportunities include:* An internship program is available. *Placement services include:* Career counseling/planning, job interviews arranged, and resume preparation.

EXPENSES *Tuition (state resident):* Full-time: $7302. Part-time: $406 per credit. *Tuition (nonresident):* Full-time: $17,911. Part-time: $995 per credit. *Tuition (international):* Full-time: $17,911. Part-time: $995 per credit. Tuition and/or fees vary by local reciprocity agreements. *Graduate housing:* Room and board costs vary by number of occupants, type of accommodation, and type of board plan. *Typical cost:* $5500 (including board), $3500 (room only).

FINANCIAL AID (2007–08) Loans. Aid is available to part-time students. *Financial aid application deadline:* 4/15.

Financial Aid Contact Mr. Ron Ronnenberg, Director of Financial Aid, 2420 Nicolet Drive, Green Bay, WI 54311-7001. *Phone:* 920-465-2075. *Fax:* 920-465-5754. *E-mail:* ronnenbr@uwgb.edu.

INTERNATIONAL STUDENTS 5% of students enrolled are international students. *Services and facilities:* Counseling/support services, Housing location assistance, International student organization. Financial aid is available to international students. *Required with application:* TOEFL with recommended score of 213 (computer) or 550 (paper); proof of adequate funds; proof of health/immunizations.

International Student Contact Brent Blahnik, Director of International Education, Rose Hall 310, 2420 Nicolet Drive, Green Bay, WI 54311-7001. *Phone:* 920-465-2889. *Fax:* 920-465-2949. *E-mail:* blahnikb@uwgb.edu.

APPLICATION *Required:* Application form, baccalaureate/first degree, essay, 3 letters of recommendation, personal statement, transcripts of college work. School will accept GMAT and GRE. *Application fee:* $55. Applications for domestic and international students are processed on a rolling basis.

Application Contact Don McCartney, Interim Chair, Wood Hall 460, 2420 Nicolet Drive, Green Bay, WI 54311-7001. *Phone:* 920-465-2520. *Fax:* 920-465-2123. *E-mail:* mccartnd@uwgb.edu.

University of Wisconsin–La Crosse
College of Business Administration

La Crosse, Wisconsin

Phone: 608-785-8067 **E-mail:** kiefer.kath@uwlax.edu

Business Program(s) Web Site: http://www.uwlax.edu/ba/graduate

Graduate Business Unit Enrollment *Total:* 51 (14 full-time; 37 part-time; 17 women; 7 international).

Graduate Business Faculty 15 full-time.

Admissions *Applied:* 35. *Admitted:* 29. *Enrolled:* 18. *Average GMAT:* 530. *Average GPA:* 3.4

Academic Calendar Semesters.

Accreditation AACSB—The Association to Advance Collegiate Schools of Business.

DEGREE   MBA

MBA—Master of Business Administration Full-time and part-time. Distance learning option. 30 to 60 total credits required. 18 to 36 months to complete program. *Concentration:* general MBA.

RESOURCES AND SERVICES 700 on-campus PCs are available to graduate business students. Access to Internet/World Wide Web and online grade reports available. *Personal computer requirements:* Graduate business students are strongly recommended to purchase or lease a personal computer. *Placement services include:* Alumni network, career placement, career counseling/planning, electronic job bank, resume referral, career fairs, resume preparation, and career library.

EXPENSES *Tuition (state resident):* Full-time: $7588. Part-time: $664 per credit. *Tuition (nonresident):* Full-time: $18,200. Part-time: $1007 per credit. *Tuition (international):* Full-time: $18,200. Part-time: $1007 per credit. Tuition and/or fees vary by academic program.

FINANCIAL AID (2007–08) 12 students received aid, including grants, loans, research assistantships, scholarships, and work study. Aid is available to part-time students. *Financial aid application deadline:* 3/15.

Financial Aid Contact Director of Financial Aid, 1725 State Street, La Crosse, WI 54601-3742. *Phone:* 608-785-8604.

INTERNATIONAL STUDENTS 14% of students enrolled are international students. *Services and facilities:* Counseling/support services, ESL/language courses, Housing location assistance, International student housing, International student organization, Language tutoring, Orientation, Visa Services. Financial aid is available to international students. *Required with application:* TOEFL with recommended score of 213 (computer) or 550 (paper); proof of adequate funds; proof of health/immunizations.

International Student Contact Mr. Jay Lokken, Director, Office of International Education, 1725 State Street, La Crosse, WI 54601-3742. *Phone:* 608-785-8016.

APPLICATION *Required:* GMAT, application form, baccalaureate/first degree, transcripts of college work. *Recommended:* Letter(s) of recommendation, 3 years of work experience. *Application fee:* $45. Applications for domestic and international students are processed on a rolling basis.

Application Contact Kathy Kiefer, Admissions Director, 1725 State Street, La Crosse, WI 54601-3742. *Phone:* 608-785-8067. *E-mail:* kiefer.kath@uwlax.edu.

See full description on page 756.

University of Wisconsin–Madison
Wisconsin School of Business

Madison, Wisconsin

Phone: 608-262-4000 **Fax:** 608-265-4192 **E-mail:** ssweeney@bus.wisc.edu

Business Program(s) Web Site: http://www.bus.wisc.edu

Graduate Business Unit Enrollment *Total:* 601 (375 full-time; 226 part-time; 206 women; 134 international). *Average Age:* 31.

Graduate Business Faculty *Total:* 91 (78 full-time; 13 part-time).

Admissions *Applied:* 1,177. *Admitted:* 400. *Enrolled:* 310. *Average GMAT:* 656. *Average GPA:* 3.37

Academic Calendar Semesters.

Accreditation AACSB—The Association to Advance Collegiate Schools of Business.

After Graduation (Class of 2006–07) *Employed within 3 months of graduation:* 96%. *Average starting salary:* $82,000.

DEGREES   EMBA • M Acc • MBA • MS • PhD/MBA

EMBA—Executive Master of Business Administration Full-time. 8 to 10 years of work experience required and pre-requisite basic accounting course. 18 months to complete program. *Concentration:* management.

M Acc—Master of Accountancy Full-time. 54 total credits required. 21 months to complete program. *Concentrations:* accounting, taxation.

MBA—Evening Master of Business Administration Part-time. Interview required. 50 total credits required. 32 months to complete program. *Concentration:* management.

MBA—Full-Time Master of Business Administration Full-time. 53 to 60 total credits required. 21 months to complete program. *Concentrations:* arts administration/management, banking, entrepreneurship, finance, human resources management, insurance, investments and securities, management information systems, management science, marketing, marketing research, operations management, real estate, risk management, supply chain management, technology management.

MS—Master of Science in Business Full-time. GMAT or GRE. 48 to 51 total credits required. 18 to 24 months to complete program. *Concentration:* finance.

MS—Master of Science in Business Full-time. GMAT or GRE. 30 to 50 total credits required. 12 to 24 months to complete program. *Concentration:* actuarial science.

PhD/MBA—PhD in Business Full-time. 32 to 50 total credits required. 48 to 60 months to complete program. *Concentrations:* accounting, actuarial science, human resources management, information systems, insurance, investments and securities, marketing, real estate, risk management.

RESOURCES AND SERVICES 614 on-campus PCs are available to graduate business students. Access to Internet/World Wide Web, online (class) registration, and online grade reports available. *Personal computer requirements:* Graduate business students are strongly recommended to purchase or lease a personal computer. *Special opportunities include:* An internship program is available. *Placement services include:* Alumni network, career placement, job search course, career counseling/planning, electronic job bank, resume referral, career fairs, job interviews arranged, resume preparation, and career library.

EXPENSES *Tuition (state resident):* Full-time: $10,240.32. Part-time: $14,939.68 per year. *Tuition (nonresident):* Full-time: $25,678. Part-time: $14,939.68 per year. *Tuition (international):* Full-time: $25,678.40. Part-time: $14,939.68 per year. *Required fees:* Full-time: $858.08. Part-time: $966.32 per year. Tuition and/or fees vary by academic program and local reciprocity agreements. *Graduate housing:* Room and board costs vary by campus location, number of occupants, type of accommodation, and type of board plan. *Typical cost:* $10,520 (including board).

FINANCIAL AID (2007–08) 223 students received aid, including fellowships, research assistantships, scholarships, and teaching assistantships. Aid is available to part-time students.

Financial Aid Contact Seann Sweeney, Assistant Director of MBA Marketing and Recruiting, 975 University Avenue, 2400 Grainger Hall, Madison, WI 53706. *Phone:* 608-262-4000. *Fax:* 608-265-4192. *E-mail:* mba@bus.wisc.edu.

INTERNATIONAL STUDENTS 22% of students enrolled are international students. *Services and facilities:* Counseling/support services,

ESL/language courses, Housing location assistance, International student housing, International student organization, Language tutoring, Orientation, Visa Services. Financial aid is available to international students. *Required with application:* TOEFL with recommended score of 600 (paper) or 100 (Internet); proof of adequate funds.

International Student Contact Jen Smet, Assistant Director, Career Services, 975 University Avenue, 2400 Grainger Hall, Madison, WI 53706. *Phone:* 608-265-2353. *Fax:* 608-265-4192. *E-mail:* jsmet@bus.wisc.edu.

APPLICATION *Required:* GMAT, application form, baccalaureate/first degree, essay, 3 letters of recommendation, resume/curriculum vitae, transcripts of college work, 2 years of work experience. *Recommended:* Interview. *Application fee:* $45. Applications for domestic and international students are processed on a rolling basis.

Application Contact Seann Sweeney, Assistant Director of MBA Marketing and Recruiting, 975 University Avenue, 2400 Grainger Hall, Madison, WI 53706. *Phone:* 608-262-4000. *Fax:* 608-265-4192. *E-mail:* ssweeney@bus.wisc.edu.

See full description on page 756.

University of Wisconsin–Milwaukee

Sheldon B. Lubar School of Business

Milwaukee, Wisconsin

Phone: 414-229-5403 **Fax:** 414-229-2372 **E-mail:** uwmbusmasters@csd.uwm.edu

Business Program(s) Web Site: http://www4.uwm.edu/business

Graduate Business Unit Enrollment *Total:* 669 (669 part-time; 268 women; 50 international). *Average Age:* 27.

Graduate Business Faculty *Total:* 62 (41 full-time; 21 part-time).

Admissions *Applied:* 454. *Admitted:* 279. *Enrolled:* 204. *Average GMAT:* 555. *Average GPA:* 3.25

Academic Calendar Semesters.

Accreditation AACSB—The Association to Advance Collegiate Schools of Business.

After Graduation (Class of 2006–07) *Employed within 3 months of graduation:* 85%. *Average starting salary:* $55,000.

DEGREES MBA • MS

MBA—Executive Master of Business Administration Full-time. At least 40 total credits required. 22 months to complete program. *Concentration:* executive programs.

MBA—Master of Business Administration Full-time and part-time. 36 to 39 total credits required. 24 to 84 months to complete program. *Concentration:* general MBA.

MS—Master of Science in Management Full-time and part-time. 30 to 33 total credits required. 24 to 84 months to complete program. *Concentrations:* accounting, electronic commerce (E-commerce), finance, management information systems, marketing, taxation.

RESOURCES AND SERVICES 175 on-campus PCs are available to graduate business students. Access to Internet/World Wide Web, online (class) registration, and online grade reports available. *Personal computer requirements:* Graduate business students are not required to have a personal computer. *Special opportunities include:* An international exchange program and an internship program are available. *Placement services include:* Alumni network, career placement, career counseling/planning, electronic job bank, resume referral, career fairs, job interviews arranged, resume preparation, and career library.

EXPENSES *Tuition (state resident):* Part-time: $675 per credit. *Tuition (nonresident):* Part-time: $1577 per credit. *Tuition (international):* Part-time: $1577 per credit. Tuition and/or fees vary by campus location and academic program. *Graduate housing:* Room and board costs vary by

type of accommodation and type of board plan. *Typical cost:* $4600 (including board), $1800 (room only).

FINANCIAL AID (2007–08) 172 students received aid, including fellowships, grants, loans, research assistantships, scholarships, teaching assistantships, and work study. Aid is available to part-time students. *Financial aid application deadline:* 3/1.

Financial Aid Contact Jane Hojan-Clark, Financial Aid and Student Employment, PO Box 469, Milwaukee, WI 53201. *Phone:* 414-229-4541. *Fax:* 414-229-5699. *E-mail:* finaid@uwm.edu.

INTERNATIONAL STUDENTS 7% of students enrolled are international students. *Services and facilities:* Counseling/support services, ESL/language courses, Housing location assistance, International student organization, Orientation, Visa Services. Financial aid is not available to international students. *Required with application:* TOEFL with recommended score of 213 (computer), 550 (paper), or 79 (Internet); proof of adequate funds.

International Student Contact Ms. Jennifer Singer, Graduate Evaluator, Center for International Education, PO Box 413, Milwaukee, WI 53201. *Phone:* 414-229-5321. *Fax:* 414-229-3750. *E-mail:* jksinger@uwm.edu.

APPLICATION *Required:* GMAT, application form, baccalaureate/first degree, personal statement, transcripts of college work. School will accept GRE. *Application fee:* $45, $85 (international). Applications for domestic and international students are processed on a rolling basis.

Application Contact Sarah M. Sandin, MBA/MS Program Manager, PO Box 742, Milwaukee, WI 53201-0742. *Phone:* 414-229-5403. *Fax:* 414-229-2372. *E-mail:* uwmbusmasters@csd.uwm.edu.

University of Wisconsin–Oshkosh

College of Business

Oshkosh, Wisconsin

Phone: 920-424-1436 **Fax:** 920-424-7413 **E-mail:** mba@uwosh.edu

Business Program(s) Web Site: http://www.uwosh.edu/coba

Graduate Business Faculty *Total:* 43 (40 full-time; 3 part-time).

Admissions *Average GMAT:* 540. *Average GPA:* 3.1

Academic Calendar Semesters.

Accreditation AACSB—The Association to Advance Collegiate Schools of Business.

After Graduation (Class of 2006–07) *Employed within 3 months of graduation:* 97%.

DEGREES MBA • MSIS

MBA—Global MBA Program *Concentration:* international business.

MBA—MBA Consortium Full-time and part-time. Distance learning option. 30 to 49 total credits required. 18 to 84 months to complete program. *Concentration:* general MBA.

MBA—Master of Business Administration Full-time and part-time. Distance learning option. 30 to 49 total credits required. 18 to 84 months to complete program. *Concentration:* general MBA.

MSIS—Master of Science in Information Systems Full-time and part-time. 30 to 49 total credits required. 18 to 84 months to complete program. *Concentration:* management information systems.

RESOURCES AND SERVICES 500 on-campus PCs are available to graduate business students. Access to Internet/World Wide Web, online (class) registration, and online grade reports available. *Personal computer requirements:* Graduate business students are strongly recommended to purchase or lease a personal computer. *Placement services include:* Alumni network, career placement, career counseling/planning, resume referral, career fairs, job interviews arranged, resume preparation, and career library.

University of Wisconsin–Oshkosh (continued)

FINANCIAL AID (2007–08) Loans, research assistantships, and work study. Aid is available to part-time students. *Financial aid application deadline:* 3/15.

Financial Aid Contact Beatriz Contreras, Director of Financial Aid, Financial Aid Office, Oshkosh, WI 54901. *Phone:* 920-424-3377. *Fax:* 920-424-0284. *E-mail:* fao@uwosh.edu.

INTERNATIONAL STUDENTS *Services and facilities:* Counseling/ support services, International student housing, International student organization, Orientation. Financial aid is available to international students. *Required with application:* TOEFL with recommended score of 213 (computer) or 550 (paper); proof of adequate funds; proof of health/immunizations.

International Student Contact Ms. Judy Jaeger, International Student Advisor, Dean of Students Office, Oshkosh, WI 54901. *Phone:* 920-424-3100. *Fax:* 920-424-7317. *E-mail:* jaeger@uwosh.edu.

APPLICATION *Required:* GMAT, application form, baccalaureate/first degree, transcripts of college work. School will accept GRE. *Recommended:* 3 years of work experience. *Application fee:* $45. Applications for domestic and international students are processed on a rolling basis.

Application Contact Amy Pinkston, MBA Advisor, 800 Algoma Boulevard, Oshkosh, WI 54901. *Phone:* 920-424-1436. *Fax:* 920-424-7413. *E-mail:* mba@uwosh.edu.

See full description on page 756.

FINANCIAL AID (2007–08) Fellowships, loans, scholarships, and work study. Aid is available to part-time students.

Financial Aid Contact Mr. Randy McCready, Director of Financial Aid, 900 Wood Road, Box 2000, Kenosha, WI 53141-2000. *Phone:* 262-595-2195. *E-mail:* randall.mccready@uwp.edu.

INTERNATIONAL STUDENTS 8% of students enrolled are international students. *Services and facilities:* Counseling/support services, ESL/language courses, Housing location assistance, International student organization, Language tutoring, Orientation, Visa Services, International advisor. Financial aid is available to international students. *Required with application:* TOEFL with recommended score of 213 (computer) or 550 (paper); proof of adequate funds.

International Student Contact Dirk Baldwin, Associate Dean and MBA Director, 900 Wood Road, Box 2000, Kenosha, WI 53141-2000. *Phone:* 262-595-2046. *Fax:* 262-595-2680. *E-mail:* dirk.baldwin@uwp.edu.

APPLICATION *Required:* GMAT, application form, baccalaureate/first degree, 2 letters of recommendation, resume/curriculum vitae, transcripts of college work. *Recommended:* Work experience. *Application fee:* $45. Applications for domestic and international students are processed on a rolling basis.

Application Contact Dirk Baldwin, Associate Dean and MBA Director, 900 Wood Road, Box 2000, Kenosha, WI 53141-2000. *Phone:* 262-595-2046. *Fax:* 262-595-2680. *E-mail:* dirk.baldwin@uwp.edu.

See full description on page 756.

University of Wisconsin–Parkside
School of Business and Technology

Kenosha, Wisconsin

Phone: 262-595-2046 **Fax:** 262-595-2680 **E-mail:** dirk.baldwin@uwp.edu

Business Program(s) Web Site: http://www.uwp.edu/departments/business.technology/

Graduate Business Unit Enrollment *Total:* 77 (8 full-time; 69 part-time; 33 women; 6 international). *Average Age:* 26.

Graduate Business Faculty 20 full-time.

Admissions *Applied:* 26. *Admitted:* 23. *Enrolled:* 21. *Average GMAT:* 440. *Average GPA:* 3.4

Academic Calendar Semesters.

Accreditation AACSB—The Association to Advance Collegiate Schools of Business.

After Graduation (Class of 2006–07) *Employed within 3 months of graduation:* 98%.

DEGREE MBA

MBA—Master of Business Administration Full-time and part-time. At least 32 total credits required. 12 to 84 months to complete program. *Concentration:* general MBA.

RESOURCES AND SERVICES 100 on-campus PCs are available to graduate business students. Access to Internet/World Wide Web, online (class) registration, and online grade reports available. *Personal computer requirements:* Graduate business students are strongly recommended to purchase or lease a personal computer. *Special opportunities include:* An internship program is available. *Placement services include:* Career placement, career counseling/planning, electronic job bank, career fairs, resume preparation, and career library.

EXPENSES *Tuition (state resident):* Full-time: $7100. Part-time: $396.30 per credit. *Tuition (nonresident):* Full-time: $17,710. Part-time: $985.74 per credit. *Tuition (international):* Full-time: $17,710. Part-time: $985.74 per credit. *Required fees:* Full-time: $277. Part-time: $31 per credit. *Graduate housing:* Room and board costs vary by number of occupants, type of accommodation, and type of board plan. *Typical cost:* $4600 (including board), $3600 (room only).

University of Wisconsin–Stout
Program in Training and Development

Menomonie, Wisconsin

Phone: 715-232-1322 **Fax:** 715-232-2413 **E-mail:** johnsona@uwstout.edu

Business Program(s) Web Site: http://www.uwstout.edu/programs/mstd/

Graduate Business Unit Enrollment *Total:* 67 (15 full-time; 52 part-time; 44 women; 7 international). *Average Age:* 35.

Graduate Business Faculty 9 full-time.

Admissions *Applied:* 27. *Admitted:* 23. *Enrolled:* 15.

Academic Calendar Semesters.

DEGREE MS

MS—Master of Science in Training and Development Full-time and part-time. At least 30 total credits required. Maximum of 84 months to complete program. *Concentration:* training and development.

RESOURCES AND SERVICES 500 on-campus PCs are available to graduate business students. Access to online (class) registration available. *Personal computer requirements:* Graduate business students are not required to have a personal computer. *Special opportunities include:* An international exchange program and an internship program are available. *Placement services include:* Alumni network, career placement, job search course, career counseling/planning, electronic job bank, resume referral, career fairs, job interviews arranged, resume preparation, and career library.

EXPENSES *Tuition (state resident):* Part-time: $331.62 per credit. *Tuition (nonresident):* Part-time: $553.46 per credit.

FINANCIAL AID (2007–08) Grants, research assistantships, scholarships, teaching assistantships, and work study. Aid is available to part-time students. *Financial aid application deadline:* 4/1.

Financial Aid Contact Beth Boisen, Interim Director of Financial Aid, Room 210, Bowman Hall, Menomonie, WI 54751-0790. *Phone:* 715-232-1363. *Fax:* 715-232-5246. *E-mail:* finaid1@uwstout.edu.

INTERNATIONAL STUDENTS 10% of students enrolled are international students. *Services and facilities:* Counseling/support services, International student housing, Visa Services. Financial aid is available to international students. *Required with application:* TOEFL with recommended score of 173 (computer), 500 (paper), or 61 (Internet); proof of adequate funds.

International Student Contact Vickie Kuester, Senior Administrative Program Specialist, Room 421, Bowman Hall, Menomonie, WI 54751-0790. *Phone:* 715-232-2132. *Fax:* 715-232-2500. *E-mail:* kuesterv@uwstout.edu.

APPLICATION *Required:* Application form, baccalaureate/first degree, transcripts of college work. *Recommended:* Resume/curriculum vitae. *Application fee:* $45. Applications for domestic and international students are processed on a rolling basis.

Application Contact Anne Johnson, Graduate Student Evaluator, Room 130, Bowman Hall, Menomonie, WI 54751. *Phone:* 715-232-1322. *Fax:* 715-232-2413. *E-mail:* johnsona@uwstout.edu.

University of Wisconsin–Whitewater
College of Business and Economics
Whitewater, Wisconsin

Phone: 262-472-1945 **Fax:** 262-472-4863 **E-mail:** zahnd@uww.edu

Business Program(s) Web Site: http://www.uww.edu/business/

Accreditation AACSB—The Association to Advance Collegiate Schools of Business.

DEGREES   MBA • MPA

MBA—MBA—Master of Business Administration Full-time and part-time. Distance learning option. 36 to 51 total credits required. 24 to 36 months to complete program. *Concentrations:* administration of technological information, finance, human resources management, information management, international business, management, marketing, operations management.

MPA—Graduate Business Program Full-time and part-time. Minimum GMAT score of 450 required. 30 to 60 total credits required. 24 to 84 months to complete program. *Concentration:* accounting.

RESOURCES AND SERVICES 500 on-campus PCs are available to graduate business students. Access to Internet/World Wide Web, online (class) registration, and online grade reports available. *Personal computer requirements:* Graduate business students are not required to have a personal computer. *Special opportunities include:* An international exchange program and an internship program are available. *Placement services include:* Career placement, job search course, career counseling/planning, electronic job bank, resume referral, career fairs, job interviews arranged, resume preparation, and career library.

Application Contact Donald Zahn, Associate Dean, Carlson Hall, Whitewater, WI 53190. *Phone:* 262-472-1945. *Fax:* 262-472-4863. *E-mail:* zahnd@uww.edu.

WYOMING

University of Wyoming
College of Business
Laramie, Wyoming

Phone: 307-766-2449 **Fax:** 307-766-4028 **E-mail:** mba@uwyo.edu

Business Program(s) Web Site: http://business.uwyo.edu/mba

Graduate Business Unit Enrollment *Total:* 80 (10 full-time; 70 part-time; 38 women; 4 international).

Graduate Business Faculty 29 full-time.

Admissions *Applied:* 50. *Admitted:* 45. *Enrolled:* 45. *Average GMAT:* 500. *Average GPA:* 3.0

Academic Calendar Semesters.

Accreditation AACSB—The Association to Advance Collegiate Schools of Business.

After Graduation (Class of 2006–07) *Employed within 3 months of graduation:* 70%. *Average starting salary:* $42,000.

DEGREES   EMBA • MBA

EMBA—Executive MBA Part-time. Distance learning option. Work experience required. 30 total credits required. 24 to 72 months to complete program. *Concentrations:* administration, business policy/strategy, business studies, general MBA, management, marketing.

MBA—MBA—Master of Business Administration Full-time. Distance learning option. See application requirement at: http://uwadmnweb.uwyo.edu/UWGrad/. 40 to 54 total credits required. 12 to 72 months to complete program. *Concentrations:* entrepreneurship, executive programs, technology management.

RESOURCES AND SERVICES 229 on-campus PCs are available to graduate business students. Access to Internet/World Wide Web, online (class) registration, and online grade reports available. *Personal computer requirements:* Graduate business students are required to have a personal computer. *Special opportunities include:* An internship program is available. *Placement services include:* Alumni network, career placement, career counseling/planning, electronic job bank, resume referral, career fairs, job interviews arranged, resume preparation, and career library.

FINANCIAL AID (2007–08) 10 students received aid, including loans, research assistantships, scholarships, and work study. Aid is available to part-time students. *Financial aid application deadline:* 2/1.

Financial Aid Contact Student Financial Aid, Department 3335, 1000 East University Avenue, Laramie, WY 82071. *Phone:* 307-766-2116. *Fax:* 307-766-3800. *E-mail:* finaid@uwyo.edu.

INTERNATIONAL STUDENTS 5% of students enrolled are international students. *Services and facilities:* Counseling/support services, ESL/language courses, Housing location assistance, International student organization, Language tutoring, Orientation, Visa Services, Newsletter, Student exchange program. Financial aid is available to international students. *Required with application:* TOEFL with recommended score of 207 (computer), 540 (paper), or 80 (Internet); proof of adequate funds; proof of health/immunizations.

International Student Contact Jill Johnson, Manager, International Student and Scholars Office, Department 3228, 1000 East University Avenue, Laramie, WY 82071. *Phone:* 307-766-5193. *Fax:* 307-766-4053. *E-mail:* wecnhelp@uwyo.edu.

APPLICATION *Required:* GMAT, application form, baccalaureate/first degree, essay, 3 letters of recommendation, resume/curriculum vitae, transcripts of college work. *Recommended:* Personal statement, 2 years of work experience. *Application fee:* $50. *Deadlines:* 3/1 for fall, 2/1 for summer, 2/1 for fall (international).

Application Contact Stuart K. Webster, Director, MBA Program, Department #3275, 1000 East University Avenue, Laramie, WY 82071. *Phone:* 307-766-2449. *Fax:* 307-766-4028. *E-mail:* mba@uwyo.edu.

Canada

Athabasca University
Centre for Innovative Management

Athabasca, Alberta, Canada

Phone: 780-459-1144 **Fax:** 780-459-2093 **E-mail:** cimoffice@athabascau.ca

Business Program(s) Web Site: http://www.mba.athabascau.ca

DEGREES EMBA • MBA

EMBA—MBA with Policing Electives Part-time. Distance learning option. For those in policing/security roles only. At least 48 total credits required. 24 to 60 months to complete program. *Concentrations:* leadership, operations management, other, public policy and administration, strategic management.

MBA—Executive Master of Business Administration Part-time. Distance learning option. At least 48 total credits required. 24 to 60 months to complete program. *Concentrations:* administration, executive programs, general MBA, leadership, management, operations management, organizational management, strategic management.

MBA—MBA with Energy Electives Part-time. Distance learning option. At least 48 total credits required. 24 to 60 months to complete program. *Concentrations:* general MBA, industrial administration/management, resources management.

MBA—Master of Business Administration in Project Management Part-time. Distance learning option. Project management certification or significant practical experience. At least 48 total credits required. 24 to 60 months to complete program. *Concentrations:* management, organizational management, project management, strategic management.

RESOURCES AND SERVICES Access to Internet/World Wide Web and online (class) registration available. *Personal computer requirements:* Graduate business students are required to have a personal computer. *Placement services include:* Alumni network.

Application Contact Ms. Shannon Larose, Customer Service Representative, 301 Grandin Park Plaza, 22 Sir Winston Churchill Avenue, St. Albert, AB T8N 1B4, Canada. *Phone:* 780-459-1144. *Fax:* 780-459-2093. *E-mail:* cimoffice@athabascau.ca.

Brock University
Faculty of Business

St. Catharines, Ontario, Canada

Phone: 905-688-5550 Ext. 5362 **Fax:** 905-688-4286 **E-mail:** mba@brocku.ca

Business Program(s) Web Site: http://www.bus.brocku.ca/current/graduate/

Graduate Business Unit Enrollment *Total:* 185 (149 full-time; 36 part-time; 106 international). *Average Age:* 27.

Graduate Business Faculty 69 full-time.

Admissions *Applied:* 462. *Admitted:* 203. *Enrolled:* 123. *Average GMAT:* 600. *Average GPA:* 77/100 scale

Academic Calendar Trimesters.

Accreditation AACSB—The Association to Advance Collegiate Schools of Business.

After Graduation (Class of 2006–07) *Employed within 3 months of graduation:* 97%. *Average starting salary:* 61,000 Canadian dollars.

DEGREES M Ac • M Sc • MBA

M Ac—Master of Accountancy Full-time. Undergraduate degree with concentration in accounting required. 5 total credits required. 12 to 36 months to complete program. *Concentrations:* accounting, information systems, taxation.

M Sc—Master of Science in Management Full-time. GMAT score at least 550 or a minimum score in the 70th percentile on the GRE General Test required. 5 total credits required. 20 to 36 months to complete program. *Concentrations:* accounting, finance, management science, marketing.

MBA—Master of Business Administration Full-time and part-time. Minimum GMAT score of 550 required for traditional MBA. 5 to 10 total credits required. 8 to 72 months to complete program. *Concentrations:* accounting, finance, human resources management, management, marketing.

RESOURCES AND SERVICES 34 on-campus PCs are available to graduate business students. Access to Internet/World Wide Web, online (class) registration, and online grade reports available. *Personal computer requirements:* Graduate business students are strongly recommended to purchase or lease a personal computer. *Special opportunities include:* An international exchange program and an internship program are available. *Placement services include:* Career placement, job search course, career counseling/planning, electronic job bank, career fairs, job interviews arranged, resume preparation, and career library.

EXPENSES *Tuition, province resident:* Full-time: 8000 Canadian dollars. Part-time: 786 Canadian dollars per course. *Tuition (international):* Full-time: 17,500 Canadian dollars. *Required fees:* Full-time: 500 Canadian dollars. Part-time: 250 Canadian dollars per year. Tuition and/or fees vary by number of courses or credits taken and academic program. *Graduate housing:* Room and board costs vary by type of accommodation. *Typical cost:* 5000 Canadian dollars (room only).

FINANCIAL AID (2007–08) 40 students received aid, including research assistantships, scholarships, and teaching assistantships.

INTERNATIONAL STUDENTS 57% of students enrolled are international students. *Services and facilities:* Counseling/support services, ESL/language courses, Orientation, Visa Services, Accent reduction program. Financial aid is available to international students. *Required with application:* IELT with recommended score of 6.5; TOEFL with recommended score of 213 (computer) or 550 (paper); TWE with recommended score of 4.5.

International Student Contact Ms. Jingtao Teresa Feng, International Coordinator, 500 Glenridge Avenue, St. Catharines, ON L2S 3A1, Canada. *Phone:* 905-688-5550 Ext. 4157. *Fax:* 905-688-4286. *E-mail:* mba@brocku.ca.

APPLICATION *Required:* GMAT, application form, baccalaureate/first degree, 3 letters of recommendation, personal statement, resume/curriculum vitae, transcripts of college work. *Recommended:* Interview, work experience. *Application fee:* 100 Canadian dollars. Applications for domestic and international students are processed on a rolling basis.

Application Contact Ms. Andrea Navin, Graduate Recruitment Officer, 500 Glenridge Avenue, St. Catharines, ON L2S 3A1, Canada. *Phone:* 905-688-5550 Ext. 5362. *Fax:* 905-688-4286. *E-mail:* mba@brocku.ca.

Cape Breton University
School of Business

Sydney, Nova Scotia, Canada

Phone: 902-563-1664 **Fax:** 902-562-0075 **E-mail:** anne_chiasson@capebretonu.ca

Business Program(s) Web Site: http://www.cbu.ca

Graduate Business Unit Enrollment *Total:* 139 (34 full-time; 105 part-time; 74 women; 33 international). *Average Age:* 28.

Graduate Business Faculty *Total:* 18 (11 full-time; 7 part-time).

Admissions *Average GMAT:* 540. *Average GPA:* 3.0

Academic Calendar Semesters.

MBA—Master of Business Administration in Community Economic Development Full-time and part-time. At least 48 total credits required. Minimum of 12 months to complete program. *Concentrations:* developmental economics, international development management, international management, leadership.

RESOURCES AND SERVICES 150 on-campus PCs are available to graduate business students. Access to Internet/World Wide Web, online (class) registration, and online grade reports available. *Personal computer requirements:* Graduate business students are not required to have a personal computer. *Special opportunities include:* An international exchange program is available. *Placement services include:* Alumni network, career placement, career counseling/planning, resume referral, career fairs, resume preparation, and career library.

EXPENSES *Tuition, province resident:* Full-time: 11,840 Canadian dollars. Part-time: 1184 Canadian dollars per course. *Tuition, Canadian resident:* Full-time: 11,840 Canadian dollars. Part-time: 1184 Canadian dollars per course. *Tuition (international):* Full-time: 17,500 Canadian dollars. Part-time: 1750 Canadian dollars per course. *Required fees:* Full-time: 100 Canadian dollars. Part-time: 50 Canadian dollars per semester. Tuition and/or fees vary by class time, number of courses or credits taken, campus location, academic program, and local reciprocity agreements. *Graduate housing:* Room and board costs vary by number of occupants, type of accommodation, and type of board plan. *Typical cost:* 7000 Canadian dollars (including board), 4100 Canadian dollars (room only).

FINANCIAL AID (2007–08) 6 students received aid, including scholarships. *Financial aid application deadline:* 2/28.

Financial Aid Contact Ms. Beverley Patterson, Student Loans Officer, PO Box 5300, Sydney, NS B1P 6L2, Canada. *Phone:* 902-563-1420. *Fax:* 902-563-1371. *E-mail:* bpatterson@uccb.ns.ca.

INTERNATIONAL STUDENTS 24% of students enrolled are international students. *Services and facilities:* Counseling/support services, ESL/language courses, Housing location assistance, International student organization, Language tutoring, Orientation. Financial aid is available to international students. *Required with application:* Proof of adequate funds; proof of health/immunizations. *Recommended with application:* IELT with recommended score of 7; TOEFL with recommended score of 220 (computer) or 550 (paper).

International Student Contact Ms. Elaine Delaney, International Student Advisor, PO Box 5300, Sydney, NS B1P 6L2, Canada. *Phone:* 902-563-1671. *Fax:* 902-563-1371. *E-mail:* elaine_delaney@cbu.ca.

APPLICATION *Required:* GMAT, application form, baccalaureate/first degree, essay, 3 letters of recommendation, personal statement, resume/curriculum vitae, transcripts of college work. School will accept GRE. *Application fee:* 80 Canadian dollars. Applications for domestic and international students are processed on a rolling basis.

Application Contact Ms. Anne Michele Chiasson, Coordinator, PO Box 5300, Sydney, NS B1P 6L2, Canada. *Phone:* 902-563-1664. *Fax:* 902-562-0075. *E-mail:* anne_chiasson@capebretonu.ca.

Carleton University
Eric Sprott School of Business
Ottawa, Ontario, Canada

Phone: 613-520-2807 **Fax:** 613-520-7507 **E-mail:** mba_info@sprott.carleton.ca

Business Program(s) Web Site: http://sprott.carleton.ca/mba/

Graduate Business Unit Enrollment *Total:* 145 (145 full-time; 70 women; 60 international).

Graduate Business Faculty 55 full-time.

Admissions *Average GMAT:* 600. *Average GPA:* 9.7/12 scale

Academic Calendar Canadian Standard Year.

MBA—Master of Business Administration Full-time and part-time. Honours bachelor degree with "B" average required. 7 to 9 total credits required. 12 to 60 months to complete program. *Concentrations:* financial management/planning, international business, organizational management, technology management.

RESOURCES AND SERVICES 700 on-campus PCs are available to graduate business students. Access to Internet/World Wide Web, online (class) registration, and online grade reports available. *Personal computer requirements:* Graduate business students are strongly recommended to purchase or lease a personal computer. *Special opportunities include:* An internship program is available. *Placement services include:* Alumni network, career placement, job search course, career counseling/planning, electronic job bank, career fairs, resume preparation, and career library.

Financial Aid Contact Faculty of Graduate Studies and Research, 512 Tory Building, 1125 Colonel By Drive, Ottawa, ON K1S 5B6, Canada. *Phone:* 613-520-2525. *Fax:* 613-520-4049. *E-mail:* graduate_studies@carleton.ca.

INTERNATIONAL STUDENTS 41% of students enrolled are international students. *Services and facilities:* Counseling/support services, ESL/language courses, Housing location assistance, International student organization, Language tutoring, Orientation, Visa Services. *Required with application:* IELT with recommended score of 7; TOEFL with recommended score of 213 (computer), 550 (paper), or 86 (Internet).

International Student Contact Liane Mazzulli, Graduate Promotions Officer, 1125 Colonel By Drive, 310 Dunton Tower, Ottawa, ON K1S 5B6, Canada. *Phone:* 613-520-2807. *Fax:* 613-520-7507. *E-mail:* mba_info@sprott.carleton.ca.

APPLICATION *Required:* GMAT, application form, transcripts of college work, 2 years of work experience. *Recommended:* Resume/curriculum vitae. *Application fee:* 75 Canadian dollars.

Application Contact Liane Mazzulli, Graduate Promotions Officer, 1125 Colonel By Drive, 310 Dunton Tower, Ottawa, ON K1S 5B6, Canada. *Phone:* 613-520-2807. *Fax:* 613-520-7507. *E-mail:* mba_info@sprott.carleton.ca.

Dalhousie University
Faculty of Management
Halifax, Nova Scotia, Canada

Phone: 902-494-1814 **Fax:** 902-494-7154 **E-mail:** mba.admissions@dal.ca

Business Program(s) Web Site: http://www.dal.ca/mba

Graduate Business Unit Enrollment *Total:* 196 (174 full-time; 22 part-time; 78 women; 18 international). *Average Age:* 26.

Graduate Business Faculty *Total:* 50 (37 full-time; 13 part-time).

Admissions *Applied:* 232. *Admitted:* 141. *Enrolled:* 105. *Average GMAT:* 590. *Average GPA:* 3.6/4.3 scale

Academic Calendar Semesters.

Accreditation AACSB—The Association to Advance Collegiate Schools of Business.

After Graduation (Class of 2006–07) *Employed within 3 months of graduation:* 80%. *Average starting salary:* 65,000 Canadian dollars.

DEGREES MBA • MBA/LL B • MBA/M Eng • MBA/MHA • MBA/MLS

MBA—Master of Business Administration in Financial Services Full-time and part-time. Distance learning option. Must be recommended through employer bank. Minimum 5 years of management experience required. At least 27 total credits required. Maximum of 60 months to complete program. *Concentration:* banking.

MBA—Master of Business Administration Full-time and part-time. Work experience may be waived. Minimum requirements: GMAT score of

Dalhousie University (continued)

550 and a GPA of 3.0 during last 2 years of undergraduate study. 17 to 20 total credits required. 20 to 72 months to complete program. *Concentrations:* finance, international business, marketing.

MBA/LL B—Master of Business Administration/LL B Master of Business Administration/Bachelor of Laws Full-time. Applicant must apply to and be accepted by both programs separately, but may apply (by deadlines) from within the first year of one program to add the other as a joint degree. 40 to 50 total credits required. 48 to 72 months to complete program. *Concentrations:* finance, international business, marketing.

MBA/M Eng—Master of Business Administration/Master's in Engineering Full-time. Applicant must apply to and be accepted by both programs separately, but may apply (by deadlines) from within the first year of one program to add the other as a joint degree. 22 total credits required. 24 to 72 months to complete program. *Concentrations:* combined degrees, engineering, finance, general MBA, international business, marketing.

MBA/MHA—Master of Business Administration/Master of Health Services Administration Full-time. Applicant must apply to and be accepted by both programs separately, but may apply (by deadlines) from within the first year of one program to add the other as a joint degree. 37 to 40 total credits required. 40 to 72 months to complete program. *Concentrations:* finance, international business, marketing.

MBA/MLS—Master of Business Administration/Master of Library and Information Studies Full-time. Applicant must apply to and be accepted by both programs separately, but may apply (by deadlines) from within the first year of one program to add the other as a joint degree. 40 to 50 total credits required. 30 to 72 months to complete program. *Concentrations:* finance, international business, marketing.

RESOURCES AND SERVICES 300 on-campus PCs are available to graduate business students. Access to Internet/World Wide Web, online (class) registration, and online grade reports available. *Personal computer requirements:* Graduate business students are strongly recommended to purchase or lease a personal computer. *Special opportunities include:* An international exchange program and an internship program are available. *Placement services include:* Alumni network, career placement, job search course, career counseling/planning, resume referral, career fairs, resume preparation, and career library.

EXPENSES *Tuition, province resident:* Full-time: 6750 Canadian dollars.

FINANCIAL AID (2007–08) 34 students received aid, including grants, research assistantships, scholarships, and teaching assistantships. *Financial aid application deadline:* 4/1.

Financial Aid Contact Marianne Hagen, MBA Admissions and Program Officer, 6100 University Avenue, Halifax, NS B3H 3J5, Canada. *Phone:* 902-494-1814. *Fax:* 902-494-7154. *E-mail:* mba.admissions@dal.ca.

INTERNATIONAL STUDENTS 9% of students enrolled are international students. *Services and facilities:* Counseling/support services, Housing location assistance, International student housing, International student organization, August International Student Preparation Program. Financial aid is available to international students. *Required with application:* TOEFL with recommended score of 237 (computer), 580 (paper), or 92 (Internet); proof of adequate funds. *Recommended with application:* IELT with recommended score of 7; proof of health/immunizations.

International Student Contact Melissa Ferguson, Advisor, International Students, Student Services Killam Library Room G25, 6225 University Avenue, Halifax, NS B3H 4H8, Canada. *Phone:* 902-494-1735. *Fax:* 902-494-6848. *E-mail:* melissa.ferguson@dal.ca.

APPLICATION *Required:* GMAT, application form, baccalaureate/first degree, 2 letters of recommendation, personal statement, resume/curriculum vitae, transcripts of college work. *Recommended:* 3 years of work experience. *Application fee:* 70 Canadian dollars. *Deadlines:* 6/1 for fall, 4/1 for fall (international).

Application Contact Ms. Marianne Hagen, MBA Admissions and Program Officer, 6100 University Avenue, Halifax, NS B3H 3J5, Canada. *Phone:* 902-494-1814. *Fax:* 902-494-7154. *E-mail:* mba.admissions@dal.ca.

HEC Montreal
Master's Program in Business Administration and Management
Montréal, Quebec, Canada

Phone: 514-340-6136 **Fax:** 514-340-6411 **E-mail:** mba@hec.ca

Business Program(s) Web Site: http://www.hec.ca/en/programs/mba/

Graduate Business Unit Enrollment *Total:* 2,645 (1,362 full-time; 1,283 part-time; 1,229 women; 271 international).

Graduate Business Faculty *Total:* 620 (250 full-time; 370 part-time).

Admissions *Applied:* 546. *Admitted:* 338. *Enrolled:* 241. *Average GMAT:* 600.

Academic Calendar Trimesters.

Accreditation AACSB—The Association to Advance Collegiate Schools of Business.

After Graduation (Class of 2006–07) *Employed within 3 months of graduation:* 69%. *Average starting salary:* 70,000 Canadian dollars.

DEGREE MBA

MBA—Master of Business Administration Full-time and part-time. At least 57 total credits required. 12 to 36 months to complete program. *Concentrations:* entrepreneurship, finance, human resources management, information technology, international business, management, marketing, supply chain management.

RESOURCES AND SERVICES 169 on-campus PCs are available to graduate business students. Access to Internet/World Wide Web, online (class) registration, and online grade reports available. *Personal computer requirements:* Graduate business students are required to have a personal computer. *Special opportunities include:* An international exchange program is available. *Placement services include:* Alumni network, career placement, job search course, career counseling/planning, electronic job bank, resume referral, career fairs, job interviews arranged, and resume preparation.

EXPENSES *Tuition, province resident:* Full-time: 3557 Canadian dollars. *Tuition, Canadian resident:* Full-time: 10,226 Canadian dollars. *Tuition (international):* Full-time: 16,647 Canadian dollars. *Required fees:* Full-time: 2577 Canadian dollars. Tuition and/or fees vary by academic program and local reciprocity agreements. *Graduate housing:* Room and board costs vary by number of occupants and type of accommodation. *Typical cost:* 5146 Canadian dollars (room only).

FINANCIAL AID (2007–08) 43 students received aid, including grants and scholarships.

Financial Aid Contact Mme. Mariam Ladha, Student Services, 3000 Chemin de la Cote-Sainte-Catherine, Montreal, QC H3T 2A7, Canada. *Phone:* 514-340-6168. *Fax:* 514-340-5636. *E-mail:* mariam.ladha@hec.ca.

INTERNATIONAL STUDENTS 10% of students enrolled are international students. *Services and facilities:* Counseling/support services, ESL/language courses, Housing location assistance. Financial aid is available to international students. *Required with application:* IELT with recommended score of 7; TOEFL with recommended score of 250 (computer) or 600 (paper). *Recommended with application:* Proof of adequate funds.

International Student Contact Mme. Jacqueline Lemay, International Exchange Program Coordinator, 3000 Chemin de la Cote-Sainte-Catherine, Montreal, QC H3T 2A7, Canada. *Phone:* 514-340-6840. *Fax:* 514-340-7100. *E-mail:* baei@hec.ca.

APPLICATION *Required:* GMAT, application form, baccalaureate/first degree, essay, 2 letters of recommendation, resume/curriculum vitae, transcripts of college work, 3 years of work experience. *Application fee:* 75 Canadian dollars. *Deadlines:* 3/15 for fall, 10/1 for winter. Applications for international students are processed on a rolling basis.

Application Contact Mme. Stephanie de Celles, Administrative Director of MBA Program, 3000 Chemin de la Cote-Sainte-Catherine, Montreal, QC H3T 2A7, Canada. *Phone:* 514-340-6136. *Fax:* 514-340-6411. *E-mail:* mba@hec.ca.

Laurentian University
School of Commerce and Administration
Sudbury, Ontario, Canada

Phone: 705-675-1151 Ext. 2135 **Fax:** 705-673-6518 **E-mail:** apegoraro@laurentian.ca

Business Program(s) Web Site: http://www.laurentian.ca/commerce

Graduate Business Unit Enrollment *Total:* 70 (28 full-time; 42 part-time; 29 women; 32 international).

Graduate Business Faculty *Total:* 12 (9 full-time; 3 part-time).

Admissions *Applied:* 42. *Admitted:* 28. *Enrolled:* 22. *Average GMAT:* 590.

Academic Calendar Trimesters.

After Graduation (Class of 2006–07) *Employed within 3 months of graduation:* 100%.

DEGREE MBA

MBA—Master of Business Administration Full-time and part-time. Distance learning option. At least 60 total credits required. 12 to 96 months to complete program. *Concentrations:* general MBA, sports/entertainment management.

RESOURCES AND SERVICES 300 on-campus PCs are available to graduate business students. Access to Internet/World Wide Web and online grade reports available. *Personal computer requirements:* Graduate business students are strongly recommended to purchase or lease a personal computer. *Special opportunities include:* An international exchange program is available. *Placement services include:* Alumni network, electronic job bank, and job interviews arranged.

FINANCIAL AID (2007–08) 12 students received aid, including fellowships, grants, and teaching assistantships. *Financial aid application deadline:* 9/1.

Financial Aid Contact Linda Weber, Secretary, Graduate Studies, Ramsey Lake Road, Sudbury, ON P3E 2C6, Canada. *Phone:* 705-675-1151 Ext. 3204. *Fax:* 705-671-3840. *E-mail:* lweber@laurentian.ca.

INTERNATIONAL STUDENTS 46% of students enrolled are international students. *Services and facilities:* Counseling/support services, ESL/language courses, Housing location assistance, International student organization, Language tutoring, Orientation. Financial aid is available to international students. *Required with application:* TOEFL with recommended score of 213 (computer) or 550 (paper).

International Student Contact Melissa Keeping, Director, Laurentian International, Ramsey Lake Road, Sudbury, ON P3E 2C6, Canada. *Phone:* 705-675-1151 Ext. 1556. *Fax:* 705-671-3833. *E-mail:* mkeeping@laurentian.ca.

APPLICATION *Required:* GMAT, application form, baccalaureate/first degree, 2 letters of recommendation, personal statement, transcripts of college work, 2 years of work experience. *Application fee:* 50 Canadian dollars. *Deadlines:* 5/31 for fall, 2/1 for fall (international).

Application Contact Dr. Ann Pegoraro, Coordinator, MBA Program, Ramsey Lake Road, Sudbury, ON P3E 2C6, Canada. *Phone:* 705-675-1151 Ext. 2135. *Fax:* 705-673-6518. *E-mail:* apegoraro@laurentian.ca.

McGill University
Desautels Faculty of Management
Montréal, Quebec, Canada

Phone: 514-398-4066 **Fax:** 514-398-2499 **E-mail:** antoinette.molino@mcgill.ca

Business Program(s) Web Site: http://www.mcgill.ca/mba

Graduate Business Unit Enrollment *Total:* 642 (340 full-time; 302 part-time; 224 women).

Graduate Business Faculty *Total:* 85 (78 full-time; 7 part-time).

Admissions *Applied:* 339. *Admitted:* 111. *Enrolled:* 57. *Average GMAT:* 650. *Average GPA:* 3.3

Academic Calendar Semesters.

After Graduation (Class of 2006–07) *Employed within 3 months of graduation:* 86%. *Average starting salary:* 87,700 Canadian dollars.

DEGREES EMM • JD/MBA • MBA • MD/MBA • MMM

EMM—International Master's Programs in Practising Management (IMPM) Part-time. Significant managerial work experience. 45 total credits required. 24 months to complete program. *Concentration:* international management.

EMM—International Master's in Health Management (IMHL) Part-time. Managerial experience in the health care industry. 45 total credits required. 24 months to complete program. *Concentration:* international management.

JD/MBA—Juris Doctor/Master of Business Administration Full-time. Admission to Faculty of Law. At least 138 total credits required. 48 to 60 months to complete program. *Concentration:* combined degrees.

MBA—Master of Business Administration Full-time and part-time. At least 51 total credits required. 15 to 20 months to complete program. *Concentrations:* finance, information systems, international business, international management, marketing, strategic management.

MD/MBA Full-time. Admission to Faculty of Medicine. 265 total credits required. 60 months to complete program. *Concentration:* combined degrees.

MMM—Master of Manufacturing Management Full-time and part-time. GRE or GMAT required. At least 60 total credits required. Minimum of 16 months to complete program. *Concentrations:* engineering, logistics, management, manufacturing management, supply chain management.

RESOURCES AND SERVICES 180 on-campus PCs are available to graduate business students. Access to Internet/World Wide Web, online (class) registration, and online grade reports available. *Personal computer requirements:* Graduate business students are strongly recommended to purchase or lease a personal computer. *Special opportunities include:* An international exchange program and an internship program are available. *Placement services include:* Alumni network, career placement, job search course, career counseling/planning, electronic job bank, resume referral, career fairs, job interviews arranged, resume preparation, and career library.

EXPENSES *Tuition:* Full-time: 20,000 Canadian dollars. *Tuition (international):* Full-time: 5141 Canadian dollars. *Required fees:* Full-time: 2724 Canadian dollars.

FINANCIAL AID (2007–08) 33 students received aid, including fellowships, loans, and scholarships. *Financial aid application deadline:* 3/15.

Financial Aid Contact Antoinette Molino, Associate Director of MBA Admissions, 1001 Sherbrooke Street, West, Suite 300, Montreal, QC H3A 1G5, Canada. *Phone:* 514-398-4066. *Fax:* 514-398-2499. *E-mail:* antoinette.molino@mcgill.ca.

INTERNATIONAL STUDENTS *Services and facilities:* Counseling/support services, ESL/language courses, Housing location assistance, International student organization, Orientation. Financial aid is available to international students. *Required with application:* TOEFL with recommended score of 250 (computer), 600 (paper), or 100 (Internet); proof of adequate funds; proof of health/immunizations.

International Student Contact Antoinette Molino, Associate Director of MBA Admissions, 1001 Sherbrooke Street, West, Suite 300, Montreal, QC H3A 1G5, Canada. *Phone:* 514-398-4066. *E-mail:* mba.mgmt@mcgill.ca.

APPLICATION *Required:* GMAT, application form, baccalaureate/first degree, essay, interview, 2 letters of recommendation, personal statement, resume/curriculum vitae, transcripts of college work, 2 years of work

McGill University (continued)

experience. *Application fee:* 100 Canadian dollars. Applications for domestic and international students are processed on a rolling basis.

Application Contact Antoinette Molino, Associate Director of MBA Admissions, 1001 Sherbrooke Street, West, Suite 300, Montreal, QC H3A 1G5, Canada. *Phone:* 514-398-4066. *Fax:* 514-398-2499. *E-mail:* antoinette.molino@mcgill.ca.

See full description on page 658.

McMaster University
DeGroote School of Business
Hamilton, Ontario, Canada

Phone: 905-525-9140 Ext. 26565 **Fax:** 905-528-0907 **E-mail:** mbaadmissions@mcmaster.ca

Business Program(s) Web Site: http://www.degroote.mcmaster.ca

Graduate Business Unit Enrollment *Total:* 352 (240 full-time; 112 part-time; 110 women; 26 international). *Average Age:* 28.

Graduate Business Faculty *Total:* 97 (66 full-time; 31 part-time).

Admissions *Applied:* 359. *Admitted:* 219. *Enrolled:* 155. *Average GMAT:* 630. *Average GPA:* 3.3

Academic Calendar Trimesters.

After Graduation (Class of 2006–07) *Employed within 3 months of graduation:* 85%. *Average starting salary:* 69,000 Canadian dollars.

DEGREES MBA

MBA—Master of Business Administration Full-time and part-time. B average in all required business/commerce courses from previous Business degree. At least 10 total credits required. 8 to 36 months to complete program. *Concentrations:* accounting, electronic commerce (E-commerce), finance, general MBA, marketing, risk management, supply chain management, technology management.

MBA—Master of Business Administration Full-time and part-time. At least 20 total credits required. 20 to 96 months to complete program. *Concentrations:* accounting, electronic commerce (E-commerce), finance, general MBA, health care, marketing, risk management, supply chain management, technology management.

RESOURCES AND SERVICES 90 on-campus PCs are available to graduate business students. Access to Internet/World Wide Web, online (class) registration, and online grade reports available. *Personal computer requirements:* Graduate business students are strongly recommended to purchase or lease a personal computer. *Special opportunities include:* An international exchange program and an internship program are available. *Placement services include:* Alumni network, job search course, career counseling/planning, electronic job bank, career fairs, job interviews arranged, resume preparation, and career library.

EXPENSES *Tuition, province resident:* Full-time: 12,000 Canadian dollars. Part-time: 1400 Canadian dollars per course. *Tuition, Canadian resident:* Full-time: 12,000 Canadian dollars. Part-time: 1400 Canadian dollars per course. *Tuition (international):* Full-time: 25,000 Canadian dollars. Part-time: 3000 Canadian dollars per course. Tuition and/or fees vary by academic program.

FINANCIAL AID (2007–08) Loans, scholarships, teaching assistantships, and work study. *Financial aid application deadline:* 6/15.

Financial Aid Contact Ms. Tracie Long, Manager, Student Financial Aid, GH, Room 120, 1280 Main Street West, Hamilton, ON L8S 4L8, Canada. *Phone:* 905-525-9140 Ext. 23230. *Fax:* 905-521-9565. *E-mail:* traciel@mcmaster.ca.

INTERNATIONAL STUDENTS 7% of students enrolled are international students. *Services and facilities:* Counseling/support services, ESL/language courses, Housing location assistance, International student organization, Language tutoring, Orientation, Visa Services. Financial aid is not available to international students. *Required with application:*

TOEFL with recommended score of 250 (computer), 600 (paper), or 100 (Internet). *Recommended with application:* IELT with recommended score of 7.5.

International Student Contact Mr. Marcos Costa, International Students Advisor, Gilmour Hall, Room 104, 1280 Main Street West, Hamilton, ON L8S 4L8, Canada. *Phone:* 905-525-9140 Ext. 27701. *Fax:* 905-527-6510. *E-mail:* costama@mcmaster.ca.

APPLICATION *Required:* GMAT, application form, 2 letters of recommendation, personal statement, resume/curriculum vitae, transcripts of college work, 1 year of work experience. *Recommended:* Baccalaureate/first degree, interview. *Application fee:* 150 Canadian dollars. Applications for domestic and international students are processed on a rolling basis.

Application Contact Isabella Piatek, Co-Administrator, MBA Admissions, MBA Office, 1280 Main Street W, Hamilton, ON L8S 4M4, Canada. *Phone:* 905-525-9140 Ext. 26565. *Fax:* 905-528-0907. *E-mail:* mbaadmissions@mcmaster.ca.

Memorial University of Newfoundland
Faculty of Business Administration
St. John's, Newfoundland and Labrador, Canada

Phone: 709-737-8522 **Fax:** 709-737-2467 **E-mail:** mba@mun.ca

Business Program(s) Web Site: http://www.business.mun.ca

Graduate Business Unit Enrollment *Total:* 109 (30 full-time; 79 part-time; 54 women; 12 international).

Graduate Business Faculty *Total:* 29 (28 full-time; 1 part-time).

Admissions *Applied:* 78. *Admitted:* 30. *Enrolled:* 24. *Average GMAT:* 580. *Average GPA:* 3.5

Academic Calendar Semesters.

Accreditation AACSB—The Association to Advance Collegiate Schools of Business.

After Graduation (Class of 2006–07) *Employed within 3 months of graduation:* 95%.

DEGREES MBA

MBA—Master of Business Administration Full-time and part-time. 30 to 60 total credits required. 8 to 84 months to complete program. *Concentration:* general MBA.

MBA—Thesis Option Full-time and part-time. 30 to 60 total credits required. 8 to 84 months to complete program. *Concentrations:* finance, human resources management, international business, marketing, strategic management.

RESOURCES AND SERVICES 55 on-campus PCs are available to graduate business students. Access to Internet/World Wide Web, online (class) registration, and online grade reports available. *Personal computer requirements:* Graduate business students are strongly recommended to purchase or lease a personal computer. *Special opportunities include:* An international exchange program is available. *Placement services include:* Alumni network, career placement, career counseling/planning, electronic job bank, career fairs, and resume preparation.

EXPENSES *Tuition, province resident:* Full-time: 2199 Canadian dollars. Part-time: 2187 Canadian dollars per semester. *Tuition (international):* Full-time: 2859 Canadian dollars. Part-time: 2844 Canadian dollars per semester. *Required fees:* Full-time: 1096 Canadian dollars. Part-time: 345 Canadian dollars per semester. *Graduate housing:* Room and board costs vary by campus location, number of occupants, type of accommodation, and type of board plan. *Typical cost:* 8100 Canadian dollars (including board), 4440 Canadian dollars (room only).

FINANCIAL AID (2007–08) 10 students received aid, including scholarships.

Financial Aid Contact Ms. Lisa Savage, MBA Program Secretary, St. John's, NF A1B 3X5, Canada. *Phone:* 709-737-8522. *Fax:* 709-737-2467. *E-mail:* mba@mun.ca.

INTERNATIONAL STUDENTS 11% of students enrolled are international students. *Services and facilities:* Counseling/support services, ESL/language courses, Housing location assistance, International student housing, International student organization, Language tutoring, Orientation. Financial aid is available to international students. *Required with application:* TOEFL with recommended score of 237 (computer) or 580 (paper); proof of adequate funds. *Recommended with application:* TWE with recommended score of 4; proof of health/immunizations.

International Student Contact Ms. Lisa Savage, MBA Program Secretary, St. John's, NF A1B 3X5, Canada. *Phone:* 709-737-8522. *Fax:* 709-737-2467. *E-mail:* mba@mun.ca.

APPLICATION *Required:* GMAT, application form, baccalaureate/first degree, essay, 3 letters of recommendation, personal statement, resume/curriculum vitae, transcripts of college work. *Recommended:* Work experience. *Application fee:* 40 Canadian dollars. *Deadline:* 2/1 for fall (international). Applications for domestic students are processed on a rolling basis.

Application Contact Ms. Lisa Savage, MBA Program Secretary, St. John's, NF A1B 3X5, Canada. *Phone:* 709-737-8522. *Fax:* 709-737-2467. *E-mail:* mba@mun.ca.

Royal Military College of Canada
Department of Business Administration

Kingston, Ontario, Canada

Phone: 613-541-6000 Ext. 6259 **Fax:** 613-541-6315 **E-mail:** essaddam-n@rmc.ca

Business Program(s) Web Site: http://www.rmc.ca/academic/grad/calendar/arts/busadm_e.html

Graduate Business Unit Enrollment *Total:* 42 (20 full-time; 22 part-time; 16 women). *Average Age:* 35.

Graduate Business Faculty *Total:* 17 (15 full-time; 2 part-time).

Admissions *Applied:* 120. *Admitted:* 12. *Enrolled:* 10. *Average GMAT:* 550. *Average GPA:* 3.3

Academic Calendar Semesters.

After Graduation (Class of 2006–07) *Employed within 3 months of graduation:* 100%. *Average starting salary:* 75,000 Canadian dollars.

DEGREES MA • MBA

MA—Public Administration Full-time and part-time. Distance learning option. 12 total credits required. 12 to 18 months to complete program. *Concentration:* public policy and administration.

MBA—Master of Business Administration Full-time and part-time. Distance learning option. 20 total credits required. 24 months to complete program. *Concentrations:* general MBA, logistics.

RESOURCES AND SERVICES 50 on-campus PCs are available to graduate business students. Access to Internet/World Wide Web available. *Personal computer requirements:* Graduate business students are strongly recommended to purchase or lease a personal computer. *Placement services include:* Resume referral.

EXPENSES *Tuition, province resident:* Full-time: 5200 Canadian dollars. Part-time: 1050 Canadian dollars per course. *Tuition (international):* Full-time: 12,000 Canadian dollars. Part-time: 2000 Canadian dollars per course. *Required fees:* Full-time: 420 Canadian dollars. Tuition and/or fees vary by number of courses or credits taken and local reciprocity agreements.

FINANCIAL AID (2007–08) 7 students received aid, including scholarships.

INTERNATIONAL STUDENTS Financial aid is not available to international students.

APPLICATION *Required:* Application form, baccalaureate/first degree, 3 letters of recommendation, personal statement, resume/curriculum vitae, transcripts of college work, 5 years of work experience. School will accept GMAT. *Application fee:* 50 Canadian dollars. Applications for domestic students are processed on a rolling basis.

Application Contact Dr. N. Essaddam, Chair of MBA Program, PO Box 17000, Station Forces, Kingston, ON K7K 7B4, Canada. *Phone:* 613-541-6000 Ext. 6259. *Fax:* 613-541-6315. *E-mail:* essaddam-n@rmc.ca.

Royal Roads University
Faculty of Management

Victoria, British Columbia, Canada

Phone: 800-788-8028 **E-mail:** learn.more@royalroads.ca

Business Program(s) Web Site: http://www.royalroads.ca/programs/faculties-schools-centres/faculty-management/

Graduate Business Unit Enrollment *Total:* 217 (217 full-time; 104 women; 1 international). *Average Age:* 38.

Graduate Business Faculty *Total:* 113 (13 full-time; 100 part-time).

Admissions *Applied:* 494. *Admitted:* 296. *Enrolled:* 217. *Average GPA:* 3.2

Academic Calendar Continuous.

After Graduation (Class of 2006–07) *Employed within 3 months of graduation:* 95%.

DEGREES MBA

MBA—Digital Technologies Management Distance learning option. Formal education/professional experience in digital technologies required. At least 64 total credits required. 24 months to complete program. *Concentrations:* general MBA, technology management.

MBA—Executive Management Distance learning option. At least 64 total credits required. 24 months to complete program. *Concentrations:* general MBA, management, strategic management.

MBA—Human Resources Management Distance learning option. Formal education/professional experience in human resources required. At least 64 total credits required. 24 months to complete program. *Concentrations:* general MBA, human resources management.

MBA—Leadership Distance learning option. At least 64 total credits required. 24 months to complete program. *Concentrations:* general MBA, leadership, management.

MBA—Management Consulting Distance learning option. At least 64 total credits required. 24 months to complete program. *Concentrations:* general MBA, management consulting.

MBA—Public Relations and Communication Management Distance learning option. Formal education/professional experience in public relations/communications required. At least 64 total credits required. 24 months to complete program. *Concentrations:* general MBA, public relations.

RESOURCES AND SERVICES 155 on-campus PCs are available to graduate business students. Access to Internet/World Wide Web, online (class) registration, and online grade reports available. *Personal computer requirements:* Graduate business students are required to have a personal computer. *Placement services include:* Alumni network, career counseling/planning, electronic job bank, and resume preparation.

EXPENSES *Tuition, province resident:* Full-time: 18,000 Canadian dollars. *Tuition, Canadian resident:* Full-time: 18,000 Canadian dollars. *Tuition (international):* Full-time: 26,800 Canadian dollars. *Required fees:* Full-time: 725 Canadian dollars. Tuition and/or fees vary by campus location and academic program.

FINANCIAL AID (2007–08) 32 students received aid, including grants, loans, and scholarships. Aid is available to part-time students.

Royal Roads University (continued)

Financial Aid Contact Gwen Campden, Coordinator, Financial Aid and Awards, University Life, 2005 Sooke Road, Victoria, BC V9B 5Y2, Canada. *Phone:* 250-391-2502. *Fax:* 250-391-2500. *E-mail:* rrufinancialaid@royalroads.ca.

INTERNATIONAL STUDENTS 0.5% of students enrolled are international students. *Services and facilities:* Counseling/support services, ESL/language courses, Housing location assistance, Language tutoring, Orientation, Friendship and Cultural Exchange (volunteer mentor group). Financial aid is available to international students. *Required with application:* TOEFL with recommended score of 233 (computer) or 570 (paper); proof of health/immunizations. *Recommended with application:* IELT with recommended score of 6.5; proof of adequate funds.

International Student Contact Ms. Cheryl-Lynn Townsin, International MBA Coordinator, MBA International Programs, 2005 Sooke Road, Victoria, BC V9B 5Y2, Canada. *Phone:* 250-391-2600 Ext. 4403. *Fax:* 250-391-2610. *E-mail:* cheryl-lynn.townsin@royalroads.ca.

APPLICATION *Required:* Application form, 2 letters of recommendation, personal statement, resume/curriculum vitae, transcripts of college work, 7 years of work experience. *Recommended:* Baccalaureate/first degree. *Application fee:* 100 Canadian dollars. Applications for domestic and international students are processed on a rolling basis.

Application Contact Ms. Michelle Tai, Manager, Admissions and Enrollment Services, Office of Admissions, 2005 Sooke Road, Victoria, BC V9B 5Y2, Canada. *Phone:* 800-788-8028. *E-mail:* learn.more@royalroads.ca.

Simon Fraser University
Faculty of Business Administration

Burnaby, British Columbia, Canada

Phone: 778-782-7857 **Fax:** 778-782-5122 **E-mail:** sharon_hummel@sfu.ca

Business Program(s) Web Site: http://business.sfu.ca/segal/

Graduate Business Unit Enrollment *Total:* 372 (117 full-time; 255 part-time; 116 women; 57 international). *Average Age:* 30.

Graduate Business Faculty *Total:* 54 (33 full-time; 21 part-time).

Admissions *Applied:* 479. *Admitted:* 201. *Enrolled:* 141. *Average GMAT:* 600. *Average GPA:* 3.3

Academic Calendar Trimesters.

Accreditation AACSB—The Association to Advance Collegiate Schools of Business.

After Graduation (Class of 2006–07) *Employed within 3 months of graduation:* 95%. *Average starting salary:* 75,000 Canadian dollars.

DEGREES Dipl-Kfm • MBA • MBF

Dipl-Kfm—Graduate Diploma in Business Administration Full-time and part-time. Distance learning option. 24 total credits required. 12 to 36 months to complete program. *Concentration:* management.

MBA—Executive Master of Business Administration Part-time. 54 to 60 total credits required. 20 months to complete program. *Concentration:* executive programs.

MBA—Global Asset and Wealth Management Full-time and part-time. 42 total credits required. 16 to 28 months to complete program. *Concentration:* financial management/planning.

MBA—Management of Technology/Biotechnology Part-time. 46 to 54 total credits required. 24 months to complete program. *Concentration:* technology management.

MBA—Master of Business Administration Full-time. 45 total credits required. 12 months to complete program. *Concentration:* general MBA.

MBF—Master of Financial Risk Management Full-time. 42 total credits required. 12 months to complete program. *Concentration:* finance.

RESOURCES AND SERVICES 35 on-campus PCs are available to graduate business students. Access to Internet/World Wide Web, online (class) registration, and online grade reports available. *Personal computer requirements:* Graduate business students are strongly recommended to purchase or lease a personal computer. *Special opportunities include:* An internship program is available. *Placement services include:* Career placement, job search course, career counseling/planning, electronic job bank, resume referral, career fairs, job interviews arranged, resume preparation, and career library.

EXPENSES *Tuition, province resident:* Full-time: 27,000 Canadian dollars. *Tuition, Canadian resident:* Full-time: 27,000 Canadian dollars. *Tuition (international):* Full-time: 27,000 Canadian dollars. *Required fees:* Full-time: 900 Canadian dollars. Tuition and/or fees vary by number of courses or credits taken and academic program. *Graduate housing:* Room and board costs vary by campus location, number of occupants, type of accommodation, and type of board plan. *Typical cost:* 12,000 Canadian dollars (including board).

FINANCIAL AID (2007–08) 30 students received aid, including fellowships, scholarships, and teaching assistantships. Aid is available to part-time students. *Financial aid application deadline:* 8/1.

Financial Aid Contact Alan Wiseman, Graduate Awards Manager, Office of the Dean of Graduate Studies, MBC 1100, 8888 University Drive, Burnaby, BC V5A 1S6, Canada. *Phone:* 778-782-8499. *Fax:* 778-782-3080. *E-mail:* alan_wiseman@sfu.ca.

INTERNATIONAL STUDENTS 15% of students enrolled are international students. *Services and facilities:* Counseling/support services, ESL/language courses, Housing location assistance, International student organization, Orientation. Financial aid is available to international students. *Required with application:* TOEFL with recommended score of 230 (computer), 570 (paper), or 88 (Internet); TWE with recommended score of 5.

International Student Contact Kate Jennings, Acting Co-Director, SFU International, MBC 1200, 8888 University Drive, Burnaby, BC V5A 1S6, Canada. *Phone:* 778-782-4232. *Fax:* 778-782-5880. *E-mail:* kjenning@sfu.ca.

APPLICATION *Required:* GMAT, application form, baccalaureate/first degree, essay, 3 letters of recommendation, personal statement, resume/curriculum vitae, transcripts of college work. *Recommended:* 2 years of work experience. *Application fee:* 75 Canadian dollars. Applications for domestic and international students are processed on a rolling basis.

Application Contact Ms. Sharon Hummel, Admissions Advisor, Graduate Business Programs, Segal Graduate School of Business, 3990-500 Granville Street, Vancouver, BC V6C 1W6, Canada. *Phone:* 778-782-7857. *Fax:* 778-782-5122. *E-mail:* sharon_hummel@sfu.ca.

Université de Moncton
Faculty of Administration

Moncton, New Brunswick, Canada

Phone: 506-858-4218 **Fax:** 506-858-4093 **E-mail:** tania.morris@umoncton.ca

Business Program(s) Web Site: http://www.umoncton.ca/administration/

Graduate Business Unit Enrollment *Total:* 189 (47 full-time; 142 part-time; 80 women; 30 international). *Average Age:* 28.

Graduate Business Faculty *Total:* 20 (14 full-time; 6 part-time).

Admissions *Applied:* 82. *Admitted:* 62. *Enrolled:* 26. *Average GPA:* 3.0

Academic Calendar Semesters.

After Graduation (Class of 2006–07) *Employed within 3 months of graduation:* 100%. *Average starting salary:* 42,000 Canadian dollars.

DEGREES MBA • MBA/LL B

MBA—Multimedia Master of Business Administration Part-time. Distance learning option. At least 45 total credits required. 36 to 60 months to complete program. *Concentration:* general MBA.

MBA—Master of Business Administration Full-time and part-time. At least 45 total credits required. 20 to 28 months to complete program. *Concentration:* general MBA.

MBA/LL B—Master of Business Administration/Bachelor of Laws Full-time. At least 122 total credits required. 48 to 60 months to complete program. *Concentration:* combined degrees.

RESOURCES AND SERVICES 120 on-campus PCs are available to graduate business students. Access to Internet/World Wide Web, online (class) registration, and online grade reports available. *Personal computer requirements:* Graduate business students are strongly recommended to purchase or lease a personal computer. *Special opportunities include:* An international exchange program and an internship program are available. *Placement services include:* Alumni network, career placement, job search course, career counseling/planning, electronic job bank, resume referral, job interviews arranged, and resume preparation.

EXPENSES *Tuition, province resident:* Full-time: 9945 Canadian dollars. Part-time: 573 Canadian dollars per credit. *Tuition (international):* Full-time: 14,805 Canadian dollars. Part-time: 897 Canadian dollars per credit. *Graduate housing:* Room and board costs vary by campus location and type of board plan. *Typical cost:* 5543 Canadian dollars (including board), 3583 Canadian dollars (room only).

FINANCIAL AID (2007–08) 6 students received aid, including fellowships and scholarships. *Financial aid application deadline:* 10/15.

Financial Aid Contact Renée Savoie-Power, Service des Bourses et de L'Aide Financiere, Moncton, NB E1A 3E9, Canada. *Phone:* 506-858-3731. *Fax:* 506-858-4492. *E-mail:* renee.savoie-power@umoncton.ca.

INTERNATIONAL STUDENTS 16% of students enrolled are international students. *Services and facilities:* Counseling/support services, Housing location assistance, International student organization. Financial aid is not available to international students. *Required with application:* Proof of adequate funds; proof of health/immunizations. *Recommended with application:* TWE.

International Student Contact Hermel Deschenes, Service aux étudiantes et étudiant internationaux, Moncton, NB E1A3E9, Canada. *Phone:* 506-858-3713. *Fax:* 506-858-4492. *E-mail:* hermel.deschenes@umoncton.ca.

APPLICATION *Required:* GRE, application form, baccalaureate/first degree, 2 letters of recommendation, personal statement, resume/curriculum vitae, transcripts of college work. *Recommended:* Interview, 2 years of work experience. *Application fee:* 39 Canadian dollars. *Deadlines:* 6/1 for fall, 11/15 for winter, 3/31 for spring, 3/31 for summer, 2/1 for fall (international), 9/1 for winter (international), 1/1 for spring (international), 1/1 for summer (international).

Application Contact Dr. Tania Morris, MBA Program Director, Moncton, NB E1A 3E9, Canada. *Phone:* 506-858-4218. *Fax:* 506-858-4093. *E-mail:* tania.morris@umoncton.ca.

Université du Québec en Outaouais
Program in Financial Services
Gatineau, Quebec, Canada

Phone: 819-773-1769 **Fax:** 819-773-1637 **E-mail:** suzanne.jolicoeur@uqo.ca

Business Program(s) Web Site: http://www.uqo.ca/programmes-etudes/programmes/3457.htm

DEGREE MBA

MBA—Master of Business Administration in Financial Services Full-time and part-time. 4 years of work experience required. 30 to 45 total credits required. 2 to 4 months to complete program. *Concentration:* finance.

RESOURCES AND SERVICES Access to Internet/World Wide Web, online (class) registration, and online grade reports available. *Personal computer requirements:* Graduate business students are strongly recom-

mended to purchase or lease a personal computer. *Placement services include:* Career placement and career fairs.

Application Contact Ms. Suzanne Jolicoeur, Graduate Students Office, 101 Saint-Jean-Bosco Street, Room B-0164, Gatineau, QC J8X 3X7, Canada. *Phone:* 819-773-1769. *Fax:* 819-773-1637. *E-mail:* suzanne.jolicoeur@uqo.ca.

University of Alberta
School of Business
Edmonton, Alberta, Canada

Phone: 780-492-3946 **Fax:** 780-492-7825 **E-mail:** mba@ualberta.ca

Business Program(s) Web Site: http://www.mba.net/

Accreditation AACSB—The Association to Advance Collegiate Schools of Business.

DEGREES MBA • MBA/LL B • MBA/M Ag • MBA/M Eng • MBA/MF

MBA—Executive Master of Business Administration Full-time. 54 total credits required. 20 months to complete program. *Concentration:* executive programs.

MBA—Master of Business Administration Full-time and part-time. 57 total credits required. 16 to 72 months to complete program. *Concentration:* general MBA.

MBA—Master of Business Administration in International Business Full-time and part-time. 57 total credits required. 16 to 72 months to complete program. *Concentration:* international business.

MBA—Master of Business Administration in Leisure and Sport Management Full-time and part-time. 57 total credits required. 16 to 72 months to complete program. *Concentration:* sports/entertainment management.

MBA—Master of Business Administration in Natural Resources and Energy Full-time and part-time. 57 total credits required. 20 to 72 months to complete program. *Concentrations:* environmental economics/management, resources management.

MBA—Master of Business Administration in Technology Commercialization Full-time and part-time. 57 total credits required. 16 to 72 months to complete program. *Concentration:* technology management.

MBA—Master of Business Administration with Public Management Stream Full-time and part-time. 57 total credits required. 16 to 72 months to complete program. *Concentration:* public management.

MBA/LL B—Master of Business Administration/Bachelor of Law Full-time. 122 total credits required. 44 to 72 months to complete program. *Concentrations:* combined degrees, general MBA.

MBA/M Ag—Master of Business Administration/Master of Agriculture Full-time and part-time. Undergraduate degree in agriculture or equivalent required. 63 total credits required. 20 to 72 months to complete program. *Concentrations:* combined degrees, general MBA.

MBA/M Eng—Master of Business Administration/Master of Engineering Full-time and part-time. Undergraduate degree in engineering required. 63 to 69 total credits required. 20 to 72 months to complete program. *Concentrations:* combined degrees, general MBA.

MBA/MF—Master of Business Administration/Master of Forestry Full-time and part-time. Undergraduate degree in forestry or equivalent required. 63 total credits required. 20 to 72 months to complete program. *Concentrations:* combined degrees, general MBA.

RESOURCES AND SERVICES 25 on-campus PCs are available to graduate business students. Access to Internet/World Wide Web, online (class) registration, and online grade reports available. *Personal computer requirements:* Graduate business students are not required to have a personal computer. *Special opportunities include:* An international exchange program and an internship program are available. *Placement services include:* Alumni network, career placement, career counseling/

University of Alberta (continued)

planning, electronic job bank, resume referral, career fairs, job interviews arranged, resume preparation, and career library.

Application Contact Joan White, Executive Director, MBA Programs, 2-30 Business Building, Edmonton, AB T6G 2R6, Canada. *Phone:* 780-492-3946. *Fax:* 780-492-7825. *E-mail:* mba@ualberta.ca.

The University of British Columbia
Sauder School of Business

Vancouver, British Columbia, Canada

Phone: 604-822-8422 **Fax:** 604-822-9030 **E-mail:** mba@sauder.ubc.ca

Business Program(s) Web Site: http://www.sauder.ubc.ca/mba

Graduate Business Unit Enrollment *Total:* 425 (350 full-time; 75 part-time).

Graduate Business Faculty *Total:* 72 (48 full-time; 24 part-time).

Admissions *Average GMAT:* 620. *Average GPA:* 3.3

Academic Calendar Continuous.

Accreditation AACSB—The Association to Advance Collegiate Schools of Business.

After Graduation (Class of 2006–07) *Employed within 3 months of graduation:* 94%. *Average starting salary:* 80,000 Canadian dollars.

DEGREES IMBA • MBA • MBA/LL B • MBA/MA • MM • MS

IMBA—International Master of Business Administration Full-time and part-time. At least 41 total credits required. Minimum of 24 months to complete program. *Concentration:* general MBA.

MBA—Master of Business Administration Full-time and part-time. At least 51 total credits required. 15 to 30 months to complete program. *Concentrations:* entrepreneurship, environmental economics/management, finance, general MBA, human resources management, management information systems, marketing, organizational behavior/development, strategic management, supply chain management.

MBA/LL B—Master of Business Administration/Bachelor of Laws Full-time. Application to the Joint LLB/MBA program involves applying separately to each of the MBA and the LLB programs. Candidates are required to meet all of the admission requirements and deadlines for both. At least 136 total credits required. 48 to 60 months to complete program. *Concentrations:* entrepreneurship, environmental economics/management, finance, general MBA, human resources management, management information systems, marketing, organizational behavior/development, strategic management, supply chain management.

MBA/MA—MBA/MA in Asia Pacific Policy Studies Full-time. Application to the Joint MBA/MAPPS program involves applying separately to each of the MBA and the MAPPS programs. Candidates are required to meet all of the admission requirements and deadlines for b. 75 total credits required. 20 to 24 months to complete program. *Concentrations:* entrepreneurship, environmental economics/management, finance, general MBA, information technology, marketing, organizational behavior/development, strategic management, supply chain management.

MM—Early Career Master's Full-time. 30 total credits required. 8 to 12 months to complete program. *Concentration:* management.

MM—Master of Management Full-time and part-time. 30 to 36 total credits required. 12 to 24 months to complete program. *Concentration:* operations management.

MS—Master of Science in Business Administration Full-time. At least 30 total credits required. 12 to 36 months to complete program. *Concentrations:* finance, management information systems, management science, transportation management.

RESOURCES AND SERVICES 84 on-campus PCs are available to graduate business students. Access to Internet/World Wide Web, online (class) registration, and online grade reports available. *Personal computer requirements:* Graduate business students are strongly recommended to purchase or lease a personal computer. *Special opportunities include:* An international exchange program and an internship program are available. *Placement services include:* Alumni network, career placement, job search course, career counseling/planning, electronic job bank, resume referral, career fairs, job interviews arranged, resume preparation, and career library.

FINANCIAL AID (2007–08) 49 students received aid, including fellowships, grants, loans, research assistantships, scholarships, teaching assistantships, and work study. *Financial aid application deadline:* 4/30.

Financial Aid Contact Ms. Lindsay Johnson, Manager, Admissions and Recruitment, 160—2053 Main Mall, Vancouver, BC V6T 1Z2, Canada. *Phone:* 604-822-8422. *Fax:* 604-822-9030. *E-mail:* mba@sauder.ubc.ca.

INTERNATIONAL STUDENTS *Services and facilities:* Counseling/ support services, ESL/language courses, International student housing, International student organization, Orientation, Visa Services, Cultural adaptation program. Financial aid is available to international students. *Required with application:* IELT with recommended score of 6.5; TOEFL with recommended score of 250 (computer), 600 (paper), or 100 (Internet).

International Student Contact Ms. Lindsay Johnson, Manager, Admissions and Recruitment, 160—2053 Main Mall, Vancouver, BC V6T 1Z2, Canada. *Phone:* 604-822-8422. *Fax:* 604-822-9030. *E-mail:* mba@sauder.ubc.ca.

APPLICATION *Required:* GMAT, application form, baccalaureate/first degree, essay, interview, 3 letters of recommendation, personal statement, resume/curriculum vitae, transcripts of college work. *Recommended:* 2 years of work experience. *Application fee:* 125 Canadian dollars. Applications for domestic and international students are processed on a rolling basis.

Application Contact Ms. Lindsay Johnson, Manager, Admissions and Recruitment, 160—2053 Main Mall, Vancouver, BC V6T 1Z2, Canada. *Phone:* 604-822-8422. *Fax:* 604-822-9030. *E-mail:* mba@sauder.ubc.ca.

University of Calgary
Haskayne School of Business

Calgary, Alberta, Canada

Phone: 403-220-8757 **Fax:** 403-282-0095 **E-mail:** mbarequest@haskayne.ucalgary.ca

Business Program(s) Web Site: http://www.haskayne.ucalgary.ca

Accreditation AACSB—The Association to Advance Collegiate Schools of Business.

DEGREES MBA

MBA—Executive Master of Business Administration Part-time. At least 60 total credits required. Minimum of 20 months to complete program. *Concentration:* executive programs.

MBA—Haskayne MBA Full-time and part-time. 24 to 60 total credits required. 16 to 72 months to complete program. *Concentrations:* combined degrees, entrepreneurship, finance, general MBA, marketing, other, student designed.

RESOURCES AND SERVICES 150 on-campus PCs are available to graduate business students. Access to Internet/World Wide Web, online (class) registration, and online grade reports available. *Personal computer requirements:* Graduate business students are strongly recommended to purchase or lease a personal computer. *Special opportunities include:* An international exchange program and an internship program are available. *Placement services include:* Alumni network, career placement, job search course, career counseling/planning, electronic job bank, resume referral, career fairs, job interviews arranged, resume preparation, and career library.

Application Contact Shahauna Siddiqui, Associate Director, MBA Programs, 2500 University Drive, NW, Scurfield Hall, Calgary, AB T2N 1N4, Canada. *Phone:* 403-220-8757. *Fax:* 403-282-0095. *E-mail:* mbarequest@haskayne.ucalgary.ca.

University of Guelph
Faculty of Management
Guelph, Ontario, Canada

Phone: 519-824-4120 Ext. 56607 **Fax:** 519-836-0661 **E-mail:** plago@uoguelph.ca

Business Program(s) Web Site: http://www.mba.uoguelph.ca

Graduate Business Unit Enrollment *Total:* 80 (80 full-time; 29 women; 1 international). *Average Age:* 35.

Graduate Business Faculty *Total:* 44 (37 full-time; 7 part-time).

Admissions *Applied:* 78. *Admitted:* 43. *Enrolled:* 35. *Average GPA:* 3.0

Academic Calendar Semesters.

DEGREES MA • MBA

MA—MA (Leadership) Full-time. Minimum of five years of professional experience in leadership. This is an online offering geared toward midcareer professionals. 24 months to complete program. *Concentration:* leadership.

MBA—Master of Business Administration Full-time. Distance learning option. Professional experience in Agribusiness or Hospitality and Tourism required. 12 to 36 months to complete program. *Concentrations:* agribusiness, hospitality management.

RESOURCES AND SERVICES 250 on-campus PCs are available to graduate business students. Access to Internet/World Wide Web, online (class) registration, and online grade reports available. *Personal computer requirements:* Graduate business students are required to have a personal computer.

FINANCIAL AID (2007–08) 24 students received aid, including grants, loans, research assistantships, scholarships, and teaching assistantships.

Financial Aid Contact Ms. Patti Lago, Manager, Executive Programs, College of Management and Economics, 150 Research Lane, Suite #205, Guelph, ON N1H 4T2, Canada. *Phone:* 519-824-4120 Ext. 56607. *Fax:* 519-836-0661. *E-mail:* plago@uoguelph.ca.

INTERNATIONAL STUDENTS 1% of students enrolled are international students. *Services and facilities:* Counseling/support services, ESL/language courses, Housing location assistance, International student housing, International student organization, Language tutoring, Orientation, Visa Services, international student advisor. Financial aid is available to international students. *Required with application:* TOEFL with recommended score of 213 (computer), 550 (paper), or 89 (Internet); proof of adequate funds.

International Student Contact Ms. Patti Lago, Manager, Executive Programs, College of Management and Economics, 150 Research Lane, Suite #205, Guelph, ON N1H 4T2, Canada. *Phone:* 519-824-4120 Ext. 56607. *Fax:* 519-836-0661. *E-mail:* plago@uoguelph.ca.

APPLICATION *Required:* Application form, baccalaureate/first degree, interview, 2 letters of recommendation, personal statement, resume/curriculum vitae, transcripts of college work, 3 years of work experience. School will accept GMAT. *Application fee:* 150 Canadian dollars. Applications for domestic and international students are processed on a rolling basis.

Application Contact Ms. Patti Lago, Manager, Graduate Programs, College of Management and Economics, 150 Research Lane, Suite #205, Guelph, ON N1H 4T2, Canada. *Phone:* 519-824-4120 Ext. 56607. *Fax:* 519-836-0661. *E-mail:* plago@uoguelph.ca.

University of Manitoba
Faculty of Management
Winnipeg, Manitoba, Canada

Phone: 204-474-8448 **Fax:** 204-474-7544 **E-mail:** emorphy@ms.umanitoba.ca

Business Program(s) Web Site: http://www.umanitoba.ca/asper

Graduate Business Unit Enrollment *Total:* 180 (50 full-time; 130 part-time; 75 women; 25 international). *Average Age:* 32.

Graduate Business Faculty *Total:* 45 (43 full-time; 2 part-time).

Admissions *Applied:* 160. *Admitted:* 110. *Enrolled:* 90. *Average GMAT:* 580. *Average GPA:* 3.5/4.5 scale

Academic Calendar Trimesters.

Accreditation AACSB—The Association to Advance Collegiate Schools of Business.

After Graduation (Class of 2006–07) *Employed within 3 months of graduation:* 75%. *Average starting salary:* 75,000 Canadian dollars.

DEGREES M Sc • MBA

M Sc—Master's of Science in Management Full-time and part-time. Undergraduate Degree, GMAT. 18 to 36 total credits required. 12 to 60 months to complete program. *Concentrations:* administration, business policy/strategy, business studies, human resources development, human resources management, industrial administration/management, industrial/labor relations, international marketing, logistics, manufacturing management, marketing, operations management, organizational behavior/development, organizational management, production management, quality management, supply chain management, training and development.

MBA—Master of Business Administration Full-time and part-time. 60 to 66 total credits required. 11 to 72 months to complete program. *Concentrations:* administration, finance, general MBA, health administration, human resources management, management, marketing, supply chain management.

RESOURCES AND SERVICES 125 on-campus PCs are available to graduate business students. Access to Internet/World Wide Web and online grade reports available. *Personal computer requirements:* Graduate business students are strongly recommended to purchase or lease a personal computer. *Special opportunities include:* An internship program is available. *Placement services include:* Alumni network, career placement, job search course, career counseling/planning, electronic job bank, resume referral, career fairs, job interviews arranged, resume preparation, and career library.

EXPENSES *Tuition, province resident:* Full-time: 19,100 Canadian dollars. *Tuition (international):* Full-time: 27,100 Canadian dollars. Tuition and/or fees vary by academic program. *Graduate housing:* Room and board costs vary by campus location, number of occupants, type of accommodation, and type of board plan.

FINANCIAL AID (2007–08) 5 students received aid, including fellowships, grants, loans, research assistantships, scholarships, and teaching assistantships. Aid is available to part-time students. *Financial aid application deadline:* 4/1.

Financial Aid Contact Mrs. Jane Lastra, Director, Financial Aid and Awards, Room 421, University Centre Building, Winnipeg, MB R3T 2N2, Canada. *Phone:* 204-474-6382. *Fax:* 204-474-7554. *E-mail:* jane_lastra@umanitoba.ca.

INTERNATIONAL STUDENTS 14% of students enrolled are international students. *Services and facilities:* Counseling/support services, ESL/language courses, Housing location assistance, International student housing, International student organization, Language tutoring, Orientation, Visa Services. Financial aid is available to international students. *Required with application:* TOEFL with recommended score of 213 (computer), 550 (paper), or 80 (Internet); proof of adequate funds; proof of health/immunizations.

University of Manitoba (continued)

International Student Contact Director, International Student Center, 541 University Center, Winnipeg, MB R3T 2N2, Canada. *Phone:* 204-474-8501. *Fax:* 204-474-7562. *E-mail:* ics@cc.umanitoba.ca.

APPLICATION *Required:* GMAT, application form, baccalaureate/first degree, 2 letters of recommendation, resume/curriculum vitae, transcripts of college work, 3 years of work experience. *Recommended:* Interview, personal statement. *Application fee:* 75 Canadian dollars, 90 Canadian dollars (international). Applications for domestic and international students are processed on a rolling basis.

Application Contact Ms. Ewa Morphy, Graduate Program Manager, 324 Drake Centre, Winnipeg, MB R3T 5V4, Canada. *Phone:* 204-474-8448. *Fax:* 204-474-7544. *E-mail:* emorphy@ms.umanitoba.ca.

University of New Brunswick Fredericton

Faculty of Business Administration

Fredericton, New Brunswick, Canada

Phone: 506-451-6817 **Fax:** 506-453-3561 **E-mail:** mbacontact@unb.ca

Business Program(s) Web Site: http://www.business.unbf.ca

Graduate Business Unit Enrollment *Total:* 80 (35 full-time; 45 part-time; 36 women; 16 international). *Average Age:* 30.

Graduate Business Faculty *Total:* 42 (38 full-time; 4 part-time).

Admissions *Applied:* 114. *Admitted:* 51. *Enrolled:* 42. *Average GMAT:* 560. *Average GPA:* 3.4

Academic Calendar Semesters.

After Graduation (Class of 2006–07) *Average starting salary:* 49,000 Canadian dollars.

DEGREES MBA • MBA/LL B • MBA/M Eng

MBA—MBA in Sport and Recreation Management Full-time and part-time. At least 60 total credits required. Maximum of 24 months to complete program. *Concentration:* sports/entertainment management.

MBA—Master of Business Administration Full-time and part-time. Applicants may apply to have GMAT requirements waived if they have 10 years of work experience or a GPA of 3.5 and above. At least 60 total credits required. Maximum of 24 months to complete program. *Concentration:* general MBA.

MBA/LL B—Master of Business Administration/Bachelor of Laws Full-time and part-time. Applicants must separately apply to and be accepted by both the MBA and LLB programs. At least 120 total credits required. Minimum of 48 months to complete program. *Concentration:* combined degrees.

MBA/M Eng—MBA in Engineering Management Full-time. 54 total credits required. *Concentration:* engineering.

RESOURCES AND SERVICES 800 on-campus PCs are available to graduate business students. Access to Internet/World Wide Web, online (class) registration, and online grade reports available. *Personal computer requirements:* Graduate business students are strongly recommended to purchase or lease a personal computer. *Special opportunities include:* An internship program is available. *Placement services include:* Alumni network, career counseling/planning, electronic job bank, career fairs, and career library.

EXPENSES *Tuition, province resident:* Full-time: 7380 Canadian dollars. Part-time: 3690 Canadian dollars per semester. *Tuition, Canadian resident:* Full-time: 7380 Canadian dollars. Part-time: 3690 Canadian dollars per semester. *Tuition (international):* Full-time: 11,260 Canadian dollars. Part-time: 5630 Canadian dollars per semester. *Required fees:* Full-time: 1758 Canadian dollars. *Graduate housing:* Room and board costs vary by campus location, number of occupants, type of accommodation, and type of board plan.

FINANCIAL AID (2007–08) 17 students received aid, including research assistantships, scholarships, and teaching assistantships. *Financial aid application deadline:* 8/31.

Financial Aid Contact Karen P. Hansen, MBA Secretary, PO Box 4400, Fredericton, NB E3B 5A3, Canada. *Phone:* 506-451-6817. *Fax:* 506-453-3561. *E-mail:* mbacontact@unb.ca.

INTERNATIONAL STUDENTS 20% of students enrolled are international students. *Services and facilities:* Counseling/support services, ESL/language courses, Housing location assistance, International student housing, International student organization, Language tutoring, Orientation. Financial aid is available to international students. *Required with application:* TOEFL with recommended score of 237 (computer) or 580 (paper); TWE with recommended score of 4.

International Student Contact Kay Nandlall, Director, International Student Advisor, International Student Advisor's Office, PO Box 4400, NB, Canada. *Phone:* 506-453-4860. *Fax:* 506-453-5005. *E-mail:* nandlall@unb.ca.

APPLICATION *Required:* GMAT, application form, baccalaureate/first degree, 3 letters of recommendation, personal statement, resume/ curriculum vitae, transcripts of college work. *Recommended:* 5 years of work experience. *Application fee:* 50 Canadian dollars. Applications for domestic and international students are processed on a rolling basis.

Application Contact Karen P. Hansen, MBA Secretary, PO Box 4400, Fredericton, NB E3B 5A3, Canada. *Phone:* 506-451-6817. *Fax:* 506-453-3561. *E-mail:* mbacontact@unb.ca.

University of New Brunswick Saint John

Faculty of Business

Saint John, New Brunswick, Canada

Phone: 506-648-5806 **Fax:** 506-648-5574 **E-mail:** mba@unbsj.ca

Business Program(s) Web Site: http://www.mba.unbsj.ca

DEGREE MBA

MBA—Master of Business Administration Full-time and part-time. At least 64 total credits required. 12 to 72 months to complete program. *Concentrations:* Asian business studies, Chinese business studies, electronic commerce (E-commerce), European business studies, general MBA, information technology, international and area business studies, international business, international management, international trade, Latin American business studies, management, new venture management, other, student designed, technology management, telecommunications management.

RESOURCES AND SERVICES 300 on-campus PCs are available to graduate business students. Access to Internet/World Wide Web, online (class) registration, and online grade reports available. *Personal computer requirements:* Graduate business students are strongly recommended to purchase or lease a personal computer. *Special opportunities include:* An international exchange program and an internship program are available. *Placement services include:* Alumni network, career placement, job search course, career counseling/planning, electronic job bank, resume referral, career fairs, job interviews arranged, resume preparation, and career library.

Application Contact Ms. Tammy Morin, MBA Admissions, PO Box 5050, 100 Tucker Park Road, NB, Canada. *Phone:* 506-648-5806. *Fax:* 506-648-5574. *E-mail:* mba@unbsj.ca.

See full description on page 724.

University of Ottawa

Telfer School of Management

Ottawa, Ontario, Canada

Phone: 613-562-5884 **Fax:** 613-562-5912 **E-mail:** charette@management.uottawa.ca

Business Program(s) Web Site: http://www.telfer.uOttawa.ca/

Graduate Business Unit Enrollment *Total:* 242 (61 full-time; 181 part-time; 85 women; 32 international). *Average Age:* 31.

Graduate Business Faculty *Total:* 70 (37 full-time; 33 part-time).

Admissions *Applied:* 239. *Admitted:* 158. *Enrolled:* 118. *Average GMAT:* 611. *Average GPA:* 3.1

Academic Calendar Trimesters.

Accreditation AACSB—The Association to Advance Collegiate Schools of Business.

After Graduation (Class of 2006–07) *Employed within 3 months of graduation:* 92%. *Average starting salary:* 72,222 Canadian dollars.

DEGREES   EMBA • MBA

EMBA—Executive Master of Business Administration Full-time. At least 54 total credits required. 24 months to complete program. *Concentrations:* general MBA, management.

MBA—Master of Business Administration Full-time and part-time. At least 54 total credits required. 12 to 36 months to complete program. *Concentrations:* general MBA, international management, management, technology management.

RESOURCES AND SERVICES 180 on-campus PCs are available to graduate business students. Access to Internet/World Wide Web, online (class) registration, and online grade reports available. *Personal computer requirements:* Graduate business students are strongly recommended to purchase or lease a personal computer. *Special opportunities include:* An international exchange program is available. *Placement services include:* Alumni network, career placement, job search course, career counseling/ planning, electronic job bank, resume referral, career fairs, job interviews arranged, resume preparation, and career library.

EXPENSES *Tuition, province resident:* Full-time: 16,200 Canadian dollars. Part-time: 292.46 Canadian dollars per credit. *Tuition (international):* Full-time: 29,472 Canadian dollars. Part-time: 468 Canadian dollars per credit. *Graduate housing:* Room and board costs vary by number of occupants, type of accommodation, and type of board plan.

FINANCIAL AID (2007–08) 25 students received aid, including loans, research assistantships, scholarships, and teaching assistantships. Aid is available to part-time students. *Financial aid application deadline:* 4/1.

Financial Aid Contact Ms. Manon Gauvreau, Administrator, School of Graduate and Postdoctoral Studies, Hagen Building, 115 Séraphin Marion, Ottawa, ON K1N 6N5, Canada. *Phone:* 613-562-5800 Ext. 1248. *Fax:* 613-562-5992. *E-mail:* manong@uottawa.ca.

INTERNATIONAL STUDENTS 13% of students enrolled are international students. *Services and facilities:* Counseling/support services, ESL/language courses, Housing location assistance, International student housing, International student organization, Language tutoring, Orientation. Financial aid is available to international students. *Required with application:* TOEFL with recommended score of 250 (computer), 600 (paper), or 100 (Internet); TWE with recommended score of 5; proof of adequate funds; proof of health/immunizations. *Recommended with application:* IELT with recommended score of 7.

International Student Contact Ms. Sylvie Seguin-Jak, Administrator, International Exchange Programs, Desmarais Building, 55 Laurier Avenue East, Ottawa, ON K1N 6N5, Canada. *Phone:* 613-562-5821. *Fax:* 613-562-5167. *E-mail:* seguin@management.uottawa.ca.

APPLICATION *Required:* GMAT, application form, baccalaureate/first degree, 2 letters of recommendation, personal statement, resume/ curriculum vitae, transcripts of college work, 2 years of work experience. *Recommended:* Interview. *Application fee:* 75 Canadian dollars. Applications for domestic and international students are processed on a rolling basis.

Application Contact Ms. Danielle Charette, Admission and Registration Officer, Desmarais Building, 55 Laurier Avenue East, Ottawa, ON K1N 6N5, Canada. *Phone:* 613-562-5884. *Fax:* 613-562-5912. *E-mail:* charette@management.uottawa.ca.

University of Phoenix–Vancouver Campus
College of Graduate Business and Management

Burnaby, British Columbia, Canada

Phone: 480-317-6200 **Fax:** 480-643-1479 **E-mail:** beth.barilla@phoenix.edu

Business Program(s) Web Site: http://www.phoenix.edu

DEGREES   M Mgt • MA • MBA

M Mgt—Human Resource Management Full-time. At least 39 total credits required. *Concentration:* human resources management.

MA—Master of Arts in Organizational Management Full-time. At least 40 total credits required. *Concentration:* organizational management.

MBA—Global Management Full-time. At least 45 total credits required. *Concentration:* international business.

MBA—Human Resource Management Full-time. At least 45 total credits required. *Concentration:* human resources management.

MBA—Master of Business Administration Full-time. At least 45 total credits required. *Concentration:* administration.

RESOURCES AND SERVICES Access to online grade reports available. *Personal computer requirements:* Graduate business students are strongly recommended to purchase or lease a personal computer. *Placement services include:* Alumni network.

Application Contact Beth Barilla, Associate Vice President of Student Admissions and Services, Mail Stop AA-K101, 4615 East Elwood Street, Phoenix, AZ 85040-1958. *Phone:* 480-317-6200. *Fax:* 480-643-1479. *E-mail:* beth.barilla@phoenix.edu.

University of Regina
Kenneth Levene Graduate School of Business

Regina, Saskatchewan, Canada

Phone: 306-585-4735 **Fax:** 306-585-5361 **E-mail:** levene.gradschool@uregina.ca

Business Program(s) Web Site: http://www.uregina.ca/admin/academic/ graduate_school/index.htm

DEGREES   EMBA • MBA • MHRM

EMBA—Master of Business Administration—Executive Route Part-time. Minimum of 5 years of full-time management experience or a minimum of 7 years of full-time management experience if lacking an undergraduate degree. 36 total credits required. 16 to 20 months to complete program. *Concentration:* management.

MBA—Master of Business Administration Full-time and part-time. GMAT score minimum 500 and a minimum of 2 years of professional experience required. 30 total credits required. 10 to 72 months to complete program. *Concentration:* management.

MHRM—Master of Human Resources Management Full-time and part-time. Distance learning option. 2 years of human resource management experience required. 30 total credits required. 10 to 72 months to complete program. *Concentration:* human resources management.

RESOURCES AND SERVICES 120 on-campus PCs are available to graduate business students. Access to Internet/World Wide Web, online (class) registration, and online grade reports available. *Personal computer requirements:* Graduate business students are strongly recommended to

University of Regina (continued)

purchase or lease a personal computer. *Placement services include:* Alumni network, career placement, job search course, career counseling/ planning, electronic job bank, career fairs, job interviews arranged, and resume preparation.

Application Contact Ms. Annette Marche, Graduate Academic Advisor, Faculty of Business Administration, 3737 Wascana Parkway, Regina, SK S4S 0A2, Canada. *Phone:* 306-585-4735. *Fax:* 306-585-5361. *E-mail:* levene.gradschool@uregina.ca.

University of Saskatchewan
Edwards School of Business

Saskatoon, Saskatchewan, Canada

Phone: 306-966-2557 **Fax:** 306-966-2515 **E-mail:** kretzer@edwards.usask.ca

Business Program(s) Web Site: http://www.edwardsmba.ca

Graduate Business Unit Enrollment *Total:* 19 (19 full-time; 7 women; 3 international). *Average Age:* 38.

Graduate Business Faculty 27 full-time.

Admissions *Applied:* 70. *Admitted:* 25. *Enrolled:* 25. *Average GMAT:* 510. *Average GPA:* 77

Academic Calendar Trimesters.

After Graduation (Class of 2006–07) *Employed within 3 months of graduation:* 92.31%. *Average starting salary:* 66,779 Canadian dollars.

DEGREES M Sc • MBA • MP Acc • MS

M Sc—Master of Science in Accounting—Thesis Program Full-time and part-time. Degree in accounting required. At least 18 total credits required. 8 to 60 months to complete program. *Concentration:* accounting.

MBA—Master of Business Administration Full-time and part-time. 42 total credits required. 12 to 60 months to complete program. *Concentrations:* agribusiness, health administration, international and area business studies, other, technology management.

MP Acc—Master of Professional Accountancy Part-time. Degree in accounting required. At least 34 total credits required. 12 months to complete program. *Concentration:* accounting.

MS—Master of Science in Finance Full-time. A degree in finance is preferred. At least 18 total credits required. 16 to 60 months to complete program. *Concentration:* finance.

RESOURCES AND SERVICES 100 on-campus PCs are available to graduate business students. Access to Internet/World Wide Web, online (class) registration, and online grade reports available. *Personal computer requirements:* Graduate business students are required to have a personal computer, the cost of which is included in tuition or other required fees. *Special opportunities include:* An internship program is available. *Placement services include:* Alumni network, career placement, job search course, career counseling/planning, electronic job bank, resume referral, career fairs, job interviews arranged, resume preparation, and career library.

EXPENSES *Tuition, province resident:* Full-time: 23,550 Canadian dollars. *Tuition (international):* Full-time: 31,750 Canadian dollars. *Required fees:* Full-time: 3475 Canadian dollars.

FINANCIAL AID (2007–08) 8 students received aid, including fellowships, scholarships, and teaching assistantships. Aid is available to part-time students.

Financial Aid Contact Chandra Kretzer, Administrative Assistant, MBA Program, 25 Campus Drive, Saskatoon, SK S7N 5A7, Canada. *Phone:* 306-966-2557. *Fax:* 306-966-2515. *E-mail:* kretzer@edwards.usask.ca.

INTERNATIONAL STUDENTS 16% of students enrolled are international students. *Services and facilities:* Counseling/support services, ESL/language courses, International student organization, Orientation.

Financial aid is available to international students. *Required with application:* TOEFL with recommended score of 250 (computer) or 600 (paper).

International Student Contact Mr. Kurt Tischler, Director of International Student Office, 1 Campus Drive, Room 60, Place Riel, Saskatoon, SK S7N 5A3, Canada. *Phone:* 306-966-4923. *Fax:* 306-966-5081. *E-mail:* tischler@admin.usask.ca.

APPLICATION *Required:* GMAT, application form, baccalaureate/first degree, essay, interview, 3 letters of recommendation, personal statement, resume/curriculum vitae, transcripts of college work, 3 years of work experience. *Application fee:* 75 Canadian dollars. Applications for domestic and international students are processed on a rolling basis.

Application Contact Ms. Chandra Kretzer, Administrative Assistant, Graduate Programs, 25 Campus Drive, Saskatoon, SK S7N 5A7, Canada. *Phone:* 306-966-2557. *Fax:* 306-966-2515. *E-mail:* kretzer@edwards.usask.ca.

University of Toronto
Joseph L. Rotman School of Management

Toronto, Ontario, Canada

Phone: 416-978-3499 **Fax:** 416-978-5812 **E-mail:** mba@rotman.utoronto.ca

Business Program(s) Web Site: http://www.rotman.utoronto.ca

Graduate Business Unit Enrollment *Total:* 719 (541 full-time; 178 part-time; 199 women; 270 international). *Average Age:* 27.

Graduate Business Faculty *Total:* 138 (102 full-time; 36 part-time).

Admissions *Applied:* 1,350. *Admitted:* 400. *Enrolled:* 360. *Average GMAT:* 660. *Average GPA:* 3.4

Academic Calendar Quarters.

Accreditation AACSB—The Association to Advance Collegiate Schools of Business.

After Graduation (Class of 2006–07) *Employed within 3 months of graduation:* 93%. *Average starting salary:* 83,067 Canadian dollars.

DEGREES JD/MBA • MBA • MF • MMPA

JD/MBA—Juris Doctor/Master of Business Administration Full-time. At least 60 total credits required. 44 months to complete program. *Concentrations:* economics, finance, management, marketing, operations management, organizational behavior/development, research and development administration.

MBA—Three-Year Master of Business Administration Part-time. Four years of work experience preferred. At least 60 total credits required. 36 months to complete program. *Concentrations:* economics, entrepreneurship, finance, management, marketing, operations management, organizational behavior/development, strategic management.

MBA—Two-Year (Full-Time) Master of Business Administration Full-time. Two years of full-time work experience required. At least 60 total credits required. 20 to 42 months to complete program. *Concentrations:* banking, economics, entrepreneurship, finance, financial engineering, general MBA, health administration, human resources management, international management, management, management consulting, marketing, operations management, organizational behavior/development, risk management, strategic management.

MF—Master of Finance Part-time. Two years of full-time work experience in finance or in a finance-related field required. At least 42 total credits required. 20 months to complete program. *Concentrations:* finance, financial management/planning.

MMPA—Master of Management and Professional Accounting Full-time. At least 70 total credits required. 16 to 27 months to complete program. *Concentrations:* accounting, management.

RESOURCES AND SERVICES Access to Internet/World Wide Web available. *Personal computer requirements:* Graduate business students are required to have a personal computer. *Special opportunities include:* An international exchange program is available. *Placement services include:* Alumni network, career placement, job search course, career counseling/planning, resume referral, career fairs, job interviews arranged, resume preparation, and career library.

EXPENSES *Tuition, province resident:* Full-time: 32,000 Canadian dollars. Part-time: 22,000 Canadian dollars per year. *Tuition (international):* Full-time: 87,000 Canadian dollars. Part-time: 30,000 Canadian dollars per year. *Required fees:* Full-time: 1000 Canadian dollars. Part-time: 1000 Canadian dollars per year. Tuition and/or fees vary by class time, number of courses or credits taken, academic program, and local reciprocity agreements.

FINANCIAL AID (2007–08) 85 students received aid, including fellowships, grants, loans, research assistantships, scholarships, and teaching assistantships. Aid is available to part-time students. *Financial aid application deadline:* 4/30.

Financial Aid Contact Ms. Cheryl Millington, Director, MBA Recruiting and Admissions, 105 Saint George Street, Toronto, ON M5S 3E6, Canada. *Phone:* 416-978-3499. *Fax:* 416-978-5812. *E-mail:* mba@rotman.utoronto.ca.

INTERNATIONAL STUDENTS 38% of students enrolled are international students. *Services and facilities:* Counseling/support services, ESL/language courses, Housing location assistance, International student housing, International student organization, Orientation, Visa Services, Health insurance program. Financial aid is available to international students. *Required with application:* TOEFL with recommended score of 250 (computer) or 600 (paper); TWE with recommended score of 5; proof of adequate funds.

International Student Contact Ms. Cheryl Millington, Director, MBA Recruiting and Admissions, 105 Saint George Street, Toronto, ON M5S 3E6, Canada. *Phone:* 416-978-3499. *Fax:* 416-978-5812. *E-mail:* mba@rotman.utoronto.ca.

APPLICATION *Required:* GMAT, application form, baccalaureate/first degree, essay, 2 letters of recommendation, personal statement, resume/curriculum vitae, transcripts of college work, 2 years of work experience. *Recommended:* Interview. *Application fee:* 150 Canadian dollars. Applications for domestic and international students are processed on a rolling basis.

Application Contact Ms. Cheryl Millington, Director, MBA Recruiting and Admissions, 105 Saint George Street, Toronto, ON M5S 3E6, Canada. *Phone:* 416-978-3499. *Fax:* 416-978-5812. *E-mail:* mba@rotman.utoronto.ca.

University of Victoria
Faculty of Business

Victoria, British Columbia, Canada

Phone: 250-721-6075 **Fax:** 250-721-7066 **E-mail:** hranson@uvic.ca

Business Program(s) Web Site: http://www.business.uvic.ca/mba/

Graduate Business Unit Enrollment *Total:* 109 (85 full-time; 24 part-time; 46 women; 39 international). *Average Age:* 29.

Graduate Business Faculty *Total:* 20 (17 full-time; 3 part-time).

Admissions *Applied:* 210. *Admitted:* 115. *Enrolled:* 54. *Average GMAT:* 559. *Average GPA:* 3.3

Academic Calendar Semesters.

After Graduation (Class of 2006–07) *Employed within 3 months of graduation:* 90%. *Average starting salary:* 74,000 Canadian dollars.

DEGREES MBA • MBA/LL B • MBA/M Eng • MBA/MCS

MBA—Master of Business Administration Full-time and part-time. At least 21 total credits required. 17 to 60 months to complete program. *Concentrations:* entrepreneurship, general MBA, international business, other.

MBA/LL B—Master of Business Administration/Bachelor of Laws Full-time. Acceptance to both the Faculty of Law and the Faculty of Graduate Studies required. At least 131 total credits required. Minimum of 44 months to complete program. *Concentration:* general MBA.

MBA/M Eng—MBA/MEng Full-time. Applicants must be admitted to Business and Engineering and have an undergraduate degree in Engineering. 40 total credits required. 24 to 60 months to complete program. *Concentrations:* engineering, general MBA.

MBA/MCS—MBA/MSc Full-time. Applicants must be admitted to Business and Science and have an undergraduate degree in science. 31 to 32 total credits required. 24 to 60 months to complete program. *Concentration:* combined degrees.

RESOURCES AND SERVICES 450 on-campus PCs are available to graduate business students. Access to Internet/World Wide Web, online (class) registration, and online grade reports available. *Personal computer requirements:* Graduate business students are strongly recommended to purchase or lease a personal computer. *Special opportunities include:* An international exchange program and an internship program are available. *Placement services include:* Alumni network, career placement, job search course, career counseling/planning, electronic job bank, resume referral, career fairs, job interviews arranged, resume preparation, and career library.

EXPENSES *Tuition, province resident:* Full-time: 10,260.40 Canadian dollars. *Tuition, Canadian resident:* Full-time: 10,260 Canadian dollars. *Tuition (international):* Full-time: 11,146.80 Canadian dollars. *Required fees:* Full-time: 2381.27 Canadian dollars. *Graduate housing:* Room and board costs vary by number of occupants, type of accommodation, and type of board plan. *Typical cost:* 13,600 Canadian dollars (including board).

FINANCIAL AID (2007–08) 100 students received aid, including fellowships, loans, research assistantships, scholarships, teaching assistantships, and work study. Aid is available to part-time students.

Financial Aid Contact Ms. Heather Ranson, Marketing Manager, MBA Program, MBA Program, PO Box 1700, STN CSC, Victoria, BC V8W 2Y2, Canada. *Phone:* 250-721-6075. *Fax:* 250-721-7066. *E-mail:* hranson@uvic.ca.

INTERNATIONAL STUDENTS 36% of students enrolled are international students. *Services and facilities:* Counseling/support services, ESL/language courses, Housing location assistance, International student organization, Language tutoring, Orientation. Financial aid is available to international students. *Required with application:* IELT with recommended score of 7; TOEFL with recommended score of 233 (computer) or 575 (paper). *Recommended with application:* TWE with recommended score of 3.5.

International Student Contact Ms. Cindy Bruckel, MBA Program Receptionist, MBA Program, PO Box 1700, STN CSC, Victoria, BC V8W 2Y2, Canada. *Phone:* 250-472-4278. *Fax:* 250-721-7066. *E-mail:* mbarecep@uvic.ca.

APPLICATION *Required:* GMAT, application form, baccalaureate/first degree, essay, 2 letters of recommendation, personal statement, resume/curriculum vitae, transcripts of college work. *Recommended:* Interview, 2 years of work experience. *Application fee:* 100 Canadian dollars, 125 Canadian dollars (international). Applications for domestic and international students are processed on a rolling basis.

Application Contact Ms. Heather Ranson, Marketing Manager, MBA Program, MBA Program, PO Box 1700, STN CSC, Victoria, BC V8W 2Y2, Canada. *Phone:* 250-721-6075. *Fax:* 250-721-7066. *E-mail:* hranson@uvic.ca.

University of Waterloo
Graduate Studies

Waterloo, Ontario, Canada

Phone: 519-888-4567 Ext. 6030 **Fax:** 519-746-3051 **E-mail:** sinclair@uwaterloo.ca

University of Waterloo (continued)

Business Program(s) Web Site: http://www.grad.uwaterloo.ca

DEGREES   M Sc • M Tax • MA • MAES • MBET

M Sc—Master of Science in Management Sciences Full-time and part-time. GRE or GMAT required. Minimum of 12 months to complete program. *Concentrations:* information management, information systems, management information systems, management science, management systems analysis, technology management.

M Sc—Master of Science in Management Sciences Part-time. Distance learning option. 12 to 60 months to complete program. *Concentrations:* information systems, management information systems, management science, management systems analysis, organizational behavior/development, organizational management, technology management.

M Tax—Master of Taxation Full-time and part-time. Interview and GMAT may be required. 20 to 24 months to complete program. *Concentrations:* accounting, law, taxation.

MA—Master of Arts in Economics Full-time and part-time. Undergraduate statistics and calculus required; co-op program available. 12 to 16 months to complete program. *Concentrations:* economics, financial economics.

MA—Master of Arts in Planning Full-time and part-time. Must complete additional planning application. 12 to 20 months to complete program. *Concentrations:* city/urban administration, developmental economics, environmental economics/management, international development management.

MAES—Master of Applied Environmental Studies in Local Economic Development Full-time and part-time. 24 to 36 months to complete program. *Concentration:* environmental economics/management.

MBET—Master of Business, Entrepreneurship and Technology Full-time. At least 1 year of prior work experience required. Minimum of 12 months to complete program. *Concentrations:* business information science, electronic commerce (E-commerce), entrepreneurship, technology management.

RESOURCES AND SERVICES Access to Internet/World Wide Web, online (class) registration, and online grade reports available. *Personal computer requirements:* Graduate business students are not required to have a personal computer. *Special opportunities include:* An international exchange program and an internship program are available. *Placement services include:* Alumni network, job search course, career counseling/planning, electronic job bank, career fairs, resume preparation, and career library.

Application Contact Ms. Tracey Sinclair, Graduate Studies Recruitment Manager, Graduate Studies Office, Room 2072, Needles Hall, 200 University Avenue, West, Waterloo, ON N2L 3G1, Canada. *Phone:* 519-888-4567 Ext. 6030. *Fax:* 519-746-3051. *E-mail:* sinclair@uwaterloo.ca.

The University of Western Ontario
Richard Ivey School of Business

London, Ontario, Canada

Phone: 519-661-3419 **Fax:** 519-661-3431 **E-mail:** nhealey@ivey.uwo.ca

Business Program(s) Web Site: http://www.ivey.uwo.ca/mba

DEGREES   MBA • MBA/LL B

MBA—Full-Time MBA Full-time. At least 12 total credits required. 12 months to complete program. *Concentrations:* accounting, Asian business studies, banking, business information science, economics, entrepreneurship, European business studies, finance, human resources management, international and area business studies, management science, marketing, operations management, organizational behavior/development, production management, strategic management, taxation.

MBA/LL B—Master of Business Administration/Bachelor of Laws Full-time. Must apply to both Law and Business schools. 36 months to complete program. *Concentration:* law.

RESOURCES AND SERVICES 15 on-campus PCs are available to graduate business students. Access to Internet/World Wide Web, online (class) registration, and online grade reports available. *Personal computer requirements:* Graduate business students are required to have a personal computer. *Special opportunities include:* An international exchange program is available. *Placement services include:* Alumni network, career placement, job search course, career counseling/planning, electronic job bank, resume referral, career fairs, job interviews arranged, resume preparation, and career library.

Application Contact Ms. Niki Healey, Manager, MBA Recruitment, 1151 Richmond Street North, London, ON N6A 3K7, Canada. *Phone:* 519-661-3419. *Fax:* 519-661-3431. *E-mail:* nhealey@ivey.uwo.ca.

University of Windsor
Odette School of Business

Windsor, Ontario, Canada

Phone: 519-253-3000 Ext. 3097 **Fax:** 519-973-7073 **E-mail:** mba@uwindsor.ca

Business Program(s) Web Site: http://www.mba.uwindsor.ca

DEGREES   MBA • MBA/LL B

MBA—Master of Business Administration Co-op Full-time. 30 to 63 total credits required. 12 to 23 months to complete program. *Concentrations:* business policy/strategy, entrepreneurship, finance, human resources management, industrial administration/management, industrial/labor relations, international and area business studies, international business, management science, marketing, production management.

MBA/LL B—Master of Business Administration/Bachelor of Laws Full-time. Must apply separately to Faculty of Graduate Studies and Faculty of Law. 111 to 144 total credits required. 36 to 48 months to complete program. *Concentrations:* business policy/strategy, entrepreneurship, finance, human resources management, industrial administration/management, industrial/labor relations, international and area business studies, international business, management science, marketing, production management.

RESOURCES AND SERVICES 245 on-campus PCs are available to graduate business students. Access to Internet/World Wide Web, online (class) registration, and online grade reports available. *Personal computer requirements:* Graduate business students are not required to have a personal computer. *Special opportunities include:* An international exchange program and an internship program are available. *Placement services include:* Alumni network, career placement, job search course, career counseling/planning, electronic job bank, resume referral, job interviews arranged, resume preparation, and career library.

Application Contact Sue Skrobiak, Graduate Secretary, 401 Sunset Avenue, Windsor, ON N9B 3P4, Canada. *Phone:* 519-253-3000 Ext. 3097. *Fax:* 519-973-7073. *E-mail:* mba@uwindsor.ca.

Vancouver Island University
Program in Business Administration

Nanaimo, British Columbia, Canada

Phone: 250-740-6384 **E-mail:** kellyj@mala.bc.ca

Business Program(s) Web Site: http://www.mala.ca/mba/index.asp

---

DEGREES   MBA

MBA—International Masters in Business Administration Full-time. Undergraduate degree must be in a business discipline. 180 total credits required. 12 months to complete program. *Concentration:* international business.

MBA—Master of Business Administration Full-time. Undergraduate degree in a discipline other than business and students must pass the summer pre-MBA program. 180 total credits required. 12 months to complete program. *Concentrations:* general MBA, human resources management, marketing.

RESOURCES AND SERVICES 90 on-campus PCs are available to graduate business students. Access to Internet/World Wide Web and online grade reports available. *Personal computer requirements:* Graduate business students are required to have a personal computer. *Special opportunities include:* An international exchange program is available. *Placement services include:* Alumni network, job search course, career counseling/planning, career fairs, resume preparation, and career library.

Application Contact Ms. Jane Kelly, Admissions Manager, Faculty of International Education, 900 Fifth Street, Nanaimo, BC V9R 5S5, Canada. *Phone:* 250-740-6384. *E-mail:* kellyj@mala.bc.ca.

Wilfrid Laurier University
School of Business and Economics

Waterloo, Ontario, Canada

Phone: 519-884-0710 Ext. 6220 **Fax:** 519-884-6016 **E-mail:** mferraro@wlu.ca

Business Program(s) Web Site: http://www.wlu.ca/mba

Graduate Business Unit Enrollment *Total:* 524 (105 full-time; 419 part-time; 158 women; 24 international).

Graduate Business Faculty *Total:* 165 (100 full-time; 65 part-time).

Admissions *Applied:* 477. *Admitted:* 443. *Enrolled:* 358. *Average GMAT:* 620. *Average GPA:* 9.5/12 scale

Academic Calendar Semesters.

Accreditation AACSB—The Association to Advance Collegiate Schools of Business.

After Graduation (Class of 2006–07) *Employed within 3 months of graduation:* 97%. *Average starting salary:* 65,000 Canadian dollars.

DEGREES MA • MBA

MA—Master of Arts in Business Economics Full-time. 4 year Honours Economics Undergraduate Degree or equivalent, with a B average in last year or last five full credits. Individual Economics course grades must be a B or better. 12 to 18 months to complete program. *Concentration:* economics.

MBA—MBA Full-Time with Co-op Full-time. Four year undergraduate degree, with final GPA of B+ or better, and GMAT score of 600 or better required. At least 20 total credits required. 20 months to complete program. *Concentrations:* accounting, business policy/strategy, entrepreneurship, finance, financial management/planning, general MBA, management, marketing, operations management, organizational management, strategic management, supply chain management.

MBA—MBA with CFA® Option, Part-Time, Weekend Program (Toronto Campus) Part-time. Four year or equivalent undergraduate degree, with GPA of B or better, GMAT score of 550 or better, and two years full-time work experience required. At least 20 total credits required. 39 to 60 months to complete program. *Concentration:* finance.

MBA—MBA with CMA Option, Part-Time, Weekend Program (Toronto Campus) Part-time. Four year or equivalent undergraduate degree, with a final GPA of B or better, and a GMAT score of 550 or better, two years of full-time work experience required. At least 20 total credits required. 39 to 60 months to complete program. *Concentration:* accounting.

MBA—MBA, Full-Time, Weekday Program (Waterloo Campus) Full-time. Four year or equivalent undergraduate degree, with a final GPA of B or better, and a GMAT score of 550 or better, two years of full-time work experience required. At least 20 total credits required. 12 to 60 months to complete program. *Concentrations:* accounting, business policy/strategy, entrepreneurship, finance, general MBA, management, marketing, operations management, organizational management, strategic management, supply chain management.

MBA—MBA, Part-Time, Evening Program (Waterloo Campus) Part-time. Four year or equivalent undergraduate degree, with a final GPA of B or better, and a GMAT score of 550 or better, two years of full-time work experience required. At least 20 total credits required. 22 to 60 months to complete program. *Concentrations:* accounting, business policy/strategy, entrepreneurship, finance, general MBA, management, marketing, operations management, organizational management, strategic management, supply chain management.

MBA—MBA, Part-Time, Weekend Program (Toronto Campus) Part-time. Four year or equivalent undergraduate degree, with a final GPA of B or better, and a GMAT score of 550 or better, two years of full-time work experience required. At least 20 total credits required. 22 to 60 months to complete program. *Concentrations:* business policy/strategy, entrepreneurship, finance, general MBA, management, marketing, operations management, organizational management, strategic management, supply chain management.

RESOURCES AND SERVICES 170 on-campus PCs are available to graduate business students. Access to Internet/World Wide Web, online (class) registration, and online grade reports available. *Personal computer requirements:* Graduate business students are strongly recommended to purchase or lease a personal computer. *Special opportunities include:* An international exchange program and an internship program are available. *Placement services include:* Alumni network, career placement, job search course, career counseling/planning, electronic job bank, resume referral, career fairs, job interviews arranged, resume preparation, and career library.

EXPENSES *Tuition, province resident:* Full-time: 20,000 Canadian dollars. Part-time: 1000 Canadian dollars per course. *Tuition, Canadian resident:* Full-time: 20,000 Canadian dollars. Part-time: 1000 Canadian dollars per course. *Tuition (international):* Full-time: 26,250 Canadian dollars. *Required fees:* Full-time: 1962 Canadian dollars.

FINANCIAL AID (2007–08) 31 students received aid, including fellowships, loans, research assistantships, scholarships, and teaching assistantships. Aid is available to part-time students. *Financial aid application deadline:* 11/1.

Financial Aid Contact Pauline Wong, Director of Student Awards, 75 University Avenue West, Waterloo, ON N2L 3C5, Canada. *Phone:* 519-884-0710 Ext. 6094. *Fax:* 519-884-7615. *E-mail:* pgwong@wlu.ca.

INTERNATIONAL STUDENTS 5% of students enrolled are international students. *Services and facilities:* Counseling/support services, Housing location assistance, International student organization, Orientation, Visa Services. Financial aid is available to international students. *Required with application:* TOEFL with recommended score of 230 (computer), 573 (paper), or 89 (Internet). *Recommended with application:* IELT with recommended score of 7.

International Student Contact Janet Doner, Manager, Laurier International Program and Services, 75 University Avenue West, Waterloo, ON N2L 3C5, Canada. *Phone:* 519-884-0710 Ext. 6842. *Fax:* 519-886-4507. *E-mail:* jdoner@wlu.ca.

APPLICATION *Required:* GMAT, application form, baccalaureate/first degree, essay, 3 letters of recommendation, personal statement, resume/ curriculum vitae, transcripts of college work, 2 years of work experience. *Application fee:* 100 Canadian dollars. Applications for domestic and international students are processed on a rolling basis.

Application Contact Maureen Ferraro, MBA Marketing Coordinator, 75 University Avenue West, Waterloo, ON N2L 3C5, Canada. *Phone:* 519-884-0710 Ext. 6220. *Fax:* 519-884-6016. *E-mail:* mferraro@wlu.ca.

See full description on page 766.

York University
Schulich School of Business

Toronto, Ontario, Canada

Phone: 416-736-5060 **Fax:** 416-650-8174 **E-mail:** cpattend@schulich.yorku.ca

Business Program(s) Web Site: http://www.schulich.yorku.ca

DEGREES IMBA • MBA • MBA/LL B • MBA/MA • MPA

IMBA—International Master of Business Administration Full-time. International experience and advanced foreign language skills required. At least 71 total credits required. 20 months to complete program. *Concentrations:* accounting, arts administration/management, Asian business studies, Chinese business studies, economics, entrepreneurship, environmental economics/management, European business studies, finance, financial engineering, financial management/planning, health administration, industrial/labor relations, information management, international and area business studies, international business, Japanese business studies, Latin American business studies, management information systems, management science, marketing, nonprofit management, operations management, organizational behavior/development, public management, real estate, strategic management.

MBA—Master of Business Administration Full-time and part-time. At least 60 total credits required. 8 to 72 months to complete program. *Concentrations:* accounting, arts administration/management, economics, entrepreneurship, environmental economics/management, finance, financial engineering, financial management/planning, health administration, industrial/labor relations, information management, international business, management information systems, management science, marketing, nonprofit management, operations management, organizational behavior/development, public management, quantitative analysis, real estate, strategic management.

MBA/LL B—MBA/LLB—Master of Business Administration/ Bachelor of Laws Full-time. At least 122 total credits required. 48 months to complete program. *Concentrations:* accounting, arts administration/ management, economics, entrepreneurship, environmental economics/ management, finance, financial management/planning, health administration, industrial/labor relations, international business, management information systems, management science, marketing, nonprofit management, operations management, organizational behavior/development, public management, quantitative analysis, real estate, strategic management.

MBA/MA—Master of Business Administration/Master of Arts in Fine Arts Full-time. 4 year undergraduate degree in Fine Arts and relevant work experience in arts/cultural industries required. At least 75 total credits required. 36 months to complete program. *Concentrations:* accounting, arts administration/management, economics, entrepreneurship, environmental economics/management, finance, financial engineering, financial management/planning, health administration, industrial/labor relations, information management, international business, management information systems, management science, marketing, nonprofit management, operations management, organizational behavior/development, public management, real estate, strategic management.

MPA—Master of Public Administration Full-time and part-time. At least 60 total credits required. 8 to 72 months to complete program. *Concentrations:* accounting, economics, entrepreneurship, environmental economics/management, finance, financial management/planning, health administration, industrial/labor relations, information management, organizational behavior/development, public management, public policy and administration.

RESOURCES AND SERVICES 130 on-campus PCs are available to graduate business students. Access to Internet/World Wide Web, online (class) registration, and online grade reports available. *Personal computer requirements:* Graduate business students are required to have a personal computer. *Special opportunities include:* An international exchange program and an internship program are available. *Placement services include:* Alumni network, career placement, job search course, career counseling/planning, electronic job bank, resume referral, career fairs, job interviews arranged, resume preparation, and career library.

Application Contact Carol Pattenden, Assistant Director, Admissions, 4700 Keele Street, Toronto, ON M3J 1P3, Canada. *Phone:* 416-736-5060. *Fax:* 416-650-8174. *E-mail:* cpattend@schulich.yorku.ca.

See full description on page 772.

International

AUSTRALIA

Bond University

School of Business

Gold Coast, Australia

Phone: 617-55952266 **Fax:** 617-55952209 **E-mail:** tmerrots@bond.edu.au

Business Program(s) Web Site: http://www.bond.edu.au/bus/index.htm

---

DEGREES EMBA • M Acc • MB • MBA

EMBA—Executive Master of Business Administration Part-time. The entry requirements for this program require a minimum 8 years work experience with 3 years in a management role. The GMAT is desirable (mandatory for students without a first degree). At least 12 total credits required. Minimum of 13 months to complete program. *Concentrations:* accounting, entrepreneurship, finance, management, marketing.

M Acc—Master of Accounting Full-time and part-time. Must have completed an undergraduate or postgraduate degree in any discipline other than accounting or hold a non-degree professional accounting qualification with at least 5 years of work experience. At least 12 total credits required. Minimum of 12 months to complete program. *Concentration:* accounting.

MB—Master of Business (Finance) Full-time and part-time. Must have completed a quality undergraduate degree from a recognised institution in any discipline or have considerable work experience. At least 12 total credits required. Minimum of 12 months to complete program.

MB—Master of Business (International Business) Full-time and part-time. A quality undergraduate degree from a recognised institution in any discipline or considerable work experience. At least 12 total credits required. Minimum of 12 months to complete program.

MB—Master of Business (Marketing) Full-time and part-time. An undergraduate degree from a recognised institution in any discipline or considerable work experience. At least 12 total credits required. Minimum of 12 months to complete program.

MBA—Master of Business Administration Full-time. 3 years of work experience, an undergraduate degree from a recognized university or exceptional professional achievement where no previous tertiary study has been undertaken. GMAT is required. At least 12 total credits required. Minimum of 12 months to complete program. *Concentrations:* accounting, business law, electronic commerce (E-commerce), entrepreneurship, finance, international business, management, marketing.

RESOURCES AND SERVICES Access to Internet/World Wide Web and online (class) registration available. *Personal computer requirements:* Graduate business students are strongly recommended to purchase or lease a personal computer. *Special opportunities include:* An international exchange program and an internship program are available. *Placement services include:* Alumni network, career placement, career counseling/planning, electronic job bank, resume referral, career fairs, job interviews arranged, resume preparation, and career library.

Application Contact Mrs. Tanya Merrotsy, Postgraduate Program Adviser, Bond University, Faculty of Business, Technology and Sustainable Development, Queensland, Australia. *Phone:* 617-55952266. *Fax:* 617-55952209. *E-mail:* tmerrots@bond.edu.au.

Central Queensland University

Faculty of Business and Informatics

Rockhampton, Australia

Phone: 61-7-49309358 **Fax:** 61-7-49309925 **E-mail:** s.christensen@cqu.edu.au

Business Program(s) Web Site: http://www.fbi.cqu.edu.au/

Graduate Business Unit Enrollment *Total:* 2,647 (2,482 full-time; 165 part-time; 860 women; 2424 international). *Average Age:* 26-34.

Graduate Business Faculty *Total:* 190 (50 full-time; 140 part-time).

Admissions *Applied:* 761. *Admitted:* 663. *Enrolled:* 534.

Academic Calendar Trimesters.

After Graduation (Class of 2006–07) *Employed within 3 months of graduation:* 85%. *Average starting salary:* 75,294 Australian dollars.

DEGREE MBA

MBA—Master of Business Administration Full-time and part-time. Distance learning option. Prior undergraduate degree and two years management experience required. 96 total credits required. *Concentrations:* accounting, financial management/planning, human resources management, management, marketing.

RESOURCES AND SERVICES 250 on-campus PCs are available to graduate business students. Access to Internet/World Wide Web, online (class) registration, and online grade reports available. *Personal computer requirements:* Graduate business students are strongly recommended to purchase or lease a personal computer. *Special opportunities include:* An international exchange program is available. *Placement services include:* Alumni network, career counseling/planning, electronic job bank, career fairs, resume preparation, and career library.

EXPENSES *Tuition:* Full-time: 8100 Australian dollars. *Tuition (international):* Full-time: 14,220 Australian dollars. Tuition and/or fees vary by number of courses or credits taken and campus location. *Typical graduate housing cost:* 13,910 Australian dollars (including board).

FINANCIAL AID (2007–08) 11 students received aid, including scholarships.

Financial Aid Contact Postgraduate Program Advisor, Building 34/G.19, Bruce Highway, Rockhampton QLD, 4702, Australia. *Phone:* 61-7-49309358. *Fax:* 61-7-49309925. *E-mail:* papg-bus-fbi@cqu.edu.au.

INTERNATIONAL STUDENTS 92% of students enrolled are international students. *Services and facilities:* Counseling/support services, ESL/language courses, Housing location assistance, International student housing, International student organization, Language tutoring, Orientation. Financial aid is available to international students. *Required with application:* IELT with recommended score of 6; proof of adequate funds; proof of health/immunizations.

International Student Contact International Student Support Coordinator, Bruce Highway, Rockhampton QLD, 4702, Australia. *Phone:* 61-7-49306370. *Fax:* 61-7-49309366. *E-mail:* international-support@cqu.edu.au.

APPLICATION *Required:* Application form, baccalaureate/first degree, personal statement, transcripts of college work, 2 years of work experience. *Recommended:* Resume/curriculum vitae. Applications for domestic and international students are processed on a rolling basis.

Application Contact Sue Christensen, Student Liaison Officer, Bruce Highway, Rockhampton, 4702, Australia. *Phone:* 61-7-49309358. *Fax:* 61-7-49309925. *E-mail:* s.christensen@cqu.edu.au.

Deakin University

Deakin Business School

Geelong, Australia

Phone: 61-3-52272216 **Fax:** 61-3-52272655 **E-mail:** dbs-enquiries@deakin.edu.au

Business Program(s) Web Site: http://www.deakin.edu.au/dbs

Graduate Business Unit Enrollment *Total:* 1,252 (195 full-time; 1,057 part-time; 372 women; 272 international).

Graduate Business Faculty *Total:* 87 (75 full-time; 12 part-time).

Admissions *Applied:* 1,345. *Admitted:* 983.

Academic Calendar Semesters.

DEGREES IMBA • M Comm • MB • MBA • MCL • MIB • MIS

IMBA—Master of Business Administration (International) Full-time and part-time. Distance learning option. Minimum 65% GPA and 3-year bachelor's degree required. 12 total credits required. 12 to 84 months to complete program. *Concentrations:* accounting, administration, arts administration/management, business education, economics, electronic commerce (E-commerce), finance, financial management/planning, human resources management, information systems, insurance, international and area business studies, international business, law, leadership, management, marketing, public policy and administration, strategic management, supply chain management.

M Comm—Master of Commerce Full-time and part-time. Distance learning option. 12 total credits required. 18 to 84 months to complete program. *Concentrations:* accounting, arts administration/management, business law, commerce, economics, electronic commerce (E-commerce), finance, financial management/planning, information systems, insurance, international and area business studies, international business, international management, international trade, management, management information systems, marketing.

MB—Master of Business (Sports Management) Full-time and part-time. 12 total credits required. 24 to 84 months to complete program. *Concentration:* sports/entertainment management.

MBA—Master of Business Administration Full-time and part-time. Distance learning option. Minimum 2 years relevant work experience required. 12 total credits required. 12 to 84 months to complete program. *Concentrations:* accounting, arts administration/management, business education, economics, electronic commerce (E-commerce), finance, financial management/planning, general MBA, human resources management, information systems, insurance, international and area business studies, international business, international trade, law, leadership, management, marketing, public management, public policy and administration, strategic management, supply chain management.

MCL—Master of Commercial Law Full-time and part-time. Distance learning option. Applicants must hold a bachelor's degree and a total of four years of tertiary study. 8 total credits required. 12 to 60 months to complete program. *Concentration:* law.

MCL—Master of Laws (LL M) Full-time and part-time. Distance learning option. Applicants must hold a bachelor law degree and a total of 4 years of tertiary study. 8 total credits required. 12 to 60 months to complete program. *Concentration:* law.

MIB—Master of International Business Full-time and part-time. 12 total credits required. 18 to 84 months to complete program. *Concentrations:* international and area business studies, international business, international management, international trade.

MIS—Master of Information Systems Full-time and part-time. Distance learning option. 12 total credits required. 18 to 84 months to complete program. *Concentration:* information systems.

RESOURCES AND SERVICES 211 on-campus PCs are available to graduate business students. Access to Internet/World Wide Web, online (class) registration, and online grade reports available. *Personal computer requirements:* Graduate business students are strongly recommended to purchase or lease a personal computer. *Special opportunities include:* An

international exchange program and an internship program are available. *Placement services include:* Alumni network, career placement, career counseling/planning, electronic job bank, resume preparation, and career library.

INTERNATIONAL STUDENTS 22% of students enrolled are international students. *Services and facilities:* Counseling/support services, ESL/language courses, Housing location assistance, International student housing, International student organization, Language tutoring, Orientation, Visa Services. Financial aid is not available to international students. *Required with application:* IELT with recommended score of 6.5; proof of adequate funds; proof of health/immunizations.

International Student Contact Deakin International, 221 Burwood Highway, Burwood, Victoria, 3125, Australia. *Phone:* 61-3-92445095. *Fax:* 61-3-92445094. *E-mail:* dconnect@deakin.edu.au.

APPLICATION *Required:* Application form, baccalaureate/first degree, resume/curriculum vitae, transcripts of college work, 2 years of work experience. *Recommended:* 2 letters of recommendation, personal statement. Applications for domestic and international students are processed on a rolling basis.

Application Contact Admissions Office, Pigdons Road, Waurn Ponds, Victoria, 3217, Australia. *Phone:* 61-3-52272216. *Fax:* 61-3-52272655. *E-mail:* dbs-enquiries@deakin.edu.au.

Edith Cowan University

Faculty of Business and Public Management

Churchlands, Australia

Phone: 61-8-92738673 **Fax:** 61-8-92738810 **E-mail:** postgraduatebusiness@ecu.edu.au

Business Program(s) Web Site: http://www.business.ecu.edu.au/

DEGREES M Mktg • MB • MBA • MBA equivalent • MHRM • MIB • MM • MPA • MSS

M Mktg—Master of Professional Marketing Full-time and part-time. Undergraduate degree other than a marketing major required. 18 to 48 months to complete program. *Concentrations:* international marketing, marketing, marketing research, public relations.

MB—Master of Business Full-time and part-time. 24 to 48 months to complete program. *Concentrations:* accounting, economics, finance, human resources management, information management, management, marketing.

MBA—Master of Business Administration Full-time and part-time. Distance learning option. At least 5 years professional work experience required. 18 to 48 months to complete program. *Concentrations:* accounting, finance, health care, human resources management, information management, international business, legal administration, management, marketing, marketing research, organizational behavior/development, sports/entertainment management, travel industry/tourism management.

MBA equivalent—Master of e-Business Full-time and part-time. Distance learning option. 18 to 48 months to complete program. *Concentrations:* electronic commerce (E-commerce), information systems.

MHRM—Master of Human Resources Management Full-time and part-time. 18 to 48 months to complete program. *Concentration:* human resources management.

MIB—Master of International Business Full-time and part-time. 18 to 48 months to complete program. *Concentrations:* Asian business studies, international business.

MM—Master of Sport Management Full-time and part-time. Distance learning option. 18 to 48 months to complete program. *Concentrations:* management, sports/entertainment management.

MPA—Master of Professional Accounting Full-time and part-time. 18 to 48 months to complete program. *Concentrations:* accounting, taxation.

MSS—Master of Social Science (Leisure Science) Full-time and part-time. Distance learning option. 18 to 48 months to complete program. *Concentration:* social work.

RESOURCES AND SERVICES 52 on-campus PCs are available to graduate business students. Access to Internet/World Wide Web, online (class) registration, and online grade reports available. *Personal computer requirements:* Graduate business students are not required to have a personal computer. *Special opportunities include:* An international exchange program is available. *Placement services include:* Alumni network, career counseling/planning, resume referral, career fairs, and resume preparation.

Application Contact Higher Degrees Coordinator, Research and Higher Degrees Office, Pearson Street, Western Australia, Australia. *Phone:* 61-8-92738673. *Fax:* 61-8-92738810. *E-mail:* postgraduatebusiness@ecu.edu.au.

Flinders University
Flinders Business School
Adelaide, Australia

Phone: 61-8-82013074 **Fax:** 61-8-82012644 **E-mail:** amanda.banytis@flinders.edu.au

Business Program(s) Web Site: http://business.flinders.edu.au

Graduate Business Unit Enrollment *Total:* 50 (40 full-time; 10 part-time; 12 women; 37 international).

Graduate Business Faculty 5 full-time.

Admissions *Applied:* 62. *Admitted:* 50. *Enrolled:* 26.

Academic Calendar Semesters.

DEGREES   MBA

MBA Full-time and part-time. Bachelor's degree plus 2 years work experience required. 72 total credits required. 4 to 6 months to complete program. *Concentration:* management.

MBA—MBA (Biotechnology) Full-time and part-time. Bachelor's degree in life sciences-related field plus 2 years work experience required. 72 total credits required. 4 to 6 months to complete program. *Concentration:* technology management.

MBA—MBA (Education) Full-time and part-time. Bachelor's degree in education-related field plus 2 years work experience required. 4 to 6 total credits required. 72 months to complete program. *Concentration:* training and development.

MBA—MBA (Finance) Full-time and part-time. Bachelor's degree plus 2 years work experience required. 72 total credits required. 4 to 6 months to complete program. *Concentration:* finance.

MBA—MBA (Health Management) Full-time and part-time. Bachelor's degree plus 4 years work experience required. 72 total credits required. 4 to 6 months to complete program. *Concentration:* health administration.

MBA—MBA (International Business) Full-time and part-time. Bachelor's degree plus 2 years work experience required. 72 total credits required. 4 to 6 months to complete program. *Concentration:* international business.

MBA—MBA (Tourism) Full-time and part-time. Bachelor's degree plus 2 years work experience required. 72 total credits required. 4 to 6 months to complete program. *Concentration:* travel industry/tourism management.

RESOURCES AND SERVICES 26 on-campus PCs are available to graduate business students. Access to Internet/World Wide Web, online (class) registration, and online grade reports available. *Personal computer requirements:* Graduate business students are strongly recommended to purchase or lease a personal computer. *Special opportunities include:* An international exchange program and an internship program are available. *Placement services include:* Alumni network, career counseling/planning, electronic job bank, career fairs, and resume preparation.

EXPENSES *Tuition:* Full-time: 27,000 Australian dollars. *Tuition (international):* Full-time: 34,800 Australian dollars.

FINANCIAL AID (2007–08) Loans and scholarships.

INTERNATIONAL STUDENTS 74% of students enrolled are international students. *Services and facilities:* Counseling/support services, ESL/language courses, Housing location assistance, International student housing, International student organization, Language tutoring, Orientation, Visa Services. Financial aid is not available to international students. *Required with application:* IELT with recommended score of 6.5; TOEFL with recommended score of 230 (computer) or 550 (paper). *Recommended with application:* Proof of adequate funds; proof of health/immunizations.

International Student Contact International Student Office, GPO Box 2100, Adelaide, 5001, Australia. *Phone:* 61-8-82012768. *Fax:* 61-8-82013177. *E-mail:* intl.office@flinders.edu.au.

APPLICATION *Required:* Application form, baccalaureate/first degree, 2 letters of recommendation, resume/curriculum vitae, transcripts of college work, 2 years of work experience. *Recommended:* Personal statement. Applications for domestic and international students are processed on a rolling basis.

Application Contact Ms. Amanda Banytis, Admissions Office, GPO Box 2100, Adelaide, 5001, Australia. *Phone:* 61-8-82013074. *Fax:* 61-8-82012644. *E-mail:* amanda.banytis@flinders.edu.au.

James Cook University
Faculty of Law, Business, and the Creative Arts—Townsville
Cairns, Australia

Phone: 07-47815601 **Fax:** 07-47815988 **E-mail:** internationalstudentcentre@jcu.edu.au

Business Program(s) Web Site: http://www.jcu.edu.au/flbca/public/faculty/

DEGREES   MBA • MBA/MIT • MBA/MPA

MBA—Master of Business Administration Full-time. 12 to 18 months to complete program. *Concentration:* general MBA.

MBA/MIT—Master of Business Administration/Master of Information Technology Full-time. 18 to 24 months to complete program. *Concentration:* combined degrees.

MBA/MPA—MPA/MBA Full-time. Up to 4 total credits required. 18 to 24 months to complete program. *Concentrations:* accounting, general MBA.

RESOURCES AND SERVICES 120 on-campus PCs are available to graduate business students. Access to Internet/World Wide Web, online (class) registration, and online grade reports available. *Personal computer requirements:* Graduate business students are strongly recommended to purchase or lease a personal computer. *Placement services include:* Career counseling/planning, career fairs, and job interviews arranged.

Application Contact Admission Officer, International Student Centre, James Cook University, Townsville, 4811, Australia. *Phone:* 07-47815601. *Fax:* 07-47815988. *E-mail:* internationalstudentcentre@jcu.edu.au.

Macquarie University
Macquarie Graduate School of Management
Sydney, Australia

Phone: 61-02-98509017 Ext. 9017 **Fax:** 61-02-98509022 Ext. 9022 **E-mail:** mgsminfo@mgsm.edu.au

Business Program(s) Web Site: http://www.mgsm.edu.au

Macquarie University (continued)

Graduate Business Unit Enrollment *Total:* 2,090 (155 full-time; 1,935 part-time; 786 women; 646 international). *Average Age:* 34.

Graduate Business Faculty *Total:* 54 (36 full-time; 18 part-time).

Admissions *Applied:* 1,385. *Admitted:* 1,248. *Enrolled:* 1,022.

Academic Calendar Quarters.

After Graduation (Class of 2006–07) *Employed within 3 months of graduation:* 92%. *Average starting salary:* 146,063 Australian dollars.

DEGREES M Mgt • MBA

M Mgt—Master of Management Full-time and part-time. 3-5 years managerial/professional work experience and first degree required. 40 total credits required. 9 to 18 months to complete program. *Concentrations:* financial management/planning, human resources management, information management, international management, management, management information systems, marketing, operations management, strategic management, technology management.

MBA—Master of Business Administration Full-time and part-time. 5 years managerial/professional work experience and first degree required. 64 total credits required. 12 to 36 months to complete program. *Concentrations:* financial management/planning, general MBA, human resources management, information technology, international management, logistics, management, marketing, operations management, strategic management, technology management.

RESOURCES AND SERVICES 116 on-campus PCs are available to graduate business students. Access to Internet/World Wide Web and online grade reports available. *Personal computer requirements:* Graduate business students are required to have a personal computer. *Special opportunities include:* An international exchange program and an internship program are available. *Placement services include:* Alumni network, career placement, job search course, career counseling/planning, electronic job bank, resume referral, career fairs, job interviews arranged, resume preparation, and career library.

EXPENSES *Tuition (state resident):* Full-time: 48,000 Australian dollars. Part-time: 3000 Australian dollars per unit. *Tuition (international):* Full-time: 48,000 Australian dollars. Part-time: 3000 Australian dollars per unit. *Required fees:* Full-time: 370 Australian dollars. *Graduate housing:* Room and board costs vary by number of occupants and type of accommodation. *Typical cost:* 14,000 Australian dollars (room only).

FINANCIAL AID (2007–08) 5 students received aid, including scholarships and work study. Aid is available to part-time students.

Financial Aid Contact Fees Executive, New South Wales, Australia. *E-mail:* sscadvice@mgsm.edu.au.

INTERNATIONAL STUDENTS 31% of students enrolled are international students. *Services and facilities:* Counseling/support services, ESL/language courses, Housing location assistance, International student housing, International student organization, Language tutoring, Orientation, Visa Services, Health coverage, Social activities, Career development, Academic consulting. Financial aid is available to international students. *Required with application:* IELT with recommended score of 6.5; TOEFL with recommended score of 237 (computer) or 580 (paper); TWE with recommended score of 5; proof of adequate funds; proof of health/immunizations.

International Student Contact Vice-Chancellor, Recruitment and Admissions, New South Wales, Australia. *E-mail:* iso@mq.edu.au.

APPLICATION *Required:* Application form, baccalaureate/first degree, 3 letters of recommendation, personal statement, resume/curriculum vitae, transcripts of college work, 5 years of work experience. *Application fee:* 0 Australian dollars, 110 Australian dollars (international). Applications for domestic and international students are processed on a rolling basis.

Application Contact Admissions, New South Wales, Australia. *Phone:* 61-02-98509017 Ext. 9017. *Fax:* 61-02-98509022 Ext. 9022. *E-mail:* mgsminfo@mgsm.edu.au.

Monash University
MBA Programme

Caulfield East, Australia

Phone: 61-3-99031166 **Fax:** 61-3-99031168 **E-mail:** mba@buseco.monash.edu.au

Business Program(s) Web Site: http://www.mba.monash.edu.au

Graduate Business Unit Enrollment *Total:* 471 (116 full-time; 355 part-time; 160 women; 63 international). *Average Age:* 34.

Graduate Business Faculty *Total:* 56 (50 full-time; 6 part-time).

Admissions *Applied:* 523. *Admitted:* 264. *Enrolled:* 157. *Average GPA:* 3.0

Academic Calendar Semesters.

After Graduation (Class of 2006–07) *Employed within 3 months of graduation:* 85%. *Average starting salary:* 120,000 Australian dollars.

DEGREES MBA • MBA/LLM • MBA/MPA

MBA—MBA/Master of Corporate Environmental and Sustainability Management Full-time and part-time. 120 total credits required. 24 to 72 months to complete program. *Concentration:* environmental economics/management.

MBA—Master of Business Administration/Master of Applied Finance Full-time and part-time. International students must be enrolled full-time. At least 120 total credits required. 24 to 72 months to complete program. *Concentrations:* finance, financial management/planning, general MBA.

MBA—Master of Business Administration/Master of Business Law Full-time and part-time. International students must be enrolled full-time. At least 120 total credits required. 24 to 72 months to complete program. *Concentrations:* business law, general MBA.

MBA—Master of Business Administration/Master of Commercial Law Full-time and part-time. International students must be enrolled full-time. At least 120 total credits required. 24 to 72 months to complete program. *Concentrations:* business law, general MBA.

MBA—Master of Business Administration/Master of Health Services Management Full-time and part-time. International students must be enrolled full-time. At least 120 total credits required. 24 to 72 months to complete program. *Concentrations:* general MBA, health administration, health care.

MBA—Master of Business Administration/Master of Human Resource Management Full-time and part-time. International students must be enrolled full-time. At least 120 total credits required. 24 to 72 months to complete program. *Concentrations:* general MBA, human resources management, management.

MBA—Master of Business Administration/Master of Marketing Full-time and part-time. International students must be enrolled full-time. At least 120 total credits required. 24 to 72 months to complete program. *Concentrations:* advertising, general MBA, international marketing, logistics, marketing, marketing research, supply chain management.

MBA—Master of Business Administration/Master of Risk Management Full-time and part-time. International students must be enrolled full-time. At least 120 total credits required. 24 to 72 months to complete program. *Concentrations:* general MBA, risk management.

MBA—Master of Business Administration Full-time and part-time. At least 96 total credits required. 16 to 72 months to complete program. *Concentrations:* accounting, administration, agribusiness, arts administration/management, Asian business studies, banking, business education, business ethics, business information science, business law, business policy/strategy, business studies, Chinese business studies, commerce, conflict resolution management, corporate accounting, decision sciences, economics, electronic commerce (E-commerce), engineering, entrepreneurship, environmental economics/management, European business studies, executive programs, finance, financial management/planning, general MBA, health administration, health care, human resources management, industrial administration/management, industrial/labor relations, information management, information systems, international and area business studies, international banking, international business, international economics, international finance, international logistics, international management, international marketing, international trade, law, leadership, legal administration, logistics, management, management consulting, management information systems, managerial economics, marketing, medicine, new venture management, operations management, organizational behavior/development, organizational management, pharmaceutical management, project management, public and private management, public policy and administration, quality management, quantitative analysis, risk management, strategic management, supply chain management, taxation, transportation management.

MBA/LLM—MBA/Master of Laws in Commercial Law Full-time and part-time. 120 total credits required. 24 to 72 months to complete program. *Concentration:* commerce.

MBA/LLM—Master of Business Administration/Master of Laws Full-time and part-time. International students must be enrolled full-time. At least 120 total credits required. 24 to 72 months to complete program. *Concentrations:* business law, general MBA.

MBA/MPA—Master of Business Administration/Master of Professional Accounting Full-time and part-time. Distance learning option. At least 120 total credits required. 24 to 72 months to complete program. *Concentrations:* accounting, administration, business ethics, business law, business policy/strategy, corporate accounting, credit management, economics, entrepreneurship, finance, financial management/planning, general MBA, information management, international business, law, leadership, logistics, marketing, new venture management, organizational behavior/development, organizational management, quantitative analysis, risk management, statistics, strategic management, supply chain management.

RESOURCES AND SERVICES 30 on-campus PCs are available to graduate business students. Access to Internet/World Wide Web, online (class) registration, and online grade reports available. *Personal computer requirements:* Graduate business students are strongly recommended to purchase or lease a personal computer. *Special opportunities include:* An international exchange program is available. *Placement services include:* Alumni network, job search course, career counseling/planning, electronic job bank, resume referral, resume preparation, and career library.

EXPENSES *Tuition (state resident):* Full-time: 21,920 Australian dollars. Part-time: 10,960 Australian dollars per year. *Tuition (international):* Full-time: 25,200 Australian dollars. Part-time: 12,600 Australian dollars per year. Tuition and/or fees vary by academic program. *Graduate housing:* Room and board costs vary by campus location, number of occupants, and type of accommodation. *Typical cost:* 14,000 Australian dollars (including board), 10,000 Australian dollars (room only).

FINANCIAL AID (2007–08) 5 students received aid, including scholarships. Aid is available to part-time students.

INTERNATIONAL STUDENTS 13% of students enrolled are international students. *Services and facilities:* Counseling/support services, ESL/language courses, Housing location assistance, International student housing, International student organization, Language tutoring, Orientation, Visa Services. Financial aid is available to international students. *Required with application:* IELT with recommended score of 7; TOEFL with recommended score of 250 (computer), 600 (paper), or 100 (Internet); TWE with recommended score of 4.5; proof of health/immunizations.

International Student Contact Ms. Christine Tuason, Senior Admissions Officer, International Recruitment Services, 871 Dandenong Road, Caulfield East, Victoria, 3145, Australia. *Phone:* 61-3-99034720. *Fax:* 61-3-99034779. *E-mail:* christine.tuason@adm.monash.edu.au.

APPLICATION *Required:* Application form, baccalaureate/first degree, 2 letters of recommendation, personal statement, resume/curriculum vitae, transcripts of college work, 4 years of work experience. School will accept GMAT. Applications for domestic and international students are processed on a rolling basis.

Application Contact Graduate School of Business, 27 Sir John Monash Drive, Caulfield East, Victoria, 3145, Australia. *Phone:* 61-3-99031166. *Fax:* 61-3-99031168. *E-mail:* mba@buseco.monash.edu.au.

Queensland University of Technology
Brisbane Graduate School of Business
Brisbane, Australia

Phone: 61-7-38641473 **Fax:** 61-7-38641055 **E-mail:** bgsbenq@qut.edu.au

Business Program(s) Web Site: http://www.bgsb.qut.edu.au

DEGREES EMBA • IMBA • MBA

EMBA—Executive Master of Business Administration Part-time. Required: minimum of 5 years senior management experience with a degree or 10 years senior management experience without a degree. At least 144 total credits required. Minimum of 22 months to complete program. *Concentrations:* international business, leadership.

IMBA—International Master of Business Administration Full-time. At least 144 total credits required. Minimum of 18 months to complete program. *Concentrations:* accounting, economics, entrepreneurship, finance, human resources management, information technology, international business, leadership, management communication, marketing, new venture management, nonprofit management, project management, strategic management.

MBA—Master of Business Administration (Major) Full-time and part-time. At least 192 total credits required. 18 to 72 months to complete program. *Concentrations:* accounting, economics, entrepreneurship, finance, information management, research and development administration.

MBA—Master of Business Administration Full-time and part-time. At least 144 total credits required. 12 to 60 months to complete program. *Concentrations:* accounting, economics, entrepreneurship, finance, human resources management, information technology, international business, leadership, management communication, marketing, new venture management, nonprofit management, project management, strategic management.

RESOURCES AND SERVICES 850 on-campus PCs are available to graduate business students. Access to Internet/World Wide Web, online (class) registration, and online grade reports available. *Personal computer requirements:* Graduate business students are strongly recommended to purchase or lease a personal computer. *Special opportunities include:* An international exchange program and an internship program are available. *Placement services include:* Alumni network, career placement, job search course, career counseling/planning, electronic job bank, career fairs, and resume preparation.

Application Contact Student Services Coordinator, GPO Box 2434, Brisbane, Queensland, 4001, Australia. *Phone:* 61-7-38641473. *Fax:* 61-7-38641055. *E-mail:* bgsbenq@qut.edu.au.

Southern Cross University
Graduate College of Management
Lismore, Australia

Phone: 61-2-66203851 **Fax:** 61-2-66203227 **E-mail:** jasquith@scu.edu.au

Business Program(s) Web Site: http://www.scu.edu.au/schools/gcm/

DEGREE MBA

MBA—Master of Business Administration Full-time and part-time. Distance learning option. At least 144 total credits required. 12 to 60 months to complete program. *Concentrations:* accounting, entrepreneurship, finance, general MBA, health administration, hospitality management, human resources management, international business, management information systems, marketing, sports/entertainment management, travel industry/tourism management.

RESOURCES AND SERVICES 40 on-campus PCs are available to graduate business students. Access to Internet/World Wide Web, online

Southern Cross University (continued)

(class) registration, and online grade reports available. *Personal computer requirements:* Graduate business students are required to have a personal computer. *Special opportunities include:* An international exchange program is available. *Placement services include:* Alumni network, career counseling/planning, career fairs, and resume preparation.

Application Contact Jo Asquith, Manager, PO Box 157, Lismore, New South Wales, 2480, Australia. *Phone:* 61-2-66203851. *Fax:* 61-2-66203227. *E-mail:* jasquith@scu.edu.au.

Swinburne University of Technology

Australian Graduate School of Entrepreneurship (AGSE)

Hawthorne, Australia

Phone: 1300-368-777 **Fax:** 61-3-98192117 **E-mail:** postgrad@swin.edu.au

Business Program(s) Web Site: http://www.swin.edu.au/business

DEGREES   MBA • MBA equivalent

MBA—Master of Business Administration Full-time and part-time. Minimum of 3 years relevant work experience. At least 200 total credits required. 18 to 48 months to complete program. *Concentrations:* accounting, business policy/strategy, electronic commerce (E-commerce), entrepreneurship, finance, general MBA, information management, international management, leadership, management, management information systems, marketing, new venture management, organizational behavior/development, strategic management.

MBA equivalent—Master of Entrepreneurship and Innovation Full-time and part-time. Demonstrated entrepreneurial activity and characteristics usually over a period of 4 years. At least 150 total credits required. 18 to 36 months to complete program. *Concentrations:* business policy/strategy, entrepreneurship, finance, financial management/planning, international business, international finance, international management, international marketing, international trade, leadership, legal administration, management, marketing, marketing research, new venture management, nonprofit management, risk management.

RESOURCES AND SERVICES 150 on-campus PCs are available to graduate business students. Access to Internet/World Wide Web, online (class) registration, and online grade reports available. *Personal computer requirements:* Graduate business students are required to have a personal computer. *Special opportunities include:* An international exchange program is available. *Placement services include:* Alumni network, job search course, career counseling/planning, electronic job bank, resume referral, job interviews arranged, resume preparation, and career library.

Application Contact Information Hotline, Postgraduate Information, Australian Graduate School of Entrepreneurship, PO Box 218, Hawthorn, Victoria, Australia. *Phone:* 1300-368-777. *Fax:* 61-3-98192117. *E-mail:* postgrad@swin.edu.au.

The University of Adelaide

The University of Adelaide Business School

Adelaide, Australia

Phone: 61-8-83035525 **Fax:** 61-8-82234782 **E-mail:** mba.international@adelaide.edu.au

Business Program(s) Web Site: http://www.business.adelaide.edu.au

Graduate Business Unit Enrollment *Total:* 1,798 (874 full-time; 924 part-time; 804 women; 1171 international). *Average Age:* 26.

Graduate Business Faculty *Total:* 92 (58 full-time; 34 part-time).

Admissions *Applied:* 1,908. *Admitted:* 1,568. *Enrolled:* 867.

Academic Calendar Trimesters.

After Graduation (Class of 2006–07) *Employed within 3 months of graduation:* 95%.

DEGREES   EVEMBA • M Comm • MBA • PhD/MBA

EVEMBA—Evening Master of Business Administration Full-time and part-time. 2 years of managerial experience required. At least 36 total credits required. 12 to 80 months to complete program. *Concentration:* general MBA.

M Comm—Master of Commerce Full-time and part-time. *Concentrations:* accounting, finance, management, marketing.

MBA—Master of Business Administration Full-time and part-time. 2 years of relevant work experience required. At least 36 total credits required. 12 to 72 months to complete program. *Concentration:* general MBA.

MBA—Master of Business Administration (Advanced) Full-time and part-time. 2 years of relevant work experience required. At least 48 total credits required. 16 to 84 months to complete program. *Concentrations:* Asian business studies, finance, international management, marketing.

PhD/MBA—Doctor of Philosophy Full-time and part-time. *Concentration:* business studies.

RESOURCES AND SERVICES 80 on-campus PCs are available to graduate business students. Access to Internet/World Wide Web, online (class) registration, and online grade reports available. *Personal computer requirements:* Graduate business students are not required to have a personal computer. *Special opportunities include:* An international exchange program and an internship program are available. *Placement services include:* Alumni network, career counseling/planning, electronic job bank, resume referral, career fairs, and resume preparation.

EXPENSES *Tuition (state resident):* Full-time: 22,896 Australian dollars. Part-time: 2544 Australian dollars per trimester. *Tuition (international):* Full-time: 24,561 Australian dollars. Part-time: 2729 Australian dollars per trimester. Tuition and/or fees vary by campus location and academic program.

FINANCIAL AID (2007–08) Scholarships. *Financial aid application deadline:* 8/1.

Financial Aid Contact Ms. Linda Rust, Web and International Communications Officer, South Australia, Australia. *Phone:* 61-8-83035525. *Fax:* 61-8-82234782. *E-mail:* mba.international@adelaide.edu.au.

INTERNATIONAL STUDENTS 65% of students enrolled are international students. *Services and facilities:* Counseling/support services, ESL/language courses, Housing location assistance, International student housing, International student organization, Language tutoring, Orientation, Visa Services, Student learning support, Career counseling. Financial aid is available to international students. *Required with application:* IELT with recommended score of 6.5; TOEFL with recommended score of 230 (computer) or 575 (paper); TWE with recommended score of 4.5; proof of adequate funds.

International Student Contact Ms. Linda Rust, Web and International Communications Officer, South Australia, Australia. *Phone:* 61-8-83035525. *Fax:* 61-8-82234782. *E-mail:* mba.international@adelaide.edu.au.

APPLICATION *Required:* Application form, baccalaureate/first degree, 2 letters of recommendation, resume/curriculum vitae, transcripts of college work, 2 years of work experience. *Recommended:* Interview, personal statement. Applications for domestic and international students are processed on a rolling basis.

Application Contact Ms. Carol McHugh, Admissions Executive Officer, South Australia, Australia. *Phone:* 61-8-83035525. *Fax:* 61-8-82234782. *E-mail:* mba.international@adelaide.edu.au.

University of Melbourne

Melbourne Business School

Melbourne, Australia

Phone: 61-3-93498131 **Fax:** 61-3-93498377 **E-mail:** w.hill@mbs.edu

Business Program(s) Web Site: http://www.mbs.edu

Graduate Business Unit Enrollment *Total:* 614 (228 full-time; 386 part-time; 386 women; 386 international). *Average Age:* 30.

Graduate Business Faculty *Total:* 73 (50 full-time; 23 part-time).

Admissions *Applied:* 356. *Admitted:* 135. *Enrolled:* 69. *Average GMAT:* 650.

Academic Calendar Trimesters.

After Graduation (Class of 2006–07) *Employed within 3 months of graduation:* 94%. *Average starting salary:* 126,075 Australian dollars.

DEGREE MBA

MBA—Master of Business Administration Full-time and part-time. At least 20 total credits required. 16 to 60 months to complete program. *Concentrations:* accounting, entrepreneurship, finance, general MBA, human resources management, international management, management, marketing, organizational management, public management, strategic management, technology management.

RESOURCES AND SERVICES 20 on-campus PCs are available to graduate business students. Access to Internet/World Wide Web and online grade reports available. *Personal computer requirements:* Graduate business students are required to have a personal computer. *Special opportunities include:* An international exchange program and an internship program are available. *Placement services include:* Alumni network, career placement, job search course, career counseling/planning, electronic job bank, resume referral, career fairs, job interviews arranged, resume preparation, and career library.

EXPENSES *Tuition:* Full-time: 37,500 Australian dollars. Part-time: 15,000 Australian dollars per year. *Tuition (international):* Full-time: 37,500 Australian dollars.

FINANCIAL AID (2007–08) 45 students received aid, including scholarships. Aid is available to part-time students. *Financial aid application deadline:* 11/30.

Financial Aid Contact Ms. Wendy Hill, Admissions Manager, 200 Leicester Street, Carlton, Victoria, Australia. *Phone:* 61-3-93498131. *Fax:* 61-3-93498377. *E-mail:* w.hill@mbs.edu.

INTERNATIONAL STUDENTS 63% of students enrolled are international students. *Services and facilities:* Counseling/support services, ESL/language courses, Housing location assistance, International student housing, International student organization, Orientation, Visa Services, International Student Web Forum. Financial aid is available to international students. *Required with application:* IELT with recommended score of 6.5. *Recommended with application:* TOEFL with recommended score of 253 (computer), 610 (paper), or 90 (Internet).

International Student Contact Ms. Anna Parkin, General Manager, Marketing and Admissions, 200 Leicester Street, Carlton, Victoria, Australia. *Phone:* 61-3-93498283. *Fax:* 61-3-93498377. *E-mail:* a.parkin@mbs.edu.

APPLICATION *Required:* GMAT, application form, baccalaureate/first degree, essay, 2 letters of recommendation, personal statement, resume/curriculum vitae, transcripts of college work, 2 years of work experience. *Recommended:* Interview. *Application fee:* 0 Australian dollars. Applications for domestic and international students are processed on a rolling basis.

Application Contact Ms. Wendy Hill, Admissions Manager, 200 Leicester Street, Carlton, Victoria, Australia. *Phone:* 61-3-93498131. *Fax:* 61-3-93498377. *E-mail:* w.hill@mbs.edu.

University of Newcastle
Graduate School of Business

Callaghan, Australia

Phone: 61-2-49218749 **Fax:** 61-2-49217398 **E-mail:** ngsb@newcastle.edu.au

Business Program(s) Web Site: http://www.newcastle.edu.au/school/ngsb/index.html

---

DEGREES M Mktg • MAF • MBA • MEntr • MHRMIR • MIB • MIT • MM • MTD

M Mktg—Master of Marketing Full-time and part-time. At least 8 total credits required. Minimum of 12 months to complete program. *Concentrations:* entrepreneurship, marketing, marketing research.

MAF—Master of Applied Finance Full-time and part-time. At least 8 total credits required. Minimum of 12 months to complete program. *Concentrations:* accounting, banking, economics, finance, financial economics.

MBA—Master of Business Administration Full-time and part-time. Distance learning option. At least 12 total credits required. Minimum of 12 months to complete program. *Concentrations:* accounting, commerce, economics, entrepreneurship, finance, financial economics, human resources management, industrial/labor relations, international business, management, management information systems, marketing, quantitative analysis.

MEntr—Master of Entrepreneurship Full-time and part-time. At least 8 total credits required. Minimum of 12 months to complete program. *Concentrations:* accounting, business ethics, economics, entrepreneurship, financial economics, human resources management, management, marketing.

MHRMIR—Master of Human Resource Management and Industrial Relations Full-time and part-time. At least 8 total credits required. Minimum of 12 months to complete program. *Concentrations:* human resources management, industrial/labor relations, organizational behavior/development.

MIB—Master of International Business Full-time and part-time. At least 8 total credits required. Minimum of 12 months to complete program. *Concentrations:* accounting, economics, entrepreneurship, financial economics, human resources management, international business, marketing.

MIT—Master of Information Technology Full-time and part-time. Distance learning option. At least 12 total credits required. Minimum of 18 months to complete program. *Concentrations:* information management, management information systems, quantitative analysis.

MM—Master in Environmental and Business Management Full-time and part-time. Distance learning option. Minimum of 12 months to complete program. *Concentration:* environmental economics/management.

MM—Master of Applied Management in Aviation Full-time and part-time. Distance learning option. Minimum of 12 months to complete program. *Concentration:* aviation management.

MM—Master of Applied Management in Education Full-time and part-time. Distance learning option. Minimum of 12 months to complete program. *Concentration:* training and development.

MM—Master of Applied Management in Health Full-time and part-time. Distance learning option. Minimum of 12 months to complete program. *Concentration:* health care.

MTD—Master of Trade and Development Full-time and part-time. Bachelor's degree with Economics component required. At least 8 total credits required. Minimum of 12 months to complete program. *Concentrations:* developmental economics, economics.

RESOURCES AND SERVICES 80 on-campus PCs are available to graduate business students. Access to Internet/World Wide Web, online (class) registration, and online grade reports available. *Personal computer requirements:* Graduate business students are not required to have a personal computer. *Special opportunities include:* An international exchange program is available. *Placement services include:* Alumni network, career placement, career counseling/planning, career fairs, resume preparation, and career library.

Application Contact Administrative Officer, Level 3, University House, Corner of King and Auckland Streets, NSW, Australia. *Phone:* 61-2-49218749. *Fax:* 61-2-49217398. *E-mail:* ngsb@newcastle.edu.au.

The University of New England

The Graduate School of Business Administration

Armidale, Australia

Phone: 61-2-67733382 **Fax:** 61-2-67733461 **E-mail:** gsb@une.edu.au

Business Program(s) Web Site: http://www.gsb.une.edu.au

DEGREE MBA

MBA—Master of Business Administration Full-time and part-time. Distance learning option. At least 72 total credits required. 12 to 72 months to complete program. *Concentrations:* accounting, agribusiness, Asian business studies, business law, general MBA, human resources management, information technology, international management, marketing, nonprofit management, public management, student designed.

RESOURCES AND SERVICES Access to Internet/World Wide Web and online grade reports available. *Personal computer requirements:* Graduate business students are required to have a personal computer. *Placement services include:* Alumni network, career counseling/planning, and career fairs.

Application Contact Admissions, Armidale, New South Wales, 2351, Australia. *Phone:* 61-2-67733382. *Fax:* 61-2-67733461. *E-mail:* gsb@une.edu.au.

University of New South Wales

Australian School of Business

Kensington, Australia

Phone: 61-2-99319490 **Fax:** 61-2-99319206 **E-mail:** admissions@agsm.edu.au

Business Program(s) Web Site: http://www.agsm.edu.au

Graduate Business Unit Enrollment *Total:* 1,595 (121 full-time; 1,474 part-time; 510 women; 166 international). *Average Age:* 33.

Graduate Business Faculty *Total:* 164 (29 full-time; 135 part-time).

Admissions *Applied:* 1,239. *Admitted:* 892. *Enrolled:* 743. *Average GMAT:* 660. *Average GPA:* 3.0

Accreditation AACSB—The Association to Advance Collegiate Schools of Business.

After Graduation (Class of 2006–07) *Employed within 3 months of graduation:* 77%. *Average starting salary:* 121,628 Australian dollars.

DEGREES EMBA • MBA

EMBA—Executive Master of Business Administration Part-time. Undergraduate degree, 2 years professional work experience (or 6 years of work experience in lieu of a degree), currently employed in management and Australian residency. At least 96 total credits required. 30 to 84 months to complete program. *Concentration:* general MBA.

MBA—Master of Business Administration Full-time. Undergraduate degree, minimum 2 years work experience, minimum GMAT score of 550, minimum GPA of 2.0, 2 referee reports, leadership potential and curriculum vitae. At least 96 total credits required. 12 to 16 months to complete program. *Concentration:* general MBA.

RESOURCES AND SERVICES 60 on-campus PCs are available to graduate business students. Access to Internet/World Wide Web, online (class) registration, and online grade reports available. *Personal computer requirements:* Graduate business students are required to have a personal computer. *Special opportunities include:* An international exchange program and an internship program are available. *Placement services include:* Alumni network, career placement, job search course, career counseling/planning, electronic job bank, resume referral, career fairs, job interviews arranged, resume preparation, and career library.

EXPENSES *Tuition (state resident):* Full-time: 57,120 Australian dollars. *Tuition (international):* Full-time: 57,120 Australian dollars. *Required fees:* Full-time: 469 Australian dollars. *Graduate housing:* Room and board costs vary by campus location, number of occupants, type of accommodation, and type of board plan. *Typical cost:* 11,266 Australian dollars (including board), 9360 Australian dollars (room only).

FINANCIAL AID (2007–08) 31 students received aid, including scholarships. Aid is available to part-time students.

Financial Aid Contact Admissions Office, AGSM MBA Programs, New South Wales, Australia. *Phone:* 61-2-99319490. *Fax:* 61-2-99319206. *E-mail:* admissions@agsm.edu.au.

INTERNATIONAL STUDENTS 10% of students enrolled are international students. *Services and facilities:* Counseling/support services, ESL/language courses, Housing location assistance, International student housing, International student organization, Orientation, Visa Services, Career management program. Financial aid is available to international students. *Required with application:* IELT with recommended score of 6.5; TOEFL with recommended score of 250 (computer), 600 (paper), or 100 (Internet).

International Student Contact Sharyn Roberts, Director, AGSM MBA Programs, AGSM MBA Programs, New South Wales, Australia. *Phone:* 61-2-99319546. *Fax:* 61-2-99319206. *E-mail:* sharynr@agsm.edu.au.

APPLICATION *Required:* GMAT, application form, baccalaureate/first degree, essay, interview, 2 letters of recommendation, personal statement, resume/curriculum vitae, 2 years of work experience. *Application fee:* 100 Australian dollars. Applications for domestic and international students are processed on a rolling basis.

Application Contact Admissions Office, AGSM MBA Programs, New South Wales, Australia. *Phone:* 61-2-99319490. *Fax:* 61-2-99319206. *E-mail:* admissions@agsm.edu.au.

University of the Sunshine Coast

Faculty of Business

Maroochydore, Australia

Business Program(s) Web Site: http://www.usc.edu.au/Students/Handbook/Postgrad/

Graduate Business Unit Enrollment *Total:* 320 (45 full-time; 275 part-time; 144 women; 175 international). *Average Age:* 38.

Graduate Business Faculty *Total:* 14 (12 full-time; 2 part-time).

Admissions *Average GPA:* 4.5/7 scale

Academic Calendar Trimesters.

After Graduation (Class of 2006–07) *Employed within 3 months of graduation:* 95%. *Average starting salary:* 50,000 Australian dollars.

DEGREES M Mgt • MBA • MF

M Mgt—Master of Management Full-time and part-time. Distance learning option. At least 12 total credits required. 12 to 48 months to complete program. *Concentration:* management.

MBA—Master of Business Administration Full-time and part-time. Distance learning option. At least 12 total credits required. 12 to 48 months to complete program. *Concentration:* general MBA.

MF—Master of Financial Planning Full-time and part-time. Distance learning option. Interest in Australian financial regulations required. At least 12 total credits required. 12 to 48 months to complete program. *Concentration:* financial management/planning.

RESOURCES AND SERVICES 50 on-campus PCs are available to graduate business students. Access to Internet/World Wide Web, online (class) registration, and online grade reports available. *Personal computer requirements:* Graduate business students are strongly recommended to purchase or lease a personal computer. *Special opportunities include:* An international exchange program and an internship program are available.

Placement services include: Alumni network, career counseling/planning, electronic job bank, career fairs, and career library.

EXPENSES *Tuition:* Full-time: 21,000 Australian dollars. Part-time: 7000 Australian dollars per trimester. *Tuition (international):* Full-time: 21,000 Australian dollars. Part-time: 7000 Australian dollars per trimester.

FINANCIAL AID (2007–08) 2 students received aid, including scholarships.

Financial Aid Contact PELS, Canberra, Australia. *Phone:* 61-1-800020108. *E-mail:* pels@hecs.gov.au.

INTERNATIONAL STUDENTS 55% of students enrolled are international students. *Services and facilities:* Counseling/support services, ESL/language courses, Housing location assistance, International student housing, International student organization, Orientation. Financial aid is available to international students. *Required with application:* IELT with recommended score of 6.5; TOEFL with recommended score of 230 (computer), 575 (paper), or 88 (Internet).

International Student Contact Mr. John McKelvey, Manager, Graduate Studies, Maroochydore, DC, Queensland, 4558, Australia. *Phone:* 61-7-54301239. *Fax:* 61-7-54301231. *E-mail:* jmckelve@usc.edu.au.

APPLICATION *Required:* Application form, resume/curriculum vitae, transcripts of college work, 3 years of work experience. *Recommended:* Baccalaureate/first degree. Applications for domestic and international students are processed on a rolling basis.

Application Contact John McKelvey, Maroochydore DC, 4558, Australia.

The University of Western Australia
Business School
Nedlands, Australia

Phone: 61-8-64883980 **Fax:** 61-8-64881072 **E-mail:** renu.burr@uwa.edu.au

Business Program(s) Web Site: http://www.business.uwa.edu.au

Graduate Business Unit Enrollment *Total:* 620 (136 full-time; 484 part-time; 195 women; 199 international). *Average Age:* 28.

Graduate Business Faculty *Total:* 92 (68 full-time; 24 part-time).

Admissions *Applied:* 420. *Admitted:* 381. *Enrolled:* 234. *Average GMAT:* 605.

Academic Calendar Trimesters or semesters.

After Graduation (Class of 2006–07) *Employed within 3 months of graduation:* 95%. *Average starting salary:* 65,000 Australian dollars.

DEGREES EMBA • IMBA/MBA • MBA

EMBA—Executive Master of Business Administration Part-time. 5 years of managerial experience required. 12 total credits required. 24 months to complete program. *Concentration:* executive programs.

IMBA/MBA—International Master of Business Administration Full-time and part-time. 16 total credits required. 16 to 72 months to complete program. *Concentrations:* international and area business studies, international business.

MBA—Master of Business Administration (Advanced) Full-time and part-time. 16 total credits required. 16 to 72 months to complete program. *Concentrations:* entrepreneurship, financial management/planning, general MBA, international business, international management, leadership, management, marketing.

MBA—Master of Business Administration Full-time and part-time. 12 total credits required. 12 to 60 months to complete program. *Concentration:* general MBA.

RESOURCES AND SERVICES 140 on-campus PCs are available to graduate business students. Access to Internet/World Wide Web, online (class) registration, and online grade reports available. *Personal computer requirements:* Graduate business students are strongly recommended to

purchase or lease a personal computer. *Special opportunities include:* An international exchange program is available. *Placement services include:* Alumni network, career placement, job search course, career counseling/planning, electronic job bank, resume referral, resume preparation, and career library.

EXPENSES Tuition and/or fees vary by number of courses or credits taken, campus location, and academic program. *Graduate housing:* Room and board costs vary by campus location, number of occupants, type of accommodation, and type of board plan.

FINANCIAL AID (2007–08) 20 students received aid, including loans, scholarships, and work study. Aid is available to part-time students. *Financial aid application deadline:* 12/8.

Financial Aid Contact Dr. Renu Burr, MBA Program Director, M404, 35 Stirling Highway, Western Australia, Australia. *Phone:* 61-8-64883980. *Fax:* 61-8-64881072. *E-mail:* renu.burr@uwa.edu.au.

INTERNATIONAL STUDENTS 32% of students enrolled are international students. *Services and facilities:* Counseling/support services, ESL/language courses, Housing location assistance, International student housing, International student organization, Language tutoring, Orientation, Visa Services, International advisor. Financial aid is not available to international students. *Required with application:* IELT with recommended score of 6.5; proof of adequate funds; proof of health/immunizations. *Recommended with application:* TOEFL with recommended score of 230 (computer), 570 (paper), or 90 (Internet).

International Student Contact Ms. Kaye MacPherson-Smith, International Student Coordinator, M404, 35 Stirling Highway, Western Australia, Australia. *Phone:* 61-8-64883980. *Fax:* 61-8-64881072. *E-mail:* kaye.macpherson-smith@uwa.edu.au.

APPLICATION *Required:* Application form, baccalaureate/first degree, personal statement, transcripts of college work, 2 years of work experience. School will accept GMAT. *Recommended:* 2 letters of recommendation, resume/curriculum vitae. Applications for domestic and international students are processed on a rolling basis.

Application Contact Dr. Renu Burr, MBA Program Director, M404, 35 Stirling Highway, Western Australia, Australia. *Phone:* 61-8-64883980. *Fax:* 61-8-64881072. *E-mail:* renu.burr@uwa.edu.au.

University of Western Sydney
Sydney Graduate School of Management
Campbelltown, Australia

Phone: 612-88335999 **Fax:** 612-98915899 **E-mail:** marketing@sgsm.com.au

Business Program(s) Web Site: http://www.sgsm.com.au

Academic Calendar Quarters.

DEGREE MBA

MBA—Master of Business Administration Full-time and part-time. 12 to 36 months to complete program. *Concentration:* general MBA.

RESOURCES AND SERVICES Access to Internet/World Wide Web and online grade reports available. *Personal computer requirements:* Graduate business students are required to have a personal computer. *Special opportunities include:* An international exchange program is available. *Placement services include:* Alumni network, career counseling/planning, career fairs, resume preparation, and career library.

FINANCIAL AID (2007–08) Scholarships. Aid is available to part-time students.

INTERNATIONAL STUDENTS *Services and facilities:* Counseling/support services, ESL/language courses, Housing location assistance, International student housing, International student organization, Language tutoring, Orientation, Visa Services. Financial aid is available to international students. *Required with application:* IELT with recommended score of 6.5; TOEFL with recommended score of 250 (computer) or 600 (paper); proof of adequate funds; proof of health/immunizations.

University of Western Sydney (continued)

International Student Contact Client Services Centre, PO Box 6145, New South Wales, Australia. *Phone:* 612-88335999. *Fax:* 612-98915899. *E-mail:* marketing@sgsm.com.au.

APPLICATION *Required:* Application form, baccalaureate/first degree, 2 letters of recommendation, personal statement, resume/curriculum vitae, transcripts of college work, 3 years of work experience. Applications for domestic and international students are processed on a rolling basis.

Application Contact Client Services Centre, PO Box 6145, New South Wales, Australia. *Phone:* 612-88335999. *Fax:* 612-98915899. *E-mail:* marketing@sgsm.com.au.

AUSTRIA

The International University, Vienna

MBA Programs

Vienna, Austria

Phone: 43-1-7185068 Ext. 19 **Fax:** 43-1-7185068 Ext. 9 **E-mail:** marketing@iuvienna.edu

Business Program(s) Web Site: http://www.iuvienna.edu/412_EN-International-University-Academics.5B134F0e0be5fa9a7e5cd06e6cce147831bb55

Graduate Business Unit Enrollment *Total:* 38 (37 full-time; 1 part-time; 18 women).

Graduate Business Faculty *Total:* 22 (5 full-time; 17 part-time).

Admissions *Applied:* 10. *Admitted:* 7. *Enrolled:* 6.

Academic Calendar Semesters.

After Graduation (Class of 2006–07) *Employed within 3 months of graduation:* 90%.

DEGREES MBA • MIB

MBA—Master of Business Administration Full-time and part-time. Distance learning option. 45 total credits required. 15 to 24 months to complete program. *Concentration:* general MBA.

MIB—Master of International Business Full-time and part-time. Distance learning option. 39 total credits required. 15 to 24 months to complete program. *Concentration:* international business.

RESOURCES AND SERVICES 15 on-campus PCs are available to graduate business students. Access to Internet/World Wide Web available. *Personal computer requirements:* Graduate business students are strongly recommended to purchase or lease a personal computer. *Special opportunities include:* An international exchange program and an internship program are available. *Placement services include:* Alumni network, career placement, and career fairs.

EXPENSES *Tuition:* Full-time: 10,000 euros.

FINANCIAL AID (2007–08) 20 students received aid, including loans, scholarships, and work study. Aid is available to part-time students.

Financial Aid Contact Dr. Linda Boyer, Administrative Vice President, Mondscheingasse 16, Vienna, A-1070, Austria. *Phone:* 43-1-7185068 Ext. 11. *Fax:* 43-1-7185068 Ext. 9. *E-mail:* lboyer@iuvienna.edu.

INTERNATIONAL STUDENTS *Services and facilities:* Counseling/support services, ESL/language courses, Housing location assistance, International student housing, Language tutoring, Orientation, Visa Services. Financial aid is available to international students. *Required with application:* TOEFL with recommended score of 213 (computer), 550 (paper), or 79 (Internet); proof of adequate funds. *Recommended with application:* IELT with recommended score of 6.

International Student Contact Sabrina Nill, Marketing Director, Mondscheingasse 16, Vienna, A-1070, Austria. *Phone:* 43-1-7185068 Ext. 19. *Fax:* 43-1-7185068 Ext. 9. *E-mail:* marketing@iuvienna.edu.

APPLICATION *Required:* Application form, baccalaureate/first degree, essay, 2 letters of recommendation, personal statement, transcripts of college work. *Recommended:* 3 years of work experience. *Application fee:* $60.

Application Contact Sabrina Nill, Marketing Director, Mondscheingasse 16, Vienna, A-1070, Austria. *Phone:* 43-1-7185068 Ext. 19. *Fax:* 43-1-7185068 Ext. 9. *E-mail:* marketing@iuvienna.edu.

Vienna University of Economics and Business Administration

WU Wien MBA

Vienna, Austria

Phone: 43-1-31336 Ext. 4327 **Fax:** 43-1-31336 Ext. 790 **E-mail:** emba@wu-wien.ac.at

Business Program(s) Web Site: http://www.executiveacademy.at

Graduate Business Unit Enrollment *Total:* 250 (250 part-time; 75 women; 100 international). *Average Age:* 35.

Graduate Business Faculty *Total:* 290 (90 full-time; 200 part-time).

Admissions *Applied:* 550. *Admitted:* 300. *Enrolled:* 250. *Average GMAT:* 620. *Average GPA:* 3.5

Academic Calendar Semesters.

DEGREES EMBA • MBA • MBA equivalent

EMBA—Executive MBA Part-time. Undergraduate university degree (equivalent to a bachelor's degree) and a minimum of 5 years relevant work experience. Minimum of 14 months to complete program. *Concentrations:* executive programs, general MBA, international business, international management, leadership, management, organizational management.

MBA—Professional MBA Accounting & Taxation Part-time. Undergraduate university degree (equivalent to a bachelor's degree) and a minimum of 2 years relevant work experience. Minimum of 18 months to complete program. *Concentrations:* accounting, corporate accounting, taxation.

MBA—Professional MBA Banking & Insurance Part-time. Undergraduate university degree (equivalent to a bachelor's degree) and a minimum of 2 years relevant work experience. Minimum of 18 months to complete program. *Concentrations:* banking, finance, financial management/planning, insurance, international banking, international finance, risk management.

MBA—Professional MBA Controlling & Finance Part-time. Undergraduate university degree (equivalent to a bachelor's degree) and a minimum of 2 years relevant work experience. Minimum of 18 months to complete program. *Concentrations:* corporate accounting, finance, financial economics, financial engineering, financial management/planning, international finance.

MBA—Professional MBA Energy Management Part-time. Undergraduate university degree (equivalent to a bachelor's degree) and a minimum of 2 years relevant work experience. Minimum of 15 months to complete program. *Concentration:* general MBA.

MBA—Professional MBA Entrepreneurship and Innovation Part-time. Undergraduate university degree (equivalent to a bachelor's degree) and a minimum of 2 years of significant professional experience. Minimum of 18 months to complete program. *Concentrations:* engineering, entrepreneurship, new venture management.

MBA—Professional MBA Health Care Management Part-time. Undergraduate university degree (equivalent to a bachelor's degree) and a minimum of 2 years relevant work experience. At least 90 total credits required. Minimum of 24 months to complete program. *Concentrations:*

health administration, health care, medicine, organizational management, pharmaceutical management, public management, rehabilitation administration.

MBA—Professional MBA IT & Business Process Management Part-time. Undergraduate university degree (equivalent to a bachelor's degree) and a minimum of 2 years relevant work experience. Minimum of 18 months to complete program. *Concentrations:* information systems, information technology, management information systems.

MBA—Professional MBA Marketing & Sales Part-time. Undergraduate university degree (equivalent to a bachelor's degree) and a minimum of 2 years relevant work experience. At least 90 total credits required. Minimum of 18 months to complete program. *Concentrations:* advertising, international marketing, marketing, marketing research.

MBA—Professional MBA Project and Process Management Part-time. Undergraduate university degree (equivalent to a bachelor's degree) and a minimum of 2 years of significant professional experience in project, program and/or process management. At least 90 total credits required. Minimum of 18 months to complete program. *Concentration:* project management.

MBA—Professional MBA Social Management Part-time. Undergraduate university degree (equivalent to a bachelor's degree) and a minimum of 2 years relevant work experience. Minimum of 24 months to complete program. *Concentrations:* nonprofit management, nonprofit organization, social work.

MBA—Professional MBA Tourism Management Full-time and part-time. Undergraduate university degree (equivalent to a bachelor's degree) and a minimum of 2 years relevant work experience. 18 to 24 months to complete program. *Concentrations:* hospitality management, international hospitality and restaurant business, international hotel and resort management, travel industry/tourism management.

MBA equivalent—Professional MBA Public Auditing Part-time. Undergraduate university degree (equivalent to a bachelor's degree) and a minimum of 2 years relevant work experience. Minimum of 18 months to complete program. *Concentrations:* accounting, corporate accounting, public finance.

RESOURCES AND SERVICES 60 on-campus PCs are available to graduate business students. Access to Internet/World Wide Web available. *Personal computer requirements:* Graduate business students are required to have a personal computer. *Special opportunities include:* An international exchange program is available. *Placement services include:* Alumni network, career placement, career counseling/planning, electronic job bank, resume referral, career fairs, resume preparation, and career library.

FINANCIAL AID (2007–08) Fellowships, loans, scholarships, and teaching assistantships.

Financial Aid Contact Ms. Regine Eitelbös, Program Manager, WU Executive Academy, Nordbergstrasse 15, Vienna, A-1090, Austria. *Phone:* 43 1 31336 Ext. 4327. *Fax:* 43 1 31336 Ext. 790. *E-mail:* regine.eitelboes@wu-wien.ac.at.

INTERNATIONAL STUDENTS 40% of students enrolled are international students. *Services and facilities:* Counseling/support services, Housing location assistance, Orientation, Visa Services, Internet-based preparation for part-time students. *Recommended with application:* IELT with recommended score of 7.

International Student Contact Ms. Regine Eitelbös, Program Manager, WU Executive Academy, Nordbergstrasse 15, Vienna, A-1090, Austria. *Phone:* 43-1-31336 Ext. 4327. *Fax:* 43-1-31336 Ext. 790. *E-mail:* emba@wu-wien.ac.at.

APPLICATION *Required:* Application form, baccalaureate/first degree, essay, interview, 2 letters of recommendation, personal statement, resume/curriculum vitae, transcripts of college work, 2 years of work experience. Applications for domestic and international students are processed on a rolling basis.

Application Contact Ms. Regine Eitelbös, Program Manager, WU Executive Academy, Nordbergstrasse 15, Vienna, A-1090, Austria. *Phone:* 43-1-31336 Ext. 4327. *Fax:* 43-1-31336 Ext. 790. *E-mail:* emba@wu-wien.ac.at.

BELGIUM

Antwerp International Business School

Graduate Programs in Business

Antwerp, Belgium

Business Program(s) Web Site: http://www.aibs.be

Graduate Business Faculty 25 part-time.

Academic Calendar Quarters.

After Graduation (Class of 2006–07) *Employed within 3 months of graduation:* 80%.

DEGREES IMBA • MIB

IMBA—International Master of Business Administration Full-time and part-time. Distance learning option. 60 to 80 total credits required. 9 to 12 months to complete program. *Concentrations:* business studies, entrepreneurship, executive programs, financial management/planning, general MBA, human resources management, international business, international hospitality and restaurant business, international logistics, international management, international marketing, marketing, operations management, production management, public relations, resources management, sports/entertainment management, strategic management, transportation management, travel industry/tourism management.

MIB—International Master in Business Studies Full-time and part-time. Distance learning option. 60 to 80 total credits required. 9 to 12 months to complete program. *Concentrations:* business studies, entrepreneurship, European business studies, executive programs, financial management/planning, general MBA, hospitality management, human resources management, international banking, international hospitality and restaurant business, international logistics, international management, international marketing, international trade, leadership, management communication, management information systems, marketing, organizational management, sports/entertainment management, transportation management.

RESOURCES AND SERVICES Access to Internet/World Wide Web, online (class) registration, and online grade reports available. *Personal computer requirements:* Graduate business students are strongly recommended to purchase or lease a personal computer. *Special opportunities include:* An international exchange program and an internship program are available. *Placement services include:* Alumni network, career placement, job search course, career counseling/planning, electronic job bank, resume referral, career fairs, job interviews arranged, resume preparation, and career library.

EXPENSES *Tuition (state resident):* Full-time: 8775 euros. Part-time: 350 euros per course. *Tuition (nonresident):* Full-time: 8775 euros. Part-time: 350 euros per course. *Tuition (international):* Full-time: 8775 euros. Part-time: 350 euros per course. *Graduate housing:* Room and board costs vary by campus location, number of occupants, type of accommodation, and type of board plan.

FINANCIAL AID (2007–08) Scholarships.

INTERNATIONAL STUDENTS *Services and facilities:* Counseling/support services, ESL/language courses, Housing location assistance, International student housing, International student organization, Language tutoring, Orientation, Visa Services. *Required with application:* Proof of adequate funds; proof of health/immunizations.

International Student Contact Mr. F Kirschstein, Director, International Admissions Department, Grote Steenweg 42, Laakdal, 2431, Belgium. *Phone:* 32-14545043. *E-mail:* info@antwerp.uibs.org.

APPLICATION *Required:* Application form, letter(s) of recommendation, personal statement, resume/curriculum vitae, transcripts of college work. *Application fee:* 200 ECU. Applications for domestic and international students are processed on a rolling basis.

European Business Management School

MBA Programmes

Antwerp, Belgium

Phone: 32-2-32185431 **Fax:** 32-2-32185868 **E-mail:** info@ebms.edu

Business Program(s) Web Site: http://www.EBMS.edu

DEGREE MBA

MBA—Master of Business Administration Full-time and part-time. 12 to 36 months to complete program. *Concentration:* general MBA.

RESOURCES AND SERVICES 25 on-campus PCs are available to graduate business students. Access to Internet/World Wide Web and online (class) registration available. *Personal computer requirements:* Graduate business students are strongly recommended to purchase or lease a personal computer. *Special opportunities include:* An international exchange program and an internship program are available. *Placement services include:* Alumni network and career counseling/planning.

Application Contact Freddy Kirschstein, Dean, Frederik de Merodestraat 10-16 2600 Antwerp, rue de livourne 116—120, Brussels, 1000, Belgium. *Phone:* 32-2-32185431. *Fax:* 32-2-32185868. *E-mail:* info@ebms.edu.

The International Management Institute

International Business School

Antwerp, Belgium

Phone: 32-3-2185431 **Fax:** 32-3-2185868 **E-mail:** info@timi.edu

Business Program(s) Web Site: http://www.timi.edu

DEGREES MA • MBA • MS • MTL

MA—Master of Arts in Business Communications and Public Relations Full-time and part-time. 12 to 36 months to complete program. *Concentration:* public relations.

MBA—Master of Business Administration Full-time and part-time. Distance learning option. 12 to 36 months to complete program. *Concentrations:* business information science, finance, international business, international marketing, management.

MS—Master of Science in Information Systems Full-time and part-time. 12 to 36 months to complete program. *Concentration:* management information systems.

MTL—Master of Transportation and Logistics Full-time and part-time. 12 to 36 months to complete program. *Concentration:* logistics.

RESOURCES AND SERVICES 60 on-campus PCs are available to graduate business students. Access to Internet/World Wide Web available. *Personal computer requirements:* Graduate business students are strongly recommended to purchase or lease a personal computer. *Special opportunities include:* An international exchange program and an internship program are available. *Placement services include:* Alumni network, career placement, career counseling/planning, electronic job bank, career fairs, job interviews arranged, and resume preparation.

Application Contact Luc Van Mele, Director of MBA Admissions, Laarstraat 16 Blok C, Antwerp, 2610, Belgium. *Phone:* 32-3-2185431. *Fax:* 32-3-2185868. *E-mail:* info@timi.edu.

Katholieke Universiteit Leuven

Leuven School of Business and Economics

Leuven, Belgium

Phone: 32-16-663219 **Fax:** 32-16-663220 **E-mail:** michel.vanbuggenum@econ.kuleuven.ac.be

Business Program(s) Web Site: http://www.econ.kuleuven.ac.be/lsbe

DEGREES M Sc • MAS • MS

M Sc—Master of Advanced Studies in Economics Full-time and part-time. 10 to 22 months to complete program. *Concentrations:* developmental economics, economics, financial economics, industrial/labor relations, international banking, international economics, international finance, public management.

MAS—Master of Financial and Actuarial Engineering Full-time and part-time. University degree in mathematics, physics, applied economics, economics, engineering, commercial engineering or equivalent required. 10 to 60 months to complete program. *Concentrations:* actuarial science, insurance, quantitative analysis, risk management.

MS—Master of Advanced Business Studies Full-time and part-time. TOEFL or British Council Test required. 10 to 60 months to complete program. *Concentration:* economics.

MS—Master of Financial Economics Full-time and part-time. TOEFL or British Council Test required. 10 to 60 months to complete program. *Concentrations:* banking, financial economics, international banking, international finance.

MS—Master of International Business Economics Full-time and part-time. TOEFL or British Council Test required. 10 to 60 months to complete program. *Concentrations:* European business studies, international business, international management, managerial economics.

RESOURCES AND SERVICES 120 on-campus PCs are available to graduate business students. Access to Internet/World Wide Web available. *Personal computer requirements:* Graduate business students are required to have a personal computer. *Special opportunities include:* An international exchange program is available. *Placement services include:* Alumni network, electronic job bank, career fairs, and job interviews arranged.

Application Contact Mrs. Michèle Van Buggenum, Program Coordinator, Naamsestraat 69, Leuven, B-3000, Belgium. *Phone:* 32-16-663219. *Fax:* 32-16-663220. *E-mail:* michel.vanbuggenum@econ.kuleuven.ac.be.

United Business Institutes

MBA Program

Brussels, Belgium

Phone: 32-2-5480480 **Fax:** 32-2-5480489 **E-mail:** info@ubi.edu

Business Program(s) Web Site: http://www.ubi.edu/programs-mba.htm

Graduate Business Unit Enrollment *Total:* 260 (80 full-time; 180 part-time; 104 women; 208 international). *Average Age:* 32.

Graduate Business Faculty *Total:* 75 (14 full-time; 61 part-time).

Admissions *Applied:* 340. *Admitted:* 128. *Enrolled:* 102. *Average GMAT:* 550. *Average GPA:* 3.26

Academic Calendar Trimesters.

After Graduation (Class of 2006–07) *Employed within 3 months of graduation:* 95%. *Average starting salary:* 50,000 euros.

DEGREE MBA

MBA—Master of Business Administration *Concentrations:* information technology, international business, leadership.

RESOURCES AND SERVICES 28 on-campus PCs are available to graduate business students. Access to Internet/World Wide Web available.

Personal computer requirements: Graduate business students are required to have a personal computer. *Special opportunities include:* An international exchange program and an internship program are available. *Placement services include:* Alumni network, job search course, career counseling/planning, electronic job bank, resume referral, and job interviews arranged.

EXPENSES *Tuition:* Full-time: 10,500 euros. Part-time: 700 euros per course. *Tuition (international):* Full-time: 10,500 euros. Part-time: 700 euros per course.

INTERNATIONAL STUDENTS 80% of students enrolled are international students. *Services and facilities:* Counseling/support services, ESL/language courses, Housing location assistance, Language tutoring, Orientation. Financial aid is not available to international students. *Required with application:* TOEFL with recommended score of 600 (paper).

International Student Contact François A. d'Anethan, Dean, Avenue Marnix, 20, Brussels, B-1000, Belgium. *Phone:* 32-2-5480480. *Fax:* 32-2-5480489. *E-mail:* thedean@ubi.edu.

APPLICATION *Required:* GMAT, application form, baccalaureate/first degree, essay, 2 letters of recommendation, personal statement, resume/curriculum vitae, transcripts of college work, 4 years of work experience. *Recommended:* Interview. *Application fee:* 0 euros. Applications for domestic and international students are processed on a rolling basis.

Application Contact François A. d'Anethan, Dean, Avenue Marnix, 20, Brussels, B-1000, Belgium. *Phone:* 32-2-5480480. *Fax:* 32-2-5480489. *E-mail:* info@ubi.edu.

Universite Libre de Bruxelles
Solvay Business School

Brussels, Belgium

Phone: 32-2-6504167 **Fax:** 32-2-6504199 **E-mail:** leclercq@ulb.ac.be

Business Program(s) Web Site: http://www.solvay.edu/mba

DEGREE MA/MBA

MA/MBA—Master of Business Administration Full-time and part-time. Application form, university degree, GMAT, interview, TOEFL, 2-3 years of work experience and 2 letters of reference required. At least 60 total credits required. 10 to 20 months to complete program. *Concentrations:* accounting, business information science, entrepreneurship, European business studies, finance, general MBA, marketing, strategic management, technology management.

RESOURCES AND SERVICES Access to Internet/World Wide Web and online (class) registration available. *Personal computer requirements:* Graduate business students are strongly recommended to purchase or lease a personal computer. *Special opportunities include:* An international exchange program is available. *Placement services include:* Alumni network, career placement, job search course, career counseling/planning, electronic job bank, resume referral, career fairs, job interviews arranged, resume preparation, and career library.

Application Contact Ms. Claudie Leclercq, Programme Coordinator, Avenue F.D. Roosevelt 21, Brussels, 1050, Belgium. *Phone:* 32-2-6504167. *Fax:* 32-2-6504199. *E-mail:* leclercq@ulb.ac.be.

University of Antwerp
University of Antwerp Management School

Antwerp, Belgium

Phone: 32-3-2204471 **Fax:** 32-3-2204953 **E-mail:** cathy.boesmans@ua.ac.be

Business Program(s) Web Site: http://www.uams.be/

Graduate Business Unit Enrollment *Total:* 3,550 (200 full-time; 3,350 part-time; 1,450 women; 80 international).

Graduate Business Faculty *Total:* 300 (50 full-time; 250 part-time).

Admissions *Applied:* 600. *Admitted:* 340. *Enrolled:* 285. *Average GMAT:* 590.

Academic Calendar Semesters.

After Graduation (Class of 2006–07) *Employed within 3 months of graduation:* 95%. *Average starting salary:* 35,000 euros.

DEGREES MBA • MEntr • MF • MIM

MBA—Master of Business Administration Full-time. 60 total credits required. 12 months to complete program. *Concentration:* general MBA.

MEntr—Master in Product Innovation and Entrepreneurship Full-time. 60 total credits required. 10 months to complete program. *Concentrations:* entrepreneurship, strategic management.

MF—Master of Finance Full-time. 60 total credits required. 9 months to complete program. *Concentrations:* banking, finance, financial management/planning, international banking, international finance.

MIM—Master of Global Management Full-time. 60 total credits required. 10 months to complete program. *Concentrations:* Asian business studies, European business studies, international and area business studies, international business.

RESOURCES AND SERVICES 400 on-campus PCs are available to graduate business students. Access to Internet/World Wide Web available. *Personal computer requirements:* Graduate business students are strongly recommended to purchase or lease a personal computer. *Special opportunities include:* An international exchange program and an internship program are available. *Placement services include:* Alumni network, career placement, job search course, career counseling/planning, electronic job bank, resume referral, career fairs, job interviews arranged, resume preparation, and career library.

EXPENSES *Tuition (international):* Full-time: 5770 euros.

INTERNATIONAL STUDENTS 2% of students enrolled are international students. *Services and facilities:* Counseling/support services, ESL/language courses, Housing location assistance, International student housing, International student organization, Orientation, Career management services. Financial aid is not available to international students. *Required with application:* Proof of adequate funds. *Recommended with application:* IELT with recommended score of 6.5; TOEFL.

International Student Contact Cathy Boesmans, Program Assistant, St-Jacobsmarkt 13, Antwerp, 2000, Belgium. *Phone:* 32-3-2204471. *Fax:* 32-3-2204953. *E-mail:* cathy.boesmans@ua.ac.be.

APPLICATION *Required:* Application form, baccalaureate/first degree, essay, interview, resume/curriculum vitae, transcripts of college work. *Recommended:* 2 letters of recommendation, personal statement. *Application fee:* 0 euros. Applications for domestic and international students are processed on a rolling basis.

Application Contact Cathy Boesmans, Program Assistant, St-Jacobsmarkt 13, Antwerp, 2000, Belgium. *Phone:* 32-3-2204471. *Fax:* 32-3-2204953. *E-mail:* cathy.boesmans@ua.ac.be.

Vlerick Leuven Gent Management School
MBA Programmes

Ghent, Belgium

Phone: 32-9-2109231 **Fax:** 32-9-2109700 **E-mail:** marike.vanderstaak@vlerick.be

Business Program(s) Web Site: http://www.vlerick.be/mba/

Graduate Business Unit Enrollment *Total:* 495 (253 full-time; 242 part-time; 116 women; 121 international). *Average Age:* 33.

Graduate Business Faculty *Total:* 81 (42 full-time; 39 part-time).

Vlerick Leuven Gent Management School (continued)

Admissions *Applied:* 835. *Admitted:* 429. *Enrolled:* 370. *Average GMAT:* 640.

Academic Calendar Semesters.

After Graduation (Class of 2006–07) *Employed within 3 months of graduation:* 83%. *Average starting salary:* 76,000 euros.

DEGREES IMBA/MBA • M Mgt • M Mktg • MF

IMBA/MBA—International Master of Business Administration/Master of Business Administration Full-time and part-time. 60 total credits required. 11 to 20 months to complete program. *Concentrations:* entrepreneurship, European business studies, general MBA, technology management.

M Mgt—Master of General Management Full-time. 60 total credits required. 10 to 12 months to complete program. *Concentration:* general MBA.

M Mktg—Master of Marketing Management Full-time. 60 total credits required. 10 to 12 months to complete program. *Concentrations:* international marketing, marketing.

MF—Master of Financial Management Full-time. 60 total credits required. 10 to 12 months to complete program. *Concentrations:* finance, international finance.

RESOURCES AND SERVICES 85 on-campus PCs are available to graduate business students. Access to Internet/World Wide Web and online (class) registration available. *Personal computer requirements:* Graduate business students are not required to have a personal computer. *Special opportunities include:* An international exchange program and an internship program are available. *Placement services include:* Alumni network, career placement, career counseling/planning, electronic job bank, career fairs, job interviews arranged, resume preparation, and career library.

EXPENSES *Tuition:* Full-time: 17,500 euros. Part-time: 23,000 euros per degree program. *Tuition (international):* Full-time: 17,500 euros. Part-time: 23,000 euros per degree program. Tuition and/or fees vary by academic program.

FINANCIAL AID (2007–08) 32 students received aid, including scholarships. *Financial aid application deadline:* 3/31.

Financial Aid Contact Mr. Peter Rafferty, International Development Director, Vlamingenstraat 83, Leuven, 3000, Belgium. *Phone:* 32-16-248887. *Fax:* 32-16-248800. *E-mail:* peter.rafferty@vlerick.be.

INTERNATIONAL STUDENTS 24% of students enrolled are international students. *Services and facilities:* Counseling/support services, ESL/language courses, Housing location assistance, Orientation, Visa Services. Financial aid is available to international students. *Required with application:* TOEFL with recommended score of 250 (computer), 600 (paper), or 100 (Internet); proof of adequate funds; proof of health/immunizations.

International Student Contact Ms. Charlotte De Volder, Full-Time MBA Coordinator, Vlamingenstraat 83, Leuven, 3000, Belgium. *Phone:* 32-16-248889. *Fax:* 32-16-248800. *E-mail:* charlotte.devolder@vlerick.be.

APPLICATION *Required:* GMAT, application form, baccalaureate/first degree, essay, interview, 2 letters of recommendation, resume/curriculum vitae, transcripts of college work, 3 years of work experience. *Application fee:* 50 euros. Applications for domestic and international students are processed on a rolling basis.

Application Contact Ms. Marike Van der Staak, Student Administrator, Reep 1, Gent, 9000, Belgium. *Phone:* 32-9-2109231. *Fax:* 32-9-2109700. *E-mail:* marike.vanderstaak@vlerick.be.

CHINA

China Europe International Business School

MBA Programme

Shanghai, China

Phone: 86-21-28905308 **Fax:** 86-21-28905200 **E-mail:** jsteven@ceibs.edu

Business Program(s) Web Site: http://www.ceibs.edu/

Graduate Business Unit Enrollment *Total:* 5,757 (1,613 full-time; 4,144 part-time; 396 international).

Graduate Business Faculty 31 full-time.

Admissions *Applied:* 1,578. *Admitted:* 612. *Enrolled:* 612. *Average GMAT:* 688.

Academic Calendar 6-week modules.

After Graduation (Class of 2006–07) *Employed within 3 months of graduation:* 90.9%. *Average starting salary:* 312,852 Chinese yuans.

DEGREES MBA

MBA—Executive Master of Business Administration Part-time. 8 years of work experience (including 5 years managerial), employer support for time away from job, fluency in English required. 24 months to complete program. *Concentration:* general MBA.

MBA—Master of Business Administration Full-time. Bachelor's degree or equivalent, minimum of 2 years of full-time work experience, balanced GMAT score, proficiency in English, 2 letters of recommendation, interview, and 3 essays required. 18 months to complete program. *Concentration:* general MBA.

RESOURCES AND SERVICES 69 on-campus PCs are available to graduate business students. Access to Internet/World Wide Web and online (class) registration available. *Personal computer requirements:* Graduate business students are required to have a personal computer. *Special opportunities include:* An international exchange program and an internship program are available. *Placement services include:* Alumni network, career placement, job search course, career counseling/planning, electronic job bank, career fairs, job interviews arranged, resume preparation, and career library.

EXPENSES *Tuition:* Full-time: $17,747. Part-time: $26,478 per degree program. *Tuition (international):* Full-time: $23,333. Part-time: $26,478 per degree program. *Graduate housing:* Room and board costs vary by number of occupants. *Typical cost:* $1717 (room only).

FINANCIAL AID (2007–08) 65 students received aid, including grants, loans, and scholarships. *Financial aid application deadline:* 5/11.

Financial Aid Contact Mr. Steven Ji, Senior Admissions Manager (MBA), 699 Hongfeng Road, Pudong, New District, Shanghai, 201206, China. *Phone:* 86-21-28905308. *Fax:* 86-21-28905200. *E-mail:* jsteven@ceibs.edu.

INTERNATIONAL STUDENTS 7% of students enrolled are international students. *Services and facilities:* Counseling/support services, ESL/language courses, Housing location assistance, International student housing, International student organization, Language tutoring, Orientation, Visa Services, School search for students' children, Assistance with health check-ups, Airport pick-up, Special catering services (for those with special diets), Church/temple search. Financial aid is available to international students. *Required with application:* Proof of health/immunizations. *Recommended with application:* IELT; TOEFL.

International Student Contact Mr. Steven Ji, Acting Senior Admissions Manager, 699 Hongfeng Road, Pudong, New District, Shanghai, 201206, China. *Phone:* 86-21-28905308. *Fax:* 86-21-28905200. *E-mail:* jsteven@ceibs.edu.

APPLICATION *Required:* GMAT, application form, baccalaureate/first degree, essay, interview, 2 letters of recommendation, personal statement, resume/curriculum vitae, transcripts of college work, 2 years of work experience. *Application fee:* $70, $80 (international). Applications for domestic and international students are processed on a rolling basis.

Application Contact Mr. Steven Ji, Senior Admissions Manager (MBA), 699 Hongfeng Road, Pudong, New District, Shanghai, 201206, China. *Phone:* 86-21-28905308. *Fax:* 86-21-28905200. *E-mail:* jsteven@ceibs.edu.

The Chinese University of Hong Kong
Faculty of Business Administration

Hong Kong, China

Phone: 852-26097777 **Fax:** 852-26036289 **E-mail:** hkchan@baf.msmail.cuhk.edu.hk

Business Program(s) Web Site: http://www.baf.cuhk.edu.hk/

Accreditation AACSB—The Association to Advance Collegiate Schools of Business.

DEGREES EMBA • JD/IMBA • JD/MBA • M Acc • M Phil • M Sc • MBA • MS

EMBA—EMBA (Asia Pacific) Part-time. At least 48 total credits required. 24 to 48 months to complete program. *Concentrations:* accounting, business law, business policy/strategy, electronic commerce (E-commerce), finance, human resources management, information technology, international management, leadership, management, managerial economics, marketing, strategic management, supply chain management.

EMBA—EMBA (Xian) Programme Part-time. At least 48 total credits required. 24 to 48 months to complete program. *Concentrations:* accounting, business law, business policy/strategy, electronic commerce (E-commerce), finance, international management, leadership, management, managerial economics, marketing, strategic management, supply chain management.

EMBA—Executive Master of Business Administration Part-time. 48 total credits required. 24 to 48 months to complete program. *Concentrations:* business policy/strategy, business studies, Chinese business studies, finance, general MBA, leadership, management, managerial economics, marketing, organizational management, strategic management.

EMBA—OneMBA, Global Executive MBA Part-time. At least 48 total credits required. 21 to 48 months to complete program. *Concentration:* international and area business studies.

JD/IMBA—JD/MBA Program (Part-Time) Part-time. At least 96 total credits required. 60 to 90 months to complete program. *Concentrations:* accounting, Chinese business studies, decision sciences, entrepreneurship, finance, international business, management, managerial economics, marketing.

JD/MBA—JD/MBA Program (Full-Time) Full-time. At least 102 total credits required. 36 to 60 months to complete program. *Concentrations:* accounting, Chinese business studies, decision sciences, entrepreneurship, finance, international business, management, managerial economics, marketing.

M Acc—Master of Accountancy Program Part-time. At least 30 total credits required. 24 to 36 months to complete program. *Concentration:* accounting.

M Phil—Master of Philosophy in Business Administration Full-time and part-time. At least 12 total credits required. 24 to 60 months to complete program. *Concentrations:* accounting, decision sciences, finance, hospitality management, international business, management, managerial economics, marketing.

M Sc—Executive Master of Professional Accountancy Part-time. At least 36 total credits required. 24 to 36 months to complete program. *Concentration:* accounting.

M Sc—Master of Science in Finance Part-time. At least 30 total credits required. 16 to 48 months to complete program. *Concentration:* finance.

M Sc—Master of Science in Information and Technology Management Part-time. 27 to 33 total credits required. 18 to 48 months to complete program. *Concentration:* management information systems.

MBA—Full-Time MBA Program Full-time. At least 54 total credits required. 16 to 48 months to complete program. *Concentrations:* accounting, Chinese business studies, decision sciences, entrepreneurship, finance, international business, management, managerial economics, marketing.

MBA—MBA Program (Evening and Weekend Modes) Part-time. At least 48 total credits required. 24 to 60 months to complete program. *Concentrations:* accounting, Chinese business studies, decision sciences, entrepreneurship, finance, international business, management, managerial economics, marketing.

MBA—MBA Programme in Finance Part-time. At least 48 total credits required. Minimum of 24 months to complete program. *Concentration:* finance.

MBA—MBA Programme in Health Care Full-time and part-time. At least 49 total credits required. 36 to 60 months to complete program. *Concentrations:* accounting, Chinese business studies, decision sciences, finance, health care, international business, management, managerial economics, marketing.

MS—Master of Science in Marketing Part-time. At least 30 total credits required. Minimum of 18 months to complete program. *Concentrations:* advertising, Chinese business studies, electronic commerce (E-commerce), international marketing, management, marketing, marketing research, strategic management.

RESOURCES AND SERVICES Access to Internet/World Wide Web, online (class) registration, and online grade reports available. *Personal computer requirements:* Graduate business students are strongly recommended to purchase or lease a personal computer. *Special opportunities include:* An international exchange program and an internship program are available. *Placement services include:* Alumni network, career placement, job search course, career counseling/planning, electronic job bank, resume referral, job interviews arranged, resume preparation, and career library.

Application Contact Mr. Lawrence Chan, Administrative Director of Marketing and Student Recruiting, MBA Programmes, Shatin, NT, Hong Kong. *Phone:* 852-26097777. *Fax:* 852-26036289. *E-mail:* hkchan@baf.msmail.cuhk.edu.hk.

City University of Hong Kong
Faculty of Business

Hong Kong SAR, China

Phone: 852-21942658 **Fax:** 852-27887182 **E-mail:** fbsng@cityu.edu.hk

Business Program(s) Web Site: http://www.fb.cityu.edu.hk/postgrad/

Graduate Business Unit Enrollment *Total:* 1,681 (176 full-time; 1,505 part-time).

Graduate Business Faculty *Total:* 238 (203 full-time; 35 part-time).

Admissions *Applied:* 3,190. *Admitted:* 1,181. *Enrolled:* 782. *Average GMAT:* 550. *Average GPA:* 3/4.3 scale

Academic Calendar Trimesters.

DEGREES DBA • EMBA • M Sc • MA • MBA • MSF • MSISM • PhD/Mphil

DBA—Doctor of Business Administration Part-time. A recognized master's degree in business or related disciplines plus 10 years of work experience required. At least 57 total credits required. 48 to 72 months to complete program. *Concentration:* administration.

City University of Hong Kong (continued)

EMBA—Executive Master of Business Administration Part-time. At least 40 total credits required. 24 to 48 months to complete program. *Concentrations:* Chinese business studies, leadership.

M Sc—Master of Science in Applied Economics Full-time and part-time. At least 30 total credits required. *Concentration:* economics.

M Sc—Master of Science in Banking Full-time and part-time. At least 30 total credits required. *Concentration:* banking.

M Sc—Master of Science in Business Information Systems Full-time and part-time. At least 30 total credits required. *Concentration:* information systems.

M Sc—Master of Science in Electronic Business and Knowledge Management Full-time and part-time. At least 30 total credits required. *Concentrations:* electronic commerce (E-commerce), management.

M Sc—Master of Science in Electronic Commerce Full-time and part-time. At least 36 total credits required. *Concentration:* electronic commerce (E-commerce).

M Sc—Master of Science in Financial Engineering Full-time and part-time. At least 30 total credits required. *Concentration:* financial engineering.

M Sc—Master of Science in Professional Accounting and Corporate Governance Full-time and part-time. At least 36 total credits required. *Concentration:* accounting.

MA—Master of Arts in Global Business Management Full-time and part-time. At least 30 total credits required. *Concentrations:* human resources management, international business.

MA—Master of Arts in Operations and Supply Chain Management Full-time and part-time. At least 30 total credits required. *Concentrations:* operations management, supply chain management.

MA—Master of Arts in Quantitative Analysis for Business Full-time and part-time. At least 30 total credits required. *Concentrations:* management science, quantitative analysis.

MBA—Master of Business Administration Full-time and part-time. At least 40 total credits required. 12 to 48 months to complete program. *Concentration:* general MBA.

MSF—Master of Science in Finance Full-time and part-time. At least 30 total credits required. *Concentration:* finance.

MSISM—Master of Science in Information Systems Management Full-time and part-time. At least 30 total credits required. *Concentrations:* information systems, management information systems.

PhD/Mphil—Doctor of Philosophy/Master of Philosophy *Concentrations:* accounting, advertising, banking, business ethics, business policy/strategy, Chinese business studies, decision sciences, economics, electronic commerce (E-commerce), entrepreneurship, finance, financial engineering, financial management/planning, human resources management, information management, information systems, international banking, international business, international economics, international finance, international logistics, international trade, investments and securities, management, management information systems, management science, operations management, organizational behavior/development, quantitative analysis, risk management, statistics, strategic management, taxation, technology management, training and development.

RESOURCES AND SERVICES 1,281 on-campus PCs are available to graduate business students. Access to Internet/World Wide Web, online (class) registration, and online grade reports available. *Personal computer requirements:* Graduate business students are strongly recommended to purchase or lease a personal computer. *Special opportunities include:* An international exchange program and an internship program are available. *Placement services include:* Alumni network, career placement, career counseling/planning, and career library.

EXPENSES *Tuition (state resident):* Full-time: 116,550 Hong Kong dollars. Part-time: 116,550 Hong Kong dollars per degree program. Tuition and/or fees vary by number of courses or credits taken and academic program. *Graduate housing:* Room and board costs vary by number of occupants. *Typical cost:* 37,500 Hong Kong dollars (room only).

FINANCIAL AID (2007–08) 42 students received aid, including scholarships. Aid is available to part-time students. *Financial aid application deadline:* 9/1.

Financial Aid Contact Ms. Stephanie Ng, Executive Officer, G7502, 7/F, Academic Building Green, 83 Tat Chee Avenue, Kowloon Tong, Hong Kong, China. *Phone:* 852-21942658. *Fax:* 852-27887182. *E-mail:* fbsng@cityu.edu.hk.

INTERNATIONAL STUDENTS *Services and facilities:* Counseling/support services, ESL/language courses, Housing location assistance, International student housing, International student organization, Language tutoring, Orientation, Visa Services. Financial aid is not available to international students. *Required with application:* IELT with recommended score of 6.5; TOEFL with recommended score of 213 (computer), 550 (paper), or 79 (Internet).

International Student Contact Ms. Stephanie Ng, Executive Officer, G7502, 7/F, Academic Building Green, 83 Tat Chee Avenue, Kowloon Tong, Hong Kong, China. *Phone:* 852-21942658. *Fax:* 852-27887182. *E-mail:* fbsng@cityu.edu.hk.

APPLICATION *Required:* Application form, baccalaureate/first degree, interview, transcripts of college work, 3 years of work experience. School will accept GMAT and GRE. *Recommended:* Essay, personal statement, resume/curriculum vitae. *Application fee:* 100 Hong Kong dollars. Applications for domestic and international students are processed on a rolling basis.

Application Contact Ms. Stephanie Ng, Executive Officer, G7502, 7/F, Academic Building Green, 83 Tat Chee Avenue, Kowloon Tong, Hong Kong, China. *Phone:* 852-21942658. *Fax:* 852-27887182. *E-mail:* fbsng@cityu.edu.hk.

Hong Kong Baptist University
School of Business

Hong Kong, China

Phone: 852-34117929 **Fax:** 852-34115133 **E-mail:** rpgs@hkbu.edu.hk

Business Program(s) Web Site: http://www.hkbu.edu.hk/~bus

Graduate Business Faculty *Total:* 83 (72 full-time; 11 part-time).

Admissions *Average GMAT:* 500.

Academic Calendar Semesters or trimesters (course specific).

DEGREES DBA • MBA • MS • PhD/Mphil

DBA—Doctor of Business Administration Part-time. Applicant should have a minimum of 10 years of managerial or professional experience at appropriate level. At least 48 total credits required. Minimum of 36 months to complete program. *Concentrations:* business education, business studies.

MBA—Master of Business Administration Full-time and part-time. At least 37 total credits required. 12 to 24 months to complete program. *Concentration:* general MBA.

MS—MSc in Applied Accounting and Finance Part-time. Bachelor's degree with honours in Business from a recognized university or comparable institution, or a professional qualification deemed to be equivalent (e.g. Qualification in accounting & finance). At least 30 total credits required. Minimum of 18 months to complete program. *Concentrations:* accounting, finance.

MS—MSc in Corporate Governance and Directorship Full-time and part-time. At least 29 total credits required. 12 to 18 months to complete program. *Concentrations:* administration, business ethics, business policy/strategy, other.

MS—MSc in Strategic Human Resources Management Part-time. At least 33 total credits required. Minimum of 24 months to complete program. *Concentration:* human resources management.

PhD/Mphil—Doctor of Philosophy/Master of Philosophy Full-time and part-time. 36 to 60 months to complete program. *Concentrations:* accounting, economics, finance, human resources management, law, marketing.

RESOURCES AND SERVICES 110 on-campus PCs are available to graduate business students. Access to Internet/World Wide Web, online (class) registration, and online grade reports available. *Personal computer requirements:* Graduate business students are not required to have a personal computer. *Special opportunities include:* An international exchange program is available. *Placement services include:* Alumni network, career placement, career counseling/planning, and electronic job bank.

FINANCIAL AID (2007–08) Fellowships and scholarships. *Financial aid application deadline:* 4/30.

Financial Aid Contact Ms. Ice Or, Admissions, Scholarship and Financial Aid Section, Academic Registry, Kowloon Tong, Hong Kong, China. *Phone:* 852-34117844. *Fax:* 852-34117373.

INTERNATIONAL STUDENTS *Services and facilities:* Counseling/ support services, ESL/language courses, Housing location assistance, International student housing, Orientation. Financial aid is available to international students. *Recommended with application:* TOEFL with recommended score of 550 (paper).

International Student Contact Mr. Benny Petty, International Student Exchange Officer, Undergraduate Studies Section, Academic Registry, Kowloon Tong, Hong Kong, China. *Phone:* 852-34115347. *Fax:* 852-34115568. *E-mail:* blpetty@hkbu.edu.hk.

APPLICATION *Required:* GMAT, application form, baccalaureate/first degree, interview, 2 letters of recommendation, transcripts of college work, 2 years of work experience. *Application fee:* 150 Hong Kong dollars. *Deadlines:* 6/30 for fall, 4/30 for fall (international).

Application Contact Ms. Cecilia Tsui, Executive Officer I, Office of Graduate School, Kowloon Tong, Hong Kong, China. *Phone:* 852-34117929. *Fax:* 852-34115133. *E-mail:* rpgs@hkbu.edu.hk.

The Hong Kong University of Science and Technology
School of Business and Management

Hong Kong, China

Phone: 852-23587539 **Fax:** 852-27059596 **E-mail:** mba@ust.hk

Business Program(s) Web Site: http://www.bm.ust.hk

Graduate Business Unit Enrollment *Total:* 1,125.

Graduate Business Faculty *Total:* 85 (76 full-time; 9 part-time).

Admissions *Average GMAT:* 643.

Academic Calendar Semesters.

Accreditation AACSB—The Association to Advance Collegiate Schools of Business.

After Graduation (Class of 2006–07) *Employed within 3 months of graduation:* 98%. *Average starting salary:* $78,000.

DEGREES EMBA • M Econ • M Sc • MBA • MBA/MS • MS • UA Undergraduate Associate

---

EMBA—Executive Master of Business Administration Part-time. A strong bachelor's degree, minimum 10 years of work experience, and company sponsorship and support are required; GMAT (if applicable). At least 30 total credits required. 16 months to complete program. *Concentrations:* executive programs, general MBA.

M Econ—Master of Economics Full-time. A strong bachelor's degree and satisfied GMAT/GRE Score are required; TOEFL score (if applicable). At least 30 total credits required. 12 to 60 months to complete program. *Concentration:* economics.

M Sc—Master of Science in Global Finance Part-time. A strong bachelor's degree with good GPA, minimum 5 years full time working experience and two recommendation letters are required; GMAT and TOEFL score (if applicable). At least 24 total credits required. Minimum of 12 months to complete program. *Concentration:* international finance.

MBA—Master of Business Administration Full-time and part-time. A strong bachelor's degree and GMAT score are required; minimum 1 year of work experience for full-time, 3 years for part-time are required; TOEFL score (if applicable). 45 to 52 total credits required. 12 to 60 months to complete program. *Concentrations:* Chinese business studies, finance, general MBA, management information systems.

MBA/MS—Master of Business Administration/Master of Science in Financial Analysis Part-time. Minimum 3 years of work experience, and other admission requirements of the part time MBA and MSc(FA) programs are required to be fulfilled. At least 61 total credits required. 36 to 60 months to complete program. *Concentrations:* Chinese business studies, finance, financial management/planning, general MBA.

MBA/MS—Master of Business Administration/Master of Science in Information Systems Management Part-time. Minimum 3 years of work experience, and other admission requirement of the part time MBA and MSc(IS) are required to be fulfilled. At least 61 total credits required. 36 to 60 months to complete program. *Concentrations:* Chinese business studies, finance, general MBA, management information systems.

MBA/MS—Master of Business Administration/Master of Science in Investment Management Part-time. Minimum 3 years of work experience, and other admissions requirements of the part time MBA and MSc(IM) are required to be fulfilled. At least 61 total credits required. 36 to 60 months to complete program. *Concentrations:* Chinese business studies, finance, general MBA, investments and securities, management information systems.

MS—Master of Science in Information Systems Management Part-time. A strong bachelor's degree, minimum 2 years of professional working experience, and satisfied GMAT/GRE score are required; TOEFL score (if applicable). At least 30 total credits required. 16 to 60 months to complete program. *Concentration:* information systems.

MS—Master of Science in Investment Management Part-time. A strong bachelor's degree with second class honors or above, and satisfied GMAT score are required; work experience is strongly preferred; TOEFL score (if applicable). At least 30 total credits required. 18 to 60 months to complete program. *Concentration:* investments and securities.

UA Undergraduate Associate—Master of Science in Financial Analysis Part-time. A strong bachelor's degree with second class honors or above, and satisfied GMAT score are required; work experience is strongly preferred; TOEFL score (if applicable). At least 30 total credits required. 18 to 60 months to complete program. *Concentrations:* finance, investments and securities.

RESOURCES AND SERVICES 330 on-campus PCs are available to graduate business students. Access to Internet/World Wide Web, online (class) registration, and online grade reports available. *Personal computer requirements:* Graduate business students are strongly recommended to purchase or lease a personal computer. *Special opportunities include:* An international exchange program and an internship program are available. *Placement services include:* Alumni network, career placement, job search course, career counseling/planning, electronic job bank, resume referral, career fairs, job interviews arranged, resume preparation, and career library.

EXPENSES *Typical graduate housing cost:* $4600 (room only).

FINANCIAL AID (2007–08) Scholarships.

INTERNATIONAL STUDENTS *Services and facilities:* Counseling/ support services, ESL/language courses, Housing location assistance, International student housing, International student organization, Orientation, Visa Services, 10 language courses and cultural activities. Financial aid is available to international students.

APPLICATION *Required:* GMAT, application form, baccalaureate/first degree, essay, interview, 2 letters of recommendation, transcripts of college work, work experience. *Recommended:* Resume/curriculum vitae. *Application fee:* $64. *Deadlines:* 12/15 for winter (international), 3/12 for spring (international).

The Hong Kong University of Science and Technology (continued)

Application Contact MBA Program Office, Room 5601, 5/F, Annex, Clearwater Bay, Kowloon, Hong Kong. *Phone:* 852-23587539. *Fax:* 852-27059596. *E-mail:* mba@ust.hk.

Nanjing University
School of Business

Nanjing, China

Phone: 86-25-83621006 **Fax:** 86-25-83317769 **E-mail:** zmmba@nju.edu.cn

Business Program(s) Web Site: http://www.nju.edu.cn/cps/site/NJU/njue/dep/business/index.htm

Graduate Business Unit Enrollment *Total:* 1,350 (420 full-time; 930 part-time; 530 women; 18 international).

Graduate Business Faculty *Total:* 153 (103 full-time; 50 part-time).

Admissions *Applied:* 1,439. *Admitted:* 483. *Enrolled:* 477.

Academic Calendar Semesters.

After Graduation (Class of 2006–07) *Employed within 3 months of graduation:* 90%. *Average starting salary:* 120,000 Chinese yuans.

DEGREES EMBA • IEMBA • IMBA • MBA

EMBA—Executive Master of Business Administration Part-time. At least 2 years of top management experiences, college level degree. At least 42 total credits required. Minimum of 20 months to complete program. *Concentration:* general MBA.

IEMBA—International Executive Master of Business Administration Part-time. 3 years of top management experiences, college level degree, proficient English. At least 45 total credits required. Minimum of 20 months to complete program. *Concentration:* general MBA.

IMBA—International Master of Business Administration Full-time. National MBA Exam, GPA 3.0, TOEFL 550, GMAT 500. At least 50 total credits required. Minimum of 24 months to complete program. *Concentration:* general MBA.

MBA—Master of Business Administration Full-time and part-time. 3 years of work experience and exposure to high mathematics required. 44 to 60 total credits required. 21 to 60 months to complete program. *Concentrations:* accounting, advertising, banking, executive programs, financial management/planning, general MBA, human resources management, leadership, marketing, organizational behavior/development, strategic management.

RESOURCES AND SERVICES 300 on-campus PCs are available to graduate business students. Access to Internet/World Wide Web, online (class) registration, and online grade reports available. *Personal computer requirements:* Graduate business students are strongly recommended to purchase or lease a personal computer. *Special opportunities include:* An international exchange program and an internship program are available. *Placement services include:* Alumni network, career placement, career counseling/planning, electronic job bank, career fairs, job interviews arranged, and resume preparation.

EXPENSES *Tuition:* Full-time: 28,000 Chinese yuans. Part-time: 28,000 Chinese yuans per year. *Tuition (international):* Full-time: 28,000 Chinese yuans. Part-time: 28,000 Chinese yuans per year. *Required fees:* Full-time: 800 Chinese yuans. Part-time: 800 Chinese yuans per year.

FINANCIAL AID (2007–08) 60 students received aid, including fellowships, scholarships, teaching assistantships, and work study.

Financial Aid Contact Bingnan Sang, Deputy Director of MBA Educational Center, Hankou Road #22, Nanjing, Jiangsu Province, 210093, China. *Phone:* 86-25-83592461. *Fax:* 86-25-83592461. *E-mail:* sangbn@nju.edu.cn.

INTERNATIONAL STUDENTS 1% of students enrolled are international students. *Services and facilities:* Counseling/support services, ESL/language courses, Housing location assistance, International student housing, International student organization, Language tutoring, Orientation, Visa Services. Financial aid is available to international students. *Required with application:* Proof of health/immunizations. *Recommended with application:* TOEFL with recommended score of 550 (paper); proof of adequate funds.

International Student Contact Wanwen Dai, Director of International Business Center, Hankou Road #22, Nanjing, Jiangsu Province, 210093, China. *Phone:* 86-25-83592401. *Fax:* 86-25-83260037. *E-mail:* wwdai@nju.edu.cn.

APPLICATION *Required:* Application form, baccalaureate/first degree, essay, 2 letters of recommendation, personal statement, resume/curriculum vitae, transcripts of college work, 3 years of work experience. *Recommended:* Interview. *Application fee:* $40, $60 (international). *Deadlines:* 10/20 for fall, 10/20 for spring. Applications for international students are processed on a rolling basis.

Application Contact Ming Gong, MBA Educational Center, Hankou Road #22, Nanjing, Jiangsu Province, 210093, China. *Phone:* 86-25-83621006. *Fax:* 86-25-83317769. *E-mail:* zmmba@nju.edu.cn.

CYPRUS

Cyprus International Institute of Management
MBA Programme

Nicosia, Cyprus

Phone: 357-22462246 **Fax:** 357-22331121 **E-mail:** theodora@ciim.ac.cy

Business Program(s) Web Site: http://www.ciim.ac.cy

Graduate Business Unit Enrollment *Total:* 275 (100 full-time; 175 part-time; 118 women; 60 international). *Average Age:* 28.

Graduate Business Faculty *Total:* 47 (12 full-time; 35 part-time).

Admissions *Applied:* 450. *Admitted:* 200. *Enrolled:* 150. *Average GMAT:* 650. *Average GPA:* 3.2

Academic Calendar Modular.

After Graduation (Class of 2006–07) *Employed within 3 months of graduation:* 90%. *Average starting salary:* $45,000.

DEGREES MBA • MPA

MBA—Master of Business Administration Full-time and part-time. At least 105 total credits required. 12 to 36 months to complete program. *Concentrations:* combined degrees, entrepreneurship, executive programs, finance, general MBA, human resources management, marketing, organizational behavior/development, strategic management.

MPA—Master in Public Sector Management Full-time and part-time. At least 105 total credits required. 12 to 36 months to complete program. *Concentrations:* public and private management, public management, public policy and administration.

RESOURCES AND SERVICES 40 on-campus PCs are available to graduate business students. Access to Internet/World Wide Web, online (class) registration, and online grade reports available. *Personal computer requirements:* Graduate business students are strongly recommended to purchase or lease a personal computer. *Special opportunities include:* An international exchange program and an internship program are available. *Placement services include:* Alumni network, career placement, job search course, career counseling/planning, electronic job bank, resume referral, career fairs, job interviews arranged, resume preparation, and career library.

EXPENSES *Tuition:* Full-time: 14,560 euros. *Tuition (international):* Full-time: 14,560 euros. *Required fees:* Full-time: 200 euros. *Graduate*

housing: Room and board costs vary by number of occupants and type of accommodation. *Typical cost:* 7000 euros (including board), 3000 euros (room only).

FINANCIAL AID (2007–08) 45 students received aid, including grants, loans, research assistantships, scholarships, and work study. Aid is available to part-time students. *Financial aid application deadline:* 7/30.

Financial Aid Contact Mrs. Maria Ioannou, Graduate Course Administrator, 21 Akademias Avenue, PO Box 20378, Nicosia, 2151, Cyprus. *Phone:* 357-22-462246. *Fax:* 357-22-331121. *E-mail:* mioannou@ciim.ac.cy.

INTERNATIONAL STUDENTS 22% of students enrolled are international students. *Services and facilities:* Counseling/support services, Housing location assistance, International student housing, International student organization, Language tutoring, Orientation, Visa Services, Career services. Financial aid is available to international students. *Required with application:* Proof of adequate funds; proof of health/immunizations. *Recommended with application:* IELT with recommended score of 6.5; TOEFL with recommended score of 237 (computer) or 580 (paper).

International Student Contact Mr. Marios Siathas, Head of International Office, 21 Akademias Avenue, PO Box 20378, Aglandjia, Nicosia, 2151, Cyprus. *Phone:* 357-22462246. *Fax:* 357-22331121. *E-mail:* marios@ciim.ac.cy.

APPLICATION *Required:* Application form, baccalaureate/first degree, interview, 2 letters of recommendation, personal statement, transcripts of college work. School will accept GMAT and GRE. *Recommended:* Resume/curriculum vitae, 2 years of work experience. *Application fee:* 50 euros. Applications for domestic and international students are processed on a rolling basis.

Application Contact Mrs. Theodora Petasi, Admissions Officer, 21 Akademias Avenue, PO Box 20378, Aglandjia, Nicosia, 2151, Cyprus. *Phone:* 357-22462246. *Fax:* 357-22331121. *E-mail:* theodora@ciim.ac.cy.

DENMARK

The Aarhus School of Business

Faculty of Business Administration

Aarhus, Denmark

Phone: 45-89486688 **E-mail:** mbainfo@asb.dk

Business Program(s) Web Site: http://www.asb.dk

Graduate Business Unit Enrollment *Average Age:* 40.

Admissions *Applied:* 40. *Admitted:* 25. *Enrolled:* 25.

Academic Calendar Semesters.

DEGREES EMBA • MBA/LLM • MBC

EMBA—Executive Master of Business Administration with Focus on Change Management Part-time. 24 months to complete program. *Concentrations:* administration, business policy/strategy, commerce, entrepreneurship, executive programs, general MBA, human resources management, leadership, management, organizational behavior/development, organizational management.

MBA/LLM—LLM in VAT and Other In-Direct Taxes Part-time. 24 months to complete program. *Concentrations:* administration, business law, law, other, public policy and administration, taxation.

MBC—Master of Corporate Communication Part-time. 24 months to complete program. *Concentrations:* commerce, information management, leadership, management, management communication, management consulting, management science, media administration, strategic management.

RESOURCES AND SERVICES Access to Internet/World Wide Web and online grade reports available. *Personal computer requirements:* Graduate business students are strongly recommended to purchase or lease a personal computer. *Placement services include:* Alumni network.

APPLICATION *Required:* Application form, essay, interview, 2 letters of recommendation, resume/curriculum vitae, 3 years of work experience. Applications for domestic students are processed on a rolling basis.

Application Contact Louise Rechnitzer Lauridsen, Admissions, Fuglesangs Allé 4, Århus V, 8210, Denmark. *Phone:* 45-89486688. *E-mail:* mbainfo@asb.dk.

Copenhagen Business School

Faculty of Economics and Business Administration

Copenhagen, Denmark

Phone: 45-3815-3016 **Fax:** 45-3815-3010 **E-mail:** lm.mba@cbs.dk

Business Program(s) Web Site: http://www.cbs.dk/

Graduate Business Unit Enrollment *Total:* 7,000 (5,000 full-time; 2,000 part-time). *Average Age:* 31.

Admissions *Applied:* 120. *Admitted:* 50. *Enrolled:* 36. *Average GMAT:* 600.

Academic Calendar Semesters.

After Graduation (Class of 2006–07) *Employed within 3 months of graduation:* 91%.

DEGREES MB • MBA • MPA • MS

MB—Master of Corporate Communication Part-time. Minimum three years of work experience, proficiency in English required. 24 months to complete program. *Concentrations:* advertising, marketing, media administration, organizational management.

MBA—Executive MBA Program Part-time. 5 years of relevant full-time work experience and proficiency in Danish and English required. 21 months to complete program. *Concentrations:* entrepreneurship, leadership, strategic management.

MBA—Full-Time MBA Full-time. Minimum 2 years of work experience; proficiency in English required. 12 months to complete program. *Concentrations:* entrepreneurship, leadership, strategic management.

MBA—Master of Business Administration in Shipping and Logistics Part-time. Bachelor's degree, proficiency in English and personal recommendations required. 24 months to complete program. *Concentrations:* human resources management, law, logistics, management, port/maritime management.

MBA—Master of Management Development Part-time. Bachelor's degree, minimum of 5 years of relevant full-time work experience and proficiency in Danish and English required. 24 months to complete program. *Concentration:* management.

MPA—Master of Public Administration Part-time. Minimum of 5 years of work experience; proficiency in Danish and English required. 24 months to complete program. *Concentrations:* public management, public policy and administration, strategic management.

MS—Master of Science in Business Administration and Commercial Law Full-time. Proficiency in Danish required. 24 to 70 months to complete program. *Concentrations:* business law, economics, finance, organizational behavior/development, taxation.

MS—Master of Science in Business Administration and Computer Science Full-time. Proficiency in Danish required. 24 to 70 months to complete program. *Concentrations:* economics, information management, management information systems, organizational behavior/development, project management.

MS—Master of Science in Business Administration and Management Science Full-time. Proficiency in Danish required. 24 to 70 months to

Copenhagen Business School (continued)

complete program. *Concentrations:* economics, finance, management science, management systems analysis, marketing research, quantitative analysis.

MS—Master of Science in Business Administration and Modern Language Full-time. Proficiency in English and German, French, Spanish, Russian or Japanese required. 24 to 70 months to complete program. *Concentrations:* developmental economics, international and area business studies, international business, international management.

MS—Master of Science in Business Administration and Philosophy Full-time. Proficiency in Danish required. 24 to 70 months to complete program. *Concentrations:* business ethics, business policy/strategy, economics, management.

MS—Master of Science in Business Economics and Auditing Full-time. Proficiency in Danish required. 24 to 70 months to complete program. *Concentrations:* accounting, business law, taxation.

MS—Master of Science in Economics and Business Administration Full-time. Proficiency in Danish/English required. 24 to 70 months to complete program. *Concentrations:* economics, finance, human resources management, international business, international economics, international logistics, international management, international marketing, organizational behavior/development, organizational management, strategic management, supply chain management, technology management.

RESOURCES AND SERVICES 500 on-campus PCs are available to graduate business students. Access to Internet/World Wide Web available. *Personal computer requirements:* Graduate business students are required to have a personal computer. *Placement services include:* Alumni network, job search course, career counseling/planning, career fairs, and resume preparation.

EXPENSES *Tuition (state resident):* Full-time: 245,000 Danish kroner. *Tuition (nonresident):* Full-time: 245,000 Danish kroner. *Tuition (international):* Full-time: 245,000 Danish kroner.

FINANCIAL AID (2007–08) 14 students received aid, including scholarships. *Financial aid application deadline:* 5/1.

Financial Aid Contact Mr. Lee Milligan, Full-time MBA Admissions Manager, Dalgas Have 15, Frederiksberg, 2000, Denmark. *Phone:* 45-3815-3016. *Fax:* 45-3815-3016. *E-mail:* lm.mba@cbs.dk.

INTERNATIONAL STUDENTS *Services and facilities:* Counseling/support services, ESL/language courses, Housing location assistance, International student housing, International student organization, Orientation. Financial aid is available to international students.

International Student Contact Ms. Line Nørman Christensen, Full-Time MBA Program Manager, Dalgas Have 15, Frederiksberg, 2000, Denmark. *Phone:* 45-3815-3015. *Fax:* 45-3815-3017. *E-mail:* lnc.mba@cbs.dk.

APPLICATION *Required:* GMAT, application form, baccalaureate/first degree, essay, interview, 2 letters of recommendation, resume/curriculum vitae, transcripts of college work, work experience. Applications for domestic and international students are processed on a rolling basis.

Application Contact Mr. Lee Milligan, Full-time MBA Admissions Manager, Dalgas Have 15, Frederiksberg, 2000, Denmark. *Phone:* 45-3815-3016. *Fax:* 45-3815-3010. *E-mail:* lm.mba@cbs.dk.

EGYPT

The American University in Cairo

School of Business, Economics and Communication

Cairo, Egypt

Phone: 202-2-7975612 **Fax:** 202-2-7957565 **E-mail:** emallawany@aucegypt.edu

Business Program(s) Web Site: http://www.aucegypt.edu

Graduate Business Unit Enrollment *Total:* 200 (121 full-time; 79 part-time; 70 women; 7 international). *Average Age:* 28.

Graduate Business Faculty *Total:* 49 (25 full-time; 24 part-time).

Admissions *Applied:* 278. *Admitted:* 56. *Enrolled:* 47. *Average GMAT:* 500. *Average GPA:* 3.25

Academic Calendar Semesters.

DEGREES   MA • MBA • MPA

MA—Program in Economics Full-time and part-time. GRE required. 36 total credits required. 18 to 60 months to complete program. *Concentrations:* developmental economics, economics, financial economics, industrial/labor relations, international economics, quantitative analysis.

MBA—Master of Business Administration Full-time and part-time. 33 to 48 total credits required. 24 to 72 months to complete program. *Concentrations:* business law, information systems, international banking, international marketing, international trade, management, marketing research, operations management, project management, strategic management.

MPA—Master of Public Administration Full-time and part-time. Up to 3 pre-requisite courses required. Interview is preferred. 27 to 33 total credits required. 18 to 60 months to complete program. *Concentrations:* city/urban administration, environmental economics/management, international and area business studies, organizational behavior/development, public policy and administration, research and development administration, system management.

RESOURCES AND SERVICES 265 on-campus PCs are available to graduate business students. Access to Internet/World Wide Web, online (class) registration, and online grade reports available. *Personal computer requirements:* Graduate business students are strongly recommended to purchase or lease a personal computer. *Placement services include:* Alumni network, career counseling/planning, resume referral, career fairs, job interviews arranged, resume preparation, and career library.

FINANCIAL AID (2007–08) 69 students received aid, including fellowships, research assistantships, scholarships, teaching assistantships, and work study. Aid is available to part-time students. *Financial aid application deadline:* 9/15.

Financial Aid Contact Ms. Samia S. El Shazly, Director, Student Financial Affairs, 113 Kasr El Aini Street, PO Box 2511, Cairo, 11511, Egypt. *Phone:* 20-2-27975691. *Fax:* 20-2-27957565. *E-mail:* shazly@aucegypt.edu.

INTERNATIONAL STUDENTS 4% of students enrolled are international students. *Services and facilities:* Counseling/support services, ESL/language courses, International student organization, Orientation, Visa Services, International graduate programs office. Financial aid is available to international students. *Required with application:* TOEFL with recommended score of 79 (Internet); TWE with recommended score of 4.2; proof of adequate funds; proof of health/immunizations.

International Student Contact Ms. Sawsan Mardini, International Graduate Program Coordinator, Office of Graduate Studies and Research, 113 Kasr El Aini Street, Cairo, Egypt. *Phone:* 20-2-27975530. *Fax:* 20-2-27957565. *E-mail:* aucgrad@aucegypt.edu.

APPLICATION *Required:* GMAT, application form, baccalaureate/first degree, 2 letters of recommendation, personal statement, resume/curriculum vitae, transcripts of college work, 2 years of work experience. *Recommended:* Interview. *Application fee:* $50. Applications for domestic and international students are processed on a rolling basis.

Application Contact Ms. Eman Osama El Mallawany, International Graduate Student Recruitment and Admission, Office of Graduate Studies and Research, 113 Kasr El Aini Street, PO Box 2511, Cairo, 11511, Egypt. *Phone:* 202-2-7975612. *Fax:* 202-2-7957565. *E-mail:* emallawany@aucegypt.edu.

FINLAND

University of Vaasa
Faculty of Business Administration

Vaasa, Finland

Phone: +358-6-3248111 **Fax:** +358-6-3248350 **E-mail:** helena.etelaaho@uwasa.fi

Business Program(s) Web Site: http://www.uwasa.fi/samjay/b_admin/index.html

---
DEGREE EMBA

EMBA—MBA Part-time. *Concentration:* general MBA.

RESOURCES AND SERVICES *Personal computer requirements:* Graduate business students are strongly recommended to purchase or lease a personal computer.

Application Contact Ms. Helena Etelaaho, Training Manager, PO Box 700, 65101 Vaasa, Finland. *Phone:* +358-6-3248111. *Fax:* +358-6-3248350. *E-mail:* helena.etelaaho@uwasa.fi.

FRANCE

École Nationale des Ponts et Chaussées
ENPC MBA

Paris, France

Phone: 33-1-44582852 **Fax:** 33-1-40159347 **E-mail:** admissions@enpcmbaparis.com

Business Program(s) Web Site: http://www.enpcmbaparis.com

Graduate Business Unit Enrollment *Total:* 47 (44 full-time; 3 part-time; 15 women; 28 international).

Graduate Business Faculty *Total:* 38 (7 full-time; 31 part-time).

Admissions *Applied:* 200. *Admitted:* 75. *Enrolled:* 47. *Average GMAT:* 600. *Average GPA:* 3.0

Academic Calendar Semesters.

After Graduation (Class of 2006–07) *Employed within 3 months of graduation:* 60%. *Average starting salary:* 65,000 euros.

DEGREES EMBA • MBA

EMBA—Executive MBA *Concentration:* executive programs.

MBA—Master of Business Administration in International Business Full-time and part-time. At least 18 total credits required. 10 months to complete program. *Concentrations:* administration of technological information, Asian business studies, business ethics, business law, business policy/strategy, business studies, decision sciences, economics, electronic commerce (E-commerce), entrepreneurship, European business studies, executive programs, finance, financial management/planning, general MBA, international and area business studies, international banking, international business, international development management, international economics, international finance, international logistics, international management, international marketing, international trade, Japanese business studies, leadership, logistics, management, management consulting, management information systems, marketing, operations management, organizational behavior/development, organizational management, profit management, project management, quality management,

quantitative analysis, resources management, risk management, strategic management, supply chain management, taxation, technology management, telecommunications management, transportation management.

RESOURCES AND SERVICES 40 on-campus PCs are available to graduate business students. Access to Internet/World Wide Web available. *Personal computer requirements:* Graduate business students are strongly recommended to purchase or lease a personal computer. *Special opportunities include:* An international exchange program and an internship program are available. *Placement services include:* Alumni network, career placement, job search course, career counseling/planning, electronic job bank, resume referral, career fairs, job interviews arranged, resume preparation, and career library.

FINANCIAL AID (2007–08) 11 students received aid, including scholarships. Aid is available to part-time students. *Financial aid application deadline:* 7/15.

Financial Aid Contact Miss Michela Tagliaferri, Marketing and Admissions Coordinator, 28 rue des Saints-Pères, Paris, 75343, France. *Phone:* 33-1-44582852. *Fax:* 33-1-40159347. *E-mail:* admissions@enpcmbaparis.com.

INTERNATIONAL STUDENTS 60% of students enrolled are international students. *Services and facilities:* Counseling/support services, Housing location assistance, Orientation, Career development services. Financial aid is available to international students. *Required with application:* IELT with recommended score of 7; TOEFL with recommended score of 240 (computer) or 550 (paper). *Recommended with application:* Proof of adequate funds; proof of health/immunizations.

International Student Contact Mrs. Michela Tagliaferri, Marketing and Admissions Coordinator, 28 Rue des Saints-Pères, Paris, 75343, France. *Phone:* 33-1-44582852. *Fax:* 33-1-40159347. *E-mail:* admissions@enpcmbaparis.com.

APPLICATION *Required:* GMAT, application form, essay, interview, 3 letters of recommendation, personal statement, resume/curriculum vitae, transcripts of college work, 3 years of work experience. *Recommended:* Baccalaureate/first degree. *Application fee:* 100 euros. Applications for domestic and international students are processed on a rolling basis.

Application Contact Ms. Michela Tagliaferri, Marketing and Admissions Manager, 28 rue des Saints-Pères, Paris, 75343, France. *Phone:* 33-1-44582852. *Fax:* 33-1-40159347. *E-mail:* admissions@enpcmbaparis.com.

ESCP-EAP European School of Management
ESCP-EAP European School of Management

Paris, France

Phone: 33-1-49232115 **Fax:** 33-1-49232012 **E-mail:** leparmentier@escp-eap.net

Business Program(s) Web Site: http://www.escp-eap.eu

Graduate Business Unit Enrollment *Total:* 3,500 (3,100 full-time; 400 part-time).

Graduate Business Faculty *Total:* 167 (121 full-time; 46 part-time).

Admissions *Applied:* 6,200. *Admitted:* 1,050. *Enrolled:* 777.

Academic Calendar Continuous.

Accreditation AACSB—The Association to Advance Collegiate Schools of Business.

DEGREES EMBA • MBA • MEB • MS

EMBA—European Executive Master of Business Administration in Paris, London, Madrid and Berlin Part-time. Modular Program in English delivered across 4 campuses; at least 5 years of relevant experience required. Maximum of 18 months to complete program. *Concentrations:* financial management/planning, human resources man-

ESCP-EAP European School of Management (continued)

agement, management, managerial economics, marketing, strategic management, technology management.

MBA—International Master of Business Administration in Paris Full-time. Proficiency in English, minimum GMAT score of 600 and 3 years of relevant work experience required. At least 60 total credits required. Minimum of 12 months to complete program. *Concentrations:* international business, international management, management, strategic management.

MEB—Master in European Business Full-time. Mobility (two 6-month periods in 2 countries); Languages (depends on countries chosen—any combination of English, French, German, or Spanish required). 12 to 15 months to complete program. *Concentrations:* business studies, European business studies, international business, international management.

MS—Master of Science in Management Full-time. Mobility and Languages: 2 year International Track (English and French required); 3 year European Track (English, French plus either German or Spanish required). 24 to 36 months to complete program. *Concentrations:* business studies, European business studies, international business, international management, management.

MS—Mastere Spécialise Full-time. Specialized master's programs are taught in Paris in French (some courses are taught in English). 12 to 14 months to complete program. *Concentrations:* entrepreneurship, finance, financial engineering, human resources management, marketing, organizational management, project management, quality management, strategic management.

RESOURCES AND SERVICES 450 on-campus PCs are available to graduate business students. Access to Internet/World Wide Web available. *Personal computer requirements:* Graduate business students are required to have a personal computer. *Special opportunities include:* An international exchange program and an internship program are available. *Placement services include:* Alumni network, job search course, career counseling/planning, electronic job bank, resume referral, career fairs, job interviews arranged, resume preparation, and career library.

FINANCIAL AID (2007–08) Research assistantships and scholarships. *Financial aid application deadline:* 10/15.

Financial Aid Contact Mrs. Sophia Bensoula, Students Assistant Administrator, Paris Campus, 79 avenue de la République, Paris, 75543, France. *Phone:* 33-1- 49232026. *Fax:* 33-1-49232012. *E-mail:* sbensoula@escp-eap.net.

INTERNATIONAL STUDENTS *Services and facilities:* Counseling/support services, Housing location assistance, Language tutoring, Orientation. Financial aid is available to international students. *Required with application:* TOEFL with recommended score of 250 (computer) or 600 (paper); proof of adequate funds. *Recommended with application:* IELT with recommended score of 6.5.

International Student Contact Ms. Dina Brassart, Promotion Administrator, ESCP-EAP Paris Campus, 79 avenue de la République, Paris, 75543, France. *Phone:* 33-1-49232145. *Fax:* 33-1-49232012. *E-mail:* dbrassart@escp-eap.net.

APPLICATION *Required:* GMAT, application form, baccalaureate/first degree, essay, interview, 2 letters of recommendation, personal statement, resume/curriculum vitae, transcripts of college work, work experience. *Application fee:* 175 euros. Applications for domestic and international students are processed on a rolling basis.

Application Contact Mrs. Marion Leparmentier, Admissions Manager, Paris Campus, 79 avenue de la République, Paris, 75543, France. *Phone:* 33-1-49232115. *Fax:* 33-1-49232012. *E-mail:* leparmentier@escp-eap.net.

European Institute of Purchasing Management

MBA Programs

Archamps, France

Phone: 33-4-50315678 **Fax:** 33-4-50315680 **E-mail:** gmeignan@eipm.org

Business Program(s) Web Site: http://www.eipm.org

Graduate Business Unit Enrollment *Total:* 20 (20 part-time; 8 women; 15 international). *Average Age:* 37.

Graduate Business Faculty *Total:* 48 (8 full-time; 40 part-time).

Admissions *Applied:* 25. *Admitted:* 18. *Enrolled:* 18.

DEGREES EMBA • MSM-SC/MBA

EMBA—Executive Master of Business Administration with a Focus on Purchasing and Supply Chain Management Part-time. 18 to 36 months to complete program. *Concentration:* supply chain management.

MSM-SC/MBA—Executive Master of Science in Purchasing and Supply Chain Part-time. 12 to 18 months to complete program. *Concentration:* supply chain management.

RESOURCES AND SERVICES 3 on-campus PCs are available to graduate business students. Access to Internet/World Wide Web available. *Personal computer requirements:* Graduate business students are strongly recommended to purchase or lease a personal computer. *Placement services include:* Alumni network.

INTERNATIONAL STUDENTS 75% of students enrolled are international students. *Services and facilities:* Counseling/support services, Housing location assistance, Orientation. *Required with application:* TOEFL with recommended score of 600 (paper); proof of adequate funds.

International Student Contact Gwenaelle Meignan, Training and MBA Coordinator, French Geneva Campus, Bât Le Mont Blanc II, Archamps, 74160, France. *Phone:* 33-4-50315678. *Fax:* 33-4-50315680. *E-mail:* gmeignan@eipm.org.

APPLICATION *Required:* GMAT, application form, interview, 2 letters of recommendation, personal statement, resume/curriculum vitae, 8 years of work experience. Applications for domestic and international students are processed on a rolling basis.

Application Contact Gwenaelle Meignan, Training and MBA Coordinator, French Geneva Campus, Bât Le Mont Blanc II, Archamps, 74160, France. *Phone:* 33-4-50315678. *Fax:* 33-4-50315680. *E-mail:* gmeignan@eipm.org.

Groupe CERAM

Ceram ESC Nice School of Management

Sophia Antipolis, France

E-mail: admissions@ecft.nl

Business Program(s) Web Site: http://www.ceram.edu/xfm

DEGREES EMBA • M Sc • MSCIB • MSCIF

EMBA—XFM Part-time. Work experience required. *Concentrations:* finance, financial economics, financial engineering, financial information systems, financial management/planning.

M Sc—Master of Science in Business Tourism Full-time. *Concentration:* travel industry/tourism management.

MSCIB—Master of Science in International Business Full-time. Minimum of 10 months to complete program. *Concentration:* international business.

MSCIF—Master of Science in International Finance Full-time. Minimum of 10 months to complete program. *Concentration:* international finance.

RESOURCES AND SERVICES *Personal computer requirements:* Graduate business students are required to have a personal computer. *Special opportunities include:* An international exchange program and an internship program are available. *Placement services include:* Alumni network, career placement, job interviews arranged, and resume preparation.

Application Contact Admissions Office, BP 085, Sophia Antipolis Cedex, 06902, France. *E-mail:* admissions@ecft.nl.

HEC Paris
HEC MBA Program

Jouy-en-Josas, France

Phone: 33-1-39679546 **Fax:** 33-1-39677465 **E-mail:** admissionmba@hec.fr

Business Program(s) Web Site: http://www.hec.fr/hec/eng/mba/index.html

Graduate Business Unit Enrollment *Total:* 200 (200 full-time; 67 women).

Graduate Business Faculty *Total:* 173 (106 full-time; 67 part-time).

Admissions *Applied:* 1,391. *Admitted:* 306. *Enrolled:* 200. *Average GMAT:* 660.

Academic Calendar Four 4-month periods.

Accreditation AACSB—The Association to Advance Collegiate Schools of Business.

After Graduation (Class of 2006–07) *Employed within 3 months of graduation:* 63%. *Average starting salary:* 79,215 euros.

DEGREE MBA

MBA—The Full-Time MBA Program Full-time. 120 to 128 total credits required. 16 months to complete program. *Concentrations:* accounting, business law, corporate accounting, economics, entrepreneurship, European business studies, finance, financial economics, financial management/planning, human resources management, international banking, international business, international economics, international finance, international management, international marketing, management, management consulting, managerial economics, marketing, organizational behavior/development, production management, project management, public and private management, strategic management, supply chain management.

The HEC MBA Program trains high-potential managers to take on positions of international business leadership. Located in the heart of Europe, HEC Paris offers the best of all worlds: its human class size of 200 participants, combined with its ideal sixteen-month program length, allows participants to engage in a transformative experience of personal and professional development. Fully accredited by AMBA, EQUIS, and AACSB, the HEC MBA Program is consistently ranked among the top ten European M.B.A. programs and among the top twenty programs worldwide. In the Financial Times 2008 Global MBA Ranking, HEC ranked eighteenth worldwide, earning stellar marks for international mobility (second) and career progress (eighth).

The HEC MBA Program is divided into two 8-month periods: the Core Phase and the Personalized Phase. During Core Phase, participants develop the fundamental management knowledge and techniques that equip them to advance in their careers.

In the Personalized Phase, participants customize their curriculum by choosing electives and selecting a specialized track in entrepreneurship, finance, marketing, strategy. They may also gain corporate exposure through M.B.A. fieldwork by completing an Individual Professional Project, a Company Consulting Project, a Creative Academic Project, or a Mission And Action Project. Participants may further expand their international perspective and network by participating in an exchange or dual-degree program with one of HEC's prestigious partner institutions. The comprehensive, personalized HEC MBA Program allows participants to broaden their knowledge base, expand their management competencies, and enhance their expertise in a chosen field, thus bridging the gap between course work and real-life, practical experience.

The HEC MBA Program is taught in English, with opportunities to learn and carry out course work in French. For those with no background in French skills, an intensive pre-M.B.A. course is offered in Paris before arrival on the HEC campus; language courses are also available throughout the academic year.

RESOURCES AND SERVICES 30 on-campus PCs are available to graduate business students. Access to Internet/World Wide Web and online (class) registration available. *Personal computer requirements:* Graduate business students are strongly recommended to purchase or lease a personal computer. *Special opportunities include:* An international exchange program is available. *Placement services include:* Alumni network, career placement, job search course, career counseling/planning, electronic job bank, resume referral, career fairs, job interviews arranged, resume preparation, and career library.

FINANCIAL AID (2007–08) 82 students received aid, including loans and scholarships. *Financial aid application deadline:* 5/7.

Financial Aid Contact Financial Aid Officer, 1 rue de la Liberation, Jouy-en-Josas, 78351, France. *Phone:* 33-1-39677380. *Fax:* 33-1-39677465.

INTERNATIONAL STUDENTS *Services and facilities:* Counseling/support services, ESL/language courses, Housing location assistance, International student housing, International student organization, Language tutoring, Orientation, Visa Services, Personal managerial profiling and group interaction. Financial aid is available to international students. *Required with application:* IELT; TOEFL with recommended score of 250 (computer).

International Student Contact Joshua Kobb, Development Director, 1 rue de la Liberation, Jouy-en-Josas, 78351, France. *Phone:* 33-1-39677383. *Fax:* 33-1-39677465. *E-mail:* kobb@hec.fr.

APPLICATION *Required:* GMAT, application form, baccalaureate/first degree, essay, interview, 2 letters of recommendation, resume/curriculum vitae, transcripts of college work. *Application fee:* 100 euros. Applications for domestic and international students are processed on a rolling basis.

Application Contact Isabelle Cota, Director of Admissions and Development, 1 rue de la Liberation, Jouy-en-Josas, 78351, France. *Phone:* 33-1-39679546. *Fax:* 33-1-39677465. *E-mail:* admissionmba@hec.fr.

See full description on page 632.

Institut d'Etudes Politiques de Paris
MBA Programme

Paris, France

Phone: 33-1-45448743 **Fax:** 33-1-45448892 **E-mail:** mba@sciences-po.fr

Business Program(s) Web Site: http://mba.sciences-po.fr

DEGREE MBA

MBA—Master of Business Administration *Concentration:* general MBA.

RESOURCES AND SERVICES 30 on-campus PCs are available to graduate business students. Access to Internet/World Wide Web available. *Personal computer requirements:* Graduate business students are required to have a personal computer. *Placement services include:* Alumni network, career placement, job search course, career counseling/planning, career fairs, and resume preparation.

Application Contact Prof. Rosa Jean-Jacques, Dean, 174 boulevard Saint Germain, Paris, 75006, France. *Phone:* 33-1-45448743. *Fax:* 33-1-45448892. *E-mail:* mba@sciences-po.fr.

Rouen School of Management
Postgraduate Programmes

Mount Saint Aignan, France

Phone: 33-2-32825849 **Fax:** 33-2-32825830 **E-mail:** mba@groupe-esc-rouen.fr

Rouen School of Management (continued)

Business Program(s) Web Site: http://www.groupe-esc-rouen.fr

Graduate Business Unit Enrollment *Total:* 155 (125 full-time; 30 part-time; 85 women; 31 international).

Graduate Business Faculty *Total:* 312 (62 full-time; 250 part-time).

Admissions *Applied:* 465. *Admitted:* 180. *Enrolled:* 155. *Average GMAT:* 600. *Average GPA:* 3.5

Academic Calendar Trimesters.

After Graduation (Class of 2006–07) *Employed within 3 months of graduation:* 95%. *Average starting salary:* 36,000 euros.

DEGREES MBA • MBC • MBF • MEB • MIB • MIS • MM

MBA—Normandy Master of Business Administration Full-time. English language programme with French instruction. Open to University graduates with significant managerial experience. GMAT and TOEFL required. 9 to 15 months to complete program. *Concentration:* management.

MBC—Master in Corporate Communication Strategies Part-time. Taught in French. 11 months to complete program. *Concentration:* management communication.

MBF—Master in International Financial Management Full-time. Taught in French. 10 to 15 months to complete program. *Concentration:* international finance.

MBF—Master of Business Finance Part-time. Program conducted in Poland (Gdansk). 11 to 15 months to complete program. *Concentration:* international finance.

MEB—Master in European Management Full-time. Taught in English. 14 to 16 months to complete program. *Concentration:* European business studies.

MIB—Master in International Development Strategies Full-time. Taught in French. 11 to 15 months to complete program. *Concentration:* international development management.

MIS—Master in Business Information Systems Full-time. Taught in English. 11 to 15 months to complete program. *Concentration:* information management.

MM—Master in Market Research and Marketing Management Full-time and part-time. Taught in French. 11 to 15 months to complete program. *Concentration:* marketing.

RESOURCES AND SERVICES 250 on-campus PCs are available to graduate business students. Access to Internet/World Wide Web available. *Personal computer requirements:* Graduate business students are not required to have a personal computer. *Special opportunities include:* An international exchange program and an internship program are available. *Placement services include:* Alumni network, career placement, job search course, career counseling/planning, electronic job bank, resume referral, career fairs, job interviews arranged, resume preparation, and career library.

EXPENSES *Tuition:* Full-time: 18,000 euros.

FINANCIAL AID (2007–08) Loans.

INTERNATIONAL STUDENTS 20% of students enrolled are international students. *Services and facilities:* Counseling/support services, ESL/language courses, Housing location assistance, International student housing, International student organization, Language tutoring, Orientation, Visa Services. Financial aid is not available to international students. *Required with application:* IELT with recommended score of 6; TOEFL with recommended score of 250 (computer) or 600 (paper); TWE with recommended score of 5; proof of adequate funds.

International Student Contact Mrs. Elisabeth Neu, International Contact, BP 188, 1 rue Maréchal Juin, Mont Saint Aignan, 76825, France. *Phone:* 33-2-32825719. *Fax:* 33-2-32825836. *E-mail:* international@groupe-esc-rouen.fr.

APPLICATION *Required:* Application form, baccalaureate/first degree, essay, interview, 2 letters of recommendation, personal statement, resume/curriculum vitae, transcripts of college work, 3 years of work experience. School will accept GMAT. *Application fee:* 75 euros. Applications for domestic and international students are processed on a rolling basis.

Application Contact Mrs. Muriel Leguillon, French Contact, BP 188, 1 rue Maréchal Juin, Mont Saint Aignan, 76825, France. *Phone:* 33-2-32825849. *Fax:* 33-2-32825830. *E-mail:* mba@groupe-esc-rouen.fr.

Schiller International University

MBA Program Paris, France

Paris, France

Phone: 727-736-5082 Ext. 240 **Fax:** 727-734-0359 **E-mail:** admissions@schiller.edu

Business Program(s) Web Site: http://www.schiller.edu

Graduate Business Unit Enrollment *Total:* 590 (240 full-time; 350 part-time). *Average Age:* 23.

Graduate Business Faculty *Total:* 14 (4 full-time; 10 part-time).

Admissions *Average GPA:* 3.0

Academic Calendar Semesters.

After Graduation (Class of 2006–07) *Employed within 3 months of graduation:* 94%.

DEGREE MBA

MBA—Master of Business Administration in International Business Full-time and part-time. Distance learning option. At least 45 total credits required. 12 to 36 months to complete program. *Concentration:* international business.

RESOURCES AND SERVICES 10 on-campus PCs are available to graduate business students. Access to Internet/World Wide Web available. *Personal computer requirements:* Graduate business students are required to have a personal computer. *Special opportunities include:* An international exchange program and an internship program are available. *Placement services include:* Alumni network, career placement, job search course, career counseling/planning, electronic job bank, resume referral, resume preparation, and career library.

EXPENSES *Tuition:* Full-time: 15,600 euros. Part-time: 1300 euros per course. *Tuition (international):* Full-time: 15,600 euros. Part-time: 1300 euros per course. *Required fees:* Full-time: 230 euros. Part-time: 230 euros per year. *Graduate housing:* Room and board costs vary by campus location.

FINANCIAL AID (2007–08) Grants, loans, scholarships, and work study. *Financial aid application deadline:* 4/1.

Financial Aid Contact Ms. Jennifer Fraser, Financial Aid Officer, 300 East Bay Drive, Largo, FL 33770. *Phone:* 727-736-5082 Ext. 253. *Fax:* 727-734-0359. *E-mail:* financial_aid@schiller.edu.

INTERNATIONAL STUDENTS *Services and facilities:* Counseling/support services, ESL/language courses, Housing location assistance, International student housing, Language tutoring, Orientation, Visa Services. Financial aid is available to international students. *Required with application:* Proof of adequate funds. *Recommended with application:* TOEFL with recommended score of 213 (computer), 550 (paper), or 73 (Internet).

International Student Contact Ms. Stephanie Givens, Admissions, 300 East Bay Drive, Largo, FL 33770. *Phone:* 727-736-5082 Ext. 411. *Fax:* 727-734-0359. *E-mail:* admissions@schiller.edu.

APPLICATION *Required:* Application form, baccalaureate/first degree, essay, transcripts of college work. *Recommended:* Resume/curriculum vitae, work experience. *Application fee:* $65. Applications for domestic and international students are processed on a rolling basis.

Application Contact Ms. Kamala Dontamsetti, Assistant Director of Admissions, 300 East Bay Drive, Largo, FL 33770. *Phone:* 727-736-5082 Ext. 240. *Fax:* 727-734-0359. *E-mail:* admissions@schiller.edu.

See full description on page 684.

Schiller International University

MBA Program, Strasbourg, France Campus

Strasbourg, France

Phone: 727-736-5082 Ext. 240 **Fax:** 727-734-0359 **E-mail:** admissions@schiller.edu

Business Program(s) Web Site: http://www.schiller.edu/

DEGREE MBA

MBA—Master of Business Administration in International Business Part-time. Distance learning option. At least 45 total credits required. 12 to 24 months to complete program. *Concentration:* international business.

RESOURCES AND SERVICES 3 on-campus PCs are available to graduate business students. Access to Internet/World Wide Web available. *Personal computer requirements:* Graduate business students are strongly recommended to purchase or lease a personal computer. *Special opportunities include:* An international exchange program and an internship program are available. *Placement services include:* Alumni network, career placement, career counseling/planning, electronic job bank, resume referral, job interviews arranged, and resume preparation.

Application Contact Ms. Kamala Dontamsetti, Assistant Director of Admissions, 300 East Bay Drive, Largo, FL 33770. *Phone:* 727-736-5082 Ext. 240. *Fax:* 727-734-0359. *E-mail:* admissions@schiller.edu.

See full description on page 684.

GERMANY

Bayerische Julius-Maximilians University of Wuerzburg

MBA Program

Wuerzburg, Germany

Phone: 49-931-3501250 **Fax:** 49-931-312955 **E-mail:** info@businessintegration.de

Business Program(s) Web Site: http://www.businessintegration.de/

Graduate Business Unit Enrollment *Total:* 60 (60 part-time; 15 women). *Average Age:* 36.

Graduate Business Faculty 90 part-time.

Admissions *Applied:* 70. *Admitted:* 25. *Enrolled:* 25. *Average GMAT:* 300. *Average GPA:* 3.0

Academic Calendar Semesters.

After Graduation (Class of 2006–07) *Employed within 3 months of graduation:* 100%. *Average starting salary:* 75,000 euros.

DEGREE MBA

MBA—MBA in Business Integration Part-time. Distance learning option. 75 total credits required. 24 to 36 months to complete program. *Concentrations:* business education, business information science, business policy/strategy, business studies, commerce, electronic commerce (E-commerce), European business studies, finance, financial engineering, general MBA, industrial administration/management, information management, information systems, information technology, international development management, leadership, management communication, marketing, production management, project management, risk management, strategic management.

RESOURCES AND SERVICES 100 on-campus PCs are available to graduate business students. Access to Internet/World Wide Web, online (class) registration, and online grade reports available. *Personal computer requirements:* Graduate business students are required to have a personal computer. *Special opportunities include:* An international exchange program is available. *Placement services include:* Alumni network, career placement, and career fairs.

EXPENSES *Tuition:* Part-time: 3500 euros per semester. *Tuition (international):* Part-time: 3500 euros per semester.

Financial Aid Contact Mrs. Jutta Thomas, Management Assistant, MBA Business Integration, Lehrstuhl Professor Thome, Sanderring 2, Wuerzburg, D-97070, Germany. *Phone:* 49-931-3501250. *Fax:* 49-931-312955. *E-mail:* info@businessintegration.de.

INTERNATIONAL STUDENTS *Services and facilities:* Counseling/support services, ESL/language courses, Housing location assistance, Language tutoring, Orientation. Financial aid is not available to international students. *Required with application:* TOEFL with recommended score of 200 (computer) or 400 (paper).

International Student Contact Mr. Marcus Pauli, International Director, MBA Business Integration, Lehrstuhl Professor Thome, Sanderring 2, Wuerzburg, D-97070, Germany. *Phone:* 49-931-3501250. *Fax:* 49-931-312955. *E-mail:* info@businessintegration.de.

APPLICATION *Required:* Application form, baccalaureate/first degree, essay, interview, 1 letter of recommendation, personal statement, resume/curriculum vitae, transcripts of college work, 3 years of work experience. School will accept GMAT. *Application fee:* 0 euros. Applications for domestic and international students are processed on a rolling basis.

Application Contact Mr. Michael Doerflein, Managing Director, MBA Business Integration, Lehrstuhl Professor Thome, Sanderring 2, Wuerzburg, D-97070, Germany. *Phone:* 49-931-3501250. *Fax:* 49-931-312955. *E-mail:* info@businessintegration.de.

Fachhochschule Offenburg

MBA International Business Consulting

Offenburg, Germany

Phone: 49-7803-969843 **Fax:** 49-7803-969857 **E-mail:** ibc@fh-offenburg.de

Business Program(s) Web Site: http://www.mba-ibc.com

Graduate Business Unit Enrollment *Total:* 19 (19 full-time; 9 women; 18 international). *Average Age:* 27.

Graduate Business Faculty *Total:* 30 (8 full-time; 22 part-time).

Admissions *Applied:* 129. *Admitted:* 27. *Enrolled:* 15. *Average GMAT:* 565. *Average GPA:* 3.15

Academic Calendar Semesters.

After Graduation (Class of 2006–07) *Employed within 3 months of graduation:* 80%.

DEGREE MBA

MBA—Master of Business Administration in International Business Consulting Full-time. Bachelor's degree and 2 years of work experience required. 90 to 94 total credits required. 15 to 24 months to complete program. *Concentration:* international business.

RESOURCES AND SERVICES 61 on-campus PCs are available to graduate business students. Access to Internet/World Wide Web and online (class) registration available. *Personal computer requirements:* Graduate business students are strongly recommended to purchase or lease a personal computer. *Special opportunities include:* An international exchange program and an internship program are available. *Placement services include:* Alumni network, job search course, career counseling/planning, electronic job bank, career fairs, and resume preparation.

FINANCIAL AID (2007–08) 9 students received aid, including scholarships and work study. *Financial aid application deadline:* 5/31.

Fachhochschule Offenburg (continued)

Financial Aid Contact Alexandra Raunig, MBA Coordinator, Klosterstr. 14, Gengenbach, 77723, Germany. *Phone:* 49-7803-969843. *Fax:* 49-7803-969857. *E-mail:* ibc@fh-offenburg.de.

INTERNATIONAL STUDENTS 95% of students enrolled are international students. *Services and facilities:* Counseling/support services, ESL/language courses, Housing location assistance, Language tutoring, Orientation, Personal tutoring, Trips, Get-togethers with German citizens. Financial aid is available to international students. *Required with application:* IELT with recommended score of 6.5; TOEFL with recommended score of 213 (computer), 550 (paper), or 79 (Internet). *Recommended with application:* Proof of adequate funds.

International Student Contact Alexandra Raunig, MBA Coordinator, Klosterstr. 14, Gengenbach, 77723, Germany. *Phone:* 49-7803-969843. *Fax:* 49-7803-969857. *E-mail:* ibc@fh-offenburg.de.

APPLICATION *Required:* GMAT, application form, baccalaureate/first degree, 2 letters of recommendation, personal statement, resume/curriculum vitae, transcripts of college work, 2 years of work experience. *Application fee:* 0 euros. Applications for domestic and international students are processed on a rolling basis.

Application Contact Alexandra Raunig, MBA Coordinator, Klosterstr. 14, Gengenbach, 77723, Germany. *Phone:* 49-7803-969843. *Fax:* 49-7803-969857. *E-mail:* ibc@fh-offenburg.de.

GISMA Business School
Graduate Programs

Hannover, Germany

Phone: 49-511-5460936 **Fax:** 49-511-5460954 **E-mail:** info@gisma.com

Business Program(s) Web Site: http://www.gisma.com

Graduate Business Unit Enrollment *Total:* 124 (49 full-time; 75 part-time; 34 women; 94 international). *Average Age:* 30.

Graduate Business Faculty *Total:* 45 (30 full-time; 15 part-time).

Admissions *Applied:* 125. *Admitted:* 70. *Enrolled:* 50. *Average GMAT:* 620. *Average GPA:* 3.5

Academic Calendar Five 8-week modules.

Accreditation AACSB—The Association to Advance Collegiate Schools of Business.

After Graduation (Class of 2006–07) *Employed within 3 months of graduation:* 91%. *Average starting salary:* 60,000 euros.

DEGREES EMBA • MBA

EMBA—International Master in Management Part-time. 5 years of work experience required. 48 total credits required. 22 months to complete program. *Concentration:* general MBA.

MBA—Full-Time Master of Business Administration Full-time. 48 to 54 total credits required. 11 months to complete program. *Concentration:* general MBA.

RESOURCES AND SERVICES 25 on-campus PCs are available to graduate business students. Access to Internet/World Wide Web, online (class) registration, and online grade reports available. *Personal computer requirements:* Graduate business students are required to have a personal computer. *Special opportunities include:* An international exchange program is available. *Placement services include:* Alumni network, career placement, job search course, career counseling/planning, electronic job bank, resume referral, career fairs, job interviews arranged, resume preparation, and career library.

EXPENSES *Tuition:* Full-time: 25,000 euros. Part-time: 52,500 euros per degree program. *Tuition (international):* Full-time: 25,000 euros. Part-time: 52,500 euros per degree program.

FINANCIAL AID (2007–08) 30 students received aid, including loans, scholarships, and teaching assistantships. *Financial aid application deadline:* 5/31.

Financial Aid Contact Monika Baer, Recruitment Manager, Feodor-Lynen-Strasse 27, Hannover, 30625, Germany. *Phone:* 49-511-5460936. *Fax:* 49-511-5460954. *E-mail:* mbaer@gisma.com.

INTERNATIONAL STUDENTS 76% of students enrolled are international students. *Services and facilities:* Counseling/support services, ESL/language courses, Housing location assistance, International student organization, Language tutoring, Orientation, Visa Services, Health insurance, Working permit service. *Required with application:* IELT with recommended score of 6.5; TOEFL with recommended score of 213 (computer), 550 (paper), or 77 (Internet). *Recommended with application:* Proof of adequate funds.

International Student Contact Monika Baer, Recruitment Manager, Feodor-Lynen-Strasse 27, Hannover, 30625, Germany. *Phone:* 49-511-5460936. *Fax:* 49-511-5460954. *E-mail:* info@gisma.com.

APPLICATION *Required:* GMAT, application form, baccalaureate/first degree, essay, 2 letters of recommendation, personal statement, resume/curriculum vitae, transcripts of college work, 2 years of work experience. School will accept GRE. *Recommended:* Interview. *Application fee:* $60. Applications for domestic and international students are processed on a rolling basis.

Application Contact Monika Baer, Recruitment Manager, Feodor-Lynen-Strasse 27, Hannover, 30625, Germany. *Phone:* 49-511-5460936. *Fax:* 49-511-5460954. *E-mail:* info@gisma.com.

HfB—Business School of Finance and Management
Frankfurt School of Finance and Management

Frankfurt, Germany

Phone: 49-69-154008254 **Fax:** 49-69-1540084254 **E-mail:** d.jansen@frankfurt-school.de

Business Program(s) Web Site: http://www.frankfurt-school.de

Graduate Business Unit Enrollment *Total:* 235 (120 full-time; 115 part-time; 66 women; 59 international). *Average Age:* 32.

Graduate Business Faculty *Total:* 82 (32 full-time; 50 part-time).

Admissions *Applied:* 250. *Admitted:* 210. *Enrolled:* 195. *Average GPA:* 2.2

Academic Calendar Semesters.

After Graduation (Class of 2006–07) *Employed within 3 months of graduation:* 100%. *Average starting salary:* 70,000 euros.

DEGREES DBA • EMBA • M Sc • MA • MBA/LLM

DBA—PhD Program Full-time and part-time. 36 months to complete program. *Concentrations:* accounting, banking, business ethics, business information science, business law, business policy/strategy, business studies, Chinese business studies, decision sciences, developmental economics, economics, entrepreneurship, environmental economics/management, finance, financial economics, financial engineering, financial management/planning, health administration, human resources development, human resources management, information management, information systems, international banking, international development management, international economics, international finance, international management, investments and securities, management, management systems analysis, managerial economics, public finance, quantitative analysis, risk management, statistics, taxation.

EMBA—Master of Business Administration in International Hospital and Healthcare Management Part-time. Distance learning option. 80 total credits required. 18 months to complete program. *Concentrations:* general MBA, health administration.

M Sc—Master of Accounting and Taxation Full-time and part-time. 90 total credits required. 18 months to complete program. *Concentrations:* accounting, taxation.

M Sc—Master of Banking Full-time and part-time. 90 total credits required. 18 months to complete program. *Concentration:* banking.

M Sc—Master of Development Finance Full-time. Up to 120 total credits required. 24 months to complete program. *Concentrations:* banking, business ethics, business policy/strategy, developmental economics, economics, finance, international banking, international economics, international finance, leadership.

M Sc—Master of Finance Full-time and part-time. 90 total credits required. 18 months to complete program. *Concentration:* finance.

M Sc—Master of Quantitative Finance Part-time. 60 total credits required. 24 months to complete program. *Concentrations:* finance, financial engineering, quantitative analysis.

MA—Master of International Business Full-time. 120 total credits required. 24 months to complete program. *Concentrations:* Asian business studies, Chinese business studies, developmental economics, economics, European business studies, international and area business studies, international business, international management, leadership, management.

MBA/LLM—Master of International Business and Tax Law Part-time. 60 total credits required. 24 months to complete program. *Concentrations:* business law, European business studies, international business, taxation.

MBA/LLM—Master of Mergers and Acquisitions Part-time. 60 total credits required. 24 months to complete program. *Concentrations:* finance, law.

RESOURCES AND SERVICES 30 on-campus PCs are available to graduate business students. Access to Internet/World Wide Web, online (class) registration, and online grade reports available. *Personal computer requirements:* Graduate business students are strongly recommended to purchase or lease a personal computer. *Special opportunities include:* An international exchange program and an internship program are available. *Placement services include:* Alumni network, career placement, career counseling/planning, electronic job bank, resume referral, career fairs, job interviews arranged, and resume preparation.

EXPENSES *Tuition:* Full-time: 22,000 euros. Part-time: 22,000 euros per degree program. *Tuition (international):* Full-time: 22,000 euros. Part-time: 22,000 euros per degree program. *Required fees:* Full-time: 1000 euros. Part-time: 1000 euros per hour. Tuition and/or fees vary by number of courses or credits taken and academic program.

FINANCIAL AID (2007–08) 15 students received aid, including grants, loans, and research assistantships. Aid is available to part-time students. *Financial aid application deadline:* 12/31.

Financial Aid Contact Dr. Detlef Jansen, Program Director, Sonnemannstrasse 9—11, Frankfurt, 60314, Germany. *Phone:* 49-69-154008254. *Fax:* 49-69-1540084254. *E-mail:* d.jansen@frankfurt-school.de.

INTERNATIONAL STUDENTS 25% of students enrolled are international students. *Services and facilities:* Counseling/support services, Housing location assistance, International student organization, Language tutoring, Orientation. Financial aid is available to international students. *Required with application:* TOEFL with recommended score of 80 (Internet); proof of adequate funds.

International Student Contact Dr. Detlef Jansen, Program Director, Sonnemannstrasse 9—11, Frankfurt, 60314, Germany. *Phone:* 49-69-154008254. *Fax:* 49-69-1540084254. *E-mail:* d.jansen@frankfurt-school.de.

APPLICATION *Required:* Application form, baccalaureate/first degree, interview, personal statement, resume/curriculum vitae, transcripts of college work. *Recommended:* Work experience. *Application fee:* 0 euros. Applications for domestic and international students are processed on a rolling basis.

Application Contact Dr. Detlef Jansen, Program Director, Sonnemannstrasse 9—11, Frankfurt, 60314, Germany. *Phone:* 49-69-154008254. *Fax:* 49-69-1540084254. *E-mail:* d.jansen@frankfurt-school.de.

HHL—Leipzig Graduate School of Management

MBA Program

Leipzig, Germany

Phone: 49-341-9851 Ext. 730 **Fax:** 49-341-9851 Ext. 731 **E-mail:** petra.spanka@hhl.de

Business Program(s) Web Site: http://www.hhl.de

Graduate Business Unit Enrollment *Total:* 296 (247 full-time; 49 part-time; 72 women; 95 international). *Average Age:* 29.

Graduate Business Faculty *Total:* 32 (12 full-time; 20 part-time).

Admissions *Applied:* 356. *Admitted:* 109. *Enrolled:* 78. *Average GMAT:* 600. *Average GPA:* 3.5

Academic Calendar Quarters.

After Graduation (Class of 2006–07) *Employed within 3 months of graduation:* 95%. *Average starting salary:* 75,000 euros.

DEGREES MBA • MSM

MBA—International Management Full-time. 116 to 150 total credits required. 12 to 15 months to complete program. *Concentrations:* general MBA, international management, leadership, management.

MBA—International Management Part-time. 3 years of work experience required. 116 to 125 total credits required. 24 to 27 months to complete program. *Concentrations:* general MBA, international management, leadership, management.

MSM—Master of Science in Management Full-time. HHL-Entry test required. 120 to 150 total credits required. 18 to 24 months to complete program. *Concentrations:* accounting, finance, international marketing, management, strategic management, supply chain management.

RESOURCES AND SERVICES 64 on-campus PCs are available to graduate business students. Access to Internet/World Wide Web, online (class) registration, and online grade reports available. *Personal computer requirements:* Graduate business students are not required to have a personal computer. *Special opportunities include:* An international exchange program and an internship program are available. *Placement services include:* Alumni network, career placement, job search course, career counseling/planning, electronic job bank, resume referral, career fairs, job interviews arranged, resume preparation, and career library.

EXPENSES *Tuition:* Full-time: 18,000 euros. Part-time: 12,600 euros per year. *Tuition (international):* Full-time: 18,000 euros. Part-time: 12,600 euros per year. *Required fees:* Full-time: 200 euros. Part-time: 150 euros per year. Tuition and/or fees vary by academic program. *Graduate housing:* Room and board costs vary by type of accommodation. *Typical cost:* 6000 euros (including board), 2500 euros (room only).

FINANCIAL AID (2007–08) 9 students received aid, including loans and scholarships. *Financial aid application deadline:* 4/1.

Financial Aid Contact Frank Hoffmann, Director of International Relations, Jahnallee 59, Leipzig, 04109, Germany. *Phone:* 49-341-9851 Ext. 626. *Fax:* 49-341 9851 Ext. 810. *E-mail:* hoffmann@hhl.de.

INTERNATIONAL STUDENTS 32% of students enrolled are international students. *Services and facilities:* Counseling/support services, ESL/language courses, Housing location assistance, International student organization, Language tutoring, Orientation, Visa Services. Financial aid is available to international students. *Required with application:* TOEFL with recommended score of 250 (computer), 550 (paper), or 100 (Internet).

International Student Contact Petra Spanka, Administrative Director, Jahnallee 59, Leipzig, 04109, Germany. *Phone:* 49-341-9851 Ext. 730. *Fax:* 49-341-9851 Ext. 731. *E-mail:* petra.spanka@hhl.de.

APPLICATION *Required:* GMAT, application form, baccalaureate/first degree, essay, 2 letters of recommendation, personal statement, resume/curriculum vitae, transcripts of college work, 1 year of work experience.

HHL—Leipzig Graduate School of Management (continued)

School will accept GRE. *Recommended:* Interview. *Application fee:* 0 euros. Applications for domestic and international students are processed on a rolling basis.

Application Contact Petra Spanka, Administrative Director, Jahnallee 59, Leipzig, 04109, Germany. *Phone:* 49-341-9851 Ext. 730. *Fax:* 49-341-9851 Ext. 731. *E-mail:* petra.spanka@hhl.de.

Schiller International University

MBA Programs, Heidelberg, Germany

Heidelberg, Germany

Phone: 727-736-5082 Ext. 240 **Fax:** 727-734-0359 **E-mail:** admissions@schiller.edu

Business Program(s) Web Site: http://www.schiller.edu/

Graduate Business Unit Enrollment *Average Age:* 23.

Graduate Business Faculty *Total:* 16 (4 full-time; 12 part-time).

Admissions *Average GMAT:* 350. *Average GPA:* 3.0

Academic Calendar Semesters.

After Graduation (Class of 2006–07) *Employed within 3 months of graduation:* 90%.

DEGREES MBA • MIM

MBA—Master of Business Administration in International Business Full-time and part-time. Distance learning option. At least 45 total credits required. 12 to 24 months to complete program. *Concentration:* international business.

MBA—Master of Business Administration in Management of Information Technology Full-time and part-time. Distance learning option. At least 45 total credits required. 12 to 24 months to complete program. *Concentration:* management information systems.

MIM—Master of International Management in International Business Full-time and part-time. At least 45 total credits required. 12 to 24 months to complete program. *Concentrations:* international business, international management.

RESOURCES AND SERVICES 26 on-campus PCs are available to graduate business students. Access to Internet/World Wide Web available. *Personal computer requirements:* Graduate business students are required to have a personal computer. *Special opportunities include:* An international exchange program and an internship program are available. *Placement services include:* Alumni network, career placement, job search course, career counseling/planning, electronic job bank, resume referral, resume preparation, and career library.

FINANCIAL AID (2007–08) Grants, loans, scholarships, and work study. *Financial aid application deadline:* 4/1.

Financial Aid Contact Ms. Jennifer Fraser, Financial Aid Officer, 300 East Bay Drive, Largo, FL 33770. *Phone:* 727-736-5082 Ext. 253. *Fax:* 727-738-8405. *E-mail:* financial_aid@schiller.edu.

INTERNATIONAL STUDENTS *Services and facilities:* Counseling/support services, ESL/language courses, Housing location assistance, International student housing, Language tutoring, Orientation, Visa Services. Financial aid is available to international students. *Required with application:* Proof of adequate funds. *Recommended with application:* TOEFL with recommended score of 213 (computer), 550 (paper), or 73 (Internet).

International Student Contact Ms. Lilian Prado, Admissions Representative, 300 East Bay Drive. *Phone:* 727-736-5082 Ext. 410. *E-mail:* admissions@schiller.edu.

APPLICATION *Required:* Application form, baccalaureate/first degree, essay, transcripts of college work. *Recommended:* Work experience. *Application fee:* $65. Applications for domestic and international students are processed on a rolling basis.

Application Contact Ms. Kamala Dontamsetti, Associate Director of Admissions, 300 East Bay Drive, Largo, FL 33770. *Phone:* 727-736-5082 Ext. 240. *Fax:* 727-734-0359. *E-mail:* admissions@schiller.edu.

See full description on page 684.

University of Applied Sciences Esslingen

Graduate School

Esslingen, Germany

Phone: 49-711-3974464 **Fax:** 49-711-3974477 **E-mail:** mba@hs-esslingen.de

Business Program(s) Web Site: http://www.graduate-school.de/mba

Graduate Business Unit Enrollment *Total:* 22 (22 full-time; 11 women; 22 international). *Average Age:* 27.

Graduate Business Faculty *Total:* 66 (24 full-time; 42 part-time).

Admissions *Applied:* 188. *Admitted:* 33. *Enrolled:* 15. *Average GMAT:* 580.

Academic Calendar Semesters.

After Graduation (Class of 2006–07) *Employed within 3 months of graduation:* 80%. *Average starting salary:* 38,000 euros.

DEGREE MBA

MBA—Master of Business Administration in International Industrial Management Full-time. At least 90 total credits required. Minimum of 18 months to complete program. *Concentrations:* industrial administration/management, international management, manufacturing management, operations management.

RESOURCES AND SERVICES 30 on-campus PCs are available to graduate business students. Access to Internet/World Wide Web available. *Personal computer requirements:* Graduate business students are strongly recommended to purchase or lease a personal computer. *Special opportunities include:* An internship program is available. *Placement services include:* Alumni network, job search course, resume referral, career fairs, job interviews arranged, and resume preparation.

EXPENSES *Tuition (state resident):* Full-time: 1200 euros. *Tuition (nonresident):* Full-time: 1200 euros. *Tuition (international):* Full-time: 1200 euros. *Typical graduate housing cost:* 1600 euros (room only).

Financial Aid Contact Ms. Tudao Luong, MBA Program Manager, Flandernstrasse 101, BW, Germany. *Phone:* 49-711-3974464. *Fax:* 49-711-3974477. *E-mail:* mba@hs-esslingen.de.

INTERNATIONAL STUDENTS 100% of students enrolled are international students. *Services and facilities:* Counseling/support services, ESL/language courses, Housing location assistance, International student housing, International student organization, Language tutoring, Orientation, Visa Services, German language courses, Cultural program with excursions. Financial aid is not available to international students. *Required with application:* IELT with recommended score of 6.5; TOEFL with recommended score of 213 (computer), 550 (paper), or 79 (Internet); TWE. *Recommended with application:* Proof of adequate funds.

International Student Contact Ms. Tudao Luong, MBA Program Manager, Flandernstrasse 101, BW, Germany. *Phone:* 49-711-3974464. *Fax:* 49-711-3974477. *E-mail:* mba@hs-esslingen.de.

APPLICATION *Required:* GMAT, application form, baccalaureate/first degree, essay, 2 letters of recommendation, personal statement, resume/curriculum vitae, transcripts of college work, 2 years of work experience. Applications for domestic and international students are processed on a rolling basis.

Application Contact Ms. Tudao Luong, MBA Program Manager, Flandernstrasse 101, BW, Germany. *Phone:* 49-711-3974464. *Fax:* 49-711-3974477. *E-mail:* mba@hs-esslingen.de.

WHU—Otto Beisheim School of Management

WHU—Otto Beisheim School of Management

Vallendar, Germany

Phone: 49-261-6509-141 **Fax:** 49-261-6509-149 **E-mail:** heidrun.hoffmann@whu.edu

Business Program(s) Web Site: http://www.whu.edu

Graduate Business Unit Enrollment *Total:* 480 (385 full-time; 95 part-time; 114 women; 109 international). *Average Age:* 29.

Graduate Business Faculty *Total:* 115 (26 full-time; 89 part-time).

Admissions *Applied:* 668. *Admitted:* 257. *Enrolled:* 250. *Average GMAT:* 610.

Academic Calendar Semesters.

After Graduation (Class of 2006–07) *Employed within 3 months of graduation:* 98%. *Average starting salary:* 55,000 euros.

DEGREES Dipl-Kfm • MBA • MBA/LLM

Dipl-Kfm—German Diploma Program (Master equivalent) Full-time. Maximum of 48 months to complete program. *Concentrations:* economics, entrepreneurship, finance, international economics, international finance, marketing, production management, technology management.

MBA—Kellogg-WHU Executive MBA Part-time. Minimum 5 years' management level work experience required. All candidates must be in full-time employment and have the support of their company. This program is for international managers. At least 64 total credits required. Maximum of 24 months to complete program. *Concentrations:* entrepreneurship, finance, general MBA, leadership, marketing, operations management, other, project management, strategic management.

MBA Full-time. 2 years' work experience required. At least 100 total credits required. 16 months to complete program. *Concentrations:* finance, general MBA, leadership, marketing, strategic management, supply chain management.

MBA/LLM—Bucerius/WHU Master of Law and Business Full-time. The program is particularly designed for graduates in law or business/economics and young professionals with some working experience. Graduates with different academic backgrounds are also welcome. At least 60 total credits required. Minimum of 12 months to complete program. *Concentrations:* business law, business studies, corporate legal counseling, economics, law, management.

RESOURCES AND SERVICES 44 on-campus PCs are available to graduate business students. Access to Internet/World Wide Web, online (class) registration, and online grade reports available. *Personal computer requirements:* Graduate business students are strongly recommended to purchase or lease a personal computer. *Special opportunities include:* An international exchange program and an internship program are available. *Placement services include:* Alumni network, career placement, career counseling/planning, electronic job bank, resume referral, career fairs, job interviews arranged, and resume preparation.

EXPENSES Tuition and/or fees vary by academic program.

FINANCIAL AID (2007–08) 23 students received aid, including fellowships, grants, loans, research assistantships, and scholarships.

Financial Aid Contact Stefanie Schweins, Director, International Programmes, Burgplatz 2, Vallendar, 56179, Germany. *Phone:* 49-261-6509160. *Fax:* 49-261-6509169. *E-mail:* stefanie.schweins@whu.edu.

INTERNATIONAL STUDENTS 23% of students enrolled are international students. *Services and facilities:* Counseling/support services, ESL/language courses, Housing location assistance, International student housing, International student organization, Language tutoring, Orientation, Visa Services, Assistance with internship organization and work permits. Financial aid is available to international students. *Required with*

application: TOEFL with recommended score of 250 (computer), 600 (paper), or 100 (Internet); proof of adequate funds.

International Student Contact Stefanie Schweins, Director, International Programmes, Burgplatz 2, Vallendar, 56179, Germany. *Phone:* 49-261-6509160. *Fax:* 49-261-6509169. *E-mail:* stefanie.schweins@whu.edu.

APPLICATION *Required:* GMAT, application form, baccalaureate/first degree, interview, 2 letters of recommendation, resume/curriculum vitae, transcripts of college work, 2 years of work experience. *Application fee:* 90 euros. Applications for domestic and international students are processed on a rolling basis.

Application Contact Heidrun Hoffmann, Program Manager, Burgplatz 2, Vallendar, 56179, Germany. *Phone:* 49-261-6509-141. *Fax:* 49-261-6509-149. *E-mail:* heidrun.hoffmann@whu.edu.

GREECE

American College of Thessaloniki

Department of Business Administration

Pylea, Greece

Phone: 3-02310398239 Ext. 239 **E-mail:** admissions@act.edu

Business Program(s) Web Site: http://www.act.edu

Graduate Business Unit Enrollment *Total:* 50 (6 full-time; 44 part-time; 33 women; 17 international). *Average Age:* 28.

Graduate Business Faculty *Total:* 16 (6 full-time; 10 part-time).

Admissions *Applied:* 30. *Admitted:* 29. *Enrolled:* 24. *Average GPA:* 7.5/10 scale

Academic Calendar Quarters.

After Graduation (Class of 2006–07) *Employed within 3 months of graduation:* 35%.

DEGREES EMBA • MBA

EMBA—Joint Program ALBA/ACT Part-time. 3 or more years of working experience required. 45 total credits required. 24 months to complete program. *Concentration:* executive programs.

MBA—Master of Business Administration Full-time and part-time. English language proficiency required. 48 to 60 total credits required. 12 to 48 months to complete program. *Concentrations:* banking, entrepreneurship, management, marketing.

RESOURCES AND SERVICES 170 on-campus PCs are available to graduate business students. Access to Internet/World Wide Web and online grade reports available. *Personal computer requirements:* Graduate business students are strongly recommended to purchase or lease a personal computer. *Special opportunities include:* An internship program is available. *Placement services include:* Alumni network, career placement, career counseling/planning, resume referral, career fairs, job interviews arranged, and resume preparation.

EXPENSES *Tuition:* Full-time: 11,520 euros. *Tuition (international):* Full-time: 11,520 euros.

FINANCIAL AID (2007–08) 14 students received aid, including scholarships. Aid is available to part-time students. *Financial aid application deadline:* 8/15.

Financial Aid Contact Mrs. Ifigenia Sougaraki, Director of Scholarships and Gifts, PO Box 21021, Pylea, Thessaloniki, 555 10, Greece. *Phone:* 3-02310398249 Ext. 249. *E-mail:* ics@act.edu.

INTERNATIONAL STUDENTS 34% of students enrolled are international students. *Services and facilities:* Counseling/support services, Housing location assistance, Language tutoring, Orientation, Visa Services, Scholarship assistance. Financial aid is available to international

---

American College of Thessaloniki (continued)

students. *Recommended with application:* TOEFL with recommended score of 180 (computer), 510 (paper), or 64 (Internet).

International Student Contact Dr. Archontis Pantsios, Assistant Dean for Academic and Student Affairs and International Programs, PO Box 21021, Pylea, Thessaloniki, 555 10, Greece. *Phone:* 3-02310398228 Ext. 228. *E-mail:* apantsio@act.edu.

APPLICATION *Required:* Application form, baccalaureate/first degree, interview, 2 letters of recommendation, resume/curriculum vitae, transcripts of college work. School will accept GMAT and GRE. *Recommended:* Essay, personal statement, work experience. *Application fee:* 70 euros. Applications for domestic and international students are processed on a rolling basis.

Application Contact Mrs. Roula Lebetli, Director of Admissions, PO Box 21021, Pylea, Thessaloniki, 555 10, Greece. *Phone:* 3-02310398239 Ext. 239. *E-mail:* admissions@act.edu.

Athens Laboratory of Business Administration

MBA Program

Athens, Greece

Phone: +30-2108964531 Ext. 250 **Fax:** +30-2108962139 **E-mail:** lkomnino@alba.edu.gr

Business Program(s) Web Site: http://www.alba.edu.gr/academic/mba/message/

DEGREES   MBA

MBA—MBA in Banking Part-time. 24 to 48 months to complete program. *Concentration:* banking.

MBA—MBA in Shipping Part-time. 23 months to complete program. *Concentration:* general MBA.

MBA—Professional MBA Part-time. 24 to 48 months to complete program. *Concentration:* general MBA.

MBA—Master of Business Administration Full-time. 12 to 24 months to complete program. *Concentration:* general MBA.

RESOURCES AND SERVICES 40 on-campus PCs are available to graduate business students. Access to Internet/World Wide Web available. *Personal computer requirements:* Graduate business students are required to have a personal computer. *Special opportunities include:* An international exchange program is available. *Placement services include:* Alumni network, career placement, career counseling/planning, electronic job bank, resume referral, career fairs, job interviews arranged, resume preparation, and career library.

Application Contact Ms. Lida Komninou, MBA Department, Athinas Ave. & 2A Areos Str., Vouliagmeni, 166 71, Greece. *Phone:* +30-2108964531 Ext. 250. *Fax:* +30-2108962139. *E-mail:* lkomnino@alba.edu.gr.

INDIA

Indian Institute of Management, Ahmedabad

Post-Graduate Programme in Management

Gujarat, India

Phone: 91-79-66324817 **Fax:** 91-79-66326896 **E-mail:** admission@iimahd.ernet.in

Business Program(s) Web Site: http://www.iimahd.ernet.in

Graduate Business Unit Enrollment *Total:* 675 (675 full-time; 95 women; 7 international). *Average Age:* 23.

Graduate Business Faculty *Total:* 148 (87 full-time; 61 part-time).

Admissions *Average GMAT:* 763. *Average GPA:* 8.1/10 scale

Academic Calendar Trimesters.

After Graduation (Class of 2006–07) *Employed within 3 months of graduation:* 100%. *Average starting salary:* 1,370,000 Indian rupees.

DEGREES   EMBA • MBA equivalent

EMBA—One-Year Post-Graduate Diploma in Public Management and Policy Full-time. Admission through GMAT/GRE/CAT or a test conducted by the Institute. 25 to 27 total credits required. 12 months to complete program. *Concentrations:* general MBA, public management, public policy and administration.

EMBA—Post-Graduate Program for Executives Full-time. GMAT required for all applicants. 27 total credits required. 12 months to complete program. *Concentrations:* executive programs, general MBA.

MBA equivalent—Post-Graduate Program in Management Full-time. GMAT required for foreign students. 35 to 37 total credits required. 22 months to complete program. *Concentration:* general MBA.

RESOURCES AND SERVICES 680 on-campus PCs are available to graduate business students. Access to Internet/World Wide Web and online (class) registration available. *Personal computer requirements:* Graduate business students are required to have a personal computer. *Special opportunities include:* An international exchange program and an internship program are available. *Placement services include:* Alumni network, career placement, career counseling/planning, electronic job bank, career fairs, job interviews arranged, and resume preparation.

EXPENSES *Tuition:* Full-time: 125,000 Indian rupees. *Tuition (international):* Full-time: 500,817 Indian rupees. *Required fees:* Full-time: 99,183 Indian rupees. *Typical graduate housing cost:* 44,183 Indian rupees (including board), 20,000 Indian rupees (room only).

FINANCIAL AID (2007–08) 160 students received aid, including scholarships. *Financial aid application deadline:* 7/20.

Financial Aid Contact Prof. Ajay Pandey, Professor, Vastrapur, Ahmedabad, Gujarat, 380015, India. *Phone:* 91-79-66324879. *Fax:* 91-79-66326896. *E-mail:* apandey@iimahd.ernet.in.

INTERNATIONAL STUDENTS 1% of students enrolled are international students. *Services and facilities:* Counseling/support services, ESL/language courses, Housing location assistance, International student housing, Orientation. Financial aid is not available to international students. *Required with application:* Proof of health/immunizations.

International Student Contact Prof. Anurag K. Agarwal, Assistant Professor, Vastrapur, Ahmedabad, Gujarat, 380015, India. *Phone:* 91-79-66324916. *Fax:* 91-79-66326896. *E-mail:* akagarwal@iimahd.ernet.in.

APPLICATION *Required:* Application form, baccalaureate/first degree, interview, transcripts of college work. School will accept GMAT. *Application fee:* 1100 Indian rupees, 4500 Indian rupees (international). *Deadlines:* 9/5 for fall, 12/15 for fall (international).

Application Contact Prof. Satish Y. Deodhar, Associate Professor, Vastrapur, Ahmedabad, Gujarat, 380015, India. *Phone:* 91-79-66324817. *Fax:* 91-79-66326896. *E-mail:* admission@iimahd.ernet.in.

Indian School of Business

MBA Program

Andhra Pradesh, India

Phone: 91-40-23187474 **Fax:** 91-40-23007099 **E-mail:** admissions@isb.edu

Business Program(s) Web Site: http://www.isb.edu/pgp

Graduate Business Unit Enrollment *Total:* 442 (442 full-time; 105 women; 19 international). *Average Age:* 28.

Graduate Business Faculty *Total:* 136 (31 full-time; 105 part-time).

Admissions *Applied:* 3,486. *Admitted:* 545. *Enrolled:* 442. *Average GMAT:* 714.

Academic Calendar Eight 6-week terms.

After Graduation (Class of 2006–07) *Employed within 3 months of graduation:* 100%. *Average starting salary:* $138,600.

DEGREE MBA equivalent

MBA equivalent—Post-Graduate Programme in Management Full-time. GMAT,TOEFL/IELTS and work experience of two years or more required. 33 to 35 total credits required. 12 months to complete program. *Concentrations:* accounting, economics, entrepreneurship, finance, information technology, leadership, logistics, management information systems, managerial economics, marketing, operations management, organizational behavior/development, public policy and administration, real estate, risk management, statistics, strategic management, system management, technology management.

RESOURCES AND SERVICES 30 on-campus PCs are available to graduate business students. Access to Internet/World Wide Web, online (class) registration, and online grade reports available. *Personal computer requirements:* Graduate business students are required to have a personal computer. *Special opportunities include:* An international exchange program is available. *Placement services include:* Alumni network, career placement, job search course, career counseling/planning, electronic job bank, resume referral, job interviews arranged, resume preparation, and career library.

EXPENSES *Graduate housing:* Room and board costs vary by number of occupants, type of accommodation, and type of board plan.

FINANCIAL AID (2007–08) 52 students received aid, including scholarships. *Financial aid application deadline:* 12/1.

Financial Aid Contact Mr. Srinath V, Manager, Admissions and Financial Aid, ISB Campus, Gachibowli, Hyderabad, 500032, India. *Phone:* 91-40-23187474. *Fax:* 91-40-23007099. *E-mail:* admissions@isb.edu.

INTERNATIONAL STUDENTS 4% of students enrolled are international students. *Services and facilities:* Counseling/support services, Housing location assistance, International student housing, Orientation. Financial aid is available to international students. *Recommended with application:* IELT with recommended score of 7; TOEFL with recommended score of 250 (computer); proof of health/immunizations.

International Student Contact Mr. Sharat Kumar, Senior Executive, Admissions and Financial Aid, ISB Campus, Gachibowli, Hyderabad, 500032, India. *Phone:* 91-40-23187453. *Fax:* 91-40-23007099. *E-mail:* sharat_kumar@isb.edu.

APPLICATION *Required:* GMAT, application form, baccalaureate/first degree, essay, interview, 2 letters of recommendation, resume/curriculum vitae, transcripts of college work, 2 years of work experience. *Application fee:* $75. *Deadline:* 12/1 for summer. Applications for international students are processed on a rolling basis.

Application Contact Mr. Srinath V, Manager, Admissions, ISB Campus, Gachibowli, Hyderabad, 500032, India. *Phone:* 91-40-23187474. *Fax:* 91-40-23007099. *E-mail:* admissions@isb.edu.

IRELAND

National University of Ireland, Dublin

The Michael Smurfit Graduate School of Business

Blackrock, Ireland

Phone: 353-1-7168862 **Fax:** 353-1-7168965 **E-mail:** mba@ucd.ie

Business Program(s) Web Site: http://www.smurfitschool.ie

Graduate Business Unit Enrollment *Total:* 1,207 (805 full-time; 402 part-time; 200 international).

Graduate Business Faculty *Total:* 85 (62 full-time; 23 part-time).

Admissions *Applied:* 299. *Admitted:* 180. *Enrolled:* 108. *Average GMAT:* 615.

Academic Calendar Semesters.

Accreditation AACSB—The Association to Advance Collegiate Schools of Business.

After Graduation (Class of 2006–07) *Employed within 3 months of graduation:* 85%. *Average starting salary:* 67,571 euros.

DEGREES EMBA • M Mgt • M Sc • MBA • MBS • MS • MSMP

EMBA—Executive Master of Business Administration Part-time. At least 21 total credits required. Maximum of 24 months to complete program. *Concentrations:* accounting, entrepreneurship, finance, human resources management, management information systems, marketing.

M Mgt—Master in Management Full-time and part-time. Distance learning option. Non-business undergraduate degree required. 12 to 24 months to complete program. *Concentrations:* accounting, administration, business policy/strategy, finance, human resources management, management, marketing, organizational behavior/development, strategic management.

M Sc—Business Analytics Full-time and part-time. Engineering and/or strong mathematical aptitude required. 12 to 24 months to complete program. *Concentrations:* information management, information technology, management consulting, management information systems, management systems analysis, operations management, project management, system management, technology management.

M Sc—Master of Science (varying specialisations) Full-time. Undergraduate business degree required. Minimum of 12 months to complete program. *Concentrations:* information systems, international business, management, marketing.

MBA—Master of Business Administration Full-time. At least 21 total credits required. Maximum of 12 months to complete program. *Concentrations:* accounting, business law, economics, entrepreneurship, finance, human resources management, insurance, international and area business studies, international marketing, management information systems, manufacturing management, marketing, organizational behavior/development, strategic management.

MBS—Master of Business Studies Full-time and part-time. Undergraduate business degree or a degree in a cognate discipline required. 12 to 24 months to complete program. *Concentrations:* actuarial science, finance, human resources management, international and area business studies, international business, international marketing, management information systems, manufacturing management, marketing, marketing research, organizational behavior/development, strategic management, travel industry/tourism management.

MS—Master of Science in Quantitative Finance Full-time and part-time. 12 to 24 months to complete program. *Concentrations:* finance, financial economics, financial management/planning, international finance, management.

National University of Ireland, Dublin (continued)

MSMP—Master of Science Marketing Practice Full-time. Undergraduate degree in business marketing required. 12 months to complete program. *Concentrations:* marketing, marketing research.

RESOURCES AND SERVICES Access to Internet/World Wide Web, online (class) registration, and online grade reports available. *Personal computer requirements:* Graduate business students are required to have a personal computer. *Special opportunities include:* An international exchange program and an internship program are available. *Placement services include:* Alumni network, job search course, career counseling/planning, resume referral, career fairs, job interviews arranged, resume preparation, and career library.

FINANCIAL AID (2007–08) Scholarships. Aid is available to part-time students.

Financial Aid Contact Ms. Elaine McAree, MBA Admissions Manager, Blackrock, County Dublin, Ireland. *Phone:* 353-1-7168891. *Fax:* 353-1-7168965. *E-mail:* mba@ucd.ie.

INTERNATIONAL STUDENTS 17% of students enrolled are international students. *Services and facilities:* Counseling/support services, Housing location assistance, International student housing, International student organization. Financial aid is available to international students. *Required with application:* IELT with recommended score of 6.5; TOEFL with recommended score of 250 (computer) or 600 (paper).

International Student Contact Ms. Elaine McAree, MBA Admissions Officer, Blackrock, County Dublin, Ireland. *Phone:* 353-1-7168862. *Fax:* 353-1-7168965. *E-mail:* mba@ucd.ie.

APPLICATION *Required:* GMAT, application form, baccalaureate/first degree, essay, interview, 2 letters of recommendation, personal statement, resume/curriculum vitae, transcripts of college work, 3 years of work experience. *Application fee:* 25 euros. Applications for domestic and international students are processed on a rolling basis.

Application Contact Ms. Elaine McAree, MBA Admissions Manager, Blackrock, County Dublin, Ireland. *Phone:* 353-1-7168862. *Fax:* 353-1-7168965. *E-mail:* mba@ucd.ie.

ISRAEL

Bar-Ilan University

Graduate School of Business

Ramat-Gan, Israel

Phone: 972-3-5317914 **Fax:** 972-3-7384040 **E-mail:** imba@mail.biu.ac.il

Business Program(s) Web Site: http://www.biu.ac.il/imba

Graduate Business Unit Enrollment *Total:* 36 (30 full-time; 6 part-time; 9 women; 5 international). *Average Age:* 27.

Graduate Business Faculty 22 full-time.

Admissions *Applied:* 60. *Admitted:* 45. *Enrolled:* 35. *Average GMAT:* 650. *Average GPA:* 3.4

Academic Calendar 7-week course cycle.

After Graduation (Class of 2006–07) *Employed within 3 months of graduation:* 90%.

DEGREE MBA

MBA—International Master of Business Administration Full-time and part-time. 22 to 30 total credits required. 13 to 26 months to complete program. *Concentrations:* economics, entrepreneurship, finance, international and area business studies, management, management information systems, marketing.

RESOURCES AND SERVICES 25 on-campus PCs are available to graduate business students. Access to Internet/World Wide Web and online grade reports available. *Personal computer requirements:* Graduate business students are strongly recommended to purchase or lease a personal computer. *Placement services include:* Alumni network, career placement, job search course, career counseling/planning, and resume preparation.

EXPENSES *Tuition:* Full-time: $21,900. *Tuition (international):* Full-time: $21,900.

FINANCIAL AID (2007–08) 5 students received aid, including scholarships.

Financial Aid Contact Ms. Cindy Sinvani, Coordinator, International MBA, Ramat Gan, 52900, Israel. *Phone:* 972-3-5317914. *Fax:* 972-3-7384040. *E-mail:* imba@mail.biu.ac.il.

INTERNATIONAL STUDENTS 14% of students enrolled are international students. *Services and facilities:* Counseling/support services. Financial aid is available to international students.

International Student Contact Cindy Sinvani, Coordinator, International MBA, Ramat Gan, 52900, Israel. *Phone:* 972-3-5317914. *Fax:* 972-3-7384040. *E-mail:* imba@mail.biu.ac.il.

APPLICATION *Required:* GMAT, application form, baccalaureate/first degree, essay, interview, 2 letters of recommendation, transcripts of college work. *Recommended:* Work experience. *Application fee:* $100. Applications for domestic and international students are processed on a rolling basis.

Application Contact Shmuel Stashevsky, Director, International MBA, Ramat Gan, 52900, Israel. *Phone:* 972-3-5317914. *Fax:* 972-3-7384040. *E-mail:* imba@mail.biu.ac.il.

Technion-Israel Institute of Technology

Technion Graduate School

Haifa, Israel

Phone: 972-4-8294248 **Fax:** 972-4-8294453 **E-mail:** mba@ie.technion.ac.il

Business Program(s) Web Site: http://www.mba.technion.ac.il

DEGREE MBA

MBA—Master of Business Administration Part-time. GMAT, work experience and an undergraduate degree are required. 48 to 60 total credits required. 20 to 36 months to complete program. *Concentration:* technology management.

RESOURCES AND SERVICES 50 on-campus PCs are available to graduate business students. Access to Internet/World Wide Web and online grade reports available. *Personal computer requirements:* Graduate business students are strongly recommended to purchase or lease a personal computer. *Special opportunities include:* An international exchange program is available. *Placement services include:* Alumni network, electronic job bank, and career fairs.

Application Contact Hanna Shapira, Coordinator, MBA Student Services, Faculty of Industrial Engineering and Management, Technion City, Haifa, 32000, Israel. *Phone:* 972-4-8294248. *Fax:* 972-4-8294453. *E-mail:* mba@ie.technion.ac.il.

ITALY

Bocconi University
SDA Bocconi
Milan, Italy

Phone: 39-0258363297 **Fax:** 39-0258363275 **E-mail:** admissions@sdabocconi.it

Business Program(s) Web Site: http://www.sdabocconi.it/

Graduate Business Unit Enrollment *Total:* 252 (109 full-time; 143 part-time; 71 women; 85 international).

Graduate Business Faculty *Total:* 119 (92 full-time; 27 part-time).

Admissions *Applied:* 402. *Admitted:* 150. *Enrolled:* 109. *Average GMAT:* 660.

Academic Calendar Phases.

After Graduation (Class of 2006–07) *Employed within 3 months of graduation:* 87%.

DEGREE MBA

MBA—Master of Business Administration Full-time. Maximum of 12 months to complete program. *Concentrations:* finance, marketing, strategic management.

RESOURCES AND SERVICES 140 on-campus PCs are available to graduate business students. Access to Internet/World Wide Web available. *Personal computer requirements:* Graduate business students are required to have a personal computer. *Special opportunities include:* An international exchange program and an internship program are available. *Placement services include:* Alumni network, career placement, job search course, career counseling/planning, electronic job bank, resume referral, career fairs, job interviews arranged, resume preparation, and career library.

FINANCIAL AID (2007–08) 37 students received aid, including loans and scholarships. *Financial aid application deadline:* 4/30.

Financial Aid Contact Rossana Camera, Admissions and Financial Aid Officer, Via Balilla 18, Milano, 20136, Italy. *Phone:* 39-0258363297. *Fax:* 39-0258363275. *E-mail:* rossana.camera@sdabocconi.it.

INTERNATIONAL STUDENTS 34% of students enrolled are international students. *Services and facilities:* Counseling/support services, ESL/language courses, Housing location assistance, Language tutoring, Orientation, Visa Services. Financial aid is available to international students. *Required with application:* TOEFL with recommended score of 250 (computer), 600 (paper), or 100 (Internet); proof of adequate funds.

International Student Contact Simone Consonni, Student and Internal Relations, Via Balilla 18, Milano, 20136, Italy. *Phone:* 39-0258363271. *Fax:* 39-0258363275. *E-mail:* simone.consonni@sdabocconi.it.

APPLICATION *Required:* GMAT, application form, baccalaureate/first degree, essay, interview, 2 letters of recommendation, resume/curriculum vitae, transcripts of college work, 2 years of work experience. *Application fee:* 100 euros. Applications for domestic and international students are processed on a rolling basis.

Application Contact Rossana Camera, Admissions Officer, Via Balilla 18, Milano, 20136, Italy. *Phone:* 39-0258363297. *Fax:* 39-0258363275. *E-mail:* admissions@sdabocconi.it.

European School of Economics
MBA Programme
Lucca, Italy

Phone: 39-058305-10-22 Ext. 211 **Fax:** 39-058305-02-87

Business Program(s) Web Site: http://www.eselondon.ac.uk/campuses/lucca-florence-business-school

Admissions *Average GMAT:* 590. *Average GPA:* 3.2

Academic Calendar Four 10-12 week terms.

After Graduation (Class of 2006–07) *Employed within 3 months of graduation:* 90%.

DEGREES IMBA

IMBA—International Master of Business Administration in Finance and Banking Full-time and part-time. At least 96 total credits required. 12 to 18 months to complete program. *Concentrations:* banking, business ethics, business law, corporate accounting, economics, finance, financial management/planning, general MBA, human resources management, international banking, international finance, leadership, marketing, operations management.

IMBA—International Master of Business Administration in Marketing Management Full-time and part-time. At least 96 total credits required. 12 to 18 months to complete program. *Concentrations:* advertising, business ethics, business law, commerce, decision sciences, economics, entrepreneurship, general MBA, human resources management, information management, international business, international finance, international management, international marketing, international trade, marketing, marketing research, operations management, strategic management, supply chain management.

RESOURCES AND SERVICES 250 on-campus PCs are available to graduate business students. Access to Internet/World Wide Web available. *Personal computer requirements:* Graduate business students are strongly recommended to purchase or lease a personal computer. *Special opportunities include:* An international exchange program and an internship program are available. *Placement services include:* Alumni network, career placement, career counseling/planning, electronic job bank, resume referral, career fairs, job interviews arranged, resume preparation, and career library.

FINANCIAL AID (2007–08) Fellowships, scholarships, and teaching assistantships.

Financial Aid Contact Director of Financial Aid, Via Nieri 51, Lucca, 55100, Italy. *Phone:* 39-058305-10-22. *Fax:* 39-058305-02-87.

INTERNATIONAL STUDENTS *Services and facilities:* Counseling/support services, ESL/language courses, Housing location assistance, International student housing, International student organization, Language tutoring, Visa Services. Financial aid is available to international students. *Required with application:* IELT; TOEFL with recommended score of 550 (paper). *Recommended with application:* Proof of adequate funds.

International Student Contact Director of Graduate Studies, Via Nieri 51, Lucca, 55100, Italy. *Phone:* 39-058305-10-22. *Fax:* 39-058305-02-87.

APPLICATION *Required:* GMAT, application form, essay, 2 letters of recommendation, resume/curriculum vitae, transcripts of college work, 2 years of work experience. *Application fee:* 50 euros. Applications for domestic and international students are processed on a rolling basis.

Application Contact International Admissions Coordinator, Via Nieri 51, Lucca, 55040, Italy. *Phone:* 39-058305-10-22 Ext. 211. *Fax:* 39-058305-02-87.

See full description on page 608.

European School of Economics
MBA Programme
Milan, Italy

Phone: 39-02-365-04-235 **Fax:** 39-02-365-04-236 **E-mail:** ese.milano@uniese.it

Business Program(s) Web Site: http://www.eselondon.ac.uk/campuses/milan-business-school

European School of Economics (continued)

Academic Calendar Four 10-12 week terms.

DEGREE   MBA

MBA—Master of Business Administration Full-time and part-time. 12 to 18 months to complete program. *Concentrations:* general MBA, international finance, marketing.

RESOURCES AND SERVICES *Special opportunities include:* An internship program is available. *Placement services include:* Career placement, career counseling/planning, electronic job bank, job interviews arranged, resume preparation, and career library.

FINANCIAL AID (2007–08) Fellowships, scholarships, and teaching assistantships.

INTERNATIONAL STUDENTS *Required with application:* IELT; TOEFL with recommended score of 550 (paper). *Recommended with application:* Proof of adequate funds.

APPLICATION *Required:* GMAT, application form, essay, 2 letters of recommendation, resume/curriculum vitae, transcripts of college work, 2 years of work experience. *Application fee:* 50 British pounds. Applications for domestic and international students are processed on a rolling basis.

Application Contact Admission Office, Corso di Porta Vittoria, 16, Milan, 20122, Italy. *Phone:* 39-02-365-04-235. *Fax:* 39-02-365-04-236. *E-mail:* ese.milano@uniese.it.

See full description on page 608.

European School of Economics
MBA Programme

Rome, Italy

Phone: +39-0583-0510-22 **E-mail:** c.tighe@uniese.it

Business Program(s) Web Site: http://www.eselondon.ac.uk/campuses/rome-business-school

Academic Calendar Four 10-12 week terms.

DEGREES   MBA • MS

MBA—Master of Business Administration Full-time and part-time. 15 to 18 months to complete program. *Concentrations:* international finance, international marketing.

MS—Master of Science Full-time and part-time. 15 to 18 months to complete program. *Concentrations:* international finance, international management, international marketing.

RESOURCES AND SERVICES *Special opportunities include:* An internship program is available. *Placement services include:* Career placement, career counseling/planning, electronic job bank, job interviews arranged, resume preparation, and career library.

FINANCIAL AID (2007–08) Fellowships, scholarships, and teaching assistantships.

Financial Aid Contact Student Financial Services, Via Nieri, 51, Lucca, 55100, Italy. *Phone:* 39-0583-0510-22. *E-mail:* info@uniese.it.

INTERNATIONAL STUDENTS *Required with application:* IELT; TOEFL with recommended score of 550 (paper). *Recommended with application:* Proof of adequate funds.

International Student Contact Amanda Batarseh, Student Counseling, Via Nieri 51, Lucca, 55100, Italy. *Phone:* 39-0583-0510-22. *Fax:* 39-0583-0502-87. *E-mail:* b.amanda@uniese.it.

APPLICATION *Required:* GMAT, application form, essay, 2 letters of recommendation, resume/curriculum vitae, transcripts of college work, 2 years of work experience. *Application fee:* 50 British pounds. Applications for domestic and international students are processed on a rolling basis.

Application Contact Carrie Tighe, Admissions Office, Via Nieri, 51, Lucca, 55100, Italy. *Phone:* +39-0583-0510-22. *E-mail:* c.tighe@uniese.it.

See full description on page 608.

JAPAN

International University of Japan
Graduate School of International Management

Minami Uonuma-gu, Japan

Phone: 81-25-779-1500 **Fax:** 81-25-779-1187 **E-mail:** admgsim@iuj.ac.jp

Business Program(s) Web Site: http://ibs.iuj.ac.jp/

Graduate Business Unit Enrollment *Total:* 133 (133 full-time; 43 women; 109 international). *Average Age:* 29.

Graduate Business Faculty *Total:* 30 (10 full-time; 20 part-time).

Admissions *Applied:* 162. *Admitted:* 113. *Enrolled:* 76. *Average GMAT:* 608. *Average GPA:* 3.2

Academic Calendar Trimesters.

After Graduation (Class of 2006–07) *Employed within 3 months of graduation:* 93%. *Average starting salary:* 8,500,000 Japanese yen.

DEGREES   MBA • MBA equivalent

MBA—MBA Program Full-time. At least 54 total credits required. 21 to 48 months to complete program. *Concentrations:* accounting, advertising, Asian business studies, banking, business education, business ethics, business law, business policy/strategy, business studies, Chinese business studies, corporate accounting, economics, entrepreneurship, finance, financial economics, financial management/planning, general MBA, human resources development, human resources management, international banking, international business, international economics, international finance, international management, international marketing, international trade, investments and securities, Japanese business studies, leadership, logistics, management, management communication, management consulting, management science, managerial economics, manufacturing management, marketing, marketing research, new venture management, operations management, organizational behavior/development, organizational management, production management, risk management, statistics, strategic management, supply chain management, taxation.

MBA equivalent—e-Business Management Program Full-time. At least 30 total credits required. 12 to 24 months to complete program. *Concentrations:* accounting, business education, business ethics, business information science, business law, business policy/strategy, business studies, commerce, corporate accounting, electronic commerce (E-commerce), entrepreneurship, finance, financial economics, financial information systems, financial management/planning, human resources management, information management, information systems, international business, international finance, international marketing, management, management communication, management information systems, management systems analysis, marketing, marketing research, new venture management, operations management, organizational behavior/development, organizational management, project management, strategic management, supply chain management, telecommunications management.

RESOURCES AND SERVICES 100 on-campus PCs are available to graduate business students. Access to Internet/World Wide Web, online (class) registration, and online grade reports available. *Personal computer requirements:* Graduate business students are not required to have a personal computer. *Special opportunities include:* An international exchange program and an internship program are available. *Placement* services include: Alumni network, career placement, job search course, career counseling/planning, resume referral, career fairs, job interviews arranged, resume preparation, and career library.

EXPENSES *Tuition:* Full-time: 1,900,000 Japanese yen. Tuition and/or fees vary by academic program. *Graduate housing:* Room and board costs vary by type of accommodation. *Typical cost:* 744,000 Japanese yen (including board), 384,000 Japanese yen (room only).

FINANCIAL AID (2007–08) 35 students received aid, including research assistantships, scholarships, and teaching assistantships. *Financial aid application deadline:* 3/28.

Financial Aid Contact Ms. Miyoko Wada, Deputy Manager, Admissions and Curriculum Service Center, 777 Kokusai-cho, Minami Uonuma-shi, Niigata, Japan. *Phone:* 81-25-779-1500. *Fax:* 81-25-779-1187. *E-mail:* admgsim@iuj.ac.jp.

INTERNATIONAL STUDENTS 82% of students enrolled are international students. *Services and facilities:* Counseling/support services, ESL/language courses, Housing location assistance, International student housing, International student organization, Language tutoring, Orientation, Visa Services, Career counseling and services. Financial aid is available to international students. *Required with application:* TOEFL with recommended score of 250 (computer), 600 (paper), or 100 (Internet); proof of adequate funds; proof of health/immunizations.

International Student Contact Ms. Fumiko Hirasawa, Advisor, Admissions and Curriculum Service Center, 777 Kokusai-cho, Minami Uonuma-shi, Niigata, Japan. *Phone:* 81-25-779-1104. *Fax:* 81-25-779-1188. *E-mail:* info@iuj.ac.jp.

APPLICATION *Required:* GMAT, application form, baccalaureate/first degree, essay, 2 letters of recommendation, personal statement, transcripts of college work. *Recommended:* Resume/curriculum vitae, work experience. *Application fee:* 30,000 Japanese yen. *Deadlines:* 11/16 for fall, 2/1 for winter, 3/21 for spring, 5/2 for summer, 2/8 for winter (international), 3/28 for spring (international).

Application Contact Ms. Miyoko Wada, Deputy Manager, Admissions and Curriculum Service Center, 777 Kokusai-cho, Minami Uonuma-shi, Niigata, Japan. *Phone:* 81-25-779-1500. *Fax:* 81-25-779-1187. *E-mail:* admgsim@iuj.ac.jp.

Keio University
Keio Business School

Yokohama-shi, Japan

E-mail: gakukbs@info.keio.ac.jp

Business Program(s) Web Site: http://www.kbs.keio.ac.jp/

Graduate Business Unit Enrollment *Total:* 187 (187 full-time; 36 women; 7 international).

Graduate Business Faculty *Total:* 36 (26 full-time; 10 part-time).

Admissions *Applied:* 288. *Admitted:* 111. *Enrolled:* 96.

Academic Calendar Trimesters.

Accreditation AACSB—The Association to Advance Collegiate Schools of Business.

After Graduation (Class of 2006–07) *Employed within 3 months of graduation:* 90%.

DEGREE MBA

MBA—Master of Business Administration Full-time. At least 40 total credits required. Minimum of 24 months to complete program. *Concentration:* general MBA.

RESOURCES AND SERVICES 48 on-campus PCs are available to graduate business students. Access to Internet/World Wide Web available. *Personal computer requirements:* Graduate business students are strongly recommended to purchase or lease a personal computer. *Special opportunities include:* An international exchange program is available. *Placement services include:* Alumni network and career fairs.

FINANCIAL AID (2007–08) Loans and scholarships.

INTERNATIONAL STUDENTS 4% of students enrolled are international students. *Services and facilities:* Housing location assistance. Financial aid is not available to international students. *Required with application:* Proof of health/immunizations.

International Student Contact International Services, 2-1-1 Hiyoshi-honcho, Kohoku-ku, Yokohama, 223-8523, Japan. *Phone:* 45-564-2441. *Fax:* 45-562-3502. *E-mail:* gakukbs@info.keio.ac.jp.

APPLICATION *Required:* Application form, personal statement, resume/curriculum vitae, transcripts of college work. *Recommended:* Baccalaureate/first degree, essay, interview. *Application fee:* 35,000 Japanese yen. *Deadlines:* 9/11 for fall, 1/9 for spring.

Application Contact International Services, 2-1-1 Hiyoshi-honcho, Kohoku-ku, Yokohama, 223-8523, Japan. *E-mail:* gakukbs@info.keio.ac.jp.

Waseda University
Graduate School of Commerce

Tokyo, Japan

Phone: 81-3-52863877 **Fax:** 81-3-52724533 **E-mail:** wbs@list.waseda.jp

Business Program(s) Web Site: http://www.waseda.jp/wbs/index_en.html

Graduate Business Unit Enrollment *Total:* 450 (450 full-time). *Average Age:* 32.

Academic Calendar Quarters.

DEGREES MBA • MOT

MBA—Master of Business Administration Full-time. At least 50 total credits required. 12 to 48 months to complete program. *Concentrations:* accounting, Asian business studies, business information science, business policy/strategy, entrepreneurship, finance, information management, international finance, international management, Japanese business studies, logistics, management systems analysis, marketing, operations management, production management, strategic management, system management.

MOT—Master in Management of Technology Full-time. At least 50 total credits required. 12 to 48 months to complete program. *Concentration:* technology management.

RESOURCES AND SERVICES Access to Internet/World Wide Web available. *Personal computer requirements:* Graduate business students are not required to have a personal computer. *Special opportunities include:* An international exchange program and an internship program are available. *Placement services include:* Alumni network, career placement, career counseling/planning, electronic job bank, career fairs, and career library.

EXPENSES *Tuition:* Full-time: 1,650,000 Japanese yen. *Required fees:* Full-time: 263,000 Japanese yen. Tuition and/or fees vary by class time and academic program.

FINANCIAL AID (2007–08) 92 students received aid, including grants, scholarships, and teaching assistantships.

Financial Aid Contact Mr. Eng Seng Tan, Financial Aid Officer, Nishi-Waseda Building 7F, 1-21-1 Nishi-Waseda, Shinjuku-ku, Tokyo, 169-0051, Japan. *Phone:* 81-3-52863877. *Fax:* 81-3-52724533. *E-mail:* wbs@list.waseda.jp.

INTERNATIONAL STUDENTS *Services and facilities:* Counseling/support services, ESL/language courses, Housing location assistance, International student housing, International student organization, Language tutoring, Orientation, Visa Services. Financial aid is available to international students. *Required with application:* IELT; TOEFL; proof of adequate funds.

Waseda University (continued)

International Student Contact Yuichi Hasegawa, Admissions Officer, Nishi-Waseda Building 7F, 1-21-1 Nishi-Waseda, Shinjuku-ku, Japan. *Phone:* 81-3-52863877. *Fax:* 81-3-52724533. *E-mail:* wbs@ list.waseda.jp.

APPLICATION *Required:* GMAT, application form, essay, interview, 2 letters of recommendation, personal statement, transcripts of college work. School will accept GRE. *Recommended:* Baccalaureate/first degree, 3 years of work experience. *Application fee:* 35,000 Japanese yen. *Deadlines:* 9/18 for fall, 1/23 for winter, 4/18 for spring, 9/18 for fall (international), 1/23 for winter (international), 4/18 for spring (international).

Application Contact Yuichi Hasegawa, Admissions Officer, Nishi-Waseda Building 7F, 1-21-1 Nishi-Waseda, Shinjuku-ku, Tokyo, 169-0051, Japan. *Phone:* 81-3-52863877. *Fax:* 81-3-52724533. *E-mail:* wbs@list.waseda.jp.

LEBANON

American University of Beirut
MBA Program

Beirut, Lebanon

Phone: 961-1-374374 Ext. 3160 **Fax:** 961-1-750775 **E-mail:** sk00@aub.edu.lb

Business Program(s) Web Site: http://sb.aub.edu.lb

Graduate Business Unit Enrollment *Total:* 106 (19 full-time; 87 part-time; 61 women; 12 international). *Average Age:* 24.

Graduate Business Faculty *Total:* 75 (47 full-time; 28 part-time).

Admissions *Applied:* 86. *Admitted:* 33. *Enrolled:* 21. *Average GMAT:* 600. *Average GPA:* 3.3

Academic Calendar Semesters.

After Graduation (Class of 2006–07) *Employed within 3 months of graduation:* 87.3%. *Average starting salary:* $16,500.

DEGREES EMBA • MBA

EMBA—EMBA—Executive Master of Business Administration Full-time. 48 total credits required. 20 months to complete program. *Concentration:* executive programs.

MBA—Master of Business Administration Full-time and part-time. 42 to 60 total credits required. 14 to 48 months to complete program. *Concentration:* general MBA.

RESOURCES AND SERVICES 119 on-campus PCs are available to graduate business students. Access to Internet/World Wide Web, online (class) registration, and online grade reports available. *Personal computer requirements:* Graduate business students are not required to have a personal computer. *Placement services include:* Alumni network, career placement, career counseling/planning, electronic job bank, resume referral, career fairs, job interviews arranged, and resume preparation.

EXPENSES *Tuition (international):* Full-time: $14,232. Part-time: $593 per credit. Tuition and/or fees vary by number of courses or credits taken and academic program. *Graduate housing:* Room and board costs vary by number of occupants and type of accommodation. *Typical cost:* $2814 (room only).

FINANCIAL AID (2007–08) 21 students received aid, including research assistantships and scholarships. Aid is available to part-time students. *Financial aid application deadline:* 2/2.

Financial Aid Contact Dr. Salim Chahine, Director of the MBA Program, Bliss Street, PO Box 11-0236, Riad El-Solh 1107 2020, Beirut, Lebanon. *Phone:* 961-1-374444 Ext. 3722. *Fax:* 961-1-750214. *E-mail:* sc09@ aub.edu.lb.

INTERNATIONAL STUDENTS 11% of students enrolled are international students. *Services and facilities:* Counseling/support services, ESL/language courses, Housing location assistance, International student housing, International student organization, Language tutoring, Orientation, Visa Services. Financial aid is available to international students. *Required with application:* TOEFL with recommended score of 250 (computer) or 600 (paper); proof of health/immunizations.

International Student Contact Ms. Rania Murr, Coordinator of International Student Services, International Student Services Office, Bliss Street, PO Box 11-0236, Riad El-Solh 1107 2020, Beirut, Lebanon. *Phone:* 961-1-374374 Ext. 3176. *Fax:* 961-1-744-478. *E-mail:* rm64@ aub.edu.lb.

APPLICATION *Required:* GMAT, application form, baccalaureate/first degree, 2 letters of recommendation, resume/curriculum vitae, transcripts of college work, 2 years of work experience. *Recommended:* Essay, interview, personal statement. *Application fee:* 75,000 Lebanese pounds. Applications for domestic and international students are processed on a rolling basis.

Application Contact Dr. Salim Kanaan, Director of Admissions and Financial Aid, Bliss Street, College Hall, PO Box 11-0236, Riad El-Solh 1107 2020, Beirut, Lebanon. *Phone:* 961-1-374374 Ext. 3160. *Fax:* 961-1-750775. *E-mail:* sk00@aub.edu.lb.

LITHUANIA

Vytautas Magnus University
Faculty of Business and Management

Kaunus, Lithuania

Phone: 370-37-327855 **Fax:** 370-37-327857 **E-mail:** mba@evf.vdu.lt

DEGREE MBA

MBA—Master of Business Administration in Marketing and International Commerce Full-time. Bachelor's degree in Business, Management or Economics related subject required. At least 95 total credits required. Minimum of 12 months to complete program. *Concentration:* international business.

RESOURCES AND SERVICES 25 on-campus PCs are available to graduate business students. Access to Internet/World Wide Web, online (class) registration, and online grade reports available. *Personal computer requirements:* Graduate business students are not required to have a personal computer. *Special opportunities include:* An international exchange program is available. *Placement services include:* Alumni network, job search course, career counseling/planning, and career fairs.

Application Contact Ms. Jone Sakalyte, International Programs Coordinator, Daukanto 28, Kaunas, 44246, Lithuania. *Phone:* 370-37-327855. *Fax:* 370-37-327857. *E-mail:* mba@evf.vdu.lt.

MACAO

Asia International Open University
MBA Program

Macau, Macao

Phone: 853-28781698 **Fax:** 853-28781691 **E-mail:** genoffice@aiou.edu
Business Program(s) Web Site: http://www.aiou.edu/eng/mba_cur.htm

DEGREE MBA

MBA—Master of Business Administration Part-time. 60 total credits required. 15 to 48 months to complete program. *Concentration:* administration.

RESOURCES AND SERVICES Access to Internet/World Wide Web available. *Personal computer requirements:* Graduate business students are strongly recommended to purchase or lease a personal computer. *Placement services include:* Alumni network.

Application Contact Miss Linda Chan, Assistant Registrar, 3 andar, Edificio Royal Centre, Av. do Dr. Rodrigo Rodrigues, Macau, China. *Phone:* 853-28781698. *Fax:* 853-28781691. *E-mail:* genoffice@aiou.edu.

MACEDONIA

Saints Cyril and Methodius University
Faculty of Economics

Skopje, Macedonia

Phone: 389-2-3286839 **Fax:** 389-2-3118701 **E-mail:** pecen@eccf.ukim.edu.mk

Business Program(s) Web Site: http://www.eccf.ukim.edu.mk/

DEGREES MBA • MS

MBA—Master of Business Administration Full-time and part-time. 27 total credits required. 12 to 28 months to complete program. *Concentration:* general MBA.

MS—Accounting and Auditing Full-time. 60 total credits required. 12 to 18 months to complete program. *Concentration:* accounting.

MS—Business Economics Full-time. 60 total credits required. 12 to 18 months to complete program. *Concentration:* business education.

MS—Economic Development and International Finances Full-time. 60 total credits required. 12 to 18 months to complete program. *Concentrations:* developmental economics, international finance.

MS—European Studies Full-time. 60 total credits required. 12 to 18 months to complete program. *Concentration:* European business studies.

MS—Insurance Management Full-time. 60 total credits required. 12 to 18 months to complete program. *Concentration:* insurance.

MS—International Trade Full-time. 60 total credits required. 12 to 18 months to complete program. *Concentration:* international and area business studies.

MS—Marketing Full-time. 60 total credits required. 12 to 18 months to complete program. *Concentration:* marketing.

MS—Monetary Economics Full-time. 60 total credits required. 12 to 18 months to complete program. *Concentration:* financial economics.

RESOURCES AND SERVICES 103 on-campus PCs are available to graduate business students. Access to Internet/World Wide Web available. *Personal computer requirements:* Graduate business students are strongly recommended to purchase or lease a personal computer. *Placement services include:* Career counseling/planning and career fairs.

Application Contact Mr. Pece Borko Nedanoski, PhD, Vice-Dean of the Faculty of Economics Skopje, Boulevard Krste Misirkov bb, Skopje, 1 000, Macedonia. *Phone:* 389-2-3286839. *Fax:* 389-2-3118701. *E-mail:* pecen@eccf.ukim.edu.mk.

MALAYSIA

University of Malaya
Graduate School of Business

Kuala Lumpur, Malaysia

Phone: 60-3-26173044 **Fax:** 60-3-26173050 **E-mail:** gsb_fpp2@um.edu.my

Business Program(s) Web Site: http://www.um.edu.my/FPP

DEGREES MBA • MM

MBA—Master of Business Administration Full-time and part-time. At least 51 total credits required. 18 to 60 months to complete program. *Concentrations:* accounting, finance, health care, hospitality management, human resources management, international business, management information systems, marketing, organizational behavior/development, travel industry/tourism management.

MM—MM—Master of Management Part-time. At least 43 total credits required. 24 to 60 months to complete program. *Concentration:* management.

RESOURCES AND SERVICES 221 on-campus PCs are available to graduate business students. Access to Internet/World Wide Web and online (class) registration available. *Personal computer requirements:* Graduate business students are strongly recommended to purchase or lease a personal computer. *Special opportunities include:* An international exchange program is available. *Placement services include:* Alumni network, career placement, and resume referral.

Application Contact Miss Rafiza Hashim, Assistant Registrar, Graduate School of Business, Faculty Business and Accountancy, Level 4, Block C, City Campus, Jalan Tun Ismail, Kuala Lumpur, 50480, Malaysia. *Phone:* 60-3-26173044. *Fax:* 60-3-26173050. *E-mail:* gsb_fpp2@um.edu.my.

MEXICO

Alliant International University–México City
Marshall Goldsmith School of Management

Mexico City, Mexico

Phone: 52-5552642187 Ext. 108 **Fax:** 52-5552642188 **E-mail:** vquiroz@alliant.edu

Business Program(s) Web Site: http://www.alliant.edu/wps/wcm/connect/website/Home/About+Alliant/Schools+%26+Colleges/Marshall+Goldsmith+School+of+Management+%28MGSM%29/Business+%26

Admissions *Average GMAT:* 500. *Average GPA:* 3.0

Academic Calendar Semesters.

After Graduation (Class of 2006–07) *Employed within 3 months of graduation:* 70%.

DEGREE MBA

MBA—Igor Ansoff Strategic Management MBA/MIBA Full-time. 39 total credits required. *Concentration:* strategic management.

RESOURCES AND SERVICES 12 on-campus PCs are available to graduate business students. Access to Internet/World Wide Web available. *Personal computer requirements:* Graduate business students are strongly

Alliant International University–México City (continued)

recommended to purchase or lease a personal computer. *Special opportunities include:* An international exchange program and an internship program are available. *Placement services include:* Alumni network.

EXPENSES *Tuition:* Full-time: $14,400. Part-time: $7200 per semester. *Tuition (international):* Full-time: $14,400. Part-time: $7200 per semester. *Required fees:* Full-time: $450. Part-time: $450 per semester. Tuition and/or fees vary by academic program.

FINANCIAL AID (2007–08) Grants and loans.

Financial Aid Contact Vania Quiroz, General Operations Manager, Alvaro Obregón 110, Colonia Roma,, Mexico, Mexico. *Phone:* 52-5552642187 Ext. 108. *Fax:* 52-5552642188. *E-mail:* vquiroz@alliant.edu.

INTERNATIONAL STUDENTS *Services and facilities:* ESL/language courses, Housing location assistance, Language tutoring, Orientation. Financial aid is not available to international students. *Required with application:* TOEFL with recommended score of 213 (computer) or 550 (paper).

International Student Contact Eric A. Pearse, Program Director, Álvaro Obregón 110 (corner of Orizaba), Col. Roma, Mexico, 06700, Mexico. *Phone:* 52-5552642187 Ext. 105. *Fax:* 52-5552642188. *E-mail:* epearse@alliant.com.mx.

APPLICATION *Required:* Application form, baccalaureate/first degree, essay, 2 letters of recommendation, personal statement, transcripts of college work. *Application fee:* $55. Applications for domestic and international students are processed on a rolling basis.

Application Contact Vania Quiroz, General Operations Manager, Alvaro Obregón 110, Colonia Roma,, Mexico, 06700, Mexico. *Phone:* 52-5552642187 Ext. 108. *Fax:* 52-5552642188. *E-mail:* vquiroz@alliant.edu.

Instituto Tecnológico y de Estudios Superiores de Monterrey, Campus Ciudad Juárez

Program in Business Administration

Ciudad Juárez, Mexico

Phone: 656-629-9100 Ext. 2402 **Fax:** 656-629-9101 **E-mail:** jorge.montes@itesm.mx

Business Program(s) Web Site: http://www.cdj.itesm.mx/maestrias

Graduate Business Unit Enrollment *Total:* 480 (400 full-time; 80 part-time; 200 women; 10 international). *Average Age:* 42.

Graduate Business Faculty *Total:* 34 (4 full-time; 30 part-time).

Admissions *Applied:* 75. *Admitted:* 50. *Enrolled:* 30. *Average GPA:* 88/100 scale

Academic Calendar Trimesters.

After Graduation (Class of 2006–07) *Employed within 3 months of graduation:* 99%. *Average starting salary:* 25,000 Mexican pesos.

DEGREE MBA

MBA—Master in Business Administration Full-time and part-time. Distance learning option. 192 total credits required. 18 to 60 months to complete program. *Concentrations:* finance, human resources management, manufacturing management, marketing.

RESOURCES AND SERVICES 100 on-campus PCs are available to graduate business students. Access to Internet/World Wide Web, online (class) registration, and online grade reports available. *Personal computer requirements:* Graduate business students are required to have a personal computer. *Special opportunities include:* An international exchange program is available. *Placement services include:* Alumni network, career placement, electronic job bank, and career fairs.

EXPENSES *Tuition:* Full-time: 75,000 Mexican pesos. Part-time: 37,500 Mexican pesos per course. *Tuition (international):* Full-time: 75,000 Mexican pesos. Part-time: 37,500 Mexican pesos per course. Tuition and/or fees vary by number of courses or credits taken.

FINANCIAL AID (2007–08) 210 students received aid, including fellowships, loans, and scholarships. Aid is available to part-time students. *Financial aid application deadline:* 8/4.

Financial Aid Contact Lic. Irma Romero, Financial Aid Coordinator, PO Box 10482, El Paso, TX 79995-0482. *Phone:* 656-629-9100 Ext. 3703. *Fax:* 656-629-9101. *E-mail:* irma.romero@itesm.mx.

INTERNATIONAL STUDENTS 2% of students enrolled are international students. *Services and facilities:* Counseling/support services, ESL/language courses, Orientation. Financial aid is available to international students. *Required with application:* TOEFL with recommended score of 500 (paper).

International Student Contact Ms. Ewa Stankowska, International Programs Coordinator, PO Box 10482, El Paso, TX 79995-0482. *Phone:* 656-629-9100 Ext. 2553. *Fax:* 656-629-9101. *E-mail:* eva.stankowska@itesm.mx.

APPLICATION *Required:* Application form, baccalaureate/first degree, transcripts of college work. School will accept GMAT and GRE. *Recommended:* Interview, resume/curriculum vitae, 2 years of work experience. *Application fee:* 500 Mexican pesos. *Deadlines:* 9/1 for fall, 1/5 for spring, 7/10 for summer, 9/1 for fall (international), 1/5 for spring (international), 7/10 for summer (international).

Application Contact Jorge Arturo Montes Figueroa, Admissions Coordinator, PO Box 10482, El Paso, TX 79995-0482. *Phone:* 656-629-9100 Ext. 2402. *Fax:* 656-629-9101. *E-mail:* jorge.montes@itesm.mx.

MONACO

The International University of Monaco

Graduate Programs

Monte Carlo, Monaco

Phone: 377-97-986986 **Fax:** 377-92-052830 **E-mail:** info@monaco.edu

Business Program(s) Web Site: http://www.monaco.edu

Graduate Business Unit Enrollment *Total:* 211 (210 full-time; 1 part-time; 98 women; 209 international). *Average Age:* 30.

Graduate Business Faculty *Total:* 33 (23 full-time; 10 part-time).

Admissions *Applied:* 220. *Admitted:* 170. *Enrolled:* 130. *Average GMAT:* 528. *Average GPA:* 3.3

Academic Calendar Trimesters.

After Graduation (Class of 2006–07) *Employed within 3 months of graduation:* 100%. *Average starting salary:* 79,000 euros.

DEGREES EMBA • M Sc • MBA

EMBA—Executive Master of Business Administration Full-time. Distance learning option. Combination of residency and distance education; 6 weeks of residency in Monaco over 15 months. Up to 54 total credits required. 15 to 30 months to complete program. *Concentration:* general MBA.

M Sc—Master of Science in Luxury Goods and Services Full-time and part-time. 60 total credits required. 10 months to complete program. *Concentration:* other.

M Sc—Master's in Finance Full-time. At least 60 total credits required. 10 months to complete program. *Concentrations:* banking, finance, financial engineering, financial management/planning, international banking, international finance, investments and securities.

MBA—MonacoMBA Full-time. GMAT required. At least 69 total credits required. 10 months to complete program. *Concentrations:* finance, general MBA, international marketing, other.

RESOURCES AND SERVICES 35 on-campus PCs are available to graduate business students. Access to Internet/World Wide Web and online grade reports available. *Personal computer requirements:* Graduate business students are strongly recommended to purchase or lease a personal computer. *Special opportunities include:* An international exchange program and an internship program are available. *Placement services include:* Alumni network, career placement, job search course, career counseling/planning, electronic job bank, resume referral, job interviews arranged, and resume preparation.

EXPENSES *Tuition:* Full-time: 19,900 euros. *Tuition (international):* Full-time: 19,900 euros. *Required fees:* Full-time: 2400 euros.

FINANCIAL AID (2007–08) 9 students received aid, including scholarships and work study. *Financial aid application deadline:* 5/1.

Financial Aid Contact Ms. Leila Bello, Admissions Coordinator, 2, avenue Albert II, Monte Carlo, MC 98000, Monaco. *Phone:* 377-97-986986. *Fax:* 377-92-052830. *E-mail:* info@monaco.edu.

INTERNATIONAL STUDENTS 99% of students enrolled are international students. *Services and facilities:* Counseling/support services, ESL/language courses, Housing location assistance, Language tutoring, Orientation, Visa Services. Financial aid is available to international students. *Required with application:* IELT with recommended score of 6; TOEFL with recommended score of 213 (computer) or 550 (paper). *Recommended with application:* Proof of adequate funds.

International Student Contact Ms. Leila Bello, Admissions Coordinator, 2, avenue Albert II, Monte Carlo, MC 98000, Monaco. *Phone:* 377-97-986986. *Fax:* 377-92-052830. *E-mail:* lbello@monaco.edu.

APPLICATION *Required:* Application form, baccalaureate/first degree, essay, 2 letters of recommendation, resume/curriculum vitae, transcripts of college work, 3 years of work experience. School will accept GMAT and GRE. *Recommended:* Interview, personal statement. *Application fee:* 100 euros. Applications for domestic and international students are processed on a rolling basis.

Application Contact Ms. Leila Bello, Admissions Coordinator, 2, avenue Albert II, Monte Carlo, MC 98000, Monaco. *Phone:* 377-97-986986. *Fax:* 377-92-052830. *E-mail:* info@monaco.edu.

NETHERLANDS

Erasmus University Rotterdam

Rotterdam School of Management

Rotterdam, Netherlands

Phone: 31-10-4082222 **Fax:** 31-10-4529509 **E-mail:** mba.info@rsm.nl

Business Program(s) Web Site: http://www.rsm.nl

Accreditation AACSB—The Association to Advance Collegiate Schools of Business.

DEGREES MBA

MBA—Executive Master of Business Administration Part-time. 24 months to complete program. *Concentrations:* electronic commerce (E-commerce), entrepreneurship, general MBA, international business, international finance, international management, international marketing, management consulting, management information systems, strategic management.

MBA—Full-Time International Master of Business Administration Full-time. 15 months to complete program. *Concentrations:* electronic commerce (E-commerce), entrepreneurship, general MBA, international business, international finance, international marketing, management information systems, strategic management.

MBA—Global Executive OneMBA Part-time. Distance learning option. 21 months to complete program. *Concentrations:* general MBA, international business, international finance, international management, international marketing, leadership, organizational management, strategic management.

RESOURCES AND SERVICES 80 on-campus PCs are available to graduate business students. Access to Internet/World Wide Web and online (class) registration available. *Personal computer requirements:* Graduate business students are required to have a personal computer. *Special opportunities include:* An international exchange program and an internship program are available. *Placement services include:* Alumni network, career placement, job search course, career counseling/planning, electronic job bank, resume referral, career fairs, job interviews arranged, resume preparation, and career library.

Application Contact Admissions Office, Admissions Office, J-Building, Burgemeester Oudlaan 50, Rotterdam, 3062 PA, Netherlands. *Phone:* 31-10-4082222. *Fax:* 31-10-4529509. *E-mail:* mba.info@rsm.nl.

The Hague University

Faculty of Economics and Management

The Hague, Netherlands

Phone: 31-70-4458284 **Fax:** 31-70-4457951 **E-mail:** p.p.l.a.baart@hhs.nl

Business Program(s) Web Site: http://www.thehagueuniversity.nl

DEGREES MBA • MM • MMPA

MBA—Full-Time International Master of Business Administration Full-time and part-time. Undergraduate degree in a business related field, TOEFL and GMAT and/or pre-MBA required. 60 total credits required. 12 to 30 months to complete program. *Concentrations:* accounting, finance, general MBA, human resources management, marketing, project management.

MBA—Part-Time Executive Master of Business Administration Full-time and part-time. 2 years of work experience, TOEFL and GMAT and/or pre-MBA required. 60 total credits required. 12 to 30 months to complete program. *Concentrations:* accounting, finance, human resources management, marketing, project management.

MM—Master in Facility Management Part-time. Proficiency in Dutch language required. 60 total credits required. 12 to 30 months to complete program. *Concentrations:* accounting, administration, facilities management, finance, hospitality management, international business, marketing, nonprofit organization, organizational behavior/development, sports/entertainment management, strategic management.

MMPA—Master in Accounting and Controlling Full-time and part-time. Undergraduate education and experience in accounting and controlling required. 60 total credits required. 12 to 28 months to complete program. *Concentrations:* accounting, electronic commerce (E-commerce), finance, financial information systems, human resources management, information management.

RESOURCES AND SERVICES 500 on-campus PCs are available to graduate business students. Access to Internet/World Wide Web, online (class) registration, and online grade reports available. *Personal computer requirements:* Graduate business students are strongly recommended to purchase or lease a personal computer. *Special opportunities include:* An internship program is available. *Placement services include:* Alumni network, resume referral, resume preparation, and career library.

Application Contact Mr. Peter-Paul L.A. Baart, MBA Course Manager, Master Studies, Room ST3.19, J. Westerdijkplein 75, The Hague, 2521 EN, Netherlands. *Phone:* 31-70-4458284. *Fax:* 31-70-4457951. *E-mail:* p.p.l.a.baart@hhs.nl.

See full description on page 628.

Hotel Management School Maastricht

MBA Program

Maastricht, Netherlands

Phone: 31-43-3528282 Ext. 210 **Fax:** 31-43-3528285 **E-mail:** admissions@mbahoteltourism.com

Business Program(s) Web Site: http://www.mbahoteltourism.com

Graduate Business Unit Enrollment *Total:* 22 (22 full-time; 12 women; 15 international).

Graduate Business Faculty *Total:* 34 (4 full-time; 30 part-time).

Admissions *Applied:* 43. *Admitted:* 27. *Enrolled:* 22.

Academic Calendar Trimesters.

After Graduation (Class of 2006–07) *Employed within 3 months of graduation:* 100%.

DEGREES MBA • MIIM

MBA—Master of Business Administration in Hotel and Tourism Management Full-time and part-time. 3 years of work experience required. 60 to 72 total credits required. 12 to 48 months to complete program. *Concentrations:* hospitality management, international business, international hospitality and restaurant business, international hotel and resort management, management, travel industry/tourism management.

MIIM—Innovative Hospitality Management Full-time. 60 total credits required. 12 months to complete program. *Concentrations:* hospitality management, international hospitality and restaurant business, international hotel and resort management, management, travel industry/tourism management.

RESOURCES AND SERVICES 80 on-campus PCs are available to graduate business students. Access to Internet/World Wide Web available. *Personal computer requirements:* Graduate business students are strongly recommended to purchase or lease a personal computer. *Special opportunities include:* An international exchange program and an internship program are available. *Placement services include:* Alumni network, career placement, career counseling/planning, career fairs, and job interviews arranged.

Financial Aid Contact Mr. Matt Heckman, Resources Manager, PO Box 3900, Maastricht, 6202 NX, Netherlands. *Phone:* 31-43-3528282 Ext. 220. *Fax:* 31-43-3528285. *E-mail:* resources@mbahoteltourism.com.

INTERNATIONAL STUDENTS 68% of students enrolled are international students. *Services and facilities:* Counseling/support services, ESL/language courses, Housing location assistance, International student housing, Language tutoring, Orientation, Visa Services. Financial aid is not available to international students. *Required with application:* TOEFL with recommended score of 213 (computer) or 550 (paper); proof of health/immunizations.

International Student Contact MBA Service Desk, PO Box 3900, Maastricht, 6202 NX, Netherlands. *Phone:* 31-43-3528282. *Fax:* 31-43-3528285. *E-mail:* info@mbahoteltourism.com.

APPLICATION *Required:* Application form, baccalaureate/first degree, essay, interview, 2 letters of recommendation, personal statement, transcripts of college work, 3 years of work experience. *Recommended:* Resume/curriculum vitae. *Application fee:* 150 euros. Applications for domestic and international students are processed on a rolling basis.

Application Contact Ms. Carol L. Stijnen, MBA Office, PO Box 3900, Maastricht, 6202 NX, Netherlands. *Phone:* 31-43-3528282 Ext. 210. *Fax:* 31-43-3528285. *E-mail:* admissions@mbahoteltourism.com.

Nyenrode Business Universiteit

Netherlands Business School

Breukelen, Netherlands

Phone: 31-346-291291 **Fax:** 31-346-291450 **E-mail:** v.bressers@nyenrode.nl

Business Program(s) Web Site: http://www.nyenrode.nl/

Graduate Business Unit Enrollment *Total:* 4,672.

Graduate Business Faculty *Total:* 143 (54 full-time; 89 part-time).

Admissions *Average GMAT:* 580. *Average GPA:* 3.5

Academic Calendar Blocks.

After Graduation (Class of 2006–07) *Average starting salary:* 60,000 euros.

DEGREES M Sc • MBA

M Sc—Master of Science in Management Full-time and part-time. Bachelor's degree or equivalent, maximum two years' work experience required. 16 months to complete program. *Concentrations:* entrepreneurship, finance, international management, management, management information systems, marketing, operations management, organizational behavior/development, statistics, supply chain management.

MBA—International Master of Business Administration Full-time. A minimum of 3 years of work experience required. At least 80 total credits required. Maximum of 13 months to complete program. *Concentrations:* entrepreneurship, international management, management, management information systems, marketing, operations management, organizational behavior/development, statistics, supply chain management.

MBA—Part-Time Master of Business Administration Part-time. Distance learning option. 4 years of work experience required. At least 69 total credits required. Maximum of 21 months to complete program. *Concentrations:* entrepreneurship, facilities management, finance, international management, management, marketing, operations management, statistics, supply chain management, technology management.

RESOURCES AND SERVICES 90 on-campus PCs are available to graduate business students. Access to Internet/World Wide Web, online (class) registration, and online grade reports available. *Personal computer requirements:* Graduate business students are strongly recommended to purchase or lease a personal computer. *Special opportunities include:* An internship program is available. *Placement services include:* Alumni network, career placement, job search course, career counseling/planning, electronic job bank, resume referral, career fairs, job interviews arranged, resume preparation, and career library.

EXPENSES Tuition and/or fees vary by class time, number of courses or credits taken, and academic program. *Graduate housing:* Room and board costs vary by number of occupants, type of accommodation, and type of board plan.

FINANCIAL AID (2007–08) Scholarships. Aid is available to part-time students. *Financial aid application deadline:* 7/1.

Financial Aid Contact Mrs. Bianca van Eunen, Scholarship Officer, Nyenrode Scholarship and Financial Aid Office, Straatweg 25, PO Box 130, Breukelen, 3620 AC, Netherlands. *Phone:* 31-346-291720. *Fax:* 31-346-291450. *E-mail:* scholarships@nyenrode.nl.

INTERNATIONAL STUDENTS *Services and facilities:* Counseling/support services, International student housing, International student organization, Orientation, Visa Services, Housing provided on campus. Financial aid is available to international students. *Required with application:* IELT with recommended score of 6.5; TOEFL with recommended score of 250 (computer), 600 (paper), or 100 (Internet); proof of adequate funds; proof of health/immunizations.

International Student Contact Mrs. Yamit Gutman, MBA Programs Manager, MBA Office, Straatweg 25, PO Box 130, Breukelen, 3620 AC, Netherlands. *Phone:* 31-346-291618. *Fax:* 31-346-291450. *E-mail:* y.gutman@nyenrode.nl.

APPLICATION *Required:* GMAT, application form, baccalaureate/first degree, essay, interview, 2 letters of recommendation, resume/curriculum vitae, transcripts of college work, 3 years of work experience. *Recommended:* Personal statement. *Application fee:* 80 euros. Applications for domestic and international students are processed on a rolling basis.

Application Contact Mrs. Victoria Bressers, Head of Admissions, MBA Office, Straatweg 25, PO Box 130, Breukelen, 3620 AC, Netherlands. *Phone:* 31-346-291291. *Fax:* 31-346-291450. *E-mail:* v.bressers@ nyenrode.nl.

Open University of the Netherlands
Business Programs
Heerlen, Netherlands

Phone: +31-43-3884619 **Fax:** +31-43-3884970 **E-mail:** information@euromba.org

Business Program(s) Web Site: http://www.euromba.org

DEGREE MBA

MBA—Euro Master of Business Administration Part-time. Distance learning option. Proficiency in English required. 24 to 36 months to complete program. *Concentrations:* business law, European business studies, human resources management, international business, international finance, international management, international marketing, public policy and administration, strategic management, technology management.

RESOURCES AND SERVICES Access to Internet/World Wide Web, online (class) registration, and online grade reports available. *Personal computer requirements:* Graduate business students are required to have a personal computer. *Special opportunities include:* An international exchange program is available. *Placement services include:* Alumni network, electronic job bank, career fairs, resume preparation, and career library.

Application Contact Dr. Stuart Dixon, Academic Director, Euro MBA Programme, UMBS/Euro MBA, Tongersestraat 53, PO Box 616, Maastricht, 6200 MD, Netherlands. *Phone:* +31-43-3884619. *Fax:* +31-43-3884970. *E-mail:* information@euromba.org.

NEW ZEALAND

Manukau Institute of Technology
Manukau Business School
Auckland, New Zealand

Phone: 649-9687789 **Fax:** 649-9687783 **E-mail:** mba@manukau.ac.nz

Business Program(s) Web Site: http://www.manukau.ac.nz/mba

DEGREES MBA • MIB

MBA—Master of Business Administration Part-time. Distance learning option. 1 year of management experience required. *Concentration:* general MBA.

MIB—Master of International Business Part-time. Distance learning option. 1 year of management experience required. *Concentrations:* international business, international management.

RESOURCES AND SERVICES Access to Internet/World Wide Web available. *Personal computer requirements:* Graduate business students are strongly recommended to purchase or lease a personal computer. *Placement services include:* Alumni network.

Application Contact Mrs. Elly Forsyth, MBA Programme Manager, Manukau Institute of Technology, Manukau Business School, Private Bag 94006, Manukau City, 1730, New Zealand. *Phone:* 649-9687789. *Fax:* 649-9687783. *E-mail:* mba@manukau.ac.nz.

University of Canterbury
Department of Management
Christchurch, New Zealand

Phone: 3-364-2657 **Fax:** 3-364-2925 **E-mail:** venkat.pulakanam@canterbury.ac.nz

Business Program(s) Web Site: http://www.mba.canterbury.ac.nz

Graduate Business Faculty 20 full-time.

Academic Calendar Semesters.

DEGREE MBA

MBA—Master of Business Administration Full-time and part-time. 15 to 30 months to complete program. *Concentrations:* accounting, economics, finance, human resources management, management, management information systems, marketing, organizational behavior/ development, production management, quantitative analysis, strategic management.

RESOURCES AND SERVICES 30 on-campus PCs are available to graduate business students. *Personal computer requirements:* Graduate business students are not required to have a personal computer. *Placement services include:* Career placement and career counseling/planning.

FINANCIAL AID (2007–08) Grants, loans, and scholarships.

Financial Aid Contact MBA Secretary, Private Bag 4800, Christchurch, 8041, New Zealand. *Phone:* 3-364-2657. *Fax:* 3-364-2925.

INTERNATIONAL STUDENTS Financial aid is available to international students. *Required with application:* IELT; TOEFL with recommended score of 600 (paper); TWE.

International Student Contact International Office, Private Bag 4800, Christchurch, 8041, New Zealand. *Phone:* 3-364-2459. *Fax:* 3-364-2171. *E-mail:* international@canterbury.ac.nz.

APPLICATION *Required:* Application form, baccalaureate/first degree, interview, 3 letters of recommendation, personal statement, resume/ curriculum vitae, transcripts of college work, 5 years of work experience. School will accept GMAT. *Application fee:* 25,000 New Zealand dollars, 39,900 New Zealand dollars (international). *Deadlines:* 12/15 for winter, 11/15 for winter (international).

Application Contact Dr. Venkat Pulakanam, MBA Director, College of Business and Economics, Private Bag 4800, Christchurch, New Zealand. *Phone:* 3-364-2657. *Fax:* 3-364-2925. *E-mail:* venkat.pulakanam@ canterbury.ac.nz.

University of Otago
School of Business
Dunedin, New Zealand

Phone: 64-3-4798046 **Fax:** 64-3-4798045 **E-mail:** mbainfo@business.otago.ac.nz

Business Program(s) Web Site: http://www.otagomba.co.nz

Admissions *Average GMAT:* 590.

Academic Calendar Quarters.

After Graduation (Class of 2006–07) *Employed within 3 months of graduation:* 92%.

DEGREES MBA

MBA—Executive Master of Business Administration Part-time. 5 years of work experience required. 24 to 48 months to complete program. *Concentration:* executive programs.

MBA—Master of Business Administration Full-time. 3 years of work experience required. 16 to 48 months to complete program. *Concentrations:* international business, strategic management.

University of Otago (continued)

RESOURCES AND SERVICES 500 on-campus PCs are available to graduate business students. Access to Internet/World Wide Web available. *Personal computer requirements:* Graduate business students are not required to have a personal computer. *Special opportunities include:* An international exchange program and an internship program are available. *Placement services include:* Alumni network, career counseling/planning, resume referral, resume preparation, and career library.

EXPENSES *Tuition (state resident):* Full-time: 22,275 New Zealand dollars. *Tuition (international):* Full-time: 28,800 New Zealand dollars. *Required fees:* Full-time: 600 New Zealand dollars. Tuition and/or fees vary by academic program. *Graduate housing:* Room and board costs vary by campus location, number of occupants, type of accommodation, and type of board plan. *Typical cost:* 11,000 New Zealand dollars (including board), 8500 New Zealand dollars (room only).

FINANCIAL AID (2007–08) Research assistantships, scholarships, teaching assistantships, and work study. *Financial aid application deadline:* 6/30.

Financial Aid Contact MBA Admissions Office, PO Box 56, Dunedin, New Zealand. *Phone:* 64-3-4798046. *Fax:* 64-3-4798045. *E-mail:* mbainfo@business.otago.ac.nz.

INTERNATIONAL STUDENTS *Services and facilities:* Counseling/support services, ESL/language courses, Housing location assistance, International student housing, International student organization, Language tutoring, Orientation, Visa Services, Airport pickup on arrival. Financial aid is not available to international students. *Required with application:* IELT with recommended score of 6.5; TOEFL with recommended score of 280 (computer) or 650 (paper). *Recommended with application:* Proof of adequate funds; proof of health/immunizations.

International Student Contact MBA Admissions Office, PO Box 56, Dunedin, New Zealand. *Phone:* 64-3-4798046. *Fax:* 64-3-4798045. *E-mail:* mbainfo@business.otago.ac.nz.

APPLICATION *Required:* GMAT, application form, baccalaureate/first degree, essay, interview, 2 letters of recommendation, personal statement, resume/curriculum vitae, transcripts of college work, 3 years of work experience. School will accept GRE. *Application fee:* 100 New Zealand dollars. Applications for domestic and international students are processed on a rolling basis.

Application Contact MBA Admissions Office, PO Box 56, Dunedin, New Zealand. *Phone:* 64-3-4798046. *Fax:* 64-3-4798045. *E-mail:* mbainfo@business.otago.ac.nz.

NORWAY

Norwegian School of Management
Graduate School

Sandvika, Norway

Phone: 47-46410083 **Fax:** 47-21048000 **E-mail:** kristin.olberg@bi.no

Business Program(s) Web Site: http://www.bi.edu

Graduate Business Unit Enrollment *Total:* 1,720 (900 full-time; 820 part-time; 760 women; 100 international). *Average Age:* 32.

Graduate Business Faculty *Total:* 124 (100 full-time; 24 part-time).

Admissions *Applied:* 2,212. *Admitted:* 1,902. *Enrolled:* 1,720. *Average GMAT:* 600.

Academic Calendar Semesters.

After Graduation (Class of 2006–07) *Employed within 3 months of graduation:* 87%. *Average starting salary:* 550,000 Norwegian kroners.

DEGREES EMBA • MBA • MS

EMBA—Executive Master of Business Administration Part-time. 120 total credits required. 18 months to complete program. *Concentrations:* business studies, combined degrees, executive programs, finance, leadership, strategic management.

MBA—Full-Time Master of Business Administration Full-time. 120 total credits required. 11 months to complete program. *Concentrations:* Chinese business studies, finance, general MBA, leadership, strategic management.

MS—Master of Science Full-time. At least 40 total credits required. 12 to 36 months to complete program. *Concentrations:* administration, Asian business studies, combined degrees, corporate accounting, economics, entrepreneurship, European business studies, financial economics, human resources management, international business, international management, international marketing, leadership, marketing, organizational behavior/development, other, strategic management.

RESOURCES AND SERVICES 75 on-campus PCs are available to graduate business students. Access to Internet/World Wide Web, online (class) registration, and online grade reports available. *Personal computer requirements:* Graduate business students are strongly recommended to purchase or lease a personal computer. *Special opportunities include:* An international exchange program is available. *Placement services include:* Alumni network, job search course, career counseling/planning, electronic job bank, resume referral, career fairs, resume preparation, and career library.

EXPENSES *Tuition:* Full-time: 60,800 Norwegian kroners. Part-time: 62,000 Norwegian kroners per year. *Tuition (international):* Full-time: 60,800 Norwegian kroners. Part-time: 62,000 Norwegian kroners per year. *Required fees:* Full-time: 440 Norwegian kroners. Tuition and/or fees vary by class time, number of courses or credits taken, and academic program.

FINANCIAL AID (2007–08) 38 students received aid, including grants, loans, research assistantships, scholarships, and teaching assistantships. *Financial aid application deadline:* 4/15.

Financial Aid Contact Ms. Kristin Ølberg, Director of Studies MBA Programmes, Nydalsveien 37, NO-0442 Oslo, Oslo, 0442, Norway. *Phone:* 47-46410083. *Fax:* 47-21048000. *E-mail:* kristin.olberg@bi.no.

INTERNATIONAL STUDENTS 6% of students enrolled are international students. *Services and facilities:* Counseling/support services, ESL/language courses, Housing location assistance, International student housing, International student organization, Language tutoring, Orientation, Visa Services, airport collection service for exchange students. Financial aid is available to international students. *Required with application:* Proof of adequate funds. *Recommended with application:* TWE.

International Student Contact Mrs. Ellen Tobiasson, International Coordinator, BI Norwegian School of Management, Nydalsveien 37, NO-0442 Oslo, Oslo, 0442, Norway. *Phone:* 47-06600. *Fax:* 47 21048000. *E-mail:* ellen.tobiasson@bi.no.

APPLICATION *Required:* GMAT, application form, baccalaureate/first degree, interview, 2 letters of recommendation, personal statement, resume/curriculum vitae, transcripts of college work, 3 years of work experience. *Recommended:* Essay. *Application fee:* 0 Norwegian kroners. Applications for domestic and international students are processed on a rolling basis.

Application Contact Ms. Kristin Ølberg, Director of Studies MBA Programmes, Nydalsveien 37, NO-0042 Oslo, Oslo, 0042, Norway. *Phone:* 47-46410083. *Fax:* 47-21048000. *E-mail:* kristin.olberg@bi.no.

PAKISTAN

Lahore University of Management Sciences

Graduate School of Business Administration

Lahore Cantt, Pakistan

Phone: 92-42-5722670 Ext. 2107 **Fax:** 92-42-5722591 **E-mail:** skhan@lums.edu.pk

Business Program(s) Web Site: http://www.lums.edu.pk/schools%20%26%20Programs/grad_school/MBA/mba_overview.asp

DEGREE MBA

MBA—Master of Business Administration Full-time. Minimum of 24 months to complete program. *Concentration:* general MBA.

RESOURCES AND SERVICES 650 on-campus PCs are available to graduate business students. Access to Internet/World Wide Web and online (class) registration available. *Personal computer requirements:* Graduate business students are strongly recommended to purchase or lease a personal computer. *Special opportunities include:* An international exchange program and an internship program are available. *Placement services include:* Alumni network, career placement, job search course, career counseling/planning, electronic job bank, resume referral, career fairs, job interviews arranged, resume preparation, and career library.

Application Contact Mr. Sajid M. Khan, Head, Admissions and Financial Aid, Opposite Sector U, Phase II LCCHS, Punjab, Pakistan. *Phone:* 92-42-5722670 Ext. 2107. *Fax:* 92-42-5722591. *E-mail:* skhan@lums.edu.pk.

PERU

Escuela de Administracion de Negocios para Graduados

Programa Magister—MBA Programs

Lima, Peru

Phone: 51-1-3451332 Ext. 2280 **Fax:** 51-1-3451276 **E-mail:** preveggino@esan.edu.pe

Business Program(s) Web Site: http://www.esan.edu.pe

DEGREES MA/MBA • MBA

MA/MBA—Magíster en Administración Full-time. 2 years of work experience required. At least 84 total credits required. Maximum of 14 months to complete program. *Concentrations:* finance, general MBA, information technology, international management, management, marketing.

MBA—Magíster en Administración Part-time. 3 years of work experience required. At least 84 total credits required. Minimum of 24 months to complete program. *Concentrations:* finance, international business, management, management information systems, marketing.

RESOURCES AND SERVICES 70 on-campus PCs are available to graduate business students. Access to Internet/World Wide Web, online (class) registration, and online grade reports available. *Personal computer requirements:* Graduate business students are required to have a personal computer, the cost of which is included in tuition or other required fees. *Special opportunities include:* An international exchange program and an

internship program are available. *Placement services include:* Alumni network, career counseling/planning, electronic job bank, resume referral, job interviews arranged, resume preparation, and career library.

Application Contact Mrs. Patricia Reveggino, Head of Admissions, Alonso de Molina 1652, Monterrico Chico, Surco, Lima, 100, Peru. *Phone:* 51-1-3451332 Ext. 2280. *Fax:* 51-1-3451276. *E-mail:* preveggino@esan.edu.pe.

PHILIPPINES

Asian Institute of Management

Master Programs

Makati City, Philippines

Phone: 2-8924011 Ext. 227 **Fax:** 2-8937631 **E-mail:** admissions@aim.edu

Business Program(s) Web Site: http://www.aim.edu

Graduate Business Unit Enrollment *Total:* 233 (233 full-time; 52 women; 147 international). *Average Age:* 32.

Graduate Business Faculty *Total:* 89 (42 full-time; 47 part-time).

Admissions *Applied:* 452. *Admitted:* 226. *Enrolled:* 149. *Average GMAT:* 644. *Average GPA:* 2.5

Academic Calendar Continuous.

After Graduation (Class of 2006–07) *Employed within 3 months of graduation:* 82%. *Average starting salary:* $20,000.

DEGREE MBA equivalent

MBA equivalent—Master in Business Management Full-time. At least 2 years work experience required. 71 total credits required. 16 months to complete program. *Concentrations:* finance, management, marketing.

RESOURCES AND SERVICES 14 on-campus PCs are available to graduate business students. Access to Internet/World Wide Web available. *Personal computer requirements:* Graduate business students are strongly recommended to purchase or lease a personal computer. *Special opportunities include:* An international exchange program and an internship program are available. *Placement services include:* Alumni network, career placement, job search course, career counseling/planning, resume referral, career fairs, job interviews arranged, and resume preparation.

EXPENSES *Tuition:* Full-time: $16,130. *Tuition (international):* Full-time: $16,130. *Required fees:* Full-time: $7870. Tuition and/or fees vary by academic program. *Graduate housing:* Room and board costs vary by number of occupants. *Typical cost:* $7600 (including board), $2700 (room only).

FINANCIAL AID (2007–08) 34 students received aid, including scholarships. *Financial aid application deadline:* 5/30.

Financial Aid Contact Mr. Rey R. Reyes, Associate Managing Director, Student Services, Admissions and Registration, Joseph R. McMicking Campus, 123 Paseo de Roxas, Makati City, 1260, Philippines. *Phone:* 2-8924011 Ext. 227. *Fax:* 2-8937631. *E-mail:* admissions@aim.edu.

INTERNATIONAL STUDENTS 63% of students enrolled are international students. *Services and facilities:* Counseling/support services, Housing location assistance, International student housing, Orientation, Visa Services. Financial aid is available to international students. *Required with application:* Proof of adequate funds. *Recommended with application:* IELT with recommended score of 7.

International Student Contact Mr. Rey R. Reyes, Associate Managing Director, Student Services, Admissions and Registration, Joseph R.

Asian Institute of Management (continued)

McMicking Campus, 123 Paseo de Roxas, Makati City, 1260, Philippines. *Phone:* 2-8924011 Ext. 227. *Fax:* 2-8937631. *E-mail:* admissions@aim.edu.

APPLICATION *Required:* Application form, baccalaureate/first degree, essay, interview, 2 letters of recommendation, transcripts of college work, 2 years of work experience. School will accept GMAT. *Recommended:* Personal statement, resume/curriculum vitae. *Application fee:* $20. Applications for domestic and international students are processed on a rolling basis.

Application Contact Mr. Rey R. Reyes, Associate Managing Director, Student Services, Admissions and Registration, Joseph R. McMicking Campus, 123 Paseo de Roxas, Makati City, 1260, Philippines. *Phone:* 2-8924011 Ext. 227. *Fax:* 2-8937631. *E-mail:* admissions@aim.edu.

PORTUGAL

Universidade Nova de Lisboa

Faculdade de Economia-Gestao

Lisbon, Portugal

Phone: 351-217225077 **E-mail:** belen.vicente@mbacatolicanova.com

Business Program(s) Web Site: http://www.mbacatolicanova.com and www.thelisbonmba.com

Graduate Business Unit Enrollment *Total:* 93 (14 women; 5 international). *Average Age:* 31.

Admissions *Average GMAT:* 615.

Academic Calendar Trimesters.

DEGREES MBA

MBA—MBA Catolica Nova Part-time. 24 months to complete program. *Concentration:* general MBA.

MBA—The Lisbon MBA Full-time. 12 months to complete program. *Concentration:* general MBA.

RESOURCES AND SERVICES Access to Internet/World Wide Web, online (class) registration, and online grade reports available. *Personal computer requirements:* Graduate business students are strongly recommended to purchase or lease a personal computer. *Special opportunities include:* An international exchange program is available. *Placement services include:* Alumni network, career placement, job search course, career counseling/planning, resume referral, job interviews arranged, and resume preparation.

EXPENSES *Tuition (state resident):* Full-time: 30,000 euros. Part-time: 19,000 euros per degree program.

FINANCIAL AID (2007–08) Grants. *Financial aid application deadline:* 6/30.

Financial Aid Contact Belen Vicente, MBA Executive Director, Palacete Henrique de Mendonça, Rua Marquês da Fronteira, 20, Lisbon, 1099-038, Portugal. *Phone:* 351-217225077. *E-mail:* belen.vicente@mbacatolicanova.com.

INTERNATIONAL STUDENTS 5% of students enrolled are international students. *Services and facilities:* Counseling/support services, ESL/language courses, Housing location assistance, Orientation. Financial aid is available to international students. *Required with application:* TOEFL.

International Student Contact Belen Vicente, MBA Executive Director, Palacete Henrique de Mendonça, Rua Marquês da Fronteira,20, Lisbon, 1099-038, Portugal. *Phone:* 351-217225077. *E-mail:* belen.vicente@mbacatolicanova.com.

APPLICATION *Required:* GMAT, application form, baccalaureate/first degree, essay, interview, 2 letters of recommendation, personal statement, resume/curriculum vitae, transcripts of college work, 3 years of work experience. *Application fee:* 100 euros. Applications for domestic and international students are processed on a rolling basis.

Application Contact Belen Vicente, MBA Executive Director, Palacete Henrique de Mendonça, Rua Marquês da Fronteira,20, Lisbon, 1099-038, Portugal. *Phone:* 351-217225077. *E-mail:* belen.vicente@mbacatolicanova.com.

REPUBLIC OF KOREA

KDI School of Public Policy and Management

MBA Program

Seoul, Republic of Korea

Phone: 82-2-3299-1281 **Fax:** 82-2-3299-1223 **E-mail:** admissions@kdischool.ac.kr

Business Program(s) Web Site: http://www.kdischool.ac.kr

DEGREE MBA

MBA—Master of Business Administration Full-time and part-time. At least 36 total credits required. 18 to 24 months to complete program. *Concentrations:* banking, finance, international management, strategic management.

RESOURCES AND SERVICES 33 on-campus PCs are available to graduate business students. Access to Internet/World Wide Web, online (class) registration, and online grade reports available. *Personal computer requirements:* Graduate business students are not required to have a personal computer. *Special opportunities include:* An international exchange program and an internship program are available. *Placement services include:* Alumni network, career placement, career counseling/planning, resume referral, resume preparation, and career library.

Application Contact Office of Admissions, 207-43 Cheongnyangri 2-dong, Dondaemun-gu, Seoul, 130-868, Republic of Korea. *Phone:* 82-2-3299-1281. *Fax:* 82-2-3299-1223. *E-mail:* admissions@kdischool.ac.kr.

RUSSIAN FEDERATION

The International Management Institute of St. Petersburg

International Management Institute of St. Petersburg

St. Petersburg, Russian Federation

Phone: 812-323-92-00 **Fax:** 812-325-63-48 **E-mail:** bondarevskaya@imisp.ru

Business Program(s) Web Site: http://www.imisp.ru

Graduate Business Unit Enrollment *Total:* 1,022 (7 full-time; 1,015 part-time; 453 women; 7 international). *Average Age:* 33.

Graduate Business Faculty *Total:* 62 (39 full-time; 23 part-time).

Admissions *Applied:* 108. *Admitted:* 81. *Enrolled:* 81. *Average GMAT:* 610.

Academic Calendar Semesters.

DEGREE MBA

MBA—Master of Business Administration Part-time. 2 years of work experience required. 50 to 70 total credits required. 24 to 28 months to complete program. *Concentration:* management.

RESOURCES AND SERVICES 38 on-campus PCs are available to graduate business students. Access to Internet/World Wide Web available. *Personal computer requirements:* Graduate business students are not required to have a personal computer. *Placement services include:* Alumni network.

EXPENSES *Tuition:* Full-time: 9400 euros.

INTERNATIONAL STUDENTS 0.7% of students enrolled are international students. *Services and facilities:* Counseling/support services. Financial aid is not available to international students. *Required with application:* TOEFL with recommended score of 500 (paper).

International Student Contact Mr. Fedor Ragin, Vice Rector for International Projects, 50, Liniya 9, Vasilievsky Ostrov, St. Petersburg, 199004, Russian Federation. *Phone:* 812-320-45-08. *Fax:* 812-325-63-48. *E-mail:* ragin@imisp.ru.

APPLICATION *Required:* Application form, baccalaureate/first degree, essay, interview, 2 letters of recommendation, 3 years of work experience. School will accept GMAT. *Deadlines:* 11/3 for winter, 4/1 for spring, 11/3 for winter (international), 4/1 for spring (international).

Application Contact Dr. Elena Bondarevskaya, Director of MBA Programmes, 50, Liniya 9, Vasilievsky Ostrov, St. Petersburg, 199004, Russian Federation. *Phone:* 812-323-92-00. *Fax:* 812-325-63-48. *E-mail:* bondarevskaya@imisp.ru.

SINGAPORE

Nanyang Technological University
Nanyang Business School
Singapore, Singapore

Phone: 65-67905681 **Fax:** 65-67913561 **E-mail:** nbsmba@ntu.edu.sg

Business Program(s) Web Site: http://www.nanyangmba.ntu.edu.sg

Graduate Business Unit Enrollment *Total:* 581 (374 full-time; 207 part-time; 187 women; 304 international). *Average Age:* 32.

Graduate Business Faculty *Total:* 105 (94 full-time; 11 part-time).

Admissions *Applied:* 1,589. *Admitted:* 480. *Enrolled:* 356. *Average GMAT:* 653.

Academic Calendar Trimesters.

After Graduation (Class of 2006–07) *Employed within 3 months of graduation:* 91%. *Average starting salary:* 79,867 Singapore dollars.

DEGREE MBA

MBA—Master of Business Administration Full-time and part-time. At least 54 total credits required. 16 to 24 months to complete program. *Concentrations:* accounting, banking, finance, general MBA, information technology, international business, marketing, strategic management, technology management.

RESOURCES AND SERVICES 210 on-campus PCs are available to graduate business students. Access to Internet/World Wide Web, online (class) registration, and online grade reports available. *Personal computer requirements:* Graduate business students are not required to have a personal computer. *Special opportunities include:* An international

exchange program and an internship program are available. *Placement services include:* Alumni network, career placement, job search course, career counseling/planning, electronic job bank, resume referral, career fairs, job interviews arranged, resume preparation, and career library.

EXPENSES *Tuition (state resident):* Full-time: 26,000 Singapore dollars. Part-time: 30,000 Singapore dollars per degree program. *Tuition (international):* Full-time: 26,000 Singapore dollars. *Required fees:* Full-time: 280 Singapore dollars. Tuition and/or fees vary by academic program. *Graduate housing:* Room and board costs vary by number of occupants. *Typical cost:* 4200 Singapore dollars (room only).

FINANCIAL AID (2007–08) 10 students received aid, including scholarships. *Financial aid application deadline:* 12/31.

Financial Aid Contact Dr. Lai Hong Chung, Director, Nanyang Avenue, S3-B3a-01, Singapore, 639798, Singapore. *Phone:* 65-67904655. *Fax:* 65-67913561. *E-mail:* nbsmba@ntu.edu.sg.

INTERNATIONAL STUDENTS 52% of students enrolled are international students. *Services and facilities:* Counseling/support services, ESL/language courses, Housing location assistance, International student housing, International student organization, Orientation, Visa Services, optional internship. Financial aid is available to international students. *Required with application:* TOEFL with recommended score of 250 (computer) or 600 (paper); proof of adequate funds; proof of health/immunizations.

International Student Contact Lindsay Tan, Senior Manager, Nanyang Avenue, S3-B3a-01, Singapore, 639798, Singapore. *Phone:* 65-67906101. *Fax:* 65-67913561. *E-mail:* nbsmba@ntu.edu.sg.

APPLICATION *Required:* GMAT, application form, baccalaureate/first degree, essay, interview, 2 letters of recommendation, personal statement, transcripts of college work, 2 years of work experience. School will accept GRE. *Recommended:* Resume/curriculum vitae. *Application fee:* 50 Singapore dollars. Applications for domestic and international students are processed on a rolling basis.

Application Contact Rachel Ng, Senior Manager, Nanyang Avenue, S3-B3a-01, Singapore, 639798, Singapore. *Phone:* 65-67905681. *Fax:* 65-67913561. *E-mail:* nbsmba@ntu.edu.sg.

See full description on page 662.

SOUTH AFRICA

University of the Witwatersrand
Graduate School of Business Administration
Wits, South Africa

Phone: 27-11-7173537 **Fax:** 27-11-6432336 **E-mail:** yelland.c@wbs.wits.ac.za

Business Program(s) Web Site: http://wbs.mgmt.wits.ac.za

DEGREE MBA

MBA—Master of Business Administration Full-time and part-time. 14 to 36 months to complete program. *Concentrations:* accounting, economics, entrepreneurship, finance, human resources management, industrial/labor relations, international business, international economics, international finance, international management, international marketing, management information systems, marketing, operations management, production management, public and private management, quantitative analysis, strategic management.

RESOURCES AND SERVICES 66 on-campus PCs are available to graduate business students. Access to Internet/World Wide Web available. *Personal computer requirements:* Graduate business students are not required to have a personal computer. *Special opportunities include:* An international exchange program is available. *Placement services include:*

University of the Witwatersrand (continued)

Alumni network, career placement, career counseling/planning, job interviews arranged, resume preparation, and career library.

Application Contact Mrs. Chris Yelland, Course Coordinator, PO Box 98, Witwatersrand, 2050, South Africa. *Phone:* 27-11-7173537. *Fax:* 27-11-6432336. *E-mail:* yelland.c@wbs.wits.ac.za.

SPAIN

Barcelona Business School

Graduate Programs in Business

Barcelona, Spain

Phone: 003-4-934522230 **Fax:** 003-4-934522228 **E-mail:** info@barcelona.uibs.org

Business Program(s) Web Site: http://www.bbs-edu.org

Graduate Business Faculty 35 part-time.

Academic Calendar Quarters.

After Graduation (Class of 2006–07) *Employed within 3 months of graduation:* 80%.

DEGREES IMBA • MA/MBA • MBA/MS

IMBA—International MBA—International Management Full-time and part-time. Distance learning option. At least 60 total credits required. *Concentrations:* business education, business ethics, business studies, entrepreneurship, financial management/planning, general MBA, human resources management, information systems, international and area business studies, international business, international economics, international finance, international management, international marketing, international trade, leadership, management, management communication, managerial economics, marketing, operations management, organizational behavior/development, quantitative analysis, strategic management.

IMBA—International MBA—e-Business Full-time and part-time. Distance learning option. At least 60 total credits required. *Concentrations:* commerce, electronic commerce (E-commerce), general MBA, logistics, new venture management, supply chain management, technology management.

MA/MBA—Master of Arts in Business Communication and Public Relations Full-time and part-time. Distance learning option. At least 60 total credits required. *Concentrations:* general MBA, management communication, public relations.

MA/MBA—Master of Arts in Tourism and Hospitality Management Full-time and part-time. Distance learning option. 60 to 80 total credits required. 9 to 12 months to complete program. *Concentrations:* general MBA, hospitality management, international hospitality and restaurant business, international hotel and resort management, resort management, travel industry/tourism management.

MBA/MS—Master of Science in European Business and Management Full-time and part-time. Distance learning option. At least 60 total credits required. *Concentrations:* business studies, European business studies, general MBA, international and area business studies, management.

MBA/MS—Master of Science in Global Banking and Financial Markets Full-time and part-time. Distance learning option. At least 60 total credits required. *Concentrations:* banking, economics, financial economics, general MBA, international banking, international economics, international finance, international trade, investments and securities.

MBA/MS—Master of Science in Sports Management Full-time and part-time. Distance learning option. At least 60 total credits required. *Concentrations:* general MBA, leadership, sports/entertainment management.

MBA/MS—Master of Science in Transportation and Logistics Management Full-time and part-time. Distance learning option. At least 60 total credits required. *Concentrations:* general MBA, logistics, port/maritime management, production management, supply chain management, transportation management.

RESOURCES AND SERVICES Access to Internet/World Wide Web, online (class) registration, and online grade reports available. *Personal computer requirements:* Graduate business students are strongly recommended to purchase or lease a personal computer. *Special opportunities include:* An international exchange program and an internship program are available. *Placement services include:* Alumni network, career placement, job search course, career counseling/planning, electronic job bank, resume referral, career fairs, job interviews arranged, resume preparation, and career library.

EXPENSES *Tuition:* Full-time: 13,500 euros. Part-time: 525 euros per course. *Tuition (international):* Full-time: 13,500 euros. Part-time: 525 euros per course. *Graduate housing:* Room and board costs vary by campus location, number of occupants, type of accommodation, and type of board plan.

FINANCIAL AID (2007–08) Scholarships.

Financial Aid Contact Mr. F Kirschstein, Director, Calle Aragón 182, Barcelona, 08011, Spain. *Phone:* 003-4-934522230. *E-mail:* info@barcelona.uibs.org.

INTERNATIONAL STUDENTS *Services and facilities:* Counseling/support services, ESL/language courses, Housing location assistance, International student housing, International student organization, Language tutoring, Orientation, Visa Services. Financial aid is available to international students. *Required with application:* Proof of adequate funds; proof of health/immunizations. *Recommended with application:* IELT with recommended score of 6; TOEFL with recommended score of 550 (paper).

International Student Contact Ms. Maricelle Ruiz-Calderón, Associate Dean, Calle Aragón 182, Barcelona, 08011, Spain. *Phone:* 003-4-934522230. *Fax:* 003-4-934522228. *E-mail:* info@barcelona.uibs.org.

APPLICATION *Required:* Application form, baccalaureate/first degree, 2 letters of recommendation, personal statement, resume/curriculum vitae, transcripts of college work. School will accept GMAT, GRE, and MAT. *Application fee:* 200 euros. Applications for domestic and international students are processed on a rolling basis.

Application Contact Mr. F Kirschstein, Director, Calle Aragón 182, Barcelona, 08011, Spain. *Phone:* 003-4-934522230. *Fax:* 003-4-934522228. *E-mail:* info@barcelona.uibs.org.

EADA International Management Development Center

Business Programs

Barcelona, Spain

Phone: 34-93-4520844 **Fax:** 34-93-3237317 **E-mail:** bcamba@eada.edu

Business Program(s) Web Site: http://www.eada.edu

Graduate Business Unit Enrollment *Total:* 197 (197 full-time; 88 women; 136 international).

Graduate Business Faculty 33 full-time.

Admissions *Applied:* 687. *Admitted:* 389. *Enrolled:* 241. *Average GMAT:* 640. *Average GPA:* 3.5

Academic Calendar Trimesters.

After Graduation (Class of 2006–07) *Employed within 3 months of graduation:* 90%. *Average starting salary:* $75,000.

DEGREES EMM • M Mktg • MBA • MF • MHR • MS

EMM—International Master in Management Full-time. Program taught in English. 9 months to complete program. *Concentration:* management.

M Mktg—International Master in Marketing Full-time. Program available in English or Spanish. 9 months to complete program. *Concentration:* marketing.

MBA—Executive Master of Business Administration Part-time. Fluency in Spanish and a minimum 5 years of management experience required. 18 months to complete program. *Concentration:* management.

MBA—International Master of Business Administration Full-time. Program available in English or Spanish; 2 years relevant work experience requested. 10 months to complete program. *Concentration:* management.

MBA—MBA Part-Time Part-time. 15 months to complete program. *Concentration:* management.

MF—International Master in Finance Full-time. Program available in Spanish. 9 months to complete program. *Concentration:* finance.

MHR—International Master in Human Resources Full-time. Program available in Spanish and English. 9 months to complete program. *Concentration:* human resources management.

MS—Master in Tourism Full-time. 8 months to complete program. *Concentration:* travel industry/tourism management.

RESOURCES AND SERVICES 87 on-campus PCs are available to graduate business students. Access to Internet/World Wide Web available. *Personal computer requirements:* Graduate business students are strongly recommended to purchase or lease a personal computer. *Special opportunities include:* An international exchange program and an internship program are available. *Placement services include:* Alumni network, career placement, job search course, career counseling/planning, electronic job bank, resume referral, career fairs, job interviews arranged, resume preparation, and career library.

FINANCIAL AID (2007–08) 13 students received aid, including grants and loans. *Financial aid application deadline:* 4/30.

Financial Aid Contact Bibiana Camba, Programmes Information Department, Arago 204, Barcelona, 08011, Spain. *Phone:* 34-93-4520844. *Fax:* 34-93-3237317. *E-mail:* bcamba@eada.edu.

INTERNATIONAL STUDENTS 69% of students enrolled are international students. *Services and facilities:* Counseling/support services, ESL/language courses, Housing location assistance, International student housing, Language tutoring, Orientation, Visa Services. Financial aid is available to international students. *Recommended with application:* IELT; TOEFL with recommended score of 250 (computer) or 550 (paper).

International Student Contact Bibiana Camba, Programmes Information Department, Arago 204, Barcelona, 08011, Spain. *Phone:* 34-93-4520844. *Fax:* 34-93-3237317. *E-mail:* bcamba@eada.edu.

APPLICATION *Required:* GMAT, application form, baccalaureate/first degree, essay, interview, 2 letters of recommendation, personal statement, resume/curriculum vitae, transcripts of college work, 3 years of work experience. *Application fee:* 25,500 euros. *Deadline:* 5/31 for fall (international). Applications for domestic students are processed on a rolling basis.

Application Contact Bibiana Camba, Programmes Information Department, Arago 204, Barcelona, 08011, Spain. *Phone:* 34-93-4520844. *Fax:* 34-93-3237317. *E-mail:* bcamba@eada.edu.

IE Business School

Business School

Madrid, Spain

Phone: 34-91-5689610 **Fax:** 34-91-5689710 **E-mail:** admissions@ie.edu

Business Program(s) Web Site: http://www.ie.edu

Accreditation AACSB—The Association to Advance Collegiate Schools of Business.

DEGREES EMIB • IMBA

EMIB—International Executive Master of Business Administration Part-time. Distance learning option. 3 years of work experience in a management position, application form and essays are required. Maximum of 13 months to complete program. *Concentrations:* accounting, administration, advertising, banking, business education, business ethics, business information science, business law, business policy/strategy, business studies, commerce, conflict resolution management, corporate accounting, developmental economics, economics, electronic commerce (E-commerce), entrepreneurship, finance, financial economics, human resources management, information management, information systems, international and area business studies, international banking, international business, international economics, international finance, international management, international marketing, international trade, Latin American business studies, leadership, management, management consulting, managerial economics, marketing, nonprofit management, nonprofit organization, operations management, organizational behavior/development, production management, project management, risk management, statistics, supply chain management, system management.

IMBA—International Master of Business Administration Full-time. Distance learning option. Application form, essays and GMAT are required. Maximum of 15 months to complete program. *Concentrations:* accounting, administration, advertising, banking, business ethics, business law, business studies, commerce, corporate accounting, economics, electronic commerce (E-commerce), entrepreneurship, environmental economics/management, European business studies, finance, financial economics, financial management/planning, general MBA, human resources management, information management, information systems, international and area business studies, international banking, international business, international economics, international finance, international management, international marketing, international trade, Latin American business studies, leadership, logistics, management, management consulting, management information systems, management systems analysis, managerial economics, marketing, nonprofit management, nonprofit organization, operations management, organizational behavior/development, organizational management, production management, project management, public policy and administration, quantitative analysis, risk management, statistics, strategic management, supply chain management, transportation management.

RESOURCES AND SERVICES 250 on-campus PCs are available to graduate business students. Access to Internet/World Wide Web, online (class) registration, and online grade reports available. *Personal computer requirements:* Graduate business students are strongly recommended to purchase or lease a personal computer. *Special opportunities include:* An international exchange program is available. *Placement services include:* Alumni network, career placement, job search course, career counseling/planning, electronic job bank, resume referral, career fairs, job interviews arranged, resume preparation, and career library.

Application Contact Deise Leobet, Admissions Department, C/ Maria de Molina 11, 13 y 15, Madrid, 28006, Spain. *Phone:* 34-91-5689610. *Fax:* 34-91-5689710. *E-mail:* admissions@ie.edu.

See full description on page 636.

Schiller International University

MBA Program, Madrid, Spain

Madrid, Spain

Phone: 727-736-5082 Ext. 240 **Fax:** 727-734-0359 **E-mail:** admissions@schiller.edu

Business Program(s) Web Site: http://www.schillermadrid.edu/

Graduate Business Unit Enrollment *Total:* 590 (240 full-time; 350 part-time). *Average Age:* 23.

Graduate Business Faculty *Total:* 8 (1 full-time; 7 part-time).

Admissions *Average GPA:* 3.0

Academic Calendar Semesters.

After Graduation (Class of 2006–07) *Employed within 3 months of graduation:* 89%.

Schiller International University (continued)

DEGREE MBA

MBA—Master of Business Administration in International Business Full-time and part-time. Distance learning option. At least 45 total credits required. 12 to 24 months to complete program. *Concentration:* international business.

RESOURCES AND SERVICES 21 on-campus PCs are available to graduate business students. Access to Internet/World Wide Web available. *Personal computer requirements:* Graduate business students are required to have a personal computer. *Special opportunities include:* An international exchange program and an internship program are available. *Placement services include:* Alumni network, career placement, career counseling/planning, electronic job bank, resume referral, resume preparation, and career library.

EXPENSES *Tuition:* Part-time: 1300 euros per course. *Tuition (international):* Part-time: 1300 euros per course. Tuition and/or fees vary by campus location.

FINANCIAL AID (2007–08) Grants, loans, scholarships, and work study. *Financial aid application deadline:* 4/1.

Financial Aid Contact Ms. Jennifer Fraser, Financial Aid Officer, 300 East Bay Drive, Largo, FL 33770. *Phone:* 727-736-5082 Ext. 253. *Fax:* 727-738-8405. *E-mail:* financial_aid@schiller.edu.

INTERNATIONAL STUDENTS *Services and facilities:* Counseling/support services, ESL/language courses, Housing location assistance, International student housing, Language tutoring, Orientation, Visa Services. Financial aid is available to international students. *Required with application:* Proof of adequate funds. *Recommended with application:* TOEFL with recommended score of 213 (computer), 550 (paper), or 73 (Internet).

International Student Contact Ms. Stephanie Givens, Admissions Representative, 300 East Bay Drive. *Phone:* 727-736-5082 Ext. 411. *Fax:* 727-734-0359. *E-mail:* admissions@schiller.edu.

APPLICATION *Required:* Application form, baccalaureate/first degree, essay, transcripts of college work. *Recommended:* Resume/curriculum vitae, work experience. *Application fee:* 65 euros. Applications for domestic and international students are processed on a rolling basis.

Application Contact Ms. Kamala Dontamsetti, Assistant Director of Admissions, 300 East Bay Drive, Largo, FL 33770. *Phone:* 727-736-5082 Ext. 240. *Fax:* 727-734-0359. *E-mail:* admissions@schiller.edu.

See full description on page 684.

Universitat Pompeu Fabra

Department of Business and Economics, MBA Program

Barcelona, Spain

Phone: 34-935422912 **Fax:** 34-935421827 **E-mail:** sylvia.busquets@idec.upf.edu

Business Program(s) Web Site: http://www.idec.upf.edu/mba

Graduate Business Faculty *Total:* 203 (104 full-time; 99 part-time).

Admissions *Applied:* 50. *Admitted:* 42. *Enrolled:* 25. *Average GMAT:* 550.

Academic Calendar Quarters.

After Graduation (Class of 2006–07) *Employed within 3 months of graduation:* 80%.

DEGREES MBA

MBA—Master in Business Administration Part-time. 100 total credits required. 15 months to complete program. *Concentration:* general MBA.

MBA—Master of Business Administration Full-time. GMAT, TOEFL. 100 total credits required. 15 months to complete program. *Concentration:* general MBA.

RESOURCES AND SERVICES 60 on-campus PCs are available to graduate business students. Access to Internet/World Wide Web available. *Personal computer requirements:* Graduate business students are required to have a personal computer. *Special opportunities include:* An international exchange program and an internship program are available. *Placement services include:* Alumni network, career placement, job search course, career counseling/planning, electronic job bank, resume referral, career fairs, job interviews arranged, resume preparation, and career library.

FINANCIAL AID (2007–08) 30 students received aid, including grants, loans, scholarships, and teaching assistantships.

Financial Aid Contact Sylvia Busquets, MBA Marketing and Admissions Director, Balmes 132-134, Barcelona, 08008, Spain. *Phone:* 34-935422639. *Fax:* 34-935421805. *E-mail:* sylvia.busquets@idec.upf.edu.

INTERNATIONAL STUDENTS *Services and facilities:* Counseling/support services, ESL/language courses, Housing location assistance, International student organization, Language tutoring, Orientation, Assist in the process of getting the Student ID Card with the Spanish authorities. Financial aid is available to international students. *Required with application:* IELT with recommended score of 6.5; TOEFL with recommended score of 220 (computer) or 82 (Internet). *Recommended with application:* Proof of adequate funds; proof of health/immunizations.

International Student Contact Ms. Sylvia Busquets, MBA Marketing and Admissions Director, Balmes 132-134, Barcelona, 08008, Spain. *Phone:* 34-935422912. *Fax:* 34-935421827. *E-mail:* sylvia.busquets@idec.upf.edu.

APPLICATION *Required:* GMAT, application form, baccalaureate/first degree, interview, 2 letters of recommendation, personal statement, resume/curriculum vitae, transcripts of college work, 2 years of work experience. *Application fee:* 0 euros. Applications for domestic and international students are processed on a rolling basis.

Application Contact Sylvia Busquets, MBA Marketing and Admissions Director, Balmes 132-134, Barcelona, 08008, Spain. *Phone:* 34-935422912. *Fax:* 34-935421827. *E-mail:* sylvia.busquets@idec.upf.edu.

University of Deusto

Faculty of Economics and Business Administration

Bilbao, Spain

Phone: 34-944-139262 **Fax:** 34-944-457381 **E-mail:** emp-mba@unicomer.deusto.es

Business Program(s) Web Site: http://www.lacomercial.deusto.es

DEGREE MBA

MBA—European MBA Full-time. Good command of the English language and knowledge of Spanish/French required. At least 90 total credits required. 13 to 16 months to complete program. *Concentrations:* European business studies, general MBA, international management.

RESOURCES AND SERVICES 98 on-campus PCs are available to graduate business students. Access to Internet/World Wide Web, online (class) registration, and online grade reports available. *Personal computer requirements:* Graduate business students are not required to have a personal computer. *Special opportunities include:* An international exchange program and an internship program are available. *Placement services include:* Alumni network, career placement, electronic job bank, and career fairs.

Application Contact María Ugarte, MBA Secretary, Hermanos Aguirre, 2, Bilbao, 48014, Spain. *Phone:* 34-944-139262. *Fax:* 34-944-457381. *E-mail:* emp-mba@unicomer.deusto.es.

SWEDEN

Stockholm School of Economics
Department of Business Administration

Stockholm, Sweden

Phone: 46-8-7369799 **Fax:** 46-8-318186 **E-mail:** anna.sundmark@hhs.se

Business Program(s) Web Site: http://www.sse.edu/ssemba

DEGREES EMBA • MA Sc • MBA • MS

EMBA—Executive Master of Business Administration in General Management, Business Development and IT Part-time. Minimum Bachelor's degree & relevant professional experience of at least 5 years required. At least 45 total credits required. Minimum of 24 months to complete program. *Concentrations:* administration of technological information, business education, business ethics, business information science, business law, business policy/strategy, business studies, conflict resolution management, corporate accounting, economics, electronic commerce (E-commerce), entrepreneurship, European business studies, executive programs, finance, financial economics, financial information systems, general MBA, human resources management, information management, information technology, international banking, international business, international economics, international finance, international management, international marketing, international trade, law, leadership, management, management communication, marketing, new venture management, operations management, organizational behavior/development, organizational management, profit management, quality management, resources management, risk management, statistics, strategic management, supply chain management, system management, telecommunications management.

MA Sc—Master of Arts in Management Sciences—Business Administration Full-time and part-time. This program is conducted primarily in Swedish. 160 total credits required. 48 months to complete program. *Concentrations:* accounting, administration, administration of technological information, advertising, arts administration/management, banking, business education, business ethics, business information science, business law, business policy/strategy, business studies, combined degrees, commerce, conflict resolution management, contract management, corporate accounting, developmental economics, economics, entrepreneurship, environmental economics/management, European business studies, finance, financial economics, financial management/planning, human resources management, industrial administration/management, industrial/labor relations, information management, information technology, international and area business studies, international banking, international business, international development management, international economics, international finance, international management, international marketing, international trade, leadership, logistics, management, management consulting, management science, management systems analysis, managerial economics, manufacturing management, marketing, marketing research, media administration, new venture management, operations management, organizational management, profit management, project management, public policy and administration, quantitative analysis, resources management, risk management, strategic management, supply chain management, system management.

MBA—Master of Business Administration Full-time. The full-time SSE MBA is offered in English only. Minimum Bachelor's degree, three years professional experience required. At least 48 total credits required. 11 months to complete program. *Concentrations:* banking, business education, business ethics, business law, business policy/strategy, business studies, economics, entrepreneurship, European business studies, finance, financial management/planning, general MBA, management, management communication.

MS—Master of Science in International Economics and Business This program is conducted in English. At least 60 total credits required.

Minimum of 18 months to complete program. *Concentrations:* administration, economics, European business studies, finance, financial economics.

RESOURCES AND SERVICES Access to Internet/World Wide Web, online (class) registration, and online grade reports available. *Personal computer requirements:* Graduate business students are required to have a personal computer. *Special opportunities include:* An internship program is available. *Placement services include:* Alumni network, career placement, career counseling/planning, resume referral, career fairs, job interviews arranged, and resume preparation.

Application Contact Ms. Anna Sundmark, Admissions Director, PO Box 6501, Stockholm, SE-113 83, Sweden. *Phone:* 46-8-7369799. *Fax:* 46-8-318186. *E-mail:* anna.sundmark@hhs.se.

SWITZERLAND

American Graduate School of Business
International Business Administration Program

La Tour-de-Peilz, Switzerland

Phone: 41-21-9449501 **Fax:** 41-21-9449504 **E-mail:** info@agsb.ch

Business Program(s) Web Site: http://www.agsb.ch/

DEGREE MIBA

MIBA—Master of International Business Administration Full-time and part-time. At least 39 total credits required. 12 to 24 months to complete program. *Concentration:* international business.

RESOURCES AND SERVICES 10 on-campus PCs are available to graduate business students. Access to Internet/World Wide Web and online grade reports available. *Personal computer requirements:* Graduate business students are strongly recommended to purchase or lease a personal computer. *Special opportunities include:* An international exchange program and an internship program are available. *Placement services include:* Alumni network, career placement, career counseling/planning, resume referral, job interviews arranged, and resume preparation.

Application Contact Mr. Amyn Lalani, MSC, Director of Academic Programs, Place des Anciens-Fosses 6, La Tour-de-Peilz, 1814, Switzerland. *Phone:* 41-21-9449501. *Fax:* 41-21-9449504. *E-mail:* info@agsb.ch.

Business School Lausanne
MBA Programs

Lausanne, Switzerland

Phone: 41-21-6190606 **Fax:** 41-21-6190600 **E-mail:** admissions@bsl-lausanne.ch

Graduate Business Unit Enrollment *Total:* 60 (30 full-time; 30 part-time; 20 women; 40 international).

Graduate Business Faculty 15 part-time.

Academic Calendar Trimesters.

Accreditation ACBSP—The American Council of Business Schools and Programs.

After Graduation (Class of 2006–07) *Employed within 3 months of graduation:* 80%.

Business School Lausanne (continued)

DEGREE MBA

MBA—Master of Business Administration Full-time and part-time. Bachelor's degree in a business-related area required. 30 to 42 total credits required. 12 months to complete program. *Concentration:* management.

RESOURCES AND SERVICES 30 on-campus PCs are available to graduate business students. Access to Internet/World Wide Web available. *Personal computer requirements:* Graduate business students are strongly recommended to purchase or lease a personal computer. *Placement services include:* Alumni network, electronic job bank, career fairs, and resume preparation.

FINANCIAL AID (2007–08) 1 student received aid, including scholarships.

Financial Aid Contact Mr. Massimiliano Baroni, Accountant, PO Box 160, Lausanne, 1001, Switzerland. *Phone:* 41-21-6190606. *Fax:* 41-21-6190600. *E-mail:* mb@bsl-lausanne.ch.

INTERNATIONAL STUDENTS 67% of students enrolled are international students. *Services and facilities:* Counseling/support services, ESL/language courses, Housing location assistance, International student housing, Orientation, Visa Services. Financial aid is not available to international students. *Required with application:* TOEFL with recommended score of 210 (computer) or 550 (paper); proof of adequate funds.

International Student Contact Ms. Marjorie Schönauer, Receptionist, PO Box 160, Lausanne, 1001, Switzerland. *Phone:* 41-21-6190606. *Fax:* 41-21-6190600. *E-mail:* admissions@bsl-lausanne.ch.

APPLICATION *Required:* Application form, baccalaureate/first degree, interview, 2 letters of recommendation, resume/curriculum vitae, transcripts of college work, 2 years of work experience. School will accept GMAT. *Application fee:* 200 Swiss francs, 600 Swiss francs (international). Applications for domestic and international students are processed on a rolling basis.

Application Contact Ms. Marjorie Schönauer, Receptionist, PO Box 160, Lausanne, 1001, Switzerland. *Phone:* 41-21-6190606. *Fax:* 41-21-6190600. *E-mail:* admissions@bsl-lausanne.ch.

European University
Center for Management Studies

Montreux-Fontanivent, Switzerland

Phone: 41-21-9648464 **Fax:** 41-21-9648468 **E-mail:** c.grimaitre@euruni.edu

Business Program(s) Web Site: http://www.euruni.edu

Graduate Business Unit Enrollment *Total:* 800 (650 full-time; 150 part-time; 180 women; 750 international).

Graduate Business Faculty *Total:* 68 (16 full-time; 52 part-time).

Admissions *Applied:* 620. *Admitted:* 580. *Enrolled:* 580. *Average GMAT:* 500. *Average GPA:* 3.0

Academic Calendar Trimesters.

After Graduation (Class of 2006–07) *Employed within 3 months of graduation:* 90%.

DEGREE EMBA

EMBA—Executive Master of Business Administration Full-time and part-time. Distance learning option. 45 total credits required. 15 to 24 months to complete program. *Concentrations:* accounting, administration, arts administration/management, business studies, commerce, economics, European business studies, executive programs, finance, general MBA, health care, hospitality management, human resources management, information systems, international finance, international management, international marketing, management, management information systems, marketing, organizational behavior/development, public relations, technology management, telecommunications management.

RESOURCES AND SERVICES 10 on-campus PCs are available to graduate business students. Access to Internet/World Wide Web available. *Personal computer requirements:* Graduate business students are required to have a personal computer. *Special opportunities include:* An international exchange program is available. *Placement services include:* Alumni network, career placement, job search course, career counseling/planning, resume referral, career fairs, job interviews arranged, and resume preparation.

Financial Aid Contact Dr. Dirk Leonard Craen, President, Grand-Rue 3, Montreux 2, 1820, Switzerland. *Phone:* 41-21-9648464. *Fax:* 41-21-9648468. *E-mail:* d.craen@euruni.edu.

INTERNATIONAL STUDENTS 94% of students enrolled are international students. *Services and facilities:* Counseling/support services, Housing location assistance, International student organization, Visa Services. Financial aid is not available to international students. *Required with application:* TOEFL with recommended score of 213 (computer) or 550 (paper).

International Student Contact Cinta Grimaitre, Admission Officer, Grand-Rue 3, Montreux 2, 1820, Switzerland. *Phone:* 41-21-9648464. *Fax:* 41-21-9648468. *E-mail:* c.grimaitre@euruni.edu.

APPLICATION *Required:* GMAT, GRE, baccalaureate/first degree, essay, 2 letters of recommendation, personal statement, resume/curriculum vitae, transcripts of college work. *Recommended:* Interview, 3 years of work experience. *Application fee:* 200 Swiss francs. Applications for domestic and international students are processed on a rolling basis.

Application Contact Cinta Grimaitre, Admission Officer, Grand-Rue 3, Montreux 2, 1820, Switzerland. *Phone:* 41-21-9648464. *Fax:* 41-21-9648468. *E-mail:* c.grimaitre@euruni.edu.

Graduate School of Business Administration Zurich
Executive Management Programs

Zurich, Switzerland

Phone: 41-44-2269944 **Fax:** 41-44-2269945 **E-mail:** info@gsba.ch

Business Program(s) Web Site: http://www.gsba.ch

Graduate Business Unit Enrollment *Total:* 880 (880 part-time; 170 women; 567 international). *Average Age:* 35.

Graduate Business Faculty 52 part-time.

Admissions *Applied:* 930. *Admitted:* 470. *Enrolled:* 440. *Average GMAT:* 660. *Average GPA:* 3.5

Academic Calendar Modules.

After Graduation (Class of 2006–07) *Employed within 3 months of graduation:* 99%. *Average starting salary:* 200,000 Swiss francs.

DEGREES M Sc • MA/MS • MBA

M Sc—Master of Science in Finance Part-time. 60 to 100 total credits required. 12 to 24 months to complete program. *Concentrations:* accounting, corporate accounting, credit management, executive programs, finance, financial economics, financial information systems, financial management/planning, international banking, international finance, management.

M Sc—Master of Science in Logistics Part-time. 60 to 100 total credits required. 12 to 24 months to complete program. *Concentrations:* business policy/strategy, corporate accounting, executive programs, international logistics, international management, logistics, management information systems, marketing, operations management.

M Sc—Master of Science in Management Information Systems and Information Technology Part-time. 60 to 100 total credits required. 12 to 24 months to complete program. *Concentrations:* administration of technological information, information management, information systems, management systems analysis, system management.

M Sc—Master of Science in Marketing Part-time. 60 to 100 total credits required. 12 to 24 months to complete program. *Concentrations:* accounting, economics, executive programs, international marketing, management, management communication, marketing, marketing research.

MA/MS—Master of Science in Human Resource Management Part-time. 60 to 100 total credits required. 12 to 24 months to complete program. *Concentrations:* business ethics, conflict resolution management, executive programs, human resources development, human resources management, information systems, international business, leadership, management.

MBA—Executive Master of Business Administration Part-time. 60 to 120 total credits required. 12 to 48 months to complete program. *Concentrations:* accounting, financial management/planning, human resources management, international business, international development management, international economics, international finance, international logistics, international management, international marketing, management information systems, management systems analysis, operations management, organizational behavior/development, strategic management.

RESOURCES AND SERVICES 150 on-campus PCs are available to graduate business students. Access to Internet/World Wide Web, online (class) registration, and online grade reports available. *Personal computer requirements:* Graduate business students are not required to have a personal computer. *Special opportunities include:* An international exchange program is available. *Placement services include:* Alumni network, career placement, job search course, career counseling/planning, resume referral, career fairs, job interviews arranged, and resume preparation.

EXPENSES *Tuition:* Part-time: 89,000 Swiss francs per degree program. *Tuition (international):* Part-time: 89,000 Swiss francs per degree program. *Required fees:* Part-time: 1100 Swiss francs per semester. Tuition and/or fees vary by campus location and academic program. *Graduate housing:* Room and board costs vary by number of occupants. *Typical cost:* 1100 Swiss francs (room only).

FINANCIAL AID (2007–08) 5 students received aid, including grants.

Financial Aid Contact Beat Herren, Chief Financial Officer, Hirsackerstrasse 46, PO Box 324, Horgen-Zurich, 8810, Switzerland. *Phone:* 41-44-7289900. *Fax:* 41-44-7289998. *E-mail:* b.herren@gsba.ch.

INTERNATIONAL STUDENTS 64% of students enrolled are international students. *Services and facilities:* Counseling/support services, ESL/language courses, Housing location assistance, International student housing, Orientation, Visa Services, Career assistance. Financial aid is not available to international students. *Required with application:* TOEFL with recommended score of 200 (computer) or 500 (paper).

International Student Contact Dr. Albert Stähli, Dean, Hirsackerstrasse 46, PO Box 324, Horgen-Zurich, 8810, Switzerland. *Phone:* 41-44-7289944. *Fax:* 41-44-7289945. *E-mail:* info@gsba.ch.

APPLICATION *Required:* GMAT, application form, baccalaureate/first degree, interview, personal statement, resume/curriculum vitae, 5 years of work experience. *Recommended:* 2 letters of recommendation, transcripts of college work. *Application fee:* 300 Swiss francs. Applications for domestic and international students are processed on a rolling basis.

Application Contact Dr. Albert Stähli, Dean, Hirsackerstrasse 46, PO Box 324, Horgen, 8810, Switzerland. *Phone:* 41-44-2269944. *Fax:* 41-44-2269945. *E-mail:* info@gsba.ch.

IMD International Institute for Management Development
IMD International
Lausanne, Switzerland

Phone: 41-21-6180298 **Fax:** 41-21-6180615 **E-mail:** mbainfo@imd.ch

Business Program(s) Web Site: http://www.imd.ch/mba

Graduate Business Unit Enrollment *Total:* 90 (90 full-time; 20 women; 87 international). *Average Age:* 31.

Graduate Business Faculty *Total:* 40 (30 full-time; 10 part-time).

Admissions *Applied:* 425. *Admitted:* 110. *Enrolled:* 90. *Average GMAT:* 671.

Academic Calendar Blocks/project based.

Accreditation AACSB—The Association to Advance Collegiate Schools of Business.

After Graduation (Class of 2006–07) *Employed within 3 months of graduation:* 99%. *Average starting salary:* $130,000.

DEGREE MBA

MBA—Master of Business Administration Full-time. 11 months to complete program. *Concentrations:* entrepreneurship, general MBA, international management, leadership, management.

RESOURCES AND SERVICES 50 on-campus PCs are available to graduate business students. Access to Internet/World Wide Web available. *Personal computer requirements:* Graduate business students are strongly recommended to purchase or lease a personal computer. *Placement services include:* Alumni network, career placement, job search course, career counseling/planning, electronic job bank, resume referral, career fairs, job interviews arranged, resume preparation, and career library.

EXPENSES *Tuition:* Full-time: 58,000 Swiss francs. *Tuition (international):* Full-time: 58,000 Swiss francs. *Required fees:* Full-time: 21,500 Swiss francs.

FINANCIAL AID (2007–08) 27 students received aid, including loans and scholarships. *Financial aid application deadline:* 9/30.

Financial Aid Contact MBA Admissions Office, Chemin de Bellerive 23, PO Box 915, Lausanne, CH-1001, Switzerland. *Phone:* 41-21-6180298. *Fax:* 41-21-6180615. *E-mail:* mbainfo@imd.ch.

INTERNATIONAL STUDENTS 97% of students enrolled are international students. *Services and facilities:* Counseling/support services, Housing location assistance, Orientation, Visa Services, Partner Program. Financial aid is available to international students.

International Student Contact MBA Admissions Office, Chemin de Bellerive 23, PO Box 915, Lausanne, CH-1001, Switzerland. *Phone:* 41-21-6180298. *Fax:* 41-21-6180615. *E-mail:* mbainfo@imd.ch.

APPLICATION *Required:* GMAT, application form, baccalaureate/first degree, essay, interview, 3 letters of recommendation, personal statement, transcripts of college work, 5 years of work experience. *Application fee:* 350 Swiss francs. Applications for domestic and international students are processed on a rolling basis.

Application Contact MBA Admissions Office, Chemin de Bellerive 23, PO Box 915, Lausanne, CH-1001, Switzerland. *Phone:* 41-21-6180298. *Fax:* 41-21-6180615. *E-mail:* mbainfo@imd.ch.

International University in Geneva
MBA Program
Geneva, Switzerland

Phone: 41-22-7107110 Ext. 12 **Fax:** 41-22-7107111 **E-mail:** admissions@iun.ch

Business Program(s) Web Site: http://www.iun.ch

Graduate Business Unit Enrollment *Total:* 80 (20 full-time; 60 part-time; 31 women; 35 international). *Average Age:* 27.

Graduate Business Faculty *Total:* 38 (13 full-time; 25 part-time).

Admissions *Applied:* 114. *Admitted:* 89. *Enrolled:* 56. *Average GMAT:* 500. *Average GPA:* 3.1

Academic Calendar Trimesters.

After Graduation (Class of 2006–07) *Employed within 3 months of graduation:* 75%. *Average starting salary:* 105,000 Swiss francs.

International University in Geneva (continued)

DEGREE MBA

MBA—Master of Business Administration Full-time. Up to 50 total credits required. 15 months to complete program. *Concentrations:* accounting, banking, business policy/strategy, electronic commerce (E-commerce), European business studies, finance, general MBA, human resources management, information management, international business, international finance, international management, international marketing, management communication, marketing, organizational behavior/development, organizational management, public relations, telecommunications management.

RESOURCES AND SERVICES 38 on-campus PCs are available to graduate business students. Access to Internet/World Wide Web available. *Personal computer requirements:* Graduate business students are strongly recommended to purchase or lease a personal computer. *Special opportunities include:* An international exchange program is available. *Placement services include:* Alumni network, career placement, job search course, career counseling/planning, career fairs, resume preparation, and career library.

EXPENSES *Tuition:* Full-time: 36,200 Swiss francs.

FINANCIAL AID (2007–08) 5 students received aid, including scholarships. *Financial aid application deadline:* 6/28.

INTERNATIONAL STUDENTS 44% of students enrolled are international students. *Services and facilities:* Counseling/support services, ESL/language courses, Housing location assistance, Language tutoring, Orientation, Visa Services. Financial aid is available to international students. *Required with application:* TOEFL with recommended score of 80 (Internet).

International Student Contact Miss Marthe Muller, International Admissions Officer, 20 Route de Pré-Bois, Geneva, 1215, Switzerland. *Phone:* 41-22-7107110. *Fax:* 41-22-7107111. *E-mail:* info@iun.ch.

APPLICATION *Required:* GMAT, application form, baccalaureate/first degree, 2 letters of recommendation, resume/curriculum vitae, transcripts of college work. *Recommended:* Essay, interview. *Application fee:* 150 Swiss francs. Applications for domestic and international students are processed on a rolling basis.

Application Contact Ms. Sanela Pavlovic, Admissions Officer, 20 Route de Pré-Bois, Geneva, 1215, Switzerland. *Phone:* 41-22-7107110 Ext. 12. *Fax:* 41-22-7107111. *E-mail:* admissions@iun.ch.

See full description on page 640.

LES ROCHES, Swiss Hotel Association, School of Hotel Management

Graduate Programmes

Bluche, Switzerland

Phone: 41-21-989-2655 **Fax:** 41-21-989-2645 **E-mail:** claudia.toletti@les-roches.ch

Business Program(s) Web Site: http://www.lesroches.edu

Graduate Business Unit Enrollment *Total:* 55 (55 full-time; 28 women; 53 international). *Average Age:* 25.

Graduate Business Faculty *Total:* 12 (8 full-time; 4 part-time).

Admissions *Applied:* 32. *Admitted:* 32. *Enrolled:* 26. *Average GPA:* 80/100 scale

Academic Calendar Quarters.

After Graduation (Class of 2006–07) *Employed within 3 months of graduation:* 90%. *Average starting salary:* 60,000 Swiss francs.

DEGREES MBA

MBA—Master of Business Administration in Hospitality Finance Full-time. 46 total credits required. 18 months to complete program. *Concentration:* hospitality management.

MBA—Master of Business Administration in Hospitality Marketing Full-time. 46 total credits required. 18 months to complete program. *Concentration:* hospitality management.

RESOURCES AND SERVICES 2 on-campus PCs are available to graduate business students. Access to Internet/World Wide Web available. *Personal computer requirements:* Graduate business students are required to have a personal computer. *Special opportunities include:* An internship program is available. *Placement services include:* Alumni network, career placement, career counseling/planning, resume referral, career fairs, job interviews arranged, and career library.

EXPENSES *Tuition:* Full-time: 39,900 Swiss francs. *Tuition (international):* Full-time: 39,900 Swiss francs. *Required fees:* Full-time: 54,100 Swiss francs. Tuition and/or fees vary by local reciprocity agreements. *Graduate housing:* Room and board costs vary by number of occupants and type of accommodation. *Typical cost:* 14,000 Swiss francs (including board).

FINANCIAL AID (2007–08) Scholarships. *Financial aid application deadline:* 5/15.

Financial Aid Contact Mr. René Maillard, Registrar, 118 rue du Lac, Clarens, 1815, Switzerland. *Phone:* 41-21-989-2608. *Fax:* 41-21-989-2645. *E-mail:* maillard@glion.ch.

INTERNATIONAL STUDENTS 96% of students enrolled are international students. *Services and facilities:* Counseling/support services, ESL/language courses, Housing location assistance, International student housing, Language tutoring, Orientation, Visa Services, Alumni association. Financial aid is available to international students. *Required with application:* TOEFL with recommended score of 213 (computer), 550 (paper), or 80 (Internet); proof of adequate funds; proof of health/immunizations. *Recommended with application:* IELT with recommended score of 5.5.

International Student Contact Ms. Frances Drury, Online Recruitment Manager, 118 rue du Lac, Clarens, 1815, Switzerland. *Phone:* 41-21-989-2636. *Fax:* 41-21-989-2645. *E-mail:* frances.drury@les-roches.ch.

APPLICATION *Required:* Application form, baccalaureate/first degree, essay, 2 letters of recommendation, personal statement, resume/curriculum vitae, transcripts of college work, 3 years of work experience. *Recommended:* Interview. *Application fee:* 100 Swiss francs. Applications for domestic and international students are processed on a rolling basis.

Application Contact Mrs. Claudia Toletti, Senior Admissions Manager, 118 rue du Lac, Clarens, 1815, Switzerland. *Phone:* 41-21-989-2655. *Fax:* 41-21-989-2645. *E-mail:* claudia.toletti@les-roches.ch.

Schiller International University, American College of Switzerland

MBA Program

Leysin, Switzerland

Phone: 727-736-5082 Ext. 240 **Fax:** 727-734-0359 **E-mail:** admissions@schiller.edu

Business Program(s) Web Site: http://www.schiller.edu

Graduate Business Unit Enrollment *Total:* 590 (240 full-time; 350 part-time). *Average Age:* 23.

Graduate Business Faculty *Total:* 12 (4 full-time; 8 part-time).

Admissions *Average GPA:* 3.0

Academic Calendar Semesters.

After Graduation (Class of 2006–07) *Employed within 3 months of graduation:* 100%.

DEGREE MBA

MBA—Master of Business Administration in International Business Full-time and part-time. Distance learning option. At least 45 total credits required. 12 to 24 months to complete program. *Concentration:* international business.

RESOURCES AND SERVICES 15 on-campus PCs are available to graduate business students. Access to Internet/World Wide Web available. *Personal computer requirements:* Graduate business students are required to have a personal computer. *Special opportunities include:* An international exchange program and an internship program are available. *Placement services include:* Alumni network, career placement, job search course, career counseling/planning, electronic job bank, resume referral, and resume preparation.

EXPENSES *Tuition:* Full-time: 27,600 Swiss francs. Part-time: 2300 Swiss francs per course. *Tuition (international):* Full-time: 27,600 Swiss francs. Part-time: 2300 Swiss francs per course. *Required fees:* Full-time: 960 Swiss francs.

FINANCIAL AID (2007–08) Grants, loans, scholarships, and work study. *Financial aid application deadline:* 4/1.

Financial Aid Contact Ms. Jennifer Fraser, Financial Aid Officer, 300 East Bay Drive, Largo, FL 33770. *Phone:* 727-736-5082 Ext. 253. *Fax:* 727-738-8405. *E-mail:* financial_aid@schiller.edu.

INTERNATIONAL STUDENTS *Services and facilities:* Counseling/support services, ESL/language courses, Housing location assistance, International student housing, Language tutoring, Orientation, Visa Services. Financial aid is available to international students. *Required with application:* Proof of adequate funds. *Recommended with application:* TOEFL with recommended score of 213 (computer), 550 (paper), or 73 (Internet).

International Student Contact Ms. Stephanie Givens, Admissions, 300 East Bay Drive, Largo, FL 33770. *Phone:* 727-736-5082 Ext. 411. *Fax:* 727-734-0359. *E-mail:* admissions@schiller.edu.

APPLICATION *Required:* Application form, baccalaureate/first degree, essay, transcripts of college work. *Recommended:* Resume/curriculum vitae, work experience. *Application fee:* $65. Applications for domestic and international students are processed on a rolling basis.

Application Contact Ms. Kamala Dontamsetti, Assistant Director of Admissions, 300 East Bay Drive, Largo, FL 33770. *Phone:* 727-736-5082 Ext. 240. *Fax:* 727-734-0359. *E-mail:* admissions@schiller.edu.

See full description on page 684.

University of Geneva
MBA Program

Geneva, Switzerland

Fax: 41-22-3798120 **E-mail:** iomba@hec.unige.ch

Business Program(s) Web Site: http://www.iomba.ch

Graduate Business Unit Enrollment *Total:* 500 (100 full-time; 400 part-time; 280 women; 350 international). *Average Age:* 32.

Graduate Business Faculty *Total:* 45 (25 full-time; 20 part-time).

Admissions *Applied:* 150. *Admitted:* 35. *Enrolled:* 30. *Average GMAT:* 650.

Academic Calendar Semesters.

After Graduation (Class of 2006–07) *Employed within 3 months of graduation:* 90%.

DEGREE IMBA

IMBA—International Organizations Master of Business Administration Full-time. 90 to 120 total credits required. 12 months to complete program. *Concentrations:* international development management, international management, international trade, management, nonprofit management, nonprofit organization, public policy and administration.

RESOURCES AND SERVICES 600 on-campus PCs are available to graduate business students. Access to Internet/World Wide Web available. *Personal computer requirements:* Graduate business students are strongly recommended to purchase or lease a personal computer. *Special opportunities include:* An international exchange program is available. *Placement services include:* Alumni network, career placement, job search course, career counseling/planning, electronic job bank, resume referral, career fairs, job interviews arranged, and resume preparation.

FINANCIAL AID (2007–08) 10 students received aid, including scholarships. *Financial aid application deadline:* 11/15.

Financial Aid Contact Kasia Wasiukiewicz, Finance Officer, 16, Chemin de la Voie Creuse, Geneva, CH-1202, Switzerland. *E-mail:* wasiukiewicz@hec.unige.ch.

INTERNATIONAL STUDENTS 70% of students enrolled are international students. *Services and facilities:* Counseling/support services, ESL/language courses, Housing location assistance, International student organization, Language tutoring, Orientation, Visa Services. Financial aid is available to international students. *Required with application:* TOEFL with recommended score of 250 (computer) or 600 (paper); proof of health/immunizations. *Recommended with application:* Proof of adequate funds.

International Student Contact Daniele Alesani, Coordinator, International Organizations MBA, 16, Chemin de la Voie Creuse, CH-1202, Geneva, CH-1202, Switzerland. *Fax:* 41-22-3798120. *E-mail:* iomba@hec.unige.ch.

APPLICATION *Required:* GMAT, application form, baccalaureate/first degree, essay, 2 letters of recommendation, personal statement, transcripts of college work, 3 years of work experience. *Recommended:* Resume/curriculum vitae. *Application fee:* 75 euros. Applications for domestic and international students are processed on a rolling basis.

Application Contact Admissions Office, 16, Chemin de la Voie Creuse, Geneva, CH-1202, Switzerland. *Fax:* 41-22-3798120. *E-mail:* iomba@hec.unige.ch.

University of St. Gallen
Business School

St. Gallen, Switzerland

Phone: 41-71-224-73-55 **Fax:** 41-71-224-24-73 **E-mail:** mba@unisg.ch

Business Program(s) Web Site: http://www.mba.unisg.ch/

Graduate Business Unit Enrollment *Total:* 34 (34 full-time; 8 women; 32 international). *Average Age:* 29.

Graduate Business Faculty 23 part-time.

Admissions *Applied:* 250. *Admitted:* 80. *Enrolled:* 40. *Average GMAT:* 680.

Academic Calendar Quarters.

Accreditation AACSB—The Association to Advance Collegiate Schools of Business.

After Graduation (Class of 2006–07) *Employed within 3 months of graduation:* 90%. *Average starting salary:* 126,000 Swiss francs.

DEGREE MBA

MBA—MBA—HSG Full-time. Minimum GMAT 650. 12 months to complete program. *Concentration:* general MBA.

RESOURCES AND SERVICES Access to Internet/World Wide Web available. *Personal computer requirements:* Graduate business students are required to have a personal computer. *Special opportunities include:* An international exchange program and an internship program are available. *Placement services include:* Alumni network, career placement, job search course, career counseling/planning, electronic job bank, resume referral, career fairs, and resume preparation.

EXPENSES *Tuition (state resident):* Full-time: 60,000 Swiss francs. Part-time: 67,000 Swiss francs per degree program. *Tuition (nonresident):*

University of St. Gallen (continued)

Full-time: 60,000 Swiss francs. Part-time: 67,000 Swiss francs per degree program. *Tuition (international):* Full-time: 60,000 Swiss francs. Part-time: 67,000 Swiss francs per degree program. *Typical graduate housing cost:* 20,000 Swiss francs (including board), 9000 Swiss francs (room only).

FINANCIAL AID (2007–08) 34 students received aid, including loans and scholarships. Aid is available to part-time students. *Financial aid application deadline:* 6/1.

Financial Aid Contact Ms. Barbara Fricker, Admissions Manager, MBA-HSG, Blumenbergplatz 9, St. Gallen, CH-9000, Switzerland. *Phone:* 41-71-224-73-55. *Fax:* 41-71-224-24-73. *E-mail:* mba@unisg.ch.

INTERNATIONAL STUDENTS 94% of students enrolled are international students. *Services and facilities:* Counseling/support services, ESL/language courses, Housing location assistance, International student organization, Language tutoring, Orientation, Visa Services, specialist career services. Financial aid is available to international students. *Recommended with application:* TOEFL with recommended score of 260 (computer) or 107 (Internet).

International Student Contact Ms. Barbara Fricker, Admissions Manager, MBA-HSG, Blumenbergplatz 9, St. Gallen, CH-9000, Switzerland. *Phone:* 41-71-224-73-55. *Fax:* 41-71-224-24-73. *E-mail:* mba@unisg.ch.

APPLICATION *Required:* GMAT, application form, baccalaureate/first degree, essay, interview, 2 letters of recommendation, personal statement, transcripts of college work, 4 years of work experience. School will accept GRE. *Recommended:* Resume/curriculum vitae. *Application fee:* 0 Swiss francs. *Deadlines:* 6/1 for fall, 6/1 for fall (international).

Application Contact Ms. Barbara Fricker, Admissions Manager, MBA-HSG, Blumenbergplatz 9, St. Gallen, CH-9000, Switzerland. *Phone:* 41-71-224-73-55. *Fax:* 41-71-224-24-73. *E-mail:* mba@unisg.ch.

THAILAND

Asian Institute of Technology
School of Management

Pathumthani, Thailand

Phone: 66-2-5245665 **Fax:** 66-2-5245667 **E-mail:** somadmissions@ait.ac.th

Business Program(s) Web Site: http://www.som.ait.ac.th/

Graduate Business Unit Enrollment *Total:* 350 (200 full-time; 150 part-time; 160 women; 280 international). *Average Age:* 26.

Graduate Business Faculty *Total:* 35 (20 full-time; 15 part-time).

Admissions *Applied:* 750. *Admitted:* 105. *Enrolled:* 85. *Average GMAT:* 500. *Average GPA:* 3.2

Academic Calendar Semesters.

After Graduation (Class of 2006–07) *Employed within 3 months of graduation:* 70%. *Average starting salary:* 600,000 Thai bahts.

DEGREES DBA • EMBA • MBA • PhD/Mphil

DBA—DBA for Executives (5 country locations) Part-time. MBA or EMBA degree with 10 years of work experience required. 84 total credits required. 36 to 60 months to complete program. *Concentration:* management.

EMBA Part-time. 6 years of relevant working experience required. 54 total credits required. 20 to 36 months to complete program. *Concentration:* executive programs.

MBA—MBA Program Full-time and part-time. TOEFL; 4-years bachelor's degree with above average GPA required. 51 to 52 total credits required. 15 to 22 months to complete program. *Concentrations:* entrepreneurship, finance, general MBA, human resources management, international business, international management, marketing, public management, technology management.

PhD/Mphil—PhD Program Full-time and part-time. Minimum GPA of 3.5 or equivalent at graduate level in management or economics required. 84 total credits required. 36 to 84 months to complete program. *Concentration:* management.

RESOURCES AND SERVICES 80 on-campus PCs are available to graduate business students. Access to Internet/World Wide Web, online (class) registration, and online grade reports available. *Personal computer requirements:* Graduate business students are strongly recommended to purchase or lease a personal computer. *Special opportunities include:* An international exchange program and an internship program are available. *Placement services include:* Alumni network, career placement, career fairs, and job interviews arranged.

EXPENSES *Tuition:* Full-time: 376,000 Thai bahts. *Tuition (international):* Full-time: 376,000 Thai bahts. *Typical graduate housing cost:* 138,000 Thai bahts (including board), 36,000 Thai bahts (room only).

FINANCIAL AID (2007–08) 50 students received aid, including fellowships, scholarships, and teaching assistantships. *Financial aid application deadline:* 3/28.

Financial Aid Contact Ms. Wilaiporn Cherngchawano, Senior Program Officer, Km. 42 Paholyothin Highway, Klong Luang, PO Box 4, Pathumthani, 12120, Thailand. *Phone:* 66-2-5245665. *Fax:* 66-2-5245667. *E-mail:* somadmissions@ait.ac.th.

INTERNATIONAL STUDENTS 80% of students enrolled are international students. *Services and facilities:* Counseling/support services, ESL/language courses, Housing location assistance, International student housing, International student organization, Language tutoring, Orientation, Visa Services, International phone booths, Banking service, International cuisine. Financial aid is available to international students. *Required with application:* TOEFL with recommended score of 213 (computer) or 550 (paper); proof of adequate funds; proof of health/immunizations. *Recommended with application:* IELT with recommended score of 6.

International Student Contact Ms. Jaram Hanpol, Program Officer, SOM-AIT, Km. 42 Paholyothin Highway, Klong Luang, PO Box 4, Pathumthani, 12120, Thailand. *Phone:* 66-2-5246018. *Fax:* 66-2-5245667. *E-mail:* mba-france@ait.ac.th.

APPLICATION *Required:* Application form, baccalaureate/first degree, essay, 2 letters of recommendation, personal statement, transcripts of college work. School will accept GMAT. *Recommended:* Interview, resume/curriculum vitae, 2 years of work experience. *Application fee:* 800 Thai bahts, 1000 Thai bahts (international). *Deadlines:* 6/30 for fall, 6/30 for fall (international).

Application Contact Ms. Ms. Wilaiporn Cherngchawano, Senior Program Officer, Km. 42 Paholyothin Highway, Klong Luang, PO Box 4, Pathumthani, 12120, Thailand. *Phone:* 66-2-5245665. *Fax:* 66-2-5245667. *E-mail:* somadmissions@ait.ac.th.

Chulalongkorn University
Sasin Graduate Institute of Business Administration

Bangkok, Thailand

Phone: 66-2-2183856 **Fax:** 66-2-2161312 **E-mail:** lalida.ruangtrakool@sasin.edu

Business Program(s) Web Site: http://www.sasin.edu

DEGREES MBA • MSHR

MBA—Executive MBA Program Part-time. Minimum of 7 years work experience required. At least 72 total credits required. 24 to 48 months to complete program. *Concentration:* management.

MBA—Master of Business Administration Full-time. 1 year of full-time work experience required. At least 76 total credits required. 20 to 48 months to complete program. *Concentrations:* entrepreneurship, finance, international business, marketing, strategic management.

MSHR—Master of Science in Human Resources Part-time. At least 52 total credits required. 18 to 48 months to complete program. *Concentration:* human resources management.

RESOURCES AND SERVICES 36 on-campus PCs are available to graduate business students. Access to Internet/World Wide Web available. *Personal computer requirements:* Graduate business students are required to have a personal computer. *Special opportunities include:* An international exchange program and an internship program are available. *Placement services include:* Alumni network, job search course, resume referral, career fairs, job interviews arranged, and resume preparation.

Application Contact Mrs. Lalida Ruangtrakool, Head of Admissions Section, Sasa Patasala Building, Soi Chula 12, Phyathai Road, Bangkok, 10330, Thailand. *Phone:* 66-2-2183856. *Fax:* 66-2-2161312. *E-mail:* lalida.ruangtrakool@sasin.edu.

TURKEY

Koc University
Graduate School of Business
Istanbul, Turkey

Phone: 90-212-3381307 **Fax:** 90-212-3381652 **E-mail:** iunlusoy@ku.edu.tr

Business Program(s) Web Site: http://www.gsb.ku.edu.tr

Graduate Business Unit Enrollment *Total:* 109 (68 full-time; 41 part-time; 44 women; 4 international). *Average Age:* 24.

Graduate Business Faculty *Total:* 42 (32 full-time; 10 part-time).

Admissions *Applied:* 152. *Admitted:* 119. *Enrolled:* 75. *Average GMAT:* 624. *Average GPA:* 3.0

Academic Calendar Semesters.

After Graduation (Class of 2006–07) *Employed within 3 months of graduation:* 55%. *Average starting salary:* $28,000.

DEGREES MAF • MBA

MAF—MS in Finance Part-time. Work experience required. 30 total credits required. 12 to 24 months to complete program. *Concentration:* finance.

MBA—Executive Master of Business Administration Part-time. Minimum 5 years of full-time work experience required. 50 total credits required. 13 to 26 months to complete program. *Concentration:* executive programs.

MBA—Master of Business Administration Full-time. 54 total credits required. 10 to 15 months to complete program. *Concentration:* general MBA.

RESOURCES AND SERVICES 15 on-campus PCs are available to graduate business students. Access to Internet/World Wide Web, online (class) registration, and online grade reports available. *Personal computer requirements:* Graduate business students are not required to have a personal computer. *Special opportunities include:* An international exchange program and an internship program are available. *Placement services include:* Alumni network, career placement, job search course, career counseling/planning, electronic job bank, resume referral, career fairs, job interviews arranged, resume preparation, and career library.

EXPENSES *Tuition:* Full-time: $20,000. Part-time: $29,000 per year. *Tuition (international):* Full-time: $20,000. Part-time: $29,000 per year. *Required fees:* Full-time: $60. Part-time: $60 per year. Tuition and/or fees

vary by academic program. *Graduate housing:* Room and board costs vary by number of occupants, type of accommodation, and type of board plan. *Typical cost:* $1500 (including board).

FINANCIAL AID (2007–08) 20 students received aid, including scholarships and work study. *Financial aid application deadline:* 6/30.

Financial Aid Contact ASUMAN AKCA, Assistant to the Director, Rumeli FeneriI Yolu, Sariyer, Istanbul, 34450, Turkey. *Phone:* 90-212-3381307. *Fax:* 90-212-3381652. *E-mail:* iunlusoy@ku.edu.tr.

INTERNATIONAL STUDENTS 4% of students enrolled are international students. *Services and facilities:* Counseling/support services, ESL/language courses, Housing location assistance, Orientation, Visa Services. Financial aid is not available to international students. *Required with application:* TOEFL with recommended score of 213 (computer), 550 (paper), or 80 (Internet); TWE with recommended score of 4; proof of health/immunizations. *Recommended with application:* Proof of adequate funds.

International Student Contact ASUMAN AKCA, Assistant to the Director, Rumeli FeneriI Yolu, Sariyer, Istanbul, 34450, Turkey. *Phone:* 90-212-3381307. *Fax:* 90-212-3381652. *E-mail:* iunlusoy@ku.edu.tr.

APPLICATION *Required:* GMAT, application form, baccalaureate/first degree, essay, interview, 2 letters of recommendation, transcripts of college work. *Recommended:* Personal statement, resume/curriculum vitae, 2 years of work experience. *Application fee:* $60. Applications for domestic and international students are processed on a rolling basis.

Application Contact ASUMAN AKCA, Assistant to the Director, Rumeli FeneriI Yolu, Sariyer, Istanbul, 34450, Turkey. *Phone:* 90-212-3381307. *Fax:* 90-212-3381652. *E-mail:* iunlusoy@ku.edu.tr.

Middle East Technical University
Department of Business Administration
Ankara, Turkey

Phone: 90-312-2102010 **Fax:** 90-312-2107962 **E-mail:** nazli@metu.edu.tr

Business Program(s) Web Site: http://www.ba.metu.edu.tr/

Graduate Business Unit Enrollment *Total:* 66 (66 full-time; 33 women). *Average Age:* 28.

Graduate Business Faculty *Total:* 29 (19 full-time; 10 part-time).

Admissions *Applied:* 318. *Admitted:* 60. *Enrolled:* 32.

Academic Calendar Semesters.

DEGREES EMBA • MBA • PhD/Mphil

EMBA—Executive Master of Business Administration Part-time. At least 30 total credits required. 15 to 30 months to complete program. *Concentration:* executive programs.

MBA—Master of Business Administration—non-thesis Full-time. At least 57 total credits required. 24 to 36 months to complete program. *Concentration:* general MBA.

PhD/Mphil—Doctor of Philosophy in Business Administration Full-time and part-time. 30 to 51 total credits required. 48 to 96 months to complete program. *Concentrations:* accounting, finance.

RESOURCES AND SERVICES 80 on-campus PCs are available to graduate business students. Access to Internet/World Wide Web, online (class) registration, and online grade reports available. *Personal computer requirements:* Graduate business students are strongly recommended to purchase or lease a personal computer. *Special opportunities include:* An international exchange program is available.

Financial Aid Contact Prof. Nazli S Wasti-Pamuksuz, Chairperson, Inonu Bulvari, Ankara, 06531, Turkey. *Phone:* 90-312-2102010. *Fax:* 90-312-2107962. *E-mail:* nazli@metu.edu.tr.

INTERNATIONAL STUDENTS *Recommended with application:* TOEFL.

Middle East Technical University (continued)

International Student Contact Prof. Nazli S Wasti-Pamuksuz, MBA Advisor, Inonu Bulvari, Ankara, 06531, Turkey. *Phone:* 90-312-2102010. *Fax:* 90-312-2107962. *E-mail:* nguner@ba.metu.edu.tr.

APPLICATION School will accept GMAT. *Deadline:* 4/26 for fall.

Application Contact Prof. Nazli S Wasti-Pamuksuz, MBA Advisor, Inonu Bulvari, Ankara, 06531, Turkey. *Phone:* 90-312-2102010. *Fax:* 90-312-2107962. *E-mail:* nazli@metu.edu.tr.

UNITED ARAB EMIRATES

The American University in Dubai
MBA Program

Dubai, United Arab Emirates

Phone: 971-4-3999000 Ext. 170 **Fax:** 971-4-3998899 **E-mail:** cmaalouf@aud.edu

Business Program(s) Web Site: http://www.aud.edu/Academic_Programs/graduate.asp

DEGREE MBA

MBA—Master of Business Administration Full-time and part-time. GMAT score 500 or higher; undergraduate GPA 3.0 or higher; two years work experience. At least 36 total credits required. Minimum of 10 months to complete program. *Concentrations:* international finance, international marketing.

RESOURCES AND SERVICES 150 on-campus PCs are available to graduate business students. Access to Internet/World Wide Web, online (class) registration, and online grade reports available. *Personal computer requirements:* Graduate business students are strongly recommended to purchase or lease a personal computer. *Special opportunities include:* An international exchange program and an internship program are available. *Placement services include:* Alumni network, career placement, resume referral, career fairs, job interviews arranged, and resume preparation.

Application Contact Mrs. Carol Maalouf, Associate Director of Admissions, PO Box 28282, Dubai, United Arab Emirates. *Phone:* 971-4-3999000 Ext. 170. *Fax:* 971-4-3998899. *E-mail:* cmaalouf@aud.edu.

American University of Sharjah
School of Business and Management

Sharjah, United Arab Emirates

Business Program(s) Web Site: http://www.aus.edu/sbm/mba/index.php

Graduate Business Unit Enrollment *Total:* 88 (28 full-time; 60 part-time; 48 women; 63 international). *Average Age:* 28-35.

Graduate Business Faculty 20 full-time.

Admissions *Applied:* 30. *Admitted:* 24. *Enrolled:* 21. *Average GPA:* 3.3

Academic Calendar Semesters.

DEGREE MBA

MBA—Master of Business Administration Full-time and part-time. 30 to 51 total credits required. 12 to 60 months to complete program. *Concentrations:* finance, human resources management, supply chain management.

RESOURCES AND SERVICES 100 on-campus PCs are available to graduate business students. Access to Internet/World Wide Web, online

(class) registration, and online grade reports available. *Personal computer requirements:* Graduate business students are required to have a personal computer. *Special opportunities include:* An international exchange program and an internship program are available. *Placement services include:* Alumni network, career placement, career counseling/planning, career fairs, and resume preparation.

EXPENSES *Tuition:* Part-time: 8000 United Arab Emirates dirhams per credit. *Tuition (international):* Part-time: 8000 United Arab Emirates dirhams per credit. Tuition and/or fees vary by number of courses or credits taken.

FINANCIAL AID (2007–08) 20 students received aid, including research assistantships and work study. Aid is available to part-time students. *Financial aid application deadline:* 4/30.

INTERNATIONAL STUDENTS 72% of students enrolled are international students. *Services and facilities:* Counseling/support services, ESL/language courses, Language tutoring, Orientation, Visa Services. Financial aid is available to international students. *Required with application:* TOEFL with recommended score of 213 (computer), 550 (paper), or 80 (Internet); proof of health/immunizations.

International Student Contact Mrs. Fatima Zaidi, PO Box 26666, Sharjah, United Arab Emirates. *Phone:* 971-6-515-2028. *E-mail:* fzaidi@aus.edu.

APPLICATION *Required:* GMAT, application form, baccalaureate/first degree, personal statement, transcripts of college work. *Recommended:* 2 years of work experience. *Application fee:* 200 United Arab Emirates dirhams. Applications for domestic and international students are processed on a rolling basis.

UNITED KINGDOM

American InterContinental University–London
School of Business

London, United Kingdom

Business Program(s) Web Site: http://www.aiulondon.ac.uk/
See full description on page 564.

Ashridge
Ashridge Executive MBA Program

Berkhamsted, United Kingdom

Phone: 44-1442-841143 **Fax:** 44-1442-841144 **E-mail:** mba@ashridge.org.uk

Business Program(s) Web Site: http://www.ashridge.com/mba

Accreditation AACSB—The Association to Advance Collegiate Schools of Business.

DEGREES MBA

MBA—Executive Master of Business Administration Part-time. Maximum of 24 months to complete program. *Concentrations:* business ethics, finance, human resources management, international and area business studies, international finance, international marketing, leadership, logistics, management consulting, marketing, operations management, organizational behavior/development, project management, strategic management, technology management.

MBA—Master of Business Administration Full-time. Maximum of 12 months to complete program. *Concentrations:* accounting, economics, finance, human resources management, international business, management, management information systems, marketing, operations management, organizational behavior/development, quantitative analysis.

RESOURCES AND SERVICES 30 on-campus PCs are available to graduate business students. Access to Internet/World Wide Web and online (class) registration available. *Personal computer requirements:* Graduate business students are strongly recommended to purchase or lease a personal computer. *Special opportunities include:* An international exchange program and an internship program are available. *Placement services include:* Alumni network, career counseling/planning, electronic job bank, resume referral, career fairs, resume preparation, and career library.

Application Contact Ms. Amy Barrow, Director of Marketing Strategy, Hertfordshire, United Kingdom. *Phone:* 44-1442-841143. *Fax:* 44-1442-841144. *E-mail:* mba@ashridge.org.uk.

Aston University
Aston Business School
Birmingham, United Kingdom

Phone: 44-121-2043096 Ext. 3096 **Fax:** 44-121-2043224 Ext. 3224 **E-mail:** j.m.evans@aston.ac.uk

Business Program(s) Web Site: http://www.abs.aston.ac.uk/pg

Accreditation AACSB—The Association to Advance Collegiate Schools of Business.

DEGREES M Sc • MBA • MSC

M Sc—Master of Science in Business Studies Full-time. Minimum of 10 months to complete program. *Concentrations:* accounting, finance, human resources management, international business, management, operations management, organizational behavior/development, statistics, strategic management.

M Sc—Master of Science in Business and Information Technology Full-time. Minimum of 12 months to complete program. *Concentrations:* decision sciences, information systems, operations management, organizational behavior/development, strategic management.

M Sc—Master of Science in Finance and Investments Full-time. Candidates must have a good level of quantitative and analytical skills and must have studied Finance or Economics at the undergraduate level. Minimum of 10 months to complete program. *Concentrations:* accounting, finance, financial management/planning, international finance, management, operations management, quantitative analysis, strategic management.

M Sc—Master of Science in Human Resource Management and Business Full-time and part-time. Minimum of 12 months to complete program. *Concentrations:* human resources management, industrial/labor relations, management, organizational behavior/development, strategic management.

M Sc—Master of Science in International Business Full-time. Minimum of 10 months to complete program. *Concentrations:* international business, international finance, international management, international marketing, management, operations management, organizational behavior/development, quality management, strategic management.

M Sc—Master of Science in Managing Public Services Full-time and part-time. 12 to 60 months to complete program. *Concentrations:* health care, nonprofit management, public management, public policy and administration.

M Sc—Master of Science in Marketing Management Full-time. Minimum of 10 months to complete program. *Concentrations:* accounting, advertising, international marketing, management, marketing, marketing research, public relations, strategic management.

M Sc—Master of Science in Operational Research and Management Studies Full-time. Candidates will need to provide evidence of aptitude for mathematical analysis. Minimum of 10 months to complete program. *Concentrations:* financial management/planning, marketing, operations management, organizational behavior/development, statistics.

M Sc—Master of Science in Operational Research and Performance Management Full-time. Candidates will need to provide evidence of aptitude for mathematical analysis. Maximum of 10 months to complete program. *Concentrations:* marketing, operations management, organizational behavior/development, quantitative analysis, statistics.

M Sc—Master of Science in Work Psychology and Business Full-time. First degree in psychology required. Minimum of 12 months to complete program. *Concentrations:* accounting, human resources management, industrial/labor relations, marketing, operations management, organizational behavior/development, strategic management, training and development.

M Sc—Master of Science in e-Business Full-time. Minimum of 10 months to complete program. *Concentrations:* business studies, commerce, electronic commerce (E-commerce), entrepreneurship, international business, logistics, marketing, strategic management.

MBA—Master of Business Administration in Public Services Management Full-time and part-time. 12 to 60 months to complete program. *Concentrations:* health care, nonprofit management, organizational behavior/development, public management, public policy and administration, strategic management.

MBA—Master of Business Administration Full-time and part-time. Distance learning option. A UK honours degree, an overseas degree recognized by Aston University, or a degree equivalent professional qualification required. 12 to 60 months to complete program. *Concentrations:* accounting, economics, entrepreneurship, European business studies, finance, financial economics, financial management/planning, general MBA, health care, human resources management, industrial administration/management, international business, management, marketing, operations management, organizational behavior/development, public policy and administration, quality management, quantitative analysis, strategic management.

MSC—Master of Science in Commerce—Accounting and Business Minimum of 10 months to complete program. *Concentrations:* accounting, finance, international finance, marketing, operations management.

RESOURCES AND SERVICES 350 on-campus PCs are available to graduate business students. Access to Internet/World Wide Web available. *Personal computer requirements:* Graduate business students are not required to have a personal computer. *Special opportunities include:* An international exchange program and an internship program are available. *Placement services include:* Alumni network, job search course, career counseling/planning, resume referral, career fairs, job interviews arranged, resume preparation, and career library.

Application Contact Mrs. Jenny Evans, MBA Office Manager, MBA Programme, Nelson Building, NB432, Birmingham, B4 7ET, United Kingdom. *Phone:* 44-121-204-3096 Ext. 3096. *Fax:* 44-121-2043224 Ext. 3224. *E-mail:* j.m.evans@aston.ac.uk.

Cardiff University
Cardiff Business School
Cardiff, United Kingdom

Phone: 44-29-20874557 **Fax:** 44-29-20874130 **E-mail:** dillonr@cardiff.ac.uk

Business Program(s) Web Site: http://www.cf.ac.uk/carbs.html

Graduate Business Unit Enrollment *Total:* 813 (692 full-time; 121 part-time; 297 women; 577 international). *Average Age:* 27.

Graduate Business Faculty *Total:* 160 (142 full-time; 18 part-time).

Admissions *Applied:* 5,003. *Admitted:* 1,972. *Enrolled:* 684.

Academic Calendar Semesters.

DEGREES M Sc • MBA

M Sc—Master of Science in Financial Economics Full-time. 12 months to complete program. *Concentration:* financial economics.

M Sc—Master of Science in Human Resource Management Full-time. 12 months to complete program. *Concentration:* human resources management.

M Sc—Master of Science in International Economics, Banking and Finance Full-time. 12 to 24 months to complete program. *Concentrations:* international banking, international economics, international finance.

M Sc—Master of Science in Lean Operations Part-time. 24 to 36 months to complete program. *Concentration:* operations management.

MBA—Master of Business Administration Full-time and part-time. 12 to 24 months to complete program. *Concentrations:* environmental economics/management, international and area business studies, management, organizational management, public and private management.

RESOURCES AND SERVICES 404 on-campus PCs are available to graduate business students. Access to Internet/World Wide Web available. *Personal computer requirements:* Graduate business students are strongly recommended to purchase or lease a personal computer. *Placement services include:* Alumni network, career placement, job search course, career counseling/planning, resume referral, career fairs, job interviews arranged, resume preparation, and career library.

Financial Aid Contact Ms. Rosemarie Dillon, Senior Assistant Registrar, PO Box 495, Cardiff, CF10 3XD, United Kingdom. *Phone:* 44-29-20874557. *Fax:* 44-29-20874130. *E-mail:* dillonr@cardiff.ac.uk.

INTERNATIONAL STUDENTS 71% of students enrolled are international students. *Services and facilities:* Counseling/support services, ESL/language courses, Housing location assistance, International student housing, International student organization, Language tutoring, Orientation, Visa Services. Financial aid is not available to international students. *Required with application:* IELT with recommended score of 6.5; TOEFL with recommended score of 230 (computer) or 570 (paper); proof of adequate funds.

International Student Contact Miss Sarah Rees, International Recruitment Manager, Aberconway Building, Colum Drive, Cardiff, CF10 3EU, United Kingdom. *Phone:* 44-29-20875095. *Fax:* 44-29-20874417. *E-mail:* reess15@cardiff.ac.uk.

APPLICATION *Required:* Application form, baccalaureate/first degree, 2 letters of recommendation, transcripts of college work. School will accept GMAT and GRE. *Recommended:* Personal statement, resume/curriculum vitae, work experience. Applications for domestic and international students are processed on a rolling basis.

Application Contact Ms. Rosemarie Dillon, Senior Assistant Registrar, PO Box 495, Cardiff, CF10 3XO, United Kingdom. *Phone:* 44-29-20874557. *Fax:* 44-29-20874130. *E-mail:* dillonr@cardiff.ac.uk.

Cranfield University

Cranfield School of Management

Cranfield, United Kingdom

Phone: 44-1234-754431 **Fax:** 44-1234-752439 **E-mail:** e.fisher@cranfield.ac.uk

Business Program(s) Web Site: http://www.cranfield.ac.uk/som

Graduate Business Unit Enrollment *Total:* 591 (289 full-time; 302 part-time; 180 women; 387 international). *Average Age:* 32.

Graduate Business Faculty 99 full-time.

Admissions *Applied:* 462. *Admitted:* 220. *Enrolled:* 129. *Average GMAT:* 660.

Academic Calendar Quarters.

Accreditation AACSB—The Association to Advance Collegiate Schools of Business.

After Graduation (Class of 2006–07) *Employed within 3 months of graduation:* 97%. *Average starting salary:* 53,500 British pounds.

DEGREES M Sc • MBA • MS

M Sc—Modular Master of Science in Managing Organisational Performance Part-time. 24 months to complete program. *Concentrations:* management, organizational management.

MBA—Executive Modular Master of Business Administration Part-time. At least 280 total credits required. 24 months to complete program. *Concentrations:* executive programs, general MBA, management.

MBA—Executive Part-Time Master of Business Administration Part-time. At least 288 total credits required. 24 months to complete program. *Concentrations:* executive programs, general MBA, management.

MBA—Full-Time Master of Business Administration Full-time. At least 282 total credits required. 12 months to complete program. *Concentrations:* general MBA, management.

MBA—MBA Defence (Executive) Part-time. 24 months to complete program. *Concentration:* executive programs.

MBA—MBA Defence (Full-Time) Full-time. 12 months to complete program. *Concentration:* general MBA.

MS—Executive Master of Science in Logistics and Supply Chain Management Part-time. 24 months to complete program. *Concentrations:* executive programs, logistics, supply chain management.

MS—Master of Science in Finance and Management Full-time. 12 months to complete program. *Concentration:* finance.

MS—Master of Science in Logistics and Supply Chain Management Full-time. 12 months to complete program. *Concentrations:* logistics, supply chain management.

MS—Master of Science in Strategic Marketing Full-time. 12 months to complete program. *Concentration:* marketing.

MS—Modular Master of Science by Research in Leading Learning and Change 24 months to complete program. *Concentrations:* leadership, organizational behavior/development.

MS—Modular Master of Science in International HR Management Part-time. 24 months to complete program. *Concentration:* human resources management.

MS—Modular Master of Science in International Human Resource Management Defence Part-time. 24 to 36 months to complete program. *Concentrations:* human resources management, management.

MS—Modular Master of Science in Program and Project Management Part-time. 36 months to complete program. *Concentrations:* management, project management.

MS—Modular Master of Science in Strategic Marketing Part-time. 36 months to complete program. *Concentrations:* marketing, strategic management.

RESOURCES AND SERVICES 213 on-campus PCs are available to graduate business students. Access to Internet/World Wide Web, online (class) registration, and online grade reports available. *Personal computer requirements:* Graduate business students are required to have a personal computer, the cost of which is included in tuition or other required fees. *Special opportunities include:* An international exchange program is available. *Placement services include:* Alumni network, career placement, job search course, career counseling/planning, electronic job bank, resume referral, career fairs, job interviews arranged, resume preparation, and career library.

EXPENSES *Tuition (state resident):* Full-time: 28,000 British pounds. Part-time: 28,000 British pounds per degree program. *Tuition (international):* Full-time: 28,000 British pounds. Part-time: 28,000 British pounds per degree program. *Graduate housing:* Room and board costs vary by number of occupants, type of accommodation, and type of board plan.

FINANCIAL AID (2007–08) 129 students received aid, including grants and scholarships. Aid is available to part-time students. *Financial aid application deadline:* 5/1.

Financial Aid Contact Mrs. Eileen Fisher, Admissions Executive, Cranfield, Bedfordshire, MK43 OAL, United Kingdom. *Phone:* 44-1234-754431. *Fax:* 44-1234-752439. *E-mail:* e.fisher@cranfield.ac.uk.

INTERNATIONAL STUDENTS 65% of students enrolled are international students. *Services and facilities:* Counseling/support services, ESL/language courses, Housing location assistance, International student organization, Language tutoring, Orientation, Visa Services. Financial aid is available to international students. *Required with application:* IELT with recommended score of 7; TOEFL with recommended score of 250 (computer), 600 (paper), or 100 (Internet); proof of adequate funds.

International Student Contact Mrs. Lesley Smith, MBA Marketing, Cranfield, Bedfordshire, MK43 OAL, United Kingdom. *Phone:* 44-1234-754386. *Fax:* 44-1234-752439. *E-mail:* l.a.smith@cranfield.ac.uk.

APPLICATION *Required:* GMAT, application form, baccalaureate/first degree, essay, interview, 2 letters of recommendation, 3 years of work experience. Applications for domestic and international students are processed on a rolling basis.

Application Contact Mrs. Eileen Fisher, Admissions Executive, Cranfield, Bedfordshire, MK43 OAL, United Kingdom. *Phone:* 44-1234-754431. *Fax:* 44-1234-752439. *E-mail:* e.fisher@cranfield.ac.uk.

European School of Economics
MBA Programme
London, United Kingdom

Phone: 44-207-2456148 **Fax:** 44-207-2456164 **E-mail:** julianne.stanhope@eselondon.ac.uk

Business Program(s) Web Site: http://www.eselondon.ac.uk/postgraduate/international/index.asp

Admissions *Average GMAT:* 640. *Average GPA:* 3.6

Academic Calendar Four 10-12 week terms.

After Graduation (Class of 2006–07) *Employed within 3 months of graduation:* 78%.

DEGREE IMBA

IMBA—International Master of Business Administration Full-time and part-time. 96 total credits required. 12 to 18 months to complete program. *Concentrations:* electronic commerce (E-commerce), entrepreneurship, finance, general MBA, international finance, international marketing, marketing.

RESOURCES AND SERVICES 20 on-campus PCs are available to graduate business students. Access to Internet/World Wide Web available. *Personal computer requirements:* Graduate business students are strongly recommended to purchase or lease a personal computer. *Special opportunities include:* An international exchange program and an internship program are available. *Placement services include:* Career placement, career counseling/planning, electronic job bank, job interviews arranged, resume preparation, and career library.

EXPENSES *Tuition:* Full-time: 13,000 British pounds.

FINANCIAL AID (2007–08) Fellowships, grants, loans, scholarships, and teaching assistantships. Aid is available to part-time students.

INTERNATIONAL STUDENTS *Services and facilities:* Counseling/support services, Housing location assistance, Language tutoring, Orientation, Visa Services. Financial aid is available to international students. *Required with application:* IELT; TOEFL with recommended score of 550 (paper). *Recommended with application:* Proof of adequate funds.

International Student Contact Ms. Julianne Stanhope, Marketing and Admissions, 8/9 Grosvenor Place, London, SW1X7SH, United Kingdom. *Phone:* 44-207-2456148. *Fax:* 44-207-2456164. *E-mail:* julianne.stanhope@eselondon.ac.uk.

APPLICATION *Required:* GMAT, application form, essay, 2 letters of recommendation, resume/curriculum vitae, transcripts of college work, 2

years of work experience. *Application fee:* 50 British pounds. Applications for domestic and international students are processed on a rolling basis.

Application Contact Julianne Stanhope, Marketing and Admissions, 8/9 Grosvenor Place, London, SW1X7SH, United Kingdom. *Phone:* 44-207-2456148. *Fax:* 44-207-2456164. *E-mail:* julianne.stanhope@eselondon.ac.uk.

See full description on page 608.

Kingston University
Kingston Business School
Kingston upon Thames, United Kingdom

Phone: 44-20-85477120 **Fax:** 44-20-85477452 **E-mail:** mba@kingston.ac.uk

Business Program(s) Web Site: http://www.kingston.ac.uk/mba/

DEGREES MA • MBA

MA—Master of Arts in Accounting and Finance Full-time. Minimum of 24 months to complete program. *Concentration:* accounting.

MA—Master of Arts in Business Management Full-time. 12 to 30 months to complete program. *Concentration:* management.

MA—Master of Arts in Employment Relations and Law Part-time. Minimum of 24 months to complete program. *Concentration:* human resources management.

MA—Master of Arts in Managing Human Resources Part-time. Minimum of 24 months to complete program. *Concentration:* human resources management.

MA—Master of Arts in Marketing Full-time and part-time. 12 to 24 months to complete program. *Concentration:* marketing.

MA—Master of Arts in Personnel Management Full-time and part-time. 12 to 24 months to complete program. *Concentration:* human resources management.

MA—Master of Arts in Strategic Financial Management Part-time. Minimum of 24 months to complete program. *Concentration:* finance.

MBA—Master of Business Administration Part-time. Minimum of 24 months to complete program. *Concentration:* general MBA.

RESOURCES AND SERVICES *Placement services include:* Alumni network, career counseling/planning, resume preparation, and career library.

Application Contact MBA Administrator, Kingston Hill, Kingston upon Thames, KT2 7LB, United Kingdom. *Phone:* 44-20-85477120. *Fax:* 44-20-85477452. *E-mail:* mba@kingston.ac.uk.

Lancaster University
Management School
Lancaster, United Kingdom

Phone: 44-1524-594068 **Fax:** 44-1524-592417 **E-mail:** mba@lancaster.ac.uk

Business Program(s) Web Site: http://www.lums.lancs.ac.uk/

Graduate Business Unit Enrollment *Total:* 1,400 (700 full-time; 700 part-time; 600 women; 700 international).

Graduate Business Faculty *Total:* 142 (136 full-time; 6 part-time).

Admissions *Applied:* 5,750. *Admitted:* 2,430. *Enrolled:* 1,370. *Average GMAT:* 640.

Academic Calendar Trimesters.

After Graduation (Class of 2006–07) *Employed within 3 months of graduation:* 93%. *Average starting salary:* $104,000.

Lancaster University (continued)

DEGREES EMBA • MA • MBA • MPA • MS

EMBA—Executive Master of Business Administration Part-time. 5 years of postgraduate work experience required. 24 months to complete program. *Concentrations:* accounting, administration, general MBA, human resources management, information management, international business, international management, leadership, management, marketing, marketing research, organizational management, project management, strategic management, training and development.

MA—Management Learning and Leadership Part-time. 24 months to complete program. *Concentrations:* human resources management, leadership, management, management communication, organizational behavior/development, organizational management.

MA—Master of Arts in Human Resource Development and Consulting Full-time. 12 months to complete program. *Concentrations:* business education, human resources management, international management, management, organizational management, training and development.

MA—Master of Arts in Human Resource and Knowledge Management Full-time. 12 months to complete program. *Concentrations:* human resources management, industrial administration/management, industrial/labor relations, management, organizational behavior/development, organizational management, research and development administration.

MBA—Master of Business Administration Full-time. At least three years' work experience required. 12 to 18 months to complete program. *Concentrations:* accounting, business ethics, commerce, electronic commerce (E-commerce), entrepreneurship, financial management/planning, general MBA, human resources management, international management, leadership, management, project management, quantitative analysis, strategic management.

MPA—Master of Public Administration Full-time. 12 months to complete program. *Concentrations:* accounting, administration, financial management/planning, legal administration, organizational management, public finance, public management, public policy and administration.

MS—Logistics and Supply Chain Management Full-time. 12 months to complete program. *Concentrations:* logistics, management, management science, supply chain management.

MS—Management Science and Market Analysis Full-time. 12 months to complete program. *Concentrations:* decision sciences, management information systems, management science, management systems analysis, marketing research, quantitative analysis, statistics, supply chain management.

MS—Management and Law Full-time. 12 months to complete program. *Concentrations:* accounting, business law, economics, financial management/planning, law, management, new venture management, organizational behavior/development.

MS—Management and Marketing Full-time. 12 months to complete program. *Concentrations:* accounting, economics, financial management/planning, marketing, marketing research, new venture management.

MS—Management and the Environment Full-time. 12 months to complete program. *Concentrations:* accounting, economics, environmental economics/management, management, project management, quality management, risk management.

MS—Master of Science in Accounting and Financial Management Full-time. 12 months to complete program. *Concentrations:* accounting, finance, financial management/planning, international finance.

MS—Master of Science in Advanced Marketing Management Full-time. Significant academic or work-based marketing experience required. 12 months to complete program. *Concentration:* marketing.

MS—Master of Science in Finance Full-time. 12 months to complete program. *Concentrations:* finance, international finance.

MS—Master of Science in Information Technology, Management and Organizational Change Full-time. 12 months to complete program. *Concentrations:* information management, information systems, leadership, management, management information systems, organizational behavior/development, organizational management, system management, technology management, training and development.

MS—Master of Science in International Business Full-time. 12 months to complete program. *Concentrations:* commerce, economics, financial economics, international business, international finance, international marketing, managerial economics, research and development administration.

MS—Master of Science in Management Full-time. 12 months to complete program. *Concentrations:* accounting, entrepreneurship, financial management/planning, management, marketing, organizational management.

MS—Master of Science in Operational Research and Management Science Full-time. 12 months to complete program. *Concentrations:* logistics, management science, operations management.

MS—Master of Science in Project Management Part-time. 12 to 24 months to complete program. *Concentrations:* administration, contract management, industrial administration/management, leadership, operations management, organizational management, project management.

MS—Master of Science in e-Business and Innovation Full-time. 12 months to complete program. *Concentrations:* combined degrees, information technology, management.

MS—Money, Banking and Finance Full-time. 12 months to complete program. *Concentrations:* finance, financial economics, international banking.

MS—Project Management Part-time. 24 months to complete program. *Concentration:* project management.

RESOURCES AND SERVICES 100 on-campus PCs are available to graduate business students. Access to Internet/World Wide Web available. *Personal computer requirements:* Graduate business students are required to have a personal computer. *Special opportunities include:* An international exchange program and an internship program are available. *Placement services include:* Alumni network, job search course, career counseling/planning, electronic job bank, resume referral, career fairs, job interviews arranged, resume preparation, and career library.

EXPENSES *Tuition (state resident):* Full-time: 18,500 British pounds. Part-time: 17,500 British pounds per degree program. *Tuition (nonresident):* Full-time: 18,500 British pounds. Part-time: 17,500 British pounds per degree program. *Tuition (international):* Full-time: 18,500 British pounds. Part-time: 17,500 British pounds per degree program. Tuition and/or fees vary by academic program. *Graduate housing:* Room and board costs vary by number of occupants and type of accommodation. *Typical cost:* 4590 British pounds (room only).

FINANCIAL AID (2007–08) Research assistantships and scholarships. Aid is available to part-time students. *Financial aid application deadline:* 5/15.

Financial Aid Contact Ms. Julie Gabriel-Clarke, Programme Manager, The MBA Office, Lancaster, LA1 4YX, United Kingdom. *Phone:* 44-1524-594068. *Fax:* 44-1524-592417. *E-mail:* mba@lancaster.ac.uk.

INTERNATIONAL STUDENTS 50% of students enrolled are international students. *Services and facilities:* Counseling/support services, ESL/language courses, Housing location assistance, International student organization, Language tutoring, Orientation, Religious facilities. Financial aid is available to international students. *Required with application:* IELT with recommended score of 7; TOEFL with recommended score of 250 (computer), 600 (paper), or 100 (Internet); proof of adequate funds. *Recommended with application:* Proof of health/immunizations.

International Student Contact Susan Lucas, International Officer, Lancaster, LA1 4YX, United Kingdom. *Phone:* 44-1524-594059. *Fax:* 44-1524-592652. *E-mail:* s.lucas@lancaster.ac.uk.

APPLICATION *Required:* GMAT, application form, baccalaureate/first degree, interview, 2 letters of recommendation, personal statement, transcripts of college work, 3 years of work experience. *Recommended:* Essay, resume/curriculum vitae. Applications for domestic and international students are processed on a rolling basis.

Application Contact Ms. Angela Graves, MBA Admissions Coordinator, The MBA Office, Lancaster, LA1 4YX, United Kingdom. *Phone:* 44-1524-594068. *Fax:* 44-1524-592417. *E-mail:* mba@lancaster.ac.uk.

London Metropolitan University

Department of Management and Professional Development

London, United Kingdom

Phone: 44-20-71334200 **Fax:** 44-20-71332678 **E-mail:** admissions@londonmet.ac.uk

Business Program(s) Web Site: http://www.londonmet.ac.uk/

DEGREE MBA

MBA—Master of Business Administration Full-time and part-time. Undergraduate degree and 3 years management experience required. 220 total credits required. 12 to 60 months to complete program. *Concentration:* general MBA.

RESOURCES AND SERVICES 400 on-campus PCs are available to graduate business students. Access to Internet/World Wide Web available. *Personal computer requirements:* Graduate business students are strongly recommended to purchase or lease a personal computer. *Placement services include:* Alumni network and career fairs.

Application Contact Admissions, 236-250 Holloway Road, London, N7 6PP, United Kingdom. *Phone:* 44-20-71334200. *Fax:* 44-20-71332678. *E-mail:* admissions@londonmet.ac.uk.

London School of Economics and Political Science

The Graduate School

London, United Kingdom

Phone: 44-207-9556613 **Fax:** 44-207-9556001 **E-mail:** stu.rec@lse.ac.uk

Business Program(s) Web Site: http://www.lse.ac.uk/collections/graduateadmissions

Graduate Business Unit Enrollment *Average Age:* 22.

Academic Calendar Trimesters.

After Graduation (Class of 2006–07) *Employed within 3 months of graduation:* 98%. *Average starting salary:* 27,000 British pounds.

DEGREES EMBA • M Sc • MPA • MS

EMBA—TRIUM Global EMBA Part-time. *Concentrations:* business policy/strategy, executive programs, management.

M Sc—MSc in Accounting and Finance Full-time and part-time. All applicants must submit a GMAT score. 9 to 21 months to complete program. *Concentrations:* accounting, finance, international finance.

M Sc—MSc in Analysis, Design, and Management of Information Systems Full-time and part-time. 12 to 24 months to complete program. *Concentrations:* information management, information systems.

M Sc—MSc in Decision Sciences Full-time and part-time. 12 to 24 months to complete program. *Concentration:* decision sciences.

M Sc—MSc in Development Management Full-time and part-time. 12 to 24 months to complete program. *Concentration:* international development management.

M Sc—MSc in Econometrics and Mathematical Economics Full-time and part-time. Graduates of non-UK institutions must submit a GRE score. 9 to 21 months to complete program. *Concentration:* economics.

M Sc—MSc in Economics Full-time and part-time. One year/research—all graduates of non-UK institutions must submit a GRE score. Two year—all applicants must submit a GRE score. 10 to 22 months to complete program. *Concentrations:* economics, international economics.

M Sc—MSc in Finance and Economics Full-time. All applicants must submit a GRE or GMAT score. 10 months to complete program. *Concentrations:* economics, finance, international economics, international finance.

M Sc—MSc in Information Systems and Organisations (Research) Full-time and part-time. 12 to 24 months to complete program. *Concentrations:* information management, information systems.

M Sc—MSc in International Management (CEMS/IMEX) Full-time. All applicants must submit a GRE (preferred) or GMAT score. 12 months to complete program. *Concentration:* international management.

M Sc—MSc in Management (two-year programme) Full-time. Graduates of non-UK institutions must submit a GRE (preferred) or GMAT score. 22 months to complete program. *Concentration:* management.

M Sc—MSc in Management and Regulation of Risk Full-time. Graduates of non-UK institutions must submit a GMAT (preferred) or GRE score. GMAT also recommended for UK graduates. 12 months to complete program. *Concentration:* risk management.

M Sc—MSc in Management and Strategy Full-time. All applicants must submit a GRE (preferred) or GMAT score. 12 months to complete program. *Concentrations:* management, management science, strategic management.

M Sc—MSc in Non-Governmental Organizations and Development Full-time and part-time. 12 to 24 months to complete program. *Concentrations:* management, nonprofit management, nonprofit organization.

M Sc—MSc in Operational Research Full-time and part-time. 12 to 24 months to complete program. *Concentrations:* decision sciences, operations management, system management.

M Sc—MSc in Public Management and Governance Full-time. 12 months to complete program. *Concentrations:* management, public management, public policy and administration.

M Sc—MSc in Public Policy and Administration Full-time and part-time. 12 to 24 months to complete program. *Concentration:* public policy and administration.

MPA—Master of Public Administration—Public Policy and Management Full-time. 21 months to complete program. *Concentrations:* organizational management, public policy and administration.

MPA—Master of Public Administration—Public and Economic Policy Full-time. 21 months to complete program. *Concentrations:* economics, public policy and administration.

MS—MSc in Human Resource Management Full-time and part-time. 12 to 24 months to complete program. *Concentrations:* human resources management, industrial/labor relations.

MS—MSc in International Employment Relations and Human Resource Management Full-time and part-time. 12 to 24 months to complete program. *Concentrations:* human resources management, industrial/labor relations.

MS—MSc in Management and Economics Full-time. Graduates of non-UK institutions must submit a GRE or GMAT score. 10 months to complete program. *Concentrations:* economics, management.

MS—MSc in Management, Organisations and Governance Full-time and part-time. Graduates of non-UK institutions must submit a GRE or GMAT score. 12 to 24 months to complete program. *Concentrations:* management, organizational management.

MS—MSc in Real Estate Economics and Finance Full-time and part-time. Graduates of non-UK institutions must submit a GRE (preferred) or GMAT score. 12 to 24 months to complete program. *Concentrations:* economics, finance, real estate.

RESOURCES AND SERVICES 1,300 on-campus PCs are available to graduate business students. Access to Internet/World Wide Web, online (class) registration, and online grade reports available. *Personal computer requirements:* Graduate business students are not required to have a personal computer. *Special opportunities include:* An international exchange program and an internship program are available. *Placement services include:* Alumni network, career placement, career counseling/planning, electronic job bank, career fairs, resume preparation, and career library.

London School of Economics and Political Science (continued)

FINANCIAL AID (2007–08) Grants, loans, and scholarships. *Financial aid application deadline:* 4/27.

Financial Aid Contact Financial Support Office, Houghton Street, London, WC2A 2AE, United Kingdom. *Phone:* 44-207-9557155. *Fax:* 44-207-9556099. *E-mail:* financial-support@lse.ac.uk.

INTERNATIONAL STUDENTS *Services and facilities:* Counseling/support services, ESL/language courses, Housing location assistance, International student housing, International student organization, Language tutoring, Orientation, Visa Services. Financial aid is available to international students. *Required with application:* IELT with recommended score of 7; TOEFL with recommended score of 263 (computer), 627 (paper), or 107 (Internet). *Recommended with application:* Proof of adequate funds.

International Student Contact Mr. Will Breare-Hall, International Student Recruitment Manager, Houghton Street, London, WC2A 2AE, United Kingdom. *Phone:* 44-207-9556613. *Fax:* 44-207-9556001. *E-mail:* stu.rec@lse.ac.uk.

APPLICATION *Required:* Application form, baccalaureate/first degree, 2 letters of recommendation, personal statement, transcripts of college work. School will accept GMAT and GRE. *Application fee:* 30 British pounds. Applications for domestic and international students are processed on a rolling basis.

Application Contact Student Recruitment Office, Houghton Street, London, WC2A 2AE, United Kingdom. *Phone:* 44-207-9556613. *Fax:* 44-207-9556001. *E-mail:* stu.rec@lse.ac.uk.

Loughborough University

The Business School—Postgraduate Office

Loughborough, United Kingdom

Phone: 44-1509-223398 **Fax:** 44-1509-228052 **E-mail:** mba@lboro.ac.uk

Business Program(s) Web Site: http://www.lboro.ac.uk/departments/bs/

DEGREES EMBA • M Sc

EMBA—Master of Business Administration Part-time. At least 180 total credits required. 36 to 96 months to complete program. *Concentration:* general MBA.

M Sc—Master of Science in Management Full-time. At least 150 total credits required. Minimum of 12 months to complete program. *Concentration:* management.

RESOURCES AND SERVICES 200 on-campus PCs are available to graduate business students. Access to Internet/World Wide Web available. *Personal computer requirements:* Graduate business students are not required to have a personal computer. *Placement services include:* Alumni network, career counseling/planning, and career library.

Application Contact Ms. Linda Smith, MBA Administrator, Leicestershire, United Kingdom. *Phone:* 44-1509-223398. *Fax:* 44-1509-228052. *E-mail:* mba@lboro.ac.uk.

Napier University

Napier Business School

Edinburgh, United Kingdom

Phone: 44-131-455-4535 **Fax:** 44-131-455-4537 **E-mail:** s.ferrier@napier.ac.uk

Business Program(s) Web Site: http://www.napier.ac.uk

Graduate Business Unit Enrollment *Total:* 904 (220 full-time; 684 part-time; 398 women; 40 international).

Graduate Business Faculty *Total:* 193 (144 full-time; 49 part-time).

Academic Calendar Trimesters.

DEGREES MBA

MBA—Flexible Learning Master of Business Administration Part-time. 36 to 48 months to complete program. *Concentration:* general MBA.

MBA—Full-Time Master of Business Administration Full-time. 12 to 18 months to complete program. *Concentration:* general MBA.

RESOURCES AND SERVICES 1,060 on-campus PCs are available to graduate business students. Access to Internet/World Wide Web available. *Personal computer requirements:* Graduate business students are strongly recommended to purchase or lease a personal computer. *Placement services include:* Alumni network, career counseling/planning, career fairs, and career library.

INTERNATIONAL STUDENTS 4% of students enrolled are international students. *Services and facilities:* Counseling/support services, ESL/language courses, Housing location assistance, International student housing, International student organization, Language tutoring, Orientation, Visa Services. Financial aid is not available to international students. *Required with application:* IELT with recommended score of 6. *Recommended with application:* TOEFL with recommended score of 213 (computer), 550 (paper), or 80 (Internet).

International Student Contact Mrs. Sheila Ferrier, Programme Administrator, Craiglockhart Campus, Edinburgh, EH14 1DJ, United Kingdom. *Phone:* 44-131-455-4535. *Fax:* 44-131-455-4537. *E-mail:* s.ferrier@napier.ac.uk.

APPLICATION *Required:* Application form, personal statement, resume/curriculum vitae, transcripts of college work, work experience. *Recommended:* Baccalaureate/first degree, interview, letter(s) of recommendation. Applications for domestic and international students are processed on a rolling basis.

Application Contact Mrs. Sheila Ferrier, Programme Administrator, Craiglockhart Campus, Edinburgh, EH14 1DJ, United Kingdom. *Phone:* 44-131-455-4535. *Fax:* 44-131-455-4537. *E-mail:* s.ferrier@napier.ac.uk.

Nottingham Trent University

Nottingham Business School

Nottingham, United Kingdom

Phone: 44-115-8486198 **Fax:** 44-115-8484707 **E-mail:** helen.trivett@ntu.ac.uk

Business Program(s) Web Site: http://www.ntu.ac.uk/nbs

DEGREES MBA • MSC

MBA—Master of Business Administration Part-time. A first degree or relevant professional/academic qualification of first degree standing, 4 years of work experience including operational responsibilities and employment in an organization required. 12 to 24 months to complete program. *Concentrations:* business ethics, business policy/strategy, business studies, general MBA, human resources management, leadership, management, marketing, strategic management.

MSC—MSc Management and Investment Strategy Full-time. A good honours degree or equivalent from a respected University is required. 12 months to complete program. *Concentrations:* accounting, corporate accounting, finance, human resources management, information management, international business, management, marketing, organizational management, research and development administration, strategic management, system management.

MSC—MSc Marketing Full-time. A good honours degree or equivalent from a respected University required. 12 months to complete program. *Concentrations:* advertising, electronic commerce (E-commerce), marketing, nonprofit organization, production management, strategic management.

MSC—MSc in Management Full-time. A good honours degree or equivalent from a respected University required. 12 months to complete program. *Concentrations:* accounting, electronic commerce (E-commerce), entrepreneurship, finance, financial management/planning, human resources management, information management, information systems, international business, international economics, management, marketing, organizational management, research and development administration, strategic management, system management.

MSC—MSc in Management and Human Resources Management Full-time. A good honours degree or equivalent from a respected University required. 12 months to complete program. *Concentrations:* accounting, finance, human resources management, information management, international finance, marketing, organizational management, research and development administration, strategic management, system management, training and development.

MSC—MSc in Management and Information Systems Full-time. A good honours degree or equivalent from a respected University required. 12 months to complete program. *Concentrations:* accounting, electronic commerce (E-commerce), finance, human resources management, information management, information systems, information technology, international business, marketing, organizational management, strategic management, system management.

MSC—MSc in Management and International Business Full-time. A good honours degree or equivalent from a respected University required. 12 months to complete program. *Concentrations:* accounting, business policy/strategy, finance, financial management/planning, human resources management, information management, international business, international finance, international management, international marketing, management, marketing, research and development administration, strategic management.

MSC—MSc in Management and Marketing Full-time. A good honours degree or equivalent from a respected University required. 12 months to complete program. *Concentrations:* accounting, finance, human resources management, information management, international business, management, marketing, organizational management, research and development administration, strategic management, system management.

RESOURCES AND SERVICES Access to Internet/World Wide Web available. *Personal computer requirements:* Graduate business students are strongly recommended to purchase or lease a personal computer. *Placement services include:* Alumni network, career counseling/planning, career fairs, and resume preparation.

Application Contact Ms. Helen Trivett, Senior Programme Administrator, Burton Street, Nottingham, NG1 4BU, United Kingdom. *Phone:* 44-115-8486198. *Fax:* 44-115-8484707. *E-mail:* helen.trivett@ntu.ac.uk.

Open University
Business School
Milton Keynes, United Kingdom

Phone: 44-8700-100311 **Fax:** 44-1908-654806 **E-mail:** oubs-ilgen@open.ac.uk

Business Program(s) Web Site: http://www3.open.ac.uk/oubs/

DEGREES M Sc • MBA • MPA

M Sc—Master of Science in Human Resource Management Part-time. Distance learning option. 120 to 180 total credits required. 24 to 90 months to complete program. *Concentration:* human resources management.

M Sc—Master of Science in International Finance and Management Part-time. Distance learning option. 90 to 180 total credits required. 30 to 120 months to complete program. *Concentrations:* international finance, international management.

M Sc—Master of Science in Management and Business Research Methods Full-time and part-time. Distance learning option. At least 180 total credits required. 36 to 120 months to complete program. *Concentrations:* management, research and development administration.

MBA—Master of Business Administration Part-time. Distance learning option. Minimum age 25 years. 90 to 180 total credits required. 30 to 120 months to complete program. *Concentration:* general MBA.

MBA—Master of Business Administration in Life Sciences Part-time. Distance learning option. Minimum age 25 years. 90 to 180 total credits required. 30 to 120 months to complete program. *Concentration:* other.

MBA—Master of Business Administration in Technology Management Part-time. Distance learning option. Minimum age 25 years. 90 to 180 total credits required. 30 to 120 months to complete program. *Concentration:* technology management.

MPA—Master of Public Administration Part-time. Distance learning option. Minimum age 25 years. 90 to 180 total credits required. 24 to 120 months to complete program. *Concentration:* public policy and administration.

RESOURCES AND SERVICES 10 on-campus PCs are available to graduate business students. Access to Internet/World Wide Web, online (class) registration, and online grade reports available. *Personal computer requirements:* Graduate business students are required to have a personal computer. *Placement services include:* Alumni network and career counseling/planning.

Application Contact Mr. Paul King, Information Team, Customer Contact Centre, Walton Hall, Milton Keynes, MK7 6AA, United Kingdom. *Phone:* 44-8700-100311. *Fax:* 44-1908-654806. *E-mail:* oubs-ilgen@open.ac.uk.

Queen Margaret University College, Edinburgh
School of Business and Enterprise
Edinburgh, United Kingdom

Phone: 44-131-4740000 **Fax:** 44-131-4740001 **E-mail:** admissions@qmu.ac.uk

Business Program(s) Web Site: http://www.qmu.ac.uk/be/default.htm

Admissions *Average GPA:* 3.0

Academic Calendar Semesters.

After Graduation (Class of 2006–07) *Employed within 3 months of graduation:* 94%.

DEGREES MBA • MBA/MS

MBA—Master of Business Administration Full-time. Distance learning option. At least 180 total credits required. Minimum of 12 months to complete program. *Concentration:* general MBA.

MBA—Master of Business Administration in Entrepreneurship Full-time. Distance learning option. At least 180 total credits required. Minimum of 12 months to complete program. *Concentration:* entrepreneurship.

MBA—Master of Business Administration in Golf and Country Club Management Full-time. Distance learning option. At least 180 total credits required. Minimum of 12 months to complete program. *Concentration:* sports/entertainment management.

MBA—Master of Business Administration in Hospitality Management Full-time. Distance learning option. At least 180 total credits required. Minimum of 12 months to complete program. *Concentration:* hospitality management.

MBA—Master of Business Administration in Public Service Management Full-time. Distance learning option. At least 180 total credits required. Minimum of 12 months to complete program. *Concentration:* public management.

Queen Margaret University College, Edinburgh (continued)

MBA—Master of Business Administration in eTourism Management Full-time. Distance learning option. At least 180 total credits required. Minimum of 12 months to complete program. *Concentration:* travel industry/tourism management.

MBA/MS—Master of Business Administration/Master of Arts in Cultural Management Full-time. Distance learning option. At least 180 total credits required. Minimum of 12 months to complete program. *Concentration:* arts administration/management.

RESOURCES AND SERVICES 1,000 on-campus PCs are available to graduate business students. Access to Internet/World Wide Web available. *Personal computer requirements:* Graduate business students are not required to have a personal computer. *Special opportunities include:* An international exchange program is available. *Placement services include:* Alumni network, career counseling/planning, resume referral, resume preparation, and career library.

EXPENSES *Tuition (international):* Full-time: 9975 British pounds. *Typical graduate housing cost:* 4812.50 British pounds (room only).

FINANCIAL AID (2007–08) Scholarships. *Financial aid application deadline:* 10/6.

INTERNATIONAL STUDENTS *Services and facilities:* Counseling/support services, ESL/language courses, Housing location assistance, International student housing, International student organization, Language tutoring, Orientation, Visa Services, International student trips. Financial aid is available to international students. *Required with application:* IELT with recommended score of 6; TOEFL with recommended score of 237 (computer) or 580 (paper); proof of adequate funds.

International Student Contact Mr. Alan McLachlan, Student Recruitment and Liaison Manager, Queen Margaret University Drive, Musselburgh, EH21 6UU, United Kingdom. *Phone:* 44-131-4740000. *Fax:* 44-131-4740001. *E-mail:* rilo@qmu.ac.uk.

APPLICATION *Required:* Application form, baccalaureate/first degree, 2 letters of recommendation, personal statement, transcripts of college work, 2 years of work experience. School will accept GMAT, GRE, and MAT. *Recommended:* Resume/curriculum vitae. *Deadlines:* 6/30 for fall, 6/30 for fall (international).

Application Contact Mrs. Margaret Parratt, Head of Recruitment and Admissions, Queen Margaret University Drive, Musselburgh, EH21 6UU, United Kingdom. *Phone:* 44-131-4740000. *Fax:* 44-131-4740001. *E-mail:* admissions@qmu.ac.uk.

Schiller International University

Graduate Programs, London

London, United Kingdom

Phone: 877-748-4338 **Fax:** 727-738-6376 **E-mail:** admissions@schiller.edu

Business Program(s) Web Site: http://www.schiller.edu/

Graduate Business Unit Enrollment *Total:* 152 (123 full-time; 29 part-time; 44 women; 150 international).

Graduate Business Faculty *Total:* 38 (8 full-time; 30 part-time).

Academic Calendar Semesters.

After Graduation (Class of 2006–07) *Employed within 3 months of graduation:* 90%.

DEGREES MA • MBA

MA—Master of Arts in Business Communication Full-time and part-time. At least 36 total credits required. 12 to 24 months to complete program. *Concentrations:* business studies, media administration, public relations.

MA—Master of Arts in International Hotel and Tourism Management Full-time. At least 45 total credits required. 12 to 24 months to complete program. *Concentrations:* hospitality management, travel industry/tourism management.

MBA—Master of Business Administration in International Business Full-time and part-time. Distance learning option. At least 45 total credits required. 12 to 24 months to complete program. *Concentration:* international business.

MBA—Master of Business Administration in International Hotel and Tourism Management Full-time and part-time. At least 45 total credits required. 12 to 24 months to complete program. *Concentrations:* hospitality management, travel industry/tourism management.

MBA—Master of Business Administration in Management of Information Technology Full-time and part-time. Distance learning option. At least 45 total credits required. 12 to 24 months to complete program. *Concentration:* management information systems.

MBA—Master of Business Administration in Public Administration Full-time and part-time. At least 45 total credits required. 12 to 24 months to complete program. *Concentration:* public policy and administration.

RESOURCES AND SERVICES 39 on-campus PCs are available to graduate business students. Access to Internet/World Wide Web available. *Personal computer requirements:* Graduate business students are strongly recommended to purchase or lease a personal computer. *Special opportunities include:* An international exchange program and an internship program are available. *Placement services include:* Alumni network, career placement, career counseling/planning, electronic job bank, resume referral, career fairs, resume preparation, and career library.

FINANCIAL AID (2007–08) Grants, loans, scholarships, and work study. *Financial aid application deadline:* 4/1.

Financial Aid Contact Ms. Jennifer Cox, Financial Aid Officer, 300 East Bay Drive, Largo, FL 33770. *Phone:* 727-736-5082 Ext. 223. *Fax:* 727-734-0359. *E-mail:* jennifer_cox@schiller.edu.

INTERNATIONAL STUDENTS 99% of students enrolled are international students. *Services and facilities:* Counseling/support services, ESL/language courses, Housing location assistance, International student housing, Language tutoring, Orientation, Visa Services. Financial aid is available to international students. *Required with application:* Proof of adequate funds. *Recommended with application:* TOEFL with recommended score of 213 (computer) or 550 (paper).

International Student Contact Ms. Stephanie Givens, 300 East Bay Drive, Largo, FL 33770. *Phone:* 877-748-4338. *Fax:* 727-738-6376. *E-mail:* admissions@schiller.edu.

APPLICATION *Required:* GMAT, application form, baccalaureate/first degree, essay, transcripts of college work. *Recommended:* Resume/curriculum vitae, work experience. *Application fee:* 35 British pounds. Applications for domestic and international students are processed on a rolling basis.

Application Contact Ms. Stephanie Givens, 300 Edgewater Drive, Largo, FL 33770. *Phone:* 877-748-4338. *Fax:* 727-738-6376. *E-mail:* admissions@schiller.edu.

See full description on page 684.

Thames Valley University

Faculty of Professional Studies

Slough, United Kingdom

Phone: 44-20-85795000 **Fax:** 44-20-85661353 **E-mail:** learning.advice@tvu.ac.uk

Business Program(s) Web Site: http://www.tvu.ac.uk

DEGREES MA • MA/MBA • MSC

MA—Counseling Part-time. A qualification in Counseling and Psychotherapy at the postgraduate level. Currently practicing as a qualified counselor/psychotherapist and with a minimum case load of 100 hours per year. 12 months to complete program. *Concentration:* health care.

MA—Human Resource Management Full-time and part-time. First degree or equivalent professional qualifications required. 12 to 24 months to complete program. *Concentration:* human resources management.

MA—Information Management Full-time and part-time. First degree or equivalent professional qualifications required. 12 to 24 months to complete program. *Concentration:* information management.

MA—Master of Arts in Hospitality Management Full-time and part-time. A hospitality first degree from a UK university, or its equivalent from overseas. A hospitality HND and 2 years of appropriate work experience required. 12 to 24 months to complete program. *Concentration:* hospitality management.

MA—Master of Arts in Information Management (Library and Information Services) Full-time and part-time. A good degree from a UK university, or its equivalent from overseas is required. 12 to 24 months to complete program. *Concentrations:* information management, management.

MA—Master of Arts in Leading, Managing and Partnership Working Part-time. Distance learning option. A first degree or equivalent professional qualification, plus significant professional experience related to the intended course of study required. 12 to 84 months to complete program. *Concentration:* health care.

MA—Master of Arts in Learning and Teaching Part-time. A first degree, or an equivalent Level 2 professional knowledge related to the intended area of teaching and practice required. 36 to 60 months to complete program. *Concentration:* training and development.

MA—Master of Arts in Tourism Management Full-time and part-time. Any tourism first degree, or equivalent professional qualification. Any tourism HND, plus at least 2 years of relevant work experience required. 12 to 24 months to complete program. *Concentration:* travel industry/tourism management.

MA/MBA—Master of Arts/Master of Business Administration Full-time and part-time. A good first degree or equivalent professional qualification, pre-masters programme and substantial relevant work experience required. 12 to 24 months to complete program. *Concentration:* general MBA.

MSC—Advancing Practice in Health and Social Care Part-time. 24 to 84 months to complete program. *Concentration:* health care.

MSC—Applied Computing for Enterprise Full-time and part-time. First degree in a computing subject or engineering degree with a significant level of computing required. 12 to 24 months to complete program. *Concentration:* information technology.

MSC—Exercise and Behavioral Medicine Part-time. 24 months to complete program. *Concentration:* health care.

MSC—Financial and Legal Management Full-time and part-time. First degree in accounting, economics, business or law, or equivalent professional qualifications required. 15 to 27 months to complete program. *Concentration:* financial management/planning.

MSC—Information Management Full-time and part-time. First degree or equivalent professional qualifications required. 12 to 24 months to complete program. *Concentration:* information management.

MSC—Information Systems Full-time and part-time. First degree in a computing subject or engineering degree with a significant level of computing required. 12 to 24 months to complete program. *Concentration:* information systems.

RESOURCES AND SERVICES 600 on-campus PCs are available to graduate business students. Access to Internet/World Wide Web available. *Personal computer requirements:* Graduate business students are not required to have a personal computer. *Placement services include:* Alumni network, career placement, career counseling/planning, career fairs, resume preparation, and career library.

Application Contact Learning Advice Centre, Walpole House, 18-22 Bond Street, Ealing, London, W5 5AA, United Kingdom. *Phone:* 44-20-85795000. *Fax:* 44-20-85661353. *E-mail:* learning.advice@tvu.ac.uk.

University of Abertay Dundee
Dundee Business School
Dundee, United Kingdom

Phone: 44-1382-308080 **Fax:** 44-1382-308081 **E-mail:** sro@abertay.ac.uk

Business Program(s) Web Site: http://www.abertay.ac.uk/Schools/DBS/index.cfm?Key=002.003

Graduate Business Unit Enrollment *Total:* 1,353 (1,181 full-time; 172 part-time; 732 women; 850 international).

Graduate Business Faculty 25 full-time.

Admissions *Applied:* 139. *Admitted:* 102. *Enrolled:* 63.

Academic Calendar Semesters.

After Graduation (Class of 2006–07) *Employed within 3 months of graduation:* 100%.

DEGREES M Sc • MBA

M Sc—MSc International Business Full-time. Minimum of 12 months to complete program. *Concentration:* international business.

MBA—Master of Business Administration Full-time and part-time. 12 to 36 months to complete program. *Concentrations:* finance, general MBA, human resources management, international management, marketing, other, sports/entertainment management.

RESOURCES AND SERVICES 1,000 on-campus PCs are available to graduate business students. Access to Internet/World Wide Web, online (class) registration, and online grade reports available. *Personal computer requirements:* Graduate business students are not required to have a personal computer. *Placement services include:* Alumni network, career counseling/planning, career fairs, resume preparation, and career library.

EXPENSES *Tuition (international):* Full-time: 10,000 British pounds. Tuition and/or fees vary by number of courses or credits taken and academic program. *Graduate housing:* Room and board costs vary by type of accommodation. *Typical cost:* 3000 British pounds (room only).

FINANCIAL AID (2007–08) 5 students received aid, including scholarships. *Financial aid application deadline:* 9/30.

Financial Aid Contact Student Recruitment Office, Bell Street, Dundee, Scotland, DD1 1HG, United Kingdom. *Phone:* 44-1382-308080. *Fax:* 44-1382-308081. *E-mail:* sro@abertay.ac.uk.

INTERNATIONAL STUDENTS 63% of students enrolled are international students. *Services and facilities:* Counseling/support services, ESL/language courses, Housing location assistance, International student housing, International student organization, Language tutoring, Orientation, Visa Services. Financial aid is available to international students. *Required with application:* IELT with recommended score of 6; TOEFL with recommended score of 223 (computer), 563 (paper), or 85 (Internet). *Recommended with application:* Proof of adequate funds; proof of health/immunizations.

International Student Contact Student Recruitment Office, Bell Street, Dundee, Scotland, DD1 1HG, United Kingdom. *Phone:* 44-1382-308080. *Fax:* 44-1382-308081. *E-mail:* sro@abertay.ac.uk.

APPLICATION *Required:* Application form, baccalaureate/first degree, 2 letters of recommendation, personal statement, resume/curriculum vitae, transcripts of college work, 3 years of work experience. *Application fee:* 0 British pounds, 25 British pounds (international). Applications for domestic and international students are processed on a rolling basis.

Application Contact Student Recruitment Office, Bell Street, Dundee, Scotland, DD1 1HG, United Kingdom. *Phone:* 44-1382-308080. *Fax:* 44-1382-308081. *E-mail:* sro@abertay.ac.uk.

University of Bath
School of Management
Bath, United Kingdom

Phone: 44-1225-383431 **Fax:** 44-1225-386210 **E-mail:** mba-admit@management.bath.ac.uk

University of Bath (continued)

Business Program(s) Web Site: http://www.bath.ac.uk/management

---

DEGREES   M Phil • M Sc • MBA • MBA equivalent • MS • PhD/Mphil

---

M Phil—Master of Research in Management (MRes) Full-time and part-time. A first class or good second class (2:1) degree or international equivalent. At least 90 total credits required. 12 to 24 months to complete program. *Concentration:* research and development administration.

M Sc—Master of Science in Management Full-time. Minimum 2nd class honors degree required. At least 60 total credits required. 12 to 15 months to complete program. *Concentration:* management.

M Sc—Master of Science in Management with Finance Full-time. Minimum 2nd class honors degree required. At least 90 total credits required. 12 months to complete program. *Concentration:* finance.

M Sc—Master of Science in Management with Human Resource Management Full-time. Minimum 2nd class honors degree required. At least 90 total credits required. 12 months to complete program. *Concentrations:* human resources management, management.

M Sc—Master of Science in Management with Information Management Full-time. Minimum 2nd class honors degree required. At least 90 total credits required. 12 months to complete program. *Concentrations:* management, management information systems.

M Sc—Master of Science in Management with Marketing Full-time. Minimum 2nd class honors degree required. At least 90 total credits required. 12 months to complete program. *Concentrations:* management, marketing.

M Sc—Master of Science in Management with Operations Management Full-time. Minimum 2nd class honors degree required. At least 90 total credits required. 12 months to complete program. *Concentrations:* management, operations management.

M Sc—Master of Science in Responsibility and Business Practice Part-time. Minimum age 24. Applicants need to show an interest and commitment to the issues studied, ie. Ecology, Sustainability and the Environment. At least 75 total credits required. 24 to 30 months to complete program. *Concentrations:* business ethics, environmental economics/management.

MBA—Full-Time Master of Business Administration Full-time. Degree at First or Second Class Honours level or equivalent classification/GPA, awarded by an approved institution or a final qualification of a professional body accepted to the University. At least 90 total credits required. 12 months to complete program. *Concentrations:* business policy/strategy, entrepreneurship, financial information systems, financial management/planning, general MBA, human resources management, international business, international management, leadership, management, management consulting, management information systems, non-profit management, public and private management, public management, strategic management, supply chain management.

MBA—Part-Time Executive Master of Business Administration (Modular) Part-time. Degree at First or Second Class Honours level or equivalent classification/GPA, awarded by an approved institution or a final qualification of a professional body accepted to the University. At least 90 total credits required. 24 to 60 months to complete program. *Concentrations:* business policy/strategy, executive programs, financial management/planning, general MBA, human resources management, information management, information systems, international business, international management, leadership, management, management consulting, management information systems, nonprofit management, organizational behavior/development, organizational management, public management, strategic management, supply chain management.

MBA equivalent—Doctor of Business Administration in Higher Education Management Part-time. Relevant postgraduate degree or equivalent. 36 to 96 months to complete program.

MBA equivalent—Post-Graduate Certificate in Engineering Management Part-time. Distance learning option. A degree which has been accredited by a UK professional engineering or scientific institution, or awarded by an approved institution, and at least two years acceptable industrial experience. 12 to 24 months to complete program. *Concentrations:* engineering, management.

MS—MSc in Accounting and Finance Full-time. Minimum 2nd class honors degree required. At least 90 total credits required. 12 months to complete program. *Concentrations:* accounting, finance.

MS—MSc in Advanced Management Practice Full-time. At least 90 total credits required. 12 months to complete program. *Concentrations:* operations management, organizational management, project management, strategic management.

MS—MSc in Marketing Full-time. Candidates should have some previous experience of marketing or business, either from a related first degree (2:1 or above or its international equivalent) or from work experience. At least 90 total credits required. 12 months to complete program. *Concentrations:* marketing, marketing research.

MS—Msc in Innovation and Technology Management Full-time. NEW FOR 2008. A 2:1 or above (or its international equivalent). At least 90 total credits required. 12 months to complete program. *Concentration:* management.

PhD/Mphil—Engineering Doctorate (EngD) in Systems Part-time. Researchers will normally be based in industry, and will have at least a 2.1 or equivalent first degree in a relevant subject. 60 to 180 total credits required. 48 months to complete program. *Concentration:* engineering.

PhD/Mphil—MPhil and PhD Degrees in Management Full-time and part-time. Please see our website at www.bath.ac.uk/management/courses/mphil_phd/ for details. 12 to 72 months to complete program. *Concentrations:* combined degrees, management.

RESOURCES AND SERVICES 468 on-campus PCs are available to graduate business students. Access to Internet/World Wide Web, online (class) registration, and online grade reports available. *Personal computer requirements:* Graduate business students are strongly recommended to purchase or lease a personal computer. *Placement services include:* Alumni network, career placement, job search course, career counseling/planning, electronic job bank, resume referral, career fairs, job interviews arranged, resume preparation, and career library.

Application Contact Ms. Maggi Preddy, MBA Admissions and Marketing Manager, Claverton Down, Bath, BA2 7AY, United Kingdom. *Phone:* 44-1225-383431. *Fax:* 44-1225-386210. *E-mail:* mba-admit@management.bath.ac.uk.

University of Birmingham
Birmingham Business School
Birmingham, United Kingdom

Phone: 44-121-4146693 **Fax:** 44-121-4143553 **E-mail:** mba@bham.ac.uk

Business Program(s) Web Site: http://mba.bham.ac.uk

Graduate Business Unit Enrollment *Total:* 691 (164 full-time; 527 part-time; 299 women; 578 international).

Graduate Business Faculty *Total:* 67 (60 full-time; 7 part-time).

Academic Calendar Semesters.

After Graduation (Class of 2006–07) *Employed within 3 months of graduation:* 94%.

DEGREES   MBA

MBA—Full-Time Master of Business Administration Full-time. 12 to 24 months to complete program. *Concentrations:* international business, strategic management.

MBA—Master of Business Administration Joint Program with ESC Montpellier Full-time and part-time. 12 to 24 months to complete program. *Concentration:* management.

MBA—Master of Business Administration in International Banking and Finance Full-time. 12 to 24 months to complete program. *Concentrations:* international banking, international business.

MBA—Part-Time Master of Business Administration Part-time. 24 to 48 months to complete program. *Concentrations:* international business, strategic management.

MBA—Sports Management Part-time. 12 to 48 months to complete program. *Concentrations:* business studies, sports/entertainment management.

RESOURCES AND SERVICES Access to Internet/World Wide Web and online (class) registration available. *Personal computer requirements:* Graduate business students are not required to have a personal computer. *Special opportunities include:* An international exchange program is available. *Placement services include:* Alumni network, career placement, job search course, career counseling/planning, electronic job bank, resume referral, career fairs, job interviews arranged, resume preparation, and career library.

EXPENSES *Tuition (state resident):* Full-time: 16,600 British pounds. *Tuition (nonresident):* Full-time: 16,600 British pounds. *Tuition (international):* Full-time: 16,600 British pounds.

Financial Aid Contact Paul Forrester, Admission Tutor, University House, Edgbaston Park Road, Birmingham, B15 2TY, United Kingdom. *Phone:* 44-121-4146693. *Fax:* 44-121-4143553. *E-mail:* mba@bham.ac.uk.

INTERNATIONAL STUDENTS 84% of students enrolled are international students. *Services and facilities:* Counseling/support services, ESL/language courses, Housing location assistance, International student housing, International student organization, Language tutoring, Orientation, Visa Services, Career management. Financial aid is not available to international students. *Required with application:* IELT with recommended score of 6.5; TOEFL with recommended score of 237 (computer) or 580 (paper); proof of adequate funds.

International Student Contact Paul Forrester, Admission Tutor, University House, Edgbaston Park Road, Birmingham, B15 2TY, United Kingdom. *Phone:* 44-121-4146693. *Fax:* 44-121-4143553. *E-mail:* mba@bham.ac.uk.

APPLICATION *Required:* Application form, 2 letters of recommendation, transcripts of college work, 5 years of work experience. School will accept GMAT. *Recommended:* Personal statement, resume/curriculum vitae. Applications for domestic and international students are processed on a rolling basis.

Application Contact Paul Forrester, Admission Tutor, University House, Edgbaston Park Road, Birmingham, B15 2TY, United Kingdom. *Phone:* 44-121-4146693. *Fax:* 44-121-4143553. *E-mail:* mba@bham.ac.uk.

University of Durham

Durham Business School

Durham, United Kingdom

Phone: 191-3345533 **Fax:** 191-3345136 **E-mail:** pg.bus@durham.ac.uk

Business Program(s) Web Site: http://www.dur.ac.uk/dbs/

Graduate Business Unit Enrollment *Total:* 815 (552 full-time; 263 part-time). *Average Age:* 27.

Graduate Business Faculty *Total:* 90 (70 full-time; 20 part-time).

Academic Calendar Semesters.

DEGREES M Mktg • MA • MBA • MBF • MF • MHRM

M Mktg—MA—Marketing Full-time. Distance learning option. 12 to 48 months to complete program. *Concentration:* marketing.

MA—MA—Management Full-time. Distance learning option. 12 to 48 months to complete program. *Concentrations:* business studies, commerce, international management, management.

MBA—MBA (Finance) Full-time. 12 months to complete program. *Concentrations:* finance, general MBA.

MBA—Master of Business Administration Full-time and part-time. Distance learning option. 12 to 96 months to complete program. *Concentration:* general MBA.

MBF—MSc—International Banking and Finance Full-time. 12 months to complete program. *Concentrations:* banking, finance, financial economics, financial engineering, financial information systems, financial management/planning, international banking, international finance, investments and securities.

MF—MA—Financial Management Full-time. 12 months to complete program. *Concentration:* financial management/planning.

MF—MSc—Accounting and Finance Full-time. 12 months to complete program. *Concentrations:* finance, financial economics, financial management/planning, international finance, investments and securities.

MF—MSc—Corporate and International Finance Full-time. 12 months to complete program. *Concentrations:* finance, financial information systems, financial management/planning, international finance, investments and securities.

MF—MSc—Economics and Finance Full-time. 12 months to complete program. *Concentrations:* economics, finance, financial economics, international finance, investments and securities.

MF—MSc—Finance Full-time. 12 months to complete program. *Concentrations:* economics, finance, financial economics, financial engineering, financial information systems, financial management/planning, international finance.

MF—MSc—Finance and Investment Full-time. 12 months to complete program. *Concentrations:* finance, financial economics, financial engineering, financial information systems, financial management/planning, investments and securities.

MF—MSc—International Money, Finance and Investment Full-time. 12 months to complete program. *Concentrations:* finance, financial economics, financial engineering, financial management/planning, international finance, investments and securities.

MHRM—MA—Human Resource Management Full-time. 12 months to complete program. *Concentration:* human resources management.

RESOURCES AND SERVICES 68 on-campus PCs are available to graduate business students. Access to Internet/World Wide Web and online (class) registration available. *Personal computer requirements:* Graduate business students are strongly recommended to purchase or lease a personal computer. *Special opportunities include:* An international exchange program is available. *Placement services include:* Alumni network, job search course, career counseling/planning, electronic job bank, career fairs, resume preparation, and career library.

EXPENSES *Tuition:* Full-time: 20,500 British pounds. Part-time: 11,600 British pounds per year. *Tuition (international):* Full-time: 20,500 British pounds. Part-time: 11,600 British pounds per year. *Typical graduate housing cost:* 4600 British pounds (room only).

FINANCIAL AID (2007–08) Scholarships. Aid is available to part-time students. *Financial aid application deadline:* 8/31.

Financial Aid Contact Ms. Lindsay Duke, Postgraduate Student Recruitment Manager, Mill Hill Lane, Durham, DH1 3LB, United Kingdom. *Phone:* 191-3345533. *Fax:* 191-3345136. *E-mail:* pg.bus@durham.ac.uk.

INTERNATIONAL STUDENTS *Services and facilities:* Counseling/support services, ESL/language courses, Housing location assistance, International student housing, International student organization, Language tutoring, Orientation. *Required with application:* IELT with recommended score of 7; TOEFL with recommended score of 600 (paper); TWE with recommended score of 5; proof of adequate funds.

International Student Contact International Officer, International Office, University Office, Durham, DH1 3HP, United Kingdom. *Phone:* 44-191-334-6328. *Fax:* 44-191-334-6326. *E-mail:* international.office@durham.ac.uk.

APPLICATION *Required:* Application form, baccalaureate/first degree, 2 letters of recommendation, personal statement, resume/curriculum vitae, transcripts of college work, 3 years of work experience. *Recommended:*

University of Durham (continued)

Interview. *Application fee:* 500 British pounds. Applications for domestic and international students are processed on a rolling basis.

Application Contact Ms. Lindsay Duke, Postgraduate Student Recruitment Manager, Mill Hill Lane, Durham, DH1 3LB, United Kingdom. *Phone:* 191-334-5533. *Fax:* 191-334-5136. *E-mail:* pg.bus@durham.ac.uk.

University of Edinburgh
Edinburgh University Management School

Edinburgh, United Kingdom

Phone: 44-131-6508066 **Fax:** 44-131-6506501 **E-mail:** edinburgh.mba@ed.ac.uk

Business Program(s) Web Site: http://www.man.ed.ac.uk/

Graduate Business Unit Enrollment *Total:* 569 (479 full-time; 90 part-time; 430 international). *Average Age:* 28.

Graduate Business Faculty *Total:* 93 (81 full-time; 12 part-time).

Admissions *Applied:* 2,489. *Admitted:* 1,282. *Enrolled:* 439.

Academic Calendar Semesters.

After Graduation (Class of 2006–07) *Employed within 3 months of graduation:* 93%. *Average starting salary:* 63,750 British pounds.

DEGREES MBA • MS

MBA—Full-Time Master of Business Administration Full-time. 180 total credits required. 12 months to complete program. *Concentrations:* entrepreneurship, finance, international business, international management, international trade, management, marketing, nonprofit management, nonprofit organization, operations management, organizational behavior/development, strategic management.

MBA—Master of Business Administration in International Business Full-time. 180 total credits required. 15 months to complete program. *Concentrations:* Asian business studies, entrepreneurship, finance, international and area business studies, international business, international management, international marketing, international trade, management, marketing, operations management, organizational behavior/development, strategic management.

MBA—Modular Master of Business Administration Full-time. 180 total credits required. 24 to 48 months to complete program. *Concentrations:* entrepreneurship, finance, international business, international management, international trade, management, marketing, nonprofit management, nonprofit organization, operations management, organizational behavior/development, strategic management.

MBA—Part-Time Master of Business Administration Part-time. 180 total credits required. 30 months to complete program. *Concentrations:* entrepreneurship, finance, international business, management, marketing, nonprofit management, operations management, organizational behavior/development, strategic management, technology management.

MS—Accounting and Finance Full-time. 12 months to complete program. *Concentrations:* accounting, international finance, investments and securities, statistics.

MS—Carbon Management Full-time. 12 months to complete program. *Concentrations:* business ethics, environmental economics/management, other, resources management, strategic management.

MS—Economics Full-time. 12 months to complete program. *Concentrations:* economics, financial economics.

MS—Finance and Investment Full-time. 12 months to complete program. *Concentrations:* banking, finance, financial management/planning, international banking, international finance, investments and securities, risk management, statistics.

MS—International Business and Emerging Markets Full-time. 12 months to complete program. *Concentrations:* accounting, international business, international development management, international economics, international finance, international management, international marketing, international trade.

MS—Management Full-time. 12 months to complete program. *Concentrations:* accounting, economics, entrepreneurship, finance, marketing, organizational management, strategic management.

RESOURCES AND SERVICES 48 on-campus PCs are available to graduate business students. Access to Internet/World Wide Web and online (class) registration available. *Personal computer requirements:* Graduate business students are strongly recommended to purchase or lease a personal computer. *Special opportunities include:* An international exchange program and an internship program are available. *Placement services include:* Alumni network, job search course, career counseling/planning, electronic job bank, resume referral, career fairs, resume preparation, and career library.

EXPENSES *Tuition (state resident):* Full-time: 22,800 British pounds. Part-time: 16,450 British pounds per degree program. *Tuition (nonresident):* Full-time: 22,800 British pounds. Part-time: 16,450 British pounds per degree program. *Tuition (international):* Full-time: 22,800 British pounds. Part-time: 16,450 British pounds per degree program. *Typical graduate housing cost:* 8190 British pounds (including board), 4316 British pounds (room only).

FINANCIAL AID (2007–08) 20 students received aid, including scholarships. *Financial aid application deadline:* 4/30.

Financial Aid Contact Mrs. Trish Fraser, Admissions Administrator, 7 Bristo Square, Scotland, United Kingdom. *Phone:* 44-131-6508066. *Fax:* 44-131-6506501. *E-mail:* trish.fraser@ed.ac.uk.

INTERNATIONAL STUDENTS 76% of students enrolled are international students. *Services and facilities:* Counseling/support services, ESL/language courses, Housing location assistance, International student housing, International student organization, Language tutoring, Orientation, Visa Services, Skills training. Financial aid is available to international students. *Required with application:* IELT with recommended score of 7; TOEFL with recommended score of 250 (computer) or 600 (paper); TWE with recommended score of 5; proof of adequate funds; proof of health/immunizations.

International Student Contact Mrs. Trish Fraser, Applications Coordinator, 7 Bristo Square, Scotland, United Kingdom. *Phone:* 44-131-6508066. *Fax:* 44-131-6506501. *E-mail:* edinburgh.mba@ed.ac.uk.

APPLICATION *Required:* GMAT, application form, essay, 2 letters of recommendation, personal statement, resume/curriculum vitae, transcripts of college work, 3 years of work experience. *Recommended:* Baccalaureate/first degree, interview. Applications for domestic and international students are processed on a rolling basis.

Application Contact Mrs. Trish Fraser, Admissions Coordinator, 7 Bristo Square, Scotland, United Kingdom. *Phone:* 44-131-6508066. *Fax:* 44-131-6506501. *E-mail:* edinburgh.mba@ed.ac.uk.

University of Glasgow
University of Glasgow Business School

Glasgow, United Kingdom

Phone: 44-141-3303993 **Fax:** 44-141-3304939 **E-mail:** i.docherty@lbss.gla.ac.uk

Business Program(s) Web Site: http://www.glasgow.ac.uk/business

Graduate Business Unit Enrollment *Total:* 492 (423 full-time; 69 part-time; 229 women; 400 international). *Average Age:* 26.

Graduate Business Faculty *Total:* 100 (90 full-time; 10 part-time).

Admissions *Applied:* 4,364. *Admitted:* 2,803. *Enrolled:* 475.

Academic Calendar Semesters.

After Graduation (Class of 2006–07) *Employed within 3 months of graduation:* 85%.

DEGREES M Acc • M Phil • M Sc • MBA • MF • MS

M Acc—International Accounting and Financial Management Full-time. 12 months to complete program. *Concentrations:* accounting, finance.

M Phil—Contemporary Economic History Full-time and part-time. 12 to 24 months to complete program. *Concentrations:* business studies, economics.

M Sc—Management Full-time. Honours degree or equivalent required. 180 total credits required. 12 to 24 months to complete program. *Concentrations:* business studies, entrepreneurship, finance, management, operations management, organizational management, real estate, strategic management.

MBA—Master of Business Administration Full-time. Honours degree or professional equivalent, minimum 3 years managerial work experiencerequired. 180 total credits required. 12 months to complete program. *Concentrations:* business policy/strategy, economics, entrepreneurship, finance, general MBA, international management, marketing, organizational behavior/development, public management, strategic management.

MBA—Master of Business Administration Part-time. Honours degree or professional equivalent, minimum 3 years managerial work experience required. 180 total credits required. 24 to 36 months to complete program. *Concentrations:* business policy/strategy, economics, entrepreneurship, finance, general MBA, international management, marketing, organizational behavior/development, public management, strategic management.

MF—International Finance and Financial Institutions Full-time. 12 months to complete program. *Concentrations:* finance, financial management/planning.

MS—Human Resource Management Full-time. Honours degree or equivalent with considerable human resource management content required. 180 total credits required. 12 months to complete program. *Concentration:* human resources management.

MS—International Banking and Finance Full-time and part-time. 12 to 24 months to complete program. *Concentrations:* banking, finance.

MS—International Finance and Economic Policy Full-time and part-time. 12 to 24 months to complete program. *Concentrations:* developmental economics, economics, finance, financial economics, international economics, international finance.

MS—International Management and Entrepreneurship Full-time. Honours degree or equivalent with considerable international business content required. 180 total credits required. 12 months to complete program. *Concentrations:* business studies, entrepreneurship, international business, international development management.

MS—Monetary Economics and Finance Full-time and part-time. 12 to 24 months to complete program. *Concentrations:* economics, finance, financial economics.

MS—Strategic Human Resource Management and Organisational Change Part-time. Degree or professional qualification and relevant work experience required. 180 total credits required. 24 months to complete program. *Concentration:* human resources management.

MS—Strategic Marketing Full-time. Honours degree or equivalent with substantial marketing content required. 180 total credits required. 12 months to complete program. *Concentrations:* international marketing, marketing.

RESOURCES AND SERVICES 300 on-campus PCs are available to graduate business students. Access to Internet/World Wide Web, online (class) registration, and online grade reports available. *Personal computer requirements:* Graduate business students are required to have a personal computer, the cost of which is included in tuition or other required fees. *Special opportunities include:* An international exchange program is available. *Placement services include:* Alumni network, job search course, career counseling/planning, electronic job bank, resume referral, career fairs, resume preparation, and career library.

EXPENSES *Tuition (state resident):* Full-time: 13,000 British pounds. Part-time: 6500 British pounds per year. *Tuition (international):* Full-time: 16,000 British pounds. Part-time: 6500 British pounds per year. Tuition

and/or fees vary by academic program and local reciprocity agreements. *Graduate housing:* Room and board costs vary by type of accommodation and type of board plan. *Typical cost:* 4713 British pounds (room only).

FINANCIAL AID (2007–08) 20 students received aid, including grants and scholarships. Aid is available to part-time students. *Financial aid application deadline:* 6/30.

INTERNATIONAL STUDENTS 81% of students enrolled are international students. *Services and facilities:* Counseling/support services, ESL/language courses, Housing location assistance, International student housing, International student organization, Language tutoring, Orientation, Visa Services, Learning support services. Financial aid is available to international students. *Required with application:* IELT with recommended score of 6.5; proof of adequate funds; proof of health/immunizations.

International Student Contact Mrs. Ann Wilber, Postgraduate Recruitment and Marketing Officer, International and Postgraduate Service, Number 1 The Square, Scotland, United Kingdom. *Phone:* 44-141-3304515. *Fax:* 44-141-3304045. *E-mail:* pgadmissions@admin.gla.ac.uk.

APPLICATION *Required:* Application form, baccalaureate/first degree, interview, 2 letters of recommendation, personal statement, resume/curriculum vitae, transcripts of college work, 3 years of work experience. Applications for domestic and international students are processed on a rolling basis.

Application Contact Dr. Iain Docherty, MBA Programmes Director, Gilbert Scott Building, Scotland, United Kingdom. *Phone:* 44-141-3303993. *Fax:* 44-141-3304939. *E-mail:* i.docherty@lbss.gla.ac.uk.

University of Hertfordshire
University of Hertfordshire Business School
Hatfield, United Kingdom

Phone: 44-1707-284800 **Fax:** 44-1707-284870 **E-mail:** admissions@herts.ac.uk

Business Program(s) Web Site: http://www.herts.ac.uk/business/

Graduate Business Unit Enrollment *Total:* 750 (500 full-time; 250 part-time).

Graduate Business Faculty *Total:* 150 (100 full-time; 50 part-time).

Academic Calendar Semesters.

DEGREES MBA • MMS • MSCIB

MBA—Master of Business Administration Full-time and part-time. Bachelor's degree and at least 2 years of work experience with some responsibility required. At least 180 total credits required. 12 to 36 months to complete program. *Concentration:* general MBA.

MMS—Master of Arts in Management Studies Full-time and part-time. Bachelor's degree in any discipline required. At least 180 total credits required. 12 to 36 months to complete program. *Concentration:* management.

MSCIB—Master of Science in International Business Full-time. Bachelor's degree in a business related discipline required. At least 180 total credits required. 12 to 36 months to complete program. *Concentration:* international business.

RESOURCES AND SERVICES 1,600 on-campus PCs are available to graduate business students. Access to Internet/World Wide Web and online grade reports available. *Personal computer requirements:* Graduate business students are strongly recommended to purchase or lease a personal computer. *Placement services include:* Alumni network, career counseling/planning, career fairs, resume preparation, and career library.

EXPENSES *Tuition:* Full-time: 3800 British pounds. Part-time: 310 British pounds per unit. *Tuition (international):* Full-time: 9500 British pounds. Tuition and/or fees vary by number of courses or credits taken and academic program.

FINANCIAL AID (2007–08) Scholarships.

University of Hertfordshire (continued)

Financial Aid Contact Central Admissions Department, Hatfield, Hertfordshire, AL10 9AB, United Kingdom. *Phone:* 44-1707-284800.

INTERNATIONAL STUDENTS *Services and facilities:* Counseling/support services, ESL/language courses, Housing location assistance, International student housing, International student organization, Language tutoring, Orientation, Visa Services. Financial aid is not available to international students. *Required with application:* IELT with recommended score of 6.5; TOEFL with recommended score of 237 (computer) or 580 (paper); proof of adequate funds; proof of health/immunizations.

International Student Contact Central Admissions Department, Hatfield, Hertfordshire, AL10 9AB, United Kingdom. *Phone:* 44-1707-284800.

APPLICATION *Required:* Application form, baccalaureate/first degree, 2 letters of recommendation, personal statement, resume/curriculum vitae, transcripts of college work, 2 years of work experience. Applications for domestic and international students are processed on a rolling basis.

Application Contact Central Admissions Department, Hatfield, Hertfordshire, AL10 9AB, United Kingdom. *Phone:* 44-1707-284800. *Fax:* 44-1707-284870. *E-mail:* admissions@herts.ac.uk.

University of Hull
School of Management
Hull, United Kingdom

Phone: 44-01482-46 Ext. 3331 **E-mail:** b.anand@hull.ac.uk

Business Program(s) Web Site: http://www.hull.ac.uk/hubs

Graduate Business Unit Enrollment *Total:* 774 (489 full-time; 285 part-time).

Graduate Business Faculty *Total:* 102 (86 full-time; 16 part-time).

Academic Calendar Semesters.

DEGREES MBA

MBA—MBA Executive Part-time. 24 to 26 months to complete program. *Concentrations:* business studies, management.

MBA—Master of Business Administration Full-time. 180 total credits required. Maximum of 12 months to complete program. *Concentrations:* financial management/planning, information management, management, marketing, travel industry/tourism management.

RESOURCES AND SERVICES Access to Internet/World Wide Web available. *Personal computer requirements:* Graduate business students are strongly recommended to purchase or lease a personal computer. *Special opportunities include:* An international exchange program is available. *Placement services include:* Alumni network, career placement, job search course, career counseling/planning, electronic job bank, career fairs, job interviews arranged, resume preparation, and career library.

EXPENSES *Tuition (state resident):* Full-time: 13,500 British pounds.

FINANCIAL AID (2007–08) Scholarships. *Financial aid application deadline:* 5/31.

Financial Aid Contact Ms. Bella Anand, Admissions Manager, Hull University Business School, Cottingham Road, East Yorkshire, United Kingdom. *Phone:* 44-01482-46 Ext. 3331. *E-mail:* b.anand@hull.ac.uk.

INTERNATIONAL STUDENTS *Services and facilities:* Counseling/support services, ESL/language courses, Housing location assistance, International student housing, International student organization, Language tutoring, Orientation, Visa Services. Financial aid is available to international students. *Required with application:* IELT with recommended score of 6; TOEFL with recommended score of 214 (computer), 550 (paper), or 79 (Internet); proof of adequate funds.

International Student Contact Ms. Bella Anand, Admissions Manager, Hull University Business School, Cottingham Road, Hull, HU6 7RX, United Kingdom. *Phone:* 44-01482-46 Ext. 3331. *E-mail:* b.anand@hull.ac.uk.

APPLICATION *Required:* Application form, baccalaureate/first degree, 2 letters of recommendation, resume/curriculum vitae, transcripts of college work, 3 years of work experience. School will accept GMAT. *Recommended:* Essay, personal statement. *Application fee:* 0 British pounds. Applications for domestic and international students are processed on a rolling basis.

Application Contact Ms. Bella Anand, Admissions Manager, Hull University Business School, Cottingham Road, East Yorkshire, United Kingdom. *Phone:* 44-01482-46 Ext. 3331. *E-mail:* b.anand@hull.ac.uk.

University of London
London Business School
London, United Kingdom

Phone: 44-20-7000-7511 **Fax:** 44-20-7000-7001 **E-mail:** mbainfo@london.edu

Business Program(s) Web Site: http://www.london.edu

Graduate Business Unit Enrollment *Total:* 1,547 (896 full-time; 651 part-time).

Graduate Business Faculty *Total:* 123 (90 full-time; 33 part-time).

Admissions *Average GMAT:* 690.

Academic Calendar Trimesters.

Accreditation AACSB—The Association to Advance Collegiate Schools of Business.

After Graduation (Class of 2006–07) *Employed within 3 months of graduation:* 96%. *Average starting salary:* 59,982 British pounds.

DEGREES EMBA • MBA • MF • MSM

EMBA—EMBA—Global Asia in conjunction with Columbia Business School and Hong Kong University Part-time. Core classes take place in Hong Kong, London and New York. 16 to 20 months to complete program. *Concentration:* executive programs.

MBA—Dubai-London Executive MBA Part-time. Classes alternate between Dubai and London. Minimum of 20 months to complete program. *Concentration:* executive programs.

MBA—EMBA—Global Europe and Americas Part-time. Joint MBA degree with Columbia University Graduate School of Business. Classes alternate between New York and London. At least 28 total credits required. Minimum of 20 months to complete program. *Concentration:* executive programs.

MBA—Executive Master of Business Administration Part-time. Alternate weekends and part-time; based in London. Minimum of 20 months to complete program. *Concentration:* executive programs.

MBA—Full-Time Master of Business Administration Full-time. 15 to 21 months to complete program. *Concentration:* general MBA.

MF—Master of Finance—Full-Time Full-time. 10 months to complete program. *Concentration:* finance.

MF—Master of Finance—Part-Time Part-time. 22 months to complete program. *Concentration:* finance.

MSM—Sloan Fellowship MSc Full-time. 11 months to complete program. *Concentration:* management.

RESOURCES AND SERVICES 400 on-campus PCs are available to graduate business students. Access to Internet/World Wide Web, online (class) registration, and online grade reports available. *Personal computer requirements:* Graduate business students are strongly recommended to purchase or lease a personal computer. *Special opportunities include:* An international exchange program and an internship program are available. *Placement services include:* Alumni network, career placement, job search course, career counseling/planning, electronic job bank, resume referral, career fairs, job interviews arranged, resume preparation, and career library.

FINANCIAL AID (2007–08) Loans and scholarships. Aid is available to part-time students. *Financial aid application deadline:* 5/27.

Financial Aid Contact Financial Aid Officer, Regent's Park, London, NW1 4SA, United Kingdom. *Phone:* 44-20-7000-7000. *Fax:* 44-20-7000-7001. *E-mail:* financialaid@london.edu.

INTERNATIONAL STUDENTS *Services and facilities:* Counseling/support services, Housing location assistance, Language tutoring, Orientation, Disability Support Officer, More than 50 student clubs including student governance known as the London Business School Student Association. Financial aid is available to international students. *Required with application:* TOEFL with recommended score of 110 (Internet). *Recommended with application:* IELT with recommended score of 7.

International Student Contact Information Officer, MBA Programme, Regent's Park, London, NW1 4SA, United Kingdom. *Phone:* 44-20-7000-7511. *Fax:* 44-20-7000-7001. *E-mail:* mbainfo@london.edu.

APPLICATION *Required:* GMAT, application form, baccalaureate/first degree, essay, interview, 2 letters of recommendation, personal statement, resume/curriculum vitae, transcripts of college work, 3 years of work experience. *Application fee:* 145 British pounds. *Deadlines:* 10/19 for fall, 1/4 for winter, 2/28 for spring, 5/2 for summer, 10/19 for fall (international), 1/4 for winter (international), 2/28 for spring (international), 5/4 for summer (international).

Application Contact Information Officer, MBA Programme Office, Regent's Park, London, NW1 4SA, United Kingdom. *Phone:* 44-20-7000-7511. *Fax:* 44-20-7000-7001. *E-mail:* mbainfo@london.edu.

University of Oxford
Saïd Business School

Oxford, United Kingdom

Phone: 44-1865-278804 **Fax:** 44-1865-288831 **E-mail:** enquiries@sbs.ox.ac.uk

Business Program(s) Web Site: http://www.sbs.oxford.edu

Graduate Business Unit Enrollment *Average Age:* 27.

Graduate Business Faculty *Total:* 94 (63 full-time; 31 part-time).

Admissions *Average GMAT:* 680.

Academic Calendar Three 10-week terms and a summer business project, internship, or additional electives.

After Graduation (Class of 2006–07) *Employed within 3 months of graduation:* 90%. *Average starting salary:* 65,000 British pounds.

DEGREES   EMBA • MBA • MF • MS

EMBA—Executive MBA Part-time. Distance learning option. Minimum of 21 months to complete program. *Concentration:* general MBA.

MBA—Master of Business Administration Full-time. Minimum undergraduate GPA of 2.1 and minimum GMAT score of 600 required. Minimum of 12 months to complete program. *Concentration:* general MBA.

MF—MSc in Financial Economics Full-time. Minimum of 9 months to complete program. *Concentration:* financial economics.

MS—MSc in Major Programme Management Part-time. Distance learning option. Minimum 5 years work experience in project management. Maximum of 24 months to complete program. *Concentration:* project management.

MS—Master of Science in Management Research Full-time. Minimum of 12 months to complete program. *Concentration:* management science.

RESOURCES AND SERVICES 60 on-campus PCs are available to graduate business students. Access to Internet/World Wide Web available. *Personal computer requirements:* Graduate business students are strongly recommended to purchase or lease a personal computer. *Special opportunities include:* An internship program is available. *Placement services include:* Alumni network, career placement, job search course, career counseling/planning, electronic job bank, resume referral, career fairs, job interviews arranged, resume preparation, and career library.

EXPENSES *Tuition (state resident):* Full-time: 28,000 British pounds. *Tuition (nonresident):* Full-time: 28,000 British pounds. *Tuition (international):* Full-time: 28,000 British pounds. *Required fees:* Full-time: 3500 British pounds. *Graduate housing:* Room and board costs vary by number of occupants and type of accommodation. *Typical cost:* 10,000 British pounds (including board), 4500 British pounds (room only).

FINANCIAL AID (2007–08) 20 students received aid, including scholarships. *Financial aid application deadline:* 1/10.

Financial Aid Contact Admissions Office, Park End Street, Oxford, OX1 1HP, United Kingdom. *Phone:* 44-1865-278804. *Fax:* 44-1865-288831. *E-mail:* enquiries@sbs.ox.ac.uk.

INTERNATIONAL STUDENTS *Services and facilities:* Counseling/support services, Housing location assistance, International student housing. Financial aid is available to international students. *Required with application:* IELT with recommended score of 7.5; TOEFL with recommended score of 250 (computer) or 600 (paper); proof of adequate funds.

International Student Contact Ms. Anna Farrus, Admissions Manager, Park End Street, Oxford, OX1 1HP, United Kingdom. *Phone:* 44-1865-278804. *Fax:* 44-1865-288831. *E-mail:* enquiries@sbs.ox.ac.uk.

APPLICATION *Required:* GMAT, application form, baccalaureate/first degree, essay, interview, 2 letters of recommendation, personal statement, transcripts of college work, 2 years of work experience. School will accept GRE. *Application fee:* 100 British pounds. *Deadlines:* 10/27 for fall, 1/12 for winter, 3/23 for spring, 5/25 for summer, 10/27 for fall (international), 1/12 for winter (international), 3/23 for spring (international), 5/25 for summer (international).

Application Contact Ms. Anna Farrus, Admissions Manager, Park End Street, Oxford, OX1 1HP, United Kingdom. *Phone:* 44-1865-278804. *Fax:* 44-1865-288831. *E-mail:* enquiries@sbs.ox.ac.uk.

University of Plymouth
Plymouth Business School

Plymouth, United Kingdom

Phone: 44-1752-232800 **Fax:** 44-1752-232853

Business Program(s) Web Site: http://www.pbs.plym.ac.uk/

Academic Calendar Semesters.

DEGREES   M Sc • MA • MS

M Sc—Finance Full-time and part-time. *Concentration:* finance.

M Sc—International Supply Chain Management Full-time. *Concentrations:* international business, supply chain management.

MA—Personnel and Development Full-time and part-time. *Concentration:* human resources development.

MS—Master of Science in Business Management Full-time. At least 120 total credits required. 12 months to complete program. *Concentrations:* accounting, commerce, economics, entrepreneurship, finance, human resources management, international business, international trade, law, logistics, management, marketing, operations management.

RESOURCES AND SERVICES 1,250 on-campus PCs are available to graduate business students. Access to Internet/World Wide Web available. *Personal computer requirements:* Graduate business students are strongly recommended to purchase or lease a personal computer. *Special opportunities include:* An international exchange program is available. *Placement services include:* Alumni network, career placement, career fairs, job interviews arranged, resume preparation, and career library.

FINANCIAL AID (2007–08) Scholarships. *Financial aid application deadline:* 5/1.

Financial Aid Contact Faculty Marketing Officer, Drake Circus, Devon, United Kingdom. *Phone:* 44-1752-232800. *Fax:* 44-1752-232853.

University of Plymouth (continued)

INTERNATIONAL STUDENTS *Services and facilities:* Counseling/support services, Housing location assistance, International student organization, Language tutoring, Orientation, Visa Services. Financial aid is available to international students. *Required with application:* IELT with recommended score of 6.5; TOEFL with recommended score of 570 (paper).

International Student Contact Faculty Marketing Officer, Drake Circus, Devon, United Kingdom. *Phone:* 44-1752-232800. *Fax:* 44-1752-232853.

APPLICATION *Required:* Application form, baccalaureate/first degree, 2 letters of recommendation, personal statement. School will accept GMAT. *Recommended:* Interview, resume/curriculum vitae, transcripts of college work, work experience. *Deadlines:* 8/30 for fall, 6/30 for fall (international).

Application Contact Faculty Marketing Officer, Drake Circus, Devon, United Kingdom. *Phone:* 44-1752-232800. *Fax:* 44-1752-232853.

University of Reading

ICMA Centre

Reading, United Kingdom

Phone: 44-118-3788239 **Fax:** 44-118-9314741 **E-mail:** k.mountford@icmacentre.ac.uk

Business Program(s) Web Site: http://www.icmacentre.ac.uk

Graduate Business Unit Enrollment *Total:* 178 (178 full-time; 62 women; 110 international).

Graduate Business Faculty *Total:* 26 (15 full-time; 11 part-time).

Admissions *Applied:* 948. *Admitted:* 392. *Enrolled:* 178. *Average GMAT:* 600. *Average GPA:* 3.3

Academic Calendar Three 10-week terms.

After Graduation (Class of 2006–07) *Employed within 3 months of graduation:* 70%. *Average starting salary:* 32,000 British pounds.

DEGREES M Sc

M Sc—Capital Markets, Regulation and Compliance Full-time. Distance learning option. 10 to 24 months to complete program. *Concentrations:* finance, international banking.

M Sc—Corporate Finance Full-time. Distance learning option. 10 to 24 months to complete program. *Concentration:* finance.

M Sc—Finance and Real Estate Full-time. Distance learning option. 10 to 24 months to complete program. *Concentrations:* finance, international banking, investments and securities, real estate.

M Sc—Financial Engineering Full-time. Distance learning option. 10 months to complete program. *Concentrations:* finance, financial engineering, international banking, quantitative analysis.

M Sc—Financial Risk Management Full-time. Distance learning option. 10 to 24 months to complete program. *Concentrations:* finance, international banking, quantitative analysis.

M Sc—International Securities, Investment and Banking Full-time. Distance learning option. 10 to 24 months to complete program. *Concentrations:* finance, international banking, investments and securities.

M Sc—Investment Banking and Islamic Finance Full-time. 12 months to complete program. *Concentrations:* finance, international banking, international finance, investments and securities.

M Sc—Investment Management Full-time. Distance learning option. 10 to 24 months to complete program. *Concentrations:* finance, international banking, investments and securities.

RESOURCES AND SERVICES 120 on-campus PCs are available to graduate business students. Access to Internet/World Wide Web and online grade reports available. *Personal computer requirements:* Graduate business students are not required to have a personal computer. *Placement*

services include: Alumni network, job search course, career counseling/planning, electronic job bank, career fairs, resume preparation, and career library.

EXPENSES *Tuition:* Full-time: 15,000 British pounds. *Tuition (international):* Full-time: 15,000 British pounds. *Graduate housing:* Room and board costs vary by type of accommodation and type of board plan.

FINANCIAL AID (2007–08) 12 students received aid, including scholarships. *Financial aid application deadline:* 7/25.

Financial Aid Contact Mrs. Kim Mountford, Admissions Officer, Whiteknights, Reading, RG6 6BA, United Kingdom. *Phone:* 44-118-3788239. *Fax:* 44-118-9314741. *E-mail:* k.mountford@icmacentre.ac.uk.

INTERNATIONAL STUDENTS 62% of students enrolled are international students. *Services and facilities:* Counseling/support services, ESL/language courses, International student housing, International student organization, Language tutoring. Financial aid is available to international students. *Required with application:* IELT with recommended score of 7; TOEFL with recommended score of 250 (computer) or 600 (paper); TWE with recommended score of 4.5; proof of adequate funds.

International Student Contact Mrs. Kim Mountford, Admissions Officer, Whiteknights, Reading, RG6 6BA, United Kingdom. *Phone:* 44-118-3788239. *Fax:* 44-118-9314741. *E-mail:* k.mountford@icmacentre.ac.uk.

APPLICATION *Required:* Application form, baccalaureate/first degree, 2 letters of recommendation, personal statement, transcripts of college work. School will accept GMAT. *Recommended:* Resume/curriculum vitae. *Application fee:* 30 British pounds. Applications for domestic and international students are processed on a rolling basis.

Application Contact Mrs. Kim Mountford, Admissions Officer, Whiteknights, Reading, RG6 6BA, United Kingdom. *Phone:* 44-118-3788239. *Fax:* 44-118-9314741. *E-mail:* k.mountford@icmacentre.ac.uk.

University of Salford

Salford Business School

Salford, United Kingdom

Phone: 44-161-2955594 **Fax:** 44-161-2955022 **E-mail:** go-sbs@salford.ac.uk

Business Program(s) Web Site: http://www.business.salford.ac.uk

Graduate Business Unit Enrollment *Total:* 700 (400 full-time; 300 part-time; 350 women; 350 international).

Graduate Business Faculty *Total:* 150 (130 full-time; 20 part-time).

Admissions *Applied:* 4,500. *Admitted:* 1,200. *Enrolled:* 700. *Average GPA:* 2.75

Academic Calendar Semesters.

DEGREES MBA • MS

MBA—Master of Business Administration Full-time. Work experience at significant level of responsibility is required and will be taken into account on application. 12 months to complete program. *Concentration:* general MBA.

MS—Master of Science Full-time and part-time. We offer a range of mainly specialised programmes requiring at least 2nd class Honours (or equivalent) UK Bachelor's degree. 12 to 60 months to complete program. *Concentrations:* administration, administration of technological information, banking, business information science, business policy/strategy, business studies, corporate accounting, decision sciences, finance, financial economics, financial information systems, financial management/planning, hospitality management, human resources management, industrial administration/management, industrial/labor relations, information management, information systems, information technology, international banking, international business, international economics, international finance, international logistics, international management, international marketing, international trade, logistics, management communication, management consulting, management information systems, management science, management systems analysis, managerial economics, manpower administration, manufacturing management, marketing, marketing research, materials management, nonprofit management, nonprofit organization, operations management, organizational behavior/development, organizational management, production management, project management, quality management, quantitative analysis, risk management, strategic management, supply chain management, taxation, technology management, training and development, transportation management, travel industry/tourism management.

RESOURCES AND SERVICES 2,500 on-campus PCs are available to graduate business students. Access to Internet/World Wide Web available. *Personal computer requirements:* Graduate business students are strongly recommended to purchase or lease a personal computer. *Special opportunities include:* An international exchange program is available. *Placement services include:* Alumni network, career placement, job search course, career counseling/planning, electronic job bank, resume referral, career fairs, resume preparation, and career library.

FINANCIAL AID (2007–08) Loans, scholarships, and teaching assistantships. *Financial aid application deadline:* 3/30.

Financial Aid Contact Dr. Grazyna Rembielak-Vitchev, Director of Admissions, The Crescent, Salford, Greater Manchester, United Kingdom. *Phone:* 44-161-2955594. *Fax:* 44-161-2955022. *E-mail:* go-sbs@salford.ac.uk.

INTERNATIONAL STUDENTS 50% of students enrolled are international students. *Services and facilities:* Counseling/support services, ESL/language courses, Housing location assistance, International student housing, International student organization, Language tutoring, Orientation, Visa Services, Students within Greater Manchester have easy access to facilities: libraries, student societies and clubs, etc, of all three major universities there. Financial aid is available to international students. *Required with application:* IELT with recommended score of 6.5; TOEFL with recommended score of 235 (computer) or 575 (paper); TWE with recommended score of 4; proof of adequate funds; proof of health/immunizations.

International Student Contact Ms. Debbie Cartwright, Admissions Officer, The Crescent, Salford, Greater Manchester, United Kingdom. *Phone:* 44-161-2955530. *Fax:* 44-161-2953821. *E-mail:* d.cartwright@salford.ac.uk.

APPLICATION *Required:* Application form, baccalaureate/first degree, 2 letters of recommendation, personal statement, transcripts of college work. *Recommended:* Resume/curriculum vitae. Applications for domestic and international students are processed on a rolling basis.

Application Contact Dr. Grazyna Rembielak-Vitchev, Director of Admissions, The Crescent, Salford, Greater Manchester, United Kingdom. *Phone:* 44-161-2955594. *Fax:* 44-161-2955022. *E-mail:* go-sbs@salford.ac.uk.

University of Strathclyde

University of Strathclyde Graduate School of Business

Glasgow, United Kingdom

Phone: 44-141-5536056 **Fax:** 44-141-5536162 **E-mail:** admissions@gsb.strath.ac.uk

Business Program(s) Web Site: http://www.gsb.strath.ac.uk

Accreditation AACSB—The Association to Advance Collegiate Schools of Business.

DEGREES IMBA • M Sc • MBA • MBA/MS

IMBA—Part-Time Master of Business Administration Part-time. Distance learning option. Minimum age of 24 required. 180 total credits required. 30 to 42 months to complete program. *Concentrations:* international business, strategic management.

M Sc—Master of Science in Business Information Technology Systems Full-time. Must be a recent Honors degree graduate. 180 total credits required. 12 months to complete program. *Concentrations:* information management, information systems, strategic management.

M Sc—Master of Science in Business and Management Full-time. Honors degree required. 180 total credits required. 12 months to complete program. *Concentrations:* management, strategic management.

MBA—Master of Business Administration Full-time and part-time. Distance learning option. Minimum age of 24 required. 180 total credits required. 12 to 72 months to complete program. *Concentrations:* international business, strategic management.

MBA/MS—Master of Business Administration/Master of Science Distance learning option. Minimum age of 24 required. 180 total credits required. 36 to 72 months to complete program. *Concentrations:* leadership, strategic management.

RESOURCES AND SERVICES 40 on-campus PCs are available to graduate business students. Access to Internet/World Wide Web available. *Personal computer requirements:* Graduate business students are strongly recommended to purchase or lease a personal computer. *Placement services include:* Alumni network, career placement, career counseling/planning, resume referral, job interviews arranged, resume preparation, and career library.

Application Contact Lucy Reynolds, Admissions Officer, 199 Cathedral Street, Scotland, United Kingdom. *Phone:* 44-141-5536056. *Fax:* 44-141-5536162. *E-mail:* admissions@gsb.strath.ac.uk.

University of the West of England, Bristol

Bristol Business School

Bristol, United Kingdom

Phone: 44-117-3443445 **Fax:** 44-117-3442925 **E-mail:** business@uwe.ac.uk

Business Program(s) Web Site: http://www.uwe.ac.uk

Graduate Business Unit Enrollment *Total:* 777 (202 full-time; 575 part-time; 399 women; 69 international).

Graduate Business Faculty 28 full-time.

Admissions *Applied:* 209. *Admitted:* 78. *Enrolled:* 55.

Academic Calendar Trimesters.

DEGREES M Sc • MA • MBA • MSC

M Sc—Master of Science in Management Accounting Full-time and part-time. Minimum of 12 months to complete program. *Concentrations:* accounting, business policy/strategy, finance, financial management/planning, international finance.

MA—Master of Arts in Human Resource Management Full-time and part-time. Minimum of 12 months to complete program. *Concentrations:* business ethics, business law, human resources management, industrial/labor relations, manpower administration.

MA—Master of Arts in Management Part-time. 24 to 33 months to complete program. *Concentrations:* finance, human resources management, information management, marketing, operations management, strategic management.

MA—Master of Arts in Marketing Full-time and part-time. 12 to 24 months to complete program. *Concentrations:* advertising, international marketing, marketing, marketing research.

MBA—Master of Business Administration European Route Full-time. 3 years of management experience required. 12 months to complete program. *Concentrations:* accounting, business policy/strategy, economics, entrepreneurship, European business studies, finance, human resources management, international finance, international marketing, management, management information systems, marketing, operations

University of the West of England, Bristol (continued)

management, organizational behavior/development, project management, public policy and administration, quantitative analysis, strategic management, taxation.

MBA—Master of Business Administration UK Route Full-time. 3 years of management experience required. 12 months to complete program. *Concentrations:* accounting, business policy/strategy, economics, entrepreneurship, finance, human resources management, international finance, international marketing, management, management information systems, marketing, operations management, organizational behavior/development, project management, public policy and administration, quantitative analysis, strategic management, taxation.

MBA—Master of Business Administration Full-time and part-time. 3 years of management experience required. Minimum of 30 months to complete program. *Concentrations:* accounting, business policy/strategy, finance, human resources management, international marketing, management, management information systems, marketing, operations management, organizational behavior/development, project management, strategic management.

MSC—Master of Science in Commerce—International Management Full-time. 12 months to complete program. *Concentrations:* accounting, business policy/strategy, human resources management, information management, information systems, international business, international economics, international finance, international management, international marketing.

MSC—Master of Science in Financial Accounting Full-time and part-time. Minimum of 12 months to complete program. *Concentrations:* accounting, business policy/strategy, finance, financial management/planning, international finance.

RESOURCES AND SERVICES Access to Internet/World Wide Web available. *Personal computer requirements:* Graduate business students are not required to have a personal computer. *Special opportunities include:* An international exchange program is available.

Financial Aid Contact Centre for Student Affairs, Frenchay Campus, Bristol, BS16 1QY, United Kingdom. *Phone:* 44-117-9656261. *Fax:* 44-117-9763851.

INTERNATIONAL STUDENTS 9% of students enrolled are international students. Financial aid is not available to international students.

International Student Contact MBA Admissions Officer, Frenchay Campus, Bristol, BS16 1QY, United Kingdom. *Phone:* 44-117-3442857. *Fax:* 44-117-3442925. *E-mail:* business@uwe.ac.uk.

Application Contact MBA Admissions Officer, Frenchay Campus, Bristol, BS16 1QY, United Kingdom. *Phone:* 44-117-3443445. *Fax:* 44-117-3442925. *E-mail:* business@uwe.ac.uk.

to 24 months to complete program. *Concentrations:* business policy/strategy, entrepreneurship, information management, leadership, management, strategic management.

M Sc—Postgraduate Diploma/Master of Science in Business Improvement Part-time. 3 years of work experience in a management position required. 16 to 24 months to complete program. *Concentrations:* business policy/strategy, finance, financial management/planning, leadership, management, risk management, strategic management.

MBA—Master of Business Administration Full-time and part-time. 3 years of work experience required. 12 to 36 months to complete program. *Concentrations:* accounting, economics, entrepreneurship, finance, management, management information systems, marketing.

RESOURCES AND SERVICES 1,000 on-campus PCs are available to graduate business students. Access to Internet/World Wide Web and online grade reports available. *Personal computer requirements:* Graduate business students are strongly recommended to purchase or lease a personal computer. *Placement services include:* Alumni network, career placement, career counseling/planning, electronic job bank, career fairs, resume preparation, and career library.

EXPENSES *Tuition (state resident):* Full-time: 8700 British pounds. *Tuition (international):* Full-time: 10,700 British pounds. *Graduate housing:* Room and board costs vary by campus location, number of occupants, and type of accommodation.

FINANCIAL AID (2007–08) *Financial aid application deadline:* 7/31.

Financial Aid Contact Ms. Marjorie Coulter, Director of Graduate School of Business and Management, Shore Road, County Antrim, United Kingdom. *Phone:* 28-9-0368129. *E-mail:* me.coulter@ulster.ac.uk.

INTERNATIONAL STUDENTS *Services and facilities:* Counseling/support services, ESL/language courses, Housing location assistance, International student housing, International student organization, Language tutoring, Orientation, Visa Services. Financial aid is available to international students. *Required with application:* IELT with recommended score of 6; proof of adequate funds. *Recommended with application:* TOEFL with recommended score of 550 (paper).

International Student Contact Marjorie Coulter, Room 03G03, County Antrim, United Kingdom. *Phone:* 1232-366-805. *Fax:* 1232-368-129. *E-mail:* me.coulter@ulst.ac.uk.

APPLICATION *Required:* Application form, baccalaureate/first degree, 2 letters of recommendation, transcripts of college work, 3 years of work experience. School will accept GMAT. *Recommended:* Personal statement, resume/curriculum vitae. Applications for domestic and international students are processed on a rolling basis.

Application Contact Mr. Nicholas Read, Postgraduate Programmes Manager, Shore Road, County Antrim, United Kingdom. *Phone:* 28-9-0368880. *Fax:* 1232-366-843. *E-mail:* n.read@ulster.ac.uk.

University of Ulster at Jordanstown
Faculty of Business and Management
Newtown Abbey, United Kingdom

Phone: 28-9-0368880 **Fax:** 1232-366-843 **E-mail:** n.read@ulster.ac.uk

Business Program(s) Web Site: http://www.ulster.ac.uk/mba

Graduate Business Unit Enrollment *Average Age:* 32.

Graduate Business Faculty 80 full-time.

Admissions *Average GMAT:* 500.

Academic Calendar Semesters.

After Graduation (Class of 2006–07) *Employed within 3 months of graduation:* 100%.

DEGREES   M Sc • MBA

M Sc—Executive Program/Master of Science in Executive Leadership Part-time. 7 years of management experience at a senior level required. 16

University of Wales, Aberystwyth
School of Management and Business
Ceredigion, United Kingdom

Phone: 44-1970-622523 **Fax:** 44-1970-622524 **E-mail:** mbainfo@aber.ac.uk

Business Program(s) Web Site: http://www.aber.ac.uk/smba/

DEGREES   MBA • MSC

MBA—Master of Business Administration Full-time and part-time. Minimum 3 years professional management experience. 180 total credits required. 12 months to complete program. *Concentrations:* general MBA, management.

MSC—Master of Science in Accounting and Finance (Specialist/Research) Full-time. Undergraduate (honours) degree in a related subject area. 180 total credits required. 12 months to complete program. *Concentrations:* accounting, finance.

MSC—Master of Science in International Business Management Full-time. 180 total credits required. 12 months to complete program. *Concentrations:* international business, international management, management.

MSC—Master of Science in International Finance (Specialist/ Research) Full-time. Distance learning option. Undergraduate (honours) degree in a related subject area. 180 total credits required. 12 months to complete program. *Concentration:* international finance.

MSC—Master of Science in Management Full-time. 180 total credits required. 12 months to complete program. *Concentration:* management.

MSC—Master of Science in Management and Finance Full-time. 180 total credits required. 12 months to complete program. *Concentrations:* finance, management.

MSC—Master of Science in Management and Marketing Full-time. 180 total credits required. 12 months to complete program. *Concentrations:* management, marketing.

RESOURCES AND SERVICES 650 on-campus PCs are available to graduate business students. Access to Internet/World Wide Web and online grade reports available. *Personal computer requirements:* Graduate business students are not required to have a personal computer. *Placement services include:* Alumni network, job search course, career counseling/ planning, resume referral, resume preparation, and career library.

Application Contact Mrs. Sarah Norrington-Davies, Postgraduate Administrator, Cledwyn Building, Penglais Campus, Aberystwyth, Ceredigion, SY23 3DD, United Kingdom. *Phone:* 44-1970-622523. *Fax:* 44-1970-622524. *E-mail:* mbainfo@aber.ac.uk.

University of Warwick
Warwick Business School
Coventry, United Kingdom

Phone: 44-2476-524100 **Fax:** 44-2476-574400 **E-mail:** warwickmba@wbs.ac.uk

Business Program(s) Web Site: http://www.wbs.ac.uk

Graduate Business Unit Enrollment *Total:* 3,403 (658 full-time; 2,745 part-time; 989 women; 1704 international). *Average Age:* 32.

Graduate Business Faculty *Total:* 185 (172 full-time; 13 part-time).

Admissions *Applied:* 300. *Admitted:* 150. *Enrolled:* 72. *Average GMAT:* 610.

Academic Calendar Trimesters.

Accreditation AACSB—The Association to Advance Collegiate Schools of Business.

After Graduation (Class of 2006–07) *Employed within 3 months of graduation:* 96%. *Average starting salary:* 47,285 British pounds.

DEGREES M Sc • MA • MBA • MPA • MS • PhD/MBA

M Sc—Business Analytics and Consulting Full-time. 12 months to complete program. *Concentrations:* decision sciences, information management, management consulting, management science.

M Sc—Master of Science in Finance Full-time. 12 months to complete program. *Concentration:* finance.

M Sc—Master of Science in Finance and Economics Full-time. 12 months to complete program. *Concentrations:* economics, finance.

M Sc—Master of Science in Financial Mathematics Full-time. 12 months to complete program. *Concentration:* finance.

M Sc—Master of Science in Management Full-time. This generalist master's is NOT open to bachelor's graduates in business studies. 12 months to complete program. *Concentration:* management.

M Sc—Master of Science in Management Science and Operational Research Full-time and part-time. 12 to 24 months to complete program. *Concentration:* management.

MA—Master of Arts in European Industrial Relations Full-time and part-time. 12 to 24 months to complete program. *Concentration:* industrial/labor relations.

MA—Master of Arts in Industrial Relations and Personnel Management Full-time and part-time. 12 to 24 months to complete program. *Concentration:* human resources management.

MA—Master of Arts in Organization Studies Full-time and part-time. 12 to 24 months to complete program. *Concentration:* organizational management.

MBA—Distance Learning Master of Business Administration Distance learning option. 4 years of relevant work experience required. 36 to 96 months to complete program. *Concentration:* general MBA.

MBA—Executive MBA Part-time. 4 years of relevant work experience required. 36 to 96 months to complete program. *Concentration:* general MBA.

MBA—Full-Time Master of Business Administration Full-time. A good balanced GMAT score; at least 3 years' relevant work experience required. 12 months to complete program. *Concentration:* general MBA.

MPA—Modular Study Master of Public Administration Full-time and part-time. Current employment at executive level required. 36 months to complete program. *Concentration:* public policy and administration.

MS—Master of Science in Information Systems and Management Full-time. 12 months to complete program. *Concentrations:* information systems, management.

MS—Master of Science in Marketing and Strategy Full-time. 12 months to complete program. *Concentrations:* marketing, strategic management.

PhD/MBA—Doctoral Programme Full-time and part-time. Master's degree relevant to subject to be studied required. 36 to 60 months to complete program. *Concentrations:* management, other.

RESOURCES AND SERVICES 185 on-campus PCs are available to graduate business students. Access to Internet/World Wide Web, online (class) registration, and online grade reports available. *Personal computer requirements:* Graduate business students are not required to have a personal computer. *Special opportunities include:* An international exchange program and an internship program are available. *Placement services include:* Alumni network, career placement, job search course, career counseling/planning, electronic job bank, resume referral, career fairs, job interviews arranged, resume preparation, and career library.

EXPENSES *Tuition (state resident):* Full-time: 20,400 British pounds. Part-time: 4800 British pounds per year. *Tuition (nonresident):* Full-time: 20,400 British pounds. Part-time: 4800 British pounds per year. *Tuition (international):* Full-time: 20,400 British pounds. Part-time: 4800 British pounds per year. Tuition and/or fees vary by class time and academic program. *Graduate housing:* Room and board costs vary by number of occupants, type of accommodation, and type of board plan. *Typical cost:* 5450 British pounds (room only).

FINANCIAL AID (2007–08) 20 students received aid, including scholarships. Aid is available to part-time students.

Financial Aid Contact Ms. Heather Broadbent, Assistant Marketing and Recruitment Manager, Coventry, CV4 7AL, United Kingdom. *Phone:* 44-2476-524100. *Fax:* 44-2476-574400. *E-mail:* warwickmba@wbs.ac.uk.

INTERNATIONAL STUDENTS 50% of students enrolled are international students. *Services and facilities:* Counseling/support services, ESL/language courses, Housing location assistance, International student housing, International student organization, Language tutoring, Orientation, Visa Services. Financial aid is available to international students. *Required with application:* IELT with recommended score of 7. *Recommended with application:* TOEFL with recommended score of 260 (computer), 620 (paper), or 105 (Internet); proof of adequate funds; proof of health/immunizations.

International Student Contact Mrs. Ann Jackson, International and External Relations Officer, Coventry, CV4 7AL, United Kingdom. *Phone:* 44-2476-524306. *Fax:* 44-2476-523719. *E-mail:* enquiries@wbs.ac.uk.

APPLICATION *Required:* GMAT, application form, baccalaureate/first degree, essay, interview, 2 letters of recommendation, personal statement,

University of Warwick (continued)

resume/curriculum vitae, transcripts of college work, 3 years of work experience. *Application fee:* 80 British pounds. Applications for domestic and international students are processed on a rolling basis.

Application Contact Ms. Heather Broadbent, Assistant Marketing and Recruitment Manager, Coventry, CV4 7AL, United Kingdom. *Phone:* 44-2476-524100. *Fax:* 44-2476-574400. *E-mail:* warwickmba@ wbs.ac.uk.

CLOSE-UPS OF GRADUATE-LEVEL BUSINESS PROGRAMS

Adelphi University

Garden City, New York

THE DEAN'S MESSAGE

▶ *Adelphi University's School of Business creates managers, leaders, and entrepreneurs who can flourish amidst unprecedented change. The School believes that the best business leaders are those who enjoy an intellectual challenge, have a deep appreciation of the theoretical and the practical, understand today's realities and tomorrow's possibilities, and see the link between the skills they learn and the character they display.*

Traditional pedagogy is enhanced by many guest speakers, internship opportunities, and the Distinguished Executive Lecture Series.

—Anthony F. Libertella, Dean, School of Business

Programs and Curricular Focus

Adelphi's M.B.A. program requires a minimum of 33 credits and a maximum of 66 and accommodates students with varied academic backgrounds. It meets state, regional, and national accreditation standards and is designed to serve middle-level professionals seeking advancement in management careers. The curriculum integrates contemporary management issues and business fundamentals, enabling students to perform with distinction in the global environment. Its mission is to produce intellectually well-rounded, effective communicators who are aware of societal issues and responsibilities and have a thorough understanding of the legal, environmental, technological, and social issues that affect an organization's operation. Candidates are required to fulfill or waive graduate prerequisites in financial accounting, computer applications, and mathematics for managers.

The curriculum begins with a 24-credit foundation core consisting of studies in the legal and ethical environment, macroeconomics, microeconomics, corporate finance, management theory, marketing management, management information systems, and statistical methods. The 21-credit advanced core includes accounting for managerial analysis, entrepreneurship/intrapreneurship; communication and negotiations, building shareholder value, developing human resources, leadership and innovation, technology management, and total quality management. Specializations are available in accounting, corporate finance, health services administration, human resources, management information systems (MIS), and marketing.

Students with four years' managerial experience may elect the GOAL M.B.A. program. This accelerated program requires fourteen courses taken two courses per term

over seven 8-week terms. Courses are held on Saturdays only. The School also offers an innovative joint M.B.A. in management/M.S. in nursing administration. A post-master's certificate in human resource management is open to students with master's degrees in any field.

Students and the M.B.A. Experience

The School's 251 graduate students form a diverse and vibrant community. They come from across the United States and represent twelve other countries. Undergraduate majors range from anthropology and economics to nursing and fine arts, and students' professional backgrounds range from bank officer and senior accountant to government officials and entrepreneurs. Almost three quarters (73 percent) are part-time students. Of students who started in fall 2004, close to two thirds completed their degree in three years. Students' average age is 32, and 50.6 percent are women. Guest speakers, internship opportunities, and the Distinguished Executive Lecture Series further enhance the learning environment. Professional clubs and organizations provide forums to exchange ideas. The School has been granted a charter for the Beta Xi chapter of Delta Mu Delta, one of the oldest national honor societies in business administration. Delta Mu Delta is a member of the Association of College Honor Societies.

Special Features

Most graduate students in the School of Business attend part-time and are working full-time. To accommodate their busy schedules and make it easier for them to complete their degrees, courses are offered at both the main Garden City campus and the Hauppauge Center. Courses for all

graduate degree and certificate programs are scheduled Monday through Thursday evenings and Saturday mornings in Garden City. Each course meets once a week. Qualified students may also select the fast-track GOAL M.B.A. program option.

The Faculty

There are 37 full-time faculty members in the School of Business, all with advanced degrees. The faculty is known for its teaching excellence. Over the past few years, the School has hired a number of new faculty members with specialties in management, marketing, and decision sciences; accounting and law; and finance and economics. Students should visit http://adelphi.edu/faculty/profiles for complete faculty information. Anthony Libertella, Ph.D., Ohio State University, and J.D., St. John's University, is Dean of the School of Business, Special Assistant to the President for Business Development, and Professor of Management and Law.

The Business School Network

The alumni network is global, and the School enjoys especially close ties in the New York metropolitan area. More than 100 business leaders have spoken to Adelphi's students in a variety of formal and informal settings, and many are Adelphi University graduates. Recent guests include John Phelan Jr., former CEO, NYSE; Bob Catell, CEO, Keyspan; Bob Willumstad, former President, Citigroup; Dan Craig, General Manager/Vice President, Nordstrom Department Store; Ray Jansen, former Publisher, President, and CEO, *Newsday*; and Chris McCann, President, 1-800-FLOWERS.com.

The School's Business Advisory Board includes Vincent Fusco, Field Vice President, New York Region, Allstate Insurance Company; Roslyn Goldmacher, President and CEO, Long Island Development Corporation; Douglas McKenna, retired and former Vice President and General Manager, AGT&T Northeast Region, Federal Express; Jason McKenna, Advisor, UBS Paine Webber; Stephen Mischo, Vice President Special Assets Department, State Bank of New York; Paul Salerno, Partner, Pricewaterhouse-Coopers; Michael Watt, Executive Director, Long Island Partnership; and Michael Schwartz, Partner, Schwartz and Co., LLP.

The College and Environs

Located in historic Garden City, New York, 45 minutes from Manhattan and 20 minutes from Queens, Adelphi's 75-acre suburban campus is known for the beauty of its landscape and architecture. The campus is a short walk from the Long Island Railroad and convenient to New York's major airports and several major highways. Off-campus centers are located in Manhattan, Hauppauge, and Poughkeepsie. Students enjoy the benefits of being close to the financial, medical, and technological centers and cultural and sporting facilities of Manhattan and Long Island. The campus is close to fine restaurants and shopping and 15 minutes from Long Island's beautiful beaches.

Technology Environment

The Office of Information Technology and Resources provides technology-related services to the academic and administrative sectors of the University. Students have access to general and special-purpose computer labs across the University, including the business building. The Information Commons in Swirbul Library has extensive computer facilities. The Commuter Student Lounge in the University Center also provides computers and Internet access.

Placement

Career-related activities are coordinated by the University's Center for Career Development, which oversees on-campus recruitment and aims to prepare students well ahead of that process by encouraging them to schedule individual career interviews and attend career workshops as they proceed through their studies. The Center holds special receptions for employers and students as well as career seminars on resume writing and interviewing. On-campus events feature guest speakers from various corporations, who discuss career paths and opportunities. Internships place qualified students in part-time positions in their field of study, for which they earn academic credit by completing independent projects.

Admission

Applicants must have a bachelor's degree from an accredited college or university and provide official academic transcripts, an essay, GMAT scores, and two letters of recommendation from academic or professional sources. Additional requirements for international students may be found at http://admissions.adelphi.edu/international.

Finances

The 2007–08 tuition rate was $730 per credit hour. University fees ranged from about $250 to $300 per semester. Students should also plan for expenditures associated with books, travel, and personal items. Financial aid counseling is available. Students may qualify for federal and state aid programs, scholarships, and fellowship programs, including a limited number of graduate assistantships.

Application Facts and Dates

The School of Business accepts applicants on a rolling basis.

Application deadlines for international students are May 1 for the fall semester and November 1 for the spring semester.

For more information, students should contact:

Office of Admissions
Adelphi University
1 South Avenue
Garden City, New York 11530-4299
Phone: 516-877-4670
        (School of Business)
    516-877-3050
        (University Admissions)
    800-ADELPHI (toll-free)
        (University Admissions)
E-mail: admissions@adelphi.edu
Web site: http://www.adelphi.edu

Alfred University

Alfred, New York

THE ADVANTAGES OF AN ALFRED UNIVERSITY M.B.A.

"The principle goal of education in the schools should be creating men and women who are capable of doing new things, not simply repeating what other generations have done; men and women who are creative, inventive and discovers, who can be critical and verify, and not accept, everything they are offered." —Jean Piaget, quoted in Education for Democracy, *Proceedings from the Cambridge School Conference on Progressive Education.*

Piaget captures the essence of what will be your educational experience at Alfred. We will build a leader who is able to take complex problems and solve them through creative means, by thinking outside the box, and by bringing others into the solution through the use of teamwork and individual empowerment.

The College of Business' M.B.A. Program, accredited by AACSB-International, truly produces Individuals. Inspired.

Programs and Curricular Focus

The College of Business at Alfred University awards the Master of Business Administration (M.B.A.) degree. The program, which may be completed in one to two years depending on previous course work, leads to a general management degree that emphasizes leadership development.

The Alfred M.B.A. program is designed to prepare managers for the changing, global work environment of the twenty-first century and features team-oriented classes designed to develop leadership, teamwork, and a high level of camaraderie among students.

The curriculum has three components: foundation courses, the integrated core, and graduate electives. Foundation courses feature fundamentals of business knowledge that can be completed at the undergraduate level prior to starting the program or as part of the program. Typically, students who have an undergraduate degree in business (or a similar field) have already completed most, if not all, foundation requirements.

The integrated cross-disciplinary core reflects the current and emerging trends in management. Core courses have a balance of qualitative and quantitative course work to prepare students for effective leadership and management.

In addition to the required core, students must complete four electives as part of the program. Elective courses are designed to help students explore particular facets of business with an emphasis on strategic management.

Alfred University offers several options for completing the M.B.A. degree. For students who have completed all of the foundation requirements, the M.B.A. program can be completed in one year on a full-time basis. For students who have not completed any foundation requirements, the program can take up to four semesters or two years to complete. Students can also study on a part-time basis and take one to three courses per semester. To accommodate both part-time and full-time students, each course meets once weekly, typically in the late afternoon or early evening.

Students and the M.B.A. Experience

The average size of an M.B.A. class is 15 students. The average age of full-time students is 23. Approximately 60 percent are women, and the majority of full-time students have an undergraduate business degree. Part-time students average 22 years of age and are equally divided among business, engineering, and liberal arts backgrounds.

Alfred University's M.B.A. program offers an interdisciplinary approach to management education and focuses on practice and skill development. M.B.A. students find small classes and close interaction with faculty and peers. The College of Business is accredited by AACSB International–The Association to Advance Collegiate Schools of Business.

The Faculty

M.B.A. students benefit from faculty members who have significant practical experiences in their field of interest. The faculty members are constantly engaged in research, which enriches the classroom learning process. All College of Business graduate faculty members hold doctorates in their field.

The Business School Network

The M.B.A. program at Alfred University is supported by an advisory board composed of executives from leading companies. These corporate leaders provide significant input as to the relevance of the curriculum and trends in management practice. Students also have access to the Saxon Career Network, which is a partner network of alumni in encouraging the success of AU students and other alumni through mentoring and network opportunities.

The University and Environs

Founded in 1836, Alfred University is the oldest coeducational institution in New York State and the second oldest in the nation. Alfred grants bachelor's, master's, and doctoral degrees. The fifty-nine-building, 232-acre hillside campus adjoins the village of Alfred. The University comprises the College of Business, the College of Liberal Arts and Sciences, and the New York State College of Ceramics, which houses the School of Art and Design as well as the Inamori School of Engineering. In addition to the graduate programs in each of these colleges and schools, the graduate programs in school psychology are administered by the Division of School Psychology within the Graduate School.

Alfred University is consistently ranked among the top comprehensive universities in the Northeast.

Facilities

The College of Business is housed in the F. W. Olin Building. This $5.6-million facility offers outstanding classroom, lecture, conferencing, and laboratory facilities. The M.B.A. program is supported by three networked classrooms, as well as an advanced computer laboratory for projects. All computers have Internet access in addition to a variety of commonly used software and specialized software. Additionally, all classrooms are equipped with computers and LCD projection systems. In fall 2006, the College of Business unveiled a trading room equipped with a stock ticker and stock tracker as well as software to provide stock quotes.

The University maintains two libraries, Scholes Library of Ceramics, which supports engineering and arts programs, as well as Herrick Library, which supports liberal arts and sciences, professional studies, and the College of Business. The libraries hold more than 328,000 volumes, with more than 1,500 periodicals in print and more than 95,000 units of microforms, 4,000 units of audiovisual materials, and 170,000 slides. Library facilities provide workstations for access to the Internet and electronic subscriptions to more than 14,000 additional journal titles. Both libraries maintain online public-access catalogs.

Placement

Alfred University's Career Development Center provides students with a range of services to assist with all aspects of career development and job searching. The career development center provides individual career assistance such as resume and cover letter writing, job searching, effective interviewing, salary negotiation, and how to survive the first year of one's first job. In recent years, Alfred's M.B.A. program has experienced a very good employment rate, with graduates working at Corning Incorporated, Dresser Rand, Eli Lilly & Co., Lockheed Martin, NYSEG, Toro Energy, Wal-Mart, Alanx Composite Armor, First Investors Corporation, Guardian Fiberglass, Gunlocke, Pentair, and Wells Fargo Financial.

Admission

To be eligible for admission, an applicant must hold a four-year baccalaureate degree from an accredited college or university, and the undergraduate record must clearly indicate ability to perform credibly at the graduate level. Admission to the M.B.A. program is based on an assessment of each student's academic and professional accomplishments. To apply, students must submit a completed application form, official transcripts of all undergraduate and graduate course work, GMAT scores, and a brief personal statement. Official TOEFL scores are required from international students who have not received a baccalaureate degree from an institution in the U.S.

Finances

Tuition for the 2007–08 academic year was $30,784. Students in the M.B.A. program have access to a range of opportunities and resources. All qualified, full-time students are eligible for a half-time assistantship. This assistantship provides students with the opportunity to work with faculty members on special projects for 7.5 hours per week. For example, the College of Business hosts an annual conference in a developing country in conjunction with the United Nations International Trade Centre. Students working on this project have the opportunity to travel with the conference representative to countries such as China, Ecuador, Turkey, and the Philippines. Similar opportunities are available in other areas of business.

Financial aid, typically in the form of loans, is available. Information can be obtained from the Office of Student Financial Aid at 607-871-2159.

Application Facts and Dates

Students can apply for fall, spring, or summer admission. Applications are accepted on a rolling basis. For more information, students should contact:

Lori Hollenbeck, Director, M.B.A.
    Program
College of Business
Alfred University
One Saxon Drive
Alfred, New York 14802

Phone: 607-871-2630
Fax: 607-871-2114
E-mail: mba@alfred.edu
Web site:
    http://business.alfred.edu/mba.html

For applications, students should contact:

Office of Graduate Admissions
Alfred University
One Saxon Drive
Alfred, New York 14802-1232

Phone: 607-871-2141
        800-541-9229 (toll-free)
E-mail: gradinquiry@alfred.edu
Web site:
    http://www.alfred.edu/gradschool

American InterContinental University

Atlanta, Georgia; Weston, Florida; Houston, Texas; London, England; and Dubai, United Arab Emirates

▶ **DEVELOPING BUSINESS LEADERS FOR THE TWENTY-FIRST CENTURY**

American InterContinental University (AIU) offers an M.B.A. with an emphasis on team-based learning that embraces the talents of its diverse student population. Instructors with both advanced degrees in their disciplines and practical experience teach courses that effectively leverage students' varied business and educational backgrounds. Course work allows opportunities for application of theory in project-based instruction that is firmly grounded in the paradigm of the contemporary employment market.

—Dr. Terry Dixon, Provost and Chief Academic Officer

Programs and Curricular Focus

The Master of Business Administration (M.B.A.) is offered at the Atlanta (Dunwoody and Buckhead) and Fort Lauderdale campuses. This eight-course, 48-quarter-credit-hour M.B.A. program is designed to give students the knowledge, skills, and practical experience-based education necessary to accelerate their careers. The program is based on adult learning theory and concepts. This team-based learning model focuses on team collaboration and problem solving, providing students with the skills today's businesses need most.

AIU offers flexible schedules with options for online, on-campus, and a blended learning component consisting of both models. This allows students maximum scheduling convenience and program course offerings.

The M.B.A. foundation courses must be completed prior to being admitted to the full M.B.A. program. Interested students should contact the admissions department at their campus of choice for the list of courses offered at a specific location.

AIU is proud to provide students with a university education that is career-oriented and industry-current. Therefore, curriculum is frequently updated to continuously reflect the skills and knowledge required by industry. All programs of study are subject to change without notice.

The campuses in Fort Lauderdale, Buckhead, and Dunwoody feature more than 1,000 ports to deliver voice, data, and video throughout the building. Classrooms and team rooms are wired, allowing students to connect their laptop computers to the Internet and AIU's network. Smaller team rooms provide space for collaborative learning, allowing students to work together to solve real business problems. Each campus houses a media center, including a library.

Students and the M.B.A. Experience

Business in the global community is increasingly important in today's organizations, and the curriculum at AIU emphasizes a global perspective and uses the diversity of the student body to enhance global learning. AIU is proud of the diversity of its students, including both the ethnic variety represented in the M.B.A. programs across the various campus locations and the representation of students from more than thirty different countries. Applications are received from around the world. Students typically represent such fields as telecommunications, health care, manufacturing, finance, information technology, retail, and service organizations.

AIU students are highly motivated and dedicated; many attend classes while maintaining careers, working at part-time jobs, and raising families. Interactions with class and team members, including working on assigned projects, teach collaboration in real time and ultimately create lasting friendships, contacts, and networks for years to come.

The Business School Network

AIU relies on business and industry to identify what skills employers require and develops curriculum to meet those needs. The Advisory Council has been instrumental in the development of this market-driven curriculum, and regular, periodic reviews of the curriculum help students receive the most current skills needed in the marketplace. AIU uses both a theoretical and hands-on approach to learning, which is designed to provide students with background understanding and practical application. Students frequently discuss and solve real-life problems in classes and projects. With the variety of work experience represented in the student body, M.B.A. students are exposed to many different applications and business approaches to decision making and problem solving.

AIU's adjunct faculty members are experts in their various fields, with years of consulting and corporate experience to share with students. M.B.A. students are able to work with practitioners currently engaged in their fields and apply the most current information to their research and projects. When combined with the international diversity of the M.B.A. student body, this leading-edge information provides many varied and exceptional approaches to business problems and solutions.

The University and Environs

American InterContinental University is a coeducational, nondenominational institution with a reputation for global academic excellence that offers global career-oriented education to a diverse student body. The University was first established in 1970 in Europe and has since grown into a network of campuses.

The Atlanta (Dunwoody and Buckhead) campuses are located in the growing business community of the city of Atlanta. In the metropolitan area of Fort Lauderdale, long known for its international flavor and beaches, the campus is located in the community of Weston. The London campus is located in central London, the design, media, and business capital of Europe. In Dubai, students can experience both beautiful beaches and a thriving business center that is a blend of modern conveniences and colorful traditions.

At the campus in Dubai, students have the option of residing in modern, attractively furnished apartments with a variety of amenities that may include swimming pools, tennis courts, and a clubhouse on site.

The Faculty

The level of professional expertise of the faculty members enhances the quality of the M.B.A. program. AIU uses both full-time faculty and adjunct professors in the M.B.A. programs. This provides both continuity from faculty members and information on current business practices and experience from practitioners in the field. All AIU faculty members integrate conceptual knowledge with practical application to maximize the learning experience for all students.

Placement

The AIU Career Services department works actively with students on all aspects of the job search process, from assessment of current skills and resume and cover letter development to interview preparation and career management. Career services are a combination of both in-class seminars and individualized career counseling. On-campus career fairs are hosted during the year to provide students with the opportunity to meet with a variety of recruiters. Full-time professionals dedicated solely to providing career opportunities at their campus staff the Career Services department.

Admission

A major difference between AIU and many other colleges and universities is the culturally diverse student population. AIU students come from many different countries and backgrounds and bring a wide range of viewpoints, special interests, and talents to enrich the learning community. Selection of students is based on an individual assessment of each applicant. For more information or to enroll online, students should visit http://www.aiuniv.edu.

Finances

AIU offers federal and state programs to eligible students to assist in the financing of their education. Students should contact the appropriate campus to obtain further information about financial assistance.

International Students

AIU welcomes international students. Approximately 5 percent (or more) of the AIU student population is composed of international students. Many different countries are represented in the student body at AIU, and each campus has an international flavor that enables the program to be highly effective and popular with the students.

Application Facts and Dates

AIU—Atlanta-Dunwoody Campus
660 Peachtree Dunwoody Road
500 Embassy Row
Atlanta, Georgia 30328
Phone: 404-965-6500
          888-353-1744 (toll-free)
Fax: 404-965-6501
Web site: http://www.aiudunwoody.com

AIU—Atlanta-Buckhead Campus
3330 Peachtree Road NE
Atlanta, Georgia 30326
Phone: 404-965-5700
          888-999-4248 (toll-free)
Fax: 404-965-5701
Web site: http://www.aiubuckhead.com

AIU—Fort Lauderdale Campus
2250 North Commerce Parkway,
    Suite 100
Weston, Florida 33324
Phone: 954-446-6100
Web site: http://www.aiufl.edu

AIU—London
110 Marylebone High Street
London W1U 4RY, England
Phone: 44-207-467-5600
Fax: 44-207-935-8144
Web site: http://www.aiulondon.ac.uk

AIU—Dubai Campus
P.O. Box 28282
Dubai, United Arab Emirates
Phone: 971-4-399-9000
Fax: 971-4-399-8899
Web site: http://www.aiuniv.edu

Argosy University

PRACTICAL COMPETENCIES FOR TODAY'S GLOBAL ECONOMY

> Argosy focuses on developing the interpersonal competencies and solutions-focused analytical skills that make a difference to students as individuals and to the organizations for which they work. The result is an M.B.A. program geared toward our students' success.
>
> —Tom Vonk, Dean, College of Business, Argosy University

Programs and Curricular Focus

The key to success in today's complex business environment is finding workable solutions and taking personal actions as well as motivating the appropriate others to move toward the same goal. The College of Business at Argosy University builds personal competencies and technical skills in preparing managers to solve problems and take action to benefit their organizations and their communities.

The M.B.A. program requires the student to develop the necessary technical skills in a chosen discipline and especially focuses on the means to get things done, drawing on appropriate technology, providing necessary motivation and coaching to colleagues, and having the confidence to implement effective solutions.

The University's faculty combines practical professional experience with formal academic training to develop the expertise and judgment demanded by organizations.

The M.B.A. program enhances current or future career potential. For students committed to a philosophy of lifelong learning, the M.B.A. also prepares students for further study (e.g., D.B.A. programs or executive doctoral programs). The degree also serves the needs of talented students regardless of their undergraduate degrees, providing appropriate foundational training options for those who seek the M.B.A. without formal academic business training. The College of Business welcomes and encourages students from diverse academic backgrounds to continue their education and raise their career potential.

The M.B.A. program consists of eight core courses and four concentration courses, for a total of twelve courses, or 36 semester credit hours. After completing the core course requirements, students develop expertise and specific insights in a chosen area of concentration. Students must select one of the following concentrations offered within the M.B.A. program: customized professional concentration, finance, health-care administration, information systems management, international business, management, or marketing. Regardless of the concentration selected, the M.B.A. program culminates in a capstone project that integrates core competencies with concentration-area applications.

Argosy University is accredited by the Higher Learning Commission and is a member of the North Central Association (NCA, 30 North LaSalle Street, Suite 2400, Chicago, Illinois 60602; 800-621-7440 (toll-free); http://www.ncahlc.org).

Students and the M.B.A. Experience

Argosy University provides a supportive educational environment with convenient class options that enable students to earn a degree while fulfilling other life responsibilities. All of the programs are thoroughly oriented to the practical working world, focusing on developing technical proficiency in each field of study as well as fundamental management competencies.

The M.B.A. program is designed to help graduates enter the workforce with the skills necessary to be competitive and achieve success in today's complex business environment.

Argosy University offers unique opportunities for student involvement beyond individual programs of study. Most faculty committees include a student representative. In addition, a student group meets with faculty members and administrators regularly to discuss pertinent campus-related issues.

Special Features

Faculty and staff members believe that education, experience, and enthusiasm are the keys to success in career and life. Full-time students and working professionals gain the extensive knowledge and range of skills necessary for effective performance in their chosen field.

Argosy University is a private institution with nineteen locations across the nation, offering degree programs that focus on the human side of success alongside professional competence. It just may be the answer for students who seek a more personal approach to education. Argosy University provides students with a network of resources found at larger universities, including a career resources office, an academic resources center, and extensive information access for research. The school offers students the resources of a large university and the friendliness and personal attention of a small campus.

Argosy University's innovative M.B.A. program features dynamic, relevant, and practical curricula delivered in flexible class formats. Students enjoy scheduling options that make it easy to fit school into their busy lives. They can choose from day and evening courses, either on campus or online. Most students find a combination of both to be the most effective way of continuing their education while meeting family and professional demands.

The Faculty

The Argosy University faculty consists of working professionals who are eager to help students succeed. Members bring real-world experience and the latest practice innovations to the academic setting. Instructor experience ranges from running a family business to leading a multinational corporation.

The diverse faculty is widely recognized for contributions to the business field. Most hold doctoral degrees. They provide a substantive education that combines comprehensive knowledge with critical skills and practical workplace relevance. Above all, faculty members of the College of Business are committed to their students' personal and professional development.

The College and Environs

The M.B.A. program is offered at all of the following nineteen Argosy University College of Business locations:

Atlanta, 980 Hammond Drive, Suite 100, Atlanta, Georgia 30328; phone: 770-671-1200 or 888-671-4777 (toll-free)

Chicago, 225 North Michigan Avenue, Suite 1300, Chicago, Illinois 60601; phone: 312-777-7600 or 800-626-4123 (toll-free)

Dallas, 8080 Park Lane, Suite 400A, Dallas, Texas 75231; phone: 214-890-9900 or 866-954-9900 (toll-free)

Denver, 1200 Lincoln Street, Denver, Colorado 80203; phone: 303-248-2700 or 866-431-5981 (toll-free)

Hawai'i, 400 ASB Tower, 1001 Bishop Street, Honolulu, Hawaii 96813; phone: 808-536-5555 or 888-323-2777 (toll-free)

Inland Empire, 636 East Brier Drive, Suite 120, San Bernardino, California 92408; phone: 909-915-3800 or 866-217-9075 (toll-free)

Los Angeles, 2950 31st Street, Santa Monica, California 90405; phone: 310-866-4000 or 866-505-0332 (toll-free)

Nashville, 100 Centerview Drive, Suite 225, Nashville, Tennessee 37214; phone: 615-525-2800 or 866-833-6598 (toll-free)

Orange County, 3501 West Sunflower Avenue, Suite 110, Santa Ana, California 92704; phone: 714-338-6200 or 800-716-9598 (toll-free)

Phoenix, 2233 West Dunlap Avenue, Phoenix, Arizona 85021; phone: 602-216-2600 or 866-216-2777 (toll-free)

Salt Lake City, 121 Election Road, Suite 300, Draper, Utah 84020; phone: 888-639-4756 (toll-free)

San Diego, 7650 Mission Valley Road, San Diego, California 92108; phone: 858-598-1900 or 866-505-0333 (toll-free)

San Francisco Bay Area, 1005 Atlantic Avenue, Alameda, California 94501; phone: 510-217-4700 or 866-215-2777 (toll-free)

Sarasota, 5250 17th Street, Sarasota, Florida 34235; phone: 941-379-0404 or 800-331-5995 (toll-free)

Schaumburg, 999 North Plaza Drive, Suite 111, Schaumburg, Illinois 60173-5403; phone: 847-969-4900 or 866-290-2777 (toll-free)

Seattle, 2601-A Elliott Avenue, Seattle, Washington 98121; phone: 206-283-4500 or 888-283-2777 (toll-free)

Tampa, Parkside at Tampa Bay Park, 4401 North Hines Avenue, Suite 150, Tampa, Florida 33614; phone: 813-393-5290 or 800-850-6488 (toll-free)

Twin Cities, 1515 Central Parkway, Eagan, Minnesota 55121; phone: 651-846-2882 or 888-844-2004 (toll-free)

Washington DC, 1550 Wilson Boulevard, Suite 600, Arlington, Virginia 22209; phone: 703-526-5800 or 866-703-2777 (toll-free)

Facilities

Argosy University libraries provide curriculum support and educational resources, including current text materials, diagnostic training documents, reference materials and databases, journals and dissertations, and major and current titles in program areas. There is an online public-access catalog of library resources available throughout the Argosy University system. Students have full remote access to the campus library database, enabling them to study and conduct research at home. Academic databases offer dissertation abstracts, academic journals, and professional periodicals. All library computers are Internet accessible. Software applications include Word, Excel, PowerPoint, SPSS, and various test-scoring programs.

Placement

Students can register with the University's online career-services system and use select services from a distance, such as degree-specific career e-mail lists, national job posts, and virtual job fairs. Students should contact the University for more information.

Admission

Admission requirements include a bachelor's degree from a regionally accredited institution, a nationally accredited institution approved and documented by the faculty and dean of the College of Business, or an appropriately certified international institution; either a grade point average of at least 3.0 (on a scale of 4.0) for the last 60 hours of course work (including graduate work) or a minimum 2.7 cumulative grade point average; and a minimum TOEFL score of 550 (paper version), 213 (computer version), or 79 (Internet version) for all applicants whose native language is not English or who have not graduated from an institution at which English is the language of instruction.

Students who do not meet the minimum GPA requirement are also required to submit a personal/professional goal statement with a self-appraisal of qualifications for the profession, a current resume, and the names and contact information of 3 professional and/or academic references.

All applications for admission must be submitted to the Admissions Department. An admissions representative is available to help applicants complete the following required documentation: an Application for Admission Form, the application fee (nonrefundable, except in California), and official transcripts from all postsecondary schools attended.

Finances

A wide range of financial aid options is available to students who qualify. Argosy University offers access to federal and state aid programs, merit-based awards, grants, loans, and work-study. As a first step, students should complete the Free Application for Federal Student Aid (FAFSA). Prospective students can apply electronically at http://www.fafsa.ed.gov or in person at the campus. To receive consideration for the maximum amount of aid and ensure timely receipt of funds, it is best for applicants to submit an application promptly. Students should contact Argosy University for tuition information.

Application Facts and Dates

Argosy University accepts students year-round on a rolling admissions basis, depending on availability of required courses. Applications for admission are available online or by contacting the campus.

Argosy University Administrative Office
Phone: 800-377-0617 (toll-free)
Web site: http://www.argosy.edu

Auburn University

College of Business

Auburn University, Alabama

EDUCATION FOR SUCCESS IN THE TWENTY-FIRST CENTURY

At one time, a successful student in a business school graduated after having accumulated new knowledge almost exclusively. The emergence of technology, increasing global competition, multimillion-dollar corporate ethical lapses, the rate of speed at which business is changing, and many other factors dictate that knowledge alone is not sufficient. Business schools must now integrate around a new triad that includes the mastery of a variety of skill sets and the ability to interpret and understand the organizational context as well as learning business knowledge. The Auburn M.B.A. is grounded in the practical, where theory and practice must converge. We believe that the practitioner, whether a business leader, an entrepreneur, or a governmental official, has valuable insights into the roles, practice, and environment of business that need to be shared with our M.B.A. students. We see the curriculum, extracurricular activities, faculty members, and the practitioners all working together to provide an exceptional value for our students. We invite you to learn more about the values that set the Auburn graduates apart from their contemporaries.

—Paul M. Bobrowski, Dean

Programs and Curricular Focus

Auburn University's Master of Business Administration program is fully accredited by AACSB International–The Association to Advance Collegiate Schools of Business. The Auburn M.B.A. Program was ranked sixty-ninth (out of 400 public universities) by *U.S. News & World Report* for 2006. The M.B.A. program is designed to prepare students for positions of leadership in public and private enterprise. The program consists of a minimum of 36 semester hours of course work. At Auburn, the focus is on the core analytical and communication skills that best prepare students for an uncertain future. The program incorporates a mix of theory with practical applications and supplements traditional lectures with case analyses. While the program keeps abreast of the latest trends, it is not trendy. The curriculum has staying power; it reflects the broad, fundamental knowledge upon which students can build a successful career, while allowing students to specialize and develop further expertise in a particular area of concentration.

Students take eight core courses in the program and four electives. Students may choose their electives to earn a concentration in a variety of functional areas, which can include agribusiness, economics, finance, health care, logistics, management information systems, management of technology, marketing, natural resources management, operations management, and supply chain management. A team-based strategy case analysis is the capstone requirement for the degree. Core M.B.A. classes typically have

55 students in them. Most students can complete the program in three semesters of full-time work plus a summer internship (optional for students who have two or more years of full-time work experience). All Auburn M.B.A. students are required to have taken undergraduate courses in calculus and statistics prior to entering the program. In addition, students must have acquired an adequate background in the fundamentals of business principles, which is met through completion of course work in accounting, economics, finance, management, and marketing. In lieu of completing undergraduate courses in each of these fields, students may choose to take certificate courses and pass competency examinations purchased from and administered through the M.B.A. office (Business Certificate Series self-study courses).

Since 1990, the Auburn M.B.A. has also been available off campus through the video-based Graduate Outreach Program. More than 1,350 students have completed their degrees through this flexible, innovative program. This program offers professionals the opportunity to earn a graduate business degree while maintaining full-time employment, travel, and personal responsibilities wherever they may be located in the United States and Canada and on U.S. military bases. Outreach M.B.A. students receive the same instruction with the same faculty members as on-campus students and complete all class assignments and tests (via a proctor at their location). Students from across the United States in Fortune 500 companies, small firms, and all branches of

the military are currently earning an Auburn M.B.A. through the Graduate Outreach Program. Only one 5-day campus residency is required, immediately prior to completing the online degree program.

The most recent program additions are the Executive M.B.A. (E.M.B.A.) and the Physicians Executive M.B.A. (PEMBA) degree options (with health care and technology concentrations). These tracks were designed to give full-time working professionals the opportunity to earn a fully accredited M.B.A. degree in less than two years. Both the E.M.B.A. and the PEMBA combine video-based classes with the traditional, on-campus experience. Students receive DVD-based instruction coupled with several campus residency experiences and an international study trip. These programs offer the innovation and flexibility necessary to create a cohesive learning environment.

Students and the M.B.A. Experience

There are approximately 450 students in Auburn's M.B.A. program. Ninety of these students are enrolled in the on-campus full-time M.B.A. program. The average GMAT for the entering class in the fall of 2007 was 637, with an average GPA of 3.43. Thirty-one percent of the students are women, and 34 percent are international students. Degree backgrounds include business (33 percent), engineering (33 percent), and liberal arts (15 percent), with the remainder a mix of other disciplines.

While full-time work experience is not a requirement for admission, it is strongly encouraged. Many on-campus students have significant business experience to bring to the classroom. For those students who do not, a summer-term internship while in the program is required. While teamwork is a strong focus within the curriculum, individual responsibility and accountability are stressed as well. There are a number of professional student associations on campus, including an active M.B.A. student association that sponsors many activities of professional networking exposure as well as social events throughout the year.

The Faculty

The M.B.A. faculty members of Auburn University's College of Business excel as instructors and researchers. All are full-time

tenure-track faculty members who have doctoral degrees, and all are actively involved in research and consulting, keeping at the forefront of their disciplines. Good teaching is taken seriously, and that is reflected in the quality of classroom instruction. By keeping the classes small, professors can take the time to work with the students individually. By making themselves available outside of the classroom, the faculty members provide a supportive atmosphere for learning while at the same time challenging students to succeed.

The Business School Network

Interactions with the business community, through guest executives, company visits, and case analyses, are as important a component of an M.B.A. as the classroom lecture. That interaction strengthens the context in which students develop their understanding of theory as well as practical applications. The Auburn program is constantly developing new networks and linkages for the students.

Corporate Partnerships

The Auburn M.B.A. Alumni Advisory Board, comprising 30 prominent business leaders throughout the United States, works closely with the M.B.A. program to provide both programmatic advice and financial support. In addition, they actively work to identify and expand placement and internship opportunities, serve as guest lecturers for the classroom, recruit companies to host site visits, and participate in team-based strategic analyses. They also cosponsor social events throughout the year, including football tailgate events and other informal gatherings that provide students opportunities to discuss various business issues one-on-one with experienced professionals.

Prominent Alumni

Auburn M.B.A. graduates hold senior positions in local, national, and international companies, including BellSouth, Chevron, Eastman Chemical, The Home Depot, BearingPoint, IBM, KPGM, Hewlett-Packard, Boeing, McDonnell Douglas, Southern Company, Michelin, and many others.

The College and Environs

Auburn University, ranked by *U.S. News & World Report* as one of the nation's top fifty public universities in 2006–07, is a land-grant institution dedicated to serving Alabama and the nation through instruction, research, and extension.

Chartered in 1856, the University is located in the friendly, small-town environment of Auburn, Alabama. The University's beautiful 1,900-acre campus is home to 23,700 students (including 3,900 business students), 1,100 faculty members, a library with almost 3 million volumes, and more than fifty major academic buildings.

Auburn is approximately a 2-hour drive from the metropolitan areas of Atlanta, Georgia, and Birmingham, Alabama, and a 4-hour drive from the Gulf Coast beaches and Florida Panhandle.

Facilities

Classes are held in a $15-million facility that is one of the most modern structures of its type in the United States. The building includes curved and tiered classrooms, a large executive conference room designed as a formal reception area to entertain business guests and host small meetings, four video M.B.A. classrooms, and six audiovisual classrooms linked to the Auburn University satellite system. All classrooms are equipped with computer teaching terminals and data projectors to support the highest level of interactive instruction. The quality of the educational environment provided by the building is among the finest in the country. There are six computer labs and a wireless network available throughout the building.

Placement

The Auburn University and M.B.A. placement offices provide students with personal help on developing interview skills, resume preparation, alumni networking, and access to on-campus corporate recruiting. In addition, placement efforts within the M.B.A. program include direct contacts with businesses and position notifications for internships and full-time employment in addition to career fairs and hosting of visiting companies.

Admission

The Auburn M.B.A. program accepts applications for the on-campus program for fall semester only. Applications for the distance M.B.A. program are accepted for fall and spring semesters. Applicants must submit transcripts of all previous college work, current GMAT and TOEFL scores, completed Graduate School and M.B.A. applications, a resume, two essays, and three letters of recommendation with a $25 application fee ($50 for international students). Prior work experience is a plus, and personal interviews are required, either in person or via telephone.

Finances

On-campus tuition per semester for the 2007–08 academic year was $2625 for in-state students and $7875 for out-of-state students. Fees for the video-based M.B.A. program were $598 per credit hour. All M.B.A. classes are 3 semester credit hours each.

Application Facts and Dates

Applications are accepted for fall semester only for the on-campus program. The application deadline for the fall semester is March 1. Applications are accepted for the fall and spring semesters for the distance M.B.A. program. The application deadline for the spring semester is September 1. Students are strongly encouraged to submit completed applications well in advance of these deadlines. E.M.B.A. and PEMBA applications are due July 1. International students should apply earlier if possible.

Completed applications are reviewed by the M.B.A. Admission Committee on a competitive admissions basis, and students are generally informed within six to eight weeks of the deadline date. For more information, students should contact:

M.B.A. Program Admissions
415 W. Magnolia Avenue, Suite 503
Auburn University
Auburn, Alabama 36849

Phone: 334-844-4060
Fax: 334-844-2964
E-mail: mbainfo@auburn.edu
Web site: http://www.mba.business.
auburn.edu

Babson College

EDUCATING THE WORLD'S FUTURE ENTREPRENEURIAL LEADERS

The Graduate School of Business at Babson College is committed to educating entrepreneurial leaders. Entrepreneurial leadership is a way of thinking and acting to create opportunities. Recognized as the world leader in entrepreneurial education and as a leader in integrated curriculum design, Babson is a very special place to study. Students are noted for their creativity, teamwork, and ability to see business problems from a holistic perspective. I know that as you read more about Babson, you will want to become a part of this unique educational community.

Programs and Curricular Focus

The F. W. Olin Graduate School of Business at Babson College cultivates entrepreneurial thinking that students can apply in start-up ventures and the corporate environment. There are four degree programs that prepare students to become superior managers and meet the needs of progressive organizations.

The full-time Two-Year M.B.A. program features a modular curriculum that integrates the functional disciplines of business into one cohesive program. First-year course work and activities take students through each step of the business development cycle. The first-year curriculum, which emphasizes teamwork, employs varied approaches to address entrepreneurial thinking within established corporate environments as well as in start-ups, innovation as a strategic tool, the importance of effective leadership in bringing about change, the value of teamwork, the importance of having a global advantage, and quality as a competitive advantage.

The highlight of the first year of study is the Babson Consulting Alliance Program, which assigns student teams to yearlong projects with local businesses. In the second year, elective courses let students focus on their specific career goals and interests.

The One-Year M.B.A. is an accelerated program that allows students with an undergraduate business degree to complete their M.B.A. in three rigorous full-time semesters. Beginning each May, students enroll in a series of integrated modules for their first semester and then join the second-year M.B.A. students to complete the equivalent of fifteen courses in one calendar year. Candidates who work in the Boston area may complete the summer modules full-time, return to work in September, and finish the remainder of the program on a part-time basis in two years.

The Evening M.B.A. is a part-time program for working professionals that provides an integrated learning approach to the key functional areas, which students can immediately apply to their work. The Evening M.B.A. program begins each fall and spring and builds on a more compact core of courses, four of which are fully integrated. These integrated courses feature a cross-disciplinary approach designed to encourage students to analyze how management works. The Evening M.B.A. program not only provides increased flexibility, but also enables students to complete the degree in approximately three years. Students can complete their degrees even faster if they opt for full-time status.

The Fast Track M.B.A. program is a hybrid-format M.B.A. program that enables students to earn their M.B.A. in twenty-four months while remaining on the job. Course work and activities trace the business development cycle, from recognizing and assessing a business opportunity and formulating a strategy to creating and implementing the delivery system and, finally, to evolving the strategy and systems as conditions change over time.

Students and the M.B.A. Experience

Students in the Two-Year M.B.A. program are, on average, 28 years old and have five years of work experience. GMAT scores range from 510 to 760. Women make up 29 percent of the class. Students come from such diverse industries as banking and investment institutions to biotechnology, high technology, hospitality, nonprofit businesses, and consulting. The Two-Year M.B.A. class is international and represents twenty-six countries.

Global Focus

Global business perspectives are not new at Babson. To complete the Global Man-

agement Concentration, students participate in international course work or internships, as well as courses that emphasize a global perspective. The Global Management Program places students in structured field-consulting projects with corporations around the world. International electives combine intensive classroom experience with industry-based projects in international settings. International internships, electives, and study-abroad opportunities are open to students in all Babson M.B.A. programs.

Special Features

Babson fosters the entrepreneurial spirit through a variety of activities and opportunities, including electives, endowed chairs in entrepreneurship, induction of innovative businesspeople into the Academy of Distinguished Entrepreneurs on Founder's Day, the Douglass Foundation Entrepreneurial Prizes, and the Babson Entrepreneurial Group, an organization that is dedicated to promoting, cultivating, and nurturing the entrepreneurial spirit that is unique to Babson.

The Faculty

Babson's faculty is an internationally and professionally diverse group, representing nations in Asia, Australia, Europe, and North and South America and with backgrounds in pharmaceuticals, banking, high technology, retailing, and other industries. They are practitioners and scholars, executives and teachers, and researchers and consultants who have lived and worked in international settings.

The Business School Network
Corporate Partnerships

Successful business partnerships have always been a major component of Babson's programs. First-year student teams consult with Boston-area organizations through the yearlong Babson Consulting Alliance Program. The Management Consulting Field Experience offers a variety of second-year consulting projects, which can range from Fortune 500 companies to small, privately held firms, and from entrepreneurial ventures to nonprofits.

The College and Environs

Babson College, founded in 1919 by financier and entrepreneur Roger W. Babson, is

Building on the strength of more than seventy-five years of excellence in management education, Babson College embraces new challenges and opportunities and furthers successes.

located on 370 acres of woods, rolling hills, and carefully landscaped grounds in Wellesley, Massachusetts, just 14 miles from Boston. Nearby Boston, renowned for its history and cultural and intellectual life, is an exciting and lively setting for the student experience.

Facilities

Babson students have access to an extensive business collection of print, media, and electronic resources. A staff of professionals is available to help students find the information they need and to offer instruction in the use of those databases on which business practitioners rely.

The library subscribes to a browsing collection of 700 periodicals and newspapers; thousands more are available from any computer on campus through Internet subscriptions with Dow Jones Interactive, InfoTrac Web, Lexis/Nexis Universe, ProQuest Direct, FirstSearch, and Primark's Global Access.

Within Horn Library, students may access a variety of electronic resources, such as Bloomberg, Reuters, Bridge, Compustat, and Morningstar, for economics, financial information, marketing, accounting, and entrepreneurship. Group study rooms linked to Babson's computer network provide space for team meetings and individual study.

Students can select books in both management and liberal arts topics from Babson's stacks or for delivery from other area college libraries. If a resource is not available at Horn Library, students may request copies through free interlibrary loan and document delivery services.

Financial resources are also showcased in the Stephen D. Cutler Investment Man-

agement Center in the library. The center provides Babson students, faculty members, and alumni with access to state-of-the-art information resources and technology used by investment professionals in the marketplace. Some of the market data information services available include Bloomberg, Thomson One Banker, Compustat, and Baseline.

Technology Environment

The Horn Computer Center is equipped with computer workstations that run a diversified library of business-oriented programs in a Windows environment. The Horn center operates a 24-hour computer lab. The campus has over 9,000 wired network ports that support access speeds up to 100 Mb/sec. In addition to the wired network, Babson also offers wireless access in all of the residence halls, Horn Library and Computer Center, Olin Hall, Reynolds Campus Center, and Babson Executive Conference Center. All of Babson's classrooms are equipped with a robust suite of built-in multimedia technology, which includes data projection. Babson expects that entering students are comfortable with basic spreadsheet and word-processing operations.

Placement

The Center for Career Development's Relationship Management team works with students in planning a career strategy, including developing a personal marketing communication plan and preparing for networking activities and interviews.

Admission

Students are admitted to the program based on a careful evaluation of academic records, professional qualifications, GMAT scores,

and personal attributes. Interviews are required for admission to full-time M.B.A. programs. The current class's GMAT scores are in the 510 to 760 range, and the average undergraduate GPA is 3.2. International students must submit TOEFL results and official English translations of all academic documents. A minimum score of 100 (Internet-based version), 250 (computer-based version), or 600 (paper-based version) on the TOEFL is required. All candidates should have strong mathematics, computer, economics, and business writing skills.

Finances

Nine-month academic-year cost estimates for 2007–08 for the first year of the Two-Year M.B.A. program are $35,110 for tuition, $2270 for books and supplies, and approximately $18,200 for living expenses.

Twelve-month academic-year cost estimates for 2007–08 for the One-Year M.B.A. program are $48,688 for tuition and fees, $2632 for books and supplies, and approximately $24,000 for living expenses. Fast Track tuition estimate for students enrolling in September 2007 is approximately $49,800. Per-credit tuition for the Evening M.B.A. program is $1041. Merit awards include Olin Fellowships and Scholarships, Babson Fellowships and Scholarships, Forte Foundation Fellowships, Women's Leadership Awards, and several awards based on entrepreneurial accomplishments.

International Students

International students make up 44 percent of current Two-Year M.B.A. enrollment. The pre-M.B.A. orientation for international students begins two weeks before Module I classes. This intensive program consists of familiarization with the campus, library, computer center, and other services and workshops. Also, Babson faculty members present a basic introduction to economics, marketing, and the case method. Recreational and social events are also scheduled.

Application Facts and Dates

Application deadlines for the Two-Year M.B.A. program are November 15, January 15, March 15, and April 15. International applications should be submitted by January 15. Application deadlines and decision dates for all programs may be found at http://cmweb.babson.edu/MBA/admissions/applynow_timetable.aspx. For more information, applicants should contact:

Office of Graduate Admission
F. W. Olin Graduate School of Business
Babson Park, Massachusetts 02457-0310
Phone: 781-239-4317
    800-488-4512 (toll-free within
    the U.S.)
Fax: 781-239-4194
E-mail: mbaadmission@babson.edu
Web site: http://www.babson.edu/mba

Baker College

Flint, Michigan

DEVELOPING LEADERS IN THE TWENTY-FIRST CENTURY

"Executives are problem solvers; at best, they are visionaries, developing and implementing strategies for the twenty-first century." I read that definition in someone's catalog in the past. I thought then that it was a marvelous way of introducing a graduate program in business. I still do! In fact, these words are so important to the accurate description of what we do at the Baker Center for Graduate Studies that we have formulated our vision statement along the same lines: "Developing leaders, thinkers, visionaries, and problem solvers who can effectively empower both self and others in a dynamic and global economic environment."

The business programs at Baker College are the product of years of planning and are updated each year. We asked our students, our faculty and staff members, and the employers in our communities to tell us what they wanted in their leadership teams. We then set out to make sure we gave them the very best possible programs to support all those constituencies. We've even added a computer component to make the M.B.A. experience a memorable one. Most importantly, we continue to support and implement the marvelous mission and purpose statements of this organization. The M.B.A. programs at Baker College have been specifically designed with your experience, goals, and aspirations in mind.

Whether you are a manager, a professional, or an entrepreneur seeking to improve your business or leadership skills, Baker College offers you adult-oriented, practical, convenient, and efficient programs tailored for your lifestyle and needs.

—Chuck Gurden, Vice President, Graduate Admissions

Programs and Curricular Focus

Baker College's program seeks to combine the best of conventional academic training with the best of field-based learning. Most typical business disciplines are represented in the curriculum because the College believes that a successful manager must be conversant with different aspects of running any of today's organizations or companies. Thus, the standard curriculum addresses accounting, computers, finance, communications, ethics, marketing, and management. This M.B.A. program is organized into six areas of concentration: communications and information systems, research and analytical support, economic and financial applications, issues within and outside the organization, leadership and the management process, and emphasis in the chosen concentration area. Students may elect to focus their studies in one of the following areas: computer information systems, health-care management, human resource management, industrial management, international business, leadership studies, marketing, accounting, or finance.

The curriculum at Baker College is offered in two different models, which are designed to accommodate the schedules of almost all working adults. The concentration model requires a total of 50 quarter hours. A student in this program can complete their academic program in eighteen months by enrolling in two concurrent classes each term if they choose to complete it quickly. Students are expected to produce a portfolio, which is designed as both a research tool during the program and a good reference tool once the student completes the degree.

The M.B.A. programs are offered through Baker College Online and are available 24 hours a day, seven days a week from virtually anywhere in the world.

Students and the M.B.A. Experience

Baker College students bring a wide range of experience and backgrounds to the classroom. Typically, experiences represented are in areas such as business, education, psychology, engineering, and medicine. These diverse backgrounds and experiences are valued highly by Baker and are incorporated into the curriculum of the M.B.A. program.

Fifty-one percent of graduate students at Baker are women, 20 percent are members of minority groups, and about 12 percent are international students. Baker is also proud to support the educational needs of enlisted service members as part of GoArmyEd, SOC, and eArmyU.

Special Features

Baker College, a recognized leader in the development of market-worthy educational and training opportunities, stands in the unique position of being able to meet the special needs of working adults. The tradition of quality with flexibility has enabled Baker to establish accredited degree programs in a variety of nontraditional settings.

In meeting with this tradition, students take courses online in six-week sessions with no on-campus classroom requirements. As long as they have access to the Internet, they are able to attend courses—from virtually anywhere in the world.

The Faculty

Baker College faculty members know their business. Faculty members are selected for both their business experience and their academic credentials and bring great breadth and depth to the program. The flexibility of course offerings allows Baker to expose graduate students to instructors from all over the United States. This cadre of professionals, known as Baker's National Faculty, brings experience from their industries and is committed to the best education program possible.

The focus of Baker's faculty is somewhat different from traditional universities. Instead of placing an emphasis on empirical research, Baker values practitioner-oriented education. Faculty members remain continually active in their professions by consulting, conducting seminars, running their own businesses, writing, volunteering in their communities, and even working for other organizations.

The Business School Network
Corporate Partnerships

An advisory board of community leaders is established for every discipline at Baker College. These advisory boards give advice on current and future curricula, program needs or changes, employment opportunities for students, and other general advice on college activities. Students have the ability to interact with community leaders outside the classroom through the Baker College Leadership Institute.

The College and Environs

The Baker College System has evolved from schools that have been providing high-quality and practitioner-oriented degree programs in Michigan for more than a century.

The oldest of the system schools was founded in 1888 by Woodbridge Ferris in Muskegon. In 1911, Eldon Baker established Baker Business University in Flint. These two institutions merged to form the Baker College System in 1986; it is now the largest private not-for-profit independent college in the state of Michigan. Total enrollment figures, including outreach operations, for the system exceed 35,000 students. The Center for Graduate Studies has approximately 1,100 students located throughout the system and the world via Baker Online.

Facilities

The Baker College Library System is part of the PALnet system, a consortium of libraries based in Flint that supports an online catalog database of more than 750,000 holdings of the Baker College System Libraries, Kettering University, Mott Community College, and the eighteen branches of the Genesee District libraries. Baker also participates in the Online Computer Library Center interlibrary loan subsystem. The library facility also features INFOTRAC periodical indexing databases, the UMI/ProQuest General Periodicals On-Disc and Business Periodicals On-Disc full-article imaging station,

and Books-in-Print with Reviews, to name just a few of the technologies available. Fiche and microfilm collections provide additional document retrieval resources for a student who happens to be close to one of the thirteen campus locations.

Technology Environment

Every Baker College student is assigned an e-mail account. Students may also use their accounts to access the World Wide Web. Through the World Wide Web, students are able to communicate with each other and their instructors as well as members of the graduate school staff. There are more than 3,000 microcomputers in student labs available for student use.

Admission

To qualify for admission to Baker College's M.B.A. program, a student must have a bachelor's degree from a regionally accredited institution, have a 2.5 or better GPA in their undergraduate work, be able to display appropriate written communication skills, submit three letters of reference, submit a current resume, and have completed no less than three years of full-time work experience with progressive responsibility. A TOEFL score is required for all applicants for whom English is not the

native language. Once submitted, the applicant's record is evaluated by an admissions committee for the final acceptance decision.

Finances

Tuition for the 2006–07 school year was approximately $300 per quarter hour. The total program cost is approximately $15,000. The cost of books ranges from $150 to $200 each quarter.

Application Facts and Dates

Baker College uses a rolling admissions process, so there are no deadlines for applications, and students are able to begin at any quarter. Once the Admissions Committee receives an application, applicants usually receive a decision in approximately four weeks.

Chuck Gurden
Vice President for Graduate Admissions
Center for Graduate Studies
Baker College
1116 West Bristol Road
Flint, Michigan 48507-9843
Phone: 810-766-4390
   800-469-3165 (toll-free)
Fax: 810-766-4399
E-mail: chuck@baker.edu
Web site: http://online.baker.edu

 **Baylor University**

Hankamer School of Business

Waco, Texas

LEAD WITH INTEGRITY

Where you choose to attain your M.B.A. degree is an important decision. Any reputable business program can enhance your career prospects, but Baylor University can be a valuable partner on your journey in achieving your highest personal and professional potential. Baylor's Hankamer School of Business offers M.B.A. students the exceptional resources of a premier institution recognized worldwide for high academic quality, superior teaching, and a reputation for graduating students of both competence and character. At Baylor, making a difference matters.

While an M.B.A. student at Baylor, you can participate in case competitions, manage a live investment portfolio, work on live projects for actively functioning companies, study abroad, and pursue an internship at home or abroad.

We invest in promising students, offering both scholarship and assistantship awards. Baylor offers numerous financial opportunities that can make your graduate education a reality.

Come see for yourself. Experience the day as a Baylor M.B.A. student and see how the Hankamer School of Business can make a difference in your career.

—Gary Carini, Associate Dean for Graduate Programs

Programs and Curricular Focus

The Hankamer School of Business offers several M.B.A degrees designed to meet different career goals. These are the Master of Business Administration (M.B.A.), Master of Business Administration in International Management (M.B.A.-IM), and the Master of Business Administration in Information Systems (M.B.A.-ISM). Baylor also offers a joint Doctor of Jurisprudence/Master of Business Administration (J.D./M.B.A.) degree program in cooperation with Baylor School of Law. Other joint-degree programs available are business administration and information systems (M.B.A./M.S.I.S.), business administration and engineering (M.B.A./M.E.), and business administration and computer science (M.B.A./M.C.S.).

Two areas of specialization within the M.B.A. degree are health-care administration and entrepreneurship. Both specializations offer a defined series of elective courses in conjunction with the core M.B.A. classes. For more information, prospective students should go online to http://www.baylor.edu/mba/degreeoptions.

The fully integrated curriculum incorporates multidisciplinary theory and application throughout three core semesters. Students move through the core courses as a unit, creating a team approach to learning and camaraderie among class members.

Students with an undergraduate degree in business complete the three core semesters plus a summer internship in sixteen months. Students with a non-business undergraduate degree start Baylor's M.B.A. program with a semester of business prerequisites called the Integrated Management Seminar. More information can be found online at http://www.baylor.edu/mba/IMS.

Students and the M.B.A. Experience

Every day Baylor M.B.A. students are challenged to think deeper, consider a greater range of perspectives, debate alternatives intelligently, and defend their opinions boldly—gaining confidence in the process. Fellow classmates may be experienced professionals returning to school to move into advanced levels of management, or they may be recent graduates who know that an M.B.A. degree can strengthen their resume and increase their career options. A classmate may also be an international student attending Baylor who recognizes the intrinsic value advanced managerial skills bear on any given profession. Baylor M.B.A.'s use their business skills to give back to the community. More than 25 M.B.A.'s volunteer alongside business executives to help prisoners who are part of the Prison Entrepreneurship Program (PEP) prepare business plans.

The Faculty

Baylor M.B.A. students can expect a personalized and integrative educational experience administered by a highly supportive academic and administrative community. Its world-class M.B.A. faculty members are accessible, involved, and intent on students' success. Baylor Business faculty members are dedicated scholars who, collectively, publish numerous papers, books, and journal articles each year. For more information, prospective students should visit http://www.baylor.edu/mba/corefaculty.

The College and Environs

Baylor's distinctiveness lies in the University's continual pursuit of intellectual excellence and a faithfulness to the Christian tradition, which, together, inspire action on behalf of the world.

Located in Waco, Texas, Baylor's main campus is ideally situated in the center of the Lone Star State within 150 miles of four major metropolitan cities: Dallas, Houston, Austin, and San Antonio. The Waco metropolitan area offers a wealth of industry, culture, and

recreation while maintaining the charm and hospitality of a smaller town. The city itself has a population of 208,000 people and features excellent restaurants, shopping, and cultural events. Chartered in 1845 by the Republic of Texas, Baylor University is the oldest institution of higher learning in continuous operation in the state. Baylor has grown to a 735-acre campus with 14,000 students.

Facilities

A total of 170,000 square feet of educational facilities are located in the three-story Hankamer School of Business building, built in 1959, in wings added to the original building over the years and in the five story Cashion Academic Center, built in 1988. The complex provides state-of-the-art classrooms and offices for administrative staff and faculty and also houses the Kayser Auditorium (seats 256), John Graham Jones Student Center, Blume Conference Center, Southwest Securities Financial Markets Center, Graduate Center, Advanced Technology Lab, KPMG Tax Library, and banquet facilities. The central libraries, special libraries, and resource centers of Baylor house more than 1.5 million bound volumes, more than 2 million microforms and government document pieces, and thousands of audiovisual items, maps, charts, and photographs. Information is stored on microfilm, microfiche, CD-ROM, computer disks, videotape, compact discs, and cassette tapes in addition to traditional print books and journals. Students take advantage of the online catalog *Bear Cat* to search and view the libraries' vast holdings. Students can also search and download from more than 2,000 scholarly business journals onto their notebook computers for class research.

Technology Environment

Baylor's wireless data network, AirBear, is available throughout the campus. With AirBear, students as well as faculty and staff members can connect their notebook computers to the Internet from any location on campus. All M.B.A. students are required to use a notebook computer throughout their graduate business program.

Placement

A pivotal function of Baylor's Career Management is matching graduates with the perfect job opportunity. To accomplish this objective, each M.B.A. student meets personally with a Career Management staff member to determine a personalized plan of action based on his or her unique qualifications, talents, experiences, and vocational leanings.

Each semester, all M.B.A. students take a Career Management seminar class that provides important tools to help students manage their job search. The seminars address critical areas such as self-assessment, job-search strategies, and resume development, as well as provide valuable instruction on appropriate interviewing behavior, successful negotiating techniques, and how to accept a job offer in a professional manner. Topics such as "Strategy-Driven Career Plans," "Cover Letters that Work," and "Pounding the Pavement" are presented by recruiters, alumni, and career professionals who have volunteered to share strategies that can facilitate a student's professional success. Baylor's Career Management has established relationships with an impressive list of prominent corporations headquartered worldwide—ensuring significant opportunities for Baylor students in every business function and specialty. More information can be found online at http://www.baylor.edu/mba/careermanagement.

Admission

Admission to Baylor's M.B.A. program is competitive. Baylor is looking for individuals with professional work experience, outstanding scholarship, a commitment to community service, and a motivation to pursue an intense graduate business program. M.B.A. candidates should have strong analytical capabilities and communication skills. For more information, prospective students should visit http://www.baylor.edu/mba/admissions.

Finances

Baylor offers numerous graduate scholarships, assistantships, and financial aid packages that can make a graduate education a reality. Scholarships and graduate assistantships are awarded to qualified students each semester on a competitive basis. Additional information can be found online at http://www.baylor.edu/mba/expenses.

International Students

About a quarter of Baylor's M.B.A. student population is composed of international students representing myriad countries and cultures. This exciting mix of diverse perspectives both inside and outside the classroom broadens the learning experience by adding texture to discussions, exposing students to the world's people, and providing valuable insight into the subtle differences of working in an international marketplace. For additional information, students should visit http://www.baylor.edu/mba/internationalstudents.

Application Facts and Dates

The deadline for applications for admission for fall entrance is June 15; for spring entrance, November 15; and for summer entrance, April 15. Applications for admission and scholarships are processed on a rolling basis. To be competitive for scholarships and assistantships, students should submit applications by the following dates: for fall entrance, April 15; for spring entrance, October 15; and for summer entrance, February 15.

For more information, students should contact:

Laurie Wilson, Director of Graduate
    Business Degree Programs
Hankamer School of Business
Baylor University
One Bear Place #98103
Waco, Texas 76798-8013
Phone: 254-710-4163
    800-583-0622 (toll-free)
Fax: 254-710-1066
E-mail: mba_info@baylor.edu
Web site: http://www.baylor.edu/mba

Bellevue University

Bellevue, Nebraska

ONLINE EDUCATION FOR AN ONLINE WORLD

The mission of the College of Business M.B.A. program is to inspire, enable, and actively engage learners to pursue a high-quality graduate education addressing the full range of advanced business processes, strategies, and functions. To this end, College of Business faculty members use active learning online and in class, with team activities, role playing, computer simulations, case analyses, presentations, readings in the current literature, and other activities that require the student to think critically and exchange ideas with other members of the class.

Our curriculum stresses theory and application; students learn to apply business theories, concepts, practices, and standards to activities in real-world business situations.

—Donna N. McDaniel, J.D., Dean

Programs and Curricular Focus

The Master of Business Administration (M.B.A.) degree program provides students with the tools and methods required to run a business. Both the entrepreneur and the mid- to upper-level manager learn techniques to build business knowledge. The degree is composed of an 18-credit-hour core covering business managerial topics, such as financial strategy, organizational behavior, operations management, accounting, marketing, and strategic management. Nine to 12 credit hours of business electives are used to earn an M.B.A. concentration option in accounting, acquisition and contract management, executive coaching, finance, health care, human resource management, international management, management information systems, marketing, or supply chain management. The Master of Business Administration is open to any student with a bachelor's degree from an accredited college or university. However, in most cases, those who do not have an undergraduate degree in business take the foundation—9 credit hours of courses that prepare students to participate in business courses at the master's degree level.

The Master of Business Administration degree program has been accredited by the International Assembly of Collegiate Business Education (IACBE), a professional business accrediting institution.

Bellevue University also offers an Executive Master of Business Administration (eMBA), intended for mid- to senior-level managers with direct profit and loss responsibility and a desire to engage with others at the same level globally. The eMBA is a 36-credit-hour program with admission requirements that include at least five years of managerial or en-

trepreneurial experience, including profit and loss responsibility, and two letters of recommendation.

Students and the M.B.A. Experience

Bellevue University now serves nearly 8,000 students, and its diverse student body includes students from seventy-two different countries.

Since the majority of students are adult learners, they are invited to bring their work experiences to the classroom. As a result, class members learn about current business practices and problems from each other, with a better understanding of how principles are being applied in both profit and nonprofit environments.

Through Cyber-Active® Learning, the online M.B.A. utilizes the same learning model as the classroom. In fact, Bellevue University was the first accredited university to offer its entire M.B.A. program online. A supportive learning environment emphasizes principles of active learning, which exposes students to both theoretical knowledge and practical application. Traditional teacher-to-learner lectures are replaced by active involvement in the learning, using applied workplace projects through library and database research, interaction with teachers and other students, and supplementary multimedia.

Special Features

The M.B.A. program offers in-class or online options and has no prerequisite course work, regardless of a student's undergraduate degree. The degree can be completed in eighteen months and has concentrations in accounting, acquisition and contract management, executive coaching, finance, health care, human resource management, international manage-

ment, management information systems, marketing, and supply chain management.

A concentration in accounting may fulfill the educational requirements to sit for the CPA exam and for professionals to earn continuing professional education hours. Most states require 150 credit hours to sit for the exam, in addition to the completion of accounting and business courses, which may be met via online courses.

Through Access Plus, it is possible for international students to be admitted directly into the M.B.A. program.

The Faculty

The professors provide fundamental knowledge, practical applications, and a supportive environment that facilitates the learning process. Fifty percent of the faculty members are women, and all faculty members hold or are working toward terminal degrees.

Faculty List

Donna N. McDaniel, J.D., Dean.
Steve Farner, Ph.D., Interim Associate Dean.
Linda T. Thomas, Ph.D., Director of Graduate Programs.

Accounting
Pamela Dinville, M.B.A., Director of Accounting Programs; CPA, CMA.
Monica McElhaney, M.B.A., M.S.M.I.S., CPA, CMA.
Cynthia Nye, M.S., Director of Adjunct Faculty; CPA, CMA.

Business
Kevin S. Schieuer, Ph.D., Director of Undergraduate Programs.
Myra Jo Bates, M.B.A., Ph.D. candidate.
Douglas L. Brown, D.B.A.
Anthony J. Clarke, Ph.D.
Steven L. Farner Jr., Ph.D.
David L. Levy, Ph.D.
Paul Poppler, Ph.D.
Jena Shafai-Asgarpoor, Ph.D.
Carolyn Youssef, Ph.D.

The Business School Network

Local business leaders help advise the Dean and faculty members on the curriculum and content in the M.B.A. program. Progressive companies recognize the need for employees with a technological aptitude and vision for change. Bellevue University forges strategic alliances for educational and management development with corporate partners, extending its reach with regional and national partnerships, including Defense Acquisition Univer-

Bellevue University.

sity, Boys Town, Army Corps of Engineers, and First National Bank.

The College and Environs

Since 1966, when 409 students began classes in a single campus building, Bellevue University has catered to the nontraditional student by providing both day and evening class schedules and services. The University offers classes and degree programs at several locations in Nebraska and Iowa, as well as online.

Bellevue, the state's oldest city, shares its borders with Omaha, the Missouri River, and Offutt Air Force Base. Bellevue is proud of its small-town atmosphere in the state of Nebraska. In addition to its deep-rooted Western heritage, Nebraska also features top-rated attractions, including a world-class zoo and the College World Series.

Facilities

The University strives to provide a high-quality physical learning environment for its students. Regional centers include the Lozier Professional Center in northwest Omaha; the Lakeside Center in southwest Omaha; the Lincoln, Nebraska, Center; programs and services in Grand Island, Nebraska; McCook, Nebraska; North Platte, Nebraska; Sioux City, Iowa; Council Bluffs, Iowa; and the newest sites in the Kansas City metro area. All facilities on the main Bellevue campus are new or have been renovated since 1991, and major renovations have recently been completed in the Humanities Center and the Student Center. In fall 2006, the University opened its state-of-the-art, 70,000-square-foot Educational Services Building.

The library is the primary center for support of academic research and information services. The University Library is technologically advanced, with numerous electronic services, including online-assisted searches. Qualified staff members are available to assist students with research and information retrieval.

The collection is available via the Internet through any of the library's workstations or any personal computer. WEBCat, Bellevue University Online's library catalog, provides access to all resources held in the Bellevue University Library plus nine other Nebraska libraries. Customers can search a variety of databases on CD-ROM and the Internet.

Placement

Career counseling, job search programs, and numerous resources help students develop and achieve their career goals. The Career Center assists in arranging internship opportunities for current students and graduates. Students seeking full-time or part-time employment while completing their education find numerous resources and materials to assist with their job search. Up-to-date job listings, general employment information, and files containing specific company information on many employers are available.

Books, periodicals, and handouts address such topics as resumes and cover letters, interviewing, salary negotiations, using the Internet, and other strategies for conducting a successful job search.

Students may complete their M.B.A. online or on campus.

Admission

All applicants are required to submit an application and a nonrefundable application fee. Candidates must possess an undergraduate degree from a regionally accredited college or university or a U.S. equivalent degree from a nationally or internationally accredited college or university, have maintained a GPA of 2.5 or better for the most recent 60 credits of undergraduate course work, have a cumulative GPA of 3.0 or better for prior graduate work, and submit essays in response to the Life Experience Summary questions. Because there are different admission requirements for the Executive MBA, students should visit http://www.bellevue.edu for details.

Finances

Both on-site and online tuition are $405 per semester credit hour. Fees include a nonrefundable application fee of $75, a general College fee of $45 per term, and a graduation fee of $100.

Financial assistance is available from the federal and state government, the institution, and private sources, including grants, scholarships, work-study programs, and student loans. Grants and scholarships do not have to be repaid. Student loans and loans to parents for the student must be repaid.

International Students

In addition to the regular admission requirements, international students must also provide an affidavit of support form with supporting documentation and, for students from non-English-speaking countries, TOEFL test results. Bellevue University offers Access Plus and ESL programs, which provide a multilevel English-language skills and acquisition program for international students.

Application Facts and Dates

Bellevue University has a policy of open admission, with students admitted on a space-available basis. Notification of acceptance or rejection is made in writing as soon as possible after an applicant has completed admission procedures. For more information, applicants should contact:

Director of Graduate Admissions
Bellevue University
1000 Galvin Road South
Bellevue, Nebraska 68005

Phone: 800-756-7920 (toll-free)
Fax: 402-293-3730
E-mail: info@bellevue.edu
Web site: http://www.bellevue.edu

Bentley College

Waltham, Massachusetts

BENTLEY: THE BUSINESS COLLEGE

Bentley has transformed into a premier business school over the past decade, and at the center of that transformation is the McCallum School of Business. The business school education offered by Bentley goes deep and wide to address the complex questions that surface in today's business environment. What are the ethical guidelines that drive an organization's accounting procedures? Does the new customer relationship marketing program violate consumer privacy laws? Can the target audience effectively navigate a company's new software program? Students explore the answers to these and other questions in depth at the McCallum Graduate School.

Programs and Curricular Focus

The McCallum Graduate School of Business presents the Bentley Portfolio 360, which offers comprehensive graduate business programs that are flexible to fit every student's schedule, streamlined to build on their personal background, and easily customized to meet the demands of their careers. In other words, a graduate business degree just the way students want it. The College's M.B.A. and eight Master of Science (M.S.) programs integrate business, technology, ethics, and global understanding focused through experiential learning, so that students are fluent in the principles and practices that drive corporate decision-making today.

The M.B.A. program at the McCallum Graduate School of Business prepares its graduates to excel and lead in an information-driven, ever-changing business world. The program develops strong skills in decision making, communication, leadership, and teamwork. Students gain the depth and breadth of expertise critical to move ahead in their current field or change careers—at an institution whose resources and focus are fully committed to the study of business.

Bentley offers specialized Master of Science (M.S.) programs that combine in-depth knowledge of the theory and tools critical to each discipline, while also exploring how each specialty relates to other functional areas within an organization. In today's global economy, demand is high for professionals with an expertise in virtually every field of business—from capital markets to e-commerce to systems development. M.S. programs are available in accountancy, finance, financial planning, human factors in information design, information technology, marketing analytics, real estate management, and taxation.

The innovative M.S.+M.B.A. program is designed for those who wish to become effective leaders in high-level knowledge-based organizations, with a particular emphasis on state-of-the-art information technology solutions (M.S.I.T.) or consistent and highly appealing user experience (M.S.H.F.I.D.). The M.S.+M.B.A. integrates in-depth knowledge of user needs and/or technology solutions with strong business-management skills. With full-time study, graduates earn two credentials: the M.S. (ensuring technical knowledge and skills) and the Day M.B.A. (ensuring strategic, organizational, and leadership skills) in the time it previously took to earn the M.B.A.

Students and the M.B.A. Experience

Bentley, one of the largest graduate schools of business in New England, brings together approximately 1,300 students representing fifty countries. This includes 350 full-time and 950 part-time students; 44 percent are women.

Global Focus

A focus on the global economy permeates the Bentley curriculum. Specific subjects and courses that explore international themes in all graduate programs are offered. Students interested in studying abroad can enroll in seven- to ten-day study tour courses to countries that include Australia, Austria, China, Estonia, France, Japan, and the Netherlands. Intermediate business language courses are offered in French, Spanish, and Italian.

The Faculty

To advance the frontiers of knowledge, foster curricular innovation, enhance teaching, and inform and improve business practice, Bentley professors pursue a rigorous agenda of scholarship and applied research. Much of this work is transdisciplinary; faculty members from the business disciplines and the arts and sciences collaborate with one another as well as with outside scholars and business leaders. Their research and scholarship focuses largely on, though is by no means limited to, Bentley's four strategic domains: arts and sciences in the business university, business and information technology, business ethics and social responsibility, and global commerce and culture.

The Business School Network

The business community supports both curriculum design and student networking at Bentley. The Graduate School Business Advisory Council, made up of key executives from the Boston area's multinational, national, and regional firms, provides ongoing corporate input for program development. Bentley brings a real-world approach to the educational process through activities that promote interaction among graduate students and business professionals. The Graduate Student Association, in particular, sponsors a number of organizations that provide leadership opportunities and key networking contacts in a variety of fields, including finance, information systems, management, marketing, financial planning, and taxation.

Corporate Partnerships

Strong partnerships between Bentley and the corporate community are a valuable resource for students. Bentley is one of only four schools to be selected as a premier partner of the NASDAQ Stock Market. The NASDAQ program, designed to enhance the understanding of financial markets through education, includes awards for a faculty member and a student.

The College and Environs

Founded in 1917, Bentley is an independent, coeducational institution recognized internationally for its excellence in professional business education. In addition to the students at the Graduate School, more than 3,000 undergraduates are enrolled in business and liberal arts. Bentley is accredited by AACSB International–The Association to Advance Collegiate Schools of Business and regionally accredited by the New England Association of Schools and Colleges (NEASC).

Located in Waltham, Massachusetts, in the heart of the region's high-technology sector, the 163-acre suburban campus is minutes from Boston's business, financial, and cultural resources; 30 minutes from Logan International Airport; and a 3-hour drive from New York City.

Facilities

The library houses more than 200,000 volumes, receives more than 1,700 periodicals, and has 155,000 microform titles. Study rooms, computer terminals, and various databases (e.g., LexisNexis, Dow Jones News Retrieval Service, and InfoTrac) are available for student use. The media services department provides television facilities, conferencing telephones, videoconferencing, and recordings for both instruction and group-work support.

Bentley offers limited on-campus housing for graduate students, located in Bentley's new north campus. Interested applicants should request a housing application through the Graduate Admissions Office.

The Dana Physical Education Center houses an Olympic-size swimming pool, exercise rooms, an indoor track, basketball courts, racquetball courts, and a dance studio.

Technology Environment

Bentley's business-oriented, high-tech academic centers and learning labs give students hands-on experience with the latest hardware and software in finance, marketing, accounting, and languages. Most classes incorporate projects and assignments that make use of the specialized software available in these facilities, allowing students to apply concepts learned in class. The centers and labs, including the Center for Marketing Technology, the Hughey Center for Financial Services, the Accounting Center for Electronic Learning and Business Measurement, and the Design and Usability Testing Center—all among the first of their kind in higher education—feature the same high-end hardware and software that businesses use today. Many of the labs benefit the corporate community as well, offering consulting and employee education.

Placement

The Miller Center for Career Services at Bentley College helps graduate students learn how to leverage a graduate degree in the job market, fine-tune personal and professional goals, and connect with leading employers in a range of industries. Through the Graduate Student Workshop series, the Miller Center for Career Services offers guidance on a full spectrum of job search topics, including interview preparation, cover letter writing, and salary negotiation. The career-counseling staff is well versed in job-market trends and able to provide valuable insight on career-development issues. The center also offers one-on-one advising with an experienced counselor to help sharpen career-development goals. In addition, the Career Management series offers a structured group of career-development workshops customized by academic degree program, class level, and concentration. An active campus recruiting program links graduate students with top U.S. companies, such as Arthur Andersen Consulting, Deloitte & Touche, and Forrester Research.

Admission

The McCallum Graduate School of Business seeks highly motivated individuals with outstanding professional and educational credentials who can contribute to the learning experience of other graduate students. An undergraduate degree is required for admission to the McCallum Graduate School of Business. Generally, only current students of the Graduate School may attend classes. International students must submit TOEFL results and official English translations of all academic documents. All candidates should have strong mathematics, computer, economics, and business writing skills.

Applications for the Day M.B.A. program are accepted only for the fall term. Applications for the Evening M.B.A. or any M.S. program are accepted on a rolling basis; students may begin study either in September or January.

Finances

Tuition for the 2007–08 academic year was $2958 per 3-credit course. Payment for tuition is due by the start of classes each semester and may be paid by check, MasterCard, VISA, or Discover. Bentley offers two payment plan options; for additional information, students should contact the Student Accounts Office at 781-891-2171.

Bentley awards scholarships to highly qualified, full-time and part-time graduate students. Awards are based primarily on academic, professional, and personal merit, with consideration given to the contributions that each individual can make to the diversity of the graduate student population, usually without regard to financial need. Some scholarships may have a work requirement in the form of a graduate or research assistantship.

Need-based financial aid programs at Bentley assist students whose resources are insufficient to meet the costs of attendance. These programs consist of grants and loans. All awards are based on financial need as determined by the Free Application for Federal Student Aid (FAFSA) and the Bentley Graduate Aid application. In addition, the Bentley Financial Aid Office assists students in identifying potential alternative loan resources.

International Students

Bentley supports international students through a seminar series on the academic, cultural, and social aspects of the U.S. graduate school experience. Individual tutoring in language skills is available. In addition, the Joseph M. Cronin International Center has a full-time information student adviser and staff to meet the social and academic needs of international students. The Nathan R. Miller Center for Career Services also conducts seminars on immigration regulations and U.S. employment and labor certification and provides information on overseas job postings.

Application Facts and Dates

For the fall start in September, the deadline for all full-time applicants for all programs is December 1. The second-round deadline for all full-time applicants is January 15; the third-round deadline is March 15. The priority deadline for all part-time applications is May 1. The final deadline for all applications is June 1 with rolling admission (space permitting) after this date. For spring start in January, the deadline for international candidates or those wishing an early decision is October 1.

For more information, applicants should contact:

Office of Graduate Admissions
McCallum Graduate School of Business
Bentley College
175 Forest Street
Waltham, Massachusetts 02452-4705
Phone: 781-891-2108
     800-442-4723 (toll-free)
Fax: 781-891-2472
Web site: http://www.bentley.edu

Boston College

Carroll School of Management Graduate Programs

Chestnut Hill, Massachusetts

AN INVESTMENT IN SUCCESS

The foundation of the M.B.A. experience at Boston College's Carroll School is a rigorous academic curriculum that provides each student with a breadth of knowledge in the disciplines of management, a depth of knowledge in a management specialization, and a wealth of practical management experiences. Overlaying this curriculum are opportunities for you to grow and develop personally as well as professionally.

The M.B.A. Program at the Carrol School is designed to prepare each individual for a successful career in the management profession. This professional perspective, and the attention to lifelong development, begins on the first day that you arrive on campus and will guide you throughout your career. Our small class sizes allow you to work closely with faculty and staff members beginning with the admissions process, through the development of a personalized education plan and career strategy.

The environment at the Carroll School is competitive but collegial. Our motto is "Through cooperation and integrity we prosper." We believe this motto, and we live it.

We thank you for considering the M.B.A. program at the Carroll School. We encourage you to investigate the opportunities that we provide for you to further your development as a management professional.

— Jeffrey L. Ringuest, Associate Dean of Graduate Programs

Programs and Curricular Focus

The M.B.A. program at Boston College's Carroll School of Management (CSOM) provides students with the skills and perspectives necessary for success in today's global and technology-based business environment. In addition to receiving a thorough education in the functional areas of business, students have numerous opportunities to apply their knowledge in real-world settings. Students grapple with actual management problems through innovative classroom exercises, consulting projects, and new venture planning activities. This unique combination of classroom and applied learning gives Boston College M.B.A. students a distinct career advantage.

The curriculum is designed not only to provide an understanding of the fundamentals of management but also to offer abundant opportunities to tailor the program to meet specific needs and career goals. After completing the core study, students have many opportunities to explore possible career paths through electives, industry-specific programs, independent studies, and other options. These options include professional specializations in the traditional functional areas as well as interdisciplinary concentrations in such areas as asset management, change leadership, competitive service delivery, corporate finance, entrepreneurial management, financial reporting and controls, global management, marketing and information analytics, product and brand management, and tailored specialization.

The School also offers more than fifteen dual-degree programs: the M.B.A./J.D.; the M.B.A./M.S.F.; the M.B.A./M.S.W.; the M.B.A./Ph.D. in sociology or management with a concentration in finance; the M.B.A./M.A. in mathematics, political science, linguistics, Slavic studies, French studies, Italian studies, Hispanic studies, or Russian studies; the M.B.A./M.S. in biology, geology/geophysics, or nursing; the M.B.A./M.A. in pastoral ministry; and the M.B.A./M.A. in higher education. Offered on a full- or part-time (evening) basis, the M.B.A. program at Boston College's Carroll School of Management is part of a portfolio of programs that includes a Master of Science in finance and accounting and a Ph.D. in management, with concentrations in finance and organization studies.

Students and the M.B.A. Experience

There are 200 full-time and 575 evening M.B.A. students. Approximately 35 percent of students in the M.B.A. program are women. Full-time M.B.A. students have an average of 4.7 years of full-time work experience; evening M.B.A. students have an average of 5.2 years.

Global Focus

Boston College's M.B.A. curriculum is global in its outlook. Global management issues are woven throughout the curriculum so that course work across the spectrum of functional areas routinely addresses the international dimensions of business. Moreover, with approximately one third of the entering full-time class typically made up of international students, a global perspective comes naturally to the program. Students develop worldwide perspectives in a kind of learning laboratory that is much like the business environment into which they will graduate.

The Boston College Carroll School of Management maintains an extensive program of international study opportunities. The International Management Experience (IME) elective allows M.B.A. students to study a region of the world and see firsthand how business is conducted. During the three weeks of travel, students visit corporations, major commercial centers, and government agencies. The IMEs have included Asia, Europe, and Latin America. Global management is the focus of a special dual degree the Boston College M.B.A. program offers with Strasbourg (France) Graduate School of Management. Other international study opportunities include the International Consulting Project and a number of exchange programs maintained with leading management schools around the world and a semester in China option offered through the Beijing International Management Center.

Special Features

The Boston College M.B.A. program develops new programs to meet emerging managerial challenges. In spring 2002, the Investment Management Business course was launched. Via a comprehensive, reality-based program of classroom instruction, practical training, guest lectures, and field trips, students are afforded a unique opportunity to develop deep-industry knowledge that culminates in a "live-money" portfolio management experience for qualifying teams.

Outside the classroom, student-mentor relationships are leveraged with business leaders through the Wall Street Executive Fellows program. Developed as a full tuition scholarship, a limited number of M.B.A. students with exceptional academic and professional achievements are selected as Fellows. These students have the privilege and opportunity to meet with a Boston College graduate who has achieved success and recognition on Wall Street or in the broader financial community. Mentors have included Charles Clough, former Chief Investment Strategist, Merrill Lynch, and Peter Lynch, Vice Chairman of Fidelity Management & Research Company.

The Faculty

The members of the Carroll School of Management faculty represent a vibrant mix of knowledge, experience, and professional dedication. Many of them bring extensive industry backgrounds and contacts directly into the classroom, which adds to the real-world aspect of the learning experience. The Carroll School seeks faculty members who are able to balance scholarship and teaching excellence.

The Business School Network
Corporate Partnerships

Top executives regularly visit the Carroll School of Management. Inside the Manager's Studio, an executive lecture series, gives students the chance to interact directly with leaders in the business and nonprofit worlds.

The Board of Advisors, a group of senior executives from leading companies, consults regularly with the Carroll School of Management on program and curricular issues. The Carroll School also sponsors the Chief Executives' Club of Boston, one of the nation's top business speaking forums.

In addition, members participate in the Board of Advisors Mentoring Program, which offers all Carroll School M.B.A. students the opportunity to meet one-on-one with an executive or another successful practitioner in his or her area of interest. Participation in this program affords students several benefits, including deeper functional knowledge of organizations, insights into current trends in market environments, and assistance in developing their professional identities and career strategies.

The College and Environs

Located on 185 acres on the Boston line, Boston College is just a short ride by car or subway from downtown Boston, a world-renowned center of culture, learning, and industry.

Boston College is a coeducational, two-campus university with four undergraduate schools and six graduate and professional schools. The University offers fourteen degree programs and two certificate programs and enrolls 8,900 full-time undergraduates and 4,800 graduate students. Established in 1863, Boston College is the largest Jesuit-affiliated university in the country.

Facilities

Fulton Hall, which houses the Carroll School of Management, is a state-of-the-art center for management education. Among Fulton's advantages: many classrooms outfitted with advanced computer and audiovisual technologies, including wireless Internet access; abundant space for meetings, study groups, and gatherings, including a dramatic five-story atrium that functions as the School's "town square"; and its location in the heart of Boston College's Chestnut Hill campus, close to the libraries, the recreation complex, and the student union.

Computer facilities are available to M.B.A. students in the graduate computer lab in Fulton Hall and in the O'Neill Computing Facility, which provide access to a wide variety of hardware, software, and peripherals.

The University's libraries offer a wealth of resources to support research, teaching, and learning. The book collections exceed 1.7 million volumes, and approximately 20,000 serial titles are currently received. The library holds 2.7 million microforms. In addition, Boston College libraries provide access to more than 500 databases, including many in business and economics.

Graduate housing is not provided on campus; however, the Office of University Housing provides off-campus listings and suggestions for interested students.

Placement

Boston College's Carroll School of Management is committed to helping students achieve the best possible career outcomes. Graduate Management Career Strategies provides M.B.A. students with the means to achieve their career goals through placement initiatives, career coaching, and other services. The office also serves as a bridge to corporations through its outreach activities and links to Boston College's worldwide alumni network.

Admission

The Carroll School of Management welcomes applications from graduates of accredited colleges and universities. For the M.B.A. program, the Admissions Committee considers applicants with academic backgrounds from virtually all areas of study.

Courses in business administration or management are not required for admission to the Carroll School of Management M.B.A. program. However, students are expected to be proficient in English and mathematics. In addition, all applicants are expected to take the GMAT. International students must have the equivalent of a U.S.

bachelor's degree and a minimum score of 600 on the TOEFL exam.

The Admissions Committee looks for evidence of academic and management potential. Work experience and prior academic performance are significant criteria in their evaluation. In general, students enter the program after at least four years of full-time work experience. Leadership and community involvement are also important factors in admissions decisions.

Finances

Tuition for the 2007–08 academic year is $1126 per credit hour. Books and supplies average $1500 per year and medical insurance is $1500. Personal expenses currently average $4000 per year.

The graduate program offers graduate assistantships and scholarships to full-time M.B.A. classes. Awardees usually have two or more years of full-time work experience, a score of 660 or above on the GMAT, a grade point average of 3.3 or above, and a strong set of application materials. Graduate assistantships involve research or administrative duties in exchange for tuition remission. A portion of assistantship awards is subject to tax.

In addition to the assistantships and scholarships offered through CSOM, the University Financial Aid Office provides a variety of programs to help students finance their education.

Application Facts and Dates

The evening M.B.A. program admits students in September and January; the full-time M.B.A. program begins only in September. For the full-time M.B.A. program, application deadlines are November 15 for Round 1, February 15 for Round 2, and March 15 for Round 3. For the Evening M.B.A. program, application deadline dates are May 1 and June 1 for September admission and October 15 for January admission. Prospective students may apply online to the Boston College M.B.A. program at http://bc.edu/csom. For more information, applicants should contact:

Office of Graduate Management
    Admissions
Carroll School of Management
Fulton Hall, Room 315
Boston College
140 Commonwealth Avenue
Chestnut Hill, Massachusetts 02467-
    3808
Phone: 617-552-3920
Fax: 617-552-8078
E-mail: bcmba@bc.edu
Web site: http://www.bc.edu/mba

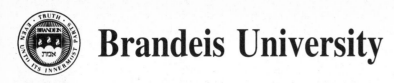

Brandeis University

> ### PREPARING PROFESSIONALS FOR THE GLOBAL ECONOMY
>
> *The Brandeis International Business School is the first school at a major U.S. university to focus on global markets, the best possible preparation for professional careers in the global economy. Our degree programs, with their strong analytical and financial orientations, will equip you with the practical and conceptual skills that are necessary to be successful in doing business across borders. Classes are small—we accept about 140 students per year—but very diverse, as more than fifty countries are represented. The internationally known faculty comprises a dynamic teaching and research team that works closely with M.B.A. students in course work as well as on projects outside the classroom. Our approach is thoroughly international and includes a semester of study overseas with one of our twenty partner exchange schools.*
>
> *—Bruce Magid, Ph.D., Dean, and Martin and Ahuva Gross Chair in Financial Markets and Institutions*

Programs and Curricular Focus

The Brandeis International Business School (IBS) offers innovative master's and Ph.D. programs for students preparing for careers in international business, finance, and economics. IBS offers full-time programs, including the Master of Business Administration/international (M.B.A.), the Master of Arts in international economics and finance (MAief), and the M.S./Ph.D. in international economics and finance. IBS also offers an innovative Master of Science in Finance program (M.S.F.).

The M.B.A.'s global orientation, multicultural training, and international experience distinguish it from "generic" M.B.A. programs. Although students study all subjects covered in a traditional M.B.A. program, they are learned in a global context. The M.B.A. prepares students for business careers in multinational enterprises, smaller firms operating across borders, and consulting firms that serve international enterprises. A unique feature of the M.B.A. is a semester of study with one of twenty business schools in Europe, Asia, or Latin America. Demonstrated proficiency in a language other than English is required.

IBS also offers the MAief degree, a highly specialized degree that combines aspects of international business and international affairs. Designed for recent college graduates and experienced professionals, this program provides the greatest benefit to students who seek careers in international finance and economic policy.

The M.S.F. consists of ten courses and can be completed on a part- or full-time basis. An elective may include a one-week field-study course given on location in a major international financial market.

The M.S./Ph.D. program provides advanced training in theory, research, and creative problem solving for students interested in careers in research, teaching, and policymaking. Admissions are open every other year.

Students and the M.B.A. Experience

The M.B.A./international program at the International Business School at Brandeis University develops expertise in doing business across borders. IBS provides a cosmopolitan yet intimate environment that supports students in developing and reaching their goals. Each entering class is limited to 125 master's students, affording every individual the opportunity to get to know and interact with classmates, faculty members, and administrators through a variety of academic and extracurricular activities. The student body is diverse, with about 70 percent of the students coming from outside the United States; typically, more than fifty nations are represented at the School. About 45 percent of the students are women and about 15 percent are members of minority groups.

Global Focus

Since the entire curriculum is focused on developing skills for use in the global marketplace and since the students are from such diverse international backgrounds, each class becomes an international learning experience. Students often work in multicultural teams with a faculty of internationally known experts, and differences in perspectives and cultural norms are actively discussed.

Special Features

The M.B.A. program is the only professional program in the U.S. that requires a semester of graduate study overseas. Students choose to study at one of twenty partner schools and in so doing develop a firsthand understanding of the business and economic systems of a major international country. Many students take course work in the local language, attaining the foreign language proficiency required for graduation. This semester abroad also allows participants to develop friendships and networks that usually intensify and expand after graduation.

The Faculty

The faculty includes several internationally known authorities on business management, exchange rates and trade policy, patents and technology transfer, and Asian economies and business. Other members conduct research with a focus on international finance. In addition, several high-level executives from Boston's business, finance, and legal communities offer their expertise in applied technical areas as adjunct professors.

Many of the faculty members conduct research in the School's Asia Pacific Center for Economics and Business using grant funding provided by prestigious international agencies, such as the Center for Global Partnership, the Luce Foundation, the United Nations, and the World Bank. IBS has also been designated as one of thirteen official Asia Pacific Economic Cooperation (APEC) Study Centers in the U.S. and is the only such center in New England.

Faculty List

Full-Time
Stephen Cecchetti, Ph.D., Berkeley. Macroeconomics, monetary theory.
Benjamin Gomes-Casseres, D.B.A., Harvard. Alliance management.
Gary Jefferson, Ph.D., Yale. Economic development.
Blake LeBaron, Ph.D., Chicago. International finance.
Catherine Mann, Ph.D., MIT. International trade, globalization of information technology.
Rachel McCulloch, Ph.D., Chicago. Foreign investment, international economic policy.

The Business School Network

IBS has developed an extensive network of partnerships with financial and multinational corporations and with professionals in the finance and economics professions. Corporate partners include the Federal Reserve Bank, JP Morgan Chase, UBS/Paine Webber, AT&T, and Accenture. The multinational Board of Overseers of the School includes executives from Andersen, the Bank of Tokyo-Mitsubishi Ltd., Erving Industries, Fuji Xerox Co., Goldman Sachs, ICI, Mellon Bank, the Monitor Company, the Ssangyong Business Group of Korea, and the World Bank. Visitors from these companies and many others provide opportunities to address important issues through informal lectures, conferences, and seminars. The School also runs an Executive Education Program in alliance strategy.

The College and Environs

Founded in 1948, Brandeis is one of the leading private research universities in the United States, with approximately 3,000 undergraduates and 1,200 graduate students. The University is situated on a parklike campus 10 miles west of Boston and Cambridge, while IBS is located in a wooded corner of the campus in the Lemberg Academic Center and Sachar International Center. The University has superb sports and theater facilities and brings a series of distinguished lecturers, artists, and performance groups to the campus. Public transportation provides quick access to Boston's cultural and educational amenities and to nearby ocean and New England rural attractions.

Facilities

Master's students frequently participate in faculty research and in seminars and discussions with visiting scholars and practitioners. As an APEC Study Center, there are special opportunities for those interested in Asian economics and business.

The School operates its own IBM-compatible computer network, with access to current software, databases, LexisNexis, and the World Wide Web. Students have access to university libraries and to other resources through the Boston Library Consortium and through exchange agreements with other leading colleges and universities in the area.

Placement

Virtually all graduates of the program are employed in positions utilizing their economic, financial, and international training. Leading employers include Citibank, PricewaterhouseCoopers, JP Morgan Chase, Goldman Sachs, and the U.S. Federal Reserve Banks. Graduates from recent classes have received offers from consulting firms such as the Boston Consulting Group, McKinsey & Co., and Accenture and from corporations such as Lycos and Corning International. Students work closely with the Office of Career Services to learn about career alternatives and to implement an effective career development strategy during their time at Brandeis.

Admission

Applicants for all master's programs are required to have an American bachelor's degree or the equivalent international degree. Prior training in a modern foreign language is highly desirable. All applications should include official copies of transcripts and three letters of recommendation. All international applicants must submit TOEFL scores.

Applicants to the M.B.A. and M.S.F. programs should have some prior work experience and must submit scores from the GMAT (not the GRE).

For the MAief program, prior course work should include at least two semesters of economics and one semester of international relations or politics. MAief applicants must also submit scores from either the general GRE or the GMAT. The M.S./Ph.D. program admits students every other year, with the next intake date of fall 2008.

Finances

Tuition charges for full-time students for 2007–08 are $34,566 per year for M.B.A. and M.A. students. Tuition rates for the part-time M.S.F. program are $3200 per course. Ten-month living expenses in the area are estimated to range from $9000 to $12,000 for a single student. Limited on-campus housing is available; most students live within a short commute of the campus.

Candidates may apply for tuition scholarships, assistantships, and loans, which are available to American and international students. Special American Leadership Awards are available to U.S. citizens or permanent resident applicants who exhibit outstanding potential for international careers.

International Students

Approximately 60 percent of the graduate students are international, typically coming from more than fifty nations. Well-represented areas include Asia, Africa, Latin America, and Central and Eastern Europe. The University also has a large international population and provides support through the International Students Office and via an active International Student Association.

Application Facts and Dates

Application deadlines are November 15, February 15, and April 15. For the Ph.D. program, the next application deadline is January 15. Candidates applying for financial aid are urged to meet the February 15 deadline. For further information, students should contact:

Holly L. Chase
Assistant Dean for Admission
International Business School
Brandeis University
Waltham, Massachusetts 02454-9110
Phone: 781-736-2252
        800-878-8866 (toll-free in the
        U.S. only)
Fax: 781-736-2263
E-mail:
    admission@lemberg.brandeis.edu
Web site: http://www.brandeis.edu/global

Carnegie Mellon University

Tepper School of Business

Pittsburgh, Pennsylvania

THE NEXT GENERATION OF LEADERS

The demand for leaders able to effectively guide organizations is a reality that we face now as well as in the future of a global economy. Tepper M.B.A. students receive an intensive background in analytical decision making that serves as the foundation for competitive advantage. The program's analytical underpinning prepares students for the dynamic and complex business situations they will face in changing business environments. At Carnegie Mellon, our students, faculty members, and alumni have mastered change in global markets because they often are the source of it.

—Kenneth B. Dunn, Dean

Programs and Curricular Focus

The Tepper School of Business offers one of the world's highest-rated graduate business degrees, owing its success to an unrelenting focus on innovation throughout all aspects of its program. The School's M.B.A. degree program features an analytic approach to global business management. Founded in 1949, Carnegie Mellon's business school is recognized as the pioneer of management science with a reputation for creating new ways to transfer knowledge. The School's proud heritage includes six Nobel laureates. Its groundbreaking research, particularly in the areas of corporate finance, macroeconomics, and operations research continues to serve as the basis for many business decisions and academic models.

The Tepper M.B.A. is a two-year, full-time program that features an interdisciplinary approach to business management. Students do not simply learn by absorbing information—they actively experience the challenge of participating in day-to-day business operations. Through course work and dynamic academic exercises, students are trained to effectively direct a range of challenging business issues in a fast-paced team environment. The program revolves around the School's popular mini-semesters—a model that provides students with exposure to a wide range of courses every eight weeks. Upon graduation, students have completed thirty-two courses, half of which are electives in areas students wish to customize according to their personal and professional goals.

The program's philosophy embraces a rigorous academic experience. In year one, the program emphasizes a strong foundation of introductory and functional knowledge necessary for business management. In addition, students gain a solid understanding of core business principles, including operations management, finance, marketing, orga-

nizational behavior, and accounting. The first year culminates in an optional, but recommended, internship program coordinated by the School's Career Opportunities Center. With a placement track record among the highest of any leading business school, the Tepper School of Business works closely with multinational-national corporations to identify meaningful internship opportunities for students.

During students' second year, the program's focus advances toward integrating various functional business arenas. With a solid foundation from the previous year's introduction to business techniques and principles, students are ready to concentrate on a range of challenging and contemporary business issues. Among the unique experiences for students is the program's capstone course, Management Game, an applied strategic management exercise in which teams of students act as senior managers of companies for three simulated years.

A part-time, three-year M.B.A. option is also available to students with an opportunity to earn a graduate degree while continuing their careers. Unlike many other M.B.A. programs, the part-time program curriculum is virtually identical to the full-time experience. Additional graduate degree programs include an eighteen-month (full-time) Master of Science in Computational Finance (M.S.C.F.), twenty-month Master in Business Management and Software Engineering (M.B.M.S.E.), two-year Master of Science in Civil Engineering and Management (MSCEM), two-year Master of Science in Environmental Engineering and Management, and collaborative course work and degree programming in conjunction with Carnegie Mellon's prestigious Heinz School of Public Policy and Management.

Students and the M.B.A. Experience

The student body exhibits diverse backgrounds, with undergraduate degrees split almost evenly between technical and non-technical majors. All parts of the U.S. and more than thirty countries are represented in the average entering class. The majority of students have full-time postgraduate work experience, with an average of four years each. This mix of students invigorates the educational experience, where teamwork and student interaction play a larger role than at virtually any other top business school.

Special Features

Concentrations under the general management curriculum include accounting, biotechnology, communications, economics, entrepreneurship, finance, information systems, international business, management and strategy, marketing, operations research, organizational behavior, and production/operations management.

Tepper School of Business also offers depth tracks as part of the full-time M.B.A. program. This course of study combines a general management education with rigorous, focused study in specific areas, such as analytical marketing strategy, biotechnology, entrepreneurship in organizations, global enterprise management, management of innovation and product development, and technology leadership.

Depth track programs, which are conducted jointly with other departments, research centers, and schools on campus, prepare students for leadership in specific industries, exposing them to leading academic thinkers, innovative research, and top students from across the University to provide a true cross-campus educational experience that has no departmental boundaries.

The Faculty

Faculty members at Tepper School of Business have received international acclaim for their research in the areas of artificial intelligence, consumer marketing, finance, operations research, and organizational theory. These valued faculty members embody the University's interdisciplinary spirit, often collaborating with colleagues at other schools and programs on campus. The small size of the student body allows for an enviable student-professor ratio (5:1) that is among the best of any top ten graduate business programs.

True to its heritage, the University commits significant resources to continuing research that influences business practice and theory. Students have an opportunity to study with professors who spearhead research programs, such as the Carnegie Bosch Institute for Applied Studies in International Management; the Carnegie Mellon Electricity Industry Center; the Center for Analytical Research in Technology; the Center for Behavioral Decision Research; the Center for Business Communication; the Center for Business Solutions; the Center for E-Business Innovation; the Center for Financial Markets; the Center for the Interdisciplinary Research on Teams; the Center for International Corporate Responsibility; the Center for the Management of Technology; the Center for Organizational Learning, Innovation, and Performance; the Donald H. Jones Center for Entrepreneurship; the Gailliot Center for Public Policy; the Green Design Institute; and the Teaching Innovation Center.

The Business School Network

Students have a multitude of opportunities to interact with business executives while in the program. Project courses allow students to gain hands-on experience solving real-world problems for company clients. Top executives are frequent guests on campus and share their experiences with students both inside and outside the classroom. Career forums, workshops, and the corporate presentation series provide venues for students to explore career issues through the experience of successful professionals.

The College and Environs

Carnegie Mellon is a decidedly small university of nearly 10,000 students; almost half are graduate students. Nearly 600 faculty members hold full-time teaching positions and another 60 are scientists on research staffs.

Pittsburgh is a big-league city that values its small-town feel. Low crime rates, tree-lined streets, three major sports teams, sparkling rivers underlining green hillsides, and affordable housing in popular neighborhoods are a few of the reasons why Pittsburgh is one of the top fifteen corporate headquarters locations in the U.S. Pittsburgh International Airport is one of the most modern airports in the country, serving hundreds of international locations.

Technology Environment

Carnegie Mellon is consistently ranked as the most wired campus in America. Wireless access is available in all buildings and classrooms, as well as in outdoor areas, including on campus parks and recreational areas. Satellite downlinks are in classrooms, and Carnegie Mellon is one of the few M.B.A. programs that have successfully introduced live, interactive classroom teaching into the curriculum.

Placement

The Career Opportunities Center provides excellent resources for every student's job search. Individual counseling and workshops help students plot their job search strategies and polish resume writing, interviewing, and salary negotiation skills. Career forums bring corporate representatives from various fields to campus, and students are encouraged to contact alumni who have succeeded in their areas of interest. The School's Career Opportunities Center works with more than 350 multinational corporations and companies throughout the year, and Tepper maintains an impressive employment rate compared to other leading business schools. Recruiting forums provide students with opportunities to talk to firms in various parts of the U.S. and the world. Students have access to numerous other resources, including a World Wide Web recruiting system, alumni database, and interactive searches. Alumni are active in providing mock interviews, resume reviews, and mentoring relationships.

Admission

Tepper School of Business welcomes diversity; nearly 30 percent of its student population comprises international students. The University encourages applicants who have studied in a variety of fields. The School seeks students who are highly motivated, self-directed, and innovative. The applicant's academic potential and promise for a productive career in business leadership are central factors.

The University's admission process is thorough and personal. The entire academic record, grade trends, full- and part-time work records, GMAT scores, and letters of recommendation are examined. Essays are used to judge an applicant's ability to communicate and to understand each student's individual goals.

Finances

The 2008–09 costs include tuition, $47,000; activity fee, $254; off-campus room and board, $13,500; and books and supplies, $5800. The Tepper School of Business provides a variety of scholarships and financial aid possibilities to maximize educational opportunities.

Application Facts and Dates

Admissions are conducted on a rolling basis. Students who apply by the November deadline are notified by late January; students who apply by the January deadline are notified by late March; students who apply by the March deadline are notified by late May; and students who apply by the May deadline are notified by late June. (The May deadline is reserved for U.S. citizens and permanent residents. International applicants for the full-time M.B.A. program must apply by the March deadline.) Interested students should contact:

M.B.A. Admissions Office
Posner Hall
Tepper School of Business
Carnegie Mellon University
5000 Forbes Avenue
Pittsburgh, Pennsylvania 15213
Phone: 412-268-2272
        800-850-4742 (toll-free inside
            the United States)
Fax: 412-268-4209
E-mail:
    mba-admissions@andrew.cmu.edu
Web site:
    http://www.tepper.cmu.edu/

Chapman University

DEAN'S MESSAGE

The George L. Argyros School of Business and Economics at Chapman University offers an integrated business education taught by faculty members deeply committed to student learning. Students graduate with a strong understanding of how American business operates in the world and how they can contribute to it. The School is accredited by AACSB International–The Association to Advance Collegiate Schools of Business.

Students are challenged in academic programs that stress economics and the functional areas of business, reinforced by analytical and behavioral skills within a pragmatic framework. Entrepreneurship and ethics as well as written and oral communication skills are integrated throughout the curriculum, along with elements of international business. In addition, students have unmatched access to a faculty of active scholars and a network of business community leaders, all of whom are driving the changes happening in business today. This close interaction gives students the insights and tools they need to become successful corporate leaders.

—Arthur Kraft, Dean

Programs and Curricular Focus

The Master of Business Administration (M.B.A.) gives students the skills they need to succeed as business leaders. Combining a strong theoretical foundation with applied skills training in finance, economics, marketing, management, information technology, and statistics, the program also stresses effective leadership and communication techniques. To earn the degree, students must complete 33 credits in core courses, 15 units in elective courses, and 4 units in a capstone course that integrates core material with a global perspective.

The Executive M.B.A. offers mid- to senior-level executives the chance to improve their mastery of business without interrupting their careers. The comprehensive curriculum encompasses finance, accounting, marketing, economics, information systems, management, international business, and strategy, stressing theoretical knowledge as well as practical business applications. Students complete 49 units over twenty-one months.

The Argyros School also offers the M.B.A. in conjunction with other degrees. The J.D./M.B.A. program allows students to earn both the J.D. and M.B.A. degrees more quickly than pursuing the degrees separately. The program requires four years of full-time study and completion of 125 credits. The Integrated Five-Year Undergraduate M.B.A. Program allows Chapman's undergraduate students who have completed 75 units or more of their course work to earn 9 credit hours of M.B.A. course work and complete an internship opportunity. The joint M.B.A./

M.F.A. in film and television producing gives students the opportunity to obtain both an M.B.A. degree and a Master of Fine Arts in film and television producing. The program is designed for individuals seeking a management or executive-level position at a production company, talent agency, studio, or television network.The school also offers the M.B.A. in conjunction with other degrees. The J.D./M.B.A. program allows students to earn both the J.D. and M.B.A. degrees more expeditiously than pursuing the degrees separately. The program requires four years of full-time study and completion of 125 credits. The Integrated Five-Year Undergraduate M.B.A. Program allows undergraduate students who have completed 75 units or more of their course work to earn 9 credit hours of M.B.A. course work and complete an internship opportunity. The joint M.B.A./M.F.A. in film and television producing gives students the opportunity to obtain both an M.B.A. degree and a Master of Fine Arts in film and television producing. The program is designed for individuals seeking a management or executive-level position at a production company, talent agency, studio, or television network.

Students and the M.B.A. Experience

On entering the program, students participate in a comprehensive orientation during the first week, where they meet their professors and classmates. During the program, students take part in team projects and study groups.

The Argyros School prefers students with at least two years of business-related work experience. Students who do not meet this standard are strongly encouraged to gain relevant experience through an internship position while enrolled in the program.

The Faculty

There are about 39 professors on the faculty; 93 percent of these professors hold terminal degrees, the highest available in their fields. Faculty members are engaged in scholarly business research in addition to their teaching duties. The student-faculty ratio is 14:1, with the average M.B.A. class having 22 students.

The Business School Network

The Distinguished Speaker Series exposes students to the latest ideas and most captivating minds in business and provides an opportunity to network at the highest levels. Speakers include Fortune 500 chairs, CEOs, and founders of successful startup companies who may speak in intimate roundtable discussions over dinner or to large gatherings that include alumni, faculty members, and members of the Board of Counselors. Recent speakers include current and former executives from Bank of America, Fluor Corporation, Ingram Micro, and other multinational corporations.

The College and Environs

Founded in 1861, Chapman University is one of California's oldest, most prestigious private universities. Recognized for its unwavering commitment to academic excellence, Chapman is rated a Top School by *U.S. News and World Report*'s America's Best Colleges.

Chapman is located in Orange County, California, about 35 minutes from Los Angeles. A vibrant economic center fueling improved salaries and outstanding job opportunities for students, Orange County is home to several large corporations, including Allergan, Broadcom, Disneyland Resort, Mazda, and Ingram Micro, making it a haven for budding entrepreneurs. Chapman is also conveniently located near local entertainment hotspots and minutes from Southern California's beaches and mountains.

Facilities

The Ralph W. Leatherby Center for Entrepreneurship and Business Ethics enables

students to gain experience in starting and maintaining new businesses. Students study entrepreneurship, receive career mentoring, participate in an internship program, and compete in entrepreneurship contests. The Walter Schmid Center for International Business provides leadership in internationalizing business education, trains students to assume leadership roles in global business, and provides a resource for local businesses to assess opportunities in the global marketplace. The A. Gary Anderson Center for Economic Research encourages faculty members and students to engage in economic and business research and disseminate the results to local communities.

Placement

The MBA Career Management Center addresses the placement and career management needs of M.B.A. and EMBA candidates, offering effective career management tools to current students and assisting alumni with ongoing career transition or career management needs. It provides a number of services, including individual counseling, interview coaching, a career resource library, and business-card printing services.

Admission

Applicants are evaluated on academic performance, leadership potential, work experience, and communication skills. Ideally, students should have at least two years' work experience.

Prospective students must submit a completed application, official transcripts from all colleges previously attended, official GMAT scores, an essay stating their reasons for wanting to enroll in the Argyros School, two letters of recommendation, and a $50 application fee. Some applicants may be required to complete an interview with the Assistant Dean; interviews are by invitation only for the M.B.A. program.

Applicants are notified of a decision as soon as possible after the application has been received.

Finances

In 2007–08, tuition was $770 per academic credit for M.B.A. students. EMBA students paid $61,250 for the entire program, including tuition, laptop computer, lodging and food, books, registration fees, and parking.

Students who require financial assistance may secure loans through the Stafford Loan Program, which may provide up to $20,500 per year, or under the Graduate PLUS Loan Program. Other loans may be available from private lenders.

International Students

Approximately 11 percent of students are from other countries. The International Students Services office acts as a source of information and assistance for these students. The office sponsors an orientation program; counseling on academic, financial, and personal matters; assistance in class registration; information on immigration requirements; and information on social and cultural events.

Application Facts and Dates

The Graduate Admissions Committee attempts to make admissions decisions on a rolling basis; therefore, applicants are encouraged to apply early. The recommended deadline is May 1 for fall admission and October 15 for spring admission.

Applicants may request an admissions packet or other information by contacting:

Debra Gonda, Associate Director,
     Graduate and Executive Programs
Office of Graduate Programs
The George L. Argyros School of
     Business and Economics
Chapman University
One University Drive
Orange, California 92866

Phone: 714-997-6745
Fax: 714-997-6757
E-mail: gonda@chapman.edu
Web site: http://www.chapman.edu/
     argyros/

City University of Seattle

Graduate School of Management Professions

Bellevue, Washington

DEVELOPING BUSINESS LEADERS IN THE TWENTY-FIRST CENTURY

Innovation, responsiveness, and commitment to excellence have been City University of Seattle's standards since our founding in 1973, and our M.B.A. program exemplifies these standards. Well-respected and well-established, the M.B.A. program at City University of Seattle assists learners in achieving excellence in their chosen field via teaching and learning communities that foster exploration, examination, and extension of professional theory and practice. Students are compelled to reach inward to achieve personal leadership and to reach forward to embrace changes and challenges—today and tomorrow.

—Dean, School of Management

Programs and Curricular Focus

City University of Seattle's M.B.A. program is oriented toward adult learners who are self-starters, who seek recognition as leaders, and whose intellectual curiosity takes them beyond the simple solutions to advanced inquiries.

The innovative M.B.A. program provides students with knowledge and skills they can apply immediately in today's workplace. The program was designed after surveying employers in the U.S., Canada, Europe, and China to determine what they look for when hiring and promoting M.B.A.'s. With a focus on leadership, the program moves students through a series of skill-based assessment tasks clustered around specific business content areas. Students learn to build their own businesses through ongoing business simulations; work in teams to arrive at sound, ethical business decisions; and apply the knowledge and skills learned in the program to a business application project done in the community with an organization of choice. Throughout the duration of the program, students maintain an e-portfolio documenting the knowledge and skills gained during the course of the program.

Students and the M.B.A. Experience

Of the students enrolled in the M.B.A. program during 2007, 43 percent were women, 15 percent represented members of minority groups, and 22 percent were students from outside the U.S. The average age of the students was 36 years. Consequently, students who enter City University of Seattle's M.B.A. program typically have several years of work experience.

Course work combines textbook theory with current, real-world study. Research and in-class discussion are significant components of all courses. Faculty members encourage discussion over straight lecture. Students also engage in team projects and student presentations. The average class size is 12 students.

As a global institution, City University of Seattle offers students opportunities to experience different perspectives, whether through online classroom exchange with students from around the globe or through more traditional study-abroad experiences.

Special Features

Students may take classes in the day or evenings, via online distance learning, or through a combination of multiple delivery schedules.

The Faculty

The City University of Seattle faculty consists of distinguished practitioners in the fields of business, education, government, and human services. Instructors' qualifications combine strong academic preparation and active professional careers in the fields in which they teach. The School of Management employs 15 full-time faculty members and more than 510 adjunct faculty members. Of these, 30 percent are women and 12 percent are members of minority groups.

The Business School Network

City University of Seattle prides itself on the successful relationships it has established with the corporate community. Corporate representatives are an integral part of the community advisory groups that help the University to update course content, relate courses to current trends in the marketplace, and ensure that programs provide students with skills employers are seeking.

The College and Environs

City University of Seattle opened its doors in 1973 with one primary purpose: to provide educational opportunities for those segments of the population not being fully served through traditional means. This purpose has guided the University's growth from an institution in a single-room facility in Seattle, Washington, to an international leader in education with locations in Washington, Western Canada, Europe, and China. City University of Seattle's administrative and academic headquarters are located in Bellevue, Washington. Students who attend one of the University's sites in the Pacific Northwest enjoy a temperate climate, beautiful landscape, and clean and cultured cities.

City University of Seattle is accredited by the Northwest Commission on Colleges and Universities and offers more than seventy-five degree and certificate programs at the undergraduate and graduate levels.

Facilities

City University of Seattle's library offers an abundance of information resources in paper, microfiche, and electronic formats. Its holdings include more than 1,403 periodical titles, ERIC documents on microfiche and online, and more than 44,000 books and curriculum materials. Most resources are indexed on the University's Web site. Reference and interlibrary loan services are offered to all students through the library's toll-free telephone number and e-mail. To serve certain education programs, the library maintains branches in Bellevue, Everett, Tacoma, and Vancouver, Washington. In addition, City University of Seattle has formed cooperative agreements with appropriate libraries to extend library privileges to students in selected cities.

Technology Environment

The University requires students to have access to a computer. Students are expected to use computer technology in the development of research papers; certain M.B.A. courses require computerized data manipulation as well. Computer lab facilities are available for students at all North American sites.

Admission

Admission to City University of Seattle graduate programs requires that students hold a baccalaureate degree or the equivalent from an accredited or otherwise recognized institution. No specific undergraduate emphasis or major is required for entrance into a particular graduate program.

Scores on standardized entrance examinations such as the Graduate Record Examinations (GRE), the Miller Analogies Test (MAT), and the Graduate Management Admission Test (GMAT) are not required.

Finances

Standard tuition rates for graduate courses for the 2007–08 academic year were $500 per credit, or $1500 per 3-credit course. Although the number of required texts and other course materials vary with each course, textbooks typically cost $100 to $150 each. Other fees may apply, depending on the specific course of study.

City University of Seattle does not provide student housing. In the Seattle area, rental expenses for a one-bedroom apartment are approximately $950 per month.

For information about financial assistance, students should contact the Financial Aid Office.

International Students

The University's International Student Services Office helps international students adjust to life and study in the United States, offering assistance with procedures related to the issuance and maintenance of student visas, counseling in academic matters, and student referral to appropriate agencies for health and other services.

Application Facts and Dates

A rolling admissions policy governs most City University of Seattle programs. That is, the University accepts applications and announces admissions decisions continuously throughout the year. Most degree programs may be commenced in the fall, winter, spring, or summer quarter. For more information, students should contact:

Office of Admissions
City University of Seattle
11900 NE First Street
Bellevue, Washington 98005

Phone: 425-637-1010
            888-422-4898 (toll-free)
            425-450-4660 (TYY/TDD)
Fax: 425-709-5361
E-mail: info@cityu.edu
Web site: http://www.cityu.edu

Financial Engineering
Claremont Graduate University

Claremont Graduate University

Claremont, California

A FUSION OF LEADERSHIP, STRATEGY, AND MANAGEMENT

The Peter F. Drucker and Masatoshi Ito Graduate School of Management is committed to developing and enriching tomorrow's leaders by weaving Peter Drucker's philosophy of management—that management is very much a human enterprise—throughout the Drucker School experience. You will be able to tailor your program of study to your needs, either on a part-time or a full-time basis. Most importantly, you will be valued as an individual with a unique set of personal and professional talents. A Drucker School M.B.A. provides you with both personal enrichment and professional growth.

—Ira A. Jackson, Dean

Programs and Curricular Focus

The Drucker M.B.A. is made up of 60 academic units (with 4 units allotted to a typical course). The program takes between eighteen and thirty-six months to complete, depending on whether a student attends full- or part-time. The curriculum instills a powerful knowledge base from the required core courses, yet provides the opportunity to concentrate elective courses in one of six areas: leadership, strategy, finance, marketing, global management, or entrepreneurship.

Unique, relative to other management schools, the Drucker M.B.A. embodies the philosophies of management pioneer Peter F. Drucker, a longtime faculty member and prolific writer and lecturer on management. The program is based on the belief that management is not only about tasks, but it is also about people—motivating them and leading them. The curriculum provides students with substantial value to complement their unique talents, undergraduate course work, and work experience. The classroom experience is enriched through student participation and faculty blending of theory and practice.

As part of the Claremont College consortium, a Drucker student may earn a dual degree with any of the other schools of Claremont Graduate University (CGU). Some of the most popular dual-degree programs include the M.B.A./Ph.D. in economics; the M.B.A./M.A. in human resources design, and the M.B.A./M.S. in information systems. In addition, the Drucker School offers joint degrees with the School of Mathematics (M.S. in financial engineering) and the School of Arts and Humanities (M.A. in arts and cultural management). The M.S. in financial engineering program at Claremont Graduate University is ranked among the top financial engineering programs in the United States.

In addition to the M.B.A., the Drucker School offers an Executive M.B.A., a Master of Arts in Management (M.A.M.) and a Master of Science in Advanced Management (M.S.A.M.). These programs are designed for experienced managers who are looking for a classroom experience that updates their leadership and strategy skills to match their changing responsibilities.

Students and the M.B.A. Experience

The Drucker M.B.A. program enrolls approximately 200 students with a variety of educational and work experiences. Approximately 25 percent of the students are fully employed and enrolled as part-time students. These students bring their daily work experience into the classroom and, together with the faculty, relate business theory to practice. A number of the Drucker full-time students are sponsored by their overseas employers and bring global realities to the Drucker experience. The average Drucker M.B.A. student is 28 years old with five years of work experience. Women make up approximately 40 percent of the student body.

The small-class format (average class size is 25 students) provides students with an intimate, educational experience while enjoying the benefits provided by the facilities of the Claremont Graduate University.

Special Features

Drucker students are able to study at Oxford University (England), University of St. Gallen (Switzerland), Rotterdam School of Management (the Netherlands), Hitotsubashi Business School (Japan), and Inha University (South Korea).

Full-time students may pursue internships between the spring term of their first year and the fall term of their second year with assistance from the Office of Career Services and Corporate Relations.

The Faculty

Drucker alumni reflecting on their M.B.A experience generally mention outstanding teaching and courses as some of the unique characteristics of the Drucker experience. World-renowned authors, such as Mihalii Csiksentmihlayi (*Flow* and *Creativity and Innovation*) and Jean Lipman-Blumen (*Toxic Leadership* and *Connective Leadership*) teach inimitable courses based on their cutting-edge research. The Drucker School's faculty members are selected for the high quality of their academic training and research, their knowledge of management and leadership practice, and their superior teaching skills. Most of the full-time faculty members are experienced consultants or have significant managerial experience.

The Business School Network

Through Drucker School institutes, faculty research, and consulting alliances, the Drucker School maintains key relationships in the business community. The School's Board of Visitors includes CEOs and other prominent businesspeople who provide guidance and financial resources to further the Drucker School's programs. A broad range of leading corporate partners sponsor research, collaborate with the Drucker School faculty members, and regularly recruit Drucker School M.B.A. interns and graduates. In order to connect students with valuable alumni, the Drucker School has an active Drucker Alumni Association that holds numerous events annually.

The College and Environs

The Claremont Colleges are a group of small and distinguished liberal arts colleges. Claremont Graduate University, founded in 1925, was the second member of The Claremont Colleges. CGU enrolls approximately 2,200 students in seven schools or centers. The mission of Claremont Graduate University is to prepare a diverse group of outstanding individuals to assume leadership

The Peter F. Drucker and Masatoshi Ito Graduate School of Management at Claremont.

roles in the worldwide community through research, teaching, and practice in selected fields.

Claremont is a beautiful residential community of 34,000 located 35 miles east of Los Angeles, close to skiing, the beach, the desert, and other recreational areas. This pleasant college town with an Ivy League atmosphere is situated in the foothills of the San Gabriel Mountains.

Technology Environment

Claremont Graduate University has an academic computing center reserved for student use where IBM, Apple, and Digital Equipment computers are provided. Most software packages utilized in instruction are Microsoft products, but many other software packages are available. The Claremont Colleges' Honnold-Mudd Library is advanced in electronic access and CD-ROM capability. CGU also has wireless laptop capabilities in some buildings and courtyards.

Placement

The Office of Career Services and Corporate Relations helps students and alumni effectively manage their career paths to ensure long-term success in their chosen fields. Beginning with their first day on campus, Drucker students meet individually with a Career Services staff member who gets to know the student's aptitude and interests. Ongoing workshops with alumni and local employers help prepare the students for a successful career.

Career Services and leaders within the Drucker School conduct a consistent marketing and corporate communications program to solicit additional placement opportunities in areas of interest to CGU students and alumni. Career Services maintains an aggressive program of flexible and tailored response to potential employers based on a state-of-the-art resume database. Career Services also offers a variety of services, including one-on-one counseling, resume and cover letter critiquing, networking opportunities, individual job listings, on- and off-campus recruiting, a career resources library, and career skills workshops.

Admission

Applicants to the Drucker M.B.A. program must submit a completed application, a GMAT score, undergraduate and graduate school transcripts, three letters of reference, a resume, a personal statement, and the application fee to the Admissions Office of the Claremont Graduate University. Prospective students may apply online at the School's Web site.

Finances

Tuition and fees for the 2007–08 academic year were $1376 per unit in the M.B.A. program and $1580 per unit in the Executive Management Program. Living expenses were about $12,360 for on-campus residents and $16,000 for off-campus residents.

Approximately 50 percent of Drucker M.B.A. students receive fellowships, assistantships, or other grants, with the average award amounting to about $12,000 a year. Institutional aid programs based on both academic merit and financial need are available, as are loans and work-study programs.

International Students

To support a global learning environment, approximately 40 percent of Drucker M.B.A. students are international. Starting in summer and continuing into fall, the International Fellows program is an excellent intensive pre-M.B.A. program for nonnative English speakers. The International Place of the Claremont Colleges offers many services to international students, including airport pickup and apartment hunting, and helps students adjust to their new environment. The Claremont Colleges excel in helping these students feel welcome and receive maximum benefit from their degrees. In this intimate and collegial environment, domestic and international students share their experiences and perspectives for a truly global graduate education.

Application Facts and Dates

The Drucker School utilizes a rolling admissions process for fall, spring, and summer admissions. Applicants generally are notified of the decision within four weeks of applying.

Peter F. Drucker and Masatoshi Ito
    Graduate School of Management
Claremont Graduate University
1021 North Dartmouth Avenue
Claremont, California 91711-6184
Phone: 909-607-7811
       800-944-4312 (toll-free)
Fax: 909-607-9104
E-mail: drucker@cgu.edu
Web site: http://www.drucker.cgu.edu

Clark University

Worcester, Massachusetts

AN M.B.A. FOR THE GLOBAL ECONOMY

Clark University combines three features that will make your experience here unique. First, we are small—300 students, 19 full-time faculty members. The extraordinary accessibility of our faculty builds a rapport with students that enhances the learning environment. Second, we are internationally focused. Our curriculum reflects a deep commitment to preparing you to manage effectively in the global marketplace. Third, our faculty is research oriented. We share a dedication to staying at the forefront of our disciplines. This means that you will learn best practices and state-of-the-art techniques for today's business world plus how to develop the new best practices needed for tomorrow's world.

—Ed Ottensmeyer, Dean

Programs and Curricular Focus

Accredited by AACSB International–The Association to Advance Collegiate Schools of Business, Clark University Graduate School of Management offers a personal setting for a multinational management education, attracting students from more than thirty countries.

Clark's integrated M.B.A. curriculum goes far beyond offering the fundamentals. Through projects and internships, the program provides students with rich opportunities to work on multidisciplinary teams with people from all over the world. Students solve complex business problems designed to develop an understanding of global marketplace trends, sharpen leadership skills, and acquire essential practical experience.

Clark's M.B.A. curriculum is designed to provide students with strong analytical foundations and critical management judgment. What sets Clark apart is its emphasis on courses that reflect the way the world does business: teams of managers bringing together diverse cultures, skills, and experiences to meet the toughest business challenges.

Other curricular features include concentrations in accounting, finance, global business, international development/community/environment, management, management information systems, and marketing; an expanded accounting concentration that qualifies students to sit for the CPA exam; a Master of Science in Finance (M.S.F.) program; international exchange programs in Europe; and the opportunity to audit one course per semester in other divisions of the University.

Students and the M.B.A. Experience

Clark's M.B.A. program attracts a diverse student body. Hailing from many different states and countries, students come together to form a microcosm of the contemporary business arena. They work together in teams in many courses, notably the Management Consulting Projects course. This course offers students the opportunity to work as a member of a consulting team on actual management problems facing area corporations.

The average full-time student has three years of full-time professional work experience, along with a record of strong undergraduate achievement. Approximately 35 percent of all entering students have an undergraduate business background. Women make up 42 percent of the population, and approximately 45 percent of the students come from outside the United States. Because of the program's small size, students readily form lasting friendships with their classmates and professors; these friendships are truly meaningful, especially as students enter the business world in both the U.S. and abroad.

Global Focus

Students' understanding of the world's way of doing business is not limited to just a few courses at Clark. Clark has intentionally created a curriculum that reflects the world's rapidly changing business environment, and international issues are addressed in many courses. Students also develop a personal understanding of global topics by getting to know colleagues from all over the world.

The Faculty

The Graduate School of Management emphasizes excellence in both teaching and research. The School's reputation in the United States and abroad is maintained, in large measure, through respect for the intellectual contributions of its faculty members. The School is a true community, and it fosters collegiality and close relationships between students and faculty members.

The Business School Network

Faculty consulting and research activities ensure Clark's link to the business community. Semester after semester, area corporations, Fortune 500 firms among them, turn to Clark for assistance in addressing management issues. The School's advisory council, made up of prominent CEOs and other top executives, ensures that the M.B.A. curriculum is continually refined to reflect the dynamic nature of business.

The College and Environs

A teaching and research institution founded in 1887, Clark University is one of the oldest graduate institutions in the nation. Clark is one of only three New England universities, with Harvard and Yale, to be a founding member of the Association of American Universities. Clark University is located in Worcester, Massachusetts, the second-largest city in New England, just 1 hour from Boston and 3 hours from New

York City. Worcester is a center of the high-technology, biotechnology, health-care, and financial services industries.

Placement

Because of the program's small size, students have outstanding access to career management services for a university of Clark's quality. From the first day of orientation, career services staff members are ready to help students assess their skills, research career options, develop experience, prepare their resumes, and meet employers.

Alumni mentoring, individual advising, and on-campus recruiting are just a few of the many career services readily available. The staff members are keenly aware that students' primary motivating factor in seeking an M.B.A. is to improve employment prospects.

Admission

Clark seeks students who add to the vitality of the interactions between faculty members and students. Applications from men and women with diverse educational and professional backgrounds are encouraged. The Admission Review Committee at the Graduate School of Management considers the entire application for offering admission and granting scholarships. GMAT or GRE test scores, a student's records of undergraduate academic achievement, and a current resume, along with letters of recommendation and a personal statement, are considered. A minimum TOEFL score of 80 (Internet-based), 213 (computer-based), or 550 (paper-based) is required for international students.

Finances

Tuition is calculated on a per-course basis rather than per semester. For the 2008–09 academic year, tuition per course is $3180. Activity, service, and insurance fees are estimated at $2305. Living and personal expenses are estimated at $9500, with books and supplies costing an additional $1000.

The Graduate School of Management offers scholarships based exclusively on merit to both U.S. and international students.

Awards range from 25 percent to 100 percent of tuition. Graduate assistantship positions are also awarded on merit. All applicants are considered for these merit-based awards.

International Students

Clark University is an exceptionally hospitable place for international students. With students from more than seventy countries, the University prides itself on the range of support services available to these students. Clark maintains a department dedicated to the service of international students, assisting them with visa issues and with the social, cultural, and academic adjustments to life at an American university.

Application Facts and Dates

For M.B.A applicants, the fall semester priority admission deadline for full-time students who would like to be considered for merit-based scholarships is April 1; the final deadline is June 1. For the spring semester, the deadline for full-time applicants is November 1.

For more information, students should contact:

Ms. Lynn Davis
Director of Enrollment and Marketing
Graduate School of Management
Clark University
950 Main Street
Worcester, Massachusetts 01610-1477

Phone: 508-793-7406
Fax: 508-421-3825
E-mail: clarkmba@clarku.edu
Web site: http://www.clarku.edu/gsom

The College of Saint Rose

Albany, New York

TOOLS FOR SUCCESS IN THE TWENTY-FIRST CENTURY

Today's increasingly competitive business environment requires that an M.B.A. program provide students with opportunities to acquire cutting-edge knowledge, analytical abilities, and practical application skills to prepare business managers for productive and efficient leadership. The Saint Rose M.B.A. curriculum is designed to meet these requirements. The Saint Rose M.B.A. program includes course work that addresses leadership, communication, production and quality management, finance, technology, human resource management, and marketing.

The business world of the twenty-first century presents managers with more challenges than ever before. Graduates of our M.B.A. program are equipped with the tools they need to meet these challenges successfully.

—Severin Carlson, Dean, School of Business

Programs and Curricular Focus

The College of Saint Rose M.B.A. program, which is accredited by the Association of Collegiate Business Schools and Programs, balances theoretical instruction, case-study simulations, and the opportunity to work with existing businesses. The M.B.A. program's courses are designed to teach students how to lead and communicate on the job and in the community. The educational approach of the Saint Rose School of Business is to emphasize results-oriented management. Faculty members apply a variety of teaching methods, such as group discussion, computer-aided instruction, seminars by members of the business community, and individual and team projects.

The School of Business offers part-time, full-time, and one-year M.B.A. program options, all of which share the goal of preparing M.B.A. students to be effective, innovative managers. The part-time M.B.A. option allows students the flexibility of taking one or two courses per semester and completing the program at their own pace. Or, students may take more than two courses per semester, plus summer sessions, to complete the part-time program in two calendar years. The one-year M.B.A. curriculum program combines intensive course work with career development opportunities, including internships and a competitive executive mentor program. Students may transfer up to 12 degree-applicable graduate credits from another accredited institution.

The Saint Rose M.B.A. requires a minimum of 36 credits of course work to complete the degree. Applicants may be required to complete program prerequisites.

The Saint Rose M.B.A. Plus requires a minimum of 45 credits of course work to complete the degree. Students who choose

to pursue this option are awarded a Master of Business Administration and an advanced certificate in one of three specialized content areas: computer information systems, financial planning, and not-for-profit management.

Students can also pursue the advanced certificates as stand-alone certificates to gain specialized knowledge in a business field. Each certificate consists of five 3-credit courses.

The Advanced Certificate in Computer Information Systems provides prospective and current managers with a theoretical and practical understanding of critical aspects of managing, communicating, and decision making related to computer information systems. The minimum length of time to complete the program is one calendar year, including fall, spring, and summer sessions.

The Advanced Certificate in Financial Planning provides students and professionals with high-quality financial planning education that fulfills the requirements to sit for the CFP Certification Examination administered by the CFP Board. The curriculum includes study of income tax management, employee benefits, retirement planning, insurance, estate planning, and investments. The minimum length of time to complete the program is one calendar year, including fall, spring, and summer sessions.

The Advanced Certificate in Not-For-Profit Management provides not-for-profit professionals with the formal training and credentials needed to move ahead in their careers. The certificate fulfills the education requirement for the Certified Association Executive comprehensive examination sponsored by the American Society of Association Executives (ASAE) and covers five major content areas: governance and structure,

leadership process, management and administration, internal and external relations, and programs and services. The minimum length of time to complete the program is one calendar year, including fall, spring, and summer sessions.

The College of Saint Rose offers a joint law/business program with Albany Law School to provide students with the opportunity to complete both the M.B.A. and the J.D. degree in less than four years of full-time study. Applicants must first satisfy the admission requirements of Albany Law School.

The College's 30-credit M.S. in accounting program qualifies graduates to sit for the CPA examination in New York state provided they have at least 60 credits of liberal arts and the requisite number of undergraduate and graduate business courses. The degree is also geared toward students who already work in accounting but who want to advance in their field and students who want to enter the field of accounting for the first time. Emphasis is on the development of conceptual knowledge and analytical skills in business with a specialized concentration in the specific functions of accounting. The program takes place in the evenings, can be completed on a full- or part-time basis, and is registered by the New York State Board of Regents and the State Education Department's Office of Professions.

Students and the M.B.A. Experience

The M.B.A. program is structured to accommodate the needs of a wide range of students, including those with substantial knowledge of business, those without an undergraduate business degree or previous business experience, and those returning to advanced study after an absence. Classes for the M.B.A. are conveniently scheduled in the evenings and on weekends to fit into the schedules of students who work full-time or have other commitments during the day. Students enrolled in the intensive one-year M.B.A. program attend some classes during the day. Class size is kept to an average of 16 students in order to facilitate interaction in the classroom. Approximately 50 percent of M.B.A. students are women.

The Faculty

Graduate business faculty members are professionals with significant experience who have built strong relationships with members of the business community and remain involved with private companies, not-for-profit organizations, and government agencies in a variety of capacities. All M.B.A. courses are taught by full-time faculty members or experts from the local business community. Ninety-three percent of the faculty members in the School of Business hold a doctorate or professional certification in their area of expertise, and 50 percent of the faculty members are women.

The Business School Network

Recent distinguished lecturers include Mario Gabelli, Chairman, CEO, and CIO, Gabelli Asset Management, Inc.; William J. McDonough, President, Federal Reserve Bank of New York; Mary Farrell, Managing Director, Paine Webber; Hugh Johnson Jr., Chairman and President, First Albany Asset Management Corporation; and Joseph J. Plumeri, Chairman and CEO, Willis Group Holdings, Ltd.

The College and Environs

Founded in 1920 by the Sisters of Saint Joseph of Carondelet, Saint Rose is a private, independent, coeducational institution serving more than 5,000 graduate and undergraduate students. Located in Albany's historic Pine Hills neighborhood, the College enjoys all the advantages of a major metropolitan area; a variety of restaurants, shops, museums, and theaters are easily accessible. The College is just a short ride away from many destinations, including New York City, Boston, and Montreal; the Adirondack and Catskill Mountains of New York; and the Green Mountains of Vermont.

Facilities

The campus features historic and contemporary buildings, including the Thelma P. Lally School of Education, Neil Hellman Library, Science Center, Learning Center, Joy Emery Educational and Clinical Services Center, Massry Center for the Arts, Picotte Hall Art Center, Events and Athletics Center, and renovated Victorian homes.

Two classrooms designed to facilitate faculty-student interaction are reserved for use by M.B.A. classes. Both classrooms feature state-of-the-art technology that allows faculty members to utilize computer-based instructional support.

The Neil Hellman Library houses 233,258 volumes, 680 periodical subscriptions, 313,340 titles on microform, 2,564

DVD/VHS, 1,200 audio CDs, 35,000 e-books, 50 database subscriptions, and a collection of rare books and provides access to 30,000 full-text periodical titles.

The College's Office of Residence Life assists graduate students in locating suitable off-campus housing.

Technology Environment

The use of computers is integral to the course work of the Saint Rose M.B.A. program. Many assignments require proficiency with word processing, spreadsheet, and presentation software. Students have access to computer labs and up-to-date software packages, as well as Internet and World Wide Web service. Smart classrooms are equipped with full multimedia, making classroom instruction interactive and allowing students to create and demonstrate professional presentations. The College's on-site copy center aids students in creating full-color slide presentations and bound proposals.

Placement

The College's Career Center provides students and alumni with a resource center consisting of job banks, information about job fairs, career assessment and counseling, a computer-assisted career guidance and job searching system, resume preparation assistance and referral, credential files, on-campus interviews, videotaped mock interviews, and workshops. These services are available to all M.B.A. students and alumni free of charge.

Admission

Admission to the M.B.A. and advanced certificate program options is dependent on the completion of an undergraduate degree program at an accredited college or university. An applicant with a background in any undergraduate major is qualified to apply; however, students must meet M.B.A. program prerequisites prior to beginning their studies.

Applicants must file a completed application form, official transcripts from all colleges and universities attended, a personal essay, and two letters of recommendation for graduate study. There is a nonrefundable application fee of $35. Only individuals with an undergraduate GPA of less than 3.0 must submit Graduate Management Admission Test (GMAT) scores. Applicants whose native language is not English must submit TOEFL scores, official

English translations of all transcripts, a grading key, and a copy of a diploma.

Finances

Tuition for the 2008–09 academic year is $596 per semester hour of credit. There is a technology fee of $21 and a student records fee of $50 per year. Saint Rose serves graduate students through a comprehensive program of federal, state, and institutional financial aid, which may include Federal Stafford Student Loans (subsidized and unsubsidized), the New York State Tuition Assistance Program (TAP), graduate assistantships, graduate multicultural and international scholarships, or graduate merit scholarships, if the applicant qualifies. Applicants are required to submit the Free Application for Federal Student Aid (FAFSA), the New York State Tuition Assistance application, and signed copies of federal and state income tax documents and W-2 wage statements.

International Students

An International Student Organization is active on campus. The Director of International Studies coordinates activities and programs for international students studying at Saint Rose, including orientation, immigration and personal advisement, language assessment and assistance, and the coordination of on- and off-campus community programs. In addition, the Learning Center also offers English for speakers of other languages (ESOL) tutorial support.

Application Facts and Dates

Preferred application deadlines are October 15 for the spring semester, March 15 for the summer semester, and June 1 for the fall semester.

M.B.A. Program Director
School of Business
The College of Saint Rose
Albany, New York 12203-1490
Phone: 518-454-5143
Fax: 518-458-5479
E-mail: mba@strose.edu

Graduate and Continuing Education
 Admissions
The College of Saint Rose
432 Western Avenue
Albany, New York 12203-1490
Phone: 518-454-5143
Fax: 518-458-5479
E-mail: grad@strose.edu
Web site: http://www.strose.edu

Colorado State University

Fort Collins, Colorado

DEAN'S MESSAGE

The College of Business has enjoyed significant growth and national attention in its climb toward becoming a world-class institution. Several hallmarks denote the quality of our programs, including this year's ranking as one of U.S. News & World Report's top 100 best undergraduate business schools, number one in the Princeton Review's Best 237 Business Schools 2007 Best Administered category and ranked as one of Business Week's top 100 Best Colleges of Business. Then add the facts that business administration, the University's largest major, has grown 46 percent in the last five years and that its students have the University's highest cumulative GPA (3.2). Next, consider that more than 70 percent of the business faculty members received their doctoral degrees from the nation's top fifty and premier-tier institutions.

Our path for the next level of excellence includes lofty goals in program development, student services, external rankings, fundraising, and alumni involvement. This is an exciting time for the College of Business. Share the success; come with us on the journey!

—Ajay Menon, Dean

Programs and Curricular Focus

The College of Business aims to be the college of choice for its two major stakeholders—students and employers. The College provides a superior applied educational experience to on-campus and distance students, with an emphasis on global leadership, entrepreneurship, and corporate citizenship. The Master of Business Administration (M.B.A.) degree programs are fully accredited by AACSB International–The Association to Advance Collegiate Schools of Business—and rank among the top 20 percent of business programs in the United States. The Distance M.B.A. Program from Colorado State University (CSU), now more than 40 years old, is one of the only AACSB International–accredited Distance M.B.A. programs available, and it is delivered to distance students via multimedia DVD technology and the recently introduced video streaming to offer students around the world even faster access to course materials. Students benefit from viewing the entire lecture, including the Power-Point slides, presentations by guest lecturers, class discussions, and student questions. The full classroom environment is delivered to each distance student, thus increasing their level of interest and retention of the material presented. Nearly 2,000 students have earned their M.B.A. degrees from CSU.

Students may earn their M.B.A. through three program options—the on-campus Professional M.B.A. Program, the Distance M.B.A. Program, or the Denver Executive M.B.A. Program.

The Professional M.B.A. Program is designed to serve the needs of working professionals and provide a fresh, relevant approach to graduate business education. This 36-credit program takes twenty-one months to complete, including one summer session. All classes meet in the early evening, just two days per week, to minimize the impact on busy work schedules and personal lives.

The Colorado State University Denver Executive M.B.A. Program was launched in 1988 and was the first such program in Denver. It offers full-time professionals an alternative educational delivery option while they pursue full-time careers. The Denver Executive M.B.A. Program targets advancing managers and emerging leaders, individuals who want to go beyond the theory and application of their learning to the strategic level of thinking. This program allows students to complete their M.B.A. degree in twenty-one months, with classes only two evenings per week, thereby minimizing impact on their weekends. Students feel as if they are meeting with a very diverse and accomplished board of directors twice a week, because the high experience level of the participants provides such a vibrant cohort program.

The Distance M.B.A. Program is designed to deliver a high-quality education while providing students with the flexibility they need. Each class is recorded on DVD in a specially designed, state-of-the-art, multimedia classroom. Via DVDs, students in the Distance M.B.A. Program view the class exactly as it progresses on campus, benefiting from the full lecture, class discussions, and the all-important questions asked by the on-campus students. The DVDs are supplemented with an exclusive M.B.A. intranet for communication with professors, classmates, and the University's student-support services and library. Introduced in late 2007, video streaming is available to all Distance M.B.A. Program students regardless of location around the world. The video streaming, called BizCast, gives students nearly no delay in viewing the full classroom dynamic. With two 16-week semesters per year, each divided into two 8-week sessions, the program can

be completed in as little as twenty-one months or may be extended to four or five years. There is no on-campus attendance required; however, more than half of the Distance M.B.A. Program graduates come to the campus each year for commencement. There is no residency requirement for individuals in the Distance M.B.A. Program.

Students and the M.B.A. Experience

The average business experience reported by the class entering in 2008 totaled twelve years. The diversity of professional disciplines represented in the entering class spanned a great variety of corporate and business departments and skill sets, including finance, marketing, human resources, Internet technology, sales, organizational management, supply chain management, accounting, manufacturing, and product development. A number of students were private business owners and consultants. The class members' undergraduate degrees ranged from business and finance to psychology, life sciences, physics, engineering, and history.

Most distance M.B.A. students are working professionals with more than twelve years of work experience. They are drawn from all fifty states, several Canadian provinces, and many countries around the world, with an average age of 33 and an average GMAT score of 580. A large number of U.S. military personnel stationed around the world are active in the Distance M.B.A. Program.

Students entering the Denver Executive M.B.A. Program last year had broad business experience, with eight to thirty years of professional work. The 2008 graduating class had an average GPA above 3.6, reflective of the impact of cross-group executive team support and a highly leveraged learning environment. Executives from some of Denver's most progressive firms have graduated from this program, including Denver Community Federal Credit Union, Ericsson, Excel Energy, First Data, Frontier Airlines, Galileo, Hein & Associates, the Medtronic Surgical, Sybase, Nortel, University of Colorado Health Science Center, and Teledyne WaterPik.

The Faculty

Graduate study offered at Colorado State University comprises programs of excellence. What differentiates these programs from the others is the high quality of the faculty members, who integrate real-world experiences into their courses. The vast majority of professors who teach in the M.B.A. programs are full-time faculty members with Ph.D.'s in their disciplines; those who do not hold a Ph.D. have excellent specialized industry experience and bring a unique expertise to the classroom. Many of the professors also continue to work in their respective industries as consultants.

The Business School Network

Fort Collins is the center for a wide range of high-tech and production firms, including Agilent, Anheuser-Busch, Hewlett-Packard, Intel, Kodak, LSI-Logic, Teledyne WaterPik, and Woodward Governor.

Colorado State graduates have gone on to win Pulitzer Prizes, become leaders of industry and education, and carry on important scholarly work.

College of Business M.B.A. students are connected to each other on campus and around the world through an M.B.A. intranet. This communications platform provides students with an avenue to "talk" with their professors, classmates, and team members; detailed discussions are encouraged in threaded discussions and chat rooms. In addition, M.B.A. program alumni have an opportunity to stay connected with other alumni and professors to bring added value for networking after graduation.

The College and Environs

The mission of the College of Business is to provide a diverse set of students with the knowledge, skills, and functional competencies needed to become effective decision makers and leaders in a business environment that is becoming more global, competitive, and dynamic and to give those students the knowledge and resources that are useful to the business community, their fellow scholars, and other constituencies seeking expertise.

The College of Business is part of Colorado State University, a land-grant university founded in 1870, with an enrollment of more than 24,000 students. CSU has a tradition of research excellence, being cited by both the Carnegie Commission and the Association of Research Libraries as one of the top 100 research universities in the United States.

Colorado State University is located in Fort Collins, a community of 132,000 located 65 miles north of Denver. Fort Collins is nestled against the foothills of the Front Range of the Rocky Mountains. The city is a business and retail center for the Northern Front Range region, an area that encompasses Loveland and Greeley, Colorado, and Cheyenne, Wyoming.

Facilities

The on-campus M.B.A. program is housed in a classroom to be envied. The double-horseshoe boardroom-style setup encourages discussion and interaction among the students and the professor. The modified stadium seating allows for everyone to be seen and heard. The technology in this room is excellent, from the four commercial-quality production cameras (to capture all the activity in the classroom for the Distance M.B.A. Program students) to the downloadable SMART Board and, finally, to the sensitive microphones around the room to capture the questions and ideas from the students. All M.B.A. students in the CSU program have access to the excellent library resources through the College of Business portal.

The CSU library provides services to Distance M.B.A. participants comparable to those available to the on-campus community. It provides remote access to databases and the library catalog, document delivery, reference help, and instruction sessions. Through the portal, students can use all but a few of the databases listed on the library's Web site. Distance M.B.A. students can request books and paper articles to be sent to them. In addition, all M.B.A. students have direct access to M.B.A. program advising services, program support personnel, and technical support. In addition, there is a career liaison to assist with resume preparation and advice on career moves. Colorado State University makes a point of treating all students as if they were on campus.

The Denver Executive M.B.A. Program's downtown location, in 410 Republic Square, is in the business heart of Denver. It offers an executive learning environment with expanded classrooms, new class technology, and business-to-business connections. In the new facilities, the College uses the Harvard executive forum format, with students positioned in a U-shaped management meeting room setup. The class uses wireless Internet and SMART Board technology to build on team collaboration and group communication. The facility provides executives and faculty members with easy access throughout the Denver metropolitan and Front Range areas.

Admission

Admission to the Professional M.B.A. Program is in the fall semester, with an application deadline of May 1. Because there are a limited number of openings each year, students should apply as early as possible. The Distance M.B.A. Program accepts applications in the fall and spring semesters, with submission deadlines of July 15 and December 8, respectively. The Denver Executive M.B.A. Program accepts applications through July 15 of each year for a fall start. Both the Distance M.B.A. and the Denver Executive M.B.A. Programs admit students on a rolling basis, whereas the Professional M.B.A. Program uses competitive admission criteria because of space limitations.

A primary goal of the Colorado State University M.B.A. programs is to select a set of richly diverse students with various undergraduate degrees and professional experiences; therefore, applicants with all types of undergraduate backgrounds are encouraged to apply. Admission decisions are based on an evaluation of the candidate's potential for successfully completing the graduate business program, the candidate's ability to add to the perspective of the class, and the school's ability to accommodate a limited number of students. Applicants for the Professional or Distance M.B.A. Programs must have a minimum of four years' full-time professional work experience. Applicants must submit a resume, a cover letter that reflects the applicant's carefully considered reasons for pursuing a business degree at the master's level, GMAT scores (petitions for GMAT waivers are considered), TOEFL scores (for international students), the College of Business Applicant Data Sheet, three completed recommendation forms in sealed envelopes, two copies of official transcripts in sealed envelopes, a completed Graduate School Web Application, and a $50 application fee. If the applicant's grade point average is below 3.0, a separate letter that explains the circumstances must be included.

Finances

For the 2008–09 academic year, tuition and fees for state residents enrolled in the Professional M.B.A. Program are about $22,000. Nonresidents pay about $29,000 for the program. The total tuition for the twenty-one-month Executive M.B.A. Program in Denver is $49,000. The current tuition for the Distance M.B.A. Program is $620 per credit, or about $22,000 for the total program, which includes the costs of the mixed-media DVDs sent directly to the students, access to the video streaming, the exclusive M.B.A. intranet, and all other student-support services. There were no additional program costs, except for books and materials. The University imposes a technology fee of $15 each semester.

All active-duty military, reservist, National Guard members, and veterans are granted a 10 percent reduction in their tuition when enrolling in the Distance M.B.A. Program. In addition, those in the federal and state governments also are extended this same tuition discount.

The College of Business has a limited number of assistantships available to graduate students enrolled in on-campus programs. The graduate assistantship award, based on the student's residency classification, includes either full in-state tuition, or half out-of-state tuition and a stipend for the fall and spring semester (not the summer term). Graduate assistantships are awarded on a semester basis, with students working with a faculty member or administrator in the College of Business for 10 hours per week during the fall and/or spring semesters. The student's supervisor evaluates the student's performance and determines the renewal of student contracts. Students must maintain a minimum 3.0 grade point average to keep their assistantship. To apply for an assistantship, students must complete the assistantship application available from the College of Business. A resume must be submitted with the application. Priority is given to those students who apply before April 1. Students must be accepted to a master's program in the College of Business before being offered an assistantship. This assistance is available to all graduate students, except for those in the Distance M.B.A. and Denver Executive M.B.A. Programs.

Federal financial aid is available to qualified students admitted to the M.B.A. programs who take at least 5 credits per semester. More information can be obtained from the Financial Aid Office at http://sfs.colostate.edu/B2000.cfm or by calling 800-491-4622 Ext 7 (toll-free). Students may also apply for financial aid on the Web at http://www.fafsa.gov. Students interested in using their Montgomery GI Bill or tuition assistance will find well-trained, helpful individuals to help them.

Application Facts and Dates

Applications for the Professional M.B.A. Program must be submitted by May 1. The application deadlines for the Distance M.B.A. Program are July 15 and December 8 for the fall and spring semesters, respectively. Those applying to the Executive M.B.A. Program in Denver must do so by July 15 for the fall semester.

Completed application packets should be sent to:

Rachel Stoll
College of Business Graduate Admissions
Colorado State University
1270 Campus Delivery
Fort Collins, Colorado 80523-1270

Phone: 800-491-4662 (toll-free)
Fax: 970-491-3481
E-mail: rachel.stoll@colostate.edu
Web site: http://www.CSUmba.com

Cornell University

Johnson Graduate School of Management

Ithaca, New York

REAL IMPACT

▶ *At the Johnson School, our M.B.A. graduates are exceptionally skilled, highly focused leaders who are ready to make an impact in the business world. The Johnson School is a competitive, collaborative community where future leaders learn to motivate organizations, guide them to success, and steward their continued growth in the marketplace. Our M.B.A. education speaks to the mission and traditions of the Johnson School: applying knowledge, advancing ideas, and sparking innovation—and our process combines a focus on performance-based education, a small and dynamic community, and the ability to leverage the vast resources of Cornell, one of the world's top research institutions. Within our walls exists an integrated, cross-functional, global community that truly mirrors today's business environment. The Johnson School community is a microcosm of today's business environment: cross-functional, global, diverse. Our renowned faculty—strong in research, applied practice, and teaching—interacts and works closely with a dynamic student body from myriad nations and walks of life. Students develop their own course of study, draw on the resources of a world-famous research institution, and participate in innovative, hands-on projects, such as student-run venture capital fund. They graduate ready to make an immediate impact and deliver lasting results.*

Program and Curricular Focus

The Johnson School program combines rigor and flexibility. A first-year core includes integration among functional areas and a heavy emphasis on financial analysis, case analysis, and strategic topics. Also included in the core curriculum is the development of leadership, team building, strategic thinking, and communication skills.

One prime example of this is the Integrative Case Competition, which requires students to integrate materials covered during the semester and apply that knowledge to a complex business problem. Teams of students discuss a real-life case study and formulate a plan of action, presenting their case to a panel of judges. The competition, a part of the Managerial Finance and Strategy core courses, counts toward the students' final course grades.

Core courses are scheduled so students may take electives during their first year and gain advanced training prior to the summer internship. Most students participate in the acclaimed immersion courses, which are currently offered in strategic operations, managerial finance, investment banking, capital markets and asset management entrepreneurship and private equity, brand management, and sustainable global enterprise. Immersion courses offer an integrated, real-world focus, which has made them vastly popular with students and recruiters alike.

The Parker Center for Investment Research and the Center for Sustainable Global Enterprise are leading-edge institutions for the research and study of these areas vital to business. Future centers will focus on business in entrepreneurship and business in science and technology.

There are many opportunities for students to apply their skills in their area of interest. For example, the Cayuga Fund LLC and the BR Ventures capital fund give students opportunities to work on investment funds in a hands-on way. Johnson School students are also encouraged to make full use of Cornell's other internationally renowned programs, such as industrial and labor relations, biotechnology, law, engineering, public policy, international development, hotel administration, and advanced computing. A significant portion of the credits required to complete the M.B.A. program may be fulfilled with any graduate-level course at Cornell.

Students and the M.B.A. Experience

The Johnson School tradition of working and socializing together leads to an unusually strong sense of community and collegiality. The average age of the students is 25, and the average work experience is five years. Women make up 25 percent of the class; members of minority groups, 20 percent; and international students, 34 percent. About one third of the M.B.A. students are married.

Global Focus

The Johnson School features a student body with approximately one third international students, myriad opportunities for classroom learning in international business, and a wealth of international activities. The wide variety of courses in international subjects features prominent guest speakers from around the world.

Experiential learning opportunities in the international management area include study trips to such places as the European Union,

Asia, Latin America, and many transition economies. Students can pursue a joint M.B.A./M.A. in Asian studies. In addition, second-year students in the Johnson School's resident two-year M.B.A. program can participate in exchange programs with seventeen international schools of business, including two through which dual M.B.A. degrees are awarded.

Extracurricular symposia, conferences, and speaker programs bring top international executives to the campus; activities such as the monthly WorldSmarts dinners and International Week provide informal social settings for networking and learning. Students have opportunities to attend internationally oriented conferences, and several student clubs are dedicated to international and regional issues.

The School's Career Management Center includes a full-time staff member dedicated to assisting international students and U.S. students targeting careers abroad. Johnson School's international mentorship program matches students with its powerful and diverse international alumni for one-on-one career assistance.

Special Features

The highly competitive two-year, full-tuition plus stipend Park Fellowships, open only to U.S. citizens, are awarded to up to 25 entering two-year M.B.A. students each year. Park Fellows receive enriched leadership opportunities and are required to complete a leadership project.

The Accelerated M.B.A. allows individuals who hold graduate degrees in scientific or technical fields and who have proven quantitative skills to complete an accelerated core curriculum during the summer (May to August) and join the second-year class in the fall.

The Johnson School offers dual-degree programs that confer an M.B.A. plus a degree in human resources management, engineering, law, Asian studies, or medicine. It is possible to pursue a dual-degree option with most master's programs at Cornell.

Two executive options to the M.B.A. program are offered, both taught by regular faculty members and resulting in a full Johnson School M.B.A. First, the Executive M.B.A. (E.M.B.A.) program, taught on alternative weekends in the New York City area, is an intensive year-round program that takes twenty-two months to complete. Second, the Johnson School's sixteen-month Cornell-Queen's Executive M.B.A., given in partnership with Queen's School of Business (Kingston, Ontario), uses a combination of on-campus sessions and interactive multipoint videoconferencing to deliver program material to learning teams located at sites in the U.S. and Canada; graduating students receive M.B.A. degrees from both Cornell and Queen's.

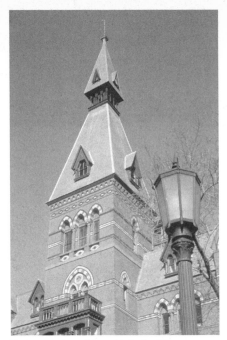

The renovation of Sage Hall, the Johnson School's home, has turned one of Cornell's most dramatic buildings into one of the most technologically advanced management education centers in the world.

Students in both executive programs must have substantial management experience and be sponsored by their employers. For more information about the E.M.B.A. program, prospective students should e-mail emba@cornell.edu; for the Cornell-Queen's program, cqemba@cornell.edu.

The Faculty

Johnson School faculty members consistently receive high marks for the quality of their research and teaching. The Johnson School believes that world-class research translates into leading-edge teaching. Because of their links with the business world, the faculty members are also a good resource for career advice.

The Business School Network
Corporate Partnerships

The Visiting Executives Program, the Durland Lecture Series, the Roy H. Park Leadership Speakers Program, and the Leadership Skills Program as well as the large number of conferences, symposia, career treks, and networking events organized by the student organizations provide a wide variety of formal and informal opportunities to interact with successful business leaders.

Recent executive speakers have included Wyeth chairman and CEO, Robert Essner; Honeywell, China, president Shane Tedjarati; Kraft CEO, Irene Rosenfeld; and Citigroup head of global cards, Global Consumer Group, Faith Massingale. Corporate advisory boards, and often corporate sponsorships, exist for a number of programs, including the Parker Center, the Center for Sustainable Global Enterprise, the Business of Science and Technology Initiative, the entrepreneurship program, and the immersion learning courses. Corporate leaders also sit on the Johnson School Advisory Council.

Another option for Corporate Partners is to participate in the school's Business Diversity Partnership (BDP) program. Designed to help corporations increase diversity in their ranks and throughout the business world, the BDP program assists organizations in reaching women and underrepresented groups. The BDP program consolidates the Johnson School's various diversity initiatives, letting corporations reach students across a spectrum of programs, rather than single events. Corporations can distribute their contributions across initiatives involving students from different age groups—from teens to current M.B.A. candidates.

The College and Environs

Cornell is an Ivy League university, and its more than 19,000 students come from more than 100 countries. Ithaca, with its combination of cosmopolitan sophistication and small-town accessibility, offers residents the best of both worlds—diverse cultural offerings and recreational activities in a beautiful setting of lakes, waterfalls, forests, and countryside. Students with families find it a hospitable place for balancing family and career; the public school system is excellent.

Facilities

Sage Hall, the Johnson School's home, is located in the center of the Cornell campus. The $38.2-million historic renovation project has turned one of Cornell's original and most dramatic buildings into one of the most technologically advanced management education centers in the world.

Technology Environment

Sage Hall's state-of-the-art technology infrastructure includes fiber-optic cable throughout the building; 1,600 computer ports including 802.11a/b/g wireless connectivity, distance learning, and teleconferencing capabilities; a student computing lab; a student business service center; a business simulation lab; and access to live electronic data feeds from the top financial information services. The Parker Center's "trading room" is equipped with $2 million of sophisticated analyst software. Students are required to own a laptop computer.

Placement

The Career Management Center (CMC) of Cornell's Johnson Graduate School of Management introduces students to an integrated career-management program as soon as the new class arrives on campus.

There are 5 professional staff members, 28 career/work group facilitators, and 30 peer career assistants available to offer personalized career assistance, advice, and coaching for on- and off-campus job searches. A member of the CMC staff is dedicated to serving international students, and additional programming targets their special needs. There are 10,000 Johnson School alumni and 250,000 Cornell alumni around the world who can offer information and career advice. Students are encouraged to network with alumni, are taught effective networking techniques, and have full access to the online alumni directories.

The CMC manages an extensive on-campus recruiting program for both summer internships and full-time employment. During the 2006–07 academic year, 175 companies hired Johnson School students. Every year, about two thirds of the students obtain their jobs through on-campus recruitment activities.

The Johnson School also participates in a variety of career forums and corporate recruiting events worldwide.

Admission

The Admissions Committee considers an applicant's prior academic performance, GMAT scores, breadth and depth of work experience, demonstrated leadership, interpersonal and communication skills, extracurricular and community involvement, career aspirations, recommendations, and previous professional achievements. For the two-year class of 2009, the median GMAT score was 690; the average undergraduate GPA, 3.3; and the median TOEFL score, 650 (paper-based) or 273 (computer-based). For the Accelerated M.B.A. class of 2008, the median GMAT score was 710; the average undergraduate GPA, 3.6; and the median TOEFL score, 267 (computer based). Interviews are set at the discretion of the Office of Admissions, and staff member, student, and alumni interviews are given equal weight. All applicants are encouraged to visit the Johnson School; the Office of Admissions arranges for a student host.

Finances

For 2007–08, tuition is $40,700. Student health insurance is $1430, books and computer allowance are $4100, and housing and food cost approximately $10,750 (based on the cost of sharing a moderately priced apartment). Johnson School has more than $1 million in merit-based scholarship funds to award each year to new and returning students in addition to federal, institutional, and private educational loan funds. International applicants receive similar consideration as U.S. citizens for merit-based scholarships and may apply for the School's international loan program with Citibank. The Park Leadership Fellows Program provides up to twenty-five full-tuition awards plus stipend each year. This two-year fellowship program is founded on a leadership theme that emphasizes professional achievements as well as personal contribution. The Park Leadership Fellows Program is limited to U.S. citizens.

Application Facts and Dates

Application deadlines for the two-year program and the Twelve-Month M.B.A. Option are the same: November 9, December 9, January 9, and March 9. For more information, students should contact:

Office of Admissions and Financial Aid
111 Sage Hall
Cornell University
Ithaca, New York 14853-6201
Phone: 607-255-4526
         800-847-2082 (toll-free in the U.S. and Canada)
Fax: 607-255-0065
E-mail: mba@cornell.edu
Web site:
    http://www.johnson.cornell.edu/

Dominican University

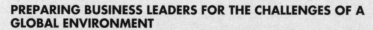
River Forest, Illinois

> ### PREPARING BUSINESS LEADERS FOR THE CHALLENGES OF A GLOBAL ENVIRONMENT
>
> *At the Brennan School of Business, we focus on educating ethical business leaders who will make a significant difference in their business communities. Our goal is to prepare our graduates to respond to complex business issues thoughtfully—with clarity, confidence, and integrity.*
>
> *This preparation begins with excellent teaching. We have an outstanding faculty comprised of highly qualified academics and practicing business professionals. The curriculum provides a solid global focus, because we recognize that ethical decision making requires today's business leaders to have an understanding of the economic, political, and cultural dimensions of the countries in which they do business.*
>
> *At the Brennan School of Business, we believe that ethical business leaders make a difference in their business communities and have the capacity to make the world a better place. We invite you to learn more about us.*

Programs and Curricular Focus

The Brennan School of Business M.B.A. curriculum is intended for students entering business and management professions or continuing their professional development. A candidate for the M.B.A. normally needs eighteen courses to complete the degree. The eighteen-course curriculum consists of six foundation courses, eight core courses, and four electives. However, depending upon the candidate's undergraduate preparation, one to all of the foundation courses may be waived. The M.B.A. program offers a choice of nine areas of concentration: accounting, entrepreneurship, finance, general management, health-care administration, human resource management, international business, management information systems, and marketing.

Master's degrees are also offered in accounting, computer information systems, knowledge management, and management information systems.

In addition, the Brennan School of Business offers several joint-degree programs. The M.B.A./J.D. program is awarded in partnership with the John Marshall Law School of Chicago. The M.B.A./M.L.I.S. is awarded in cooperation with Dominican University's Graduate School of Library and Information Science. The five-year B.A./M.B.A. is offered to qualified Dominican University seniors.

Students and the M.B.A. Experience

While students choose the Brennan School of Business for its faculty and its curriculum, they also select it for its flexibility and accessibility. Classes are conveniently offered in the evenings and on Saturdays. During the fall and spring semesters, classes are offered once a week for fifteen weeks. The summer semester is divided into three sessions to allow students to pursue their studies while still taking time off if they choose.

Coming from more than thirty different countries, Brennan students bring a wide variety of cultural experiences and perspectives to the classroom. Students also have diverse work experiences. Many have been in business for some time and have returned for an M.B.A. or other graduate degree to advance their careers. Others have entered Brennan's graduate programs immediately after earning their undergraduate degrees. Brennan students recognize that the more they understand about each other's perspective, the more valuable they are as managers in today's global business environment.

Special Features

Over the past ten years, the Brennan School of Business has developed a distinctive reputation for its global focus. It has established Executive M.B.A. programs in partnership with top-ranked universities in the Czech Republic and Poland and it has cooperative programs with universities in China and India. Brennan M.B.A. students are offered courses involving intensive study in Europe, Asia, and South America. The global focus of the business curriculum is further enhanced by the international students, whose perspectives add depth to classroom discussions.

Since its inception, the Brennan School of Business has been committed to offering a curriculum that addresses issues of business ethics. The establishment of the Christopher Chair in Business Ethics in 2003 and, more recently, the development of a Center for Global Peace through Commerce reflect the School's commitment to preparing students to have a positive impact in their communities and around the world.

Entrepreneurship is another long-standing strength of the Brennan School of Business and is one of the areas of concentration available to M.B.A. students. Recognition and support in this area have been given by the Coleman Foundation as well as the Kaufman Foundation. Both graduate and undergraduate students regularly work with entrepreneurial companies at a variety of stages in the start-up and growth process.

The Faculty

The Brennan School of Business faculty is composed of scholars with significant teaching, consulting, researching, and publishing backgrounds. Full-time professors with doctoral degrees teach more than 70 percent of the courses. Part-time faculty members are selectively chosen based on their education, career success, and particular expertise within the business community. All courses are taught by professors, not graduate assistants, and a low student-faculty ratio facilitates the kind of relationships among students and faculty members that add value in the academic setting.

The Business School Network

The majority of the Brennan School of Business alumni work within the greater Chicago area. This creates a significant and accessible Dominican University network of business professionals working in diverse fields. The Graduate Business Career Center orchestrates a variety of events that bring these alumni and other business professionals into contact with students. In addition, faculty members often invite corporate executives to campus to provide their perspectives on current business issues, thereby providing meaningful opportunities for students to interact with business leaders.

The College and Environs

Dominican University is a comprehensive, Catholic university offering degrees to approximately 3,300 students. It offers

bachelor's degrees in more than fifty areas of study and master's degrees from its schools of library and information science, business, education, and social work. *U.S. News & World Report* consistently ranks Dominican in the top tier of Midwest master's-level universities and as a "best value."

Founded in 1977, the School of Business was named in 2006 in honor of Edward A. Brennan, retired chairman and chief executive officer of Sears, Roebuck and Co., and his wife Lois Brennan, an alumna of Dominican. Today the Brennan School of Business is one of the leading small business programs in the Chicago metropolitan area. Approximately 600 students pursue undergraduate and graduate degrees in the fields of accounting, business, economics, international business, and information systems.

Located on Dominican's main campus in River Forest, the Brennan School of Business is just 10 miles west of Chicago's Loop. Students appreciate the School's proximity to one of the world's largest and most diverse economies, and they recognize the enormous business and cultural opportunities that Chicago offers.

Technology Environment

Dominican University's Technology Center and computer labs are available to all students. In these facilities, students can use Dominican's software, send and receive e-mail, and search the Internet. In addition, networked desktop computers are located on every level of the Rebecca Crown Library. These workstations provide access to laser jet printers and the Internet. Wireless access is available throughout the library as well as in a variety of other locations on campus.

Placement

Dominican's Graduate Business Career Center works with students as well as alumni to help them reach their career goals. The center provides individual career assessments and job leads. It also assists with job search skills such as resume writing, networking, and interviewing. It develops connections with employers and develops partnerships and programs that promote employment opportunities. The center maintains an Alumni Career Network that provides valuable career assistance, mentoring, and job resources.

Admission

Admission to the Brennan School of Business graduate programs is open to those who hold a bachelor's degree in any field from an accredited institution. No prior business courses are required. The Committee on Graduate Admissions bases its decision on the applicant's total academic record, satisfactory scores on the GMAT (or the GRE for students applying to the Master of Science in Computer Information Systems (M.S.C.I.S.) program), letters of reference, and other information from the student's application. Students may enter the program at the beginning of the fall, spring, or summer terms.

The Brennan School of Business welcomes applications from international students. For those who were educated outside the United States, an official TOEFL score or IELTS score is also required. All international students are required to show proof of financial support for one year.

Finances

Tuition for the 2008–09 year is $2280 per 3-credit-hour course. Room and board for the 2008–09 year is approximately $7250, depending on the meal plan chosen. There is a student fee of $10 per course as well as a one-time matriculation fee of $25.

International Students

The classroom experience is strengthened by a strong international student community. An international student adviser helps students with the application and admissions process as well as with issues associated with living in another country. An adviser assists students in complying with the regulations of the U.S. Immigration and Naturalization Service and the U.S. Department of State, including regulations that govern on-campus and off-campus employment. The active International Student Organization sponsors a variety of events for all graduate business students.

Application Facts and Dates

Applications are accepted on a rolling basis for all semesters. All application materials for U.S. students should be submitted at least one month before the beginning of the semester in which the student desires admission. Materials for international students should be submitted two months before the beginning of the semester. Applicants may apply online at the Brennan School of Business Web site. For additional information, students should contact:

Linda Puvogel
Assistant Dean
Brennan School of Business
Dominican University
7900 West Division Street
River Forest, Illinois 60305-1066

Phone: 708-524-6507
Fax: 708-524-6939
E-mail: gradbus@dom.edu
Web site: http://www.business.dom.edu

EAST CAROLINA UNIVERSITY

COLLEGE of BUSINESS

East Carolina University

College of Business

Greenville, North Carolina

AN M.B.A. WITH ADVANTAGES

Of all the pieces that make up your career puzzle, perhaps the biggest piece is your education. Earning your M.B.A. can provide you with opportunities not otherwise available. The East Carolina University M.B.A. program is of recognized quality and provides exceptional value. Your program is extremely flexible and can be completed full-time, part-time, or online.

—Frederick Niswander, Dean

Programs and Curricular Focus

The M.B.A. program at East Carolina University (ECU) is one of approximately 455 graduate business programs accredited by AACSB International–The Association to Advance Collegiate Schools of Business. It was the second program to be accredited by the AACSB in North Carolina and is one of approximately 140 M.B.A. programs that belong to the Graduate Management Admissions Council.

The goal of the ECU M.B.A. is to prepare men and women for managerial leadership in both profit and nonprofit organizations. Required and elective courses are taught from a managerial perspective with a blend of teaching methods, including lectures, discussions, computer simulations, team projects, cases, and independent study, to develop critical-thinking and human relations skills. The average class size is 27 students.

The ECU M.B.A. is individually tailored to each student's background and needs. Students who previously took business classes at the undergraduate level and received high grades can exempt from some or all of the first-year classes. Such waivers can reduce the program to a minimum of 30 semester hours, or one year full-time. The maximum program length is 60 semester hours, or two years.

Students may begin the M.B.A. program in any term—fall, spring, or summer. Spring or summer entrance presents no scheduling problems since all required courses are offered in all terms. The availability of two terms each summer allows students to accelerate the completion of their program.

This program can accommodate a wide range of student needs, including full-time, part-time, and distance education students. All required course work is available in afternoon, night, and online sections, and students may use any combination of classes in any semester to accommodate their schedules. Students may also work at their own pace, taking as little as one class (3 credit hours) to a maximum of five classes (15 credit hours) per semester. Full-time students may finish the program in as little as one year, while most part-time students finish in two to five years.

The ECU Brody School of Medicine and the College of Business offer a joint M.D./M.B.A. dual-degree program. The M.D./M.B.A. is also available to students who are accepted to or enrolled in other accredited medical schools and medical residents whose training program allows one year away from clinical responsibilities. Students enter in late June and complete the M.B.A. twelve months later. A part-time schedule is also available. The GMAT requirement is waived for applicants with M.D. degrees or students from accredited medical schools.

The College of Business offers a Master of Science in Accounting (M.S.A.) program to prepare students for the CPA exam and careers in public and management accounting. The M.S.A. for students with an undergraduate degree in accounting is typically 30–60 semester hours, depending on undergraduate courses and grades. For students with degrees in fields other than accounting, the M.S.A. is generally 60 semester hours. Current enrollment in the M.S.A. program is approximately 100 students. A concentration in taxation is also available.

Students and the M.B.A. Experience

East Carolina's M.B.A. students are drawn from a wide variety of educational and business backgrounds. Approximately 229 attend full-time, while 229 work full-time and attend part-time. In addition, 304 students attend entirely online. The typical student is 28 years old and has five years of work experience. The 2005–06 student body included 44 percent women and 18 percent members of minority groups. Approximately 50 percent have undergraduate degrees in disciplines other than business, with 20 percent in engineering, science, social science, and health professions, including 8 to 10 students with M.D. degrees. Students hail from approximately 220 different undergraduate institutions.

Special Features

In addition to elective courses in the traditional business subjects, East Carolina's M.B.A. program offers eleven optional concentrations. Approximately 20 percent of the students take their electives in other ECU professional schools and receive a certificate from that school in conjunction with their M.B.A. Optional concentrations include development and environmental planning, finance, health-care management, hospitality management, international management, management information systems, professional investment management and operations, school business management, security studies (homeland security), sport management, and supply chain management. There is an additional application for the international management option, as fluency in a second language and international experience are required. M.S.A. candidates may earn an optional concentration in taxation in addition to those listed above.

The Faculty

ECU is committed to high-quality teaching. Faculty members' backgrounds are diverse and cosmopolitan and include extensive business, consulting, teaching, and research experience. The business faculty members hold graduate degrees from institutions such as Arizona State, Chicago, Duke, Florida, Georgetown, Georgia, Harvard, Illinois, Indiana, Michigan State, North Carolina, Tennessee, Texas, Texas A&M, Virginia, and Wisconsin. Professors are dedicated to providing meaningful, challenging experiences for ECU's M.B.A. students and are readily available for discussion and assistance outside the classroom.

The Business School Network

Many M.B.A. students work full-time for major organizations and attend graduate school part-time. Full- and part-time students are in class together and work on projects that enhance learning and networking opportunities. Eastern North Carolina

A class in the ECU College of Business.

is home to scores of major corporations, including Abbott Laboratories, Black & Decker, Bosch, DuPont, Firestone, Frigidaire, NACCO, Sara Lee, TRW, and Weyerhaeuser.

Students are also able to get hands-on experience consulting with local businesses through the Small Business Institute, the Small Business Technology and Development Center, and other not-for-profit entities.

In addition, the College of Business is served by a distinguished Business Advisory Council of 35 senior executives who advise the dean on a broad range of issues. These executives participate as guest lecturers in many courses each year.

The College and Environs

East Carolina University, which was founded in 1907, is the third-largest campus of the University of North Carolina System. Current enrollment is 23,164 students, including 5,150 graduate students and 286 medical students. The ECU Brody School of Medicine is one of the top producers of primary-care physicians in the nation.

Quality of life during the M.B.A. experience is an important consideration. Greenville is a comfortable city of 60,000 with a reasonable cost of living, a temperate climate, and a relaxed outdoor lifestyle. It is an educational, commercial, industrial, medical, and cultural center for eastern North Carolina, with the beaches 90 minutes away and the mountains and skiing just a half-day's drive. Greenville is 45 miles from I-95 and is served by regional airports.

Facilities

The M.B.A. program is housed in a modern facility, which was completed in 1988 and includes a large, comfortable M.B.A. student lounge, group and individual study areas, and a graduate computer lab. ECU's Joyner Library holds 1.2 million bound volumes plus microforms and periodicals.

Technology Environment

Computing for M.B.A. students is also available in all other College of Business computer labs, with more than 100 Windows-based computers that are connected to a fiber-optic campus network with a high-speed link to the Internet. A variety of software packages and databases are available.

Placement

The College of Business Career Services Office provides career and placement services to M.B.A. students and recent alumni. Resume preparation, interviewing skills workshops, internship placement, and computerized databases are all part of the services offered, while career fairs and on-campus recruiting are augmented by business contacts through the College of Business.

The office also assists M.B.A. students in preparing for and securing career-related temporary employment, usually of a semester's duration. This is particularly valuable for students who do not have extensive full-time work experience. With ECU's flexible M.B.A. program, co-op jobs do not create scheduling problems because students can easily suspend and resume their programs.

Admission

The ECU M.B.A. program is open to applicants with baccalaureate degrees from accredited institutions in business and non-business fields. Work experience is recommended but not required. Ability is evaluated based on the applicant's prior undergraduate record and performance on the Graduate Management Admission Test (GMAT). The average GMAT score is approximately 525 in any given semester, and the College offers a GMAT review course twice a year through the Division of Professional Programs.

Applicants from non-English-speaking countries must submit results of the Test of English as a Foreign Language (TOEFL). The minimum acceptable TOEFL score is 550 for the paper-based test or 213 for the computer-based test.

Finances

Value is a function of quality and cost. East Carolina provides a substantial accredited M.B.A. program at a reasonable cost. Full-time tuition and fees are $2782 per semester for North Carolina residents and $7940 per semester for nonresidents, with additional charges for optional summer sessions. Tuition and fees for part-time students are lower. In addition, waivers of business core classes may provide additional value by eliminating tuition, fees, and living expenses for one or more semesters.

Off-campus housing, which is estimated at $6000 per calendar year, is readily available and is used by most graduate students. University housing is also available.

The College of Business offers approximately 125 graduate assistantships, which are awarded based on academic merit. Students may earn between $3750 and $7500 per year working 10 to 20 hours each week assisting professors in research or working with undergraduates in computer labs. In addition, the College awards ten $10,000 scholarships each academic year.

International Students

The ECU M.B.A. program welcomes international students. During 2005–06, there were students from Argentina, China, Germany, India, Indonesia, Jordan, Morocco, Nigeria, Pakistan, Paraguay, Romania, Slovenia, South Africa, Taiwan, and Venezuela.

Application Facts and Dates

Applications are accepted for any term. Early applications are strongly encouraged because of the rolling admission process.

Len Rhodes
Assistant Dean for Graduate Programs
College of Business
East Carolina University
Greenville, North Carolina 27858-4353

Phone: 252-328-6970
Fax: 252-328-2106
E-mail: gradbus@ecu.edu
Web site:
    http://www.business.ecu.edu/grad/

Embry-Riddle Aeronautical University

Business Administration Department

Daytona Beach, Florida

THE M.B.A.

Contemporary organizations all over the world recognize the value of professional management. The hallmark of the professional manager is the M.B.A. The Embry-Riddle M.B.A. provides graduates with a world-class management education in an aviation/aerospace context. Professional managers who have earned their M.B.A. at Embry-Riddle Aeronautical University (ERAU) understand the imperatives of change, globalization, technological innovation, and increasingly sophisticated and demanding customers that mark the strategic and operational environments of today's enterprises. They appreciate the challenges these imperatives represent and face them with confidence armed with state-of-the-art tools and behaviors that effective managers need to lead their organizations successfully. Our managers are committed to improving the industry they know so well and are also prepared to apply performance-tested management principles to the fascinating problems shared by all of today's enterprises. M.B.A. students interact with colleagues who share an affinity for the aviation/aerospace industry and dedication to developing world-class management abilities and are representative of a truly global industry. Faculty members combine first-rate academic credentials with deep industry experience and commitment. The M.B.A. at ERAU's Daytona Beach campus represents an exciting, challenging opportunity to learn and develop as twenty-first-century professional managers.

—Dr. Daniel Petree, Department Chair, Business Administration

Programs and Curricular Focus

The Master of Business Administration (M.B.A.) degree program is designed to develop managers who can apply the concepts of modern management techniques to the challenges of the aviation/aerospace industry. The M.B.A. is offered as a full-time residential program on the Daytona Beach campus and as a degree via distance learning.

The M.B.A. curriculum combines a strong traditional business core with specializations in airport management, airline management, aviation policy and planning, aviation human resources, and aviation system management. The development of versatility and analytical resourcefulness are two of the key aims of the M.B.A. program. The program is fashioned to stress pragmatic solutions to the managerial, technical, and operational problems likely to arise in the aviation/aerospace industry as a result of the frequent and sweeping changes that occur in technology as well as in the domestic and international regulations with which the industry must abide.

M.B.A. degree candidates must complete a minimum of 39 credit hours of course work consisting of 27 hours of core curriculum and 12 hours of specified electives. The M.B.A. degree residential program can usually be completed in eighteen to twenty-four months.

Students and the M.B.A. Experience

ERAU's graduate programs currently enroll approximately 400 students in residential graduate degree programs in Daytona where 25 percent are from other countries, 25 percent are women, and 23 percent are members of U.S. minority groups. On the Prescott campus, 32 residential graduate students are enrolled in the Master of Science in Safety Science program. Approximately 12 percent of the campus-based graduate students are employed full-time; many hold professional positions in the aviation industry. The M.B.A. program attracts students with diverse academic backgrounds and common scholastic abilities that enrich the program. The majority of incoming students have business degrees. The average age of incoming students is 28.

In addition, the Worldwide Campus enrolls about 3,500 students in graduate degree programs off campus at more than 130 locations throughout the United States and Europe.

The Faculty

The College of Business faculty takes pride in bringing relevant, real-world problems, issues, and experiences into the classrooms. Faculty members give a high priority to preparing students for the leadership roles they will eventually assume. They accomplish this not only by excellence in teaching but also by advising students on their business research and consulting projects. Many members of the faculty serve as consultants to a variety of industries, and their diverse backgrounds provide a rich, multicultural teaching field, with an emphasis on global standards and practices.

Faculty List

Ahmed Abdelghany, Ph.D., Texas at Austin

Anke Arnaud, Ph.D., Central Florida

Massoud Bazargan, Ph.D., New South Wales (Australia).

Vedapuri Raghavan, Ph.D., Washington State

Rosemarie Reynolds, Ph.D., South Florida.

Dawna Rhoades, Ph.D., Houston.

Janet Tinoco, Ph.D., Central Florida

Bijan Vasigh, Ph.D., NYU.

Blaise Waguespack, Program Coordinator; Ph.D., North Texas.

Michael Williams, Ph.D., Nova.

Seth Young, Ph.D., Berkeley.

Bert Zarb, Ph.D., Argosy.

The Business School Network

The Embry-Riddle Industry Advisory Committee (Daytona Beach campus) provides key input to the M.B.A. program by helping to develop the program curriculum on a continual basis to meet the current demands of the industry. Through this process, Embry-Riddle is able to shape the curriculum as necessary to provide students with the skills and educational background that suit the current needs of the aviation/aerospace industry. The Embry-Riddle Industry Advisory Committee, which is composed of various distinguished representatives from throughout the industry, participates directly with the M.B.A. program by providing key guest speakers and lecturers for industry colloquiums and specialized classroom lectures. Through these events, students are able to further nurture their talents and develop contacts within the industry itself.

The College and Environs

Since its founding in 1926, Embry-Riddle Aeronautical University has built a reputation for high-quality education within the field of aviation and has become a world leader in aerospace higher education. The University is composed of the western campus in Prescott, Arizona; the eastern campus in Daytona Beach, Florida; and the Worldwide Campus, with off-campus programs.

The Prescott, Arizona, campus is set in a mile-high town nestled between the rugged Bradshaw and Mingus mountain ranges. Known for its western flair and friendly spirit, the mile-high city offers a warm, friendly, and safe environment where students can live and learn. The Daytona Beach, Florida, campus is located next to the Daytona Beach International Airport and 10 minutes from the Daytona beaches. Within an hour's drive are Disney World and EPCOT, Kennedy Space Center, SeaWorld, Universal Studios, and St. Augustine. The Worldwide Campus resident centers are located in thirty-seven states and seven other nations. Prospective students may visit http://www.erau.edu/ec for a location map.

Technology Environment

A cluster of mainframes (UNIX and IBM) and PCs supported by a telecommunications network provide the faculty and students with the latest advances in information management and computing facilities. These are augmented by academic student labs, the Airway Science Simulation Lab, and the Aviation Human Factors Research Lab. Extensive modern computer facilities and Internet access are available to all students.

Placement

In addition to contacts gained from internships, the M.B.A. degree program conducts placement activities for its graduates. Years of research and consulting have allowed the faculty to cultivate contacts within the aviation industry, and its network provides job opportunities for graduates. The Career Services Office sponsors an annual industry Career Expo, which attracts more than 100 major companies such as Boeing, Federal Express, Delta, and United Airlines. In addition, the Career Resource Center offers corporate profiles, job postings, and development information. The office also assists with resume development and interview preparation.

Admission

The desired minimum bachelor degree cumulative GPA is 3.0 on a 4.0 scale. A minimum score of 500 on the GMAT is a requirement for admissions consideration for the M.B.A. program.

Finances

In 2008–09, tuition costs for the residential M.B.A. program are $1100 per credit hour; tuition for the distance learning M.B.A. program is $690 per credit hour. The estimated cost of books and supplies is $500 per semester. On-campus housing is not usually available to graduate students on the Daytona Beach campus. Single students who share rent and utility expenses can expect off-campus room and board expenses of $6000. Scholarships are awarded to outstanding graduate students during the admissions process. Assistantships are also available on a limited basis. Students may apply for financial aid by calling 800-943-6279 (toll-free). All graduate programs are approved for U.S. Veterans Administration education benefits.

Application Facts and Dates

Applications are accepted on a rolling basis and should be completed sixty days prior to the start of a semester for U.S. citizens, resident aliens, and international students.

Prospective residential and distance learning M.B.A. students should contact:

Office of International and Graduate Admissions
Embry-Riddle Aeronautical University
600 South Clyde Morris Boulevard
Daytona Beach, Florida 32114-3900
Phone: 386-226-6176 (outside the U.S.)
        800-388-3728 (toll-free, within the U.S.)
Fax: 386-226-7070
E-mail: graduate.admissions@erau.edu
Web site: http://www.embryriddle.edu/graduate

Emory University

Roberto C. Goizueta Business School

Atlanta, Georgia

THE NATION'S STRONGEST LEADERSHIP PROGRAM

Our leadership development program is not one class. It is not just a weekend retreat or a special colloquium. It is a personal journey that is mapped out for the entire M.B.A. experience. Our M.B.A. ensures that you have the analytical expertise yet also the leadership abilities to make an impact on an organization—and on the world.

—Dr. Steve Walton, Interim Associate Dean

Programs and Curricular Focus

Goizueta Business School's M.B.A. program offers students the opportunity to pursue an M.B.A. in a flexible, innovative environment. Students are encouraged to work closely with professors, to individualize a course of study, and to customize career goals. The core curriculum includes the "flex core," which allows students to prioritize the sequencing of core courses. In addition, Lead Week, an introduction to each semester, consists of an analytical problem-solving boot camp and focused minicourses in the fall terms and international travel modules in the spring terms. Faculty members use teaching methods that are best suited to the course material, including cases, lectures, class discussions, student presentations, team and field projects, and computer simulations, with a balanced emphasis on quantitative and qualitative approaches.

During the first year, students complete a core curriculum that stresses the fundamental building blocks of business and the basic principles in each of the primary functional areas. Goizueta Plus, which is required during the first year, is a coordinated program for developing essential competencies in communication skills and leadership. During the second year, students have the opportunity to develop an area of concentration in a wide range of areas, including decision and information analysis, brand management, customer relationship management, marketing consulting, entrepreneurship, leadership, management consulting, financial analysis, global financial reporting and analysis, professional accounting, corporate finance, real estate, capital markets, and global management.

In addition to the full-time Two-Year M.B.A. program, four other formats of the M.B.A. program are offered. The accelerated One-Year M.B.A. program allows students to complete the M.B.A. in twelve months. Students who are interested in the One-Year M.B.A. program must have an undergraduate degree in business or, depending on the university attended and the course work completed, economics. In addition, applicants with strong quantitative backgrounds (e.g., engineering or math majors) who have business experience and some business course work may qualify for this program (determined on a case-by-case basis). Students begin this program in May and complete it in one calendar year. Goizueta Business School also offers a part-time, three-year Evening M.B.A. program for working professionals and an Executive M.B.A. program for candidates with significant managerial experience. Weekend (sixteen months) and modular (twenty months) formats are available. Joint-degree programs are available with the Law School, J.D./M.B.A. (four years); the School of Public Health, M.P.H./M.B.A. (five semesters); the Candler School of Theology, M.B.A./M.Div. (four years); and the Division of Physical Therapy, D.P.T./M.B.A. (four years).

Students and the M.B.A. Experience

Goizueta Business School consists of 400 full-time and 250 part-time M.B.A. students, who come from a wide variety of academic disciplines, geographic regions, and professions. For the full-time programs, the average length of post-undergraduate work is five years, with the majority of students typically having three or more years of work experience. More than 30 percent of the students are women, and more than a third of the class is composed of students who come from outside of the U.S.

Global Focus

The Goizueta M.B.A. program exposes students to global issues on many levels. The Global Perspectives elective course serves as an introduction using a multidisciplinary, integrated approach. By bringing all the functional disciplines together, the course helps students learn to operate in a global environment and develop their understanding of varied political, cultural, ethical, and geographic perspectives. There are other international course electives in finance, accounting, management, and marketing.

Students may also choose to study abroad for the summer, a semester, or a full year as part of their M.B.A. experience. Goizueta currently offers more than twenty programs in such countries as China, Chile, England, Finland, France, Germany, Mexico, Singapore, Spain, and Venezuela. Through specialized area studies tracks in Soviet, post-Soviet, and East European studies and Latin American studies at Emory University, students can gain valuable multidisciplinary experience. Through four double-degree programs, they can opt to earn two master's degrees simultaneously by studying at one of Goizueta's partner institutions in Spain, France, Austria, or the Netherlands.

Special Features

Goizueta Business School students are very involved in the Atlanta community. Projects such as volunteer days and fund-raising events for organizations such as Hands on Atlanta and Children's Healthcare of Atlanta allow students to make an impact in the lives of those in need. Goizueta Games, Goizueta Gives, and Goizueta Follies are just a few of the School's extracurricular traditions. The Goizueta Marketing Strategy Competition gives students the opportunity to apply marketing research and strategy development skills to real business challenges for such companies as the Coca-Cola Company, Kodak, IBM, SunTrust, Cingular Wireless, Georgia-Pacific Corporation, UPS, and BellSouth.

All full-time M.B.A. students participate in the Goizueta Leadership Academy, which focuses on developing personal leadership skills and takes students through real leadership opportunities. Students who have demonstrated a strong interest in further developing their leadership skills may apply to the Goizueta Advanced Leadership Academy (GALA). The goal of GALA is to support the School's mission of developing Principled Leaders for Global Enterprise by providing supplemental developmental and experiential opportunities for those chosen to become Academy Fellows.

The Faculty

While Emory places teaching first, scholarly research and service to the business community are also highly valued components of the faculty profile. Faculty members have joined the Business School from such institutions as Harvard, Northwestern, Pennsylvania (Wharton), and Stanford. Their professional experiences include companies such as PWC, Deloitte, Microsoft, Coca-Cola, Morgan Stanley, General Motors, and Ernst & Young.

The College and Environs

The city of Atlanta is the business, cultural, and international center of the southeastern United States. According to a recent study, Atlanta ranks third in the nation among cities with Fortune 500 headquarters. The moderate climate and reasonable cost of living, in addition to an impressive array of cultural and recreational offerings, attract people from all over the world.

Emory University is located 6 miles from downtown Atlanta on the northeast side of the city. The campus consists of 550 heavily wooded acres in a residential neighborhood. Emory offers students access to the resources of a cosmopolitan university community with more than 11,000 students. The diverse learning environment is enhanced by specialized centers and affiliates, such as the Carter Center, the Law and Economics Center, Scholars Press, the Yerkes Primate Center, and the Centers for Disease Control and Prevention (CDC).

Facilities

The Goizueta Business School moved into its current home on Emory's campus in 1997. The building is 119,000 square feet, with state-of-the-art technology throughout the facility. The five-story structure has a strategic design that facilitates an interactive teaching and research environment. In 2005, the facilities were expanded to include a 90,000-square-foot, five-story addition, including five classrooms, a broadcast studio, and a research lab. Both buildings are immediately adjacent to one another and connected by a walkway. All facilities have fully integrated wired and wireless networking, which extends to the beautiful outdoor courtyard and café.

Technology Environment

Information technology at Goizueta Business School is comprehensive, with modern facilities, a professional staff, and extensive documentation. Extensive library resources are available to students, with online databases such as ABI/Inform business magazine index, LexisNexis, and Dow Jones News/Retrieval Service.

Placement

The mission of the Career Management Center is centered on assisting students in pragmatically focusing on particular abilities, experiences, and interests toward a career goal and helping each student develop an individual strategy for marketing himself or herself in order to conduct an effective job search. Workshops, speakers, internships, mentors, interview coaching, and alumni are some of the resources available to students. The median starting salary for the full-time M.B.A. class of 2006 was $90,000.

Admission

Admission to the M.B.A. program is highly selective. Each candidate is evaluated on the basis of his or her ability to perform in an academically rigorous environment as well as contribute to classroom discussions based on work and/or life experiences. Candidates must also present demonstrated leadership through professional excellence and meaningful involvement in their communities. Diversity and international perspectives are highly valued in the admission process. To apply to Goizueta Business School, a student must submit the results of the Graduate Management Admission Test (GMAT), official transcripts from all previous undergraduate and graduate institutions attended, an updated resume, two letters of recommendation, and the completed application form, including statistical data, work history, essays, and an application fee. Applicants from non-English-speaking countries must also submit scores from the Test of English as a Foreign Language (TOEFL). A personal interview is required for admission.

Finances

Estimated tuition for the 2007–08 academic year at Goizueta Business School is $18,600 per semester. The estimated annual living expenses and fees for a student living on or off campus total $16,000. Students who complete an application by February 1 are automatically considered for merit-based scholarships. Need-based aid in the form of loans is available to students. Applicants should file the FAFSA and the Financial Aid PROFILE for loan consideration. To contact Emory University's Financial Aid Office, students should call 404-727-1141 or visit http://www.emory.edu/FINANCIAL_AID/.

International Students

International students are encouraged to apply by December 15. Good communication skills are essential to the program. Applicants whose native language is not English must score a minimum of 250 on the TOEFL (600 on the paper-based test). International students are eligible for merit-based scholarship awards as well as loans that do not require a United States citizen to be a cosigner.

Application Facts and Dates

Applications are reviewed on a rolling basis. However, prospective students are strongly advised to consider the following dates. Full-time M.B.A. applicants who wish to receive earliest consideration should apply by November 1. International applicants are encouraged to apply by December 15. All One-Year M.B.A. applicants, and any full-time applicants interested in receiving scholarship consideration, should apply by February 1. The final deadline for the Two-Year M.B.A. is March 1. The Evening M.B.A. program deadline is June 1. The Executive M.B.A. program deadlines are October 31 (weekend format) and July 1 (modular format). Access to online applications is available via the School's Web site. Students may also obtain applications and admissions information from:

Goizueta Business School
Emory University
Atlanta, Georgia 30322-2712

Phone: 404-727-6311
Fax: 404-727-4612
E-mail: admissions@bus.emory.edu
Web site: http://www.goizueta.emory.edu

Master of Business Administration

London, England

> ### DEFINING INDIVIDUAL SUCCESS IN THE GLOBAL MARKETPLACE
>
> *A university can no longer limit itself to providing textbook knowledge; it should also prepare students to adapt to the changing needs of the global market while inspiring them to seek fulfillment in their professional and personal lives.*
>
> *The European School of Economics (ESE) prepares young entrepreneurs and managers to lead their organizations with the cultural versatility, intellectual abilities, practical skills, and moral qualities sought in today's business world. With campuses in the United States, the United Kingdom, and Italy, we offer comprehensive international programs that combine the fundamentals of business with specialized training in cutting-edge business sectors.*
>
> *Because ESE maintains close relationships with the world's largest companies, our students are able to participate in meaningful internships during their programs and then find gainful employment. The end result is a generation of business leaders who conduct business in a manner that fosters cooperation, encourages ethical behavior, and supports individual career advancement.*
>
> —Elio D'Anna, President

Programs and Curricular Focus

M.B.A. students benefit from a variety of innovative teaching methods, from independent study and class discussions to seminars and computer-aided business simulations. Courses have a strong international approach and are carefully calibrated to achieve a fine balance between conceptual and experiential learning. The program requires twelve months of full-time study or eighteen months of part-time study. The curriculum is divided into four terms, each of which lasts ten to twelve weeks.

The first and second terms consist of ten core courses. The first term provides the tools needed to manage and lead organizations, with courses in financial accounting, e-commerce, and international marketing. The second term brings together the various threads of business activity to focus on the overall strategy of international organizations; courses include international business law, operations management, and managing people. The third term consists of elective modules chosen by the students according to their particular interests and professional objectives. Electives include courses in international strategic management and business ethics or from one of two specialization areas: international finance or marketing management. Students also complete the Integrity Seminar. The fourth term consists of a three- to six-month internship, followed by a dissertation.

Students and the M.B.A. Experience

The individual attention given to each student is one of the aspects that set the European School of Economics apart from other universities. In order to maintain this level of attention, the School limits attendance to 100 students per campus each year. These students come from around the world, including Europe, Asia, the United States, and South America, allowing for a robust exchange of ideas, experiences, and culture.

One of the defining features of ESE is the integration of theory and practice into its curriculum. In the classroom, the theory of business is presented by experienced faculty members with whom students interact on a first-name basis. Internships are designed to equip students with the skills necessary for achieving success in today's complex business environment. In addition, international lecturers, economic and political experts, and other renowned world figures are a constant presence at ESE, participating in meetings, seminars, and academic ceremonies.

The Faculty

ESE Business Schools' faculties in Europe and the United States comprise prestigious, internationally known figures, including professors chosen from the best European and American universities. In addition to teaching at ESE London, many faculty members work at some of the city's most prominent corporations and law firms, or they own and operate their own companies.

Faculty List

Kamran Abers. Business development, strategic development, corporate finance, mergers and acquisitions.

Stephen Acunto. Politics, international relations.

Marco Allegrini. Financial reporting, internal auditing.

Marco Arcari. Alternative investment, specifically private equity and venture capital.

Sabbia Auriti. Women's studies, Italian-American relations.

Stefano Baldi. Fashion and fair marketing, event management.

Jean Blanquart. Research methods of social sciences, advanced business structures.

Lance Brofman. Mutual funds, portfolio theory, derivatives, econometrics.

George Brown. Treasury management, strategic planning, finance and risk management.

Sara Bucciarelli. Humanities, philosophy, anthropology, history.

Theresa Joy Buell. Assessing new and emerging markets; analyzing data; researching competitors; evaluating financial, economic, and strategic business impacts.

Stefano D'Anna. Economics, sociology.

Fergal De Clar. Corporate finance.

Dario De Pietro. Physics, engineering, mathematics, chemistry.

Giuseppe Di Donna. Economics, communications.

Fabio Frigo-Mosca. Managing operations, operation management.

Marialuisa Galbiati. Business law.

Marco E. L. Guidi. History of economics thought.

Sergio Ianni. International strategic management and strategic marketing.

Jennifer Kirklys. Management, marketing.

Aroop Mahanty. Competitive strategies in global markets, new-product development, impact of culture on consumer behaviors, holistic approach to utility maximization, new interactive pedagogy, distance learning technology.

Michele Montresoro. Managerial statistics, finance.

Sydney A. Passey. Teaching English as a second language.

Ivo Pezzuto. Marketing management, international marketing, marketing strategy, marketing of services, financial services marketing, business and corporate strategy, cross-cultural management, consumer finance, credit risk management, e-marketing, distance learning programs.

Carolina Rincon Ponze. Spanish pedagogia.

Philip Reid. French, German, English.

Dominique Roux. Management consulting.

Barbara Steadman. Business law within a national and international environment.

Enrico Stecchi. Luxury-goods management.

Eugene Stepanov. Pure mathematics, applied stochastic financial mathematics, economics, risk management.

Lisa Sweetman. Marketing administration, psychotherapy.

Diana Tomai. Business management, strategic marketing, communications, branding.

Anna Maria Variato. Economics.

David Ward. Strategic management, qualitative business methods, international marketing, managing multinational companies.

John Wyse. Entrepreneurial management, product and service innovation, new-product launch, management issues related to Japanese business world.

Yuen. Structuring and oversight of investment programs utilizing third-party managers.

The Business School Network

The European School of Economics takes pride in its close ties to the business world. Its pragmatic approach to education prepares students to step right into their professional careers. Faculty members hold management positions in world-renowned companies and law firms, and their real-world experience complements classroom discussions about business fundamentals.

ESE strives to make sure students are also applying their knowledge in the international business world. Each year, the School dedicates a large part of its operations to placing more than 1,000 students in internships with some of the leading companies and institutions worldwide, including General Motors, Salomon Smith Barney, Unilever, Virgin Records, and Walt Disney Co. These internships are recognized as an integral part of the M.B.A. program and provide the opportunity to work in an environment related to their specialized course of study; many of these interns become full-time employees upon graduation.

The College and Environs

Students can move freely between the centers on either a semester or yearly basis, having the possibility of attending the same programs in London, New York, Rome, Milan, and Lucca/Florence. The ESE Business School in London has its location in the very heart of the city and offers the double benefit of an intimate and highly personal classroom atmosphere amid a cosmopolitan backdrop featuring great diversity. New York City ESE Business School is located in the heart of Manhattan. Outside the classroom, New York City's unique mix of languages and cultures offers students an education unto itself, with nearly 200 nationalities represented among its 8 million residents. ESE Rome Business School is located in the center of the city, adjoining the city's political and business centers. As a world center for fashion and commerce, Milan exudes creativity, hard work, and fun—a reflection of ESE's philosophy toward education and personal development. ESE's international business school sits in Lucca, a beautiful small town just 30 minutes from Pisa's international airport.

Facilities

The European School of Economics campuses are situated in some of the world's most beautiful settings. These include a Victorian building overlooking the gardens of London's Buckingham Palace; a state-of-the-art facility in New York's famous Empire State Building, with a breathtaking view of Manhattan; a seventeenth-century neoclassical palace (former residence of Marquis Gaspare Ordono de Rosales) in Milan; a historic residence in Rome, near the famous via Veneto, the heart of Dolce Vita; and Palazzo Poleschi (a former art gallery) in Lucca (Florence).

Placement

Each ESE campus has a placement department that maintains close relationships with students and companies in order to match students with the jobs and organizations that are best suited to their specific talents and career objectives. The student services department assists students with interview and resume preparation, and a careers notice board lists current internships and job opportunities.

Admission

All applicants should have a minimum of two years' work experience. Exceptions are possible if the candidate shows an exceptional record of community service and a high maturity level. Prior study in statistics, accounting, and economics is not required for admission, but students are encouraged to complete introductory courses in these subjects prior to entrance.

Candidates must submit the completed application form and essays, a copy of the undergraduate degree and transcript, three passport-size photographs, a photocopy of a passport/ID, a current resume, two letters of recommendation, official GMAT scores of 550 or higher, official TOEFL or IELTS scores, a financial statement for those applicants who are applying for scholarships, and a £50 application fee.

Finances

In 2008, tuition for London's M.B.A. program is £13,000. Registration and application fees are £800, and student medical insurance is £200.

Approximately one half of all full-time students receive some form of assistance. Through both need- and merit-based matching funds programs, international scholarships are offered to encourage academic excellence and student leadership and to continue the ESE tradition of enrolling a community of scholars from every cultural background. Fellowships are available for first-time applicants who demonstrate outstanding scholastic achievement, leadership qualities, and community involvement. A number of graduate assistantships are awarded, based on achievement and merit, to full-time students.

ESE works in partnership with a private agency to provide a range of housing options for students. Apartments and home-sharing situations are located near public transportation and are available for both short- and long-term stays. Prices range from £79 per week for a shared triple room to £149 for a single room in an apartment. Homestay options range from £79 for a shared room to £163 for a single room with breakfast.

Application Facts and Dates

Applications are accepted year-round on a first-come, first-served basis. In all five ESE centers, students may start in September or January.

Applications for admission or additional information can be requested by contacting the university at:

European School of Economics
8/9 Grosvenor Place
London SW1X7SH
United Kingdom
Phone: 44-207-245-61-48
Fax: 44-207-245-61-64
E-mail: info@eselondon.ac.uk
Web site: http://www.eselondon.ac.uk/

ESE New York
350 Fifth Avenue, 33rd Floor
New York, New York 10118
Phone: 212-400-1440
Fax: 212-400-1441
E-mail: info@ese.edu

ESE Milan
Corso di Porta Vittoria, 16
20122 Milan
Italy
Phone: 39-02-365-04-235
Fax: 39-02-365-04-236
E-mail: ese.milano@uniese.it

ESE Rome
Via Quintino Sella, 67/69
00187 Rome
Italy
Phone: 39-06-97-27-07-10

Excelsior College

Albany, New York

> ### ► EARN A REAL-WORLD M.B.A. ONLINE FROM EXCELSIOR COLLEGE
>
> *The Excelsior College M.B.A.: Managing in the Global Economy is framed within a work-related global setting to increase understanding of business topics, improve career prospects, and expand individual horizons. This program will successfully equip you to further your career through enhanced knowledge and application of international strategies. You will learn about every aspect of worldwide business and then put your knowledge to work in a challenging capstone course. More importantly, you will study with some of the nation's leading business faculty members in a program designed by professors at respected business schools around the world. Immerse yourself in a rigorous real-world program specially developed for the global arena. Through a cutting-edge curriculum, online learning services, and supportive academic advisement, you will earn an M.B.A. that equips you with the essential knowledge and the required credentials to move ahead in your career in a challenging international environment.*
>
> *The program continues the long-standing Excelsior College model for adult higher education, which recognizes prior learning and enables flexible, self-paced study. Students entering the program may transfer up to 24 approved graduate-level credits toward the 48 credits required for graduation. They complete the remaining degree requirements by taking Excelsior College online courses and approved courses from other accredited institutions. All in all, the program delivers an M.B.A. education that is flexible, affordable, and applicable to the real world.*

Programs and Curricular Focus

Enrolled M.B.A. students work with Excelsior College academic advisers to create degree plans that meet their needs and conform to the academic policies and course requirements of the program. The program is designed to be flexible and ensure student success by providing many options for earning credit, including online Excelsior College courses, M.B.A. courses from other approved colleges and universities, and American Council on Education (ACE)–approved course alternatives, such as business or military training. Excelsior College courses are offered in fifteen-week and accelerated eight-week sessions and begin every other month.

Excelsior College advisers help students determine the options that meet their academic and career objectives, preferred learning styles, and current lifestyles. The diversity of educational alternatives makes this program unique and helps to ensure that additional alternatives in graduate business education are provided to populations that are traditionally underserved by higher education.

The required courses include accounting for managers (3 credits), business communications* (3 credits), business electives (9 credits), change management (3 credits), finance (3 credits), global environment (3 credits), human resources management (3 credits), information technology (3 credits), leadership (3 credits), marketing (3 credits), operations management (3 credits), organizational behavior (3 credits), quantitative analysis (3 credits), and strategy and policy–capstone* (3 credits). The courses noted with an asterisk (*) must be completed through Excelsior College.

The Faculty

The business faculty members of Excelsior College are drawn from some of the foremost business programs in the world. They establish and monitor academic policies and standards, determine degree requirements and the ways in which credit can be earned, develop the content for all examinations, review the records of students to verify their degree requirement completion, and recommend degree conferral. The School of Business and Technology also employs qualified, experienced teaching faculty members to lead instruction for Excelsior College online courses at the graduate level.

The College and Environs

As an accredited world leader in distance education, Excelsior College has helped busy working adults earn their college degrees since 1971. Because it has no residency requirement, the College accepts a broad array of prior college-level credit in transfer. With more than 125,000 graduates, the College's associate, baccalaureate, and master's degree programs are accessible worldwide. This enables students to work at their own pace while maintaining a full-time work schedule and family and civic responsibilities.

Facilities

As a distance education program, Excelsior College provides a variety of guided learning services to students, such as virtual online library services, an online bookstore, and an Electronic Peer Network (EPN), which provides the opportunity for enrolled students to interact online. The College maintains a database of distance courses that are available from accredited institutions. Academic advisers are available to provide services to students by telephone, fax, computer, and mail.

Placement

Detailed career resources are provided to enrolled students on the College's Web site, including self-assessment and career exploration guidance and job-search resources. In addition, resources provided to alumni include a resume critique service, career services, and online professional connections.

Admission

Students with a bachelor's degree from an accredited institution may be admitted into the Excelsior College M.B.A. program. The GMAT is not required. Graduate-level course work completed within ten years of the enrollment date may be used to satisfy the requirements of the M.B.A. degree program if approved by the Excelsior College faculty. Students may transfer up to 24 credits into this 48-credit program. There is no on-campus requirement; study may be completed entirely at a distance.

Finances

Students applying to the M.B.A. program pay an application fee of $100. Upon matriculation, a Student Service Fee of $215 is due. This fee is due annually while the student is enrolled in the program. Tuition is $410 per credit hour; because all Excelsior College M.B.A. courses are 3 credits each, the total tuition comes to $1230 per course. Upon completion of the program, a fee of $130 is due to cover costs associated with the awarding of the degree.

Different fees and fee structures apply to students who choose to pay their Excelsior College enrollment expenses via the College's FACTS Payment Plan. Federal Financial Aid is available to eligible students. Detailed fee schedules are available in hard copy and on the College's Web site. Additional costs depend on the amount of credit students need to earn and what credit sources they choose. Students should also figure in costs for books and other learning materials, travel, postage, online resources, and miscellaneous charges and supplies. Students seeking financial aid should contact the Excelsior College Financial Aid Office before enrolling.

Application Facts and Dates

More information about the Excelsior College M.B.A. program, including an enrollment form, is available online at http://mba.excelsior.edu. Students can start their program at any time. Enrollments are accepted year-round.

M.B.A. Program
School of Business and Technology
Excelsior College
7 Columbia Circle
Albany, New York 12203-5159
Phone: 518-464-8500
        888-647-2388, press 2-7 at the
            automated greeting (toll-free
            in the U.S.)
        518-464-8501 (TTY/TDD)
Fax: 518-464-8777
E-mail: admissions@excelsior.edu
Web site: http://www.excelsior.edu

Fairleigh Dickinson University

Silberman College of Business

Teaneck and Madison, New Jersey

AN M.B.A. WITH A GLOBAL PERSPECTIVE

The Silberman Master of Business Administration (M.B.A.) recognizes the new reality of a career in business. The program prepares graduates for leadership in a global business community characterized by multiculturalism and rapid technological and social changes.

Today's business school graduates no longer rely on organizations for career security but instead look to their own employability. Whether employed by a large organization or in one's own business, today's M.B.A. graduate is expected to bring an entrepreneurial outlook to an international marketplace.

The Silberman M.B.A. provides students with the skills to identify and capitalize on these opportunities. The work of the faculty members in developing a curriculum that meets the needs of the individual who has chosen business as a career, received national attention in 2006 when Entrepreneur Magazine and The Princeton Review named Silberman among the top best business schools in the nation for entrepreneurs (seventh in the country for undergraduate study and nineteenth for graduate study). Silberman has recruited an internationally diverse faculty and student body, integrated global themes throughout its programs of study, and forged international partnerships with universities throughout Asia, South America, and Europe.

The College's internationally prepared and high-quality teaching faculty members employ an innovative curriculum developed for the contemporary business environment. This combination is designed to give each Silberman M.B.A. graduate the competitive edge necessary to succeed in a global business community.

Programs and Curricular Focus

Accredited by AACSB International–The Association to Advance Collegiate Schools of Business, the Silberman College of Business has been dedicated to providing high-quality innovative programs for more than forty years. The College strives to develop graduates who are prepared to compete in a rapidly changing business environment. The Master of Business Administration curriculum reflects the integrated, cross-functional manner in which contemporary business operates and focuses on linking theory and practice through innovation.

The program is designed to address the complex demands placed on organizations and the individuals who manage them. Global perspectives and ethical concerns of business are integrated into all courses. The development and refinement of student communication skills is an important component of the integrative courses that form the program core. Topics critical to the value creation process, such as entrepreneurship, creativity, and strategic thinking, are introduced early in the program. The influences of demographic diversity, environment, law, politics, society, and technology are integrated throughout the program.

The Silberman College of Business offers a streamlined curriculum, which enables students to complete their degree in as few as 30 credits but no more than 48 credits. The introductory course, Executive Communication and Leadership, emphasizes the development of strong verbal, writing, leadership, and presentation skills in a business environment.

The six core courses are designed to ensure that all M.B.A. students have an understanding of fundamental principles before pursuing advanced business studies. The core courses include Financial Accounting: An End-User Approach, Economic Analysis, Organizational Behavior, Financial Analysis, Marketing Concepts, and Applied Statistical Analysis. Any or all of the core courses can be waived if a student meets the appropriate criteria.

The breadth courses expose students to the key business areas that are essential to success in every business environment. The breadth courses include Social, Political and Legal Environment of Business; Information Systems and Technology Management; Entrepreneurship and Strategy; and Production and Operations Management.

After completion of most core and breadth courses, students pursue four courses in one the following major fields of study: entrepreneurial studies, finance, human resource management, international business, management, management with concentra-

tions in corporate communication or information systems, marketing, or pharmaceutical management.

Other M.B.A. options include an Executive M.B.A. and a full-time M.B.A. in global business management. The College also offers the M.S. in accounting (M.S.A.) and the M.S. in taxation (M.S.T.) as well as four-course postgraduate certificate programs in nine subject areas for individuals already holding an M.B.A.

Students and the M.B.A. Experience
Global Focus

In addition to international business courses offered on the New Jersey campuses, M.B.A. students can experience the business of other countries through Silberman's international business seminars at partner institutions in Europe, Asia, and South America. The College has an impressive network of educational partners around the world, including universities in Belize, Brazil, China, France, Germany, Greece, Lebanon, Malaysia, South Korea, Switzerland, and Thailand, as well as the International University in Monaco and the Institute of Management Technology in India. Through these programs, students become immersed in different cultures and are able to view international business from a different perspective.

Fairleigh Dickinson has a special relationship with the United Nations. The University is one of only four universities to receive nongovernmental organization (NGO) status from the UN. As a result, faculty members and students enjoy special access to UN facilities and programs. Through the UN Pathways Program, ambassadors and diplomats make regular on-campus presentations.

Special Features

All students enrolled in the College's graduate business programs participate in at least one course on entrepreneurship offered by the Rothman Institute of Entrepreneurial Studies. Students may choose to select a sequence of courses in this area. Internship opportunities with new ventures are available.

In addition to traditional majors, the College offers an M.B.A. in pharmaceutical management, one of the first programs of its kind in the nation.

The Faculty

The College's faculty comes from sixteen countries and brings a combination of industry experience and academic training to the classroom. The faculty is committed to excellence in teaching. Faculty research interests concentrate on application of theory to business practice and are supported by research centers that include the Institute of Forensic Science Administration, Institute for Sustainable Enterprise, Center for Human Resource Management, and the Rothman Institute of Entrepreneurial Studies.

The Business School Network
Corporate Partnerships

Each of the academic departments is guided by a corporate advisory board that works with the faculty in developing the curriculum. Members of the advisory boards are often guest lecturers.

Prominent Alumni

The College counts among its alumni a number of leading corporate executives, including Patrick Zenner, President and CEO, Hoffman-LaRoche, Inc.; Stephen Sudovar, Senior Vice President, Pharmaceuticals Division, Hoffman-LaRoche, Inc.; Ron Dorfler, Senior Vice President and Chief Financial Officer, Capital Cities/ABC Inc.; Dennis Strigl, President and Chief Executive Officer, Bell Atlantic NYNEX Mobile; Richard Swift, Chairman, President, and Chief Executive Officer, Foster Wheeler Corp.; and Ronald Brill, Executive Vice President and Chief Administrative Officer, Home Depot.

The College and Environs

The 88-acre Metropolitan Campus in Teaneck, New Jersey, stretches along the east and west banks of the Hackensack River. Robison Hall, the Weiner Library, and Alumni Hall sit on the river's east edge, while the Silberman College of Business, located in Dickinson Hall, sits on the west edge. The College of Florham in Madison, New Jersey, is a beautifully landscaped parklike setting of 166 acres. Its Georgian-style buildings have been adapted to the educational needs of the University. Both Fairleigh Dickinson University (FDU) campuses are located in attractive residential suburbs close to local theaters, restaurants, and sports arenas. Students can easily reach the business, cultural, and social offerings of New York City by private or public transportation.

Wroxton College, the overseas campus of the University, was originally built as an abbey and became the home of Lord North in the 1700s. It is centrally located in England between Oxford and Stratford-upon-Avon.

Fairleigh Dickinson also offers undergraduate business studies at its newest international location in Vancouver, British Columbia, Canada.

Facilities

In recent years, the University has made extensive renovations to its facilities. On the Metropolitan Campus, the College resides in a building that features executive classrooms, three computer laboratories, and a comprehensive business reference library, which includes general and international business reference volumes, annual reports, subject CD-ROMs, business indexes, and online search services.

At the College of Florham, Silberman College occupies a major part of a 100-room mansion designed by Stanford White, as well as part of a new academic building where every classroom is hardwired for computers and Internet access. Weekend classes in the Executive M.B.A. in management and the Executive M.B.A. in health care and life sciences are offered at the Hamilton Park Hotel and Conference Center, a world-class executive facility located adjacent to the College at Florham.

Technology Environment

The University maintains a range of computer laboratories for students, including the latest in personal computer technology and software, as well as Compaq Alpha, Sun E450, Sun E250, and Cisco Power Network. There also is a wide variety of software for use independent of campus or location. There are several PC laboratories on each campus. All PCs are connected to a central file server through a local area network with access to the University-wide network and the Internet.

Placement

The Career Management Center offers career and employment services to all M.B.A. students and alumni. A large network of corporate contacts augments on-campus recruiting programs and career fairs. Computerized databases and job search strategy workshops are a regular part of the services offered to M.B.A. students.

Admission

The College considers each candidate's academic record, GMAT score, and professional experience in the admission process. International students whose native language is not English are required to submit a TOEFL score. It is recommended that students have a basic knowledge of statistics; computer usage, including spreadsheets and word processing; and mathematics, including calculus.

Finances

Tuition for most graduate programs in 2008–09 is $921 per credit hour. Approximately twenty-five graduate assistantships are available to qualified candidates, offering tuition remission. A number of graduate business programs, such as the Executive M.B.A. in management, the Executive M.B.A. in health care and life sciences, and the Global M.B.A. have comprehensive flat rates.

International Students

International students from twenty-nine countries represent 17 percent of all graduate business students at Silberman College. Extensive English language preparation and assistance programs are available. An international scholarship program is offered for non-U.S. full-time students.

Application Facts and Dates

Applications for domestic students are accepted on a rolling basis for fall, spring, and summer sessions. International student applications for the fall semester are due by July 1, and applications for the spring semester are due by December 1. For additional information, students should contact:

Fairleigh Dickinson University
1000 River Road, T.KB1.01
Teaneck, New Jersey 07666
Web site: http://www.fdu.edu
          http://www.fdu.edu/business
          (Business)

Office of Graduate Admissions
  (domestic students)
Phone: 201-692-2554
E-mail: grad@fdu.edu

Office of International Admissions
  (international students)
Phone: 201-692-2205
E-mail: global@fdu.edu

Felician College

DEVELOPING BUSINESS LEADERS FOR THE TWENTY-FIRST CENTURY

Our primary objective is to create a learning environment that will enable and encourage each student to participate, teach, learn, and develop the skills needed to fulfill his or her life and career dreams. We believe that students learn best by doing. Our overall goal is to assist each student in becoming a skilled practitioner who can successfully and ethically practice in the business world. To achieve this goal, we use an integrated learning approach. This approach offers each class member the opportunity to improve his or her competencies related to ethical decision making, critical reasoning, communication, quantitative reasoning, and teamwork.

Felician business students should not expect their professors to dominate the class experience with lectures. Instead, they can expect to be encouraged to share significant experiences and opinions that help inform the course content. In class, they will participate in various learning activities, debates, discussions, and experiential self-development exercises. We believe that when each class member participates fully in this manner, a great synergy is created that adds depth and life to the curriculum.

As Dean of the Division of Business and Management Sciences, I am committed to helping students achieve their educational goals and objectives. To accomplish this I am dedicated, and maintain a consistent resolve, to providing high-quality programs and courses. The Division operates in a culture of continuous improvement, and both the program and the students within it are expected to evolve and grow. Student feedback is used regularly to update and modify our content and methodologies. Our overarching goal is to create curriculum and a learning environment that helps students achieve their full potential. You can expect dedicated, professional, and caring faculty members; individualized academic advising; small class sizes; and a positive nurturing environment. We simply put "Students First."

—Beth Castiglia, Dean

Program and Curricular Focus

Felician College offers an M.B.A. that focuses on innovation and entrepreneurship. This program has an approach unlike other M.B.A. programs—it focuses on the development of competencies through the delivery of academic content, allowing students to become competent, ethical, articulate, and creative leaders. Students can earn their degrees in one of two tracks—innovation and entrepreneurship or accounting. The program uses a unique combination of classroom and online learning intertwined with hands-on practical application. The goal of the program is to create visionary thinking and innovative leadership for individuals who wish to start their own businesses or be agents of change within their corporations.

Specially tailored to meet the needs of working adults, the program meets only one night a week, from 6 to 10, and allows students to complete the 36-credit degree in just two years. The program is conveniently located at the Felician College campuses in Lodi and Rutherford and several branch campuses across the state.

Students and the M.B.A. Experience

The cohort-based program allows students to progress with a cohesive learning team so they can grow and benefit from teamwork and the support and guidance of an academic learning community. The curriculum prepares students with both the technical knowledge they need for solving complex problems and the core competencies that will equip them with the survival skills necessary for the competitive business world. The Felician M.B.A. core competencies, which are intertwined with content in every course, include critical reasoning, effective communication, emotional intelligence, teamwork, ethical decision making, and creativity.

The Faculty

All courses are taught by fully qualified faculty members with advanced degrees, who are dedicated to teaching, advising, and continued involvement in their disciplines. The student-faculty ratio of 19:1 facilitates close working relationships and the devel-

opment of individualized programs of instruction. The faculty is composed of both lay and religious men and women who are committed to the intellectual and spiritual growth of every student.

The College and Environs

Felician College, a coeducational liberal arts college, is a Catholic, private, independent institution for students representing diverse religious, racial, and ethnic backgrounds. The College is one of the institutions of higher learning operated by the Felician Sisters in the United States. Its mission is to provide a values-oriented education based in the liberal arts while it prepares students for meaningful lives and careers in contemporary society. To meet the needs of students and to provide personal enrichment courses to matriculated and nonmatriculated students, Felician College offers day, evening, and weekend programs. The College is accredited by the Middle States Association of Colleges and Schools and carries program accreditation from the National League for Nursing Accrediting Commission, the National Accrediting Agency for Clinical Laboratory Sciences, and the International Assembly for Collegiate Business Education.

Felician College operates on campuses in Lodi and Rutherford, New Jersey. The College's Lodi campus, located on the banks of the Saddle River on a beautifully landscaped campus of 27 acres, offers a collegiate setting in suburban Bergen County, within easy driving distance of New York City. The Rutherford campus is set on 10½ beautifully landscaped acres in the heart of the historic community of Rutherford, New Jersey. Only 15 minutes from the Lodi campus, the Rutherford complex includes student residences, classroom buildings, a student center, and a gymnasium. The campus is a short distance from downtown Rutherford, where there are many shops and businesses of interest to students.

Facilities

The library is a two-story building that serves the needs of students, faculty and staff members, and alumni, with more than 110,000 books and more than 800 periodical subscriptions. This collection is enhanced by large holdings of materials in microform, which can be used on the library's reader/printer equipment. With its computers linked to information services such as Dialog and

OCLC, and as a member of the New Jersey Library Network and VALE, the library locates and obtains information, journal articles, and books from sources all across the country. Computerized databases can also be accessed directly by users through the online FirstSearch workstation, where up-to-date information on 40 million books and an index of 15,000 periodicals are available. The library is also connected to the Internet and has several CD-ROM workstations. Through EBSCOhost, Bell & Howell's ProQuest, CINAHL, and other services, students have access to numerous online journal indexes—as well as the articles from thousands of periodicals—from anywhere on the campus network or from their home computers. An experienced staff of professional librarians is available to assist users.

Technology Environment

The College's computer facilities include an academic and administrative network, four computerized labs, a computerized learning center, and two computer centers for stu-dents, with a total of about 200 computers available for student and faculty use. All classrooms, offices, and facilities are wired for Internet and e-mail.

Placement

Graduates are positioned as change agents who are able to lead and succeed within their organizations with ethical integrity as their guide.

Admission

Admission to Felician College is as person-alized as the College's educational pro-grams. Each application is holistically re-viewed, including careful consideration of the applicant's academic achievement, work history, motivation, and suitability. Students must submit the completed application, the $40 nonrefundable application fee, official transcripts, GMAT scores, a resume, and a personal statement. Upon the discretion of the division admission committee, the GMAT requirement may be waived for those students with significant and progressive postgraduate professional experience.

Finances

In 2006–07, graduate tuition was $675 per credit. Fees were additional. On-campus room and board ranged between $3200 and $5500 per semester. Scholarships, fellow-ships, work-study programs, and loans are available. To qualify for financial aid, a student must complete the Free Application for Federal Student Aid (FAFSA).

Application Facts and Dates

Applications are processed on a rolling basis.

Department of Admissions
Felician College
262 South Main Street
Lodi, New Jersey 07644-2117
Phone: 201-559-6131 (Admissions)
     201-559-6092 (Business
     Division)
Fax: 201-559-6120
Web site: http://www.felician.edu/
     business/index.asp

Fielding Graduate University

Santa Barbara, California

DEAN'S MESSAGE

Fielding Graduate University's programs in organization management and development offer online cohort-based master's degrees and graduate certificates for professionals and decision makers in the networked economy. The program is dedicated to fostering new ways of leading and working with organizational change and transitions, leadership and complexity, virtual work teams and work design, and employee and team development within corporations, profit and nonprofit agencies, education, and government.

We offer fully accredited, high-quality graduate education programs that are rigorous and demanding. Our outstanding faculty members will challenge you in many ways as they help prepare you for the life of the scholar-practitioner. As a Fielding student, you will become part of a community of scholars dispersed throughout the country and around the world. This community is committed to transforming graduate education and research to advance individuals, organizations, and society.

Fielding students and graduates are self-directed, academically talented men and women who combine their practical experience with scholarly pursuits and make contributions in highly meaningful ways.

—Charles McClintock, Ph.D., Dean

Programs and Curricular Focus

The twenty-month, online master's program in organization management and development (OMD) offers midcareer adults the opportunity to develop and expand their professional skills through the study and practical application of organizational science, management, and behavior in order to lead change that matters.

OMD students and graduates enhance their ability to create organizational excellence and act as change agents through the study of adult development, complex adaptive systems, virtual practices, distributed teams, and innovative models of leadership, management, and organization development.

The program prepares students to keep pace with organizational challenges, from rapidly expanding and contracting markets and organization changes to issues of globalization, virtual team management, and leadership development and the call to create sustainability.

Throughout the program, students apply their educational experiences to the real-world situations they face on a continual basis. By immediately relating their new knowledge to the workplace, students put theories into practice and are able to see the results of their educational investment as they study.

Collaborative learning, student-centered focus, flexibility, and convenience are just a few distinguishing features of the master's degree and graduate-level certificate programs in organization management and development. In this program, students can study any time, any place. OMD graduates experience professional development and career distinctiveness.

As a preeminent leader in distance learning for more than thirty years, Fielding has designed the OMD program to integrate adult learning principles and its extensive experience in online community development with contemporary models of leadership, management, and organization development practices. During their course of study, OMD students work with faculty members who are recognized professionals in their fields; apply day-to-day professional experience to their course work; enhance leadership skills to manage change in complex organizations; create innovative work solutions to support organizational mission and goals; develop the competence to design and lead virtual networked teams; build competencies to be an effective instrument of change with individuals, groups, organizations, and communities; and become members of Fielding's global network of professionals and scholar-practitioners.

Students in the M.A. and graduate-level certificate programs are experienced professionals participating in a flexible and collaborative learning environment. Students in the master's degree program complete ten courses to earn an M.A. degree. The program consists of four core courses, four elective courses, and a two-course master's project.

In addition to the M.A. degree program in organization management and development, there are three graduate-level certificates in organization management and development, integral studies, and evidence-based coaching. The graduate-level certificate programs consist of four courses overall—two core courses and two electives selected from the master's degree curriculum.

Fielding's total student population is more than 1,500. The 160 students in the master's-level programs are a diverse group of individuals who form a worldwide professional network. Fielding scholars are practitioners with varied experience in areas such as consulting, the corporate arena, profit and nonprofit agencies, education, and government. The average age of the OMD student is 42, with a range from 26 to 68.

The Fielding Graduate University student community consists primarily of adult learners who have a self-directed, independent learning style and are geographically dispersed, as are the members of the faculty.

Special Features

Custom programs and courses for business, nonprofits, government agencies, education, and human services are available in the aforementioned areas as well as in coaching and mentoring, community development, health-care systems and management, public administration, knowledge management, and conflict resolution and negotiation. Fielding Graduate University works in partnership with businesses and organizations to deliver customized online learning solutions or blended learning approaches that combine online and face-to-face delivery. The flexibility of the programs is what makes them truly customized to the needs of the learners.

The Faculty

The master's faculty consists of an international group of scholar-practitioners representing multiple disciplines and with active professional lives across all sectors of society. These instructors are skilled at facilitating online conversations and helping students develop real-time solutions to real-life business and organizational problems. Fielding faculty members promote an interactive, individualized approach to guided practice.

Faculty List

Candido Trujillo, Ph.D., Program Director.
Jim Beaubien, Ph.D.
Marcella Benson-Quaziena, Ph.D.
Sean Esbjorn-Hargens, Ph.D.
Gary M. Fontaine, Ph.D.
Jeff Frakes, Ph.D.
Bo Gyllenpalm, Ph.D.
Barclay Hudson, Ed.D.
Ruth Middleton House, Ed.D.
Randy Martin, Ph.D.
Rena Palloff, Ph.D.
Leni Wildflower, Ph.D.

The College and Environs

Founded in 1974, Fielding Graduate University is a world leader in graduate-level, networked education for professionals. Fielding is dedicated to providing high-quality, accredited programs through a combination of face-to-face and online interactions between accomplished students and nationally recognized faculty members. The student-centered programs combine theory with practice and are designed to support flexible, independent learning and competency development. This flexibility allows students to apply their graduate studies to their professional work. The Fielding community is dedicated to lifelong learning, innovation, and change for individuals, communities, organizations, and social justice.

Fielding Graduate University's administrative offices are located in Santa Barbara, California. The students and faculty members create a global Fielding community, with students located in the United States and thirty-one other countries.

Facilities

Fielding's library services are designed to serve the complex needs of busy professionals by offering substantial research tools via the Web. The library collection and services include a database of Internet resources, a subsidized document delivery service, a catalog of available dissertations and electronic books, and access to numerous online library databases and journals.

Finances

Fielding Graduate University participates in the Federal Stafford Student Loan Program, making subsidized and unsubsidized loans available based on financial need. Fielding also participates in veterans' assistance programs. In 2007–08, Fielding Graduate University administered approximately $18 million in aid to about 75 percent of its graduate students.

The 2007–08 tuition for the M.A. and certificate programs was $681 per credit for full-time students. Tuition and fee rates are subject to change each academic year. Current tuition information can be found at http://www.fielding.edu/tuition. Given that Fielding Graduate University students work independently and live in various parts of the United States and beyond, costs in addition to tuition vary per student. Considerations include computer equipment, books and materials, and required travel to one regional session in preparation for the master's project. Students start the M.A. program with a two-week introductory course prior to the first term of enrollment.

Application Facts and Dates

Students may enter the master's degree program in January, May, or September. Applicants must submit a $75 nonrefundable fee, an online application form, a resume, a statement of purpose, one letter of recommendation, and sealed official undergraduate transcripts for consideration.

Admission Office
Fielding Graduate University
2112 Santa Barbara Street
Santa Barbara, California 93105
Phone: 800-340-1099 (toll-free)
E-mail: admission@fielding.edu
Web site: http://www.fielding.edu

Florida International University

Alvah H. Chapman, Jr., Graduate School of Business

Miami, Florida

THE BUSINESS SCHOOL FOR THE AMERICAS

The Alvah H. Chapman Jr., Graduate School of Business in the College of Business Administration (CBA) at Florida International University (FIU) is south Florida's most important resource for global business education, technology, and research, and is especially noted for its unique expertise in Latin American commerce, entrepreneurship, and information technology. Its distinctive and successful M.B.A. programs offer integrated, international, multicultural, and technology-supported curricula tailored to address the needs of the specific student groups each is designed to serve.

Regardless of the specific graduate program, however, students emerge with a broad and deep understanding of global strategic management and of enterprisewide, process-oriented, and customer-driven organizations. Graduates become effective members of such enterprises, able to blend pragmatism and creativity in solving increasingly complex business problems. In short, they are ready to exercise global business leadership in the twenty-first century.

—Joyce J. Elam, Dean

Programs and Curricular Focus

The Chapman School offers academic programs leading to the Master of Accounting (M.Acc.), the Master of Business Administration (M.B.A.), the Master in International Business (M.I.B.), the Master of Science in Finance (M.S.F.), the Master of Science in Human Resource Management (M.S.H.R.M.), the Master of Science in Management Information Systems (M.S.M.I.S.), and the Master of Science in International Real Estate (M.S.I.R.E.). It offers an Executive Master of Science in Taxation (E.M.S.T.) and programs that lead to the Doctor of Philosophy (Ph.D.) degree in business administration, with concentrations in accounting, finance, international business, management, management information systems, and marketing. All of its degree programs are accredited by the AACSB International–The Association to Advance Collegiate Schools of Business.

Options for students interested in pursuing an M.B.A. degree include the International M.B.A. (IMBA), the Executive M.B.A. (EMBA), the Downtown M.B.A. (DtMBA), the Professional M.B.A. (PMBA), and the Evening M.B.A. (EveMBA). All require 42 to 55 credit hours of graduate course work.

The IMBA, the Chapman School's only full-time M.B.A. program, is an intensive, twelve-month, lock-step program with daytime classes. It features international study and internship components and is especially designed for recent college graduates or international students interested in pursuing full-time study to further their international business careers.

The EMBA, tailored to the mid-level executive with at least eight years of professional experience, is a twenty-month, lock-step program that meets on Saturdays.

The PMBA, designed for working professionals with at least five years of professional experience, offers classes on Saturdays through a twenty-month, lock-step program.

The DtMBA serves working professionals in the downtown Miami area, offering classes two evenings per week in an eighteen-month, lock-step program.

The EVEMBA program, which serves working professionals in the South Florida community, offers nightly classes (Monday through Thursday), with each course meeting once a week. Students taking six courses per year can complete their degrees in about three years.

Through its five academic departments and six top-notch research and service centers, the College also provides a broad range of graduate, professional, and executive education; customized training and certificate programs; seminars, short courses, and conferences; and study-abroad and global programs.

Students and the M.B.A. Experience

The Chapman School's uniquely diverse and multicultural student body generally reflects the international demographics of South Florida: Hispanic American, 45 percent; African American, 7 percent; Caucasian, 15 percent; Asian American, 4 percent; and international, 18 percent. The student population is 39 percent women. The average age

of the beginning graduate student is 28, while the average age of the advanced graduate student is 37. Many international students are from the Latin American and Caribbean regions.

Students in the accelerated, full-time IMBA program include recent college graduates from all over the world as well as those who have been in the international workforce for a while and are returning to pursue an advanced degree. This blend of personal and business backgrounds enriches the learning experience for all students.

Most of the students in the EVEMBA and DtMBA programs are from South Florida, are bilingual, and have personal and business ties with one or more Latin American countries. Their academic work is augmented by their active involvement in the Chapman Graduate School, which, in addition to social and seminar activities, maintains close contact with alumni and the business community.

The EMBA program includes managers from large multinational corporations, entrepreneurs, and officers of small firms. Because they represent a variety of countries, industries, and professional expertise, they draw and build upon one another's skills and experiences.

Designed for the working professional with a minimum of five years of professional work experience, the PMBA program offers a fast-paced, intense program in which the student can network with his or her peers and learn from each other in a dynamic environment. Students are assigned to study teams, which function as support groups throughout the program. The twenty-month program allows students to complete their M.B.A. without interrupting their careers.

All M.B.A. programs combine classroom lecture and discussion with case analyses, field work, computer modeling and analysis,

e-business technologies, group research projects, computer simulations, role playing, and both written and oral presentations. They also incorporate professional development sessions on teamwork, managing diversity, leadership, and communication.

The Faculty

A dynamic force for excellence, the roster of 118 College faculty members who teach in the Chapman School's graduate programs includes 6 Eminent Scholars and a cadre of internationally known experts in information systems, e-commerce, operations research, knowledge management, financial derivatives, international trade, consumer research, multinational corporations, international management, and corporate responsibility.

The Business School Network

All students benefit from the international character of Chapman's many partners and alumni in Miami's business community. Because the city links the two Americas with the rest of the global economy, it serves as regional headquarters for hundreds of multinational companies. A major center for international trade, finance, banking, and real estate, the area also supports a healthy travel and tourism industry, a substantial number of entrepreneurial technology firms, and a growing entertainment industry. If not already working in this environment, students can participate in it through internships, mentorships, special research projects, field trips, lectures by top executives, and international business forums.

The College of Business Administration is one of only thirty-one business schools to have received a Department of Education grant to support its Center for International Business, Education and Research (CIBER). Its other research and service centers—such as the Center for Accounting, Auditing, and Tax Studies; the Knight Ridder Center for Excellence in Management; the Jerome Bain Real Estate Institute; and the Ryder Center for Supply Chain Systems—also give students opportunities for involvement in industry and professional associations.

The College and Environs

The College of Business Administration is the second largest of Florida International University's professional schools, enrolling about 3,000 undergraduate and 1,200 graduate students each year. The University, a member of the State University System of Florida, is a comprehensive, urban research institution founded in 1972 and has 38,000 students, 1,100 faculty members, and more than 100,000 alumni from around the world. It offers more than 190 academic degree programs and is the largest university in south Florida.

The College and Chapman School are headquartered on the University Park campus, a 344-acre tract located about 10 miles west of downtown Miami.

Technology Environment

The Chapman School's sizeable investments in its Technology Center, computer labs, and wireless multimedia case classrooms provide state-of-the-art IT support for students. The College has received more than $1 million in software, training, and technical support to integrate a business-process perspective through its partnerships and grants it has received. It also relies on Oracle, Rational Rose, PL/SQL, Cold Fusion, UML, XML, Java, and a host of other technologies.

Placement

The mission of the Chapman School's Career Management Services office is to partner with, and provide extensive services to, students so that they can become active participants in their own continuing development, evaluation, and implementation of personal career plans. By assisting students in the management of their own expectations, students become their own success story.

This includes offering students high-quality, accessible, extensive, and well-coordinated services and information designed for career success. Workshop topics include resume preparation, acing the interview, job search strategies, and effective networking. In addition, the office provides students with self-assessment tools, one-on-one advising, resume referral, and on-campus interviews for internships and permanent employment opportunities.

The Career Management Office is a partner with the FIU Career Services Office and with other M.B.A. alliances for on-campus interviews, career fairs, and/or other career development related activities.

Admission

Applicants who are considered for admission to the Chapman School programs must submit a formal application and application fee and must have, at a minimum, a bachelor's degree from a regionally accredited college or university; official transcripts from every college or university attended; a resume; an essay stating goals and reason for attending the program; and a minimum score of 500 on the Graduate Management Admission Test (GMAT) or a combined score of 1000 on the quantitative and verbal sections of the Graduate Record Examinations (GRE) and a minimum 3.0 upper-division grade point average (GPA). Exceptions may be made on the GMAT or GRE tests for EMBA, PMBA, and M.S.H.R.M. applicants. Students whose native language is not English must also obtain a minimum score of 550 (paper), 213 (computer-based), or 80 (iBT) on the TOEFL. Additional criteria vary and reflect the nature of the specific program.

Finances

Tuition and fees vary by program and are also determined by residency status. All fees are subject to change without notice. Financial aid is available to qualifying students.

Application Facts and Dates

For program and application information and materials, please contact:

Marketing and Recruiting
Chapman Graduate School of Business
Florida International University
11200 SW 8th Street
Miami, Florida 33199

Phone: 305-348-7398
        800-955-8771 (TDD via FRS,
        toll-free)
E-mail: chapman@fiu.edu
Web site: http://business.fiu.edu

Fordham University

DEAN'S MESSAGE

Fordham's Graduate School of Business is committed to providing its students with access—access to New York City, to an international perspective, to a world-class education, and to new professional opportunities.

Located in New York City, the Fordham Graduate School of Business offers students a front-row seat in the global business arena. With frequent guest lecturers from prominent corporations, students gain new perspectives and invaluable contacts that supplement the rigorous course work from our prestigious faculty.

Our goal is to provide a strong foundation for our students' careers and to continue career advancement opportunities after graduation through alumni services and programs. We go out of our way to get to know our students, advise them on a personal basis, and support the development of their unique goals, both in business and in life.

—Howard P. Tuckman, Dean

Programs and Curricular Focus

Quality is a major focus for Fordham's M.B.A. program. Students acquire the knowledge and skills necessary to become leaders in business. In the classroom, faculty members teach fundamental theory and current research tied to pragmatic solutions, so students master both abstract and applied methods of thinking.

Students develop expertise in specific fields by selecting a concentration pertaining to areas of business that interest them, including accounting and taxation, communications and media management, finance, information systems, management systems, and marketing.

The designations offered along with the concentrations add a stronger foundation to the student's base of study. Students can pursue a designation in global sustainability, electronic business, entrepreneurship, and international business.

The course of study at the Business School is organized on a trimester (three terms per year) academic year that begins in September and goes through April. A full-time student can finish the program within fifteen to eighteen months, whereas a part-time student can take from three to four years, depending on the number of credits taken per term and waivers granted.

The 69-credit M.B.A. degree program has three prerequisite courses and eight business core courses included in the curriculum. The business core classes range from accounting to management. All upper-level courses can be used, either in the concentration area or the breadth-elective and free-elective areas, filling out the remaining requirements for the M.B.A.

degree. Students can also pursue a dual concentration, getting a concentration in two business areas.

Fordham's Graduate School of Business also offers four specialized M.S. degree programs. The courses are current, relevant to the real world, and taught by the same renowned faculty members who teach in Fordham's M.B.A. program. Students who are looking to expand their skill set with a highly focused graduate degree program may choose from M.S. degree programs in information systems, media management, quantitative finance, or taxation.

Fordham offers a Global Professional M.B.A. program that culminates in an international experience, a joint J.D./M.B.A. program with Fordham Law School, and a 99-credit Master in Taxation and Accounting program (MTA), which awards the M.B.A. in professional accounting and the M.S. in taxation. The M.B.A. prepares students for the CPA exam, while the M.S. in taxation prepares students to be taxation professionals.

The Executive M.B.A. (E.M.B.A.) is an executive-style program for students who either have five or more years of business experience or are on a fast track to upper-level managerial positions. Classes are held one weekend per month at the Lincoln Center campus.

There are international options available to students through partnerships with Peking University in Beijing, China, and ESADE in Barcelona, Spain.

Students and the M.B.A. Experience

The total student population of Fordham's graduate business school is 1,432, with 686 attending on a full-time basis, 746 attending on a part-time basis, and 25 participating in a new full-time cohort. The average age is 25; 39 percent are women. Students representing more than thirty countries compose nearly 26 percent of the full-time student body.

On average, Fordham business students have had five years of work experience. As a consequence, many classroom discussions are enriched by students contributing their own on-the-job experiences.

The Faculty

Fordham has 92 full-time faculty members, 98 percent of whom hold a Ph.D. or a similar terminal degree. Women compose 32 percent of the group. The adjunct faculty pool totals 200.

Many members of the faculty serve as consultants to a variety of industries as well as to international governments and institutions. The diverse backgrounds of the faculty members provide a multicultural teaching field, with an emphasis on global standards and practices.

The Business School Network

Because of Fordham's graduate business school's location in New York City, which many consider the business capital of the world, students have easy access to a "who's who" of corporate leaders and Wall Street executives who visit the campus regularly. In addition, with an alumni networking organization, the World Wise Network, students are constantly exposed to alumni who offer their expertise and guidance.

Corporate Partnerships

In addition to guest speakers in classes, at seminars, and in panel discussions, students are able to take advantage of two formal programs that provide business contacts: the M.B.A. Consulting Program, in which teams of students solve problems for real corporate assignments, and the MTA Program, funded largely by the accounting and tax industries, which then hire the program's graduates.

The College and Environs

Fordham's Graduate School of Business was established in 1969 and is founded on the

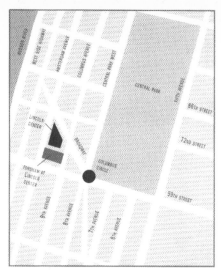

Fordham at Lincoln Center, with Columbus Circle and Central Park.

Jesuit tradition of rigorous education. Fordham's business school is located at Lincoln Center on a 7-acre green campus that marks the southern border of the cultural heart of New York City.

The Lincoln Center campus consists of the academic building, the residence hall, and the School of Law, all of which are connected by a central plaza that serves as an island of calm in a city of skyscrapers. It is one block from Central Park and Columbus Circle, a major transportation hub in midtown Manhattan.

Placement

Fordham's Career Services Office offers individual counseling, workshops, and mock interview sessions to guide students in the subtleties of networking, information gathering, and interviewing. Panel discussions by industry representatives provide the chance to learn about career opportunities and trends in particular areas of academic concentration. On-campus and off-campus recruitment opportunities are also available throughout the year.

Admission

The principal elements that define a Fordham student are academic and professional accomplishments, clearly defined career objectives, motivation, and personal integrity. Each candidate must possess the U.S. equivalent of a four-year baccalaureate degree and must have taken the Graduate Management Admission Test (GMAT). The candidate's academic record, GMAT scores, personal statements, professional recommendations, and work experience are considered in the admission process.

Applicants from non-English-speaking countries must submit the results of the Test of English as a Foreign Language (TOEFL). The minimum TOEFL score accepted is 100 on the Internet-based test, 250 on the computer-based test, or 600 on the paper-based test.

Finances

The annual tuition for a full-time student in 2008–09 is $30,300 for 30 credit hours of study ($1010 per credit hour). The average part-time student completes 18 credits per year, which cost $18,180 in 2008–09. The estimated cost of fees, insurance, books, and supplies is $1575 per year. Off-campus housing, although greatly varied, is estimated to cost at least $15,000.

Fordham uses the Free Application for Federal Student Aid (FAFSA) to determine the need of each student for any scholarship, graduate assistantship, or loan, thus the FAFSA should be filed as soon as possible. Deadlines and requirements differ based on the specific aid program.

International Students

Twenty-six percent of Fordham's full-time M.B.A. student population comes from other countries; more than thirty countries are represented in the School.

Application Facts and Dates

Application deadlines are June 1 for the September trimester, November 1 for the January trimester, and March 1 for the April trimester. Full- and part-time students may apply for both the fall and spring trimesters. Only part-time applicants are eligible to apply for the summer trimester. Decisions are made on a rolling basis. Notification is usually within one month after application is completed.

International students are asked to submit their application one month prior to the regular deadlines, and they must also provide documentation that they have the resources to pay for their studies prior to receiving their visa. For more information, students should contact:

Director of Admissions
Graduate School of Business
Fordham University
33 West 60th Street, 4th Floor
New York, New York 10023
Phone: 212-636-6200
        800-823-4422 (toll-free)
Fax: 212-636-7076
E-mail: admissionsgb@fordham.edu
Web site: http://www.bnet.fordham.edu

The George Washington University

MANAGEMENT THAT MATTERS

Situated just steps from the World Bank, the International Monetary Fund, the State Department, the Federal Reserve, and the White House, the School of Business at the George Washington University (GW) provides students the opportunity to make a difference. GW business students have access to an exceptional array of guest speakers and internship opportunities. Combining the tremendous resources of Washington, D.C., with high-quality teaching and research, GW offers M.B.A. students an unparalleled management education.

In spring 2006, GW opened its doors to a new building for the School of Business. Ric and Dawn Duques Hall is designed to provide the GW management community with technology-rich classrooms, student meeting space, faculty offices, a capital markets room, and a new auditorium. The building will provide the University with a commanding presence on one of Washington's most prestigious avenues.

Perhaps the greatest strength of the School of Business is the depth and breadth of its academic offerings. One of the largest schools in the nation in terms of specialized (non-M.B.A.) management degrees in areas such as accountancy, finance, information systems, and project management, GW offers many truly unique courses that allow a deeper understanding of the various functional areas of business.

We are looking for M.B.A. candidates who will act responsibly, lead passionately, and think globally. Our new curriculum, set to launch in fall 2008, is designed to take advantage of tremendous resources both internally with outstanding faculty members and externally, as our university is located in the heart of the nation's capital.

—Dr. Murat Tarimcilar, Associate Dean, Graduate Programs

Programs and Curricular Focus

The George Washington University Master of Business Administration is designed to deliver a strong general management education through core and integrative courses while maintaining an array of options and opportunities that can be packaged differently for each student.

The full-time Global M.B.A. program (57 credit hours) is designed with a first-year cohort experience structured to promote teamwork; it provides opportunities to approach problems and issues across the curriculum and is enhanced by a series of cocurricular activities that are designed to support and expand upon classroom concepts. An international practicum and a capstone course, designed to integrate the M.B.A. courses, are also required. Students may pursue any of seventeen areas of interest (accounting; finance and investments; health services administration; environmental policy and management; human resources management; information systems management; international business; supply chain management; management decision making; management of science, technology, and innovation; marketing; nonprofit organization management; organizational behavior and development; real estate and urban development; small business and

entrepreneurship; strategic management and public policy; and tourism and hospitality management) or craft an individualized concentration. Electives provide flexibility and opportunities for additional depth and breadth.

There are a number of options for students whose lives do not permit full-time study. The accelerated M.B.A. program provides a fast-paced cohort option for employed students. Students attend this program (48–52.5 credits) on a year-round basis, and this option includes residencies as well as applied and integrated projects. The self-paced M.B.A. program (also 48–52.5 credits) is the most flexible, permitting enrollment in any combination of semesters and at any credit load as long as the program is completed in five years. Electives, which constitute half of the program, help students position themselves for immediate and long-range opportunities. The Executive M.B.A. program, a 56-hour, twenty-one month cohort program, is designed for middle- and senior-level managers who seek an intensive program to enhance their career development. The program consists of courses taught on alternate Fridays and Saturdays, plus three residencies, including one mul-

ticity international experience. The curriculum emphasis is on strategic leadership in a complex world.

Through a special credit-hour transfer arrangement between the School of Business and GW's School of Law, students can complete both the M.B.A. and J.D. degrees within four years. (Part-time students must do it in five.) Also, students may pursue degrees in the School of Business and GW's Elliott School of International Affairs simultaneously, receiving the M.B.A. and M.A. in two to three years. In addition, the School of Business offers a joint M.B.A./M.S. in Finance.

In addition to the M.B.A., the GW School of Business offers the Master of Accountancy; the Master of Science in finance, information systems management, and project management; and the Master of Tourism Administration. The Ph.D. is offered in accountancy, business administration, and management and technology.

Students and the M.B.A. Experience

GW M.B.A. students are intellectually mature people who have exhibited a strong potential for management and leadership. The average student is 27 years old. Of the M.B.A. students, 45 percent are women, 13 percent are members of U.S. minority groups, and 36 percent are international students.

More than 90 percent of GW M.B.A. students possess substantial business experience before beginning their graduate work. They come from domestic and foreign corporations, family-owned companies, nonprofit organizations, private practices, and the arts. Many work on Capitol Hill or in one of the businesses headquartered in the Washington area.

Global Focus

With students from sixty-nine countries, GW offers a culturally diverse environment for learning about life and business around the world. In addition to the core course, The World Economy and Multinational Corporations, students are required to take at least one additional elective that adds international background. For students who choose to study abroad, exchange programs have been established in Europe, Asia, and South America.

The School of Business is located within a few blocks of the World Bank, the International Monetary Fund, and embassies from around the world, offering GW M.B.A. students a unique opportunity to gain a global perspective. In addition to internships with international agencies in the Washington area, students may develop opportunities for internships in other countries. For example, a student recently interned at an advertising agency in Ecuador and another in South Africa with USAID in small business and economic development.

The Faculty

The program faculty members form a diverse group of highly respected experts, many of whom have achieved national and international prominence for their research, writing, and professional accomplishments. These experienced executives, managers, and consultants bring an incisive knowledge of current issues to the classroom. In addition to working closely with students, faculty members work together to address themes that cut across all aspects of business, such as management communication, business ethics, cross-cultural management, and career development. This collaborative effort makes it easier for students to integrate their knowledge.

The Business School Network

Students of the School of Business develop an extraordinary loyalty to their alma mater, as evidenced by more than 30,000 alumni in the fifty states and seventy countries. This extensive network is the key to helping graduating students establish contacts in the area in which they plan to settle. Through the mentor program, alumni offer guidance in their various areas of expertise, serve on panels to help students make intelligent career decisions, and evaluate students' performance in workshops and case studies.

The Dean's Associates Council includes leaders from both the private and public sectors. These partnerships provide direction for the School of Business and opportunities for students to meet and learn from today's business leaders.

The College and Environs

Unquestionably one of the most exciting cities in the world, Washington, D.C., is a global center of power and influence. Courses and faculty members provide opportunities for access to, and the development

of, insider perspectives. Living in Washington means enjoying the beauty of four glorious seasons and being in the midst of a region filled with historic sites and natural beauty. Attracting interesting people from all over the world, Washington boasts the highest percentage of college graduates of any metropolitan area in the country. In addition to a wide array of Fortune 500 companies and technology-based industries, the area provides a wealth of cultural and recreational attractions that few cities can match.

Located five blocks from the White House in the historic Foggy Bottom area of northwest Washington, The George Washington University is an integral part of the city. Modern and efficient public transportation makes it easy to participate in the exciting life of the capital city.

Placement

Career services are available to GW M.B.A. students from a variety of resources. The School's Graduate Career Center offers comprehensive career planning and placement services. The M.B.A. Association and the Alumni Association regularly sponsor networking activities and career panels. Cooperative education opportunities and internships become an excellent network for future career opportunities. M.B.A. students find faculty members ready and willing to provide career advice and networking opportunities. These resources allow each student to develop an aggressive strategy for finding the best opportunities after graduation.

Admission

The School of Business seeks candidates who have demonstrated potential for management and who have the intellectual ability, maturity, initiative, and creativity to fully participate in the challenging interdisciplinary environment. Applicants must have a bachelor's degree from a regionally accredited college or university. Selection is based upon the applicant's academic record, work experience, statement of purpose, recommendations, and scores on the required Graduate Management Admission Test (GMAT).

Applications from international students are welcome. Proficiency in reading, writing, and speaking English must be demonstrated by all students from countries where English is not an official language. International students, in addition to the above listed requirements, must submit certified English

translations of all academic records of course work corresponding to a bachelor's degree in the United States; scores for the Test of English as a Foreign Language (TOEFL), with a total score of 250 or higher (computer-based); and a financial certificate, which is required of any applicant who plans to enter or remain in the United States to study and whose immigration status will be either F-1 (student) or J-1 (exchange visitor).

Finances

Tuition for academic year 2008–09 is $1150 per credit hour, including University fees. The application fee is $60. Full-time students normally take 15–18 credits per semester during the first year and 12–15 during the second year. Part-time students generally register for 4 to 8 credit hours per semester. Books, supplies, and health insurance cost approximately $1700 per year. Estimated costs for room, board, and miscellaneous personal expenses total about $10,000 per academic year. The majority of graduate students live off campus.

A number of graduate assistantships and fellowships are available based on academic merit. To be considered, applicants must complete the admissions application process no later than January 15. Additional aid sources are available on the Web site.

Application Facts and Dates

The full-time Global M.B.A. program accepts applications only for fall of each year. The first deadline for priority scholarship consideration is December 3, and the final deadline is May 1. Students who wish to be considered for scholarships must complete the application process no later than January 15. The part-time M.B.A. program admits student in both the fall and spring semesters. The deadlines are May 15 for fall and November 15 for spring. For more information, students should contact the Office of Graduate Programs and indicate the M.B.A. option of interest.

Albert Razick
Director of Admissions
M.B.A. Programs
School of Business
The George Washington University
2201 G Street NW, Suite 550
Washington, D.C. 20052
Phone: 202-994-1212
Fax: 202-994-3571
E-mail: gosbgrad@gwu.edu
Web site: http://www.gwu.edu/business

Georgia Institute of Technology

College of Management

Atlanta, Georgia

ACHIEVE. LEAD. SUCCEED.
THE BUSINESS SCHOOL AT GEORGIA TECH

The intersection of business and technology has always been at the heart of the Georgia Tech College of Management. Our nationally ranked business school teaches students how to take advantage of the many business opportunities made possible by emerging technologies as well as how to succeed in an increasingly global economy.

Thanks to the College's location in Technology Square—the center of Atlanta's high-tech business community—opportunities abound for our students and faculty members to explore synergies between management and technology. This state-of-the-art setting ensures that students have access to all the latest learning tools and enables them to attend classes just around the corner from companies where they find fulfilling and challenging internships, co-op jobs, and careers.

Much more important than this high-tech environment are, of course, the College of Management's people—its greatest resource. Our professors enjoy a world-class reputation for their research and teaching, and our top-notch students go on to be entrepreneurs and corporate leaders who are successful at bridging the worlds of business and technology.

With the right people and programs in the right place, we're creating a new standard in business education

—Steven Salbu, Dean

Programs and Curricular Focus

Georgia Tech's M.B.A. program, now offered in both full-time and evening formats, helps students develop the skills they will need to succeed in the rapidly changing world of high-tech business. The program exposes students to the social, environmental, political, and international factors that shape the global marketplace. Thanks to the entrepreneurial spirit pervading the entire Georgia Tech campus, its M.B.A. students gain valuable insight into entrepreneurship and the process of technology innovation and commercialization. Georgia Tech students have numerous opportunities to explore a wide variety of career paths.

The traditional Georgia Tech M.B.A. is a two-year, full-time program admitting about 75 students into each class. Both the school's full-time and Evening M.B.A. formats offer small class sizes to foster a close-knit community and enrich student/faculty relationships. The Evening M.B.A. program enables interested students to earn a Georgia Tech M.B.A. while advancing their careers. Most Evening M.B.A. students take two courses each semester, completing the program in approximately three years.

The curriculum for the Evening M.B.A. program mirrors that of the full-time program. In either case, the return on investment of a Georgia Tech M.B.A. is outstanding, making it one of the best education values among M.B.A. programs nationally.

Both full-time and evening students come from many different backgrounds, bringing a variety of perspectives to the program. Georgia Tech welcomes applicants with accredited undergraduate degrees from all academic backgrounds.

The business school at Georgia Tech also offers two executive degrees in a weekend format: the Executive M.B.A. in Management of Technology and the Global Executive M.B.A. Both programs are designed for professionals with five to fifteen years of experience who want to advance their careers without interrupting them.

The EMBA in Management of Technology program is an innovative nineteen-month program for individuals pursuing management careers in technology-intensive environments. In addition to traditional business fundamentals, this program emphasizes entrepreneurial leadership and technological innovation.

The seventeen-month Global Executive M.B.A. is designed to fine-tune the skills and knowledge of business leaders who want to shift their careers toward international business and/or understand global issues.

The College also offers a variety of certificate and custom programs for executives, professionals, and corporations.

Special Features

One week before the start of class every August, first-year M.B.A. students in the full-time program gather for orientation. New students get acquainted with one another, and learn more about the program and Georgia Tech. The week features group interaction and exercises to encourage team building and creative thinking. Leadership Development, a daylong event held in the North Georgia Mountains, provides an opportunity to work in teams with classmates before the rigors of academic life begin.

Students in the Evening M.B.A. program may begin their studies in either the fall or spring semesters following orientation.

Executive M.B.A. in Management of Technology students begin the nineteen-month program every May with a week of classes at Georgia Tech. Then they meet every other weekend for all-day Friday and Saturday classes until December, when there is another week of classes at Georgia Tech. Students conclude the program a year later with a two-week trip to China focused on cross-cultural business and leadership issues.

Global Executive M.B.A. students begin the seventeen-month program in August with a week of classes at Georgia Tech. Then they meet every weekend for Friday evening and Saturday classes. They go on two international trips during the course of the program (the countries visited varying from class to class).

Students in all of Georgia Tech College of Management's M.B.A. programs have numerous opportunities to extend their educational experience through participation in speaker series, conferences, lectures, and presentations by highly successful entrepreneurs and visionary leaders from business, government, and education. Many of these events focus on technology entrepreneurship, innovation, commercialization, and leadership.

The College's many exceptional opportunities for students include the Technological Innovation: Generating Economic Results (TI: GER program). This nationally recognized program teams M.B.A., law, science, and engineering students who work on commercializing the research of Ph.D. students.

The College's new high-tech, $1-million Trading Floor is a rarity at all but the best business schools. Preparing students for careers in investment banking and financial services, the 2,000-square-foot Trading Floor includes the financial analysis and electronic trading tools used by professional brokerage firms.

The College's Net Impact chapter plays an important role in the business school's growing emphasis on sustainable, environmentally friendly business practices and corporate social responsibility. Net Impact is an international network of graduate students using the power of business to effect positive economic, environmental, and social change.

The Faculty

The faculty members for the graduate programs are a diverse, internationally recognized team with strengths in both teaching and research. They are dedicated to creating an optimal learning environment. Many faculty members are active consultants to national and international corporations or have developed their own entrepreneurial ventures.

The Business School Network

Georgia Tech business students share in the international reputation of Georgia Institute of Technology, earned through high academic standards and the Institute's commitment to excellence. Students regularly receive invitations to Institute and College alumni events, which are excellent opportunities for network building.

The Georgia Tech Business Network is an active and growing alumni association, which graduates can use to continue their professional education, extend their network, and develop their careers.

The Jones MBA Career Center is an active liaison to the business community. Frequent contact with hundreds of companies keeps an open line between employers and M.B.A. students.

The College and Environs

Georgia Tech was established in 1888 with 129 students. Today, the Institute is a leading center for research and technological development. Georgia Tech's international reputation in engineering, computer, and science programs contributes to its vibrant and exciting position as a leader in technology entrepreneurship and commercialization. Approximately 13,000 students are enrolled, more than 3,000 of whom are seeking graduate degrees.

Established in 1913, the business school at Georgia Tech has earned a place among the most highly respected business programs in the world.

Facilities

In 2003, Georgia Tech College of Management moved into a state-of-the-art new building in Technology Square, the heart of Midtown Atlanta's high-tech business community. Technology Square is about making connections—linking entrepreneurs and innovators, corporate leaders and promising minds, and today's ideas with tomorrow's reality.

As the cornerstone of Technology Square, the College enjoys the unique ability to access the resources of its neighbors, including the 252 guest rooms at the Georgia Tech Hotel and Conference Center; the tiered classrooms, amphitheaters, and distance learning tools of the Global Learning Center; and the Barnes &

Noble at Georgia Tech bookstore as well as other retail stores and restaurants. Technology Square is also home to Georgia Tech's Economic Development Institute; the Center for Quality Growth and Regional Development; and one of the nation's top technology incubators, the Advanced Technology Development Center, which is devoted to helping entrepreneurs launch and build successful companies.

Georgia Tech's Executive M.B.A. programs are held in the state-of-the-art Huang Executive Education Center. Designed to meet the special requirements of executive education, the Huang center offers high-quality meeting space with the latest technological tools in a comfortable business environment.

Technology Environment

The College harnesses and blends advanced technology throughout the curriculum. Common classroom activities include interactive polls, electronic discussions, and access to network resources and videoconferencing.

Students have access to a high-speed digital and wireless network and take advantage of the latest multimedia and distance learning equipment accessible in each classroom. Faculty members have the latest technology available to them to aid in instruction. All graduate students are required to have an up-to-date laptop computer.

Admission

All materials submitted for admission to the College of Management graduate programs are carefully reviewed. Factors considered in determining eligibility for the M.B.A. program include undergraduate performance, GMAT and TOEFL scores, letters of recommendation, responses to essay questions, an evaluative interview, and full-time work experience.

Admission decisions for Executive M.B.A. programs are made on a rolling basis and are determined by the applicant's overall profile of academic and professional accomplishments. These include undergraduate and/or graduate academic performance, career performance trajectory, letters of recommendation, company support, and performance on the GMAT. In addition, an assessment is made as to whether the program would likely enhance the applicant's career and the applicant's readiness to undertake the program. Additional personal interviews may also be requested during the application process.

Finances

For the full-time M.B.A. program, current annual in-state tuition and fees are $8908, and out-of-state tuition and fees are $32,076. The College awards graduate research assistantships based on academic merit, GMAT scores, and the needs of the College. Other sources of funding include graduate assistantships in other areas of the Institute and other forms of financial assistance.

Current tuition for the Evening M.B.A. is $676 per credit hour for Georgia residents ($1248 for nonresidents). Estimated tuition and fees for the entire program is approximately $41,800 ($72,700 for nonresidents).

The Executive M.B.A. in Management of Technology program costs $67,900 for students starting in May 2009. Tuition and fees for the Global Executive M.B.A. program are $69,500 for the class starting in August 2009.

While many students in these master's programs receive financial support from their employers, it is not a requirement for enrollment. Applicants may be eligible for financial aid through the Georgia Tech Financial Aid Office. For more information regarding financial aid assistance or to request an application package, students should contact the Georgia Tech Office of Scholarships and Financial Aid at 404-894-4160.

Tuition costs in these programs are subject to change from year to year.

Application Facts and Dates

The application deadlines for the full-time M.B.A. program are January 15, to be considered for graduate assistantships and for international applicants; March 15, the final deadline for priority consideration for U.S. and permanent residents; and May 1, the space-available deadline.

To start the Evening M.B.A. in fall 2009, May 1 is the priority deadline, and June 15 is the final deadline. To start in spring 2010, October 1 is the deadline.

Applications for the two Executive M.B.A. programs are reviewed and accepted throughout the year, and applicants are encouraged to submit their completed applications early. The Executive M.B.A. in Management of Technology program begins in mid-May, and applications should be received by March 1 (early acceptance) or April 15 (final deadline). The Global Executive M.B.A. program begins in early August, and applications should be received by April 1 (early acceptance) or June 1 (final deadline). Applications received after these deadlines are accepted on a space-available basis.

International candidates should submit applications as soon as possible to ensure adequate time to process student visas and transcript requests.

For more information, students should contact:

M.B.A. Program
Graduate Office
College of Management
Georgia Institute of Technology
800 West Peachtree Street, NW
Atlanta, Georgia 30308-0520

Phone: 404-894-8722 (M.B.A. program)
     800-869-1014 (toll-free)
     800-815-7662 (toll-free, for
       Executive Degree Programs)
Web site: http://mgt.gatech.edu/

Georgia State University

Atlanta, Georgia

CONNECTING YOU WITH THE KNOWLEDGE AND TOOLS TO SUCCEED

Being centered in Atlanta, one of the nation's most dynamic business centers, is just one advantage of attending the J. Mack Robinson College of Business. Others include a renowned faculty, an alumni network of more than 60,000, a very deep and diverse curriculum, and rankings that demonstrate the Robinson College is one of the nation's premier business schools.

Ranked for twelve straight years in the top 10 of the U.S. News and World Report "Part-Time M.B.A." rankings, Robinson College is also listed among the "Best in the World" in the Financial Times E.M.B.A. rankings, in BusinessWeek's "Part-Time M.B.A." rankings, and in a variety of other publications. Overall the College has eight programs ranked by sixteen leading publications.

The College also has a worldwide reach. In addition to having locations throughout the Atlanta area, the College partners with leading institutions around the world, including the Sorbonne in Paris and COPPEAD in Rio de Janiero.

From corporate CEOs to some of the world's most successful entrepreneurs, J. Mack Robinson College of Business has had a hand in molding those who shape the future. Whether your goal is to land a job here or abroad or to better your position within your current company, Robinson College can connect you with the knowledge and tools to succeed.

—H. Fenwick Huss, Dean

Programs and Curricular Focus

Business schools are not known for flexibility and allowing students personal choice. However, Georgia State is not like most business schools. The J. Mack Robinson College of Business is not so specialized that students can't find classes to match their interests. At the same time, the College is a recognized leader in such fields as accounting, computer information systems, real estate management, and risk management among others.

The College offers the M.B.A. degree in four formats, as well as eighteen specialized master's programs. Students can earn an M.B.A. with a major or concentration in one of eighteen areas. Classes are offered during the daytime and evenings and on Saturdays. Georgia State's part-time M.B.A. program was ranked among the top ten in *U.S. News & World Report*'s 2007 listing of the nation's best graduate schools—the eleventh consecutive year the program has been in the top ten.

The Flexible M.B.A. offers the greatest choice of day, evening, and Saturday courses for both full- and part-time students. Students plan course schedules to fit their needs and can start in any semester. The Executive M.B.A. (E.M.B.A.) is a lockstep, two-year program designed for managers with significant career experience, with classes on Fridays and Saturdays.

The College's newest program is the Professional M.B.A. (PMBA). Designed for high-potential performers with three or more years of business experience, the PMBA is offered predominantly on Saturdays. Students spend their first year in a lock-step core curriculum and their second year taking electives from as many as nineteen diverse areas. They also have an opportunity to extend their program to acquire a concentration or major or to participate in an international or domestic residency.

The Flexible M.B.A. student can earn a concentration (four courses) and/or a major (seven courses) in the following areas: accounting, actuarial science, decision sciences, economics, electronic commerce, entrepreneurship, finance, general business, health administration, hospitality administration, human resource management, information systems, international business, management, marketing, personal financial planning, real estate, and risk management and insurance. The College also has five career paths in the M.B.A. program. Career paths are composed of two complementary concentrations that prepare students for specialized careers. For more information about the career paths, students should visit http://robinson.gsu.edu/academic/oaa/career_paths.html.

While the M.B.A. is a general management degree, the College's specialized master's degrees allow students to focus on one functional business area. The Master of Science is offered with majors in business economics, computer information systems, decision sciences, finance, human resource management, management, marketing, personal financial planning, and risk management and insurance.

Other specialized degrees include the Master of International Business, which requires that students become proficient in another language and intern overseas; Master of Actuarial Science; Master of Professional Accountancy; Master of Science in Health Administration; Master of Science in Real Estate; and Master of Taxation as well as joint programs such as the M.B.A./Master of Health Administration and M.B.A./J.D.

Students and the M.B.A. Experience

Business students at Georgia State learn not only from the faculty members but also from each other. That's because the average master's student is 29 years old and has five years of full-time work experience. Students discover that this work experience, and that of their colleagues, is a vital component of the Georgia State program. There are about 1,212 M.B.A. students and 484 specialized master's students. Of all master's students, 44 percent are women, 21 percent are members of minority groups, and 23 percent are international. The program is large and offers numerous classes in specialized fields not found at other schools. This allows students the opportunity to explore their areas of interest and meet their career goals

Global Focus

Today's competitive global marketplace has created a need for business leaders with a demonstrated understanding of the challenges involved in conducting business on a global level. To meet this growing need, Robinson College has teamed up with leading business schools in Paris (the Sorbonne) and Rio de Janeiro (the COPPEAD Graduate School of Business, Federal University of Rio de Janeiro) to offer a new Global Partners M.B.A. The program enables students to learn and experience firsthand the intricacies of doing business globally.

This unique program features a fourteen-month curriculum with a combination of courses from Robinson's nationally ranked

Robinson students attend classes in the four-story Aderhold Learning Center. This state-of-the-art building includes classrooms with computer ports, two 200-seat lecture halls, a computer lab, and a cyber café.

M.B.A. program and meetings and presentations from business leaders, members of academia, and government officials within each of the four continents. During the first six months, students divide their time between Atlanta, Paris, and Rio and have two additional weeks in China. The final four months are dedicated to an International Field Service/Internship. The program attracts students from all over the world. Graduates receive their M.B.A. from Robinson College.

The Faculty

The College's 179 full-time faculty members are teachers, researchers, authors, and leaders. Georgia State business faculty members take pride in bringing relevant, real-world problems, issues, and experiences into the classroom. With degrees from schools such as Harvard, MIT, Wharton, and Northwestern, Robinson faculty members also attract students to one of the largest doctoral programs in the nation.

The Business School Network

As graduates of the largest business program in the Atlanta area, Robinson's approximately 60,000 business alumni serve as a great network. The College's own Board of Advisors includes more than 40 top CEOs, presidents, partners, and entrepreneurs from the Atlanta area and around the U.S.

Prominent Alumni

Some of the nation's top executives are among the College's alumni. They include Ken Lewis, Chairman, CEO, and President of Bank of America Corporation; David

Stonecipher, retired Chairman and CEO of Jefferson-Pilot Corporation; James Copeland, retired CEO of Deloitte & Touche, LLP; and Mackey MacDonald, Chairman of VF Corporation.

The College and Environs

Located in the heart of downtown Atlanta's business and financial district, Georgia State University is home to more than 27,000 students, making it one of the two largest of the state's universities. The 28-acre main campus includes the Pullen Library, which houses more than 1.4 million volumes. In addition to the main campus, graduate evening and weekend classes are also offered at the University's Alpharetta Center in North Fulton County, the Georgia State Brookhaven Center in Atlanta's Brookhaven-Buckhead area, and the Georgia State Henry County Center in McDonough, Georgia. The College has also just opened a new Executive Education Center in Buckhead, which will be home to Robinson's top-ranked Executive M.B.A.

Facilities

Just across the street from the city's rapid rail hub, Robinson College is located in the historic Citizens and Southern National Bank Building, which was donated to the College by NationsBank (now Bank of America). The building houses all College faculty and administrative offices, including the Office of Graduate Student and Alumni Services.

Placement

The Graduate Career Management Office offers comprehensive career services, in-

cluding an employer library and lists of job and internship opportunities as well as computer terminals for online and database job searches. The office offers workshops to help students in their job search and also hosts the annual Business Career Expo, which attracts more than 100 employers and almost 1,000 students. Career counselors are also available to provide individual assessments of students' career goals and opportunities. For more information, students should visit http://robinson.gsu.edu/career.

Admission

Admission into the College's graduate programs is competitive, with each applicant being evaluated individually in relation to the current group of candidates. The Master's Admissions Committee considers previous academic performance and educational background, work experience, and GMAT scores. The College's average GMAT score for the past year was 610. The average undergraduate GPA was 3.39. Previous academic work in business is not required.

Finances

Graduate tuition for the fall 2007 through summer 2008 semesters was $281 per credit hour for residents and $1019 for nonresidents. For 12 or more hours, in-state tuition was $3372, and $12,228 for out-of-state students. Students also paid $494 per semester for student activity, recreation, transportation, health, and athletics fees. Tuition rates are subject to change.

The University awards a limited number of merit and need-based scholarships to eligible students and sponsors various institutional and government loan programs. Full-time students are eligible for research assistantships and a limited number of nonresident fee waivers, which are awarded based on academic performance in graduate course work. For information on scholarship and loan opportunities, students should contact the Office of Student Financial Aid at 404-413-2400. For information on graduate assistantships, students should contact the Office of Graduate Student and Alumni Services.

Application Facts and Dates

Individuals who have earned undergraduate degrees from a regionally accredited institution may apply for graduate admission for any semester (except for the E.M.B.A. and Global Partners M.B.A.). For an application and admission information, students should contact:

Office of Graduate Student and Alumni Services
J. Mack Robinson College of Business
P.O. Box 3988
Georgia State University
Atlanta, Georgia 30302-3988

Phone: 404-413-7130
Fax: 404-413-7162
Web site: http://robinson.gsu.edu

The Hague University

Master Studies

The Hague, Netherlands

THE HAGUE WAY TO THE M.B.A.

No one should believe that doing this master's degree is easy. It isn't. Much time and energy will be invested in class hours, assignments, meetings, presentations, discussions, reports, and exams. Thousands of people worldwide opt to invest in the best possible education to improve their quality of life. I hope you accept the challenge.

—Drs. Frans Dijkstra, Master Programmes, The Hague University

Programs and Curricular Focus

The Hague University (THU) M.B.A. curriculum is composed of five main stages: Phase 0, MBA Foundation Course; Phase 1, The Manager as a Team Member; Phase 2, The Manager as a Group Leader; Phase 3, Manager of Strategic Change; and Phase 4, The Business Report (the final dissertation).

At THU, students can study the M.B.A. course on a full- or part-time basis. Whichever way they choose, they gain the skills needed to work in a demanding—and fulfilling—international management role.

What makes the THU M.B.A. experience stand out is the importance the University places on the values of knowledge, talent, and diversity. The Hague University believes that knowledge is something to be shared, not just with its own students, but with the outside world. The University is always looking for new opportunities to exchange knowledge with people from other places, and it teaches its own students to do the same.

Having knowledge is not enough. Students have to know how to use it, how to adapt it, and how to apply it to real situations. Practical experience and independent thinking are a big part of The Hague University experience.

To discover new ways of thinking, students have to explore other people's perspectives. The University believes that diversity is essential to progress and welcomes different viewpoints through cross-cultural debate and collaboration.

Students and the M.B.A. Experience

The Hague University's M.B.A. program caters to budding business managers at every stage. The average student is 34 years old and is recruited from about twenty-six different countries. The program is structured as a series of courses that link together to build up students' core management skills. Each course section equips them with the business acumen needed to fulfill their career ambitions.

Students progress through each phase of the M.B.A. by completing various modules. Each of these modules addresses different aspects of life as a working manager with a personal and hands-on experience. The University expects students to leave the course as strategists, free thinkers, and true team players.

Global Focus

For students who aspire to work in a global business, the M.B.A. for international students—an intensive twelve-month program—helps them acclimatize to living and working abroad in a multicultural setting. Students gain a true-to-life experience.

The Faculty

M.B.A. students at The Hague University gain new professional and academic training from the highly skilled staff members, who all have experience in the field as consultants and researchers. The M.B.A. staff team is made up of 20 faculty members. Of these experts, 6 are permanent THU faculty members, and 14 are staff lecturers. There is representation from seven different nationalities on the team.

The Business School Network

The Hague University has close links within industry. As members of a business school network, the University is able to match students to management positions in international companies and organizations. Students are exposed to as many international and cross-cultural experiences as possible, having access to more than 150 partner institutions all over the globe.

The College and Environs

The Hague is a global hub. It is a city of global stature despite its relatively small size. As the home of the International Criminal Court, Peace Palace, War Crimes Tribunal, and Europol, it is rightly known as an International City of Peace, Justice, and Security. It is also the political capital of The Netherlands and home to its royal family.

The Hague is a city for day-to-day life, too, with the benefits of a big city but with a small-town feel. Visitors can wander the streets soaking up all the wonderful historic architecture while following in the footsteps of Mondrian and Vermeer. Or they can sit on the sandy beaches soaking up the sun or gazing out over the water.

The Hague University is located next to the international railway station and close to the city center. The campus complex covers more than 84,000 square meters (21 acres) and is entirely surrounded by water, a kind of city within a city. There are always events going on, from celebrations and social gatherings to conferences and symposia, from local to international.

Life on campus revolves around the magnificent oval atrium hall, with its soaring glass ceiling. Nearly 17,000 students and 1,600 staff members pass through the hall every day.

THU was formed in 1985 from a merger of fourteen smaller institutions in The Hague. Its master's programs started in 1991, with the part-time M.B.A. being the first. THU has more than 17,000 students reading economics, management, marketing, accounting, engineering, health care, behavioral and social sciences, information sciences and technology, education, sport, and languages.

Facilities

THU has a state-of-the-art library, computer facilities, media labs, and science labs to help students study. There are several restaurants, extensive sports facilities, and student lounges to help them unwind and meet friends. There are also an international office and student housing office for anyone who needs help getting settled.

Placement

Because The Hague's professional partnerships stretch round the globe, students spend time working for international organizations on real-life projects as part of their school experience. There is also an extensive recruitment program right on the campus.

After graduation, students become members of the distinguished alumni association, The Hague Masters, with its significant network of contacts and opportunities.

Graduates are employed across every sector in private, public, profit, and not-for-profit enterprises. THU follows its students' careers closely as they progress. Current M.B.A. alumni are working in companies across The Netherlands and around the world in Belgium, Canada, China, Colombia, Cyprus, France, Germany, Iceland, India, Indonesia, Ireland, Israel, Italy, Malaysia, Mexico, Nigeria, Russia, South Africa, Spain, Taiwan, Thailand, United Kingdom, the U.S.A., and Vietnam.

Admission

From around 250 applicants for the M.B.A. program, the University accepts 60 successful candidates. To apply, candidates must be 22 years old or over. Applicants should have a degree from a Netherlands university/polytechnic or any accredited university and at least one semester of work experience during or after graduation or an equivalent recognized professional qualification with the appropriate work experience.

For entry into Phase 1, applicants must have experience as a manager, with at least four years' experience in a professional or administrative position and a track record of company training.

For Phase 2 entry, an applicant must have either a business degree or a major with a significant business component from a recognized university/institution or a postgraduate degree in a management or business major and a minimum of two years' management experience.

The program is taught in English, so students should be able to speak the language well. Students whose native language is not English should have a minimum score of 550 on the Test of English as a Foreign Language (TOEFL) or a minimum score of 213 on the International English Language Testing System (IELTS). The Graduate Management Admission Test (GMAT) is also recommended for students without much work experience or if their undergraduate degree was not in English or a business subject. A GMAT score can be submitted instead of a TOEFL score when applying.

A student study visa is required for those who are from the United States, a non–European Union country, Canada, or Switzerland.

Finances

The tuition fee, which includes textbooks, is €16,500. Classes on the MBA Foundation Course (Phase 0) can be taken individually at a fee of €50 per hour session.

Application Facts and Dates

For more information about the M.B.A. course, students should contact:

Frank H. Fox
Master Studies, Room ST3.01
The Hague University
Johanna Westerdijkplein 75
2521 EN The Hague
Netherlands
Phone: 31-70-445-8900
Fax: 31-70-445-7591
E-mail: info-masters@hhs.nl
Web site:
    http://www.thehagueuniversity.nl

Hawai'i Pacific University

Honolulu, Hawaii

MEETING TODAY'S GLOBAL CHALLENGE

Hawai'i Pacific University's (HPU) M.B.A. enhances the career development of today's business professional. The HPU student body is culturally diverse, representing Hawaii, the U.S. mainland, and more than 100 countries. HPU offers the skills, knowledge, and training required in today's highly competitive global business environment.

Academic programs combine practice, theory, and the skills needed in modern career fields. Students learn to implement the latest developments in computer technology, business simulations, communications theory, and strategic planning. Our graduates are well prepared for success in today's rapidly changing marketplace.

—Dr. John Kearns, Interim Dean, College of Business Administration

Programs and Curricular Focus

The Hawai'i Pacific University M.B.A. program requires 45 semester hours of graduate work (fifteen courses). Core requirements (27 semester hours) include accounting, economics, finance, human resource management, information systems, international business management, law, marketing, and quantitative methods. Elective courses (12 semester hours) may be taken in twelve different areas. The last area is the capstone series (6 semester hours), which includes Management Policy and Strategy Formulation and completion of the Professional Paper.

There are six joint-degree program (66 semester hours) options: the M.B.A./Master of Arts in human resource management, the M.B.A./Master of Arts in organizational change, the M.B.A./Master of Arts in global leadership and sustainable development, the M.B.A./Master of Arts in communication, the M.B.A./Master of Science in Information Systems (M.S.I.S.), and the M.B.A./Master of Science in Nursing (M.S.N.).

Full-time students have a flexible schedule that allows them to complete the program in twelve to twenty-four months. Part-time students can attend evening, day, or weekend classes and have a choice of seven start dates throughout the year. Students can design a flexible sequencing of certain core courses as well as a choice of electives. All students must complete the Professional Paper within seven years of initial enrollment in graduate courses and within one year from first enrollment in the Professional Paper course.

Hawai'i Pacific University is an independent, not-for-profit, coeducational, nonsectarian, career-oriented postsecondary institution founded in 1965. It is accredited by the Accrediting Commission for Senior Colleges and Universities of the Western Association of Schools and Colleges. The University is a member of AACSB International–the Association to Advance Collegiate Schools of Business and also a member of the Executive M.B.A. Council. HPU is recognized by the Hawaii Commission of Postsecondary Education, approved for veteran's benefits, and authorized to issue I-20 documents to international students.

Students and the M.B.A. Experience

The average age of graduate students at Hawai'i Pacific University is 26 years of age. Students represent more than eighty countries. Teamwork is an essential ingredient of the M.B.A. program. In various courses throughout the program, students are formed into teams to solve problems collectively and to achieve a better understanding of group dynamics and challenges while producing specific desired results. Hands-on experience is gained through internships with leading Honolulu corporations. For example, students work in accounting, human resource management, and marketing internships, to name a few.

The Faculty

The M.B.A. program at Hawai'i Pacific University permits students to study with some of the most distinguished professors in the Pacific region. Faculty members have contemporary experience with leading corporations, outstanding academic credentials, and a dedication to teaching. The graduate faculty includes 40 full-time and 18 part-time professors. Ninety percent of the faculty members hold a doctorate or its equivalent. Average class size is 20. Four full-time academic advisers are available to assist students.

The Business School Network

The Honolulu business community plays an integral role in the Hawai'i Pacific University M.B.A. program. Honolulu's leading corporations sponsor students for internships, many of which eventually result in offers of full-time employment. Senior executives of local investment firms, health-care systems, banks, schools, law firms, and trust companies serve on the University Board of Trustees, providing vision and direction for the future. Other HPU M.B.A. graduates serve on the Alumni Board, helping to maintain a base of future employment contacts for new graduates as well as supporting the University. HPU also integrates the business community into the curriculum through the use of guest speakers with individual areas of expertise in appropriate academic disciplines, exposing students to current issues and emerging trends.

The College and Environs

With three campuses on the island of Oahu, Hawai'i Pacific University combines the excitement of an urban downtown campus with a pristine marine institute and the serenity of a residential campus set in the green foothills of the Koolau Mountains. The main campus is ideally located in downtown Honolulu, the business and financial center of the Pacific. Eight miles away, situated on 135 acres in Kaneohe, the windward Hawai'i Loa campus is the site of environmental sciences, marine biology, nursing, oceanography, and several liberal arts programs. Students can travel between the two campuses on a convenient HPU shuttle service. The third campus, Oceanic Institute, is an applied aquaculture research facility located on a 56-acre site at Makapuu Point on the windward coast of Oahu, Hawaii, with facilities on the Big Island of Hawaii as well. There are also eight military campus programs located at Pearl Harbor, Barbers Point, Hickam Air Force Base, Schofield Barracks, Fort Shafter, Tripler Army Medical Center, Kaneohe Marine Corps Air Station, and Camp Smith.

Facilities

Meader Library and Atherton Library are available to HPU students. Total holdings include 153,000 volumes, 205,000 microforms, and 1,700 current periodical subscriptions. Other in-house, business-related, and commercially vendored databases support specialized information needs. CD-ROM players are available for graduate student use. Access is provided to online bibliographic retrieval services.

Technology Environment

Located at the downtown campus, the Frear Center contains classrooms and labs equipped with state-of-the-art equipment. Throughout the Frear Center, technology is utilized to assist in the training of students and to enhance their education experience. All students have free access to the Internet. Computer labs are open from 8 a.m. to 9 p.m. daily and from 8 a.m. to 5 p.m. on weekends.

Placement

Hawai'i Pacific University's Career Services Center provides, free of charge, one sponsored job fair per year, job-search preparation, seminars, on-campus recruiters, employer visits, workshops, job placement, national computerized resume referral services, a career resource library, internships, and campus employment opportunities. International student advisers are available to provide current information regarding visas, passports, F-1 regulations, work permits, and other concerns critical to international students.

Admission

Admission requirements include a completed application, official transcripts from each postsecondary school attended (sent directly to HPU), a document showing conferral of the bachelor's degree, two letters of reference, and GMAT results. International students should submit certified copies of A-level (or similar postsecondary) examinations directly to HPU. The Test of English as a Foreign Language (TOEFL) is recommended unless students have completed a bachelor's degree from an accredited American college or university with a grade point average of 2.7 or above.

Hawai'i Pacific University seeks students with academic promise, outstanding career potential, and high motivation.

Finances

For the 2007–08 academic year, graduate tuition was $13,440, housing expenses were approximately $10,280, and other expenses (books and insurance) were approximately $2560; the total cost was $26,280. Part-time cost was $560 per credit hour.

Rooms are available to students at an average cost of $9840 per year, including board. The typical monthly cost of living in one-bedroom off-campus housing not owned by the University is $900 to $1200. For further graduate housing information, students should contact Student Housing at 808-544-1430.

Financial aid is available to both full-time and part-time students. The University participates in all federal financial aid programs designated for graduate students. These programs provide aid in the form of subsidized (need-based) and unsubsidized (non-need-based) Federal Stafford Student Loans. Through these loans, funds may be available to cover a student's entire cost of education. To apply for aid, students must submit the Free Application for Federal Student Aid (FAFSA) after January 1. Mailing of student award letters usually begins by the end of March. For further financial aid information, students should call 808-544-0253.

International Students

The International Student Office provides a variety of services to international students, including advising on personal, interpersonal, cultural, and academic matters; assisting on immigration matters, especially F-1 requirements, I-20 extensions, and work authorization; advising on money management and housing needs; conducting orientation programs to facilitate academic and social adjustment; and providing medical insurance information. An International Day is held each year to highlight the contributions of HPU's diverse student population. There are more than fifteen different country-specific organizations on campus.

Application Facts and Dates

Admission decisions for the M.B.A. program are made on a rolling basis, and applicants are notified between one and two weeks after all documents have been submitted. Completed applications should be sent to:

Graduate Admissions
1164 Bishop Street, Suite 911
Honolulu, Hawaii 96813
Phone: 808-544-1135
        866-GRAD-HPU (toll-free)
Fax: 808-544-0280
E-mail: graduate@hpu.edu
Web site: http://www.hpu.edu/grad

HEC Paris

HEC. THE M.B.A. THAT BUILDS CHARACTER

Since its founding in 1881, HEC Paris has educated thousands of leaders who play an active role in international business. The HEC M.B.A. Program offers a transformative learning experience at the cutting edge of international management education. Our world-renowned faculty of over 100 full-time professors offers participants a solid foundation in fundamental business subjects during the Core Phase and advanced expertise in a range of specialized tracks during the Personalized Phase. At HEC, our approach to management training is ACE: Analytical, Critical, and Experiential. We take a hands-on approach to learning that allows our participants to test their leadership potential and define their personal visions of leadership.

Diversity is a hallmark of our program: our participants represent over 50 nationalities and pool more than 1,000 years of professional experience in a wide range of industries and functions. Our multicultural learning environment renders HEC M.B.A. graduates uniquely qualified to take on leadership positions in global organizations. In fact, 92 percent of our graduates are in positions of international scope, with 63 percent working outside their home country.

HEC M.B.A. participants have direct access to the 40,000-strong network of HEC alumni, many of whom hold executive positions in businesses and organizations worldwide. The HEC M.B.A. offers a unique opportunity to transform your profile, learn to make ethical business decisions, and build enduring relationships in the heart of the European business community.

—Valérie Gauthier, Ph.D., HEC M.B.A. Associate Dean

Programs and Curricular Focus

During the first eight months of the HEC M.B.A. Program (the Core Phase), participants develop a solid foundation in management techniques and business fundamentals such as finance, strategy, statistics, marketing, management, and economics. Participants also attend a series of executive seminars, including a business simulation known as NEGOSIM, which tests their skills in real-life situations. In addition, they are required to attend a yearlong series of seminars called Visions of Leadership, which draws CEOs, entrepreneurs, and leadership analysts to the HEC campus to share their knowledge and experience in dedicated sessions with M.B.A. participants. Visions of Leadership represents a core element of the HEC M.B.A. curriculum that allows participants to explore the analytical, critical, and experiential aspects of being a leader.

During the second eight months of the program (the Personalized Phase), participants enhance their managerial competencies by selecting a specialized track and choosing from more than eighty electives, including Global Business and International Human Rights, Marketing and Strategies in Luxury, Indispensable Asia, and Psychology & Economics. Participants may also gain hands-on experience through a range of M.B.A. fieldwork options and enhance their global perspectives by participating in an international exchange or dual-degree program.

French is not a requirement for admission, and most HEC M.B.A. participants choose to take their classes in English; however, it is possible to do some course work in French. For those who would like to gain some basic French skills before arrival, HEC offers an intensive pre-M.B.A. language workshop in Paris. Additional language courses are also available during the academic year.

Students and the M.B.A. Experience

Each year, HEC M.B.A. participants host the European M.B.A. Tournament (MBAT), a three-day sporting event that has become the largest annual gathering of international business school students. Two thousand M.B.A. participants from twelve leading European business schools competed in the 2007 MBAT, which included twenty-four sporting events. Organized exclusively by HEC M.B.A. participants, the MBAT creates an environment of mutual recognition that enables participants to establish lasting personal relationships and valuable professional networks. The involvement of individuals from over seventy nationalities makes for a challenging and educational atmosphere characterized by teamwork, competition, and networking.

All participants are encouraged to take advantage of the HEC M.B.A. Program's wide range of professional clubs, which allow members to optimize their M.B.A. experience, explore new career paths, and enhance their personal and professional networks. Student-run professional clubs include the Finance Club, the Entrepreneurship Club, the Marketing and Luxury Club, and the Consulting Club. In 2005, a group of M.B.A. participants launched the HEC chapter of Net Impact, an international network of more than 13,000 students, teachers, and professionals that seeks to advance sustainable business development and practices worldwide. Net Impact HEC recently hosted on-campus a Sustainable Development Conference dedicated to the "Positive Power of Business."

With the support of student-run professional clubs like Women in Leadership, the HEC M.B.A. encourages women participants to reach their full potential and sensitizes the entire M.B.A. community to issues that are of particular relevance to women in business, such as maintaining a work/life balance and managing diversity. Women currently comprise approximately 30 percent of the HEC M.B.A. student body, and this number will no doubt continue to rise as the program maintains its commitment to diversity and equal opportunity.

The Faculty

The HEC full-time faculty consists of more than 100 professors from the world's most renowned universities. HEC's international teaching staff includes over 35 visiting professors from a worldwide network of partner institutions, as well as 20 affiliate professors and 450 adjunct lecturers, most of whom are business executives. HEC's full-time faculty members hold doctorates from the world's leading research universities, and in the last five years, 40 percent of new faculty members have been hired from abroad.

HEC boasts a number of distinguished professors whose publications and research are world renowned, such as Jean-Noël Kapferer, a professor of marketing whose work on strategic brand management has become a touchstone for the field. Many HEC M.B.A. professors serve on the editorial boards of international management journals, and faculty members maintain close ties with the business community through research, consulting, and designing executive development programs.

The Global Network

With a network of 40,000 alumni worldwide, HEC offers its graduates a direct link to some of the business world's most influential decision makers. The HEC alumni community also provides a framework for building ongoing relationships between companies and participants. For example, HEC alumni in the United States have created active regional chapters that organize relevant events and services for their members. Direct access to a global network of

HEC alumni puts HEC M.B.A. graduates in a strong position to achieve their career objectives.

The HEC Foundation brings together over forty prestigious multinational companies that help to guide the school's strategic orientation, support its ambitions, and foster links between the academic and business worlds. This corporate network promotes research programs in the management sciences and supports major international development projects. The HEC Foundation includes such leading companies as Apple, Capgemini, Hewlett-Packard, McKinsey & Company, Ogilvy, Reuters, Suez, and Toshiba.

The University and Environs
HEC is located on a 300-acre wooded campus, 10 miles (16 kilometers) southwest of Paris, where the culture, history, and myriad attractions of the capital city are easily accessible. The campus is also close to La Défense, the largest business district in Europe, which houses the headquarters of 1,500 multinational companies. These nearby international firms interact with HEC as both partners and potential recruiters.

Most M.B.A. participants choose to live on the fully autonomous campus, which offers such amenities as computer facilities with Wi-Fi access, a well-equipped gymnasium, a library, and a full-service dining hall. The M.B.A. residence offers 177 individual furnished rooms and twenty-four apartments reserved for couples and families. This facility also includes meeting rooms, a common area, laundry machines, a piano bar, and other conveniences. The M.B.A. Partners Club helps participants' partners and families to adapt to life in France and on the HEC campus.

Placement
When seeking internships, project partners, and employers, HEC M.B.A. participants benefit from the full integration of the program's Career Development Service. Each M.B.A. participant receives customized job-search advice from alumni, consultants, coaches, and peers before they are exposed to the hundreds of recruiters who visit campus every year. In addi-

tion, three major on-campus job fairs collectively attract more than 200 recruiting multinational companies each year.

The HEC M.B.A. Career Development Service provides job-search workshops, seminars, counseling, and an extensive documentation center as well as contacts with the worldwide HEC alumni network and privileged access to firms actively supporting the school. Numerous seminars, as well as group and individual counseling sessions, are organized throughout the year, along with company presentations, on- and off-campus job fairs, and alumni events. Career advising is available one-on-one, in small groups, and in collaboration with HEC alumni.

The M.B.A. Career Development Service publishes the M.B.A. Business Card Profiles brochure, which enables recruiters to view the diverse backgrounds and talents of incoming students, as well as the annual *M.B.A. Profiles Book*, which contains the bilingual resumes of all M.B.A. participants along with their contact details. The Profiles Book is sent electronically or mailed to approximately 1,000 international recruiters, who can conduct online resume searches based on a wide range of variables and criteria.

The Career Development Service also keeps track of the employment history of HEC M.B.A. participants after graduation. For the 2007 graduating class, 92 percent were recruited into positions of international scope, 63 percent found employment outside their home country, and 55 percent of non-European graduates found jobs in Europe. By sector, 40 percent of the 2007 graduating students were recruited into industry and manufacturing; 25 percent, into finance and banking; 18 percent, into consulting; and 17 percent, into services.

Admission
The HEC M.B.A. attracts exceptional students from around the world, with more than fifty nationalities represented in the current graduating class. Academic excellence is maintained through a rigorous selection process that seeks an overall balance between academic achievement, professional experience, international exposure, and personal motivation. Knowledge of French is not an entry requirement; however,

participants are strongly encouraged to have a basic knowledge of French at the start of the program.

In addition to completing the online application form, candidates must submit their university transcripts; official GMAT test scores; TOEFL, IELTS, or TOEIC results, if applicable; two letters of recommendation; and essay responses. Preselected candidates are invited to attend evaluation interviews conducted on the HEC campus or in designated locations around the world.

Finances
For applicants joining the program in September 2008, tuition fees are €42,000 for the duration of the sixteen-month M.B.A. program. Estimated expenses, including an on-campus room, books, and meals, total approximately €16,686.

The HEC M.B.A. Program offers need- and merit-based scholarships in addition to an Honorship Fund. Admitted candidates are invited to fill out the online scholarship application through their application account. Various country and region-specific scholarships are also available. The HEC M.B.A. has established partnerships with leading French banks that enable participants to obtain educational loans at competitive rates. All of HEC's banking partners have local branches with ATM machines in the area, which has a sizeable international population.

Application Facts and Dates
The HEC M.B.A. welcomes two intakes per year, in September and January. Admission is on a rolling basis, so candidates can apply to either the September or January intake throughout the year, without having to wait for the set deadlines. In addition, the HEC M.B.A. offers a unique Candidate Profile Evaluation that enables candidates to receive preliminary feedback on their application directly from the admissions team. This free-of-charge, no-obligation form is quick and easy to fill out and can be found on the HEC M.B.A. Web site. When completing their online application form, applicants receive a secure PIN and password, so they can work on their applications over several sessions.

Prospective participants are encouraged to visit the HEC campus to discover what makes the HEC M.B.A. community so unique. Formal visits are organized regularly throughout the year, and further information is available on the HEC M.B.A. Web site. Campus visits offer valuable insight into the HEC M.B.A. Program and allow candidates to attend an M.B.A. class, meet current participants and faculty members, and participate in an admissions discussion.

Applicants are encouraged to apply early. For further information on the application process, students should contact:

Isabelle Cota
Director of Admissions & Development,
    HEC M.B.A. Program
1 rue de la Libération
F-78351 Jouy-en-Josas Cedex
France
Phone: 33-0-1-39-67-95-46
Fax: 33-0-1-39-67-74-65
E-mail: admissionmba@hec.fr
Web site: http://www.mba.hec.edu

HULT International Business School

Hult International Business School

HULT'S TOP-RANKED INTERNATIONAL ONE-YEAR M.B.A.

Founded in 1964, Hult International Business School offers a top-ranked one-year U.S. M.B.A. program in four key locations: Boston, London, Dubai, and Shanghai. Campus rotation is an integral part of Hult's international M.B.A. experience that allows students to gain unique insight into the world's key economies. Hult is ranked first for Post-Graduation Salary Increase, 21st in the U.S. overall, and 39th in the world by The Economist. The Hult M.B.A. prepares experienced professionals for managerial and leadership responsibilities and gives them the tools to be successful in the global business world.

Hult is the M.B.A. program of choice for those who seek a one-year M.B.A. program from a U.S. institution but also want a truly international experience. Hult has an international student body from more than forty different countries and faculty members who have taught at Harvard, Wharton, INSEAD, and MIT. Furthermore the program helps students develop superior skills in managing diverse teams, clients, and vendors in today's global economy.

Programs and Curricular Focus

Hult offers an M.B.A. degree with options to specialize in entrepreneurship, finance, marketing, and other fields of interest. The program has a very practical orientation as students learn through a combination of case studies, lectures, business simulations, and field study projects. Comprising four modules, which cover all the functional areas of business, the program helps students develop a broad managerial perspective, and require students to apply their skills in an intense Action Learning Project where they work with real companies solving their real business issues.

Students and the M.B.A. Experience

One of the leading attributes of the program is the depth of the professional experience of the students. Participants generally have seven years of work experience and the average age is 30. In addition, the student body is international, comprising students from more than forty countries in the Americas, Europe, Asia, Middle East, and Africa.

Global Focus

The diversity of the class provides a unique opportunity to learn and practice the skills of international business management by working closely with their colleagues. The students represent a broad diversity of cultures and a wide range of industry and functional expertise. Courses and projects are designed to incorporate teamwork and team building as an approach to developing cross-cultural managerial skills. The campus rotation available during the last two modules also provides unique opportunity for Hult students to go global—gaining exposure to and insight about the world's key economies.

Special Features

At the heart of Hult's one-year M.B.A. is an innovative curriculum called "Action Learning," which melds theory and practice. This approach means that learning is hands-on. Concepts and theories that students learn in the classroom are reinforced by field-study projects, business simulations, and team exercises. This is the most effective way to train business leaders in the practical realities of running and growing businesses.

Hult also offers pre-M.B.A. preparation courses in foundation skills and intensive English.

The Faculty

Hult attracts professors who have both strong academic credentials and decades of real-world experience leading and consulting for some of the world's top companies. The faculty includes professors who have taught or concurrently teach at Harvard, Wharton, Duke, Cornell, Babson, Boston University, Northeastern University, and Tel-Aviv University. Revealing Hult's real-world orientation, its faculty also includes professors who are partners at Monitor and Arthur D. Little and who have consulted for Xerox, Siemens, and other major multinational companies.

Placement

Hult has established a global career services network with dedicated resources in key job markets to support international careers. Career services teams are based in Boston, London, Dubai, and Shanghai. In addition, the School works individually with each participant to develop a career strategy. A Career Management Course (CMC) is designed to enhance skill development regarding the job-search process. CMC is complemented by workshops to further enhance job-search skills and provide opportunities to practice these new techniques. CMC provides individual career counseling, presentations of industry panels, and access to networking events.

Admission

Applicants for the M.B.A. program are considered on the basis of a qualitative evaluation of the relevance of work experience and career objectives, academic records, strength of recommendations, personal motivation, and quantitative and analytical ability. Submission of a GMAT score is required of all candidates, and a TOEFL score must be submitted where appropriate.

Finances

Tuition for the one-year M.B.A. program is $42,780. Financial aid and scholarships are also available for all applicants, including international students, who meet certain criteria. Hult scholarships range from $2000 to $16,000. Hult partners with Erika Loans, which can finance up to 70 percent of the M.B.A. tuition. In addition, Hult partners with the Massachusetts Educational Financing Authority, which offers financing for up to 100 percent of tuition and living expenses.

International Students

Hult is among the best global M.B.A. programs in the world and is known for its international and mature student body composed of experienced professionals from more than forty countries. Current students come from countries as diverse as Germany, Japan, Vietnam, Venezuela, Ukraine, Cameroon, and Kazakhstan; they are on average 30 years old with seven years of professional experience.

Application Facts and Dates

The School utilizes a rolling admissions process for its start dates every September. Early application is suggested, as enrollment is limited. Correspondence should be directed to:

Alice Huang
Global Head of Recruiting
Hult International Business School
1 Education Street
Cambridge, Massachusetts 02141
Phone: 617-746-1990
Fax: 617-746-1991
E-mail: admissions@hult.edu
Web site: http://www.hult.edu

IE Business School

Madrid, Spain

THE DEAN'S MESSAGE

I would like to thank you for your interest in IE Business School. We are confident that in selecting IE Business School for your master's degree studies, you are taking the first step toward success in your professional and personal development.

IE Business School's objective is to train leaders in the fields of entrepreneurship, business management, and corporate counsel—leaders who create collective value by instigating competitive business projects without losing sight of their responsibilities and commitments to their environment. The enormous changes taking place in society have made our mission all the more intense and exciting as we rise to the challenge of upholding our firm commitment to continuous innovation and the pursuit of excellence.

Here at IE Business School we are fully aware of the new business opportunities opened up by information and communication technologies. They constitute an integral part our programs not only as mere work tools but also in the form of training material in each area. We also recognize the inexorable globalization process taking place, which now extends far beyond multinationals as small family-run businesses begin to feel its effects.

IE Business School's international focus is a direct response to our belief that only globally oriented business initiatives will be able to survive into the future. Our student body comprises more than seventy-three nationalities at any given time, and the enormous diversity of nationalities among our teaching faculty makes us one of the most international business schools in the world.

We are convinced that the successful business models of the future will be those that best know how to interact with an increasingly sophisticated and demanding social environment, accepting with full responsibility their role in the collective creation of value. This philosophy is present in our attitude, our vision, and in our understanding of how to prepare professionals for the business environment.

—Santiago Iñiguez, Dean, IE Business School

Programs and Curricular Focus

IE Business School offers three types of M.B.A. programs—the International M.B.A., the Global M.B.A., and the International Executive M.B.A.

The International M.B.A. is a one-year program intended for people with aspirations, ambitions, and drive. An international program in all senses of the word, it gives a head start in a career or helps reroute a professional future, developing theoretical and practical knowledge, honing soft skills, and expanding professional networks and horizons. Students receive a second-to-none business education complemented by the cultural experience of studying at an international school with a truly international student body, all against the backdrop of Spain's capital city. The International M.B.A. at IE affords the opportunities, inspiration, and experience necessary for international professional success.

IE's Global M.B.A. has raised the benchmark for online M.B.A. programs. The program includes the full M.B.A. syllabus and a highly innovative online methodology in which IE's professors—themselves experts in their fields—and technology combine to enhance the learning experience, furthering students' skills and career prospects. Diversity is an intrinsic part of the Global M.B.A., and the program develops a truly global network encompassing professionals, classmates, and alumni, opening the door to the wider international business community.

Catering to the international management community, the International Executive M.B.A. offers the utmost flexibility required by the working executive. The program offers two timetabling options: the online program combines periods of both on-campus and online training, and the presential (face-to-face), part-time schedule (classes held in Madrid every other week) allows students to obtain a high-quality and prestigious M.B.A. without having to leave their place of residence for prolonged periods of time. Equipping students with the knowledge and tools that today's top-level company executives require, the International Executive M.B.A. is consistently ranked high in the top business school rankings, including the *Financial Times* and *The Economist.*

Students and the M.B.A. Experience

The diversity in IE's student body is almost unparalleled, with seventy-three nationalities on campus and graduates occupying management positions in more than 100 countries. The backgrounds of IE's students are as varied academically and professionally as they are geographically and culturally. Each program counts on the participation of exceptional students from every sector who have studied at a broad range of institutions and who have degrees in a plethora of subjects. The wealth of perspectives brought to the program by students from diverse academic backgrounds contributes greatly to IE Business School's programs.

IE adopts a remarkably practical approach based on the case method. Students work as part of a team, mentored by professors as they develop solutions to complicated international cases and issues. Students work in teams with others from all over the world, learn to look at things in a new way and appreciate different cultures and perspectives, and develop an international network of friends.

There are currently 236 International M.B.A. students, including 93 percent international students (33 percent women) with an average age of 29 and average work experience of 4½ years; 20 Global M.B.A. students, including 70 percent international students (30 percent women) with an average age of 30 and average work experience of six years; and 30 International Executive M.B.A. students, including 81 percent international students (22 percent women) with an average age of 37 and average work experience of eleven years.

Special Features

The International M.B.A. incorporates a number of programs to ensure that students get the best out of their M.B.A. and the IE experience. It features the ACCELERATE Program, which builds soft skills; Venture Lab (entrepreneurial workshops); more than sixty elective courses; international exchange programs; and dual-degree programs.

The Global M.B.A. features Integration Days, which are two-day events held around the globe that bring students together and complement the predominately online training.

The International Executive M.B.A. features trips to Madrid and Shanghai. A truly flexible program that offers two timetabling options; students may choose between a completely asynchronous online version or a biweekly part-time version with classes in Madrid every other weekend.

The Faculty

IE's world-class faculty members come from around the world. There are 90 full-time professors and 200 part-time professors. Thirty-one percent of IE's faculty members are women, and 89 percent have doctoral degrees.

The Business School Network

IE prides itself on its close ties to the corporate world. Over its thirty-five-year existence, IE has nurtured close relationships with a constantly expanding network of professionals and companies across the globe.

Corporate Partnerships

The corporate relationships continue to develop, and students are able to take advantage of the expertise and contacts provided by this network, which now includes Accenture, Banesto, BBVA, Boulanger, Carrefour, Danone, Decathlon, Deloitte, Deutsche Post, Deutsche Telecom, Ferrovial, France Telecom, General Electric, Hertz, Ing Direct, JP Morgan, Kimberly Clark, KPMG, Kraft, Leroy Merlin, LG, L'Oreal, McKinsey, Microsoft, Philips, Procter & Gamble, PWC, Schering Plough, Deloitte, Ernst & Young, Freshfields, KPMG, and Landwell.

The College and Environs

Founded in 1973, the IE campus is situated in the heart of Madrid. Students can experience in full everything the city has to offer. Madrid, the capital of Spain, has a rich heritage in the arts and a cultural experience like few others in the world. The city offers a host of museums, parks and gardens, palaces, and modern and historic architecture as well as being surrounded by Spain's other treasures, such as the Alhambra in Granada, the University of Salamanca, and the ancient city of Córdoba.

Facilities

Students at IE are able to take advantage of well-appointed lecture theaters and workrooms for meeting with the team for group work as well as the library for researching projects and assignments. A wireless Internet connection is available that covers all of IE's urban campus, keeping students connected at all hours of the day.

Placement

The Careers Management Center is an active partner in helping students map their career paths, teaching the skills needed to rise to the challenges they will face in the labor market and achieve their career goals. The center facilitates the job search of all students and alumni by providing access to a range of resources and remains available for the rest of their professional lives.

The Careers Management Center provides the following assistance: individual career planning and coaching sessions with members of the center; seminars and workshops led by members of the center and external specialists on career orientation, market research, effective interviewing, networking, CV and cover letter preparation, and salary negotiation; an interactive Web page and a virtual library that provides access to a large number of online resources; training and advisory service; a job bank; the IE career fair; club support; company presentations; and the CV book.

Admission

General requirements for admission include the completed application form, a bachelor's degree credential or equivalent, proof of professional work experience, GMAT or IE Admissions Test results, English language certificate (where applicable), and an interview. Students should visit the Web site for specific requirements for each M.B.A. program.

Following the interview, the application is subject to a final analysis by the Admissions Committee. The Admissions Committee evaluates all aspects of the candidature as a whole and subsequently communicates its decision in writing.

Finances

Tuition is €45,000 for the International M.B.A., €35,000 for the Global M.B.A., and €46,000 for the International Executive M.B.A. Additional fees are €1050.

Financial aid is available to all students and must be applied for after acceptance in a program of study. For more details, students should visit the IE Scholarships Web page.

International Students

The Student Office at IE looks after the needs of all students, particularly those from outside Madrid. The Student Office assists students with immigration issues, provides language classes for further integration into Spanish life, and helps find accommodation for the duration of study, whether it be for a full year or for the part-time and online programs. With up to 93 percent international participation in the M.B.A. programs, the School is well-versed in attending to students from abroad.

Application Facts and Dates

IE Business School operates a rolling admissions process. Due to the quantity of applications received as well as the limited number of places, it is strongly recommended that candidates apply up to a year in advance. This is especially important if the student intends to apply for a scholarship, as only accepted students may apply for financial aid.

Admissions Department
IE Business School
María de Molina 11
28006, Madrid,
Spain
Phone: +34 915 689 610
　　　　+34 915 689 710
E-mail: admissions@ie.edu
Web site:
　　http://www.ie.edu/business/index_en.
　　php?&ns_campaign=_corp_sinpr_
　　sinc_int_mun_20080400_cc_en&ns_
　　mchannel=profile&ns_source=
　　petersons&ns

Illinois State University

Normal, Illinois

THE ILLINOIS STATE M.B.A. PROGRAM—ADDING VALUE TO A DIVERSE STUDENT BODY

At Illinois State University, our M.B.A. program welcomes students prepared to embark on the important path of learning and personal and professional growth. We offer an excellent professional program in an outstanding new College of Business building with state-of-the-art technology, a corporate presence, special-use rooms and classrooms, and other features that provide an outstanding learning environment. The Illinois State M.B.A. program was recognized by Princeton Review in the 2008 edition of Best Business Schools for the second consecutive year. Identifying the major commitment required to earn an M.B.A., our program has been structured to allow you to develop the skills and to achieve the knowledge base needed for success in this very competitive and challenging global business environment. Our faculty members are among the best—both in the mastery of their disciplines and in their commitment to a learning environment that will help you achieve your goals. Our class sizes are small, so faculty members are accessible and willing to mentor students both inside and outside the classroom. Our graduates consistently rate our faculty as one of the greatest strengths of the M.B.A. program. We welcome your interest and your application.

—Dr. S. J. Chang, Program Director

Programs and Curricular Focus

Illinois State has both a traditional, evening M.B.A. program and an accelerated, weekend-formatted corporate M.B.A. program. Both full- and part-time students are accepted into the traditional program. Full-time students in the traditional evening program typically take three classes, and part-time students, one or two, per academic semester, attending each class only one night a week over the fifteen-week semester. Students in the corporate program often complete as many as 9-hours of academic course work during an academic semester while continuing to work full-time, attending classes on Friday evening and the subsequent Saturday every other weekend for three weekends to complete a 3-hour course. After completing a course in the corporate program, students take two weekends off before starting their next course in this lock-step-formatted program. In both programs, students benefit from the synergies generated through class discussions and group activities.

The curriculum in both the traditional and corporate programs has three interrelated parts: foundation, core, and elective courses. Graduate-level foundation courses are designed for the student with no previous university-level business course work in order to prepare the student for graduate-level core courses. Students who have earned an undergraduate business degree typically take few, if any, of the seven foundation courses. Proficiency exams to waive foundation requirements are available for those who qualify.

Students needing foundation preparation in the corporate, lock-step weekend-formatted program must start their M.B.A. course work at the beginning of the program. Students in the corporate program meeting all foundation requirements begin their course work at the beginning of the core curriculum.

The core and elective course requirements for the program consist of 36 semester hours of study (twelve courses). The nine core courses are designed to build analytical, critical thinking, decision-making, team, and communication skills across the functional areas of business, culminating with an integrative capstone course on organizational strategy and planning.

Students may choose to concentrate or diversify the three elective courses in the areas of agribusiness, arts management, finance, human resources, insurance, marketing, and project management. Accounting and business information systems also are concentration options for those with significant undergraduate course work in the area. Full-time students without significant business experience are encouraged to complete an internship experience as one elective.

Students in the corporate M.B.A. program choose their electives as a learning cohort.

The College also offers graduate programs leading to the Master of Science in Accountancy and the Master of Professional Accountancy.

Students and the M.B.A. Experience

Illinois State M.B.A. alumni give the program a 95 percent satisfaction rating. A supportive environment encourages students to reach their potential during and beyond their program. The College is committed to providing the best student-centered education in business, serving the needs of business and society by giving students the time and support needed as they progress toward their degrees and by preparing students for lifelong learning. This student-centered approach is reflected in small class sizes (averaging fewer than 25 students in core courses), faculty members who are accessible to students and who challenge them to broaden their business perspectives, and active alumni and student organizations designed to enhance networking and professional skills.

A diverse student body adds to the quality of the M.B.A. experience. Approximately 200 part-time and full-time students, whose professional and academic backgrounds vary widely, take classes together. Although work experience is not a requirement for admission to the traditional or corporate program, the average full-time work experience is approximately five years for those in the traditional program and approximately seven years for those in the corporate program. Small classes and M.B.A. Association activities allow students to learn from each other as they exchange perspectives reflecting different cultures, professions, and industries.

The M.B.A. Association also allows students to develop leadership and organizational skills through service as officers or M.B.A. ambassadors. The association sponsors professional, philanthropic, and social activities.

The Faculty

The graduate faculty members hold degrees from major universities throughout the nation. The faculty members combine a strong student-centered orientation with their personal involvement in relevant research. These faculty dimensions foster a stimulating learning environment within which to study contemporary business topics. During exit interviews, graduating M.B.A. students consistently list student-professor relationships, accessibility of professors, and high quality of the courses offered as areas of particular strength for the Illinois State M.B.A. program.

The Business School Network
Corporate Partnerships

A $9.5-million grant provided by State Farm Insurance and matched by the state of Illinois provided for a new $27-million College of Business building, which opened in January of 2005. In addition, grants from major corporate partners, such as Caterpillar, Archer Daniels Midland Company, and MassMutual Insurance, have enabled the College to complete major updates in the computer labs and in classroom technology. The M.B.A. program has been offered, on-site, on a contractual basis to employees of Ameren IP, Archer Daniels Midland Company, Bridgestone-Firestone, Caterpillar, Inc., and a number of other smaller businesses and is currently being offered in Bloomington-Normal through a cooperative arrangement with the McLean County Chamber of Commerce. College faculty members also developed and teach a two-week overseas study program for the Lloyd's of London APEX Programme. In addition, the College is home to the Katie Insurance School. With funding in excess of $3 million from insurance companies, the Katie Insurance School is devoted to providing the finest undergraduate and graduate insurance programs in the country and sponsors a number of continuing education and professional development programs.

Prominent Alumni

The Illinois State University M.B.A. program counts among its alumni a number of notable business leaders, including Ann Baughan, Assistant Vice President, State Farm Insurance; Robert English, President, English & Associates; John Franklin, Owner, Innotech Communications; Karl Heien, Vice President, Smith Barney Inc.; Phil Maughan, Vice President, The Northern Trust Company; Warren Schmidgall, Executive Vice President, Hill's Pet Nutrition Inc.; James C. Tyree, Chairman and CEO, Mesirow Financial Group; Sheila Jayaraj, Vice President, Pro-Pharmaceuticals Inc.; Mike Baroni and Terry Stoa, Vice Presidents, Archer Daniels Midland Company; Tony J. Sorcic, President and CEO, Citizens First National Bank and Princeton National Bancorp, Inc.; and Jack Hartung, Vice President and CFO, Chipotle.

The College and Environs

Founded in 1857 as the first public institution of higher education in the state, Illinois State has developed into a major university. It prides itself on providing personalized instruction of high quality and developing student potential through superior teaching. Yale's *Insider's Guide to the Colleges* has reported that students at Illinois State University praise the small-school feeling they get from this large university and the incredible opportunities they encounter. Also, *Kiplinger* magazine recently ranked Illinois State seventy-third in the 100 best values in public colleges in the country. Further, Illinois State's M.B.A. Program has been recognized by *Princeton Review* as one of the Best Business Schools for 2008.

Bloomington-Normal was recognized by *Money* magazine as one of the nation's most livable communities. In addition, *Forbes* magazine ranked Bloomington-Normal fifteenth in the country for best small places for business and careers. Five major highways intersect in the Twin Cities, which are in McLean County midway between St. Louis and Chicago. An Amtrak train station is just two blocks from the Illinois State campus, and major airlines serve the Central Illinois Regional Airport, the fastest growing downstate air transportation provider.

The community is one of the state's fastest growing, with a population of 110,000. Firms with national headquarters in central Illinois include State Farm Insurance Companies, Caterpillar Inc., Mitsubishi Motor Manufacturing, Archer Daniels Midland Company, and Country

Financial. Other major employers in the Twin Cities include BroMenn Healthcare; OSF St. Joseph Medical Center; Bridgestone/Firestone OTR; General Electric; Beer Nuts, Inc.; and Verizon.

Facilities

The University library contains more than 1.8 million items, including more than 5,000 journals, 16,500 electronic journals, and 85,000 titles in business and economics. Business publications are located on a single floor in the library. Students can access the library system remotely for online searching of fifty-two databases in business and economics, full-text databases covering more than 375 journals, the *Business Periodicals Index,* and other indexes on CD-ROM. The Library Computer System online catalog provides access to the collections of eighty-five other university and college libraries in Illinois.

Technology Environment

The new College of Business building maintains computer labs with hundreds of personal computers with Pentium IV processors and featuring the current software programs students are likely to encounter in the business world. The College of Business has more than 1,700 wired ports, and wireless access is also available throughout the building. Computer labs are available each day from 7:30 a.m. to 11 p.m. At no cost to students, the computer center offers numerous seminars on software packages and current computing topics. New projects include clicker response systems, Bloomberg Financials, and doubling of network Web and storage services.

Placement

The University's Career Center assists students with career decisions, resumes, and finding positions after graduation. A Web-based resume and job posting service serves both current M.B.A. students and alumni. In addition, the M.B.A. office sponsors seminars on career topics and "Update Your M.B.A." programs, both of which bring alumni back to campus and remotely service their need to learn about developments in business theory and practice that have occurred since they completed their programs of study. M.B.A. Alumni Network members assist students in a variety of ways, including mentoring. More than 80 percent of Illinois State M.B.A. students are employed when they complete their degrees. The average starting salary for Illinois State's M.B.A. graduates is competitive with that of most other Midwestern M.B.A. programs.

Admission

Admission is limited to holders of baccalaureate degrees who demonstrate high promise of success in graduate business study. All undergraduate majors are acceptable. Criteria considered in the evaluation of applicants are Graduate Management Admission Test (GMAT) score, GPA earned during the last 60 credit hours of undergraduate work, letters of recommendation, personal essays, and the experience base that applicants bring with them to the program. This includes work experience, supervisory/managerial experience, client/customer-service experience, and international experience.

Applicants need to submit an M.B.A. application and related essays, a resume, and two letters of recommendation to the M.B.A. office. In addition, official GMAT scores, Test of English as a Foreign Language (TOEFL) scores (if applicable), the graduate school application, a $40 application processing fee, and official transcripts must be submitted to the graduate school.

Recently admitted students have an average GPA of 3.45 (target minimum 3.0) and GMAT score of 560 (target minimum 500). A TOEFL score is required of all students whose native language is not English (minimum: 600, paper-based; 250, computer-based; 83, Internet-based).

Finances

In-state tuition and fees for fall 2007 were $2419 per semester for students taking three courses. Out-of-state tuition is $4309 for three courses. The corporate M.B.A. program is fee-based rather than tuition-based, and the current cost for the 36-hour program is slightly less than $18,500.

Graduate assistantships, tuition waivers, scholarships, student loans, and veterans assistance programs are available to students in the traditional program. Applications are reviewed in late March for fall graduate assistantship appointments, tuition waivers, and other financial aid and in October for the spring semester.

International Students

Nineteen percent of current M.B.A. students are international students, hailing from Africa, Asia, Australia, Canada, Europe, Mexico, and South America. The University provides a week-long orientation for international students, an International House dormitory, and married student housing. The Intensive English Language Institute offers programs for family members who are building their language skills.

Application Facts and Dates

Students in the traditional evening M.B.A. program may begin their studies during any of the three semesters. Full consideration for financial aid and for advance class registration is given to those submitting completed applications by February 1 for summer/fall admission and September 1 for spring admission. Therefore, early submission of application materials is encouraged.

Also noteworthy is that the M.B.A. program now utilizes a rolling admission policy. Applications are reviewed as completed for admitting students to the traditional program. However, to guarantee a seat in a particular semester, the applicant must have all materials on file by the following dates: spring semester, December 1; summer semester, April 1; fall semester, July 1.

For further information, applicants should contact:

The M.B.A. Program
College of Business
Campus Box 5570
Illinois State University
Normal, Illinois 61790-5570
Phone: 309-438-8388
Fax: 309-438-7255
E-mail: isumba@exchange.cob.ilstu.edu
Web site: http://www.mba.ilstu.edu

International University in Geneva

Geneva, Switzerland

AN INTERNATIONAL PERSPECTIVE

▶ *The international business world has become a rapidly evolving environment. New challenges that business leaders are facing include standards of corporate social responsibility, sustainable development, resource and energy efficiency, and emerging markets. The business leader of tomorrow has to work within a context that extends far beyond the classic economic disciplines to consider such aspects as relationships with civil society and the media. Studying in a multicultural atmosphere brings several advantages to an education that takes these new dimensions into account. In this regard, Geneva as a city can hardly be matched. Geneva is the European seat of the United Nations and government representations from all over the world. Geneva and its surroundings also host the headquarters of a variety of large multinational corporations, nongovernmental organizations, the World Economic Forum, and the World Business Council for Sustainable Development. Lively interaction between these organizations and the business world create a cutting-edge innovation and learning. The faculty and the student body of the University represent a diversity of nationalities and cultures providing a lifetime enriching experience. The curricula are likewise based on a variety of business models, case studies, and theories in a context of interactive and experiential learning. Thus the University's mission responds to the leadership needs and managerial skills of the future. I am looking forward to welcoming you to our University.*

—The Chancellor

Programs and Curricular Focus

Education at International University in Geneva is a combination of the American and European academic curriculum, resulting in a unique approach based on high-quality learning. The multicultural and dynamic environment of the University and the international faculty members contribute to the creation of a framework in which the students acquire global experience. Classes are small in order to allow group discussion and provide more individualized attention.

IUG is committed to helping students reach their full potential. All of the professors have solid practical experience in industry and business at senior levels combined with strong academic backgrounds.

The M.B.A. full-time program at International University in Geneva is held over fifteen months.

The methods of instruction at IUG are innovative and underline the importance of gaining an international perspective on management and communication issues. For example, the use of business simulations ensures the development of analytical skills, which are critical in today's competitive and rapidly changing world.

The University emphasizes the importance of interpersonal skills, such as leadership, communication, and the ability to work in a multicultural team, by encour-

aging active class preparation and making regular presentations about various management topics. In that spirit, the students are expected to work in groups in order to stimulate a situation in which they develop a proactive attitude and master effectiveness in communication. The academic philosophy stresses the development of an entrepreneurial attitude relevant to both small companies as well as large, multinational corporations.

The University aims to bridge the gap between theory and practice and build the skills necessary to compete in a global marketplace.

The University has three majors available, in finance, human resources, and marketing.

Students and the M.B.A. Experience

The M.B.A. program is composed of a highly multicultural student body, representing a diversity of academic and professional experiences. The average student is 27 years old with four years of work experience. Women comprise 39 percent of the class. The campus culture is enriched by international students from fifty-two countries.

Special Features

International University in Geneva has developed educational affiliation agreements

with the following universities: University of Connecticut, Indiana University of Pennsylvania, Tulane University (New Orleans, Louisiana), and Monterey Institute of International Studies (California) in the U.S.A.; ESIC, Madrid, in Spain; ISC, Paris, in France; Universidad de San Ignacio de Loyola, Lima, in Peru; and Anahuac University, Mexico City, in Mexico

The Faculty

The faculty at IUG is multidisciplinary in professional training, international in experience, practical in orientation, and focused on their teaching. The full-time faculty members are organized into unit coordinators, and the adjunct faculty members are drawn from other educational institutions in the area and from the business community.

The Business School Network

The University has a network of corporate partners in the Geneva area, which is the European headquarter of many multinational companies.

During the academic year, guest lecturers from the business community are invited to the University.

Several European CEOs of large multinationals, such as Hewlett-Packard, Procter and Gamble, and Du Pont de Nemours, are members of the Advisory Council of the University.

Through contacts with the alumni of the University, students have access to a large number of businesses in Geneva.

The College and Environs

The College of Business Administration and Media and Communication is located in a modern building in Geneva.

Geneva belongs to a select group of truly international cities of the world, making it an ideal place to study international management. The city is host to the United Nations and specialized agencies, such as the World Trade Organization, and is often referred to as the capital of peace and diplomacy.

Many multinationals are located in the region, due to the excellent logistical network and the central location of Geneva at the heart of Europe, only 1 hour by air from London, Paris, Brussels, and Milan. Geneva is well-known as one of the world's major international financial centers, especially for the management of private capital assets.

The quality and variety of Geneva's cultural life, with its numerous theaters, museums, and international conferences, makes it the right place to obtain a global education. The city is a showcase for the most celebrated names in fashion, jewelry, and watchmaking and is home to Rolex and Patek Philippe, among others.

Ideally situated on the shores of Lake Leman at the foot of the Alps, Geneva offers excellent outdoor sporting activities.

Technology Environment

Students have access to a range of information resources and networks as well as an online library system and the Internet. The computers are regularly updated with the latest software and all use ADSL technology, which increases the transmission speed. Most of the classrooms are equipped with beamers as well as Internet and video connections.

Placement

The University regularly invites executives from companies to present career opportunities to the students. In addition, seminars relating to job searches are held throughout the year. Company visits are part of the program. A career counselor is available throughout the year.

Admission

Applicants are admitted on the basis of academic and professional accomplishments, scores on the GMAT, individual career goals, written recommendations, and responses to interview and application essay questions. The median GMAT score is 500. Class size is limited to 45 students.

The Test of English as a Foreign Language (TOEFL) is required of all applicants whose native language is not English and who graduated from an educational institution where the language of instruction was not English. The minimum TOEFL score required is 80 (Internet-based test).

The University has four intakes during the academic year: September, December, March, and June.

Finances

The 2008–09 tuition and fees are 36,200 Swiss francs.

International Students

The student body at International University in Geneva is multicultural, representing fifty-two countries.

Application Facts and Dates

For more information about application and deadlines, students should contact:

International University in Geneva
Ms. Sanela Pavlovic
Admission Office
ICC, Route de Pré-Bois 20
1215 Geneva 15
Switzerland
Phone: (+41 +22) 710 71 10-12
Fax: (+41 +22) 710 71 11
E-mail: admissions@iun.ch
Web site: http://www.iun.ch

Iona College

LEADERSHIP—THE HAGAN M.B.A. PROGRAM

The Hagan School of Business seeks to cultivate an intellectually rigorous learning environment in which all students can develop practices and competencies necessary for effective and ethical leadership.

—Vincent J. Calluzzo, Dean

Programs and Curricular Focus

The goal of the Hagan School of Business M.B.A. program is to produce graduates and future leaders who understand business and its challenges in the twenty-first century. It seeks to graduate women and men who have the skills to work productively in a high-technology society, demonstrate sensitivity to the global and multicultural character of business, provide strategic leadership in a competitive environment, and subscribe to high ethical standards in the practice of their profession.

The M.B.A. curriculum consists of core courses in the functional areas of business perspectives (an integrated overview), followed by a major concentration allowing for specialized study, with advanced electives that provide students an opportunity to custom design the breadth component of the curriculum and a capstone course.

Computer applications are integrated into the program, as are the development of presentation and communication skills. Case studies, team projects, computer simulation games, experiential exercises, and lectures are the commonly used methods of teaching.

The calendar follows a trimester schedule of twelve weeks each, with two summer sessions, allowing students to earn more credits within the year. Classes meet once a week in the evening, Monday through Thursday, from 6:30 p.m. to 9:30 p.m. In addition, there is a wide selection of Internet distance learning courses available.

The number of credits required for the degree is 57 before waivers and transfer credits are applied. There is a six-year limit to finish the program. A typical M.B.A. student takes 39 credits and completes the program in 2½ years on a part-time basis or eighteen months full-time.

In addition to the traditional M.B.A., the College also offers a Fast Track program. Geared toward people who want to gain an edge in their chosen field, the Fast Track M.B.A. shaves ten months off the length of traditional M.B.A. programs by offering courses in a sequence that guarantees a speedy graduation. This program is open to all college graduates—regardless of undergraduate major. The Fast Track program is especially designed for non-business students who want a business background prior to entering graduate or professional school and for professional school graduates who would like an M.B.A. before starting a residency. Courses may be offered in an online distance-learning format, in a traditional classroom setting, or in hybrid format that utilizes both online and in-person class meetings.

Students and the M.B.A. Experience

Almost all of the students in the program hold full-time jobs at Fortune 500 companies, major brokerage houses, large commercial banks, and insurance companies. Midsize and small companies are also well represented. Some students hold middle-management positions in blue-chip firms such as IBM, Chase Manhattan Bank, Kraft-General Foods, and Lederle Laboratories, to cite a few.

The average age of the students is 28. They have, on the average, about four years of full-time work experience in various industries. It is this maturity, diverse corporate background, and significant work experience that they bring to the program and contribute to the overall quality of the learning process.

The student body is represented by approximately the same number of women and men. Most come from the tri-state area of New York, New Jersey, and Connecticut. International students represent all continents.

Global Focus

The institutional thrust toward global education and the international character of the faculty members strengthen the goal dimension of the M.B.A. curriculum. Students are encouraged to participate in a variety of courses offered abroad.

The Faculty

The Hagan School of Business faculty members are dedicated teachers and professionals. As teacher-scholars, they keep current in their fields of expertise, doing research, publishing, and giving presentations at academic conferences. As professionals, they blend theory and practice, drawing upon their own and their students' business experience. Among them are internationally recognized experts in such diverse fields as artificial intelligence, case writing, corporate values, and business ethics.

With very few exceptions, those who teach in the M.B.A. program are full-time, with appropriate terminal degrees earned at America's top universities. Students recognize them for their teaching excellence and seek their advice on career matters.

The Business School Network
Corporate Partnerships

The Hagan School has created partnerships with several corporations in Westchester and Rockland Counties. Through these partnerships, business has a real opportunity to influence the strategic direction of the School. It is mechanisms of this kind that allow the School to be responsive to the needs of the business community and offer a relevant curriculum. The Executive of the Day Program brings successful alumni as well as prominent local business executives to the campus to give lectures on current issues to the student body. The *Hagan Report* keeps alumni and students informed.

Prominent Alumni

The Hagan School is proud to count among its distinguished alumni senior executives and business leaders from America's largest and best corporations. Some prominent alumni include the chairman and CEO of AOL, Director of the New York Stock Exchange, and President of NASDAQ.

A view of campus.

The College and Environs

Iona College was founded in 1940 by the Congregation of Christian Brothers. Its main campus is located in New Rochelle, a small city on the Long Island Sound in Westchester County, about 20 minutes north of Manhattan. The M.B.A. program is also offered in Rockland County, a few miles west of the Hudson River.

With its strategic locations and proximity to New York City, the Hagan School of Business enables students to benefit from the rich, diversified environment that is attuned to the advances and innovations of the global market. The New York metropolitan area is home to many major national and multinational corporations, such as IBM, MasterCard International, and PepsiCo, as well as many of the nation's largest banks, brokerage houses, and insurance firms.

Technology Environment

In fall 2007, groundbreaking took place for a library expansion and renovation that will provide a multimedia seminar room and group study facilities equipped for students to collaborate on podcasts and digital projects—all while enjoying a Starbucks from the library's café (one of two outlets on campus). The library has already installed fifty-two dual-boot iMacs, which can run both Microsoft Windows and the latest Mac OS, making Iona one of a handful of colleges to invest in the cutting-edge technology. Iona College features fully wireless facilities offering students high-speed access to the Internet and possesses more than 700 networked computers and two fully networked computer labs located at Iona's graduate center in Rockland County. Computer lab assistants are available to help students with their questions, and one lab stays open 24-hours-a-day, seven days a week.

The M.B.A. courses incorporate the use of computers both in and out of the classroom. Each student is provided with a computer account, an e-mail address, and access to the system. Many students also take advantage of Iona's distance learning courses that enable them to log on and complete course assignments at their convenience.

Placement

The College's Gerri Ripp Center for Career Development provides students with career counseling and job search assistance. It alerts students to job openings and positions in companies and to the organizations that seek graduates of the College. Resume referral, mock interviews, and counseling for alumni are among the services available to students.

Admission

Admission is selective and based on an evaluation of the student's academic record, scores on the Graduate Management Admission Test (GMAT), references, and work experience. Applications and credentials should be sent to the Graduate Admissions Office of the Hagan School of Business.

Candidates may enter the graduate program in the fall (September), winter (November), or spring (March) trimester and summer sessions. The completed application, with fee, must be supported by official transcripts from each institution of higher education attended, two letters of recommendation, and Graduate Management Admission Test (GMAT) scores. All required documents should be received no later than two weeks prior to the start of the trimester or summer session for which the candidate is applying. TOEFL scores are required for all students whose native language is not English. International students must provide evidence of adequate funds to cover all expenses.

Finances

Tuition per credit in 2008–09 is $755. Books and supplies can cost, on average, $1500 per year. There are no boarding facilities on campus for graduate students. Living expense estimates range from $10,000 to $12,000 for ten months, not including vacation periods.

Tuition scholarships are awarded based on exceptional GMAT scores.

Application Facts and Dates

For more information, students should contact:

M.B.A. Office
Hagan School of Business
Iona College
715 North Avenue
New Rochelle, New York 10801-1890

Phone: 914-633-2288
Fax: 914-633-2012
E-mail: jfleurismond@iona.edu
Web site: http://www.iona.edu/hagan/

M.B.A. Admissions Office
Rockland Graduate Center
Iona College
2 Blue Hill Plaza
Concourse Level
Pearl River, New York 10965

Phone: 845-620-1350
Fax: 845-620-1260
E-mail: rockland@iona.edu

Iowa State University

Ames, Iowa

YOUR AMBITION, OUR M.B.A.

The pace of business today requires a new M.B.A.—one that is innovative and prepares you to outperform the competition. The Iowa State M.B.A. will give you an educational experience linking theory with practice while offering the choices you—the discerning education consumer—want. Our course work provides you with the needed skills to organize, discern, and more effectively manage and lead today's complex organizations.

You will be taught by nationally recognized faculty members who are committed to your success. Iowa State offers an unparalleled environment with a friendly, welcoming Midwestern atmosphere on a campus recognized as one of the most beautiful in the nation. You will have access to a wide variety of organizations, events, and experiences. And you can experience your M.B.A. education in the state-of-the-art Gerdin Business Building.

It's your goal and your ambition. Make your choice an Iowa State M.B.A.

—Labh S. Hira, Dean

Programs and Curricular Focus

The Iowa State University M.B.A. program attracts students worldwide who aspire to become twenty-first-century business leaders in today's globally diverse, technology-driven business environment. The University challenges M.B.A. students to become their best and grow individually and collectively through their classroom experiences and beyond. M.B.A. students learn and succeed together in diverse work teams, maximizing each member's contributions through their varied academic backgrounds, degrees of work experience, personal strengths and skills, genders and ethnicities, and countries of origin. Enrollment in the program is kept low and class sizes are small. Students are given the personal attention that they need and deserve from accessible faculty members and dedicated academic and career services support staff.

M.B.A. candidates may pursue their graduate management degree through a full-time program or, to accommodate employed students, part-time by taking classes on Saturdays in Ames or in the evenings in Des Moines. The 48-credit-hour M.B.A. program consists of an integrated core curriculum and 24 credit hours of electives. Teamwork is an integral part of the first half of the M.B.A. experience and entering students are placed on diverse work teams for the duration of the core curriculum. During the second half of the program, students tailor their course work to meet individual academic and career goals, choosing from a wide array of M.B.A.

electives. M.B.A. students may opt to concentrate their studies in a particular area or pursue a general management degree. Areas of specialization include accounting, agribusiness, family financial planning, finance, international business, management information systems, marketing, and supply chain management. A minor in sustainable agriculture is also offered.

Students and the M.B.A. Experience

The 300 graduate business students at Iowa State reflect diverse educational, cultural, and professional backgrounds. Drawing upon the University's international stature, the Iowa State M.B.A. program attracts students worldwide. International students represent nearly 40 percent of the M.B.A. student body. About 30 percent of Iowa State M.B.A. students bring an undergraduate degree in business to their graduate experience. Almost half reflect a background in engineering and the sciences. Social sciences, arts and humanities, and other degrees illustrate the other varying backgrounds of undergraduates who enroll in the College of Business for graduate work. Iowa State's part-time M.B.A. candidates represent industry sectors throughout the state of Iowa, including agriculture, education, financial services, information technology, health and human services, manufacturing, and small business.

Students are encouraged to be active participants in the M.B.A. Association. This organization promotes career development

activities, plans social events, and serves as a representative body for M.B.A. students in the College.

Global Focus

Iowa State M.B.A. students can add an international dimension to their studies by participating in a summer study-abroad program. Iowa State University is a member of an international education consortium that offers a summer graduate program in Asolo, Italy. Part-time M.B.A. students may participate in an intensive, two-week international experience through the European Summer School of Advanced Management (ESSAM) in Aarhus, Denmark. International study tours are arranged annually by M.B.A. faculty. Other international study opportunities are available through the Iowa State University Study Abroad Office.

Special Features

M.B.A. students culminate their first year of study in an internal case competition. M.B.A. student teams are given 24 hours to analyze a comprehensive business case and present their findings and recommendations to panel of judges the following day. Scholarships are awarded to top-performing teams and individuals. Iowa State M.B.A. teams also actively participate in external case competitions throughout the country.

M.B.A. students may enhance their educational experience through the College's close association with various academic and outreach centers. The Pappajohn Center for Entrepreneurship offers educational and outreach programs aimed at developing the entrepreneurial interests and capabilities of M.B.A. students. M.B.A. students may be given the opportunity to provide research support and consulting services to Iowa small businesses through the Iowa Small Business Development Center.

The Faculty

College of Business faculty members have broad backgrounds in industry and education. They possess doctoral degrees from leading business schools across the nation. Faculty members conduct research that keeps them on the leading edge of business theory and practice. Many have international experience. College of Business faculty members are accommodating, accessible, and available to advise and help students in achieving their academic and career goals.

The Business School Network
Corporate Partnerships
Iowa State University places immense importance on the exchange of ideas between corporate and academic environments. The College of Business Dean's Advisory Council meets regularly to share its members' expertise and ideas for the M.B.A. program. M.B.A. students visit local and regional facilities to observe businesses in action. Through the College's Executive-in-Residence program, M.B.A. students interact with prominent business leaders who visit the campus yearly. The M.B.A. Executive Speaker Series gives students the opportunity to regularly dialogue with successful business people on a variety of pertinent topics.

The College and Environs
Founded in 1858, Iowa State University is the first land-grant university to have been established under the Morrill Land-Grant Act. The University embraces its land-grant heritage with an institutional orientation toward science and technology. Iowa State is a University of international stature that is deeply rooted in its tradition of learning, discovery, and engagement.

M.B.A. students can experience the Midwest at its best at Iowa State University. The nearly 2,000-acre, park-like campus is recognized as one of the most beautiful in America. More than 26,000 undergraduate and graduate students are enrolled at the University. It is located in Ames, Iowa, which is ranked among the top small cities in the nation. It is located just 35 miles north of the state's capital, Des Moines. It is a safe, friendly community of 50,000 residents. In addition, Ames and the adjoining Iowa State campus offer a wealth of recreational activities, splendid parks, NCAA Big XII sports, theater and performing arts, fine dining, cultural events, concerts, and other exciting entertainment.

Facilities
The Gerdin Business Building offers Iowa State M.B.A. students the latest in instructional and computer technology, private study and work areas, and first-rate academic and career services accommodations. Multiple spaces are designated for student use, including team rooms, student organization space, a career services resource area, a commons area, office space for graduate

assistants, and a graduate student lounge. This beautiful 111,000-square-foot facility was made possible by a $10-million lead gift from Russ and Ann Gerdin of North Liberty, Iowa. Mr. Gerdin is president, chairman, and chief executive officer of Heartland Express, Inc.

Technology Environment
Iowa State University is home to the world's first electronic digital computer. M.B.A. students experience the rich tradition of technological inventiveness in their classrooms, computer labs, and residences today. Iowa State provides a wide range of computer hardware and software support services, such as e-mail, wireless Internet access, computer consulting, and instructional courses and workshops. Kiosks are located across the campus for students to access personal and University information 24 hours a day. The state-of-the-art Gerdin Business Building has wireless network access throughout the facility. All classrooms are equipped with full multimedia capability. The building contains three computer laboratories, a computer networking laboratory, and a trading laboratory.

Placement
Job placement is the ultimate goal for most M.B.A. students, and the placement success rate for Iowa State M.B.A. graduates ranks among the highest for M.B.A. programs nationwide. The College of Business offers comprehensive career management services to help students reach their career goals. Preparing students for placement success begins during orientation and continues into the first semester with a professional skills development course. One of the nation's largest business career fairs takes place at Iowa State in the fall and spring semesters. A full-time director provides individual career services support to M.B.A. students throughout their two years of study.

Admission
Each applicant is carefully assessed in terms of his or her intellectual potential, academic achievement, work and professional involvement, interpersonal communication skills, career goals, and motivation. Although it is not required, work experience is strongly preferred for candidacy. Educational records are reviewed from official transcripts, as well as scores from the Graduate Management Admission Test (GMAT) and TOEFL (for international students). Three letters of recommendation,

a resume, and the candidate's responses to the essay portion of the application are also required.

Finances
The College of Business offers a number of graduate assistantships to qualified M.B.A. students. Graduate assistants pay resident tuition fees and receive a monthly stipend. Various scholarships are also offered to qualified M.B.A. applicants. Admitted M.B.A. students who are members of ethnic minority groups and U.S. citizens may seek financial assistance through the Graduate Minority Assistantship Program. The Office of Student Financial Aid offers financial assistance through low-interest loans of various types and employment assistance.

International Students
International Education Services (IES) provides orientation and advising to new international students. IES is a resource through which international students can utilize local community services. It also serves as a liaison with the U.S. Information Agency and the Immigration and Naturalization Service to bring visiting scholars and students to Iowa State University.

Application Facts and Dates

M.B.A. students are encouraged to submit their application materials by June 1 (March 1 for international students) for priority consideration for full-time admission and financial assistance. An admission decision can be expected within two weeks after receipt of all application materials. Full-time M.B.A. admission is granted for fall semester entry only. Admission into the part-time M.B.A. programs is granted for fall, spring, or summer semesters.

To learn more about the Iowa State M.B.A. and how to apply, students should contact the College of Business or visit the Web site.

Director of M.B.A. Recruitment and Marketing
Dr. Charles B. Handy Graduate Programs Office
College of Business
1360 Gerdin Business Building
Iowa State University
Ames, Iowa 50011-1350
Phone: 515-294-8118
877-ISU-4MBA (toll-free)
Fax: 515-294-2446
E-mail: busgrad@iastate.edu
Web site: http://www.bus.iastate.edu/mba

Johns Hopkins University

Baltimore, Maryland, and Washington, D.C.

DEAN'S MESSAGE

With its innovative approach to graduate education, the Johns Hopkins University Carey Business School is preparing a new generation of leaders with the breadth of knowledge, ethical principles, and teamwork techniques to advance professionally and bring enduring value to their employers and their communities. Combining rigorous theory and best practices, the Johns Hopkins hallmark model brings highly motivated student colleagues together with academic and practitioner faculty members—oftentimes nationally recognized researchers and prominent business leaders. Programs of study include a team-based approach to business and management cases, practical experiences in the business arena, and access to the rich resources of the Johns Hopkins community, including interdisciplinary programs with other renowned schools and divisions of the Johns Hopkins University.

— Yash Gupta, Dean, Carey Business School

Programs and Curricular Focus

The Carey Business School offers the M.B.A., a variety of specialized master's degrees, and several joint-degree programs with other distinguished Johns Hopkins schools. Most degrees are offered in flexible full-time, part-time, or Saturday formats. The Carey Business School also offers the M.B.A. Fellows Program, a project-based M.B.A. combining residencies and an online component, specifically designed for professionals in leadership positions whose schedules don't allow regular class time.

The Johns Hopkins M.B.A. features a broad-based, up-to-date curriculum that emphasizes the latest research and practical applications. It combines quantitative and qualitative approaches to give students a broader perspective and stronger set of skills attuned to the complex environment they face. Students also participate in an innovative ethics curriculum that spans the entire program and takes them beyond the traditional business school approaches.

Studying either full- or part-time, students first complete core courses that provide a thorough grounding in business theory and practice. They can then customize their path of study, choosing from ten concentration areas—accounting, competitive intelligence, finance, human resources, information security management, information technology, international business, management, marketing management, and nonprofit management. The program offers a wide array of electives, including courses unique to the Carey Business School. The final course of the program is the capstone—an innovative

exercise that gives students an opportunity to synthesize and apply the knowledge and skills acquired in prior courses to a real world situation.

Johns Hopkins Carey School offers M.B.A. degrees in life sciences, medical services management, and organization development (part-time only). Also offered are dual M.B.A./M.A. degrees in communication (full- and part-time) and government (full- and part-time) and M.B.A./M.S. degrees in biotechnology (part-time only) and information and telecommunication systems (full- and part-time, with a concentration in information systems). In addition, the dual M.B.A./Master of Public Health (M.P.H.) degree (full-time only) and the M.B.A./Master of Science in Nursing (M.S.N.) degree (full- and part-time) are offered.

Specialized Master of Science (M.S.) programs are available in information and telecommunications systems for business, marketing, and real estate. A Master of Science in Finance (M.S.F.) is also offered.

Johns Hopkins students benefit from the University's unique ability to attract practitioner faculty members from the top ranks of business, government, and nonprofit organizations located in the Philadelphia-Baltimore-Washington-Northern Virginia corridor. Along with Johns Hopkins' regular full-time faculty members, these experts offer students a depth and breadth of knowledge and experience that is unavailable in most parts of the country or at most universities.

Johns Hopkins University's history is a tradition of innovation. The Carey School's programs are similarly innovative—in content and delivery.

For example, the capstone experiences at the end of the M.B.A. program and the M.S. programs in marketing and in information and telecommunications systems are based on an interdisciplinary case from a business, nonprofit, or government organization. Along with a team of student colleagues, a student puts his or her talents to the test in a hands-on opportunity to address actual management challenges faced by a real-world organization. The team presents its findings to key executives in the organization and receives valuable feedback and experience in the process.

Students and the M.B.A. Experience

Of the total student body of 2,182, 399 students are full-time. The average student is 34 years old, and about 44 percent of the students are women.

The Faculty

The Carey School's blend of academic and practitioner faculty members provides a powerful learning climate for its students. The Carey School also calls on faculty members from other schools at Johns Hopkins University to offer students an even broader base of expertise. This rich environment provides a solid theoretical foundation in business and in the application of theory to relevant, timely issues. Approximately 200 part-time faculty members lend their expertise to 25 full-time faculty members.

The Business School Network

The relationships between the University and business, government, and nonprofit communities are important to the graduate business programs. Johns Hopkins has strong connections with many of the world's leading companies, consultancies, and governmental and nonprofit organizations.

The College and Environs

Johns Hopkins University was founded in Baltimore in 1876 and was the first American university dedicated to both advanced study and scientific research. There are nine academic divisions within the

University, including the top-ranked School of Medicine and the Bloomberg School of Public Health. In recent years, Johns Hopkins has won more federal research and development funding than any other university. The University has academic facilities at several campuses in Baltimore; Washington, D.C.; Howard and Montgomery Counties, Maryland; Nanjing, China; and Bologna, Italy.

Facilities

The University's main campus is situated on 140 beautiful acres in residential north Baltimore. The Carey Business School offers classes at four convenient locations in the Baltimore-Washington metropolitan area. The Downtown Center in Baltimore, located in the heart of Baltimore's historic financial district. The Columbia Center, just off I-95 in Howard County, is located midway between Baltimore and Washington. The Montgomery County Campus is located in Rockville in the I-270 information and biomedical technology corridor just north of the nation's capital. The Washington D.C. Center is located at the Johns Hopkins University complex on embassy row near Dupont Circle.

The Eisenhower Library and seven additional on-campus libraries make 2.8 million volumes, 3.8 million microforms, and more than 19,000 periodical subscriptions available to Hopkins' students.

Technology Environment

Johns Hopkins provides a full-service information technology environment to support its students' educational objectives. Complementing these resources are communications and networking services that provide remote access to the University's Eisenhower Library, e-mail, the Internet, online class registration and grade reports, and numerous specialized software packages and databases. Graduate business students have access to 275 on-campus PCs, although personal computers are required of all students.

Placement

The Career Services program provides assistance in all phases of career development, including self-assessment, career counseling and planning, career fairs, career decision-making, resume preparation, job search, an electronic job bank, resume referral, and career placement. Students and alumni also have access to Hopkins InCircle, the worldwide Hopkins Alumni Network.

Ninety-three percent of the class of 2006–07 were employed within three months of graduation.

Admission

To be considered for admission to an M.B.A. program, applicants must submit an online application, transcripts from all schools attended, two letters of recommendation, GMAT or GRE scores, professional resume/ curriculum vitae, personal essay, and the application fee. Since specific admission requirements vary by program, applicants should contact the Office of Admissions for details.

For the fall 2007 class, the Carey Business School received 826 applications. Of these applicants, 486 were admitted and 385 enrolled.

Though not required, a personal interview is recommended. Previous work experience is also highly recommended.

Finances

Though tuition and fees vary across programs and locations, the average cost for a part-time student is $720 per credit hour. Students should contact the Office of Admissions for complete, detailed information on costs and fees.

For 2007–08, 427 students received financial aid that included loans and scholarships. For further information about financial aid, students should contact Ms. Laura Donnelly, the Director of Financial Aid (Professional Schools Administration, 6740 Alexander Bell Drive, Suite 110, Columbia, Maryland 21046-2101; telephone: 410-516-9808; fax: 410-516-9799).

International Students

International students add an important dimension to Johns Hopkins programs. The University offers counseling and support services, visa services, and international student organizations.

International students can get additional information from Ms. Ann Roeder, the Director of International and Disability Services (10 North Charles Street, Baltimore, Maryland 21201; telephone: 410-516-9740; fax: 410-516-9748).

Application Facts and Dates

Students generally may begin their program of study in the fall or spring terms; applications are reviewed on a rolling basis. Applicants should submit completed applications at least ten weeks in advance to allow adequate time for review. For more information, students should contact the Office of Admissions. The application deadline for financial aid is June 1.

For international students, the application deadlines are May 1 (fall enrollment) and October 15 (spring enrollment). International students must submit TOEFL scores, proof of adequate funds, and proof of health/immunizations. Minimum TOEFL scores are 250 (computer-based test), 600 (paper-based test), or 100 (Internet-based test), and the test must have been taken within the last two years.

Ms. Sondra Smith
Carey Business School
Johns Hopkins University
100 North Charles Street
Baltimore, Maryland 21201

Phone: 410-516-4234
        877-88CAREY (toll-free)
Fax: 410-516-0826
E-mail: careyinfo@jhu.edu
Web site: http://www.carey.jhu.edu

Johnson & Wales University

> ### UNIVERSITY MISSION
> *The mission of Johnson & Wales University is to empower its diverse student body to succeed in today's dynamic world by integrating general education, professional skills, and career-focused education.*

Programs and Curricular Focus

The M.B.A. in Global Business Program of the Alan Shawn Feinstein Graduate School is driven by the theme "learning that gets results worldwide." Graduates apply the knowledge attained from the M.B.A. programs to their workplaces and throughout their careers. Core courses provide students with the fundamental concepts, analytical tools, and professional skills that industry requires in M.B.A. graduates.

In addition to achieving solid mastery of the basic knowledge and skills needed to be leaders in today's enterprises, all M.B.A. in Global Business students are given the opportunity to develop a special area of expertise in one of the following areas of concentration: marketing, financial management, international trade, organizational leadership, and accounting. Each concentration is designed in partnership with industry to ensure that graduates develop the specific advanced skills that employers are seeking in M.B.A. graduates.

The M.B.A. in Hospitality Program provides students with a similar core of management concepts. Added to this is a focus of hospitality-specific courses that are aimed at assisting managers in maximizing yield, refining strategies in the industry, and strengthening their skills as creative problem solvers and agents of change.

The Alan Shawn Feinstein Graduate School of Education offers an M.A.T. degree in teacher education, with dual certification in business/food service education and elementary education and special education.

Students and the M.B.A. Experience

The international reputation of the M.B.A. programs enables the Graduate School to recruit and carefully select a distinctly global student body. The graduate students at Johnson & Wales (J&W) represent diverse cultural, professional, and academic backgrounds. The average student is 28 years old, with four to eight years of work-related experience. The enrollment mix includes students from sixty-one countries, with women representing 46 percent of the enrollment population. The majority of American students come from the Northeast (72 percent). Another 46 percent of the graduate enrollment is composed of international students. Most of the students have undergraduate degrees in business, with many others having backgrounds in education, science, or liberal arts. Employers provide tuition reimbursement for 34 percent of American students, and 72 percent of American students are working while pursuing their graduate degrees.

Special Features

There are convenient afternoon and evening classes to accommodate most schedules, accelerated schedules that allow a student to graduate in less time, and three terms instead of semesters, allowing the student to complete more courses in less time. There is a diverse student population, representing sixty-two countries; a student-focused faculty with esteemed academic and professional experience; creative tuition-payment arrangements; specialized programs with career opportunities; and an outstanding career-placement department that offers lifetime placement services.

The Faculty

The Feinstein Graduate School faculty consists of individuals with excellent teaching skills who focus on professional development and provide a learning environment that encourages student participation. The faculty members are selected based on their academic achievements and professional experiences. They are devoted to preparing students for success in the workplace and go through extensive training on working with a diverse student population and staying informed on the latest technology. The graduate faculty members either hold terminal or professional degrees or are working toward these degrees.

The Business School Network
Corporate Partnerships

Johnson & Wales University is continuously expanding its relationship with corporate America. As University guests, local business leaders meet with students to discuss current business trends and developments. Brainstorming and problem-solving skills are sharpened as real-life situations are addressed. As the alumni base grows, many return and discuss how their course work applies to their daily routine.

Prominent Alumni

Johnson & Wales University prides itself on preparing men and women for leadership roles, often as entrepreneurs in business, industry, and education. Alumni hold top positions in a variety of businesses that range from finance to food. Some prominent alumni are Ira Kaplan, President, Servolift Eastern Corporation; Leonard Pinault, President, Foxboro National Bank; Joseph Damore, President, Food Systems IDBA, Inc.; Tracey Trosko, President, First National Network, Inc.; and William Francis, President, Marbil Enterprises, Inc.

The College and Environs

Johnson & Wales University's main campus is located in Providence, Rhode Island. Providence is New England's second-largest city, but it retains its historic charm in combination with the resources of a cultural, business, and industrial center. An hour from the city of Boston, Massachusetts, and less than 4 hours from New York City, Providence is also within easy reach of such well-known vacation spots as Newport, Rhode Island, and Cape Cod, Massachusetts.

A true city campus, Johnson & Wales's facilities are located throughout Providence, a city that provides students with a wide variety of cultural, educational, recreational, and social activities. Students enjoy the local restaurants and shops and are able to take advantage of a myriad of theater, music, and performance opportunities. From museums to sports events and Broadway shows to shopping, the city offers something for everyone.

Interstate buses and trains are near Johnson & Wales's downtown campus, and the T. F. Green Airport, served by most major U.S. airlines, is adjacent to the J&W's Radisson Airport Hotel in nearby Warwick, Rhode Island.

Technology Environment

Johnson & Wales University's three computer centers feature IBM-compatible com-

puters. In addition, translation software is available to convert Macintosh-based files for printing in the labs. All computers feature the MS Office suite and offer black-and-white and color printing.

Placement

The Career Development Office (CDO) of Johnson & Wales University provides assistance to graduate students as soon as they enroll. The CDO sponsors workshops on resume writing, company research, and interviewing, as well as guest speakers. A job hotline also provides postings of full- and part-time jobs on and off campus. Ninety-eight percent of Johnson & Wales students find work after college in their chosen field. Global companies, such as Walt Disney; hotel chains, such as Four Seasons, Marriott, and Hyatt; resorts, such as Canyon Ranch; casinos, such as Caesars Palace; and well-known companies, such as Abraham & Straus, have all hired Johnson & Wales students.

Admission

All applicants must submit a signed application, official college transcripts, and two letters of recommendation to the Feinstein Graduate Admissions Office. The Admissions Office also suggests that applicants submit a statement of purpose. In addition, all international students must submit a TOEFL score (unless they wish to be placed in the University's ESL program), a declaration of financial support, and a financial statement that supports the information given in the declaration of financial support.

Finances

Tuition for 2008–09 is $304 per quarter credit hour ($1368 per course). All master's programs are 54 to 76.5 quarter credits; each course is 4.5 quarter credits (3 semester credits are equal to 4.5 quarter credits). Books and supplies cost approximately $950 per year.

Although most graduate students choose to live in independent housing near the campus, limited room and board options are available for international graduate students at the University. The University estimates that living expenses for an academic year for a student living off campus are $8000. For more information about room and board, students should contact the Office of Residential Life (401-598-1132). For assistance and information regarding independent housing, students should contact Elaine Petronio at epetronio@jwu.edu.

International Students

The uniqueness of Johnson & Wales's Feinstein Graduate School attracts professionals and students from across the country and around the globe. Forty-six percent of the students attending the Graduate School are international students, representing sixty-two countries. The University offers international students courses in English as a second language, academic counseling, advice on Immigration and Naturalization Service rules, and assistance with off-campus housing. In addition, the University organizes an international ambassador program and supports international associations.

Application Facts and Dates

Applications are reviewed on a rolling admission basis. Once all application requirements are met, the Feinstein Graduate Admissions staff takes pride in processing the application materials in a timely manner. Enrollment is very limited, and applicants are encouraged to submit required documents at least eight weeks prior to the chosen start date for each of the fall, winter, spring, and summer terms. All twelve-month programs start in the fall term only. For more information, students should contact:

Graduate Admissions
Johnson & Wales University
8 Abbott Park Place
Providence, Rhode Island 02903

Phone: 401-598-1015
Fax: 401-598-1286
E-mail: admissions.grad@jwu.edu
Web site:
    http://www.jwu.edu/admiss/grad/

Keller Graduate School of Management

Master of Business Administration Program

Oakbrook Terrace, Illinois

DEVELOPING BUSINESS LEADERS FOR THE TWENTY-FIRST CENTURY

In today's rapidly changing business environment, managers' responsibilities are increasingly complex. Technological advances, increasing demographic diversity, and global competition have prompted an ever-growing need for highly skilled and adaptive managers in all fields.

At DeVry University's Keller Graduate School of Management, students participate in an M.B.A. curriculum that equips them with the very skills companies seek in order to meet ever-evolving business challenges. Our dynamic faculty of practicing business managers brings to the classroom a wealth of experience and years of proven success in the business world. As one of the nation's largest and most respected M.B.A. programs, designed for working professionals, Keller's curriculum provides a unique blend of management theories and concepts and helps students apply these to the realities of everyday business. The result? Better managers and more profitable businesses.

—Timothy H. Ricordati, Dean

Programs and Curricular Focus

Geared toward working adults, Keller's programs teach students to master the special skills and concepts businesses demand from today's management professionals. Graduates are able to blend management theory with real-world applications in a multitude of business settings.

Each Keller student receives a solid background in every important business discipline. The School also builds flexibility into that sturdy foundation by offering a wide range of electives. That way, students can customize their degrees to suit personal and professional interests.

The M.B.A. program requires successful completion of sixteen courses (3 semester-credit hours each). These include four management core, one quantitative, and five program-specific courses, including the culminating Business Planning Seminar. Also required are six electives, which may be chosen in accounting, educational management, human resources, finance, information security, information systems, general management, marketing, health services, network and communications management, e-commerce, international business, project management, public administration, and security management.

Other graduate degree programs offered at DeVry University's Keller Graduate School include the Master of Accounting and Financial Management, Master of Human Resource Management, Master of Project Management, Master of Information Systems Management, Master of Network and Com-

munications Management, and the Master of Public Administration.

Class hours are designed to accommodate work and family responsibilities. Classes are offered in eight-week sessions during each of three semesters per year. They meet once a week for 3½ hours, either on weekday evenings or Saturdays.

DeVry University offers graduate programs at more than seventy locations nationwide as well as online, enabling students to continue their education after job transfers, temporary assignments, or other relocations with the least possible disruption to their academic schedules.

For students who wish to complete their M.B.A. in less than 1½ years without disrupting their work week, the M.B.A. program is offered in an accelerated format on Saturdays. The curriculum requires successful completion of sixteen prescribed courses that provide a solid business management foundation in critical areas, such as leadership, information technology, project and change management, and new product development.

Students who prefer the Internet can complete graduate degree programs through DeVry University's Online Center (http://online.keller.edu). Students receive a solid education enhanced by the latest in interactive information technology (computer-mediated e-mail and threaded conversations, videotapes, and the Internet) that enables them to send and receive feedback from instructors as well as to participate in various group and team activities with fellow online students.

Distance learning courses demand the same dedicated student efforts as traditional classroom-based courses. Online students read course materials, write papers, conduct applied research, and take exams. Students have access to the same full range of support services they would receive if they were attending a traditional location.

Students and the M.B.A. Experience

Students attending Keller Graduate School are working adults who bring their diverse experiences to the classroom. They want, and insist on, useful and relevant instruction. Academic knowledge is meant to be practiced in real-world situations, and that "practitioner orientation" colors everything that is done at the School. Whatever their ultimate career goals, students come to Keller for flexible, personalized instruction that equips them for the challenges of a complex, competitive, and rapidly changing working environment.

The Faculty

Keller faculty members practice what they teach. They are working professionals who deal with cutting-edge business and management issues both inside and outside the classroom. They bring their expertise to the classroom, emphasizing theories, practices, and issues that most benefit students in the working world. When students learn from instructors who work in the field in which they teach, they get as close to real-world learning as possible.

The Business School Network

Keller's faculty consists of practicing business professionals—leaders in the corporate community as well as in the classroom. These professionals bring business contacts as well as hands-on knowledge and experience to graduate students.

Keller's faculty includes both part- and full-time instructors who are effective communicators, coaches, and mentors as well as practitioners with extensive management experience. Those who teach full-time commit most of their working hours to teaching and curricula development while remaining actively involved in business as consultants and participants in professional organizations. Part-time instructors are full-time managers whose teaching provides adult

students with vital professional enrichment and perspectives. All faculty members have developed contacts and relationships with a variety of academic and professional fields and geographic locations. The relationships students develop with these instructors often lead to mentoring arrangements, professional contacts, and even job offers.

The College and Environs

Keller Graduate School of Management was founded in 1973 on the idea that the most important components of management education are effective teaching and student mastery of practical management skills. Centers are located in major metropolitan areas and near accessible transportation routes, keeping commuting time to a minimum. There are one or more centers in each of the following states: Arizona, California, Colorado, Florida, Georgia, Illinois, Indiana, Maryland, Minnesota, Missouri, Nevada, New York, North Carolina,

Ohio, Oklahoma, Oregon, Pennsylvania, Tennessee, Texas, Utah, Virginia, Washington, and Wisconsin.

Facilities

A variety of accommodations are offered at multiple locations, and all provide comfortable areas in which to study, relax, and learn. Most centers include spacious classrooms in handy locations, vending areas, student lounges, and convenient hours for computer labs and information centers. The information centers offer Internet access to 300 databases, alternative texts, student study guides, career service materials, and periodicals.

Placement

Career Services helps management-level students and graduates acquire professional development skills and identify currently available career opportunities.

Admission

For regular admission, applicants must hold a baccalaureate degree from a U.S. institution accredited by, or in candidacy status with, a regional accrediting agency recognized by the U.S. Department of Education (international applicants must hold a degree equivalent to a U.S. baccalaureate degree); pass the Graduate Management Admission Test or the Graduate Record Examinations or Keller's alternative admission test; complete a personal interview with an admissions representative; and complete a written application.

Applicants with postbaccalaureate degrees from accredited graduate schools must complete an application and an interview as well as document their degree. An admissions test is not required for these applicants.

Finances

At current rates, tuition per course (3 semester credit hours) differs by state, ranging from $1845 to $2100 per course. After acceptance, new students pay a $100 deposit, which is credited toward the first term's tuition. Tuition is payable in full at registration or in installments of two or three payments (with small handling fees for the latter two choices). Books and materials average $175 per course.

Application Facts and Dates

Students may begin their program in either of two 8-week sessions offered each semester. There are three full semesters each year beginning in July, November, and March. There is no application fee. For more information, students should contact:

DeVry University
Keller Graduate School of Management
One Tower Lane, 9th Floor
Oakbrook Terrace, Illinois 60181

Phone: 630-571-1960
Web site: http://www.keller.edu

Lake Forest
Graduate School of Management

Chicago, Schaumburg, and Lake Forest, Illinois

LAKE FOREST M.B.A.—BROAD THINKERS. STRONG LEADERS.

If your professional goals include advancing your career through a richer understanding of the key areas of business, I invite you to consider the benefits of an M.B.A. from Lake Forest Graduate School of Management (LFGSM).

Before I introduce you to the Lake Forest M.B.A., allow me to share some insights I often provide when asked how a person can find the right M.B.A. program. My recommendation is that you evaluate the following criteria: what you will be learning, the credentials and experience of the people teaching, the quality and experience of the classmates you will be collaborating with, and whether the School feels like the right fit for you.

At LFGSM, we've created an M.B.A. program that truly delivers on the needs of today's experienced, working professionals. The combined strengths of our curriculum, faculty, students, and administration are what set us apart in Chicago's M.B.A. community.

Our general management curriculum equips you with broad-based business competencies to maximize your managerial flexibility and advance your career. Our 100-percent-business-leader faculty facilitates your learning process and your understanding of what really works in business today. Our students are serious about their careers and their education and are valuable team members on your group projects and worthy contributors in classroom discussions. Our administration values the personal touch and is responsive to your needs as a working professional. Our program is designed with your busy lifestyle in mind, incorporating leading-edge technology to enhance your learning experience and provide scheduling flexibility.

I hope that the insights above, combined with the information provided in the remainder of this profile, are helpful to you in determining your personal selection criteria and making the right decision regarding your M.B.A.

—Arlene Mayzel, Vice President & Dean–Degree Programs

Programs and Curricular Focus

The courses in the Lake Forest M.B.A. curriculum are designed to build upon one another, gradually increasing each student's skills and confidence while deepening their understanding of the relationships among disciplines. Timeless management principles are the foundation of the program, but the courses are continually refined to reflect current business issues and practices. Courses that expose students to functional areas outside their own are designed to broaden their thinking. Courses that explore change management, leadership styles, ethical business decisions, diversity, and strategic management develop them into the kind of strong leader who gets noticed and gets results.

Recognizing the increasingly important challenges in global business, the Lake Forest M.B.A. provides opportunities to study international management abroad. Within the general management M.B.A. curriculum are elective courses featuring challenging, on-site project work for actual businesses in the region. Courses are offered in Asia, Europe, and Latin America.

Lake Forest M.B.A. courses are created with specific learning outcomes to facilitate students' introduction, development, and measured competence in critical learning areas. The learning outcomes for each course are listed in full at the Lake Forest M.B.A. Web site. Degrees can be completed in two, three, or four years. Because the program is geared for experienced working professionals, all classes are held in the evening and on Saturday. Successful completion of sixteen course units is required to obtain the degree.

LFGSM also offers specializations in international management, organizational behavior, and health-care management. LFGSM and the Chicago School of Professional Psychology offer a dual-degree program for students pursuing both the M.B.A. and the Master of Arts (M.A.) in organizational and industrial psychology. Students should consult an LFGSM program catalog for full details.

Students and the M.B.A. Experience

LFGSM students are working professionals who bring an average of thirteen years' work experience to the classroom. All are employed full-time, and participants must live and work in the Chicago area. Thirty-six percent of the students are women. The average student is 37 years old, and 74 percent have nonbusiness undergraduate degrees. Their diverse backgrounds might come as a surprise. A typical class can include IT professionals, entrepreneurs, financial analysts, human resources managers, engineers, sales professionals, and scientists. They come to class ready

and willing to share their practical experience and past successes. A profile of the 2007 entering class is listed on page 5 of the Lake Forest catalog, which is available on the Web site at http://www.LakeForestMBA.edu.

LFGSM takes a proven, pragmatic approach to business education, called Leadership Learning®. This three-point approach to management education can be described as "preparation with purpose." It readies students for greater workplace success through developing competence in critical disciplines; providing the confidence to use the related skills, tools, and knowledge in the workplace; and, therefore, creating the ability to make significant contributions to their organizations. Students use the interactive, creative, and challenging environment at LFGSM as their "practice field" for success in their career.

LFGSM is an independent, not-for-profit business school, solely focused on creating more effective business leaders. Educating working professionals and facilitating students' transitions back to the classroom is LFGSM's specialty. At LFGSM, the work is hard, but the experience of working with LFGSM is not.

The Faculty

Lake Forest courses are led by a 100-percent-practitioner faculty of business leaders and successful professionals, many of whom are entrusted with major P&L responsibility. They bring

—Arlene Mayzel, Vice President and Dean– Degree Programs, Lake Forest Graduate School of Management

The Lake Forest M.B.A. program is taught by a faculty of more than 150 business leaders, like Iwona Bochenska, International Trade Specialist, Office of Trade and Investment, State of Illinois. Faculty members have an average of twenty-seven years of professional experiences and pride themselves in providing a practical business education.

experience that can only come from making real decisions that affect real companies.

Theories are supported by real business examples and contemporary applications. This means that the students get their business education from business leaders, not from teaching assistants or research-focused professors.

LFGSM faculty members represent a wide variety of organizations, industries, and functions and have a wide range of job titles, such as Partner, Vice President, Director, Consultant, and CEO. Lake Forest faculty members have extensive practical experience in the subject areas they teach and are uniquely qualified to deliver compelling, contemporary course content. They have in common a strong desire to share their knowledge, facilitate learning, and help students achieve measurable success. Most of all, they're at Lake Forest because they love to teach.

The Business School Network
LFGSM was founded in 1946 as a partnership between business and education and has maintained its strong ties to the business community since then. More than 7,200 alumni, 832 students, and 150 faculty members work for Chicago's finest companies, including Abbott Laboratories; Allstate Corporation; Baxter Healthcare; Blue Cross Blue Shield; CDW; Federal Reserve Bank of Chicago; HSBC; Motorola, Inc.; and Grainger.

The Board of Directors of Lake Forest Graduate School of Management comprises top management executives from major Chicago-area businesses and organizations. This active board provides governance and guidance over LFGSM's policymaking, strategic planning, and growth initiatives.

LFGSM's executive training business, Lake Forest Corporate Education (LFCE), further strengthens the School's ties to the business community. LFCE builds critical management skills through targeted training programs that deliver measurable business results. Clients include Ace Hardware Corporation, Allstate Insurance, Brunswick, Federal Reserve Bank of Chicago, HSBC, Peoples Energy, Symantec, Walgreens, and WMS Gaming.

The School and Environs
Lake Forest Graduate School of Management offers full programs at three campus locations in the Chicago area: downtown Chicago, Schaumburg, and Lake Forest.

The downtown Chicago campus is located in the Federal Reserve Bank Building, in the heart of Chicago's financial district. The Schaumburg campus is located in the Galvin Center at Motorola, Inc., in the northwest suburbs, just 25 miles (30 minutes) northwest of Chicago. The Lake Forest campus is only 30 minutes north of downtown Chicago in Lake Forest's Conway Park.

In addition to the three campuses, classes are also offered on-site at several local corporations and at locations in Grayslake and Glenview.

Facilities
All LFGSM campuses are modern facilities in thriving corporate environments. In addition to multimedia classrooms, facilities provide dedicated space for student study groups, dining, and computer access.

Technology Environment
LFGSM's courses use a Web-based course-management system, Blackboard, to complement the in-person classroom experience and learning. All Lake Forest M.B.A. students are required to have unlimited access to at least a Pentium-class personal computer with broadband or DSL Internet access, a CD-ROM drive, and e-mail. All specialized software needed for course work is provided to students.

LFGSM provides access to the Electric Library from student computers located at each of the three campuses and remotely via the Internet. The Electric Library has content from six sources, totaling millions of documents: reference books, magazines, newspapers, TV/radio transcripts, maps, and photographs. The resources are updated daily. The library features a powerful, easy-to-use search engine with online help.

Each campus is located near additional reference resources, including the Harold Washington Library Center in Chicago, the Schaumburg Township District Library, and the North Suburban Library Consortium.

Placement
Lake Forest M.B.A. students are full-time working professionals, but they can receive assistance with career management and planning through LFGSM's online Career Management Center, offered in partnership with global outplacement leader Drake Beam Morin.

Admission
The general M.B.A. program has three start dates, in August, February, and April of each school year. Applications are accepted on a rolling basis. To be considered for admission, LFGSM requires a bachelor's degree, undergraduate transcripts, GMAT test scores, an interview with an admissions counselor, a minimum of four years of professional work experience, and two letters of recommendation. No prerequisite courses are needed for the Lake Forest M.B.A. program, regardless of the applicant's undergraduate degree.

LFGSM values the professional work experience students bring to the classroom. Students may be eligible for a standardized test waiver based on significant years of professional work experience, an earned graduate degree, and, in some cases, their cumulative undergraduate GPA.

While undergraduate grades and entrance exam scores are a factor, LFGSM also places a great emphasis on the student's current professional work experience and achievements. Given the collaborative and interactive nature of the Lake Forest M.B.A. learning experience, the admissions department looks for a student's ability to contribute to classroom discussions of contemporary business challenges. Applicants must demonstrate communication and leadership skills, as well as the ability to work productively as part of a team.

Finances
Tuition for the 2007–08 academic year was $2585 per course. A majority of LFGSM students receive tuition reimbursement from their employers.

For the most complete information about scholarships, loans, and veterans' benefits, students should visit the Lake Forest M.B.A. Web site or call the Alternative Financing Coordinator, Terry Hamlin, at 847-574-5184.

Application Facts and Dates

There are four 10-week terms per year and three start dates for new students—late August, early February, and mid-April. Applicants are encouraged to begin the admissions process a minimum of six weeks prior to start dates. Each start date for new students begins with a stimulating one-day (Saturday) Kickoff, where deans and faculty members lead interactive workshops focusing on group dynamics, team building, and assessment of personal skills. The day provides a great opportunity for students to become acquainted and prepares them to begin graduate studies. Books and materials for classes are given out at the end of Kickoff.

Downtown Chicago Campus
230 South La Salle Street
Chicago, Illinois 60604

Phone: 312-435-5330
Fax: 312-435-5333
E-mail: admissionsinfo@lfgsm.edu
Web site: http://www.LakeForestMBA.edu

Lake Forest Campus
1905 West Field Court
Lake Forest, Illinois 60604

Phone: 847-234-5005
Fax: 847-295-3656
E-mail: admissionsinfo@lfgsm.edu
Web site: http://www.LakeForestMBA.edu

Schaumburg Campus
1295 East Algonquin Road
Schaumburg, Illinois 60604

Phone: 847-576-1212
Fax: 847-576-1213
E-mail: admissionsinfo@lfgsm.edu
Web site: http://www.LakeForestMBA.edu

Lawrence Technological University

Southfield, Michigan

DEVELOPING TOMORROW'S LEADERS TODAY

The College of Management at Lawrence Tech is committed to improving the quality of life tomorrow by developing the managerial and leadership skills of students today. Its distinctive management programs are aligned with the college's mission to help maximize students' human potential and create a more humane, sustainable world community led by global thinkers and leaders. The linkage of theory and practice has always been a core value, and one of the College's primary strengths is the ability to respond quickly to the ever-changing needs of students and the business community. Since 1998, the College of Management has consistently ranked among the nation's highest in student satisfaction surveys.

—Louis A. DeGennaro, Dean

Programs and Curricular Focus

Melding theory and practice with the creation of real-world workshops is the primary focus of the college's graduate programs. Lawrence Tech's accredited graduate programs, conveniently offered during the day, in the evenings, and on weekends, were developed with input from industry advisory boards to provide students with the practical tools needed to succeed in a competitive environment.

Lawrence Tech's 36-credit Master of Business Administration (M.B.A.) program consists of nine core classes and three electives. Students can select one of seven areas of concentration to help expand their experiences and meet future goals: finance, global leadership and management, human resources, management information systems, nonprofit management, operations management, and project management. The Lawrence Tech M.B.A. can be obtained in as few as two years of day, evening, weekend, and/or online study.

Tomorrow's leaders must be prepared to meet the challenges of the twenty-first century, which include global competition and advanced technology. Lawrence Tech's Master of Business Administration/Global Leadership and Management (M.B.A./GLM) is a dual degree designed to prepare managers in global organizations for senior-level positions by deepening their knowledge of the global economy and the diverse societies that make up today's world. The program consists of core courses from the M.B.A. program and the GLM program. Upon completion, students receive two master's degrees, one in business administration and the other in global leadership and management. The College of Management also offers dual-degree programs in M.B.A./Engineering Man-

agement, M.B.A./Information Systems, and M.B.A./Operations Management.

Developed for mid-level managers who work or aspire to work in organizations that operate across national boundaries, the Master of Business Administration International (MBAI) is a 20-month program with classes meeting on alternating weekends. The curriculum consists of 36 credit hours of course work organized into twelve modules, each consisting of a core business component delivered in workshops, seminars, exercises, case analyses, and other forms of instruction. Designed to provide students with access to executives of global companies, governmental officials, internationally recognized faculty members, and other experts, Lawrence Tech's MBAI also includes international travel.

Information technology is a key enabler for economic growth and organizational re-engineering. The Master of Science in Information Systems (M.S.I.S.) program is designed to prepare students for leadership roles with both technical and managerial course work. Students enter the M.S.I.S. program with a background in the foundations of business, management information systems, and programming. Students acquire a core set of business and technology skills with courses that include leading organizational change, project management, database models, analysis and design, and telecommunications. Students take a minimum of three courses to specialize in one of these concentrations: enterprise resource planning, enterprise security management, or project management. Students finish their core studies with a capstone course designed to integrate their learning experience. An evening program, the M.S.I.S. requires 30 credit hours for graduation.

The Master of Science in Operations Management (M.S.O.M.) is a unique program that combines real-life learning with a strong theo-

retical base in operations and high-level management. Designed for working professionals seeking to enhance their abilities in the management of capital and human resources, the M.S.O.M. can be completed in as few as eighteen months. The curriculum consists of 30 hours of course work, including 21 hours of core courses and 9 hours of electives in manufacturing operations, service operations, or project management. The M.S.O.M., offered in the evenings and on Saturdays, prepares students for management positions with consulting firms, start-up companies, or large-scale construction projects.

Lawrence Tech's Doctor of Business Administration (D.B.A.) program is unique because it is one of the nation's few on-campus, part-time, practitioner/scholar-focused programs designed for the working professional. The program is appropriate for those interested in broadening and deepening their leadership skills for executive-level positions in industry and consulting or for those seeking faculty positions at universities that emphasize theory and practice. The curriculum consists of 36 hours of course work and 24 equivalent hours of research toward a doctoral dissertation and can be completed within four years. Course work falls in two categories, namely the D.B.A. core and research. Research toward a dissertation is conducted on a topic within one of the following three areas: leadership and organization development, business economics and finance, and international business.

Lawrence Tech's Doctor of Management in Information Technology (D.M.I.T.) program is the only program in the region for the practitioner/scholar. Intensive and part-time, the D.M.I.T. is designed specifically for working professionals with high levels of experience and expertise in management and technology, who possess strong analytical skills and a desire to make a contribution to the field. The D.M.I.T. program consists of 36 credit hours of course work, including a tailored specialization of 9 credit hours and 24 credit hours of dissertation course work.

Students and the M.B.A. Experience

More than 800 graduate students a year pursue degrees through Lawrence Tech's College of Management. The average length of work experience is more than seven years. Approximately 36 percent of students are women. The College offers graduate degree

programs throughout the state in Southfield, Detroit, Clinton Township, Auburn Hills, Livonia, Warren, Traverse City, and Petoskey as well as onsite in a number of companies. Programs are also delivered in Canada and Asia.

The Faculty

Lawrence Tech faculty members are dedicated to providing students with a high-quality education and practical career preparation. Their emphasis is on what works and what is around the corner. All of Lawrence Tech's full-time graduate faculty members (and most of the adjunct faculty members) have terminal degrees in specialized areas. In addition to academic preparation from leading universities throughout the world, faculty members have managerial and executive experience. Many have published and received recognition for research and consulting. Most importantly, the faculty members understand what works in practice as well as in theory. Smaller classes mean more individualized attention, and each student has a personal faculty adviser to help make curriculum decisions and address any concerns.

The Business School Network

The University is situated in proximity to some of the world's leading industrial, technological, business, and scientific enterprises. More than 200 Fortune 500 corporations have their headquarters or major operations within a half hour of the campus. The American Society of Employers ranks Lawrence Tech first in its class as a preferred provider of graduates to southeast Michigan. Standard & Poor's also ranks Lawrence Tech in the top one third of all colleges and universities providing the leaders of America's most successful businesses.

The College and Environs

The College of Management is headquartered in the Wayne H. Buell Management Building. Convenient for students due to its location at the heart of campus, this building includes classrooms, faculty and departmental offices, computer labs, the University library, dining commons, and the bookstore. University housing (apartment-style living) can accommodate up to 600 students. Abundant free parking is available in paved, lighted, and patrolled campus lots. Lawrence Tech's modern 102-acre campus is situated on the northwest corner of the intersection of West Ten Mile Road and Northwestern Highway/Lodge Freeway (M-10), less than a half mile south of I-696 and easily accessible from other major freeways.

Facilities

Course work relies heavily on computers. Lawrence Tech, Michigan's first wireless laptop campus, provides all undergraduates laptop or tablet computers. Graduate students can opt to participate in this program. Students also have ready access to PCs and the College's state-of-the-art computer lab. Many students find it convenient to work on campus or log on from home or work.

Placement

More than 95 percent of graduate students hold a full-time job while attending school. The Office of Career Services facilitates the job search process by assisting students and alumni in their search for employment. Services include on-campus interviews and job postings through the electronic job board. In addition, counseling is available for a variety of career development needs, including job-search strategies and interviewing skills. An online resume service is provided for students who choose to register with the office.

Admission

Students can start their degree programs in September, January, or May, except for the Master of Business Administration International and doctoral programs (students should visit the Web site for start dates and admission requirements). Applicants to graduate degree programs are expected to be working or to have work experience. Lawrence Tech requires transcripts sent directly from all colleges or universities attended, and applicants must have a baccalaureate degree or the equivalent. Lawrence Tech also requires one of the following: a GPA of 3.0 or higher in the student's last 60 credit hours of undergraduate work or a master's degree from an accredited institution.

Satisfactory completion of courses fundamental to the selected graduate degree program also may be required. Complete information on admission procedures is available from the University's Office of Admissions (telephone: 800-CALL-LTU, Ext. 1, toll-free). Students may also transfer into the program from another accredited program. If previous graduate course work is similar in content to that offered at Lawrence Tech, up to 12 semester hours of graduate credit may transfer in the M.B.A. program and 9 in the M.S.I.S. and M.S.O.M. programs.

Finances

The 2007–08 tuition rate for a graduate business course was $710 per credit hour. For 2008–09 tuition rates, students should visit the Web site. The registration fee for each term is $115. Students interested in financial aid should contact the Office of Financial Aid at 248-204-2120.

Application Facts and Dates

The application deadlines are August 15 for fall, January 4 for spring, and May 1 for summer. International students must submit their application two months prior to the start of the semester. For more information, students should contact:

College of Management
Lawrence Technological University
21000 West Ten Mile Road
Southfield, Michigan 48075-1058

Phone: 248-204-3050
        800-CALL-LTU Ext. 74
        (toll-free)
E-mail: mgtdean@ltu.edu
Web site: http://www.ltu.edu

Lehigh University

PARTNERING WITH THE BEST

Today's business requirements are rapidly changing. For more than fifty years, Lehigh's M.B.A. program has anticipated and adapted to meet those needs. The College of Business and Economics continues to develop degrees that reflect a complex business landscape. Our innovative joint-degree programs and market-driven certificate programs give students the added flexibility to create a niche in their companies. Our curriculum is continually reviewed, renewed, and refreshed to increase the integration and richness of educational options. We take well-established, highly reputed programs and combine the elements necessary to meet the demands of business in the twenty-first century. We continue to evaluate business needs and respond with innovative programs. We refuse to stand still. Business does not.

Our programs are cutting edge. Supported by research that is theoretically relevant, but also managerially useful, courses are taught by a superb faculty with extensive research and industry experience. Faculty members are experts in their fields. Just as we add new programs to address business requirements, we also continue to add faculty members that bring valuable expertise to all of our M.B.A. offerings. Experienced faculty is important.

Lehigh's M.B.A. program has earned and maintained AACSB accreditation for more than forty years. It is an important distinction, of which we are proud.

If innovation, a highly credentialed faculty, AACSB accreditation and market-driven programs are important considerations in your selection process for an M.B.A. program—Lehigh is a perfect fit. I invite you to join us.

—Paul R. Brown, Dean

Programs and Curricular Focus

Lehigh's M.B.A. program focuses on the impact of business strategies, challenges, and solutions on all areas of the company. These issues, taught from the perspective of the firm as a whole, are addressed through an integrated core curriculum team taught by faculty members from multiple areas of expertise.

The 36-credit-hour M.B.A. program begins with a two-day orientation in which teaming, negotiation, and global issues are addressed. Flexibly formatted, the M.B.A. can be pursued either part-time or full-time, both on campus and via satellite, through Lehigh's corporate partner companies and public sites. Six core courses emphasize strategic decision making required across multiple disciplines and functions and stress leadership and ethical practices in the business environment. The capstone course uses a business simulation that requires students to analyze and compare a real company against a fictional one, thus providing the opportunity to apply the body of knowledge acquired in the core.

Both on campus and via satellite, the compact and integrated nature of the core curriculum offers increased flexibility for tailoring the program to fit individual career goals. On-campus students may select a concentration in corporate entrepreneurship, finance, international business, marketing, and supply chain management. M.B.A. students may also simultaneously pursue certificates in corporate entrepreneurship, project management, and supply chain management.

Lehigh students bring a rich depth of experience in a variety of industries and disciplines into the classroom. Students have an average of seven years of work experience, and 25 percent have master's degrees or doctorates in areas other than business. Class discussions encourage students to share their experiences, broadening their knowledge base by exposure to a variety of practices within business and industry.

Lehigh's M.B.A. program has been accredited by AACSB International–The Association to Advance Collegiate Schools of Business for more than forty years and provides the cornerstone for career advancement.

Students and the M.B.A. Experience

Lehigh's College of Business and Economics enrolls approximately 350 students in its graduate degree programs. They come from a variety of academic and professional backgrounds and bring a wide range of qualities to the program.

Thirty percent of M.B.A. students come from undergraduate backgrounds in business and economics, 61 percent from engineering and applied science, and 9 percent from liberal arts. Women comprise about 29 percent of the M.B.A. population.

Eighty-five percent of Lehigh M.B.A. students attend classes part-time and are an important part of the learning environment. Their business experience and sense of purpose enhance the educational experience of all students.

Special Features

Anticipating the diverse needs of business and industry, Lehigh's College of Business and Economics offers two joint degrees with the M.B.A. program: the M.B.A. and Engineering and the M.B.A. and Educational Leadership. Featuring a core curriculum in each of the disciplines, these degrees combine business skills with the skills needed to excel in their respective fields.

The MBA*Plus* program gives Lehigh's M.B.A. graduates the opportunity to enroll in current courses at less than one third of the regular cost. Graduates gain ongoing, cost-effective access to courses that can enhance their professional development and advance their careers; they are able to keep current in their fields and acquire new skills.

The Faculty

Lehigh University's College of Business and Economics faculty members are experts in their fields and are regularly called upon by national and international media for commentary on business trends and events. Ninety-nine percent of the College's full-time faculty members hold doctorates and have researched and published extensively in their fields, and many have coauthored textbooks used internationally.

Aside from being experts in their fields, the M.B.A. core faculty members bring extensive practical experience from industry into the classroom. Coupled with Professors of Practice whose unique blend of theory and practical knowledge enhance the learning experience, Lehigh's M.B.A. faculty offers relevant real-world solutions to today's business challenges.

Faculty members play an important role in the educational and research activities of

Rauch Business Center.

interdisciplinary centers and institutes both inside and outside of Lehigh, ensuring students receive exposure to the latest information. Students are also exposed to the applications experience of carefully chosen business practitioners.

The Iacocca Institute, Value Chain Institute, Small Business Development Center (SBDC), and six other centers complement the activities of its academic departments. They host conferences such as the annual Pharmaceutical Conference and the Martindale Centers Speakers on global economic conditions and visiting experts, sponsor faculty and student research, and provide services to business firms and the educational community.

The Business School Network

Lehigh maintains extensive relationships with the corporate community. The Board of Advisors consists of highly accomplished business leaders who are active in committees on curriculum, alumni relations, and distance learning, providing a direct link between the College of Business and Economics and the business world. Members are among the visiting executives who interact with students in conferences, major lectures, classroom sessions, and informal discussions.

Lehigh's distance learning initiative enables employees of its partners to complete a Lehigh M.B.A. while taking their classes at the corporate site via satellite. These students interact with the class on campus through voice communication, a computer message center, fax, and interactive white boards.

The Small Business Development Center provides opportunities for students to serve as business analysts, providing consulting services for small and medium-sized businesses in northeast Pennsylvania. M.B.A. students also may complete field projects with SBDC's clients and the International Trade Development Program.

The College and Environs

Lehigh University, founded in 1865, consists of three distinctive, contiguous areas totaling more than 1,600 acres. Located 90 miles southwest of New York City and 50 miles north of Philadelphia, the Lehigh Valley is Pennsylvania's fourth-largest metropolitan area. Bethlehem, one of three principal cities of the Lehigh Valley, is a center of industry, high technology, culture, and education.

Facilities

A state-of-the-art, wireless Financial Services Laboratory allows students to experience the financial markets in a real-time environment. Equipped with laptops, this twenty-seven-seat classroom is designed to simulate a Wall Street trading environment for application towards the financial services industry.

The Rauch Business Center, headquarters of the College of Business and Economics, is a modern, dynamic, professional environment for learning and teaching. There are forty well-equipped classrooms, computer labs, an auditorium, and conference rooms with advanced computing and audiovisual capabilities. The Clayton Conference Center wing has excellent facilities for executive education programs, conferences, seminars, and other special programs.

Technology Environment

Along with books and journals, Lehigh's library system includes electronic databases and microfilm, computer software, and media collections. Via the campus-wide integrated voice and data communication network, users can access the Internet, the libraries' online catalog, and hundreds of national and international electronic databases and can submit reference inquiries, place orders, request media services, and request delivery of documents electronically.

The campus network provides access to mainframe computers, the Integrated Library System, and other computers on campus. The Computing Center houses several mainframes and maintains hundreds of microcomputers in sites across the campus.

Placement

Lehigh's Career Services Office offers a variety of career-enhancing services from resume polishing to seminars and networking events designed to provide M.B.A. students (both full- and part-time) with exclusive access to prominent industry executives. Electronic databases and resume delivery systems are available to students and potential employers to facilitate on- and off-campus recruiting.

The Lehigh University Career Advisory Network is a group of more than 800 alumni volunteers. These individuals have agreed to act as advisers to current students, graduate students, and alumni seeking information about career paths and specific industries. A wide variety of corporations and government agencies recruit M.B.A. students through on-campus interviews, which are conducted in the fall and spring. Career prospects for graduates of Lehigh's graduate management programs are excellent. The Office of Career Services offers a full range of services to support students' career search efforts.

Admission

Candidates must have completed four years in an undergraduate program at an accredited college or university and have at least two years of full-time, professional work experience. International students must have sixteen years of formal education, including four years at the university level. A TOEFL score is required of all applicants for whom English is not the native language. The credentials evaluated by the faculty admission committee include the candidate's undergraduate background, GMAT scores, personal essay, letters of recommendation, and relevant professional work experience.

Finances

Tuition charges for the 2008–09 academic year are $700 per credit hour. On-campus housing costs range from $485 to $640 per month. Off-campus listings are available through the Department of Residential Services.

Several types of financial aid are available, including M.B.A. scholarships, teaching assistantships (which cover tuition and pay a stipend for the academic year), and business analyst posts in the Small Business Development Center. Those wishing to be considered for financial aid should submit all application materials, including GMAT scores, by January 15 for the upcoming academic year.

Application Facts and Dates

Lehigh evaluates applications on a rolling basis and usually notifies applicants of admission decisions within three weeks of receiving a completed application. Deadlines for regular students are July 15 for fall semester, December 1 for spring semester, April 30 for summer session I, and June 15 for summer session II. Associate students may apply up to two weeks before classes begin in any semester or summer session. For more information, students should contact:

Director of Recruitment and Admissions
College of Business and Economics
Lehigh University
621 Taylor Street
Bethlehem, Pennsylvania 18015
Phone: 610-758-3418
Fax: 610-758-5283
E-mail: mba.admissions@lehigh.edu
Web site: http://www.lehigh.edu/mba

McGill University

Desautels Faculty of Management

Montreal, Quebec, Canada

REINVENT: YOURSELF, YOUR IDEAS, YOUR FUTURE

At the Desautels Faculty of Management, we have a successful tradition of innovative teaching and research and work closely with members of Montreal's business community to incorporate industry practices into the learning process. Known for the diversity and global outlook of our students and professors, the Faculty prepares graduates to assume leadership positions with dynamic organizations anywhere in the world. We have redesigned the M.B.A. program for a planned launch in the 2008–09 academic year in order to maintain our position as one of the top 100 business schools globally.

— Peter Todd, Dean and Professor

The McGill M.B.A. learning experience is fun, challenging, and engaging. It provides amazing opportunities to work collaboratively with a truly international group of fellow students. The program allows students to connect with business leaders in a variety of industries and also offers the opportunity to participate in many clubs and other activities. Through McGill's affiliations with top schools in Asia, Europe, and Latin America, M.B.A. students at the Desautels Faculty of Management can study overseas and develop new insight into other cultures while increasing their professional network at a global level.

— Andrea Wolfson, President, M.B.A. Students Association

Programs and Curricular Focus

The McGill M.B.A. is an internationally renowned graduate business program designed to provide students with a comprehensive understanding of the concepts of business, specialized knowledge in their chosen field, and the international perspective needed to meet the challenges of today's complex business environment.

Building on traditional strengths in functional areas, the McGill M.B.A. program takes the learning experience one step further. Not only are students provided with a strong grounding in the basic business disciplines, they are also provided with the intangible skills explicitly sought by employers today—the ability to apply their knowledge for the greatest benefit to the organization, to make effective decisions, to both work in teams and lead others, and to adapt to nonstructured situations.

In September 2008, McGill is launching a redesigned M.B.A. program. The twenty-month program will feature a fully integrated and shortened core curriculum. Some students will be invited to attend preparatory modules to refresh their quantitative skills; these modules will be held during the last three weeks of August each year, immediately prior to the start of the program. Beginning in the second semester, students are free to choose from four streams, thus tailoring their studies to meet their specific career goals and interests. Choosing from more than forty elective courses, students pursue in-depth study in one of the following four areas: finance, global leadership, marketing, or technological innovation, operations and information management. To complete their McGill M.B.A. degree, students then have the

option of participating in an international exchange or an internship or completing a practicum.

Students may complete the program on either a full-time or part-time basis. An accelerated study option is also available for those who have completed an undergraduate degree in business in North America. The accelerated option allows students to complete a 45-credit program as opposed to the usual 51 credit program.

Students and the M.B.A. Experience

Students typically hail from every corner of the globe, come from a wide variety of cultures and backgrounds, and possess highly diversified educational and work-related experience. Students also share a number of common characteristics—intelligence, inquisitiveness, an openness to learning and embracing new ideas, and a high degree of motivation.

Of the 70 full-time students in the 2007–08 incoming class, the average age was 28 and the ratio of women to men was 1:1. Students came from fourteen different countries, with 54 percent having English as their mother tongue, 14 percent having French, and 32 percent another language. Students also came from a cross section of universities, with 40 percent from institutions located outside of Canada. Twelve percent of the total was American, and a quarter came from Canadian universities outside of Quebec. Of the M.B.A. students in the 2007–08 incoming class, 19 percent held a B.A., 23 percent a B.Sc., 23 percent a B.Eng., and 35 percent a B.Com./B.B.A.

M.B.A. activities, such as the CEO Speakers Series, the Management Graduate Business Conference, and the M.B.A. Business Luncheon, put students in direct contact with leading businesspeople. For those who enjoy the thrill of competition, Case Competitions match student's case-

M.B.A. CURRICULUM (as of September 2008)		
Pre-work	**CORE Semester**	**Streams (choice of):**
Statistics	Global Leadership	1) Finance
Math for Finance	Business Tools	2) Global Leadership
Financial Accounting Basics	Managing Resources	3) Marketing
	Value Creation	4) Technological Innovation,
	Markets and Globalization	Operations and Information Management

analysis skills against those of other M.B.A. programs. Students also participate in the annual rugby and soccer matches and the Investment Fund Challenge.

Special Features

McGill is world renowned as a leader in international management education. All students acquire an inherent understanding of international commerce and an appreciation for other cultures in McGill's multicultural learning environment, and those interested in international business enjoy exceptional opportunities to network and acquire experience.

McGill M.B.A. students can further expand on the international experiences provided through the program by participating in the Faculty's international student exchange program. Students earn academic credit while studying at one of thirty-one world-class universities located in the Americas, Asia, Europe, and Australia.

Through the many cross-disciplinary and joint-degree programs offered with the M.B.A. program, students have the opportunity to gain specialized knowledge in today's leading fields and benefit greatly from the contact and interaction they have with others attracted to these programs. Programs offered include the Master in Manufacturing Management (M.M.M.), management and medicine (M.B.A./M.D.), and management and law (M.B.A./Law).

The Faculty

The Desautels Faculty of Management has an eclectic team of international faculty members who enjoy the challenges that the M.B.A. program affords them. They represent fifteen nationalities and have all lived, studied, and worked in countries around the world. They bring direct experience of business practices in other countries to the classroom, and many have proven themselves to be in the forefront of research in cross-cultural and multinational business issues.

The Business School Network
Corporate Partnerships

McGill's learning environment includes involvement with businesses of every size in every industry sector, as well as government agencies and departments.

Through various projects and events and a range of faculty and student initiatives, students interact with CEOs, entrepreneurs, consultants, managers, government officials, conference delegates, and visiting faculty members from around the world. They benefit from exceptional opportunities to learn, contribute, network, and explore career directions.

The Desautels Faculty of Management continually benefits from valuable counsel of its International Advisory Board, whose members include 27 prominent businesspeople.

The College and Environs

McGill is recognized around the world for its high standards in teaching and research, and it has achieved international renown for its Faculties of Agriculture, Dentistry, Engineering, Law, Management, and Medicine. It is Canada's leading university and one of the top 25 in the world (source: London Times Higher Education supplement).

Founded in 1821, McGill University has fifty institutional buildings and eleven faculties on 75 acres in downtown Montreal. A leading center for high-tech R&D and home to innovative companies operating in the aviation, transportation, telecommunications, pharmaceutical, and computer/software industries, Montreal is one of North America's most cosmopolitan cities.

McGill has an undergraduate enrollment of more than 33,000 and a graduate enrollment of more than 6,000.

Facilities

The Desautels Faculty of Management occupies the Samuel Bronfman Building, and its classrooms have been refurbished with state-of-the-art computers, video cameras, and 3M data display units that allow professors to select from a variety of teaching media. Each classroom features wireless laptop capabilities. Facilities available to M.B.A. students include a lounge and study area, the M.B.A. Computer Lab, and an impressive library featuring electronic database searching services and a number of networked databases. Students also have access to more than 3 million volumes housed in the University's comprehensive system of libraries and specialized collections.

Students enjoy excellent sports facilities, efficient housing services, a graduate house, and a health service.

Placement

Placement starts in Orientation Week, when the Management Career Center holds the first of many networking occasions. Students seeking both permanent and summer employment benefit from workshops, videotaped mock interviews, one-on-one career counseling, a resource library, and an alumni reference database.

The center provides job listings, holds an annual M.B.A. Career Day, publishes a graduating class book that is distributed to prospective employers in Canada and abroad, and follows up on interviews with both students and employers.

Continual interaction with companies has made McGill's Management Career Center a valued resource for employers and students alike.

Admission

Admission is competitive. Decisions are based on many factors: solid academic credentials (minimum 3.0 CGPA, average 3.4), a strong GMAT score (average 650), a TOEFL score of at least 600 (250 computer-based or 100 Internet-based) if English was not the language of university education, a minimum of two years of relevant work experience (students average 4.5 years of experience), professional and extracurricular achievements, and letters of reference. All qualified applicants are invited to an interview.

Finances

Tuition fees for the 2007–08 academic year were Can$1768 for Quebec residents, Can$5140 for other Canadian citizens, and Can$20,000 for international students. There were also student service and society fees of Can$1583 and a health insurance fee of Can$639 for international students. Bilateral agreements exist with several countries to obtain an international fee waiver.

All accepted candidates are automatically considered for financial aid and fellowships.

A minimal figure for living expenses per academic year is Can$15,000 for single students and Can$18,500 for married students.

International Students

International students are warmly received and supported in the Faculty's multicultural environment. Typically, 45 to 50 percent of incoming students are international. In addition, the University runs a combined Student Aid/International Advisor's Office to handle all nonacademic matters of concern, such as visa status, immigration procedures, health insurance requirements, and cost estimates for Foreign Exchange boards.

Application Facts and Dates

Applications for the full-time program are accepted for September only. The application deadline is March 15. The application fee is Can$100.

For more information, applicants should contact:

McGill M.B.A.
Desautels Faculty of Management
McGill University
1001 Sherbrooke Street West
Montreal, Quebec H3A 1G5
Canada
Phone: 514-398-4066
Fax: 514-398-2499
E-mail: mba.mgmt@mcgill.ca
Web site: http://www.mcgill.ca/mba

MONTEREY INSTITUTE
MONTEREY INSTITUTE OF INTERNATIONAL STUDIES
An affiliate of Middlebury College

Monterey Institute of International Studies

Fisher Graduate School of International Business

Monterey, California

GOING GLOBAL WITH THE MONTEREY M.B.A.

The Fisher Graduate School of International Business prepares professionals to operate successfully in the global business environment of the twenty-first century. Our core competencies include not only the traditional business skills but also development of a global mindset, cross-cultural teamwork, language skills, and international business planning. We consider each student's background and career interests in designing his or her course of study. Our class sizes are small, and students and faculty and staff members form an intimate international learning community. Even our career assessment and job/internship search activities are personalized for each M.B.A. student.

The Monterey Institute provides a microcosm of the international business environment. Business students are surrounded by other graduate students who will launch international careers as commercial diplomats, trade negotiators, interpreters, and language instructors. Approximately half of our student body is from overseas, and all our students are multilingual. When walking across campus, one overhears conversations on important global issues being discussed in many different languages. Our campus provides a learning environment that is rich and challenging, which prepares graduates with an experience, perspective, and a network of contacts that promote success in international business.

—Dr. Ernest Scalberg, Dean

Programs and Curricular Focus

The Monterey M.B.A. program prepares students for leadership in international business by developing competence in basic business disciplines, communication skills in at least one foreign language, and interpersonal skills, including problem solving and cross-cultural teamwork. The Monterey Institute offers a two-year M.B.A. program and a one-year advanced-entry M.B.A. program. It also offers a Master's International M.B.A. program as a joint venture with the Peace Corps. Students may enroll in these programs in August or January.

The two-year M.B.A. program enrolls students with prior study in nonbusiness fields, work experience, and a minimum of two years of university-level foreign language. The one-year advanced-entry M.B.A. program enrolls students with previous formal undergraduate business education, significant work experience, and a minimum of three years' university-level foreign language. Concentrations within both M.B.A. programs are offered in entrepreneurship, global business management, international economics and finance, international marketing, international trade management, regional business environments, environmental management, corporate social responsibility, and international business strategy. Students may also design their own specializations.

Students and the M.B.A. Experience

The Monterey M.B.A. program emphasizes the development of skills for effective teamwork in multicultural settings, both in individual courses and in the International Business Plan (IBP). The

IBP is a culminating project that integrates the functional disciplines of management through the development of a detailed international business plan for a sponsoring company. It exposes students to the unique aspects of international business environments, hones communication and presentation skills, and develops a strong entrepreneurial orientation. Plans are accomplished in close consultation with a team of experienced faculty members. Students also develop strong relationships with experienced executives at sponsoring companies.

Monterey Institute's M.B.A. program is also the nation's first and only business program to develop a federally funded business globalization and localization center (GLOBE). The GLOBE Center offers Monterey students a unique opportunity to gain valuable resume-building experience by participating in real-world international research and consulting engagements.

Fifty percent of the M.B.A. students are citizens of other countries. Fifty percent are women, and about 12 percent of American students are members of minority groups.

Global Focus

The Monterey M.B.A. program has a distinctive emphasis on cross-cultural communication and effectiveness. During the program, students combine business courses with language study in Arabic, Chinese, English, French, German, Japanese, Russian, or Spanish. Although fluency in English is required of all students, one of the Institute's unique opportunities is the availability of electives taught in other languages.

The Faculty

The small size of the program creates a sense of intimacy and cohesion between students and faculty members, who encourage lively classroom interaction. The faculty members maintain an active intellectual and professional agenda and close involvement with corporate contacts.

Faculty List

Harvey Arbeláez, Professor; Ph.D., Temple. Capital budgeting, political risk, emerging markets, dollarization, Latin America.

Canri Chan, Assistant Professor; Ph.D., Flinders (Australia); CPA. Financial, managerial, and international accounting.

Eddine Dahel, Associate Professor; Ph.D., IIT. Production and operations management, quantitative analysis, supply chain management.

Scott Hoenig, Visiting Professor; M.Phil., Ph.D., Columbia. Marketing strategy, management of innovation, marketing metrics, determinants of sustainable corporate financial performance, international business planning.

Fredric Kropp, Assistant Professor; Ph.D., Oregon. International marketing, consumer psychology, entrepreneurship, social marketing.

Steve Landry, Associate Professor; Ph.D., Colorado; CPA, CMA, CFM. Financial accounting, managerial accounting, auditing, management control systems, government and nonprofit accounting.

Robert McCleery, Associate Professor; Ph.D., Stanford. Empirical issues in trade and trade policy, economic integration and preferential trade agreements, East and Southeast Asia, Mexico and U.S.–Mexico trade, investment, and immigration issues.

David Roberts, Professor; Ph.D., USC. Economic theory, policy, and application; quantitative analysis.

Yuwei Shi, Associate Professor; Ph.D., Texas. Strategic management, global strategic development, e-business and business technology management.

Thomas J. Urich, Associate Professor; M.B.A., Ph.D., NYU. International financial markets, investments, sovereign bond markets, international equity markets, metals markets and fixed-income analysis.

Adjunct Faculty

Tobi Adams, M.B.A., California State. Marketing, strategy and management.

Herbert Aspbury, B.A., Villanova. Cross-border leadership and management, international finance.

Alan Bird, Ph.D., Oregon. Leadership and organizational change, organizational behavior, Japanese business, human resource management.

Vassilis Dalakas, Ph.D., Oregon. Advertising, cross-cultural consumer behavior, international marketing and marketing communications.

Greg Elofson, Ph.D., Arizona. Artificial intelligence, information technology strategy, object-oriented systems, analysis and design.

John Jenkins, D.Phil., Oxford. Political/economic geography, market research, economics.

Leonard Lane, M.B.A., USC. Leadership development, organizational structuring, strategic planning.

Janet Marks, Ph.D., NYU. Anthropology, cross-cultural communication, leadership development, organizational behavior.

Hillel Maximon, M.B.A., NYU; CPA. Financial and management accounting, financial statement analysis, real estate finance.

Hugh McAllister, Ph.D., Rensselaer. Corporate finance, foreign direct investment, international capital markets, international finance.

Joyce Osland, Ph.D., Case Western Reserve. Cross-border leadership and management, cross-cultural communication, expatriate managers, global leadership, leadership development, organizational behavior.

Bruce Paton, Ph.D., California, Santa Cruz. Social impact management, sustainable business strategy, environmental management.

Ronald Schill, Ph.D., Oregon. International marketing, strategic partnerships.

Cary Simon, Ph.D., US International. Cross-border leadership and management, leadership development, strategic planning.

Luc Soenen, Ph.D., Harvard. International finance, treasury management, foreign exchange management.

Eli Zelkha, M.B.A., Stanford. Market development, strategic management, venture capital.

The Business School Network
Corporate Partnerships

Dynamic, innovative companies form partnerships with the Monterey Institute to manage expansion, localize products or services, explore international markets, and experiment with new business concepts. Corporate partnerships include business-plan sponsorship, internships, job placement, and guest speakers. Business executives provide feedback that is part of the continuous improvement of the program. Prominent international corporate partnerships include HSBC, Lexmark, Hisense, The Pebble Beach Company, and Cisco Systems.

The Middlebury College Partnership

The learning options at the Monterey Institute of International Studies are now even more varied, thanks to a powerful new partnership. In 2005, the Monterey Institute became an affiliate of Middlebury College, in Vermont. One of the world's premier colleges, Middlebury is renowned for its summer Language Schools and Schools Abroad programs. This partnership cre-

ates a unique chance for both schools to build even greater global connectedness.

Prominent Alumni

Monterey M.B.A. alumni live and work around the world and provide a global network that is available for business and social contact. This network is an enduring asset for Monterey graduates. Alumni often maintain supportive relationships with the faculty and administration.

The College and Environs

Opened in 1955 with summer classes in language and culture, the Monterey Institute of Foreign Studies was the first institute dedicated to the concept that a living language should be taught as such: French in French, German in German, etc. Full-year degree programs began in 1961. By 1979, the Institute had grown to international distinction and was renamed the Monterey Institute of International Studies. It is situated in one of the most spectacular natural environments in the world. The Monterey Peninsula is 130 miles south of San Francisco on California's central coast, surrounded by ocean and mountains. It has a population of 100,000. The area combines a variety of rich cultural resources and agricultural activities. Students benefit from exposure to Silicon Valley companies, hospitality industries, and agribusiness enterprises.

Facilities

The McGowan International Business Center is a state-of-the-art learning facility for the students and faculty at the Fisher School. Students utilize its sophisticated multimedia capabilities during their business plan presentations. The classrooms are purposely designed to facilitate interactive case discussion, drawing the students, faculty, and staff together in a dynamic learning community. The Center includes two high-tech, multitiered, case-teaching rooms; seminar and executive education classrooms; faculty and staff offices; and lounge areas. The Max Kade Language and Technology Center is a fully equipped language-learning center. It provides multimedia classrooms and conference rooms with state-of-the-art-technology, including a telecommunications studio and a pronunciation and accent reduction lab. The Institute's specialized international library has a collection of more than 80,000 volumes and maintains 500 periodicals, 400 online journals, plus 35 daily and weekly newspapers.

Technology Environment

The entire campus is wireless, allowing students to access the Internet and campus networks and print from remote locations. Computer laboratories are available for course-related computing in accounting, finance, quantitative methods, and decision sciences. They also offer workshops, individual assistance, and free Internet access.

Placement

The Fisher School's M.B.A. Career Management Center plays an important role in planning, locating, and assisting students in obtaining professional employment. This process is dependent upon clarity of career goals, level of experience, and a committed effort to find the right position. The center conducts workshops covering resume preparation, interviewing skills, salary negotiation strategies, and effective networking techniques. The office also provides personal coach-

ing, individualized resume reviews, and videotaped mock interviews. Students have access to an extensive online selection of career resources, including one of the largest Webliographies of career-related Web sites available. Students are also connected to the Institute's global M.B.A. alumni, who are available to discuss students' career interests and job hunting in their fields and geographic areas.

Admission

Applicants must have a U.S. bachelor's degree or the equivalent. All M.B.A. applicants must submit the GMAT score report and demonstrate foreign language proficiency or extend their program with summer language study. Nonnative speakers of English must submit a minimum TOEFL score of 550 (paper-based test), 213 (computer-based test), or 80 (Internet-based test) for the two-year program and a minimum of 600 (paper), 250 (computer), or 100 (Internet) for the advanced-entry program.

Finances

Tuition for 2007–08 is $27,500. The cost of fees, books, and supplies is estimated to be $1100. Housing, transportation, and living expenses for the academic year are estimated to be $11,920. Health Insurance is $1690 for the year.

Candidates with a minimum GPA of 3.3 on a 4.0 scale (or equivalent) are considered for scholarships up to $14,000 per year. Scholarships are renewable for a second year depending on the recipient's program and academic performance. Numerous part-time jobs are available on campus, and some faculty members employ research assistants. Some of these opportunities are awarded with scholarships, and others are available when students enroll. U.S. citizens and permanent residents may apply for need-based financial aid programs, including low-interest loans.

International Students

In recent years, the largest numbers of international M.B.A. students have come from Norway, Japan, China, Germany, India, Russia, and the former Soviet Union states. Nonnative speakers of English must use English as their language of study to fulfill the language component. Students who demonstrate exceptionally high levels of written and oral English may take other elective courses in English or study a third language if they qualify. In addition to the required orientation for all new students, there is a supplementary orientation for international students and other workshops during the academic year.

Application Facts and Dates

Application may be made at any time, provided it is received at least one month prior to the applicant's proposed semester of enrollment or three months in advance for international students residing in their home countries. For more information on the Monterey M.B.A. program, including admission requirements, application procedures, and deadlines for scholarship and financial aid, students should contact:

Monterey Institute of International Studies
460 Pierce Street
Monterey, California 93940

Phone: 831-647-4123
Fax: 831-647-6405
E-mail: admit@miis.edu
Web site: http://fisher.miis.edu

Nanyang Technological University

Singapore

ASIA'S GLOBAL M.B.A.

Nanyang Business School was ranked among the World's Top 100 by Economist Intelligence Unit (EIU) for 2004–2006. It is among the top three in Asia. Its commitment to excellence in teaching and quality research has earned the accreditation from AACSB International–The Association to Advance Collegiate Schools of Business and EQUIS (European Quality Improvement System). The Nanyang M.B.A. program offers a unique mix of global perspective with a strong Asian focus, keeping you abreast of the latest business trends and technology. As an industry-oriented business school, we create opportunities for you to network with business leaders, professionals, and entrepreneurs. You will also have the flexibility of specializing in an area that adds depth to your portfolio or graduating with a general M.B.A. for a broader business outlook.

—Associate Professor Ooi Lee Lee, Director, M.B.A. Program

Programs and Curricular Focus

The Nanyang M.B.A. trains future business leaders to be strategic and innovative and have a solid understanding of Asian and global business and cultural perspectives. The program also provides graduates with the best of East and West in business education through its curricula and equips them with competencies to lead organizations to the forefront of global competition.

The program's emphasis on industry orientation provides participants with ample opportunities to interact and network with entrepreneurs, professionals, and business leaders—both in and out of the classroom. A team of highly qualified international faculty members helps participants to develop a strong integration of skills, knowledge, and professional competencies.

Participants have the flexibility of graduating with a general M.B.A. for a broader business outlook or choosing an area of specialization that provides depth and adds value to their marketability. They are required to complete sixteen subjects, including nine core subjects, and submit a dissertation or complete an overseas Business Study Mission (BSM) or complete two additional subjects. To maintain high standards, the intake for each specialization is kept small to create a dynamic environment for study.

The program offers a general and specialized M.B.A. in accountancy, banking and finance, international business, marketing, strategy, and technology. The Nanyang Business School has received both AACSB–International and EQUIS accreditations and is the first and only business school in Singapore to do so.

Students and the M.B.A. Experience

The Nanyang M.B.A. student body exhibits a richness and diversity of experience and culture. The class of 2006 included participants from twenty-four countries, who averaged seven years of work experience and hold middle- to senior-management positions in multinational corporations or small and medium enterprises (SMEs). Thirty-five percent had engineering degrees, 30 percent had business/accountancy degrees, 20 percent had science and technology degrees, 13 percent had arts and social science degrees, and 2 percent had degrees from other disciplines. Women made up 32 percent and international participants made up 60 percent of the M.B.A. student population. This diverse student body invigorates the educational experience at Nanyang Business School, where teamwork and student interaction are emphasized.

Special Features

The Nanyang M.B.A. offers a unique mix of global perspective with an Asian focus, keeping participants abreast of the latest business trends and technologies. In addition to an international exchange program with forty institutions worldwide and an international student body, participants have the opportunity to take part in the unique Business Study Missions (BSMs) that are organized on a twice-yearly basis. These trips provide firsthand experience of business practices in different cultural environments around the world. Also, the choice of Asian-related courses and BSMs to Asian countries provides an in-depth understanding of economic changes and social developments in the Asia Pacific region. The Asian Business Case Centre also helps promote the use of Asian cases in teaching and Asian case-writing.

Exclusive to the Nanyang M.B.A. is the Double Master's Program with the University of St. Gallen in Switzerland, the ESSEC Business School in France, and the Waseda University in Japan. Participants gain the best of both Asian and European managerial skills and perspectives and high-tech, cutting-edge technologies from the NTU-Waseda programme. The M.B.A. (Accountancy) qualification is professionally recognized by the Institute of Certified Public Accountants of Singapore (ICPAS) and by CPA Australia, subject to preadmission requirements. For information about the Nanyang M.B.A., students should visit http://www.nanyangmba.ntu.edu.sg. Additional information regarding the Double Master's Programs can be found at http://www.waseda.ntu.edu.sg (NTU-Waseda), http://www.nanyangmba.ntu.edu.sg/essec.asp (NTU-ESSEC), and http://www.nanyangmba.ntu.edu.sg/stG.asp (NTU-St. Gallen).

The Faculty

The school has 160 highly qualified faculty members, many of whom have extensive

professional and managerial work experience prior to joining the school. Faculty members actively participate in conferences and seminars around the world, and their research can be found in reputable local and international scholarly journals. All faculty members are encouraged to keep abreast of developments in business and industry through specialized consultancy work.

The Business School Network

The effectiveness of the M.B.A. curriculum depends on a good understanding of the prevailing economic, social, and political realities and trends, as well as the changing demands of industry. An international advisory committee provides this guidance and includes some of the most prominent members in industry, as well as Nanyang Business School alumni.

The College and Environs

Singapore is known for its resilient economy, open and sound government policies, excellent infrastructure, high corporate credibility, and state-of-the-art technology. It is also one of the great learning centers in the Asian region. The University's sprawling 200-hectare campus is situated in the southwestern part of the island. It has a modern campus with conveniently located residences, recreational amenities, and up-to-date teaching and research facilities. This lushly landscaped, high-technology environment provides staff members and students with an inspiring environment for learning and research.

Facilities

There is a wide range of facilities and services available at the University, including a library with a collection of nearly 491,000 volumes of books and bound periodicals, as well as 2,200 titles of current periodicals. To bring the library collections to users' desktops, the library launched i-GEMS (i-Gateway to Educational and Media Services) to provide one-stop access to a variety of information resources such as online databases, CD-ROM databases, electronic journals and books, multimedia CD-ROMs, audiovisuals, and Internet resources. In addition, the University has more than 8,000 networked PCs and workstations, a

comprehensive sports complex that offers both indoor and outdoor recreational facilities, banking facilities, and a Medical Centre, all conveniently located on campus. On-campus housing is also available to faculty members and participants.

Technology Environment

The Financial Trading Rooms at the University are equipped with state-of-the-art hardware, software technology, and a video-conferencing facility, coupled with the Reuters 3000 Xtra, to support teaching and research activities in financial engineering and other areas of high-technology finance. One of the Financial Trading Rooms also serves as a laboratory for teaching and research in e-commerce. In addition, Nanyang Technological University is one of the first universities in Asia to offer a high-speed campuswide wireless computer network system.

Placement

The Career Development Service (CDS) provides professional career development and job placement services to current participants and alumni. Seminars and workshops are organized throughout the year, in addition to one-on-one career counseling, resume editing, and recruitment talks/fairs. The CDS office maintains close contact with industry and serves as a liaison for career development. An optional internship program is also available for full-time participants to further gain valuable industry exposure and experience.

Admission

Candidates must have a bachelor's degree, with at least two years of management or professional work experience at the time of admission and a minimum GMAT score of 600. For applicants whose medium of instruction was not in English, a TOEFL score of at least 600 is required (250 for computer-based testing).

Finances

Tuition fees are S$26,000 for full-time and S$30,000 for part-time participants, including a S$1000 enrollment fee. On average, a full-time participant takes about

four trimesters to complete the program and a part-time participant about six to eight trimesters.

Information on available scholarships and financial aid can be found on the University's Web site (http://www.nanyang-mba.ntu.edu.sg) by first clicking on Application and then on Scholarships & Loans.

International Students

Before the start of the program, a four-day induction session is organized for all new participants. International students may either select on-campus accommodation or find their own off-campus accommodation. Married quarters on campus are also available. In 2005–06, the international student body included participants from Asia (84 percent), Europe (15 percent), and North America (1 percent).

Application Facts and Dates

The application deadline for August admission is the end of March. Rolling admission in November and March are on request. For more information, students should contact:

The Nanyang M.B.A.
Nanyang Business School
Nanyang Technological University
S3-B3A-08 Nanyang Avenue
Singapore 639798

Phone: 65-6790-6055 or 6183
Fax: 65-6791-3561
E-mail: nbsmba@ntu.edu.sg
Web site:
   http://www.nanyangmba.ntu.edu.sg

North Carolina State University

College of Management

Raleigh, North Carolina

DEAN'S MESSAGE

Our M.B.A. program has four unique factors that have enabled us to grow and be successful. Technology is a key to the future as well as the economic engine that drives growth in the Research Triangle Park (RTP) region. Our focus on technology, a core strength of NC State University, and the management of technology enables our M.B.A. program to benefit from RTP's growth and the resulting new job opportunities for our graduates. We emphasize real projects with real companies for real learning. We know this approach provides a superior student experience. Cross-functional teamwork is an essential part of business today, and we have made it a key part of our M.B.A. program. Our faculty has formed cross-campus collaborations and joint programs that enable our M.B.A. students to learn and work with students from many of the disciplines on campus, including those in the Colleges of Engineering, Textiles, Design, and Life Sciences. When you come to NC State's M.B.A. program, you're going to learn about value: how to create it and how to estimate it. Here's a simple definition. It's the ratio of what you get compared to what you pay. Looking at our M.B.A. program, you'll find that it's the best value in management education today.

—Steven G. Allen, Ph.D., Associate Dean for Graduate Programs and Research

Programs and Curricular Focus

The Master of Business Administration (M.B.A.) at NC State emphasizes the management of innovation and technology. Students take an integrated core curriculum, with a focus on technology, business processes, and practical applications, in a collaborative learning environment. Through simulations, case studies, and projects, students learn from real-world examples and experiences. Both full- and part-time students take a course in managerial effectiveness, which emphasizes communication skills, networking, negotiations, team skills, ethics, and social responsibility.

Students begin the program by taking core courses. Students then choose a concentration from biotech/pharmaceuticals, finance, information technology management, marketing management, product innovation management, services management, supply chain management, and technology entrepreneurship. Full-time students complete the program in twenty-one months; part-time students complete the program in thirty-three months.

The technology focus of the program comes from three sources. First, all students take core courses related to technology, including strategy, operations, and managing people in a high-technology environment. Even courses in traditional management subjects, such as economics and marketing, have a technology slant through the choice of cases and projects used in the course. Second, the concentrations focus on the interface between management and technology, with classes team-taught with faculty members from engineering and other colleges. Third, most students have a strong technology background and seek careers with high-technology companies.

Students and the M.B.A. Experience

Almost all M.B.A. students have professional work experience, many in high-technology industries, such as telecommunications or software, and others in industries such as health care or financial services, in which technology is the key to a competitive advantage. A technical background is not essential for the M.B.A., but all students must be willing to learn about technology and the management challenges it creates. More than 70 percent of M.B.A. students have undergraduate degrees in business, computer science, or engineering. The rest come from a variety of fields, including the social sciences and humanities.

Management education is highly interactive. The program challenges students to become active participants in their education through interaction with faculty members, peers, and the business community. Many professors formulate their courses around case discussions, which give students an opportunity to confront real business problems and practice the art of business communication. Class simulations and team projects also create realistic environments for decision making. During the first semester, students are assigned to a peer group of 4 or 5 people who collaborate for a large portion of assignments, class projects, and outside study. The team environment exposes students to a wealth of contrasting experiences and perspectives and helps build relationships.

The average full-time M.B.A. student has four years of work experience. The average part-time student has seven years of professional experience. Women comprise approximately 30 percent of each entering class; members of minority groups account for approximately 15 percent; international students account for approximately 33 percent of the full-time class.

Special Features

BioPharma management is an exciting new area of specialization at NC State. Life sciences comprise one of today's fastest-growing business sectors, offering new opportunities for those who can provide managerial leadership in a technology-focused environment. This concentration was designed and is taught by faculty members with extensive experience in biotechnology and pharmaceuticals, working closely with industry leaders located right in the Research Triangle Park.

Services management is another new area of concentration. Services are dominating the economy, providing about three-fourths of all jobs—a rising share of which are highly skilled and technology-intensive. This is fueling a growing need for managers skilled in outsourcing, consulting, and process re-engineering. NC State's management and engineering faculties are at the forefront of curriculum development and research in the evolving discipline of services science, management and engineering (SSME), working with IBM and a growing list of other company partners. Two tracks are offered: relationship management and innovation management.

The Supply Chain Resource Consortium (SCRC) is dedicated to achieving innovation and excellence in the practice of supply chain management. The SCRC is a corporately funded organization charged with providing access to cutting-edge supply chain research and intelligence to its corporate partners. Member companies actively recruit M.B.A. students for internships and permanent positions. Bank of America Distinguished University Professor Robert Handfield directs the SCRC and works closely with the member companies to keep the program on the cutting edge.

The Technology, Education, and Commercialization (TEC) program within the M.B.A. teaches students how to turn technologies into business, using real technologies as live case studies. Supported by the National Science Foundation, the Kenan Institute, and several other organizations, graduate students and faculty members in the College of Management work closely in teams with their counterparts in the science and engineering disciplines to identify, evaluate, and commercialize promising technologies. The TEC curriculum follows the complete product-development cycle. Students gain evaluation skills for commercializing new technologies, along with an understanding of what it takes to start and run a high-technology business. Students also interact with business experts and entrepreneurs from outside the University.

The Faculty

The graduate faculty members of the M.B.A. program are outstanding teachers and researchers. In recent years, faculty members have been selected for the University of North Carolina Board of Governors' Award, Alumni Distinguished Professorships, and the NC State Academy of Outstanding Teachers. They match their teaching methods to the subject material, using case discussions, group projects, lectures, class discussions, and guest speakers as appropriate. Several faculty members serve on the editorial boards of journals in accounting, finance, marketing, operations, project management, and strategy. They have been ranked in the top twenty nationally for publishing in the top economics and finance journals.

Many faculty members held positions in management before receiving their doctoral degrees and stay in touch with today's business world through consulting and executive education.

The Business School Network

M.B.A. students have multiple opportunities to network with businesses. Some of these opportunities are built into the courses. Through the Supply Chain Resource Cooperative, students interact with member companies through student projects, internships, and biannual conferences. Students in the TEC program interact extensively with venture capitalists, entrepreneurs, and lawyers to learn how to launch a high-technology enterprise. Many TEC projects involve technologies that are under consideration at local companies. Based on his experience with TEC, Jeffrey Glass, Director of Research and Development at Kobe Steel USA in Research Triangle Park, said, "I think the concept is fantastic. There is a real void in teaching product development in high-tech. So I think this program will be great for industry." The practicum requirement also gives students the opportunity to interact with local companies.

Outside the classroom, many full-time students help finance their graduate study and gain valuable work experience in co-op positions at the leading companies in the Research Triangle area, such as IBM, Nortel, GlaxoSmithKline, and Ericsson. These positions can be obtained either through the University or by networking with classmates. Another key part of the M.B.A. network is the College of Management's Board of Advisors, which includes representatives from the leading companies in the region, including IBM, Nortel, Wachovia, and Progress Energy.

The College and Environs

NC State was founded in 1889 as a land-grant institution. Within 100 years, it has become one of the nation's leading research universities. Located in the Research Triangle, a world-renowned center of research, industry, technology, and education, the College of Management is housed on the 623-acre main campus of NC State, which lies just west of downtown Raleigh, the state capital. NC State comprises eleven colleges and schools serving a total student population of 28,000. More than 5,000 of those students are in graduate programs.

Facilities

The College of Management is headquartered in Nelson Hall, which houses classrooms, computer labs, and the offices of the faculty members and students. Classrooms feature tiered seating, laptop connections, a wireless network, and complete multimedia facilities. The College of Management's computer lab houses 100 microcomputers connected to a campuswide network. Students have access to a wide range of spreadsheet, word processing, database, statistical, and econometric software, along with several large databases. D. H. Hill Library, which is located near the center of the campus, offers access to millions of volumes of books and journals and an extensive and growing collection of CD-ROM and electronic databases. Graduate students also have borrowing privileges at Duke University, North Carolina Central University, and the University of North Carolina at Chapel Hill.

Placement

The Career Services Center is dedicated to educating full- and part-time students and to guiding their search for employment opportunities. The staff teaches students the skills required for a self-directed search, enabling them to secure post-M.B.A. employment and to manage their career.

The placement and promotion of graduates is the strongest testament to the value of the NC State M.B.A. program. The program's alumni include managers, entrepreneurs, and innovators in all fields and in all sizes of companies. Recent employers include SAS Institute, IBM, Progress Energy, Red Hat,

John Deere, GlaxoSmithKline, Cisco Systems, and several local start-up ventures.

Admission

M.B.A. students must have a baccalaureate degree from an accredited college or university and are strongly encouraged to have had courses in calculus, statistics, accounting, and economics. Calculus must be completed prior to enrollment, with a grade of C or better. Admissions decisions are based on previous academic performance, GMAT scores, essays, letters of reference, and previous work and volunteer experience. Applicants whose native language is not English, regardless of citizenship, must also submit TOEFL scores of at least 250 (computer-based); applicants to the part-time programs may apply for a TOEFL waiver. Interviews are by invitation.

Finances

The budget for M.B.A. students depends on the number of credit hours the student takes and the student's residency status. For full-time students who are North Carolina residents, tuition and fees in 2007–08 are $6130 per semester; the estimated total for living expenses, including tuition and fees, books, medical insurance, housing, food, clothing, transportation, and other miscellaneous items, is $14,000 per semester. Tuition and fees for full-time nonresidents are $12,092 per semester, with estimated total living expenses of $20,200 per semester. Part-time students who are North Carolina residents pay $3387 per semester for tuition and fees only; nonresidents pay $8308. Graduate assistantships and scholarships are available to full-time students through the College of Management. Grants and loan programs are available through the Graduate School and the University's Financial Aid Office.

Application Facts and Dates

The NC State M.B.A. program accepts applications for the fall semester only for the full-time program, with application deadlines of October 15, January 7, and March 3. Part-time students may enter the program in either fall or spring, with application deadlines of October 15 for spring entry and February 4 and April 7 for fall entry. Once an application has been received and is complete, it is reviewed for admission. This rolling admission process allows an applicant to receive an admission decision within six weeks of receipt of a completed application.

Ms. Pam Bostic
Director
M.B.A. Program
North Carolina State University
Box 7229
Raleigh, North Carolina 27695
Phone: 919-515-5584
Fax: 919-515-5073
E-mail: mba@ncsu.edu
Web site: http://www.mba.ncsu.edu

Nova Southeastern University

H. Wayne Huizenga School of Business and Entrepreneurship

Fort Lauderdale, Florida

> ### STRONG LEADERSHIP, A UNIQUE PERSPECTIVE, AND A VISION FOR THE FUTURE
>
> *The Huizenga School continues to transform, transgress, and transcend business education. Today, we are offering a fully integrated, philosophical approach to managing and leading, which we call value-driven management. You will discover how to add value to yourself, your career, your organization, and your future. You will master the professional competencies required to manage and excel in this rapidly changing global environment. Our programs are designed for individuals who want to enhance their business sense, who want to pursue their entrepreneurial spirit, and who want to be tomorrow's successful leaders and managers. If you share our enthusiasm about the future of business education in the twenty-first century, you will find this program an unparalleled value.*
>
> —Randolph A. Pohlman, Ph.D., Dean

Programs and Curricular Focus

The H. Wayne Huizenga School of Business and Entrepreneurship at Nova Southeastern University (NSU) is committed to fostering within its students the ability to work as a team, the tools to manage change and become innovative thinkers, and the freedom to cultivate their entrepreneurial spirit. There are a variety of M.B.A. programs to suit the students' needs and lifestyles. Concentrations in entrepreneurship, finance, and real estate development are available. The Working Track program allows students to take classes online or on campus on alternate weekends to complete their degree in only eighteen months.

The M.B.A. One-Year Program, designed for full-time students and professionals who are retraining for a career change, is conducted during weekdays at the main campus in Fort Lauderdale, Florida. Students attend three or four classes per semester for four semesters. Cohorts start in January, April, July, and October, with an academic orientation program facilitating the students' introduction to the program. In addition to the M.B.A. curriculum, the program also includes a course in computer technology skills and career development workshops (resume writing, business communication, interviewing).

For many years, the online M.B.A. programs have provided the same quality curricula as the on-campus M.B.A. programs, using the latest interactive Internet-based technologies to make them more accessible to a wider range of students. Class sizes are limited to ensure personal attention, and the Huizenga School hosts its own courses and uses custom-developed software.

Students and the M.B.A. Experience

The typical weekend graduate student in a Huizenga School's master's degree program is 30–35 years old. Most work full-time in mid- to upper-level management positions and are engaged in study for the purpose of professional development and advancement. The average age of full-time students is 23.

The Graduate Business Student Association (GBSA) is an organization within the Huizenga School that was established for students to promote group interaction, social networking, professional development, and entry into the local business community. The GBSA provides an opportunity for students to interact with local business and government leaders through forums, debates, and educational programs. Recent activities have included textbook exchanges, "Lunch and Learn" workshops, business etiquette dinners, a graduation cruise, holiday dessert mixers with fund-raising raffles for the Jack & Jill Children's Center, and a barbecue event honoring Dean Pohlman. The GBSA Board is composed of at least 4 elected M.B.A. students, and elections are held annually in October. Together with other M.B.A. student volunteers, they meet regularly to plan and execute events. A Huizenga School faculty member and a staff administrator oversee the GBSA.

Special Features

The Huizenga School has offered custom on-site bachelor's and master's degree programs for such companies as American Express; AT&T; DHL; First Data; BellSouth; Citibank; Disney World; Federal Express; Florida Power and Light; GATX;

GTE Data Services; Lucent Technologies; Modcomp; Rockwell International; Royal Caribbean Cruise Lines; Sears, Roebuck and Co.; Seimens; Westinghouse Savannah River Company; and ZPMC, Co., LTD.

The Faculty

The faculty comprises some of the best minds and most dedicated professionals in the industry. Their extensive experience in both the academic and business realms makes them sought after as consultants in industry, government, and the nonprofit sector. They bring a dynamic, global perspective to the classroom and provide the support and guidance necessary for academic success. Most faculty members hold a doctoral degree.

Faculty List

Rebecca Abraham
Russell Abratt
H. Young Baek
F. Barry Barnes
James M. Barry
Michael Bendixen
Charles W. Blackwell
Nicholas Castaldo
Frank Cavico
Ramdas Chandra
Ruth Clarke
Charles D. Collver
Barbara D. Dastoor
Peter T. Di Paolo
J. Wayne Falbey
Peter S. Finley
Jeffrey J. Fountain
Jane Whitney Gibson
Baiyun "Claire" Gong
Regina Greenwood
Thomas Griffin
George L. Hanbury II
Charles W. Harrington
William J. Harrington
Judith A. Harris
Michael Hoffman
J. Preston Jones
Joung Kim
Barbara Landau
Terrell G. Manyak
Timothy O. McCartney
Karen McKenzie
Walter B. Moore
Bahaudin G. Mujtaba
Ronald E. Needleman
Ordean G. Olson
Kathleen O'Leary

Pedro F. Pellet
Jack Pinkowski
Randolph A. Pohlman
Robert C. Preziosi
Randall W. Rentfro
Cynthia Ruppel
Robert J. Sellani
John T. Sennetti
Belay Seyoum
Randi L. Sims
Leslie C. Tworoger
Tom M. Tworoger
Art J. Weinstein
Albert Williams
Pan G. Yatrakis

The Business School Network

Wayne Huizenga, the business school's namesake and benefactor, has a long history of strong leadership and an unparalleled ability to build businesses. A self-made businessman who turned his first enterprise into a multimillion dollar business, Huizenga now acts as chair of AutoNation, Inc.; Extended Stay America; Republic Services, Inc.; Huizenga Holdings, Inc., and the Miami Dolphins.

Internships are an integral part of the M.B.A. One-Year Program. Students choose to learn in a corporate or government setting and apply their M.B.A. skills, gaining practical experience and establishing important contacts within the business community. Career Networking Evenings are held biannually to establish important networking contacts with corporations and other students.

The College and Environs

The main campus of Nova Southeastern University is located on a 300-acre campus in Broward County, Florida, and is part of the Fort Lauderdale-Miami metropolitan area. The area supports both high-tech manufacturing and recreational industries. Cultural attractions and sports are available throughout the metropolitan area. NSU has more than 26,000 students and is the largest independent institution of higher education in Florida. It is the sixth-largest independent, not-for-profit institution nationally.

Facilities

The Carl DeSantis Building, home to the H. Wayne Huizenga School of Business and Entrepreneurship, opened in early 2004. The 261,000-square-foot, five-story facility gives business students and faculty members increased access to technology, resources, and space and has hosted numerous lectures and conferences. The building includes general-purpose classrooms, compressed videoconferencing/teleconferencing classrooms, a lecture theater, computer labs, multipurpose facilities, conference facilities, a business services/copy center, and a full-service café. It is also equipped with administrative and student offices with support facilities.

Library and information services are offered via traditional and technology-driven approaches in the libraries, which are stocked with carefully selected print materials and provide access to readily available electronic resources. The NSU libraries are nationally known for their excellent services to distance education students. With its 325,000 square feet—the largest library building in Florida—the Alvin Sherman Library, Research, and Information Technology Center has individual study rooms, large conference rooms, exhibit areas, electronic classrooms, a café, and the Rose and Alfred Miniaci 500-seat Performing Arts Center.

Placement

Widely respected regional, national, and international companies that employ Huizenga School graduates include Alamo; American Broadcast Company (ABC); American Express; American University; AT&T; AutoNation USA; Bank of America; Baptist Hospital; Beckman Coulter Electronics; BellSouth; BellSouth Mobility; Blockbuster Entertainment; Boeing Aircraft; Burger King; Busch Gardens; CALA; Chrysler Credit; Citicorp; the City of Fort Lauderdale; the City of Houston; Coca-Cola; Computer Sciences Corporation; CSX; the Department of Energy; Digital Equipment Corporation; DisneyWorld; EG&G; Exxon-Mobil; Federal Express; First Data; Florida Power; Ford Motor Company; FPL; General Electric; General Mills; General Motors; GlaxoSmithKlein; Hewlett-Packard; Hughes Aerospace; Humana Health Care Plus; Hyundai Electronics; IBM; Jackson Memorial Hospital; John Alden Financial; Johnson & Johnson; Johnson & Johnson Cordis; Kaiser Engineering; Knight-Ridder; Lenox; Lucent Technologies; Martin Marietta; McDonald's; Microsoft; Modcomp; Motorola; NASA; Northern Telecom; Parke-Davis; Pepsico; Perrier; Petro Canada; Price Waterhouse Coopers; Quaker Oats; Raymond James and Associates; Rexall Sundown; Rockwell Collins; Royal Caribbean Cruise Lines; Rubbermaid; Ryder; Sears, Roebuck and Co.; Sensormatic; Siemens; TVA Tropicana; Unisys; United Parcel Service; the U.S. Military (Air Force, Army, Coast Guard, Marines, National Guard, Navy); United Technologies; Verizon; Xerox; Westinghouse Savannah River Company, Inc.; and ZPMC, Co., LTD.

Admission

The Huizenga School considers applicants on both quantitative and qualitative data. Applicants must submit a completed graduate admission application form with the nonrefundable application fee and provide official transcripts in English, showing degrees conferred and all undergraduate course work from all colleges and universities attended. Candidates applying must have unrestricted access to a PC. Applicants may be considered for admission through corporate sponsorship, which indicates that the applicant has been identified as eligible for reimbursement, is currently in a senior management position with significant responsibilities, and has adequate preparation to complete the graduate program. A letter on company letterhead verifying corporate sponsorship, signed by the corporate tuition benefits officer or an appropriate human resources official, must accompany the application.

Finances

In 2008–09, the M.B.A. tuition ranges from $570 to $646 per credit hour, depending on program format and location. NSU offers various loans, student employment, and scholarships to graduate students. Although administered by the colleges, many scholarships are funded by private individuals and institutions. Financial aid awards are based on the completion of the Free Application for Federal Student Aid (FAFSA), the accuracy and timeliness of information, the receipt of appropriate documentation, and the availability of funds. More information is available online.

International Students

The Huizenga School community includes a large number of students who come from many different countries and provide diversity, both welcomed and vital. The professional and cultural experiences of international students enhance this community, offering depth and character to the curriculum and environment. All international students who reside in the United States must attend classes on the Fort Lauderdale campus and fulfill specific requirements.

Application Facts and Dates

Students are admitted on a year-round basis and may begin classes in any of the four terms (January, April, July, and October). Application materials may be obtained by writing or calling the Admission Office, by contacting a site coordinator for a field location, or by visiting the Huizenga School's Web site at http://www.nova.edu/business. The application fee is $50.

H. Wayne Huizenga School of Business
    and Entrepreneurship
Nova Southeastern University
Carl DeSantis Building
3301 College Avenue
Ft. Lauderdale, Florida 33314-7196
Phone: 954-262-5168
        800-672-7223 Ext. 25168 (toll-
        free)
E-mail: info@huizenga.nova.edu
Web site: http://www.nova.edu/business

Philadelphia University

FULL-TIME, ONE-YEAR DAY M.B.A.

The one-year, full-time Day M.B.A. program attracts students who are coming either directly out of their undergraduate experience or who recently completed their bachelor's degrees. The program offers these students opportunities that are not available anywhere else, including paid internships, an international business trip, and interaction with a student-focused faculty that includes our full-time School of Business instructors, as well as renowned visiting instructors from institutions throughout the world; all in a small cohort class setting and completed in one year.

—MarySheila McDonald, Assistant Dean of Graduate Business Programs

Programs and Curricular Focus

The fastest-growing M.B.A. program at Philadelphia University is the one-year, full-time Day M.B.A program. The program is designed to provide students coming directly from their undergraduate degree programs, or those who recently completed their bachelor's degree, with the skills and abilities that employers are looking for. The program offers a global perspective, including a two-week international business trip to locations such as Budapest, Prague, Italy, Hong Kong, India, China, and Singapore. Students may begin the program in August of each year. The curriculum responds to the global and managerial skills needed to be successful after completing the M.B.A.

The program comprises eleven courses (33 credits), including Global Managing in the 21st Century, Management of Information through Technology, Strategic Planning in the Global Environment, and an internship (many of which involve paying positions). Students are able to integrate academic theory with practical work experience in a variety of fields. Internships develop increased expertise and networking opportunities.

Students in the Day M.B.A. program at Philadelphia University have completed internships at Aramark, Subaru, DuPont, QVC, and PNC Bank, among others. Graduates of the programs have reported back that employers hired them specifically because they came to them not only with an M.B.A. but with previous employment experience gained through their internships in the Day M.B.A. program.

The international business trip is another key component of the Day M.B.A. program. Students on these trips have visited businesses such as Jaguar and City Corp in Britain, Salomon Smith Barney in Hong Kong, Coca-Cola and Honeywell in Singapore, and Deloitte & Touche and Rohm and Haas in France. The ability to visit the overseas headquarters of these international companies in coordinated visits, in addition to the remarkable cultural experience of visiting other countries, makes the international business trip one of the most popular features of the Day M.B.A. program.

The design of the Day M.B.A. program, which offers a combination of in-class work with the intern experience, results in an excellent preparation for a business career. The internships that supplement classroom education often lead to full-time employment. The Day M.B.A. program provides a challenging opportunity to work with and learn from professionals drawn from varied business backgrounds and academicians in the field of business administration. A blend of theory and practice is the core of this dynamic graduate program that prepares students for today's business careers.

Students and the M.B.A. Experience

Students come from throughout the United States and abroad to study in the M.B.A. programs at Philadelphia University. The international students have come to the University from places such as Germany, India, Korea, Mexico, Taiwan, and The Netherlands. More than half of the students in this full-time program are women, and the average age is 24.

The Faculty

Philadelphia University is a teaching institution where the primary focus is the students. Classes are small (average size is 15), which allows for extensive faculty-student interaction. The M.B.A. faculty combines both full-time professors and business leaders from the Philadelphia area, as well as visiting professors from universities throughout the world. This unique combination provides an interesting mix of real-world experiences and applied research in the classroom.

The College and Environs

Founded in 1884, Philadelphia University is an independent, career-oriented institution that offers both graduate and undergraduate programs of study. Currently, Philadelphia University offers twelve professionally oriented graduate programs, each providing a blend of academic theory and real-world application.

On a small, coeducational college campus, Philadelphia University fosters close relationships between faculty members and students and enrolls a student body that is academically and culturally diverse. The University is primarily a teaching institution that also encourages research as a service to industry and as a vehicle for faculty and student development. The 100-acre campus is situated 15 minutes from Center City Philadelphia, the fifth-largest city in the nation.

Facilities

The sixty-one buildings on the University's 100-acre campus range from historic Victorian mansions to contemporary facilities, including the Kanbar Student Center—the new 72,000-square-foot addition to the Philadelphia University campus where students come together for a bite to eat, to meet with fellow graduate students, or to connect with other students and faculty and staff members.

The University's Tuttleman Center, with twelve high-technology classrooms plus a 200-seat auditorium, provides the best teaching technology available. The auditorium offers dual projection screens, dual podiums, a full projection booth for slides and video, and automated lighting controls. In addition, each seat is wired to provide electrical power for laptops and offers wireless networking for data connectivity. The standard technology classrooms in the

Tuttleman Center offer an array of projected media equipment, including a built-in PC, laptop connection, DVD, VCR, and document camera (projects both transparent and opaque images). Stereo sound, an automated projection screen, and dimmable lighting are located in each room.

Placement

Graduates of Philadelphia University are guaranteed lifetime assistance with career counseling. Last year, more than 200 companies visited the campus, well above the national average of 23 recruiters per year. Full-time graduate students may take advantage of the extensive on-campus recruiting schedule. Evening hours are also available twice a week, and workshops in resume writing, interview skills, and job search tips are scheduled regularly throughout the semester. In addition, the one-year, full-time Day M.B.A. program offers internships as part of the curriculum. Students maintain a part-time internship throughout the program.

Admission

Candidates who seek admission are reviewed based on the merit of their academic record, work experience, and the required Graduate Management Admission Test (GMAT). Depending on the applicant's academic background, foundation courses may be required.

International students may begin in either the spring or fall semester. A minimum TOEFL score of 550 on the paper-based test, 213 on the computer-based test, or 79 on the Internet-based test is required for students for whom English is not their native language. International students must provide proof of adequate funds to cover the cost of tuition, room and board, and expenses.

Philadelphia University requires all international students to provide, as part of their application, an official transcript evaluation from an NACES-accredited evaluation agency. A full listing of these agencies is available at http://www.naces.org. The evaluations provide security for both the institution and the individual in that all transcripts are individually reviewed and verified for accuracy. This is particularly helpful in guaranteeing the applicant will receive full credit for all courses taken prior to their application to Philadelphia University. Another benefit to the applicant is that these reports are permanently on file with the evaluating agency, and the applicant can have official evaluations sent anywhere at any time in the future. This is helpful not only for future academic endeavors but also for possible employment opportunities, as many employers require confirmation of academic degree completion.

Finances

The cost for full-time enrollment in the Day M.B.A. program for 2007–08 was $24,618. For the part-time M.B.A. programs, the cost for 2007–08 was $746 per credit. Books and supplies cost approximately $750 per semester. Philadelphia University is unique in offering academic scholarships to qualified students entering the M.B.A. or M.S. in taxation programs. These scholarships are offered through the School of Business Administration. The amounts range from $50 to $200 per graduate credit. Students are automatically considered for the awards upon receipt of their application and all supporting credentials.

International Students

Thirteen percent of M.B.A. students at Philadelphia University come from outside the United States. International students must take the English language placement exam prior to registering for classes. The International Society is one of the largest groups on campus. It provides students with a network of support for problem solving, social activities, and general advising.

Application Facts and Dates

Applications are accepted for the Day M.B.A. program in the fall term only. All other programs admit in the fall, spring, and summer semesters and are reviewed on a rolling basis. International applicants to the online programs may also apply for the summer term, but all other programs are limited to fall or spring admission. International students should send completed applications by June 1 for fall semester. For more information, applicants should contact:

Jack Klett
Director of Graduate Admissions
Philadelphia University
School House Lane and Henry Avenue
Philadelphia, Pennsylvania 19144
Phone: 215-951-2943
Fax: 215-951-2907
E-mail: gradadm@PhilaU.edu
Web site: http://www.philau.edu/graduate

Rensselaer Polytechnic Institute

Lally School of Management and Technology

Troy, New York

THE LALLY M.B.A.: ADVANCING BUSINESS THROUGH INNOVATION

Our mission is to develop technologically sophisticated business leaders who are prepared to guide their organizations in the integration of technology for new products, new businesses, and new systems.

—David A. Gautschi, Dean

Programs and Curricular Focus

The Lally M.B.A. program prepares business leaders with the skills and thinking that are essential for meeting the day-to-day, real-world challenges of running a business within the evolving dynamics of the global economy. Through experiential hands-on instruction, students acquire an overall understanding of the new sources of value creation brought about by the convergence of globalization and the information technology (IT) revolution.

The curriculum is built on streams of knowledge, enabling students to gain critical expertise in launching, running, and growing a successful business. The streams include creating and managing an enterprise; value creation, managing networks, and driving innovation; developing innovative products and services; formulating and executing competitive business strategies; and managing the business implications of emerging technologies. These streams of knowledge focus on critical business issues in today's global marketplace and integrate all discreet business functions, from finance and operations to global marketing and supply chain management, within the dynamics of each course experience.

The Pathfinders M.B.A. program at the Lally School of Management and Technology at Rensselaer is designed for the recent graduating senior of an engineering, science, or math program. The Pathfinders M.B.A. program allows the student to attend M.B.A. classes on the Rensselaer campus during Year 1, get experience and get paid through participation in a one-year co-op program in the United States or abroad in Year 2, and return to campus to complete the second year of the M.B.A. program for Year 3. Both the classes and the co-op program reflect the tenets of a Lally School education—Experience in Global Innovation and Technological Entrepreneurship.

To ensure that each M.B.A. student graduates with the necessary in-depth business skills, key modules complement the streams of knowledge. Modules include global business, decision models, social responsibility and business ethics, and succeeding in knowledge-intensive organizations. Students also have the opportunity to specialize in one of five areas: strategy and entrepreneurship, management of information systems, finance, new product development and marketing, and production and operations management.

Students and the M.B.A. Experience

Unique to Rensselaer and the 60-credit-hour Lally M.B.A. are two seminars that set the tone for leadership and entrepreneurial skills building. The program opens with an introductory seminar, Heroes, Leaders, and Innovators, which highlights the key characteristics of people who have successfully led change and driven innovation in a variety of settings—both inside and outside business. It concludes with a special seminar entitled Managing on the Edge, which places students in nonlinear, unstable, and uncertain situations and challenges them to use their newly acquired tools to develop innovative solutions to unanticipated business problems. Upon completion of the program, graduates enter the global economy with confidence, knowing how to work across business functions, manage risk and uncertainty, and work effectively in high-performance, cross-cultural teams.

As part of the Lally experience, students have access to projects and cooperative work programs with companies in the Rensselaer Incubator Program or located in the Rensselaer Technology Park as well as throughout the region. Firms include GE, Corning, AT&T, Lockheed Martin, Allied Signal, First Albany, IBM, Albany Molecular Research, and many leading-edge research centers and small research and development companies in the emerging Tech Valley region of New York State.

Building on Rensselaer's core strengths in engineering and the sciences, the curriculum also leverages the technical savvy of Lally M.B.A. students and helps them fully understand the business implications of such emerging fields as nanotechnology, biotechnology, and IT. In addition, practical experience is integrated into Developing Innovative Products and Services, in which students develop and market their own business concepts as part of high-performance teams in research design, manufacturing, and service settings.

During the two-year program, all M.B.A. students also develop their own business portfolio—a tangible set of deliverables—which includes a business plan, a corporate strategy assessment, a marketing plan, and a financial analysis of a designated firm. This enables students to demonstrate how they can deliver business results to recruiters and prospective employers.

The Faculty

Lally faculty members are recruited for their world-class capabilities in teaching and research. Strong emphasis is placed on the delivery of the M.B.A. and Ph.D. instructional programs. These programs build upon the Lally School's state-of-the-art research foci: technological entrepreneurship, new product development and radical innovation, management of information systems, financial technology, and global management of technology. Many full-time faculty members have substantial managerial experience in business or government. Biotech-entrepreneurship, an emerging focus at the Lally School, is closely tied to Rensselaer's major initiatives in supporting a world-class research program in biotechnology.

During the two-year program, relationships with faculty members become strong and extensive. Faculty members guide students as they work together on specific innovative projects for local and global companies. They open new knowledge and commercial networks to students and foster personal and professional development through one-on-one mentoring.

The Business School Network

Students can take advantage of the many programs conducted by the Paul J. '69 and Kathleen M. Severino Center for Technological Entrepreneurship, established at the Lally School in 1998. The center helps foster new generations of budding and successful entrepreneurs through its outreach programs, education, and research. Its mission is to integrate educational and research programs by exposing Rensselaer students to the practices and principles of entrepreneurship, infusing the fundamentals of entrepreneurship throughout the Rensselaer curriculum, extending Rensselaer's leadership and national prominence in technological entrepreneurship, and enhancing the synergy between entrepreneurship and IT.

Activities include business forums on technology incubation, high-technology entrepreneurship, and venture capital funding; the Rensselaer Entrepreneurship Internship Program; an annual Women in Entrepreneurship seminar; and the Tech Valley Collegiate Business Plan Competition.

In 2008, the Lally School of Management and Technology's graduate entrepreneurship program ranked twenty-third in the nation, up from twenty-sixth the previous year, according to *U.S. News and World Report*'s "America's Best Graduate Schools."

The College and Environs

While quiet and parklike, Rensselaer's 275-acre campus has all the conveniences of a self-contained city. The campus setting is a blend of modern style and classic charm. Built into a hillside, the campus overlooks the historic city of Troy and the Hudson River. With red brick buildings dating from the early 1900s adjacent to state-of-the-art research and teaching facilities, Rensselaer's campus reflects a majestic past and exciting future. The Lally School is nationally accredited by AACSB International–The Association to Advance Collegiate Schools of Business.

The campus is only 10 minutes from Albany, the capital city of New York, and a 2½-hour commute to New York City. It is within a few hours' driving distance of Boston and Montreal. These and other major metropolitan areas are also easily accessible via Amtrak and Albany International Airport, each of which is a short drive from the campus.

The Capital Region is a major center for government, industry, research, and academic life, and is gaining visibility as Tech Valley, a name recognized nationally for one of the fastest growing technology clusters in nanotechnology, energy, IT, and biotechnology research and development. In 2004, the region was recognized as third in the nation for quality of education in *Forbes*.

Technology Environment

The Lally School is housed in the Pittsburgh Building, a 43,000-square-foot teaching and research facility. The building provides technology-intensive multimedia classrooms, distance learning facilities, and student lounges with laptop connectivity. Management students are encouraged to build their own online systems (such as inventory, enterprise portals, e-commerce applications, order processing) and, to this end, the Lally School provides enterprise databases, Web servers, portals, commerce servers, and a host of other programs to assist students.

The Lally School learning environment is built upon team building and team teaching. Admissions criteria result in the development of a strong cohort of students with a diverse body of professional work experience, which offers an excellent opportunity for close peer-to-peer team building. In addition, Lally's team-teaching approach allows students to gain knowledge and understanding of critical business issues from many perspectives.

Placement

The Lally MBA Career Resources Office works with all Lally students to clarify their career goals and assist them in developing productive job-search strategies. Lally M.B.A. students receive an array of services, including on-campus interviews, alumni networking, and workshops on resume writing, interviewing, and salary negotiation. Students also benefit from an online resume directory, which is promoted to more than 1,200 employers. The Career Resources Office also executes a year-round employer relations outreach that helps brand the Lally M.B.A. among the best employers in the world.

Admission

The admissions review of Lally M.B.A. applicants is very thorough and examines all aspects of what makes an applicant a good fit for the unique program. In addition to valuing strong academic credentials and intellectual curiosity, importance is placed on previous work experience. Therefore, GMAT scores of 600 or better and applicants who have three or more years of work experience are preferred. Each year, a limited number of highly qualified applicants are admitted directly into the M.B.A. program from an undergraduate program. Applicants to the evening M.B.A. program with less than three years of work experience can be considered. International students are required to take the TOEFL and must obtain a minimum score of 600.

Finances

Rensselaer is committed to providing full-time graduate students with the opportunity for tuition support combined with a stipend awarded on a competitive basis and based on merit. Additional fellowships and other financial support also may be available. Expenses for the 2008–09 academic year are estimated at $50,630 for full-time students. This includes a flat rate of $36,950 for tuition and $13,680 for estimated living expenses, books, health and dental services and insurance, and miscellaneous fees.

Application Facts and Dates

Applications are accepted year-round for a fall semester start date, and admission decisions are made on a rolling basis. Early submission is strongly encouraged for tuition support and stipend consideration, preferably by March 15.

To request additional information or to schedule a visit, prospective students should contact:

Jill M. Terry
Assistant Dean of Master's Programs
Lally School of Management and
    Technology
Rensselaer Polytechnic Institute
Pittsburgh Building
110 8th Street
Troy, New York 12180-3590

Phone: 518-276-6565
Fax: 518-276-2665
E-mail: lallymba@rpi.edu
Web site: http://www.lallyschool.rpi.edu

Robert Morris University

Graduate Programs in Business

Moon Township, Pennsylvania

AN INVITATION FROM THE DEAN

Contemporary, exciting, connected, personal education is the hallmark of the Robert Morris University (RMU) M.B.A. Building on relationships with the business and nonprofit communities, RMU's faculty members partner with students to develop real-time solutions to actual management problems. The value of our approach is demonstrated by an extensive alumni network and very high placement rates. Designed to meet the needs of the working adult, our program facilitates completion time and flexibility through customized study plans. Emphasizing continuous improvement, the faculty members at RMU actively interact with organizations throughout the region to learn about and develop cutting-edge experiential education. We welcome your interest in Robert Morris University and invite you to our state-of-the-art facilities for a personal visit with our attentive faculty and staff members.

—Derya A. Jacobs, Ph.D., Dean, School of Business

Programs and Curricular Focus

Robert Morris University's School of Business offers a highly respected M.B.A. program that is one of the most sought-after degree programs in the region. This intensive part-time program provides value-added education primarily to midlevel, midcareer managers who are seeking professional advancement. The 36-credit, twelve-course M.B.A. program is designed to challenge and stimulate the working professional through a curriculum that stresses continuous professional improvement based on current best practices, thereby providing employers with knowledgeable workers who are capable of moving the organization forward.

Courses are scheduled one night a week and delivered in intensive eight-week sessions. This format allows students to complete two 3-credit courses during the fall and spring semesters and one 3-credit course during the summer semester, for a total of five courses per year. At this pace, a student can complete the M.B.A. program in twenty-eight months. Students may also elect to accelerate or decelerate their pace through the program as workload and personal life needs change.

The Robert Morris University M.B.A. model is divided into three phases. These phases provide foundational course material in phase one, examine the specific internal needs of organizations in phase two, and promote the customization of the students' programs to support specialty areas in phase three.

Students and the M.B.A. Experience

Students who enroll in the Robert Morris University M.B.A. program are, typically, proven middle-level professionals who desire to make a larger impact on their company or organization. This program does not preclude senior-level professionals from enrolling and gaining additional insight, and it is ideal for students who do not have undergraduate degrees in business and who seek to advance to management-level positions.

Students learn in a contemporary, interactive environment. Professors rely on their professional experience and encourage team projects throughout the program. This style of learning, coupled with the diversity of the students, makes this a very attractive and distinctive M.B.A. program.

There are a total of 166 students in the program. The average age of an M.B.A. student is 30. Many of the students have one or more years of professional experience, and women comprise 38 percent of the M.B.A. student body. In fall 2005, the average GPA of entering students was 3.02.

Students come from diverse professional backgrounds. Accountants, bankers, computer and information specialists, communicators, educators, lawyers, and marketers are common professionals in the Robert Morris University M.B.A. program.

The Faculty

Each faculty member brings expertise in teaching and in the chosen field of study. This experience brings a great measure of wisdom into each course, giving the students a clearer and more rewarding experience. The M.B.A. faculty has experience in multiple disciplines, including banking, consulting, management, and marketing.

The Business School Network

At the heart of the Robert Morris University M.B.A. program are the close-knit ties to the business and corporate communities throughout the northeast region of the United States. Robert Morris University brings a real-world approach to the educational process through gifted faculty members and a strong curriculum.

The University hosts an annual career fair for its students, which has been embraced by many national business leaders who come to the campus to recruit both undergraduate and graduate students. In addition, nearly 22,000 University alumni work and live throughout the western Pennsylvania region, giving each graduate a valuable networking resource. The University also has a very active Career Center that has had an average graduate placement rate of 94 percent over the past five years.

The University and Environs

Robert Morris University, founded in 1921, is a four-year private institution offering thirty undergraduate and nineteen master's and doctoral degree programs. The University's main campus rests upon 230 acres in suburban Moon Township, Pennsylvania, 17 miles from downtown Pittsburgh and just a 15-minute drive from Pittsburgh International Airport. The M.B.A. and other graduate and adult programs are offered at RMU's Center for Adult and Continuing Education, located in downtown Pittsburgh. Select programs offer courses at a satellite location in suburban Cranberry.

Facilities

State-of-the-art computer facilities are available for students at both campus locations. The main campus provides a variety of learning facilities, including a traditional library with more than 120,000 bound volumes, more than 320,000 items on microfilm, and nearly 600 current periodical subscriptions. The library also houses an extensive tax library and specializes in business information and materials. Nu-

merous online research databases are available to M.B.A. students at both on- and off-campus locations.

Placement

The PPG Industries Career and Leadership Development Center provides career advising, a comprehensive on-campus recruiting program, resume referral service, and resources to support the job search. More than 150 local, national, and international employers visit Robert Morris University annually to recruit students. Over the past five years, 94 percent of Robert Morris University graduates have gained employment in their chosen field within six months of graduation.

Admission

Students who are interested in studying in the Robert Morris University M.B.A. program must submit an application for admission, official undergraduate transcripts, two letters of recommendation, and an official GMAT score that is no more than five years old to the Office of Graduate Admissions.

Finances

Tuition and fees for the 2008–09 academic year are $700 per credit. Financial aid is available in the form of student loans. A limited number of graduate assistantships are available for highly qualified applicants. These assistantships consist of a partial-tuition waiver and, possibly, a stipend in exchange for work in a variety of University office settings. Financial aid is not available for international students.

International Students

The University has a growing international student community at the undergraduate and graduate levels. Three percent of Robert Morris University students are international students. Robert Morris University's Office of International Programs and Services assists international students with their personal and academic adjustments and offers counseling and support services for each international student.

Application Facts and Dates

With a rolling admission structure, students are encouraged to submit their application and $35 application fee as early as possible. Students may also apply online for free at http://www.rmu.edu. Consideration for entrance into the M.B.A. program is given to each student until the start of the academic year. Students may also enter the program at midterm in the fall and spring semesters if all entrance requirements are met.

International students must have a minimum TOEFL score of 550 on the paper-based version of the test, 213 on the computer-based version, or 79 on the Internet-based version and proof of adequate financial resources.

For additional information and requirements for application, students should contact:

Kellie Laurenzi, Dean of Admissions
Robert Morris University
6001 University Boulevard
Moon Township, Pennsylvania 15108
Phone: 412-397-5200
        800-762-0097 (toll-free)
Fax: 412-397-2425
E-mail: admissions@rmu.edu
Web site: http://www.rmu.edu

Rollins College

Crummer Graduate School of Business

Winter Park/Orlando, Florida

TAKING THE LEAD

Students seek an M.B.A. not only to increase their base of knowledge but also to enhance their career opportunities. By pursuing an M.B.A. degree, they are taking the lead in managing their own futures. Similarly, the Crummer School has taken the lead in graduate management study by developing its curriculum into four M.B.A. programs that meet the needs of today's students. Depending on your academic and professional background, the Crummer School has an M.B.A. program that suits you, and I encourage you to learn more about these innovative opportunities.

—Craig McAllaster, Dean

Programs and Curricular Focus

The Crummer Graduate School of Business at Rollins College is among a select group of elite business schools in the nation that have been accredited at the graduate level and is distinguished by its faculty and the academic and business successes of its alumni. The Crummer School offers four M.B.A. programs. Each is designed to provide a general management education with the opportunity to earn a concentration in a chosen business discipline through selection of the elective courses.

The Early Advantage M.B.A. (EAMBA) program has been recognized as the number 1 full-time M.B.A. program in Florida. The four-semester program is designed for recent college graduates without work experience, as well as career changers who seek career management support and academic advising in addition to experiential learning and internship opportunities. Classes are limited in size and students go through the program as a group. The EAMBA program allows students to explore a variety of career options before committing to a specific professional direction. Upon graduation, students are prepared to enter the workforce with the kind of practical experience that employers seek. All applicants are automatically considered for a merit-based scholarship, including corporate, endowed, and school scholarships.

The Rollins Professional M.B.A. (PMBA) is consistently ranked the number 1 part-time M.B.A. program in Florida. This program is designed for working professionals who have chosen to pursue an M.B.A. in a part-time, evening format. Rollins PMBA students have the distinct advantage of being able to apply the business thinking skills learned in the classroom directly to their current and future positions, increasing their value to their employers and bolstering the learning process through hands-on application. This thirty-two-month cohort program does not require an undergraduate degree in business. Students in this program also have the option of an integrative experiential focus in either leadership or entrepreneurship to help align their course of study to their career plans after graduation.

The Rollins Saturday M.B.A. (SMBA) is an intensive nineteen-month program designed for managers and executives who have at least five years of full-time work experience. One of the major advantages of the SMBA Program is the caliber of the students, making for a dynamic classroom environment. In this program, students learn as much from their classmates as they do from the distinguished professors of the Crummer Graduate School of Business. The SMBA Program starts once every January. Classes meet on Saturdays, from 8 a.m. to 5 p.m., in an exclusive cohort experience.

The Rollins Corporate M.B.A. (CMBA) program is composed of successful managers, entrepreneurs, and professionals who represent diverse industries. The Corporate M.B.A. program consists of a twenty-two-month program, with classes held on alternating Fridays and Saturdays. The program is tailored to the fast-paced schedule of today's mid-to-upper managers and executives who have a minimum of ten years of experience. Students are engaged in a blend of courses intended to enhance their skills with selected analytical methods and introduce them to advanced areas of managerial decision making. The CMBA is an exclusive cohort experience that also includes an international study trip to one or more major foreign locations. Students study management practices in an international setting, offering a truly global classroom.

Students and the M.B.A. Experience

The Crummer School enrolls 80 EAMBA students, 80 PMBA students, 40 SMBA students, and 40 CMBA students each year. As a result of the lock-step format, more than 90 percent of the matriculated students graduate each year.

Crummer classes average 16 percent international students (full-time only) and 36 percent women. Approximately one third of Crummer students have business undergraduate degrees; other disciplines include engineering, humanities, computer science, and the social sciences.

Students earning the Rollins M.B.A. learn and implement the Crummer Method for Applied Business Thinking^{SM} that defines the learning culture at the Crummer Graduate School of Business. A wide variety of programs and courses in entrepreneurship, leadership, and philanthropy encourage students to think differently and analytically and apply these learned methodologies to real-world business challenges. Offering a truly global classroom, the Rollins M.B.A. seeks to diversify the way its students learn and apply business thinking strategies. Rollins M.B.A. students participate in practicums in countries

Global Research and Study Project (GRASP) trip.

Gateway to the College's main entrance.

around the world in real business environments solving real business problems.

Global Focus

International components are incorporated into every course to stress its importance in today's growing global emphasis in business. Each Crummer student also completes a required international business course as part of the core curriculum. In addition, all EAMBA, SMBA, and CMBA students travel on a seven- to ten-day international study trip as part of their core curriculum.

To further students' experience with multinational corporations, the Crummer School offers all students the opportunity to apply to be on a team of 5 to 7 students for a Global Consulting Project. Students work with a company that has operations overseas to solve a business problem. After conducting research, students travel overseas to meet with business executives and employees to study the problem in greater detail. The students then present their analysis, recommendations, and suggestions for implementation to the company.

Special Features

The Crummer School provides each student with a notebook computer upon enrollment. The computer is used extensively both in and out of the classroom for spreadsheet and database development, presentation graphics, and online research. Students also use the Internet extensively for research and communication via e-mail.

In addition, the Crummer School is one of only twenty-five schools in the United States and forty-three schools in the world accredited by AACSB International at the graduate level only. This means that all of the School's facilities, career management services, and faculty members are devoted exclusively to M.B.A. students.

The Faculty

The Crummer School hires only experienced faculty members with proven track records and doctoral degrees. Because of the integrative nature of the Crummer curriculum, faculty members work closely together to ensure that each class builds upon the others, thereby avoiding a redundancy of material and creating an interdisciplinary approach to education. Class sizes are intentionally kept small, so faculty-student

interaction remains high and provides as much value to the student as possible.

In addition to their teaching experience, faculty members maintain close ties with the business community through consulting work and research. This brings the theoretical material to life in the classroom and encourages immediate application of the course material.

As a further testament to the in-depth knowledge each professor brings to the classroom, Crummer faculty members are also prolific writers. Among them, they have authored more than ninety textbooks, many of which are the leading text used for the subject matter, as well as countless journal articles.

The Business School Network
Corporate Partnerships

Because of its location in Orlando, one of the nation's fastest-growing business communities, the Crummer School has forged ties with business leaders from a variety of industries. These relationships not only result in financial support in the form of scholarships and resources but also provide Crummer students with role models in the Crummer Mentor Program and in the career management process. These relationships also provide members of the Crummer faculty and administration with crucial insight into the skills that companies seek from M.B.A. graduates.

Prominent Alumni

Hundreds of alumni from the Crummer Graduate School of Business now hold positions as CEOs, CFOs, presidents, and vice presidents and other essential roles in some of the world's most prestigious companies, including The Walt Disney Company, Lockheed Martin, Darden Restaurants, Tupperware, and many others.

The College and Environs

As the oldest university in the state of Florida, Rollins College carries a long history of providing excellent liberal arts education. Located in the charming city of Winter Park, the small, private college is just 5 miles from downtown Orlando, a booming business community. In addition to the well-known theme park attractions, the Orlando area is home to many international headquarters, including Harris Corporation, AAA, Tupperware, and Lockheed Martin and more.

Facilities

Crummer Hall houses all Crummer classrooms as well as all faculty and administrative offices. The executive-style classrooms feature the latest technology in projection equipment and access to the Internet via wireless and LAN connections. The building also features a student lounge, study rooms, and a computer lab—all equipped with plasma screen TVs, so students may plug in their laptops and view presentations on a larger screen. This tool has proven to be a welcome asset to student teams as they prepare for classroom projects.

Technology Environment

The Crummer School provides each student with a notebook computer, and the entire Rollins College campus is wireless, providing easy access to today's technology. M.B.A. students may also elect to expand their knowledge of continuous business improvement by taking a course on Six Sigma to receive a Green Belt Certification. Six Sigma is the in-depth strategy that seeks to identify, reduce, and eliminate defects from every product, process, and transaction. Many organizations begin Six Sigma deployments by training

Champions and Black Belts and quickly realize the need to involve a larger critical mass of people to achieve breakthrough-level results from their Six Sigma initiative. Green Belt training is an excellent way to enhance the effectiveness of both process owners and team members as they learn to apply tools and methods used in the Six Sigma methodology.

Placement

The Career Management Center is devoted exclusively to Crummer students. All full-time students complete a career management course as part of their core curriculum. In addition, one-on-one counseling sessions, videotaped mock interviews, corporate information sessions, and networking and recruiting events are available to assist students with their job search. A variety of resources are also offered for the School's working professional students who are currently enrolled in the CMBA, PMBA, or SMBA program, including career strategies seminars.

Admission

The Crummer School evaluates each candidate on an individual basis, seeking a balance among the various application criteria. Each applicant to the Crummer School is required to submit a formal application, an application fee, a score on the Graduate Management Admission Test (GMAT), all undergraduate and graduate transcripts, and two to three letters of recommendation. Work experience is evaluated for all but the EAMBA Program. The average full-time student enters the program with a 3.2 undergraduate GPA and a 597 on the GMAT.

Finances

Total tuition is $59,200 ($14,800 per term) for the Early Advantage M.B.A. Program; $49,600 ($6200 per term) for the Professional M.B.A. Program; $62,540 for the Corporate M.B.A. Program; and $59,360 for the Saturday M.B.A. Program. All tuition costs include the notebook computer, and tuition for the EAMBA, SMBA, and CMBA Programs includes the Global Research and Study Project. Living expenses are not included in any of the tuition figures.

Full-time, enrolled M.B.A. students are eligible for placement in graduate housing. Rollins College maintains a limited number of apartments that are used to provide housing accommodations. In addition, apartments near the school are abundant. The estimated cost of living for one year is $18,200 for full-time students.

Scholarships are available to full-time students. Each application is automatically reviewed for these awards.

Application Facts and Dates

Admission is granted on a rolling basis for each program, and early application is encouraged. The CMBA program begins in July, the EAMBA and PMBA programs start in September and January, and the Saturday M.B.A. program begins in January. For additional information, students should direct correspondence to the appropriate program director at the following address:

Director of Admission
Crummer Graduate School of Business
Rollins College
1000 Holt Avenue
Winter Park, Florida 32789-4499

Phone: 407-646-2405
      800-866-2405 (toll-free)
Web site:
      http://www.crummer.rollins.edu

Roosevelt University

Walter E. Heller College of Business Administration

Chicago and Schaumburg, Illinois

THE ROOSEVELT UNIVERSITY M.B.A.

The Master of Business Administration degree is designed for students who wish to prepare for executive and managerial positions in both the private and public sectors. The degree includes a broad preparation in business administration, while allowing for a concentration in a specific business-related area. Emphasis is placed on the development of problem-solving and decision-making abilities.

The faculty members at Roosevelt University offer the most innovative M.B.A. in the Chicago area. Roosevelt's M.B.A. represents a complete rethinking of what is taught and how it is taught. The focus of the learning process is a shared responsibility of the student and the instructor. Our classes are small, and the contact is personal. We stress teamwork and group projects, with case analyses that include written and oral presentations. Above all, we expect each student to contribute to the education of his/her colleagues, because adult learners often have considerable expertise to share with classmates.

Programs and Curricular Focus

The emphasis of the program is to integrate business core competencies with specialized education to create essential skills expertise in one of the functional areas of business. A concentration from other graduate programs within the University is an option. Some of these areas include hospitality and tourism management, integrated marketing communications, and training and development.

The M.B.A. program accepts students with liberal arts and other nonbusiness baccalaureate degrees as well as those with a bachelor's degree in business administration. The 37-semester-hour program consists of thirteen courses. The first is an online "boot camp" (BADM 401, Graduate Business Orientation), which is taken during the first semester of study. The six modules provide an overview of basic business subjects. Thereafter, all students take eight core courses. Each course is a self-contained analysis of the stated topic; no prior exposure to the subject is required beyond the boot camp. Students whose academic preparation and/or work experience has given them a high degree of expertise in a specific subject may petition to substitute a more advanced course in that subject for the required course. In addition to BADM 401 and the core classes, each M.B.A. student completes a concentration of three courses and one elective to complete the M.B.A. degree.

Students and the M.B.A. Experience

More than 800 graduate business students attend classes in the Heller College, where they study for the M.B.A. as well as the Master of Science in accounting (MSA), human resource management (MSHRM), information systems (MSIS), international business (MSIB), and real estate (MSRE). Students of varied backgrounds and ages, from many states and more than fifty countries, pursue graduate studies at Roosevelt University. Most work part- or full-time and find evening and weekend classes well suited to their schedules. Full-time students can also attend class in the evening and on the weekend, in addition to weekday classes.

Special Features

Roosevelt University is among the few universities to offer an M.B.A. with a concentration in real estate. The Chicago School of Real Estate's mission is to raise the quality bar within the real estate profession. Its aim is to create career opportunities and enhance the resource base for the industry through a diversified program that attracts the best and the brightest of individuals to the school. Through the accounting department, a concentration in business forensics, which covers the prevention and detection of business fraud, is also offered in the M.B.A.

The Faculty

Roosevelt University has a diverse faculty representing the culture and vibrancy of the metropolitan area. The business faculty includes approximately 30 full-time professors and more than 60 part-time instructors.

Faculty List

Terri L. Friel, Dean.
Undine Stinnette, Associate Dean.
Connie Wells, Assistant Dean of Graduate Studies.
Marilyn Nance, Assistant Dean and M.B.A. Program Director.

Full-Time Faculty
Joseph D. Ament, J.D., John Marshall Law.
Lisa Amoroso, Ph.D., Northwestern.
Donald S. Bernstein, Ph.D., IIT.
Joseph O. Chan, Ph.D., Illinois at Chicago.
Shamsul Chowdhury, Ph.D., Linköping (Sweden).
Sofia Dermisi, D.Des., Harvard.
Gilbert R. Ghez, Ph.D., Columbia.
Rifat Gorener.
Michael I. Groner, Ph.D., Illinois at Urbana-Champaign.
Ralph Haug, Ph.D., Wisconsin–Milwaukee.
Thomas C. Head, Ph.D., Texas A&M.
Donald A. Hoppa, M.S.A., Roosevelt.
Wayne Jones, Ph.D., Hawaii.
Josetta McLaughlin, Ph.D., Virginia Tech.
Sumaria Mohan-Neill, Ph.D., Illinois at Chicago.
Marilyn Nance.
David Nickerson, Ph.D., Northwestern.
Charles Noty, Ph.D., Loyola.

The Albert A. Robin Campus in Schaumburg is architecturally modern with a horizontal profile that encompasses 225,000 square feet and complements the suburban landscape.

Gordon L. Patzer, Ph.D., Virginia Tech.
Deborah Pavelka, Ph.D., Missouri.
Richard F. Ruby, J.D., John Marshall Law.
Henry Silverman.
Undine M. Stinnette, M.S.A., Roosevelt.
Donald Swanton, Ph.D., Northwestern.
Steven Tippins, Ph.D., Florida State.
Paul M. Wellen, Ph.D., IIT.
Connie Wells, Ph.D., Minnesota.
Carolyn Wiley, Ph.D., UCLA.
Carl Witte, Ph.D., Nebraska.

The College and Environs

From its founding as a private university in 1945, Roosevelt pioneered the education of adult and nontraditional students, creating a diverse learning environment for all students, with an emphasis on social justice. Today, its educational programs are recognized nationwide, and students from all races and ethnicities throughout metropolitan Chicago and from around the world pursue degrees at its two campuses. Roosevelt's characteristics provide a number of graduate educational benefits: small classes that encourage an open exchange of ideas, outstanding faculty members, excellent academic programs, scheduling flexibility to accommodate working students, and counseling and career planning services.

Roosevelt University's mission is to educate socially conscious citizens for active and dedicated lives as leaders in their professions and their communities. The mission of Walter E. Heller College of Business Administration is to give students a career-oriented business education that emphasizes personal and professional integrity and stresses the social responsibility of business.

Roosevelt University has two campuses. The Chicago Campus is in the heart of the downtown and is accessible by car or public transportation. Students can take advantage of the many events and activities in the city. The Albert A. Robin Campus is located in northwest suburban Schaumburg, approximately 30 miles from downtown Chicago. The University shuttle service provides daily transport to convenient public transportation so students and faculty and staff members can travel between campuses. In addition to the two campus locations, Roosevelt is continually expanding its course offerings through partnerships with community colleges and corporations and through its Internet-based RU Online program. Currently, the Master of Arts in Teacher Leadership and the Master of Arts in Training and Development are available in fully online formats as well as on campus.

Facilities

The Murray-Green Library holds more than 225,000 volumes and a variety of research materials, including print and electronic journals and reference subscriptions and microforms. A full staff is on duty to assist student researchers at the Chicago Campus, and research services are also available at the Schaumburg Campus. Roosevelt University is a member of the Illinois Library Computer Services Organization (ILCSO), which operates a statewide online circulation system embracing forty-five of the largest libraries in Illinois. It is also backed up by the OCLC international bibliographic network and subscribes to numerous online electronic database services.

Placement

Roosevelt University maintains an active placement service for graduates of all of its professional programs. Placement opportunities for graduates are enhanced by the University's location in the Chicago area, where employment opportunities are many and varied. The Office of Career Services assists students in finding part-time, full-time, and second-career positions. Its services remain available to Roosevelt graduates, who may take advantage of a full range of career counseling and planning services.

Admission

Admission to the M.B.A. program depends on previous academic success and work experience. Domestic students have three options. With a bachelor's degree from a regionally accredited college or university and a GPA of 3.25 or higher (4.0 scale) or a graduate degree in any discipline, they are granted direct admission. Applicants whose GPA is 2.8 to 3.24 must submit a detailed work history, a letter of career goals and objectives, or the results of the Graduate Management Admission Test (GMAT). Admission is determined after review of the submitted documents. The third option is for applicants whose grade point average is below 2.8; they must submit work history, a letter of career objectives and goals, and a GMAT score. Admission is determined after review of these documents.

International students seeking admission to the M.B.A. program must submit a transcript of college-level work, GMAT score, and results of both the Test of English as a Foreign Language (TOEFL) and the Test of Written English (TWE). Visa services, TOEFL scores of at least 550 on paper-based test or 213 on the computer-based test, and a TWE of 4.5 or higher are required for enrollment. Admission is based on a weighted combination of these measures of ability and aptitude.

Finances

Tuition for 2008–09 is $737 per graduate semester hour or $14,730 per year for full-time students (9–12 credits/semester). Scholarships are available that provide grants to cover a partial cost of tuition. A limited number of graduate assistantships, which cover tuition and provide a cash stipend of approximately $5000 for the academic year, are offered by the University to full-time students. Loans, including Federal Perkins Loans (formerly National Direct Student Loan Program) are available. A number of business firms in the Chicago area have employee tuition-reimbursement programs, and many of Roosevelt University's students matriculate under these arrangements.

The historic Auditorium Building, which overlooks Grant Park and Lake Michigan, is the center of the Chicago Campus.

International Students

International students constitute about 7 percent of the graduate student body. Support services include the English Language Program, which provides language tutoring through ESL courses.

Application Facts and Dates

Applicants should write to the Office of Admissions indicating their field of interest. For domestic applicants, the priority deadlines for admission are March 31 for the fall semester, December 1 for the spring semester, and April 15 for the summer sessions. The application fee is $25. International students must apply at least three months prior to the intended semester, leaving additional time for visas. The international application fee is $35. For more information, students should contact:

Chicago Campus Office of Admission
Roosevelt University
430 South Michigan Avenue
Chicago, Illinois 60605-1394

Phone: 877-APPLY RU (877-277-5978)
    (toll-free)
       312-341-3531 (international)
Fax: 312-341-3523
       312-341-6377 (international)

Schaumburg Campus Office of Admission
Roosevelt University
1400 North Roosevelt Boulevard
Schaumburg, Illinois 60173-4348

Phone: 877-APPLY RU (877-277-5978)
    (toll-free)
Fax: 847-619-8636
E-mail: applyRU@roosevelt.edu
    internat@roosevelt.edu
    (international)
    mbadvise@roosevelt.edu
    (College of Business)
Web site: http://www.roosevelt.edu

Rutgers, The State University of New Jersey

RUTGERS
Rutgers Business School
Newark and New Brunswick

Rutgers Business School—Newark and New Brunswick

Newark and New Brunswick, New Jersey

BUSINESS AND SCIENCE

Rutgers Business School (RBS) offers strong partnerships with global businesses, faculty members with an international reputation for the high quality of their teaching and research, a highly diverse student body, and a curriculum that emphasizes experiential learning—providing students with the advantage of innovative, industry-relevant knowledge and real-world, international experiences.

As a Rutgers Business School student, you will become part of a prestigious institution rich in resources and history, with a large network of successful alumni. I am honored to have this opportunity to use my experience as a CEO to further align our programs with industry by strengthening our corporate partnerships, in order to provide you with a powerful RBS experience.

Rutgers Business School is favorably positioned in one of the world's leading corporate centers, within one of the nation's oldest and most highly regarded institutions of higher education—Rutgers University. By combining our proximity to a wealth of industry and a multidisciplinary emphasis, I look forward to leading Rutgers Business School to taking on an even more integral role within New Jersey and the world beyond while we become recognized as a premier business school.

—Michael R. Cooper, Ph.D., Dean

Programs and Curricular Focus

Steeped in academic excellence, with a distinguished faculty, Rutgers Business School is highly ranked by the *Financial Times, U.S. News & World Report, Business Week,* and the *Wall Street Journal.* It is recognized as one of the top three business schools in the greater New York metropolitan area, and in 2008 was ranked number 10 nationwide for Most Competitive Students by the *Princeton Review.*

Rutgers arms its M.B.A. students with the business knowledge and real-world skills required to achieve excellence in their careers. Students are exposed to an array of decision-making and problem-solving tools that have broad applicability in business situations, through classroom study as well as team projects, internships, and a variety of other experiential learning opportunities.

With more than 270 Rutgers University degree programs to partner with, RBS is uniquely capable of delivering cutting-edge, multidisciplinary curricula that combine the mix of business and science required by today's leading corporations.

Geographically situated in an epicenter of global business, Rutgers Business School has high access to the top executives leading the world's largest corporations. Its partnerships with these companies are central to the Rutgers Business School experience and offers students distinct career advantages, evidenced by the success of the School's alumni.

The M.B.A. curriculum is offered on a full-time basis at the School's Newark, New Jersey, campus and on a part-time basis at the School's two main campuses—Newark and New Brunswick, New Jersey. In addition, part-time students may begin the program at three convenient off-campus locations—Princeton, Jersey City, and Morristown, New Jersey.

The M.B.A. degree requires completion of no less than 60 credit hours, 28 of which cover a core curriculum of general business courses, including the MBA Team Consulting course requirement. The remaining credits are taken as electives, allowing students advanced study in subjects relevant to their interests. Advanced standing credits may be awarded for prior academic work or for successfully passing "challenge exams."

Concentrations are available in finance, information technology, management and global business, marketing, pharmaceutical management, and supply chain management. Students may alternately pursue other specialized interests by developing a customized concentration.

The School's M.B.A. in pharmaceutical management is offered through a partnership with seven of the nation's leading drug manufacturers. Students who are selected each year for the prestigious Industry Scholars Program receive full-tuition scholarships, a paid summer internship in the industry, and the opportunity to learn from senior pharmaceutical executives.

Rutgers Business School also offers an undergraduate program; a twenty-month Executive M.B.A. program; three International Executive M.B.A. programs (in Shanghai and Beijing, China, and in Singapore); a fourteen-month M.B.A. program in professional accounting; and other graduate degree options that include the Master of Information Technology; the Master of Quantitative Finance; the Master of Accountancy (M.Accy.) in financial accounting, governmental accounting, and taxation; and a Ph.D. in management.

In addition, the School offers a variety of innovative, multidisciplinary dual-degree and joint-degree programs, enabling students to pursue an accelerated undergraduate and an M.B.A. degree or to earn an M.B.A. while pursuing a graduate degree in another discipline.

Beginning with the fall 2008 semester, Rutgers Business School plans to offer two new accelerated bachelor's/M.B.A. degrees that will enable students to obtain undergraduate and graduate degrees, as well as valuable work experience through a required internship, in as little as 5½ years: the Bachelor of Science in business/M.B.A. and the Science M.B.A. The Bachelor of Science in business/M.B.A., open to Rutgers' top business students, provides internships, team consulting, and cooperative employment opportunities, giving students a competitive edge for launching their careers. The Science M.B.A. is designed specifically for undergraduate students with an interest in science, to open up doors to leadership jobs and careers. Rutgers Business School is the only business school in New Jersey that equips M.B.A. students with such powerful real-world experiences.

Longstanding dual-degree programs include the B.S./M.B.A. and B.A./M.B.A. programs offered in conjunction with Rutgers' Newark and New Brunswick Schools of Arts and Sciences. Masters-level dual-degree programs include a J.D./M.B.A. and a J.D./M.B.A. in professional accounting offered in conjunction with the Rutgers School of Law in Newark. A dual-degree Master's of Public Planning (M.P.P./M.B.A.) is offered in conjunction with Rutgers' Bloustein School of Planning and Public Policy. Other joint-degree programs are available in public health M.P.H./M.B.A. and biomedical sciences (M.S./M.B.A.), and an M.D./M.B.A. is offered with the University of Medicine and Dentistry New Jersey (UMDNJ).

Students and the M.B.A. Experience

Current Rutgers M.B.A. students come from nearly 100 different U.S. colleges and universities and more than sixty schools in twenty-nine countries. Their average age is 27, and the average student arrives at Rutgers with five years of work experience. The diversity of the student body is enhanced by the number of part-time students who bring to the classroom the issues and situations that they face in their jobs on a daily basis.

The cohort format enables students to forge lasting friendships and to gain an appreciation of different cultures and business practices from their fellow classmates.

The M.B.A. curriculum stresses teamwork and an integrated, cross-functional view of business. An example of this is MBA Team Consulting, a required capstone course, which gives students the opportunity to work on a consulting assignment for corporate clients while allowing them to synthesize the concepts and tools that they have learned in the classroom. Students interact with senior management to define the scope of the assignment, work as a team to find an appropriate solution, and are given a real situation in which to hone their oral and written presentation skills.

Rutgers further supplements its classroom lessons with numerous other forms of experiential learning opportunities, including corporate internships, case-study competitions, industry-sponsored student clubs, mentoring by business executives, involvement with the Rutgers Business School Boards of Advisers, presentations by distinguished guest speakers, and international study-abroad programs.

The Faculty

The quality of what an M.B.A. student takes from the classroom is reflected in what the faculty members bring to it. The professors at the Rutgers Business School are internationally renowned scholars, editors of prestigious academic journals, award-winning teachers, and top consultants to industry and government. Nationally, Rutgers ranks among the top business schools for research. This means that Rutgers professors bring to the classroom the latest, most forward-thinking ideas in business today. By pushing the frontiers of business knowledge, their goal is to enable students to think beyond traditional functional boundaries and ignite in them the confidence to meet any business challenge.

The Business School Network

The Rutgers M.B.A. program brings the real world of business to the classroom, and capitalizes on the fact that the School is located in a global business epicenter, and amid the largest concentration of corporate headquarters in the United States.

RBS students and faculty access a strong network of corporate partnerships and more than 27,000 Rutgers Business School alumni. Through a multidisciplinary approach with other Rutgers schools and departments, they also tap into a network of over 380,000 Rutgers University alumni.

Each year, CEOs and prominent executives participate in a variety of forums—including in-class lectures as well as symposia and conferences—providing students with the opportunity to engage high-level business leaders in an open exchange.

Corporate partners also work to arrange internships and play a leadership role in forging links between the University and the business community.

Among those are participants in the School's Executives-in-Residence program, which brings a number of these corporate leaders onto its faculty. Each contributes a significant amount of time and energy to the program, offering a wealth of experience and wisdom to M.B.A. students through classroom lectures, mentoring, and career counseling sessions.

The School also has an active Board of Advisers, comprising 50 distinguished executives from a variety of industries. Advisers provide critical input into the programs of the School, generate internship and placement opportunities for students, and find ways to improve the resources for promoting and enhancing learning.

The Global Financial Markets Center is a state-of-the-art stock trading and financial research classroom on Rutgers Business School's Newark campus.

The College and Environs

Rutgers, The State University of New Jersey, was chartered in 1766. One of the nation's oldest and most distinguished institutions of higher learning, from its roots as a colonial college and land-grant institution it has developed into one of America's leading public research universities. New Jersey's state university fulfills its three-part mission of instruction, research, and service by educating a diverse student body of almost 50,000 on its three campuses, by creating new knowledge, and by contributing to the economic and cultural vitality of the state. Rutgers continues to strengthen its tradition of teaching and research excellence as one of the select members of the prestigious Association of American Universities. Founded in 1929, Rutgers Business School has been accredited since 1941 by AACSB International–The Association to Advance Collegiate Schools of Business—the hallmark of excellence in management education.

Both of the School's main campuses are accessible by bus, train, or car and are convenient to Newark Liberty International Airport. Northern New Jersey is home to five professional sports franchises and a variety of outstanding cultural and recreational resources. In addition, New York City's midtown and Wall Street are both less than 30 minutes by train from the Newark campus. Midtown Manhattan is an hour by train from New Brunswick.

Placement

Through the aggressive effort of its full-time professional staff, Rutgers Business School's Office of Career Management not only taps into its extensive network of corporate recruiters on behalf of Rutgers students, but also actively partners with students in every phase of their job search so that they acquire life-long career management skills. From the moment that M.B.A. students register with the Office of Career Management, they participate in a comprehensive career planning program to acquire skills that carry them through to graduation and beyond. From the basics of resume writing, cover letter preparation, and interview survival to mentoring and coaching, the Office of Career Management assists the student throughout the entire career management process.

Among the services provided to Rutgers M.B.A. students are on-campus recruiting, internship career fairs, individual career coaching, and career planning and skills workshops. In addition, M.B.A. students receive an account with eRecruiting, a leading online recruitment and resume-posting service, and the Career Manage-

ment office publishes the Rutgers MBA Résumé Book, providing corporate recruiters nationwide with student resumes packaged in a convenient electronic format.

As a first step, full-time M.B.A. students participate in a mandatory, nine-week Career Management Program, designed to help students explore, develop, evaluate, and attain their career goals. Part-time M.B.A. students participate in a mandatory, weekend Career Managment Workshop that prepares them for the competitive job-search process.

All M.B.A.'s are required to meet with a Career Management Specialist for resume approval and a mock interview in order to participate in the M.B.A. Recruiting Program.

Admission

Rutgers Business School admits those students who show promise of succeeding in the program. Primary consideration is given to the applicant's scholastic record, including the distribution and quality of work as well as the GMAT score and work experience. Other considerations include civic leadership, progressively responsible work experience, and clearly defined goals. The Test of English as a Foreign Language (TOEFL) is required of students whose native language is not English. The average GMAT score for the class entering in fall 2007 was 637. The average undergraduate GPA was 3.3.

Finances

Tuition for the 2007–08 academic year was $18,928 for full-time in-state students, $31,494 for full-time out-of-state students, $657.35 per credit hour for part-time in-state students, and $1133.50 per credit hour for part-time out-of-state students. Fees were $1448 for full-time students and $254.50 to $331.50 for part-time students, depending on the number of credit hours.

International Students

Twenty-seven percent of the School's M.B.A. students are international, representing more than thirty countries. The Rutgers–Newark campus, which for eleven years straight has been rated by *U.S. News & World Report* as the most diverse of any university campus in America, holds this distinction, in part, because of the large number of international students studying there. The proximity of Newark Liberty International Airport and Manhattan make the School's location particularly attractive to international students.

Application Facts and Dates

The application deadline for admission to the full- or part-time program is May 1 for classes starting the following fall. International students must apply by March 15. Students wishing to complete the program on a part-time basis may also apply by November 15 for classes starting the following spring. Candidates may apply online at http://www.gradstudy.rutgers.edu or http://www.embark.com. For more information, prospective students may contact:

Rutgers Business School
Office of Graduate Admissions
190 University Avenue
Newark, New Jersey 07102-1813

Phone: 973-353-1234
E-mail: admit@business.rutgers.edu
Web site:
    http://www.business.rutgers.edu

St. John's University

THE PETER J. TOBIN COLLEGE OF BUSINESS

The Peter J. Tobin College of Business

Queens, New York

THE PETER J. TOBIN COLLEGE OF BUSINESS

For nearly eighty years, the Tobin College of Business has offered future business leaders a strong foundation in management education with a focus on developing individuals for the most senior corporate positions in the world. "I am very excited about the opportunities at the Tobin College," says Dean Steven D. Papamarcos. "Our mission at Tobin is to develop men and women of character able to lead the way in today's rapidly globalizing economy. With campuses in Queens, Manhattan, Staten Island, and Rome, Italy, we prepare students with state-of-the-art problem solving, communications, and leadership skills benefiting all stakeholders. It is an honor to be a small part of their lives."

—Steven D. Papamarcos, Dean

Programs and Curricular Focus

The Tobin College has a long history of providing a strong educational foundation to individuals who have risen to senior executive positions all over the world. The College's educational philosophy is grounded in the importance of not just conveying business understandings but also developing leaders who appreciate the need to think, and often act, globally and who realize and appreciate the role that social responsibility plays in successful business practice.

St. John's early recognition of the important role that the globalization of business holds for future business leaders is represented by its having been one of the first American business schools to establish a physical presence beyond U.S. shores in Rome, Italy. Today, the campus there is a thriving center for students who are interested primarily in the intersection of business and international markets.

St. John's extensive alumni network, talented and dedicated faculty members, outstanding resources, and commitment to a values-based business education all make the Tobin College unique in not just providing management education to master's degree candidates and working executives but also developing business leadership skills for life. The Tobin College is fully accredited for business and accounting programs by AACSB International–The Association to Advance Collegiate Schools of Business.

The M.B.A. degree is offered with specializations in accounting, taxation, decision sciences, executive management, finance, financial services, international business, international finance, marketing management, insurance financial management, risk management, and computer information systems for managers. Successful completion requires a minimum of 36 credits; additional credits may be required, depending on previous course work that has been completed in business and economics. Individual plans of study are developed for each student in consultation with advisers and faculty members in the College. The degree may be completed on either a part-time or full-time basis and includes study in the M.B.A. core, specialization courses, and electives. The Master of Science (M.S.) degree is offered in management of risk, accounting, and taxation. Advanced Professional Certificates (APCs) are available to individuals who have completed the M.B.A. degree. These are designed to enable such students to accrue additional knowledge or skills in another field or update and enhance skills in their current field. Eighteen credits are required for completion of the APC.

The Rome campus offers the M.B.A. degree in international finance and marketing.

Students and the M.B.A. Experience

With a student enrollment that reflects the cultural diversity present within actual business settings and the very special business center that is Manhattan in proximity, the Tobin College has succeeded in launching the careers of more than 35,000 business leaders worldwide.

Classes focus on the application of business theory to real-world situations. Graduate students are exposed to the dynamics of business and group interaction using simulated and real-world business situations, and through these, they are able to finely hone skills in the areas of communication, presentation, negotiation, persuasion, motivation, and working effectively in a team environment. The College's focus on the importance of global awareness is emphasized throughout the program, and students are encouraged to take advantage of opportunities to complete some of their degree requirements at St. John's center in Rome or through special opportunities offered in other business centers.

Special opportunities exist for students to network with alumni of the College for the purposes of career information and development and internships. Graduate programs offered in historic Queens, Staten Island, and the Manhattan financial district provide for an exceedingly large number of opportunities for professional, social, and cultural activities that are unique to New York, including Broadway and the world center of finance that is Wall Street.

Special Features

In addition to extensive opportunities to study abroad, selected students may participate in the Executive-in-Residence program, which provides students with special opportunities to obtain hands-on and real-world consulting experience while they are simultaneously studying for the master's degree. The program is designed to help students develop a deeper understanding of corporate leadership and the complexities of organizational decision making.

The Financial Information Lab enhances the education provided to students through the establishment of a learning environment that brings real-time news, market information, financial data, and analysis to students and faculty members. This type of facility enables students to learn about and live in financial markets and business environments and situations throughout the world.

A Student Management Investment Fund also enables students to obtain hands-on investing experience under the guidance of seasoned faculty members and alumni with successful Wall Street careers. The College operates in a highly sophisticated technological environment with wireless capabilities and student access to highly sophisticated databases for the purpose of research.

The Faculty

Tobin College faculty members are selected for their commitment to teaching and their understanding of the real world of business. Ninety percent of the faculty members hold the highest terminal degree in the field, and together they possess an internationally diverse portfolio of business experience. Six members of the faculty are internationally recognized Fulbright Scholars; numerous others are frequent consultants to business and the business news media.

The Business School Network

One of the greatest strengths of the Tobin College is its extensive and loyal network of more than 35,000 alumni worldwide, many of whom hold the most senior executive positions in major business and nonprofit organizations. There is a strong partnership with business both within and outside the U.S., and events such as the Executive Speaker Series and the Henry George and Colman Mockler Lectures bring together distinguished speakers, business leaders, faculty members, and students for discussions that are critical in today's global economy. The Dean's Advisory Board is a regular presence at the College and is made up of business leaders who provide their insights and expertise to students and faculty members alike.

The College and Environs

In the New York metropolitan area, the Tobin College has campuses in historic Queens, on Staten Island, and in downtown Manhattan, within the financial district. All of these campuses provide students with easy access to the enormous resources of the world center of business that is New York City. The campus in Rome is located in the heart of the Eternal City and provides students with a perfect setting in which to pursue graduate business study.

Facilities

The Main Library of the University is in St. Augustine Hall, located on the Queens campus. Together with the collections of the Loretto Memorial Library on the Staten Island campus, the Law School Library, the Oakdale Campus Library, the Kathryn and Shelby Cullom Davis Library in Manhattan, and the Rome campus library, the total University library collection numbers 1.7 million volumes and includes more than 6,000 periodical subscriptions. These materials support course offerings as well as students' cultural and recreational interests.

The collection includes government documents and audiovisual materials.

Specific support for the study of business is provided by a collection of more than 63,420 book titles and 645 business periodicals subscriptions. There is also an extensive collection of indexes, abstracts, and full-text databases.

Technology Environment

St. John's University is committed to preparing its students with the technological skills that are necessary to meet the challenges of the twenty-first-century marketplace. The University was recently named one of the top ten campuses in Intel's *100 Most Unwired Campuses* in recognition of the establishment of its wireless environment.

The University's wireless network enables each microcomputer to access a wide range of software, e-mail, and the Internet throughout the campus. St. John's Central is the University portal that supports courseware, instruction, and communication. Students also have access to four newly upgraded microcomputer laboratories, more than 100 multimedia classrooms, microcomputer classrooms, library patron computers, and a newly added cyber lounge for resident students. Deployment of desktop computers to these facilities now totals more than 1,200 Intel-based workstations and more than 125 high-end Macintosh computers.

The University has recently added a Financial Information Lab to its Queens campus. This lab enhances the education provided to students through the establishment of a learning environment that brings real-time news, market information, financial data, and analysis to the students and faculty members. It enables students to learn about and live in financial markets and business environments and situations throughout the world.

Placement

The Career Center's professional placement programs offer a wide variety of services that are designed to give each graduate student and alumnus the competitive edge. Services and resources include career advisement, an on-campus recruiting program, full-time and part-time employment opportunities, a career resource library, resume

preparation and interview techniques, a videotape library, and mock interview sessions.

Admission

All applicants must possess a baccalaureate degree from an accredited institution or the international equivalent. The candidate should submit, in addition to the $40 nonrefundable application fee, official transcripts from all undergraduate, graduate, and professional schools attended. In addition, results of the Graduate Management Admission Test (GMAT) taken within the last five years, a resume, letters of recommendation, and a personal statement should be submitted with the application. Details of these requirements may be obtained from the Office of Graduate Admissions of the Tobin College. Applicants whose native language is not English must also submit the results of the TOEFL.

Finances

Tuition for 2008–09 is $880 per credit. An additional $150 general fee per term is due at the time of registration. A limited number of graduate assistantships are awarded, based on academic merit.

Living expenses in the New York metropolitan area vary widely, depending on housing and lifestyle. St. John's offers students some limited housing opportunities. Information about these opportunities can be obtained through the Office of Residence Life. Through the University's Housing Service, students can find comfortable and convenient off-campus housing in surrounding neighborhoods. All inquiries concerning off-campus housing should be directed to the Office of Student Life at 718-990-6257.

Application Facts and Dates

For applications and additional information, students should contact:

St. John's University
8000 Utopia Parkway
Queens, New York 11439
Phone: 877-STJ-5550 Ext. T1345B
(toll-free)
Fax: 718-990-5242
E-mail: mbaadmissions@stjohns.edu
Web site: http://www.stjohns.edu/
learnmore/01405.stj

Saint Peter's College

M.B.A. Programs

Jersey City, New Jersey

> ### EDUCATION. ONE STUDENT AT A TIME.
>
> *With an M.B.A. from Saint Peter's College, you can go anywhere you choose. Our 48-credit M.B.A. is taught on a flexible trimester schedule, which means you can complete the program faster than students on a traditional semester calendar.*
>
> *An M.B.A. student may receive credit for prior undergraduate and graduate work, up to 12 credits, with approval from the M.B.A. Coordinator and Adviser. Thus, individuals with undergraduate credit in accounting, statistics, computer science, or economics may complete the M.B.A. program in 36 credits.*

Program and Curricular Focus

The M.B.A. program at Saint Peter's College offers five areas of study: finance, management, management information systems, marketing, and international business. The M.B.A. is a 48-credit program that encompasses a sharpened risk management and compliance focus.

Saint Peter's College utilizes the trimester calendar so students can earn their degrees quickly. This unique scheduling pattern offers students three 10-week sessions in one academic year—fall, winter, and spring. Summer sessions are available, as are one-week course formats.

Students and the M.B.A. Experience

Total enrollment at Saint Peter's exceeds 3,300. Of this number, more than 700 are graduate students. Of the students enrolled in graduate business programs, 88 percent attend part-time, 44 percent are women, 6 percent are international students, and 41 percent are members of minority groups. The average age of students in the business program is 33.

The Faculty

In addition to being dedicated teachers, the faculty members at Saint Peter's College hold Ph.D.'s from leading universities and are scholars and researchers in their fields. The faculty utilizes a variety of teaching approaches, including lectures, classroom discussions, case studies, team projects, simulation exercises, and independent study.

The College and Environs

Saint Peter's College, founded in 1872, is a Jesuit, Catholic, coeducational liberal arts college in an urban setting that seeks to develop the whole person in preparation for a lifetime of learning, leadership, and service in a diverse and global society. Committed to academic excellence and individual attention, Saint Peter's College provides education informed by values.

Saint Peter's College offers two campuses with convenient locations. The main campus has long been a landmark on Kennedy Boulevard in Jersey City, New Jersey. The College's atmosphere, architecture, and activity reflect a dynamic, vital, urban institution that offers important intellectual resources to the community. The New York City skyline, visible from Jersey City, is a constant reminder of the College's proximity to a major cultural and financial center. The branch campus at Englewood Cliffs in Bergen County, New Jersey, was established as a college for adults. The campus is perched on a bluff overlooking northern Manhattan and the Hudson River, located on the Palisades, 1 mile north of the George Washington Bridge. Saint Peter's College has off-site locations at the Jersey City Waterfront and in South Amboy, New Jersey. These additional sites afford graduate students the opportunity to take business classes at convenient locations.

Facilities

The libraries of Saint Peter's College provide extensive services and research facilities to the College community at both campuses. The Theresa and Edward O'Toole Library in Jersey City is fully automated, and the catalog is accessible via the campus network. The Jersey City and Englewood Cliffs libraries hold more than 300,000 volumes. Both libraries provide access to databases in business, nursing, and the humanities.

Students enjoy the small class sizes and personal attention that are the hallmarks of a Saint Peter's College education.

Technology Environment

Every student has a computer ID that permits access to eighteen computer labs, the campus computer network, e-mail, and the Internet. All classrooms are wired for computer access, enabling faculty members to use a wide variety of instructional resources. The Blackboard Classroom System makes class material available online 24 hours a day, seven days a week, and facilitates communication between students and professors.

Placement

Saint Peter's College guides students toward a successful career, a career change, or advancement in their current professions. Services range from career counseling and resume review to current job listings.

A Standard & Poor's survey of 56,000 business leaders ranked Saint Peter's College in the top twenty liberal arts colleges that have graduated America's leading corporate officers. Saint Peter's College has an alumni network of 20,000 active members across the country and abroad.

Saint Peter's College has four convenient locations that are close to where students work and live.

Admission

To apply for admission, a candidate completes an application form and submits official college transcripts (in English) showing completion of a bachelor's degree. In addition to this, international applicants must provide evidence of English language proficiency. The College reserves the right to request additional information in order to strengthen an application. An initial review of the complete application for admission is conducted by the Office of Graduate Admissions. The file is then forwarded to the M.B.A. Program Director for an admission decision. All correspondence should be conducted with the Office of Graduate Admissions.

Finances

To make financing an education possible, Saint Peter's financial aid advisers help students explore the best means of affording their degree. Options include tuition deferment and installment plans, employer-sponsored tuition reimbursement plans, and student loans. Interested students should call a financial aid adviser at 201-915-9308.

The cost of tuition for graduate study in 2008–09 is $885 per credit.

Application Facts and Dates

For more information, students should contact:

Office of Graduate Admissions
Saint Peter's College
2641 Kennedy Boulevard
Jersey City, New Jersey 07306

Phone: 201-761-6470
Fax: 201-435-5270
E-mail: gradadmit@spc.edu
Web site: http://www.spc.edu

Schiller International University

Largo, Florida; London, United Kingdom; Paris and Strasbourg, France; Leysin, Switzerland; Heidelberg, Germany; and Madrid, Spain

BUILDING THE INTERNATIONAL THEME AT SIU

For more than four decades Schiller has been known for its serious commitment to international education. Schiller is an American university with campuses in six countries, an international program of study, a multinational faculty, and students from more than 100 countries. This means that students can expect a stimulating multicultural environment and a unique opportunity to study in more than one country in the same university in most fields of specialization. Particularly for students whose career goals include work in an international firm or environment, Schiller's graduate programs provide an excellent foundation.

As a graduate student, you can expect challenging course work in programs that aim to develop each student's theoretical understanding of the subject area and provide grounding in practical applications of the subject matter. Please contact our admissions offices should you have further questions.

—Cathy Eberhart, Dr.Phil., Provost

Programs and Curricular Focus

Schiller students have the opportunity to study the M.B.A program with concentrations in financial planning, international business, international hotel and tourism management, and management of information technology. Program courses involve theoretical and practical applications, strategic decision making, teamwork and group mobilization, understanding diverse interdependent environmental forces, and incorporating ethical standards into business decisions.

The M.B.A. is a free-standing degree program of 36 hours and is available online and at every campus.

However, the 45-semester-credit programs may be completed during two semesters and a summer session on a full-time basis, or in two years on a part-time basis. Students must complete fifteen M.B.A. courses including seven core courses; one of each in the areas of advanced accounting, finance, information technology, international management, international marketing, managerial statistics, and methods of research and analysis. The remaining course requirements include eight electives from approved M.B.A. courses and a final comprehensive examination. The overall GPA for all graduate courses completed must be at least 3.0.

The M.B.A. in international hotel and tourism management is directed to students in the fields of business, hotel/restaurant management, and tourism and related areas who wish to earn an advanced business degree. The course work, comprising five international hotel and tourism management courses, in addition to ten M.B.A. courses, provides the credentials to enter the industry at management level. The degree is offered at the London-Waterloo campus and also at the Florida Campus of SIU. It can be completed in two semesters and a summer session of full-time study, and working professionals can earn this degree on a part-time basis in two to four years. The program consists of fifteen 3-credit courses, plus a final comprehensive examination. The overall GPA must be at least 3.0.

The M.B.A. in information technology is also available online.

The M.B.A. in financial planning is available at the Florida campus and is conducted in conjunction with Kaplan College.

Schiller International University also offers an M.B.A. in IT management.

The Master of Science in computer engineering is one of the newer graduate programs. Interested students should consult the catalog for this program's admission requirements.

M.B.A. programs are offered at SIU's Largo, Florida; London, England; Paris and Strasbourg, France; Madrid, Spain; Heidelberg, Germany; and Leysin, Switzerland campuses as well as online.

Students and the M.B.A. Experience

Schiller is a university where each student counts and is taken seriously and where faculty members know students by name. The close attention paid to each individual student is one of the hallmarks of an SIU education.

The Schiller philosophy is based on the conviction that the give and take between students and their teachers is the very essence of education and can never be replaced, not even by the best technical equipment. It is from this personal relationship that students receive inspiration.

The Faculty

The real assets of Schiller are the high quality of its students and their dedication to serious study as well as the excellence of its instructors. Schiller faculty members are carefully selected not only for the quality of their educational background but also for their practical experience in their fields of expertise.

The educational process puts particular emphasis on developing international and cross-cultural competencies through foreign language skills, facility, intercampus transfer, and other international academic opportunities as well as an intense interaction among people with diverse backgrounds.

The Business School Network

The Office of Alumni Affairs coordinates the University's relationships with former SIU students around the world. Using a computerized list, which is continuously updated, the Alumni Affairs Office issues a University newsletter to all former students and organizes an alumni network to assist potential SIU students. This office is also responsible for collecting evaluations of its own effectiveness. SIU maintains Alumni Affairs staff in the United States to help students and parents in assessing and selecting study abroad opportunities as well as assisting alumni in maintaining their sharing and alumni networking options. An alumni directory is available at each campus.

The College and Environs

Schiller International University was established in 1964, laying the foundation of what was to become a small, independent university offering its students an education of high quality. During the 1960s, when many large universities emerged as mass institutions in which the individual student often felt lost in a crowd, the founding of Schiller was a conscious departure from the growing anonymity of such institutions. With alumni from more than 130 countries and with men and women from more than 100 nations currently enrolled, SIU offers students the unique opportunity to gain an American education in an international setting.

English is the language of instruction online and at all of SIU's campuses in six countries, where students are prepared for careers in academic institutions, business and management, governmental agencies, multinational organizations, and social services or for further education in their chosen field. Through enrollment in both practical and theoretical courses and through discussions in small classes with instructors and classmates of multicultural backgrounds, students gain firsthand knowledge of business and cultural relations among the peoples of the world.

SIU students have the unique opportunity to transfer among SIU's campuses without losing any credits while continuing their chosen program of study. SIU's campuses are in Largo (Tampa area), Florida; central London, England; Paris and Strasbourg, France; Heidelberg, Germany; Leysin, Switzerland; and Madrid, Spain.

Admission

Admissions requirements include completion of a bachelor's degree with a business specialization (i.e., accounting, economics, finance and management, law, marketing, statistics) or a bachelor's degree in a nonbusiness field followed by business studies at diploma-level or a preparatory program. The average GPA for all graduate courses completed must be at least 3.0. The GMAT is not required for admission, but is required for graduation. The GMAT must be taken and scores submitted to Schiller before completion of the student's last term.

To ensure that distance learning applicants feel comfortable with e-mail composition, file attachments, downloading and uploading files, and the use of discussion forums and chat room, the admissions requirements include the completion of two surveys, *Student Self-Evaluation Checklist* and *Survey of Student Technology Experience*, located on the distance learning page of the SIU Web site at http://www.schiller.edu. These surveys must be downloaded as a Word document and returned to the Florida Admissions Office (Susan_Russeff@schiller.edu) as an e-mail attachment. Other admissions requirements for all distance learning students are the same as those as for traditional students.

Finances

Schiller International University is an independent institution with limited funds for financial aid. Students are encouraged to seek assistance through private or governmental loans and scholarship programs before applying to the University.

Students wishing to apply for financial assistance from SIU should request a scholarship application form when applying for admission.

Graduate fees for the one-year program (two semesters and the summer session) of fifteen courses are $21,300.

International Students

From its founding, the University has dedicated itself to the encouragement and active development of international understanding. Schiller study programs have a distinct international focus. Its student body, which is presently from more than 150 nations, has the invaluable experience of studying together with students from many different national and cultural backgrounds and the opportunity to form lifelong relationships. Personal initiative is encouraged throughout. The development of an entrepreneurial spirit is another hallmark of a Schiller education.

Application Facts and Dates

Applications are processed on a rolling basis. For further information, students should contact:

Susan Russeff
Associate Director of Admissions
Schiller International University
300 Edgewater Drive
Largo, Florida 33770
Phone: 727-736-5082
          800-336-4133 (toll-free in the U.S.)
E-mail: admissions@schiller.edu
Web site: http://www.schiller.edu/

Seton Hall University

Stillman School of Business

South Orange, New Jersey

> ▶ **THE PRACTICAL M.B.A.**
> **HIGHLY ACCREDITED, COMPLETELY ACCEPTED, TOTALLY PRACTICAL**
>
> *Program highlights include a 42-credit M.B.A. program that can be completed in as few as eighteen months for full-time students and a full schedule of evening classes to accommodate working professionals. The M.B.A. program at Seton Hall allows students to choose from eight different areas of specialization, including accounting, finance, information technology management, international business, management, marketing, pharmaceutical management, and sport management. Unique dual-degree programs are available with the Seton Hall School of Law (M.B.A./J.D.), the School of Diplomacy and International Relations (M.B.A./M.A.D.I.R.), and the College of Nursing (M.B.A./M.S. in nursing).*
>
> *—Karen E. Boroff, Ph.D., Dean*

Programs and Curricular Focus

The Stillman School of Business at Seton Hall University offers graduate education geared toward the needs of business leaders in a rapidly changing environment. The Master of Business Administration (M.B.A.) program provides the business-discipline knowledge and management skills necessary to lead organizations and manage the effects of technology and globalization. The Master of Science (M.S.) programs focus on accounting, professional accounting, and taxation—fields requiring the support of "retooled" managers with updated skills and knowledge in their respective areas.

The focus of the Stillman School is on transforming concepts into practice, developing in its students the business skills necessary to identify problems, research relevant information, and determine and evaluate alternative courses of action. As the business school of a major Catholic university, the School has a curriculum that also stresses the importance of ethical and socially responsible decision making. The Stillman School is the only New Jersey M.B.A. program and one of only four New York metropolitan area M.B.A. programs in the Global Top 100 ranking by the Aspen Institute for Excellence on Social and Environmental Issues

Developed by corporate partners and Stillman faculty members, students, and alumni, the M.B.A. program enables a select group of students to engage in an intensive study of the critical aspects of business management. The curriculum provides a foundation in accounting, finance, economics, and the behavioral and quantitative sciences as well as the functional areas of business. The first three levels of the

program form the basis from which students choose one of eight areas of specialization: accounting, finance, information technology management, international business, marketing, management, pharmaceutical management, and sport management. Students also have the ability to add a second area of specialization to their degree programs. To address the growing interest of graduate students in starting their own business, the School's Center for Entrepreneurial Studies now offers a certificate in entrepreneurship.

Classes are often team-taught by Stillman faculty members, who are chosen for their strong academic credentials, practical business knowledge, and innovative teaching methods.

Students and the M.B.A. Experience

A Stillman M.B.A. student experiences a program that can best be described as a combination of innovative program development paired with a unique classroom delivery system. The emphasis on transforming concepts into practice, continued faculty development, and the integration of technology into the learning process have come together to form the strong foundation on which the program is built.

The graduate student population has an average of five years corporate work experience upon entering the program. The average age of the M.B.A. and M.S. candidates ranges from 27 to 30. The types of students that the Stillman School attracts work in a variety of industries. Some of the corporations that employ Stillman School students are Johnson & Johnson; JP Morgan Chase; Ernst & Young; Continental Airlines; National Sports Network; Schering-Plough; Nissan North America, Inc.; and Prudential

Financial. The Stillman graduate degree has always been recognized in the corporate arena as being superior in its ability to prepare working professionals for the challenges of a dynamic global marketplace.

Global Focus

The Stillman School of Business recognized the need for the integration of global business practices into its curriculum long before it became a '90's catchphrase. The Institute of International Business was established in 1964 and facilitated the development of relationships with international universities in China, the Dominican Republic, France, Russia, Poland, Ireland, and Italy. The Institute, which sponsors international academic scholars, is also responsible for developing and implementing a joint-degree program with the John C. Whitehead School of Diplomacy and International Relations. The School has also maintained an alliance with the University of International Business and Economics in Beijing for nearly three decades, as well as partnered with Shanghai Institute for Foreign Trade and Macau University.

The Faculty

Stillman School's faculty members facilitate professional business education through a variety of teaching methods, including lectures, seminars, "live" and simulated business cases, and the integration of technology. The School's low student-faculty ratio and small class size encourage one-on-one interaction. Its faculty members have expertise in all areas of business, have their works published regularly in nationally and internationally recognized business journals, and are often contacted by the media.

Jubilee Hall, home of the Stillman School of Business.

The Business School Network

Seton Hall's network of corporate partners and alumni is extensive. Alumni commitment is ongoing through active participation in the Stillman School of Business Advisory Boards, which are nested in the School's disciplines and unique initiatives, such as the Center for Securities Trading and Analysis, the Center for Sport Management, and the Center for Entrepreneurial Studies. When the School has needed the input of business leaders in program development, alumni have willingly contributed their time and shared their expertise.

The College and Environs

Seton Hall's heritage has provided the School with the foundation for its success. Founded in 1856, Seton Hall is the oldest diocesan Catholic university in the nation and maintains regional accreditation through the Middle States Association of Colleges and Schools. Located on 58 acres in the suburban village of South Orange, New Jersey, the University is 14 miles from New York City and less than one half mile from the Midtown Direct train.

The Stillman School of Business, founded in 1950, earned national recognition when it became the first private business school in New Jersey to earn accreditation by AACSB International–The Association to Advance Collegiate Schools of Business. Most recently, the School is listed as one of the *Princeton Review*'s Best 290 Business Schools for having outstanding academic offerings with the M.B.A. program.

Facilities

The state-of-the-art Jubilee Hall, housing the Stillman School, has corporate-style breakout and multimedia rooms, a student lounge, a computer lab and technical support services solely for business students, and an amphitheater. Another facility that confirms Seton Hall's commitment to innovation is the 155,000-square-foot Walsh Library, which is open 24 hours a day, Monday through Friday. It seats more than 1,100 and contains CD-ROM databases (both index and full-text), multimedia computer labs, audiovisual installations, an electronic visual aid (scanner-reader), and Setoncat, the online catalog of holdings accessible both on-site and via the campus network.

Technology Environment

The Center for Securities Trading and Analysis, also known as the Trading Room, offers students a genuine feel for Wall Street and prepares them to track, analyze, and model transactions across a variety of securities, including stocks, bonds, options, exchange rates, and commodities. The Trading Room provides access to the latest financial market data, including Bloomberg and Reuters data feeds. Data display boards, trading desks, dual-display computers, Web cameras, and other interactive multimedia features create regular interaction between students, faculty members, and Wall Street industry professionals.

The Center for Sport Management is home to the Seton Hall Sports Poll. Conducted by The Sharkey Institute, it is the first University-based ongoing polling service to delve into the multibillion-dollar sport industry, and its findings—which have garnered national media attention—serve as a barometer of public opinion on the many issues confronting sports today.

Placement

The Career Center at Seton Hall University offers programs that help students develop the skills necessary to achieve professional success. Offering students the ability to create a career development and management plan, the Career Center has been instrumental in helping students secure summer internships and gain employment with top companies. These internships and job opportunities are the result of strong partnerships with employers in the New York and New Jersey metropolitan areas. Corporations are also afforded the opportunity to recruit Stillman graduates online and to participate in on-campus career events throughout the year. Some past events included networking forums and an annual career fair. More than 300 organizations actively participate in on-campus events each year and many more place job ads online through the University-wide eRecruiting database.

Admission

Admission to the Stillman School of Business is selective. For consideration, applicants must hold a baccalaureate degree from an accredited college or university. The Stillman School welcomes applicants from business and nonbusiness undergraduate majors. Although all applications are considered based on individual merit, a minimum undergraduate GPA of 3.0 (on a 4.0 scale) is required. The average GMAT score is 560. (Students should note that seasoned managers may be eligible for a GMAT waiver.) An application is considered complete and is reviewed by the graduate admissions office upon receipt of the completed application form, required letters of recommendation (academic and/or business), a current resume, a 250- to 500-word personal statement, official transcripts from all undergraduate and graduate institutions attended, GMAT scores, TOEFL scores (international applicants only), and a $75 application fee. Students who are in the process of completing an application and wish to take classes may do so by entering the Stillman School as a nonmatriculated student. Non-matriculated students are advised by the Office of Graduate Admissions and may take up to 12 credits in any given program. Students applying to one of the dual-degree programs (M.B.A./M.S.N., M.B.A./J.D., M.B.A./M.A.D.I.R.) must meet the admission standards and be accepted by each school in order to enter the program.

Finances

Graduate tuition for the 2008–09 academic year is $941 per credit. Students are also charged a University fee ($85 for part-time students and $105 for full-time students) as well as a technology fee ($100 for part-time students and $200 for full-time students) each semester. All domestic students are eligible to submit a FAFSA form to the Financial Aid Office to determine what types of federal loans and grants they are qualified to receive. Full-time students may also want to apply for a Graduate Assistantship position by visiting the Graduate Admissions Web site at http://www.shu.edu/applying/graduate. These positions offer students tuition remission up to a certain number of credits per semester and a small monthly stipend in exchange for working on campus. Both of these financial options may be pursued only after the student has applied and been accepted to a graduate program.

International Students

Applications from international students interested in full-time studies are encouraged. The University's Office of International Programs (OIP) provides and organizes a wide variety of supportive services. The Stillman School of Business's Institute for International Business works closely with visiting dignitaries and scholars. For more information, students should visit the OIP Web site at http://academic.shu.edu/oip/ or the International Admissions Web site at http://www.shu.edu/applying/graduate/international.cfm.

Application Facts and Dates

Although graduate applications are considered on a rolling basis, the priority deadlines are May 31 for fall admission, March 31 for summer admission, and October 31 for spring admission. To apply online or download an application, students should visit the Stillman School of Business Web site at http://business.shu.edu. For further information, students should contact:

Stillman School of Business
Office of Graduate Admissions
Seton Hall University
400 South Orange Avenue
South Orange, New Jersey 07079-2692

Phone: 973-761-9262
Fax: 973-761-9208
E-mail: stillman@shu.edu
Web site: http://business.shu.edu

SMU ⬛ COX Southern Methodist University

Edwin L. Cox School of Business

Dallas, Texas

▶ TRANSFORMING THE WORLD OF BUSINESS—ONE PERSON AT A TIME

The M.B.A. program at the Cox School of Business in Dallas, Texas, is positioned to provide you with all of the benefits of an exciting and rewarding business career. Through our unique combination of programs and extensive connections to the business community, the Cox School will prepare you to be a leader in this rapidly changing and globally oriented economy. The American Airlines Global Leadership Program will provide you with a hands-on experience in one of the four major business regions of the world—China, India, Latin America, and Europe. Cox's unique Business Leadership Center hones your leadership and management skills, and our Associate Board Executive Mentoring Program matches you with a senior-level business executive who can act as a career coach and role model. Only the M.B.A. program at the Cox School offers these programs to enhance your career, provide hands-on business learning, and enrich your personal experience.

—Albert W. Niemi Jr., Dean

Programs and Curricular Focus

The Cox M.B.A. program provides an integrated curriculum that helps students establish a solid foundation for success in business. The small class size encourages students to work closely with faculty members and individualize their M.B.A. experience. Located in Dallas, a national and international business center, the Cox M.B.A. program offers nationally recognized faculty members, a global focus, and close ties with the business community. At Cox, students gain much more than a business education—they gain a personalized business experience.

The M.B.A. curriculum is composed of 61 credit hours that include a global experience and a modular curriculum. The Cox School's program builds a strong portfolio of diverse international perspectives and course offerings for the Cox M.B.A. student.

First-year students complete a series of core courses in business fundamentals, the Global Leadership Program (GLP), required career and communication skills seminars, and business elective courses. Students commence their summer internships after they return from the GLP travel-abroad experience.

Second-year students take courses from the elective concentration curriculum. The modular curriculum allows students to take multiple courses each term, which is divided into two sets of eight-week courses. Some of the courses are closely integrated, while others are stand-alone courses. This design provides students with greater curriculum

flexibility, which allows them to build depth in an area of emphasis or create breadth for a broader perspective of business.

M.B.A. students can choose to concentrate in the following areas: finance, with a specialization in alternative asset management, corporate finance, or investments; marketing, with a specialization in marketing consulting or product and brand management; strategy and entrepreneurship; strategic leadership; information technology and operations management; accounting,

with a specialization in financial statement analysis; financial consulting; and general management.

In addition, two joint-degree programs are available: the M.A. in arts administration/M.B.A. (two years) in conjunction with the Meadows School of the Arts and the Juris Doctor/M.B.A. (four years) in conjunction with the Dedman School of Law.

Cox's distinguished Business Leadership Center (BLC) complements the classroom curriculum throughout the two-year period. The BLC's innovative program is designed to help students develop effective management skills through seminars that center on interpersonal and communication skills, team building, and negotiation skills. Courses are organized by business leaders and taught by outside consultants from some of today's most progressive corporations.

In addition to the full-time, two-year M.B.A. program, Cox offers a part-time, two-year Professional M.B.A. program developed for working professionals and a twenty-one-month Executive M.B.A. program for candidates with significant managerial experience.

Students and the M.B.A. Experience

Cox students come from all regions of the United States and the world. The M.B.A. program consists of approximately 175 full-time students, with 25 percent coming from countries other than the U.S. Students have a wide variety of academic disciplines and professional experiences. The average amount of work experience prior to entering the M.B.A. program is four years, and the average age is approximately 28. Women make up nearly 30 percent of the population, and members of minority groups account for 20 percent of the student body.

Cox's small size not only promotes collaboration among students, it also creates a close and supportive environment for students and faculty and staff members. The small size also gives students significant opportunities to assume leadership roles in M.B.A. student organizations, such as the Finance Club, the Buyside Club, the Marketing Club, the Consulting Club, and Women in Business.

Global Focus

Today's business leaders must be global thinkers. At Cox, global thinking is incorpo-

EDWIN L. COX SCHOOL OF BUSINESS

rated into the M.B.A. curriculum. The Global Leadership Program is a mandatory yearlong learning experience that culminates in a two-week travel-abroad course. Transportation, lodging, and most meals are provided to all students at no cost thanks in part to the generosity of American Airlines and additional sponsors. All first-year students travel to one of four regions of the world—China, India, Europe, or Latin America—to meet with business and government leaders. The goal is to allow students to experience how business is conducted globally. In addition, the School's location at the gateway to NAFTA and Latin America is well positioned for enhancing international perspectives.

An international exchange program allows select students to experience their international business education firsthand by studying abroad. Cox has relationships with schools in Argentina, Australia, Belgium, Brazil, China, Denmark, England, France, Germany, Italy, Japan, Mexico, Singapore, Spain, and Venezuela.

Special Features

Like the Business Leadership Center, Cox institutes provide a forum for students, faculty members, and the business community to participate in interactive programs and research. Two of Cox's most prominent institutes include the Caruth Institute of Entrepreneurship, which focuses on entrepreneurship, and the Maguire Oil & Gas Institute, which promotes the study of oil and gas industry issues.

The Faculty

Cox students benefit from a nationally recognized faculty that is approachable and accessible and is as dedicated to teaching as it is to research. Classes are taught using a variety of teaching methods that are best suited for the course material, including cases, lectures, class discussions, student presentations, team and field projects, and computer simulations. The Cox M.B.A. curriculum is developed to equally emphasize quantitative and qualitative skills.

The Business School Network
Corporate Partnerships

At Cox, interaction with the business community is encouraged and formalized for students. The School established the Associate Board Executive Mentoring Program with nearly 250 top business executives who actively serve as mentors to Cox M.B.A. students.

In addition to being a valuable source of business contacts, a mentor relationship provides students with insightful career advice, an inside track on current business trends, and a valuable perspective from an experienced businessperson.

Prominent Alumni

Prominent Cox alumni include Thaddeus F. Arroyo, CIO, Cingular Wireless; C. Fred Ball, Chairman and CEO, Bank of Texas; Thomas W. Horton, EVP Finance and Planning and CFO, AMR Corporation; Ruth Ann Marshall, President of the Americas, MasterCard International; and James Mac-Naughton, Managing Director, Rothschild, Inc.

The College and Environs

SMU, established in 1911, has six different schools and graduate programs in addition to its undergraduate program. The total undergraduate and graduate population is approximately 11,000 students.

The University's location in one of the world's major centers of commerce gives students an excellent advantage. The Dallas/Fort Worth metroplex ranks high both in the United States and globally as a site of multinational corporate headquarters. Dallas offers a wide variety of cultural events and opportunities, from major-league sports to the nationally renowned Myerson Symphony Center and the Dallas Museum of Art.

Technology Environment

From state-of-the-art classrooms to the Business Information Center, the Cox School offers the latest in business technologies. The Cox School offers wireless networking, which allows students to use their laptop computers on the network from a classroom, a study room, or throughout the buildings. Students utilize an in-house network (accessible from home) to communicate with other students and faculty members, connect with the Internet to conduct classroom assignments, and access numerous business databases and research tools. All new Cox M.B.A. students are required to own or have access to a laptop computer for use in their M.B.A. courses.

Placement

The M.B.A. Career Management Center (CMC) partners with students to help develop and implement successful career strategies. This is accomplished by creating and implementing an individualized Career Development Plan tailored to meet each individual student's needs. The personalized approach to each student's career is what is most distinctive about the Cox CMC.

Admission

Admission to the M.B.A. programs at the Cox School of Business is highly selective. The Admissions Committee seeks to admit students who represent various geographic, economic, religious, and ethnic groups and have a diverse set of work experiences and educational backgrounds.

Successful applicants are well-rounded individuals who have clearly demonstrated academic achievement in addition to a commitment and capacity for leadership in today's dynamic business world.

Finances

The cost of tuition and fees for 2007–08 was $39,010; books and supplies were approximately $2000. Off-campus housing generally costs between $600 and $1200 per month. Scholarships are available and are awarded strictly on merit.

Application Facts and Dates

Students enter the full-time program in the fall semester only (orientation is held in mid-August). Application deadlines for all applicants to the full-time M.B.A. program are as follows: November 15, January 15, March 1, and April 15. To be given priority consideration for scholarships, students should submit a complete application by March 1. International students are strongly encouraged to apply by January 15. Starting April 16, new applications are considered on a space-available basis.

Students enter the part-time M.B.A. program in the fall (orientation is held in August) or spring (orientation is held in January). The application deadline for fall admission is June 10 and for spring admission, November 18.

Patti Cudney, Director of M.B.A.
  Admissions
Edwin L. Cox School of Business
Southern Methodist University
P.O. Box 750333
Dallas, Texas 75275-0333
Phone: 214-768-1214
    800-472-3622 (toll-free)
Fax: 214-768-3956
E-mail: mbainfo@cox.smu.edu
Web site: http://www.coxmba.com

Southern New Hampshire University

Manchester, New Hampshire

REAL-WORLD MANAGEMENT—THE GLOBAL M.B.A. AT SOUTHERN NEW HAMPSHIRE UNIVERSITY

The number of emerging markets and companies doing business around the world has increased exponentially in the last decade. So if you're not thinking globally, you're missing out.

Southern New Hampshire University has been graduating business leaders for more than seventy years. Our Global M.B.A., the only one of its kind in northern New England, offers the broad management knowledge of an M.B.A. with a global focus and the opportunity to earn a second credential by delving deeper into specific fields.

At Southern New Hampshire University's School of Business, we pay attention to the qualities industry leaders tell us they want in employees. As a result, our graduates are equipped with the knowledge, skills, and wisdom to benefit any organization. We've often been told that our graduates contribute from day one on the job.

—Dr. Martin Bradley, Dean

Programs and Curricular Focus

Southern New Hampshire University students get an impressive degree and a global perspective that is valuable in any workplace. The University's Global M.B.A., the only one in northern New England, offers the broad management knowledge of an M.B.A. with a global focus and the opportunity to delve deeper into specific fields.

The School of Business' Global M.B.A. goes beyond a traditional M.B.A. to include a global perspective and the opportunity to use electives to earn a second credential—a graduate certificate—specific to students' interests. Students tailor their M.B.A. to fit their needs. No other school in northern New England offers this option. Options include finance, human resource management, integrated marketing communications, international business, international finance, international sport management, information technology, operations management, sport administration, and taxation.

Southern New Hampshire University's Global M.B.A. program offers students a range of program options and learning experiences to accommodate the needs of the diverse student body. Both full-time and part-time options are available, and courses may be taken on campus, at one of School's locations throughout New Hampshire and in Maine, or completely online. The Global M.B.A. can be completed in as little as two years.

Southern New Hampshire University is accredited by the Association of Collegiate Business Schools and Programs (ACBSP).

The emphasis of the University is on excellence in teaching, reflected in the combined academic and professional application approach of all of its business programs.

Students and the M.B.A. Experience

The philosophy at Southern New Hampshire University is that there are no limits to what its students can achieve. With a culture that inspires every person, every day, to do more, learn more, try harder, and exceed expectations, everyone at the University is dedicated to helping students realize their potential.

Southern New Hampshire University is a premier university with a small-college feel. Here students find caring, credentialed faculty members; high-quality academic programs; small classes; state-of-the-art facilities; and an exciting campus culture.

The School's diverse student body—students and alumni come from more than seventy countries, and many of the faculty members come from or have taught in other countries—creates a dynamic atmosphere for learning. While some of the students enter the program directly out of college, most have two or more years of work experience to share in the classroom. The University realizes the need for students to gain a world view of business and has been successful in recruiting students from more than twenty-five countries.

Students range in age from 21 to 64 and represent a broad spectrum of academic backgrounds and disciplines.

Global Focus

Southern New Hampshire University's Global M.B.A. program includes students from around the world. Canada, Colombia, Egypt, India, Japan, Kenya, Mexico, Russia, South Africa, South Korea, Spain, Sweden, Taiwan, and Turkey are among the countries represented in the program.

In small-class settings, students are exposed to one another's cultural backgrounds and business practices, significantly enhancing their Global M.B.A. experience.

The Global M.B.A. curriculum is developed to incorporate the program's international perspective. Case studies and practical applications in required course work provide students with a critical understanding of global business issues.

Students wishing to develop a more intensive global focus may pursue a certificate in international business or the M.S. in international business in combination with the M.B.A. degree.

The Faculty

The School of Business's full-time faculty members (more than 60, the most of any school in northern New England) have worked and taught all over the world and bring an expertise that cannot be duplicated. A few examples are Dr. Massood Samii, former chief economist for OPEC; Dr. Bulent Aybar, a multinational finance expert with consulting customers throughout the United States and Europe; Dr. Yusaf Akbar, a trade expert who has taught in Bulgaria, Hungary, France, and England; and Dr. Jane Legacy, a leadership and education expert who has taught in the United Arab Emirates, Greece, and Malaysia.

The Business School Network Corporate Partnerships

Since its inception, Southern New Hampshire University has developed extensive links to local, regional, national, and international corporate entities. Advisory boards made up of corporate leaders consistently assist the School in developing programs that match the needs of the business community. An international alumni network that is linked to many of the world's leading corporations provides students with contacts who assist them throughout their working careers.

The College and Environs

The University is located on the Merrimack River in Manchester, New Hampshire, northern New England's largest city and the "most livable" city in the East, according to *Money* magazine. Downtown Manchester, just minutes away, is home to a number of fine and casual ethnically diverse restaurants, clubs, cultural attractions, sports venues, and the Verizon Wireless Arena. It is an hour's drive from Boston and the state's coast, lakes, and mountain recreational areas.

Facilities

The School of Business is housed in Webster Hall on the main campus in Manchester. The building contains modern lecture halls, classrooms, and seminar and conference rooms. The building houses a computer center, classroom PCs are networked, and students have access to the Internet with their own accounts. Wireless access is available. Centers, which also offer the Global M.B.A., are equipped with library access, computer labs, student resource areas, and more.

Technology Environment

Southern New Hampshire University's computing resource center supports a variety of business programming languages. Statistical and analytical packages such as SPSS and simulation and modeling software, including Arena, are also accessible, along with specialized programs in marketing, production, accounting, artificial intelligence/ expert systems, and other disciplines. PROLOG and SQL are used in certain courses, and personal computer software used in courses includes EXSYS/ReSolver, Office 97/2000, System Architect, and other Windows-based application software. The School is the headquarters of the *Journal of Educational Computing Research.*

Placement

Southern New Hampshire University's Career Development Center provides extensive on-campus recruitment opportunities. In addition, internships for credit are available to full-time degree candidates approved by the faculty. Additional services include career advising and assistance in resume preparation.

Admission

Students with bachelor's degrees from accredited institutions are invited to apply to Southern New Hampshire University's Global M.B.A. program. Although many applicants have work experience in business or other professional settings, students who are just completing their undergraduate careers are also encouraged to apply.

Unconditional admission to the Global M.B.A. program requires that the student has previously completed specific business-related courses. Students lacking the courses may be required to take graduate business foundation courses. International students whose native language is not English must submit TOEFL results.

Finances

Graduate tuition for the 2007–08 academic year ranged from $699 to $1434 per course.

Application Facts and Dates

Admissions decisions are made on a rolling basis. For more information, students should contact:

Graduate Admission and Enrollment Services
Southern New Hampshire University
2500 North River Road
Manchester, New Hampshire 03106-1045

Phone: 603-644-3102
Fax: 603-644-3144
E-mail: graduateprograms@snhu.edu
Web site: http://www.snhu.edu

International students can obtain applications online or from:

International Admissions
Southern New Hampshire University

Phone: 603-645-9629
Fax: 603-645-9603
E-mail: s.harvey@snhu.edu

Syracuse University

Syracuse, New York

THE WHITMAN EXPERIENCE

With a 160,000-square-foot state-of-the-art facility, the Whitman School continues to aim high by partnering in the greater community to develop ever-more-relevant learning experiences for students. At the same time, we work with practitioners to tackle business challenges and strengthen economic development. These partnerships not only make for a vibrant learning environment; they are also increasing our national visibility.

Whitman continues to develop excellent academic programs for our students and give them the resources they need to enter the real world. Our far-reaching network of alumni and friends has proven to be a great source of inspiration and support for our students–in fact, this year, Whitman has partnered with alumni and friends as never before, to lead international trips to India and Chile, launch the Brand Management Summit, and place more curricular emphasis on experiential learning.

Whitman has increased recruiting partnerships and remains focused on making global experiences a priority for its students. Whitman continues to be a diverse learning community, developing leaders in an era of global competitiveness and technological advancements. Whitman is an exceptional place to learn and grow, offering students experiences that promote intellectual engagement, personal and professional growth, and lifelong scholarship.

—Melvin T. Stith, Dean

Programs and Curricular Focus

The M.B.A. curriculum is based on the premise that all managers need broad knowledge and skills, as well as functional expertise.

The heart of the curriculum is its integrated group of professional core courses that introduce the concepts of the functional areas of business and the relationships that exist among them. Elective courses are also integral to the program, offering students the opportunity to tailor the program to their own professional and career interests.

Concentrations are offered in six areas: accounting, entrepreneurship, finance, general management, marketing management, and supply chain management. A few elective courses may also be selected from other graduate programs at Syracuse University. Joint-degree programs may also be pursued that combine a master's degree in another graduate program with the M.B.A.

The M.B.A. program is completed in 54 credits. During the first year, students follow a prescribed sequence that includes personal skills

courses and most professional core courses. During the second year, students complete their required core courses as well as electives. There is an accelerated M.B.A. program for those who hold an undergraduate degree in management from an AACSB International–accredited program and have significant work experience.

Additional graduate degree programs include the Master of Science (M.S.) in accounting, M.S. in finance, M.S. in media management (offered jointly with the S. I. Newhouse School of Public Communications), and a part-time executive independent-study M.B.A. (iMBA) program (a limited-residency distance learning program). Joint-degree programs include the Juris Doctor (J.D./M.B.A. and J.D./M.S. in accounting) in cooperation with the College of Law and the Master of Public Administration (M.P.A./M.B.A.) with the Maxwell School of Citizenship and Public Affairs as well as with other graduate programs at Syracuse University.

Students and the M.B.A. Experience

The Whitman School of Management M.B.A. program has a diverse, talented, and interactive student body. Nearly one third of the 150 full-time M.B.A. students are women, and approximately 50 percent are from outside the United States. The majority of the M.B.A. students have worked full-time for at least one year prior to enrolling; the average is three years.

Undergraduate majors include such diverse areas as history, engineering, nursing, accounting, and economics. Small classes, averaging 30 students or fewer, help create a feeling of intimacy within a large collegiate environment

of 18,500 students and prepare graduates for today's team-oriented organizational environment.

Global Focus

Courses incorporate international and global perspectives throughout the entire curriculum. Another important aspect of the program is that the student body—half of whom are international students representing twenty countries—naturally acquires familiarity with international and intercultural aspects of business through classroom discussion and group project work.

Students may also take advantage of international internship opportunities. Most recently, students completed internships in London, Madrid, Shanghai, Singapore, and Hong Kong.

Special Features

New students begin the fall semester with Learning Is a Team Effort (LITE) Week, a five-day orientation program; participants include the faculty and distinguished business leaders. LITE Week offers new students opportunities for building teams and support groups and an introduction to other personal skills areas, including managing conflict, communication, ethics in management, and teamwork and groups.

The Faculty

The members of the faculty of the Whitman School are distinguished by their accomplishments in research and consulting, their effectiveness in the classroom, and their genuine concern for students. Teaching methods vary from subject to subject, as appropriate. Methods of instruction include lectures, student presentations, class discussions, case studies, small-group projects, computer and management simulations, and other techniques. Instructional methods take full advantage of the program's small group structure and unique experience base represented by the students in the program.

Faculty List

Michel Benaroch, Ph.D., NYU. Knowledge modeling, knowledge systems.

Chung Chen, Ph.D., Wisconsin. Time-series modeling, forecasting methods.

Ravi Dharwadkar, Ph.D., Cincinnati. International management issues in emerging markets.

Fernando Diz, Ph.D., Cornell. Trading, market volatility, derivative securities.

Fred Easton, Ph.D., Washington (Seattle). Capacity management issues in service and manufacturing organizations.

David G. Harris, Ph.D., Michigan. Effects of taxation on business decisions.

Maurice Harris, Ph.D., Syracuse. Market microstructure, asset volatility, corporate finance.

Donald Harter, Ph.D., Carnegie Mellon. Management information decision sciences.

Peter Koveos, Ph.D., Penn State. International financial market behavior, especially as it pertains to economic systems in transition; theory and practice of financial system reform.

E. Scott Lathrop, Ph.D., Cornell. Adaptive decision-making process, decision making in complex choice tasks, behavioral consequences of brand equity.

Michael Morris, Chris Witting Chair of Entrepreneurship; Ph.D., Virginia Tech. Entrepreneurship and emerging enterprises.

Kira Reed, Ph.D., Connecticut. Intellectual capital in organizations, issues in strategic human resource management.

Minet Schindehutte, Ph.D., South Africa. Entrepreneurship and emerging enterprises.

William Walsh, M.B.A., Syracuse. Taxes for closely held businesses.

David Wilemon, Ph.D., Michigan State. Managing innovative markets, technology teams.

The Business School Network

"In considering new hires," says Peter M. Sturtevant, a vice president of Xerox Corporation, "one of the qualities we look for is the ability to be a quick study—to get a good understanding of the company quickly."

Whitman M.B.A. graduates are quick studies, because they can draw on broad exposure to business and business practitioners. Corporate ties are woven throughout the fabric of the program, affording contact with managers in every relevant field and specialty. Whitman graduates find themselves at home in today's complex corporate environment.

The College and Environs

Founded in 1870, Syracuse University is a private, nonsectarian liberal arts institution and is one of the largest and most comprehensive independent universities in the nation. The Whitman School of Management, in existence since 1919, has offered graduate programs since 1947.

Syracuse is a moderately sized, friendly city located in upstate New York. Boston, New York City, Cleveland, Philadelphia, Pittsburgh, Toronto, and Montreal are all less than a half-day's drive away. Most importantly, being so close to these major metropolitan centers provides ease of access for graduates to the vast northeastern U.S. job market.

Facilities

The University libraries serve the informational and research needs of the entire Syracuse University community. The library system is one of the largest in the country and ranks in the top 2 percent of university libraries nationally. It contains more than 10 million books, periodicals, and pieces of microform information housed in the main Ernest Stevenson Bird Library and five branch libraries.

The state-of-the-art Whitman facility incorporates the newest technology available, including videoconferencing, multimedia classrooms, high-tech team meeting rooms, and wireless access throughout. The University's resources also include sixteen computer clusters of approximately fifty computers each as well as wireless access throughout the campus.

Placement

The Career Center provides students with personal help on developing interview skills, resume preparation, alumni networking, access to on-campus corporate recruiting, and a number of specialized career fairs. Employers of the class of 2007 included such diverse organizations as Accenture, BDO Seidman, Bear Stearns, Ernst & Young, NBT Bank, and PetCareRX.

Admission

Applicants must submit transcripts of all previous college work, GMAT and TOEFL scores, a completed application for admission, two letters of recommendation, and responses to a group of personal history and essay questions, together with a $65 application fee. Prior work experience is strongly preferred, and personal interviews are encouraged. An online application can be found at https://apply.embark.com/grad/syracuse/37/.

Finances

Tuition in 2008–09 is $1069 per credit. Books and other course materials are estimated at $1325 per academic year.

Approximately 80 percent of the M.B.A. students receive merit-based assistance in the form of scholarships or a fellowship. Scholarships vary from partial to full tuition remission. The fellowship includes full remittance of tuition plus a stipend.

Application Facts and Dates

Applications for admission to the full-time programs should be submitted no later than March 1 for international students and May 1 for all other applicants for fall admission.

For more information, applicants should contact:

For the master's programs:
Carol J. Swanberg
Director of Admissions and Financial Aid
M.B.A. and M.S. Programs
Martin J. Whitman School of Management
721 University Avenue, Suite 315
Syracuse University
Syracuse, New York 13244-2450
Phone: 315-443-9214
Fax: 315-443-9517
E-mail: MBAinfo@syr.edu
Web site: http://whitman.syr.edu/mba

For the Ph.D. program:
Ravi Dharwadkar
Director, Ph.D. Program
Martin J. Whitman School of Management
721 University Avenue
Syracuse University
Syracuse, New York 13244-2450
Phone: 315-443-3549
Fax: 315-443-5584
E-mail: srhiemst@syr.edu
Web site: http://whitman.syr.edu/phd

Texas Christian University

Neeley School of Business

Fort Worth, Texas

THE NEELEY ADVANTAGE

There are real differences among nationally recognized M.B.A. programs. At the Neeley School, our focus is on individual development. We believe that innovative solutions to complex business problems can best be developed by teams of individuals who bring different perspectives, not by groups of people who have been trained to think alike. Our program will help you build on your strengths, develop new skills and perspectives, and enhance your ability to work with others. By emphasizing experiential learning, our program helps you learn how to translate your knowledge into action. As a result, our graduates are recognized for the ability to make meaningful differences within the organizations that they join. Simply stated, Texas Christian University (TCU) makes a difference in the lives of people who make a difference in business.

—Daniel G. Short, Dean

Programs and Curricular Focus

The Neeley School brings together highly motivated professionals and exceptional faculty members in a personalized, interactive environment. TCU's Texas location in the Dallas/Fort Worth metroplex—home to hundreds of leading companies—gives students frequent and meaningful interaction with business leaders. Learning goes beyond the classroom to hands-on experiences that impact the bottom line. Neeley is committed to an experience that is personal, connected, and real.

At Neeley, the M.B.A. is not a one-size-fits-all program. Recognizing that students have different backgrounds and career goals, several options are available. The twelve-month Accelerated M.B.A. is targeted to individuals with significant academic and professional backgrounds in business looking to move forward within their career field. Neeley is one of an elite group of accredited business schools to offer this M.B.A. option. The Full-time M.B.A. is a comprehensive two-year program that allows students to explore career options to make a broader career change. The Professional M.B.A. is an evening program that allows students to earn a business degree without putting their careers on hold.

The Neeley M.B.A. is more than a collection of classes—it is an integrated experience. Core faculty members meet regularly to coordinate topics, schedules, and projects to ensure that students gain a well-rounded strategic perspective of business and can assimilate the information into problem-solving skills. Concentrations are available in accounting, business consulting, entrepreneurship, finance/corporate finance, finance/investments, general management,

marketing/product and brand management, marketing/managing customer relationships, and supply chain management.

Students and the M.B.A. Experience

The Neeley Full-time M.B.A. entering class includes a select group, typically of 50 to 65 students from a wide variety of cultural, geographic, professional, and academic backgrounds. The small class size creates an interactive team-based learning environment that encourages different points of view. On average, Neeley students bring four to five years of previous professional experience to the program, allowing them to share a rich mix of professional perspectives. Academic backgrounds of the students are varied: business, liberal arts, engineering, health services, technology, and education.

At Neeley, the focus is on experiential learning. Students gain real experiences that are both attractive to recruiters and key to exploring new career interests. Students serve as corporate consultants, learn hands-on financial modeling and forecasting, manage a $2-million investment portfolio, experience career-building internships, and learn global business practices in China, Chile, Germany, India, Italy, Japan, or Korea.

Global Focus

Neeley's international-experience electives provide students the opportunity to learn firsthand about the issues related to global business. The courses are taught in English by Neeley faculty members and are offered between regular semesters to make them more convenient. Students travel to major and emerging world markets, usually for ten to fourteen days, to participate in company

visits, presentations by local business and civic leaders, and lectures by local scholars. Students choose among courses taught in Chile, China, India, Italy, Germany, Japan, or Korea.

Special Features

Through Neeley & Associates (N&A) Consulting, leading-edge instruction on consulting practices is combined with consulting practice. Student teams are hired by corporate clients to tackle issues ranging from marketing to real estate to supply chain. Each team is mentored by one of the N&A principals, who are second-year students selected as program leaders. In addition, consultants from major global consulting organizations provide mentoring and coaching to the teams.

The Neeley School is home to the nation's second-oldest student-run investment portfolio. Students in the Educational Investment Fund (EIF) manage more than $2 million and are the ultimate decision makers.

Leadership development is recognized at the Neeley School as essential to career advancement. Neeley combines many of the same leadership assessment tools used by major companies with feedback from expert staff members and industry leaders to relate the assessment results to the student's professional development. Through workshops, online tools, and one-on-one coaching sessions, each student creates an individual plan for development.

The Faculty

The Neeley School's nationally recognized faculty comprises expert educators who bring both academic and real-world perspectives to the classroom. They are respected researchers and frequent consultants to industry. Neeley faculty members are dedicated, accessible teachers and mentors who take an active interest in the professional development of their students.

The Business School Network

From day one of their Neeley M.B.A. experience, students have frequent and meaningful interaction with important business contacts. Whether through the Executive Speaker Series or guest classroom speakers, Neeley students are kept abreast of the latest industry trends. They are coached

and mentored by alumni and other executives through leadership development programs, career development sessions, and the M.B.A. Mentor Program. Neeley students are challenged to think on their feet and provide tangible results as they interact with corporate clients in consulting projects as well as get feedback on cases from recruiters, national competitions, and the Integrative Project.

The College and Environs

Founded in 1873, Texas Christian University (TCU) is an independent private university. TCU limits its total undergraduate and graduate enrollment to about 9,000 students so all may benefit from personalized programs and services. The University has a long-standing reputation for excellence in teaching and research and is accredited by all major accreditation associations. With one of the fifty-largest university endowments in the United States, TCU is able to provide a first-class faculty and outstanding educational resources to its students.

Located 5 minutes from downtown Fort Worth in the city's cultural and park district, TCU's 237-acre campus has some of the most outstanding academic, living, and athletic facilities in the nation. In addition to being a top business location, the Dallas/Fort Worth metroplex offers a great lifestyle, with access to world-class arts, exciting nightlife, major league sports teams, and year-round recreation on area lakes and golf courses.

Placement

Even before the first classes meet, the Neeley Graduate Career Service Center (GCSC) begins working with M.B.A. students to enhance their marketability. Neeley's experienced career-management professionals work with students in key areas such as resume preparation, interviewing and networking skills, salary negotiation, and job search strategies. The staff maintains important connections with top employers from the region, national employers, and international companies to proactively showcase Neeley M.B.A. students. In addition to myriad networking opportunities on campus and in the Dallas/Fort Worth community, Neeley students are sponsored by GCSC to attend major national career fairs. GCSC also provides sponsorships for career outreach experiences, such as networking trips to meet with investment firms on Wall Street or major marketing firms in Chicago.

Admission

The Neeley School seeks to bring together highly motivated and academically talented students from a broad range of backgrounds. Admission is competitive, and the School seeks excellence in its applicants. Candidates should be proactive individuals who can contribute in a highly interactive, team-based learning environment and who have meaningful life and professional experiences upon which to draw. Most of all, the Neeley School seeks focused, motivated students who are dedicated to success.

Finances

For 2008–09, combined tuition and fees for the Full-time M.B.A. program are $29,235 per year. The Neeley School offers a comprehensive scholarship program available to students of all nationalities. Last year, more than 90 percent of the Full-time M.B.A. students were awarded either scholarships or graduate assistantships. In addition, numerous loans and grants are available to U.S. citizens with demonstrated financial need.

International Students

The Neeley School recognizes that a global perspective is essential to good business and warmly welcomes students from across the globe to its M.B.A. program. Typically, international students make up 25 percent of the Full-time M.B.A. class.

Application Facts and Dates

Application deadlines are as follows: November 15 and January 15 (early decision and scholarship priority), March 1 (general admission and scholarship deadline), and April 15 (extended admission and scholarship deadline). After these dates, applications are accepted on a space-available basis. Due to the limited class size, students are encouraged to apply early.

For more information, applicants should contact:

Ms. Peggy Conway
Director of M.B.A. Admissions
Neeley School of Business
Texas Christian University
P.O. Box 298540
Fort Worth, Texas 76139
Phone: 817-257-7531
    800-828-3764 Ext. 7531
    (toll-free)
Fax: 817-257-6431
E-mail: mbainfo@tcu.edu
Web site: http://www.mba.tcu.edu

UCLA Anderson School of Management

Los Angeles, California

UCLA ANDERSON SCHOOL

UCLA Anderson was founded over seventy years ago with a mission to provide business education and thought leadership for Los Angeles and Southern California. Today, we are recognized internationally as an innovator in management education and research. As a leader in advancing knowledge about business models, decision making, and market behavior, UCLA Anderson's faculty and research centers are influential in shaping theoretical and practical developments in critical areas ranging from global capital markets, information technology management, and organizational strategy to entrepreneurship and leadership. Our alumni network is vast, reaching the highest levels of business, government, and nonprofit organizations across the world, affirming the value of a UCLA Anderson education and a community that is so well connected.

The intellectual capital of our world-renowned faculty is a key distinguishing feature of all of our programs and is essential to who we are as a leading business school. We have created a culture built on integrity, teamwork, and an entrepreneurial spirit and are nimble in adapting to emerging business challenges and opportunities. Using our extensive network of faculty and staff members, alumni, leading executives on our board of visitors, and corporate partners throughout the world, we constantly create new forums and learning programs that challenge conventional thinking about business and management. The opportunities presented by the vibrant and rapidly changing Southern California region add a special advantage and are leveraged into powerful learning and immersion experiences woven throughout our programs.

If you are stimulated by joining a learning partnership to explore what is on the horizon in business and are motivated by rigorous academics, then UCLA Anderson is the place for you. Our faculty members and students are focused on the market forces and technological developments that are transforming global business today. We started with a promise to prepare our students to lead organizations. Today, we are a global leader, transforming how business people think and act.

—Judy D. Olian, Dean and John E. Anderson Chair in Management

Programs and Curricular Focus

The UCLA Anderson School M.B.A. Program is designed for highly motivated, exceptional students and is structured to ensure that each graduate leaves with a leadership-level knowledge of all key management disciplines as well as the conceptual and analytical frameworks underlying those disciplines. Consisting of three components—the management core, advanced electives, and the management field study—the curriculum is regularly updated to address the evolving challenges today's business managers must meet.

UCLA Anderson School's M.B.A. program has a general management focus that enables students to tailor individual discipline-based programs of study rather than declare a major or concentration. There are nine specialized areas of study and several interdisciplinary studies.

All students are required to take the management core, a set of ten courses that provides the base knowledge for the major functional fields of management. The management core provides the first building blocks on which advanced study in a variety of areas can be developed. The ten core courses are integrated and sequential, so that each successive course builds upon the knowledge gained in prior courses.

Twelve courses of the M.B.A. curriculum are composed of advanced electives chosen from any of the nine disciplines: accounting, business economics, decision sciences, finance, human resources and organizational behavior, information systems, marketing, operations and technology management, and strategy and organization, as well as the interdisciplinary areas of study: entrepreneurial studies, entertainment management, international business and comparative management, and real estate.

The ratio of electives to core courses and the flexibility that students can practice in choosing electives adds breadth to each student's program of study.

The Management Field Study is the capstone requirement of the M.B.A. program and is conducted during the second year of the program. In this project, students integrate and apply their knowledge and skills in a professional setting outside the classroom.

UCLA Anderson provides three M.B.A. programs for individuals whose professional goals require that they remain employed while completing their M.B.A. degree. The Fully Employed M.B.A. Program is targeted toward emerging managers who seek to take on increased levels of responsibility and expanded management roles within their organizations. The Executive M.B.A. Program is an intensive twenty-four-month program designed for midcareer professionals seeking to develop broad-based management skills, while balancing jobs with high levels of responsibility. The UCLA-NUS Global Executive M.B.A. program is designed to train top executives for the global marketplace. Students of this dual-degree program enter two of the world's leading graduate management schools: UCLA Anderson and National University of Singapore Business School.

Students and the M.B.A. Experience

The UCLA Anderson School of Management has a vibrant student body whose extraordinary intellectual, cultural, social, and athletic energies spill out of the classroom into a plethora of nonacademic activities. The average full-time student is 28 years old, with a little more than 4½ years of full-time work experience. Women make up 35 percent of the student population, members of minority groups make up 21 percent, and international students make up 33 percent.

From day one, UCLA Anderson teaches students how to work effectively with others to transform ideas into realities. Teamwork is part of everyday life at Anderson. Students work together in study groups, on class assignments or field study, and other projects.

Global Focus

UCLA Anderson offers students a wide range of exciting opportunities to increase their international perspectives, from working on group projects with peers from among the forty-five countries represented at Anderson to studying abroad and from enrolling in the International Management Fellows Program to touring a factory in Prague.

UCLA Anderson encourages students to become involved in academic exchange programs with universities located abroad. Currently, the school participates in more than fifty academic foreign exchange programs.

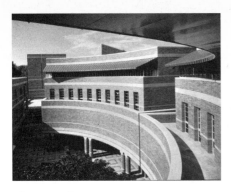

The Faculty

The mainstay of UCLA Anderson's high-quality management education programs is its esteemed faculty. Each year, UCLA Anderson faculty members demonstrate the caliber of their intellectual abilities by publishing groundbreaking research in leading scholarly journals. The scholarly success that UCLA Anderson faculty members achieve sets the stage for the curriculum they implement in the classroom. Through their scholarship in fundamental areas as finance, marketing, operations and technology management, organizational behavior, global economics, and strategy, the faculty members help create the enduring value of a UCLA Anderson M.B.A., helping graduates achieve continual success in business.

UCLA Anderson has a total of 116 faculty members and twenty-three chaired professorships.

The Business School Network
Corporate Partnerships

The UCLA Anderson School Board of Visitors (BOV) comprises more than 70 highly successful entrepreneurs and business executives from around the world who bring a wealth of expertise and experience to the leadership and advancement of management education. The BOV actively assists the dean in the ongoing qualitative growth of the School. Among them are John E. Anderson, the School's namesake and President of Topa Equities, Ltd.; Jeffrey Berg, Chairman and CEO of International Creative Management; B. Kipling Hagopian, founder of venture capitalist firm Brentwood Associates; Lester B. Korn, founder of Korn/Ferry International; and Zuisho Hayashi, President and Chairman of the Board of the Japan-based HUMAX Corporation.

Prominent Alumni

UCLA Anderson alumni make up an eclectic body of talented business leaders and research professionals, from corporate executives to entrepreneurs and from management consultants to film producers and entertainment executives. UCLA Anderson alumni enjoy lifelong bonds with fellow graduates, current students, and faculty and staff members through an extensive agenda of programs worldwide. Events that typically were social in nature have been refocused to address career and personal development issues.

Hire Anderson is an Anderson Alumni Association initiative to assist graduating students and alumni seeking career opportunities in an increasingly competitive job market. The list of prominent alumni includes Jeff Henley ('67), Chairman of Oracle Corporation; Mitch Kupchak ('87), General Manager of the Los Angeles Lakers; Laurie Younger ('83), President, Buena Vista Worldwide Television; Kelly Perdew ('95), winner of "The Apprentice;" and Steve Wadsworth ('88), President, Walt Disney Internet Group.

The College and Environs

Strolling to classes through the serene gardens on UCLA's campus, it is easy to forget that the UCLA Anderson School is located in the middle of the second-largest city in the United States. For UCLA Anderson students, Los Angeles offers the best of many worlds. Beach, mountain, and desert recreation areas are plentiful and easily accessible by car. Los Angeles museums and theaters offer the world's most acclaimed entertainment. In addition, Westwood Village, which adjoins the UCLA campus to the south, offers shopping, dining, and a wide range of services.

Facilities

UCLA Anderson's management education complex is a testament to the school's vision of the growing importance of superior management education. UCLA Anderson students and faculty and staff members have the latest and finest technological resources, including wireless, to maximize their research, teaching, investment, and commitment to management education. Classrooms, conference rooms, and auditoriums are equipped with computers and video projection systems for multimedia presentations, and every seat in every classroom, the library, and every student breakout room is wired for laptop computer use. Rosenfeld Library is the information partner of UCLA Anderson and an integral part of Anderson Computing and Information Services. One of the thirteen UCLA libraries, it is ranked a leading academic business library in the *College and University Business Libraries Statistics.*

Placement

Career planning begins before students enter UCLA Anderson and becomes increasingly focused during the M.B.A. program. Starting in the summer before students enroll, extending into Orientation Week, and continuing throughout graduation, UCLA Anderson's John E. Parker Career Management Center (Parker CMC) helps students define their career objectives, identify resources, strategize opportunities, hone interviewing skills, and make critical connections. The center's skilled professional staff assists UCLA Anderson M.B.A. students and alumni in creating personal career development strategies and connecting to employment opportunities worldwide by leveraging a powerful global network of professional business executives. The Parker CMC also partners with M.B.A. recruiters and their firms throughout the world to ensure that they receive the timely services and guidance needed to fill important positions within their organizations.

Admission

The UCLA Anderson admissions policy emphasizes academic ability, leadership, work experience, and breadth of life experiences. UCLA Anderson students come from diverse backgrounds yet share important qualities such as superior intelligence, the ability to think broadly and analytically, strong interpersonal skills, and a desire to solve complex problems. The Admissions Committee evaluates applicants' prospects as future leaders and their projected ability to succeed and profit from the M.B.A. program. The committee carefully considers biographical and academic background information, GMAT and TOEFL (for most international applicants) scores, achievements, awards and honors, employment history, letters of recommendation, and college and community involvement, especially where candidates have served in a leadership capacity.

Finances

Tuition for the full-time UCLA Anderson M.B.A. program during the 2008–09 academic year is $31,760 for California residents and $39,050 for nonresidents.

Room and board for the 2008–09 academic year are $13,407. Books and supplies are $11,230 (including the cost of a laptop computer). Transportation, entertainment, and miscellaneous costs are $6180. These costs are for students living off campus in shared housing. Additional costs may include support of dependents and medical expenses. Married students should expect to budget about $4000 in additional costs from personal resources, as financial aid only covers the student's costs.

Application Facts and Dates

Applicants may apply for fall admission beginning in September of the previous year. The Admissions Committee begins considering applications in November of each year. For more information, students should contact:

Mae Jennifer Shores
Assistant Dean and Director of M.B.A.
    Admissions and Financial Aid
UCLA Anderson School of Management
110 Westwood Plaza, Suite B201
Box 951481
Los Angeles, California 90095-1481
Phone: 310-825-6944
Fax: 310-825-8582
E-mail:
    mba.admissions@anderson.ucla.edu
Web site: http://www.anderson.ucla.edu/

University of California, Riverside

The A. Gary Anderson Graduate School of Management

Riverside, California

DEVELOPING FUTURE LEADERS

The A. Gary Anderson Graduate School of Management (AGSM) is all about growth. We are the program of choice for students, recruiters, and faculty members who wish to focus on how to identify and evaluate growth opportunities and how to launch and develop, as well as manage and sustain, those opportunities. AGSM faces the important growth markets of the future along the Pacific Rim, in Asia, and in South America. All of the growth industries of the future are in our backyard: biotechnology, nanotechnology, information technology, communications, and health-care services. At AGSM, you are a part of a living laboratory in which you can see and experience firsthand the issues, opportunities, and problems associated with growth. You will also interact with one of the most diverse student bodies found in any university. Growth requires a willingness to embrace diversity—diversity in markets, diversity in the workforce, diversity in the community. AGSM is also about personal growth; we challenge our students to grow as individuals, as leaders, as managers, and as contributors to community. We invite you to come grow with us.

Programs and Curricular Focus

At AGSM, students receive a thorough grounding in the fundamental concepts of business that lead them to explore elective areas specific to their future success. The faculty focuses on entrepreneurship, technology transfer, e-commerce, supply chain management, information technology, health-care management, communications, and international business. The program also prepares students to excel in a competitive international environment. The curriculum stresses the interdependencies among functional areas, emphasizing the development of superior management skills based on a strong theoretical foundation. Students learn how to integrate analytical techniques with practical skills to develop solutions. Teamwork and effective communication are underscored.

The curriculum has six major components, including a communication workshop, core courses, electives, an internship, and a capstone course.

The core courses provide the foundation in analytical and managerial skills, while electives allow students to customize their M.B.A. experience based on their individual interests. Students can choose electives from different areas, including accounting, entrepreneurial management, finance, general management, human resources management/organizational behavior, international management,

management information systems, management science/operations management, and marketing.

As part of the M.B.A. program, students are required to participate in an internship. Students work with AGSM Career Services to choose an internship in their area of interest.

Students conclude the twenty-course, 80-unit program with a capstone management course or thesis.

The program is designed to accommodate the unique requirements of both career professionals and full-time students. Sufficient sections of courses are offered in the evenings to permit career professionals to complete the M.B.A. on a part-time basis.

Students and the M.B.A. Experience

UC Riverside has a diverse student population that creates a dynamic learning experience. While some of the students enter the program directly out of college, the average student has about three years of work experience and is 27 years old. Students come from a wide variety of backgrounds and undergraduate studies, which adds to the diversity of the M.B.A. experience and the intellectual environment at AGSM.

Significant emphasis is placed on teamwork, which is accomplished through

study groups and team projects. Students in the M.B.A. program learn to communicate, build relationships, and accomplish a shared objective with their teams.

Special Features

UC Riverside does not view a student's lack of work experience as a negative, and, in fact, it welcomes applications. The M.B.A. program is specifically designed for those who may have limited work experience. As part of the M.B.A. program, students are required to participate in an internship that enhances their learning and solidifies the management concepts taught in the classroom. Students who are working professionals can complete their internships with their current employers.

Currently, AGSM also offers an M.B.A. program in entrepreneurial management at UC Riverside's Palm Desert Graduate Center. The curriculum provides students with the same fundamental concepts as the on-campus/Riverside program.

The Faculty

The A. Gary Anderson Graduate School of Management follows in the tradition of excellence and high standards of the University of California in attracting and recruiting renowned faculty members who represent excellence in their respective areas. Faculty members have doctorates from world-class universities and have published compelling research in top journals in their fields.

The College and Environs

The 1,200-acre Riverside campus of the University of California is conveniently located some 50 miles east of Los Angeles, within easy driving distance of most of the major cultural and recreational offerings in southern California. It is equally close to the beach, the desert, and the mountains.

Southern California can only grow in one direction. UC Riverside and AGSM are directly in the path of that growth.

The Inland Empire in which AGSM resides is one of the fastest-growing regions of the United States. With a population of more than 4 million, it has more people than twenty-four states. The U.S Department of Commerce has forecast that the Inland Empire will grow faster than any other area in the United States over the next decade.

Technology Environment

UC Riverside is a leader in infusing technology into the learning process. The University's students and professors have the world's resources available to them at the click of the mouse. The California Digital Library connects the libraries of all UC campuses through the Internet. The award-winning GROWL allows students to take care of academic business in a one-stop Web portal. Intel rated UC Riverside among the top twenty U.S. university campuses for wireless computer accessibility.

The AGSM Computing Facility provides resources for academic course work and related activities. The facility operates on a convenient schedule and includes fifty Intel-based desktop computers running Windows, several high-capacity printers, and a scanner. Knowledgeable consultants are always available to students. The facility is conveniently located in the south wing of the Anderson complex.

Placement

A full range of career planning placement services is offered through the Career Services Center. The center is staffed by professional counselors who can address the specific career needs of graduate business students. Available services include on-campus interviews, career seminars and workshops, individual counseling, an alumni career network, and an extensive career library offering computerized employment databases. The staff members of the AGSM Career Services get to know students personally and can uniquely individualize partnerships between the business community and students.

The M.B.A. Academic Internship Program at the A. Gary Anderson Graduate School of Management was designed to provide students with an opportunity to gain meaningful work experience by exploring jobs in various industries and work environments. The internship also allows students to combine academic knowledge and skills acquired in the classroom and apply them in a business setting, working on real-world projects. The learning experience gives students an opportunity to demonstrate and stretch their capacity to bring serious analytical thinking to problems of strategic importance in business.

Admission

Admission is open to eligible students from all undergraduate majors. Applications are accepted for admission in the fall quarter only. Admission is based on several criteria, including the quality of previous academic work as measured by the GPA for the last two years of undergraduate work; scores on the Graduate Management Admission Test (GMAT) and TOEFL (for international applicants); letters of recommendation; meeting general requirements for graduate status, as set forth in UC Riverside's General Catalog; and potential for success in the program. The program seeks promising individuals who have potential for future leadership.

Finances

Tuition and fees for the 2007–08 academic year for full-time students were $24,231 for California residents and $36,476 for nonresidents. Part-time fees were $13,390.50 for California residents and $19,425.50 for nonresidents. The approximate cost for books, supplies, board, and personal expenses was estimated to be $10,850 per year for full-time residents and $3675 for part-time students.

Several kinds of financial assistance are available. These include fellowships, teaching assistantships, and research assistantships. Loans and work-study may be applied for through the University Financial Aid Office.

Application Facts and Dates

Applications are accepted for the fall quarter only. The application deadline for domestic students is May 1, and it is February 1 for international students.

Applications are processed and decisions are made when files are complete. For further information, applicants should contact:

A. Gary Anderson Graduate School of Management
University of California, Riverside
Riverside, California 92521-0203
Phone: 951-827-6200
E-mail: mba@ucr.edu
Web site: http://www.agsm.ucr.edu

University of California, San Diego

Rady School of Management

San Diego, California

THE RADY SCHOOL: INNOVATION TO IMPACT

Here at Rady, we think of our impact in terms of discoveries brought to the marketplace, products launched, new service models established, and companies started or reinvented. We are a community focused intently on intellectual discovery and learning—and on action. We develop leaders for organizations that are driven by constant innovation and for industries that are transforming the world.

—Robert S. Sullivan, Dean

Programs and Curricular Focus

The Rady School of Management at the University of California, San Diego (UC San Diego), educates global leaders for innovation-driven organizations. A leading professional school within one of the top-ranked institutions in the U.S. for higher education and research, the Rady School offers a full-time M.B.A. program and a FlexMBA program for working professionals in two formats: FlexEvening and FlexWeekend.

The M.B.A. curriculum places a special emphasis on issues faced by innovation-driven organizations, with a focus on the life sciences and technology industries, allowing Rady M.B.A.'s to develop expertise in these key industry sectors. The School works collaboratively with the business community and with the UC San Diego campus. In the Rady program, students work in teams alongside faculty members and mentors from the business community.

The Rady M.B.A. programs combine a rigorous core curriculum with electives focused on business and management issues faced by emerging and innovative organizations. The core curriculum culminates in Lab to Market, a three-course sequence that begins in the classroom and moves into a project-based environment. Students develop the skills necessary to take an idea to market and gain exposure to commercialization opportunities at the world's leading research institutes.

Students may take selected graduate courses in other academic departments at UC San Diego to support their educational and career goals.

Students and the M.B.A. Experience

Rady students come from a wide variety of academic, professional, and personal backgrounds. What they have in common is a passion for innovation. Rady M.B.A. students are driven to innovate and are passionately interested in the ways business and the world are being transformed by discovery and development in science and technology. They explore, seeking ideas and opportunities, and want to learn how to launch ideas into the marketplace.

The School promotes an active, collaborative learning environment, reaching beyond the School to the campus and the business community. Students work in teams, undertake real-world projects, and collaborate with students from other UC San Diego graduate programs.

The Faculty

Rady School faculty members draw upon their research and passion for innovation to educate the next generation of leaders who will shape the practice of business globally. Rady School faculty members are recognized experts in their fields, always seeking new knowledge and new practices for business. They are dedicated to education and to ensuring that Rady M.B.A.'s have the knowledge and skills to be effective as managers and leaders in an ever-changing business world. For up-to-date information on faculty appointments, students should visit the Rady School Web site at http://rady.ucsd.edu/faculty/.

The Business School Network

San Diego is a great place to study—and a great place to live. The University, research institutions, and innovative business community are a magnet for attracting smart, successful people to the region. The San Diego area is home to more than 400 life science companies and 500 technology companies, and UC San Diego itself is an engine for regional economic growth. UC San Diego faculty members and alumni have spun off more than 250 local companies, including many of the region's biotechnology companies.

The Rady School is a critical node in the San Diego innovation network and a catalyst for building bridges and enhancing relationships. Collaborations are common in the region, which has a track record of amazing innovation—especially in life sciences, high technology, and communications. Organizations are making generous commitments to the Rady School—industry executives participate as speakers and serve as mentors to Rady students.

Beyond the region, the Rady School has strong relationships with companies that find its focus on innovation-driven organizations appealing. Internationally renowned corporations hire Rady students for internships and career positions.

UC San Diego has more than 90,000 alumni, with active alumni association chapters throughout the country and abroad. The Rady School also has its own Alumni Association, which gives Rady M.B.A.'s an extended network for both social and professional development.

The College and Environs

The Rady School is located on a campus that is at the forefront of scientific discovery and technological innovation. UC San Diego has rapidly become one of the top institutions in the nation for higher education and research. UC San Diego was named the "hottest school for science" by *Newsweek* magazine and ranks seventh in the nation for National Academy of Sciences membership. *U.S. News & World Report* ranks UC San Diego as the seventh-best public university in the nation, and the National Research Council ranks it tenth in the nation in quality of its faculty and graduate programs. The University has been home to 16 Nobel Laureates (former and current faculty members).

The UC San Diego campus is nestled along the Pacific Ocean on 1,200 acres of coastal woodland. Known for its near-idyllic climate, San Diego offers 70 miles of pristine beaches for Rady students to enjoy.

Technology Environment

The Rady School actively promotes the use of technology as a learning tool. The School's learning management system serves as a portal to the academic program, and the School's intranet links students to the School community. The School's IT support provides access to the latest technology, including wireless access in the School's facilities and across the campus.

Placement

Rady's MBA Career Connections Office provides a comprehensive career management program. MBA Career Connections begins working with full-time M.B.A. students early in the first year of the program, providing career assessment and individual and group career advising/coaching, as well as a comprehensive series of career workshops, including resume writing, behavioral and case interviewing, job and company research methods, and salary negotiation. Career Connections also offers assistance with job and internship searches, including an on-campus interviewing program, job postings, company information sessions, industry nights, and corporate networking events. Career Connections actively works to increase students' access to opportunities in southern California and beyond.

Admission

The Rady School is looking for intelligent risk-takers who are determined to make an impact—people who demonstrate passion and understanding and focus on working in innovation-driven organizations. The School seeks individuals who want to create their own education, who are ready to accelerate their careers, and who will be stakeholders in the future of the Rady School.

Rady full-time M.B.A.'s have the potential to be managers, leaders, and innovators in business and the community. Rady FlexMBAs have demonstrated their leadership abilities, and they have made significant contributions and are ready to have even more impact in their organizations and in business. All are intellectually capable, and many students in both programs have earned a master's or doctoral degree and are finding that their specialized degree has taken them just so far. All see the value a Rady M.B.A. can have for their careers and plan to be active contributors in the classroom, their study groups and teams, the Rady community, and beyond.

Finances

Tuition and fees for the full-time M.B.A. program for 2007–08 were approximately $23,900 for California residents and $36,100 for nonresidents. The FlexMBA program fee for 2007–08 was $37,500. The admissions committee awards merit-based fellowships to highly competitive applicants for the full-time M.B.A. Need-based loans are available to all eligible domestic and international applicants.

International Students

The Rady School welcomes applicants from outside the United States. The School provides focused support services to assist international students.

Application Facts and Dates

The Rady School M.B.A. application and updated information on the School and its programs are available at the School's Web site.

M.B.A. Admissions
Rady School of Management
University of California, San Diego
9500 Gilman Drive, MC 0554
La Jolla, California 92093-0554

Phone: 858-534-0864
E-mail: MBAadmissions@ucsd.edu
Web site: http://rady.ucsd.edu/

University of Colorado at Boulder

Boulder, Colorado

DEAN'S MESSAGE

It is difficult to convey in print the spirit of innovation and dynamic culture that you will find at the Leeds School of Business. We hope you will visit our Web site, ask questions, and engage with the current students, faculty, and staff to learn more.

Success at Leeds comes in many forms: through national and international competitions, you will have the opportunity to test your knowledge against teams from other universities; new business ventures are vetted by students like yourself as they look for market opportunities; and there opportunities to work side-by-side with executives in entrepreneurial environments.

The Leeds faculty is at the forefront of knowledge creation. With outstanding research records and extensive private sector experience, they bring the latest thinking into their classes, along with practical applications of business knowledge.

The University and surrounding community are reflective of the entrepreneurial spirit. New companies are created through technologies created in the campus labs, and the community's entrepreneurial environment has spawned companies including Crocs® footwear and Sambazon® juices, both started by Leeds alumni. The University's excellence has been honored by having 4 faculty members named as Nobel prize winners since 2000.

I hope this message has piqued your interest, and you are ready to learn more. Please know that for every example of the School's creative and innovative spirit, there are hundreds more that you will find when you join the Leeds community.

— Dennis A. Ahlburg, Dean

Programs and Curricular Focus

The Leeds School of Business offers an M.B.A. program with a flexibility that allows the student to design an M.B.A. that will support his or her personal and professional goals. The M.B.A. curriculum provides a comprehensive general management education through the core courses while adding breadth and depth of knowledge through electives.

The M.B.A. requires 55 credits with a minimum GPA for graduation. The required core courses create a strong foundation in business theory and application (28 credits). Electives allow students to develop breadth and depth in a functional area of expertise (finance, marketing, systems, or management) balanced with options in Leeds' niche areas of specialization: entrepreneurship, real estate, and the newest focus—sustainability.

The J.D./M.B.A., the M.B.A./M.S. in telecommunications, M.B.A./M.A. in fine arts, M.B.A./M.A. in theater and dance, M.B.A./M.A. in Germanic languages, M.B.A./M.S. in environmental studies, M.B.A./M.S. in computer science, and M.B.A./M.A. in anthropology dual-degree programs give students specialization options to supplement their management backgrounds.

Students and the M.B.A. Experience

Students in the program come from all over the world, sharing the perspectives and experience they bring from around the globe. Students are broadened by the multicultural experience that takes place within and beyond the classroom. A typical class is 30 percent women and 20 percent international students. The average student is 28 years old with an average of five years of professional experience. The M.B.A. class includes a wealth of diverse professional backgrounds, ranging from consulting to financial services to nonprofit management and from engineering to real estate development to biotechnology.

Special Features

The Robert H. and Beverly A. Deming Center for Entrepreneurship continues to take its place among the top nationally recognized programs. The Deming Center has been ranked among the top 20 entrepreneurship programs for seven consecutive years (*U.S. News & World Report,* 2000 through 2006). Much of the entrepreneurship program's success is the result of the strong connections between the Leeds faculty and the Boulder/Denver business community. By offering entrepreneurially

focused activities, specialized classroom and in-company experiences, and renowned entrepreneurship faculty members and resources, the entrepreneurship center provides an exclusive opportunity for students to expand their entrepreneurial thinking.

The CU Real Estate Center develops leaders in the real estate industry by providing a world-class academic curriculum, internships at major firms, and mentoring relationships with regional industry professionals. The Real Estate Council, a group of more than 270 industry leaders, works closely with the center to ensure that students receive the education and skills needed to excel in the job market. Course offerings include all aspects of real estate, including finance, development, marketing, construction management, architecture, urban planning, environmental law, and growth management. In addition, the Real Estate Center gives students the opportunity to meet with real estate professionals and academics at an annual conference and at a variety of educational and networking events.

The Richard M. Burridge Center for Securities Analysis and Valuation's first mission is to facilitate the exchange of ideas and knowledge between professional investment managers, finance scholars, policy makers, and the investing public. In support of this mission, the center has held an annual research conference and is actively seeking additional outreach opportunities to augment the School's curriculum.

The Faculty

As world-class academics involved in business research, private consulting, and international teaching opportunities, Leeds faculty members are at the frontier of knowledge creation. These top scholars know that they have to gain the respect of established thought-leaders before they can innovate and challenge conventional thinking. Therefore professors use a blend of formal lectures, class discussions, case studies, and company-based consulting projects to offer students a comprehensive understanding of core business fundamentals. Their strong ties to the business community bring a current perspective to the classroom, giving students a strong education built on management theory and real-world business applications.

The University of Colorado at Boulder, nestled in the foothills of the Rocky Mountains, offers a beautiful environment in which to pursue a graduate education.

The Business School Network

By partnering with the business community, the M.B.A. program facilitates critical relationships between students and industry professionals. Advisory boards, comprising prominent executives, work with students to provide mentoring and support.

Students gain pragmatic experience by interacting with regional and international firms. Colorado's unique business environment provides a setting in which established corporations enjoy success, and entrepreneurial ventures flourish. The region has business niches in the computer, telecommunications, and biotechnology industries as well as the renewable energy sector and the natural foods business.

The College and Environs

The University of Colorado at Boulder ranks tenth among public research universities and third among rising research universities in the public sector. The campus is strategically located near the mountains and city, so students can drive west and be atop the Continental Divide or drive east to Denver.

Acres of protected open space surround Boulder, providing beautiful hiking, biking, and riding trails. The city of Boulder hosts a variety of cultural and recreational activities, including the Colorado Shakespeare Festival, the Colorado Music Festival, and the Bolder Boulder 10K run.

Placement

The Business Career Center helps students choose their professional paths. The center offers individual counseling, strategic career assessment, and help with internship and post-M.B.A. placement and sponsors a variety of seminars and professional activities to help students meet their professional goals.

Whether a student is making a major career transition or accelerating his or her current career path, the Business Career Center takes a proactive role in preparing each student for his or her long-term career goals. Beginning with resume work, continuing with industry seminars and individual career planning, and through the internship and post-M.B.A. job search, the Business Career Center works with students during every step of their professional journey.

The Business Career Center helps students discover professional opportunities in their local business communities and works with them to search outside of the School's geographical area, tapping established contacts and alumni who are connected with the School.

Admission

In the admissions process Leeds' mission is to select the brightest, most talented and diverse candidates each year—looking for a balance of qualitative elements and quantitative strengths and a richness of cultural, ethnic, professional, and personal perspectives as well as the right attitude and lots of potential. As a result, the admission process is not held hostage by numbers and statistics. Instead the focus is on selecting those applicants who will thrive at Leeds and add value to the programs.

Finances

Full-time tuition per year in 2006–07 was $8982 for residents and $24,156 for nonresidents. Students paid annual fees of approximately $1200. Approximately half of CU–Boulder's students receive offers of fellowship funding. Other funding sources available to graduate students are loans, federal grants, and work-study.

Application Facts and Dates

The deadline for candidates requesting early decision is December 1. International students and applicants requesting fellowship consideration are encouraged to apply by February 1. The final deadline for all applications is April 1. For additional information, students should contact:

M.B.A. and Executive Programs
Leeds School of Business
UCB 419
University of Colorado at Boulder
Boulder, Colorado 80309-0419

Phone: 303-492-8397
Fax: 303-492-1727
E-mail: leedsmba@colorado.edu
Web site: http://leeds.colorado.edu/mba

University of Colorado at Colorado Springs

Graduate School of Business Administration

Colorado Springs, Colorado

DEAN'S MESSAGE

The M.B.A. program at the University of Colorado at Colorado Springs (UCCS) is dedicated to providing an exceptional learning environment for current and future business leaders. Our culture emphasizes collaborative excellence. Our professors balance superior teaching with cutting-edge research. What distinguishes us from other graduate business programs is our blend of business practice and research in every aspect of the program. Whether you are expanding into international markets, entering into strategic alliances, or deciding how to pursue new technologies, our highly personalized programs will meet your professional needs. The M.B.A. program trains students in business fundamentals and allows them to pursue specialty areas that mirror their specific interests and address the issues affecting business today. And it offers the flexibility necessary to complete the program successfully and in time. We are also very much excited about our recognition three years in a row by the readers of the Colorado Springs Business Journal as the Best Business School in the region. It is a real honor to be recognized by our business community members and leaders as a school that adds value to our community. Our AACSB International accreditation goes a long way in ensuring that our students get the best-quality education possible.

—Venkat K. Reddy, Dean

Programs and Curricular Focus

The M.B.A. program at the University of Colorado at Colorado Springs allows students the opportunity to explore cutting-edge issues that challenge businesses, and it offers the ultimate in flexible delivery of courses. The Graduate School of Business Administration is recognized as one of the premier graduate business programs in the region and is the only graduate program in southern Colorado to independently earn accreditation by AACSB International–The Association to Advance Collegiate Schools of Business. Full-time, doctorally qualified faculty members enrich students' classroom experience with their own experience in research, academic publishing, community involvement, and industry consulting.

The M.B.A. program offers a broad business foundation that also allows students to concentrate on specialized areas of emphasis or select courses to design a curriculum that fits their personal and professional goals. To earn the degree, students must complete a total of 36 to 51 credit hours, depending on academic background. Courses may be taken on campus or online. Fifteen credits are taken in preparatory courses in accounting, economics, statistics, and business communications, if needed. Twenty-one credits are earned in core courses that cover competency areas directly applicable in today's business world, including financial management, information systems, and marketing strategy.

Students can then complete 15 credits in an area of emphasis that allows them to develop expertise in a chosen specialization. Areas of emphasis in the on-campus program include accounting, finance, homeland defense, inter-national business, management, marketing, operations management, service management, and technology management. The distance program offers students the opportunity to pursue areas of emphasis in finance, health-care administration, homeland defense, information systems, international business, management, project management, and technology management.

The M.B.A. program curriculum is designed for students of all undergraduate academic backgrounds. Up to 15 credits in preparatory courses may be required for students whose academic backgrounds lack certain course material, but these preparatory courses are waived based on equivalent undergraduate course work.

Students and the M.B.A. Experience

There are 225 students enrolled in the campus M.B.A. program and another 225 in the distance M.B.A. program; about 60 percent are men. Approximately half of all students hold undergraduate degrees in business, while other students hold degrees in engineering, science, humanities, social science, education, law, dentistry, and medicine. The average student works 40 hours a week, but 20 percent of students are enrolled full-time. While work experience is not required for admission, the average student starts the program at age 31 and has nine years of work experience.

The M.B.A. program meets the needs of working professionals by offering opportunities for both part-time and full-time study in both on-campus and distance formats. Both formats are available to all admitted M.B.A. students, and students may take courses in either or both mediums. Students taking courses on campus meet once a week in the evening. In the summer, classes meet twice a week during eight-week sessions and four times a week during four-week sessions.

Online M.B.A. classes are asynchronous, allowing students to complete their weekly course work at a time that fits their schedule and still meet course deadlines. The distance M.B.A. degree may be completed entirely online and does not have an on-campus residency requirement.

Students may begin the M.B.A. program during any semester.

The Faculty

The faculty members are doctorally qualified academic scholars from preeminent universities and leaders in their fields, including technology management, global competitiveness, and strategic planning. They also serve as consultants for Fortune 500 companies, conduct research in their business specialty, and author and edit peer-reviewed journals and textbooks.

Faculty List

Thomas W. Gruen, Professor and Chair, Marketing Department; Ph.D., Indiana, 1997.

Ann M. Hickey, Associate Professor of Information Systems and Associate Dean, College of Business; Ph.D., Arizona, 1999.

Clark L. Maxam, El Pomar Chair of Entrepreneurial Finance; Ph.D., Indiana, 1996.

Venkateshwar K. Reddy, Professor of Finance and Dean, College of Business; Ph.D., Penn State, 1992.

Thomas J. Zwirlein, Professor and Chair, Information Systems, Accounting, and Finance Department; Ph.D., Oregon, 1985.

The Business School Network

Faculty members at the UCCS Graduate School of Business Administration have extensive experience in the business world and share their experiences with the students. In addition, many local businesses participate in career fairs at the University and conduct job interviews with students and alumni.

The School maintains a close relationship with the very dynamic Pikes Peak business community. The area is home to leading firms, such as Agilent, FedEx, Front Range Solutions, Hewlett Packard, and Oracle. Close ties to these and other companies are critical to the School's ability to tailor its curriculum to meet emerging business trends. The School also interacts with the business and military communities through its various outreach activities, including Entrepreneur in Residence, Colorado Springs Technology Incubator, the Small Business Development Center (SBDC), Southern Colorado Economic Forum, Colorado Institute for Technology Transfer and Implementation (CITTI), and the Center for Entrepreneurship.

The College and Environs

The University of Colorado at Colorado Springs is situated on a bluff facing a panoramic vista of the Rocky Mountains. It was founded in 1965 and is part of the University of Colorado system. Approximately 8,000 students are enrolled in six colleges. The University provides a full range of academic programs, from bachelor's degrees to doctoral degrees.

Colorado Springs is a beautiful city of 500,000 residents 60 miles south of Denver. With more than 300 days of sunshine annually and four distinct seasons, it is an ideal place to live. Students take advantage of many opportunities for golfing, hiking, rock climbing, mountain biking, skiing, and rafting. In addition, world-class ski resorts are just a 2-hour drive from the campus.

Facilities

The Kraemer Family Library has a collection of 371,900 volumes, 451,500 microforms, 368,800 government documents/maps, 705 current journals in print, and 28,000 journals online in full text.

Technology Environment

The Columbine Hall computer lab operates a fifty-two-station computing lab and seven computerized classrooms. Each computerized classroom is equipped with Windows XP Professional work stations and a laser printer. The El Pomar Information Commons contains 135 PCs, four Macs, and nine black-and-white laser printers.

Placement

The University's Career Center offers a number of services that assist students and alumni in setting career goals and finding employment. Services include on-campus career fairs, career-development workshops, and employer visits that can include on-campus interviewing. Alumni of the program work in a variety of industries, corporations, nonprofit institutions, and government organizations around the globe. They can be found managing project teams, entire corporations, and entrepreneurial ventures.

Admission

A candidate's application should include a completed application for admission, two official transcripts from all colleges previously attended, official GRE or GMAT scores, a current resume, a formal statement indicating the reasons for attending the program, and a $60 application fee. Letters of recommendation are welcome but not required. The application process should begin two to four months prior to the application deadline. The Admissions Committee looks at a number of factors, including prior work experience and academic performance. On average, students enter the program with a GPA of 3.0 or higher, GMAT scores between 540 and 580, or combined GRE scores of 1000.

Finances

Tuition for the M.B.A. program is $607 for the first credit and $397 for each additional credit ($920 for nonresidents). Students in the distance M.B.A. program pay $1971 per 3-credit course. Students may borrow under the Federal Perkins Loan and Stafford Loan programs or secure a loan from a private lender. Colorado residents may be eligible for a Colorado Graduate Grant or a UCCS Tuition Grant; other scholarships may be available from the University or other sources. To qualify for financial aid, students must file the Free Application for Federal Student Aid (FAFSA) before March 1.

Estimated student living expenses in Colorado Springs are $11,000 per calendar year.

International Students

The International Student Services (ISS) office provides international students with a check-in process to introduce them to the University and the campus. ISS also sponsors INFO WEEK, which helps students adjust to life in the United States, and assists with INS requirements. In addition to other application materials, applicants from other countries must submit the international application supplement, an affidavit of financial support, and a $75 application fee. The ISS Office may be reached by telephone at 719-262-3819 or by e-mail at imartine@uccs.edu.

Application Facts and Dates

The Graduate School of Business Administration welcomes applications on an ongoing basis for admission into the fall, spring, or summer session. Regular application deadlines for admission to the M.B.A. program are June 1 for the fall semester, November 1 for the spring semester, and April 1 for the summer semester. Applicants are notified of the admission decision within one month of their application completion date.

Application materials and program information can be requested by contacting:

Graduate School of Business Administration
University of Colorado at Colorado Springs
1420 Austin Bluffs Parkway
Colorado Springs, Colorado 80918

Phone: 719-262-3408
Fax: 719-262-3100
E-mail: mba@uccs.edu
Web site: http://www.business.uccs.edu/landing/petersons2.html

University of Colorado Denver

FLEXIBLE PROGRAMS . . . BUSINESS PARTNERSHIPS . . . WORLD-CLASS TEACHING AND RESEARCH

The University of Colorado Denver (UCD) offers future business leaders a unique combination of flexibility in program schedules, including our 11-Month M.B.A.; faculty committed to excellence in both teaching and research; and close relationship with the Denver business community. This, combined with the vast cultural, recreational, and networking opportunities the thriving downtown Denver environment offers, makes UCD an ideal place for graduate business education. I cordially invite you to learn more about us at the School's home page on the World Wide Web.

—Sueann Ambron, Dean

Programs and Curricular Focus

The Business School at the University of Colorado Denver (UCD) is recognized as one of the premier graduate business programs in the Rocky Mountain region. Graduate programs include a number of flexible options for pursuing the Master of Business Administration (M.B.A.) degree: the Professional M.B.A., the innovative 11-Month M.B.A., the M.B.A. with an emphasis in health administration, the Executive M.B.A, and the Executive M.B.A. with an emphasis in health administration. Focused areas in business-to-consumer marketing, business-to-business marketing, marketing, change management, decision sciences, human resources management, enterprise technology management, entrepreneurship, investment management, information systems, services management, business strategy, international business, corporate financial management, and financial analysis are available as part of the Professional M.B.A.

In addition, Master of Science (M.S.) degrees in seven focused fields of study are offered. For a more specialized business program, students may choose the Master of Science degree in accounting, finance, health administration, information systems, international business, marketing, or management.

All business programs are accredited by AACSB International–The Association to Advance Collegiate Schools of Business. Both the Master of Business Administration with an emphasis in health administration and the Master of Science in health administration are also accredited by the Accrediting Commission on Education for Health Services Administration (ACEHSA). The Master of Science in accounting is one

of a few accounting programs to earn a separate accreditation by AACSB International.

The sixteen-course, 48-credit-hour Professional M.B.A. and the M.B.A. with an emphasis in health administration programs consist of ten core courses that provide an introduction to all functional areas of business management. The emphasis is on integrating the functional area courses through application of theory to real business problems. Skills in both qualitative and quantitative methods of analysis are taught, since both are important for making competitive business decisions. In addition to the functional core, students take elective and special topics courses along with one required international business course. Applications are accepted for fall, spring, and summer, and courses are offered in the evening and/or online, which allows students to work full-time while completing either M.B.A.

The innovative 11-Month M.B.A. is an accelerated, full-time program that enables highly motivated students to complete all M.B.A. requirements in five 8-week sessions plus an international business course abroad. The accelerated format, structured for those students who are not working, provides the same excellent curriculum as the Professional M.B.A. program. The 11-Month M.B.A. program begins in late August, and the degree is completed in mid-July of the following year.

The University of Colorado Executive M.B.A. program is taught in downtown Denver. The executive program invites business executives to participate in a specialized program of seminars with prominent business faculty members from all three University of Colorado campuses.

Classes meet once a week, alternating Fridays and Saturdays, for two academic years.

Dual-degree programs are also available, combining the M.B.A. with any Master of Science degree except the M.S. in health administration (a separate M.B.A. with an emphasis in health administration is offered). Selected graduate study in other schools within the University may also be combined with the M.B.A. In addition, the Business School offers a dual Master of Business Administration/Master of International Management (M.B.A./M.I.M.) degree in cooperation with Thunderbird, the Garvin School of International Management in Glendale, Arizona. Furthermore, students can complete an entire M.B.A., M.S. in finance, or M.S. in information systems online, if so desired.

Students and the M.B.A. Experience

M.B.A. students at UCD are adult learners with an average age of 33. Many students have five to ten years of work experience. More than 75 percent continue to be employed full-time as they complete their degree programs. The Business School seeks diversity in the student body. Approximately 12 percent of the students represent more than thirty countries around the world. UCD is a recognized center of international business, and, as an integral part of the greater Denver community, UCD is committed to including international perspectives in all programs. Services to international students, including assistance with housing, orientation, and immigration concerns, are provided through the Office of International Education. A team of graduate advisers assists all students in the M.B.A. and M.S. programs with degree planning.

The Faculty

M.B.A. and M.S. programs are designed to help students achieve learning and career objectives through interaction with a high-quality, diverse faculty committed to teaching and research. More than 60 full-time faculty members, along with distinguished business professionals, work with students to create a dynamic learning environment. UCD faculty members rank among the top business scholars in the country, conducting leading research directly related to the courses they teach. As a group, the faculty is on the

cutting edge of business knowledge, publishing an average of 100 articles per year in scholarly business journals. Several faculty members have written textbooks used by universities around the world, and many are reviewers or editors for scholarly journals.

The University of Colorado Denver's business students also benefit from the faculty's extensive managerial and consulting experience. In addition, the faculty members of the Business School rank among the best teachers on campus. Several business faculty members have received the prestigious "Outstanding Teacher of the Year" award from UCD.

The Business School Network

The Business School is privileged to have the support of a 45-member Advisory Board, comprising CEOs and senior executives from the greater Denver business community, many of whom are graduates of its programs. The board serves in an advisory capacity to the dean and the faculty on matters concerning curriculum; outreach programs, such as mentoring and internships; and the development of strong ties with the local business community.

Throughout the school year, within the classroom experience, students have the opportunity to participate in more than 120 projects with businesses in the Denver metro area.

The College and Environs

The University of Colorado Denver campus is located in downtown Denver. The mild climate and the city's proximity to the Rocky Mountains contribute to Denver's status as one of the most beautiful and dynamic cities in the country. Students in the Business School benefit from close ties to Colorado's business community through UCD's Executive-in-Residence Program, classroom projects, and numerous networking events.

Technology Environment

Four computer labs on campus (one reserved exclusively for business students) are equipped with IBM-compatible computers that are part of a local area network and linked to the Internet. The Auraria Library houses more than 600,000 books, videos, government publications, and media items, with subscriptions to more than 3,300 journals, magazines, and newspapers. Hundreds of periodicals are accessible full-text via the Auraria Online Information System. Within the library, students have access to more than 250 online and CD-ROM commercial databases and the Internet. With a PC, registered students may access many of these databases from home. The library is a depository of Colorado and U.S. government publications.

Placement

The Business School has a dedicated Business Career Center Advisor and provides many opportunities to bring students and businesses together. A full-service career planning and internship advisory office is also available on campus to all students at UCD. The Career Center offers information and support to students seeking internships with companies in the greater Denver area. Along with providing career counseling and workshops on resume preparation and interview techniques, the Career Center serves as a clearinghouse for employer connections and job vacancy announcements. A computer-assisted resume referral service allows prospective employers to review the qualifications of students and graduates registered with the program and informs students of job openings.

Admission

The Business School admits qualified students for the fall, spring, and summer semesters. A two-part application form, resume, personal essay, GMAT score, two original transcripts in sealed envelopes sent directly from each institution of higher education attended, and an application fee (M.B.A., $50 domestic, $75 international; M.B.A./M.S. dual program, $80 domestic, $95 international) must be submitted by published deadlines. International students whose native language is not English must submit TOEFL scores. Two letters of recommendation are required for all international applicants and also for the 11-Month M.B.A. and the M.B.A. with an emphasis in health administration. The M.B.A. with an emphasis in health administration also requires a personal interview.

Finances

In 2007–08, Colorado resident students in business paid $470 per graduate credit hour; nonresidents in business paid $1118 per credit hour. Full-time graduate business tuition (covering a tuition discount of 12 credit hours) was $4392 for Colorado residents and $9319 for nonresidents. Required student fees totaled approximately $250 per semester. Student health insurance purchased through the University group policy, required for international students, was $1760 per calendar year.

Single students should budget approximately $1000 per month for housing, food, books, and moderate entertainment expenses. UCD provides on-campus housing. Reasonably priced accommodations are also available in nearby neighborhoods.

Financial aid may be available to U.S. citizens through the Financial Aid Office. In addition, graduate scholarships are available to graduate students in business administration through the M.B.A. program or through one of the seven specialized Master of Science programs. Information about scholarships is available at http://cudenver. edu/business.

Application Facts and Dates

The Business School welcomes applications on an ongoing basis for admission in the fall, spring, or summer semester. The 11-Month M.B.A. accepts applications for the fall semester only.

Domestic application deadlines for admission are June 1 for the fall semester, November 1 for spring, and April 1 for summer. International applications should be received by March 15 (fall enrollment), October 1 (spring enrollment), and January 15 (summer enrollment). Completed applications for the 11-Month M.B.A. program must be received by June 15. UCD's programs are competitive; early application is encouraged. Application materials and all program information may be accessed at the School's Web site. For further information, students should contact:

Graduate Admission Office
Business School
University of Colorado Denver
Campus Box 165
P.O. Box 173364
Denver, Colorado 80217-3364

Phone: 303-556-5900
Fax: 303-556-5904
E-mail: grad.business@cudenver.edu
Web site: http://www.cudenver.edu/
business

University of Connecticut

School of Business

Storrs, Connecticut

UCONN M.B.A.—THE DIFFERENCE IS EXPERIENTIAL LEARNING

Educating leaders for more than 125 years, the University of Connecticut (UConn) has grown from a strong regional school in recent years to a prominent national academic institution. In fact, since 1999, U.S. News & World Report consistently ranks UConn among the top public universities in the country as well as the number one public university in New England. In addition, the UConn School of Business ranks among the "Best B-schools" in the nation by Business Week and the Wall Street Journal. UConn's highly regarded M.B.A. program is known for its innovative curriculum design that incorporates distinctive learning accelerators to leverage traditional academic instruction with high-profile corporate partnering in solving practical, real-time challenges. Learning accelerators include edgelab, in partnership with General Electric (GE); SS&C Technologies Financial Accelerator; Student Managed Investment Fund; and M.B.A. Integration Project. Corporate partners in recent years have included Aetna, Pitney Bowes, Pratt & Whitney, Xerox Engineering Systems, GE, WellPoint, and Hamilton Sundstrand. UConn students study in a $27-million research and learning facility. Recognized as one of the most technologically advanced business school buildings in New England, the four-story, 100,000-square-foot facility houses the School's five academic departments (accounting, finance, management, marketing, and operations and information management) as well as classrooms that are outfitted with broad multimedia capability, including a document camera, a microcomputer, and a telephone hybrid system designed to aid in guest lecturer and distance learning scenarios. Each room also includes high-speed Internet connections at every seat, reflecting the School's commitment to meet the demands of the information era. These competitive advantages—the experiential learning component and state-of-the-art facilities and resources—produce M.B.A. graduates who have it all: the fundamental knowledge, skills, and practical experience necessary to compete in business today. Visit us on the Web at http://mba.uconn.edu.

—P. Christopher Earley, Dean

Programs and Curricular Focus

UConn's M.B.A. program integrates experiential learning across all functional business disciplines. The M.B.A. curriculum requires a total of nineteen courses (57 credits) to earn the degree, which takes two academic years.

There are a number of ways in which UConn's M.B.A program distinguishes itself from other highly ranked M.B.A. programs. For instance, UConn's M.B.A. program was one of the first programs worldwide to have a laptop computer requirement as a tool of the trade. However, the greatest differentiating factor of UConn's M.B.A. program is the integration of innovative learning accelerators into the curriculum. These dynamic multipartner initiatives create a real-world environment that significantly leverages the learning process, allowing students to acquire a business education like no other.

One of UConn's earliest experiential learning opportunities was the integration project component. First-year M.B.A. students are assigned to teams and work together throughout their first year as members of these cross-functional teams. The spring semester of the first year culminates in a live, real-company integration project that draws upon all formal course instruction as well as the students' work experiences. Presentations are made to faculty members and business leaders, and students are given structured feedback to hone their technical, analytical, and interpersonal skills. Partnering companies have included Aetna, Pitney Bowes, Xerox, GE, among many others.

A second experiential opportunity is UConn's $2-million student-managed equities fund (SMF). Reporting to the University's investment oversight board, the SMF gives M.B.A. students majoring in finance the opportunity to serve as actual portfolio managers—investing $2 million of the University's endowment funds. As in the case of the laptop requirement, UConn was again one of the first schools in the country to provide real money for student investing experience.

In addition to the student integration project and student-managed equities fund is *edgelab*. Unprecedented in graduate business education, *edgelab* is a strategic alliance between GE and the University of Connecticut School of Business that offers incomparable research facilities and unmatched learning and applied research experience for M.B.A. students. Working in an intensive research environment, M.B.A. students collaborate directly with UConn faculty members and GE executives to generate team-based solutions to real-time, complex, business problems that provide educational value for the students and tangible business value to GE. Teams are typically composed of 3 to 5 students, 2 cross-disciplinary

faculty members, a GE program manager, and GE subject-matter experts. Offering exciting projects that impact real-time needs of GE businesses, *edgelab* has become a center of excellence for new product introductions, stochastic/financial modeling, emerging technologies research, process improvement, risk management, and business development.

UConn's SS&C Technologies Financial Accelerator is a robust multipartner environment in which students, faculty members, and business executives utilize the latest financial technologies and real-time databases to develop solutions to real insurance and financial challenges. Using technology as an aid, the School's faculty members, students, and business partners investigate alternative markets and trader support tools, study insider trading identification and control, review alternative auction market mechanisms, design financial product bundling alternatives that enhance competitive advantage, evaluate emerging technologies, and create specialized algorithms and business processes that increase efficiency, reduce costs, and increase revenues.

Students and the M.B.A. Experience

The type of student a program attracts is an essential ingredient in the quality of the academic experience, and UConn actively recruits the best. The learning environment is also enhanced by the diversity of cultural, geographic, and work backgrounds, creating a microcosm of the business world.

Through paid summer internships with major corporations and smaller entrepreneurial businesses, with which UConn has partnerships, many M.B.A. students acquire additional relevant work experience that augments the academic program by developing effective managerial skills within the students.

The Graduate Business Association (GBA) rapidly becomes an integral part of M.B.A. life. Completely organized and governed by the students, the GBA coordinates corporate

meet and greets with prospective employers, an Executive Speaker Series that brings leading executives to campus for up-close and personal discussions, resume workshops, international dinners, and numerous other events.

Faculty List

Accounting: Stanley F. Biggs, Ph.D., Minnesota. Amy Dunbar, Ph.D., Texas at Austin. Lawrence J. Gramling, Ph.D., Maryland. Robert E. Hoskin, Ph.D., Cornell. Richard Hurley, Ph.D., Connecticut. Mohamed E. Hussein, Ph.D., Pittsburgh. Cliff Nelson, D.B.A., Illinois. Jose Oaks, M.B.A., NYU. Ed O'Donnell, Ph.D., North Texas. John Phillips, Ph.D., Iowa. George Plesko, Ph.D., Wisconsin–Madison. Michael Redemske, M.S., DePaul. Andrew J. Rosman, Ph.D., North Carolina at Chapel Hill. Gim S. Seow, Ph.D., Oregon. Michael Willenborg, Ph.D., Penn State.

Finance: John M. Clapp, Ph.D., Columbia. Walter Dolde, Ph.D., Yale. Assaf Eisdorfer, Ph.D., Rochester. Chinmoy Ghosh, Ph.D., Penn State. Carmelo Giaccotto, Ph.D., Kentucky. Joseph Golec, Ph.D., Washington (St. Louis). John P. Harding, Ph.D., Berkeley. Shantaram P. Hegde, Ph.D., Massachusetts. Ray Kehrhahn, M.B.A., Connecticut. Linda S. Klein, Ph.D., Florida State. John Knopf, Ph.D., NYU. Jeffrey Kramer, Ph.D., Connecticut. Norman H. Moore, Ph.D., Florida State. Kenneth P. Nunn, Ph.D., Massachusetts. Thomas J. O'Brien, Ph.D., Florida. Katherine Pancak, J.D., Boston College. Rexford Santerre, Ph.D., Connecticut. James Sfiridis, Ph.D., Connecticut. C. F. Sirmans, Ph.D., Georgia. John Vernon, Ph.D., Pennsylvania.

Management: Lane Barrow, M.A., Harvard. Kathleen Dechant, Ed.D., Columbia. Richard N. Dino, Associate Dean; Ph.D., SUNY at Buffalo. Juan Florin, Ph.D., Connecticut. Steven W. Floyd, Ph.D., Colorado. Eric Gedajlovic, Ph.D., Concordia (Montreal). Lucy L. Gilson, Ph.D., Georgia Tech. Jodi Goodman, Ph.D., Georgia Tech. Michael H. Lubatkin, Ph.D., Tennessee. Nora Madjar, Ph.D., Illinois. John E. Mathieu, Ph.D., Old Dominion. David D. Palmer, Ph.D., SUNY at Buffalo. Gary N. Powell, Ph.D., Massachusetts. Eugene M. Salorio, D.B.A., Harvard. Zeki Simsek, Ph.D. candidate, Connecticut. John F. Veiga, D.B.A., Kent State.

Marketing and Business Law: Robert Bird, J.D., Boston University. Vincent A. Carrafiello, J.D., Connecticut. Robin A. Coulter, Ph.D., Pittsburgh. Mark DeAngelis, J.D., Suffolk. Karla H. Fox, J.D., Duke. Wynd Harris, Ph.D., Oklahoma. Subhash C. Jain, Ph.D., Oregon. V. Kumar, Ph.D., Texas at Austin. Joseph Pancras, Ph.D., NYU. Charles Peterson, M.B.A., NYU. Girish N. Punj, Ph.D., Carnegie Mellon. Samuel Schrager,

J.D., Miami (Florida). Murphy A. Sewall, Ph.D., Washington (St. Louis). Susan Spiggle, Ph.D., Connecticut. Narasimhan Srinivasan, Ph.D., SUNY at Buffalo. S. Sriram, Ph.D., Purdue. Rajkumar Venkatesan, Ph.D., Houston.

Operations and Information Management: Sulin Ba, Ph.D., Texas at Austin. Ravi Bapna, Ph.D., Connecticut. Sudip Bhattacharjee, Ph.D., SUNY at Buffalo. Jose Cruz, Ph.D., Massachusetts. Robert Day, Ph.D., Maryland–College Park. Moustapha V. Diaby, Ph.D., SUNY at Buffalo. Timothy J. Dowding, Ph.D., Connecticut. Robert S. Garfinkel, Ph.D., Johns Hopkins. Paulo B. Goes, Ph.D., Rochester. Ram Gopal, Ph.D., SUNY at Buffalo. Wei-Kuang Huang, Ph.D., Rutgers. Robert E. Johnson, Ph.D., Rochester. Cuihong Li, Ph.D., Carnegie Mellon. Xinxin Li, Ph.D., Pennsylvania. James R. Marsden, Ph.D., Purdue. Suresh K. Nair, Ph.D., Northwestern. Manuel A. Nunez, Ph.D., MIT. Jeffrey Rummel, Ph.D., Rochester. George M. Scott, Ph.D., Washington (Seattle). Jan Stallaert, Ph.D., UCLA. Lakshman S. Thakur, Eng.Sc.D., Columbia. Yung-Chin Tung, Ph.D., Kentucky. Michael Vertefeuille, B.A., Central Connecticut State. Fang Yin, Ph.D., Texas. Zhongju (John) Zhang, Ph.D., Washington (Seattle).

The Business School Network

Connecticut is located in a major center for financial services, a major manufacturing area with a strong involvement in international trade, and the incredible retail market for the highest per capita income population of any state. One third of the Fortune 500 companies and hundreds of small and medium-sized firms have their headquarters in the unique corporate corridor connecting New York City and Boston, and many of them employ the School's alumni. This greatly facilitates both placement and maintenance of a state-of-the-art curriculum.

The College and Environs

The University of Connecticut is a large, multifaceted institution with nationally recognized professional schools of business, dentistry, engineering, law, and medicine. The University is one of the nation's major public research universities, with 28,000 students, 170,000 alumni, and 120 major buildings on 3,100 acres at the main campus in Storrs.

All of the academic, library, computer, social, and cultural opportunities and facilities of a major university are readily available to all M.B.A. students. Compared to most major universities, UConn's campus is a safe and very scenic environment. The cost of living is substantially less than in most metropolitan areas. The capital and metropolitan area of Hartford is half an hour away, Boston is a 1½-hour drive, and New York City is a 3-hour drive.

Placement

For most M.B.A. students, building and developing a challenging and satisfying manage-

ment career is their primary purpose in attending an M.B.A. program. The University of Connecticut M.B.A. program provides the education, training, support, and opportunities to advance toward this goal. Activities in career planning begin during orientation and continue throughout the two academic years. Career coaching and opportunities to practice specific skills, such as developing effective resumes and cover letters, interview techniques, arranging interviews, and networking, are available to all M.B.A. students. Mock interviews with supportive but tough alumni executives make a significant difference in preparing students for successful interviews.

Admission

Admission is very competitive. The minimum requirements for admission include two years of postgraduate professional work experience; a minimum 3.0 GPA on a 4.0 scale, or the equivalent, from a four-year institution; and a total GMAT score of at least 560. For international students whose native language is not English, a TOEFL score of at least 233 (computer-based) is required.

Finances

The 2006–07 tuition and fees for the full-time M.B.A. program at Storrs for the academic year (two semesters) were $9510 for Connecticut residents and $22,290 for nonresidents. Housing and living costs vary among candidates, but current costs are approximately $4948 for graduate resident housing and $3916 for meals. Additional costs, including required health insurance, textbooks, mobile computer, laundry, and incidentals (estimated at $7000) bring the total yearly cost of attending the M.B.A. program to approximately $25,000 for Connecticut residents and $37,000 for nonresidents.

Financial aid is available in the form of loans, scholarships, and graduate assistantships. Graduate assistantships normally involve working with faculty members, departments, or partnering corporations in research or administrative activities. Offers of graduate assistantships are made to those admitted students with the best qualifications in the School's pool as of April 1.

Application Facts and Dates

Admission into UConn's full-time M.B.A. program is available for the fall semester only. The application deadline for international applicants is March 1 and for domestic applicants, April 15. Admission decisions are made as completed applications are received; therefore, early submission is strongly encouraged.

M.B.A. Program
University of Connecticut
2100 Hillside Road, Unit 1041
Storrs, Connecticut 06269-1041

Phone: 860-486-2872
Fax: 860-486-5222
E-mail: uconnmba@business.uconn.edu
Web site: http://www.business.uconn.edu

University of Dallas

Irving, Texas

THE GRADUATE SCHOOL OF MANAGEMENT IN THE GLOBAL ARENA

Relevance. Rigor. Convenience. Choice. What do those words have to do with selecting the right business school? Everything. With so many business schools to choose from today, it is important to carefully consider the quality of the education you will receive and how well it prepares you to become a leader in your field.

The Harvard Business Review recently published an article about how business schools have lost their way by hiring professors who are qualified to teach but have never engaged in the actual practice of running a business. The Graduate School of Management (GSM) at the University of Dallas (UD) was one of only four business schools the article cited in a favorable light because of our commitment to utilizing faculty members who have actually done what they teach. Our online courses are taught by the same professors who teach our on-ground courses. You get the benefit of faculty experience along with the flexibility of completing any core course or selecting concentrations online or combining online courses with on-campus courses to complete your degree requirements.

When you attend the Graduate School of Management, you will find we offer a rare combination of relevance, rigor, convenience, and choice. This means you can find the program you want—delivered when and where you need it. I invite you to take a closer look at what we can offer you and let us help you find the right program to fit your future plans.

—J. Lee Whittington, Ph.D., Dean

Programs and Curricular Focus

The Graduate School of Management offers a variety of programs and concentrations.

The M.B.A. is a 41-credit-hour* program that provides management education covering both the functional areas of business and critical knowledge and skills required of managers. The curriculum is divided into three components: the value creation core, 17 credit hours (eight courses); concentration/electives, 15 credit hours (five courses); and the integrative core, 9 credit hours (three courses).

Students who wish to develop more specific skills or focus on a particular business environment may select from one of the twenty-one M.B.A. concentrations: accounting, business management, corporate finance, engineering management, entrepreneurship, financial services, global business, health services management, human resource management, information assurance, information technology, information technology service management, interdisciplinary option, marketing management, not-for-profit management, organization development, project management, service management, sports and entertainment management, strategic leadership, and supply chain management.

On GSM's twelve-week trimester system, most full-time M.B.A. students can com-plete their degree requirements in less than two years; part-time students typically complete their degree in 2½–3 years.

The Master of Science (M.S.) is a 31-credit-hour* program designed for students who seek in-depth practical and technical knowledge in a specific field. The M.S. is currently offered in accounting, information assurance, information technology, and information technology service management. The Graduate School of Management also offers an M.S./M.B.A. dual degree (http://www.udallas.edu/gsm/msmba.cfm).

Students who have already earned an M.B.A. may pursue a second master's degree, the Master of Management (M.M.). Adding an M.M. to an M.B.A. can strengthen students' academic credentials and help them stay current in today's and tomorrow's workplace. The Master of Management is a 30-credit-hour* program that provides profession-specific education to those who already hold an M.B.A. from a regionally accredited U.S. college or university or a comparable foreign degree. Students can select from eighteen concentration areas (http://www.udallas.edu/gsm/mm.cfm).

The Graduate Certificate is a 15- to 18-credit-hour* program for individuals looking to acquire specialized knowledge without completing a graduate degree. Each Graduate Certificate consists of five or six graduate-level courses, and students can select from one of twenty concentration areas.

GSM's noncredit Pre-M.B.A. and Intensive English Language Programs allow international students to prepare for graduate studies in business while becoming acclimated to life in the United States. The Pre-M.B.A. Program is an intensive, thirteen-week preparatory program that is designed to enhance communication skills and teach fundamental business concepts. This program is specifically designed to meet the needs of international students who may not have an undergraduate degree in business.

The full-time Intensive English Program utilizes the focal-skills method of instruction, allowing students to progress at their own pace through classes in listening, reading, writing, and immersion, which focuses on all skill areas. Students continuing into a graduate program may take a business fluency course designed to prepare them for oral presentations and writing research papers.

*Depending on previous course work, students may be responsible for satisfying additional requirements.

Students and the M.B.A. Experience

The Graduate School of Management attracts working professionals. The average GSM student is 34 years old and has 7–10 years of work experience. The student profile is 41 percent women, 25 percent members of minority groups, and 20 percent international students from more than fifty countries.

Global Focus

The Graduate School of Management has long recognized the importance of global education. In addition to offering a concentration in global business, the University also offers international study tours, which include faculty-guided study in international business arenas. Also available are student exchange programs offered with partnering universities.

Special Features

The Graduate School of Management was the first business school in the region to assign students to actual consulting projects for local, national, and international firms.

Through the Capstone Experience, students conduct full-scale projects by applying what they have learned to help organizations solve real-world business issues. Unlike other business schools, the Capstone Experience is required for all students in the M.B.A. and M.M. programs. In the past thirty years, Capstone consulting teams have completed classroom-based projects for more than 600 clients.

In addition to its world class curricula, the Graduate School of Management has four academic centers that connect the academic programs and students to the business community by offering essential research services and information resources. These centers are the Center for Global Sustainability and Ethics (http://www.udallas.edu/gsm/cr/ccse.cfm), the Center for Entrepreneurship (http://www.udallas.edu/gsm/ep/center.cfm), the Center for Information Assurance (http://www.udallas.edu/gsm/ia/cia.cfm), and the Center for Professional Development (http://www.udallas.edu/gsm/cpd/).

The Graduate School of Management also has a Corporate Partners Program (http://www.udallas.edu/gsm/cr/corpprtnr.cfm).

The Faculty

GSM's faculty provides a rare mix of competence in both the theoretical aspects of management and the applied working knowledge of its practical aspects. Comprising both full-time professors and part-time adjunct professors, the faculty members all have extensive backgrounds in business. Full-time faculty members also have additional experience in teaching, applied research, and consulting. The adjunct faculty consists of practicing managers, attorneys, accountants, consultants, and other professionals. Because of the professors' expertise, GSM students are able to learn from scholar-practitioners—teachers who actually do what they teach. This provides a more complete and relevant learning experience.

The College and Environs

The University of Dallas is a Catholic, coeducational, liberal arts university with just over 3,000 students enrolled in undergraduate and graduate programs through the Constantin College of Liberal Arts, the College of Business (includes the Graduate School of Management), the Braniff Graduate School of Liberal Arts, and the School of Ministry.

The Graduate School of Management was founded in 1966 as an evening graduate school for individuals who were already employed in business and the professions. Over the years, the School's educational scope has broadened to serve a diverse student population, while its programs have remained focused on the practical realities of managerial and executive life. Today, the GSM alumni network includes more than 14,500 alumni in ninety-six countries.

The University of Dallas' main campus is located in the suburban community of Irving, Texas, part of the Dallas–Fort Worth Metroplex (DFW), and is within 10 miles of downtown Dallas and the Dallas–Fort Worth International Airport. The scenic campus is located on more than 600 acres of rolling hills. In addition, UD has two satellite campuses located in Frisco and North Richland Hills, both cities in the Dallas–Fort Worth Metroplex.

The DFW area has 3.4 million people and is one of the fastest-growing population centers in the country. Its diversified economy includes important industries in electronics, aerospace, insurance, and banking. The moderate climate and abundance of lakes and parks in the surrounding area offer numerous recreational opportunities. The Metroplex also provides rich cultural and entertainment opportunities.

Technology Environment

Faulkner's Communications Infodisk, Computer Select, the National Trade Data Base, Compact Disclosure, and the ABI-Inform full text system are a few of the technical resources available in the University of Dallas Blakley Library. Students also have access to the resources of many other public and university libraries in north Texas. All students are required to have a laptop computer.

Placement

The University of Dallas Career Management Office assists students with their job search and offers workshops on resume preparation and interviewing skills. Students participate in job fairs on- and off-campus, and many corporations seek out GSM students for professional internships.

Admission

Information pertaining to admission can be found at http://www.thedallasmba.com.

Finances

Graduate tuition (for credit) is $541 per credit hour; graduate tuition (not-for-credit) is $750 per course. More information about tuition costs can be found at http://www.udallas.edu/gsm/admissions/tuition.cfm

International Students

International students make up roughly 20 percent of the GSM student body, and many join a regional or country-specific student organization.

Application Facts and Dates

GSM has a rolling admission process and accepts applications for all three trimesters throughout the year. Applications from outside the United States should be sent at least eight weeks before the trimester desired. The nonrefundable application fee is $50 for U.S. and permanent resident applicants and $100 for International applicants.

For more information on the University of Dallas Graduate School of Management, applicants should contact:

Office of Admissions
The Graduate School of Management
University of Dallas
1845 East Northgate Drive
Irving, Texas 75062-4799

Phone: 800-832-5622 (toll-free)
Fax: 972-721-4009
E-mail: admiss@gsm.udallas.edu
Web site: http://www.thedallasmba.com

The University of Delaware

Alfred Lerner College of Business and Economics

Newark and Wilmington, Delaware

SMALL CLASSES AND OUTSTANDING FACULTY

I am very pleased you are considering the University of Delaware in your search to find an M.B.A. program that is right for you. If you want an M.B.A. program that offers small class sizes, an outstanding faculty, and the challenge of working with other well-qualified students and the management of some of the world's most innovative companies, then pursuing an M.B.A. at the University of Delaware may be the answer for you. All of our M.B.A. programs are accredited by AACSB International, and the College of Business at the University of Delaware is a member of the Graduate Management Admission Council.

I encourage you to visit our Web site and hope you will be intrigued by what you learn about our M.B.A. programs. If you have any questions, please contact us by telephone or e-mail. We are pleased that you are considering pursuing your M.B.A. at the University of Delaware.

—Conrado (Bobby) Gempesaw, Dean

Programs and Curricular Focus

The Alfred Lerner College of Business and Economics offers rigorous programs for superior students leading to M.B.A., M.S./M.B.A., and M.A./M.B.A. degrees. The special combination of academically accomplished faculty, highly qualified students, and ideal location—a small university town in the midst of the large eastern megalopolis—provides the necessary ingredients for an outstanding experience in graduate business education.

The Lerner M.B.A. curriculum is made up of 48 credits of course work: 30 credits of core and required courses and 18 credits of electives. The core curriculum covers a number of topics and skill areas including capable leadership, effective team building, group decision making, strategic use of technology, power negotiating, creative problem-solving techniques, international business considerations, e-business, entrepreneurship, and ethical business conduct.

Elective courses complement the traditional courses in accounting, economics, finance, operations, and marketing and are used to provide either broad or in-depth coverage of subjects in students' particular areas of interest. Students who wish to pursue more in-depth course work are offered the option of concentrating in finance, marketing, new venture creation, international business, information technology, and even in museum leadership and management.

As an alternative to concentrations, students may pursue a specialization. These are self-designed courses of study in which Lerner M.B.A. students can, in consultation with a faculty adviser, customize their program to more closely match their specific career interest. Examples of approved specializations have included sport management, hotel restaurant and institutional management, operations management, public administration, pharmaceutical and biotechnology innovation, and information technology in accounting. Specializations allow M.B.A. students tremendous flexibility in designing a course of study, and electives may be selected both from the variety of M.B.A. program electives and from those offered by other graduate degree programs at the University.

Both concentrations and specializations are made up of 12 credit hours (usually four courses) of course work. The remaining 6 credits of electives may be any graduate elective courses outside of one's area of concentration or specialization. Finally, at least one elective must have an international focus.

The 48-credit professional M.B.A. program can normally be completed in eighteen to twenty-one months. The program can also be completed on a part-time basis, taking between three and five years. An Executive M.B.A. program allows students with a minimum of five years of professional experience to complete the degree in nineteen months by taking classes Friday evenings and Saturdays. The combination of small class sizes, problem-based learning, and students' practical experiences creates a stimulating environment for the analysis of today's business world and its mastery.

Students and the M.B.A. Experience

For fall 2007, the average length of full-time work experience represented in the incoming class was five years, and the average age was 32.6. Of the 355 total M.B.A. students as of September 2007, 73 percent were part-time, 35 percent were women, 23 percent were members of minority groups, and 30 percent were international students, including students from many South American countries, Bosnia, Bulgaria, China, Ghana, India, Poland, and Russia. The diversity of the student body adds to the interactive learning environment in the classroom.

Special Features

All Delaware M.B.A. students are given an Internet account and are introduced to its many tools over the course of the program. The M.B.A. program has its own interactive Web site that is used for information sharing and a variety of other functions. Some M.B.A. classes also use news groups and the World Wide Web as additional learning environments. E-mail is the preferred form of communication between students, faculty members, and administrators.

The Faculty

Faculty members who teach M.B.A. classes hold doctoral degrees in their disciplines. Through widely respected research and publishing efforts, they have earned national reputations in their fields. M.B.A. faculty members have also enhanced their respective skills through consulting positions with major national and international corporations, a good number of which are headquartered in Delaware near the University.

The Business School Network

Because of the excellent reputation of the Delaware M.B.A., positive program relations exist with members of the corporate community, including DuPont, Vanguard, Endo Pharmaceuticals, Bank of New York, J. P. Morgan Chase, ICI America, W. L. Gore & Associates, and AstraZeneca. These relationships have fostered the development of internship opportunities for Delaware M.B.A. students at these and other firms (e.g., Hewlett-Packard, AAA Mid-Atlantic, Arco, and Cyanamid). The College has also developed an innovative Corporate Associates program that partners with the corporate community to provide a mutually beneficial financial aid package for full-time students. The College's Visiting Board, composed of high-ranking corporate executives from major corporations, serves as an advisory group to the Dean of the College on various matters, including those pertaining to the M.B.A. program.

The College and Environs

The University of Delaware, founded in 1743 as a small liberal arts school, now ranks among the finest of the nation's medium-sized universities, with approximately 16,000 undergraduate and 3,000 graduate students. Included in the Lerner College of Business and Economics are four departments: accounting and MIS, business administration, economics, and finance.

The University of Delaware is located in Newark, a suburban community of approximately 30,000 residents, and there is also a campus in Wilmington. Newark is in the northwest corner of Delaware within 3 miles of the Pennsylvania and Maryland borders. It is located within easy driving distance of Philadelphia (45 miles); Baltimore (50 miles); Washington, D.C. (100 miles); and New York City (130 miles). It is also less than 100 miles from the Delaware and New Jersey beaches. The Wilmington campus location is ideal for many of the part-time M.B.A. students whose jobs are located nearby. The Executive M.B.A. program is offered exclusively on the Wilmington campus. Wilmington is a major center for credit banking and the chemical industry. Eighty percent of all Fortune 500 companies are incorporated in Delaware, which allows the College to maintain strong ties with the corporate sector.

Facilities

The University library is a modern research facility with more than 2 million volumes, is a member of the Association of Research Libraries, and is a depository for U.S. government documents and patents. All computing at the University is built on top of a high-speed fiber-optic network that connects all buildings, laboratories, offices, and student housing on campus. Connected to the network are an array of computing resources, ranging from NT servers to supercomputing clusters. The College has a high-speed network, computing labs, com-

puter classrooms, a variety of NT servers, an SAP environment, multimedia conferencing, and a behavioral research facility. M.B.A. classes are held both on the main campus in Newark and on the Wilmington campus in proximity to the center of Delaware's business community. Wireless Internet hubs assure convenient Internet connectivity at both locations. In addition, networked stations are placed in common areas for easy Internet and e-mail access.

Placement

In addition to M.B.A. job fairs and on-campus interviews, the M.B.A. program participates in two M.B.A. consortia in Philadelphia and Washington, D.C. Along with graduates from other top M.B.A. schools, Delaware's M.B.A. graduates network and arrange interviews with a number of prospective employers. Employers of recent graduates include Colgate Palmolive, DuPont, IBM, Lockheed Martin, Bank of America, Stanley Works, and W. L. Gore.

Admission

A student must submit official copies of all undergraduate and graduate transcripts, GMAT scores, a current resume, and two letters of recommendation. For qualified applicants, a personal interview is also required. While a minimum GMAT score is not strictly enforced, a score of 550 or above is preferred, and the scores of entering classes typically average 600. In addition, students who hold undergraduate GPAs that are a minimum of 2.7 are preferred. Entering classes for the past several years have about a 3.0 GPA. A score that is a minimum of 100 is required on the TOEFL for all students for whom English is not their native language. At least two years of full-time work experience is required. Although no prerequisite courses are required, it is assumed that applicants possess basic skills in written and oral communication, mathematics, and computers.

Finances

In 2007–08, the yearly tuition for full-time M.B.A. students was $18,594 ($9000 for Delaware residents). Part-time study was $500 per credit hour for Delaware residents and $1033 per credit hour for nonresident students. Rental costs for shared occupancy in a graduate student complex are $450 per

month. University and privately owned apartments, furnished and unfurnished, are available at costs ranging from $700 to $1200 per month.

Numerous financial aid packages are available to superior full-time M.B.A. students. These include graduate assistantships, corporate assistantships, and tuition grants that are awarded on a competitive basis regardless of nationality or financial need. Awards to first-year students are based on prior work experience and academic performance. Awards to second-year students are based on academic performance in the program and professional experience.

A typical aid package may include a $7000 per year stipend and/or a 50 percent waiver of tuition. These awards are administered by the Graduate and Executive Programs Office. Information on other possible sources of aid can be found on the M.B.A. Web site or can be obtained by writing to the University's Office of Scholarships and Student Financial Aid.

International Students

Nearly 37 percent of the full-time student body is international. International student orientation is designed to prepare students for active participation in the highly interactive M.B.A. classroom. The University also offers a Pre-M.B.A. Program for international students via the English Language Institute. Countries represented by the international students include France, Germany, Ghana, Greece, India, the Netherlands, the People's Republic of China, Singapore, Sweden, Taiwan, and Turkey.

Application Facts and Dates

Applications for the fall semester should be submitted by May 1. Students seeking financial aid should submit their applications by February 1. Students pursuing both full- and part-time study are also admitted in the spring semester. Applications for the spring should be submitted by November 1.

M.B.A. Program Admissions
Lerner College of Business and
Economics
103 Alfred Lerner Hall
University of Delaware
Newark, Delaware 19716
Phone: 302-831-2221
Fax: 302-831-3329
E-mail: mbaprogram@udel.edu
Web site: http://www.mba.udel.edu

The University of Iowa

Henry B. Tippie School of Management

Iowa City, Iowa

LEARNING AND WORKING TOGETHER

The Iowa M.B.A. program is designed for people who like to learn and work together. Often, assignments are completed by students working in teams, and group presentations are the rule rather than the exception. The program is small enough so that our students get to know our faculty and staff members and each other very well.

Through the newly created Business Solutions Center, students partner with national and multinational companies as part of the M.B.A. curriculum. These real-world consulting opportunities complement the theory taught through typical course work, producing a skill-set that is sought after by employers.

The Pomerantz Center, opened in 2006, provides a world-class learning environment for full-time M.B.A. students. This new facility enhances the sense of community at Tippie and provides an exceptional learning experience through M.B.A. group-study rooms, offices for student organizations, and dedicated M.B.A. classrooms equipped with the latest technology. The fourth floor houses M.B.A. Career Services and Student Services, the M.B.A. Resource Library, a roof-top deck, and The Exchange—a gathering area with a flat screen plasma TV that is the perfect spot for full-time M.B.A. students to relax and mingle with their peers. The Pappajohn Building is a high-tech, state-of-the-art environment complete with Bloomberg financial markets technology, Bridge Telerate, LexisNexis, and a real-time trading room. In addition to all the desirable learning tools, we also provide lockers, an ATM machine, parking under the building after 4:30 p.m. on weekdays and all weekend, and an in-house restaurant.

The unique combination of a top-notch M.B.A. program situated in a safe and cosmopolitan small city make The University of Iowa's Henry B. Tippie School of Management an excellent choice for anyone.

—William C. (Curt) Hunter, Dean

Programs and Curricular Focus

The Henry B. Tippie M.B.A. program at the University of Iowa provides students with a solid foundation for future growth and flexibility in business management. The curriculum is rigorous, but learning takes place in a collaborative environment that builds teamwork while encouraging independent problem solving.

Students tailor individual course portfolios to combine analytical skills, broad-based knowledge, and professional experiences into a package that will advance their personal career goals.

Concentrations are available in accounting, corporate finance, investment management, marketing research, operations management, product management, and strategic management and consulting. Specialty concentrations are completed in conjunction with a primary concentration. Specialty concentrations are available in entrepreneurship, international business, management information systems, and nonprofit management. Students may also create their own concentration, incorporating courses from the University's other colleges, or pursue a dual-degree program in health management policy, nursing, law, or medicine.

Students and the M.B.A. Experience

IMPACT, a week long orientation program for entering M.B.A. students, links students with one another and with faculty members even before course work begins. This collaborative atmosphere is sustained throughout the program through team projects, student organization activities, alumni functions, corporate visits, and daily communication. Dedicated and diverse, Tippie M.B.A. students come from top undergraduate institutions worldwide and hold degrees and honors in disciplines ranging from English to engineering.

The average student is 26 years old and has approximately three years of professional experience. Women compose 23 percent of the student population, and international students make up 31 percent.

Global Focus

The Tippie M.B.A. program offers many opportunities for developing a global business perspective. Students may join one of the International Executive M.B.A. classes offered in Hong Kong as part of the Experience China program. In the international projects course, students serve as consultants for a firm planning international expansion and visit the target country during spring break. Corporate partners include

Fortune 100 companies with multi-national operations and middle-market businesses with extensive import/export activities. These companies provide internship and consulting opportunities and willingly share their knowledge of global markets and emerging economies.

The Iowa Institute for International Business (IIIB) fosters multicultural awareness and cooperation through ongoing student support. IIIB also assists students in arranging international internships and study-abroad opportunities.

Special Features

Information technology is dramatically altering the way business is conducted. Managers now have nearly instantaneous access to information about changing financial markets, customer demand, and competitive conditions in international and domestic markets. In addition to a state-of-the-art computer lab and trading room, Tippie M.B.A. students and faculty members benefit from the program's substantial investment in information technology: students have access to real-time information and benefit from the incorporation of new concepts and technology throughout the curriculum. Videoconferencing facilities provide communication with business leaders throughout the world.

The Faculty

Tippie M.B.A. faculty members are accomplished, dynamic, and dedicated to providing a comprehensive business education to students. Holding Ph.D.'s from some of the world's top educational institutions, all can apply practical experiences gained in such places as the Federal Deposit Insurance Corporation, Motorola, the Federal Reserve Bank, and United Parcel Service to the M.B.A. classroom.

Beyond their impressive credentials, Tippie M.B.A. faculty members are dedicated professionals who share a passion for teaching. They are enthusiastic about challenging students to excel, and they interact with students both inside and outside the classroom. This personal approach to management education is not often available to students in larger M.B.A. programs.

The Business School Network
Corporate Partnerships

The Tippie School of Management is fortunate to have excellent ties to and communication with the business community. Prominent business leaders often visit campus to talk about issues facing their industries. In addition, the newly created Business Solutions Center connects Tippie students with prominent local, re-

The Pomerantz Center at The University of Iowa brings together a number of academic and career-related services.

gional, and national companies to help the participating organization tackle a real business challenge facing their company. The center not only exposes students to consulting opportunities that allow them to put theory into practice in a real world setting, but also introduces the students to top executives in their areas of interest. In some cases the result is a continuing role in the company's success through an internship or full-time job offer.

The College and Environs

Iowa City is a uniquely wonderful community. Here, students and members of the faculty and community work and play together harmoniously.

The University of Iowa is the very heart of Iowa City, both in fact and spirit. The oldest of Iowa's three state universities, it includes, in addition to the College of Business Administration, the Colleges of Dentistry, Education, Engineering, Law, Liberal Arts, Medicine, Nursing, and Pharmacy. There are approximately 28,000 students, of whom 6,000 are pursuing graduate study.

Chicago, Minneapolis, St. Louis, and Kansas City are almost equidistant from the Iowa campus, providing urban advantages when desired. The Iowa City community itself offers an impressive array of cultural and recreational diversions.

Facilities

The M.B.A. program is housed in the newly constructed Pomerantz Center and the John Pappajohn Business Building. These modern buildings provide a beautiful, functional, and up-to-date setting that fosters interpersonal and technological interactions. The classrooms, restaurant, and informal spaces encourage one-on-one communication, group discussion, and the impromptu exchange of ideas between students and faculty members.

Technology Environment

In addition to the global information and video-conferencing capabilities of the M.B.A. facilities, the Pappajohn Business Building houses the largest student computing facility on the University of Iowa campus. Three computing classrooms, available for M.B.A. student use, complement a laboratory of nearly 100 workstations. Technology in the computer laboratory, library, and classrooms provides direct links to the global community, ranging from real-time national and international stock market feeds and information databases to a full spectrum of electronic resources.

Placement

The M.B.A. career services staff provides everything from resources to referrals. Beginning early in each student's program, staff members help them get "job ready" through an M.B.A. Competitive Prep course and one-on-one career counseling. Through a far-reaching alumni network, referral services, and video conferencing capabilities, Tippie M.B.A. career services personnel work with students to find internships and employment opportunities in the students' chosen fields and geographic locations. Interviews are arranged at on-campus locations, employer offices, and national job fairs. The Career Resource Center, exclusively for M.B.A. student use, provides access to career development information and employer databases, plus computer, telephone, fax, and copier equipment, to facilitate the job search process.

Admission

Each applicant's entire portfolio is considered. The admissions committee reviews each file individually and in full, looking for candidates who are a good match with the Tippie program. Students are asked to submit a completed application form, transcripts of all undergraduate and graduate work, a resume, responses to essay questions, GMAT scores, three references, and an application fee. Work experience is a key factor. Admission is only available for the fall term (mid-August). April 15 is both the priority consideration date and the application deadline for international applicants. Applications received between April 15 and July 15 are reviewed on a space-available basis. Application reviews begin in December.

Results from either the Test of English as a Foreign Language (TOEFL) or the International English Language Testing System (IELTS) must be provided by candidates whose native language is not English. The minimum acceptable TOEFL score is 250 computer-based, 600 paper-based, or 100 Internet-based. Information on the TOEFL is available at http//:www.toefl.org. The minimum acceptable total IELTS score is 7.0, with no sub-score less than 6.0. All IELTS test-takers are required to take the on-campus English Proficiency Evaluation. International students must present proof of adequate funds to cover the first year of study.

Finances

Tuition and fees for 2008–09 are $14,387 for Iowa residents and $25,717 for non-residents and are subject to change. Estimates provided by the Office of Student Financial Aid suggest that M.B.A. students budget approximately $940 per month for living expenses.

Merit-based aid, consisting of graduate assistantships and scholarships, is available to M.B.A. students. Graduate assistantships provide resident tuition, pay approximately $8000 per year, and cover 90 percent of health-care costs. In return, students work 10 hours per week for a department on campus. Scholarships average approximately $5000 and are awarded in place of, or in addition to, graduate assistantships. Awards are based on information found within the application portfolio, including GMAT scores, GPA, work experience, leadership potential, and results of the admission interview. Students are also encouraged to apply for need-based financial assistance through the University Office of Student Financial Aid.

International Students

International students and issues are integrated into the Tippie M.B.A. program as critical elements of the learning process. Built-in global connections occur within the classroom when discussion takes place between international and domestic students under the direction of knowledgeable faculty members who weave global issues into the fabric of their courses.

Application Facts and Dates

Admission preference for the full-time program (fall entrance) is given to those applications completed by April 15. Electronic applications are available through the M.B.A. Web site at http://www.biz.uiowa.edu/fulltimemba.

Henry B. Tippie School of Management
100 Pomerantz Center
Suite C432
The University of Iowa
Iowa City, Iowa 52242-7700
Phone: 319-335-1039
　　　　800-622-4692 (toll-free)
E-mail: tippiemba@uiowa.edu
Web site: http://www.biz.uiowa.edu/mba

University of Kentucky

A WORLD-READY M.B.A.

Thank you for your interest in the Gatton College of Business and Economics. I would like to extend a personal invitation for you to consider our M.B.A. offerings.

At the Gatton College our M.B.A. programs are designed to make you world-ready—ready to be recruited by major corporations, ready to become an entrepreneur, and ready to meet the challenges of the ever-changing international business landscape. Our one-year M.B.A. program provides an accelerated format where you'll be embedded and engaged in an environment rich in projects, real-world skill development, and cross-disciplinary thinking designed to accelerate your career path. In less than one year, you will have the comprehensive knowledge, hands-on business experience, and emergent leadership skills that employers worldwide seek. You can also gain the same leadership skills through our more traditional evening M.B.A. program designed for the working individual.

If you are looking for an innovative school that is leading the way in M.B.A. education, then consider us. Our M.B.A. staff is poised to help you answer any questions. Feel free to contact us to find out how the Gatton College of Business and Economics can help you achieve your career goals. Wishing you the best as you engage in making this important decision.

D. Sudharshan, Dean

Programs and Curricular Focus

The Gatton College of Business and Economics was named for Carol Martin Gatton, a distinguished alumnus, after he contributed the single largest gift in the history of the University of Kentucky (UK). Graduate programs include the Ph.D. in business administration and economics and the master's degree in business administration, accounting, and economics. Joint degrees are offered between the Master of Business Administration program and the Juris Doctorate, Bachelor's of Engineering, and Pharmaceutical Doctoral programs.

The M.B.A. program enrolls approximately 100 new students each year; the entering class size is deliberately limited to ensure personal contact with graduate faculty members and individualized attention. The program is designed to provide students with the education needed to prepare them for upper-level managerial responsibilities.

In July of 2005, the University of Kentucky proudly launched a revolutionary new M.B.A. program: the One Year Immersive M.B.A. Program. This eleven-month M.B.A. program was designed by real-world savvy faculty members with significant input from corporate friends. At the Gatton College M.B.A. program, students do not find the traditional "silos" in accounting, finance, or marketing courses. Instead, they plunge into learning laboratories that provide opportunities to discover and apply a wide variety of disciplinary concepts and tools. They focus on the key business processes—new product development, supply-chain management, and mergers and acquisitions—that are critical foundations to any firm's success. Designed to meet corporate and social needs, the program offers clinical experiences, including the Venture Studio and workshops that focus on managerial ethics, teamwork, corporate governance, and personal and professional development. The program offers certification in new product development and Green Belt certification in Six Sigma.

Most M.B.A. programs give students an internship opportunity between the first and second years of course work, thus offering the chance to put those theories into practice, experience the realities of a business environment, and acquire knowledge about a specific firm and industry. Gatton has redefined internships by integrating them into the body of its immersive curriculum. Gatton's Project Connect Program pairs teams of students with a high-ranking corporate executive. Over the course of twenty-three weeks, each executive provides the team with three projects of importance to the executive's company—one involving new product development, another supply chain management, and the third, mergers and acquisitions. Each project culminates with a real-world formal presentation to the executives' management team.

Individual development, personal achievement, teamwork, leadership, social responsibility—the University's Evening M.B.A. Program is designed for the working professional looking to succeed in a wide variety of professional contexts: as an individual, a team player, and a leader within his or her organization. Anchored by a series of rigorous foundation courses in economics, finance, marketing, management, accounting, and information systems, this M.B.A. curriculum enhances participants' skills, perspective, and contribution in the business marketplace. The curriculum is developed around twelve courses. Students can complete the program in as little as two years by completing three courses per semester. Most part-time students take two courses a semester, requiring three years to complete their degrees.

Students and the M.B.A. Experience

In 2007–08, the College enrolled 181 graduate students. Of the 2007 M.B.A. class, women represented 27 percent; international students, 8 percent; and members of minority groups, 10 percent of the student body. Fifty-seven percent of the students were part-time. The average student's age was 27, the average work experience was 3.4 years, and the average GMAT score was 603.4. The program offers a judicious mix of teamwork and individual projects, case study, and lectures designed to improve analytical, technical, and communication skills. Students are selected on the basis of proven academic excellence and a commitment to succeeding.

The Faculty

The College, headed by Dean Devanathan Sudharshan and Associate Dean Merle Hackbart consists of three divisions: the School of Accountancy, with 17 faculty members; the School of Management, incorporating the areas of decision sciences and information systems, finance, management, and marketing, with a total of 46 faculty members under the direction of Dr. Scott Kelley; and the Department of Economics, with 21 faculty members under the chairmanship of Dr. John Garen. Faculty members have achieved both national and international recognition for excellence in teaching and research as well as for service to the commonwealth of Kentucky and the business community. Many of the faculty members are presently actively engaged in joint research projects with faculty members at institutions around the world including Austria, England, China, Indonesia, Kazakhstan, Sweden, and Croatia.

The Business School Network
Corporate Partnerships
The College's University of Kentucky Business Partnership Foundation consists of prominent individuals in the business and academic communities. The Board of Directors of the Foundation fulfills an important role in assessing the present and future needs of the business world and in advising the College on how to provide the education necessary to meet those needs in a manner consistent with the College's missions of excellence in teaching, research, and service. Guest speakers from the business community visit the college on a regular basis throughout the year.

Prominent Alumni
There are more than 1,400 M.B.A. alumni in all fifty states and in twenty-two other countries. Prominent alumni of the College include the presidents and CEOs of numerous corporations including public companies listed on the NYSE, including James E. Rogers, Chairman, President, and CEO, Cinergy Corp.; Chris Sullivan, Chairman, Outback Steakhouse; Paul Varga, CEO, Brown Forman; Gretchen Price, VP Finance and Accounting, Global Operations, P&G; and Rodney Lanthom, President, Kyocera International, Inc.

The College and Environs
The UK campus and the Gatton College of Business and Economics are close to the heart of downtown Lexington, a city with a population of 243,000, where many of the cultural and recreational amenities of a large city are combined with the charm and traditions of a small town. Famed for its horse farms, Lexington lies within a 500-mile radius of nearly three fourths of the manufacturing, employment, retail sales, and population of the United States. Established in 1865, the University of Kentucky has more than 26,000 students, of whom approximately 7,000 are graduate students. Founded in 1925 as the College of Commerce, the Gatton College of Business and Economics occupies a modern building with all the facilities needed to fulfill the mission of excellence in teaching, research, and service. The College is accredited by AACSB International–The Association to Advance Collegiate Schools of Business.

Technology Environment
As befits a Carnegie Foundation Research University of the first class, the University of Kentucky has excellent facilities. The $58-million William T. Young Library, which opened in spring 1998, contains more than 2.5 million volumes and receives more than 27,000 periodical and serial titles. The M. I. King Library houses several special and rare books collections. The Computing Center has several high-level systems supporting research and networking needs. Within the College are the electronic Business Information Center for state-of-the-art business database access and seven centers of research that serve as resources to the state, local, and international business community. At sites throughout the campus, computer workstations cater to the computing needs of all students.

Placement
MBA Career Services at the Gatton College of Business and Economics offers a host of career development and job search services in individual and group sessions. Staff members help in areas of career assessment, career decision making, resume writing, job-search strategies, interview preparation, salary negotiation, business etiquette, and first-year on-the-job assistance. MBA Career Services partners with the University of Kentucky's James W. Stuckert Career Center, which is a state-of-the-art facility. The Career Center helps to expand recruiting relationships with employers through career fairs, networking receptions, employer information sessions, on-campus interviews, resume books, and Wildcat CareerLink, a Web-based job posting and recruitment system.

Major corporations, such as Affiliated Computer Services; Alltech; Ashland Oil; BB&T; Crow Chizek and Co., LLP; Eli Lilly; Fifth Third Bank; General Electric; Lexmark; Humana; IBM; Procter & Gamble; PricewaterhouseCoopers, LLP; Tempur-Pedic; and Toyota, are among the impressive list of companies that recruit graduates of the University of Kentucky's Master of Business Administration program.

Admission
Admission to the One Year Immersive M.B.A. and the Evening M.B.A. programs is for the fall semester only. An undergraduate degree with a minimum GPA of 2.75 is required. The Evening M.B.A. Program requires the following course work: two principles of accounting courses (financial, managerial), two principles of economics courses (micro, macro), a course in statistics and probability, and an elementary calculus course. All prerequisite courses should be equivalent to at least 3 semester hours. Applicants to both programs must also submit GMAT scores, and international applicants must also present a minimum TOEFL score of 550 (paper-based) or 213 (computer-based) overall and a minimum Test of Written English (TWE) score of 4.5. Academic background, GMAT score, personal recommendations, and the applicant's statement of purpose are all considered in the evaluation for admission. Demonstrated academic ability and potential for subsequent success in the business world are qualities that are looked for in applicants.

Finances
The College and Graduate School offer merit-based scholarships and fellowships. The University of Kentucky operates on the semester system. For the 2006–07 school year, in-state tuition for the One Year Program was $14,212, which includes the $6000 program fee. Nonresidents paid $23,700, which includes the $7000 program fee. On-campus housing rent ranged from $424 to $665 per month.

Tuition for the Evening M.B.A. student is charged per credit hour. In-state students pay $468.12 per credit hour. A $750 program fee per semester and $15.55 registration fee per credit hour is assessed. Out-of-state students in the Evening M.B.A. program pay $1046.43 per credit hour. An $1100 program fee per semester and $155.55 registration fee per credit hour are assessed.

Application Facts and Dates
Admission to the College's graduate business programs is achieved by applying to both the Graduate School and the M.B.A. program. The M.B.A. program accepts applicants only in the fall. Deadlines for applying are as follows: international students, February 1; financial aid, April 1; One Year Program, June 1; and the Evening M.B.A. Program, July 1.

Applicants are usually notified two to four weeks after the receipt of all required documentation. For information, applicants should contact:

Ms. Beverly Kemper
M.B.A. Center
Gatton College of Business and
    Economics
University of Kentucky
Lexington, Kentucky 40506
Phone: 859-257-7722
Fax: 859-323-9971
E-mail: kemper@uky.edu

For application materials, students should contact:

Admissions
M.B.A. Center
Gatton College of Business and
    Economics
University of Kentucky
Lexington, Kentucky 40506
Phone: 859-257-1306
Fax: 859-323-9971
E-mail: ukmba@uky.edu
Web site: http://gatton.uky.edu/

University of Miami

M.B.A. PROGRAMS AT THE UNIVERSITY OF MIAMI

The School of Business Administration is a premier school for business education. As a student, you can look forward to having classmates from all over the world whose diverse backgrounds and perspectives will enhance your learning. Your classes will be taught by our renowned faculty members, leading educators, and consultants to major corporations. Job placement is a priority at the University of Miami (UM). Our modern placement center provides personalized career development, on-campus interviews, career fairs, and forums. Join us . . . the business ideas and skills you'll acquire at UM will benefit you for a lifetime.

—Dr. Barbara E. Kahn, Dean

Programs and Curricular Focus

The University of Miami School of Business Administration is a comprehensive business school offering undergraduate business, full-time M.B.A., Executive M.B.A., Master of Professional Accounting, M.S. in Taxation, Ph.D., and nondegree executive education programs.

The University of Miami offers an M.B.A. program that is innovative, flexible, and career focused. It is designed to meet the needs of the student with an undergraduate background in business as well as the student who is just entering the business arena. The curriculum not only prepares business leaders of the future but also adds a valuable dimension to other professions.

The University of Miami offers a full-time, two-year M.B.A. program (48 credits). This program consists of twenty-four courses, nine of which are electives that may be used toward a concentration. Students register for three courses per term, for a total of six courses per semester. There are four semesters in total. The first year of the program is lockstep and cohort in nature, where classes are predetermined and taken with the same group of 30 to 37 students. In the fall semester of the first year, students focus on building management skills, while classes in the spring semester educate students in making management decisions. The second year permits a flexible schedule, allowing students to enroll in elective courses, which may be used to obtain a concentration. The fall semester focuses on expanding career opportunities, while the spring semester teaches the "executive perspective."

The curriculum may be customized. Students in the two-year program may choose from seven concentrations: accounting, computer information systems, finance, international business, management, management science, and marketing. Elective offerings required to complete a concentration are based on student demand. J.D./M.B.A. and M.D./M.B.A. degrees can be earned, requiring admission to both the law or medical school and the M.B.A. program. Waivers are permitted if the student passes waiver exams. Course transfers are not permitted.

All students are encouraged to take advantage of the summer internship opportunities available through the Ziff Graduate Career Services Center.

Students and the M.B.A. Experience

Located in Coral Gables, Florida, a major hub of international trade and commerce, the School of Business Administration is acclaimed for the global orientation and diversity of its faculty, students, and curriculum. Nearly a third of the students are international. Approximately half of the students' undergraduate majors are from areas other than business. Entering students average 25 years of age, with two years of work experience.

Special Features

The Graduate Business Student Association (GBSA) is a professional, social student-run organization that is available to all graduate business students enrolled in the M.B.A. program. The GBSA organizes presentations by executives from the business community on topics of interest to graduate students and sponsors numerous social events and activities that encourage and support career goals. M.B.A. students may also participate in the M.B.A. Consultants Program and offer business expertise to local nonprofit organizations, alongside a business mentor.

Professional organizations sponsored by the School include American Marketing Association, Real Estate Business Leaders, Alpha Kappa Psi, Beta Gamma Sigma, Phi Beta Lambda, Delta Sigma Pi, International Business Association, Entrepreneurship Club, Propeller Club, and Human Resource Advocates. In addition, numerous campuswide student clubs and organizations are available.

The Faculty

Faculty members at the University of Miami's School of Business Administration have a strong commitment to the students. Their courses offer a blend of case studies and theory and emphasize practical application to the modern business world. All full-time, tenured faculty members hold a doctorate or the highest degree in their fields. In addition to teaching and conducting leading-edge business research, the School's distinguished faculty members are active in management consulting and serve on corporate boards across the globe.

The Business School Network
Corporate Partnerships

The School of Business Administration maintains close ties to both local and international business communities. Miami has emerged as a critical node in the global business network, and corporate affiliate–sponsored events are open to all graduate students. Students use these opportunities to meet with top corporate executives in small-group and seminar settings. Through an annual membership commitment, participating corporations provide valuable support to the School.

The Mentor Program pairs University of Miami alumni and other professionals with graduate business students. Mentors serve as advisers, supporters, sponsors, tutors, and coaches. These relationships provide a link between academic theories and the realities of the business world, create a feeling of community involvement, bolster the students' sense of confidence, and provide them with a benchmark to strive for.

The College and Environs

Founded in 1925, the University of Miami is a private, independent, international research university. The first Master of Business Administration degree was offered in 1948. The University of Miami's School of

Business Administration offers state-of-the-art facilities located on a 260-acre campus in Coral Gables, Florida, minutes from metropolitan Miami. There are 15,670 degree-seeking students in approximately 120 undergraduate, 108 master's, forty-nine doctoral, and two professional areas of study. There are currently 2,226 full-time faculty members, whose ranks include Guggenheim Fellows, Fulbright Scholars, and National Science Foundation award recipients. Of this distinguished faculty, 97 percent hold doctorates or the highest degree in their fields.

Facilities

The School of Business Administration is housed in a modern complex surrounding a tropical courtyard and encompasses the George W. Jenkins Building and the William and Elsa Stubblefield Classroom Building. The Stubblefield Building contains classrooms outfitted with the latest in audiovisual equipment, faculty offices, administrative areas, and conference rooms. The Ziff Graduate Career Services Center and the Alma Jennings Foundation/Carlos and Rose de la Cruz Study Center make up the ground floor of the Jenkins Building.

The 48,000-square-foot addition to the business school complex, completed in 2000, includes graduate classrooms, the 300-seat Storer Auditorium, the James W. McLamore Executive Education Center, the M.B.A. student lounge, and a state-of-the-art computer lab. The auditorium accommodates business guest lecturers and student and faculty presentations. Classrooms dedicated exclusively to graduate programs have full computer network access at every student's seat and projectors linked to a lectern with built-in computer and Internet access. The five-story, 12,000-square-foot Kosar/Epstein faculty office wing was completed in fall 2003 and contains thirty-six faculty offices and meeting rooms. The faculty office wing was made possible through a lead naming gift from 1994 Alumnus of Distinction Bernie Kosar (B.B.A. '85) and his business associate David L. Epstein, founder of Precision Research Corporation.

Technology Environment

With its $3-million endowment, the Judi Prokop Newman Business Information Center functions as a "virtual library," emphasizing the use of computer technology. Laptops are permanently installed at each table, giving students access to business research databases such as Bloomberg, Compustat, Disclosure, Hoover's, LexisNexis, and more. The center's staff members provide expert advice to students. In addition, the center conducts monthly workshops for students on topics such as company, industry, and legal research.

The School's modern computer labs feature IBM PCs with access to the Internet

and the University's other online resources. Current software programs are available, including word processing, database management, presentation graphics, and statistical packages. Additional computer facilities are located at the University's Ungar Computer Center.

Placement

The Ziff Graduate Career Services Center is dedicated to helping students realize their career goals. Offering a variety of services, from career counseling to resume preparation, the center is dedicated to preparing students to effectively compete for high-quality jobs as well as creating employment opportunities.

Admission

The Graduate Admissions Committee welcomes applications from individuals whose undergraduate degrees are from accredited colleges or universities. Attendance at orientation prior to the start of the student's first term is mandatory. Programs start in August and January.

A completed application file contains an application form, a resume, a nonrefundable $50 application fee, GMAT scores (less than five years old), and academic credentials, including an official transcript from each college or university attended (even for only one course). An additional final transcript showing the degree conferred and date of graduation should be sent after completion of any course work still in progress at the time of admission. Work experience is strongly recommended for admission. A letter of recommendation from a professor or employer is required. Applicants from international institutions should provide statements by the officials of the institutions attended indicating the courses taken, grades earned, and classification of degree. If not in English, international credentials must be accompanied by certified translations. International applicants whose native language is not English and/or who did not earn an undergraduate degree from an English-speaking institution must submit a TOEFL score with their application. The TOEFL should have been taken within two years prior to application for admission; a minimum score of 550 (paper-based), 213 (computer-based), or 59 (Internet-based) is required.

Prospective students are encouraged to attend the Campus Visit Program, offered once per month. This is an excellent opportunity to learn about the program, meet current students, and speak one-on-one with admissions and placement staff members.

Finances

Tuition for 2008–09 is $1424 per credit hour. There are a limited number of merit-based graduate assistantships. Typically, a graduate assistantship covers 60 to 75 percent of the student's tuition and includes a stipend of $1500 per semester.

The student is assigned to a particular department and is expected to carry 12 semester credit hours and work 15 hours per week on assigned research or special projects. Merit-based scholarships and fellowships are also available. Early application is recommended for those requesting a graduate assistantship, scholarship, or fellowship.

Students applying for need-based assistance must submit the Free Application for Federal Student Aid (FAFSA). Federal Perkins Loans, Federal Stafford Student Loans, and the Federal Work-Study Program are based upon the financial need of applicants and the availability of funds. Stafford loans are available to students enrolled in 6 or more credit hours. The unsubsidized Stafford loan is a non-need-based federal loan program. The FAFSA must be completed and submitted to the processors by students requesting this loan, even if no need is demonstrated.

International Students

The Department of International Student and Scholar Services (ISSS) serves as the central resource for international students and scholars at the University of Miami. ISSS assists the international student or scholar in complying with the regulations of the U.S. Immigration and Naturalization Service and the Department of State, including regulations that govern on-campus and off-campus employment. ISSS also advises students and scholars on personal, academic, and professional concerns and provides opportunities for cross-cultural experiences. International students are encouraged to contact ISSS at 305-284-2928 or ISSS@miami.edu.

Application Facts and Dates

Applicants are encouraged to submit their application in advance of the set deadline for each round. Decisions for admission are made four to five weeks after the deadline for each round. For full consideration for scholarships, fellowships, and assistantships, applicants are strongly encouraged to apply by the first round. For questions regarding application deadlines, admission requirements, or the status of an application, students should contact:

Recruiting and Admissions
Graduate Business Programs
School of Business Administration
221 Jenkins Building
University of Miami
P.O. Box 248505
Coral Gables, Florida 33124-6524

Phone: 305-284-4607
          800-531-7137 (toll-free, U.S. only)
Fax: 305-284-1878
E-mail: mba@miami.edu
Web site: http://www.bus.miami.edu/grad

University of Missouri–Columbia

Columbia, Missouri

THE GORDON E. CROSBY, JR., M.B.A. PROGRAM—DESIGNED TO MEET YOUR GOALS

Besides being challenging and contemporary, the Crosby M.B.A. program is flexible and friendly, with small class sizes and individualized attention from faculty and staff members. Our format allows you the flexibility to join the program at a time that better fits your schedule and the freedom to tailor your program of study to satisfy your personal interests and career goals. Crosby M.B.A. candidates are top caliber. Our admission standards are high and the curriculum is rigorous; you'll graduate with the knowledge, skills, and values necessary for success in the business world. Our M.B.A. program, with classes taught by the College's award-winning faculty, will provide the foundation you need to realize your professional goals.

—Bruce J. Walker, Dean

Programs and Curricular Focus

Flexibility, individuality, and collaboration are the hallmarks of the Crosby M.B.A. program at the University of Missouri (MU). The Crosby M.B.A. provides graduate professional business education to talented students from diverse backgrounds, while allowing them to prepare for specific career paths.

The Crosby M.B.A. program permits broad flexibility, enabling students to tailor programs of study to meet their specific needs and interests. Students may concentrate electives in the business areas of finance, marketing, management, and management information systems, or they may individualize their programs with outside course work in areas as diverse as law, engineering, journalism, public relations, health services management, or computer science.

To complement the foundation courses and advanced electives, the Crosby M.B.A. offers skill-enhancing experiences in communication, leadership, and teamwork. A professional perspective is infused through small-group meetings with executives, summer internships, real-world case experiences, and professional development seminars designed specifically for M.B.A. students.

A student may enter the Crosby M.B.A. program in the fall, spring, or summer semesters. Students complete a minimum of 32 and a maximum of 59 semester hours; foundation-level courses may be waived for students having prior equivalent course work. Prerequisite course work in statistics and microeconomic theory can be completed prior to or concurrent with entering the program. Joint-degree programs are also available for students wishing to pursue an M.B.A. degree simultaneously with a J.D.,

Master of Health Administration, or Master of Science in Industrial Engineering degree.

Students and the M.B.A. Experience

Admission to the Crosby M.B.A. program is selective; students admitted to the program are committed to and capable of academic and professional success. The program is kept relatively small, with approximately 200 students enrolled. Crosby M.B.A. students typically represent nearly thirty colleges in twenty states and fifteen countries; they hold undergraduate degrees in more than twenty different disciplines. Managerial experience is not a prerequisite for admission, but most students have acquired significant work experience.

Global Focus

Students can study abroad through MU's formal relationships with various international universities and selected exchange programs. Crosby M.B.A. students who are interested in international business can attend summer class in Asolo, Italy, as part of an International Business Studies Consortium or can explore the London and Paris business communities as part of an international marketing class. The Crosby M.B.A. network of alumni stretches to nations all around the globe.

Special Features

The Crosby M.B.A. program welcomes students with a one-week orientation program designed to introduce them to the program, the University, and, most importantly, to one another. Highlights include business and internship panels with a focus on the new M.B.A. student's career search, opportu-

nities to meet and interact with faculty members, and an extensive array of social activities. Academic modules in finance, marketing, and statistics are offered by outstanding M.B.A. faculty members to prepare students for a challenging and exciting curriculum.

Throughout their time in the Crosby M.B.A. program, students have the opportunity to know their instructors and actively participate in and out of class. They might attend a reception at the home of a faculty member, have lunch with a visiting executive, help design a business plan for a small local business, or intern with a large company or a start-up firm. Students gain real-world experience in team case project and consulting case courses, which require consultation with a local or regional business.

By becoming a member of the student-led M.B.A. Association, a student has many opportunities to develop the skills needed for the future. Crosby M.B.A. students participate in service projects and frequently socialize with fellow M.B.A. students after an executive presentation. These opportunities promote involvement in the M.B.A. program and provide a personal touch difficult to find in larger, lock-step programs.

The Faculty

Excellence in teaching is a priority among Trulaske College of Business faculty members, many of whom have won national and campus awards in recognition of their teaching. Innovative classroom techniques, computer technology, and effective class materials strengthen the learning process. In addition to the high quality of its classroom instruction, the College's faculty, which includes a large number of young, doctorally qualified instructors along with well-known senior professors, is recognized for its research productivity.

The Business School Network
Corporate Partnerships

Collaboration between business leaders and M.B.A. students is facilitated through the College's Executive-in-Residence, Professor-for-a-Day, and M.B.A. Professional Development Seminar programs. In addition, corporate site visits give students the opportunity to meet key company representatives and learn about company culture, products, services, and business strategy in an interactive environment.

Prominent Alumni

The College's more than 29,000 alumni contribute their expertise to organizations in every state and a multitude of other countries. *Business Week* magazine ranked MU as the number-one producer of corporate CEOs in both the state of Missouri and the Midwest, while *Fortune* ranked MU in the top fifteen nationally. The College has seven advisory boards that bring CEOs, CFOs, and other top officials from Fortune 500 companies back to "Mizzou" for regular visits and support.

The College and Environs

MU is the oldest state university west of the Mississippi River and the largest of the four campuses of the University of Missouri System. The University, which enrolls more than 28,250 students, offers many cultural and sports events. Columbia is a warm, friendly, cosmopolitan, and safe college community with a population in excess of 84,000. Columbia's growing economy and low unemployment rate offer job opportunities for student family members. The community includes a large number of private apartment complexes, oriented to both students and professionals, that are conveniently located near campus. Sidewalk restaurants, pubs, coffeehouses, and the quaint downtown shopping district are within three blocks of MU and help make the community a very pleasant place to live.

Facilities

A state-of-the-art building, Cornell Hall houses the Trulaske College of Business. Crosby M.B.A. students enjoy use of a designated lounge for pre-class readings, group study, and socialization. Flexible teaching spaces, including classrooms and breakout rooms that facilitate class interaction, teamwork, research, and small-group activities, are emphasized throughout the building.

The MU libraries, including Ellis Library, house 3.2 million volumes, 6.8 million microforms, and more than 19,746 serial titles. Friendly, professional staff members are available to answer questions, help solve research problems, and support numerous online and CD-ROM databases. MU has excellent recreational facilities as well as residence halls for men and women students. University apartments are available for married student families and single graduate students.

Technology Environment

The Trulaske College of Business features state-of-the-practice technologies, including a building-wide wireless network; several three-station e-mail kiosks, building directory kiosks, and a distance learning classroom with two-way video capabilities; computer classrooms; teaching rooms equipped with dedicated networked computer, a wireless keyboard and mouse, a ceiling-hung projector, a DVD/VCR, a document camera, a laptop, and Internet and cable TV connectivity; behavioral lab rooms with cameras, microphones, VCRs, and monitors; a thirty-station laptop cart; computer labs containing the latest versions of a wide variety of business software and online databases; and student checkout equipment, including wireless laptops, a digital camera, a digital camcorder, and a teleconference phone. Computer labs contain the latest versions of business software.

Online databases available to graduate students include the Wharton Data Management System, including CRSP (Daily Stocks, Monthly Stocks, Mutual Funds, Monthly U.S. Treasuries), Compustat (Annual Quarterly Industrial, Business and Geographic, Canadian Industrial Annual and Quarterly Executive Compensation, Global), I/B/E/S, NYSE TAQ, ISSM, Thomson Financial, Eventus, Audit Analytics, IRRC, and First Call along with a number of other databases. The College also subscribes to AICPA, ARN, FARS, FEN, ERN, Government Account Research System, LIPPER, SDC Platinum, and Stock Trak.

Placement

The College's Career Services Office brings more than 200 recruiting firms to campus each year. Recent Crosby M.B.A. graduates have accepted employment throughout the United States, with annual starting salaries ranging from $40,000 to $100,000. Internships allow many students the opportunity to preview positions and companies prior to accepting employment. The Career Services Office also sponsors a career fair each fall and an internship fair each spring, coordinates and schedules on-campus interviews, maintains a job listing service for employers, and holds career development workshops and seminars. In addition to individualized career counseling services, students may also take advantage of the Alumni Mentorship Program and numerous site visits to business enterprises.

Admission

Admission depends primarily on the quality of the applicant's undergraduate work, the score received on the Graduate Management Admission Test (GMAT), and professional work experience, if any. The average entering grade point average is 3.41, and the average GMAT score is 624. The Test of English as a Foreign Language (TOEFL) is required of applicants whose native language is other than English and who do not have a degree from an institution in the United States.

Finances

In 2007–08, Missouri residents and out-of-state graduate students paid educational fees of $286.90 and $740.80 per credit hour, respectively. Other miscellaneous fees of approximately $400 per semester and a supplemental College of Business fee of $33.20 per credit hour are also assessed. (Fees are subject to change without notice.) Graduate assistantships, partial or complete waivers of tuition fees, and scholarships ranging from $1000 to $10,000 per year are awarded to Crosby M.B.A. students competitively on the basis of their academic and professional achievements. Graduate assistants receive a stipend of over $4700 per year and work 10 hours per week in a variety of positions in the College, including teaching, research, technology services, public relations, and business consulting. Scholarships, grants, and loans are also available through the MU Financial Aid Office. International students with the highest qualifications may qualify for financial assistance. Once enrolled at MU, they can also apply for a Curator's Grant-in-Aid that allows them to waive certain educational fees.

Application Facts and Dates

Students may enter the Crosby M.B.A. program in the fall semester (August), spring semester (January), or summer session (June). Application deadlines are August 1, December 1, and May 1, respectively, although earlier application is strongly encouraged. International students should apply by April 1, October 1, and March 1 so that travel documents can be prepared. Admissions decisions are made on a rolling basis, usually within one month of receipt of all application materials. Exceptions to deadlines are possible if GMAT scores and transcripts are available. For more information, applicants should contact:

Ms. Barbara Schneider
Coordinator of Recruiting and
  Admissions
Graduate Studies in Business
Robert J. Trulaske, Sr. College of
  Business
213 Cornell Hall
University of Missouri
Columbia, Missouri 65211
Phone: 573-882-2750
Fax: 573-882-6838
E-mail: mba@missouri.edu
Web site: http://mba.missouri.edu

UNLV University of Nevada, Las Vegas

College of Business

Las Vegas, Nevada

> ### EDUCATION FOR LIFE'S CAREER
>
> *As we enter the twenty-first century, business leaders face unprecedented challenges. Markets are becoming increasingly competitive and globalized, and society is becoming much more multiculturally diverse. Advances in information and communication technology are reshaping market structures and demanding entirely new business strategies. To be successful in the changing business environment, tomorrow's business leaders, more than ever before, must be solidly grounded in all functional areas of business. The University of Nevada, Las Vegas (UNLV) College of Business offers innovative M.B.A. programs to provide the foundation for those who seek global career and leadership opportunities. The faculty and staff at UNLV are very proud to be your partners in building a successful career.*
>
> —Dr. Paul Jarley, College of Business

Programs and Curricular Focus

The keys to success in this competitive, fast-paced world are sound academic preparation, specialized knowledge and communication skills. To provide students with the best academic setting, the faculty embraces a combination of teaching methods. Lectures, group discussions, seminars, case studies, computer simulations, and individual and group research projects are frequently used within courses and across the curriculum. Through professional analysis of and recommendations for case situations, students' communication and interpersonal skills are enhanced. Students develop sensitivity to the context of each management issue and become more aware of the ethical issues that challenge managers.

The integrative M.B.A. curriculum, aligned with the changing demands of global business, provides students with the needed skills to become innovative and creative business leaders. The curriculum integrates practical business application with leading-edge research. It provides the right blend of theory and practice, offering a comprehensive and integrated education. The M.B.A. program accommodates the needs of full- and part-time students by offering a full-time day program and an evening program.

The Executive M.B.A. (E.M.B.A.) program of study offers a dynamic combination of theory and practice and provides an opportunity for executives, professionals, and leaders to optimize their potential in their careers and sharpen their leadership skills. The intensive sessions bring other executives and professionals from diverse industries to add depth to the learning environment. Students are able to pursue their M.B.A. degree in this eighteen-month program without interrupting their professional career. Classes meet every other Friday and Saturday from 8:30 to 5:30.

The dual M.B.A. and M.S. degree in hotel administration is designed for those who seek career and business leadership opportunities in hotel administration. The core M.B.A. program is designed to advance the knowledge and practice of business and administration. The M.S. in hotel administration portion of the dual degree is designed to provide the industry-specific teaching and learning program. The program takes advantage of the natural learning environment that is created by the Las Vegas economy, the entertainment capital of the world. Students receive a dual degree, an M.B.A./M.S. in hotel administration.

The College of Business at UNLV and the William S. Boyd School of Law offer a dual M.B.A. and Juris Doctor (M.B.A./J.D.) degree program that allows students to be admitted to both programs to achieve both degrees simultaneously.

The UNLV College of Business and the School of Dental Medicine at UNLV offer a dual M.B.A. and Doctorate of Dental Medicine (M.B.A./D.D.M.) degree program. Students must satisfy the admission requirements for both programs.

Students and the M.B.A. Experience

Since UNLV has taken the position that an M.B.A. candidate is best served with a broad general education, students from all academic majors are welcome in the program. The average age of students entering the M.B.A. programs (including the dual programs) is 29 years, with five years of full-time work experience. The age range is 24 to 62 years. Women compose 40 percent of the class; members of minority groups, 10 percent; international students, 12 percent; and 9 percent of the students already have advanced degrees. The average age of students entering the

E.M.B.A. program is 38 years, with fourteen years of work experience.

The M.B.A. program values teamwork as an integral part of the learning experience. The M.B.A. program office and the M.B.A. student association plan events each semester to facilitate interaction between M.B.A. administrators, faculty members, alumni, and students outside the classroom. Events begin before the first day of class at the new student orientation and assist in the development of valuable relationships by providing informal discussions that enhance the students' learning experience.

Special Features

All programs that are offered by the College of Business have been fully accredited by AACSB International–The Association to Advance Collegiate Schools of Business. AACSB accreditation certifies a high-quality education with high standards and is widely recognized within academic and business professional circles.

The Faculty

The UNLV College of Business faculty members are dedicated to student development. They are committed to excellence in teaching and to ensuring that all courses are intellectually rigorous and relevant to today's business practices. Faculty members value a smaller, more student-focused atmosphere created by the small faculty-student ratio. They are active in research and publish in high-quality journals across the business disciplines. Faculty members are as diverse as the students they teach. With a vibrant mix of cultural heritage and business experiences, all faculty members hold doctoral degrees in their field of specialization from leading academic institutions. They bring their expertise, talent, and dedication to the classroom. They are dedicated to high-quality innovative instruction, which promotes an environment that fosters learning.

The Business School Network

The College of Business enjoys a strong relationship with the business community. There are several advisory boards composed of executives with senior leadership experience from diverse corporate backgrounds. They provide the College of Business, as well as the individual departments, with invaluable insight on current and innovative business practices that enhances the curriculum and increases the effectiveness of teaching and learning.

The College also has an active alumni group. The M.B.A. Alumni Council, along with the College of Business Alumni Association, plans a number of events for current students and alumni to interact.

The College and Environs

While the University of Nevada, Las Vegas is relatively young, it has experienced rapid growth in recent years. More than 180 graduate and undergraduate programs are now offered on the 337-acre campus. Student enrollment has reached 29,000 students, including 7,500 graduate students. Las Vegas is one of the fastest-growing cities in the United States and is the primary shopping and business district for more than 1.9 million people. The University is located less than 2 miles from McCarran International Airport, one of the world's most efficient and well-connected airports. Along with the appealing desert temperatures and 320 days of sunshine, the beauty of the desert makes southern Nevada a very attractive place for outdoor recreation any time of year.

Technology Environment

Computer technology applications and information sources are on the forefront of management theory and practice. The College offers full support of an information technology infrastructure, which provides students with networking experiences for their team projects. The Business Information Center laboratory is fully equipped with an integrated network computer system. Business and educational software, electronic mail, and statistical analysis software are standard.

The 302,000-square-foot Lied Library, completed in 2001, is one of the most technically sophisticated university libraries in the United States. The five-story Lied Library features hundreds of computer workstations; the Lied Automatic Storage and Retrieval (LASR) System; an information commons, featuring ninety-six personal computers; and a number of group study areas.

Placement

Beginning with the new student orientation, the M.B.A. program's goal is to position every student for successful career placement. The M.B.A. Career Services office serves both students and alumni, and acts as liaison between employers and M.B.A. students seeking employment. The office assists students with many career decisions. M.B.A. students and alumni can use Career Services to explore opportunities, build or polish career management skills, and connect with real-world business challenges. The office assists in developing career strategies and offers coaching, resources, connections, and opportunities that can help students and alumni achieve their career goals. The Career Center offers a variety of programs and services for employers who wish to recruit students for employment. The College of Business sponsors campus interviewing, panel presentations, and job postings.

Admission

The College of Business M.B.A. Program and the UNLV Graduate College conduct admission to the M.B.A. program. Applicants must hold a bachelor's degree from an accredited college or university. The M.B.A. program welcomes applications from college graduates in all disciplines. Applicants are evaluated based upon demonstrated academic ability as evidenced by a strong performance on the Graduate Management Admission Test (GMAT), maturity, motivation, leadership, communication skills, and interest in professional management. The average GMAT score of accepted students during the last two years is about 600, with each component more than the 25th percentile. The Graduate College requires that international students must also have a minimum score of 550 (paper-based), 213 (com-

puter-based), or 80 (Internet-based) on the Test of English as a Second Language (TOEFL). In addition, the M.B.A. program recommends two years of relevant work experience. The application procedure for the dual programs and the E.M.B.A. program are different.

Finances

For the fall 2007 to summer 2008 academic year, the graduate resident tuition and registration fee was $172.25 per credit hour; part-time nonresidents paid $361.75 per credit hour. Full-time nonresidents paid $5405 plus the $172.25 per-credit-hour graduate fee per semester. Students may apply for graduate assistant positions. These positions are very competitive and are filled on the basis of a student's merit and the University's needs. Both University and private housing are available. Housing costs vary from $600 to $1000 per month.

International Students

The Office of International Students and Scholars assists all UNLV international students and faculty and staff members to make smooth transitions into successful academic, professional, and social experiences. The office provides arrival information, immigration advising and related documents, personal and academic advice, and cultural/social programming. The office also provides a very important international student orientation. For additional information, students should e-mail isssc@unlv.edu or visit the Web site at http://www.unlv.edu/studentlife/international/. There are approximately 900 international students who come from more than eighty countries. For international students who need to reinforce their language skills, the English Language Center provides beginning-, intermediate-, and advanced-level English as a second language courses. For additional information regarding these courses, students should contact the center at 702-895-3925 or vholmes@unlv.edu.

Application Facts and Dates

The day program admits in the fall only. Round 1 deadline is January 30, round 2 is February 28, round 3 is March 30, and the final deadline is June 1. The final day to submit an application for the evening program for the fall semester is June 1. All international application materials must be completed and received by May 1. The final day to submit an application for the evening program for the spring semester is November 15. All international application materials must be completed and received by October 1. For additional information, students should contact the M.B.A. program:

College of Business M.B.A. Program
University of Nevada, Las Vegas
4505 South Maryland Parkway, Box 456031
Las Vegas, Nevada 89154-6031
Phone: 702-895-3655
Fax: 702-895-3632
E-mail: cobmba@unlv.edu
Web site: http://business.unlv.edu

University of New Brunswick Saint John

Faculty of Business

Saint John, New Brunswick, Canada

DEAN'S MESSAGE

The Faculty of Business at the University of New Brunswick Saint John (UNBSJ) offers a twelve-month M.B.A. program focused on developing innovative and entrepreneurial leaders who are equipped to manage in the global marketplace. UNB Saint John offers students the opportunity to learn in a diverse and dynamic environment. Innovation and Technology Management M.B.A. students work in a high-tech business, while International Business M.B.A. students complete two study modules in different trade regions—one in North America and one in either Europe or Asia. Graduates of the UNB Saint John M.B.A. program not only have an appreciation of the challenges and opportunities the international business environment affords but also have access to a global network of colleagues and contacts that are invaluable in business today. A highly qualified team of faculty and staff members work together to deliver a unique curriculum along with a comprehensive skills-development program that enables students to develop the managerial prowess necessary to compete effectively in a global information-based business environment.

—Regena Farnsworth, Ph.D., Dean

Programs and Curricular Focus

The UNB Saint John M.B.A. offers the career-oriented individual unique and rewarding learning experiences—experiences that help them realize their career goals and aspirations. The M.B.A. program produces knowledgeable leaders who are adaptable and comfortable with innovation and who can successfully lead companies in a globally competitive economy. The UNB Saint John M.B.A. program offers two streams: International Business (IB) and Innovation and Technology Management (ITM). After the first three of the nine-week modules (October–May), International Business students study two of three trade options: the North American Free Trade Agreement (NAFTA) in Saint John during the summer term and, during the fall term, either the European Union (EU) in France or the Asian trade region in either India or China. At the end of May, Innovation and Technology students begin a project term working with one of the University's industry partners in an IT company. ITM students return to UNB Saint John for the final module as IB students continue their studies abroad.

The program can be completed both on a full-time (twelve months) or a part-time (approximately three years) basis. Students should note that the study-abroad term in the IB specialization adds three months to the degree program. In addition to studying a competitive and challenging curriculum, students may follow up with an optional three-month internship at the end of their program. In addition, each student is assigned an industry mentor from the executive ranks of the Saint John business community. Students also benefit from extensive individual and group-oriented professional development throughout the program.

The M.B.A. program rewards students' dedication and commitment. Because the program is only twelve to fifteen months long, graduates return to the job market with an M.B.A. degree sooner and start earning money earlier than those in a traditional two-year program. In each program module, full-time students enroll in five courses. Each course requires a 4-hour weekly classroom commitment, with a total of 20 contact hours with professors per week. This high number of classroom hours gives students ample time to have questions addressed and to have in-depth discussions amongst peers and instructors.

Students and the M.B.A. Experience

The M.B.A. program is delivered in a close-knit environment. Students have the opportunity to get to know all of their peers in a supportive and social learning environment and form friendships that will last a lifetime. Because of the small class sizes, students are ensured access to professors and instructors for additional help outside of the classroom. The professor-student ratio is 1:2, which is highly appealing. The faculty members are dedicated to providing their students with the necessary individual attention that helps them grasp complex concepts and succeed in their course work. The UNB Saint John M.B.A. environment provides an ideal venue for effective social, cultural, and career growth.

The average age of students in the program is 28; candidates typically have an average of five years' work experience. Core classes can have up to 50 students per course, while electives can be held with 10 to 15 students in each class. In addition, students can expect that 30 to 35 percent of the course work is team-based, stimulating cross-cultural learning as the program tends to have up to twelve different countries represented in its classes each year.

Special Features

The UNB Saint John M.B.A. program is short, but it achieves a great deal during that period. To augment classroom work, students are exposed to the business environment through networking events, panel discussions, seminars, and projects led by corporate executives; internships; and a mentorship program. In addition, students have the opportunity to go abroad to study or work internationally. After they complete their degrees, students may choose an optional three-month internship in Canada.

Course work, internships, the mentorship program, and international study exchanges are all supplemented and supported through an integrated and customized professional development program. At the outset of each M.B.A. year, students meet individually with the M.B.A. Director and Professional Development Consultant to discuss their career and life goals. A mix of in-class seminars, small-group work, and one-on-one coaching is used to assist students in developing the appropriate mix of skills to meet their career goals. Previous seminar topics have included self-assessment and goal setting, effective communication, team development, leading and influencing, effective business presentations, problem solving and decision making, developing and communicating a vision, living with and managing change, project management, time and workload management, and business writing.

The Faculty

The M.B.A. courses are taught by international faculty members who have exceptional reputations in their respective fields. The dedicated faculty members are involved in innovative regional, national, and international research projects sponsored by both government and private organizations and often collaborate with their peers from universities from around the globe.

UNBSJ's professors are doing research in such areas as business and the natural environment, consumer experience in interactive markets, corporate governance, cultural and heritage tourism, game theory, high-involvement work systems, how businesses use Weblogs and podcasts to communicate internally and externally, implications of WTO membership, international competitiveness, international financial management, measuring service quality in electronic environments, occupational health and safety, quality of work life, stakeholder theory and business ethics, supply chain management, and use of green space in an urban setting.

Understanding the importance of staying connected to industry and the community, professors often provide consultative services to private- and public-sector organizations and are involved in international projects in North America, Asia, and Europe.

The Business School Network

The M.B.A. program has strong business partnerships with regional and national organizations such as Anywhere Group; Bell Aliant Inc.; Deloitte Inc.; Exxon Mobil; the government of New Brunswick; Innovatia; Irving Group of Companies, including J.D. Irving Limited and Irving Oil Limited; Kinek Technologies, Inc.; Mariner Partners; Royal Bank of Canada; Scotiabank; and Xwave. Organizations such as these cooperate with the M.B.A. program on research, employment, and delivery of innovative credit and noncredit courses. Throughout the program, students have ample opportunity to interact with local, regional, and national business leaders through seminars and competitions and develop a close network of business leaders to build upon throughout their future careers.

The College and Environs

Saint John is located in southern New Brunswick. The city has been nationally recognized on numerous occasions for its beauty, its high quality of life, and its low cost of living. As New Brunswick's largest municipality, with a population of approximately 135,000, greater Saint John is a key commercial centre with rapidly growing high-tech and energy sectors. The city offers a lifestyle to suit everyone, with many of the assets of a large city combined with the friendliness and safety of a small community.

Students from out of town quickly become familiar with the world-renowned maritime hospitality. Saint John residents are welcoming and supportive of all cultures—a quality reflected in the diversity of city residents.

Facilities

The Ward Chipman Library and computer labs are integral to success in UNBSJ M.B.A. studies. The library is a place to study, conduct research, and learn how to research. In addition to the collection in the library, students have access to more than 10,000 academic journals, with full-text journal articles to use for research papers and supplementary course material. The library can also be accessed online off campus or in any one of the University's state-of-the-art computer labs equipped with laser printers and scanners or the laptop program operated in the wireless environment of the library. Students are also given their own storage space on the network servers for personal Web pages and e-mail to stay in touch with family and friends.

The Jeux Canada Games Stadium features a 400-metre track and a grass field used for varsity and intramural soccer and other sports, such as flag football and cricket. The G. Forbes Elliott Athletics Centre features fitness rooms with aerobic and weight-training equipment and a table tennis room with five tables. The gymnasium has a new indoor track and a variety of courts that allow users to play everything from soccer and basketball to volleyball and tennis or badminton— all at the same time. Several recreational opportunities are available to all UNBSJ students and faculty and staff members, including badminton, basketball, cricket, soccer (indoor and outdoor), special events, table tennis, and various fitness classes led by certified instructors.

Student Life and Support Services provides students assistance in personal and career counseling, employment services, financial aid and scholarship advising, and developing study skills as well as a math help centre, services for students with disabilities, and a writing centre. In addition, from the on-campus residences to apartments in beautiful uptown Saint John to homestays with families, there are housing options to fit every student's taste, style, and budget.

Technology Environment

The M.B.A. program integrates computer literacy and communication skills in as many courses as possible. Students have unlimited access to the wireless network connection that provides seamless access to the Internet, the University intranet, e-mail, research, and course material.

Placement

Industry-experienced staff members in the M.B.A. Professional Development Program offer one-on-one coaching and a series of seminars designed to help students set and meet their career goals. Staff members also coordinate internships, projects in industry settings, and an individualized graduate placement process.

Admission

Applicants for the UNB Saint John M.B.A. program need to meet the following minimum admission requirements: a four-year undergraduate degree with a minimum cumulative average of B (3.0 out of 4.3) or the equivalent; a Graduate Management Admissions Test (GMAT) score of at least 550 (candidates with a CGPA of 3.2 or higher out of 4.3 are eligible for a GMAT waiver); two years of relevant professional work experience; and, for international students only, a TOEFL (or other English language test) score.

With their M.B.A. application form, prospective students should submit a personal statement on why they wish to join the M.B.A. program, a resume reflecting their work experience, three references, official copies of their transcripts and test scores, and an application fee of Can$100.

If candidates are uncertain whether they meet the requirements of the program, they may submit a pre-application form along with a resume and unofficial transcript of their marks. This form is available at http://www.mba.unbsj.ca/apply/documents/PreApplicationMBA_000.pdf. The Admissions Office responds to inquiries within two business days. All application materials are available at http://www.mba.unbsj.ca/apply/AdmissionApplication.html.

The official application is reviewed only when all parts of the application package have been received by the University. The application fee can be paid either by bank draft, money order, wire transfer, or certified cheque payable to University of New Brunswick Saint John. The University also accepts payment with Visa, AMEX, or MasterCard credit cards.

Finances

Tuition fees for full-time M.B.A. students are Can$18,000 for Canadian students and Can$24,500 for international students. Students typically spend an additional Can$2000 to Can$2500 on books (used textbooks are available). A nonrefundable deposit of Can$1000 is deducted from tuition fees upon enrolment. Part-time tuition for the 2008–09 academic year is Can$738 per course for Canadian students and Can$1126 for international students.

The Faculty of Business provides a limited number of bursaries of up to Can$5000 to the top full-time candidates providing completed applications by May 31 prior to the subsequent October intake. Bursaries are applied directly against the second tuition installment, payable in March.

Living costs in Saint John are relatively inexpensive compared with other major Canadian cities. Aside from housing costs, Saint John is fortunate to be able to provide residents with energy, food, transportation, and entertainment costs similar to or below most major municipalities in the country. As a result, residents enjoy all of the amenities one would expect from a city of similar size but at an affordable cost. Students should expect to pay approximately Can$1000 per month for accommodations, food, transportation, and other living expenses. Total estimated expenses for the year (including tuition, fees, and books) are between Can$32,000 and Can$38,000.

International Students

Students in the M.B.A. program come from diverse backgrounds. They are engineers, accountants, researchers, and managers. They have experience in the energy sector, natural resources, government, and telecommunications. They come from all over the world, including Africa, Asia, Europe, the Middle East, North America, and South America. More than 50 percent of the students are from countries other than Canada. The students' diversity allows them to learn with and from peers who accurately reflect today's global business environment.

Application Facts and Dates

The application deadline for all full-time students is May 31 of each year in order to be eligible for bursaries. Part-time applicants can submit their application at any time during the year and begin their study in any one of the five modules.

UNBSJ continues to accept applications into July and August until all seats are filled with qualified students. However, international candidates are encouraged to have their applications in by June 30. By using a rolling admission process, applications are reviewed as soon as they are complete. Applicants hear from the committee within two to four weeks of the completion date.

For more information about the UNB Saint John M.B.A. program, prospective candidates should contact:

M.B.A. Admission
Faculty of Business
University of New Brunswick Saint John
P.O. Box 5050
Saint John, New Brunswick E2L 4L5
Canada
Phone: 506-648-5746
   800-50-UNBSJ (508-6275; toll-free
      in North America)
Fax: 506-648-5574
E-mail: mba@unbsj.ca
Web site: http://mba.unbsj.ca

University of New Hampshire

The Whittemore School of Business and Economics

Durham, New Hampshire

MBA PREPARES LEADERS FOR CHANGING ECONOMY

The mission of the Whittemore School of Business and Economics is to prepare graduates for professional roles at the forefront of emerging business strategies, techniques, and technologies, and to prepare them to lead others in an ever-changing global business environment. The School is committed to a curriculum that is designed to develop problem solvers who are adept in change management and leadership. The learning environment emphasizes problem-based learning through continuous interaction with the business community and other external entities.

—Daniel Innis, Dean

Programs and Curricular Focus

The Whittemore School offers students three models in which to pursue the M.B.A.: full-time, part-time evening, or executive weekend. All classes are intentionally small (30 to 40 students) to foster a close association between students and faculty members. The small size allows classes to be informal and maximizes student involvement within each program.

The intensive, one-year, full-time M.B.A. program begins each fall with a cohort of 40 students. The program begins with an orientation designed to introduce students to team development, case analysis, business communication, ethics, and professional development. Ten core courses and four electives (one is an internship if the student has less than three years of work experience) are required. The program culminates with a corporate consulting project with a local business, requiring students to participate in small groups or as individuals, applying concepts and skills to real-world challenges in the business world.

The part-time, two-year evening program is offered in both Durham and Manchester. Required core courses are typically taken two at a time during the first and second years, and each course meets one evening a week. Students have ten core courses and six electives. Specializations in general management, marketing and supply chain management, entrepreneurial venture creation, and financial management are available.

The executive model is the third option. This nineteen-month program allows working professionals to attend classes every other Friday and Saturday while continuing full-time employment. Applicants must have a minimum of five years of professional work experience to apply to the program. Since this program has a housing option at the University's Conference Center, students come from a variety of professional back-grounds from across the greater New England region. In addition to the alternating class weekends, there are three required residency periods. The first residency of four days is held on campus at the beginning of the program and provides an introduction to the University, the program, classes, and team development. As part of the finance class, students in the second year participate in a three-day visit to Wall Street in New York City. The program culminates with a ten-day trip abroad as part of the international management course. In the second year, students choose between two tracks: entrepreneurial venture creation or technological innovation.

Another graduate-level program in the Whittemore School is a one-year, full-time M.S. in Accounting (M.S.A.) program. This program is intended for students with undergraduate majors in accounting who wish to meet the recommended professional level of education. There is also a two-year option available for non-accounting majors.

The M.A. and Ph.D. in economics are also offered to students interested in research and academic careers.

Students and the M.B.A. Experience

While 60 percent of students in the full-time M.B.A. program are from the local region, the remaining 40 percent are split between other New England regions, the rest of the United States, and other countries. Half of the students are prepared in the liberal arts and social science disciplines, while a quarter of each entering class has been prepared in the physical sciences and business and economics. Half of the students are women, and the average age of the entering class is 25.

Specializations are offered in the part-time M.B.A. program only. However, students in the full-time M.B.A. have the opportunity to take elective courses in these areas. The specialization in marketing and supply chain management covers all aspects from market research and analysis and new products and services concept development to production and final delivery. A cross-functional approach is used to teach students how to manage the fundamental value processes involved in producing and marketing goods and services. This specialization is unique in its integrative emphasis on meeting customer and market needs in an optimally effective and efficient manner given technological and operational constraints.

The specialization in entrepreneurial venture creation provides opportunities to learn about the high-growth entrepreneurial venture process of value creation through an application of technology in a dynamic environment. The school fosters an entrepreneurial culture and focuses on experiential, real-world and real-time learning in the high-growth environment. It requires active student participation, field trips to entrepreneurial ventures, guest speakers, case studies, and a final project that focuses on the creation of a new venture. From this specialization select students are given the opportunity to participate in the annual Holloway Entrepreneurial Business Plan Competition.

The financial management specialization provides students the opportunity to study the discipline in greater depth. A finance specialization provides career opportunities in a wide variety of areas such as banking, insurance, corporate finance, investment management, and risk management. Students in the full-time program choose electives from these areas, but they do not have the opportunity to complete a specialization due to the intensive format of the program.

The Faculty

The faculty members of the Whittemore School are both researchers and teachers, performing both jobs at a high level of excellence. The 59 faculty members in the school support the accounting, business management, economics, and hospitality management programs. The Whittemore School also brings in Executives-in-Residence. These executives teach classes and act as mentors or general resources in their field of expertise. Executives-in-Residence are chosen for their high levels of professional experience and their willingness to complement the academic strengths of the School. The Whittemore School does not use graduate assistants to teach master's- or doctoral-level classes.

The Business School Network
Corporate Partnerships

The Whittemore School Executive Board is made up of 40 senior officers from many of the top businesses in the Northeast and Atlantic regions of the United States. These senior officers interact with the schools' leadership and students to provide an educational experience that is both up-to-date and real-world.

The University and Environs

The University of New Hampshire, founded in 1866, is located in Durham—a small town in a semirural area that retains many traces of its colonial past. The 200-acre campus is surrounded by more than 3,000 acres of fields, farms, and woodlands owned by the University. A stream running through a large wooded area in the middle of the campus enhances a sense of openness and natural beauty. The University enrolls more than 13,500 students in both its undergraduate and graduate programs and as such is the largest academic institution in the state. The accessibility of Boston's cultural opportunities (65 miles south); the skiing, hiking, and scenery of the White Mountains (60 miles north); and the sandy beaches and rocky coast of New Hampshire and Maine (10 miles east) make it an ideal location to live and study.

Placement

The Whittemore School offers individualized placement for all graduate students. Two career fairs are held each year that attract regional and national companies, and an active alumni database is available to students interested in networking. The University also maintains a comprehensive full-time career planning office. In cooperation with the University Career Services office, the school conducts a number of workshops throughout the year that include resume writing, interviewing techniques, salary negotiations, and overviews of the current employment market.

Admission

The crucial requirement for admission to any of the M.B.A. programs is a history that demonstrates that the applicant has the potential and desire for graduate study in business. All students must have completed a bachelor's degree before beginning the M.B.A. program. The focus of the applicant's undergraduate studies is of less importance than evidence of academic ability and potential for becoming a responsible manager and leader. The GMAT exam is required of all applicants, along with the TOEFL exam for all international applicants. In recent years, the average GMAT score was 550 and the average grade point average was 3.34. The minimum TOEFL score is 550 (paper-based test) or 213 (computer-based test).

Applicants to the full-time M.B.A. program can be considered for admission without work experience but must demonstrate excellence in all other aspects of their application. Part-time applicants must have a minimum of two years of professional experience, and applicants to the executive M.B.A. must have a minimum of five years.

Finances

Yearly tuition for the full-time M.B.A. program in 2008–09 is proposed to be $29,450 for out-of-state students and $18,170 for in-state students. A single room cost $5654 in the graduate student dorm, Babcock Hall. Students may remain in Babcock Hall during the summer for an additional cost. Limited on-campus housing is available for married students. Prices for efficiencies and one- and two-bedroom apartments ranged from $706 to $935 per month. For more information, students should visit the Web site at http://www.unh.edu/housing.

Tuition scholarships are competitive and awarded to full-time applicants who demonstrate high academic achievement and professional promise. Students who are eligible for federal aid are also encouraged to apply for low-interest loans through the Financial Aid Office (Web site: http://www.unh.edu/financial-aid/).

Yearly tuition and fees for part-time students (Durham and Manchester) for 2008–09 are proposed to be $1860 per course for New Hampshire residents and $2151 per course for nonresidents. Mandatory fees were $34.50 for 1–3 credits, $233.50 for 6 credits, and $427 per term for 9 credits.

Program costs for the executive M.B.A. for 2008–09 are proposed to be $46,730 with housing and $41,810 without housing. The program fee includes tuition, fees, materials and books, a one-week residency in the first year, a ten-day international residency (excluding airfare), a three-day New York City Wall Street residence, and lunches/snacks while classes are in session. Housing rates include overnight accommodations on Friday nights when class is in session.

Application Facts and Dates

Application deadlines are July 1 for the full-time program for U.S. nationals and April 1 for international applicants. Full-time applicants who wish to be considered for graduate assistantships and tuition scholarships should submit their applications by March 1. The deadline for applicants to the executive program is July 31. The fall deadline for part-time applications is July 31 and November 15 for winter. For information, applicants should contact:

Graduate Programs Office
The Whittemore School of Business
116 McConnell Hall
University of New Hampshire
15 Academic Way
Durham, New Hampshire 03824-3593

Phone: 603-862-1367
Fax: 603-862-4468
E-mail: wsbe.grad.@unh.edu
Web site: http://www.wsbe.unh.edu/grad

University of New Haven

AN UPDATED M.B.A. FOR TODAY'S PROFESSIONAL

The working environment is changing, becoming more global and more competitive. Information technology has revolutionized the way we do business. New service-based corporations and industries are forming, and established industries such as banking, health care, and energy are being reshaped. Professional success in today's world requires knowledge and skills in all of the basic business functional areas plus the ability to lead in a multicultural society, to build effective functionally integrated teams, and, most importantly, to successfully manage constant change. Because of these changes in the business environment and the increasingly robust economy, employers are intensifying their recruitment of M.B.A. graduates. The job market for new hires is expanding, and the possibilities for advancement abound. Now is the time to prepare for these new opportunities.

Upon graduation, you will join more than 15,000 alumni from the University of New Haven (UNH) College of Business who work in businesses throughout the world.

Programs and Curricular Focus

The primary objective of the M.B.A. program at the University of New Haven is the development of leadership skills and a global perspective, required in today's complex business environment. Additional objectives include development of analytical skills and specialization training that produces effective performance in a range of organizations, from entrepreneurial to high technology and global. Many courses require cases, group projects, and in-class presentations. Since many students in the program are currently working in high-technology and multinational firms operating in Connecticut, class discussions reflect this rich mix.

The M.B.A. curriculum has three components that include a total of seventeen courses (51 credits). Students with prior studies in business might be able to reduce their requirements to as little as eleven courses (33 credits). Full-time students can complete their studies within twelve to twenty-two months. Part-time students typically take three to four years.

The first component is six courses covering core competencies. Although some students will need all six, those with a strong coverage of core undergraduate business studies may be able to waive most.

The second component consists of courses in seven required areas: communication, product creation, valuation, global issues, organizational change, business and society, and strategic vision.

The concluding component is four advanced electives. These may be used to explore a mix of interests or to form a concentration from one of several areas:

accounting, business policy and strategic leadership, finance, human resources management, global marketing and e-commerce, and management of sports industries.

Students and the M.B.A. Experience

Nearly 500 students, many holding full-time jobs, are enrolled in the M.B.A. program at the University of New Haven. Most students are from the northeastern United States, but the University has made a strong commitment to maintain a diverse student body. Women make up 51 percent of the student population, and 16 percent are international students, representing approximately fifty countries.

Special Features

Trimester scheduling allows students to accelerate progress toward their degree, and, while a complete curriculum is available to full-time students, there are evening and weekend classes suitable for working adults. Several courses are now offered online as distance learning courses.

Students can enrich their personal and professional competences by selecting a concentration in a particular discipline, and some departments offer students the opportunity to obtain additional credit and practical experience by participation in an internship program.

The MBA for Emerging Leaders Program is designed for busy adults, in a format conducive to their lifestyles, which allows students to complete a master's degree quickly without sacrificing quality. In less than two years, a cohort of 15 to 25 students

can complete an M.B.A. degree that develops the skills, knowledge, and values today's manager must possess to be successful. The program is a modular lock-step curriculum that includes core and advanced courses. Students take and complete one course at a time in five-week increments. Each course is a building block for the next. The same group of students remains together for the entire program in a seminar style. Classes break for all the major holidays and for a five- to six-week break in the summer.

Benefits of the MBA for Emerging Leaders Program include development and improvement of managerial and supervisory skills, 18 credits of introductory courses designed to build a foundation of general knowledge in key business areas, 33 credits of advanced courses designed to develop skills and enhance training of the individual and group in a work-related collaborative environment, immediate company and employee benefit from work-related assignments, real-world curriculum, the cohort style, and the ability to earn a high-quality M.B.A. in less than two years without career interruptions.

The Faculty

The highly qualified faculty represents a combination of full-time academics who hold doctoral degrees in their specialties from a variety of prestigious institutions and part-time faculty members chosen from managers who have demonstrated a high degree of leadership and who have received national recognition for their applied research. Each brings practical insight and experience to the classroom.

Class size is relatively small, averaging less than 15 students. Classes are kept small to allow for interaction and personal attention. The faculty members at UNH get to know students and act as advisers in discussions about business decisions and plans for personal and professional growth and development. UNH faculty members have international, national, and regional reputations in their fields through outstanding accomplishments in research and writing and as visiting lecturers.

The Business School Network

Most students in the M.B.A program hold full-time positions in regional businesses and nonprofit corporations; that experience allows the classroom to become a mechanism for extending students' learning into varied practical environments. Ongoing interaction with the business community also occurs through the Executive-in-Residence Program. Additional networking occurs through students' participation in the UNH chapter of Sigma Beta Delta, the National Honor Society in business, management, and administration.

Each fall and spring, the Bartels' Fellowship Lecture Series brings a successful CEO or entrepreneur to campus to lecture and interact with faculty and students. Some Distinguished Bartels' Fellows have been Dr. David Ebsworth, former President of Bayer Corporation; Robert Beavers Jr., Senior Vice President of McDonald's Corporation; Francis Freidman, former CEO of GCI Group, Grey Advertising; Ronald G. Shaw, President and CEO of Pilot Pen; and William J. Weisz, former CEO of Motorola, Inc.

The College and Environs

The University's 80-acre campus is located in south-central Connecticut, on a hillside in West Haven that overlooks Long Island Sound and downtown New Haven. The area is semisuburban and is easily accessible by car, bus, train, or plane. The campus, located near the intersection of Interstate Highways 95 and 91, is 75 miles northeast of New York City and 135 miles southwest of Boston.

New Haven, just 10 minutes from the campus, is a city where arts and cultural activities flourish and coexist with science and business. Settled in the early 1600s and rich in history and heritage, the New Haven area is proud of its past, prouder of its present, and actively planning for its future. The city, considered by many as the "Gateway to New England," is a manufacturing center, a deep-water port, a major arts center, and a college town with seven colleges and universities in the immediate area.

Facilities

The University of New Haven provides facilities for a full complement of student services, including career development and placement services; academic, vocational,

and personal counseling; alumni relations; health services; international student services; veterans' affairs; minority affairs; and services for students with disabilities. In addition, there are athletic facilities and a campus store for the students' use and convenience. There is no housing on campus for graduate students

Technology Environment

The UNH Center for Computing Services provides both administrative and academic computing support. Clusters of terminals and personal computers for student use are spread throughout the campus. Access to the Internet, graphics terminals, printing and plotting devices, laser printing, and a wide variety of data files and software and simulation packages are available.

Placement

The University of New Haven provides career development and placement services as well as academic, vocational, and personal counseling.

Admission

Admission decisions are based primarily on an applicant's undergraduate record. Candidates for admission to the Emerging Leaders Program are required to meet the same criteria as the traditional Master of Business Administration. The MBA for Emerging Leaders Program requires a bachelor's degree and two or more years of business or professional experience. An interview may be arranged at the request of the applicant; for detailed information, students should contact the Director of the Emerging Leaders Program.

In support of their applications, students should submit scores from the Graduate Management Admission Test (GMAT). Students for whom English is not their native language must present a TOEFL score. International students must submit official, certified documents showing sufficient financial support from personal or sponsor's funds or a scholarship.

Finances

For the 2007–08 academic year, the tuition rate was $1890 per 3-credit course, plus a

Graduate Student Council fee of $20 per term and a technology fee of $20 per term. There is a nonrefundable application fee of $50 and an additional nonrefundable acceptance fee of $200 for international students not on scholarship. Students should calculate additional expenses for books, supplies, and housing.

Financial aid is available for domestic students, including loans and assistantships. Financial aid is not available for international students. Teaching, research, or administrative assistantships are available to full-time students. Compensation includes $7.65 per hour as well as a 50 percent tuition reduction; students typically work 15–20 hours per week.

International Students

Qualified international students are welcome in the M.B.A. program at the University of New Haven. Ten percent of the students currently enrolled are from approximately fifty countries outside the United States. To qualify, a prospective student must have completed an acceptable undergraduate degree program. All transcripts must be submitted in English.

The University has an Office of International Student Services that provides a full range of support services for international students.

To facilitate preparation for admission by international students, the University is currently planning to bring a branch of an internationally known English as a second language (ESL) school to campus.

Application Facts and Dates

For more information or applications, students should contact:

Eloise Gormley
Director of Graduate Admissions
University of New Haven
300 Boston Post Road
West Haven, Connecticut 06516
Phone: 203-932-7133
    800-DIAL-UNH Ext. 7133
       (toll-free)
E-mail: gradinfo@newhaven.edu
Web site: http://www.newhaven.edu

The University of North Carolina at Charlotte

Belk College of Business Administration

Charlotte, North Carolina

THE DEAN'S MESSAGE

Thank you for your interest in the Belk College of Business M.B.A. program. The Belk College is Charlotte's leader in business education. Since the College's founding in 1970, we have created a culture of innovation and responsiveness; we were the first business school in the Charlotte region to offer an M.B.A. and the first to attain AACSB accreditation. With the addition of our Ph.D. program in 2006, UNC Charlotte became just the third university in North Carolina—and the only one exclusively serving the Charlotte region—to offer bachelor's, master's, and doctoral degrees in business administration.

Within the Belk College's responsive and innovative academic environment, you will find challenging academic programs, an outstanding faculty, strong community partnerships, global impact, international accreditation, and extensive business and alumni networks. The Belk College is committed to developing the next generation of business leaders by offering programs that stress academic rigor, real-world solutions, and global perspective. I encourage you to take a look at the advantages that the Belk College M.B.A. offers.

—Steven Ott, Interim Dean

Programs and Curricular Focus

The Belk College of Business at UNC Charlotte offers an exciting M.B.A. program designed for students in both full-time and flexible (evening) formats. At the Belk College of Business, students find that classrooms are alive with the exchange of real-world ideas and strategies, preparing future leaders to thrive in today's global business economy. Whether students are just starting out in the business world or contemplating the next step in an established career, UNC Charlotte offers an M.B.A. program to meet their individual needs and goals.

The Full-Time M.B.A. is designed as a cohort program and follows a set schedule. Core courses are offered during the day on the main UNC Charlotte campus. Students who select a concentration may also take courses at UNC Charlotte Uptown. This seventeen-month program begins in August and concludes the following December. During the summer term, students may choose to participate in professional internships or study-abroad programs. Spaces are limited in this highly selective program.

With the Flexible M.B.A. program at UNC Charlotte, professionals can continue a full-time career as they earn an advanced degree. The Flexible M.B.A. at UNC Charlotte allows students to begin the program during any semester and structure their course loads around work, family, and other commitments. Courses are held in the evening and meet once a week. Some students finish in less than two years, while others take longer. The program can be structured to meet the needs of each individual.

The Belk College adds a contemporary approach to the traditional course of study. The M.B.A. was originally envisioned as a gener-alist degree to ensure that a graduate emerged with a wide range of skills to advance to leadership positions. This idea is taken a step further with a curriculum that allows students to develop a specialty or concentration in a business discipline. Students are exposed to major decision areas through core courses, and with electives, students explore specific topics. Concentrations provide a depth of knowledge in a specific function or business area, such as finance, marketing, economics, information technology, management, or real estate development. The UNC Charlotte M.B.A. is a 37-credit-hour program. Additional preparatory courses may be required for students who do not hold an undergraduate degree in business.

The M.B.A. in sports marketing and management is designed to address the growing need for highly skilled business professionals in sports-related organizations. The program is delivered in a full-time, two-year, cohort-based format combining the strength and rigor of the M.B.A. with the application of this knowledge geared directly to the sports industry. A full-time six-month internship is required during the second year of the M.B.A. program, providing valuable hands-on experience from seasoned pros.

The Belk College has earned the ultimate citation for excellence in business education—accreditation by AACSB International–The Association to Advance Collegiate Schools of Business. AACSB International accreditation represents the highest standard of achievement for business schools worldwide; only about one third of U.S. institutions hold this designation. A rigorous and comprehensive peer review of the M.B.A. and other academic programs con-firms the Belk College's commitment to quality and continuous improvement.

Students and the M.B.A. Experience

The Belk College M.B.A. program is designed for both the Full-Time and Flexible M.B.A. student and attracts a remarkably diverse student body—diverse in age, race, gender, national origin, educational background, and work experience.

More than three fourths of the students are working professionals, with an average of six to eight years' work experience. Approximately one third of the students are women. Students range in age from 22 to 57, with an average age of 29. Approximately 10 percent of the students identify themselves as members of minority groups. International students make up 7 percent of the total enrollment. More than 200 companies are represented by alumni of the program.

Although nearly half of the students earned an undergraduate degree in business, students from a variety of educational backgrounds, including engineering, psychology, computer science, English, and science, bring their unique perspectives to the program.

Global Focus

In today's interconnected world, it is imperative that students develop an understanding of the international arena. To support this critical component of a modern business education, the Belk College has established strong ties with top business schools around the world

The Faculty

The College's distinguished faculty members create theoretical and practical solutions used by business leaders to solve problems and make advances in their industries. The Belk College has more than 80 professors, who have all met the rigorous appointment process to the graduate faculty. All hold doctoral degrees and have met standards of academic achievement and scholarship. The faculty members are housed in six different departments: accounting, business information systems and operations management, economics, finance and business law, management, and marketing. These talented teachers are published scholars, top researchers, active consultants, and successful business professionals.

The Business School Network

The Belk College is committed to maintaining strong connections to its 17,000 graduates, most of whom live in the Charlotte region. Many dedicated alumni give back to UNC Charlotte and the Belk College, not only through their

financial contributions, but also by serving as guest lecturers in classes, mentoring students, providing internships, and hiring graduates.

Corporate Partnerships
Charlotte is an energetic business city that has embraced the Belk College and shown unflagging support for its ambitions and initiatives. From the Center for Real Estate to the TIAA-CREF Economic Forecast to the prominent and engaged advisory boards, connections run deep and provide unparalleled opportunities for students and faculty members. UNC Charlotte M.B.A. students have the opportunity to interact with influential leaders in business, government, health care, and technology. The program features guest lecturers and panelists from local, regional, national, and multinational companies. It also sponsors networking opportunities with fellow M.B.A. students and UNC Charlotte alumni.

The College and Environs
UNC Charlotte has been educating business leaders since 1965 and has offered an M.B.A. since 1970. Today, with more than 2,500 undergraduate students, 500 graduate students, and 17,000 alumni, the Belk College of Business is one of the Carolinas' largest business programs.

UNC Charlotte's main campus is located in the booming University City area of Charlotte, a metropolitan area of more than 1.2 million. The campus is easily accessible from major interstates and thoroughfares. UNC Charlotte has a second campus located in uptown, the heart of the center city. The University has had an uptown presence since 1995 to respond to the educational needs and demands of the approximately 50,000 people who work in or live near uptown Charlotte.

Facilities
The Belk College makes its home in the Friday Building on the main campus of UNC Charlotte. Constructed in 1982 and expanded in 1995, the building holds lecture halls, classrooms, faculty and administrative offices, computer labs,

and a study and lounge area for graduate business students. Other facilities at UNC Charlotte include the J. Murray Atkins Library. The library contains more than 1 million volumes and microforms and subscribes to 20,000 periodicals, with three fourths having electronic accessibility. It also houses a 7,782-volume rare-book collection and an estimated 3.3 million documents in its manuscript collection. The library provides state-of-the-art information technologies, including 1,200 data drops, 1,800 reader seats, and 250 public computer stations for research. Atkins Library is a member of ASERL (Association of Southeastern Research Libraries).

Technology Environment
The Belk College responds to technological changes by teaching the skills needed to incorporate these changes into overall business strategies. The UNC Charlotte campuses are equipped with voice, data, and video connectivity, essential for creating and supporting a fully interactive learning environment.

Placement
M.B.A. students have access to all career services available to UNC Charlotte students as well as the support of a full-time M.B.A. program staff member dedicated to career and professional development. Services include individual counseling and advising (especially for career changers), resume critiques or counseling sessions, Career Fall and Spring Expos, national Career Conferences of America in select cities, campus professional job resume database, and resume referral services. The University Career Center (UCC) and M.B.A. program staff members are committed to helping students develop a job search, internship search, or career-enhancement strategy that meets their individual needs. Professional job coaches are hired by the M.B.A. program to further assist with the career development process. Postgraduation rates consistently show 100 percent regional, national, and global employment rates for UNC Charlotte M.B.A.'s.

Admission
The UNC Charlotte M.B.A. program seeks a diverse body of students that encompasses various academic, cultural, and professional backgrounds. Applications are evaluated on the basis of a number of factors, including previous academic performance, GMAT scores, work experience (preferred but not required), and references. The average GMAT score is 591. The average GPA is 3.34.

Completed applications must include official transcripts from all colleges and universities attended, official GMAT scores, three letters of recommendation, a resume or description of work experiences, a statement of purpose, and the application fee. Students applying to the M.B.A. in sports marketing and management program have additional essays and interview requirements. Students whose native language is not English must submit TOEFL, IELTS, or MELAB scores to demonstrate English proficiency.

Finances
The 2007–08 tuition and fees for a full-time North Carolina resident were $4773 per semester ($9877 per semester for nonresidents). Tuition and fees for a part-time resident ranged from $1241 to $3449 per semester, depending on number of credit hours taken.

On-campus housing, including a campus meal plan, ranged from $3000 to $4000 per semester for the academic year 2007–08. Private apartments are also available near the University. Housing, food, and miscellaneous living expenses in the Charlotte area compare favorably with national averages.

The College offers a limited number of graduate assistantships to students. Applicants should have an excellent academic record. In 2007–08, the stipend was $10,000 for a 20-hour-per-week position for the nine-month academic year.

International Students
In fall 2007, international students composed about 10 percent of the students enrolled in the M.B.A. program. Support services for international students are provided through the UNC Charlotte International Student Scholar Office. These students may attend evening classes along with the part-time students but on a full-time basis, or they may choose the full-time program.

Application Facts and Dates
Applications to the Flexible (evening) M.B.A. are reviewed on a continuous basis. The recommended deadlines are May 1 for fall admission, October 1 for spring admission, and April 1 for summer admission. The application deadlines for international students are May 1 for fall admission and October 1 for spring admission. The Full-Time M.B.A. program admits students only in the fall, with a May 1 deadline.

Applications to the M.B.A. in sports marketing and management are reviewed only for fall admission. The deadline for priority consideration is January 15, with a secondary deadline of March 1 as space remains available.

To develop a personalized application schedule to address their individual circumstances, students should contact the M.B.A. office.

M.B.A. Office
UNC Charlotte
9201 University City Boulevard
Charlotte, North Carolina 28223

Phone: 704-687-7566
Fax: 704-687-2809
E-mail: mba@uncc.edu
Web site: http://www.mba.uncc.edu

Graduate Admissions
Allison Brinkley

Phone: 704-687-2633
Fax: 704-687-3279
E-mail: abrinkley@uncc.edu
Web site: http://www.uncc.edu/gradmiss

International Admissions
Allison Brinkley

Phone: 704-687-2633
Fax: 704-687-6340
E-mail: abrinkley@uncc.edu
Web site: http://www.uncc.edu/intradmn

University of Oregon

Charles H. Lundquist College of Business

Eugene, Oregon

ONE STUDENT AT A TIME

The Oregon M.B.A. educates one student at a time. By combining business fundamentals with hands-on learning through skills workshops and team consulting projects with our business partners, we prepare our students for advanced courses and careers in innovation and entrepreneurship, securities analysis, sports business, and sustainable business practices. The state-of-art Lillis Business Complex provides the perfect educational environment for our small and select student cohorts.

—James Bean, Dean

Programs and Curricular Focus

The Oregon M.B.A. seeks to develop business leaders—women and men who have the intellectual curiosity, professional training, and ethical demeanor to stand out in a crowd, regardless of industry, functional area, or organizational level. Effective leaders must possess superior strategic, analytical, and communication skills to identify opportunities and mobilize others to implement important business initiatives. The Oregon M.B.A. combines leadership training, experiential education, and business theory in order to inculcate these skills. Through its four signature centers, the Oregon M.B.A. offers curricular tracks, experiential learning, and networking opportunities in innovation and entrepreneurship, securities analysis (finance/accounting), sports business, and sustainable business practices.

The regular full-time M.B.A. program combines a solid foundation of core business courses with more specialized electives in each of the four tracks. Students take courses in one or more of the tracks and avail themselves of the industry contacts and opportunities for practical projects provided by the centers. Starting with an extended orientation, the focus is also on team building, written and oral communication, and practical business skills. In the second year, students are challenged to apply these skills and their industry knowledge to their Strategic Planning Projects, which are team-based consulting projects arranged by the four centers with businesses in the Northwest.

Students with strong undergraduate backgrounds in finance and accounting are eligible for the accelerated program, which requires the completion of fifteen advanced courses. With intensive study, accelerated students may graduate in nine or eleven months; alternatively, they may study part-time.

In addition to the full-time twenty-one-month program and the full- or part-time accelerated M.B.A. programs, the Lundquist College offers the following degree programs: J.D./M.B.A., M.Acc., and Ph.D.

Students and the M.B.A. Experience

Small entering classes (a maximum of 60 regular and 15 accelerated students) make the Oregon M.B.A. a boutique program. Not surprisingly, students are drawn to the Oregon M.B.A. not only by the center-based curriculum but also by its human scale and diversity. They can count on the personal attention of instructors, administrators, and staff members, who all give generously of their time and energy.

Despite its small size, the Oregon M.B.A. program has students from half the states in the U.S. and from ten to twelve countries. Women account for 35 to 40 percent of the class; the proportion of international students ranges from 15 to 25 percent. About a third of the entering students have undergraduate business degrees, while more than 40 percent hail from the humanities and social sciences. Their work experience is diverse, both in kind and in length—rarely less than two years, with an average of four.

Oregon M.B.A. students prize and learn from this variety of cultural, educational, and professional backgrounds. The result is a genuine esprit de corps that shuns fierce competition in favor of friendly collaboration and that lets students work actively and constructively toward collective and programmatic improvements.

Special Features

The opportunity to work with the centers' business partners and to apply classroom learning sets the Oregon M.B.A. program apart from other programs. In their second year, student teams of 4 members each work with Northwest companies to develop solutions—real, not hypothetical—for a new business opportunity or challenge. At the end, the teams must present their recommendations to senior management.

During the summer, Technology Entrepreneurship Fellows—select students from business, law, and the sciences—explore the commercial feasibility of technologies developed at the University and elsewhere. Technologies that pass the test and ideas developed by students on their own are developed into full-fledged business plans in the fall of the second year under the auspices of the Lundquist Center for Entrepreneurship (LCE). The best teams participate in national business plan competitions, including the New Venture Championship organized by LCE in Portland in the spring; prize money in excess of $60,000 attracts teams from the best business schools in the country and abroad.

For anyone interested in pursuing a career in the sports and entertainment business, the Warsaw Sports Marketing Center has become the preeminent place in the world. In addition to taking courses in sports business and hearing from prominent speakers, second-year students also spend a week in New York meeting with the chief executives of all major-league sports and sports media.

Drawing on its recognized strengths in finance and accounting as well as the strong financial support of Wall Street and the West Coast investment community, the Lundquist College has created a new curricular track and launched a Securities Analysis Center, which provides practical experience and contacts for any M.B.A. student wanting to embark on a successful career in international finance.

In keeping with the values and policies of the state of Oregon, the environmentally friendly and LEED-certified design of the Lillis Business Complex, and the growing presence of innovative businesses in this field, sustainable business practices have become the focus of a fourth center and of the Oregon M.B.A. program.

The Faculty

The Lundquist faculty consists of 42 tenured or tenure-track members as well as numerous instructors and adjunct professors, many of whom have extensive practical business experience and contacts. Those chosen to teach in the M.B.A. program stand out for their commitment to the program and good teaching as well as ready accessibility to their students. Above all, they expect their students to be active contributors rather than passive consumers.

More information on individual faculty members, their research, and their teaching interests can be found at the College's Web site.

The Business School Network

Regardless of the school attended, most M.B.A. graduates are recruited and hired by companies located in the same region as their school. While the Oregon M.B.A.'s network of consulting clients, business sponsors, corporate recruiters, and alumni is strongest on the West Coast in general and in the Pacific Northwest in particular, it also extends to the Midwest and East Coast as well as abroad. Students get a glimpse of that network through their summer internships, strategic planning projects, and company visits and the centers' industry contacts. Silicon Forest, the region between San Francisco and Seattle and the home of high-tech companies such as Intel, Hewlett-Packard, Tektronix, and Xerox, has provided happy hunting grounds for many Oregon M.B.A. graduates. Portland-area sports marketers such as Nike, Adidas, and Yakima are desired destinations for some Warsaw Center students, while others find luck with professional teams and other prominent employers throughout the country. Oregon M.B.A. finance graduates find open doors at prominent banks and investment firms on either coast. Most importantly, however, Oregon M.B.A. alumni at these and other firms are helpful in guiding current students, identifying promising opportunities, and advising the program on improvements and changes. Students and alumni alike are part of the Oregon M.B.A. Web-based network that provides permanent e-mail addresses and serves as a lifetime networking vehicle.

The College and Environs

Founded in 1876 and one of only sixty-three members of the prestigious Association of American Universities, the University of Oregon is located in an intimate, parklike setting of 295 acres. M.B.A. students can count on up-to-the-minute business sources and information through the Northwest's second-largest library. Eugene/Springfield, with a population of 200,000, has very good schools, low crime, affordable housing, and wonderful recreational opportunities. Wooded hills, green open spaces, and two rivers

provide the backdrop for year-round outdoor activities. The mild, temperate climate and relaxed way of life create a congenial environment for learning and living. The spectacular Oregon coast and snow-covered Cascade Mountains are each an hour's drive from the campus.

The University and Eugene's Holt Center for the Performing Arts, numerous galleries, cafes, and other venues offer events to suit any taste, and Portland, Seattle, and San Francisco are big-city getaways within easy travel distance.

Technology Environment

The Lillis Business Complex provides the latest in technological advances, including wireless and wired access throughout the business school and videotaping and video-conferencing as well as a multimedia studio. The small-group workrooms that are part of the newly renovated graduate programs area—bright and airy Peterson Hall—are equipped with flat-screen wall monitors. The Oregon M.B.A. program and its students are also served by the Lundquist College Business Technology Center.

Placement

Thanks to the small size of each entering class, the Career Services Office offers personal attention and a customized approach for each student. Workshops and individual coaching focus on resume writing, networking, interviewing, negotiation, and job-search strategies. The office identifies internship and employment opportunities, coordinates recruiters' visits, organizes company visitations, and hosts alumni workshops and receptions both on and off campus. For the past several years, job placement for those seeking employment has ranged between 80 and 100 percent within three months of graduation.

Admission

To be eligible for admission, applicants must have a bachelor's degree or its equivalent and take the GMAT. Chances of admission are greatly improved by a GMAT score above 600, a GPA of 3.0 or better, and at least two years of meaningful work experience. Applicants with degrees from non-English-speaking countries and institutions should finish the Internet-based TOEFL with a score of 96 or better (22 for speaking). Personal interviews are required.

Admitted students must have completed college-level calculus before they can enroll. The math prerequisite can also be satisfied

by placing in the 60th percentile or better in the quantitative section of the GMAT. An online program provides tutorials in accounting, economics, finance, and statistics for all entering students.

Finances

The Oregon M.B.A. is considered a "best buy" in graduate business education. Tuition for the 2007–08 academic year was $13,887 for Oregon residents and $18,909 for nonresidents. All applicants are automatically considered for merit scholarships. Second-year students are eligible for graduate teaching fellowships and academic merit scholarships. The University's Financial Aid Office is responsible for loan programs and work-study certification.

Off-campus housing ranges from $4500 to $6000; campus housing starts at $5750. Personal expenses, books, and supplies are estimated at $3000. Oregon has no sales tax. Students ride buses free of charge.

International Students

Eugene is well known for its tolerance and celebration of cultural and ethnic diversity. International students and their families from almost ninety countries find the University of Oregon and Eugene a warmly welcoming and safe place. The University has the highest percentage of international students of any public university. The International Affairs office and a large number of international student organizations provide support and fellowship.

Application Facts and Dates

Applications are reviewed on a rolling basis. Applicants receive a decision by December 15 if they submit their completed applications by November 15. The deadline for international applications is February 15. The domestic deadline is March 15. Thereafter, applications are accepted until May 15, subject to space availability. Interviews are recommended.

For more information, students should contact:

Ms. Perri McGee, Oregon M.B.A.
Charles H. Lundquist College of
   Business
1208 University of Oregon
Eugene, Oregon 97403-1208
Phone: 541-346-3306
Fax: 541-346-0073
E-mail: mbainfo@oregonmba.com
Web site: http://www.oregonmba.com

University of Rhode Island

College of Business Administration

Kingston, Rhode Island

EDUCATION WITH CURRENCY AND RELEVANCY

The environment for business has changed, with both globalization and geopolitical factors having a dramatic impact on the world economy. Our graduate programs are aimed toward individuals who are interested in management and leadership positions. The programs draw on an outstanding faculty with education and professional experience who challenge our students and allow them to achieve their career objectives. The faculty members combine theoretical knowledge with real-world business issues to foster a dynamic classroom environment. Our small classes enable faculty members to work with the students to develop their oral and written communication skills and provide for a more personalized approach to graduate education. Our focus on the student learner along with our dedicated faculty and staff differentiates us from other M.B.A. programs. I hope you will find our programs worthy of additional consideration.

—Mark Higgins, Dean and Alfred J. Verrecchia-Hasbro Inc. Leadership Chair in Business

Programs and Curricular Focus

The College of Business Administration at the University of Rhode Island (URI) currently offers two master's programs in business administration: a one-year full-time M.B.A. and an evening part-time M.B.A. The one-year program in Kingston integrates course work, career planning and development, and work experience within a one-calendar-year period. A group of up to 25 students begins the program in August and finishes during the following summer with two required courses and an internship or two electives. The program consists of fifteen courses, with students working in teams on projects and presentations throughout the year. Students are also required to participate in a consulting project with a nonprofit organization, with assistance from a faculty mentor.

The Providence evening M.B.A. program is aimed at individuals who want to pursue a degree while maintaining their professional commitments. This program requires the completion of 45 credits, or fifteen courses. Waivers are available for students with previous business courses or by taking waiver exams. Students can waive up to 36 credits.

Classes (with a maximum of 30 students) meet one night a week during the fall, spring, and summer sessions in Providence or Kingston. Concentrations include finance, management, marketing, and supply chain management. Web-based and Saturday courses are available for matriculated M.B.A. students and alumni.

Students and the M.B.A. Experience

The M.B.A. experience at URI combines case studies, lectures, simulations, team and individual projects, and presentations to develop the skills needed to excel in business. Students come from a diverse range of majors, industries, and job categories—making for a great learning and networking experience.

The fall 2007 entering class for the Kingston one-year M.B.A. had average GMAT scores of 550 and an average undergraduate GPA of 3.34. Twenty-nine percent were women and 33 percent were international students. The average age was 26. The breakdown of undergraduate degrees was 24 percent in social science, 47 percent in business, 24 percent in engineering, and 5 percent in math/science. The fall 2007 entering class for the Providence evening M.B.A. had average GMAT scores of 558 and an average undergraduate GPA of 3.18. Thirty-eight percent were women and 12 percent had an advanced degree. The average age was 28. The breakdown of undergraduate degrees was 12 percent in social science, 40 percent in business, 26 percent in engineering, 6 percent in economics, and 16 percent in math/science.

The Faculty

The College of Business Administration at URI consists of 46 faculty members. In addition to teaching, faculty members take part in a variety of research and consulting projects as well as participate in other professional and public service activities. Some are corporate board members. Faculty members use a variety of teaching methods. Class size is kept small for interaction amongst students and faculty members.

The Business School Network

The College of Business Administration is the headquarters for institutes that specialize in academic and business research. The Research Institute for Telecommunications and Information Marketing is a leader in the generation and dissemination of knowledge of telecommunications and information marketing. It does so through lectures by visiting executives, class projects, and research grants. The Research Center in Business and Economics brings together resources from various departments to assist business, nonprofit, and government agencies in formulating, conducting, and evaluating research projects. The Center also conducts statewide consumer confidence surveys. The Pacific-Basin Capital Markets Research Center creates, maintains, and distributes capital market data for eleven nations in the Pacific Basin region. It provides an international forum for global communities of business and government to exchange ideas and information.

The College and Environs

URI was founded as a land-grant college in 1892. The University enrolls more than 11,000 undergraduate students and 3,000 graduate students. One of the seven colleges at URI, the College of Business Administration, which was 80 years old in 2000, offers the B.S., the M.B.A., the M.S. in accounting, and the Ph.D. in business administration. The Kingston M.B.A. takes place on the main campus in Kingston, Rhode Island—15 miles from scenic Newport and the Atlantic Ocean. It is only 30 miles south of the capital of Providence, where the evening M.B.A. program is held.

Facilities

URI offers a wide variety of facilities on all campuses. The library collection of more than 1 million bound volumes and 1.5 million microforms is housed in the University libraries in Kingston and Providence. Online public access is available to all students. The Decision Support Lab provides access to the University's extensive mainframe computer and superminicomputer facilities. Three Mac labs are also available for student use. E-mail addresses are given to each student upon arrival, providing participants with the ability to access the Web through ISP addresses in various locations.

A large athletic complex with an indoor track, multipurpose courts, a swimming facility, a gymnastics training center, and two fitness rooms is available on the Kingston campus. An ice arena has also been constructed. In addition, graduate housing, an international students' office, disability services, and special tutoring are available.

The College of Business is housed in Ballentine Hall, renovated in 2003 with state-of-the-art equipment in all classrooms. Projectors, electronic shades, and auto-dimming lights create the perfect experience for both the lecturer and the class.

Technology Environment

The Sherman Trading Room, named for Bruce S. Sherman, a 1969 graduate and the founder of Private Capital Management, provides access to financial data and information that gives students a distinct advantage over graduates of other business schools. Students are able to simulate stock trades and purchases as well as analyze financial information from markets around the globe.

Placement

URI helps students assess their goals, develop skills, and implement career objectives through the Career Services Department. Professional career advisers and planning specialists provide individual advising, noncredit workshops, on-campus interviews, and semester job fairs with leading global organizations. The staff members help students explore internships, job and career inquiries, resumes and cover letters, job search methods, and research concerning potential employers.

A dedicated internship coordinator resides in the College of Business Administration to help undergraduate and M.B.A. students find an internship.

Admission

All candidates for admission are required to provide a completed online application that consists of a statement of purpose, official scores from the Graduate Management Admission Test (GMAT), official transcripts from all universities attended, two letters of recommendation, a resume, and $50 application fee. In addition, a residency form is required for in-state residents. Applicants for whom English is not the native language are required to score 575 or above on the paper-based version of the TOEFL or 90 or above on the Internet-based version.

Finances

Tuition for the 2007–08 academic year for the entire Kingston one-year program was $12,711 for Rhode Island residents and $34,914 for nonresidents. Additional University fees were $2000 for the year. Tuition for the Providence M.B.A. program for Rhode Island residents was $385 per credit, $1058 per credit for nonresidents. Fees were approximately $50 per semester.

Limited graduate assistantships are available for all full-time students. Students who work 10 hours per week receive half tuition plus a stipend; students who work 20 hours per week receive full tuition plus a stipend.

Application Facts and Dates

The application deadline for the Kingston one-year M.B.A. program is April 15 for U.S. citizens and February 15 for international students. Providence M.B.A. program applications are due June 1 for September admission and October 1 for January admission. For more information, applicants should contact:

Graduate Programs Office
College of Business Administration
7 Lippitt Road, Ballentine Hall
University of Rhode Island
Kingston, Rhode Island 02881
Phone: 401-874-5000
Fax: 401-874-4312
E-mail: mba@uri.edu
Web site: http://www.cba.uri.edu/mba

University of Rochester

SIMON—WHERE THINKERS BECOME LEADERS

The Simon School's integrated, cross-functional approach to management is enhanced by our small size and significant international composition. The School's small size promotes communication among faculty members and students that is very difficult to achieve in a large, departmentalized school. The international student body, combined with the School's emphasis on student teams, brings the global workplace to life for the Simon School student.

—Mark Zupan, Dean

Programs and Curricular Focus

The Simon School's M.B.A. programs are designed to train individuals to solve management problems as members of a study-team structure. The curriculum emphasizes learning the principles of economics and effective decision making through a mix of lecture, case study, and project courses.

The degree program requires 67 hours (twenty courses) and can be completed in six quarters of full-time study. Three core courses are required in the underlying disciplines of economics, accounting, and management and information systems. In addition, a two-course sequence teaches students to frame, analyze, and communicate (F.A.Ct.) solutions to unstructured business problems. One course must be taken in each of the functional areas of finance, marketing, operations management, and organization theory. A course in business communications is required of all full-time students.

Eleven elective courses are required. Students may connect these electives to develop expertise in one or two concentrations. The fifteen concentrations offered are corporate accounting, public accounting, accounting and information systems, business environment and public policy, business systems consulting, competitive and organizational strategy, computers and information systems, electronic commerce, entrepreneurship, finance, health sciences management, international management, marketing, operations management–manufacturing, and operations management–services. Students may select one or more concentrations to customize their course of study in preparation for specific career objectives.

Students and the M.B.A. Experience

Each September approximately 100 students enter the Simon community as members of a cohort. Another 50–60 students join their classmates in January. Each cohort takes core classes together. September entrants complete the first-year core courses during the fall, winter, and spring quarters; January entrants typically complete core courses during the winter, spring, and summer quarters. Within each cohort, students are assigned to a study team of 4 or 5 members. Each team typically includes representatives from at least three countries and a variety of personal, professional, and academic backgrounds.

Simon students enter the program with a wide range of educational, professional, and geographic backgrounds. Undergraduate majors include economics, humanities, social sciences, business and commerce, engineering, and math and science. The class of 2008 includes 30 percent women and 18 percent members of under-represented U.S. minority groups. Prior full-time work experience averages 4.5 years, and the average age is 27, with approximately one third enrolling with fewer than three years of postbaccalaureate work experience.

Global Focus

Of the leading U.S. business schools, the Simon School is one of the most geographically diverse. More than 40 percent of its students come from outside the United States. In the class of 2008, seventeen countries are represented. Approximately one third of its alumni reside and work outside of the U.S., and about one third of its tenure-track faculty members have non-U.S. backgrounds. A Simon School education combines rigorous training in the business disciplines and functions with cross-cultural training and lifelong professional contact with an international alumni network.

During regularly scheduled Broaden Your Horizons seminars, students present lunch hour talks about their various countries' cultures, economies, political environments, and business protocols. International ex-change programs are offered with schools in nine countries, each approved by a faculty committee for compatibility with Simon M.B.A. program objectives. Interested students may pursue study abroad during one quarter of their second year of study.

Special Features

During the two-week Orientation Program, students participate in self-assessment exercises, personal selling and communication skills instruction, corporate leadership training, and one-on-one career counseling. The goals of the orientation include acclimating students to campus life, assessing and building on specific skills, and introducing the valuable programs of the Career Management Center. Students also participate in several VISION modules designed to enhance leadership skills in the areas of team building, training in diversity issues, ethical decision making, and social responsibility. The School also offers a five-day leadership development course during orientation each September.

The Faculty

The Simon School faculty is known internationally for leading scholarship in management education. There is a long tradition at Simon of coordinating teaching and research as well as integrating knowledge from all of the functional areas into the curriculum. Teaching awards for the best professors are presented annually by each M.B.A. class, and teaching is improved continuously through a formal faculty peer review. Leading-edge research is intrinsic to teaching the basic scientific principles of management. Many research findings used by the Simon faculty members in classroom study have served as foundations for corporate practices in use today. Simon faculty members serve as editors on four major academic journals, and recent studies of research productivity rank them among the top five faculties in the United States.

The Business School Network
Corporate Partnerships

The Frederick Kalmbach Executive Seminar Series features senior corporate executives who lecture annually on current issues in management. Each year speakers include members or professional associates of Simon's internationally prominent Executive

Advisory Committee. Simon students organize and participate in annual marketing-case competitions and consulting-case competitions. Students work directly with worldwide corporations, such as Johnson & Johnson and Eastman Kodak Company, in project courses offered as part of the academic curriculum.

Prominent Alumni

The long list of successful Simon alumni includes Robert J. Keegan, CEO and President of Goodyear Tire and Rubber Company; Mark B. Grier, Executive Vice President, the Prudential Insurance Company of America; Thomas J. Hartman, Partner, Accenture, LLP; Stephen E. Rogers, Managing Director, Barclays Global Investors; Dag Skattum, Managing Director, JPMorgan-Chase; Larry Aiello, President and CEO, Corning, Inc.; Lance Drummond, Senior Vice President, Bank of America; Eduardo Centola, Managing Director, Goldman, Sachs & Co.; Andrew Thomas, CEO, Heineken USA; and Alan Heuer, CFO, MasterCard International.

The College and Environs

The Simon School is part of the University of Rochester, a leading research university offering graduate study in approximately fifty fields, with a combined enrollment of undergraduate and graduate students totaling approximately 8,730. Situated near Lake Ontario, one of the Great Lakes, the metropolitan Rochester area (population 1 million) is home to many major international industries and entrepreneurial ventures, including Eastman Kodak Company, Bausch & Lomb, and Xerox Corporation's marketing group. Numerous cultural and recreational opportunities include the Rochester Philharmonic Orchestra and the University's own Eastman School of Music.

Facilities

Schlegel Hall, opened in 1991, is the Simon School's classroom and student services building. It contains case-style classrooms equipped with state-of-the-art technology and rear projection equipment, study rooms, a student lounge, and its own Computing Center. The center provides a wireless network for student's laptops, laser printing via local area networks, and access to several external data sources, such as Bloomberg and *Business News*. James S. Gleason Hall, a 38,000-square-foot addition, was completed in October 2001. On-campus graduate housing, both high-rise apartments and town houses, is available to Simon students. Off-campus housing is also available.

Placement

The Career Management Center offers one-on-one career counseling, targeted education, and the development of a personalized job-search strategy. Simon students are poised to secure meaningful internships and full-time opportunities in finance, investment banking, consulting, marketing, technology, and operations.

Admission

A Simon School Admissions Committee reads each application individually and evaluates recommendations, teamwork and communication skills, the nature and scope of prior work experience, the undergraduate academic record, GMAT scores, TOEFL scores as an indicator of English-language skills, evidence of leadership and maturity, and career focus. English language proficiency is critically important for successful interaction in the Simon School's geographically diverse study-team structure. Potential contributions to Simon classmates and to the world's business community are carefully considered. All undergraduate majors are represented in the program.

Finances

Tuition is $1228 per credit hour, or $36,840 per year, for 2007–08. The cost of books and supplies averages $1500 a year, and living expenses (rent, food supplies, personal expenses, and health insurance) are estimated at less than $14,000 for the 2007–08 academic year. Both U.S. and international applicants are eligible for scholarship support.

International Students

There is an active support network for international students in Rochester. The University of Rochester's International Services Office provides professional guidance to incoming international students. They are assisted by an independent, but University-affiliated, community volunteer group, the Rochester International Friendship Council, which locates host families for interested Simon students and helps students' spouses in language instruction and acculturation. Social outings and cultural adjustment workshops are offered during late-August orientation for all University international students. Instruction in English as a second language and orientation to U.S. culture are also available through the Simon English Language and U.S. Culture Program (ELUSC) offered each June, July, and October.

Application Facts and Dates

Application deadlines are November 1, December 1, January 8, April 1, and June 1 for September enrollment and August 1 and October 15 for January enrollment. For additional information, students should contact:

Gregory V. MacDonald
Executive Director for M.B.A.
    Admissions and Administration
William E. Simon Graduate School of
    Business Administration
University of Rochester
Rochester, New York 14627-0107
Phone: 585-275-3533
Fax: 585-271-3907
E-mail: admissions@simon.rochester.edu
Web site:
    http://www.simon.rochester.edu

University of St. Thomas

Minneapolis and St. Paul, Minnesota

HIGHLY PRINCIPLED GLOBAL BUSINESS LEADERS

Take a step back and look at the world. It is more competitive, faster paced, more complex, and less forgiving than ever before. This is especially true of business. To excel in this world we must be visionary, global strategic thinkers and principled leaders who inspire commitment from others. As business leaders, we face enormous challenges and enormous opportunities.

The University of St. Thomas M.B.A. offers an excellent, relevant business education that helps tomorrow's business leaders form the foundation for success. Our advantage is that we provide a high-quality education within a personal environment. As students, you have unlimited opportunities for personal interaction with classmates and professors within a rigorous, collegial, and team-oriented setting. The faculty members have extensive research and consulting experience, but they also act as learning coaches while partnering with you as you apply concepts to the real world. This combination of academic and practical expertise results in a dynamic and motivating learning environment. All of this is accomplished with a curriculum that is infused with ethics. The UST M.B.A. challenges your thinking about the role of business in society, creating a perspective that incorporates ethics and values.

An M.B.A. degree from a leading business school can help you stand out from the crowd and give you the skills to help your company do the same. I am confident that the UST M.B.A. will be a top choice for anyone seeking an excellent, relevant business education that develops highly principled global business leaders.

—Christopher P. Puto, Ph.D., Dean

Programs and Curricular Focus

The Opus College of Business at the University of St. Thomas (UST) offers the Full-time UST M.B.A. (twenty-one months), the Evening UST M.B.A. for working professionals, an Executive UST M.B.A., and the Health Care UST M.B.A. for physicians and health-care professionals. The goal of the Opus College of Business is to be recognized nationally and internationally for its overall excellence in educating highly principled global business leaders. Faculty members are leading scholars in their fields who also understand the value of practical experience. This recognized combination of theory and practice gives students the relevance necessary for rapid advancement in their careers.

The Full-time UST M.B.A. offers a traditional business core curriculum augmented by unique learning laboratories that prepare students with advanced analytical, communications, and problem-solving skills. Special attention is given to understanding the process of ethical decision making in today's complicated global environment. Elective options cover a wide variety of career tracks, and students have access to extensive career counseling and a network of successful alumni. This program includes special Professional Friday activities and an

active student association that includes numerous clubs, competitions, and social events.

The Evening UST M.B.A. offers flexible class schedules to accommodate working professionals. Classes meet one night per week, with selected courses available on Saturdays. A similar variety of elective tracks enables students to tailor the program to support their career interests. The typical time to complete the degree is approximately four years. Industrious part-time students can finish in less than four years.

The Health Care UST M.B.A. program offers course delivery through a combination of distance learning technology and intensive residencies to accommodate working health-care professionals from throughout the continental United States and Canada.

The Executive UST M.B.A. is designed for leaders and managers who have the flexibility to attend class on a Friday and Saturday, one weekend per month.

All programs feature smaller class sizes designed to enable each student to have regular interactions with members of the highly talented faculty. The Full-time UST M.B.A., the Executive UST M.B.A., and the Health Care UST M.B.A. are all cohort-based programs.

Cocurricular activities include an investment management course in which

students actively manage $2 million and a venture capital fund that invests in technology-based start-up businesses. Other activities include M.B.A. clubs and organizations, such as the Accounting and Finance club, Marketing club, National Society of Hispanic MBAs, and National Society of Women MBAs.

Students and the M.B.A. Experience

St. Thomas's Opus College of Business has more than 2,000 students in its degree programs. Yet classes are purposely kept small and personal. Students come from a wide range of educational and professional backgrounds, with most from the region around the Twin Cities. The student body is composed of 42 percent women. The College also has significant representation of minorities and international students. The M.B.A. programs have students from a broad array of backgrounds, vocations, and experiences. Postundergraduate work experience varies accordingly, and current students are employed at more than 1,000 companies. This diversity in the student body greatly enhances the educational experience through the different perspectives brought to team projects, classroom discussions, and other activities.

Global Focus

In the fall of 2004, the Opus College of Business celebrated its twentieth anniversary of excellence in international business education. International issues are addressed in the curricula across the degree programs. In addition, students can take advantage of several study-abroad courses designed to provide firsthand experience with international business venues.

Special Features

St. Thomas has been emphasizing the role of ethics in managing businesses for more than thirty years. Ethics is not a recent addition to the curriculum. Rather, it is integrated throughout the curriculum and beyond. Business leaders must have a sound moral compass to guide them through the difficult ethical dilemmas that confront them. In the UST M.B.A., students go beyond discussing responsible business leadership by practicing making complex choices in the ethics and leadership laboratories. UST M.B.A. students have the opportunity to visit the ethics divisions of a Fortune 500 company. They also hear from executives about how ethics is put into practice in their companies. As the job search process begins, consultants help match students with companies that share similar values. When students finish the program, they know how to use their own moral compasses and how to recognize and resolve complex ethical situations.

The Faculty

St. Thomas's full-time and adjunct faculty members, many of whom are leaders in their industries, bring a unique combination of business and academic experience to the classroom. This mixture of theory and practice results in the relevance that makes a St. Thomas degree so valued in the business community.

Students also benefit from faculty expertise because of the accessibility that accompanies small class sizes, along with the mentoring and advisory roles many faculty members assume.

The Business School Network

The Opus College of Business is highly regarded in the business community and benefits from the support and involvement of leaders in multiple sectors of that community in a variety of ways. Many teach as adjunct faculty members, serve as guest lecturers, sponsor internships, or host students at their facilities. In addition, many serve on boards advising the school and its various degree programs and concentrations, thus ensuring a dialogue between the school and its corporate partners that results in curricula and programming that truly meet the demands of a competitive, rapidly changing marketplace. Several companies have sponsored endowed chairs in business ethics, family business, risk and insurance management, international management, management, and entrepreneurship.

The Opus College of Business also has professional development centers and institutes that have strong affiliations with many companies and professional organizations through advice and consulting services and sponsorship of custom and joint programming. St. Thomas's Small Business Development Center, in affiliation with the Small Business Administration and the local business community, offers students opportunities to consult for growing small businesses.

UST M.B.A. students also are connected to a powerful network of more than 70,000 St. Thomas alumni. Through events and activities, students have many opportunities to meet alumni who hold a wide range of top positions across a broad spectrum of organizations, from Fortune 100 companies to entrepreneurial ventures.

The College and Environs

Founded in 1885, the University of St. Thomas is a comprehensive Catholic university made up of more than 10,000 graduate and undergraduate students. Colleges and schools of the University include Arts and Sciences, Business, Education, Law, Social Work, Engineering, and Divinity, and there are also graduate programs in professional psychology and software engineering. Main campuses are located in St. Paul and Minneapolis, Minnesota, with satellite campuses in several Minnesota communities and in Rome, Italy.

Facilities

Students have access to state-of-the-art computing stations, which, in turn, provide access to the Internet, e-mail system, electronic databases, and other library resources. Comprehensive library resources, with more than 300,000 volumes, are located on both the St. Paul and Minneapolis campuses. Full-time M.B.A. students have their own student commons, complete with study rooms, meeting rooms, lockers, mailboxes, an informal lounge, and access to TV financial news networks. An 86,000-square-foot School of Entrepreneurship opened in fall 2005, which houses a 320-seat state-of-the-art auditorium, multiple conference and meeting rooms, a 425-seat dining room, an entrepreneurship lab, and connections to the Minneapolis skyway system.

Placement

UST M.B.A.'s Career Services provides powerful tools and resources to plan and build a career at every stage of students' M.B.A. studies and professional lives. These include networking skills and access to a built-in network; resume and cover letter writing skills; interviewing skills; access to GradBiz Recruiting, an online job recruiting system, and CareerLeader, the business career interest inventory from Harvard Business School; effective job search techniques; and one-on-one coaching.

The focus of UST M.B.A.'s Career Services goes beyond getting that perfect internship or ideal job. While those things are important, the focus is also on developing the career planning and job search skills necessary for a lifetime of professional success. It starts with the kind of individual attention only a small program can offer. Career Services staff members work closely with students to identify specific opportunities well-suited to their individual career goals. Career Services is invested in each student's success.

Admission

In general, programs require GMAT scores above the 50th percentile and, for nonnative

speakers of English, TOEFL scores of at least 550 on the paper-based version or 213 on the computer-based version. The average undergraduate GPA of incoming students is 3.2, based on official transcripts from applicants' schools.

Finances

Tuition for 2007–08 ranged from $708 to $1242 per credit hour for all graduate programs. Expenses for course materials and fees vary by program and course. Both need-based and non-need-based financial aid is available through a variety of private, institutional, and federal programs. The Opus College of Business awards multiple scholarships for students who demonstrate superior academic performance. A diversity scholarship is available to students who bring distinctive personal characteristics and/or demonstrate resilience in overcoming significant hardships.

International Students

International students are welcomed at the University of St. Thomas, and the International Student Services Office has several programs to assist with counseling and support services, housing, visa services, and ESL courses, as well as many other special needs. Programs are available to help students become quickly acclimated to the school and the local community and to help them make the most of their educational experience.

Application Facts and Dates

Students can apply online at the College's Web site or through traditional application forms available on the Internet or from the program office. Applications are considered on a rolling basis; most programs adhere to a semester schedule, but cohort programs, such as the Full-time UST M.B.A., Executive UST M.B.A., and Health Care UST M.B.A., may have different start times. The full-time UST M.B.A. offers fall admission only, but applications are considered in five rounds, beginning in November. The other programs offer fall and spring admission. For specific information and application materials, students should contact the College of Business.

Opus College of Business M.B.A.
  Programs
University of St. Thomas
1000 LaSalle Avenue, TMH100
Minneapolis, Minnesota 55403-2005
Phone: 651-962-8800 (Full-time)
        651-962-4200 (Evening)
        651-962-4230 (Executive)
        651-962-4128 (Health Care)
Fax: 651-962-4129
E-mail: cob@stthomas.edu
Web site: http://www.stthomas.edu/
        business

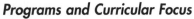

University of South Carolina

Moore School of Business

Columbia, South Carolina

THE WORLD IS OUR CLASSROOM

As the world's economies continue to intertwine, corporations worldwide are searching for professionals who are multilingual and have knowledge of other cultures and experience working in multiple countries. The International M.B.A. program at the Moore School of Business prepares students for today's competitive business world through a blend of academic and real-world experience. In addition to experiencing an internationalized core curriculum, students gain practical experience during a required four- to five-month internship with a global company, typically overseas.

Through 30 years of growth and continuous improvement, the Moore School's expertise in international business and breadth of programs has remained unmatched and has been consistently ranked among the top two business schools in the world with an international business specialty by U.S. News & World Report since its rankings began in 1989.

The Moore School of Business provides an international business education that you will not find anywhere else. Our internationalized curriculum, foreign language instruction, and global internships make a real difference. No matter where our graduates work—in the United States or abroad—they are able to think and act globally.

—Dr. Hildy J. Teegen, Dean

Students enjoy networking in the Moore School lobby.

and members of minority groups represent 10 percent. The typical entering student is 27 years old and has approximately 3½ years of work experience.

Programs and Curricular Focus

The School offers an International Master of Business Administration (I.M.B.A.) degree with two program options: the Language Track and the Global Track.

Regardless of the option chosen, all students study the same internationalized core of course work. The core courses emphasize the global aspects of the various functional areas, consistent with the program's mission to provide students with an expertise in the international dimensions of business.

Because fluency in another language is often critical for success in the business world, students selecting the Language Track combine their business education with intensive language training in one of eight languages: Arabic, Chinese, French, German, Italian, Japanese, Portuguese, or Spanish. In addition to language training, students have an internship in a country where the language they have studied is spoken. All language tracks are two years, with the exception of Chinese, Japanese, and Arabic, which require three years of study to give students added exposure to the more complex languages and cultures of these countries.

Alternatively, students who want a more holistic global orientation can choose the Global Track. Course work in this track focuses on the political, socioeconomic, cultural, and business factors affecting the investment climate of various regions throughout the world, such as Europe, Latin

America, Southeast Asia, and Africa. Global Track students have an internship with a multinational company in the U.S., in a country where English is the native language, or in a foreign language–speaking country with an English-speaking multinational organization. After their internships are completed, students in both the Language and Global Tracks return to the Moore School of Business in Columbia, South Carolina, to continue their business education. Alternatively, elective course work may be completed at one of the many international partner exchange schools for one of the two remaining semesters. During the second year of the program, students obtain depth in their areas of interest and take elective classes. All students have the opportunity to have a concentration in a designated area, such as finance, marketing, supply chain management, sustainable enterprise, marketing, or other areas. This depth of knowledge, combined with their global training and international experience, gives students the competitive advantage they need in today's workplace.

Students and the I.M.B.A. Experience

The students in the I.M.B.A. program come from a wide variety of backgrounds. Enrollment in the I.M.B.A. 2007 incoming class was 107 students. Women represent 35 percent of this student population, international students make up 25 percent,

The Faculty

The faculty members at the Moore School of Business have strong research interests that have won national and international visibility. Faculty members have nearly 100 articles and more than a dozen books published in a typical year and are editors of or are on editorial boards of many leading business and professional journals, including the *Journal of International Business Studies, Journal of Financial Research,* the *Journal of International Management,* the *Journal of Management,* the *Journal of Management Mathematics,* and the *Economics of Education Journal.*

The Business School Network

The School's ties to the business and alumni communities are strong, and these ties play several critical roles in the educational process. Relationships with local, national, and international corporations lead to internships and consulting projects for students and to employment opportunities for all graduates. The University of South Carolina Business Partnership Foundation is composed of business and academic leaders who play an active leadership role for the Moore School and are an integral part of the review process for curriculum and other program innovations. Moore School alumni include active and prominent executives who have the opportunity to stay connected via the private online alumni community.

The College and Environs

Founded in 1801, the University of South Carolina's main campus (and the Moore School of Business) is located in downtown Columbia, the state's capital. The University has a total enrollment of more than 40,889 students, including the University's eight other campuses. Carolina is a progressive, comprehensive institution committed to excellence in education and public service. Development of the University's InnoVista is well under way. InnoVista has been designed with the sole purpose of setting the new standard for integrating public- and private-sector research and researchers within a vibrant, contemporary urban landscape. This stimulating "innovation district" will be the centerpiece of a thriving intellectual ecosystem that creates an inspiring lifestyle for those who live and work in South Carolina. On the Columbia campus, fourteen degree-granting colleges and schools offer more than 350 degree programs. The commitment extends to the continued development and support of graduate education, and research is a priority. This commitment has led to growth in the variety and number of graduate programs available. Currently, the University enrolls more than 6,900 graduate students.

The city of Columbia is the seat of state government, is rich in culture and history, and is considered one of the most progressive cities in the Southeast. The current population of the Columbia metropolitan area is roughly 704,000. The state's economy includes benefits from the tourism industry, international and domestic business, and industry giants. Government and industry are working together to provide excellent employment opportunities throughout the state.

South Carolinians appreciate the fine arts and are committed to the cultivation of the arts throughout the state. Columbia is the home of several outstanding art and history museums and the nationally ranked Riverbanks Zoo and Gardens. Diverse vacation spots are abundant throughout the state, including ocean resorts, historic cities, and the Blue Ridge Mountains.

The Moore School.

Facilities

The Moore School of Business is housed in the connected complex of the H. William Close and Francis M. Hipp buildings. Within the complex, the School is relatively self-sufficient, with its business library, computer center, classrooms, TV studio classrooms, presentation rooms, and faculty offices. The library features a circulation collection that includes business and industrial directories and publications, with approximately 100 current subscriptions and back issues of selected magazines and newspapers and nearly 500 journals in microfilm format. Students also have access to the University's main library, which seats 2,500 users at one time and allows access to more than 7 million volumes, microfilm entries, manuscripts, and periodicals. The computer center has 150 interactive workstations, three computer teaching rooms, and graduate student labs. In addition, students have the option of linking into a building-wide wireless network.

Placement

The Office of Career Management at Moore is a full-service career center providing services and processes that best meet the needs of students and employers. In addition to on-campus interviewing opportunities, students benefit from a structured professional development curriculum, including the Birkman Method career assessment, to develop a career roadmap for lifelong use. Moore School has partnered with Lee Hecht Harrison, a preeminent global career man-

agement company, to provide professional career coaching and expertise in interviewing, job search, resume preparation, networking, and negotiating. The active network of alumni contributes to the job and internship search.

Admission

Every applicant's complete file, including his or her academic record, resume, required essays, and GMAT scores, is evaluated through comparison with the current applicant pool for the appropriate program. Average GMAT scores and GPAs vary; currently, the average GMAT score is 639 and the average GPA is 3.43. Interviews are required upon request.

Finances

The Program Fee for the I.M.B.A. Language and Global Tracks is $35,500 for South Carolina residents and $52,000 for nonresidents. Participants pay a stipulated percentage of these totals at the beginning of each semester of study until they are paid in full by the start of the last semester of study. Other fees and charges include an international student fee, technology fee, books, and health insurance. All fees and costs are subject to change without notice. Financial assistance is available in the forms of merit-based fellowships, fee reductions, and work grants. In 2007, more than 80 percent of incoming students received financial assistance.

Application Facts and Dates

Students should apply online at http://www.gradschool.sc.edu and adhere to the deadlines listed on the Web site.

Graduate Admissions
Moore School of Business
University of South Carolina
Columbia, South Carolina 29208
Phone: 803-777-4346
        800-236-6427
Fax: 803-777-0414
E-mail: gradadmit@moore.sc.edu
Web site: http://mooreschool.sc.edu

The University of Tampa

College of Business

Tampa, Florida

ARE YOU READY TO LEAD A TWENTY-FIRST-CENTURY ENTERPRISE?

The University of Tampa's (UT) graduate business programs teach essential knowledge for business success. From day one, students sharpen strategic leadership skills through advanced courses taught by dedicated professors, all with doctoral degrees and real-world experience. UT offers students personalized attention from faculty and staff members, small classes, and innovative approaches to learning that help students progress faster in the classroom. Located in downtown Tampa, UT offers students internships and job opportunities in one of Florida's fastest growing job markets.

Programs and Curricular Focus

The program theme of the John H. Sykes College of Business M.B.A. Program, "Creating Value Through Strategic Leadership," helps students develop the sophisticated strategic perspectives and mindset demonstrated by successful top executives.

The Fast Start Workshop is a 2½-day weekend program that introduces students to their new colleagues. Students participate in a team-based business simulation that demonstrates essential business concepts and perspectives, how to work in and lead a team, and how to make effective oral and written presentations.

The Leadership Development Program has several program elements that improve the student's leadership capacity after graduation. Elements include Fast Start Workshop, Leading for Performance course, Leadership Coaching program, video series, speaker series, and the online Leadership Resource Guide.

In the Leading for Performance course, students have the opportunity to work with a skilled faculty team with expertise in management, exercise science, psychology, and nutrition. The result is a Personal Commitment Plan that sets personal and leadership goals to implement during the student's M.B.A. program.

In the Leadership Coaching Program, students work one-on-one with business executives from the local community and with M.B.A. alumni and faculty members to develop leadership and interpersonal skills.

Students are provided a stream of information and resources that may be organized into a personal reference guide. The Web-based Leadership Resource Guide is continuously updated, and remains available for use after graduation. The information ranges from academic themes and concepts to suggestions for applying effective leadership behavior.

The Developing Software Competencies course is required of all students in their first semester to help enhance their skills in Microsoft Office products. A waiver exam is available for students who possess at least intermediate-level skills.

Students entering the M.B.A. program without prior business course work take the Foundation Course Sequence. This set of half- and full-semester courses in accounting, economics, finance, management, marketing, and statistics provide a solid foundation that prepares students to succeed in the Integrated Core courses.

The Integrated Core is a series of twelve half-semester course modules designed to develop the practical, hands-on business knowledge and tools required to lead the value creation process. Students acquire both the basic tools and the sophisticated conceptual frameworks necessary to focus and refocus a business, drive performance, and align key functions with the core strategy of a business.

In addition to the foundation skills and strategic mindset developed through the previous courses, students deepen business knowledge of specific topics by taking 12 credits in any one of nine different M.B.A. concentrations: accounting, economics, entrepreneurship, finance, international business, information systems management, management, marketing, or nonprofit management and innovation. The finance concentration has tracks in investment analysis and CFA®, corporate financial strategy and management, and general finance. Students electing not to declare an M.B.A. concentration may take their 12 credits from two or more of the concentration areas.

In the Capstone Experience, students work in teams to perform a strategic business assessment and create an oral and written presentation for the top leadership of an actual company. Student teams have helped take companies into new international markets, redirect marketing and financial strategies, and restructure entire organizations—well beyond textbook case studies and solutions.

In addition to the M.B.A. program, the University offers four additional graduate business programs: Master of Science in Accounting, Master of Science in Finance, Master of Science in Innovation Management, and Master of Science in Marketing.

Students and the M.B.A. Experience

Faculty members are not the only ones who teach. The students represent a talented pool of real-world experience and professional knowledge. The average M.B.A. student has four years of experience. Learning occurs as much outside the classroom as in it, as students develop new relationships with their classmates.

For the fall 2007 semester, the Sykes College of Business consisted of 415 M.B.A. students. Women make up 40 percent of the students, and 20 percent are international students.

Special Features

With hectic schedules, business obligations, and personal and professional deadlines, students need the flexibility of the program as they pursue their degree. In short, students may complete the M.B.A. program at their own pace.

All M.B.A. classes are offered at times when students can take full advantage of them. Full-time students can complete the core curriculum in as few as sixteen months in the Accelerated Full-Time Day Program. Students who work full-time can complete the course work in less than three years in the Flex Part-Time Evening Program. The Saturday M.B.A. program offers a convenient schedule for experienced working professionals. The program can be completed in less than two years. It is important to note, however, that students have up to seven years from their time of entry in which to complete the entire program.

The Faculty

The College's highest priority is on the teaching and mentoring role of its faculty members. Students are never anonymous numbers. The College maintains a low student-faculty ratio to fulfill its commitment to working with students individually and ensuring that they get the best education possible. Faculty members have offices in the Sykes College of Business Building.

All of the M.B.A. faculty members have Ph.D. degrees. They are well equipped to meet the educational needs of the students, as evidenced by their degrees, professional research, and experience in a variety of private and public organizations. Many of the graduate faculty members have won awards for teaching and professional excellence.

The Business School Network

More than 700 business and community leaders serve on nineteen different campus boards and advisory councils. Local, national, and international organizations participate in University programs that provide students with real-world business experience.

The John H. Sykes College of Business at the University of Tampa.

The University also sponsors numerous business and community events that give students the opportunity to meet and learn from local business leaders, complementing their academic learning. Among the discussion and speaker groups that meet regularly on campus are the Fellows Forum, Business Network Symposium, Distinguished Practitioner Speaker Series, and M.B.A. Alumni Association as well as college, department, and center advisory boards.

The College and Environs
The John H. Sykes College of Business is accredited by AACSB International–The Association to Advance Collegiate Schools of Business. The University is also accredited by the Commission on Colleges of the Southern Association of Colleges and Schools to award associate, baccalaureate, and master's degrees.

The 100-acre University of Tampa campus offers a full-service educational setting that includes a comprehensive library, a broad range of technology and support, an active Career Services and Placement Center, and many student programs. The campus is located adjacent to downtown Tampa.

Tampa is Florida's west coast center for the arts, banking, real estate, law, transportation, international business, education, communications, and health and scientific research.

Facilities
The 80,000-square-foot facility has several wireless areas for high-speed networking and access to the Internet. Students can log onto the information highway in all thirty classrooms,

the student lounge, three computer labs, and even in the hallways and vending area. Students use the Internet for electronic access to class materials, information, cases for class assignments, and to communicate with professors, classmates, and students on the campus and around the world.

The Huizenga Family Foundation Trading Center is one of the technological centerpieces of the building, providing a significant hands-on dimension to finance education. For M.B.A. students who are managing portfolios and investments using Bloomberg Professional™ real-time trading information, the Trading Center's cutting-edge technology offers a unique real-world experience.

Placement
M.B.A. students can expect individualized attention from the professional staff members in the Office of Career Services. Typical M.B.A. services include resume critique, design and referral, personal career advising, interview skills refreshers, on-campus interview opportunities, and informational interviews with business professionals from the greater Tampa Bay area.

Whether M.B.A. students are looking for employment while enrolled, at graduation, or as alumni, the innovative HIRE-UT Job Listing System and Resume Database is available 24 hours a day, seven days a week. Since its inception in September 1999, more than 900 employers have registered with the HIRE-UT program. With its combination of a resume database, internships, online employer access, and job listings, the HIRE-UT system is the epitome of online career services, perfectly suited for today's busy professionals.

Some of the companies that have hired graduate business students and recruited on campus include: Citibank, Coca-Cola, Deloitte, Ernst & Young, ESPN, Franklin Templeton, Hilton Vacations, Home Shopping Network, HSBC, M & I Bank, Merck Pharmaceuticals, USAA, Verizon, and Wachovia.

Admission
Admission to UT's M.B.A. program is competitive and is based on a number of important factors. Admission to the full- and part-time programs can be effective with either fall, spring, or, on a limited basis, during the summer sessions. Application deadlines for the fall semester are: priority, June 1; deadline, July 15; international, June 1. Application deadlines for the fall semester are: priority, June 1; deadline, July 15; international, June 1. Application deadlines for the spring semester are: priority, November 1; deadline, December 15; international, November 1. Students should contact the Graduate Studies Office for details about summer and Saturday M.B.A. admission deadlines.

Individual interviews are encouraged, but not required. All students admitted to the M.B.A. program must have earned four-year undergraduate degrees from a regionally accredited college or university. A specific undergraduate major is not required.

Finances
Tuition for 2007–08 is $450 per credit hour. The Saturday M.B.A. tuition is $565 per credit hour. Tuition is payable at registration each semester. In addition, a $35 student services fee is required each term. The cost of books, supplies, health insurance, parking, and personal expenses is additional. More than fifty graduate assistantships, which include a tuition waiver and stipend, are available to qualified, full-time students each academic year. The graduate and financial aid offices assist students with preparation of necessary application forms.

International Students
All international applicants must submit a Test of English as a Foreign Language (TOEFL) score report with a minimum score of 577 (230 computer-based; 90 Internet-based) or an International English Language Testing System (IELTS) score report (minimum score 7.5).

In addition, international students must submit transcripts from all previously attended colleges (printed in English), and financial certification with appropriate supporting documents.

Application Facts and Dates

Applications are not reviewed until all required materials are received by the Graduate Studies Office. Students are notified of the admission decision after materials have been received and evaluated.

Applicants need to submit the following documents: a completed application, $40 application fee, official transcripts of all previous college work received directly from each institution, two professional reference forms completed by individuals that attest to the applicants professional background and academic potential, a resume, a personal statement, TOEFL or IELTS score report (international applicants only), and Graduate Management Admission Test (GMAT) score report. Individual interviews are recommended but not required.

Applicants should submit materials to:

Graduate Studies
The University of Tampa
Box O
401 West Kennedy Boulevard
Tampa, Florida 33606-1490

Phone: 813-258-7409
Fax: 813-259-5403
E-mail: utgrad@ut.edu
Web site: http://grad.ut.edu

University of Tennessee

College of Business Administration

Knoxville, Tennessee

WANTED: BOLD, INNOVATIVE THINKERS AND LEADERS

The University of Tennessee College of Business Administration is proud of our innovative, seventeen-month M.B.A. program. We believe that we have created a unique program that is a "win" for our students, industry, and our alumni.

Our program emphasizes the managerial skills that are required to coordinate and integrate business functions both within organizations as well as across an integrated value chain of businesses. The program prepares students by going beyond business basics to include additional training in resource, supply chain, information, and relationship management. We believe that this knowledge is essential for every manager, regardless of industry or specific business function.

Once again, the University of Tennessee is "setting new standards" in M.B.A. education.

—Sarah Gardial, Associate Dean

Programs and Curricular Focus

The University of Tennessee (UT) has designed a seventeen-month program that reflects today's globally connected business world. From the cutting-edge, integrated curriculum to intense team-building exercises and leadership development, students learn the skills they need to successfully chart their transition from the classroom to the networked business world.

The program is built on a foundation of basic business skills, ones that every global manager needs to know. Because alliances and partnerships are an integral part of business success, the first-year core curriculum includes an emphasis on integrated value chain (IVC) management that provides students with the tools and skills for interfirm and intrafirm management. The IVC model illustrates how global relationships among business partners, suppliers, customers, and even competitors are used to achieve more dramatic results more quickly.

Utilizing a multimodal mix of applied-learning methodologies, UT's approach to M.B.A. education gives its graduates a competitive edge when applying business school knowledge and skills to real-world situations. From team-building exercises to cross-functional, team-taught course modules, the program is built around learning modes that are specifically developed to meet students' educational needs.

Core I (first of August, three weeks) lays the business basics foundation, essential computer skills, team building, and communication skills.

Core II (August–December), a 15-hour integrated class, consists of two parallel tracks: What Every Global Manager Needs to Know, regarding business basics, and What Every Global Manager Needs to Know About Integrated Value Chain Management, both within and across firms in the value chain. In addition, there is a 1-hour career-development course designed to ensure a successful internship and full-time job search.

Core III (January–mid-March) is a 9-hour course that continues the two tracks from the fall semester. Also, students are required to participate in an international experience (trip) in order to enhance their understanding of the global business environment.

For HUB I and II (mid-March), students enroll in their first concentration and elective courses. By receiving additional in-depth training in their concentrations prior to the Summer Internship, students enhance their internship experience.

During the Summer Internship (May–August), students are required to secure an internship with a company or organization to apply their knowledge and skills in a real-world environment, which adds value to their overall learning experience.

Fall II (final semester) is when students complete concentration and elective courses, plus a 1-hour capstone course and a 3-hour global business strategy course. Included in the courses are finance, innovation and entrepreneurship, logistics, marketing, and operations management. Innovative support areas include global business, information management, and sport management.

Joint programs include J.D./M.B.A. degree (four years), an M.B.A./M.S. degree in engineering (two years plus one summer session), and an M.B.A./M.S. degree in sport management (two years).

Students and the M.B.A. Experience

Diversity defines the student profile of the UT M.B.A. student. Tennessee M.B.A. students bring a wealth of experiences, both professional and personal, which enrich the learning environment. The average student has 3½ years of professional work experience; 83 percent have more than one year of experience. Their professional experiences include the private, public, and nonprofit domain with a number of students also having been entrepreneurs.

About 45 percent have backgrounds in the arts and sciences, with 10 percent having engineering degrees. The average class size is 86; about 35 percent are women, 8 percent are members of minority groups, and 17 percent are foreign nationals from multiple countries.

Global Focus

Throughout their M.B.A. careers, students apply what they learn to a global context. In the final semester, students are required to take a global business strategy class and can select elective courses in global business in order to gain deeper exposure to international management, finance, marketing, logistics, and related issues. Students are also required to participate in an M.B.A.-sponsored weeklong international trip for an additional cost.

Special Features

Students may take an optional one-week prep course covering accounting, economics, finance, and statistics prior to orientation.

There are also numerous student organizations that add great value to the students' M.B.A. education, and students are encouraged to join several. The Tennessee Organization of M.B.A.'s (TOMBA) is a must. Other organizations include New Ventures Now for aspiring entrepreneurs; the Global Business Club for students with international experience or aspirations; an investment club for students with their sights set on Wall Street; Corporate Connections, an organization that puts M.B.A. students in front of leaders of major businesses to describe the vitality and value of the UT M.B.A. program and its students; Community Connections, an organization of M.B.A. students committed to public service;

a marketing club; and the Women's Organization of M.B.A.'s, which addresses issues specific to women.

The Faculty

Faculty members who teach in the M.B.A. program are selected for their outstanding teaching, research, and experience working with corporations. Many of the UT M.B.A. faculty members are instructors in the executive education programs delivered through the Center for Executive Education. Working with corporate leaders, faculty members learn the kinds of skills and talents companies currently value and what they are likely to need in the future. They bring these concepts into the classroom to more accurately prepare M.B.A. students for the competitive world they will enter after graduation.

The Business School Network

Faculty, administration, and students are committed to maintaining active relationships with the local, national, and international business communities. M.B.A. administrators are committed to maintaining strong business relationships as well as developing additional industry partnerships.

Corporate Partnerships

The UT M.B.A. program is enriched by the close ties held with the College's Center for Executive Education, which trains approximately 1,000 corporate executives yearly, as well as the close ties held with the Senior Executive M.B.A. Program, which enrolls close to 40 international executives each year. More than 30 guest executives visit UT annually as part of the Executive-in-Residence classes offered to M.B.A. students. The Dean maintains an Advisory Board consisting of executives from many national companies who meet with students and faculty once a year to assess the status and currency of the M.B.A. curriculum. In addition, a select group of M.B.A. students are chosen each year to serve on the Corporate Connections team, which serves as a means to market the M.B.A. program to the national business community.

The College and Environs

The University of Tennessee in Knoxville, a federal land-grant institution that began its tradition of service in 1794, is one of the nation's twenty largest universities, enrolling approximately 27,000 students, including more than 7,000 graduate students. The College of Business Administration is the second-largest college of the University, enrolling over 3,500 students.

Knoxville lies within a metropolitan area of approximately 600,000 that houses major corporate headquarters and numerous industrial and commercial operations. Many cultural and entertainment activities are available year-round, and the nearby Great Smoky Mountains National Park offers year-round recreational opportunities. Knoxville is consistently rated as one of the top ten cities in the country in providing gracious amenities and a high quality of life.

Facilities

The University of Tennessee is the home of one of the finest library facilities in the nation. The Hodges Library has more than 2.7 million volumes and subscribes to 22,000 journals. In addition, the library has state-of-the-art electronic resources available for student research, communication, and information retrieval. M.B.A. classes are generally held in two classrooms specially reserved for the M.B.A. program located in the new state-of-the-art Business School building. The University itself also has excellent cultural, recreational, fitness, and sports facilities.

Technology Environment

The chancellor of the University of Tennessee has challenged the school to become the "information university" for the state of Tennessee. Accordingly, the campus has an excellent information infrastructure for the M.B.A. program to use. Given the intense use of information technology in the M.B.A. program, each student is required to have his/her own laptop computer for document preparation, spreadsheet analysis, database design, computer graphics, and Internet and e-mail connections.

Placement

The UT M.B.A. Career Services Office coordinates with the campuswide Career Services Office for on-campus interviews and interviews via video teleconferencing. In addition to the required career development course, services delivered exclusively to M.B.A. students include resume referrals for both intern and full-time searches, membership and participation in several University-business consortia, resume writing workshops, videotaped interviews, and career management classes aimed at developing students' skills in such areas as job/intern search strategies, salary negotiation techniques, and leadership development.

Admission

Applications are accepted for fall semester only. The Admission Committee considers the applicant's academic record, with particular emphasis on the last two years of undergraduate work and any previous graduate studies; scores on the GMAT and TOEFL (if applicable); full-time professional work experience (three years preferred); and other activities that demonstrate leadership potential. Personal interviews are strongly recommended but not required.

Finances

The 2007–08 educational expense for first-year students was approximately $20,000 to $30,000, including about $12,000 annually for in-state tuition and $24,000 annually for out-of-state tuition. The total annual amount quoted includes M.B.A.-specific fees, books, supplies, room, board, and other miscellaneous costs. Merit-based fellowships and assistantships are awarded by the College. Assistantships carry a University tuition waiver and a monthly stipend. Federal and state programs for student loans and grants and the Student Employment Service are administered by the Office of Financial Aid, 115 Student Services Building, 865-974-3131. The priority deadline is February 1.

International Students

There is a significant international student population at the University of Tennessee, Knoxville. The M.B.A. program has 17 percent international students, with several nationalities represented. The University's Center for International Education and the International House provide resources and programs to meet the cultural, social, and professional interests of the international students.

Application Facts and Dates

The M.B.A. program application deadline (fall entrance only) for domestic and international applicants is February 1. Admission decisions are made on a rolling basis. In general, applicants receive a decision approximately four to six weeks after the M.B.A. Program Office receives a completed application. For additional information, students should contact:

M.B.A. Admissions Director
University of Tennessee
527 Stokely Management Center
Knoxville, Tennessee 37996-0552

Phone: 865-974-5033
Fax: 865-974-3826
E-mail: mba@utk.edu
Web site: http://mba.utk.edu

The University of Texas at Arlington

QUALITY, VALUE, AND FLEXIBILITY

Our goal is to continue to offer one of the best business educational experiences in America. The M.B.A. curriculum aligns the expertise of our faculty members with the educational outcomes that corporations seek. This approach enables us to keep pace with emerging technology and best practices. Our strategic location in the center of the dynamic Dallas/Fort Worth metroplex provides enriched and seldom-matched educational and professional opportunities for both full-time and part-time students. Classrooms in the College of Business Administration are equipped with cutting-edge instructional technologies that are second to none. Students completing the M.B.A. program develop the ability to effectively function on teams and task forces, leverage global opportunities, formulate and execute leadership initiatives, apply new technologies to complex processes, and design integrated solutions for organizational challenges.

—Daniel Himarios, Dean

Programs and Curricular Focus

Students from a wide variety of academic backgrounds choose the M.B.A. at the University of Texas at Arlington (UT Arlington) because of its flexibility and academic rigor. Students now have four program options: the Flexible Format M.B.A., the Professional Cohort M.B.A., the Online M.B.A., and the Executive M.B.A.

The Flexible Format program allows students with limited academic business backgrounds to begin with up to 18 hours of core course work. Students who have had business classes within the past ten years may waive core and deficiency courses (similar courses in which they earned a grade of B or better) and complete their advanced studies in as few as sixteen months. The College's weekday evening class schedule makes the program convenient for working adults. Students may select from specializations in accounting, finance, information systems, management, operations management, marketing, or real estate and tailor their program to include skill-building electives that are appropriate for their chosen functional area, level, and industry. Students with professional degrees may select electives in their professional areas such as engineering, science, or environmental studies. Students wishing to expand their career opportunities may complete reduced requirements for a dual (second) degree in business, engineering, architecture, nursing, social work, or urban affairs.

The College's Professional Cohort M.B.A. program is designed for working professionals with no prior academic background in business. Courses are taught in accelerated mini-sessions that allow part-time students to take up to 21 hours per year and complete their degrees in twenty-four months. This program is currently offered at UT Arlington Fort Worth.

UT Arlington offers the University of Texas System M.B.A. Online Program. This innovative general management M.B.A. program is designed for students whose busy lifestyle, geographic isolation, or other restrictions prevent them from participating in a traditional M.B.A. residence program. The entire M.B.A. online program is offered using the Internet and supplemental materials such as videotapes, audiotapes, and CD-ROMs.

UT Arlington's newest M.B.A. option is the Executive M.B.A. (E.M.B.A.). This program is designed for middle- and upper-level managers and is available in Fort Worth, China, and Taiwan.

Each M.B.A. option provides students with a competitive advantage through their expanded ability to effectively perform on challenging team, consulting, and leadership assignments that must deal with advanced technologies, organizational change, and emerging markets.

Students and the M.B.A. Experience

The student body in fall 2007 consisted of 457 students. Nearly 80 percent of the students have industry experience, with the average being five years. Slightly less than half of the students have degrees outside of business, with engineering and science making up the largest group (20 percent). The student diversity makes the M.B.A. experience an innovative approach to learning about business teams in the global village. Thirty-nine percent of the students are women, 18 percent come from other countries on every continent, and more than 21 percent are members of minority groups. Every year, students may participate in exchange programs in Australia, England, France, Germany, Korea, Mexico, or Norway and in other study-abroad opportunities. These experiences allow students to perform at a broader level in the global village.

Special Features

Students may participate in a comprehensive careers program that begins with a careers class (MANA 5338) that provides extensive individual assessment, analysis of career options, and guidance in networking with key people in possible future career fields. Once a career orientation is evaluated, the student is advised on recommended electives and encouraged to discuss options with advisers, key faculty members, and alumni. Students are then assisted in locating paid internships that will provide hands-on experiences in their chosen fields.

The Faculty

The College has 126 faculty members, of whom 100 are full-time. More than 80 percent of full-time faculty members hold doctoral degrees from some of the most prestigious business schools in the U.S. Full-time faculty members are growing in both number and diversity; currently, they include 32 women and 15 racial and ethnic minority individuals. Faculty members are assigned to six departments.

Faculty List

Accounting: Larry Walther, Ph.D., Oklahoma State.
Economics: Daniel Himarios, Ph.D., Virginia Tech.
Finance and Real Estate: J. David Diltz, Ph.D., Illinois.
Information Systems and Operations Management: R. C. Baker, Ph.D., Texas A&M.
Management: Jeff McGee, Ph.D., Georgia.
Marketing: Larry Chonko, Ph.D., Houston.

The Business School Network

In addition to an active College Advisory Council, the College of Business Administration also has departmental- and program-level advisory councils and boards that serve as advocacy groups for the College, providing advice and support on such matters as curriculum, internship programs, facilities enhancements, career services for students, and staff and faculty recruitment. The Small Business Institute also helps match the research needs of small businesses with M.B.A. students' interests and academic experience. Each year the college hosts "Business Leadership Week," featuring guest speakers from leading corporations. These councils, boards, and events provide personal contacts between the members of the College and the business community, which greatly assists in the shaping of the school's programs and the leaders of tomorrow.

The College and Environs

The Dallas/Fort Worth metroplex is a large market and distribution center, a major convention site, a growing financial and cultural center, and the tenth-largest market in the U.S. Arlington, located midway between these larger cities, is a busy suburban city of more than 365,000 that contains many of the top entertainment sites in the state. The University, located on a peaceful 392-acre campus, has flourished for more than 100 years and has grown to become one of the top 100 universities based on enrollment in the U.S. The College of Business Administration, one of the largest in the nation, with more than 5,000 graduate and undergraduate students, is housed in a modern facility that contains research centers, numerous computer labs, electronic classrooms, special libraries, and modern advising facilities.

Facilities

The College's student-centered environment features a comprehensive student service center that houses advising and career services, a library extension with online library access, a student study area, and offices for student organizations. In addition to modern computer labs, classrooms are equipped with state-of-the-art multimedia instruments, including ceiling-mounted monitors and wireless technology.

Technology Environment

Though students can conduct much of their library research through their PC and modem, the College houses six laboratory facilities with more than 211 computers and related software libraries. Currently, all of the PCs run on Windows XP. In addition to a standard package of MS Office 2007 (Access, Excel, FrontPage, InfoPath, Power-Point, Publisher, and Word) and Internet Explorer 6.x, Adobe Reader, and Symantic AntiVirus 10.x, additional software is based on the business discipline and courses offered. Students also have access to several Microsoft products at a greatly reduced cost. All students have a computer account and access to the Internet and are able to complete advising and registration via the Internet.

Placement

The Dallas/Fort Worth metroplex provides a fertile lab for the exploration and pursuit of hundreds of career alternatives. Each fall and spring, the University hosts one of the largest "job fair events" in Texas, which attracts top employers throughout the region. These events help maintain a large database of excellent full-and part-time employment opportunities and internships. A core of career professionals participates in a comprehensive M.B.A. for-credit careers program, which presents an array of class sessions designed to increase the candidate's self-knowledge and extend his or her professional network. A state-of-the-art virtual mock interview system is available as well as an interactive resume and job listing data bank, which complement traditional on-campus interviews.

Admission

While managerial or supervisory experience is preferred, it is not required. Prerequisites for admission to this program include a bachelor's degree from an accredited university, a satisfactory GMAT score, past academic performance that demonstrates the potential for graduate work, three letters of recommendation that reflect an ability to perform at a high level, and a personal essay that persuasively outlines the student's academic goals, strengths, and weaknesses. An entering class of students will normally have an average GMAT score of 550 and an average GPA of 3.2.

Finances

Modest tuition rates and fees make this M.B.A. a great selection for students seeking the greatest return on their investment. The estimated annual tuition and fees rate for the 2007–08 year for 30 semester hours of graduate course work was $10,703 for in-state residents and $19,035 for out-of-state residents. The annual cost for textbooks and supplies is approximately $900. The annual costs (twelve months) for room, board, and incidentals may cost an additional $11,400 (lower if shared living). A vehicle may be necessary to take full advantage of internships and work opportunities. Students are encouraged to participate in the M.B.A. loans program when necessary.

International Students

International students from every continent participate in the M.B.A. program. The University provides a Graduate English Skills Program that helps international students adjust to the culture and helps polish verbal skills that are vital to success in the M.B.A. classroom. International students should have a TOEFL score of at least 550 (paper-based test); 213 (computer-based test), 79 (Internet based test, with minimums of writing: 22, speaking: 21, reading: 20, listening: 16) or a minimum IELTS score of 6.5.

Application Facts and Dates

Applications may be submitted for fall, spring, and summer semesters. Application deadlines are generally as follows: for U.S. students for fall semester, the deadline is June 8; for spring semester, the deadline is November 15; and for summer semester, the deadline is April 15. For international students, the deadline for fall semester is April 1; for spring semester, the deadline is September 1; and for summer semester, the deadline is January 1.

Detailed information on application requirements and steps to take after acceptance are all explained on the University's Web site. Application materials may be accessed and submitted electronically via the Web.

Graduate Business Services Office
University of Texas at Arlington
UTA Box 19376
Arlington, Texas 76019-0376
Phone: 817-272-3005
Fax: 817-272-5799
E-mail: admit@uta.edu
Web site: http://www.uta.edu/gradbiz

The University of Texas at Dallas

MANAGEMENT EDUCATION—A HIGH PRIORITY

▶ *The University of Texas at Dallas' (UT Dallas) School of Management, distinguished in many ways, is especially proud of its talented group of faculty members, many of whom have achieved national and international recognition. Based on publications in the top 24 business journals spanning all areas of business, our faculty ranks in the top 20 in research productivity among business school faculties nationwide. The UT Dallas campus, located in a dynamic and growing area where health-care, technology, and transportation start-ups transform the local and global economy, offers the benefits of living in a thriving community where twenty-four of the nation's Fortune 500 companies are headquartered. This gives the School of Management a unique competitive advantage and permits us to recruit an active Advisory Council. And because the University of Texas at Dallas is a young university, focused on excellence and dedicated to ensuring management education is an area of high priority, we offer students an environment in which we can deliver the highest-quality education to our students.*

—Hasan Pirkul, Dean of the School of Management and Caruth Professor of Management Information Systems

Programs and Curricular Focus

The M.B.A. programs at the School of Management address the challenges faced by businesses in today's dynamic, technology-driven, global society. The quality of M.B.A. education the School of Management delivers is attested to by the places its M.B.A. graduates go to work—from Fortune 500 companies, many located in the Dallas–Fort Worth area, to high-tech start-ups to Wall Street firms to federal agencies in Washington, D.C. UT Dallas' School of Management is fully accredited by AACSB International–The Association to Advance Collegiate Schools of Business.

The School of Management offers six paths to earn an M.B.A. in addition to its Executive M.B.A. program, which is ranked number one in Texas by *Financial Times*. All M.B.A.'s require 53 credit hours. Depending upon the program, students may earn the hours in classrooms on campus, online in a semester-based timeframe, or with a combination of the two. The School of Management prides itself in its vigorous analytical approach and its strong 29-hour core curriculum. Area and international businesses—from multinationals to high-tech start-ups—find this rigorous curriculum prepares graduates for the challenges they face in the real world.

UT Dallas' M.B.A. programs enroll almost 1,300 students. With more than 100 faculty members, the School of Management can schedule more graduate business courses than any university in the Dallas–Fort Worth area. Being convenient to several major transportation hubs, the campus is easily accessed from companies headquartered along the Telecom Corridor, in downtown Dallas, or in the corporate offices ringing the city's northern suburbs.

The Professional M.B.A. is the School of Management's largest M.B.A. program and caters to those who work full-time. Most classes are offered in the evening, and students generally complete their degree in about three years. Another option, the Full-Time M.B.A., takes eighteen months to complete, primarily with daytime classes taught in cohort fashion, and was recently ranked among the nation's top 60 full-time programs and among the top 25 at public universities. Full-Time M.B.A. students have an average of four years of management experience and strong GMAT scores. Students take part in an internship during the summer between their second and third semesters of class work.

The Global M.B.A. Online offers highly interactive, flexible online courses in a semester-length format to part-time students, who may also be enrolled in the Professional M.B.A. program. The Global M.B.A. Online program is taught by the same faculty members and with the same material as on-campus classes, and students receive the same diploma.

The School of Management's Executive M.B.A. program was ranked by *Financial Times* as number one in Texas this year and tied with Georgetown University for number ten in the nation. The twenty-one-month Executive M.B.A. program requires three days per month of class work on campus and includes a personal coach, a ten-day international study tour, and a curriculum that focuses on leadership, managing for change, and developing skills to solve real-world business issues. Most participants are executives with at least six years of management experience.

The School offers three other Executive M.B.A. programs, including its Global Leadership Executive M.B.A. (GLEMBA), cited by *Forbes* as one of the best on the Web. GLEMBA's classes, designed for working professionals with at least five years of executive experience who are particularly interested in the global component of businesses today, are taught combining online and on-site class work. This program includes a ten-day international study tour.

The School of Management is one of the few campuses nationwide with a certified project management program. Students interested in project management have several educational avenues open to them. After completing a 21-hour core curriculum, students earn a Project Management Institute certificate. With an additional 18 hours of class work, students attain a Master of Science with a project management concentration; with a total of 53 hours, students earn an M.B.A. with an emphasis in project management. The course work can either be taken online or on campus, and students typically have solid experience in project management. *PM Network* magazine listed the UT Dallas program as one of the "Best Bets" worldwide for project managers seeking graduate and continuing education.

The Healthcare Management Executive M.B.A. is a part-time program for physicians offered jointly with the UT Southwestern Medical School. Student-physicians typically complete the health-care management class work in eighteen months, while an additional eight general business classes are taken online.

Admittance to any M.B.A. program does not require a previous business degree.

Students and the M.B.A. Experience

Students at UT Dallas study alongside working professionals who have significant experience and strong educational credentials in an environment that is both challenging and naturally diverse. The typical

graduate student takes 6 or 7 hours each semester, though the number of hours taken is flexible, with a third of the graduate students taking 9 or more hours per semester.

UT Dallas offers an on-campus apartment complex called Waterview Park that is operated by a private company. These apartments offer a variety of floor plans and are competitively priced. Students should visit http://www.utdallas.edu for information about on-campus housing. In addition, many off-campus housing options in the surrounding metropolitan area are available. An array of shopping and dining establishments, representing everything from large chains to small, single proprietor-run shops, are within bicycling distance of the campus.

The Faculty

The University of Texas at Dallas' School of Management faculty members teach all master's-level classes. Because the School has more than 100 faculty members, it can schedule more graduate-level business classes than any other program in the Dallas–Fort Worth area. Many professors are leading scholars in their area, serve as editors of professional journals, and have received awards for teaching excellence. Faculty members frequently team-teach selected courses and often are joined, in selected courses, by faculty members from other disciplines at the University of Texas at Dallas. In addition, many M.B.A. classes enjoy supplemental teaching from local corporate executives, who often provide case problems for student participation.

The Business School Network

The School of Management receives support and counsel from the business community through its Advisory Council and President's Leadership Circle. The council provides essential feedback on programs and curriculum in the School of Management. Members frequently speak in the classroom, at School-sponsored conferences, and at all graduate student retreats. Local and area business leaders are involved in the School's Centers of Excellence, which tackle issues ranging from corporate governance to supply chain management.

The College and Environs

Before being established in 1969, the University of Texas at Dallas operated as the privately funded Southwest Center for Advanced Studies. When the University opened its new campus buildings in 1975, the existing academic programs were organized into the Schools of Natural Sciences and Mathematics, Management, and Human Development. New programs were later introduced through the Schools of Arts and Humanities, General Studies, and Social Sciences. The School of Management, the largest college on the UT Dallas campus, enrolls about 5,000 students a year, almost evenly split between its undergraduate and graduate programs. The School of Management is fully accredited by AACSB International.

Facilities

The University of Texas at Dallas campus, in Richardson, is within a 2-minute drive of the George Bush Turnpike and Central Expressway and just minutes from Dallas North Tollway and LBJ Freeway (Interstate 635). This nearby network of highways provides rapid access to the northern tier of Dallas suburbs, including Frisco, McKinney, Allen, Prosper, and Fairview. The campus has easily accessible parking near all its main buildings, including the newly constructed School of Management.

The School of Management occupies a 204,000-square-foot building, which opened in 2003. Each classroom is fully wired, and the building has Wi-Fi access throughout. Computer labs offer a broad range of software, and various research centers operating from the School of Management seek graduate students to run studies and conduct research for corporate clients, offering students a high level of interaction with real-life business issues during their time in school.

Admission

Prerequisites for all graduate admissions include completion of an undergraduate calculus class and personal computer proficiency; spreadsheet proficiency is a must. Completion of a baccalaureate degree from an accredited institution is required; previous undergraduate work in business courses is not a requirement. Additional requirements for all but the Executive M.B.A. program include GMAT or GRE scores, a complete application, and three recent letters of reference. A TOEFL score is required from those for whom English is not the native language. Applicants are evaluated on personal qualities and academic backgrounds, following admission formula guidelines of the International Association for Management Education. Personal interviews are not required. Admission deadlines vary by program. To receive an application, students should e-mail grad-admission@utdallas.edu.

Part-time students may start their studies in the fall, spring, or summer semester. The deadline for spring admission is November 1; summer is April 1. The deadline for the Full-Time M.B.A. and other specialized master's programs is July 1. Admission decisions are made in the order of receipt of a complete application.

Finances

Texas resident graduate student tuition for fall 2008 is $4145 for full-time (9 hours) students and $1831 per 3 hours for part-time students; nonresident tuition is $7122 for full-time (9 hours) students and $2864 per 3 hours for part-time students. Online courses carry an $80-per-hour surcharge. The total cost for an M.B.A. is roughly $25,000 for in-state students and $43,000 for nonresidents.

The UT Dallas School of Management Scholarship Committee awards many scholarships each fall. Applications are available from the UT Dallas Office of Financial Aid. The University participates in most federal and state aid programs. Short-term loans are also available. In addition, students can apply for the Dean's Excellence Scholarship, several of which are awarded each semester. The School offers scholarships to master's students with strong academic potential. Prospective students should visit the School of Management's Web site at http://som.utdallas.edu.

Application Facts and Dates

For information, students should contact:

Doug Eckel, Assistant Dean
School of Management, SM 42
The University of Texas at Dallas
800 West Campbell Road
Richardson, Texas 75080-3021

Phone: 972-883-5923
Fax: 972-883-4095
E-mail: doug.eckel@utdallas.edu
Web site: http://som.utdallas.edu

College of Business

The University of Texas at San Antonio

San Antonio, Texas

KNOWLEDGE FOR A NEW WORLD

Welcome to the University of Texas at San Antonio (UTSA) College of Business. The College of Business is one of the nation's best business schools, developing transformational leaders with Knowledge for a New World™. We are uniquely positioned to integrate the new world business issues of emerging markets, security, and cultural pluralism. Our unparalleled set of strategic alliances, centers, and programs prepares students to assume transformational leadership roles—through experiences and opportunities not available anywhere else.

UTSA's College of Business offers a portfolio of programs that are on the leading edge of business education. Whether you are looking for a basic M.B.A. or for a tailored program in accounting, economics, or technology, this is the place to be. Our flexible-format programs include a Noon M.B.A., Online M.B.A., M.B.A. International, and Executive M.B.A. (E.M.B.A.). Our graduate programs are undergoing innovative changes to address knowledge leadership for global challenges. The graduate program's strength is in its diversity. Study with top-notch faculty members from diverse cultures, interact with students who possess a variety of life experiences, and select a degree program that matches your needs.

The College has received national recognition for our accomplishments. Our Flex M.B.A. program was ranked third in the Southwest and twenty-sixth in the nation by BusinessWeek. For the third straight year, the College was named one of the top 10 M.B.A. programs for minorities by the Princeton Review, and our doctoral faculty were ranked in the top 10 nationally for their research productivity in business administration.

The UTSA College of Business is dedicated to creating, applying, and sharing knowledge that translates theory to practice, combines rigor with relevance, and provides innovative solutions to global business challenges. Join us in this new world venture.

—Lynda de la Viña, Dean

Programs and Curricular Focus

The College of Business is accredited by AACSB International–The Association to Advance Collegiate Schools of Business. A separate accreditation for the undergraduate and graduate accounting programs further distinguishes the College among its peer institutions. This accreditation addresses curriculum issues, credentials of professors, student-teacher ratios, and educational resources.

UTSA's graduate business program offers twenty-six degree choices in a wide variety of areas, such as the traditional M.B.A. and a renowned E.M.B.A. program, which was featured in *Fast Company*. In the past several years, several new programs have been approved, including master's degrees in management of technology, finance, and information technology; M.B.A. concentrations in real estate finance and tourism destination development; and Ph.D.'s in accounting, applied statistics, finance, information technology, marketing, and organization and management studies.

UTSA's College of Business graduate program is known for its high quality and affordability. College features include a talented, dedicated faculty; a $30-million, state-of-the-art

Business Building; a diverse student body; and its Center for Professional Excellence, Center for Global Entrepreneurship, and Center for Innovation and Technology Entrepreneurship.

Advanced business degrees include an M.B.A. (with concentration choices in accounting, business economics, finance, health-care management, information assurance, information systems, management science, management of technology, marketing management, project management, real estate finance, and tourism destination development); M.B.A. International; Online M.B.A.; Master of Arts in economics; Master of Accountancy (with tracks available in either accounting or taxation); Master of Science in finance (with a concentration in real estate finance); Master of Science in information technology (with a concentration in infrastructure assurance); Master of Science in management of technology; Master of Science in statistics; Executive M.B.A. (exclusively for professionals with an average of ten years of full-time work experience who are seeking a program with an emphasis on leading in times of great change); Ph.D. in applied statistics; and Ph.D. in business administration, with

emphasis in accounting, finance, information technology, marketing, and organization and management studies.

Students and the M.B.A. Experience

UTSA has a graduate business enrollment of approximately 700. In the M.B.A., the students' average age is 30, and 38 percent of the students are women. Approximately 71 percent of the M.B.A. students attend graduate school part-time. The classroom experience is further enhanced by the "real-world" contributions of these graduate business students who have an average of four years' work experience. Thirty-four percent of M.B.A. students are members of minority groups, and 14 percent are international students.

Global Focus

Located in San Antonio, the College has enjoyed a strategic advantage in offering opportunities to effectively integrate global business issues. A number of strong faculty and student exchange relationships have been developed with top institutions. They include partnerships with universities in the People's Republic of China and Hong Kong, and other programs in Italy, the United Kingdom, Mexico, and Canada. One of the premier exchange programs in the College is the Liu's Family Foundation U.S.–China Business Education Initiative, which sponsors exchanges in excess of 30 students, scholars, and executives each academic year, while fostering additional customized programs, such as an ongoing short-term banking program for Chinese bankers. The College's Business Studies for the Americas (BSA) program gives strategic focus to the College's Latin American initiatives. BSA programs develop the professional and academic skills of students and executives and include academic course work, internship, immersion programs, and professional development opportunities. Two unique programs for graduate students include a Strategies for the Border course that studies border business issues and a trilateral academic exchange program with Canadian and Mexican universities that studies the effects of the North American Free Trade Agreement. Both the College and the University provide special program support through their International Programs Offices.

Special Features

A young and dynamic institution, UTSA is one of the forty-largest business schools in the nation and has offered graduate courses since 1973. The College's enrollment of 6,000 has afforded it the latitude to offer more than twenty-six graduate degree choices. The Office of Graduate Studies offers personalized academic advis-

The UTSA College of Business Flex M.B.A. is ranked as one of the top three programs in the Southwest and twenty-sixth nationwide by *BusinessWeek*.

ing from professional advisers and program faculty members, as well as tailored career-development counseling from the Assistant Director of Graduate Business Career Services. Program choices, combined with flexible scheduling plans, are available for virtually anyone who is seriously interested in pursuing a business graduate education. Programs have been developed that focus on the top-level executive looking for a challenging peer-group experience, the midlevel manager returning for the tools necessary for promotion, and the more traditional full-time graduate student. A strong student organization, the M.B.A. Association, is only one of the many opportunities available for graduate students to enrich their academic experience and to enhance their professional network.

The Faculty

UTSA has built an outstanding business faculty with Ph.D.'s from leading business schools nationwide, including Harvard, MIT, Berkeley, and Rice. Forty-six percent of the faculty members are women or members of minority groups. Successful recruiting has created a broad and diverse faculty with a balanced approach to teaching, research, and service. The majority of business classes are taught by full-time professors, many of whom have practical business experience. Highly qualified professionals from the business community supplement the faculty in special topic categories.

The Business School Network

The College enjoys an extensive corporate community network. Faculty members and students alike engage in professional organization affiliations and classroom projects, strengthening their ties to the business community. A 30-member Business Advisory Council of top-level executives from the global business community is committed to the College through recruiting,

classroom interaction, financial support, and participation in social and academic activities.

The College and Environs

San Antonio, Texas, is the nation's eighth-largest city. It is a city rich in history and culture and has close to 20 million visitors a year. The tourism, medical, financial, and defense industries, along with a growing communications and technology sector, make it a dynamic business community. The University, with an enrollment of approximately 28,500, is respected as an energetic, growing metropolitan university. UTSA is the second-largest component of the University of Texas system and one of the state's fastest-growing public universities. The University includes a 600-acre campus located in northwest San Antonio, neighboring the famous Texas Hill Country. The UTSA Downtown Campus and the Institute of Texan Cultures are located in the heart of San Antonio.

Facilities

The College of Business is housed in the 205,000-square-foot, $30-million Business Building on the UTSA 1604 Campus. It features five student computer labs, a digital forensics lab, two high-quality theaters, and a bistro. UTSA students benefit from the growth of the University, and the Business Building is one of the University's premier facilities. The UTSA Downtown Campus, located in the heart of San Antonio, is home to a growing population of more than 5,000 students.

Technology Environment

The University continues to make significant capital investments in equipment, creating new ways for students to retrieve information more quickly and easily, and expanding its training, distance learning, and computer support programs. Most recently, the Business Building has become wireless, allowing students to connect to online resources from a laptop computer at several hot spots throughout the building. The building also features distance education and teleconference facilities, specialized networking and statistics computer labs, computer classrooms, and a 200-seat general student computing facility.

Placement

In addition to the University Career Services Office, the College of Business has established a Center for Student Professional Development that complements the College's current academic programming with enhanced professional development resources and services for students. By combining theory with practice, students can develop a well-rounded portfolio of academic, career readiness, and leadership training programs to place them on the path to success in their professional careers through personalized internship and job placement.

Admission

A bachelor's degree from an accredited institution is the basic requirement for admission to graduate study at UTSA. For admission to most graduate programs, applicants must meet University-wide graduate admission requirements.

Applicants are evaluated on the basis of demonstrated potential for success in graduate study in business administration, as indicated by a combination of prior academic achievement, Graduate Management Admission Test (GMAT) scores, personal statement, resume (optional), and references (optional). GMAT results are only accepted if the test was taken no more than five years before the date of application. Students recently admitted to the M.B.A. program have an average GMAT score of 580. International students are also required to show proof of adequate funds, and proof of health/immunizations is recommended. International students whose native language is not English must submit TOEFL results, with a minimum score of 500.

Finances

In fall 2007, full-time tuition (9 semester hours) and fees for residents were $3190. For nonresidents, they were approximately $8193. Tuition and fee amounts are subject to change by legislative action or by action of the Board of Regents of the University of Texas system. Changes in tuition and fees are effective upon the date of enactment. Students should refer to each semester's schedule of classes for current tuition and fee amounts.

The Border County Program is available for Mexican citizens and permanent residents with limited financial resources. Mexican students who qualify for admission to bachelor's or master's degree programs, who cannot afford to pay nonresident tuition but can afford to pay resident tuition rates, are charged resident tuition rates. This program is designed to encourage Mexican students of more limited means to attend public universities in Texas.

Financial aid is available in the form of fellowships, research assistantships, grants, scholarships, work-study, and loans. Financial aid is available to international students.

International Students

Services and facilities for international students include the international student office, international student center, international student housing, visa services, ESL courses, and counseling/support services.

Application Facts and Dates

For domestic applicants, applications and any required documents for the master's degree programs should be filed by July 1 for the fall semester, November 1 for the spring semester, and May 1 for the summer sessions. Deadlines for international students submitting applications for admission are April 1 for the fall semester, September 1 for the spring semester, and March 1 for the summer sessions.

For applications and instructions for completion, students should contact:

Graduate School
The University of Texas at San Antonio
One UTSA Circle
San Antonio, Texas 78249
Phone: 210-458-4330
Fax: 210-458-4332
E-mail: graduatestudies@utsa.edu
Web site: http://www.utsa.edu/graduate

University of the Pacific

Stockton, California

START HERE. LEAD ANYWHERE.

As a business school with a global orientation, we offer highly interactive classes that encourage close working relationships between students and faculty members, enabling our professors to challenge students to achieve their full potential. Our unique curricula also emphasize experience in the workplace, which we achieve through class consulting projects, a required internship, and travel overseas to study global markets. The Eberhardt School of Business Eighteen-Month M.B.A. is designed for students who want to make a difference. The Eberhardt School is committed to cultivating the leadership skills and innovative spirit of our students, in addition to training them in state-of-the-art technical business applications.

—Chuch Williams, Dean

Programs and Curricular Focus

The Eberhardt M.B.A. at the University of the Pacific is designed to place young managers on the fast track to a successful and rewarding career. Rigorous and challenging courses provide a firm foundation in the fundamental business areas, integrating the technological innovation, leadership, global perspective, and team-building aspects of business.

The average class size is 15 students. The faculty team uses a variety of teaching methodologies in small, seminar-style classes. Faculty members know each student and work with the entire M.B.A. team to make sure that students' studies correspond with the progression of their management career path. Faculty members are accessible, involved, and dedicated to teaching. They offer personalized attention to assure a mastery of the business and management techniques critical to career success.

The Eberhardt M.B.A. is fully accredited by AACSB International–The Association to Advance Collegiate Schools of Business. The program has continually met the high standards AACSB sets for curriculum content, admissions, faculty members, and instructional methodology.

The program includes advanced course work that allows students to specialize in finance, marketing, general management, or entrepreneurship. In the advanced classes, students expand their leadership skills and integrate their foundation knowledge and decision-making skills. A capstone strategy competition provides a team-based experience in real-world decision making and problem solving focused on developing strategic plans through an exercise of analysis and strategy development with a corporate advisory board of professionals.

International competency is an essential element of success in today's global economy. Understanding globalization and its implications for business is a requirement for future managers. Eberhardt M.B.A. students travel overseas in a simulated business trip, which may include a consulting project and corporate site visits. Since 1996, groups have traveled to countries in Asia, Europe, and Latin America, including Taipei, Taiwan; Singapore, Malaysia; Lyon, France; Mardrid, Spain; Helsinki, Finland; Talinn, Estonia; and Santiago, Chile.

The Eberhardt Eighteen-Month M.B.A. offers a choice of four specialized tracks: entrepreneurship, finance, general management, and marketing. Dual-degree programs are offered in law (J.D./M.B.A.) and pharmacy (Pharm.D./M.B.A.). In addition, a cooperative Master's International Program is offered in conjunction with the Peace Corps.

Students and the M.B.A. Experience

The highest percentage of the students in the Eighteen-Month M.B.A. program have academic backgrounds in business, management, or economics, but the range of academic preparation typically encompasses engineering, pharmacy, natural sciences, social sciences, and the humanities. The blending of professional and liberal arts students provides a unique opportunity to develop teamwork and leadership skills in an academically diverse environment.

The entering classes are organized around cohort groups of approximately 35 students. The Eberhardt M.B.A. provides a friendly, supportive environment that helps each individual adapt to the challenges of graduate management studies. A cohort approach also provides a format that fosters close student-faculty interaction. The average full-time student is 25 years of age, with less than two years of work experience. Women represent 40 percent of the student body, while 15 percent are international students.

The MBA Student Association (MBASA) is responsible for developing high-quality extracurricular activities for M.B.A. students. It provides formal and informal social events, professional programs, and student representation on governance committees within the business school and the University structure as a whole.

Special Features

The Eighteen-Month M.B.A. program provides the opportunity for students to achieve an M.B.A. degree with a quick payback and high return on invested time and money.

Leadership development components during the program include the assessment of individual competencies, creation of a personal development plan, and collaborative coaching.

Real-world learning opportunities are offered through the Global Business Competition course, the $1-million Student Investment Fund, the *Wall Street Journal* academic partnership, and strategic business competitions, where Eberhardt M.B.A. students often take top honors.

The Faculty

The Eberhardt School of Business faculty members are committed to teaching excellence. Consulting and research complement this teaching mission, enabling faculty members to offer instruction that is relevant and current. They integrate their real-world business experience with their extensive teaching experience to provide classroom and experiential learning aimed at developing professional skills and knowledge. Faculty members establish lasting, close relationships with their students.

The Eberhardt School of Business is proud of its top-rated faculty members, who are distinguished and internationally known for work in their respective areas of expertise. The faculty members are firmly engaged in the business community and provide students with exceptional opportunities for experiential learning. They are dedicated to assisting students to reach their highest level of academic and professional achievement. Because of the student-centered approach, students keep in touch with their professors long after graduation.

Faculty List

Thomas Brierton, Associate Professor; J.D., Northern Illinois.

Michael L. Canniff, Lecturer; M.S., Syracuse.

Lucien J. Dhooge, Associate Professor; LL.M., Georgetown.

Cynthia F. Eakin, Assistant Professor; Ph.D., Florida State.

Joel Herche, Associate Professor; Ph.D., Oregon.

Ronald A. Hoverstad, Associate Professor and Associate Dean for M.B.A. Programs; Ph.D., Minnesota.

Albert H. Huang, Associate Professor; Ph.D., North Texas.

Benjamas Jirasakuldech, Assistant Professor; Ph.D., Nebraska.

Sacha M. Joseph, Assistant Professor; Ph.D., Florida State.

John R. Knight, Professor; Ph.D., LSU.
Unro Lee, Professor; Ph.D., Purdue.
Jeffrey A. Miles, Associate Professor; Ph.D., Ohio State.
Stefanie E. Naumann, Assistant Professor; Ph.D., LSU.
Newman S. Peery Jr., Professor; Ph.D., Washington (Seattle).
Gerald V. Post, Professor; Ph.D., Iowa State.
Willard T. Price, Professor; Ph.D., Pittsburgh.
Sean Snaith, Associate Professor and Director of the Business Forecasting Center; Ph.D., Pennsylvania.
Ray Sylvester, Professor and Associate Dean for Undergraduate Programs; Ph.D., Michigan.
Dara M. Szyliowicz, Assistant Professor; Ph.D., Illinois.
Eric Typpo, Associate Professor; Ph.D., Florida State.
Richard Vargo, Professor; Ph.D., Washington (Seattle).
R. Daniel Wahdwani, Assistant Professor; Ph.D., Pennsylvania.
Suzanne B. Walchli, Assistant Professor; Ph.D., Northwestern.
Cynthia Wagner Weick, Professor; Ph.D., Pennsylvania.
Stephen W. Wheeler, Professor; Ph.D., Arizona State.
Chuck Williams, Professor and Dean; Ph.D., Michigan State.

The Business School Network
Corporate Partnerships

The Eberhardt School of Business at University of the Pacific has built strong relationships with the corporate regional and national partners and strives to integrate the classroom experience with the business world in a variety of ways, including the Pacific Business Forum, which brings nationally and internationally recognized corporate or government leaders to the campus; the recently developed Business Forecasting Center, a vibrant source of business and economic information for regional and state decision makers; the Invention Evaluation Service, which assists aspiring inventors and entrepreneurs with the commercialization of their ideas; the Westgate Center for Management Development, which provides management training for the regional business community; the Institute for Family Business, which assists family-owned businesses in finding and developing solutions to their unique business challenges; the Business Advisory Board, which includes 25 executives from local, regional, and national businesses who work closely with the dean and faculty members, integrating the business school and the business world; and an internship program, which provides business exposure for students, either on an individual basis or as part of a consulting team.

The College and Environs

The Eberhardt School of Business is located on the main campus of University of the Pacific,

with its red-brick buildings and ivy-covered walls, which is now in its 156th year. Centrally located in the heart of California, Pacific is near Yosemite National Park, Lake Tahoe, Napa Valley, and the California coastline where limitless activities, world-class cuisine, and unparalleled beauty abound. The campus is only 80 miles east of San Francisco and 45 miles south of Sacramento, allowing students direct access to companies and career opportunities in the dynamic business environments of the Silicon Valley and State Capital. The campus is nestled in the midst of the rapidly growing Central Valley, providing a dynamic economy and entrepreneurial culture that offer unique learning opportunities. The University also includes the Arthur A. Dugoni School of Dentistry in San Francisco and the McGeorge School of Law in Sacramento.

Technology Environment

The University has substantial academic computing resources available to students, with multiple laboratories across the campus, including a dedicated lab and classroom in the Eberhardt School. Wireless access is available throughout the campus, providing Internet connections for laptop users.

Placement

The Career Services Office is an integral part of each student's experience in the Eberhardt M.B.A. Students begin the process of launching their professional careers during orientation and continue year-round with workshops, mock interviews, on- and off-campus recruiting events, and internship placements. In addition to career development sessions, students have an online application and job-posting system available. Eighty-six percent of 2005–06 Eberhardt M.B.A. graduates accepted jobs within a few months of graduation, with medial total compensation of $52,688.

Admission

Admission to the Eberhardt M.B.A. program is competitive and based on criteria that indicate significant promise for a successful academic and professional career. Qualified candidates are admitted to the program on a rolling basis for the fall semester each year. The Eighteen-Month M.B.A. enrolls a cohort class of 35 students. A personalized review of each applica-

tion is conducted, with each candidate's file evaluated on the basis of previous academic record and grade trends, standardized test scores (GMAT), professional and personal accomplishments, personal statements, letters of recommendation, and a required interview. The typical undergraduate GPA is 3.0 or higher, and GMAT scores are generally 540 and above. A score of 80 (Internet-based test) or better on the TOEFL is required for all international students for whom English is not their native language. In addition, international students must present proof of adequate funds to cover expenses for the first year of the M.B.A. program. On-campus informational interviews are required and by invitation only. Telephone interviews can be scheduled as required with administrative staff members, faculty members, and students.

Finances

The tuition for the entire Eighteen-Month M.B.A. program is approximately $47,000 or $890 per unit. The cost of living in Stockton is relatively low for California, and students can find housing for about $800 to $1000 per month. Room and board on the campus are approximately $10,500 per year, depending on the housing and meal plan options chosen. Additional student recreation and health center fees are required of all full-time students.

Financial assistance is available through several scholarships, graduate assistantships, and loans. Merit-based scholarships and graduate assistantships are available directly from the Eberhardt School. Fifty percent of M.B.A. students receive some form of financial assistance from the school. Federal and private loans are also available. These awards are generally determined by May 1; students should submit an admission application by March 1 to ensure consideration.

Application Facts and Dates

The application deadline is March 1 for the fall semester. Applicants seeking priority consideration are advised to submit their applications by January 15. M.B.A. admissions decisions are made on a rolling basis, and applicants are notified immediately when decisions have been made. To ensure a timely response, application packages should be submitted as a complete package. For more information, students should contact:

Christopher R. Lozano
Director of Student Recruitment and
  Admissions
Eberhardt School of Business
University of the Pacific
3601 Pacific Avenue
Stockton, California 95211
Phone: 209-946-2629
Fax: 209-946-2586
E-mail: clozano@pacific.edu
Web site:
  http://www.business.pacific.edu/mba

University of Washington

Seattle, Washington

Programs and Curricular Focus

The Foster School of Business offers a full-time M.B.A. program and a Global M.B.A. program. In the two-year, full-time Master of Business Administration program, University of Washington (UW) students are immersed in one of the most innovative M.B.A. experiences in the world, a program designed to deliver a personalized education for each student. Students begin with a first-year integrated curriculum that focuses on core business concepts and the enhancement of vital business skills. Students have frequent contact with the business community and participate in formal professional development and leadership training.

UW M.B.A. students can study a broad range of subjects in various areas, such as finance or international marketing, and they can choose from certificate programs in entrepreneurship, global business, environmental management, global trade and logistics, and real estate. Students also have the option to pursue dual-degrees with other departments.

In the first year of the M.B.A., students are offered an integrated core of fundamental business concepts, skills, and tools. At the beginning of the program, students design a personal study plan that includes academic courses, career planning efforts, and plans for experiential learning, such as internships. In the spring quarter, students begin to take electives to help them dive deeper into subject areas before they start summer internships. During the summer between first and second year, students complete an internship to demonstrate their ability to apply M.B.A. skills to real-life situations. Students secure internships with exciting local and national companies as well as international organizations.

In year two, students focus more on their particular career objectives. Students can choose from traditional areas of concentration, such as investment banking, or newly emerging fields, such as nanotechnology. Students take a required course on corporate ethics along with a macroeconomics course and complete the remainder of the curriculum choosing from elective courses within the School of Business or in another school or college at the UW.

UW allows students to forge their own unique career paths. Students can customize their M.B.A. by choosing to focus a majority of their elective options in one traditional area; pursuing a nontraditional concentration or range of concentrations; completing a certificate along with their unique, personal M.B.A. degree; or by obtaining a second graduate degree in addition to the M.B.A.

The Global M.B.A. program offers an accelerated one-year, full-time option for professionals with international business experience and an undergraduate education that includes extensive business and economics course work or the equivalent. The Global M.B.A. attracts students from every part of the world.

This program is ideal for those who are looking to gain knowledge and experience in global business. The compressed structure of the program is designed for those who have clearly focused career goals and intend to explore internationally focused career opportunities post-M.B.A.

The four–quarter program begins in June with an accelerated summer M.B.A. core curriculum. Students then complete three academic quarters of course work, including studies in cross-cultural communication, ethics, corporate governance, and an optional course in U.S. business practices. Ten elective courses, including two in global business, complete the program. The program also includes a two-week international study tour.

Students and the M.B.A. Experience

Each M.B.A. class includes people with unique strengths as well as impressive academic and professional qualifications. More than 25 percent of the students have undergraduate liberal arts degrees and 30 percent have science and technical backgrounds. The program attracts students from throughout the U.S. and the world. The most recent classes included 38 percent women, 19 percent members of minority groups, and 34 percent international students.

Global Focus

The Foster School of Business at the University of Washington (formerly the UW Business School) is a recognized leader in global management education. International business concepts are integrated throughout the curriculum. In addition to the many courses with international business components, the program offers a range of electives focused on global management issues. Students can also study abroad in eighteen different exchange programs, pursue international internships, complete overseas study tours, and participate in weekly, on-campus, foreign language conversation sessions.

Special Features

In addition to their degree, M.B.A. students can earn a business school certificate in global business or entrepreneurship. The internationally recognized Global Business Center (GBC) and the Center for Innovation and Entrepreneurship (CIE) both encourage students to explore new opportunities through course work, clubs, internships, speaker series, competitions, and special events on and off campus. Students also have the opportunity to learn about economic development issues through the Business and Economic Development Center.

Nearly all M.B.A. students participate in club activities. Many first-year students complete a project with the Business Consulting Network while also participating in clubs focused on technology, consulting, investments, marketing, public speaking, community service, or socially-responsible business practices.

The Faculty

The University of Washington M.B.A. philosophy emphasizes a partnership between students and faculty members. Professors at the Foster School of Business have achieved recognition for both teaching and research. M.B.A. students praise the faculty's active involvement in student learning and their integration of research and teaching. Professors take a personal interest in their students and, in return, they demand a high level of student effort and commitment.

The Business School Network

The M.B.A. program enjoys a strong relationship with the business community. Proximity to cutting-edge industries and businesses in Seattle makes it easy for prominent business leaders and entrepreneurs to serve as guest speakers, visiting lecturers, and mentors. Faculty members invite executives into the classroom for perspectives on current issues, and students interact with executives through lecture series, consulting and business plan competitions, off-site business projects, and networking events. The School's Advisory Board includes representatives from prominent employers such as Accenture, Alaska Airlines, Deloitte & Touche, Expedia, Ford Motor Company, Hewlett-Packard, Hitachi Consulting, IBM, Intel, Microsoft, Nike, Starbucks, T-Mobile, Washington Mutual, and Weyerhaeuser. A large alumni network provides information from a wide range of careers and geographical locales.

The College and Environs

The University of Washington was founded in 1861 and enjoys a long-standing reputation for excellence in education and research. It has received more government research funding over the past twenty-six years than any other public university in the nation. UW employs a faculty of approximately 3,300 members, with several winning such prestigious prizes as the Nobel Prize and National Book Award.

Its sixteen schools and colleges provide education to 34,000 students, who can choose from more than 100 academic disciplines and 5000 courses. UW has 218 buildings on 693 acres in north-central Seattle, with two other campuses in Tacoma and Bothell. But the low faculty-to-student ratio and collaborative culture create a dynamic entrepreneurial learning community where connections are easily made. Each graduating class from the M.B.A. program has about 100 students, also fostering a close knit community.

The University of Washington's main campus is located in Seattle, a major city in the Pacific Northwest. With a population of more than 500,000, Seattle is one of the world's most vibrant, diverse, and beautiful cities and is a center for creativity and entrepreneurial activity—especially in the field of technology. It is a world of opportunity. In Seattle, Pacific Rim business opportunities meet Pacific Northwest quality of life. International and ethnic diversity characterize the greater Seattle area. The city offers amenities such as fine dining and art galleries while the temperate climate and natural beauty of the west coast allow residents to indulge in numerous outdoor recreational activities year round.

The region's dynamic economy is a hotbed for business development across industrial sectors and is an ideal laboratory for real-world practice. The UW M.B.A. program gives students access to prominent regional, national, and international business leaders and builds connections with top companies, including Apple, Starbucks, Nintendo, Wells Fargo, Safeco, Goldman Sachs, and PricewaterhouseCoopers. Washington is ranked fourth nationally and first on a per capita basis for total value of exports, primarily to Pacific Rim nations.

Facilities

The University of Washington library system is the twelfth largest in the nation and houses more than 5.4 million volumes. The School of Business's Foster Library holds a comprehensive collection of books, periodicals, reference materials, newspapers, pamphlets, CD-ROMs, videotapes, microfiche, and corporate annual reports. The library also offers a multitude of online search services and worldwide databases.

Placement

The M.B.A. program has an excellent career placement rate of more than 95 percent of its graduating students. The Business Connections Center facilitates connections between students, employers, alumni, and faculty members and offers an array of services to M.B.A. students. The career planning process begins prior to starting the program, through early meetings with a personal program counselor, and ends with successful completion of an integrated two-year plan executed throughout the M.B.A. program. Whether students seek major career change or accelerated career advancement, the Business Connections Center offers programs and coaching in resume writing, interviewing, and salary negotiation. Students have access to the highly respected Mentor Program, M.B.A. career forums, and internship fairs. Employers such as Accenture, Alaska Airlines, Deloitte & Touche, Expedia, Ford Motor Company, Hewlett-Packard, Hitachi Consulting, IBM, Intel, Microsoft, Nike, Starbucks, T-Mobile, Washington Mutual, and Weyerhaeuser are represented in the membership of the Career Services Advisory Board.

Admission

The Foster School of Business believes that personal connections are essential to business education, just as they are to business. Counseling in advance of applying for admission is strongly advised. The M.B.A. program encourages prospective students to meet face-to-face with admissions staff or to attend a reception held in cities worldwide. Applicants must complete the equivalent of a four–year U.S. bachelor's degree from an accredited college or university, demonstrate quantitative aptitude, take the GMAT, possess minimum English language skills, and, if pursuing a dual degree, apply to each school, college, or department of interest. Students must take the TOEFL if they are permanent residents or international applicants who do not hold a degree from a college or university in the U.S., Canada, the U.K., Ireland, Australia, or New Zealand.

Finances

Out–of–state tuition for the two-year M.B.A. is $9667 per quarter. Washington residents pay $6433. Other annual expenses (e.g., room and board, books, computers and supplies, local transportation, personal expenses, M.B.A. association and club dues, and health insurance) are estimated at $26,354. Tuition for the four-quarter Global M.B.A. program is $37,000, and other expenses are estimated at $26,354.

Financial aid is available from the University of Washington and the Foster School of Business in the form of loans, scholarships, and academic employment. Students should visit the UW Office of Student Financial aid Web site at http://www.washington.edu/students/osfa for more information on financial aid.

International Students

International students are drawn to the University of Washington by the beauty, diversity, dynamism, and relative safety of Seattle and the Pacific Northwest region. It is a supportive and welcoming place, not only for students, but for their families as well. The program currently enrolls approximately 60 international students who compose 29 percent of the student body. Current international students came to UW from seventeen countries, including China, Czech Republic, Ecuador, France, Germany, India, Japan, Korea, Philippines, Taiwan, Thailand, Turkey, Uruguay, and Venezuela.

Application Facts and Dates

The Foster School of Business has four application filing dates: October 15, November 15, January 15, and March 15. International students applying to the full-time M.B.A. program and all Global M.B.A. applicants must submit their online application and supplemental materials no later than January 15. U.S. citizens and permanent residents must submit complete applications by March 15. Students submitting TOEFL scores should obtain a minimum score of 600 (paper-based test), 250 (computer-based test), or 100 (Internet-based test) before applying. All students pay the $75 application fee and complete the application online.

M.B.A. Admissions
Michael G. Foster School of Business
110 Mackenzie Hall, Box 353200
University of Washington
Seattle, Washington 98195-3200
Phone: 206-543-4661
Fax: 206-616-7351
E-mail: mba@u.washington.edu
Web site:
    http://foster.washington.edu/mba

University of Wisconsin–M.B.A. Consortium

M.B.A. Consortium

Eau Claire, Wisconsin

DEAN'S MESSAGE

The University of Wisconsin–M.B.A. Consortium is an association of four business schools accredited by AACSB International–The Association to Advance Collegiate Schools of Business: the University of Wisconsin–Eau Claire, the University of Wisconsin–La Crosse, the University of Wisconsin–Oshkosh, and the University of Wisconsin–Parkside. Located in America's heartland, the universities are part of the University of Wisconsin (UW) system, one of the largest and most prestigious higher education systems in the United States. Our on-campus M.B.A. programs are some of the finest graduate programs in our region. Collectively, we have more than 100 years of experience in the field of graduate education. Using the knowledge gained from managing our own on-campus M.B.A. programs, we have come together to develop the first collaborative online M.B.A. program offered by the UW system.

As a student in our M.B.A. program, you will gain a broad, practical understanding of business and the dynamic global environment in which it operates. You will develop the skills and entrepreneurial spirit needed to manage change and recognize the opportunities it creates. And you will learn guidelines for confronting situations in an ethical and socially responsible manner. Our M.B.A. curriculum balances theory with application, number crunching with interpersonal skill development, and team projects with individual assignments. We are accredited by AACSB International, the oldest and most distinguished international accrediting body specifically for schools of business. Fewer than 25 percent of all business schools in the United States have achieved this highly sought-after recognition.

Programs and Curricular Focus

This 30-credit online program consists of a required core of 16 credits of interdisciplinary modules and 1 credit of leadership/teamwork, with the remaining 13 credits chosen from elective offerings. Individuals without baccalaureate business degrees must complete preliminary M.B.A. foundation courses. M.B.A. students enroll in 4 to 6 credits per semester and 1 to 3 credits in the summer session. All M.B.A. modules and electives are offered online. Using the latest in Web-based course work, faculty members teach each course and conduct virtual office hours. Grades are based on class participation, projects, written case studies and reports, quizzes, and examinations. The consortium's M.B.A. program enables students with multiple commitments to make reasonably paced progress toward their degree. The degree can be completed within two years after M.B.A. foundation requirements have been met.

The 16 interdisciplinary credits are divided into four 4-credit courses composed of themes and skill development activities. This required core of study consists of integrated team-taught modules to give today's business leader a comprehensive perspective of the big picture. Successful leaders must be able to think outside their areas of expertise, synthesize ideas and concepts from other disciplines, and understand how decisions made in one functional area impact the entire firm.

The four M.B.A. modules reflect the situations managers face as their organizations move through the business cycle. Each module is taught by a team of 3 to 4 graduate faculty members from the four University of Wisconsin–M.B.A. Consortium schools.

The first module, Strategies for Managing Ongoing Operations, focuses on the strategies needed to manage the day-to-day operations of an organization and the interplay among the various functional areas of business.

The second module, Developing New Products and Services, introduces students to the complexities involved in launching new products/services, business ventures, subsidiaries, or divisions within existing businesses. Two themes predominate in this module: a marketing theme focusing on the identification and fulfillment of customer needs and a financial theme exploring capital budgeting and long-term financial issues.

The required 1-credit minimodule is taken concurrently with Module 2 and focuses on leadership and teamwork, leading students to examine the challenges and responsibilities inherent in the role of leadership.

Managing Strategically in a Global Environment is the third module. In this course, students develop the critical skills and integrated knowledge necessary to function effectively in today's global environment. Course work involves analyzing the impact of multinational corporate lobbying on geopolitical issues and discussing how global agreements, changing technologies, global institutions, and evolving political patterns affect the conduct of global business.

The fourth module, Focusing on the Future, builds on the previous modules by preparing students to consider present conditions and analyze possible future events during their careers. Participants identify and analyze trends in business and project their potential impact on managerial practice.

Electives are 1- to 2-credit courses in which students participate in brief explorations into topics relevant to their particular needs and interests. Upcoming electives include such topics as business process simulation, decision analysis, project management, strategy and tactics of pricing, international marketing research, introduction to assurance services, regional marketing agreements and emerging markets, selling ideas at work, reengineering financial performance measures, and enterprise resource planning. Elective offerings vary from semester to semester, and new electives are added each term.

Students requiring preliminary foundation courses work with the M.B.A. Director to determine the appropriate foundation courses needed.

Students and the M.B.A. Experience

This M.B.A. program enrolls working professionals as well as students seeking direct admission from their undergraduate programs.

Online classes are similar to traditional college courses in many ways: students have a professor, textbooks, classmates, assignments, quizzes, and tests. Courses are held during a specific time frame, varying from three weeks to sixteen weeks, based on the number of credits, and have deadlines for assignments and discussions at regular intervals. The difference between the two methods is that everything is done online. Participants are able to access lecture notes, reference materials, and assignments at any time from anywhere they can make an Internet connection. Courses are offered in exciting new technological environments that are easy to navigate.

Special Features

The Consortium has its own design team dedicated to working with faculty members on course development. Students have access to advising, library services, career services, online textbook ordering, and both phone and e-mail technology support through the Consortium's managing partner, UW–Eau Claire.

The Faculty

Faculty members have Ph.D.'s and strong academic credentials. They are professionally active in consulting and applied research and serve on boards of corporate and nonprofit organizations. Most are also teaching in the face-to-face environment on their own campuses as well as participating in the online program.

Admission

Requirements for admission to the M.B.A. program include a baccalaureate degree from an accredited college or university, a cumulative GPA of at least 2.75, completion of the M.B.A. foundation courses if necessary, a Graduate Management Admission Test (GMAT) score of at least 475 or a comparable score on the Graduate Record Examinations (GRE), and, for students whose native language is not English, a score on the Test of English as a Foreign Language (TOEFL) of at least 550 on the paper-based test or 213 on the computer-based test. Applications from international students are welcomed.

In addition, the online courses require home access to the Internet, a computer capable of playing and saving multimedia files, and a modem. More in-depth information about technology requirements and skills needed for the online program is provided on the consortium's Web site.

Finances

Tuition for the online M.B.A. for 2007–08 was $600 per credit. There are several forms of financial aid assistance available to graduate students.

Application Facts and Dates

Students can officially begin the M.B.A. program in either the fall or the spring semester by enrolling in Module 1. Students who wish to start prior to Module 1 may take elective courses during the summer session. Applications are submitted through UW–Eau Claire and can be found online at http://apply.wisconsin.edu/graduate/eau. There is a $45 application fee.

Application fees and official transcripts should be sent to the following address:

UW–M.B.A. Consortium Program
c/o UW–Eau Claire
Schofield Hall, Room 112
P.O. Box 4004
Eau Claire, Wisconsin 54702-4004
Phone: 715-836-6019
Web site:
    http://www.wisconsinonlinemba.org/

Vanderbilt University

> ## DISCOVER THIS PLACE, SHAPE YOUR WORLD
>
> *Vanderbilt Owen Graduate School of Management is a business school unlike others. Our goal is to provide an outstanding, relevant, practical business education to fully prepare you for your roles as ethical business leaders of tomorrow. Here you will find a rigorous, career-focused program of study in a unique and intimate atmosphere that is supportive and collegial. You'll find support as you shape your future, discover lifelong friends and mentors, and open doors to new possibilities. As a prospective student looking to catapult your career, you have Our Promise: a promise to do everything within our power to help you achieve your professional goals.*
>
> — Jim Bradford, Dean, Vanderbilt Owen Graduate School of Management, and Ralph Owen Professor for the Practice of Management

Programs and Curricular Focus

Each August, a diverse group of 175 to 200 talented students from around the world enrolls in Owen's full-time M.B.A. program. Students come from a wide variety of academic, professional, and personal backgrounds and have worked for an average of five years before enrolling.

All Owen students start with the required courses in the core—an intense and immediate immersion in the fundamentals of management. Recruiters value the Owen core, because it produces M.B.A.'s who have that extra something: exceptional analytical skills, a solid strategic foundation, outstanding teamwork, and drive and determination.

Small classes and a low student-faculty ratio promote effective learning in the classroom and help each student focus on topics of special interest and natural aptitude.

Flexibility is a hallmark of the Vanderbilt M.B.A. curriculum. The seven-week modular calendar gives students a fast start by allowing them to complete significant study in their chosen career field before beginning a summer internship. Students also have multiple options to customize their degree to their personal career goals, including market-driven specializations, and concentrations.

Specializations are intensive programs that require a minimum of 20 credit hours of course work beyond the core. These programs are designed to meet specific market needs, including brand management, corporate finance, health care, human and organizational performance, investment management, and operations. A concentration represents a minimum of 12 hours in a single discipline that is usually the foundation for the student's chosen career. Areas of concentration include accounting, finance, general management, human and organizational per-

formance, information technology, marketing, operations, and strategy.

Students can also earn credits toward their M.B.A. degree outside of Owen by taking classes in another graduate or professional school at the University or by spending a semester abroad at one of many international exchange partners.

Owen offers an M.B.A. degree with a health-care specialization, a groundbreaking program that combines the core business education with active learning through real-world health-care experience. The School also offers a law and business program, which gives students an opportunity to take interdisciplinary courses at Vanderbilt Law School.

Vanderbilt offers several dual-degree programs in conjunction with other schools on campus, and many individuals take advantage of the opportunity to obtain a dual degree. Current dual-degree programs include M.B.A./J.D. (law), M.B.A./M.D. (medicine), M.B.A./M.S.N. (nursing), M.B.A./M.A.L.A.S. (Latin American studies), M.B.A./M.Div (divinity), and M.B.A./Ph.D. (biomedical engineering). Interested students must be admitted to each school separately.

Vanderbilt M.B.A. course work requires regular contact with faculty members, research partners, and the business community—often through teams that mirror those used by today's successful businesses. Outside of the classroom, students further develop enhanced personal effectiveness and teamwork skills through group study, team projects, and experiential learning opportunities.

Students and the M.B.A. Experience

The Vanderbilt M.B.A. program enrolls approximately 360 full-time students who bring a great diversity of experience and a wide

range of interests to the classroom. The average full-time student is 29 years old with five years of work experience. Women make up approximately 25 percent of the student population. About 75 percent of students come from outside of the southeastern United States, including international students (15–20 percent of the student population) representing more than twenty-five countries.

Special Features

Vanderbilt M.B.A. faculty members perform collaborative research with industry partners through the School's research centers: Financial Markets Research Center (FMRC), the Owen Entrepreneurship Center, the Cal Turner Program for Moral Leadership in the Professions, and Vanderbilt Center for Environmental Management Studies (VCEMS).

Vanderbilt offers opportunities for M.B.A. students to participate in exchange programs with partner schools around the world. Most exchanges take place in the fall of the second year, and applications are due in the spring of the first year.

The Faculty

The finest scholars, researchers, teachers, and practitioners make up Vanderbilt's accomplished faculty. Educated at the best universities and seasoned with significant experience, these faculty members are in demand as conference speakers and panelists, consultants, authors and referees for prominent academic journals, and experts for leading media outlets. A few professors of note include Bill Christie, whose research on pricing and trading practices in the financial markets resulted in a sweeping reform of the NASDAQ market; Luke Froeb, who recently completed a term as Director of the Bureau of Economics at the Federal Trade Commission; Bob Whaley, who developed three market indexes for the Chicago Board Options Exchange; Dawn Iacobucci, an award-winning expert on customer satisfaction and service marketing; and Nancy Lea Hyer, an award-winning author nationally recognized for her cutting-edge research into cellular manufacturing. Vanderbilt professors infuse the classroom with academic research and professional experience to create a cutting-edge and relevant learning environment. The Vanderbilt M.B.A. program exposes students to important theories and applications using a balanced mix of lectures, classroom discussions, case studies, and group projects. In order to shape successful business managers and insightful leaders, Vanderbilt combines these time-tested methods and its teaching excellence in the classroom with experiential learning opportunities in the business community. The spirit of respect and intellectual curiosity leads to many lifelong faculty-student friendships.

The Business School Network
Corporate Partnerships
Corporate partners play a vital role in the success of the Vanderbilt Owen Graduate School of Management. There are numerous opportunities to partner with Owen. Many organizations choose to help sustain and improve the M.B.A. program through financial donations. These gifts may be unrestricted or designated for a specific purpose—funding a Center of Excellence, endowing a chair or scholarship, or sponsoring an academic event. Other organizations provide enormous value through direct involvement with students, including participation in the Distinguished Speaker Series, class presentations, case competitions, mock interviews, recruiting/internships, mentoring, student club activities, and consulting projects. In return, companies receive direct access to top M.B.A. talent, world-class management expertise and research, and a unique opportunity to make a difference.

Prominent Alumni
Vanderbilt M.B.A. alumni are a close network of individuals who demonstrate their commitment to the Owen community by volunteering to serve on committees that help the School in many of its activities, including corporate relations, recruiting, development, and networking. Alumni often cite that giving back is a reflection of the personal help they received from alumni and faculty and staff members at Owen.

Prominent alumni include Nancy Abbott, Vice President of Human Resources, GE Commercial Finance; Tom Barr, Vice President, Starbucks; John Bogle, President, Bogle Investment Management; Josue Gomes da Silva, President, Coteminas; David Farr, Emerson Electric Company; Adena Friedman, EVP, Corporate Strategy and Data Products, NASDAQ; Sara Gates, Vice President, Sun Microsystems; David Ingram, Chairman/President, Ingram Entertainment, Inc.; John Ingram, Chairman, Ingram Distribution Holdings; David Kloeppel, EVP/CFO, Gaylord Entertainment Company; Bill Levisay, Senior Vice President, Coca-Cola; Doug Parker, Chairman/President/CEO, U.S. Airways; Maria Renz, Vice President, Amazon.com; Karen Rogers, Vice President of U.S. Marketing, FedEx; and Craig Savage, Vice President, Private Wealth Management, Goldman Sachs.

The College and Environs
Vanderbilt University is located on a beautiful 330-acre campus that is also a national arboretum, complete with paths that wind among magnificent, centuries-old trees. Vanderbilt is in Nashville, Tennessee, a major southern city and the Tennessee state capital. Nashville has a population of more than 1.5 million and was recently ranked first in *Kiplinger*'s Top 50 Smart Places to Live survey. A center for banking, finance, health care, publishing, entertainment, distribution, automobile manufacturing, and insurance, Nashville is home base for many national and international corporations. Long known as the "Athens of the South," Nashville boasts a rich cultural life. Many museums and historic sites provide ample opportunities for leisure-time excursions or scholarly exploration. Nashville's mild weather, acres of green space, sense of history, and dynamic business climate create an ideal environment for learning and leisure.

Facilities
All support services for Vanderbilt M.B.A. students are located in Management Hall, a spacious, modern, multilevel building containing classrooms, seminar rooms, faculty and staff member offices, study rooms, a student lounge, a wireless computer network, and a world-class library. These facilities are devoted solely to the Vanderbilt graduate business community.

Technology Environment
In addition to leading-edge research and groundbreaking course work, Vanderbilt M.B.A. students learn firsthand about new technology through practically oriented classes, consulting projects with research center sponsors, and involvement with the surrounding business community.

Vanderbilt features a technology-savvy environment that makes it easy for students to meet the day-to-day challenges of communicating at a top-tier business school. One of the first business schools in the country to go wireless, Owen requires students to participate in the wireless laptop program. The high-speed wireless network conveniently extends to the Starbucks across the street. Owen has implemented a sophisticated intranet that provides access to Web-based course materials, discussion boards, virtual chat, and online library databases.

Placement
Owen offers a highly personal approach to career management, ensuring that each student receives individual attention and access to the knowledge, resources, and guidance required to accomplish their career goals. The Career Management Center supports students with counseling, negotiation assistance, industry seminars, on-campus interviews, recruiter feedback, networking trips, and more. Salaries for Vanderbilt M.B.A.s are highly competitive with other top business schools, and graduates are highly prized by recruiters. "Owen graduates enter the workforce with a good mix of quantitative/analytical skills, general business knowledge, and communication/leadership abilities," says James Rile of Deloitte Consulting. "The high quality of the student body and strong support of the Career Management Center continue to demonstrate high value to Deloitte." The rigorous curriculum, extensive recruiting contacts, global alumni network, and reputation for creating well-rounded managers help propel graduates into successful careers in many different industries, functional areas, and geographic regions. In addition, the relationships built at Owen will support and enhance career opportunities for years to come.

Admission
Candidates for the Vanderbilt M.B.A. program must have a U.S. bachelor's degree or its equivalent from an accredited four-year college or university. Evaluation for admission is very competitive. The Admissions Committee considers many factors, including work experience, GMAT scores, undergraduate record, recommendations, required essays, and the personal interview.

Finances
For 2007–08, tuition was estimated at $37,834, and a nine-month budget included the following estimates: housing, $8644; meals, $3412; personal expenses, including student health insurance, $4706; average transportation costs, $1656; books and supplies, $2150; loan origination fees, $626; orientation fee, $350; and wireless laptop, $1550.

Permanent residents and U.S. citizens are eligible for a variety of loan programs. All applicants are automatically considered for merit-based scholarships.

Application Facts and Dates

The application is considered complete and ready for review by the Admissions Committee following receipt of a completed online application, unofficial transcripts, unofficial test scores, resume, two essays, two recommendations, and the application fee. Well-qualified candidates are required to interview with an admissions officer prior to receiving a decision. To learn more about the Vanderbilt M.B.A., students should contact:

M.B.A. Admissions Office
Owen Graduate School of Management
Vanderbilt University
401 21st Avenue South
Nashville, Tennessee 37203

Phone: 615-322-6469
　　　800-288-OWEN (6936; toll-free)
Fax: 615-343-1175
E-mail:
　　admissions@owen.vanderbilt.edu
Web site:
　　http://www.owen.vanderbilt.edu

Wayne State University

Detroit, Michigan

THE WAYNE STATE M.B.A.—A PROGRAM FOR YOUR FUTURE

The M.B.A. program at Wayne State University is one of the oldest in the United States and, we believe, one of the finest. The School has assembled graduate faculty members who publish regularly in their discipline's most prestigious journals and who are dedicated to the highest teaching standards. The excellent academic credentials and impressive professional backgrounds of the students in the M.B.A. program serve not only to attract and retain our fine faculty but also to enrich the educational experience in the program through the insights they bring to the classroom.

The faculty and staff members of the School of Business Administration have worked hard to make the graduate study of business an enjoyable and exciting experience for our M.B.A. students. Thank you for taking a closer look!

—David Williams, Dean

Programs and Curricular Focus

The accelerated Master of Business Administration (M.B.A.) program at Wayne State University (WSU) is designed to incorporate the fluid nature of business and industry in the twenty-first century. By emphasizing functional and conceptual knowledge, the comprehensive, high-impact M.B.A. program is intended to prepare men and women for leadership and management positions in business, government, and other types of organizations.

The core and elective requirements for the program consist of 36 semester hours of study (twelve courses). Applicants with a baccalaureate degree in business administration usually meet all of the program's foundation requirements. Applicants with baccalaureate degrees in fields other than business administration may have to complete certain foundation requirements in the following areas: accounting, economics, finance, management, management information systems, marketing, mathematics, production management, and statistics. Special accelerated foundation courses have been developed to help entering M.B.A. students meet these requirements.

In addition to taking six core courses, the M.B.A. student may select from an extensive number of elective courses in accounting, finance, industrial relations, international business, management and organizational behavior, management information systems, marketing, personnel/human resources management, and taxation. Graduate-level courses in other schools and colleges of the University may also be elected with special approval of the M.B.A. program director. Students interested in pursuing a J.D./M.B.A. should contact an adviser in the Office of Student Services.

The academic year is divided into two 15-week semesters and a split spring/summer semester. A full schedule of graduate courses is offered each term. Courses are taught in convenient suburban locations as well as on campus and online.

Students and the M.B.A. Experience

Wayne State M.B.A. students bring cross-cultural diversity and a broad range of employment experiences to the program. More than 93 percent of the students are employed full- or part-time, with an average of five years of work experience. Half of the M.B.A. students hold supervisory positions within their corporations.

The average student is 27 years old, with women making up 41 percent of the student base. International students compose 5 percent of the M.B.A. population, bringing to the program valued input on business in their regions of the world.

Students in the Wayne State M.B.A. program find its strength to be the real-world experience their peers bring to classroom discussions and projects, combined with relevant business theory presented by the faculty. While 55 percent of current M.B.A. students hold undergraduate degrees in business, the remaining 45 percent are made up of engineering, liberal arts, fine arts, and science graduates.

The Faculty

Faculty members of Wayne State's School of Business Administration are recruited from the finest graduate programs both in America and abroad, and the excellent quality of both the graduate and undergraduate students has proven to be a powerful force in retaining this talented group. The business school faculty members publish approximately 100 works, including books, journal articles, and scholarly papers each year. They are regular contributors to the finest academic journals in the business disciplines.

In addition, the School of Business is proud of the energetic group of business executives who teach as adjunct faculty members in the M.B.A. program. These experienced professional managers are consistently well received by their graduate students.

The Business School Network
Corporate Partnerships

Among the strong partnerships that have been established between the School of Business Administration and prominent local and international corporations are relationships with Chrysler, Ford Motor Company, General Motors, Google, Lear, and National City Bank.

Prominent Alumni

The School of Business Administration at Wayne State University counts among its alumni a number of notable business leaders, including Lin Cummins, Senior Vice President-Communications, Arvin-Meritor; George Johnson, Managing Director, George Johnson & Company; David Meador, Executive Vice President and Chief Financial Officer, DTE Energy; Sandra Pierce, President and Chief Executive Officer, Charter One Bank, Michigan and Indiana; Anne Regling, Vice President and Controller, Blue Cross Blue Shield of Michigan; Terry Reiley, President, Rehabilitation Institute of Michigan; Mark Schmid, Vice President-Trust Investments and Chief Investment Officer, Boeing; James Vandenberghe, Vice Chairman and Chief Financial Officer, Lear Corporation; and Tom Wilson, President and Chief Executive Officer, Palace Sports and Entertainment.

The College and Environs

Since Wayne State University was founded in 1868, it has continued growing to meet educational needs. In 1994, Wayne State became one of only eighty-eight Carnegie Research I Universities out of a total of 3,600 accredited universities in the U.S. It offers a broad range of baccalaureate programs while demonstrating a commitment to graduate education and a significant capacity for research. Wayne State University is Michigan's only urban research university, filling a unique niche by providing access to a world-class education at a great value. Wayne State's eleven schools and colleges offer more than 350 major subject areas to its 33,000 graduate and undergraduate students.

WSU is located in the heart of Detroit's University Cultural Center, the home of renowned museums, galleries, and theaters—most within walking distance. The WSU main campus encompasses 203 acres of beautifully landscaped walkways and gathering spots, linking 100 education and research buildings. The five extension centers in the metropolitan area provide convenient access to a wide selection of courses.

Also near the campus are the Engineering Society of Detroit, the Detroit Medical Center, the Charles H. Wright Museum, the Merrill Palmer Institute, and the General Motors World Headquarters. Detroit and southeastern Michigan provide extensive opportunities for study, research, cultural enjoyment, and employment.

Facilities

The Wayne State University School of Business Administration offers a wide range of computing resources to students. The School has a dedicated computer laboratory exclusively for business school students. It is equipped with the latest PC workstations, network printers, and cutting-edge business software. In addition, the distance learning classrooms link WSU's main campus in Detroit with the Oakland Center campus in Farmington Hills, and new software products allow faculty members to record lectures that students can view from any computer with Internet access. Most M.B.A. courses are available online. On campus, high-speed wireless Internet is accessible throughout the business school's buildings, including classrooms, and in and around all libraries and many other classroom buildings on campus.

Wayne State University has a high-speed, fiber-optic gigabit Ethernet network interconnecting buildings on its main and medical campuses. With high-performance connections to the commercial Internet, Internet2, and the Michigan LambdaRail (MiLR) research network, WSU's network infrastructure supports the reach of University research and collaboration to academic institutions around the country and abroad, including national laboratories and supercomputing centers.

Wayne State also operates a centrally managed Grid-enabled computing system, which houses research-related projects involving high-speed computation, data management, statistical analysis, and other computationally intensive applications. The WSU Grid infrastructure is designed to allow students access to many different programs and data-storage options, depending on the research being performed. More information about the WSU Grid is available online at https://www.grid.wayne.edu.

The University Library System provides access to many business resources, including electronic indexes with abstracts and full-text and subject guides that focus on specific areas of research. Many of these resources can be accessed directly through the Library System Web site at http://www.lib.wayne.edu. The library system provides open-access computing labs for the entire campus community. These labs include more than 800 computers with a variety of applications in support of student learning. The 24-hour Extended Study Center is open during the fall and winter semesters.

Placement

The School of Business Administration's Career Planning and Placement Office regularly places M.B.A. students in permanent positions locally, nationally, and internationally. Employers post positions daily and students apply for jobs on the School's exclusive Web site, WayneBizCareers.com—designed solely for students and alumni of the School of Business Administration. The School hosts an annual Career Day, providing students with an opportunity to meet recruiters from dozens of national and international business, manufacturing, and service corporations. The School's Career Planning and Placement Office also offers information on major corporations, job searching, interviewing, and resume writing.

Admission

Admission to the Master of Business Administration program is open to students who have a baccalaureate degree in any discipline from a regionally accredited institution and who demonstrate a high promise of success in the graduate study of business. A minimum 2.5 overall undergraduate honor point average (HPA) or 2.75 honor point average in the last half of the undergraduate program is required. In addition, a minimum GMAT score of 450 is required. No decision regarding a student's admission will be made without the GMAT results. Students should visit http://www.mba.com for more information about the GMAT test.

International students must have completed an appropriate four-year university-level program and, in addition to the above requirements, achieve a minimum score of 550 (paper-based) or 213 (computer-based) on the Test of English as a Foreign Language (TOEFL) or a score of at least 85 on the Michigan English Language Assessment Battery (MELAB).

Finances

The Office of Scholarships and Financial Aid provides students with information regarding sources of funds. Graduate research assistantships are offered through the School's academic departments. Stipends for 2008–09 average $14,172 for nine-month appointments. University graduate and professional scholarships are also available.

In 2008, tuition for Michigan residents is $467.60 per credit hour, and non-Michigan residents pay $954.50 per credit hour.

International Students

International students constitute 5 percent of the M.B.A. student body. The Office of International Students and Scholars offers assistance to all students with their new surroundings. The International Business Association also offers students an opportunity to meet their fellow classmates and develop international networks through special events and business functions.

Application Facts and Dates

Application deadlines for graduate admission are July 1 for the fall term, November 1 for the winter term, and March 15 for the spring/summer term. To apply, prospective students must submit a completed application for graduate admission online at http://www.gradadmissions.wayne.edu. An application fee, official transcripts from all collegiate institutions attended, and GMAT results must be submitted before the application can be processed. International students must provide required materials four months prior to the beginning of the term. For more information, students should address inquiries to:

Office of Student Services
School of Business Administration
Wayne State University
Detroit, Michigan 48202
Phone: 313-577-4510
        800-910-EARN (toll-free)
Fax: 313-577-5299
Web site: http://www.business.wayne.edu

Webber International University

Babson Park, Florida

DEVELOPING BUSINESS LEADERS FOR THE TWENTY-FIRST CENTURY

Webber International University's M.B.A. program is designed to utilize in-class instruction, modern information technology, team projects, and practical consulting experience to prepare its graduates for global business competition. Our commitment at Webber is to advance the business careers of our partners—the students. We believe that human development is of critical importance and that growth is nurtured by interdependence. Students are encouraged to take advantage of our close-knit, friendly environment. Interactions between faculty members and students are not the exception but the rule.

The design and delivery of our curriculum emphasizes action rather than lecture. We make use of live cases, not just paper cases. The focus fosters team building, imagination, and innovation as students learn to apply conceptual theory to real-life situations. Leadership, entrepreneurship, ethics, communication, and global perspective are interwoven in our interdisciplinary curriculum.

—Dr. Nikos Orphanoudakis, Dean

Programs and Curricular Focus

The Webber International University Graduate School of Business offers a unique nineteen-month, full-time program leading to a Master of Business Administration with an option in accounting, management, or sport management. The degree consists of 36 credit hours, with courses offered one night a week over six 10-week periods. The University is accredited by the Southern Association of Colleges and Schools (SACS) and the International Assembly for Collegiate Business Education (IACBE).

The Webber M.B.A. aims to assist students in enhancing their managerial skills through the delivery of techniques and best practices that integrate academic theory with contemporary applications. The program places a premium level of focus on developing students' critical-thinking skills so that they may more easily adapt to paradigm shifts within business.

The Webber International University Graduate School of Business offers an M.B.A. program that focuses on the interdisciplinary nature of business practices. The program capitalizes on the faculty's ability to focus on proven traditional methods of teaching that integrate the various facets of effective business administration, while utilizing information technology to enhance problem-solving skills.

Through the practicum course(s), students undertake group-based consulting projects that give them the opportunity to test theoretical concepts in an applied setting.

Students and the M.B.A. Experience

The Graduate School of Business is small in size, with approximately 65 graduate students. The small class sizes provide ample opportunity for students to exchange ideas with other students and interact closely with the faculty.

The students are distinguished by the diversity of their professional and ethnic backgrounds. The average age of the students in the M.B.A. program is 30, and approximately 55 percent of the class have had one year or more of professional, full-time employment experience. Students come from several states as well as several different countries. About half are women, and approximately 60 percent are employed full- or part-time.

The Faculty

The Webber International University Graduate School of Business faculty members bring both professional and academic expertise to the classroom. The faculty members are distinguished in their fields and are dedicated to teaching.

The Webber International University Graduate School of Business emphasizes strong faculty-student interaction, indicated by the small class size and the nature of the course work.

The Business School Network

Webber International University has developed strong ties with the business community. Webber's proximity to Orlando is an asset for the M.B.A. program.

The Graduate School of Business is counseled by the Business Advisory Board. The Board is composed of a group of business professionals who provide faculty members with advice on curricula and updated information on industry needs and trends, as well as provide students with field experience opportunities.

In addition to the Business Advisory Board, the Graduate School is a member of several Chambers of Commerce in the area that, together with local businesses, provide the opportunity for students to apply and test theoretical concepts through consulting activities with the practicum.

The College and Environs

Webber International University was founded in 1927 by Grace Knight and Roger W. Babson as a women's college, with the exclusive purpose of teaching women about business. It was the first school chartered under the educational and charitable laws of the state of Florida as a nonprofit organization. In 1971, the first men were admitted to the University. The Graduate School of Business was established in 1997 and granted its first degrees in 1999.

Webber International University is a small college with a total student body of approximately 650. The small size aids the students in getting to know the president as well as the faculty and staff members. It is located on a beautiful 110-acre campus along the shoreline of Crooked Lake, approximately 45 minutes south of Orlando. The town of Babson Park, a small, rural residential community, is located in the heart of Florida's citrus county near a chain of freshwater lakes. Babson Park is conveniently located near many major recreational facilities and national tourist attractions in central Florida.

Facilities

The Roger Babson Learning Center, located in the central part of the campus, is a modern and comprehensive library facility that contains extensive collections of ref-erence, research, and reserve materials keyed to business research. The center also offers access to several external data sources, such as EbscoHost, LexisNexis Academic Universe, LIRN-Library, and several others.

The computer resource center is a data processing center and teaching facility whose microcomputers offer the latest modern technology for developing student excellence in business, communication, and creativity.

Placement

Webber International University's career services professionals are available to advise and assist students in developing and attaining their career goals. Career management services available to M.B.A. students include an annual career day, a career expo, an alumni database, on-campus recruiting, career information and advising, a resume book, and seminars and interviews throughout the year by employment recruiters on campus.

While career services are available to all students, international students should be aware that job opportunities in the United States are limited by the type of visa they hold.

Admission

Men and women with baccalaureate degrees from regionally accredited colleges or uni-versities are eligible for consideration for admission. Admission to the Graduate School of Business is based on both quantitative and qualitative criteria. In addition to the application, the applicant must submit a resume, an essay, and a list of references. Academic qualifications are determined by evaluation of student performance at previous higher education institutions, and the GMAT may be required. In addition, international applicants are required to submit results from the TOEFL, unless they have obtained a degree from a college or university where English is the language of instruction.

Finances

The tuition for the 2007–08 academic year was $485 per credit hour. Book expenses vary by course.

On-campus housing is available to graduate students. Housing costs range from $1000 to $1230 per ten-week term. A meal plan is available for $685 per ten-week term.

Financial aid is available in the form of student loans for eligible students. In addition, many employers provide for, or subsidize, their employees' tuition expenses. For more information, students should contact the financial aid office (telephone: 863-638-2929).

Application Facts and Dates

The standard academic year for the full-time M.B.A. program begins in late August and ends in mid-July. Options for other times of enrollment are also available. Applications are considered on a first-come, first-served basis. Applications may be obtained by mail or downloaded from the School's Web site. For additional information or questions regarding the Webber International University Graduate School of Business, students should contact:

M.B.A. Coordinator
Graduate School of Business
Webber International University
1201 North Scenic Highway
P.O. Box 96
Babson Park, Florida 33827-0096

Phone: 863-638-2927
Fax: 863-638-1591
E-mail: mba@webber.edu
Web site: http://www.webber.edu

Widener University

Chester, Pennsylvania

> ### THE PHILOSOPHY BEHIND WIDENER'S BUSINESS PROGRAMS
>
> *Widener's AACSB-accredited graduate business programs provide unique, fully integrative curricula for aspiring business leaders to gain the knowledge and skills they need to succeed in today's business environment. The completely redesigned M.B.A. has a comprehensive core program that is taught by a team of full-time faculty members and industry executives. This program is not confined by the barriers of traditional business functions but is built on the concept of process innovation for performance excellence leading to sustainable growth—key drivers to success in today's business world.*
>
> —Savas Özatalay, Dean

Programs and Curricular Focus

Whether the goal is career advancement, improved salary, or gaining a better understanding of one's field, Widener's School of Business Administration has graduate programs that give its students the credentials, knowledge, and insight they need to succeed.

Over the past four decades, Widener has prepared more than 4,000 graduates for leadership roles in assorted industries in the business community. Full-time students mix with part-time students who bring years of work experience across a broad spectrum of industries. These diverse backgrounds create a rich learning environment, providing fresh approaches to problem solving as well as excellent networking opportunities. Whether working on case studies or group projects or during regular classroom discussions, students have a wealth of real-world experiences from which to draw.

Widener's graduate business programs are accredited by AACSB International–The Association to Advance Collegiate Schools of Business, which is a status that only about a third of all business schools in the country can claim. In addition, the School's programs for health-care professionals are accredited by the Commission on Accreditation of Healthcare Management Education (CAHME). As a result, Widener's graduate business students have the unique advantage of studying at one of only a few schools in the United States that offer programs carrying both AACSB International and CAHME accreditation.

Degree programs offered are the Master of Business Administration (M.B.A.), the Master of Business Administration in Health Care Management (M.B.A.–HCM), the Master of Science in Information Systems (M.S.I.S.), the Master of Science in Human Resource and Organizational Leadership (M.S.H.R.O.L.), and the Master of Science in Taxation and Financial Planning. Aspiring financial planning professionals can fulfill the academic requirements to sit for the Certified Financial Planner (CFP™) certification examination through this program.

Dual-degree programs are offered in conjunction with the School of Law (J.D./M.B.A.), School of Engineering (M.E./M.B.A.), Institute for Graduate Clinical Psychology (Psy.D./M.B.A., Psy.D./M.B.A.–HCM, and Psy.D./M.S.H.R.O.L.), and Jefferson Medical College of Thomas Jefferson University (M.D./M.B.A.–HCM).

Students and the M.B.A. Experience

Part- and full-time students enter the M.B.A. program in the fall semester. Grouped into cohorts, the students move as a group through the integrated core program. Full-time students complete the program in one year, part-time students in two years. The 18-hour integrated core curriculum is designed and taught by a team of 8 full-time faculty members, augmented by industry executives. Students also complete 12 credits of elective courses. In addition to the required and elective courses, students must attend 12 hours of noncredit career-development workshops. These sessions are an excellent forum for honing career skills and networking with peers and alumni.

Special Features

The integrated core allows students to see traditional functional areas as part of business as a whole. Concentrations within the general M.B.A. are available in business process management, enterprise resource planning, financial planning, human resources, and marketing.

As a university alliance member of SAP, Widener also offers students the opportunity to obtain a Certificate of Recognition from SAP by completing at least three courses with significant SAP content.

The Faculty

The faculty members at Widener understand business through firsthand experience. They stay current in their field through involvement in research, consulting, and professional organizations, helping them expose students to the latest techniques and concepts as well as established business theories and practices.

The M.B.A. integrated core team was selected for excellence in teaching and research. Members of the team have earned the Lindback Award for Excellence in Teaching and Scholarship and the School of Business Administration Distinguished Teaching Award.

The Business School Network

Widener's School of Business Administration provides excellent opportunities for networking. Current Widener M.B.A. students hold positions at more than 200 different companies, including AstraZeneca, Boeing, Children's Hospital of Philadelphia,

The Leslie C. Quick Jr. Center houses Widener's School of Business.

DuPont, General Electric, IDS Scheer, PFPC, the Vanguard Group, and Verizon.

The College and Environs

Widener University is a multicampus, independent, metropolitan institution located in and accredited by the commonwealth of Pennsylvania and the state of Delaware. Founded in 1821, Widener offers doctoral, master's, baccalaureate, and associate degrees through its eight schools and colleges, which include the College of Arts and Sciences, the School of Business Administration, the School of Engineering, the School of Hospitality Management, the School of Human Service Professions, the School of Law, the School of Nursing, and University College. As part of its mission, the University seeks to inspire its students to be citizens of character as well as professional and civic leaders.

Facilities

Graduate business students take classes on the Main Campus in Chester, Pennsylvania, in the Leslie C. Quick Jr. Center, the school's dedicated home. Opened in fall 2002, this state-of-the-art wireless building includes multimedia classrooms, a student lounge, an information systems lab, an executive education center in which seminars and conferences are held, and a simulated Wall Street trading room.

Placement

Graduate advisers are available to help merge career goals with programs offered. A professionally staffed Career Advising and Planning Services (CAPS) Office on the Main Campus is available to all students.

Admission

Interested holders of baccalaureate degrees can apply for admission by completing the application, submitting payment of the nonrefundable application fee, submitting two letters of recommendation, and having their transcripts forwarded. In addition, students must take the GMAT or an alternative test, as determined by the program. International students from non-English-speaking countries must take the Test of English as a Foreign Language (TOEFL) and submit a transcript evaluation.

Finances

For the 2008–09 academic year, students in the graduate business programs pay a tuition fee of $755 per credit. A limited number of graduate assistantships are available for full-time students. Graduate assistants aid the faculty members in research projects and work approximately 20 hours per week. Assistantships are compensated by a stipend and tuition remission for up to 9 credits per semester.

Application Facts and Dates

Applications for the M.B.A. program must be received by May 1 (April 1 for international students).

Non-M.B.A. applicants may enroll in the fall semester, spring semester, or summer sessions, with application deadlines of August 1, December 1, and April 1, respectively. Prospective students should note that applications from international students must be received four months prior to these dates.

For more information, students should contact:

Graduate Programs
School of Business Administration
Widener University
One University Place
Chester, Pennsylvania 19013

Phone: 610-499-4305
Fax: 610-499-4615
E-mail: sbagradv@mail.widener.edu
Web site: http://www.widener.edu/sba

Wilfrid Laurier University

Waterloo and Toronto, Ontario, Canada

CHANGING THE FACE OF BUSINESS

At Laurier we are all about developing leaders who are innovative and adaptive and who can make a real difference to business enterprise and not-for-profit organizations throughout the world. Through our innovative integrated curriculum and our strategic partnerships with influential corporations and professional associations, you can customize your M.B.A. to fulfill your unique specific career aspirations. And you can do all this while you balance your home and work commitments. Come and visit us in our M.B.A. classroom, and you'll discover what sets up apart.

—Ginny Dybenko, Dean

Programs and Curricular Focus

The Laurier M.B.A. programs stress the skills and abilities required to take effective action and to develop managers who know about management. Central to this philosophy is the belief that management must be problem solving and opportunity centered. While it is essential that managers know the theories and concepts of management, it is in handling the real challenges that businesses face that contributions are measured.

The learning environment at Laurier enables students to develop the skills needed to be effective decision makers. The presentation and defense of students' ideas, the exchange of ideas, and the critical evaluation by their peers form an important part of the classroom process.

Seven M.B.A. programs are offered at Laurier: a full-time twelve-month program, a full-time with co-op twenty-month program, an M.B.A. in innovation and entrepreneurship, a part-time evening program at the Waterloo campus, and three weekend-format programs at the Toronto campus, which include the general M.B.A., the M.B.A./Certified Management Accountant (CMA), and the M.B.A./Chartered Financial Analyst (CFA). They provide a broad overview of the major areas of business activities and consist of eight required half-credit core courses, ten half-credit elective courses, and two research consulting credits. Laurier now offers students the opportunity to specialize their M.B.A. degree with ten different areas of concentration: accounting, brand communication, innovation and entrepreneurship, financial management, international business management, management and organizational behaviour, marketing, operations management, strategic management, and supply chain management.

The core component of the full-time program is delivered in an integrated format that emulates the multidimensional nature of the business world. The full-time program begins in mid-August and continues for twelve months. The full-time with co-op program also begins

in mid-August and continues for twenty months, including three full-time academic terms and two co-op work terms.

The part-time program, offered through late afternoon and evening courses, normally consists of two courses per term for three terms per year. The program takes approximately three years and one term to complete.

The Toronto programs are offered Friday evenings and all day Saturday on alternate weekends over a ten-term period. The academic cycle begins in early spring. A break is scheduled during the summer months of July and August and again from mid-December to January.

One of the Toronto programs, developed in partnership with Certified Management Accountant Canada-Ontario, is a combined M.B.A. with the CMA option. In this format, M.B.A. students can acquire both the M.B.A. degree and the Certified Management Accountant designation at the same time. The other Toronto pro-

gram is the M.B.A. with the Chartered Financial Analyst option. Students can complete the requirements for both their M.B.A. degree and the CFA exams concurrently. Successful candidates graduate with an M.B.A. degree with an expertise in investment analysis and portfolio management, while preparing for the three levels of CFA examinations.

Laurier's School of Business & Economics also offers an M.A. in business economics that prepares economists for a career in the private or public sector.

Students and the M.B.A. Experience

The Laurier M.B.A. program is one of the most innovative in Canada. Students come from a diverse range of academic and employment backgrounds. International students make up fifteen percent of the student body; women 40 percent of the class. The average student age is 34, and all students enter the Laurier M.B.A. program with successful track records in their work and technical backgrounds in their chosen fields.

Global Focus

Students have the opportunity to be involved in projects that prepare them to manage in the complexities of the global marketplace. Optional International Study Tours offer an opportunity to combine field study with in-class components. Prior to the field-study component, students conduct background research into a

A full M.B.A. in the heart of downtown Toronto.

The Schlegel Centre for Entrepreneurship, Waterloo Campus.

country's economic, regulatory, and political environments. The experience culminates in a two-week international excursion to the region under investigation.

The Faculty

Faculty members at Laurier are committed to the interplay between teaching and research. The combination of current research and innovative teaching provides Laurier Business & Economics students with an engaging, dynamic environment that stimulates learning. It also provides industry partners with valuable competitive intelligence.

Laurier has one of the largest business and economics faculties in Canada and, with the establishment of specialized chairs, Laurier offers tremendous breadth and depth in research and teaching expertise. More than 135 full- and part-time faculty members publish and consult worldwide, bringing industry experience and a global perspective to the classroom. This strongly positions students for future business endeavours and teaches them to capitalize on new, relevant, and late-breaking business trends.

The Business School Network

Strong ties have been developed between Laurier and the corporate community. Whether through research centres, an Integrated Case Exercise, a Speaker Series, the M.B.A. Industry Dinner, or the Laurier Business Leader of the Year Award, Laurier provides students with opportunities to connect and build relationships with local, national, and international business leaders.

Students take advantage of the University's connections and partnerships when choosing applied research projects. For example, the Applied Business Research initiative provides students with an opportunity to apply the techniques they have learned in the classroom to solve practical strategic management issues. Students work in teams on a live consulting project that matches their skills and interests to a corporate client. Staff support is provided to assign the teams to their projects.

The College and Environs

Laurier has an ideal location in the hub of Canada's Technology Triangle, one of the most prosperous areas in the country, and just 1 hour west of metropolitan Toronto. Laurier's main campus is located in the city of Waterloo in the province of Ontario, Canada. The twin cities of Kitchener-Waterloo, with a combined population of approximately 300,000, are located 112 kilometers west of Toronto and 128 kilometers northwest of Niagara Falls. Residents of the region of Waterloo enjoy a rich cultural heritage, industry, and a high quality of life. Laurier's Toronto M.B.A. programs are presented at St. Andrews Club and Conference Centre (Sun Life Building), 150 King Street West (at University), 27th floor, Toronto.

Technology Environment

First-class computing facilities are provided through a voluntary student-funded organization. All labs are equipped with Pentium computers and have Internet access. The School also provides notebook computers for overnight/weekend sign out. The Schlegel Centre for Entrepreneurship offers a wireless network for M.B.A. students.

Placement

Career Services provides assistance to all students both on an individual and group basis. The services are part of students' activities from their first term through graduation and beyond (with the Alumni Referral Service). A graduate student employment adviser works directly with the graduate students to provide one-on-one and group assistance. The adviser also helps market Laurier's M.B.A. graduates to prospective employers.

Throughout the academic year, Career Services workshops are offered on a regular basis on topics such as resume writing, job search techniques, networking, and informational interviewing. Programs and special events are scheduled throughout the academic year. These include an annual M.B.A. Fair and Employer Information Sessions. Each fall and winter semester, representatives from business, industry, government, and social services visit the campus to interview students for permanent employment available following graduation.

Admission

Admission to the M.B.A. program is competitive and is based on the following criteria: a recognized four-year undergraduate degree (or its equivalent), with a minimum B average in the final year or most recent ten university degree courses of study (73 percent, a 3.0 GPA, or second-class honours); a minimum GMAT score of 550; full-time work experience (two years or its equivalent in a recognized co-op program); and three letters of reference (if the applicant's degree is less than five years old, one academic and two professional references are required). For students applying to the M.B.A. with co-op program, no work experience is required. Applicants to the M.B.A. with co-op must have completed a four-year undergraduate degree from a recognized institution, with a minimum B+ average in the final year or most recent ten university degree courses of study (77 percent, first-class honours), and have a minimum GMAT score of 600. For students whose undergraduate degree was conferred by a non-English-language institution, TOEFL (minimum score 573 paper-based or 230 computer-based test), IELTS (minimum score 7), MELAB (minimum score 90), or CAEL (minimum score 70) results are also required.

Finances

Tuition for the 2007–08 academic year was approximately Can$20,000 for both the one-year full-time and the ten-term part-time programs in Waterloo. Tuition for the M.B.A with co-op program was also Can$20,000 for the academic terms and approximately Can$1500 for the co-op work-term fees. Tuition costs for international full-time M.B.A. students were approximately Can$24,500. Student fees, books, case materials, and supplies for all students were approximately Can$6400 per year for full-time students and approximately Can$2135 per year for part-time students.

The total tuition for Laurier's Toronto M.B.A. program was Can$45,000, inclusive of materials, fees, and food. The total tuition for Laurier's Toronto M.B.A. with the CMA option was approximately Can$53,000, inclusive of CMA fees, and for the Toronto M.B.A. with the CFA option, Can$50,000, inclusive of materials and fees except for the CFA exam fees, which are paid directly to the CFA. All Laurier tuition fees are payable on an installment basis, three times per year.

Financial assistance is available to qualified applicants.

Application Facts and Dates

Application for the Waterloo-based programs should be received by May 1 for a fall start. Applications for the Toronto-based programs should be received by February 15 for a spring start. The international application deadline is January 30. For further information, students should contact:

Maureen Ferraro
M.B.A. Marketing Coordinator
School of Business & Economics
Wilfrid Laurier University
75 University Avenue West
Waterloo, Ontario N2L 3C5
Canada
Phone: 519-884-0710 Ext. 6220
Fax: 519-884-6016
E-mail: mferraro@wlu.ca
        wlumba@wlu.ca
Web site: http://www.wlu.ca/mba

Willamette University

Salem, Oregon

EMPOWER YOURSELF WITH THE EARLY CAREER M.B.A.

As a Willamette Early Career M.B.A. student, you will participate in an M.B.A. program noted for excellent teaching and experiential learning. You will have multiple opportunities to learn, "to do," and to build your resume of professional experience. While the distinct design of the Early Career M.B.A. develops the real-world experience and interpersonal skills sought by employers, the curriculum offers the added benefit of more choices—you can pursue your individual career goals in a variety of areas of management and prepare for careers in business, government, or not-for-profit enterprises.

—Debra J. Ringold, Interim Dean

Programs and Curricular Focus

Willamette University's Early Career M.B.A. program is specifically designed to prepare students for career entry or career change in a wide variety of industries and organizations. The program emphasizes experiential learning and builds the knowledge and real-world experience employers value. In just twenty-one months, students develop an in-depth understanding of management, refine their career goals, and build a resume of professional experience.

The curriculum is project based and cross-functional. From the first day of class, students learn the tools that support management decision making and apply what they learn to real organizations. Class consulting projects, internships, in-depth case studies, the Student Investment Fund, the Ethics in Business project, and the PaCE program (where teams of students serve as consultants for non-profit organizations, develop a plan for an entrepreneurial venture, and can start their own businesses) offer powerful opportunities for learning and professional development.

Elective areas of interest include accounting, finance, general management, human resources, information systems, international management, marketing, organizational analysis, public management, and quantitative analysis/management science.

A four-year M.B.A./J.D. joint degree program is available in cooperation with Willamette University's College of Law.

International exchange programs are also available with Copenhagen Business School (Denmark) and Bordeaux Business School (France).

Students and the M.B.A. Experience

Willamette Early Career M.B.A. students come from across the United States and around the world. The average student is 25 years of age

and has from zero to three years of full-time work experience. Forty percent of the students are women, and 60 percent are men. Thirty percent are international students, and 16 percent are members of minority groups. Undergraduate major areas of study include business, social science, liberal arts, economics, engineering, math, and science.

Willamette's size and collegial atmosphere facilitate a high degree of interaction between faculty members and students. The learning environment emphasizes excellent teaching, teamwork, and the practical application of knowledge. The program is demanding and requires 60 to 70 hours of academic work per week—but the rewards are life changing.

Special Features

The Early Career M.B.A. program is dually accredited for business and public administration. As one of only two M.B.A. programs in the world accredited for both business (AACSB International) and public administration (NASPAA), the Willamette Early Career M.B.A. prepares students for careers in business, government, and not-for-profit organizations.

Willamette is a national leader in early-career M.B.A. education. Willamette M.B.A. students build the knowledge and work experience they need to jump start their careers through internships, class consulting projects, leadership and networking opportunities, and a complete program of career services.

Professional organizations are available for students interested in accounting, finance, marketing, human resources, and public management. Other organizations include the international graduate student association, business women's forum, M.B.A./J.D. association, Beta Gamma Sigma (international honor society for management), and Pi Alpha Alpha (national honor society for public management).

The M.B.A. for Professionals is an evening M.B.A. program available in Portland and Sa-

lem for practicing managers with three or more years of work experience. Information about the M.B.A. for Professionals is available at http://www.willamette.edu/agsm/pmba/.

The Faculty

Willamette M.B.A. faculty members are excellent teachers who share an intense commitment to the academic and professional success of their students. One hundred percent of full-time M.B.A. faculty members have doctorate degrees, and all have professional work experience. They are also respected scholars, recipients of awards for outstanding teaching and research, leaders of professional and community organizations, authors of books and articles, and consultants to business and government organizations.

Three endowed faculty chairs (business, public policy, and international management) provide additional resources for faculty members to pursue teaching innovation and scholarly research.

The Business School Network
Corporate Partnerships

Interaction with leaders of business, government, and not-for-profit organizations is frequent and occurs through class projects, faculty/student consulting projects, internships, the visiting executive program, guest speakers, mentorship program, career services seminars, and company site visits.

Prominent Alumni

Willamette M.B.A. alumni work and succeed in exceptionally diverse settings, including sole proprietorships, mid-market companies, Fortune 500 companies, government entities, not-for-profits, and service firms. Employers describe alumni as down-to-earth communicators, approachable leaders, collaborative team players, and creative problem solvers who see the big picture of managerial issues.

Seventy percent of Willamette M.B.A. alumni live in the Pacific Northwest. Thirty percent are located elsewhere throughout the United States and internationally.

More information about alumni is available at the School's Web site.

The College and Environs

Willamette University is widely recognized for excellence and innovation in academic and professional education. Willamette is an independent coeducational university with a total of 2,500 students enrolled in the College of Liberal Arts (B.A.), College of Law (J.D.), Atkinson Graduate School of Management (M.B.A.), and School of Education (M.A.T.). The University was founded in 1842 and is located in Salem, Oregon. The Salem location offers an excellent quality of life, friendly people, mild climate, and quick access to the resources of the beautiful Pacific Northwest. Students can ski the Cascade Mountains, enjoy the beaches of the Pacific Ocean, hike the Willamette National Forest, windsurf the Columbia River Gorge, and enjoy the big-city excitement of Portland. Portland is recognized as one of the fastest-growing cities of highly educated people between the ages of 25 and 34, and is the home of Willamette University's new Portland Center and M.B.A. for Pro-

fessionals Program. Professionally, the Portland-Salem area provides easy access to a multitude of businesses, including Northwest legends Nike, Intel, and Tektronix, and hosts a variety of government and not-for-profit organizations.

Technology Environment

M.B.A. students are required to have a laptop computer with wireless LAN capability and a standard suite of software. Wireless access to the Internet, e-mail, and local network services are available 24 hours per day. The local network provides statistical database forecasting and other specialty software and printing services. University library resources include books, periodicals, journals, and specialized computerized information databases.

Placement

The Willamette M.B.A. offers a complete program of career services and places a high priority on career development. In fact, the school's Career Roadmap (a month-by-month program of the best practices of career management) is part of the required curriculum. Career services help students develop strategic career management skills, identify career opportunities, improve job search skills, interview and negotiate for salaries, and obtain internships and employment. Employers of recent graduates and interns include Columbia Sportswear; Ernst & Young; Gallup Organization; Hewlett Packard Company; Intel Corporation; KPMG; Mentor Graphics; Merrill Lynch; Microsoft Corporation; Morgan Stanley; Nike, Inc.; Moss Adams LLP; Nautilus; Nordstrom; Providence Health Systems; Russell Investments; State of Oregon; Tektronix, Inc.; the United Nations; and more.

Admission

The extensive real-world, experiential nature of Willamette's Early Career M.B.A. makes it an excellent choice for recent college graduates seeking their first professional position or career change. Admission is based on academic ability and managerial potential, and no work experience is required. All applicants must submit the online application form, essays, two letters of reference, official transcripts of all college/university course work, and an official GMAT or GRE score. An interview is part of the selection process.

Finances

Tuition for the Early Career M.B.A. program for the 2007–08 academic year was $25,200 ($12,600 per semester). Books/fees totaled approximately $1280. Living expenses ranged from $7400 to $11,355 per year, depending on personal lifestyle. Merit-based scholarships ranging from 25 percent to 100 percent of tuition and educational loans are available to qualified students.

International Students

With 30 percent of students coming from countries outside the United States, the Willamette M.B.A. provides a global environment for learning. Class teams represent a microcosm of the world marketplace and enhance understanding of management issues. International aspects of management are weaved throughout the curriculum, and elective courses in international management are available. The International Graduate Student Association (IGSA) serves the interests of students interested in international management, and the University's International Student Advisor assists international students with personal, social, cultural, and immigration-related questions.

Application Facts and Dates

Early Action applicants receive priority consideration for admission and scholarship assistance. Early action deadlines are January 11 and March 1. The final deadline is May 1. Students can apply online from Willamette's Web site at http://www.willamette.edu/mba. Applications are reviewed on a rolling basis. For further information, students should contact:

Director of Admission
Atkinson Graduate School of
    Management
Willamette University
Salem, Oregon 97301
Phone: 503-370-6167
            866-MBA-AGSM (toll-free in the
            U.S.)
Fax: 503-370-3011
E-mail: mba-admission@willamette.edu
Web site: http://www.willamette.edu/mba

Worcester Polytechnic Institute

Worcester, Massachusetts

THE MANAGEMENT OF TECHNOLOGY

At Worcester Polytechnic Institute (WPI), the integration of business and technology drives every aspect of our graduate management programs. We believe the future of management lies in leveraging the power of technology to optimize business opportunities. WPI stays ahead of the curve, giving students the knowledge to combine sound strategies with cutting-edge innovation and the confidence to contribute meaningfully within a global competitive environment.

Our location in the heart of New England's high-tech corridor and our outstanding facilities, dedicated faculty members, and superior record of our graduates' successes highlight why WPI enjoys a nationally recognized reputation as one of the most respected names in technology-based management education.

—McRae C. Banks, Professor of Management and Department Head

Programs and Curricular Focus

Worcester Polytechnic Institute offers a variety of graduate management programs focusing on the intersection of business and technology. WPI's Master of Business Administration (M.B.A.) program (49 credits) is a highly integrated, applications-oriented M.B.A. that provides students with both the big-picture perspective required of successful upper-level managers and the hands-on knowledge needed to meet the daily demands in the workplace. WPI's focus on managing technology comes from the recognition that rapidly changing technology is driving the pace of business.

Students enjoy extensive opportunities to expand their networks through associations with their peers and leading high-tech organizations. They also benefit from the latest available technologies and an institution that is one of the nation's most wired universities. The program's strong emphasis on interpersonal and communications skills prepares students to be leaders in any organization, while the global threads throughout the curriculum ensure that students understand the global imperative facing all businesses. Whether dealing with information technology, biotechnology, financial markets, information security, supply-chain management, manufacturing, or a host of other technology-oriented industries, the real world is part of the classroom, and students explore up-to-the-minute challenges faced by actual companies through hands-on projects and teamwork. WPI promotes an active learning process designed to develop the very best managers, leaders, and executives in a technology-dependent world.

WPI's M.B.A. program features a 15-credit core of five cross-functional courses designed to give students a larger framework for understanding disciplinary material that is critical for managers in a globally competitive technological world. Core courses include Interpersonal and Leadership Skills for Technological Managers, Creating and Implementing Strategy in Technological Organizations, Designing Processes for Technological Organizations, Business Analysis for Technological Managers, and Legal and Ethical Context of Technological Organizations. Most of the core courses have prerequisite requirements from within an 18-credit foundation. The purpose of the foundation is to ensure that students have a solid understanding of the basic functions carried out in organizations and of the environment in which they operate as well as an introduction to the tools used to analyze business problems. Foundation courses consist of the following nine 2-credit courses, each of which covers a major functional area of business: Financial Accounting, Finance, Organizational Behavior, Operations Management, Quantitative Methods, Principles of Marketing, Management Information Systems, Economics of the Firm, and Domestic and Global Economic Environment of Business. Foundation-level courses are potentially waivable, based on prior graduate or undergraduate course work.

The M.B.A. program also features a capstone Graduate Qualifying Project (GQP), which provides students with a hands-on, real-world opportunity to apply and enhance their classroom experience.

M.B.A. students are required to complete 12 credit hours of free elective course work. Elective concentration areas include entrepreneurship, information security management, information technology, operations management, process design, supply chain management, technological innovation, and technology marketing. In addition, students may choose a 6-credit option for specialization, which requires 6 additional credits in a particular functional area in combination with at least 6 credits of the free electives in the chosen area.

WPI also offers three highly specialized Master of Science (M.S.) programs specifically designed for individuals seeking advanced academic training in a particular area: the M.S. in Information Technology (35 credits), the M.S. in Marketing and Technological Innovation (32 credits), and the M.S. in Operations Design and Leadership (35 credits).

All graduate management degree programs provide internship, thesis, and independent study options. Part-time students typically complete the M.B.A. program in three to four years, dependent upon prior academic background, whereas full-time students typically complete the M.B.A. program in two years. An M.S. degree program is typically completed in two to three years part-time or 1 ½ years full-time.

Students and the M.B.A. Experience

Approximately 240 students are currently enrolled in WPI's graduate management programs. The majority are working professionals pursuing their degrees part-time in the evening. WPI students average seven years of prior full-time work experience when they commence their programs. Many students are practicing managers from the region's leading high-technology employers, including Bose, EMC, Intel, Raytheon, Staples, and United Technologies. This creates a dynamic peer-to-peer educational experience and also presents outstanding networking opportunities. Students bring to class their backgrounds in, among others, the computer, electronics, biotechnology, machine tool, chemical, software, and defense industries, facilitating in-class discussions grounded in real-world experience.

Students choose WPI for its practical, hands-on approach to management that provides them with an environment where they can develop and practice their ideas. Students frequently cite the immediate benefits of their WPI education in their daily work and place great value on the relevance of their classroom experience.

Twenty-two countries are represented in WPI's graduate management programs.

Women make up 30 percent of the student population; students range in age from 21 to 55, with an average age of 32.

Special Features

Tailored to meet the challenges of working professionals, WPI offers full- and part-time graduate management study at its campus in Worcester, Massachusetts, as well as worldwide online via its Advanced Distance Learning Network (ADLN).

WPI is a leader in high-quality distance learning. The entire M.B.A. curriculum has been available via distance learning since 1979, making WPI one of the first universities in the U.S. to deliver a distance M.B.A. An M.B.A. earned through ADLN is equivalent to one earned on campus in both its content and its value in the job market. Online M.B.A. students fully participate in all aspects of each course, including case discussions, team projects, and project presentations. Through the use of the Blackboard course management and communication tool, ADLN students receive course materials online and interact with their professors and fellow students, both on campus and off, via chat rooms, shared whiteboards, and discussion forums. Students may complete all or part of the M.B.A. programs via ADLN. There is no on-campus residency requirement.

The Faculty

The WPI management faculty is dedicated to academic excellence through scholarship and teaching. Faculty members approach the study of management from both theoretical and applications-oriented perspectives and use the classroom as a forum for exploring traditional management principles and practices and current management topics. Case studies, lectures, discussions, and computer simulations all contribute to a stimulating and challenging instructional program.

In addition to teaching, the Department of Management's faculty members are involved in a variety of sponsored research and consulting work covering a wide spectrum of topics. Particular strength may be found in the following areas: information quality, organizational impacts of enterprise systems, Web accessibility, data envelopment analysis, supply-chain management, lean manufacturing, organizational innovation, and the emerging field of organizational aesthetics.

The Business School Network
Prominent Alumni

Students enjoy a strong alumni network. Prominent WPI alumni include Paul Allaire, former chairman and CEO, Xerox Corporation; Judith Nitsch, Judith Nitsch Engineering, Inc.; Windle Priem, president and CEO, Korn/Ferry International; and Stephen Rubin, president and CEO, Intellution, Inc.

The College and Environs

WPI is set on an 80-acre hilltop campus in a residential section of Worcester, Massachusetts, a city of 176,000. Located in the heart of New England, Worcester is the third-largest city in the six-state region. WPI is located near many national and international businesses and industries and enjoys close working relationships with a number of major firms.

Worcester is well known for its many colleges and for such cultural centers as the Worcester Art Museum, which houses one of the finest collections in the country, and the world-renowned American Antiquarian Society, both of which are adjacent to WPI. Also nearby are the historic Higgins Armory Museum, the Worcester Center for Crafts, and the New England Science Center. Music is well represented by several excellent choruses, a symphony orchestra, and concerts performed by internationally recognized artists in the beautifully restored Mechanics Hall, one of the finest concert halls in the U.S. The city is home to several theater companies, and the 15,500-seat DCU Center and the Worcester Convention Center host a wide variety of entertainment events and meetings.

The city is within an easy drive of many historical sites, cultural centers, and recreational facilities. These include Boston's Freedom Trail, Old Sturbridge Village (a living museum depicting 1830s village life), the beaches of Cape Cod and Maine, the ski slopes of New Hampshire and Vermont, the splendid country charm of the Berkshires, and several major metropolitan areas that feature world-class museums, concert halls, and professional sports teams.

Facilities

Computing services at WPI include powerful Unix workstations, high-performance computing, electronic classrooms, a campuswide high-speed data network, high-speed Internet connections, extensive roaming wireless coverage that lets students with wireless-enabled laptops or PDAs to work "unplugged," and a Web-based information system. WPI is also one of only about 200 universities in the United States that is connected to Internet2; it built and operates the Goddard GigaPop, one of only 29 in the nation. The speed and reliability of Internet2 allow WPI faculty and students to do remarkable things that will transform research and education at WPI.

Gordon Library is home to more than 275,000 bound volumes and subscribes to more than 2,200 periodicals, supporting all graduate areas. The library provides online search services to hundreds of databases, interlibrary loan services, technical support, Internet access, CD-ROM databases, and a variety of other research and support services.

Placement

The services of WPI's Career Development Center (CDC) are available to all WPI students and alumni. In a typical year, recruiters from more than 250 organizations, including large and small business firms, government, and civic and professional organizations, visit the campus. The CDC maintains a large reference library for WPI students and alumni. The CDC is also involved in on-campus recruiting, hotline job listings, resume referral, and corporate presentations. The average starting salary for M.B.A. graduates is $92,000.

Admission

Admission to WPI's graduate management programs is competitive. Admission is granted to applicants whose academic and professional records indicate the likelihood of success in a challenging academic program and whose career aspirations are in line with the focus of the program.

Applicants should have the analytic aptitude and academic preparation necessary to complete a technology-oriented management program. This includes a minimum of three semesters of college-level math or two semesters of college-level calculus. Applicants are also required to have an understanding of computer systems.

Current students have an average GMAT score of 620 and an average undergraduate GPA of 3.35. The minimum TOEFL requirement is 213.

Finances

The estimated tuition and fees for full-time graduate students are $33,000 per academic year. Books and supplies average $800 per year. Local apartment rentals average $750 per month. The 2008–09 tuition rate is $1089 per credit hour.

A limited number of assistantships are available for full-time students. Students should contact the Director of Graduate Management Programs for details.

Application Facts and Dates

Applicants are required to submit a formal application, a nonrefundable $70 application fee (waived for WPI alumni), official transcripts of all college work, three letters of recommendation, a resume, a GMAT score report (GRE may be substituted for M.S. applicants), and a TOEFL score if applicable. Applicants are accepted on a rolling admissions basis. Applicants should contact:

Norman D. Wilkinson, Director of
 Graduate Management Programs
Worcester Polytechnic Institute
100 Institute Road
Worcester, Massachusetts 01609

Phone: 508-831-5218
Fax: 508-831-5720
E-mail: gmp@wpi.edu
Web site: http://www.mgt.wpi.edu/
 Graduate/

York University

> **GLOBAL FOCUS. INNOVATIVE PROGRAMMING. DIVERSE PERSPECTIVES.**
>
> *Business today is global—your M.B.A. degree should be too. At Schulich, you will join a select group of men and women with diverse backgrounds and proven leadership ability. They are bright, accomplished, and ambitious. Make no mistake, you will be challenged here—challenged by our award-winning faculty, by the rigor and intensity of our programs, by the drive and passion of your classmates. Our mission here at Schulich is clear and compelling: to graduate men and women who will become business leaders of the highest calibre and to prepare them to succeed in a constantly changing world.*
>
> —Dezsö J. Horváth, Dean

Programs and Curricular Focus

Schulich is transforming business education through its global thinking. At York University's Schulich School of Business, students have unparalleled choice, flexible programming, and countless ways to meet changing career needs and lifestyle demands through its innovative programs. Students can choose a Master of Business Administration (M.B.A.), International Master of Business Administration (I.M.B.A.), Master of Finance (M.F.), joint Kellogg-Schulich Executive M.B.A. (E.M.B.A.), M.B.A./Bachelor of Laws (M.B.A./L.L.B.), M.B.A./Master of Fine Arts/ Master of Arts (M.B.A./M.F.A./M.A.), Master of Public Administration (M.P.A.), or Ph.D. in Administration.

The Schulich M.B.A. curriculum combines academic rigour with real-world relevance. It provides action-learning opportunities to develop critical qualitative skills. In Year 1, the program provides a solid grounding in management fundamentals. In Year 2, it offers numerous opportunities to specialize in management functions, industry sectors, and issues such as sustainability and corporate social responsibility. Students can study year-round and complete the Schulich M.B.A. in just sixteen months. Those with an approved B.B.A. or B.C.O.M. degree and two years of postdegree work experience may qualify for the Schulich Accelerated M.B.A. (eight months in length). In Schulich's six-month capstone Strategy Field Study, student teams develop a comprehensive strategic consulting project for real-world organizations.

Schulich's I.M.B.A. is the ideal choice for students who want to launch a global career or grow an existing one. The program is designed for a borderless world, and allows students to broaden their horizons and push personal and geographic boundaries. Students leverage their Canadian and international experience by specializing in global trading regions as well as work and study abroad. As a result, second-language skills become a competitive advantage. The Schulich I.M.B.A. offers a balanced program of formal study and firsthand real-world experience, including a four-month term abroad working in an international language.

Students and the M.B.A. Experience

"Be involved. Be active." That is a recurring message in the advice given by Schulich students. "Get involved with the Schulich community. Get involved with student causes and social functions. Get involved with recruiting events. Take advantage of countless opportunities to enrich formal in-class learning with extracurricular activities." Schulich alumni often say that in terms of academic value, Schulich offers excellent education, and what students do outside the classroom contributes in making the Schulich M.B.A. priceless. It is these extracurricular activities that help build lifelong friendships and create those treasured memories that last a lifetime.

The average Schulich student is 29 years old. Of the entire Schulich student body, 37 percent are women, 73 percent carry two passports, nearly 57 percent are international, and each student has an average of more than six years of work experience. According to the 2008 *Financial Times* (of London) M.B.A. ranking, Schulich is the most internationally diverse school in North America.

Special Features

Students love the choice and flexibility offered by Schulich. At Schulich, students can choose what to study, when to study, and where to study. Students can select from more than 100 courses and eighteen different specialized streams. These include management functions such as accounting, economics, finance, marketing, operations management and information systems, organizations, and strategic management; industry sectors such as arts and media administration, financial engineering, financial services, health-industry management, nonprofit management and leadership, public sector management and real estate and infrastructure; and special management topics such as business and sustainability, business consulting, entrepreneurial studies, and international business.

The Faculty

Schulich faculty members are leading scholars from the world's top universities and are passionate about their chosen fields, dedicated to their students, and committed to award-winning research. As pioneers in areas such as risk management, business and sustainability, global marketing, and entrepreneurism, they draw on their research findings to enrich every class. Many professors are also working practitioners and believe that a combination of active and interactive learning leads to the most effective teaching process. Schulich faculty members draw on a range of pedagogical approaches, including lectures, group work, case studies, simulations, and real-world projects.

The Business School Network
Corporate Partnerships

Schulich's location in Toronto, the financial, business, and cultural centre of Canada and one of the world's great multicultural cities, gives access to head offices of many organizations, which has allowed Schulich to build strong linkages to the corporate community. A number of the country's leading executives act as advisers on Schulich's board, teach in the classrooms, and provide guidance and counsel to students.

The Dean's Advisory Council, Dean's International Advisory Council, and nine other advisory boards, consisting of close to 200 distinguished CEOs, leading academics, and senior government representatives, offer advice and networks to support strategic planning for Schulich programs and countless mentorship and networking opportunities for Schulich students.

The College and Environs

Location is important in choosing a business school. Toronto, the most culturally and ethnically diverse city in Canada, gives Schu-

The Schulich School of Business and Executive Learning Centre.

lich students great benefits. As Schulich is situated in the cultural and entertainment capital of Canada with numerous parks, restaurants, and recreational activities, Schulich students are able to work and play hard.

Facilities

Students can choose to attend classes in Schulich's state-of-the-art $104-million home on York's main campus or in the heart of Toronto's financial district at King and Bay, in the Miles S. Nadal Management Centre. York University houses five libraries with considerable resources, including a book collection of more than 2.5 million volumes and more than 205,000 serials (periodicals, magazines, reports and digests, collections of microfiche, maps, videos, films, sound recordings, compact discs, and databases). In addition, Schulich has one of the best business reference collections in metropolitan Toronto.

Technology Environment

Schulich is a completely wireless facility. Students have access to a number of computer labs and desktop computers in Schulich's business library. All classrooms are designed to facilitate the use of laptops and are equipped with state-of-the-art LCD projectors and audio-visual equipment. Schulich offers students full computing services, including user, technical, Web, and application services.

Placement

Part of the Schulich advantage is to accelerate career opportunities. At Schulich, career management is a lifetime investment. Schulich's Career Development Centre works closely with students to identify career choices and objectives, develop a proactive career plan, and hone skill sets. Students can take advantage of the training, counseling expertise, and networking opportunities. Schulich boasts that 91 percent of graduates land their first job offer within three months of graduation. Schulich alumni are among award recipients in the Caldwell Partner's national program that honours Canadians under the age of 40 who have reached a significant level of success. Schulich M.B.A. graduates

are recruited by leading world-class companies such as Amex, CIBC, Ernst & Young, General Mills, IBM, Imperial Oil, Microsoft, Pfizer, Proctor and Gamble, RBC, Scotiabank, TD Canada Trust, and Telus.

Admission

Students must have an undergraduate degree from a recognized university, with a minimum B average in the last two full years of study, acceptable scores on all GMAT measures (not required for the E.M.B.A.), and at least two years of full-time work or life experience (postundergraduate degree). Schulich also looks for leadership qualities, communication skills, creativity, and innovation. Nonbaccalaureate candidates must have at least eight years of high-quality management experience and must have demonstrated a strong upward progression in their careers.

Finances

Schulich offers a large number of bursaries, scholarships, and awards to domestic and international students. Students may also apply for graduate and teaching assistantships. Students pay fees each semester according to whether they are enrolled on a full-time or part-time basis. The 2008–09 full-time tuition is approximately $11,000 per term for Canadian residents and $15,000 per term for nonresidents. Tuition for the entire two-year Executive M.B.A. is $100,000 for both Canadian and international students. On-campus housing is available at reasonable rates. Travel and personal expenses vary with each student but range from $6500 to $7100 per semester. All costs are in Canadian dollars.

Application Facts and Dates

Application deadlines for M.B.A., I.M.B.A., and M.P.A. programs are February 1 (to be first considered for scholarships and for all international students) and May 1 (domestic students) for the fall term. For the winter term, the deadlines are September 1 (international students) and October 1 (domestic students). For the summer term, the deadline is February 1 (domestic part-time students only). There are two application deadlines for the joint M.B.A./L.L.B. program that begins in September: the law application is due November 1 and the M.B.A. application is due May 1. The E.M.B.A. offers January admission only. The application deadline for the Ph.D. (fall only) program is January 15.

Division of Student Services and
    International Relations
Schulich School of Business
York University
4700 Keele Street
Toronto, Ontario M3J 1P3
Canada
Phone: 416-736-5059
Fax: 416-650-8174
E-mail:
    intladmissions@schulich.yorku.ca
Web site: http://www.schulich.yorku.ca

INDEXES

Areas of Concentration

In this index the page locations of the **Profiles** are printed in regular type, **Profiles** with **Announcements** in *italic* type, and **Close-Ups** in **bold** type.

ACCOUNTING

Abilene Christian University, College of Business Administration, Abilene (TX) 404

American Jewish University, David Lieber School of Graduate Studies, Bel Air (CA) 63

American University, Kogod School of Business, Washington (DC) 118

Angelo State University, Department of Management and Marketing, San Angelo (TX) 405

Anna Maria College, Program in Business Administration, Paxton (MA) 219

Antioch University New England, Department of Organization and Management, Keene (NH) 277

Appalachian State University, John A. Walker College of Business, Boone (NC) 322

Argosy University, Atlanta, College of Business, Atlanta (GA) 141, **566**

Argosy University, Chicago, College of Business, Chicago (IL) 158, **566**

Argosy University, Denver, College of Business, Denver (CO) 100, **566**

Argosy University, Hawai'i, College of Business, Honolulu (HI) 153, **566**

Argosy University, Inland Empire, College of Business, San Bernardino (CA) 65, **566**

Argosy University, Los Angeles, College of Business, Santa Monica (CA) 65, **566**

Argosy University, Nashville, College of Business, Nashville (TN) 395, **566**

Argosy University, Orange County, College of Business, Santa Ana (CA) 65, **566**

Argosy University, Phoenix, College of Business, Phoenix (AZ) 54, **566**

Argosy University, Salt Lake City, College of Business, Draper (UT) 430, **566**

Argosy University, San Diego, College of Business, San Diego (CA) 65, **566**

Argosy University, San Francisco Bay Area, College of Business, Alameda (CA) 66, **566**

Argosy University, Sarasota, College of Business, Sarasota (FL) 122, **566**

Argosy University, Schaumburg, College of Business, Schaumburg (IL) 158, **566**

Argosy University, Seattle, College of Business, Seattle (WA) 447, **566**

Argosy University, Tampa, College of Business, Tampa (FL) 122, **566**

Argosy University, Twin Cities, College of Business, Eagan (MN) 248, **566**

Argosy University, Washington DC, College of Business, Arlington (VA) 436, **566**

Arizona State University, W.P. Carey School of Business, Tempe (AZ) 54

Arizona State University at the West campus, School of Global Management and Leadership, Phoenix (AZ) 55

Arkansas State University, College of Business, Jonesboro (AR) 61

Ashridge, Ashridge Executive MBA Program, Berkhamsted (United Kingdom) 538

Assumption College, Department of Business Studies, Worcester (MA) 219

Aston University, Aston Business School, Birmingham (United Kingdom) 539

Auburn University Montgomery, School of Business, Montgomery (AL) 46

Aurora University, Dunham School of Business, Aurora (IL) 158

Avila University, School of Business, Kansas City (MO) 258

Baker College Center for Graduate Studies, Graduate Programs, Flint (MI) 236, **572**

Baldwin-Wallace College, Division of Business, Berea (OH) 337

Barry University, Andreas School of Business, Miami Shores (FL) 123

Bellevue University, College of Business, Bellevue (NE) 271, **576**

Belmont University, Jack C. Massey Graduate School of Business, Nashville (TN) 395

Benedictine College, Executive Master of Business Administration Program, Atchison (KS) 193

Benedictine University, Graduate Programs, Lisle (IL) 158

Bentley College, The Elkin B. McCallum Graduate School of Business, Waltham (MA) 221, **578**

Bernard M. Baruch College of the City University of New York, Zicklin School of Business, New York (NY) 296

Boise State University, College of Business and Economics, Boise (ID) 155

Bond University, School of Business, Gold Coast (Australia) 483

Boston College, The Carroll School of Management, Chestnut Hill (MA) 221, **580**

Bowling Green State University, College of Business Administration, Bowling Green (OH) 338

Bradley University, Foster College of Business Administration, Peoria (IL) 159

Brandeis University, International Business School, Waltham (MA) 224, **582**

Brenau University, School of Business and Mass Communication, Gainesville (GA) 143

Brigham Young University, Marriott School of Management, Provo (UT) 431

Brock University, Faculty of Business, St. Catharines (Canada) 466

Butler University, College of Business Administration, Indianapolis (IN) 180

Caldwell College, Program in Business Administration, Caldwell (NJ) 281

California National University for Advanced Studies, College of Business Administration, Northridge (CA) 67

California Polytechnic State University, San Luis Obispo, Orfalea College of Business, San Luis Obispo (CA) 68

California State University, East Bay, College of Business and Economics, Hayward (CA) 69

California State University, Fullerton, College of Business and Economics, Fullerton (CA) 70

California State University, Long Beach, College of Business Administration, Long Beach (CA) 71

California State University, Los Angeles, College of Business and Economics, Los Angeles (CA) 71

California State University, Sacramento, College of Business Administration, Sacramento (CA) 72

California State University, San Bernardino, College of Business and Public Administration, San Bernardino (CA) 73

Canisius College, Richard J. Wehle School of Business, Buffalo (NY) 296

Carnegie Mellon University, Tepper School of Business, Pittsburgh (PA) 363, **584**

Case Western Reserve University, Weatherhead School of Management, Cleveland (OH) 338

Central Queensland University, Faculty of Business and Informatics, Rockhampton (Australia) 483

Charleston Southern University, Program in Business, Charleston (SC) 390

The Chinese University of Hong Kong, Faculty of Business Administration, Hong Kong (China) 497

Christian Brothers University, School of Business, Memphis (TN) 396

City University of Hong Kong, Faculty of Business, Hong Kong (China) 497

Clarion University of Pennsylvania, College of Business Administration, Clarion (PA) 364

Clark Atlanta University, School of Business Administration, Atlanta (GA) 143

Clark University, Graduate School of Management, Worcester (MA) 224, **592**

Cleary University, Program in Business Administration, Ann Arbor (MI) 236

Clemson University, College of Business and Behavioral Science, Clemson (SC) 391

Cleveland State University, Nance College of Business Administration, Cleveland (OH) 340

College of Charleston, School of Business and Economics, Charleston (SC) 391

College of St. Catherine, Program in Organizational Leadership, St. Paul (MN) 249

The College of Saint Rose, School of Business, Albany (NY) 298, **594**

Colorado State University, College of Business, Fort Collins (CO) 101, **596**

Columbia Union College, MBA Program, Takoma Park (MD) 213

Columbia University, Graduate School of Business, New York (NY) 298

Copenhagen Business School, Faculty of Economics and Business Administration, Copenhagen (Denmark) 501

Dallas Baptist University, Graduate School of Business, Dallas (TX) 406

Davenport University, Sneden Graduate School, Grand Rapids (MI) 237

Deakin University, Deakin Business School, Geelong (Australia) 484

Delta State University, College of Business, Cleveland (MS) 254

DePaul University, Charles H. Kellstadt Graduate School of Business, Chicago (IL) 159

DeSales University, Department of Business, Center Valley (PA) 365

DeVry University, Keller Graduate School of Management, Phoenix (AZ) 56

DeVry University, Keller Graduate School of Management, Fremont (CA) 76

DeVry University, Keller Graduate School of Management, Long Beach (CA) 76

DeVry University, Keller Graduate School of Management, Palmdale (CA) 76

DeVry University, Keller Graduate School of Management, Pomona (CA) 77

DeVry University, Keller Graduate School of Management, San Diego (CA) 77

DeVry University, Keller Graduate School of Management, Colorado Springs (CO) 102

DeVry University, Keller Graduate School of Management, Miami (FL) 124

DeVry University, Keller Graduate School of Management, Miramar (FL) 124

DeVry University, Keller Graduate School of Management, Orlando (FL) 124

DeVry University, Keller Graduate School of Management, Tampa (FL) 124

DeVry University, Keller Graduate School of Management, Alpharetta (GA) 144

DeVry University, Keller Graduate School of Management, Atlanta (GA) 144

DeVry University, Keller Graduate School of Management, Decatur (GA) 144

DeVry University, Keller Graduate School of Management, Duluth (GA) 145

DeVry University, Keller Graduate School of Management, Elgin (IL) 160

DeVry University, Keller Graduate School of Management, Gurnee (IL) 161

DeVry University, Keller Graduate School of Management, Lincolnshire (IL) 161

DeVry University, Keller Graduate School of Management, Oakbrook Terrace (IL) 161, **650**

DeVry University, Keller Graduate School of Management, Schaumburg (IL) 162

DeVry University, Keller Graduate School of Management, Tinley Park (IL) 162

DeVry University, Keller Graduate School of Management (IN) 180

DeVry University, Keller Graduate School of Management, Merrillville (IN) 180

DeVry University, Keller Graduate School of Management, Kansas City (MO) 259

DeVry University, Keller Graduate School of Management, St. Louis (MO) 259

DeVry University, Keller Graduate School of Management (NV) 275

DeVry University, Keller Graduate School of Management (NC) 323

DeVry University, Keller Graduate School of Management, Columbus (OH) 341

DeVry University, Keller Graduate School of Management, Seven Hills (OH) 341

DeVry University, Keller Graduate School of Management (OR) 356

DeVry University, Keller Graduate School of Management (PA) 365

DeVry University, Keller Graduate School of Management, Fort Washington (PA) 365

DeVry University, Keller Graduate School of Management, Pittsburgh (PA) 365

DeVry University, Keller Graduate School of Management (TX) 406

DeVry University, Keller Graduate School of Management, Irving (TX) 407

DeVry University, Keller Graduate School of Management, Arlington (VA) 437

DeVry University, Keller Graduate School of Management, McLean (VA) 437

DeVry University, Keller Graduate School of Management, Bellevue (WA) 447

DeVry University, Keller Graduate School of Management, Federal Way (WA) 448

Dominican University, Edward A. and Lois L. Brennan School of Business, River Forest (IL) 162, **600**

Drake University, College of Business and Public Administration, Des Moines (IA) 189

Drexel University, LeBow College of Business, Philadelphia (PA) 366

Drury University, Breech School of Business Administration, Springfield (MO) 259

Duke University, The Fuqua School of Business, Durham (NC) 323

Duquesne University, John F. Donahue Graduate School of Business, Pittsburgh (PA) 367

Eastern Illinois University, Lumpkin College of Business and Applied Sciences, Charleston (IL) 163

Eastern Kentucky University, College of Business and Technology, Richmond (KY) 199

Eastern Mennonite University, Program in Business Administration, Harrisonburg (VA) 438

Eastern Michigan University, College of Business, Ypsilanti (MI) 237

Eastern University, Graduate Business Programs, St. Davids (PA) 368

Eastern Washington University, College of Business and Public Administration, Cheney (WA) 448

East Tennessee State University, College of Business and Technology, Johnson City (TN) 396

Edgewood College, Program in Business, Madison (WI) 458

Edith Cowan University, Faculty of Business and Public Management, Churchlands (Australia) 484

Elmhurst College, Program in Business Administration, Elmhurst (IL) 163

Emory University, Roberto C. Goizueta Business School, Atlanta (GA) 145, **606**

Emporia State University, School of Business, Emporia (KS) 193

European University, Center for Management Studies, Montreux-Fontanivent (Switzerland) 532

Everest University, Graduate School of Business, Clearwater (FL) 126

Everest University, Program in Business Administration, Lakeland (FL) 126

Everest University, Program in Business Administration, Orlando (FL) 126

Fairfield University, Charles F. Dolan School of Business, Fairfield (CT) 109

Fairleigh Dickinson University, College at Florham, Silberman College of Business, Madison (NJ) 282, **612**

Fairleigh Dickinson University, Metropolitan Campus, Silberman College of Business, Teaneck (NJ) 282, **612**

Felician College, Program in Business, Lodi (NJ) 283, **614**

Fitchburg State College, Division of Graduate and Continuing Education, Fitchburg (MA) 225

Florida Atlantic University, College of Business, Boca Raton (FL) 126

Florida International University, Alvah H. Chapman, Jr. Graduate School of Business, Miami (FL) 128, **618**

Florida State University, College of Business, Tallahassee (FL) 129

Fontbonne University, Department of Business Administration, St. Louis (MO) 260

Fordham University, Graduate School of Business Administration, New York (NY) 301, **620**

Franciscan University of Steubenville, Department of Business, Steubenville (OH) 341

Frostburg State University, College of Business, Frostburg (MD) 213

Gannon University, School of Business, Erie (PA) 368

Gardner-Webb University, Graduate School of Business, Boiling Springs (NC) 325

George Mason University, School of Management, Fairfax (VA) 438

The George Washington University, School of Business, Washington (DC) 119, **622**

Georgia College & State University, The J. Whitney Bunting School of Business, Milledgeville (GA) 145

Georgia Institute of Technology, College of Management, Atlanta (GA) 146, **624**

Georgia Southern University, College of Business Administration, Statesboro (GA) 146

Georgia State University, J. Mack Robinson College of Business, Atlanta (GA) 147, **626**

Golden Gate University, Ageno School of Business, San Francisco (CA) 78

Gonzaga University, School of Business Administration, Spokane (WA) 448

Governors State University, College of Business and Public Administration, University Park (IL) 164

Graduate School of Business Administration Zurich, Executive Management Programs, Zurich (Switzerland) 532

Grand Canyon University, College of Business, Phoenix (AZ) 56

Grand Valley State University, Seidman College of Business, Allendale (MI) 238

The Hague University, Faculty of Economics and Management, The Hague (Netherlands) 521, **628**

Harding University, College of Business Administration, Searcy (AR) 61

Hawai'i Pacific University, College of Business Administration, Honolulu (HI) 153, **630**

HEC Paris, HEC MBA Program, Jouy-en-Josas (France) *505*, **632**

HfB—Business School of Finance and Management, Frankfurt School of Finance and Management, Frankfurt (Germany) 508

HHL—Leipzig Graduate School of Management, MBA Program, Leipzig (Germany) 509

Hofstra University, Frank G. Zarb School of Business, Hempstead (NY) 302

Hong Kong Baptist University, School of Business, Hong Kong (China) 498

Hood College, Department of Economics and Management, Frederick (MD) 214

Howard University, School of Business, Washington (DC) 120

Hult International Business School, Graduate Program, Cambridge (MA) *227*, **634**

Idaho State University, College of Business, Pocatello (ID) 156

IE Business School, Business School, Madrid (Spain) 529, **636**

Illinois State University, College of Business, Normal (IL) 165, **638**

Indiana State University, College of Business, Terre Haute (IN) 181

Indiana Tech, Program in Business Administration, Fort Wayne (IN) 181

Indiana University Bloomington, Kelley School of Business, Bloomington (IN) 182

Indiana University–Purdue University Indianapolis, Kelley School of Business, Indianapolis (IN) 184

Indiana University South Bend, School of Business and Economics, South Bend (IN) 184

Indian School of Business, MBA Program, Andhra Pradesh (India) 512

Inter American University of Puerto Rico, San Germán Campus, Department of Business Administration, San Germán (PR) 385

International University in Geneva, MBA Program, Geneva (Switzerland) 533, **640**

International University of Japan, Graduate School of International Management, Minami Uonuma-gu (Japan) 516

Iona College, Hagan School of Business, New Rochelle (NY) 303, **642**

Iowa State University of Science and Technology, College of Business, Ames (IA) 189, **644**

Ithaca College, School of Business, Ithaca (NY) 303

Jackson State University, School of Business, Jackson (MS) 255

Jacksonville State University, College of Commerce and Business Administration, Jacksonville (AL) 47

James Cook University, Faculty of Law, Business, and the Creative Arts—Townsville, Cairns (Australia) 485

John Carroll University, John M. and Mary Jo Boler School of Business, University Heights (OH) 342

Johnson & Wales University, The Alan Shawn Feinstein Graduate School, Providence (RI) 388, **648**

Jones International University, Graduate School of Business Administration, Centennial (CO) 103

Kansas State University, College of Business Administration, Manhattan (KS) 194

Kean University, College of Business and Public Administration, Union (NJ) 284

Kennesaw State University, Michael J. Coles College of Business, Kennesaw (GA) 148

Kent State University, Graduate School of Management, Kent (OH) 342

Kingston University, Kingston Business School, Kingston upon Thames (United Kingdom) 541

Lakeland College, Graduate Studies Division, Sheboygan (WI) 459

Lamar University, College of Business, Beaumont (TX) 408

Lancaster University, Management School, Lancaster (United Kingdom) 541

La Salle University, School of Business, Philadelphia (PA) 370

Lehigh University, College of Business and Economics, Bethlehem (PA) 371, **656**

Lenoir-Rhyne College, Charles M. Snipes School of Business, Hickory (NC) 326

Lewis University, College of Business, Romeoville (IL) 166

Liberty University, School of Business, Lynchburg (VA) 439

Lincoln University, College of Business and Professional Studies (MO) 260

Lindenwood University, Division of Management, St. Charles (MO) 261

Lipscomb University, MBA Program, Nashville (TN) 397

London School of Economics and Political Science, The Graduate School, London (United Kingdom) 543

Long Island University, Brooklyn Campus, School of Business, Public Administration and Information Sciences, Brooklyn (NY) 304

Long Island University, C.W. Post Campus, College of Management, Brookville (NY) 305

Louisiana State University and Agricultural and Mechanical College, E. J. Ourso College of Business, Baton Rouge (LA) 204

Louisiana Tech University, College of Administration and Business, Ruston (LA) 205

Loyola College in Maryland, Sellinger School of Business and Management, Baltimore (MD) 215

Loyola Marymount University, College of Business Administration, Los Angeles (CA) 81

Loyola University Chicago, Graduate School of Business, Chicago (IL) 167

Marquette University, Graduate School of Management, Milwaukee (WI) 459

Maryville University of Saint Louis, The John E. Simon School of Business, St. Louis (MO) 262

McMaster University, DeGroote School of Business, Hamilton (Canada) 470

McNeese State University, College of Business, Lake Charles (LA) 206

Mercy College, Division of Business and Accounting, Dobbs Ferry (NY) 307

Miami University, Farmer School of Business, Oxford (OH) 343

Michigan State University, Eli Broad Graduate School of Management, East Lansing (MI) 240

Middle East Technical University, Department of Business Administration, Ankara (Turkey) 537

Millsaps College, Else School of Management, Jackson (MS) 255

Misericordia University, Division of Behavioral Science, Education, and Business, Dallas (PA) 372

Mississippi College, School of Business Administration, Clinton (MS) 256

Mississippi State University, College of Business and Industry, Mississippi State (MS) 256

Missouri State University, College of Business Administration, Springfield (MO) *262*

Monash University, MBA Programme, Clayton (Australia) 486

Monmouth University, School of Business Administration, West Long Branch (NJ) 284

Montana State University, College of Business, Bozeman (MT) 271

Montclair State University, School of Business, Montclair (NJ) 285

Monterey Institute of International Studies, Fisher Graduate School of International Business, Monterey (CA) 82, **660**

Mount St. Mary's University, Program in Business Administration, Emmitsburg (MD) 215

Murray State University, College of Business and Public Affairs, Murray (KY) 200

Nanjing University, School of Business, Nanjing (China) 500

Nanyang Technological University, Nanyang Business School, Singapore (Singapore) 527, **662**

National University, School of Business and Management, La Jolla (CA) 82

National University of Ireland, Dublin, The Michael Smurfit Graduate School of Business, Blackrock (Ireland) 513

New Mexico State University, College of Business, Las Cruces (NM) 293

New York Institute of Technology, School of Management (NY) 308

New York University, Leonard N. Stern School of Business (NY) 309

North Carolina State University, College of Management, Raleigh (NC) 328, **664**

North Dakota State University, College of Business, Fargo (ND) 335

Northeastern Illinois University, College of Business and Management, Chicago (IL) 169

Northeastern University, Graduate School of Business Administration, Boston (MA) 228

Northern Arizona University, College of Business Administration, Flagstaff (AZ) 57

Northern Illinois University, College of Business, De Kalb (IL) 169

Northern Kentucky University, College of Business, Highland Heights (KY) 201

Northwestern Polytechnic University, School of Business and Information Technology, Fremont (CA) 84

Northwestern University, Kellogg School of Management, Evanston (IL) 171

Northwest Missouri State University, Melvin and Valorie Booth College of Business and Professional Studies, Maryville (MO) 263

Nottingham Trent University, Nottingham Business School, Nottingham (United Kingdom) 544

Nova Southeastern University, H. Wayne Huizenga School of Business and Entrepreneurship, Fort Lauderdale (FL) 130, **666**

Nyack College, School of Business, Nyack (NY) 310

Oakland University, School of Business Administration, Rochester (MI) 241

The Ohio State University, Max M. Fisher College of Business, Columbus (OH) 344

Oklahoma City University, Meinders School of Business, Oklahoma City (OK) 352

Old Dominion University, College of Business and Public Administration, Norfolk (VA) 441

Oral Roberts University, School of Business, Tulsa (OK) 353

Pace University, Lubin School of Business, New York (NY) 310

Pacific States University, College of Business, Los Angeles (CA) 85

Philadelphia University, School of Business Administration, Philadelphia (PA) 375, **668**

Pittsburg State University, Kelce College of Business, Pittsburg (KS) 195

Pontifical Catholic University of Puerto Rico, College of Business Administration, Ponce (PR) 386

Portland State University, School of Business Administration, Portland (OR) 358

Prairie View A&M University, College of Business, Prairie View (TX) 410

Providence College, School of Business, Providence (RI) 388

Purdue University, Krannert School of Management, West Lafayette (IN) 185

Purdue University Calumet, School of Management, Hammond (IN) 186

Queensland University of Technology, Brisbane Graduate School of Business, Brisbane (Australia) 487

Quinnipiac University, School of Business, Hamden (CT) 109

Regis University, College for Professional Studies, Denver (CO) 103

Rhodes College, Department of Economics/Business Administration, Memphis (TN) 398

The Richard Stockton College of New Jersey, Program in Business Administration, Pomona (NJ) 286

Rochester Institute of Technology, E. Philip Saunders College of Business, Rochester (NY) 312

Rockford College, Program in Business Administration, Rockford (IL) 171

Rockhurst University, Helzberg School of Management, Kansas City (MO) 264

Roosevelt University, Walter E. Heller College of Business Administration, Chicago (IL) 172, **676**

Rowan University, William G. Rohrer College of Business, Glassboro (NJ) 287

Rutgers, The State University of New Jersey, Rutgers Business School–Newark and New Brunswick, Newark and New Brunswick (NJ) 288, **678**

Rutgers, The State University of New Jersey, Camden, School of Business, Camden (NJ) 288

Sacred Heart University, John F. Welch College of Business, Fairfield (CT) 110

Saginaw Valley State University, College of Business and Management, University Center (MI) 242

St. Ambrose University, Program in Business Administration, Davenport (IA) 190

St. Bonaventure University, School of Business, St. Bonaventure (NY) 313

St. Edward's University, The School of Management and Business, Austin (TX) 410

Saint Francis University, Master of Business Administration Program, Loretto (PA) 377

St. John's University, The Peter J. Tobin College of Business, Queens (NY) 314, **680**

Saint Joseph's University, Erivan K. Haub School of Business, Philadelphia (PA) 377

Saint Leo University, Graduate Business Studies, Saint Leo (FL) 132

Saint Louis University, John Cook School of Business, St. Louis (MO) *264*

Saint Martin's University, Division of Economics and Business Administration, Lacey (WA) 450

St. Mary's University, Bill Greehey School of Business (TX) 411

Saint Peter's College, MBA Programs, Jersey City (NJ) 289, **682**

Saints Cyril and Methodius University, Faculty of Economics, Skopje (Macedonia) 519

St. Thomas University, Department of Business Administration, Miami Gardens (FL) 132

Samford University, School of Business, Birmingham (AL) 47

San Diego State University, College of Business Administration, San Diego (CA) 86

San Francisco State University, College of Business, San Francisco (CA) 87

San Jose State University, Lucas Graduate School of Business, San Jose (CA) 87

Santa Clara University, Leavey School of Business, Santa Clara (CA) 88

Seattle University, Albers School of Business and Economics, Seattle (WA) 451

Seton Hall University, Stillman School of Business, South Orange (NJ) 290, **686**

Southeastern Louisiana University, College of Business, Hammond (LA) 207

Southeastern University, College of Graduate Studies, Washington (DC) 121

Southeast Missouri State University, Harrison College of Business, Cape Girardeau (MO) 265

Southern Adventist University, School of Business and Management, Collegedale (TN) 398

Southern Cross University, Graduate College of Management, Coffs Harbour (Australia) 487

Southern Illinois University Carbondale, College of Business and Administration, Carbondale (IL) 173

Southern Illinois University Edwardsville, School of Business, Edwardsville (IL) *174*

Southern Methodist University, Cox School of Business, Dallas (TX) 411, **688**

Southern New Hampshire University, School of Business, Manchester (NH) 279, **690**

Southern Utah University, School of Business, Cedar City (UT) 431

Southwestern Adventist University, Business Department, Graduate Program, Keene (TX) 412

State University of New York at Binghamton, School of Management, Binghamton (NY) 315

State University of New York at New Paltz, School of Business, New Paltz (NY) 316

State University of New York at Oswego, School of Business, Oswego (NY) 316

State University of New York Institute of Technology, School of Business, Utica (NY) 317

Stephen F. Austin State University, College of Business, Nacogdoches (TX) 413

Stockholm School of Economics, Department of Business Administration, Stockholm (Sweden) 531

Suffolk University, Sawyer Business School, Boston (MA) 230

Swinburne University of Technology, Australian Graduate School of Entrepreneurship (AGSE), Hawthorne (Australia) 488

Syracuse University, Martin J. Whitman School of Management, Syracuse (NY) 318, **692**

Tarleton State University, College of Business Administration, Stephenville (TX) 413

Temple University, Fox School of Business and Management, Philadelphia (PA) 379

Tennessee State University, College of Business, Nashville (TN) 399

Tennessee Technological University, College of Business, Cookeville (TN) 399

Texas A&M International University, College of Business Administration, Laredo (TX) 414

Texas A&M University, Mays Business School, College Station (TX) 414

Texas A&M University–Corpus Christi, College of Business, Corpus Christi (TX) 416

Texas A&M University–Texarkana, College of Business, Texarkana (TX) 416

Texas Christian University, The Neeley School of Business at TCU, Fort Worth (TX) 416, **694**

Texas Wesleyan University, School of Business, Fort Worth (TX) 419

Trinity University, Department of Business Administration, San Antonio (TX) 419

Troy University, College of Business, Troy (AL) 48

Troy University Dothan, College of Business Administration, Dothan (AL) 49

Truman State University, School of Business, Kirksville (MO) 266

Tulane University, A. B. Freeman School of Business, New Orleans (LA) 207

Universite Libre de Bruxelles, Solvay Business School, Brussels (Belgium) 495

University at Albany, State University of New York, School of Business, Albany (NY) 319

University at Buffalo, the State University of New York, School of Management, Buffalo (NY) 320

The University of Adelaide, The University of Adelaide Business School, Adelaide (Australia) 488

The University of Akron, College of Business Administration, Akron (OH) 346

The University of Alabama, Manderson Graduate School of Business, Tuscaloosa (AL) 49

The University of Alabama at Birmingham, School of Business, Birmingham (AL) 50

The University of Alabama in Huntsville, College of Business Administration, Huntsville (AL) 51

The University of Arizona, Eller College of Management, Tucson (AZ) 58

University of Arkansas, Sam M. Walton College of Business Administration, Fayetteville (AR) 62

University of Baltimore, Merrick School of Business, Baltimore (MD) 216

University of Bath, School of Management, Bath (United Kingdom) 547

University of Bridgeport, School of Business, Bridgeport (CT) 111

University of California, Berkeley, Haas School of Business, Berkeley (CA) 89

University of California, Davis, Graduate School of Management, Davis (CA) 90

University of California, Los Angeles, UCLA Anderson School of Management, Los Angeles (CA) 91, **696**

University of California, Riverside, A. Gary Anderson Graduate School of Management, Riverside (CA) 93, **698**

University of Canterbury, Department of Management, Christchurch (New Zealand) 523

University of Central Arkansas, College of Business, Conway (AR) 62

University of Central Florida, College of Business Administration, Orlando (FL) 133

University of Central Missouri, Harmon College of Business Administration, Warrensburg (MO) 266

University of Chicago, Graduate School of Business, Chicago (IL) 175

University of Cincinnati, College of Business, Cincinnati (OH) 346

University of Colorado at Boulder, Leeds School of Business, Boulder (CO) 104, **702**

University of Colorado at Colorado Springs, Graduate School of Business Administration, Colorado Springs (CO) 105, **704**

University of Colorado Denver, Business School, Denver (CO) 105, **706**

University of Connecticut, School of Business, Storrs (CT) 112, **708**

University of Dallas, Graduate School of Management, Irving (TX) 420, **710**

University of Dayton, School of Business Administration, Dayton (OH) 347

University of Delaware, Alfred Lerner College of Business and Economics, Newark (DE) 116, **712**

University of Denver, Daniels College of Business, Denver (CO) 106

University of Detroit Mercy, College of Business Administration, Detroit (MI) 243

University of Edinburgh, Edinburgh University Management School, Edinburgh (United Kingdom) 550

The University of Findlay, College of Business, Findlay (OH) 348

University of Georgia, Terry College of Business, Athens (GA) 151

University of Glasgow, University of Glasgow Business School, Glasgow (United Kingdom) 550

University of Hartford, Barney School of Business, West Hartford (CT) 113

University of Hawaii at Manoa, Shidler College of Business, Honolulu (HI) 154

University of Houston, Bauer College of Business, Houston (TX) 420

University of Houston–Clear Lake, School of Business, Houston (TX) 421

University of Houston–Victoria, School of Business Administration, Victoria (TX) 421

University of Idaho, College of Business and Economics, Moscow (ID) 156

University of Illinois at Chicago, Liautaud Graduate School of Business, Chicago (IL) 176

University of Illinois at Urbana–Champaign, College of Business, Champaign (IL) 176

The University of Iowa, Henry B. Tippie College of Business, Iowa City (IA) 191, **714**

University of Kansas, School of Business, Lawrence (KS) 196

University of Kentucky, Gatton College of Business and Economics, Lexington (KY) 202, **716**

University of La Verne, College of Business and Public Management, La Verne (CA) 94

University of Louisiana at Lafayette, Graduate School, Lafayette (LA) 208

University of Louisville, College of Business, Louisville (KY) 203

University of Malaya, Graduate School of Business, Kuala Lumpur (Malaysia) 519

University of Mary, Program in Management, Bismarck (ND) 335

University of Maryland, College Park, Robert H. Smith School of Business, College Park (MD) 217

University of Maryland University College, Graduate School of Management and Technology, Adelphi (MD) 218

University of Mary Washington, College of Graduate and Professional Studies, Fredericksburg (VA) 444

University of Massachusetts Amherst, Isenberg School of Management, Amherst (MA) 231

University of Massachusetts Boston, College of Management, Boston (MA) 232

University of Massachusetts Lowell, College of Management, Lowell (MA) 233

University of Melbourne, Melbourne Business School, Melbourne (Australia) 488

University of Memphis, Fogelman College of Business and Economics, Memphis (TN) 400

University of Miami, School of Business Administration, Coral Gables (FL) 135, **718**

University of Michigan, Ross School of Business at the University of Michigan, Ann Arbor (MI) 244

University of Michigan–Dearborn, School of Management, Dearborn (MI) 245

University of Michigan–Flint, School of Management, Flint (MI) 246

University of Minnesota, Twin Cities Campus, Carlson School of Management, Minneapolis (MN) 252

University of Mississippi, School of Business Administration, Oxford (MS) 257

University of Missouri–Columbia, Robert J. Trulaske, Sr. College of Business, Columbia (MO) 267, **720**

University of Missouri–Kansas City, Henry W. Bloch School of Business and Public Administration, Kansas City (MO) 267

University of Missouri–St. Louis, College of Business Administration, St. Louis (MO) *268*

University of Nebraska at Kearney, College of Business and Technology, Kearney (NE) 273

University of Nebraska–Lincoln, College of Business Administration, Lincoln (NE) 274

University of Nevada, Las Vegas, College of Business, Las Vegas (NV) 275, **722**

University of Nevada, Reno, College of Business Administration, Reno (NV) 276

University of Newcastle, Graduate School of Business, Callaghan (Australia) 489

The University of New England, The Graduate School of Business Administration, Armidale (Australia) 490

University of New Hampshire, Whittemore School of Business and Economics, Durham (NH) 280, **726**

University of New Haven, School of Business, West Haven (CT) 113, **728**

University of New Mexico, Robert O. Anderson Graduate School of Management, Albuquerque (NM) 294

University of New Orleans, College of Business Administration, New Orleans (LA) 209

University of North Alabama, College of Business, Florence (AL) 52

The University of North Carolina at Chapel Hill, Kenan-Flagler Business School, Chapel Hill (NC) 330

The University of North Carolina at Charlotte, Belk College of Business Administration, Charlotte (NC) 330, **730**

The University of North Carolina Wilmington, School of Business, Wilmington (NC) 332

University of North Dakota, College of Business and Public Administration, Grand Forks (ND) 336

University of Northern Iowa, College of Business Administration, Cedar Falls (IA) 192

University of North Florida, Coggin College of Business, Jacksonville (FL) 136

University of North Texas, College of Business Administration, Denton (TX) 422

University of Notre Dame, Mendoza College of Business, Notre Dame (IN) 187

University of Oklahoma, Michael F. Price College of Business, Norman (OK) 355

University of Oregon, Charles H. Lundquist College of Business, Eugene (OR) 359, **732**

University of Pennsylvania, Wharton School, Philadelphia (PA) 380

University of Phoenix, College of Graduate Business and Management, Phoenix (AZ) 59

University of Phoenix–Bay Area Campus, College of Graduate Business and Management, Pleasanton (CA) 94

University of Phoenix–Central Florida Campus, College of Graduate Business and Management, Maitland (FL) 137

University of Phoenix–Charlotte Campus, College of Graduate Business and Management, Charlotte (NC) 332

University of Phoenix–Cincinnati Campus, College of Graduate Business and Management, West Chester (OH) 348

University of Phoenix–Columbus Georgia Campus, College of Graduate Business and Management, Columbus (GA) 152

University of Phoenix–Dallas Campus, College of Graduate Business and Management, Dallas (TX) 423

University of Phoenix–Denver Campus, College of Graduate Business and Management, Lone Tree (CO) 107

University of Phoenix–Eastern Washington Campus, College of Graduate Business and Management, Spokane Valley (WA) 451

University of Phoenix–Hawaii Campus, College of Graduate Business and Management, Honolulu (HI) 155

University of Phoenix–Idaho Campus, College of Graduate Business and Management, Meridian (ID) 157

University of Phoenix–Indianapolis Campus, College of Graduate Business and Management, Indianapolis (IN) 187

University of Phoenix–Kansas City Campus, College of Graduate Business and Management, Kansas City (MO) 268

University of Phoenix–Louisiana Campus, College of Graduate Business and Management, Metairie (LA) 210

University of Phoenix–New Mexico Campus, College of Graduate Business and Management, Albuquerque (NM) 294

University of Phoenix–North Florida Campus, College of Graduate Business and Management, Jacksonville (FL) 137

University of Phoenix–Oklahoma City Campus, College of Graduate Business and Management, Oklahoma City (OK) 355

University of Phoenix–Oregon Campus, College of Graduate Business and Management, Tigard (OR) 360

University of Phoenix–Phoenix Campus, College of Graduate Business and Management, Phoenix (AZ) 59

University of Phoenix–Pittsburgh Campus, College of Graduate Business and Management, Pittsburgh (PA) 381

University of Phoenix–Puerto Rico Campus, College of Graduate Business and Management, Guaynabo (PR) 387

University of Phoenix–Sacramento Valley Campus, College of Graduate Business and Management, Sacramento (CA) 95

University of Phoenix–San Diego Campus, College of Graduate Business and Management, San Diego (CA) 95

University of Phoenix–Southern Arizona Campus, College of Graduate Business and Management, Tucson (AZ) 60

University of Phoenix–Southern California Campus, College of Graduate Business and Management, Costa Mesa (CA) 96

University of Phoenix–Southern Colorado Campus, College of Graduate Business and Management, Colorado Springs (CO) 107

University of Phoenix–South Florida Campus, College of Graduate Business and Management, Fort Lauderdale (FL) 137

University of Phoenix–Tulsa Campus, College of Graduate Business and Management, Tulsa (OK) 355

University of Phoenix–Utah Campus, College of Graduate Business and Management, Salt Lake City (UT) 432

University of Phoenix–Washington Campus, College of Graduate Business and Management, Seattle (WA) 452

University of Phoenix–West Florida Campus, College of Graduate Business and Management, Temple Terrace (FL) 138

University of Phoenix–West Michigan Campus, College of Graduate Business and Management, Walker (MI) 246

University of Phoenix–Wisconsin Campus, College of Graduate Business and Management, Brookfield (WI) 461

University of Pittsburgh, Joseph M. Katz Graduate School of Business, Pittsburgh (PA) 381

University of Plymouth, Plymouth Business School, Plymouth (United Kingdom) 553

University of Rhode Island, College of Business Administration, Kingston (RI) 389, **734**

University of Rochester, William E. Simon Graduate School of Business Administration, Rochester (NY) 321, **736**

University of St. Thomas, Opus College of Business (MN) 253, **738**

University of St. Thomas, Cameron School of Business (TX) 424

University of San Diego, School of Business Administration, San Diego (CA) 96

University of Saskatchewan, Edwards School of Business, Saskatoon (Canada) 478

The University of Scranton, Program in Business Administration, Scranton (PA) 382

University of Sioux Falls, John T. Vucurevich School of Business, Sioux Falls (SD) 394

University of South Alabama, Mitchell College of Business, Mobile (AL) 52

University of South Carolina, Moore School of Business, Columbia (SC) *392,* **740**

The University of South Dakota, School of Business, Vermillion (SD) 395

University of Southern California, School of Business, Los Angeles (CA) 98

University of Southern Maine, School of Business, Portland (ME) 212

University of Southern Mississippi, College of Business, Hattiesburg (MS) 257

University of South Florida, College of Business Administration, Tampa (FL) 138

The University of Tampa, John H. Sykes College of Business, Tampa (FL) 139, **742**

The University of Tennessee, College of Business Administration, Knoxville (TN) *401,* **744**

The University of Tennessee at Chattanooga, College of Business, Chattanooga (TN) 402

The University of Texas at Arlington, College of Business Administration, Arlington (TX) 424, **746**

The University of Texas at Austin, Programs in MBA, Austin (TX) 425

The University of Texas at Dallas, School of Management, Richardson (TX) *426,* **748**

The University of Texas at San Antonio, College of Business, San Antonio (TX) 427, **750**

The University of Texas at Tyler, College of Business and Technology, Tyler (TX) 428

The University of Texas of the Permian Basin, School of Business, Odessa (TX) 428

The University of Texas–Pan American, College of Business Administration, Edinburg (TX) 428

University of the District of Columbia, School of Business and Public Administration, Washington (DC) 122

University of the West of England, Bristol, Bristol Business School, Bristol (United Kingdom) 555

University of the Witwatersrand, Graduate School of Business Administration, Wits (South Africa) 527

The University of Toledo, College of Business Administration, Toledo (OH) 349

University of Toronto, Joseph L. Rotman School of Management, Toronto (Canada) 478

University of Tulsa, College of Business Administration, Tulsa (OK) 356

University of Ulster at Jordanstown, Faculty of Business and Management, Newtown Abbey (United Kingdom) 556

University of Wales, Aberystwyth, School of Management and Business, Ceredigion (United Kingdom) 556

University of Washington, Michael G. Foster School of Business, Seattle (WA) 452, **754**

University of Waterloo, Graduate Studies, Waterloo (Canada) 479

The University of Western Ontario, Richard Ivey School of Business, London (Canada) 480

University of West Florida, College of Business, Pensacola (FL) 139

University of West Georgia, Richards College of Business, Carrollton (GA) 152

University of Wisconsin–Eau Claire, College of Business, Eau Claire (WI) 461, **756**

University of Wisconsin–Madison, Wisconsin School of Business, Madison (WI) 462, **756**

University of Wisconsin–Milwaukee, Sheldon B. Lubar School of Business, Milwaukee (WI) 463

University of Wisconsin–Whitewater, College of Business and Economics, Whitewater (WI) 465

Upper Iowa University, Online Master's Programs, Fayette (IA) 192

Valparaiso University, College of Business Administration, Valparaiso (IN) 188

Vanderbilt University, Owen Graduate School of Management, Nashville (TN) 403, **758**

Vienna University of Economics and Business Administration, WU Wien MBA, Vienna (Austria) 492

Villanova University, Villanova School of Business, Villanova (PA) 382

Virginia Commonwealth University, School of Business, Richmond (VA) 445

Virginia Polytechnic Institute and State University, Pamplin College of Business, Blacksburg (VA) 446

Wagner College, Department of Business Administration, Staten Island (NY) 321

Walsh College of Accountancy and Business Administration, Graduate Programs, Troy (MI) 247

Waseda University, Graduate School of Commerce, Tokyo (Japan) 517

Washington State University, College of Business, Pullman (WA) 453

Washington University in St. Louis, Olin Business School, St. Louis (MO) 269

Wayne State University, School of Business Administration, Detroit (MI) 247, **760**

Webber International University, Graduate School of Business, Babson Park (FL) 140, **762**

Weber State University, John B. Goddard School of Business and Economics, Ogden (UT) 432

Western Carolina University, College of Business, Cullowhee (NC) 333

Western Illinois University, College of Business and Technology, Macomb (IL) 178

Western Michigan University, Haworth College of Business, Kalamazoo (MI) 248

Western New England College, School of Business, Springfield (MA) 234

Westminster College, The Bill and Vieve Gore School of Business, Salt Lake City (UT) 433

West Texas A&M University, College of Business, Canyon (TX) 430

Wheeling Jesuit University, Department of Business, Wheeling (WV) 457

Widener University, School of Business Administration, Chester (PA) 384, **764**

Wilfrid Laurier University, School of Business and Economics, Waterloo (Canada) 481, **766**

Wilkes University, College of Arts, Humanities and Social Sciences, Wilkes-Barre (PA) 384

Willamette University, George H. Atkinson Graduate School of Management, Salem (OR) 361, **768**

William Paterson University of New Jersey, Christos M. Cotsakos College of Business, Wayne (NJ) 292

William Woods University, Graduate and Adult Studies, Fulton (MO) 271

Winthrop University, College of Business Administration, Rock Hill (SC) 393

Woodbury University, School of Business and Management, Burbank (CA) 100

Wright State University, Raj Soin College of Business, Dayton (OH) 350

York College of Pennsylvania, Department of Business Administration, York (PA) 385

York University, Schulich School of Business, Toronto (Canada) 482, **772**

Youngstown State University, Warren P. Williamson Jr. College of Business Administration, Youngstown (OH) 351

ACTUARIAL SCIENCE

Georgia State University, J. Mack Robinson College of Business, Atlanta (GA) 147, **626**

Katholieke Universiteit Leuven, Leuven School of Business. and Economics, Leuven (Belgium) 494

National University, School of Business and Management, La Jolla (CA) 82

National University of Ireland, Dublin, The Michael Smurfit Graduate School of Business, Blackrock (Ireland) 513

Otterbein College, Department of Business, Accounting and Economics, Westerville (OH) 345

Temple University, Fox School of Business and Management, Philadelphia (PA) 379

University of Wisconsin–Madison, Wisconsin School of Business, Madison (WI) 462, **756**

ADMINISTRATION

The Aarhus School of Business, Faculty of Business Administration, Aarhus (Denmark) 501

American Jewish University, David Lieber School of Graduate Studies, Bel Air (CA) 63

Angelo State University, Department of Management and Marketing, San Angelo (TX) 405

Antioch University New England, Department of Organization and Management, Keene (NH) 277

Asia International Open University, MBA Program, Macau (Macao) 518

Athabasca University, Centre for Innovative Management, Athabasca (Canada) 466

City University of Hong Kong, Faculty of Business, Hong Kong (China) 497

Cleveland State University, Nance College of Business Administration, Cleveland (OH) 340

Deakin University, Deakin Business School, Geelong (Australia) 484

European University, Center for Management Studies, Montreux-Fontanivent (Switzerland) 532

Grand Canyon University, College of Business, Phoenix (AZ) 56

The Hague University, Faculty of Economics and Management, The Hague (Netherlands) 521, **628**

Hong Kong Baptist University, School of Business, Hong Kong (China) 498

Hope International University, Program in Business Administration, Fullerton (CA) 79

IE Business School, Business School, Madrid (Spain) 529, **636**

Lancaster University, Management School, Lancaster (United Kingdom) 541

Madonna University, School of Business, Livonia (MI) 240

Monash University, MBA Programme, Clayton (Australia) 486

National University of Ireland, Dublin, The Michael Smurfit Graduate School of Business, Blackrock (Ireland) 513

New York University, Robert F. Wagner Graduate School of Public Service (NY) 309

Northeastern University, Graduate School of Business Administration, Boston (MA) 228

Norwegian School of Management, Graduate School, Sandvika (Norway) 524

Notre Dame de Namur University, Department of Business Administration, Belmont (CA) 84

Saint Mary's University of Minnesota, Schools of Graduate and Professional Programs, Winona (MN) 251

Southern Adventist University, School of Business and Management, Collegedale (TN) 398

Southwest Baptist University, College of Business and Computer Science, Bolivar (MO) 265

Southwestern College, Professional Studies Programs, Winfield (KS) 196

Stockholm School of Economics, Department of Business Administration, Stockholm (Sweden) 531

Texas A&M University, Mays Business School, College Station (TX) 414

University of Management and Technology, Graduate Business Programs, Arlington (VA) 443

University of Manitoba, Faculty of Management, Winnipeg (Canada) 475

University of Phoenix, College of Graduate Business and Management, Phoenix (AZ) 59

University of Phoenix–Atlanta Campus, College of Graduate Business and Management, Sandy Springs (GA) 151

University of Phoenix–Bay Area Campus, College of Graduate Business and Management, Pleasanton (CA) 94

University of Phoenix–Boston Campus, College of Graduate Business and Management, Braintree (MA) 233

University of Phoenix–Central Florida Campus, College of Graduate Business and Management, Maitland (FL) 137

University of Phoenix–Central Massachusetts Campus, College of Graduate Business and Management, Westborough (MA) 234

University of Phoenix–Charlotte Campus, College of Graduate Business and Management, Charlotte (NC) 332

University of Phoenix–Chicago Campus, College of Graduate Business and Management, Schaumburg (IL) 177

University of Phoenix–Cincinnati Campus, College of Graduate Business and Management, West Chester (OH) 348

University of Phoenix–Cleveland Campus, College of Graduate Business and Management, Independence (OH) 348

University of Phoenix–Columbus Georgia Campus, College of Graduate Business and Management, Columbus (GA) 152

University of Phoenix–Columbus Ohio Campus, College of Graduate Business and Management, Columbus (OH) 349

University of Phoenix–Dallas Campus, College of Graduate Business and Management, Dallas (TX) 423

University of Phoenix–Denver Campus, College of Graduate Business and Management, Lone Tree (CO) 107

University of Phoenix–Eastern Washington Campus, College of Graduate Business and Management, Spokane Valley (WA) 451

University of Phoenix–Hawaii Campus, College of Graduate Business and Management, Honolulu (HI) 155

University of Phoenix–Houston Campus, College of Graduate Business and Management, Houston (TX) 423

University of Phoenix–Idaho Campus, College of Graduate Business and Management, Meridian (ID) 157

University of Phoenix–Indianapolis Campus, College of Graduate Business and Management, Indianapolis (IN) 187

University of Phoenix–Kansas City Campus, College of Graduate Business and Management, Kansas City (MO) 268

University of Phoenix–Las Vegas Campus, College of Graduate Business and Management, Las Vegas (NV) 276

University of Phoenix–Little Rock Campus, College of Graduate Business and Management, Little Rock (AR) 63

University of Phoenix–Louisiana Campus, College of Graduate Business and Management, Metairie (LA) 210

University of Phoenix–Maryland Campus, College of Graduate Business and Management, Columbia (MD) 219

University of Phoenix–Metro Detroit Campus, College of Graduate Business and Management, Troy (MI) 246

University of Phoenix–Nashville Campus, College of Graduate Business and Management, Nashville (TN) 401

University of Phoenix–New Mexico Campus, College of Graduate Business and Management, Albuquerque (NM) 294

University of Phoenix–North Florida Campus, College of Graduate Business and Management, Jacksonville (FL) 137

University of Phoenix–Oklahoma City Campus, College of Graduate Business and Management, Oklahoma City (OK) 355

University of Phoenix–Oregon Campus, College of Graduate Business and Management, Tigard (OR) 360

University of Phoenix–Philadelphia Campus, College of Graduate Business and Management, Wayne (PA) 380

University of Phoenix–Phoenix Campus, College of Graduate Business and Management, Phoenix (AZ) 59

University of Phoenix–Pittsburgh Campus, College of Graduate Business and Management, Pittsburgh (PA) 381

University of Phoenix–Puerto Rico Campus, College of Graduate Business and Management, Guaynabo (PR) 387

University of Phoenix–Sacramento Valley Campus, College of Graduate Business and Management, Sacramento (CA) 95

University of Phoenix–St. Louis Campus, College of Graduate Business and Management, St. Louis (MO) 269

University of Phoenix–San Diego Campus, College of Graduate Business and Management, San Diego (CA) 95

University of Phoenix–Southern Arizona Campus, College of Graduate Business and Management, Tucson (AZ) 60

University of Phoenix–Southern California Campus, College of Graduate Business and Management, Costa Mesa (CA) 96

University of Phoenix–Southern Colorado Campus, College of Graduate Business and Management, Colorado Springs (CO) 107

University of Phoenix–South Florida Campus, College of Graduate Business and Management, Fort Lauderdale (FL) 137

University of Phoenix–Tulsa Campus, College of Graduate Business and Management, Tulsa (OK) 355

University of Phoenix–Utah Campus, College of Graduate Business and Management, Salt Lake City (UT) 432

University of Phoenix–Vancouver Campus, College of Graduate Business and Management, Burnaby (Canada) 477

University of Phoenix–Washington Campus, College of Graduate Business and Management, Seattle (WA) 452

University of Phoenix–West Florida Campus, College of Graduate Business and Management, Temple Terrace (FL) 138

University of Phoenix–West Michigan Campus, College of Graduate Business and Management, Walker (MI) 246

University of Phoenix–Wichita Campus, College of Graduate Business and Management, Wichita (KS) 196

University of Phoenix–Wisconsin Campus, College of Graduate Business and Management, Brookfield (WI) 461

University of Salford, Salford Business School, Salford (United Kingdom) 554

The University of Texas at Tyler, College of Business and Technology, Tyler (TX) 428

The University of Toledo, College of Business Administration, Toledo (OH) 349

University of Wyoming, College of Business, Laramie (WY) 465

Whitworth University, School of Global Commerce and Management, Spokane (WA) 455

ADMINISTRATION OF TECHNOLOGICAL INFORMATION

Baker College Center for Graduate Studies, Graduate Programs, Flint (MI) 236, **572**

École Nationale des Ponts et Chaussées, ENPC MBA, Paris (France) 503

Graduate School of Business Administration Zurich, Executive Management Programs, Zurich (Switzerland) 532

James Madison University, College of Business, Harrisonburg (VA) 438

Monterey Institute of International Studies, Fisher Graduate School of International Business, Monterey (CA) 82, **660**

Pontifical Catholic University of Puerto Rico, College of Business Administration, Ponce (PR) 386

Stockholm School of Economics, Department of Business Administration, Stockholm (Sweden) 531

University of Phoenix, College of Graduate Business and Management, Phoenix (AZ) 59

University of Rochester, William E. Simon Graduate School of Business Administration, Rochester (NY) 321, **736**

University of Salford, Salford Business School, Salford (United Kingdom) 554

University of Wisconsin–Whitewater, College of Business and Economics, Whitewater (WI) 465

ADVERTISING

Aston University, Aston Business School, Birmingham (United Kingdom) 539

Bernard M. Baruch College of the City University of New York, Zicklin School of Business, New York (NY) 296

The Chinese University of Hong Kong, Faculty of Business Administration, Hong Kong (China) 497

City University of Hong Kong, Faculty of Business, Hong Kong (China) 497

Cleveland State University, Nance College of Business Administration, Cleveland (OH) 340

ADVERTISING

Copenhagen Business School, Faculty of Economics and Business Administration, Copenhagen (Denmark) 501

European School of Economics, MBA Programme (Italy) 515, **608**

The George Washington University, School of Business, Washington (DC) 119, **622**

IE Business School, Business School, Madrid (Spain) 529, **636**

Illinois Institute of Technology, Stuart School of Business, Chicago (IL) 164

International University of Japan, Graduate School of International Management, Minami Uonuma-gu (Japan) 516

Monash University, MBA Programme, Clayton (Australia) 486

Nanjing University, School of Business, Nanjing (China) 500

Nottingham Trent University, Nottingham Business School, Nottingham (United Kingdom) 544

Roosevelt University, Walter E. Heller College of Business Administration, Chicago (IL) 172, **676**

Stockholm School of Economics, Department of Business Administration, Stockholm (Sweden) 531

University of Missouri–Columbia, Robert J. Trulaske, Sr. College of Business, Columbia (MO) 267, **720**

University of Rochester, William E. Simon Graduate School of Business Administration, Rochester (NY) 321, **736**

University of the West of England, Bristol, Bristol Business School, Bristol (United Kingdom) 555

Vienna University of Economics and Business Administration, WU Wien MBA, Vienna (Austria) 492

AGRIBUSINESS

Auburn University, College of Business, Auburn University (AL) 45, **568**

California Polytechnic State University, San Luis Obispo, Orfalea College of Business, San Luis Obispo (CA) 68

Illinois State University, College of Business, Normal (IL) 165, **638**

Iowa State University of Science and Technology, College of Business, Ames (IA) 189, **644**

Monash University, MBA Programme, Clayton (Australia) 486

New Mexico State University, College of Business, Las Cruces (NM) 293

Santa Clara University, Leavey School of Business, Santa Clara (CA) 88

Tarleton State University, College of Business Administration, Stephenville (TX) 413

Texas A&M University, Mays Business School, College Station (TX) 414

Texas Tech University, Jerry S. Rawls College of Business Administration, Lubbock (TX) 418

University of Guelph, Faculty of Management, Guelph (Canada) 475

University of Missouri–Columbia, Robert J. Trulaske, Sr. College of Business, Columbia (MO) 267, **720**

University of Nebraska–Lincoln, College of Business Administration, Lincoln (NE) 274

The University of New England, The Graduate School of Business Administration, Armidale (Australia) 490

University of Saskatchewan, Edwards School of Business, Saskatoon (Canada) 478

Western Illinois University, College of Business and Technology, Macomb (IL) 178

West Texas A&M University, College of Business, Canyon (TX) 430

AGRICULTURAL ECONOMICS

California Polytechnic State University, San Luis Obispo, Orfalea College of Business, San Luis Obispo (CA) 68

North Carolina State University, College of Management, Raleigh (NC) 328, **664**

Northwest Missouri State University, Melvin and Valorie Booth College of Business and Professional Studies, Maryville (MO) 263

University of Missouri–Columbia, Robert J. Trulaske, Sr. College of Business, Columbia (MO) 267, **720**

ARCHITECTURE

California Polytechnic State University, San Luis Obispo, Orfalea College of Business, San Luis Obispo (CA) 68

University of Nebraska–Lincoln, College of Business Administration, Lincoln (NE) 274

Washington University in St. Louis, Olin Business School, St. Louis (MO) 269

ARTS ADMINISTRATION/ MANAGEMENT

Aquinas College, School of Management, Grand Rapids (MI) 235

Bellevue University, College of Business, Bellevue (NE) 271, **576**

Case Western Reserve University, Weatherhead School of Management, Cleveland (OH) 338

Claremont Graduate University, Peter F. Drucker and Masatoshi Ito Graduate School of Management, Claremont (CA) 75, **590**

Deakin University, Deakin Business School, Geelong (Australia) 484

Doane College, Program in Management, Crete (NE) 273

European University, Center for Management Studies, Montreux-Fontanivent (Switzerland) 532

Florida Atlantic University, College of Business, Boca Raton (FL) 126

Illinois State University, College of Business, Normal (IL) 165, **638**

Lindenwood University, Division of Management, St. Charles (MO) 261

Monash University, MBA Programme, Clayton (Australia) 486

New York University, Robert F. Wagner Graduate School of Public Service (NY) 309

Oklahoma City University, Meinders School of Business, Oklahoma City (OK) 352

Point Park University, School of Business, Pittsburgh (PA) 375

Queen Margaret University College, Edinburgh, School of Business and Enterprise, Edinburgh (United Kingdom) 545

Rutgers, The State University of New Jersey, Rutgers Business School–Newark and New Brunswick, Newark and New Brunswick (NJ) 288, **678**

Saint Mary's University of Minnesota, Schools of Graduate and Professional Programs, Winona (MN) 251

Southern Methodist University, Cox School of Business, Dallas (TX) 411, **688**

Stockholm School of Economics, Department of Business Administration, Stockholm (Sweden) 531

University of Delaware, Alfred Lerner College of Business and Economics, Newark (DE) 116, **712**

University of Wisconsin–Madison, Wisconsin School of Business, Madison (WI) 462, **756**

York University, Schulich School of Business, Toronto (Canada) 482, **772**

ASIAN BUSINESS STUDIES

École Nationale des Ponts et Chaussées, ENPC MBA, Paris (France) 503

Edith Cowan University, Faculty of Business and Public Management, Churchlands (Australia) 484

HfB—Business School of Finance and Management, Frankfurt School of Finance and Management, Frankfurt (Germany) 508

International University of Japan, Graduate School of International Management, Minami Uonuma-gu (Japan) 516

Monash University, MBA Programme, Clayton (Australia) 486

Monterey Institute of International Studies, Fisher Graduate School of International Business, Monterey (CA) 82, **660**

Norwegian School of Management, Graduate School, Sandvika (Norway) 524

The University of Adelaide, The University of Adelaide Business School, Adelaide (Australia) 488

University of Antwerp, University of Antwerp Management School, Antwerp (Belgium) 495

University of California, Berkeley, Haas School of Business, Berkeley (CA) 89

University of Connecticut, School of Business, Storrs (CT) 112, **708**

University of Edinburgh, Edinburgh University Management School, Edinburgh (United Kingdom) 550

University of Hawaii at Manoa, Shidler College of Business, Honolulu (HI) 154

University of Michigan, Ross School of Business at the University of Michigan, Ann Arbor (MI) 244

University of New Brunswick Saint John, Faculty of Business, Saint John (Canada) 476, **724**

The University of New England, The Graduate School of Business Administration, Armidale (Australia) 490

University of Pennsylvania, Wharton School, Philadelphia (PA) 380

The University of Western Ontario, Richard Ivey School of Business, London (Canada) 480

Waseda University, Graduate School of Commerce, Tokyo (Japan) 517

Washington University in St. Louis, Olin Business School, St. Louis (MO) 269

York University, Schulich School of Business, Toronto (Canada) 482, **772**

AVIATION MANAGEMENT

Dowling College, School of Business, Oakdale (NY) 300

Embry-Riddle Aeronautical University, College of Business, Daytona Beach (FL) 125, **604**

Embry-Riddle Aeronautical University Worldwide, Department of Management, Daytona Beach (FL) 125

Lynn University, School of Business, Boca Raton (FL) 130

University of Newcastle, Graduate School of Business, Callaghan (Australia) 489

BANKING

American College of Thessaloniki, Department of Business Administration, Pylea (Greece) 511

Athens Laboratory of Business Administration, MBA Program, Athens (Greece) 512

Barcelona Business School, Graduate Programs in Business, Barcelona (Spain) 528

Case Western Reserve University, Weatherhead School of Management, Cleveland (OH) 338

Christian Brothers University, School of Business, Memphis (TN) 396

City University of Hong Kong, Faculty of Business, Hong Kong (China) 497

Cleveland State University, Nance College of Business Administration, Cleveland (OH) 340

Dalhousie University, Faculty of Management, Halifax (Canada) 467

DePaul University, Charles H. Kellstadt Graduate School of Business, Chicago (IL) 159

Dowling College, School of Business, Oakdale (NY) 300

European School of Economics, MBA Programme (Italy) 515, **608**

HfB—Business School of Finance and Management, Frankfurt School of Finance and Management, Frankfurt (Germany) 508

IE Business School, Business School, Madrid (Spain) 529, **636**

International University in Geneva, MBA Program, Geneva (Switzerland) 533, **640**

International University of Japan, Graduate School of International Management, Minami Uonuma-gu (Japan) 516

The International University of Monaco, Graduate Programs, Monte Carlo (Monaco) 520

Katholieke Universiteit Leuven, Leuven School of Business and Economics, Leuven (Belgium) 494

KDI School of Public Policy and Management, MBA Program, Seoul (Republic of Korea) 526

Mercy College, Division of Business and Accounting, Dobbs Ferry (NY) 307

Monash University, MBA Programme, Clayton (Australia) 486

Nanjing University, School of Business, Nanjing (China) 500

Nanyang Technological University, Nanyang Business School, Singapore (Singapore) 527, **662**

New York University, Leonard N. Stern School of Business (NY) 309

Stockholm School of Economics, Department of Business Administration, Stockholm (Sweden) 531

Suffolk University, Sawyer Business School, Boston (MA) 230

The University of Alabama, Manderson Graduate School of Business, Tuscaloosa (AL) 49

University of Antwerp, University of Antwerp Management School, Antwerp (Belgium) 495

University of California, Berkeley, Haas School of Business, Berkeley (CA) 89

University of Durham, Durham Business School, Durham (United Kingdom) 549

University of Edinburgh, Edinburgh University Management School, Edinburgh (United Kingdom) 550

University of Glasgow, University of Glasgow Business School, Glasgow (United Kingdom) 550

University of Kentucky, Gatton College of Business and Economics, Lexington (KY) 202, **716**

University of Mississippi, School of Business Administration, Oxford (MS) 257

University of Missouri–Columbia, Robert J. Trulaske, Sr. College of Business, Columbia (MO) 267, **720**

University of Newcastle, Graduate School of Business, Callaghan (Australia) 489

University of Salford, Salford Business School, Salford (United Kingdom) 554

University of Toronto, Joseph L. Rotman School of Management, Toronto (Canada) 478

The University of Western Ontario, Richard Ivey School of Business, London (Canada) 480

University of Wisconsin–Madison, Wisconsin School of Business, Madison (WI) 462, **756**

Vienna University of Economics and Business Administration, WU Wien MBA, Vienna (Austria) 492

BUSINESS EDUCATION

Barcelona Business School, Graduate Programs in Business, Barcelona (Spain) 528

Bayerische Julius-Maximilians University of Wuerzburg, MBA Program, Wuerzburg (Germany) 507

Bloomsburg University of Pennsylvania, College of Business, Bloomsburg (PA) 362

Colorado State University, College of Business, Fort Collins (CO) 101, **596**

Concordia University Wisconsin, Graduate Programs, Mequon (WI) 458

Deakin University, Deakin Business School, Geelong (Australia) 484

Hong Kong Baptist University, School of Business, Hong Kong (China) 498

IE Business School, Business School, Madrid (Spain) 529, **636**

Indiana University of Pennsylvania, Eberly College of Business and Information Technology, Indiana (PA) 369

Inter American University of Puerto Rico, San Germán Campus, Department of Business Administration, San Germán (PR) 385

International University of Japan, Graduate School of International Management, Minami Uonuma-gu (Japan) 516

Jackson State University, School of Business, Jackson (MS) 255

Lancaster University, Management School, Lancaster (United Kingdom) 541

Leadership Institute of Seattle, School of Applied Behavioral Science, Kenmore (WA) 449

Monash University, MBA Programme, Clayton (Australia) 486

OGI School of Science & Engineering at Oregon Health & Science University, Department of Management in Science and Technology, Beaverton (OR) 358

Saints Cyril and Methodius University, Faculty of Economics, Skopje (Macedonia) 519

Stockholm School of Economics, Department of Business Administration, Stockholm (Sweden) 531

University of Missouri–Columbia, Robert J. Trulaske, Sr. College of Business, Columbia (MO) 267, **720**

Vanderbilt University, Owen Graduate School of Management, Nashville (TN) 403, **758**

BUSINESS ETHICS

American Jewish University, David Lieber School of Graduate Studies, Bel Air (CA) 63

Antioch University Santa Barbara, Program in Organizational Management, Santa Barbara (CA) 64

Ashridge, Ashridge Executive MBA Program, Berkhamsted (United Kingdom) 538

Barcelona Business School, Graduate Programs in Business, Barcelona (Spain) 528

Bentley College, The Elkin B. McCallum Graduate School of Business, Waltham (MA) 221, **578**

Christian Brothers University, School of Business, Memphis (TN) 396

City University of Hong Kong, Faculty of Business, Hong Kong (China) 497

Copenhagen Business School, Faculty of Economics and Business Administration, Copenhagen (Denmark) 501

Duquesne University, John F. Donahue Graduate School of Business, Pittsburgh (PA) 367

École Nationale des Ponts et Chaussées, ENPC MBA, Paris (France) 503

European School of Economics, MBA Programme (Italy) 515, **608**

The George Washington University, School of Business, Washington (DC) 119, **622**

Gonzaga University, School of Business Administration, Spokane (WA) 448

Graduate School of Business Administration Zurich, Executive Management Programs, Zurich (Switzerland) 532

HfB—Business School of Finance and Management, Frankfurt School of Finance and Management, Frankfurt (Germany) 508

Hong Kong Baptist University, School of Business, Hong Kong (China) 498

IE Business School, Business School, Madrid (Spain) 529, **636**

International University of Japan, Graduate School of International Management, Minami Uonuma-gu (Japan) 516

Lancaster University, Management School, Lancaster (United Kingdom) 541

Leadership Institute of Seattle, School of Applied Behavioral Science, Kenmore (WA) 449

Loyola University Chicago, Graduate School of Business, Chicago (IL) 167

Mercy College, Division of Business and Accounting, Dobbs Ferry (NY) 307

Monash University, MBA Programme, Clayton (Australia) 486

Monterey Institute of International Studies, Fisher Graduate School of International Business, Monterey (CA) 82, **660**

National University, School of Business and Management, La Jolla (CA) 82

North Central College, Department of Business, Naperville (IL) *168*

Nottingham Trent University, Nottingham Business School, Nottingham (United Kingdom) 544

Penn State Great Valley, Graduate Studies, Malvern (PA) 373

Saint Mary's University of Minnesota, Schools of Graduate and Professional Programs, Winona (MN) 251

Stockholm School of Economics, Department of Business Administration, Stockholm (Sweden) 531

University of Bath, School of Management, Bath (United Kingdom) 547

University of Denver, Daniels College of Business, Denver (CO) 106

University of Edinburgh, Edinburgh University Management School, Edinburgh (United Kingdom) 550

University of Newcastle, Graduate School of Business, Callaghan (Australia) 489

University of South Florida, College of Business Administration, Tampa (FL) 138

University of the West of England, Bristol, Bristol Business School, Bristol (United Kingdom) 555

BUSINESS INFORMATION SCIENCE

Bayerische Julius-Maximilians University of Wuerzburg, MBA Program, Wuerzburg (Germany) 507

California State University, Los Angeles, College of Business and Economics, Los Angeles (CA) 71

Cleveland State University, Nance College of Business Administration, Cleveland (OH) 340

DePaul University, Charles H. Kellstadt Graduate School of Business, Chicago (IL) 159

HfB—Business School of Finance and Management, Frankfurt School of Finance and Management, Frankfurt (Germany) 508

IE Business School, Business School, Madrid (Spain) 529, **636**

Indiana University–Purdue University Indianapolis, Kelley School of Business, Indianapolis (IN) 184

The International Management Institute, International Business School, Antwerp (Belgium) 494

International University of Japan, Graduate School of International Management, Minami Uonuma-gu (Japan) 516

Michigan State University, Eli Broad Graduate School of Management, East Lansing (MI) 240

Monash University, MBA Programme, Clayton (Australia) 486

National University, School of Business and Management, La Jolla (CA) 82

North Central College, Department of Business, Naperville (IL) *168*

Penn State Great Valley, Graduate Studies, Malvern (PA) 373

Rensselaer Polytechnic Institute, Lally School of Management and Technology, Troy (NY) 311, **670**

Southern Illinois University Edwardsville, School of Business, Edwardsville (IL) *174*

Stockholm School of Economics, Department of Business Administration, Stockholm (Sweden) 531

Universite Libre de Bruxelles, Solvay Business School, Brussels (Belgium) 495

University of California, Berkeley, Haas School of Business, Berkeley (CA) 89

University of Dayton, School of Business Administration, Dayton (OH) 347

University of Denver, Daniels College of Business, Denver (CO) 106

University of Florida, Hough Graduate School of Business, Gainesville (FL) 134

University of Missouri–Columbia, Robert J. Trulaske, Sr. College of Business, Columbia (MO) 267, **720**

University of Salford, Salford Business School, Salford (United Kingdom) 554

University of Waterloo, Graduate Studies, Waterloo (Canada) 479

The University of Western Ontario, Richard Ivey School of Business, London (Canada) 480

Walden University, School of Management, Minneapolis (MN) 253

Waseda University, Graduate School of Commerce, Tokyo (Japan) 517

BUSINESS LAW

The Aarhus School of Business, Faculty of Business Administration, Aarhus (Denmark) 501

The American University in Cairo, School of Business, Economics and Communication, Cairo (Egypt) 502

Baylor University, Hankamer School of Business, Waco (TX) 405, **574**

Bond University, School of Business, Gold Coast (Australia) 483

California State University, Northridge, College of Business and Economics, Northridge (CA) 72

The Chinese University of Hong Kong, Faculty of Business Administration, Hong Kong (China) 497

Copenhagen Business School, Faculty of Economics and Business Administration, Copenhagen (Denmark) 501

Deakin University, Deakin Business School, Geelong (Australia) 484

Eastern Mennonite University, Program in Business Administration, Harrisonburg (VA) 438

École Nationale des Ponts et Chaussées, ENPC MBA, Paris (France) 503

European School of Economics, MBA Programme (Italy) 515, **608**

HEC Paris, HEC MBA Program, Jouy-en-Josas (France) *505*, **632**

HfB—Business School of Finance and Management, Frankfurt School of Finance and Management, Frankfurt (Germany) 508

IE Business School, Business School, Madrid (Spain) 529, **636**

International University of Japan, Graduate School of International Management, Minami Uonuma-gu (Japan) 516

Lancaster University, Management School, Lancaster (United Kingdom) 541

Loyola Marymount University, College of Business Administration, Los Angeles (CA) 81

Loyola University Chicago, Graduate School of Business, Chicago (IL) 167

Monash University, MBA Programme, Clayton (Australia) 486

National University of Ireland, Dublin, The Michael Smurfit Graduate School of Business, Blackrock (Ireland) 513

Open University of the Netherlands, Business Programs, Heerlen (Netherlands) 523

Rutgers, The State University of New Jersey, Camden, School of Business, Camden (NJ) 288

Seattle University, Albers School of Business and Economics, Seattle (WA) 451

Stockholm School of Economics, Department of Business Administration, Stockholm (Sweden) 531

Suffolk University, Sawyer Business School, Boston (MA) 230

Temple University, Fox School of Business and Management, Philadelphia (PA) 379

The University of New England, The Graduate School of Business Administration, Armidale (Australia) 490

University of South Carolina, Moore School of Business, Columbia (SC) *392,* **740**

University of the West of England, Bristol, Bristol Business School, Bristol (United Kingdom) 555

University of Washington, Michael G. Foster School of Business, Seattle (WA) 452, **754**

Vanderbilt University, Owen Graduate School of Management, Nashville (TN) 403, **758**

WHU—Otto Beisheim School of Management, WHU—Otto Beisheim School of Management, Vallendar (Germany) 511

BUSINESS POLICY/STRATEGY

The Aarhus School of Business, Faculty of Business Administration, Aarhus (Denmark) 501

Bayerische Julius-Maximilians University of Wuerzburg, MBA Program, Wuerzburg (Germany) 507

California National University for Advanced Studies, College of Business Administration, Northridge (CA) 67

Case Western Reserve University, Weatherhead School of Management, Cleveland (OH) 338

The Chinese University of Hong Kong, Faculty of Business Administration, Hong Kong (China) 497

City University of Hong Kong, Faculty of Business, Hong Kong (China) 497

Cleveland State University, Nance College of Business Administration, Cleveland (OH) 340

Copenhagen Business School, Faculty of Economics and Business Administration, Copenhagen (Denmark) 501

École Nationale des Ponts et Chaussées, ENPC MBA, Paris (France) 503

The George Washington University, School of Business, Washington (DC) 119, **622**

Graduate School of Business Administration Zurich, Executive Management Programs, Zurich (Switzerland) 532

HfB—Business School of Finance and Management, Frankfurt School of Finance and Management, Frankfurt (Germany) 508

Hong Kong Baptist University, School of Business, Hong Kong (China) 498

Hult International Business School, Graduate Program, Cambridge (MA) *227*, **634**

IE Business School, Business School, Madrid (Spain) 529, **636**

International University in Geneva, MBA Program, Geneva (Switzerland) 533, **640**

International University of Japan, Graduate School of International Management, Minami Uonuma-gu (Japan) 516

Leadership Institute of Seattle, School of Applied Behavioral Science, Kenmore (WA) 449

London School of Economics and Political Science, The Graduate School, London (United Kingdom) 543

Monash University, MBA Programme, Clayton (Australia) 486

Monterey Institute of International Studies, Fisher Graduate School of International Business, Monterey (CA) 82, **660**

National University, School of Business and Management, La Jolla (CA) 82

National University of Ireland, Dublin, The Michael Smurfit Graduate School of Business, Blackrock (Ireland) 513

New York Institute of Technology, School of Management (NY) 308

Nottingham Trent University, Nottingham Business School, Nottingham (United Kingdom) 544

Point Loma Nazarene University, Program in Business Administration, San Diego (CA) 86

Purdue University, Krannert School of Management, West Lafayette (IN) 185

Rensselaer Polytechnic Institute, Lally School of Management and Technology, Troy (NY) 311, **670**

Saint Michael's College, Program in Administration and Management, Colchester (VT) 434

Southern Methodist University, Cox School of Business, Dallas (TX) 411, **688**

Stockholm School of Economics, Department of Business Administration, Stockholm (Sweden) 531

Swinburne University of Technology, Australian Graduate School of Entrepreneurship (AGSE), Hawthorne (Australia) 488

The University of Alabama, Manderson Graduate School of Business, Tuscaloosa (AL) 49

University of Bath, School of Management, Bath (United Kingdom) 547

University of California, Berkeley, Haas School of Business, Berkeley (CA) 89

University of Detroit Mercy, College of Business Administration, Detroit (MI) 243

University of Florida, Hough Graduate School of Business, Gainesville (FL) 134

University of Glasgow, University of Glasgow Business School, Glasgow (United Kingdom) 550

University of Manitoba, Faculty of Management, Winnipeg (Canada) 475

University of New Haven, School of Business, West Haven (CT) 113, **728**

University of New Mexico, Robert O. Anderson Graduate School of Management, Albuquerque (NM) 294

University of Salford, Salford Business School, Salford (United Kingdom) 554

University of the West of England, Bristol, Bristol Business School, Bristol (United Kingdom) 555

University of Ulster at Jordanstown, Faculty of Business and Management, Newtown Abbey (United Kingdom) 556

University of Windsor, Odette School of Business, Windsor (Canada) 480

University of Wyoming, College of Business, Laramie (WY) 465

Waseda University, Graduate School of Commerce, Tokyo (Japan) 517

Wilfrid Laurier University, School of Business and Economics, Waterloo (Canada) 481, **766**

BUSINESS STUDIES

Anna Maria College, Program in Business Administration, Paxton (MA) 219

Antwerp International Business School, Graduate Programs in Business, Antwerp (Belgium) 493

Aston University, Aston Business School, Birmingham (United Kingdom) 539

Barcelona Business School, Graduate Programs in Business, Barcelona (Spain) 528

Bayerische Julius-Maximilians University of Wuerzburg, MBA Program, Wuerzburg (Germany) 507

Baylor University, Hankamer School of Business, Waco (TX) 405, **574**

Bellevue University, College of Business, Bellevue (NE) 271, **576**

Benedictine College, Executive Master of Business Administration Program, Atchison (KS) 193

The Chinese University of Hong Kong, Faculty of Business Administration, Hong Kong (China) 497

Concordia University, St. Paul, College of Business and Organizational Leadership, St. Paul (MN) 250

École Nationale des Ponts et Chaussées, ENPC MBA, Paris (France) 503

ESCP-EAP European School of Management, ESCP-EAP European School of Management (France) 503

European University, Center for Management Studies, Montreux-Fontanivent (Switzerland) 532

Grand Valley State University, Seidman College of Business, Allendale (MI) 238

HfB—Business School of Finance and Management, Frankfurt School of Finance and Management, Frankfurt (Germany) 508

Hong Kong Baptist University, School of Business, Hong Kong (China) 498

IE Business School, Business School, Madrid (Spain) 529, **636**

International University of Japan, Graduate School of International Management, Minami Uonuma-gu (Japan) 516

Jones International University, Graduate School of Business Administration, Centennial (CO) 103

Leadership Institute of Seattle, School of Applied Behavioral Science, Kenmore (WA) 449

Madonna University, School of Business, Livonia (MI) 240

Monash University, MBA Programme, Clayton (Australia) 486

National University, School of Business and Management, La Jolla (CA) 82

Northeastern University, Graduate School of Business Administration, Boston (MA) 228

Norwegian School of Management, Graduate School, Sandvika (Norway) 524

Nottingham Trent University, Nottingham Business School, Nottingham (United Kingdom) 544

Pontifical Catholic University of Puerto Rico, College of Business Administration, Ponce (PR) 386

Salve Regina University, Graduate Studies, Newport (RI) 389

Schiller International University, Graduate Programs, London (United Kingdom) 546, **684**

Stockholm School of Economics, Department of Business Administration, Stockholm (Sweden) 531

Texas Southern University, Jesse H. Jones School of Business, Houston (TX) 417

The University of Adelaide, The University of Adelaide Business School, Adelaide (Australia) 488

University of Birmingham, Birmingham Business School, Birmingham (United Kingdom) 548

University of Durham, Durham Business School, Durham (United Kingdom) 549

University of Glasgow, University of Glasgow Business School, Glasgow (United Kingdom) 550

University of Hull, School of Management, Hull (United Kingdom) 552

University of Illinois at Chicago, Liautaud Graduate School of Business, Chicago (IL) 176

University of Manitoba, Faculty of Management, Winnipeg (Canada) 475

University of Salford, Salford Business School, Salford (United Kingdom) 554

University of Wyoming, College of Business, Laramie (WY) 465

Wagner College, Department of Business Administration, Staten Island (NY) 321

Wayland Baptist University, Graduate Programs, Plainview (TX) 429

Webster University, School of Business and Technology, St. Louis (MO) 270

WHU—Otto Beisheim School of Management, WHU—Otto Beisheim School of Management, Vallendar (Germany) 511

CHINESE BUSINESS STUDIES

The Chinese University of Hong Kong, Faculty of Business Administration, Hong Kong (China) 497

City University of Hong Kong, Faculty of Business, Hong Kong (China) 497

HfB—Business School of Finance and Management, Frankfurt School of Finance and Management, Frankfurt (Germany) 508

The Hong Kong University of Science and Technology, School of Business and Management, Hong Kong (China) 499

International University of Japan, Graduate School of International Management, Minami Uonuma-gu (Japan) 516

Louisiana State University and Agricultural and Mechanical College, E. J. Ourso College of Business, Baton Rouge (LA) 204

Monash University, MBA Programme, Clayton (Australia) 486

Monterey Institute of International Studies, Fisher Graduate School of International Business, Monterey (CA) 82, **660**

Norwegian School of Management, Graduate School, Sandvika (Norway) 524

University of Hawaii at Manoa, Shidler College of Business, Honolulu (HI) 154

University of New Brunswick Saint John, Faculty of Business, Saint John (Canada) 476, **724**

University of Pennsylvania, Wharton School, Philadelphia (PA) 380

York University, Schulich School of Business, Toronto (Canada) 482, **772**

CITY/URBAN ADMINISTRATION

The American University in Cairo, School of Business, Economics and Communication, Cairo (Egypt) 502

Brigham Young University, Marriott School of Management, Provo (UT) 431

California Polytechnic State University, San Luis Obispo, Orfalea College of Business, San Luis Obispo (CA) 68

California State University, Sacramento, College of Business Administration, Sacramento (CA) 72

East Carolina University, College of Business, Greenville (NC) 324, **602**

Eastern Washington University, College of Business and Public Administration, Cheney (WA) 448

The George Washington University, School of Business, Washington (DC) 119, **622**

New York University, Robert F. Wagner Graduate School of Public Service (NY) 309

Old Dominion University, College of Business and Public Administration, Norfolk (VA) 441

University of California, Los Angeles, UCLA Anderson School of Management, Los Angeles (CA) 91, **696**

University of Waterloo, Graduate Studies, Waterloo (Canada) 479

COMBINED DEGREES

Arizona State University, W.P. Carey School of Business, Tempe (AZ) 54

Barry University, Andreas School of Business, Miami Shores (FL) 123

Benedictine University, Graduate Programs, Lisle (IL) 158

Bentley College, The Elkin B. McCallum Graduate School of Business, Waltham (MA) 221, **578**

Bernard M. Baruch College of the City University of New York, Zicklin School of Business, New York (NY) 296

Boston College, The Carroll School of Management, Chestnut Hill (MA) 221, **580**

Boston University, School of Management, Boston (MA) 223

Bowling Green State University, College of Business Administration, Bowling Green (OH) 338

Brandeis University, The Heller School for Social Policy and Management (MA) 223

Brigham Young University, Marriott School of Management, Provo (UT) 431

California Polytechnic State University, San Luis Obispo, Orfalea College of Business, San Luis Obispo (CA) 68

Capital University, School of Management, Columbus (OH) 338

Chapman University, The George L. Argyros School of Business and Economics, Orange (CA) 74, **586**

Clemson University, College of Business and Behavioral Science, Clemson (SC) 391

Cleveland State University, Nance College of Business Administration, Cleveland (OH) 340

The College of Saint Rose, School of Business, Albany (NY) 298, **594**

Columbia University, Graduate School of Business, New York (NY) 298

Cornell University, Johnson Graduate School of Management, Ithaca (NY) 299, **598**

Creighton University, Eugene C. Eppley College of Business Administration, Omaha (NE) 272

Cyprus International Institute of Management, MBA Programme, Nicosia (Cyprus) 500

Dalhousie University, Faculty of Management, Halifax (Canada) 467

Dartmouth College, Tuck School of Business at Dartmouth, Hanover (NH) 277

DePaul University, Charles H. Kellstadt Graduate School of Business, Chicago (IL) 159

DeSales University, Department of Business, Center Valley (PA) 365

Drake University, College of Business and Public Administration, Des Moines (IA) 189

Duquesne University, John F. Donahue Graduate School of Business, Pittsburgh (PA) 367

Eastern University, Graduate Business Programs, St. Davids (PA) 368

Emory University, Roberto C. Goizueta Business School, Atlanta (GA) 145, **606**

Florida International University, Alvah H. Chapman, Jr. Graduate School of Business, Miami (FL) 128, **618**

Georgetown University, McDonough School of Business, Washington (DC) 119

The George Washington University, School of Business, Washington (DC) 119, **622**

Georgia State University, J. Mack Robinson College of Business, Atlanta (GA) 147, **626**

Gonzaga University, School of Business Administration, Spokane (WA) 448

Grand Valley State University, Seidman College of Business, Allendale (MI) 238

Howard University, School of Business, Washington (DC) 120

Illinois Institute of Technology, Stuart School of Business, Chicago (IL) 164

Indiana University–Purdue University Indianapolis, Kelley School of Business, Indianapolis (IN) 184

James Cook University, Faculty of Law, Business, and the Creative Arts—Townsville, Cairns (Australia) 485

The Johns Hopkins University, Carey Business School, Baltimore (MD) 214, **646**

Kean University, College of Business and Public Administration, Union (NJ) 284

Kent State University, Graduate School of Management, Kent (OH) 342

Lancaster University, Management School, Lancaster (United Kingdom) 541

Lewis University, College of Business, Romeoville (IL) 166

Long Island University, C.W. Post Campus, College of Management, Brookville (NY) 305

Loyola University New Orleans, Joseph A. Butt, S.J., College of Business, New Orleans (LA) 205

Massachusetts Institute of Technology, Sloan School of Management, Cambridge (MA) 227

McGill University, Desautels Faculty of Management, Montréal (Canada) 469, **658**

Monterey Institute of International Studies, Fisher Graduate School of International Business, Monterey (CA) 82, **660**

New York University, Leonard N. Stern School of Business (NY) 309

North Carolina Central University, School of Business, Durham (NC) 327

Northeastern University, Graduate School of Business Administration, Boston (MA) 228

Northern Kentucky University, College of Business, Highland Heights (KY) 201

North Park University, School of Business and Nonprofit Management, Chicago (IL) 170

Norwegian School of Management, Graduate School, Sandvika (Norway) 524

Pace University, Lubin School of Business, New York (NY) 310

Pacific Lutheran University, School of Business, Tacoma (WA) 449

Penn State Great Valley, Graduate Studies, Malvern (PA) 373

Pontifical Catholic University of Puerto Rico, College of Business Administration, Ponce (PR) 386

Saint Louis University, John Cook School of Business, St. Louis (MO) *264*

Samford University, School of Business, Birmingham (AL) 47

San Diego State University, College of Business Administration, San Diego (CA) 86

San Jose State University, Lucas Graduate School of Business, San Jose (CA) 87

Seton Hall University, Stillman School of Business, South Orange (NJ) 290, **686**

SIT Graduate Institute, Master's Programs in Intercultural Service, Leadership, and Management, Brattleboro (VT) 434

Southern Illinois University Carbondale, College of Business and Administration, Carbondale (IL) 173

Southern New Hampshire University, School of Business, Manchester (NH) 279, **690**

Stanford University, Graduate School of Business, Stanford (CA) 88

Stevens Institute of Technology, Wesley J. Howe School of Technology Management, Hoboken (NJ) 290

Stockholm School of Economics, Department of Business Administration, Stockholm (Sweden) 531

Suffolk University, Sawyer Business School, Boston (MA) 230

Temple University, Fox School of Business and Management, Philadelphia (PA) 379

Texas Christian University, The Neeley School of Business at TCU, Fort Worth (TX) 416, **694**

Texas Southern University, Jesse H. Jones School of Business, Houston (TX) 417

Texas Tech University, Jerry S. Rawls College of Business Administration, Lubbock (TX) 418

Université de Moncton, Faculty of Administration, Moncton (Canada) 472

University at Buffalo, the State University of New York, School of Management, Buffalo (NY) 320

The University of Akron, College of Business Administration, Akron (OH) 346

The University of Alabama, Manderson Graduate School of Business, Tuscaloosa (AL) 49

The University of Alabama at Birmingham, School of Business, Birmingham (AL) 50

University of Alberta, School of Business, Edmonton (Canada) 473

University of Bath, School of Management, Bath (United Kingdom) 547

University of Calgary, Haskayne School of Business, Calgary (Canada) 474

University of California, Los Angeles, UCLA Anderson School of Management, Los Angeles (CA) 91, **696**

University of Cincinnati, College of Business, Cincinnati (OH) 346

University of Colorado at Boulder, Leeds School of Business, Boulder (CO) 104, **702**

University of Connecticut, School of Business, Storrs (CT) 112, **708**

University of Denver, Daniels College of Business, Denver (CO) 106

University of Houston–Clear Lake, School of Business, Houston (TX) 421

University of Idaho, College of Business and Economics, Moscow (ID) 156

University of Illinois at Urbana–Champaign, College of Business, Champaign (IL) 176

The University of Iowa, Henry B. Tippie College of Business, Iowa City (IA) 191, **714**

University of Kentucky, Gatton College of Business and Economics, Lexington (KY) 202, **716**

University of Louisville, College of Business, Louisville (KY) 203

University of Maryland, College Park, Robert H. Smith School of Business, College Park (MD) 217

University of Mary Washington, College of Graduate and Professional Studies, Fredericksburg (VA) 444

University of Memphis, Fogelman College of Business and Economics, Memphis (TN) 400

University of Miami, School of Business Administration, Coral Gables (FL) 135, **718**

University of Michigan, Ross School of Business at the University of Michigan, Ann Arbor (MI) 244

University of Missouri–Columbia, Robert J. Trulaske, Sr. College of Business, Columbia (MO) 267, **720**

University of Nevada, Las Vegas, College of Business, Las Vegas (NV) 275, **722**

University of New Brunswick Fredericton, Faculty of Business Administration, Fredericton (Canada) 476

The University of North Carolina at Chapel Hill, Kenan-Flagler Business School, Chapel Hill (NC) 330

The University of North Carolina at Greensboro, Bryan School of Business and Economics, Greensboro (NC) 331

University of Oklahoma, Michael F. Price College of Business, Norman (OK) 355

University of Oregon, Charles H. Lundquist College of Business, Eugene (OR) 359, **732**

University of Pittsburgh, Joseph M. Katz Graduate School of Business, Pittsburgh (PA) 381

University of Richmond, Richard S. Reynolds Graduate School, Richmond (VA) 444

University of San Diego, School of Business Administration, San Diego (CA) 96

University of San Francisco, Masagung Graduate School of Management, San Francisco (CA) 97

University of Southern California, School of Business, Los Angeles (CA) 98

The University of Texas at Tyler, College of Business and Technology, Tyler (TX) 428

University of the Incarnate Word, H-E-B School of Business and Administration (TX) 429

The University of Toledo, College of Business Administration, Toledo (OH) 349

University of Tulsa, College of Business Administration, Tulsa (OK) 356

University of Victoria, Faculty of Business, Victoria (Canada) 479

Villanova University, Villanova School of Business, Villanova (PA) 382

Virginia Commonwealth University, School of Business, Richmond (VA) 445

Virginia Polytechnic Institute and State University, Pamplin College of Business, Blacksburg (VA) 446

Washington State University, College of Business, Pullman (WA) 453

Washington University in St. Louis, Olin Business School, St. Louis (MO) 269

Wichita State University, W. Frank Barton School of Business, Wichita (KS) 197

Widener University, School of Business Administration, Chester (PA) 384, **764**

Wright State University, Raj Soin College of Business, Dayton (OH) 350

Xavier University, Williams College of Business, Cincinnati (OH) 350

Yale University, Yale School of Management, New Haven (CT) 114

COMMERCE

The Aarhus School of Business, Faculty of Business Administration, Aarhus (Denmark) 501

Aston University, Aston Business School, Birmingham (United Kingdom) 539

Barcelona Business School, Graduate Programs in Business, Barcelona (Spain) 528

Bayerische Julius-Maximilians University of Wuerzburg, MBA Program, Wuerzburg (Germany) 507

Deakin University, Deakin Business School, Geelong (Australia) 484

European School of Economics, MBA Programme (Italy) 515, **608**

European University, Center for Management Studies, Montreux-Fontanivent (Switzerland) 532

IE Business School, Business School, Madrid (Spain) 529, **636**

International University of Japan, Graduate School of International Management, Minami Uonuma-gu (Japan) 516

Lancaster University, Management School, Lancaster (United Kingdom) 541

Mississippi College, School of Business Administration, Clinton (MS) 256

Monash University, MBA Programme, Clayton (Australia) 486

Monterey Institute of International Studies, Fisher Graduate School of International Business, Monterey (CA) 82, **660**

Stockholm School of Economics, Department of Business Administration, Stockholm (Sweden) 531

University of Durham, Durham Business School, Durham (United Kingdom) 549

University of Newcastle, Graduate School of Business, Callaghan (Australia) 489

University of Plymouth, Plymouth Business School, Plymouth (United Kingdom) 553

CONFLICT RESOLUTION MANAGEMENT

American Jewish University, David Lieber School of Graduate Studies, Bel Air (CA) 63

Baker University, School of Professional and Graduate Studies, Baldwin City (KS) 193

Boise State University, College of Business and Economics, Boise (ID) 155

College of St. Catherine, Program in Organizational Leadership, St. Paul (MN) 249

Dallas Baptist University, Graduate School of Business, Dallas (TX) 406

The George Washington University, School of Business, Washington (DC) 119, **622**

Graduate School of Business Administration Zurich, Executive Management Programs, Zurich (Switzerland) 532

IE Business School, Business School, Madrid (Spain) 529, **636**

Jones International University, Graduate School of Business Administration, Centennial (CO) 103

Leadership Institute of Seattle, School of Applied Behavioral Science, Kenmore (WA) 449

Lipscomb University, MBA Program, Nashville (TN) 397

Monash University, MBA Programme, Clayton (Australia) 486

Monterey Institute of International Studies, Fisher Graduate School of International Business, Monterey (CA) 82, **660**

National University, School of Business and Management, La Jolla (CA) 82

North Park University, School of Business and Nonprofit Management, Chicago (IL) 170

SIT Graduate Institute, Master's Programs in Intercultural Service, Leadership, and Management, Brattleboro (VT) 434

Stockholm School of Economics, Department of Business Administration, Stockholm (Sweden) 531

TUI University, College of Business Administration, Cypress (CA) 89

CONSTRUCTION MANAGEMENT

University of Cincinnati, College of Business, Cincinnati (OH) 346

University of Denver, Daniels College of Business, Denver (CO) 106

University of North Florida, Coggin College of Business, Jacksonville (FL) 136

CONTRACT MANAGEMENT

Bellevue University, College of Business, Bellevue (NE) 271, **576**

Lancaster University, Management School, Lancaster (United Kingdom) 541

Naval Postgraduate School, School of Business and Public Policy, Monterey (CA) 83

Stockholm School of Economics, Department of Business Administration, Stockholm (Sweden) 531

University of La Verne, College of Business and Public Management, La Verne (CA) 94

University of Management and Technology, Graduate Business Programs, Arlington (VA) 443

University of Mary Washington, College of Graduate and Professional Studies, Fredericksburg (VA) 444

CORPORATE ACCOUNTING

European School of Economics, MBA Programme (Italy) 515, **608**

Florida State University, College of Business, Tallahassee (FL) 129

Graduate School of Business Administration Zurich, Executive Management Programs, Zurich (Switzerland) 532

HEC Paris, HEC MBA Program, Jouy-en-Josas (France) *505*, **632**

IE Business School, Business School, Madrid (Spain) 529, **636**

Illinois Institute of Technology, Stuart School of Business, Chicago (IL) 164

International University of Japan, Graduate School of International Management, Minami Uonuma-gu (Japan) 516

Mercy College, Division of Business and Accounting, Dobbs Ferry (NY) 307

Monash University, MBA Programme, Clayton (Australia) 486

Northeastern University, Graduate School of Business Administration, Boston (MA) 228

Norwegian School of Management, Graduate School, Sandvika (Norway) 524

Nottingham Trent University, Nottingham Business School, Nottingham (United Kingdom) 544

Old Dominion University, College of Business and Public Administration, Norfolk (VA) 441

Rice University, Jesse H. Jones Graduate School of Management, Houston (TX) 410

Rochester Institute of Technology, E. Philip Saunders College of Business, Rochester (NY) 312

Stockholm School of Economics, Department of Business Administration, Stockholm (Sweden) 531

University of Denver, Daniels College of Business, Denver (CO) 106

University of Rochester, William E. Simon Graduate School of Business Administration, Rochester (NY) 321, **736**

University of Salford, Salford Business School, Salford (United Kingdom) 554

University of San Diego, School of Business Administration, San Diego (CA) 96

Vienna University of Economics and Business Administration, WU Wien MBA, Vienna (Austria) 492

CORPORATE LEGAL COUNSELING

WHU—Otto Beisheim School of Management, WHU—Otto Beisheim School of Management, Vallendar (Germany) 511

CREDIT MANAGEMENT

Graduate School of Business Administration Zurich, Executive Management Programs, Zurich (Switzerland) 532

Monash University, MBA Programme, Clayton (Australia) 486

DECISION SCIENCES

Aston University, Aston Business School, Birmingham (United Kingdom) 539

California State University, Fullerton, College of Business and Economics, Fullerton (CA) 70

The Chinese University of Hong Kong, Faculty of Business Administration, Hong Kong (China) 497

City University of Hong Kong, Faculty of Business, Hong Kong (China) 497

Clark Atlanta University, School of Business Administration, Atlanta (GA) 143

Columbia University, Graduate School of Business, New York (NY) 298

Duke University, The Fuqua School of Business, Durham (NC) 323

École Nationale des Ponts et Chaussées, ENPC MBA, Paris (France) 503

European School of Economics, MBA Programme (Italy) 515, **608**

The George Washington University, School of
Business, Washington (DC) 119, **622**

Georgia State University, J. Mack Robinson
College of Business, Atlanta (GA) 147, **626**

HfB—Business School of Finance and
Management, Frankfurt School of Finance and
Management, Frankfurt (Germany) 508

Lancaster University, Management School,
Lancaster (United Kingdom) 541

London School of Economics and Political
Science, The Graduate School, London (United
Kingdom) 543

Millsaps College, Else School of Management,
Jackson (MS) 255

Monash University, MBA Programme, Clayton
(Australia) 486

Monterey Institute of International Studies, Fisher
Graduate School of International Business,
Monterey (CA) 82, **660**

National University, School of Business and
Management, La Jolla (CA) 82

Northwestern University, Kellogg School of
Management, Evanston (IL) 171

Old Dominion University, College of Business and
Public Administration, Norfolk (VA) 441

Rensselaer Polytechnic Institute, Lally School of
Management and Technology, Troy
(NY) 311, **670**

St. John's University, The Peter J. Tobin College
of Business, Queens (NY) 314, **680**

Saint Joseph's University, Erivan K. Haub School
of Business, Philadelphia (PA) 377

Salem State College, Program in Business
Administration, Salem (MA) 229

San Francisco State University, College of
Business, San Francisco (CA) 87

Southern Illinois University Edwardsville, School
of Business, Edwardsville (IL) *174*

The University of Alabama, Manderson Graduate
School of Business, Tuscaloosa (AL) 49

University of California, Los Angeles, UCLA
Anderson School of Management, Los Angeles
(CA) 91, **696**

University of Colorado at Boulder, Leeds School
of Business, Boulder (CO) 104, **702**

University of Detroit Mercy, College of Business
Administration, Detroit (MI) 243

University of Illinois at Urbana–Champaign,
College of Business, Champaign (IL) 176

University of Maryland, College Park, Robert H.
Smith School of Business, College Park
(MD) 217

University of North Texas, College of Business
Administration, Denton (TX) 422

University of Salford, Salford Business School,
Salford (United Kingdom) 554

The University of Texas at Arlington, College of
Business Administration, Arlington
(TX) 424, **746**

University of Warwick, Warwick Business School,
Coventry (United Kingdom) 557

University of Washington, Michael G. Foster
School of Business, Seattle (WA) 452, **754**

Virginia Commonwealth University, School of
Business, Richmond (VA) 445

DEVELOPMENTAL ECONOMICS

The American University in Cairo, School of
Business, Economics and Communication,
Cairo (Egypt) 502

Auburn University, College of Business, Auburn
University (AL) 45, **568**

Cape Breton University, School of Business,
Sydney (Canada) 466

Copenhagen Business School, Faculty of
Economics and Business Administration,
Copenhagen (Denmark) 501

The George Washington University, School of
Business, Washington (DC) 119, **622**

HfB—Business School of Finance and
Management, Frankfurt School of Finance and
Management, Frankfurt (Germany) 508

IE Business School, Business School, Madrid
(Spain) 529, **636**

Katholieke Universiteit Leuven, Leuven School of
Business and Economics, Leuven
(Belgium) 494

New York University, Robert F. Wagner Graduate
School of Public Service (NY) 309

Saints Cyril and Methodius University, Faculty of
Economics, Skopje (Macedonia) 519

Stockholm School of Economics, Department of
Business Administration, Stockholm
(Sweden) 531

University of Detroit Mercy, College of Business
Administration, Detroit (MI) 243

University of Glasgow, University of Glasgow
Business School, Glasgow (United Kingdom)
550

University of Houston–Victoria, School of
Business Administration, Victoria (TX) 421

University of Newcastle, Graduate School of
Business, Callaghan (Australia) 489

University of Waterloo, Graduate Studies,
Waterloo (Canada) 479

ECONOMICS

The American University in Cairo, School of
Business, Economics and Communication,
Cairo (Egypt) 502

Antioch University New England, Department of
Organization and Management, Keene
(NH) 277

Arizona State University, W.P. Carey School of
Business, Tempe (AZ) 54

Arkansas State University, College of Business,
Jonesboro (AR) 61

Ashridge, Ashridge Executive MBA Program,
Berkhamsted (United Kingdom) 538

Assumption College, Department of Business
Studies, Worcester (MA) 219

Aston University, Aston Business School,
Birmingham (United Kingdom) 539

Auburn University, College of Business, Auburn
University (AL) 45, **568**

Auburn University Montgomery, School of
Business, Montgomery (AL) 46

Barcelona Business School, Graduate Programs in
Business, Barcelona (Spain) 528

Bar-Ilan University, Graduate School of Business,
Ramat-Gan (Israel) 514

Bentley College, The Elkin B. McCallum
Graduate School of Business, Waltham
(MA) 221, **578**

Bernard M. Baruch College of the City University
of New York, Zicklin School of Business, New
York (NY) 296

Brandeis University, International Business School,
Waltham (MA) 224, **582**

California National University for Advanced
Studies, College of Business Administration,
Northridge (CA) 67

California State University, East Bay, College of
Business and Economics, Hayward (CA) 69

California State University, Fullerton, College of
Business and Economics, Fullerton (CA) 70

California State University, Los Angeles, College
of Business and Economics, Los Angeles
(CA) 71

California State University, Northridge, College of
Business and Economics, Northridge (CA) 72

Carnegie Mellon University, Tepper School of
Business, Pittsburgh (PA) 363, **584**

Case Western Reserve University, Weatherhead
School of Management, Cleveland (OH) 338

City University of Hong Kong, Faculty of
Business, Hong Kong (China) 497

Claremont Graduate University, Peter F. Drucker
and Masatoshi Ito Graduate School of
Management, Claremont (CA) 75, **590**

Clarion University of Pennsylvania, College of
Business Administration, Clarion (PA) 364

Columbia University, Graduate School of
Business, New York (NY) 298

Copenhagen Business School, Faculty of
Economics and Business Administration,
Copenhagen (Denmark) 501

Deakin University, Deakin Business School,
Geelong (Australia) 484

Delta State University, College of Business,
Cleveland (MS) 254

DePaul University, Charles H. Kellstadt Graduate
School of Business, Chicago (IL) 159

Drexel University, LeBow College of Business,
Philadelphia (PA) 366

Duquesne University, John F. Donahue Graduate
School of Business, Pittsburgh (PA) 367

Eastern Mennonite University, Program in
Business Administration, Harrisonburg
(VA) 438

Eastern University, Graduate Business Programs,
St. Davids (PA) 368

École Nationale des Ponts et Chaussées, ENPC
MBA, Paris (France) 503

Edith Cowan University, Faculty of Business and
Public Management, Churchlands
(Australia) 484

European School of Economics, MBA Programme
(Italy) 515, **608**

European University, Center for Management
Studies, Montreux-Fontanivent
(Switzerland) 532

Florida Atlantic University, College of Business,
Boca Raton (FL) 126

The George Washington University, School of
Business, Washington (DC) 119, **622**

Georgia State University, J. Mack Robinson
College of Business, Atlanta (GA) 147, **626**

Graduate School of Business Administration
Zurich, Executive Management Programs,
Zurich (Switzerland) 532

Hawai'i Pacific University, College of Business
Administration, Honolulu (HI) 153, **630**

HEC Paris, HEC MBA Program, Jouy-en-Josas
(France) *505*, **632**

HfB—Business School of Finance and
Management, Frankfurt School of Finance and
Management, Frankfurt (Germany) 508

Hong Kong Baptist University, School of
Business, Hong Kong (China) 498

The Hong Kong University of Science and
Technology, School of Business and
Management, Hong Kong (China) 499

Hult International Business School, Graduate
Program, Cambridge (MA) *227*, **634**

IE Business School, Business School, Madrid
(Spain) 529, **636**

Indian School of Business, MBA Program, Andhra
Pradesh (India) 512

International University of Japan, Graduate School
of International Management, Minami
Uonuma-gu (Japan) 516

Katholieke Universiteit Leuven, Leuven School of
Business and Economics, Leuven
(Belgium) 494

Kent State University, Graduate School of Management, Kent (OH) 342

Lancaster University, Management School, Lancaster (United Kingdom) 541

Lehigh University, College of Business and Economics, Bethlehem (PA) 371, **656**

London School of Economics and Political Science, The Graduate School, London (United Kingdom) 543

Louisiana State University and Agricultural and Mechanical College, E. J. Ourso College of Business, Baton Rouge (LA) 204

Louisiana Tech University, College of Administration and Business, Ruston (LA) 205

Loyola University Chicago, Graduate School of Business, Chicago (IL) 167

Marquette University, Graduate School of Management, Milwaukee (WI) 459

Miami University, Farmer School of Business, Oxford (OH) 343

Mississippi State University, College of Business and Industry, Mississippi State (MS) 256

Monash University, MBA Programme, Clayton (Australia) 486

Montclair State University, School of Business, Montclair (NJ) 285

Murray State University, College of Business and Public Affairs, Murray (KY) 200

National University of Ireland, Dublin, The Michael Smurfit Graduate School of Business, Blackrock (Ireland) 513

New Mexico State University, College of Business, Las Cruces (NM) 293

New York University, Leonard N. Stern School of Business (NY) 309

North Carolina State University, College of Management, Raleigh (NC) 328, **664**

North Park University, School of Business and Nonprofit Management, Chicago (IL) 170

Norwegian School of Management, Graduate School, Sandvika (Norway) 524

Oakland University, School of Business Administration, Rochester (MI) 241

Old Dominion University, College of Business and Public Administration, Norfolk (VA) 441

Pace University, Lubin School of Business, New York (NY) 310

Providence College, School of Business, Providence (RI) 388

Queensland University of Technology, Brisbane Graduate School of Business, Brisbane (Australia) 487

Quinnipiac University, School of Business, Hamden (CT) 109

Roosevelt University, Walter E. Heller College of Business Administration, Chicago (IL) 172, **676**

Saginaw Valley State University, College of Business and Management, University Center (MI) 242

St. Cloud State University, G.R. Herberger College of Business, St. Cloud (MN) 251

St. John's University, The Peter J. Tobin College of Business, Queens (NY) 314, **680**

Saint Louis University, John Cook School of Business, St. Louis (MO) *264*

Seattle University, Albers School of Business and Economics, Seattle (WA) 451

Southeastern University, College of Graduate Studies, Washington (DC) 121

Southern Illinois University Edwardsville, School of Business, Edwardsville (IL) *174*

Stockholm School of Economics, Department of Business Administration, Stockholm (Sweden) 531

The University of Alabama, Manderson Graduate School of Business, Tuscaloosa (AL) 49

The University of Arizona, Eller College of Management, Tucson (AZ) 58

University of Arkansas, Sam M. Walton College of Business Administration, Fayetteville (AR) 62

University of California, Berkeley, Haas School of Business, Berkeley (CA) 89

University of California, Los Angeles, UCLA Anderson School of Management, Los Angeles (CA) 91, **696**

University of Canterbury, Department of Management, Christchurch (New Zealand) 523

University of Central Florida, College of Business Administration, Orlando (FL) 133

University of Chicago, Graduate School of Business, Chicago (IL) 175

University of Delaware, Alfred Lerner College of Business and Economics, Newark (DE) 116, **712**

University of Detroit Mercy, College of Business Administration, Detroit (MI) 243

University of Durham, Durham Business School, Durham (United Kingdom) 549

University of Edinburgh, Edinburgh University Management School, Edinburgh (United Kingdom) 550

University of Georgia, Terry College of Business, Athens (GA) 151

University of Glasgow, University of Glasgow Business School, Glasgow (United Kingdom) 550

University of Louisiana at Lafayette, Graduate School, Lafayette (LA) 208

University of Memphis, Fogelman College of Business and Economics, Memphis (TN) 400

University of Miami, School of Business Administration, Coral Gables (FL) 135, **718**

University of Mississippi, School of Business Administration, Oxford (MS) 257

University of Missouri–Columbia, Robert J. Trulaske, Sr. College of Business, Columbia (MO) 267, **720**

University of Nevada, Las Vegas, College of Business, Las Vegas (NV) 275, **722**

University of Nevada, Reno, College of Business Administration, Reno (NV) 276

University of Newcastle, Graduate School of Business, Callaghan (Australia) 489

University of New Hampshire, Whittemore School of Business and Economics, Durham (NH) 280, **726**

The University of North Carolina at Charlotte, Belk College of Business Administration, Charlotte (NC) 330, **730**

University of North Florida, Coggin College of Business, Jacksonville (FL) 136

University of Pennsylvania, Wharton School, Philadelphia (PA) 380

University of Plymouth, Plymouth Business School, Plymouth (United Kingdom) 553

University of Rochester, William E. Simon Graduate School of Business Administration, Rochester (NY) 321, **736**

University of South Carolina, Moore School of Business, Columbia (SC) *392*, **740**

University of South Florida, College of Business Administration, Tampa (FL) 138

The University of Tampa, John H. Sykes College of Business, Tampa (FL) 139, **742**

The University of Tennessee, College of Business Administration, Knoxville (TN) *401*, **744**

The University of Texas at Arlington, College of Business Administration, Arlington (TX) 424, **746**

The University of Texas at San Antonio, College of Business, San Antonio (TX) 427, **750**

University of the West of England, Bristol, Bristol Business School, Bristol (United Kingdom) 555

University of the Witwatersrand, Graduate School of Business Administration, Wits (South Africa) 527

University of Toronto, Joseph L. Rotman School of Management, Toronto (Canada) 478

University of Ulster at Jordanstown, Faculty of Business and Management, Newtown Abbey (United Kingdom) 556

University of Warwick, Warwick Business School, Coventry (United Kingdom) 557

University of Washington, Michael G. Foster School of Business, Seattle (WA) 452, **754**

University of Waterloo, Graduate Studies, Waterloo (Canada) 479

The University of Western Ontario, Richard Ivey School of Business, London (Canada) 480

Virginia Commonwealth University, School of Business, Richmond (VA) 445

Walsh College of Accountancy and Business Administration, Graduate Programs, Troy (MI) 247

Western Illinois University, College of Business and Technology, Macomb (IL) 178

Westminster College, The Bill and Vieve Gore School of Business, Salt Lake City (UT) 433

West Texas A&M University, College of Business, Canyon (TX) 430

WHU—Otto Beisheim School of Management, WHU—Otto Beisheim School of Management, Vallendar (Germany) 511

Wilfrid Laurier University, School of Business and Economics, Waterloo (Canada) 481, **766**

Woodbury University, School of Business and Management, Burbank (CA) 100

Wright State University, Raj Soin College of Business, Dayton (OH) 350

York University, Schulich School of Business, Toronto (Canada) 482, **772**

ELECTRONIC COMMERCE (E-COMMERCE)

Adelphi University, School of Business, Garden City (NY) 295, **560**

American University, Kogod School of Business, Washington (DC) 118

Arkansas State University, College of Business, Jonesboro (AR) 61

Aston University, Aston Business School, Birmingham (United Kingdom) 539

Barcelona Business School, Graduate Programs in Business, Barcelona (Spain) 528

Bayerische Julius-Maximilians University of Wuerzburg, MBA Program, Wuerzburg (Germany) 507

Benedictine University, Graduate Programs, Lisle (IL) 158

Bernard M. Baruch College of the City University of New York, Zicklin School of Business, New York (NY) 296

Bond University, School of Business, Gold Coast (Australia) 483

California State University, East Bay, College of Business and Economics, Hayward (CA) 69

California State University, Fullerton, College of Business and Economics, Fullerton (CA) 70

Carnegie Mellon University, Tepper School of Business, Pittsburgh (PA) 363, **584**

Case Western Reserve University, Weatherhead School of Management, Cleveland (OH) 338

The Chinese University of Hong Kong, Faculty of
Business Administration, Hong Kong
(China) 497

City University of Hong Kong, Faculty of
Business, Hong Kong (China) 497

Columbia Southern University, MBA Program,
Orange Beach (AL) 46

Dallas Baptist University, Graduate School of
Business, Dallas (TX) 406

Deakin University, Deakin Business School,
Geelong (Australia) 484

DePaul University, Charles H. Kellstadt Graduate
School of Business, Chicago (IL) 159

DeSales University, Department of Business,
Center Valley (PA) 365

DeVry University, Keller Graduate School of
Management, Alpharetta (GA) 144

DeVry University, Keller Graduate School of
Management, Oakbrook Terrace (IL) 161, **650**

DeVry University, Keller Graduate School of
Management, Arlington (VA) 437

Eastern Michigan University, College of Business,
Ypsilanti (MI) 237

École Nationale des Ponts et Chaussées, ENPC
MBA, Paris (France) 503

Edith Cowan University, Faculty of Business and
Public Management, Churchlands
(Australia) 484

Erasmus University Rotterdam, Rotterdam School
of Management, Rotterdam (Netherlands) 521

European School of Economics, MBA Programme
(United Kingdom) 541, **608**

Fordham University, Graduate School of Business
Administration, New York (NY) 301, **620**

The George Washington University, School of
Business, Washington (DC) 119, **622**

The Hague University, Faculty of Economics and
Management, The Hague
(Netherlands) 521, **628**

Hawai'i Pacific University, College of Business
Administration, Honolulu (HI) 153, **630**

IE Business School, Business School, Madrid
(Spain) 529, **636**

Illinois Institute of Technology, Stuart School of
Business, Chicago (IL) 164

Indiana State University, College of Business,
Terre Haute (IN) 181

International University in Geneva, MBA Program,
Geneva (Switzerland) 533, **640**

International University of Japan, Graduate School
of International Management, Minami
Uonuma-gu (Japan) 516

The Johns Hopkins University, Carey Business
School, Baltimore (MD) 214, **646**

Kean University, College of Business and Public
Administration, Union (NJ) 284

Lancaster University, Management School,
Lancaster (United Kingdom) 541

LeTourneau University, Graduate and Professional
Studies, Longview (TX) 409

Lewis University, College of Business, Romeoville
(IL) 166

Lynn University, School of Business, Boca Raton
(FL) 130

Madonna University, School of Business, Livonia
(MI) 240

Maryville University of Saint Louis, The John E.
Simon School of Business, St. Louis (MO) 262

McMaster University, DeGroote School of
Business, Hamilton (Canada) 470

Monash University, MBA Programme, Clayton
(Australia) 486

Monterey Institute of International Studies, Fisher
Graduate School of International Business,
Monterey (CA) 82, **660**

Murray State University, College of Business and
Public Affairs, Murray (KY) 200

National University, School of Business and
Management, La Jolla (CA) 82

New Jersey Institute of Technology, School of
Management, Newark (NJ) 285

New York Institute of Technology, School of
Management (NY) 308

New York University, Leonard N. Stern School of
Business (NY) 309

Northcentral University, MBA Program, Prescott
Valley (AZ) 56

Northwestern University, Kellogg School of
Management, Evanston (IL) 171

Notre Dame de Namur University, Department of
Business Administration, Belmont (CA) 84

Nottingham Trent University, Nottingham Business
School, Nottingham (United Kingdom) 544

Pace University, Lubin School of Business, New
York (NY) 310

Pepperdine University, Graziadio School of
Business and Management, Los Angeles
(CA) 85

Purdue University, Krannert School of
Management, West Lafayette (IN) 185

Regis University, College for Professional Studies,
Denver (CO) 103

Rochester Institute of Technology, E. Philip
Saunders College of Business, Rochester
(NY) 312

San Diego State University, College of Business
Administration, San Diego (CA) 86

San Francisco State University, College of
Business, San Francisco (CA) 87

Seattle Pacific University, School of Business and
Economics, Seattle (WA) 450

Seattle University, Albers School of Business and
Economics, Seattle (WA) 451

Southern Illinois University Edwardsville, School
of Business, Edwardsville (IL) *174*

Southern Methodist University, Cox School of
Business, Dallas (TX) 411, **688**

Stevens Institute of Technology, Wesley J. Howe
School of Technology Management, Hoboken
(NJ) 290

Stockholm School of Economics, Department of
Business Administration, Stockholm
(Sweden) 531

Swinburne University of Technology, Australian
Graduate School of Entrepreneurship
(AGSE), Hawthorne (Australia) 488

University at Buffalo, the State University of New
York, School of Management, Buffalo
(NY) 320

The University of Akron, College of Business
Administration, Akron (OH) 346

University of California, Berkeley, Haas School of
Business, Berkeley (CA) 89

University of Dayton, School of Business
Administration, Dayton (OH) 347

University of Denver, Daniels College of
Business, Denver (CO) 106

University of Florida, Hough Graduate School of
Business, Gainesville (FL) 134

University of Georgia, Terry College of Business,
Athens (GA) 151

University of Maryland, College Park, Robert H.
Smith School of Business, College Park
(MD) 217

University of Maryland University College,
Graduate School of Management and
Technology, Adelphi (MD) 218

University of Massachusetts Boston, College of
Management, Boston (MA) 232

University of Missouri–Columbia, Robert J.
Trulaske, Sr. College of Business, Columbia
(MO) 267, **720**

University of Missouri–St. Louis, College of
Business Administration, St. Louis
(MO) *268*

University of New Brunswick Saint John, Faculty
of Business, Saint John (Canada) 476, **724**

The University of North Carolina at Chapel Hill,
Kenan-Flagler Business School, Chapel Hill
(NC) 330

University of Pennsylvania, Wharton School,
Philadelphia (PA) 380

University of Phoenix–Bay Area Campus, College
of Graduate Business and Management,
Pleasanton (CA) 94

University of Phoenix–Central Florida Campus,
College of Graduate Business and
Management, Maitland (FL) 137

University of Phoenix–Charlotte Campus, College
of Graduate Business and Management,
Charlotte (NC) 332

University of Phoenix–Chicago Campus, College
of Graduate Business and Management,
Schaumburg (IL) 177

University of Phoenix–Cincinnati Campus, College
of Graduate Business and Management, West
Chester (OH) 348

University of Phoenix–Cleveland Campus, College
of Graduate Business and Management,
Independence (OH) 348

University of Phoenix–Columbus Georgia
Campus, College of Graduate Business and
Management, Columbus (GA) 152

University of Phoenix–Dallas Campus, College of
Graduate Business and Management, Dallas
(TX) 423

University of Phoenix–Denver Campus, College of
Graduate Business and Management, Lone
Tree (CO) 107

University of Phoenix–Hawaii Campus, College of
Graduate Business and Management, Honolulu
(HI) 155

University of Phoenix–Houston Campus, College
of Graduate Business and Management,
Houston (TX) 423

University of Phoenix–Idaho Campus, College of
Graduate Business and Management, Meridian
(ID) 157

University of Phoenix–Kansas City Campus,
College of Graduate Business and
Management, Kansas City (MO) 268

University of Phoenix–Las Vegas Campus, College
of Graduate Business and Management, Las
Vegas (NV) 276

University of Phoenix–Louisiana Campus, College
of Graduate Business and Management,
Metairie (LA) 210

University of Phoenix–Maryland Campus, College
of Graduate Business and Management,
Columbia (MD) 219

University of Phoenix–Metro Detroit Campus,
College of Graduate Business and
Management, Troy (MI) 246

University of Phoenix–Nashville Campus, College
of Graduate Business and Management,
Nashville (TN) 401

University of Phoenix–New Mexico Campus,
College of Graduate Business and
Management, Albuquerque (NM) 294

University of Phoenix–North Florida Campus,
College of Graduate Business and
Management, Jacksonville (FL) 137

University of Phoenix–Oklahoma City Campus,
College of Graduate Business and
Management, Oklahoma City (OK) 355

University of Phoenix–Oregon Campus, College of Graduate Business and Management, Tigard (OR) 360

University of Phoenix–Philadelphia Campus, College of Graduate Business and Management, Wayne (PA) 380

University of Phoenix–Phoenix Campus, College of Graduate Business and Management, Phoenix (AZ) 59

University of Phoenix–Pittsburgh Campus, College of Graduate Business and Management, Pittsburgh (PA) 381

University of Phoenix–Puerto Rico Campus, College of Graduate Business and Management, Guaynabo (PR) 387

University of Phoenix–Sacramento Valley Campus, College of Graduate Business and Management, Sacramento (CA) 95

University of Phoenix–St. Louis Campus, College of Graduate Business and Management, St. Louis (MO) 269

University of Phoenix–San Diego Campus, College of Graduate Business and Management, San Diego (CA) 95

University of Phoenix–Southern Arizona Campus, College of Graduate Business and Management, Tucson (AZ) 60

University of Phoenix–Southern California Campus, College of Graduate Business and Management, Costa Mesa (CA) 96

University of Phoenix–Southern Colorado Campus, College of Graduate Business and Management, Colorado Springs (CO) 107

University of Phoenix–South Florida Campus, College of Graduate Business and Management, Fort Lauderdale (FL) 137

University of Phoenix–Tulsa Campus, College of Graduate Business and Management, Tulsa (OK) 355

University of Phoenix–Utah Campus, College of Graduate Business and Management, Salt Lake City (UT) 432

University of Phoenix–Washington Campus, College of Graduate Business and Management, Seattle (WA) 452

University of Phoenix–West Florida Campus, College of Graduate Business and Management, Temple Terrace (FL) 138

University of Phoenix–Wisconsin Campus, College of Graduate Business and Management, Brookfield (WI) 461

University of Rochester, William E. Simon Graduate School of Business Administration, Rochester (NY) 321, **736**

The University of Texas at Arlington, College of Business Administration, Arlington (TX) 424, **746**

The University of Texas at Dallas, School of Management, Richardson (TX) *426, 748*

University of Washington, Michael G. Foster School of Business, Seattle (WA) 452, **754**

University of Waterloo, Graduate Studies, Waterloo (Canada) 479

University of Wisconsin–Milwaukee, Sheldon B. Lubar School of Business, Milwaukee (WI) 463

Woodbury University, School of Business and Management, Burbank (CA) 100

Worcester Polytechnic Institute, Department of Management, Worcester (MA) 234, **770**

Xavier University, Williams College of Business, Cincinnati (OH) 350

ENGINEERING

Baylor University, Hankamer School of Business, Waco (TX) 405, **574**

Boise State University, College of Business and Economics, Boise (ID) 155

California National University for Advanced Studies, College of Business Administration, Northridge (CA) 67

California Polytechnic State University, San Luis Obispo, Orfalea College of Business, San Luis Obispo (CA) 68

Carnegie Mellon University, Tepper School of Business, Pittsburgh (PA) 363, **584**

Clemson University, College of Business and Behavioral Science, Clemson (SC) 391

Dalhousie University, Faculty of Management, Halifax (Canada) 467

Drexel University, LeBow College of Business, Philadelphia (PA) 366

Kettering University, Graduate School, Flint (MI) 238

Lehigh University, College of Business and Economics, Bethlehem (PA) 371, **656**

Loyola Marymount University, College of Business Administration, Los Angeles (CA) 81

Marquette University, Graduate School of Management, Milwaukee (WI) 459

McGill University, Desautels Faculty of Management, Montréal (Canada) 469, **658**

Monash University, MBA Programme, Clayton (Australia) 486

The Ohio State University, Max M. Fisher College of Business, Columbus (OH) 344

Rochester Institute of Technology, E. Philip Saunders College of Business, Rochester (NY) 312

University of Bath, School of Management, Bath (United Kingdom) 547

University of Dallas, Graduate School of Management, Irving (TX) 420, **710**

University of Louisville, College of Business, Louisville (KY) 203

University of Massachusetts Amherst, Isenberg School of Management, Amherst (MA) 231

University of Missouri–Columbia, Robert J. Trulaske, Sr. College of Business, Columbia (MO) 267, **720**

University of New Brunswick Fredericton, Faculty of Business Administration, Fredericton (Canada) 476

University of North Texas, College of Business Administration, Denton (TX) 422

The University of Texas at Tyler, College of Business and Technology, Tyler (TX) 428

University of Victoria, Faculty of Business, Victoria (Canada) 479

Vienna University of Economics and Business Administration, WU Wien MBA, Vienna (Austria) 492

Villanova University, Villanova School of Business, Villanova (PA) 382

Winthrop University, College of Business Administration, Rock Hill (SC) 393

ENTREPRENEURSHIP

The Aarhus School of Business, Faculty of Business Administration, Aarhus (Denmark) 501

Alvernia College, Department of Business, Reading (PA) 361

American College of Thessaloniki, Department of Business Administration, Pylea (Greece) 511

American Public University System, AMU/APU Graduate Programs, Charles Town (WV) 455

American University, Kogod School of Business, Washington (DC) 118

Andrew Jackson University, Brian Tracy College of Business and Entrepreneurship, Birmingham (AL) 45

Anna Maria College, Program in Business Administration, Paxton (MA) 219

Antwerp International Business School, Graduate Programs in Business, Antwerp (Belgium) 493

Ashland University, Dauch College of Business and Economics, Ashland (OH) 337

Asian Institute of Technology, School of Management, Pathumthani (Thailand) 536

Aston University, Aston Business School, Birmingham (United Kingdom) 539

Babson College, F. W. Olin Graduate School of Business, Wellesley (MA) *220*, **570**

Baldwin-Wallace College, Division of Business, Berea (OH) 337

Ball State University, Miller College of Business, Muncie (IN) 179

Barcelona Business School, Graduate Programs in Business, Barcelona (Spain) 528

Bar-Ilan University, Graduate School of Business, Ramat-Gan (Israel) 514

Baylor University, Hankamer School of Business, Waco (TX) 405, **574**

Belmont University, Jack C. Massey Graduate School of Business, Nashville (TN) 395

Benedictine University, Graduate Programs, Lisle (IL) 158

Bentley College, The Elkin B. McCallum Graduate School of Business, Waltham (MA) 221, **578**

Bernard M. Baruch College of the City University of New York, Zicklin School of Business, New York (NY) 296

Boise State University, College of Business and Economics, Boise (ID) 155

Bond University, School of Business, Gold Coast (Australia) 483

Boston College, The Carroll School of Management, Chestnut Hill (MA) 221, **580**

Boston University, School of Management, Boston (MA) 223

California State University, East Bay, College of Business and Economics, Hayward (CA) 69

California State University, Fresno, Craig School of Business, Fresno (CA) 70

California State University, Fullerton, College of Business and Economics, Fullerton (CA) 70

California State University, San Bernardino, College of Business and Public Administration, San Bernardino (CA) 73

Cameron University, Office of Graduate Studies, Lawton (OK) 352

Carlos Albizu University, Miami Campus, Graduate Programs, Miami (FL) 123

Carnegie Mellon University, Tepper School of Business, Pittsburgh (PA) 363, **584**

Case Western Reserve University, Weatherhead School of Management, Cleveland (OH) 338

Centenary College of Louisiana, Frost School of Business, Shreveport (LA) 204

The Chinese University of Hong Kong, Faculty of Business Administration, Hong Kong (China) 497

Chulalongkorn University, Sasin Graduate Institute of Business Administration, Bangkok (Thailand) 536

City University of Hong Kong, Faculty of Business, Hong Kong (China) 497

Claremont Graduate University, Peter F. Drucker and Masatoshi Ito Graduate School of Management, Claremont (CA) 75, **590**

Clemson University, College of Business and Behavioral Science, Clemson (SC) 391

The College of William and Mary, Mason School of Business, Williamsburg (VA) 436

Columbia University, Graduate School of Business, New York (NY) 298

Copenhagen Business School, Faculty of Economics and Business Administration, Copenhagen (Denmark) 501

Cyprus International Institute of Management, MBA Programme, Nicosia (Cyprus) 500

DePaul University, Charles H. Kellstadt Graduate School of Business, Chicago (IL) 159

Dominican University, Edward A. and Lois L. Brennan School of Business, River Forest (IL) 162, **600**

Drake University, College of Business and Public Administration, Des Moines (IA) 189

Drexel University, LeBow College of Business, Philadelphia (PA) 366

Drury University, Breech School of Business Administration, Springfield (MO) 259

Duke University, The Fuqua School of Business, Durham (NC) 323

Eastern Michigan University, College of Business, Ypsilanti (MI) 237

Eastern Washington University, College of Business and Public Administration, Cheney (WA) 448

École Nationale des Ponts et Chaussées, ENPC MBA, Paris (France) 503

Elon University, Martha and Spencer Love School of Business, Elon (NC) 324

Emory University, Roberto C. Goizueta Business School, Atlanta (GA) 145, **606**

Erasmus University Rotterdam, Rotterdam School of Management, Rotterdam (Netherlands) 521

ESCP-EAP European School of Management, ESCP-EAP European School of Management (France) 503

European School of Economics, MBA Programme (Italy) 515, **608**

European School of Economics, MBA Programme (United Kingdom) 541, **608**

Fairleigh Dickinson University, College at Florham, Silberman College of Business, Madison (NJ) 282, **612**

Fairleigh Dickinson University, Metropolitan Campus, Silberman College of Business, Teaneck (NJ) 282, **612**

Fayetteville State University, Program in Business Administration, Fayetteville (NC) 325

Felician College, Program in Business, Lodi (NJ) 283, **614**

Florida Atlantic University, College of Business, Boca Raton (FL) 126

Florida International University, Alvah H. Chapman, Jr. Graduate School of Business, Miami (FL) 128, **618**

George Mason University, School of Management, Fairfax (VA) 438

The George Washington University, School of Business, Washington (DC) 119, **622**

Georgia Institute of Technology, College of Management, Atlanta (GA) 146, **624**

Georgia State University, J. Mack Robinson College of Business, Atlanta (GA) 147, **626**

Gonzaga University, School of Business Administration, Spokane (WA) 448

Hardin-Simmons University, The Acton MBA in Entrepreneurship, Austin (TX) 407

HEC Montreal, Master's Program in Business Administration and Management, Montréal (Canada) 468

HEC Paris, HEC MBA Program, Jouy-en-Josas (France) *505*, **632**

HfB—Business School of Finance and Management, Frankfurt School of Finance and Management, Frankfurt (Germany) 508

Howard University, School of Business, Washington (DC) 120

Hult International Business School, Graduate Program, Cambridge (MA) *227*, **634**

IE Business School, Business School, Madrid (Spain) 529, **636**

Illinois Institute of Technology, Stuart School of Business, Chicago (IL) 164

IMD International Institute for Management Development, IMD International, Lausanne (Switzerland) 533

Indiana University Bloomington, Kelley School of Business, Bloomington (IN) 182

Indian School of Business, MBA Program, Andhra Pradesh (India) 512

International University of Japan, Graduate School of International Management, Minami Uonuma-gu (Japan) 516

Jones International University, Graduate School of Business Administration, Centennial (CO) 103

King College, School of Business and Economics, Bristol (TN) 396

Lamar University, College of Business, Beaumont (TX) 408

Lancaster University, Management School, Lancaster (United Kingdom) 541

Lehigh University, College of Business and Economics, Bethlehem (PA) 371, **656**

Lincoln University, College of Business and Professional Studies (MO) 260

Lindenwood University, Division of Management, St. Charles (MO) 261

Louisiana State University and Agricultural and Mechanical College, E. J. Ourso College of Business, Baton Rouge (LA) 204

Loyola Marymount University, College of Business Administration, Los Angeles (CA) 81

Loyola University Chicago, Graduate School of Business, Chicago (IL) 167

Massachusetts Institute of Technology, Sloan School of Management, Cambridge (MA) 227

Monash University, MBA Programme, Clayton (Australia) 486

Monterey Institute of International Studies, Fisher Graduate School of International Business, Monterey (CA) 82, **660**

National University, School of Business and Management, La Jolla (CA) 82

National University of Ireland, Dublin, The Michael Smurfit Graduate School of Business, Blackrock (Ireland) 513

New York University, Leonard N. Stern School of Business (NY) 309

North Carolina State University, College of Management, Raleigh (NC) 328, **664**

Northeastern University, Graduate School of Business Administration, Boston (MA) 228

Northern Kentucky University, College of Business, Highland Heights (KY) 201

Northwestern University, Kellogg School of Management, Evanston (IL) 171

Norwegian School of Management, Graduate School, Sandvika (Norway) 524

Nottingham Trent University, Nottingham Business School, Nottingham (United Kingdom) 544

Nova Southeastern University, H. Wayne Huizenga School of Business and Entrepreneurship, Fort Lauderdale (FL) 130, **666**

Nyenrode Business Universiteit, Netherlands Business School, Breukelen (Netherlands) 522

Oakland University, School of Business Administration, Rochester (MI) 241

Oral Roberts University, School of Business, Tulsa (OK) 353

Pace University, Lubin School of Business, New York (NY) 310

Pacific Lutheran University, School of Business, Tacoma (WA) 449

Park University, Program in Business Administration, Parkville (MO) 264

Penn State Great Valley, Graduate Studies, Malvern (PA) 373

Penn State University Park, The Mary Jean and Frank P. Smeal College of Business Administration, State College (PA) 374

Pepperdine University, Graziadio School of Business and Management, Los Angeles (CA) 85

Portland State University, School of Business Administration, Portland (OR) 358

Queen Margaret University College, Edinburgh, School of Business and Enterprise, Edinburgh (United Kingdom) 545

Queensland University of Technology, Brisbane Graduate School of Business, Brisbane (Australia) 487

Regent University, School of Global Leadership and Entrepreneurship, Virginia Beach (VA) 442

Rensselaer at Hartford, Lally School of Management and Technology, Hartford (CT) 110

Rensselaer Polytechnic Institute, Lally School of Management and Technology, Troy (NY) 311, **670**

Rice University, Jesse H. Jones Graduate School of Management, Houston (TX) 410

Rider University, College of Business Administration, Lawrenceville (NJ) 287

Rochester Institute of Technology, E. Philip Saunders College of Business, Rochester (NY) 312

Rollins College, Crummer Graduate School of Business, Winter Park (FL) 131, **674**

Rowan University, William G. Rohrer College of Business, Glassboro (NJ) 287

Saginaw Valley State University, College of Business and Management, University Center (MI) 242

St. Edward's University, The School of Management and Business, Austin (TX) 410

Saint Louis University, John Cook School of Business, St. Louis (MO) *264*

San Diego State University, College of Business Administration, San Diego (CA) 86

San Francisco State University, College of Business, San Francisco (CA) 87

Santa Clara University, Leavey School of Business, Santa Clara (CA) 88

Seattle University, Albers School of Business and Economics, Seattle (WA) 451

Seton Hill University, Program in Business Administration, Greensburg (PA) 378

Simmons College, Simmons School of Management, Boston (MA) 230

Southeastern University, College of Graduate Studies, Washington (DC) 121

Southern Cross University, Graduate College of Management, Coffs Harbour (Australia) 487

Southern Methodist University, Cox School of Business, Dallas (TX) 411, **688**

Stevens Institute of Technology, Wesley J. Howe School of Technology Management, Hoboken (NJ) 290

Stockholm School of Economics, Department of Business Administration, Stockholm (Sweden) 531

Stratford University, Graduate Business Programs, Falls Church (VA) 443

Suffolk University, Sawyer Business School, Boston (MA) 230

Swinburne University of Technology, Australian Graduate School of Entrepreneurship (AGSE), Hawthorne (Australia) 488

Syracuse University, Martin J. Whitman School of Management, Syracuse (NY) 318, **692**

Texas Tech University, Jerry S. Rawls College of Business Administration, Lubbock (TX) 418

Thunderbird School of Global Management, Graduate Programs, Glendale (AZ) 57

TUI University, College of Business Administration, Cypress (CA) 89

Universite Libre de Bruxelles, Solvay Business School, Brussels (Belgium) 495

The University of Akron, College of Business Administration, Akron (OH) 346

The University of Alabama, Manderson Graduate School of Business, Tuscaloosa (AL) 49

University of Antwerp, University of Antwerp Management School, Antwerp (Belgium) 495

The University of Arizona, Eller College of Management, Tucson (AZ) 58

University of Arkansas, Sam M. Walton College of Business Administration, Fayetteville (AR) 62

University of Baltimore, Merrick School of Business, Baltimore (MD) 216

University of Baltimore/Towson University, Joint University of Baltimore/Towson University (UB/Towson) MBA Program, Baltimore (MD) 217

University of Bath, School of Management, Bath (United Kingdom) 547

The University of British Columbia, Sauder School of Business, Vancouver (Canada) 474

University of Calgary, Haskayne School of Business, Calgary (Canada) 474

University of California, Berkeley, Haas School of Business, Berkeley (CA) 89

University of California, Davis, Graduate School of Management, Davis (CA) 90

University of California, Los Angeles, UCLA Anderson School of Management, Los Angeles (CA) 91, **696**

University of California, Riverside, A. Gary Anderson Graduate School of Management, Riverside (CA) 93, **698**

University of California, San Diego, Rady School of Management, La Jolla (CA) 93, **700**

University of Central Florida, College of Business Administration, Orlando (FL) 133

University of Chicago, Graduate School of Business, Chicago (IL) 175

University of Colorado at Boulder, Leeds School of Business, Boulder (CO) 104, **702**

University of Dallas, Graduate School of Management, Irving (TX) 420, **710**

University of Dayton, School of Business Administration, Dayton (OH) 347

University of Denver, Daniels College of Business, Denver (CO) 106

University of Edinburgh, Edinburgh University Management School, Edinburgh (United Kingdom) 550

University of Florida, Hough Graduate School of Business, Gainesville (FL) 134

University of Georgia, Terry College of Business, Athens (GA) 151

University of Glasgow, University of Glasgow Business School, Glasgow (United Kingdom) 550

University of Hawaii at Manoa, Shidler College of Business, Honolulu (HI) 154

University of Houston–Victoria, School of Business Administration, Victoria (TX) 421

University of Illinois at Chicago, Liautaud Graduate School of Business, Chicago (IL) 176

University of Kansas, School of Business, Lawrence (KS) 196

University of Louisville, College of Business, Louisville (KY) 203

University of Maryland, College Park, Robert H. Smith School of Business, College Park (MD) 217

University of Melbourne, Melbourne Business School, Melbourne (Australia) 488

University of Michigan, Ross School of Business at the University of Michigan, Ann Arbor (MI) 244

University of Minnesota, Twin Cities Campus, Carlson School of Management, Minneapolis (MN) 252

University of Missouri–Kansas City, Henry W. Bloch School of Business and Public Administration, Kansas City (MO) 267

University of Newcastle, Graduate School of Business, Callaghan (Australia) 489

University of New Hampshire, Whittemore School of Business and Economics, Durham (NH) 280, **726**

University of New Mexico, Robert O. Anderson Graduate School of Management, Albuquerque (NM) 294

The University of North Carolina at Chapel Hill, Kenan-Flagler Business School, Chapel Hill (NC) 330

The University of North Carolina Wilmington, School of Business, Wilmington (NC) 332

University of Notre Dame, Mendoza College of Business, Notre Dame (IN) 187

University of Oklahoma, Michael F. Price College of Business, Norman (OK) 355

University of Oregon, Charles H. Lundquist College of Business, Eugene (OR) 359, **732**

University of Pennsylvania, Wharton School, Philadelphia (PA) 380

University of Plymouth, Plymouth Business School, Plymouth (United Kingdom) 553

University of Portland, Dr. Robert B. Pamplin, Jr. School of Business, Portland (OR) 360

University of Rochester, William E. Simon Graduate School of Business Administration, Rochester (NY) 321, **736**

University of St. Thomas, Opus College of Business (MN) 253, **738**

University of San Francisco, Masagung Graduate School of Management, San Francisco (CA) 97

University of South Carolina, Moore School of Business, Columbia (SC) *392*, **740**

University of Southern California, School of Business, Los Angeles (CA) 98

University of South Florida, College of Business Administration, Tampa (FL) 138

The University of Tampa, John H. Sykes College of Business, Tampa (FL) 139, **742**

The University of Texas at Austin, Programs in MBA, Austin (TX) 425

University of the Pacific, Eberhardt School of Business, Stockton (CA) 99, **752**

University of the West of England, Bristol, Bristol Business School, Bristol (United Kingdom) 555

University of the Witwatersrand, Graduate School of Business Administration, Wits (South Africa) 527

The University of Toledo, College of Business Administration, Toledo (OH) 349

University of Toronto, Joseph L. Rotman School of Management, Toronto (Canada) 478

University of Ulster at Jordanstown, Faculty of Business and Management, Newtown Abbey (United Kingdom) 556

University of Victoria, Faculty of Business, Victoria (Canada) 479

University of Washington, Michael G. Foster School of Business, Seattle (WA) 452, **754**

University of Waterloo, Graduate Studies, Waterloo (Canada) 479

The University of Western Australia, Business School, Nedlands (Australia) 491

The University of Western Ontario, Richard Ivey School of Business, London (Canada) 480

University of Windsor, Odette School of Business, Windsor (Canada) 480

University of Wisconsin–Madison, Wisconsin School of Business, Madison (WI) 462, **756**

University of Wyoming, College of Business, Laramie (WY) 465

Vienna University of Economics and Business Administration, WU Wien MBA, Vienna (Austria) 492

Vlerick Leuven Gent Management School, MBA Programmes, Ghent (Belgium) 495

Wake Forest University, Babcock Graduate School of Management, Winston-Salem (NC) 332

Walden University, School of Management, Minneapolis (MN) 253

Waseda University, Graduate School of Commerce, Tokyo (Japan) 517

Washington State University Tri-Cities, College of Business, Richland (WA) 453

Washington University in St. Louis, Olin Business School, St. Louis (MO) 269

Wayne State University, School of Business Administration, Detroit (MI) 247, **760**

Western Carolina University, College of Business, Cullowhee (NC) 333

Westminster College, The Bill and Vieve Gore School of Business, Salt Lake City (UT) 433

WHU—Otto Beisheim School of Management, WHU—Otto Beisheim School of Management, Vallendar (Germany) 511

Wichita State University, W. Frank Barton School of Business, Wichita (KS) 197

Wilfrid Laurier University, School of Business and Economics, Waterloo (Canada) 481, **766**

Wilkes University, College of Arts, Humanities and Social Sciences, Wilkes-Barre (PA) 384

Willamette University, George H. Atkinson Graduate School of Management, Salem (OR) 361, **768**

Worcester Polytechnic Institute, Department of Management, Worcester (MA) 234, **770**

York University, Schulich School of Business, Toronto (Canada) 482, **772**

ENVIRONMENTAL ECONOMICS/ MANAGEMENT

The American University in Cairo, School of Business, Economics and Communication, Cairo (Egypt) 502

Antioch University New England, Department of Organization and Management, Keene (NH) 277

Cardiff University, Cardiff Business School, Cardiff (United Kingdom) 539

Clarkson University, School of Business, Potsdam (NY) 297

Clark University, Graduate School of Management, Worcester (MA) 224, **592**

Dominican University of California, Division of Business and International Studies, San Rafael (CA) 77

Duquesne University, John F. Donahue Graduate School of Business, Pittsburgh (PA) 367

The George Washington University, School of Business, Washington (DC) 119, **622**

HfB—Business School of Finance and Management, Frankfurt School of Finance and Management, Frankfurt (Germany) 508

IE Business School, Business School, Madrid (Spain) 529, **636**

Illinois Institute of Technology, Stuart School of Business, Chicago (IL) 164

Kean University, College of Business and Public Administration, Union (NJ) 284

Lancaster University, Management School, Lancaster (United Kingdom) 541

Lipscomb University, MBA Program, Nashville (TN) 397

Monash University, MBA Programme, Clayton (Australia) 486

Monterey Institute of International Studies, Fisher Graduate School of International Business, Monterey (CA) 82, **660**

New York University, Robert F. Wagner Graduate School of Public Service (NY) 309

Southeast Missouri State University, Harrison College of Business, Cape Girardeau (MO) 265

Stockholm School of Economics, Department of Business Administration, Stockholm (Sweden) 531

University of Alberta, School of Business, Edmonton (Canada) 473

University of Bath, School of Management, Bath (United Kingdom) 547

The University of British Columbia, Sauder School of Business, Vancouver (Canada) 474

University of Edinburgh, Edinburgh University Management School, Edinburgh (United Kingdom) 550

University of Houston–Clear Lake, School of Business, Houston (TX) 421

University of Massachusetts Boston, College of Management, Boston (MA) 232

University of Newcastle, Graduate School of Business, Callaghan (Australia) 489

The University of North Carolina at Chapel Hill, Kenan-Flagler Business School, Chapel Hill (NC) 330

University of Pennsylvania, Wharton School, Philadelphia (PA) 380

University of Waterloo, Graduate Studies, Waterloo (Canada) 479

Webster University, School of Business and Technology, St. Louis (MO) 270

York University, Schulich School of Business, Toronto (Canada) 482, **772**

EUROPEAN BUSINESS STUDIES

Antwerp International Business School, Graduate Programs in Business, Antwerp (Belgium) 493

Aston University, Aston Business School, Birmingham (United Kingdom) 539

Barcelona Business School, Graduate Programs in Business, Barcelona (Spain) 528

Bayerische Julius-Maximilians University of Wuerzburg, MBA Program, Wuerzburg (Germany) 507

École Nationale des Ponts et Chaussées, ENPC MBA, Paris (France) 503

ESCP-EAP European School of Management, ESCP-EAP European School of Management (France) 503

European University, Center for Management Studies, Montreux-Fontanivent (Switzerland) 532

The George Washington University, School of Business, Washington (DC) 119, **622**

HEC Paris, HEC MBA Program, Jouy-en-Josas (France) *505*, **632**

HfB—Business School of Finance and Management, Frankfurt School of Finance and Management, Frankfurt (Germany) 508

IE Business School, Business School, Madrid (Spain) 529, **636**

International University in Geneva, MBA Program, Geneva (Switzerland) 533, **640**

Katholieke Universiteit Leuven, Leuven School of Business and Economics, Leuven (Belgium) 494

Monash University, MBA Programme, Clayton (Australia) 486

National University, School of Business and Management, La Jolla (CA) 82

Norwegian School of Management, Graduate School, Sandvika (Norway) 524

Open University of the Netherlands, Business Programs, Heerlen (Netherlands) 523

Pepperdine University, Graziadio School of Business and Management, Los Angeles (CA) 85

Rouen School of Management, Postgraduate Programmes, Mount Saint Aignan (France) 505

Saints Cyril and Methodius University, Faculty of Economics, Skopje (Macedonia) 519

Stockholm School of Economics, Department of Business Administration, Stockholm (Sweden) 531

Universite Libre de Bruxelles, Solvay Business School, Brussels (Belgium) 495

University of Antwerp, University of Antwerp Management School, Antwerp (Belgium) 495

University of California, Berkeley, Haas School of Business, Berkeley (CA) 89

University of Connecticut, School of Business, Storrs (CT) 112, **708**

University of Deusto, Faculty of Economics and Business Administration, Bilbao (Spain) 530

University of Kentucky, Gatton College of Business and Economics, Lexington (KY) 202, **716**

University of Missouri–Columbia, Robert J. Trulaske, Sr. College of Business, Columbia (MO) 267, **720**

University of New Brunswick Saint John, Faculty of Business, Saint John (Canada) 476, **724**

University of Pennsylvania, Wharton School, Philadelphia (PA) 380

University of the West of England, Bristol, Bristol Business School, Bristol (United Kingdom) 555

The University of Western Ontario, Richard Ivey School of Business, London (Canada) 480

Vlerick Leuven Gent Management School, MBA Programmes, Ghent (Belgium) 495

York University, Schulich School of Business, Toronto (Canada) 482, **772**

EXECUTIVE PROGRAMS

The Aarhus School of Business, Faculty of Business Administration, Aarhus (Denmark) 501

Alaska Pacific University, Business Administration Department, Anchorage (AK) 53

American College of Thessaloniki, Department of Business Administration, Pylea (Greece) 511

American University of Beirut, MBA Program, Beirut (Lebanon) 518

Antwerp International Business School, Graduate Programs in Business, Antwerp (Belgium) 493

Arizona State University, W.P. Carey School of Business, Tempe (AZ) 54

Arkansas State University, College of Business, Jonesboro (AR) 61

Asian Institute of Technology, School of Management, Pathumthani (Thailand) 536

Athabasca University, Centre for Innovative Management, Athabasca (Canada) 466

Auburn University, College of Business, Auburn University (AL) 45, **568**

Baldwin-Wallace College, Division of Business, Berea (OH) 337

Baylor University, Hankamer School of Business, Waco (TX) 405, **574**

Bellarmine University, W. Fielding Rubel School of Business, Louisville (KY) 198

Bellevue University, College of Business, Bellevue (NE) 271, **576**

Benedictine College, Executive Master of Business Administration Program, Atchison (KS) 193

Benedictine University, Graduate Programs, Lisle (IL) 158

Boston University, School of Management, Boston (MA) 223

Bowling Green State University, College of Business Administration, Bowling Green (OH) 338

Brandeis University, International Business School, Waltham (MA) 224, **582**

Brigham Young University, Marriott School of Management, Provo (UT) 431

California State University, Sacramento, College of Business Administration, Sacramento (CA) 72

Centenary College of Louisiana, Frost School of Business, Shreveport (LA) 204

Chapman University, The George L. Argyros School of Business and Economics, Orange (CA) 74, **586**

Claremont Graduate University, Peter F. Drucker and Masatoshi Ito Graduate School of Management, Claremont (CA) 75, **590**

Colorado State University, College of Business, Fort Collins (CO) 101, **596**

Cornell University, Johnson Graduate School of Management, Ithaca (NY) 299, **598**

Cranfield University, Cranfield School of Management, Cranfield (United Kingdom) 540

Cyprus International Institute of Management, MBA Programme, Nicosia (Cyprus) 500

École Nationale des Ponts et Chaussées, ENPC MBA, Paris (France) 503

European University, Center for Management Studies, Montreux-Fontanivent (Switzerland) 532

Fairleigh Dickinson University, College at Florham, Silberman College of Business, Madison (NJ) 282, **612**

Fairleigh Dickinson University, Metropolitan Campus, Silberman College of Business, Teaneck (NJ) 282, **612**

Florida International University, Alvah H. Chapman, Jr. Graduate School of Business, Miami (FL) 128, **618**

George Fox University, School of Management, Newberg (OR) 357

George Mason University, School of Management, Fairfax (VA) 438

Georgetown University, McDonough School of Business, Washington (DC) 119

The George Washington University, School of Business, Washington (DC) 119, **622**

Georgia Institute of Technology, College of Management, Atlanta (GA) 146, **624**

Georgian Court University, School of Business, Lakewood (NJ) 283

Georgia State University, J. Mack Robinson College of Business, Atlanta (GA) 147, **626**

Golden Gate University, Ageno School of Business, San Francisco (CA) 78

Graduate School of Business Administration Zurich, Executive Management Programs, Zurich (Switzerland) 532

Grand Canyon University, College of Business, Phoenix (AZ) 56

Hawai'i Pacific University, College of Business Administration, Honolulu (HI) 153, **630**

The Hong Kong University of Science and Technology, School of Business and Management, Hong Kong (China) 499

Hope International University, Program in Business Administration, Fullerton (CA) 79

Indiana University of Pennsylvania, Eberly College of Business and Information Technology, Indiana (PA) 369

Indian Institute of Management, Ahmedabad, Post-Graduate Programme in Management, Gujarat (India) 512

Kent State University, Graduate School of Management, Kent (OH) 342

Koc University, Graduate School of Business, Istanbul (Turkey) 537

Leadership Institute of Seattle, School of Applied Behavioral Science, Kenmore (WA) 449

London School of Economics and Political Science, The Graduate School, London (United Kingdom) 543

Louisiana State University and Agricultural and Mechanical College, E. J. Ourso College of Business, Baton Rouge (LA) 204

Loyola College in Maryland, Sellinger School of Business and Management, Baltimore (MD) 215

Loyola Marymount University, College of Business Administration, Los Angeles (CA) 81

Loyola University Chicago, Graduate School of Business, Chicago (IL) 167

Marquette University, Graduate School of Management, Milwaukee (WI) 459

Middle East Technical University, Department of Business Administration, Ankara (Turkey) 537

Monash University, MBA Programme, Clayton (Australia) 486

Nanjing University, School of Business, Nanjing (China) 500

National University, School of Business and Management, La Jolla (CA) 82

Northeastern University, Graduate School of Business Administration, Boston (MA) 228

Northern Illinois University, College of Business, De Kalb (IL) 169

Norwegian School of Management, Graduate School, Sandvika (Norway) 524

The Ohio State University, Max M. Fisher College of Business, Columbus (OH) 344

Purdue University, Krannert School of Management, West Lafayette (IN) 185

Purdue University Calumet, School of Management, Hammond (IN) 186

Queens University of Charlotte, McColl Graduate School of Business, Charlotte (NC) 329

Rider University, College of Business Administration, Lawrenceville (NJ) 287

Rochester Institute of Technology, E. Philip Saunders College of Business, Rochester (NY) 312

Saint Joseph's University, Erivan K. Haub School of Business, Philadelphia (PA) 377

Saint Mary's University of Minnesota, Schools of Graduate and Professional Programs, Winona (MN) 251

San Diego State University, College of Business Administration, San Diego (CA) 86

Santa Clara University, Leavey School of Business, Santa Clara (CA) 88

Seattle University, Albers School of Business and Economics, Seattle (WA) 451

Simon Fraser University, Faculty of Business Administration, Burnaby (Canada) 472

Southern Illinois University Carbondale, College of Business and Administration, Carbondale (IL) 173

State University of New York at Binghamton, School of Management, Binghamton (NY) 315

Stockholm School of Economics, Department of Business Administration, Stockholm (Sweden) 531

Suffolk University, Sawyer Business School, Boston (MA) 230

Temple University, Fox School of Business and Management, Philadelphia (PA) 379

Texas Christian University, The Neeley School of Business at TCU, Fort Worth (TX) 416, **694**

The University of Alabama, Manderson Graduate School of Business, Tuscaloosa (AL) 49

University of Alberta, School of Business, Edmonton (Canada) 473

The University of Arizona, Eller College of Management, Tucson (AZ) 58

University of Bath, School of Management, Bath (United Kingdom) 547

University of Calgary, Haskayne School of Business, Calgary (Canada) 474

University of California, Irvine, The Paul Merage School of Business, Irvine (CA) 91

University of California, Los Angeles, UCLA Anderson School of Management, Los Angeles (CA) 91, **696**

University of California, San Diego, Rady School of Management, La Jolla (CA) 93, **700**

University of Central Florida, College of Business Administration, Orlando (FL) 133

University of Charleston, Executive Business Administration Program, Charleston (WV) 456

University of Chicago, Graduate School of Business, Chicago (IL) 175

University of Colorado Denver, Business School, Denver (CO) 105, **706**

University of Connecticut, School of Business, Storrs (CT) 112, **708**

University of Delaware, Alfred Lerner College of Business and Economics, Newark (DE) 116, **712**

University of Denver, Daniels College of Business, Denver (CO) 106

University of Detroit Mercy, College of Business Administration, Detroit (MI) 243

University of Hawaii at Manoa, Shidler College of Business, Honolulu (HI) 154

University of Illinois at Urbana–Champaign, College of Business, Champaign (IL) 176

University of Indianapolis, Graduate Business Programs, Indianapolis (IN) 186

The University of Iowa, Henry B. Tippie College of Business, Iowa City (IA) 191, **714**

University of London, London Business School, London (United Kingdom) 552

University of Mary, Program in Management, Bismarck (ND) 335

University of Maryland, College Park, Robert H. Smith School of Business, College Park (MD) 217

University of Maryland University College, Graduate School of Management and Technology, Adelphi (MD) 218

University of Memphis, Fogelman College of Business and Economics, Memphis (TN) 400

University of Nevada, Las Vegas, College of Business, Las Vegas (NV) 275, **722**

University of New Haven, School of Business, West Haven (CT) 113, **728**

University of New Orleans, College of Business Administration, New Orleans (LA) 209

The University of North Carolina at Chapel Hill, Kenan-Flagler Business School, Chapel Hill (NC) 330

The University of North Carolina at Charlotte, Belk College of Business Administration, Charlotte (NC) 330, **730**

University of Notre Dame, Mendoza College of Business, Notre Dame (IN) 187

University of Otago, School of Business, Dunedin (New Zealand) 523

University of Pennsylvania, Wharton School, Philadelphia (PA) 380

University of Phoenix–Bay Area Campus, College of Graduate Business and Management, Pleasanton (CA) 94

University of Phoenix–Central Florida Campus, College of Graduate Business and Management, Maitland (FL) 137

University of Phoenix–Denver Campus, College of Graduate Business and Management, Lone Tree (CO) 107

University of Phoenix–North Florida Campus, College of Graduate Business and Management, Jacksonville (FL) 137

University of Rochester, William E. Simon Graduate School of Business Administration, Rochester (NY) 321, **736**

University of St. Thomas, Opus College of Business (MN) 253, **738**

University of San Francisco, Masagung Graduate School of Management, San Francisco (CA) 97

University of South Carolina, Moore School of Business, Columbia (SC) *392*, **740**

University of South Florida, College of Business Administration, Tampa (FL) 138

The University of Tennessee, College of Business Administration, Knoxville (TN) *401*, **744**

The University of Tennessee at Chattanooga, College of Business, Chattanooga (TN) 402

The University of Texas at Austin, Programs in MBA, Austin (TX) 425

The University of Texas at Dallas, School of Management, Richardson (TX) *426*, **748**

The University of Texas at San Antonio, College of Business, San Antonio (TX) 427, **750**

The University of Western Australia, Business School, Nedlands (Australia) 491

University of Wisconsin–Milwaukee, Sheldon B. Lubar School of Business, Milwaukee (WI) 463

University of Wyoming, College of Business, Laramie (WY) 465

Vienna University of Economics and Business Administration, WU Wien MBA, Vienna (Austria) 492

Villanova University, Villanova School of Business, Villanova (PA) 382

Virginia Polytechnic Institute and State University, Pamplin College of Business, Blacksburg (VA) 446

Wagner College, Department of Business Administration, Staten Island (NY) 321

Wake Forest University, Babcock Graduate School of Management, Winston-Salem (NC) 332

Washington University in St. Louis, Olin Business School, St. Louis (MO) 269

Wichita State University, W. Frank Barton School of Business, Wichita (KS) 197

Winthrop University, College of Business Administration, Rock Hill (SC) 393

Xavier University, Williams College of Business, Cincinnati (OH) 350

FACILITIES MANAGEMENT

California Polytechnic State University, San Luis Obispo, Orfalea College of Business, San Luis Obispo (CA) 68

The Hague University, Faculty of Economics and Management, The Hague (Netherlands) 521, **628**

Nyenrode Business Universiteit, Netherlands Business School, Breukelen (Netherlands) 522

FINANCE

Adelphi University, School of Business, Garden City (NY) 295, **560**

Alliant International University, Marshall Goldsmith School of Management, San Diego (CA) 63

American InterContinental University Online, Program in Business Administration, Hoffman Estates (IL) 157

American Public University System, AMU/APU Graduate Programs, Charles Town (WV) 455

American University, Kogod School of Business, Washington (DC) 118

American University of Sharjah, School of Business and Management, Sharjah (United Arab Emirates) 538

Andrew Jackson University, Brian Tracy College of Business and Entrepreneurship, Birmingham (AL) 45

Anna Maria College, Program in Business Administration, Paxton (MA) 219

Argosy University, Atlanta, College of Business, Atlanta (GA) 141, **566**

Argosy University, Chicago, College of Business, Chicago (IL) 158, **566**

Argosy University, Dallas, College of Business, Dallas (TX) 405, **566**

Argosy University, Denver, College of Business, Denver (CO) 100, **566**

Argosy University, Hawai'i, College of Business, Honolulu (HI) 153, **566**

Argosy University, Inland Empire, College of Business, San Bernardino (CA) 65, **566**

Argosy University, Los Angeles, College of Business, Santa Monica (CA) 65, **566**

Argosy University, Nashville, College of Business, Nashville (TN) 395, **566**

Argosy University, Orange County, College of Business, Santa Ana (CA) 65, **566**

Argosy University, Phoenix, College of Business, Phoenix (AZ) 54, **566**

Argosy University, Salt Lake City, College of Business, Draper (UT) 430, **566**

Argosy University, San Diego, College of Business, San Diego (CA) 65, **566**

Argosy University, San Francisco Bay Area, College of Business, Alameda (CA) 66, **566**

Argosy University, Sarasota, College of Business, Sarasota (FL) 122, **566**

Argosy University, Schaumburg, College of Business, Schaumburg (IL) 158, **566**

Argosy University, Seattle, College of Business, Seattle (WA) 447, **566**

Argosy University, Tampa, College of Business, Tampa (FL) 122, **566**

Argosy University, Twin Cities, College of Business, Eagan (MN) 248, **566**

Argosy University, Washington DC, College of Business, Arlington (VA) 436, **566**

Arizona State University, W.P. Carey School of Business, Tempe (AZ) 54

Arizona State University at the West campus, School of Global Management and Leadership, Phoenix (AZ) 55

Arkansas State University, College of Business, Jonesboro (AR) 61

Ashland University, Dauch College of Business and Economics, Ashland (OH) 337

Ashridge, Ashridge Executive MBA Program, Berkhamsted (United Kingdom) 538

Asian Institute of Management, Master Programs, Makati City (Philippines) 525

Asian Institute of Technology, School of Management, Pathumthani (Thailand) 536

Assumption College, Department of Business Studies, Worcester (MA) 219

Aston University, Aston Business School, Birmingham (United Kingdom) 539

Auburn University, College of Business, Auburn University (AL) 45, **568**

Auburn University Montgomery, School of Business, Montgomery (AL) 46

Avila University, School of Business, Kansas City (MO) 258

Azusa Pacific University, School of Business and Management, Azusa (CA) 66

Baker College Center for Graduate Studies, Graduate Programs, Flint (MI) 236, **572**

Baker University, School of Professional and Graduate Studies, Baldwin City (KS) 193

Ball State University, Miller College of Business, Muncie (IN) 179

Bar-Ilan University, Graduate School of Business, Ramat-Gan (Israel) 514

Barry University, Andreas School of Business, Miami Shores (FL) 123

Bayerische Julius-Maximilians University of Wuerzburg, MBA Program, Wuerzburg (Germany) 507

Baylor University, Hankamer School of Business, Waco (TX) 405, **574**

Bellevue University, College of Business, Bellevue (NE) 271, **576**

Belmont University, Jack C. Massey Graduate School of Business, Nashville (TN) 395

Benedictine University, Graduate Programs, Lisle (IL) 158

Bentley College, The Elkin B. McCallum Graduate School of Business, Waltham (MA) 221, **578**

Bernard M. Baruch College of the City University of New York, Zicklin School of Business, New York (NY) 296

Bocconi University, SDA Bocconi, Milan (Italy) 515

Boise State University, College of Business and Economics, Boise (ID) 155

Bond University, School of Business, Gold Coast (Australia) 483

Boston College, The Carroll School of Management, Chestnut Hill (MA) 221, **580**

Boston University, School of Management, Boston (MA) 223

Bowling Green State University, College of Business Administration, Bowling Green (OH) 338

Bradley University, Foster College of Business Administration, Peoria (IL) 159

Brandeis University, International Business School, Waltham (MA) 224, **582**

Brigham Young University, Marriott School of Management, Provo (UT) 431

Brock University, Faculty of Business, St. Catharines (Canada) 466

Butler University, College of Business Administration, Indianapolis (IN) 180

California Lutheran University, School of Business, Thousand Oaks (CA) 67

California National University for Advanced Studies, College of Business Administration, Northridge (CA) 67

California State University, Dominguez Hills, College of Business Administration and Public Policy, Carson (CA) 69

California State University, East Bay, College of Business and Economics, Hayward (CA) 69

California State University, Fresno, Craig School of Business, Fresno (CA) 70

California State University, Fullerton, College of Business and Economics, Fullerton (CA) 70

California State University, Long Beach, College of Business Administration, Long Beach (CA) 71

California State University, Los Angeles, College of Business and Economics, Los Angeles (CA) 71

California State University, Northridge, College of Business and Economics, Northridge (CA) 72

California State University, Sacramento, College of Business Administration, Sacramento (CA) 72

California State University, San Bernardino, College of Business and Public Administration, San Bernardino (CA) 73

Canisius College, Richard J. Wehle School of Business, Buffalo (NY) 296

Carnegie Mellon University, Tepper School of Business, Pittsburgh (PA) 363, **584**

Case Western Reserve University, Weatherhead School of Management, Cleveland (OH) 338

Centenary College, Program in Business Administration, Hackettstown (NJ) 281

Charleston Southern University, Program in Business, Charleston (SC) 390

The Chinese University of Hong Kong, Faculty of Business Administration, Hong Kong (China) 497

Christian Brothers University, School of Business, Memphis (TN) 396

Chulalongkorn University, Sasin Graduate Institute of Business Administration, Bangkok (Thailand) 536

City University of Hong Kong, Faculty of Business, Hong Kong (China) 497

Claremont Graduate University, Peter F. Drucker and Masatoshi Ito Graduate School of Management, Claremont (CA) 75, **590**

Clarion University of Pennsylvania, College of Business Administration, Clarion (PA) 364

Clark Atlanta University, School of Business Administration, Atlanta (GA) 143

Clark University, Graduate School of Management, Worcester (MA) 224, **592**

Clemson University, College of Business and Behavioral Science, Clemson (SC) 391

Cleveland State University, Nance College of Business Administration, Cleveland (OH) 340

College for Financial Planning, Program in Financial Planning, Greenwood Village (CO) 101

College of Santa Fe, Department of Business Administration, Santa Fe (NM) 292

The College of William and Mary, Mason School of Business, Williamsburg (VA) 436

Columbia Southern University, MBA Program, Orange Beach (AL) 46

Columbia University, Graduate School of Business, New York (NY) 298

Concordia University Wisconsin, Graduate Programs, Mequon (WI) 458

Copenhagen Business School, Faculty of Economics and Business Administration, Copenhagen (Denmark) 501

Cranfield University, Cranfield School of Management, Cranfield (United Kingdom) 540

Creighton University, Eugene C. Eppley College of Business Administration, Omaha (NE) 272

Long Island University, Brooklyn Campus, School of Business, Public Administration and Information Sciences, Brooklyn (NY) 304

Long Island University, Rockland Graduate Campus, Program in Business Administration, Orangeburg (NY) 305

Louisiana State University and Agricultural and Mechanical College, E. J. Ourso College of Business, Baton Rouge (LA) 204

Louisiana Tech University, College of Administration and Business, Ruston (LA) 205

Loyola College in Maryland, Sellinger School of Business and Management, Baltimore (MD) 215

Loyola Marymount University, College of Business Administration, Los Angeles (CA) 81

Loyola University Chicago, Graduate School of Business, Chicago (IL) 167

Marquette University, Graduate School of Management, Milwaukee (WI) 459

Marylhurst University, Department of Business Administration, Marylhurst (OR) 357

Marymount University, School of Business Administration, Arlington (VA) 440

Massachusetts Institute of Technology, Sloan School of Management, Cambridge (MA) 227

McGill University, Desautels Faculty of Management, Montréal (Canada) 469, **658**

McMaster University, DeGroote School of Business, Hamilton (Canada) 470

Memorial University of Newfoundland, Faculty of Business Administration, St. John's (Canada) 470

Mercy College, Division of Business and Accounting, Dobbs Ferry (NY) 307

Metropolitan State University, College of Management, St. Paul (MN) 250

Michigan State University, Eli Broad Graduate School of Management, East Lansing (MI) 240

Middle East Technical University, Department of Business Administration, Ankara (Turkey) 537

Millsaps College, Else School of Management, Jackson (MS) 255

Mills College, Graduate School of Business, Oakland (CA) 81

Mississippi State University, College of Business and Industry, Mississippi State (MS) 256

Missouri State University, College of Business Administration, Springfield (MO) *262*

Monash University, MBA Programme, Clayton (Australia) 486

Monmouth University, School of Business Administration, West Long Branch (NJ) 284

Montclair State University, School of Business, Montclair (NJ) 285

Monterey Institute of International Studies, Fisher Graduate School of International Business, Monterey (CA) 82, **660**

Mount St. Mary's University, Program in Business Administration, Emmitsburg (MD) 215

Murray State University, College of Business and Public Affairs, Murray (KY) 200

Nanyang Technological University, Nanyang Business School, Singapore (Singapore) 527, **662**

National University, School of Business and Management, La Jolla (CA) 82

National University of Ireland, Dublin, The Michael Smurfit Graduate School of Business, Blackrock (Ireland) 513

New Jersey Institute of Technology, School of Management, Newark (NJ) 285

Newman University, School of Business, Wichita (KS) 194

New York Institute of Technology, School of Management (NY) 308

New York University, Leonard N. Stern School of Business (NY) 309

New York University, Robert F. Wagner Graduate School of Public Service (NY) 309

North Dakota State University, College of Business, Fargo (ND) 335

Northeastern University, Graduate School of Business Administration, Boston (MA) 228

Northern Arizona University, College of Business Administration, Flagstaff (AZ) 57

Northern Kentucky University, College of Business, Highland Heights (KY) 201

North Park University, School of Business and Nonprofit Management, Chicago (IL) 170

Northwestern University, Kellogg School of Management, Evanston (IL) 171

Norwegian School of Management, Graduate School, Sandvika (Norway) 524

Notre Dame de Namur University, Department of Business Administration, Belmont (CA) 84

Nottingham Trent University, Nottingham Business School, Nottingham (United Kingdom) 544

Nova Southeastern University, H. Wayne Huizenga School of Business and Entrepreneurship, Fort Lauderdale (FL) 130, **666**

Nyack College, School of Business, Nyack (NY) 310

Nyenrode Business Universiteit, Netherlands Business School, Breukelen (Netherlands) 522

Oakland University, School of Business Administration, Rochester (MI) 241

The Ohio State University, Max M. Fisher College of Business, Columbus (OH) 344

Oklahoma City University, Meinders School of Business, Oklahoma City (OK) 352

Oklahoma Wesleyan University, Professional Studies Division, Bartlesville (OK) 353

Old Dominion University, College of Business and Public Administration, Norfolk (VA) 441

Oral Roberts University, School of Business, Tulsa (OK) 353

Ottawa University, Graduate Studies-Arizona (AZ) 57

Otterbein College, Department of Business, Accounting and Economics, Westerville (OH) 345

Pace University, Lubin School of Business, New York (NY) 310

Pacific States University, College of Business, Los Angeles (CA) 85

Penn State Great Valley, Graduate Studies, Malvern (PA) 373

Penn State University Park, The Mary Jean and Frank P. Smeal College of Business Administration, State College (PA) 374

Pepperdine University, Graziadio School of Business and Management, Los Angeles (CA) 85

Philadelphia University, School of Business Administration, Philadelphia (PA) 375, **668**

Piedmont College, School of Business, Demorest (GA) 149

Pontifical Catholic University of Puerto Rico, College of Business Administration, Ponce (PR) 386

Portland State University, School of Business Administration, Portland (OR) 358

Providence College, School of Business, Providence (RI) 388

Purdue University, Krannert School of Management, West Lafayette (IN) 185

Queensland University of Technology, Brisbane Graduate School of Business, Brisbane (Australia) 487

Queens University of Charlotte, McColl Graduate School of Business, Charlotte (NC) 329

Quinnipiac University, School of Business, Hamden (CT) 109

Regis University, College for Professional Studies, Denver (CO) 103

Rensselaer at Hartford, Lally School of Management and Technology, Hartford (CT) 110

Rensselaer Polytechnic Institute, Lally School of Management and Technology, Troy (NY) 311, **670**

Rice University, Jesse H. Jones Graduate School of Management, Houston (TX) 410

Rider University, College of Business Administration, Lawrenceville (NJ) 287

Rochester Institute of Technology, E. Philip Saunders College of Business, Rochester (NY) 312

Rockford College, Program in Business Administration, Rockford (IL) 171

Rockhurst University, Helzberg School of Management, Kansas City (MO) 264

Rollins College, Crummer Graduate School of Business, Winter Park (FL) 131, **674**

Roosevelt University, Walter E. Heller College of Business Administration, Chicago (IL) 172, **676**

Rowan University, William G. Rohrer College of Business, Glassboro (NJ) 287

Rutgers, The State University of New Jersey, Rutgers Business School–Newark and New Brunswick, Newark and New Brunswick (NJ) 288, **678**

Rutgers, The State University of New Jersey, Camden, School of Business, Camden (NJ) 288

Sacred Heart University, John F. Welch College of Business, Fairfield (CT) 110

Sage Graduate School, Department of Management, Troy (NY) 313

Saginaw Valley State University, College of Business and Management, University Center (MI) 242

St. Ambrose University, Program in Business Administration, Davenport (IA) 190

St. Bonaventure University, School of Business, St. Bonaventure (NY) 313

St. Edward's University, The School of Management and Business, Austin (TX) 410

Saint Francis University, Master of Business Administration Program, Loretto (PA) 377

St. John's University, The Peter J. Tobin College of Business, Queens (NY) 314, **680**

Saint Joseph's University, Erivan K. Haub School of Business, Philadelphia (PA) 377

Saint Louis University, John Cook School of Business, St. Louis (MO) *264*

Saint Mary's University of Minnesota, Schools of Graduate and Professional Programs, Winona (MN) 251

Saint Peter's College, MBA Programs, Jersey City (NJ) 289, **682**

St. Thomas Aquinas College, Division of Business Administration, Sparkill (NY) 315

Saint Xavier University, Graham School of Management, Chicago (IL) 173

San Diego State University, College of Business Administration, San Diego (CA) 86

San Francisco State University, College of Business, San Francisco (CA) 87

Santa Clara University, Leavey School of Business, Santa Clara (CA) 88

Seattle Pacific University, School of Business and Economics, Seattle (WA) 450

Seattle University, Albers School of Business and Economics, Seattle (WA) 451

University of Nevada, Las Vegas, College of Business, Las Vegas (NV) 275, **722**

University of Newcastle, Graduate School of Business, Callaghan (Australia) 489

University of New Hampshire, Whittemore School of Business and Economics, Durham (NH) 280, **726**

University of New Haven, School of Business, West Haven (CT) 113, **728**

University of New Mexico, Robert O. Anderson Graduate School of Management, Albuquerque (NM) 294

University of New Orleans, College of Business Administration, New Orleans (LA) 209

University of North Alabama, College of Business, Florence (AL) 52

The University of North Carolina at Chapel Hill, Kenan-Flagler Business School, Chapel Hill (NC) 330

The University of North Carolina at Charlotte, Belk College of Business Administration, Charlotte (NC) 330, **730**

The University of North Carolina Wilmington, School of Business, Wilmington (NC) 332

University of North Florida, Coggin College of Business, Jacksonville (FL) 136

University of North Texas, College of Business Administration, Denton (TX) 422

University of Notre Dame, Mendoza College of Business, Notre Dame (IN) 187

University of Oklahoma, Michael F. Price College of Business, Norman (OK) 355

University of Oregon, Charles H. Lundquist College of Business, Eugene (OR) 359, **732**

University of Pennsylvania, Wharton School, Philadelphia (PA) 380

University of Pittsburgh, Joseph M. Katz Graduate School of Business, Pittsburgh (PA) 381

University of Plymouth, Plymouth Business School, Plymouth (United Kingdom) 553

University of Portland, Dr. Robert B. Pamplin, Jr. School of Business, Portland (OR) 360

University of Reading, ICMA Centre, Reading (United Kingdom) 554

University of Redlands, School of Business, Redlands (CA) 96

University of Rhode Island, College of Business Administration, Kingston (RI) 389, **734**

University of Rochester, William E. Simon Graduate School of Business Administration, Rochester (NY) 321, **736**

University of St. Thomas, Opus College of Business (MN) 253, **738**

University of St. Thomas, Cameron School of Business (TX) 424

University of Salford, Salford Business School, Salford (United Kingdom) 554

University of San Diego, School of Business Administration, San Diego (CA) 96

University of San Francisco, Masagung Graduate School of Management, San Francisco (CA) 97

University of Saskatchewan, Edwards School of Business, Saskatoon (Canada) 478

The University of Scranton, Program in Business Administration, Scranton (PA) 382

University of South Carolina, Moore School of Business, Columbia (SC) *392,* **740**

University of Southern California, School of Business, Los Angeles (CA) 98

University of Southern Mississippi, College of Business, Hattiesburg (MS) 257

University of South Florida, College of Business Administration, Tampa (FL) 138

The University of Tampa, John H. Sykes College of Business, Tampa (FL) 139, **742**

The University of Tennessee, College of Business Administration, Knoxville (TN) *401,* **744**

The University of Texas at Arlington, College of Business Administration, Arlington (TX) 424, **746**

The University of Texas at Austin, Programs in MBA, Austin (TX) 425

The University of Texas at Dallas, School of Management, Richardson (TX) *426,* **748**

The University of Texas at San Antonio, College of Business, San Antonio (TX) 427, **750**

The University of Texas at Tyler, College of Business and Technology, Tyler (TX) 428

University of the District of Columbia, School of Business and Public Administration, Washington (DC) 122

University of the Pacific, Eberhardt School of Business, Stockton (CA) 99, **752**

University of the West, Department of Business Administration, Rosemead (CA) 99

University of the West of England, Bristol, Bristol Business School, Bristol (United Kingdom) 555

University of the Witwatersrand, Graduate School of Business Administration, Wits (South Africa) 527

The University of Toledo, College of Business Administration, Toledo (OH) 349

University of Toronto, Joseph L. Rotman School of Management, Toronto (Canada) 478

University of Tulsa, College of Business Administration, Tulsa (OK) 356

University of Ulster at Jordanstown, Faculty of Business and Management, Newtown Abbey (United Kingdom) 556

University of Wales, Aberystwyth, School of Management and Business, Ceredigion (United Kingdom) 556

University of Warwick, Warwick Business School, Coventry (United Kingdom) 557

University of Washington, Michael G. Foster School of Business, Seattle (WA) 452, **754**

The University of Western Ontario, Richard Ivey School of Business, London (Canada) 480

University of Windsor, Odette School of Business, Windsor (Canada) 480

University of Wisconsin–Eau Claire, College of Business, Eau Claire (WI) 461, **756**

University of Wisconsin–Madison, Wisconsin School of Business, Madison (WI) 462, **756**

University of Wisconsin–Milwaukee, Sheldon B. Lubar School of Business, Milwaukee (WI) 463

University of Wisconsin–Whitewater, College of Business and Economics, Whitewater (WI) 465

Vanderbilt University, Owen Graduate School of Management, Nashville (TN) 403, **758**

Vienna University of Economics and Business Administration, WU Wien MBA, Vienna (Austria) 492

Villanova University, Villanova School of Business, Villanova (PA) 382

Virginia Commonwealth University, School of Business, Richmond (VA) 445

Virginia Polytechnic Institute and State University, Pamplin College of Business, Blacksburg (VA) 446

Vlerick Leuven Gent Management School, MBA Programmes, Ghent (Belgium) 495

Wagner College, Department of Business Administration, Staten Island (NY) 321

Wake Forest University, Babcock Graduate School of Management, Winston-Salem (NC) 332

Walden University, School of Management, Minneapolis (MN) 253

Walsh College of Accountancy and Business Administration, Graduate Programs, Troy (MI) 247

Waseda University, Graduate School of Commerce, Tokyo (Japan) 517

Washington University in St. Louis, Olin Business School, St. Louis (MO) 269

Waynesburg University, Graduate and Professional Studies, Waynesburg (PA) 383

Wayne State University, School of Business Administration, Detroit (MI) 247, **760**

Webster University, School of Business and Technology, St. Louis (MO) 270

Western Illinois University, College of Business and Technology, Macomb (IL) 178

Western International University, Graduate Programs in Business, Phoenix (AZ) 60

Western Michigan University, Haworth College of Business, Kalamazoo (MI) 248

Westminster College, The Bill and Vieve Gore School of Business, Salt Lake City (UT) 433

West Texas A&M University, College of Business, Canyon (TX) 430

WHU—Otto Beisheim School of Management, WHU—Otto Beisheim School of Management, Vallendar (Germany) 511

Wichita State University, W. Frank Barton School of Business, Wichita (KS) 197

Wilfrid Laurier University, School of Business and Economics, Waterloo (Canada) 481, **766**

Wilkes University, College of Arts, Humanities and Social Sciences, Wilkes-Barre (PA) 384

Willamette University, George H. Atkinson Graduate School of Management, Salem (OR) 361, **768**

William Paterson University of New Jersey, Christos M. Cotsakos College of Business, Wayne (NJ) 292

Wilmington University, Division of Business, New Castle (DE) 117

Winthrop University, College of Business Administration, Rock Hill (SC) 393

Woodbury University, School of Business and Management, Burbank (CA) 100

Wright State University, Raj Soin College of Business, Dayton (OH) 350

Xavier University, Williams College of Business, Cincinnati (OH) 350

Yale University, Yale School of Management, New Haven (CT) 114

York College of Pennsylvania, Department of Business Administration, York (PA) 385

York University, Schulich School of Business, Toronto (Canada) 482, **772**

Youngstown State University, Warren P. Williamson Jr. College of Business Administration, Youngstown (OH) 351

FINANCIAL ECONOMICS

The American University in Cairo, School of Business, Economics and Communication, Cairo (Egypt) 502

Aston University, Aston Business School, Birmingham (United Kingdom) 539

Barcelona Business School, Graduate Programs in Business, Barcelona (Spain) 528

Brandeis University, International Business School, Waltham (MA) 224, **582**

California State University, Los Angeles, College of Business and Economics, Los Angeles (CA) 71

Cardiff University, Cardiff Business School, Cardiff (United Kingdom) 539

Graduate School of Business Administration Zurich, Executive Management Programs, Zurich (Switzerland) 532

Groupe CERAM, Ceram ESC Nice School of Management, Sophia Antipolis (France) 504

HEC Paris, HEC MBA Program, Jouy-en-Josas (France) *505*, **632**

HfB—Business School of Finance and Management, Frankfurt School of Finance and Management, Frankfurt (Germany) 508

IE Business School, Business School, Madrid (Spain) 529, **636**

Illinois Institute of Technology, Stuart School of Business, Chicago (IL) 164

International University of Japan, Graduate School of International Management, Minami Uonuma-gu (Japan) 516

Katholieke Universiteit Leuven, Leuven School of Business and Economics, Leuven (Belgium) 494

Kent State University, Graduate School of Management, Kent (OH) 342

Lancaster University, Management School, Lancaster (United Kingdom) 541

Marquette University, Graduate School of Management, Milwaukee (WI) 459

National University, School of Business and Management, La Jolla (CA) 82

National University of Ireland, Dublin, The Michael Smurfit Graduate School of Business, Blackrock (Ireland) 513

New York University, Leonard N. Stern School of Business (NY) 309

Norwegian School of Management, Graduate School, Sandvika (Norway) 524

Saints Cyril and Methodius University, Faculty of Economics, Skopje (Macedonia) 519

Southern Illinois University Edwardsville, School of Business, Edwardsville (IL) *174*

Stockholm School of Economics, Department of Business Administration, Stockholm (Sweden) 531

Tulane University, A. B. Freeman School of Business, New Orleans (LA) 207

The University of Alabama, Manderson Graduate School of Business, Tuscaloosa (AL) 49

University of California, Berkeley, Haas School of Business, Berkeley (CA) 89

University of Durham, Durham Business School, Durham (United Kingdom) 549

University of Edinburgh, Edinburgh University Management School, Edinburgh (United Kingdom) 550

University of Georgia, Terry College of Business, Athens (GA) 151

University of Glasgow, University of Glasgow Business School, Glasgow (United Kingdom) 550

University of Newcastle, Graduate School of Business, Callaghan (Australia) 489

University of Oxford, Saïd Business School, Oxford (United Kingdom) 553

University of Salford, Salford Business School, Salford (United Kingdom) 554

The University of Texas at Arlington, College of Business Administration, Arlington (TX) 424, **746**

University of Waterloo, Graduate Studies, Waterloo (Canada) 479

Vienna University of Economics and Business Administration, WU Wien MBA, Vienna (Austria) 492

Virginia Commonwealth University, School of Business, Richmond (VA) 445

FINANCIAL ENGINEERING

Bayerische Julius-Maximilians University of Wuerzburg, MBA Program, Wuerzburg (Germany) 507

City University of Hong Kong, Faculty of Business, Hong Kong (China) 497

Claremont Graduate University, Peter F. Drucker and Masatoshi Ito Graduate School of Management, Claremont (CA) 75, **590**

ESCP-EAP European School of Management, ESCP-EAP European School of Management (France) 503

Groupe CERAM, Ceram ESC Nice School of Management, Sophia Antipolis (France) 504

HfB—Business School of Finance and Management, Frankfurt School of Finance and Management, Frankfurt (Germany) 508

Illinois Institute of Technology, Stuart School of Business, Chicago (IL) 164

The International University of Monaco, Graduate Programs, Monte Carlo (Monaco) 520

Lehigh University, College of Business and Economics, Bethlehem (PA) 371, **656**

National University, School of Business and Management, La Jolla (CA) 82

Stevens Institute of Technology, Wesley J. Howe School of Technology Management, Hoboken (NJ) 290

Temple University, Fox School of Business and Management, Philadelphia (PA) 379

University of California, Berkeley, Haas School of Business, Berkeley (CA) 89

University of Durham, Durham Business School, Durham (United Kingdom) 549

University of Maryland, College Park, Robert H. Smith School of Business, College Park (MD) 217

University of Reading, ICMA Centre, Reading (United Kingdom) 554

University of Toronto, Joseph L. Rotman School of Management, Toronto (Canada) 478

University of Tulsa, College of Business Administration, Tulsa (OK) 356

Vienna University of Economics and Business Administration, WU Wien MBA, Vienna (Austria) 492

Washington University in St. Louis, Olin Business School, St. Louis (MO) 269

York University, Schulich School of Business, Toronto (Canada) 482, **772**

FINANCIAL INFORMATION SYSTEMS

Graduate School of Business Administration Zurich, Executive Management Programs, Zurich (Switzerland) 532

Groupe CERAM, Ceram ESC Nice School of Management, Sophia Antipolis (France) 504

The Hague University, Faculty of Economics and Management, The Hague (Netherlands) 521, **628**

Illinois Institute of Technology, Stuart School of Business, Chicago (IL) 164

International University of Japan, Graduate School of International Management, Minami Uonuma-gu (Japan) 516

National University, School of Business and Management, La Jolla (CA) 82

Oakland University, School of Business Administration, Rochester (MI) 241

OGI School of Science & Engineering at Oregon Health & Science University, Department of Management in Science and Technology, Beaverton (OR) 358

Penn State Great Valley, Graduate Studies, Malvern (PA) 373

Rensselaer Polytechnic Institute, Lally School of Management and Technology, Troy (NY) 311, **670**

Stevens Institute of Technology, Wesley J. Howe School of Technology Management, Hoboken (NJ) 290

Stockholm School of Economics, Department of Business Administration, Stockholm (Sweden) 531

Texas A&M University, Mays Business School, College Station (TX) 414

Tulane University, A. B. Freeman School of Business, New Orleans (LA) 207

University of Bath, School of Management, Bath (United Kingdom) 547

University of California, Berkeley, Haas School of Business, Berkeley (CA) 89

University of Durham, Durham Business School, Durham (United Kingdom) 549

University of Salford, Salford Business School, Salford (United Kingdom) 554

FINANCIAL MANAGEMENT/ PLANNING

The American College, Richard D. Irwin Graduate School, Bryn Mawr (PA) 362

Antwerp International Business School, Graduate Programs in Business, Antwerp (Belgium) 493

Aston University, Aston Business School, Birmingham (United Kingdom) 539

Barcelona Business School, Graduate Programs in Business, Barcelona (Spain) 528

Bentley College, The Elkin B. McCallum Graduate School of Business, Waltham (MA) 221, **578**

Boise State University, College of Business and Economics, Boise (ID) 155

Brigham Young University, Marriott School of Management, Provo (UT) 431

California Lutheran University, School of Business, Thousand Oaks (CA) 67

California National University for Advanced Studies, College of Business Administration, Northridge (CA) 67

Carleton University, Eric Sprott School of Business, Ottawa (Canada) 467

Central Queensland University, Faculty of Business and Informatics, Rockhampton (Australia) 483

City University of Hong Kong, Faculty of Business, Hong Kong (China) 497

College for Financial Planning, Program in Financial Planning, Greenwood Village (CO) 101

The College of Saint Rose, School of Business, Albany (NY) 298, **594**

Creighton University, Eugene C. Eppley College of Business Administration, Omaha (NE) 272

Deakin University, Deakin Business School, Geelong (Australia) 484

DePaul University, Charles H. Kellstadt Graduate School of Business, Chicago (IL) 159

DeVry University, Keller Graduate School of Management, Phoenix (AZ) 56

DeVry University, Keller Graduate School of Management, Fremont (CA) 76

DeVry University, Keller Graduate School of Management, Long Beach (CA) 76

DeVry University, Keller Graduate School of Management, Palmdale (CA) 76

DeVry University, Keller Graduate School of Management, Pomona (CA) 77

DeVry University, Keller Graduate School of Management, San Diego (CA) 77

DeVry University, Keller Graduate School of Management, Colorado Springs (CO) 102

DeVry University, Keller Graduate School of Management, Miami (FL) 124

DeVry University, Keller Graduate School of Management, Miramar (FL) 124

DeVry University, Keller Graduate School of Management, Orlando (FL) 124

DeVry University, Keller Graduate School of Management, Tampa (FL) 124

DeVry University, Keller Graduate School of Management, Alpharetta (GA) 144

DeVry University, Keller Graduate School of Management, Atlanta (GA) 144

DeVry University, Keller Graduate School of Management, Decatur (GA) 144

DeVry University, Keller Graduate School of Management, Duluth (GA) 145

DeVry University, Keller Graduate School of Management, Elgin (IL) 160

DeVry University, Keller Graduate School of Management, Gurnee (IL) 161

DeVry University, Keller Graduate School of Management, Lincolnshire (IL) 161

DeVry University, Keller Graduate School of Management, Schaumburg (IL) 162

DeVry University, Keller Graduate School of Management, Tinley Park (IL) 162

DeVry University, Keller Graduate School of Management (IN) 180

DeVry University, Keller Graduate School of Management, Merrillville (IN) 180

DeVry University, Keller Graduate School of Management, Kansas City (MO) 259

DeVry University, Keller Graduate School of Management, St. Louis (MO) 259

DeVry University, Keller Graduate School of Management (NV) 275

DeVry University, Keller Graduate School of Management (NC) 323

DeVry University, Keller Graduate School of Management, Columbus (OH) 341

DeVry University, Keller Graduate School of Management, Seven Hills (OH) 341

DeVry University, Keller Graduate School of Management (OR) 356

DeVry University, Keller Graduate School of Management (PA) 365

DeVry University, Keller Graduate School of Management, Fort Washington (PA) 365

DeVry University, Keller Graduate School of Management, Pittsburgh (PA) 365

DeVry University, Keller Graduate School of Management (TX) 406

DeVry University, Keller Graduate School of Management, Irving (TX) 407

DeVry University, Keller Graduate School of Management, Arlington (VA) 437

DeVry University, Keller Graduate School of Management, McLean (VA) 437

DeVry University, Keller Graduate School of Management, Bellevue (WA) 447

DeVry University, Keller Graduate School of Management, Federal Way (WA) 448

École Nationale des Ponts et Chaussées, ENPC MBA, Paris (France) 503

ESCP-EAP European School of Management, ESCP-EAP European School of Management (France) 503

European School of Economics, MBA Programme (Italy) 515, **608**

Florida Atlantic University, College of Business, Boca Raton (FL) 126

Florida International University, Alvah H. Chapman, Jr. Graduate School of Business, Miami (FL) 128, **618**

Georgia State University, J. Mack Robinson College of Business, Atlanta (GA) 147, **626**

Golden Gate University, Ageno School of Business, San Francisco (CA) 78

Graduate School of Business Administration Zurich, Executive Management Programs, Zurich (Switzerland) 532

Groupe CERAM, Ceram ESC Nice School of Management, Sophia Antipolis (France) 504

HEC Paris, HEC MBA Program, Jouy-en-Josas (France) *505*, **632**

HfB—Business School of Finance and Management, Frankfurt School of Finance and Management, Frankfurt (Germany) 508

The Hong Kong University of Science and Technology, School of Business and Management, Hong Kong (China) 499

IE Business School, Business School, Madrid (Spain) 529, **636**

Illinois Institute of Technology, Stuart School of Business, Chicago (IL) 164

Indiana State University, College of Business, Terre Haute (IN) 181

International University of Japan, Graduate School of International Management, Minami Uonuma-gu (Japan) 516

The International University of Monaco, Graduate Programs, Monte Carlo (Monaco) 520

Iowa State University of Science and Technology, College of Business, Ames (IA) 189, **644**

Johnson & Wales University, The Alan Shawn Feinstein Graduate School, Providence (RI) 388, **648**

Lamar University, College of Business, Beaumont (TX) 408

Lancaster University, Management School, Lancaster (United Kingdom) 541

Lincoln University, Business Administration Program, Oakland (CA) 80

Lindenwood University, Division of Management, St. Charles (MO) 261

Lipscomb University, MBA Program, Nashville (TN) 397

Macquarie University, Macquarie Graduate School of Management, Sydney (Australia) 485

Massachusetts Institute of Technology, Sloan School of Management, Cambridge (MA) 227

Missouri State University, College of Business Administration, Springfield (MO) *262*

Monash University, MBA Programme, Clayton (Australia) 486

Nanjing University, School of Business, Nanjing (China) 500

National University, School of Business and Management, La Jolla (CA) 82

National University of Ireland, Dublin, The Michael Smurfit Graduate School of Business, Blackrock (Ireland) 513

Naval Postgraduate School, School of Business and Public Policy, Monterey (CA) 83

North Carolina State University, College of Management, Raleigh (NC) 328, **664**

North Central College, Department of Business, Naperville (IL) *168*

Northcentral University, MBA Program, Prescott Valley (AZ) 56

Northeastern University, Graduate School of Business Administration, Boston (MA) 228

Nottingham Trent University, Nottingham Business School, Nottingham (United Kingdom) 544

OGI School of Science & Engineering at Oregon Health & Science University, Department of Management in Science and Technology, Beaverton (OR) 358

Old Dominion University, College of Business and Public Administration, Norfolk (VA) 441

Pace University, Lubin School of Business, New York (NY) 310

Penn State University Park, The Mary Jean and Frank P. Smeal College of Business Administration, State College (PA) 374

St. Mary's University, Bill Greehey School of Business (TX) 411

Saint Xavier University, Graham School of Management, Chicago (IL) 173

Salem State College, Program in Business Administration, Salem (MA) 229

San Diego State University, College of Business Administration, San Diego (CA) 86

Simon Fraser University, Faculty of Business Administration, Burnaby (Canada) 472

Southeastern University, College of Graduate Studies, Washington (DC) 121

Stockholm School of Economics, Department of Business Administration, Stockholm (Sweden) 531

Swinburne University of Technology, Australian Graduate School of Entrepreneurship (AGSE), Hawthorne (Australia) 488

Texas A&M University, Mays Business School, College Station (TX) 414

Texas Tech University, Jerry S. Rawls College of Business Administration, Lubbock (TX) 418

Thames Valley University, Faculty of Professional Studies, Slough (United Kingdom) 546

Tulane University, A. B. Freeman School of Business, New Orleans (LA) 207

University of Antwerp, University of Antwerp Management School, Antwerp (Belgium) 495

University of Bath, School of Management, Bath (United Kingdom) 547

University of California, Berkeley, Haas School of Business, Berkeley (CA) 89

University of Dallas, Graduate School of Management, Irving (TX) 420, **710**

University of Durham, Durham Business School, Durham (United Kingdom) 549

University of Edinburgh, Edinburgh University Management School, Edinburgh (United Kingdom) 550

University of Florida, Hough Graduate School of Business, Gainesville (FL) 134

University of Glasgow, University of Glasgow Business School, Glasgow (United Kingdom) 550

University of Hull, School of Management, Hull (United Kingdom) 552

University of Massachusetts Amherst, Isenberg School of Management, Amherst (MA) 231

University of Mississippi, School of Business Administration, Oxford (MS) 257

University of St. Thomas, Opus College of Business (MN) 253, **738**

University of Salford, Salford Business School, Salford (United Kingdom) 554

University of San Diego, School of Business Administration, San Diego (CA) 96

University of Southern California, School of Business, Los Angeles (CA) 98

The University of Texas at Arlington, College of Business Administration, Arlington (TX) 424, **746**

The University of Texas at Austin, Programs in MBA, Austin (TX) 425

University of the Sunshine Coast, Faculty of Business, Maroochydore (Australia) 490

University of the West of England, Bristol, Bristol Business School, Bristol (United Kingdom) 555

University of Toronto, Joseph L. Rotman School of Management, Toronto (Canada) 478

University of Tulsa, College of Business Administration, Tulsa (OK) 356

University of Ulster at Jordanstown, Faculty of Business and Management, Newtown Abbey (United Kingdom) 556

The University of Western Australia, Business School, Nedlands (Australia) 491

Upper Iowa University, Online Master's Programs, Fayette (IA) 192

Vienna University of Economics and Business Administration, WU Wien MBA, Vienna (Austria) 492

Walsh College of Accountancy and Business Administration, Graduate Programs, Troy (MI) 247

Weber State University, John B. Goddard School of Business and Economics, Ogden (UT) 432

Widener University, School of Business Administration, Chester (PA) 384, **764**

Wilfrid Laurier University, School of Business and Economics, Waterloo (Canada) 481, **766**

York University, Schulich School of Business, Toronto (Canada) 482, **772**

FORENSIC ACCOUNTING

Florida Atlantic University, College of Business, Boca Raton (FL) 126

Georgia Southern University, College of Business Administration, Statesboro (GA) 146

National University, School of Business and Management, La Jolla (CA) 82

Roosevelt University, Walter E. Heller College of Business Administration, Chicago (IL) 172, **676**

Saint Xavier University, Graham School of Management, Chicago (IL) 173

GENERAL MBA

The Aarhus School of Business, Faculty of Business Administration, Aarhus (Denmark) 501

Alaska Pacific University, Business Administration Department, Anchorage (AK) 53

Albertus Magnus College, Program in Management, New Haven (CT) 108

Alcorn State University, School of Business, Alcorn State (MS) 254

Alfred University, College of Business, Alfred (NY) 295, **562**

Alvernia College, Department of Business, Reading (PA) 361

Amberton University, Department of Business Administration, Garland (TX) 404

American InterContinental University, School of Business, Weston (FL) 122, **564**

American InterContinental University Buckhead Campus, School of Business, Atlanta (GA) 141, **564**

American InterContinental University Dunwoody Campus, School of Business, Atlanta (GA) 141, **564**

American University of Beirut, MBA Program, Beirut (Lebanon) 518

Anderson University, Falls School of Business, Anderson (IN) 178

Antwerp International Business School, Graduate Programs in Business, Antwerp (Belgium) 493

Appalachian State University, John A. Walker College of Business, Boone (NC) 322

Arizona State University, W.P. Carey School of Business, Tempe (AZ) 54

Asian Institute of Technology, School of Management, Pathumthani (Thailand) 536

Aston University, Aston Business School, Birmingham (United Kingdom) 539

Athabasca University, Centre for Innovative Management, Athabasca (Canada) 466

Athens Laboratory of Business Administration, MBA Program, Athens (Greece) 512

Auburn University, College of Business, Auburn University (AL) 45, **568**

Auburn University Montgomery, School of Business, Montgomery (AL) 46

Augusta State University, Hull College of Business, Augusta (GA) 142

Aurora University, Dunham School of Business, Aurora (IL) 158

Babson College, F. W. Olin Graduate School of Business, Wellesley (MA) *220*, **570**

Baker College Center for Graduate Studies, Graduate Programs, Flint (MI) 236, **572**

Ball State University, Miller College of Business, Muncie (IN) 179

Barcelona Business School, Graduate Programs in Business, Barcelona (Spain) 528

Barry University, Andreas School of Business, Miami Shores (FL) 123

Bayerische Julius-Maximilians University of Wuerzburg, MBA Program, Wuerzburg (Germany) 507

Belhaven College, Program in Business, Jackson (MS) 254

Bellarmine University, W. Fielding Rubel School of Business, Louisville (KY) 198

Bellevue University, College of Business, Bellevue (NE) 271, **576**

Belmont University, Jack C. Massey Graduate School of Business, Nashville (TN) 395

Benedictine University, Graduate Programs, Lisle (IL) 158

Bernard M. Baruch College of the City University of New York, Zicklin School of Business, New York (NY) 296

Berry College, Campbell School of Business, Mount Berry (GA) 142

Biola University, Crowell School of Business, La Mirada (CA) 66

Bloomsburg University of Pennsylvania, College of Business, Bloomsburg (PA) 362

Boise State University, College of Business and Economics, Boise (ID) 155

Boston University, School of Management, Boston (MA) 223

Bowling Green State University, College of Business Administration, Bowling Green (OH) 338

Bryant University, Graduate School, Smithfield (RI) 387

California Baptist University, Program in Business Administration, Riverside (CA) 67

California Polytechnic State University, San Luis Obispo, Orfalea College of Business, San Luis Obispo (CA) 68

California State University, Bakersfield, School of Business and Public Administration, Bakersfield (CA) 68

California State University, Dominguez Hills, College of Business Administration and Public Policy, Carson (CA) 69

California State University, Fresno, Craig School of Business, Fresno (CA) 70

California State University, Fullerton, College of Business and Economics, Fullerton (CA) 70

California State University, Long Beach, College of Business Administration, Long Beach (CA) 71

California State University, Stanislaus, College of Business Administration, Turlock (CA) 74

California University of Pennsylvania, School of Graduate Studies and Research, California (PA) 363

Cameron University, Office of Graduate Studies, Lawton (OK) 352

Campbellsville University, School of Business and Economics, Campbellsville (KY) 199

Campbell University, Lundy-Fetterman School of Business, Buies Creek (NC) 323

Canisius College, Richard J. Wehle School of Business, Buffalo (NY) 296

Capital University, School of Management, Columbus (OH) 338

Capitol College, Graduate Programs, Laurel (MD) 212

Cardinal Stritch University, College of Business and Management, Milwaukee (WI) 457

Carnegie Mellon University, Tepper School of Business, Pittsburgh (PA) 363, **584**

Case Western Reserve University, Weatherhead School of Management, Cleveland (OH) 338

Chadron State College, Department of Business and Economics, Chadron (NE) 272

Chapman University, The George L. Argyros School of Business and Economics, Orange (CA) 74, **586**

Chatham University, Program in Business Administration, Pittsburgh (PA) 364

China Europe International Business School, MBA Programme, Shanghai (China) 496

The Chinese University of Hong Kong, Faculty of Business Administration, Hong Kong (China) 497

Christian Brothers University, School of Business, Memphis (TN) 396

The Citadel, The Military College of South Carolina, Citadel Graduate College, Charleston (SC) 390

City University of Hong Kong, Faculty of Business, Hong Kong (China) 497

City University of Seattle, School of Management, Bellevue (WA) 447, **588**

Claremont Graduate University, Peter F. Drucker and Masatoshi Ito Graduate School of Management, Claremont (CA) 75, **590**

Clarion University of Pennsylvania, College of Business Administration, Clarion (PA) 364

Clarke College, Program in Business Administration, Dubuque (IA) 188

Clarkson University, School of Business, Potsdam (NY) 297

Clark University, Graduate School of Management, Worcester (MA) 224, **592**

Clemson University, College of Business and Behavioral Science, Clemson (SC) 391

Cleveland State University, Nance College of Business Administration, Cleveland (OH) 340

College of St. Joseph, Program in Master of Business Administration, Rutland (VT) 433

The College of Saint Rose, School of Business, Albany (NY) 298, **594**

The College of St. Scholastica, Department of Management, Duluth (MN) 249

Colorado Christian University, Program in Business Administration, Lakewood (CO) 101

Colorado State University, College of Business, Fort Collins (CO) 101, **596**

Columbia College, Program in Business Administration, Columbia (MO) 258

Columbia Southern University, MBA Program, Orange Beach (AL) 46

Columbia Union College, MBA Program, Takoma Park (MD) 213

Columbia University, Graduate School of Business, New York (NY) 298

Columbus State University, College of Business, Columbus (GA) 143

Concordia University, St. Paul, College of Business and Organizational Leadership, St. Paul (MN) 250

Cornell University, Johnson Graduate School of Management, Ithaca (NY) 299, **598**

Cranfield University, Cranfield School of Management, Cranfield (United Kingdom) 540

Creighton University, Eugene C. Eppley College of Business Administration, Omaha (NE) 272

Cyprus International Institute of Management, MBA Programme, Nicosia (Cyprus) 500

Dalhousie University, Faculty of Management, Halifax (Canada) 467

Dartmouth College, Tuck School of Business at Dartmouth, Hanover (NH) 277

Deakin University, Deakin Business School, Geelong (Australia) 484

Delta State University, College of Business, Cleveland (MS) 254

DePaul University, Charles H. Kellstadt Graduate School of Business, Chicago (IL) 159

DeVry University, Keller Graduate School of Management, Colorado Springs (CO) 102

DeVry University, Keller Graduate School of Management, Alpharetta (GA) 144

DeVry University, Keller Graduate School of Management, Atlanta (GA) 144

DeVry University, Keller Graduate School of Management (NC) 323

DeVry University, Keller Graduate School of Management (TX) 406

DeVry University, Keller Graduate School of Management, Arlington (VA) 437

DeVry University, Keller Graduate School of Management, Bellevue (WA) 447

Dominican University of California, Division of Business and International Studies, San Rafael (CA) 77

Drexel University, LeBow College of Business, Philadelphia (PA) 366

Duke University, The Fuqua School of Business, Durham (NC) 323

Duquesne University, John F. Donahue Graduate School of Business, Pittsburgh (PA) 367

East Carolina University, College of Business, Greenville (NC) 324, **602**

Eastern Illinois University, Lumpkin College of Business and Applied Sciences, Charleston (IL) 163

Eastern Kentucky University, College of Business and Technology, Richmond (KY) 199

Eastern Michigan University, College of Business, Ypsilanti (MI) 237

Eastern New Mexico University, College of Business, Portales (NM) 292

Eastern Washington University, College of Business and Public Administration, Cheney (WA) 448

East Tennessee State University, College of Business and Technology, Johnson City (TN) 396

École Nationale des Ponts et Chaussées, ENPC MBA, Paris (France) 503

Edgewood College, Program in Business, Madison (WI) 458

Elmhurst College, Program in Business Administration, Elmhurst (IL) 163

Elon University, Martha and Spencer Love School of Business, Elon (NC) 324

Emory University, Roberto C. Goizueta Business School, Atlanta (GA) 145, **606**

Emporia State University, School of Business, Emporia (KS) 193

Endicott College, Program in Business Administration, Beverly (MA) 225

Erasmus University Rotterdam, Rotterdam School of Management, Rotterdam (Netherlands) 521

Escuela de Administracion de Negocios para Graduados, Programa Magister—MBA Programs, Lima (Peru) 525

European Business Management School, MBA Programmes, Antwerp (Belgium) 494

European School of Economics, MBA Programme (NY) 301, **608**

European School of Economics, MBA Programme (Italy) 515, **608**

European School of Economics, MBA Programme, Milan (Italy) 515, **608**

European School of Economics, MBA Programme (United Kingdom) 541, **608**

European University, Center for Management Studies, Montreux-Fontanivent (Switzerland) 532

Everest University, Program in Business Administration, Orlando (FL) 126

Excelsior College, School of Business and Technology, Albany (NY) 301, **610**

Fairleigh Dickinson University, College at Florham, Silberman College of Business, Madison (NJ) 282, **612**

Fairleigh Dickinson University, Metropolitan Campus, Silberman College of Business, Teaneck (NJ) 282, **612**

Fayetteville State University, Program in Business Administration, Fayetteville (NC) 325

Florida Atlantic University, College of Business, Boca Raton (FL) 126

Florida Institute of Technology, College of Business, Melbourne (FL) 128

Florida International University, Alvah H. Chapman, Jr. Graduate School of Business, Miami (FL) 128, **618**

Florida State University, College of Business, Tallahassee (FL) 129

Fontbonne University, Department of Business Administration, St. Louis (MO) 260

Framingham State College, Program in Business Administration, Framingham (MA) 226

Francis Marion University, School of Business, Florence (SC) 392

Gannon University, School of Business, Erie (PA) 368

Geneva College, Department of Business, Accounting and Management, Beaver Falls (PA) 369

George Fox University, School of Management, Newberg (OR) 357

Georgetown University, McDonough School of Business, Washington (DC) 119

The George Washington University, School of Business, Washington (DC) 119, **622**

Georgia College & State University, The J. Whitney Bunting School of Business, Milledgeville (GA) 145

Georgia Institute of Technology, College of Management, Atlanta (GA) 146, **624**

Georgian Court University, School of Business, Lakewood (NJ) 283

Georgia Southern University, College of Business Administration, Statesboro (GA) 146

Georgia Southwestern State University, School of Business Administration, Americus (GA) 147

Georgia State University, J. Mack Robinson College of Business, Atlanta (GA) 147, **626**

GISMA Business School, Graduate Programs, Hannover (Germany) 508

Golden Gate University, Ageno School of Business, San Francisco (CA) 78

Goldey-Beacom College, Graduate Program, Wilmington (DE) 116

Gonzaga University, School of Business Administration, Spokane (WA) 448

Grantham University, Mark Skousen School of Business, Kansas City (MO) 260

The Hague University, Faculty of Economics and Management, The Hague (Netherlands) 521, **628**

Hardin-Simmons University, Kelley College of Business, Abilene (TX) 407

HfB—Business School of Finance and Management, Frankfurt School of Finance and Management, Frankfurt (Germany) 508

HHL—Leipzig Graduate School of Management, MBA Program, Leipzig (Germany) 509

High Point University, Norcross Graduate School, High Point (NC) 326

Hong Kong Baptist University, School of Business, Hong Kong (China) 498

The Hong Kong University of Science and Technology, School of Business and Management, Hong Kong (China) 499

Houston Baptist University, College of Business and Economics, Houston (TX) 408

Howard University, School of Business, Washington (DC) 120

Hult International Business School, Graduate Program, Cambridge (MA) 227, **634**

Humboldt State University, School of Business, Arcata (CA) 80

Idaho State University, College of Business, Pocatello (ID) 156

IE Business School, Business School, Madrid (Spain) 529, **636**

Illinois Institute of Technology, Stuart School of Business, Chicago (IL) 164

IMD International Institute for Management Development, IMD International, Lausanne (Switzerland) 533

Indiana University Northwest, School of Business and Economics, Gary (IN) 183

Indiana University of Pennsylvania, Eberly College of Business and Information Technology, Indiana (PA) 369

Indiana University–Purdue University Fort Wayne, School of Business and Management Sciences, Fort Wayne (IN) 183

Indiana University South Bend, School of Business and Economics, South Bend (IN) 184

Indian Institute of Management, Ahmedabad, Post-Graduate Programme in Management, Gujarat (India) 512

Institut d'Etudes Politiques de Paris, MBA Programme, Paris (France) 505

Inter American University of Puerto Rico, San Germán Campus, Department of Business Administration, San Germán (PR) 385

International University in Geneva, MBA Program, Geneva (Switzerland) 533, **640**

International University of Japan, Graduate School of International Management, Minami Uonuma-gu (Japan) 516

The International University of Monaco, Graduate Programs, Monte Carlo (Monaco) 520

The International University, Vienna, MBA Programs, Vienna (Austria) 492

ITT Technical Institute, Online MBA Program, Indianapolis (IN) 185

Jackson State University, School of Business, Jackson (MS) 255

James Cook University, Faculty of Law, Business, and the Creative Arts—Townsville, Cairns (Australia) 485

James Madison University, College of Business, Harrisonburg (VA) 438

The Johns Hopkins University, Carey Business School, Baltimore (MD) 214, **646**

Kansas State University, College of Business Administration, Manhattan (KS) 194

Keio University, Keio Business School, Yokohama-shi (Japan) 517

Kennesaw State University, Michael J. Coles College of Business, Kennesaw (GA) 148

Kettering University, Graduate School, Flint (MI) 238

Kingston University, Kingston Business School, Kingston upon Thames (United Kingdom) 541

Koc University, Graduate School of Business, Istanbul (Turkey) 537

Kutztown University of Pennsylvania, College of Business, Kutztown (PA) 369

Lahore University of Management Sciences, Graduate School of Business Administration, Lahore Cantt (Pakistan) 525

Lake Forest Graduate School of Management, MBA Program, Lake Forest (IL) 166, **652**

Lancaster University, Management School, Lancaster (United Kingdom) 541

La Salle University, School of Business, Philadelphia (PA) 370

Laurentian University, School of Commerce and Administration, Sudbury (Canada) 469

Lebanon Valley College, Program in Business Administration, Annville (PA) 371

Lehigh University, College of Business and Economics, Bethlehem (PA) 371, **656**

Le Moyne College, Division of Management, Syracuse (NY) 304

Lenoir-Rhyne College, Charles M. Snipes School of Business, Hickory (NC) 326

Liberty University, School of Business, Lynchburg (VA) 439

Lindenwood University, Division of Management, St. Charles (MO) 261

Lipscomb University, MBA Program, Nashville (TN) 397

London Metropolitan University, Department of Management and Professional Development, London (United Kingdom) 543

Long Island University, C.W. Post Campus, College of Management, Brookville (NY) 305

Loughborough University, The Business School— Postgraduate Office, Loughborough (United Kingdom) 544

Louisiana State University and Agricultural and Mechanical College, E. J. Ourso College of Business, Baton Rouge (LA) 204

Loyola College in Maryland, Sellinger School of Business and Management, Baltimore (MD) 215

Loyola University New Orleans, Joseph A. Butt, S.J., College of Business, New Orleans (LA) 205

Lynchburg College, School of Business and Economics, Lynchburg (VA) 439

Macquarie University, Macquarie Graduate School of Management, Sydney (Australia) 485

Manukau Institute of Technology, Manukau Business School, Auckland (New Zealand) 523

Marist College, School of Management, Poughkeepsie (NY) 306

Marquette University, Graduate School of Management, Milwaukee (WI) 459

Marylhurst University, Department of Business Administration, Marylhurst (OR) 357

McMaster University, DeGroote School of Business, Hamilton (Canada) 470

McNeese State University, College of Business, Lake Charles (LA) 206

Medaille College, Accelerated Learning Programs (NY) 307

Memorial University of Newfoundland, Faculty of Business Administration, St. John's (Canada) 470

Mercer University, Eugene W. Stetson School of Business and Economics (GA) 149

Mercy College, Division of Business and Accounting, Dobbs Ferry (NY) 307

Meredith College, John E. Weems Graduate School, Raleigh (NC) 327

Mesa State College, Department of Business, Grand Junction (CO) 103

Michigan State University, Eli Broad Graduate School of Management, East Lansing (MI) 240

Michigan Technological University, School of Business and Economics, Houghton (MI) 241

Middle East Technical University, Department of Business Administration, Ankara (Turkey) 537

Middle Tennessee State University, College of Business, Murfreesboro (TN) 397

Millersville University of Pennsylvania, Department of Business Administration, Millersville (PA) 372

Mills College, Graduate School of Business, Oakland (CA) 81

Mississippi State University, College of Business and Industry, Mississippi State (MS) 256

Missouri State University, College of Business Administration, Springfield (MO) *262*

Monash University, MBA Programme, Clayton (Australia) 486

Monmouth University, School of Business Administration, West Long Branch (NJ) 284

Montreat College, School of Professional and Adult Studies, Montreat (NC) 327

Moravian College, The Moravian MBA, Bethlehem (PA) 373

Morehead State University, College of Business, Morehead (KY) 200

Nanjing University, School of Business, Nanjing (China) 500

Nanyang Technological University, Nanyang Business School, Singapore (Singapore) 527, **662**

Napier University, Napier Business School, Edinburgh (United Kingdom) 544

National-Louis University, College of Management and Business, Chicago (IL) 168

National University, School of Business and Management, La Jolla (CA) 82

Naval Postgraduate School, School of Business and Public Policy, Monterey (CA) 83

New York University, Leonard N. Stern School of Business (NY) 309

Nicholls State University, College of Business Administration, Thibodaux (LA) 206

Nichols College, Graduate Program in Business Administration, Dudley (MA) 228

North Carolina Central University, School of Business, Durham (NC) 327

Northcentral University, MBA Program, Prescott Valley (AZ) 56

Northeastern Illinois University, College of Business and Management, Chicago (IL) 169

Northeastern University, Graduate School of Business Administration, Boston (MA) 228

Northern Illinois University, College of Business, De Kalb (IL) 169

Northwest Christian College, School of Business and Management, Eugene (OR) 358

Northwest Missouri State University, Melvin and Valorie Booth College of Business and Professional Studies, Maryville (MO) 263

Northwood University, Richard DeVos Graduate School of Management, Midland (MI) 241

Norwegian School of Management, Graduate School, Sandvika (Norway) 524

Norwich University, Distance MBA Program, Northfield (VT) 433

Nottingham Trent University, Nottingham Business School, Nottingham (United Kingdom) 544

Nyack College, School of Business, Nyack (NY) 310

Oakland City University, School of Adult and Extended Learning, Oakland City (IN) 185

The Ohio State University, Max M. Fisher College of Business, Columbus (OH) 344

Ohio University, College of Business, Athens (OH) 344

Old Dominion University, College of Business and Public Administration, Norfolk (VA) 441

Open University, Business School, Milton Keynes (United Kingdom) 545

Ottawa University, Graduate Studies-Arizona (AZ) 57

Ottawa University, Graduate Studies-Kansas City, Ottawa (KS) 195

Otterbein College, Department of Business, Accounting and Economics, Westerville (OH) 345

Pacific Lutheran University, School of Business, Tacoma (WA) 449

Park University, Program in Business Administration, Parkville (MO) 264

Penn State Great Valley, Graduate Studies, Malvern (PA) 373

Penn State Harrisburg, School of Business Administration, Middletown (PA) 373

Pepperdine University, Graziadio School of Business and Management, Los Angeles (CA) 85

Pittsburg State University, Kelce College of Business, Pittsburg (KS) 195

Point Loma Nazarene University, Program in Business Administration, San Diego (CA) 86

Portland State University, School of Business Administration, Portland (OR) 358

Prairie View A&M University, College of Business, Prairie View (TX) 410

Purdue University, Krannert School of Management, West Lafayette (IN) 185

Purdue University Calumet, School of Management, Hammond (IN) 186

Queen Margaret University College, Edinburgh, School of Business and Enterprise, Edinburgh (United Kingdom) 545

Queens University of Charlotte, McColl Graduate School of Business, Charlotte (NC) 329

Quinnipiac University, School of Business, Hamden (CT) 109

Radford University, College of Business and Economics, Radford (VA) 441

Regent University, School of Global Leadership and Entrepreneurship, Virginia Beach (VA) 442

Regis University, College for Professional Studies, Denver (CO) 103

The Richard Stockton College of New Jersey, Program in Business Administration, Pomona (NJ) 286

Rivier College, Department of Business Administration, Nashua (NH) 279

Robert Morris University, Program in Business Administration, Moon Township (PA) 376, **672**

Rockford College, Program in Business Administration, Rockford (IL) 171

Rosemont College, Accelerated Program in Management, Rosemont (PA) 376

Rowan University, William G. Rohrer College of Business, Glassboro (NJ) 287

Royal Military College of Canada, Department of Business Administration, Kingston (Canada) 471

Royal Roads University, Faculty of Management, Victoria (Canada) 471

Rutgers, The State University of New Jersey, Rutgers Business School–Newark and New Brunswick, Newark and New Brunswick (NJ) 288, **678**

Saginaw Valley State University, College of Business and Management, University Center (MI) 242

St. John Fisher College, The Ronald L. Bittner School of Business, Rochester (NY) 314

Saint Joseph's University, Erivan K. Haub School of Business, Philadelphia (PA) 377

Saint Leo University, Graduate Business Studies, Saint Leo (FL) 132

Saint Martin's University, Division of Economics and Business Administration, Lacey (WA) 450

St. Mary's University, Bill Greehey School of Business (TX) 411

Saints Cyril and Methodius University, Faculty of Economics, Skopje (Macedonia) 519

St. Thomas Aquinas College, Division of Business Administration, Sparkill (NY) 315

Saint Xavier University, Graham School of Management, Chicago (IL) 173

Salem State College, Program in Business Administration, Salem (MA) 229

Salisbury University, Franklin P. Perdue School of Business, Salisbury (MD) 216

Salve Regina University, Graduate Studies, Newport (RI) 389

Samford University, School of Business, Birmingham (AL) 47

San Diego State University, College of Business Administration, San Diego (CA) 86

San Francisco State University, College of Business, San Francisco (CA) 87

San Jose State University, Lucas Graduate School of Business, San Jose (CA) 87

Seattle University, Albers School of Business and Economics, Seattle (WA) 451

Shenandoah University, Byrd School of Business, Winchester (VA) 442

Shippensburg University of Pennsylvania, John L. Grove College of Business, Shippensburg (PA) 379

Shorter College, School of Business, Rome (GA) 150

Simmons College, Simmons School of Management, Boston (MA) 230

Simon Fraser University, Faculty of Business Administration, Burnaby (Canada) 472

Southeastern Louisiana University, College of Business, Hammond (LA) 207

Southeastern Oklahoma State University, School of Business, Durant (OK) 353

Southern Connecticut State University, School of Business, New Haven (CT) 111

Southern Cross University, Graduate College of Management, Coffs Harbour (Australia) 487

Southern Illinois University Edwardsville, School of Business, Edwardsville (IL) *174*

Southern New Hampshire University, School of Business, Manchester (NH) 279, **690**

Southern Oregon University, School of Business, Ashland (OR) 359

Southern Utah University, School of Business, Cedar City (UT) 431

Southwestern Adventist University, Business Department, Graduate Program, Keene (TX) 412

Spring Arbor University, School of Business and Management, Spring Arbor (MI) 243

Spring Hill College, Division of Business and Management, Mobile (AL) 48

Stanford University, Graduate School of Business, Stanford (CA) 88

State University of New York at Binghamton, School of Management, Binghamton (NY) 315

State University of New York at New Paltz, School of Business, New Paltz (NY) 316

State University of New York at Oswego, School of Business, Oswego (NY) 316

Stephen F. Austin State University, College of Business, Nacogdoches (TX) 413

Stevens Institute of Technology, Wesley J. Howe School of Technology Management, Hoboken (NJ) 290

Stockholm School of Economics, Department of Business Administration, Stockholm (Sweden) 531

Swinburne University of Technology, Australian Graduate School of Entrepreneurship (AGSE), Hawthorne (Australia) 488

Syracuse University, Martin J. Whitman School of Management, Syracuse (NY) 318, **692**

Taylor University Fort Wayne, Master of Business Administration Program, Fort Wayne (IN) 186

Temple University, Fox School of Business and Management, Philadelphia (PA) 379

Texas A&M University, Mays Business School, College Station (TX) 414

Texas A&M University–Commerce, College of Business and Technology, Commerce (TX) 415

Texas A&M University–Corpus Christi, College of Business, Corpus Christi (TX) 416

Texas A&M University–Texarkana, College of Business, Texarkana (TX) 416

Texas Christian University, The Neeley School of Business at TCU, Fort Worth (TX) 416, **694**

Texas Southern University, Jesse H. Jones School of Business, Houston (TX) 417

Texas Woman's University, School of Management, Denton (TX) 419

Thames Valley University, Faculty of Professional Studies, Slough (United Kingdom) 546

Thomas College, Programs in Business, Waterville (ME) 211

Thomas Edison State College, School of Business and Management, Trenton (NJ) 291

Thomas More College, Program in Business Administration, Crestview Hills (KY) 201

Tiffin University, Program in Business Administration, Tiffin (OH) 345

TUI University, College of Business Administration, Cypress (CA) 89

Union Graduate College, School of Management, Schenectady (NY) 319

Universidade Nova de Lisboa, Faculdade de Economia-Gestao, Lisbon (Portugal) 526

Universitat Pompeu Fabra, Department of Business and Economics, MBA Program, Barcelona (Spain) 530

Université de Moncton, Faculty of Administration, Moncton (Canada) 472

Universite Libre de Bruxelles, Solvay Business School, Brussels (Belgium) 495

University at Albany, State University of New York, School of Business, Albany (NY) 319

University at Buffalo, the State University of New York, School of Management, Buffalo (NY) 320

University of Abertay Dundee, Dundee Business School, Dundee (United Kingdom) 547

The University of Adelaide, The University of Adelaide Business School, Adelaide (Australia) 488

The University of Akron, College of Business Administration, Akron (OH) 346

The University of Alabama, Manderson Graduate School of Business, Tuscaloosa (AL) 49

The University of Alabama at Birmingham, School of Business, Birmingham (AL) 50

University of Alberta, School of Business, Edmonton (Canada) 473

University of Antwerp, University of Antwerp Management School, Antwerp (Belgium) 495

The University of Arizona, Eller College of Management, Tucson (AZ) 58

University of Arkansas, Sam M. Walton College of Business Administration, Fayetteville (AR) 62

University of Baltimore/Towson University, Joint University of Baltimore/Towson University (UB/Towson) MBA Program, Baltimore (MD) 217

University of Bath, School of Management, Bath (United Kingdom) 547

The University of British Columbia, Sauder School of Business, Vancouver (Canada) 474

University of Calgary, Haskayne School of Business, Calgary (Canada) 474

University of California, Berkeley, Haas School of Business, Berkeley (CA) 89

University of California, Davis, Graduate School of Management, Davis (CA) 90

University of California, Irvine, The Paul Merage School of Business, Irvine (CA) 91

University of California, Los Angeles, UCLA Anderson School of Management, Los Angeles (CA) 91, **696**

University of California, San Diego, Rady School of Management, La Jolla (CA) 93, **700**

University of Central Arkansas, College of Business, Conway (AR) 62

University of Central Florida, College of Business Administration, Orlando (FL) 133

University of Central Oklahoma, College of Business Administration, Edmond (OK) 354

University of Colorado at Boulder, Leeds School of Business, Boulder (CO) 104, **702**

University of Colorado at Colorado Springs, Graduate School of Business Administration, Colorado Springs (CO) 105, **704**

University of Colorado Denver, Business School, Denver (CO) 105, **706**

University of Delaware, Alfred Lerner College of Business and Economics, Newark (DE) 116, **712**

University of Denver, Daniels College of Business, Denver (CO) 106

University of Deusto, Faculty of Economics and Business Administration, Bilbao (Spain) 530

University of Dubuque, School of Business, Dubuque (IA) 190

University of Durham, Durham Business School, Durham (United Kingdom) 549

University of Florida, Hough Graduate School of Business, Gainesville (FL) 134

University of Georgia, Terry College of Business, Athens (GA) 151

University of Glasgow, University of Glasgow Business School, Glasgow (United Kingdom) 550

University of Hartford, Barney School of Business, West Hartford (CT) 113

University of Hertfordshire, University of Hertfordshire Business School, Hatfield (United Kingdom) 551

University of Houston, Bauer College of Business, Houston (TX) 420

University of Illinois at Urbana–Champaign, College of Business, Champaign (IL) 176

University of Indianapolis, Graduate Business Programs, Indianapolis (IN) 186

The University of Iowa, Henry B. Tippie College of Business, Iowa City (IA) 191, **714**

University of Kansas, School of Business, Lawrence (KS) 196

University of Kentucky, Gatton College of
  Business and Economics, Lexington
  (KY) 202, **716**
University of London, London Business School,
  London (United Kingdom) 552
University of Louisville, College of Business,
  Louisville (KY) 203
University of Management and Technology,
  Graduate Business Programs, Arlington
  (VA) 443
University of Manitoba, Faculty of Management,
  Winnipeg (Canada) 475
University of Maryland, College Park, Robert H.
  Smith School of Business, College Park
  (MD) 217
University of Maryland University College,
  Graduate School of Management and
  Technology, Adelphi (MD) 218
University of Massachusetts Amherst, Isenberg
  School of Management, Amherst (MA) 231
University of Massachusetts Dartmouth, Charlton
  College of Business, North Dartmouth
  (MA) 232
University of Massachusetts Lowell, College of
  Management, Lowell (MA) 233
University of Melbourne, Melbourne Business
  School, Melbourne (Australia) 488
University of Memphis, Fogelman College of
  Business and Economics, Memphis (TN) 400
University of Michigan, Ross School of Business
  at the University of Michigan, Ann Arbor
  (MI) 244
University of Michigan–Dearborn, School of
  Management, Dearborn (MI) 245
University of Michigan–Flint, School of
  Management, Flint (MI) 246
University of Minnesota, Duluth, Labovitz School
  of Business and Economics, Duluth (MN) 252
University of Mississippi, School of Business
  Administration, Oxford (MS) 257
University of Missouri–Columbia, Robert J.
  Trulaske, Sr. College of Business, Columbia
  (MO) 267, **720**
University of Missouri–St. Louis, College of
  Business Administration, St. Louis
  (MO) *268*
University of Mobile, School of Business, Mobile
  (AL) 51
University of Nebraska at Kearney, College of
  Business and Technology, Kearney (NE) 273
University of Nevada, Reno, College of Business
  Administration, Reno (NV) 276
University of New Brunswick Fredericton, Faculty
  of Business Administration, Fredericton
  (Canada) 476
University of New Brunswick Saint John, Faculty
  of Business, Saint John (Canada) 476, **724**
The University of New England, The Graduate
  School of Business Administration, Armidale
  (Australia) 490
University of New Hampshire, Whittemore School
  of Business and Economics, Durham
  (NH) 280, **726**
University of New Haven, School of Business,
  West Haven (CT) 113, **728**
University of New Orleans, College of Business
  Administration, New Orleans (LA) 209
University of New South Wales, Australian School
  of Business, Kensington (Australia) 490
University of North Alabama, College of Business,
  Florence (AL) 52
The University of North Carolina at Charlotte,
  Belk College of Business Administration,
  Charlotte (NC) 330, **730**

The University of North Carolina at Greensboro,
  Bryan School of Business and Economics,
  Greensboro (NC) 331
The University of North Carolina at Pembroke,
  Graduate Studies, Pembroke (NC) 331
University of Oklahoma, Michael F. Price College
  of Business, Norman (OK) 355
University of Ottawa, Telfer School of
  Management, Ottawa (Canada) 476
University of Oxford, Saïd Business School,
  Oxford (United Kingdom) 553
University of Redlands, School of Business,
  Redlands (CA) 96
University of Rhode Island, College of Business
  Administration, Kingston (RI) 389, **734**
University of Richmond, Richard S. Reynolds
  Graduate School, Richmond (VA) 444
University of St. Gallen, Business School, St.
  Gallen (Switzerland) 535
University of Salford, Salford Business School,
  Salford (United Kingdom) 554
The University of Scranton, Program in Business
  Administration, Scranton (PA) 382
University of Sioux Falls, John T. Vucurevich
  School of Business, Sioux Falls (SD) 394
University of South Alabama, Mitchell College of
  Business, Mobile (AL) 52
University of Southern Maine, School of Business,
  Portland (ME) 212
The University of Tampa, John H. Sykes College
  of Business, Tampa (FL) 139, **742**
The University of Tennessee at Chattanooga,
  College of Business, Chattanooga (TN) 402
The University of Tennessee at Martin, College of
  Business and Public Affairs, Martin (TN) 402
The University of Texas at Arlington, College of
  Business Administration, Arlington
  (TX) 424, **746**
The University of Texas at Austin, Programs in
  MBA, Austin (TX) 425
The University of Texas at Brownsville, School of
  Business, Brownsville (TX) 426
The University of Texas at Tyler, College of
  Business and Technology, Tyler (TX) 428
The University of Texas–Pan American, College of
  Business Administration, Edinburg (TX) 428
University of the Incarnate Word, H-E-B School
  of Business and Administration (TX) 429
University of the Sacred Heart, Department of
  Business Administration, San Juan (PR) 387
University of the Sunshine Coast, Faculty of
  Business, Maroochydore (Australia) 490
University of the Virgin Islands, Division of
  Business Administration, Saint Thomas
  (VI) 435
University of Toronto, Joseph L. Rotman School
  of Management, Toronto (Canada) 478
University of Vaasa, Faculty of Business
  Administration, Vaasa (Finland) 503
University of Vermont, School of Business
  Administration, Burlington (VT) 435
University of Victoria, Faculty of Business,
  Victoria (Canada) 479
University of Wales, Aberystwyth, School of
  Management and Business, Ceredigion (United
  Kingdom) 556
University of Warwick, Warwick Business School,
  Coventry (United Kingdom) 557
University of Washington, Michael G. Foster
  School of Business, Seattle (WA) 452, **754**
The University of Western Australia, Business
  School, Nedlands (Australia) 491
University of Western Sydney, Sydney Graduate
  School of Management, Campbelltown
  (Australia) 491

University of West Florida, College of Business,
  Pensacola (FL) 139
University of West Georgia, Richards College of
  Business, Carrollton (GA) 152
University of Wisconsin–La Crosse, College of
  Business Administration, La Crosse
  (WI) 462, **756**
University of Wisconsin–Milwaukee, Sheldon B.
  Lubar School of Business, Milwaukee
  (WI) 463
University of Wisconsin–Oshkosh, College of
  Business, Oshkosh (WI) 463, **756**
University of Wisconsin–Parkside, School of
  Business and Technology, Kenosha
  (WI) 464, **756**
University of Wyoming, College of Business,
  Laramie (WY) 465
Valdosta State University, Langdale College of
  Business Administration, Valdosta (GA) 153
Vancouver Island University, Program in Business
  Administration, Nanaimo (Canada) 480
Vanguard University of Southern California,
  School of Business and Management, Costa
  Mesa (CA) 100
Vienna University of Economics and Business
  Administration, WU Wien MBA, Vienna
  (Austria) 492
Villanova University, Villanova School of
  Business, Villanova (PA) 382
Virginia Commonwealth University, School of
  Business, Richmond (VA) 445
Vlerick Leuven Gent Management School, MBA
  Programmes, Ghent (Belgium) 495
Wake Forest University, Babcock Graduate School
  of Management, Winston-Salem (NC) 332
Walden University, School of Management,
  Minneapolis (MN) 253
Warner Southern College, School of Business,
  Lake Wales (FL) 140
Washburn University, School of Business, Topeka
  (KS) *197*
Washington State University, College of Business,
  Pullman (WA) 453
Washington State University Tri-Cities, College of
  Business, Richland (WA) 453
Washington State University Vancouver, Program
  in Business Administration, Vancouver
  (WA) 454
Washington University in St. Louis, Olin Business
  School, St. Louis (MO) 269
Wayne State College, School of Business and
  Technology, Wayne (NE) 274
Weber State University, John B. Goddard School
  of Business and Economics, Ogden (UT) 432
Webster University, School of Business and
  Technology, St. Louis (MO) 270
West Chester University of Pennsylvania, College
  of Business and Public Affairs, West Chester
  (PA) 383
Western Carolina University, College of Business,
  Cullowhee (NC) 333
Western Connecticut State University, Ancell
  School of Business, Danbury (CT) 114
Western International University, Graduate
  Programs in Business, Phoenix (AZ) 60
Western Kentucky University, Gordon Ford
  College of Business, Bowling Green (KY) 203
Western Michigan University, Haworth College of
  Business, Kalamazoo (MI) 248
Western New England College, School of
  Business, Springfield (MA) 234
Western Washington University, College of
  Business and Economics, Bellingham
  (WA) 454
Westminster College, The Bill and Vieve Gore
  School of Business, Salt Lake City (UT) 433

West Texas A&M University, College of Business, Canyon (TX) 430

West Virginia Wesleyan College, Department of Business and Economics, Buckhannon (WV) 456

Wheeling Jesuit University, Department of Business, Wheeling (WV) 457

WHU—Otto Beisheim School of Management, WHU—Otto Beisheim School of Management, Vallendar (Germany) 511

Wichita State University, W. Frank Barton School of Business, Wichita (KS) 197

Widener University, School of Business Administration, Chester (PA) 384, **764**

Wilfrid Laurier University, School of Business and Economics, Waterloo (Canada) 481, **766**

Willamette University, George H. Atkinson Graduate School of Management, Salem (OR) 361, **768**

William Carey University, School of Business, Hattiesburg (MS) 258

William Paterson University of New Jersey, Christos M. Cotsakos College of Business, Wayne (NJ) 292

Winthrop University, College of Business Administration, Rock Hill (SC) 393

Worcester Polytechnic Institute, Department of Management, Worcester (MA) 234, **770**

Xavier University, Williams College of Business, Cincinnati (OH) 350

York College of Pennsylvania, Department of Business Administration, York (PA) 385

HEALTH ADMINISTRATION

Adelphi University, School of Business, Garden City (NY) 295, **560**

Alaska Pacific University, Business Administration Department, Anchorage (AK) 53

Andrew Jackson University, Brian Tracy College of Business and Entrepreneurship, Birmingham (AL) 45

Argosy University, Chicago, College of Business, Chicago (IL) 158, **566**

Argosy University, Dallas, College of Business, Dallas (TX) 405, **566**

Argosy University, Denver, College of Business, Denver (CO) 100, **566**

Argosy University, Hawai'i, College of Business, Honolulu (HI) 153, **566**

Argosy University, Los Angeles, College of Business, Santa Monica (CA) 65, **566**

Argosy University, Nashville, College of Business, Nashville (TN) 395, **566**

Argosy University, Orange County, College of Business, Santa Ana (CA) 65, **566**

Argosy University, Phoenix, College of Business, Phoenix (AZ) 54, **566**

Argosy University, Salt Lake City, College of Business, Draper (UT) 430, **566**

Argosy University, San Francisco Bay Area, College of Business, Alameda (CA) 66, **566**

Argosy University, Sarasota, College of Business, Sarasota (FL) 122, **566**

Argosy University, Schaumburg, College of Business, Schaumburg (IL) 158, **566**

Argosy University, Seattle, College of Business, Seattle (WA) 447, **566**

Argosy University, Tampa, College of Business, Tampa (FL) 122, **566**

Argosy University, Twin Cities, College of Business, Eagan (MN) 248, **566**

Argosy University, Washington DC, College of Business, Arlington (VA) 436, **566**

Arizona State University, W.P. Carey School of Business, Tempe (AZ) 54

Auburn University, College of Business, Auburn University (AL) 45, **568**

Bellevue University, College of Business, Bellevue (NE) 271, **576**

Benedictine University, Graduate Programs, Lisle (IL) 158

Boise State University, College of Business and Economics, Boise (ID) 155

Boston University, School of Management, Boston (MA) 223

Case Western Reserve University, Weatherhead School of Management, Cleveland (OH) 338

Clemson University, College of Business and Behavioral Science, Clemson (SC) 391

Cleveland State University, Nance College of Business Administration, Cleveland (OH) 340

The College of St. Scholastica, Department of Management, Duluth (MN) 249

Columbia Southern University, MBA Program, Orange Beach (AL) 46

DePaul University, Charles H. Kellstadt Graduate School of Business, Chicago (IL) 159

DeVry University, Keller Graduate School of Management, Alpharetta (GA) 144

Duke University, The Fuqua School of Business, Durham (NC) 323

Duquesne University, John F. Donahue Graduate School of Business, Pittsburgh (PA) 367

Elon University, Martha and Spencer Love School of Business, Elon (NC) 324

Fairleigh Dickinson University, Metropolitan Campus, Silberman College of Business, Teaneck (NJ) 282, **612**

Flinders University, Flinders Business School, Adelaide (Australia) 485

Florida Atlantic University, College of Business, Boca Raton (FL) 126

Franklin Pierce University, Graduate Studies, Rindge (NH) 278

Frostburg State University, College of Business, Frostburg (MD) 213

The George Washington University, School of Business, Washington (DC) 119, **622**

Georgia College & State University, The J. Whitney Bunting School of Business, Milledgeville (GA) 145

Georgia State University, J. Mack Robinson College of Business, Atlanta (GA) 147, **626**

Grand Canyon University, College of Business, Phoenix (AZ) 56

Grand Valley State University, Seidman College of Business, Allendale (MI) 238

HfB—Business School of Finance and Management, Frankfurt School of Finance and Management, Frankfurt (Germany) 508

Kean University, College of Business and Public Administration, Union (NJ) 284

Lamar University, College of Business, Beaumont (TX) 408

Lehigh University, College of Business and Economics, Bethlehem (PA) 371, **656**

Long Island University, Brooklyn Campus, School of Business, Public Administration and Information Sciences, Brooklyn (NY) 304

Midwestern State University, College of Business Administration, Wichita Falls (TX) 409

Monash University, MBA Programme, Clayton (Australia) 486

Moravian College, The Moravian MBA, Bethlehem (PA) 373

New England College, Program in Management, Henniker (NH) 278

New York University, Robert F. Wagner Graduate School of Public Service (NY) 309

Northcentral University, MBA Program, Prescott Valley (AZ) 56

Northeastern University, Graduate School of Business Administration, Boston (MA) 228

North Park University, School of Business and Nonprofit Management, Chicago (IL) 170

Northwestern University, Kellogg School of Management, Evanston (IL) 171

OGI School of Science & Engineering at Oregon Health & Science University, Department of Management in Science and Technology, Beaverton (OR) 358

Ohio University, College of Business, Athens (OH) 344

Pacific Lutheran University, School of Business, Tacoma (WA) 449

Park University, Program in Business Administration, Parkville (MO) 264

Penn State Great Valley, Graduate Studies, Malvern (PA) 373

Regis University, College for Professional Studies, Denver (CO) 103

Roosevelt University, Walter E. Heller College of Business Administration, Chicago (IL) 172, **676**

Rush University, Department of Health Systems Management, Chicago (IL) 172

Saint Leo University, Graduate Business Studies, Saint Leo (FL) 132

Saint Mary's University of Minnesota, Schools of Graduate and Professional Programs, Winona (MN) 251

St. Thomas University, Department of Business Administration, Miami Gardens (FL) 132

Saint Vincent College, Alex G. McKenna School of Business, Economics, and Government, Latrobe (PA) 378

Salve Regina University, Graduate Studies, Newport (RI) 389

Seton Hall University, Stillman School of Business, South Orange (NJ) 290, **686**

Siena Heights University, Graduate College, Adrian (MI) 242

Southeastern University, College of Graduate Studies, Washington (DC) 121

Southeast Missouri State University, Harrison College of Business, Cape Girardeau (MO) 265

Southern Cross University, Graduate College of Management, Coffs Harbour (Australia) 487

Southwest Baptist University, College of Business and Computer Science, Bolivar (MO) 265

State University of New York Institute of Technology, School of Business, Utica (NY) 317

Suffolk University, Sawyer Business School, Boston (MA) 230

Texas Southern University, Jesse H. Jones School of Business, Houston (TX) 417

University at Buffalo, the State University of New York, School of Management, Buffalo (NY) 320

University of California, Berkeley, Haas School of Business, Berkeley (CA) 89

University of Colorado Denver, Business School, Denver (CO) 105, **706**

University of Louisiana at Monroe, College of Business Administration, Monroe (LA) 209

University of Manitoba, Faculty of Management, Winnipeg (Canada) 475

University of Massachusetts Boston, College of Management, Boston (MA) 232

University of Miami, School of Business Administration, Coral Gables (FL) 135, **718**

University of Michigan–Dearborn, School of Management, Dearborn (MI) 245

University of Missouri–Columbia, Robert J. Trulaske, Sr. College of Business, Columbia (MO) 267, **720**

University of North Texas, College of Business Administration, Denton (TX) 422

University of Rochester, William E. Simon Graduate School of Business Administration, Rochester (NY) 321, **736**

University of Saskatchewan, Edwards School of Business, Saskatoon (Canada) 478

University of Southern California, School of Business, Los Angeles (CA) 98

University of Toronto, Joseph L. Rotman School of Management, Toronto (Canada) 478

University of Washington, Michael G. Foster School of Business, Seattle (WA) 452, **754**

Vienna University of Economics and Business Administration, WU Wien MBA, Vienna (Austria) 492

Villanova University, Villanova School of Business, Villanova (PA) 382

Wagner College, Department of Business Administration, Staten Island (NY) 321

Walsh University, Program in Business Administration, North Canton (OH) 350

Webster University, School of Business and Technology, St. Louis (MO) 270

Wichita State University, W. Frank Barton School of Business, Wichita (KS) 197

Widener University, School of Business Administration, Chester (PA) 384, **764**

York University, Schulich School of Business, Toronto (Canada) 482, **772**

HEALTH CARE

Alvernia College, Department of Business, Reading (PA) 361

American InterContinental University, Program in Business Administration, Los Angeles (CA) 63, **564**

American InterContinental University Online, Program in Business Administration, Hoffman Estates (IL) 157

Aquinas College, School of Management, Grand Rapids (MI) 235

Argosy University, Atlanta, College of Business, Atlanta (GA) 141, **566**

Argosy University, Inland Empire, College of Business, San Bernardino (CA) 65, **566**

Aston University, Aston Business School, Birmingham (United Kingdom) 539

Auburn University, College of Business, Auburn University (AL) 45, **568**

Avila University, School of Business, Kansas City (MO) 258

Baker College Center for Graduate Studies, Graduate Programs, Flint (MI) 236, **572**

Baldwin-Wallace College, Division of Business, Berea (OH) 337

Barry University, Andreas School of Business, Miami Shores (FL) 123

Baylor University, Hankamer School of Business, Waco (TX) 405, **574**

Belmont University, Jack C. Massey Graduate School of Business, Nashville (TN) 395

Benedictine University, Graduate Programs, Lisle (IL) 158

Bernard M. Baruch College of the City University of New York, Zicklin School of Business, New York (NY) 296

Boston University, School of Management, Boston (MA) 223

Brandeis University, The Heller School for Social Policy and Management (MA) 223

Brenau University, School of Business and Mass Communication, Gainesville (GA) 143

California National University for Advanced Studies, College of Business Administration, Northridge (CA) 67

California State University, Long Beach, College of Business Administration, Long Beach (CA) 71

California State University, Los Angeles, College of Business and Economics, Los Angeles (CA) 71

Capital University, School of Management, Columbus (OH) 338

Carnegie Mellon University, Tepper School of Business, Pittsburgh (PA) 363, **584**

Case Western Reserve University, Weatherhead School of Management, Cleveland (OH) 338

Chatham University, Program in Business Administration, Pittsburgh (PA) 364

The Chinese University of Hong Kong, Faculty of Business Administration, Hong Kong (China) 497

Christian Brothers University, School of Business, Memphis (TN) 396

College of St. Catherine, Program in Organizational Leadership, St. Paul (MN) 249

Columbia University, Graduate School of Business, New York (NY) 298

Dallas Baptist University, Graduate School of Business, Dallas (TX) 406

Davenport University, Sneden Graduate School, Grand Rapids (MI) 237

DeSales University, Department of Business, Center Valley (PA) 365

DeVry University, Keller Graduate School of Management, Alpharetta (GA) 144

DeVry University, Keller Graduate School of Management, Oakbrook Terrace (IL) 161, **650**

DeVry University, Keller Graduate School of Management, Arlington (VA) 437

Dominican University, Edward A. and Lois L. Brennan School of Business, River Forest (IL) 162, **600**

Dowling College, School of Business, Oakdale (NY) 300

Drake University, College of Business and Public Administration, Des Moines (IA) 189

Drury University, Breech School of Business Administration, Springfield (MO) 259

Duquesne University, John F. Donahue Graduate School of Business, Pittsburgh (PA) 367

East Carolina University, College of Business, Greenville (NC) 324, **602**

Eastern University, Graduate Business Programs, St. Davids (PA) 368

Eastern Washington University, College of Business and Public Administration, Cheney (WA) 448

Edith Cowan University, Faculty of Business and Public Management, Churchlands (Australia) 484

European University, Center for Management Studies, Montreux-Fontanivent (Switzerland) 532

Fayetteville State University, Program in Business Administration, Fayetteville (NC) 325

Francis Marion University, School of Business, Florence (SC) 392

Gardner-Webb University, Graduate School of Business, Boiling Springs (NC) 325

The George Washington University, School of Business, Washington (DC) 119, **622**

Georgian Court University, School of Business, Lakewood (NJ) 283

Georgia Southern University, College of Business Administration, Statesboro (GA) 146

Governors State University, College of Business and Public Administration, University Park (IL) 164

Grand Canyon University, College of Business, Phoenix (AZ) 56

Harding University, College of Business Administration, Searcy (AR) 61

Idaho State University, College of Business, Pocatello (ID) 156

Illinois Institute of Technology, Stuart School of Business, Chicago (IL) 164

Indiana University–Purdue University Indianapolis, Kelley School of Business, Indianapolis (IN) 184

James Madison University, College of Business, Harrisonburg (VA) 438

Jones International University, Graduate School of Business Administration, Centennial (CO) 103

Lake Forest Graduate School of Management, MBA Program, Lake Forest (IL) 166, **652**

Lewis University, College of Business, Romeoville (IL) 166

Lindenwood University, Division of Management, St. Charles (MO) 261

Lipscomb University, MBA Program, Nashville (TN) 397

Loyola University Chicago, Graduate School of Business, Chicago (IL) 167

Lynn University, School of Business, Boca Raton (FL) 130

Marylhurst University, Department of Business Administration, Marylhurst (OR) 357

Marymount University, School of Business Administration, Arlington (VA) 440

McMaster University, DeGroote School of Business, Hamilton (Canada) 470

Missouri State University, College of Business Administration, Springfield (MO) *262*

Monash University, MBA Programme, Clayton (Australia) 486

Monmouth University, School of Business Administration, West Long Branch (NJ) 284

Moravian College, The Moravian MBA, Bethlehem (PA) 373

New England College, Program in Management, Henniker (NH) 278

The New School: A University, Milano The New School for Management and Urban Policy, New York (NY) 308

New York Institute of Technology, School of Management (NY) 308

New York University, Robert F. Wagner Graduate School of Public Service (NY) 309

Northeastern University, Graduate School of Business Administration, Boston (MA) 228

North Park University, School of Business and Nonprofit Management, Chicago (IL) 170

Northwestern University, Kellogg School of Management, Evanston (IL) 171

Notre Dame de Namur University, Department of Business Administration, Belmont (CA) 84

Oakland University, School of Business Administration, Rochester (MI) 241

Oklahoma City University, Meinders School of Business, Oklahoma City (OK) 352

Old Dominion University, College of Business and Public Administration, Norfolk (VA) 441

Penn State Great Valley, Graduate Studies, Malvern (PA) 373

Pfeiffer University, Program in Business Administration, Misenheimer (NC) 329

Philadelphia University, School of Business Administration, Philadelphia (PA) 375, **668**

Piedmont College, School of Business, Demorest (GA) 149

Portland State University, School of Business Administration, Portland (OR) 358

Providence College, School of Business, Providence (RI) 388

Quinnipiac University, School of Business, Hamden (CT) 109

Rider University, College of Business Administration, Lawrenceville (NJ) 287

Rivier College, Department of Business Administration, Nashua (NH) 279

Rockhurst University, Helzberg School of Management, Kansas City (MO) 264

Roosevelt University, Walter E. Heller College of Business Administration, Chicago (IL) 172, **676**

Rutgers, The State University of New Jersey, Camden, School of Business, Camden (NJ) 288

Sage Graduate School, Department of Management, Troy (NY) 313

St. Ambrose University, Program in Business Administration, Davenport (IA) 190

Saint Francis University, Master of Business Administration Program, Loretto (PA) 377

Saint Joseph's University, Erivan K. Haub School of Business, Philadelphia (PA) 377

Saint Vincent College, Alex G. McKenna School of Business, Economics, and Government, Latrobe (PA) 378

Saint Xavier University, Graham School of Management, Chicago (IL) 173

San Diego State University, College of Business Administration, San Diego (CA) 86

Silver Lake College, Program in Management and Organizational Behavior, Manitowoc (WI) 460

Southeastern Louisiana University, College of Business, Hammond (LA) 207

Southern Adventist University, School of Business and Management, Collegedale (TN) 398

State University of New York at Binghamton, School of Management, Binghamton (NY) 315

Stevens Institute of Technology, Wesley J. Howe School of Technology Management, Hoboken (NJ) 290

Stony Brook University, State University of New York, W. Averell Harriman School for Management and Policy, Stony Brook (NY) 317

Suffolk University, Sawyer Business School, Boston (MA) 230

Temple University, Fox School of Business and Management, Philadelphia (PA) 379

Tennessee State University, College of Business, Nashville (TN) 399

Texas A&M University–Corpus Christi, College of Business, Corpus Christi (TX) 416

Texas Tech University, Jerry S. Rawls College of Business Administration, Lubbock (TX) 418

Thames Valley University, Faculty of Professional Studies, Slough (United Kingdom) 546

Union Graduate College, School of Management, Schenectady (NY) 319

The University of Akron, College of Business Administration, Akron (OH) 346

The University of Alabama, Manderson Graduate School of Business, Tuscaloosa (AL) 49

The University of Alabama at Birmingham, School of Business, Birmingham (AL) 50

University of Baltimore, Merrick School of Business, Baltimore (MD) 216

University of Baltimore/Towson University, Joint University of Baltimore/Towson University (UB/Towson) MBA Program, Baltimore (MD) 217

University of California, Berkeley, Haas School of Business, Berkeley (CA) 89

University of California, Irvine, The Paul Merage School of Business, Irvine (CA) 91

University of Colorado at Colorado Springs, Graduate School of Business Administration, Colorado Springs (CO) 105, **704**

University of Colorado Denver, Business School, Denver (CO) 105, **706**

University of Connecticut, School of Business, Storrs (CT) 112, **708**

University of Dallas, Graduate School of Management, Irving (TX) 420, **710**

The University of Findlay, College of Business, Findlay (OH) 348

University of Hartford, Barney School of Business, West Hartford (CT) 113

University of Houston–Clear Lake, School of Business, Houston (TX) 421

The University of Iowa, Henry B. Tippie College of Business, Iowa City (IA) 191, **714**

University of La Verne, College of Business and Public Management, La Verne (CA) 94

University of Louisiana at Lafayette, Graduate School, Lafayette (LA) 208

University of Maine, The Maine Business School, Orono (ME) 211

University of Malaya, Graduate School of Business, Kuala Lumpur (Malaysia) 519

University of Mary, Program in Management, Bismarck (ND) 335

University of Michigan–Flint, School of Management, Flint (MI) 246

University of Minnesota, Twin Cities Campus, Carlson School of Management, Minneapolis (MN) 252

University of Newcastle, Graduate School of Business, Callaghan (Australia) 489

University of New Haven, School of Business, West Haven (CT) 113, **728**

University of New Orleans, College of Business Administration, New Orleans (LA) 209

University of Pennsylvania, Wharton School, Philadelphia (PA) 380

University of Portland, Dr. Robert B. Pamplin, Jr. School of Business, Portland (OR) 360

University of Rochester, William E. Simon Graduate School of Business Administration, Rochester (NY) 321, **736**

University of St. Francis, College of Business, Joliet (IL) 177

University of St. Thomas, Opus College of Business (MN) 253, **738**

University of Sioux Falls, John T. Vucurevich School of Business, Sioux Falls (SD) 394

The University of South Dakota, School of Business, Vermillion (SD) 395

The University of Texas at Arlington, College of Business Administration, Arlington (TX) 424, **746**

The University of Texas at Dallas, School of Management, Richardson (TX) *426,* **748**

The University of Texas at San Antonio, College of Business, San Antonio (TX) 427, **750**

The University of Texas at Tyler, College of Business and Technology, Tyler (TX) 428

University of the Incarnate Word, H-E-B School of Business and Administration (TX) 429

Vanderbilt University, Owen Graduate School of Management, Nashville (TN) 403, **758**

Vienna University of Economics and Business Administration, WU Wien MBA, Vienna (Austria) 492

Virginia Commonwealth University, School of Business, Richmond (VA) 445

Wayland Baptist University, Graduate Programs, Plainview (TX) 429

Waynesburg University, Graduate and Professional Studies, Waynesburg (PA) 383

Webster University, School of Business and Technology, St. Louis (MO) 270

Western Carolina University, College of Business, Cullowhee (NC) 333

Western Connecticut State University, Ancell School of Business, Danbury (CT) 114

West Texas A&M University, College of Business, Canyon (TX) 430

Widener University, School of Business Administration, Chester (PA) 384, **764**

Wilkes University, College of Arts, Humanities and Social Sciences, Wilkes-Barre (PA) 384

William Woods University, Graduate and Adult Studies, Fulton (MO) 271

Wilmington University, Division of Business, New Castle (DE) 117

HOSPITALITY MANAGEMENT

Antwerp International Business School, Graduate Programs in Business, Antwerp (Belgium) 493

Barcelona Business School, Graduate Programs in Business, Barcelona (Spain) 528

The Chinese University of Hong Kong, Faculty of Business Administration, Hong Kong (China) 497

Columbia Southern University, MBA Program, Orange Beach (AL) 46

East Carolina University, College of Business, Greenville (NC) 324, **602**

European University, Center for Management Studies, Montreux-Fontanivent (Switzerland) 532

Florida State University, College of Business, Tallahassee (FL) 129

Georgia State University, J. Mack Robinson College of Business, Atlanta (GA) 147, **626**

The Hague University, Faculty of Economics and Management, The Hague (Netherlands) 521, **628**

Hotel Management School Maastricht, MBA Program, Maastricht (Netherlands) 522

Johnson & Wales University, The Alan Shawn Feinstein Graduate School, Providence (RI) 388, **648**

LES ROCHES, Swiss Hotel Association, School of Hotel Management, Graduate Programmes, Bluche (Switzerland) 534

Lynn University, School of Business, Boca Raton (FL) 130

Michigan State University, Eli Broad Graduate School of Management, East Lansing (MI) 240

Queen Margaret University College, Edinburgh, School of Business and Enterprise, Edinburgh (United Kingdom) 545

Roosevelt University, Walter E. Heller College of Business Administration, Chicago (IL) 172, **676**

San Francisco State University, College of Business, San Francisco (CA) 87

Schiller International University, MBA Programs, Florida (FL) 133, **684**

Schiller International University, Graduate Programs, London (United Kingdom) 546, **684**

Southern Cross University, Graduate College of Management, Coffs Harbour (Australia) 487

Southern New Hampshire University, School of Business, Manchester (NH) 279, **690**

Thames Valley University, Faculty of Professional Studies, Slough (United Kingdom) 546

University of Delaware, Alfred Lerner College of Business and Economics, Newark (DE) 116, **712**

University of Denver, Daniels College of Business, Denver (CO) 106

The University of Findlay, College of Business, Findlay (OH) 348

University of Guelph, Faculty of Management, Guelph (Canada) 475

University of Houston, Bauer College of Business, Houston (TX) 420

University of Malaya, Graduate School of Business, Kuala Lumpur (Malaysia) 519

University of Massachusetts Amherst, Isenberg School of Management, Amherst (MA) 231

University of Missouri–Columbia, Robert J. Trulaske, Sr. College of Business, Columbia (MO) 267, **720**

University of New Orleans, College of Business Administration, New Orleans (LA) 209

University of North Texas, College of Business Administration, Denton (TX) 422

University of Salford, Salford Business School, Salford (United Kingdom) 554

Vienna University of Economics and Business Administration, WU Wien MBA, Vienna (Austria) 492

HUMAN RESOURCES DEVELOPMENT

Antioch University New England, Department of Organization and Management, Keene (NH) 277

Bellevue University, College of Business, Bellevue (NE) 271, **576**

California National University for Advanced Studies, College of Business Administration, Northridge (CA) 67

Graduate School of Business Administration Zurich, Executive Management Programs, Zurich (Switzerland) 532

HfB—Business School of Finance and Management, Frankfurt School of Finance and Management, Frankfurt (Germany) 508

International University of Japan, Graduate School of International Management, Minami Uonuma-gu (Japan) 516

Leadership Institute of Seattle, School of Applied Behavioral Science, Kenmore (WA) 449

National University, School of Business and Management, La Jolla (CA) 82

Ottawa University, Graduate Studies-Arizona (AZ) 57

Pontifical Catholic University of Puerto Rico, College of Business Administration, Ponce (PR) 386

Regent University, School of Global Leadership and Entrepreneurship, Virginia Beach (VA) 442

University of Manitoba, Faculty of Management, Winnipeg (Canada) 475

University of Mary Washington, College of Graduate and Professional Studies, Fredericksburg (VA) 444

University of Missouri–Columbia, Robert J. Trulaske, Sr. College of Business, Columbia (MO) 267, **720**

University of Phoenix, College of Graduate Business and Management, Phoenix (AZ) 59

University of Plymouth, Plymouth Business School, Plymouth (United Kingdom) 553

Waynesburg University, Graduate and Professional Studies, Waynesburg (PA) 383

Webster University, School of Business and Technology, St. Louis (MO) 270

Widener University, School of Business Administration, Chester (PA) 384, **764**

HUMAN RESOURCES MANAGEMENT

The Aarhus School of Business, Faculty of Business Administration, Aarhus (Denmark) 501

Adelphi University, School of Business, Garden City (NY) 295, **560**

Alvernia College, Department of Business, Reading (PA) 361

American InterContinental University, Program in Business Administration, Los Angeles (CA) 63, **564**

American InterContinental University Online, Program in Business Administration, Hoffman Estates (IL) 157

American University of Sharjah, School of Business and Management, Sharjah (United Arab Emirates) 538

Andrew Jackson University, Brian Tracy College of Business and Entrepreneurship, Birmingham (AL) 45

Anna Maria College, Program in Business Administration, Paxton (MA) 219

Antioch University Los Angeles, Program in Organizational Management, Culver City (CA) 64

Antioch University New England, Department of Organization and Management, Keene (NH) 277

Antioch University Santa Barbara, Program in Organizational Management, Santa Barbara (CA) 64

Antwerp International Business School, Graduate Programs in Business, Antwerp (Belgium) 493

Ashland University, Dauch College of Business and Economics, Ashland (OH) 337

Ashridge, Ashridge Executive MBA Program, Berkhamsted (United Kingdom) 538

Asian Institute of Technology, School of Management, Pathumthani (Thailand) 536

Assumption College, Department of Business Studies, Worcester (MA) 219

Aston University, Aston Business School, Birmingham (United Kingdom) 539

Auburn University Montgomery, School of Business, Montgomery (AL) 46

Aurora University, Dunham School of Business, Aurora (IL) 158

Baker College Center for Graduate Studies, Graduate Programs, Flint (MI) 236, **572**

Baker University, School of Professional and Graduate Studies, Baldwin City (KS) 193

Baldwin-Wallace College, Division of Business, Berea (OH) 337

Barcelona Business School, Graduate Programs in Business, Barcelona (Spain) 528

Barry University, Andreas School of Business, Miami Shores (FL) 123

Bellevue University, College of Business, Bellevue (NE) 271, **576**

Benedictine University, Graduate Programs, Lisle (IL) 158

Bernard M. Baruch College of the City University of New York, Zicklin School of Business, New York (NY) 296

Brescia University, Program in Management, Owensboro (KY) 198

Brigham Young University, Marriott School of Management, Provo (UT) 431

Brock University, Faculty of Business, St. Catharines (Canada) 466

California National University for Advanced Studies, College of Business Administration, Northridge (CA) 67

California State University, Dominguez Hills, College of Business Administration and Public Policy, Carson (CA) 69

California State University, East Bay, College of Business and Economics, Hayward (CA) 69

California State University, Fresno, Craig School of Business, Fresno (CA) 70

California State University, Long Beach, College of Business Administration, Long Beach (CA) 71

California State University, Sacramento, College of Business Administration, Sacramento (CA) 72

Canisius College, Richard J. Wehle School of Business, Buffalo (NY) 296

Cardiff University, Cardiff Business School, Cardiff (United Kingdom) 539

Case Western Reserve University, Weatherhead School of Management, Cleveland (OH) 338

The Catholic University of America, Metropolitan College, Washington (DC) 118

Centenary College, Program in Business Administration, Hackettstown (NJ) 281

Central Queensland University, Faculty of Business and Informatics, Rockhampton (Australia) 483

The Chinese University of Hong Kong, Faculty of Business Administration, Hong Kong (China) 497

Christian Brothers University, School of Business, Memphis (TN) 396

Chulalongkorn University, Sasin Graduate Institute of Business Administration, Bangkok (Thailand) 536

City University of Hong Kong, Faculty of Business, Hong Kong (China) 497

Claremont Graduate University, Peter F. Drucker and Masatoshi Ito Graduate School of Management, Claremont (CA) 75, **590**

Cleveland State University, Nance College of Business Administration, Cleveland (OH) 340

The College of St. Scholastica, Department of Management, Duluth (MN) 249

College of Santa Fe, Department of Business Administration, Santa Fe (NM) 292

Columbia Southern University, MBA Program, Orange Beach (AL) 46

Columbia University, Graduate School of Business, New York (NY) 298

Concordia University, St. Paul, College of Business and Organizational Leadership, St. Paul (MN) 250

Concordia University Wisconsin, Graduate Programs, Mequon (WI) 458

Copenhagen Business School, Faculty of Economics and Business Administration, Copenhagen (Denmark) 501

Cranfield University, Cranfield School of Management, Cranfield (United Kingdom) 540

Cyprus International Institute of Management, MBA Programme, Nicosia (Cyprus) 500

Dallas Baptist University, Graduate School of Business, Dallas (TX) 406

Davenport University, Sneden Graduate School, Grand Rapids (MI) 237

Deakin University, Deakin Business School, Geelong (Australia) 484

DePaul University, Charles H. Kellstadt Graduate School of Business, Chicago (IL) 159

DeVry University, Keller Graduate School of Management, Phoenix (AZ) 56

DeVry University, Keller Graduate School of Management, Fremont (CA) 76

DeVry University, Keller Graduate School of Management, Long Beach (CA) 76

DeVry University, Keller Graduate School of Management, Palmdale (CA) 76

DeVry University, Keller Graduate School of Management, Pomona (CA) 77

DeVry University, Keller Graduate School of Management, San Diego (CA) 77

DeVry University, Keller Graduate School of Management, Colorado Springs (CO) 102

DeVry University, Keller Graduate School of Management, Miami (FL) 124

DeVry University, Keller Graduate School of Management, Miramar (FL) 124

DeVry University, Keller Graduate School of Management, Orlando (FL) 124

DeVry University, Keller Graduate School of Management, Tampa (FL) 124

DeVry University, Keller Graduate School of Management, Alpharetta (GA) 144

DeVry University, Keller Graduate School of Management, Atlanta (GA) 144

DeVry University, Keller Graduate School of Management, Decatur (GA) 144

DeVry University, Keller Graduate School of Management, Duluth (GA) 145

DeVry University, Keller Graduate School of Management, Elgin (IL) 160

DeVry University, Keller Graduate School of Management, Gurnee (IL) 161

DeVry University, Keller Graduate School of Management, Lincolnshire (IL) 161

DeVry University, Keller Graduate School of Management, Oakbrook Terrace (IL) 161, **650**

DeVry University, Keller Graduate School of Management, Schaumburg (IL) 162

DeVry University, Keller Graduate School of Management, Tinley Park (IL) 162

DeVry University, Keller Graduate School of Management (IN) 180

DeVry University, Keller Graduate School of Management, Merrillville (IN) 180

DeVry University, Keller Graduate School of Management, Kansas City (MO) 259

DeVry University, Keller Graduate School of Management, St. Louis (MO) 259

DeVry University, Keller Graduate School of Management (NV) 275

DeVry University, Keller Graduate School of Management (NC) 323

DeVry University, Keller Graduate School of Management, Columbus (OH) 341

DeVry University, Keller Graduate School of Management, Seven Hills (OH) 341

DeVry University, Keller Graduate School of Management (OR) 356

DeVry University, Keller Graduate School of Management (PA) 365

DeVry University, Keller Graduate School of Management, Fort Washington (PA) 365

DeVry University, Keller Graduate School of Management, Pittsburgh (PA) 365

DeVry University, Keller Graduate School of Management, Irving (TX) 407

DeVry University, Keller Graduate School of Management, Arlington (VA) 437

DeVry University, Keller Graduate School of Management, McLean (VA) 437

DeVry University, Keller Graduate School of Management, Bellevue (WA) 447

DeVry University, Keller Graduate School of Management, Federal Way (WA) 448

Dominican University, Edward A. and Lois L. Brennan School of Business, River Forest (IL) 162, **600**

Drake University, College of Business and Public Administration, Des Moines (IA) 189

Duquesne University, John F. Donahue Graduate School of Business, Pittsburgh (PA) 367

EADA International Management Development Center, Business Programs, Barcelona (Spain) 528

Eastern Mennonite University, Program in Business Administration, Harrisonburg (VA) 438

Eastern Michigan University, College of Business, Ypsilanti (MI) 237

Edith Cowan University, Faculty of Business and Public Management, Churchlands (Australia) 484

Emmanuel College, Graduate and Professional Programs, Boston (MA) 225

Emory University, Roberto C. Goizueta Business School, Atlanta (GA) 145, **606**

ESCP-EAP European School of Management, ESCP-EAP European School of Management (France) 503

European School of Economics, MBA Programme (Italy) 515, **608**

European University, Center for Management Studies, Montreux-Fontanivent (Switzerland) 532

Everest University, Graduate School of Business, Clearwater (FL) 126

Everest University, Program in Business Administration, Lakeland (FL) 126

Everest University, Program in Business Administration, Orlando (FL) 126

Fairfield University, Charles F. Dolan School of Business, Fairfield (CT) 109

Fairleigh Dickinson University, College at Florham, Silberman College of Business, Madison (NJ) 282, **612**

Fairleigh Dickinson University, Metropolitan Campus, Silberman College of Business, Teaneck (NJ) 282, **612**

Fitchburg State College, Division of Graduate and Continuing Education, Fitchburg (MA) 225

Florida International University, Alvah H. Chapman, Jr. Graduate School of Business, Miami (FL) 128, **618**

Franklin Pierce University, Graduate Studies, Rindge (NH) 278

Gannon University, School of Business, Erie (PA) 368

Gardner-Webb University, Graduate School of Business, Boiling Springs (NC) 325

The George Washington University, School of Business, Washington (DC) 119, **622**

Georgia State University, J. Mack Robinson College of Business, Atlanta (GA) 147, **626**

Golden Gate University, Ageno School of Business, San Francisco (CA) 78

Goldey-Beacom College, Graduate Program, Wilmington (DE) 116

Governors State University, College of Business and Public Administration, University Park (IL) 164

Graduate School of Business Administration Zurich, Executive Management Programs, Zurich (Switzerland) 532

The Hague University, Faculty of Economics and Management, The Hague (Netherlands) 521, **628**

Hawai'i Pacific University, College of Business Administration, Honolulu (HI) 153, **630**

HEC Montreal, Master's Program in Business Administration and Management, Montréal (Canada) 468

HEC Paris, HEC MBA Program, Jouy-en-Josas (France) 505, **632**

HfB—Business School of Finance and Management, Frankfurt School of Finance and Management, Frankfurt (Germany) 508

Hofstra University, Frank G. Zarb School of Business, Hempstead (NY) 302

Hong Kong Baptist University, School of Business, Hong Kong (China) 498

Hood College, Department of Economics and Management, Frederick (MD) 214

Houston Baptist University, College of Business and Economics, Houston (TX) 408

Howard University, School of Business, Washington (DC) 120

Hult International Business School, Graduate Program, Cambridge (MA) 227, **634**

IE Business School, Business School, Madrid (Spain) 529, **636**

Illinois State University, College of Business, Normal (IL) 165, **638**

Indiana Tech, Program in Business Administration, Fort Wayne (IN) 181

Instituto Tecnológico y de Estudios Superiores de Monterrey, Campus Ciudad Juárez, Program in Business Administration, Ciudad Juárez (Mexico) 520

Inter American University of Puerto Rico, San Germán Campus, Department of Business Administration, San Germán (PR) 385

International University in Geneva, MBA Program, Geneva (Switzerland) 533, **640**

International University of Japan, Graduate School of International Management, Minami Uonuma-gu (Japan) 516

Iona College, Hagan School of Business, New Rochelle (NY) 303, **642**

The Johns Hopkins University, Carey Business School, Baltimore (MD) 214, **646**

Johnson & Wales University, The Alan Shawn Feinstein Graduate School, Providence (RI) 388, **648**

Kansas State University, College of Business Administration, Manhattan (KS) 194

Kent State University, Graduate School of Management, Kent (OH) 342

King College, School of Business and Economics, Bristol (TN) 396

Kingston University, Kingston Business School, Kingston upon Thames (United Kingdom) 541

Kutztown University of Pennsylvania, College of Business, Kutztown (PA) 369

Lancaster University, Management School, Lancaster (United Kingdom) 541

La Roche College, School of Graduate Studies and Adult Education, Pittsburgh (PA) 370

La Salle University, School of Business, Philadelphia (PA) 370

Lawrence Technological University, College of Management, Southfield (MI) 239, **654**

Leadership Institute of Seattle, School of Applied Behavioral Science, Kenmore (WA) 449

LeTourneau University, Graduate and Professional Studies, Longview (TX) 409

Lewis University, College of Business, Romeoville (IL) 166

Liberty University, School of Business, Lynchburg (VA) 439

Lindenwood University, Division of Management, St. Charles (MO) 261

London School of Economics and Political Science, The Graduate School, London (United Kingdom) 543

Long Island University, Brooklyn Campus, School of Business, Public Administration and Information Sciences, Brooklyn (NY) 304

Louisiana State University and Agricultural and Mechanical College, E. J. Ourso College of Business, Baton Rouge (LA) 204

Loyola Marymount University, College of Business Administration, Los Angeles (CA) 81

Loyola University Chicago, Graduate School of Business, Chicago (IL) 167

Macquarie University, Macquarie Graduate School of Management, Sydney (Australia) 485

Madonna University, School of Business, Livonia (MI) 240

Manhattanville College, School of Graduate and Professional Studies, Purchase (NY) 306

Marquette University, Graduate School of Management, Milwaukee (WI) 459

Marymount University, School of Business Administration, Arlington (VA) 440

Memorial University of Newfoundland, Faculty of Business Administration, St. John's (Canada) 470

Mercy College, Division of Business and Accounting, Dobbs Ferry (NY) 307

Michigan State University, Eli Broad Graduate School of Management, East Lansing (MI) 240

Misericordia University, Division of Behavioral Science, Education, and Business, Dallas (PA) 372

Monash University, MBA Programme, Clayton (Australia) 486

Nanjing University, School of Business, Nanjing (China) 500

National University, School of Business and Management, La Jolla (CA) 82

National University of Ireland, Dublin, The Michael Smurfit Graduate School of Business, Blackrock (Ireland) 513

New Mexico Highlands University, School of Business, Las Vegas (NM) 293

New York Institute of Technology, School of Management (NY) 308

North Central College, Department of Business, Naperville (IL) *168*

Northcentral University, MBA Program, Prescott Valley (AZ) 56

North Park University, School of Business and Nonprofit Management, Chicago (IL) 170

Norwegian School of Management, Graduate School, Sandvika (Norway) 524

Notre Dame de Namur University, Department of Business Administration, Belmont (CA) 84

Nottingham Trent University, Nottingham Business School, Nottingham (United Kingdom) 544

Nova Southeastern University, H. Wayne Huizenga School of Business and Entrepreneurship, Fort Lauderdale (FL) 130, **666**

Nyack College, School of Business, Nyack (NY) 310

Oakland University, School of Business Administration, Rochester (MI) 241

The Ohio State University, Max M. Fisher College of Business, Columbus (OH) 344

Oklahoma Wesleyan University, Professional Studies Division, Bartlesville (OK) 353

Old Dominion University, College of Business and Public Administration, Norfolk (VA) 441

Open University, Business School, Milton Keynes (United Kingdom) 545

Open University of the Netherlands, Business Programs, Heerlen (Netherlands) 523

Ottawa University, Graduate Studies-Arizona (AZ) 57

Ottawa University, Graduate Studies-Kansas City, Ottawa (KS) 195

Otterbein College, Department of Business, Accounting and Economics, Westerville (OH) 345

Pace University, Lubin School of Business, New York (NY) 310

Purdue University, Krannert School of Management, West Lafayette (IN) 185

Queensland University of Technology, Brisbane Graduate School of Business, Brisbane (Australia) 487

Regis University, College for Professional Studies, Denver (CO) 103

Robert Morris University, Program in Business Administration, Moon Township (PA) 376, **672**

Rochester Institute of Technology, E. Philip Saunders College of Business, Rochester (NY) 312

Roosevelt University, Walter E. Heller College of Business Administration, Chicago (IL) 172, **676**

Royal Roads University, Faculty of Management, Victoria (Canada) 471

Rutgers, The State University of New Jersey, New Brunswick, School of Management and Labor Relations, New Brunswick (NJ) 289

Sage Graduate School, Department of Management, Troy (NY) 313

St. Ambrose University, Program in Business Administration, Davenport (IA) 190

St. Cloud State University, G.R. Herberger College of Business, St. Cloud (MN) 251

St. Edward's University, The School of Management and Business, Austin (TX) 410

Saint Francis University, Master of Business Administration Program, Loretto (PA) 377

Saint Joseph's University, Erivan K. Haub School of Business, Philadelphia (PA) 377

Saint Leo University, Graduate Business Studies, Saint Leo (FL) 132

Saint Mary's University of Minnesota, Schools of Graduate and Professional Programs, Winona (MN) 251

Saint Michael's College, Program in Administration and Management, Colchester (VT) 434

St. Thomas University, Department of Business Administration, Miami Gardens (FL) 132

San Diego State University, College of Business Administration, San Diego (CA) 86

Seattle Pacific University, School of Business and Economics, Seattle (WA) 450

Siena Heights University, Graduate College, Adrian (MI) 242

Southern Cross University, Graduate College of Management, Coffs Harbour (Australia) 487

Southern Illinois University Edwardsville, School of Business, Edwardsville (IL) *174*

Southern New Hampshire University, School of Business, Manchester (NH) 279, **690**

State University of New York Institute of Technology, School of Business, Utica (NY) 317

Stockholm School of Economics, Department of Business Administration, Stockholm (Sweden) 531

Stony Brook University, State University of New York, W. Averell Harriman School for Management and Policy, Stony Brook (NY) 317

Tarleton State University, College of Business Administration, Stephenville (TX) 413

Temple University, Fox School of Business and Management, Philadelphia (PA) 379

Tennessee Technological University, College of Business, Cookeville (TN) 399

Texas A&M University, Mays Business School, College Station (TX) 414

Texas Wesleyan University, School of Business, Fort Worth (TX) 419

Thames Valley University, Faculty of Professional Studies, Slough (United Kingdom) 546

Thomas College, Programs in Business, Waterville (ME) 211

Thomas Edison State College, School of Business and Management, Trenton (NJ) 291

Troy University, College of Business, Troy (AL) 48

Troy University Dothan, College of Business Administration, Dothan (AL) 49

TUI University, College of Business Administration, Cypress (CA) 89

University at Albany, State University of New York, School of Business, Albany (NY) 319

University of Abertay Dundee, Dundee Business School, Dundee (United Kingdom) 547

The University of Akron, College of Business Administration, Akron (OH) 346

The University of Alabama, Manderson Graduate School of Business, Tuscaloosa (AL) 49

The University of Arizona, Eller College of Management, Tucson (AZ) 58

University of Baltimore, Merrick School of Business, Baltimore (MD) 216

University of Baltimore/Towson University, Joint University of Baltimore/Towson University (UB/Towson) MBA Program, Baltimore (MD) 217

University of Bath, School of Management, Bath (United Kingdom) 547

The University of British Columbia, Sauder School of Business, Vancouver (Canada) 474

University of California, Berkeley, Haas School of Business, Berkeley (CA) 89

University of California, Los Angeles, UCLA Anderson School of Management, Los Angeles (CA) 91, **696**

University of California, Riverside, A. Gary Anderson Graduate School of Management, Riverside (CA) 93, **698**

University of Canterbury, Department of Management, Christchurch (New Zealand) 523

University of Central Florida, College of Business Administration, Orlando (FL) 133

University of Chicago, Graduate School of Business, Chicago (IL) 175

University of Dallas, Graduate School of Management, Irving (TX) 420, **710**

University of Denver, Daniels College of Business, Denver (CO) 106

University of Detroit Mercy, College of Business Administration, Detroit (MI) 243

University of Durham, Durham Business School, Durham (United Kingdom) 549

The University of Findlay, College of Business, Findlay (OH) 348

University of Florida, Hough Graduate School of Business, Gainesville (FL) 134

University of Glasgow, University of Glasgow Business School, Glasgow (United Kingdom) 550

University of Hawaii at Manoa, Shidler College of Business, Honolulu (HI) 154

University of Houston–Clear Lake, School of Business, Houston (TX) 421

University of Illinois at Urbana–Champaign, College of Business, Champaign (IL) 176

University of Kansas, School of Business, Lawrence (KS) 196

University of La Verne, College of Business and Public Management, La Verne (CA) 94

University of Malaya, Graduate School of Business, Kuala Lumpur (Malaysia) 519

University of Manitoba, Faculty of Management, Winnipeg (Canada) 475

University of Mary, Program in Management, Bismarck (ND) 335

University of Massachusetts Boston, College of Management, Boston (MA) 232

University of Melbourne, Melbourne Business School, Melbourne (Australia) 488

University of Michigan, Ross School of Business at the University of Michigan, Ann Arbor (MI) 244

University of Michigan–Dearborn, School of Management, Dearborn (MI) 245

University of Mississippi, School of Business Administration, Oxford (MS) 257

University of Missouri–Columbia, Robert J. Trulaske, Sr. College of Business, Columbia (MO) 267, **720**

University of Nebraska at Kearney, College of Business and Technology, Kearney (NE) 273

University of Nebraska–Lincoln, College of Business Administration, Lincoln (NE) 274

University of Newcastle, Graduate School of Business, Callaghan (Australia) 489

The University of New England, The Graduate School of Business Administration, Armidale (Australia) 490

University of New Haven, School of Business, West Haven (CT) 113, **728**

University of New Mexico, Robert O. Anderson Graduate School of Management, Albuquerque (NM) 294

University of New Orleans, College of Business Administration, New Orleans (LA) 209

University of North Florida, Coggin College of Business, Jacksonville (FL) 136

University of Pennsylvania, Wharton School, Philadelphia (PA) 380

University of Phoenix, College of Graduate Business and Management, Phoenix (AZ) 59

University of Phoenix–Atlanta Campus, College of Graduate Business and Management, Sandy Springs (GA) 151

University of Phoenix–Bay Area Campus, College of Graduate Business and Management, Pleasanton (CA) 94

University of Phoenix–Central Florida Campus, College of Graduate Business and Management, Maitland (FL) 137

University of Phoenix–Chicago Campus, College of Graduate Business and Management, Schaumburg (IL) 177

University of Phoenix–Cincinnati Campus, College of Graduate Business and Management, West Chester (OH) 348

University of Phoenix–Cleveland Campus, College of Graduate Business and Management, Independence (OH) 348

University of Phoenix–Columbus Georgia Campus, College of Graduate Business and Management, Columbus (GA) 152

University of Phoenix–Columbus Ohio Campus, College of Graduate Business and Management, Columbus (OH) 349

University of Phoenix–Dallas Campus, College of Graduate Business and Management, Dallas (TX) 423

University of Phoenix–Denver Campus, College of Graduate Business and Management, Lone Tree (CO) 107

University of Phoenix–Eastern Washington Campus, College of Graduate Business and Management, Spokane Valley (WA) 451

University of Phoenix–Hawaii Campus, College of Graduate Business and Management, Honolulu (HI) 155

University of Phoenix–Houston Campus, College of Graduate Business and Management, Houston (TX) 423

University of Phoenix–Idaho Campus, College of Graduate Business and Management, Meridian (ID) 157

University of Phoenix–Indianapolis Campus, College of Graduate Business and Management, Indianapolis (IN) 187

University of Phoenix–Kansas City Campus, College of Graduate Business and Management, Kansas City (MO) 268

University of Phoenix–Las Vegas Campus, College of Graduate Business and Management, Las Vegas (NV) 276

University of Phoenix–Louisiana Campus, College of Graduate Business and Management, Metairie (LA) 210

University of Phoenix–Metro Detroit Campus, College of Graduate Business and Management, Troy (MI) 246

University of Phoenix–Nashville Campus, College of Graduate Business and Management, Nashville (TN) 401

University of Phoenix–New Mexico Campus, College of Graduate Business and Management, Albuquerque (NM) 294

University of Phoenix–North Florida Campus, College of Graduate Business and Management, Jacksonville (FL) 137

University of Phoenix–Oklahoma City Campus, College of Graduate Business and Management, Oklahoma City (OK) 355

University of Phoenix–Oregon Campus, College of Graduate Business and Management, Tigard (OR) 360

University of Phoenix–Puerto Rico Campus, College of Graduate Business and Management, Guaynabo (PR) 387

University of Phoenix–Sacramento Valley Campus, College of Graduate Business and Management, Sacramento (CA) 95

University of Phoenix–St. Louis Campus, College of Graduate Business and Management, St. Louis (MO) 269

University of Phoenix–San Diego Campus, College of Graduate Business and Management, San Diego (CA) 95

University of Phoenix–Southern Arizona Campus, College of Graduate Business and Management, Tucson (AZ) 60

University of Phoenix–Southern California Campus, College of Graduate Business and Management, Costa Mesa (CA) 96

University of Phoenix–Southern Colorado Campus, College of Graduate Business and Management, Colorado Springs (CO) 107

University of Phoenix–South Florida Campus, College of Graduate Business and Management, Fort Lauderdale (FL) 137

University of Phoenix–Tulsa Campus, College of Graduate Business and Management, Tulsa (OK) 355

University of Phoenix–Utah Campus, College of Graduate Business and Management, Salt Lake City (UT) 432

University of Phoenix–Vancouver Campus, College of Graduate Business and Management, Burnaby (Canada) 477

University of Phoenix–Washington Campus, College of Graduate Business and Management, Seattle (WA) 452

University of Phoenix–West Florida Campus, College of Graduate Business and Management, Temple Terrace (FL) 138

University of Phoenix–West Michigan Campus, College of Graduate Business and Management, Walker (MI) 246

University of Pittsburgh, Joseph M. Katz Graduate School of Business, Pittsburgh (PA) 381

University of Plymouth, Plymouth Business School, Plymouth (United Kingdom) 553

University of Regina, Kenneth Levene Graduate School of Business, Regina (Canada) 477

University of St. Thomas, Opus College of Business (MN) 253, **738**

University of Salford, Salford Business School, Salford (United Kingdom) 554

University of South Carolina, Moore School of Business, Columbia (SC) *392*, **740**

The University of Tennessee, College of Business Administration, Knoxville (TN) *401*, **744**

The University of Texas at Arlington, College of Business Administration, Arlington (TX) 424, **746**

University of the Sacred Heart, Department of Business Administration, San Juan (PR) 387

University of the West of England, Bristol, Bristol Business School, Bristol (United Kingdom) 555

University of the Witwatersrand, Graduate School of Business Administration, Wits (South Africa) 527

University of Toronto, Joseph L. Rotman School of Management, Toronto (Canada) 478

University of Warwick, Warwick Business School, Coventry (United Kingdom) 557

University of Washington, Michael G. Foster School of Business, Seattle (WA) 452, **754**

The University of Western Ontario, Richard Ivey School of Business, London (Canada) 480

University of Windsor, Odette School of Business, Windsor (Canada) 480

University of Wisconsin–Green Bay, Program in Management, Green Bay (WI) 461

University of Wisconsin–Madison, Wisconsin School of Business, Madison (WI) 462, **756**

University of Wisconsin–Whitewater, College of Business and Economics, Whitewater (WI) 465

Upper Iowa University, Online Master's Programs, Fayette (IA) 192

Vancouver Island University, Program in Business Administration, Nanaimo (Canada) 480

Vanderbilt University, Owen Graduate School of Management, Nashville (TN) 403, **758**

Virginia Commonwealth University, School of Business, Richmond (VA) 445

Walden University, School of Management, Minneapolis (MN) 253

Walsh College of Accountancy and Business Administration, Graduate Programs, Troy (MI) 247

Washington State University Tri-Cities, College of Business, Richland (WA) 453

Wayland Baptist University, Graduate Programs, Plainview (TX) 429

Wayne State University, School of Business Administration, Detroit (MI) 247, **760**

Webster University, School of Business and Technology, St. Louis (MO) 270

Western Carolina University, College of Business, Cullowhee (NC) 333

Westminster College, The Bill and Vieve Gore School of Business, Salt Lake City (UT) 433

Widener University, School of Business Administration, Chester (PA) 384, **764**

Wilkes University, College of Arts, Humanities and Social Sciences, Wilkes-Barre (PA) 384

Willamette University, George H. Atkinson Graduate School of Management, Salem (OR) 361, **768**

William Woods University, Graduate and Adult Studies, Fulton (MO) 271

Wilmington University, Division of Business, New Castle (DE) 117

York College of Pennsylvania, Department of Business Administration, York (PA) 385

INDUSTRIAL ADMINISTRATION/ MANAGEMENT

Aston University, Aston Business School, Birmingham (United Kingdom) 539

Athabasca University, Centre for Innovative Management, Athabasca (Canada) 466

INDUSTRIAL/LABOR RELATIONS

INFORMATION MANAGEMENT

National University, School of Business and Management, La Jolla (CA) 82

National University of Ireland, Dublin, The Michael Smurfit Graduate School of Business, Blackrock (Ireland) 513

North Central College, Department of Business, Naperville (IL) *168*

Northeastern University, Graduate School of Business Administration, Boston (MA) 228

Nottingham Trent University, Nottingham Business School, Nottingham (United Kingdom) 544

Penn State Great Valley, Graduate Studies, Malvern (PA) 373

Queensland University of Technology, Brisbane Graduate School of Business, Brisbane (Australia) 487

Regis University, College for Professional Studies, Denver (CO) 103

Rensselaer Polytechnic Institute, Lally School of Management and Technology, Troy (NY) 311, **670**

Rider University, College of Business Administration, Lawrenceville (NJ) 287

Rouen School of Management, Postgraduate Programmes, Mount Saint Aignan (France) 505

Saint Leo University, Graduate Business Studies, Saint Leo (FL) 132

Southeastern University, College of Graduate Studies, Washington (DC) 121

Southern Illinois University Edwardsville, School of Business, Edwardsville (IL) *174*

Southern Methodist University, Cox School of Business, Dallas (TX) 411, **688**

Southern New Hampshire University, School of Business, Manchester (NH) 279, **690**

Stevens Institute of Technology, Wesley J. Howe School of Technology Management, Hoboken (NJ) 290

Stockholm School of Economics, Department of Business Administration, Stockholm (Sweden) 531

Swinburne University of Technology, Australian Graduate School of Entrepreneurship (AGSE), Hawthorne (Australia) 488

Texas A&M University, Mays Business School, College Station (TX) 414

Texas Southern University, Jesse H. Jones School of Business, Houston (TX) 417

Thames Valley University, Faculty of Professional Studies, Slough (United Kingdom) 546

Troy University, College of Business, Troy (AL) 48

TUI University, College of Business Administration, Cypress (CA) 89

University at Albany, State University of New York, School of Business, Albany (NY) 319

The University of Alabama, Manderson Graduate School of Business, Tuscaloosa (AL) 49

University of Arkansas, Sam M. Walton College of Business Administration, Fayetteville (AR) 62

University of Bath, School of Management, Bath (United Kingdom) 547

University of California, Berkeley, Haas School of Business, Berkeley (CA) 89

University of California, San Diego, Rady School of Management, La Jolla (CA) 93, **700**

University of Central Missouri, Harmon College of Business Administration, Warrensburg (MO) 266

University of Cincinnati, College of Business, Cincinnati (OH) 346

University of Colorado at Boulder, Leeds School of Business, Boulder (CO) 104, **702**

University of Colorado Denver, Business School, Denver (CO) 105, **706**

University of Dallas, Graduate School of Management, Irving (TX) 420, **710**

University of Delaware, Alfred Lerner College of Business and Economics, Newark (DE) 116, **712**

University of Denver, Daniels College of Business, Denver (CO) 106

University of Hawaii at Manoa, Shidler College of Business, Honolulu (HI) 154

University of Hull, School of Management, Hull (United Kingdom) 552

University of Illinois at Urbana–Champaign, College of Business, Champaign (IL) 176

University of Kansas, School of Business, Lawrence (KS) 196

University of Kentucky, Gatton College of Business and Economics, Lexington (KY) 202, **716**

University of La Verne, College of Business and Public Management, La Verne (CA) 94

University of Maryland University College, Graduate School of Management and Technology, Adelphi (MD) 218

University of Minnesota, Twin Cities Campus, Carlson School of Management, Minneapolis (MN) 252

University of Mississippi, School of Business Administration, Oxford (MS) 257

University of Missouri–Columbia, Robert J. Trulaske, Sr. College of Business, Columbia (MO) 267, **720**

University of Newcastle, Graduate School of Business, Callaghan (Australia) 489

University of New Mexico, Robert O. Anderson Graduate School of Management, Albuquerque (NM) 294

University of Pennsylvania, Wharton School, Philadelphia (PA) 380

University of Redlands, School of Business, Redlands (CA) 96

University of St. Thomas, Opus College of Business (MN) 253, **738**

University of Salford, Salford Business School, Salford (United Kingdom) 554

University of South Carolina, Moore School of Business, Columbia (SC) *392,* **740**

University of Southern California, School of Business, Los Angeles (CA) 98

University of Strathclyde, University of Strathclyde Graduate School of Business, Glasgow (United Kingdom) 555

The University of Tampa, John H. Sykes College of Business, Tampa (FL) 139, **742**

The University of Tennessee, College of Business Administration, Knoxville (TN) *401,* **744**

The University of Texas at Arlington, College of Business Administration, Arlington (TX) 424, **746**

The University of Texas at Austin, Programs in MBA, Austin (TX) 425

The University of Texas at Dallas, School of Management, Richardson (TX) *426,* **748**

University of the West of England, Bristol, Bristol Business School, Bristol (United Kingdom) 555

University of Ulster at Jordanstown, Faculty of Business and Management, Newtown Abbey (United Kingdom) 556

University of Warwick, Warwick Business School, Coventry (United Kingdom) 557

University of Washington, Michael G. Foster School of Business, Seattle (WA) 452, **754**

University of Waterloo, Graduate Studies, Waterloo (Canada) 479

University of Wisconsin–Eau Claire, College of Business, Eau Claire (WI) 461, **756**

University of Wisconsin–Whitewater, College of Business and Economics, Whitewater (WI) 465

Virginia Commonwealth University, School of Business, Richmond (VA) 445

Walden University, School of Management, Minneapolis (MN) 253

Waseda University, Graduate School of Commerce, Tokyo (Japan) 517

Webster University, School of Business and Technology, St. Louis (MO) 270

Western Illinois University, College of Business and Technology, Macomb (IL) 178

Westminster College, The Bill and Vieve Gore School of Business, Salt Lake City (UT) 433

Willamette University, George H. Atkinson Graduate School of Management, Salem (OR) 361, **768**

Worcester Polytechnic Institute, Department of Management, Worcester (MA) 234, **770**

York University, Schulich School of Business, Toronto (Canada) 482, **772**

INFORMATION SYSTEMS

Adelphi University, School of Business, Garden City (NY) 295, **560**

The American University in Cairo, School of Business, Economics and Communication, Cairo (Egypt) 502

Argosy University, Atlanta, College of Business, Atlanta (GA) 141, **566**

Argosy University, Chicago, College of Business, Chicago (IL) 158, **566**

Argosy University, Dallas, College of Business, Dallas (TX) 405, **566**

Argosy University, Denver, College of Business, Denver (CO) 100, **566**

Argosy University, Hawai'i, College of Business, Honolulu (HI) 153, **566**

Argosy University, Inland Empire, College of Business, San Bernardino (CA) 65, **566**

Argosy University, Los Angeles, College of Business, Santa Monica (CA) 65, **566**

Argosy University, Nashville, College of Business, Nashville (TN) 395, **566**

Argosy University, Orange County, College of Business, Santa Ana (CA) 65, **566**

Argosy University, Phoenix, College of Business, Phoenix (AZ) 54, **566**

Argosy University, Salt Lake City, College of Business, Draper (UT) 430, **566**

Argosy University, San Diego, College of Business, San Diego (CA) 65, **566**

Argosy University, San Francisco Bay Area, College of Business, Alameda (CA) 66, **566**

Argosy University, Sarasota, College of Business, Sarasota (FL) 122, **566**

Argosy University, Schaumburg, College of Business, Schaumburg (IL) 158, **566**

Argosy University, Seattle, College of Business, Seattle (WA) 447, **566**

Argosy University, Tampa, College of Business, Tampa (FL) 122, **566**

Argosy University, Twin Cities, College of Business, Eagan (MN) 248, **566**

Argosy University, Washington DC, College of Business, Arlington (VA) 436, **566**

Arizona State University, W.P. Carey School of Business, Tempe (AZ) 54

Arkansas State University, College of Business, Jonesboro (AR) 61

Aston University, Aston Business School, Birmingham (United Kingdom) 539

Auburn University Montgomery, School of Business, Montgomery (AL) 46

Baker University, School of Professional and Graduate Studies, Baldwin City (KS) 193

Roosevelt University, Walter E. Heller College of Business Administration, Chicago (IL) 172, **676**

San Diego State University, College of Business Administration, San Diego (CA) 86

San Francisco State University, College of Business, San Francisco (CA) 87

Stevens Institute of Technology, Wesley J. Howe School of Technology Management, Hoboken (NJ) 290

Stony Brook University, State University of New York, W. Averell Harriman School for Management and Policy, Stony Brook (NY) 317

Stratford University, Graduate Business Programs, Falls Church (VA) 443

Suffolk University, Sawyer Business School, Boston (MA) 230

Tarleton State University, College of Business Administration, Stephenville (TX) 413

Texas A&M International University, College of Business Administration, Laredo (TX) 414

Texas A&M University, Mays Business School, College Station (TX) 414

Thames Valley University, Faculty of Professional Studies, Slough (United Kingdom) 546

Troy University, College of Business, Troy (AL) 48

The University of Alabama, Manderson Graduate School of Business, Tuscaloosa (AL) 49

University of Bath, School of Management, Bath (United Kingdom) 547

University of California, Los Angeles, UCLA Anderson School of Management, Los Angeles (CA) 91, **696**

University of California, San Diego, Rady School of Management, La Jolla (CA) 93, **700**

University of Cincinnati, College of Business, Cincinnati (OH) 346

University of Colorado at Boulder, Leeds School of Business, Boulder (CO) 104, **702**

University of Colorado at Colorado Springs, Graduate School of Business Administration, Colorado Springs (CO) 105, **704**

University of Colorado Denver, Business School, Denver (CO) 105, **706**

University of Delaware, Alfred Lerner College of Business and Economics, Newark (DE) 116, **712**

University of Denver, Daniels College of Business, Denver (CO) 106

University of Detroit Mercy, College of Business Administration, Detroit (MI) 243

University of Kansas, School of Business, Lawrence (KS) 196

University of Mary, Program in Management, Bismarck (ND) 335

University of Maryland, College Park, Robert H. Smith School of Business, College Park (MD) 217

University of Massachusetts Lowell, College of Management, Lowell (MA) 233

University of Miami, School of Business Administration, Coral Gables (FL) 135, **718**

University of Missouri–Columbia, Robert J. Trulaske, Sr. College of Business, Columbia (MO) 267, **720**

University of Missouri–St. Louis, College of Business Administration, St. Louis (MO) *268*

University of Nebraska at Kearney, College of Business and Technology, Kearney (NE) 273

University of Nevada, Las Vegas, College of Business, Las Vegas (NV) 275, **722**

University of Salford, Salford Business School, Salford (United Kingdom) 554

University of South Carolina, Moore School of Business, Columbia (SC) *392,* **740**

University of Southern California, School of Business, Los Angeles (CA) 98

University of Strathclyde, University of Strathclyde Graduate School of Business, Glasgow (United Kingdom) 555

University of the West of England, Bristol, Bristol Business School, Bristol (United Kingdom) 555

The University of Toledo, College of Business Administration, Toledo (OH) 349

University of Warwick, Warwick Business School, Coventry (United Kingdom) 557

University of Washington, Michael G. Foster School of Business, Seattle (WA) 452, **754**

University of Waterloo, Graduate Studies, Waterloo (Canada) 479

University of Wisconsin–Madison, Wisconsin School of Business, Madison (WI) 462, **756**

Vienna University of Economics and Business Administration, WU Wien MBA, Vienna (Austria) 492

Villanova University, Villanova School of Business, Villanova (PA) 382

Virginia Commonwealth University, School of Business, Richmond (VA) 445

Webber International University, Graduate School of Business, Babson Park (FL) 140, **762**

Webster University, School of Business and Technology, St. Louis (MO) 270

Worcester Polytechnic Institute, Department of Management, Worcester (MA) 234, **770**

Xavier University, Williams College of Business, Cincinnati (OH) 350

INFORMATION TECHNOLOGY

American InterContinental University, School of Business, Weston (FL) 122, **564**

American InterContinental University Dunwoody Campus, School of Business, Atlanta (GA) 141, **564**

American Public University System, AMU/APU Graduate Programs, Charles Town (WV) 455

Bayerische Julius-Maximilians University of Wuerzburg, MBA Program, Wuerzburg (Germany) 507

Bellevue University, College of Business, Bellevue (NE) 271, **576**

Benedictine University, Graduate Programs, Lisle (IL) 158

Bentley College, The Elkin B. McCallum Graduate School of Business, Waltham (MA) 221, **578**

Boise State University, College of Business and Economics, Boise (ID) 155

California State University, Dominguez Hills, College of Business Administration and Public Policy, Carson (CA) 69

California State University, East Bay, College of Business and Economics, Hayward (CA) 69

California State University, Fullerton, College of Business and Economics, Fullerton (CA) 70

Canisius College, Richard J. Wehle School of Business, Buffalo (NY) 296

Case Western Reserve University, Weatherhead School of Management, Cleveland (OH) 338

The Chinese University of Hong Kong, Faculty of Business Administration, Hong Kong (China) 497

College of St. Catherine, Program in Organizational Leadership, St. Paul (MN) 249

Creighton University, Eugene C. Eppley College of Business Administration, Omaha (NE) 272

Escuela de Administracion de Negocios para Graduados, Programa Magister—MBA Programs, Lima (Peru) 525

Florida Atlantic University, College of Business, Boca Raton (FL) 126

Gannon University, School of Business, Erie (PA) 368

Georgia Institute of Technology, College of Management, Atlanta (GA) 146, **624**

Golden Gate University, Ageno School of Business, San Francisco (CA) 78

Harding University, College of Business Administration, Searcy (AR) 61

HEC Montreal, Master's Program in Business Administration and Management, Montréal (Canada) 468

Indian School of Business, MBA Program, Andhra Pradesh (India) 512

The Johns Hopkins University, Carey Business School, Baltimore (MD) 214, **646**

Jones International University, Graduate School of Business Administration, Centennial (CO) 103

Kansas State University, College of Business Administration, Manhattan (KS) 194

Kean University, College of Business and Public Administration, Union (NJ) 284

Kettering University, Graduate School, Flint (MI) 238

Lancaster University, Management School, Lancaster (United Kingdom) 541

Lindenwood University, Division of Management, St. Charles (MO) 261

Macquarie University, Macquarie Graduate School of Management, Sydney (Australia) 485

Marymount University, School of Business Administration, Arlington (VA) 440

Moravian College, The Moravian MBA, Bethlehem (PA) 373

Nanyang Technological University, Nanyang Business School, Singapore (Singapore) 527, **662**

National University, School of Business and Management, La Jolla (CA) 82

National University of Ireland, Dublin, The Michael Smurfit Graduate School of Business, Blackrock (Ireland) 513

New Mexico Highlands University, School of Business, Las Vegas (NM) 293

North Carolina State University, College of Management, Raleigh (NC) 328, **664**

Northcentral University, MBA Program, Prescott Valley (AZ) 56

Northwestern Polytechnic University, School of Business and Information Technology, Fremont (CA) 84

Northwest Missouri State University, Melvin and Valorie Booth College of Business and Professional Studies, Maryville (MO) 263

Nottingham Trent University, Nottingham Business School, Nottingham (United Kingdom) 544

Old Dominion University, College of Business and Public Administration, Norfolk (VA) 441

Ottawa University, Graduate Studies-Arizona (AZ) 57

Pacific States University, College of Business, Los Angeles (CA) 85

Penn State Great Valley, Graduate Studies, Malvern (PA) 373

Queensland University of Technology, Brisbane Graduate School of Business, Brisbane (Australia) 487

Regis University, College for Professional Studies, Denver (CO) 103

Rutgers, The State University of New Jersey, Rutgers Business School–Newark and New Brunswick, Newark and New Brunswick (NJ) 288, **678**

Saginaw Valley State University, College of Business and Management, University Center (MI) 242

Southeastern University, College of Graduate Studies, Washington (DC) 121

Southern New Hampshire University, School of Business, Manchester (NH) 279, **690**

Stevens Institute of Technology, Wesley J. Howe School of Technology Management, Hoboken (NJ) 290

Stockholm School of Economics, Department of Business Administration, Stockholm (Sweden) 531

Stratford University, Graduate Business Programs, Falls Church (VA) 443

Temple University, Fox School of Business and Management, Philadelphia (PA) 379

Thames Valley University, Faculty of Professional Studies, Slough (United Kingdom) 546

United Business Institutes, MBA Program, Brussels (Belgium) 494

University at Albany, State University of New York, School of Business, Albany (NY) 319

The University of Alabama at Birmingham, School of Business, Birmingham (AL) 50

University of Arkansas, Sam M. Walton College of Business Administration, Fayetteville (AR) 62

The University of British Columbia, Sauder School of Business, Vancouver (Canada) 474

University of California, San Diego, Rady School of Management, La Jolla (CA) 93, **700**

University of Dallas, Graduate School of Management, Irving (TX) 420, **710**

University of Delaware, Alfred Lerner College of Business and Economics, Newark (DE) 116, **712**

University of Denver, Daniels College of Business, Denver (CO) 106

University of Georgia, Terry College of Business, Athens (GA) 151

University of Illinois at Urbana–Champaign, College of Business, Champaign (IL) 176

University of Indianapolis, Graduate Business Programs, Indianapolis (IN) 186

University of Management and Technology, Graduate Business Programs, Arlington (VA) 443

University of Massachusetts Boston, College of Management, Boston (MA) 232

University of Missouri–Columbia, Robert J. Trulaske, Sr. College of Business, Columbia (MO) 267, **720**

University of New Brunswick Saint John, Faculty of Business, Saint John (Canada) 476, **724**

The University of New England, The Graduate School of Business Administration, Armidale (Australia) 490

The University of North Carolina at Charlotte, Belk College of Business Administration, Charlotte (NC) 330, **730**

University of North Texas, College of Business Administration, Denton (TX) 422

University of Redlands, School of Business, Redlands (CA) 96

University of Salford, Salford Business School, Salford (United Kingdom) 554

University of South Carolina, Moore School of Business, Columbia (SC) *392*, **740**

The University of Texas at Dallas, School of Management, Richardson (TX) *426*, **748**

The University of Texas at San Antonio, College of Business, San Antonio (TX) 427, **750**

University of the West, Department of Business Administration, Rosemead (CA) 99

Vienna University of Economics and Business Administration, WU Wien MBA, Vienna (Austria) 492

Villanova University, Villanova School of Business, Villanova (PA) 382

Walden University, School of Management, Minneapolis (MN) 253

Woodbury University, School of Business and Management, Burbank (CA) 100

Worcester Polytechnic Institute, Department of Management, Worcester (MA) 234, **770**

INSURANCE

Deakin University, Deakin Business School, Geelong (Australia) 484

Florida State University, College of Business, Tallahassee (FL) 129

Georgia State University, J. Mack Robinson College of Business, Atlanta (GA) 147, **626**

Illinois State University, College of Business, Normal (IL) 165, **638**

Katholieke Universiteit Leuven, Leuven School of Business and Economics, Leuven (Belgium) 494

National University of Ireland, Dublin, The Michael Smurfit Graduate School of Business, Blackrock (Ireland) 513

St. John's University, The Peter J. Tobin College of Business, Queens (NY) 314, **680**

Saints Cyril and Methodius University, Faculty of Economics, Skopje (Macedonia) 519

State University of New York Maritime College, Program in International Transportation Management, Throggs Neck (NY) 317

Temple University, Fox School of Business and Management, Philadelphia (PA) 379

University of Georgia, Terry College of Business, Athens (GA) 151

University of Hartford, Barney School of Business, West Hartford (CT) 113

University of Mary Washington, College of Graduate and Professional Studies, Fredericksburg (VA) 444

University of Mississippi, School of Business Administration, Oxford (MS) 257

University of Pennsylvania, Wharton School, Philadelphia (PA) 380

University of Wisconsin–Madison, Wisconsin School of Business, Madison (WI) 462, **756**

Vienna University of Economics and Business Administration, WU Wien MBA, Vienna (Austria) 492

INTERNATIONAL AND AREA BUSINESS STUDIES

The American University in Cairo, School of Business, Economics and Communication, Cairo (Egypt) 502

Ashridge, Ashridge Executive MBA Program, Berkhamsted (United Kingdom) 538

Barcelona Business School, Graduate Programs in Business, Barcelona (Spain) 528

Bar-Ilan University, Graduate School of Business, Ramat-Gan (Israel) 514

Brandeis University, International Business School, Waltham (MA) 224, **582**

Cardiff University, Cardiff Business School, Cardiff (United Kingdom) 539

The Chinese University of Hong Kong, Faculty of Business Administration, Hong Kong (China) 497

Christian Brothers University, School of Business, Memphis (TN) 396

Cleveland State University, Nance College of Business Administration, Cleveland (OH) 340

Copenhagen Business School, Faculty of Economics and Business Administration, Copenhagen (Denmark) 501

Deakin University, Deakin Business School, Geelong (Australia) 484

DeVry University, Keller Graduate School of Management, Alpharetta (GA) 144

DeVry University, Keller Graduate School of Management, Arlington (VA) 437

Doane College, Program in Management, Crete (NE) 273

École Nationale des Ponts et Chaussées, ENPC MBA, Paris (France) 503

HfB—Business School of Finance and Management, Frankfurt School of Finance and Management, Frankfurt (Germany) 508

Hult International Business School, Graduate Program, Cambridge (MA) 227, **634**

IE Business School, Business School, Madrid (Spain) 529, **636**

Lakeland College, Graduate Studies Division, Sheboygan (WI) 459

Lenoir-Rhyne College, Charles M. Snipes School of Business, Hickory (NC) 326

Madonna University, School of Business, Livonia (MI) 240

Monash University, MBA Programme, Clayton (Australia) 486

Monterey Institute of International Studies, Fisher Graduate School of International Business, Monterey (CA) 82, **660**

National University, School of Business and Management, La Jolla (CA) 82

National University of Ireland, Dublin, The Michael Smurfit Graduate School of Business, Blackrock (Ireland) 513

Northeastern University, Graduate School of Business Administration, Boston (MA) 228

Rollins College, Crummer Graduate School of Business, Winter Park (FL) 131, **674**

Saint Mary's University of Minnesota, Schools of Graduate and Professional Programs, Winona (MN) 251

Saints Cyril and Methodius University, Faculty of Economics, Skopje (Macedonia) 519

Salve Regina University, Graduate Studies, Newport (RI) 389

State University of New York Maritime College, Program in International Transportation Management, Throggs Neck (NY) 317

Stockholm School of Economics, Department of Business Administration, Stockholm (Sweden) 531

Texas A&M University, Mays Business School, College Station (TX) 414

University of Antwerp, University of Antwerp Management School, Antwerp (Belgium) 495

The University of Arizona, Eller College of Management, Tucson (AZ) 58

University of California, Berkeley, Haas School of Business, Berkeley (CA) 89

University of Central Florida, College of Business Administration, Orlando (FL) 133

University of Detroit Mercy, College of Business Administration, Detroit (MI) 243

University of Edinburgh, Edinburgh University Management School, Edinburgh (United Kingdom) 550

University of Hawaii at Manoa, Shidler College of Business, Honolulu (HI) 154

University of Kentucky, Gatton College of Business and Economics, Lexington (KY) 202, **716**

University of Michigan, Ross School of Business at the University of Michigan, Ann Arbor (MI) 244

University of Minnesota, Twin Cities Campus, Carlson School of Management, Minneapolis (MN) 252

University of Missouri–Columbia, Robert J. Trulaske, Sr. College of Business, Columbia (MO) 267, **720**

University of New Brunswick Saint John, Faculty of Business, Saint John (Canada) 476, **724**

University of Pennsylvania, Wharton School, Philadelphia (PA) 380

University of Saskatchewan, Edwards School of Business, Saskatoon (Canada) 478

University of South Carolina, Moore School of Business, Columbia (SC) *392,* **740**

University of Southern California, School of Business, Los Angeles (CA) 98

University of Washington, Michael G. Foster School of Business, Seattle (WA) 452, **754**

The University of Western Australia, Business School, Nedlands (Australia) 491

The University of Western Ontario, Richard Ivey School of Business, London (Canada) 480

University of Windsor, Odette School of Business, Windsor (Canada) 480

Upper Iowa University, Online Master's Programs, Fayette (IA) 192

Wilkes University, College of Arts, Humanities and Social Sciences, Wilkes-Barre (PA) 384

York University, Schulich School of Business, Toronto (Canada) 482, **772**

INTERNATIONAL BANKING

The American University in Cairo, School of Business, Economics and Communication, Cairo (Egypt) 502

Antwerp International Business School, Graduate Programs in Business, Antwerp (Belgium) 493

Barcelona Business School, Graduate Programs in Business, Barcelona (Spain) 528

Brandeis University, International Business School, Waltham (MA) 224, **582**

Cardiff University, Cardiff Business School, Cardiff (United Kingdom) 539

City University of Hong Kong, Faculty of Business, Hong Kong (China) 497

Dowling College, School of Business, Oakdale (NY) 300

École Nationale des Ponts et Chaussées, ENPC MBA, Paris (France) 503

European School of Economics, MBA Programme (Italy) 515, **608**

Florida International University, Alvah H. Chapman, Jr. Graduate School of Business, Miami (FL) 128, **618**

Graduate School of Business Administration Zurich, Executive Management Programs, Zurich (Switzerland) 532

HEC Paris, HEC MBA Program, Jouy-en-Josas (France) *505,* **632**

HfB—Business School of Finance and Management, Frankfurt School of Finance and Management, Frankfurt (Germany) 508

IE Business School, Business School, Madrid (Spain) 529, **636**

International University of Japan, Graduate School of International Management, Minami Uonuma-gu (Japan) 516

The International University of Monaco, Graduate Programs, Monte Carlo (Monaco) 520

Katholieke Universiteit Leuven, Leuven School of Business and Economics, Leuven (Belgium) 494

Lancaster University, Management School, Lancaster (United Kingdom) 541

Madonna University, School of Business, Livonia (MI) 240

Monash University, MBA Programme, Clayton (Australia) 486

Monterey Institute of International Studies, Fisher Graduate School of International Business, Monterey (CA) 82, **660**

National University, School of Business and Management, La Jolla (CA) 82

Stockholm School of Economics, Department of Business Administration, Stockholm (Sweden) 531

Texas A&M International University, College of Business Administration, Laredo (TX) 414

University of Antwerp, University of Antwerp Management School, Antwerp (Belgium) 495

The University of Arizona, Eller College of Management, Tucson (AZ) 58

University of Birmingham, Birmingham Business School, Birmingham (United Kingdom) 548

University of Durham, Durham Business School, Durham (United Kingdom) 549

University of Edinburgh, Edinburgh University Management School, Edinburgh (United Kingdom) 550

University of Kentucky, Gatton College of Business and Economics, Lexington (KY) 202, **716**

University of Pennsylvania, Wharton School, Philadelphia (PA) 380

University of Reading, ICMA Centre, Reading (United Kingdom) 554

University of Salford, Salford Business School, Salford (United Kingdom) 554

Vienna University of Economics and Business Administration, WU Wien MBA, Vienna (Austria) 492

INTERNATIONAL BUSINESS

American Graduate School of Business, International Business Administration Program, La Tour-de-Peilz (Switzerland) 531

American InterContinental University Online, Program in Business Administration, Hoffman Estates (IL) 157

American University, Kogod School of Business, Washington (DC) 118

Antioch University Santa Barbara, Program in Organizational Management, Santa Barbara (CA) 64

Antwerp International Business School, Graduate Programs in Business, Antwerp (Belgium) 493

Aquinas College, School of Management, Grand Rapids (MI) 235

Argosy University, Atlanta, College of Business, Atlanta (GA) 141, **566**

Argosy University, Chicago, College of Business, Chicago (IL) 158, **566**

Argosy University, Dallas, College of Business, Dallas (TX) 405, **566**

Argosy University, Denver, College of Business, Denver (CO) 100, **566**

Argosy University, Hawai'i, College of Business, Honolulu (HI) 153, **566**

Argosy University, Inland Empire, College of Business, San Bernardino (CA) 65, **566**

Argosy University, Los Angeles, College of Business, Santa Monica (CA) 65, **566**

Argosy University, Nashville, College of Business, Nashville (TN) 395, **566**

Argosy University, Orange County, College of Business, Santa Ana (CA) 65, **566**

Argosy University, Phoenix, College of Business, Phoenix (AZ) 54, **566**

Argosy University, Salt Lake City, College of Business, Draper (UT) 430, **566**

Argosy University, San Diego, College of Business, San Diego (CA) 65, **566**

Argosy University, San Francisco Bay Area, College of Business, Alameda (CA) 66, **566**

Argosy University, Sarasota, College of Business, Sarasota (FL) 122, **566**

Argosy University, Schaumburg, College of Business, Schaumburg (IL) 158, **566**

Argosy University, Seattle, College of Business, Seattle (WA) 447, **566**

Argosy University, Tampa, College of Business, Tampa (FL) 122, **566**

Argosy University, Twin Cities, College of Business, Eagan (MN) 248, **566**

Argosy University, Washington DC, College of Business, Arlington (VA) 436, **566**

Ashland University, Dauch College of Business and Economics, Ashland (OH) 337

Ashridge, Ashridge Executive MBA Program, Berkhamsted (United Kingdom) 538

Asian Institute of Technology, School of Management, Pathumthani (Thailand) 536

Assumption College, Department of Business Studies, Worcester (MA) 219

Aston University, Aston Business School, Birmingham (United Kingdom) 539

Avila University, School of Business, Kansas City (MO) 258

Azusa Pacific University, School of Business and Management, Azusa (CA) 66

Baker College Center for Graduate Studies, Graduate Programs, Flint (MI) 236, **572**

Baker University, School of Professional and Graduate Studies, Baldwin City (KS) 193

Barcelona Business School, Graduate Programs in Business, Barcelona (Spain) 528

Barry University, Andreas School of Business, Miami Shores (FL) 123

Benedictine University, Graduate Programs, Lisle (IL) 158

Bentley College, The Elkin B. McCallum Graduate School of Business, Waltham (MA) 221, **578**

Bernard M. Baruch College of the City University of New York, Zicklin School of Business, New York (NY) 296

Bond University, School of Business, Gold Coast (Australia) 483

Boston University, School of Management, Boston (MA) 223

Brandeis University, International Business School, Waltham (MA) 224, **582**

Brescia University, Program in Management, Owensboro (KY) 198

Butler University, College of Business Administration, Indianapolis (IN) 180

California Lutheran University, School of Business, Thousand Oaks (CA) 67

California National University for Advanced Studies, College of Business Administration, Northridge (CA) 67

California State University, Dominguez Hills, College of Business Administration and Public Policy, Carson (CA) 69

California State University, East Bay, College of Business and Economics, Hayward (CA) 69

California State University, Fresno, Craig School of Business, Fresno (CA) 70

California State University, Fullerton, College of Business and Economics, Fullerton (CA) 70

California State University, Los Angeles, College of Business and Economics, Los Angeles (CA) 71

California State University, Northridge, College of Business and Economics, Northridge (CA) 72

Canisius College, Richard J. Wehle School of Business, Buffalo (NY) 296

Carleton University, Eric Sprott School of Business, Ottawa (Canada) 467

The Chinese University of Hong Kong, Faculty of Business Administration, Hong Kong (China) 497

Chulalongkorn University, Sasin Graduate Institute of Business Administration, Bangkok (Thailand) 536

City University of Hong Kong, Faculty of Business, Hong Kong (China) 497

Claremont Graduate University, Peter F. Drucker and Masatoshi Ito Graduate School of Management, Claremont (CA) 75, **590**

Clarion University of Pennsylvania, College of Business Administration, Clarion (PA) 364

Clark University, Graduate School of Management, Worcester (MA) 224, **592**

Clemson University, College of Business and Behavioral Science, Clemson (SC) 391

Columbia University, Graduate School of Business, New York (NY) 298

Concordia University Wisconsin, Graduate Programs, Mequon (WI) 458

Copenhagen Business School, Faculty of Economics and Business Administration, Copenhagen (Denmark) 501

Creighton University, Eugene C. Eppley College of Business Administration, Omaha (NE) 272

Dalhousie University, Faculty of Management, Halifax (Canada) 467

Dallas Baptist University, Graduate School of Business, Dallas (TX) 406

Deakin University, Deakin Business School, Geelong (Australia) 484

DePaul University, Charles H. Kellstadt Graduate School of Business, Chicago (IL) 159

DeVry University, Keller Graduate School of Management, Oakbrook Terrace (IL) 161, **650**

Dominican University, Edward A. and Lois L. Brennan School of Business, River Forest (IL) 162, **600**

Dominican University of California, Division of Business and International Studies, San Rafael (CA) 77

Drexel University, LeBow College of Business, Philadelphia (PA) 366

Duquesne University, John F. Donahue Graduate School of Business, Pittsburgh (PA) 367

D'Youville College, Department of Business, Buffalo (NY) 300

East Carolina University, College of Business, Greenville (NC) 324, **602**

Eastern Mennonite University, Program in Business Administration, Harrisonburg (VA) 438

Eastern Michigan University, College of Business, Ypsilanti (MI) 237

Eastern Washington University, College of Business and Public Administration, Cheney (WA) 448

École Nationale des Ponts et Chaussées, ENPC MBA, Paris (France) 503

Edgewood College, Program in Business, Madison (WI) 458

Edith Cowan University, Faculty of Business and Public Management, Churchlands (Australia) 484

Emory University, Roberto C. Goizueta Business School, Atlanta (GA) 145, **606**

Erasmus University Rotterdam, Rotterdam School of Management, Rotterdam (Netherlands) 521

ESCP-EAP European School of Management, ESCP-EAP European School of Management (France) 503

Escuela de Administracion de Negocios para Graduados, Programa Magister—MBA Programs, Lima (Peru) 525

European School of Economics, MBA Programme (Italy) 515, **608**

Everest University, Graduate School of Business, Clearwater (FL) 126

Everest University, Program in Business Administration, Lakeland (FL) 126

Fachhochschule Offenburg, MBA International Business Consulting, Offenburg (Germany) 507

Fairfield University, Charles F. Dolan School of Business, Fairfield (CT) 109

Fairleigh Dickinson University, College at Florham, Silberman College of Business, Madison (NJ) 282, **612**

Fairleigh Dickinson University, Metropolitan Campus, Silberman College of Business, Teaneck (NJ) 282, **612**

Flinders University, Flinders Business School, Adelaide (Australia) 485

Florida Atlantic University, College of Business, Boca Raton (FL) 126

Florida International University, Alvah H. Chapman, Jr. Graduate School of Business, Miami (FL) 128, **618**

Fordham University, Graduate School of Business Administration, New York (NY) 301, **620**

Gardner-Webb University, Graduate School of Business, Boiling Springs (NC) 325

The George Washington University, School of Business, Washington (DC) 119, **622**

Georgia Institute of Technology, College of Management, Atlanta (GA) 146, **624**

Georgian Court University, School of Business, Lakewood (NJ) 283

Georgia Southern University, College of Business Administration, Statesboro (GA) 146

Georgia State University, J. Mack Robinson College of Business, Atlanta (GA) 147, **626**

Golden Gate University, Ageno School of Business, San Francisco (CA) 78

Governors State University, College of Business and Public Administration, University Park (IL) 164

Graduate School of Business Administration Zurich, Executive Management Programs, Zurich (Switzerland) 532

Groupe CERAM, Ceram ESC Nice School of Management, Sophia Antipolis (France) 504

The Hague University, Faculty of Economics and Management, The Hague (Netherlands) 521, **628**

Harding University, College of Business Administration, Searcy (AR) 61

Hawai'i Pacific University, College of Business Administration, Honolulu (HI) 153, **630**

HEC Montreal, Master's Program in Business Administration and Management, Montréal (Canada) 468

HEC Paris, HEC MBA Program, Jouy-en-Josas (France) *505*, **632**

HfB—Business School of Finance and Management, Frankfurt School of Finance and Management, Frankfurt (Germany) 508

Hofstra University, Frank G. Zarb School of Business, Hempstead (NY) 302

Hotel Management School Maastricht, MBA Program, Maastricht (Netherlands) 522

Howard University, School of Business, Washington (DC) 120

Hult International Business School, Graduate Program, Cambridge (MA) **227**, **634**

IE Business School, Business School, Madrid (Spain) 529, **636**

Illinois Institute of Technology, Stuart School of Business, Chicago (IL) 164

The International Management Institute, International Business School, Antwerp (Belgium) 494

International University in Geneva, MBA Program, Geneva (Switzerland) 533, **640**

International University of Japan, Graduate School of International Management, Minami Uonuma-gu (Japan) 516

The International University, Vienna, MBA Programs, Vienna (Austria) 492

Iowa State University of Science and Technology, College of Business, Ames (IA) 189, **644**

John Carroll University, John M. and Mary Jo Boler School of Business, University Heights (OH) 342

Katholieke Universiteit Leuven, Leuven School of Business and Economics, Leuven (Belgium) 494

Kent State University, Graduate School of Management, Kent (OH) 342

King College, School of Business and Economics, Bristol (TN) 396

Kutztown University of Pennsylvania, College of Business, Kutztown (PA) 369

Lake Forest Graduate School of Management, MBA Program, Lake Forest (IL) 166, **652**

Lancaster University, Management School, Lancaster (United Kingdom) 541

La Salle University, School of Business, Philadelphia (PA) 370

Lawrence Technological University, College of Management, Southfield (MI) 239, **654**

Lehigh University, College of Business and Economics, Bethlehem (PA) 371, **656**

LeTourneau University, Graduate and Professional Studies, Longview (TX) 409

Lewis University, College of Business, Romeoville (IL) 166

Liberty University, School of Business, Lynchburg (VA) 439

Lincoln University, Business Administration Program, Oakland (CA) 80

Lindenwood University, Division of Management, St. Charles (MO) 261

Long Island University, Brooklyn Campus, School of Business, Public Administration and Information Sciences, Brooklyn (NY) 304

Loyola College in Maryland, Sellinger School of Business and Management, Baltimore (MD) 215

Loyola Marymount University, College of Business Administration, Los Angeles (CA) 81

Loyola University Chicago, Graduate School of Business, Chicago (IL) 167

Lynn University, School of Business, Boca Raton (FL) 130

Madonna University, School of Business, Livonia (MI) 240

Maine Maritime Academy, Department of Graduate Studies, Castine (ME) 210

Manhattanville College, School of Graduate and Professional Studies, Purchase (NY) 306

Manukau Institute of Technology, Manukau Business School, Auckland (New Zealand) 523

Marquette University, Graduate School of Management, Milwaukee (WI) 459

Marymount University, School of Business Administration, Arlington (VA) 440

McGill University, Desautels Faculty of Management, Montréal (Canada) 469, **658**

Memorial University of Newfoundland, Faculty of Business Administration, St. John's (Canada) 470

Mercer University, Eugene W. Stetson School of Business and Economics (GA) 149

Mercy College, Division of Business and Accounting, Dobbs Ferry (NY) 307

Michigan State University, Eli Broad Graduate School of Management, East Lansing (MI) 240

Millsaps College, Else School of Management, Jackson (MS) 255

Mills College, Graduate School of Business, Oakland (CA) 81

Missouri State University, College of Business Administration, Springfield (MO) *262*

Monash University, MBA Programme, Clayton (Australia) 486

Montclair State University, School of Business, Montclair (NJ) 285

Monterey Institute of International Studies, Fisher Graduate School of International Business, Monterey (CA) 82, **660**

Nanyang Technological University, Nanyang Business School, Singapore (Singapore) 527, **662**

National University, School of Business and Management, La Jolla (CA) 82

National University of Ireland, Dublin, The Michael Smurfit Graduate School of Business, Blackrock (Ireland) 513

Newman University, School of Business, Wichita (KS) 194

New Mexico Highlands University, School of Business, Las Vegas (NM) 293

New Mexico State University, College of Business, Las Cruces (NM) 293

New York Institute of Technology, School of Management (NY) 308

New York University, Leonard N. Stern School of Business (NY) 309

Northcentral University, MBA Program, Prescott Valley (AZ) 56

Northeastern University, Graduate School of Business Administration, Boston (MA) 228

Northern Kentucky University, College of Business, Highland Heights (KY) 201

North Park University, School of Business and Nonprofit Management, Chicago (IL) 170

Northwestern University, Kellogg School of Management, Evanston (IL) 171

Norwegian School of Management, Graduate School, Sandvika (Norway) 524

Nottingham Trent University, Nottingham Business School, Nottingham (United Kingdom) 544

Nova Southeastern University, H. Wayne Huizenga School of Business and Entrepreneurship, Fort Lauderdale (FL) 130, **666**

Nyack College, School of Business, Nyack (NY) 310

Oakland University, School of Business Administration, Rochester (MI) 241

OGI School of Science & Engineering at Oregon Health & Science University, Department of Management in Science and Technology, Beaverton (OR) 358

The Ohio State University, Max M. Fisher College of Business, Columbus (OH) 344

Old Dominion University, College of Business and Public Administration, Norfolk (VA) 441

Open University of the Netherlands, Business Programs, Heerlen (Netherlands) 523

Oral Roberts University, School of Business, Tulsa (OK) 353

Ottawa University, Graduate Studies-Arizona (AZ) 57

Pace University, Lubin School of Business, New York (NY) 310

Pacific States University, College of Business, Los Angeles (CA) 85

Palm Beach Atlantic University, Rinker School of Business, West Palm Beach (FL) 131

Park University, Program in Business Administration, Parkville (MO) 264

Pepperdine University, Graziadio School of Business and Management, Los Angeles (CA) 85

Pfeiffer University, Program in Business Administration, Misenheimer (NC) 329

Philadelphia University, School of Business Administration, Philadelphia (PA) 375, **668**

Pittsburg State University, Kelce College of Business, Pittsburg (KS) 195

Point Park University, School of Business, Pittsburgh (PA) 375

Pontifical Catholic University of Puerto Rico, College of Business Administration, Ponce (PR) 386

Portland State University, School of Business Administration, Portland (OR) 358

Providence College, School of Business, Providence (RI) 388

Purdue University, Krannert School of Management, West Lafayette (IN) 185

Queensland University of Technology, Brisbane Graduate School of Business, Brisbane (Australia) 487

Quinnipiac University, School of Business, Hamden (CT) 109

Regis University, College for Professional Studies, Denver (CO) 103

Rice University, Jesse H. Jones Graduate School of Management, Houston (TX) 410

Rider University, College of Business Administration, Lawrenceville (NJ) 287

Rochester Institute of Technology, E. Philip Saunders College of Business, Rochester (NY) 312

Rockhurst University, Helzberg School of Management, Kansas City (MO) 264

Roosevelt University, Walter E. Heller College of Business Administration, Chicago (IL) 172, **676**

Rutgers, The State University of New Jersey, Rutgers Business School–Newark and New Brunswick, Newark and New Brunswick (NJ) 288, **678**

Rutgers, The State University of New Jersey, Camden, School of Business, Camden (NJ) 288

Saginaw Valley State University, College of Business and Management, University Center (MI) 242

St. Bonaventure University, School of Business, St. Bonaventure (NY) 313

St. Edward's University, The School of Management and Business, Austin (TX) 410

St. John's University, The Peter J. Tobin College of Business, Queens (NY) 314, **680**

Saint Joseph's University, Erivan K. Haub School of Business, Philadelphia (PA) 377

Saint Louis University, John Cook School of Business, St. Louis (MO) *264*

Saint Mary's University of Minnesota, Schools of Graduate and Professional Programs, Winona (MN) 251

Saint Peter's College, MBA Programs, Jersey City (NJ) 289, **682**

St. Thomas University, Department of Business Administration, Miami Gardens (FL) 132

Salem International University, School of Business, Salem (WV) 455

Salem State College, Program in Business Administration, Salem (MA) 229

San Diego State University, College of Business Administration, San Diego (CA) 86

San Francisco State University, College of Business, San Francisco (CA) 87

Santa Clara University, Leavey School of Business, Santa Clara (CA) 88

Schiller International University, MBA Programs, Florida (FL) 133, **684**

Schiller International University, MBA Program Paris, France, Paris (France) 506, **684**

Schiller International University, MBA Program, Strasbourg, France Campus, Strasbourg (France) 507, **684**

Schiller International University, MBA Programs, Heidelberg, Germany (Germany) 510, **684**

Schiller International University, MBA Program, Madrid, Spain (Spain) 529, **684**

Schiller International University, Graduate Programs, London (United Kingdom) 546, **684**

Schiller International University, American College of Switzerland, MBA Program, Leysin (Switzerland) 534, **684**

Seattle University, Albers School of Business and Economics, Seattle (WA) 451

Seton Hall University, Stillman School of Business, South Orange (NJ) 290, **686**

Silver Lake College, Program in Management and Organizational Behavior, Manitowoc (WI) 460

SIT Graduate Institute, Master's Programs in Intercultural Service, Leadership, and Management, Brattleboro (VT) 434

Southeast Missouri State University, Harrison College of Business, Cape Girardeau (MO) 265

Southern Cross University, Graduate College of Management, Coffs Harbour (Australia) 487

Southern Illinois University Carbondale, College of Business and Administration, Carbondale (IL) 173

Southern Illinois University Edwardsville, School of Business, Edwardsville (IL) *174*

Southern New Hampshire University, School of Business, Manchester (NH) 279, **690**

State University of New York Maritime College, Program in International Transportation Management, Throggs Neck (NY) 317

Stockholm School of Economics, Department of Business Administration, Stockholm (Sweden) 531

Suffolk University, Sawyer Business School, Boston (MA) 230

Swinburne University of Technology, Australian Graduate School of Entrepreneurship (AGSE), Hawthorne (Australia) 488

Temple University, Fox School of Business and Management, Philadelphia (PA) 379

Tennessee Technological University, College of Business, Cookeville (TN) 399

Texas A&M International University, College of Business Administration, Laredo (TX) 414

Texas A&M University, Mays Business School, College Station (TX) 414

Texas A&M University–Corpus Christi, College of Business, Corpus Christi (TX) 416

Texas Christian University, The Neeley School of Business at TCU, Fort Worth (TX) 416, **694**

Texas Tech University, Jerry S. Rawls College of Business Administration, Lubbock (TX) 418

Texas Wesleyan University, School of Business, Fort Worth (TX) 419

TUI University, College of Business Administration, Cypress (CA) 89

United Business Institutes, MBA Program, Brussels (Belgium) 494

University at Buffalo, the State University of New York, School of Management, Buffalo (NY) 320

University of Abertay Dundee, Dundee Business School, Dundee (United Kingdom) 547

The University of Akron, College of Business Administration, Akron (OH) 346

The University of Alabama, Manderson Graduate School of Business, Tuscaloosa (AL) 49

University of Alberta, School of Business, Edmonton (Canada) 473

University of Antwerp, University of Antwerp Management School, Antwerp (Belgium) 495

The University of Arizona, Eller College of Management, Tucson (AZ) 58

University of Baltimore, Merrick School of Business, Baltimore (MD) 216

University of Baltimore/Towson University, Joint University of Baltimore/Towson University (UB/Towson) MBA Program, Baltimore (MD) 217

University of Bath, School of Management, Bath (United Kingdom) 547

University of Birmingham, Birmingham Business School, Birmingham (United Kingdom) 548

University of Bridgeport, School of Business, Bridgeport (CT) 111

University of California, Berkeley, Haas School of Business, Berkeley (CA) 89

University of California, Los Angeles, UCLA Anderson School of Management, Los Angeles (CA) 91, **696**

University of Chicago, Graduate School of Business, Chicago (IL) 175

University of Cincinnati, College of Business, Cincinnati (OH) 346

University of Colorado at Colorado Springs, Graduate School of Business Administration, Colorado Springs (CO) 105, **704**

University of Colorado Denver, Business School, Denver (CO) 105, **706**

University of Connecticut, School of Business, Storrs (CT) 112, **708**

University of Dallas, Graduate School of Management, Irving (TX) 420, **710**

University of Dayton, School of Business Administration, Dayton (OH) 347

University of Delaware, Alfred Lerner College of Business and Economics, Newark (DE) 116, **712**

University of Edinburgh, Edinburgh University Management School, Edinburgh (United Kingdom) 550

The University of Findlay, College of Business, Findlay (OH) 348

University of Florida, Hough Graduate School of Business, Gainesville (FL) 134

University of Georgia, Terry College of Business, Athens (GA) 151

University of Glasgow, University of Glasgow Business School, Glasgow (United Kingdom) 550

University of Hartford, Barney School of Business, West Hartford (CT) 113

University of Hawaii at Manoa, Shidler College of Business, Honolulu (HI) 154

University of Hertfordshire, University of Hertfordshire Business School, Hatfield (United Kingdom) 551

University of Houston, Bauer College of Business, Houston (TX) 420

University of Houston–Clear Lake, School of Business, Houston (TX) 421

University of Houston–Victoria, School of Business Administration, Victoria (TX) 421

University of Illinois at Urbana–Champaign, College of Business, Champaign (IL) 176

University of Kansas, School of Business, Lawrence (KS) 196

University of Kentucky, Gatton College of Business and Economics, Lexington (KY) 202, **716**

University of La Verne, College of Business and Public Management, La Verne (CA) 94

University of Malaya, Graduate School of Business, Kuala Lumpur (Malaysia) 519

University of Maryland, College Park, Robert H. Smith School of Business, College Park (MD) 217

University of Miami, School of Business Administration, Coral Gables (FL) 135, **718**

University of Michigan, Ross School of Business at the University of Michigan, Ann Arbor (MI) 244

University of Michigan–Dearborn, School of Management, Dearborn (MI) 245

University of Michigan–Flint, School of Management, Flint (MI) 246

University of Minnesota, Twin Cities Campus, Carlson School of Management, Minneapolis (MN) 252

University of Mississippi, School of Business Administration, Oxford (MS) 257

University of Missouri–Columbia, Robert J. Trulaske, Sr. College of Business, Columbia (MO) 267, **720**

University of Missouri–Kansas City, Henry W. Bloch School of Business and Public Administration, Kansas City (MO) 267

University of Nebraska–Lincoln, College of Business Administration, Lincoln (NE) 274

University of New Brunswick Saint John, Faculty of Business, Saint John (Canada) 476, **724**

University of Newcastle, Graduate School of Business, Callaghan (Australia) 489

University of New Haven, School of Business, West Haven (CT) 113, **728**

University of New Mexico, Robert O. Anderson Graduate School of Management, Albuquerque (NM) 294

University of New Orleans, College of Business Administration, New Orleans (LA) 209

University of North Alabama, College of Business, Florence (AL) 52

The University of North Carolina at Chapel Hill, Kenan-Flagler Business School, Chapel Hill (NC) 330

The University of North Carolina Wilmington, School of Business, Wilmington (NC) 332

University of North Dakota, College of Business and Public Administration, Grand Forks (ND) 336

University of North Florida, Coggin College of Business, Jacksonville (FL) 136

University of Otago, School of Business, Dunedin (New Zealand) 523

University of Pennsylvania, Wharton School, Philadelphia (PA) 380

University of Phoenix, College of Graduate Business and Management, Phoenix (AZ) 59

University of Phoenix–Atlanta Campus, College of Graduate Business and Management, Sandy Springs (GA) 151

University of Phoenix–Boston Campus, College of Graduate Business and Management, Braintree (MA) 233

University of Phoenix–Central Florida Campus, College of Graduate Business and Management, Maitland (FL) 137

University of Phoenix–Central Massachusetts Campus, College of Graduate Business and Management, Westborough (MA) 234

University of Phoenix–Charlotte Campus, College of Graduate Business and Management, Charlotte (NC) 332

University of Phoenix–Chicago Campus, College of Graduate Business and Management, Schaumburg (IL) 177

University of Phoenix–Cincinnati Campus, College of Graduate Business and Management, West Chester (OH) 348

University of Phoenix–Columbus Georgia Campus, College of Graduate Business and Management, Columbus (GA) 152

University of Phoenix–Columbus Ohio Campus, College of Graduate Business and Management, Columbus (OH) 349

University of Phoenix–Dallas Campus, College of Graduate Business and Management, Dallas (TX) 423

University of Phoenix–Hawaii Campus, College of Graduate Business and Management, Honolulu (HI) 155

University of Phoenix–Houston Campus, College of Graduate Business and Management, Houston (TX) 423

University of Phoenix–Idaho Campus, College of Graduate Business and Management, Meridian (ID) 157

University of Phoenix–Kansas City Campus, College of Graduate Business and Management, Kansas City (MO) 268

University of Phoenix–North Florida Campus, College of Graduate Business and Management, Jacksonville (FL) 137

University of Phoenix–Oregon Campus, College of Graduate Business and Management, Tigard (OR) 360

University of Phoenix–Puerto Rico Campus, College of Graduate Business and Management, Guaynabo (PR) 387

University of Phoenix–Sacramento Valley Campus, College of Graduate Business and Management, Sacramento (CA) 95

University of Phoenix–St. Louis Campus, College of Graduate Business and Management, St. Louis (MO) 269

University of Phoenix–Utah Campus, College of Graduate Business and Management, Salt Lake City (UT) 432

University of Phoenix–Vancouver Campus, College of Graduate Business and Management, Burnaby (Canada) 477

University of Phoenix–Washington Campus, College of Graduate Business and Management, Seattle (WA) 452

University of Phoenix–West Michigan Campus, College of Graduate Business and Management, Walker (MI) 246

University of Phoenix–Wichita Campus, College of Graduate Business and Management, Wichita (KS) 196

University of Phoenix–Wisconsin Campus, College of Graduate Business and Management, Brookfield (WI) 461

University of Pittsburgh, Joseph M. Katz Graduate School of Business, Pittsburgh (PA) 381

University of Plymouth, Plymouth Business School, Plymouth (United Kingdom) 553

University of Portland, Dr. Robert B. Pamplin, Jr. School of Business, Portland (OR) 360

University of Redlands, School of Business, Redlands (CA) 96

University of St. Thomas, Cameron School of Business (TX) 424

University of Salford, Salford Business School, Salford (United Kingdom) 554

University of San Diego, School of Business Administration, San Diego (CA) 96

University of San Francisco, Masagung Graduate School of Management, San Francisco (CA) 97

The University of Scranton, Program in Business Administration, Scranton (PA) 382

University of South Carolina, Moore School of Business, Columbia (SC) *392,* **740**

University of Southern California, School of Business, Los Angeles (CA) 98

University of South Florida, College of Business Administration, Tampa (FL) 138

University of Strathclyde, University of Strathclyde Graduate School of Business, Glasgow (United Kingdom) 555

The University of Tampa, John H. Sykes College of Business, Tampa (FL) 139, **742**

The University of Texas at Arlington, College of Business Administration, Arlington (TX) 424, **746**

The University of Texas at Austin, Programs in MBA, Austin (TX) 425

The University of Texas at Dallas, School of Management, Richardson (TX) *426,* **748**

The University of Texas at San Antonio, College of Business, San Antonio (TX) 427, **750**

University of the District of Columbia, School of Business and Public Administration, Washington (DC) 122

University of the Incarnate Word, H-E-B School of Business and Administration (TX) 429

University of the West, Department of Business Administration, Rosemead (CA) 99

University of the West of England, Bristol, Bristol Business School, Bristol (United Kingdom) 555

University of the Witwatersrand, Graduate School of Business Administration, Wits (South Africa) 527

The University of Toledo, College of Business Administration, Toledo (OH) 349

University of Victoria, Faculty of Business, Victoria (Canada) 479

University of Wales, Aberystwyth, School of Management and Business, Ceredigion (United Kingdom) 556

University of Washington, Michael G. Foster School of Business, Seattle (WA) 452, **754**

The University of Western Australia, Business School, Nedlands (Australia) 491

University of Windsor, Odette School of Business, Windsor (Canada) 480

University of Wisconsin–Oshkosh, College of Business, Oshkosh (WI) 463, **756**

University of Wisconsin–Whitewater, College of Business and Economics, Whitewater (WI) 465

Vancouver Island University, Program in Business Administration, Nanaimo (Canada) 480

Vienna University of Economics and Business Administration, WU Wien MBA, Vienna (Austria) 492

Villanova University, Villanova School of Business, Villanova (PA) 382

Vytautas Magnus University, Faculty of Business and Management, Kaunus (Lithuania) 518

Wagner College, Department of Business Administration, Staten Island (NY) 321

Walsh College of Accountancy and Business Administration, Graduate Programs, Troy (MI) 247

Wayne State University, School of Business Administration, Detroit (MI) 247, **760**

Webster University, School of Business and Technology, St. Louis (MO) 270

Western Illinois University, College of Business and Technology, Macomb (IL) 178

Western International University, Graduate Programs in Business, Phoenix (AZ) 60

Western Michigan University, Haworth College of Business, Kalamazoo (MI) 248

Westminster College, The Bill and Vieve Gore School of Business, Salt Lake City (UT) 433

Whitworth University, School of Global Commerce and Management, Spokane (WA) 455

Wichita State University, W. Frank Barton School of Business, Wichita (KS) 197

Winthrop University, College of Business Administration, Rock Hill (SC) 393

Woodbury University, School of Business and Management, Burbank (CA) 100

Wright State University, Raj Soin College of Business, Dayton (OH) 350

Xavier University, Williams College of Business, Cincinnati (OH) 350

York University, Schulich School of Business, Toronto (Canada) 482, **772**

INTERNATIONAL DEVELOPMENT MANAGEMENT

Bayerische Julius-Maximilians University of Wuerzburg, MBA Program, Wuerzburg (Germany) 507

Cape Breton University, School of Business, Sydney (Canada) 466

Clark University, Graduate School of Management, Worcester (MA) 224, **592**

Eastern University, Graduate Business Programs, St. Davids (PA) 368

École Nationale des Ponts et Chaussées, ENPC MBA, Paris (France) 503

The George Washington University, School of Business, Washington (DC) 119, **622**

Graduate School of Business Administration Zurich, Executive Management Programs, Zurich (Switzerland) 532

HfB—Business School of Finance and Management, Frankfurt School of Finance and Management, Frankfurt (Germany) 508

Hope International University, Program in Business Administration, Fullerton (CA) 79

London School of Economics and Political Science, The Graduate School, London (United Kingdom) 543

Monterey Institute of International Studies, Fisher Graduate School of International Business, Monterey (CA) 82, **660**

National University, School of Business and Management, La Jolla (CA) 82

New York University, Robert F. Wagner Graduate School of Public Service (NY) 309

Northwestern Polytechnic University, School of Business and Information Technology, Fremont (CA) 84

Rouen School of Management, Postgraduate Programmes, Mount Saint Aignan (France) 505

SIT Graduate Institute, Master's Programs in Intercultural Service, Leadership, and Management, Brattleboro (VT) 434

Stockholm School of Economics, Department of Business Administration, Stockholm (Sweden) 531

Thunderbird School of Global Management, Graduate Programs, Glendale (AZ) 57

The University of Arizona, Eller College of Management, Tucson (AZ) 58

University of California, Berkeley, Haas School of Business, Berkeley (CA) 89

University of Edinburgh, Edinburgh University Management School, Edinburgh (United Kingdom) 550

University of Geneva, MBA Program, Geneva (Switzerland) 535

University of Glasgow, University of Glasgow Business School, Glasgow (United Kingdom) 550

University of Kentucky, Gatton College of Business and Economics, Lexington (KY) 202, **716**

The University of Texas at Dallas, School of Management, Richardson (TX) *426,* **748**

University of Waterloo, Graduate Studies, Waterloo (Canada) 479

INTERNATIONAL ECONOMICS

The American University in Cairo, School of Business, Economics and Communication, Cairo (Egypt) 502

Barcelona Business School, Graduate Programs in Business, Barcelona (Spain) 528

Brandeis University, International Business School, Waltham (MA) 224, **582**

Brescia University, Program in Management, Owensboro (KY) 198

California State University, Los Angeles, College of Business and Economics, Los Angeles (CA) 71

Cardiff University, Cardiff Business School, Cardiff (United Kingdom) 539

City University of Hong Kong, Faculty of Business, Hong Kong (China) 497

Claremont Graduate University, Peter F. Drucker and Masatoshi Ito Graduate School of Management, Claremont (CA) 75, **590**

Colorado State University, College of Business, Fort Collins (CO) 101, **596**

Copenhagen Business School, Faculty of Economics and Business Administration, Copenhagen (Denmark) 501

École Nationale des Ponts et Chaussées, ENPC MBA, Paris (France) 503

The George Washington University, School of Business, Washington (DC) 119, **622**

Graduate School of Business Administration Zurich, Executive Management Programs, Zurich (Switzerland) 532

HEC Paris, HEC MBA Program, Jouy-en-Josas (France) *505,* **632**

HfB—Business School of Finance and Management, Frankfurt School of Finance and Management, Frankfurt (Germany) 508

IE Business School, Business School, Madrid (Spain) 529, **636**

Illinois Institute of Technology, Stuart School of Business, Chicago (IL) 164

International University of Japan, Graduate School of International Management, Minami Uonuma-gu (Japan) 516

Katholieke Universiteit Leuven, Leuven School of Business and Economics, Leuven (Belgium) 494

London School of Economics and Political Science, The Graduate School, London (United Kingdom) 543

Madonna University, School of Business, Livonia (MI) 240

Marquette University, Graduate School of Management, Milwaukee (WI) 459

Monash University, MBA Programme, Clayton (Australia) 486

Monterey Institute of International Studies, Fisher Graduate School of International Business, Monterey (CA) 82, **660**

National University, School of Business and Management, La Jolla (CA) 82

Nottingham Trent University, Nottingham Business School, Nottingham (United Kingdom) 544

Pace University, Lubin School of Business, New York (NY) 310

Stockholm School of Economics, Department of Business Administration, Stockholm (Sweden) 531

Texas A&M International University, College of Business Administration, Laredo (TX) 414

The University of Alabama, Manderson Graduate School of Business, Tuscaloosa (AL) 49

The University of Arizona, Eller College of Management, Tucson (AZ) 58

University of California, Los Angeles, UCLA Anderson School of Management, Los Angeles (CA) 91, **696**

University of Edinburgh, Edinburgh University Management School, Edinburgh (United Kingdom) 550

University of Georgia, Terry College of Business, Athens (GA) 151

University of Glasgow, University of Glasgow Business School, Glasgow (United Kingdom) 550

University of Kentucky, Gatton College of Business and Economics, Lexington (KY) 202, **716**

University of Pennsylvania, Wharton School, Philadelphia (PA) 380

University of Salford, Salford Business School, Salford (United Kingdom) 554

University of the West of England, Bristol, Bristol Business School, Bristol (United Kingdom) 555

University of the Witwatersrand, Graduate School of Business Administration, Wits (South Africa) 527

University of Washington, Michael G. Foster School of Business, Seattle (WA) 452, **754**

WHU—Otto Beisheim School of Management, WHU—Otto Beisheim School of Management, Vallendar (Germany) 511

INTERNATIONAL FINANCE

Alaska Pacific University, Business Administration Department, Anchorage (AK) 53

American University, Kogod School of Business, Washington (DC) 118

The American University in Dubai, MBA Program, Dubai (United Arab Emirates) 538

Ashridge, Ashridge Executive MBA Program, Berkhamsted (United Kingdom) 538

Aston University, Aston Business School, Birmingham (United Kingdom) 539

Barcelona Business School, Graduate Programs in Business, Barcelona (Spain) 528

Brandeis University, International Business School, Waltham (MA) 224, **582**

Cardiff University, Cardiff Business School, Cardiff (United Kingdom) 539

City University of Hong Kong, Faculty of Business, Hong Kong (China) 497

Dowling College, School of Business, Oakdale (NY) 300

École Nationale des Ponts et Chaussées, ENPC MBA, Paris (France) 503

Erasmus University Rotterdam, Rotterdam School of Management, Rotterdam (Netherlands) 521

European School of Economics, MBA Programme (NY) 301, **608**

European School of Economics, MBA Programme (Italy) 515, **608**

European School of Economics, MBA Programme, Milan (Italy) 515, **608**

European School of Economics, MBA Programme, Rome (Italy) 516, **608**

European School of Economics, MBA Programme (United Kingdom) 541, **608**

European University, Center for Management Studies, Montreux-Fontanivent (Switzerland) 532

The George Washington University, School of Business, Washington (DC) 119, **622**

Graduate School of Business Administration Zurich, Executive Management Programs, Zurich (Switzerland) 532

Groupe CERAM, Ceram ESC Nice School of Management, Sophia Antipolis (France) 504

HEC Paris, HEC MBA Program, Jouy-en-Josas (France) *505*, **632**

HfB—Business School of Finance and Management, Frankfurt School of Finance and Management, Frankfurt (Germany) 508

The Hong Kong University of Science and Technology, School of Business and Management, Hong Kong (China) 499

Hult International Business School, Graduate Program, Cambridge (MA) *227*, **634**

IE Business School, Business School, Madrid (Spain) 529, **636**

Illinois Institute of Technology, Stuart School of Business, Chicago (IL) 164

International University in Geneva, MBA Program, Geneva (Switzerland) 533, **640**

International University of Japan, Graduate School of International Management, Minami Uonuma-gu (Japan) 516

The International University of Monaco, Graduate Programs, Monte Carlo (Monaco) 520

Katholieke Universiteit Leuven, Leuven School of Business and Economics, Leuven (Belgium) 494

Lancaster University, Management School, Lancaster (United Kingdom) 541

London School of Economics and Political Science, The Graduate School, London (United Kingdom) 543

Madonna University, School of Business, Livonia (MI) 240

Monash University, MBA Programme, Clayton (Australia) 486

Monterey Institute of International Studies, Fisher Graduate School of International Business, Monterey (CA) 82, **660**

National University, School of Business and Management, La Jolla (CA) 82

National University of Ireland, Dublin, The Michael Smurfit Graduate School of Business, Blackrock (Ireland) 513

New York Institute of Technology, School of Management (NY) 308

New York University, Robert F. Wagner Graduate School of Public Service (NY) 309

Nottingham Trent University, Nottingham Business School, Nottingham (United Kingdom) 544

Oklahoma City University, Meinders School of Business, Oklahoma City (OK) 352

Open University, Business School, Milton Keynes (United Kingdom) 545

Open University of the Netherlands, Business Programs, Heerlen (Netherlands) 523

Pepperdine University, Graziadio School of Business and Management, Los Angeles (CA) 85

Rouen School of Management, Postgraduate Programmes, Mount Saint Aignan (France) 505

St. John's University, The Peter J. Tobin College of Business, Queens (NY) 314, **680**

Saints Cyril and Methodius University, Faculty of Economics, Skopje (Macedonia) 519

Stockholm School of Economics, Department of Business Administration, Stockholm (Sweden) 531

Suffolk University, Sawyer Business School, Boston (MA) 230

Swinburne University of Technology, Australian Graduate School of Entrepreneurship (AGSE), Hawthorne (Australia) 488

Texas A&M International University, College of Business Administration, Laredo (TX) 414

Thunderbird School of Global Management, Graduate Programs, Glendale (AZ) 57

The University of Akron, College of Business Administration, Akron (OH) 346

University of Antwerp, University of Antwerp Management School, Antwerp (Belgium) 495

The University of Arizona, Eller College of Management, Tucson (AZ) 58

University of California, Berkeley, Haas School of Business, Berkeley (CA) 89

University of California, Los Angeles, UCLA Anderson School of Management, Los Angeles (CA) 91, **696**

University of Durham, Durham Business School, Durham (United Kingdom) 549

University of Edinburgh, Edinburgh University Management School, Edinburgh (United Kingdom) 550

University of Glasgow, University of Glasgow Business School, Glasgow (United Kingdom) 550

University of Kentucky, Gatton College of Business and Economics, Lexington (KY) 202, **716**

University of Maryland University College, Graduate School of Management and Technology, Adelphi (MD) 218

University of Pennsylvania, Wharton School, Philadelphia (PA) 380

University of Reading, ICMA Centre, Reading (United Kingdom) 554

University of Salford, Salford Business School, Salford (United Kingdom) 554

University of South Carolina, Moore School of Business, Columbia (SC) *392*, **740**

University of Southern California, School of Business, Los Angeles (CA) 98

University of the West of England, Bristol, Bristol Business School, Bristol (United Kingdom) 555

University of the Witwatersrand, Graduate School of Business Administration, Wits (South Africa) 527

University of Tulsa, College of Business Administration, Tulsa (OK) 356

University of Wales, Aberystwyth, School of Management and Business, Ceredigion (United Kingdom) 556

University of Washington, Michael G. Foster School of Business, Seattle (WA) 452, **754**

Vienna University of Economics and Business Administration, WU Wien MBA, Vienna (Austria) 492

Vlerick Leuven Gent Management School, MBA Programmes, Ghent (Belgium) 495

Waseda University, Graduate School of Commerce, Tokyo (Japan) 517

WHU—Otto Beisheim School of Management, WHU—Otto Beisheim School of Management, Vallendar (Germany) 511

INTERNATIONAL HOSPITALITY AND RESTAURANT BUSINESS

Antwerp International Business School, Graduate Programs in Business, Antwerp (Belgium) 493

Barcelona Business School, Graduate Programs in Business, Barcelona (Spain) 528

Hotel Management School Maastricht, MBA Program, Maastricht (Netherlands) 522

Vienna University of Economics and Business Administration, WU Wien MBA, Vienna (Austria) 492

INTERNATIONAL HOTEL AND RESORT MANAGEMENT

Barcelona Business School, Graduate Programs in Business, Barcelona (Spain) 528

Hotel Management School Maastricht, MBA Program, Maastricht (Netherlands) 522

Vienna University of Economics and Business Administration, WU Wien MBA, Vienna (Austria) 492

INTERNATIONAL LOGISTICS

Antwerp International Business School, Graduate Programs in Business, Antwerp (Belgium) 493

City University of Hong Kong, Faculty of Business, Hong Kong (China) 497

Copenhagen Business School, Faculty of Economics and Business Administration, Copenhagen (Denmark) 501

École Nationale des Ponts et Chaussées, ENPC MBA, Paris (France) 503

Graduate School of Business Administration Zurich, Executive Management Programs, Zurich (Switzerland) 532

Maine Maritime Academy, Department of Graduate Studies, Castine (ME) 210

Monash University, MBA Programme, Clayton (Australia) 486

National University, School of Business and Management, La Jolla (CA) 82

State University of New York Maritime College, Program in International Transportation Management, Throggs Neck (NY) 317

The University of Arizona, Eller College of Management, Tucson (AZ) 58

University of Salford, Salford Business School, Salford (United Kingdom) 554

University of Washington, Michael G. Foster School of Business, Seattle (WA) 452, **754**

INTERNATIONAL MANAGEMENT

American University, Kogod School of Business, Washington (DC) 118

Antioch University Santa Barbara, Program in Organizational Management, Santa Barbara (CA) 64

Antwerp International Business School, Graduate Programs in Business, Antwerp (Belgium) 493

Arizona State University, W.P. Carey School of Business, Tempe (AZ) 54

Asian Institute of Technology, School of Management, Pathumthani (Thailand) 536

Aston University, Aston Business School, Birmingham (United Kingdom) 539

Baldwin-Wallace College, Division of Business, Berea (OH) 337

Barcelona Business School, Graduate Programs in Business, Barcelona (Spain) 528

Baylor University, Hankamer School of Business, Waco (TX) 405, **574**

Bellevue University, College of Business, Bellevue (NE) 271, **576**

Boston College, The Carroll School of Management, Chestnut Hill (MA) 221, **580**

Boston University, School of Management, Boston (MA) 223

Brandeis University, International Business School, Waltham (MA) 224, **582**

Cape Breton University, School of Business, Sydney (Canada) 466

Carnegie Mellon University, Tepper School of Business, Pittsburgh (PA) 363, **584**

Case Western Reserve University, Weatherhead School of Management, Cleveland (OH) 338

Centenary College, Program in Business Administration, Hackettstown (NJ) 281

The Chinese University of Hong Kong, Faculty of Business Administration, Hong Kong (China) 497

Claremont Graduate University, Peter F. Drucker and Masatoshi Ito Graduate School of Management, Claremont (CA) 75, **590**

Columbia Southern University, MBA Program, Orange Beach (AL) 46

Copenhagen Business School, Faculty of Economics and Business Administration, Copenhagen (Denmark) 501

Deakin University, Deakin Business School, Geelong (Australia) 484

Duquesne University, John F. Donahue Graduate School of Business, Pittsburgh (PA) 367

East Carolina University, College of Business, Greenville (NC) 324, **602**

École Nationale des Ponts et Chaussées, ENPC MBA, Paris (France) 503

Erasmus University Rotterdam, Rotterdam School of Management, Rotterdam (Netherlands) 521

ESCP-EAP European School of Management, ESCP-EAP European School of Management (France) 503

Escuela de Administracion de Negocios para Graduados, Programa Magister—MBA Programs, Lima (Peru) 525

European School of Economics, MBA Programme (Italy) 515, **608**

European School of Economics, MBA Programme, Rome (Italy) 516, **608**

European University, Center for Management Studies, Montreux-Fontanivent (Switzerland) 532

Everest University, Program in Business Administration, Orlando (FL) 126

Florida International University, Alvah H. Chapman, Jr. Graduate School of Business, Miami (FL) 128, **618**

Georgia State University, J. Mack Robinson College of Business, Atlanta (GA) 147, **626**

Graduate School of Business Administration Zurich, Executive Management Programs, Zurich (Switzerland) 532

HEC Paris, HEC MBA Program, Jouy-en-Josas (France) *505*, **632**

HfB—Business School of Finance and Management, Frankfurt School of Finance and Management, Frankfurt (Germany) 508

HHL—Leipzig Graduate School of Management, MBA Program, Leipzig (Germany) 509

Hult International Business School, Graduate Program, Cambridge (MA) *227*, **634**

IE Business School, Business School, Madrid (Spain) 529, **636**

IMD International Institute for Management Development, IMD International, Lausanne (Switzerland) 533

International University in Geneva, MBA Program, Geneva (Switzerland) 533, **640**

International University of Japan, Graduate School of International Management, Minami Uonuma-gu (Japan) 516

Jones International University, Graduate School of Business Administration, Centennial (CO) 103

Katholieke Universiteit Leuven, Leuven School of Business and Economics, Leuven (Belgium) 494

KDI School of Public Policy and Management, MBA Program, Seoul (Republic of Korea) 526

Lancaster University, Management School, Lancaster (United Kingdom) 541

London School of Economics and Political Science, The Graduate School, London (United Kingdom) 543

Macquarie University, Macquarie Graduate School of Management, Sydney (Australia) 485

Madonna University, School of Business, Livonia (MI) 240

Manukau Institute of Technology, Manukau Business School, Auckland (New Zealand) 523

McGill University, Desautels Faculty of Management, Montréal (Canada) 469, **658**

Michigan State University, Eli Broad Graduate School of Management, East Lansing (MI) 240

Monash University, MBA Programme, Clayton (Australia) 486

Monterey Institute of International Studies, Fisher Graduate School of International Business, Monterey (CA) 82, **660**

National University, School of Business and Management, La Jolla (CA) 82

New York University, Robert F. Wagner Graduate School of Public Service (NY) 309

Northeastern University, Graduate School of Business Administration, Boston (MA) 228

Norwegian School of Management, Graduate School, Sandvika (Norway) 524

Nottingham Trent University, Nottingham Business School, Nottingham (United Kingdom) 544

Nyenrode Business Universiteit, Netherlands Business School, Breukelen (Netherlands) 522

OGI School of Science & Engineering at Oregon Health & Science University, Department of Management in Science and Technology, Beaverton (OR) 358

Open University, Business School, Milton Keynes (United Kingdom) 545.

Open University of the Netherlands, Business Programs, Heerlen (Netherlands) 523

Portland State University, School of Business Administration, Portland (OR) 358

Saint Mary's University of Minnesota, Schools of Graduate and Professional Programs, Winona (MN) 251

Saint Michael's College, Program in Administration and Management, Colchester (VT) 434

Schiller International University, MBA Programs, Heidelberg, Germany (Germany) 510, **684**

SIT Graduate Institute, Master's Programs in Intercultural Service, Leadership, and Management, Brattleboro (VT) 434

Stanford University, Graduate School of Business, Stanford (CA) 88

Stockholm School of Economics, Department of Business Administration, Stockholm (Sweden) 531

Swinburne University of Technology, Australian Graduate School of Entrepreneurship (AGSE), Hawthorne (Australia) 488

Temple University, Fox School of Business and Management, Philadelphia (PA) 379

Texas A&M University, Mays Business School, College Station (TX) 414

Thunderbird School of Global Management, Graduate Programs, Glendale (AZ) 57

Tulane University, A. B. Freeman School of Business, New Orleans (LA) 207

University of Abertay Dundee, Dundee Business School, Dundee (United Kingdom) 547

INTERNATIONAL MARKETING

Lancaster University, Management School, Lancaster (United Kingdom) 541

Madonna University, School of Business, Livonia (MI) 240

Monash University, MBA Programme, Clayton (Australia) 486

Monterey Institute of International Studies, Fisher Graduate School of International Business, Monterey (CA) 82, **660**

National University, School of Business and Management, La Jolla (CA) 82

National University of Ireland, Dublin, The Michael Smurfit Graduate School of Business, Blackrock (Ireland) 513

Norwegian School of Management, Graduate School, Sandvika (Norway) 524

Nottingham Trent University, Nottingham Business School, Nottingham (United Kingdom) 544

Oklahoma City University, Meinders School of Business, Oklahoma City (OK) 352

Open University of the Netherlands, Business Programs, Heerlen (Netherlands) 523

Pepperdine University, Graziadio School of Business and Management, Los Angeles (CA) 85

Saint Joseph's University, Erivan K. Haub School of Business, Philadelphia (PA) 377

Stockholm School of Economics, Department of Business Administration, Stockholm (Sweden) 531

Suffolk University, Sawyer Business School, Boston (MA) 230

Swinburne University of Technology, Australian Graduate School of Entrepreneurship (AGSE), Hawthorne (Australia) 488

Thunderbird School of Global Management, Graduate Programs, Glendale (AZ) 57

The University of Arizona, Eller College of Management, Tucson (AZ) 58

University of California, Los Angeles, UCLA Anderson School of Management, Los Angeles (CA) 91, **696**

University of Edinburgh, Edinburgh University Management School, Edinburgh (United Kingdom) 550

University of Glasgow, University of Glasgow Business School, Glasgow (United Kingdom) 550

University of Hawaii at Manoa, Shidler College of Business, Honolulu (HI) 154

University of Kentucky, Gatton College of Business and Economics, Lexington (KY) 202, **716**

University of Manitoba, Faculty of Management, Winnipeg (Canada) 475

University of Maryland University College, Graduate School of Management and Technology, Adelphi (MD) 218

University of Pennsylvania, Wharton School, Philadelphia (PA) 380

University of Salford, Salford Business School, Salford (United Kingdom) 554

University of South Carolina, Moore School of Business, Columbia (SC) *392*, **740**

University of the West of England, Bristol, Bristol Business School, Bristol (United Kingdom) 555

University of the Witwatersrand, Graduate School of Business Administration, Wits (South Africa) 527

University of Washington, Michael G. Foster School of Business, Seattle (WA) 452, **754**

Vienna University of Economics and Business Administration, WU Wien MBA, Vienna (Austria) 492

Vlerick Leuven Gent Management School, MBA Programmes, Ghent (Belgium) 495

INTERNATIONAL TRADE

The American University in Cairo, School of Business, Economics and Communication, Cairo (Egypt) 502

Antwerp International Business School, Graduate Programs in Business, Antwerp (Belgium) 493

Barcelona Business School, Graduate Programs in Business, Barcelona (Spain) 528

City University of Hong Kong, Faculty of Business, Hong Kong (China) 497

Clemson University, College of Business and Behavioral Science, Clemson (SC) 391

Deakin University, Deakin Business School, Geelong (Australia) 484

École Nationale des Ponts et Chaussées, ENPC MBA, Paris (France) 503

European School of Economics, MBA Programme (Italy) 515, **608**

IE Business School, Business School, Madrid (Spain) 529, **636**

International University of Japan, Graduate School of International Management, Minami Uonuma-gu (Japan) 516

Johnson & Wales University, The Alan Shawn Feinstein Graduate School, Providence (RI) 388, **648**

Madonna University, School of Business, Livonia (MI) 240

Maine Maritime Academy, Department of Graduate Studies, Castine (ME) 210

Monash University, MBA Programme, Clayton (Australia) 486

Monterey Institute of International Studies, Fisher Graduate School of International Business, Monterey (CA) 82, **660**

State University of New York Maritime College, Program in International Transportation Management, Throggs Neck (NY) 317

Stockholm School of Economics, Department of Business Administration, Stockholm (Sweden) 531

Swinburne University of Technology, Australian Graduate School of Entrepreneurship (AGSE), Hawthorne (Australia) 488

Texas A&M International University, College of Business Administration, Laredo (TX) 414

The University of Arizona, Eller College of Management, Tucson (AZ) 58

University of Detroit Mercy, College of Business Administration, Detroit (MI) 243

University of Edinburgh, Edinburgh University Management School, Edinburgh (United Kingdom) 550

University of Geneva, MBA Program, Geneva (Switzerland) 535

University of Kentucky, Gatton College of Business and Economics, Lexington (KY) 202, **716**

University of Maryland University College, Graduate School of Management and Technology, Adelphi (MD) 218

University of New Brunswick Saint John, Faculty of Business, Saint John (Canada) 476, **724**

University of Pennsylvania, Wharton School, Philadelphia (PA) 380

University of Plymouth, Plymouth Business School, Plymouth (United Kingdom) 553

University of Salford, Salford Business School, Salford (United Kingdom) 554

University of South Carolina, Moore School of Business, Columbia (SC) *392*, **740**

University of Washington, Michael G. Foster School of Business, Seattle (WA) 452, **754**

INVESTMENTS AND SECURITIES

Arizona State University at the West campus, School of Global Management and Leadership, Phoenix (AZ) 55

Barcelona Business School, Graduate Programs in Business, Barcelona (Spain) 528

City University of Hong Kong, Faculty of Business, Hong Kong (China) 497

Creighton University, Eugene C. Eppley College of Business Administration, Omaha (NE) 272

Florida International University, Alvah H. Chapman, Jr. Graduate School of Business, Miami (FL) 128, **618**

HfB—Business School of Finance and Management, Frankfurt School of Finance and Management, Frankfurt (Germany) 508

The Hong Kong University of Science and Technology, School of Business and Management, Hong Kong (China) 499

Illinois Institute of Technology, Stuart School of Business, Chicago (IL) 164

International University of Japan, Graduate School of International Management, Minami Uonuma-gu (Japan) 516

The International University of Monaco, Graduate Programs, Monte Carlo (Monaco) 520

National University, School of Business and Management, La Jolla (CA) 82

Pace University, Lubin School of Business, New York (NY) 310

University of Durham, Durham Business School, Durham (United Kingdom) 549

University of Edinburgh, Edinburgh University Management School, Edinburgh (United Kingdom) 550

University of Missouri–Columbia, Robert J. Trulaske, Sr. College of Business, Columbia (MO) 267, **720**

University of Notre Dame, Mendoza College of Business, Notre Dame (IN) 187

University of Oklahoma, Michael F. Price College of Business, Norman (OK) 355

University of Reading, ICMA Centre, Reading (United Kingdom) 554

The University of Texas at Austin, Programs in MBA, Austin (TX) 425

University of Wisconsin–Madison, Wisconsin School of Business, Madison (WI) 462, **756**

Virginia Polytechnic Institute and State University, Pamplin College of Business, Blacksburg (VA) 446

JAPANESE BUSINESS STUDIES

École Nationale des Ponts et Chaussées, ENPC MBA, Paris (France) 503

International University of Japan, Graduate School of International Management, Minami Uonuma-gu (Japan) 516

University of California, Berkeley, Haas School of Business, Berkeley (CA) 89

University of Hawaii at Manoa, Shidler College of Business, Honolulu (HI) 154

University of Pennsylvania, Wharton School, Philadelphia (PA) 380

Waseda University, Graduate School of Commerce, Tokyo (Japan) 517

York University, Schulich School of Business, Toronto (Canada) 482, **772**

LATIN AMERICAN BUSINESS STUDIES

The George Washington University, School of Business, Washington (DC) 119, **622**

IE Business School, Business School, Madrid (Spain) 529, **636**

IMD International Institute for Management Development, IMD International, Lausanne (Switzerland) 533

Indian School of Business, MBA Program, Andhra Pradesh (India) 512

International University of Japan, Graduate School of International Management, Minami Uonuma-gu (Japan) 516

Johnson & Wales University, The Alan Shawn Feinstein Graduate School, Providence (RI) 388, **648**

Jones International University, Graduate School of Business Administration, Centennial (CO) 103

Lancaster University, Management School, Lancaster (United Kingdom) 541

Leadership Institute of Seattle, School of Applied Behavioral Science, Kenmore (WA) 449

Lehigh University, College of Business and Economics, Bethlehem (PA) 371, **656**

Lenoir-Rhyne College, Charles M. Snipes School of Business, Hickory (NC) 326

LeTourneau University, Graduate and Professional Studies, Longview (TX) 409

Liberty University, School of Business, Lynchburg (VA) 439

Lindenwood University, Division of Management, St. Charles (MO) 261

Lipscomb University, MBA Program, Nashville (TN) 397

Madonna University, School of Business, Livonia (MI) 240

Manhattanville College, School of Graduate and Professional Studies, Purchase (NY) 306

Marymount University, School of Business Administration, Arlington (VA) 440

Medaille College, Accelerated Learning Programs (NY) 307

Mercy College, Division of Business and Accounting, Dobbs Ferry (NY) 307

Michigan State University, Eli Broad Graduate School of Management, East Lansing (MI) 240

Monash University, MBA Programme, Clayton (Australia) 486

Nanjing University, School of Business, Nanjing (China) 500

National University, School of Business and Management, La Jolla (CA) 82

New England College, Program in Management, Henniker (NH) 278

Newman University, School of Business, Wichita (KS) 194

New York University, Leonard N. Stern School of Business (NY) 309

New York University, Robert F. Wagner Graduate School of Public Service (NY) 309

North Central College, Department of Business, Naperville (IL) *168*

Northeastern State University, College of Business and Technology, Tahlequah (OK) 352

North Park University, School of Business and Nonprofit Management, Chicago (IL) 170

Norwegian School of Management, Graduate School, Sandvika (Norway) 524

Nottingham Trent University, Nottingham Business School, Nottingham (United Kingdom) 544

Nova Southeastern University, H. Wayne Huizenga School of Business and Entrepreneurship, Fort Lauderdale (FL) 130, **666**

OGI School of Science & Engineering at Oregon Health & Science University, Department of Management in Science and Technology, Beaverton (OR) 358

Ottawa University, Graduate Studies-Arizona (AZ) 57

Penn State Great Valley, Graduate Studies, Malvern (PA) 373

Pepperdine University, Graziadio School of Business and Management, Los Angeles (CA) 85

Pfeiffer University, Program in Business Administration, Misenheimer (NC) 329

Philadelphia Biblical University, School of Business and Leadership, Langhorne (PA) 374

Piedmont College, School of Business, Demorest (GA) 149

Point Park University, School of Business, Pittsburgh (PA) 375

Queensland University of Technology, Brisbane Graduate School of Business, Brisbane (Australia) 487

Regent University, School of Global Leadership and Entrepreneurship, Virginia Beach (VA) 442

Regis College, Department of Management and Leadership, Weston (MA) 229

Regis University, College for Professional Studies, Denver (CO) 103

Rensselaer Polytechnic Institute, Lally School of Management and Technology, Troy (NY) 311, **670**

Roberts Wesleyan College, Division of Business, Rochester (NY) 312

Rochester Institute of Technology, E. Philip Saunders College of Business, Rochester (NY) 312

Roosevelt University, Walter E. Heller College of Business Administration, Chicago (IL) 172, **676**

Royal Roads University, Faculty of Management, Victoria (Canada) 471

St. Bonaventure University, School of Business, St. Bonaventure (NY) 313

Saint Joseph's College of Maine, Program in Business Administration, Standish (ME) 211

Salve Regina University, Graduate Studies, Newport (RI) 389

Santa Clara University, Leavey School of Business, Santa Clara (CA) 88

Shorter College, School of Business, Rome (GA) 150

Siena Heights University, Graduate College, Adrian (MI) 242

SIT Graduate Institute, Master's Programs in Intercultural Service, Leadership, and Management, Brattleboro (VT) 434

Southern Nazarene University, School of Business, Bethany (OK) 354

Southwestern Adventist University, Business Department, Graduate Program, Keene (TX) 412

Stanford University, Graduate School of Business, Stanford (CA) 88

State University of New York at Binghamton, School of Management, Binghamton (NY) 315

Stockholm School of Economics, Department of Business Administration, Stockholm (Sweden) 531

Stratford University, Graduate Business Programs, Falls Church (VA) 443

Suffolk University, Sawyer Business School, Boston (MA) 230

Swinburne University of Technology, Australian Graduate School of Entrepreneurship (AGSE), Hawthorne (Australia) 488

Texas A&M University, Mays Business School, College Station (TX) 414

Thomas Edison State College, School of Business and Management, Trenton (NJ) 291

Tiffin University, Program in Business Administration, Tiffin (OH) 345

Troy University, College of Business, Troy (AL) 48

United Business Institutes, MBA Program, Brussels (Belgium) 494

University of Baltimore/Towson University, Joint University of Baltimore/Towson University (UB/Towson) MBA Program, Baltimore (MD) 217

University of Bath, School of Management, Bath (United Kingdom) 547

University of California, Davis, Graduate School of Management, Davis (CA) 90

University of California, Los Angeles, UCLA Anderson School of Management, Los Angeles (CA) 91, **696**

University of Dallas, Graduate School of Management, Irving (TX) 420, **710**

University of Denver, Daniels College of Business, Denver (CO) 106

University of Guelph, Faculty of Management, Guelph (Canada) 475

University of Indianapolis, Graduate Business Programs, Indianapolis (IN) 186

University of La Verne, College of Business and Public Management, La Verne (CA) 94

University of Maryland, College Park, Robert H. Smith School of Business, College Park (MD) 217

University of Missouri–Kansas City, Henry W. Bloch School of Business and Public Administration, Kansas City (MO) 267

University of San Diego, School of Business Administration, San Diego (CA) 96

University of South Florida, College of Business Administration, Tampa (FL) 138

University of Strathclyde, University of Strathclyde Graduate School of Business, Glasgow (United Kingdom) 555

The University of Toledo, College of Business Administration, Toledo (OH) 349

University of Ulster at Jordanstown, Faculty of Business and Management, Newtown Abbey (United Kingdom) 556

The University of Western Australia, Business School, Nedlands (Australia) 491

University of Wisconsin–Green Bay, Program in Management, Green Bay (WI) 461

Vienna University of Economics and Business Administration, WU Wien MBA, Vienna (Austria) 492

Walden University, School of Management, Minneapolis (MN) 253

Washington University in St. Louis, Olin Business School, St. Louis (MO) 269

Waynesburg University, Graduate and Professional Studies, Waynesburg (PA) 383

Wesley College, Business Program, Dover (DE) 117

Western International University, Graduate Programs in Business, Phoenix (AZ) 60

WHU—Otto Beisheim School of Management, WHU—Otto Beisheim School of Management, Vallendar (Germany) 511

Wilkes University, College of Arts, Humanities and Social Sciences, Wilkes-Barre (PA) 384

Worcester Polytechnic Institute, Department of Management, Worcester (MA) 234, **770**

Yale University, Yale School of Management, New Haven (CT) 114

LEGAL ADMINISTRATION

Cleveland State University, Nance College of Business Administration, Cleveland (OH) 340

Edith Cowan University, Faculty of Business and Public Management, Churchlands (Australia) 484

Lancaster University, Management School, Lancaster (United Kingdom) 541

Marymount University, School of Business Administration, Arlington (VA) 440

Monash University, MBA Programme, Clayton (Australia) 486

National University, School of Business and Management, La Jolla (CA) 82

Northcentral University, MBA Program, Prescott Valley (AZ) 56

Swinburne University of Technology, Australian Graduate School of Entrepreneurship (AGSE), Hawthorne (Australia) 488

Texas Tech University, Jerry S. Rawls College of Business Administration, Lubbock (TX) 418

The University of Arizona, Eller College of Management, Tucson (AZ) 58

University of La Verne, College of Business and Public Management, La Verne (CA) 94

University of Washington, Michael G. Foster School of Business, Seattle (WA) 452, **754**

LOGISTICS

Ashridge, Ashridge Executive MBA Program, Berkhamsted (United Kingdom) 538

Aston University, Aston Business School, Birmingham (United Kingdom) 539

Barcelona Business School, Graduate Programs in Business, Barcelona (Spain) 528

Bellevue University, College of Business, Bellevue (NE) 271, **576**

Copenhagen Business School, Faculty of Economics and Business Administration, Copenhagen (Denmark) 501

Cranfield University, Cranfield School of Management, Cranfield (United Kingdom) 540

Duquesne University, John F. Donahue Graduate School of Business, Pittsburgh (PA) 367

École Nationale des Ponts et Chaussées, ENPC MBA, Paris (France) 503

The George Washington University, School of Business, Washington (DC) 119, **622**

Graduate School of Business Administration Zurich, Executive Management Programs, Zurich (Switzerland) 532

IE Business School, Business School, Madrid (Spain) 529, **636**

Indian School of Business, MBA Program, Andhra Pradesh (India) 512

The International Management Institute, International Business School, Antwerp (Belgium) 494

International University of Japan, Graduate School of International Management, Minami Uonuma-gu (Japan) 516

Kutztown University of Pennsylvania, College of Business, Kutztown (PA) 369

Lancaster University, Management School, Lancaster (United Kingdom) 541

Macquarie University, Macquarie Graduate School of Management, Sydney (Australia) 485

Maine Maritime Academy, Department of Graduate Studies, Castine (ME) 210

McGill University, Desautels Faculty of Management, Montréal (Canada) 469, **658**

Michigan State University, Eli Broad Graduate School of Management, East Lansing (MI) 240

Monash University, MBA Programme, Clayton (Australia) 486

Naval Postgraduate School, School of Business and Public Policy, Monterey (CA) 83

New Jersey Institute of Technology, School of Management, Newark (NJ) 285

The Ohio State University, Max M. Fisher College of Business, Columbus (OH) 344

Purdue University, Krannert School of Management, West Lafayette (IN) 185

Royal Military College of Canada, Department of Business Administration, Kingston (Canada) 471

State University of New York Maritime College, Program in International Transportation Management, Throggs Neck (NY) 317

Stockholm School of Economics, Department of Business Administration, Stockholm (Sweden) 531

Texas A&M International University, College of Business Administration, Laredo (TX) 414

TUI University, College of Business Administration, Cypress (CA) 89

University of Arkansas, Sam M. Walton College of Business Administration, Fayetteville (AR) 62

University of Delaware, Alfred Lerner College of Business and Economics, Newark (DE) 116, **712**

University of Manitoba, Faculty of Management, Winnipeg (Canada) 475

University of Maryland, College Park, Robert H. Smith School of Business, College Park (MD) 217

University of North Florida, Coggin College of Business, Jacksonville (FL) 136

University of North Texas, College of Business Administration, Denton (TX) 422

University of Plymouth, Plymouth Business School, Plymouth (United Kingdom) 553

University of Salford, Salford Business School, Salford (United Kingdom) 554

Waseda University, Graduate School of Commerce, Tokyo (Japan) 517

MANAGEMENT

The Aarhus School of Business, Faculty of Business Administration, Aarhus (Denmark) 501

Adelphi University, School of Business, Garden City (NY) 295, **560**

Albertus Magnus College, Program in Management, New Haven (CT) 108

Amberton University, Department of Business Administration, Garland (TX) 404

American College of Thessaloniki, Department of Business Administration, Pylea (Greece) 511

American InterContinental University, Program in Business Administration, Los Angeles (CA) 63, **564**

American InterContinental University Online, Program in Business Administration, Hoffman Estates (IL) 157

The American University in Cairo, School of Business, Economics and Communication, Cairo (Egypt) 502

Andrew Jackson University, Brian Tracy College of Business and Entrepreneurship, Birmingham (AL) 45

Andrews University, School of Business, Berrien Springs (MI) 235

Antioch University McGregor, Program in Management, Yellow Springs (OH) 336

Antioch University New England, Department of Organization and Management, Keene (NH) 277

Antioch University Santa Barbara, Program in Organizational Management, Santa Barbara (CA) 64

Argosy University, Atlanta, College of Business, Atlanta (GA) 141, **566**

Argosy University, Chicago, College of Business, Chicago (IL) 158, **566**

Argosy University, Dallas, College of Business, Dallas (TX) 405, **566**

Argosy University, Denver, College of Business, Denver (CO) 100, **566**

Argosy University, Hawai'i, College of Business, Honolulu (HI) 153, **566**

Argosy University, Inland Empire, College of Business, San Bernardino (CA) 65, **566**

Argosy University, Los Angeles, College of Business, Santa Monica (CA) 65, **566**

Argosy University, Nashville, College of Business, Nashville (TN) 395, **566**

Argosy University, Orange County, College of Business, Santa Ana (CA) 65, **566**

Argosy University, Phoenix, College of Business, Phoenix (AZ) 54, **566**

Argosy University, Salt Lake City, College of Business, Draper (UT) 430, **566**

Argosy University, San Diego, College of Business, San Diego (CA) 65, **566**

Argosy University, San Francisco Bay Area, College of Business, Alameda (CA) 66, **566**

Argosy University, Sarasota, College of Business, Sarasota (FL) 122, **566**

Argosy University, Schaumburg, College of Business, Schaumburg (IL) 158, **566**

Argosy University, Seattle, College of Business, Seattle (WA) 447, **566**

Argosy University, Tampa, College of Business, Tampa (FL) 122, **566**

Argosy University, Twin Cities, College of Business, Eagan (MN) 248, **566**

Argosy University, Washington DC, College of Business, Arlington (VA) 436, **566**

Arizona State University, W.P. Carey School of Business, Tempe (AZ) 54

Arizona State University at the West campus, School of Global Management and Leadership, Phoenix (AZ) 55

Arkansas State University, College of Business, Jonesboro (AR) 61

Ashland University, Dauch College of Business and Economics, Ashland (OH) 337

Ashridge, Ashridge Executive MBA Program, Berkhamsted (United Kingdom) 538

Asian Institute of Management, Master Programs, Makati City (Philippines) 525

Asian Institute of Technology, School of Management, Pathumthani (Thailand) 536

Assumption College, Department of Business Studies, Worcester (MA) 219

Aston University, Aston Business School, Birmingham (United Kingdom) 539

Athabasca University, Centre for Innovative Management, Athabasca (Canada) 466

Auburn University Montgomery, School of Business, Montgomery (AL) 46

Averett University, Program in Business Administration, Danville (VA) 436

Avila University, School of Business, Kansas City (MO) 258

Babson College, F. W. Olin Graduate School of Business, Wellesley (MA) 220, **570**

Baker College Center for Graduate Studies, Graduate Programs, Flint (MI) 236, **572**

Barcelona Business School, Graduate Programs in Business, Barcelona (Spain) 528

Bar-Ilan University, Graduate School of Business, Ramat-Gan (Israel) 514

Barry University, Andreas School of Business, Miami Shores (FL) 123

Bellevue University, College of Business, Bellevue (NE) 271, **576**

Belmont University, Jack C. Massey Graduate School of Business, Nashville (TN) 395

Benedictine University, Graduate Programs, Lisle (IL) 158

Fayetteville State University, Program in Business Administration, Fayetteville (NC) 325

Fitchburg State College, Division of Graduate and Continuing Education, Fitchburg (MA) 225

Flinders University, Flinders Business School, Adelaide (Australia) 485

Florida Gulf Coast University, Lutgert College of Business, Fort Myers (FL) 127

Florida International University, Alvah H. Chapman, Jr. Graduate School of Business, Miami (FL) 128, **618**

Fontbonne University, Department of Business Administration, St. Louis (MO) 260

Fordham University, Graduate School of Business Administration, New York (NY) 301, **620**

Francis Marion University, School of Business, Florence (SC) 392

Frostburg State University, College of Business, Frostburg (MD) 213

George Fox University, School of Management, Newberg (OR) 357

The George Washington University, School of Business, Washington (DC) 119, **622**

Georgian Court University, School of Business, Lakewood (NJ) 283

Georgia State University, J. Mack Robinson College of Business, Atlanta (GA) 147, **626**

Golden Gate University, Ageno School of Business, San Francisco (CA) 78

Goldey-Beacom College, Graduate Program, Wilmington (DE) 116

Governors State University, College of Business and Public Administration, University Park (IL) 164

Graduate School of Business Administration Zurich, Executive Management Programs, Zurich (Switzerland) 532

Harvard University, Business School, Cambridge (MA) 226

Hawai'i Pacific University, College of Business Administration, Honolulu (HI) 153, **630**

HEC Montreal, Master's Program in Business Administration and Management, Montréal (Canada) 468

HEC Paris, HEC MBA Program, Jouy-en-Josas (France) 505, **632**

Heidelberg College, Program in Business, Tiffin (OH) 342

HfB—Business School of Finance and Management, Frankfurt School of Finance and Management, Frankfurt (Germany) 508

HHL—Leipzig Graduate School of Management, MBA Program, Leipzig (Germany) 509

Hofstra University, Frank G. Zarb School of Business, Hempstead (NY) 302

Holy Names University, Department of Business, Oakland (CA) 79

Hope International University, Program in Business Administration, Fullerton (CA) 79

Hotel Management School Maastricht, MBA Program, Maastricht (Netherlands) 522

Hult International Business School, Graduate Program, Cambridge (MA) 227, **634**

Idaho State University, College of Business, Pocatello (ID) 156

IE Business School, Business School, Madrid (Spain) 529, **636**

Illinois Institute of Technology, Stuart School of Business, Chicago (IL) 164

Illinois State University, College of Business, Normal (IL) 165, **638**

IMD International Institute for Management Development, IMD International, Lausanne (Switzerland) 533

Indiana Tech, Program in Business Administration, Fort Wayne (IN) 181

Indiana University Bloomington, Kelley School of Business, Bloomington (IN) 182

Indiana University Kokomo, School of Business, Kokomo (IN) 182

Indiana University Northwest, School of Business and Economics, Gary (IN) 183

Indiana University–Purdue University Indianapolis, Kelley School of Business, Indianapolis (IN) 184

The International Management Institute, International Business School, Antwerp (Belgium) 494

The International Management Institute of St. Petersburg, International Management Institute of St. Petersburg, St. Petersburg (Russian Federation) 526

International University of Japan, Graduate School of International Management, Minami Uonuma-gu (Japan) 516

Iona College, Hagan School of Business, New Rochelle (NY) 303, **642**

Ithaca College, School of Business, Ithaca (NY) 303

John Carroll University, John M. and Mary Jo Boler School of Business, University Heights (OH) 342

The Johns Hopkins University, Carey Business School, Baltimore (MD) 214, **646**

Johnson & Wales University, The Alan Shawn Feinstein Graduate School, Providence (RI) 388, **648**

Kean University, College of Business and Public Administration, Union (NJ) 284

Keuka College, Program in Management, Keuka Park (NY) 304

Kingston University, Kingston Business School, Kingston upon Thames (United Kingdom) 541

Lamar University, College of Business, Beaumont (TX) 408

Lancaster University, Management School, Lancaster (United Kingdom) 541

La Salle University, School of Business, Philadelphia (PA) 370

Leadership Institute of Seattle, School of Applied Behavioral Science, Kenmore (WA) 449

Lehigh University, College of Business and Economics, Bethlehem (PA) 371, **656**

LeTourneau University, Graduate and Professional Studies, Longview (TX) 409

Lewis University, College of Business, Romeoville (IL) 166

Liberty University, School of Business, Lynchburg (VA) 439

Lincoln University, Business Administration Program, Oakland (CA) 80

Lincoln University, College of Business and Professional Studies (MO) 260

Lindenwood University, Division of Management, St. Charles (MO) 261

London School of Economics and Political Science, The Graduate School, London (United Kingdom) 543

Long Island University, Brooklyn Campus, School of Business, Public Administration and Information Sciences, Brooklyn (NY) 304

Long Island University, Rockland Graduate Campus, Program in Business Administration, Orangeburg (NY) 305

Loughborough University, The Business School—Postgraduate Office, Loughborough (United Kingdom) 544

Louisiana Tech University, College of Administration and Business, Ruston (LA) 205

Loyola College in Maryland, Sellinger School of Business and Management, Baltimore (MD) 215

Loyola Marymount University, College of Business Administration, Los Angeles (CA) 81

Loyola University Chicago, Graduate School of Business, Chicago (IL) 167

Macquarie University, Macquarie Graduate School of Management, Sydney (Australia) 485

Manhattanville College, School of Graduate and Professional Studies, Purchase (NY) 306

Marylhurst University, Department of Business Administration, Marylhurst (OR) 357

Marymount University, School of Business Administration, Arlington (VA) 440

Maryville University of Saint Louis, The John E. Simon School of Business, St. Louis (MO) 262

Massachusetts Institute of Technology, Sloan School of Management, Cambridge (MA) 227

McGill University, Desautels Faculty of Management, Montréal (Canada) 469, **658**

Mercy College, Division of Business and Accounting, Dobbs Ferry (NY) 307

Miami University, Farmer School of Business, Oxford (OH) 343

Michigan State University, Eli Broad Graduate School of Management, East Lansing (MI) 240

Midwestern State University, College of Business Administration, Wichita Falls (TX) 409

Millsaps College, Else School of Management, Jackson (MS) 255

Minot State University, College of Business, Minot (ND) 334

Misericordia University, Division of Behavioral Science, Education, and Business, Dallas (PA) 372

Missouri State University, College of Business Administration, Springfield (MO) *262*

Monash University, MBA Programme, Clayton (Australia) 486

Montclair State University, School of Business, Montclair (NJ) 285

Moravian College, The Moravian MBA, Bethlehem (PA) 373

Mount St. Mary's University, Program in Business Administration, Emmitsburg (MD) 215

Murray State University, College of Business and Public Affairs, Murray (KY) 200

National-Louis University, College of Management and Business, Chicago (IL) 168

National University, School of Business and Management, La Jolla (CA) 82

National University of Ireland, Dublin, The Michael Smurfit Graduate School of Business, Blackrock (Ireland) 513

Naval Postgraduate School, School of Business and Public Policy, Monterey (CA) 83

New Jersey Institute of Technology, School of Management, Newark (NJ) 285

Newman University, School of Business, Wichita (KS) 194

New York Institute of Technology, School of Management (NY) 308

New York University, Leonard N. Stern School of Business (NY) 309

New York University, Robert F. Wagner Graduate School of Public Service (NY) 309

North Central College, Department of Business, Naperville (IL) *168*

Northcentral University, MBA Program, Prescott Valley (AZ) 56

North Dakota State University, College of Business, Fargo (ND) 335

Northeastern State University, College of Business and Technology, Tahlequah (OK) 352

Northeastern University, Graduate School of Business Administration, Boston (MA) 228

Northern Arizona University, College of Business Administration, Flagstaff (AZ) 57

Northwestern University, Kellogg School of Management, Evanston (IL) 171

Northwood University, Richard DeVos Graduate School of Management, Midland (MI) 241

Nottingham Trent University, Nottingham Business School, Nottingham (United Kingdom) 544

Nyenrode Business Universiteit, Netherlands Business School, Breukelen (Netherlands) 522

OGI School of Science & Engineering at Oregon Health & Science University, Department of Management in Science and Technology, Beaverton (OR) 358

Oklahoma City University, Meinders School of Business, Oklahoma City (OK) 352

Open University, Business School, Milton Keynes (United Kingdom) 545

Oral Roberts University, School of Business, Tulsa (OK) 353

Ottawa University, Graduate Studies-Kansas City, Ottawa (KS) 195

Pace University, Lubin School of Business, New York (NY) 310

Palm Beach Atlantic University, Rinker School of Business, West Palm Beach (FL) 131

Penn State Great Valley, Graduate Studies, Malvern (PA) 373

Pepperdine University, Graziadio School of Business and Management, Los Angeles (CA) 85

Pfeiffer University, Program in Business Administration, Misenheimer (NC) 329

Philadelphia University, School of Business Administration, Philadelphia (PA) 375, **668**

Pittsburg State University, Kelce College of Business, Pittsburg (KS) 195

Plymouth State University, Department of Graduate Studies in Business, Plymouth (NH) 279

Point Park University, School of Business, Pittsburgh (PA) 375

Pontifical Catholic University of Puerto Rico, College of Business Administration, Ponce (PR) 386

Providence College, School of Business, Providence (RI) 388

Purdue University, Krannert School of Management, West Lafayette (IN) 185

Quinnipiac University, School of Business, Hamden (CT) 109

Regis University, College for Professional Studies, Denver (CO) 103

Rensselaer Polytechnic Institute, Lally School of Management and Technology, Troy (NY) 311, **670**

Rice University, Jesse H. Jones Graduate School of Management, Houston (TX) 410

Rider University, College of Business Administration, Lawrenceville (NJ) 287

Rochester Institute of Technology, E. Philip Saunders College of Business, Rochester (NY) 312

Rockford College, Program in Business Administration, Rockford (IL) 171

Rockhurst University, Helzberg School of Management, Kansas City (MO) 264

Rollins College, Crummer Graduate School of Business, Winter Park (FL) 131, **674**

Roosevelt University, Walter E. Heller College of Business Administration, Chicago (IL) 172, **676**

Rosemont College, Accelerated Program in Management, Rosemont (PA) 376

Rouen School of Management, Postgraduate Programmes, Mount Saint Aignan (France) 505

Rowan University, William G. Rohrer College of Business, Glassboro (NJ) 287

Royal Roads University, Faculty of Management, Victoria (Canada) 471

Rutgers, The State University of New Jersey, Rutgers Business School–Newark and New Brunswick, Newark and New Brunswick (NJ) 288, **678**

Rutgers, The State University of New Jersey, Camden, School of Business, Camden (NJ) 288

Sacred Heart University, John F. Welch College of Business, Fairfield (CT) 110

Sage Graduate School, Department of Management, Troy (NY) 313

Saginaw Valley State University, College of Business and Management, University Center (MI) 242

St. Bonaventure University, School of Business, St. Bonaventure (NY) 313

St. Edward's University, The School of Management and Business, Austin (TX) 410

St. John's University, The Peter J. Tobin College of Business, Queens (NY) 314, **680**

Saint Joseph's University, Erivan K. Haub School of Business, Philadelphia (PA) 377

Saint Leo University, Graduate Business Studies, Saint Leo (FL) 132

Saint Louis University, John Cook School of Business, St. Louis (MO) *264*

Saint Mary's University of Minnesota, Schools of Graduate and Professional Programs, Winona (MN) 251

Saint Michael's College, Program in Administration and Management, Colchester (VT) 434

Saint Peter's College, MBA Programs, Jersey City (NJ) 289, **682**

St. Thomas Aquinas College, Division of Business Administration, Sparkill (NY) 315

St. Thomas University, Department of Business Administration, Miami Gardens (FL) 132

Saint Xavier University, Graham School of Management, Chicago (IL) 173

Salve Regina University, Graduate Studies, Newport (RI) 389

Samford University, School of Business, Birmingham (AL) 47

San Diego State University, College of Business Administration, San Diego (CA) 86

San Francisco State University, College of Business, San Francisco (CA) 87

Seattle Pacific University, School of Business and Economics, Seattle (WA) 450

Seattle University, Albers School of Business and Economics, Seattle (WA) 451

Seton Hall University, Stillman School of Business, South Orange (NJ) 290, **686**

Seton Hill University, Program in Business Administration, Greensburg (PA) 378

Simmons College, Simmons School of Management, Boston (MA) 230

Simon Fraser University, Faculty of Business Administration, Burnaby (Canada) 472

SIT Graduate Institute, Master's Programs in Intercultural Service, Leadership, and Management, Brattleboro (VT) 434

Southeastern University, College of Graduate Studies, Washington (DC) 121

Southeast Missouri State University, Harrison College of Business, Cape Girardeau (MO) 265

Southern Adventist University, School of Business and Management, Collegedale (TN) 398

Southern Illinois University Carbondale, College of Business and Administration, Carbondale (IL) 173

Southern Illinois University Edwardsville, School of Business, Edwardsville (IL) *174*

Southern Methodist University, Cox School of Business, Dallas (TX) 411, **688**

Southern Nazarene University, School of Business, Bethany (OK) 354

Southern Oregon University, School of Business, Ashland (OR) 359

Southern Wesleyan University, Program in Management, Central (SC) 392

Southwestern Adventist University, Business Department, Graduate Program, Keene (TX) 412

Southwestern College, Professional Studies Programs, Winfield (KS) 196

Stanford University, Graduate School of Business, Stanford (CA) 88

State University of New York Maritime College, Program in International Transportation Management, Throggs Neck (NY) 317

Stephen F. Austin State University, College of Business, Nacogdoches (TX) 413

Stevens Institute of Technology, Wesley J. Howe School of Technology Management, Hoboken (NJ) 290

Stockholm School of Economics, Department of Business Administration, Stockholm (Sweden) 531

Stony Brook University, State University of New York, W. Averell Harriman School for Management and Policy, Stony Brook (NY) 317

Stratford University, Graduate Business Programs, Falls Church (VA) 443

Swinburne University of Technology, Australian Graduate School of Entrepreneurship (AGSE), Hawthorne (Australia) 488

Tarleton State University, College of Business Administration, Stephenville (TX) 413

Tennessee Technological University, College of Business, Cookeville (TN) 399

Texas A&M International University, College of Business Administration, Laredo (TX) 414

Texas A&M University, Mays Business School, College Station (TX) 414

Texas Christian University, The Neeley School of Business at TCU, Fort Worth (TX) 416, **694**

Texas Tech University, Jerry S. Rawls College of Business Administration, Lubbock (TX) 418

Thames Valley University, Faculty of Professional Studies, Slough (United Kingdom) 546

Tiffin University, Program in Business Administration, Tiffin (OH) 345

Troy University, College of Business, Troy (AL) 48

Troy University Dothan, College of Business Administration, Dothan (AL) 49

Tulane University, A. B. Freeman School of Business, New Orleans (LA) 207

Union Graduate College, School of Management, Schenectady (NY) 319

University at Albany, State University of New York, School of Business, Albany (NY) 319

University at Buffalo, the State University of New York, School of Management, Buffalo (NY) 320

The University of Adelaide, The University of Adelaide Business School, Adelaide (Australia) 488

The University of Akron, College of Business Administration, Akron (OH) 346

The University of Alabama, Manderson Graduate School of Business, Tuscaloosa (AL) 49

University of Alaska Anchorage, College of Business and Public Policy, Anchorage (AK) 53

University of Alaska Fairbanks, School of Management, Fairbanks (AK) 54

The University of Arizona, Eller College of Management, Tucson (AZ) 58

University of Baltimore, Merrick School of Business, Baltimore (MD) 216

University of Bath, School of Management, Bath (United Kingdom) 547

University of Birmingham, Birmingham Business School, Birmingham (United Kingdom) 548

University of Bridgeport, School of Business, Bridgeport (CT) 111

The University of British Columbia, Sauder School of Business, Vancouver (Canada) 474

University of California, Berkeley, Haas School of Business, Berkeley (CA) 89

University of California, Davis, Graduate School of Management, Davis (CA) 90

University of California, Los Angeles, UCLA Anderson School of Management, Los Angeles (CA) 91, **696**

University of California, Riverside, A. Gary Anderson Graduate School of Management, Riverside (CA) 93, **698**

University of California, San Diego, Rady School of Management, La Jolla (CA) 93, **700**

University of Canterbury, Department of Management, Christchurch (New Zealand) 523

University of Chicago, Graduate School of Business, Chicago (IL) 175

University of Cincinnati, College of Business, Cincinnati (OH) 346

University of Colorado at Boulder, Leeds School of Business, Boulder (CO) 104, **702**

University of Colorado at Colorado Springs, Graduate School of Business Administration, Colorado Springs (CO) 105, **704**

University of Colorado Denver, Business School, Denver (CO) 105, **706**

University of Connecticut, School of Business, Storrs (CT) 112, **708**

University of Dallas, Graduate School of Management, Irving (TX) 420, **710**

University of Delaware, Alfred Lerner College of Business and Economics, Newark (DE) 116, **712**

University of Detroit Mercy, College of Business Administration, Detroit (MI) 243

University of Durham, Durham Business School, Durham (United Kingdom) 549

University of Edinburgh, Edinburgh University Management School, Edinburgh (United Kingdom) 550

University of Florida, Hough Graduate School of Business, Gainesville (FL) 134

University of Geneva, MBA Program, Geneva (Switzerland) 535

University of Glasgow, University of Glasgow Business School, Glasgow (United Kingdom) 550

University of Hartford, Barney School of Business, West Hartford (CT) 113

University of Hawaii at Manoa, Shidler College of Business, Honolulu (HI) 154

University of Hertfordshire, University of Hertfordshire Business School, Hatfield (United Kingdom) 551

University of Houston–Victoria, School of Business Administration, Victoria (TX) 421

University of Hull, School of Management, Hull (United Kingdom) 552

University of Illinois at Chicago, Liautaud Graduate School of Business, Chicago (IL) 176

University of Illinois at Urbana–Champaign, College of Business, Champaign (IL) 176

University of Indianapolis, Graduate Business Programs, Indianapolis (IN) 186

University of Kansas, School of Business, Lawrence (KS) 196

University of La Verne, College of Business and Public Management, La Verne (CA) 94

University of London, London Business School, London (United Kingdom) 552

University of Louisiana at Lafayette, Graduate School, Lafayette (LA) 208

University of Louisiana at Monroe, College of Business Administration, Monroe (LA) 209

University of Maine, The Maine Business School, Orono (ME) 211

University of Malaya, Graduate School of Business, Kuala Lumpur (Malaysia) 519

University of Management and Technology, Graduate Business Programs, Arlington (VA) 443

University of Manitoba, Faculty of Management, Winnipeg (Canada) 475

University of Mary, Program in Management, Bismarck (ND) 335

University of Mary Hardin-Baylor, College of Business, Belton (TX) 422

University of Maryland University College, Graduate School of Management and Technology, Adelphi (MD) 218

University of Mary Washington, College of Graduate and Professional Studies, Fredericksburg (VA) 444

University of Melbourne, Melbourne Business School, Melbourne (Australia) 488

University of Miami, School of Business Administration, Coral Gables (FL) 135, **718**

University of Michigan–Dearborn, School of Management, Dearborn (MI) 245

University of Minnesota, Twin Cities Campus, Carlson School of Management, Minneapolis (MN) 252

University of Mississippi, School of Business Administration, Oxford (MS) 257

University of Missouri–Columbia, Robert J. Trulaske, Sr. College of Business, Columbia (MO) 267, **720**

University of Missouri–Kansas City, Henry W. Bloch School of Business and Public Administration, Kansas City (MO) 267

University of Missouri–St. Louis, College of Business Administration, St. Louis (MO) *268*

University of Nebraska–Lincoln, College of Business Administration, Lincoln (NE) 274

University of New Brunswick Saint John, Faculty of Business, Saint John (Canada) 476, **724**

University of Newcastle, Graduate School of Business, Callaghan (Australia) 489

University of New Haven, School of Business, West Haven (CT) 113, **728**

University of New Mexico, Robert O. Anderson Graduate School of Management, Albuquerque (NM) 294

University of North Alabama, College of Business, Florence (AL) 52

The University of North Carolina at Chapel Hill, Kenan-Flagler Business School, Chapel Hill (NC) 330

The University of North Carolina at Charlotte, Belk College of Business Administration, Charlotte (NC) 330, **730**

University of Northern Iowa, College of Business Administration, Cedar Falls (IA) 192

University of North Florida, Coggin College of Business, Jacksonville (FL) 136

University of Notre Dame, Mendoza College of Business, Notre Dame (IN) 187

University of Ottawa, Telfer School of Management, Ottawa (Canada) 476

University of Pennsylvania, Wharton School, Philadelphia (PA) 380

University of Phoenix–Atlanta Campus, College of Graduate Business and Management, Sandy Springs (GA) 151

University of Phoenix–Bay Area Campus, College of Graduate Business and Management, Pleasanton (CA) 94

University of Phoenix–Central Florida Campus, College of Graduate Business and Management, Maitland (FL) 137

University of Phoenix–Chicago Campus, College of Graduate Business and Management, Schaumburg (IL) 177

University of Phoenix–Columbus Georgia Campus, College of Graduate Business and Management, Columbus (GA) 152

University of Phoenix–Dallas Campus, College of Graduate Business and Management, Dallas (TX) 423

University of Phoenix–Denver Campus, College of Graduate Business and Management, Lone Tree (CO) 107

University of Phoenix–Hawaii Campus, College of Graduate Business and Management, Honolulu (HI) 155

University of Phoenix–Houston Campus, College of Graduate Business and Management, Houston (TX) 423

University of Phoenix–Kansas City Campus, College of Graduate Business and Management, Kansas City (MO) 268

University of Phoenix–Las Vegas Campus, College of Graduate Business and Management, Las Vegas (NV) 276

University of Phoenix–Little Rock Campus, College of Graduate Business and Management, Little Rock (AR) 63

University of Phoenix–Louisiana Campus, College of Graduate Business and Management, Metairie (LA) 210

University of Phoenix–Maryland Campus, College of Graduate Business and Management, Columbia (MD) 219

University of Phoenix–Metro Detroit Campus, College of Graduate Business and Management, Troy (MI) 246

University of Phoenix–New Mexico Campus, College of Graduate Business and Management, Albuquerque (NM) 294

University of Phoenix–Oklahoma City Campus, College of Graduate Business and Management, Oklahoma City (OK) 355

University of Phoenix–Oregon Campus, College of Graduate Business and Management, Tigard (OR) 360

University of Phoenix–Philadelphia Campus, College of Graduate Business and Management, Wayne (PA) 380

University of Phoenix–Phoenix Campus, College of Graduate Business and Management, Phoenix (AZ) 59

University of Phoenix–Pittsburgh Campus, College of Graduate Business and Management, Pittsburgh (PA) 381

University of Phoenix–Sacramento Valley Campus, College of Graduate Business and Management, Sacramento (CA) 95

University of Phoenix–St. Louis Campus, College of Graduate Business and Management, St. Louis (MO) 269

University of Phoenix–San Diego Campus, College of Graduate Business and Management, San Diego (CA) 95

University of Phoenix–Southern Arizona Campus, College of Graduate Business and Management, Tucson (AZ) 60

University of Phoenix–Southern California Campus, College of Graduate Business and Management, Costa Mesa (CA) 96

University of Phoenix–Southern Colorado Campus, College of Graduate Business and Management, Colorado Springs (CO) 107

University of Phoenix–South Florida Campus, College of Graduate Business and Management, Fort Lauderdale (FL) 137

University of Phoenix–Utah Campus, College of Graduate Business and Management, Salt Lake City (UT) 432

University of Phoenix–Washington Campus, College of Graduate Business and Management, Seattle (WA) 452

University of Phoenix–West Florida Campus, College of Graduate Business and Management, Temple Terrace (FL) 138

University of Phoenix–Wisconsin Campus, College of Graduate Business and Management, Brookfield (WI) 461

University of Pittsburgh, Joseph M. Katz Graduate School of Business, Pittsburgh (PA) 381

University of Plymouth, Plymouth Business School, Plymouth (United Kingdom) 553

University of Portland, Dr. Robert B. Pamplin, Jr. School of Business, Portland (OR) 360

University of Redlands, School of Business, Redlands (CA) 96

University of Regina, Kenneth Levene Graduate School of Business, Regina (Canada) 477

University of Rhode Island, College of Business Administration, Kingston (RI) 389, **734**

University of Rochester, William E. Simon Graduate School of Business Administration, Rochester (NY) 321, **736**

University of St. Francis, College of Business, Joliet (IL) 177

University of St. Thomas, Opus College of Business (MN) 253, **738**

University of San Diego, School of Business Administration, San Diego (CA) 96

University of Sioux Falls, John T. Vucurevich School of Business, Sioux Falls (SD) 394

University of South Carolina, Moore School of Business, Columbia (SC) **392**, **740**

University of Southern California, School of Business, Los Angeles (CA) 98

University of Southern Mississippi, College of Business, Hattiesburg (MS) 257

University of South Florida, College of Business Administration, Tampa (FL) 138

University of Strathclyde, University of Strathclyde Graduate School of Business, Glasgow (United Kingdom) 555

The University of Tampa, John H. Sykes College of Business, Tampa (FL) 139, **742**

The University of Texas at Arlington, College of Business Administration, Arlington (TX) 424, **746**

The University of Texas at Austin, Programs in MBA, Austin (TX) 425

The University of Texas at Tyler, College of Business and Technology, Tyler (TX) 428

The University of Texas of the Permian Basin, School of Business, Odessa (TX) 428

University of the District of Columbia, School of Business and Public Administration, Washington (DC) 122

University of the Pacific, Eberhardt School of Business, Stockton (CA) 99, **752**

University of the Sunshine Coast, Faculty of Business, Maroochydore (Australia) 490

University of the West of England, Bristol, Bristol Business School, Bristol (United Kingdom) 555

The University of Toledo, College of Business Administration, Toledo (OH) 349

University of Toronto, Joseph L. Rotman School of Management, Toronto (Canada) 478

University of Tulsa, College of Business Administration, Tulsa (OK) 356

University of Ulster at Jordanstown, Faculty of Business and Management, Newtown Abbey (United Kingdom) 556

University of Virginia, Darden Graduate School of Business Administration, Charlottesville (VA) 445

University of Wales, Aberystwyth, School of Management and Business, Ceredigion (United Kingdom) 556

University of Warwick, Warwick Business School, Coventry (United Kingdom) 557

University of Washington, Michael G. Foster School of Business, Seattle (WA) 452, **754**

The University of Western Australia, Business School, Nedlands (Australia) 491

University of Wisconsin–Eau Claire, College of Business, Eau Claire (WI) 461, **756**

University of Wisconsin–Green Bay, Program in Management, Green Bay (WI) 461

University of Wisconsin–Madison, Wisconsin School of Business, Madison (WI) 462, **756**

University of Wisconsin–Whitewater, College of Business and Economics, Whitewater (WI) 465

University of Wyoming, College of Business, Laramie (WY) 465

Vanderbilt University, Owen Graduate School of Management, Nashville (TN) 403, **758**

Vienna University of Economics and Business Administration, WU Wien MBA, Vienna (Austria) 492

Virginia Polytechnic Institute and State University, Pamplin College of Business, Blacksburg (VA) 446

Wagner College, Department of Business Administration, Staten Island (NY) 321

Wake Forest University, Babcock Graduate School of Management, Winston-Salem (NC) 332

Walsh University, Program in Business Administration, North Canton (OH) 350

Warner Southern College, School of Business, Lake Wales (FL) 140

Washington State University Tri-Cities, College of Business, Richland (WA) 453

Washington University in St. Louis, Olin Business School, St. Louis (MO) 269

Wayland Baptist University, Graduate Programs, Plainview (TX) 429

Wayne State University, School of Business Administration, Detroit (MI) 247, **760**

Webber International University, Graduate School of Business, Babson Park (FL) 140, **762**

Webster University, School of Business and Technology, St. Louis (MO) 270

Wesley College, Business Program, Dover (DE) 117

Western Illinois University, College of Business and Technology, Macomb (IL) 178

Western International University, Graduate Programs in Business, Phoenix (AZ) 60

Western Michigan University, Haworth College of Business, Kalamazoo (MI) 248

West Texas A&M University, College of Business, Canyon (TX) 430

WHU—Otto Beisheim School of Management, WHU—Otto Beisheim School of Management, Vallendar (Germany) 511

Widener University, School of Business Administration, Chester (PA) 384, **764**

Wilfrid Laurier University, School of Business and Economics, Waterloo (Canada) 481, **766**

Wilkes University, College of Arts, Humanities and Social Sciences, Wilkes-Barre (PA) 384

Willamette University, George H. Atkinson Graduate School of Management, Salem (OR) 361, **768**

Wingate University, Program in Business Administration, Wingate (NC) 334

Woodbury University, School of Business and Management, Burbank (CA) 100

Worcester Polytechnic Institute, Department of Management, Worcester (MA) 234, **770**

Wright State University, Raj Soin College of Business, Dayton (OH) 350

York College of Pennsylvania, Department of Business Administration, York (PA) 385

Youngstown State University, Warren P. Williamson Jr. College of Business Administration, Youngstown (OH) 351

MANAGEMENT COMMUNICATION

The Aarhus School of Business, Faculty of Business Administration, Aarhus (Denmark) 501

Antwerp International Business School, Graduate Programs in Business, Antwerp (Belgium) 493

Barcelona Business School, Graduate Programs in Business, Barcelona (Spain) 528

Bayerische Julius-Maximilians University of Wuerzburg, MBA Program, Wuerzburg (Germany) 507

California Polytechnic State University, San Luis Obispo, Orfalea College of Business, San Luis Obispo (CA) 68

Graduate School of Business Administration Zurich, Executive Management Programs, Zurich (Switzerland) 532

International University in Geneva, MBA Program, Geneva (Switzerland) 533, **640**

International University of Japan, Graduate School of International Management, Minami Uonuma-gu (Japan) 516

Lancaster University, Management School, Lancaster (United Kingdom) 541

Leadership Institute of Seattle, School of Applied Behavioral Science, Kenmore (WA) 449

Murray State University, College of Business and Public Affairs, Murray (KY) 200

National University, School of Business and Management, La Jolla (CA) 82

Penn State Great Valley, Graduate Studies, Malvern (PA) 373

Queensland University of Technology, Brisbane Graduate School of Business, Brisbane (Australia) 487

Rouen School of Management, Postgraduate Programmes, Mount Saint Aignan (France) 505

Stockholm School of Economics, Department of Business Administration, Stockholm (Sweden) 531

University of Colorado at Boulder, Leeds School of Business, Boulder (CO) 104, **702**

University of St. Thomas, Opus College of Business (MN) 253, **738**

University of Salford, Salford Business School, Salford (United Kingdom) 554

MANAGEMENT CONSULTING

The Aarhus School of Business, Faculty of Business Administration, Aarhus (Denmark) 501

Antioch University New England, Department of Organization and Management, Keene (NH) 277

Ashridge, Ashridge Executive MBA Program, Berkhamsted (United Kingdom) 538

Benedictine University, Graduate Programs, Lisle (IL) 158

Boston College, The Carroll School of Management, Chestnut Hill (MA) 221, **580**

École Nationale des Ponts et Chaussées, ENPC MBA, Paris (France) 503

Erasmus University Rotterdam, Rotterdam School of Management, Rotterdam (Netherlands) 521

The George Washington University, School of Business, Washington (DC) 119, **622**

HEC Paris, HEC MBA Program, Jouy-en-Josas (France) *505*, **632**

Hult International Business School, Graduate Program, Cambridge (MA) *227*, **634**

IE Business School, Business School, Madrid (Spain) 529, **636**

International University of Japan, Graduate School of International Management, Minami Uonuma-gu (Japan) 516

Leadership Institute of Seattle, School of Applied Behavioral Science, Kenmore (WA) 449

Monash University, MBA Programme, Clayton (Australia) 486

National University, School of Business and Management, La Jolla (CA) 82

National University of Ireland, Dublin, The Michael Smurfit Graduate School of Business, Blackrock (Ireland) 513

The Ohio State University, Max M. Fisher College of Business, Columbus (OH) 344

Rensselaer Polytechnic Institute, Lally School of Management and Technology, Troy (NY) 311, **670**

Rice University, Jesse H. Jones Graduate School of Management, Houston (TX) 410

Royal Roads University, Faculty of Management, Victoria (Canada) 471

Southern Methodist University, Cox School of Business, Dallas (TX) 411, **688**

Stockholm School of Economics, Department of Business Administration, Stockholm (Sweden) 531

Texas A&M University, Mays Business School, College Station (TX) 414

Texas Christian University, The Neeley School of Business at TCU, Fort Worth (TX) 416, **694**

University at Buffalo, the State University of New York, School of Management, Buffalo (NY) 320

University of Bath, School of Management, Bath (United Kingdom) 547

University of Connecticut, School of Business, Storrs (CT) 112, **708**

University of Maryland, College Park, Robert H. Smith School of Business, College Park (MD) 217

The University of North Carolina at Chapel Hill, Kenan-Flagler Business School, Chapel Hill (NC) 330

University of Salford, Salford Business School, Salford (United Kingdom) 554

University of Southern California, School of Business, Los Angeles (CA) 98

University of Toronto, Joseph L. Rotman School of Management, Toronto (Canada) 478

University of Warwick, Warwick Business School, Coventry (United Kingdom) 557

Wake Forest University, Babcock Graduate School of Management, Winston-Salem (NC) 332

Washington University in St. Louis, Olin Business School, St. Louis (MO) 269

MANAGEMENT INFORMATION SYSTEMS

Alliant International University, Marshall Goldsmith School of Management, San Diego (CA) 63

American University, Kogod School of Business, Washington (DC) 118

Antwerp International Business School, Graduate Programs in Business, Antwerp (Belgium) 493

Ashridge, Ashridge Executive MBA Program, Berkhamsted (United Kingdom) 538

Auburn University, College of Business, Auburn University (AL) 45, **568**

Avila University, School of Business, Kansas City (MO) 258

Azusa Pacific University, School of Business and Management, Azusa (CA) 66

Bar-Ilan University, Graduate School of Business, Ramat-Gan (Israel) 514

Barry University, Andreas School of Business, Miami Shores (FL) 123

Benedictine University, Graduate Programs, Lisle (IL) 158

Bentley College, The Elkin B. McCallum Graduate School of Business, Waltham (MA) 221, **578**

Bernard M. Baruch College of the City University of New York, Zicklin School of Business, New York (NY) 296

Boston College, The Carroll School of Management, Chestnut Hill (MA) 221, **580**

Boston University, School of Management, Boston (MA) 223

Bowling Green State University, College of Business Administration, Bowling Green (OH) 338

Brigham Young University, Marriott School of Management, Provo (UT) 431

California National University for Advanced Studies, College of Business Administration, Northridge (CA) 67

California State University, Fresno, Craig School of Business, Fresno (CA) 70

California State University, Fullerton, College of Business and Economics, Fullerton (CA) 70

California State University, Long Beach, College of Business Administration, Long Beach (CA) 71

California State University, Los Angeles, College of Business and Economics, Los Angeles (CA) 71

California State University, Northridge, College of Business and Economics, Northridge (CA) 72

California State University, Sacramento, College of Business Administration, Sacramento (CA) 72

Carnegie Mellon University, Tepper School of Business, Pittsburgh (PA) 363, **584**

Case Western Reserve University, Weatherhead School of Management, Cleveland (OH) 338

Charleston Southern University, Program in Business, Charleston (SC) 390

The Chinese University of Hong Kong, Faculty of Business Administration, Hong Kong (China) 497

City University of Hong Kong, Faculty of Business, Hong Kong (China) 497

Clark University, Graduate School of Management, Worcester (MA) 224, **592**

Clemson University, College of Business and Behavioral Science, Clemson (SC) 391

Cleveland State University, Nance College of Business Administration, Cleveland (OH) 340

Colorado State University, College of Business, Fort Collins (CO) 101, **596**

Concordia University Wisconsin, Graduate Programs, Mequon (WI) 458

Copenhagen Business School, Faculty of Economics and Business Administration, Copenhagen (Denmark) 501

Creighton University, Eugene C. Eppley College of Business Administration, Omaha (NE) 272

Dallas Baptist University, Graduate School of Business, Dallas (TX) 406

Deakin University, Deakin Business School, Geelong (Australia) 484

DePaul University, Charles H. Kellstadt Graduate School of Business, Chicago (IL) 159

Dominican University, Edward A. and Lois L. Brennan School of Business, River Forest (IL) 162, **600**

Drexel University, LeBow College of Business, Philadelphia (PA) 366

Duquesne University, John F. Donahue Graduate School of Business, Pittsburgh (PA) 367

East Carolina University, College of Business, Greenville (NC) 324, **602**

Eastern Michigan University, College of Business, Ypsilanti (MI) 237

École Nationale des Ponts et Chaussées, ENPC MBA, Paris (France) 503

Emory University, Roberto C. Goizueta Business School, Atlanta (GA) 145, **606**

Erasmus University Rotterdam, Rotterdam School of Management, Rotterdam (Netherlands) 521

Escuela de Administracion de Negocios para Graduados, Programa Magister—MBA Programs, Lima (Peru) 525

European University, Center for Management Studies, Montreux-Fontanivent (Switzerland) 532

Fairfield University, Charles F. Dolan School of Business, Fairfield (CT) 109

Fairleigh Dickinson University, College at Florham, Silberman College of Business, Madison (NJ) 282, **612**

Fairleigh Dickinson University, Metropolitan Campus, Silberman College of Business, Teaneck (NJ) 282, **612**

Florida International University, Alvah H. Chapman, Jr. Graduate School of Business, Miami (FL) 128, **618**

Florida State University, College of Business, Tallahassee (FL) 129

Gardner-Webb University, Graduate School of Business, Boiling Springs (NC) 325

George Mason University, School of Management, Fairfax (VA) 438

The George Washington University, School of Business, Washington (DC) 119, **622**

Gonzaga University, School of Business Administration, Spokane (WA) 448

Governors State University, College of Business and Public Administration, University Park (IL) 164

Graduate School of Business Administration Zurich, Executive Management Programs, Zurich (Switzerland) 532

Hofstra University, Frank G. Zarb School of Business, Hempstead (NY) 302

The Hong Kong University of Science and Technology, School of Business and Management, Hong Kong (China) 499

Howard University, School of Business, Washington (DC) 120

Idaho State University, College of Business, Pocatello (ID) 156

IE Business School, Business School, Madrid (Spain) 529, **636**

Illinois State University, College of Business, Normal (IL) 165, **638**

Indiana University South Bend, School of Business and Economics, South Bend (IN) 184

Indian School of Business, MBA Program, Andhra Pradesh (India) 512

Inter American University of Puerto Rico, San Germán Campus, Department of Business Administration, San Germán (PR) 385

The International Management Institute, International Business School, Antwerp (Belgium) 494

International University of Japan, Graduate School of International Management, Minami Uonuma-gu (Japan) 516

Iona College, Hagan School of Business, New Rochelle (NY) 303, **642**

Iowa State University of Science and Technology, College of Business, Ames (IA) 189, **644**

The Johns Hopkins University, Carey Business School, Baltimore (MD) 214, **646**

Kean University, College of Business and Public Administration, Union (NJ) 284

Kent State University, Graduate School of Management, Kent (OH) 342

Lamar University, College of Business, Beaumont (TX) 408

Lancaster University, Management School, Lancaster (United Kingdom) 541

La Salle University, School of Business, Philadelphia (PA) 370

Lawrence Technological University, College of Management, Southfield (MI) 239, **654**

Lewis University, College of Business, Romeoville (IL) 166

Lincoln University, Business Administration Program, Oakland (CA) 80

Lindenwood University, Division of Management, St. Charles (MO) 261

Long Island University, Brooklyn Campus, School of Business, Public Administration and Information Sciences, Brooklyn (NY) 304

Louisiana State University and Agricultural and Mechanical College, E. J. Ourso College of Business, Baton Rouge (LA) 204

Loyola College in Maryland, Sellinger School of Business and Management, Baltimore (MD) 215

Loyola Marymount University, College of Business Administration, Los Angeles (CA) 81

Loyola University Chicago, Graduate School of Business, Chicago (IL) 167

Macquarie University, Macquarie Graduate School of Management, Sydney (Australia) 485

Manhattanville College, School of Graduate and Professional Studies, Purchase (NY) 306

Massachusetts Institute of Technology, Sloan School of Management, Cambridge (MA) 227

Metropolitan State University, College of Management, St. Paul (MN) 250

Michigan State University, Eli Broad Graduate School of Management, East Lansing (MI) 240

Midwestern State University, College of Business Administration, Wichita Falls (TX) 409

Missouri State University, College of Business Administration, Springfield (MO) *262*

Monash University, MBA Programme, Clayton (Australia) 486

Montclair State University, School of Business, Montclair (NJ) 285

National University, School of Business and Management, La Jolla (CA) 82

National University of Ireland, Dublin, The Michael Smurfit Graduate School of Business, Blackrock (Ireland) 513

Naval Postgraduate School, School of Business and Public Policy, Monterey (CA) 83

New Jersey Institute of Technology, School of Management, Newark (NJ) 285

Newman University, School of Business, Wichita (KS) 194

New York Institute of Technology, School of Management (NY) 308

New York University, Leonard N. Stern School of Business (NY) 309

North Central College, Department of Business, Naperville (IL) *168*

Northcentral University, MBA Program, Prescott Valley (AZ) 56

Northern Illinois University, College of Business, De Kalb (IL) 169

Northern Kentucky University, College of Business, Highland Heights (KY) 201

Notre Dame de Namur University, Department of Business Administration, Belmont (CA) 84

Nyenrode Business Universiteit, Netherlands Business School, Breukelen (Netherlands) 522

Oakland University, School of Business Administration, Rochester (MI) 241

The Ohio State University, Max M. Fisher College of Business, Columbus (OH) 344

Oklahoma City University, Meinders School of Business, Oklahoma City (OK) 352

Oklahoma Wesleyan University, Professional Studies Division, Bartlesville (OK) 353

Old Dominion University, College of Business and Public Administration, Norfolk (VA) 441

Palm Beach Atlantic University, Rinker School of Business, West Palm Beach (FL) 131

Penn State Great Valley, Graduate Studies, Malvern (PA) 373

Penn State Harrisburg, School of Business Administration, Middletown (PA) 373

Pontifical Catholic University of Puerto Rico, College of Business Administration, Ponce (PR) 386

Providence College, School of Business, Providence (RI) 388

Purdue University, Krannert School of Management, West Lafayette (IN) 185

Quinnipiac University, School of Business, Hamden (CT) 109

Regis University, College for Professional Studies, Denver (CO) 103

Rensselaer at Hartford, Lally School of Management and Technology, Hartford (CT) 110

Rensselaer Polytechnic Institute, Lally School of Management and Technology, Troy (NY) 311, **670**

Rochester Institute of Technology, E. Philip Saunders College of Business, Rochester (NY) 312

Roosevelt University, Walter E. Heller College of Business Administration, Chicago (IL) 172, **676**

Rutgers, The State University of New Jersey, Camden, School of Business, Camden (NJ) 288

St. Ambrose University, Program in Business Administration, Davenport (IA) 190

St. Cloud State University, G.R. Herberger College of Business, St. Cloud (MN) 251

St. Edward's University, The School of Management and Business, Austin (TX) 410

St. John's University, The Peter J. Tobin College of Business, Queens (NY) 314, **680**

Saint Louis University, John Cook School of Business, St. Louis (MO) *264*

Saint Michael's College, Program in Administration and Management, Colchester (VT) 434

Saint Peter's College, MBA Programs, Jersey City (NJ) 289, **682**

Santa Clara University, Leavey School of Business, Santa Clara (CA) 88

Schiller International University, MBA Programs, Florida (FL) 133, **684**

Schiller International University, MBA Programs, Heidelberg, Germany (Germany) 510, **684**

Schiller International University, Graduate Programs, London (United Kingdom) 546, **684**

Seattle Pacific University, School of Business and Economics, Seattle (WA) 450

Seton Hall University, Stillman School of Business, South Orange (NJ) 290, **686**

Southeastern Louisiana University, College of Business, Hammond (LA) 207

Southern Cross University, Graduate College of Management, Coffs Harbour (Australia) 487

Southern Illinois University Carbondale, College of Business and Administration, Carbondale (IL) 173

Southern Illinois University Edwardsville, School of Business, Edwardsville (IL) *174*

Southern Polytechnic State University, Department of Business Administration, Marietta (GA) 150

State University of New York at Binghamton, School of Management, Binghamton (NY) 315

State University of New York Maritime College, Program in International Transportation Management, Throggs Neck (NY) 317

Swinburne University of Technology, Australian Graduate School of Entrepreneurship (AGSE), Hawthorne (Australia) 488

Tarleton State University, College of Business Administration, Stephenville (TX) 413

Temple University, Fox School of Business and Management, Philadelphia (PA) 379

Tennessee State University, College of Business, Nashville (TN) 399

Tennessee Technological University, College of Business, Cookeville (TN) 399

Texas A&M University, Mays Business School, College Station (TX) 414

Texas Tech University, Jerry S. Rawls College of Business Administration, Lubbock (TX) 418

Texas Wesleyan University, School of Business, Fort Worth (TX) 419

Troy University Dothan, College of Business Administration, Dothan (AL) 49

Tulane University, A. B. Freeman School of Business, New Orleans (LA) 207

University at Albany, State University of New York, School of Business, Albany (NY) 319

University at Buffalo, the State University of New York, School of Management, Buffalo (NY) 320

The University of Akron, College of Business Administration, Akron (OH) 346

The University of Alabama, Manderson Graduate School of Business, Tuscaloosa (AL) 49

The University of Alabama in Huntsville, College of Business Administration, Huntsville (AL) 51

The University of Arizona, Eller College of Management, Tucson (AZ) 58

University of Baltimore, Merrick School of Business, Baltimore (MD) 216

University of Baltimore/Towson University, Joint University of Baltimore/Towson University (UB/Towson) MBA Program, Baltimore (MD) 217

University of Bath, School of Management, Bath (United Kingdom) 547

University of Bridgeport, School of Business, Bridgeport (CT) 111

The University of British Columbia, Sauder School of Business, Vancouver (Canada) 474

University of California, Berkeley, Haas School of Business, Berkeley (CA) 89

University of California, Davis, Graduate School of Management, Davis (CA) 90

University of California, Los Angeles, UCLA Anderson School of Management, Los Angeles (CA) 91, **696**

University of California, Riverside, A. Gary Anderson Graduate School of Management, Riverside (CA) 93, **698**

University of California, San Diego, Rady School of Management, La Jolla (CA) 93, **700**

University of Canterbury, Department of Management, Christchurch (New Zealand) 523

University of Central Florida, College of Business Administration, Orlando (FL) 133

University of Colorado at Boulder, Leeds School of Business, Boulder (CO) 104, **702**

University of Dayton, School of Business Administration, Dayton (OH) 347

University of Delaware, Alfred Lerner College of Business and Economics, Newark (DE) 116, **712**

University of Denver, Daniels College of Business, Denver (CO) 106

University of Detroit Mercy, College of Business Administration, Detroit (MI) 243

University of Florida, Hough Graduate School of Business, Gainesville (FL) 134

University of Georgia, Terry College of Business, Athens (GA) 151

University of Hartford, Barney School of Business, West Hartford (CT) 113

University of Hawaii at Manoa, Shidler College of Business, Honolulu (HI) 154

University of Houston–Clear Lake, School of Business, Houston (TX) 421

University of Illinois at Chicago, Liautaud Graduate School of Business, Chicago (IL) 176

University of Illinois at Urbana–Champaign, College of Business, Champaign (IL) 176

University of Malaya, Graduate School of Business, Kuala Lumpur (Malaysia) 519

University of Management and Technology, Graduate Business Programs, Arlington (VA) 443

University of Maryland, College Park, Robert H. Smith School of Business, College Park (MD) 217

University of Massachusetts Boston, College of Management, Boston (MA) 232

University of Memphis, Fogelman College of Business and Economics, Memphis (TN) 400

University of Michigan, Ross School of Business at the University of Michigan, Ann Arbor (MI) 244

University of Michigan–Dearborn, School of Management, Dearborn (MI) 245

University of Minnesota, Twin Cities Campus, Carlson School of Management, Minneapolis (MN) 252

University of Mississippi, School of Business Administration, Oxford (MS) 257

University of Missouri–Columbia, Robert J. Trulaske, Sr. College of Business, Columbia (MO) 267, **720**

University of Missouri–Kansas City, Henry W. Bloch School of Business and Public Administration, Kansas City (MO) 267

University of Nebraska–Lincoln, College of Business Administration, Lincoln (NE) 274

University of Nevada, Las Vegas, College of Business, Las Vegas (NV) 275, **722**

University of Newcastle, Graduate School of Business, Callaghan (Australia) 489

University of New Mexico, Robert O. Anderson Graduate School of Management, Albuquerque (NM) 294

University of New Orleans, College of Business Administration, New Orleans (LA) 209

University of North Alabama, College of Business, Florence (AL) 52

The University of North Carolina Wilmington, School of Business, Wilmington (NC) 332

University of Oklahoma, Michael F. Price College of Business, Norman (OK) 355

University of Pittsburgh, Joseph M. Katz Graduate School of Business, Pittsburgh (PA) 381

University of Redlands, School of Business, Redlands (CA) 96

University of Rochester, William E. Simon Graduate School of Business Administration, Rochester (NY) 321, **736**

University of St. Thomas, Cameron School of Business (TX) 424

University of Salford, Salford Business School, Salford (United Kingdom) 554

The University of Scranton, Program in Business Administration, Scranton (PA) 382

University of South Carolina, Moore School of Business, Columbia (SC) 392, **740**

University of Southern California, School of Business, Los Angeles (CA) 98

University of South Florida, College of Business Administration, Tampa (FL) 138

The University of Texas at Arlington, College of Business Administration, Arlington (TX) 424, **746**

The University of Texas at Dallas, School of Management, Richardson (TX) 426, **748**

The University of Texas at San Antonio, College of Business, San Antonio (TX) 427, **750**

University of the Sacred Heart, Department of Business Administration, San Juan (PR) 387

University of the West of England, Bristol, Bristol Business School, Bristol (United Kingdom) 555

University of the Witwatersrand, Graduate School of Business Administration, Wits (South Africa) 527

University of Tulsa, College of Business Administration, Tulsa (OK) 356

University of Ulster at Jordanstown, Faculty of Business and Management, Newtown Abbey (United Kingdom) 556

University of Washington, Michael G. Foster School of Business, Seattle (WA) 452, **754**

University of Waterloo, Graduate Studies, Waterloo (Canada) 479

University of Wisconsin–Madison, Wisconsin School of Business, Madison (WI) 462, **756**

University of Wisconsin–Milwaukee, Sheldon B. Lubar School of Business, Milwaukee (WI) 463

University of Wisconsin–Oshkosh, College of Business, Oshkosh (WI) 463, **756**

Vanderbilt University, Owen Graduate School of Management, Nashville (TN) 403, **758**

Vienna University of Economics and Business Administration, WU Wien MBA, Vienna (Austria) 492

Villanova University, Villanova School of Business, Villanova (PA) 382

Virginia Commonwealth University, School of Business, Richmond (VA) 445

Virginia Polytechnic Institute and State University, Pamplin College of Business, Blacksburg (VA) 446

Washington State University Tri-Cities, College of Business, Richland (WA) 453

Wayland Baptist University, Graduate Programs, Plainview (TX) 429

Wayne State University, School of Business Administration, Detroit (MI) 247, **760**

Western International University, Graduate Programs in Business, Phoenix (AZ) 60

Western Michigan University, Haworth College of Business, Kalamazoo (MI) 248

West Texas A&M University, College of Business, Canyon (TX) 430

Widener University, School of Business Administration, Chester (PA) 384, **764**

Wilmington University, Division of Business, New Castle (DE) 117

Worcester Polytechnic Institute, Department of Management, Worcester (MA) 234, **770**

Wright State University, Raj Soin College of Business, Dayton (OH) 350

York University, Schulich School of Business, Toronto (Canada) 482, **772**

MANAGEMENT SCIENCE

The Aarhus School of Business, Faculty of Business Administration, Aarhus (Denmark) 501

Brock University, Faculty of Business, St. Catharines (Canada) 466

California State University, Fullerton, College of Business and Economics, Fullerton (CA) 70

California State University, Northridge, College of Business and Economics, Northridge (CA) 72

City University of Hong Kong, Faculty of Business, Hong Kong (China) 497

Copenhagen Business School, Faculty of Economics and Business Administration, Copenhagen (Denmark) 501

The George Washington University, School of Business, Washington (DC) 119, **622**

Hult International Business School, Graduate Program, Cambridge (MA) 227, **634**

Illinois Institute of Technology, Stuart School of Business, Chicago (IL) 164

International University of Japan, Graduate School of International Management, Minami Uonuma-gu (Japan) 516

Lancaster University, Management School, Lancaster (United Kingdom) 541

Leadership Institute of Seattle, School of Applied Behavioral Science, Kenmore (WA) 449

London School of Economics and Political Science, The Graduate School, London (United Kingdom) 543

Massachusetts Institute of Technology, Sloan School of Management, Cambridge (MA) 227

National University, School of Business and Management, La Jolla (CA) 82

Pace University, Lubin School of Business, New York (NY) 310

Regis University, College for Professional Studies, Denver (CO) 103

Rensselaer Polytechnic Institute, Lally School of Management and Technology, Troy (NY) 311, **670**

SIT Graduate Institute, Master's Programs in Intercultural Service, Leadership, and Management, Brattleboro (VT) 434

Stockholm School of Economics, Department of Business Administration, Stockholm (Sweden) 531

The University of Alabama, Manderson Graduate School of Business, Tuscaloosa (AL) 49

The University of British Columbia, Sauder School of Business, Vancouver (Canada) 474

University of California, Los Angeles, UCLA Anderson School of Management, Los Angeles (CA) 91, **696**

University of California, Riverside, A. Gary Anderson Graduate School of Management, Riverside (CA) 93, **698**

University of Detroit Mercy, College of Business Administration, Detroit (MI) 243

University of Illinois at Urbana–Champaign, College of Business, Champaign (IL) 176

University of Maryland, College Park, Robert H. Smith School of Business, College Park (MD) 217

University of Massachusetts Amherst, Isenberg School of Management, Amherst (MA) 231

University of Miami, School of Business Administration, Coral Gables (FL) 135, **718**

University of Minnesota, Twin Cities Campus, Carlson School of Management, Minneapolis (MN) 252

University of Oxford, Saïd Business School, Oxford (United Kingdom) 553

University of Salford, Salford Business School, Salford (United Kingdom) 554

University of South Carolina, Moore School of Business, Columbia (SC) *392,* **740**

The University of Tennessee, College of Business Administration, Knoxville (TN) *401,* **744**

The University of Texas at Arlington, College of Business Administration, Arlington (TX) 424, **746**

The University of Texas at San Antonio, College of Business, San Antonio (TX) 427, **750**

University of Warwick, Warwick Business School, Coventry (United Kingdom) 557

University of Waterloo, Graduate Studies, Waterloo (Canada) 479

The University of Western Ontario, Richard Ivey School of Business, London (Canada) 480

University of Windsor, Odette School of Business, Windsor (Canada) 480

University of Wisconsin–Madison, Wisconsin School of Business, Madison (WI) 462, **756**

Webster University, School of Business and Technology, St. Louis (MO) 270

Willamette University, George H. Atkinson Graduate School of Management, Salem (OR) 361, **768**

York University, Schulich School of Business, Toronto (Canada) 482, **772**

MANAGEMENT SYSTEMS ANALYSIS

Copenhagen Business School, Faculty of Economics and Business Administration, Copenhagen (Denmark) 501

Graduate School of Business Administration Zurich, Executive Management Programs, Zurich (Switzerland) 532

HfB—Business School of Finance and Management, Frankfurt School of Finance and Management, Frankfurt (Germany) 508

IE Business School, Business School, Madrid (Spain) 529, **636**

International University of Japan, Graduate School of International Management, Minami Uonuma-gu (Japan) 516

Lancaster University, Management School, Lancaster (United Kingdom) 541

Leadership Institute of Seattle, School of Applied Behavioral Science, Kenmore (WA) 449

Maine Maritime Academy, Department of Graduate Studies, Castine (ME) 210

National University of Ireland, Dublin, The Michael Smurfit Graduate School of Business, Blackrock (Ireland) 513

Penn State Great Valley, Graduate Studies, Malvern (PA) 373

Rensselaer Polytechnic Institute, Lally School of Management and Technology, Troy (NY) 311, **670**

Rivier College, Department of Business Administration, Nashua (NH) 279

Southern Illinois University Edwardsville, School of Business, Edwardsville (IL) *174*

Stockholm School of Economics, Department of Business Administration, Stockholm (Sweden) 531

Texas A&M University, Mays Business School, College Station (TX) 414

University of Salford, Salford Business School, Salford (United Kingdom) 554

The University of Texas at Arlington, College of Business Administration, Arlington (TX) 424, **746**

University of Waterloo, Graduate Studies, Waterloo (Canada) 479

Waseda University, Graduate School of Commerce, Tokyo (Japan) 517

MANAGERIAL ECONOMICS

Antioch University Santa Barbara, Program in Organizational Management, Santa Barbara (CA) 64

Barcelona Business School, Graduate Programs in Business, Barcelona (Spain) 528

The Chinese University of Hong Kong, Faculty of Business Administration, Hong Kong (China) 497

ESCP-EAP European School of Management, ESCP-EAP European School of Management (France) 503

HEC Paris, HEC MBA Program, Jouy-en-Josas (France) *505,* **632**

HfB—Business School of Finance and Management, Frankfurt School of Finance and Management, Frankfurt (Germany) 508

IE Business School, Business School, Madrid (Spain) 529, **636**

Indian School of Business, MBA Program, Andhra Pradesh (India) 512

International University of Japan, Graduate School of International Management, Minami Uonuma-gu (Japan) 516

Katholieke Universiteit Leuven, Leuven School of Business and Economics, Leuven (Belgium) 494

Lancaster University, Management School, Lancaster (United Kingdom) 541

Loyola University Chicago, Graduate School of Business, Chicago (IL) 167

Mercy College, Division of Business and Accounting, Dobbs Ferry (NY) 307

Monash University, MBA Programme, Clayton (Australia) 486

New York Institute of Technology, School of Management (NY) 308

Northwestern University, Kellogg School of Management, Evanston (IL) 171

Stockholm School of Economics, Department of Business Administration, Stockholm (Sweden) 531

University of California, Berkeley, Haas School of Business, Berkeley (CA) 89

University of California, Los Angeles, UCLA Anderson School of Management, Los Angeles (CA) 91, **696**

University of Chicago, Graduate School of Business, Chicago (IL) 175

University of Mississippi, School of Business Administration, Oxford (MS) 257

University of Salford, Salford Business School, Salford (United Kingdom) 554

The University of Texas at Dallas, School of Management, Richardson (TX) *426,* **748**

University of Washington, Michael G. Foster School of Business, Seattle (WA) 452, **754**

Wayne State University, School of Business Administration, Detroit (MI) 247, **760**

MANPOWER ADMINISTRATION

California National University for Advanced Studies, College of Business Administration, Northridge (CA) 67

National University, School of Business and Management, La Jolla (CA) 82

Naval Postgraduate School, School of Business and Public Policy, Monterey (CA) 83

Southern Illinois University Edwardsville, School of Business, Edwardsville (IL) *174*

University of Salford, Salford Business School, Salford (United Kingdom) 554

University of the West of England, Bristol, Bristol Business School, Bristol (United Kingdom) 555

MANUFACTURING MANAGEMENT

California Polytechnic State University, San Luis Obispo, Orfalea College of Business, San Luis Obispo (CA) 68

Instituto Tecnológico y de Estudios Superiores de Monterrey, Campus Ciudad Juárez, Program in Business Administration, Ciudad Juárez (Mexico) 520

International University of Japan, Graduate School of International Management, Minami Uonuma-gu (Japan) 516

Kettering University, Graduate School, Flint (MI) 238

Lawrence Technological University, College of Management, Southfield (MI) 239, **654**

McGill University, Desautels Faculty of Management, Montréal (Canada) 469, **658**

Michigan State University, Eli Broad Graduate School of Management, East Lansing (MI) 240

National University of Ireland, Dublin, The Michael Smurfit Graduate School of Business, Blackrock (Ireland) 513

Northwestern University, Kellogg School of Management, Evanston (IL) 171

OGI School of Science & Engineering at Oregon Health & Science University, Department of Management in Science and Technology, Beaverton (OR) 358

Penn State University Park, The Mary Jean and Frank P. Smeal College of Business Administration, State College (PA) 374

Purdue University, Krannert School of Management, West Lafayette (IN) 185

Rensselaer Polytechnic Institute, Lally School of Management and Technology, Troy (NY) 311, **670**

Rochester Institute of Technology, E. Philip Saunders College of Business, Rochester (NY) 312

Stockholm School of Economics, Department of Business Administration, Stockholm (Sweden) 531

Texas A&M University, Mays Business School, College Station (TX) 414

University at Buffalo, the State University of New York, School of Management, Buffalo (NY) 320

The University of Alabama, Manderson Graduate School of Business, Tuscaloosa (AL) 49

University of Applied Sciences Esslingen, Graduate School, Esslingen (Germany) 510

MARKETING

DeSales University, Department of Business, Center Valley (PA) 365

DeVry University, Keller Graduate School of Management, Alpharetta (GA) 144

DeVry University, Keller Graduate School of Management, Oakbrook Terrace (IL) 161, **650**

DeVry University, Keller Graduate School of Management, Arlington (VA) 437

Dominican University, Edward A. and Lois L. Brennan School of Business, River Forest (IL) 162, **600**

Drexel University, LeBow College of Business, Philadelphia (PA) 366

Duke University, The Fuqua School of Business, Durham (NC) 323

Duquesne University, John F. Donahue Graduate School of Business, Pittsburgh (PA) 367

EADA International Management Development Center, Business Programs, Barcelona (Spain) 528

Eastern Mennonite University, Program in Business Administration, Harrisonburg (VA) 438

Eastern Michigan University, College of Business, Ypsilanti (MI) 237

Eastern Washington University, College of Business and Public Administration, Cheney (WA) 448

École Nationale des Ponts et Chaussées, ENPC MBA, Paris (France) 503

Edgewood College, Program in Business, Madison (WI) 458

Edith Cowan University, Faculty of Business and Public Management, Churchlands (Australia) 484

Elon University, Martha and Spencer Love School of Business, Elon (NC) 324

Emory University, Roberto C. Goizueta Business School, Atlanta (GA) 145, **606**

ESCP-EAP European School of Management, ESCP-EAP European School of Management (France) 503

Escuela de Administracion de Negocios para Graduados, Programa Magister—MBA Programs, Lima (Peru) 525

European School of Economics, MBA Programme (NY) 301, **608**

European School of Economics, MBA Programme (Italy) 515, **608**

European School of Economics, MBA Programme, Milan (Italy) 515, **608**

European School of Economics, MBA Programme (United Kingdom) 541, **608**

European University, Center for Management Studies, Montreux-Fontanivent (Switzerland) 532

Fairfield University, Charles F. Dolan School of Business, Fairfield (CT) 109

Fairleigh Dickinson University, College at Florham, Silberman College of Business, Madison (NJ) 282, **612**

Fairleigh Dickinson University, Metropolitan Campus, Silberman College of Business, Teaneck (NJ) 282, **612**

Florida Atlantic University, College of Business, Boca Raton (FL) 126

Florida Gulf Coast University, Lutgert College of Business, Fort Myers (FL) 127

Florida International University, Alvah H. Chapman, Jr. Graduate School of Business, Miami (FL) 128, **618**

Florida State University, College of Business, Tallahassee (FL) 129

Fordham University, Graduate School of Business Administration, New York (NY) 301, **620**

Gannon University, School of Business, Erie (PA) 368

George Mason University, School of Management, Fairfax (VA) 438

The George Washington University, School of Business, Washington (DC) 119, **622**

Georgia Institute of Technology, College of Management, Atlanta (GA) 146, **624**

Georgian Court University, School of Business, Lakewood (NJ) 283

Georgia State University, J. Mack Robinson College of Business, Atlanta (GA) 147, **626**

Golden Gate University, Ageno School of Business, San Francisco (CA) 78

Goldey-Beacom College, Graduate Program, Wilmington (DE) 116

Gonzaga University, School of Business Administration, Spokane (WA) 448

Governors State University, College of Business and Public Administration, University Park (IL) 164

Graduate School of Business Administration Zurich, Executive Management Programs, Zurich (Switzerland) 532

Grand Canyon University, College of Business, Phoenix (AZ) 56

The Hague University, Faculty of Economics and Management, The Hague (Netherlands) 521, **628**

Hawai'i Pacific University, College of Business Administration, Honolulu (HI) 153, **630**

HEC Montreal, Master's Program in Business Administration and Management, Montréal (Canada) 468

HEC Paris, HEC MBA Program, Jouy-en-Josas (France) *505*, **632**

Hofstra University, Frank G. Zarb School of Business, Hempstead (NY) 302

Holy Names University, Department of Business, Oakland (CA) 79

Hong Kong Baptist University, School of Business, Hong Kong (China) 498

Hood College, Department of Economics and Management, Frederick (MD) 214

Howard University, School of Business, Washington (DC) 120

Hult International Business School, Graduate Program, Cambridge (MA) 227, **634**

Idaho State University, College of Business, Pocatello (ID) 156

IE Business School, Business School, Madrid (Spain) 529, **636**

Illinois Institute of Technology, Stuart School of Business, Chicago (IL) 164

Illinois State University, College of Business, Normal (IL) 165, **638**

Indiana Tech, Program in Business Administration, Fort Wayne (IN) 181

Indiana University Bloomington, Kelley School of Business, Bloomington (IN) 182

Indiana University–Purdue University Indianapolis, Kelley School of Business, Indianapolis (IN) 184

Indian School of Business, MBA Program, Andhra Pradesh (India) 512

Instituto Tecnológico y de Estudios Superiores de Monterrey, Campus Ciudad Juárez, Program in Business Administration, Ciudad Juárez (Mexico) 520

Inter American University of Puerto Rico, San Germán Campus, Department of Business Administration, San Germán (PR) 385

International University in Geneva, MBA Program, Geneva (Switzerland) 533, **640**

International University of Japan, Graduate School of International Management, Minami Uonuma-gu (Japan) 516

Iona College, Hagan School of Business, New Rochelle (NY) 303, **642**

Iowa State University of Science and Technology, College of Business, Ames (IA) 189, **644**

John Carroll University, John M. and Mary Jo Boler School of Business, University Heights (OH) 342

The Johns Hopkins University, Carey Business School, Baltimore (MD) 214, **646**

Johnson & Wales University, The Alan Shawn Feinstein Graduate School, Providence (RI) 388, **648**

Kean University, College of Business and Public Administration, Union (NJ) 284

Kent State University, Graduate School of Management, Kent (OH) 342

Kingston University, Kingston Business School, Kingston upon Thames (United Kingdom) 541

Kutztown University of Pennsylvania, College of Business, Kutztown (PA) 369

Lakeland College, Graduate Studies Division, Sheboygan (WI) 459

Lancaster University, Management School, Lancaster (United Kingdom) 541

La Salle University, School of Business, Philadelphia (PA) 370

Lehigh University, College of Business and Economics, Bethlehem (PA) 371, **656**

LeTourneau University, Graduate and Professional Studies, Longview (TX) 409

Lewis University, College of Business, Romeoville (IL) 166

Lindenwood University, Division of Management, St. Charles (MO) 261

Long Island University, Brooklyn Campus, School of Business, Public Administration and Information Sciences, Brooklyn (NY) 304

Louisiana State University and Agricultural and Mechanical College, E. J. Ourso College of Business, Baton Rouge (LA) 204

Louisiana Tech University, College of Administration and Business, Ruston (LA) 205

Loyola College in Maryland, Sellinger School of Business and Management, Baltimore (MD) 215

Loyola Marymount University, College of Business Administration, Los Angeles (CA) 81

Loyola University Chicago, Graduate School of Business, Chicago (IL) 167

Lynn University, School of Business, Boca Raton (FL) 130

Macquarie University, Macquarie Graduate School of Management, Sydney (Australia) 485

Madonna University, School of Business, Livonia (MI) 240

Marquette University, Graduate School of Management, Milwaukee (WI) 459

Marylhurst University, Department of Business Administration, Marylhurst (OR) 357

Marymount University, School of Business Administration, Arlington (VA) 440

Maryville University of Saint Louis, The John E. Simon School of Business, St. Louis (MO) 262

McGill University, Desautels Faculty of Management, Montréal (Canada) 469, **658**

McMaster University, DeGroote School of Business, Hamilton (Canada) 470

Memorial University of Newfoundland, Faculty of Business Administration, St. John's (Canada) 470

Mercy College, Division of Business and Accounting, Dobbs Ferry (NY) 307

Metropolitan State University, College of Management, St. Paul (MN) 250

Michigan State University, Eli Broad Graduate School of Management, East Lansing (MI) 240

Millsaps College, Else School of Management, Jackson (MS) 255

Mills College, Graduate School of Business, Oakland (CA) 81

Milwaukee School of Engineering, Rader School of Business, Milwaukee (WI) 460

Misericordia University, Division of Behavioral Science, Education, and Business, Dallas (PA) 372

Missouri State University, College of Business Administration, Springfield (MO) *262*

Monash University, MBA Programme, Clayton (Australia) 486

Montclair State University, School of Business, Montclair (NJ) 285

Monterey Institute of International Studies, Fisher Graduate School of International Business, Monterey (CA) 82, **660**

Mount St. Mary's University, Program in Business Administration, Emmitsburg (MD) 215

Murray State University, College of Business and Public Affairs, Murray (KY) 200

Nanjing University, School of Business, Nanjing (China) 500

Nanyang Technological University, Nanyang Business School, Singapore (Singapore) 527, **662**

National University, School of Business and Management, La Jolla (CA) 82

National University of Ireland, Dublin, The Michael Smurfit Graduate School of Business, Blackrock (Ireland) 513

New Jersey Institute of Technology, School of Management, Newark (NJ) 285

New York Institute of Technology, School of Management (NY) 308

New York University, Leonard N. Stern School of Business (NY) 309

North Carolina State University, College of Management, Raleigh (NC) 328, **664**

North Central College, Department of Business, Naperville (IL) *168*

North Dakota State University, College of Business, Fargo (ND) 335

Northeastern University, Graduate School of Business Administration, Boston (MA) 228

Northern Arizona University, College of Business Administration, Flagstaff (AZ) 57

Northern Kentucky University, College of Business, Highland Heights (KY) 201

North Park University, School of Business and Nonprofit Management, Chicago (IL) 170

Northwestern Polytechnic University, School of Business and Information Technology, Fremont (CA) 84

Northwestern University, Kellogg School of Management, Evanston (IL) 171

Norwegian School of Management, Graduate School, Sandvika (Norway) 524

Notre Dame de Namur University, Department of Business Administration, Belmont (CA) 84

Nottingham Trent University, Nottingham Business School, Nottingham (United Kingdom) 544

Nova Southeastern University, H. Wayne Huizenga School of Business and Entrepreneurship, Fort Lauderdale (FL) 130, **666**

Nyack College, School of Business, Nyack (NY) 310

Nyenrode Business Universiteit, Netherlands Business School, Breukelen (Netherlands) 522

Oakland University, School of Business Administration, Rochester (MI) 241

OGI School of Science & Engineering at Oregon Health & Science University, Department of Management in Science and Technology, Beaverton (OR) 358

The Ohio State University, Max M. Fisher College of Business, Columbus (OH) 344

Oklahoma City University, Meinders School of Business, Oklahoma City (OK) 352

Oklahoma Wesleyan University, Professional Studies Division, Bartlesville (OK) 353

Oral Roberts University, School of Business, Tulsa (OK) 353

Ottawa University, Graduate Studies-Arizona (AZ) 57

Pace University, Lubin School of Business, New York (NY) 310

Palm Beach Atlantic University, Rinker School of Business, West Palm Beach (FL) 131

Penn State Great Valley, Graduate Studies, Malvern (PA) 373

Penn State University Park, The Mary Jean and Frank P. Smeal College of Business Administration, State College (PA) 374

Pepperdine University, Graziadio School of Business and Management, Los Angeles (CA) 85

Philadelphia University, School of Business Administration, Philadelphia (PA) 375, **668**

Pontifical Catholic University of Puerto Rico, College of Business Administration, Ponce (PR) 386

Portland State University, School of Business Administration, Portland (OR) 358

Providence College, School of Business, Providence (RI) 388

Purdue University, Krannert School of Management, West Lafayette (IN) 185

Queensland University of Technology, Brisbane Graduate School of Business, Brisbane (Australia) 487

Queens University of Charlotte, McColl Graduate School of Business, Charlotte (NC) 329

Quinnipiac University, School of Business, Hamden (CT) 109

Regis University, College for Professional Studies, Denver (CO) 103

Rensselaer Polytechnic Institute, Lally School of Management and Technology, Troy (NY) 311, **670**

Rice University, Jesse H. Jones Graduate School of Management, Houston (TX) 410

Rider University, College of Business Administration, Lawrenceville (NJ) 287

Rivier College, Department of Business Administration, Nashua (NH) 279

Roberts Wesleyan College, Division of Business, Rochester (NY) 312

Rochester Institute of Technology, E. Philip Saunders College of Business, Rochester (NY) 312

Rockford College, Program in Business Administration, Rockford (IL) 171

Rockhurst University, Helzberg School of Management, Kansas City (MO) 264

Rollins College, Crummer Graduate School of Business, Winter Park (FL) 131, **674**

Roosevelt University, Walter E. Heller College of Business Administration, Chicago (IL) 172, **676**

Rouen School of Management, Postgraduate Programmes, Mount Saint Aignan (France) 505

Rowan University, William G. Rohrer College of Business, Glassboro (NJ) 287

Rutgers, The State University of New Jersey, Rutgers Business School–Newark and New Brunswick, Newark and New Brunswick (NJ) 288, **678**

Rutgers, The State University of New Jersey, Camden, School of Business, Camden (NJ) 288

Sage Graduate School, Department of Management, Troy (NY) 313

St. Ambrose University, Program in Business Administration, Davenport (IA) 190

St. Bonaventure University, School of Business, St. Bonaventure (NY) 313

St. Edward's University, The School of Management and Business, Austin (TX) 410

Saint Francis University, Master of Business Administration Program, Loretto (PA) 377

St. John's University, The Peter J. Tobin College of Business, Queens (NY) 314, **680**

Saint Joseph's University, Erivan K. Haub School of Business, Philadelphia (PA) 377

Saint Louis University, John Cook School of Business, St. Louis (MO) *264*

Saint Mary's University of Minnesota, Schools of Graduate and Professional Programs, Winona (MN) 251

Saint Michael's College, Program in Administration and Management, Colchester (VT) 434

Saint Peter's College, MBA Programs, Jersey City (NJ) 289, **682**

Saints Cyril and Methodius University, Faculty of Economics, Skopje (Macedonia) 519

St. Thomas Aquinas College, Division of Business Administration, Sparkill (NY) 315

Saint Xavier University, Graham School of Management, Chicago (IL) 173

Salem State College, Program in Business Administration, Salem (MA) 229

San Diego State University, College of Business Administration, San Diego (CA) 86

San Francisco State University, College of Business, San Francisco (CA) 87

Santa Clara University, Leavey School of Business, Santa Clara (CA) 88

Seattle University, Albers School of Business and Economics, Seattle (WA) 451

Seton Hall University, Stillman School of Business, South Orange (NJ) 290, **686**

Southeastern Louisiana University, College of Business, Hammond (LA) 207

Southeastern University, College of Graduate Studies, Washington (DC) 121

Southern Adventist University, School of Business and Management, Collegedale (TN) 398

Southern Cross University, Graduate College of Management, Coffs Harbour (Australia) 487

Southern Illinois University Carbondale, College of Business and Administration, Carbondale (IL) 173

Southern Illinois University Edwardsville, School of Business, Edwardsville (IL) *174*

Southern Methodist University, Cox School of Business, Dallas (TX) 411, **688**

Southern New Hampshire University, School of Business, Manchester (NH) 279, **690**

Southern Polytechnic State University, Department of Business Administration, Marietta (GA) 150

State University of New York at Binghamton, School of Management, Binghamton (NY) 315

State University of New York Institute of Technology, School of Business, Utica (NY) 317

Stockholm School of Economics, Department of Business Administration, Stockholm (Sweden) 531

Stony Brook University, State University of New York, W. Averell Harriman School for Management and Policy, Stony Brook (NY) 317

Stratford University, Graduate Business Programs, Falls Church (VA) 443

Suffolk University, Sawyer Business School, Boston (MA) 230

Swinburne University of Technology, Australian Graduate School of Entrepreneurship (AGSE), Hawthorne (Australia) 488

Syracuse University, Martin J. Whitman School of Management, Syracuse (NY) 318, **692**

Tarleton State University, College of Business Administration, Stephenville (TX) 413

Temple University, Fox School of Business and Management, Philadelphia (PA) 379

Texas A&M International University, College of Business Administration, Laredo (TX) 414

Texas A&M University, Mays Business School, College Station (TX) 414

Texas Christian University, The Neeley School of Business at TCU, Fort Worth (TX) 416, **694**

Texas Tech University, Jerry S. Rawls College of Business Administration, Lubbock (TX) 418

Tulane University, A. B. Freeman School of Business, New Orleans (LA) 207

Universite Libre de Bruxelles, Solvay Business School, Brussels (Belgium) 495

University at Albany, State University of New York, School of Business, Albany (NY) 319

University at Buffalo, the State University of New York, School of Management, Buffalo (NY) 320

University of Abertay Dundee, Dundee Business School, Dundee (United Kingdom) 547

The University of Adelaide, The University of Adelaide Business School, Adelaide (Australia) 488

The University of Akron, College of Business Administration, Akron (OH) 346

The University of Alabama, Manderson Graduate School of Business, Tuscaloosa (AL) 49

The University of Arizona, Eller College of Management, Tucson (AZ) 58

University of Arkansas, Sam M. Walton College of Business Administration, Fayetteville (AR) 62

University of Baltimore, Merrick School of Business, Baltimore (MD) 216

University of Baltimore/Towson University, Joint University of Baltimore/Towson University (UB/Towson) MBA Program, Baltimore (MD) 217

University of Bath, School of Management, Bath (United Kingdom) 547

University of Bridgeport, School of Business, Bridgeport (CT) 111

The University of British Columbia, Sauder School of Business, Vancouver (Canada) 474

University of Calgary, Haskayne School of Business, Calgary (Canada) 474

University of California, Berkeley, Haas School of Business, Berkeley (CA) 89

University of California, Davis, Graduate School of Management, Davis (CA) 90

University of California, Los Angeles, UCLA Anderson School of Management, Los Angeles (CA) 91, **696**

University of California, Riverside, A. Gary Anderson Graduate School of Management, Riverside (CA) 93, **698**

University of Canterbury, Department of Management, Christchurch (New Zealand) 523

University of Central Florida, College of Business Administration, Orlando (FL) 133

University of Central Missouri, Harmon College of Business Administration, Warrensburg (MO) 266

University of Chicago, Graduate School of Business, Chicago (IL) 175

University of Cincinnati, College of Business, Cincinnati (OH) 346

University of Colorado at Boulder, Leeds School of Business, Boulder (CO) 104, **702**

University of Colorado at Colorado Springs, Graduate School of Business Administration, Colorado Springs (CO) 105, **704**

University of Colorado Denver, Business School, Denver (CO) 105, **706**

University of Connecticut, School of Business, Storrs (CT) 112, **708**

University of Dallas, Graduate School of Management, Irving (TX) 420, **710**

University of Dayton, School of Business Administration, Dayton (OH) 347

University of Delaware, Alfred Lerner College of Business and Economics, Newark (DE) 116, **712**

University of Denver, Daniels College of Business, Denver (CO) 106

University of Detroit Mercy, College of Business Administration, Detroit (MI) 243

University of Durham, Durham Business School, Durham (United Kingdom) 549

University of Edinburgh, Edinburgh University Management School, Edinburgh (United Kingdom) 550

The University of Findlay, College of Business, Findlay (OH) 348

University of Florida, Hough Graduate School of Business, Gainesville (FL) 134

University of Georgia, Terry College of Business, Athens (GA) 151

University of Glasgow, University of Glasgow Business School, Glasgow (United Kingdom) 550

University of Hartford, Barney School of Business, West Hartford (CT) 113

University of Hawaii at Manoa, Shidler College of Business, Honolulu (HI) 154

University of Houston–Clear Lake, School of Business, Houston (TX) 421

University of Houston–Victoria, School of Business Administration, Victoria (TX) 421

University of Hull, School of Management, Hull (United Kingdom) 552

University of Illinois at Chicago, Liautaud Graduate School of Business, Chicago (IL) 176

University of Illinois at Urbana–Champaign, College of Business, Champaign (IL) 176

University of Indianapolis, Graduate Business Programs, Indianapolis (IN) 186

University of Kansas, School of Business, Lawrence (KS) 196

University of Kentucky, Gatton College of Business and Economics, Lexington (KY) 202, **716**

University of La Verne, College of Business and Public Management, La Verne (CA) 94

University of Louisiana at Lafayette, Graduate School, Lafayette (LA) 208

University of Malaya, Graduate School of Business, Kuala Lumpur (Malaysia) 519

University of Manitoba, Faculty of Management, Winnipeg (Canada) 475

University of Maryland, College Park, Robert H. Smith School of Business, College Park (MD) 217

University of Massachusetts Amherst, Isenberg School of Management, Amherst (MA) 231

University of Massachusetts Boston, College of Management, Boston (MA) 232

University of Melbourne, Melbourne Business School, Melbourne (Australia) 488

University of Miami, School of Business Administration, Coral Gables (FL) 135, **718**

University of Michigan, Ross School of Business at the University of Michigan, Ann Arbor (MI) 244

University of Michigan–Dearborn, School of Management, Dearborn (MI) 245

University of Minnesota, Twin Cities Campus, Carlson School of Management, Minneapolis (MN) 252

University of Mississippi, School of Business Administration, Oxford (MS) 257

University of Missouri–Columbia, Robert J. Trulaske, Sr. College of Business, Columbia (MO) 267, **720**

University of Missouri–Kansas City, Henry W. Bloch School of Business and Public Administration, Kansas City (MO) 267

University of Missouri–St. Louis, College of Business Administration, St. Louis (MO) *268*

University of Nebraska–Lincoln, College of Business Administration, Lincoln (NE) 274

University of Nevada, Las Vegas, College of Business, Las Vegas (NV) 275, **722**

University of Newcastle, Graduate School of Business, Callaghan (Australia) 489

The University of New England, The Graduate School of Business Administration, Armidale (Australia) 490

University of New Haven, School of Business, West Haven (CT) 113, **728**

University of New Mexico, Robert O. Anderson Graduate School of Management, Albuquerque (NM) 294

University of New Orleans, College of Business Administration, New Orleans (LA) 209

University of North Alabama, College of Business, Florence (AL) 52

The University of North Carolina at Chapel Hill, Kenan-Flagler Business School, Chapel Hill (NC) 330

The University of North Carolina at Charlotte, Belk College of Business Administration, Charlotte (NC) 330, **730**

The University of North Carolina Wilmington, School of Business, Wilmington (NC) 332

University of North Florida, Coggin College of Business, Jacksonville (FL) 136

University of North Texas, College of Business Administration, Denton (TX) 422

University of Notre Dame, Mendoza College of Business, Notre Dame (IN) 187

University of Pennsylvania, Wharton School, Philadelphia (PA) 380

University of Phoenix, College of Graduate Business and Management, Phoenix (AZ) 59

University of Phoenix–Bay Area Campus, College of Graduate Business and Management, Pleasanton (CA) 94

University of Phoenix–Central Florida Campus, College of Graduate Business and Management, Maitland (FL) 137

University of Phoenix–Cincinnati Campus, College of Graduate Business and Management, West Chester (OH) 348

University of Phoenix–Cleveland Campus, College of Graduate Business and Management, Independence (OH) 348

University of Phoenix–Columbus Georgia Campus, College of Graduate Business and Management, Columbus (GA) 152

York College of Pennsylvania, Department of Business Administration, York (PA) 385

York University, Schulich School of Business, Toronto (Canada) 482, **772**

Youngstown State University, Warren P. Williamson Jr. College of Business Administration, Youngstown (OH) 351

MARKETING RESEARCH

The American University in Cairo, School of Business, Economics and Communication, Cairo (Egypt) 502

Arizona State University at the West campus, School of Global Management and Leadership, Phoenix (AZ) 55

Aston University, Aston Business School, Birmingham (United Kingdom) 539

Bernard M. Baruch College of the City University of New York, Zicklin School of Business, New York (NY) 296

The Chinese University of Hong Kong, Faculty of Business Administration, Hong Kong (China) 497

Clemson University, College of Business and Behavioral Science, Clemson (SC) 391

Copenhagen Business School, Faculty of Economics and Business Administration, Copenhagen (Denmark) 501

DePaul University, Charles H. Kellstadt Graduate School of Business, Chicago (IL) 159

Edith Cowan University, Faculty of Business and Public Management, Churchlands (Australia) 484

European School of Economics, MBA Programme (Italy) 515, **608**

The George Washington University, School of Business, Washington (DC) 119, **622**

Graduate School of Business Administration Zurich, Executive Management Programs, Zurich (Switzerland) 532

Hofstra University, Frank G. Zarb School of Business, Hempstead (NY) 302

Illinois Institute of Technology, Stuart School of Business, Chicago (IL) 164

International University of Japan, Graduate School of International Management, Minami Uonuma-gu (Japan) 516

Lancaster University, Management School, Lancaster (United Kingdom) 541

Mercy College, Division of Business and Accounting, Dobbs Ferry (NY) 307

Monash University, MBA Programme, Clayton (Australia) 486

National University of Ireland, Dublin, The Michael Smurfit Graduate School of Business, Blackrock (Ireland) 513

Rochester Institute of Technology, E. Philip Saunders College of Business, Rochester (NY) 312

Southern Illinois University Edwardsville, School of Business, Edwardsville (IL) *174*

Stockholm School of Economics, Department of Business Administration, Stockholm (Sweden) 531

Swinburne University of Technology, Australian Graduate School of Entrepreneurship (AGSE), Hawthorne (Australia) 488

Texas A&M University, Mays Business School, College Station (TX) 414

The University of Alabama, Manderson Graduate School of Business, Tuscaloosa (AL) 49

The University of Arizona, Eller College of Management, Tucson (AZ) 58

University of Bath, School of Management, Bath (United Kingdom) 547

University of Denver, Daniels College of Business, Denver (CO) 106

University of Georgia, Terry College of Business, Athens (GA) 151

University of Newcastle, Graduate School of Business, Callaghan (Australia) 489

University of Rochester, William E. Simon Graduate School of Business Administration, Rochester (NY) 321, **736**

University of Salford, Salford Business School, Salford (United Kingdom) 554

The University of Texas at Arlington, College of Business Administration, Arlington (TX) 424, **746**

University of the West of England, Bristol, Bristol Business School, Bristol (United Kingdom) 555

University of Wisconsin–Madison, Wisconsin School of Business, Madison (WI) 462, **756**

Vienna University of Economics and Business Administration, WU Wien MBA, Vienna (Austria) 492

MATERIALS MANAGEMENT

Maine Maritime Academy, Department of Graduate Studies, Castine (ME) 210

University of Georgia, Terry College of Business, Athens (GA) 151

University of Salford, Salford Business School, Salford (United Kingdom) 554

Webster University, School of Business and Technology, St. Louis (MO) 270

MEDIA ADMINISTRATION

The Aarhus School of Business, Faculty of Business Administration, Aarhus (Denmark) 501

Columbia University, Graduate School of Business, New York (NY) 298

Copenhagen Business School, Faculty of Economics and Business Administration, Copenhagen (Denmark) 501

Fordham University, Graduate School of Business Administration, New York (NY) 301, **620**

Lynn University, School of Business, Boca Raton (FL) 130

New York University, Leonard N. Stern School of Business (NY) 309

Northwestern University, Kellogg School of Management, Evanston (IL) 171

St. Edward's University, The School of Management and Business, Austin (TX) 410

Schiller International University, Graduate Programs, London (United Kingdom) 546, **684**

Stockholm School of Economics, Department of Business Administration, Stockholm (Sweden) 531

Syracuse University, Martin J. Whitman School of Management, Syracuse (NY) 318, **692**

Webster University, School of Business and Technology, St. Louis (MO) 270

MEDICINE

Boston University, School of Management, Boston (MA) 223

Drexel University, LeBow College of Business, Philadelphia (PA) 366

The Johns Hopkins University, Carey Business School, Baltimore (MD) 214, **646**

Monash University, MBA Programme, Clayton (Australia) 486

Northeastern University, Graduate School of Business Administration, Boston (MA) 228

Vienna University of Economics and Business Administration, WU Wien MBA, Vienna (Austria) 492

NEW VENTURE MANAGEMENT

Barcelona Business School, Graduate Programs in Business, Barcelona (Spain) 528

Clarkson University, School of Business, Potsdam (NY) 297

The George Washington University, School of Business, Washington (DC) 119, **622**

Indiana University–Purdue University Indianapolis, Kelley School of Business, Indianapolis (IN) 184

International University of Japan, Graduate School of International Management, Minami Uonuma-gu (Japan) 516

Lancaster University, Management School, Lancaster (United Kingdom) 541

Massachusetts Institute of Technology, Sloan School of Management, Cambridge (MA) 227

Monash University, MBA Programme, Clayton (Australia) 486

National University, School of Business and Management, La Jolla (CA) 82

Northeastern University, Graduate School of Business Administration, Boston (MA) 228

OGI School of Science & Engineering at Oregon Health & Science University, Department of Management in Science and Technology, Beaverton (OR) 358

Penn State Great Valley, Graduate Studies, Malvern (PA) 373

Queensland University of Technology, Brisbane Graduate School of Business, Brisbane (Australia) 487

Rensselaer Polytechnic Institute, Lally School of Management and Technology, Troy (NY) 311, **670**

Stockholm School of Economics, Department of Business Administration, Stockholm (Sweden) 531

Swinburne University of Technology, Australian Graduate School of Entrepreneurship (AGSE), Hawthorne (Australia) 488

Texas A&M University, Mays Business School, College Station (TX) 414

University at Albany, State University of New York, School of Business, Albany (NY) 319

University of California, Berkeley, Haas School of Business, Berkeley (CA) 89

University of California, Los Angeles, UCLA Anderson School of Management, Los Angeles (CA) 91, **696**

University of California, San Diego, Rady School of Management, La Jolla (CA) 93, **700**

University of Nevada, Las Vegas, College of Business, Las Vegas (NV) 275, **722**

University of New Brunswick Saint John, Faculty of Business, Saint John (Canada) 476, **724**

The University of North Carolina at Chapel Hill, Kenan-Flagler Business School, Chapel Hill (NC) 330

University of St. Thomas, Opus College of Business (MN) 253, **738**

University of San Diego, School of Business Administration, San Diego (CA) 96

University of Southern California, School of Business, Los Angeles (CA) 98

Vienna University of Economics and Business Administration, WU Wien MBA, Vienna (Austria) 492

Worcester Polytechnic Institute, Department of Management, Worcester (MA) 234, **770**

NONPROFIT MANAGEMENT

American Jewish University, David Lieber School of Graduate Studies, Bel Air (CA) 63

Andrews University, School of Business, Berrien Springs (MI) 235

Antioch University New England, Department of Organization and Management, Keene (NH) 277

Antioch University Santa Barbara, Program in Organizational Management, Santa Barbara (CA) 64

Aston University, Aston Business School, Birmingham (United Kingdom) 539

Boston University, School of Management, Boston (MA) 223

Brandeis University, The Heller School for Social Policy and Management (MA) 223

Brigham Young University, Marriott School of Management, Provo (UT) 431

Case Western Reserve University, Weatherhead School of Management, Cleveland (OH) 338

Cleary University, Program in Business Administration, Ann Arbor (MI) 236

The College of Saint Rose, School of Business, Albany (NY) 298, **594**

Columbia University, Graduate School of Business, New York (NY) 298

DeVry University, Keller Graduate School of Management, Alpharetta (GA) 144

Drake University, College of Business and Public Administration, Des Moines (IA) 189

Eastern Michigan University, College of Business, Ypsilanti (MI) 237

Eastern University, Graduate Business Programs, St. Davids (PA) 368

Eastern Washington University, College of Business and Public Administration, Cheney (WA) 448

Gannon University, School of Business, Erie (PA) 368

The George Washington University, School of Business, Washington (DC) 119, **622**

Hope International University, Program in Business Administration, Fullerton (CA) 79

IE Business School, Business School, Madrid (Spain) 529, **636**

Illinois Institute of Technology, Stuart School of Business, Chicago (IL) 164

Kean University, College of Business and Public Administration, Union (NJ) 284

Lawrence Technological University, College of Management, Southfield (MI) 239, **654**

Leadership Institute of Seattle, School of Applied Behavioral Science, Kenmore (WA) 449

Lipscomb University, MBA Program, Nashville (TN) 397

London School of Economics and Political Science, The Graduate School, London (United Kingdom) 543

Madonna University, School of Business, Livonia (MI) 240

Marylhurst University, Department of Business Administration, Marylhurst (OR) 357

Mills College, Graduate School of Business, Oakland (CA) 81

Monterey Institute of International Studies, Fisher Graduate School of International Business, Monterey (CA) 82, **660**

New England College, Program in Management, Henniker (NH) 278

New Mexico Highlands University, School of Business, Las Vegas (NM) 293

The New School: A University, Milano The New School for Management and Urban Policy, New York (NY) 308

New York University, Robert F. Wagner Graduate School of Public Service (NY) 309

North Park University, School of Business and Nonprofit Management, Chicago (IL) 170

Northwestern University, Kellogg School of Management, Evanston (IL) 171

Oral Roberts University, School of Business, Tulsa (OK) 353

Otterbein College, Department of Business, Accounting and Economics, Westerville (OH) 345

Queensland University of Technology, Brisbane Graduate School of Business, Brisbane (Australia) 487

Regis University, College for Professional Studies, Denver (CO) 103

Robert Morris University, Program in Business Administration, Moon Township (PA) 376, **672**

Roosevelt University, Walter E. Heller College of Business Administration, Chicago (IL) 172, **676**

Saint Joseph's University, Erivan K. Haub School of Business, Philadelphia (PA) 377

Saint Michael's College, Program in Administration and Management, Colchester (VT) 434

Saint Xavier University, Graham School of Management, Chicago (IL) 173

SIT Graduate Institute, Master's Programs in Intercultural Service, Leadership, and Management, Brattleboro (VT) 434

Southeastern University, College of Graduate Studies, Washington (DC) 121

Suffolk University, Sawyer Business School, Boston (MA) 230

Swinburne University of Technology, Australian Graduate School of Entrepreneurship (AGSE), Hawthorne (Australia) 488

University of Bath, School of Management, Bath (United Kingdom) 547

University of California, Berkeley, Haas School of Business, Berkeley (CA) 89

University of California, Los Angeles, UCLA Anderson School of Management, Los Angeles (CA) 91, **696**

University of Dallas, Graduate School of Management, Irving (TX) 420, **710**

University of Edinburgh, Edinburgh University Management School, Edinburgh (United Kingdom) 550

University of Geneva, MBA Program, Geneva (Switzerland) 535

University of Maine, The Maine Business School, Orono (ME) 211

University of Massachusetts Boston, College of Management, Boston (MA) 232

University of Missouri–Columbia, Robert J. Trulaske, Sr. College of Business, Columbia (MO) 267, **720**

The University of New England, The Graduate School of Business Administration, Armidale (Australia) 490

University of New Mexico, Robert O. Anderson Graduate School of Management, Albuquerque (NM) 294

University of Notre Dame, Mendoza College of Business, Notre Dame (IN) 187

University of St. Thomas, Opus College of Business (MN) 253, **738**

University of Salford, Salford Business School, Salford (United Kingdom) 554

The University of Tampa, John H. Sykes College of Business, Tampa (FL) 139, **742**

University of the West, Department of Business Administration, Rosemead (CA) 99

Vienna University of Economics and Business Administration, WU Wien MBA, Vienna (Austria) 492

Whitworth University, School of Global Commerce and Management, Spokane (WA) 455

Willamette University, George H. Atkinson Graduate School of Management, Salem (OR) 361, **768**

Yale University, Yale School of Management, New Haven (CT) 114

York University, Schulich School of Business, Toronto (Canada) 482, **772**

NONPROFIT ORGANIZATION

Alvernia College, Department of Business, Reading (PA) 361

American Jewish University, David Lieber School of Graduate Studies, Bel Air (CA) 63

Antioch University Santa Barbara, Program in Organizational Management, Santa Barbara (CA) 64

Carlos Albizu University, Miami Campus, Graduate Programs, Miami (FL) 123

Concordia University Wisconsin, Graduate Programs, Mequon (WI) 458

Eastern Washington University, College of Business and Public Administration, Cheney (WA) 448

The Hague University, Faculty of Economics and Management, The Hague (Netherlands) 521, **628**

IE Business School, Business School, Madrid (Spain) 529, **636**

Leadership Institute of Seattle, School of Applied Behavioral Science, Kenmore (WA) 449

London School of Economics and Political Science, The Graduate School, London (United Kingdom) 543

Metropolitan State University, College of Management, St. Paul (MN) 250

Monterey Institute of International Studies, Fisher Graduate School of International Business, Monterey (CA) 82, **660**

New York University, Robert F. Wagner Graduate School of Public Service (NY) 309

North Park University, School of Business and Nonprofit Management, Chicago (IL) 170

Nottingham Trent University, Nottingham Business School, Nottingham (United Kingdom) 544

Regis University, College for Professional Studies, Denver (CO) 103

Rockford College, Program in Business Administration, Rockford (IL) 171

St. Ambrose University, Program in Business Administration, Davenport (IA) 190

Siena Heights University, Graduate College, Adrian (MI) 242

SIT Graduate Institute, Master's Programs in Intercultural Service, Leadership, and Management, Brattleboro (VT) 434

Southern Adventist University, School of Business and Management, Collegedale (TN) 398

University of California, Berkeley, Haas School of Business, Berkeley (CA) 89

University of Edinburgh, Edinburgh University Management School, Edinburgh (United Kingdom) 550

University of Geneva, MBA Program, Geneva (Switzerland) 535

University of Michigan, Ross School of Business at the University of Michigan, Ann Arbor (MI) 244

University of Missouri–Columbia, Robert J. Trulaske, Sr. College of Business, Columbia (MO) 267, **720**

University of Salford, Salford Business School, Salford (United Kingdom) 554

University of the West, Department of Business Administration, Rosemead (CA) 99

Vienna University of Economics and Business Administration, WU Wien MBA, Vienna (Austria) 492

OPERATIONS MANAGEMENT

American InterContinental University Online, Program in Business Administration, Hoffman Estates (IL) 157

The American University in Cairo, School of Business, Economics and Communication, Cairo (Egypt) 502

Anna Maria College, Program in Business Administration, Paxton (MA) 219

Antwerp International Business School, Graduate Programs in Business, Antwerp (Belgium) 493

Ashridge, Ashridge Executive MBA Program, Berkhamsted (United Kingdom) 538

Aston University, Aston Business School, Birmingham (United Kingdom) 539

Athabasca University, Centre for Innovative Management, Athabasca (Canada) 466

Auburn University, College of Business, Auburn University (AL) 45, **568**

Aurora University, Dunham School of Business, Aurora (IL) 158

Ball State University, Miller College of Business, Muncie (IN) 179

Barcelona Business School, Graduate Programs in Business, Barcelona (Spain) 528

Benedictine University, Graduate Programs, Lisle (IL) 158

Bentley College, The Elkin B. McCallum Graduate School of Business, Waltham (MA) 221, **578**

Bernard M. Baruch College of the City University of New York, Zicklin School of Business, New York (NY) 296

Boston College, The Carroll School of Management, Chestnut Hill (MA) 221, **580**

California Polytechnic State University, San Luis Obispo, Orfalea College of Business, San Luis Obispo (CA) 68

California State University, East Bay, College of Business and Economics, Hayward (CA) 69

Cardiff University, Cardiff Business School, Cardiff (United Kingdom) 539

Carnegie Mellon University, Tepper School of Business, Pittsburgh (PA) 363, **584**

Case Western Reserve University, Weatherhead School of Management, Cleveland (OH) 338

City University of Hong Kong, Faculty of Business, Hong Kong (China) 497

Cleveland State University, Nance College of Business Administration, Cleveland (OH) 340

The College of William and Mary, Mason School of Business, Williamsburg (VA) 436

Columbia University, Graduate School of Business, New York (NY) 298

DePaul University, Charles H. Kellstadt Graduate School of Business, Chicago (IL) 159

Drexel University, LeBow College of Business, Philadelphia (PA) 366

Duke University, The Fuqua School of Business, Durham (NC) 323

Eastern Mennonite University, Program in Business Administration, Harrisonburg (VA) 438

École Nationale des Ponts et Chaussées, ENPC MBA, Paris (France) 503

Emory University, Roberto C. Goizueta Business School, Atlanta (GA) 145, **606**

European School of Economics, MBA Programme (Italy) 515, **608**

Florida Atlantic University, College of Business, Boca Raton (FL) 126

The George Washington University, School of Business, Washington (DC) 119, **622**

Georgia Institute of Technology, College of Management, Atlanta (GA) 146, **624**

Georgia State University, J. Mack Robinson College of Business, Atlanta (GA) 147, **626**

Golden Gate University, Ageno School of Business, San Francisco (CA) 78

Graduate School of Business Administration Zurich, Executive Management Programs, Zurich (Switzerland) 532

Hult International Business School, Graduate Program, Cambridge (MA) *227*, **634**

IE Business School, Business School, Madrid (Spain) 529, **636**

Illinois Institute of Technology, Stuart School of Business, Chicago (IL) 164

Indiana University Bloomington, Kelley School of Business, Bloomington (IN) 182

Indian School of Business, MBA Program, Andhra Pradesh (India) 512

International University of Japan, Graduate School of International Management, Minami Uonuma-gu (Japan) 516

Kansas State University, College of Business Administration, Manhattan (KS) 194

Kettering University, Graduate School, Flint (MI) 238

Lancaster University, Management School, Lancaster (United Kingdom) 541

Lawrence Technological University, College of Management, Southfield (MI) 239, **654**

Lewis University, College of Business, Romeoville (IL) 166

London School of Economics and Political Science, The Graduate School, London (United Kingdom) 543

Loyola University Chicago, Graduate School of Business, Chicago (IL) 167

Macquarie University, Macquarie Graduate School of Management, Sydney (Australia) 485

Madonna University, School of Business, Livonia (MI) 240

Maine Maritime Academy, Department of Graduate Studies, Castine (ME) 210

Massachusetts Institute of Technology, Sloan School of Management, Cambridge (MA) 227

Michigan State University, Eli Broad Graduate School of Management, East Lansing (MI) 240

Milwaukee School of Engineering, Rader School of Business, Milwaukee (WI) 460

Monash University, MBA Programme, Clayton (Australia) 486

National University, School of Business and Management, La Jolla (CA) 82

National University of Ireland, Dublin, The Michael Smurfit Graduate School of Business, Blackrock (Ireland) 513

New Jersey Institute of Technology, School of Management, Newark (NJ) 285

New York University, Leonard N. Stern School of Business (NY) 309

North Park University, School of Business and Nonprofit Management, Chicago (IL) 170

Northwestern University, Kellogg School of Management, Evanston (IL) 171

Nyenrode Business Universiteit, Netherlands Business School, Breukelen (Netherlands) 522

Oakland University, School of Business Administration, Rochester (MI) 241

OGI School of Science & Engineering at Oregon Health & Science University, Department of Management in Science and Technology, Beaverton (OR) 358

The Ohio State University, Max M. Fisher College of Business, Columbus (OH) 344

Purdue University, Krannert School of Management, West Lafayette (IN) 185

Regis University, College for Professional Studies, Denver (CO) 103

Rensselaer at Hartford, Lally School of Management and Technology, Hartford (CT) 110

Rensselaer Polytechnic Institute, Lally School of Management and Technology, Troy (NY) 311, **670**

Rutgers, The State University of New Jersey, Camden, School of Business, Camden (NJ) 288

St. Edward's University, The School of Management and Business, Austin (TX) 410

Saint Vincent College, Alex G. McKenna School of Business, Economics, and Government, Latrobe (PA) 378

San Diego State University, College of Business Administration, San Diego (CA) 86

San Francisco State University, College of Business, San Francisco (CA) 87

Southern Methodist University, Cox School of Business, Dallas (TX) 411, **688**

Southern New Hampshire University, School of Business, Manchester (NH) 279, **690**

Southern Polytechnic State University, Department of Business Administration, Marietta (GA) 150

State University of New York at Binghamton, School of Management, Binghamton (NY) 315

Stockholm School of Economics, Department of Business Administration, Stockholm (Sweden) 531

Texas A&M University, Mays Business School, College Station (TX) 414

The University of Alabama, Manderson Graduate School of Business, Tuscaloosa (AL) 49

University of Applied Sciences Esslingen, Graduate School, Esslingen (Germany) 510

The University of Arizona, Eller College of Management, Tucson (AZ) 58

University of Bath, School of Management, Bath (United Kingdom) 547

The University of British Columbia, Sauder School of Business, Vancouver (Canada) 474

University of California, Berkeley, Haas School of Business, Berkeley (CA) 89

University of California, Los Angeles, UCLA Anderson School of Management, Los Angeles (CA) 91, **696**

University of California, Riverside, A. Gary Anderson Graduate School of Management, Riverside (CA) 93, **698**

University of Chicago, Graduate School of Business, Chicago (IL) 175

University of Cincinnati, College of Business, Cincinnati (OH) 346

University of Colorado at Boulder, Leeds School of Business, Boulder (CO) 104, **702**

University of Colorado at Colorado Springs, Graduate School of Business Administration, Colorado Springs (CO) 105, **704**

University of Connecticut, School of Business, Storrs (CT) 112, **708**

University of Dayton, School of Business Administration, Dayton (OH) 347

University of Delaware, Alfred Lerner College of Business and Economics, Newark (DE) 116, **712**

University of Detroit Mercy, College of Business Administration, Detroit (MI) 243

University of Edinburgh, Edinburgh University Management School, Edinburgh (United Kingdom) 550

University of Georgia, Terry College of Business, Athens (GA) 151

University of Glasgow, University of Glasgow Business School, Glasgow (United Kingdom) 550

University of Illinois at Urbana–Champaign, College of Business, Champaign (IL) 176

University of Manitoba, Faculty of Management, Winnipeg (Canada) 475

University of Massachusetts Boston, College of Management, Boston (MA) 232

University of Michigan, Ross School of Business at the University of Michigan, Ann Arbor (MI) 244

University of Minnesota, Twin Cities Campus, Carlson School of Management, Minneapolis (MN) 252

University of Mississippi, School of Business Administration, Oxford (MS) 257

University of Missouri–Kansas City, Henry W. Bloch School of Business and Public Administration, Kansas City (MO) 267

University of Missouri–St. Louis, College of Business Administration, St. Louis (MO) *268*

University of New Mexico, Robert O. Anderson Graduate School of Management, Albuquerque (NM) 294

University of North Texas, College of Business Administration, Denton (TX) 422

University of Pennsylvania, Wharton School, Philadelphia (PA) 380

University of Pittsburgh, Joseph M. Katz Graduate School of Business, Pittsburgh (PA) 381

University of Plymouth, Plymouth Business School, Plymouth (United Kingdom) 553

University of Rochester, William E. Simon Graduate School of Business Administration, Rochester (NY) 321, **736**

University of Salford, Salford Business School, Salford (United Kingdom) 554

The University of Scranton, Program in Business Administration, Scranton (PA) 382

University of South Carolina, Moore School of Business, Columbia (SC) *392,* **740**

University of Southern California, School of Business, Los Angeles (CA) 98

The University of Tennessee, College of Business Administration, Knoxville (TN) *401,* **744**

The University of Texas at Arlington, College of Business Administration, Arlington (TX) 424, **746**

The University of Texas at Austin, Programs in MBA, Austin (TX) 425

The University of Texas at Dallas, School of Management, Richardson (TX) *426,* **748**

University of the West of England, Bristol, Bristol Business School, Bristol (United Kingdom) 555

University of the Witwatersrand, Graduate School of Business Administration, Wits (South Africa) 527

The University of Toledo, College of Business Administration, Toledo (OH) 349

University of Toronto, Joseph L. Rotman School of Management, Toronto (Canada) 478

University of Washington, Michael G. Foster School of Business, Seattle (WA) 452, **754**

The University of Western Ontario, Richard Ivey School of Business, London (Canada) 480

University of Wisconsin–Madison, Wisconsin School of Business, Madison (WI) 462, **756**

University of Wisconsin–Whitewater, College of Business and Economics, Whitewater (WI) 465

Vanderbilt University, Owen Graduate School of Management, Nashville (TN) 403, **758**

Wake Forest University, Babcock Graduate School of Management, Winston-Salem (NC) 332

Waseda University, Graduate School of Commerce, Tokyo (Japan) 517

WHU—Otto Beisheim School of Management, WHU—Otto Beisheim School of Management, Vallendar (Germany) 511

Wichita State University, W. Frank Barton School of Business, Wichita (KS) 197

Wilfrid Laurier University, School of Business and Economics, Waterloo (Canada) 481, **766**

Willamette University, George H. Atkinson Graduate School of Management, Salem (OR) 361, **768**

Worcester Polytechnic Institute, Department of Management, Worcester (MA) 234, **770**

Yale University, Yale School of Management, New Haven (CT) 114

York University, Schulich School of Business, Toronto (Canada) 482, **772**

ORGANIZATIONAL BEHAVIOR/DEVELOPMENT

The Aarhus School of Business, Faculty of Business Administration, Aarhus (Denmark) 501

American Public University System, AMU/APU Graduate Programs, Charles Town (WV) 455

The American University in Cairo, School of Business, Economics and Communication, Cairo (Egypt) 502

Antioch University Los Angeles, Program in Organizational Management, Culver City (CA) 64

Antioch University New England, Department of Organization and Management, Keene (NH) 277

Aquinas College, School of Management, Grand Rapids (MI) 235

Ashridge, Ashridge Executive MBA Program, Berkhamsted (United Kingdom) 538

Aston University, Aston Business School, Birmingham (United Kingdom) 539

Azusa Pacific University, School of Business and Management, Azusa (CA) 66

Barcelona Business School, Graduate Programs in Business, Barcelona (Spain) 528

Bernard M. Baruch College of the City University of New York, Zicklin School of Business, New York (NY) 296

Boston College, The Carroll School of Management, Chestnut Hill (MA) 221, **580**

Bowling Green State University, College of Business Administration, Bowling Green (OH) 338

Brenau University, School of Business and Mass Communication, Gainesville (GA) 143

Brigham Young University, Marriott School of Management, Provo (UT) 431

California Lutheran University, School of Business, Thousand Oaks (CA) 67

California National University for Advanced Studies, College of Business Administration, Northridge (CA) 67

Carnegie Mellon University, Tepper School of Business, Pittsburgh (PA) 363, **584**

Case Western Reserve University, Weatherhead School of Management, Cleveland (OH) 338

Charleston Southern University, Program in Business, Charleston (SC) 390

City University of Hong Kong, Faculty of Business, Hong Kong (China) 497

City University of Seattle, School of Management, Bellevue (WA) 447, **588**

Claremont Graduate University, Peter F. Drucker and Masatoshi Ito Graduate School of Management, Claremont (CA) 75, **590**

Cleveland State University, Nance College of Business Administration, Cleveland (OH) 340

The College of St. Scholastica, Department of Management, Duluth (MN) 249

Concordia University, St. Paul, College of Business and Organizational Leadership, St. Paul (MN) 250

Copenhagen Business School, Faculty of Economics and Business Administration, Copenhagen (Denmark) 501

Cranfield University, Cranfield School of Management, Cranfield (United Kingdom) 540

Cyprus International Institute of Management, MBA Programme, Nicosia (Cyprus) 500

Eastern Michigan University, College of Business, Ypsilanti (MI) 237

École Nationale des Ponts et Chaussées, ENPC MBA, Paris (France) 503

Edith Cowan University, Faculty of Business and Public Management, Churchlands (Australia) 484

Emory University, Roberto C. Goizueta Business School, Atlanta (GA) 145, **606**

European University, Center for Management Studies, Montreux-Fontanivent (Switzerland) 532

The George Washington University, School of Business, Washington (DC) 119, **622**

Georgia Institute of Technology, College of Management, Atlanta (GA) 146, **624**

Graduate School of Business Administration Zurich, Executive Management Programs, Zurich (Switzerland) 532

The Hague University, Faculty of Economics and Management, The Hague (Netherlands) 521, **628**

Hawai'i Pacific University, College of Business Administration, Honolulu (HI) 153, **630**

HEC Paris, HEC MBA Program, Jouy-en-Josas (France) *505,* **632**

Hult International Business School, Graduate Program, Cambridge (MA) *227,* **634**

IE Business School, Business School, Madrid (Spain) 529, **636**

Illinois State University, College of Business, Normal (IL) 165, **638**

Indian School of Business, MBA Program, Andhra Pradesh (India) 512

International University in Geneva, MBA Program, Geneva (Switzerland) 533, **640**

International University of Japan, Graduate School of International Management, Minami Uonuma-gu (Japan) 516

The Johns Hopkins University, Carey Business School, Baltimore (MD) 214, **646**

Lake Forest Graduate School of Management, MBA Program, Lake Forest (IL) 166, **652**

Lancaster University, Management School, Lancaster (United Kingdom) 541

Leadership Institute of Seattle, School of Applied Behavioral Science, Kenmore (WA) 449

Lindenwood University, Division of Management, St. Charles (MO) 261

Loyola University Chicago, Graduate School of Business, Chicago (IL) 167

Maine Maritime Academy, Department of Graduate Studies, Castine (ME) 210

Marylhurst University, Department of Business Administration, Marylhurst (OR) 357

Marymount University, School of Business Administration, Arlington (VA) 440

Medaille College, Accelerated Learning Programs (NY) 307

Mercy College, Division of Business and Accounting, Dobbs Ferry (NY) 307

Michigan State University, Eli Broad Graduate School of Management, East Lansing (MI) 240

Monash University, MBA Programme, Clayton (Australia) 486

Nanjing University, School of Business, Nanjing (China) 500

National University, School of Business and Management, La Jolla (CA) 82

National University of Ireland, Dublin, The Michael Smurfit Graduate School of Business, Blackrock (Ireland) 513

New York University, Leonard N. Stern School of Business (NY) 309

North Park University, School of Business and Nonprofit Management, Chicago (IL) 170

Northwestern University, Kellogg School of Management, Evanston (IL) 171

Norwegian School of Management, Graduate School, Sandvika (Norway) 524

Nyenrode Business Universiteit, Netherlands Business School, Breukelen (Netherlands) 522

OGI School of Science & Engineering at Oregon Health & Science University, Department of Management in Science and Technology, Beaverton (OR) 358

Pace University, Lubin School of Business, New York (NY) 310

Philadelphia Biblical University, School of Business and Leadership, Langhorne (PA) 374

Point Loma Nazarene University, Program in Business Administration, San Diego (CA) 86

Purdue University, Krannert School of Management, West Lafayette (IN) 185

Queens University of Charlotte, McColl Graduate School of Business, Charlotte (NC) 329

Roosevelt University, Walter E. Heller College of Business Administration, Chicago (IL) 172, **676**

Saint Michael's College, Program in Administration and Management, Colchester (VT) 434

Siena Heights University, Graduate College, Adrian (MI) 242

Southern Illinois University Carbondale, College of Business and Administration, Carbondale (IL) 173

Southern Methodist University, Cox School of Business, Dallas (TX) 411, **688**

Stockholm School of Economics, Department of Business Administration, Stockholm (Sweden) 531

Stratford University, Graduate Business Programs, Falls Church (VA) 443

Suffolk University, Sawyer Business School, Boston (MA) 230

Swinburne University of Technology, Australian Graduate School of Entrepreneurship (AGSE), Hawthorne (Australia) 488

Texas A&M University, Mays Business School, College Station (TX) 414

Tulane University, A. B. Freeman School of Business, New Orleans (LA) 207

University of Bath, School of Management, Bath (United Kingdom) 547

The University of British Columbia, Sauder School of Business, Vancouver (Canada) 474

University of California, Berkeley, Haas School of Business, Berkeley (CA) 89

University of California, Davis, Graduate School of Management, Davis (CA) 90

University of California, Los Angeles, UCLA Anderson School of Management, Los Angeles (CA) 91, **696**

University of California, Riverside, A. Gary Anderson Graduate School of Management, Riverside (CA) 93, **698**

University of Canterbury, Department of Management, Christchurch (New Zealand) 523

University of Chicago, Graduate School of Business, Chicago (IL) 175

University of Dallas, Graduate School of Management, Irving (TX) 420, **710**

University of Delaware, Alfred Lerner College of Business and Economics, Newark (DE) 116, **712**

University of Edinburgh, Edinburgh University Management School, Edinburgh (United Kingdom) 550

University of Glasgow, University of Glasgow Business School, Glasgow (United Kingdom) 550

University of Hartford, Barney School of Business, West Hartford (CT) 113

University of Illinois at Urbana–Champaign, College of Business, Champaign (IL) 176

University of Malaya, Graduate School of Business, Kuala Lumpur (Malaysia) 519

University of Manitoba, Faculty of Management, Winnipeg (Canada) 475

University of Mary Washington, College of Graduate and Professional Studies, Fredericksburg (VA) 444

University of Massachusetts Amherst, Isenberg School of Management, Amherst (MA) 231

University of Michigan, Ross School of Business at the University of Michigan, Ann Arbor (MI) 244

University of Mississippi, School of Business Administration, Oxford (MS) 257

University of Newcastle, Graduate School of Business, Callaghan (Australia) 489

University of New Mexico, Robert O. Anderson Graduate School of Management, Albuquerque (NM) 294

The University of North Carolina Wilmington, School of Business, Wilmington (NC) 332

University of North Texas, College of Business Administration, Denton (TX) 422

University of St. Francis, College of Business, Joliet (IL) 177

University of Salford, Salford Business School, Salford (United Kingdom) 554

University of South Carolina, Moore School of Business, Columbia (SC) *392,* **740**

The University of Texas at Dallas, School of Management, Richardson (TX) *426,* **748**

University of the West of England, Bristol, Bristol Business School, Bristol (United Kingdom) 555

University of Toronto, Joseph L. Rotman School of Management, Toronto (Canada) 478

University of Washington, Michael G. Foster School of Business, Seattle (WA) 452, **754**

University of Waterloo, Graduate Studies, Waterloo (Canada) 479

The University of Western Ontario, Richard Ivey School of Business, London (Canada) 480

University of Wisconsin–Green Bay, Program in Management, Green Bay (WI) 461

Upper Iowa University, Online Master's Programs, Fayette (IA) 192

Vanderbilt University, Owen Graduate School of Management, Nashville (TN) 403, **758**

Washington University in St. Louis, Olin Business School, St. Louis (MO) 269

Westminster College, The Bill and Vieve Gore School of Business, Salt Lake City (UT) 433

Willamette University, George H. Atkinson Graduate School of Management, Salem (OR) 361, **768**

Worcester Polytechnic Institute, Department of Management, Worcester (MA) 234, **770**

York University, Schulich School of Business, Toronto (Canada) 482, **772**

ORGANIZATIONAL MANAGEMENT

The Aarhus School of Business, Faculty of Business Administration, Aarhus (Denmark) 501

Antioch University Los Angeles, Program in Organizational Management, Culver City (CA) 64

Antioch University New England, Department of Organization and Management, Keene (NH) 277

Antwerp International Business School, Graduate Programs in Business, Antwerp (Belgium) 493

Athabasca University, Centre for Innovative Management, Athabasca (Canada) 466

Boise State University, College of Business and Economics, Boise (ID) 155

Brenau University, School of Business and Mass Communication, Gainesville (GA) 143

Brescia University, Program in Management, Owensboro (KY) 198

Cardiff University, Cardiff Business School, Cardiff (United Kingdom) 539

Carleton University, Eric Sprott School of Business, Ottawa (Canada) 467

Carlos Albizu University, Miami Campus, Graduate Programs, Miami (FL) 123

The Chinese University of Hong Kong, Faculty of Business Administration, Hong Kong (China) 497

City University of Seattle, School of Management, Bellevue (WA) 447, **588**

Claremont Graduate University, Peter F. Drucker and Masatoshi Ito Graduate School of Management, Claremont (CA) 75, **590**

Cleveland State University, Nance College of Business Administration, Cleveland (OH) 340

Concordia University, St. Paul, College of Business and Organizational Leadership, St. Paul (MN) 250

Copenhagen Business School, Faculty of Economics and Business Administration, Copenhagen (Denmark) 501

Cranfield University, Cranfield School of Management, Cranfield (United Kingdom) 540

Drexel University, LeBow College of Business, Philadelphia (PA) 366

Eastern Connecticut State University, School of Education and Professional Studies/Graduate Division, Willimantic (CT) 108

École Nationale des Ponts et Chaussées, ENPC MBA, Paris (France) 503

Erasmus University Rotterdam, Rotterdam School of Management, Rotterdam (Netherlands) 521

ESCP-EAP European School of Management, ESCP-EAP European School of Management (France) 503

Fielding Graduate University, Programs in Organizational Management and Organizational Development, Santa Barbara (CA) 77, **616**

Fresno Pacific University, Graduate Programs, Fresno (CA) 78

Georgia State University, J. Mack Robinson College of Business, Atlanta (GA) 147, **626**

Harding University, College of Business Administration, Searcy (AR) 61

Wilmington University, Division of Business, New Castle (DE) 117

Worcester Polytechnic Institute, Department of Management, Worcester (MA) 234, **770**

PHARMACEUTICAL MANAGEMENT

Columbia University, Graduate School of Business, New York (NY) 298

Creighton University, Eugene C. Eppley College of Business Administration, Omaha (NE) 272

Drake University, College of Business and Public Administration, Des Moines (IA) 189

Drexel University, LeBow College of Business, Philadelphia (PA) 366

Fairleigh Dickinson University, College at Florham, Silberman College of Business, Madison (NJ) 282, **612**

Fairleigh Dickinson University, Metropolitan Campus, Silberman College of Business, Teaneck (NJ) 282, **612**

Monash University, MBA Programme, Clayton (Australia) 486

North Carolina State University, College of Management, Raleigh (NC) 328, **664**

Penn State Great Valley, Graduate Studies, Malvern (PA) 373

Rutgers, The State University of New Jersey, Rutgers Business School–Newark and New Brunswick, Newark and New Brunswick (NJ) 288, **678**

Saint Joseph's University, Erivan K. Haub School of Business, Philadelphia (PA) 377

Seton Hall University, Stillman School of Business, South Orange (NJ) 290, **686**

Stevens Institute of Technology, Wesley J. Howe School of Technology Management, Hoboken (NJ) 290

University of California, San Diego, Rady School of Management, La Jolla (CA) 93, **700**

University of Rochester, William E. Simon Graduate School of Business Administration, Rochester (NY) 321, **736**

Vienna University of Economics and Business Administration, WU Wien MBA, Vienna (Austria) 492

PORT/MARITIME MANAGEMENT

Barcelona Business School, Graduate Programs in Business, Barcelona (Spain) 528

Copenhagen Business School, Faculty of Economics and Business Administration, Copenhagen (Denmark) 501

Maine Maritime Academy, Department of Graduate Studies, Castine (ME) 210

Old Dominion University, College of Business and Public Administration, Norfolk (VA) 441

PRODUCTION MANAGEMENT

Antwerp International Business School, Graduate Programs in Business, Antwerp (Belgium) 493

Auburn University, College of Business, Auburn University (AL) 45, **568**

Barcelona Business School, Graduate Programs in Business, Barcelona (Spain) 528

Bayerische Julius-Maximilians University of Wuerzburg, MBA Program, Wuerzburg (Germany) 507

California Polytechnic State University, San Luis Obispo, Orfalea College of Business, San Luis Obispo (CA) 68

Drexel University, LeBow College of Business, Philadelphia (PA) 366

Eastern Mennonite University, Program in Business Administration, Harrisonburg (VA) 438

HEC Paris, HEC MBA Program, Jouy-en-Josas (France) *505*, **632**

IE Business School, Business School, Madrid (Spain) 529, **636**

International University of Japan, Graduate School of International Management, Minami Uonuma-gu (Japan) 516

North Carolina State University, College of Management, Raleigh (NC) 328, **664**

Nottingham Trent University, Nottingham Business School, Nottingham (United Kingdom) 544

Rensselaer Polytechnic Institute, Lally School of Management and Technology, Troy (NY) 311, **670**

Southern Illinois University Carbondale, College of Business and Administration, Carbondale (IL) 173

Texas A&M University, Mays Business School, College Station (TX) 414

Texas Tech University, Jerry S. Rawls College of Business Administration, Lubbock (TX) 418

The University of Alabama, Manderson Graduate School of Business, Tuscaloosa (AL) 49

University of California, Los Angeles, UCLA Anderson School of Management, Los Angeles (CA) 91, **696**

University of California, Riverside, A. Gary Anderson Graduate School of Management, Riverside (CA) 93, **698**

University of Canterbury, Department of Management, Christchurch (New Zealand) 523

University of Chicago, Graduate School of Business, Chicago (IL) 175

University of Georgia, Terry College of Business, Athens (GA) 151

University of Illinois at Urbana–Champaign, College of Business, Champaign (IL) 176

University of Manitoba, Faculty of Management, Winnipeg (Canada) 475

University of Michigan, Ross School of Business at the University of Michigan, Ann Arbor (MI) 244

University of Salford, Salford Business School, Salford (United Kingdom) 554

The University of Tennessee, College of Business Administration, Knoxville (TN) *401*, **744**

University of the Witwatersrand, Graduate School of Business Administration, Wits (South Africa) 527

The University of Western Ontario, Richard Ivey School of Business, London (Canada) 480

University of Windsor, Odette School of Business, Windsor (Canada) 480

Waseda University, Graduate School of Commerce, Tokyo (Japan) 517

WHU—Otto Beisheim School of Management, WHU—Otto Beisheim School of Management, Vallendar (Germany) 511

Worcester Polytechnic Institute, Department of Management, Worcester (MA) 234, **770**

PROFIT MANAGEMENT

École Nationale des Ponts et Chaussées, ENPC MBA, Paris (France) 503

Stockholm School of Economics, Department of Business Administration, Stockholm (Sweden) 531

PROJECT MANAGEMENT

American InterContinental University Online, Program in Business Administration, Hoffman Estates (IL) 157

The American University in Cairo, School of Business, Economics and Communication, Cairo (Egypt) 502

Ashland University, Dauch College of Business and Economics, Ashland (OH) 337

Ashridge, Ashridge Executive MBA Program, Berkhamsted (United Kingdom) 538

Athabasca University, Centre for Innovative Management, Athabasca (Canada) 466

Bayerische Julius-Maximilians University of Wuerzburg, MBA Program, Wuerzburg (Germany) 507

Benedictine University, Graduate Programs, Lisle (IL) 158

Brenau University, School of Business and Mass Communication, Gainesville (GA) 143

Christian Brothers University, School of Business, Memphis (TN) 396

City University of Seattle, School of Management, Bellevue (WA) 447, **588**

Columbia Southern University, MBA Program, Orange Beach (AL) 46

Copenhagen Business School, Faculty of Economics and Business Administration, Copenhagen (Denmark) 501

Cranfield University, Cranfield School of Management, Cranfield (United Kingdom) 540

DeVry University, Keller Graduate School of Management, Phoenix (AZ) 56

DeVry University, Keller Graduate School of Management, Fremont (CA) 76

DeVry University, Keller Graduate School of Management, Long Beach (CA) 76

DeVry University, Keller Graduate School of Management, Palmdale (CA) 76

DeVry University, Keller Graduate School of Management, Pomona (CA) 77

DeVry University, Keller Graduate School of Management, San Diego (CA) 77

DeVry University, Keller Graduate School of Management, Colorado Springs (CO) 102

DeVry University, Keller Graduate School of Management, Miami (FL) 124

DeVry University, Keller Graduate School of Management, Miramar (FL) 124

DeVry University, Keller Graduate School of Management, Orlando (FL) 124

DeVry University, Keller Graduate School of Management, Tampa (FL) 124

DeVry University, Keller Graduate School of Management, Alpharetta (GA) 144

DeVry University, Keller Graduate School of Management, Atlanta (GA) 144

DeVry University, Keller Graduate School of Management, Decatur (GA) 144

DeVry University, Keller Graduate School of Management, Duluth (GA) 145

DeVry University, Keller Graduate School of Management, Elgin (IL) 160

DeVry University, Keller Graduate School of Management, Gurnee (IL) 161

DeVry University, Keller Graduate School of Management, Lincolnshire (IL) 161

DeVry University, Keller Graduate School of Management, Oakbrook Terrace (IL) 161, **650**

DeVry University, Keller Graduate School of Management, Schaumburg (IL) 162

DeVry University, Keller Graduate School of Management, Tinley Park (IL) 162

DeVry University, Keller Graduate School of Management (IN) 180

DeVry University, Keller Graduate School of Management, Merrillville (IN) 180

DeVry University, Keller Graduate School of Management, Kansas City (MO) 259

DeVry University, Keller Graduate School of Management, St. Louis (MO) 259

DeVry University, Keller Graduate School of Management (NV) 275

DeVry University, Keller Graduate School of Management (NC) 323

DeVry University, Keller Graduate School of Management, Columbus (OH) 341

DeVry University, Keller Graduate School of Management, Seven Hills (OH) 341

DeVry University, Keller Graduate School of Management (OR) 356

DeVry University, Keller Graduate School of Management (PA) 365

DeVry University, Keller Graduate School of Management, Fort Washington (PA) 365

DeVry University, Keller Graduate School of Management, Pittsburgh (PA) 365

DeVry University, Keller Graduate School of Management (TX) 406

DeVry University, Keller Graduate School of Management, Irving (TX) 407

DeVry University, Keller Graduate School of Management, Arlington (VA) 437

DeVry University, Keller Graduate School of Management, McLean (VA) 437

DeVry University, Keller Graduate School of Management, Bellevue (WA) 447

DeVry University, Keller Graduate School of Management, Federal Way (WA) 448

École Nationale des Ponts et Chaussées, ENPC MBA, Paris (France) 503

Elon University, Martha and Spencer Love School of Business, Elon (NC) 324

Embry-Riddle Aeronautical University Worldwide, Department of Management, Daytona Beach (FL) 125

ESCP-EAP European School of Management, ESCP-EAP European School of Management (France) 503

Fayetteville State University, Program in Business Administration, Fayetteville (NC) 325

George Mason University, School of Management, Fairfax (VA) 438

The George Washington University, School of Business, Washington (DC) 119, **622**

Georgia State University, J. Mack Robinson College of Business, Atlanta (GA) 147, **626**

Grantham University, Mark Skousen School of Business, Kansas City (MO) 260

The Hague University, Faculty of Economics and Management, The Hague (Netherlands) 521, **628**

HEC Paris, HEC MBA Program, Jouy-en-Josas (France) *505*, **632**

IE Business School, Business School, Madrid (Spain) 529, **636**

Illinois State University, College of Business, Normal (IL) 165, **638**

International University of Japan, Graduate School of International Management, Minami Uonuma-gu (Japan) 516

Jones International University, Graduate School of Business Administration, Centennial (CO) 103

Lancaster University, Management School, Lancaster (United Kingdom) 541

Lawrence Technological University, College of Management, Southfield (MI) 239, **654**

Lehigh University, College of Business and Economics, Bethlehem (PA) 371, **656**

Lewis University, College of Business, Romeoville (IL) 166

Louisiana State University and Agricultural and Mechanical College, E. J. Ourso College of Business, Baton Rouge (LA) 204

Marymount University, School of Business Administration, Arlington (VA) 440

Metropolitan State University, College of Management, St. Paul (MN) 250

Milwaukee School of Engineering, Rader School of Business, Milwaukee (WI) 460

Mississippi State University, College of Business and Industry, Mississippi State (MS) 256

Monash University, MBA Programme, Clayton (Australia) 486

National University of Ireland, Dublin, The Michael Smurfit Graduate School of Business, Blackrock (Ireland) 513

Naval Postgraduate School, School of Business and Public Policy, Monterey (CA) 83

New England College, Program in Management, Henniker (NH) 278

Northern Kentucky University, College of Business, Highland Heights (KY) 201

Northwestern Polytechnic University, School of Business and Information Technology, Fremont (CA) 84

Notre Dame de Namur University, Department of Business Administration, Belmont (CA) 84

OGI School of Science & Engineering at Oregon Health & Science University, Department of Management in Science and Technology, Beaverton (OR) 358

Penn State Great Valley, Graduate Studies, Malvern (PA) 373

Queensland University of Technology, Brisbane Graduate School of Business, Brisbane (Australia) 487

Regis University, College for Professional Studies, Denver (CO) 103

Saint Mary's University of Minnesota, Schools of Graduate and Professional Programs, Winona (MN) 251

Southern Illinois University Edwardsville, School of Business, Edwardsville (IL) *174*

Southern New Hampshire University, School of Business, Manchester (NH) 279, **690**

Stevens Institute of Technology, Wesley J. Howe School of Technology Management, Hoboken (NJ) 290

Stockholm School of Economics, Department of Business Administration, Stockholm (Sweden) 531

University of Bath, School of Management, Bath (United Kingdom) 547

University of Colorado at Colorado Springs, Graduate School of Business Administration, Colorado Springs (CO) 105, **704**

University of Dallas, Graduate School of Management, Irving (TX) 420, **710**

University of Management and Technology, Graduate Business Programs, Arlington (VA) 443

University of Mary Washington, College of Graduate and Professional Studies, Fredericksburg (VA) 444

University of Oxford, Saïd Business School, Oxford (United Kingdom) 553

University of Salford, Salford Business School, Salford (United Kingdom) 554

The University of Texas at Dallas, School of Management, Richardson (TX) *426*, **748**

The University of Texas at San Antonio, College of Business, San Antonio (TX) 427, **750**

University of the West of England, Bristol, Bristol Business School, Bristol (United Kingdom) 555

Vienna University of Economics and Business Administration, WU Wien MBA, Vienna (Austria) 492

Walden University, School of Management, Minneapolis (MN) 253

Walsh College of Accountancy and Business Administration, Graduate Programs, Troy (MI) 247

Western Carolina University, College of Business, Cullowhee (NC) 333

WHU—Otto Beisheim School of Management, WHU—Otto Beisheim School of Management, Vallendar (Germany) 511

Worcester Polytechnic Institute, Department of Management, Worcester (MA) 234, **770**

Wright State University, Raj Soin College of Business, Dayton (OH) 350

PUBLIC AND PRIVATE MANAGEMENT

Antioch University Santa Barbara, Program in Organizational Management, Santa Barbara (CA) 64

Birmingham-Southern College, Program in Public and Private Management, Birmingham (AL) 46

Cardiff University, Cardiff Business School, Cardiff (United Kingdom) 539

Cleveland State University, Nance College of Business Administration, Cleveland (OH) 340

Cyprus International Institute of Management, MBA Programme, Nicosia (Cyprus) 500

HEC Paris, HEC MBA Program, Jouy-en-Josas (France) *505*, **632**

Monash University, MBA Programme, Clayton (Australia) 486

Saint Mary's University of Minnesota, Schools of Graduate and Professional Programs, Winona (MN) 251

Saint Xavier University, Graham School of Management, Chicago (IL) 173

TUI University, College of Business Administration, Cypress (CA) 89

University of Bath, School of Management, Bath (United Kingdom) 547

University of Management and Technology, Graduate Business Programs, Arlington (VA) 443

University of the Witwatersrand, Graduate School of Business Administration, Wits (South Africa) 527

Willamette University, George H. Atkinson Graduate School of Management, Salem (OR) 361, **768**

PUBLIC FINANCE

HfB—Business School of Finance and Management, Frankfurt School of Finance and Management, Frankfurt (Germany) 508

Lancaster University, Management School, Lancaster (United Kingdom) 541

National University, School of Business and Management, La Jolla (CA) 82

New York University, Robert F. Wagner Graduate School of Public Service (NY) 309

Vienna University of Economics and Business Administration, WU Wien MBA, Vienna (Austria) 492

PUBLIC MANAGEMENT

Argosy University, Dallas, College of Business, Dallas (TX) 405, **566**

Argosy University, Denver, College of Business, Denver (CO) 100, **566**

Argosy University, Inland Empire, College of Business, San Bernardino (CA) 65, **566**

Argosy University, Los Angeles, College of Business, Santa Monica (CA) 65, **566**

Asian Institute of Technology, School of Management, Pathumthani (Thailand) 536

Aston University, Aston Business School, Birmingham (United Kingdom) 539

Carnegie Mellon University, Tepper School of Business, Pittsburgh (PA) 363, **584**

The Catholic University of America, Metropolitan College, Washington (DC) 118

Cleveland State University, Nance College of Business Administration, Cleveland (OH) 340

Columbia University, Graduate School of Business, New York (NY) 298

Copenhagen Business School, Faculty of Economics and Business Administration, Copenhagen (Denmark) 501

Cyprus International Institute of Management, MBA Programme, Nicosia (Cyprus) 500

Deakin University, Deakin Business School, Geelong (Australia) 484

Gannon University, School of Business, Erie (PA) 368

Governors State University, College of Business and Public Administration, University Park (IL) 164

Hood College, Department of Economics and Management, Frederick (MD) 214

Illinois Institute of Technology, Stuart School of Business, Chicago (IL) 164

Indian Institute of Management, Ahmedabad, Post-Graduate Programme in Management, Gujarat (India) 512

Katholieke Universiteit Leuven, Leuven School of Business and Economics, Leuven (Belgium) 494

Lancaster University, Management School, Lancaster (United Kingdom) 541

Lindenwood University, Division of Management, St. Charles (MO) 261

London School of Economics and Political Science, The Graduate School, London (United Kingdom) 543

Metropolitan State University, College of Management, St. Paul (MN) 250

New York University, Robert F. Wagner Graduate School of Public Service (NY) 309

Notre Dame de Namur University, Department of Business Administration, Belmont (CA) 84

Old Dominion University, College of Business and Public Administration, Norfolk (VA) 441

Queen Margaret University College, Edinburgh, School of Business and Enterprise, Edinburgh (United Kingdom) 545

Rockford College, Program in Business Administration, Rockford (IL) 171

Saint Mary's University of Minnesota, Schools of Graduate and Professional Programs, Winona (MN) 251

St. Thomas University, Department of Business Administration, Miami Gardens (FL) 132

Stanford University, Graduate School of Business, Stanford (CA) 88

Suffolk University, Sawyer Business School, Boston (MA) 230

University at Buffalo, the State University of New York, School of Management, Buffalo (NY) 320

University of Alberta, School of Business, Edmonton (Canada) 473

University of Bath, School of Management, Bath (United Kingdom) 547

The University of Findlay, College of Business, Findlay (OH) 348

University of Glasgow, University of Glasgow Business School, Glasgow (United Kingdom) 550

University of Hartford, Barney School of Business, West Hartford (CT) 113

University of Melbourne, Melbourne Business School, Melbourne (Australia) 488

The University of New England, The Graduate School of Business Administration, Armidale (Australia) 490

University of the District of Columbia, School of Business and Public Administration, Washington (DC) 122

Vienna University of Economics and Business Administration, WU Wien MBA, Vienna (Austria) 492

Willamette University, George H. Atkinson Graduate School of Management, Salem (OR) 361, **768**

Yale University, Yale School of Management, New Haven (CT) 114

York University, Schulich School of Business, Toronto (Canada) 482, **772**

PUBLIC POLICY AND ADMINISTRATION

The Aarhus School of Business, Faculty of Business Administration, Aarhus (Denmark) 501

The American University in Cairo, School of Business, Economics and Communication, Cairo (Egypt) 502

Andrew Jackson University, Brian Tracy College of Business and Entrepreneurship, Birmingham (AL) 45

Argosy University, Orange County, College of Business, Santa Ana (CA) 65, **566**

Argosy University, Salt Lake City, College of Business, Draper (UT) 430, **566**

Argosy University, San Diego, College of Business, San Diego (CA) 65, **566**

Argosy University, San Francisco Bay Area, College of Business, Alameda (CA) 66, **566**

Argosy University, Seattle, College of Business, Seattle (WA) 447, **566**

Argosy University, Tampa, College of Business, Tampa (FL) 122, **566**

Argosy University, Twin Cities, College of Business, Eagan (MN) 248, **566**

Aston University, Aston Business School, Birmingham (United Kingdom) 539

Athabasca University, Centre for Innovative Management, Athabasca (Canada) 466

Belhaven College, Program in Business, Jackson (MS) 254

Boise State University, College of Business and Economics, Boise (ID) 155

Brandeis University, The Heller School for Social Policy and Management (MA) 223

California State University, Sacramento, College of Business Administration, Sacramento (CA) 72

Clemson University, College of Business and Behavioral Science, Clemson (SC) 391

Columbia Southern University, MBA Program, Orange Beach (AL) 46

Concordia University Wisconsin, Graduate Programs, Mequon (WI) 458

Copenhagen Business School, Faculty of Economics and Business Administration, Copenhagen (Denmark) 501

Cyprus International Institute of·Management, MBA Programme, Nicosia (Cyprus) 500

Deakin University, Deakin Business School, Geelong (Australia) 484

DeVry University, Keller Graduate School of Management, Phoenix (AZ) 56

DeVry University, Keller Graduate School of Management, Fremont (CA) 76

DeVry University, Keller Graduate School of Management, Long Beach (CA) 76

DeVry University, Keller Graduate School of Management, Pomona (CA) 77

DeVry University, Keller Graduate School of Management, San Diego (CA) 77

DeVry University, Keller Graduate School of Management, Colorado Springs (CO) 102

DeVry University, Keller Graduate School of Management, Miami (FL) 124

DeVry University, Keller Graduate School of Management, Miramar (FL) 124

DeVry University, Keller Graduate School of Management, Orlando (FL) 124

DeVry University, Keller Graduate School of Management, Tampa (FL) 124

DeVry University, Keller Graduate School of Management, Alpharetta (GA) 144

DeVry University, Keller Graduate School of Management, Atlanta (GA) 144

DeVry University, Keller Graduate School of Management, Decatur (GA) 144

DeVry University, Keller Graduate School of Management, Duluth (GA) 145

DeVry University, Keller Graduate School of Management, Elgin (IL) 160

DeVry University, Keller Graduate School of Management, Gurnee (IL) 161

DeVry University, Keller Graduate School of Management, Lincolnshire (IL) 161

DeVry University, Keller Graduate School of Management, Oakbrook Terrace (IL) 161, **650**

DeVry University, Keller Graduate School of Management, Schaumburg (IL) 162

DeVry University, Keller Graduate School of Management, Tinley Park (IL) 162

DeVry University, Keller Graduate School of Management (IN) 180

DeVry University, Keller Graduate School of Management, Merrillville (IN) 180

DeVry University, Keller Graduate School of Management, Kansas City (MO) 259

DeVry University, Keller Graduate School of Management, St. Louis (MO) 259

DeVry University, Keller Graduate School of Management (NV) 275

DeVry University, Keller Graduate School of Management (NC) 323

DeVry University, Keller Graduate School of Management, Columbus (OH) 341

DeVry University, Keller Graduate School of Management, Seven Hills (OH) 341

DeVry University, Keller Graduate School of Management (OR) 356

DeVry University, Keller Graduate School of Management (PA) 365

DeVry University, Keller Graduate School of Management, Fort Washington (PA) 365

DeVry University, Keller Graduate School of Management, Pittsburgh (PA) 365

DeVry University, Keller Graduate School of Management, Arlington (VA) 437

DeVry University, Keller Graduate School of Management, McLean (VA) 437

DeVry University, Keller Graduate School of Management, Bellevue (WA) 447

DeVry University, Keller Graduate School of Management, Federal Way (WA) 448

Drake University, College of Business and Public Administration, Des Moines (IA) 189

Eastern Washington University, College of Business and Public Administration, Cheney (WA) 448

Gannon University, School of Business, Erie (PA) 368

The George Washington University, School of Business, Washington (DC) 119, **622**

Golden Gate University, Ageno School of Business, San Francisco (CA) 78

IE Business School, Business School, Madrid (Spain) 529, **636**

Illinois Institute of Technology, Stuart School of Business, Chicago (IL) 164

Indian Institute of Management, Ahmedabad, Post-Graduate Programme in Management, Gujarat (India) 512

Indian School of Business, MBA Program, Andhra Pradesh (India) 512

Lancaster University, Management School, Lancaster (United Kingdom) 541

Lincoln University, College of Business and Professional Studies (MO) 260

London School of Economics and Political Science, The Graduate School, London (United Kingdom) 543

Louisiana State University and Agricultural and Mechanical College, E. J. Ourso College of Business, Baton Rouge (LA) 204

Marquette University, Graduate School of Management, Milwaukee (WI) 459

Monash University, MBA Programme, Clayton (Australia) 486

The New School: A University, Milano The New School for Management and Urban Policy, New York (NY) 308

New York University, Leonard N. Stern School of Business (NY) 309

New York University, Robert F. Wagner Graduate School of Public Service (NY) 309

Northcentral University, MBA Program, Prescott Valley (AZ) 56

Nova Southeastern University, H. Wayne Huizenga School of Business and Entrepreneurship, Fort Lauderdale (FL) 130, **666**

Old Dominion University, College of Business and Public Administration, Norfolk (VA) 441

Open University, Business School, Milton Keynes (United Kingdom) 545

Open University of the Netherlands, Business Programs, Heerlen (Netherlands) 523

Pepperdine University, Graziadio School of Business and Management, Los Angeles (CA) 85

Rochester Institute of Technology, E. Philip Saunders College of Business, Rochester (NY) 312

Roosevelt University, Walter E. Heller College of Business Administration, Chicago (IL) 172, **676**

Royal Military College of Canada, Department of Business Administration, Kingston (Canada) 471

Saint Mary's University of Minnesota, Schools of Graduate and Professional Programs, Winona (MN) 251

Schiller International University, Graduate Programs, London (United Kingdom) 546, **684**

Siena Heights University, Graduate College, Adrian (MI) 242

Stockholm School of Economics, Department of Business Administration, Stockholm (Sweden) 531

Texas A&M University, Mays Business School, College Station (TX) 414

University of California, Berkeley, Haas School of Business, Berkeley (CA) 89

University of Geneva, MBA Program, Geneva (Switzerland) 535

University of Maine, The Maine Business School, Orono (ME) 211

University of Management and Technology, Graduate Business Programs, Arlington (VA) 443

University of Mary Washington, College of Graduate and Professional Studies, Fredericksburg (VA) 444

University of Massachusetts Amherst, Isenberg School of Management, Amherst (MA) 231

University of Miami, School of Business Administration, Coral Gables (FL) 135, **718**

University of Michigan, Ross School of Business at the University of Michigan, Ann Arbor (MI) 244

University of Missouri–Columbia, Robert J. Trulaske, Sr. College of Business, Columbia (MO) 267, **720**

University of New Haven, School of Business, West Haven (CT) 113, **728**

University of New Mexico, Robert O. Anderson Graduate School of Management, Albuquerque (NM) 294

University of Pennsylvania, Wharton School, Philadelphia (PA) 380

University of Phoenix, College of Graduate Business and Management, Phoenix (AZ) 59

University of Phoenix–Bay Area Campus, College of Graduate Business and Management, Pleasanton (CA) 94

University of Phoenix–Central Florida Campus, College of Graduate Business and Management, Maitland (FL) 137

University of Phoenix–Cincinnati Campus, College of Graduate Business and Management, West Chester (OH) 348

University of Phoenix–Cleveland Campus, College of Graduate Business and Management, Independence (OH) 348

University of Phoenix–Columbus Ohio Campus, College of Graduate Business and Management, Columbus (OH) 349

University of Phoenix–Dallas Campus, College of Graduate Business and Management, Dallas (TX) 423

University of Phoenix–Eastern Washington Campus, College of Graduate Business and Management, Spokane Valley (WA) 451

University of Phoenix–Hawaii Campus, College of Graduate Business and Management, Honolulu (HI) 155

University of Phoenix–Houston Campus, College of Graduate Business and Management, Houston (TX) 423

University of Phoenix–Idaho Campus, College of Graduate Business and Management, Meridian (ID) 157

University of Phoenix–Kansas City Campus, College of Graduate Business and Management, Kansas City (MO) 268

University of Phoenix–Las Vegas Campus, College of Graduate Business and Management, Las Vegas (NV) 276

University of Phoenix–New Mexico Campus, College of Graduate Business and Management, Albuquerque (NM) 294

University of Phoenix–North Florida Campus, College of Graduate Business and Management, Jacksonville (FL) 137

University of Phoenix–Oregon Campus, College of Graduate Business and Management, Tigard (OR) 360

University of Phoenix–Sacramento Valley Campus, College of Graduate Business and Management, Sacramento (CA) 95

University of Phoenix–San Diego Campus, College of Graduate Business and Management, San Diego (CA) 95

University of Phoenix–Southern California Campus, College of Graduate Business and Management, Costa Mesa (CA) 96

University of Phoenix–South Florida Campus, College of Graduate Business and Management, Fort Lauderdale (FL) 137

University of Phoenix–Utah Campus, College of Graduate Business and Management, Salt Lake City (UT) 432

University of Phoenix–West Florida Campus, College of Graduate Business and Management, Temple Terrace (FL) 138

University of Phoenix–West Michigan Campus, College of Graduate Business and Management, Walker (MI) 246

University of Rochester, William E. Simon Graduate School of Business Administration, Rochester (NY) 321, **736**

University of the District of Columbia, School of Business and Public Administration, Washington (DC) 122

University of the West of England, Bristol, Bristol Business School, Bristol (United Kingdom) 555

University of Warwick, Warwick Business School, Coventry (United Kingdom) 557

Upper Iowa University, Online Master's Programs, Fayette (IA) 192

Webster University, School of Business and Technology, St. Louis (MO) 270

Western International University, Graduate Programs in Business, Phoenix (AZ) 60

Willamette University, George H. Atkinson Graduate School of Management, Salem (OR) 361, **768**

Wilmington University, Division of Business, New Castle (DE) 117

York University, Schulich School of Business, Toronto (Canada) 482, **772**

PUBLIC RELATIONS

Antwerp International Business School, Graduate Programs in Business, Antwerp (Belgium) 493

Aston University, Aston Business School, Birmingham (United Kingdom) 539

Barcelona Business School, Graduate Programs in Business, Barcelona (Spain) 528

Edith Cowan University, Faculty of Business and Public Management, Churchlands (Australia) 484

European University, Center for Management Studies, Montreux-Fontanivent (Switzerland) 532

Golden Gate University, Ageno School of Business, San Francisco (CA) 78

Illinois Institute of Technology, Stuart School of Business, Chicago (IL) 164

The International Management Institute, International Business School, Antwerp (Belgium) 494

International University in Geneva, MBA Program, Geneva (Switzerland) 533, **640**

Roosevelt University, Walter E. Heller College of Business Administration, Chicago (IL) 172, **676**

Royal Roads University, Faculty of Management, Victoria (Canada) 471

Schiller International University, Graduate Programs, London (United Kingdom) 546, **684**

University of Missouri–Columbia, Robert J. Trulaske, Sr. College of Business, Columbia (MO) 267, **720**

University of New Haven, School of Business, West Haven (CT) 113, **728**

QUALITY MANAGEMENT

Anna Maria College, Program in Business Administration, Paxton (MA) 219

Aston University, Aston Business School, Birmingham (United Kingdom) 539

California National University for Advanced Studies, College of Business Administration, Northridge (CA) 67

Cleveland State University, Nance College of Business Administration, Cleveland (OH) 340

École Nationale des Ponts et Chaussées, ENPC MBA, Paris (France) 503

ESCP-EAP European School of Management, ESCP-EAP European School of Management (France) 503

Fordham University, Graduate School of Business Administration, New York (NY) 301, **620**

Hofstra University, Frank G. Zarb School of Business, Hempstead (NY) 302

Illinois Institute of Technology, Stuart School of Business, Chicago (IL) 164

Lancaster University, Management School, Lancaster (United Kingdom) 541

Leadership Institute of Seattle, School of Applied Behavioral Science, Kenmore (WA) 449

Madonna University, School of Business, Livonia (MI) 240

Marquette University, Graduate School of Management, Milwaukee (WI) 459

Milwaukee School of Engineering, Rader School of Business, Milwaukee (WI) 460

Monash University, MBA Programme, Clayton (Australia) 486

Northwest Missouri State University, Melvin and Valorie Booth College of Business and Professional Studies, Maryville (MO) 263

OGI School of Science & Engineering at Oregon Health & Science University, Department of Management in Science and Technology, Beaverton (OR) 358

Rensselaer Polytechnic Institute, Lally School of Management and Technology, Troy (NY) 311, **670**

Rivier College, Department of Business Administration, Nashua (NH) 279

Rochester Institute of Technology, E. Philip Saunders College of Business, Rochester (NY) 312

Stockholm School of Economics, Department of Business Administration, Stockholm (Sweden) 531

The University of Alabama, Manderson Graduate School of Business, Tuscaloosa (AL) 49

University of Manitoba, Faculty of Management, Winnipeg (Canada) 475

University of Miami, School of Business Administration, Coral Gables (FL) 135, **718**

University of Salford, Salford Business School, Salford (United Kingdom) 554

Upper Iowa University, Online Master's Programs, Fayette (IA) 192

Wayne State University, School of Business Administration, Detroit (MI) 247, **760**

QUANTITATIVE ANALYSIS

The American University in Cairo, School of Business, Economics and Communication, Cairo (Egypt) 502

Ashridge, Ashridge Executive MBA Program, Berkhamsted (United Kingdom) 538

Aston University, Aston Business School, Birmingham (United Kingdom) 539

Barcelona Business School, Graduate Programs in Business, Barcelona (Spain) 528

Bentley College, The Elkin B. McCallum Graduate School of Business, Waltham (MA) 221, **578**

Bernard M. Baruch College of the City University of New York, Zicklin School of Business, New York (NY) 296

California National University for Advanced Studies, College of Business Administration, Northridge (CA) 67

Carnegie Mellon University, Tepper School of Business, Pittsburgh (PA) 363, **584**

City University of Hong Kong, Faculty of Business, Hong Kong (China) 497

Copenhagen Business School, Faculty of Economics and Business Administration, Copenhagen (Denmark) 501

École Nationale des Ponts et Chaussées, ENPC MBA, Paris (France) 503

Emory University, Roberto C. Goizueta Business School, Atlanta (GA) 145, **606**

Georgia Institute of Technology, College of Management, Atlanta (GA) 146, **624**

HfB—Business School of Finance and Management, Frankfurt School of Finance and Management, Frankfurt (Germany) 508

Hult International Business School, Graduate Program, Cambridge (MA) 227, **634**

IE Business School, Business School, Madrid (Spain) 529, **636**

Illinois Institute of Technology, Stuart School of Business, Chicago (IL) 164

Katholieke Universiteit Leuven, Leuven School of Business and Economics, Leuven (Belgium) 494

Lancaster University, Management School, Lancaster (United Kingdom) 541

Louisiana Tech University, College of Administration and Business, Ruston (LA) 205

Monash University, MBA Programme, Clayton (Australia) 486

Rensselaer Polytechnic Institute, Lally School of Management and Technology, Troy (NY) 311, **670**

Stockholm School of Economics, Department of Business Administration, Stockholm (Sweden) 531

The University of Alabama, Manderson Graduate School of Business, Tuscaloosa (AL) 49

University of California, Berkeley, Haas School of Business, Berkeley (CA) 89

University of Canterbury, Department of Management, Christchurch (New Zealand) 523

University of Cincinnati, College of Business, Cincinnati (OH) 346

University of Detroit Mercy, College of Business Administration, Detroit (MI) 243

University of Mississippi, School of Business Administration, Oxford (MS) 257

University of Newcastle, Graduate School of Business, Callaghan (Australia) 489

University of Reading, ICMA Centre, Reading (United Kingdom) 554

University of Salford, Salford Business School, Salford (United Kingdom) 554

University of South Carolina, Moore School of Business, Columbia (SC) *392,* **740**

University of the West of England, Bristol, Bristol Business School, Bristol (United Kingdom) 555

University of the Witwatersrand, Graduate School of Business Administration, Wits (South Africa) 527

University of Washington, Michael G. Foster School of Business, Seattle (WA) 452, **754**

Washington University in St. Louis, Olin Business School, St. Louis (MO) 269

Willamette University, George H. Atkinson Graduate School of Management, Salem (OR) 361, **768**

York University, Schulich School of Business, Toronto (Canada) 482, **772**

REAL ESTATE

American University, Kogod School of Business, Washington (DC) 118

Bentley College, The Elkin B. McCallum Graduate School of Business, Waltham (MA) 221, **578**

Clemson University, College of Business and Behavioral Science, Clemson (SC) 391

Cleveland State University, Nance College of Business Administration, Cleveland (OH) 340

Columbia University, Graduate School of Business, New York (NY) 298

DePaul University, Charles H. Kellstadt Graduate School of Business, Chicago (IL) 159

Duquesne University, John F. Donahue Graduate School of Business, Pittsburgh (PA) 367

Emory University, Roberto C. Goizueta Business School, Atlanta (GA) 145, **606**

Florida Atlantic University, College of Business, Boca Raton (FL) 126

Florida International University, Alvah H. Chapman, Jr. Graduate School of Business, Miami (FL) 128, **618**

Florida State University, College of Business, Tallahassee (FL) 129

The George Washington University, School of Business, Washington (DC) 119, **622**

Georgia State University, J. Mack Robinson College of Business, Atlanta (GA) 147, **626**

Indian School of Business, MBA Program, Andhra Pradesh (India) 512

The Johns Hopkins University, Carey Business School, Baltimore (MD) 214, **646**

London School of Economics and Political Science, The Graduate School, London (United Kingdom) 543

Louisiana State University and Agricultural and Mechanical College, E. J. Ourso College of Business, Baton Rouge (LA) 204

Marquette University, Graduate School of Management, Milwaukee (WI) 459

Marylhurst University, Department of Business Administration, Marylhurst (OR) 357

Monmouth University, School of Business Administration, West Long Branch (NJ) 284

Northwestern University, Kellogg School of Management, Evanston (IL) 171

The Ohio State University, Max M. Fisher College of Business, Columbus (OH) 344

Pacific States University, College of Business, Los Angeles (CA) 85

Portland State University, School of Business Administration, Portland (OR) 358

Rice University, Jesse H. Jones Graduate School of Management, Houston (TX) 410

Roosevelt University, Walter E. Heller College of Business Administration, Chicago (IL) 172, **676**

San Diego State University, College of Business Administration, San Diego (CA) 86

Texas A&M University, Mays Business School, College Station (TX) 414

The University of Alabama, Manderson Graduate School of Business, Tuscaloosa (AL) 49

University of California, Berkeley, Haas School of Business, Berkeley (CA) 89

University of California, Los Angeles, UCLA Anderson School of Management, Los Angeles (CA) 91, **696**

University of Cincinnati, College of Business, Cincinnati (OH) 346

University of Colorado at Boulder, Leeds School of Business, Boulder (CO) 104, **702**

University of Connecticut, School of Business, Storrs (CT) 112, **708**

University of Denver, Daniels College of Business, Denver (CO) 106

University of Florida, Hough Graduate School of Business, Gainesville (FL) 134

University of Georgia, Terry College of Business, Athens (GA) 151

University of Glasgow, University of Glasgow Business School, Glasgow (United Kingdom) 550

University of Illinois at Chicago, Liautaud Graduate School of Business, Chicago (IL) 176

University of Kentucky, Gatton College of Business and Economics, Lexington (KY) 202, **716**

University of Memphis, Fogelman College of Business and Economics, Memphis (TN) 400

University of Michigan, Ross School of Business at the University of Michigan, Ann Arbor (MI) 244

University of Mississippi, School of Business Administration, Oxford (MS) 257

University of Missouri–Columbia, Robert J. Trulaske, Sr. College of Business, Columbia (MO) 267, **720**

The University of North Carolina at Chapel Hill, Kenan-Flagler Business School, Chapel Hill (NC) 330

The University of North Carolina at Charlotte, Belk College of Business Administration, Charlotte (NC) 330, **730**

University of North Texas, College of Business Administration, Denton (TX) 422

University of Pennsylvania, Wharton School, Philadelphia (PA) 380

University of Reading, ICMA Centre, Reading (United Kingdom) 554

University of St. Thomas, Opus College of Business (MN) 253, **738**

University of San Diego, School of Business Administration, San Diego (CA) 96

University of South Carolina, Moore School of Business, Columbia (SC) *392,* **740**

University of Southern California, School of Business, Los Angeles (CA) 98

The University of Texas at Arlington, College of Business Administration, Arlington (TX) 424, **746**

The University of Texas at San Antonio, College of Business, San Antonio (TX) 427, **750**

University of Washington, Michael G. Foster School of Business, Seattle (WA) 452, **754**

University of Wisconsin–Madison, Wisconsin School of Business, Madison (WI) 462, **756**

Virginia Commonwealth University, School of Business, Richmond (VA) 445

York University, Schulich School of Business, Toronto (Canada) 482, **772**

REHABILITATION ADMINISTRATION

Salve Regina University, Graduate Studies, Newport (RI) 389

Vienna University of Economics and Business Administration, WU Wien MBA, Vienna (Austria) 492

RESEARCH AND DEVELOPMENT ADMINISTRATION

The American University in Cairo, School of Business, Economics and Communication, Cairo (Egypt) 502

Lancaster University, Management School, Lancaster (United Kingdom) 541

Nottingham Trent University, Nottingham Business School, Nottingham (United Kingdom) 544

Open University, Business School, Milton Keynes (United Kingdom) 545

Queensland University of Technology, Brisbane Graduate School of Business, Brisbane (Australia) 487

Rensselaer Polytechnic Institute, Lally School of Management and Technology, Troy (NY) 311, **670**

University of Bath, School of Management, Bath (United Kingdom) 547

University of California, San Diego, Rady School of Management, La Jolla (CA) 93, **700**

University of Toronto, Joseph L. Rotman School of Management, Toronto (Canada) 478

RESORT MANAGEMENT

Barcelona Business School, Graduate Programs in Business, Barcelona (Spain) 528

RESOURCES MANAGEMENT

American Jewish University, David Lieber School of Graduate Studies, Bel Air (CA) 63

Antwerp International Business School, Graduate Programs in Business, Antwerp (Belgium) 493

Athabasca University, Centre for Innovative Management, Athabasca (Canada) 466

École Nationale des Ponts et Chaussées, ENPC MBA, Paris (France) 503

Lawrence Technological University, College of Management, Southfield (MI) 239, **654**

Michigan Technological University, School of Business and Economics, Houghton (MI) 241

Naval Postgraduate School, School of Business and Public Policy, Monterey (CA) 83

SIT Graduate Institute, Master's Programs in Intercultural Service, Leadership, and Management, Brattleboro (VT) 434

Stockholm School of Economics, Department of Business Administration, Stockholm (Sweden) 531

University of Alberta, School of Business, Edmonton (Canada) 473

University of Edinburgh, Edinburgh University Management School, Edinburgh (United Kingdom) 550

Westminster College, The Bill and Vieve Gore School of Business, Salt Lake City (UT) 433

RISK MANAGEMENT

Bayerische Julius-Maximilians University of Wuerzburg, MBA Program, Wuerzburg (Germany) 507

Bentley College, The Elkin B. McCallum Graduate School of Business, Waltham (MA) 221, **578**

City University of Hong Kong, Faculty of Business, Hong Kong (China) 497

Columbia University, Graduate School of Business, New York (NY) 298

Concordia University Wisconsin, Graduate Programs, Mequon (WI) 458

École Nationale des Ponts et Chaussées, ENPC MBA, Paris (France) 503

Florida State University, College of Business, Tallahassee (FL) 129

Georgia State University, J. Mack Robinson College of Business, Atlanta (GA) 147, **626**

HfB—Business School of Finance and Management, Frankfurt School of Finance and Management, Frankfurt (Germany) 508

Hult International Business School, Graduate Program, Cambridge (MA) *227,* **634**

IE Business School, Business School, Madrid (Spain) 529, **636**

Illinois Institute of Technology, Stuart School of Business, Chicago (IL) 164

Indian School of Business, MBA Program, Andhra Pradesh (India) 512

International University of Japan, Graduate School of International Management, Minami Uonuma-gu (Japan) 516

Katholieke Universiteit Leuven, Leuven School of Business and Economics, Leuven (Belgium) 494

Lancaster University, Management School, Lancaster (United Kingdom) 541

London School of Economics and Political Science, The Graduate School, London (United Kingdom) 543

Loyola University Chicago, Graduate School of Business, Chicago (IL) 167

McMaster University, DeGroote School of Business, Hamilton (Canada) 470

Monash University, MBA Programme, Clayton (Australia) 486

North Carolina State University, College of Management, Raleigh (NC) 328, **664**

St. John's University, The Peter J. Tobin College of Business, Queens (NY) 314, **680**

Southwestern College, Professional Studies Programs, Winfield (KS) 196

Stockholm School of Economics, Department of Business Administration, Stockholm (Sweden) 531

Swinburne University of Technology, Australian Graduate School of Entrepreneurship (AGSE), Hawthorne (Australia) 488

Temple University, Fox School of Business and Management, Philadelphia (PA) 379

Tennessee Technological University, College of Business, Cookeville (TN) 399

The University of Alabama, Manderson Graduate School of Business, Tuscaloosa (AL) 49

University of California, Berkeley, Haas School of Business, Berkeley (CA) 89

University of Edinburgh, Edinburgh University Management School, Edinburgh (United Kingdom) 550

University of Georgia, Terry College of Business, Athens (GA) 151

University of Mary Washington, College of Graduate and Professional Studies, Fredericksburg (VA) 444

University of Missouri–Columbia, Robert J. Trulaske, Sr. College of Business, Columbia (MO) 267, **720**

University of Oklahoma, Michael F. Price College of Business, Norman (OK) 355

University of Pennsylvania, Wharton School, Philadelphia (PA) 380

University of St. Thomas, Opus College of Business (MN) 253, **738**

University of Salford, Salford Business School, Salford (United Kingdom) 554

University of Toronto, Joseph L. Rotman School of Management, Toronto (Canada) 478

University of Tulsa, College of Business Administration, Tulsa (OK) 356

University of Ulster at Jordanstown, Faculty of Business and Management, Newtown Abbey (United Kingdom) 556

University of Wisconsin–Madison, Wisconsin School of Business, Madison (WI) 462, **756**

Vienna University of Economics and Business Administration, WU Wien MBA, Vienna (Austria) 492

Virginia Commonwealth University, School of Business, Richmond (VA) 445

Walden University, School of Management,
Minneapolis (MN) 253

SOCIAL WORK

Edith Cowan University, Faculty of Business and
Public Management, Churchlands
(Australia) 484

University at Buffalo, the State University of New
York, School of Management, Buffalo
(NY) 320

University of Maryland, College Park, Robert H.
Smith School of Business, College Park
(MD) 217

Vienna University of Economics and Business
Administration, WU Wien MBA, Vienna
(Austria) 492

Washington University in St. Louis, Olin Business
School, St. Louis (MO) 269

SPORTS/ENTERTAINMENT MANAGEMENT

Antwerp International Business School, Graduate
Programs in Business, Antwerp (Belgium) 493

Arizona State University, W.P. Carey School of
Business, Tempe (AZ) 54

Auburn University, College of Business, Auburn
University (AL) 45, **568**

Barcelona Business School, Graduate Programs in
Business, Barcelona (Spain) 528

Columbia Southern University, MBA Program,
Orange Beach (AL) 46

Concordia University, St. Paul, College of
Business and Organizational Leadership, St.
Paul (MN) 250

Deakin University, Deakin Business School,
Geelong (Australia) 484

East Carolina University, College of Business,
Greenville (NC) 324, **602**

Edith Cowan University, Faculty of Business and
Public Management, Churchlands
(Australia) 484

Florida Atlantic University, College of Business,
Boca Raton (FL) 126

The George Washington University, School of
Business, Washington (DC) 119, **622**

Gonzaga University, School of Business
Administration, Spokane (WA) 448

The Hague University, Faculty of Economics and
Management, The Hague
(Netherlands) 521, **628**

Hofstra University, Frank G. Zarb School of
Business, Hempstead (NY) 302

Laurentian University, School of Commerce and
Administration, Sudbury (Canada) 469

Lindenwood University, Division of Management,
St. Charles (MO) 261

Loyola University Chicago, Graduate School of
Business, Chicago (IL) 167

Lynn University, School of Business, Boca Raton
(FL) 130

Manhattanville College, School of Graduate and
Professional Studies, Purchase (NY) 306

Northcentral University, MBA Program, Prescott
Valley (AZ) 56

Ohio University, College of Business, Athens
(OH) 344

Point Park University, School of Business,
Pittsburgh (PA) 375

Queen Margaret University College, Edinburgh,
School of Business and Enterprise, Edinburgh
(United Kingdom) 545

Saint Leo University, Graduate Business Studies,
Saint Leo (FL) 132

St. Thomas University, Department of Business
Administration, Miami Gardens (FL) 132

Seton Hall University, Stillman School of
Business, South Orange (NJ) 290, **686**

Southern Cross University, Graduate College of
Management, Coffs Harbour (Australia) 487

Southern New Hampshire University, School of
Business, Manchester (NH) 279, **690**

Tiffin University, Program in Business
Administration, Tiffin (OH) 345

University of Abertay Dundee, Dundee Business
School, Dundee (United Kingdom) 547

University of Alberta, School of Business,
Edmonton (Canada) 473

University of Baltimore/Towson University, Joint
University of Baltimore/Towson University
(UB/Towson) MBA Program, Baltimore
(MD) 217

University of Birmingham, Birmingham Business
School, Birmingham (United Kingdom) 548

University of California, Los Angeles, UCLA
Anderson School of Management, Los Angeles
(CA) 91, **696**

University of Central Florida, College of Business
Administration, Orlando (FL) 133

University of Dallas, Graduate School of
Management, Irving (TX) 420, **710**

University of Delaware, Alfred Lerner College of
Business and Economics, Newark
(DE) 116, **712**

University of Florida, Hough Graduate School of
Business, Gainesville (FL) 134

University of Massachusetts Amherst, Isenberg
School of Management, Amherst (MA) 231

University of New Brunswick Fredericton, Faculty
of Business Administration, Fredericton
(Canada) 476

University of New Haven, School of Business,
West Haven (CT) 113, **728**

The University of North Carolina at Charlotte,
Belk College of Business Administration,
Charlotte (NC) 330, **730**

University of Oregon, Charles H. Lundquist
College of Business, Eugene (OR) 359, **732**

University of the Incarnate Word, H-E-B School
of Business and Administration (TX) 429

Webber International University, Graduate School
of Business, Babson Park (FL) 140, **762**

Western Carolina University, College of Business,
Cullowhee (NC) 333

Western New England College, School of
Business, Springfield (MA) 234

STATISTICS

Aston University, Aston Business School,
Birmingham (United Kingdom) 539

Bernard M. Baruch College of the City University
of New York, Zicklin School of Business, New
York (NY) 296

City University of Hong Kong, Faculty of
Business, Hong Kong (China) 497

Clemson University, College of Business and
Behavioral Science, Clemson (SC) 391

HfB—Business School of Finance and
Management, Frankfurt School of Finance and
Management, Frankfurt (Germany) 508

IE Business School, Business School, Madrid
(Spain) 529, **636**

Indian School of Business, MBA Program, Andhra
Pradesh (India) 512

International University of Japan, Graduate School
of International Management, Minami
Uonuma-gu (Japan) 516

Lancaster University, Management School,
Lancaster (United Kingdom) 541

Monash University, MBA Programme, Clayton
(Australia) 486

New Mexico State University, College of
Business, Las Cruces (NM) 293

New York University, Leonard N. Stern School of
Business (NY) 309

Nyenrode Business Universiteit, Netherlands
Business School, Breukelen (Netherlands) 522

Rensselaer Polytechnic Institute, Lally School of
Management and Technology, Troy
(NY) 311, **670**

Stockholm School of Economics, Department of
Business Administration, Stockholm
(Sweden) 531

Temple University, Fox School of Business and
Management, Philadelphia (PA) 379

Texas Tech University, Jerry S. Rawls College of
Business Administration, Lubbock (TX) 418

The University of Alabama, Manderson Graduate
School of Business, Tuscaloosa (AL) 49

University of California, Berkeley, Haas School of
Business, Berkeley (CA) 89

University of Chicago, Graduate School of
Business, Chicago (IL) 175

University of Edinburgh, Edinburgh University
Management School, Edinburgh (United
Kingdom) 550

University of Miami, School of Business
Administration, Coral Gables (FL) 135, **718**

University of Missouri–Columbia, Robert J.
Trulaske, Sr. College of Business, Columbia
(MO) 267, **720**

University of Pennsylvania, Wharton School,
Philadelphia (PA) 380

University of South Carolina, Moore School of
Business, Columbia (SC) *392*, **740**

The University of Tennessee, College of Business
Administration, Knoxville (TN) *401*, **744**

The University of Texas at San Antonio, College
of Business, San Antonio (TX) 427, **750**

University of Wisconsin–Green Bay, Program in
Management, Green Bay (WI) 461

Western Illinois University, College of Business
and Technology, Macomb (IL) 178

STRATEGIC MANAGEMENT

The Aarhus School of Business, Faculty of
Business Administration, Aarhus
(Denmark) 501

Alliant International University, Marshall
Goldsmith School of Management, San Diego
(CA) 63

Alliant International University–México City,
Marshall Goldsmith School of Management,
Mexico City (Mexico) 519

The American University in Cairo, School of
Business, Economics and Communication,
Cairo (Egypt) 502

Andrew Jackson University, Brian Tracy College
of Business and Entrepreneurship, Birmingham
(AL) 45

Anna Maria College, Program in Business
Administration, Paxton (MA) 219

Antwerp International Business School, Graduate
Programs in Business, Antwerp (Belgium) 493

Ashridge, Ashridge Executive MBA Program,
Berkhamsted (United Kingdom) 538

Aston University, Aston Business School,
Birmingham (United Kingdom) 539

Athabasca University, Centre for Innovative
Management, Athabasca (Canada) 466

Azusa Pacific University, School of Business and
Management, Azusa (CA) 66

Barcelona Business School, Graduate Programs in
Business, Barcelona (Spain) 528

Bayerische Julius-Maximilians University of
Wuerzburg, MBA Program, Wuerzburg
(Germany) 507

Bernard M. Baruch College of the City University of New York, Zicklin School of Business, New York (NY) 296

Bocconi University, SDA Bocconi, Milan (Italy) 515

Boise State University, College of Business and Economics, Boise (ID) 155

Boston College, The Carroll School of Management, Chestnut Hill (MA) 221, **580**

Boston University, School of Management, Boston (MA) 223

Brescia University, Program in Management, Owensboro (KY) 198

California State University, East Bay, College of Business and Economics, Hayward (CA) 69

Carnegie Mellon University, Tepper School of Business, Pittsburgh (PA) 363, **584**

Centenary College of Louisiana, Frost School of Business, Shreveport (LA) 204

The Chinese University of Hong Kong, Faculty of Business Administration, Hong Kong (China) 497

Chulalongkorn University, Sasin Graduate Institute of Business Administration, Bangkok (Thailand) 536

City University of Hong Kong, Faculty of Business, Hong Kong (China) 497

Claremont Graduate University, Peter F. Drucker and Masatoshi Ito Graduate School of Management, Claremont (CA) 75, **590**

College of St. Catherine, Program in Organizational Leadership, St. Paul (MN) 249

Copenhagen Business School, Faculty of Economics and Business Administration, Copenhagen (Denmark) 501

Cranfield University, Cranfield School of Management, Cranfield (United Kingdom) 540

Cyprus International Institute of Management, MBA Programme, Nicosia (Cyprus) 500

Davenport University, Sneden Graduate School, Grand Rapids (MI) 237

Deakin University, Deakin Business School, Geelong (Australia) 484

Drexel University, LeBow College of Business, Philadelphia (PA) 366

Drury University, Breech School of Business Administration, Springfield (MO) 259

Duke University, The Fuqua School of Business, Durham (NC) 323

Eastern Mennonite University, Program in Business Administration, Harrisonburg (VA) 438

École Nationale des Ponts et Chaussées, ENPC MBA, Paris (France) 503

Emory University, Roberto C. Goizueta Business School, Atlanta (GA) 145, **606**

Erasmus University Rotterdam, Rotterdam School of Management, Rotterdam (Netherlands) 521

ESCP-EAP European School of Management, ESCP-EAP European School of Management (France) 503

European School of Economics, MBA Programme (Italy) 515, **608**

The George Washington University, School of Business, Washington (DC) 119, **622**

Georgia Institute of Technology, College of Management, Atlanta (GA) 146, **624**

Graduate School of Business Administration Zurich, Executive Management Programs, Zurich (Switzerland) 532

The Hague University, Faculty of Economics and Management, The Hague (Netherlands) 521, **628**

HEC Paris, HEC MBA Program, Jouy-en-Josas (France) *505*, **632**

HHL—Leipzig Graduate School of Management, MBA Program, Leipzig (Germany) 509

Hult International Business School, Graduate Program, Cambridge (MA) *227*, **634**

IE Business School, Business School, Madrid (Spain) 529, **636**

Illinois Institute of Technology, Stuart School of Business, Chicago (IL) 164

Indian School of Business, MBA Program, Andhra Pradesh (India) 512

International University of Japan, Graduate School of International Management, Minami Uonuma-gu (Japan) 516

KDI School of Public Policy and Management, MBA Program, Seoul (Republic of Korea) 526

Lancaster University, Management School, Lancaster (United Kingdom) 541

Leadership Institute of Seattle, School of Applied Behavioral Science, Kenmore (WA) 449

London School of Economics and Political Science, The Graduate School, London (United Kingdom) 543

Loyola University Chicago, Graduate School of Business, Chicago (IL) 167

Macquarie University, Macquarie Graduate School of Management, Sydney (Australia) 485

Manhattanville College, School of Graduate and Professional Studies, Purchase (NY) 306

Massachusetts Institute of Technology, Sloan School of Management, Cambridge (MA) 227

McGill University, Desautels Faculty of Management, Montréal (Canada) 469, **658**

Memorial University of Newfoundland, Faculty of Business Administration, St. John's (Canada) 470

Monash University, MBA Programme, Clayton (Australia) 486

Nanjing University, School of Business, Nanjing (China) 500

Nanyang Technological University, Nanyang Business School, Singapore (Singapore) 527, **662**

National University of Ireland, Dublin, The Michael Smurfit Graduate School of Business, Blackrock (Ireland) 513

New England College, Program in Management, Henniker (NH) 278

New Jersey Institute of Technology, School of Management, Newark (NJ) 285

New York University, Leonard N. Stern School of Business (NY) 309

Northwestern University, Kellogg School of Management, Evanston (IL) 171

Norwegian School of Management, Graduate School, Sandvika (Norway) 524

Nottingham Trent University, Nottingham Business School, Nottingham (United Kingdom) 544

OGI School of Science & Engineering at Oregon Health & Science University, Department of Management in Science and Technology, Beaverton (OR) 358

Open University of the Netherlands, Business Programs, Heerlen (Netherlands) 523

Penn State University Park, The Mary Jean and Frank P. Smeal College of Business Administration, State College (PA) 374

Pepperdine University, Graziadio School of Business and Management, Los Angeles (CA) 85

Purdue University, Krannert School of Management, West Lafayette (IN) 185

Queensland University of Technology, Brisbane Graduate School of Business, Brisbane (Australia) 487

Regent University, School of Global Leadership and Entrepreneurship, Virginia Beach (VA) 442

Regis University, College for Professional Studies, Denver (CO) 103

Rice University, Jesse H. Jones Graduate School of Management, Houston (TX) 410

Rockford College, Program in Business Administration, Rockford (IL) 171

Roosevelt University, Walter E. Heller College of Business Administration, Chicago (IL) 172, **676**

Royal Roads University, Faculty of Management, Victoria (Canada) 471

Sage Graduate School, Department of Management, Troy (NY) 313

Southern Methodist University, Cox School of Business, Dallas (TX) 411, **688**

Stockholm School of Economics, Department of Business Administration, Stockholm (Sweden) 531

Swinburne University of Technology, Australian Graduate School of Entrepreneurship (AGSE), Hawthorne (Australia) 488

Temple University, Fox School of Business and Management, Philadelphia (PA) 379

Texas A&M University, Mays Business School, College Station (TX) 414

TUI University, College of Business Administration, Cypress (CA) 89

Universite Libre de Bruxelles, Solvay Business School, Brussels (Belgium) 495

The University of Alabama, Manderson Graduate School of Business, Tuscaloosa (AL) 49

University of Antwerp, University of Antwerp Management School, Antwerp (Belgium) 495

University of Bath, School of Management, Bath (United Kingdom) 547

University of Birmingham, Birmingham Business School, Birmingham (United Kingdom) 548

The University of British Columbia, Sauder School of Business, Vancouver (Canada) 474

University of California, Berkeley, Haas School of Business, Berkeley (CA) 89

University of California, Los Angeles, UCLA Anderson School of Management, Los Angeles (CA) 91, **696**

University of Canterbury, Department of Management, Christchurch (New Zealand) 523

University of Chicago, Graduate School of Business, Chicago (IL) 175

University of Denver, Daniels College of Business, Denver (CO) 106

University of Edinburgh, Edinburgh University Management School, Edinburgh (United Kingdom) 550

University of Glasgow, University of Glasgow Business School, Glasgow (United Kingdom) 550

University of Illinois at Urbana–Champaign, College of Business, Champaign (IL) 176

University of Kansas, School of Business, Lawrence (KS) 196

University of Massachusetts Amherst, Isenberg School of Management, Amherst (MA) 231

University of Melbourne, Melbourne Business School, Melbourne (Australia) 488

University of Michigan, Ross School of Business at the University of Michigan, Ann Arbor (MI) 244

University of Minnesota, Twin Cities Campus, Carlson School of Management, Minneapolis (MN) 252

University of Nebraska–Lincoln, College of Business Administration, Lincoln (NE) 274

University of North Texas, College of Business Administration, Denton (TX) 422

University of Otago, School of Business, Dunedin (New Zealand) 523

University of Pennsylvania, Wharton School, Philadelphia (PA) 380

University of Phoenix–Atlanta Campus, College of Graduate Business and Management, Sandy Springs (GA) 151

University of Phoenix–Hawaii Campus, College of Graduate Business and Management, Honolulu (HI) 155

University of Phoenix–Phoenix Campus, College of Graduate Business and Management, Phoenix (AZ) 59

University of Phoenix–San Diego Campus, College of Graduate Business and Management, San Diego (CA) 95

University of Phoenix–Southern Colorado Campus, College of Graduate Business and Management, Colorado Springs (CO) 107

University of Phoenix–Utah Campus, College of Graduate Business and Management, Salt Lake City (UT) 432

University of Rochester, William E. Simon Graduate School of Business Administration, Rochester (NY) 321, **736**

University of Salford, Salford Business School, Salford (United Kingdom) 554

University of South Carolina, Moore School of Business, Columbia (SC) *392, **740***

University of Southern California, School of Business, Los Angeles (CA) 98

University of Strathclyde, University of Strathclyde Graduate School of Business, Glasgow (United Kingdom) 555

The University of Texas at Austin, Programs in MBA, Austin (TX) 425

The University of Texas at Dallas, School of Management, Richardson (TX) *426*, **748**

University of the West of England, Bristol, Bristol Business School, Bristol (United Kingdom) 555

University of the Witwatersrand, Graduate School of Business Administration, Wits (South Africa) 527

University of Toronto, Joseph L. Rotman School of Management, Toronto (Canada) 478

University of Ulster at Jordanstown, Faculty of Business and Management, Newtown Abbey (United Kingdom) 556

University of Warwick, Warwick Business School, Coventry (United Kingdom) 557

University of Washington, Michael G. Foster School of Business, Seattle (WA) 452, **754**

The University of Western Ontario, Richard Ivey School of Business, London (Canada) 480

Vanderbilt University, Owen Graduate School of Management, Nashville (TN) 403, **758**

Waseda University, Graduate School of Commerce, Tokyo (Japan) 517

Washington University in St. Louis, Olin Business School, St. Louis (MO) 269

WHU—Otto Beisheim School of Management, WHU—Otto Beisheim School of Management, Vallendar (Germany) 511

Wilfrid Laurier University, School of Business and Economics, Waterloo (Canada) 481, **766**

Yale University, Yale School of Management, New Haven (CT) 114

York University, Schulich School of Business, Toronto (Canada) 482, **772**

STUDENT DESIGNED

California Polytechnic State University, San Luis Obispo, Orfalea College of Business, San Luis Obispo (CA) 68

Florida Gulf Coast University, Lutgert College of Business, Fort Myers (FL) 127

The George Washington University, School of Business, Washington (DC) 119, **622**

Hult International Business School, Graduate Program, Cambridge (MA) *227*, **634**

Point Loma Nazarene University, Program in Business Administration, San Diego (CA) 86

Roosevelt University, Walter E. Heller College of Business Administration, Chicago (IL) 172, **676**

University of Calgary, Haskayne School of Business, Calgary (Canada) 474

University of California, San Diego, Rady School of Management, La Jolla (CA) 93, **700**

University of Illinois at Chicago, Liautaud Graduate School of Business, Chicago (IL) 176

University of New Brunswick Saint John, Faculty of Business, Saint John (Canada) 476, **724**

The University of New England, The Graduate School of Business Administration, Armidale (Australia) 490

University of Pennsylvania, Wharton School, Philadelphia (PA) 380

University of Southern California, School of Business, Los Angeles (CA) 98

SUPPLY CHAIN MANAGEMENT

American University of Sharjah, School of Business and Management, Sharjah (United Arab Emirates) 538

Arizona State University, W.P. Carey School of Business, Tempe (AZ) 54

Auburn University, College of Business, Auburn University (AL) 45, **568**

Barcelona Business School, Graduate Programs in Business, Barcelona (Spain) 528

Boise State University, College of Business and Economics, Boise (ID) 155

Brigham Young University, Marriott School of Management, Provo (UT) 431

California Polytechnic State University, San Luis Obispo, Orfalea College of Business, San Luis Obispo (CA) 68

California State University, East Bay, College of Business and Economics, Hayward (CA) 69

California State University, San Bernardino, College of Business and Public Administration, San Bernardino (CA) 73

Canisius College, Richard J. Wehle School of Business, Buffalo (NY) 296

Case Western Reserve University, Weatherhead School of Management, Cleveland (OH) 338

The Chinese University of Hong Kong, Faculty of Business Administration, Hong Kong (China) 497

City University of Hong Kong, Faculty of Business, Hong Kong (China) 497

Clarkson University, School of Business, Potsdam (NY) 297

Clemson University, College of Business and Behavioral Science, Clemson (SC) 391

Copenhagen Business School, Faculty of Economics and Business Administration, Copenhagen (Denmark) 501

Cranfield University, Cranfield School of Management, Cranfield (United Kingdom) 540

Deakin University, Deakin Business School, Geelong (Australia) 484

Duquesne University, John F. Donahue Graduate School of Business, Pittsburgh (PA) 367

East Carolina University, College of Business, Greenville (NC) 324, **602**

Eastern Michigan University, College of Business, Ypsilanti (MI) 237

École Nationale des Ponts et Chaussées, ENPC MBA, Paris (France) 503

Elmhurst College, Program in Business Administration, Elmhurst (IL) 163

European Institute of Purchasing Management, MBA Programs, Archamps (France) 504

European School of Economics, MBA Programme (Italy) 515, **608**

Florida State University, College of Business, Tallahassee (FL) 129

The George Washington University, School of Business, Washington (DC) 119, **622**

Gonzaga University, School of Business Administration, Spokane (WA) 448

HEC Montreal, Master's Program in Business Administration and Management, Montréal (Canada) 468

HEC Paris, HEC MBA Program, Jouy-en-Josas (France) *505*, **632**

HHL—Leipzig Graduate School of Management, MBA Program, Leipzig (Germany) 509

Howard University, School of Business, Washington (DC) 120

IE Business School, Business School, Madrid (Spain) 529, **636**

Indiana University Bloomington, Kelley School of Business, Bloomington (IN) 182

International University of Japan, Graduate School of International Management, Minami Uonuma-gu (Japan) 516

Iowa State University of Science and Technology, College of Business, Ames (IA) 189, **644**

Kutztown University of Pennsylvania, College of Business, Kutztown (PA) 369

Lancaster University, Management School, Lancaster (United Kingdom) 541

Lehigh University, College of Business and Economics, Bethlehem (PA) 371, **656**

Maine Maritime Academy, Department of Graduate Studies, Castine (ME) 210

McGill University, Desautels Faculty of Management, Montréal (Canada) 469, **658**

McMaster University, DeGroote School of Business, Hamilton (Canada) 470

Michigan State University, Eli Broad Graduate School of Management, East Lansing (MI) 240

Monash University, MBA Programme, Clayton (Australia) 486

Monterey Institute of International Studies, Fisher Graduate School of International Business, Monterey (CA) 82, **660**

Moravian College, The Moravian MBA, Bethlehem (PA) 373

Naval Postgraduate School, School of Business and Public Policy, Monterey (CA) 83

North Carolina State University, College of Management, Raleigh (NC) 328, **664**

Northeastern University, Graduate School of Business Administration, Boston (MA) 228

Nyenrode Business Universiteit, Netherlands Business School, Breukelen (Netherlands) 522

OGI School of Science & Engineering at Oregon Health & Science University, Department of Management in Science and Technology, Beaverton (OR) 358

Penn State University Park, The Mary Jean and Frank P. Smeal College of Business Administration, State College (PA) 374

Portland State University, School of Business Administration, Portland (OR) 358

Purdue University, Krannert School of Management, West Lafayette (IN) 185

Rochester Institute of Technology, E. Philip Saunders College of Business, Rochester (NY) 312

Rutgers, The State University of New Jersey, Rutgers Business School–Newark and New Brunswick, Newark and New Brunswick (NJ) 288, **678**

Saint Louis University, John Cook School of Business, St. Louis (MO) *264*

Santa Clara University, Leavey School of Business, Santa Clara (CA) 88

State University of New York Maritime College, Program in International Transportation Management, Throggs Neck (NY) 317

Stockholm School of Economics, Department of Business Administration, Stockholm (Sweden) 531

Syracuse University, Martin J. Whitman School of Management, Syracuse (NY) 318, **692**

Tennessee State University, College of Business, Nashville (TN) 399

Texas A&M University, Mays Business School, College Station (TX) 414

Texas Christian University, The Neeley School of Business at TCU, Fort Worth (TX) 416, **694**

The University of Akron, College of Business Administration, Akron (OH) 346

University of Arkansas, Sam M. Walton College of Business Administration, Fayetteville (AR) 62

University of Bath, School of Management, Bath (United Kingdom) 547

The University of British Columbia, Sauder School of Business, Vancouver (Canada) 474

University of California, Los Angeles, UCLA Anderson School of Management, Los Angeles (CA) 91, **696**

University of Dallas, Graduate School of Management, Irving (TX) 420, **710**

University of Denver, Daniels College of Business, Denver (CO) 106

University of Florida, Hough Graduate School of Business, Gainesville (FL) 134

University of La Verne, College of Business and Public Management, La Verne (CA) 94

University of Manitoba, Faculty of Management, Winnipeg (Canada) 475

University of Maryland, College Park, Robert H. Smith School of Business, College Park (MD) 217

University of Miami, School of Business Administration, Coral Gables (FL) 135, **718**

University of Michigan–Dearborn, School of Management, Dearborn (MI) 245

University of Minnesota, Twin Cities Campus, Carlson School of Management, Minneapolis (MN) 252

University of Missouri–St. Louis, College of Business Administration, St. Louis (MO) *268*

University of New Hampshire, Whittemore School of Business and Economics, Durham (NH) 280, **726**

The University of North Carolina at Chapel Hill, Kenan-Flagler Business School, Chapel Hill (NC) 330

University of North Texas, College of Business Administration, Denton (TX) 422

University of Oklahoma, Michael F. Price College of Business, Norman (OK) 355

University of Oregon, Charles H. Lundquist College of Business, Eugene (OR) 359, **732**

University of Plymouth, Plymouth Business School, Plymouth (United Kingdom) 553

University of Rhode Island, College of Business Administration, Kingston (RI) 389, **734**

University of Salford, Salford Business School, Salford (United Kingdom) 554

University of San Diego, School of Business Administration, San Diego (CA) 96

University of South Carolina, Moore School of Business, Columbia (SC) *392*, **740**

University of Southern California, School of Business, Los Angeles (CA) 98

The University of Texas at Dallas, School of Management, Richardson (TX) *426*, **748**

University of Wisconsin–Madison, Wisconsin School of Business, Madison (WI) 462, **756**

Walden University, School of Management, Minneapolis (MN) 253

Washington University in St. Louis, Olin Business School, St. Louis (MO) 269

Western Illinois University, College of Business and Technology, Macomb (IL) 178

WHU—Otto Beisheim School of Management, WHU—Otto Beisheim School of Management, Vallendar (Germany) 511

Wilfrid Laurier University, School of Business and Economics, Waterloo (Canada) 481, **766**

Worcester Polytechnic Institute, Department of Management, Worcester (MA) 234, **770**

Wright State University, Raj Soin College of Business, Dayton (OH) 350

SYSTEM MANAGEMENT

The American University in Cairo, School of Business, Economics and Communication, Cairo (Egypt) 502

Baldwin-Wallace College, Division of Business, Berea (OH) 337

Baylor University, Hankamer School of Business, Waco (TX) 405, **574**

Fairleigh Dickinson University, Metropolitan Campus, Silberman College of Business, Teaneck (NJ) 282, **612**

Graduate School of Business Administration Zurich, Executive Management Programs, Zurich (Switzerland) 532

IE Business School, Business School, Madrid (Spain) 529, **636**

Indian School of Business, MBA Program, Andhra Pradesh (India) 512

Jackson State University, School of Business, Jackson (MS) 255

Lancaster University, Management School, Lancaster (United Kingdom) 541

Leadership Institute of Seattle, School of Applied Behavioral Science, Kenmore (WA) 449

London School of Economics and Political Science, The Graduate School, London (United Kingdom) 543

Loyola Marymount University, College of Business Administration, Los Angeles (CA) 81

Metropolitan State University, College of Management, St. Paul (MN) 250

National University of Ireland, Dublin, The Michael Smurfit Graduate School of Business, Blackrock (Ireland) 513

Nottingham Trent University, Nottingham Business School, Nottingham (United Kingdom) 544

Penn State Great Valley, Graduate Studies, Malvern (PA) 373

Regis University, College for Professional Studies, Denver (CO) 103

Saint Joseph's University, Erivan K. Haub School of Business, Philadelphia (PA) 377

Southern Illinois University Edwardsville, School of Business, Edwardsville (IL) *174*

Stockholm School of Economics, Department of Business Administration, Stockholm (Sweden) 531

Texas A&M University, Mays Business School, College Station (TX) 414

University of California, San Diego, Rady School of Management, La Jolla (CA) 93, **700**

University of Maryland University College, Graduate School of Management and Technology, Adelphi (MD) 218

University of Memphis, Fogelman College of Business and Economics, Memphis (TN) 400

University of Mississippi, School of Business Administration, Oxford (MS) 257

The University of Texas at Arlington, College of Business Administration, Arlington (TX) 424, **746**

Virginia Polytechnic Institute and State University, Pamplin College of Business, Blacksburg (VA) 446

Waseda University, Graduate School of Commerce, Tokyo (Japan) 517

Western International University, Graduate Programs in Business, Phoenix (AZ) 60

TAXATION

The Aarhus School of Business, Faculty of Business Administration, Aarhus (Denmark) 501

American University, Kogod School of Business, Washington (DC) 118

Appalachian State University, John A. Walker College of Business, Boone (NC) 322

Arizona State University, W.P. Carey School of Business, Tempe (AZ) 54

Bentley College, The Elkin B. McCallum Graduate School of Business, Waltham (MA) 221, **578**

Bernard M. Baruch College of the City University of New York, Zicklin School of Business, New York (NY) 296

Boise State University, College of Business and Economics, Boise (ID) 155

Brigham Young University, Marriott School of Management, Provo (UT) 431

Brock University, Faculty of Business, St. Catharines (Canada) 466

Bryant University, Graduate School, Smithfield (RI) 387

California Polytechnic State University, San Luis Obispo, Orfalea College of Business, San Luis Obispo (CA) 68

California State University, East Bay, College of Business and Economics, Hayward (CA) 69

California State University, Fullerton, College of Business and Economics, Fullerton (CA) 70

Case Western Reserve University, Weatherhead School of Management, Cleveland (OH) 338

City University of Hong Kong, Faculty of Business, Hong Kong (China) 497

Clemson University, College of Business and Behavioral Science, Clemson (SC) 391

Copenhagen Business School, Faculty of Economics and Business Administration, Copenhagen (Denmark) 501

DePaul University, Charles H. Kellstadt Graduate School of Business, Chicago (IL) 159

East Carolina University, College of Business, Greenville (NC) 324, **602**

Eastern Michigan University, College of Business, Ypsilanti (MI) 237

École Nationale des Ponts et Chaussées, ENPC MBA, Paris (France) 503

Edith Cowan University, Faculty of Business and Public Management, Churchlands (Australia) 484

Fairfield University, Charles F. Dolan School of Business, Fairfield (CT) 109

Fairleigh Dickinson University, College at Florham, Silberman College of Business, Madison (NJ) 282, **612**

Florida Atlantic University, College of Business, Boca Raton (FL) 126

Florida International University, Alvah H. Chapman, Jr. Graduate School of Business, Miami (FL) 128, **618**

Florida State University, College of Business, Tallahassee (FL) 129

Fontbonne University, Department of Business Administration, St. Louis (MO) 260

Fordham University, Graduate School of Business Administration, New York (NY) 301, **620**

Gardner-Webb University, Graduate School of Business, Boiling Springs (NC) 325

The George Washington University, School of Business, Washington (DC) 119, **622**

Georgia State University, J. Mack Robinson College of Business, Atlanta (GA) 147, **626**

Golden Gate University, Ageno School of Business, San Francisco (CA) 78

Gonzaga University, School of Business Administration, Spokane (WA) 448

Grand Valley State University, Seidman College of Business, Allendale (MI) 238

HfB—Business School of Finance and Management, Frankfurt School of Finance and Management, Frankfurt (Germany) 508

Hofstra University, Frank G. Zarb School of Business, Hempstead (NY) 302

International University of Japan, Graduate School of International Management, Minami Uonuma-gu (Japan) 516

Long Island University, Brooklyn Campus, School of Business, Public Administration and Information Sciences, Brooklyn (NY) 304

Long Island University, C.W. Post Campus, College of Management, Brookville (NY) 305

Michigan State University, Eli Broad Graduate School of Management, East Lansing (MI) 240

Mississippi State University, College of Business and Industry, Mississippi State (MS) 256

Monash University, MBA Programme, Clayton (Australia) 486

National University, School of Business and Management, La Jolla (CA) 82

Northeastern University, Graduate School of Business Administration, Boston (MA) 228

Northern Illinois University, College of Business, De Kalb (IL) 169

Nova Southeastern University, H. Wayne Huizenga School of Business and Entrepreneurship, Fort Lauderdale (FL) 130, **666**

Pace University, Lubin School of Business, New York (NY) 310

Philadelphia University, School of Business Administration, Philadelphia (PA) 375, **668**

Robert Morris University, Program in Business Administration, Moon Township (PA) 376, **672**

Rutgers, The State University of New Jersey, Rutgers Business School–Newark and New Brunswick, Newark and New Brunswick (NJ) 288, **678**

St. John's University, The Peter J. Tobin College of Business, Queens (NY) 314, **680**

San Diego State University, College of Business Administration, San Diego (CA) 86

San Jose State University, Lucas Graduate School of Business, San Jose (CA) 87

Seton Hall University, Stillman School of Business, South Orange (NJ) 290, **686**

Southeastern University, College of Graduate Studies, Washington (DC) 121

Southern New Hampshire University, School of Business, Manchester (NH) 279, **690**

Suffolk University, Sawyer Business School, Boston (MA) 230

Texas A&M University, Mays Business School, College Station (TX) 414

Texas Tech University, Jerry S. Rawls College of Business Administration, Lubbock (TX) 418

Truman State University, School of Business, Kirksville (MO) 266

Tulane University, A. B. Freeman School of Business, New Orleans (LA) 207

University at Albany, State University of New York, School of Business, Albany (NY) 319

The University of Akron, College of Business Administration, Akron (OH) 346

University of Baltimore, Merrick School of Business, Baltimore (MD) 216

University of Central Florida, College of Business Administration, Orlando (FL) 133

University of Colorado at Boulder, Leeds School of Business, Boulder (CO) 104, **702**

University of Denver, Daniels College of Business, Denver (CO) 106

University of Georgia, Terry College of Business, Athens (GA) 151

University of Hartford, Barney School of Business, West Hartford (CT) 113

University of Illinois at Urbana–Champaign, College of Business, Champaign (IL) 176

University of Kansas, School of Business, Lawrence (KS) 196

University of Memphis, Fogelman College of Business and Economics, Memphis (TN) 400

University of Miami, School of Business Administration, Coral Gables (FL) 135, **718**

University of Michigan–Dearborn, School of Management, Dearborn (MI) 245

University of Minnesota, Twin Cities Campus, Carlson School of Management, Minneapolis (MN) 252

University of New Haven, School of Business, West Haven (CT) 113, **728**

University of New Mexico, Robert O. Anderson Graduate School of Management, Albuquerque (NM) 294

University of New Orleans, College of Business Administration, New Orleans (LA) 209

The University of North Carolina at Charlotte, Belk College of Business Administration, Charlotte (NC) 330, **730**

University of North Florida, Coggin College of Business, Jacksonville (FL) 136

University of North Texas, College of Business Administration, Denton (TX) 422

University of Notre Dame, Mendoza College of Business, Notre Dame (IN) 187

University of Salford, Salford Business School, Salford (United Kingdom) 554

University of San Diego, School of Business Administration, San Diego (CA) 96

University of Southern California, School of Business, Los Angeles (CA) 98

The University of Tennessee, College of Business Administration, Knoxville (TN) *401*, **744**

The University of Texas at Arlington, College of Business Administration, Arlington (TX) 424, **746**

The University of Texas at Austin, Programs in MBA, Austin (TX) 425

The University of Texas at San Antonio, College of Business, San Antonio (TX) 427, **750**

University of the Sacred Heart, Department of Business Administration, San Juan (PR) 387

University of the West of England, Bristol, Bristol Business School, Bristol (United Kingdom) 555

University of Tulsa, College of Business Administration, Tulsa (OK) 356

University of Washington, Michael G. Foster School of Business, Seattle (WA) 452, **754**

University of Waterloo, Graduate Studies, Waterloo (Canada) 479

The University of Western Ontario, Richard Ivey School of Business, London (Canada) 480

University of Wisconsin–Madison, Wisconsin School of Business, Madison (WI) 462, **756**

University of Wisconsin–Milwaukee, Sheldon B. Lubar School of Business, Milwaukee (WI) 463

Vienna University of Economics and Business Administration, WU Wien MBA, Vienna (Austria) 492

Villanova University, Villanova School of Business, Villanova (PA) 382

Virginia Commonwealth University, School of Business, Richmond (VA) 445

Walsh College of Accountancy and Business Administration, Graduate Programs, Troy (MI) 247

Wayne State University, School of Business Administration, Detroit (MI) 247, **760**

Weber State University, John B. Goddard School of Business and Economics, Ogden (UT) 432

Western Illinois University, College of Business and Technology, Macomb (IL) 178

Widener University, School of Business Administration, Chester (PA) 384, **764**

TECHNOLOGY MANAGEMENT

Antioch University Santa Barbara, Program in Organizational Management, Santa Barbara (CA) 64

Arizona State University, W.P. Carey School of Business, Tempe (AZ) 54

Ashridge, Ashridge Executive MBA Program, Berkhamsted (United Kingdom) 538

Asian Institute of Technology, School of Management, Pathumthani (Thailand) 536

Auburn University, College of Business, Auburn University (AL) 45, **568**

Babson College, F. W. Olin Graduate School of Business, Wellesley (MA) *220*, **570**

Barcelona Business School, Graduate Programs in Business, Barcelona (Spain) 528

Benedictine University, Graduate Programs, Lisle (IL) 158

Boise State University, College of Business and Economics, Boise (ID) 155

California University of Pennsylvania, School of Graduate Studies and Research, California (PA) 363

Carleton University, Eric Sprott School of Business, Ottawa (Canada) 467

Case Western Reserve University, Weatherhead School of Management, Cleveland (OH) 338

City University of Hong Kong, Faculty of Business, Hong Kong (China) 497

City University of Seattle, School of Management, Bellevue (WA) 447, **588**

Cleveland State University, Nance College of Business Administration, Cleveland (OH) 340

Copenhagen Business School, Faculty of Economics and Business Administration, Copenhagen (Denmark) 501

Creighton University, Eugene C. Eppley College of Business Administration, Omaha (NE) 272

Dallas Baptist University, Graduate School of Business, Dallas (TX) 406

École Nationale des Ponts et Chaussées, ENPC MBA, Paris (France) 503

Embry-Riddle Aeronautical University Worldwide, Department of Management, Daytona Beach (FL) 125

ESCP-EAP European School of Management, ESCP-EAP European School of Management (France) 503

European University, Center for Management Studies, Montreux-Fontanivent (Switzerland) 532

Flinders University, Flinders Business School, Adelaide (Australia) 485

The George Washington University, School of Business, Washington (DC) 119, **622**

Georgia Institute of Technology, College of Management, Atlanta (GA) 146, **624**

Grand Valley State University, Seidman College of Business, Allendale (MI) 238

Hawai'i Pacific University, College of Business Administration, Honolulu (HI) 153, **630**

Illinois Institute of Technology, Stuart School of Business, Chicago (IL) 164

Indian School of Business, MBA Program, Andhra Pradesh (India) 512

The Johns Hopkins University, Carey Business School, Baltimore (MD) 214, **646**

Lancaster University, Management School, Lancaster (United Kingdom) 541

Lehigh University, College of Business and Economics, Bethlehem (PA) 371, **656**

Macquarie University, Macquarie Graduate School of Management, Sydney (Australia) 485

Marymount University, School of Business Administration, Arlington (VA) 440

Massachusetts Institute of Technology, Sloan School of Management, Cambridge (MA) 227

McMaster University, DeGroote School of Business, Hamilton (Canada) 470

Nanyang Technological University, Nanyang Business School, Singapore (Singapore) 527, **662**

National University of Ireland, Dublin, The Michael Smurfit Graduate School of Business, Blackrock (Ireland) 513

New Jersey Institute of Technology, School of Management, Newark (NJ) 285

North Carolina State University, College of Management, Raleigh (NC) 328, **664**

Northcentral University, MBA Program, Prescott Valley (AZ) 56

Northeastern University, Graduate School of Business Administration, Boston (MA) 228

Northwestern University, Kellogg School of Management, Evanston (IL) 171

Nyenrode Business Universiteit, Netherlands Business School, Breukelen (Netherlands) 522

OGI School of Science & Engineering at Oregon Health & Science University, Department of Management in Science and Technology, Beaverton (OR) 358

Old Dominion University, College of Business and Public Administration, Norfolk (VA) 441

Open University, Business School, Milton Keynes (United Kingdom) 545

Open University of the Netherlands, Business Programs, Heerlen (Netherlands) 523

Pacific Lutheran University, School of Business, Tacoma (WA) 449

Penn State Great Valley, Graduate Studies, Malvern (PA) 373

Pepperdine University, Graziadio School of Business and Management, Los Angeles (CA) 85

Portland State University, School of Business Administration, Portland (OR) 358

Regis University, College for Professional Studies, Denver (CO) 103

Rensselaer at Hartford, Lally School of Management and Technology, Hartford (CT) 110

Rensselaer Polytechnic Institute, Lally School of Management and Technology, Troy (NY) 311, **670**

Rochester Institute of Technology, E. Philip Saunders College of Business, Rochester (NY) 312

Royal Roads University, Faculty of Management, Victoria (Canada) 471

Santa Clara University, Leavey School of Business, Santa Clara (CA) 88

Simon Fraser University, Faculty of Business Administration, Burnaby (Canada) 472

Southern Methodist University, Cox School of Business, Dallas (TX) 411, **688**

Southern Polytechnic State University, Department of Business Administration, Marietta (GA) 150

Stevens Institute of Technology, Wesley J. Howe School of Technology Management, Hoboken (NJ) 290

Technion-Israel Institute of Technology, Technion Graduate School, Haifa (Israel) 514

Texas A&M University, Mays Business School, College Station (TX) 414

Universite Libre de Bruxelles, Solvay Business School, Brussels (Belgium) 495

The University of Akron, College of Business Administration, Akron (OH) 346

The University of Alabama in Huntsville, College of Business Administration, Huntsville (AL) 51

University of Alberta, School of Business, Edmonton (Canada) 473

University of Baltimore, Merrick School of Business, Baltimore (MD) 216

University of California, Berkeley, Haas School of Business, Berkeley (CA) 89

University of California, Davis, Graduate School of Management, Davis (CA) 90

University of California, Los Angeles, UCLA Anderson School of Management, Los Angeles (CA) 91, **696**

University of California, San Diego, Rady School of Management, La Jolla (CA) 93, **700**

University of Colorado at Boulder, Leeds School of Business, Boulder (CO) 104, **702**

University of Colorado at Colorado Springs, Graduate School of Business Administration, Colorado Springs (CO) 105, **704**

University of Connecticut, School of Business, Storrs (CT) 112, **708**

University of Dallas, Graduate School of Management, Irving (TX) 420, **710**

University of Delaware, Alfred Lerner College of Business and Economics, Newark (DE) 116, **712**

University of Edinburgh, Edinburgh University Management School, Edinburgh (United Kingdom) 550

University of Florida, Hough Graduate School of Business, Gainesville (FL) 134

University of Houston–Clear Lake, School of Business, Houston (TX) 421

University of Maryland University College, Graduate School of Management and Technology, Adelphi (MD) 218

University of Mary Washington, College of Graduate and Professional Studies, Fredericksburg (VA) 444

University of Melbourne, Melbourne Business School, Melbourne (Australia) 488

University of New Brunswick Saint John, Faculty of Business, Saint John (Canada) 476, **724**

University of New Hampshire, Whittemore School of Business and Economics, Durham (NH) 280, **726**

University of New Mexico, Robert O. Anderson Graduate School of Management, Albuquerque (NM) 294

University of New Orleans, College of Business Administration, New Orleans (LA) 209

University of Ottawa, Telfer School of Management, Ottawa (Canada) 476

University of Pennsylvania, Wharton School, Philadelphia (PA) 380

University of Salford, Salford Business School, Salford (United Kingdom) 554

University of Saskatchewan, Edwards School of Business, Saskatoon (Canada) 478

University of Southern California, School of Business, Los Angeles (CA) 98

The University of Tampa, John H. Sykes College of Business, Tampa (FL) 139, **742**

The University of Texas at Arlington, College of Business Administration, Arlington (TX) 424, **746**

The University of Texas at Dallas, School of Management, Richardson (TX) *426*, **748**

The University of Texas at San Antonio, College of Business, San Antonio (TX) 427, **750**

The University of Texas at Tyler, College of Business and Technology, Tyler (TX) 428

The University of Toledo, College of Business Administration, Toledo (OH) 349

University of Washington, Michael G. Foster School of Business, Seattle (WA) 452, **754**

University of Waterloo, Graduate Studies, Waterloo (Canada) 479

University of Wisconsin–Madison, Wisconsin School of Business, Madison (WI) 462, **756**

University of Wyoming, College of Business, Laramie (WY) 465

Vlerick Leuven Gent Management School, MBA Programmes, Ghent (Belgium) 495

Walden University, School of Management, Minneapolis (MN) 253

Waseda University, Graduate School of Commerce, Tokyo (Japan) 517

Washington State University Tri-Cities, College of Business, Richland (WA) 453

Westminster College, The Bill and Vieve Gore School of Business, Salt Lake City (UT) 433

WHU—Otto Beisheim School of Management, WHU—Otto Beisheim School of Management, Vallendar (Germany) 511

Worcester Polytechnic Institute, Department of Management, Worcester (MA) 234, **770**

TELECOMMUNICATIONS MANAGEMENT

DeVry University, Keller Graduate School of Management, Oakbrook Terrace (IL) 161, **650**

École Nationale des Ponts et Chaussées, ENPC MBA, Paris (France) 503

European University, Center for Management Studies, Montreux-Fontanivent (Switzerland) 532

International University in Geneva, MBA Program, Geneva (Switzerland) 533, **640**

International University of Japan, Graduate School of International Management, Minami Uonuma-gu (Japan) 516

The Johns Hopkins University, Carey Business School, Baltimore (MD) 214, **646**

Murray State University, College of Business and Public Affairs, Murray (KY) 200

Rochester Institute of Technology, E. Philip Saunders College of Business, Rochester (NY) 312

Saint Mary's University of Minnesota, Schools of Graduate and Professional Programs, Winona (MN) 251

Southern Methodist University, Cox School of Business, Dallas (TX) 411, **688**

Stevens Institute of Technology, Wesley J. Howe School of Technology Management, Hoboken (NJ) 290

Stockholm School of Economics, Department of Business Administration, Stockholm (Sweden) 531

Texas A&M University, Mays Business School, College Station (TX) 414

University of Arkansas, Sam M. Walton College of Business Administration, Fayetteville (AR) 62

University of California, San Diego, Rady School of Management, La Jolla (CA) 93, **700**

University of Colorado at Boulder, Leeds School of Business, Boulder (CO) 104, **702**

University of Dallas, Graduate School of Management, Irving (TX) 420, **710**

University of Management and Technology, Graduate Business Programs, Arlington (VA) 443

University of Maryland University College, Graduate School of Management and Technology, Adelphi (MD) 218

University of Missouri–St. Louis, College of Business Administration, St. Louis (MO) *268*

University of New Brunswick Saint John, Faculty of Business, Saint John (Canada) 476, **724**

The University of Texas at Dallas, School of Management, Richardson (TX) *426,* **748**

Webster University, School of Business and Technology, St. Louis (MO) 270

Worcester Polytechnic Institute, Department of Management, Worcester (MA) 234, **770**

THEOLOGY/DIVINITY

Hope International University, Program in Business Administration, Fullerton (CA) 79

TRAINING AND DEVELOPMENT

Aston University, Aston Business School, Birmingham (United Kingdom) 539

Boise State University, College of Business and Economics, Boise (ID) 155

California National University for Advanced Studies, College of Business Administration, Northridge (CA) 67

City University of Hong Kong, Faculty of Business, Hong Kong (China) 497

Flinders University, Flinders Business School, Adelaide (Australia) 485

Lancaster University, Management School, Lancaster (United Kingdom) 541

Leadership Institute of Seattle, School of Applied Behavioral Science, Kenmore (WA) 449

Lindenwood University, Division of Management, St. Charles (MO) 261

Nottingham Trent University, Nottingham Business School, Nottingham (United Kingdom) 544

Roosevelt University, Walter E. Heller College of Business Administration, Chicago (IL) 172, **676**

Saint Xavier University, Graham School of Management, Chicago (IL) 173

Siena Heights University, Graduate College, Adrian (MI) 242

Silver Lake College, Program in Management and Organizational Behavior, Manitowoc (WI) 460

Southern New Hampshire University, School of Business, Manchester (NH) 279, **690**

Thames Valley University, Faculty of Professional Studies, Slough (United Kingdom) 546

University of Manitoba, Faculty of Management, Winnipeg (Canada) 475

University of Newcastle, Graduate School of Business, Callaghan (Australia) 489

University of Salford, Salford Business School, Salford (United Kingdom) 554

University of Wisconsin–Stout, Program in Training and Development, Menomonie (WI) 464

TRANSPORTATION MANAGEMENT

Antwerp International Business School, Graduate Programs in Business, Antwerp (Belgium) 493

Barcelona Business School, Graduate Programs in Business, Barcelona (Spain) 528

California Polytechnic State University, San Luis Obispo, Orfalea College of Business, San Luis Obispo (CA) 68

École Nationale des Ponts et Chaussées, ENPC MBA, Paris (France) 503

IE Business School, Business School, Madrid (Spain) 529, **636**

Maine Maritime Academy, Department of Graduate Studies, Castine (ME) 210

Michigan State University, Eli Broad Graduate School of Management, East Lansing (MI) 240

Missouri State University, College of Business Administration, Springfield (MO) *262*

Monash University, MBA Programme, Clayton (Australia) 486

Naval Postgraduate School, School of Business and Public Policy, Monterey (CA) 83

New York University, Robert F. Wagner Graduate School of Public Service (NY) 309

San Jose State University, Lucas Graduate School of Business, San Jose (CA) 87

State University of New York Maritime College, Program in International Transportation Management, Throggs Neck (NY) 317

The University of British Columbia, Sauder School of Business, Vancouver (Canada) 474

University of Salford, Salford Business School, Salford (United Kingdom) 554

The University of Tennessee, College of Business Administration, Knoxville (TN) *401,* **744**

University of Washington, Michael G. Foster School of Business, Seattle (WA) 452, **754**

Wilmington University, Division of Business, New Castle (DE) 117

TRAVEL INDUSTRY/TOURISM MANAGEMENT

Antwerp International Business School, Graduate Programs in Business, Antwerp (Belgium) 493

Barcelona Business School, Graduate Programs in Business, Barcelona (Spain) 528

Black Hills State University, College of Business and Technology, Spearfish (SD) 394

Delta State University, College of Business, Cleveland (MS) 254

EADA International Management Development Center, Business Programs, Barcelona (Spain) 528

Edith Cowan University, Faculty of Business and Public Management, Churchlands (Australia) 484

Flinders University, Flinders Business School, Adelaide (Australia) 485

The George Washington University, School of Business, Washington (DC) 119, **622**

Groupe CERAM, Ceram ESC Nice School of Management, Sophia Antipolis (France) 504

Hawai'i Pacific University, College of Business Administration, Honolulu (HI) 153, **630**

Hotel Management School Maastricht, MBA Program, Maastricht (Netherlands) 522

National University of Ireland, Dublin, The Michael Smurfit Graduate School of Business, Blackrock (Ireland) 513

Queen Margaret University College, Edinburgh, School of Business and Enterprise, Edinburgh (United Kingdom) 545

Schiller International University, MBA Programs, Florida (FL) 133, **684**

Schiller International University, Graduate Programs, London (United Kingdom) 546, **684**

Southern Cross University, Graduate College of Management, Coffs Harbour (Australia) 487

Thames Valley University, Faculty of Professional Studies, Slough (United Kingdom) 546

University of Denver, Daniels College of Business, Denver (CO) 106

University of Hull, School of Management, Hull (United Kingdom) 552

University of Malaya, Graduate School of Business, Kuala Lumpur (Malaysia) 519

University of New Orleans, College of Business Administration, New Orleans (LA) 209

University of Salford, Salford Business School, Salford (United Kingdom) 554

The University of Texas at San Antonio, College of Business, San Antonio (TX) 427, **750**

Vienna University of Economics and Business Administration, WU Wien MBA, Vienna (Austria) 492

Alphabetical Listing of Schools

In this index the page locations of the **Profiles** are printed in regular type, **Profiles** with **Announcements** in *italic* type, and **Close-Ups** in **bold** type.

East Carolina University, College of Business, Greenville (NC) 324, **602**

Eastern Connecticut State University, School of Education and Professional Studies/Graduate Division, Willimantic (CT) 108

Eastern Illinois University, Lumpkin College of Business and Applied Sciences, Charleston (IL) 163

Eastern Kentucky University, College of Business and Technology, Richmond (KY) 199

Eastern Mennonite University, Program in Business Administration, Harrisonburg (VA) 438

Eastern Michigan University, College of Business, Ypsilanti (MI) 237

Eastern New Mexico University, College of Business, Portales (NM) 292

Eastern University, Graduate Business Programs, St. Davids (PA) 368

Eastern Washington University, College of Business and Public Administration, Cheney (WA) 448

East Tennessee State University, College of Business and Technology, Johnson City (TN) 396

Eberhardt School of Business
See University of the Pacific

Eberly College of Business and Information Technology
See Indiana University of Pennsylvania

École Nationale des Ponts et Chaussées, ENPC MBA, Paris (France) 503

Edgewood College, Program in Business, Madison (WI) 458

Edinburgh University Management School
See University of Edinburgh

Edith Cowan University, Faculty of Business and Public Management, Churchlands (Australia) 484

E. J. Ourso College of Business
See Louisiana State University and Agricultural and Mechanical College

Eli Broad Graduate School of Management
See Michigan State University

The Elkin B. McCallum Graduate School of Business
See Bentley College

Eller College of Management
See The University of Arizona

Elmhurst College, Program in Business Administration, Elmhurst (IL) 163

Elon University, Martha and Spencer Love School of Business, Elon (NC) 324

Else School of Management
See Millsaps College

Embry-Riddle Aeronautical University, College of Business, Daytona Beach (FL) 125, **604**

Embry-Riddle Aeronautical University Worldwide, Department of Management, Daytona Beach (FL) 125

Emmanuel College, Graduate and Professional Programs, Boston (MA) 225

Emory University, Roberto C. Goizueta Business School, Atlanta (GA) 145, **606**

Emporia State University, School of Business, Emporia (KS) 193

Endicott College, Program in Business Administration, Beverly (MA) 225

ENPC MBA
See École Nationale des Ponts et Chaussées

Erasmus University Rotterdam, Rotterdam School of Management, Rotterdam (Netherlands) 521

Eric Sprott School of Business
See Carleton University

Erivan K. Haub School of Business
See Saint Joseph's University

ESCP-EAP European School of Management, ESCP-EAP European School of Management (France) 503

Escuela de Administracion de Negocios para Graduados, Programa Magister—MBA Programs, Lima (Peru) 525

Eugene W. Stetson School of Business and Economics
See Mercer University

European Business Management School, MBA Programmes, Antwerp (Belgium) 494

European Institute of Purchasing Management, MBA Programs, Archamps (France) 504

European School of Economics, MBA Programme (NY) 301, **608**

European School of Economics, MBA Programme (Italy) 515, **608**

European School of Economics, MBA Programme, Milan (Italy) 515, **608**

European School of Economics, MBA Programme, Rome (Italy) 516, **608**

European School of Economics, MBA Programme (United Kingdom) 541, **608**

European University, Center for Management Studies, Montreux-Fontanivent (Switzerland) 532

Everest University, Graduate School of Business, Clearwater (FL) 126

Everest University, Program in Business Administration, Lakeland (FL) 126

Everest University, Program in Business Administration, Orlando (FL) 126

Excelsior College, School of Business and Technology, Albany (NY) 301, **610**

Executive Business Administration Program
See University of Charleston

Fachhochschule Offenburg, MBA International Business Consulting, Offenburg (Germany) 507

Faculdade de Economia-Gestao
See Universidade Nova de Lisboa

Fairfield University, Charles F. Dolan School of Business, Fairfield (CT) 109

Fairleigh Dickinson University, College at Florham, Silberman College of Business, Madison (NJ) 282, **612**

Fairleigh Dickinson University, Metropolitan Campus, Silberman College of Business, Teaneck (NJ) 282, **612**

Fayetteville State University, Program in Business Administration, Fayetteville (NC) 325

Felician College, Program in Business, Lodi (NJ) 283, **614**

Fielding Graduate University, Programs in Organizational Management and Organizational Development, Santa Barbara (CA) 77, **616**

Fisher Graduate School of International Business
See Monterey Institute of International Studies

Fitchburg State College, Division of Graduate and Continuing Education, Fitchburg (MA) 225

Flinders University, Flinders Business School, Adelaide (Australia) 485

Florida Atlantic University, College of Business, Boca Raton (FL) 126

Florida Gulf Coast University, Lutgert College of Business, Fort Myers (FL) 127

Florida Institute of Technology, College of Business, Melbourne (FL) 128

Florida International University, Alvah H. Chapman, Jr. Graduate School of Business, Miami (FL) 128, **618**

Florida State University, College of Business, Tallahassee (FL) 129

Fogelman College of Business and Economics
See University of Memphis

Fontbonne University, Department of Business Administration, St. Louis (MO) 260

Fordham University, Graduate School of Business Administration, New York (NY) 301, **620**

Foster College of Business Administration
See Bradley University

Fox School of Business and Management
See Temple University

Framingham State College, Program in Business Administration, Framingham (MA) 226

Franciscan University of Steubenville, Department of Business, Steubenville (OH) 341

Francis Marion University, School of Business, Florence (SC) 392

Frank G. Zarb School of Business
See Hofstra University

Franklin Pierce University, Graduate Studies, Rindge (NH) 278

Franklin P. Perdue School of Business
See Salisbury University

Fresno Pacific University, Graduate Programs, Fresno (CA) 78

Frostburg State University, College of Business, Frostburg (MD) 213

Frost School of Business
See Centenary College of Louisiana

The Fuqua School of Business
See Duke University

F. W. Olin Graduate School of Business
See Babson College

Gannon University, School of Business, Erie (PA) 368

Gardner-Webb University, Graduate School of Business, Boiling Springs (NC) 325

Gatton College of Business and Economics
See University of Kentucky

Geneva College, Department of Business, Accounting and Management, Beaver Falls (PA) 369

George Fox University, School of Management, Newberg (OR) 357

George H. Atkinson Graduate School of Management
See Willamette University

The George L. Argyros School of Business and Economics
See Chapman University

George Mason University, School of Management, Fairfax (VA) 438

Georgetown University, McDonough School of Business, Washington (DC) 119

The George Washington University, School of Business, Washington (DC) 119, **622**

Georgia College & State University, The J. Whitney Bunting School of Business, Milledgeville (GA) 145

Georgia Institute of Technology, College of Management, Atlanta (GA) 146, **624**

Georgian Court University, School of Business, Lakewood (NJ) 283

Georgia Southern University, College of Business Administration, Statesboro (GA) 146

Georgia Southwestern State University, School of Business Administration, Americus (GA) 147

Georgia State University, J. Mack Robinson College of Business, Atlanta (GA) 147, **626**

GISMA Business School, Graduate Programs, Hannover (Germany) 508

Golden Gate University, Ageno School of Business, San Francisco (CA) 78

Goldey-Beacom College, Graduate Program, Wilmington (DE) 116

Gonzaga University, School of Business Administration, Spokane (WA) 448

Miami University, Farmer School of Business, Oxford (OH) 343

Michael F. Price College of Business
See University of Oklahoma

Michael J. Coles College of Business
See Kennesaw State University

Michigan State University, Eli Broad Graduate School of Management, East Lansing (MI) 240

Michigan Technological University, School of Business and Economics, Houghton (MI) 241

Middle East Technical University, Department of Business Administration, Ankara (Turkey) 537

Middle Tennessee State University, College of Business, Murfreesboro (TN) 397

Midwestern State University, College of Business Administration, Wichita Falls (TX) 409

Milano The New School for Management and Urban Policy
See The New School: A University

Millersville University of Pennsylvania, Department of Business Administration, Millersville (PA) 372

Millsaps College, Else School of Management, Jackson (MS) 255

Mills College, Graduate School of Business, Oakland (CA) 81

Milwaukee School of Engineering, Rader School of Business, Milwaukee (WI) 460

Minot State University, College of Business, Minot (ND) 334

Misericordia University, Division of Behavioral Science, Education, and Business, Dallas (PA) 372

Mississippi College, School of Business Administration, Clinton (MS) 256

Mississippi State University, College of Business and Industry, Mississippi State (MS) 256

Missouri State University, College of Business Administration, Springfield (MO) *262*

Mitchell College of Business
See University of South Alabama

Monash University, MBA Programme, Clayton (Australia) 486

Monmouth University, School of Business Administration, West Long Branch (NJ) 284

Montana State University, College of Business, Bozeman (MT) 271

Montclair State University, School of Business, Montclair (NJ) 285

Monterey Institute of International Studies, Fisher Graduate School of International Business, Monterey (CA) 82, **660**

Montreat College, School of Professional and Adult Studies, Montreat (NC) 327

Moore School of Business
See University of South Carolina

Moravian College, The Moravian MBA, Bethlehem (PA) 373

The Moravian MBA
See Moravian College

Morehead State University, College of Business, Morehead (KY) 200

Mount St. Mary's University, Program in Business Administration, Emmitsburg (MD) 215

Murray State University, College of Business and Public Affairs, Murray (KY) 200

Nance College of Business Administration
See Cleveland State University

Nanjing University, School of Business, Nanjing (China) 500

Nanyang Business School
See Nanyang Technological University

Nanyang Technological University, Nanyang Business School, Singapore (Singapore) 527, **662**

Napier Business School
See Napier University

Napier University, Napier Business School, Edinburgh (United Kingdom) 544

National-Louis University, College of Management and Business, Chicago (IL) 168

National University, School of Business and Management, La Jolla (CA) 82

National University of Ireland, Dublin, The Michael Smurfit Graduate School of Business, Blackrock (Ireland) 513

Naval Postgraduate School, School of Business and Public Policy, Monterey (CA) 83

The Neeley School of Business at TCU
See Texas Christian University

Netherlands Business School
See Nyenrode Business Universiteit

New England College, Program in Management, Henniker (NH) 278

New Jersey Institute of Technology, School of Management, Newark (NJ) 285

Newman University, School of Business, Wichita (KS) 194

New Mexico Highlands University, School of Business, Las Vegas (NM) 293

New Mexico State University, College of Business, Las Cruces (NM) 293

The New School: A University, Milano The New School for Management and Urban Policy, New York (NY) 308

New York Institute of Technology, School of Management (NY) 308

New York University, Leonard N. Stern School of Business (NY) 309

New York University, Robert F. Wagner Graduate School of Public Service (NY) 309

Nicholls State University, College of Business Administration, Thibodaux (LA) 206

Nichols College, Graduate Program in Business Administration, Dudley (MA) 228

North Carolina Central University, School of Business, Durham (NC) 327

North Carolina State University, College of Management, Raleigh (NC) 328, **664**

North Central College, Department of Business, Naperville (IL) *168*

Northcentral University, MBA Program, Prescott Valley (AZ) 56

North Dakota State University, College of Business, Fargo (ND) 335

Northeastern Illinois University, College of Business and Management, Chicago (IL) 169

Northeastern State University, College of Business and Technology, Tahlequah (OK) 352

Northeastern University, Graduate School of Business Administration, Boston (MA) 228

Northern Arizona University, College of Business Administration, Flagstaff (AZ) 57

Northern Illinois University, College of Business, De Kalb (IL) 169

Northern Kentucky University, College of Business, Highland Heights (KY) 201

North Park University, School of Business and Nonprofit Management, Chicago (IL) 170

Northwest Christian College, School of Business and Management, Eugene (OR) 358

Northwestern Polytechnic University, School of Business and Information Technology, Fremont (CA) 84

Northwestern University, Kellogg School of Management, Evanston (IL) 171

Northwest Missouri State University, Melvin and Valorie Booth College of Business and Professional Studies, Maryville (MO) 263

Northwood University, Richard DeVos Graduate School of Management, Midland (MI) 241

Norwegian School of Management, Graduate School, Sandvika (Norway) 524

Norwich University, Distance MBA Program, Northfield (VT) 433

Notre Dame de Namur University, Department of Business Administration, Belmont (CA) 84

Nottingham Business School
See Nottingham Trent University

Nottingham Trent University, Nottingham Business School, Nottingham (United Kingdom) 544

Nova Southeastern University, H. Wayne Huizenga School of Business and Entrepreneurship, Fort Lauderdale (FL) 130, **666**

Nyenrode Business Universiteit, Netherlands Business School, Breukelen (Netherlands) 522

Oakland City University, School of Adult and Extended Learning, Oakland City (IN) 185

Oakland University, School of Business Administration, Rochester (MI) 241

Odette School of Business
See University of Windsor

OGI School of Science & Engineering at Oregon Health & Science University, Department of Management in Science and Technology, Beaverton (OR) 358

The Ohio State University, Max M. Fisher College of Business, Columbus (OH) 344

Ohio University, College of Business, Athens (OH) 344

Oklahoma City University, Meinders School of Business, Oklahoma City (OK) 352

Oklahoma Wesleyan University, Professional Studies Division, Bartlesville (OK) 353

Old Dominion University, College of Business and Public Administration, Norfolk (VA) 441

Olin Business School
See Washington University in St. Louis

Open University, Business School, Milton Keynes (United Kingdom) 545

Open University of the Netherlands, Business Programs, Heerlen (Netherlands) 523

Oral Roberts University, School of Business, Tulsa (OK) 353

Orfalea College of Business
See California Polytechnic State University, San Luis Obispo

Ottawa University, Graduate Studies-Arizona (AZ) 57

Ottawa University, Graduate Studies-Kansas City, Ottawa (KS) 195

Otterbein College, Department of Business, Accounting and Economics, Westerville (OH) 345

Owen Graduate School of Management
See Vanderbilt University

Pace University, Lubin School of Business, New York (NY) 310

Pacific Lutheran University, School of Business, Tacoma (WA) 449

Pacific States University, College of Business, Los Angeles (CA) 85

Palm Beach Atlantic University, Rinker School of Business, West Palm Beach (FL) 131

Pamplin College of Business
See Virginia Polytechnic Institute and State University

Park University, Program in Business Administration, Parkville (MO) 264

Penn State Great Valley, Graduate Studies, Malvern (PA) 373

Penn State Harrisburg, School of Business Administration, Middletown (PA) 373

Penn State University Park, The Mary Jean and Frank P. Smeal College of Business Administration, State College (PA) 374

University of Missouri–Columbia, Robert J. Trulaske, Sr. College of Business, Columbia (MO) 267, **720**

University of Missouri–Kansas City, Henry W. Bloch School of Business and Public Administration, Kansas City (MO) 267

University of Missouri–St. Louis, College of Business Administration, St. Louis (MO) *268*

University of Mobile, School of Business, Mobile (AL) 51

University of Nebraska at Kearney, College of Business and Technology, Kearney (NE) 273

University of Nebraska–Lincoln, College of Business Administration, Lincoln (NE) 274

University of Nevada, Las Vegas, College of Business, Las Vegas (NV) 275, **722**

University of Nevada, Reno, College of Business Administration, Reno (NV) 276

University of New Brunswick Fredericton, Faculty of Business Administration, Fredericton (Canada) 476

University of New Brunswick Saint John, Faculty of Business, Saint John (Canada) 476, **724**

University of Newcastle, Graduate School of Business, Callaghan (Australia) 489

The University of New England, The Graduate School of Business Administration, Armidale (Australia) 490

University of New Hampshire, Whittemore School of Business and Economics, Durham (NH) 280, **726**

University of New Haven, School of Business, West Haven (CT) 113, **728**

University of New Mexico, Robert O. Anderson Graduate School of Management, Albuquerque (NM) 294

University of New Orleans, College of Business Administration, New Orleans (LA) 209

University of New South Wales, Australian School of Business, Kensington (Australia) 490

University of North Alabama, College of Business, Florence (AL) 52

The University of North Carolina at Chapel Hill, Kenan-Flagler Business School, Chapel Hill (NC) 330

The University of North Carolina at Charlotte, Belk College of Business Administration, Charlotte (NC) 330, **730**

The University of North Carolina at Greensboro, Bryan School of Business and Economics, Greensboro (NC) 331

The University of North Carolina at Pembroke, Graduate Studies, Pembroke (NC) 331

The University of North Carolina Wilmington, School of Business, Wilmington (NC) 332

University of North Dakota, College of Business and Public Administration, Grand Forks (ND) 336

University of Northern Iowa, College of Business Administration, Cedar Falls (IA) 192

University of North Florida, Coggin College of Business, Jacksonville (FL) 136

University of North Texas, College of Business Administration, Denton (TX) 422

University of Notre Dame, Mendoza College of Business, Notre Dame (IN) 187

University of Oklahoma, Michael F. Price College of Business, Norman (OK) 355

University of Oregon, Charles H. Lundquist College of Business, Eugene (OR) 359, **732**

University of Otago, School of Business, Dunedin (New Zealand) 523

University of Ottawa, Telfer School of Management, Ottawa (Canada) 476

University of Oxford, Saïd Business School, Oxford (United Kingdom) 553

University of Pennsylvania, Wharton School, Philadelphia (PA) 380

University of Phoenix, College of Graduate Business and Management, Phoenix (AZ) 59

University of Phoenix–Atlanta Campus, College of Graduate Business and Management, Sandy Springs (GA) 151

University of Phoenix–Bay Area Campus, College of Graduate Business and Management, Pleasanton (CA) 94

University of Phoenix–Boston Campus, College of Graduate Business and Management, Braintree (MA) 233

University of Phoenix–Central Florida Campus, College of Graduate Business and Management, Maitland (FL) 137

University of Phoenix–Central Massachusetts Campus, College of Graduate Business and Management, Westborough (MA) 234

University of Phoenix–Charlotte Campus, College of Graduate Business and Management, Charlotte (NC) 332

University of Phoenix–Chicago Campus, College of Graduate Business and Management, Schaumburg (IL) 177

University of Phoenix–Cincinnati Campus, College of Graduate Business and Management, West Chester (OH) 348

University of Phoenix–Cleveland Campus, College of Graduate Business and Management, Independence (OH) 348

University of Phoenix–Columbus Georgia Campus, College of Graduate Business and Management, Columbus (GA) 152

University of Phoenix–Columbus Ohio Campus, College of Graduate Business and Management, Columbus (OH) 349

University of Phoenix–Dallas Campus, College of Graduate Business and Management, Dallas (TX) 423

University of Phoenix–Denver Campus, College of Graduate Business and Management, Lone Tree (CO) 107

University of Phoenix–Eastern Washington Campus, College of Graduate Business and Management, Spokane Valley (WA) 451

University of Phoenix–Hawaii Campus, College of Graduate Business and Management, Honolulu (HI) 155

University of Phoenix–Houston Campus, College of Graduate Business and Management, Houston (TX) 423

University of Phoenix–Idaho Campus, College of Graduate Business and Management, Meridian (ID) 157

University of Phoenix–Indianapolis Campus, College of Graduate Business and Management, Indianapolis (IN) 187

University of Phoenix–Kansas City Campus, College of Graduate Business and Management, Kansas City (MO) 268

University of Phoenix–Las Vegas Campus, College of Graduate Business and Management, Las Vegas (NV) 276

University of Phoenix–Little Rock Campus, College of Graduate Business and Management, Little Rock (AR) 63

University of Phoenix–Louisiana Campus, College of Graduate Business and Management, Metairie (LA) 210

University of Phoenix–Maryland Campus, College of Graduate Business and Management, Columbia (MD) 219

University of Phoenix–Metro Detroit Campus, College of Graduate Business and Management, Troy (MI) 246

University of Phoenix–Nashville Campus, College of Graduate Business and Management, Nashville (TN) 401

University of Phoenix–New Mexico Campus, College of Graduate Business and Management, Albuquerque (NM) 294

University of Phoenix–North Florida Campus, College of Graduate Business and Management, Jacksonville (FL) 137

University of Phoenix–Oklahoma City Campus, College of Graduate Business and Management, Oklahoma City (OK) 355

University of Phoenix–Oregon Campus, College of Graduate Business and Management, Tigard (OR) 360

University of Phoenix–Philadelphia Campus, College of Graduate Business and Management, Wayne (PA) 380

University of Phoenix–Phoenix Campus, College of Graduate Business and Management, Phoenix (AZ) 59

University of Phoenix–Pittsburgh Campus, College of Graduate Business and Management, Pittsburgh (PA) 381

University of Phoenix–Puerto Rico Campus, College of Graduate Business and Management, Guaynabo (PR) 387

University of Phoenix–Sacramento Valley Campus, College of Graduate Business and Management, Sacramento (CA) 95

University of Phoenix–St. Louis Campus, College of Graduate Business and Management, St. Louis (MO) 269

University of Phoenix–San Diego Campus, College of Graduate Business and Management, San Diego (CA) 95

University of Phoenix–Southern Arizona Campus, College of Graduate Business and Management, Tucson (AZ) 60

University of Phoenix–Southern California Campus, College of Graduate Business and Management, Costa Mesa (CA) 96

University of Phoenix–Southern Colorado Campus, College of Graduate Business and Management, Colorado Springs (CO) 107

University of Phoenix–South Florida Campus, College of Graduate Business and Management, Fort Lauderdale (FL) 137

University of Phoenix–Tulsa Campus, College of Graduate Business and Management, Tulsa (OK) 355

University of Phoenix–Utah Campus, College of Graduate Business and Management, Salt Lake City (UT) 432

University of Phoenix–Vancouver Campus, College of Graduate Business and Management, Burnaby (Canada) 477

University of Phoenix–Washington Campus, College of Graduate Business and Management, Seattle (WA) 452

University of Phoenix–West Florida Campus, College of Graduate Business and Management, Temple Terrace (FL) 138

University of Phoenix–West Michigan Campus, College of Graduate Business and Management, Walker (MI) 246

University of Phoenix–Wichita Campus, College of Graduate Business and Management, Wichita (KS) 196

University of Phoenix–Wisconsin Campus, College of Graduate Business and Management, Brookfield (WI) 461

Notes

Notes

Notes

Notes

Notes

Notes

Notes

Notes

FIND YOUR IDEAL BUSINESS SCHOOL.

Use our MBA Search at Petersons.com/mba.

Discover the perfect MBA program for you with help
from these resources at Petersons.com:

- Business school search by program choice or other criteria
- Online courses and practice tests
- Free information from schools you contact
- Financial aid information
- Advice articles
- Monthly e-newsletters

VISIT PETERSONS.COM/MBA TODAY.

© 2008 Nelnet, Inc. All rights reserved. Nelnet and Peterson's are registered service marks of Nelnet, Inc.

PETERSON'S

A **nelnet** COMPANY

Peterson's
Book Satisfaction Survey

Give Us Your Feedback

Thank you for choosing Peterson's as your source for personalized solutions for your education and career achievement. Please take a few minutes to answer the following questions. Your answers will go a long way in helping us to produce the most user-friendly and comprehensive resources to meet your individual needs.

When completed, please tear out this page and mail it to us at:

Publishing Department
Peterson's, a Nelnet company
2000 Lenox Drive
Lawrenceville, NJ 08648

You can also complete this survey online at **www.petersons.com/booksurvey.**

1. **What is the ISBN of the book you have purchased? (The ISBN can be found on the book's back cover in the lower right-hand corner.)** _____

2. **Where did you purchase this book?**
   ❏ Retailer, such as Barnes & Noble
   ❏ Online reseller, such as Amazon.com
   ❏ Petersons.com
   ❏ Other (please specify) _____

3. **If you purchased this book on Petersons.com, please rate the following aspects of your online purchasing experience on a scale of 4 to 1 (4 = Excellent and 1 = Poor).**

	4	3	2	1
Comprehensiveness of Peterson's Online Bookstore page	❏	❏	❏	❏
Overall online customer experience	❏	❏	❏	❏

4. **Which category best describes you?**

   ❏ High school student
   ❏ Parent of high school student
   ❏ College student
   ❏ Graduate/professional student
   ❏ Returning adult student

   ❏ Teacher
   ❏ Counselor
   ❏ Working professional/military
   ❏ Other (please specify) _____

5. **Rate your overall satisfaction with this book.**

Extremely Satisfied	Satisfied	Not Satisfied
❏	❏	❏

6. Rate each of the following aspects of this book on a scale of 4 to 1 (4 = Excellent and 1 = Poor).

	4	3	2	1
Comprehensiveness of the information	❏	❏	❏	❏
Accuracy of the information	❏	❏	❏	❏
Usability	❏	❏	❏	❏
Cover design	❏	❏	❏	❏
Book layout	❏	❏	❏	❏
Special features *(e.g., CD, flashcards, charts, etc.)*	❏	❏	❏	❏
Value for the money	❏	❏	❏	❏

7. This book was recommended by:
- ❏ Guidance counselor
- ❏ Parent/guardian
- ❏ Family member/relative
- ❏ Friend
- ❏ Teacher
- ❏ Not recommended by anyone—I found the book on my own
- ❏ Other (please specify) _____

8. Would you recommend this book to others?

Yes	Not Sure	No
❏	❏	❏

9. Please provide any additional comments.

_____

_____

_____

_____

_____

Remember, you can tear out this page and mail it to us at:

Publishing Department
Peterson's, a Nelnet company
2000 Lenox Drive
Lawrenceville, NJ 08648

or you can complete the survey online at **www.petersons.com/booksurvey.**

Your feedback is important to us at Peterson's, and we thank you for your time!

If you would like us to keep in touch with you about new products and services, please include your e-mail address here: _____